Get connected to the power of the Internet

McDougal Littell's online resources for teachers provide time-saving planning, instruction, and assessment support.

classzone.com

- Links correlated to the text
- Web Research Guide
- Self-scoring quizzes
- Interactive activities, games, and simulations
- Links to current events
- Test practice
- Teacher Center

You have immediate access to *ClassZone's* teacher resources.

MCD5UBQ2IQZHI

Use this code to create your own username and password.

easyPlanner Plus ONLINE

- Customizable lesson plans
- Trackable standards correlated to each lesson

Visit classzone.com for purchasing information and free demos

eEdition Plus ONLINE

- Online version of the text
- Interactive features to explore American history

eTest Plus ONLINE

- Customizable assessment tool
- Automatically grades tests
- Generates reports correlated to standards

Now it all clicks!™

CLASSZONE.COM

McDougal Littell

McDOUGAL LITTELL

TEACHER'S EDITION

Creating America

A History of the United States

Beginnings through Reconstruction

Acknowledgments begin on page R84.

ISBN 0-618-37699-2

Printed in the United States of America
1 2 3 4 5 6 7 8 9-VJM-06 05 04

Creating America

Contents

Creating America

Motivate students to interact with history.

Students are much more motivated to study history when they are actively involved in their learning. *Creating America* provides this motivation by bringing history alive through interactive exercises and hands-on activities. Through these interactive approaches, students will make personal connections to the people, events, and issues that form the panorama of American history.

2

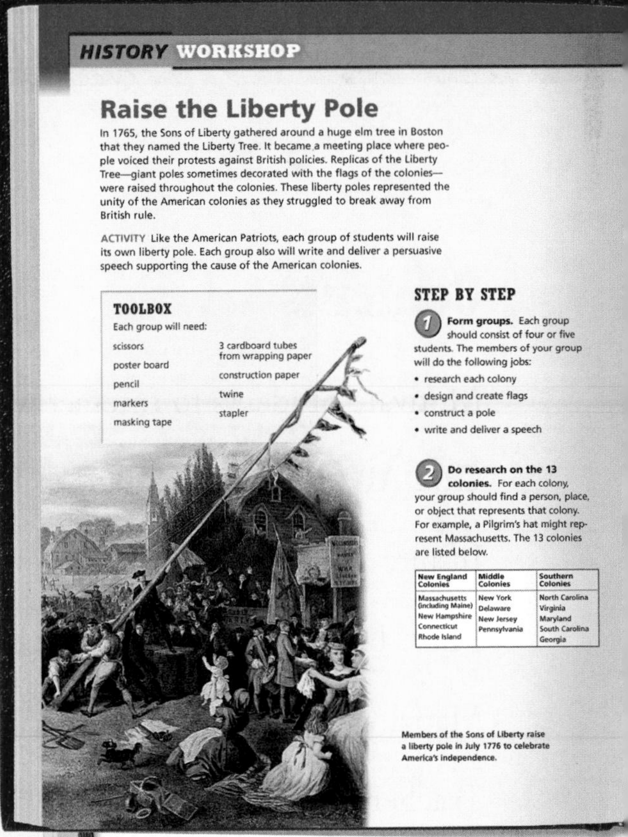

HISTORY WORKSHOP

Raise the Liberty Pole

In 1765, the Sons of Liberty gathered around a huge elm tree in Boston that they named the Liberty Tree. It became a meeting place where people voiced their protests against British policies. Replicas of the Liberty Tree—giant poles sometimes decorated with the flags of the colonies—were raised throughout the colonies. These liberty poles represented the unity of the American colonies as they struggled to break away from British rule.

ACTIVITY Like the American Patriots, each group of students will raise its own liberty pole. Each group also will write and deliver a persuasive speech supporting the cause of the American colonies.

TOOLBOX

Each group will need:

scissors

poster board

pencil

markers

masking tape

3 cardboard tubes from wrapping paper

construction paper

twine

stapler

STEP BY STEP

1 Form groups. Each group should consist of four or five students. The members of your group will do the following jobs:

- research each colony
- design and create flags
- construct a pole
- write and deliver a speech

2 Do research on the 13 colonies. For each colony, your group should find a person, place, or object that represents that colony. For example, a Pilgrim's hat might represent Massachusetts. The 13 colonies are listed below.

New England Colonies	Middle Colonies	Southern Colonies
Massachusetts (including Maine) New Hampshire Connecticut Rhode Island	New York Delaware New Jersey Pennsylvania	North Carolina Virginia Maryland South Carolina Georgia

Members of the Sons of Liberty raise a liberty pole in July 1776 to celebrate America's independence.

CHAPTER 6

The Road to Revolution 1763–1776

Section 1 Tighter British Control

Section 2 Colonial Resistance Grows

Section 3 The Road to Lexington and Concord

Section 4 Declaring Independence

Angry colonists watch the arrival of British troops in Boston.

1

Interact with History

A colonist reads a copy of a new British tax law.

Tax stamps are burned.

Protesters include men, women, and children.

The year is 1765. Your neighbors are enraged by Britain's attempt to tax them without their consent. Britain has never done this before. Everyone will be affected by the tax. There are protests in many cities. You have to decide what you would do.

What Do You Think?

- What is the best way to show opposition to policies you consider unjust?
- Is there anything to be gained by protesting? Anything to be lost?
- Does government have the right to tax without consent of the people? Why or why not?

Would you join the protest?

USA

World

1763

1763 Proclamation of 1763 becomes law.

1765 Stamp Act is passed.

1767 Townshend Acts are passed.

1769 Spanish begin to establish military posts and missions in California.

1770 Boston Massacre

1773 Boston Tea Party

1774 Intolerable Acts are passed; First Continental Congress meets.

1775 Battles of Lexington and Concord

1776 Declaration of Independence is signed.

1763 Treaty of Paris ends Seven Years' War in Europe.

1765 Chinese forces invade Burma.

1772 Captain Cook explores the South Pacific.

1774 Reign of Louis XVI begins in France.

1776

1 Interact with History

In an interactive situation at the beginning of every chapter, students face the difficult problems and decisions that faced real people in American history. By putting themselves into these actual situations, students learn to analyze issues and make decisions. Also, history becomes more relevant to students.

2 History Workshops

In these engaging hands-on activities, students learn about the daily life of the past. In each of the nine Workshops in the textbook, students work in cooperative learning groups to create a historical product and present their product to the class. In creating that product, students explore the social history of the period in a highly interactive way.

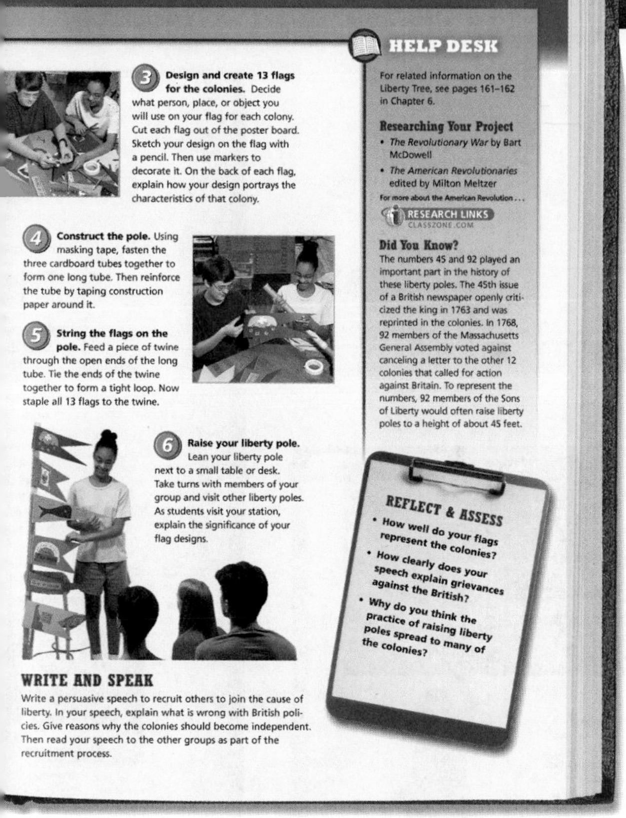
HELP DESK
For related information on the Liberty Tree, see pages 161–162 in Chapter 6.
Researching Your Project
• The Revolutionary War by Bart McDowell
• The American Revolutionaries edited by Milton Meltzer
RESEARCH LINKS
CLASSZONE.COM
Did You Know?
The numbers 45 and 92 played an important part in the history of these liberty poles. The 45th issue of a British newspaper openly criticized the king in 1763 and was reprinted in the colonies. In 1768, 92 members of the Massachusetts General Assembly voted against canceling a letter to the other 12 colonies that called for action against Britain. To represent the numbers, 92 members of the Sons of Liberty would often raise liberty poles to a height of about 45 feet.
3 Design and create 13 flags for the colonies. Decide what person, place, or object you will use on your flag for each colony. Cut each flag out of the poster board. Sketch your design on the flag with a pencil. Then use markers to decorate it. On the back of each flag, explain how your design portrays the characteristics of that colony.
4 Construct the pole. Using masking tape, fasten the three cardboard tubes together to form one long tube. Then reinforce the tube by taping construction paper around it.
5 String the flags on the pole. Feed a piece of twine through the open ends of the long tube. Tie the ends of the twine together to form a tight loop. Now staple all 13 flags to the twine.
6 Raise your liberty pole. Lean your liberty pole next to a small table or desk. Take turns with members of your group and visit other liberty poles. As students visit your station, explain the significance of your flag designs.
REFLECT & ASSESS
• How well do your flags represent the colonies?
• How clearly does your speech explain grievances against the British?
• Why do you think the practice of raising liberty poles spread to many of the colonies?
WRITE AND SPEAK
Write a persuasive speech to recruit others to join the cause of liberty. In your speech, explain what is wrong with British policies. Give reasons why the colonies should become independent. Then read your speech to the other groups as part of the recruitment process.

4

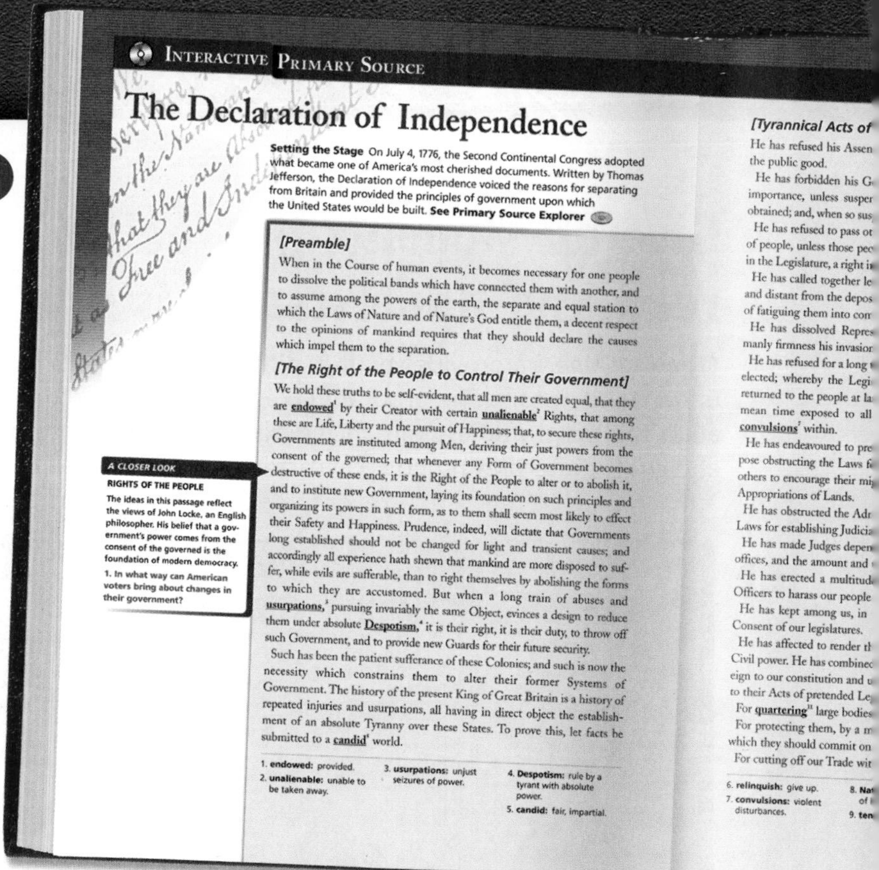
INTERACTIVE PRIMARY SOURCE
The Declaration of Independence
Setting the Stage On July 4, 1776, the Second Continental Congress adopted what became one of America's most cherished documents. Written by Thomas Jefferson, the Declaration of Independence voiced the reasons for separating from Britain and provided the principles of government upon which the United States would be built. See Primary Source Explorer
[Preamble]
When in the Course of human events, it becomes necessary for one people to dissolve the political bands which have connected them with another, and to assume among the powers of the earth, the separate and equal station to which the Laws of Nature and of Nature's God entitle them, a decent respect to the opinions of mankind requires that they should declare the causes which impel them to the separation.
[The Right of the People to Control Their Government]
We hold these truths to be self-evident, that all men are created equal, that they are endowed by their Creator with certain unalienable Rights, that among these are Life, Liberty and the pursuit of Happiness; that, to secure these rights, Governments are instituted among Men, deriving their just powers from the consent of the governed; that whenever any Form of Government becomes destructive of these ends, it is the Right of the People to alter or to abolish it, and to institute new Government, laying its foundation on such principles and organizing its powers in such form, as to them shall seem most likely to effect their Safety and Happiness. Prudence, indeed, will dictate that Governments long established should not be changed for light and transient causes; and accordingly all experience hath shewn that mankind are more disposed to suffer, while evils are sufferable, than to right themselves by abolishing the forms to which they are accustomed. But when a long train of abuses and usurpations, pursuing invariably the same Object, evinces a design to reduce them under absolute Despotism, it is their right, it is their duty, to throw off such Government, and to provide new Guards for their future security.
Such has been the patient sufferance of these Colonies; and such is now the necessity which constrains them to alter their former Systems of Government. The history of the present King of Great Britain is a history of repeated injuries and usurpations, all having in direct object the establishment of an absolute Tyranny over these States. To prove this, let facts be submitted to a candid world.
A CLOSER LOOK
RIGHTS OF THE PEOPLE
The ideas in this passage reflect the views of John Locke, an English philosopher. His belief that a government's power comes from the consent of the governed is the foundation of modern democracy.
1. In what way can American voters bring about changes in their government?
1. endowed: provided.
2. unalienable: unable to be taken away.
3. usurpations: unjust seizures of power.
4. Despotism: rule by a tyrant with absolute power.
5. candid: fair, impartial.
[Tyrannical Acts of

Section 2 Assessment

1. Terms & Names

Explain the significance of:
- Crispus Attucks
- Townshend Acts
- writs of assistance
- Samuel Adams
- Boston Massacre
- John Adams
- committee of correspondence
- Boston Tea Party

2. Taking Notes

Create a time line like the one below to show the significant people and events described in this section.

1767 — 1773

Which event do you think was the most important? Explain.

3. Main Ideas

a. Why did colonists oppose the Townshend Acts?

b. Why were British troops sent to Boston?

c. What prompted the Boston Tea Party?

4. Critical Thinking

Drawing Conclusions
Do you think colonial outrage over the Boston Massacre was justified? Explain.

THINK ABOUT
- how the British troops were taunted
- whether troops have the right to fire on citizens

3

ACTIVITY OPTIONS

SPEECH
TECHNOLOGY

Read more about the Boston Massacre or the Boston Tea Party. Present an **oral report** or plan a **multimedia presentation** about the event.

3 Activity Options

Every **Section Assessment** includes **Activity Options**—short culminating activities for the section. These interdisciplinary activities allow students to demonstrate, in a variety of ways, that they have understood the historical concepts taught in the section.

4 Interactive Primary Sources and Primary Source Explorer

Creating America features 17 of the key primary source documents of American history. Side notes entitled **A Closer Look** rephrase the important ideas of the document and ask students critical thinking questions. Each document is also featured on the **Primary Source Explorer** CD-ROM. The CD-ROM contains numerous activities—including creating multimedia presentations—that invite students to interact with each of the primary sources.

Creating America

Give all students the tools to read and understand history.

Creating America provides built-in aids to help students read and understand history. The program takes a flexible approach to teaching all of the social studies skills, including map reading, interpreting graphs and charts, interpreting political cartoons, and other skills.

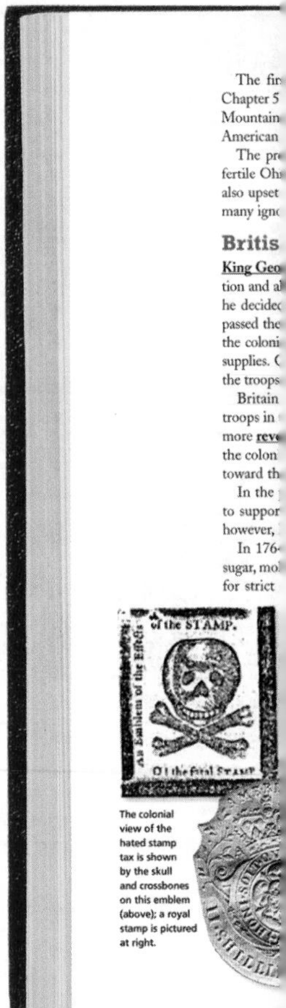

1

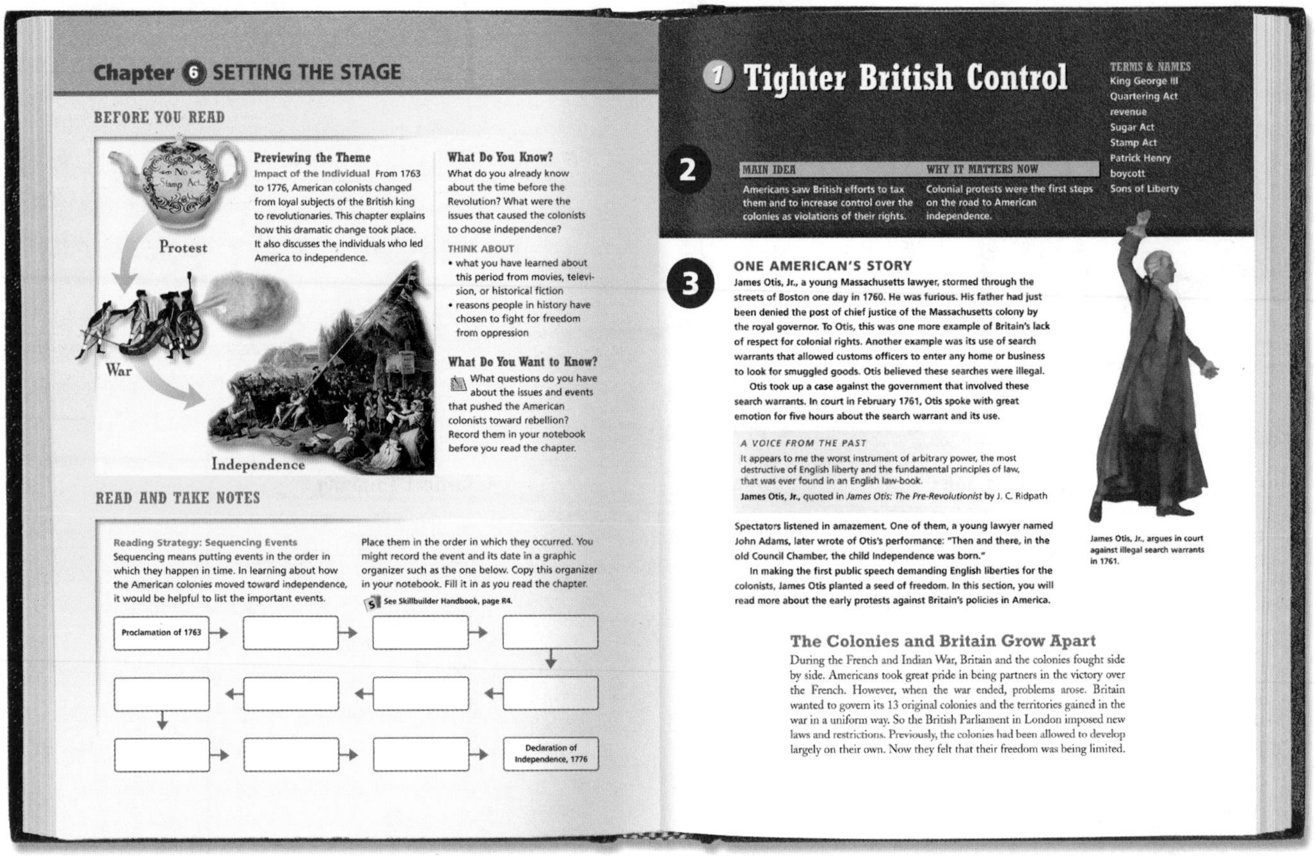

1 Setting the Stage

This page follows Interact with History at the beginning of every chapter. The page features the widely used K-W-L strategy, asking students what they **know** about the historical period, and **what** they would like to know. The Chapter Assessment asks students what they **learned.** The page also teaches students a reading strategy and provides a graphic organizer to help students take notes.

2 Main Idea and Why It Matters Now

By addressing the age-old issue "Why it matters now," students begin to understand that historical events have influenced their own lives. Every section of *Creating America* clearly tells students what the main idea is and why the history of that period matters today.

3 One American's Story and A Voice from the Past

Creating America tells the varied stories of people who helped to create America through the force of their ideas or the heroism of their actions. **One American's Story** begins every section with a story of one of these people. **A Voice from the Past** incorporates primary source material into the narrative of the textbook, giving American history a human voice.

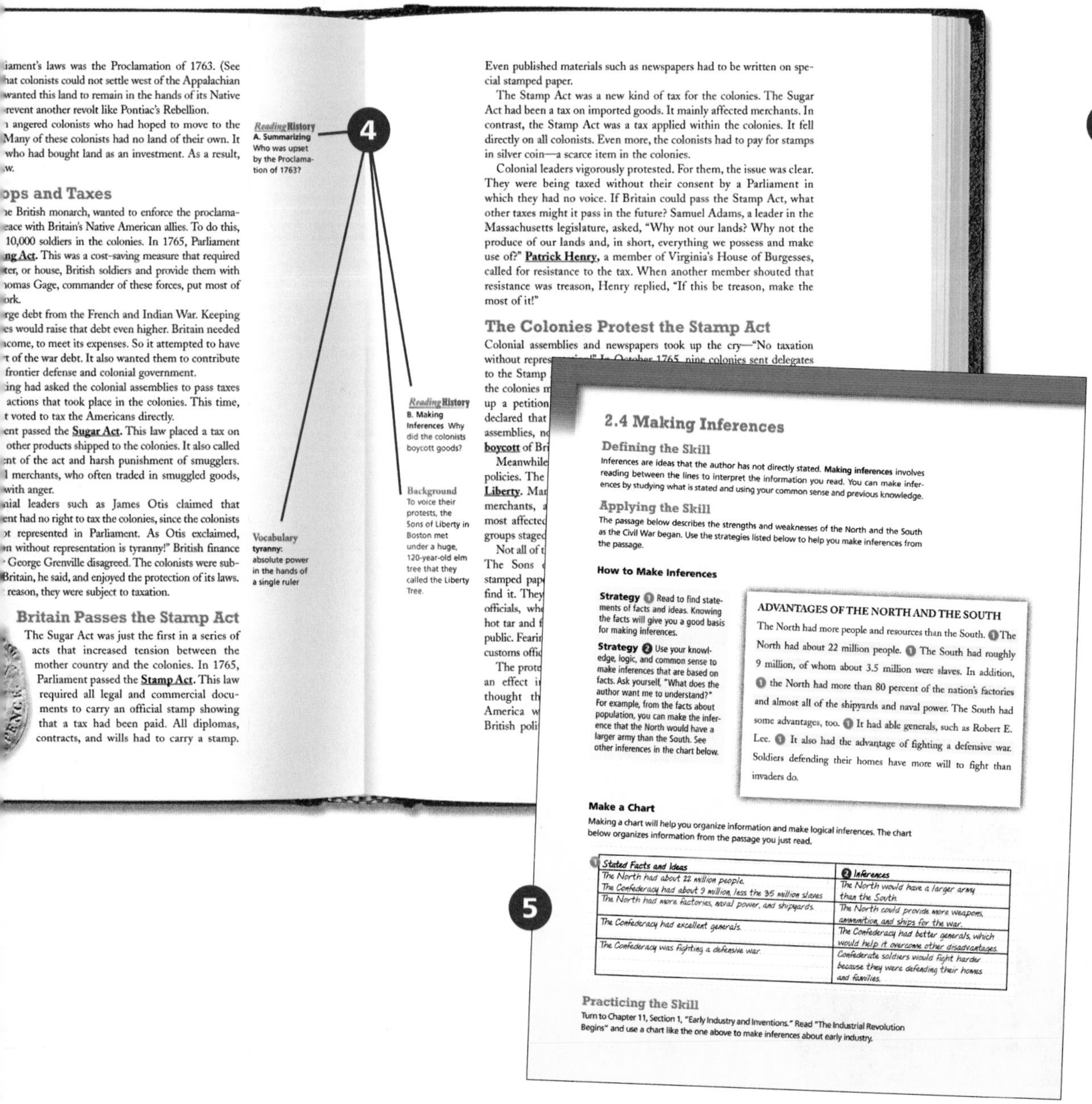

1 Stated Facts and Ideas	2 Inferences
The North had about 22 million people. The Confederacy had about 9 million, less the 3.5 million slaves. The North had more factories, naval power, and shipyards.	The North would have a larger army than the South. The North could provide more weapons, ammunition, and ships for the war.
The Confederacy had excellent generals.	The Confederacy had better generals, which would help it overcome other disadvantages.
The Confederacy was fighting a defensive war.	Confederate soldiers would fight harder because they were defending their homes and families.

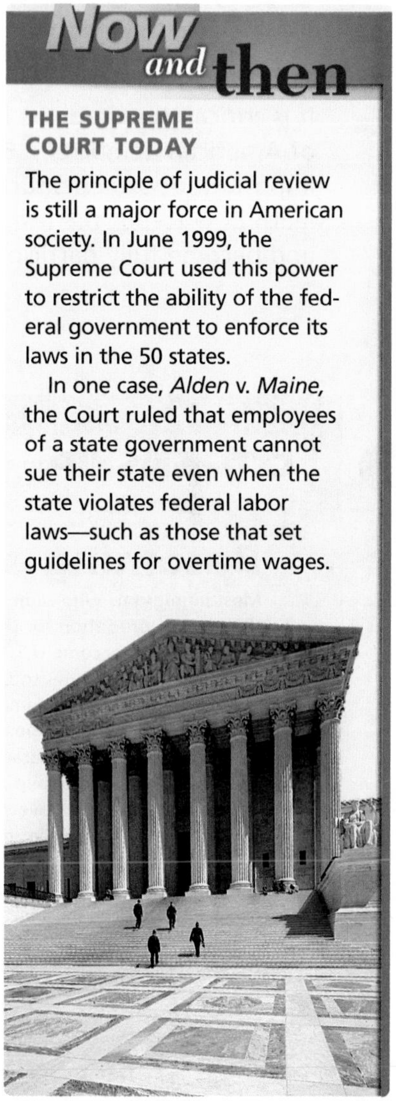

6
Now and then
THE SUPREME COURT TODAY
The principle of judicial review is still a major force in American society. In June 1999, the Supreme Court used this power to restrict the ability of the federal government to enforce its laws in the 50 states.
In one case, Alden v. Maine, the Court ruled that employees of a state government cannot sue their state even when the state violates federal labor laws—such as those that set guidelines for overtime wages.

4 Reading History, Vocabulary, and Background Notes

Creating America provides reading support for students as they read. Side-column notes on every page support student comprehension at point of use. **Reading History** notes ask students comprehension and critical thinking questions. **Vocabulary** notes define important vocabulary words at point of use. **Background** notes provide vital historical information that helps to clarify events for students.

5 Skillbuilder Handbook

To develop their abilities in critical thinking, reading maps, and other social studies skills, students need access to direct and clear explanations of skills. *Creating America* provides this access in its unique **Skillbuilder Handbook,** found in the reference section of the textbook. The handbook teaches students 30 essential social studies skills. References throughout the textbook suggest when students should access the handbook.

6 Now and Then

Students understand history better when they see how it affects their lives today. **Now and Then** connects past events to contemporary issues and events.

Creating America

Inspire students to become active citizens.

It is critical that students learn about the foundations of American democracy. By studying our heritage and important documents such as the Constitution, they will learn how to put the lessons of the past into action today and become fully participating citizens in our democracy.

1

CITIZENSHIP TODAY

Becoming a Citizen

Most immigrants who came to America in the 1800s shared one thing: an appreciation for the nation's values and laws. As a result, many chose to become U.S. citizens.

This trend continues today. In recent decades, more than half a million Vietnamese have immigrated to the United States. Many became citizens of their new country. One of them was Lam Ton, who is a successful restaurant owner in Chicago. Ton viewed U.S. citizenship as both a privilege and a duty. "We have to stick to this country and help it do better," he said.

Each year, immigrants from around the world are sworn in as U.S. citizens on Citizenship Day, September 17. But first they must pass a test on English, the U.S. political system, and the rights and duties of citizenship.

This young immigrant proudly holds up his certificate of citizenship.

How Does Someone Become a Citizen?

1. In a small group, discuss what questions you would ask those seeking to become U.S. citizens.
2. Create a citizenship test using your questions.
3. Have another group take the test and record their scores.
4. Use the McDougal Littell nternet site to link to the actual U.S. citizenship test. Compare it to your test.

See Citizenship Handbook, page 281.

For more about becoming a U.S. citizen . . .

RESEARCH LINKS
CLASSZONE.COM

2

Citizenship HANDBOOK

The Role of the Citizen

Citizens of the United States enjoy many basic rights and freedoms. Freedom of speech and religion are examples. These rights are guaranteed by the Constitution, the Bill of Rights, and other amendments to the Constitution. Along with these rights, however, come responsibilities. Obeying rules and laws, voting, and serving on juries are some examples.

Active citizenship is not limited to adults. Younger citizens can help their communities become better places. The following pages will help you to learn about your rights and responsibilities. Knowing them will help you to become an active and involved citizen of your community, state, and nation.

In this book you will find examples of active citizenship by young people like yourself. **Look for the Citizenship Today features.**

Citizen → KNOW YOUR RIGHTS → BE RESPONSIBLE → STAY INFORMED → MAKE GOOD DECISIONS → PARTICIPATE IN YOUR COMMUNITY → Model Citizen

President John F. Kennedy urged all Americans to become active citizens and work to improve their communities.

The weather was sunny but cold on January 20, 1961—the day that John F. Kennedy became the 35th president of the United States. In his first speech as president, he urged all Americans to serve their country. Since then, Kennedy's words have inspired millions of Americans to become more active citizens.

"Ask not what your country can do for you—ask what you can do for your country!"

—JOHN F. KENNEDY

What Is a Citizen?

A citizen is a legal member of a nation and pledges loyalty to that nation. A citizen has certain guaranteed rights, protections, and responsibilities. A citizen is a member of a community and wants to make it a good place to live.

Today in the United States there are a number of ways to become a citizen. The most familiar are citizenship by birth and citizenship by naturalization. All citizens have the right to equal protection under the law.

1 Citizenship Today

This feature focuses on young Americans who have made a difference in their communities. By reading about the community activities of other young people, students learn about positive role models, and they learn important lessons about being American citizens. A community-based activity concludes each **Citizenship Today** feature.

2 Citizenship Handbook

This special section of the textbook teaches students about their responsibilities as citizens, the role that government plays, and the many ways in which students can get involved in helping their own communities.

3 Constitution Handbook and The Living Constitution

Creating America presents the Constitution in a highly interactive way that is firmly grounded in history yet connects the Constitution to important issues today. The **Constitution Handbook** begins by explaining the seven principles of the Constitution. The Constitution itself is then presented in a highly interactive format, including side-column notes entitled **A Closer Look**. The Constitution is also featured on the **Primary Source Explorer** CD-ROM, with additional resources and activities.

3

Constitution **HANDBOOK**

The Living Constitution

The Framers of the Constitution created a flexible plan for governing the United States far into the future. They also described ways to allow changes in the Constitution. For over 200 years, the Constitution has guided the American people. It remains a "living document." The Constitution still thrives, in part, because it echoes the principles the delegates valued. Each generation of Americans renews the meaning of the Constitution's timeless ideas. These two pages show you some ways in which the Constitution has shaped events in American history. **See Primary Source Explorer**

"In framing a system which we wish to last for ages, we should not lose sight of the changes which ages will produce."

—JAMES MADISON, CONSTITUTIONAL CONVENTION

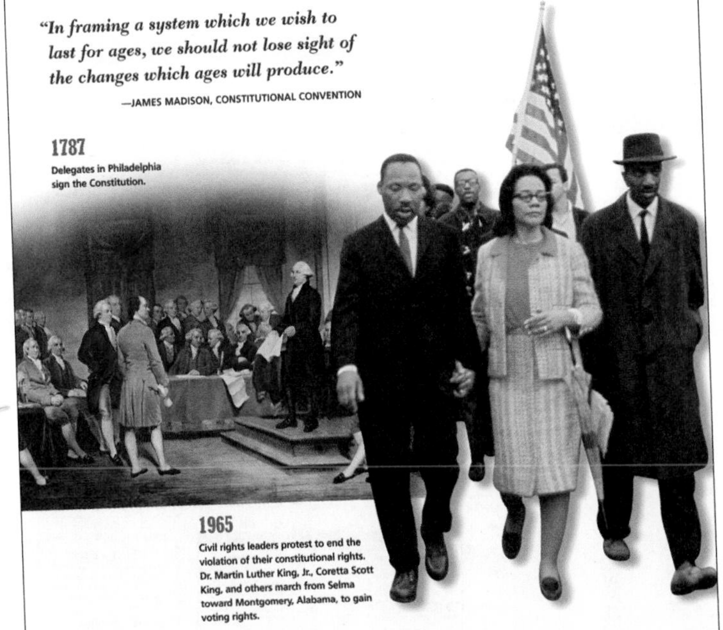

1787

Delegates in Philadelphia sign the Constitution.

1965

Civil rights leaders protest to end the violation of their constitutional rights. Dr. Martin Luther King, Jr., Coretta Scott King, and others march from Selma toward Montgomery, Alabama, to gain voting rights.

4

AMERICA'S **HISTORY MAKERS**

ELIZABETH CADY STANTON

1815–1902

Elizabeth Cady Stanton's first memory was the birth of a sister when she was four. So many people said, "What a pity it is she's a girl!" that Stanton felt sorry for the new baby. She later wrote, "I did not understand at that time that girls were considered an inferior order of beings."

When Stanton was 11, her only brother died. Her father said, "Oh, my daughter, I wish you were a boy!" That sealed Stanton's determination to prove that girls were just as important as boys.

How did Stanton's childhood experiences motivate her to help other people besides herself?

5

HISTORIC DECISIONS *OF THE SUPREME COURT*

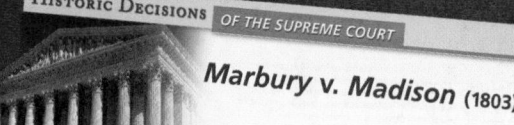

Marbury v. *Madison* (1803)

THE ISSUE **Judicial Review**

ORIGINS OF THE CASE **In 1801, just before he left office, President John Adams appointed dozens of Federalists as judges. Most of these "midnight justices" took their posts before Thomas Jefferson, Adams's Democratic-Republican successor, took office. Jefferson ordered his secretary of state, James Madison, to block the remaining appointees from taking their posts. One of these appointees, William Marbury, asked the Supreme Court to issue an order forcing Madison to recognize the appointments.**

THE RULING **The Court ruled that the law under which Marbury had asked the Supreme Court to act was unconstitutional.**

The Legal Arguments

Chief Justice John Marshall wrote the Court's opinion, stating that Marbury had every right to receive his appointment. Further, Marshall noted, the Judiciary Act of 1789 gave Marbury the right to file his claim directly with the Supreme Court. But Marshall questioned whether the Court had the power to act. The answer, he argued, rested on the kinds of cases that could be argued directly in the Supreme Court without first being heard by a lower court.

Article 3 of the Constitution clearly identified those cases that the Court could hear directly. A case like Marbury's was not one of them. The Judiciary Act, therefore, was at odds with the Constitution. Which one should be upheld? Marshall's response was clear:

> . . . **[T]he particular phraseology of the Constitution of the United States confirms and strengthens the principle . . . that a law repugnant to the Constitution is void; and that *courts* . . . are bound by that instrument.**

Since Section 13 of the Judiciary Act violated the Constitution, Marshall concluded, it could not be enforced. The Court, therefore, could not issue the order. With this decision, Marshall appeared to limit the powers of the Supreme Court. In fact, the decision increased the Court's power because it established the principle of judicial review. This holds that the courts—most notably the Supreme Court—have the power to decide if laws are unconstitutional.

William Marbury received his appointment as a reward for his loyal support of John Adams in the 1800 presidential election.

LEGAL *Sources*

U.S. CONSTITUTION/LEGISLATION

Article 3, Section 2 (1789)
"In all cases affecting ambassadors, other public ministers and consuls, and those in which a state shall be party, the Supreme Court shall have original jurisdiction. In all other cases . . . the Supreme Court shall have appellate jurisdiction."

Judiciary Act, Section 13 (1789)
"The Supreme Court . . . shall have power to issue . . . writs of *mandamus*, in cases warranted by the principles and usages of law."

RELATED CASES

***Fletcher* v. *Peck* (1810)**
For the first time, the Supreme Court ruled a state law unconstitutional.

***Cohens* v. *Virginia* (1821)**
For the first time, the Court overturned a state court decision.

4 America's History Makers

These features focus on Americans who made an impact on American history through their leadership and decision making. A question at the end of each feature challenges students to think about the qualities of citizenship and leadership.

5 Historic Decisions of the Supreme Court

This feature explores nine of the most important Supreme Court decisions in U.S. history. The cases included are:

- *Marbury* v. *Madison*
- *McCulloch* v. *Maryland*
- *Gibbons* v. *Ogden*
- *Dred Scott* v. *Sandford*
- *Plessy* v. *Ferguson*
- *Schenck* v. *United States*
- *Brown* v. *Board of Education*
- *Reynolds* v. *Sims*
- *Regents* v. *Bakke*

Creating America

Make interdisciplinary connections.

Students see history as more relevant when they see how it connects to other subjects they are studying. *Creating America* makes numerous interdisciplinary connections through activities and features that show how history relates to literature, art, science, mathematics, and other subjects.

2

1

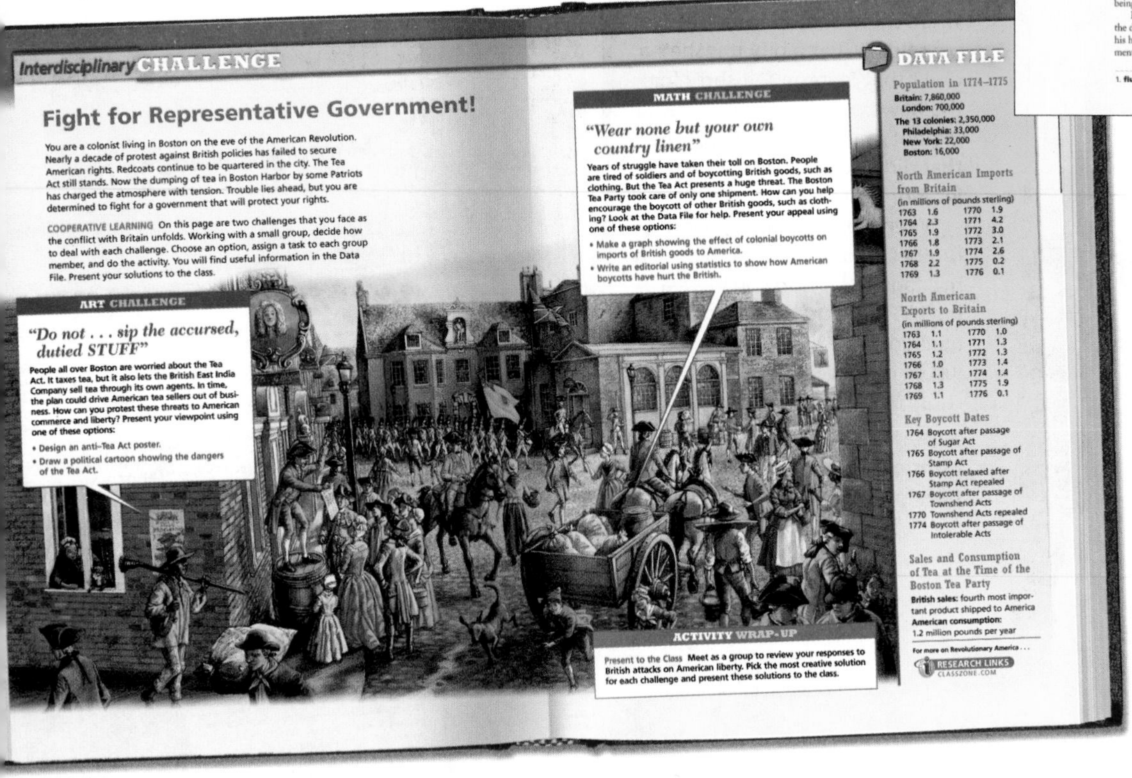

3

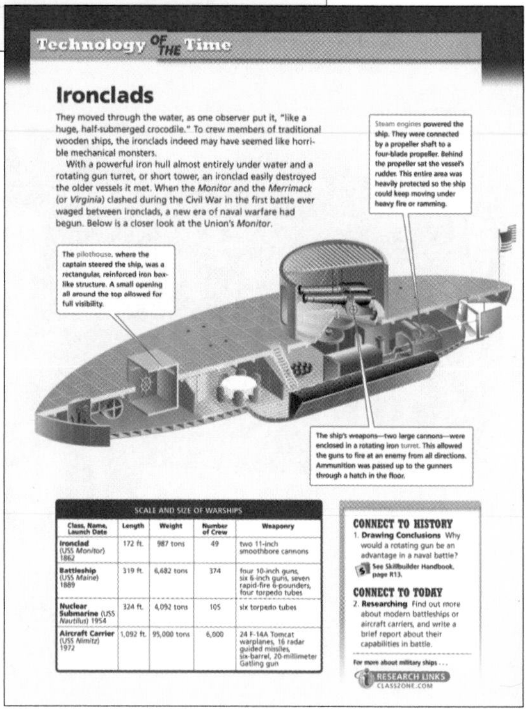

1 Interdisciplinary Challenge

These interactive features place students into historical situations and challenge them to solve problems by making connections to other disciplines. Every **Interdisciplinary Challenge** includes a **Data File** of historical information that students use in solving the problems.

2 Literature Connections

To emphasize the drama and human dimension of history, *Creating America* presents excerpts from important historical literature, showing how history has been presented in fiction. All excerpts are from the **Literature Connections** series of books from McDougal Littell.

3 Technology of the Time

Students see the critical role that science and technology have played in American history in this highly visual feature. Each feature concludes with **Connect to History** and **Connect to Today,** providing opportunities for critical thinking and research. Links on McDougal Littell's Web site (classzone.com) give students access to information on the Internet.

Map a course through history.

The numerous colorful maps in *Creating America* help students build their skills in geography and see its important connection to history.

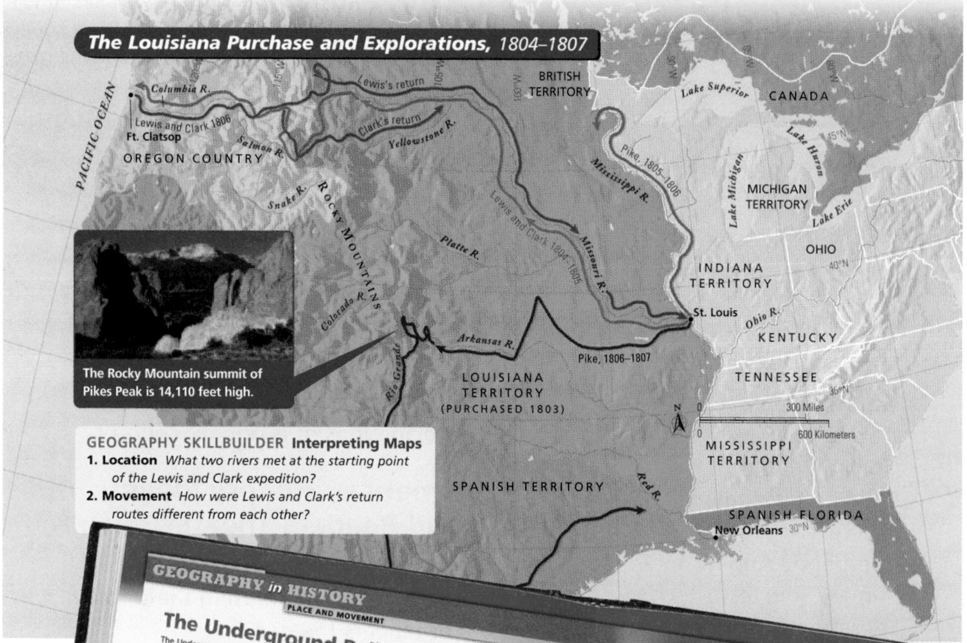

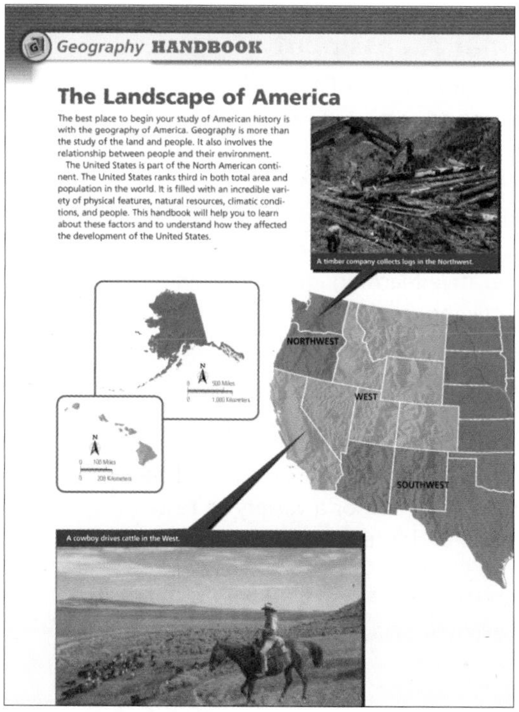

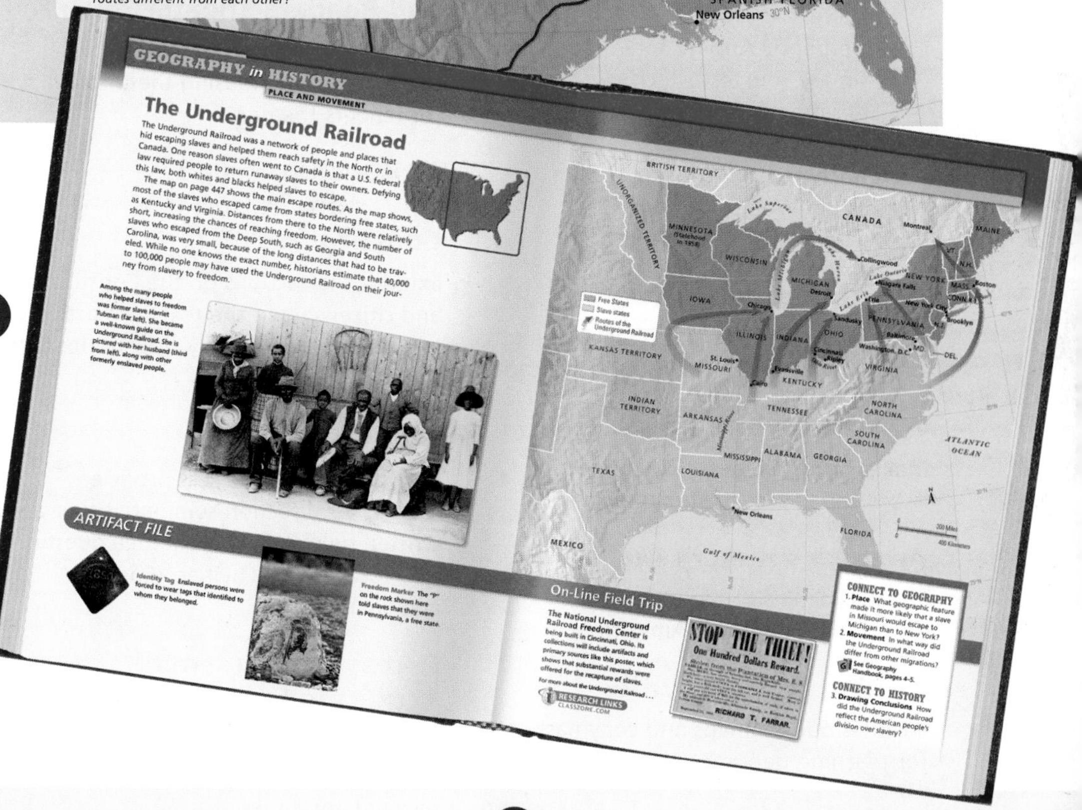

1 The Geography Handbook

This handbook at the beginning of *Creating America* teaches students the basics of map reading and gives them an overview of the physical geography and human geography of the United States.

2 Realistic Maps

The maps in *Creating America* have been created with the latest technology, resulting in maps that are realistic and three-dimensional in appearance.

3 Geography in History

These features show dramatically how geography has played a major role in key events in American history. Each of these features includes an **Artifact File** with an **Online Field Trip** to a local or regional museum.

Creating America

Teacher's Resource Package

Creating America offers a wide variety of resources to help teachers manage their classroom and support students as they interact with history. The complete range of options will help teachers meet the needs of all the students in the classroom.

In-Depth Resources

- Setting the Stage
- Tracing Themes
- Guided Reading
- Building Vocabulary
- SkillBuilder Practice
- Geography Applications
- Primary Sources
- Literature Selections
- Reteaching Activities
- Enrichment Activities
- History Workshop Resources
- Answer Key

Interdisciplinary Projects

Includes projects for language arts, math, science, art, music, and physical education

Why It Matters Now

Makes history relevant by connecting issues and events to students' lives

America's History Makers

Provides extensive biographies of historically significant Americans

Outline Map Activities

Includes outline maps and copymasters for teaching geography skills

Economics in History

Features worksheets with in-depth explanations of economic concepts

American History Plays and Readers Theater

Includes plays based on key historical events and tips on using the textbook for readers theater

Citizenship Today: Government and the Constitution

Extends the sections on the Constitution and citizenship in the text with activities in which students apply citizenship skills

Reading Study Guide Workbook

Provides support for less-proficient readers with section summaries that are written below level, main idea questions, and vocabulary activities. (English and Spanish)

Access for Students Acquiring English: Spanish Translations

Contains Spanish translations of selected ancillaries

Presidential Elections Handbook

Includes supplementary information on each presidential election

Formal Assessment

Offers three levels of tests for each chapter and section quizzes

Integrated Assessment

Provides explanations and forms for a variety of assessment options, including cooperative learning, group discussion, role-playing, oral presentations, peer assessment, self-assessment, and portfolio assessment

Strategies for Test Preparation

Contains strategies and exercises to help prepare students for a variety of test-taking experiences

Strategies for Test Preparation Teacher's Manual

Planning for Block Schedules

Includes a pacing guide, chapter teaching models, organization charts, and suggestions for addressing multiple learning styles

Library of Professional Resources

- Cooperative Learning and Conflict Resolution Skills
- Teaching for Inclusion
- Building Reading and Writing Skills

Writing Research Reports for Social Studies

Provides extra content-area writing support for students

Team Teaching: Connecting History and Literature

Provides teachers with options for integrating McDougal Littell's *Literature Connections* and *The Language of Literature* into their history lessons

Document-Based Questions Strategies and Practice: Middle School

Provides a set of document-based, constructed-response, and multiple-choice questions for each chapter allowing students to practice test-taking strategies

Modified Lesson Plans for English Learners

Includes tips for teachers on adapting lessons and activities for English Learners

Multi-Language Glossary of Social Studies Terms

Includes key terms from the text and other commonly-used social studies terms defined in English with Spanish, Cambodian, Vietnamese, Hmong, Cantonese, Portuguese, Russian, Arabic, and Haitian Creole translations

Additional Resources

Humanities Transparencies

Integrates fine art, artifacts, photographs, and political cartoons into the lessons

Geography Transparencies

Includes map transparencies for teaching geography skills

Critical Thinking Transparencies

Builds students' critical thinking skills through graphic organizers, cause-and-effect charts, and visual summaries

Test Practice Transparencies

Includes one transparency for each section of the textbook that reviews the content and familiarizes students with a variety of testing items

5-Minute Warm-up Transparencies

Features quick, motivating activities to begin the class

Creating America Workbook

Features note-taking strategies and graphic organizers for enhancing reading comprehension

Reading Toolkit for Social Studies

Offers a collection of reading support resources that includes graphic organizers, vocabulary practice and support, plus Skillbuilder transparencies

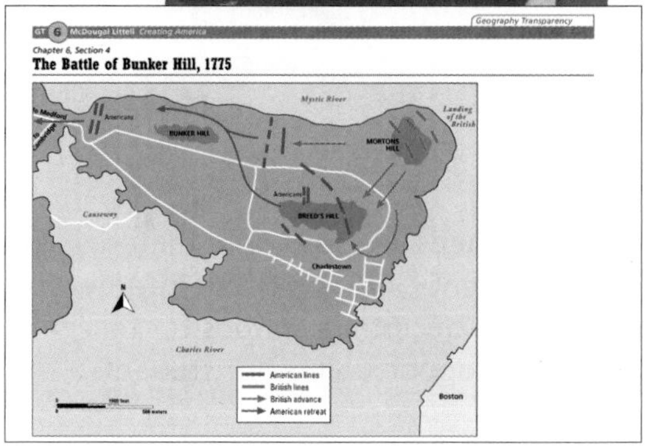

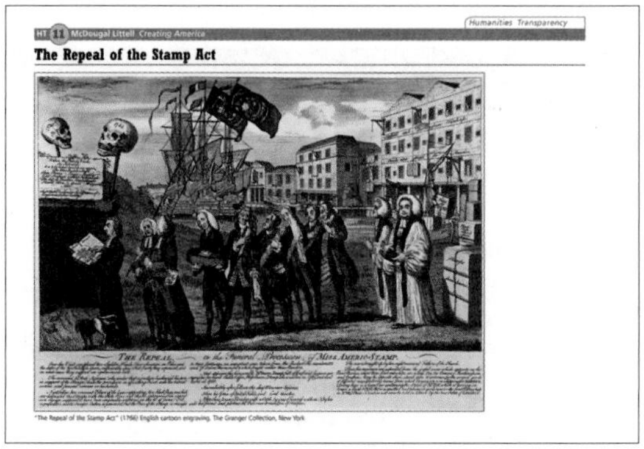

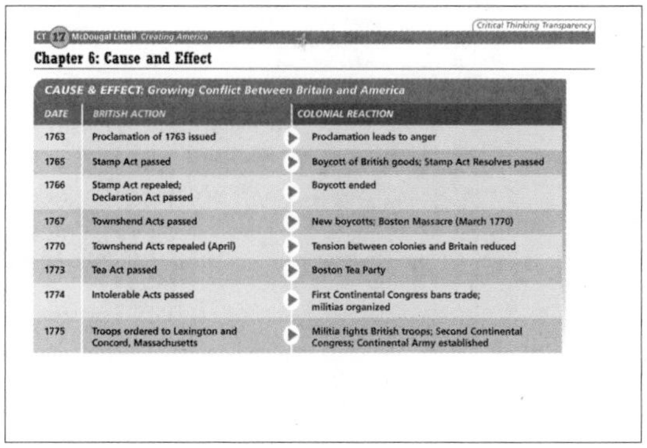
Critical Thinking Transparency

CT 17 McDougal Littell *Creating America*

Chapter 6: Cause and Effect

CAUSE & EFFECT: Growing Conflict Between Britain and America

DATE	BRITISH ACTION	COLONIAL REACTION
1763	Proclamation of 1763 issued	Proclamation leads to anger
1765	Stamp Act passed	Boycott of British goods; Stamp Act Resolves passed
1766	Stamp Act repealed; Declaration Act passed	Boycott ended
1767	Townshend Acts passed	New boycotts; Boston Massacre (March 1770)
1770	Townshend Acts repealed (April)	Tension between colonies and Britain reduced
1773	Tea Act passed	Boston Tea Party
1774	Intolerable Acts passed	First Continental Congress bans trade; militias organized
1775	Troops ordered to Lexington and Concord, Massachusetts	Militia fights British troops; Second Continental Congress; Continental Army established

Assessment Planning and Preparation

Comprehensive assessment materials in print, transparency, CD-ROM, and Internet formats offer a variety of testing options for teachers and test practice opportunities for students.

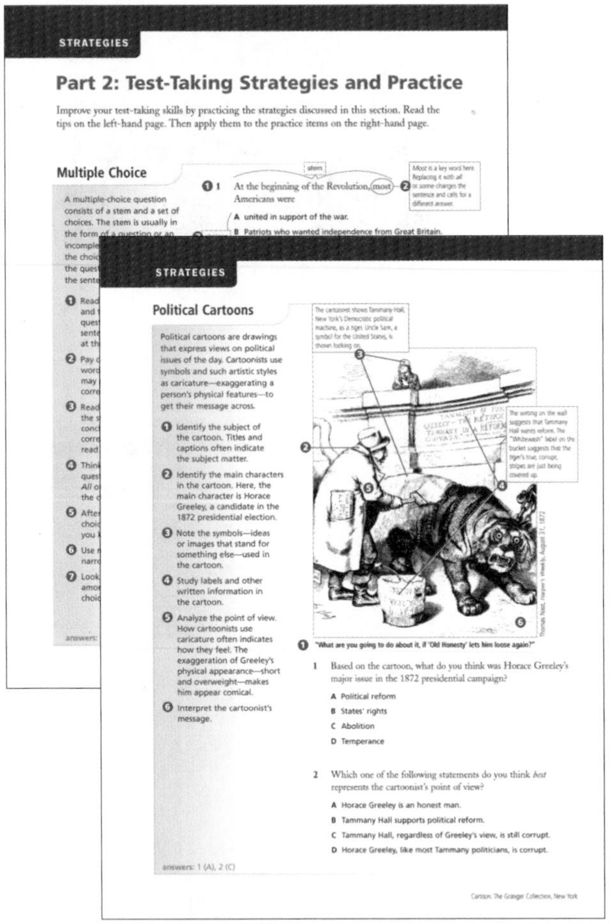
STRATEGIES

Part 2: Test-Taking Strategies and Practice

Improve your test-taking skills by practicing the strategies discussed in this section. Read the tips on the left-hand page. Then apply them to the practice items on the right-hand page.

Multiple Choice

A multiple-choice question consists of a stem and a set of choices. The stem is usually in the form of a question or an

1 At the beginning of the Revolution, most Americans were

stem

Most is a key word here. Replacing it with all or some changes the sentence and calls for a different answer.

A united in support of the war.

B Patriots who wanted independence from Great Britain.

STRATEGIES

Political Cartoons

Political cartoons are drawings that express views on political issues of the day. Cartoonists use symbols and such artistic styles as caricature—exaggerating a person's physical features—to get their message across.

1. Identify the subject of the cartoon. Titles and captions often indicate the subject matter.
2. Identify the main characters in the cartoon. Here, the main character is Horace Greeley, a candidate in the 1872 presidential election.
3. Note the symbols—ideas or images that stand for something else—used in the cartoon.
4. Study labels and other written information in the cartoon.
5. Analyze the point of view. How cartoonists use caricature often indicates how they feel. The exaggeration of Greeley's physical appearance—short and overweight—makes him appear comical.
6. Interpret the cartoonist's message.

The cartoonist shows Tammany Hall, New York's Democratic political machine, as a tiger. Uncle Sam, a symbol for the United States, is shown looking on.

The writing on the wall suggests that Tammany Hall wants reform. The "Whitewash" label on the bucket suggests that the tiger's true, corrupt, stripes are just being covered up.

Thomas Nast, Harper's Weekly, August 31, 1872

"What are you going to do about it, if 'Old Honesty' lets him loose again?"

1 Based on the cartoon, what do you think was Horace Greeley's major issue in the 1872 presidential campaign?

A Political reform
B States' rights
C Abolition
D Temperance

2 Which one of the following statements do you think *best* represents the cartoonist's point of view?

A Horace Greeley is an honest man.
B Tammany Hall supports political reform.
C Tammany Hall, regardless of Greeley's view, is still corrupt.
D Horace Greeley, like most Tammany politicians, is corrupt.

answers: 1 (A), 2 (C)

Cartoon: The Granger Collection, New York

Strategies for Taking Standardized Tests

This innovative section of the *Pupil's Edition* includes strategies for answering multiple-choice, constructed-response, extended-response, and document-based questions, and guidelines for analyzing primary and secondary sources. Each strategy is followed by a set of practice items.

Strategies for Test Preparation

The strategies and exercises in this booklet help prepare students for a variety of test-taking experiences.

Test Practice Transparencies

This booklet provides one transparency for each section of the textbook that covers the content and familiarizes students with a variety of testing items.

Formal Assessment

The formal assessment booklet provides section quizzes and three levels of tests for each chapter.

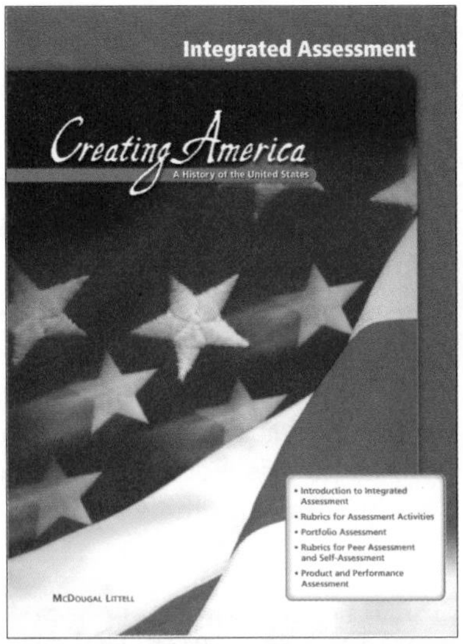

Integrated Assessment

This booklet includes rubrics for evaluating alternative assessments, including portfolios, cooperative learning activities, group discussions, and presentations.

Document-Based Questions Strategies and Practice: Middle School

This set of document-based, constructed-response, and multiple-choice questions provides students with practice and test-taking strategies for each chapter.

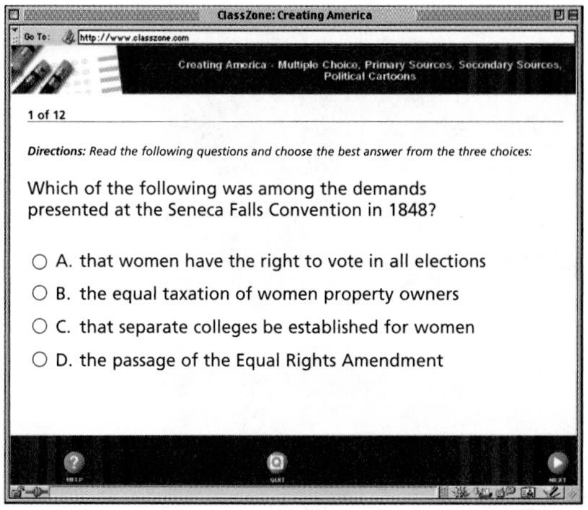

Online Test Preparation

This online, student test practice feature can be accessed through the *ClassZone* Web site. The test practice includes test-taking tips, diagnostic tests, skill-based tutorials, and skills and strategies help.

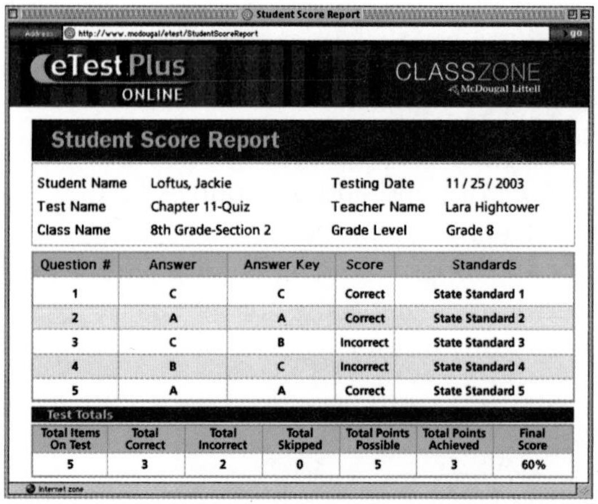

eTest Plus Online

This customizable assessment tool allows teachers to publish tests from the *Test Generator*. Students take the tests online, with results graded automatically. Individual and group score reports can be viewed, printed, and correlated to national and state standards.

Test Generator CD-ROM

This CD-ROM contains a variety of pre-made tests and a test bank of items for creating customized tests. Questions are provided in three levels: basic, average, and advanced. Tools walk the user through the searching and editing steps and help teachers correlate tests to national and state standards. Form A is available in Spanish.

English Learner Support

These print and audio resources focus on reading comprehension and offer specific support to help English learners better understand the content as they study history.

Reading Study Guide Workbook

This workbook contains chapter summaries and reading comprehension questions written at the 6–7 grade level. (English and Spanish)

Reading Study Guide Audio CDs

These audio versions of below grade-level section summaries support struggling readers. (English and Spanish).

Modified Lesson Plans for English Learners

This lesson plan booklet includes tips for teachers on adapting lessons and activities for English learners.

Access for Students Acquiring English: Spanish Translations

This English learner support book offers strategies for teaching EL students and Spanish translations of selected ancillaries.

Multi-Language Glossary of Social Studies Terms

This glossary contains key terms from the text and other commonly-used social studies terms defined in English with Spanish, Cambodian, Vietnamese, Hmong, Cantonese, Portuguese, Russian, Arabic, and Haitian Creole translations.

Reading Toolkit for Social Studies

This collection of resources provides reading support for the social studies classroom. Included are graphic organizers, vocabulary practice and support, plus Skillbuilder transparencies.

INSTRUCT: OBJECTIVE 3

The Midnight Ride

- What was the role of spies in the pre-revolutionary period?
- Why did Britain's General Gage send troops to Lexington and Concord?
- What was the mission of the midnight riders?

In-Depth Resources: Unit 2
- Literature Selection: "Paul Revere's Ride," pp. 14–17

MORE ABOUT . . .

A Revolutionary Spy
One of the most shocking spy cases of the Revolutionary period involved Dr. Benjamin Church, the colonial army's surgeon general. Church was a member of the inner circle of patriot leaders—and a British agent. Church's spying days ended after a coded message ended up in the hands of colonial leaders. This particular memo described the strength and movement of colonial troops. After serving some time in prison, Church was released due to ill health and allowed to sail to the West Indies. His ship sank during the trip, and he was lost at sea.

HISTORY FROM VISUALS

Reading the Map Point out to students the number of riders, as well as the routes each one took. Ask them who appeared to take the longest route to Lexington. **Answer** William Dawes

Extension Have students imagine they are a midnight rider, and ask them to write a brief diary entry about their ride.

Most colonial leaders believed that any fight with Britain would be short. They thought that a show of force would make Britain change its policies. Few expected a war. One who did was Patrick Henry.

A VOICE FROM THE PAST

Gentlemen may cry peace, peace—but there is no peace. The war is actually begun! The next gale that sweeps from the north will bring to our ears the clash of resounding arms! Our brethren are already in the field! Why should we idle here? . . . I know not what course others may take. But as for me, give me liberty or give me death.

Patrick Henry, quoted in *Patriots* by A. J. Langguth

Henry delivered what became his most famous speech in the Virginia House of Burgesses in March 1775.

3 The Midnight Ride

Meanwhile, spies were busy on both sides. Sam Adams had built a spy network to keep watch over British activities. The British had their spies too. They were Americans who were loyal to Britain. From them, General Gage learned that the Massachusetts militia was storing arms and ammunition in Concord, about 20 miles northwest of Boston. He also heard that Sam Adams and John Hancock were in Lexington. On the night of April 18, 1775, Gage ordered his troops to arrest Adams and Hancock in Lexington and to destroy the supplies in Concord.

The Sons of Liberty had prepared for this moment. **Paul Revere,** a Boston silversmith, and a second messenger, William Dawes, were charged with spreading the news about British troop movements. Revere had arranged a system of signals to alert colonists in Charlestown, on the shore opposite Boston. If one lantern burned in the Old North Church steeple, the British troops were coming by land; if two, they were coming by water. Revere would go across the water from Boston to Charlestown and ride to Lexington and Concord from there. Dawes would take the land route.

Reading History
B. Recognizing Effects What effect might spying have had on the people of Boston?
B. Possible Answer It might have turned them against one another.

Background
The signals were a backup system in case Revere was captured.

Skillbuilder Answers
1. Lexington and Concord
2. About six miles

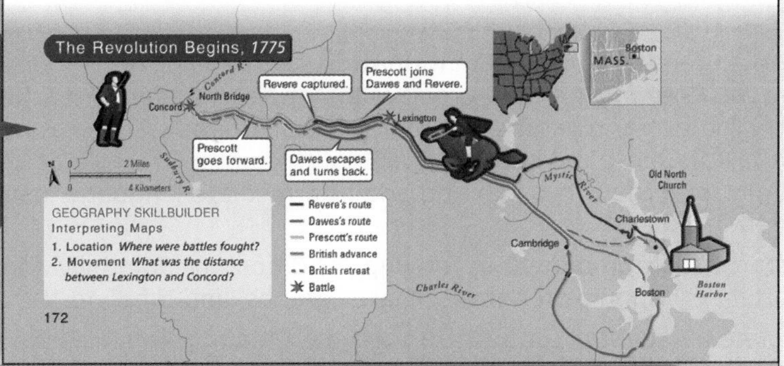

GEOGRAPHY SKILLBUILDER
Interpreting Maps
1. Location *Where were battles fought?*
2. Movement *What was the distance between Lexington and Concord?*

172

ACTIVITY OPTIONS

INDIVIDUAL NEEDS

STUDENTS ACQUIRING ENGLISH/ESL

Social Studies Vocabulary To help students understand the many social studies concept vocabulary words in this section, have the students add the following list to their personal dictionaries: *militia, musket, intolerable, committees, correspondence, continental, congress, delegate, boycott, repeal.*

Next have students look up the words in a dictionary. Help them understand each word by discussing its meaning and use. Then have them write a definition of the term in their own words in their personal dictionaries.

Have the students find the words in a sentence in the text. (The words listed are in order according to appearance.) Ask them to read the sentence aloud and explain what the sentence means. Finally, have the students write a sentence using the term.

Differentiated Instruction

Every chapter provides teaching suggestions, practice, and activities that specifically address the needs of English learners.

Teaching English Learners

Nancy Siddens
Consulting Editor,
English for Speakers of Other Languages,
McDougal Littell

McDougal Littell recognizes the challenges that English learners and their teachers face in the mainstream classroom. The trend to use English instruction in content classes (with less support in students' primary languages) and the federal legislation (No Child Left Behind) requiring instruction in content simultaneously with instruction in English, have driven the need for comprehensive, flexible support materials for teaching in English to English learners.

McDougal Littell's ***Creating America*** provides a wide range of support for these students and their teachers. This support gives teachers the tools needed to employ research-based principles for teaching standards-based curriculum to English learners while they learn the English language in meaningful historical contexts.

Research on facilitating the learning of content by students acquiring English has determined that effective instruction is built on these three principles:

- **Increase comprehension**
- **Enhance student interaction**
- **Improve thinking and study skills**

These principles, identified as effective through research by the Center for Applied Linguistics (Jameson), have guided McDougal Littell's approach to developing materials for teaching social studies and language to English learners.

Principle 1: Increase comprehension

Providing understandable information to the English learner is crucial for accessing both language and content. ***Creating America*** provides materials that enable teachers to employ practical strategies for increasing student comprehension. Verbal as well as nonverbal support is provided to make history more accessible to the English learner. The role of visual and experiential clues is especially important to beginning and intermediate language learners. Examples of nonverbal instruction include:

- A strong visual component in the Pupil's Edition, including vivid images, large maps, a variety of graphic organizers, charts, graphs, and timelines
- Complete audiovisual support through the ***Creating America*** video series, audio chapter summaries, and extensive online services
- A transparency program that includes *Geography Transparencies, Critical Thinking Transparencies,* and *Humanities Transparencies*

Examples of verbal and print support include:

- The *Reading Study Guide* in both English and Spanish, chapter summaries written below grade level accompanied by comprehension questions
- The *Multi-Language Glossary of Social Studies Terms,* a compilation of translations of the key terms from the Pupil's Edition in nine languages
- *Access for Students Acquiring English: Spanish Translations,* Spanish translations of selected ancillary support pages

Principle 2: Enhance student interaction

Research shows that language is learned through communication with others—negotiating meaning to accomplish real purposes (Long and Porter). Participants in a discussion restate, question, explain, and clarify in order to come to a common understanding. This process helps students learn social studies as well as language. ***Creating America***—and *Modified Lesson Plans* *for English Learners*, which accompanies it—provide opportunities to increase interaction in the classroom in a variety of ways, including:

- Pair activities, in which students work in pairs to compare their own experiences relating to a particular lesson or topic
- Group work such as "jigsaw" reading, in which each student takes on responsibility for presenting one part of a lesson to a small group
- Class activities such as debates, unit projects, or games
- Opportunities for family involvement

Principle 3: Improve thinking and study skills

Explicit teaching of academic skills helps develop thinking skills and "thinking language" for English learners (Chamot and O'Malley). ***Creating America*** provides materials that focus instruction on performing higher-order thinking tasks, asking critical-thinking questions, assessing learning in a manner and language consistent with instruction, and reinforcing study and test-taking skills.

In the Pupil's Edition of ***Creating America***, support for developing thinking and study skills includes:

- An emphasis on the main idea of each section before reading begins
- Graphic organizers for notetaking practice in each section
- Highlighted vocabulary terms
- Main Idea comprehension questions that reinforce important content
- Skillbuilder questions accompanying large visuals such as maps and charts
- Section and chapter assessments that provide leveled questions from Main Idea to Critical Thinking
- A skills strand woven throughout the section and chapter assessments and reinforced in the Skillbuilder Handbook
- Test practice opportunities such as the 32-page "Strategies for Taking Standardized Tests" in the front of the book and Standards-Based Assessment practice in the chapter assessments

The Teacher's Edition and ancillaries for ***Creating America*** provide additional support for developing students' skills through activities for differentiated instruction and Guided Reading and Skillbuilder Practice pages.

Creating America provides teachers with the comprehensive support they need for teaching English learners. The program provides verbal and nonverbal support to increase understanding, promotes increased interaction and opportunities for communication, and encourages the development of academic thinking and study skills. Each of these areas has been identified, through research, as crucial for promoting the success of the English learner in acquiring content knowledge as well as language.

For more information:

Chamot, A.U. and O'Malley, J.M. (1994). The CALLA Handbook: Implementing the Cognitive Academic Language Learning Approach. Addison-Wesley: Reading, MA.

Jameson, J. (1998). Three Principles for Success: English Language Learners in Mainstream Content Classes, From Theory to Practice 6, Center for Applied Linguistics: Region XIV Comprehensive Center.

Long, M. and Porter, P.A. (1985). Group Work, Interlanguage Talk, and Second Language Acquisition, in TESOL Quarterly 19: 207–227.

Integrated Technology

Creating America enables you to enrich and expand students' understanding by offering a wide array of technology, from CD-ROMs to the Internet.

CD-ROM Resources

Primary Source Explorer CD-ROM
This program helps students explore the impact of significant historical documents and create multimedia presentations. Resources include background information, full-motion video, audio, photos, art, and newspaper articles.

eEdition CD-ROM
The electronic version of the textbook allows students and teachers to access all the same features of the printed text plus interactive maps, infographics, and links to *ClassZone.*

Power Presentations CD-ROM
This multimedia presentation tool augments teachers' lectures and provides resources for students to create presentations. Detailed, multimedia lecture notes are enhanced by a gallery of photographs, maps, art, charts, and graphs.

EasyPlanner CD-ROM
This CD-ROM contains all of the teacher resources in the print ancillaries. Teachers can view, search, and print ancillaries organized by resource and chapter.

Test Generator CD-ROM
Pre-made, customizable tests with three levels of questions, including document-based questions, are correlated to national and state standards. Form A is available in Spanish. The *Test Generator* interfaces with *eTest Plus Online.*

GeoQuest: Interactive Maps for U.S. History CD-ROM
Thirty interactive geographic and historic maps engage students while reinforcing geography skills.

Audio Resources

Reading Study Guide Audio CDs
Below grade-level section summaries on audio CD support struggling readers. Available in English and Spanish.

America's Music Audio CD
Songs from American history enhance students' study of their cultural heritage.

Video Resources

***Creating America* Video Series**
This eight-part video series explores the growth and development of the United States. The 10–15 minute videos include a teacher's guide with suggestions for lessons and activities.

- *How the USA Grew: From 13 Colonies to 50 States*
- *Lewis and Clark Go West*
- *Rosa Parks and The Civil Rights Movement*
- *Harriet Tubman*
- *Creating the Federal Government*
- *The Legislative Branch*
- *The Executive Branch*
- *The Judicial Branch*

CLASSZONE.COM

The online guide to *Creating America*

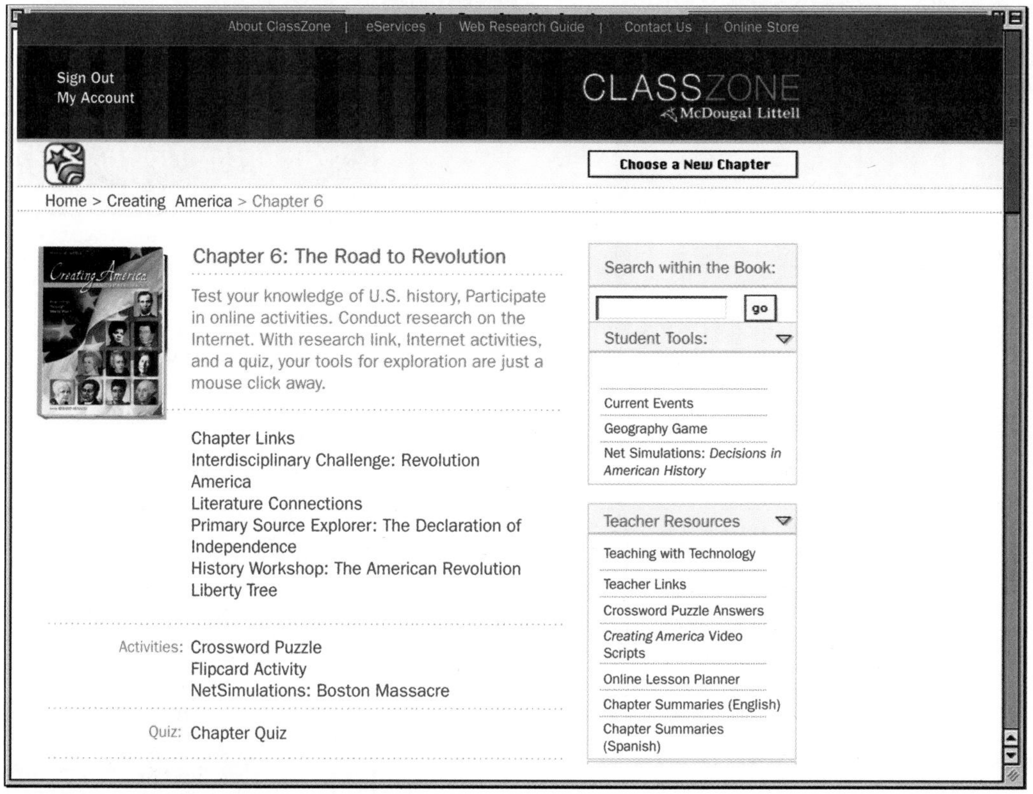

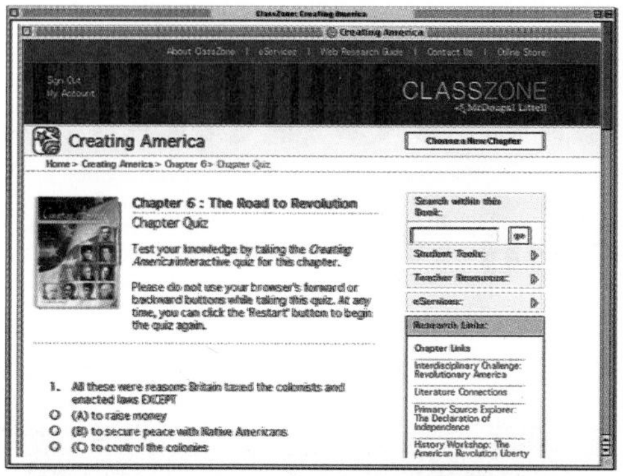

Quizzes
Check students' history knowledge with interactive quizzes.

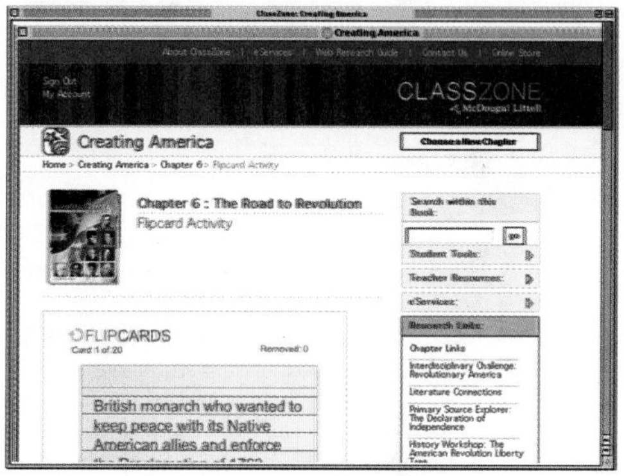

Activities
Encourage student interactivity through online games and activities.

Current Events
Create real-world connections with links to current events.

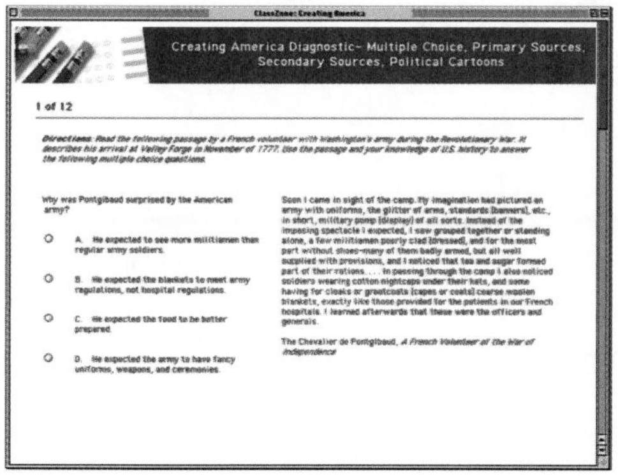

Test Practice
Support students with test-taking tips and skill-based tutorials.

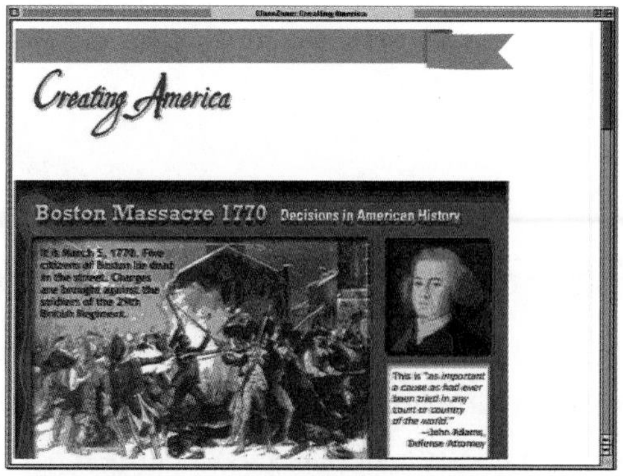

Simulations
Help students relate to history through engaging simulations of key events.

McDougal Littell eServices

Plan it

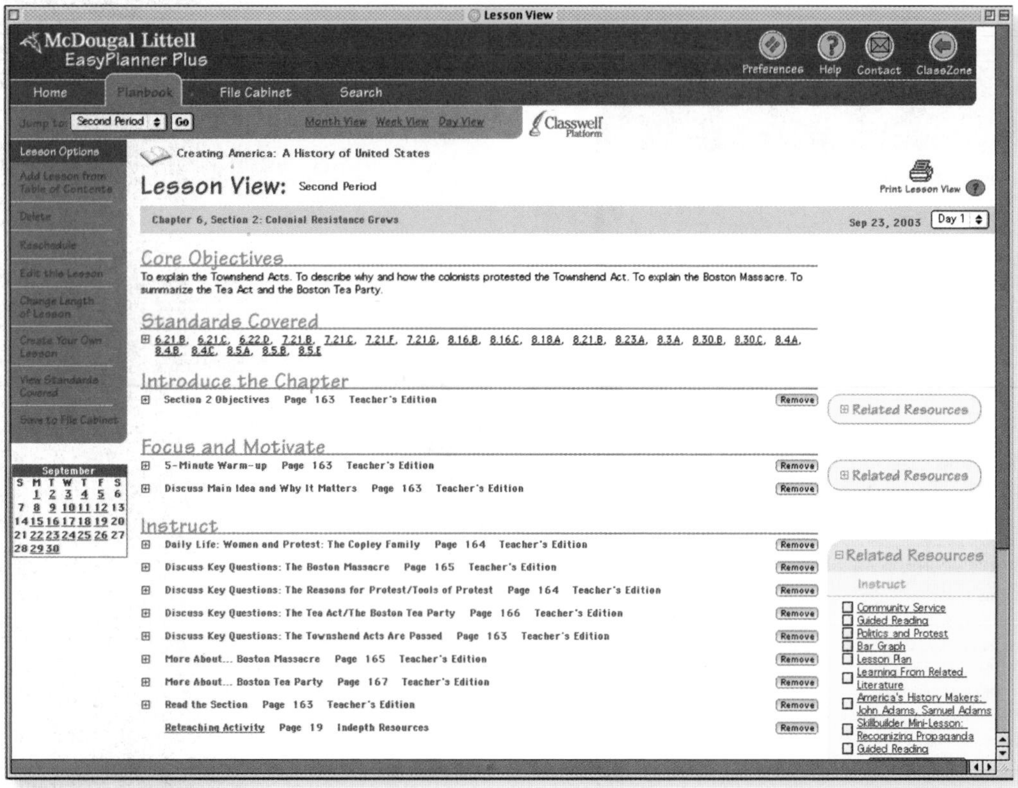

easyPlanner Plus
ONLINE

Teach it

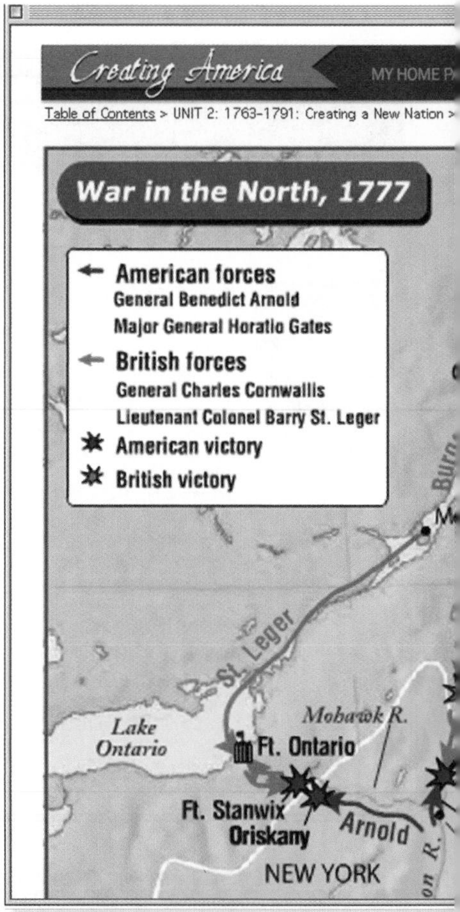

EasyPlanner Plus Online

Lesson Planning When and Where You Want It

- Customize lesson plans using all teacher resources.
- Plan a lesson, or plan the whole year.
- Access, view, and print all teacher resources.
- Print plans in daily, weekly, or monthly views.
- Track state standards correlated to each lesson.

eEdition Plus Online

A Textbook for the Internet Generati

- Access interactive textbook online.
- View animated maps and infographics.
- Take notes onscreen.
- Send and receive e-mail to build student-teacher communication.
- Post worksheets and assignments right to the student book.

Assess it

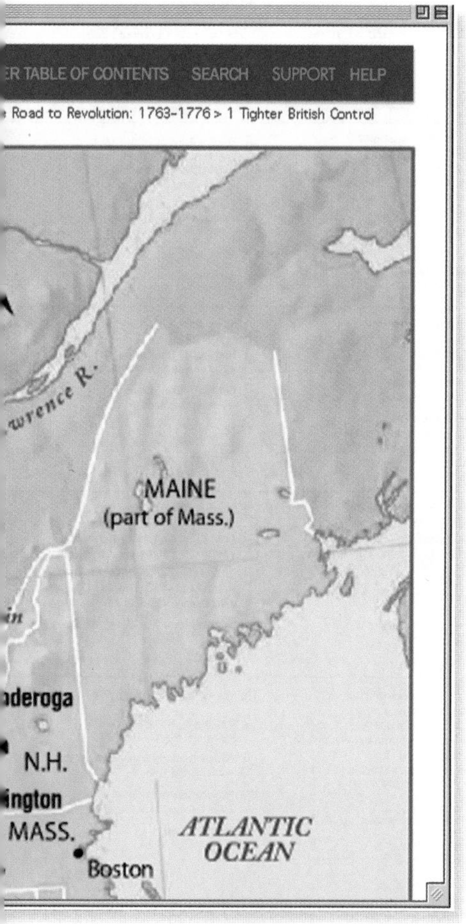

eEdition Plus ONLINE

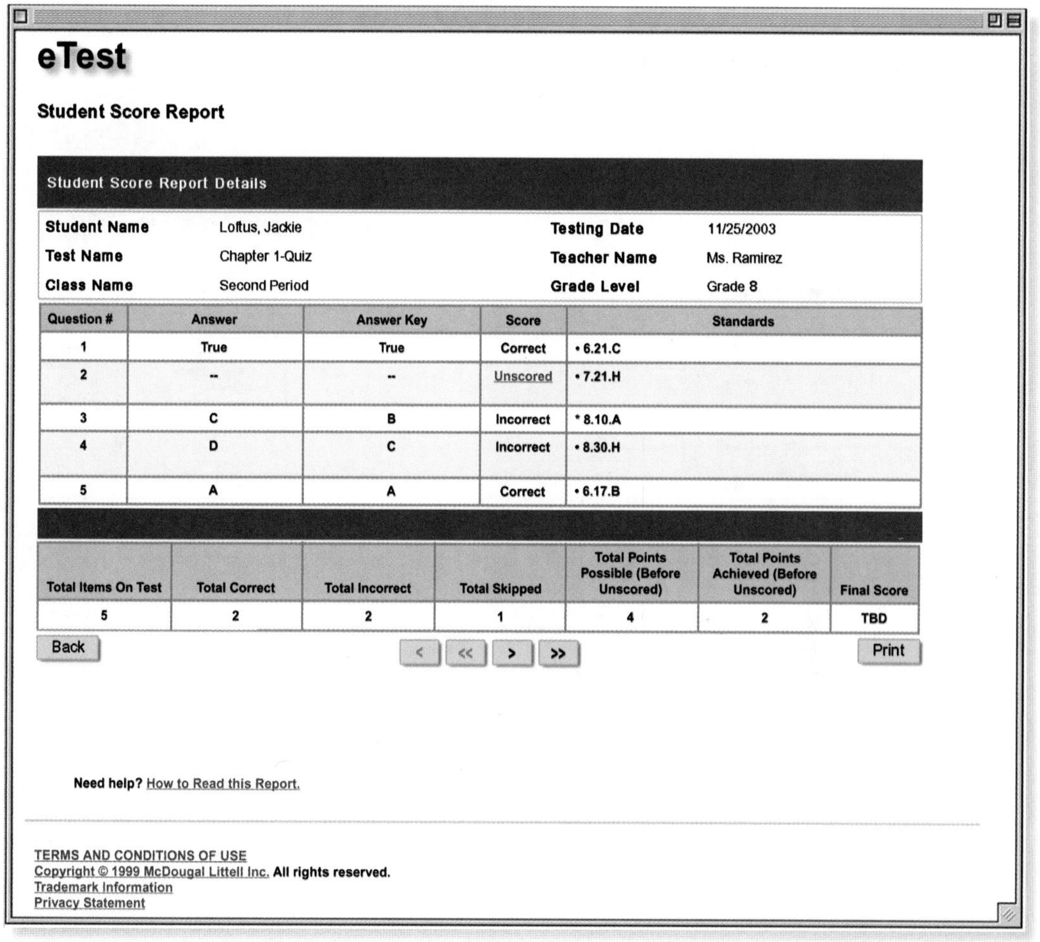

eTest

Student Score Report

Student Score Report Details

Student Name	Loftus, Jackie	**Testing Date**	11/25/2003
Test Name	Chapter 1-Quiz	**Teacher Name**	Ms. Ramirez
Class Name	Second Period	**Grade Level**	Grade 8

Question #	Answer	Answer Key	Score	Standards
1	True	True	Correct	• 6.21.C
2	--	--	Unscored	• 7.21.H
3	C	B	Incorrect	• 8.10.A
4	D	C	Incorrect	• 8.30.H
5	A	A	Correct	• 6.17.B

Total Items On Test	Total Correct	Total Incorrect	Total Skipped	Total Points Possible (Before Unscored)	Total Points Achieved (Before Unscored)	Final Score
5	2	2	1	4	2	TBD

Back < << > >> Print

Need help? How to Read this Report.

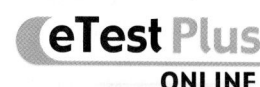

eTest Plus ONLINE

eTest Plus Online

Customized Assessment Online

- Create tests with the *Test Generator* and publish them to the e*Test Plus Online* service.
- Have students take tests online, with results graded automatically.
- View and print individual and class score reports.
- Generate reports correlated to national and state standards

Chapter Planning Guide

Every chapter of the *Creating America: Beginnings through Reconstruction* Teacher's Edition opens with a convenient two-page Planning Guide. By giving an overview of the chapter's key ideas, copymasters, technology, and assessment resources, the Planning Guide can help teachers meet the diverse needs of the classroom.

Name ____________ Date ____________

Economics in History

Chapter 6 Section 1, Tighter British Control

The Impact of British Taxes

Changes in British taxes—required payments to the government—helped bring about the American Revolution. The British began to increase taxes on American colonists after the French and Indian War (1754–1763). The war proved to be long and costly to Britain. Britain had borrowed huge sums of money to cover the costs of this war, as well as other European wars. In 1754, Britain's national debt was about £72 million. (£ is the symbol for a British pound.) By 1763, the debt nearly doubled to more than £132 million (more than $10 billion today).

After the French and Indian War, Britain stationed 10,000 troops in North America. Maintaining these troops added another heavy expense to the British treasury—about £400,000 a year. To raise money, the British Parliament passed the Sugar Act (1764) and the Stamp Act (1765). The Sugar Act and the Stamp Act marked the beginning of a series of laws that forced colonists to ask this question: Did the benefits of belonging to the British empire outweigh the benefits of becoming an independent nation?

The Sugar Act In passing the Sugar Act, Parliament's goal was to collect £100,000 a year. This amount was expected to cover about 20 percent of Britain's military costs in North America. The Sugar Act included a three-pence tax on every gallon of imported molasses from the French West Indies. Molasses was a thick, sugary syrup used in making rum. The act also taxed many other goods, such as indigo, coffee, wine, and silk. From 1766 to 1775, Britain raised about £30,000 a year in revenue.

The Sugar Act struck an economic blow to merchants and ship captains. Many colonists feared Britain was seizing powers, such as the right to tax, from the colonial legislatures.

The Stamp Act The Sugar Act did not solve Britain's financial problems. Its national debt kept increasing. In 1765, Parliament took more drastic measures and passed the Stamp Act. The goal was to raise £60,000 to £100,000 a year.

British tax stamp used in 1765.
The Granger Collection, New York

The Stamp Act was the first time that the colonists directly paid a tax on goods and services. The Stamp Act required colonists to buy specially stamped paper for printed materials, such as legal documents, pamphlets, and newspapers.

The tax affected all free men and women, both rich and poor, in the colonies. Churchgoers had to pay a stamp tax on prayer books. Engaged couples had to pay a stamp tax on their marriage licenses. African-American laborers, craft workers, small farmers, southern planters, and northern merchants—all paid the stamp tax.

Especially hard-hit were lawyers and publishers. Lawyers had to pay a 10-pound stamp tax on their law licenses. They also became alarmed about losing clients who had to pay a tax on documents, such as wills, mortgages, and deeds. Many colonial lawyers spoke out against the Stamp Act and embraced the revolutionary cause. Of the 56 men who signed the Declaration of Independence in 1776, 26 were lawyers.

The American Revolution that followed was not fought over the issue of paying taxes. Rather, the Revolution was fought, in part, over Britain's authority to impose taxes.

Activity

The British government passed the Sugar Act and the Stamp Act to pay the expense of keeping troops in North America. If you had been in charge of the British government, what would you have done to raise the needed money? Write your ideas on a piece of paper. Then exchange papers with a partner. Each of you should then write how you think the colonists would have reacted to the plan.

References to specific ancillaries help teachers to plan lessons.

CHAPTER 6 PLANNING GUIDE

The Road to Revolution 1763–1776

	1 CHAPTER OVERVIEW	COPYMASTERS 2	3 INTEGRATED TECHNOLOGY
CHAPTER RESOURCES	The chapter identifies the causes of tension between the British government and the colonists in the years 1763–1776. It explains issues and events leading up to the declaration of independence from Britain. It describes the roles played by significant individuals.	**In-Depth Resources: Unit 2** • Tracing Themes: Impact of the Individual, p. 2 • Building Vocabulary, p. 8 • History Workshop Resources, p. 23 **Interdisciplinary Projects, pp. 31–36**	• eEdition Plus Online • EasyPlanner Plus Online • eTest Plus Online • eEdition • Power Presentations • EasyPlanner • Electronic Library of Primary Sources • Test Generator • Reading Study Guide • America's Music
	1 KEY IDEAS		
SECTION 1 **Tighter British Control pp. 159–162**	• Tighter British control causes tension with American colonists. • The Stamp Act enrages the colonists. • [illegible] repeal of the Stamp Act.	**In-Depth Resources: Unit 2** • Setting the Stage, p. 1 • Guided Reading, p. 3 • Primary Source: Resolutions of the Stamp Act Congress, p. 12 • Reteaching Activity, p. 18 **Economics in History** • The Impact of British Taxes, p. 6 **Outline Map Activities** • Pre-Revolutionary North America, pp. 11–12	**Warm-Up Transparency WT6** **Humanities Transparency HT11** • The Repeal of the Stamp Act **Critical Thinking Transparency CT16** • Setting the Stage
SECTION 2 **Colonial Resistance Grows pp. 163–169**	• Townshend Acts bring new protests. • The Boston Massacre causes more tension. • Sons of Liberty protest the Tea Act.	**In-Depth Resources: Unit 2** • Setting the Stage, p. 1 • Guided Reading, p. 4 • Skillbuilder Practice: Recognizing Propaganda, p. 9 • Reteaching Activity, p. 19 **Why It Matters Now** • Politics and Protest, pp. 11–12	**Warm-Up Transparency WT6** **Humanities Transparency HT12** • *The Copley Family* by John Copley **Critical Thinking Transparency CT16** • Setting the Stage classzone.com
SECTION 3 **The Road to Lexington and Concord pp. 170–175**	• The Intolerable Acts punish the colonists. • Colonists must choose between war and peace. • Lexington and Concord become the first battles of the American Revolutionary War.	**In-Depth Resources: Unit 2** • Setting the Stage, p. 1 • Guided Reading, p. 5 • Literature Selection: "Paul Revere's Ride" by Henry Wadsworth Longfellow, pp. 14–17 • Reteaching Activity, p. 20	**Warm-Up Transparency WT6** **Critical Thinking Transparency CT16** • Setting the Stage **Critical Thinking Transparency CT17** • Cause and Effect: Growing Conflict Between Britain and America classzone.com
SECTION 4 **Declaring Independence pp. 176–185**	• Encounters between the British and colonists deepen the conflict. • *Common Sense* makes a case for independence. • American colonists declare independence from Great Britain.	**In-Depth Resources: Unit 2** • Setting the Stage, p. 1 • Guided Reading, p. 6 • Guided Reading: The Declaration of Independence, p. 7 • Geography Application, pp. 10–11 • Primary Source, p. 13 • Reteaching Activity, p. 21 **America's History Makers, pp. 23–26** **American History Plays** • *Franklin & the King* by Paul Green	**Warm-Up Transparency WT6** **Geography Transparency GT6** • Battle of Bunker Hill, 1775 **Critical Thinking Transparency CT16** • Setting the Stage **Primary Source Explorer** • *The Declaration of Independence* classzone.com

139a CHAPTER 6

1 Chapter Overview and Key Ideas

An overview summarizes the important events covered in the chapter. A chronological, section-by-section summary then lists the key ideas in the chapter.

2 Copymasters

A complete listing of reproducible materials for each section reveals the depth of resource material that is available.

3 Integrated Technology

Technology is listed for each section and includes a wealth of transparencies, the Primary Source Explorer CD-ROM, audio resources, videos, and Internet ideas.

4 Assessment Options

This column identifies pages on which section quizzes and chapter tests are available. Resources for alternative assessment are also noted.

Pupil's Edition | Overhead Transparency | CD
Copymaster | Audio Library | Internet

4

ASSESSMENT OPTIONS

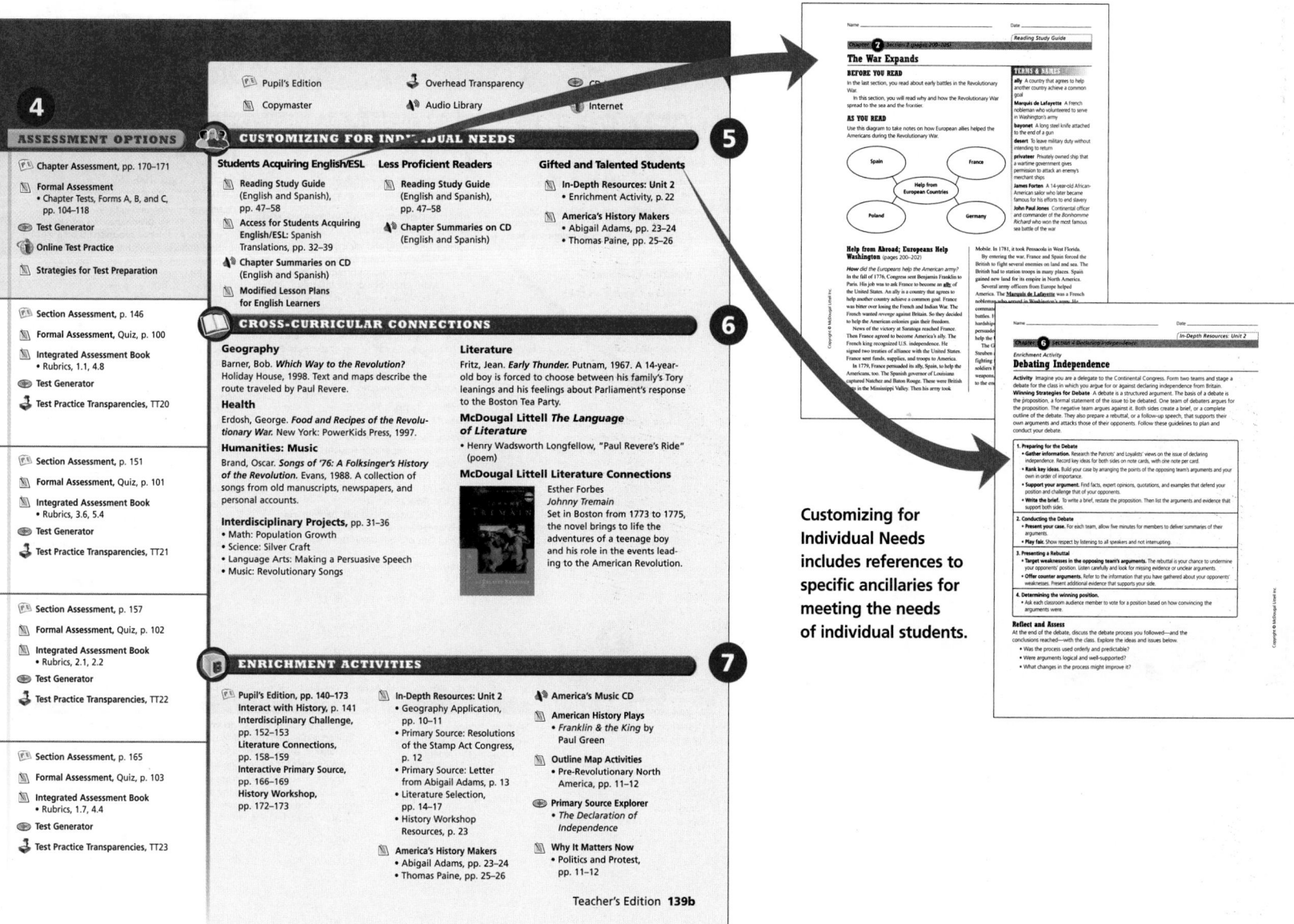

- Chapter Assessment, pp. 170–171
- Formal Assessment
  - Chapter Tests, Forms A, B, and C, pp. 104–118
- Test Generator
- Online Test Practice
- Strategies for Test Preparation

- Section Assessment, p. 146
- Formal Assessment, Quiz, p. 100
- Integrated Assessment Book
  - Rubrics, 1.1, 4.8
- Test Generator
- Test Practice Transparencies, TT20

- Section Assessment, p. 151
- Formal Assessment, Quiz, p. 101
- Integrated Assessment Book
  - Rubrics, 3.6, 5.4
- Test Generator
- Test Practice Transparencies, TT21

- Section Assessment, p. 157
- Formal Assessment, Quiz, p. 102
- Integrated Assessment Book
  - Rubrics, 2.1, 2.2
- Test Generator
- Test Practice Transparencies, TT22

- Section Assessment, p. 165
- Formal Assessment, Quiz, p. 103
- Integrated Assessment Book
  - Rubrics, 1.7, 4.4
- Test Generator
- Test Practice Transparencies, TT23

CUSTOMIZING FOR INDIVIDUAL NEEDS 5

Students Acquiring English/ESL
- Reading Study Guide (English and Spanish), pp. 47–58
- Access for Students Acquiring English/ESL: Spanish Translations, pp. 32–39
- Chapter Summaries on CD (English and Spanish)
- Modified Lesson Plans for English Learners

Less Proficient Readers
- Reading Study Guide (English and Spanish), pp. 47–58
- Chapter Summaries on CD (English and Spanish)

Gifted and Talented Students
- In-Depth Resources: Unit 2
  - Enrichment Activity, p. 22
- America's History Makers
  - Abigail Adams, pp. 23–24
  - Thomas Paine, pp. 25–26

CROSS-CURRICULAR CONNECTIONS 6

Geography
Barner, Bob. ***Which Way to the Revolution?*** Holiday House, 1998. Text and maps describe the route traveled by Paul Revere.

Health
Erdosh, George. ***Food and Recipes of the Revolutionary War.*** New York: PowerKids Press, 1997.

Humanities: Music
Brand, Oscar. ***Songs of '76: A Folksinger's History of the Revolution.*** Evans, 1988. A collection of songs from old manuscripts, newspapers, and personal accounts.

Interdisciplinary Projects, pp. 31–36
- Math: Population Growth
- Science: Silver Craft
- Language Arts: Making a Persuasive Speech
- Music: Revolutionary Songs

Literature
Fritz, Jean. ***Early Thunder.*** Putnam, 1967. A 14-year-old boy is forced to choose between his family's Tory leanings and his feelings about Parliament's response to the Boston Tea Party.

McDougal Littell *The Language of Literature*
- Henry Wadsworth Longfellow, "Paul Revere's Ride" (poem)

McDougal Littell Literature Connections

Esther Forbes
Johnny Tremain
Set in Boston from 1773 to 1775, the novel brings to life the adventures of a teenage boy and his role in the events leading to the American Revolution.

ENRICHMENT ACTIVITIES 7

- Pupil's Edition, pp. 140–173
  - Interact with History, p. 141
  - Interdisciplinary Challenge, pp. 152–153
  - Literature Connections, pp. 158–159
  - Interactive Primary Source, pp. 166–169
  - History Workshop, pp. 172–173
- In-Depth Resources: Unit 2
  - Geography Application, pp. 10–11
  - Primary Source: Resolutions of the Stamp Act Congress, p. 12
  - Primary Source: Letter from Abigail Adams, p. 13
  - Literature Selection, pp. 14–17
  - History Workshop Resources, p. 23
- America's History Makers
  - Abigail Adams, pp. 23–24
  - Thomas Paine, pp. 25–26
- America's Music CD
- American History Plays
  - *Franklin & the King* by Paul Green
- Outline Map Activities
  - Pre-Revolutionary North America, pp. 11–12
- Primary Source Explorer
  - *The Declaration of Independence*
- Why It Matters Now
  - Politics and Protest, pp. 11–12

Teacher's Edition **139b**

Name ______ Date ______

Reading Study Guide

Chapter 7 Section 2 (pages 200–205)

The War Expands

BEFORE YOU READ

In the last section, you read about early battles in the Revolutionary War.

In this section, you will read why and how the Revolutionary War spread to the sea and the frontier.

AS YOU READ

Use this diagram to take notes on how European allies helped the Americans during the Revolutionary War.

Spain | France | Help from European Countries | Poland | Germany

TERMS & NAMES

ally A country that agrees to help another country achieve a common goal
Marquis de Lafayette A French nobleman who volunteered to serve in Washington's army
bayonet A long steel knife attached to the end of a gun
desert To leave military duty without intending to return
privateer Privately owned ship that a wartime government gives permission to attack an enemy's merchant ships
James Forten A 14-year-old African-American sailor who later became famous for his efforts to end slavery
John Paul Jones Continental officer and commander of the *Bonhomme Richard* who won the most famous sea battle of the war

Help from Abroad; Europeans Help Washington (pages 200–202)

How did the Europeans help the American army?
In the fall of 1776, Congress sent Benjamin Franklin to Paris. His job was to ask France to become an ally of the United States. An ally is a country that agrees to help another country achieve a common goal. France was bitter over losing the French and Indian War. The French wanted *revenge* against Britain. So they decided to help the American colonies gain their freedom.

News of the victory at Saratoga reached France. Then France agreed to become America's ally. The French king recognized U.S. independence. He signed two treaties of alliance with the United States. France sent funds, supplies, and troops to America.

In 1779, France persuaded its ally, Spain, to help the Americans, too. The Spanish governor of Louisiana captured Natchez and Baton Rouge. These were British ...s in the Mississippi Valley. Then his army took Mobile. In 1781, it took Pensacola in West Florida.

By entering the war, France and Spain forced the British to fight several enemies on land and sea. The British had to station troops in many places. Spain gained new land for its empire in North America.

Several army officers from Europe helped America. The Marquis de Lafayette was a French nobleman who served in Washington's army. He ...

Name ______ Date ______

In-Depth Resources: Unit 2

Chapter 6 Section 4 Declaring Independence

Enrichment Activity

Debating Independence

Activity Imagine you are a delegate to the Continental Congress. Form two teams and stage a debate for the class in which you argue for or against declaring independence from Britain.

Winning Strategies for Debate A debate is a structured argument. The basis of a debate is the proposition, a formal statement of the issue to be debated. One team of debaters argues for the proposition. The negative team argues against it. Both sides create a brief, or a complete outline of the debate. They also prepare a rebuttal, or a follow-up speech, that supports their own arguments and attacks those of their opponents. Follow these guidelines to plan and conduct your debate.

1. Preparing for the Debate
- **Gather information.** Research the Patriots' and Loyalists' views on the issue of declaring independence. Record key ideas for both sides on note cards, with one note per card.
- **Rank key ideas.** Build your case by arranging the points of the opposing team's arguments and your own in order of importance.
- **Support your argument.** Find facts, expert opinions, quotations, and examples that defend your position and challenge that of your opponents.
- **Write the brief.** To write a brief, restate the proposition. Then list the arguments and evidence that support both sides.

2. Conducting the Debate
- **Present your case.** For each team, allow five minutes for members to deliver summaries of their arguments.
- **Play fair.** Show respect by listening to all speakers and not interrupting.

3. Presenting a Rebuttal
- **Target weaknesses in the opposing team's arguments.** The rebuttal is your chance to undermine your opponents' position. Listen carefully and look for missing evidence or unclear arguments.
- **Offer counter arguments.** Refer to the information that you have gathered about your opponents' weaknesses. Present additional evidence that supports your side.

4. Determining the winning position.
- Ask each classroom audience member to vote for a position based on how convincing the arguments were.

Reflect and Assess
At the end of the debate, discuss the debate process you followed—and the conclusions reached—with the class. Explore the ideas and issues below.
- Was the process used orderly and predictable?
- Were arguments logical and well-supported?
- What changes in the process might improve it?

Customizing for Individual Needs includes references to specific ancillaries for meeting the needs of individual students.

5 Customizing for Individual Needs

Here are suggested resources for teaching students acquiring English, less proficient readers, and gifted and talented students. From Spanish-language resources to Enrichment Activities designed specifically for gifted and talented students, *Creating America: Beginnings through Reconstruction* offers practical help for the classroom needs of all students.

6 Cross-Curricular Connections

This section lists resources for interdisciplinary teaching. There are always references to Interdisciplinary Projects, the component of *Creating America* designed specifically for interdisciplinary teams. In addition, resources are listed for literature, science, geography, and other subjects.

7 Enrichment Activities

These are resources in *Creating America* that will help teachers to extend and enrich their teaching of the chapter.

Block Schedule Lesson Plan Options

Block Schedule Lesson Plan Options appear immediately after the Planning Guide for every chapter in the *Creating America: Beginnings through Reconstruction* Teacher's Edition. This easy-to-use guide is a valuable aid in planning lessons for block schedules.

BLOCK SCHEDULING — LESSON PLAN OPTIONS (90-MINUTE PERIOD)

DAY 1

Interact with History, p. 141
Class Time 20 minutes

Options for pacing and variety:
- Role-Playing Have students meet in groups of four or five and act as neighbors meeting to discuss the "What Do You Think?" questions and the main questions. **Class Time** 15 minutes

Setting the Stage, p. 142
Class Time 20 minutes

Options for pacing and variety:
- Time Saver Assign the "What Do You Know?" and "What Do You Want to Know?" questions as homework so that students can get a head start on preparing to read the chapter. **Class Time** 5 minutes

Section 1, pp. 143–146
Class Time 50 minutes

Options for pacing and variety:
- Time Saver Use the political cartoon transparency, "Repeal of the Stamp Act," as a summary of the section. **Class Time** 10 minutes
- Peer Teaching Have students work in pairs to answer the Reading History questions in the section and Critical Thinking question in the Section 1 assessment. **Class Time** 15 minutes

DAY 2

Section 2, pp. 147–153
Class Time 45 minutes

Interdisciplinary Challenge, pp. 152–153
Class Time 55 minutes

Options for pacing and variety:
- Team Teaching Invite the math teacher to your class to coach student groups as they solve the Math Challenge or the Interdisciplinary Link (Math) on page 155 in the Teacher's Edition. **Class Time** 55 minutes.
- Peer Teaching Assign the content under each heading to a small group of students. Each group is responsible for explaining the information to the class. **Class Time** 30 minutes

Section 3, pp. 154–159
Class Time 45 minutes

Options for pacing and variety:
- Peer Teaching Divide students into small groups. Using the information from the chart on p. 155, create a different way to present the information to the class. **Class Time** 25 minutes
- Internet Extend students' background knowledge of the Battles at Lexington and Concord by having them visit classzone.com. **Class Time** 20 minutes

DAY 3

Section 4, pp. 160–169
Class Time 50 minutes

Options for pacing and variety:
- Peer Teaching Divide the class into small groups. Assign one group to become a living time line. Have another group become living biographies of individuals in this chapter. A third group performs the Cooperative Learning Activity on page 171. **Class Time** 50 minutes
- History on Film Extend students' background on the Revolutionary War by viewing either episode one or two, "The Conflict Ignites" or "1776," of *The American Revolution.* A&E Home Video, 1994. **Class Time** 50 minutes

History Workshop, pp. 172–173
Class Time 50 minutes

Options for pacing and variety:
- Time Saver Have students work on steps 1–5 in Raise the Liberty Pole. **Class Time** 30 minutes

Chapter 6 Assessment, pp. 170–171
Class Time 40 minutes

Options for pacing and variety:
- Peer Evaluation Have student pairs work out the answers to the Critical Thinking Questions, page 170. Then have them exchange papers with another team to evaluate their answers. **Class Time** 20 minutes
- Peer Teaching Divide the class into four groups. Assign each group one section of the Review Questions to complete. Students should exchange answers for the review questions. **Class Time** 20 minutes

TEACHER-TESTED ACTIVITY Holly West Brewer, Buena Vista Paideia Magnet School, Nashville, Tennessee

ILLUSTRATED TIME LINE

Class Time Two class periods for preparation and one for presentation

Task Creating an illustrated time line of the events leading to the American Revolution

Purpose To visualize and sequence events that led to the Revolution

Supplies Needed
- reference books and Internet sources on the American Revolution
- markers, colored pencils
- poster paper or rolls of paper

Activity Divide the class into small groups. Students should compile at least ten events that led to the Revolution. Each student should be responsible for researching two or three events. In addition, each student chooses one of the following roles: illustrator or recorder.

The illustrators should create original drawings for each event. Each event should be placed on the large time line in chronological order. In addition, the recorders should write a cause-and-effect explanation as a caption for each event. Present the time line to the class.

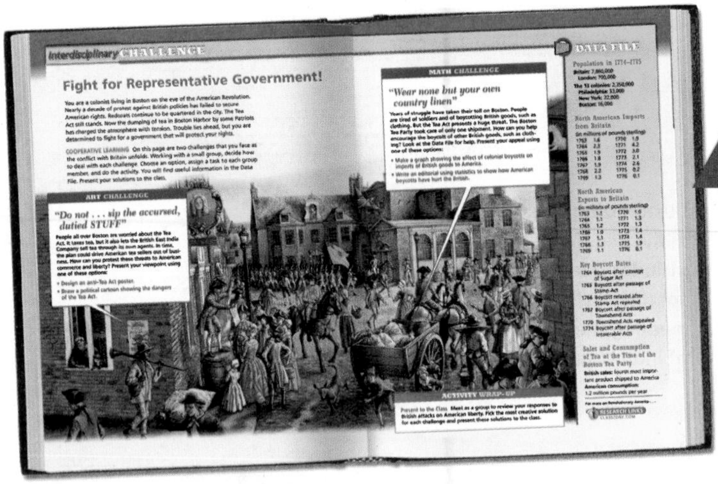

The Block Scheduling options refer to ancillaries and features—such as the Interdisciplinary Challenges—that are especially valuable for block schedules.

1 Estimated Times

The estimated time needed for each activity is provided to help you make efficient use of the block period.

2 Numerous Teaching Options

Numerous teaching options help to vary the pacing of the class and the types of activities in which students are engaged.

3 Teacher-Tested Activity

Beneath the Block Schedule Lesson Plan Options are activities written and used in the classroom by teachers.

Creating America

CHAPTER 6 TECHNOLOGY IN THE CLASSROOM

INTERNET-BASED (ELECTRONIC) FIELD TRIP

Electronic field trips are one of the most popular ways for students to use the Internet. Students generally visit a specified set of Web sites that take them to real places, such as historic sites or national parks. This type of field trip is often an excellent substitute for an actual field trip, which may be logistically impossible. **1**

ACTIVITY OUTLINE **2**

Objective By planning an electronic field trip to places important to the movement for American independence and the Revolutionary War, students will deepen their understanding of the Revolutionary Era and gain experience with the Internet.

Task Students will plan a three-day electronic field trip to learn more about the beginnings of the Revolutionary War.

Class Time Two class periods

DIRECTIONS **3** **4**

1. Have students prepare a detailed itinerary of a three-day field trip to some of the early Revolutionary War sites they have read about in Chapter 6.
2. Ask students to label the top of each slide with one of the following titles, indicating the places they will visit (here, the destinations are listed in chronological order, from the earliest event to the latest):
   a) Old State House, Boston
   b) Boston Tea Party Ship
   c) Carpenter's Hall, Philadelphia
   d) Independence Hall, Philadelphia
   e) Old North Church, Boston
   f) Paul Revere House, Boston
   g) Lexington, Massachusetts
   h) Concord, Massachusetts
   i) Fort Ticonderoga, New York
   j) Bunker Hill, Boston
3. The Web sites for this field trip are located in the Teacher Center of classzone.com.
4. For each destination, ask students to pull pictures into their presentations and to list three reasons why this place is an important destination on a Revolutionary War historical field trip. Have students determine the order in which they would visit the destinations. Have them place the destinations in order chronologically or by location.
5. Additional options:
   - Ask students to include maps of the destinations or to create them using a blank outline map of the Northeast.
   - Give students a budget for food, transportation, and accommodations, and have them provide an account of how they will allocate their money.

Technology in the Classroom

For every chapter in *Creating America: Beginnings through Reconstruction*, the Teacher's Edition includes a page that provides an innovative strategy for using the Internet and other technologies in the classroom. These strategies will help you integrate technology into your teaching of *Creating America*.

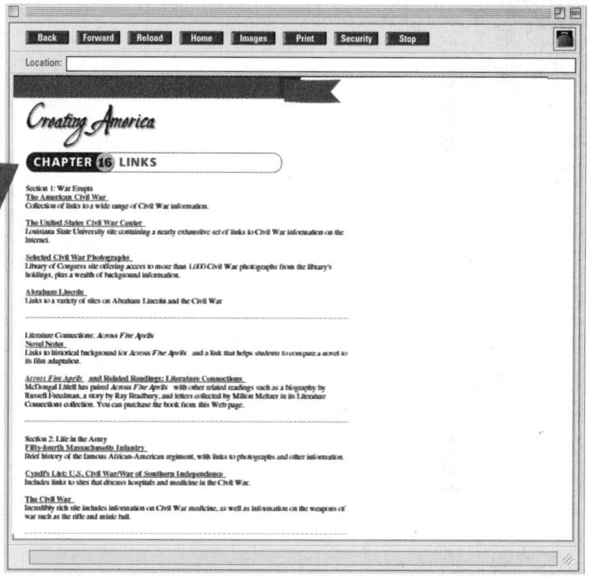

Technology in the Classroom pages refer you to links through ClassZone.

1 Overview

An overview introduces the strategy and gives an instructional rationale for using it with students.

2 Activity Outline

The activity outline states the objective of the strategy and summarizes the task in direct, easy-to-understand terms. The relevance of the activity to the content of the chapter is also explained.

3 Directions

The directions spell out, step-by-step, what students should do in the activity. These straightforward directions are specific enough to ensure that the activities will be successful in the classroom.

4 Links through classzone.com

Every web–based strategy includes links to relevant Web sites through ClassZone.

Creating America

Teacher's Edition Lesson Support

The *Creating America: Beginnings through Reconstruction* Teacher's Edition provides you with a wealth of information and practical teaching suggestions at your fingertips. Meet the needs of each student, link history to other subjects, connect the past to the present, and more.

The side columns focus on core instruction. At the bottom of the pages, you will find optional activities and teaching activities—including those for block schedules.

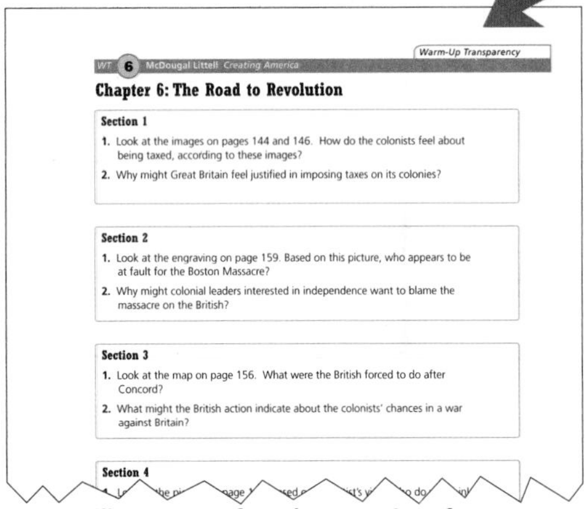

Warm-Up Transparency

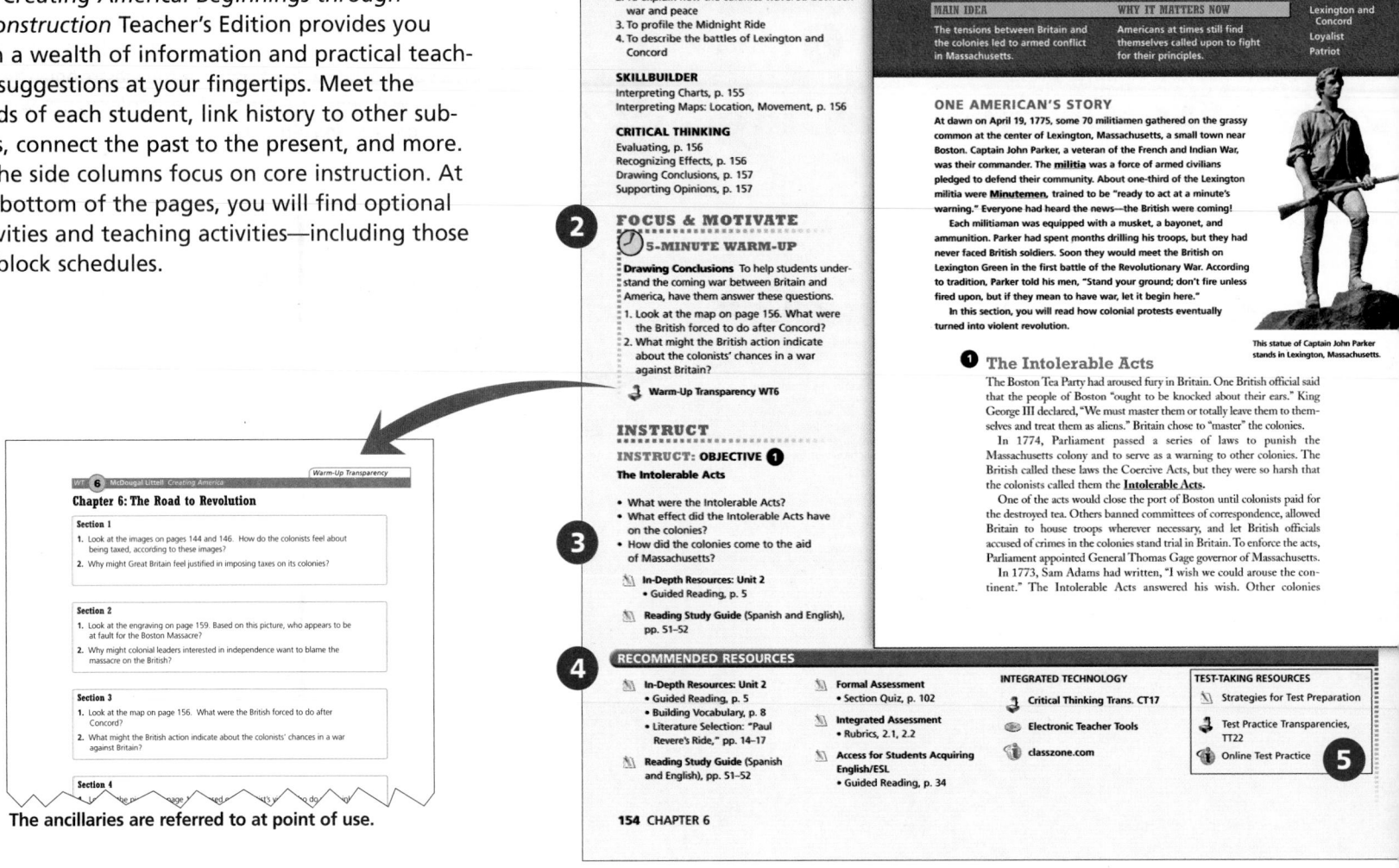

WT 6 McDougal Littell *Creating America*

Chapter 6: The Road to Revolution

Section 1

1. Look at the images on pages 144 and 146. How do the colonists feel about being taxed, according to these images?
2. Why might Great Britain feel justified in imposing taxes on its colonies?

Section 2

1. Look at the engraving on page 159. Based on this picture, who appears to be at fault for the Boston Massacre?
2. Why might colonial leaders interested in independence want to blame the massacre on the British?

Section 3

1. Look at the map on page 156. What were the British forced to do after Concord?
2. What might the British action indicate about the colonists' chances in a war against Britain?

Section 4

The ancillaries are referred to at point of use.

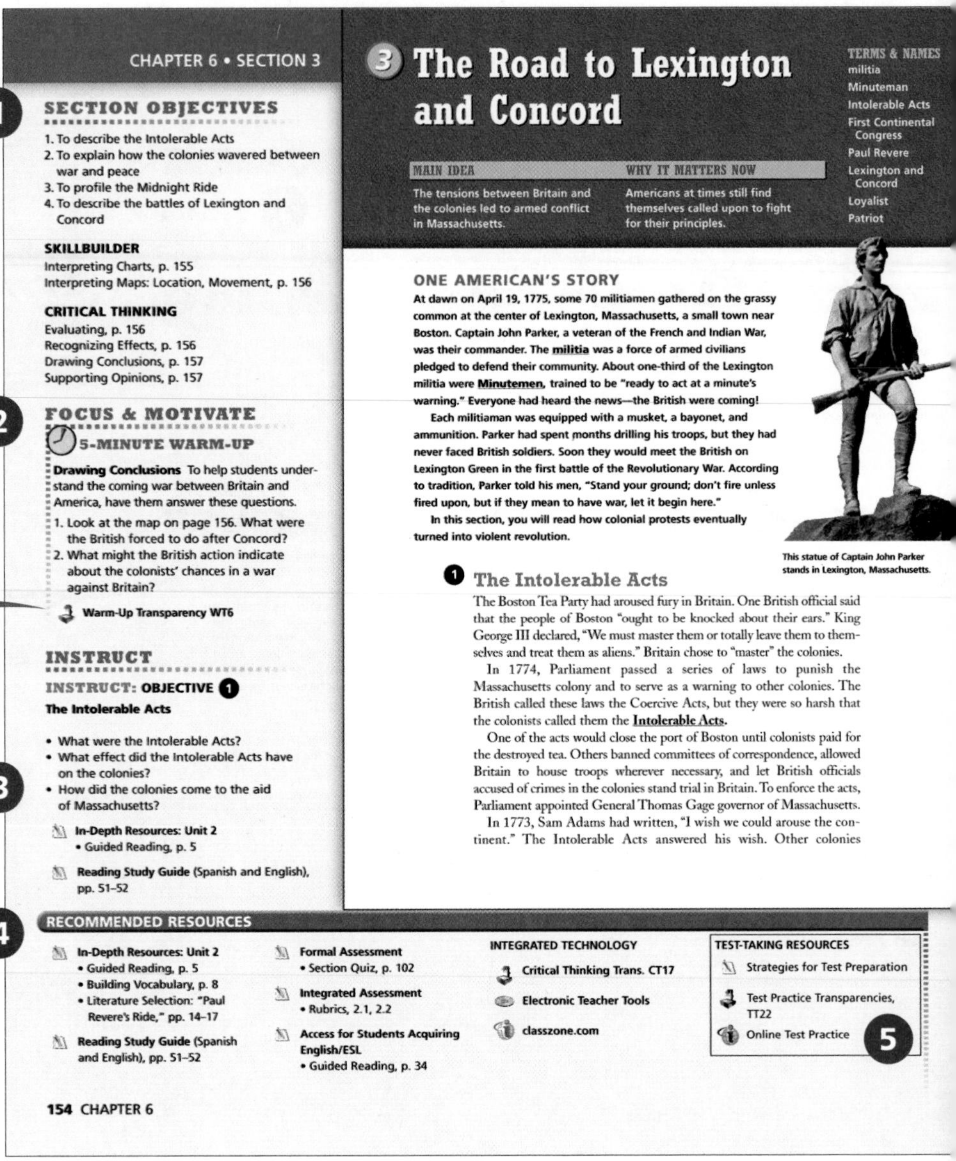

CHAPTER 6 • SECTION 3

1 **SECTION OBJECTIVES**

1. To describe the Intolerable Acts
2. To explain how the colonies wavered between war and peace
3. To profile the Midnight Ride
4. To describe the battles of Lexington and Concord

SKILLBUILDER
Interpreting Charts, p. 155
Interpreting Maps: Location, Movement, p. 156

CRITICAL THINKING
Evaluating, p. 156
Recognizing Effects, p. 156
Drawing Conclusions, p. 157
Supporting Opinions, p. 157

2 **FOCUS & MOTIVATE**

5-MINUTE WARM-UP

Drawing Conclusions To help students understand the coming war between Britain and America, have them answer these questions.

1. Look at the map on page 156. What were the British forced to do after Concord?
2. What might the British action indicate about the colonists' chances in a war against Britain?

Warm-Up Transparency WT6

INSTRUCT

INSTRUCT: OBJECTIVE 1
The Intolerable Acts

3
- What were the Intolerable Acts?
- What effect did the Intolerable Acts have on the colonies?
- How did the colonies come to the aid of Massachusetts?

In-Depth Resources: Unit 2
- Guided Reading, p. 5

Reading Study Guide (Spanish and English), pp. 51–52

3 The Road to Lexington and Concord

TERMS & NAMES
militia
Minuteman
Intolerable Acts
First Continental Congress
Paul Revere
Lexington and Concord
Loyalist
Patriot

MAIN IDEA
The tensions between Britain and the colonies led to armed conflict in Massachusetts.

WHY IT MATTERS NOW
Americans at times still find themselves called upon to fight for their principles.

ONE AMERICAN'S STORY

At dawn on April 19, 1775, some 70 militiamen gathered on the grassy common at the center of Lexington, Massachusetts, a small town near Boston. Captain John Parker, a veteran of the French and Indian War, was their commander. The **militia** was a force of armed civilians pledged to defend their community. About one-third of the Lexington militia were **Minutemen**, trained to be "ready to act at a minute's warning." Everyone had heard the news—the British were coming!

Each militiaman was equipped with a musket, a bayonet, and ammunition. Parker had spent months drilling his troops, but they had never faced British soldiers. Soon they would meet the British on Lexington Green in the first battle of the Revolutionary War. According to tradition, Parker told his men, "Stand your ground; don't fire unless fired upon, but if they mean to have war, let it begin here."

In this section, you will read how colonial protests eventually turned into violent revolution.

This statue of Captain John Parker stands in Lexington, Massachusetts.

1 **The Intolerable Acts**

The Boston Tea Party had aroused fury in Britain. One British official said that the people of Boston "ought to be knocked about their ears." King George III declared, "We must master them or totally leave them to themselves and treat them as aliens." Britain chose to "master" the colonies.

In 1774, Parliament passed a series of laws to punish the Massachusetts colony and to serve as a warning to other colonies. The British called these laws the Coercive Acts, but they were so harsh that the colonists called them the **Intolerable Acts**.

One of the acts would close the port of Boston until colonists paid for the destroyed tea. Others banned committees of correspondence, allowed Britain to house troops wherever necessary, and let British officials accused of crimes in the colonies stand trial in Britain. To enforce the acts, Parliament appointed General Thomas Gage governor of Massachusetts.

In 1773, Sam Adams had written, "I wish we could arouse the continent." The Intolerable Acts answered his wish. Other colonies

4 RECOMMENDED RESOURCES

In-Depth Resources: Unit 2
- Guided Reading, p. 5
- Building Vocabulary, p. 8
- Literature Selection: "Paul Revere's Ride," pp. 14–17

Reading Study Guide (Spanish and English), pp. 51–52

Formal Assessment
- Section Quiz, p. 102

Integrated Assessment
- Rubrics, 2.1, 2.2

Access for Students Acquiring English/ESL
- Guided Reading, p. 34

INTEGRATED TECHNOLOGY
Critical Thinking Trans. CT17
Electronic Teacher Tools
classzone.com

TEST-TAKING RESOURCES
Strategies for Test Preparation
Test Practice Transparencies, TT22
Online Test Practice 5

154 CHAPTER 6

1 Section Objectives

The objectives of the section are clearly spelled out. Each objective is number-coded to help you know when in the lesson you are teaching to that objective. The Skillbuilder skills and critical thinking skills covered in the section are also listed.

2 Focus & Motivate/ 5-Minute Warm-Up

A Warm-Up Activity begins every section to help you begin your classes in motivational ways that focus student attention on the lesson. A Warm-Up Transparency supports each Warm-Up Activity.

3 Key Questions

These questions help you reinforce students' understanding of what they read.

4 Recommended Resources

For your convenience, all of the program resources that are appropriate for teaching the section are listed at the bottom of the first page of that section.

5 Test-Taking Resources

Test-Taking Resources include Strategies for Test Preparation, Test Practice Transparencies, and the Online Test Practice.

Creating America

immediately offered Massachusetts their support. They sent food and money to Boston. The committees of correspondence also called for a meeting of colonial delegates to discuss what to do next.

❷ The First Continental Congress Meets

In September 1774, delegates from all the colonies except Georgia met in Philadelphia. At this meeting, called the **First Continental Congress,** delegates voted to ban all trade with Britain until the Intolerable Acts were repealed. They also called on each colony to begin training troops. Georgia agreed to be a part of the actions of the Congress even though it had voted not to send delegates.

The First Continental Congress marked a key step in American history. Although most delegates were not ready to call for independence, they were determined to uphold colonial rights. This meeting planted the seeds of a future independent government. John Adams called it "a nursery of American statesmen." The delegates agreed to meet in seven months, if necessary. By that time, however, fighting with Britain had begun.

Reading History
A. Evaluating Why do you think the First Continental Congress was important?
A. Possible Answer It was important because it showed that colonists were determined to uphold colonial rights.

Between War and Peace

The colonists hoped that the trade boycott would force a repeal of the Intolerable Acts. After all, past boycotts had led to the repeal of the Stamp Act and the Townshend Acts. This time, however, Parliament stood firm. It even increased restrictions on colonial trade and sent more troops.

By the end of 1774, some colonists were preparing to fight. In Massachusetts, John Hancock headed the Committee of Safety, which had the power to call out the militia. The colonial troops continued to train.

CAUSE AND EFFECT: *Growing Conflict Between Britain and America*

DATE	BRITISH ACTION	COLONIAL REACTION
1763	Proclamation of 1763 issued	Proclamation leads to anger
1765	Stamp Act passed	Boycott of British goods; Stamp Act Resolves passed
1766	Stamp Act repealed; Declaration Act passed	Boycott ended
1767	Townshend Acts passed	New boycotts; Boston Massacre (March 1770)
1770	Townshend Acts repealed (April)	Tension between colonies and Britain reduced
1773	Tea Act passed	Boston Tea Party
1774	Intolerable Acts passed	First Continental Congress bans trade; militias organized
1775	Troops ordered to Lexington and Concord, Massachusetts	Militia fights British troops; Second Continental Congress; Continental Army established

SKILLBUILDER Interpreting Charts
1. *What British action caused the first violence in the growing conflict between Britain and America?*
2. *How might the Intolerable Acts be seen as a reaction as well as an action?*

Skillbuilder Answers
1. The Townshend Acts led to the Boston Massacre.
2. The Intolerable Acts were passed as a result of the Boston Tea Party, and they caused the calling of the First Continental Congress.

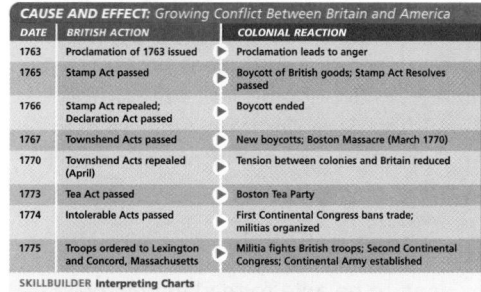

The Road to Revolution 155

CHAPTER 6 • SECTION 3

INSTRUCT: OBJECTIVE ❷
The First Continental Congress Meets/ Between War and Peace

- What happened at the First Continental Congress?
- How did the colonists protest the Intolerable Acts? How successful were they?
- What did most colonial leaders think about the prospect of war with Britain?

MORE ABOUT . . . ❻

First Continental Congress
In the first session of the Continental Congress, the delegates rejected, by a vote of six to five, Pennsylvania delegate Joseph Galloway's plan to create a union of the colonies. Galloway's Plan of Union included a Grand Council with delegates from all the colonies that would deal with issues affecting more than one colony. Legislation would be subject to Parliament's approval. The council would also have the right to reject Parliament's legislation.

HISTORY FROM VISUALS ❼

Interpreting the Chart Have students note the span of years on the chart, and explain that the graphic shows how British-American tension built up over time and did not stem from one or two incidents. Ask students how colonial leaders might use this chart to defend their desire to break free from Britain. **Possible Response** Colonial leaders might use the chart to emphasize Britain's pattern of injustice and to show how the colonies have been enduring such injustice for too long.

Extension Have students work in pairs to create a different way of showing the same information.

Critical Thinking Transparency CT17
- Cause and Effect: Growing Conflict Between Britain and America

ACTIVITY OPTIONS ❽
INTERDISCIPLINARY LINK: MATH — BLOCK SCHEDULING ❾

EFFECTS OF A BOYCOTT

Class Time 30 minutes

Task Determining a boycott's economic impact

Purpose To understand the effectiveness of boycotting as a form of protest

Supplies Needed
- Scratch paper and pencils
- Calculators

Activity Divide students into groups representing British colonial businesses (tea, woolens, foodstuffs, tinware, glass and pottery, textiles). Provide each group with a figure that represents the business's average monthly earnings (e.g., $50,000). Have each group determine the economic impact of a six-month boycott against its products by using several different assigned loss percentages (2 percent, 5 percent, 10 percent, etc.). Each group should share its findings with the class and discuss how the losses would affect the political views of the British businessmen.

Teacher's Edition notes also include:

- Assessment suggestions
- Cooperative Learning activities
- Gifted and Talented Students activities
- Less Proficient Readers activities
- Multiple Learning Styles suggestions
- Skillbuilder Lessons
- Standards for Evaluation
- Students Acquiring English/ESL activities
- Teaching Strategies

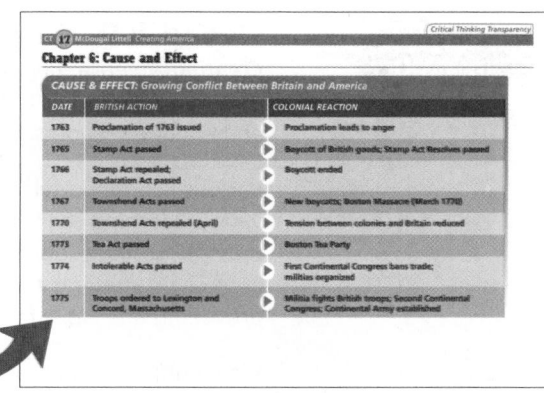

CT17 McDougal Littell Creating America — Critical Thinking Transparency

Chapter 6: Cause and Effect

CAUSE & EFFECT: Growing Conflict Between Britain and America

DATE	BRITISH ACTION	COLONIAL REACTION
1763	Proclamation of 1763 issued	Proclamation leads to anger
1765	Stamp Act passed	Boycott of British goods; Stamp Act Resolves passed
1766	Stamp Act repealed; Declaration Act passed	Boycott ended
1767	Townshend Acts passed	New boycotts; Boston Massacre (March 1770)
1770	Townshend Acts repealed (April)	Tension between colonies and Britain reduced
1773	Tea Act passed	Boston Tea Party
1774	Intolerable Acts passed	First Continental Congress bans trade; militias organized
1775	Troops ordered to Lexington and Concord, Massachusetts	Militia fights British troops; Second Continental Congress; Continental Army established

The ancillaries are referred to at point of use.

❻ More About . . .

These terrific nuggets of information occur often to supplement the text.

❼ History from Visuals

These notes provide a variety of learning strategies and extension activities to help students make the most of maps, charts, graphs, political cartoons, and historical photographs.

❽ Activity Options/ Interdisciplinary Links

Activity options at the bottom of the Teacher's Edition pages offer a range of choices. Many of these choices are Interdisciplinary Links to math, science, language arts, literature, humanities, civics, economics, and health. The amount of time required for the activity is listed.

❾ Block Scheduling

The logo labeled Block Scheduling appears wherever an Activity Option is appropriate for block schedules.

Helping Students Read History

DONNA M. OGLE
Professor, Reading and Language, National–Louis University, Evanston, Illinois; President, International Reading Association

The best learners are active and engaged readers. Successful readers connect what they are reading with what they already know. These readers:

- build associations among ideas
- create visual images of what they are reading
- continually revise their interpretations as they gather more information.

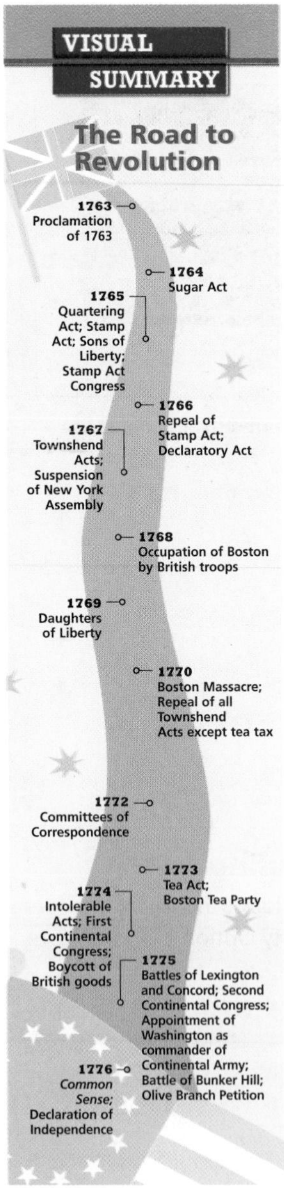

Supporting Readers

Creating America: Beginnings through Reconstruction uses many strategies to help students become active and engaged readers.

Various Learning Styles *Creating America* addresses various learning styles by including a variety of activity options, posing problems, providing graphic organizers to help students take notes, and asking thought-provoking questions for discussion.

Visual Information Many readers rely on visual information when reading unfamiliar material. In *Creating America,* photos and artifacts create a context for new ideas; maps help readers associate and compare ideas. In addition, charts of ideas and events summarize and clarify information. A visual summary at the end of each chapter provides another way of remembering ideas and events.

Personal Connections Personal stories and human connections can help to bring a subject such as history alive. *Creating America* uses personal voices throughout to support student learning.

> ***A VOICE FROM THE PAST***
>
> Gentlemen may cry peace, peace—but there is no peace. The war is actually begun! The next gale that sweeps from the north will bring to our ears the clash of resounding arms! Our brethren are already in the field! Why should we idle here? . . . I know not what course others may take. But as for me, give me liberty or give me death.
>
> **Patrick Henry,** quoted in *Patriots* by A. J. Langguth

Inner-Column Notes Inner-column notes in *Creating America* help students read the text. Vocabulary notes explain and define words and phrases. Background notes provide additional information about a person, idea, or event. Reading History questions help students to read critically.

Students Acquiring English Second-language learners need to have information and ideas presented to them in multiple ways. Being able to "see" history helps make it real for them. *Creating America* uses illustrations and visuals to present information to students in a variety of ways.

Evolving Forms of Reading

Students today need to be able to read in new ways.

Nonlinear Materials Today's students must:

- gather ideas from multiple sources—resource books, magazines, computerized databases, CD-ROMs, the Internet
- find their way through nonlinear materials, such as by deciding which area of a computer screen contains the information they want.

The Interactive Primary Sources in the textbook also appear on a separately available CD-ROM entitled Primary Source Explorer, along with resources for exploring each primary source in depth.

Graphic Layouts Today's readers must deal with informational materials that come in various formats.

- multiple columns of text with many pictures, graphs, and maps
- single-column texts with large marginal areas used for illustrations, highlighted information, and thought-provoking ideas

Creating America familiarizes students with these multiple text formats and teaches students reading strategies for effectively obtaining information from each format.

McDOUGAL LITTELL

Creating America

A History of the United States

Beginnings
through
Reconstruction

Zitkala-Ša
Native American author

Elizabeth Cady Stanton
Leader of the women's rights movement in the 1800s

Abigail Adams
Supporter of women's rights; married to President John Adams

Sam Houston
A hero of the Texas Revolution and the first president of the Republic of Texas

Juan Seguín
A hero of the Texas Revolution

Andrew Jackson
Seventh president of the United States

Harriet Tubman
Abolitionist and conductor on the Underground Railroad

Abraham Lincoln
Sixteenth president of the United States

Crispus Attucks
American colonist killed in the Boston Massacre

George Washington
First president of the United States

Creating America

A History of the United States

Beginnings through Reconstruction

Jesus Garcia

Donna M. Ogle

C. Frederick Risinger

Joyce Stevos

McDougal Littell
A DIVISION OF HOUGHTON MIFFLIN COMPANY

Senior Consultants

Jesus Garcia is Professor of Curriculum and Instruction at the University of Kentucky. A former social studies teacher, Dr. Garcia has co-authored many books and articles on subjects that range from teaching social studies in elementary school to seeking diversity in education. Dr. Garcia will serve as President of the National Council for the Social Studies in 2004–2005.

Donna M. Ogle is Professor of Reading and Language Arts at National-Louis University in Evanston, Illinois, and is a specialist in reading in the content areas with an interest in social studies. She is past president of the International Reading Association. A former social studies teacher, Dr. Ogle is also Director of a Goals 2000 grant for Reading and Thinking in the Content Areas for four Chicago high schools. She developed the K-W-L reading strategy that is so widely used in schools.

C. Frederick Risinger is Director of Professional Development and Coordinator for Social Studies Education at Indiana University. He is past president of the National Council for the Social Studies. Mr. Risinger also served on the coordinating committee for the National History Standards Project. He writes a monthly column on technology in the social studies classroom for *Social Education.*

Joyce Stevos recently retired from 36 years of service to the Providence, Rhode Island, Public Schools. For 15 of those years, she was the social studies area supervisor and developed programs on Holocaust studies, the Armenian genocide, character education, voter education, and government and law. Currently, she is a Ph.D. candidate in education focusing on how youth develop a citizen identity.

Acknowledgments begin on page R84.

ISBN 0-618-37698-4

Printed in the United States of America

1 2 3 4 5 6 7 8 9 – DWO – 07 06 05 04

iv

Consultants and Reviewers

Content Consultants

The content consultants reviewed the manuscript for historical depth and accuracy and for clarity of presentation.

Roger Beck
Department of History
Eastern Illinois University
Charleston, Illinois

David Farber
Department of History
University of New Mexico
Albuquerque, New Mexico

Cheryl Johnson-Odim
Department of History
Loyola University
Chicago, Illinois

Joseph Kett
Department of History
University of Virginia
Charlottesville, Virginia

Jack N. Rakove
Department of History
Stanford University
Stanford, California

Virginia Stewart
Department of History
University of North Carolina, Wilmington
Wilmington, North Carolina

Christopher Waldrep
Department of History
Eastern Illinois University
Charleston, Illinois

Nancy Woloch
Department of History
Barnard College
New York, New York

Multicultural Advisory Board

The multicultural advisors reviewed the manuscript for appropriate historical content.

Betty Dean
Social Studies Consultant
Pearland, Texas

Tyrone C. Howard
College of Education
The Ohio State University
Columbus, Ohio

Jose C. Moya
Department of History
University of California at Los Angeles
Los Angeles, California

Pat Payne
Office of Multicultural Education
Indianapolis Public Schools
Indianapolis, Indiana

Betto Ramirez
Former Teacher, La Joya, Texas
Social Studies Consultant
Mission, Texas

Jon Reyhner
Department of Education
Northern Arizona University
Flagstaff, Arizona

Ronald Young
Department of History
Georgia Southern University
Statesboro, Georgia

v

Consultants and Reviewers

Teacher Consultants

The following educators contributed activity options for the Pupil's Edition and teaching ideas and activities for the Teacher's Edition.

Paul C. Beavers
J. T. Moore Middle School
Nashville, Tennessee

Holly West Brewer
Buena Vista Paideia Magnet School
Nashville, Tennessee

Ron Campana
Social Studies Consultant
New York, New York

Patricia B. Carlson
Swanson Middle School
Arlington, Virginia

Ann Cotton
Ft. Worth Independent School District
Ft. Worth, Texas

Kelly Ellis
Hamilton Junior High School
Cypress, Texas

James Grimes
Middlesex County Vocational–Technical High School
Woodbridge, New Jersey

Brent Heath
De Anza Middle School
Ontario, California

Suzanne Hidalgo
Serrano Middle School
Highland, California

Barbara Kennedy
Sylvan Middle School
Citrus Heights, California

Pamela Kniffin
Navasota Junior High School
Navasota, Texas

Tammy Leiber
Navasota Junior High School
Navasota, Texas

Lori Lesslie
Cedar Bluff Middle School
Knoxville, Tennessee

Brian McKenzie
Dr. Charles R. Drew Science Magnet School
Buffalo, New York

W. W. Bear Mills
Goddard Junior High School
Midland, Texas

Lindy Poling
Millbrook High School
Raleigh, North Carolina

Jean Price
T. H. Rogers Middle School
Houston, Texas

Meg Robbins
Wilbraham Middle School
Wilbraham, Massachusetts

Philip Rodriguez
McNair Middle School
San Antonio, Texas

Leslie Schubert
Parkland School
McHenry, Illinois

Robert Sisko
Carteret Middle School
Carteret, New Jersey

Marci Smith
Hurst-Euless-Bedford Independent School District
Bedford, Texas

James Sorenson
Chippewa Middle School
Des Plaines, Illinois

Nicholas G. Sysock
Carteret Middle School
Carteret, New Jersey

Lisa Williams
Lamberton Middle School
Carlisle, Pennsylvania

Michael Yell
Hudson Middle School
Hudson, Wisconsin

vi

Teacher Panels

The following educators provided ongoing review during the development of prototypes, the table of contents, and key components of the program.

Bill Albright
Wilson Southern Junior High School
Sinking Spring, Pennsylvania

Henry Assetto
Gordon Middle School
Coatesville, Pennsylvania

James Berry
Kennedy Middle School
Grand Prairie, Texas

Ralph Burnley
Roosevelt Middle School
Philadelphia, Pennsylvania

Mary Ann Canamar
Garner Middle School
San Antonio, Texas

Zoe Carter
San Jacinto Junior High School
Midland, Texas

Stephen Cicero
Butler Area Junior High School
Butler, Pennsylvania

Charles Crescenzi
Dover Intermediate School
Dover, Pennsylvania

Sharon McDonald
Cook Junior High School
Houston, Texas

Phil Mifsud
Roosevelt Middle School
Erie, Pennsylvania

Joel Mumma
Centerville Middle School
Lancaster, Pennsylvania

September Olson
Richardson Middle School
El Paso, Texas

Donald Roberts
Frick International Studies Academy
Pittsburgh, Pennsylvania

Mary Rogers
Brookside Intermediate School
Friendswood, Texas

Lucy Sanchez
John F. Kennedy High School
San Antonio, Texas

Steve Seale
Hamilton Middle School
Houston, Texas

Yolanda Villalobos
Dallas Independent School District
Dallas, Texas

Diane Williams
Hill-Freedman Middle School
Philadelphia, Pennsylvania

Lisa Williams
Lamberton Middle School
Carlisle, Pennsylvania

Student Board

The following students reviewed pages for the textbook.

Adam Backhaus
Parkland School
McHenry, Illinois

Ben Barney
Hamilton Junior High School
Cypress, Texas

Amanda Berrier
Lamberton Middle School
Carlisle, Pennsylvania

Debra Hurwitz
T. H. Rogers Middle School
Houston, Texas

Reginald Jones
Dr. Charles R. Drew Science Magnet School
Buffalo, New York

Brendon Keinath
Wilbraham Middle School
Wilbraham, Massachusetts

Daniel MacDonald
Carteret Middle School
Carteret, New Jersey

Cameron Mote
Serrano Middle School
Highland, California

Kim Nguyen
Sylvan Middle School
Citrus Heights, California

Arianna G. Noriega
De Anza Middle School
Ontario, California

Nicholas Tofilon
Burlington Middle School
Burlington, Wisconsin

Emmanuel Zepeda
Haven Middle School
Evanston, Illinois

vii

UNIT 1 Three Worlds Meet BEGINNINGS TO 1763

viii

Pontiac

ix

UNIT 2 Creating a New Nation 1763 – 1791

George Washington

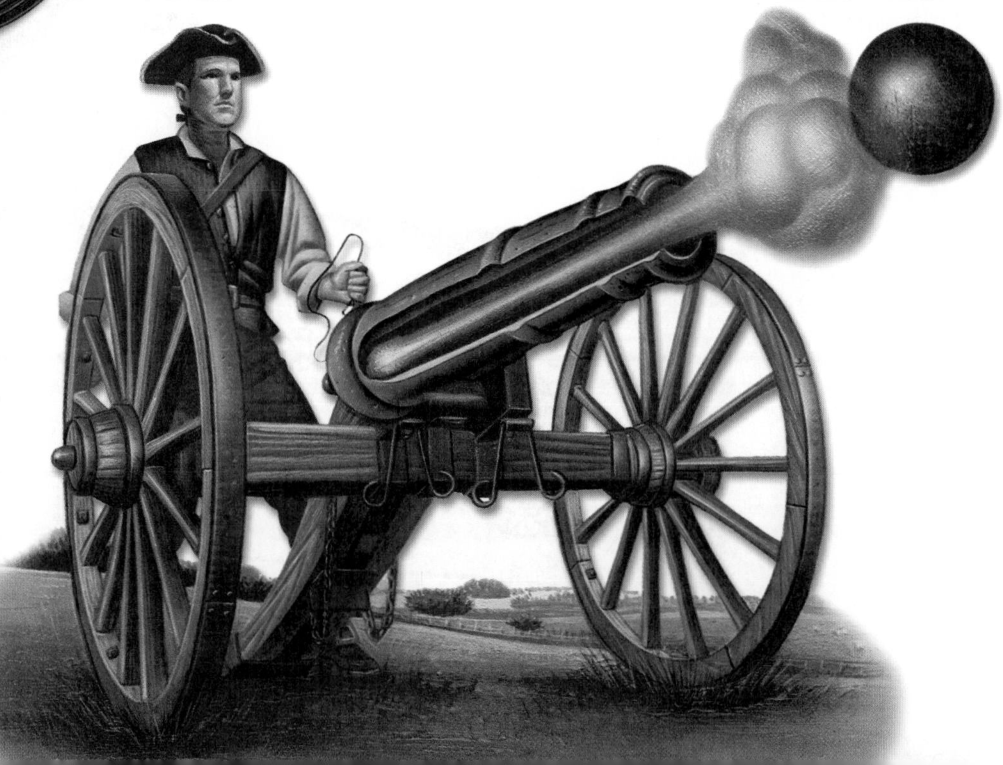

x

xi

UNIT 3 The Early Republic 1789 – 1844

xii

A Changing Nation 1810 – 1860

UNIT 4

California gold miner

Frances Ellen Watkins Harper

UNIT 5 A Nation Divided and Rebuilt 1846 – Present

Abraham Lincoln

xiv

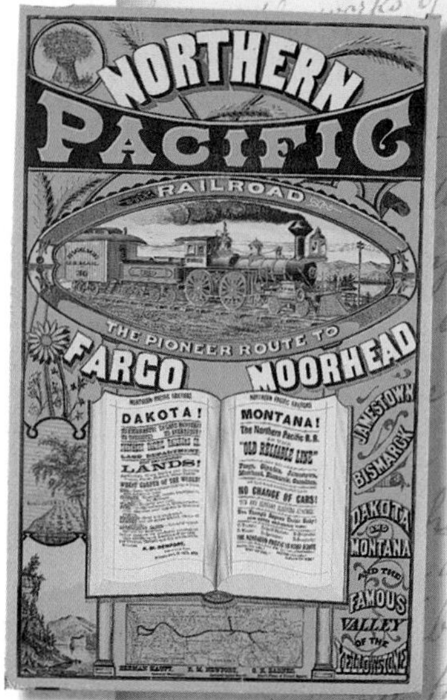

Buzz Aldrin

xv

Features

Interdisciplinary CHALLENGE

GEOGRAPHY *in* HISTORY

Technology *OF THE* Time

INTERACTIVE PRIMARY SOURCES

Literature *Connections*

HISTORY WORKSHOP

xvi

CITIZENSHIP TODAY

Economics in History

America's HERITAGE

AMERICA'S HISTORY MAKERS

xvii

Features

daily *life*

HISTORY *through* ART

Now *and* then

Connections TO

STRANGE *but* True

xviii

Voices from the Past

A VOICE FROM THE PAST

The land is the finest for cultivation that I ever in my life set foot upon, and it also abounds in trees of every description.

Henry Hudson, quoted in *Discoverers of America*

A VOICE FROM THE PAST

These, with the pictures, busts [sculptures of the head and shoulders], and prints (of which copies upon copies are spread everywhere), have made your father's face as well known as that of the moon.

Benjamin Franklin,
letter to his daughter Sally

xix

Voices from the Past

A VOICE FROM THE PAST

I overtook many sloops and schooners, beating to the windward, and parted with them as if they had been at anchor. The power of propelling boats by steam is now fully proved.

Robert Fulton,
quoted in *Robert Fulton and the "Clermont"*

xx

A VOICE FROM THE PAST

The determination of our slaveholding President to prosecute the war, and the probability of his success in wringing from the people men and money to carry it on, is made evident,...None seem willing to take their stand for peace at all risks; and all seem willing that the war should be carried on in some form or other.

Frederick Douglass,
The North Star, January 21, 1848

Chapter 14

A VOICE FROM THE PAST

The red coat was changed for one of blue and buff, a sword was held in the hand instead of a sceptre [staff of authority], the head was decorated with a cocked hat, and underneath was painted in large characters, GENERAL WASHINGTON.

Washington Irving,
"Rip Van Winkle"

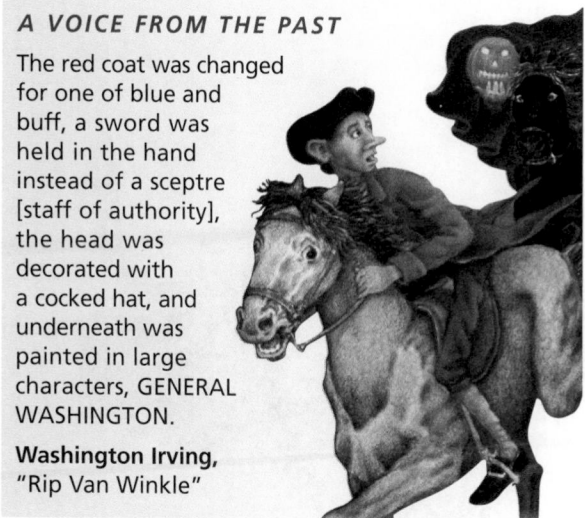

Chapter 15

A VOICE FROM THE PAST

"A house divided against itself cannot stand." I believe this government cannot endure, permanently half slave and half free. I do not expect the Union to be dissolved—I do not expect the house to fall—but I do expect it will cease to be divided. It will become all one thing, or all the other.

Abraham Lincoln,
Springfield, Illinois, June 16, 1858

Chapter 16

Chapter 17

xxi

Voices from the Past

A VOICE FROM THE PAST

This dust was once the man,
Gentle, plain, just and resolute, under whose cautious hand,
Against the foulest crime in history known in any land or age,
Was saved the Union of these States.

Walt Whitman, *This Dust Was Once the Man*

Chapter 18

Chapter 19 Epilogue

Chapter 20 Epilogue

A VOICE FROM THE PAST

I have a dream that my four little children will one day live in a nation where they will not be judged by the color of their skin but by the content of their character. I have a dream today.

Dr. Martin Luther King, Jr.,
"I Have a Dream,"
August 28, 1963

Visual Primary Sources for Assessment

xxii

Historical Maps

xxiii

Charts and Graphs

Charts

Graphs

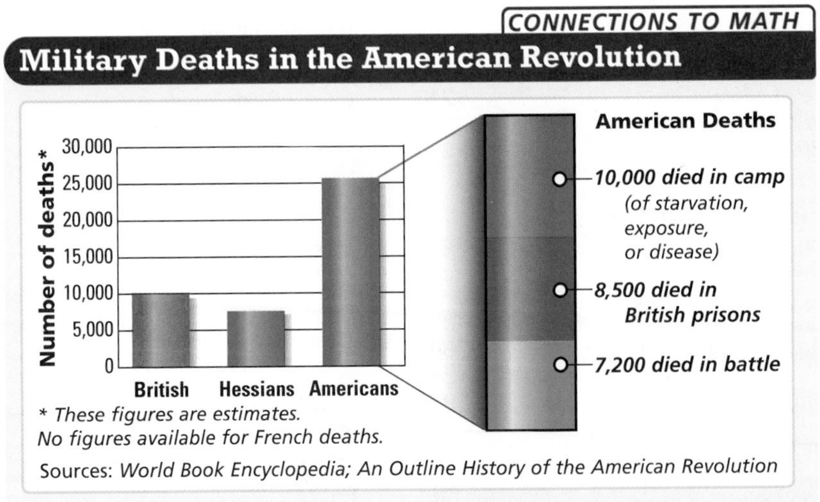

*These figures are estimates.
No figures available for French deaths.

Sources: *World Book Encyclopedia; An Outline History of the American Revolution*

xxiv

Time Lines and Infographics

Time Lines

Infographics

The Rise and Decline of Feudalism

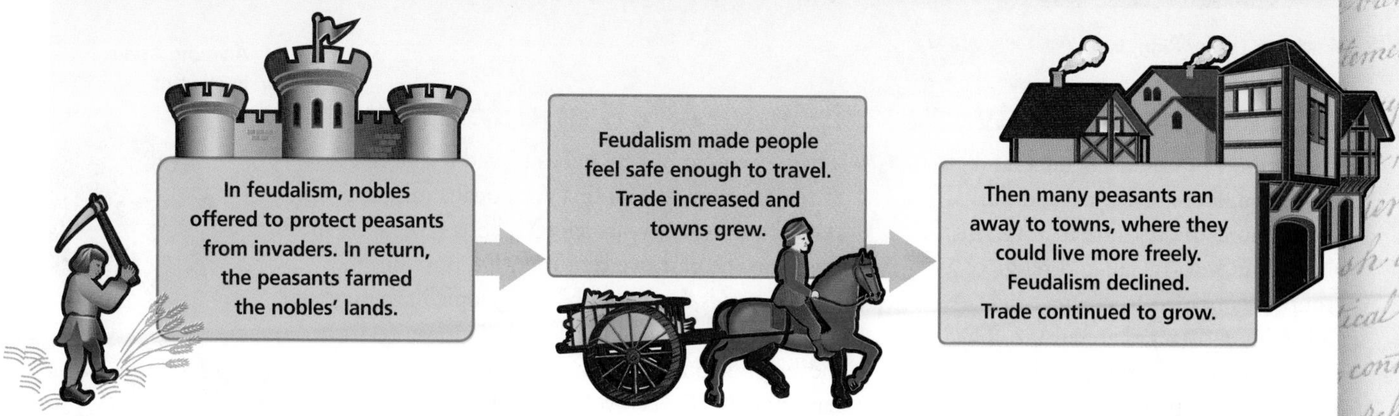

In feudalism, nobles offered to protect peasants from invaders. In return, the peasants farmed the nobles' lands.
Feudalism made people feel safe enough to travel. Trade increased and towns grew.
Then many peasants ran away to towns, where they could live more freely. Feudalism declined. Trade continued to grow.

xxv

THEMES of AMERICAN HISTORY

Imagine life in Jamestown, America's first permanent English settlement. The nation we inhabit now is a much different place than it was then, more than three centuries ago. Yet there are repeating themes—ideas and issues—in American history that tie the past and present together. This book focuses on nine significant themes in U.S. history. Understanding these themes will help you to make sense of American history.

Democratic Ideals

From the day they declared themselves citizens of a new nation, Americans have built their society around the principles of democracy. In a democracy, power lies with the people, and every individual enjoys basic rights that cannot be taken away. Throughout the nation's history, however, some Americans—mainly women and minorities—have had to struggle to gain their full rights. Still, the ideals of democracy remain the guiding principles of this land.

What right or freedom do you consider the most important? Why?

Citizenship

The citizens of the United States enjoy rights and freedoms found in very few other places in the world. Yet Americans know that with such freedoms come responsibilities and duties. Whether they stand in line to vote or spend a weekend to clean up a local river, Americans recognize that citizen participation is what keeps a democracy strong.

How do citizens that you know contribute to your community?

Dr. Martin Luther King, Jr.

Impact of the Individual

The history of the United States is the story not only of governments and laws but of individuals. Indeed, individuals have made the United States what it is today through their extraordinary achievements. American history provides a variety of examples of the impact of the individual on society in both the United States and the world.

Name several individuals who have an impact on American society today. What impact do they have?

Diversity and Unity

The United States has been a land of many peoples, cultures, and faiths. Throughout the nation's history, this blend of ethnic, racial, and religious groups has helped to create a rich and uniquely American culture. The nation's many different peoples are united in their belief in American values and ideals.

What things do you enjoy that came to the United States from other cultures?

Immigration and Migration

The movement of people has played a vital role in American history. The first Americans migrated from Asia thousands of years ago. Millions more have immigrated in the past five centuries. Even within the United States, large numbers of people have migrated to different regions of the country. However, movements to and within the United States have not always been voluntary. Africans were brought against their will to this country. Native Americans were forced from their homelands in order to make room for European settlers.

Why do you think people continue to immigrate to the United States?

A young Asian immigrant

xxvi

Expansion

When the United States declared its independence from Great Britain, it was only a collection of states along the Atlantic Ocean. But the new country would not remain that way for long. Many Americans shared a sense of curiosity, adventure, and a strong belief that their destiny was to expand all the way to the Pacific Ocean. Driven by this belief, they pushed westward. Americans' efforts to increase the size of their nation is a recurring theme in early U.S. history.

Where do you predict that the exploration of space—the final frontier—will lead?

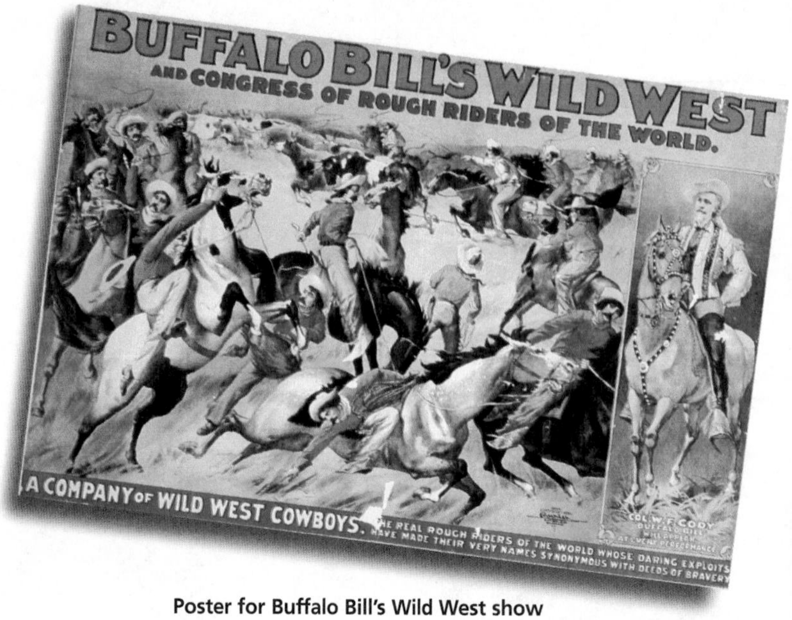

Poster for Buffalo Bill's Wild West show

America and the World

As the power and prestige of the United States have grown, the nation has played a much more active role in world affairs. Indeed, throughout the 20th century, the United States focused much of its energy on events beyond its borders. The nation fought in two world wars and tried to promote democracy, peace, and economic growth around the globe. As one of the world's political and economic leaders, the United States will continue to be a key player in world affairs throughout the new century.

What do you think the role of the United States in the world should be today?

Science and Technology

Americans have always been quick to embrace inventions and new ways of doing things. After all, this country was settled by people who turned away from old ways and tried new ones. In the past two centuries, new inventions, new technologies, and scientific breakthroughs have transformed the United States—and will continue to do so in the new century.

What recent inventions or innovations affect your life?

Economics in History

Economics has had a powerful impact on the course of U.S. history. For example, the desire for wealth led thousands to join the California Gold Rush in 1849. The nation as a whole has grown wealthy, thanks to its abundant resources and the hard work of its citizens. An important economic issue, however, has been how to make sure that all people have opportunities to share fully in the nation's wealth. This issue will continue to be important in the 21st century.

What do you think are the most exciting economic opportunities for Americans today?

Thomas Edison's first light bulb

xxvii

STRATEGIES FOR TAKING STANDARDIZED TESTS

This section of the textbook helps you develop and practice the skills you need to study history and to take standardized tests. Part 1, **Strategies for Studying History,** takes you through the features of the textbook and offers suggestions on how to use these features to improve your reading and study skills.

Part 2, **Test-Taking Strategies and Practice** offers specific strategies for tackling many of the items you'll find on a standardized test. It gives tips for answering multiple-choice, constructed-response, extended-response, and document-based questions. In addition, it offers guidelines for analyzing primary and secondary sources, maps, political cartoons, charts, graphs, and time lines. Each strategy is followed by a set of questions you can use for practice.

CONTENTS

S1

Part 1: Strategies for Studying History

Reading is the central skill in the effective study of history or any other subject. You can improve your reading skills by using helpful techniques and through practice. The better your reading skills, the more you'll remember what you read. Below you'll find several strategies that involve built-in features of *Creating America.* Careful use of these strategies will help you learn and understand history more effectively.

Preview Chapters Before You Read

Each chapter begins with a two-page chapter opener and a one-page **Setting the Stage** feature. Study the materials to help you get ready to read.

1. Read the chapter and section titles and study the chapter-opening visual. Look for clues that indicate what will be covered in the chapter.
2. Preview the time line. Note the years that the chapter covers. What important events took place during this time period?
3. Study the **Interact with History** feature. Experience what it was like to live in the past by answering **What Do You Think?** questions.
4. Read the **Setting the Stage** feature (see page S3). **What Do You Want to Know?** and **Read and Take Notes** will help focus your reading.

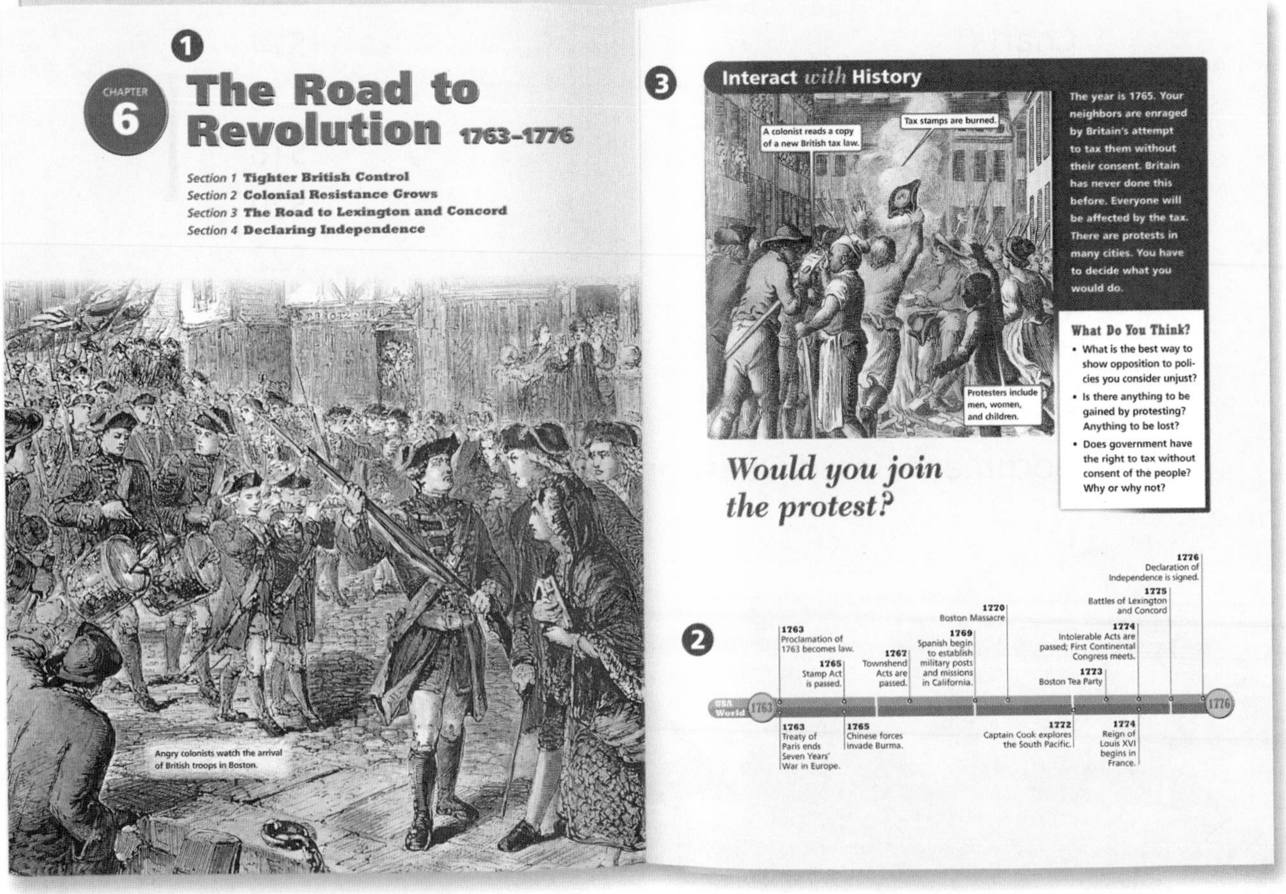
1
CHAPTER 6
The Road to Revolution 1763–1776
Section 1 Tighter British Control
Section 2 Colonial Resistance Grows
Section 3 The Road to Lexington and Concord
Section 4 Declaring Independence
Angry colonists watch the arrival of British troops in Boston.
3
Interact with History
A colonist reads a copy of a new British tax law.
Tax stamps are burned.
Protesters include men, women, and children.
The year is 1765. Your neighbors are enraged by Britain's attempt to tax them without their consent. Britain has never done this before. Everyone will be affected by the tax. There are protests in many cities. You have to decide what you would do.
What Do You Think?
• What is the best way to show opposition to policies you consider unjust?
• Is there anything to be gained by protesting? Anything to be lost?
• Does government have the right to tax without consent of the people? Why or why not?
Would you join the protest?
2
USA
World
1763
1763 Proclamation of 1763 becomes law.
1765 Stamp Act is passed.
1767 Townshend Acts are passed.
1769 Spanish begin to establish military posts and missions in California.
1770 Boston Massacre
1773 Boston Tea Party
1774 Intolerable Acts are passed; First Continental Congress meets.
1775 Battles of Lexington and Concord
1776 Declaration of Independence is signed.
1763 Treaty of Paris ends Seven Years' War in Europe.
1765 Chinese forces invade Burma.
1772 Captain Cook explores the South Pacific.
1774 Reign of Louis XVI begins in France.
1776

S2

Preview Sections Before You Read

Each chapter consists of three, four, or five sections. These sections focus on shorter periods of time or on particular historical themes. Use the section openers to help you prepare to read.

5. Study the sentences under the headings **Main Idea** and **Why It Matters Now.** These tell you what's important in the material that you're about to read.
6. Preview the **Terms & Names** list. This will give you an idea of the issues and personalities you will read about in the section.
7. Read **One American's Story** and **A Voice from the Past**. These provide one individual's view of an important issue of the time.
8. Notice how the section is divided into smaller chunks, each with a red headline. These headlines give you a quick outline of the section.

TERMS & NAMES
King George III
Quartering Act
revenue
Sugar Act
Stamp Act
Patrick Henry
boycott
Sons of Liberty

4

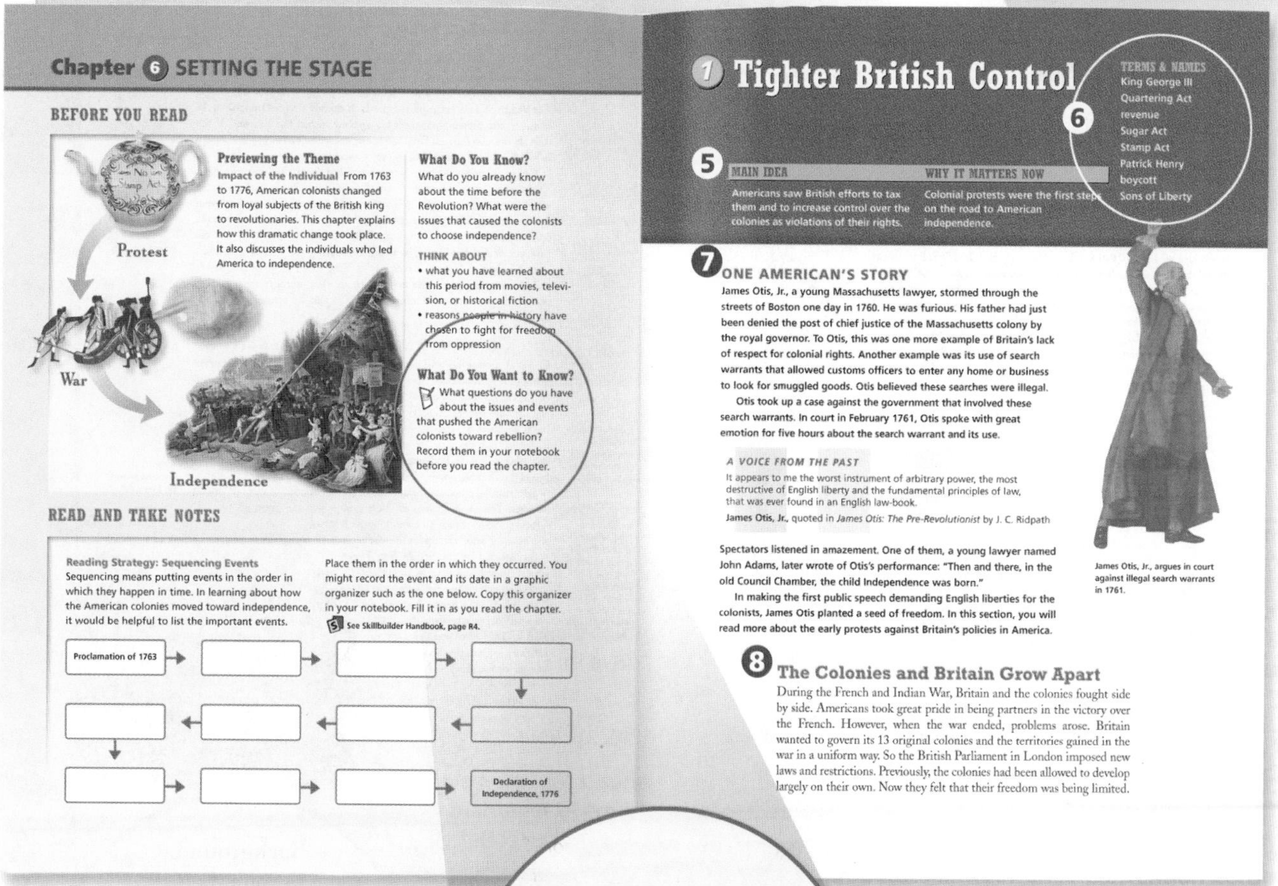

Chapter 6 SETTING THE STAGE

BEFORE YOU READ

Previewing the Theme
Impact of the Individual From 1763 to 1776, American colonists changed from loyal subjects of the British king to revolutionaries. This chapter explains how this dramatic change took place. It also discusses the individuals who led America to independence.

What Do You Know?
What do you already know about the time before the Revolution? What were the issues that caused the colonists to choose independence?

THINK ABOUT
- what you have learned about this period from movies, television, or historical fiction
- reasons people in history have chosen to fight for freedom from oppression

What Do You Want to Know?
What questions do you have about the issues and events that pushed the American colonists toward rebellion? Record them in your notebook before you read the chapter.

READ AND TAKE NOTES

Reading Strategy: Sequencing Events
Sequencing means putting events in the order in which they happen in time. In learning about how the American colonies moved toward independence, it would be helpful to list the important events. Place them in the order in which they occurred. You might record the event and its date in a graphic organizer such as the one below. Copy this organizer in your notebook. Fill it in as you read the chapter.
See Skillbuilder Handbook, page R4.

1 Tighter British Control

6
TERMS & NAMES
King George III
Quartering Act
revenue
Sugar Act
Stamp Act
Patrick Henry
boycott
Sons of Liberty

5
MAIN IDEA	WHY IT MATTERS NOW
Americans saw British efforts to tax them and to increase control over the colonies as violations of their rights.	Colonial protests were the first steps on the road to American independence.

7 **ONE AMERICAN'S STORY**
James Otis, Jr., a young Massachusetts lawyer, stormed through the streets of Boston one day in 1760. He was furious. His father had just been denied the post of chief justice of the Massachusetts colony by the royal governor. To Otis, this was one more example of Britain's lack of respect for colonial rights. Another example was its use of search warrants that allowed customs officers to enter any home or business to look for smuggled goods. Otis believed these searches were illegal.

Otis took up a case against the government that involved these search warrants. In court in February 1761, Otis spoke with great emotion for five hours about the search warrant and its use.

A VOICE FROM THE PAST
It appears to me the worst instrument of arbitrary power, the most destructive of English liberty and the fundamental principles of law, that was ever found in an English law-book.
James Otis, Jr., quoted in *James Otis: The Pre-Revolutionist* by J. C. Ridpath

Spectators listened in amazement. One of them, a young lawyer named John Adams, later wrote of Otis's performance: "Then and there, in the old Council Chamber, the child Independence was born."

In making the first public speech demanding English liberties for the colonists, James Otis planted a seed of freedom. In this section, you will read more about the early protests against Britain's policies in America.

James Otis, Jr., argues in court against illegal search warrants in 1761.

8 **The Colonies and Britain Grow Apart**
During the French and Indian War, Britain and the colonies fought side by side. Americans took great pride in being partners in the victory over the French. However, when the war ended, problems arose. Britain wanted to govern its 13 original colonies and the territories gained in the war in a uniform way. So the British Parliament in London imposed new laws and restrictions. Previously, the colonies had been allowed to develop largely on their own. Now they felt that their freedom was being limited.

What Do You Want to Know?
What questions do you have about the issues and events that pushed the American colonists toward rebellion? Record them in your notebook before you read the chapter.

S3

Use Active Reading Strategies As You Read

Now you're ready to read the chapter. Read one section at a time, from beginning to end.

1. Ask and answer questions as you read. Look for the **Reading History** questions in the margin. Answering these will show whether you understand what you've just read.
2. Try to visualize the people, places, and events you read about. Studying the pictures and any illustrated features will help you do this.
3. Read to build your vocabulary. Use the marginal **Vocabulary** notes to find the meaning of unfamiliar terms.
4. Look for the story behind the events. Read **Background** notes in the margin for additional information on people, places, events, and ideas.

*Reading*History
A. Summarizing
Who was upset by the Proclamation of 1763?

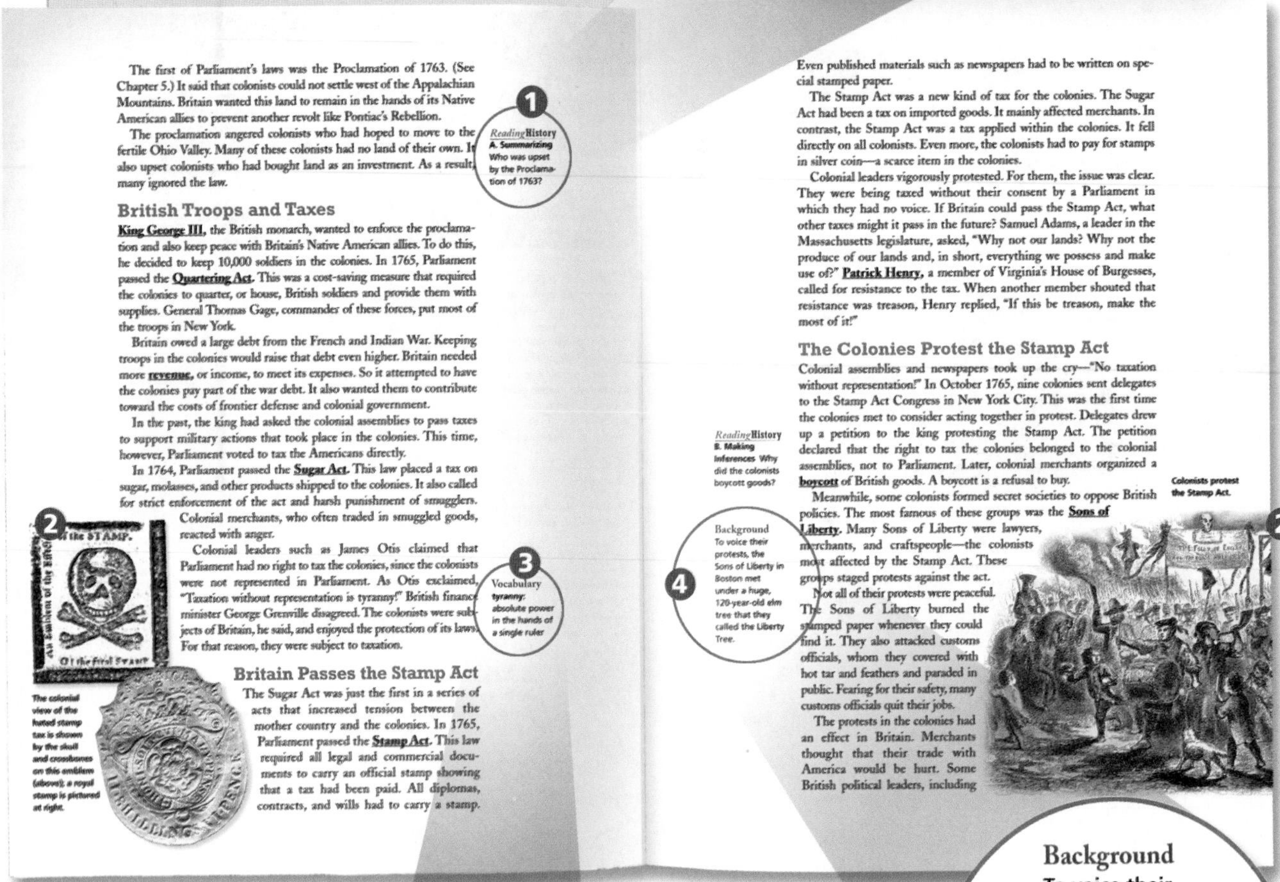
The first of Parliament's laws was the Proclamation of 1763. (See Chapter 5.) It said that colonists could not settle west of the Appalachian Mountains. Britain wanted this land to remain in the hands of its Native American allies to prevent another revolt like Pontiac's Rebellion.

The proclamation angered colonists who had hoped to move to the fertile Ohio Valley. Many of these colonists had no land of their own. It also upset colonists who had bought land as an investment. As a result, many ignored the law.

1 *Reading*History **A. Summarizing** Who was upset by the Proclamation of 1763?

British Troops and Taxes

King George III, the British monarch, wanted to enforce the proclamation and also keep peace with Britain's Native American allies. To do this, he decided to keep 10,000 soldiers in the colonies. In 1765, Parliament passed the **Quartering Act.** This was a cost-saving measure that required the colonies to quarter, or house, British soldiers and provide them with supplies. General Thomas Gage, commander of these forces, put most of the troops in New York.

Britain owed a large debt from the French and Indian War. Keeping troops in the colonies would raise that debt even higher. Britain needed more **revenue,** or income, to meet its expenses. So it attempted to have the colonies pay part of the war debt. It also wanted them to contribute toward the costs of frontier defense and colonial government.

In the past, the king had asked the colonial assemblies to pass taxes to support military actions that took place in the colonies. This time, however, Parliament voted to tax the Americans directly.

In 1764, Parliament passed the **Sugar Act.** This law placed a tax on sugar, molasses, and other products shipped to the colonies. It also called for strict enforcement of the act and harsh punishment of smugglers. Colonial merchants, who often traded in smuggled goods, reacted with anger.

Colonial leaders such as James Otis claimed that Parliament had no right to tax the colonies, since the colonists were not represented in Parliament. As Otis exclaimed, "Taxation without representation is tyranny!" British finance minister George Grenville disagreed. The colonists were subjects of Britain, he said, and enjoyed the protection of its laws. For that reason, they were subject to taxation.

3 Vocabulary **tyranny:** absolute power in the hands of a single ruler

2 The colonial view of the hated stamp tax is shown by the skull and crossbones on this emblem (above); a royal stamp is pictured at right.

Britain Passes the Stamp Act

The Sugar Act was just the first in a series of acts that increased tension between the mother country and the colonies. In 1765, Parliament passed the **Stamp Act.** This law required all legal and commercial documents to carry an official stamp showing that a tax had been paid. All diplomas, contracts, and wills had to carry a stamp. Even published materials such as newspapers had to be written on special stamped paper.

The Stamp Act was a new kind of tax for the colonies. The Sugar Act had been a tax on imported goods. It mainly affected merchants. In contrast, the Stamp Act was a tax applied within the colonies. It fell directly on all colonists. Even more, the colonists had to pay for stamps in silver coin—a scarce item in the colonies.

Colonial leaders vigorously protested. For them, the issue was clear. They were being taxed without their consent by a Parliament in which they had no voice. If Britain could pass the Stamp Act, what other taxes might it pass in the future? Samuel Adams, a leader in the Massachusetts legislature, asked, "Why not our lands? Why not the produce of our lands and, in short, everything we possess and make use of?" **Patrick Henry,** a member of Virginia's House of Burgesses, called for resistance to the tax. When another member shouted that resistance was treason, Henry replied, "If this be treason, make the most of it!"

The Colonies Protest the Stamp Act

Colonial assemblies and newspapers took up the cry—"No taxation without representation!" In October 1765, nine colonies sent delegates to the Stamp Act Congress in New York City. This was the first time the colonies met to consider acting together in protest. Delegates drew up a petition to the king protesting the Stamp Act. The petition declared that the right to tax the colonies belonged to the colonial assemblies, not to Parliament. Later, colonial merchants organized a **boycott** of British goods. A boycott is a refusal to buy.

*Reading*History **B. Making Inferences** Why did the colonists boycott goods?

Meanwhile, some colonists formed secret societies to oppose British policies. The most famous of these groups was the **Sons of Liberty.** Many Sons of Liberty were lawyers, merchants, and craftspeople—the colonists most affected by the Stamp Act. These groups staged protests against the act.

4 Background To voice their protests, the Sons of Liberty in Boston met under a huge, 120-year-old elm tree that they called the Liberty Tree.

Not all of their protests were peaceful. The Sons of Liberty burned the stamped paper whenever they could find it. They also attacked customs officials, whom they covered with hot tar and feathers and paraded in public. Fearing for their safety, many customs officials quit their jobs.

The protests in the colonies had an effect in Britain. Merchants thought that their trade with America would be hurt. Some British political leaders, including

2 Colonists protest the Stamp Act.

Background
To voice their protests, the Sons of Liberty in Boston met under a huge, 120-year-old elm tree that they called the Liberty Tree.

Vocabulary
tyranny:
absolute power in the hands of a single ruler

S4

Review and Summarize What You Have Read

When you finish reading a section, review and summarize what you've read. If necessary, go back and reread information that was not clear the first time through.

5. Reread the red headlines for a quick summary of the major points covered in the section.
6. Study any charts, graphs, and maps in the section. These visual materials usually provide a condensed version of information in the section.
7. Review the pictures and note how they relate to the section content.
8. Complete all the questions in the **Section Assessment.** They will help you think critically about what you have just read.

immediately offered Massachusetts their support. They sent food and money to Boston. The committees of correspondence also called for a meeting of colonial delegates to discuss what to do next.

5

The First Continental Congress Meets

In September 1774, delegates from all the colonies except Georgia met in Philadelphia. At this meeting, called the **First Continental Congress,** delegates voted to ban all trade with Britain until the Intolerable Acts were repealed. They also called on each colony to begin training troops. Georgia agreed to be a part of the actions of the Congress even though it had voted not to send delegates.

The First Continental Congress marked a key step in American history. Although most delegates were not ready to call for independence, they were determined to uphold colonial rights. This meeting planted the seeds of a future independent government. John Adams called it "a nursery of American statesmen." The delegates agreed to meet in seven months, if necessary. By that time, however, fighting with Britain had begun.

*Reading*History
A. Evaluating
Why do you think the First Continental Congress was important?

Between War and Peace

The colonists hoped that the trade boycott would force a repeal of the Intolerable Acts. After all, past boycotts had led to the repeal of the Stamp Act and the Townshend Acts. This time, however, Parliament stood firm. It even increased restrictions on colonial trade and sent more troops.

By the end of 1774, some colonists were preparing to fight. In Massachusetts, John Hancock headed the Committee of Safety, which had the power to call out the militia. The colonial troops continued to train.

6

CAUSE AND EFFECT: *Growing Conflict Between Britain and America*

DATE	BRITISH ACTION	COLONIAL REACTION
1763	Proclamation of 1763 issued	Proclamation leads to anger
1765	Stamp Act passed	Boycott of British goods; Stamp Act Resolves passed
1766	Stamp Act repealed; Declaration Act passed	Boycott ended
1767	Townshend Acts passed	New boycotts; Boston Massacre (March 1770)
1770	Townshend Acts repealed (April)	Tension between colonies and Britain reduced
1773	Tea Act passed	Boston Tea Party
1774	Intolerable Acts passed	First Continental Congress bans trade; militias organized
1775	Troops ordered to Lexington and Concord, Massachusetts	Militia fights British troops; Second Continental Congress; Continental Army established

SKILLBUILDER **Interpreting Charts**
1. *What British action caused the first violence in the growing conflict between Britain and America?*
2. *How might the Intolerable Acts be seen as a reaction as well as an action?*

When the British moved, so did Revere and Dawes. They galloped over the countryside on their "midnight ride," spreading the news. In Lexington, they were joined by Dr. Samuel Prescott. When Revere and Dawes were stopped by a British patrol, Prescott broke away and carried the message to Concord.

Lexington and Concord

At dawn on April 19, some 700 British troops reached Lexington. They found Captain John Parker and about 70 militiamen waiting. The British commander ordered the Americans to drop their muskets. They refused. No one knows who fired first, but within a few minutes eight militiamen lay dead. The British then marched to Concord, where they destroyed military supplies. A battle broke out at a bridge north of town, forcing the British to retreat.

Nearly 4,000 Minutemen and militiamen arrived in the area. They lined the road from Concord to Lexington and peppered the retreating redcoats with musket fire. "It seemed as if men came down from the clouds," one soldier said. Only the arrival of 1,000 more troops saved the British from destruction as they scrambled back to Boston.

Background
British losses totaled 273 soldiers compared to 95 militiamen.

Lexington and Concord were the first battles of the Revolutionary War. As Ralph Waldo Emerson later wrote, colonial troops had fired the "shot heard 'round the world." Americans would now have to choose sides and back up their political opinions by force of arms. Those who supported the British were called **Loyalists.** Those who sided with the rebels were **Patriots.** The conflict between the two sides divided communities, families, and friends. The war was on!

*Reading*History
C. Drawing Conclusions
Why did Emerson call it the "shot heard 'round the world"?

Now and then

PATRIOTS' DAY

The "shot heard 'round the world" is celebrated every year in Massachusetts and Maine. Patriots' Day, as it is called, is the third Monday of April. In Concord and nearby towns, modern-day Minutemen like those below reenact the battle that began the Revolution on April 19, 1775. The Boston Marathon is also run on Patriots' Day.

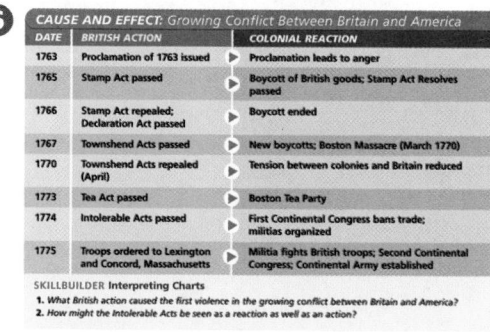

7

8

Section 3 Assessment

1. Terms & Names
Identify:
- militia
- Minuteman
- Intolerable Acts
- First Continental Congress
- Paul Revere
- Lexington and Concord
- Loyalist
- Patriot

2. Taking Notes
Use a diagram like the one below to show events that led to the Revolutionary War.

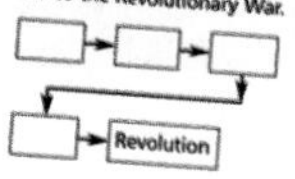

3. Main Ideas
a. Why did Britain pass the Intolerable Acts?
b. Who took part in the First Continental Congress?
c. What was the purpose of the "midnight ride"?

4. Critical Thinking
Supporting Opinions
Do you think the fighting between Britain and the colonies could have been avoided? Why or why not?
THINK ABOUT
- Britain's attitude toward the colonies
- colonial feelings about Britain

ACTIVITY OPTIONS
GEOGRAPHY
MATH
Research the Battles of Lexington and Concord. Draw a **map** of key events or create a **chart** showing statistics from the battles.

S5

USING STRATEGIES FOR . . .

Multiple Choice
Multiple-choice questions test the ability to choose the correct answer from several choices. The test taker reads each stem and decides which is the correct answer. Test takers are often asked to mark their answers on an answer sheet by filling in the circle or oval that has the same letter as the answer they have chosen.

Explain to students that they will do best on test questions that they think through carefully and by applying test-taking strategies such as the following.

1. Pay attention to introductory phrases such as "At the beginning of the Revolution" in question 1. Americans' feelings at the beginning were different from their feelings at the end, when they were generally against the British. Thus, at the beginning, most Americans were (C) against a war with Great Britain.

2. Question 2 includes *all of the above* among the choices. If you select this answer, be sure that all of the choices are correct. Since Arizona, California, and New Mexico were all ceded to the United States in the Treaty of Guadalupe Hidalgo, the correct answer is (D) all of the above.

3. In question 3, eliminate (D) because of the word *all.* Use your knowledge of history to eliminate (A), since Oklahoma was not a state at the time of the Civil War. Although (C) includes four border states, West Virginia was part of Virginia at the beginning of the Civil War. Therefore, (B) is the best answer.

General Test-Taking Tips
Share these tips with your students.
- The night before a test, make sure you get at least eight hours of sleep.
- Have a healthy breakfast or lunch before taking your test.
- Wear clothes that make you comfortable.
- Relax and enjoy the challenge!

Part 2: Test-Taking Strategies and Practice

Improve your test-taking skills by practicing the strategies discussed in this section. Read the tips on the left-hand page. Then apply them to the practice items on the right-hand page.

Multiple Choice

A multiple-choice question consists of a stem and a set of choices. The stem is usually in the form of a question or an incomplete sentence. One of the choices correctly answers the question or completes the sentence.

1. Read the stem carefully and try to answer the question or complete the sentence without looking at the choices.
2. Pay close attention to key words in the stem. They may direct you toward the correct answer.
3. Read each choice with the stem. Don't jump to conclusions about the correct answer until you've read all of the choices.
4. Think carefully about questions that include *All of the above* among the choices.
5. After reading all of the choices, eliminate any that you know are incorrect.
6. Use modifiers to help narrow your choice.
7. Look for the best answer among the remaining choices.

answers: 1 (C), 2 (D), 3 (B)

stem

❶ 1. At the beginning of the Revolution, most Americans were

❷ *Most* is a key word here. Replacing it with *all* or *some* changes the sentence and calls for a different answer.

❸ choices

A. united in support of the war.
B. Patriots who wanted independence from Great Britain.
C. against a war with Great Britain.
D. Loyalists who supported the British point of view.

2. Which of the following present-day states was ceded to the United States in the Treaty of Guadalupe Hidalgo?

A. Arizona
B. California
C. New Mexico
D. all of the above

❹ If you select this answer, be sure that all of the choices are correct.

3. At the outset of the Civil War, both the Union and the Confederacy wanted the support of the border states

A. Delaware, Maryland, Kentucky, and Oklahoma.
B. Delaware, Maryland, Kentucky, and Missouri.
C. Delaware, Maryland, West Virginia, Kentucky, and Missouri.
D. all the states bordering the Missouri Compromise line.

❺ You can eliminate **A** if you remember that Oklahoma was not a state at the time of the Civil War.

❻ Absolute words, such as *all, never, always, every,* and *only,* often signal an incorrect choice.

❼ In **C,** West Virginia did lie on the border between the Union and the Confederacy. However, it broke away from Virginia early in the war and became a state in 1863. Therefore, **B** is the correct answer.

ACTIVITY OPTIONS

INDIVIDUAL NEEDS

STUDENTS ACQUIRING ENGLISH/ESL

Social Studies Vocabulary Make sure students understand the following terms and concepts in the sample questions on these pages.

Strategy Page
Question 1 *Americans:* Europeans who came to live in the New World
Question 2 *ceded:* surrendered; given up
Question 3 *border states:* slave states that bordered states in which slavery was not legal

Practice Page
Question 1 *harrow:* a farming machine used to break up clumps of soil before planting
Question 2 *Puritans:* a religious group from England in the 16th and 17th centuries
Question 3 *foster:* encourage; promote
Question 4 *Alamo:* a mission in San Antonio, Texas, captured by Mexico in 1836

For more test practice online . . .
TEST PRACTICE
CLASSZONE.COM

Directions: Read the following questions and choose the *best* answer from the four choices.

1. New inventions that helped open the Great Plains to farming included

A. the steel windmill.
B. barbed wire.
C. the spring-tooth harrow.
D. all of the above

2. The movement of Puritans from England to North America in the 1620s and 1630s is known as the Great

A. Awakening.
B. Compromise.
C. Debate.
D. Migration.

3. During the presidency of Thomas Jefferson, the United States was able to foster westward expansion when it acquired territory in what is known as

A. Seward's Folly.
B. the Missouri Compromise.
C. the Kansas-Nebraska Act.
D. the Louisiana Purchase.

4. Who commanded the Texan forces at the Alamo?

A. James Fannin
B. David Crockett
C. William Travis
D. Sam Houston

PRACTICE QUESTIONS

Thinking It Through

Share the following explanations with students as they discuss the strategies they used to answer the practice questions.

1. This item is an example of an *All of the above* question. If any of the choices had not been an invention that helped open the Great Plains to farming between 1854 and 1880, you would have been able to eliminate that answer and *all of the above* and would have then had to choose between the other two. In this case, the correct answer is (D).
2. Use your knowledge of U.S. history to answer this question. Eliminate (A) since the Great Awakening was the revival of religious feeling in the American colonies during the 1730s and 1740s. Eliminate (B) since the Great Compromise involved an agreement in the Constitutional Convention to establish a two-house national legislature. Notice that the question asks about the Puritans' *movement* from one country to another, which means migration. The correct answer is (D).
3. This is an example of eliminating obviously incorrect answers. Seward's Folly (the acquisition of Alaska) did not occur during Jefferson's presidency, so (A) is incorrect. Neither the Missouri Compromise nor the Kansas-Nebraska Act acquired any territory for the United States, so (B) and (C) are incorrect. The correct answer is (D).
4. James Fannin led a Texas force at Goliad, so eliminate (A). Although Davy Crockett fought and died at the Alamo, he was not the commander, so eliminate (B). Sam Houston was the commander of the Texas army, but he was not at the Alamo. The correct answer is (C).

SKILLS TESTED IN THE ITEMS

STRATEGY ITEMS		PRACTICE ITEMS	
Item Number	**Skill Tested**	**Item Number**	**Skill Tested**
1.	Clarifying	**1.**	Categorizing
2.	Categorizing	**2.**	Clarifying
3.	Categorizing	**3.**	Analyzing Causes; Recognizing Effects
		4.	Clarifying

USING STRATEGIES FOR . . .

Primary Sources

Students can learn about the past by studying primary sources. As students read the primary source, have them try to answer the following questions: Who is it about? What is it about? When did it happen? Where did it happen? Why did it happen?

Explain to students that they will do best on test questions by thinking them through carefully and by applying test-taking strategies, such as the following.

1. Look at the primary source itself when answering the questions. Question 1 asks you to identify the war in which the attack takes place. You should skim the passage to find information that would help identify the war. In this case, the date (1814) in the source line is a clue to the correct answer, (D).

2. Question 2 asks you to consider what qualifies the author to write about the events discussed in the passage. The passage indicates that Dolley Madison was an eyewitness to the attack, so (B) is the correct answer.

General Test-Taking Tips

Share these tips with your students.

- Read the directions carefully before you begin to answer the questions.
- Plan the time you are given to take the test.
- Check your answers.
- Believe in yourself.

Primary Sources

Primary sources are materials written or made by people who took part in or witnessed historical events. Letters, diaries, speeches, newspaper articles, and autobiographies are all primary sources. So, too, are legal documents, such as wills, deeds, and financial records.

1. Look at the source line and identify the author. Consider what qualifies the author to write about the events discussed in the passage.
2. Skim the document to form an idea of what it is about.
3. Note special punctuation. Ellipses indicate that words or sentences have been removed from the original passage. Brackets indicate words that were not in the original. Bracketed words often are replacements for difficult or unfamiliar terms.
4. Carefully read the passage and distinguish between facts and the author's opinions. (That the groups of soldiers were wandering in all directions is a fact. The reasons for their wandering offered by Madison are her opinions.)
5. Consider for whom the author was writing. The intended audience may influence what and how an author writes.
6. Before rereading the passage, skim the questions to identify the information you need to find.

answers: 1 (D), 2 (B)

The Flight from the White House

Wednesday Morning, twelve o'clock. Since sunrise I have been turning my spy-glass in every direction, . . . but alas! I can [see] (3) only groups of military, wandering in all directions, as if there was (4) a lack of arms, or of spirit to fight for their own fireside.

(2) *Three o'clock.* Will you believe it, my sister? we have had a battle, or skirmish, near Bladensburg, and here I am still, within sound of the cannon!. . . Two messengers covered with dust come to bid me fly. . . . At this late hour a wagon has been [found], and I have had it filled with plate and the most valuable portable articles belonging to the house. Whether it will reach its destination . . . or fall into the hands of British soldiery, events must determine. Our kind friend, Mr. Carroll, has come to hasten my departure, and is in a very bad humor with me, because I insist on waiting until the large picture of General Washington is secured. . . . It is done! and the precious portrait placed in the hands of two gentlemen of New York, for safe keeping. And now, dear sister, I must leave this house. . . . When I shall again write to you, or where I shall be tomorrow, I cannot tell!

—Dolley Madison, in a letter to her sister describing her flight from the White House in August 1814

(1) The author is Dolley Madison, the wife of President James Madison. She personally oversaw the evacuation of the White House in 1814.

(5) This is a letter. If it were an official report to Congress, the style and content would be much different.

(6) 1. Dolley Madison's letter describes her preparations to flee the White House in advance of a British attack. In which war did this attack take place?

A. War of Jenkins' Ear
B. French and Indian War
C. Revolutionary War
D. War of 1812

2. Why might Dolley Madison be considered a good source of information on the British attack on Washington, D.C.?

A. She was the wife of President James Madison.
B. She was an eyewitness to the attack.
C. She helped her husband develop military policy.
D. She had intercepted British war plans.

ACTIVITY OPTIONS

INDIVIDUAL NEEDS

STUDENTS ACQUIRING ENGLISH/ESL

Social Studies Vocabulary Make sure students understand the following terms and concepts in the sample questions on these pages.

Strategy Page: Primary Source
fireside: hearth, standing for home
plate: silver-plated serving dishes and utensils
soldiery: soldiers
in a bad humor: annoyed, displeased

Practice Page: Primary Source
emphasize: make known the importance of
fellowship: brotherhood; companionship
prevailed: was felt
fashion: to create; to make

For more test practice online . . .
TEST PRACTICE
CLASSZONE.COM

Directions: Use this passage and your knowledge of U.S. history to answer questions 1 through 4.

Life in Texas, Mid-1800s

I wish that I could emphasize this feature of our early Texan life. *The spirit of helpfulness and friendly fellowship always prevailed. It was one of the best of the good things of the new country.* We were all strangers together, always willing to lend or borrow. . . . Once Mr. Van Zandt was called away from home . . . [and] another man came and took our gun and killed a deer, for he knew we needed meat. . . . When our need for things was pressing, we usually found a way for making them. One time Mr. Van Zandt needed a saddle—he made it, having only a drawing knife from which to fashion the saddle-tree from a dead sassafras tree which he cut down for the purpose. His shoes were gone and he could get no others. He bought some red leather, made a last [a foot-shaped, wooden block] and manufactured some very respectable shoes.

—Frances Cook Lipscomb Van Zandt,
Texas settler, 1839–1846

1. What was a good thing about the new Texas country that the author writes was important to her?

   A. Being hungry
   B. Being a stranger
   C. The spirit of helpfulness and friendliness
   D. Getting deer meat whenever she wanted it

2. Mr. Van Zandt used leather, wood, and simple tools to

   A. build a wagon.
   B. make goods to trade for meat.
   C. build a spinning wheel.
   D. make a saddle and shoes.

3. According to the passage, the Van Zandts and their Texas neighbors got their supplies in all of the following ways *except* by

   A. lending or borrowing things.
   B. making them by hand with simple tools.
   C. buying them from mail-order catalogs.
   D. volunteering to help each other.

4. Frances Van Zandt wrote, "We were all strangers together," to explain that hardships on the Texas frontier

   A. left people isolated and alone.
   B. drew people together to help each other.
   C. were shared only by close friends and relatives.
   D. made people suspicious of one another.

Passage from "Frances Cook Lipscomb Van Zandt Reminisces About the Early Years in Texas, 1839–1846," from the Van Zandt Folder, Mary Daggett Lake Papers, series IV, box 3, Fort Worth Public Library, Fort Worth, Texas. Courtesy of the Fort Worth Public Library, Fort Worth, Texas.

PRACTICE QUESTIONS

Thinking It Through

Share the following explanations with students as they discuss the strategies they used to answer the practice questions.

1. You may recall the answer to this question without needing to reread the passage. If not, skim the passage to identify a good thing about the new Texas country that was important to the author. In the second and third sentences, she says the spirit of helpfulness and friendly fellowship is one of the best things of the new country. So the correct answer is (C).
2. Skim the passage to find the answer to this question. (D) is the correct answer.
3. The word *except* in this question makes it an example of a question constructed in the negative. You are asked to find the way that the Van Zandt family and their neighbors did not get their supplies. To answer this item, you should first find the three ways that the family and their friends did get their supplies. The passage mentions or implies (A), (B), and (D) as ways the Van Zandt family and their neighbors got their supplies. The passage does not mention buying supplies from mail-order catalogs, so (C) is the correct answer.
4. Skim the passage to form an idea of what Van Zandt meant by "We were all strangers together." The main idea of the passage is that the hardships on the Texas frontier drew people together to help each other, so (B) is the correct answer.

SKILLS TESTED IN THE ITEMS

STRATEGY ITEMS		PRACTICE ITEMS	
Item Number	**Skill Tested**	**Item Number**	**Skill Tested**
1.	Clarifying	**1.**	Clarifying
2.	Making Inferences	**2.**	Summarizing
		3.	Clarifying
		4.	Determining Main Ideas

USING STRATEGIES FOR . . .

Secondary Sources

Explain to students that they will do best on test questions by thinking them through carefully and by applying test-taking strategies, such as the following.

1. Question 1 asks you to analyze the authors' point of view. First, use context clues in the passage to determine the meaning of *fiasco.* Next, reread the passage to find information that would help you identify why the Battle of Bladensburg was a fiasco. The authors say that "the American troops fled, virtually without firing a shot," so (A) is the correct answer.

2. Question 2 asks you to find what the British raid on Washington, D.C., accomplished. The passage indicates that besides "embarrassing and angering Americans, the Washington raid accomplished little. . . ." Therefore, (D) is the correct answer.

General Test-Taking Tips

Share these tips with your students.

- Glance over the test to determine the types and numbers of questions.
- Estimate the amount of time you have to spend on each type of question.

Secondary Sources

Secondary sources are descriptions or interpretations of historical events made by people who were not at those events. The most common types of written secondary sources are history books, encyclopedias, and biographies. A secondary source often combines information from several primary sources.

1. Read titles to preview what the passage is about.
2. Look for topic sentences. These, too, will help you preview the content of the passage.
3. As you read, use context clues to help you understand difficult or unfamiliar words. (You can tell from the description of the battle in the previous sentences that the word *fiasco* must mean something like "disaster," "failure," or "blunder.")
4. As you read, ask and answer questions that come to mind. You might ask: Why would the Washington raid embarrass and anger Americans? Why did the Washington raid achieve little?
5. Before rereading the passage, skim the questions to identify the information you need to find.

answers: 1 (A), 2 (D)

(1) **The British Offensive**

(2) Ironically, Britain's most spectacular success began as a diversion from [its main] offensive [in the North]. A British army that had come up from Bermuda entered Chesapeake Bay and on August 24, 1814, met a larger American force . . . at Bladensburg, Maryland. The Battle of Bladensburg deteriorated into the "Bladensburg Races" as the American troops fled, virtually without firing a shot. The British then descended on Washington, D.C. Madison, who had witnessed (3) the Bladensburg fiasco, fled into the Virginia hills. His wife, Dolley, loaded her silver, a bed, and a portrait of George Washington onto her carriage before joining him. British troops ate the supper prepared for the Madisons and then burned the presidential mansion (4) and other public buildings in the capital. Beyond embarrassing and angering Americans, the Washington raid accomplished little, for after a failed attack on Baltimore, the British broke off the operation.

—Paul S. Boyer, et al., *The Enduring Vision*

(5) **1.** Why do you think the authors refer to the Battle of Bladensburg as a "fiasco"?

A. because the American forces fled almost without a fight
B. because President Madison had to flee the White House
C. because it allowed the British to attack Washington, D.C.
D. because it was a famous victory for the British forces

2. What, according to the authors, did the British raid on Washington, D.C., accomplish?

A. It paved the way for the British capture of Baltimore.
B. It burned down all the public buildings in the city.
C. It helped the British offensive in the North.
D. It embarrassed and angered many Americans.

Remember to be wary of choices that contain absolutes, such as *all, every,* or *only.*

ACTIVITY OPTIONS

INDIVIDUAL NEEDS

STUDENTS ACQUIRING ENGLISH/ESL

Social Studies Vocabulary Make sure students understand the following terms and concepts in the sample sources and questions on these pages.

Strategy Page: Secondary Source
"Bladensburg Races": term used sarcastically, because the soldiers were running away from the battle so quickly

Practice Page: Secondary Source
maritime commerce: sailing as a job; trade conducted by shipping
escapees: slaves running away
Question 1 *records:* official papers

Directions: Use this passage and your knowledge of U.S. history to answer questions 1 through 3.

African-American Sailors

African Americans contributed greatly to the growth of maritime commerce in the United States. Beginning in colonial times, slaves, with their masters' permission, hired themselves out as sailors. Some served as translators on slave ships. Merchant ships also offered a means of escape for runaway slaves. A few escapees even took to the sea as pirates.

Seafaring was one of the few occupations open to free African Americans. They served on clippers, naval vessels, and whaling ships from the 1700s into the late 1800s. Federal crew lists from Atlantic seaports show that during this time African Americans made up 10 percent or more of sailors on American ships. Seafaring was an especially dangerous line of work for free blacks. They risked capture in southern ports, where they were often thrown in jail or sold into slavery.

1. What records show that African Americans made up 10 percent or more of sailors on American ships?

   A. shipyard records

   B. family Bibles

   C. federal crew lists

   D. ships' logs

2. The passage implies that free and enslaved African Americans went to sea for all of the following reasons *except* to

   A. escape slavery.

   B. live as pirates.

   C. earn wages as sailors.

   D. discover new lands.

3. The author states that life was especially dangerous for free African-American sailors because

   A. American prosperity depended on their work alone.

   B. the worst jobs on board ship were always assigned to them.

   C. they ran the risk of capture and enslavement in southern ports.

   D. they were more likely than white sailors to contract scurvy.

PRACTICE QUESTIONS

Thinking It Through

Share the following explanations with students as they discuss the strategies they used to answer the practice questions.

1. You may recall the answer to this question without needing to reread the passage. If not, you should skim the passage to identify the records that show the percentage of African-American sailors on American ships. The second paragraph identifies the "Federal crew lists" as showing the percentage of African-American sailors on American ships, so the correct answer is (C).

2. The word *except* in this question makes it an example of a question constructed in the negative. The correct answer is (D).

3. The key word *states* tells you to skim or reread the passage to find the correct answer. The correct answer is (C).

SKILLS TESTED IN THE ITEMS

STRATEGY ITEMS		PRACTICE ITEMS	
Item Number	**Skill Tested**	**Item Number**	**Skill Tested**
1.	Analyzing Causes	**1.**	Clarifying
2.	Recognizing Effects	**2.**	Making Inferences
		3.	Drawing Conclusions

USING STRATEGIES FOR . . .

Political Cartoons

Political cartoons are one kind of primary source. Remind students to analyze the political cartoon before reading the questions. They should identify the subject, note important symbols and details, interpret the message, and analyze the point of view. Then they will read the question to identify the information they need to find.

Explain to students that they will do best on test questions by thinking them through carefully and by applying test-taking strategies, such as the following.

1. Question 1 asks you to use the cartoon to identify Horace Greeley's major issue in the 1872 presidential campaign. Since the subject of the cartoon is political reform, (A) is the correct answer.

2. To answer Question 2, look at how the cartoonist uses caricature in the cartoon. Horace Greeley looks comical as he paints, or covers up, the tiger's true stripes. The cartoonist caricatures, or exaggerates, the tiger's ferocious look, showing that it is still wild and out of control. Thus, (C) is the correct answer.

General Test-Taking Tips

Share these tips with your students.

- Ask questions before the test begins.
- Know how to fill in the answer form.
- Read and listen to directions carefully.

Political Cartoons

Political cartoons are drawings that express views on political issues of the day. Cartoonists use symbols and such artistic styles as caricature—exaggerating a person's physical features—to get their message across.

1. Identify the subject of the cartoon. Titles and captions often indicate the subject matter.
2. Identify the main characters in the cartoon. Here, the main character is Horace Greeley, a candidate in the 1872 presidential election.
3. Note the symbols—ideas or images that stand for something else—used in the cartoon.
4. Study labels and other written information in the cartoon.
5. Analyze the point of view. How cartoonists use caricature often indicates how they feel. The exaggeration of Greeley's physical appearance—short and overweight—makes him appear comical.
6. Interpret the cartoonist's message.

answers: 1 (A), 2 (C)

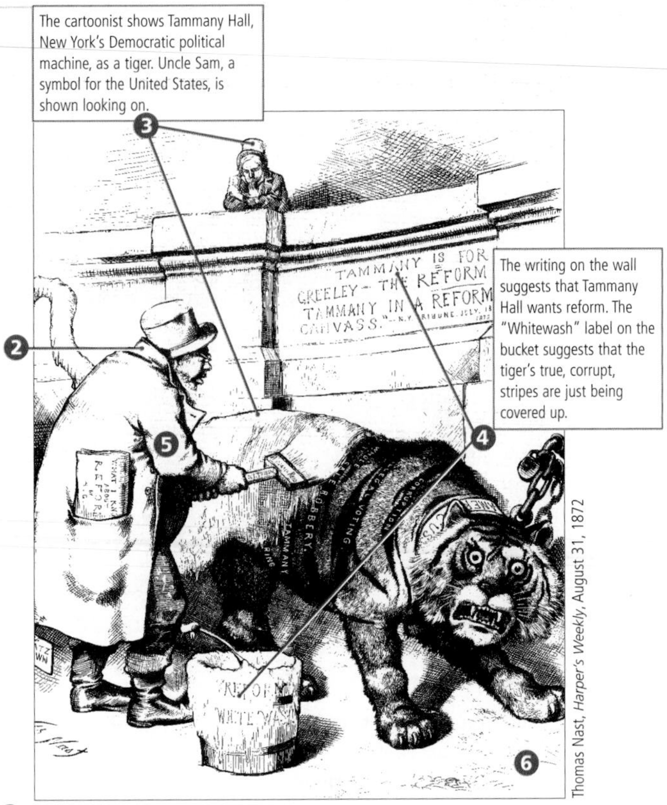

Thomas Nast, *Harper's Weekly*, August 31, 1872

1 **"What are you going to do about it, if 'Old Honesty' lets him loose again?"**

1. Based on the cartoon, what do you think was Horace Greeley's major issue in the 1872 presidential campaign?
   A. political reform
   B. states' rights
   C. abolition
   D. temperance

2. Which one of the following statements do you think *best* represents the cartoonist's point of view?
   A. Horace Greeley is an honest man.
   B. Tammany Hall supports political reform.
   C. Tammany Hall, regardless of Greeley's view, is still corrupt.
   D. Horace Greeley, like most Tammany politicians, is corrupt.

 Cartoon: The Granger Collection, New York

ACTIVITY OPTIONS

INDIVIDUAL NEEDS

STUDENTS ACQUIRING ENGLISH/ESL

Social Studies Vocabulary Make sure students understand the following terms on these pages.

Strategy Page: Political Cartoon
Tammany Hall: the name for a group of corrupt politicians in New York in the 1800s
whitewash: white paint; by extension, covering up something criminal or embarrassing
Question 1 *abolition:* the movement to end slavery
temperance: avoidance of alcohol
Question 2 *corrupt:* dishonest

Practice Page:
Question 1 *portrayed:* shown; drawn
gladiator: a person engaged in a fight to the death
Question 2 *federalism:* system in which national government and the states share government powers
Question 3 *monarchy:* government rule by a king or queen

For more test practice online . . .
TEST PRACTICE
CLASSZONE.COM

Directions: Use the cartoon and your knowledge of U.S. history to answer questions 1 through 3.

WELL! LET EM COME ON, WE'RE ARM'D.
POPULAR SOVEREIGNTY
THE MAJORITY RULE
THE LITTLE GIANT IN THE CHARACTER OF THE GLADIATOR.

Anonymous, 1858

1. Stephen A. Douglas is portrayed as a gladiator armed with the sword and shield of
   - **A.** Congress and the rule of law.
   - **B.** freedom of speech and of the press.
   - **C.** constitutional and property rights of slaveholders.
   - **D.** voting rights and self-government for the territories.

2. Popular sovereignty was used in the 1850s to address the issue of
   - **A.** states' rights.
   - **B.** federalism.
   - **C.** slavery.
   - **D.** voting rights.

3. The cartoon illustrates the fight over whether to
   - **A.** admit Kansas into the Union as a free state or a proslavery state.
   - **B.** grant freedom of the press to newspapers in the territories.
   - **C.** allow sword fighting and dueling as legal activities in the 1850s.
   - **D.** replace a system of majority rule with a monarchy.

PRACTICE QUESTIONS

Thinking It Through

Share the following explanations with students as they discuss the strategies they used to answer the practice questions.

1. This question asks you to identify the significance of the sword and shield that Stephen A. Douglas carries. The sword reads *freedom of the elective franchise,* which means voting rights. Note that the label on the shield says *popular sovereignty.* Since this term means a system in which the residents of a state or territory vote to decide an issue, the correct answer is (D).
2. *1850s* is a key term in this question. Use your knowledge of U.S. history to answer. Popular sovereignty just before the Civil War was used to address the issue of slavery in the territories and new states. The correct answer is (C).
3. You need to analyze the cartoonist's point of view and use your knowledge of U.S. history to answer this question. The correct answer is (A). Popular sovereignty was a key issue for Douglas throughout his political career.

SKILLS TESTED IN THE ITEMS

STRATEGY ITEMS		PRACTICE ITEMS	
Item Number	**Skill Tested**	**Item Number**	**Skill Tested**
1.	Analyzing Political Cartoons	1.	Clarifying
2.	Determining Main Ideas	2.	Making Inferences
		3.	Determining Main Ideas

USING STRATEGIES FOR . . .

Charts

Explain to students that they will do best on test questions by thinking them through carefully and by applying test-taking strategies such as the following.

1. Question 1 asks you to compare and contrast the information in the column headed "Best Time to Travel." Since most of the trails list spring and summer as the best time, the correct answer is (A).

2. Question 2 requires you to compare and contrast the information in the column headed "Average Daily Distance." Look down this column to find the two trails where travelers average up to 20 miles per day. Then move your eyes across the rows to the left to find the names of these trails. The correct answer is (C) because the two trails with the average daily distance of 20 miles per day are the Mormon (15–20 miles) and Santa Fe (12–20 miles) trails.

General Test-Taking Tips

Share these tips with your students.

- Use practice tests, such as the one you are taking now, to learn about your test-taking habits and weaknesses.
- Use this information to practice strategies that will help you be a successful test-taker.

Charts

Charts present information in a visual form. History textbooks use several types of charts, including tables, flow charts, Venn diagrams, and infographics. The type of chart most commonly found in standardized tests is the table. It organizes information in columns and rows for easy viewing.

1. Read the title and identify the broad subject of the chart.
2. Read the column and row headings and any other labels. This will provide more details about the subject of the chart.
3. Compare and contrast the information from column to column and row to row.
4. Try to draw conclusions from the information in the chart. Ask yourself: What patterns are apparent in the chart?
5. Read the questions and then study the chart again.

answers: 1 (A), 2 (C)

1 Trails West, 1850

Trail	Start/End Point	Distance	Time Taken	Average Daily Distance	Best Time to Travel
California Trail	Fort Hall, Id./Sutter's Fort, Calif.	700 miles	About 6 weeks	15 miles	Summer months
Mormon Trail	Iowa/Great Salt Lake, Ut.	1,300 miles	2–3 months	15–20 miles	May–September
Old Spanish Trail	Santa Fe/ Los Angeles	1,200 miles	10–12 weeks	12–15 miles	Spring–early summer
Oregon Trail	Missouri/ Oregon	2,000 miles	4–6 months	10–15 miles	April–September
Santa Fe Trail	Missouri/ Santa Fe	800 miles	6–8 weeks	12–20 miles	Early spring–early summer

Compare and contrast the distance, time taken, and average daily distance traveled for each trail. 3

1. What was the best time of year for travel on most of the trails?

A. spring and summer
B. summer and fall
C. April
D. September

2. On which trails did travelers sometimes average 20 miles per day?

A. California and Oregon trails
B. Santa Fe and Old Spanish trails
C. Mormon and Santa Fe trails
D. Oregon and Mormon trails

ACTIVITY OPTIONS

INDIVIDUAL NEEDS

STUDENTS ACQUIRING ENGLISH/ESL

Social Studies Vocabulary Make sure students understand the following terms and concepts in the sample charts and questions on these pages.

Strategy Page: Chart
column: reads down
row: reads across
flow chart: See below
Venn diagram: See below
concept web: See below

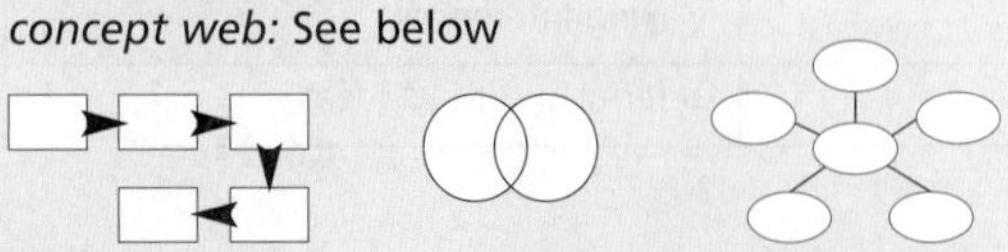

flow chart *Venn diagram* *concept web*

Practice Page: Charts
enslaved: refers to people from Africa who became slaves

For more test practice online . . .
TEST PRACTICE
CLASSZONE.COM

Directions: Use the charts and your knowledge of U.S. history to answer questions 1 through 4.

Percentage of Population Free and Enslaved, by States and Territories, 1790

North		
State/Territory	**Free**	**Enslaved**
Connecticut	98.9	1.1
Delaware	85.0	15.0
Maine	100.0	0.0
Massachusetts	100.0	0.0
New Hampshire	99.9	0.1
New Jersey	93.8	6.2
New York	93.8	6.2
Pennsylvania	99.1	0.9
Rhode Island	98.6	1.4
Vermont	100.0	0.0

South		
State/Territory	**Free**	**Enslaved**
Georgia	64.5	35.5
Kentucky	83.1	16.9
Maryland	67.8	32.2
North Carolina	74.5	25.5
South Carolina	57.0	43.0
Virginia	60.9	39.1

Source: Inter-University Consortium for Political and Social Research

1. The state with the highest percentage of enslaved people was
   - **A.** New Hampshire.
   - **B.** North Carolina.
   - **C.** Rhode Island.
   - **D.** South Carolina.

2. Which of the following *best* describes most states in the North?
   - **A.** The population was more than 98 percent free.
   - **B.** More than 10 percent of the population was enslaved.
   - **C.** Less than 60 percent of the population was free.
   - **D.** The population was more than 20 percent enslaved.

3. Which statement about the percentage of enslaved people is true?
   - **A.** It was much lower in the South.
   - **B.** It was much higher in the South.
   - **C.** There was no difference between the regions.
   - **D.** There was a slight difference between the regions.

4. What economic factor *best* explains the population differences between the regions?
   - **A.** The North focused on manufacturing.
   - **B.** The North was wealthy enough to free enslaved people.
   - **C.** The South focused on plantation agriculture.
   - **D.** The South needed enslaved people for factory work.

PRACTICE QUESTIONS

Thinking It Through

Share the following explanations with students as they discuss the strategies they used to answer the practice questions.

1. You must compare and contrast information from both charts to answer this question. Read the columns and rows headed "State/Territory" and "Enslaved" to compare and contrast the information. The key word in this question is *highest,* so look for the largest numeral in the column marked "Enslaved." The correct answer is (D).
2. *Best* and *most* are key words. *Best* indicates that more than one answer may also be in some way correct, but not the best answer to this question. *Most* indicates that the answer should refer to the majority of states, but not all. The question is asking you to look only at the chart of the North. Read each answer choice and then study the chart to see which choice is the best. The correct answer is (A).
3. This item asks you to compare information from both charts. To find the answer compare the column headed "Enslaved" on both charts. The correct answer is (B).
4. You need to use both the charts and your knowledge of United States history to answer this question. The South had a high percentage of enslaved population because slaves were used to work the region's plantation agriculture, which was its main economic activity. The correct answer is (C).

SKILLS TESTED IN THE ITEMS

STRATEGY ITEMS		PRACTICE ITEMS	
Item Number	**Skill Tested**	**Item Number**	**Skill Tested**
1.	Clarifying	**1.**	Clarifying
2.	Categorizing	**2.**	Interpreting Charts
		3.	Comparing and Contrasting
		4.	Drawing Conclusions

USING STRATEGIES FOR . . .

Line and Bar Graphs
Remind students that the vertical axis goes up and down and is normally shown on the left side of the graph. The horizontal axis runs across the bottom of the graph.

Explain to students that they will do best on test questions by thinking them through carefully and by applying test-taking strategies such as the following.

1. In question 1, begin by finding the approximate location of the population of 10,000,000 on the vertical axis. Remember, the label says the population numbers are given in thousands, and 10,000 thousand equals 10,000,000. At 10,000, move your eyes across the horizontal axis. From the dot, look down to read the corresponding date and the date after it on the horizontal axis. The correct answer is (B).

2. To answer question 2, you need to study the information in the graph and note any trends. Read the answer choices to find the sentence that best describes the trend. The population didn't increase at a very steady pace, but it did always increase, so the best answer is (A).

General Test-Taking Tips

Share these tips with your students.

- Do not spend too much time on one question.
- Skip a question you are having problems with. Go back to it later, if you have time.
- If you skip a question, be sure to skip the answer space for the same number on your answer sheet.

Line and Bar Graphs

Graphs show statistics in a visual form. Line graphs are particularly useful for showing changes over time. Bar graphs make it easy to compare numbers or sets of numbers.

1. Read the title and identify the broad subject of the graph.
2. Study the labels on the vertical and horizontal axes to see the kinds of information presented in the graph. Note the intervals between amounts and between dates. This will help you read the graph more efficiently.
3. Look at the source line and evaluate the reliability of the information in the graph. Government statistics on population tend to be reliable.
4. Study the information in the graph and note any trends.
5. Draw conclusions and make generalizations based on these trends.
6. Read the questions carefully and then study the graph again.

answers: 1 (B), 2 (A)

❶ United States Population, 1800–1850

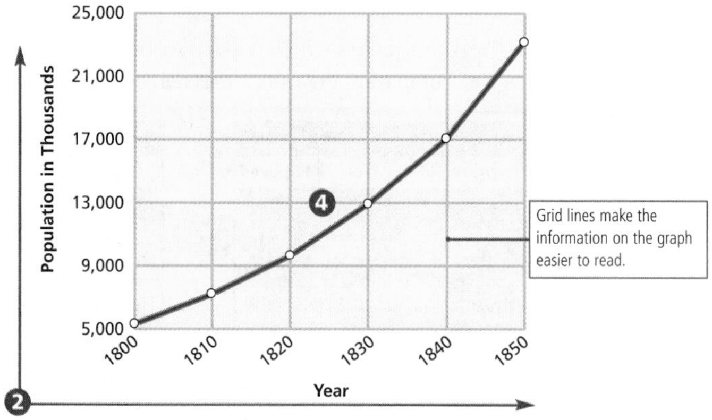

❸ **Source:** *Historical Statistics of the United States*

❻ **1.** The United States population rose above 10,000,000 between

A. 1810 and 1820.
B. 1820 and 1830.
C. 1830 and 1840.
D. 1840 and 1850.

❶ United States Urban Population, 1800–1850

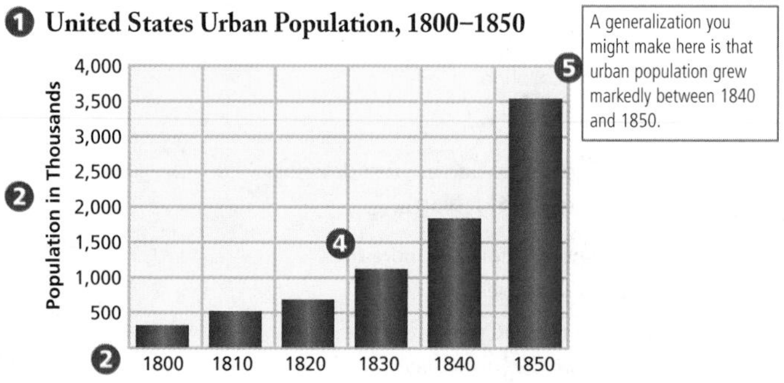

❸ **Source:** *Historical Statistics of the United States*

❻ **2.** Which of the following sentences *best* describes the trend shown in the bar graph?

A. United States urban population steadily increased.
B. United States urban population showed little change.
C. United States urban population rose and fell.
D. United States urban population decreased steadily.

ACTIVITY OPTIONS

INDIVIDUAL NEEDS

STUDENTS ACQUIRING ENGLISH/ESL

Social Studies Vocabulary Make sure students understand the following terms and concepts in the sample questions on these pages.

Strategy Page
Strategy 4 and Question 2 *trend:* a general direction or tendency

Practice Page
Question 1 *exceed:* go beyond; become more than
Question 2 *enslaved population:* the population of African Americans who were treated like property and forced to work without pay and without freedoms

For more test practice online . . .
TEST PRACTICE
CLASSZONE.COM

Directions: Use the graphs and your knowledge of U.S. history to answer questions 1 through 4.

Growth of the African-American Population, 1820–1860

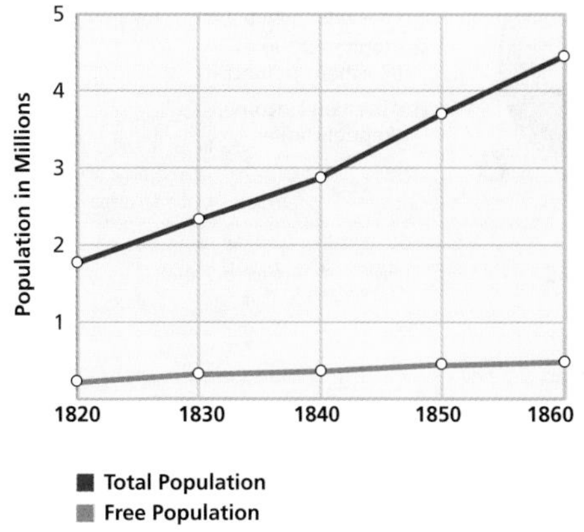

Source: Gilder Lehrman Institute of American History

Churches by Denomination, 1750

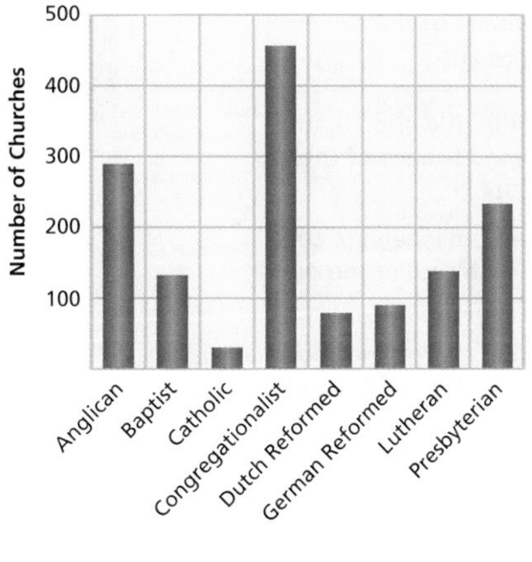

Source: Gilder Lehrman Institute of American History

1. In which decade did the total African-American population first exceed 3.5 million?

A. 1820–1830
B. 1830–1840
C. 1840–1850
D. 1850–1860

2. About how many times larger than the free African-American population was the enslaved population in 1860?

A. four
B. five
C. six
D. eight

3. Which one of the following statements accurately reflects information in the graph?

A. There were more Congregationalist churches than all other denominations combined.
B. There were more Presbyterian churches than Anglican churches.
C. The Baptists had the fewest churches.
D. The Congregationalists had the most churches.

4. In which colony might you expect the most Catholics to live?

A. Georgia
B. Maryland
C. Massachusetts
D. Virginia

PRACTICE QUESTIONS

Thinking It Through

Share the following explanations with students as they discuss the strategies they used to answer the practice questions.

1. Look at the legend to see which line on the graph stands for the total African-American population. Find the approximate location of 3.5 million on the vertical axis. From there, look to the right and down to read the corresponding date, the first year the total African-American population was higher than 3.5 million. The correct answer is (C).
2. Look at both lines of the graph to help you answer this question. First, subtract the free population in 1860 from the total population in 1860 to find the enslaved population (4.5 million -0.5 million = 4 million). Next, divide the enslaved population (4 million) by the free population (0.5 million) to find out how many times larger the enslaved population was than the free population (4 million ÷ 0.5 million = 8). (D) is the correct choice.
3. To find the accurate statement, you need to read each choice and study the bars of the graph again with that choice in mind. The correct answer is (D).
4. You need to use your knowledge of U.S. history to answer this question. Since many Catholics settled Maryland, the correct answer is (B).

SKILLS TESTED IN THE ITEMS

STRATEGY ITEMS		PRACTICE ITEMS	
Item Number	**Skill Tested**	**Item Number**	**Skill Tested**
1.	Interpreting Graphs	**1.**	Clarifying
2.	Summarizing	**2.**	Contrasting
		3.	Comparing and Contrasting
		4.	Making Inferences

USING STRATEGIES FOR . . .

Pie Graphs

Explain to students that they will do best on test questions by thinking them through carefully and by applying test-taking strategies, such as the following.

1. Question 1 asks you to interpret the results of the 1860 presidential election. You must think about the differences among the terms *landslide, plurality,* and *majority.* If you know the meanings of any two of these terms, you should be able to arrive at the correct answer once you have eliminated (D). Compare the slices of the pie. (C) is the correct answer because it is a generalization you can make based on the comparisons.

2. Use your knowledge of U.S. history to answer question 2. Eliminate choices that you know are wrong. Eliminate (B) when you notice that the Republican party received more votes than any other party. Eliminate choice (C) since the pie graph represents the popular not the electoral vote. Since the graph clearly shows the division of the Democratic party into two wings, the correct answer is (A).

General Test-Taking Tips

Share these tips with your students.

- Read the question and each answer choice before answering.
- Many items include choices that may seem right at first glance, but are actually wrong.

Pie Graphs

A pie, or circle, graph shows relationships among the parts of a whole. These parts look like slices of a pie. The size of each slice is proportional to the percentage of the whole that it represents.

1. Read the title and identify the broad subject of the pie graph.
2. Look at the legend to see what each slice of the pie represents.
3. Read the source line and note the origin of the data shown in the pie graph.
4. Compare the slices of the pie and try to make generalizations and draw conclusions from your comparisons.
5. Read the questions carefully and review difficult or unfamiliar terms.
6. Eliminate choices that you know are wrong.

answers: 1 (C), 2 (A)

1 The Popular Vote in the 1860 Presidential Election

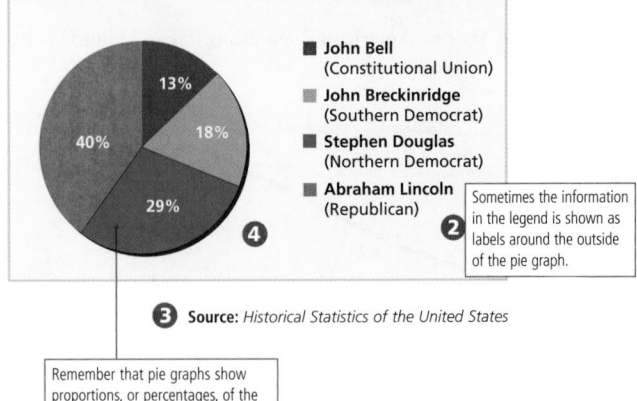

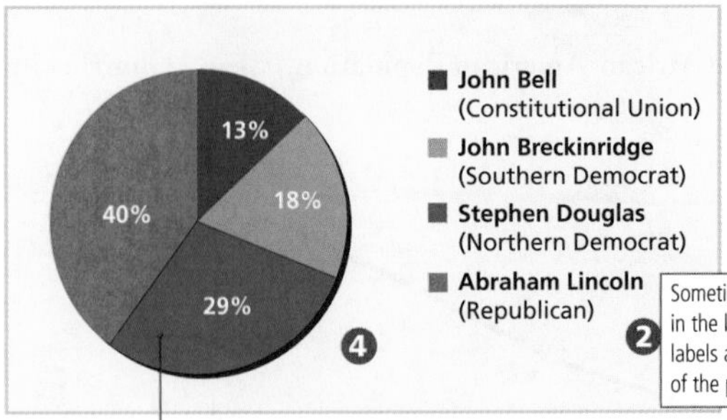

2 Sometimes the information in the legend is shown as labels around the outside of the pie graph.

3 **Source:** *Historical Statistics of the United States*

Remember that pie graphs show proportions, or percentages, of the whole, not absolute quantities.

1. In the 1860 presidential election, Abraham Lincoln won

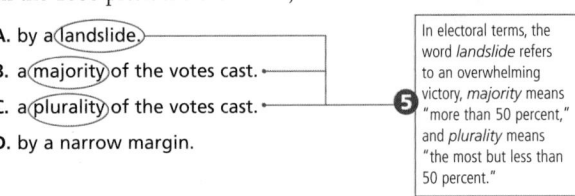

A. by a landslide.
B. a majority of the votes cast.
C. a plurality of the votes cast.
D. by a narrow margin.

5 In electoral terms, the word *landslide* refers to an overwhelming victory, *majority* means "more than 50 percent," and *plurality* means "the most but less than 50 percent."

2. What political situation in 1860 does the pie graph show?

A. The Democratic Party was split into northern and southern wings before the 1860 election.
B. The Republican Party was not yet an important force in national politics.
C. Douglas won fewer popular votes than Lincoln but won more electoral votes.
D. Because no candidate won a majority of the popular votes, the House of Representatives decided the election.

6 You can eliminate **B** when you notice that the Republican Party received more votes than any other.

ACTIVITY OPTIONS

INDIVIDUAL NEEDS

STUDENTS ACQUIRING ENGLISH/ESL

Social Studies Vocabulary Make sure students understand the following terms and concepts in the sample graphs on these pages.

Strategy Page: Pie Graph
Strategy 2 *legend:* a key; a list that tells what each slice of the pie graph represents

Practice Page: Pie Graph
ethnic makeup: the combination of groups that speak different languages and follow different customs
colonial population: the people who lived in the American colonies
Question 3 *colonized:* made into permanent settlements

For more test practice online . . .
TEST PRACTICE
CLASSZONE.COM

Directions: Use the pie graph and your knowledge of U.S. history to answer questions 1 through 4.

Ethnic Makeup of the Colonial Population, 1775

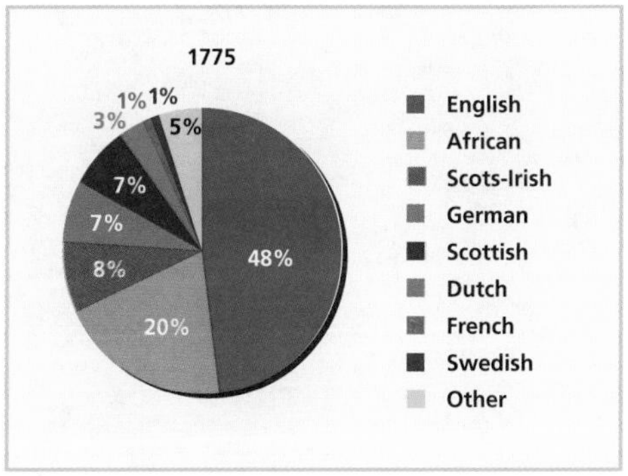

Source: Gilder Lehrman Institute of American History

1. The largest ethnic group in the colonial population of 1775 was

   A. African.
   B. Dutch.
   C. English.
   D. French.

2. What percentage of the colonial population arrived mostly against its own will?

   A. 5%
   B. 8%
   C. 20%
   D. 48%

3. The area between the Connecticut and Delaware rivers, now known as New York, was first colonized in the 1600s by the

   A. Dutch.
   B. English.
   C. Swedes.
   D. Germans.

4. What was the largest group of non-English-speaking Europeans to settle in the colonies?

   A. Swedes
   B. Dutch
   C. Germans
   D. French

PRACTICE QUESTIONS

Thinking It Through

Share the following explanations with students as they discuss the strategies they used to answer the practice questions.

1. Key words are *largest* and *1775.* Find the largest slice on the pie graph. Then look at the legend to see which ethnic group is represented by that slice's color. The correct answer is (C).
2. Key words are *against its own will.* Since African Americans were brought to the colonies against their will, look in the legend for the color labeled African. Find this color on the pie graph and read the percentage. The correct answer is (C) 20 percent.
3. You need to use your knowledge of U.S. history to answer this question. If you remember that New York was formerly known as New Amsterdam, that may give you a clue. The correct answer is (A).
4. To answer this question, look at all the slices of the pie that represent European ethnic groups except the English-speaking ethnic groups of English, Scottish, and Scots-Irish. Find the largest of those slices. The correct answer is (C) Germans.

SKILLS TESTED IN THE ITEMS

STRATEGY ITEMS		PRACTICE ITEMS	
Item Number	**Skill Tested**	**Item Number**	**Skill Tested**
1.	Interpreting Graphs	1.	Comparing and Contrasting
2.	Summarizing	2.	Making Inferences
		3.	Clarifying
		4.	Categorizing; Comparing and Contrasting

USING STRATEGIES FOR . . .

Political Maps

Explain to students that they will do best on test questions by thinking them through carefully and by applying test-taking strategies, such as the following.

1. To answer question 1, study the legend to find the meaning of symbols used on the map. Next, locate New Netherland and the English colonies on the map. Find the body of water that formed part of the border between New Netherland and the English middle colonies. Answer (C) Delaware River is the correct answer.

2. In question 2, note that if you choose (D) all of the choices must be correct. Study the legend to find the meaning of symbols used on the map. Notice you can eliminate (A) and (D) because only part of New York was part of New Netherland. Eliminate (C) because Pennsylvania was not part of New Netherland. The correct answer is (B).

General Test-Taking Tips

Share these tips with your students.

- Try to answer every question on the test.
- If you are not sure of an answer, make an educated guess.
- First eliminate the choices you are sure are not correct. Then choose from the choices that remain.

Political Maps

Political maps show countries and the political divisions within countries—states, for example. They also show the location of major cities. In addition, political maps often show physical features, such as rivers, seas, oceans, and mountain ranges.

1. Read the title to determine the subject and purpose of the map.
2. Read the labels on the map. This will reveal information about the map's subject and purpose.
3. Study the legend to find the meaning of symbols used on the map.
4. Look at the lines of latitude and longitude. This grid makes locating places much easier.
5. Use the compass rose to determine directions on the map.
6. Use the scale to estimate the distances between places shown on the map.
7. Read the questions and then carefully study the map to determine the answers.

answers: 1 (C), 2 (B)

Instead of a compass rose, some maps have a North arrow. (5)

(1) **Middle Colonies to 1700**

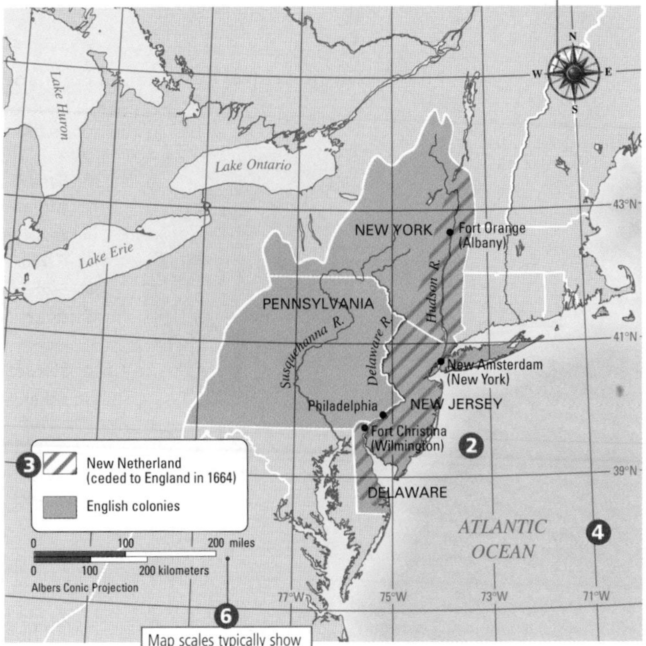

(6) Map scales typically show distances in both miles and kilometers.

(7) 1. Which of the following bodies of water formed part of the border between New Netherland and the English middle colonies?

A. Lake Erie

B. Lake Huron

C. Delaware River

D. Hudson River

2. Which entire English colony was once part of New Netherland?

A. New York

B. New Jersey

C. Pennsylvania

D. all of the above

ACTIVITY OPTIONS

INDIVIDUAL NEEDS

STUDENTS ACQUIRING ENGLISH/ESL

Social Studies Vocabulary Make sure students understand the following terms and concepts on these pages.

Strategy Page: Political Map

latitude: lines that run east-west on maps and globes

longitude: lines that run north-south on maps and globes

political: not referring to politics, but showing borders of countries, states, and the like

N, S, E, W: the directions north, south, east, and west

Practice Page

Question 1 *Union:* another name for the United States

Republic: government in which elected representatives govern

Question 3 *barge:* a flat-bottomed boat used mainly on inland waterways

Directions: Use the map and your knowledge of U.S. history to answer questions 1 through 4.

New States, 1816–1848

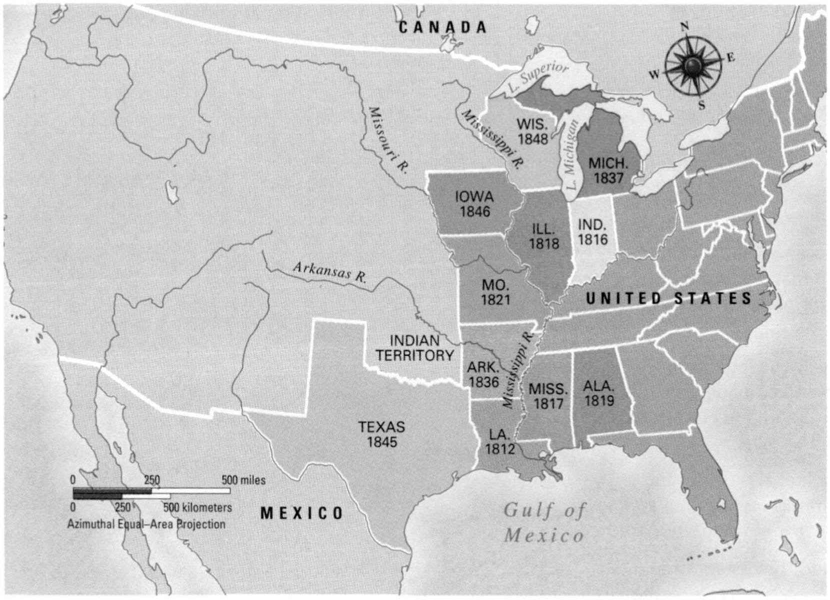

1. Which state joined the Union in 1845?
   - **A.** Iowa
   - **B.** Illinois
   - **C.** Wisconsin
   - **D.** Texas

2. The Mississippi River forms the western border of which of the following states?
   - **A.** Missouri, Arkansas, and Louisiana
   - **B.** Illinois and Mississippi
   - **C.** Iowa and Missouri
   - **D.** Iowa, Missouri, and Arkansas

3. A barge filled with logs from Wisconsin is going to the Gulf of Mexico. It is most likely traveling
   - **A.** south on the Mississippi River.
   - **B.** west across the Great Plains.
   - **C.** north on the Arkansas River.
   - **D.** southwest through Indian Territory.

4. The states admitted to the Union in the 1840s were
   - **A.** Missouri, Wisconsin, and Illinois.
   - **B.** Kansas, Texas, and Iowa.
   - **C.** Texas, Wisconsin, and Iowa.
   - **D.** Illinois, Texas, and Wisconsin.

PRACTICE QUESTIONS

Thinking It Through

Share the following explanations with students as they discuss the strategies they used to answer the practice questions.

1. To answer this question, you need to find the states listed on the map and use the labels to identify the correct state. Only Texas joined the Union in 1845. The correct answer is (D).
2. *Western* is a key word. Use the compass rose and read the labels on the map to find the Mississippi River and the states in which the river forms the western border. The correct answer is (B).
3. You need to use the labels on the map and the compass rose to answer this question. The correct answer is (A).
4. Use the labels on the map to find the states admitted to the Union in the ten-year period from 1840 to 1849. The correct answer is (C).

SKILLS TESTED IN THE ITEMS

STRATEGY ITEMS		PRACTICE ITEMS	
Item Number	**Skill Tested**	**Item Number**	**Skill Tested**
1.	Interpreting Maps	**1.**	Interpreting Maps
2.	Interpreting Maps	**2.**	Interpreting Maps
		3.	Making Inferences
		4.	Interpreting Maps

USING STRATEGIES FOR . . .

Thematic Maps

Explain to students that they will do best on test questions by thinking them through carefully and by applying test-taking strategies, such as the following.

1. To answer question 1, use the map labels and the legend. The numbers on the states tell you when each state was readmitted to the Union. Tennessee was readmitted in 1866, making it the first to be readmitted, so the correct answer is (A).

2. To answer question 2, use the map labels and the legend. Texas was in the military district commanded by General Philip Sheridan, so the correct answer is (C).

General Test-Taking Tips

Share these tips with your students.

- Think positively.
- Tell yourself that you can do it!
- If you have studied for the test, you are prepared to succeed.

Thematic Maps

A thematic map, or special-purpose map, focuses on a particular topic. The location of baseball parks, a country's natural resources, election results, and major battles in a war are all topics you might see illustrated on a thematic map.

1. Read the title to determine the subject and purpose of the map.
2. Examine the labels on the map to find more information about the map's subject and purpose.
3. Study the legend to find the meaning of the symbols and colors used on the map.
4. Look at the colors and symbols on the map and try to identify patterns.
5. Read the questions and then carefully study the map to determine the answers.

1 Southern Military Districts, 1867

3 While a thematic map focuses on one topic, it often offers several kinds of information on that topic. Therefore, the legend for a thematic map is usually very detailed.

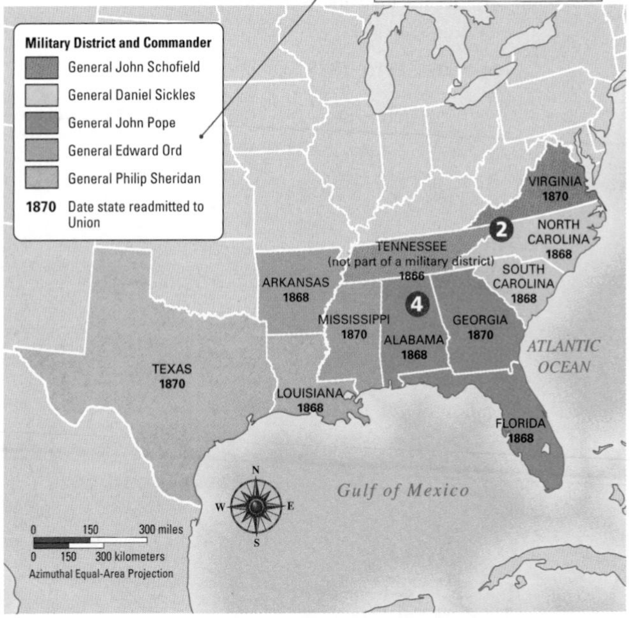

5 1. Which former Confederate state was the first to be readmitted to the Union?

A. Tennessee

B. South Carolina

C. Florida

D. Alabama

2. The military district in which Texas was located was commanded by

A. General Edward Ord.

B. General John Pope.

C. General Philip Sheridan.

D. General Daniel Sickles.

answers: 1 (A), 2 (C)

ACTIVITY OPTIONS

INDIVIDUAL NEEDS

STUDENTS ACQUIRING ENGLISH/ESL

Social Studies Vocabulary Make sure students understand the following terms and concepts in maps and questions on these pages.

Strategy Page: Thematic Map
military districts: regions of the South under the command of the U.S. military during Reconstruction

Practice Page
Question 3 *launched:* begun
Question 4 *avenged:* got even with; retaliated against

For more test practice online . . .
TEST PRACTICE
CLASSZONE.COM

Directions: Use the map and your knowledge of U.S. history to answer questions 1 through 4.

The Battle of San Jacinto, 1836

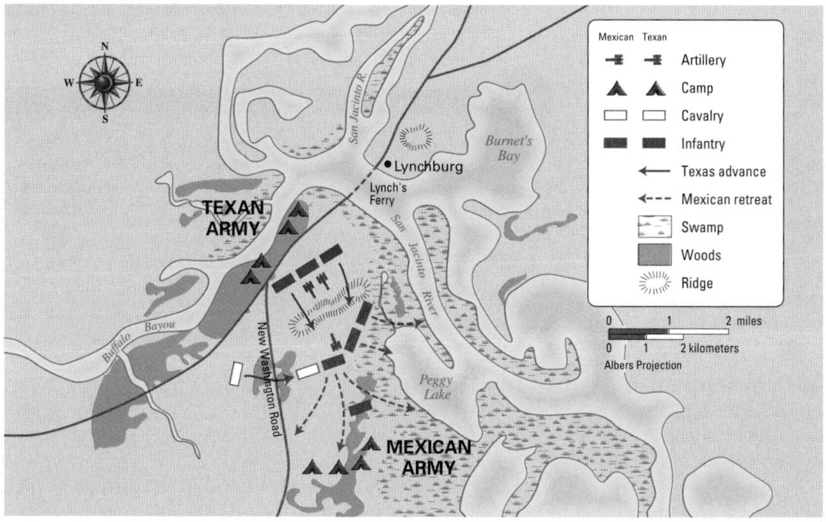

1. The Texan camp was located in what type of area?
   - **A.** swamp
   - **B.** ridge
   - **C.** woods
   - **D.** open plains

2. In which direction did the Texan forces move to attack the Mexican army?
   - **A.** directly south
   - **B.** northeast
   - **C.** directly east
   - **D.** southeast

3. An attack was launched on the Mexican forces from the west by
   - **A.** Texan artillery.
   - **B.** Texan cavalry.
   - **C.** Texan infantry.
   - **D.** all of the above

4. What was the importance of the Battle of San Jacinto?
   - **A.** Texas won its independence from Mexico.
   - **B.** It avenged the defeats at Goliad and the Alamo.
   - **C.** Texas gained U.S. support in the struggle for freedom.
   - **D.** It proved that the Texans were better fighters than the Mexicans.

PRACTICE QUESTIONS

Thinking It Through

Share the following explanations with the students as they discuss the strategies they used to answer the practice questions.

1. Use the map labels and the legend to answer this question. Read the labels to find the Texan camp. Use the legend to find the meaning of the symbols used on the map and identify the terrain where the Texan camp was located. The correct answer is (C).
2. Use the map labels, the legend, and the compass to answer this question. The Texan army was located in the northwest part of the area shown on the map. Follow the arrows that show which direction the Texan army moved. They moved southeast to attack the Mexican army. The correct answer is (D).
3. Use the map labels, the legend, and the compass to answer this question. The Texan cavalry came from the west to attack the Mexican forces. The correct answer is (B).
4. Use your knowledge of United States history to answer this question. It is true that the Battle of San Jacinto avenged the defeats at Goliad and the Alamo. But this was not the most important outcome of the battle. At the Battle of San Jacinto, Texans forced Santa Anna to surrender and sign a treaty giving Texas its independence. The correct answer is (A).

SKILLS TESTED IN THE ITEMS

STRATEGY ITEMS		PRACTICE ITEMS	
Item Number	**Skill Tested**	**Item Number**	**Skill Tested**
1.	Interpreting Maps	1.	Interpreting Maps
2.	Interpreting Maps	2.	Interpreting Maps
		3.	Interpreting Maps
		4.	Clarifying

USING STRATEGIES FOR . . .

Time Lines

Explain to students that they will do best on test questions by thinking them through carefully and by applying test-taking strategies, such as the following.

1. To answer question 1, note how the events on the time line are related to one another. Look for cause and effect relationships. Find the Townshend Acts on the time line. Look for a direct response of the colonists. The correct answer is (C).

2. To answer question 2, use your knowledge of U.S. history. Read the events on the time line and notice the time interval between the passage of the Coercive Acts and the Battles of Lexington and Concord, the first battles of the Revolutionary War. (A) is the correct answer.

General Test-Taking Tips

Share these tips with your students.

- Relax during the test.
- Several times during the test, take a few seconds to relax and breathe deeply.
- Occasional deep breaths will help relieve anxiety and keep you focused.

Time Lines

A time line is a type of chart that lists events in the order in which they occurred. In other words, time lines are a visual method of showing what happened when.

1. Read the title to discover the subject of the time line.
2. Identify the time period covered by the time line by noting the earliest and latest dates shown. On vertical time lines, the earliest date is shown at the top. On horizontal time lines, it is on the far left.
3. Read the events and their dates in sequence. Notice the intervals between events.
4. Use your knowledge of history to develop a fuller picture of the events listed in the time line. For example, you might try to identify some of the leading individuals involved in the events.
5. Note how events are related to one another. Look particularly for cause-effect relationships.
6. Use the information you have gathered from the above strategies to answer the questions.

answers: 1 (C), 2 (A)

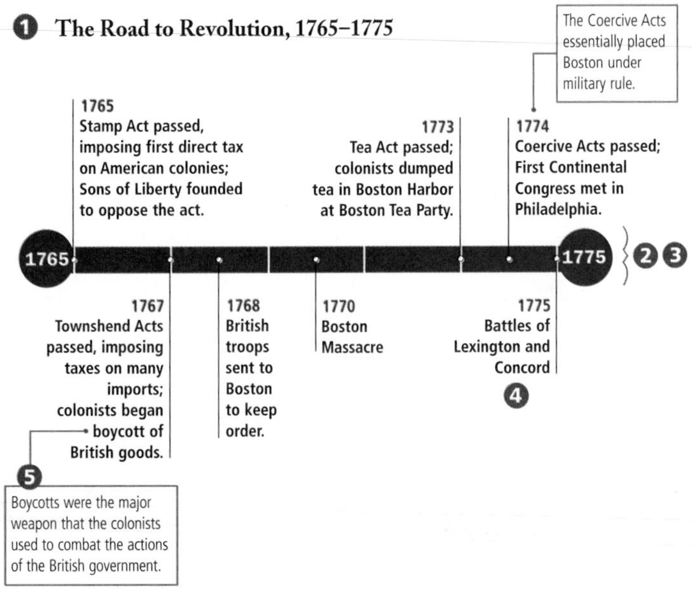

1 The Road to Revolution, 1765–1775
The Coercive Acts essentially placed Boston under military rule.
1765 Stamp Act passed, imposing first direct tax on American colonies; Sons of Liberty founded to oppose the act.
1773 Tea Act passed; colonists dumped tea in Boston Harbor at Boston Tea Party.
1774 Coercive Acts passed; First Continental Congress met in Philadelphia.
1765
1775
2 3
1767 Townshend Acts passed, imposing taxes on many imports; colonists began boycott of British goods.
1768 British troops sent to Boston to keep order.
1770 Boston Massacre
1775 Battles of Lexington and Concord
4
5
Boycotts were the major weapon that the colonists used to combat the actions of the British government.

6 **1.** How did the colonists respond to the passage of the Townshend Acts?

A. They founded the Sons of Liberty.
B. They dumped British tea in Boston Harbor.
C. They began a boycott of British goods.
D. They called the First Continental Congress.

2. About how much time passed between the Coercive Acts and the first battles of the Revolutionary War?

A. one year
B. three years
C. seven years
D. nine years

ACTIVITY OPTIONS

INDIVIDUAL NEEDS

STUDENTS ACQUIRING ENGLISH/ESL

Social Studies Vocabulary Make sure students understand the following terms and concepts in the sample time lines and questions on these pages.

Strategy Page: Time Line

Revolution: the American Revolution in which the colonists won their independence from Britain
boycott: the refusal to buy certain goods
Boston Massacre: conflict in which the British fired into a crowd and killed five colonists
First Continental Congress: meeting of colonial delegates to uphold rights of the colonists

Practice Page: Time Line

toll receipts: money paid as a tax for using a transportation system, such as a canal
bushel: a unit of dry measure

Directions: Use the time line and your knowledge of U.S. history to answer questions 1 through 3.

The Erie Canal, 1816–1840s

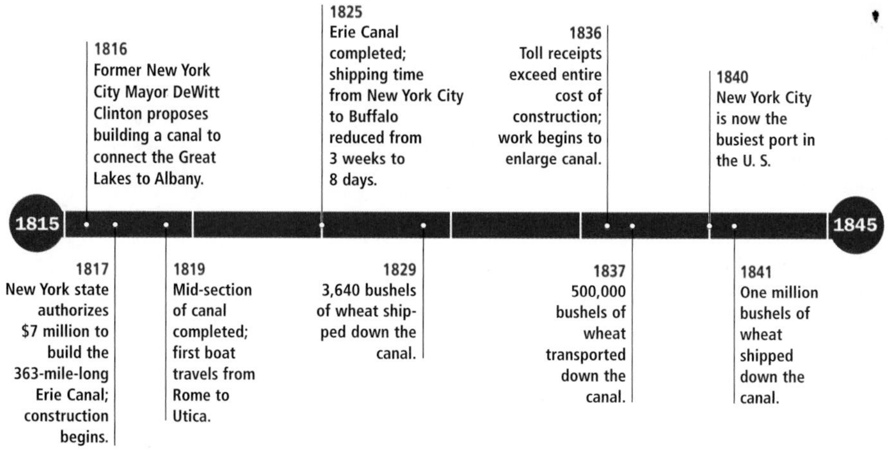

1815
1845
1816 Former New York City Mayor DeWitt Clinton proposes building a canal to connect the Great Lakes to Albany.
1817 New York state authorizes $7 million to build the 363-mile-long Erie Canal; construction begins.
1819 Mid-section of canal completed; first boat travels from Rome to Utica.
1825 Erie Canal completed; shipping time from New York City to Buffalo reduced from 3 weeks to 8 days.
1829 3,640 bushels of wheat shipped down the canal.
1836 Toll receipts exceed entire cost of construction; work begins to enlarge canal.
1837 500,000 bushels of wheat transported down the canal.
1840 New York City is now the busiest port in the U. S.
1841 One million bushels of wheat shipped down the canal.

1. The Erie Canal was completed and ready for water traffic between Buffalo and Albany in
   - **A.** 1817.
   - **B.** 1819.
   - **C.** 1825.
   - **D.** 1840.

2. About how many years after the canal was finished did work begin to enlarge it?
   - **A.** 4 years
   - **B.** 6 years
   - **C.** 11 years
   - **D.** 21 years

3. Which of the following statements about the Erie Canal is *not* true?
   - **A.** The canal greatly reduced the time it took to ship goods between the Great Lakes and New York.
   - **B.** From 1837 to 1841, the volume of wheat shipped through the canal doubled.
   - **C.** The cost of building the canal was greater than the amount of tolls collected.
   - **D.** The mid-section of the canal was completed in 1819.

PRACTICE QUESTIONS

Thinking It Through

Share the following explanations with students as they discuss the strategies they used to answer the practice questions.

1. Check each date against the time line. The key word in this question is *completed* because the entire time line is about the Erie Canal. You need to find the date when the Erie Canal was completed. The correct answer is (C).
2. First skim the time line to find the date the Erie Canal was completed. Next skim the time line to find the date work began to enlarge the canal. Then subtract the dates to determine the answer. The correct answer is (C).
3. Be careful when you answer a question that contains the word *not.* You are looking for an answer that is false. Be sure to read all the choices and compare them with the time line. Eliminate answers that are true. Answers (A), (B), and (D) are true. The correct answer is (C) because it is a false statement about the Erie Canal. According to the time line, in 1836, toll receipts exceeded construction costs.

SKILLS TESTED IN THE ITEMS

STRATEGY ITEMS		PRACTICE ITEMS	
Item Number	**Skill Tested**	**Item Number**	**Skill Tested**
1.	Recognizing Effects	**1.**	Following Chronological Order
2.	Summarizing	**2.**	Following Chronological Order
		3.	Clarifying

USING STRATEGIES FOR . . .

Constructed Response

Remind students of the following:

- In the constructed-response questions on this page, you need to use the document to answer the first question. In questions 2 and 3, you need to use your knowledge of United States history to answer the question.
- Some constructed-response questions do not include a document. Instead, you may need to use your knowledge of United States history to answer them.
- Sometimes constructed-response questions start with short-answer questions and build up to a short essay. The short answers may help you write the short essay, so try to answer the questions in the order they are asked. When your responses are scored, each part will be worth some points, but the short essay will probably be worth more than the short-answer questions.
- Useful information may be found in a title, caption, or source line as well as in the document itself.

General Test-Taking Tips

Share these tips with your students.

- Be sure to answer all parts of constructed-response questions, or as many parts as you can. Each part is worth points.
- As you answer each question, make sure that the number of the answer and the number of the question are the same.

Constructed Response

Constructed-response questions focus on various kinds of documents. Each document usually is accompanied by a series of questions. These questions call for short answers that, for the most part, can be found directly in the document. Some answers, however, require knowledge of the subject or time period addressed in the document.

1. Read the title of the document to discover the subject addressed in the questions.
2. Study and analyze the document. Take notes on what you see.
3. Read the questions and then study the document again to locate the answers.
4. Carefully write your answers. Unless the directions say otherwise, your answers need not be complete sentences.

(1) **List of Purchases Made by Meriwether Lewis for the Expedition to the West**

Item	Cost
Mathematical Instruments	$ 412.95
Arms, Ammunition, & Accouterments	182.08
Medicine, etc.	94.49
Clothing	317.73
Provision, etc.	366.70
Indian Presents	669.50
Camp Equipage	116.68
	$2,160.13

Source: National Archives and Records Administration

(2) Constructed-response questions use a wide range of documents, including short passages, cartoons, charts, graphs, maps, time lines, posters, and other visual materials. The information in this chart is taken from the records kept by Meriwether Lewis.

(3) **1.** What was the largest expense for Lewis and Clark's expedition to the West?

(4) *Indian presents*

2. Why were arms and ammunition needed for the expedition?

for protection and for hunting for food

3. Why did Lewis and Clark carry mathematical instruments with them on their expedition to the West?

President Thomas Jefferson asked Lewis and Clark to make charts and to carry out scientific studies during the expedition.

S26

ACTIVITY OPTIONS

INDIVIDUAL NEEDS

STUDENTS ACQUIRING ENGLISH/ESL

Social Studies Vocabulary Make sure students understand the following terms and concepts in the sample document on these pages.

Strategy Page: Document
expedition: a journey undertaken for a specific reason
accouterments: equipment
provision: a stock of food
equipage: equipment

Practice Page: Document
publish: print
Question 1 *amendment:* addition
Question 2 *mayor:* the elected or appointed as leader of a town or city
intersection: the place where two streets meet

For more test practice online . . .
TEST PRACTICE
CLASSZONE.COM

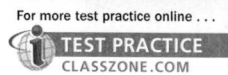

Directions: Use the chart and your knowledge of U.S. history to answer questions 1 through 3.

First Amendment Rights: the Five Basic Freedoms

Freedom of Religion	People have the right to practice the religion of their choice.
Freedom of Speech	People have the right to state their ideas.
Freedom of the Press	People have the right to publish their ideas.
Freedom of Assembly	People have the right to meet peacefully in groups.
Freedom to Petition	People have the right to petition the government.

1. Does the first amendment guarantee you the right to belong to any religion you like?

2. You write a letter to the mayor asking for a stop sign to be placed at an intersection near your school. Which of the five basic freedoms are you exercising?

3. What specific activities are covered by freedom of speech, and what activities are covered by freedom of the press? How are the two freedoms related?

PRACTICE QUESTIONS

Thinking It Through

Share the following explanations with students as they discuss the strategies they used to answer the practice questions.

1. Study the chart and use your knowledge of U.S. history to answer the question. The first amendment does guarantee the right to belong to any religious group you choose.
2. Read the question and then study the chart. The answer is that you are exercising your freedom of speech and your freedom to petition.
3. To answer this question, you must summarize what activities are covered by each freedom in one or two sentences. Then explain how they are related. Include specific details and facts to support your answer.

Scoring for Constructed-Response Questions

Constructed-response questions usually are scored using a rubric, or scoring guide. The questions on this page might be scored by giving 1 point for each question—a total score of 3 points.

SKILLS TESTED IN THE ITEMS

STRATEGY ITEMS		PRACTICE ITEMS	
Item Number	**Skill Tested**	**Item Number**	**Skill Tested**
1.	Interpreting Charts	**1.**	Interpreting Charts
2.	Making Inferences	**2.**	Categorizing
3.	Summarizing	**3.**	Clarifying

USING STRATEGIES FOR . . .

Extended Response

Remind students of the following.

- Read all the extended-response questions that go with one document before beginning to answer any questions. Look for words that tell you how to organize your answers.
- In question 1, you are to use the chart to create a time line. Make a rough sketch of the time line on a separate paper. Include a title. Place the events and their dates in sequence starting with the earliest date and ending with the latest date. Use the appropriate intervals between events. Use your knowledge of U.S. history to add important information to your time line. Make a final copy of your time line on the answer sheet.
- In question 2, you need to apply your own knowledge of U.S. history. Jot down your ideas and create an outline on a separate piece of paper. Use this outline to write a short essay to answer the question. Support your main ideas with details and examples.

General Test-Taking Tips

Share these tips with your students.

- Write in complete sentences, whenever appropriate. Extended-response essays require complete sentences.
- Use correct grammar, punctuation, and spelling to help the scorer understand your answer.
- Remember, neatness counts! If the scorer cannot read your answer, you will not get credit for it.

Extended Response

Extended-response questions, like constructed-response questions, usually focus on one kind of document. However, they are more complex and require more time to complete than typical short-answer constructed-response questions. Some extended-response questions ask you to complete a chart, graph, or diagram. Still others ask you to write an essay, a report, or some other lengthier piece based on the document.

1. Read the title of the document to get an idea of the subject.
2. Study and analyze the document. Take notes on your ideas.
3. Carefully read the extended-response questions. (Question 1 asks you to present the information in the chart in a time line. Question 2 asks you to write an essay by applying your knowledge of history to information in the chart.)
4. If the question calls for some type of diagram, make a rough sketch on scrap paper first. Then make a final copy of your diagram on the answer sheet.
5. If the question requires an extended piece of writing, jot down ideas in outline form. Use this outline to write your answer.

❶ **Ratifying the Constitution**

❷

State	Date Ratified
Connecticut	January 9, 1788
Delaware	December 7, 1787
Georgia	January 2, 1788
Maryland	April 28, 1788
Massachusetts	February 6, 1788
New Hampshire	June 21, 1788
New Jersey	December 18, 1787
New York	July 26, 1788
North Carolina	November 21, 1789
Pennsylvania	December 12, 1787
Rhode Island	May 29, 1790
South Carolina	May 23, 1788
Virginia	June 25, 1788

❹ For time lines and other diagrams, remember to include a title and all appropriate labels.

❸ **1.** Use the information in the chart and your knowledge of U.S. history to create a time line for the ratification of the Constitution.

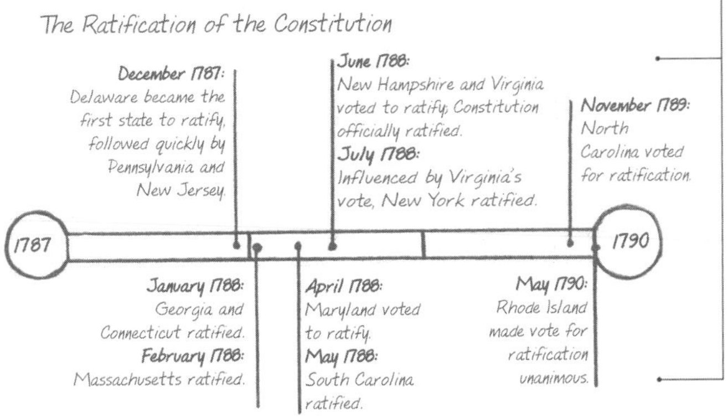

The Ratification of the Constitution
December 1787: Delaware became the first state to ratify, followed quickly by Pennsylvania and New Jersey.
June 1788: New Hampshire and Virginia voted to ratify. Constitution officially ratified.
July 1788: Influenced by Virginia's vote, New York ratified.
November 1789: North Carolina voted for ratification.
1787
1790
January 1788: Georgia and Connecticut ratified.
February 1788: Massachusetts ratified.
April 1788: Maryland voted to ratify.
May 1788: South Carolina ratified.
May 1790: Rhode Island made vote for ratification unanimous.

❸ **2.** Write a brief essay explaining the significance of the Bill of Rights to the ratification of the Constitution.

❺ **Essay Rubric** The best essays will point out that the promise of a Bill of Rights was key to getting enough support to ensure ratification of the Constitution. The vote for ratification by Virginia—the largest of the states—was contingent upon the passage of a Bill of Rights.

ACTIVITY OPTIONS

INDIVIDUAL NEEDS

STUDENTS ACQUIRING ENGLISH/ESL

Social Studies Vocabulary Make sure students understand the following terms in the documents and questions on these pages.

Strategy Page: Document
ratifying: accepting
Constitution: the written plan for U.S. government
Question 2 *Bill of Rights:* the first ten amendments of U.S. Constitution, listing citizens' rights and freedoms

Practice Page: Document
parallel: line of latitude
slave state: state in which slavery was legal
free state: state in which slavery was not legal
fugitive slave law: law to help slaveholders recapture runaway slaves
popular sovereignty: system in which residents vote to decide an issue
repeal: do away with; abolish

For more test practice online . . .
TEST PRACTICE
CLASSZONE.COM

Directions: Use the chart and your knowledge of U.S. history to answer question 1.

A Country Dividing

As the United States grew during the 1800s, Congress and the people argued about what form of government each new territory and state would have. The differences of opinion centered on one issue more than any other: slavery. Eventually, those sectional arguments led to the Civil War.

The chart below lists three acts of Congress that addressed the issue of slavery in the West. On the right are the provisions of each of these acts.

Act	Provisions
Missouri Compromise, 1820	1. Slavery was to be prohibited in the Louisiana territory north of the 36° 30′ parallel. 2. Missouri would enter the Union as a slave state. 3. Maine would enter the Union as a free state.
Compromise of 1850	1. The territories of New Mexico and Utah were created without restrictions on slavery. 2. California would enter the Union as a free state. 3. The slave trade would be prohibited in Washington, D.C. 4. Congress would pass a strong fugitive slave law for mandatory return of escaped slaves.
Kansas-Nebraska Act, 1854	1. Two new territories, Kansas and Nebraska, were created. 2. The people residing in the Kansas and Nebraska territories would have the right to decide whether their territory would enter the Union as a free or slave state (popular sovereignty). 3. The Kansas-Nebraska Act repealed the Missouri Compromise of 1820, which prohibited slavery in territories north of 36° 30′.

1. Write an essay explaining how the Missouri Compromise, the Compromise of 1850, and the Kansas-Nebraska Act promoted sectionalism.

PRACTICE QUESTION

Thinking It Through

Share the following explanations with students as they discuss the strategies they used to answer the practice question.

- Read the directions and the passage. Review the information presented in the chart.
- Apply your knowledge of United States history to write an essay explaining how the provisions of these acts promoted sectionalism.

The best essays will point out the following information:

Missouri Compromise, 1820

- This act led to sectionalism because a large part of the Louisiana Territory was closed to slavery.
- Several free states could be formed later.
- Fewer slave states could be formed from the part of the Louisiana Territory that was open to slavery.

Compromise of 1850

- Both the North and the South gave up a lot, leading to resentment.
- Fugitive Slave Act angered Northerners, who resented being required to recapture runaway slaves.
- Northerners also resented the law because many Southerners came north in search of escaped slaves, and they often captured free African Americans.

Kansas-Nebraska Act, 1854

- Angered Northerners because it repealed the Missouri Compromise, which had prohibited slavery in territories north of the 36° 30′ parallel.
- Instead, this act left the decision of slavery up to the people living in the territories. The fight over slavery turned the Kansas territory into a battlefield.

Scoring Extended-Response Questions

Extended-response questions usually are scored using a rubric, or scoring guide. The question on this page might be scored by giving the discussion of each act in the essay 2 points, for a total score of 6 points.

SKILLS TESTED IN THE ITEMS

STRATEGY ITEMS		PRACTICE ITEMS	
Item Number	**Skill Tested**	**Item Number**	**Skill Tested**
1.	Creating Charts and Graphs	**Essay Question**	Summarizing; Analyzing Issues
2.	Clarifying		

USING STRATEGIES FOR . . .

Document-Based Questions
Remind students of the following.

- Document-based questions are designed to help you work like a historian. You are given several documents from a variety of sources that you must analyze, evaluate, and synthesize in order to write an essay, much the way a historian would proceed.
- Use the information in the "Introduction" to help you organize your essay. The "Historical Context" gives you the focus of the document-based question. The document-based question shown here focuses on the development of political parties in the early American republic and their influence on policies.
- Use the information in the "Task" section to help you make a graphic organizer such as an outline, chart, or concept web to organize the information for your essay. For example, in this document-based question, "Task" explains that the essay requires you to do two things: (1) Discuss the role of the Federalist and Democratic-Republican parties. (2) Explain why George Washington believed them to be divisive. Make an outline on a piece of scratch paper. Use the following headings in the outline: I. Beliefs of President Washington; II. Views Held by the Parties; III. Policy Issues, 1789–1801.
- As you answer the "Part 1: Short Answer" questions, also complete the outline.
- To answer the "Part 2: Essay" question, use the documents, the answers to the short-answer questions, the notes in your graphic organizer, and your knowledge of history to help you write the essay.

General Test-Taking Tips

Share these tips with your students.
- Write legibly.
- Sometimes answer sheets are scanned for scoring purposes. If you do not write dark enough, they will not be readable.

Document-Based Questions

A document-based question focuses on several documents—both visual and written. These documents often are accompanied by short-answer questions. You then use the answers to these questions and information from the documents to write an essay on a specified subject.

1. Carefully read the "Historical Context" to get an indication of the issue addressed in the question.
2. Note the action words used in the "Task" section. These words tell you exactly what the essay question requires.
3. Study and analyze each document. Think about how the documents are connected to the essay question. Take notes on your ideas.
4. Read and answer each of the document-specific questions.

Introduction

1 Historical Context: During President George Washington's first term, political parties started to develop around the beliefs of two members of Washington's cabinet, Secretary of the Treasury Alexander Hamilton and Secretary of State Thomas Jefferson. Despite Washington's opposition to political parties, they had a great influence in American domestic and foreign policy.

2 Task: Discuss the role of the Federalist and the Democratic-Republican parties in the early republic, and explain why George Washington believed that political parties were divisive.

Part 1: Short Answer

Study each document carefully and answer the questions that follow.

Document 1: A Warning on Political Parties

3 Let me . . . warn you in the most solemn manner against the baneful [harmful] effects of the spirit of party generally. This spirit, unfortunately, is inseparable from our nature, having its root in the strongest passions of the human mind. . . .

It serves always to distract the public councils and enfeeble [weaken] the public administration. It agitates the community with illfounded jealousies and false alarms; kindles the animosity [hatred] of one part against another; foments occasionally riot and insurrection. It opens the door to foreign influence and corruption, which find a facilitated access [easy entry] to the government itself through the channels of party passions.

—George Washington, Farewell Address

4 Why did Washington believe that political parties would harm the nation?

He believed that political parties would have a bad effect on the nation by playing upon the jealousies of different factions and stirring up considerable trouble for the nation. Foreign governments might also find it easy to use political parties to influence our national affairs.

Washington's Farewell Address, *Annals of America, Volume 3, 1784–1796* (Chicago: Encyclopaedia Britannica, Inc., 1976), 610–11.

ACTIVITY OPTIONS

INDIVIDUAL NEEDS

STUDENTS ACQUIRING ENGLISH/ESL

Social Studies Vocabulary Make sure students understand the following terms and concepts on these pages.

Strategy Pages
Document 1 *solemn:* serious
passions: intense emotions
foments: to promote or incite
insurrection: revolt against government authority
corruption: decay of moral principles

Document 2 *interpretation:* to explain in the light of personal belief
National Bank: bank funded by nation to issue paper money

Document 2: Positions of the First United States Political Parties

Federalist Party	Democratic-Republican Party
Strong central government	Weak central government
Loose interpretation of the Constitution	Strict interpretation of the Constitution
Government should pay states' Revolutionary War debts	Each state should pay its own debts
Favored a national bank	Opposed a national bank
Favored business interests	Favored agricultural interests
Pro-British foreign policy	Pro-French foreign policy

How were the policies favored by the Federalists different from those favored by the Democratic-Republicans?

The parties held opposite views on major policy issues.

Document 3: Policy Dispute in Congress Hall, Philadelphia

The cartoon shows the two parties fighting over foreign policy. What does it imply about their ability to settle disagreements?

Their disputes, if not settled by debate, threatened to destroy the federal government.

Part 2: Essay

5 Using information from the documents, your answers to the questions in Part 1, and your knowledge of U.S. history, write an essay in which you discuss the different views the first political parties held on major issues between 1789 and 1801, and explain why Washington believed that political parties were divisive. 6

5 Carefully read the essay question. Then write an outline for your essay.

6 Write your essay. Be sure that it has an introductory paragraph that introduces your argument, main body paragraphs that explain it, and a concluding paragraph that restates your position. In your essay, include extracts or details from specific documents to support your ideas. Add other supporting facts or details that you know from your study of American history.

Essay Rubric The best essays will point out the differences between the Federalists and the Democratic-Republicans (Document 2) and will show how political disagreements, such as those portrayed in the cartoon (Document 3), supported Washington's warning in his Farewell Address (Document 1). Essays should draw upon information not specifically included in the documents that illustrates an understanding of the political debate during the Washington and Adams administrations. Students may also refer to the Alien and Sedition Acts passed by the Federalist Congress during Adams's presidency and the opposing viewpoint expressed in the Kentucky and Virginia Resolutions authored by Jefferson and Madison, respectively.

Cartoon: Prints Division, The New York Public Library, Astor, Lenox, and Tilden Foundations

Rubric for DBQ Essay

The following is a sample rubric that might be used to score a DBQ essay.

To score a 5, the DBQ essay:
- thoroughly answers all parts of Task.
- uses information from all the documents.
- is supported with relevant facts and details.
- includes relevant outside knowledge.
- is well developed and organized.
- has a strong introduction and conclusion.

To score a 4, the DBQ essay:
- answers all parts of Task.
- uses information from most of the documents.
- is supported with relevant facts and details.
- includes relevant outside knowledge.
- is well developed and organized.
- has a good introduction and conclusion.

To score a 3, the DBQ essay:
- answers most parts of Task.
- uses information from some documents.
- is supported with some relevant facts and details.
- includes little relevant outside knowledge.
- is satisfactorily developed and organized.
- restates the essay theme in the introduction and conclusion.

To score a 2, the DBQ essay:
- answers some parts of the Task or all parts in a limited way.
- uses limited information from the documents.
- uses few facts or details to support the essay.
- includes little or no relevant outside knowledge.
- is poorly organized.
- has a limited or missing intro or conclusion.

To score a 1, the DBQ essay:
- shows limited understanding of the Task.
- uses limited information from the documents.
- uses few or no facts or details to support the essay.
- includes no relevant outside knowledge.
- is poorly organized.
- has a limited or missing intro or conclusion.

To score a 0, the DBQ essay:
- does not answer the Task.
- is illegible.
- is blank or missing.

SKILLS TESTED IN THE ITEMS

STRATEGY ITEMS	
Item Number	**Skill Tested**
Document 1	Analyzing Primary Sources
Document 2	Interpreting Charts
Document 3	Analyzing Political Cartoons
Part 2: Essay	Synthesizing

PRACTICE

PRACTICE QUESTIONS

Thinking It Through
Share the following explanations with students as they discuss the strategies they used to answer the practice questions.

Part 1: Short Answers
Document 1. Analyze the picture and the caption to answer the question: The "rifle dress," according to Washington, would make the British think that the men were all "complete marksmen."
Document 2. Skim the primary source for the following answer: Thomas Paine reminds the colonists that they are fighting for freedom against tyranny.
Document 3. Read the columns and rows in both charts for the following answer: The French supplied 7,800 soldiers with General Rochambeau, and 35 ships carrying a total of 2,610 guns with Lieutenant General DeGrasse.

Part 2: Essay. Share the sample rubric on page S31 with students so they know the criteria they must meet to earn the maximum amount of points for this essay. Tell students the following.

- Use the information in the "Introduction" to help you organize your essay. Jot down things you know about the time period or theme of the question. Use the information in "Task" to help you make a graphic organizer, such as a chart with three columns: "Colonists' Beliefs," "Colonists' Military Actions," and "American Alliances with European Nations." As you answer the short-answer questions, also complete this chart.
- Use the documents, the answers to the short-answer questions, the notes in your graphic organizer, and your knowledge of history to help you write the essay.

Introduction

Historical Context: In 1775, Great Britain had an army of 48,647 men located throughout the world, about 8,000 of them in the Americas. A rebellion by the small group of 13 colonies in America did not scare the keepers of such a large colonial empire.

Task: Discuss how the colonists' beliefs and military actions contributed to their victory in the Revolution. Include the significance of the American alliances with European nations.

Part 1: Short Answer

Study each document carefully and answer the questions that follow.

Document 1: First Georgia Regiment of Infantry Continental Line, 1777

The hunting shirt, or rifle dress, shown here was recommended by George Washington in his general order of July 24, 1776. Declaring it a practical item to be given to the troops, he also claimed that ". . . it is a dress justly supposed to carry no small terror to the enemy, who think every such person a complete marksman."

Source: New-York Historical Society

What unusual military tactics did patriots like the man in the picture use to surprise and outsmart the British during the Revolution?

Document 1: *Uniforms of the American Revolution: 1st Georgia Regiment Continental Infantry, 1777, Private Field Dress,* Charles Lefferts. Watercolor, gouache on paper. Copyright © Collection of the New-York Historical Society.

ACTIVITY OPTIONS

INDIVIDUAL NEEDS

STUDENTS ACQUIRING ENGLISH/ESL

Make sure students understand the following in the documents on these pages.

Practice Pages
Documents 1 and 2
Remind students who George Washington and Thomas Paine were.

Document 3
Explain that the French fought on the American side in the Revolution.

Document 2: Philadelphia, September 12, 1777

> I close this paper with a short address to General Howe. . . . We know the cause which we are engaged in, and though a passionate fondness for it may make us grieve at every injury. . . . We are not moved by the gloomy smile of a worthless king, but by the ardent glow of generous patriotism. We fight not to enslave, but to set a country free, and to make room upon the earth for honest men to live in. In such a case we are sure that we are right; and we leave to you the despairing reflection of being the tool of a miserable tyrant.
>
> —Thomas Paine, *The American Crisis No. IV*

Although this excerpt is addressed to the British General Howe, how might it also have encouraged the colonists to continue their fight against the British?

Document 3: The Battle of Yorktown, 1781: Winning the American Revolution

Estimated American, French, and British Forces and Casualties		
Generals and Their Divisions	**Forces**	**Casualties**
General Washington (American colonies)	11,100	90
General Rochambeau (France)	7,800	250
General Cornwallis (Britain)	8,900	550

Source: U.S. Army Center of Military History

Estimated French and British Naval Strength*		
French and British Fleets	**Ships**	**Guns on Board Ship**
Admiral Graves (Britain)	25	1,450
Lieutenant General DeGrasse (France)	35	2,610

*Does not include small craft or transport ships

What support was provided by the French in the Battle of Yorktown?

Part 2: Essay

Using information from the documents, your answers to the questions in Part 1, and your knowledge of U.S. history, write an essay that discusses how the colonists' beliefs and military actions contributed to their victory in the Revolution. Include in your essay the significance of American alliances with European nations.

Rubric for Essay

The best essays will address all three parts of the question—colonists' beliefs, colonists' military tactics, and American alliances with European countries.

Colonists' Beliefs

- The colonists were engaged in a struggle against a tyrant king (Document 2).
- They were fighting a patriotic war for freedom (Document 2).
- They wanted to be represented in Parliament if Britain was going to tax them (outside knowledge).
- They wanted independence and their own form of government (outside knowledge).
- They wanted the freedom to trade with countries other than Britain (outside knowledge).
- They wanted the freedom to move west of the Appalachian Mountains (outside knowledge).

Colonists' Military Tactics

- The "rifle dress" gave the appearance of excellent marksmen to fool the British (Document 1).
- The dress also allowed the colonists to hide in the forests because their uniform blended with the surroundings (Document 1, outside knowledge).
- In the forests, the colonists could use guerrilla warfare, or hold surprise attacks, against the British (outside knowledge).

American Alliances with European Countries

- An American alliance with France provided colonists with military experts, thousands of soldiers, 35 ships loaded with many guns (Document 3).
- Essays should mention that the French provided the most assistance of any European nation (outside knowledge).
- Colonies also needed and received financial and military aid from other European nations, such as Spain and Germany (outside knowledge).

SKILLS TESTED IN THE ITEMS

PRACTICE ITEMS	
Item Number	**Skill Tested**
Document 1	Analyzing Primary Sources
Document 2	Making Inferences
Document 3	Interpreting Charts
Part 2: Essay	Synthesizing

GEOGRAPHY HANDBOOK OBJECTIVE

The student will examine the five themes of geography, explore how they aid geographic observation and analysis, and identify some ways in which the geography of the United States has affected its development.

GEOGRAPHY FROM VISUALS

Interpreting the Photographs Have students look at the photographs on pages 2 and 3. Point out that each provides information about both the physical and human geography of the region. Have student volunteers describe what each picture suggests about climate, soil, natural resources, terrain, or ways of making a living in these five regions. Ask students to find similarities in the interactions between people and their environment in the pictures. **Possible Response** In all pictures, people are using unique aspects of the environment to make a living.

Extension Have students consult an encyclopedia or a world almanac to find out how important each of the economic activities shown in the photographs is to the area in which it occurs.

MORE ABOUT . . .

Geography

The term *geography* was coined more than 2,000 years ago in ancient Greece. It combines *geo,* meaning "earth," with *graphia,* meaning a "way of writing, drawing, or describing."

The Landscape of America

The best place to begin your study of American history is with the geography of America. Geography is more than the study of the land and people. It also involves the relationship between people and their environment.

The United States is part of the North American continent. The United States ranks third in both total area and population in the world. It is filled with an incredible variety of physical features, natural resources, climatic conditions, and people. This handbook will help you to learn about these factors and to understand how they affected the development of the United States.

A timber company collects logs in the Northwest.

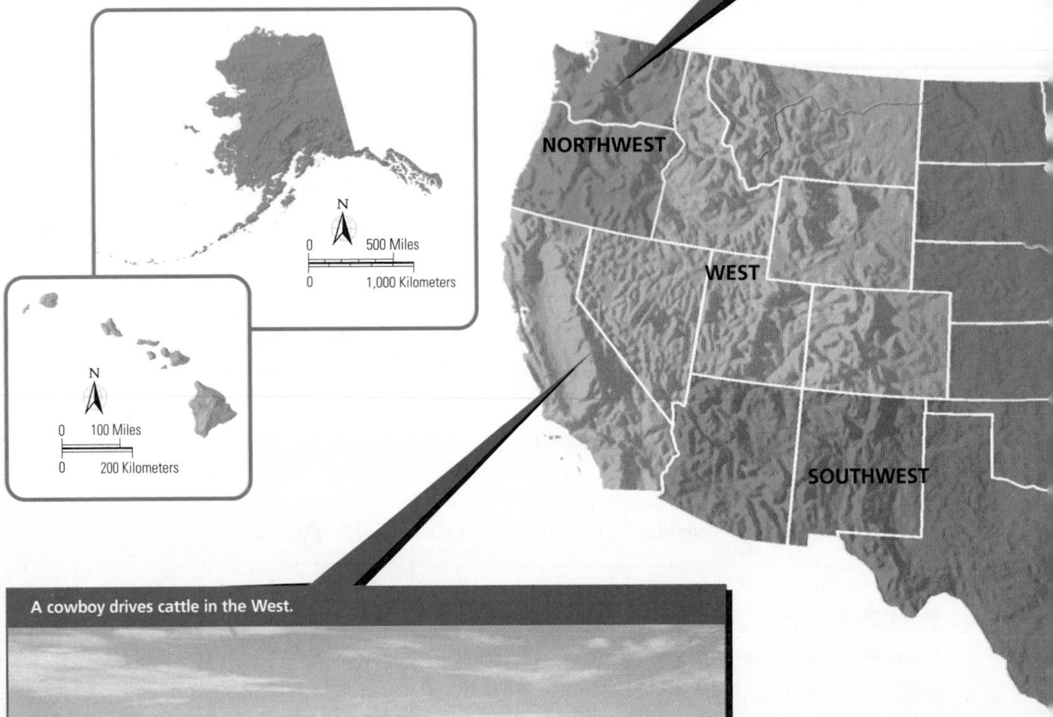

A cowboy drives cattle in the West.

2

RECOMMENDED RESOURCES

BOOKS FOR THE TEACHER

Birdsall, Stephen. ***Regional Landscapes of the United States and Canada.*** New York: John Wiley & Sons, 1999. Looks at the land and people of Canada and the United States from a geographic perspective.

De Blij, Harm J. and Peter O. Muller. ***Geography: Realms, Regions, and Concepts.*** New York: John Wiley & Sons, 1999. Introduction to world geography by one of the nation's finest geographers.

Monmonier, Mark. ***How to Lie with Maps.*** Chicago: University of Chicago Press, 1996. Examines the use and abuse of maps.

SOFTWARE

Inspirer Collection. CD-ROM. Tom Snyder, 1998. Five fast-paced map search games.

VIDEO

Basics of Geography. United Learning, 1996. Discusses water, landforms, climate, and resources.

INTERNET

For more about the Geographic Learning Site, visit . . .

classzone.com

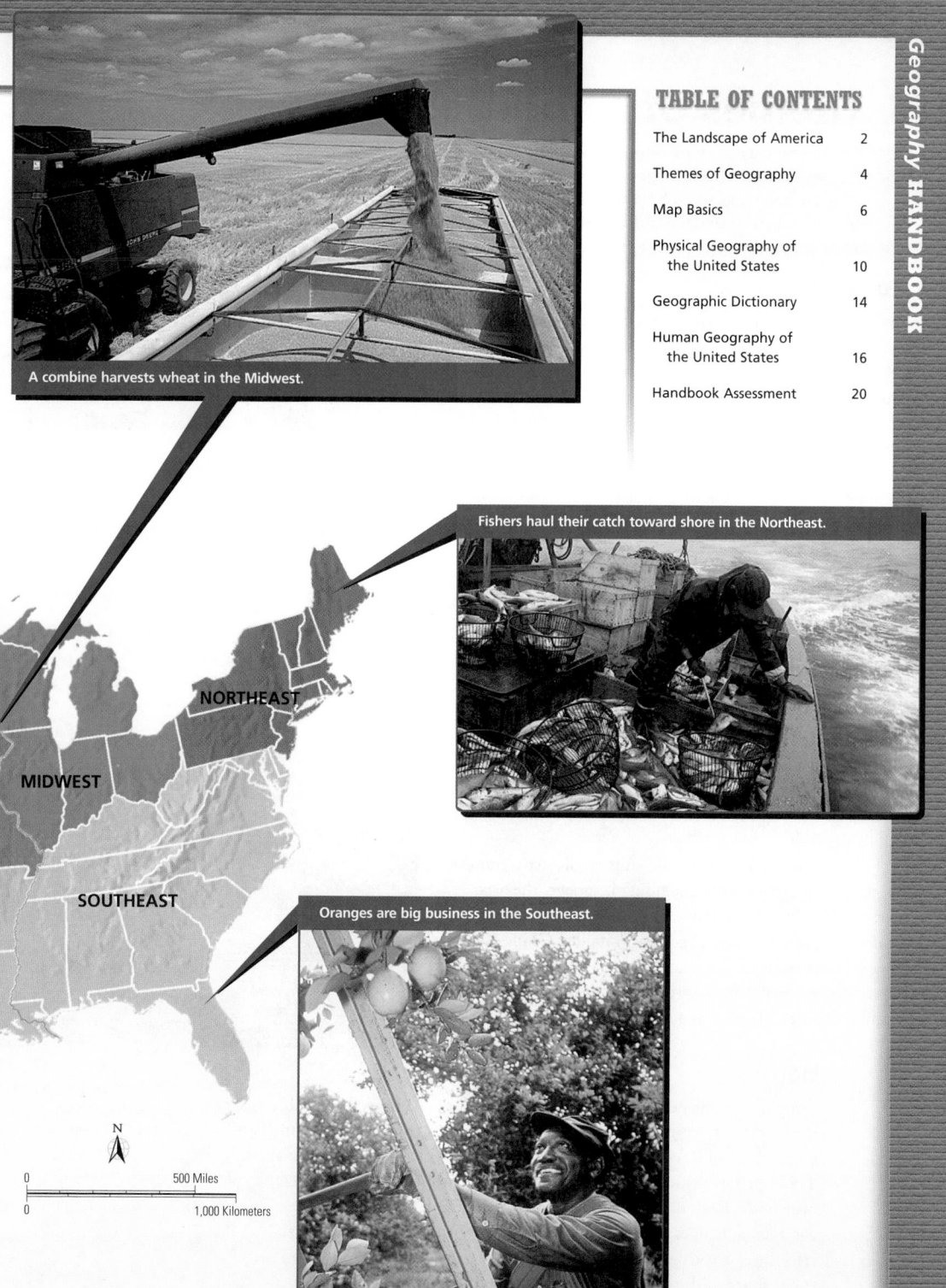

A combine harvests wheat in the Midwest.

TABLE OF CONTENTS

Fishers haul their catch toward shore in the Northeast.

Oranges are big business in the Southeast.

MORE ABOUT . . .

Massachusetts Fisheries

Fishing the offshore banks of the North Atlantic has been an important industry in the Northeast since colonial times. In the 1500s, European fishing crews crossed the Atlantic to catch cod, which could be salted and dried to keep for long periods without spoiling. Today, Massachusetts is a leading commercial fishing state. It supplies cod, ocean perch, flounder, haddock, whiting, and about half of the scallops in the United States. In the early 1990s, overfishing and poor management of cod stocks led to a sharp decline in Atlantic cod. The U.S. and Canadian governments restricted cod fishing to aid in species recovery.

MORE ABOUT . . .

Florida Citrus

Citrus fruits such as oranges, grapefruits, lemons, and limes require a warm climate. They grow best in places with almost no frost or wind. Although citrus trees yield fruit in tropical regions, they produce better fruit in a slightly cooler climate. Much of Florida has a subtropical climate with many months of frost-free weather. Like Arizona, California, and Texas, it is well suited to citrus production. Approximately three out of every four oranges and grapefruits grown in the United States are produced in Florida.

TEACHING STRATEGY

Setting the Stage Have students work in small groups to create a chart like the one here. In the first column, have students list the six regions shown on the map and discuss what they already know about the location, physical features, natural resources, climate, and people of each region. In the third column, have students list at least three questions they have about the people of each region and their environment. Have each group describe a photograph or draw a picture to illustrate the Southwest, and share both the chart and the picture suggestion with the class.

Region	What I Already Know	What I Want to Know

FOCUS & MOTIVATE

5-MINUTE WARM-UP

Finding Main Ideas To help students identify the five major themes of geography and how they apply to Boston, Massachusetts, have them answer these questions.

1. Look at the illustrations on pages 4–5. How might Boston's location on the shores of the Atlantic Ocean have affected its economic development?
2. Judging by the illustrations, how would you answer the question, "What is Boston like?"

INSTRUCT

Themes of Geography

- What is the difference between absolute and relative location?
- How might the physical characteristics of a place influence its human characteristics?
- How is technology changing the way ideas and goods move?

MORE ABOUT . . .

Place

Human characteristics of place can also include patterns of livelihood, land use and ownership, town planning, and communication and transportation networks. In earlier times, Boston was known for its outspoken patriots, who helped make it a birthplace of the American Revolution. Later, Boston's writers, thinkers, and religious leaders turned the city into a center of culture and religious thought. Today, it is known for the academic excellence of its numerous colleges, its fine museums, symphony, and variety of cultural activities as well as for its respected medical centers and its scientific and technological resources.

Themes of Geography

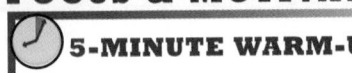

One useful way to think about geography is in terms of major themes or ideas. These pages examine the five major themes of geography and show how they apply to Boston, Massachusetts. Recognizing and understanding these themes will help you to understand all the different aspects of geography.

Boston is located on the shores of the Atlantic Ocean.

Location

"Where am I?" Your answer to this question is your *location.* One way to answer it is to use *absolute* location. That means you'll use the coordinates of longitude and latitude to give your answer (see page 8). For example, if you're in Boston, its absolute location is approximately 42° north latitude and 71° west longitude.

Like most people, however, you'll probably use *relative* location to answer the question. Relative location describes where a certain area is in relation to another area. For example, Boston lies in the northeast corner of the United States, next to the Atlantic Ocean.

THINKING ABOUT GEOGRAPHY What is the relative location of your school?

Place

"What is Boston like?" *Place* can help you answer this question. Place refers to the physical and human factors that make one area different from another. Physical characteristics are natural features, such as physical setting, plants, animals, and weather. For example, Boston sits on a hilly peninsula.

Human characteristics include cultural diversity and the things people have made—including language, the arts, and architecture. For instance, Boston includes African Americans, as well as people of Irish, Italian, Chinese, and Hispanic ancestry.

THINKING ABOUT GEOGRAPHY What physical and human characteristics make where you live unique?

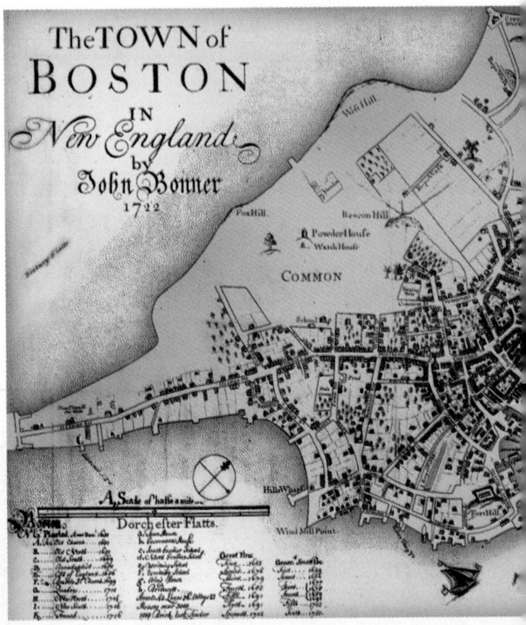

Boston has grown and changed since this 1722 map.

Region

Geographers can't easily study the whole world at one time. So they break the world into regions. A *region* can be as large as a continent or as small as a neighborhood. A region has certain shared characteristics that set it apart. These characteristics might include political division, climate, language, or religion. Boston is part of the northeast region. It shares a climate—continental temperate—with the cities of New York and Philadelphia.

THINKING ABOUT GEOGRAPHY What characteristics does your city or town share with nearby cities or towns?

4 GEOGRAPHY HANDBOOK

ACTIVITY OPTIONS

INTERDISCIPLINARY LINK: ART

BLOCK SCHEDULING

ILLUSTRATING THE FIVE THEMES OF GEOGRAPHY

Class Time One class period

Task Making a poster showing how the five themes of geography apply to a city in the United States

Purpose To use the five themes of geography to analyze and organize geographic information

Supplies Needed
- Encyclopedias and other reference materials on cities in the United States
- Internet access
- Posterboard
- Art supplies

Activity Divide students into groups of five. As a class, select a region of the United States. Within this region, have each group pick a city and create a poster that illustrates how the city chosen reflects each theme of geography. Within groups, one student can be responsible for illustrating each theme. Posters should have both pictures or drawings and captions. After each group has presented its poster to the class, have students identify the regional characteristics the cities share.

Airplanes from Boston's Logan International Airport move people and ideas around the globe.

People shop, eat, and interact at Boston's famous Quincy Market.

Movement

Movement refers to the shifting of people, goods, and ideas from one place to another. People constantly move in search of better places to live, and they trade goods with one another over great distances. Movement also causes ideas to travel from place to place. In recent years, technology has quickened the movement of ideas and goods.

Boston became known as the *Cradle of Liberty* because of the movement of ideas. The concepts of freedom and self-government that developed in Boston spread to the other colonies and helped to start the American Revolution.

THINKING ABOUT GEOGRAPHY What are some of the different ways you spread information and ideas?

Human-Environment Interaction

Human-environment interaction refers to ways people interact with their environment, such as building a dam, cutting down a tree, or even sitting in the sun.

In Boston, human-environment interaction occurred when officials filled in swampy areas to make the city larger. In other ways, the environment has forced people to act. For example, people have had to invent ways to protect themselves from extreme weather and natural disasters.

THINKING ABOUT GEOGRAPHY What are ways that people in your city or town have changed their environment?

Themes of Geography Assessment

1. Main Ideas

a. What is the relative location of your home?

b. What are three characteristics of the region in which you live?

c. What are at least three ways in which you have recently interacted with the environment?

2. Critical Thinking

Forming and Supporting Opinions Which aspect of geography described in these themes do you think has most affected your life? Explain.

THINK ABOUT

- ways that you interact with your environment
- how you travel from place to place

MORE ABOUT . . .

Movement Reshapes Boston

In the 1850s, Boston inaugurated its first horse-drawn trolleys, or horse cars. These forerunners of the electric trolley made it possible for city workers to live farther from their workplaces. The horse-car and trolley lines fueled the movement of people out of the center city and into smaller surrounding towns, such as Roxbury, Dorchester, Brighton, and Charlestown. Between 1855 and 1873, these once independent communities became a part of the larger city.

MORE ABOUT . . .

Boston's Human-Environment Interaction

When Boston was first settled, it covered the Shawmut Peninsula and was almost completely surrounded by water. Its only connection with the mainland was a narrow neck of land to the south. West of the neck was a vast area of mud flats and salt marshes, which were submerged at high tide. Throughout the 1800s, the salt flats in this area, known as the Back Bay, were filled in by cutting down hills and bringing in gravel from neighboring towns. In the 1830s, a public garden was built in the Back Bay. By century's end, the Back Bay was one of the city's best-known residential areas.

Assessment: Themes of Geography

1. Main Ideas

a. Answers should demonstrate understanding of the term *relative location.* **b.** Answers should demonstrate understanding of the term *region.* **c.** Answers should demonstrate understanding of human-environment interaction.

2. Critical Thinking

Forming and Supporting Opinions Answers should demonstrate understanding of the themes of geography.

FOCUS & MOTIVATE

5-MINUTE WARM-UP

Comparing These questions focus on the tools used by geographers.

1. Look at the illustrations of the tools of geography and read the captions on page 6. List similarities between the tools of the 19th-century surveyor and the contemporary geographer.
2. What are some reasons that might make maps out of date?

INSTRUCT

Map Basics

- How do physical, political, and historical maps differ?
- How are computers used in map making?

MORE ABOUT . . .

Global Positioning Systems

A global positioning system, or GPS, is a navigational system that uses radio signals broadcast by satellites. Airplanes, ships, and other vehicles—as well as people on foot—determine their own location by "reading" the signals through computerized radio receivers. The current GPS has been fully operational since 1995. It has 24 satellites in six orbits at a height of about 12,500 miles. The satellites send back signals to GPS receivers indicating their location and broadcast time. With this information, the GPS receiver can determine the latitude, longitude, and altitude of its location and find its own position in seconds to an accuracy of less than 50 feet.

Map Basics

Geographers use many different types of maps, and these maps all have a variety of features. The map on the next page gives you information on a historical event—the War of 1812. But you can use it to learn about different parts of a map, too.

Types of Maps

Physical maps Physical maps show mountains, hills, plains, rivers, lakes, oceans, and other physical features of an area.

Political maps Political maps show political units, such as countries, states, provinces, counties, districts, and towns. Each unit is normally shaded a different color, represented by a symbol, or shown with a different typeface.

Historical maps Historical maps illustrate such things as economic activity, migrations, battles, and changing national boundaries.

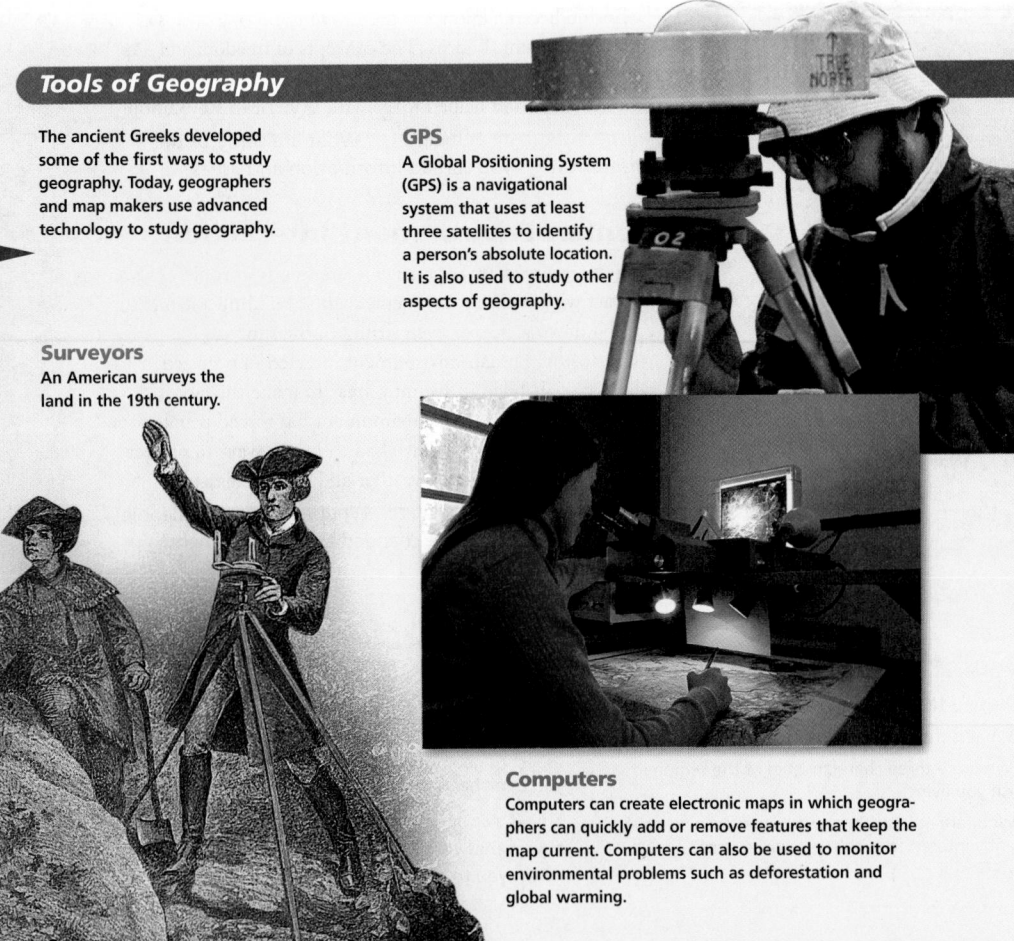

Tools of Geography

The ancient Greeks developed some of the first ways to study geography. Today, geographers and map makers use advanced technology to study geography.

GPS
A Global Positioning System (GPS) is a navigational system that uses at least three satellites to identify a person's absolute location. It is also used to study other aspects of geography.

Surveyors
An American surveys the land in the 19th century.

Computers
Computers can create electronic maps in which geographers can quickly add or remove features that keep the map current. Computers can also be used to monitor environmental problems such as deforestation and global warming.

6

TEACHING STRATEGY

Comparing Have students skim newspapers, newsmagazines, advertising circulars, travel brochures, and Internet sources for examples of different kinds of maps. Then have students identify as many types of maps as they can, such as the types of maps found in telephone books, national parks, almanacs, amusement parks, state highway visitor's centers, history books, newspapers and newsmagazines, and on television programs.

Have each student present one map to the class and explain what type of map it is, what information it provides, who might use it, and why. Have students suggest alternative ways that information on the map might be presented. After the presentations, put students into groups by the type of map they selected, and have each group list ways its maps are similar.

Reading a Map

A **Lines** Lines indicate political boundaries, roads and highways, human movement, and rivers and other waterways.

B **Symbols** Symbols represent such items as capital cities, battle sites, or economic activities.

C **Labels** Labels are words or phrases that explain various items or activities on a map.

D **Compass Rose** A compass rose shows which way the directions north (N), south (S), east (E), and west (W) point on the map.

E **Scale** A scale shows the ratio between a unit of length on the map and a unit of distance on the earth. A typical one-inch scale indicates the number of miles and kilometers that length represents on the map.

F **Colors** Colors show a variety of information on a map, such as population density or the physical growth of a country.

G **Legend or Key** A legend or key lists and explains the symbols, lines, and colors on a map.

H **Lines of Longitude** These are imaginary, north-south lines that run around the globe.
Lines of Latitude These are imaginary, east-west lines that run around the globe. Together, latitude and longitude lines form a grid on a map or globe to indicate an area's absolute location.

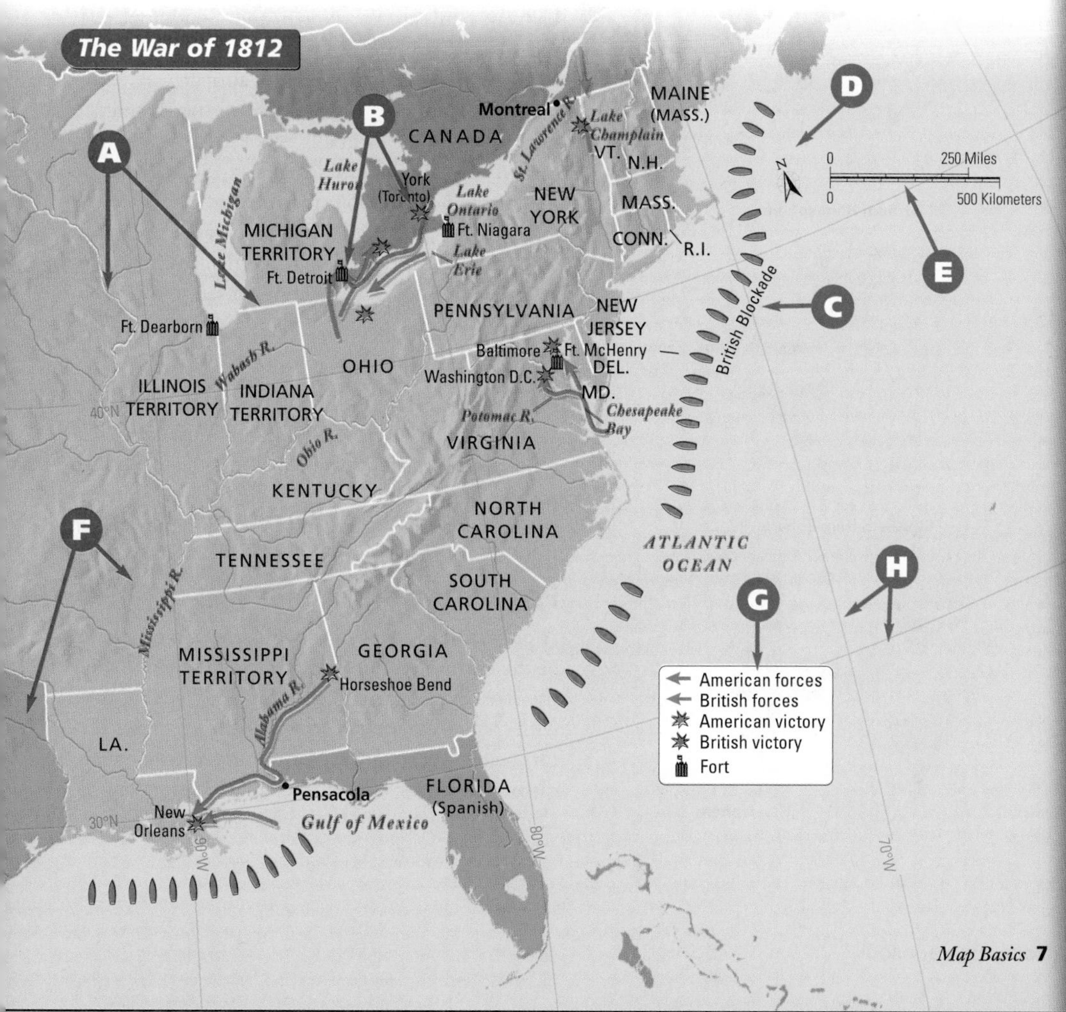

GEOGRAPHY FROM VISUALS

Reading the Map Ask students what the lines/arrows labeled "A" on the map shown stand for. **Answer** rivers, territorial boundaries. What symbols are used to represent British and American victories? **Answer** red and blue stars. What does a red arrow represent? **Answer** the direction in which British forces were moving. What does the orange color on the map indicate? **Answer** land areas that are not a part of the United States

Extension Have students look in reference books or history books to find other maps showing the War of 1812. Ask students to work in pairs to identify similarities and differences between maps.

MORE ABOUT . . .

Surveying
During colonial times and into the 1900s, the surveyor worked to determine locations and boundaries of places by measuring angles, distances, and heights with mechanical instruments. In the 20th century, newer technologies like aerial photography, infrared and radar imaging systems that perform remote sensing, global positioning systems, and computerized data systems have transformed the ways maps are made.

TEACHING STRATEGY

Comparing Maps with Different Scales To give students practice in reading and measuring scale on maps, provide small groups with two maps of the same place in two different scales. For example, you might pair a map of a city with one of the city's financial district or of a neighborhood within the city. Pair a highway map of a state with a map of a city in the state. Pair two maps of different scale of the same historical event. Have small groups of students examine paired maps, noting the scale of each, the overall size of each, and describing differences in the details that can be seen on each map. Have groups use the map scale to measure two distances on each map. Check student answers. Then have each group make up three questions about its maps that require measuring distances on the maps. Have groups exchange maps and questions.

MORE ABOUT . . .

Longitude

Parallels of latitude and meridians of longitude together form a grid that can be used to specify any point on the earth's surface. At the equator, the distance between two meridians is greatest—about 69 miles. That distance narrows as the meridians approach the North and South Poles. One degree of longitude at Miami is about 62 miles wide. Farther north, at New York City, one degree of longitude is about 55 miles wide.

MORE ABOUT . . .

Latitude

The Tropic of Cancer and the Tropic of Capricorn mark the farthest points north and south of the equator where the sun's rays fall vertically. The Arctic Circle and the Antarctic Circle mark the farthest points north and south of the equator where the sun appears above the horizon each day of the year. North of the Arctic Circle and south of the Antarctic Circle in the polar regions, the sun remains continuously visible in the sky for 24 hours a day during certain times of the year.

Longitude Lines (Meridians)

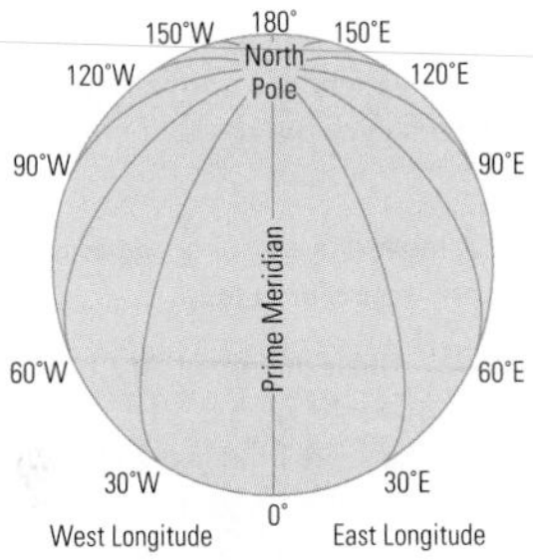

Latitude Lines (Parallels)

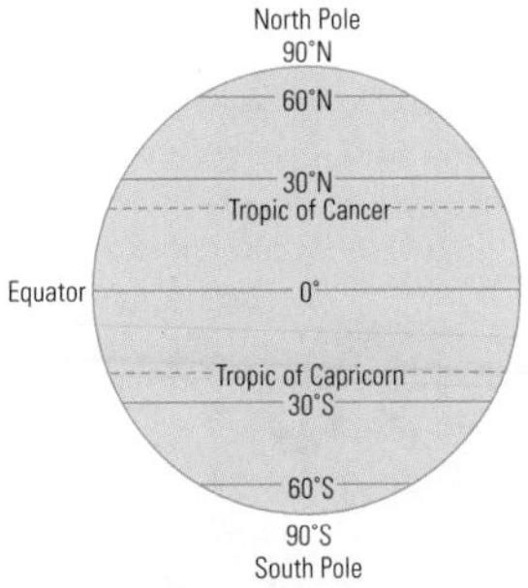

Northern Hemisphere

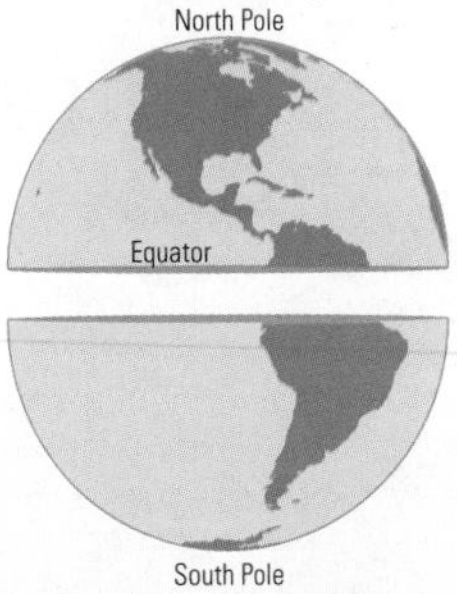

Southern Hemisphere

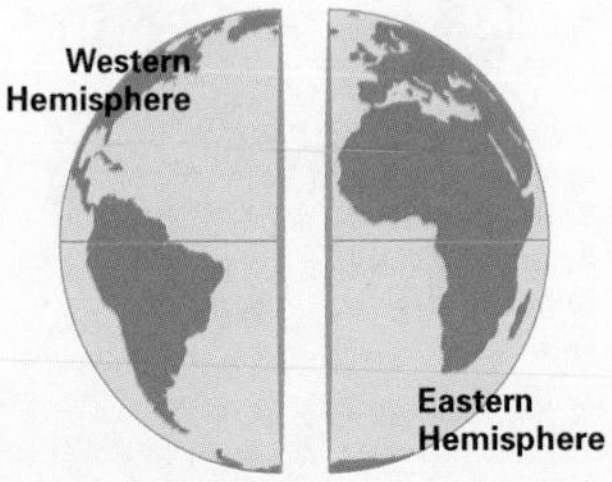

Longitude lines

- are imaginary lines that run north to south around the globe and are known as meridians
- show the distance in degrees east or west of the prime meridian

The prime meridian is a longitude line that runs from the North Pole to the South Pole. It passes through Greenwich, England, and measures 0° longitude.

Latitude lines

- are imaginary lines that run east to west around the globe and are known as parallels
- show distance in degrees north or south of the equator

The equator is a latitude line that circles the earth halfway between the North and South poles. It measures 0° latitude.

The tropics of Cancer and Capricorn are parallels that form the boundaries of the Tropics, a region that stays warm all year.

Latitude and longitude lines appear together on a map and allow you to pinpoint the absolute location of cities and other geographic features. You express this location through coordinates of intersecting lines. These are measured in degrees.

Hemisphere

Hemisphere is a term for half the globe. The globe can be divided into Northern and Southern hemispheres (separated by the equator) or into Eastern and Western hemispheres. The United States is located in the Northern and Western hemispheres.

Projections

A projection is a way of showing the curved surface of the earth on a flat map. Flat maps cannot show the size, shape, and direction of a globe all at once with total accuracy. As a result, all projections distort some aspect of the earth's surface. Some maps distort distances, while other maps distort angles. On the next page are four projections.

ACTIVITY OPTIONS

MULTIPLE LEARNING STYLES: INTERPERSONAL — **BLOCK SCHEDULING**

REVIEWING LATITUDE AND LONGITUDE

Class Time One class period

Task Identifying places by longitude and latitude

Purpose To review basics of latitude and longitude

Supplies Needed
- World atlases

Activity Divide students into teams. Have each team pick five cities, use an atlas to find the absolute location of each city, and write a clue in the following form to describe its relative location: My city is in the Eastern and Northern Hemisphere, north of the Tropic of Cancer, south of 40° N latitude, northeast of Kyoto, south of Hokkaido. *(Tokyo, Japan, 35° N, 139° E)* Have teams take turns writing their clues on the board. The first team to identify the city and its absolute location wins the round.

Mercator Projection

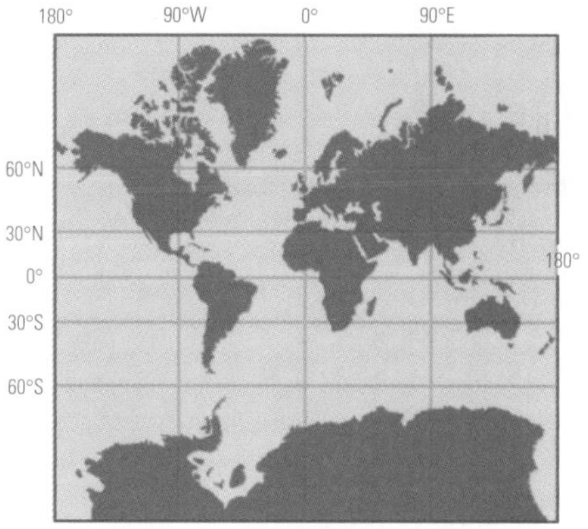

The Mercator projection shows most of the continents as they look on a globe. However, the projection stretches out the lands near the North and South poles. The Mercator is used for all kinds of navigation.

Azimuthal Projection

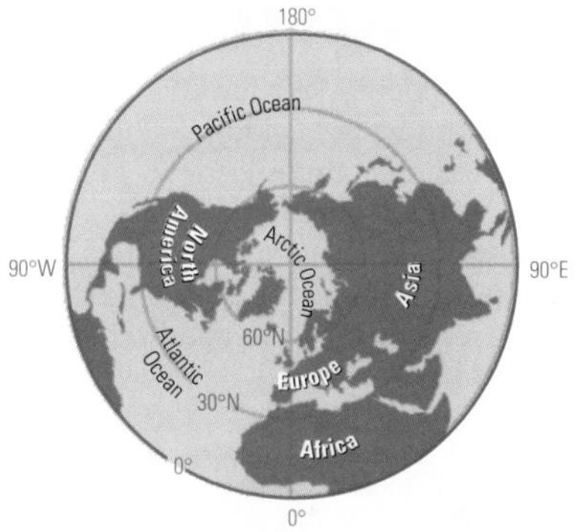

An azimuthal projection shows the earth so that a straight line from the central point to any other point on the map gives the shortest distance between the two points. Size and shape of the continents are also distorted.

Homolosine Projection

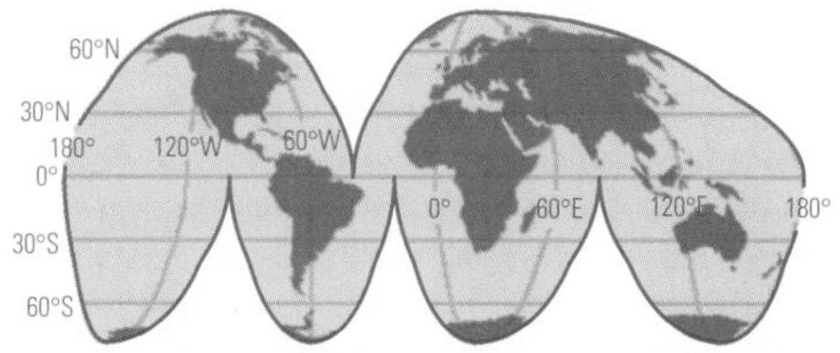

This projection shows the accurate shapes and sizes of the landmasses, but distances on the map are not correct.

Robinson Projection

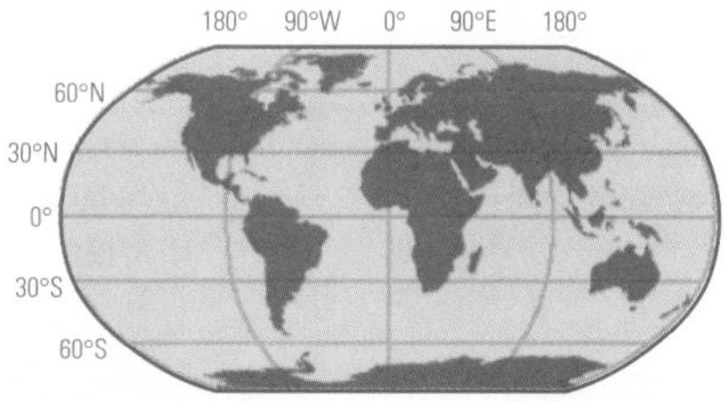

Textbook maps commonly use the Robinson projection. It shows the entire earth with nearly the true sizes and shapes of the continents and oceans. However, the shapes of the landforms near the poles appear flat.

Map Basics Assessment

1. Main Ideas

a. What is the longitude and latitude of your city or town?

b. What information is provided by the legend on the map on page 7?

c. What is a projection? Compare and contrast Antarctica on the Mercator and the Robinson projections.

2. Critical Thinking

Making Inferences Why do you think latitude and longitude are so important to sailors?

THINK ABOUT
- the landmarks you use to find your way around
- the landmarks available to sailors on the ocean

MORE ABOUT . . .

Azimuthal Projections

Only a globe can accurately represent the shape of the earth and the relationship among the earth's surface features. An azimuthal projection depicts a part of the earth as a flattened disk viewed from one of several different points. Azimuthal projections can show the earth's surface from a point at the center of the earth, on the opposite side of the earth's surface, or from a point out in space. A polar projection is an azimuthal projection from a point in space over the North or South Pole. In a polar projection, parallels of latitude are concentric circles, while meridians are straight lines.

MORE ABOUT . . .

Mercator Projection

Flemish geographer Gerhardus Mercator created the Mercator projection in 1569. It broke new ground in showing the earth on a flat sheet of paper. In a Mercator projection, the parallels of latitude, which on the globe are equal distances apart, are drawn farther and farther apart from each other as their distance from the equator increases. This preserves the shapes of land areas but distorts their size, especially those that are far from the equator. Greenland, for example, is shown with its proper shape but appears much larger than it actually is.

Assessment: Map Basics

1. Main Ideas

a. Students may check their answers in a geographical dictionary or atlas. **b.** The legend identifies the symbols used on the map. **c.** A projection is a way of showing the curved surface of the earth on a flat map. Antarctica appears larger than it is on a Mercator projection; a Robinson projection flattens the landforms of Antarctica.

2. Critical Thinking

Possible Response Latitude and longitude provide absolute location. On the open seas, sailors cannot depend on relative location because they cannot compare one part of the ocean to another.

FOCUS & MOTIVATE

5-MINUTE WARM-UP

Comparing These questions focus on the resources of the United States

1. Look at the map on page 11. Where in the country are deposits of iron ore located?
2. In which part of the nation are oil deposits found?

INSTRUCT

Physical Geography of the United States

- What natural features do physical geographers study?
- What natural resources have helped the growth of U.S. industries?
- How do human-environment interactions affect climate?
- What explains regional variations in the types of vegetation found in the United States?

MORE ABOUT . . .

Alaska's Resources

Oil production is Alaska's single most important economic activity. Oil drilled in Alaska is shipped by tanker and Trans-Alaskan pipeline to the lower 48 states. Other valuable minerals and metals found in Alaska are gold, zinc, molybdenum, and tin plus smaller quantities of antimony, chromite, copper, nickel, platinum, silver, and tungsten.

Physical Geography of the United States

From the heights of Mount McKinley (20,320 feet above sea level) in Alaska to the depths of Death Valley, California (282 feet below sea level), the geography of the United States is incredibly diverse. In between these extremes lie such varied features and conditions as scorching Arizona deserts, lush Oregon forests, freezing Vermont winters, and sunny Florida beaches. Physical geography involves all the natural features on the earth. This includes the land, resources, climate, and vegetation.

Flowers and brush cover the Coral Pink Sand Dunes in southern Utah.

Land

Separated from much of the world by two oceans, the United States covers 3,717,796 square miles and spans the entire width of North America. To the west, Hawaii stretches the United States into the Pacific Ocean. To the north, Alaska extends the United States to the Arctic Circle. On the U.S. mainland, a huge central plain separates large mountains in the West and low mountains in the East. Plains make up almost half of the country, while mountains and plateaus make up a quarter each.

An abundance of lakes—Alaska alone has three million—and rivers also dot the landscape. Twenty percent of the United States is farmed, providing the country with a steady food supply. Urban areas cover only about two percent of the nation. Refer to the map on the next page for a complete look at the U.S. landscape.

THINKING ABOUT GEOGRAPHY What is the land like around your city or state?

Oil drilled from Alaska helps power the nation's planes, trains, cars, and factories.

Resources

The United States has a variety of natural resources. Vast amounts of coal, oil, and natural gas lie underneath American soil. Valuable deposits of lead, zinc, uranium, gold, and silver also exist. These resources have helped the United States become the world's leading industrial nation—producing nearly 21 percent of the world's goods and services.

These resources have also helped the United States become both the world's largest producer of energy (natural gas, oil, coal, nuclear power, and electricity) and the world's largest consumer of it. Other natural resources include the Great Lakes, which are shared with Canada. They contain about 20 percent of the world's total supply of fresh surface water. Refer to the map on the next page to examine the nation's natural resources.

THINKING ABOUT GEOGRAPHY What are the different natural resources that you and your family use in your daily lives?

ACTIVITY OPTIONS

INTERDISCIPLINARY LINK: SCIENCE — BLOCK SCHEDULING

EXAMINING FOSSIL FUELS

Class Time One class period

Task Making a diagram showing how fossil fuels are formed and where reserves are located

Purpose To understand how fossil fuels are formed and how they are distributed worldwide

Supplies Needed

- Encyclopedias and other reference materials on fossil-fuel formation
- Graph paper
- Art supplies

Activity Divide students into groups. Have each group make a diagram that shows how either coal or oil and natural gas are formed. Diagrams should also indicate the time span for formation of these energy resources. Have groups write captions for their diagrams explaining why fossil fuels are called nonrenewable energy sources.

Miners extract such minerals as gold, silver, and copper from the Rocky Mountains.

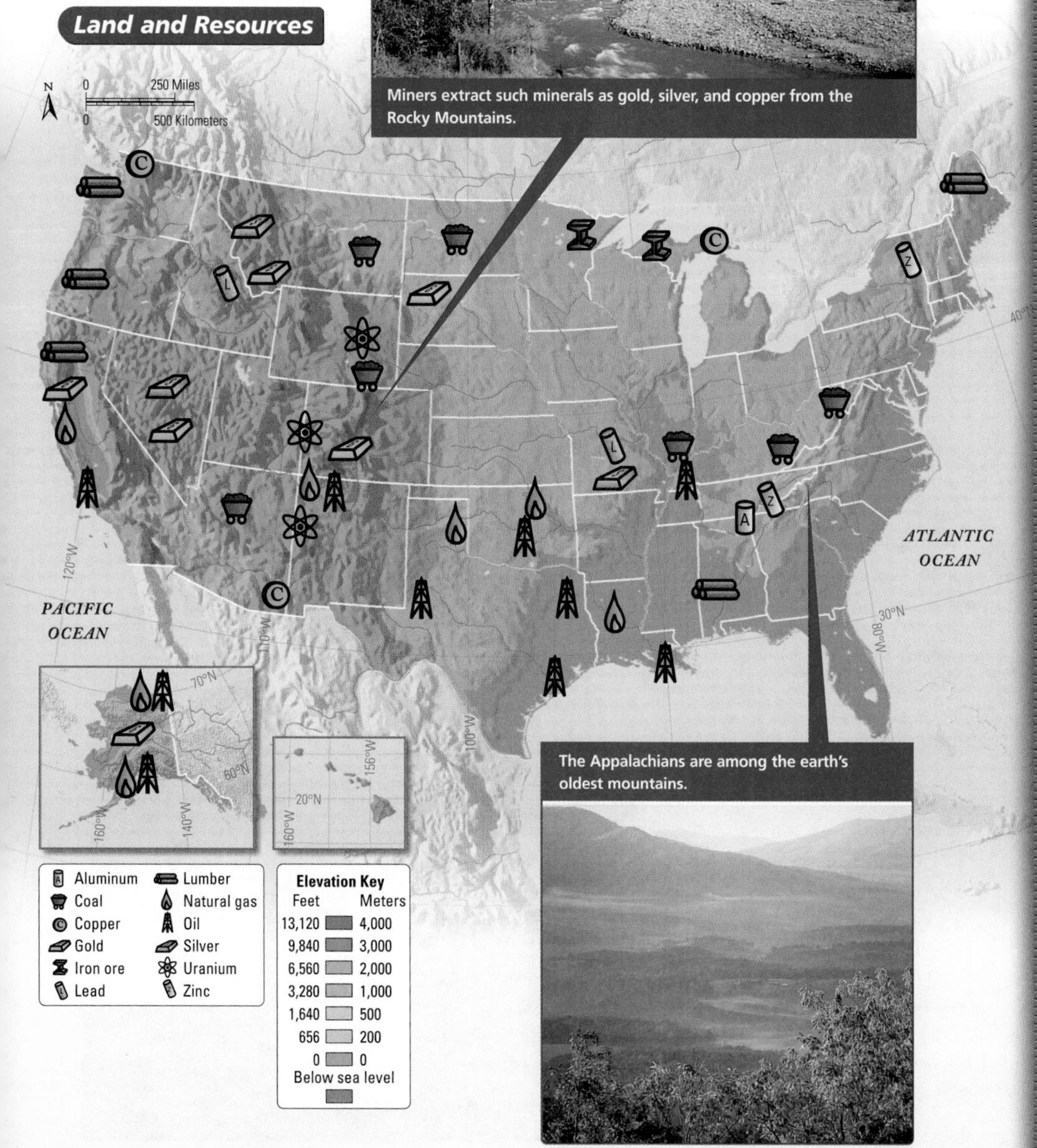

The Appalachians are among the earth's oldest mountains.

MORE ABOUT . . .

Petroleum Resources

The United States has about 22 billion barrels of oil in reserves. Most of these reserves are in Texas, Louisiana, California, Oklahoma, and Alaska. The United States is one of the world's leading producers and refiners of petroleum. Despite its leading role in production, U.S. demand for oil far exceeds domestic production, and the nation imports more than 50 percent of the oil it uses. Petroleum helps fuel the industrial economy, provides jobs for thousands of people, and is one of the nation's largest private employers.

GEOGRAPHY FROM VISUALS

Reading the Map Ask students to look at the map and the map key. Then ask the following questions: What can be learned from the map about the distribution of oil and natural gas? *(The map suggests that natural gas is usually found where oil is found.)* Judging by this map would you say that natural resources are evenly distributed? *(No, the Northeast and Midwest seem to have fewer than other regions.)* What evidence does the map provide to show that the Appalachian Mountains are older than the Rockies? *(The Rockies are higher; the Appalachians have experienced more erosion and are at lower elevations.)*

Extension Ask students to research one of the resources on the map to find how it is used in U.S. industries.

TEACHING STRATEGY

Applying Geographic Themes Have students apply the theme of human-environment interaction to the process of extracting oil, minerals, and other natural resources from the earth. The production, transportation, and use of such minerals and fossil fuels has greatly affected the environment. In many places, strip-mining has caused erosion, while offshore drilling for oil and the shipment of petroleum has at times resulted in pollution of the ocean. Have each student pick one state on the map that is rich in natural resources. Tell students to bring to class a newspaper, newsmagazine article, or article from the Internet illustrating a human-environment interaction resulting from the extraction, production, transportation, or consumption process in their chosen state.

MORE ABOUT . . .

Climate

Climates vary for many reasons. Latitude or distance from the equator affects climate, as does altitude. Surface features, such as mountains or deserts, also have an influence on climate. Because water has a moderating influence on climate, distance from oceans and large lakes can affect climate. Finally, wind patterns influence climate by distributing heat and moisture.

GEOGRAPHY FROM VISUALS

Reading the Map Have students use the key to identify climate regions of North America. Ask students to describe the location of each climate region. Then discuss with students how the diversity of climate regions within the United States might affect industry and transportation. **Possible Response** Climate diversity causes demand for different products in different parts of the country. For example, a manufacturer of snow shovels would not find customers in a tropical climate.

Extension Ask students to tell what clothes they would pack for a summer trip to southern California and northwestern Montana.

Climate

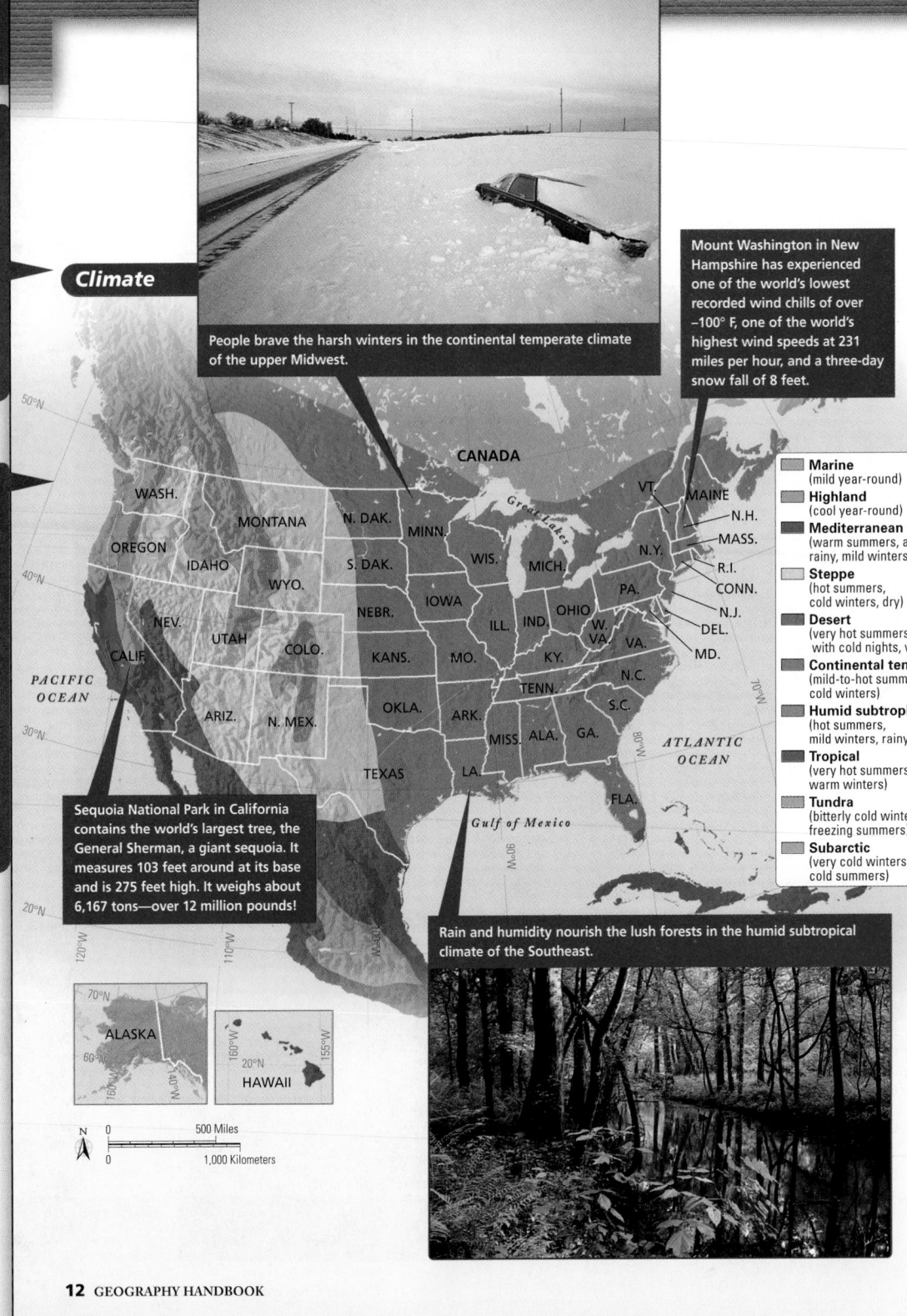

People brave the harsh winters in the continental temperate climate of the upper Midwest.

Mount Washington in New Hampshire has experienced one of the world's lowest recorded wind chills of over –100° F, one of the world's highest wind speeds at 231 miles per hour, and a three-day snow fall of 8 feet.

Sequoia National Park in California contains the world's largest tree, the General Sherman, a giant sequoia. It measures 103 feet around at its base and is 275 feet high. It weighs about 6,167 tons—over 12 million pounds!

Rain and humidity nourish the lush forests in the humid subtropical climate of the Southeast.

12 GEOGRAPHY HANDBOOK

ACTIVITY OPTIONS

INTERDISCIPLINARY LINK: GEOGRAPHY

BLOCK SCHEDULING

MAKING A CLIMATE GRAPH

Class Time One class period

Task Making a climate graph

Purpose To identify the weather patterns associated with different climate zones

Supplies Needed
- Reference materials on United States geography and climate
- Internet access
- Graph paper
- Colored pencils
- Sample climate graphs

Activity Have pairs of students pick one of the climate zones shown on the map and identify two major cities within that zone. Have students research climate data for each of their selected cities. Then have student pairs create a climate graph for each city selected. The graphs should show average monthly temperature and precipitation. When graphs are completed, have students decide which graphs most closely match the descriptions of the climate zones listed in the map key on page 12.

Tourists and residents bask in the sunshine of Waikiki Beach in Hawaii.

Climate

The United States contains a variety of climates. For example, the mean temperature in January in Miami, Florida, is 67° F, while it is 11° F in Minneapolis, Minnesota. Most of the United States experiences a continental climate, or distinct change of seasons. Some regional climatic differences include hot and humid summers in the Southeast versus hot and dry summers in the Southwest. Harsh winters and heavy snow can blanket parts of the Midwest, the Northeast, and the higher elevations of the West and Northwest. Refer to the map on the previous page to see the nation's climatic regions.

Human activities have affected the climate, too. For example, pollution from cars and factories can affect local weather conditions and may be contributing to a dangerous rise in the earth's temperature.

THINKING ABOUT GEOGRAPHY How would you describe the climate where you live?

This mountainside burns with the autumn foliage of New Hampshire.

Vegetation

Between 20,000 and 25,000 species and subspecies of plants and vegetation grow in the United States—including over 1,000 different kinds of trees. Climate often dictates the type of vegetation found in a region. For instance, cold autumns in the Northeast contribute to the brilliantly colored autumn leaves. Rain nourishes the forests in the Northwest and Southeast. The central plains, where rainfall is less heavy, are covered by grass. Cactus plants thrive in the dry southwestern deserts.

Along with natural vegetation, climate dictates the nation's variety of planted crops. For example, temperate weather in the Midwest helps wheat to grow, while warm weather nourishes citrus fruit in Florida and California.

THINKING ABOUT GEOGRAPHY What kinds of trees or plants grow in your region?

Physical Geography Assessment

1. Main Ideas

a. What are the different aspects of physical geography?

b. Which state contains the largest variety of climates?

c. What two states contain most of the country's oil resources?

2. Critical Thinking

Drawing Conclusions What do you think are the advantages of living in a country with diverse physical geography?

THINK ABOUT

- the different resources available in your region
- the variety of recreational activities in your region

MORE ABOUT . . .

Global Warming

Human activity, especially the burning of fossil fuels, such as coal, oil, and natural gas, may be changing the earth's climate. Since the late 1800s, the average temperature of the earth's surface has increased about .5°F to 1.5°F. Certain manufacturing processes and activities, such as driving cars and generating electricity, increase the amount of carbon dioxide gas in the atmosphere. This gas may be causing global warming. Scientists disagree about what effect this warming trend will have, but some fear it could affect rainfall patterns and plant and animal habitats or melt enough polar ice to raise sea levels.

Assessment: Physical Geography

1. Main Ideas

a. land, resources, climate, and vegetation **b.** California **c.** Texas and Alaska

2. Critical Thinking

Answers may include diverse resources, good recreational opportunities, and variety.

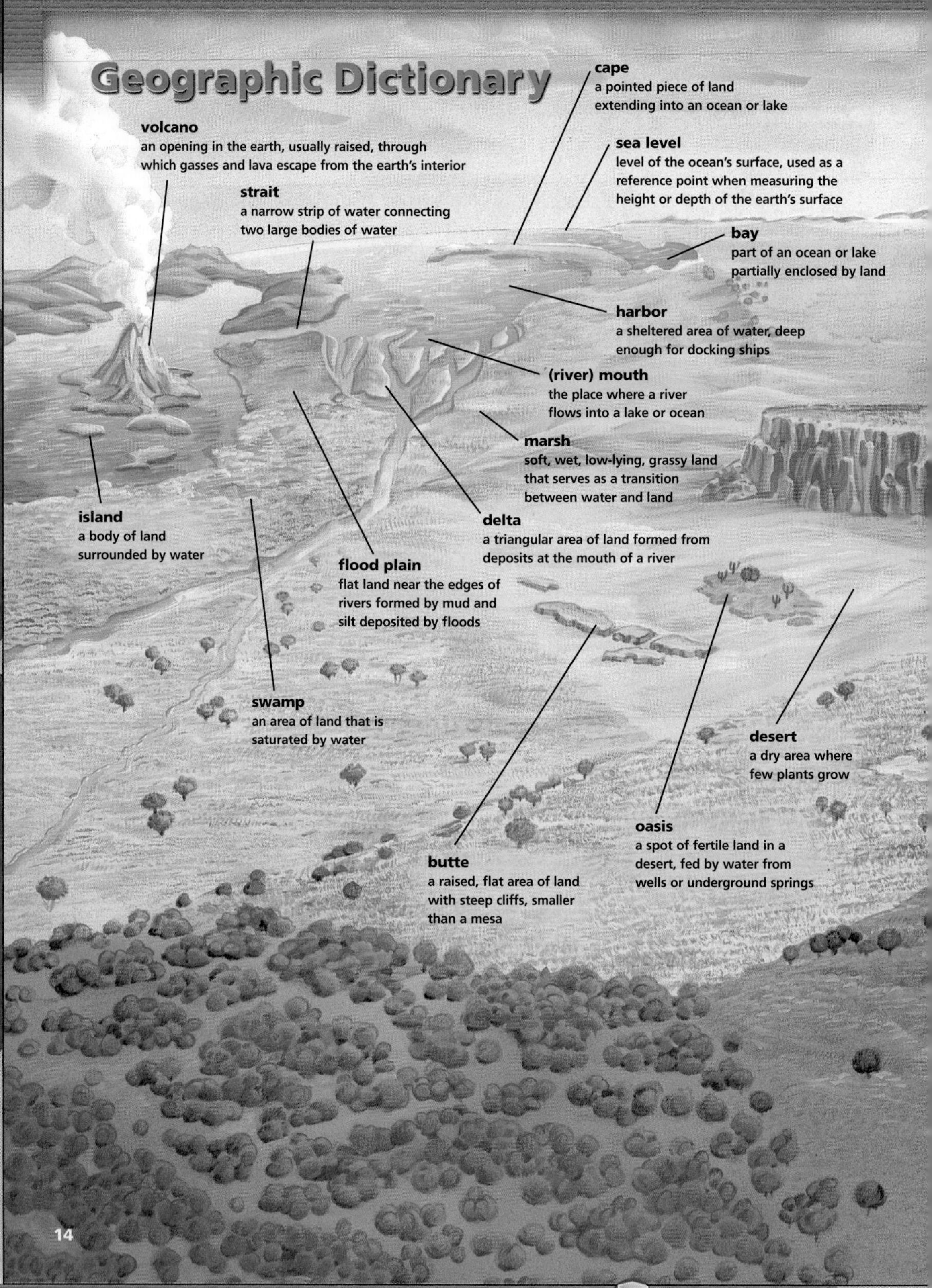
Geographic Dictionary
cape
a pointed piece of land extending into an ocean or lake
volcano
an opening in the earth, usually raised, through which gasses and lava escape from the earth's interior
sea level
level of the ocean's surface, used as a reference point when measuring the height or depth of the earth's surface
strait
a narrow strip of water connecting two large bodies of water
bay
part of an ocean or lake partially enclosed by land
harbor
a sheltered area of water, deep enough for docking ships
(river) mouth
the place where a river flows into a lake or ocean
marsh
soft, wet, low-lying, grassy land that serves as a transition between water and land
island
a body of land surrounded by water
delta
a triangular area of land formed from deposits at the mouth of a river
flood plain
flat land near the edges of rivers formed by mud and silt deposited by floods
swamp
an area of land that is saturated by water
desert
a dry area where few plants grow
oasis
a spot of fertile land in a desert, fed by water from wells or underground springs
butte
a raised, flat area of land with steep cliffs, smaller than a mesa
14

MORE ABOUT . . .

Wetlands

Many wetland areas exist throughout the United States. In wetlands areas, water stays near or above the surface of the ground during much of the year. Marshes and swamps are common in wetland areas. Freshwater marshes develop in the shallow waters of lakes and streams. Salt marshes and mangrove swamps exist in areas where freshwater and saltwater mix. Wetlands are important habitats for plants and animals. They also play a role in flood control by soaking up large amounts of water.

MORE ABOUT . . .

Everglades National Park

One of the nation's most distinctive swamps is the 1.5-million-acre Everglades in southern Florida. The northern part of the swamp is a prairie covered by shallow water and saw grass. Near the southern coast, the Everglades turn into salt marshes and mangrove swamps. The Everglades were created about 10,000 years ago, at the end of the Pleistocene Ice Age. Since the 1970s, urban development of the surrounding area and water pollution caused by chemical runoff from sugar plantations and vegetable farms have created environmental problems for the Everglades.

ACTIVITY OPTIONS

MULTIPLE LEARNING STYLES: SPATIAL — BLOCK SCHEDULING

PLAYING A GEOGRAPHY GAME

Class Time One class period

Task Identifying landforms and bodies of water visually

Purpose To recognize different types of landforms and bodies of water

Supplies Needed
- Colored markers
- Stopwatch or timer
- Small pieces of paper
- Jar or basket

Activity Write the labels from the Geographic Dictionary on small pieces of paper and put them in a jar or basket. Divide students into pairs to play "Quick-Draw Geography." In this game, pairs of students compete at the chalkboard to see how quickly one partner can name a geographic term drawn on the board by his or her partner. The student who is drawing chooses a term at random from the papers in the jar. There is no talking during this game; all clues are visual. Set a time limit for identifying the term.

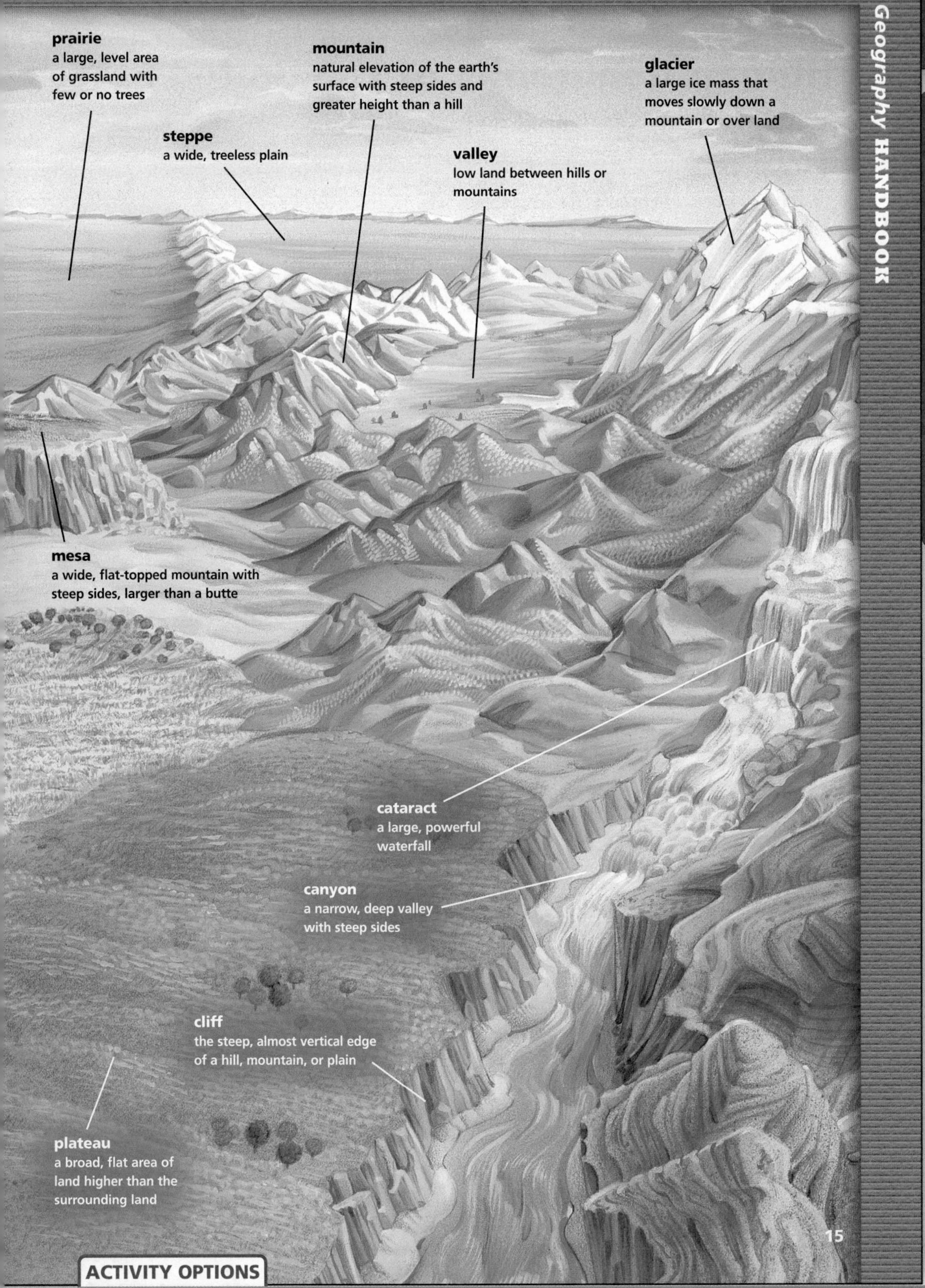
Geography HANDBOOK
prairie
a large, level area of grassland with few or no trees
mountain
natural elevation of the earth's surface with steep sides and greater height than a hill
glacier
a large ice mass that moves slowly down a mountain or over land
steppe
a wide, treeless plain
valley
low land between hills or mountains
mesa
a wide, flat-topped mountain with steep sides, larger than a butte
cataract
a large, powerful waterfall
canyon
a narrow, deep valley with steep sides
cliff
the steep, almost vertical edge of a hill, mountain, or plain
plateau
a broad, flat area of land higher than the surrounding land
15

MORE ABOUT . . .

Deserts

Deserts in the United States include Death Valley in California and Nevada, the Mojave Desert in southern California, the Painted Desert in Arizona, and the Sonoran Desert in Arizona and California. The high heat of the desert results from the fact that deserts absorb more heat from the sun than land in humid climates does. Most deserts average less than 10 inches of rain a year. In North America, many deserts developed in regions separated from the Pacific Ocean by mountains, partly because of the rain shadow effect. Moist winds blowing inland from the ocean cool and lose their moisture as they rise over the mountains. When the winds reach the leeward side, they are warm and dry with scant rainfall.

ACTIVITY OPTIONS

INDIVIDUAL NEEDS: GIFTED AND TALENTED

ADDING TO THE GEOGRAPHIC DICTIONARY

Class Time Two class periods

Task Proposing additions to the Geographic Dictionary

Purpose To expand students' geographic vocabularies

Supplies Needed
- Art supplies
- Clay

Activity Have students propose additions to the Geographic Dictionary. Students should work as a group to decide the criteria for new words to be added to the dictionary. Each student should then find one or more geographic terms that meet the criteria, write a definition of each proposed term, and make a visual representation of it, such as a drawing or clay model. Allow students to work as a group to decide where the terms should be placed on pages 14 and 15.

FOCUS & MOTIVATE

5-MINUTE WARM-UP

Finding Main Ideas These questions focus on the ways humans have adapted to their environments.

1. Look at the pictures on page 16. How did the builders of the cliff dwellings adapt to a climate of cold winters and hot summers?
2. In what ways does the dam change the environment?

INSTRUCT

Human Geography

- What is the focus of human geography?
- Which of the five themes of geography are most closely related to human geography?

MORE ABOUT . . .

The Colorado River and the Hoover Dam

Changes to the Colorado River system show some of the ways humans have adapted the natural environment to meet their needs. The Colorado River drainage basin provides hydroelectric power and water for irrigation, flood control, and recreational uses for many Western states. Hoover Dam, completed in 1936, was the first major development of the river system. The dam became not only an important energy source but also a major tourist attraction.

Human Geography of the United States

Human geography focuses on people's relationships with each other and the surrounding environment. It includes two main themes of geography: human-environment interaction and movement. The following pages will help you to better understand the link between people and geography.

Humans Adapt to Their Surroundings

Humans have always adapted to their environment. For example, in North America, many Native American tribes burned forest patches to create grazing area to attract animals and to clear area for farmland. In addition, Americans have adapted to their environment by building numerous dams, bridges, and tunnels. More recently, scientists and engineers have been developing building materials that will better withstand the earthquakes that occasionally strike California.

THINKING ABOUT GEOGRAPHY What are some of the ways in which you interact with your environment on a daily basis?

Early Americans of the Southwest protected themselves from the weather by building cliff dwellings.

The Hoover Dam, located on the Colorado River between Arizona and Nevada, provides electricity for Arizona, Nevada, and Southern California.

ACTIVITY OPTIONS

INTERDISCIPLINARY LINK: SCIENCE BLOCK SCHEDULING

RESEARCHING AN ENVIRONMENTAL ISSUE

Class Time One class period

Task Writing a position paper on an environmental issue

Purpose To analyze and form an opinion on an environmental issue

Supplies Needed
- Reference materials on the protection of salmon populations on the Snake River
- Internet access

Activity In recent years, scientists and environmentalists in Washington State have debated how best to protect diminishing salmon populations on the Snake and Columbia rivers. Scientists say several human-environment interactions have affected salmon stocks, including overfishing, construction of dams, and destruction of spawning areas. Solutions that have been proposed include breaching dams on the lower Snake River, a moratorium on fishing, or changing water- and land-use policies. Have students research this issue and write a position paper explaining the problem, alternative solutions, and recommendations for action.

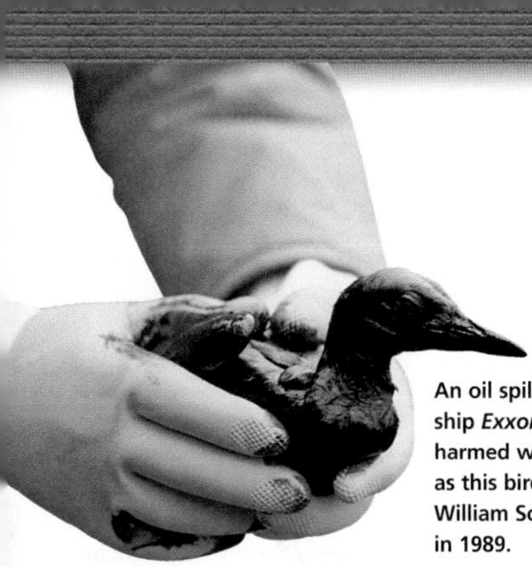

An oil spill from the ship *Exxon Valdez* harmed wildlife, such as this bird, in Prince William Sound, Alaska, in 1989.

Humans Affect the Environment

When humans interact with the environment, sometimes nature suffers. In the United States, for example, major oil leaks or spills occur each year—fouling shorelines and harming wildlife. Building suburbs and strip malls has also destroyed forests, farmland, and valuable wetlands.

THINKING ABOUT GEOGRAPHY What are some of the environmental problems in your city or town?

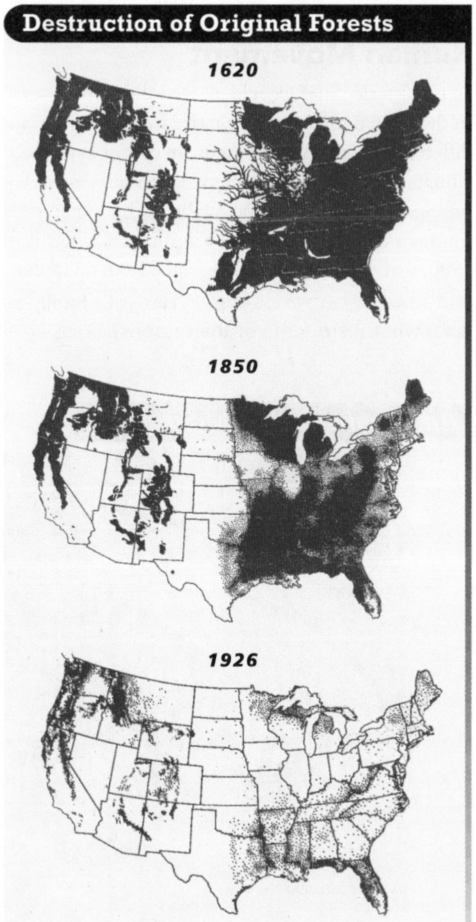

These maps show that, over the years, human beings have nearly cut down all the original forests in the United States. Each dot represents 25,000 acres.

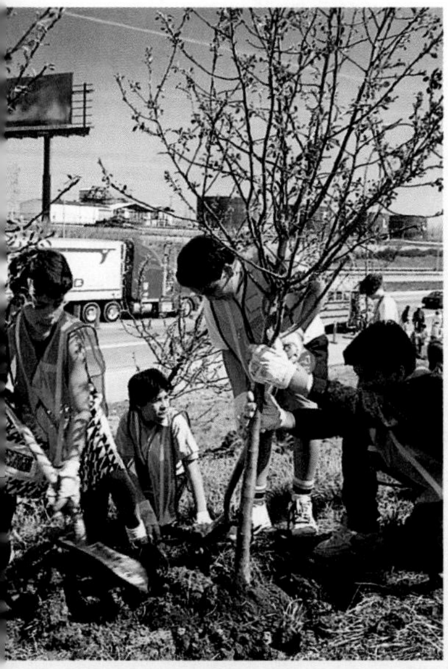

Children plant trees along a Chicago expressway.

Preserving and Restoring

Americans—as well as people all over the world—have been working hard to balance economic progress with conservation. For example, car companies in the United States and around the world are working to develop pollution-free vehicles. In 1994, the average American family of four recycled around 1,100 pounds of waste. And, in the 1990s, Americans have planted more than two million acres of new trees each year.

THINKING ABOUT GEOGRAPHY What are some of the ways in which you help the environment?

GEOGRAPHY FROM VISUALS

Reading the Map Ask students to look carefully at the maps showing the destruction of the original forests. Ask students what parts of the country were covered with original forest in 1620. **Answer** Most of the eastern half, the Northwest Coast, and some parts of the mountain region and Southwest. Ask students to compare the 1620 map to the 1850 map. What does the comparison show about settlement along the Atlantic Coast? **Possible Response** Settlement was very thick; few of the original trees remained by 1850.

Extension Ask students to write one or two sentences describing the original forests in their state in 1620, 1850, and 1926.

MORE ABOUT . . .

Exxon Valdez

On March 24, 1989, the oil tanker *Exxon Valdez* ran aground in Alaska's Prince William Sound. Delays in attempts to contain the spill, along with high winds and waves, resulted in a spill of 10.9 million gallons of crude oil. It was the biggest oil spill in U.S. history. Over time, thousands of miles of the Alaskan shoreline were polluted. Despite an intensive clean-up effort, the fragile ecosystem of the sound was damaged.

ACTIVITY OPTIONS

INTERDISCIPLINARY LINK: CIVICS

BLOCK SCHEDULING

IDENTIFYING LOCAL ENVIRONMENTAL ISSUES

Class Time One class period

Task Identifying a local environmental issue and expressing an opinion about it

Purpose To identify local issues related to human-environment interaction

Supplies Needed
- Current local newspapers
- Internet access

Activity Have students read local newspapers to identify local environmental issues. Tell students that community concerns often include such issues as waste management and disposal, land use, air and water quality, noise pollution, and treatment of animal populations. As a class, identify five local environmental issues and how humans have affected the environment in each case. Then, working in groups, have students pick one of these issues and create a political cartoon or write a letter to the editor of the school newspaper expressing an opinion on this topic.

GEOGRAPHY FROM VISUALS

Reading the Map Have students look at the map and explain the meaning of the arrows and the letters. Ask the following questions: Judging by this map, which regions have lost population since the 1970s? **Answer** Northeast and Midwest. From which region of the United States did the greatest out-migration take place? **Answer** Northeast. How has the population shift affected Arizona? The Phoenix-Mesa area now has more people than the entire state did in 1980.

Extension Have students do research about population trends in their state over the past five years.

MORE ABOUT . . .

The Sunbelt
The growth of the Sunbelt increased not only the population but also the area's economic base. The Sunbelt attracted a variety of new high-tech industries, such as aerospace, plastics, chemicals, and electronics. The space industry brought Northern transplants to Florida, Alabama, and Texas. Scientists and medical researchers also flocked to research and development zones like the Research Triangle Park in North Carolina and other facilities in Florida, Texas, and California. Many factors besides the warmer climate sparked the industrial growth of the Southeast, including land that was cheaper than in the crowded cities of the Northeast and lower labor costs because there were fewer unionized workers.

Human Movement

In prehistoric times, people roamed the earth in search of food. Today in the United States, people move from place to place for many different reasons. Among them are cost of living, job availability, and climate. Since the 1970s, many Americans—as well as many new immigrants—moved to the Sunbelt. This region runs through the southern United States from Virginia to California. Between 1950 and 1990, that region's population soared from 52 million to 118 million.

THINKING ABOUT GEOGRAPHY Has your family ever moved? If so, what were some of the reasons?

This map shows human movement in the 1970s. The information below explains some of the results of this movement in the 1990s.

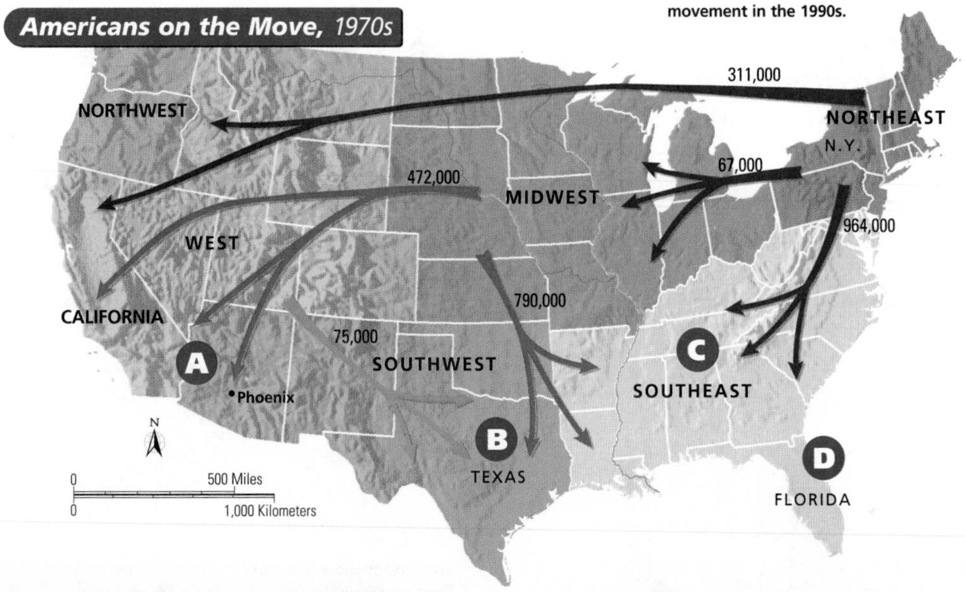

A By 1996, the Phoenix-Mesa metropolitan area reached a population of 2.75 million, more than the number of people living in the entire state in 1980.

B Between 1990 and 1994, Texas overtook New York as the nation's second most populous state, behind California.

C One of the nation's fastest growing areas was the Southeast, where population growth ranged from six to nine percent between 1990 and 1994. Jobs grew in the area by 14 percent.

D Florida's population is growing so much that it could become as populous as New York state by around 2020.

New home developments cover the desert in Las Vegas, Nevada.

ACTIVITY OPTIONS

INTERDISCIPLINARY LINK: AMERICAN HISTORY — BLOCK SCHEDULING

AMERICANS ON THE MOVE, 1990s

Class Time One class period

Task Making a map showing population change in the United States in the 1990s

Purpose To illustrate contemporary population movement

Supplies Needed
- World almanacs
- Internet access
- Outline map of the United States

Activity Have students use the most recent census data to make a three-column chart. In the first column, tell students to list the states with the greatest increases in population during the decade. In the second, have them list states with moderate to low population gain, and in the third, states with population losses. Have students color-code their chart and use the same colors on a map showing population movement and change during the 1990s.

In the late 19th century, millions of immigrants arrived on the shores of the United States.

The Sears Tower overlooks Chinatown in Chicago.

Humans Spread Ideas and Information

Throughout U.S. history, people from all over the world have come to the United States. They have brought with them food, music, language, technology, and other aspects of their culture. As a result, the United States is one of the most culturally rich and diverse nations in the world. Look around your town or city. You'll probably notice different people, languages, and foods.

Today, the spreading of ideas and customs does not rely solely on human movement. Technology—from the Internet to television to satellites—spreads ideas and information throughout the world faster than ever. This has created an ever-growing, interconnected world. As the 21st century opens, human geography will continue to play a key role in shaping the United States and the world.

THINKING ABOUT GEOGRAPHY How have computers and the Internet affected your life?

Human Geography Assessment

1. Main Ideas

a. What are some of the ways that people have helped to restore the environment?

b. What are some of the ways that residents of your region have successfully modified their landscape?

c. What are some of the reasons that people move from place to place?

2. Critical Thinking

Recognizing Effects In what ways has technology helped bring people in the world together?

THINK ABOUT

- the different ways in which people communicate today
- the speed in which people today can communicate over long distances

MORE ABOUT . . .

Immigration

Immigration patterns have greatly affected the human geography of many American cities. Patterns of immigration often shape the neighborhoods and cultures that develop in cities. When immigrants first come to a new country, they tend to settle near others with similar cultural backgrounds. As shops, grocery stores, restaurants, and houses of worship spring up to meet the needs of people in these neighborhoods, the neighborhoods themselves develop distinctive identities—as "Chinatowns" or "Little Saigons," for example—that contribute to the diversity and richness of city life.

MORE ABOUT . . .

Internet Interaction

A December 1999 *U.S. News and World Report* poll reported that most American adults used personal computers mainly for writing and sending e-mail, for searching the Internet for information, and for word processing. In the near future, small, wireless handheld devices may replace PCs for Internet use. In Finland, young and old use wireless phones with Internet connections to pay bills, buy airline and concert tickets, and shop for everything from automobiles to zithers. In the future, even grocery shopping may become obsolete, as tiny boxes in the refrigerator automatically dial up an Internet grocer to order milk when the Internet user needs a refill.

Assessment: Human Geography

1. Main Ideas

a. working to develop pollution-free vehicles, recycling, planting new trees **b.** Answers should demonstrate understanding of the concept of modifying landscapes. **c.** cost of living, job availability, climate

2. Critical Thinking

Recognizing Effects Advances in technology have brought communication devices to many more people and increased the speed of communication.

TERMS

1. **physical map,** p. 6
2. **political map,** p. 6
3. **longitude,** p. 8
4. **latitude,** p. 8
5. **hemisphere,** p. 8
6. **projection,** p. 8
7. **flood plain,** p. 14
8. **sea level,** p. 14
9. **human geography,** p. 16
10. **human movement,** p. 18

REVIEW QUESTIONS

Answers

1. Absolute location describes the location of a place using latitude and longitude, while relative location describes where a place is relative to another area.
2. Place refers to what an area looks like in both physical and human terms.
3. Movement refers to the transfer of people, goods, and ideas, while human-environment interaction includes how humans interact with their surroundings.
4. Advanced technology can help scientists and geographers keep track of serious environmental problems, and it can also improve the quality of maps.
5. physical, political, and historical maps
6. Latitude lines are imaginary lines that run east to west around the globe, and longitude lines are imaginary lines that run north to south around the globe.
7. An abundance of natural resources has aided the growth of the U.S. economy because the United States hasn't had to rely on the resources of foreign nations.
8. marine, highland, Mediterranean, steppe, desert, continental temperate, humid subtropical, tropical, tundra, subarctic
9. Human geography focuses on people's relationship with each other and the surrounding environment, while physical geography focuses on the land, natural resources, vegetation, and climate.
10. People move for a variety of reasons, including cost of living, job availability, and climate.

GEOGRAPHY HANDBOOK ASSESSMENT

TERMS

Briefly explain the significance of each of the following.

1. physical map
2. political map
3. longitude
4. latitude
5. hemisphere
6. projection
7. flood plain
8. sea level
9. human geography
10. human movement

REVIEW QUESTIONS

Themes of Geography (pages 4–5)

1. What is the difference between *absolute* location and *relative* location?
2. What is meant by the theme of place?
3. What are the themes of movement and human-environment interaction?

Map Basics (pages 6–9)

4. What do you think are some of the benefits of using technology to study geography?
5. What are the three major kinds of maps?
6. What are latitude and longitude lines?

Physical Geography (pages 10–13)

7. How have the natural resources in the United States helped its economic development?
8. What are the different climates within the United States?

Human Geography (pages 16–19)

9. How is human geography different from physical geography?
10. What aspects of human geography might cause people to move?

CRITICAL THINKING

1. **Forming and Supporting Opinions** Which of the five themes of geography do you think has had the most impact on history? Why?
2. **Analyzing Causes** How do the climate and natural resources of an area affect its economy?
3. **Drawing Conclusions** How have computers helped geographers make more accurate maps?
4. **Making Inferences** Why do you think the Mercator projection is used for all types of navigation?
5. **Recognizing Effects** How does a diverse landscape help or hurt the economy of an area?

GEOGRAPHY SKILLS

1. INTERPRETING MAPS: Movement

Basic Map Elements

a. What region of the United States is shown?

b. Compare the number of teams on the 1987 map and the 2000 map. How many more teams are on the 2000 map?

Interpreting the Map

c. What geographic theme(s) is most responsible for the increase in sports teams in this region?

d. According to the map, which sport enjoyed the biggest surge in popularity in this region?

Major League Sports in Southeast Cities

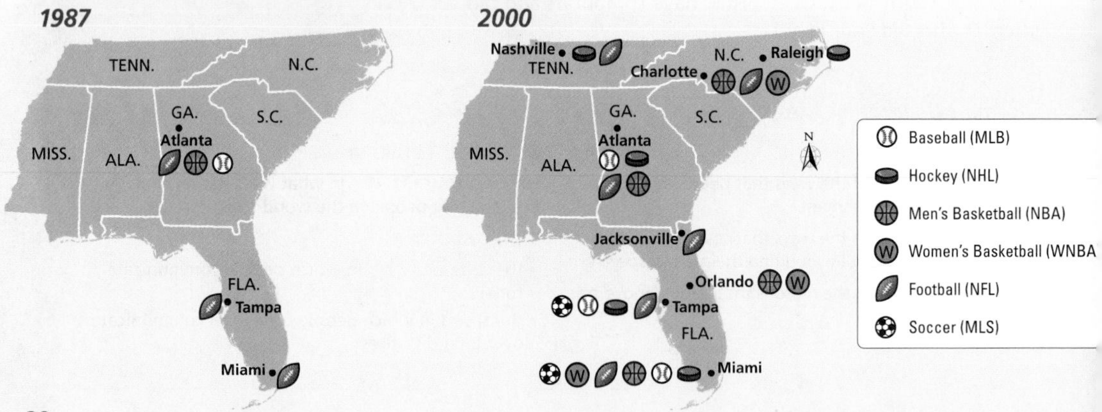

20

CRITICAL THINKING

Possible Responses

1. Some students might say location, because a civilization's location—near steady food and water supplies or surrounded by enemies—often determined whether or not it flourished. Others might say movement, because it was by moving that humans spread so many ideas and goods. Accept other reasonable responses.
2. The natural resources that are available in a region often determine an area's main economic activity. For instance, because coal is an abundant resource in the Appalachian region, coal mining is a main economic activity there. The ability to grow crops—which is determined by climate and land type—also plays a key role in an area's economic activity. Those regions that can grow oranges, for example, have made orange production an integral part of their economy.
3. Computers and satellites enable mapmakers and geographers to constantly update map information and environmental conditions.
4. It shows clearly all the landmasses as well as the large bodies of water.
5. A diverse landscape can help a region's economy by sustaining a wide variety of economic activities and by providing jobs in many different areas.

GEOGRAPHY SKILLS

2. INTERPRETING MAPS: Region

Study the map and then answer the questions.

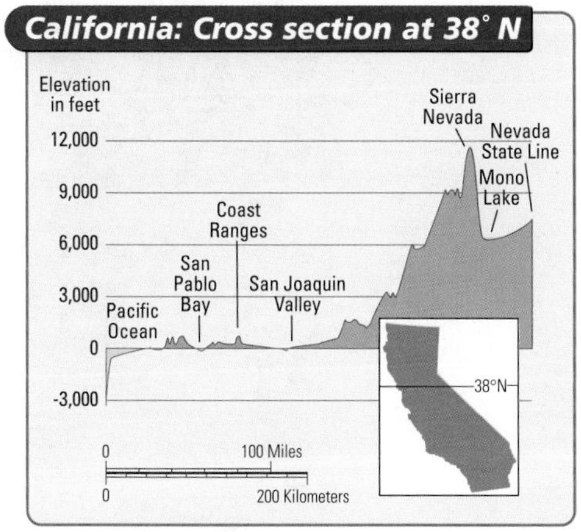

Basic Map Elements

a. What are the different landforms on the map?

Interpreting the Map

b. What is the level of the San Joaquin Valley? How many miles does it take to get from there to the highest point in California at the 38th parallel?

3. INTERPRETING PRIMARY SOURCES

In 1803, President Thomas Jefferson appointed Meriwether Lewis to explore the lands of the Louisiana Purchase. Jefferson gave him these instructions:

> The object of your mission is to explore the Missouri river . . . by its course & communication with the waters of the Pacific Ocean, may offer the most direct & practicable water communication across this continent, for the purposes of commerce. . . .
>
> Other objects worthy of notice will be the soil & face of the country, its growth & vegetable productions . . . the mineral productions of every kind. . . . climate as characterized by the thermometer . . . the dates at which particular plants put forth or lose their flowers, or leaf, times of appearance of particular birds, reptiles, or insects.
>
> **Thomas Jefferson,** quoted in *The Journals of Lewis and Clark*

a. What was Jefferson expecting to find in the West?

b. Why might the president want to know about the land's soil and vegetable production?

c. What aspect of human geography might be of interest to the president?

ALTERNATIVE ASSESSMENT

1. INTERDISCIPLINARY ACTIVITY: Math

Plotting Latitude and Longitude On a piece of graph paper, sketch a map of the United States. Be sure to draw in state boundaries, too. Then, using an atlas as a reference, draw and mark the latitude and longitude lines that cross the nation at five degree intervals. Plot the estimated longitude and latitude location of your city or town. Determine at which degrees the lines intersect where you live. Repeat this exercise for at least five different places you have visited or would like to visit within the United States.

2. COOPERATIVE LEARNING ACTIVITY

Making a Map How well do you know the neighborhood around your school? Form groups of three to four students. Then work together to draw a map of the neighborhood around your school. Include:

- streets
- residences
- stores
- geographic features
- important landmarks

The map should be accurate but not too cluttered with unnecessary details. Compare your group's map with those of the other groups in the class.

3. TECHNOLOGY ACTIVITY

Writing Directions Several Internet sites provide detailed maps of the United States. They also provide driving directions to most places in the country.

- Locate one of these map sites on the Internet.
- Think of a place in the United States that you would like to visit.
- Work with the computer to find the best route for reaching it.

Write out clear directions as well as the total mileage of your trip. Also, note the type of map it is and the features it highlights.

For more important geography sites . . .

INTERNET ACTIVITY
CLASSZONE.COM

4. HISTORY PORTFOLIO

Review your alternative assessment activities. Use comments made by your teacher or classmates to improve your work.

Additional Test Practice, pp. S1–S33

TEST PRACTICE
CLASSZONE.COM

ALTERNATIVE ASSESSMENT

1. INTERDISCIPLINARY ACTIVITY: **Math**
   Maps should
   - be clearly labeled and neatly presented.
   - include a legend and title.
   - include both latitude and longitude for all locations.

2. COOPERATIVE LEARNING ACTIVITY
   Maps should
   - be clearly labeled and neatly presented.
   - include a legend and title.
   - include landmarks in the neighborhood of the school.

3. TECHNOLOGY ACTIVITY
   Directions should
   - accurately deliver instructions to reach the designated location.
   - be logically organized.
   - include total mileage and identify map type and highlights.
   - use standard grammar, spelling, sentence structure, and punctuation.

4. HISTORY PORTFOLIO
   Revised alternative assessment activities should
   - address teacher and peer responses to the selected work.
   - solve problems present in the first versions of the work.

Formal Assessment
- Geography Handbook quizzes and tests, pp. 5–16

GEOGRAPHY SKILLS

1. INTERPRETING MAPS: MOVEMENT
   Basic Map Elements
   a. southeast
   b. 18
   Interpreting the Map
   c. movement
   d. hockey

2. INTERPRETING MAPS: REGION
   Basic Map Elements
   a. ocean, bay, valley, lake, mountains
   Interpreting the Map
   b. sea level or slightly below; about 120 miles

3. INTERPRETING PRIMARY SOURCES
   a. a water route to the Pacific Ocean
   b. to learn whether or not the land would be inhabitable for American settlers
   c. what types of—and how many—Native Americans live in the area

UNIT 1

Three Worlds Meet
Beginnings to 1763

BEFORE YOU READ

Previewing Unit 1

Unit 1 begins with the arrival of the first Americans after the last Ice Age and traces a great sweep of history through settlement by diverse groups of colonists. For the first time, complex societies of Native Americans come into contact with people from Europe and Africa. The result is a cultural mingling full of tension and adaptation for both the Native Americans and the newcomers. British colonies develop, expand, and mature. By 1763, a new American culture and sense of identity has developed.

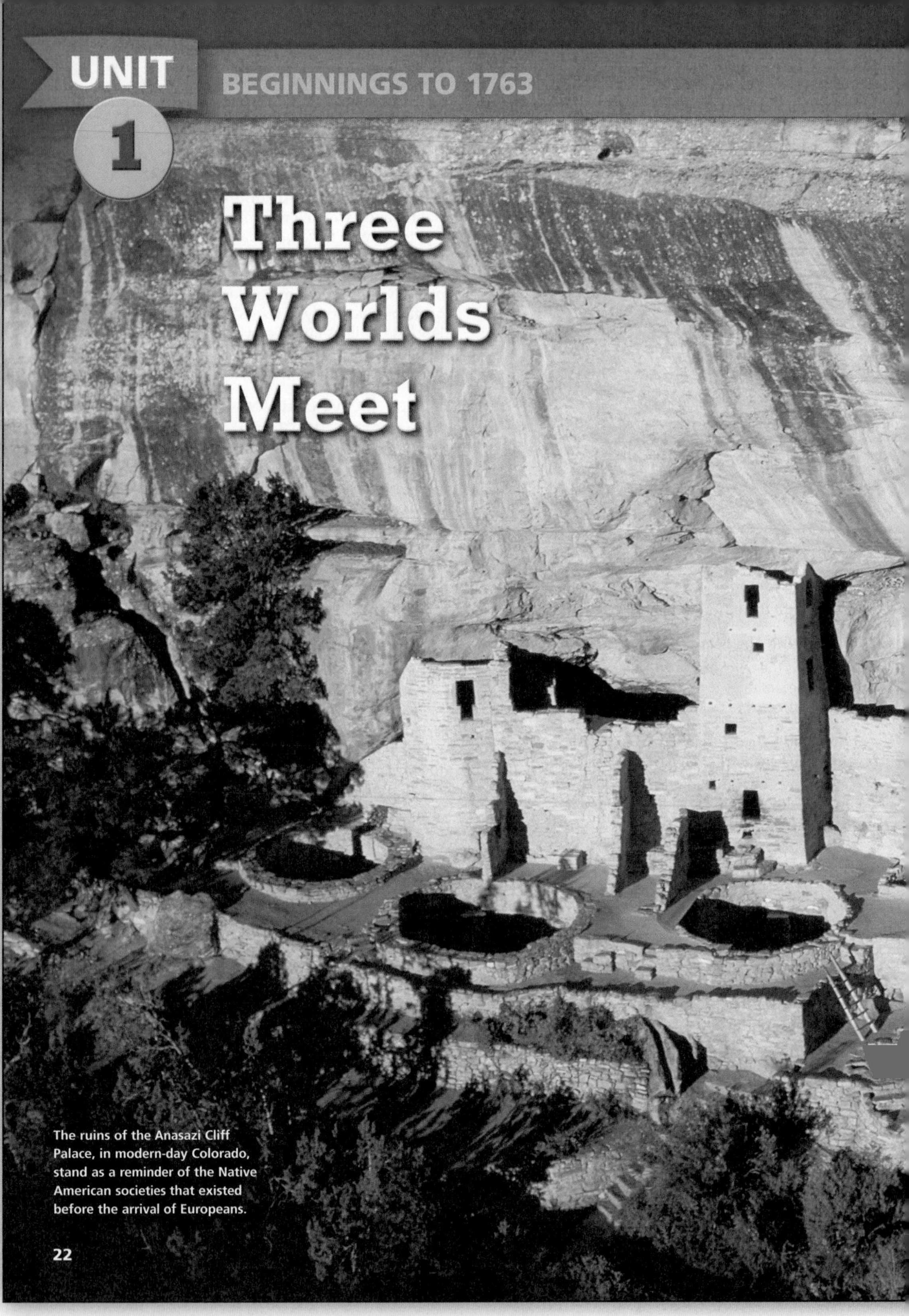

The ruins of the Anasazi Cliff Palace, in modern-day Colorado, stand as a reminder of the Native American societies that existed before the arrival of Europeans.

22

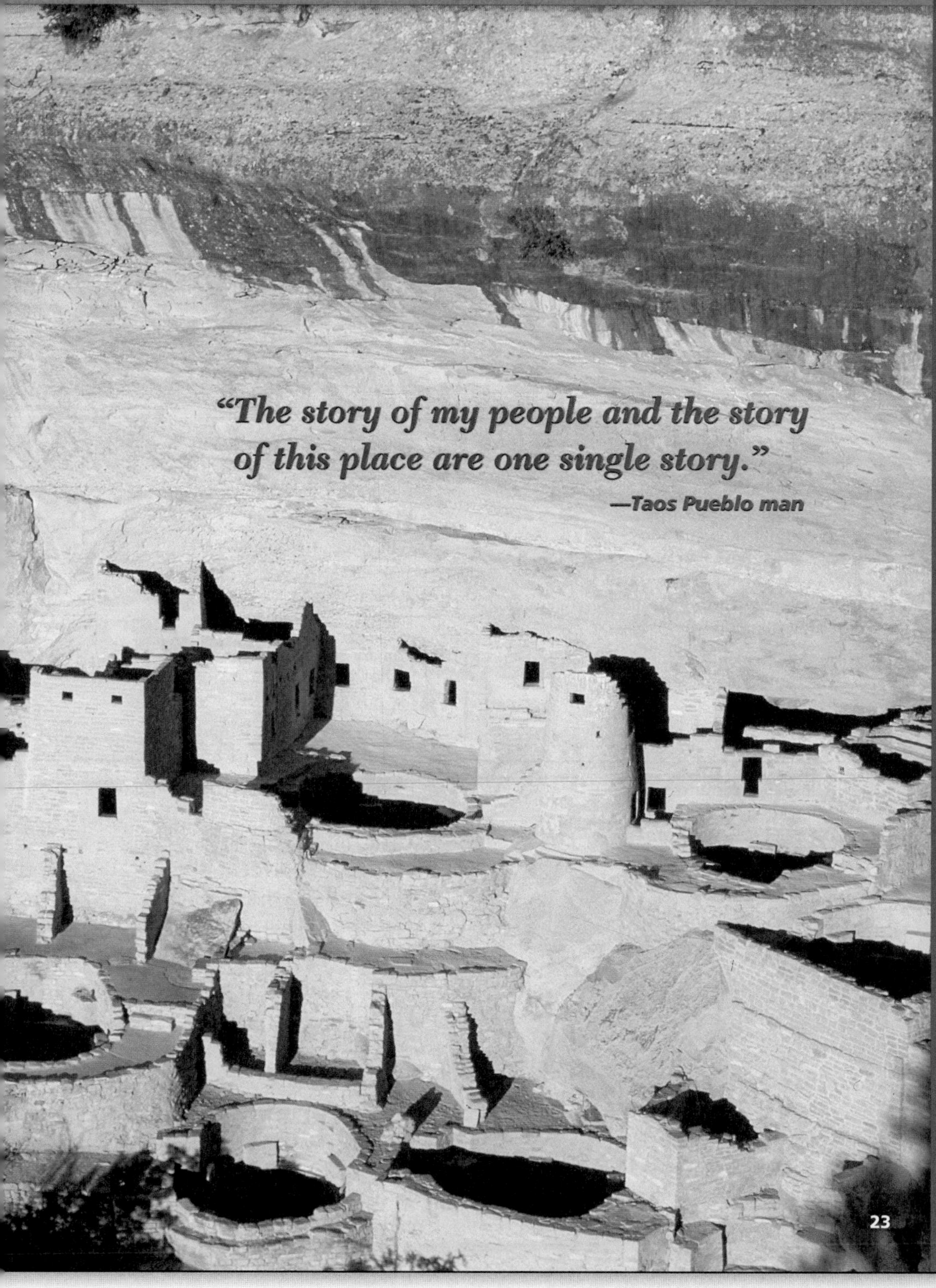
"The story of my people and the story of this place are one single story."
—Taos Pueblo man
23

HISTORY FROM VISUALS

Interpreting the Photograph Ask students to study the photograph and brainstorm ideas about the people who lived in the cliff dwellings. List students' ideas on the chalkboard. Ask students what the buildings suggest about the culture of the people who lived here. **Possible Responses** The people were well organized, understood how to construct buildings with several stories, and most likely had a sophisticated society.

Extension Ask students to find out how the Anasazi used the round pit houses, or *kivas.*

CHAPTER 1 PLANNING GUIDE
THE WORLD IN 1500 Beginnings–1500

	CHAPTER OVERVIEW	COPYMASTERS	INTEGRATED TECHNOLOGY
CHAPTER RESOURCES	The chapter discusses the migration of ancient peoples to the Americas and the development of Native American cultures. It also describes the societies of West Africa and Europe in the 1500s, and explains the motivations behind the European explorations.	**In-Depth Resources: Unit 1** • Tracing Themes: Diversity and Unity, p. 2 • Building Vocabulary, p. 6 • History Workshop Resources, p. 19 **Interdisciplinary Projects,** pp. 1–6	• eEdition Plus Online • EasyPlanner Plus Online • eTest Plus Online • eEdition • Power Presentations • EasyPlanner • Electronic Library of Primary Sources • Test Generator • Reading Study Guide • America's Music
SECTION 1 Societies of North America pp. 27–32	**KEY IDEAS** • The first people in the Americas migrate from Asia. • The use of agriculture leads these people to develop civilizations. • Native Americans create complex and diverse cultural communities. • The Aztecs build a strong empire based on conquests. • The Iroquois League brings peace to the warring tribes.	**In-Depth Resources: Unit 1** • Setting the Stage, p. 1 • Guided Reading, p. 3 • Skillbuilder Practice: Using Secondary Sources, p. 7 • Literature Selections, pp. 12–14 • Reteaching Activity, p. 15 **America's History Makers** • Deganawida, pp. 1–2 **Outline Map Activities** • Landforms of North America, pp. 1–2	**Warm-Up Transparency WT1** **Geography Transparency GT1** • Native American Lifestyles, 1500 **Humanities Transparency HT1** • Mississippian Warrior **Critical Thinking Transparency CT1** • Setting the Stage **Primary Source Explorer** • *The Iroquois Great Law of Peace* **classzone.com**
SECTION 2 Societies of West Africa and Europe pp. 33–38	• Africa's coastal ports are central to world trade. • Powerful kingdoms of Ghana, Mali, and Songhai rise to power, influenced by Islamic culture. • Feudalism dominates Europe in the Middle Ages. • The revival of trade and towns leads to a decline in feudalism. • The Renaissance and Reformation are periods of dramatic social change.	**In-Depth Resources: Unit 1** • Setting the Stage, p. 1 • Guided Reading, p. 4 • Primary Source, p. 10 • Reteaching Activity, p. 16 **Economics in History** • The Benefits of Trade, p. 1	**Warm-Up Transparency WT1** **Critical Thinking Transparency CT1** • Setting the Stage **Critical Thinking Transparency CT2** • Cause and Effect: Causes of Exploration **classzone.com**
SECTION 3 Early European Explorers PP. 39–43	• Europeans search for new trade routes. • Columbus seeks financial backing from Spain to sail across the Atlantic Ocean. • Columbus reaches islands that he believes to be Asia, but that are really the Americas, thus changing the European worldview.	**In-Depth Resources: Unit 1** • Setting the Stage, p. 1 • Guided Reading, p. 5 • Primary Source, p. 11 • Geography Application, pp. 8–9 • Reteaching Activity, p. 17 **America's History Makers,** pp. 3–4 **Why It Matters Now,** pp. 1–2	**Warm-Up Transparency WT1** **Humanities Transparency HT2** • Map of the American Southeast, 1606 **Critical Thinking Transparency CT3** • Visual Summary **classzone.com**

Pupil's Edition
Copymaster
Overhead Transparency
Audio Library
CD-ROM
Internet

ASSESSMENT OPTIONS

Chapter Assessment, pp. 44–45

Formal Assessment
- Chapter Tests, Forms A, B, and C, pp. 24–35

Test Generator

Online Test Practice

Strategies for Test Preparation

Section Assessment, p. 31

Formal Assessment, Quiz, p. 21

Integrated Assessment Book
- Rubrics, 2.1, 5.4

Test Generator

Test Practice Transparencies, TT1–TT2

Section Assessment, p. 38

Formal Assessment, Quiz, p. 22

Integrated Assessment Book
- Rubrics, 5.1, 4.8

Test Generator

Test Practice Transparencies, TT3–TT4

Section Assessment, p. 43

Formal Assessment, Quiz, p. 23

Integrated Assessment Book
- Rubrics, 2.1, 2.2

Test Generator

Test Practice Transparencies, TT5

CUSTOMIZING FOR INDIVIDUAL NEEDS

Students Acquiring English/ESL

Reading Study Guide (English and Spanish), pp. 5–12

Access for Students Acquiring English/ESL: Spanish Translations, pp. 1–6

Chapter Summaries on CD (English and Spanish)

Modified Lesson Plans for English Learners

Less Proficient Readers

Reading Study Guide (English and Spanish), pp. 5–12

Chapter Summaries on CD (English and Spanish)

Gifted and Talented Students

In-Depth Resources: Unit 1
- Enrichment Activity, p. 18

America's History Makers
- Deganawida, pp. 1–2
- Christopher Columbus, pp. 3–4

CROSS-CURRICULAR CONNECTIONS

World Cultures

Fritz, Jean, Katherine Paterson, Patricia McKissack, and Fredrick McKissack. ***The World in 1492.*** New York: Holt, 1995. A survey of world regions—Europe, Asia, Africa, Oceania, and the Americas—on the eve of the great voyages of discovery.

Koslow, Philip. **Centuries of Greatness: The West African Kingdoms, 750–1900.** New York: Chelsea, 1995. Solid, factual treatment focusing on military, economic, and political developments in more than 1,000 years of African history.

Tanaka, Shelley. ***The Lost Temple of the Aztecs: What It Was Like When the Spaniards Invaded Mexico.*** New York: Hyperion, 1998. Aztec society was fully as urban and complex as that of Spain.

Interdisciplinary Projects, pp. 1–6
- Math: Time Line—A Number Line with Dates
- Science: Surveying an Archaeological Site
- Language Arts: Oral Literature: Storytelling
- Physical Education: Playing Lacrosse

Humanities: Art

The Marshall Cavendish Illustrated History of the North American Indians. New York: Marshall Cavendish, 1996. Native Americans developed a rich variety of artistic styles.

Literature

Eboch, Chris. ***The Well of Sacrifice.*** Boston: Houghton Mifflin, 1999. Incorporates much new scholarship on the Maya in exciting fiction.

Litowinsky, Olga. ***High Voyage: The Final Crossing of Christopher Columbus.*** New York: Delacorte, 1991. Well-researched tale of Columbus's last voyage, through the eyes of his illegitimate son Fernando.

McDougal Littell *The Language of Literature*

- Joseph Bruchac, "Racing the Great Bear" (Iroquois legend)
- Robert D. San Souci, "Otoomah" (Inuit legend)

ENRICHMENT ACTIVITIES

Pupil's Edition, pp. 24–47
Interact with History, p. 25
Interactive Primary Source, p. 32
History Workshop, pp. 46–47

In-Depth Resources: Unit 1
- Geography Application: Ocean Currents, pp. 8–9
- Primary Source, p. 10
- Primary Source, p. 11
- Literature Selections, pp. 12–14
- History Workshop Resources, p. 19

America's History Makers
- Deganawida, pp. 1–2
- Christopher Columbus, pp. 3–4

Outline Map Activities
- Land Forms of North America, pp. 1–2

Primary Source Explorer
- *The Iroquois Great Law of Peace*

Why It Matters Now
- Cultural Diversity, pp. 1–2

BLOCK SCHEDULING — LESSON PLAN OPTIONS (90-MINUTE PERIOD)

DAY 1

Interact with History, p. 25
Class Time 20 minutes

Options for pacing and variety:
- Role-Playing Have students meet in groups of four or five and act as Europeans and Native Americans meeting for the first time. Have them discuss the "What Do You Think?" questions. **Class Time** 15 minutes

Setting the Stage, p. 26
Class Time 20 minutes

Options for pacing and variety:
- Time Saver For a homework assignment, have students make a three-column chart labeled "What I Know," "What I Want to Know," and "What I Learned." Have students complete the first two columns before reading the chapter. The third column can be completed as part of the Chapter Assessment. **Class Time** 10 minutes

Section 1, pp. 27–32
Class Time 50 minutes

Options for pacing and variety:
- Peer Teaching Have students work in pairs to answer the Reading History questions in the section and the Critical Thinking question in the Section 1 Assessment. **Class Time** 15 minutes
- Internet Extend students' knowledge of the early peoples of America by having them visit classzone.com **Class Time** 20 minutes

DAY 2

Section 2, pp. 33–38
Class Time 20 minutes

Options for pacing and variety:
- Peer Competition Divide the class into small groups. Have each group make up five questions that can be answered with one of the Terms & Names for the section. Have groups take turns asking the class their questions. **Class Time** 20 minutes
- Peer Evaluation Have students pairs answer the Main Ideas and Critical Thinking questions in the Section Assessment. Then have them exchange papers with another team to evaluate their answers. **Class Time** 15 minutes

Section 3, pp. 39–43
Class Time 30 minutes

Options for pacing and variety:
- Peer Evaluation Have student pairs fill in the diagram in the Section 3 Assessment. After they complete it, have them swap diagrams with another pair. Have the pairs provide suggestions and comments about the diagrams to each other. **Class Time** 30 minutes

History Workshop, pp. 56–57
Class Time 40 minutes
- Time Saver Have students work on steps 1–4 in Create and Decode a Pictograph. **Class Time** 30 minutes
- Peer Evaluation Have students complete the pictograph (steps 5 & 6). **Class Time** 10 minutes

Chapter 1 Assessment, pp. 54–55
Class Time 40 minutes

Options for pacing and variety:
- Time Saver For a homework assignment, have students complete the What I Learned column of the chart they made prior to starting the chapter on Day 1. Have them share their responses with the class. **Class Time** 20 minutes
- Peer Teaching Divide students into groups of five students each. Have each student in a group prepare answers to the Review Questions for a different section. Within groups students can exchange answers. **Class Time** 20 minutes

TEACHER-TESTED ACTIVITY **Lisa Williams, Lamberton Middle School, Carlisle, Pennsylvania**

SILENT TRADING OF GHANA

Class Time 20 minutes
Task Trading items without speaking
Purpose To understand the silent system used in the trans-Sahara trade to compensate for the lack of a common language

Supplies Needed
- Two different kinds of small items to trade (marbles, jelly beans, paper clips, mints, or such); have enough so that each student can have about ten pieces

Activity Divide the class into two groups. Give marbles to one group and jelly beans to the other. Explain that one item represents gold and the other salt. To the people of Ghana, salt was worth its weight in gold.

Set up pairs of students, one from each group. Students with the "salt" begin by silently placing what they are willing to trade on a desk, then retreating a few steps. Then the "gold" traders approach and examine the amount. They leave what they believe to be fair payment, then retreat. The salt traders return. If the payment is acceptable, they take the gold and the transaction is complete. If the trade is unacceptable, they leave the gold and the process repeats.

A GUIDED INTERNET SEARCH

An Internet search is a great way to quickly collect information on a particular topic. To reduce the amount of time needed for research and to help make these searches more effective, starting points should be suggested to guide students in the right direction and allow them to find information quickly. This particular search focuses on the possibility that some explorers may have visited the Americas before Christopher Columbus.

ACTIVITY OUTLINE

Objective A guided Internet search about early explorers will help students learn about early migrations to the Americas. It will also help students gain experience with Internet research.

Task Students will work as teams of investigators to find Internet sources that support the idea of early landings in the Americas by explorers other than Columbus.

Class Time One or two class periods

Materials Blank maps for each group that show the outlines of the continents of the Western Hemisphere. If possible, use a larger wall version of the same map, to compile information collected by each team. A blank map is available at classzone.com under *Creating America* Chapter 1 links.

DIRECTIONS

1. Divide students into small teams. If necessary, introduce students to the concept of a search engine and direct them to the recommended search engine. Tell students they will be investigating possible voyages to the Americas before Columbus ("pre-Columbian" voyages). From their knowledge of the subject and from readings in the text, have students think of a few possible search words they might use for such a search.

2. Assign two of the teams a certain key word as a beginning point. Have those teams do simultaneous searches and compare results after they complete their searches. Possible search words for each team include: Vikings, Kon-Tiki, Bering Strait, Ra II, Phoenicians, Kennewick, and Paleo-Indians. Explain to the students that they are investigating hypotheses (theories) about these voyages. They should look for evidence to prove or disprove the hypotheses.

3. Instruct students to choose Web sites that will most likely lead to useful information about the hypothesis they are investigating. Remind them that not all sites listed by a search engine will be useful. Also, remind them that not all information they find will be well written or well-researched. Have them keep a list of the sites they visit and rate the usefulness of the sites on a 10-point scale.

4. Suggest that students try to answer some questions to guide their search:
   - What evidence did you find to prove or disprove a possible landing?
   - What evidence did you find that suggests a departure point?
   - Who were the people on the voyage?
   - Why were they attempting the voyage?
   - Which scientists/researchers have studied this voyage?
   - Do you believe this voyage happened? Why or why not?

5. When the research is finished, students should review the evidence that they found. Teams that conducted simultaneous searches with the same starting search word should compare and contrast their findings.

6. Have each team plot the course of the expedition on a blank map of the Americas. For a blank map of the Western Hemisphere, go to classzone.com.

7. Finally, ask each research team to present its findings to the whole class and add those findings to a large class map. Discuss with the class which theories are the strongest. Which theories need more evidence? What kind of evidence would make the theories stronger?

CHAPTER 1 OBJECTIVE

The student will describe how events on four continents—Europe, Africa, and the Americas—led to the exploration of the Americas and the meeting of peoples from diverse cultures.

HISTORY FROM VISUALS

Interpreting the Painting Ask the students to study the painting of Native Americans looking out at the ship on the far horizon. Have them speculate about what emotions the people in the picture might have felt as they watched the ship approach. **Possible Responses** They might have been curious, frightened, or excited, depending on whether they had seen a ship before. Students could consider how prior experiences or lack of them would affect how Native Americans and Europeans thought about each other.

Extension Have the students write three questions that the Native Americans might want to ask the people on the ship and three questions the Europeans might have for the Native Americans.

CHAPTER 1

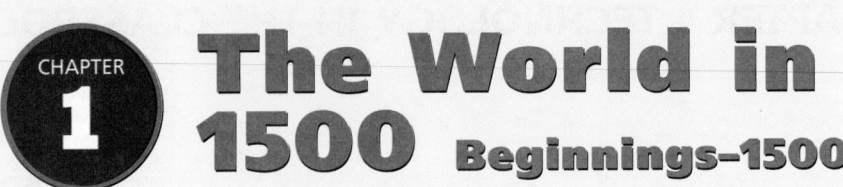

The World in 1500 Beginnings–1500

Section 1 **Societies of North America**
Section 2 **Societies of West Africa and Europe**
Section 3 **Early European Explorers**

Imagine how these Native Americans might feel at their first sight of strange ships.

RECOMMENDED RESOURCES

BOOKS FOR THE TEACHER

Davidson, Basil. ***African Kingdoms.*** New York: Time, 1966. One of the few complete histories of the subject.

Gies, Frances and Joseph. ***Life in a Medieval Village.*** New York: Harper, 1990. Detailed, vivid, and fascinating account of daily life.

Trigger, Bruce G., and Wilcomb E. Washburn. ***North America.*** New York: Cambridge Univ. Press, 1996. Authoritative reference on the history of native peoples of the Americas.

VIDEOS

Indians of North America. January Productions, Inc., 1994. Five-cassette set vividly introduces the many native cultures of North America.

Roots. Wolper Productions, Warner, 1992. Episode 1. African beginning of the much-acclaimed saga of one family.

INTERNET

For more about the first Americans or the voyage of 1492, visit . . .

classzone.com

Interact *with* History

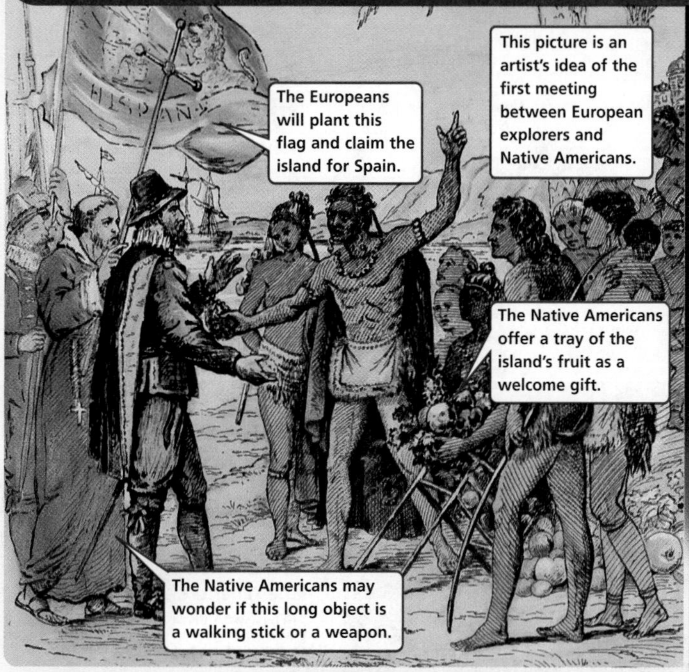

The Europeans will plant this flag and claim the island for Spain.
This picture is an artist's idea of the first meeting between European explorers and Native Americans.
The Native Americans offer a tray of the island's fruit as a welcome gift.
The Native Americans may wonder if this long object is a walking stick or a weapon.

The year is 1492, and you live on an island in the Caribbean. One day you see a giant boat topped by strange white cloths. Men climb into smaller boats and row toward you. You have never seen men like this. They have pale skin and wear heavy, colorful clothing. You wonder what will happen when they land.

What Do You Think?

- What can different societies learn from each other?
- What might they want to gain from each other?
- What positive and negative things might happen when they meet?

What happens when different societies meet?

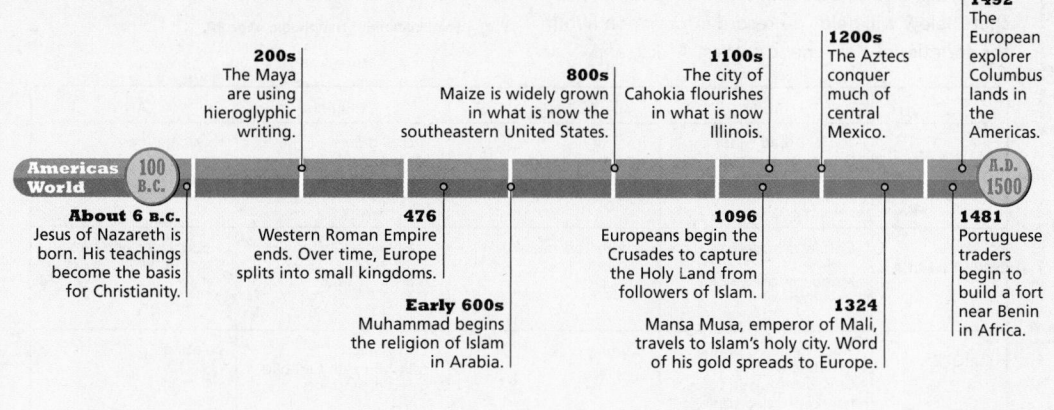

Americas / World — 100 B.C. to A.D. 1500

Americas:
- **200s** The Maya are using hieroglyphic writing.
- **800s** Maize is widely grown in what is now the southeastern United States.
- **1100s** The city of Cahokia flourishes in what is now Illinois.
- **1200s** The Aztecs conquer much of central Mexico.
- **1492** The European explorer Columbus lands in the Americas.

World:
- **About 6 B.C.** Jesus of Nazareth is born. His teachings become the basis for Christianity.
- **476** Western Roman Empire ends. Over time, Europe splits into small kingdoms.
- **Early 600s** Muhammad begins the religion of Islam in Arabia.
- **1096** Europeans begin the Crusades to capture the Holy Land from followers of Islam.
- **1324** Mansa Musa, emperor of Mali, travels to Islam's holy city. Word of his gold spreads to Europe.
- **1481** Portuguese traders begin to build a fort near Benin in Africa.

Interact *with* History

OBJECTIVES

- To identify the challenges of interactions among people of different cultures
- To differentiate between the viewpoints of the Native Americans and the European explorers

What Do You Think?

1. Ask students what these different societies might teach each other.
2. Have students explain why each society might have difficulty understanding the other.
3. Encourage students to consider how the Europeans' motives for exploration might affect the way they viewed the Native Americans they met.

What happens when different societies meet?

Encourage students to think about the ways that differences in beliefs, customs, languages, and other aspects of culture can affect the way people interact with one another and also how they resolve conflicts.

MAKING PERSONAL CONNECTIONS

Ask students to recall someone they have met who came from a different country or another part of the United States. What was their initial reaction to meeting that person? Did any misunderstandings arise? How did their impressions change as they got to know the person better?

TIME LINE DISCUSSION

Point out that this time line covers a span of 1,600 years. As indicated, events on the red line occurred in the Americas, while those on the blue line occurred in other parts of the world.

Remind students that the Americas were populated by many different groups with varying levels of development.

- Ask students what can be learned from the time line about the cultures of some of the Native American groups living in the Americas prior to contact.
Possible Response The Maya had a system of writing; people in the present-day southeastern United States knew how to grow food; people in what is now Illinois built a city; the Aztecs were sufficiently skilled in warfare to conquer others.
- Ask students to find the time period in which Europeans began overseas exploration.
Answer late 1400s

BEFORE YOU READ

Previewing the Theme: Diversity and Unity

Ask students to think about what these monumental structures suggest about the differences and similarities among the societies that built them. **Possible Responses** Students might note that the building materials, design, and sizes of the structures reflect differences in technology, available resources, religious beliefs, and artistic preferences. All three societies had sufficient resources (time, capital, and labor) and the engineering and organizational skills needed to build such structures. Moreover, all three societies considered it important to create public buildings.

What Do You Know?

Ask students to think about the organizational skills needed for such massive construction projects. Ask what such projects suggest about the power of the leaders who organized them. Point out that societies typically must meet basic needs for food, shelter, and clothing before devoting time and labor to other activities.

In-Depth Resources: Unit 1
- Tracing Themes: Diversity and Unity, p. 2

READ AND TAKE NOTES

Reading Strategy: Categorizing

Tell students that categorizing information will help them identify common characteristics among groups. Organizing that information in a chart will help students develop critical thinking skills such as comparing and contrasting. When the chart is completed, students can use it to compare the societies of the Americas, West Africa, and Europe.

In-Depth Resources: Unit 1
- Setting the Stage, p. 1

Critical Thinking Transparency CT1
- Setting the Stage

Chapter 1 SETTING THE STAGE

BEFORE YOU READ

Previewing the Theme

Diversity and Unity Chapter 1 explains that by 1500, diverse societies had developed in the Americas, West Africa, and Europe. After 1500, economic, political, social, and religious forces brought West Africans and Europeans to the Americas. Those people and Native Americans helped create the United States.

CENTRAL AMERICA This pyramid at Chichén Itzá, in what is now Mexico, was built between the 900s and 1200s.

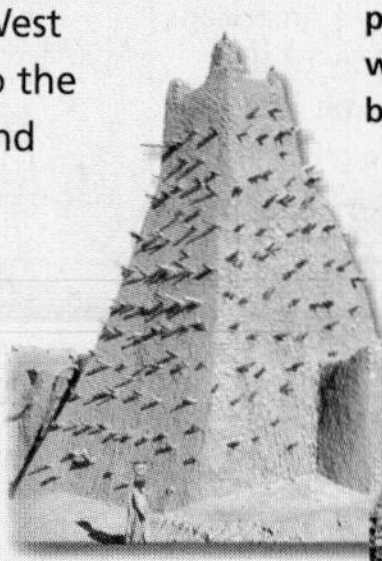

AFRICA This Muslim mosque in Timbuktu, Mali, was built in the 1300s and 1400s.

EUROPE St. Peter's Basilica (a Christian church) in Vatican City, Italy, was built in the 1500s and early 1600s.

What Do You Know?

What do you know about the history of the Americas, West Africa, and Europe? How technologically advanced must a society be to build large structures like the ones at the left?

THINK ABOUT
- what you know about other societies, such as Egypt, that built large structures
- what you've read in books

What Do You Want to Know?

What questions do you have about the past societies of the Americas, West Africa, and Europe? What do you want to know about how they met? Record those questions in your notebook before you read the chapter.

READ AND TAKE NOTES

Reading Strategy: Categorizing One way to make better sense of what you read is to categorize. To categorize is to sort information into groups. The chart below will help you record information about the societies of the Americas, West Africa, and Europe. As you read, look for information relating to the categories of trade, technology, religion, and art. Record that information on your chart.

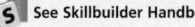

See Skillbuilder Handbook, page R6.

	Trade	Technology	Religion	Art
AMERICAS	Trade spread culture. Groups exchanged regional products.	irrigation mound building seashell and bone tools	sacred places sacred animals and natural forces	rock paintings
WEST AFRICA	Gold was traded for salt. Kingdoms grew rich on trade.	Yoruba cast metal sculpture	traditional African religions Islam	wood, ivory, and metal sculptures
EUROPE	Trade declined during Middle Ages. Crusades spurred trade. Italy controlled trade. with East.	printing press caravels	Christianity split between Catholics and Protestants	paintings

TEACHING STRATEGY

READING THE CHAPTER

This is a thematic chapter focusing on the diverse societies of the Americas, West Africa, and Europe. Encourage students to compare and contrast these societies and the reasons that brought people from each of these societies to the Americas.

ALTERNATIVE ASSESSMENT

The Chapter Assessment describes three activities for alternative assessment on page 45. You may wish to have students work on these activities during the course of the chapter and then present them at the end.

1 Societies of North America

TERMS & NAMES
culture
domestication
civilization
Mound Builders
technology
slash-and-burn agriculture
Iroquois League

MAIN IDEA

Ancient peoples came from Asia to the Americas and over time established many diverse Native American societies.

WHY IT MATTERS NOW

Some Americans today claim one or more of these cultures as part of their heritage.

ONE AMERICAN'S STORY

To do her work, Solveig Turpin must climb rugged cliffs, step over rattlesnakes, and dodge sharp cactus spines. For more than 20 years, she has searched the caves and cliffs of Texas for paintings that ancient people left on rock walls. Turpin is an archaeologist, a scientist who studies the human past by examining the things people left behind. One painting that Turpin found shows a red, 9-foot-long panther. She believes it shows a religious leader who turned himself into an animal.

A VOICE FROM THE PAST

This is the Shaman [religious leader] who transforms into the largest and most powerful animal here. . . . I like to call [the shamans] supramen because they were over everything.

Solveig Turpin, quoted in *In Search of Ancient North America*

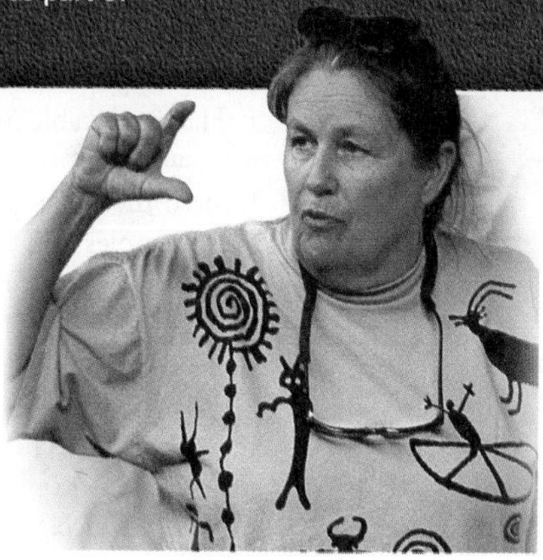

Archaeologist Solveig Turpin wears a shirt displaying the rock paintings of ancient peoples as she discusses her work.

Archaeologists make theories about the past based on what they learn from bones and artifacts. Artifacts are tools and other objects that humans made. They give clues about who ancient people were and how they lived. This section discusses some theories about early Americans.

1 The First People in America

Scientists believe that the first Americans migrated, or moved, to the Americas from Asia. They disagree, however, about how and when this movement took place. Some ancient people may have crossed a land bridge, known as Beringia, that joined Asia and North America during the last Ice Age. The Ice Age, which lasted for thousands of years, was a period of extreme cold in which glaciers trapped so much water that ocean levels dropped. The scientists who hold this theory believe the earliest Americans arrived 12,000 years ago.

Other scientists believe humans came to the Americas much earlier. They have found artifacts in South America that tests show to be 30,000 years old. These scientists believe that people came to the Americas by many routes, including by boat, over thousands of years.

SECTION OBJECTIVES

1. To explain how people first migrated to the Americas
2. To describe early Native American civilizations
3. To describe the diversity of North American societies around 1500

SKILLBUILDER

Interpreting Maps: Movement, Location, p. 30

CRITICAL THINKING

Drawing Conclusions, p. 28
Comparing, p. 31

FOCUS & MOTIVATE

5-MINUTE WARM-UP

Reading a Map Have students discuss these questions to understand the diversity of North American societies.

- Look at the map on page 30. How many different culture areas are shown?
- Which cultures seem to be less connected to others by trade?

Warm-Up Transparency WT1

INSTRUCT

INSTRUCT: OBJECTIVE 1

The First People in America / The Emergence of Civilizations

- In what ways have scientists explained the first human migrations to the Americas?
- What is the difference between a culture and a civilization?
- What were some characteristics of the Olmec civilization?

In-Depth Resources: Unit 1
- Guided Reading, p. 3

Reading Study Guide (Spanish and English), pp. 5–6

Outline Map Activities
- Landforms of North America, pp. 1–2

RECOMMENDED RESOURCES

In-Depth Resources: Unit 1
- Guided Reading, p. 3
- Building Vocabulary, p. 6
- Skillbuilder Practice, p. 7
- Literature Selection, pp. 12–14
- Reteaching Activity, p. 15

America's History Makers
- Deganawida, pp. 1–2

Reading Study Guide (Spanish and English), pp. 5–6

Outline Map Activities
- Landforms of North America, pp. 1–2

Formal Assessment
- Section Quiz, p. 21

Integrated Assessment
- Rubrics, 2.1, 5.4

Access for Students Acquiring English/ESL, pp. 1, 4

INTEGRATED TECHNOLOGY

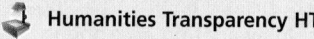

Humanities Transparency HT1

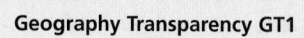

Geography Transparency GT1

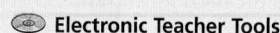

Electronic Teacher Tools

classzone.com

TEST-TAKING RESOURCES

Strategies for Test Preparation

Test Practice Transparencies, TT1–TT2

Online Test Practice

MORE ABOUT . . .

The Mayan Calendar

Mayan astronomers made highly accurate observations of the movements of the sun, moon, and stars. They used that information to create two kinds of calendars. The sacred round calendar recorded the religious year, which had 260 days. Each day had a name associated with one of 20 deities; each day also had a number from 1 to 13. Mayan priests predicted good or bad luck and the proper day for planting, marrying, and other important activities by studying the combinations of gods and numbers on the calendar. The Maya also had a 365-day solar calendar with 18 months of 20 days each. The five days at year's end were considered unlucky.

The Emergence of Civilizations

A **culture** is a way of life that people share, including arts, beliefs, and customs. The first people to live in the Americas thousands of years ago lived in hunting and gathering cultures. They hunted animals and gathered wild seeds, nuts, fruits, and berries.

In time, people in different parts of the world began planting seeds. This was the beginning of agriculture. About 5,000 years ago, humans began to domesticate plants and animals. **Domestication** is the practice of breeding plants or taming animals to meet human needs. People in central Mexico learned to grow corn, which became an important food source. Agriculture spread throughout the Americas.

Having a stable food supply changed the way people lived. Once they no longer had to travel to find food, they built permanent villages and focused their energy on many different activities. Slowly, some cultures grew complex and became civilizations. A **civilization** has five features: (1) cities that are centers of trade, (2) specialized jobs for different people, (3) organized forms of government and religion, (4) a system of record keeping, and (5) advanced tools.

Reading **History**

A. Drawing Conclusions Why would a culture need to learn agriculture before it could develop a civilization?

A. Possible Response Unless it could produce a food surplus, it could not develop specialized jobs or engage in much trade.

About 1200 B.C., an advanced civilization arose in Mesoamerica, a region that stretches from central Mexico to present-day Nicaragua. For 800 years, a people called the Olmec thrived in this region along the Gulf of Mexico. The Olmec built large cities, set up a network of trade routes, and constructed earthen mounds shaped like pyramids. Around 400 B.C., the Olmec mysteriously vanished. By then, their culture had spread along trade routes and influenced others.

By A.D. 250, about 650 years after the Olmec vanished, the Maya had developed a great civilization. Their cities were in southern Mexico and Guatemala, where they built pyramid mounds topped by temples. By 900, the Maya had abandoned many of their cities. Scientists think that revolts, disease, or crop failures may have caused their society to fail.

INSTRUCT: OBJECTIVE 2

Early Native American Civilizations

- What building activities distinguished the Hohokam and the Anasazi civilizations?
- How did different environments lead to differences in early Native American technology?

2 Early Native American Civilizations

Ancient peoples of the American Southwest used images like this to communicate with each other. Such images are called petroglyphs.

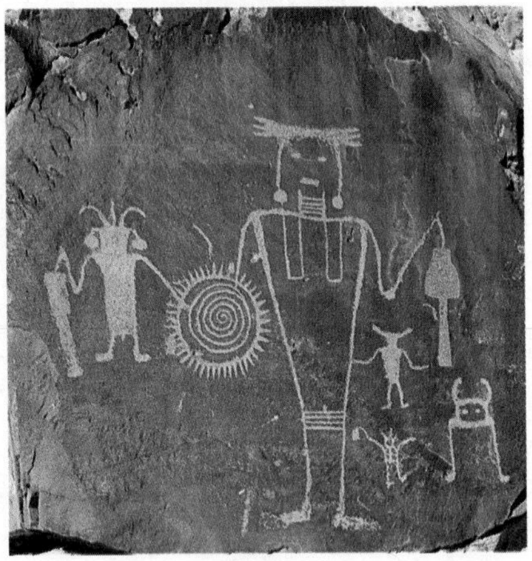

During the Mayan period, various groups of people built civilizations in the areas that would become the present-day United States. The Hohokam created a flourishing society from about 300 B.C. to A.D. 1400 in what is now Arizona. In order to farm the dry land, the Hohokam dug hundreds of miles of canals to irrigate, or water, their crops. The Hohokam also traded with peoples in neighboring regions.

Beginning about A.D. 100, the Anasazi lived in the area where Utah, Arizona, Colorado, and New Mexico now meet. Like the Hohokam, the Anasazi were mainly farmers who traded widely. Around 1300, drought or warfare caused the Anasazi to leave their homes.

ACTIVITY OPTIONS

SKILLBUILDER LESSON: USING SECONDARY SOURCES

Explaining the Skill In studying history, students must learn to use both primary and secondary sources. Primary sources are letters, diaries, speeches, and other documents by people who witnessed a historical event. Secondary sources are accounts, usually written later, by people who were not present at the original event. Secondary sources include archaeological reports, history books, and biographies. In evaluating a secondary source, it is important to know what qualification its author had for writing about the subject.

Applying the Skill After students read "A Voice from the Past" on page 27, ask:

1. Is this a primary or a secondary source? Explain. *(Secondary, the writer is not an eyewitness.)*
2. What primary sources might the author have used to create this secondary source? *(Native American artifacts)* What secondary sources? *(the works of other archaeologists)*
3. What information would help you assess the writer's qualifications? *(her occupation or expertise on this topic)*

In-Depth Resources: Unit 1

- Skillbuilder Practice, p. 7

In the eastern part of what is now the United States lived several groups of people called Mound Builders. The **Mound Builders** were Native Americans who built large earthen structures as burial mounds and temples. Mound Builder cultures included the Adena, the Hopewell, and the Mississippians. The Mississippians, who lived from A.D. 800 to 1700, built some of the first cities in North America. By the 1700s, most of the Mississippians had died from diseases they caught from Europeans.

By 1500, North America was home to hundreds of cultural groups, speaking perhaps 2,000 languages. One reason Native Americans were so diverse was that each group adapted to its own environment—whether subzero ice fields, scorching deserts, or dense forests.

Environment shaped each group's way of life. In some regions, Native Americans based their economy on farming. In others, they relied on hunting or fishing. Different environments caused technology to vary. **Technology** is the use of tools and knowledge to meet human needs. In coastal areas, farmers made tools from shells. In deserts, they used irrigation, the bringing of water to land. Environment affected religion, too. Native Americans strongly believed that certain places were sacred—and that animals, plants, and natural forces had spiritual importance.

3 Peoples of the North and West

The Aleut (uh•LOOT) and the Inuit (IHN•yoo•iht) lived in the frozen lands of the far North. The Aleut lived on islands off Alaska, and the Inuit lived near the coast. Because their climate was too cold for farming, the Inuit and Aleut were hunters. Farther south, Northwest Coast people, such as the Haida and the Kwakiutl (KWAH•kee•OOT•uhl), hunted sea mammals and fished for salmon. Living by forests, they used wood for houses, boats, and carved objects.

The peoples of the West included tribes in California, the Columbia Plateau, and the Great Basin. Much of the West is not suitable for farming. The people who lived there existed mainly by hunting and gathering. To the south, in what is now the American Southwest, lived the Pueblo people. Their ancestors were the ancient Hohokam and Anasazi. Like their ancestors, the Pueblo used irrigation to alter their desert region for farming. The Navajo and the Apache were nomadic, or wandering, hunter-gatherers who came to the region later than the Pueblo. Over time, the Navajo adopted farming and other Pueblo practices.

Reading **History**

B. Reading a Map On the map on page 30, locate the cultures of California, the Plateau, and the Great Basin. Notice why these three together are called the peoples of the West.

daily *life*

KACHINA DANCES

Every year in summer the Hopi, Zuni, and other Pueblo Indians held a religious celebration. The ceremony called on the kachinas, or spirits of the ancestors, to bring a plentiful harvest. At the festival, masked dancers played the role of different kachinas. They danced and sang songs to bring rain in the year ahead. Today, the Pueblo also carve kachina dolls, shown below, as well as hold dances.

INSTRUCT: OBJECTIVE 3

Peoples of the North and West / Peoples of Mexico

- How did climate and environment affect the way of the peoples of the North obtained food?
- What agricultural techniques did the Navajo have in common with the Hohokam?
- What two things helped the Aztecs build a strong empire?

daily *life*

Kachina Dances

According to Pueblo beliefs, the kachinas are spirits who live six months of the year in their own land known as the World Below. For the other six months, from winter to summer solstice, they come to Pueblo villages and inhabit the bodies of men. These men embody the kachinas in religious dances. While acting as a kachina, a dancer is believed to have the power to intercede on behalf of the Pueblos with their gods.

MORE ABOUT . . .

The Potlatch

From northern California to Alaska, the potlatch was central to the lives of Native American peoples. Among these groups, generosity was the key to high social standing. The community looked with suspicion and disapproval at the person who kept all his wealth to himself. European traders were bewildered by the potlatch. They considered the Indians extravagant, while the Indians considered the Europeans selfish.

ACTIVITY OPTIONS

INTERDISCIPLINARY LINK: LITERATURE — BLOCK SCHEDULING

NATIVE AMERICAN LEGENDS

Class Time One class period

Task Choosing a Native American legend to be retold or dramatized for the class

Purpose To understand the richness of Native American literature

Supplies Needed

- Anthologies of Native American literature

Activity Divide the class into groups and tell each group to choose a myth or legend and present it to the class. Presentations can take different forms such as a storyteller or a play. Each member of the group should have a task. As groups present their legends or myths, tell students to compare and contrast themes, types of characters, or lessons the stories teach.

In-Depth Resources: Unit 1

- Literature Selection: *Coyote Steals Otter's Coat,* pp. 12–13; *Song of the Sky Loom,* p. 14

HISTORY FROM VISUALS

Reading the Map Ask students to use the map to identify the major cultural groups of Native Americans in North America in 1500. Have students name the cultural region with the coldest climate and the regions likely to be hottest and driest. What effects might trade among regions have had on the way people lived? **Possible Response** Besides giving people access to resources that were lacking in their own areas, trade might have led to the exchange of technology and ideas as well as goods. How might trade between peoples of different cultural areas have spread ideas? What natural resources might have been most scarce in the Subarctic? In the Southwest?

Extension Tell students to pick one of the Native American groups shown on the map and do research to learn if members of this group still live with this region today.

Geography Transparency GT1
- Native American Lifestyles, 1500

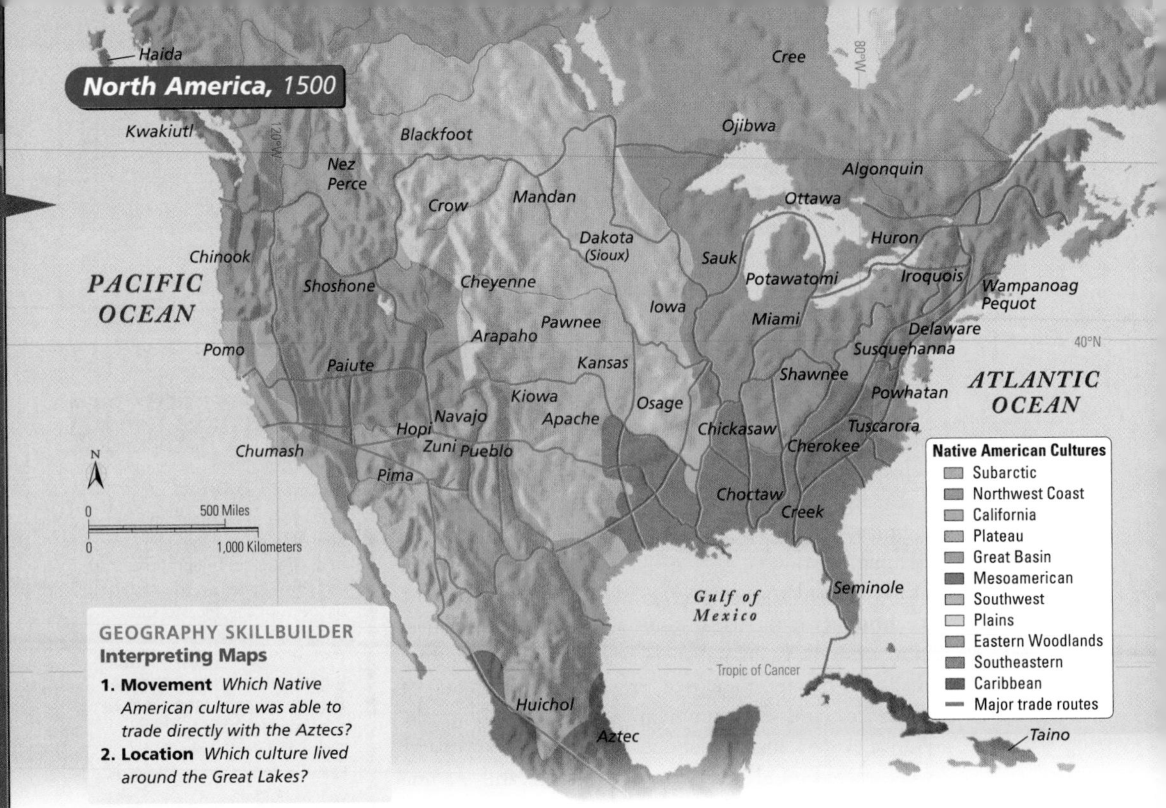

GEOGRAPHY SKILLBUILDER
Interpreting Maps
1. **Movement** *Which Native American culture was able to trade directly with the Aztecs?*
2. **Location** *Which culture lived around the Great Lakes?*

Skillbuilder Answers
1. the people of the Southwest
2. the people of the Eastern Woodlands

Peoples of Mexico

Far to the south, the Aztecs created a great civilization in what is now central Mexico. In 1325, they began to build their capital city, Tenochtitlán (teh•NAWCH•tee•TLAHN), on islands in Lake Texcoco. Two things helped the Aztecs build a strong empire. First, they drained swamps and built an irrigation system. This enabled them to grow plenty of food. Second, they were a warlike people who conquered most of their neighbors.

The Aztecs had a complex society. Rulers were the highest class. Priests and government workers ranked next. Slaves and servants were at the bottom. The Aztecs had elaborate religious ceremonies linked to their calendar and their study of the sun, moon, and stars.

4 Peoples of the Great Plains and East

The Great Plains of North America is a region of flat grasslands stretching from the Mississippi River west to the Rocky Mountains. The Native Americans that inhabited this land were a diverse group. Some were nomads. Others lived in villages by rivers, where land was easier to farm. Many Plains tribes relied on the buffalo for much of their food, clothing, and tools.

INSTRUCT: OBJECTIVE 4

Peoples of the Great Plains and East

- How did the Indians of the Great Plains and the Southeast differ in acquiring food?
- How did the Iroquois and the Algonquin use the resources of their forest environment?
- How did creation of the Iroquois League change the way the Iroquois nations lived?

ACTIVITY OPTIONS

INTERDISCIPLINARY LINK: GEOGRAPHY BLOCK SCHEDULING

INTERPRETING MAPS

Class Time 20 minutes

Task Identifying geographic features of Native American cultural regions

Purpose To draw conclusions about some of the challenges of adapting to various environments

Supplies Needed
- Physical, climate, and vegetation maps of North America

Activity Divide the class into small groups. Let each group pick a cultural region on the map and locate this area on physical, climate, and vegetation maps. Ask groups to write one paragraph about the geographic features of the region. Repeat this process using climate and vegetation maps for information on weather, plant life, and natural resources. Write another paragraph describing the challenges of life in this environment. Each group should make three inferences about how Native American groups in this region might have adapted to their environment.

The Southeast, which stretches from east Texas to the Atlantic Ocean, has mild winters and warm summers with plentiful rainfall. The long growing season allowed the Choctaw (CHAHK•taw), Chickasaw (CHIHK•uh•SAW), and other southeastern groups to become farmers.

Like the Southeast, the Northeast had plenty of fish, game, and rain. But the climate was colder with snowy winters. Forests covered much of the region, so it is called the Eastern Woodlands. Most of the people living there spoke either an Iroquoian or Algonquian language. The Iroquois adapted the forest for farming by using slash-and-burn agriculture. In **slash-and-burn agriculture,** farmers chopped down and then burned trees on a plot of land. The ashes from the fire enriched the soil.

The Iroquois often raided each other's villages for food and captives. In the late 1500s, five northern Iroquois nations took the advice of a peace-seeking man named Deganawida. They stopped warring with each other and formed an alliance. This alliance of the Cayuga, Mohawk, Oneida, Onondaga, and Seneca was the **Iroquois League.** The League brought a long period of peace to the Iroquois. A council of leaders from each nation governed the League. Though tribal leadership was male, women played important roles in Iroquois society. They nominated members of the tribal council. And if a leader did something wrong, the women of his clan could vote him out of office.

Across the Atlantic, the peoples of West Africa and Europe were also building impressive civilizations. You will read about these people and cultures in the next section.

AMERICA'S HISTORY MAKERS

DEGANAWIDA (THE PEACEMAKER)

Iroquois tradition honors Deganawida as the Peacemaker. Seeing how destructive warfare was for the Iroquois, Deganawida went from tribe to tribe and described his dream of peace. After long negotiations, the leaders of the warring nations made peace. However, Deganawida's own tribe, the Huron, did not join the League.

How did Deganawida lead the Iroquois toward peace?

Section 1 Assessment

1. Terms & Names

Explain the significance of:
- culture
- domestication
- civilization
- Mound Builders
- technology
- slash-and-burn agriculture
- Iroquois League

2. Taking Notes

Use a chart like the one below to list ancient cultures of Mesoamerica and North America and their locations.

Ancient Culture	Location

Which of these cultures was closest to where you live?

3. Main Ideas

a. How did the development of farming lead to the growth of civilization?

b. How were the Pueblo like their ancestors, the Hohokam and Anasazi?

c. How did the formation of the Iroquois League benefit its member nations?

4. Critical Thinking

Comparing How did tribes such as the Hohokam and the Iroquois adapt to living in their environment?

THINK ABOUT
- Hohokam agriculture
- Iroquois farming

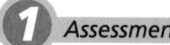

ACTIVITY OPTIONS

GEOGRAPHY
TECHNOLOGY

Review the map on page 30. Create a **map** or **electronic presentation** showing the Native American cultures and trade routes that existed in your home state.

AMERICA'S HISTORY MAKERS

Deganawida

According to legend, around 1570 Deganawida had a vision in which he saw the union of the Five Nations. Thereafter, his message was a simple one: The Iroquois must stop fighting each other and join together under a symbolic Tree of Great Peace. The Iroquois League was almost immediately successful. Within 50 years of its formation, it was the most powerful confederation of Native American peoples on the continent.

Possible Response: Deganawida was a visionary who saw the need for a peace alliance. He inspired Hiawatha to use his skills as a speaker and a negotiator to work for peace.

America's History Makers
- Deganawida, pp. 1–2

ASSESS & RETEACH

Setting the Stage Have students fill in as much as possible in the Americas row on the chapter graphic organizer.

Formal Assessment
- Section Quiz, p. 21

Critical Thinking Transparency CT1

RETEACHING ACTIVITY

Ask students to make a six-column chart on a sheet of paper. Label the columns *Cultural Region, Location, Major Tribes, Natural Resources, Shelter,* and *Adaptations to Environment.* Students can use the map on page 30 and the information in the section to complete the chart.

In-Depth Resources: Unit 1
- Reteaching Activity, p. 15

Section 1 Assessment

1. Terms & Names

culture, p. 28
domestication, p. 28
civilization, p. 28
Mound Builders, p. 29
technology, p. 29
slash-and-burn agriculture, p. 31
Iroquois League, p. 31

2. Taking Notes

Olmec—Mesoamerica
Maya—Mexico and Guatemala
Hohokam—Arizona
Anasazi—where Utah, Arizona, Colorado, and New Mexico meet
Hopewell—eastern United States
Mississippians—eastern United States

3. Main Ideas

a. Fewer people were needed to grow food, so specialized jobs developed. **b.** They used irrigation to farm. **c.** The member nations stopped fighting each other and helped defend each other.

4. Critical Thinking

The Hohokam used irrigation to farm in the desert; the Iroquois used the slash-and-burn technique.

ACTIVITY OPTIONS

Integrated Assessment
- Rubrics for a map, 2.1
- Rubrics for an electronic presentation, 5.4

INTERACTIVE PRIMARY SOURCE

OBJECTIVE
Students will analyze the introduction to the Great Law of Peace and evaluate its importance to the establishment and stability of the Iroquois League.

Primary Source Explorer
- *Iroquois Great Law of Peace*

FOCUS & MOTIVATE

Evaluating Ask students to consider the importance of symbols in any organization. What is the function of team mascots? Of national flags? How do such symbols promote unity? Tell them to identify the symbols of unity for the Iroquois League as they read and to consider why these symbols are powerful.

INSTRUCT

- How does the tree serve as a symbol for the unity of the Five Nations? What purposes do the roots of a tree serve? What purposes do the branches and leaves serve?
- Why might Deganawida believe that it takes "strength" to be peaceful?

MORE ABOUT . . .

The Great Law of Peace
The Great Law was originally handed down through oral tradition, for which a set of wampum belts served as a record. The Onondaga Nation, who live in central New York State, are the keepers of these wampum, or shell, belts. Eventually, the terms of the Great Law of Peace were recorded in writing.

INTERACTIVE PRIMARY SOURCE

The Iroquois Great Law of Peace

Setting the Stage The five nations of the Iroquois League created a constitution, called the Great Law of Peace, that had 117 laws and customs. These laws governed all aspects of life and war. In this excerpt, Deganawida introduces the Great Law by describing a tree that symbolizes the permanence and stability of the league. **See Primary Source Explorer**

1 I am Deganawida and with the Five Nations' Confederate **Lords**[1] I plant the Tree of Great Peace. I plant it in your territory, **Adodarhoh,**[2] and the Onondaga Nation, in the territory of you who are Firekeepers.

I name the tree the Tree of the Great Long Leaves. Under the shade of this Tree of the Great Peace we spread the soft white feathery down of the globe thistle as seats for you, Adodarhoh, and your cousin Lords.

We place you upon those seats, spread soft with the feathery down of the globe thistle, there beneath the shade of the spreading branches of the Tree of Peace. There shall you sit and watch the Council Fire of the **Confederacy of the Five Nations,**[3] and all the affairs of the Five Nations shall be transacted at this place before you, Adodarhoh, and your cousin Lords, by the Confederate Lords of the Five Nations.

2 Roots have spread out from the Tree of the Great Peace, one to the north, one to the east, one to the south, and one to the west. The name of these roots is The Great White Roots and their nature is Peace and Strength.

If any man or any nation outside the Five Nations shall obey the laws of the Great Peace and make known their disposition to the Lords of the Confederacy, they may trace the Roots to the Tree and if their minds are clean and they are obedient and promise to obey the wishes of the Confederate Council, they shall be welcomed to take shelter beneath the Tree of the Long Leaves.

A CLOSER LOOK
THE COUNCIL FIRE
The council fire of the Iroquois League was kept burning for about 200 years.
1. What do you think it would mean if the council fire were allowed to die?

A CLOSER LOOK
THE GREAT WHITE ROOTS
The roots of a tree help to anchor it in the ground, and they draw water and food from the soil.
2. Why might Deganawida say the nature of the roots is "Peace and Strength"?

1. **Lords:** chiefs.
2. **Adodarhoh:** the name of the office of the Onondaga chief.
3. **Confederacy of the Five Nations:** the Iroquois League.

Interactive Primary Source Assessment

1. Main Ideas
a. In what territory was the Tree of the Great Peace planted?
b. Where will the affairs of the Five Nations be conducted?
c. Where have the Tree's roots spread?

2. Critical Thinking
Making Inferences Were outsiders welcome to join the Iroquois League? Explain.
THINK ABOUT
- the phrase *they may trace the Roots to the Tree*
- the phrase *take shelter beneath the Tree*

Interactive Primary Source Assessment

1. Main Ideas
a. It was planted in the territory of the Onondaga Nation, whose chief is Adodarhoh.
b. They will meet near or in the shade of the Tree of Great Peace. They will meet before the council fire.
c. in all four directions

2. Critical Thinking
yes, if they obey the League's laws

A CLOSER LOOK
1. that the alliances of the Iroquois League had ended
2. He wants the League to be founded on those qualities.

2 Societies of West Africa and Europe

TERMS & NAMES
- Muslim
- Islam
- European Middle Ages
- feudalism
- Crusades
- Renaissance
- Reformation

MAIN IDEA

By 1500, the peoples of West Africa and Europe developed sophisticated civilizations.

WHY IT MATTERS NOW

The changes taking place in West Africa and Europe helped shape European exploration of the Americas.

ONE AFRICAN'S STORY

King Tenkaminen (TEHN•kah•MEE•nehn) of the West African empire of Ghana was a powerful ruler. He grew rich by taxing gold traders who traveled through his land. His wealth impressed visitors to his kingdom. In 1067, a geographer described the royal court.

A VOICE FROM THE PAST

The king adorns himself . . . wearing necklaces round his neck and bracelets on his forearms. . . . Behind the king stand ten pages holding shields and swords decorated with gold and on his right are the sons of the vassal [lower] kings of his country wearing splendid garments and their hair plaited [braided] with gold.

al-Bakri, quoted in *The Horizon History of Africa*

Kumasi, a modern West African chief, wears gold to show his status, just as the ancient king of Ghana did.

West Africa had several other kingdoms and empires that grew powerful through trade. Meanwhile, trade also played an increasingly significant role in Europe. This section examines life in both lands on the eve of the European explorations that would bring their worlds into contact with the Americas.

1 Africa in 1500

Africa is the world's second largest continent. (See the map on page 34.) It is home to a variety of land forms and climates. Dense rain forests stretch along the equator in central and western Africa. North and south of the rain forests are broad savannas, or flat grasslands. Beyond the savannas to the north and south are miles of desert.

By A.D. 1500, coastal ports had linked Africa with the rest of the world for many centuries. Ships from ports on the Mediterranean and the Red Sea carried goods to Arabia and Persia. On Africa's eastern coast, city-states carried on a brisk trade with ports across the Indian Ocean.

Like other parts of Africa, West Africa has rain forest along the equator and savanna to the north. Along its northern edge, West Africa borders the Sahara Desert. By A.D. 500, camel caravans led by eager merchants made regular journeys across the desert. This trade helped West African kingdoms grow wealthy.

SECTION OBJECTIVES

- To describe the geography of Africa, the continent's trade links, and the development of West African kingdoms
- To explain how Catholicism and feudalism affected life in Europe and the significance of the Renaissance and the Reformation

SKILLBUILDER

Interpreting Maps: Place, Movement, p. 34
Interpreting Charts, p. 38

CRITICAL THINKING

Clarifying, p. 34
Recognizing Effects, p. 35
Identifying Problems, p. 36
Analyzing Causes, p. 36
Making Generalizations, p. 38
Contrasting, p. 38

FOCUS & MOTIVATE

5-MINUTE WARM-UP

Drawing Conclusions To examine the importance of trade to West African empires, have students answer these questions.

1. Study the map on page 34. What port cities in northern Africa are linked to West African empires by trade routes?
2. Why would these ports be likely to trade with Europe?

Warm-Up Transparency WT1

INSTRUCT

INSTRUCT: OBJECTIVE 1

Africa in 1500 / Ghana and Islam

- What types of vegetation and landforms are found in Africa?
- How did Ghana's location help it grow rich?
- What role did Islam play in Ghana's history?

In-Depth Resources: Unit 1
- Guided Reading, p. 4

Reading Study Guide (Spanish and English), pp. 7–8

RECOMMENDED RESOURCES

In-Depth Resources: Unit 1
- Guided Reading, p. 4
- Building Vocabulary, p. 6
- Primary Source, p. 10
- Reteaching Activity, p. 16

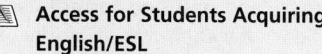

Reading Study Guide (Spanish and English), pp. 7–8

Economics in History, p. 1

Formal Assessment
- Section Quiz, p. 22

Integrated Assessment
- Rubrics, 5.1, 4.8

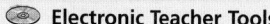

Access for Students Acquiring English/ESL
- Guided Reading, p. 2

INTEGRATED TECHNOLOGY

Critical Thinking Transparency CT2

Electronic Teacher Tools

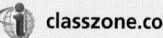

classzone.com

TEST-TAKING RESOURCES

Strategies for Test Preparation

Test Practice Transparencies, TT3–TT4

Online Test Practice

MORE ABOUT . . .

Ghana and Islam

Eager to strengthen their ties with Islamic empires in North Africa, Ghana's rulers welcomed the new religion. Although Ghana's kings and court did not at first convert to Islam, by the 11th century Ghana's rulers had Muslim advisers at court helping them run the kingdom. Eventually, many of Ghana's rulers and members of the royal court converted to Islam. However, most of the common people retained their traditional beliefs.

INSTRUCT: OBJECTIVE 2

Mali and Songhai

- What was the source of Mali's wealth and power, and who was its leader during its strongest period?
- Who were Songhai's two greatest rulers, and how did each contribute to the growth of the empire?
- What was the significance of Benin in the late 1400s?

HISTORY FROM VISUALS

Reading the Map Ghana, Mali, and Songhai are all located on the southern edge of the Sahara. How did their location help them prosper? What evidence suggests that the Sahara was not a barrier to trade? **Possible Response** They were central meeting places for merchants traveling south from ports on the Mediterranean and traders coming north bringing gold from mines or gold fields farther south. The many trade routes across the Sahara indicate that it was not a barrier to trade.

Extension Tell students to use an encyclopedia to determine what products are traded in modern West Africa.

Ghana and Islam

Ghana became the first West African kingdom to grow rich through trade. From the 700s to the mid 1000s, Ghana became a marketplace for traders going north and south in search of salt and gold. Salt was important because it helps the human body retain water in hot weather. Traders carried salt from the Saharan salt mines in the north. In Ghana's markets, they met other traders offering gold from the forests of West Africa.

Ghana's king benefited from this trade. He imposed taxes on all gold and salt passing through his kingdom. The king then used the resulting wealth to pay for an army and build an empire.

Many of the traders who came to Ghana from North Africa were **Muslims.** Muslims are followers of the religion of Islam. Founded by the prophet Muhammad in the 600s, **Islam** teaches that there is one God, named Allah. Muslims must perform such duties as praying five times a day and making a visit to the holy city of Mecca in Arabia.

The Muslim empires of North Africa sought to convert Ghana's people to Islam and to control Ghana's gold trade. In 1076, Muslim armies began invading Ghana's frontier region and the empire weakened.

*Reading*History
A. Clarifying What did Islam preach?
A. Answer There is one God, named Allah, and adherents must pray five times a day and make a pilgrimage to Mecca.

Mali and Songhai 2

By the 1200s, another West African kingdom, Mali, had taken over most of Ghana's territory. Its wealth also came from control of the gold-salt trade. By 1312, Mali had become one of the largest empires in the world.

Skillbuilder Answers
1. Songhai
2. Possible Response Tunis to Fez to Sijilmasa to Taghaza to Timbuktu

West African Empires, 800–1500

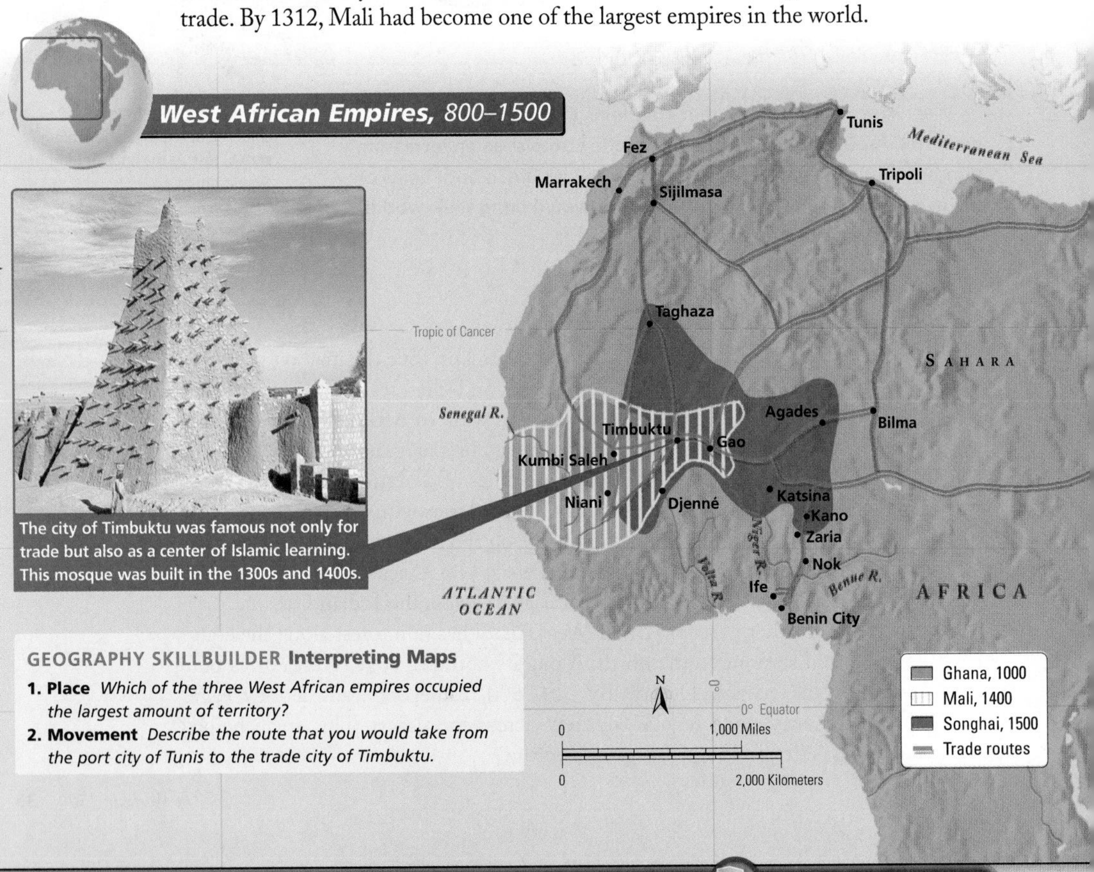

The city of Timbuktu was famous not only for trade but also as a center of Islamic learning. This mosque was built in the 1300s and 1400s.

GEOGRAPHY SKILLBUILDER Interpreting Maps

1. **Place** *Which of the three West African empires occupied the largest amount of territory?*
2. **Movement** *Describe the route that you would take from the port city of Tunis to the trade city of Timbuktu.*

ACTIVITY OPTIONS

INTERDISCIPLINARY LINK: SCIENCE/HEALTH — BLOCK SCHEDULING

GOLD AND SALT

Class Time 20 minutes

Task Finding fun facts about gold and salt

Purpose To explain why these commodities were valued in the past and to examine their current uses

Supplies Needed

- Reference materials on gold and salt
- Index cards

Activity Ask a science or health teacher to speak to the class about why the body needs salt. Divide the class in half and distribute index cards. One half will find information about salt and the other half information on gold. Students can search for information on the properties, chemical makeup, and past and current uses of each commodity. Encourage them to consider why each was so highly valued in Africa south of the Sahara. Have students write one fact about salt or gold on their index cards. Collect the cards and share the most interesting facts with the class.

Vocabulary
devout: very religious

Its leader during this period was a devout Muslim named Mansa Musa (MAHN•sah moo•SAH). Under his rule, Islamic culture spread throughout the empire. After Mansa Musa's death in 1337, Mali slowly weakened.

As the power of Mali decreased, the Songhai (SAWNG•HY) people living near the Niger River broke away from the empire's control. In 1464, under the leader Sunni Ali, they created their own empire. Sunni Ali was a Muslim, but he also practiced the traditional Songhai religion. After Sunni Ali died in 1492, Askia Muhammad rose to power. A devoted Muslim, Muhammad ably governed the empire for 35 years. He chose officials who made the government run smoothly. He also expanded trade and set up an efficient tax system. Askia Muhammad used his wealth to build mosques and support Muslim scholars. After Muhammad's reign, several weak rulers succeeded him. Eventually, the empire collapsed.

Reading **History**
B. Recognizing Effects How would Askia Muhammad's actions promote Islam in Songhai?
Possible Response by encouraging Islamic worship and study

As empires rose and fell in some parts of West Africa, small city-states arose in other parts of the region. The Hausa (HOW•suh) states emerged after A.D. 1000 in what is now Nigeria. The Yoruba (YAWR•uh•buh) lived in the forests southwest of the Niger River. They were gifted artists who carved prized wood, ivory, and metal sculptures. In the river's delta region, near a crossroad of trade routes, the kingdom of Benin emerged.

In the late 1400s, Europeans reached Benin. Portuguese arrived in ships and set up a trade center near the capital, Benin City. Trade was just one reason Europeans were sailing far beyond their lands. A number of social changes were occurring in Europe—changes that would push them to explore the world.

Now and then

AFRICAN HERITAGE

One way many African Americans show pride in their heritage is by wearing kente cloth. Kente cloth, shown below, is a colorful fabric woven by the Akan and Ewe people of Ghana.

Some African Americans celebrate the holiday of Kwanzaa in December. Based on traditional African harvest festivals, Kwanzaa lasts a week. Each day honors a value held by Africans: unity, self-determination, collective responsibility, cooperative economics, purpose, creativity, and faith.

3 Europe Undergoes Great Change

The period from the late 400s, when the Western Roman Empire collapsed, to about the 1300s, is known in Europe as the **European Middle Ages.** It was a time of great social and political instability and warfare. To survive such difficult times, Europeans developed feudalism. **Feudalism** is a political system in which a king allows nobles, or lords, to use lands that belong to him. In return, the lords owe the king military service and protection for the people living on the land.

Along with feudalism, Europeans developed the manor system. In this system, lords divided their lands into manors, or large estates, that were farmed mostly by serfs. Serfs were landless peasants who were not

Now and then

African Heritage
To celebrate Kwanzaa, families gather each night to light the candles in the *kinara,* a seven-branched candelabra, and to talk about the value honored for that day. On December 31, many families come together for a community feast called the *karamu.*

MORE ABOUT . . .

Mansa Musa
In 1324, the Muslim ruler of Mali, Mansa Musa, set out on a pilgrimage to Mecca. He traveled in a caravan with some 60,000 relatives, officials, musicians, cooks, camel drivers, servants, slaves, and hangers-on. According to one report, his treasury included 24,000 pounds (12 tons) of gold. When he arrived in Cairo, Egypt, he spent gold so freely that prices skyrocketed in all the bazaars of the city—a classic example of inflation resulting from a rapid increase in the money supply.

INSTRUCT: OBJECTIVE 3

Europe Undergoes Great Change

- How did feudalism and the manor system help Europeans survive in the Middle Ages?
- What new roles did the Roman Catholic Church play?
- What are two factors that increased trade in the Middle Ages?
- How did the bubonic plague and the growth of trade eventually lead to the rise of nations?

ACTIVITY OPTIONS

MULTIPLE LEARNING STYLES: VISUAL

MAKING A TRAVEL POSTER

Class Time One class period

Task Creating a travel poster for Ghana, Mali, or Songhai

Purpose To describe aspects of the history and culture of one of the West African kingdoms

Supplies Needed
- Reference materials on Ghana, Mali, and Songhai
- Current travel posters
- Posterboard and art supplies

Activity Students choose one of the West African kingdoms from this section and create a travel poster. In designing their posters, students may want to choose a single image or a variety of drawings showing religious sites or cities. Posters can include all or some of the following information: location, economic activities, artifacts, outstanding rulers. Display the completed posters on the bulletin board.

In-Depth Resources: Unit 1
Primary Source: from *Travels in Asia and Africa* by Ibn Battuta, p. 10

The Rise and Decline of Feudalism

In feudalism, nobles offered to protect peasants from invaders. In return, the peasants farmed the nobles' lands.
Feudalism made people feel safe enough to travel. Trade increased and towns grew.
Then many peasants ran away to towns, where they could live more freely. Feudalism declined. Trade continued to grow.

allowed to leave the manor. In return for the serfs' work, the lord promised to protect them.

Christianity was the dominant religion of Europe, and Europeans were greatly influenced by Judeo-Christian beliefs. "Judeo" refers to Judaism—the religion of the Jews. Judeo-Christian beliefs include the worth of the individual and the importance of ethical behavior. The central code of behavior is the Ten Commandments. Judeo-Christian beliefs have played an important role in the United States.

By the 1000s, feudalism had brought more stability to European society. As strong lords gained more control over their lands, long periods of peace and security followed. Merchants increasingly felt safe to travel, and trade increased. Old towns near busy trade routes revived, and new towns grew up near manor houses and churches.

War also spurred trade. In 1096, European Christians launched the **Crusades**, a series of wars to capture the Holy Land—the biblical region of Palestine in southwest Asia—from the Muslims. They ultimately failed to keep the Holy Land, but the Crusades changed European life. During the years of fighting, Europeans encountered a variety of Asian goods. After the war, they continued to demand these items.

The growth of trade and towns weakened feudalism as serfs left the manors to live in the growing towns. Beginning in 1347, a deadly disease known as bubonic plague also weakened feudalism by reducing the number of workers. Lords had to compete for laborers by paying wages to peasants.

As feudal lords lost power, kings grew stronger. Kings won the support of townspeople because they could raise large armies to enforce order. This process contributed to the gradual rise of nations.

4 The Renaissance and Reformation

Italy, which was thriving because of trade, became the birthplace of the **Renaissance**—a time of increased interest in art and learning. Renaissance is a French term meaning "rebirth." Lasting from the 1300s to 1600, the Renaissance spread from Italy throughout Europe.

Reading **History**
C. Identifying Problems What problems were Europeans trying to solve with feudalism and the manor system?
C. Answer The problems were safety from attack and providing labor for the lords' estates.

Reading **History**
D. Analyzing Causes What three causes led to the decline of feudalism?
D. Answer the growth of towns and trade, the bubonic plague, and the growing power of kings

MORE ABOUT . . .

Bubonic Plague

Between 1347 and 1352, the bubonic plague, known more dramatically as the Black Death, killed about 25 million people in Europe. (It had already killed uncounted millions in Asia.) Spread by fleas, the disease was especially devastating wherever people lived in close quarters, such as in towns or in medieval monasteries. In some Italian cities, as many as nine-tenths of the population died. The eerie cry "Bring out your dead" sounded in the streets as plague carts carried corpses off to mass graves. No other event in recorded history has killed such a large share of the world's population.

INSTRUCT: OBJECTIVE 4

The Renaissance and Reformation / Changes in Trade

- What was the Renaissance and where did it begin?
- How did the Reformation affect the Roman Catholic Church?
- How did Italians gain control of the trade in Asian goods?
- Why did other European countries begin looking for a new water route to Asia?

ACTIVITY OPTIONS

INTERDISCIPLINARY LINK: WORLD HISTORY — BLOCK SCHEDULING

FEUDALISM

Class Time 20 minutes

Task Making a diagram to show how the feudal system worked

Purpose To understand the obligations and rewards of participating in feudalism

Supplies Needed
- Reference materials on feudalism

Activity Have each student make a diagram that shows what part each level of society played in the feudal system: king, nobles, knights, peasants, serfs. On their diagrams, students should indicate the responsibilities each group had to those above and below it and how each benefited from the system. After students have shared their diagrams with the class, have them explain how this system weakened the power of kings, while strengthening the power of the nobility.

Several forces led to the Renaissance. As feudalism weakened and the plague brought great suffering, Europeans began to question what life meant. In their search for new answers, some people turned to old sources. They studied the classical writings and art of the ancient Greeks and Romans. As a result of these studies, European ideas changed.

Vocabulary
philosophy: the study of the meaning of life

1. The Greeks had praised human achievement. European scholars developed humanism, the study of human value and ideas.
2. Classical education stressed such subjects as history, philosophy, and literature. Europeans spent more time studying those subjects.
3. From classical art, Renaissance artists learned to make art more realistic. These artists created some of the world's finest paintings and statues.
4. Muslim scholars had saved classical manuscripts about science. Also, Muslim mathematicians had invented algebra. Contact with Muslim societies influenced European science and mathematics.

In about 1455, a German named Johannes Gutenberg invented the printing press. This invention prompted an increase in book printing and helped to spread Renaissance ideas more quickly.

By the early 1500s, Renaissance ideas and other forces weakened the Roman Catholic Church. Many Church leaders were corrupt. Martin Luther, a German monk, publicly posted 95 statements that criticized a number of Church practices. This protest began the **Reformation,** a movement to correct problems in the Church. The Reformation split the Church into two groups in western Europe—Catholics and Protestants. In time, Protestants divided into many different churches.

HISTORY through ART

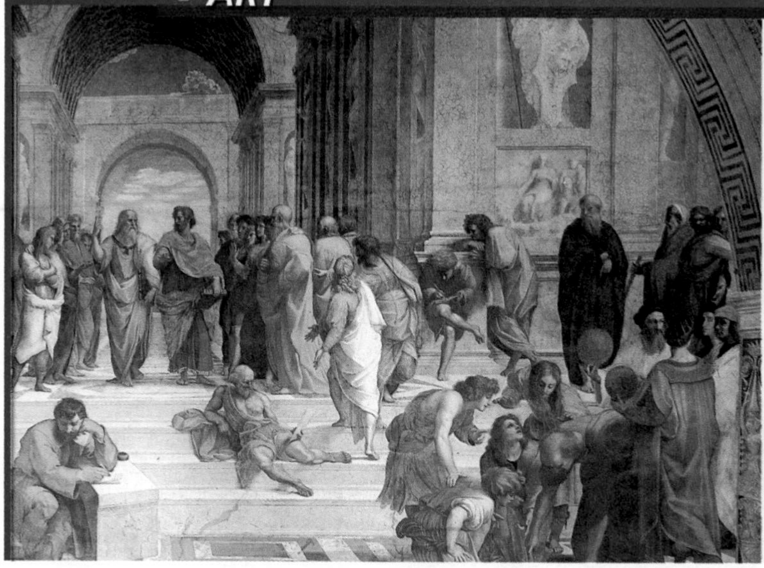

This painting, *School of Athens* by Raphael, shows many aspects of Renaissance art and culture.
- Like much Renaissance art, it looks more realistic than the art of the Middle Ages.
- It honors the Greek thinkers Aristotle and Plato, who are the two men in the center arch.
- It also honors Renaissance artists. Raphael himself is in the group to the right.

Why might Raphael have wanted to include himself in a painting with famous Greeks?

MORE ABOUT . . .

Gutenberg's Press
Both the Chinese and Koreans had some form of printing when Gutenberg invented his press. In Europe, printers had developed a method of stamping letters on various surfaces. However, Gutenberg's method of printing from movable type had several unique features. His press most closely resembled those used in making wine or paper. He also created a mold for accurately casting type and developed an oil-based printing ink.

HISTORY through ART

Interpreting the Painting By age 21, Raphael (1483–1520) was already a successful and respected painter. In 1508, Pope Julius II called him to Rome to paint a series of frescoes in the private apartments in the Vatican where the pope lived and worked. The *School of Athens* is one of these frescoes. Charming and handsome as well as talented, Raphael's popularity earned him the nickname "the prince of painters." His works have been called a perfect expression of the "classical—harmonious, beautiful and serene."

Possible Responses: He wanted to show himself as their student. He is indicating his desire to be as great as they were.

ACTIVITY OPTIONS

INDIVIDUAL NEEDS

LESS PROFICIENT READERS

Cause and Effect Point out the cause-and-effect chart on page 38. Review how an effect can become a cause that triggers a subsequent effect. Then pair a proficient reader with a less proficient reader. Have the students look at each cause and effect in the chart and identify what steps and information are implied in each combination. For example: After the Crusades, Europeans wanted Asian goods, but they needed to find a way to get goods from Asia to Europe. Italy had already developed a trade network with Asia during the Crusades, so the Italians were the first Europeans able to import goods from Asia.

Ask students to create a three-column graphic organizer. Have them write causes in the left column and effects in the right column. Then ask them to supply the implied information in the center column.

HISTORY FROM VISUALS

Interpreting the Chart Point out that events can have both intended and unintended consequences. Ask students to identify the intended and unintended consequences of the Italian domination of Asian trade. **Answer** The intended effect was to make Italy rich and powerful; the unintended effect was to make other European nations that wanted wealth and power begin to explore.

Extension Suggest that students do research to find out which Asian trade goods were most desired by Europeans.

Critical Thinking Transparency CT2
- Cause and Effect: Causes of Exploration

Economics in History
- The Benefits of Trade, p. 1

ASSESS & RETEACH

Setting the Stage Have students fill in the West Africa and Europe sections on the chapter graphic organizer.

Formal Assessment
- Section Quiz, p. 22

RETEACHING ACTIVITY

Have students write a summary of the section using the Terms & Names for the section listed on page 33.

In-Depth Resources: Unit 1
- Reteaching Activity, p. 16

CAUSE & EFFECT: *Causes of Exploration*

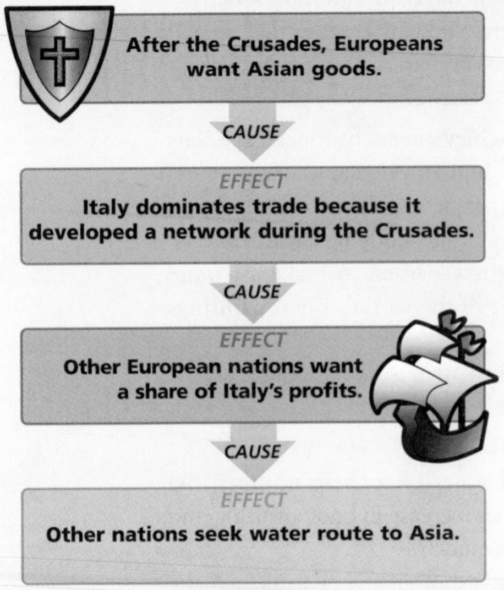

After the Crusades, Europeans want Asian goods.
CAUSE
EFFECT
Italy dominates trade because it developed a network during the Crusades.
CAUSE
EFFECT
Other European nations want a share of Italy's profits.
CAUSE
EFFECT
Other nations seek water route to Asia.

SKILLBUILDER **Interpreting Charts**
What economic activity was the primary cause of exploration?

Skillbuilder Answer trade

Changes in Trade

The Renaissance period saw not only changes in learning and religion but also in trade. As trade grew, Italian merchants needed to improve the way they did business. They began to use more exact ways of keeping track of a business's income and its costs. By subtracting the costs from the income, the merchants determined the profit.

Italian merchants made huge profits by trading in Asian goods. Italians had done business with Muslims for centuries. Thus, they had developed a special relationship. In addition, the Italians used their military strength to control the trade on the Mediterranean and did not allow other Europeans to take part in it.

Merchants in other European countries envied the profits made by Italian merchants. As a result, other Europeans began to want a share of the rich trade in Asian goods. They had to find different routes to Asia from the ones controlled by the Italians and Muslims. Other European countries began to search for a non-Mediterranean water route to Asia, as you will read in Section 3.

E. Possible Answer They will do whatever they can to find a way to undermine the first country's control.

Reading **History**
E. Making Generalizations If a country tries to completely dominate trade in a certain area, how will other countries respond?

Section 2 Assessment

1. Terms & Names
Explain the significance of:
- Muslim
- Islam
- European Middle Ages
- feudalism
- Crusades
- Renaissance
- Reformation

2. Taking Notes
On a web like the one below, list how the Renaissance changed art and learning.

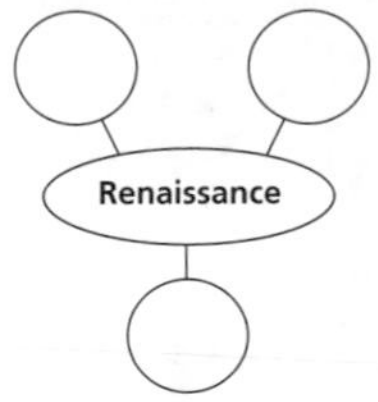

3. Main Ideas
a. How did Ghana's ruler benefit from controlling the gold-salt trade?
b. How did Islam spread within West Africa?
c. What caused feudalism to develop?

4. Critical Thinking
Contrasting How did the Renaissance differ from the European Middle Ages?
THINK ABOUT
- the economy
- how power was distributed
- the authority of the church

ACTIVITY OPTIONS
TECHNOLOGY
MUSIC
Design a **Web site** or compose a **song** advertising the great new Renaissance invention—the printing press.

Section 2 Assessment

1. Terms & Names
Muslims, p. 34
Islam, p, 34
Middle Ages, p. 35
feudalism, p. 35
Crusades, p. 36
Renaissance, p. 36
Reformation, p. 37

2. Taking Notes
- study of humanism
- increased study of history, philosophy, literature
- more realism in art
- rediscovery of classical science and exposure to algebra
- printing press, which spread learning

3. Main Ideas
a. He placed taxes on trade, which made him wealthy and enabled him to build an army and an empire.
b. through the migration of Muslim traders and scholars and the conversion of some rulers. **c.** In a time of unrest, feudalism developed as an exchange of security for land use or labor.

4. Critical Thinking
Feudalism: kings and nobles both had power; Catholic Church gained power. Renaissance: trade revived; kings gained power; Protestantism challenged Catholicism.

ACTIVITY OPTIONS
Integrated Assessment
- Rubrics for a Web site, 5.1
- Rubrics for a song, 4.8

3 Early European Explorers

TERMS & NAMES
navigator
caravel
Christopher Columbus

MAIN IDEA

As Europeans searched for sea routes to Asia, Christopher Columbus reached the Americas.

WHY IT MATTERS NOW

Columbus's journey permanently linked the Americas to the rest of the world.

ONE EUROPEAN'S STORY

Sailors seeking a route to Asia depended on the skill of their navigator. A <u>navigator</u> plans the course of a ship by using instruments to find its position. In the 1400s, Portugal had a famous prince called Henry the Navigator. Yet, Henry wasn't a navigator. He never sailed on any of the ships trying to find Asia. So how did he earn his name?

Henry lived at Sagres, on the southwestern tip of Portugal. It was a site that overlooked the Atlantic Ocean. He invited astronomers, mathematicians, mapmakers, and navigators to Sagres. There he began a school of navigation.

Henry decided to organize and pay for sailing expeditions to explore the Atlantic and the west coast of Africa. He was hoping to find African gold, to learn more about geography, and to spread Christianity. His ships traveled farther down the African coast than Europeans had ever gone. Because Henry sponsored the voyages, the English named him "the navigator." Those voyages began Europe's age of discovery. As you will read in this section, this age of discovery eventually led Europeans to the Americas.

Henry the Navigator sponsored voyages that helped Portugal find a water route to Asia.

1 A Water Route to Asia

Under Prince Henry, the Portuguese developed an improved ship called the **<u>caravel</u>.** The caravel had triangular sails as well as square sails. Square sails carried the ship forward when the wind was at its back. Triangular sails allowed the caravel to sail into the wind. The caravel was better than other European ships of the time at this type of sailing.

In January 1488, the Portuguese explorer Bartolomeu Dias (DEE•uhs) reached the southern tip of Africa. After sailing around it, he returned to Portugal at the urging of his crew. Portugal's king named the tip the Cape of Good Hope because he hoped they had found a route to Asia.

Ten years later, another Portuguese explorer, Vasco da Gama, followed Dias's route around the cape. He continued north along the eastern coast of Africa. Then he sailed east across the Indian Ocean to India. At last, someone had found an all-water route from Europe to Asia.

SECTION OBJECTIVES

1. To describe the Portuguese water route to Asia
2. To explain why Spain's rulers financed Columbus's voyages of discovery
3. To describe Columbus's first voyage
4. To evaluate the geographic knowledge Columbus brought back from his voyages

SKILLBUILDER

Interpreting Maps: Movement, Human–Environment Interaction, p. 41

CRITICAL THINKING

Comparing, p. 40
Drawing Conclusions, p. 41
Analyzing Causes, p. 42
Making Inferences, p. 43
Analyzing Points of View, p. 43

Why It Matters Now
- Cultural Diversity, pp. 1–2

FOCUS & MOTIVATE

5-MINUTE WARM-UP

Making Inferences Have students answer these questions to understand the challenges that early European explorers faced.

1. Study the painting on page 43. How does the man appear to be finding his location?
2. How do the tools that navigators use today differ from those of early explorers?

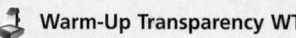

Warm-Up Transparency WT1A

INSTRUCT

INSTRUCT: OBJECTIVE 1

A Water Route to Asia

- In what way was the caravel an improvement over earlier ships?
- How did Dias's new route to Asia help Portugal?

In-Depth Resources: Unit 1
- Guided Reading, p. 5

RECOMMENDED RESOURCES

In-Depth Resources: Unit 1
- Guided Reading, p. 5
- Geog. Application, pp. 8–9
- Primary Source, p. 11
- Enrichment Activity, p. 18
- History Workshop, p. 19

America's History Makers
- Christopher Columbus, pp. 3–4

Reading Study Guide (Spanish and English), pp. 9–10

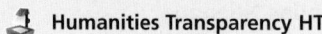

Why It Matters Now
- Cultural Diversity, pp. 1–2

Formal Assessment
- Section Quiz, p. 23

Integrated Assessment
- Rubrics, 2.1, 2.2

Access for Students Acquiring English/ESL, pp. 3, 5–6

INTEGRATED TECHNOLOGY

Humanities Transparency HT2
- Map of the American Southeast, 1606

Electronic Teacher Tools

classzone.com

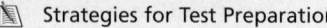

TEST-TAKING RESOURCES

Strategies for Test Preparation

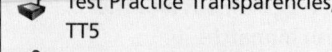

Test Practice Transparencies, TT5

Online Test Practice

AMERICA'S HISTORY MAKERS

Christopher Columbus

Today, historians argue about Columbus's character or judgment, but not his talent as a navigator. With few tools to help him cross an unknown sea, he relied upon dead reckoning, a navigation method used when few visible landmarks exist. Crossing the Atlantic, he measured latitude by the North Star. A quadrant, an instrument for measuring altitude, aided him in guessing his ship's position from the stars but only when seas were calm. He charted the ship's course with a compass, using a chart to estimate distances. A half-hour glass measured time. Estimating speed was guesswork.

Possible Responses: He showed courage, persistence, willingness to learn from others, and the ability to apply what he had learned to new situations. He was adventurous and interested in learning about the sea.

America's History Makers
- Christopher Columbus, pp. 3–4

AMERICA'S HISTORY MAKERS

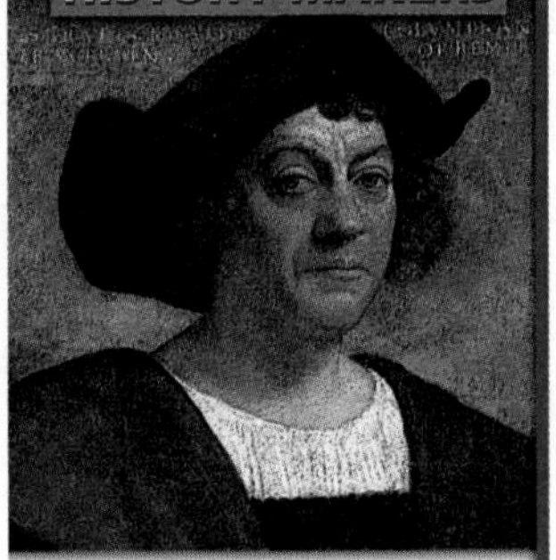

CHRISTOPHER COLUMBUS
1451–1506

Christopher Columbus's son Ferdinand wrote that his father "took to the sea at the age of 14 and followed it ever after."

Columbus's early voyages nearly cost him his life. When he was 25, pirates off the coast of Portugal sank his ship. Columbus survived by grabbing a floating oar and swimming to shore.

But he also learned a lot from sailing on Portuguese ships. The sailors taught Columbus about Atlantic wind patterns. This knowledge later helped him on his history-making voyage.

What character traits, shown in Columbus's early life, might have made him a good leader?

That route meant that the Portuguese could now trade with Asia without dealing with the Muslims or Italians. Portugal took control of the valuable spice trade. The merchants of Lisbon, Portugal's capital, grew rich. Spain and other European rivals wanted to take part in this profitable trade. They began to look for their own water routes to Asia.

Columbus's Plan ❷

By the time of da Gama's voyage, an Italian sailor named **Christopher Columbus** thought he knew a faster way to reach Asia. Europeans had known for centuries that the earth is round. Columbus decided that instead of sailing around Africa and then east, he would sail west across the Atlantic. He calculated that it would be a short journey.

But Columbus made several mistakes. First, he relied on the writings of two people—Marco Polo and a geographer named Paolo Toscanelli—who were wrong about the size of Asia. They claimed that Asia stretched farther from west to east than it really did.

Second, Columbus underestimated the distance around the globe. He thought the earth was only two thirds as large as it actually is! Because of Polo and Toscanelli, Columbus thought that Asia took up most of that distance. Therefore, he believed that the Atlantic Ocean must be small. And a voyage west to Asia would be short.

In 1483, Columbus asked the king of Portugal to finance a voyage across the Atlantic. The king's advisers opposed the plan. They argued that Columbus had miscalculated the distance to Asia. They also reminded the king of the progress that Portuguese explorers had made sailing down the coast of Africa looking for a route to Asia. The advisers persuaded the king not to finance the voyage. So in 1486, Columbus turned to Portugal's rival, Spain.

Help from Spain's Rulers

Spain's rulers, King Ferdinand and Queen Isabella, liked Columbus's plan because they wanted a share of the rich Asian trade. As a strong Catholic, the Queen also welcomed a chance to spread Christianity. But there were also reasons not to support Columbus. First, a royal council had doubts about Columbus's calculations and advised Ferdinand and Isabella not to finance him. Second, the Spanish monarchs were in the middle of a costly war to drive the Muslims out of Spain. Third, Columbus was asking a high payment for his services.

The years of waiting had made Columbus determined to profit from his explorations. As a reward for his efforts, he demanded the high title

Reading **History**

A. Comparing Compare what happened after Portugal began to control the spice trade to what happened when Italy controlled it.

A. Possible Answer In both cases, rival countries tried to find ways to end that control.

Vocabulary

monarch: a king or queen

INSTRUCT: OBJECTIVE ❷

Columbus's Plan/Help from Spain's Rulers

- What two mistakes made Columbus think that sailing west to Asia would be a short journey?
- Why did Ferdinand and Isabella support Columbus?

ACTIVITY OPTIONS

INTERDISCIPLINARY LINK: LANGUAGE ARTS

BLOCK SCHEDULING

WRITING A DIALOGUE

Class Time One class period

Task Creating a dialogue between Columbus and the Spanish monarchs

Purpose To analyze how Columbus might have attempted to persuade the rulers to back his explorations

Supplies Needed
- Reference materials on Columbus, Ferdinand, and Isabella

Activity Invite the language arts teacher to discuss techniques of persuasive writing with the class. Then as a pre-writing activity, ask students to list some arguments Columbus might have used to convince Spain's rulers to give him money. Next, let them list the possible responses the rulers might have given to each argument. Students can use these lists to help them write their dialogues. When dialogues are completed, have several volunteers read them aloud, taking the part of each speaker.

Admiral of the Ocean Sea and a percentage of any wealth he brought from Asia. He also expected to be made the ruler of the lands he found.

Finally in January of 1492, the Spanish conquered the last Muslim stronghold in Spain. The Spanish monarchs could now afford to finance Columbus but still had doubts about doing so. Columbus left the palace to return home. But after listening to a trusted adviser, the king and queen changed their minds and sent a rider on horseback to bring Columbus back. He and the rulers finally reached an agreement.

Reading **History**

B. Drawing Conclusions Did this agreement give Columbus what he was asking for? Explain.

B. Possible **Answer** Almost everything. It offers him rewards, the title he wanted, and the position of governor. There is no mention of a specific percentage of wealth.

A VOICE FROM THE PAST

Your Highnesses . . . accorded me great rewards and ennobled me so that from that time henceforth I might . . . be high admiral of the Ocean Sea and perpetual Governor of the islands and continent which I should discover.

Christopher Columbus, letter to King Ferdinand and Queen Isabella

Preparing to sail, Columbus assembled his ships—the *Niña,* the *Pinta,* and the *Santa María*—at the port of Palos de la Frontera in southern Spain.

Setting Sail ❸

At first, Columbus had trouble finding a crew. Then a respected local shipowner agreed to sign on as captain of the *Pinta.* Other crew members soon followed. About 90 men loaded the ships with enough food for one year, casks of fresh water, firewood, and other necessities.

Skillbuilder Answers

1. between 4,000 and 5,000
2. Dias was venturing into new territory, while da Gama had the knowledge acquired by Dias to guide him.

Exploration Leads to New Sea Routes, *1487–1504*

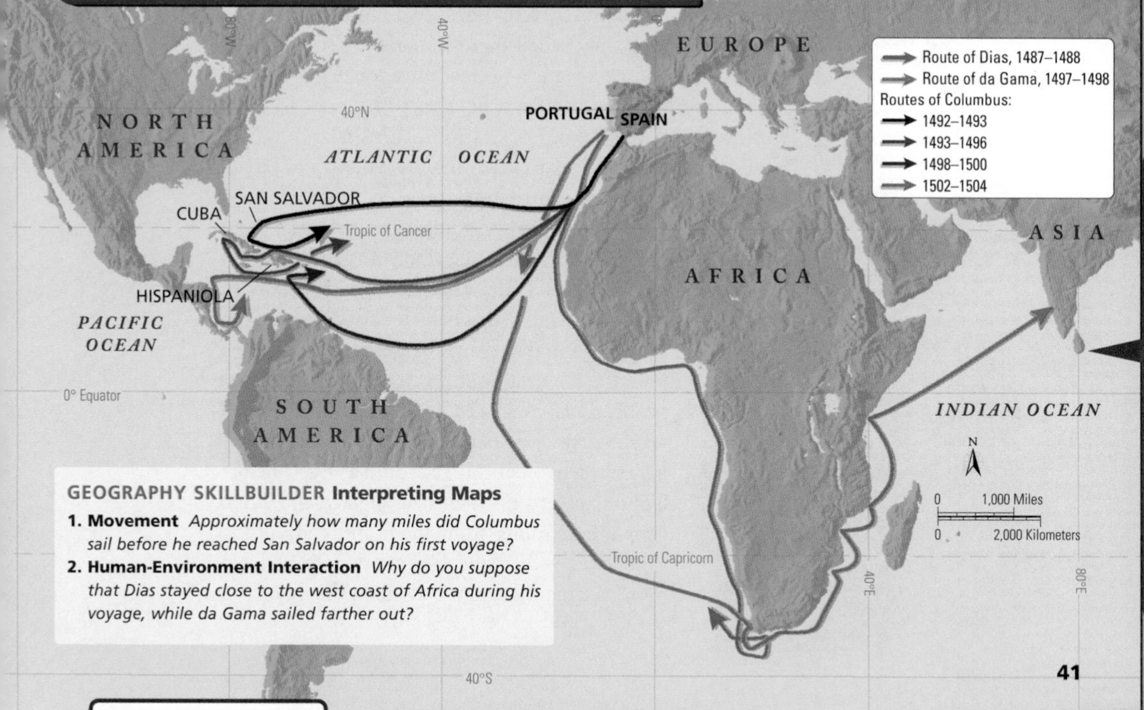

GEOGRAPHY SKILLBUILDER Interpreting Maps

1. **Movement** *Approximately how many miles did Columbus sail before he reached San Salvador on his first voyage?*
2. **Human-Environment Interaction** *Why do you suppose that Dias stayed close to the west coast of Africa during his voyage, while da Gama sailed farther out?*

41

CRITICAL THINKING ACTIVITY

Making Decisions The decision to finance Columbus's first voyage was a difficult one for Spain's rulers. The monarchs had to weigh the advice of their counselors and the possible risks to Spain's welfare. Use a decision tree to help students weigh costs and benefits.

Class Time 10 minutes

INSTRUCT: OBJECTIVE ❸

Setting Sail/Reaching the Americas

- What kinds of problems did the sailors on Columbus's ships face?
- What convinced Columbus that he had reached Asia?

In-Depth Resources: Unit 1

- Geography Application: Ocean Currents, pp. 8–9
- Primary Source: from *The Journal of Christopher Columbus,* p. 11

HISTORY FROM VISUALS

Reading the Map Ask the students to look at Columbus's four routes. Ask how the routes differ.

Possible Response Each route is slightly different. The later trips explore more areas of the West Indies. One trip goes to the land bridge connecting North and South America.

Extension Have the students research the Line of Demarcation (Treaty of Tordesillas) to understand why Portugal did not explore in the Western Hemisphere during this time.

Humanities Transparency HT2

- Map of the American Southeast, 1606

ACTIVITY OPTIONS

INDIVIDUAL NEEDS: GIFTED AND TALENTED

THE COLUMBUS CONTROVERSY

Class Time 30 minutes

Task Researching a historical controversy

Purpose To summarize the varying interpretations of Columbus as a pivotal figure in history

Supplies Needed

- Access to research sources at the library or on the Internet

Activity Have students research these topics: Should Columbus's arrival in the Americas be labeled a "discovery"? Should North and South America be called the "New World"? Excellent sources to begin this project are Marvin Lunenfeld, *1492: Discovery, Invasion, Encounter: Sources and Interpretations* (Houghton Mifflin, 1991) and Ronald Wright, *Stolen Continents: The "New World" Through Indian Eyes* (Houghton Mifflin, 1993).

In-Depth Resources: Unit 1

- Enrichment Activity, p. 18

MORE ABOUT . . .

The *Pinta*, the *Nina*, and the *Santa Maria*

By modern standards, the three ships that Columbus commanded on his first voyage were tiny indeed. The *Santa Maria* was the largest of the three; at about 100 feet in length, it carried 39 crew members. The *Pinta,* with a crew of 26, and the *Nina,* with 22, were even smaller—each about 70 feet long.

***Now and* then**

Native American View of Columbus

Harjo also had this to say about Columbus: "His story is very complex history in and of itself. Too often this history is posed as romantic myth and the uncomfortable facts . . . are eliminated. Explaining the unpleasant truths . . . does not take away from the fact that he was able to lurch over to these shores in three little boats. In fact, it gives the story of Columbus more dimension."

The tiny fleet of wooden ships glided out of the harbor on August 3, 1492. First they sailed southwest toward the Canary Islands off the northwest coast of Africa. From there, Columbus was relying on trade winds that blew toward the west to speed his ships across the ocean.

Once aboard ship, Columbus kept a log, or daily record of each day's sailing. In fact, he kept two logs. One he showed to his men and one he kept secret. Columbus's secret log recorded the truth about the journey.

A VOICE FROM THE PAST

[We] made 15 leagues [this] day and . . . [I] decided to report less than those actually traveled so in case the voyage were long the men would not be frightened and lose courage.

Christopher Columbus, quoted in *Columbus and the Age of Discovery*

By October 10, the men had lost both courage and confidence in their leader. They had been at sea for almost ten weeks and had not seen land for over a month. Afraid that they would starve if the trip went on longer, they talked of returning home. To avoid mutiny, Columbus and the crew struck a bargain. The men agreed to sail on for three more days, and Columbus promised to turn back if they had not sighted land by then. Two days later in the early morning hours of October 12, a sailor on the *Pinta* called out "Tierra, tierra" [Land, land].

Reading **History**

C. Analyzing Causes What caused Columbus to decide to keep two logs?

C. Possible Answer He was afraid his crew would be frightened if they knew the truth, so he kept a phony log to share with them.

Reaching the Americas

By noon, the ships had landed on an island in the Caribbean Sea. Columbus believed that he had reached the Indies, islands in Southeast Asia where spices grew. The islanders who greeted Columbus and his men were Taino (TY•noh) people, but Columbus mistakenly called them Indians.

Background

Today, the Indies are called the East Indies. The islands of the Caribbean are called the West Indies.

Columbus named the island San Salvador. After unfurling the royal banner and flags, he ordered his crew to "bear witness that I was taking possession of this island for the King and Queen." Eager to reach the rich country of Japan, which he believed was nearby, he left San Salvador. He took six or seven Taino with him as guides. For the next three months, he visited several of the Caribbean islands.

Finally, he reached an island that he named Española, which we call Hispaniola today. (See map on page 41.) On that island, Columbus and his men found some gold and precious objects such as pearls. This convinced Columbus that he had reached Asia. He decided to return home, leaving 39 of his men on Hispaniola. Even before Columbus left, his men had angered the Taino people by stealing from them and committing violence. By the time Columbus returned ten months later, the Taino had killed the men.

***Now and* then**

NATIVE AMERICAN VIEW OF COLUMBUS

In 1992, many Native Americans protested the 500th anniversary of Columbus's voyage. Suzan Shown Harjo, who is Cheyenne and Creek, explained why.

As Native American peoples in this red quarter of Mother Earth, we have no reason to celebrate an invasion that caused the demise [death] of so many of our people and is still causing destruction today.

The Spanish enslaved the Taino, who nearly all died from disease and bad treatment. This statue is one of the few Taino artifacts left from the 1500s.

ACTIVITY OPTIONS

MULTIPLE LEARNING STYLES: LINGUISTIC

BLOCK SCHEDULING

COLUMBUS'S LOG

Class Time One class period

Task Performing dramatic readings

Purpose To analyze Columbus's first voyage to the Americas from a reading of his log

Supplies Needed

- Selections from Columbus's log
- Audiotapes and tape recorder

Activity Instruct students to choose passages from Columbus's log that they find especially interesting and prepare short dramatic readings from the log. Each presentation can begin with two or three sentences telling at what part of the voyage these entries were made. Assign one student to be the sound engineer, who will tape students reading their selections; one student to write an introduction to the tape; and another to write a conclusion. After the class has listened to the tape, ask students how they think an account of this voyage from the perspective of a crew member might be different.

In January 1493, he sailed back to Spain. Firmly believing that he had found a new water route to Asia, he wrote to Ferdinand and Isabella. The Spanish rulers called him to the royal court to report on his voyage. Neither Columbus nor the king and queen suspected that he had landed near continents entirely unknown to Europeans.

A French map-maker uses an instrument to learn his exact position on the globe.

4 An Expanding Horizon

Columbus made three more voyages to the Americas, but never brought back the treasures he had promised Spain's rulers. He also failed to meet Queen Isabella's other goal. She wanted Christianity brought to new people. When she learned that Columbus had mistreated and enslaved the people of Hispaniola, she became angry.

After the fourth voyage, Spain's rulers refused to give Columbus any more help. He died in 1506, still believing he had reached Asia and bitter that he had not received the fame or fortune that he deserved.

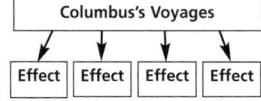

D. Possible Answer It was the body people crossed to get from one continent to the other.

In time, the geographic knowledge Columbus brought back changed European views of the world. People soon realized that Columbus had reached continents that had been unknown to them previously. And Europeans were eager to see if these continents could make them rich.

***Reading*History**
D. Making Inferences How did the Atlantic become a bridge connecting Europe, Africa, and the Americas?

For centuries, Europeans had seen the ocean as a barrier. With one voyage, Columbus changed that. Instead of a barrier, the Atlantic Ocean became a bridge that connected Europe, Africa, and the Americas. As you will learn in Chapter 2, Columbus's explorations began an era of great wealth and power for Spain. As Spain grew rich, England, France, and other European countries also began to send ships to the Americas.

Section 3 Assessment

1. Terms & Names

Explain the significance of:
- navigator
- caravel
- Christopher Columbus

2. Taking Notes

On a diagram like the one shown, list the effects of Columbus's voyages.

Columbus's Voyages			
Effect	Effect	Effect	Effect

Which effects were negative and which were positive?

3. Main Ideas

a. Why was Prince Henry eager to find an all-water route to Asia?

b. Why did Spain's king and queen decide to support Columbus's first voyage?

c. Why was Columbus disappointed by the outcome of his four voyages to the Americas?

4. Critical Thinking

Analyzing Points of View Explain how each of the following people might have viewed Columbus's first voyage. Give reasons for their points of view.

THINK ABOUT
- Columbus
- Queen Isabella
- a Taino chief

ACTIVITY OPTIONS

GEOGRAPHY
MATH

Use the map on page 41. Create an enlarged **map** of Columbus's first voyage, or measure the distance of each voyage to list on a **table.**

INSTRUCT: OBJECTIVE 4

An Expanding Horizon

- Were Columbus's voyages viewed as successful?
- How did Columbus's voyages change the way Europeans looked at the world?

ASSESS & RETEACH

Setting the Stage Tell students to review all sections on the chapter graphic organizer.

Formal Assessment
- Section Quiz, p. 23

Critical Thinking Transparency CT1
- Setting the Stage

RETEACHING ACTIVITY

Tell students to use the information in this section to create a time line of Columbus's life. As a summary, they can write a paragraph explaining how events in Columbus's life changed European history.

In-Depth Resources: Unit 1
- Reteaching Activity, p. 17

Section 3 Assessment

1. Terms & Names

navigator, p. 39
caravel, p. 39
Christopher Columbus, p. 40

2. Taking Notes

Effects: conflict with Taino; enslavement and death of Taino; failure to bring back treasures; Europeans realized Americas were a previously unknown land; Spanish colonization; further European explorations

Most students will cite the effect on the Taino as negative. Opinion about the other effects may vary.

3. Main Ideas

a. He wanted to find African gold, to learn more about geography, and to spread Christianity. **b.** They wanted a share of the Asian trade and to spread Christianity. **c.** The monarchs did not reward him as much as he thought he deserved.

4. Critical Thinking

Columbus continued to insist his voyages were a success. Isabella was disappointed that the native peoples were abused. The Taino chief wished that Columbus had never come.

ACTIVITY OPTIONS

Integrated Assessment
- Rubrics, 2.1, 2.2

TERMS & NAMES

1. **civilization,** p. 28
2. **Mound Builders,** p. 29
3. **technology,** p. 29
4. **Iroquois League,** p. 31
5. **Islam,** p. 34
6. **feudalism,** p. 35
7. **Crusades,** p. 36
8. **Renaissance,** p. 36
9. **navigator,** p. 39
10. **Christopher Columbus,** p. 40

REVIEW QUESTIONS

Possible Responses

1. that people crossed from Asia on the land bridge Beringia, which was created when the Ice Age caused ocean levels to drop, and that people came from many different places at many different times
2. as burial mounds and temples
3. They drained swamps and built irrigation canals, enabling them to grow a lot of food, and they conquered most of their neighbors and forced them to pay tribute.
4. Deganawida devised a plan for the Five Nations to be at peace and form an alliance, and Hiawatha persuaded the nations to join.
5. They were able to control and tax the profitable trade in gold and salt.
6. More. Ghana's rulers had Muslim advisers, Mali's rulers actually were Muslim, and many of Songhai's people were Muslim.
7. Lords divided their lands into manors, or large estates, which were farmed by serfs. In return for the serfs' work, the lords offered them protection.
8. The Italian ships that took Crusaders to the Middle East brought back Asian goods, which increased European desire for them.
9. because the Italians controlled the existing trade routes and would not allow others to share in the profitable trade
10. He based his calculations on incorrect sources and assumptions.

Chapter 1 ASSESSMENT

VISUAL SUMMARY

The World in 1500

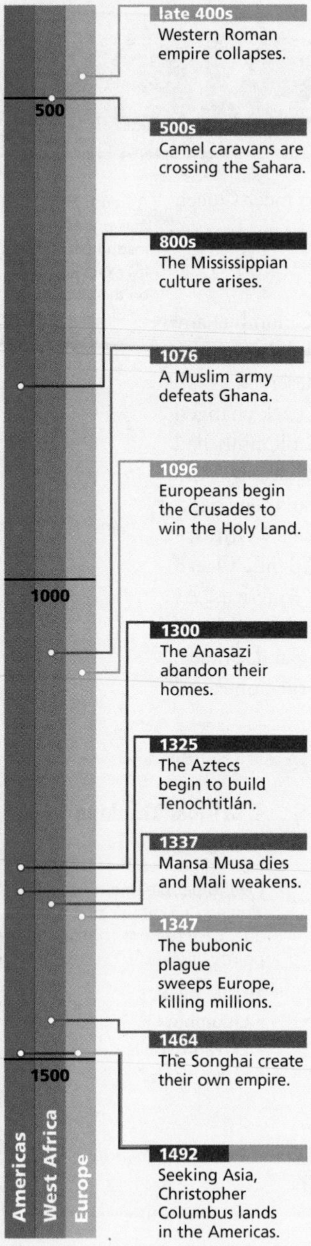

late 400s
Western Roman empire collapses.
500
500s
Camel caravans are crossing the Sahara.
800s
The Mississippian culture arises.
1076
A Muslim army defeats Ghana.
1096
Europeans begin the Crusades to win the Holy Land.
1000
1300
The Anasazi abandon their homes.
1325
The Aztecs begin to build Tenochtitlán.
1337
Mansa Musa dies and Mali weakens.
1347
The bubonic plague sweeps Europe, killing millions.
1464
The Songhai create their own empire.
1500
1492
Seeking Asia, Christopher Columbus lands in the Americas.
Americas
West Africa
Europe

TERMS & NAMES

Briefly explain the significance of each of the following.

1. civilization
2. Mound Builders
3. technology
4. Iroquois League
5. Islam
6. feudalism
7. Crusades
8. Renaissance
9. navigator
10. Christopher Columbus

REVIEW QUESTIONS

Societies of North America (pages 27–32)

1. What are two theories about migration to the Americas?
2. For what purposes did the Mound Builders construct earthen mounds?
3. What enabled the Aztecs to build a strong empire?
4. How did the Iroquois League come about?

Societies of West Africa and Europe (pages 33–38)

5. What enabled Ghana, Mali, and Songhai all to grow rich?
6. Did Islam become more or less influential in West Africa from the 700s to the 1400s? Explain.
7. How did the manor system work during the Middle Ages?
8. How did the Crusades increase European interest in trade?

Early European Explorers (pages 39–43)

9. Why did non-Italian Europeans seek new trade routes to Asia?
10. How did Columbus miscalculate the distance to Asia?

CRITICAL THINKING

1. USING YOUR NOTES

Using your completed chart, answer the questions below.

	Trade	Technology	Religion	Art
AMERICAS (Sections 1)				
WEST AFRICA (Section 2)				
EUROPE (Sections 2 and 3)				

a. What was one example of how trade spread knowledge?

b. Which of the technologies that you listed are still used today?

c. Which religions were practiced in each of the three regions?

2. ANALYZING LEADERSHIP

Do you think Columbus was a good leader or a bad one? Use details from the chapter to explain your answer.

3. THEME: DIVERSITY AND UNITY

How have Native Americans, Africans, and Europeans all influenced American culture? Give examples from your own experience.

4. MAKING GENERALIZATIONS

What types of goods are people most likely to seek through trade? Think about the trade goods mentioned in the chapter and why people wanted them.

5. APPLYING CITIZENSHIP SKILLS

Compare the Iroquois League to what you know of the U.S. government. How are they similar?

Interact *with* History

Think about the various encounters between societies mentioned in the chapter. What do you think happened when more Europeans came to the Americas and met Native Americans?

CRITICAL THINKING

Possible Responses

1. USING YOUR NOTES **a.** Trade in Mesoamerica spread knowledge of Olmec culture. **b.** irrigation, printing press **c.** America—Native American religions; Africa—African religions and Islam; Europe—Christianity
2. ANALYZING LEADERSHIP Encourage students to consider his actions in historical context.
3. THEME: DIVERSITY AND UNITY Students may cite examples such as food, art, music, religion, and dress.
4. MAKING GENERALIZATIONS People tend to seek items that are universally valued, such as gold, or items that will benefit their lives but cannot be found in their environment. Examples of this include West Africans seeking salt and Northwest Coast people seeking furs.
5. APPLYING CITIZENSHIP SKILLS In both, a leader can be voted out of office for wrongdoing.

Interact *with* History Most students will predict war and conflict, based on their own knowledge of history.

HISTORY SKILLS

1. INTERPRETING MAPS: HUMAN-ENVIRONMENT INTERACTION

Study the map. Answer the questions.

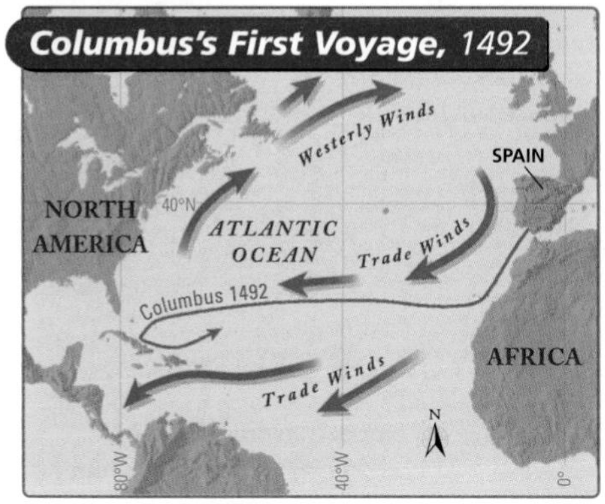

Basic Map Elements

a. What is the name of the winds blowing west across the Atlantic? blowing east?

b. In what direction did Columbus sail on his first journey from Europe?

Interpreting the Map

c. How did the winds affect Columbus's journey?

d. If Columbus's route had been farther north, would his voyage have taken more or less time? Explain.

2. INTERPRETING PRIMARY SOURCES

Drawn in 1570, this is the earliest map to show North America and South America as separate continents.

a. What are the names of any places that you recognize on this map?

b. Compare this map to the map of the world on page 41. Which continent on this map do you think looks more accurate? Explain why.

ALTERNATIVE ASSESSMENT

1. INTERDISCIPLINARY ACTIVITY: Literature

Retelling a Folk Tale Many North American Indian tales give insight into the relationship between Native Americans and their environment. Select a tale from a collection of Native American literature and retell the tale for the class.

2. COOPERATIVE LEARNING ACTIVITY

Creating a Sound Collage Columbus's log of his first voyage can be found in many public libraries. Have one or two members of your group select portions of the log for audiotaping. Other members of the group can decide on sound effects to be heard in the background. Consider using some of the following:

- sounds of the ocean or of storms
- shipboard sounds, such as bells, clanking chains, and flapping sails
- shouted commands to the crew
- seafaring songs or other music

You may want to use a sound effects tape, available in many libraries, or create your own sounds.

3. PRIMARY SOURCE EXPLORER

Choosing a Symbol Countries and alliances often use a symbol to represent who they are. The Iroquois League chose a tree. Think of a group you belong to and choose a symbol to represent it. Before you choose, use the CD-ROM, library, or Internet to find out more about why the Iroquois chose a tree.

- Think about what your group stands for. Write a list of adjectives to describe it.
- Brainstorm animals, plants, or objects that share those qualities. Choose one to be your symbol.
- Write an explanation of your symbol and why you chose it.

4. HISTORY PORTFOLIO

Review the questions that you wrote for What Do You Want to Know? on page 26. Then write a short report in which you explain the answers to your questions. If any questions were not answered, do research to answer them. Be sure to use standard grammar, spelling, sentence structure, and punctuation in your report. Add your report to your portfolio.

Additional Test Practice, pp. S1–S33

TEST PRACTICE CLASSZONE.COM

ALTERNATIVE ASSESSMENT

1. INTERDISCIPLINARY ACTIVITY: Literature

Folk tale presentations should

- have a clear introduction about the story.
- exhibit an understanding of basic concepts or ideas.
- have adequate delivery and establish rapport with the audience.

2. COOPERATIVE LEARNING ACTIVITY

Sound collages should

- clearly demonstrate an understanding of the concepts presented.
- present a concept visually.
- show technical proficiency.

3. PRIMARY SOURCE EXPLORER

Symbols should

- present a concept visually.
- clearly demonstrate an understanding of the concepts presented.
- exhibit creativity.
- demonstrate grade-level artistic skill.

4. HISTORY PORTFOLIO

Short reports should

- answer questions about the history of peoples in the Americas, West Africa, and Europe.
- use evidence to develop and support ideas.
- cite sources of information.
- use standard grammar, spelling, sentence structure, and punctuation.

Critical Thinking Transparency CT3

- Visual Summary

Formal Assessment

- Chapter Test, Forms A, B, and C, pp. 24–35

HISTORY SKILLS

Possible Responses

1. INTERPRETING MAPS

Basic Map Elements

a. the Trade Winds, the Westerly

b. southwest

Interpreting the Map

c. He used the Trade Winds, which probably made his journey faster.

d. It would have been longer, because he would not have had the wind at his back.

2. INTERPRETING PRIMARY SOURCES

a. North America, South America, Florida, Gulf of Mexico, Cuba, Atlantic Ocean, Hudson Bay

b. Students may choose either continent but should give reasons for their choice.

HISTORY WORKSHOP

OBJECTIVE
Students create and decode pictographs, analyzing how the Native Americans of the Southwest used such symbols to communicate.

BLOCK SCHEDULING

PROCEDURE

Have students assemble the materials listed in the "Toolbox." Divide the class into groups of four or five. Then review the steps for choosing a message to communicate, researching and making a pictograph, and exchanging the pictograph with another pair of students.

In-Depth Resources: Unit 1
- History Workshop Resources, p. 19

HISTORY FROM VISUALS

Interpreting the Petroglyph Ask students who or what the largest image in this petroglyph might represent and what it might be holding. **Possible Responses** The figure could be a chief, a hunter/warrior, or a god. In its hands the figure may be holding a shield and some type of weapon used in hunting; or these objects might have religious significance, with the item in the right hand perhaps representing the sun.

HISTORY **WORKSHOP**

Create and Decode a Pictograph

Native Americans of the Southwest created thousands of images to communicate with each other. These images, known as pictographs, helped people recall certain events, ideas, or information. Even if the people who created them were no longer present, others could read the messages. Most images were painted or carved on the surfaces of rock. There are three types of pictographs: petroglyphs, petrograms, and geoglyphs. (See HELP DESK on the next page.)

ACTIVITY Create a pictograph that other students will decode, or figure out. Then, acting as an anthropologist, interview students in one other group about their pictograph.

TOOLBOX

Each group will need:

- drawing paper or poster board
- markers
- regular and colored pencils
- watercolor paints and brushes (optional)
- an envelope

The Fremont culture carved this petroglyph. It is currently located in Dinosaur National Monument—most of which sits in northwestern Colorado.

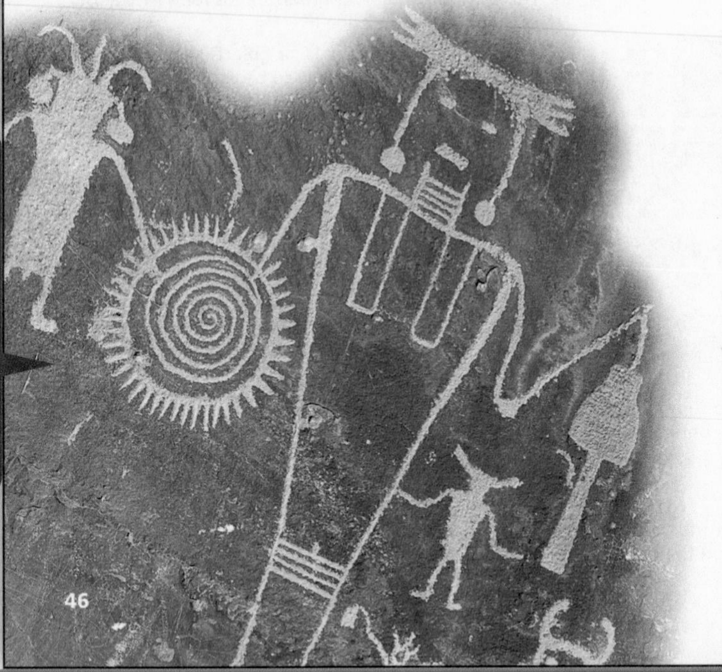

STEP BY STEP

1 Form a group of 4 or 5 students. Together, think of a message to tell someone living in the future. What might you want future generations to know about your culture, or way of life? If you're having trouble coming up with a message, copy the chart below into your notebook. Write information for each category that you think would be interesting to future generations. Then choose one of these categories for your message.

Sports	
Politics	
Fashion	
Music	
Entertainment	
Weather	
Daily Life	

2 Examine reference materials. In the library or on the Internet, research Native American pictographs. Use the information you find to help start your project. (See HELP DESK on the next page.)

46

RECOMMENDED RESOURCES

BOOKS FOR THE TEACHER

Patterson-Rudolph, Carol. ***On the Trail of the Spider Woman: Petroglyphs, Pictographs and Myths of the Southwest.*** Santa Fe, NM: Ancient City Press, 1997.

Muench, David, and Polly Schaafsma. ***Images in Stone: Southwest Rock Art.*** San Francisco, CA: BrownTrout Publishing, 1995.

VIDEO

The Ancestors. Warner Home Video, 1994. This video is part of the series *500 Nations,* which chronicles the history of Native Americans using period art, interviews with contemporary Native Americans, and computer re-creations. This video focuses on the prehistory of the Americas.

BOOKS FOR THE STUDENTS

Hucko, Bruce. ***Art on the Rocks.*** San Francisco, CA: Sierra Club Books, 1998.

Kopper, Philip. ***The Smithsonian Book of North American Indians: Before the Coming of the Europeans.*** Washington, D.C.: Smithsonian Books, 1997.

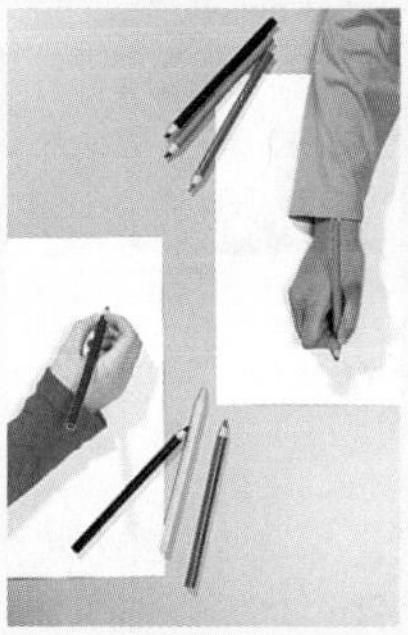

3 Create your pictograph. Communicate your message with symbols like the ones that you have researched. Sketch your pictograph on the drawing paper or poster board with a pencil first. Make the pictograph simple so that the decoders will understand your message. Remember to use symbols—not letters.

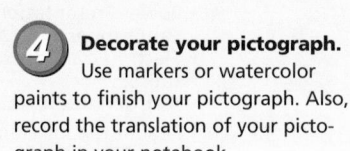

4 Decorate your pictograph. Use markers or watercolor paints to finish your pictograph. Also, record the translation of your pictograph in your notebook.

5 Exchange your pictograph with another group of students. Try to decode the message in the pictograph that the other group of students has given you. Write your translation and place it in your envelope. Give the envelope to the group whose pictograph you decoded.

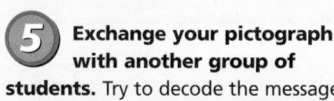

6 Compare the other students' translation with your actual message. Did the other students understand your message? Let them know how accurate they were.

WRITE AND SPEAK

Using the information in the pictograph that you decoded, write a description of the people who created the message. Use the symbols as well as the message itself to help you in your description. Explain to the class how you came to your conclusions.

HELP DESK

For related information see Chapter 1, p. 28.

Researching Your Project

- *On the Trail of Spider Woman: Petroglyphs, Pictographs, and Myths of the Southwest* by Carol Patterson-Rudolph. Shows variety of actual pictographs.
- *21 Kinds of American Folk Art and How to Make Each One* by Jean and Cle Kinney. Explains process of making pictographs.

For more about pictographs . . .

RESEARCH LINKS
CLASSZONE.COM

Did You Know?

Petroglyphs are images carved into a rock using stone tools. **Petrograms** are images painted on a rock. **Geoglyphs** are images formed on the ground by scraping away soil or by arranging stones to form an image.

REFLECT & ASSESS

- Which symbols in your pictograph were clear to the decoders? Which were not clear?
- What methods did you use to decode the messages of others?
- What did you learn about language and communication from doing this pictograph decoding activity?

MORE ABOUT . . .

Ancient Pictographs

Some of the first people to use pictographs, or picture writing, were the ancient Egyptians. They carved or painted them on tombs and monuments. In the Americas, the Aztecs developed two different kinds of pictographs. One type stood for ideas. The other stood for the sounds of syllables. The Aztecs used their pictographs mainly for tax lists, business records, and historical and religious writings.

MORE ABOUT . . .

Modern Pictographs

Today pictographs are making a comeback as icons on computer screens, automobile dashboards, and all sorts of electronic equipment. Ask students to suggest reasons for the proliferation of icons as replacements for words. What problems does the use of icons solve? What problems does it create?

Icons also appear in the form of logos for companies that make cosmetics, tennis shoes, CDs, soap, clothing, and many other products. Ask students to walk through a shopping mall, noticing the modern-day "pictographs" that advertisers use to attract consumers.

REFLECT & ASSESS

1. Ask students why certain symbols were difficult to decode. Creators might work with the decoders to design alternate symbols that everyone agrees are clearer.
2. Students may want to review mentally the sequence of steps they used to decode their message and then write these steps down.
3. Have students identify the strengths and limitations of this form of communication. Students might compare this form of communication to a writing system based on an alphabet.

STANDARDS FOR EVALUATION

HISTORY WORKSHOP

Pictographs should

- contain a message about some aspect of American culture today.
- be based on knowledge of the design and functions of real pictographs.
- use only symbols, not letters.
- be simple, clear, and readable.

WRITE AND SPEAK

Descriptions should

- clearly depict an aspect of the way of life of the people who wrote the message.
- use the symbols on the pictograph to link the message to the way of life of the people who wrote it.
- logically explain how the pictograph symbols led to the conclusions drawn.

CHAPTER 2 PLANNING GUIDE

European Exploration of the Americas 1492–1700

	CHAPTER OVERVIEW	COPYMASTERS	INTEGRATED TECHNOLOGY
CHAPTER RESOURCES	The chapter discusses the competition among European countries for control of the Americas from 1492 to 1700. It also describes the conquest of many Native American groups, the culture of Spanish colonies, and the origins of slavery in the Americas.	**In-Depth Resources: Unit 1** • Tracing Themes: Immigration and Migration, p. 21 • Building Vocabulary, p. 25 **Interdisciplinary Projects,** pp. 7–12	• eEdition Plus Online • EasyPlanner Plus Online • eTest Plus Online • eEdition • Power Presentations • EasyPlanner • Electronic Library of Primary Sources • Test Generator • Reading Study Guide • America's Music
	KEY IDEAS		
SECTION 1 **Spain Claims an Empire** **pp. 51–54**	• Spain and Portugal argue over the Line of Demarcation. • Following mercantile theory, Europe gains wealth through its colonies. • Spain sends conquistadors to conquer the Aztecs and the Incas.	**In-Depth Resources: Unit 1** • Setting the Stage, p. 20 • Guided Reading, p. 22 • Skillbuilder Practice, p. 26 • Literature Selection, pp. 31–33 • Reteaching Activity, p. 34 **Economics in History,** p. 2 **America's History Makers,** pp. 5–10 **Outline Map Activities,** pp. 3–4	**Warm-Up Transparency WT2** **Humanities Transparency HT3** • Portuguese Ship of Discovery **Geography Transparency GT2** • Cortés Marches to Tenochtitlán **Critical Thinking Transparency CT4** • Setting the Stage classzone.com
SECTION 2 **European Competition in North America** **pp. 55–58**	• France and England seek out their own claims to North America. • Spain and England clash, and England defeats the Spanish Armada. • France and the Netherlands seek wealth through the fur trade.	**In-Depth Resources: Unit 1** • Setting the Stage, p. 20 • Guided Reading, p. 23 • Reteaching Activity, p. 35 **Why It Matters Now** • The Space Race, pp. 3–4	**Warm-Up Transparency WT2** **Humanities Transparency HT4** • St. Augustine **Critical Thinking Transparency CT4** • Setting the Stage classzone.com
SECTION 3 **The Impact of Colonization** **pp. 59–63**	• Spain sets up viceroyalties to govern its colonies. • The Church and plantations are central features of Spanish colonial society. • Slavery arises in the colonies with the increasing demand for workers. • The Columbian Exchange takes plants and animals to new regions of the world.	**In-Depth Resources: Unit 1** • Setting the Stage, p. 20 • Guided Reading, p. 24 • Primary Source, pp. 29–30 • Geography Application: Spain's American Empire Expands, pp. 27–28 • Reteaching Activity, p. 36	**Warm-Up Transparency WT2** **Critical Thinking Transparency CT4** • Setting the Stage **Critical Thinking Transparency CT5** • The Columbian Exchange **Critical Thinking Transparency CT6** • Visual Summary classzone.com

Pupil's Edition
Copyman

Copymaster

Overhead Transparency

Audio Library

CD-ROM

Internet

ASSESSMENT OPTIONS

Chapter Assessment, pp. 64–65

Formal Assessment
- Chapter Tests, Forms A, B, and C, pp. 39–50

Test Generator

Online Test Practice

Strategies for Test Preparation

Section Assessment, p. 54

Formal Assessment, Quiz, p. 36

Integrated Assessment Book
- Rubrics, 1.10, 4.5

Test Generator

Test Practice Transparencies, TT6

Section Assessment, p. 58

Formal Assessment, Quiz, p. 37

Integrated Assessment Book
- Rubrics, 4.8, 5.1

Test Generator

Test Practice Transparencies, TT7

Section Assessment, p. 63

Formal Assessment, Quiz, p. 38

Integrated Assessment Book
- Rubrics, 1.3, 2.3

Test Generator

Test Practice Transparencies, TT8–TT9

CUSTOMIZING FOR INDIVIDUAL NEEDS

Students Acquiring English/ESL

Reading Study Guide (English and Spanish), pp. 13–20

Access for Students Acquiring English/ESL: Spanish Translations, pp. 7–12

Chapter Summaries on CD (English and Spanish)

Modified Lesson Plans for English Learners

Less Proficient Readers

Reading Study Guide (English and Spanish), pp. 13–20

Chapter Summaries on CD (English and Spanish)

Gifted and Talented Students

In-Depth Resources: Unit 1
- Enrichment Activity, p. 37

America's History Makers
- Amerigo Vespucci, pp. 5–6
- Hernando Cortés, pp. 7–8
- Cabeza de Vaca, pp. 9–10

CROSS-CURRICULAR CONNECTIONS

Geography

Facts on File, Inc. ***Ancient America***. New York: Facts on File, 1990. Cultural atlas.

Science/Math

DK Publishing. ***The Visual Dictionary of Ships and Sailing***. New York: DK Publishing, 1991. Detailed illustrations and cutaway diagrams.

Primary Sources

Lester, Julius. ***To Be a Slave***. New York: Dial, 1968. Easy-to-read primary source accounts assembled by noted scholar.

Interdisciplinary Projects, pp. 7–12
- Math: Calculating the Value of Wampum
- Science: Gathering and Analyzing Disease Statistics
- Language Arts: Explorers' Logs
- Art: Mexican Pyramids

Language Arts/Literature

Brown, Virginia. ***Cochula's Journey.*** Mobile: Black Belt Press, 1996. De Soto's expedition through the eyes of the 16-year-old daughter of an Alabama chief.

Fox, Paula. ***The Slave Dancer.*** New York: Bantam Doubleday Dell, 1988. Powerful story of a boy who is kidnapped and forced to play music on the deck of a slave ship.

McDougal Littell Literature Connections

Elizabeth Borton De Treviño

I, Juan de Pareja

Born a black slave in Seville, Spain, in the 1600s, Juan goes through many hardships before finding friendship and an outlet for his talents with the great painter Velázquez.

ENRICHMENT ACTIVITIES

Pupil's Edition, pp. 48–65
Interact with History, p. 49
Economics in History, p. 52

In-Depth Resources: Unit 1
- Geography Application: Spain's American Empire Expands, pp. 27–28
- Primary Source: Protesting the Mistreatment of Native Americans, p. 29
- Primary Source: from *The Interesting Narrative of the Life of Olaudah Equiano*, p. 30
- Literature Selection, pp. 31–33

America's History Makers
- Amerigo Vespucci, pp. 5–6
- Hernando Cortés, pp. 7–8
- Cabeza de Vaca, pp. 9–10

America's Music CD

Outline Map Activities
- Spain Explores the Americas, 1500s, pp. 3–4

Why It Matters Now
- Space Exploration, pp. 3–4

BLOCK SCHEDULING — LESSON PLAN OPTIONS (90-MINUTE PERIOD)

DAY 1

Interact with History, p. 49
Class Time 20 minutes

Options for pacing and variety:

- **Role-Playing** Divide students into pairs, with one student taking the part of a person eager to join an expedition and the other of a parent, sibling, or friend trying to discourage him or her from going. Have them discuss the "What Do You Think?" questions. **Class Time** 10 minutes

Setting the Stage, p. 50
Class Time 20 minutes

Options for pacing and variety:

- **Time Saver** Assign the "What Do You Know?" and "What Do You Want to Know?" questions as homework so that students can get a head start on preparing to read the chapter. **Class Time** 5 minutes

Section 1, pp. 51–54
Class Time 50 minutes

Options for pacing and variety:

- **Peer Teaching** Have students work in pairs to answer the Connect to History and Connect to Today questions in the Economics in History feature. **Class Time** 20 minutes
- **Internet** Extend students' knowledge of the *conquistadors* by having them visit classzone.com. **Class Time** 20 minutes

DAY 2

Section 2, pp. 55–58
Class Time 25 minutes

Options for pacing and variety:

- **Peer Teaching** Have students work in pairs to complete the song composition activity in the Activity Options in the Section 2 Assessment. **Class Time** 25 minutes

Section 3, pp. 59–63
Class Time 25 minutes

Options for pacing and variety:

- **Peer Teaching** Have students work in small groups to create the collage in the Activity Options in the Section 3 Assessment. **Class Time** 25 minutes
- **Peer Evaluation** Have student pairs fill in the diagram in the Section 3 assessment. After they complete it, have them swap diagrams with another pair. Have the pairs provide suggestions and comments about the diagrams to each other. **Class Time** 25 minutes

Chapter 2 Assessment, pp. 64–65
Class Time 40 minutes

Options for pacing and variety:

- **Peer Evaluation** Have student pairs work out the answers to the Critical Thinking Questions, p. 64. Then have them exchange papers with another team to evaluate their answers. **Class Time** 20 minutes
- **Peer Teaching** Divide the class into four groups. Assign each group one section of the Review Questions to complete. **Class Time** 20 minutes

TEACHER-TESTED ACTIVITY **Jim Sorenson, Chippewa Middle School, Des Plaines, Illinois**

EXPEDITION PREPARATION

Class Time Two class periods for preparation and one for presentation

Task Planning an expedition to the Americas and creating a poster illustrating these plans

Purpose To understand the complexities and dangers of undertaking an expedition to the Americas in the 1500s–1600s

Supplies Needed

- Reference books and internet sources about explorers to the Americas
- Posterboard
- Construction paper
- Colored pencils or markers

Activity Divide students into small groups. Ask each team to select an explorer discussed in Chapter 2 and make plans for an expedition led by that explorer. Each team member can consider one of these topics: skills needed by the crew for the expedition, equipment, food, water, clothing, money to finance the expedition. Teams must plan supplies and crew, based on an actual journey to the Americas made by their explorer. Have each group create a poster showing a picture of their explorer, a map of his expedition, and the supplies they should take for each category from equipment to clothing.

INTERNET-BASED (ELECTRONIC) ACTIVITY

Using transparent overlays to compare maps can be a good way to show relationships among simultaneous events that occur in different regions. Maps from the Internet or files scanned into a graphics program can be enhanced by color-coding regions or routes traveled. Enhanced maps can then be presented in a slide-show format, using presentation software. Maps can also be created in a low-tech manner, using clear transparencies and an overhead projector.

ACTIVITY OUTLINE

Objective Creating color-coded electronic maps on European exploration can help students learn about exploration and gain experience with presentation software.

Task Students will create color-coded maps of European exploration and develop a presentation based on those maps.

Class Time One class period

DIRECTIONS

1. Explain to students that they will be creating maps to show routes followed by the European explorers who reached the Americas between 1492 and 1700. They will need to carefully review the text and perhaps find additional resources for information.

2. Divide students into several small groups. If possible, have each group research the explorers from one European nation. Students should research both routes and settlements that resulted from those explorations. With greater computer access, groups can be further broken down to research individual explorers:
   a) England (color-coded blue): Hudson, Drake
   b) France (color-coded green): Cartier, Champlain
   c) Spain (color-coded yellow): Cortés, Coronado, Cabral, De Soto, Balboa, Ponce de Leon, Pizarro, Cabeza de Vaca and Estevanico (African)
   d) Portugal: (color-coded red): Cabrillo, Magellan
   e) The Netherlands (color-coded brown): Hudson
   f) Italy: (color-coded purple): Columbus, Verrazzano, Cabot

3. Each group should review Chapter 2 of *Creating America* to determine the routes of the explorers. Instruct students to note each explorer's nationality as well as the country funding the exploration. Students may need to consult other sources for additional information, such as books available in the school or public library.

4. To create color-coded routes, students should import a blank world map into a graphics program, or print the map onto a transparency. Then they can use their assigned color to highlight the explorers' routes and major areas of exploration. The blank maps can be found on classzone.com.

5. Students should then mark on a large time line the significant events for their exploration in the color they were assigned. The time line can be created using a graphics or word processing program, or manually on a long roll of paper. Divide the time line into 50-year increments.

6. Collect the maps and time lines. Work with a group of student volunteers to create an electronic or manual overlay of all the maps or an electronic slide-show, using an LCD projector or overhead projector. Have students study the overlays. Then ask students what people can learn by looking at the maps overlaid or shown in sequence that they could not learn from the individual maps. Also, ask what the maps demonstrate about the competition among European powers for territory in the Americas.

CHAPTER 2 OBJECTIVE

The student will identify the leading European explorers of North America, explain the effects of European colonization on Native Americans, and describe the origins and development of slavery in the colonies.

HISTORY FROM VISUALS

Interpreting the Illustration The 1592 engraving that opens the chapter shows the harbor of Lisbon, Portugal. Ask students to look at the city that the sailors are leaving. What can students observe about Lisbon at this time? **Possible Responses** The number of ships and piles of casks suggest busy trade. The city is walled, built of stone and brick, with church towers and large, solid buildings. The men are elaborately dressed in woven materials. One man carries a sword.

Extension Ask students to find out about the city of Lisbon in the late 1500s. What factors helped Lisbon become such an active trading center? With what parts of the world did Lisbon trade? What did the city's merchants trade for?

CRITICAL THINKING ACTIVITY

Making Inferences Present the following scenario: Scientists have discovered a new planet capable of sustaining human life and on which other life forms exist. Ask students to think of reasons why people might want to make the long, dangerous trip to explore the planet. Ask students what a nation might gain by exploring a new planet. Do students think potential explorers should consider possible harm that explorers might bring to the new planet?

Class Time 20 minutes

CHAPTER 2

European Exploration of the Americas
1492–1700

Section 1 **Spain Claims an Empire**
Section 2 **European Competition in North America**
Section 3 **The Impact of Colonization**

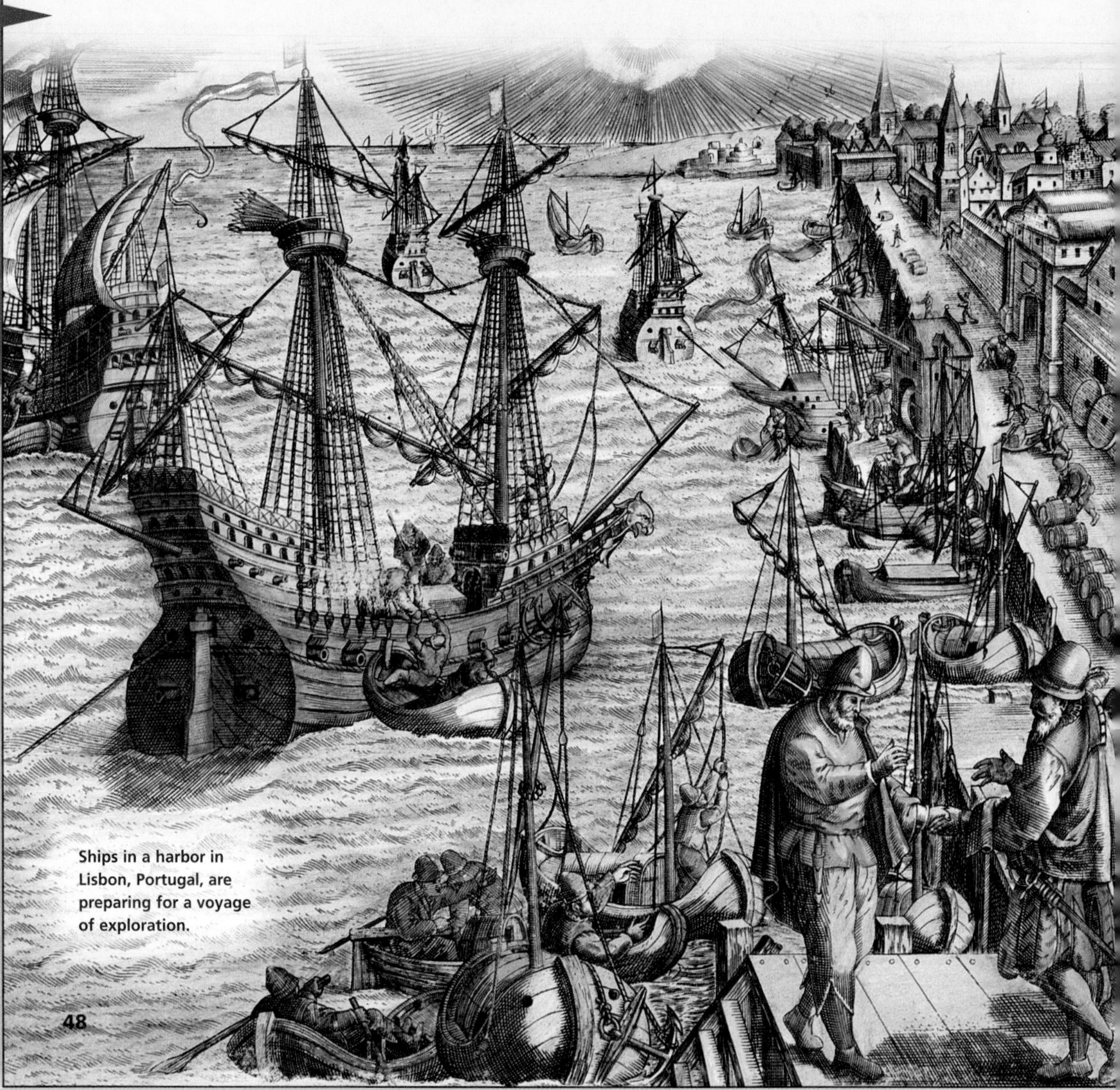

Ships in a harbor in Lisbon, Portugal, are preparing for a voyage of exploration.

48

RECOMMENDED RESOURCES

BOOKS FOR THE TEACHER

Bontemps, Arna. ***Great Slave Narratives.*** New York: Beacon Press, 1969. Classic compilation of first-hand material on slavery.

De la Vega, Garcilaso. ***Royal Commentaries of the Incas and General History of Peru.*** Tr. Harold W. Livermore. Austin: U. of Texas Press, 1987. Primary source written between 1609 and 1617.

Morison, Samuel Eliot. ***The European Discovery of America.*** New York: Oxford University Press, 1971–1974. Lively and readable, though sometimes controversial, history by a U.S. admiral.

VIDEO

America, Episode 1: The New Found Land. Midwest Tape. Part 1 of well-made series by Ken Burns.

INTERNET

For more about the slave narratives or the LaSalle shipwreck, visit . . .

classzone.com

Interact *with* History

Vasco Núñez de Balboa led expeditions to explore the Americas for Spain.
Balboa claimed the Pacific Ocean for Spain.
Balboa crossed Panama to reach the Pacific Ocean.

The year is 1510. You live in a European port town and have heard exciting tales about mysterious lands across the sea. You decide to join a voyage of exploration in search of fortune.

What Do You Think?

- What do you think led people like Balboa to explore distant lands?
- What reasons would make you want to join a voyage of exploration?
- What reasons would keep you from joining such a voyage?

Would you join a voyage of exploration?

N. America

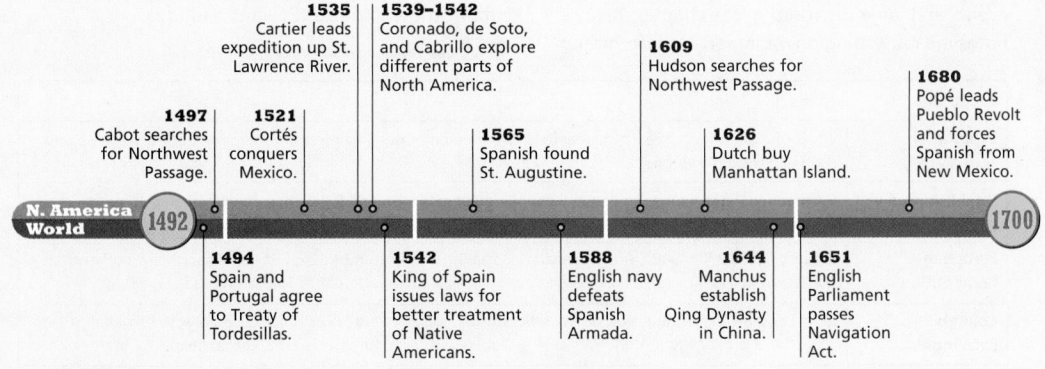

- **1497** Cabot searches for Northwest Passage.
- **1521** Cortés conquers Mexico.
- **1535** Cartier leads expedition up St. Lawrence River.
- **1539–1542** Coronado, de Soto, and Cabrillo explore different parts of North America.
- **1565** Spanish found St. Augustine.
- **1609** Hudson searches for Northwest Passage.
- **1626** Dutch buy Manhattan Island.
- **1680** Popé leads Pueblo Revolt and forces Spanish from New Mexico.

1492 — **1700**

World

- **1494** Spain and Portugal agree to Treaty of Tordesillas.
- **1542** King of Spain issues laws for better treatment of Native Americans.
- **1588** English navy defeats Spanish Armada.
- **1644** Manchus establish Qing Dynasty in China.
- **1651** English Parliament passes Navigation Act.

Interact *with* History

OBJECTIVES

- To identify European motives for exploring the Americas
- To pose and answer questions about the challenges of exploration

What Do You Think?

1. What characteristics might explorers need to be successful?
2. Have students suggest what can be gained from learning about new places.
3. Ask students to consider the effects on family members and friends who would be left behind if they went on a long and possibly dangerous trip.

Would you join a voyage of exploration?

Suggest that students weigh the possible dangers and rewards of a voyage of exploration.

MAKING PERSONAL CONNECTIONS

Ask students whether they or people they know have ever taken a long trip to a place they had never visited before. Why did they go? What kinds of questions and expectations did they have as they prepared for the trip?

TIME LINE DISCUSSION

Remind students that "in 1492, Columbus sailed the ocean blue." Point out how quickly other explorers followed him to the Americas. By 1700, European nations claimed much of North and South America.

- Ask students to identify the first major European conquest in the Americas. How many years after Columbus's voyage did that conquest take place? **Answer** Spanish under Cortés conquered Mexico by 1521, only 29 years after Columbus's voyage.
- Ask students to identify the year in which the English navy defeated the Spanish Armada. **Answer** 1588
- Why might the defeat of the Spanish Armada be important to European exploration?

Answer It may have reduced Spain's ability to explore and hold other lands.

BEFORE YOU READ

Previewing the Theme: Immigration and Migration

Ask students to speculate about why Europeans and others went to the Americas.

Europeans came to the Americas for a variety of reasons. Some came for religious reasons or for economic opportunities. However, Africans were brought to the Americas by force and served as slaves. Many Native Americans who survived the conquest by Europeans also became slaves. Their civilizations and cultures were either destroyed or greatly altered.

What Do You Know?

Tell students that by the mid-1400s, strong rulers in Spain and in England had gained much power. Competition among these rulers and others encouraged their efforts to explore and claim new territories.

In-Depth Resources: Unit 1
- Tracing Themes: Immigration and Migration, p. 21

READ AND TAKE NOTES

Reading Strategy: Taking Notes

Tell students that taking notes as they read will help them focus on main ideas and supporting details. Point out that recording notes in a chart will help them organize information in a format that is easy to reference. Remind students to note only the most important details and to take notes in a sequential order.

In-Depth Resources: Unit 1
- Setting the Stage, p. 20

Critical Thinking Transparency CT4
- Setting the Stage

Chapter 2 SETTING THE STAGE

BEFORE YOU READ

Previewing the Theme

Immigration and Migration From the 15th century to the 18th century, millions of people came to the Americas from other continents. Chapter 2 discusses why people came to the Americas and the effect that these migrations had on the people who already lived there.

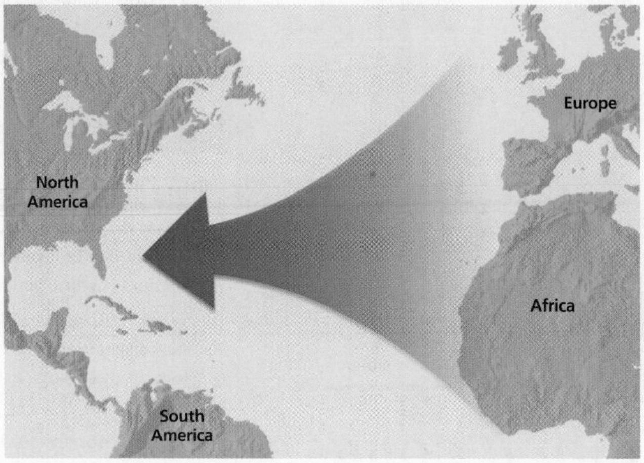

What Do You Know?

What comes to mind when someone uses the word *explorer*? Why do you think people explored different territories?

THINK ABOUT
- what you've learned about explorers from movies, school, or your parents
- reasons that people travel throughout the world today

What Do You Want to Know?

What questions do you have about exploration or the early colonization of the Americas? Write those questions in your notebook before you read the chapter.

READ AND TAKE NOTES

Reading Strategy: Taking Notes To help you remember what you read, take notes about the events and ideas discussed in the chapter. Taking notes means writing down important information.

The chart below lists the major events and ideas covered in the chapter. Use the chart to take notes about these important events and ideas.

See Skillbuilder Handbook, page R3.

Event/Idea	Notes
Exploration	Goals of exploration: spread Christianity, expand empires, gain riches. Spanish explore Central America and southern North America.
Establishing Colonies	Reasons for Spanish success: disease, weapons, alliances with some Native Americans. Life in colonies is organized around *encomiendas, haciendas,* and missions.
European Competition	Treaty of Tordesillas (1494) sets boundary for Spanish and Portuguese exploration. Spanish attack French at Fort Caroline (1564). English sea dogs attack Spanish shipping. Defeat of Spanish Armada (1588).
Columbian Exchange	Items brought to the Americas: diseases, livestock, grains, onions, citrus fruits, olives, grapes, bananas, sugar cane. Items brought to Eastern Hemisphere: tobacco, squash, turkey, peppers, cocoa, peanuts, potatoes, corn.
Origins of Slavery	Modern slavery was established in the Americas to provide labor in mines and plantations. Slave trade grew quickly between Africa and the Americas.

TEACHING STRATEGY

READING THE CHAPTER

This is a thematic chapter focusing on European exploration and conquest, European contact with Native Americans, and the origins of slavery. Encourage students to pause after reading each section to identify the main idea and supporting details of the material before continuing to the next section.

ALTERNATIVE ASSESSMENT

The Chapter Assessment describes three activities for alternative assessment on page 65. You may wish to have students work on these activities during the course of the chapter and then present them at the end.

1 Spain Claims an Empire

TERMS & NAMES
Treaty of Tordesillas
mercantilism
conquistador
Hernando Cortés
Montezuma
Francisco Pizarro

MAIN IDEA
Spain claimed a large empire in the Americas.

WHY IT MATTERS NOW
The influence of Spanish culture remains strong in modern America.

ONE EUROPEAN'S STORY

Pope Alexander VI had an important decision to make. In 1493, the rulers of Spain and Portugal wanted him to decide who would control the lands that European sailors were exploring. Ferdinand and Isabella of Spain expected Alexander VI to give Spain the rights over many of these lands. But King John II of Portugal claimed territories, too. What would the new pope do?

In May 1493, the pope issued his ruling. He drew an imaginary line around the world. It was called the Line of Demarcation. Portugal could claim all non-Christian lands to the east of the line. Spain could claim the non-Christian lands to the west. In this section, you will learn how Spain and Portugal led Europe in the race to gain colonies in the Americas.

Pope Alexander VI

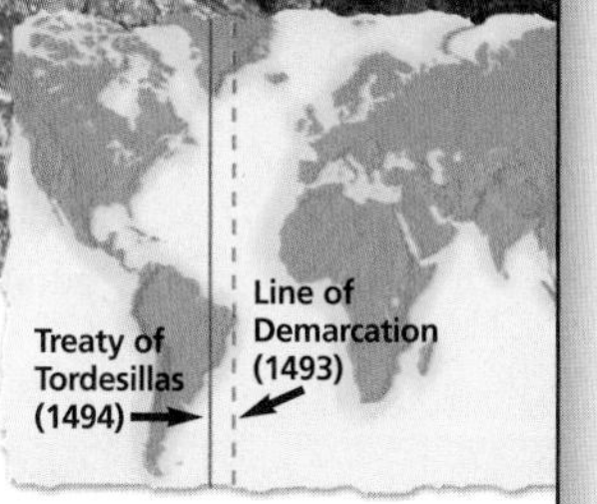

1 Spain and Portugal Compete

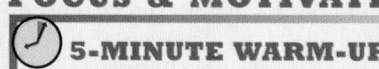

King John II was unhappy with the pope's placement of the line. He believed that it favored Spain. So he demanded that the Spanish rulers meet with him to change the pope's decision. In June 1494, the two countries agreed to the **Treaty of Tordesillas** (tawr•day•SEEL•yahs). This treaty moved the Line of Demarcation more than 800 miles farther to the west. The change eventually allowed Portugal to claim much of eastern South America, which later became the Portuguese colony of Brazil. Following this agreement, Spain and Portugal increased their voyages of exploration.

European countries had three main goals during this age of exploration. First, they wanted to spread Christianity beyond Europe. Second, they wanted to expand their empires. Third, they wanted to become rich.

By increasing their wealth, European countries could gain power and security. An economic system called **mercantilism** describes how Europeans enriched their treasuries. (See Economics in History on page 52.) Colonies helped nations grow rich in several ways. Colonies provided

SECTION OBJECTIVES

- To describe the competition between Spain and Portugal to claim foreign lands.
- To explain Spain's conquest of Mexico and the Incan Empire.
- To understand the reasons for Spanish victories.
- To identify important Spanish and Portuguese explorers.

CRITICAL THINKING
Finding Main Ideas, p. 52
Making Inferences, p. 52
Clarifying, p. 53
Drawing Conclusions, p. 54
Comparing, p. 54

FOCUS & MOTIVATE

5-MINUTE WARM-UP

Making Inferences These questions focus on the extent of European exploration in the Americas by 1700.

1. View the map on page 51. What modern country is between the broken and unbroken lines?
2. How long after Columbus's first voyage were these lines drawn?

Warm-Up Transparency WT2

INSTRUCT

INSTRUCT: OBJECTIVE 1
Spain and Portugal Compete

- Why did Spain and Portugal want to control territory in the Americas?
- How did the Treaty of Tordesillas affect Portugal?
- How did European nations use colonies to increase their wealth?

In-Depth Resources: Unit 1
- Guided Reading, p. 22
- Literature Selection: from *The High Voyage,* pp. 31–33

RECOMMENDED RESOURCES

In-Depth Resources: Unit 1
- Guided Reading, p. 22
- Building Vocabulary, p. 25
- Skillbuilder Practice, p. 26
- Literature Selection, pp. 31–33

Reading Study Guide (Spanish and English), pp. 13–14

Economics in History
- Mercantilism and Colonies, p. 2

Outline Map Activities
- Spain Explores the Americas, pp. 3–4

America's History Makers, pp. 9–10

Formal Assessment
- Section Quiz, p. 36

Integrated Assessment
- Rubrics, 1.0, 4.5

Access for Students Acquiring English/ESL, pp. 7, 10

INTEGRATED TECHNOLOGY

Geography Transparency GT2

Humanities Transparency HT3

Electronic Teacher Tools

classzone.com

TEST-TAKING RESOURCES

Strategies for Test Preparation

Test Practice Transparencies, TT6

Online Test Practice

Economics *in* History

OBJECTIVE
Students will summarize the ways mercantilism helped to create wealth.

Mercantile Governments
Mercantile governments were deeply involved in their domestic economies. They tried to ensure—through tariffs and other trade measures—that imports did not exceed exports. Those policies typically favored the economy in the home country over that of the colonies. In the 1700s, Britain tried to ensure that its North American colonies imported more goods from England than they exported.

1. **Finding Main Ideas Possible Responses** A nation needed a favorable balance of trade. Colonies enrich their country by providing precious metals, producing goods that could be traded for precious metals, and by serving as a market.
2. **Making Inferences Possible Responses** In the long run, the family would lose its possessions and its ability to buy on credit. Students most likely will say that a nation would experience a similar situation

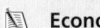

Economics in History
- Mercantilism and Colonies, p. 2

INSTRUCT: OBJECTIVE 2
Europeans Explore Foreign Lands

- Who were some of the important early European explorers?
- What feat did Magellan's crew achieve before anyone else?

Humanities Transparency HT3
- Portuguese Ship of Discovery

Economics *in* History

Mercantilism

The main goal of mercantilism was to increase the money in a country's treasury by creating a favorable balance of trade. A country had a favorable balance of trade if it had more exports than imports. Colonies helped a country have the goods to maintain a favorable balance of trade.

For example, say Spain sold $500 in sugar to France, and France sold $300 in cloth to Spain. France would also have to pay Spain $200 worth of precious metals to pay for all the sugar. Spain would then have a favorable balance of trade because the value of its exports (sugar) was greater than the value of its imports (cloth). Spain would become richer because of the precious metals it received from France.

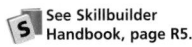

CONNECT TO HISTORY
1. **Finding Main Ideas** Under mercantilism, what did a country need to do to become rich? Discuss the way colonies enriched a country according to mercantilism.

See Skillbuilder Handbook, page R5.

CONNECT TO TODAY
2. **Making Inferences** Think about your own family budget. What do you think would happen if your family collected less money than it paid for goods for several years? Do you think this situation would be the same for a nation as it would for a family?

For more information on mercantilism . . .
RESEARCH LINKS
CLASSZONE.COM

various raw materials as well as mines that produced gold and silver. In addition, colonies served as markets for goods made in the home country.

2 Europeans Explore Foreign Lands

After Columbus's first voyage, many explorers went to sea. Italian sailor Amerigo Vespucci (vehs•POO•chee) set out in 1501 to find a sea route to Asia. Vespucci realized that the land he saw on this voyage was not Asia. A German mapmaker was impressed by Vespucci's account of the lands, so he named the continent "America" after him. Another famous explorer was the Spaniard Vasco Núñez de Balboa. In 1513, he led an expedition through the jungles of Panama and reached the Pacific Ocean.

In 1519, Portuguese sailor Ferdinand Magellan set out to reach Asia by sailing west around South America. During the long journey, he and his fellow sailors suffered great hardship. A member of the crew described what they ate.

> ***A VOICE FROM THE PAST***
> We were three months and twenty days without . . . fresh food. We ate biscuit, which was no longer biscuit, but powder of biscuits swarming with worms. . . . We drank . . . water that had been putrid for many days.
> **Antonio Pigafetta,** quoted in *The Discoverers*

Background
Magellan was killed after becoming involved in a local war in the Philippines.

Although Magellan died during the trip, his crew carried on and became the first people to sail around the world.

ACTIVITY OPTIONS
MULTIPLE LEARNING STYLES: INTERPERSONAL
BLOCK SCHEDULING

EXPLORER DIALOGUE
Class Time 40 minutes
Task Creating a dialogue among early European explorers
Purpose To gain an understanding of the motives and accomplishments of European explorers

Supplies Needed
- Reference materials about early European explorers

Activity Divide the class into groups of four. Each student in a group should play the role of an explorer cited in this section. Tell students to research their explorer. Then each group should present a dialogue with students taking the roles of the explorers. They should discuss their reasons for exploring where they went, what they found, and what happened to them after their explorations.

America's History Makers
- Amerigo Vespucci, pp. 5–6

❸ The Invasion of the Americas

While Magellan's crew was sailing around the world, the Spanish began their conquest of the Americas. Soldiers called ***conquistadors*** (kahn•KWIHS•tuh•DAWRZ), or conquerors, explored the Americas and claimed them for Spain. **Hernando Cortés** was one of these conquistadors. After landing in Central America in 1519, Cortés and his army of 508 men set their sights on conquering the mighty Aztec Empire.

The Spaniards marched inland and formed alliances (agreements with friendly peoples) with the native peoples who hated Aztec rule. Upon reaching the Aztec capital, Tenochtitlán (teh•NAWCH•tee•TLAHN), Cortés received a warm greeting from the Aztec emperor, **Montezuma.** Relations between the two sides quickly collapsed, however, as Cortés sought to take control of the empire. After several fierce clashes, the Aztecs drove the Spanish out.

Reading **History**
A. Clarifying Why did relations between the Spanish and Aztecs quickly break down?
A. Answer because Cortés wanted to conquer the empire

Despite this defeat, the Spaniards and their allies regrouped. In May 1521, Cortés led his forces back to Tenochtitlán. At this point, the Spaniards got help from an invisible ally. Many Aztecs fell victim to an outbreak of smallpox, which severely weakened their ranks. The germs that caused this disease had been brought to America by the Europeans. After months of fighting, Cortés conquered the empire.

AMERICA'S HISTORY MAKERS

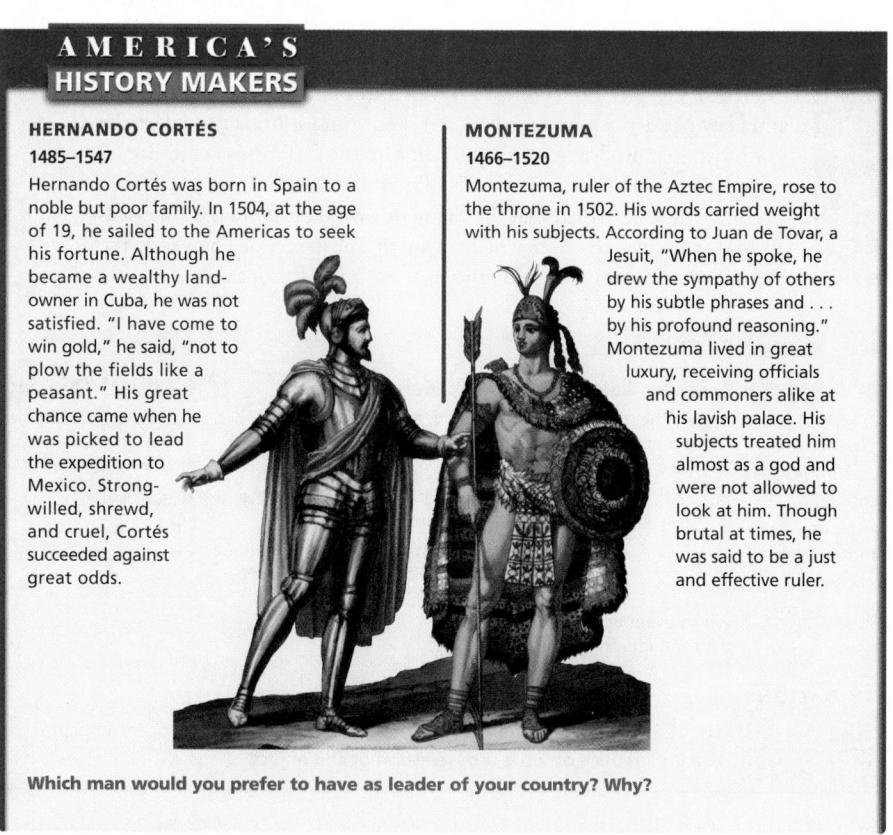

HERNANDO CORTÉS
1485–1547

Hernando Cortés was born in Spain to a noble but poor family. In 1504, at the age of 19, he sailed to the Americas to seek his fortune. Although he became a wealthy landowner in Cuba, he was not satisfied. "I have come to win gold," he said, "not to plow the fields like a peasant." His great chance came when he was picked to lead the expedition to Mexico. Strong-willed, shrewd, and cruel, Cortés succeeded against great odds.

MONTEZUMA
1466–1520

Montezuma, ruler of the Aztec Empire, rose to the throne in 1502. His words carried weight with his subjects. According to Juan de Tovar, a Jesuit, "When he spoke, he drew the sympathy of others by his subtle phrases and . . . by his profound reasoning." Montezuma lived in great luxury, receiving officials and commoners alike at his lavish palace. His subjects treated him almost as a god and were not allowed to look at him. Though brutal at times, he was said to be a just and effective ruler.

Which man would you prefer to have as leader of your country? Why?

INSTRUCT: OBJECTIVE ❸

The Invasion of the Americas

- Why were the Spanish able to defeat the Aztecs and the Incas?
- How did the Aztecs and the Incas respond to the Spanish invasion?

Geography Transparency GT2
- Cortés Marches to Tenochtitlán

MORE ABOUT . . .

Tenochtitlán

Tell students that Tenochtitlán, the Aztec capital, was a large city with hundreds of temples, government buildings, and other structures. Some scholars have estimated the population of the city and surrounding communities at about 400,000, spread over an area of more than 5 square miles (13 km), in 1519. The heart of the city lay on two islands linked by causeways to the shores of Lake Texcoco. The lake was drained in the early 1600s, and Mexico City was built on its site.

AMERICA'S HISTORY MAKERS

Hernando Cortés and Montezuma

Cortés and Montezuma were wary of each other when they met in 1519. Cortés took advantage of Montezuma's fear that the Spaniard was a legendary Aztec god. Cortés spoke directly to Montezuma, "We have come to your house in Mexico as friends. There is nothing to fear." He destroyed the Aztec Empire within two years.

Possible responses: Some students might say Cortés because he conquered the Aztecs. Others might say Montezuma because he was just.

America's History Makers
- Hernando Cortés, pp. 7–8

ACTIVITY OPTIONS

INDIVIDUAL NEEDS

BLOCK SCHEDULING

STUDENTS ACQUIRING ENGLISH/ESL

Expanding Vocabulary Write the word *ally* on the board and define it as "a partner." Begin a word pyramid with *ally* at the top. Then ask students to reread the second and third paragraphs under the heading "The Invasion of the Americas." As they read, ask them to identify words that have *ally* as the base word. Write them below ally to form a word pyramid. (alliances, allies) Define the words and then ask such questions as the following: Who did the Spanish form alliances with? What was the invisible ally?

	ally	
allied	allies	ally

INSTRUCT: OBJECTIVE 4

Other Spanish Explorers

- What lured Spanish explorers into North America?
- Which Spanish explorers led expeditions through the areas that would become the southwestern United States and Florida?

America's History Makers
- Cabeza de Vaca, pp. 9–10

Outline Map Activities
- Spain Explores the Americas, 1500s, pp. 3–4

ASSESS & RETEACH

Setting the Stage Have students complete the section of the graphic organizer on Exploration and Establishing Colonies.

Formal Assessment
- Section Quiz, p. 36

Critical Thinking Transparency CT4

RETEACHING ACTIVITY

Have students work in pairs as reporters for a newspaper covering European exploration in the Americas. Each pair should write newspaper headlines for at least four important events or individuals that helped Spain establish a large empire in the Americas. One headline should correspond to a different event or individual discussed in one of the four subsections in Section 1. As a guided review, invite students to share their headlines with the rest of the class.

In-Depth Resources: Unit 1
- Reteaching Activities, p. 34

In 1531, a *conquistador* named **Francisco Pizarro** marched on the Incas. The Incas had built a powerful and wealthy empire centered in the Cuzco Valley in what is now Peru. With an army of only 180 men, Pizarro conquered the Inca.

People have long been amazed that the great Aztec and Incan empires fell to such small groups of Spanish *conquistadors.* But Spanish success can be explained by three major reasons.

1. The spread of European diseases killed millions of Native Americans.
2. The Spanish were excellent soldiers and sailors. They also had superior weapons, such as guns.
3. Spain made alliances with Native Americans who were enemies of the Aztecs and Incas.

Having conquered the major Native American empires in Central and South America, the Spaniards began to explore other parts of North and South America.

Reading **History**

B. Drawing Conclusions What was the most important reason for the Spanish success in conquering territory in the Americas?

B. Possible responses Some students will say disease. Others might say better weapons.

Estevanico was a slave who helped the Spanish explore parts of North America. He was killed during Coronado's search for golden cities.

Other Spanish Explorers 4

The Spaniards hoped to collect treasures from North America as they had from Mexico and Peru. Rumors of golden cities kept Spanish hopes high. For example, the Spaniard Álvar Núñez Cabeza de Vaca and Estevanico, a slave of North African descent, wandered across the continent and heard Native American stories about cities of gold.

Between 1539 and 1542, three expeditions set out to find these cities. Francisco Vázquez de Coronado traveled through present-day Arizona and New Mexico. Hernando de Soto set out from Florida to explore the southeast. Juan Rodríguez Cabrillo sailed up the California coast. But all three failed to find the fabled cities of gold.

For a while, it seemed that the Spaniards would explore the Americas all by themselves. As you will read in the next section, however, the Spanish would soon face competition from other Europeans.

Section 1 Assessment

1. Terms & Names

Explain the significance of:
- Treaty of Tordesillas
- mercantilism
- *conquistador*
- Hernando Cortés
- Montezuma
- Francisco Pizarro

2. Taking Notes

Review the section and find four events to place on a time line that shows how Spain built its empire.

Spain Builds an Empire

1492 —|—|—|—|— 1542

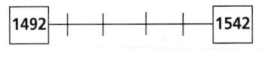

Which event do you think is the most important? Why?

3. Main Ideas

a. Why did Europeans explore different territories?

b. Why did Spain succeed in conquering so much of the Americas?

c. What was significant about the Magellan expedition?

4. Critical Thinking

Comparing What was similar about the conquests of Mexico and Peru?

THINK ABOUT
- the *conquistadors*
- the size of their armies

ACTIVITY OPTIONS

ART

LANGUAGE ARTS

Use the library or Internet to find a photograph of an Aztec or Incan artifact. Create a **replica** or write a **description** of the object.

Section 1 Assessment

1. Terms & Names

Treaty of Tordesillas, p. 51
mercantilism, p, 51
conquistador, p. 53
Hernando Cortés, p. 53
Montezuma, p. 53
Francisco Pizarro, p. 54

2. Taking Notes

1494 Treaty of Tordesillas
1513 Balboa reaches the Pacific
1521 Cortés conquers Mexico
1531 Pizarro conquers Peru

3. Main Ideas

a. to spread Christianity, expand their empires, and gain riches
b. Native Americans fell to disease; the Spanish had better weapons; the Spanish made alliances with some Native Americans; the Spanish acted brutally toward Native Americans. **c.** It was the first to travel around the world.

4. Critical Thinking

Students may note that both were led by Spanish leaders who overcame powerful Native American empires against great odds.

ACTIVITY OPTIONS

Integrated Assessment
- Rubrics for a replica, 1.10
- Rubrics for a description, 4.5

2 European Competition in North America

TERMS & NAMES
Henry Hudson
John Cabot
Giovanni da Verrazzano
Jacques Cartier
Spanish Armada
Samuel de Champlain
New France

MAIN IDEA	WHY IT MATTERS NOW
Other European countries competed with Spain for control over territory in the Americas.	European culture has strongly influenced American culture.

ONE EUROPEAN'S STORY

In 1609, an Englishman named <u>Henry Hudson</u> set sail from Europe. He sailed under the Dutch flag and hoped to find a route to China. Arriving at the coast of present-day New York, he sailed up the river that now bears his name. In his journal, Hudson described what he saw.

A VOICE FROM THE PAST

The land is the finest for cultivation that I ever in my life set foot upon, and it also abounds in trees of every description. The natives are a very good people; for, when they saw that I would not remain, they supposed that I was afraid of their bows, and taking the arrows, they broke them in pieces and threw them into the fire.

Henry Hudson, quoted in *Discoverers of America*

Hudson did not find a passage to Asia, but he led another expedition in 1610, this time sailing for the English. He made his way through ice-clogged waters in Canada and entered a large bay, today called Hudson Bay. There he sailed for months, but still found no westward passage.

After enduring a harsh winter, his crew rebelled. They put Hudson, his young son, and several loyal sailors in a small boat and set them adrift (shown at right). Hudson's party was never heard from again.

1 The Search for the Northwest Passage

Hudson's voyages showed that some European countries hoped to find a westward route to Asia as late as the 1600s. While Spain was taking control of the Americas, other Europeans were sending out expeditions to find the Northwest Passage, a water route through North America to Asia.

One of the first explorers to chart a northern route across the Atlantic in search of Asia was the Italian sailor **<u>John Cabot</u>**. In 1497, Cabot crossed the Atlantic Ocean to explore for the English. He landed in the area of Newfoundland, Canada. He was certain that he had reached Asia and claimed the land for England. The next year he set sail once more, hoping

SECTION OBJECTIVES

1. To trace the search for a water route through North America to Asia
2. To explain Spanish reaction to competition in North America and to identify effects of the defeat of the Spanish Armada
3. To describe the search for trade by the French and Dutch

CRITICAL THINKING

Drawing Conclusions, p. 53
Making Inferences, p. 54

Why It Matters Now
- Space Exploration, pp. 3–4

FOCUS & MOTIVATE

5-MINUTE WARM-UP

Recognizing Effects These questions focus on rivalries that developed among European nations.

1. Look at the painting and caption on page 53. Which nations are fighting?
2. Why might the outcome of this battle be important to the history of the Americas?

Warm-Up Transparency WT2

INSTRUCT

INSTRUCT: OBJECTIVE 1

The Search for the Northwest Passage

- What was the Northwest Passage?
- Which European nations actively sought to discover the Northwest Passage?
- Why were European nations interested in finding a Northwest Passage?

In-Depth Resources: Unit 1
- Guided Reading, p. 23
- Building Vocabulary, p. 25

Reading Study Guide (Spanish and English), pp. 15–16

RECOMMENDED RESOURCES

In-Depth Resources: Unit 1
- Guided Reading, p. 23
- Building Vocabulary, p. 25

Reading Study Guide (Spanish and English), pp. 15–16

Why It Matters Now
- Space Exploration, pp. 3–4

Formal Assessment
- Section Quiz, p. 37

Integrated Assessment
- Rubrics, 4.8, 5.1

Access for Students Acquiring English/ESL
- Guided Reading, p. 8

INTEGRATED TECHNOLOGY

Humanities Transparency HT4
- St. Augustine

Electronic Teacher Tools

classzone.com

TEST-TAKING RESOURCES

Strategies for Test Preparation

Test Practice Transparencies, TT7

Online Test Practice

HISTORY FROM VISUALS

Reading the Map Point out that many of the explorations shown on this map were confined mostly to coastal areas and areas along inland waters, such as rivers. Have students discuss why they think this often was the case. **Possible Responses** Traveling along coasts and waterways was faster and safer than traveling through unfamiliar inland regions. In addition, European explorers at this stage were still trying to determine the sizes and shapes of the new continents they had encountered.

Extension Ask students to use an encyclopedia to learn about improvements in ship design and navigation that made possible long voyages out of sight of land.

European Exploration of the Americas, 1500–1550

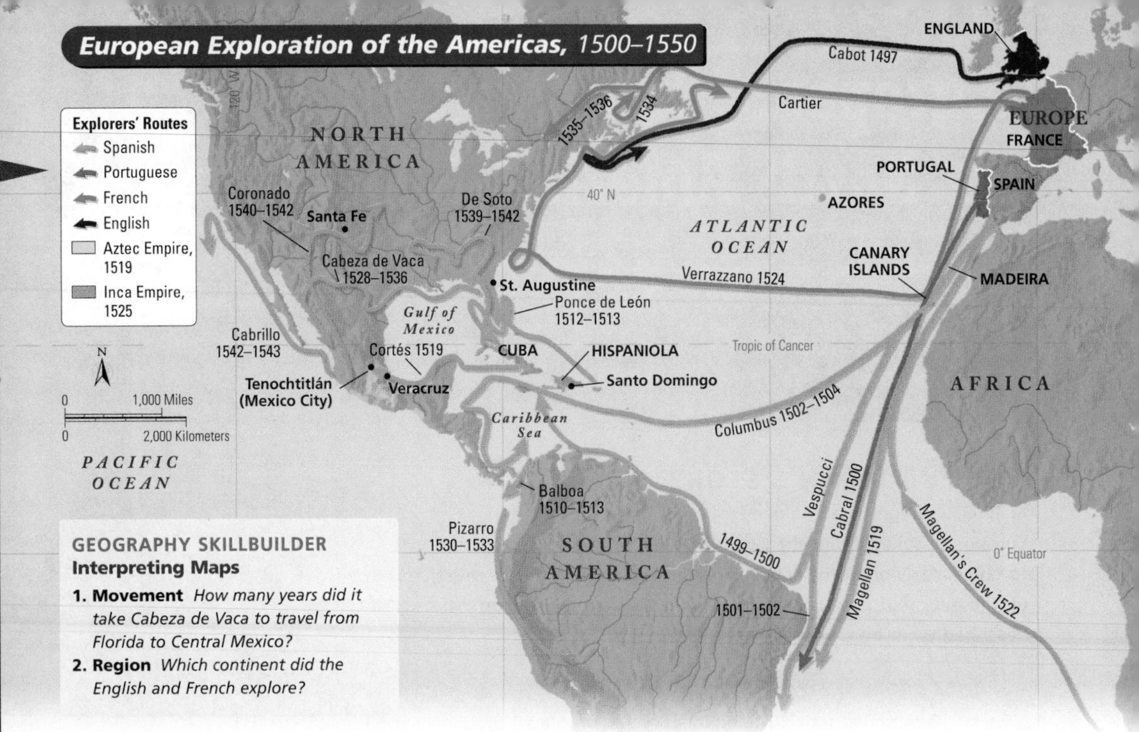

GEOGRAPHY SKILLBUILDER
Interpreting Maps

1. **Movement** *How many years did it take Cabeza de Vaca to travel from Florida to Central Mexico?*
2. **Region** *Which continent did the English and French explore?*

Skillbuilder Answers
1. Eight
2. North America

to reach Japan. He was never seen again. Even so, his voyages were the basis for future English colonies along the Atlantic shore of North America.

In 1524, another Italian, **Giovanni da Verrazzano,** set out under the French flag to find the Northwest Passage. He explored the Atlantic coastline of North America, but there was no passage to be found.

France tried again between 1534 and 1536 with the voyages of **Jacques Cartier** (ZHAHK kahr•TYAY). Cartier traveled up the St. Lawrence River to the site of present-day Montreal. At that point, rapids blocked the way and ended his search for the Northwest Passage. It would be almost 75 years before the French would return to colonize the region.

Reading **History**
A. Reading a Map Use the maps on pages 55 and 56 to see the areas Cabot, Hudson, Verrazzano, and Cartier visited.

2 Spain Responds to Competition

French and English claims to North America angered Spain, which had claimed the land under the Treaty of Tordesillas. The tensions between Spain, England, and France stemmed from religious conflicts in Europe, such as the Reformation, which you read about in Chapter 1. These conflicts also led to fighting in the Americas.

Florida was one of the battlegrounds between the Spanish and the French. In 1564, a group of French Protestants, called Huguenots (HYOO•guh•NAHTS), founded a colony called Fort Caroline. Before long, Spanish troops under the command of Pedro Menéndez de Avilés arrived in that area. "This is the armada of the King of Spain," he announced, "who has sent me [here] to burn and hang the Lutheran [Protestant] French." Menéndez built a fort, St. Augustine, a short distance away. Then he brutally massacred the French.

Vocabulary
armada: a fleet of warships

INSTRUCT: OBJECTIVE 2

Spain Responds to Competition/ Spain and England Clash/ The Defeat of the Spanish Armada

- What factors increased the tension among Spain, England, and France?
- What role did sea dogs play in the conflict between Spain and England?
- What were the effects of the defeat of the Spanish Armada?

ACTIVITY OPTIONS

INTERDISCIPLINARY LINK: LANGUAGE ARTS — BLOCK SCHEDULING

A CELEBRATORY SPEECH

Class Time 45 minutes

Task Planning a television news program

Purpose To analyze reasons for the English delight with the exploits of Francis Drake

Supplies Needed
- Reference material about Francis Drake
- Video camera and tape (optional)

Activity Divide students into groups. Tell students to plan and write copy for a television news segment on the arrival of Francis Drake in England after his trip around the world in 1580. The segment should last two minutes and include the newscaster's narration, a short welcome to Drake by a London resident, and a brief response by Drake. If the students are videotaping their segments, they should divide the tasks involved.

Spain and England Clash

Religious differences and the quest for national power also led to conflict between Spain and England. In 1558, Queen Elizabeth I, a Protestant, came to the English throne. Spain, which was Catholic, plotted to remove the Protestant queen. But Elizabeth fought to defend England and challenge Spain's power at sea.

Although England's navy was not as powerful as Spain's, the English fleet had many speedy ships with skillful sailors. Daring sailors, known as sea dogs, used these ships to attack the Spanish. The Spanish sailed bulky, slow-moving ships called galleons. These galleons brought gold and silver from the Americas to Spain.

Sir Francis Drake became the most famous of the sea dogs because of his bold adventures and attacks against the Spanish. In 1577, Drake began a three-year voyage that took him around the world. During this voyage, he raided Spanish ports and ships in South America. He stole great amounts of treasure from them. When he arrived home in 1580, he was a national hero. Not only had Drake and his men hounded the Spanish, but they were also the first Englishmen to sail around the world.

America's HERITAGE

ST. AUGUSTINE

The thick stone walls of the fort at St. Augustine (shown below) still stand guard over the Florida coast today. Founded in 1565, St. Augustine is the oldest permanent European settlement in the United States. For more than two centuries, St. Augustine was an important outpost of Spain's empire in the Americas. Many Spanish colonial buildings remain at the site. The fort is now a national monument.

The Defeat of the Spanish Armada

The attacks of Drake and other sea dogs enraged Philip II, the Spanish king. Determined to teach the English a lesson, Philip sent the **Spanish Armada** to conquer England and restore Catholicism to that nation. This fleet, made up of 130 ships, set out for England in the summer of 1588.

The English and Spanish navies met in the English Channel, which separates England from the European continent. In their smaller but faster craft, the English darted among the Spanish warships, firing deadly rounds with their cannons. Confused and crippled, the armada was retreating when it was hit by a severe storm. With half of its ships destroyed, the armada barely made it home.

Spain was still quite strong after the defeat of the armada. It quickly rebuilt its navy and maintained its large colonial possessions. But Spain would never again be as powerful as it was in 1588.

The English victory over Spain had two important effects. First, it ensured that England would remain independent and Protestant. Although England was less powerful than Spain, England proved that it could defend itself. Second, Spain's image suffered. The world saw that Spain could be beaten. Other nations joined England in challenging Spain.

B. Possible Response England remained independent, and Spain was weakened.

***Reading*History**

B. Drawing Conclusions Why was the defeat of the Spanish Armada important?

America's HERITAGE

St. Augustine

St. Augustine was named for a Roman Catholic saint. Evidence of Spanish influence in North America can be found in the names of many cities, counties, and states across the United States. Florida, for example, was named in honor of the "Feast of Flowers," the Easter celebration in Spain. Ask students to list other place names in the United States that have Spanish origins.

Humanities Transparency HT4
- St. Augustine

MORE ABOUT . . .

Queen Elizabeth I

Queen Elizabeth I was the daughter of Henry VIII. Protestant Elizabeth inherited the throne from her Catholic half-sister Mary, who had been married to Philip II of Spain. For a while, Philip hoped to marry Elizabeth. Gradually, however, it became clear that Elizabeth intended to keep England Protestant and independent of Spain. Elizabeth further angered Philip by supporting Dutch Protestants rebelling against Spanish rule.

ACTIVITY OPTIONS

INDIVIDUAL NEEDS

LESS PROFICIENT READERS

Defeat of the Spanish Armada To help students understand the links between cause and effect, have them copy the cause-and-effect diagrams shown here. Have the students read the text on page 57 under the heading "The Defeat of the Spanish Armada." Then have them find the sentences that indicate the effects.

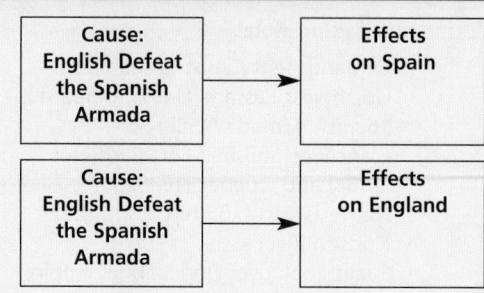

Cause: English Defeat the Spanish Armada	→	Effects on Spain
Cause: English Defeat the Spanish Armada	→	Effects on England

INSTRUCT: OBJECTIVE 3

The French and Dutch Seek Trade

- Where did the French and Dutch establish their first settlements in North America?
- In what economic activities were the French and Dutch colonies engaged?
- How did the French and Dutch settlements compare to those of the Spanish?

CRITICAL THINKING ACTIVITY

Contrasting Contrast the actions of the Spanish conquerors toward the Native Americans with those of French and Dutch settlers by using a three-column graphic organizer.

SPANISH	DUTCH	FRENCH

Class Time 10 minutes

ASSESS & RETEACH

Setting the Stage Have students complete the section of the graphic organizer on European Competition.

Formal Assessment
- Section Quiz, p. 37

RETEACHING ACTIVITY

Have students create an annotated time line showing important events discussed in this section. The annotations should include short explanations of Spanish reaction to other European explorations and the effects of the defeat of the Spanish Armada.

In-Depth Resources: Unit 1
- Reteaching Activity, p. 35

English adventurers like Drake continued to attack Spanish interests abroad. In addition, England challenged Spanish claims to lands in North America, such as California and Newfoundland. Even so, England took a cautious approach to overseas expansion. The English government refused to provide money to start colonies. Instead, private citizens had to provide the money for colonization. As a result, England did not establish a successful colony in America until after 1600.

3 The French and Dutch Seek Trade

France and the Netherlands were also looking for ways to gain wealth through exploration and colonization. At first, their goal in the Americas was to find the Northwest Passage to Asia. When that search failed, they began to focus on North America itself.

The Frenchman **Samuel de Champlain** (sham•PLAYN) explored the St. Lawrence River. In 1608, he founded a fur-trading post at Quebec. This post became the first permanent French settlement in North America. Champlain's activities opened a rich fur trade with local Native Americans. After a couple of decades, **New France,** as the colony was called, began to thrive.

At the same time, the Dutch were building a colony called New Netherland. It was located along the Hudson River in present-day New York. After Hudson's voyage up the river in 1609, the Dutch built Fort Nassau in 1614, near the site of the modern city of Albany.

In 1626, the Dutch bought Manhattan Island from Native Americans. The Dutch then founded the town of New Amsterdam on that site, where New York City is currently located. New Netherland was soon thriving from the fur trade with Native Americans.

These early French and Dutch colonies, however, were small compared to the large empire Spain was building in the Americas. You will read about Spain's empire and the impact of colonization in the next section.

C. Possible Response They were not as powerful as Spain. At first, they looked for the Northwest Passage and only set up colonies when they could not find it.

Reading **History**
C. Making Inferences Why do you think it took France and the Netherlands so long to set up colonies in the Americas?

Section 2 Assessment

1. Terms & Names

Explain the significance of:
- Henry Hudson
- John Cabot
- Giovanni da Verrazzano
- Jacques Cartier
- Spanish Armada
- Samuel de Champlain
- New France

2. Taking Notes

Use a chart like the one below to show how European nations competed for power.

England	
France	
Netherlands	
Spain	

3. Main Ideas

a. What were the English, French, and Dutch searching for in their early voyages of exploration?

b. How did England defeat the Spanish Armada?

c. Where did the French and Dutch set up their first American colonies?

4. Critical Thinking

Making Inferences Why do you think England founded colonies later than Spain did?

THINK ABOUT
- conditions in Spain and England
- the lands each country discovered

ACTIVITY OPTIONS

MUSIC / **TECHNOLOGY**: Research the life of one of the explorers discussed in this section. Compose a **song** or design a **Web page** about that person.

Section 2 Assessment

1. Terms & Names

Henry Hudson, p. 55
John Cabot, p. 55
Giovanni da Verrazzano, p. 56
Jacques Cartier, p. 56
Spanish Armada, p. 57
Samuel de Champlain, p. 58
New France, p. 58

2. Taking Notes

England: sent Cabot to search for Northwest Passage (1497); defeated Spanish Armada (1588)
France: established Fort Caroline (1564) and Quebec (1608)
Netherlands: explored along the Hudson River
Spain: took over Florida; built empire in Central and South America

3. Main Ideas

a. Northwest Passage to Asia and the spice trade **b.** The smaller, faster English ships outmaneuvered the Spanish galleons. **c.** The French set up a colony at Fort Caroline in Florida in 1564. The Dutch built Fort Nassau near modern-day Albany in 1614.

4. Critical Thinking

Spain was already much richer and more powerful. England was weaker and less willing to expand into the lands it discovered.

ACTIVITY OPTIONS

Integrated Assessment
- Rubrics for a song, 4.8
- Rubrics for a Web page, 5.1

3 The Impact of Colonization

TERMS & NAMES
- *encomienda*
- plantation
- slavery
- African Diaspora
- middle passage
- racism
- Columbian Exchange

MAIN IDEA

Spanish rule in the Americas had terrible consequences for Native Americans and Africans.

WHY IT MATTERS NOW

The effects of slavery, including racism, helped shape attitudes and social conditions in the United States.

ONE AMERICAN'S STORY

Huamán Poma, a Peruvian Native American, was angry about the abuse the Spanish heaped upon Native Americans. He wrote to King Philip III of Spain to complain about the bad treatment.

A VOICE FROM THE PAST

It is their [the Spanish] practice to collect Indians into groups and send them to forced labor without wages, while they themselves receive the payment for the work. . . . The royal administrators and the other Spaniards lord it over the Indians with absolute power.

Huamán Poma, *Letter to a King*

In his letter, Poma asked the king to help the Native Americans and uphold the rule of law in Peru. Regardless, the Spanish colonists continued to mistreat Native Americans as the Spaniards expanded their empire in the Americas. In time, colonists from Spain and other European nations would import millions of Africans to the Americas and enslave them as well. For the members of these subjected groups, American colonization was devastating.

A Spanish priest forces a Native American woman to work at a loom.

1 Life in Spanish America

The Spanish Empire grew rapidly, despite efforts by other European countries to compete with Spain. By 1700, it controlled much of the Americas. Spain took several steps to establish an effective colonial government. First, it divided its American empire into two provinces called New Spain and Peru. Each province was called a viceroyalty. The top official of each viceroyalty was called the viceroy. He ruled in the king's name.

The Spaniards made sure that people with Spanish backgrounds held power in the colonies. Just below the Spanish were the Creoles—people of Spanish descent who were born in the colonies. The next step down

SECTION OBJECTIVES

- To analyze the organization of government and society in Spanish colonies
- To explain the development of slavery
- To evaluate the treatment of slaves in European colonies in the Americas
- To understand the Columbian Exchange

SKILLBUILDER

Interpreting Maps: Location, Region, p. 60

CRITICAL THINKING

Summarizing, p. 60
Analyzing Causes, p. 62
Making Inferences, p. 63
Recognizing Effects, p. 63

FOCUS & MOTIVATE

5-MINUTE WARM-UP

Reading a Map Examining this map will help students understand the vast size of Spain's empire in the Americas.

1. Look at the map on page 60. Describe the area included in the Viceroyalty of New Spain and the Viceroyalty of Peru.
2. How do you suppose dividing Spain's vast empire into two units may have made it easier to govern?

Warm-Up Transparency WT2

INSTRUCT

INSTRUCT: OBJECTIVE 1

Life in Spanish America

- How was the Spanish colonial economy and society organized?
- How did the Spanish mistreat Native Americans?

In-Depth Resources: Unit 1
- Guided Reading, p. 24
- Geography Application: Spain's American Empire Expands, pp. 27–28

Reading Study Guide (Spanish and English), pp. 17–18

RECOMMENDED RESOURCES

In-Depth Resources: Unit 1
- Guided Reading, p. 24
- Building Vocabulary, p. 25
- Geography Application, pp. 27–28
- Primary Sources, pp. 29, 30
- Reteaching Activity, p. 36
- Enrichment Activity, p. 37

Reading Study Guide (Spanish and English), pp. 17–18

Formal Assessment
- Section Quiz, p. 38

Integrated Assessment
- Rubrics, 1.3, 2.3

Access for Students Acquiring English/ESL
- Guided Reading, p. 9
- Geography Application, pp. 11–12

INTEGRATED TECHNOLOGY

Critical Thinking Transparency CT5
- Cause and Effect: The Columbian Exchange

Electronic Teacher Tools

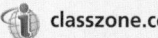

classzone.com

TEST-TAKING RESOURCES

Strategies for Test Preparation

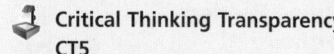

Test Practice Transparencies, TT8–TT9

Online Test Practice

HISTORY FROM VISUALS

Reading the Map Point out the large distance between the cities of Mexico City and Lima. Have students suggest the kinds of problems that the distance might cause for administrators in each city. **Possible Responses** Administrators would have difficulty. They could not keep in touch with distant areas, nor could they send troops or supplies quickly.

Extension Using an atlas, have the students identify a present-day transportation network between Mexico City and Lima.

MORE ABOUT . . .

Spanish Missions

Although many Spanish missions in the Americas were destroyed over the centuries, some survived and are popular tourist attractions. The oldest Spanish mission in the United States is Nombre de Díos, built in 1565 in St. Augustine, Florida. One of the most famous missions is San Antonio de Valero, also called the Alamo, in San Antonio, Texas. Between 1769 and 1823, Spanish priests established 21 missions in California. The southernmost mission is San Diego; the most northerly is San Francisco Solona (Sonoma Mission).

In-Depth Resources: Unit 1
- Primary Source: Protesting the Mistreatment of Native Americans, p. 29

INSTRUCT: OBJECTIVE 2

The Emergence of American Slavery

- Why did the Spanish and Portuguese enslave Africans?
- What was the middle passage?
- How did slavery influence racial attitudes among Europeans?

Spain's American Empire, 1700

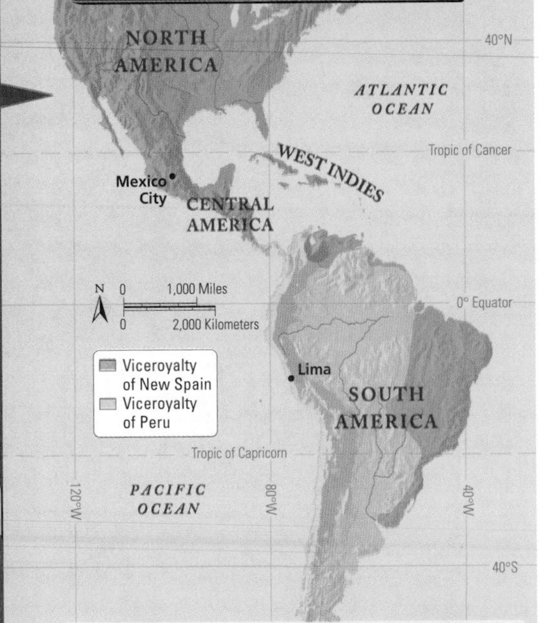

GEOGRAPHY SKILLBUILDER Interpreting Maps
1. **Location** *Which viceroyalty included the West Indies?*
2. **Region** *Which viceroyalty covered more territory?*

Skillbuilder Answers
1. New Spain
2. Peru

the social order were the *mestizos. Mestizos* are people of mixed Spanish and Native American ancestry. The people with the least power and fewest rights were Native Americans and enslaved Africans.

The Catholic Church played an important role in Spanish colonial society. In places like New Mexico and California, the church built missions, settlements that included a church, a town, and farmlands. The goal of the missions was to convert Native Americans to Christianity. The missions also increased Spanish control over the land.

Some Spanish colonists received *encomiendas* to help them make the colonies productive. An ***encomienda*** was a grant of Native American labor. The Spanish rulers also created large estates, called *haciendas,* to provide food for the colony. *Haciendas* often became **plantations,** large farms that raised cash crops, such as sugar, coffee, and cotton, which were in great demand in Europe. The Spanish forced Native Americans to work on these plantations.

Background
In precolonial America, forms of slavery were practiced by some Native Americans and differed greatly among different peoples.

Most Spaniards treated the Native Americans as little more than beasts of burden, forcing countless numbers of them to work in the fields and mines. In addition, some missionaries mistreated them by forcing them to work terribly hard. Other missionaries, though, tried to protect Native Americans from being treated cruelly.

One missionary in particular who fought for better treatment of Native Americans was Bartolomé de Las Casas. Las Casas, a Catholic priest, fought against the abuse of Native Americans, earning the title "Protector of the Indians." Due largely to his efforts, Spanish authorities passed laws providing greater protection for Native Americans. Most colonists, however, ignored the laws.

In 1680, a man named Popé led the Pueblo Indians in a rebellion against the Spanish. His forces surrounded the Spanish settlement at Santa Fe, in present-day New Mexico, and forced the colonists to flee temporarily from the region.

***Reading*History**
A. Summarizing In what ways did the Spanish mistreat Native Americans?
A. Answer by enslaving them and trying to replace their religions and traditions

2 The Emergence of American Slavery

As more and more Native Americans died from overwork and European diseases, the Spanish and Portuguese turned to another source for labor: enslaved Africans. **Slavery** is the practice of holding a person in bondage

ACTIVITY OPTIONS

INTERDISCIPLINARY LINK: CIVICS — BLOCK SCHEDULING

PETITIONS

Class Time 45 minutes

Task Writing a petition about the treatment of Native Americans

Purpose To identify and present arguments against the abuse of Native Americans in the Spanish colonies

Supplies Needed
- Textbook
- Encyclopedias or reference books about Spanish America
- Writing paper
- Color pencils

Activity Direct students to work in pairs. Have them write petitions asking the Spanish king to require colonists to stop abusing Native Americans in the colonies. Petitions should describe the treatment of Native Americans and make a case for requiring better treatment. Students might want to research some of the arguments on the subject made by Bartolomé de Las Casas and others. Students can decorate their petitions, roll them, seal them with wax, and tie them with a ribbon for presentation.

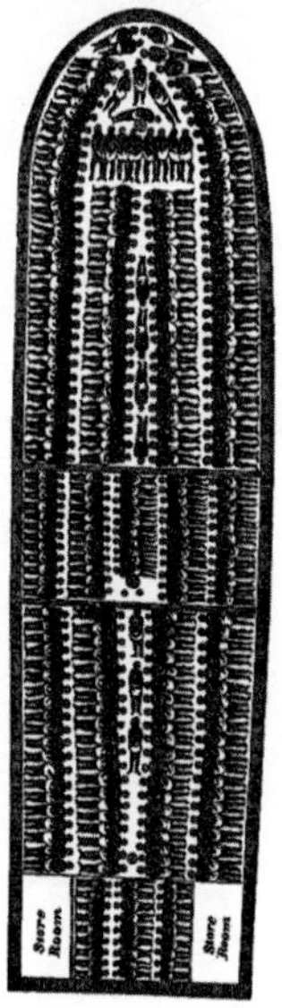

The images above show how slave traders packed enslaved Africans onto slave ships for the middle passage.

for labor. The Europeans enslaved Africans for four basic reasons. First, Africans were immune to most European diseases. Second, Africans had no friends or family in the Americas to help them resist or escape enslavement. Third, enslaved Africans provided a permanent source of cheap labor. Even their children could be held in bondage. Fourth, many Africans had worked on farms in their native lands.

In the early 1500s, European traders began bringing Africans to the Americas for slave labor. This forced removal has become known as the **African Diaspora.** Before the slave trade ended in the late 1800s, approximately 12 million Africans had been enslaved and shipped to the Western Hemisphere.

Vocabulary
diaspora: the scattering of people outside their homeland

The voyage of the slave ships from Africa to the Americas was called the **middle passage.** The voyage was given this name because it was the middle leg of the triangular trade. The triangular trade refers to the movement of trade ships between Europe, Africa, and the Americas. You will learn more about the triangular trade in Chapter 4.

Olaudah Equiano (oh•LOW•duh EHK•wee•AHN•oh) was one of these kidnapped Africans. He made this journey in the 1700s. He was about 11 years old when he was sold into slavery. Later, after he bought his freedom, he wrote his life story and described the terror of the middle passage.

A VOICE FROM THE PAST

The first object which saluted my eyes when I arrived on the coast, was the sea, and a slave ship . . . waiting for its cargo. These filled me with astonishment, which was soon converted into terror, when I was carried on board.

Olaudah Equiano, quoted in *Great Slave Narratives*

It is estimated that perhaps two million Africans died during the middle passage. Those who survived faced a hard life in the Americas. Some were taken to large homes where they worked as servants. Most were forced to do hard labor in *haciendas* or mines.

61

MORE ABOUT . . .

Slavery

Slavery was already in limited practice in various forms in West Africa when Europeans arrived. For instance, many slaves were captured during conflicts with opposing peoples.

MORE ABOUT . . .

The Middle Passage

Estimates of death rates among Africans on the slave ships have varied widely. Some recent estimates range from 10 percent to more than 30 percent, often depending on the time of year and the length of voyage. Diseases, which spread rapidly in the squalid cargo holds, killed most. Storms, shipwrecks, and disease also threatened both Africans and the captains and crews of the slave ships, and many perished at sea. Of course, the Europeans took the risks voluntarily, for the most part, unlike the enslaved Africans.

MORE ABOUT . . .

Olaudah Equiano

Equiano's ship took him to Barbados. There he saw Africans who spoke many languages. He saw his first horse and his first two-story building. Equiano was sent to a plantation in Virginia, where he worked by himself clearing weeds and rocks from the fields. He suffered greatly from loneliness. There was no one with whom he could speak. Soon he was purchased by a sea captain as a present for London cousins. Equiano eventually became a sailor and learned to read and write English. He was able to purchase his own freedom when he was 21 years old. When he was 44, he published his autobiography.

In-Depth Resources: Unit 1
- Primary Source: from *The Interesting Narrative of the Life of Olaudah Equiano,* p. 30

ACTIVITY OPTIONS

INDIVIDUAL NEEDS: GIFTED AND TALENTED

BLOCK SCHEDULING

AFRICAN DIASPORA

Class Time Two class periods

Task Finding primary source accounts of the African Diaspora

Purpose To gain an understanding of the African Diaspora from personal accounts

Supplies Needed
- Reference materials and primary sources on the African Diaspora
- Internet access for additional information

Activity Have students use reference materials and on-line resources to find additional background material about the African Diaspora. Encourage them to find personal accounts of the experience in primary source materials. Students may want to locate a copy of *Great Slave Narratives* and read quotes from other slaves. Then have students read aloud some of the narratives that they found. Have them discuss their similarities.

INSTRUCT: OBJECTIVE 3

The Columbian Exchange

- How did the Columbian Exchange contribute to the spread of disease in the Americas?
- What were some of the beneficial effects of the Columbian Exchange?

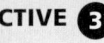

Critical Thinking Transparency CT5
- Cause and Effect: The Columbian Exchange

MORE ABOUT . . .

Diseases and History

Africans and Europeans had developed resistance to many of the same diseases—such as measles, chickenpox, and influenza—because of the long history of contact between Europe and Africa. Native Americans had little resistance or immunity to these diseases.

In addition, Africans had immunities to many diseases that proved deadly to Europeans. For example, while many African adults had some immunity to malaria, European adults exposed to the disease for the first time suffered mortality rates as high as 50 percent.

HISTORY FROM VISUALS

Interpreting the Illustration Ask students to study the illustration and identify products that Europeans brought to the Americas to cultivate for trade. Ask students which American products they think will be most valuable in Europe, Africa, and Asia. Ask students to explain the skull and crossbones on the map. **Possible Responses** Sugar cane, bananas, citrus fruits, grains, and livestock. Answers may vary but should include tomatoes, corn, and potatoes. The skull and crossbones symbolizes the danger of diseases spread by Europeans.

Extension Have students research the work of the Centers for Disease Control and Prevention in Atlanta, Georgia, in reducing the spread of the listed diseases.

Many slaves resisted slavery by running away or rebelling. To prevent rebellion, the Spanish government passed slave codes, laws to regulate the treatment of slaves. Some of these laws tried to soften the harsh conditions of slavery, but most were designed to punish slaves and keep them in bondage.

Over time, Europeans came to associate slavery with black Africans. To many Europeans, dark skin color became a sign of inferiority. Slavery, which developed to provide a labor force, led to racism. **Racism** is the belief that some people are inferior because of their race.

The slave trade lasted 400 years, from the 1500s until the 1800s. By the 1700s, all the American colonies of European countries had African slaves.

Despite the horrors of slavery, Africans survived in part by clinging to their African cultures, including their artistic heritage of dance, music, and storytelling. The slave trade brought together people from different parts of Africa with different cultural traditions. The experience of slavery helped create a common African-based culture in the Americas. African culture would become one of the forces that shaped life in the American colonies.

Reading **History**

B. Analyzing Causes What could have caused slave traders to treat other humans with such cruelty?

B. Possible Response They saw the slaves as goods that had to be kept alive but little more. Over time, racism played an important role in maintaining this attitude.

3 The Columbian Exchange

The arrival of Europeans in the Americas brought more than a clash of peoples and cultures. It also brought a movement of plants, animals, and diseases between the Eastern and Western hemispheres. This movement of living things between hemispheres is called the **Columbian Exchange.**

One result of the Columbian Exchange was the transfer of germs from Europe to the Americas. When Europeans came to America, they brought with them germs that caused diseases such as smallpox, measles, and influenza. Native Americans had no immunity to them.

The Columbian Exchange

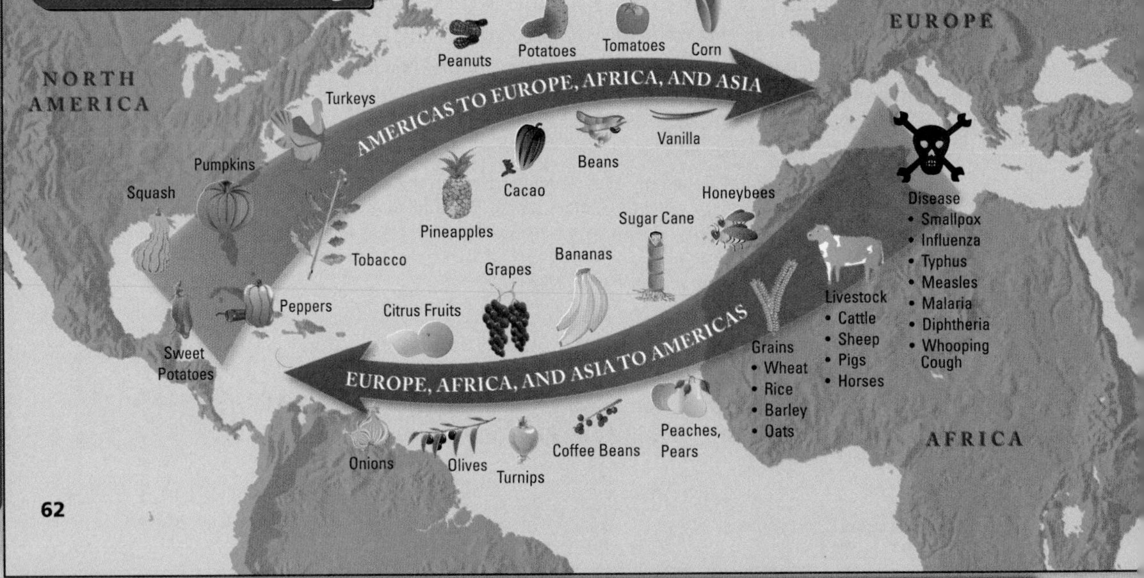

62

ACTIVITY OPTIONS

INDIVIDUAL NEEDS

LESS PROFICIENT READERS

Recognizing Effects Review with students the effects of colonization for Native Americans. Have the students create a graphic like the one shown. Have them write the textbook heading in the first box. Then identify actions that were the results of colonization and write them in the second box. Remind the students that effects can be both positive and negative.

Textbook Heading	Effect on Native Americans
Life in Spanish America	Native Americans were forced to work for colonists. Native Americans were lowest level in social order; had fewest rights.
The Columbian Exchange	Diseases killed millions of Native Americans.

Reading History

C. Making Inferences What might have happened if Native Americans had been immune to European diseases?
C. Possible Response They may not have been so easily conquered.

Although exact numbers are unknown, historians estimate that diseases brought by Europeans killed more than 20 million Native Americans in Mexico in the first century after conquest. Many scholars agree that the population of Native Americans in Central America decreased by 90 to 95 percent between the years 1519 and 1619. The result was similar in Peru and other parts of the Americas. A Spanish missionary in Mexico described the effects of smallpox on the Aztecs.

A VOICE FROM THE PAST

There was a great havoc. Very many died of it. They could not walk. . . . They could not move; they could not stir; they could not change position, nor lie on one side; nor face down, nor on their backs. And if they stirred, much did they cry out. Great was its destruction.

Bernardino de Sahagún, quoted in *Seeds of Change*

Other effects of the Columbian Exchange were more positive. The Spanish brought many plants and animals to the Americas. European livestock—cattle, pigs, and horses—all thrived in the Americas. Crops from the Eastern Hemisphere, such as grapes, onions, and wheat, also thrived in the Western Hemisphere.

The Columbian Exchange benefited Europe, too. Many American crops became part of the European diet. Two that had a huge impact were potatoes and corn. They helped feed European populations that might otherwise have gone hungry. Potatoes, for example, became an important food in Ireland, Russia, and other parts of northern Europe. Without potatoes, Europe's population might not have grown as rapidly as it did during the last five centuries.

By mixing the products of two hemispheres, the Columbian Exchange brought the world closer together. Of course, people were also moving from one hemisphere to the other. The next chapter discusses the movement of the English to the Americas and their efforts to build an empire.

Section 3 Assessment

1. Terms & Names

Explain the significance of:

- *encomienda*
- plantation
- slavery
- African Diaspora
- middle passage
- racism
- Columbian Exchange

2. Taking Notes

Use a diagram like the one below to compare the experience of Native Americans and Africans under slavery.

Native Americans	Africans

3. Main Ideas

a. What were the four levels of Spanish colonial society?

b. Why did Europeans bring Africans to the Americas?

c. How did enslaved Africans respond to their enslavement in the Americas?

4. Critical Thinking

Recognizing Effects What were the positive and negative effects of the Columbian Exchange?

THINK ABOUT
- disease
- food
- livestock

ACTIVITY OPTIONS

ART
MATH

Research some aspect of the slave trade, such as the middle passage or the number of people enslaved. Paint a **picture** or draw a **graph** to show what you learned.

MORE ABOUT . . .

Smallpox

Smallpox—which decimated Native American populations after the arrival of Europeans in the Americas was one of the most feared diseases in the world for centuries. In 1980, the World Health Assembly declared that the world was free of smallpox, thanks to a worldwide vaccination campaign. However, some countries have stockpiled smallpox germs as part of their arsenals for germ warfare. Scientists worry that if these germs are released, there will not be enough vaccine to prevent a terrible epidemic.

MORE ABOUT . . .

The Columbian Exchange

Some foods first grown in the Americas made a roundtrip from the Americas to Africa and back to the Americas. For example, the peanut first grew in South America. It was introduced to Africa by Spanish and Portuguese explorers and traders and then brought to the present-day United States by enslaved Africans. Tomatoes, which first grew in Central America, reached Italy in the 16th century. Most likely, they were a yellow or orange variety. Later, Italians brought red tomatoes to America.

ASSESS & RETEACH

Setting the Stage Have students complete the section of the chart on the Origins of Slavery and the Columbian Exchange.

Formal Assessment
- Section Quiz, p. 38

Critical Thinking Transparency CT4

RETEACHING ACTIVITY

Divide the class into groups of four. Assign one section objective to each group member. Each group member should prepare a short summary of that section's main idea. Members should then share their summaries with the rest of the group.

In-Depth Resources: Unit 1
- Reteaching Activity, p. 36

Section 3 Assessment

1. Terms & Names

ecomienda, p. 60
plantation, p. 60
slavery, p. 60
African Diaspora, p, 61
middle passage, p. 61
racism, p. 62
Columbian Exchange, p. 62

2. Taking Notes

Native Americans—could run away because friends and family were nearby; died of disease; faced hard work and abuse; were subjects of laws regulating treatment
Africans—had little opportunity to escape; immune to many European diseases; faced hard work and abuse

3. Main Ideas

a. Spanish-born, Creoles, *mestizos,* Native Americans/African slaves
b. Europeans needed labor. Enslaved Africans were immune to European diseases and had experience doing the work Europeans wanted done. **c.** Many tried to run away. They also clung to their African cultures.

4. Critical Thinking

Millions of Native Americans died from European diseases. New foods became available in both hemispheres.

ACTIVITY OPTIONS

Alternative Assessment
- Rubrics for a picture, 1.3
- Rubrics for a graph, 2.3

TERMS & NAMES

1. **mercantilism,** p. 51
2. **Hernando Cortés,** p. 53
3. **Montezuma**, p. 53
4. **Spanish Armada,** p. 57
5. **New France,** p. 58
6. ***encomienda,*** p. 60
7. **slavery,** p. 60
8. **African Diaspora,** p. 61
9. **middle passage,** p. 61
10. **Columbian Exchange,** p. 62

REVIEW QUESTIONS

Possible Responses

1. to spread Christianity, to increase national power, to win fame and riches for individual explorers
2. Two Spanish conquistadors—Cortés conquered the Aztecs and Pizarro conquered the Incas.
3. Possible responses: Spain had better weapons than Native Americans. Diseases killed millions of Native Americans. Spain made allies with some Native Americans. The Spanish acted brutally toward Native Americans.
4. a northwest route from Europe to Asia that explorers never found
5. to conquer England and return it to Catholicism
6. the fur trade
7. Native Americans died in great numbers from disease and overwork. They were enslaved and badly treated. Some converted to Christianity. Some learned to read.
8. Possible response: It introduced new foods and goods to Europe. It greatly improved European diets, helping to increase European population.
9. They needed workers to make their colonies productive. Slaves provided cheap labor.
10. European traders took goods to the coast of Africa, where African slave traders supplied captives from the African interior. These slaves were taken to the Americas and sold there.

Chapter 2 ASSESSMENT

TERMS & NAMES

Briefly explain the significance of each of the following.

1. mercantilism
2. *conquistador*
3. Hernando Cortés
4. Montezuma
5. Spanish Armada
6. New France
7. *encomienda*
8. African Diaspora
9. middle passage
10. Columbian Exchange

REVIEW QUESTIONS

Spain Claims an Empire (pages 51–54)

1. What were three reasons for the European voyages of exploration in the 1400s and 1500s?
2. Who conquered the Aztecs and Incas?
3. What three reasons explain Spain's success in building an empire in the Americas?

European Competition in North America (pages 55–58)

4. What was the Northwest Passage?
5. Why did the Spanish Armada attack England?
6. What did the French and Dutch colonists trade?

The Impact of Colonization (pages 59–63)

7. How did Spanish rule affect Native Americans?
8. How did the middle passage get its name?
9. Why did the Spanish and Portuguese use slave labor in their colonies?
10. How did the Columbian Exchange affect Europe?

CRITICAL THINKING

1. USING YOUR NOTES

Event/Idea	Notes
Exploration	
Establishing Colonies	
European Competition	
Columbian Exchange	
Origins of Slavery	

Using your completed chart, answer the questions below.

a. What causes did European competition and exploration have in common?

b. How did the establishment of colonies in the Americas lead to slavery?

c. Which concept in the chart contributed most to the Columbian Exchange?

2. ANALYZING LEADERSHIP

Think about the explorers and *conquistadors* discussed in this chapter. What qualities did they possess that made them successful in their efforts?

3. THEME: IMMIGRATION AND MIGRATION

What were the causes and effects of the migration of Europeans and Africans to the Americas?

4. APPLYING CITIZENSHIP SKILLS

What kind of values did Bartolomé de Las Casas demonstrate in his actions? How effective was he in improving his society?

Interact *with* History

Have your answers about whether or not you would join a voyage of exploration changed after reading the chapter? Explain.

VISUAL SUMMARY

European Exploration of the Americas

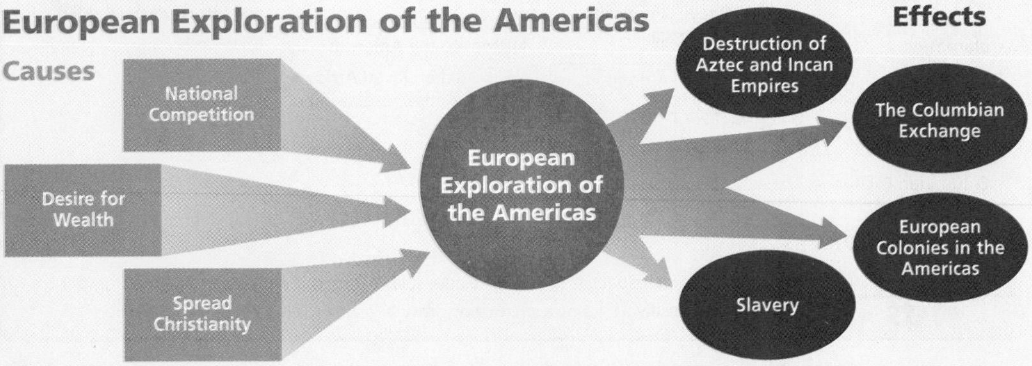

CRITICAL THINKING

Possible Responses

1. **USING YOUR NOTES** **a.** The desire for wealth and power motivated both. **b.** Europeans used slave labor on sugar plantations. **c.** Students should give evidence to support their answer.
2. **ANALYZING LEADERSHIP** strength, determination, ambition; sometimes religious devotion; sometimes brutality
3. **THEME: IMMIGRATION AND MIGRATION** Europeans migrated in search of wealth and power. Most Africans were forcibly brought to the Americas.
4. **APPLYING CITIZENSHIP SKILLS** Las Casas exhibited courage and compassion, but he neglected to help enslaved Africans. He got some laws passed to protect Native Americans, but the laws were not very effective.

Interact *with* History Students' decisions will vary but should be supported by evidence.

HISTORY SKILLS

1. INTERPRETING CHARTS

Slaves Imported to the Americas *(in thousands)* *1601–1810*

REGION/COUNTRY	1601–1700	1701–1810
British N. America	*	348
British Caribbean	263.7	1,401.3
French Caribbean	155.8	1,348.4
Spanish America	292.5	578.6
Dutch Caribbean	40	460
Danish Caribbean	4	24
Brazil (Portugal)	560	1,891.4

*=less than 1,000

Source: Philip D. Curtin, *The Atlantic Slave Trade*

Basic Chart Elements

a. What is the subject of the chart?

b. How many years are covered in each column?

Interpreting the Chart

c. Which European nation imported the most slaves in the Americas?

d. Which region imported less than 1,000 slaves before 1700?

2. INTERPRETING PRIMARY SOURCES

Bernal Díaz del Castillo was a *conquistador* who accompanied Cortés during the conquest of Mexico. Díaz described what he saw when Cortés and Montezuma met. Read the passage. Then answer the questions.

> On our arrival we entered the large court, where the great Montezuma was awaiting our Captain [Cortés]. Taking him by the hand, the prince led him to his apartment in the hall where he was to lodge, which was very richly furnished. . . . Montezuma had ready for him a very rich necklace, made of golden crabs, a marvelous piece of work, which he hung round Cortés's neck. His captains were greatly astonished at this sign of honour.
>
> **Bernal Díaz del Castillo,** from *The Conquest of New Spain*

a. What can you tell about Montezuma from this passage?

b. How would you describe the relationship between Montezuma and Cortés?

ALTERNATIVE ASSESSMENT

1. INTERDISCIPLINARY ACTIVITY: Language Arts

Writing a News Report Research an event in the conquest of the Americas, such as *La Noche Triste* or the death of Atahualpa, the Inca ruler. Write a news report about the event that explains what happened and who was involved. You should also explain when, where, why, and how the event occurred. Be sure to use standard grammar, spelling, sentence structure, and punctuation in your news report.

2. COOPERATIVE LEARNING ACTIVITY

Creating a Diorama With a group of classmates, research the communities of Spanish America in the 1600s. Then create a diorama of one of those settlements, including a mission, a hacienda, roads, and mines or sugar mills. Use elements such as drawings, maps, and written text to show significant features of life there. Display your diorama and discuss it in class.

3. TECHNOLOGY ACTIVITY

Making a Class Presentation The Columbian Exchange refers to the movement of plants and animals around the world as a result of exploration. Today, species of plants and animals continue to move across the planet. Using the library or the Internet, find diaries and news articles about the effects of this continued movement of plants and animals.

For more information on the migration of plants and animals . . .

INTERNET ACTIVITY CLASSZONE.COM

Create a class presentation about the movement of plants and animals around the world, using the suggestions below.

- Choose a specific species of plant or animal. Use a map or globe to show where that species has moved in recent years.
- Choose one specific place, and list any species that are new to the area as well as their effects on the ecology.

4. HISTORY PORTFOLIO

Review your section and chapter assessment activities. Select one that you think was your best work. Then revise your work based on the comments of your teacher or classmates and add your work to your portfolio.

Additional Test Practice, pp. S1–S33 — TEST PRACTICE CLASSZONE.COM

ALTERNATIVE ASSESSMENT

1. INTERDISCIPLINARY ACTIVITY: **Language Arts**

News reports should
- use a journalistic style.
- present information in an unbiased way.
- cover the topic adequately.
- have a headline and portray the historical events accurately.
- use correct grammar, spelling, and punctuation.

2. COOPERATIVE LEARNING ACTIVITY

Dioramas should
- accurately represent the Spanish-American community in 2- or 3-dimensional manner clear to the viewers.
- exhibit creativity.
- demonstrate grade-level artistic skill.

3. TECHNOLOGY ACTIVITY

Class presentations should
- clearly demonstrate an understanding of the concept of movement of plants and animals.
- have adequate delivery and establish rapport with the audience.
- show proficiency in the use of technology.

4. HISTORY PORTFOLIO

Revised section or chapter assessment activities should
- address teacher and peer responses to the selected work.
- solve problems present in the first versions of the work.

Critical Thinking Transparency CT6
- Visual Summary

Formal Assessment
- Chapter Test, Forms A, B, and C, pp. 39–50

HISTORY SKILLS

Possible Responses

1. INTERPRETING CHARTS

Basic Chart Elements

a. slave imports

b. 100 years in left column, 110 years in right column

Interpreting the Chart

c. Portugal

d. British North America

2. INTERPRETING PRIMARY SOURCES

a. Montezuma was wealthy and powerful. He gave Cortés a valuable gift.

b. Montezuma was trying to get on Cortés's good side.

CHAPTER 3 PLANNING GUIDE

The English Establish 13 Colonies 1585–1732

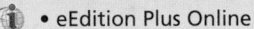

	CHAPTER OVERVIEW	COPYMASTERS	INTEGRATED TECHNOLOGY
CHAPTER RESOURCES	The chapter discusses the English colonization of North America and the leading individuals who took part in settling the colonies. It also differentiates among the three major areas of settlement on the eastern seaboard.	**In-Depth Resources: Unit 1** • Tracing Themes: Impact of the Individual, p. 39 • Building Vocabulary, p. 43 **Interdisciplinary Projects,** pp. 13–18	• eEdition Plus Online • EasyPlanner Plus Online • eTest Plus Online • eEdition • Power Presentations • EasyPlanner • Electronic Library of Primary Sources • Test Generator • Reading Study Guide • America's Music
SECTION 1 Early Colonies Have Mixed Success pp. 69–75	**KEY IDEAS** • England finances colonies through joint stock companies. • Jamestown, founded in 1607, survives under John Smith's leadership. • Bacon's Rebellion forces England to limit the powers of royal governors.	**In-Depth Resources: Unit 1** • Setting the Stage, p. 38 • Guided Reading, p. 40 • Geography Application: Roanoke Colony, pp. 45–46 • Primary Source, p. 47 • Reteaching Activity, p. 52 **America's History Makers** • Pocahontas, pp. 11–12	**Warm-Up Transparency WT3** **Humanities Transparency HT5** • John Smith Takes a Prisoner, 1624 **Critical Thinking Transparency CT7** • Setting the Stage classzone.com
SECTION 2 New England Colonies pp. 76–83	• Pilgrims and Puritans found New England colonies. • The New England Way sets standards of godliness and hard work, but also provokes challenges to its strictness. • In King Philip's War, Native Americans resist English expansion in New England.	**In-Depth Resources: Unit 1** • Setting the Stage, p. 38 • Guided Reading, p. 41 • Skillbuilder Practice, p. 44 • Literature Selection, pp. 49–51 • Reteaching Activity, p. 53 **America's History Makers** • William Bradford, pp. 13–14 **Economics in History** • Farming in the English Colonies, p. 3	**Warm-Up Transparency WT3** **Humanities Transparency HT6** • *Pilgrims Going to Church* by George Henry Boughton **Critical Thinking Transparency CT8** • Cause and Effect: King Philip's War, 1675–1676 **Primary Source Explorer** • *The Mayflower Compact* • *The Fundamental Orders of Connecticut*
SECTION 3 Founding the Middle and Southern Colonies pp. 84–87	• England takes over New York from the Dutch. • William Penn founds Pennsylvania as a colony based on religious freedom and equality. • Southern colonies thrive on economies of warm-weather crops.	**In-Depth Resources: Unit 1** • Setting the Stage, p. 38 • Guided Reading, p. 42 • Primary Source, p. 48 • Reteaching Activity, p. 54 **Why It Matters Now** • British Connections Today, pp. 5–6 **Outline Map Activities** • The 13 Colonies, pp. 5–6	**Warm-Up Transparency WT3** **Geography Transparency GT3** • European Colonies, 1650 **Critical Thinking Transparency CT9** • Visual Summary classzone.com

Pupil's Edition
Copymaster
Overhead Transparency
Audio Library
CD-ROM
Internet

ASSESSMENT OPTIONS

Chapter Assessment, pp. 88–89

Formal Assessment
- Chapter Tests, Forms A, B, and C, pp. 54–68

Test Generator

Online Test Practice

Strategies for Test Preparation

Section Assessment, p. 73

Formal Assessment, Quiz, p. 51

Integrated Assessment Book
- Rubrics, 1.1, 4.9

Test Generator

Test Practice Transparencies, TT10

Section Assessment, p. 81

Formal Assessment, Quiz, p. 52

Integrated Assessment Book
- Rubrics, 4.5, 3.6

Test Generator

Test Practice Transparencies, TT11

Section Assessment, p. 87

Formal Assessment, Quiz, p. 53

Integrated Assessment Book
- Rubrics, 4.5, 5.3

Test Generator

Test Practice Transparencies, TT12

CUSTOMIZING FOR INDIVIDUAL NEEDS

Students Acquiring English/ESL

Reading Study Guide (English and Spanish), pp. 21–28

Access for Students Acquiring English/ESL: Spanish Translations, pp. 13–18

Chapter Summaries on CD (English and Spanish)

Modified Lesson Plans for English Learners

Less Proficient Readers

Reading Study Guide (English and Spanish), pp. 21–28

Chapter Summaries on CD (English and Spanish)

Gifted and Talented Students

In-Depth Resources: Unit 1
- Enrichment Activity, p. 55

America's History Makers
- Pocahontas, pp. 11–12
- William Bradford, pp. 13–14

CROSS-CURRICULAR CONNECTIONS

Science/Math

Woods, Geraldine. ***Science of the Early Americans.*** New York: Franklin Watts, 1999.

Popular Culture

Erdosh, George. ***Food and Recipes of the Pilgrims.*** Powerkids Press, 1998.

Hale, Anna W. ***The Mayflower People: Triumphs and Tragedies.*** Niwot, CO: Rinehart, 1995. Colorful coverage of the ocean voyage filled with human detail; useful bibliography as well.

Interdisciplinary Projects, pp. 13–18

- Math: Dimensions of the *Mayflower*
- Science: Cultivating Plants
- Language Arts: Advertising for Colonists
- Home Economics: Plan a Thanksgiving Menu

Language Arts/Literature

Harragh, Madge. ***My Brother, My Enemy.*** New York: Simon & Schuster, 1997. When 14-year-old Robert Bradford finds himself caught up in Bacon's Rebellion, his loyalties and beliefs are tested to the limit.

Jacobs, Paul S. ***James Printer: A Novel of King Philip's War.*** New York: Scholastic, 1997. The story of a true-life figure, Nipmuck Indian James Printer, showing the fears, tragedies, and courage of both sides in the war.

McDougal Littell Literature Connections

Elizabeth Speare
The Witch of Blackbird Pond
Unconventional Kit Tyler does not fit well with the society of Puritan Connecticut and finds herself accused of witchcraft.

ENRICHMENT ACTIVITIES

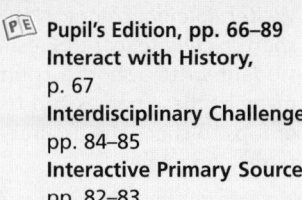

Pupil's Edition, pp. 66–89
Interact with History, p. 67
Interdisciplinary Challenge, pp. 84–85
Interactive Primary Sources, pp. 82–83

In-Depth Resources: Unit 1
- Geography Application: Roanoke Colony, pp. 45–46
- Primary Source, p. 47
- Primary Source, p. 48
- Literature Selection, pp. 49–51

America's History Makers
- Pocahontas, pp. 11–12
- William Bradford, pp. 13–14

America's Music CD

Outline Map Activities
- The 13 Colonies, pp. 5–6

Primary Source Explorer
- *The Mayflower Compact*
- *The Fundamental Orders of Connecticut*

Why It Matters Now
- British Connections Today, pp. 5–6

BLOCK SCHEDULING — LESSON PLAN OPTIONS (90-MINUTE PERIOD)

DAY 1

Interact with History, p. 67
Class Time 20 minutes

Options for pacing and variety:
- **Role-Playing** Have students suppose they are the leaders of the first colonists to arrive at Jamestown. As leaders, they need to write a short speech explaining to the other settlers why they must build a fort.
  Class Time 10 minutes

Setting the Stage, p. 68
Class Time 20 minutes

Options for pacing and variety:
- **Time Saver** For a homework assignment, have students pick one of the 13 colonies shown on the graphic organizer in Read and Take Notes and make a list of what they already know about this colony and what they would like to know. Have students share their lists with the class.
  Class Time 10 minutes

Section 1, pp. 69–75
Class Time 50 minutes

Options for pacing and variety:
- **History on Film** Extend students' background knowledge of Jamestown and other early Virginia settlements by viewing *Where America Began: Colonial Williamsburg, Jamestown, Yorktown.* Finley-Holiday.
  Class Time 60 minutes

Interdisciplinary Challenge, pp. 74–75
Options for pacing and variety:
- **Peer Evaluation** As each group presents its report to the class on how it solved the civics and economics challenges, have the other students evaluate the presentations using the guidelines in the Activity Wrap-Up. Remind students that criticism should be constructive.
  Class Time 30 minutes

DAY 2

Section 2, pp. 76–83
Class Time 45 minutes

Options for pacing and variety:
- **Internet** Extend students' background knowledge of the Pilgrims and the Plymouth Colony by taking a virtual tour of Plimoth Plantation at classzone.com
  Class Time 20 minutes

Section 3, pp. 84–87
Class Time 45 minutes

Options for pacing and variety:
- **Peer Evaluation** Have student pairs create two Reading History questions for the section and exchange them with another team to be answered. **Class Time** 15 minutes

Chapter 3 Assessment, pp. 88–89
Class Time 40 minutes

Options for pacing and variety:
- **Time Saver** Use the map "The 13 English Colonies, 1732" on page 86 to summarize the chapter. **Class Time** 10 minutes
- **Peer Competition** Divide the class into small groups. Have each group write three short "Who Am I?" paragraphs describing colony founders listed on the chart on page 88. Have teams compete to see which can provide the founder's name first. Teams can vary the game by writing "Where Am I?" descriptions. **Class Time** 30 minutes

TEACHER-TESTED ACTIVITY James G. Grimes, Middlesex County Vocational Technical High School, Woodbridge, New Jersey

WORD BY WORD

Class Time One class period

Task Writing a short report using assigned names and terms

Purpose To demonstrate understanding of key names and terms

Supplies Needed
- Dictionary
- Thesaurus

Activity Write the following words and names from Section 1 on the chalkboard, or duplicate the list and distribute it to the class: *John Smith, Powhatan, Pocahontas, John Rolfe, John White, Virginia, Jamestown, Sir Walter Raleigh, colony, Native American, persecution, joint-stock company, charter, climate, control, "starving time," indentured servant.* Have each student write a short account of the founding of Jamestown using as many of these names and terms as possible. Then assign students to small groups to check the accuracy of their accounts and the correct usage of terms and names.

AN ORAL HISTORY ACCOUNT OF JAMESTOWN

Oral histories are a great way to preserve the heritage of a generation. Most of the first British settlers of Jamestown had no opportunity to tell their stories about the daily challenges they faced, the frightening and unexpected events they experienced, or the rewards they found on the Chesapeake. In this activity, students will consider and record what they think the Jamestown colonists would tell us about life in the Jamestown colony.

ACTIVITY OUTLINE

Objective Creating audio recordings of fictional oral histories from Jamestown can help students understand life in the colony.

Task Students will use audio recording equipment to create oral histories of characters like those who were the original Jamestown colonists.

Class Time One class period

DIRECTIONS

1. Explain to students that they will be creating fictional oral history accounts that are based on fact. They must research the lives of Jamestown colonists, write a script for each character, record the story, and share their oral histories with others in the class. Divide students into groups of four students. Each group should include a narrator (interviewer), subject character, audio technician, and scriptwriter.

2. Remind students to start by reviewing Chapter 3 of *Creating America* to gather material for their oral history. Students will need to conduct additional research on the lives of the settlers to develop their character's oral history. Possible sources for information include books in the school library or Web sites on classzone.com.

3. To create the oral history, assign each group of students a character from the original Jamestown settlement roster. The characters are as follows: gentleman farmer, blacksmith, African-American servants/slaves, male indentured servants, preacher, young boy, white female servant.

4. Tell each group to look for information that can help answer these questions about daily life in the settlement for each character:
   a) What is your name and occupation?
   b) Why did you come to Jamestown?
   c) What did you bring with you and how are supplies lasting?
   d) What do you do every day?
   e) What kind of shelter do you live in?
   f) What is your diet?
   g) What are the biggest problems presently facing the colonists?
   h) What are your fears and concerns?
   i) What ideas do you have that would improve life in the settlement?

5. After completing the required research, give each group time at the computer to transcribe their ideas for the script. Suggest that each group appoint a scriptwriter, sound effects manager, narrator, and sound engineer. Encourage the groups to think about enhancements to the recordings, such as possible sound effects.

6. After the groups have completed their scripts, have the students record their oral histories. Make sure each group rehearses its narration before recording them. All students should participate in the recording session.

7. When all the oral histories have been recorded, have the groups label their tapes with the name of the character they have recorded. Collect the tapes and arrange a time to hear the oral histories of the Jamestown settlement.

CHAPTER 3 OBJECTIVE
The student will understand how the first English colonies survived and began to grow, while colonists both learned from and experienced conflict with Native Americans.

CHAPTER 3

The English Establish 13 Colonies 1585–1732

HISTORY FROM VISUALS

Interpreting the Illustration Ask the students to study the woodcut. Point out the lean-to shelter where the settlers live while building their houses. Also note the location along a river. Have students name any tools they see in the woodcut. Ask students how they can tell that members of several families are helping to build this house. Ask students who these people might be. **Possible Responses** Tools include axes, plane, sledgehammer. The people are newly arrived settlers who are clearing the land. The many adult males in this drawing suggest that this is a community effort.

Extension Have the students write one piece of advice they would give the settlers.

Early settlers build the fort at Jamestown.

RECOMMENDED RESOURCES

BOOKS FOR THE TEACHER

Hulton, Paul, ed. ***America in Fifteen Eighty-Five: The Complete Drawings of John White.*** Chapel Hill: U. of N.C. Press, 1984. A visual record of Native American life in the early contact period.

Johnson, Thomas, ed. ***Puritans: A Sourcebook.*** New York: Harper, 1965. Many primary sources, some familiar, others surprising.

Noël Hume, Ivor. ***Martin's Hundred.*** New York: Knopf, 1979. Firsthand account of an archaeological dig at the site of a 17th-century plantation in Virginia.

SOFTWARE

PilgrimQuest & PilgrimQuest II. Decision Devel. Corp. Complex simulation of Pilgrim experience from 1620 to 1626. A school version contains lessons and resources.

VIDEO

Colonial Williamsburg. Ed. Record Ctr., Inc. Life in colonial Virginia was a considerable contrast to that in colonial Massachusetts.

INTERNET

For more about Plimoth Plantation, visit . . .

classzone.com

Interact *with* History

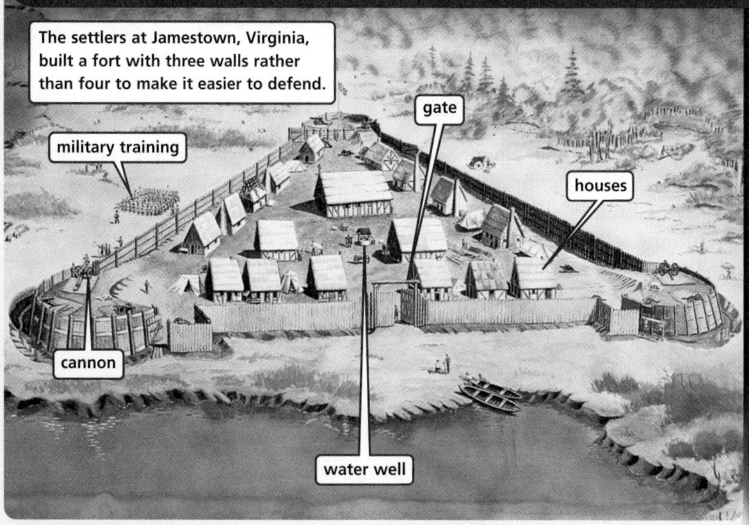
The settlers at Jamestown, Virginia, built a fort with three walls rather than four to make it easier to defend.
gate
military training
houses
cannon
water well

The year is 1607. You have just sailed across the ocean and arrived in a strange land. Your family has traveled to the eastern coast of North America in search of freedom and prosperity. Your first task in the new land is to decide what you need to do to survive.

What Do You Think?

- **What do you need to survive in the wilderness?**
- **This settlement is actually a fort, with an armed force and high fences. What reasons might there be for building a fort?**
- **What kind of settlement would you build?**

What dangers would you face as a settler?

N. America

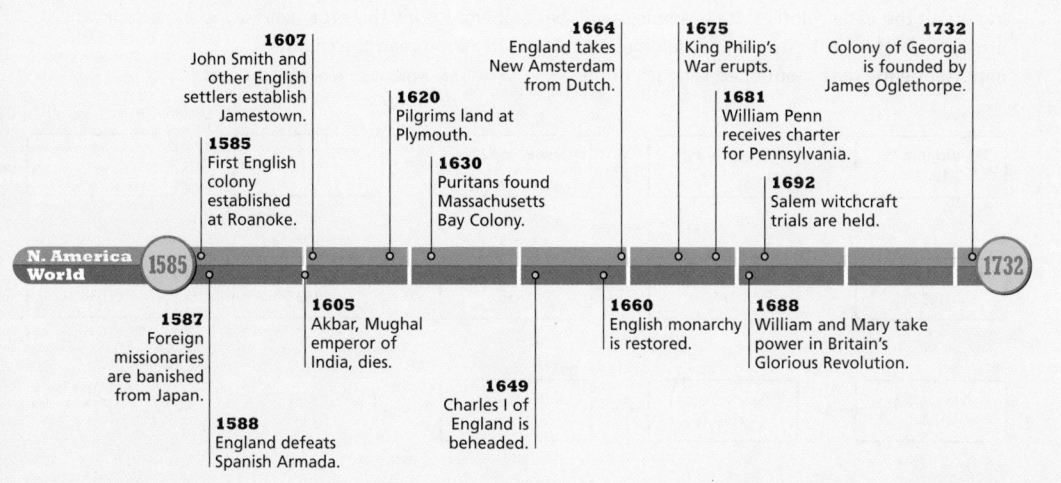

1585 First English colony established at Roanoke.

1607 John Smith and other English settlers establish Jamestown.

1620 Pilgrims land at Plymouth.

1630 Puritans found Massachusetts Bay Colony.

1664 England takes New Amsterdam from Dutch.

1675 King Philip's War erupts.

1681 William Penn receives charter for Pennsylvania.

1692 Salem witchcraft trials are held.

1732 Colony of Georgia is founded by James Oglethorpe.

World

1587 Foreign missionaries are banished from Japan.

1588 England defeats Spanish Armada.

1605 Akbar, Mughal emperor of India, dies.

1649 Charles I of England is beheaded.

1660 English monarchy is restored.

1688 William and Mary take power in Britain's Glorious Revolution.

1585 — 1732

Interact *with* History

OBJECTIVES

- To help students identify the first colonists' basic survival needs
- To help students connect with the people and events they will study in this chapter

What Do You Think?

1. Ask students to list the basic needs of survival: food, clothing, shelter, protection from wild animals and enemies.
2. Have students think about the security needs of the settlers: protection, supplies, weapons, tools, and defense of their families and land against both Native Americans and hostile European nations.
3. Ask students to think about the natural resources they can use to construct and repair their settlement, how they plan to use the surrounding land, and the climate of the area where they will build their settlement.

What dangers would you face as a settler?

Encourage students to think not only about the most obvious challenges of protecting themselves from attacks from animals and other humans but also the dangers of severe weather; of failing to get crops planted, harvested, and preserved; and of illnesses or injuries that cannot be treated with simple remedies. Conflict among settlers and failure to cooperate are also potential dangers.

MAKING PERSONAL CONNECTIONS

Ask students to think about any experiences they have had while camping or walking in forests or wilderness areas. Have students think about how their attitudes toward the wilderness might differ from those of settlers who planned to live there permanently.

TIME LINE DISCUSSION

Point out to students that during the period of English settlement in North America much political activity was occurring in England.

- Ask the students why settlement activities in North America don't seem to be affected by European activities. **Possible Answers** The events were too far away to affect the colonists, news traveled slowly, and colonists knew little about the events.
- Ask students what event shows that Spain's power in Europe was declining. **Answer** England's defeat of Spanish Armada
- Ask students to name another European group that claimed land in North America in the 1600s. **Answer** the Dutch
- Ask students how many years elapsed between the settlement of the first English colony and the founding of Georgia, the 13th colony. **Answer** 147 years

BEFORE YOU READ

Previewing the Theme:
Impact of the Individual

Remind students that both new colonies and Native American groups had some good leaders. Ask students to describe traits and skills that help a leader maintain order and get others to cooperate. Have students explain why each of these skills would be important to successful leadership.

Good leaders are often people who are fair but firm, have strong decision-making and planning skills, remain calm under pressure, and can motivate others to cooperate and work hard to reach shared goals.

What Do You Know?

Most students will be familiar with the Pilgrims, and some may also have visited re-creations of colonial settlements such as Jamestown and Plimoth Plantation. The names of colonial figures such as John Smith, Pocahontas, Peter Stuyvesant, and William Penn may also be familiar. Explore students' associations with these names.

In-Depth Resources: Unit 1
- Tracing Themes: Impact of the Individual, p. 39

READ AND TAKE NOTES

Reading Strategy: Sequencing Events

Explain to students that sequencing events, or putting them in the order in which they occurred, will make them easier to remember. Sequencing also makes it easier to understand the relationships among events. Using a sequence chart such as the one provided will allow students to see at a glance when each of the original colonies was formed.

In-Depth Resources: Unit 1
- Setting the Stage, p. 38

Critical Thinking Transparency CT7
- Setting the Stage

Chapter 3 SETTING THE STAGE

BEFORE YOU READ

Previewing the Theme Impact of the Individual

Beginning in 1585, English settlers started colonies along the eastern coast of North America. This chapter explains how the determination of a few leaders led to new colonies. It also explains how the colonies survived, gained more diverse settlers, and began to drive Native Americans (shown in the map below) off the land.

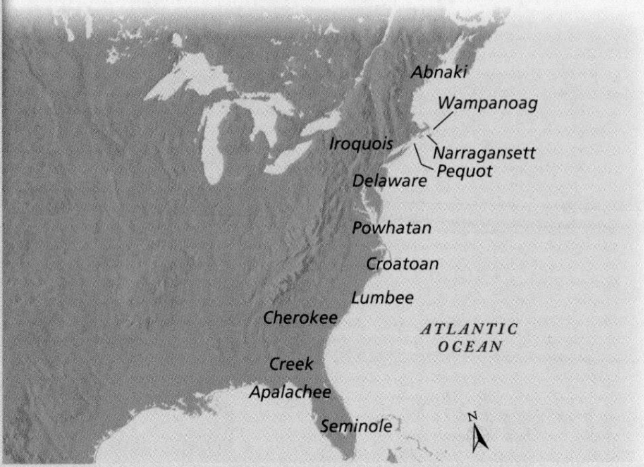

What Do You Know?

What do you already know about the American colonies? What sort of person might choose to leave his or her native country and cross the ocean to settle in a new land?

THINK ABOUT
- what you've learned about American settlers from movies, television, historical fiction, or science fiction about space travel
- opportunities and challenges offered in a new land

What Do You Want to Know?

What questions do you have about the Europeans who settled in North America? about those who were already here? Record your questions in your notebook before you read this chapter.

READ AND TAKE NOTES

Reading Strategy: Sequencing Events

Sequencing means putting events in order. In learning about the early colonies, for example, it will be useful to you to list the 13 original colonies and an important early date mentioned for each in the chapter. You might record the name and a date for each colony in a graphic organizer such as the one below. Copy this organizer in your notebook. Fill it in as you read the chapter.

See Skillbuilder Handbook, page R4.

Virginia 1607 → Massachusetts 1620 → New Hampshire 1623 → New York 1624 → Maryland 1632 → Rhode Island 1636 → Connecticut 1636 → Delaware 1638 → South Carolina 1663 → North Carolina 1663 → New Jersey 1664 → Pennsylvania 1681 → Georgia 1732

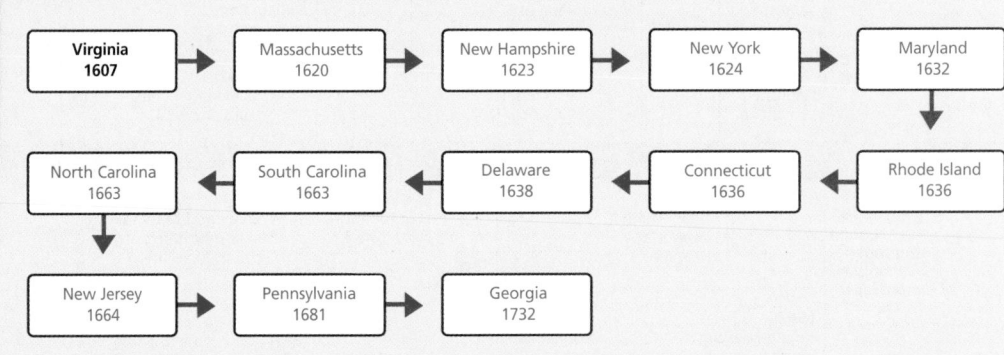

TEACHING STRATEGY

READING THE CHAPTER

This is a chronological chapter focusing on the successes and failures of the early colonies. Ask students to look for reasons why some colonies failed while others survived and grew. Encourage them to note the influence of religious groups such as the Pilgrims, the Puritans, and the Quakers on colonial development.

ALTERNATIVE ASSESSMENT

The Chapter Assessment describes two activities for alternative assessment on page 89. You may wish to have students work on these activities during the course of the chapter and then present them at the end.

1 Early Colonies Have Mixed Success

TERMS & NAMES
joint-stock company
charter
Jamestown
John Smith
indentured servant
House of Burgesses
Bacon's Rebellion

MAIN IDEA

Two early English colonies failed, but Jamestown survived—partly through individual effort and hard work.

WHY IT MATTERS NOW

Jamestown's survival led to more English colonies and a lasting English influence in the United States.

ONE AMERICAN'S STORY

John White was a talented artist. He traveled with the first English expedition to Roanoke, an island off North Carolina, in 1585. While there, he painted scenes of Native American villages. White sailed back to England in 1586 and then returned to Roanoke as governor the next year, bringing with him more than 100 settlers. White's daughter Elinor gave birth to a baby girl, Virginia Dare, during their stay. John White described the event.

A VOICE FROM THE PAST

On August 18 a daughter was born to Elinor, . . . wife of Ananias Dare. . . . The child was christened on the following Sunday and was named Virginia because she was the first Christian born in Virginia.

John White, *The New World*

In 1587, White was forced to sail back to England a second time to get needed supplies. He left the colonists, including his granddaughter, Virginia, in Roanoke. Delayed by the Spanish Armada (a fleet of ships that attempted to invade England in 1588), White did not return to Roanoke until 1590.

To his shock and grief, he found no trace of the colonists or his granddaughter, all of whom had disappeared. The only clues to their whereabouts were the letters *CRO* carved in a tree and the word *Croatoan* carved in a doorpost. White never discovered the fate of his family and the other colonists. In this section, you will learn why English settlers such as White came to America despite such hardships. You'll also learn how they lived and what they believed.

Drawing by John White of an old man of the Pomeiock tribe.

1 The English Plan Colonies

As you read in Chapter 2, religious and political rivalries increased between England and Spain in the late 1500s. Spain had many colonies in the Americas, but England had none. England began directing its resources toward establishing colonies after its defeat of the Spanish Armada in 1588.

SECTION OBJECTIVES

1. To describe early English attempts at colonizing
2. To explain English financing of a colony
3. To summarize how Jamestown was founded and grew
4. To analyze the conflicts of the Jamestown colonists both with Native Americans and among the colonists themselves

SKILLBUILDER

Interpreting Maps: Location, Human-Environment Interaction, p. 71

CRITICAL THINKING

Summarizing, p. 70
Solving Problems, p. 71
Analyzing Causes, p. 72
Finding Main Ideas, p. 72
Drawing Conclusions, p. 73

FOCUS & MOTIVATE

5-MINUTE WARM-UP

Making Inferences These questions focus on the difficulties of founding a colony.

1. Look at the map on page 71. When and where was the first English settlement?
2. Judging by the dates on the map, how long did the settlement last?

Warm-Up Transparency WT3

INSTRUCT

INSTRUCT: OBJECTIVE 1

The English Plan Colonies

- Why did Hakluyt favor founding English colonies in the Americas?
- Why did the English want to go to America?

In-Depth Resources: Unit 1
- Guided Reading, p. 40

Reading Study Guide (Spanish and English), pp. 21–22

RECOMMENDED RESOURCES

In-Depth Resources: Unit 1
- Guided Reading, p. 40
- Building Vocabulary, p. 43
- Geog. Application, pp. 45–46
- Primary Source: from *Generall Historie of Virginia* by John Smith, p. 47
- Enrichment Activity, p. 55

Reading Study Guide (Spanish and English), pp. 21–22

America's History Makers
- Pocahontas, pp. 11–12

Formal Assessment
- Section Quiz, p. 51

Integrated Assessment
- Rubrics, 1.1, 4.9

Access for Students Acquiring English/ESL, pp. 13, 17–18

INTEGRATED TECHNOLOGY

Humanities Transparency HT5
- *John Smith Takes a Prisoner,* 1624

Electronic Teacher Tools

classzone.com

TEST-TAKING RESOURCES

Strategies for Test Preparation

Test Practice Transparencies, TT10

Online Test Practice

INSTRUCT: OBJECTIVE 2

Two Early Colonies Fail/Financing a Colony

- What part did Sir Walter Raleigh play in the first English settlements?
- Why did the Roanoke colony fail?
- What did a joint-stock company have to do with colonial settlement?

In-Depth Resources: Unit 1
- Geography Application: Roanoke Colony, pp. 45–46

Now and then

The Lumbee and the Lost Colonists

Other evidence cited for Lumbee descent from the lost colonists comes from the writings of European travelers in the later 1600s. One traveler recorded meeting Native Americans familiar with European customs in what is now Robeson County in south-central North Carolina. Another told of traveling in this same area and being captured by Native Americans who spoke English. Two centuries later, in 1891, historian Stephen Weeks published a scholarly paper claiming that the distinctive dialect spoken by the Lumbee was very similar to English as it was spoken in England at the time of Queen Elizabeth. Other theories suggest that the Lumbee are descendants of the Cherokee, the Eastern Siouan, or the Iroquois-speaking Tuscarora people.

Richard Hakluyt (HAK•LOOT), an English geographer, urged England to start a colony. Hakluyt thought that colonies would provide a market for English exports. They also would serve as a source of raw materials. By having colonies, England hoped to increase its trade and build up its gold supply. This is the economic theory of mercantilism (see page 52). In mercantilism, the state controls trade and attempts to transfer wealth from colonies to the parent country. Hakluyt also thought that English colonies would help to plant the Protestant faith in the Americas.

The earliest English colonists had many reasons for going to America. The lack of economic opportunity in England forced many to seek their fortunes abroad. Stories of gold mines lured some to leave England. Others left to escape religious persecution.

Reading **History**

A. Summarizing Why did English colonists settle in America?

A. Answer They were looking for economic opportunity and religious freedom.

2 Two Early Colonies Fail

Sir Walter Raleigh was a soldier, statesman, and adventurer who served under Queen Elizabeth I of England. She gave him permission to sponsor the colony at Roanoke. He named England's first colony Virginia after the unmarried, or virgin, queen. Financed by Raleigh, the colony began in 1585 on Roanoke Island. The colonists relied on the Native Americans for food. But when the Native Americans realized that the settlers wanted their land, they cut off the colonists' food supply. Those who survived returned to England in 1586.

Vocabulary

financed: paid for; raised funds for

In 1587, artist John White convinced Raleigh to try again to establish the Roanoke colony, with the disastrous results described in One American's Story (page 69). To this day, no one knows for sure what happened. Some historians think that the colonists mingled with the neighboring Native Americans. Others believe that they moved to Chesapeake Bay and were killed by Native Americans defending their land.

Now and then

THE LUMBEE AND THE LOST COLONISTS

The Lumbee tribe lives mainly in North Carolina. Some of the Lumbee believe they are descendants of the lost colonists of Roanoke. Among the evidence cited is the fact that 41 of the 95 last names of the Lumbee were last names of the colonists.

Other Lumbee don't believe that they are descended from English ancestors. The Lumbee are trying to win federal recognition as a Native American tribe. English ancestry might weaken their claim for federal financial support.

In 1607, the Plymouth Company sponsored the Sagadahoc colony at the mouth of the Kennebec River in Maine. Some of the settlers were English convicts. One colonist wrote of George Popham, the governor, "He stocked or planted [the colony] out of all the jails of England." Within the first year, arguments among colonists, a harsh winter, fights with Native Americans, and food shortages forced most of the colonists to return to England.

Financing a Colony

Raleigh had financed the colony at Roanoke. When the colony failed, he lost his investment. The English learned from Raleigh's financial loss at Roanoke that one person could not finance a colony. To raise money, they turned to the **joint-stock company.** Joint-stock companies were backed by investors, people who put money into a project to earn profits. Each investor received pieces of ownership of the company called

ACTIVITY OPTIONS

INTERDISCIPLINARY LINK: ECONOMICS — BLOCK SCHEDULING

FORMING A JOINT-STOCK COMPANY

Class Time One class period

Task Simulating the workings of a joint-stock company

Purpose To understand the way a joint-stock company obtained funds and to understand the risks taken by investors

Supplies Needed
- Ten pennies for each student
- "Stock certificates," handwritten or photocopied
- A box or hat
- An "annual report," a card for each student indicating that his/her investment has tripled, been lost completely, or not changed

Activity Give each student ten pennies. Tell the class that you are forming a joint-stock company to fund a colony beneath the Atlantic Ocean. Ask for investors. Tell the class that each penny will represent five thousand dollars. Discuss the risks and possible rewards of such an investment. Collect the students' "investments" and give each "investor" a stock certificate for each five thousand dollars invested. Then ask students to draw an annual report card from a hat or box. Discuss the results of their investments.

shares of stock. In this way, the investors split any profits and divided any losses.

Merchants organized the Virginia Company of London and the Virginia Company of Plymouth. King James I of England granted charters to both companies in 1606. A **charter** was a written contract, issued by a government, giving the holder the right to establish a colony.

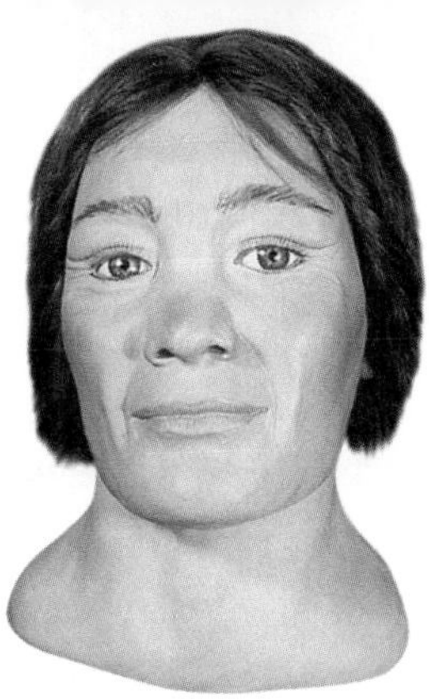

This is a computer reconstruction of the face of Mistress Forrest, believed to be the first English woman to come to Jamestown.

Skillbuilder Answers
1. Sagadahoc. Approximately 500 miles.
2. The ocean provided a source of food and a means of transportation.

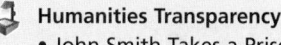

3 Jamestown Is Founded in 1607

In 1607, the Virginia Company of London financed an expedition to Chesapeake Bay that included more than 100 colonists. They sailed up the James River until they found a spot to settle. They named the first permanent English settlement **Jamestown** in honor of King James.

Background
Historians used to believe that the colony's original site had been flooded by the James River. Recent archaeological digs, however, have discovered the site on higher ground.

From the start, the Jamestown colonists endured terrible hardships. The site of the colony was swampy and full of malaria-carrying mosquitoes. This disease made the colonists sick with fever. Many also became ill from drinking the river water. To make matters worse, the London Company had incorrectly told the settlers that the colony would be rich in gold. They spent their days searching for gold rather than building houses and growing food.

The climate was also a hardship. The colonists soon learned that the summers were hot and humid and the winters bitter cold. As one colonist recalled, "There were never Englishmen left in a foreign country in such misery as we were in this newly discovered Virginia."

Jamestown Grows

By January 1608, only 38 colonists remained alive. Later that year, **John Smith,** a soldier and adventurer, took control. To make sure the colonists worked, Smith announced, "He that will not work shall not eat." Smith's methods worked. He ordered an existing wall extended around Jamestown. He also persuaded the Powhatan tribe to trade their corn to the colonists. In 1609, Smith was injured in a gunpowder explosion and returned to England. That same year, 800 more English settlers arrived in Jamestown.

B. Possible Answer
Banishment or a system of penalties and fines might have worked.

*Reading*History
B. Solving Problems If you had been John Smith, how would you have forced the colonists to work?

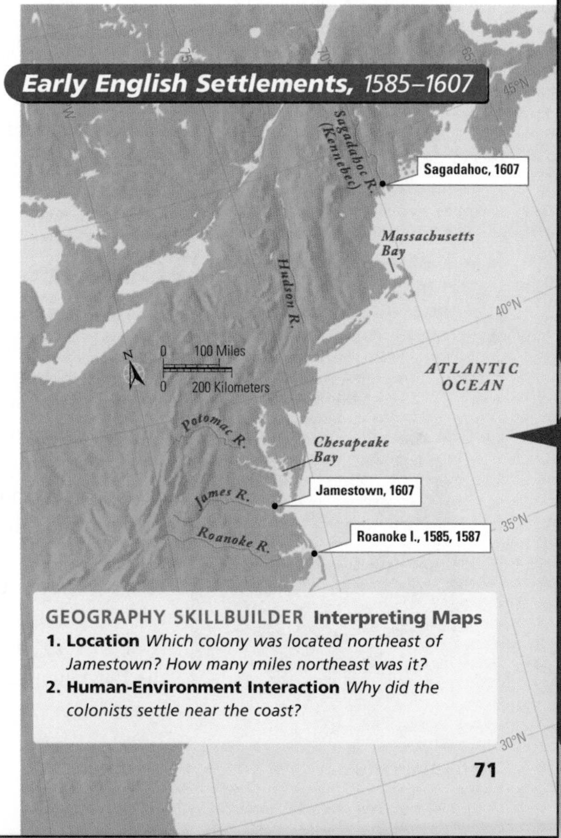

GEOGRAPHY SKILLBUILDER Interpreting Maps
1. **Location** *Which colony was located northeast of Jamestown? How many miles northeast was it?*
2. **Human-Environment Interaction** *Why did the colonists settle near the coast?*

71

INSTRUCT: OBJECTIVE 3

Jamestown Is Founded in 1607/ Jamestown Grows

- When and where was the first permanent English colony founded?
- What hardships did the colonists face in the early years of settlement?
- How did the colonists' decision to grow tobacco change Jamestown?

Humanities Transparency HT5
- John Smith Takes a Prisoner, 1624

In-Depth Resources: Unit 1
- Primary Source, p. 47

MORE ABOUT . . .

Dining at Jamestown
Jamestown colonists faced the "starving time" in the winter of 1609 in part because their main sources of food were seasonal. In a garbage pit from before 1610, archaeologists have found the bones of the animals that the colonists ate. From May to September, when the sturgeon were running, these huge fish (up to 800 pounds) kept the colony well supplied. The settlers also ate a quantity of land tortoises. In addition, they consumed oysters, birds, and raccoons. But with the cold weather, many of these fish and animals migrated to warmer areas or hibernated.

HISTORY FROM VISUALS

Reading the Map Ask students what barriers they see on the map that would make travel difficult for settlers. **Possible Responses** Mountains might create barriers to travel westward. The rivers flow toward the sea. Travel upriver might be difficult.

Extension Have students locate this segment of the coast on a map of the United States and name the states that this area covers today.

ACTIVITY OPTIONS

INDIVIDUAL NEEDS

LESS PROFICIENT READERS

Taking Notes Some students may have difficulty understanding the importance of the historical figures discussed in the section. To help them focus on the key figures and their roles, have them create a concept web for Sir Walter Raleigh, John Smith, John Rolfe, the Powhatan, and Nathaniel Bacon. You might provide a web such as the one shown as a model.

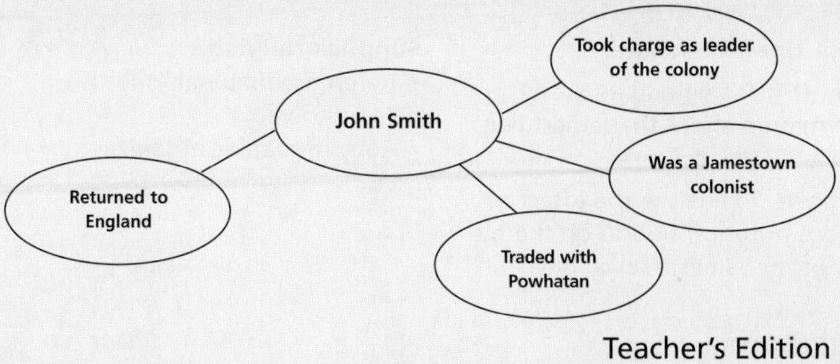

MORE ABOUT . . .

Tobacco

Not everyone in England was thrilled by the successes of the tobacco trade. King James called smoking "a custome lothsome to the eye, hatefull to the Nose, harmefull to the braine, [and] dangerous to the Lungs." He tried to prevent its spread.

AMERICA'S HISTORY MAKERS

Pocahontas

Pocahontas was famous in London long before she arrived there. Many English people had read John Smith's account of how she had saved his life. She was presented to Queen Anne and King James I at the royal court. She attended elegant parties and met famous people such as Sir Walter Raleigh. She succeeded so well in making the Virginia Company the talk of the town that the company's managers gave her a salary.

Possible Responses: Pocahontas managed to bridge the two cultures of English and Native American, as shown in her marriage to John Rolfe and her trip to England to raise money for the Jamestown colony.

America's History Makers
- Pocahontas, pp. 11–12

In-Depth Resources: Unit 1
- Enrichment Activities, p. 55

INSTRUCT: OBJECTIVE 4

Conflicts with the Powhatan/ Bacon's Rebellion in 1676

- What were the causes of conflict between English colonists and the Powhatan?
- Why did the colonists create the House of Burgesses?
- What were the causes of Bacon's Rebellion?

Because of growing tensions between the settlers and Native Americans, the Powhatan stopped trading food and attacked the settlers. The settlers did not dare leave the fort. During the "starving time," the colonists ate rats, mice, and snakes. Only 60 of the colonists were still alive when two ships arrived in 1610. Lord De La Warr, the new governor, imposed discipline, and the "starving time" ended.

In 1612, John Rolfe developed a high-grade tobacco that the colonists learned to grow. It quickly became very popular in England. The success of tobacco growing changed Jamestown in many ways. The Virginia Company thought of the colonists as employees. The colonists, however, wanted a share of the profits.

The company responded by letting settlers own land. Settlers worked harder when the land was their own. The company offered a 50-acre land grant for each man, woman, or child who could pay his or her way to the colony. In 1619, the first African Americans arrived in Jamestown. The population of Virginia jumped from about 600 in 1619 to more than 2,000 in 1621.

Even more laborers were needed. Those who could not afford passage to America were encouraged to become **indentured servants**. These men and women sold their labor to the person who paid their passage to the colony. After working for a number of years, they were free to farm or take up a trade of their own.

The colonists soon became annoyed at the strict rule of the governor, who represented the Virginia Company's interests back in London. To provide for more local control, the company decided that burgesses, or elected representatives, of the colonists would meet once a year in an assembly. The **House of Burgesses**, created in 1619, became the first representative assembly in the American colonies.

Reading History

C. Analyzing Causes What was the main reason for the various arrangements the Virginia Company came up with to bring people to America?

C. Answer The company needed people to help grow tobacco.

AMERICA'S HISTORY MAKERS

POCAHONTAS
1595?–1617

Pocahontas met John Smith when she was about 12 years old. Smith taught her English and admired her spirit. She admired Smith's bravery and saved his life twice. After Smith returned to England, she married the colonist John Rolfe in 1614. Shown below is a portrait of Pocahontas, done in 1616.

Two years later, the Rolfes went to England to raise money for the Jamestown colony. While getting ready to sail home, Pocahontas died of smallpox.

How did Pocahontas show that Native Americans and white settlers might live in peace?

4 Conflicts with the Powhatan

Cultural differences put the Powhatan and the English on a collision course. At first, the Powhatan traded food with the colonists. Then, as more colonists arrived and wanted land, relations grew worse. In an effort to improve relations between the English colonists and the Powhatan, John Rolfe married Chief Powhatan's daughter, Pocahontas, in 1614.

For a time, there was an uneasy peace. The colonists learned from the Powhatan how to grow corn, catch fish, and capture wild fowl. However, the expanding tobacco plantations took over more and more Powhatan land. In 1622, in response to land grabs by the colonists, the Powhatan killed hundreds of Jamestown's residents.

D. Answer Both groups wanted the same land.

Reading History

D. Finding Main Ideas What was the central dispute between the Powhatan and the settlers?

ACTIVITY OPTIONS

MULTIPLE LEARNING STYLES: LOGICAL-MATHEMATICAL

BLOCK SCHEDULING

JAMESTOWN SURVIVES

Class Time 20 minutes

Task Organizing and analyzing information about the Jamestown colony

Purpose To analyze the effect of various historical figures on the history of the Jamestown colony

Supplies Needed
- Reference materials on Jamestown
- Copy of graphic organizer

Activity Draw a graphic organizer like the one below on the chalkboard. Have students complete the organizer.

Person	Effect on Jamestown
John Smith	
Pocahontas	
Lord De La Warr	
John Rolfe	
Chief Powhatan	

Bacon's Rebellion in 1676

As you have seen, many of the English colonists who came to Virginia during the 1600s fought with the Native Americans. They also battled one another. By the 1670s, one-fourth of the free white men were former indentured servants. These colonists, who did not own land, resented the wealthy eastern landowners. The poor settlers lived mostly on Virginia's western frontier, where they battled the Native Americans for land.

Nathaniel Bacon and a group of landless frontier settlers opposed Governor William Berkeley. They complained about high taxes and Governor Berkeley's favoritism toward large plantation owners. Bacon demanded that Berkeley approve a war against the Native Americans to seize their land for tobacco plantations. Governor Berkeley's refusal of Nathaniel Bacon's demand sparked **Bacon's Rebellion** in 1676.

Nathaniel Bacon (right) confronts Virginia governor William Berkeley at Jamestown in 1676.

Bacon marched into Jamestown, took control of the House of Burgesses, and burned Jamestown to the ground. Bacon's sudden illness and death ended the rebellion. Berkeley hanged Bacon's followers. Angered by Berkeley's actions, King Charles II recalled the governor to England. After that incident, the House of Burgesses passed laws to prevent a royal governor from assuming such power again. The burgesses had taken an important step against tyranny. In the next section, you will read about the New England colonies and their steps toward independence.

Vocabulary
tyranny: a government in which a single ruler has absolute power

Section 1 Assessment

1. Terms & Names

Explain the significance of:
- joint-stock company
- charter
- Jamestown
- John Smith
- indentured servant
- House of Burgesses
- Bacon's Rebellion

2. Taking Notes

Use a series-of-events chain to review events that led to the founding of Jamestown.

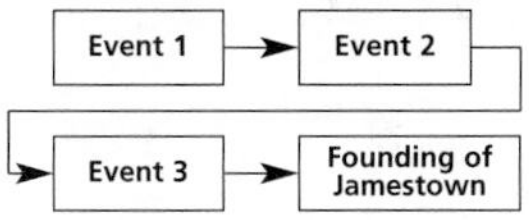

What were reasons England wanted colonies in America?

3. Main Ideas

a. Why did the first English settlement at Roanoke fail?

b. How did the English finance their colonies after 1606?

c. What was the outcome of Bacon's Rebellion?

4. Critical Thinking

Drawing Conclusions
What were the main reasons that Jamestown survived and prospered?

THINK ABOUT
- how, after the "starving time," Lord De La Warr took control
- John Rolfe's development of a high-grade tobacco plant

ACTIVITY OPTIONS

ART / LANGUAGE ARTS You need indentured servants to work on your plantation. Draw a **poster** or write an **advertisement** that will attract people to your plantation.

MORE ABOUT . . .

Bacon's Rebellion

Robert Beverley was a plantation owner and an ally of Governor Berkeley. The following is his description of Nathaniel Bacon:

"This gentleman had been brought up at one of the Inns of court in England, and had a moderate fortune. He was young, bold, active, of an inviting aspect, and powerful elocution. In a word, he was every way qualified to head a giddy and unthinking multitude."

ASSESS & RETEACH

Setting the Stage Have students complete sequencing boxes for colonies discussed in this section.

Formal Assessment
- Section Quiz, p. 51

Critical Thinking Transparency CT7
- Setting the Stage

RETEACHING ACTIVITY

Divide the class into pairs to make time lines for the settlement of the Jamestown colony. Have students pick three events from the colony's early history and write a paragraph explaining how these actions helped ensure Jamestown's survival.

In-Depth Resources: Unit 1
- Reteaching Activity, p. 52

Section 1 Assessment

1. Terms & Names

joint-stock company, p. 70
charter, p. 71
Jamestown, p. 71
John Smith, p. 71
indentured servant, p. 72
House of Burgesses, p. 72
Bacon's Rebellion, p. 73

2. Taking Notes

Event 1. England and Spain were political rivals.
Event 2. Spanish Armada defeated.
Event 3. England wanted colonies to increase trade.

England wanted colonies for religious purposes, as a market, and as a source of raw materials.

3. Main Ideas

a. It was poorly planned, it ran out of supplies, and the Spanish Armada delayed the return of the supply ships. **b.** by forming joint-stock companies **c.** The King appointed a new governor. House of Burgesses passed laws to prevent a royal governor from assuming too much power—a step toward self-government.

4. Critical Thinking

John Smith instilled discipline and made everyone work. Growing tobacco attracted new colonists and strengthened the colony.

ACTIVITY OPTIONS

Integrated Assessment
- Rubrics for a poster, 1.1
- Rubrics for an ad, 4.9

Interdisciplinary CHALLENGE

OBJECTIVE

Students will work cooperatively to meet some of the social, geographic, and economic challenges faced by colonists in adapting to their new environment in America.

BLOCK SCHEDULING

PROCEDURE

Gather supplies that students might need, such as poster boards, colored markers, pencils, and paper. For each challenge, have students form groups of three or four. Ask group members to divide the work among themselves. Then have them choose an option for presenting their solution.

CIVICS CHALLENGE

Class Time 50 minutes

Use the following suggestions to help students figure out how to get the colonists to do the work necessary for survival.

- Make a list of the tasks to be done.
- Make at least one work rule for each task and list a punishment for not following the rule.
- Pick ten rules and punishments that everyone agrees on.

POSSIBLE SOLUTIONS

Here are the ways colonial leaders got colonists to work:

- denying food to nonworkers
- forcing those who did not follow the rules to leave the community

Report from the New World

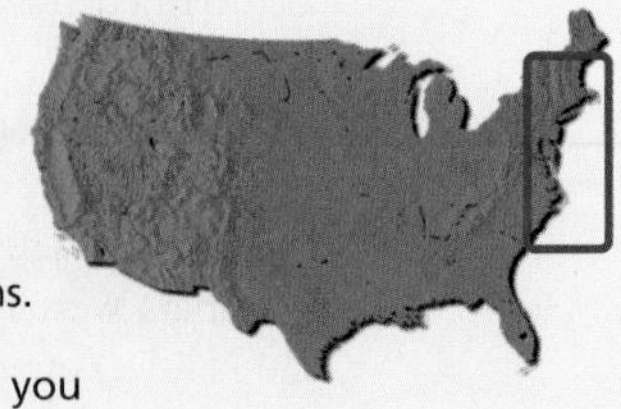

You are a settler who has landed on the wild eastern shore of North America. You and your 93 fellow colonists survived a frightening nine-week Atlantic voyage. Now you are struggling to build a new home in the wilderness. There are no roads, inns, or towns in this land. The game, berries, and fish here taste strange, sometimes unpleasant. Your only neighbors are small groups of Native Americans.

COOPERATIVE LEARNING On these pages are challenges you face as you put down roots in America. Working with a small group, decide how to deal with each challenge. Choose an option, assign a task to each group member, and do the activity. You will find useful information in the Data File. Be prepared to present your solutions to the class as part of a report to your sponsors back in England.

CIVICS CHALLENGE

"They had little or no care of any other thing, but to pamper their bellies."

As your colony takes root, most members work hard to farm, cook, wash, mend, trade, and defend the colony. But a few colonists think only of their own comfort. You call a meeting to set some rules about work. Present your solution to this problem using one of these options:

- **Make a poster for the meeting hall that states the new work rules and punishments.**
- **Write a report describing the problem and how the colony solved it.**

STANDARDS FOR EVALUATION

CIVICS CHALLENGE

Option 1 Poster of rules and punishments should

- clearly state each rule.
- list a punishment for not obeying each rule.

Option 2 Written reports should

- state the problem clearly.
- explain how the problem arose.
- include reasons that justify rules and punishments.

ECONOMICS CHALLENGE

Option 1 Role-plays of meeting should

- present different views on how to open trade.
- result in an action plan.

Option 2 Written instructions should

- logically and clearly state the duties of each team member.
- include a set of steps for the process.
- indicate the desired outcome.

GEOGRAPHY CHALLENGE

Option 1 Diagrams should

- show the placement of windows, doors, fireplace, and furniture through symbols.
- include labels to clarify the diagram.

Option 2 Written accounts should

- describe, inform, and engage.
- give details to make the account more vivid.
- have a chronological or thematic order.

ECONOMICS CHALLENGE

"A bright tin dish most pleased him."

By the time spring arrives, your stores of English foods are running low. You and your friends decide to try trading with the neighboring Native Americans. They could provide a steady supply of meat, fish, and vegetables until your harvest comes in. Develop a plan for opening trade. Present your plan using one of these options:

- As a group, role-play the meeting in which you create your trading plan.
- Write instructions for the team of colonists who will open trade with the Native Americans.

DATA FILE

The Journey

Distance: more than 5,000 nautical miles from Europe to the east coast of North America

Length: 6–14 weeks

Dangers: storms, scurvy, dysentery, malnutrition, seasickness, overcrowding

Food and Livestock Taken

barrels of salted beef, oatmeal, dried grains, cheese, oil, vinegar, and salt; seeds for peas, barley, herbs, and other crops; cows, horses, goats, pigs, sheep, and chickens

Equipment Taken

axes, hoes, nails, hooks for doors, hammers, chisels, hatchets, spades, pickaxes, iron pots, copper kettles, skillets, platters, dishes, wooden spoons, rugs

Weapons Taken

swords, muskets, daggers, gunpowder, light armor, cannon

Clothes Taken

shirts, several pairs of shoes, leather for mending, waistcoats, caps, skirts, jackets, trousers

Dangers in America

Biggest killers: typhoid, dysentery, famine

Other dangers: pneumonia, malaria, and other diseases; exposure to harsh weather; fire; wild animals; attacks by Native Americans

Benefits in America

religious and political freedom; opportunity to own land; abundant timber for shelters, forts, heat, ships, and trade; rich food resources

For more about the American colonies . . .
RESEARCH LINKS
CLASSZONE.COM

ACTIVITY WRAP-UP

Present to the class **As a group, review your solution to each challenge. Consider the following:**

- How well each solution meets its particular challenge
- Which solution shows the most creativity

Once you have made your decision, present your solutions to the class. Each group member should take part in the presentation.

ECONOMICS CHALLENGE

Class Time 50 minutes

Tell students that each person in the group should choose a part for the role play and formulate an opinion about trading with the Native Americans. Each student should then present that opinion in the role play. Each group member should speak and present ideas in the role play. Tell students to list the items they want to buy and what goods they have to trade in return. Remind them to consider the consequences of trading guns.

POSSIBLE SOLUTIONS

Typically goods were exchanged by barter. Native Americans were interested in the colonists' metal tools, utensils, and guns. Because clearing the land, planting, and harvesting took at least a year, the colonists' most pressing need was food.

ALTERNATIVE ACTIVITY

GEOGRAPHY CHALLENGE

"A . . . desolate wilderness"

Your ship reached the shores of America in raw December weather. Your leader called your new home "a hideous and desolate wilderness, full of wild beasts and wild men." You built shelters for protection. Now you are preparing a report on your first months in a new land. Present your report using one of these options:

- Make a diagram that shows your first shelter.
- Write a personal account that explains how your family survived the winter in America.

ACTIVITY WRAP-UP

Presentations should

- provide a clear, concise statement of the problem.
- give a workable solution.
- evaluate the effectiveness of the solution.
- assess the creativity of the solution.

SECTION OBJECTIVES

1. To explain why the Pilgrims established Plymouth Colony
2. To explain why the Puritans set up the Massachusetts Bay Colony
3. To identify the New England Way and to evaluate challenges to Puritan leadership
4. To summarize the causes and effects of King Philip's War and the Salem witchcraft trials

SKILLBUILDER

Interpreting Maps: Location, Place, p. 79
Interpreting Charts, p. 80

CRITICAL THINKING

Making Inferences, pp. 77, 78
Summarizing, p. 79
Forming Opinions, p. 80
Recognizing Effects, p. 81

FOCUS & MOTIVATE

5-MINUTE WARM-UP

Drawing Conclusions These questions focus on the diversity of North American societies.

1. Read the quote about Squanto on page 76. Why might the colonists need help?
2. Why might the Native Americans want to help the colonists?

Warm-Up Transparency WT3

INSTRUCT

INSTRUCT: OBJECTIVE 1

The Voyage of the *Mayflower*/ The Pilgrims Found Plymouth

- Why did the Separatists decide to leave Europe for America?
- What did the first Thanksgiving symbolize for the Pilgrims?

In-Depth Resources: Unit 1
- Guided Reading, p. 41
- Building Vocabulary, p. 43

America's History Makers
- William Bradford, pp. 13–14

2 New England Colonies

TERMS & NAMES
Pilgrims
Mayflower Compact
Puritans
Great Migration
Fundamental Orders of Connecticut
Roger Williams
Anne Hutchinson
King Philip's War

MAIN IDEA	WHY IT MATTERS NOW
Religion influenced the settlement and government of the New England colonies.	The Puritan work ethic and religious beliefs influence American culture today.

ONE AMERICAN'S STORY

In 1605, English fishermen captured and enslaved a Native American named Squanto and took him to England. While there, he learned to speak English. After a series of misadventures, including serving as a slave in Spain, Squanto returned to America in 1619. There he discovered that his Pawtuxet tribe had been wiped out by disease in the years 1616–1618. In 1621, Squanto set about helping the English plant corn, beans, and pumpkins on tribal lands. Colonist William Bradford made the following comment about Squanto.

A VOICE FROM THE PAST

Squanto . . . was a special instrument sent of God for their [the colonists'] good beyond their expectation. . . . He directed them how to set their corn, where to take fish, and to procure other commodities, and was also their pilot to bring them to unknown places.

William Bradford, quoted in *The Pilgrim Reader*

Squanto teaches the Pilgrims how to grow corn.

Thanks to Squanto, the first settlers in New England prospered and lived in peace with the Native Americans. In this section, you will learn about the Pilgrims and Puritans, their relations with the Native Americans, and their settlement of the New England colonies.

1 The Voyage of the *Mayflower*

In the early 1500s, King Henry VIII of England broke that country's ties with the Catholic Church and established the Church of England, an official state church under his control. In the early 1600s, a religious group called the Separatists called for a total break with the Church of England. They thought it was too much like the Catholic Church.

The **Pilgrims** were a Separatist group. King James attacked them for rejecting England's official church. To escape this harsh treatment, the Pilgrims fled to Holland, a country known for its acceptance of different opinions. Eventually, the Pilgrims became dissatisfied with life in Holland. They approached the Virginia Company and asked if they could settle in America "as a distinct body by themselves." The Virginia

RECOMMENDED RESOURCES

In-Depth Resources: Unit 1
- Guided Reading, p. 41
- Skillbuilder Practice, p. 44
- Literature Selection, pp. 49–51

Reading Study Guide (Spanish and English), pp. 23–24

Economics in History, p. 3

America's History Makers
- William Bradford, pp. 13–14

Formal Assessment
- Section Quiz, p. 52

Integrated Assessment
- Rubrics, 4.5, 3.6

Access for Students Acquiring English/ESL, pp. 14, 16

INTEGRATED TECHNOLOGY

Humanities Transparency HT6
- *Pilgrims Going to Church*

Critical Thinking Trans. CT8
- Cause and Effect: King Philip's War, 1675–1676

Electronic Teacher Tools

classzone.com

TEST-TAKING RESOURCES

Strategies for Test Preparation

Test Practice Transparencies, TT11

Online Test Practice

The *Mayflower* brings the Pilgrims to Plymouth in 1620.

Company arranged for them to settle on land within its boundaries on the eastern coast of North America.

On a cold, raw November day in 1620, a ship called the *Mayflower* arrived off Cape Cod on the Massachusetts coast. Blown north of its course, the *Mayflower* landed in an area that John Smith had mapped and called New England. They landed at a site that had been named Plymouth.

Because the Pilgrims landed outside the limits of the Virginia Company, their charter did not apply. For the sake of order, the men aboard the *Mayflower* signed an agreement called the **Mayflower Compact**. In it, they vowed to obey laws agreed upon for the good of the colony. The Mayflower Compact helped establish the idea of self-government and majority rule. (See Interactive Primary Sources, page 82.)

The Pilgrims Found Plymouth

Like the early settlers at Jamestown, the Pilgrims at Plymouth endured a starving time. That first winter, disease and death struck with such fury that "the living were scarce able to bury the dead." Half the group had died by spring.

However, energy, hope, and help returned. One day a Native American walked up to a group of colonists. To their astonishment, he called out, "Welcome, Englishmen." This was Samoset, a Pemaquid who had learned to speak English from European fishermen. Samoset introduced the settlers to another Native American named Squanto, a Pawtuxet, who also spoke English.

"Welcome, Englishmen."
Samoset

The Pilgrims had angered the Native Americans by taking their corn. Squanto acted as an interpreter between the Pilgrims and Chief Massasoit. He helped them to negotiate a peace treaty and showed them how to plant, hunt, and fish. While their crops grew, the colonists began trading with the Native Americans for furs and preparing lumber to ship back to England in order to make a profit.

Sometime in the fall—no one knows exactly when—the Plymouth settlement celebrated the blessings of a good harvest by holding a three-day feast. It was the first Thanksgiving. This Thanksgiving came to represent the peace that existed at that time between the Native Americans and Pilgrims.

A. Possible Answer Perhaps because his tribe had died out, Squanto wished to make himself useful to others. He may have wanted to see peaceful relations between the Native Americans and settlers.

***Reading* History**
A. Making Inferences Why do you think Squanto was so helpful to the Pilgrims?

MORE ABOUT . . .

Passengers on the *Mayflower*
Three pregnant women were among the 102 passengers who sailed on the *Mayflower.* Elizabeth Hopkins gave birth at sea to a son named Oceanus because of the circumstances of his birth. While the Pilgrims were in Provincetown Harbor, Susan White gave birth to a boy. His parents named him Peregrine, meaning "one who journeys to foreign lands." The third baby was stillborn on the *Mayflower* while the Pilgrims were building their houses at Plymouth.

Economics in History
• Farming in the English Colonies, p. 3

MORE ABOUT . . .

Native Americans
Among the Native American peoples who came into contact with the Pilgrims were the Wampanoag, a people whose name means "People of the First Light" or "Eastern People." In 1620, about 30 Wampanoag villages existed in New England. Today the Wampanoag still live in parts of southeastern Massachusetts and eastern Rhode Island. Among the best known Wampanoag groups are those living in Mashpee on Cape Cod and Gay Head on Martha's Vineyard in Massachusetts. The Gay Head Wampanoag are recognized by the federal government and are governed by the Tribal Council of Gay Head. This recognition created a government-to-government relationship between the federal government and the tribal council.

ACTIVITY OPTIONS

SKILLBUILDER LESSON: USING PRIMARY SOURCES — BLOCK SCHEDULING

Explaining the Skill Primary sources are materials that present an eyewitness account of events in the past. Visual primary sources include paintings, photographs, and video footage. Written primary sources include letters, diaries, speeches, autobiographies, and other documents produced by people who observed or participated in a historical event. Historical documents such as charters, treaties, and laws are also primary sources. In evaluating a primary source, it is important to know who wrote the piece in order to evaluate his or her qualifications for writing about this subject.

Applying the Skill Have students read the *Mayflower Compact* on page 82. Ask:

1. Is this a primary or a secondary source? Explain. (*Primary; it was written by colonists aboard the* Mayflower *in 1620.)*
2. Why is this source useful for learning about the Pilgrims? (*It provides insight into their political beliefs and their government and social organization.*)

In-Depth Resources: Unit 1
• Skillbuilder Practice, p. 44

America's HERITAGE

The First Thanksgiving

The Thanksgiving holiday as we know it today was made official by President Abraham Lincoln in 1863. Thanks for Thanksgiving goes to Sarah Josepha Hale, editor of *Godey's Lady's Book.* Beginning in 1846, this determined writer used her position at this popular periodical to lobby for creation of an official Thanksgiving holiday. Every November, Hale wrote editorials calling for recognition of the holiday. In the summer she kept the heat on with letters to the governors of every state. Almost 20 years after she started, Hale's one-woman campaign succeeded.

INSTRUCT: OBJECTIVE 2

The Puritans Come to Massachusetts Bay/ The New England Way

- Why did the Puritans decide to leave England in the 1630s?
- How was the Puritans' colonial experience different from that of the Jamestown settlers?
- What is a commonwealth?
- What was the New England Way?

Humanities Transparency HT6
- *Pilgrims Going to Church* by George Henry Boughton

CRITICAL THINKING ACTIVITY

Contrasting Have students use a Venn diagram to examine the differences and similarities between the Pilgrims and Puritans. Look at their attitudes toward the Church of England; their reasons for coming to New England; and their early experiences as colonial settlements.

Class Time 10 minutes

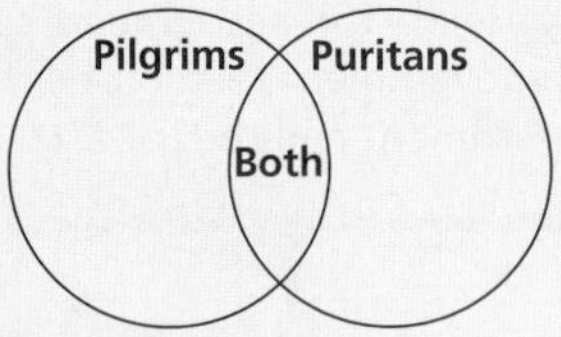

Thanks to the help of Squanto and other Native Americans, the Pilgrims learned to survive in their new environment. Soon more people would sail to New England seeking religious freedom.

America's HERITAGE

THE FIRST THANKSGIVING

It is hard to believe, but turkey was not on the menu at the first Thanksgiving. The Pilgrims and Native Americans ate venison (deer), roast duck, roast goose, clams and other shellfish, and eel (shown below). Other treats were white bread and corn bread, leeks, watercress, and salad herbs. The guests topped off their meal with wild plums and dried berries for dessert.

2 The Puritans Come to Massachusetts Bay

Between about 1630 and 1640, a religious group called the **Puritans** left England to escape bad treatment by King James I. Unlike the Separatists, who wanted to break away from the Church of England, the Puritans wanted to reform, or "purify," its practices. By the thousands, Puritan families left for the Americas. Their leaving is known as the **Great Migration.** Many thousands of Puritans left their homeland to found new settlements around the world. Of these settlers, about 20,000 crossed the Atlantic Ocean to New England.

Background During the Great Migration, the Puritans also went to Ireland, the Netherlands, the Rhineland, and the West Indies.

Many Puritan merchants had invested in the Massachusetts Bay Company. In 1629, the company received a royal charter to settle land in New England. In 1630, 11 well-supplied ships carried about 1,000 passengers to the Massachusetts Bay Colony. Unlike earlier colonists, the Puritans were well prepared and did not suffer through a starving time. John Winthrop was the colony's Puritan governor. He stated that the new colony would be a commonwealth, a community in which people work together for the good of the whole.

***Reading*History** **B. Making Inferences** After Winthrop, politicians sometimes spoke of America as "a city upon a hill." What does this phrase suggest about America's role in the world? **B. Possible Answer** The phrase suggests that America will set an example for the rest of the world.

A VOICE FROM THE PAST

So shall we keep the unity of the spirit, in the bond of peace. . . . Ten of us will be able to resist a thousand of our enemies. . . . For we must consider that we shall be as a City upon a Hill, the eyes of all people are on us.

John Winthrop, *"Model of Christian Charity"*

The New England Way

The basic unit of the commonwealth was the congregation—a group of people who belong to the same church. Each Puritan congregation set up its own town. The meetinghouse was the most important building in each town. There people gathered for town meetings, a form of self-government in which people made laws and other decisions for the community. In the Massachusetts Bay Colony, only male church members could vote or hold office. They elected representatives to a lawmaking body called the General Court, which in turn chose the governor.

By law, everyone in town had to attend church services held in the meetinghouse. The sermon, the most important part of the church service, provided instruction in the "New England Way." This was a term

ACTIVITY OPTIONS

INTERDISCIPLINARY LINK: POPULAR CULTURE — BLOCK SCHEDULING

THE FIRST THANKSGIVING

Class Time One class period

Task Comparing the first Thanksgiving with the way this event is portrayed in children's books today

Purpose To analyze the treatment of the first Thanksgiving in contemporary books for children

Supplies Needed
- Reference materials on Pilgrims; on the Wampanoag, Pequot, and Narragansett Indians; and on accounts by Pilgrims of the first Thanksgiving
- Contemporary children's books on Thanksgiving

Activity Have students read illustrated children's books about Thanksgiving to analyze the treatment of the first Thanksgiving. Ask students to compare these accounts with the actual historical event. Areas for comparison might include the implied or stated purpose of the celebration, the relationships between Pilgrims and Native Americans, the types of food eaten, and the dress and customs of the Native Americans shown participating in the celebration. Have students choose a book that accurately depicts the first Thanksgiving or a book that has historical inaccuracies and report on it to the class.

used by the Puritans to describe both their beliefs and their society, which emphasized duty, godliness, hard work, and honesty. The Puritans thought that amusements such as dancing and playing games would lead to laziness. They believed that God required them to work long and hard at their vocation.

Vocabulary
godliness: piety, reverence

The Puritan work ethic helped contribute to the rapid growth and success of the New England colonies. The New England Way also depended on education. Because the Puritans wanted everyone to be able to read the Bible, laws required that all children learn to read.

Reading **History**
C. Summarizing What were some important elements of the New England Way?
C. Answer Town meetings, church attendance, strong work ethic

Some Puritan congregations set up new colonies. In 1636, Thomas Hooker moved his congregation to the Connecticut Valley. There they wrote and adopted the **Fundamental Orders of Connecticut** in 1639 (see page 82). In effect, these laws were a constitution. The Fundamental Orders extended voting rights to nonchurch members and limited the power of the governor. They expanded the idea of representative government.

New England Settlements, 1620-1636

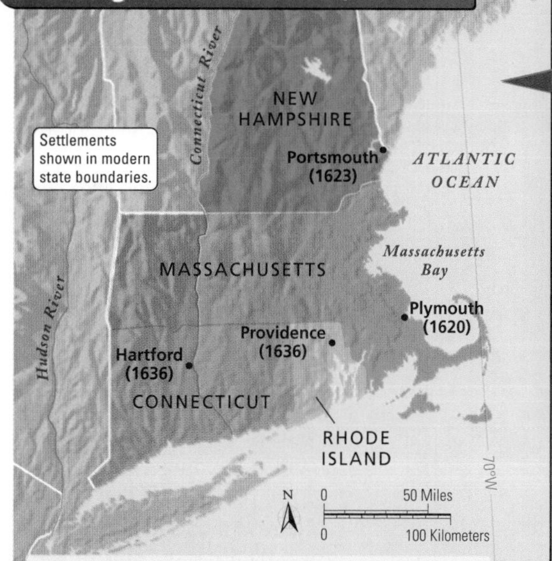

GEOGRAPHY SKILLBUILDER Interpreting Maps
1. **Location** *Which of these early colonies does the Connecticut River not flow through or touch?*
2. **Place** *What was the earliest major English settlement in the New England colonies?*

Skillbuilder Answers
1. Rhode Island
2. Plymouth, in 1620

The first European settlement in New Hampshire was a village near Portsmouth in 1623. In 1638, John Wheelwright established the town of Exeter. The town's founders drew up the Exeter Compact, which was based on the Mayflower Compact.

❸ Challenges to Puritan Leaders

Not everyone agreed with the New England Way. **Roger Williams** was a minister in Salem, Massachusetts, who founded the first Baptist church in America. He opposed forced attendance at church. He also opposed the English colonists' taking of Native American lands by force. Because of his beliefs, the General Court forced Williams to leave the colony. In 1636, he fled southward and founded the colony of Rhode Island, which guaranteed religious freedom and the separation of church and state.

Anne Hutchinson believed that a person could worship God without the help of a church, minister, or Bible. She conducted discussions in her home that challenged church authority. Hutchinson was brought to trial and forced to leave Massachusetts. In 1638, she fled to Rhode Island.

Anne Hutchinson preaches in her home in Boston.

HISTORY FROM VISUALS

Reading the Map Have students name the four settlements shown on the map. Ask students to identify two routes from Hartford to Providence.
Possible Response One route is by water down the Connecticut River to the Atlantic Ocean. The other is over land.

Extension Have students use an encyclopedia to find out what economic activities are associated with these communities today.

CRITICAL THINKING ACTIVITY

Drawing Conclusions Have students read the Mayflower Compact on page 82. Then ask: What did the Pilgrims fear might happen if they did not have a charter? If the Pilgrims had landed in the place assigned by the Virginia Company, who would have governed the colony? Discuss the importance of self-government and majority rule in a democratic government.

Class Time 10 minutes

INSTRUCT: OBJECTIVE ❸
Challenges to Puritan Leaders

- Why did some individuals and groups challenge Puritan leaders?
- How did Rhode Island differ from the Massachusetts Bay Colony?
- What beliefs and practices set the Quakers apart from the Puritans?

In-Depth Resources: Unit 1
- Literature Selection: Poems by Anne Bradstreet, pp. 49–51

ACTIVITY OPTIONS
INTERDISCIPLINARY LINK: CIVICS — BLOCK SCHEDULING

CHALLENGES TO PURITAN LEADERS

Class Time 20 minutes

Task Writing a statement describing challenges to Puritan authority or responding to such a statement

Purpose To analyze the conflict between the Puritan leaders of Massachusetts and Roger Williams or Anne Hutchinson

Supplies Needed
- Reference materials on Roger Williams, Anne Hutchinson, and the Puritans

Activity Discuss the options open to a government in dealing with citizens who disagree with its policies. Then divide the class into pairs. Direct each pair to research the conflicts that arose between the Puritan leaders of Massachusetts and Roger Williams or Anne Hutchinson. Have one member of each pair write a speech stating the reasons Puritan leaders might have given for banishing Williams or Hutchinson. The second member of the pair should write a reply that the person banished might have given.

INSTRUCT: OBJECTIVE 4

King Philip's War/ The Salem Witchcraft Trials

- How did Native Americans and Europeans differ in their views of land ownership?
- What was the outcome of King Philip's War?
- What role did the clergy play in the Salem witchcraft trials?
- What were the results of the witchcraft trials?

HISTORY FROM VISUALS

Interpreting the Chart Have students study the chart to identify the causes of the conflict. How did each of these causes lead to tensions between Native Americans and Europeans? **Possible Responses** Native Americans believed land was shared and could not be owned by individuals. Europeans believed they could claim the land for themselves. Puritans did not understand or respect the beliefs of the Native Americans. An increase in European population put pressure on Europeans to take more land used by Native Americans and claim it for themselves.

Extension Have students research the fate of the Wampanoag after the war ended, and have them make a new cause-and-effect chart on the topic of the Native American defeat.

Critical Thinking Transparency CT8
- Cause and Effect: King Philip's War, 1675–1676

Another religious group was the Quakers. Their name came from an early leader's statement that they should "tremble [quake] at the word of the Lord." Opponents coined the name as an insult. Quakers challenged the Massachusetts commonwealth. They believed that each person could know God directly through "an inner light." Neither ministers nor the Bible was needed. Quakers also believed in treating Native Americans fairly, which set them apart from other colonists. For such beliefs, Quakers were whipped, imprisoned, and hanged. Many left for Rhode Island.

*Reading***History**
D. Forming Opinions Why is it odd that the Puritans persecuted certain individuals and groups for their religious beliefs?
D. Answer The Puritans had themselves been persecuted in England for their beliefs.

4 King Philip's War

The growing population of colonists began to force the Native Americans from their land. Europeans and Native Americans defined land ownership differently. To Europeans, land could be owned by individuals. To Native Americans, land belonged to everyone. Conflict over land resulted in warfare.

In 1675–1676, the Puritan colonies fought a brutal war with the Native Americans. This was known as **King Philip's War**. "King Philip" was the English name of Metacom, leader of the Wampanoag. To help fight the war, Metacom organized an alliance of tribes. The Wampanoag lost the war. Many were killed, while others were sold into slavery in the West Indies. Those who remained lost their land and were forced to become laborers. English settlers expanded even farther into Native American land.

Background
Metacom was the son of Massasoit, friend of the Pilgrims.

CAUSE & EFFECT: *King Philip's War, 1675–1676*

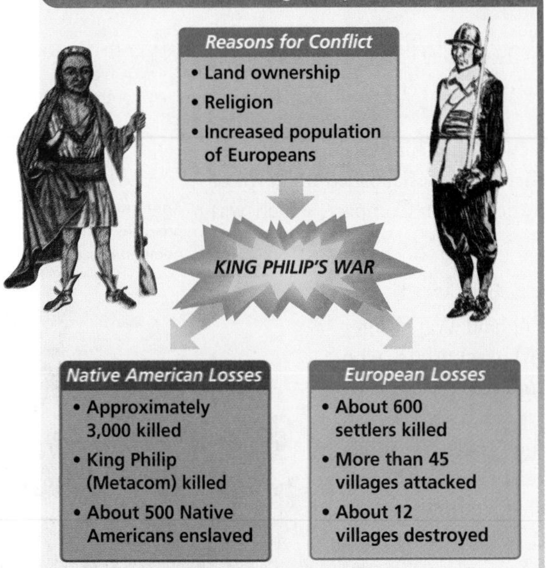

Reasons for Conflict
• Land ownership
• Religion
• Increased population of Europeans
KING PHILIP'S WAR
Native American Losses
• Approximately 3,000 killed
• King Philip (Metacom) killed
• About 500 Native Americans enslaved
European Losses
• About 600 settlers killed
• More than 45 villages attacked
• About 12 villages destroyed

Sources: *Encyclopedia Britannica, World Book Encyclopedia*

SKILLBUILDER Interpreting Charts
1. *Was there a greater loss of life among the settlers or the Native Americans?*
2. *How might the growing population of Europeans have created more conflict with the Native Americans?*

Skillbuilder Answers
1. Many more Native Americans died.
2. More settlers needed more land for their crops and livestock.

The Salem Witchcraft Trials

Puritan New England was originally a society centered on the church. By the late 1600s, however, this had begun to change. Societal changes in Puritan New England had led to an atmosphere of fear and suspicion. Then, several Salem village girls were told frightening stories about witches by Tituba, a slave from the West Indies. Pretending to be bewitched, the girls falsely accused others of witchcraft. The witch-hunts began in 1692. The clergy viewed the Salem witch-hunts and trials as a sign from God for the village to return to a strict Puritan lifestyle.

ACTIVITY OPTIONS

INDIVIDUAL NEEDS: GIFTED AND TALENTED

A BIOGRAPHY OF KING PHILIP

Class Time Two class periods

Task Writing a biography of King Philip, or Metacom, for younger students

Purpose To encourage students to use research skills and to deepen their understanding of a historical figure

Supplies Needed
- Reference materials on King Philip
- Art supplies or computer access

Activity Tell students to prepare an illustrated biography of King Philip suitable for fifth-grade students. The biography should include information about King Philip's family, his leadership of the Wampanoag, and his attempts to unite many groups of Native Americans. Tell students that many stories exist about King Philip that have not been documented by historians. Students should be sure to differentiate between fact and legend. Biographies should include a bibliography.

HISTORY *through* ART

This mid-nineteenth-century oil painting, *The Trial of George Jacobs, August 5, 1692,* was painted by T. H. Matteson in 1855. It captures the horrors of the Salem witch trials. As the young women cry out, the accused tries to defend himself against charges that he bewitched them.

Jacobs's own granddaughter testified against him. He was tried and convicted on August 5, 1692, and executed two weeks later along with four neighbors.

How accurately do you think the painting shows the strong emotions in the courtroom?

Hysteria spread through Salem. Those accused were forced to name others as witches. More than 100 people were arrested and tried. Of those, 20 were found guilty and put to death. Nineteen persons were hanged, and another was pressed to death by heavy stones when he refused to enter a plea in response to the charge of witchcraft. The panic was short-lived, and Salem came to its senses. The experience showed, however, how a society can create scapegoats for its problems.

Vocabulary
scapegoat: one that is made to bear the blame of others

In the next section, you will read about the Middle and Southern colonies, how they were founded, and how they provided the new settlers with economic opportunities.

Section 2 *Assessment*

1. Terms & Names

Explain the significance of:
- Pilgrims
- Mayflower Compact
- Puritans
- Great Migration
- Fundamental Orders of Connecticut
- Roger Williams
- Anne Hutchinson
- King Philip's War

2. Taking Notes

Use a cluster diagram to review details about the New England Way.

Which parts would you find easy to accept? Which difficult?

3. Main Ideas

a. What is the Mayflower Compact?

b. What is the meaning of the term the "Great Migration"?

c. What were some of the causes of King Philip's War?

4. Critical Thinking

Recognizing Effects What impact did the arrival of the English in New England have on the Native Americans?

THINK ABOUT
- Squanto
- Chief Massasoit
- King Philip's War

ACTIVITY OPTIONS

LANGUAGE ARTS
SPEECH

Choose one of the Puritan dissenters from this section and retell his or her story. Either write a **newspaper article** about the person or give an **oral history**.

HISTORY *through* ART

Interpreting the Illustration At the time of the Salem trials, belief in witchcraft was widespread in both Europe and America. The noted English jurist Lord Coke defined a witch as a "person who hath conference with the devil, to consult with him or to do some act." Under British law, which was the basis for the Massachusetts Bay Colony's legal system, those who were accused of working with the devil were considered felons. Their crime was punishable by hanging.

Possible Responses: Some students may say the portrayal of strong emotions is accurate because of the chaos the painting shows. Others may say it isn't accurate because a courtroom would never be so unruly.

ASSESS & RETEACH

Setting the Stage Have students complete sequencing boxes for colonies founded in this section.

Formal Assessment
- Section Quiz, p. 52

RETEACHING ACTIVITY

Have students work in pairs to make up five "Who am I?" questions about the New England settlements that follow this form: "My name is _____. I guaranteed separation of church and state in the Rhode Island colony I founded. Who am I?" Have groups exchange statements, complete them, and return them to their authors for checking.

In-Depth Resources: Unit 1
- Reteaching Activity, p. 53

Section 2 *Assessment*

1. Terms & Names

Pilgrims, p. 76
Mayflower Compact, p. 77
Puritans, p. 78
Great Migration, p. 78
Fundamental Orders of Connecticut, p. 79
Roger Williams, p. 79
Anne Hutchinson, p. 79
King Philip's War, p. 80

2. Taking Notes

Items for cluster diagram:
- Everyone attended church services.
- Amusements were frowned upon.
- Education was emphasized.
- They had a strong work ethic.

Answers will vary as to which would be easy or difficult to accept.

3. Main Ideas

a. a document written by the men aboard the *Mayflower* saying that they would obey any laws agreed upon for the good of the colony
b. a term used to describe the departure of thousands of Puritans for the Americas **c.** land ownership, and increases in European population

4. Critical Thinking

It forced the Native Americans from their land and led to King Philip's War, with heavy Native American casualties.

ACTIVITY OPTIONS

Integrated Assessment
- Rubrics for an article, 4.5
- Rubrics for an oral history, 3.6

INTERACTIVE PRIMARY SOURCES

OBJECTIVE

Students will analyze rules of settlement—the Mayflower Compact and the Fundamental Orders of Connecticut—to understand how they provided for self-government and laid a foundation for the republican government of the United States.

Primary Source Explorer
- *The Mayflower Compact*
- *The Fundamental Orders of Connecticut*

The Explorer will help students select and produce their own presentations.

Specific information about the document can be found in **A Closer Look.** To learn more about key people and events of the time, students should click on **Life in These Times. What Happened Next** will show students the impact of the document both at home and abroad, and tie the document to today.

FOCUS & MOTIVATE

Evaluating Tell students that the Pilgrims and Puritans wrote and signed these documents far from any official government. Ask students why the colonists might have felt it necessary to write down this plan. Then ask students to look in the documents for evidence about what the colonists considered important for their settlements.

MORE ABOUT . . .

Ancestors on the *Mayflower*

Some Americans proudly trace their ancestry back to passengers on the *Mayflower.* The General Society of Mayflower Descendants, which requires new members to produce strongly documented genealogies, has about 24,500 members. However, the Society estimates that about 35 million *Mayflower* descendants are alive today.

INTERACTIVE PRIMARY SOURCES

The Mayflower Compact

Setting the Stage In 1620, 41 of the colonists aboard the *Mayflower* drew up the Mayflower Compact. This document refers to the area where they landed as "Virginia" because the land grants of the Virginia Company extended into New England. The colonists provided for self-government under majority rule of the male voters. **See Primary Source Explorer**

A CLOSER LOOK

REASONS FOR VOYAGE

The three reasons the colonists give for their voyage to the eastern seaboard of North America are the glory of God, the advancement of Christianity, and the honor of the king.

1. Why might sailing to new lands advance Christianity?

We, whose names are underwritten, . . . having undertaken for the glory of God, and advancement of the Christian faith, and the honor of our King and country, a voyage to plant the first colony in the northern parts of Virginia, do by these presents, solemnly and mutually in the presence of God and one another **covenant**[1] and combine ourselves together into a civil **body politic,**[2] for our better ordering and preservation; and furtherance of the ends aforesaid . . . do enact, constitute, and frame such just and equal laws, ordinances, acts, constitutions, and offices from time to time as shall be thought most [proper] and convenient for the general good of the colony unto which we promise all due submission and obedience. In witness whereof we have hereunto subscribed our names at Cape Cod the eleventh of November, in the year of our **sovereign**[3] lord King James of England . . . Anno Domini 1620.

From B. P. Poore, ed., *The Federal and State Constitutions,* Part I, p. 931.

A CLOSER LOOK

GUIDING PURPOSE

The general good of the colony is the guiding purpose of the colonists in signing the compact.

2. What does this suggest about the relationship between the individual and the community?

1. **covenant:** promise in a binding agreement.
2. **body politic:** the people of a politically organized group.
3. **sovereign:** supreme.

The Fundamental Orders of Connecticut

Setting the Stage In January 1639, male citizens of three townships in Connecticut (Hartford, Windsor, and Wethersfield) assembled and drew up the Fundamental Orders of Connecticut. This document is often called the first written constitution in America. It contains a preamble, or introduction, and a set of laws. **See Primary Source Explorer**

Preamble

Forasmuch as it has pleased the Almighty God by the wise disposition of His Divine Providence so to order and dispose of things that we, the inhabitants and residents of Windsor, Hartford, and Wethersfield are now cohabiting

TEACHING STRATEGY

Understanding the Document Practice reading the selections with expression and then read them aloud to the class. As you read a phrase, ask for volunteers to translate the phrase into modern English. When you have read both documents to the class, ask students to compare the reasons given in both documents for their writing and signing. Ask students to copy the graphic shown to summarize their answers.

	The Mayflower Compact	The Fundamental Orders of Connecticut
Reasons for Writing this Document	for better order and for the preservation of the new colony and to further the ends for which the settlers made their voyage, the glory of God and the advancement of the Christian faith	to maintain peace and union among the settlers

and dwelling in and upon the river of Conectecotte [Connecticut] and the lands thereunto adjoining; and well knowing where a people are gathered together the Word of God requires that, to maintain the peace and union of such a people, there should be an orderly and decent government established according to God, to order and dispose of the affairs of the people at all seasons as occasion shall require; do therefore associate and **conjoin**[1] ourselves to be as one public state or commonwealth. . . . As also in our civil affairs to be guided and governed according to such laws, rules, orders, and decrees as shall be made, ordered and decreed, as follows:

Laws, Rules, and Orders

1. It is ordered, sentenced, and decreed that there shall be yearly two general assemblies or courts. . . . The first shall be called the Court of Election, wherein shall be yearly chosen . . . so many magistrates and other public officers as shall be found **requisite**.[2] . . .

4. It is ordered . . . that no person be chosen governor above once in two years, and that the governor be always a member of some approved congregation. . . .

5. It is ordered . . . that to the aforesaid Court of Election the several towns shall send their deputies. . . . Also, the other General Court in September shall be for making of laws, and any other public occasion which concerns the good of the Commonwealth. . . .

7. It is ordered . . . that after there are warrants given out for any of the said General Courts, the constable or constables of each town shall forthwith give notice distinctly to the inhabitants of the same . . . that at a place and time . . . they meet and assemble themselves together to elect and choose certain deputies to be at the General Court then following to [manage] the affairs of the Commonwealth. . . .

1. **conjoin:** unite.
2. **requisite:** required.

A CLOSER LOOK

GOOD GOVERNMENT

Good government is pleasing to God in the eyes of the colonists. An orderly and decent government helps to maintain peace and order within a community and between people.

3. How would you define good government today?

A CLOSER LOOK

THE GOVERNOR'S ROLE

The person serving as governor can serve only once every two years and must be a member of an approved congregation.

4. Why might the colonists have wished to limit the power of the chief executive?

A CLOSER LOOK

THE COURTS

The Court of Election chooses officials to serve; the General Court makes laws.

5. Why might it be a good idea to separate these two functions?

Interactive Primary Sources Assessment

1. Main Ideas

a. Whose rights did the Mayflower Compact protect?

b. Why are written documents useful in setting up a government?

c. How were the Fundamental Orders based on religion?

2. Critical Thinking

Supporting Opinions

How do you think these documents reflect the English contribution to American democracy?

THINK ABOUT

- self-government
- majority rule

Interactive Primary Sources Assessment

1. Main Ideas

a. It protected the rights of the Plymouth colonists.

b. They can provide a concrete statement of the roles and powers of the government.

c. It suggests that good government is divinely sanctioned.

2. Critical Thinking

Possible Answer In the Mayflower Compact, colonists provided for self-government under majority rule of voters. The Fundamental Orders of Connecticut describes different branches of government, limits executive power, and sets up a structure for elections.

INSTRUCT

- What was the major purpose of the Mayflower Compact and the Fundamental Orders of Connecticut?
- Describe how the Fundamental Orders of Connecticut provides for a legislature, an executive, and a system of courts.
- How do the Mayflower Compact and the Fundamental Orders of Connecticut set up governments by the people?

MAKING PERSONAL CONNECTIONS

If students were going to create a perfect community, what sort of government would it have? What laws would it have?

MORE ABOUT . . .

The Charter Oak

The Fundamental Orders of Connecticut lasted until 1662, when Charles II issued a royal charter for the Connecticut colony. In 1687, James II wanted to revoke the charter. He sent Sir Edmund Andros and an armed delegation to take the charter back, by force if necessary. Legend has it that as the king's representatives and the colony's leaders debated with the charter on a table between them, suddenly all the candles went out. When someone lit the candles again, the charter had vanished. The story continues that Joseph Wadsworth, a colonial leader, seized the charter and hid it in a hole in a large oak tree at a nearby estate. The "charter oak" remains a revered symbol of Connecticut freedom to this day.

A CLOSER LOOK

1. The colonists were looking for a better life, including economic prosperity, for themselves and their children.
2. The colonists were probably willing to put their own individual interests and opinions aside in favor of the common good of the group. The individual was expected to obey the rules of the community.
3. Most students will mention that a government should be representative, responsive, and fair.
4. They probably wished to avoid one person acquiring enough power to make him a despot or petty tyrant who could limit the freedom of the colonists.
5. By separating functions, the colonists separated the making of laws from the contest for power.

SECTION OBJECTIVES

1. To compare the founding of the four Middle Colonies
2. To trace the growth of the Middle Colonies
3. To explain how economics influenced the development of the Southern Colonies
4. To identify unique reasons for the founding of Georgia and Maryland

SKILLBUILDER

Interpreting Maps: Region, Location, p. 86

CRITICAL THINKING

Forming Opinions, p. 85
Comparing and Contrasting, p. 86
Analyzing Causes, p. 87

Why It Matters Now
- British Connections Today, pp. 5–6

FOCUS & MOTIVATE

5-MINUTE WARM-UP

Reading a Map These questions focus on how the English colonies grew.

1. Compare the map on page 86 with the one on page 71. How did the English colonies change in number and location?
2. In which set of colonies is the oldest settlement found?

Warm-Up Transparency WT3

INSTRUCT

INSTRUCT: OBJECTIVE 1

The Middle Colonies

- What attracted Catholics, Quakers, and Jews to these colonies?
- What economic activities were important in the Middle Colonies?

In-Depth Resources: Unit 1
- Guided Reading, p. 42

Reading Study Guide (Spanish and English), pp. 25–26

3 Founding the Middle and Southern Colonies

MAIN IDEA

The founding of the Middle and Southern colonies provided settlers with many economic opportunities.

WHY IT MATTERS NOW

America is still a place where immigrants seek freedom and economic opportunity.

TERMS & NAMES

Peter Stuyvesant
patroon
Duke of York
proprietary colony
William Penn
Quaker
royal colony
James Oglethorpe

ONE AMERICAN'S STORY

The Dutch had founded the colony of New Netherland (later New York) on the eastern coast of North America in 1624. **Peter Stuyvesant**, the new governor, arrived in the city of New Amsterdam in May 1647. Because of his harsh personality and rough manner, he soon lost the support of the Dutch colonists. In 1664, a British fleet ordered the city of New Amsterdam to surrender itself to British control. Stuyvesant was unable to gain the support of the Dutch colonists against the British. He surrendered and then defended his decision to his superiors back in the Netherlands.

A VOICE FROM THE PAST

Powder and provisions failing, and no relief or reinforcements being expected, we were necessitated [forced] to come to terms with the enemy, not through neglect of duty or cowardice . . . but in consequence of an absolute impossibility to defend the fort, much less the city of New Amsterdam, and still less the country.

Peter Stuyvesant, quoted in *Peter Stuyvesant and His New York*

Peter Stuyvesant, governor of the Dutch colony of New Netherland, lost his leg in 1644 during a military action against the island of St. Martin in the Caribbean.

After the surrender, Stuyvesant retired to his farm. This land later became part of New York City. In this section, you will read about the founding of the Middle Colonies (such as New York) and the Southern Colonies. You will learn who settled there and why they came.

1 The Middle Colonies

The Middle Colonies were New York, New Jersey, Pennsylvania, and Delaware. They were located between New England to the north and the Chesapeake region to the south. (See the map on page 86.) Swedes, Dutch, English, Germans, and Africans were among the groups who came to these colonies.

Religious freedom attracted many groups, including Protestants, Catholics, Quakers, and Jews. The Hudson and Delaware rivers supported shipping and commerce. The river valleys had rich soil and mild winters. These conditions were favorable for farming and raising livestock.

RECOMMENDED RESOURCES

In-Depth Resources: Unit 1
- Guided Reading, p. 42
- Building Vocabulary, p. 43
- Primary Source, p. 48

Reading Study Guide (Spanish and English), pp. 25–26

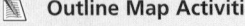

Outline Map Activities
- The 13 Colonies, pp. 5–6

Why It Matters Now
- British Connections Today, pp. 5–6

Formal Assessment
- Section Quiz, p. 53

Integrated Assessment
- Rubrics, 4.5, 5.3

Access for Students Acquiring English/ESL, p. 15

INTEGRATED TECHNOLOGY

Geography Transparency GT3
- European Colonies, 1650

Electronic Teacher Tools

classzone.com

TEST-TAKING RESOURCES

Strategies for Test Preparation

Test Practice Transparencies, TT12

Online Test Practice

❷ New Netherland Becomes New York

In 1624, Dutch settlers financed by the Dutch West India Company founded the colony of New Netherland. New Netherland included the Hudson River valley, Long Island, and the land along the Delaware River.

To attract more settlers, the Dutch West India Company employed the patroon system. A **patroon** was a person who brought 50 settlers to New Netherland. As a reward, a patroon received a large land grant. He also received special privileges in hunting, fishing, and fur trading on his land.

In the early years, many different kinds of people settled in New Netherland. Twenty-three Jewish settlers arrived in 1654, and others soon followed. Later, Africans were brought to the colony as slaves and indentured servants. Many Puritans also came.

Peter Stuyvesant, the colony's governor, wanted to add land to New Netherland. He attacked the nearby charter colony of New Sweden in 1655. This colony was located along the Delaware River. The main settlement was Fort Christina (later named Wilmington, Delaware). It had been settled by Swedes in 1638. After an attack by the Dutch, the Swedes surrendered Fort Christina.

America's HERITAGE

THE LOG CABIN

Swedish colonists living in Delaware built the first log cabin in America in 1638. The log cabin was the perfect house to build where there were many trees. Settlers needed few tools to build such cabins, which were made of round logs with curved notches at the ends. After the ends were placed in the notches, the logs were secured. After 1780, the log cabin became the typical frontier home.

Background
The Duke of York became King James II in 1685.

England's King Charles II decided that his brother, the **Duke of York,** should drive the Dutch out of New Netherland. The Dutch colony was a threat to England because of its trade. It was also a threat because of its expanding settlements and its location. There were English colonies in New England to the north and Virginia to the south. As you have seen, when the duke's ships appeared off New Amsterdam in August 1664, the colony surrendered. New Netherland became the **proprietary colony** of New York. The Duke of York was now the proprietor, or owner, of the colony.

ReadingHistory
A. Forming Opinions Why might the promise of religious freedom encourage a diverse population in a colony?
A. Answer Different sorts of people with different beliefs would be drawn to a colony that promised religious freedom.

New Jersey, Pennsylvania, and Delaware

The Duke of York had become the largest single landowner in America. He gave part of his claim, the province of New Jersey, to his friends Sir George Carteret and Lord John Berkeley in 1664. They encouraged settlers to come by promising freedom of religion. They also promised large grants of land and a representative assembly.

William Penn became another large landowner in America. Born into a wealthy English family, Penn joined the **Quakers,** to his father's disapproval. The young Penn was attacked for his Quaker beliefs. King Charles II owed the Penn family money. In repayment, in 1681 he gave Penn a large piece of land in America that came to be called Pennsylvania. The name means "Penn's woods."

INSTRUCT: OBJECTIVE ❷

New Netherland Becomes New York/ New Jersey, Pennsylvania, and Delaware

- How did the patroon system help attract settlers to New Netherland?
- How did the English acquire New Netherland?
- How did the owners of the New Jersey colony attract settlers?
- How did Penn's religious beliefs affect the way he governed Pennsylvania?

Geography Transparency GT3
- European Colonies, 1650

America's HERITAGE

The Log Cabin
The log cabin was the perfect shelter for the new colonists. It could be built easily using only an axe. After notching the logs at each end and stacking them, colonists filled in the spaces between the logs with moss, mud, or dried manure, a process known as chinking. With logs tightly fitted and cracks sealed with mud, houses were warm and snug.

MORE ABOUT . . .

William Penn
Penn's Quaker beliefs included a belief that all people are equal. He was determined to treat the Native Americans of Pennsylvania fairly. Penn purchased land from the Lenapes, also called the Delawares, the largest Native American group in the area. Penn visited Lenape villages and learned the Lenape language. Penn also set up strict rules for colonists trading with Native Americans. He made it illegal to sell alcohol to Native Americans.

ACTIVITY OPTIONS

INDIVIDUAL NEEDS

STUDENTS ACQUIRING ENGLISH/ESL

Using Proper Nouns To help students expand their use of proper nouns in relation to country of origin, pair proficient English speakers with students who are acquiring English. Invite student pairs to create charts with the headings "Country/Continent of Origin" and "Name of Group." Have students complete the chart for the groups who settled in the Middle Colonies. They can then expand the chart to include groups who have since settled in the United States.

Country/Continent of Origin	Name of Group
Sweden	Swedes
Netherlands	Dutch
England	English
Germany	Germans
Africa	Africans

HISTORY FROM VISUALS

Reading the Map Point out to students the dates of the settlements on the map. Ask students what all the settlements shown on the map except Hartford have in common. **Answer** They are all located on or near the Atlantic coast. Have students suggest reasons for this. **Possible Responses** Initial settlements were along the coast. Ports often developed into cities as they became centers of shipping and the export-import trade.

Extension Have students use a current atlas or almanac to find out which of these cities rank as major population centers in their states today.

Outline Map Activities
- The 13 Colonies, pp. 5–6

INSTRUCT: OBJECTIVE 3

The Southern Colonies/ Maryland and the Carolinas

- Why did Lord Baltimore establish Maryland?
- How did slavery begin in the Carolinas?
- In what way did Carolina change after it became a royal colony?

In-Depth Resources: Unit 1
- Primary Source, p. 48

MORE ABOUT . . .

Lord Baltimore

Charles I gave Lord Baltimore a large slice of land from the Virginia colony. The boundary for the new colony was designated as the "further bank" of the Potomac River. This meant that the new colony had been granted the entire river, including fishing rights! The ensuing "oyster war" between Maryland and Virginia crab and oyster fishermen lasted for many years. In 1785 a powerful group of Virginians including Thomas Jefferson, James Madison, and George Washington helped negotiate rights for Virginians to fish the waters of the Potomac River.

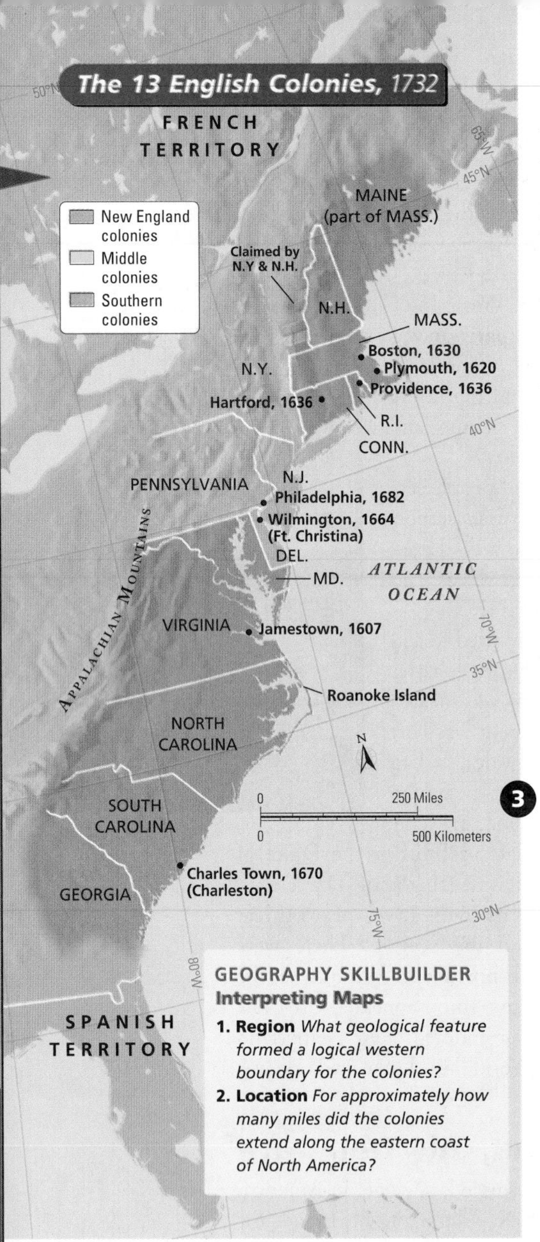

GEOGRAPHY SKILLBUILDER
Interpreting Maps
1. **Region** *What geological feature formed a logical western boundary for the colonies?*
2. **Location** *For approximately how many miles did the colonies extend along the eastern coast of North America?*

Skillbuilder Answers
1. Appalachian Mountains
2. About 1,200 miles

Penn used this land to create a colony where Quakers could live according to their beliefs. Among other things, the Quakers believed that all people should live in peace and harmony. They welcomed different religions and ethnic groups. In Pennsylvania, Penn extended religious freedom and equality to all. He especially wanted the Native Americans to be treated fairly. In a letter to them in 1681, Penn said, "May [we] always live together as neighbors and friends."

Penn's policies helped make Pennsylvania one of the wealthiest of the American colonies. Many settlers came to Pennsylvania seeking religious freedom and a better life. In 1704, Penn granted the three lower counties of Delaware their own assembly. The counties later broke away to form the colony of Delaware.

Reading **History**
B. Comparing and Contrasting How did Penn's policies toward Native Americans compare with those of other colonies you have read about?
B. Answer Penn's policies were more enlightened and tolerant than those in other colonies.

3 The Southern Colonies

The new Southern Colonies were Maryland, the Carolinas, and Georgia. The Appalachian Mountains bordered parts of these colonies in the west. In the east, the colonies bordered the Atlantic Ocean. The soil and climate of this region were suitable for warm-weather crops such as tobacco, rice, and indigo.

Maryland and the Carolinas

Lord Baltimore established Maryland in 1632 for Roman Catholics fleeing persecution in England. To attract other settlers besides Catholics, Lord Baltimore promised religious freedom. In 1649, Maryland passed the Toleration Act.

Maryland based its economy on tobacco, which required backbreaking work. Every three or four years, the tobacco crop used up the soil, and workers had to clear new land. Most laborers came as either servants or slaves. Maryland attracted few women as settlers.

In 1663, Carolina was founded as a colony. English settlers from Barbados built Charles Town, later called Charleston, in 1670. They

ACTIVITY OPTIONS

INTERDISCIPLINARY LINK: ART/LANGUAGE ARTS — BLOCK SCHEDULING

ADVERTISING THE COLONIES

Class Time One class period

Task Creating an advertising brochure

Purpose To summarize attractions of the Southern and Middle Colonies for new settlers

Supplies Needed
- Reference materials on the Middle and Southern Colonies
- Construction paper
- Art supplies

Activity Assign each student a Middle or Southern Colony. Have students create advertising brochures to attract new settlers to the colony. The brochures may highlight geographic features such as climate and soil, economic opportunities, or incentives such as land grants or freedom of religion. Tell students to identify their target audience, their message, and the action they want their readers to take before beginning to work on their brochures. Have them draw or photocopy pictures and maps for their brochures.

busied themselves cutting timber, raising cattle, and trading with the Native Americans. After 1685, Charleston became a refuge for Huguenots, French Protestants seeking religious freedom.

Vocabulary
Carolina: The name of the colony is based on a Latin form of "Charles," in honor of King Charles II.

Carolina's colonists needed laborers to grow rice and indigo. The English settlers encouraged the use of enslaved Africans. They also sold local Native Americans into slavery. As a result, wars broke out between the settlers and the Tuscarora and Yamasee tribes. The settlers' taking of tribal lands also fueled the wars.

Carolina's proprietors, or owners, refused to send help to stop a threatened Spanish attack on Charleston. Because of this, the colonists overthrew the colony's proprietary rule in 1719. In 1729, Carolina became a **royal colony.** Then it was ruled by governors appointed by the king. The colony was divided into North Carolina and South Carolina.

4 Georgia

In 1732, **James Oglethorpe** founded Georgia as a refuge for debtors. The English government wanted to use the colony as a military outpost against Spanish Florida to the south and French Louisiana to the west. In 1739, during a war between England and Spain, the Spanish tried to force the English colonists out of Georgia but were unsuccessful. English, German, Swiss, and Scottish colonists settled in Georgia. All religions were welcome. As the colony's leader, Oglethorpe set strict rules that upset the colonists. The king, in response to unrest, made Georgia a royal colony in 1752.

Reading **History**
C. Reading a Map Use the map on page 86 to check the location of Georgia in relation to the Spanish territory of Florida.

By the early 1700s, there were 13 English colonies along the eastern coast of North America. In the next chapter, you will read about how these colonies developed.

James Oglethorpe was the founder of Georgia.

Section 3 Assessment

1. Terms & Names

Explain the significance of:
- Peter Stuyvesant
- patroon
- Duke of York
- proprietary colony
- William Penn
- Quaker
- royal colony
- James Oglethorpe

2. Taking Notes

Identify an effect for each cause listed in the chart below.

Cause	Effect
New Netherland threat to English	
English attacked Quakers	
Laborers needed in Carolinas	
Oglethorpe too strict in Georgia	

3. Main Ideas

a. What were the goals of the patroon system?

b. What three Middle Colonies offered religious freedom?

c. What were three crops grown in the Southern Colonies?

4. Critical Thinking

Analyzing Causes Why did colonists in Maryland and the Carolinas enslave Native Americans and use African slaves?

THINK ABOUT
- the crops being grown
- the nature of farm work

ACTIVITY OPTIONS

LANGUAGE ARTS
SCIENCE

What are the health effects of tobacco? Write a **news article** or give a **television report** for a science show about the effects of tobacco on the body.

INSTRUCT: OBJECTIVE 4
Georgia

- Why did James Oglethorpe found Georgia?
- How did the English government intend to use the Georgia colony?

MORE ABOUT . . .

James Oglethorpe
Before coming to the Americas, James Oglethorpe was educated at Oxford University. In 1722, he entered Parliament where he headed a committee on prison reforms. His committee work led him to think about founding a colony where people who were poor and had been imprisoned for debt could start over. Oglethorpe came to Georgia in 1733 with the first settlers. During the war between England and Spain, Oglethorpe led the defense of the territory.

ASSESS & RETEACH

Setting the Stage Have students complete sequencing boxes for colonies in this section.

Formal Assessment
- Section Quiz, p. 53

Critical Thinking Transparency CT7
- Setting the Stage

RETEACHING ACTIVITY
Have the students read the introductory paragraph on the Middle Colonies. Then have students write one main idea and find two supporting statements about the Middle Colonies. Repeat for the Southern Colonies.

In-Depth Resources: Unit 1
- Reteaching Activity, p. 54

Section 3 Assessment

1. Terms & Names

Peter Stuyvesant, p. 84
patroon, p. 85
Duke of York, p. 85
proprietary colony, p. 85
William Penn, p. 85
Quaker, p. 85
royal colony, p. 87
James Oglethorpe, p. 87

2. Taking Notes

Items for effects column:
- English attacked New Netherland.
- Penn founded Pennsylvania.
- African slaves were used.
- Georgia became a royal colony.

3. Main Ideas

a. to attract settlers **b.** Pennsylvania, New Jersey, New York **c.** rice, indigo, tobacco

4. Critical Thinking

These colonies grew labor-intensive crops cultivated on large tracts of land and requiring many laborers.

ACTIVITY OPTIONS

Integrated Assessment
- Rubrics for an article, 4.5
- Rubrics for a television report, 5.3

TERMS & NAMES

1. **joint-stock company,** p. 70
2. **Jamestown,** p. 71
3. **John Smith,** p. 71
4. **House of Burgesses,** p. 72
5. **Pilgrims,** p. 76
6. **Mayflower Compact,** p. 77
7. **Great Migration,** p. 78
8. **Fundamental Orders of Connecticut,** p. 79
9. **proprietary colony,** p. 85
10. **William Penn,** p. 85

REVIEW QUESTIONS

Possible Responses

1. to provide a market for English exports, to serve as a source of raw materials, to plant the Protestant faith in America
2. to split profits and divide losses
3. He developed a high-grade tobacco, which became a basic crop.
4. He saw it as a commonwealth that would serve as a model for other people and communities.
5. Each congregation set up its own town. People gathered for town meetings in the meetinghouse. Only church members could vote or hold office. They elected the members of the General Court, which chose the governor.
6. Many settlers and Native Americans were killed, many villages were attacked and destroyed, and many Native Americans were enslaved.
7. The Dutch colony was a threat to England because of its expanding settlements, location, and trade.
8. The relations between the Native Americans and settlers in Pennsylvania were better than in any other colony.
9. This was an act passed in the colony of Maryland that promised religious freedom to attract settlers.
10. Western Europeans, Jews, Catholics, Quakers—most came for trade and farming opportunities or religious freedom. Africans, however, were brought there as slaves.

Chapter 3 ASSESSMENT

TERMS & NAMES

Briefly explain the significance of each of the following.

1. joint-stock company
2. Jamestown
3. John Smith
4. House of Burgesses
5. Pilgrims
6. Mayflower Compact
7. Great Migration
8. Fundamental Orders of Connecticut
9. proprietary colony
10. William Penn

REVIEW QUESTIONS

Early Colonies Have Mixed Success (pages 69–75)

1. What were the reasons given by Richard Hakluyt that England should start a colony?
2. Why were Jamestown and Plymouth financed by joint-stock companies?
3. How did John Rolfe change the Virginia colony?

New England Colonies (pages 76–83)

4. What was John Winthrop's vision for Massachusetts Bay?
5. What was the system of government in the Massachusetts Bay Colony?
6. What were some of the effects of King Philip's War?

Founding the Middle and Southern Colonies (pages 84–87)

7. Why did Charles II want New Netherland?
8. What were relations like between Native Americans and settlers in Pennsylvania?
9. What was the Toleration Act of 1649?
10. What ethnic and racial groups settled in the Middle Colonies and why did they do so?

CRITICAL THINKING

1. USING YOUR NOTES

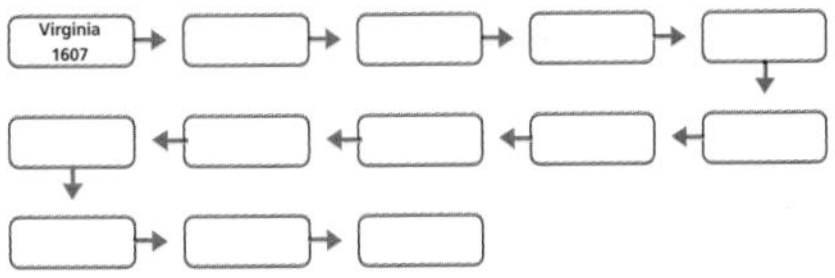

Using your completed chart, answer these questions:

a. Which was the earliest successful settlement in Virginia?

b. Which colony was founded last?

2. ANALYZING LEADERSHIP

Why do you think William Penn was a more successful leader than Peter Stuyvesant?

3. APPLYING CITIZENSHIP SKILLS

What were some of the common ideals that link the Mayflower Compact, the establishment of the House of Burgesses, and town meetings?

4. THEME: IMPACT OF THE INDIVIDUAL

How did individual effort help ensure the success of England's colonies in America?

5. ANALYZING CAUSES

What were the political, economic, and social causes for the founding of the different British colonies in North America?

Interact *with* History

How do the dangers you discussed before you read this chapter compare with the dangers people actually faced?

VISUAL SUMMARY

The 13 Colonies

	Colony	Important Early Dates	Founder(s)
New England Colonies	Massachusetts	Plymouth,1620; Mass. Bay, 1630	Pilgrims; Puritans
	New Hampshire	Portsmouth, 1623	Proprietors
	Rhode Island	Providence, 1636	Roger Williams
	Connecticut	Hartford, 1636	Thomas Hooker
Middle Colonies	New York (New Netherland)	Dutch settlers arrive, 1624	Dutch West India Company
	Delaware	Fort Christina, 1638	Swedes
	New Jersey	Duke of York establishes, 1664	George Carteret, John Berkeley
	Pennsylvania	Charles II bestows land, 1681	William Penn
Southern Colonies	Virginia	Jamestown, 1607	Virginia Company of London
	Maryland	Founded as religious haven, 1632	Lord Baltimore
	North Carolina	Founded, 1663	Proprietors
	South Carolina	Founded, 1663	Proprietors
	Georgia	Founded as debtors' refuge, 1732	James Oglethorpe

88

CRITICAL THINKING

Possible Responses

1. USING YOUR NOTES **a.** Jamestown in 1607 **b.** Georgia in 1732

2. ANALYZING LEADERSHIP Penn promised freedom of religion and equality to all settlers. He wanted to treat Native Americans fairly.

3. APPLYING CITIZENSHIP SKILLS All are based on the ideals of self-government and majority rule.

4. THEME: IMPACT OF THE INDIVIDUAL Some of the earliest individuals saved the Virginia colony through discipline, bravery, and hard work. The Pilgrims and Puritans structured communities around strict religious ideals, self-government, and hard work.

5. ANALYZING CAUSES The British wanted to increase their economic and political power compared to their European rivals. Some colonies were established to provide religious freedom.

Interact *with* History Answers will vary, but most discussions will probably center on the dangers of starvation, bad weather, shipwreck, and hostile Native Americans.

HISTORY SKILLS

1. INTERPRETING GRAPHS

Study the graph and then answer the questions.

Population of the Colonies

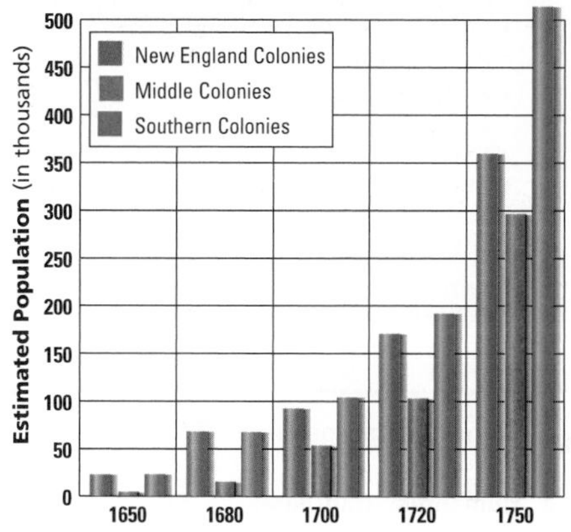

Source: *Historical Statistics of the United States,* series, Z 1–20.

a. How much did the population of the Southern colonies increase between 1720 and 1750?

b. What was the increase in the population of the New England colonies between 1700 and 1720?

c. Ask and answer a question about the geographic patterns shown in the graph.

2. INTERPRETING PRIMARY SOURCES

The early colonists used a surveyor's compass (below) to divide up the land they had come to settle.

a. What attitudes about ownership of the land are revealed by the use of a surveyor's compass?

b. How might the use of a surveyor's compass reflect differences in attitudes toward the land between European settlers and Native Americans?

ALTERNATIVE ASSESSMENT

1. INTERDISCIPLINARY ACTIVITY: Geography

Drawing a Map Draw a map of the New England, Middle, and Southern colonies. Place on the map the major cities and rivers of each colony. Show also the colonies in which people of different racial and ethnic groups settled. Explain how each region's geographic location contributed to the colonies' economic activities. Share your map with the class.

2. COOPERATIVE LEARNING ACTIVITY

Performing a Scene from a Play The "lost colonists" of Roanoke disappeared sometime between 1588 and 1590. Write and perform a play depicting a meeting of the colonists in which they try to decide what to do. John White has not returned with the supplies he promised to bring. How are the colonists to deal with food shortages, illness, and relations with the Native Americans?

Take the roles of Elinor Dare and her husband, Ananias; their child, Virginia; and other colonists. Come up with different solutions to their problems. Then vote on your preferred course of action.

3. PRIMARY SOURCE EXPLORER

Planning a Government As with any group of people living in a community, some sort of government was needed in Plymouth. The Pilgrims devised the Mayflower Compact. Using the CD-ROM, library, and Internet, find out more about the Mayflower Compact.

Create your own plan for a government using the following suggestions:

- Draw up a plan for a government that will apply to your class.
- Adapt ideas from the Mayflower Compact that you think will work for the class.
- Decide what rules are needed in your government. Decide who will hold office, how they will be appointed or selected, and how long they will serve.
- Decide whether there should be limits on majority rule in your government.

4. HISTORY PORTFOLIO

Review the chapter and write a brief report describing how different racial, ethnic, and religious groups resolved their differences in 17th- and 18th-century America. Be sure to use standard grammar, spelling, sentence structure, and punctuation in your report. Add your report to your portfolio.

Additional Test Practice, pp. S1–S33

INTERNET ACTIVITY CLASSZONE.COM

ALTERNATIVE ASSESSMENT

1. INTERDISCIPLINARY ACTIVITY: Geography
Map should
- contain major rivers and cities.
- explain the connection between location and economics.
- include clear, informative labels and captions.

2. COOPERATIVE LEARNING ACTIVITY
Scenes from plays should
- include stage directions that describe the setting, cast of characters, and props.
- contain authentic-sounding dialogue.
- dramatize moments from the meeting of the colonists.

3. PRIMARY SOURCE EXPLORER
Plans for a government should
- apply to the specific situation of the class.
- adapt some ideas from the Mayflower Compact.
- present detailed rules and ideas for choosing officers.
- address the problem of majority rule and minority rights.

4. HISTORY PORTFOLIO
Short reports should
- describe how different groups of that era resolved differences.
- use evidence to develop and support ideas.
- cite sources of information.
- use standard grammar, spelling, sentence structure, and punctuation.

Critical Thinking Transparency CT9
- Visual Summary

Formal Assessment
- Chapter Test, Forms A, B, and C, pp. 54–68

HISTORY SKILLS

Possible Responses

1. INTERPRETING GRAPHS

a. The population increased by more than 322,000.

b. The population increased by more than 78,000.

c. Question and answer should consider the growth of population in the different colonial regions.

2. INTERPRETING PRIMARY SOURCES

a. The surveyor's compass suggests that the land can be divided up and owned by individuals.

b. Native Americans did not believe that individuals could own the land.

CHAPTER 4 PLANNING GUIDE

The Colonies Develop 1700–1753

	CHAPTER OVERVIEW	COPYMASTERS	INTEGRATED TECHNOLOGY
CHAPTER RESOURCES	The chapter examines the development of the English colonies into four distinct regions: New England, the Middle Colonies, the Southern Colonies, and the Backcountry. The chapter also discusses the influence of religion on the early colonies and the increasing economic dependence on slavery in the South.	**In-Depth Resources: Unit 1** • Tracing Themes: Economics in History, p. 57 • Building Vocabulary, p. 62 **Interdisciplinary Projects,** pp. 19–24	• eEdition Plus Online • EasyPlanner Plus Online • eTest Plus Online • eEdition • Power Presentations • EasyPlanner • Electronic Library of Primary Sources • Test Generator • Reading Study Guide • America's Music
	KEY IDEAS		
SECTION 1 **New England: Commerce and Religion** **pp. 93–97**	• New England colonists depend on subsistence farming, fishing, and timber. • Trade is also a major factor in the New England economy. • Puritanism declines as a result of increasing religious diversity and the drive for economic success.	**In-Depth Resources: Unit 1** • Setting the Stage, p. 56 • Guided Reading, p. 58 • Reteaching Activity, p. 71 **Citizenship Today,** pp. 42–45	**Warm-Up Transparency WT4** **Humanities Transparency HT7** • American Colonial Hornbook, 18th Century **Geography Transparency GT4** • The Colonial Trade, 1750 **Critical Thinking Transparency CT10** • Setting the Stage classzone.com
SECTION 2 **The Middle Colonies: Farms and Cities** **pp. 98–102**	• The Middle Colonies prosper based on a wealth of resources and cash crops. • Cities thrive as trading centers in the Middle Colonies. • The Middle Colonies foster diversity of culture and religious tolerance.	**In-Depth Resources: Unit 1** • Setting the Stage, p. 56 • Guided Reading, p. 59 • Skillbuilder Practice: Creating a Map, p. 63 • Geography Application: Colonial Immigrant Groups, 1750, pp. 64–65 • Reteaching Activity, p. 72	**Warm-Up Transparency WT4** **Critical Thinking Transparency CT10** • Setting the Stage classzone.com
SECTION 3 **The Southern Colonies: Plantations and Slavery** **pp. 103–109**	• The Southern Colonies develop plantations that depend on slave labor. • The planter class dominates the Southern economy, while small landowners move west. • African Americans resist slavery, and slaveholders respond with harsh slave codes.	**In-Depth Resources: Unit 1** • Setting the Stage, p. 56 • Guided Reading, p. 60 • Literature Selection, pp. 68–70 • Reteaching Activity, p. 73 **America's History Makers** • Eliza Lucas Pinckney, pp. 15–16 **Outline Map Activities** • Colonial Products, pp. 7–8	**Warm-Up Transparency WT4** **Humanities Transparency HT8** • Maryland Plantation, 18th Century **Critical Thinking Transparency CT10** • Setting the Stage **Critical Thinking Transparency CT11** • Cause and Effect: The Slave Trade classzone.com
SECTION 4 **The Back-country** **pp. 110–113**	• The Backcountry, along the Appalachian Mountains, is a region of small farms and log cabins. • Backcountry farms are isolated, forcing settlers to be self-sufficient. • Backcountry settlers come into conflict with the area's Spanish, French, and Native American residents.	**In-Depth Resources: Unit 1** • Setting the Stage, p. 56 • Guided Reading, p. 61 • Primary Source, pp. 66–67 • Reteaching Activity, p. 74 **America's History Makers** • Alexander Spotswood, pp. 17–18 **Economics in History** • Native American Economies, p. 4 **Why It Matters Now** • Regional Differences, pp. 7–8	**Warm-Up Transparency WT4** **Critical Thinking Transparency CT10** • Setting the Stage **Critical Thinking Transparency CT12** • Visual Summary classzone.com

Pupil's Edition | Overhead Transparency | CD-ROM
Copymaster | Audio Library | Internet

ASSESSMENT OPTIONS

Chapter Assessment, pp. 114–115

Formal Assessment
- Chapter Tests, Forms A, B, and C, pp. 73–84

Test Generator

Online Test Practice

Strategies for Test Preparation

Section Assessment, p. 97

Formal Assessment, Quiz, p. 69

Integrated Assessment Book
- Rubrics, 1.9, 5.4

Test Generator

Test Practice Transparencies, TT13

Section Assessment, p. 102

Formal Assessment, Quiz, p. 70

Integrated Assessment Book
- Rubrics, 2.6, 2.1

Test Generator

Test Practice Transparencies, TT14

Section Assessment, p. 107

Formal Assessment, Quiz, p. 71

Integrated Assessment Book
- Rubrics, 1.3, 2.5

Test Generator

Test Practice Transparencies, TT15

Section Assessment, p. 113

Formal Assessment, Quiz, p. 72

Integrated Assessment Book
- Rubrics, 4.5, 1.3

Test Generator

Test Practice Transparencies, TT16

CUSTOMIZING FOR INDIVIDUAL NEEDS

Students Acquiring English/ESL

Reading Study Guide (English and Spanish), pp. 29–38

Access for Students Acquiring English/ESL: Spanish Translations, pp. 19–25

Chapter Summaries on CD (English and Spanish)

Modified Lesson Plans for English Learners

Less Proficient Readers

Reading Study Guide (English and Spanish), pp. 29–38

Chapter Summaries on CD (English and Spanish)

Gifted and Talented Students

In-Depth Resources: Unit 1
- Enrichment Activity, p. 75

America's History Makers
- Eliza Lucas Pinckney, pp. 15–16
- Alexander Spotswood, pp. 17–18

CROSS-CURRICULAR CONNECTIONS

Science/Technology

Murphy, Jim. ***Gone A-Whaling: The Lure of the Sea and the Hunt for the Great Whale.*** Boston: Houghton Mifflin, 1998.

Popular Culture

Kamensky, Jane. ***The Colonial Mosaic: American Women 1600–1760.*** The Young Oxford History of Women in the United States. New York: Oxford University Press, 1995.

Wood, Peter H. ***Strange New Land: Africans in Colonial America, 1516–1776.*** The Young Oxford History of African Americans. New York: Oxford University Press, 1996.

Interdisciplinary Projects, pp. 19–24

- Math: People of North America
- Science: Vibration and Sound
- Language Arts: American English
- Art: Dyeing Colonial Fabrics

Language Arts/Literature

Cwiklik, Robert. ***King Philip.*** New York: Silver Burdett, 1989. Novel of the life of Metacom and his 1675–1676 rebellion.

Pyle, Howard. ***Tales of Pirates and Buccaneers.*** New York: Random House, reissued 1994. Classic adventure stories based on historical pirates.

Richter, Conrad. ***The Light in the Forest.*** New York: Bantam, (1953) 1984. Acclaimed novel based on the true story of John Butler, who was captured by the Delaware Indians in 1765 and chose to stay with his captors rather than return home.

McDougal Littell Literature Connections

Walter Dean Myers

The Glory Field

Beginning with a voyage on a slave ship, this novel chronicles the saga of an African-American family from the 1700s to the present.

ENRICHMENT ACTIVITIES

Pupil's Edition, pp. 90–115
Interact with History, p. 91
Geography in History, pp. 108–109

In-Depth Resources: Unit 1
- Geography Application: Colonial Immigrant Groups, 1750, pp. 64–65
- Primary Source: Culture Clash in the Colonies, pp. 66–67
- Literature Selection: from *Roots* by Alex Haley, pp. 68–70

America's History Makers
- Eliza Lucas Pinckney, pp. 15–16
- Alexander Spotswood, pp. 17–18

Outline Map Activities
- Colonial Products, pp. 7–8

Why It Matters Now
- Regional Differences, pp. 7–8

BLOCK SCHEDULING — LESSON PLAN OPTIONS (90-MINUTE PERIOD)

DAY 1

Interact with History, p. 91
Class Time 20 minutes

Options for pacing and variety:

- **Role Playing** Have students make up identities for themselves as immigrants arriving in a port city of the 1700s. Have students write short descriptions of themselves telling where they came from, how they made a living in their homeland, and whether they hope to settle on a farm or in a town and why. **Class Time** 20 minutes

Setting the Stage, p. 92
Class Time 20 minutes

Options for pacing and variety:

- **Time Saver** For a homework assignment, have students create the Read and Take Notes graphic organizer. Remind students to complete the organizer as they read the chapter. **Class Time** 5 minutes
- **Peer Teaching** From their study of Chapter 3, students already have some knowledge of three of the colonial regions. Have them work in pairs to share their knowledge with each other and then make a list of four questions they would like to have answered. **Class Time** 15 minutes

Section 1, pp. 93–97
Class Time 50 minutes

Options for pacing and variety:

- **Internet** Extend students' background knowledge of colonial life in New England with a visit to Old Sturbridge Village at classzone.com **Class Time** 20 minutes

DAY 2

Section 2, pp. 98–102
Class Time 45 minutes

Options for pacing and variety:

- **Time Saver** Use the map The Middle Colonies, 1750 on page 99 and the chart by the same name on page 101 as graphic summaries of the section. **Class Time** 10 minutes

Section 3, pp. 103–109
Class Time 45 minutes

Options for pacing and variety:

- **Time Saver** For a homework assignment after the completion of this section, have students answer the Analyzing Leadership Critical Thinking question on page 114. Have volunteers share responses with the class. **Class Time** 20 minutes
- **History on Film** Extend students' background knowledge of the Southern Colonies by viewing *Colonial Life in the South.* Coronet. **Class Time** 20 minutes

DAY 3

Section 4, pp. 110–113
Class Time 45 minutes

Options for pacing and variety:

- **Time Saver** As a homework assignment have students complete the Read and Take Notes chart shown on page 92. Ask them to write three or four sentences telling how the Backcountry differed from other regions in resources and people. **Class Time** 10 minutes

Chapter 4 Assessment, pp. 114–115
Class Time 40 minutes

Options for pacing and variety:

- **Role Playing** Have students review the Interact with History questions on page 114 and write a response for the immigrant they role-played before they read the chapter. **Class Time** 15 minutes
- **Peer Evaluation** Have students work in groups of four to answer the Economics in History Critical Thinking question on page 114. Ask each student to answer the question for a different colonial region and let other members of the group evaluate his or her response. **Class Time** 20 minutes

TEACHER-TESTED ACTIVITY **Robert Sisko, Carteret Middle School, Carteret, New Jersey**

THE FOUR COLONIAL REGIONS

Class Time Two class periods

Task Reporting historical events as an oral presentation

Purpose To identify and describe key events of the colonial period

Supplies Needed

- Reference books and Internet sources on New England, the Middle and Southern Colonies, and the Backcountry

Activity Divide the class into small groups. Assign each group one of the four colonial regions. Tell students that they are news teams at the scene of an event that occurred in their region. Their assignment is to give a two-minute oral presentation about this event. The report should focus on the key aspects of a news story—Who, What, Where, When, Why, and How. After each group chooses its event and decides how to report it, students can select their reporter and give him or her a "pen name" by combining his or her first name with the last name of a colonial historical figure.

SLIDE-SHOW DEBATE

Presentation software is often used to help public speakers hold the attention of their audience. In this activity, students will make presentations on the value of the triangular trade for the colonies. Students will use a slide-show presentation to create talking points that support a specific argument about the triangular trade.

ACTIVITY OUTLINE

Objective Creating slide-show presentations on effects of the triangular trade will help students understand the colonial economy and gain experience with presentation software.

Task Each group will research and develop talking points to be presented in slide-show format using presentation software available.

Class Time Two class periods

DIRECTIONS

1. Explain to students that they will research the issues surrounding the triangular trade in the early days of the colonies. Divide the students into five groups. Group 1 will represent the Northern and Middle colonies. Group 2 will represent the Southern Colonies. Group 3 will represent slave traders. Group 4 will represent the European rulers of the colonies. Group 5 will represent West African leaders.

2. In a class discussion, ask students to define and explain the term *triangular trade,* as described in Chapter 4 of *Creating America.*

3. Have the groups meet to plan the research and slide show. They will also need to decide who will make their presentation.

4. In gathering information for the presentation, instruct students to address the following issues:
   a) the advantages and disadvantages of the triangle trade to their region
   b) the consequences of ending the triangular trade.

5. When each group has built its argument and created its slide show, schedule the presentations. After each presentation, the group members should answer questions from the audience and defend their point of view.

6. After all five groups have presented and defended their positions, have the audience vote on whether the triangular trade was good or bad for the colonies.

CHAPTER 4 OBJECTIVE
The student will analyze the economic and social development of the American colonies during the first half of the 18th century.

HISTORY FROM VISUALS

Interpreting the Painting Ask the students to study the painting of Philadelphia harbor or the Delaware River in 1702. Ask them to make inferences about the effect of the city's location on its economy and on its physical and social development. **Possible Responses** The city had access to a large harbor; the presence of sailing ships in the painting emphasizes the importance of trade during this period. The location probably affected its physical development because houses can be seen near the port area in the painting. Wealthy merchants and tradespeople probably built their homes close to their businesses.

Extension Have students name five occupations of citizens living in 18th-century colonial Philadelphia.

CRITICAL THINKING ACTIVITY

Making Inferences Have students make inferences about the kinds of goods that citizens of colonial Philadelphia would have imported and exported. Ask them to organize their answers on two web diagrams.

Class Time 15 minutes

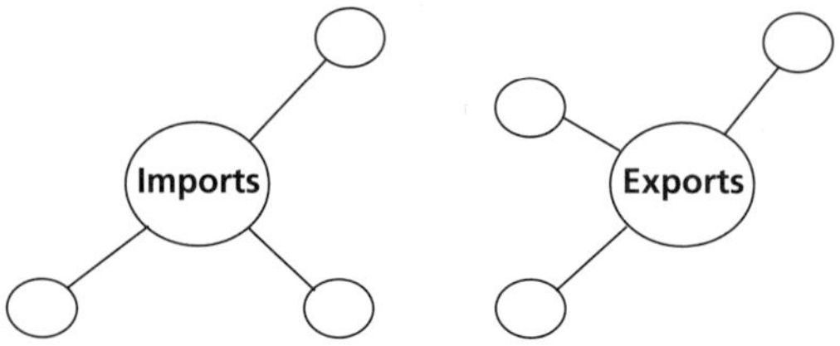

CHAPTER 4

The Colonies Develop 1700–1753

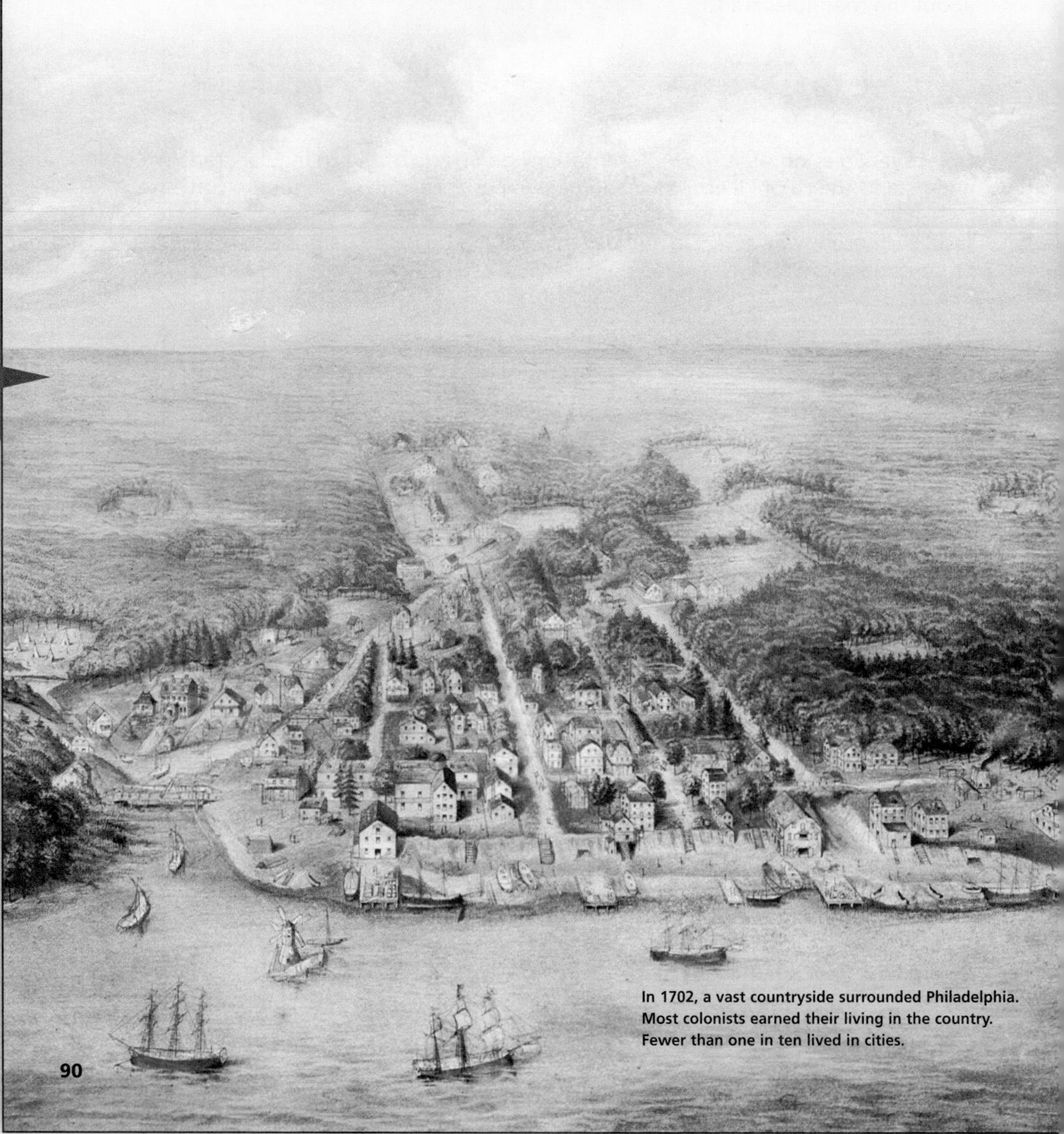

In 1702, a vast countryside surrounded Philadelphia. Most colonists earned their living in the country. Fewer than one in ten lived in cities.

90

RECOMMENDED RESOURCES

BOOKS FOR THE TEACHER

Leach, Douglas. ***Flintlock and Tomahawk: New England in King Philip's War.*** New York: Parnassus, 1992.

Merrell, James H. ***Into the American Woods.*** New York: Norton, 1999. Life on the Pennsylvania frontier.

Woodmason, Charles. ***The Carolina Backcountry on the Eve of the Revolution.*** Ed. Richard J. Hooker. Chapel Hill, NC: U. of N.C. Press, 1953. Classic account of frontier life from the journal of an itinerant minister.

SOFTWARE

Colonization. Diskette. Tom Snyder Productions/Software. Interesting presentation of colonizing process.

VIDEO

Silversmith of Williamsburg. U. Press of Va., n.d. Together with similar titles on a gunsmith and a hammerman, a useful look at the practice of some colonial crafts.

INTERNET

For more about Old Sturbridge Village, visit . . .

classzone.com

Interact *with* History

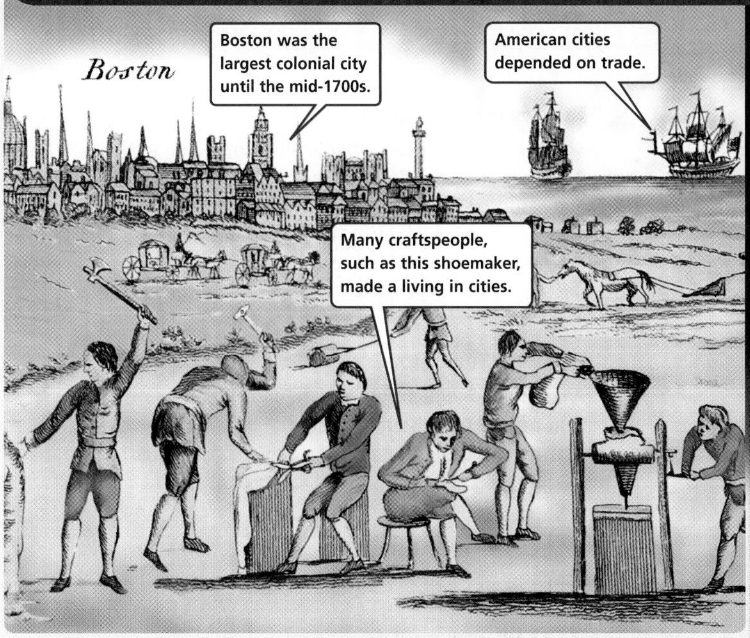
Boston
Boston was the largest colonial city until the mid-1700s.
American cities depended on trade.
Many craftspeople, such as this shoemaker, made a living in cities.

It is the early 1700s when you arrive in one of America's larger port cities. After nearly a month of ocean travel, you are thrilled to see land. As you leave the ship, you wonder where you will live and how you will earn a living.

What Do You Think?

- **Will you choose to live where other people from your homeland live? Or will you try somewhere new?**
- **How did you make a living in your old country? Will this influence your choice?**

Would you settle on a farm or in a town?

USA

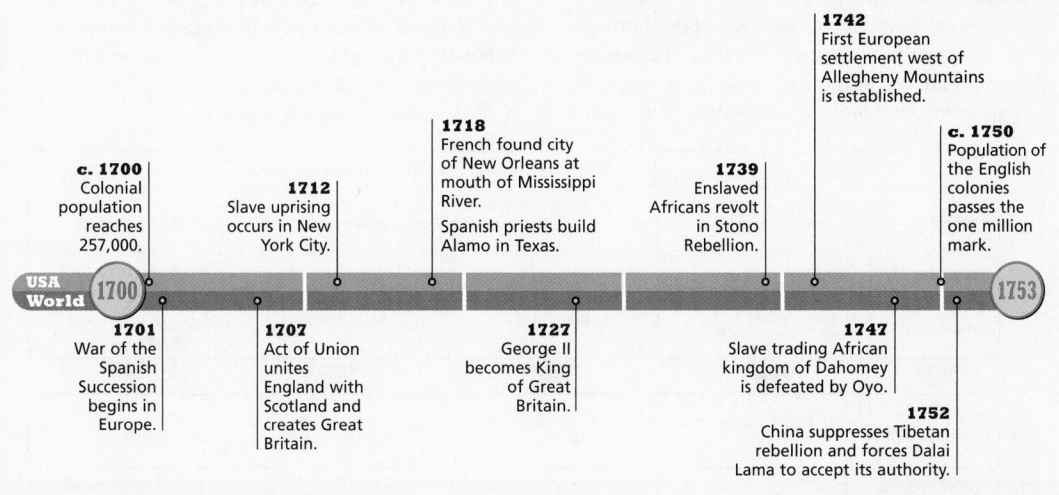

- **c. 1700** Colonial population reaches 257,000.
- **1712** Slave uprising occurs in New York City.
- **1718** French found city of New Orleans at mouth of Mississippi River. Spanish priests build Alamo in Texas.
- **1739** Enslaved Africans revolt in Stono Rebellion.
- **1742** First European settlement west of Allegheny Mountains is established.
- **c. 1750** Population of the English colonies passes the one million mark.

1700 – 1753

World

- **1701** War of the Spanish Succession begins in Europe.
- **1707** Act of Union unites England with Scotland and creates Great Britain.
- **1727** George II becomes King of Great Britain.
- **1747** Slave trading African kingdom of Dahomey is defeated by Oyo.
- **1752** China suppresses Tibetan rebellion and forces Dalai Lama to accept its authority.

Interact *with* History

OBJECTIVES

- To help students understand the economic and social problems facing immigrants to colonial America
- To help students connect with the people and events they will study in this chapter

What Do You Think?

1. Ask students why living near others from your homeland might be important.
2. Have students explain how the occupations of newcomers to America might affect where they would settle.

Would you settle on a farm or in a town?

Encourage students to think about the factors (social connections, occupations, finances) that would influence their decisions to live in a rural or an urban area.

MAKING PERSONAL CONNECTIONS

Ask students to think about experiences they might have had moving to a new country, city, or neighborhood. How would their experiences compare and contrast to those of newcomers to colonial America? What might have influenced their families' choice of a new home? Would their reasons for choosing a community be similar to or different from the reasons that influenced American colonists?

TIME LINE DISCUSSION

Remind students that the English established 13 colonies along the Atlantic Coast of North America from 1607 to 1732. Colonists were not content to remain on the seaboard. They continued to push into the continent to establish new settlements. Land and economic activity drew many immigrants, both voluntary and involuntary.

- Ask students to identify how the population of the English colonies changed between 1700 and 1750. **Answer** The population more than quadrupled from 257,000 to more than 1 million people.
- Ask students in what areas of North America settlements were being developed. **Answer** New Orleans, Texas, west of the Allegheny Mountains

BEFORE YOU READ

Previewing the Theme: Economics in History

Ask the students to think of ways that the climate, geography, and resources of a particular area affected the work of the colonists.

Point out that the climate and geography of the land along the Atlantic coast differed widely and affected the length of the growing season, the size of the farms, and the economic focus of each area. While the types of farming might differ in the four regions, nearly all the European immigrants expected to farm the land.

What Do You Know?

Point out to students that the differences in the climate influenced the economy and the way of life that developed in each region. In the North, for example, while farming remained important, industry, including manufacturing and trade, became increasingly important.

In-Depth Resources: Unit 1
- Tracing Themes: Economics in History, p. 57

READ AND TAKE NOTES

Reading Strategy: Analyzing Causes and Recognizing Effects

Tell students that analyzing causes and recognizing their effects will help them understand how and why New England and the Middle and Southern Colonies developed in unique and specific ways. Explain that factors such as climate and resources affected how people worked and survived. Point out to students that recording causes and effects in a chart will help them compare and contrast colonial development in the three regions.

In-Depth Resources: Unit 1
- Setting the Stage, p. 56

Critical Thinking Transparency CT10
- Setting the Stage

Chapter 4 SETTING THE STAGE

BEFORE YOU READ

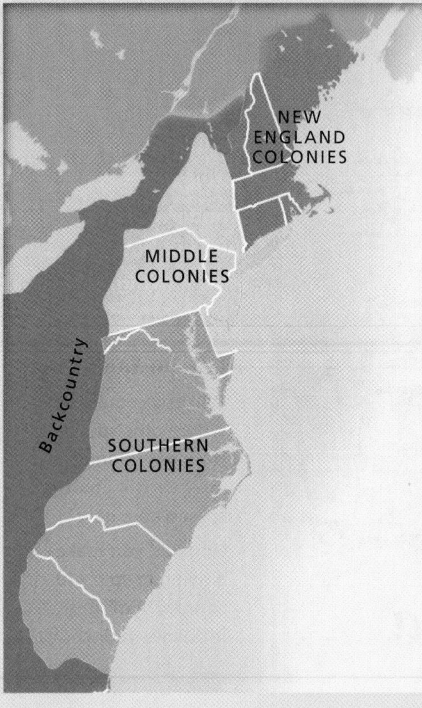

Previewing the Theme

Economics in History When immigrants came to the Americas, they settled in places with different climates and resources. These conditions affected the economic choices made by colonists. As Chapter 4 explains, those choices contributed to the formation of four different colonial regions.

What Do You Know?

What ideas and pictures come to mind when you hear people talk about "the South" or "the North"? Why do you think these distinct regions developed?

THINK ABOUT
- what you have learned about these regions from books or movies
- the way geography affects people's choices

What Do You Want to Know?

What questions do you have about how the four colonial regions developed? Record these questions in your notebook before you read the chapter.

READ AND TAKE NOTES

Reading Strategy: Analyzing Causes and Recognizing Effects As you read about history, it is important to understand not only what happened in the past, but also the reasons why it happened. Clue words that indicate cause—such as *because* and *since*—can help you look for causes of historical events. Use the chart below to list causes that contributed to the different economic developments in each of the colonial regions.

See Skillbuilder Handbook, page R11.

		NEW ENGLAND COLONIES	MIDDLE COLONIES	SOUTHERN COLONIES	BACKCOUNTRY
CAUSES	Climate	Long, cold winters and a short growing season	Shorter winters and a longer growing season	Nearly year-round growing season	Varied with latitude
	Resources	Rocky soil	Fertile soil	Fertile soil	Woods and streams
	People	English settlers	Diverse population	English and enslaved Africans	Scots-Irish and Native Americans
EFFECT	Economic Development	Small farms, fishing, and trade	Larger farms and cash crops of grain	Plantation economy	Small farms

TEACHING STRATEGY

READING THE CHAPTER

This is a thematic chapter that focuses on development of the New England, Middle, and Southern Colonies. Encourage students to use the maps in each section to help them understand each region's growth and development. Ask students to summarize each section, and then note the similarities and differences in the development of each.

ALTERNATIVE ASSESSMENT

The Chapter Assessment describes three activities for alternative assessment on page 115. You may wish to have students work on these activities during the course of the chapter and then present them at the end.

1 New England: Commerce and Religion

TERMS & NAMES
Backcountry
subsistence farming
triangular trade
Navigation Acts
smuggling

MAIN IDEA

Fishing and trade contributed to the growth and prosperity of the New England Colonies.

WHY IT MATTERS NOW

Coastal cities in New England continue to engage in trade.

ONE AMERICAN'S STORY

Peleg Folger, a New England sailor, was only 18 years old when he began whaling. Folger kept a journal that describes what whaling was like in the 1750s. In one journal entry, Folger explained what happened after whales were sighted and small boats were launched to pursue them.

A VOICE FROM THE PAST

So we row'd about a mile and a Half from the [ship], and then a whale come up under us, & [smashed in] our boat . . . and threw us every man overboard [except] one. And we all came up and Got Hold of the Boat & Held to her until the other boat (which was a mile and half off) came up and took us in, all Safe, and not one man Hurt, which was remarkable, the boat being threshed to pieces very much.

Peleg Folger, quoted in *The Sea-Hunters*

Whales hunted by New Englanders, such as Peleg Folger, might weigh as much as 50 tons and be over 60 feet in length.

When Folger and his mates did manage to kill a whale, they cut a hole in its head. Then "a man got in up to his armpits and Dipt out [barrels] of clear oil." When the ship returned to port, this oil was sold to colonists, who used it as fuel in their lamps.

Many settlers in the New England Colonies—Massachusetts, New Hampshire, Connecticut, and Rhode Island—turned to the Atlantic Ocean to make a living. The majority of New Englanders, however, were farmers.

1 Distinct Colonial Regions Develop

Between 1700 and 1750, the population of England's colonies in North America doubled and then doubled again. At the start of the century, the colonial population stood at about 257,000. By 1750, more than 1,170,000 settlers called the English colonies home.

By the 1700s, the colonies formed three distinct regions: the New England Colonies, the Middle Colonies, and the Southern Colonies. Another area was the **Backcountry**. It ran along the Appalachian Mountains through the far western part of the other regions.

SECTION OBJECTIVES

1. To explain how distinct regions developed during the colonial period
2. To describe life in the New England farms and towns
3. To describe the three types of Atlantic trade
4. To identify the reasons for changes in Puritan society

SKILLBUILDER

Interpreting Maps: Location, Region, p. 94

CRITICAL THINKING

Recognizing Effects, p. 95
Analyzing Causes, p. 96
Making Inferences, p. 97

FOCUS & MOTIVATE

5-MINUTE WARM-UP

Drawing Conclusions These questions focus on the impact of the environment on the New England Colonies.

1. Look at the map on page 94. How did New Englanders make their living from the sea?
2. What reasons might there be for no grain products shown?

Warm-Up Transparency WT4

INSTRUCT

INSTRUCT: OBJECTIVE 1

Distinct Colonial Regions Develop

- What major regions developed in the colonies by the 1700s?
- What were the key factors that made the colonial regions different from one another?
- What influenced the type of agriculture that developed in each region?

In-Depth Resources: Unit 1
- Guided Reading, p. 58

Reading Study Guide (Spanish and English), pp. 29–30

RECOMMENDED RESOURCES

In-Depth Resources: Unit 1
- Guided Reading, p. 58
- Building Vocabulary, p. 62

Reading Study Guide (Spanish and English), pp. 29–30

Citizenship Today, pp. 42–45

Formal Assessment
- Section Quiz, p. 69

Integrated Assessment
- Rubrics, 1.9, 5.4

Access for Students Acquiring English/ESL
- Guided Reading, p. 19

INTEGRATED TECHNOLOGY

Humanities Transparency HT7
- American Colonial Hornbook

Geography Transparency GT4
- The Colonial Trade, 1750

Electronic Teacher Tools

classzone.com

TEST-TAKING RESOURCES

Strategies for Test Preparation

Test Practice Transparencies, TT13

Online Test Practice

INSTRUCT: OBJECTIVE 2

The Farms and Towns of New England/ Harvesting the Sea

- How did the geography of New England affect the kind of farming practiced there?
- Describe the settlement patterns in New England.
- What role did fishing play in the economy of colonial New England?

Citizenship Today, pp. 42–45

HISTORY FROM VISUALS

Reading the Map Point out the symbols for the various economic products produced in colonial New England. Ask students why there were so many nonagricultural products produced in colonial New England. Have the students identify relationships between the kinds of products. **Possible Responses** Nonagricultural products dominated the economy because the region had direct access to the sea and because farming was difficult. Fishing and whaling were both important and depended on shipbuilding, which required timber that was abundant in the region.

Extension Have students choose one New England state and find out its chief products today. Direct students to resources such as almanacs, encyclopedias, and state pages on the Internet.

Several factors made each colonial region distinct. Some of the most important were each region's climate, resources, and people.

1. New England had long winters and rocky soil. English settlers made up the largest group in the region's population.
2. The Middle Colonies had shorter winters and fertile soil. The region attracted immigrants from all over Europe.
3. The Southern Colonies had a warm climate and good soil. There, some settlers used enslaved Africans to work their plantations.
4. The Backcountry's climate and resources varied, depending on the latitude. Many Scots-Irish immigrants settled there.

During the colonial era, the majority of people made their living by farming. However, the type of agriculture they practiced depended on the climate and resources in the region where they settled.

Vocabulary
latitude: the distance north or south of the equator, measured in degrees

2 The Farms and Towns of New England

Life in New England was not easy. The growing season was short, and the soil was rocky. Most farmers practiced **subsistence farming.** That is, they produced just enough food for themselves and sometimes a little extra to trade in town.

Most New England farmers lived near a town. This was because colonial officials usually did not sell scattered plots of land to individual

Skillbuilder Answers
1. Hudson River
2. ships, fish, and whales

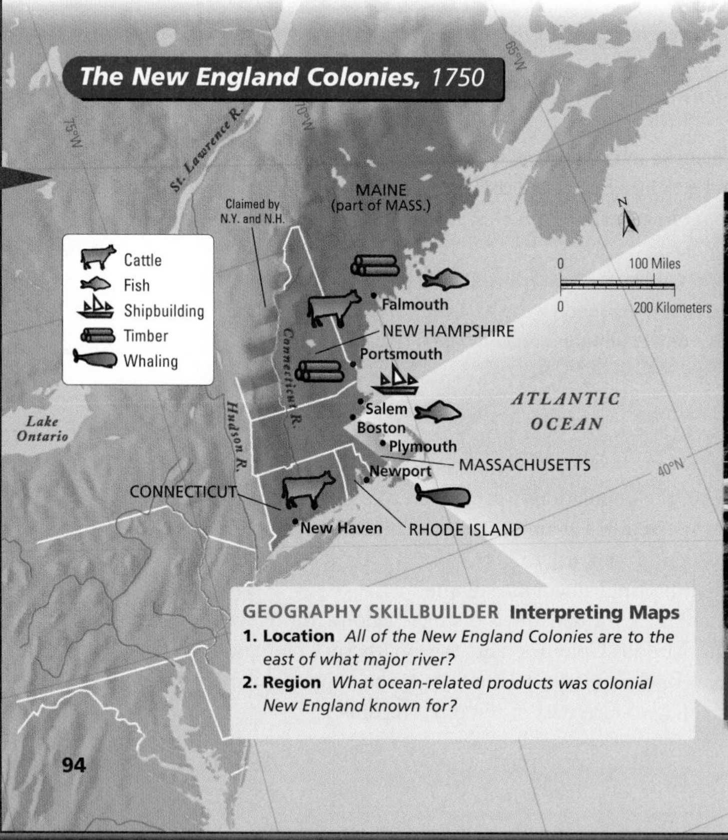

GEOGRAPHY SKILLBUILDER Interpreting Maps
1. **Location** *All of the New England Colonies are to the east of what major river?*
2. **Region** *What ocean-related products was colonial New England known for?*

This New England meetinghouse is located in Sturbridge Village, Massachusetts.

94

ACTIVITY OPTIONS

MULTIPLE LEARNING STYLES: SPATIAL

BLOCK SCHEDULING

TOWN PLANNING

Class Time One class period

Task Researching the layout of a colonial New England town

Purpose To gain understanding of how the plan of a New England town reflected its economy

Supplies Needed
- Art supplies, including rulers
- Encyclopedias, Internet access

Activity Divide the class into small groups and assign each group one of the New England towns shown on the map on this page. Tell groups to consult encyclopedias or on-line references to find information about the town's colonial history. Have students draw a diagram showing how the town was planned. Town plans should include the green, church, school, surrounding houses, shops, and farm fields.

farmers. Instead, they sold larger plots of land to groups of people—often to the congregation of a Puritan church. A congregation then settled the town and divided the land among the members of its church.

Reading **History**
A. Recognizing Effects How did the way land was sold in New England affect the way people lived?
A. Possible Response Because colonial officials sold large plots of land to groups, many New Englanders lived together in towns.

This pattern of settlement led New England towns to develop in a unique way. Usually, a cluster of farmhouses surrounded a green—a central square where a meetinghouse was located and where public activities took place. Because people lived together in small towns, shopkeepers had enough customers to make a living. Also, if the townspeople needed a blacksmith or a carpenter, they could pool their money and hire one.

Harvesting the Sea

New England's rocky soil made farming difficult. In contrast, the Atlantic Ocean offered many economic opportunities. In one story, a group of settlers was standing on a hill overlooking the Atlantic. One of them pointed out to sea and exclaimed, "There is a great pasture where our children's grandchildren will go for bread!"

The settler's prediction came true. Not far off New England's coast were some of the world's best fishing grounds. The Atlantic was filled with mackerel, halibut, cod, and many other types of fish.

New England's forests provided everything needed to harvest these great "pastures" of fish. The wood cut from iron-hard oak trees made excellent ship hulls. Hundred-foot-tall white pines were ideal for masts. Shipbuilders used about 2,500 trees to produce just one ship!

New England's fish and timber were among its most valuable articles of trade. Coastal cities like Boston, Salem, New Haven, and Newport grew rich as a result of shipbuilding, fishing, and trade.

Background
In 1742, over 16,000 people lived in Boston.

3 Atlantic Trade

New England settlers engaged in three types of trade. First was the trade with other colonies. Second was the direct exchange of goods with Europe. The third type was the triangular trade.

Triangular trade was the name given to a trading route with three stops. For example, a ship might leave New England with a cargo of rum

Triangular Trade, *1750*

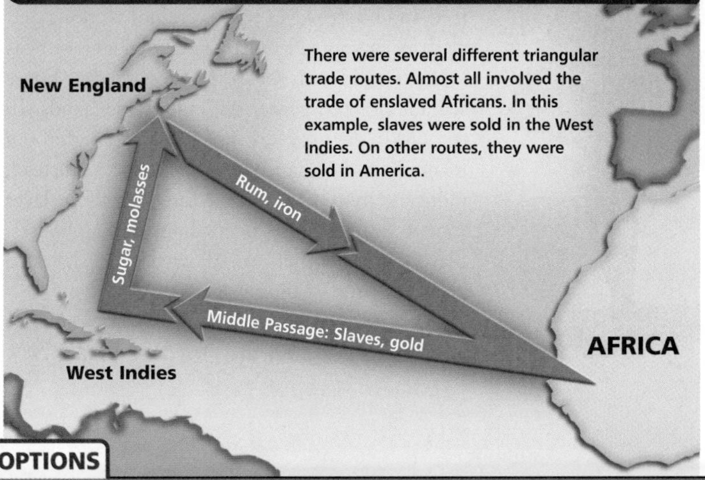
New England
There were several different triangular trade routes. Almost all involved the trade of enslaved Africans. In this example, slaves were sold in the West Indies. On other routes, they were sold in America.
Rum, iron
Sugar, molasses
Middle Passage: Slaves, gold
AFRICA
West Indies

95

MORE ABOUT . . .

Harvesting the Sea
New England fishing vessels usually headed for the Grand Banks, one of the world's richest fishing areas. The Grand Banks are a series of raised underwater plateaus off the southeast coast of Newfoundland. Many kinds of plants and fish flourish in the shallow water of the Grand Banks. In the 1960s and 1970s, however, fish stocks were declining. In 1977, Canada declared its exclusive fishing rights to most of the Grand Banks. Strict conservation measures are working to restore the populations of cod, flounder, turbot, ocean perch, haddock, and other species.

INSTRUCT: OBJECTIVE 3

**Atlantic Trade/
African Americans in New England**

- What kinds of trade did New England colonists engage in?
- What is an example of triangular trade?
- What was the purpose of the Navigation Acts?

Geography Transparency GT4
- The Colonial Trade, 1750

HISTORY FROM VISUALS

Reading the Map Point out the relative distances of the segments of the triangular trade route pictured on the map. Ask students to discuss what happened to slaves during the Middle Passage.
Possible Response Because of the length of the journey and the horrible conditions on board the ships, many people probably died on the trip.

Extension Have students do research on the experiences of enslaved Africans during the Middle Passage. Ask students to produce a monologue, journal entry, or essay about the Middle Passage.

ACTIVITY OPTIONS

INDIVIDUAL NEEDS

STUDENTS ACQUIRING ENGLISH/ESL

Understanding Prefixes Ask students to look at the map *Triangular Trade, 1750* on this page. Point out the three arrows that form a triangle. Review that a triangle is a three-sided figure and that the prefix *tri-* means "three." Discuss other words with the prefix *tri-*, and write them on the board. *(tripod, tricycle, triceps, triceratops)*

Explain that the three sides of the triangle represent three sides of a trade relationship. Help students to see the benefits of a trade arrangement with three locations. You might ask questions such as the following to prompt discussion:
- What products did Africa want from the New England Colonies?
- What products did New England colonists want from the West Indies?

STRANGE *but* True

Blackbeard the Pirate

Blackbeard's real name was Edward Teach. His nickname came from his thick, black beard. Beginning his career as a pirate around 1716, Blackbeard operated along the Virginia and Carolina coasts. By 1718, Blackbeard had established a base in a North Carolina inlet from which he collected tolls from ships passing through Pamlico Sound. He even had an agreement to share his booty with Charles Eden, governor of the North Carolina colony. Through the years, many people have searched for the treasure supposedly buried by Teach. It probably never existed.

MORE ABOUT . . .

African Americans in Whaling

African Americans played an important part in the whaling industry of New England. Many Quaker whaling captains from New Bedford or on the island of Nantucket welcomed free blacks and runaway slaves as crew members. In addition, sailors of color from the Cape Verde Islands and the Caribbean often joined New England whaling crews. Crispus Attucks, the African American killed during the Boston Massacre, spent many years as a whaler. There even were a few whalers with all African-American crews.

and iron. In Africa, the captain would trade his cargo for slaves. Slaves then endured the horrible Middle Passage to the West Indies, where they were exchanged for sugar and molasses. Traders then took the sugar and molasses back to New England. There, colonists used the molasses to make rum, and the pattern started over.

Background
See Olaudah Equiano's descriptions of the Middle Passage on page 62.

New England won enormous profits from trade. England wanted to make sure that it received part of those profits. So the English government began to pass the **Navigation Acts** in 1651. The Navigation Acts had four major provisions designed to ensure that England made money from its colonies' trade.

1. All shipping had to be done in English ships or ships made in the English colonies.
2. Products such as tobacco, wood, and sugar could be sold only to England or its colonies.
3. European imports to the colonies had to pass through English ports.
4. English officials were to tax any colonial goods not shipped to England.

But even after the passage of the Navigation Acts, England had trouble controlling colonial shipping. Merchants ignored the acts whenever possible. **Smuggling**—importing or exporting goods illegally—was common. England also had great difficulty preventing pirates—like the legendary Blackbeard—from interfering with colonial shipping.

STRANGE *but* True

BLACKBEARD THE PIRATE

Of all the pirates who attacked colonial ships, Blackbeard (shown below) was the most famous. He was a fearsome man known to stick matches in his hair to light up his face during battle.

Blackbeard's pirate career finally came to an end in 1718, when Virginia's governor sent an expedition against him. Nearly half the expedition's men died in the key battle. Blackbeard himself did not fall until he had suffered nearly 25 wounds. Before sailing back to port, sailors cut off his head and put it on the front of their ship.

African Americans in New England

There were few slaves in New England. Slavery simply was not economical in this region of small farms. Also, because the growing season was short, there was little work for slaves during the long winter months. Farmers could not afford to feed and house slaves who were not working.

***Reading*History**
B. Analyzing Causes Why were there relatively few enslaved workers in New England?
B. Possible Response Because of the small size of farms and the short growing season, slavery was not economical.

Even so, some New Englanders in larger towns and cities did own slaves. They worked as house servants, cooks, gardeners, and stable-hands. In the 1700s, slave owners seldom had enough room to house more than one or two slaves. Instead, more and more slave owners hired out their slaves to work on the docks or in shops or warehouses. Slave owners sometimes allowed their slaves to keep a portion of their wages.

Occasionally, some enslaved persons were able to save enough to buy their freedom. In fact, New

ACTIVITY OPTIONS

INTERDISCIPLINARY LINK: LANGUAGE ARTS — BLOCK SCHEDULING

WRITING EDITORIALS

Class Time 20 minutes

Task Writing a newspaper editorial

Purpose To form and express an opinion about the Navigation Acts

Supplies Needed
- Examples of editorials from school or community newspapers

Activity Have students read examples of editorials from school or community newspapers. Briefly discuss with students the characteristics of a good editorial, including the presentation of a point of view about an issue. Ask students to write editorials for an 18th-century colonial or British newspaper, either supporting or opposing the Navigation Acts. Their editorials should include reasons that support their opinions. Ask volunteers to read their editorials aloud to the group.

England was home to more free blacks than any other region. A free black man might become a merchant, sailor, printer, carpenter, or landowner. Still, white colonists did not treat free blacks as equals.

4 Changes in Puritan Society

> **"[Boston] is so conveniently Situated for Trade."**
> An observer in 1713

The early 1700s saw many changes in New England society. One of the most important was the gradual decline of the Puritan religion. There were a number of reasons for this decline.

Reading **History**
C. Making Inferences Why might an interest in material things compete with the Puritan religion?
C. Possible Response Many religions, including Puritanism, teach that too much concern with material things is wrong.

One reason was that the drive for economic success competed with Puritan ideas. Many colonists, especially those who lived along the coast, seemed to care as much about business and material things as they did about religion. One observer had this complaint.

A VOICE FROM THE PAST

[Boston] is so conveniently Situated for Trade and the Genius of the people are so inclined to merchandise, that they seek no other Education for their children than writing and Arithmetick.

An observer in 1713, quoted in *A History of American Life*

Another reason for the decline of the Puritan religion was the increasing competition from other religious groups. Baptists and Anglicans established churches in Massachusetts and Connecticut, where Puritans had once been the most powerful group.

Political changes also weakened the Puritan community. In 1691, a new royal charter for Massachusetts guaranteed religious freedom for all Protestants, not just Puritans. The new charter also granted the vote based on property ownership instead of church membership. This change put an end to the Puritan churches' ability to control elections.

To the south of New England were the Middle Colonies, which developed in quite different ways—as the next section shows.

Section 1 Assessment

1. Terms & Names

Explain the significance of:
- Backcountry
- subsistence farming
- triangular trade
- Navigation Acts
- smuggling

2. Taking Notes

Use a chart like the one shown to record how New Englanders prospered from the Atlantic Ocean.

Economic Activity	Benefits to Colonists

How did some profit illegally from the ocean?

3. Main Ideas

a. How did most people in New England earn a living?

b. Why did England pass the Navigation Acts?

c. What factors led to the decline of the Puritan religion in New England?

4. Critical Thinking

Making Inferences What advantages might there be in living near other people in small towns, such as those in New England?

THINK ABOUT
- the transportation options available to colonists
- why shopkeepers chose to open businesses in towns

ACTIVITY OPTIONS

ART
TECHNOLOGY

Read more about whaling. Make a **mobile** that shows different kinds of whales or plan a **multimedia presentation** on whaling today.

INSTRUCT: OBJECTIVE 4

Changes in Puritan Society

- How did economic success compete with Puritan ideas?
- What religious groups competed with the Puritans?
- How did the new royal charter for Massachusetts affect the Puritan community?

Humanities Transparency HT7
- American Colonial Hornbook

MORE ABOUT . . .

Puritan Practices

Leaders of Puritan churches assigned seating according to social status. The most wealthy and respected church members sat in the first rows in pews they owned themselves. Their wives sat with them, but not their children. The rest of the congregation was divided by gender—men on one side, women on the other.

ASSESS & RETEACH

Setting the Stage Have students fill in information about the New England Colonies on the chapter graphic organizer.

Formal Assessment
- Section Quiz, p. 69

Critical Thinking Transparency CT10
- Setting the Stage

RETEACHING ACTIVITY

Divide the class into four teams, representing each of the objectives for this section. Each team should create a graphic organizer that identifies the main ideas about its objective. After the teams have completed their assignments, display the graphic organizers in the classroom. Review the information on each one with the class.

In-Depth Resources: Unit 1
- Reteaching Activity, p. 71

Section 1 Assessment

1. Terms & Names

Backcountry, p. 93
subsistence farming, p. 94
triangular trade, p. 95
Navigation Acts, p. 96
smuggling, p. 96

2. Taking Notes

Fishing—Fish could be sold for consumption or export.
Whaling—Whale oil provided oil for lamps or for export.
Trading—Colonists made money from three types of Atlantic trade.
Smuggling—Smuggling was widespread, though illegal.

3. Main Ideas

a. farming **b.** England wanted to make sure that it, too, profited from its colonies' trade. **c.** People were more interested in making money; other religions began to compete; a new charter decreased the political power of the Puritan churches.

4. Critical Thinking

People could walk to the nearby locations to take care of business. Shopkeepers would have enough customers to make a living.

ACTIVITY OPTIONS

Integrated Assessment
- Rubrics for a mobile, 1.9
- Rubrics for multimedia, 5.4

SECTION OBJECTIVES

1. To identify the resources of the Middle Colonies
2. To describe the prosperity of the cities
3. To evaluate the diversity of the region
4. To analyze the treatment of African Americans

SKILLBUILDER
Interpreting Maps: Place, Movement, p. 99
Interpreting Graphs, p. 101

CRITICAL THINKING
Summarizing, p. 101
Forming Opinions, p. 102
Analyzing Causes, p. 102

FOCUS & MOTIVATE

5-MINUTE WARM-UP

Drawing Conclusions These questions focus on the economic diversity of the Middle Colonies.

1. Look at the pictures on page 100. How many occupations can you identify?
2. What can you conclude about the economy of the region from the variety of occupations represented?

Warm-Up Transparency WT4

INSTRUCT

INSTRUCT: OBJECTIVE 1

A Wealth of Resources/ The Importance of Mills

- What resources were available in the Middle Colonies?
- Why were the Middle Colonies called the "breadbasket" colonies?
- What did the immigrants contribute to the economy?

In-Depth Resources: Unit 1
- Guided Reading, p. 59
- Building Vocabulary, p. 62

2 The Middle Colonies: Farms and Cities

TERMS & NAMES
cash crop
gristmill
diversity
artisan
Conestoga wagon

MAIN IDEA	WHY IT MATTERS NOW
The people who settled in the Middle Colonies made a society of great diversity.	States in this region still boast some of the most diverse communities in the world.

ONE AMERICAN'S STORY

Elizabeth Ashbridge was only 19 years old when she arrived in America from England in the 1730s. Even though she was young, she had already been married and widowed. And although she was an indentured servant, she hoped to earn her freedom and find a way to express her strong religious feelings.

After several years, Elizabeth did gain freedom. She started to search for a religion that she could devote her life to. Finally, in the colony of Pennsylvania, she found what she was looking for—the Society of Friends, or Quakers. The new Quaker longed to share her beliefs openly.

A VOICE FROM THE PAST

I was permitted to see that all I had gone through was to prepare me for this day; and that the time was near, when it would be required of me, to go and declare to others what the God of mercy had done for my soul.

Elizabeth Ashbridge, *Some Account . . . of the Life of Elizabeth Ashbridge*

A woman speaks out at a Quaker meeting. The Society of Friends allowed women a more active role than other religions.

The Quakers believed that people of different beliefs could live together in harmony. They helped to create a climate of tolerance and acceptance in the Middle Colonies of New York, New Jersey, Pennsylvania, and Delaware. These colonies began to attract a wide variety of immigrants, as you will read in this section.

1 A Wealth of Resources

The Middle Colonies had much to offer in addition to a climate of tolerance. A Frenchman named Michel Guillaume Jean de Crèvecoeur (krehv•KUR) praised the region's "fair cities, substantial villages, extensive fields . . . decent houses, good roads, orchards, meadows, and bridges, where an hundred years ago all was wild, woody, and uncultivated."

The prosperity that Crèvecoeur described was typical of the Middle Colonies. Immigrants from all over Europe came to take advantage of this region's productive land. Their settlements soon crowded out Native Americans, who had lived in the region for thousands of years.

RECOMMENDED RESOURCES

In-Depth Resources: Unit 1
- Guided Reading, p. 59
- Skillbuilder Practice, p. 63
- Geography Application: Colonial Immigrant Groups, 1750, pp. 64–65
- Enrichment Activity, p. 75

Reading Study Guide (Spanish and English), pp. 31–32

Formal Assessment
- Section Quiz, p. 70

Integrated Assessment
- Rubrics, 2.6, 2.1

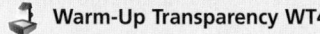

Access for Students Acquiring English/ESL
- Guided Reading, p. 20
- Skillbuilder Practice, p. 23
- Geog. Application, pp. 24–25

INTEGRATED TECHNOLOGY

Electronic Teacher Tools

classzone.com

TEST-TAKING RESOURCES

Strategies for Test Preparation

Test Practice Transparencies, TT14

Online Test Practice

Among the immigrants who came to the Middle Colonies were Dutch and German farmers. They brought the advanced agricultural methods of their countries with them. Their skills, knowledge, and hard work would soon result in an abundance of foods.

The Middle Colonies boasted a longer growing season than New England and a soil rich enough to grow **cash crops.** These were crops raised to be sold for money. Common cash crops included fruits, vegetables, and, above all, grain. The Middle Colonies produced so much grain that people began calling them the "breadbasket" colonies.

The Importance of Mills

Vocabulary
grist: another name for grain, the one-seeded fruit of cereal grasses like wheat and rye

After harvesting their crops of corn, wheat, rye, or other grains, farmers took them to a **gristmill.** There, millers crushed the grain between heavy stones to produce flour or meal. Human or animal power fueled some of these mills. But water wheels built along the region's plentiful rivers powered most of the mills.

The bread that colonists baked with these products was crucial to their diet. Colonists ate about a pound of grain in some form each day—nearly three times more than Americans eat today. Even though colonists ate a great deal of grain, they had plenty left over to send to the region's coastal markets for sale.

Skillbuilder Answers
1. Hudson, Susquehanna, and Delaware rivers
2. The rivers would enable nearby farmers to send their crops to market easily.

MORE ABOUT . . .

Mills
Building and running a mill required a large investment and many skills. The miller had to import the grinding stones from Europe, and they had to be assembled by an expert. Millers charged a fee on every bushel of grain they milled. Fees might be as high as 15 percent. However, farmers could not grind enough grain by hand to sell, so the miller became one of the most important people in a community.

The Middle Colonies, *1750*

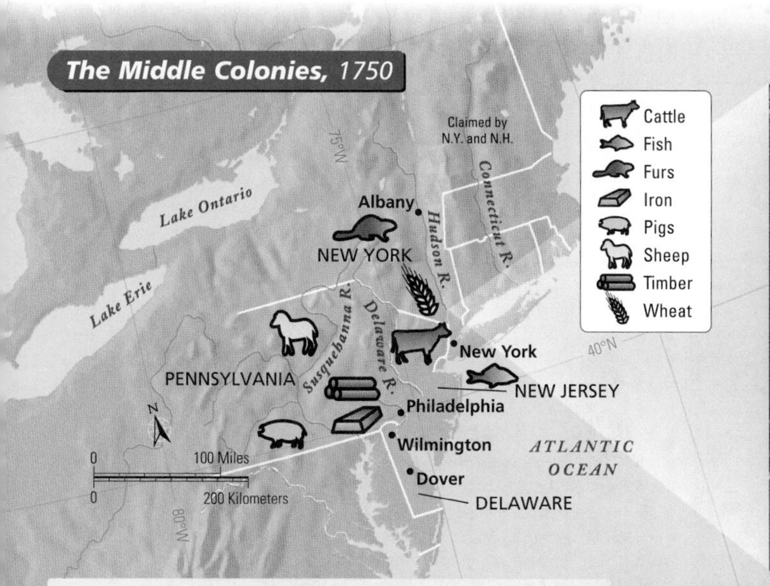

Philipsburg Manor, in Sleepy Hollow, New York, has a working 18th-century farm and a water-powered gristmill.

GEOGRAPHY SKILLBUILDER Interpreting Maps
1. **Place** *What are the three major rivers in the Middle Colonies?*
2. **Movement** *Why might the Middle Colonies' rivers that empty into the ocean be important for farmers?*

HISTORY FROM VISUALS

Reading the Map Ask students to name the Middle Colonies. Then have them name some categories of information presented on the map. **Possible Responses** products, cities, bodies of water, latitude and longitude, scale, topography

Extension Ask students to write a paragraph describing the characteristics of the Middle Colonies that made them good places to settle.

ACTIVITY OPTIONS

SKILLBUILDER LESSON: CREATING A MAP — BLOCK SCHEDULING

Explaining the Skill Maps are visual representations of information. Maps can show physical, political, or other information such as economic activities, battles, or population density. Creating a map helps students to understand information and also helps them to understand how maps are put together.

Applying the Skill Ask students to look at the maps in this chapter on pages 94, 99, and 104. Tell them to draw a map that combines the economic information from all three maps. Ask the following questions to help students prepare their maps:

1. What would you call a map that combines the three maps of colonial regions? *(The Economy of the 13 Colonies)*
2. How many items would you include in the legend if you combined the three maps? *(16)*
3. What items must you add to the legend if you show the three colonial regions in different colors? *(a color block and label identifying each color)*

In-Depth Resources: Unit 1
- Skillbuilder Practice, p. 63

INSTRUCT: OBJECTIVE 2

The Cities Prosper

- How did the geography of the Middle Colonies contribute to the growth of cities?
- Why did Philadelphia grow so quickly?

daily*life*

Names and Occupations

Links between some last names and occupations, such as Barber, are obvious. Other "occupational" last names, however, are misleading. For example, a "Farmer" was not an agricultural worker; he collected taxes. Similarly, "Banker" is not connected with finances at all. It means "dweller on a hillside."

MORE ABOUT . . .

Philadelphia

William Penn called the capital of his new colony *Philadelphia,* a Greek word meaning "brotherly love." The city benefited from the numerous contributions of its most famous citizen, Benjamin Franklin. Franklin founded a subscription library, a fire company, a hospital, a militia, and a philosophical society and was instrumental in the founding of the University of Pennsylvania.

INSTRUCT: OBJECTIVE 3

A Diverse Region/A Climate of Tolerance

- Why did so many German immigrants come to this region?
- How did their cultural diversity affect the Middle Colonies?
- What are three principles of Quaker life?

In-Depth Resources: Unit 1
- Geography Application: Colonial Immigrant Groups, 1750, pp. 64–65

2 The Cities Prosper

The excellent harbors along the coasts of the Middle Colonies were ideal sites for cities. New York City grew up at the mouth of the Hudson River, and Philadelphia was founded on the Delaware River. The merchants who lived in these growing port cities exported cash crops, especially grain, and imported manufactured goods.

Reading History
A. Reading a Map Locate New York and Philadelphia on the map on page 99. Note the rivers next to which they were built.

Because of its enormous trade, Philadelphia was the fastest growing city in the colonies. The city owed its expansion to a thriving trade in wheat and other cash crops. By 1720, it was home to a dozen large shipyards—places where ships are built or repaired.

The city's wealth also brought many public improvements. Large and graceful buildings, such as Philadelphia's statehouse—which was later renamed Independence Hall—graced the city's streets. Streetlights showed the way along paved roads. In 1748, a Swedish visitor named Peter Kalm exclaimed that Philadelphia had grown up overnight.

daily*life*

NAMES AND OCCUPATIONS

Many English colonists had names like Miller and Smith—names that reflected how their families had made a living in England. For example, a colonist named Miller probably had an ancestor who had operated a mill. Similarly, Smith probably had an ancestor who had been a blacksmith.

Sometimes colonists continued in the same occupations as their ancestors. But as time went on, colonists turned to other occupations, and their names no longer reflected how they earned a living. Yet names like Smith and Miller remain common in the United States, reflecting the country's past as English colonies.

A VOICE FROM THE PAST

And yet its natural advantages, trade, riches and power, are by no means inferior to any, even of the most ancient towns in Europe.

Peter Kalm, quoted in *America at 1750*

New York could also thank trade for its rapid growth. This bustling port handled flour, bread, furs, and whale oil. At midcentury, an English naval officer admired the city's elegant brick houses, paved streets, and roomy warehouses. "Such is this city," he said, "that very few in England can rival it in its show."

Background
In 1742, New York City's population was about 11,000, and nearly 13,000 people lived in Philadelphia.

3 A Diverse Region

Many different immigrant groups arrived in the port cities of the Middle Colonies. Soon, the region's population showed a remarkable

ACTIVITY OPTIONS

INDIVIDUAL NEEDS

LESS PROFICIENT READERS

Finding Main Ideas/Details To help students focus on the most important information in the section, suggest that they create a concept web for the main ideas and details. In the center circle have students write the label *Middle Colonies,* and in the surrounding circles have them write the main ideas *Resources, Cities, Diverse Populations,* and *Quakers.* Encourage students to add important details to each part of the web.

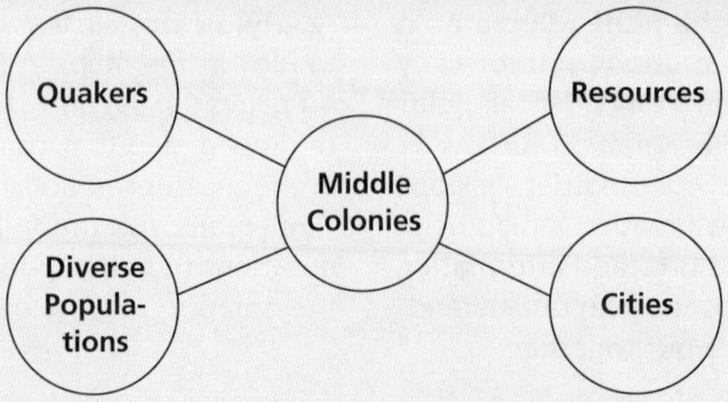

diversity, or variety, in its people. One of the largest immigrant groups in the region, after the English, was the Germans.

Many of the Germans arrived between 1710 and 1740. Most came as indentured servants fleeing religious intolerance. Known for their skillful farming, these immigrants soon made a mark on the Middle Colonies. "German communities," wrote one historian, "could be identified by the huge barns, the sleek cattle, and the stout workhorses."

Background
By the second half of the 1700s, more than one in three colonists in Pennsylvania claimed German ancestry.

Germans also brought a strong tradition of craftsmanship to the Middle Colonies. For example, German gunsmiths first developed the long rifle. Other German **artisans,** or craftspeople, became ironworkers and makers of glass, furniture, and kitchenware.

Germans built **Conestoga wagons** to carry their produce to town. These wagons used wide wheels suitable for dirt roads, and the wagons' curved beds prevented spilling when climbing up and down hills. The wagons' canvas covers offered protection from rain. Conestoga wagons would later be important in settling the West.

The Middle Colonies, *1750*

Population Diversity

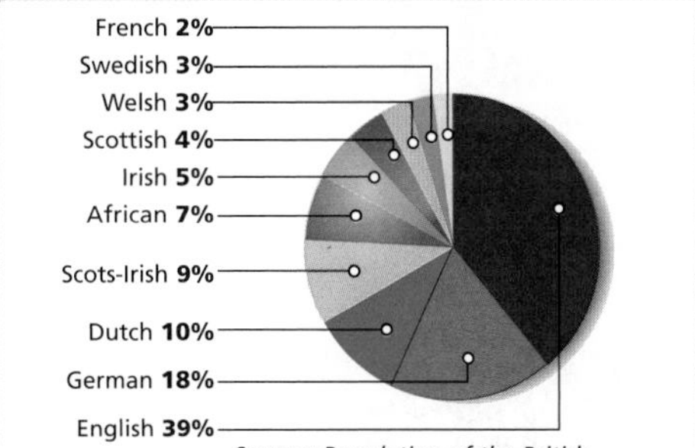

Source: *Population of the British Colonies in America Before 1776,* 1975

SKILLBUILDER **Interpreting Graphs**

1. *What group made up nearly one-fifth of the population in the Middle Colonies?*
2. *What were the two main languages spoken in the Middle Colonies?*

Skillbuilder Answers
1. Germans
2. English and German

The Middle Colonies became home to many people besides the Germans. There were also the English, Dutch, Scots-Irish, African, Irish, Scottish, Welsh, Swedish, and French. Because of the diversity in the Middle Colonies, different groups had to learn to accept, or at least tolerate, one another.

*Reading***History**
B. Summarizing How would you describe the population of the Middle Colonies?
B. Possible Response The large variety of immigrant groups made it a diverse region.

A Climate of Tolerance

While the English Puritans shaped life in the New England Colonies, many different groups contributed to the culture of the Middle Colonies. Because of the greater number of different groups, it was difficult for any single group to dominate the others. Thus, the region's diversity helped to create a climate of tolerance. Some of the region's religious groups also helped to promote tolerance.

The Middle Colonies' earliest settlers, the Dutch in New York and the Quakers in Pennsylvania, both practiced religious tolerance. That is, they honored the right of religious groups to follow their own beliefs without interference. Quakers also insisted on the equality of men and women. As a result, Quaker women served as preachers, and female missionaries traveled the world spreading the Quaker message.

HISTORY FROM VISUALS

Interpreting the Graph Point out the various ethnic groups represented on this graph. Have the students discuss which area of the world most of the immigrants to the Middle Colonies came from. **Possible Responses** northern and western Europe and the British Isles, Africa

Extension Have students study a map of the Middle Colonies to see if they can find names of cities that are similar to names found in the countries the immigrants came from.

MORE ABOUT . . .

A Climate of Tolerance
Some historians think that religious toleration in the Middle Colonies was caused by the indifference of many immigrants to organized religion. Many German and Scots-Irish immigrants, for example, did not have ministers and were slow to form churches. Because they lived among so many different sects, they could join any church of their choice or none at all. Probably fewer than one in 15 became church members.

In-Depth Resources: Unit 1
- Enrichment Activity, p. 75

ACTIVITY OPTIONS

INTERDISCIPLINARY LINK: MATH | **BLOCK SCHEDULING**

CALCULATING DIVERSITY

Class Time 20 minutes

Task Making calculations using information from a graph

Purpose To use math skills to find out the total numbers of people from various ethnic groups living in the Middle Colonies

Supplies Needed
- Calculators or paper and pencil
- Graph paper

Activity Tell students that the total population of the Middle Colonies in 1750 was 296,459. Ask students to calculate the total number of people in each of the ethnic groups shown on the graph. Ask students to display their results in a bar graph or pictograph. **Answers** Africans (free and slave)—20,736; English—115,186; Welsh—9,983; Scots-Irish—28,017; Scottish—12,704; Irish—14,454; German—53,631; Dutch—28,183; French—6,048; Swedish—7,506

INSTRUCT: OBJECTIVE 4

African Americans in the Middle Colonies

- What percentage of the population of the Middle Colonies was made up of enslaved persons?
- How was the work of African Americans in the Middle Colonies different from that in New England?
- What happened in the 1712 race riot in New York City?

CRITICAL THINKING ACTIVITY

Comparing and Contrasting Have students compare and contrast the treatment of African Americans in the Middle Colonies and the New England Colonies. Was slavery practiced in both regions? Which area had more slaves? Were there free African Americans living in the regions?

Class Time 10 minutes

ASSESS & RETEACH

Setting the Stage Have students fill in the chart with information about the Middle Colonies.

Formal Assessment
- Section Quiz, p. 70

RETEACHING ACTIVITY

Have pairs of students create two questions related to the main ideas in each section of the chapter. Students should write the questions and answers on the front and back of a 3- x 5-inch card. Ask two pairs of students to quiz each other by using the questions as flash cards.

In-Depth Resources: Unit 1
- Reteaching Activity, p. 72

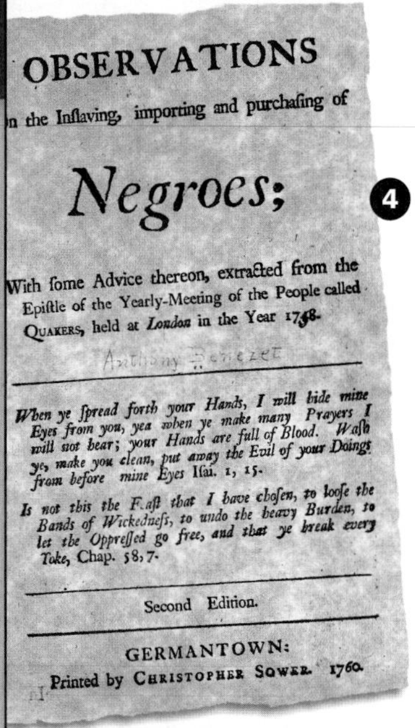

OBSERVATIONS
On the Inſlaving, importing and purchaſing of
Negroes;
With ſome Advice thereon, extracted from the Epiſtle of the Yearly-Meeting of the People called QUAKERS, held at *London* in the Year 1758.

When ye ſpread forth your Hands, I will hide mine Eyes from you, yea when ye make many Prayers I will not hear; your Hands are full of Blood. Waſh ye, make you clean, put away the Evil of your Doings from before mine Eyes Iſai. 1, 15.

Is not this the Faſt that I have choſen, to looſe the Bands of Wickedneſs, to undo the heavy Burden, to let the Oppreſſed go free, and that ye break every Yoke, Chap. 58, 7.

Second Edition.

GERMANTOWN:
Printed by CHRISTOPHER SOWER. 1760.

Most Quakers were opposed to slavery. Shown here is a Quaker antislavery pamphlet printed in the Middle Colonies.

Quakers were also the first to raise their voices against slavery. Quaker ideals influenced immigrants in the Middle Colonies—and eventually the whole nation.

4 African Americans in the Middle Colonies

The tolerant attitude of many settlers in the Middle Colonies did not prevent slavery in the region. In 1750, about 7 percent of the Middle Colonies' population was enslaved. As in New England, many people of African descent lived and worked in cities.

New York City had a larger number of people of African descent than any other city in the Northern colonies. In New York City, enslaved persons worked as manual laborers, servants, drivers, and as assistants to artisans and craftspeople. Free African-American men and women also made their way to the city, where they worked as laborers, servants, or sailors.

Tensions existed between the races in New York City, sometimes leading to violence. In 1712, for example, about 24 rebellious slaves set fire to a building. They then killed nine whites and wounded several others who came to put out the fire. Armed colonists caught the suspects, who were punished horribly. Such punishments showed that whites would resort to force and violence to control slaves. Even so, the use of violence did little to prevent the outbreak of other slave rebellions.

Force would also be used in the South, which had far more enslaved Africans than the North. In the next section, you will learn how the South's plantation economy came to depend on the labor of enslaved Africans.

Reading **History**

C. Forming Opinions Why do you think that force was needed to keep Africans enslaved?

C. Possible Response Because enslaved Africans wanted their freedom and were ready to fight for it.

Section 2 Assessment

1. Terms & Names

Explain the significance of:
- cash crop
- gristmill
- diversity
- artisan
- Conestoga wagon

2. Taking Notes

Use a cluster diagram like the one shown to indicate where different immigrants in the Middle Colonies came from.

What was the third largest group in the region?

3. Main Ideas

a. What attracted settlers to the Middle Colonies?

b. What service was performed at gristmills?

c. Why might enslaved Africans be able to join in rebellion more easily in the city than the country?

4. Critical Thinking

Analyzing Causes What factors allowed large coastal cities to develop in the Middle Colonies?

THINK ABOUT
- geography
- people
- trade

ACTIVITY OPTIONS

MATH
GEOGRAPHY

Read more about Philadelphia. Create a **database** of the city's population growth in the 1700s or draw a **map** that shows its physical growth.

Section 2 Assessment

1. Terms & Names

cash crop, p. 99
gristmill, p. 99
diversity, p. 101
artisan, p. 101
Conestoga wagon, p. 101

2. Taking Notes

Answers should include four of the following: England, Germany, Holland, Scotland, Africa, Ireland. The third largest group was the Dutch.

3. Main Ideas

a. the long growing season; fertile soil and wealth of resources; the climate of tolerance; excellent harbors **b.** grinding grain into flour and meal **c.** Communication was easier; they might not be recognized as easily as in the smaller communities.

4. Critical Thinking

excellent harbors along the coast; immigration; the profitable trade of cash crops

ACTIVITY OPTIONS

Integrated Assessment
- Rubrics for a database, 2.6
- Rubrics for a map, 2.1

3 The Southern Colonies: Plantations and Slavery

TERMS & NAMES
indigo
Eliza Lucas
William Byrd II
overseer
Stono Rebellion

MAIN IDEA

The economy of the Southern Colonies relied heavily on slave labor.

WHY IT MATTERS NOW

The existence of slavery deeply affected the South and the nation.

ONE AMERICAN'S STORY

George Mason was born to a wealthy Virginia family in 1725. Mason—who later described the slave trade as "disgraceful to mankind"—wrote about the contributions of enslaved persons on his family's plantation.

A VOICE FROM THE PAST

My father had among his slaves carpenters, coopers [barrel makers], sawyers, blacksmiths, tanners, curriers, shoemakers, spinners, weavers and knitters, and even a distiller. . . . His woods furnished timber and plank for the carpenters and coopers, and charcoal for the blacksmith; his cattle killed for his own consumption and for sale supplied skins for the tanners, curriers, and shoemakers, and his sheep gave wool and his fields produced cotton and flax for the weavers and spinners, and his orchards fruit for the distiller.

George Mason, quoted in *Common Landscape of America*

George Mason was active in local affairs in Virginia. He would later play a role in the drafting of the United States Constitution.

Because the Masons and other wealthy landowners produced all that they needed on their own plantations, they appeared to be independent. But their independence usually depended on the labor of enslaved Africans. Although planters were only a small part of the Southern population, the plantation economy and slavery shaped life in the Southern Colonies: Maryland, Virginia, the Carolinas, and Georgia.

1 The Plantation Economy

The South's soil and almost year-round growing season were ideal for plantation crops like rice and tobacco. These valuable plants required much labor to produce, but with enough workers they could be grown as cash crops. Planters had no trouble transporting their crops because the region's many waterways made it easy for oceangoing ships to tie up at plantation docks.

Like George Mason's boyhood home, most plantations were largely self-sufficient. That is, nearly everything that planters, their families, and their workers needed was produced on the plantation. Because plantations were so self-sufficient, large cities like those in the North were rare

SECTION OBJECTIVES

1. To analyze the plantation economy and the use of slaves
2. To describe plantation life
3. To understand life under slavery
4. To describe resistance to slavery

SKILLBUILDER

Interpreting Maps: Location, Place, p. 104

CRITICAL THINKING

Drawing Conclusions, p. 104
Analyzing Causes, p. 105
Recognizing Effects, p. 105
Finding Main Ideas, p. 106
Contrasting, p. 107

FOCUS & MOTIVATE

5-MINUTE WARM-UP

Making Inferences These questions will help students examine plantation life in the United States.

1. What can you infer about the people who lived in the plantation mansion shown on page 104?
2. Why did planters who lived in mansions such as this one require many workers?

Warm-Up Transparency WT4

INSTRUCT

INSTRUCT: OBJECTIVE 1

The Plantation Economy/ The Turn to Slavery

- What geographic factors made plantation crops profitable?
- Why did planters begin to use enslaved Africans for labor?
- How did the use of slaves change the population of the Southern Colonies?

In-Depth Resources: Unit 1
- Guided Reading, p. 60

RECOMMENDED RESOURCES

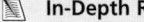

In-Depth Resources: Unit 1
- Guided Reading, p. 60
- Building Vocabulary, p. 62
- Literature Selection, pp. 68–70
- Enrichment Activity, p. 75

Reading Study Guide (Spanish and English), pp. 33–34

Outline Map Activities
- Colonial Products, pp. 7–8

America's History Makers
- Eliza Lucas Pinckney, pp. 15–16

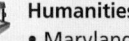

Formal Assessment
- Section Quiz, p. 71

Integrated Assessment
- Rubrics, 1.3, 2.5

Access for Students Acquiring English/ESL
- Guided Reading, p. 21

INTEGRATED TECHNOLOGY

Critical Thinking Trans. CT11
- Cause and Effect: The Rise of Slave Labor

Humanities Transparency HT8
- Maryland Plantation, 18th Century

Electronic Teacher Tools

TEST-TAKING RESOURCES

Strategies for Test Preparation

Test Practice Transparencies, TT15

Online Test Practice

HISTORY FROM VISUALS

Reading the Map Point out the map legend, then discuss the symbols and their placement on the map. Have students talk about the kinds of products provided in the Southern Colonies, and explain to them how these goods would have been transported to other colonies as well as to European nations. **Possible Responses** The products were primarily agricultural. These goods would have been transported by ship up the coast or across the Atlantic Ocean.

Extension Have students research plantations that are open to the public and report about the architecture and decoration of one of the plantation houses.

Outline Map Activities
- Colonial Products, pp. 7–8

HISTORY FROM VISUALS

Understanding the Graph Point out the differences in the U.S. slave population in the North and South between 1600 and 1750. Ask students to write a sentence describing the percentage of the population that were slaves in the North and the South in 1660. Then ask them to revise their sentences to reflect the data for 1750. **Possible Responses** In 1660, the percentage of the population in slavery in the Northern and Southern Colonies was about equal, at around 9 percent of the population. In 1750, slaves made up about 40 percent of the population of the Southern Colonies and only about 3 percent of the Northern Colonies.

Extension Have students do research to find out how much tobacco was shipped from the colonies in 1650 and in 1750.

Critical Thinking Transparency CT11
- Cause and Effect: The Rise of Slave Labor

The Southern Colonies, 1750

The Orton plantation, south of Wilmington, North Carolina, was founded around 1725. Such plantations were representative of the economic and political power held by Southern planters.

GEOGRAPHY SKILLBUILDER Interpreting Maps
1. **Location** *The Southern Colonies were south of what latitude?*
2. **Place** *Which Southern Colonies grew crops of both rice and indigo?*

Skillbuilder Answers
1. 40° North
2. South Carolina and Georgia

Southern Colonies. The port city of Charles Town (later called Charleston) in South Carolina was an early exception.

As the plantation economy continued to grow, planters began to have difficulty finding enough laborers to work their plantations. Toward the end of the 1600s, the planters began to turn to enslaved Africans for labor.

Background In 1742, Charles Town's population was 6,800.

The Turn to Slavery

For the first half of the 1600s, there were few Africans in Virginia, whether enslaved or free. In 1665, fewer than 500 Africans had been brought into the colony. At that time, African and European indentured servants worked in the fields together.

U.S. Slave Population

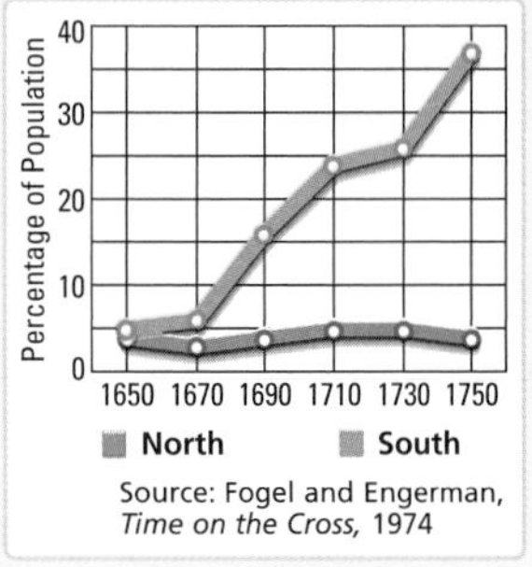

Source: Fogel and Engerman, *Time on the Cross*, 1974

Starting in the 1660s, the labor system began to change as indentured white servants started to leave the plantations. One reason they left was the large amount of land available in the Americas. It was fairly easy for white men to save enough money to buy land and start their own farms. White servants could not be kept on the plantations permanently. As Bacon's Rebellion showed, it was also politically dangerous for planters to try to keep them there (see page 73). As a result, the landowners had to find another source of labor.

A. Possible Response Question and answer should recognize the greater increase of slave population in the South than in the North.

Reading **History**
A. Reading a Graph Ask and answer a question about the geographic pattern of changes in the slave population.

ACTIVITY OPTIONS

INTERDISCIPLINARY LINK: THE ARTS BLOCK SCHEDULING

CREATE A POSTER

Class Time 30 minutes

Task Making a poster advertising land to former indentured servants in the Southern Colonies

Purpose To gain an understanding of reasons servants wanted to own land

Supplies Needed
- Drawing paper
- Art supplies

Activity Briefly discuss with the class the elements of an advertising poster: a slogan, information clearly and concisely expressed, and an interesting visual. Brainstorm with the class some reasons indentured servants wanted to own land. Tell students that posters should address those reasons.

After the students have completed their projects, display the posters in the classroom. Discuss different posters with the class.

Planters tried to force Native Americans to work for them. But European diseases caused many Native Americans to die. Those who survived usually knew the country well enough to run away.

Reading **History**
B. Analyzing Causes What factors led to the importation of enslaved Africans into the South?
B. Answer the shortage of labor

To meet their labor needs, the planters turned to enslaved Africans. As a result, the population of people of African descent began to grow rapidly. By 1750, there were over 235,000 enslaved Africans in America. About 85 percent lived in the Southern Colonies. Enslaved Africans made up about 40 percent of the South's population.

Plantations Expand ❷

The growth of slavery allowed plantation farming to expand in South Carolina and Georgia. Without slave labor, there probably would have been no rice plantations in the region's swampy lowlands.

Enslaved workers drained swamps, raked fields, burned stubble, and broke ground before planting. They also had to flood, drain, dry, hoe, and weed the same fields several times before the harvest.

The cultivation of rice required not only back-breaking labor but also considerable skill. Because West Africans had these skills, planters sought out slaves who came from Africa's rice-growing regions.

On higher ground, planters grew **indigo,** a plant that yields a deep blue dye. A young woman named **Eliza Lucas** had introduced indigo as a successful plantation crop after her father sent her to supervise his South Carolina plantations when she was 17.

The Planter Class

Slave labor allowed planters, such as the Byrd family of Virginia, to become even wealthier. These families formed an elite planter class. They had money or credit to buy the most slaves. And because they had more slaves, they could grow more tobacco, rice, or indigo to sell.

C. Possible Response The economic power of planters with large numbers of slaves allowed them to assume political power, too.

Reading **History**
C. Recognizing Effects How did the growth of slavery affect political power in the South?

Small landowners with just one or two slaves simply could not compete. Many gave up their land and moved westward. As a result, the powerful planter class gained control of the rich land along the coast. The planter class was relatively small compared to the rest of the population. However, this upper class soon took control of political and economic power in the South. A foreign traveler in the South commented that the planters "think and act precisely as do the nobility in other countries."

Some planters, following the traditions of nobility, did feel responsible for the welfare of their enslaved

AMERICA'S HISTORY MAKERS

WILLIAM BYRD II
1674–1744

William Byrd II was one of the best known of the Southern planters. His family owned a large estate in Virginia. After his father died, Byrd took on his father's responsibilities, including membership in the House of Burgesses.

But Byrd is best remembered for his writing. His most famous work is *History of the Dividing Line betwixt Virginia and North Carolina.* In it, Byrd celebrates the land and climate of the South. At times, however, he is critical of its people. Even today, the book creates a vivid picture of life in the Southern Colonies.

How did William Byrd II demonstrate his leadership abilities?

INSTRUCT: OBJECTIVE ❷
Plantations Expand/The Planter Class

- How did the growth of slavery affect farming in South Carolina and Georgia?
- How did the planter class become so powerful?
- How did the planter class treat its enslaved workers?

Humanities Transparency HT8
- Maryland Plantation, 18th Century

AMERICA'S HISTORY MAKERS

William Byrd II
William Byrd II was an avid writer throughout his life, producing letters, diaries, travel journals, and poems. In 1709, he began a secret diary that he wrote in code. When the code was finally broken in the 1940s, Byrd's secret diaries were published. They contain richly detailed information about Byrd's life, including what he ate, what he drank, how often he quarreled with his wife, even how often he forgot his prayers.

Possible Response: by becoming a member of the House of Burgesses

MORE ABOUT . . .

Indigo and Eliza Lucas
In the early 1740s, Eliza Lucas was managing her father's South Carolina plantations. Lucas was born on the Caribbean island of Antigua, where indigo was an important crop. She began to experiment with cultivating indigo and extracting its dye. Lucas was helped by white and black people from the West Indies. Her procedures for growing the plant and for processing the dye spread throughout the colony of South Carolina. Later in life, Eliza Lucas married Charles Pinckney. Their sons were important figures in the American Revolution.

America's History Makers
- Eliza Lucas Pinckney, pp. 15–16

ACTIVITY OPTIONS
INDIVIDUAL NEEDS: GIFTED AND TALENTED

LEARNING ABOUT GULLAH

Class Time One class period

Task Researching topics about Gullah

Purpose To encourage students to explore Gullah, the language of enslaved persons on the Sea Islands of Georgia and South Carolina

Supplies Needed
- Reference sources, including encyclopedias and Internet access

Activity Invite students to research Gullah, the speech of enslaved Africans and their descendants on the Sea Islands and coastal regions of South Carolina and Georgia. Ask students to prepare a report on one of these topics: origins of Gullah and Gullah words that have become part of the English language; aspects of Gullah culture; efforts to learn about and preserve Gullah.

HISTORY through ART

Interpreting the Painting Benjamin Henry Latrobe (1764–1820) was a famous architect and landscape and topographical painter of the colonial period. Born in England, he was educated in Germany and later studied engineering and architecture in London. He moved to Virginia in 1796. Latrobe was later the chief architect of public buildings in the country's capital.

Possible Response: Students may note the lounging, insolent posture of the overseer, his tobacco, and the frightened looks of the enslaved workers. From these clues they will probably decide that Latrobe opposed slavery.

HISTORY *through* ART

Benjamin Henry Latrobe's watercolor sketch, *An Overseer Doing His Duty,* shows enslaved African women on a Virginia plantation. An overseer looks on as the two women work to remove tree stumps.

What opinion do you think Latrobe had of the conditions on plantations?

workers. Power, they believed, brought with it the responsibility to do good. Many planters, though, were tyrants. They held complete authority over everyone in their households. Planters frequently used violence against slaves to enforce their will.

Vocabulary
tyrant: harsh ruler

3 Life Under Slavery

On large Southern plantations, slaves toiled in groups of about 20 to 25 under the supervision of **overseers.** Overseers were men hired by planters to watch over and direct the work of slaves. Enslaved persons performed strenuous and exhausting work, often for 15 hours a day at the peak of the harvest season. If slaves did not appear to be doing their full share of work, they were often whipped by the overseer.

Enslaved people usually lived in small, one-room cabins that were furnished only with sleeping cots. For a week's food, a slave might receive only around a quarter bushel of corn and a pound of pork. Some planters allowed their slaves to add to this meager ration by letting them raise their own potatoes, greens, fruit, or chicken.

In spite of the brutal living conditions, Africans preserved many customs and beliefs from their homelands. These included music, dances, stories, and, for a time, African religions—including Islam. African kinship customs became the basis of African-American family culture. A network of kin was a source of strength even when families were separated.

***Reading*History**
D. Finding Main Ideas What customs and beliefs from their homelands provided strength for enslaved Africans?
D. Possible Responses Music, dances, stories, Islam, and kinship customs.

4 Resistance to Slavery

At the same time that enslaved Africans struggled to maintain their own culture, they fought against their enslavement. They sometimes worked

INSTRUCT: OBJECTIVE 3
Life Under Slavery

- How did overseers treat the enslaved Africans?
- How did the enslaved people live?
- What was the effect of the plantation system on the culture of the enslaved people?

In-Depth Resources: Unit 1
- Literature Selection, pp. 68–70

INSTRUCT: OBJECTIVE 4
Resistance to Slavery

- How did enslaved Africans fight against their enslavement?
- What is the significance of the Stono Rebellion?
- In what ways did slave codes change?

ACTIVITY OPTIONS

INTERDISCIPLINARY LINK: LANGUAGE ARTS — BLOCK SCHEDULING

DIARY ENTRIES

Class Time 30 minutes

Task Creating diary entries for an enslaved African and a planter family member on a Southern plantation

Purpose To compare the experiences of Southern colonists of different groups

Supplies Needed
- Reference materials about plantation life in the colonial South

Activity Ask the language arts teacher to discuss writing diary entries. Then have students read accounts of plantation life in the colonial South.

Have students write a diary entry from the point of view of an enslaved African or from that of a member of a planter family. When the students are finished, have them read their entries aloud to a group.

slowly, damaged goods, or purposely carried out orders the wrong way. A British traveler in 1746 noted that many slaves pretended not to understand tasks they often had performed as farmers in West Africa.

A VOICE FROM THE PAST

You would really be surpriz'd at their Perseverance; let an hundred Men shew him how to hoe, or drive a wheelbarrow, he'll still take the one by the Bottom, and the other by the Wheel; and they often die before they can be conquer'd.

Edward Kimber, quoted in *White over Black*

At times, slaves became so angry and frustrated by their loss of freedom that they rose up in rebellion. One of the most famous incidents was the **Stono Rebellion.** In September 1739, about 20 slaves gathered at the Stono River just south of Charles Town. Wielding guns and other weapons, they killed several planter families and marched south, beating drums and loudly inviting other slaves to join them in their plan to seek freedom in Spanish-held Florida. By late that afternoon, however, a white militia had surrounded the group of escaping slaves. The two sides clashed, and many slaves died in the fighting. Those captured were executed.

Background
Slave codes were laws designed to control slaves and keep them in bondage.

Stono and similar revolts led planters to make slave codes even stricter. Slaves were now forbidden from leaving plantations without permission. The laws also made it illegal for slaves to meet with free blacks. Such laws made the conditions of slavery even more inhumane.

The Southern Colonies' plantation economy and widespread use of slaves set the region on a very different path from that of the New England and Middle Colonies. In the next section, you will learn how settlers used the unique resources of the Backcountry to create settlements there.

Section 3 Assessment

1. Terms & Names

Explain the significance of:
- indigo
- Eliza Lucas
- William Byrd II
- overseer
- Stono Rebellion

2. Taking Notes

Use a diagram like the one shown to review the factors that led to the use of slaves in the South.

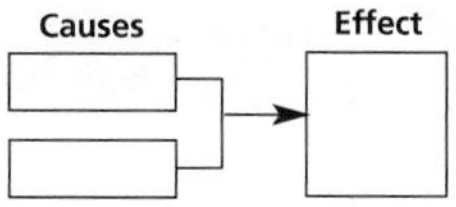

Why didn't planters use Native American workers?

3. Main Ideas

a. What percentage of the South's population was enslaved in 1750?

b. What crops did plantations in Georgia and South Carolina grow?

c. How did enslaved persons resist their slavery?

4. Critical Thinking

Contrasting How did geographic differences between the Southern Colonies and the New England Colonies affect their labor systems?

THINK ABOUT
- the climate of the regions
- the nature of the soil

ACTIVITY OPTIONS

ART
SCIENCE

Do more research on rice plantations. Draw a **diagram** of a typical plantation or write a **report** on how rice is cultivated today.

MORE ABOUT . . .

Daily Life Under Slavery

In the 1600s, the living conditions of enslaved Africans was about the same as that of their owners. However, by the 1800s, most colonists lived in houses made of brick or wood, while their slaves continued to live in rough shacks. To save money, owners gave their slaves the cheapest cloth—called Negro cloth—for their clothes. Slaves ate corn, rice, beans, salt pork, and molasses. Enslaved Africans used these ingredients to make foods that resembled foods they had known in Africa. Hoe cakes, mush, and spoon bread are foods made by slaves that entered the white Southern diet.

ASSESS & RETEACH

Setting the Stage Have students complete the chart with information about the Southern Colonies.

Formal Assessment
- Section Quiz, p. 71

RETEACHING ACTIVITY

Have students copy the graphic below and fill it in with details about life in the Southern Colonies for members of the planter class and for slaves.

Group	Details
Planter Class	
Slaves	

In-Depth Resources: Unit 1
- Reteaching Activity, p. 73

Section 3 Assessment

1. Terms & Names

indigo, p. 105
Eliza Lucas, p. 105
William Byrd II, p. 105
overseer, p. 106
Stono Rebellion, p. 107

2. Taking Notes

Causes: Labor-intensive cash crops required lots of workers; availability of land made it difficult to keep white laborers.
Effect: Planters turned to enslaved Africans for labor.

They were susceptible to European diseases and knew the country well enough to run away.

3. Main Ideas

a. about 40 percent **b.** rice; indigo
c. They worked slowly, damaged goods, and participated in violent rebellions.

4. Critical Thinking

Southern Colonies had a long growing season and fertile soil good for cash crops. New England had a short growing season and poor soil.

ACTIVITY OPTIONS

Integrated Assessment
- Rubrics for a diagram, 1.3
- Rubrics for a report, 2.5

GEOGRAPHY in HISTORY

OBJECTIVE

Students will analyze and interpret information from a map to understand the relationship between the climate and natural resources of New England and the Middle and Southern Colonies.

BLOCK SCHEDULING

MORE ABOUT . . .

Rice and Indigo

Rice and indigo were compatible crops because rice required great labor in the winter, when the fields had to be prepared. The dams, dikes, and ditches used to flood the fields had to be prepared. In early spring, workers set out the new rice plants in the flooded fields. Indigo needed little work in the winter, but it required much labor in the summer. Rice was grown in the lowest-lying fields. Indigo, on the other hand, was grown on higher ground.

INSTRUCT

- Why is the physical geography of a region important to its economy?
- How does a region's growing season affect its economy?
- How does soil quality affect a region's economy?

MAP SKILL QUESTIONS

Which map would tell you what parts of the country had the coldest and the warmest temperatures?

Use the maps to determine what physical factors enabled the Southern Colonies to prosper.

Which region produced no grain for export?

GEOGRAPHY in HISTORY

REGION AND HUMAN-ENVIRONMENT INTERACTION

Differences Among the Colonies

Many factors shape a region's economy and the way its settlers make a living. One of the most important is its physical geography—the climate, soil, and natural resources of the region. The geography of the American colonies varied from one colony to another. For example, in some areas, farmers could dig into rich, fertile soil. In others, they could not stick their shovels in the ground without hitting rocks.

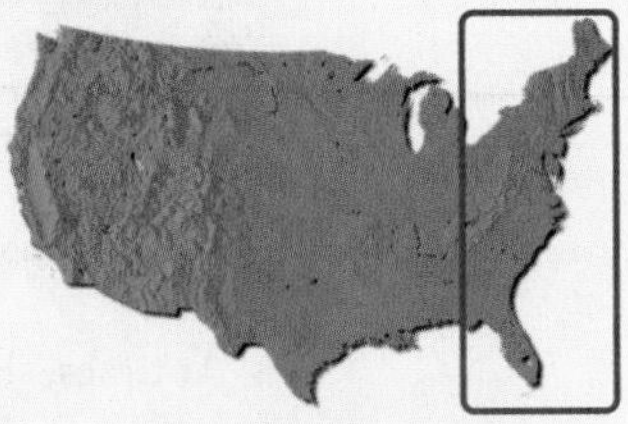

Major Regional Exports (by export value*)

NEW ENGLAND COLONIES

New England had a short growing season and rocky soil. Colonists took advantage of other opportunities in the region, especially fishing and whaling.

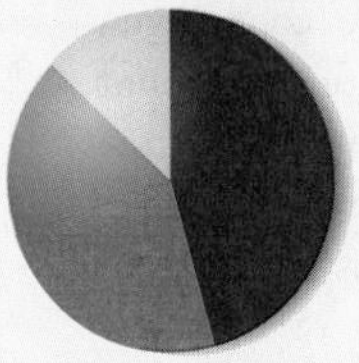

Dried Fish and Whale Oil	44%
Livestock	17%
Wood Products	13%
Other	26%

MIDDLE COLONIES

The longer growing season of the Middle Colonies—the "breadbasket colonies"—allowed farmers to grow cash crops of grain.

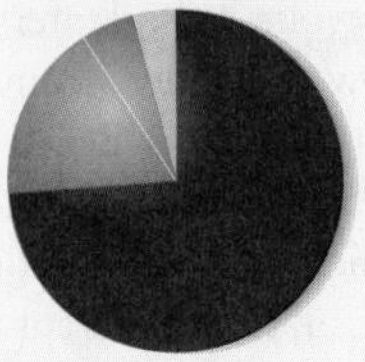

Grain	73%
Iron	5%
Wood Products	5%
Other	17%

SOUTHERN COLONIES

The South had a nearly year-round growing season. The use of enslaved Africans allowed Southern planters to produce cash crops of tobacco and rice.

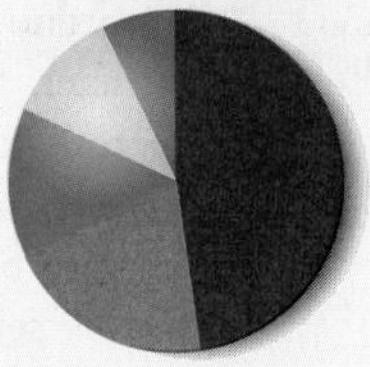

Tobacco	48%
Rice	20%
Bread, Flour, Grain (not rice)	13%
Indigo	7%
Other	12%

*Export Value in Pounds Sterling (Five-Year Average, 1768–1772)

Source: James F. Shepherd and Gary M. Walton, *Shipping, Maritime Trade, and the Economic Development of Colonial North America* (Cambridge: Cambridge University Press, 1972.)

ARTIFACT FILE

Farmer's Plow Middle colonists relied on the heavy blades of plows to cut seed rows into the region's fertile soil.

Indigo On some plantations in the South, planters grew crops of indigo plants—like the one pictured here—to produce the rich blue dyes used to color this yarn.

108 CHAPTER 4

MUSEUM CONNECTIONS

The New Bedford Whaling Museum is the country's largest museum dedicated to the whaling industry and the port of New Bedford, the greatest of the whaling ports. The museum brings to life the history of American whaling and the age of the sailing ship through displays and exhibits. The museum houses art, artifacts, and manuscripts.

The museum's Web site provides links to many whaling sites and to detailed discussions of topics such as Yankee Seafaring and Merchant Trade, New Bedford and Its People, and African Americans in New Bedford. For the Web site address, visit classzone.com.

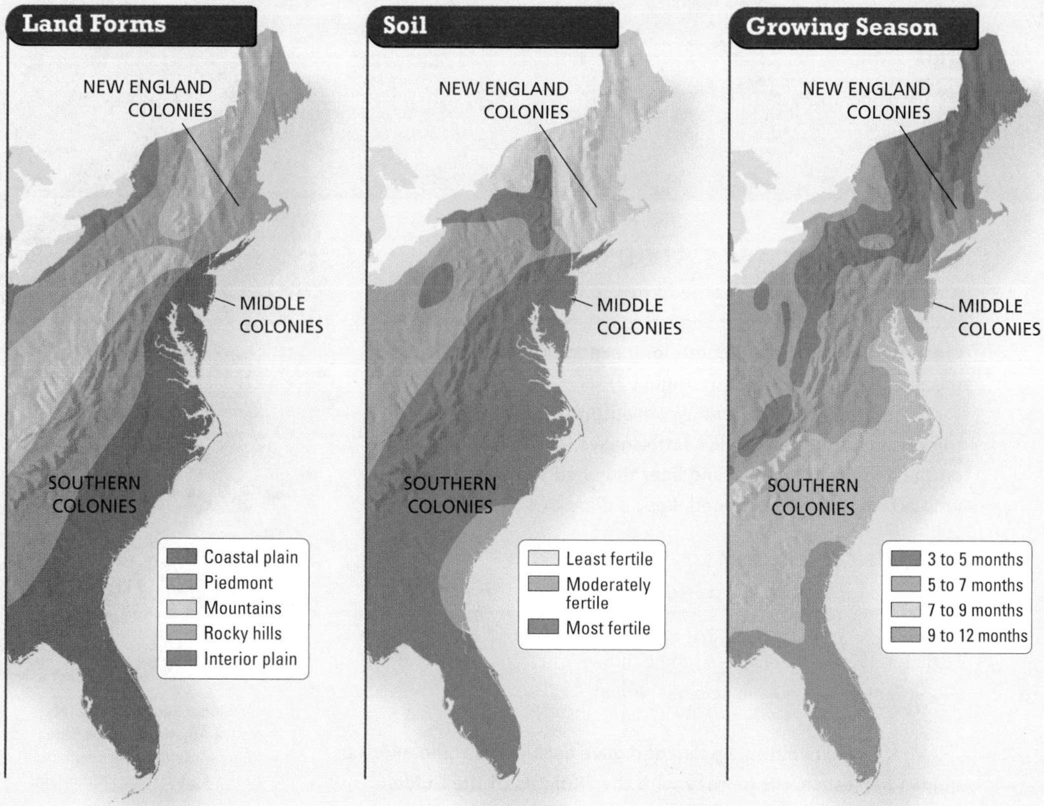

Physical Geography The maps above show the different types of land forms, soil, and growing seasons that were found in the different colonial regions. These factors helped to shape the economies of each of the regions, which were quite different, as the pie graphs show on the previous page.

On-Line Field Trip

The New Bedford Whaling Museum in Massachusetts has many objects related to whaling, including bone or ivory objects called scrimshaws. A sailor carved this whale's tooth with a jackknife or sail needle and colored the design with ink.

For more about whaling . . .

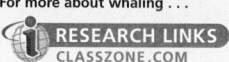

RESEARCH LINKS
CLASSZONE.COM

CONNECT TO GEOGRAPHY

1. **Region** How long was the growing season in most of the Southern Colonies?
2. **Human-Environment Interaction** How might the soil quality in the Middle Colonies have influenced the region's population?

See Geography Handbook, pages 10–13.

CONNECT TO HISTORY

3. **Analyzing Causes** Why did the land forms and soil of New England cause many to turn to the Atlantic Ocean for a living?

CRITICAL THINKING ACTIVITY

Recognizing Important Details Have students make a graphic like the one below. Then have them study the map and pie graphs and list the geographical features, natural resources, and exports of each of these colonial regions.

New England Colonies	Middle Colonies	Southern Colonies

Class Time 20 minutes

MORE ABOUT . . .

The Appalachian Mountains

Appalachia is the name for the area covered by the Appalachian Mountains. The Appalachians reach for approximately 2000 miles from Alabama to the province of Newfoundland. The Appalachians include a number of smaller mountain ranges, such as the Alleghenies, the Blue Ridge, the Great Smoky Mountains, and the Catskills.

CONNECT TO GEOGRAPHY

1. **Region** They had a short growing season, from seven to nine months.
2. **Human-Environment Interaction** Settlers used the Middle Colonies' fertile soil to form the region into a rich farming landscape.

CONNECT TO HISTORY

3. **Analyzing Causes** The rocky hills and poor soil of New England made farming difficult so people turned to skilled trade and coastal occupations.

SECTION OBJECTIVES

1. To describe the geography of the Backcountry
2. To identify Backcountry settlers and to understand Backcountry life
3. To identify other peoples in North America and explain their conflict with the English colonists

SKILLBUILDER
Interpreting Maps: Region, p. 111

CRITICAL THINKING
Analyzing Points of View, p. 111
Making Inferences, p. 112
Summarizing, p. 112
Identifying Problems, p. 113

Why It Matters Now
- Regional Differences, pp. 7–8

FOCUS & MOTIVATE

5-MINUTE WARM-UP

Making Inferences These questions focus on the interaction between settlers and Native Americans.

1. Look at the picture on page 110. What can you infer about the relationship between these Native Americans and settlers?
2. As more settlers came to the Backcountry, how do you think their relationship with the Native Americans changed?

Warm-Up Transparency WT4

INSTRUCT

INSTRUCT: OBJECTIVE 1
Geography of the Backcountry

- What are the geographical boundaries of the Backcountry?
- What attracted settlers to the Backcountry?

In-Depth Resources: Unit 1
- Guided Reading, p. 61

America's History Makers
- Alexander Spotswood, pp. 17–18

4 The Backcountry

TERMS & NAMES
Appalachian Mountains
fall line
piedmont
clan

MAIN IDEA
Settlers moved to the Backcountry because land was cheap and plentiful.

WHY IT MATTERS NOW
Backcountry settlers established a rural way of life that still exists in certain parts of the country.

ONE AMERICAN'S STORY

Alexander Spotswood governed Virginia from 1710 to 1722. He believed that the future of English colonists lay to the west. To prove his point, he led a month-long expedition over the crest of the Blue Ridge Mountains in August 1716.

During the 400-mile journey, adventurers braved dense thickets, muddy streams, and rattlesnakes. At night, they feasted on the deer, wild turkeys, and bear they had shot. John Fontaine, who accompanied Spotswood, kept a diary of the trip.

A VOICE FROM THE PAST

We had a rugged way; we passed over a great many small runs of water, some of which were very deep, and others very miry. Several of our company were dismounted, some were down with their horses, others under their horses, and some thrown off.

John Fontaine, quoted in *Colonial Virginia*

After the expedition, Spotswood gave each of his companions a golden horseshoe. His journey with the "Knights of the Golden Horseshoe" is considered a symbol of Virginia's westward expansion.

Alexander Spotswood meets Native Americans in the Blue Ridge Mountains—a segment of the Appalachians Mountains.

1 Geography of the Backcountry

Just as Spotswood predicted, settlers soon began to move into the Backcountry. This was a region of dense forests and rushing streams in or near the **Appalachian Mountains**. The Appalachians stretch from eastern Canada south to Alabama.

In the South, the Backcountry began at the **fall line**. The fall line is where waterfalls prevent large boats from moving farther upriver. Beyond the fall line is the **piedmont**. Piedmont means "foot of the mountains." It is the broad plateau that leads to the Blue Ridge Mountains of the Appalachian range.

The Backcountry's resources made it relatively easy for a family to start a small farm. The region's many springs and streams provided water, and forests furnished wood that settlers could use for log cabins and fences.

RECOMMENDED RESOURCES

In-Depth Resources: Unit 1
- Guided Reading, p. 61
- Primary Source: Culture Clash in the Colonies, pp. 66–67

Reading Study Guide, pp. 35–36

Economics in History, p. 4

America's History Makers, pp. 17–18

Why It Matters Now
- Regional Differences, pp. 7–8

Formal Assessment
- Section Quiz, p. 72

Integrated Assessment
- Rubrics, 4.5, 1.3

Access for Students Acquiring English/ESL
- Guided Reading, p. 22

INTEGRATED TECHNOLOGY
- Electronic Teacher Tools
- classzone.com

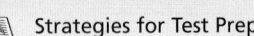

TEST-TAKING RESOURCES
- Strategies for Test Preparation
- Test Practice Transparencies, TT16
- Online Test Practice

❷ Backcountry Settlers

The first Europeans in the Backcountry made a living by trading with the Native Americans. Backcountry settlers paid for goods with deerskins. A unit of value was one buckskin or, for short, a "buck."

Vocabulary
buck: an adult male deer; the adult female is called a *doe*

Farmers soon followed the traders into the region, but they had to be cautious. As the number of settlements grew, the farmers often clashed with the Native Americans whose land they were taking.

Farmers sheltered their families in log cabins. They filled holes between the logs with mud, moss, and clay. Then they sawed out doors and windows. Lacking glass, settlers used paper smeared with animal fat to cover their windows.

***Reading* History**
A. Analyzing Points of View What was William Byrd's attitude toward Backcountry settlers?
A. Possible Response Byrd's membership in the planter class may have made him prejudiced against the lifestyle of Backcountry settlers.

William Byrd—on his expedition to establish the southern border of Virginia—described a long night that he spent in one such cabin. He complained that he and at least ten other people were "forct to pig together in a Room . . . troubled with the Squalling of peevish, dirty children into the Bargain."

Backcountry life may have been harsh, but by the late 1600s many families had chosen to move there. Some of them went to escape the plantation system, which had crowded out many small farmers closer to the seacoast. Then, in the 1700s, a new group of emigrants—the Scots-Irish—began to move into the Backcountry.

The Scots-Irish

The Scots-Irish came from the borderland between Scotland and England. Most of them had lived for a time in northern Ireland. In 1707, England and Scotland merged and formed Great Britain. The merger caused many hardships for the Scots-Irish. Poverty and crop failures made this bad situation even worse.

As a result, Scots-Irish headed to America by the thousands. After they arrived, they quickly moved into the Backcountry. The Scots-Irish brought their clan system with them to the Backcountry. **Clans** are large groups of families—sometimes in the thousands—that claim a common ancestor. Clan members were suspicious of outsiders and banded together when danger threatened. These clans helped families to deal with the dangers and problems of the Backcountry.

Vocabulary
clan: comes from an Old Irish word that means offspring, or descendants

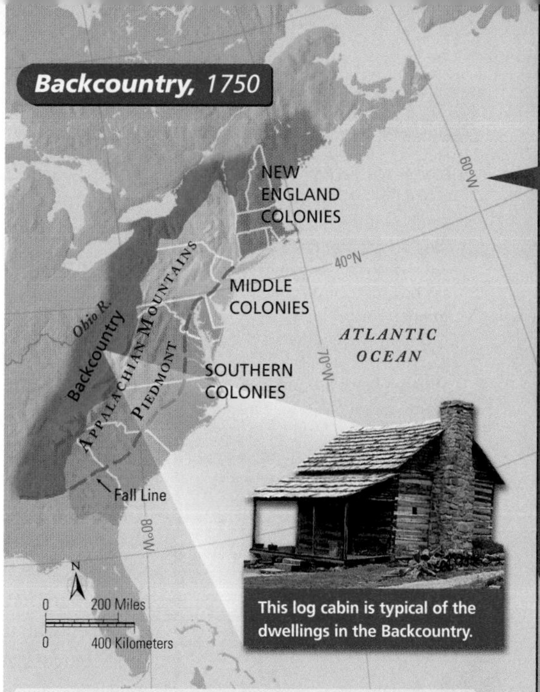

This log cabin is typical of the dwellings in the Backcountry.

GEOGRAPHY SKILLBUILDER Interpreting Maps
Region *What geographical feature did the northern and southern areas of the Backcountry have in common?*

Skillbuilder Answer
They were in or near the Appalachian Mountains.

CHAPTER 4 • SECTION 4

HISTORY FROM VISUALS

Reading the Map The Backcountry region bordered most of the American colonies. Ask the students which groups of colonies most Backcountry settlers probably came from and why. **Possible Response** The majority probably came from the Middle or Southern Colonies, since these colonies bordered most of the Backcountry. It would have been easier for colonists from these regions to resettle in the Backcountry.

Extension Have students use an atlas to identify present-day cities and towns in the Backcountry.

INSTRUCT: OBJECTIVE ❷

Backcountry Settlers/
The Scots-Irish/Backcountry Life

- How did the relationship between the settlers and the Native Americans change?
- Why did the Scots-Irish come to the Backcountry?
- How did life in the Backcountry differ from life along the seaboard?

MORE ABOUT . . .

Log Cabins
The first log cabins in the New World were built by Swedes and Finns, beginning in the mid-1600s near the Delaware River. Other groups of colonists, including English, Scots-Irish, Welsh, and Dutch settlers, adapted this easily constructed dwelling. Various types of log cabins were also built by Russians in Alaska, French in Quebec, Spaniards and Mexicans in areas of New Mexico, and French fur traders in western North America. Five American presidents claimed to have been born in log cabins: Andrew Jackson, James Polk, James Buchanan, Abraham Lincoln, and James Garfield.

ACTIVITY OPTIONS

INTERDISCIPLINARY LINK: THE ARTS — BLOCK SCHEDULING

AMERICAN QUILTS

Class Time One class period
Task Planning a quilt pattern
Purpose To research and draw a pattern for a quilt

Supplies Needed
- Reference materials about American quilts
- Art supplies, including drawing paper, pencils, ruler, colored pencils, paints

Activity Have students find reference materials about American quilts. Tell students to choose a traditional American quilt pattern and reproduce it in the colors of their choice on a large piece of drawing paper. Ask students to display their completed designs in class and discuss what they know about the design and history of their quilts.

Now and then

Backcountry Sports Today

Many Americans enjoy competing in and watching Scottish, or Highland, games. Some events in these games are very similar to those of colonial days in the Backcountry. In one event, the caber toss, competitors run with a wood pole weighing as much as 150 pounds. Then they toss the pole end over end. The toss is judged on distance and accuracy. Another event, the Farmer's Walk, requires strength and endurance. Competitors pick up and carry two 150-pound weights and then walk around pylons. The winner is the athlete who walks the farthest.

INSTRUCT: OBJECTIVE 3

Other Peoples in North America

- How did contact with the Spanish colonists affect Native American culture?
- What caused conflict between colonists and Native Americans?
- What other groups of people were establishing claims in North America?

MORE ABOUT . . .

Native Americans and Horses

The coming of horses to the Great Plains changed the culture of the Native Americans of the Plains. Young men of Plains tribes acquired status by capturing wild horses. A family's rank was determined by the number of horses it owned. Because horses could carry heavy loads, peoples of the Plains could make taller and wider tepees.

Economics in History
- Native American Economies, p. 4

Now and then

BACKCOUNTRY SPORTS TODAY

Three centuries ago, crowds in the Backcountry were thrilled by some of the same games that are now part of track and field competitions.

One of these games is the hammer throw. In this event, an athlete swings around a 16-pound metal ball on a wire-rope handle. After whirling around several times, the athlete lets go of the hammer, hoping it will travel the farthest distance.

The Scots-Irish brought other games to America, including the shotput, high jump, and long jump.

Backcountry Life

Life in the Backcountry was very different from life along the seaboard. Settlers along the coast carried on a lively trade with England. But in the Backcountry, rough roads and rivers made it almost impossible to move goods.

As a result, Backcountry farmers learned quickly to depend on themselves. They built log cabins and furnished them with cornhusk mattresses and homemade benches and tables. They fed their families with the hogs and cattle they raised and with the fish and game they killed. They grew yellow corn to feed their livestock and white corn to eat. Popcorn was probably their only snack food. To protect their precious corn from pests, daytime patrols of women, children, and the elderly served as human scarecrows.

Reading **History**

B. Making Inferences How would you describe the way people in the Backcountry lived?

B. Possible Response Because of the rough conditions in the Backcountry, settlers developed a rugged lifestyle.

Women in the Backcountry worked in the cabin and fields, but they also learned to use guns and axes. An explorer who traveled in the region described one of these hardy Backcountry women.

A VOICE FROM THE PAST

She is a very civil woman and shows nothing of ruggedness or Immodesty in her carriage, yett she will carry a gunn in the woods and kill deer, turkeys, etc., shoot doun wild cattle, catch and tye hoggs, knock down [cattle] with an ax and perform the most manfull Exercises.

A visitor to the Backcountry, quoted in *A History of American Life*

Settlers in the Backcountry often acted as if there were no other people in the region, but this was not so. In the woods and meadows that surrounded their cabins, settlers often encountered Native Americans and other groups that had made America their home.

3 Other Peoples in North America

The Backcountry settlers started a westward movement that would play a critical role in American history. Most settlers' motivation to move west was simple—the desire for land.

Yet the push to the west brought settlers into contact with other peoples of North America. Native Americans had made their homes there for thousands of years. In addition, France and Spain claimed considerable territory in North America.

Reading **History**

C. Summarizing As England's colonies expanded westward, what groups did they encounter?

C. Possible **Responses** Native Americans, Spanish, and French.

Sometimes this contact led to changes in people's cultures. For instance, North America had no horses until the Spanish colonists brought them into Mexico in the 1500s. Horses migrated north, and Native Americans caught them and made them an important part of their culture.

ACTIVITY OPTIONS

INDIVIDUAL NEEDS

LESS PROFICIENT READERS

Supporting Details To help students understand the isolated geographic position and lifestyle of the settlers in the Backcountry, write this sentence from page 112 on the board: "As a result, Backcountry farmers learned quickly to depend on themselves." After students read the sentence, ask them to find details in the text to support it. Write their responses on the board in a Main Idea/Details chart such as the one shown.

As a result, Backcountry farmers learned quickly to depend on themselves.

DETAIL	DETAIL	DETAIL	DETAIL	DETAIL
↓	↓	↓	↓	↓
made their own homes	made their own furniture	raised cattle, pigs for food	caught fish, game for food	grew corn for food

Contact also led to conflict. As English settlers pushed into the Backcountry, they put pressure on Native American tribes. Some tribes reacted by raiding isolated homesteads and small settlements. White settlers struck back, leading to more bloodshed.

This painting shows Native Americans catching wild horses. Many would later use the horses to hunt buffalo on the Great Plains.

The English colonists also came into conflict with the French. The French had colonized eastern Canada and had moved into the territories, rich with fur, along the Mississippi River. French fur traders wanted to prevent English settlers from moving west and taking away part of the trade. One Native American told an Englishman, "You and the French are like two edges of a pair of shears, and we are the cloth that is cut to pieces between them."

Vocabulary
shears: scissors

Spain also controlled large areas of North America—including territories that today form part or all of the states of Arizona, California, Colorado, Florida, Nevada, New Mexico, Texas, Utah, and Wyoming. Spanish settlers were farmers, ranchers, and priests. Priests, who established missions to convert Native Americans, built forts near the missions for protection. In 1718, Spaniards built Fort San Antonio de Bexar to guard the mission of San Antonio de Valero, later renamed the Alamo.

These different groups continued to compete—and sometimes fight—with one another. Frequently, England's colonies had to unite against these other groups. As a result, a common American identity began to take shape, as you will read in Chapter 5.

Section 4 Assessment

1. Terms & Names

Explain the significance of:
- Appalachian Mountains
- fall line
- piedmont
- clan

2. Taking Notes

Use a chart like the one shown to list some of the geographic characteristics of the Backcountry.

Backcountry Geography
1.
2.
3.
4.

3. Main Ideas

a. Which settlers migrated to the Backcountry?

b. How did clans help the Scots-Irish survive?

c. What economic activities did women carry out in the region?

4. Critical Thinking

Identifying Problems As England's colonies expanded farther west, what problems would they face?

THINK ABOUT
- other inhabitants of the Americas
- the resources desired by the colonists

ACTIVITY OPTIONS

LANGUAGE ARTS / ART

Read an account of the Backcountry written in the 1700s. Write a **newspaper article** or draw a series of **cartoons** that describe what you have read.

MORE ABOUT . . .

Diversity on the Frontier

The frontier was not so much a boundary as a zone of contact where many people encountered one another. According to one study of a northern Ohio town in the late 1700s, the population included Shawnee, Iroquois, Miami, Delaware, Cherokee, British, French, Americans, and African Americans. The residents celebrated Mardi Gras, St. Patrick's Day, Indian holidays, and the birthday of the British monarch, not to mention Christmas, New Year's Day, and—after American independence—the Fourth of July.

In-Depth Resources: Unit 1
- Primary Sources: Culture Clash in the Colonies, pp. 66–67

ASSESS & RETEACH

Setting the Stage Have students fill in the chart with the information about the Backcountry.

Formal Assessment
- Section Quiz, p. 72

Critical Thinking Transparency CT10
- Setting the Stage

RETEACHING ACTIVITY

Divide the class into four groups, assigning each group one section objective. Ask each group to produce a chart that includes the objective and three to four bulleted key ideas. Have the group illustrate the chart with a visual that supports the main objective. Display the completed graphics in class.

In-Depth Resources: Unit 1
- Reteaching Activity, p. 74

Section 4 Assessment

1. Terms & Names

Appalachian Mountains, p. 110
fall line, p. 110
piedmont, p. 110
clan, p. 111

2. Taking Notes

1. dense forests
2. rushing streams
3. near or in Appalachian Mountains
4. broad plateau

3. Main Ideas

a. small farmers who couldn't compete with wealthy plantation owners; Scots-Irish **b.** Large groups of families banded together to deal with dangers and problems. **c.** worked in the fields and in the cabin; used guns and axes

4. Critical Thinking

They would run into other inhabitants of the continent and compete with them for land, furs, and other resources.

ACTIVITY OPTIONS

Integrated Assessment
- Rubrics for a newspaper, 4.5
- Rubrics for a cartoon, 1.3

TERMS & NAMES

1. **Backcountry,** p. 93
2. **subsistence farming,** p. 94
3. **triangular trade,** p. 95
4. **Navigation Acts,** p. 96
5. **cash crop,** p. 99
6. **gristmill,** p. 99
7. **Conestoga wagon,** p. 101
8. **overseer,** p. 106
9. **Stono Rebellion,** p. 107
10. **Appalachian Mountains,** p. 110

REVIEW QUESTIONS

Possible Responses

1. They often lived near towns and practiced subsistence farming. Because of the short growing season and rocky soil, farming was challenging.
2. They became shipbuilders, traders, whalers, and fishermen.
3. A compact plot of land was often sold to a congregation, which then divided the land between members.
4. These farms often produced large cash crops.
5. The population was remarkably diverse.
6. Southern planters were self-sufficient, producing most of what they needed with the resources on their plantations. When necessary, they used nearby rivers to transport their crops.
7. Native Americans and white Europeans were unreliable sources of labor.
8. They worked slowly, damaged goods, purposely carried out orders incorrectly, and rebelled.
9. It was in or near the Appalachian Mountains in the far western part of most of the colonies.
10. Because of the Backcountry's distance from the coast, settlers there developed an independent and rugged lifestyle.

Chapter 4 ASSESSMENT

VISUAL SUMMARY

The Colonies Develop

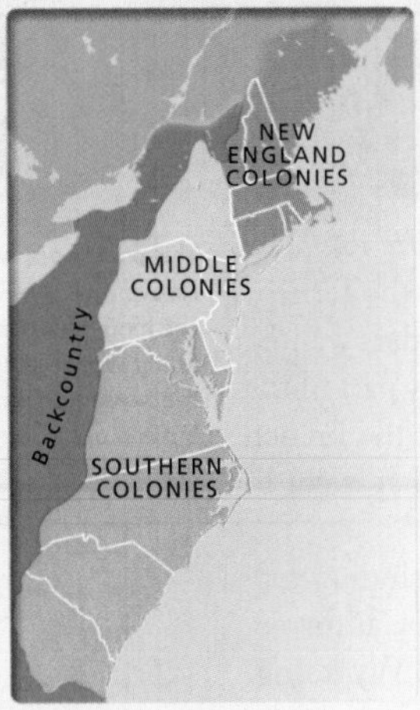

New England: Commerce and Religion

New England was distinguished by its small farming towns and profitable fishing and trade.

The Middle Colonies: Farms and Cities

The Middle Colonies' farms produced large cash crops that fueled trade in its coastal cities.

The Southern Colonies: Plantations and Slavery

The South's plantation economy and large number of enslaved Africans made it different from the other regions.

The Backcountry

The Backcountry was distant from the denser coastal populations, so settlers there developed an independent and rugged way of life.

TERMS & NAMES

Briefly explain the significance of the following.

1. Backcountry
2. subsistence farming
3. triangular trade
4. Navigation Acts
5. cash crop
6. gristmill
7. Conestoga wagon
8. overseer
9. Stono Rebellion
10. Appalachian Mountains

REVIEW QUESTIONS

New England: Commerce and Religion (pages 93–97)

1. How would you describe the life of a New England farmer?
2. In what ways did settlers in the region take advantage of the Atlantic Ocean?
3. How were New England towns settled?

The Middle Colonies: Farms and Cities (pages 98–102)

4. How were farms in the Middle Colonies different from those in New England?
5. What characterized the population of the Middle Colonies?

The Southern Colonies: Plantations and Slavery (pages 103–109)

6. Why did Southern planters infrequently travel to towns to sell their crops or to buy food and supplies?
7. Why did planters turn to enslaved Africans for labor?
8. In what ways did slaves resist?

The Backcountry (pages 110–113)

9. Where was the Backcountry located in the 1700s?
10. How was life in the Backcountry different from that along the coast?

CRITICAL THINKING

1. USING YOUR NOTES

Using your completed chart, answer the questions below.

		NEW ENGLAND COLONIES	MIDDLE COLONIES	SOUTHERN COLONIES	BACKCOUNTRY
CAUSES	Climate				
	Resources				
	People				
EFFECT	Economic Development				

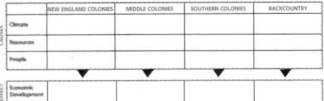

a. How was the Middle Colonies' climate different from the Backcountry's?

b. How did the South's labor system differ from the North's?

c. How did the resources of New England affect its economy?

2. ANALYZING LEADERSHIP

How did the South's plantation economy influence who became leaders in the region?

3. THEME: ECONOMICS IN HISTORY

What factors influenced the economic development of each of the four colonial regions?

4. APPLYING CITIZENSHIP SKILLS

How did the Quaker influence in the Middle Colonies contribute to the behavior of citizens of the region?

5. SEQUENCING EVENTS

What changes took place in the population and treatment of African Americans between 1650 and 1750?

Interact *with* History

How would the choice that you made at the beginning of the chapter have varied according to the region in which you lived? Would you still make the same choice?

CRITICAL THINKING

Possible Response

1. **USING YOUR NOTES a.** The shorter winters meant a longer growing season and more productive farms. **b.** The South relied much more heavily on enslaved Africans for labor than the North. **c.** The poor soil and small farms led people to economic opportunities offered by the Atlantic Ocean.
2. **ANALYZING LEADERSHIP** Because planters held all the wealth, this small class also assumed political leadership in the South.
3. **THEME: ECONOMICS IN HISTORY** climate, resources, and people
4. **APPLYING CITIZENSHIP SKILLS** Quaker religious tolerance, belief in the equality of men and women, and belief that slavery was wrong all positively influenced civic behavior.
5. **SEQUENCING EVENTS** Between 1650 and 1750, the African-American population went from 5 percent to 40 percent. By 1750, there were 235,000 enslaved Africans in America—about 85 percent lived in the South. The treatment of the enslaved African Americans worsened.

Interact *with* History Answers should acknowledge the characteristics of the region and explain reasons for their choice.

HISTORY SKILLS

1. INTERPRETING MAPS: Human-Environment Interaction

Study the map. Answer the questions.

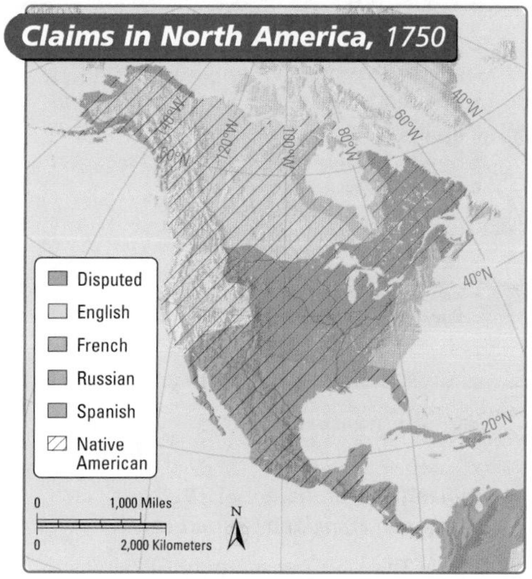

Basic Map Elements

a. What is the subject of the map?

Interpreting the Map

b. Which of the groups shown inhabited the largest area of North America?

c. Which groups claimed the northernmost territory?

2. INTERPRETING PRIMARY SOURCES

In the backwoods of North Carolina, William Byrd met a family he suspected of being escaped slaves. Read the selection below and answer the questions.

> [They] called themselves free, though by the shyness of the master of the house, who took care to keep least in sight, their freedom seemed a little doubtful. . . . Many slaves [hide] in this obscure part of the world, nor will any of their righteous neighbors discover them. On the contrary, [their neighbors profit by] settling such fugitives on some out-of-the-way corner of their land to raise stocks for a mean and inconsiderable share, well knowing their condition makes it necessary for them to [accept any pay they are offered].
>
> **William Byrd,** from *Secret History of the Dividing Line*

a. Why does Byrd suspect the family members are escaped slaves?

b. Why don't their neighbors turn them in?

ALTERNATIVE ASSESSMENT

1. INTERDISCIPLINARY ACTIVITY: Geography

Making a Map Using the library or the Internet, read more about the history of the slave trade in the 1700s. Create a map of Africa that shows countries that were major sources of enslaved persons.

For more about the history of Africa . . .

INTERNET ACTIVITY CLASSZONE.COM

2. COOPERATIVE LEARNING ACTIVITY

Building a Log Cabin Do some more research on the Backcountry and the history of log cabins. Work with others to record details about the location where you will build your cabin. Then design and construct a model of a log cabin that could be compared to the cabins in which Backcountry settlers lived.

3. TECHNOLOGY ACTIVITY

Making a Class Presentation Life on a farm in colonial New England was a real challenge. Using the library or the Internet, find accounts of how New England farm families lived. Then design a multimedia presentation about a typical New England farmer and his family. Be sure to include the social and economic contributions of women in your presentation.

For more about daily life during colonial times . . .

INTERNET ACTIVITY CLASSZONE.COM

- Create a map of the town in which the farmer and his family lived.
- Dress up like a farmer to discuss the challenges of New England agriculture.
- Create a chart that lists the differences between your family's lifestyle and the colonial family's.

4. HISTORY PORTFOLIO

Option 1 Review your section and chapter assessment activities. Select one that you think is your best work. Then use comments made by your teacher or classmates to improve your work and add it to your portfolio.

Option 2 Review the questions that you wrote for What Do You Want to Know? on page 92. Then write a short report in which you explain the answers to your questions. Add your report to your portfolio.

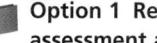

Additional Test Practice, pp. S1–S33 TEST PRACTICE CLASSZONE.COM

The Colonies Develop **115**

ALTERNATIVE ASSESSMENT

1. INTERDISCIPLINARY ACTIVITY: Geography

A map should

- include a legend and title.
- include either or both physical and political locations.
- be clearly labeled and neatly presented.
- clearly demonstrate an understanding of the sources of enslaved persons.

2. COOPERATIVE LEARNING ACTIVITY

A log cabin should

- represent the cabin in a three-dimensional manner clear to viewers.
- exhibit creativity.
- demonstrate grade-level artistic skill.

3. TECHNOLOGY ACTIVITY

Class presentations should

- utilize two or more media.
- clearly demonstrate an understanding of life on a colonial New England farm.
- engage or educate the audience about the topic.
- show technical proficiency.
- use correct grammar, spelling, and punctuation.

4. HISTORY PORTFOLIO

Option 1 Revised section or chapter assessment activities should

- address teacher and peer responses to the selected work.
- solve problems present in the first versions of the work.

Option 2 Short reports should

- answer questions about the four colonial regions.
- use evidence to develop and support ideas.
- cite sources of information.
- use standard grammar, spelling, sentence structure, and punctuation.

Critical Thinking Transparency CT12

- Visual Summary

Formal Assessment

- Chapter Test, Forms A, B, and C, pp. 73–84

HISTORY SKILLS

Possible Responses

1. INTERPRETING MAPS

Basic Map Elements

a. claims in North America in 1750

Interpreting the Map

b. Native Americans

c. Russians

2. INTERPRETING PRIMARY SOURCES

a. because they are shy and the master stayed out of sight

b. because they know that the slaves' fear of being turned in will make them work for little pay

CHAPTER 5 PLANNING GUIDE

Beginnings of an American Identity 1689–1763

	CHAPTER OVERVIEW	COPYMASTERS	INTEGRATED TECHNOLOGY
CHAPTER RESOURCES	The chapter explores the social and economic classes developing in the colonies as well as the new religious and philosophical movements. It also describes the major war that occurred between Britain and France over the settlement of western lands.	**In-Depth Resources: Unit 1** • Tracing Themes: Democratic Ideals, p. 77 • Building Vocabulary, p. 81 **Interdisciplinary Projects,** pp. 25–30	• eEdition Plus Online • EasyPlanner Plus Online • eTest Plus Online • eEdition • Power Presentations • EasyPlanner • Electronic Library of Primary Sources • Test Generator • Reading Study Guide • America's Music
	KEY IDEAS		
SECTION 1 **Early American Culture** **pp. 119–124**	• Land ownership determines social position in the colonies. • The work of women and children is essential to the colonial economy. • Schooling, literacy, the Great Awakening, and the Enlightenment influence the intellectual life of the colonies.	**In-Depth Resources: Unit 1** • Setting the Stage, p. 76 • Guided Reading, p. 78 • Skillbuilder Practice, p. 82 • Primary Source, p. 85 • Reteaching Activity, p. 90 **America's History Makers,** pp. 19–22 **Economics in History,** p. 5 **Why It Matters Now,** pp. 9–10	**Warm-Up Transparency WT5** **Humanities Transparency HT9** • *Benjamin Franklin* by Robert Feke **Critical Thinking Transparency CT13** • Setting the Stage **classzone.com**
SECTION 2 **Roots of Representative Government** **pp. 125–129**	• Colonial governments follow the English parliamentary model. • Royal governors threaten the colonies' representative governments. • England's Glorious Revolution made political liberties more secure in both England and the colonies.	**In-Depth Resources: Unit 1** • Setting the Stage, p. 76 • Guided Reading, p. 79 • Reteaching Activity, p. 91 **Citizenship Today,** pp. 1–2 **American History Plays** • *The Trial of Peter Zenger* by Paul T. Nolan	**Warm-Up Transparency WT5** **Critical Thinking Transparency CT13** • Setting the Stage **classzone.com**
SECTION 3 **The French and Indian War** **pp. 130–135**	• France and Britain go to war over western lands and trade. • Native Americans ally with France and fight against both British troops and colonists. • Britain's victory gives it control of Canada and French lands east of the Mississippi River.	**In-Depth Resources: Unit 1** • Setting the Stage, p. 76 • Guided Reading, p. 80 • Geography Application, pp. 83–84 • Primary Source, p. 86 • Literature Selection, pp. 87–89 • Reteaching Activity, p. 92 **Outline Map Activities** • Mississippi River Drainage Basin, pp. 9–10	**Warm-Up Transparency WT5** **Humanities Transparency HT10** • George Washington, 1755 **Geography Transparency GT5** • Proclamation of 1763 **Critical Thinking Transparency CT14** • Cause and Effect: The French and Indian War

Pupil's Edition | Overhead Transparency | CD-ROM
Copymaster | Audio Library | Internet

ASSESSMENT OPTIONS

Chapter Assessment, pp. 136–137

Formal Assessment
- Chapter Tests, Forms A, B, and C, pp. 88–99

Test Generator

Online Test Practice

Strategies for Test Preparation

Section Assessment, p. 124

Formal Assessment, Quiz, p. 85

Integrated Assessment Book
- Rubrics, 4.9, 1.3

Test Generator

Test Practice Transparencies, TT17

Section Assessment, p. 129

Formal Assessment, Quiz, p. 86

Integrated Assessment Book
- Rubrics, 3.6, 1.13

Test Generator

Test Practice Transparencies, TT18

Section Assessment, p. 135

Formal Assessment, Quiz, p. 87

Integrated Assessment Book
- Rubrics, 1.10, 4.8

Test Generator

Test Practice Transparencies, TT19

CUSTOMIZING FOR INDIVIDUAL NEEDS

Students Acquiring English/ESL

Reading Study Guide (English and Spanish), pp. 39–46

Access for Students Acquiring English/ESL: Spanish Translations, pp. 26–31

Chapter Summaries on CD (English and Spanish)

Modified Lesson Plans for English Learners

Less Proficient Readers

Reading Study Guide (English and Spanish), pp. 39–46

Chapter Summaries on CD (English and Spanish)

Gifted and Talented Students

In-Depth Resources: Unit 1
- Enrichment Activity, p. 93

America's History Makers
- Benjamin Franklin, pp. 19–20
- Sarah Kemble Knight, pp. 21–22

CROSS-CURRICULAR CONNECTIONS

Popular Culture
Kalman, Bobbie. ***Early Artisans.*** Early Settler Life Series. New York: Crabtree, 1983. Looks at the crafts of bookbinders, printers, co-opers, and glassblowers, among others.

Primary Sources
Smith, Carter, ed. ***The Explorers and Settlers: A Sourcebook on Colonial America*** (American Albums from the Library of Congress). Brookfield, CT: Millbrook Press, 1994.

Interdisciplinary Projects, pp. 25–30
- Math: Early Colonial Industries
- Science: Franklin's Experiments with Lightning
- Language Arts: *The New England Primer*
- Art: Colonial Furnishings

Health
Terkel, Susan N. ***Colonial American Medicine.*** New York: Franklin Watts, 1993. From the Colonial America series, this book looks at the "cures"—from herbs to leeches—with which doctors in the 1600s and 1700s treated the diseases and epidemics of their day.

Language Arts/Literature
Dorris, Michael. ***Guests.*** New York: Hyperion, 1994. Story of a young Algonquian named Moss, his quest for manhood, and his relationship with a girl named Trouble.

Durrant, Lynda. ***The Beaded Moccasins: The Story of Mary Campbell.*** New York: Clarion Books, 1998. Based on a historical incident, the story of a girl kidnapped from her Pennsylvania farm by Delaware Indians in 1759.

Longfellow, Henry W. ***Evangeline.*** LaVergne, TN: Ingram, 1999. Narrative poem relating the adventures of the Acadians and their emigration to Louisiana.

ENRICHMENT ACTIVITIES

Pupil's Edition, pp. 116–137
Interact with History, p. 117
Citizenship Today, p. 126

In-Depth Resources: Unit 1
- Geography Application: Native American Confederacies, pp. 83–84
- Primary Source, p. 85
- Primary Source, p. 86
- Literature Selection, pp. 87–89

America's History Makers
- Benjamin Franklin, pp. 19–20
- Sarah Kemble Knight, pp. 21–22

America's Music CD

American History Plays
- *The Trial of Peter Zenger* by Paul T. Nolan

Outline Map Activities
- Mississippi River Drainage Basin, pp. 9–10

Why It Matters Now
- American Identity Today, pp. 9–10

BLOCK SCHEDULING — LESSON PLAN OPTIONS (90-MINUTE PERIOD)

DAY 1

Interact with History, p. 117
Class Time 20 minutes

Options for pacing and variety:
- **Role-Playing** Have each student pick a colony and answer the "What Do You Think?" questions from the perspective of a person living in that colony.
  Class Time 15 minutes

Setting the Stage, p. 118
Class Time 20 minutes

Options for pacing and variety:
- **Time Saver** Ask students to come to class with a list of beliefs they consider to be "American." **Class Time** 10 minutes

Section 1, pp. 119–124
Class Time 50 minutes

Options for pacing and variety:
- **Peer Competition** Ask each student to make up one true and one false statement about the colonial economy, colonial education, and publishing and religion. Put the statements on the board and have students take turns identifying the true statements.
  Class Time 30 minutes

DAY 2

Section 2, pp. 125–129
Class Time 45 minutes

Options for pacing and variety:
- **History on Film** Extend students' knowledge of the Magna Carta with two 16-minute films—*Rise of the English Monarchy* and *Revolt of the Nobles and the Signing of the Charter.* Encyclopaedia Britannica.
  Class Time 35 minutes
- **Time Saver** Use the chart on page 128 to describe the key features of colonial government to students. **Class Time** 10 minutes

Section 3, pp. 130–135
Class Time: 45 minutes

Options for pacing and variety:
- **Internet** Extend students' background knowledge of the French and Indian War by learning about the battle that took place at Louisbourg at classzone.com
  Class Time 20 minutes

Chapter 5 Assessment, pp. 136–137
Class Time 40 minutes

Options for pacing and variety:
- **Peer Teaching** Working in six-member groups, students can answer the Critical Thinking questions by a round robin. Students should seat themselves in a circle. Give one person a legal-size notepad and have that person answer Question 1, then pass the paper to the next person, who adds his or her responses. When the notepad returns to the person who began it, the response is complete. Continue until all questions have been answered.
  Class Time 40 minutes

TEACHER-TESTED ACTIVITY **Leslie Schubert, Parkland School, McHenry, Illinois**

ILLUSTRATED TIME LINE

Class Time Two class periods for preparation and one for presentation

Task Creating an illustrated time line of events that occurred during the French and Indian War

Purpose To identify and understand significant events of the French and Indian War

Supplies Needed
- Reference materials and Internet sources on the French and Indian War
- Markers, colored pencils
- A roll of heavy white paper

Activity Working in small groups, students can create time lines of eight to ten events that occurred during or as a result of the French and Indian War. The time lines should include one paragraph for each event explaining its importance to the outcome of the war. The group as a whole can decide which events to include on the time line, how each should be illustrated, and why each was significant. Then some students can be illustrators and others can be writers. During their class presentations, groups should identify the event they felt was most important to the future of the European settlers in North America and why.

REPORTING ON THE FRENCH AND INDIAN WAR

War correspondents have the difficult—and often dangerous—job of reporting on war. In modern times, war correspondents use the latest technology to transmit stories from the front to the people who live far away from the fighting. In this activity, students will play the role of war correspondents, writing stories from various fronts of the French and Indian War. Even though students will rely on modern computer technology to write their reports, they should imagine that stories would have been carried by runners or riders from the front to their audience at home: British, French, American colonists, or Native Americans.

ACTIVITY OUTLINE

Objective By writing news reports on the French and Indian War, students will learn more about the war.

Task Students will file news reports about the French and Indian War for the different audiences interested in the conflict: British, French, Native Americans, and American colonists.

Class Time Two class periods

DIRECTIONS

1. Explain to students that they will be war correspondents from various fronts of the French and Indian War. They should imagine that they are observing battles and reporting the action and results to those back home. The students should cover all important issues and events that shaped the war between 1754 and 1763.
2. Students should begin by reviewing Chapter 5 of *Creating America* to gather background information on the war.
3. For additional information on the war, students can check sources in the school library or on the Internet. Helpful Web sites can be found on classzone.com under links for Chapter 5 of *Creating America.*
4. Allow students one class period, if possible, to gather information for their articles. A second class period should be spent writing short articles about causes, turning points, and outcomes of each major event in the war.
5. Articles should be presented as newspaper articles to be distributed to others to read, or as announcements by a "town crier," or perhaps as oral reports carried by a runner.
6. Finally, ask the class to compare and contrast different versions of the same event. Ask students if the articles written for different audiences showed any bias in their reporting.

CHAPTER 5 OBJECTIVE

The student will identify the political, social, and economic values shared by British colonists and learn how these values and historical events led to the growth of a representative government and a new "American" identity.

HISTORY FROM VISUALS

Interpreting the Painting Ask students to study the painting and caption. Have the students describe the expressions on the faces of the audience. Ask them what Patrick Henry might be saying. **Possible Responses** Some listeners are very intent, others look puzzled. Patrick Henry may be criticizing the king.

Extension Ask students to write a short story describing the scene portrayed in the painting.

CRITICAL THINKING ACTIVITY

Analyzing Causes What experiences might have made American colonists think they were different from the British in England? **Possible Responses** They had experiences with Native Americans, the frontier, a different style of economy, and different types of government.

Class Time 5 minutes

CHAPTER 5 Beginnings of an American Identity 1689–1763

Section 1 **Early American Culture**
Section 2 **Roots of Representative Government**
Section 3 **The French and Indian War**

Conflicts with the British government helped shape a separate identity for British colonists. Here, Patrick Henry argues against the king in 1763.

RECOMMENDED RESOURCES

BOOKS FOR THE TEACHER

Demos, John. ***The Unredeemed Captive: A Family Story from Early America.*** New York: Knopf, 1994. Highly readable story of the Williams family, captured during a raid on Deerfield, Massachusetts.

Knight, Sarah K. ***The Journal of Madam Knight.*** Washington: Scholarly Pr., 1991. The entire story of this amusing and difficult journey.

Lambert, Frank. ***Inventing "The Great Awakening."*** Princeton: Princeton U. Press, 1999. A new look at historiography.

SOFTWARE

Landmark Documents in American History, 2.0. Facts on File, 1998. Award-winning resource including over 20,000 pages.

VIDEO

Benjamin Franklin: Citizen of the World. A&E Biography. Lively life of America's first Renaissance man—inventor, writer, diplomat.

INTERNET

For more about the Fortress of Louisbourg, visit . . .

classzone.com

Interact *with* History

Conflicts with Native Americans and French colonists also helped shape the identity of British colonists. In response to attacks on the Pennsylvania frontier, Benjamin Franklin published this cartoon in 1754 urging the colonies to unite for defense.

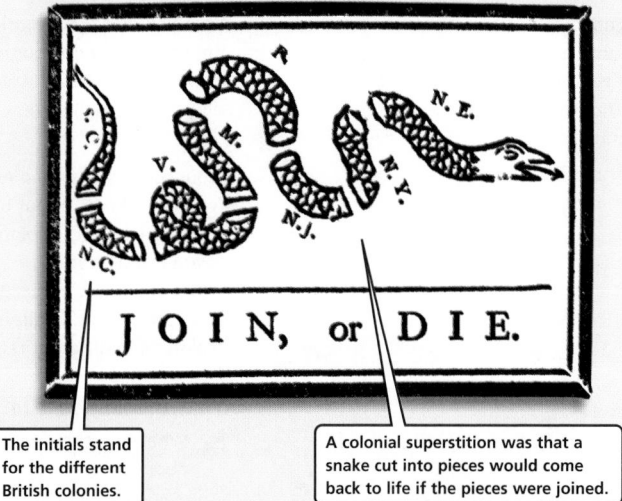

The initials stand for the different British colonies.

A colonial superstition was that a snake cut into pieces would come back to life if the pieces were joined.

What do you have in common with other British colonists?

You have seen this cartoon in the *Pennsylvania Gazette*. You are outraged by the attacks on British traders and settlers. You wonder whether it is wise to join with other colonies, though. Will it mean that Virginians or New Englanders will be able to make laws for Pennsylvania?

What Do You Think?

- What are some good reasons to join with the other British colonies?
- How great are the differences between the British colonies?
- What separates British colonists from French colonists?

USA

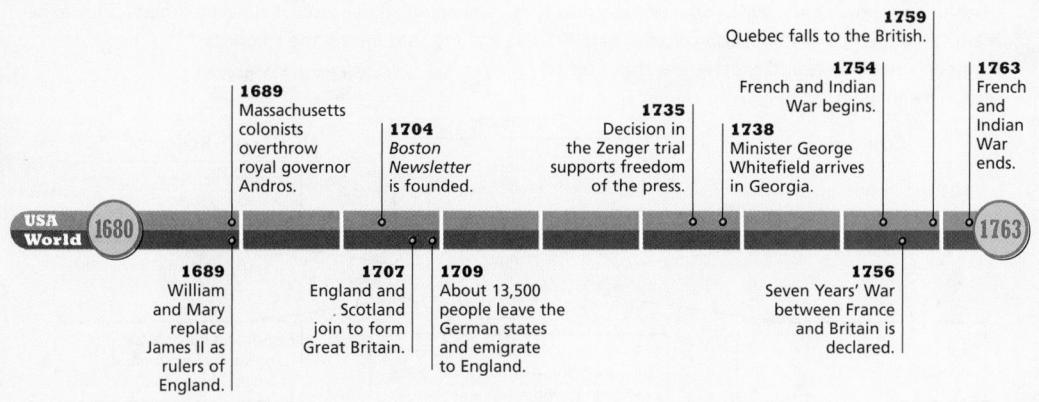

- **1689** Massachusetts colonists overthrow royal governor Andros.
- **1704** *Boston Newsletter* is founded.
- **1735** Decision in the Zenger trial supports freedom of the press.
- **1738** Minister George Whitefield arrives in Georgia.
- **1754** French and Indian War begins.
- **1759** Quebec falls to the British.
- **1763** French and Indian War ends.

1680 — 1763

World

- **1689** William and Mary replace James II as rulers of England.
- **1707** England and Scotland join to form Great Britain.
- **1709** About 13,500 people leave the German states and emigrate to England.
- **1756** Seven Years' War between France and Britain is declared.

Interact *with* History

OBJECTIVES

- To identify political loyalties of the colonists
- To analyze how colonial leaders hoped to unify the colonists' loyalties

What Do You Think?

1. Ask students to study Franklin's political cartoon. What did Franklin believe would be the result if the colonies refused to fight together?
2. Ask students whether they identify themselves as citizens of their colony, as citizens of England, or as Americans.
3. Why might French colonists' experiences be different from those of British colonists?

What do you have in common with other British colonists?

Ask students to list as many connections as they can that were shared by all British colonists. **Possible Responses** English language and customs, British government, connections to family and friends, trade with Great Britain

MAKING PERSONAL CONNECTIONS

Ask students to think about what things they have in common with students in other parts of the United States. Then ask how these experiences may be different from those of young people in other nations of the world.

TIME LINE DISCUSSION

Explain to students that the time line presents years during which a national spirit and demands for democratic government gathered force and power in the colonies. Point out that during the 1700s, the colonists began to think of themselves as American, not British.

- Ask students which world events shown on the time line might affect the colonies. Ask for reasons for their choices. **Possible Responses** succession of William and Mary, because a change in British rulers could mean a change in British colonial policy; war between Britain and France, because both countries had colonies in the Americas
- Ask students which events on the USA time line might have helped build the feeling that American colonies were different from other British colonies.

Possible Responses 1689—overthrowing the royal governor; 1735—Zenger trial

BEFORE YOU READ

Previewing the Theme: Democratic Ideals

Ask students to name some of the rights to which they feel entitled because they are Americans. Ask if they have any particular rights as citizens of their state.

What Do You Know?

Most eighth-grade students have a keen awareness of what they consider personal rights. As they volunteer answers, caution them to separate their personal desires from rights to which they are entitled by their democratic government.

In-Depth Resources: Unit 1
- Tracing Themes: Democratic Ideals, p. 77

READ AND TAKE NOTES

Reading Strategy: Finding Main Ideas

Explain to students that finding main ideas means noting the most important points in a chapter. Remind them that each section has a Main Idea statement to help them find the bigger ideas. Suggest that students use the details they find in the chapter to reinforce main ideas. Using a web diagram will help them record important details as they read.

In-Depth Resources: Unit 1
- Setting the Stage, p. 76

Critical Thinking Transparency CT13
- Setting the Stage

Chapter 5 SETTING THE STAGE

BEFORE YOU READ

Previewing the Theme

Democratic Ideals In the 1700s and even earlier, American colonists demanded protection of their "rights as Englishmen." Among these was the right to elect representatives to government. Chapter 5 explains how a heritage of English rights was one of many forces drawing the different British colonies together.

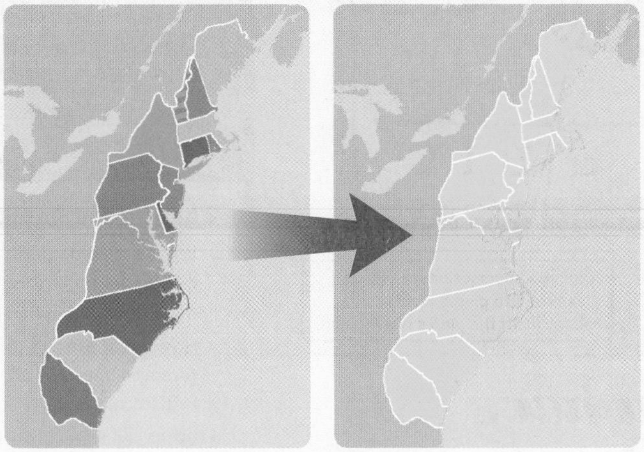

What Do You Know?

What beliefs do you consider American? How do you think people in Britain's American colonies saw themselves?

THINK ABOUT
- your own beliefs as an American
- what you know about the regions where the colonies were established
- what you know about the backgrounds and beliefs of colonists in different regions

What Do You Want to Know?

What questions do you have about colonial America in the early and middle 1700s? Write them down in your notebook before you read this chapter.

READ AND TAKE NOTES

Reading Strategy: Finding Main Ideas To recognize a main idea, you must notice how smaller details are connected. In your notebook, copy a web like the one shown here. Write brief notes about the main things people in the British colonies had in common—the beliefs and experiences that formed an American identity.

- Read and remember the Main Idea at the beginning of each section.
- At the end of each group of paragraphs under a heading, ask yourself, "Have I learned about something that united the colonists?"

See Skillbuilder Handbook, page R5.

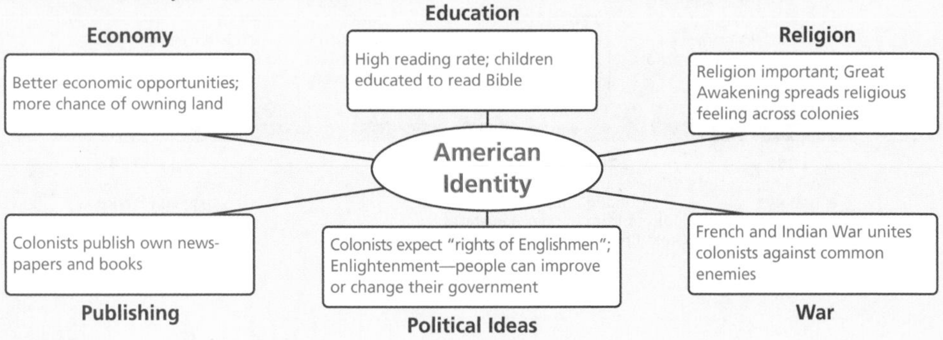

TEACHING STRATEGY

READING THE CHAPTER

This is a thematic chapter focusing on the basis for an American identity. For each section have students write summary sentences identifying distinctive American ideals, values, or behaviors. Encourage them to think about and discuss how these values have prevailed over the years.

ALTERNATIVE ASSESSMENT

The Chapter Assessment describes three activities for alternative assessment on page 137. You may wish to have students work on these activities during the course of the chapter and then present them at the end.

1 Early American Culture

TERMS & NAMES
apprentice
Great Awakening
Jonathan Edwards
George Whitefield
Enlightenment
Benjamin Franklin
John Locke

MAIN IDEA	WHY IT MATTERS NOW
The British colonies were shaped by prosperity, literacy, and new movements in religion and thought.	These forces began to create an American identity that is still developing today.

ONE AMERICAN'S STORY

On October 2, 1704, Sarah Kemble Knight set out on horseback from her home in Boston. She was riding all the way to New Haven, Connecticut. Today the ride is two hours by car, but then it took five days.

In her journal, Madam Knight described her travel hardships and commented on people she met—country girls, tobacco-chewing farmers, and rude housewives.

A VOICE FROM THE PAST

We hoped to reach the french town and Lodg there that night, but unhapily lost our way about four miles short. . . . A surly old shee Creature, not worthy the name of woman, . . . would hardly let us go into her Door, though the weather was so stormy none but shee would have turnd out a Dogg.

Sarah Kemble Knight, *The Journal of Madam Knight*

THE
JOURNAL
OF
Madam KNIGHT
By Sarah Kemble Knight
A Woman's Treacherous Journey By Horseback
From Boston to New York
In the Year 1704

This reprint of *The Journal of Madam Knight* is a 1920 edition.

Her attitude toward people from other colonies was typical. In the early 1700s, people of the different British colonies did not think of themselves as living in one country. They were separated by distance and customs. In this section, you will learn what began to draw the colonies together.

1 Land, Rights, and Wealth

At the time of Madam Knight's journey, the colonies were thriving. Cheap farmland and plentiful natural resources gave colonists a chance to prosper. They would have had less opportunity in Europe. In England, fewer than 5 percent of the people owned land. In fact, land rarely went up for sale. By contrast, in the colonies, land was plentiful—once Native American groups were forced to give up their claims. Colonists who owned land were free to use or sell whatever it produced.

Land ownership gave colonists political rights as well as prosperity. Generally, only white male landowners or property owners could vote. There were some exceptions. City dwellers could vote by paying a fee.

SECTION OBJECTIVES

1. To analyze colonial values
2. To identify roles of colonial women and children
3. To evaluate the results of a high literacy rate in the colonies
4. To identify the effects of the Great Awakening and the Enlightenment

CRITICAL THINKING

Finding Main Ideas, p. 120
Contrasting, pp. 121, 122, 124
Categorizing, p. 122
Recognizing Effects, p. 124

Why It Matters Now
- American Identity Today, pp. 9–10

FOCUS & MOTIVATE

5-MINUTE WARM-UP

Recognizing Effects These questions focus on colonial culture.

1. Look at the chart on page 120. Which groups owned land?
2. What do you think the difference was between an indentured servant and an unskilled worker?

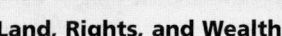

Warm-Up Transparency WT5

INSTRUCT

INSTRUCT: OBJECTIVE 1

Land, Rights, and Wealth

- What special rights did landowners enjoy?
- How did land ownership affect a colonist's place in society?

In-Depth Resources: Unit 1
- Guided Reading, p. 78
- Building Vocabulary, p. 81

America's History Makers
- Sarah Kemble Knight, pp. 21–22

Reading Study Guide (Spanish and English), pp. 39–40

RECOMMENDED RESOURCES

In-Depth Resources: Unit 1
- Guided Reading, p. 78
- Building Vocabulary, p. 81
- Skillbuilder Practice, p. 82
- Primary Source: An Indentured Servant's Plea, p. 85

Reading Study Guide, pp. 39–40

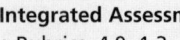

Economics in History, p. 5

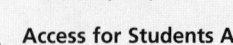

America's History Makers, pp. 19–22

Why It Matters Now
- American Identity Today, pp. 9–10

Formal Assessment
- Section Quiz, p. 85

Integrated Assessment
- Rubrics, 4.9, 1.3

Access for Students Acquiring English/ESL, pp. 26, 29

INTEGRATED TECHNOLOGY

Humanities Transparency HT9
- *Benjamin Franklin* by Robert Feke

Electronic Teacher Tools

classzone.com

TEST-TAKING RESOURCES

Strategies for Test Preparation

Test Practice Transparencies, TT17

Online Test Practice

HISTORY FROM VISUALS

Interpreting the Chart Remind students that owning land was very important in colonial society. Ask them what other kinds of property or occupation entitled a man to rank in the middle and upper classes. Also have them note which groups made up the lowest rank of the middle class. **Answers** merchants, officials in church and government, tradespeople, renters, and unskilled workers

Extension Ask students to write a story about an indentured servant who moves upward in social status, becoming a small farmer, a merchant, or a wealthy landowner. Tell students to describe what helped their character rise in society.

INSTRUCT: OBJECTIVE 2

Women and the Economy/ Young People at Work

- What work did colonial women and young people do?
- What rights were denied women?

Economics in History
- Growth of Colonial Economies, p. 5

MORE ABOUT . . .

Women's Work

Studies of colonial life have shown that in early colonial days, wives and husbands worked together to plant and harvest crops and to tend the animals. During these times, women had great authority and power within their families. As life in the colonies became more settled, women became more confined to their traditional roles and lost some of the power they had once held.

Colonial Social Ranks
HIGH
• large landowners
• church officials
• government officials
• wealthy merchants
UPPER MIDDLE
• small farmers
• tradespeople
LOWER MIDDLE
• renters
• unskilled workers
LOW
• indentured servants
• slaves

Land ownership also helped determine colonists' social position. Unlike England, America had no class of nobles whose titles passed from parent to child. But people were still divided into high, middle, and low ranks, as they were in England. Large landholders were high in rank. Small farmers who owned their land were in the middle rank. Most colonists fit this category. People who did not own land, such as servants, slaves, or hired workers, were low in rank. Colonial women held the same rank as their husbands or fathers.

Colonists showed respect to their "betters" by curtsying or tipping a hat, for example. Seats in church were assigned by rank, with wealthy families in the front pews and poor people in the back. Despite such divisions, the wealthy were expected to aid the poor.

Reading **History**
A. Finding Main Ideas What did colonists gain by owning land?
A. Answer
Prosperity, political rights, and a higher social position.

2 Women and the Economy

Although women were not landholders, their work was essential to the colonial economy. As you learned in Chapter 4, enslaved African women helped raise cash crops such as tobacco and indigo. Most white women were farm wives who performed tasks and made products their families needed. They cooked, churned butter, made soap and candles, spun fibers, wove cloth, sewed and knitted clothes, and did many other chores. They usually tended a garden and looked after farm animals. At harvest time, they often worked in the fields alongside men and older children.

Because cash was scarce, farm wives bartered, or traded, with their neighbors for goods and services. For example, a woman who nursed a sick neighbor or helped deliver a baby might be paid in sugar or cloth.

Women in towns and cities usually did the same types of housework that rural women did. In addition, some urban women ran inns or other businesses. Madam Knight, whose journey was described in One American's Story on page 119, sold writing paper, taught handwriting, and rented rooms to guests. A few women, usually the wives or widows of tradesmen, practiced trades themselves.

Reading **History**
B. Finding Main Ideas In what ways was women's work essential to the economy?
B. Answer
Women did tasks and made products necessary for their families and neighbors. They also ran some businesses.

Although women contributed to the colonial economy, they did not have many rights. Women could not vote. In most churches, they could not preach or hold office. (Quaker meetings were an exception.) A married woman could not own property without her husband's permission. By law, even the money a woman earned belonged to her husband.

Young People at Work

Children's work also supported the colonial economy. Families were large. New England families, for example, had an average of six to eight children. More children meant more workers. Children as young as three or four were expected to be useful. They might help look after farm animals, gather berries, and watch younger children.

ACTIVITY OPTIONS

SKILLBUILDER LESSON: FINDING MAIN IDEAS

BLOCK SCHEDULING

Explaining the Skill The main idea of a paragraph or section is the most important point of the writer. Finding the main idea helps the student understand the focus of a paragraph or section. The heading of every section in the textbook tells the topic of that section; the main ideas about the topic are presented in the paragraphs that follow the heads.

Applying the Skill Ask the students to find the heading "Women and the Economy." Tell students to read the section or ask for volunteers to read it aloud.

1. Ask students to summarize the section in their own words. Then ask them to identify the sentence that contains the main idea. *(the first sentence of the section)*
2. Direct students to the next section, "Young People at Work." Challenge them to find the sentence that states the main idea. *(the first sentence of the section)*

In-Depth Resources: Unit 1
- Skillbuilder Practice, p. 82

Around age six, boys were "breeched." This meant that they no longer wore the skirts or smocks of all young children but were given a pair of pants. They then began to help their fathers at work. Sons of farmers worked all day clearing land and learning to farm. Sons of craftsmen tended their fathers' shops and learned their fathers' trades.

Around age 11, many boys left their fathers to become apprentices. An **apprentice** learned a trade from an experienced craftsman. The apprentice received food, clothing, lodging, and a general education, as well as training in the specific craft or business. He worked for free, usually for four to seven years, until his contract was fulfilled. Then he could work for wages or start his own business.

Girls rarely were apprenticed. They learned sewing and other household skills from their mothers. In New England, girls of 13 or 14 often were sent away to other households to learn specialized skills such as weaving or cheese making. Orphaned girls and boys worked as servants for families who housed and fed them until adulthood.

Reading **History**
C. Contrasting How did the training of boys and girls differ?
C. Answer Boys learned from their fathers or were apprenticed to craftsmen. Girls learned from their mothers or neighbors.

3 Colonial Schooling

If land, wealth, and hard work were valued across the colonies, so was education. Most children were taught to read so that they could understand the Bible. Only children from wealthy families went beyond reading to learn writing and arithmetic. These children learned either from private tutors or in private schools. Poorer children sometimes learned to read from their mothers.

HISTORY *through* ART

This drawing shows the inside of an 18th-century one-room schoolhouse.

What does the picture suggest to you about colonial schooling?

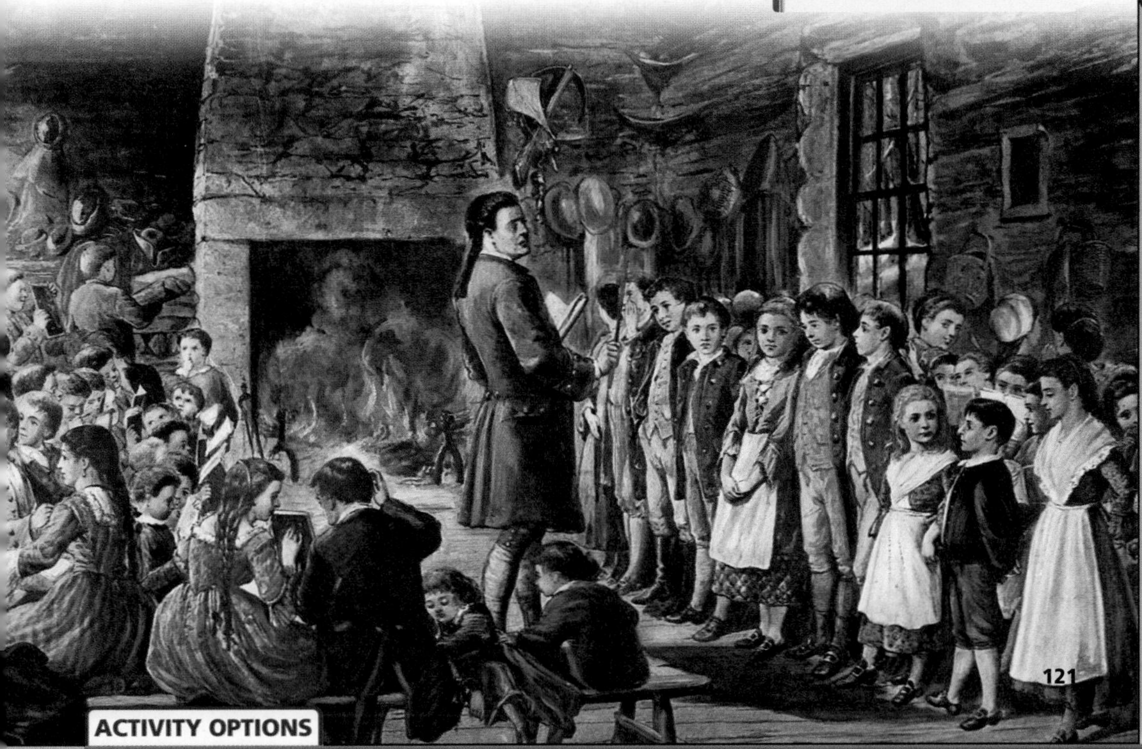

121

MORE ABOUT . . .

Apprentices
If orphan children had no relatives or neighbors willing to take them in, they were "bound out" as apprentices. In Pennsylvania and in the Southern Colonies, these orphan apprentices were treated in the same manner as indentured servants.

HISTORY *through* ART

Interpreting the Drawing Tell the students the schoolroom scene pictured here was not a common one in all colonies. Although most colonists had a great respect for education, and many were eager to establish and support free grammar schools, they often did not have resources of time and money.

Possible Response: It suggests that schoolrooms were crowded but orderly and that children of different ages learned together.

INSTRUCT: OBJECTIVE 3

Colonial Schooling/Newspapers and Books

- Why were most colonial children taught to read?
- What were some common colonial attitudes about the importance of education?
- What types of books did colonists read?

ACTIVITY OPTIONS

MULTIPLE LEARNING STYLES: KINESTHETIC — BLOCK SCHEDULING

ROLE PLAY

Class Time 30 minutes

Task Dramatizing differences between colonial and contemporary youth

Purpose To describe the daily lives of colonial children

Supplies Needed
- Textbook pages 120–121
- Props or costumes (optional)

Activity Divide the class into groups of six. In each group, designate three students as colonial young people and three students as contemporary young people. Have each group present a conversation between colonials and contemporaries. Students can discuss differences in clothing, pastimes, manners, chores, or a typical day in their lives. Students should be able to support their conversations as colonial youngsters with evidence from the painting on page 121 or from the text.

daily*life*

The School of Manners

During the 17th century, nearly all the textbooks used in the colonies were imported from England. The earliest "textbooks" printed in the colonies appeared in the late 1600s and were actually reprints of English books. Well into the 1700s, books remained scarce in the colonies, and costly.

MORE ABOUT . . .

Newspapers and Books

In 1671, royal appointee Governor William Berkeley of Virginia proudly told the king: "there are no free schools nor printing, and I hope we shall not have these . . . for learning has brought disobedience, and heresy, and sects into the world, and printing has divulged them, and libels against the best government. God keep us from both!"

Governor Berkeley's hope was not realized: By the mid-1700s, most colonies had established weekly newspapers. And, just as Berkeley had feared, the political discussions in the newspapers were highly influential in breaking down relations with the Crown—and preparing the colonists for revolution.

daily *life*

THE SCHOOL OF MANNERS

Colonial children learned proper behavior from *The School of Manners,* a book published in 1701. Here are examples of rules and an illustration from the book.

"Spit not in the Room, but in a corner, and rub it out with thy Foot, or rather go out and do it abroad."

"If thou meetest the scholars of any other School jeer not nor affront them, but show them love and respect and quietly let them pass along."

Or they attended "dame schools," where women taught the alphabet and used the Bible to teach reading. Most children finished their formal education at age seven.

Children's textbooks emphasized religion. The widely used *New England Primer* paired the letter *A* with the verse "In *Adam's* fall / We Sinned all." Beside the letter *B* was a picture of the Bible. The primer contained the Lord's Prayer and *The Shorter Catechism,* more than 100 questions and answers about religion.

Colonial America had a high literacy rate, as measured by the number of people who could sign their names. In New England, 85 percent of white men were literate, compared with 60 percent of men in England. In the Middle Colonies, 65 percent of white men were literate, and in the South, about 50 percent were. In each region of the colonies, roughly half as many white women as men were literate. Most colonists thought schooling was more important for males. Educated African Americans were rare. If they were enslaved, teaching them to read was illegal. If they were free, they were often kept out of schools.

Reading **History**

D. Contrasting How was colonial education different from education today?

D. Answer Education today lasts longer, covers more subjects, is less religious, and is available to more people.

Newspapers and Books

Colonial readers supported a publishing industry that also drew the colonies together. In the early 1700s, the colonies had only one local newspaper, the *Boston News-letter.* But over the next 70 years, almost 80 different newspapers appeared in America. Many were published for decades.

Most books in the colonies were imported from England, but colonists slowly began to publish their own books. Almanacs were very popular. A typical almanac included a calendar, weather predictions, star charts, farming advice, home remedies, recipes, jokes, and proverbs. In 1732, Benjamin Franklin began to publish *Poor Richard's Almanack.* It contained sayings that are still repeated today, such as "Haste makes waste."

Colonists also published poetry, regional histories, and autobiographies. Most personal stories told of struggles to maintain religious faith during hard times. A form of literature unique to the Americas was the captivity narrative. In it, a colonist captured by Native Americans described living among them.

Reading **History**

E. Categorizing What were some types of colonial literature?

E. Answer Newspapers, almanacs, poetry, histories, autobiographies, captivity narratives.

Mary Rowlandson's 1682 captivity narrative, *The Sovereignty and Goodness of God,* was one of the first colonial bestsellers. Native Americans attacked Rowlandson's Massachusetts village in 1676, during King Philip's War. They held her hostage for 11 weeks. During that time, she was a servant to a Narragansett chieftain, knitting stockings and making shirts for his family and others. "I told them it was Sabbath day," she recalled, "and desired them to let me rest, and told them I

ACTIVITY OPTIONS

INDIVIDUAL NEEDS: GIFTED AND TALENTED

FRANKLIN'S PROVERBS

Class Time 20 minutes

Task Writing explanations or contemporary versions of proverbs from *Poor Richard's Almanac*

Purpose To familiarize students with the literary form of the proverb and with Franklin's writings

Supplies Needed
- Copies of *Poor Richard's Almanac* or books of quotations including proverbs by Benjamin Franklin
- Paper

Activity Direct students to read some of Franklin's proverbs or read several aloud to the class. Tell students to choose one proverb and rewrite it in contemporary terms, or write a brief explanation of the proverb's meaning. Ask students to share their work. Some students may wish to make illustrated posters presenting their proverb for display.

Vocabulary
ransom: to pay for a captive's release

would do as much more tomorrow. To which they answered me, they would break my face." After townspeople raised money to ransom Rowlandson, she was released. Although she mourned a young daughter who had died in captivity, she praised God for returning her safely.

4 The Great Awakening

Mary Rowlandson's religious faith was central to her life. But in the early 1700s, many colonists feared they had lost the religious passion that had driven their ancestors to found the colonies. Religion seemed dry, dull, and distant, even to regular churchgoers.

In the 1730s and 1740s, a religious movement called the **Great Awakening** swept through the colonies. The traveling ministers of this movement preached that inner religious emotion was more important than outward religious behavior. Their sermons appealed to the heart and drew large crowds. **Jonathan Edwards,** one of the best-known preachers, terrified listeners with images of God's anger but promised they could be saved.

Background
Religious meetings with large, intensely emotional crowds remain part of American religious tradition.

A VOICE FROM THE PAST

And now you have an extraordinary opportunity, a day wherein Christ has thrown the door of mercy wide open, and stands in calling and crying with a loud voice to poor sinners. . . . How awful it is to be left behind at such a day!

Jonathan Edwards, "Sinners in the Hands of an Angry God"

The Great Awakening lasted for years and changed colonial culture. Congregations argued over religious practices and often split apart. People left their old churches and joined other Protestant groups such as Baptists. Some of these groups welcomed women, African Americans, and Native Americans. Overall, churches gained 20,000 to 50,000 new members. To train ministers, religious groups founded colleges such as Princeton and Brown.

The Great Awakening inspired colonists to help others. **George Whitefield** (HWIT•feeld) drew thousands of people with his sermons and raised funds to start a home for orphans. Other ministers taught Christianity and reading to Native Americans and African Americans. The

George Whitefield preaching to a crowd

INSTRUCT: OBJECTIVE 4

The Great Awakening/The Enlightenment

- What was the Great Awakening? How did it change colonial culture?
- How did the Enlightenment affect the colonies?
- In what ways were the Great Awakening and the Enlightenment similar? How were they different?

MORE ABOUT . . .

The Great Awakening

The preachers of the Great Awakening challenged the regular clerics of the colonies. While these clerics at first welcomed the visiting preachers, they soon found that the teachings of the traveling ministers contradicted their own. Many congregations split into two factions: "Old Lights," adherents of traditional religious teaching, and "New Lights," followers of evangelistic preachers such as George Whitefield. New Lights affected the colonial way of thinking, bringing greater tolerance for independent thinking. Far more than traditional clerics, New Lights were willing to challenge authority, including political and social authority.

ACTIVITY OPTIONS

INTERDISCIPLINARY LINK: SCIENCE — BLOCK SCHEDULING

USING *THE OLD FARMER'S ALMANAC*

Class Time 15 minutes

Task Using *The Old Farmer's Almanac* as a reference source

Purpose To allow students to explore an almanac as a reference source

Supplies Needed
- Copies of *The Old Farmer's Almanac* or Internet access: see classzone.com

Activity Remind students that almanacs were among the first books published by the colonists. Point out that almanacs such as *The Old Farmer's Almanac* are still widely used today.

Encourage students to skim the almanac and locate information for the current year about such topics as the calendar, weather predictions, star charts, or farming advice. Ask students why this information would have been important to colonists. Ask students to identify other resources where colonists might have found this kind of information.

AMERICA'S HISTORY MAKERS

Benjamin Franklin

Benjamin Franklin was a self-made, self-educated man who directed his life by using his intelligence, talents, and freedom. Franklin gained wealth and fame through his own hard work and moved upward in social class. He became the symbolic American for many Europeans of his time. He deliberately contributed to his own "frontier" image in Europe by often wearing a fur cap and always speaking in plain, direct language.

Answer: by inventing useful products, founding institutions, and promoting independence

America's History Makers
- Benjamin Franklin, pp. 19–20

Humanities Transparency HT9
- *Benjamin Franklin* by Robert Feke

ASSESS & RETEACH

Setting the Stage Have students fill in the Economy, Publishing, Education, and Religion sections on the chapter graphic organizer.

Formal Assessment
- Section Quiz, p. 85

Critical Thinking Transparency CT13
- Setting the Stage

RETEACHING ACTIVITY

Divide students into three teams. Assign each team one of the following viewpoints: that of a colonial woman, a colonial child, or a colonial minister. Have each team work together to write a description of colonial life based on the point of view assigned them. Allow time for groups to share and discuss descriptions.

In-Depth Resources: Unit 1
- Reteaching Activity, p. 90

AMERICA'S HISTORY MAKERS

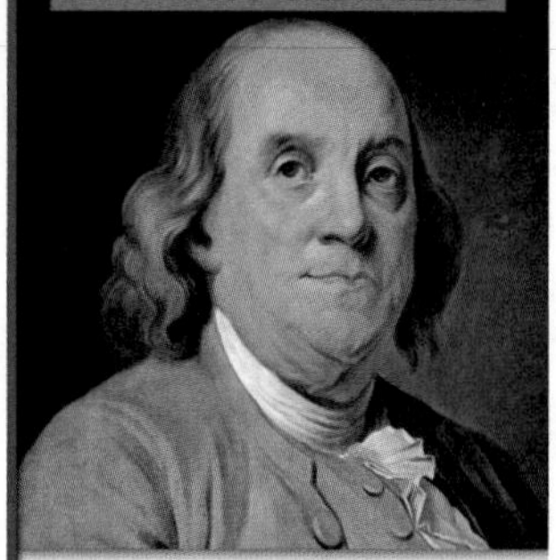

BENJAMIN FRANKLIN
1706–1790

As an Enlightenment thinker, Benjamin Franklin used reason to improve society. At 42, he retired from business to devote his life to science and public service. He proved that lightning was a form of electricity. Then he invented the lightning rod to protect buildings. The Franklin stove and bifocal eyeglasses were also his inventions. He organized a fire department, a lending library, and a society to discuss philosophy. Later he helped draft the Declaration of Independence.

How did Franklin help improve colonial society?

Great Awakening encouraged ideas of equality and the right to challenge authority. In this way, the movement contributed to the revolutionary fervor of the colonists when they declared independence from England years later.

Reading **History**
F. Recognizing Effects What were five effects of the Great Awakening?
F. Answer It encouraged religious debate, church membership, new colleges, charitable projects, and ideas of equality and independence.

The Enlightenment

Unlike the Great Awakening, which stressed religious emotion, the **Enlightenment** emphasized reason and science as the paths to knowledge. **Benjamin Franklin** was a famous American Enlightenment figure. This intellectual movement appealed mostly to wealthy, educated men. But it, too, had far-reaching effects on the colonies.

The Enlightenment began in Europe, as scientists discovered natural laws governing the universe. Isaac Newton, for example, explained the law of gravity.

Other Enlightenment thinkers applied the idea of natural law to human societies. The English philosopher **John Locke** argued that people have natural rights. These are rights to life, liberty, and property. People create governments to protect their natural rights, he claimed. If a government fails in this duty, people have the right to change it. Locke challenged the belief that kings had a God-given right to rule.

Background
Locke argued against the idea that the kings had a God-given right to rule. But he still believed that the natural rights of individuals came from God.

Enlightenment ideas of natural rights and government by agreement influenced leaders across Europe and the colonies. As you will see in Section 2, colonists began to wonder whether the British government protected their rights and freedoms. Eventually, they would rebel and form a new government.

Section 1 Assessment

1. Terms & Names

Explain the significance of:
- apprentice
- Great Awakening
- Jonathan Edwards
- George Whitefield
- Enlightenment
- Benjamin Franklin
- John Locke

2. Taking Notes

Describe the parts of colonial culture in a chart.

Economy	
Education	
Publishing	
Religion	

Why was each important in colonial culture?

3. Main Ideas

a. Why was land ownership so important to the colonists?

b. How did women and young people contribute to the colonial economy?

c. How did the Great Awakening affect the colonies?

4. Critical Thinking

Contrasting How were the Great Awakening and the Enlightenment different?

THINK ABOUT
- the ideas each movement promoted
- the people to whom each movement appealed

ACTIVITY OPTIONS

LANGUAGE ARTS
ART

Make up a **saying** that reflects some part of colonial culture, or draw an **illustration** of a saying from colonial times.

Section 1 Assessment

1. Terms & Names

apprentice, p. 121
Great Awakening, p. 123
Jonathan Edwards, p. 123
George Whitefield, p. 123
Enlightenment, p. 124
Benjamin Franklin, p. 124
John Locke, p. 124

2. Taking Notes

Econ—small farming
Edu—emphasis on religion; many colonists semiliterate
Pub—80 different newspapers
Rel—Great Awakening

Each part helped to create a new American cultural identity for the colonists.

3. Main Ideas

a. It allowed them to gain wealth and political rights. **b.** Enslaved women raised cash crops; free women ran businesses; young people learned trades. **c.** It encouraged deep religious feelings and led congregations to debate, split apart, and gain new members. It also bolstered a revolutionary attitude.

4. Critical Thinking

The Great Awakening was a religious movement that appealed to emotion. The Enlightenment was an intellectual movement that emphasized reason and science.

ACTIVITY OPTIONS

Integrated Assessment
- Rubrics for an advertisement, 4.9
- Rubrics for an illustration, 1.3

2 Roots of Representative Government

TERMS & NAMES
Magna Carta
Parliament
Edmund Andros
Glorious Revolution
English Bill of Rights
salutary neglect
John Peter Zenger

MAIN IDEA
Colonists expected their government to preserve their basic rights as English subjects.

WHY IT MATTERS NOW
U.S. citizens expect these same rights, such as the right to a trial by jury.

ONE AMERICAN'S STORY

On April 7, 1688, the famous Puritan minister Increase Mather set sail for England. He was to speak to King James II to get relief for the Massachusetts colony. The English government had canceled the charter of Massachusetts and sent a royal governor to rule.

The colonists thought that the governor trampled their rights as English subjects. Mather stayed in England for four years. During this time, he saw the king driven out and replaced by new rulers. In the end, he came home with a new charter that he hoped would satisfy the New England colonists.

This is a detail of *Increase Mather* by Jan van der Spriett.

A VOICE FROM THE PAST

For all English liberties are restored to them: No Persons shall have a Penny of their Estates taken from them; nor any Laws imposed on them, without their own Consent by Representatives chosen by themselves.

Increase Mather, quoted in *The Last American Puritan*

Mather called the new charter "a Magna Carta for New England." In this section, you will learn about the rights of English people set forth in the Magna Carta and later documents. These rights are the basis for the rights Americans enjoy today, such as the right not to be jailed without cause and the right to a jury trial.

1 The Rights of Englishmen

English colonists expected certain rights that came from living under an English government. These "rights of Englishmen" had developed over centuries.

The first step toward guaranteeing these rights came in 1215. That year, a group of English noblemen forced King John to accept the **Magna Carta** (Great Charter). The king needed the nobles' money to finance a war. This document guaranteed important rights to noblemen and freemen—those not bound to a master. They could not have their property seized by the king or his officials. They could not be taxed, in most

SECTION OBJECTIVES

1. To identify the rights that colonists expected as English subjects
2. To explain why colonies challenged the rule of Governor Edmund Andros
3. To evaluate how England's Glorious Revolution affected the colonies
4. To explain the importance of the Zenger trial verdict

SKILLBUILDER
Interpreting Charts, p. 128

CRITICAL THINKING
Comparing, p. 126
Making Inferences, p. 127
Recognizing Effects, p. 127
Drawing Conclusions, p. 129
Supporting Opinions, p. 129

FOCUS & MOTIVATE

5-MINUTE WARM-UP

Analyzing Causes These questions focus on the colonial expectation of representative government.

1. Read the quotation on page 125. Which liberties does Mather say are restored to the colonists?
2. What phrase implies that eligible colonists have the right to vote?

Warm-Up Transparency WT5

INSTRUCT

INSTRUCT: OBJECTIVE 1

The Rights of Englishmen/ Parliament and Colonial Government

- What rights does the Magna Carta guarantee?
- What was the purpose of the colonial assemblies?
- How could the king limit the power of the colonial assemblies?

In-Depth Resources: Unit 1
- Guided Reading, p. 79

RECOMMENDED RESOURCES

In-Depth Resources: Unit 1
- Guided Reading, p. 79
- Building Vocabulary, p. 81
- Enrichment Activity, p. 93

Reading Study Guide (Spanish and English), pp. 41–42

Citizenship Today, pp. 1–2

American History Plays
- *The Trial of Peter Zenger*

Formal Assessment
- Section Quiz, p. 86

Integrated Assessment
- Rubrics, 3.6, 1.13

Access for Students Acquiring English/ESL
- Guided Reading, p. 27

INTEGRATED TECHNOLOGY

Electronic Teacher Tools

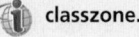

classzone.com

TEST-TAKING RESOURCES

Strategies for Test Preparation

Test Practice Transparencies, TT18

Online Test Practice

CRITICAL THINKING ACTIVITY

Contrasting Copy the following graphic onto the chalkboard. Ask students to read the paragraphs under the heading "Parliament and Colonial Government." Then have the students compare the colonists' expectation of representative government to the reality of government by the British.

Right to Representative Government	
Colonists' Expectations	**British Authority**
To elect representatives to government	Colonists did not send representatives to Parliament, but Parliament made laws that affected the colonies.

Class Time 10 minutes

cases, unless a council of prominent men agreed. They could not be put to trial based only on an official's word, without witnesses. They could be punished only by a jury of their peers, people of the same social rank.

A VOICE FROM THE PAST

No freeman shall be seized, imprisoned, dispossessed, outlawed, or exiled, . . . nor will we proceed against or prosecute him except by the lawful judgment of his peers, or by the law of the land.

Magna Carta, translated in *A Documentary History of England*

Reading **History**

A. Comparing What rights from the Magna Carta remain rights in America today?

A. Answer Trial by jury, protection from arbitrary taxation and seizure of property

The Magna Carta limited the powers of the king. Over time, the rights it listed were granted to all English people, not just noblemen and freemen.

Parliament and Colonial Government

One of the most important English rights was the right to elect representatives to government. **Parliament,** England's chief lawmaking body, was the colonists' model for representative government. Parliament was made up of two houses. Members of the House of Commons were elected by the people. Members of the House of Lords were nonelected nobles, judges, and church officials.

The king and Parliament were too far away to manage every detail of the colonies. Also, like the citizens of England, English colonists in America wanted to have a say in the laws governing them. So they formed

CITIZENSHIP TODAY

OBJECTIVE

Students will be able to explain the value of trial by jury and the importance of serving as a juror.

Serving on Juries

Jurors are selected from sources such as tax rolls, voting lists, and telephone directories. The Constitution states that jurors in a criminal trial (one that determines the guilt or innocence of a person accused of a crime) must be neutral regarding the case. In addition, a juror must be selected from the community where the crime is supposed to have happened. Every juror is questioned by both defense and prosecuting lawyers, and either lawyer may reject a juror if he/she feels the juror would not serve fairly.

Citizenship Today, pp. 1–2

CITIZENSHIP TODAY

The Importance of Juries

The right to a trial by jury, established in the Magna Carta, is an important legal right. When you become an adult, you will likely be asked to serve on a jury.

Many young people in Knox County, Illinois, have already served as jurors on a teen court (shown below, with an advisor). They decide the best punishment for other teenagers who have admitted breaking a law. For example, shoplifters might be sentenced to write an apology to the store. Knox County is one of more than 500 U.S. communities that have teen courts.

Knox County Teen Court volunteers

How Can You Serve on a Teen Court?

1. Search the library or Internet to learn more about teen courts.
2. Ask the police department whether your town has a teen court. If it does, volunteer.
3. If you want to start a teen court, seek advice from a community that has one.
4. Invite a lawyer to your class to talk about a juror's role.
5. Find a group to sponsor your court, and get support from youth officers and judges.

See the Citizenship Handbook, page 264.

For more about courts and juries . . .

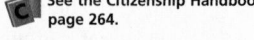

RESEARCH LINKS CLASSZONE.COM

STANDARDS FOR EVALUATION

Each student should

- engage in productive research.

Student groups should

- contact the police department and communities that have teen courts.
- prepare an invitation to a lawyer that includes an explanation of the topic for discussion.
- explore community support for a teen court by contacting youth officers and judges.

their own elected assemblies, similar to the House of Commons. Virginia's House of Burgesses was the first of these. In Pennsylvania, William Penn allowed colonists to have their own General Assembly. These Virginia and Pennsylvania assemblies imposed taxes and managed the colonies.

Although the colonists governed themselves in some ways, England still had authority over them. The king appointed royal governors to rule some colonies on his behalf. Parliament had no representatives from the colonies. Even so, it passed laws that affected the colonies. The colonists disliked these laws, and they began to clash with royal governors over how much power England should have in America. These conflicts became more intense in the late 1600s.

*Reading*History
B. Making Inferences Why did the colonists dislike laws passed by Parliament?
B. Answer They had no say in making those laws.

2 A Royal Governor's Rule

"You have no more privileges left you."
a Boston court official

The reign of James II threatened the colonies' tradition of self-government. James became king in 1685. He wanted to rule England and its colonies with total authority. One of his first orders changed the way the Northern colonies were governed. These colonies, especially Massachusetts, had been smuggling goods and ignoring the Navigation Acts (see Chapter 4). When challenged, the people of Massachusetts had claimed that England had no right to make laws for them. The previous king, Charles II, had then canceled their charter.

The colonists hated Governor Andros.

King James combined Massachusetts and the other Northern colonies into one Dominion of New England, ruled by royal governor **Edmund Andros.** Andros angered the colonists by ending their representative assemblies and allowing town meetings to be held only once a year.

*Reading*History
C. Recognizing Effects How did James II weaken self-government in the colonies?
C. Answers He put the New England colonies under one royal governor, abolished their assemblies, and limited town meetings.

With their assemblies outlawed, some colonists refused to pay taxes. They said that being taxed without having a voice in government violated their rights. Andros jailed the loudest complainers. At their trial, they were told, "You have no more privileges left you than not to be Sould [sold] for Slaves."

The colonists sent Increase Mather to England to plead with King James (see One American's Story on page 125). However, a revolution in England swept King James and Governor Andros from power.

Background
England had become Protestant in the 16th century. Catholics were kept out of high office.

3 England's Glorious Revolution

The English Parliament had decided to overthrow King James for not respecting its rights. Events came to a head in 1688. King James, a Catholic, had been trying to pack his next Parliament with officials who would overturn anti-Catholic laws. He had dismissed the last Parliament in 1685. The Protestant leaders of Parliament were outraged. They offered

INSTRUCT: OBJECTIVE 2
A Royal Governor's Rule

- Who was Edmund Andros?
- Why did he anger the residents of Massachusetts?
- What rights did Andros deny to the colonists?

MORE ABOUT . . .

Edmund Andros

Andros arrived in New England with a troop of English soldiers and a naval frigate—a clear sign of his intentions for the colonies. Andros violated colonial rights in several ways. He placed the militia under his direct control. He dispensed with juries for those accused of breaking trade laws. He also decreed that juries could be appointed by sheriffs, who were themselves appointed by royal decree. Other unpopular actions by the royal governor included converting Boston's Old South Meeting House into an Anglican church.

INSTRUCT: OBJECTIVE 3
England's Glorious Revolution

- What happened in England during the Glorious Revolution?
- What rights were guaranteed in the English Bill of Rights?
- How did colonists react to the Glorious Revolution and the new English Bill of Rights?

ACTIVITY OPTIONS

INTERDISCIPLINARY LINK: GOVERNMENT/CIVICS — BLOCK SCHEDULING

GOVERNOR ANDROS ON TRIAL

Class Time 20 minutes

Task Holding a mock trial of Governor Andros

Purpose To understand colonial displeasure with Governor Andros and to engage in a trial-like simulation

Supplies Needed
- Textbook

Activity Form students into two groups: One group (royal supporters) will defend Edmund Andros and the other (colonists) will prosecute him. Alternating from group to group, have colonists present an accusation against Andros, then ask royal supporters to respond to the accusation. When students have exhausted their accusations, call time and ask students to write on a piece of paper whether they find Andros guilty of grossly violating colonists' rights or whether they find him innocent.

INSTRUCT: OBJECTIVE 4

Shared Power in the Colonies/ The Zenger Trial

- How were most colonial governments organized after the Glorious Revolution?
- What was Parliament's policy toward the colonies after the Glorious Revolution?
- What right was at stake in the Zenger trial?

American History Plays
- *The Trial of Peter Zenger* by Paul T. Nolan

HISTORY FROM VISUALS

Reading the Chart Have students study the directional arrows, noting that only one suggests interaction. Ask students which kind of official would be most responsive to the people: one appointed by the monarch or one elected by the people. **Possible Response** Students may note that an elected official is always aware of his or her standing with the voters.

Extension Ask students to identify which parts of colonial government made laws, enforced the laws, and administered justice through the courts.

the throne to James's Protestant daughter, Mary, and her husband, William of Orange. William was the ruler of the Netherlands. Having little support from the people, James fled the country at the end of 1688. Parliament named William and Mary the new monarchs of England. This change in leadership was called England's **Glorious Revolution.**

After accepting the throne, William and Mary agreed in 1689 to uphold the **English Bill of Rights.** This was an agreement to respect the rights of English citizens and of Parliament. Under it, the king or queen could not cancel laws or impose taxes unless Parliament agreed. Free elections and frequent meetings of Parliament must be held. Excessive fines and cruel punishments were forbidden. People had the right to complain to the king or queen in Parliament without being arrested.

Background The English Bill of Rights was the model for the Bill of Rights in the U.S. Constitution.

The English Bill of Rights established an important principle: the government was to be based on laws made by Parliament, not on the desires of a ruler. The rights of English people were strengthened.

The American colonists were quick to claim these rights. When the people of Boston heard of King James's fall, they jailed Governor Andros and asked Parliament to restore their old government.

Skillbuilder Answers
1. Governor and council were appointed; assembly was elected.
2. Assembly made laws, but governor approved the laws.

Shared Power in the Colonies 4

After the Glorious Revolution, the Massachusetts colonists regained some self-government. They could again elect representatives to an assembly. However, they still had a governor appointed by the crown.

Background Massachusetts colonists also gained more religious freedom. They no longer had to be church members to vote.

Colonial Government

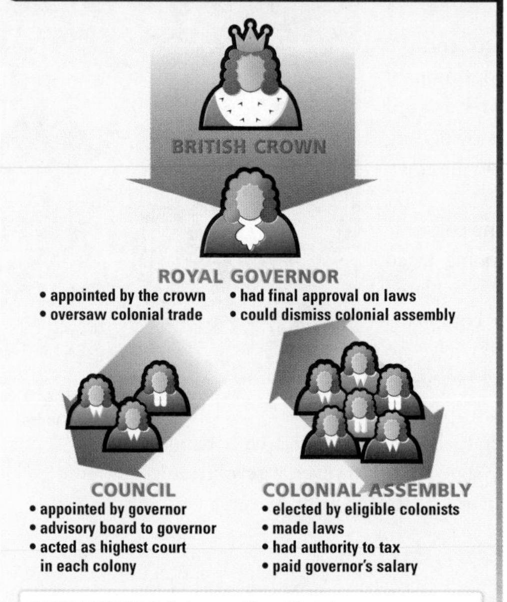

SKILLBUILDER Interpreting Charts
1. *Which officials were appointed, and which were elected?*
2. *How were lawmaking powers shared?*

The diagram on this page shows how most colonial governments were organized by 1700. Note how the royal governor, his council, and the colonial assembly shared power. The governor could strike down laws passed by the assembly, but the assembly was responsible for the governor's salary. If he blocked the assembly, the assembly might refuse to pay him.

During the first half of the 1700s, England interfered very little in colonial affairs. This hands-off policy was called **salutary neglect.** Parliament passed many laws regulating trade, the use of money, and even apprenticeships in the colonies. But governors rarely enforced these laws. The colonists got used to acting on their own.

Vocabulary salutary: healthful or beneficial

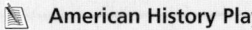

ACTIVITY OPTIONS

INDIVIDUAL NEEDS

STUDENTS ACQUIRING ENGLISH/ESL

Understanding Political Terms Write the words *appointed* and *elected* on the board. Discuss the differences between being appointed to an office and being chosen by the voting process.

Refer students to the chart *Colonial Government* on this page. Point out the appointed and the elected officials. Explain that some government officials are appointed today while others are elected by citizens. Create a chart such as the one shown in which you list current appointed and elected officials.

Appointed	Elected
Judges	President
Ambassadors	Governor
Members of Cabinet	Senator
Postmaster General	Member of Congress
	Mayor

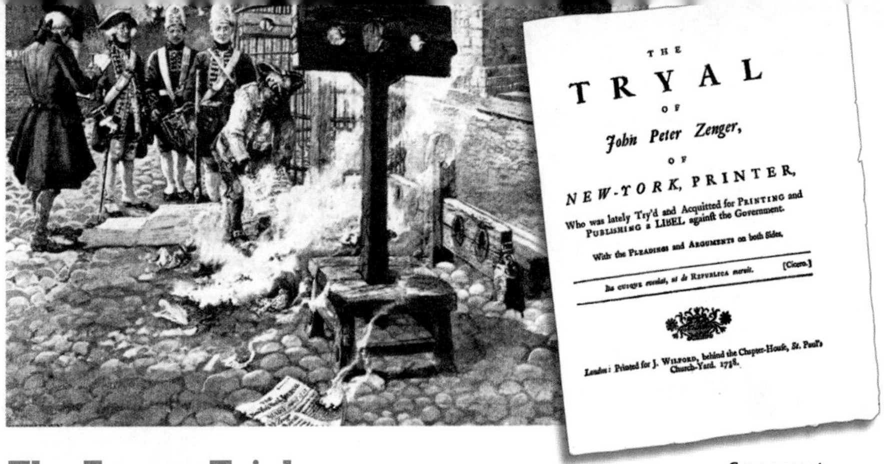

Government officials burn the *New-York Weekly Journal.*

The Zenger Trial

Colonists moved toward gaining a new right, freedom of the press, in 1735. That year, **John Peter Zenger,** publisher of the *New-York Weekly Journal,* stood trial for printing criticism of New York's governor. The governor had removed a judge and tried to fix an election.

> ***A VOICE FROM THE PAST***
>
> A Governor turns rogue [criminal], does a thousand things for which a small rogue would have deserved a halter [hanging], and because it is difficult . . . to obtain relief against him, . . . it is prudent [wise] to . . . join in the roguery.
>
> ***New-York Weekly Journal,*** quoted in *Colonial America, 1607–1763*

At that time, it was illegal to criticize the government in print. Andrew Hamilton defended Zenger at his trial, claiming that people had the right to speak the truth. The jury agreed, and Zenger was released.

English rights were part of the heritage uniting people in the British colonies. In the next section, you will read about another unifying force—a war against the French and their Indian allies.

D. Answer The jury would not punish Zenger for criticizing the government.

***Reading* History**

D. Drawing Conclusions Why was the Zenger trial a step toward freedom of the press?

Section 2 Assessment

1. Terms & Names

Explain the significance of:

- Magna Carta
- Parliament
- Edmund Andros
- Glorious Revolution
- English Bill of Rights
- salutary neglect
- John Peter Zenger

2. Taking Notes

In the boxes, show how the rights of English people developed in the three years mentioned.

English Rights: 1215 | 1689 | 1735

Which right is most important to you?

3. Main Ideas

a. What were three of the traditional rights expected by English colonists?

b. In what ways did the English government anger the colonists in the late 1600s?

c. How did England's policies toward the colonies change after the Glorious Revolution?

4. Critical Thinking

Supporting Opinions

In your opinion, who had the most power—the royal governor, the council, or the assemblies? Defend your opinion.

THINK ABOUT

- their roles in making laws
- their roles in raising money
- who had final approval in matters

ACTIVITY OPTIONS

SPEECH

ART

Deliver **closing arguments** or create a **leaflet** defending John Peter Zenger and freedom of the press.

MORE ABOUT . . .

John Peter Zenger

John Peter Zenger immigrated to New York in 1710 from Germany. A group of powerful men opposed to the actions of Governor William Cosby hired Zenger to print and publish articles critical of the governor, until Cosby had him arrested. Zenger was held in jail for ten months. Zenger expressed his view of freedom of the press in these words: "No nation ancient or modern ever lost the liberty of freely speaking, writing, or publishing their sentiments but forthwith lost their liberty in general and became slaves."

In-Depth Resources: Unit 1
- Enrichment Activity, p. 93

ASSESS & RETEACH

Setting the Stage Have students fill in the Political Ideas section on the chapter graphic organizer.

Formal Assessment
- Section Quiz, p. 86

RETEACHING ACTIVITY

Copy the graphic onto the chalkboard. Ask students to fill in the reasons the effects came about.

Problems	Reasons	Effects
Colonists disliked laws passed by Parliament that affected them.		Colonists began to clash with royal governors.
From about 1700 to 1750, the British government interfered very little in colonial affairs.		The colonists became accustomed to acting on their own.
John Peter Zenger was placed on trial for his criticism of the governor of New York.		The colonists moved toward freedom of the press.

In-Depth Resources: Unit 1
- Reteaching Activity, p. 91

Section 2 Assessment

1. Terms & Names

Magna Carta, p. 125
Parliament, p. 126
Edmund Andros, p. 127
Glorious Revolution, p. 128
English Bill of Rights, p. 128
salutary neglect, p. 128
John Peter Zenger, p. 129

2. Taking Notes

1215—King John signed the Magna Carta.
1689—English Bill of Rights established Parliament's supremacy over the Crown in making laws.
1735—Zenger trial helped establish freedom of the press.

Responses will vary.

3. Main Ideas

a. property could not be seized without reason; taxes could not be levied without representation; trial by jury; the power to elect representatives **b.** placing royal governors in charge of the colonies and outlawing assemblies **c.** England instituted a policy of salutary neglect.

4. Critical Thinking

Student answers may vary. Be sure the defense of their choice is accurate.

ACTIVITY OPTIONS

Integrated Assessment
- Rubrics for a speech, 3.6
- Rubrics for a leaflet, 1.13

SECTION OBJECTIVES

1. To identify French colonial claims
2. To trace the French and Indian War
3. To explain how the British won the French and Indian War
4. To evaluate the results of the war

SKILLBUILDER

Interpreting Maps: Place, p. 132
Interpreting Maps: Region, p. 134

CRITICAL THINKING

Recognizing Effects, p. 131
Making Inferences, p. 131
Drawing Conclusions, p. 133
Finding Main Ideas, p. 134
Analyzing Points of View, p. 135

FOCUS & MOTIVATE

5-MINUTE WARM-UP

Reading a Map These questions focus on the French and Indian War.

1. Look at the map on page 134. How many countries claimed North American territory before the French and Indian War? After?
2. Before the war, which country appears to be the biggest threat to British colonists? After?

Warm-Up Transparency WT5

INSTRUCT

INSTRUCT: OBJECTIVE 1

France Claims Western Lands/ Native American Alliances

- What parts of North America were claimed by France?
- Why did Native Americans form alliances with colonists?
- In what ways did France and England clash between 1689 and 1763?

In-Depth Resources: Unit 1
- Guided Reading, p. 80

3 The French and Indian War

TERMS & NAMES
French and Indian War
Albany Plan of Union
Battle of Quebec
Treaty of Paris
Pontiac's Rebellion
Proclamation of 1763

MAIN IDEA	WHY IT MATTERS NOW
Britain's victory in the French and Indian War forced France to give up its North American colonies.	British influence spread over North America, though French populations and place names still exist here.

ONE AMERICAN'S STORY

Charles de Langlade, born in 1729, was the son of a French fur trader and his Ottawa wife. His family controlled the fur trade around what is now Green Bay, Wisconsin.

In 1752, Charles commanded 250 Ottawa and Chippewa warriors in an attack on the village of Pickawillany, in present-day Ohio. His reason: the Miami people who lived there had stopped trading with the French and were now trading with the British. Charles and his men destroyed the village's British trading post and killed the Miami chief. This attack helped lead to the French and Indian War.

This section describes the war, in which French forces fought British forces in North America. Each side had Native American allies. Charles de Langlade led several successful attacks against the British. But in the end, he saw the British drive French armies from the continent.

This 1903 painting by Edward Deming shows Charles de Langlade attacking British forces in 1755.

1 France Claims Western Lands

As you learned in Chapters 2 and 4, the French were exploring the North American interior while English colonists were settling the eastern coast. By the late 1600s, French explorers had claimed the Ohio River valley, the Mississippi River valley, and the entire Great Lakes region. The French territory of Louisiana, claimed by the explorer La Salle in 1682, stretched from the Appalachian Mountains to the Rocky Mountains.

The French built their main settlements, Quebec and Montreal, along the St. Lawrence River in Canada. (See the map on page 132.) They also built forts along the Great Lakes and along rivers draining into the Mississippi. By 1760, the French colony, New France, had a European population of about 80,000. By contrast, the British colonies had more than a million settlers.

Some Europeans in New France were Jesuit priests. They wanted to convert Native Americans to Christianity. Other Europeans in New France worked as fur traders. Native Americans brought furs to French forts and

RECOMMENDED RESOURCES

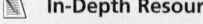

In-Depth Resources: Unit 1
- Guided Reading, p. 80
- Building Vocabulary, p. 81
- Geog. Application, pp. 83–84
- Primary Source, p. 86
- Literature Selection, pp. 87–89

Reading Study Guide (Spanish and English), pp. 43–44

Formal Assessment
- Section Quiz, p. 87

Outline Map Activities, pp. 9–10

Integrated Assessment
- Rubrics, 1.10, 4.8

Access for Students Acquiring English/ESL, pp. 28, 30–31

INTEGRATED TECHNOLOGY

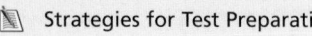

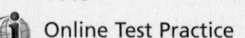

Humanities Transparency HT10
Critical Thinking Trans. CT14
Geography Transparency GT5
Electronic Teacher Tools
classzone.com

TEST-TAKING RESOURCES

Strategies for Test Preparation
Test Practice Transparencies, TT19
Online Test Practice

Background
Often French traders lived among and married Native Americans.

exchanged them for goods such as iron pots and steel knives. Many French traders carried goods by canoe into remote parts of New France.

Native American Alliances

The English competed with the French for furs. Also, different Native American groups competed to supply furs to the Europeans. The fur trade created economic and military alliances between the Europeans and their Native American trading partners. The Huron and Algonquin peoples of the Great Lakes region were allied with the French. The Iroquois of upper New York often were allied with the Dutch and, later, the English.

Background
The Iroquois were a union of six nations.

Alliances between Europeans and Native Americans led to their involvement in each other's wars. For example, by the mid-1600s, the Iroquois had trapped all the beavers in their own lands. To get more furs, they made war on their Huron and Algonquin neighbors, driving them west. Eventually the Iroquois controlled an area ranging from Maine west to the Ohio Valley and north to Lake Michigan. Iroquois expansion threatened the French fur trade. In response, the French armed the Huron and Algonquin peoples to fight the Iroquois. The Iroquois were armed by the English.

***Reading*History**
A. Recognizing Effects How did the fur trade lead to wars?
A. Answer Native American groups competed for furs, and through their alliances with European trading partners, they obtained weapons and became involved in European conflicts.

When France and England declared war on each other in Europe in 1689, French and English colonists in America also began to fight. With their Native American allies, they attacked each other's settlements and forts. During the 1700s, two more wars between France and England fueled wars in their colonies. Neither side won a clear victory in these wars. A final war, the **French and Indian War** (1754–1763), decided which nation would control the northern and eastern parts of North America.

A French trader visits a Native American family.

Conflict in the Ohio River Valley ❷

The seeds for the French and Indian War were planted when British fur traders began moving into the Ohio River valley in the 1750s. British land companies were also planning to settle colonists there. The French and their Native American allies became alarmed. To keep the British out of the valley, Charles de Langlade destroyed the village of Pickawillany and its British trading post (see One American's Story on page 130).

B. Answer To the French, it linked Canada and Louisiana and was a source of furs. To the British, it was also a source of furs and a place for new settlement.

***Reading*History**
B. Making Inferences Why was the Ohio River Valley important to the French and British governments?

The British traders left, and the French built forts to protect the region linking their Canadian and Louisiana settlements. This upset the Virginia colony, which claimed title to the land. In 1753, the lieutenant governor of Virginia sent a small group of soldiers to tell the French to

MORE ABOUT . . .

Native American Alliances
A majority of Native American groups allied with the French, although neither side totally trusted the other. All the non-Iroquois groups—Delaware, Shawnee, Abnaki, Ojibwa, Ottawa, Potawatomi—wanted protection, not only from the British, whom they viewed as arrogant and dishonest, but also from the Iroquois. The extremely powerful Iroquois Confederation hoped to dominate all other tribes, as well as play the French against English, to the destruction of both.

In-Depth Resources: Unit 1
- Geography Application: Native American Confederacies, pp. 83–84

INSTRUCT: OBJECTIVE ❷

Conflict in the Ohio River Valley/ War Begins and Spreads

- How did the French attempt to keep the English out of the Ohio Valley?
- Who are the sides in the French and Indian War?
- Why was the Albany Plan of Union significant?

Outline Map Activities
- Mississippi River Drainage Basin, pp. 9–10

ACTIVITY OPTIONS

INDIVIDUAL NEEDS

LESS PROFICIENT READERS

Sequencing Events To help students understand the events that led up to the French and Indian War and the results of the war, work with them to create a sequence chart of events as they read. Ask students to identify key dates and events and record them on the board.

1689 French and English are at war in Europe. → 1753 George Washington tells the French settlers to leave the Ohio River Valley, then builds a fort there. → 1754 French settlers and Native Americans seize the fort, which signals the beginning of the war. → 1754–1763 Battles of the war → 1763 Treaty of Paris, Proclamation of 1763 leave. Their leader was a 21-year-old major named George Washington. Washington reported the French commander's reply.

A VOICE FROM THE PAST

He told me the Country belong'd to them, that no English Man had a right to trade upon them Waters; & that he had Orders to make every Person Prisoner that attempted it on the Ohio or the Waters of it.

George Washington, *"Journey to the French Commandant"*

Virginia's lieutenant governor sent about 40 men to build a fort at the head of the Ohio River, where Pittsburgh stands today. French and Native American troops seized the partially built fort in April 1754 and completed it themselves. The French named it Fort Duquesne (du•KAYN).

War Begins and Spreads

George Washington was on his way to defend Fort Duquesne when he learned of its surrender. He and his men pushed on and built another small fort, Fort Necessity. Following Washington's surprise attack on a French force, the French and their allies attacked Fort Necessity on July 3, 1754. After Washington surrendered, the French let him march back to Virginia. The French and Indian War had begun. This war became part of the Seven Years' War (1756–1763), a worldwide struggle for empire between France and Great Britain.

Background
The Seven Years' War was fought not only in North America but also in the Caribbean, throughout Europe, and in India and Africa.

Skillbuilder Answers
1. France
2. Niagara, Frontenac, Ticonderoga, Quebec, Beauséjour, Louisbourg

MORE ABOUT . . .

The French and Indian War
The French and Indian War, at first a colonial conflict between France and Great Britain, became linked to a global war that began in 1756. This first true world war eventually involved all of Europe, India, and the Americas. France, Austria, Sweden, many small German states, and Spain were allied against Great Britain and Prussia. By the war's end, Great Britain was the dominant force both in Europe and in North America.

Critical Thinking Transparency CT14
- Cause and Effect: The French and Indian War

HISTORY FROM VISUALS

Reading the Map Point out that many of the war's battle sites were fought in hilly or rough terrain. Ask students to list some obstacles such terrain may have presented, as well as to suggest how the terrain might have prolonged the war. Also note that several battles were fought on the edge of the colonies. Ask students how those colonists living on the coast might have felt about this war. **Possible Responses** Students may note the difficulty of moving troops and supplies over rugged terrain. They may also note that colonists living in New York City or Boston would not have known about battles on the frontier until many days later.

Extension Have students create a time line for the places and dates shown on the map.

***French and Indian War,** 1754–1763*

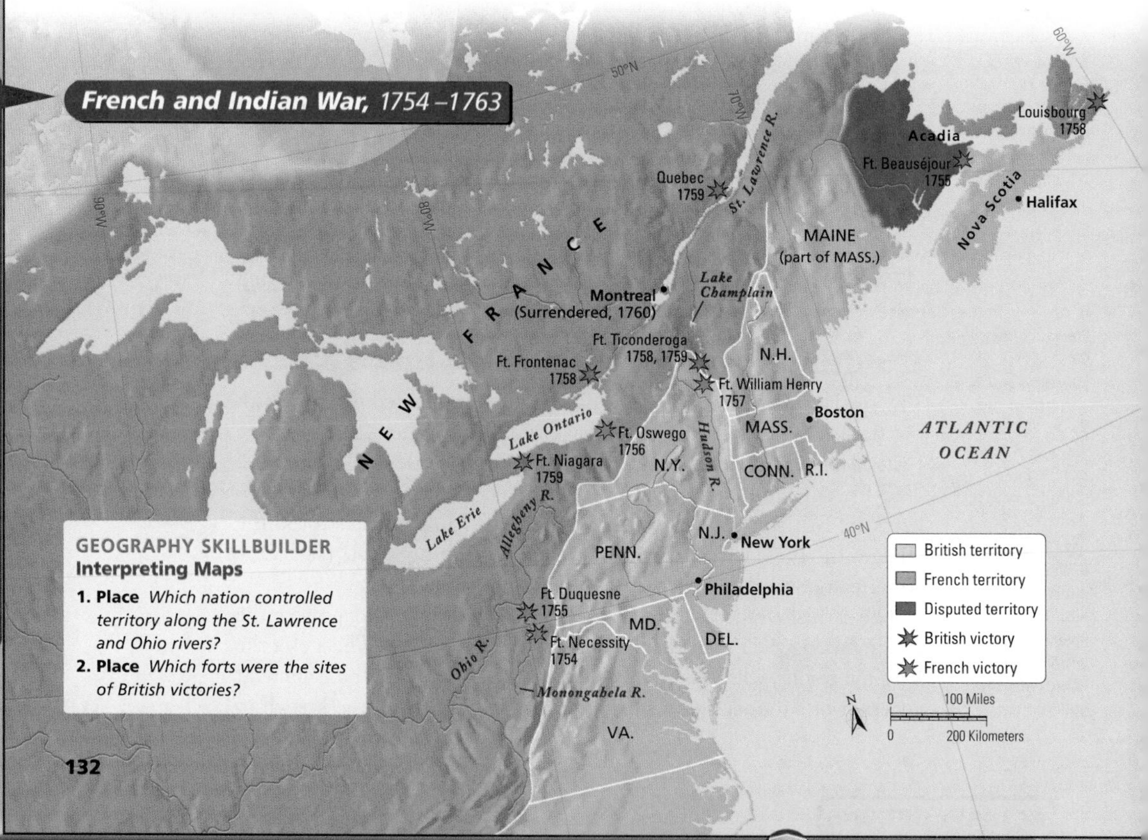

GEOGRAPHY SKILLBUILDER
Interpreting Maps
1. **Place** *Which nation controlled territory along the St. Lawrence and Ohio rivers?*
2. **Place** *Which forts were the sites of British victories?*

132

ACTIVITY OPTIONS

INTERDISCIPLINARY LINK: GEOGRAPHY — BLOCK SCHEDULING

KEY BATTLE SITES OF THE FRENCH AND INDIAN WAR

Class Time 15 minutes

Task Planning a route

Purpose To use a map to analyze the movements of French and British troops during the war

Supplies Needed
- Textbook
- Atlases
- Reference books on the French and Indian War

Activity Have students use the map on this page to plan two different tours of the battle sites of the French and Indian War. Students should plan one tour in chronological order: The first stop on the tour will be the site of the first battle, the second stop will be the site of the second battle, and so on. The second tour should be planned by geographical location, beginning with the southernmost battle site. After students have determined the stops on each tour, have them estimate which tour would take longer and why.

While Washington was surrendering Fort Necessity, representatives from the British colonies and the Iroquois nations were meeting at Albany, New York. The colonists wanted the Iroquois to fight with them against the French. The Iroquois would not commit to this alliance.

Benjamin Franklin, who admired the union of the six Iroquois nations, suggested that the colonies band together for defense. His **Albany Plan of Union** was the first formal proposal to unite the colonies. The plan called for each colony to send representatives to a Grand Council. This council would be able to collect taxes, raise armies, make treaties, and start new settlements. The leaders in Albany supported Franklin's plan, but the colonial legislatures later defeated it because they did not want to give up control of their own affairs.

3 Braddock's Defeat

Britain realized that to win the war, it could not rely solely on the colonists for funding or for troops. Therefore, the British sent General Edward Braddock and two regiments to Virginia. In 1755, Braddock marched toward the French at Fort Duquesne. George Washington was at his side. Their red-coated army of 2,100 moved slowly over the mountains, weighed down by a huge cannon.

On July 9, on a narrow trail eight miles from Fort Duquesne, fewer than 900 French and Indian troops surprised Braddock's forces. Washington suggested that his men break formation and fight from behind the trees, but Braddock would not listen. The general held his position and had four horses shot out from under him. Washington lost two horses. Four bullets went through Washington's coat, but, miraculously, none hit him. In the end, nearly 1,000 men were killed or wounded. General Braddock died from his wounds. American colonists were stunned by Braddock's defeat and by many other British losses over the next two years.

Reading **History**
C. Drawing Conclusions Why was Braddock defeated by a smaller enemy force?
C. Answer Braddock's force was unprotected and easy to see.

The British Take Quebec

In 1757, Britain had a new secretary of state, William Pitt, who was determined to win the war in the colonies. He sent the nation's best generals to America and borrowed money to pay colonial troops for fighting. The British controlled six French forts by August 1759, including Fort Duquesne (rebuilt as Fort Pitt). In late summer, the British began to attack New France at its capital, Quebec.

Background
Because the British seemed likely to win the war, some Iroquois had joined them as allies.

America's HERITAGE

ACADIANS TO CAJUNS
Braddock's defeat and other early losses in the war increased British concern about the loyalty of the French people in Acadia (now Nova Scotia). The British had won Acadia from France in 1713.

In 1755, British officers forced out 6,000 Acadians who would not take a loyalty oath. The British burned Acadian villages and spread the people to various British colonies, as shown. Eventually, some Acadians made their way to the French territory of Louisiana. There they became known as Cajuns.

INSTRUCT: OBJECTIVE 3
Braddock's Defeat/The British Take Quebec

- Why did Britain send money and men to fight in the colonies?
- What course did the war take from Braddock's defeat in 1755 to 1757?
- How did the British take Quebec?

Humanities Transparency HT10
- George Washington, 1755

America's HERITAGE

Acadians to Cajuns
The Acadians' journey to Louisiana was not easy. The English shipped some of the French Acadians to New England; others went to the West Indies. However, the Acadians found a welcome in Louisiana. They settled along the Mississippi River, Bayou Teche, Bayou Lafourche, and other streams in the southern part of the state. Many Cajuns settled in the swamplands where they became trappers and fishers. In 1971, the state of Louisiana officially recognized Acadiana: the 22-parish homeland of Cajun and Acadian culture. (Louisiana uses the French division of parish instead of county.) Tourism has become important in Acadiana. Visitors enjoy the distinctive Cajun dialect, cooking style, and music.

ACTIVITY OPTIONS

INTERDISCIPLINARY LINK: MUSIC — BLOCK SCHEDULING

CAJUN MUSIC AND ZYDECO

Class Time 30 minutes

Task Exploring Cajun music and Zydeco, a related musical form

Purpose To introduce students to one aspect of a unique American culture

Supplies Needed
- CDs or tapes of Cajun and Zydeco music

Activity Play selected Cajun songs for the class. Ask students to identify the language of the songs and the instruments being played. Then play some Zydeco music for the class. Explain that Zydeco is accordion-based Creole music of people of color and shares some similarities with Cajun music. (Creoles are people descended from French and Spanish settlers.) Ask students to compare and contrast Cajun music and Zydeco.

MORE ABOUT . . .

James Wolfe

Ambitious, brilliant, and dedicated to the art of war, Wolfe was just 32 years old at the Battle of Quebec. He wrote to Jeffrey Amherst, his commander in chief, that "an offensive, daring kind of war will awe the Indians and ruin the French. Block-houses and a trembling defense will encourage the meanest scoundrels to attack us."

INSTRUCT: OBJECTIVE 4

The Treaty of Paris/ Pontiac's Rebellion

- What were the results of the Treaty of Paris?
- Why did the British government issue the Proclamation of 1763? How did the colonists react?
- What brutal plan was used to squelch Native American uprisings?

Geography Transparency GT5
- Proclamation of 1763

In-Depth Resources: Unit 1
- Primary Source: from *Alexander Henry's Travels and Adventures*, p. 86
- Literature Selection: from *The Light in the Forest* by Conrad Richter, pp. 87–89

HISTORY FROM VISUALS

Reading the Map Ask students to study the maps and answer the following questions. Which country acquired valuable fur-trapping land along the Great Lakes? Which country gained control of New Orleans? **Answers** Britain, Spain

Extension Ask students to use atlas maps of North America to find names of geographical features or cities and towns that show the influence of the nation that claimed that territory in 1754.

Quebec sat on cliffs 300 feet above the St. Lawrence River. Cannon and thousands of soldiers guarded its thick walls. British general James Wolfe sailed around the fort for two months, unable to capture it. Then, in September, a scout found a steep, unguarded path up the cliffs to the plains just west of Quebec. At night, Wolfe and 4,000 of his men floated to the path and secretly climbed the cliffs.

When the French awoke, the British were lined up on the plains, ready to attack. In the short, fierce battle that followed, Wolfe was killed. The French commander, Montcalm, died of his wounds the next day. Quebec surrendered to the British. The **Battle of Quebec** was the turning point of the war. When Montreal fell the next year, all of Canada was in British hands.

D. Answer They surprised the French by climbing an unguarded path up to the city.

Reading **History**
D. Finding Main Ideas How were the British able to capture Quebec?

4 The Treaty of Paris

Britain and France battled in other parts of the world for almost three more years. Spain made a pact in 1761 to aid France, but its help came too late. When the Seven Years' War ended in 1763, Britain had won.

By the **Treaty of Paris,** Britain claimed all of North America east of the Mississippi River. To reward Spain for its help, France gave it New Orleans and Louisiana, the French territory west of the Mississippi. Britain, which had seized Cuba and the Philippines from Spain, gave them back in exchange for Florida. The treaty ended French power in North America.

Skillbuilder Answers
1. France, Spain
2. Britain, Spain

Background
France kept only a few islands near Newfoundland and in the West Indies.

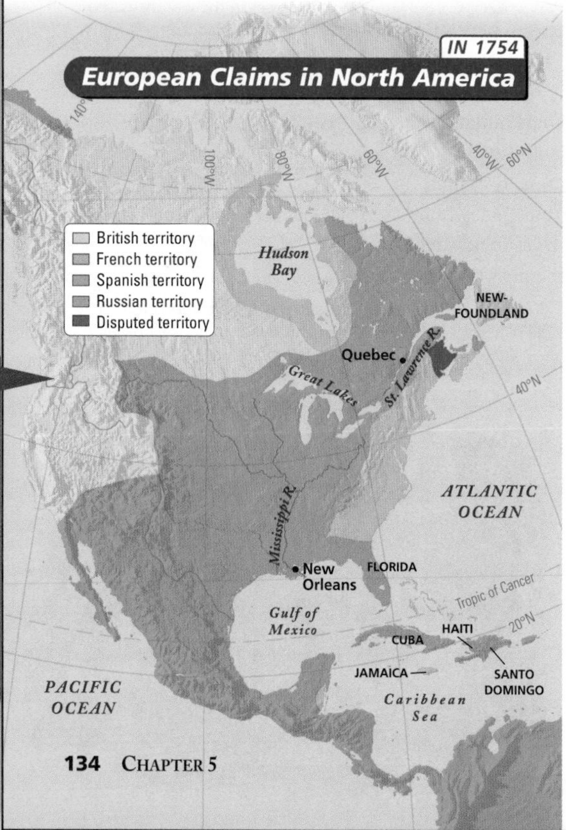

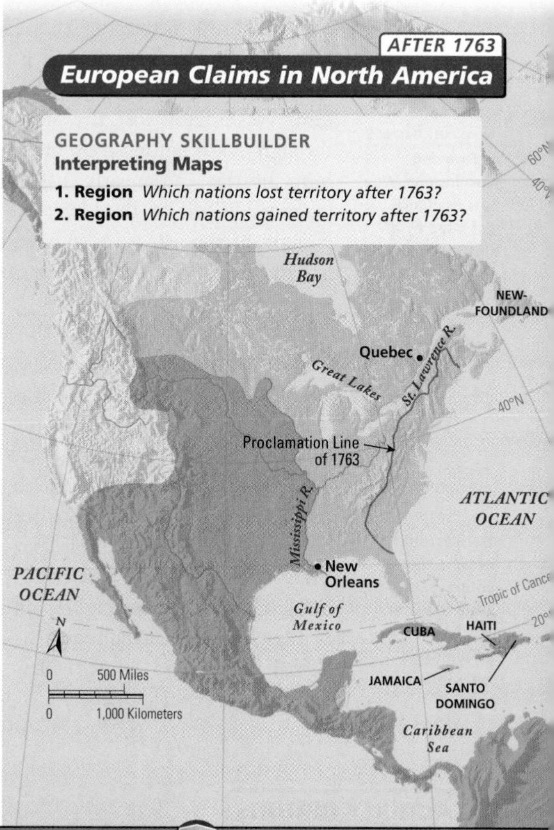

GEOGRAPHY SKILLBUILDER
Interpreting Maps
1. **Region** *Which nations lost territory after 1763?*
2. **Region** *Which nations gained territory after 1763?*

ACTIVITY OPTIONS

INTERDISCIPLINARY LINK: GEOGRAPHY/MATH — BLOCK SCHEDULING

FIGURING AREA

Class Time 15 minutes

Task Measuring distances/areas on a map

Purpose To compare approximate amounts of territory that changed hands after the French and Indian War

Supplies Needed
- Rulers

Activity Ask students to measure the scale on the map on page 134 (1/2 in. = 500 miles). Challenge them to use that measurement to determine the amounts of territory in North America that each country claimed before and after the French and Indian War. Remind students that area equals length multiplied by width (Area = length x width). Discuss various ways to make these measurements, such as picturing the territory to be measured as a rough geometric shape. Ask students to explain why their results can only be estimates, at best.

Pontiac's Rebellion

After French forces withdrew, the British took over their forts. They refused to give supplies to the Native Americans, as the French had. British settlers also moved across the mountains onto Native American land. In the spring and summer of 1763, Native American groups responded by attacking settlers and destroying almost every British fort west of the Appalachians. They surrounded the three remaining forts. This revolt was called **Pontiac's Rebellion,** although the Ottawa war leader Pontiac was only one of many organizers.

*Reading*History
E. Analyzing Points of View Why did the Native Americans attack the British?
E. Answer Settlers claimed their land, and soldiers treated them harshly.

British settlers reacted with equal viciousness, killing even Indians who had not attacked them. British officers came up with a brutal plan to end the Delaware siege at Fort Pitt.

Pontiac

A VOICE FROM THE PAST

Could it not be contrived to send the Small Pox among those disaffected [angry] tribes of Indians? We must on this occasion use every stratagem in our power to reduce them.

Major General Jeffrey Amherst, quoted in *The Conspiracy of Pontiac*

The officers invited Delaware war leaders in to talk and then gave them smallpox-infected blankets as gifts. This started a deadly outbreak.

By the fall, the Native Americans had retreated. Even so, the uprising made the British government see that defending Western lands would be costly. Therefore, the British issued the **Proclamation of 1763,** which forbade colonists to settle west of the Appalachians.

*Reading*History
F. Reading a Map Find the Proclamation Line of 1763 on the map on page 134.

The colonists were angry. They thought they had won the right to settle the Ohio River Valley. The British government was angry at the colonists, who did not want to pay for their own defense. This hostility helped cause the war for American independence, as you will read.

Section 3 Assessment

1. Terms & Names

Explain the significance of:
- French and Indian War
- Albany Plan of Union
- Battle of Quebec
- Treaty of Paris
- Pontiac's Rebellion
- Proclamation of 1763

2. Taking Notes

Write the month and year each battle occurred. Classify each as a French or British victory.

Date	Incident	Victor
	Seizure of Fort Duquesne	
	Surrender of Fort Necessity	
	Braddock's defeat	
	Battle of Quebec	

Which was most important?

3. Main Ideas

a. How did the fur trade contribute to the French and Indian War?

b. Why did the British begin to win the war after 1758?

c. What were some causes and effects of Pontiac's Rebellion?

4. Critical Thinking

Analyzing Points of View Why did the French, British, and Native Americans fight over the Ohio River Valley?

THINK ABOUT
- how the British viewed the valley
- how the French viewed it
- how the Native Americans viewed it

ACTIVITY OPTIONS

GEOGRAPHY / **MUSIC**

Learn more about the Battle of Quebec and its setting. Make a three-dimensional **model** of the battle or write a **song** about it.

MORE ABOUT . . .

Pontiac

Pontiac believed that the French would support an Indian revolt against the British and hoped to return the region to French control. When his attack on Fort Detroit failed, Pontiac moved with a small group of followers through Illinois country. In 1769, Pontiac was clubbed to death on the streets of the French village of Cahokia by a member of the Peoria tribe. The British commander of Fort De Chartres ordered that Pontiac's body should be buried in Cahokia. Stories persist that Pontiac was buried by the French in St. Louis. Another reputed burial site is in Oakland County, Michigan.

ASSESS & RETEACH

Setting the Stage Have students fill in the War section on the chapter graphic organizer.

Formal Assessment
- Section Quiz, p. 87

Critical Thinking Transparency CT13
- Setting the Stage

RETEACHING ACTIVITY

Have students compose ten True-False statements that cover the most important points of the section. Separate them into groups of four to share their statements and discuss answers.

In-Depth Resources: Unit 1
- Reteaching Activity, p. 92

Section 3 Assessment

1. Terms & Names

French and Indian War, p. 131
Albany Plan of Union, p. 133
Battle of Quebec, p. 134
Treaty of Paris, p. 134
Pontiac's Rebellion, p. 135
Proclamation of 1763, p. 135

2. Taking Notes

April 1754, French
July 1754, French
July 1755, French
September 1759, British

Student opinions may vary. Be sure they give reasons to support their opinions.

3. Main Ideas

a. British fur trade threatened French fur trade. **b.** because they sent their best generals to America and began to pay colonial troops for fighting **c.** causes—harsh treatment by British soldiers; land claims by British settlers; effects—attacks on Native Americans; the Proclamation of 1763

4. Critical Thinking

French: because it connected their settlements; British: wanted to trade and settle there; Native Americans: lived there

ACTIVITY OPTIONS

Integrated Assessment
- Rubrics for a model, 1.10
- Rubrics for a song, 4.8

TERMS & NAMES

1. **Great Awakening,** p. 123
2. **Enlightenment,** p. 124
3. **Magna Carta,** p. 125
4. **Parliament,** p. 126
5. **Edmund Andros,** p. 127
6. **Glorious Revolution,** p. 128
7. **John Peter Zenger,** p. 129
8. **French and Indian War,** p. 131
9. **Treaty of Paris,** p. 134
10. **Proclamation of 1763,** p. 135

REVIEW QUESTIONS

Possible Responses

1. to gain wealth and political rights
2. to help raise cash crops; to provide needed products and services for their families; to run some businesses
3. debate and splits within congregations; founding of colleges to train ministers; spreading of Christianity to Native Americans and African Americans; fostered revolutionary spirit
4. The king and Parliament were too far away to manage every detail of the colonies, and they wanted a voice in the making of their laws.
5. the right to a jury trial; the right not to be taxed or have property seized arbitrarily
6. The trial upheld the notion that people have the right to speak the truth.
7. William and Mary, who took the English throne during the Glorious Revolution, agreed to uphold the English Bill of Rights.
8. He told the French to leave the Ohio Valley, his surrender of Fort Necessity was one of the first battles of the war, and he behaved heroically at Braddock's defeat.
9. the former French territories of Canada and Louisiana east of the Mississippi River; Florida from Spain
10. British soldiers treated Native Americans harshly; British settlers moved onto Native American land.

Chapter 5 ASSESSMENT

VISUAL SUMMARY

Beginnings of an American Identity

Early American Culture

English colonists shared certain values, such as land ownership and hard work. The Great Awakening and the Enlightenment also drew colonists together.

Roots of Representative Government

English colonists expected the right to elect representatives to government and other political rights that had developed in England over centuries.

The French and Indian War

English colonists were also drawn together as they fought against common enemies—the French and their Native American allies.

136

TERMS & NAMES

Briefly explain the significance of each of the following.

1. Great Awakening
2. Enlightenment
3. John Peter Zenger
4. Magna Carta
5. Parliament
6. Glorious Revolution
7. Edmund Andros
8. French and Indian War
9. Treaty of Paris
10. Proclamation of 1763

REVIEW QUESTIONS

Early American Culture (pages 119–124)

1. Why did colonists want to own land?
2. What was women's role in the colonial economy?
3. What were the effects of the Great Awakening on colonial culture and politics?

Roots of Representative Government (pages 125–129)

4. Why did colonies have representative assemblies?
5. What was one important right granted in the Magna Carta?
6. How did the Zenger trial help lead to freedom of the press?
7. How was the English Bill of Rights related to the Glorious Revolution?

The French and Indian War (pages 130–135)

8. What was George Washington's role in the French and Indian War?
9. What did England gain as a result of the French and Indian War?
10. What was one reason for Pontiac's Rebellion?

CRITICAL THINKING

1. USING YOUR NOTES

Using your completed chart, answer the questions below.

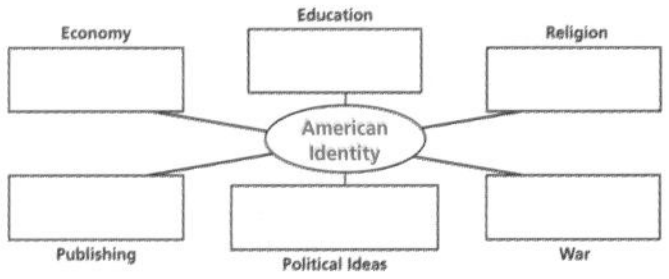

a. What were some political ideas shared by people in the American colonies?
b. How was religion important to American identity?
c. How did publishing help build an American identity?

2. THEME: DEMOCRATIC IDEALS

What democratic ideals did Americans inherit from England?

3. APPLYING CITIZENSHIP SKILLS

Why is jury duty an example of responsible citizenship?

4. CONTRASTING

How did colonial government differ from present-day government in the United States?

5. ANALYZING CAUSES

What do you think was the most important cause of the French and Indian War?

6. ANALYZING LEADERSHIP

Give an example of bad military or political leadership from the chapter. What mistake was made?

Interact *with* History

Now that you have read the chapter, what would you say British colonists in America had in common?

CRITICAL THINKING

Possible Responses

1. **USING YOUR NOTES** **a.** the right to elect representatives; people could change their government **b.** The Great Awakening paved the way for independence from England. **c.** Colonists stopped relying on British publications and published their own.
2. **THEME: DEMOCRATIC IDEALS** representative government; trial by jury; limits on the power of government; respect for individual rights
3. **APPLYING CITIZENSHIP SKILLS** Jurors are responsible for the fate of an accused person.
4. **CONTRASTING** The colonies were part of the English government, which had no colonial representatives. States are part of the federal government and have representatives.
5. **ANALYZING CAUSES** English desire for more land; France and Britain's struggle for supremacy
6. **ANALYZING LEADERSHIP** General Braddock's refusal to take cover. He was stubborn and overconfident.

Interact *with* History language; government; customs; religion

HISTORY SKILLS

1. INTERPRETING MAPS: Movement

Study the map. Answer the questions.

French Explorers on the Mississippi

Basic Map Elements

a. What do the colors indicate?

Interpreting the Map

b. Who traveled earlier?

c. Who reached the Gulf of Mexico?

d. Along whose route were Fort Detroit and New Orleans later founded?

2. INTERPRETING PRIMARY SOURCES

An unnamed Frenchman who knew Pontiac quotes a speech Pontiac gave to support an attack on British soldiers. Read the quote carefully. Answer the questions.

> When I go to see the English commander and say to him that some of our comrades are dead, instead of bewailing their death, as our French brothers do, he laughs at me and at you. If I ask anything for our sick, he refuses with the reply that he has no use for us. From all this you can well see that they are seeking our ruin. Therefore, my brothers, we must all swear their destruction and wait no longer.
>
> **Journal of Pontiac's Conspiracy,** 1763

a. Why does Pontiac want to attack the English?

b. What is Pontiac's attitude toward the French?

ALTERNATIVE ASSESSMENT

1. INTERDISCIPLINARY ACTIVITY: Language Arts

Making a Speech Do research to learn more about freedom of the press. Then make a speech to convince people that it is important.

2. COOPERATIVE LEARNING ACTIVITY

Holding a Diplomatic Council Working in a small group, review the causes of the French and Indian War, and do further research. Then hold a diplomatic council to try to prevent the war. Role-play representatives from the following groups.

- officials of the English government
- officials of the French government
- English settlers
- French fur traders
- English-allied Iroquois
- French-allied Huron or Algonquin

3. TECHNOLOGY ACTIVITY

Making a Class Presentation Colonial American culture was not like modern American culture. Using the library or the Internet, find images, literature, and informative articles that tell you about daily life in the early and middle 1700s.

For more about colonial American culture . . .

INTERNET ACTIVITY
CLASSZONE.COM

Create a class presentation about colonial culture using the suggestions below.

- Stage a fashion show that illustrates what people of different ranks and ethnic backgrounds wore.
- Create a dramatic play based on the experiences of an interesting figure from the chapter, such as Madam Sarah Knight, Benjamin Franklin, or Pontiac.
- Illustrate sayings from *Poor Richard's Almanack.*
- Give an oral book report on a colonial captivity narrative. For example, find out what happened to Mary Rowlandson among the Narragansett.

4. HISTORY PORTFOLIO

Review your section and chapter assessment activities. Select one that you think is your best work. Then use comments made by your teacher or classmates to improve your work and add it to your portfolio.

Additional Test Practice, pp. S1–S33

TEST PRACTICE
CLASSZONE.COM

ALTERNATIVE ASSESSMENT

1. INTERDISCIPLINARY ACTIVITY: **Language Arts**
   A speech should
   - reflect the student's understanding of the principles of freedom of speech.
   - have a clear introduction and conclusion.
   - have adequate delivery and establish rapport with the audience.
2. COOPERATIVE LEARNING ACTIVITY
   A diplomatic council should
   - focus on resolving the problem.
   - have students support their own positions with evidence or logic.
   - have students appropriately respond to each other's statements.
   - have students exhibit understanding of the role they are playing.
3. TECHNOLOGY ACTIVITY
   Class presentations should
   - clearly demonstrate an understanding of colonial culture.
   - utilize several sources of information.
   - have adequate delivery and establish rapport with the audience.
   - show proficiency in the use of technology.
4. HISTORY PORTFOLIO
   Revised section or chapter assessment activities should
   - address teacher and peer responses to the selected work.
   - solve problems present in the first versions of the work.

Critical Thinking Transparency CT15
- Visual Summary

Formal Assessment
- Chapter Test, Forms A, B, and C, pp. 88–99

HISTORY SKILLS

Possible Responses

1. INTERPRETING MAPS
   Basic Map Elements
   a. the voyages of La Salle and of Marquette and Joliet
   Interpreting the Map
   b. Marquette and Joliet
   c. La Salle
   d. La Salle's

2. INTERPRETING PRIMARY SOURCES
   a. because he believes the English are trying to ruin his people
   b. He seems to like the French, calling them "brothers."

UNIT 2

Creating a New Nation

1763–1791

BEFORE YOU READ

Previewing Unit 2

Unit 2 traces the increasing dissatisfaction of American colonists with their position in Great Britain's empire. The fires of revolution grow from the first sparks struck by Patriots who challenge the rule of a Parliament and a monarch across the Atlantic Ocean. The 13 colonies unite to declare themselves independent and confirm their stand by defeating Britain on the battlefield in the American Revolution. After the war, the newly independent states create a new republican government for themselves, first under the Articles of Confederation and then under the United States Constitution.

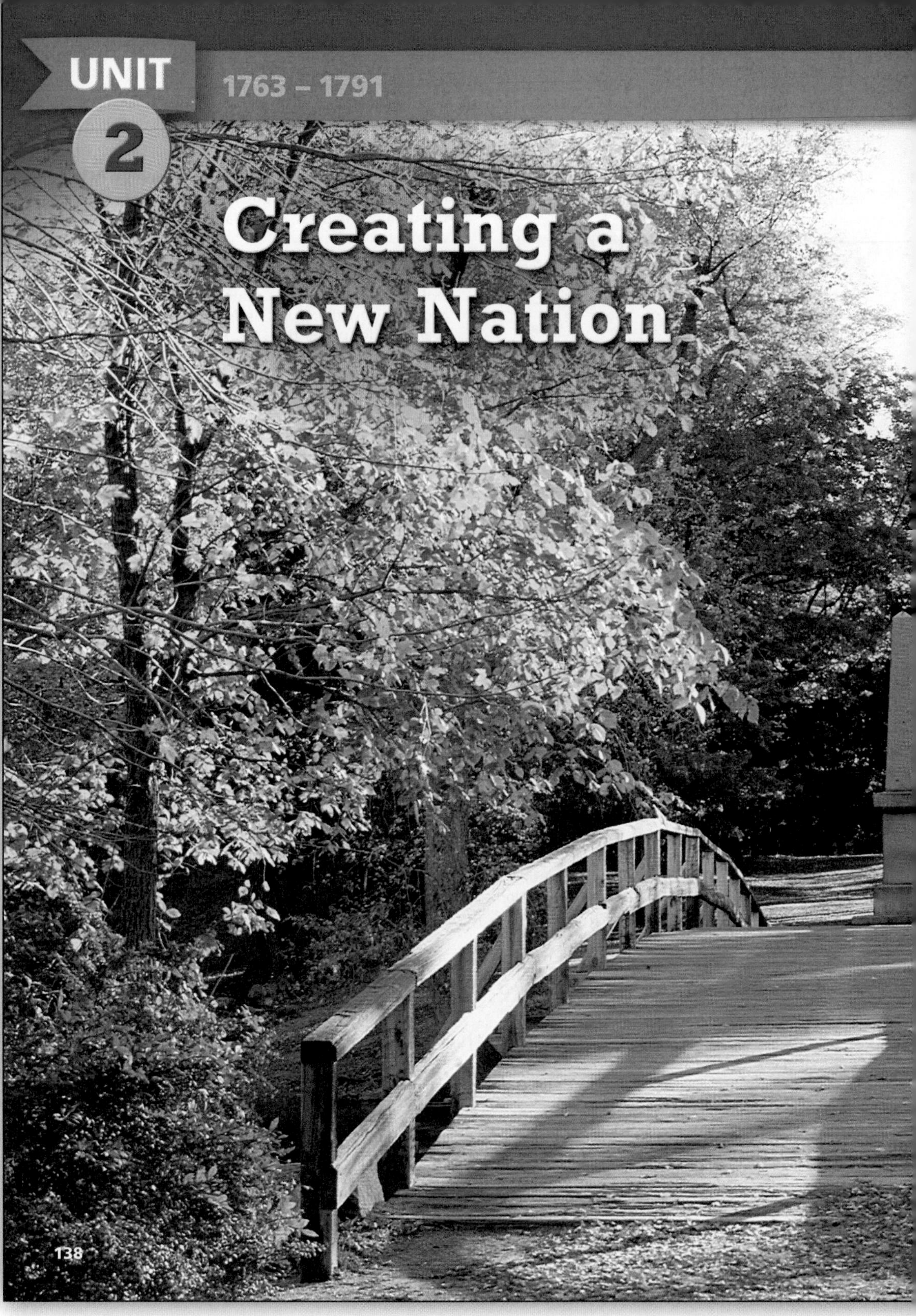

"By the rude bridge . . .
the embattled farmers
stood and fired the shot
heard round the world."
—Ralph Waldo Emerson, "Concord Hymn"

Americans battled British troops at Old North Bridge, Concord, Massachusetts, in April 1775.

HISTORY FROM VISUALS

Interpreting the Photograph Ask students to study the photograph and read the lines from the "Concord Hymn" by Ralph Waldo Emerson. Ask students to define *rude* and *embattled* in this context. Then ask them to explain why the shots fired here by the American farmers were important in other parts of the world. **Possible Responses** The American Revolution inspired democratic revolutions in other countries. The formation of the United States has affected the rest of the world in countless ways.

Extension Ask students to find the complete "Concord Hymn" and select portions to read aloud to the class.

The Road to Revolution 1763–1776

	CHAPTER OVERVIEW	COPYMASTERS	INTEGRATED TECHNOLOGY
CHAPTER RESOURCES	The chapter identifies the causes of tension between the British government and the colonists in the years 1763–1776. It explains issues and events leading up to the declaration of independence from Britain. It describes the roles played by significant individuals.	**In-Depth Resources: Unit 2** • Tracing Themes: Impact of the Individual, p. 2 • Building Vocabulary, p. 8 • History Workshop Resources, p. 23 **Interdisciplinary Projects,** pp. 31–36	• eEdition Plus Online • EasyPlanner Plus Online • eTest Plus Online • eEdition • Power Presentations • EasyPlanner • Electronic Library of Primary Sources • Test Generator • Reading Study Guide • America's Music
SECTION 1 **Tighter British Control** **pp. 159–162**	**KEY IDEAS** • Tighter British control causes tension with American colonists. • The Stamp Act enrages the colonists. • American protests force repeal of the Stamp Act.	**In-Depth Resources: Unit 2** • Setting the Stage, p. 1 • Guided Reading, p. 3 • Primary Source: Resolutions of the Stamp Act Congress, p. 12 • Reteaching Activity, p. 18 **Economics in History** • The Impact of British Taxes, p. 6 **Outline Map Activities** • Pre-Revolutionary North America, pp. 11–12	**Warm-Up Transparency WT6** **Humanities Transparency HT11** • The Repeal of the Stamp Act **Critical Thinking Transparency CT16** • Setting the Stage
SECTION 2 **Colonial Resistance Grows** **pp. 163–169**	• Townshend Acts bring new protests. • The Boston Massacre causes more tension. • Sons of Liberty protest the Tea Act.	**In-Depth Resources: Unit 2** • Setting the Stage, p. 1 • Guided Reading, p. 4 • Skillbuilder Practice: Recognizing Propaganda, p. 9 • Reteaching Activity, p. 19 **Why It Matters Now** • Politics and Protest, pp. 11–12	**Warm-Up Transparency WT6** **Humanities Transparency HT12** • *The Copley Family* by John Copley **Critical Thinking Transparency CT16** • Setting the Stage **classzone.com**
SECTION 3 **The Road to Lexington and Concord** **pp. 170–175**	• The Intolerable Acts punish the colonists. • Colonists must choose between war and peace. • Lexington and Concord become the first battles of the American Revolutionary War.	**In-Depth Resources: Unit 2** • Setting the Stage, p. 1 • Guided Reading, p. 5 • Literature Selection: "Paul Revere's Ride" by Henry Wadsworth Longfellow, pp. 14–17 • Reteaching Activity, p. 20	**Warm-Up Transparency WT6** **Critical Thinking Transparency CT16** • Setting the Stage **Critical Thinking Transparency CT17** • Cause and Effect: Growing Conflict Between Britain and America **classzone.com**
SECTION 4 **Declaring Independence** **pp. 176–185**	• Encounters between the British and colonists deepen the conflict. • *Common Sense* makes a case for independence. • American colonists declare independence from Great Britain.	**In-Depth Resources: Unit 2** • Setting the Stage, p. 1 • Guided Reading, p. 6 • Guided Reading: The Declaration of Independence, p. 7 • Geography Application, pp. 10–11 • Primary Source, p. 13 • Reteaching Activity, p. 21 **America's History Makers,** pp. 23–26 **American History Plays** • *Franklin & the King* by Paul Green	**Warm-Up Transparency WT6** **Geography Transparency GT6** • Battle of Bunker Hill, 1775 **Critical Thinking Transparency CT16** • Setting the Stage **Primary Source Explorer** • *The Declaration of Independence* **classzone.com**

Pupil's Edition | Overhead Transparency | CD-ROM
Copymaster | Audio Library | Internet

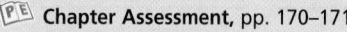

ASSESSMENT OPTIONS

Chapter Assessment, pp. 170–171

Formal Assessment
- Chapter Tests, Forms A, B, and C, pp. 104–118

Test Generator

Online Test Practice

Strategies for Test Preparation

Section Assessment, p. 146

Formal Assessment, Quiz, p. 100

Integrated Assessment Book
- Rubrics, 1.1, 4.8

Test Generator

Test Practice Transparencies, TT20

Section Assessment, p. 151

Formal Assessment, Quiz, p. 101

Integrated Assessment Book
- Rubrics, 3.6, 5.4

Test Generator

Test Practice Transparencies, TT21

Section Assessment, p. 157

Formal Assessment, Quiz, p. 102

Integrated Assessment Book
- Rubrics, 2.1, 2.2

Test Generator

Test Practice Transparencies, TT22

Section Assessment, p. 165

Formal Assessment, Quiz, p. 103

Integrated Assessment Book
- Rubrics, 1.7, 4.4

Test Generator

Test Practice Transparencies, TT23

CUSTOMIZING FOR INDIVIDUAL NEEDS

Students Acquiring English/ESL

Reading Study Guide (English and Spanish), pp. 47–58

Access for Students Acquiring English/ESL: Spanish Translations, pp. 32–39

Chapter Summaries on CD (English and Spanish)

Modified Lesson Plans for English Learners

Less Proficient Readers

Reading Study Guide (English and Spanish), pp. 47–58

Chapter Summaries on CD (English and Spanish)

Gifted and Talented Students

In-Depth Resources: Unit 2
- Enrichment Activity, p. 22

America's History Makers
- Abigail Adams, pp. 23–24
- Thomas Paine, pp. 25–26

CROSS-CURRICULAR CONNECTIONS

Geography

Barner, Bob. ***Which Way to the Revolution?*** Holiday House, 1998. Text and maps describe the route traveled by Paul Revere.

Health

Erdosh, George. ***Food and Recipes of the Revolutionary War.*** New York: PowerKids Press, 1997.

Humanities: Music

Brand, Oscar. ***Songs of '76: A Folksinger's History of the Revolution.*** Evans, 1988. A collection of songs from old manuscripts, newspapers, and personal accounts.

Interdisciplinary Projects, pp. 31–36
- Math: Population Growth
- Science: Silver Craft
- Language Arts: Making a Persuasive Speech
- Music: Revolutionary Songs

Literature

Fritz, Jean. ***Early Thunder.*** Putnam, 1967. A 14-year-old boy is forced to choose between his family's Tory leanings and his feelings about Parliament's response to the Boston Tea Party.

McDougal Littell *The Language of Literature*

- Henry Wadsworth Longfellow, "Paul Revere's Ride" (poem)

McDougal Littell Literature Connections

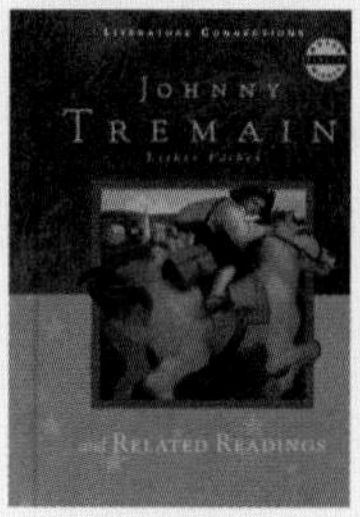

Esther Forbes
Johnny Tremain
Set in Boston from 1773 to 1775, the novel brings to life the adventures of a teenage boy and his role in the events leading to the American Revolution.

ENRICHMENT ACTIVITIES

Pupil's Edition, pp. 140–173
Interact with History, p. 141
Interdisciplinary Challenge, pp. 152–153
Literature Connections, pp. 158–159
Interactive Primary Source, pp. 166–169
History Workshop, pp. 172–173

In-Depth Resources: Unit 2
- Geography Application, pp. 10–11
- Primary Source: Resolutions of the Stamp Act Congress, p. 12
- Primary Source: Letter from Abigail Adams, p. 13
- Literature Selection, pp. 14–17
- History Workshop Resources, p. 23

America's History Makers
- Abigail Adams, pp. 23–24
- Thomas Paine, pp. 25–26

America's Music CD

American History Plays
- *Franklin & the King* by Paul Green

Outline Map Activities
- Pre-Revolutionary North America, pp. 11–12

Primary Source Explorer
- *The Declaration of Independence*

Why It Matters Now
- Politics and Protest, pp. 11–12

BLOCK SCHEDULING — LESSON PLAN OPTIONS (90-MINUTE PERIOD)

DAY 1

Interact with History, p. 141
Class Time 20 minutes

Options for pacing and variety:
- Role-Playing Have students meet in groups of four or five and act as neighbors meeting to discuss the "What Do You Think?" questions and the main questions. **Class Time** 15 minutes

Setting the Stage, p. 142
Class Time 20 minutes

Options for pacing and variety:
- Time Saver Assign the "What Do You Know?" and "What Do You Want to Know?" questions as homework so that students can get a head start on preparing to read the chapter. **Class Time** 5 minutes

Section 1, pp. 143–146
Class Time 50 minutes

Options for pacing and variety:
- Time Saver Use the political cartoon transparency, "Repeal of the Stamp Act," as a summary of the section. **Class Time** 10 minutes
- Peer Teaching Have students work in pairs to answer the Reading History questions in the section and Critical Thinking question in the Section 1 assessment. **Class Time** 15 minutes

DAY 2

Section 2, pp. 147–153
Class Time 45 minutes

Interdisciplinary Challenge, pp. 152–153
Class Time 55 minutes

Options for pacing and variety:
- Team Teaching Invite the math teacher to your class to coach student groups as they solve the Math Challenge or the Interdisciplinary Link (Math) on page 155 in the Teacher's Edition. **Class Time** 55 minutes.
- Peer Teaching Assign the content under each heading to a small group of students. Each group is responsible for explaining the information to the class. **Class Time** 30 minutes

Section 3, pp. 154–159
Class Time 45 minutes

Options for pacing and variety:
- Peer Teaching Divide students into small groups. Using the information from the chart on p. 155, create a different way to present the information to the class. **Class Time** 25 minutes
- Internet Extend students' background knowledge of the Battles at Lexington and Concord by having them visit classzone.com. **Class Time** 20 minutes

DAY 3

Section 4, pp. 160–169
Class Time 50 minutes

Options for pacing and variety:
- Peer Teaching Divide the class into small groups. Assign one group to become a living time line. Have another group become living biographies of individuals in this chapter. A third group performs the Cooperative Learning Activity on page 171. **Class Time** 50 minutes
- History on Film Extend students' background on the Revolutionary War by viewing either episode one or two, "The Conflict Ignites" or "1776," of *The American Revolution.* A&E Home Video, 1994. **Class Time** 50 minutes

History Workshop, pp. 172–173
Class Time 50 minutes

Options for pacing and variety:
- Time Saver Have students work on steps 1–5 in Raise the Liberty Pole. **Class Time** 30 minutes

Chapter 6 Assessment, pp. 170–171
Class Time 40 minutes

Options for pacing and variety:
- Peer Evaluation Have student pairs work out the answers to the Critical Thinking Questions, page 170. Then have them exchange papers with another team to evaluate their answers. **Class Time** 20 minutes
- Peer Teaching Divide the class into four groups. Assign each group one section of the Review Questions to complete. Students should exchange answers for the review questions. **Class Time** 20 minutes

TEACHER-TESTED ACTIVITY **Holly West Brewer, Buena Vista Paideia Magnet School, Nashville, Tennessee**

ILLUSTRATED TIME LINE

Class Time Two class periods for preparation and one for presentation

Task Creating an illustrated time line of the events leading to the American Revolution

Purpose To visualize and sequence events that led to the Revolution

Supplies Needed
- reference books and Internet sources on the American Revolution
- markers, colored pencils
- poster paper or rolls of paper

Activity Divide the class into small groups. Students should compile at least ten events that led to the Revolution. Each student should be responsible for researching two or three events. In addition, each student chooses one of the following roles: illustrator or recorder.

The illustrators should create original drawings for each event. Each event should be placed on the large time line in chronological order. In addition, the recorders should write a cause-and-effect explanation as a caption for each event. Present the time line to the class.

INTERNET-BASED (ELECTRONIC) FIELD TRIP

Electronic field trips are one of the most popular ways for students to use the Internet. Students generally visit a specified set of Web sites that take them to real places, such as historic sites or national parks. This type of field trip is often an excellent substitute for an actual field trip, which may be logistically impossible.

ACTIVITY OUTLINE

Objective By planning an electronic field trip to places important to the movement for American independence and the Revolutionary War, students will deepen their understanding of the Revolutionary Era and gain experience with the Internet.

Task Students will plan a three-day electronic field trip to learn more about the beginnings of the Revolutionary War.

Class Time Two class periods

DIRECTIONS

1. Have students prepare a detailed itinerary of a three-day field trip to some of the early Revolutionary War sites they have read about in Chapter 6.

2. Ask students to label the top of each slide with one of the following titles, indicating the places they will visit (here, the destinations are listed in chronological order, from the earliest event to the latest):
   a) Old State House, Boston
   b) Boston Tea Party Ship
   c) Carpenter's Hall, Philadelphia
   d) Independence Hall, Philadelphia
   e) Old North Church, Boston
   f) Paul Revere House, Boston
   g) Lexington, Massachusetts
   h) Concord, Massachusetts
   i) Fort Ticonderoga, New York
   j) Bunker Hill, Boston

3. The Web sites for this field trip are located in the Teacher Center of classzone.com.

4. For each destination, ask students to pull pictures into their presentations and to list three reasons why this place is an important destination on a Revolutionary War historical field trip. Have students determine the order in which they would visit the destinations. Have them place the destinations in order chronologically or by location.

5. Additional options:
   - Ask students to include maps of the destinations or to create them using a blank outline map of the Northeast.
   - Give students a budget for food, transportation, and accommodations, and have them provide an account of how they will allocate their money.

CHAPTER 6 OBJECTIVE
The student will understand the events that pushed Great Britain and the American colonies apart and ultimately led to the signing of the Declaration of Independence.

CHAPTER 6

The Road to Revolution 1763–1776

Section 1 **Tighter British Control**
Section 2 **Colonial Resistance Grows**
Section 3 **The Road to Lexington and Concord**
Section 4 **Declaring Independence**

HISTORY FROM VISUALS

Interpreting the Illustration Ask students to study the engraving of British troops arriving in the colonies. Have them draw conclusions about the mood of the colonists and explain why they might feel that way. **Possible Responses** The colonists were angry because they saw the influx of British troops as a sign of Britain's attempt to restrict their freedom. The colonists felt nervous and uneasy about living among so many armed British troops.

Extension Have students write a descriptive paragraph about the scene in this painting.

CRITICAL THINKING ACTIVITY

Making Inferences Have the students look at the titles of the sections in this chapter. Ask them how the images on these opening pages illustrate the ideas found in the section titles. Then ask them what images they would expect to see illustrate the rest of the chapter.

Class Time 10 minutes

Angry colonists watch the arrival of British troops in Boston.

RECOMMENDED RESOURCES

BOOKS FOR THE TEACHER

Maier, Pauline. ***American Scripture: Making the Declaration of Independence.*** New York: A. A. Knopf, 1997. A closer look at the creation of the nation's cornerstone document.

Miller, John C. ***Origins of the American Revolution.*** Stanford: SU Press, 1957. An examination of events that led to the Revolutionary War.

Morgan, Edmund S. and Helen M. ***The Stamp Act Crisis: Prologue to Revolution.*** Chapel Hill: The UNC Press, 1953. A look at one of the pivotal events leading up to the war.

Zobel, Hiller B. ***The Boston Massacre.*** New York: W. W. Norton, 1970. An examination of the famous prewar shooting incident.

VIDEOS

Liberty! The American Revolution. PBS Video, 1998. See episode one, "The Reluctant Revolutionaries."

The American Revolution. A&E Home Video, 1994. See episodes one and two, "The Conflict Ignites" and "1776."

INTERNET

For more about the American Revolution, visit . . .

classzone.com

Interact *with* History

A colonist reads a copy of a new British tax law.
Tax stamps are burned.
Protesters include men, women, and children.

The year is 1765. Your neighbors are enraged by Britain's attempt to tax them without their consent. Britain has never done this before. Everyone will be affected by the tax. There are protests in many cities. You have to decide what you would do.

What Do You Think?

- What is the best way to show opposition to policies you consider unjust?
- Is there anything to be gained by protesting? Anything to be lost?
- Does government have the right to tax without consent of the people? Why or why not?

Would you join the protest?

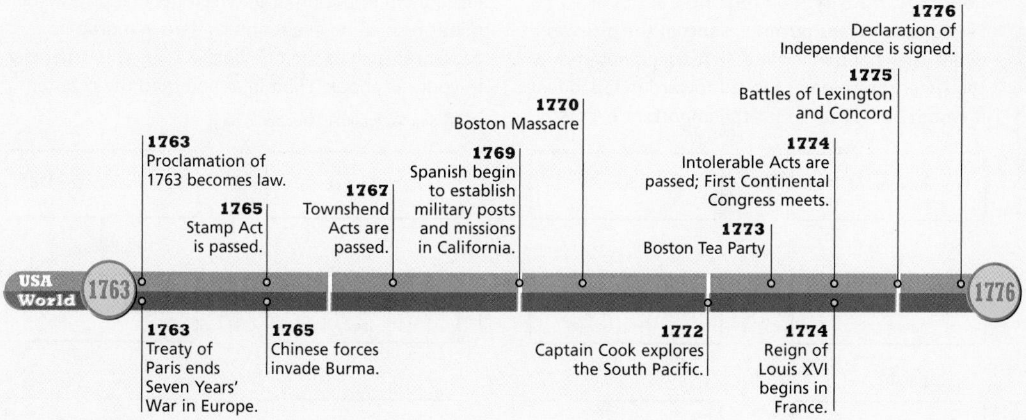
USA
World
1763
1776
1763 Proclamation of 1763 becomes law.
1765 Stamp Act is passed.
1767 Townshend Acts are passed.
1769 Spanish begin to establish military posts and missions in California.
1770 Boston Massacre
1773 Boston Tea Party
1774 Intolerable Acts are passed; First Continental Congress meets.
1775 Battles of Lexington and Concord
1776 Declaration of Independence is signed.
1763 Treaty of Paris ends Seven Years' War in Europe.
1765 Chinese forces invade Burma.
1772 Captain Cook explores the South Pacific.
1774 Reign of Louis XVI begins in France.

Interact *with* History

OBJECTIVES

- To help students identify one reason for the growing tension between Britain and the colonies
- To help students better understand the mood of the American colonists in the years before the Revolutionary War

What Do You Think?

1. Ask students how they would react if politicians collected taxes from them but ignored their views and needs.
2. Have students consider why a large public rally is an effective way to protest an unpopular policy.
3. Ask students to think about the different ways the British could react to the colonists' protest.

Would you join the protest?

Encourage students to think about the best- and worst-case scenarios facing the protesters. Possible scenarios: best—Britain repeals the tax; worst—British troops jail or beat the protesters.

MAKING PERSONAL CONNECTIONS

Ask students to think about policies either in their homes or community that they considered unjust. What did they do to protest? Did their protest achieve anything? Why or why not?

TIME LINE DISCUSSION

Explain to students that after the Seven Years' War, Great Britain was the most powerful nation in Europe. Its colonial empire included North America, holdings in the Caribbean, and India. In light of Britain's strength, the American colonists' declaration of independence seemed all the more bold and daring.

- Ask students how many years it was from Britain's passage of the Stamp Act to the Intolerable Acts. **Answer** Nine years.
- Ask students to hypothesize what colonists thought about these acts based on the events shown between 1774 and 1776.

Possible Response The colonists opposed these acts, for what followed them were fighting and a declaration of independence from British rule.

- Have students look at the time line and determine which world event and U.S. event are linked. **Possible Response** The two events in 1763 are linked. The end of the Seven Years' War set up the need for the proclamation.

BEFORE YOU READ

Previewing the Theme: Impact of the Individual

Ask students why strong and popular leaders would be so important to the colonists' attempts to gain independence from Great Britain. **Possible Response** Strong and dynamic leaders are vital to such an effort because they inspire citizens and help them to maintain their courage and determination.

What Do You Know?

Students may know that Britain and the colonists clashed over the issue of taxes. Tell them that increased taxation was just one example of Britain's attempt to achieve greater control over the colonies after the French and Indian War. Remind them that Britain had long allowed the colonies to develop with a notable degree of independence. As Britain sought to reverse this policy, however, tensions grew.

In-Depth Resources: Unit 2
- Tracing Themes: Impact of the Individual, p. 2

READ AND TAKE NOTES

Reading Strategy: Sequencing Events

Tell students that sequencing events, or arranging them in chronological order, will help them to better understand the relationship among those events. Knowing which event followed another may help students accomplish such critical-thinking tasks as analyzing causes and recognizing effects. The effect, or consequence, of one event often becomes the cause of another. By sequencing events in a chart such as the one shown here, students can more clearly see the cause-and-effect relationship among historical events.

In-Depth Resources: Unit 2
- Setting the Stage, p. 1

Critical Thinking Transparency CT16
- Setting the Stage

Chapter 6 SETTING THE STAGE

BEFORE YOU READ

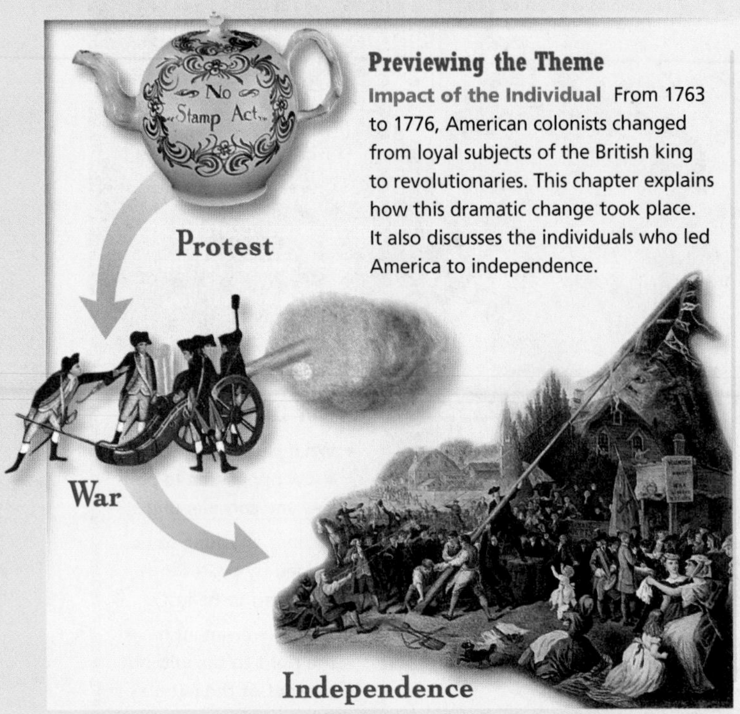

Previewing the Theme

Impact of the Individual From 1763 to 1776, American colonists changed from loyal subjects of the British king to revolutionaries. This chapter explains how this dramatic change took place. It also discusses the individuals who led America to independence.

What Do You Know?

What do you already know about the time before the Revolution? What were the issues that caused the colonists to choose independence?

THINK ABOUT
- what you have learned about this period from movies, television, or historical fiction
- reasons people in history have chosen to fight for freedom from oppression

What Do You Want to Know?

What questions do you have about the issues and events that pushed the American colonists toward rebellion? Record them in your notebook before you read the chapter.

READ AND TAKE NOTES

Reading Strategy: Sequencing Events Sequencing means putting events in the order in which they happen in time. In learning about how the American colonies moved toward independence, it would be helpful to list the important events. Place them in the order in which they occurred. You might record the event and its date in a graphic organizer such as the one below. Copy this organizer in your notebook. Fill it in as you read the chapter.

See Skillbuilder Handbook, page R4.

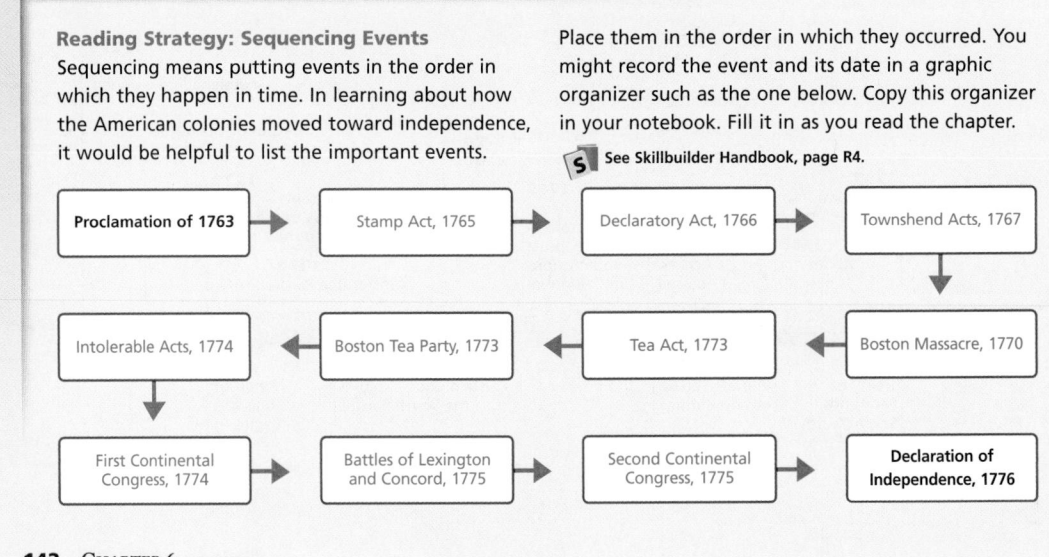

Proclamation of 1763 → Stamp Act, 1765 → Declaratory Act, 1766 → Townshend Acts, 1767 → Boston Massacre, 1770 → Tea Act, 1773 → Boston Tea Party, 1773 → Intolerable Acts, 1774 → First Continental Congress, 1774 → Battles of Lexington and Concord, 1775 → Second Continental Congress, 1775 → **Declaration of Independence, 1776**

TEACHING STRATEGY

READING THE CHAPTER

This is a chronological chapter focusing on the chain of events that led to the colonists' declaring their independence from Great Britain. Encourage students to look for the causes and effects of each event. Have them also consider how each event increased tensions between Britain and the colonies. Pause after each section to summarize the causes and effects of the main events described in the section.

ALTERNATIVE ASSESSMENT

The Chapter Assessment describes three activities for alternative assessment on page 171. You may wish to have students work on these activities during the course of the chapter and then present them at the end.

1 Tighter British Control

TERMS & NAMES
King George III
Quartering Act
revenue
Sugar Act
Stamp Act
Patrick Henry
boycott
Sons of Liberty

MAIN IDEA
Americans saw British efforts to tax them and to increase control over the colonies as violations of their rights.

WHY IT MATTERS NOW
Colonial protests were the first steps on the road to American independence.

ONE AMERICAN'S STORY

James Otis, Jr., a young Massachusetts lawyer, stormed through the streets of Boston one day in 1760. He was furious. His father had just been denied the post of chief justice of the Massachusetts colony by the royal governor. To Otis, this was one more example of Britain's lack of respect for colonial rights. Another example was its use of search warrants that allowed customs officers to enter any home or business to look for smuggled goods. Otis believed these searches were illegal.

Otis took up a case against the government that involved these search warrants. In court in February 1761, Otis spoke with great emotion for five hours about the search warrant and its use.

A VOICE FROM THE PAST

It appears to me the worst instrument of arbitrary power, the most destructive of English liberty and the fundamental principles of law, that was ever found in an English law-book.

James Otis, Jr., quoted in *James Otis: The Pre-Revolutionist* by J. C. Ridpath

James Otis, Jr., argues in court against illegal search warrants in 1761.

Spectators listened in amazement. One of them, a young lawyer named John Adams, later wrote of Otis's performance: "Then and there, in the old Council Chamber, the child Independence was born."

In making the first public speech demanding English liberties for the colonists, James Otis planted a seed of freedom. In this section, you will read more about the early protests against Britain's policies in America.

1 The Colonies and Britain Grow Apart

During the French and Indian War, Britain and the colonies fought side by side. Americans took great pride in being partners in the victory over the French. However, when the war ended, problems arose. Britain wanted to govern its 13 original colonies and the territories gained in the war in a uniform way. So the British Parliament in London imposed new laws and restrictions. Previously, the colonies had been allowed to develop largely on their own. Now they felt that their freedom was being limited.

SECTION OBJECTIVES

1. To identify why the Proclamation of 1763 angered so many colonists
2. To describe the debate over taxes and troops in the colonies
3. To explain the Stamp Act
4. To examine how the colonists forced Britain to repeal the Stamp Act

CRITICAL THINKING

Summarizing, p. 144
Making Inferences, p. 145
Drawing Conclusions, p. 146
Analyzing Points of View, p. 146

FOCUS & MOTIVATE

5-MINUTE WARM-UP

Drawing Conclusions These questions focus on the issue of taxation and the relationship between Britain and the colonies.

1. Look at the images on pages 144 and 146. How do the colonists feel about being taxed, according to these images?
2. Why might Great Britain feel justified in imposing taxes on its colonies?

Warm-Up Transparency WT6

INSTRUCT

INSTRUCT: OBJECTIVE 1
The Colonies and Britain Grow Apart

- How did Britain's policy toward its American colonies change after the French and Indian War?
- Why did the Proclamation of 1763 anger many colonists?
- What did many colonists choose to do about the proclamation?

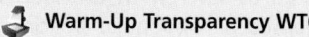

In-Depth Resources: Unit 2
- Guided Reading, p. 3

Reading Study Guide (Spanish and English), pp. 47–48

RECOMMENDED RESOURCES

In-Depth Resources: Unit 2
- Guided Reading, p. 3
- Building Vocabulary, p. 8
- Primary Source: Resolutions of the Stamp Act Congress, p. 12

Reading Study Guide (Spanish and English), pp. 47–48

Economics in History
- The Impact of British Taxes, p. 6

Outline Map Activities
- Pre-Revolutionary North America, pp. 11–12

Formal Assessment
- Section Quiz, p. 100

Integrated Assessment
- Rubrics, 1.1, 4.8

Access for Students Acquiring English/ESL, p. 32

INTEGRATED TECHNOLOGY

Humanities Transparency HT11
- The Repeal of the Stamp Act

Electronic Teacher Tools

classzone.com

TEST-TAKING RESOURCES

Strategies for Test Preparation

Test Practice Transparencies, TT20

Online Test Practice

INSTRUCT: OBJECTIVE 2

British Troops and Taxes

- What was the Quartering Act?
- Why did Parliament seek to impose greater taxes on the colonies?
- Why did the colonists oppose the Sugar Act?

Outline Map Activities
- Pre-Revolutionary North America, pp. 11–12

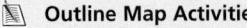

MORE ABOUT . . .

George Grenville

The colonists would have been hard pressed to find a person more unsympathetic to their plight than George Grenville. Grenville was obsessed with remedying Britain's financial difficulties after the French and Indian War. Such concerns led him to develop an intense hatred for colonial smuggling—which denied England vital tax revenues. He told an aide that smugglers should be "prosecuted and punished as severely as the law will allow." As he imposed his unpopular policies on the colonists, he showed little worry about their growing anger. Americans, he once declared, "could not hope to get any good by a controversy with the Mother Country."

INSTRUCT: OBJECTIVE 3

Britain Passes the Stamp Act

- What was the Stamp Act?
- How did the Stamp Act differ from previous taxes imposed on the colonies?
- What objection did colonial leaders voice about the Stamp Act?

Economics in History
- The Impact of British Taxes, p. 6

The first of Parliament's laws was the Proclamation of 1763. (See Chapter 5.) It said that colonists could not settle west of the Appalachian Mountains. Britain wanted this land to remain in the hands of its Native American allies to prevent another revolt like Pontiac's Rebellion.

The proclamation angered colonists who had hoped to move to the fertile Ohio Valley. Many of these colonists had no land of their own. It also upset colonists who had bought land as an investment. As a result, many ignored the law.

Reading **History**
A. Summarizing Who was upset by the Proclamation of 1763?
A. Answer colonists who wanted land of their own and those who had bought land as investments

2 British Troops and Taxes

King George III, the British monarch, wanted to enforce the proclamation and also keep peace with Britain's Native American allies. To do this, he decided to keep 10,000 soldiers in the colonies. In 1765, Parliament passed the **Quartering Act**. This was a cost-saving measure that required the colonies to quarter, or house, British soldiers and provide them with supplies. General Thomas Gage, commander of these forces, put most of the troops in New York.

Britain owed a large debt from the French and Indian War. Keeping troops in the colonies would raise that debt even higher. Britain needed more **revenue,** or income, to meet its expenses. So it attempted to have the colonies pay part of the war debt. It also wanted them to contribute toward the costs of frontier defense and colonial government.

In the past, the king had asked the colonial assemblies to pass taxes to support military actions that took place in the colonies. This time, however, Parliament voted to tax the Americans directly.

In 1764, Parliament passed the **Sugar Act.** This law placed a tax on sugar, molasses, and other products shipped to the colonies. It also called for strict enforcement of the act and harsh punishment of smugglers. Colonial merchants, who often traded in smuggled goods, reacted with anger.

Colonial leaders such as James Otis claimed that Parliament had no right to tax the colonies, since the colonists were not represented in Parliament. As Otis exclaimed, "Taxation without representation is tyranny!" British finance minister George Grenville disagreed. The colonists were subjects of Britain, he said, and enjoyed the protection of its laws. For that reason, they were subject to taxation.

Vocabulary
tyranny: absolute power in the hands of a single ruler

The colonial view of the hated stamp tax is shown by the skull and crossbones on this emblem (above); a royal stamp is pictured at right.

3 Britain Passes the Stamp Act

The Sugar Act was just the first in a series of acts that increased tension between the mother country and the colonies. In 1765, Parliament passed the **Stamp Act.** This law required all legal and commercial documents to carry an official stamp showing that a tax had been paid. All diplomas, contracts, and wills had to carry a stamp.

144

ACTIVITY OPTIONS

INDIVIDUAL NEEDS

LESS PROFICIENT READERS

Summarizing To help less proficient readers better understand the reasons for the growing tension between Britain and the colonies, have them chart the events of this section in a graphic organizer like the one shown here. Students should copy the chart and write a brief explanation of how the colonists reacted in each case. Then have the students share their answers with a more proficient reader.

Event	Colonial Response
Proclamation of 1763	
Sugar Act	
Stamp Act	

Even published materials such as newspapers had to be written on special stamped paper.

The Stamp Act was a new kind of tax for the colonies. The Sugar Act had been a tax on imported goods. It mainly affected merchants. In contrast, the Stamp Act was a tax applied within the colonies. It fell directly on all colonists. Even more, the colonists had to pay for stamps in silver coin—a scarce item in the colonies.

Colonial leaders vigorously protested. For them, the issue was clear. They were being taxed without their consent by a Parliament in which they had no voice. If Britain could pass the Stamp Act, what other taxes might it pass in the future? Samuel Adams, a leader in the Massachusetts legislature, asked, "Why not our lands? Why not the produce of our lands and, in short, everything we possess and make use of?" **Patrick Henry,** a member of Virginia's House of Burgesses, called for resistance to the tax. When another member shouted that resistance was treason, Henry reportedly replied, "If this be treason, make the most of it!"

4 The Colonies Protest the Stamp Act

Colonial assemblies and newspapers took up the cry—"No taxation without representation!" In October 1765, nine colonies sent delegates to the Stamp Act Congress in New York City. This was the first time the colonies met to consider acting together in protest. Delegates drew up a petition to the king protesting the Stamp Act. The petition declared that the right to tax the colonies belonged to the colonial assemblies, not to Parliament. Later, colonial merchants organized a **boycott** of British goods. A boycott is a refusal to buy.

B. Answer They thought Britain would fear losing trade and repeal the law.

Reading **History**
B. Making Inferences Why did the colonists boycott goods?

Meanwhile, some colonists formed secret societies to oppose British policies. The most famous of these groups was the **Sons of Liberty**. Many Sons of Liberty were lawyers, merchants, and craftspeople—the colonists most affected by the Stamp Act. These groups staged protests against the act.

Background
To voice their protests, the Sons of Liberty in Boston met under a huge, 120-year-old elm tree that they called the Liberty Tree.

Not all of their protests were peaceful. The Sons of Liberty burned the stamped paper whenever they could find it. They also attacked customs officials, whom they covered with hot tar and feathers and paraded in public. Fearing for their safety, many customs officials quit their jobs.

The protests in the colonies had an effect in Britain. Merchants thought that their trade with America would be hurt. Some British political leaders, including

Colonists protest the Stamp Act.

CONNECT TO TODAY

Tax Resistance
Point out to students that the tradition of resisting the payment of taxes began in this era and continues today. Many groups in the United States have organized to resist paying taxes for a variety of reasons. For example, the Libertarian political party has as one of its platform positions resistance to the payment of taxes. Have students do research to see if there are tax resistance groups in their own community.

INSTRUCT: OBJECTIVE 4

The Colonies Protest the Stamp Act

- In what ways did the colonists challenge the Stamp Act?
- Who were the Sons of Liberty?
- What eventually became of the Stamp Act?

In-Depth Resources: Unit 2
- Primary Source: Resolutions of the Stamp Act Congress, p. 12

MORE ABOUT . . .

The Sons of Liberty
Although we hear often about the Boston Sons of Liberty, the secret organizations were found in many colonies. In New York, the "Sons" were led by wealthy, high-born men. These men were not reluctant to use violence to resist the Stamp Act. The New York Sons of Liberty are believed to be the first in New York to die for independence. On January 18, 1775, the Sons of Liberty had an encounter with British soldiers. Several "Sons" were wounded, and one was killed.

Humanities Transparency HT11
- The Repeal of the Stamp Act

ACTIVITY OPTIONS

INTERDISCIPLINARY LINK: HUMANITIES — BLOCK SCHEDULING

PROTESTING THE STAMP ACT

Class Time 30 minutes

Task Creating protest material regarding the Stamp Act

Purpose To examine the different ways to sway public opinion

Supplies Needed
- Markers and drawing paper

Activity Break students into small groups and have them protest the Stamp Act in one of three ways: draw a poster or cartoon, create a slogan or jingle, or make a commercial. Students may focus on any aspect of the tax but should make their point clear and easy to understand. Groups that choose to draw a poster or cartoon should pick the student who is the best artist to draw the work. Have the groups display their work to the class. Groups that made a commercial should act it out, while those that created a slogan or jingle should recite it.

MORE ABOUT . . .

Tarring and Feathering

Ironically, the colonists adopted the practice of tarring and feathering from their mother country. This form of punishment reportedly began among English naval officers under the reign of King Richard the Lionhearted. English mobs occasionally performed this procedure on tax collectors and other unpopular figures. While recipients of this punishment certainly came away humiliated, they also could end up in a great deal of pain. The hot tar was known to cause third-degree burns, from which it took weeks to recover.

ASSESS & RETEACH

Setting the Stage Have students fill in the first three boxes on the graphic organizer.

Formal Assessment
- Section Quiz, p. 100

Critical Thinking Transparency CT16
- Setting the Stage

RETEACHING ACTIVITY

Have students work in pairs to perform an imaginary interview on the rising tensions between Britain and the colonies. One student should play a colonist, the other a local newspaper reporter. Have the reporter ask the colonist his or her views on the various acts and proclamations passed by the British. The reporter should write down the colonist's answers in outline form and hand them in.

In-Depth Resources: Unit 2
- Reteaching Activity, p. 18

Bostonians Paying the Taxman

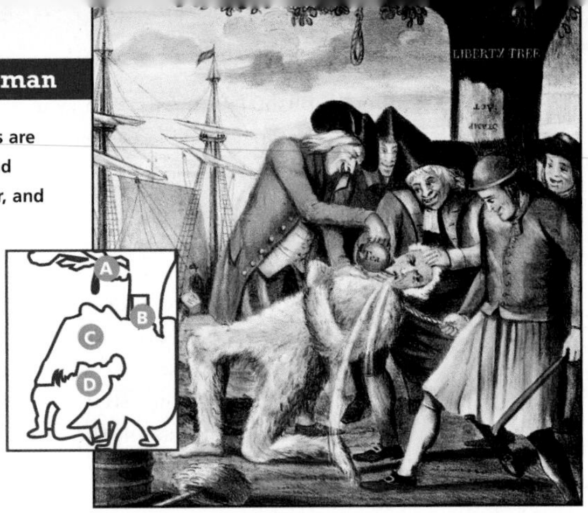

In this British political cartoon, Americans are depicted as barbarians who would tar and feather a customs official, or tax collector, and pour hot tea down his throat.

- A Liberty Tree as a gallows
- B Stamp Act posted upside down
- C Protesters in Boston
- D Customs official tarred and feathered

the popular parliamentary leader William Pitt, agreed with American thinking about taxing the colonies. Pitt spoke out against the Stamp Act.

A VOICE FROM THE PAST

The Americans have not acted in all things with prudence and [good] temper. They have been driven to madness by injustice. Will you punish them for the madness you have [caused]? . . . My opinion . . . is that the Stamp Act be repealed absolutely, totally and immediately.

William Pitt, quoted in *Patriots* by A. J. Langguth

Parliament finally saw that the Stamp Act was a mistake and repealed it in 1766. But at the same time, Parliament passed another law—the Declaratory Act. This law said that Parliament had supreme authority to govern the colonies. The Americans celebrated the repeal of the Stamp Act and tried to ignore the Declaratory Act. A great tug of war between Parliament and the colonies had begun. The central issue was control of the colonies, as you will learn in the next section.

C. Possible **Answer** It showed the colonists that even though they had won repeal of the Stamp Act, Parliament was still the supreme authority.

***Reading* History**

C. Drawing Conclusions Why was it important for Parliament to pass the Declaratory Act?

Section 1 Assessment

1. Terms & Names

Explain the significance of:
- King George III
- Quartering Act
- revenue
- Sugar Act
- Stamp Act
- Patrick Henry
- boycott
- Sons of Liberty

2. Taking Notes

Use a cluster diagram like the one below to review points of conflict between Britain and the colonies.

Which do you think was the most serious? Explain.

3. Main Ideas

a. Why did the Proclamation of 1763 anger colonists?

b. How did colonists react to the Stamp Act?

c. What was the goal of secret societies such as the Sons of Liberty?

4. Critical Thinking

Analyzing Points of View What were the two sides in the debate over British taxation of the colonies?

THINK ABOUT
- how Parliament viewed the colonies
- what concerned the colonists about taxes

ACTIVITY OPTIONS

ART / **MUSIC** Imagine that you are a colonial leader who wants to get your fellow colonists to protest British policy. Design a **poster** or write a **song of protest.**

Section 1 Assessment

1. Terms & Names

King George III, p. 144
Quartering Act, p. 144
revenue, p. 144
Sugar Act, p. 144
Stamp Act, p. 144
Patrick Henry, p. 145
boycott, p. 145
Sons of Liberty, p. 145

2. Taking Notes

Sugar Act (tax on sugar and other goods); Stamp Act (direct tax); trial without jury; Proclamation of 1763 (prevented colonists from settling in the Ohio Valley); Quartering Act (forced colonists to house soldiers). Answers will vary but should include support from the chapter.

3. Main Ideas

a. It tried to prevent them from moving west in search of land. **b.** They protested, sometimes violently, and called for its repeal. **c.** to oppose British policies and organize protests

4. Critical Thinking

The British felt the colonies should pay taxes to cover colonial expenses. The colonists said no taxes without consent and feared, once begun, taxation might never stop.

ACTIVITY OPTIONS

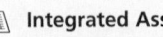

Integrated Assessment
- Rubrics for a poster, 1.1
- Rubrics for a song, 4.8

2 Colonial Resistance Grows

MAIN IDEA

Many Americans began to organize to oppose British policies.

WHY IT MATTERS NOW

Americans continue to protest what they view as wrongs and injustices.

TERMS & NAMES
Crispus Attucks
Townshend Acts
writs of assistance
Samuel Adams
Boston Massacre
John Adams
committee of correspondence
Boston Tea Party

ONE AMERICAN'S STORY

Crispus Attucks knew about the struggle for freedom. The son of an African-American father and a Native American mother, Attucks was born into slavery in Framingham, Massachusetts, around 1723. As a young man, Attucks escaped by running away to sea. He spent the next 20 years as a sailor, working on whaling boats. To avoid recapture, he used a false name, calling himself Michael Johnson.

In March 1770, Attucks found himself in Boston, where feelings against British rule were reaching a fever pitch. The words *freedom* and *liberty* seemed to be on everyone's lips. One night Attucks heard about a disturbance involving colonists and British troops and decided to investigate. He had no idea that he was about to play a key role in American history—losing his life to a British bullet in a protest that came to be known as the Boston Massacre. In this section, you will read how the tension between Britain and its colonies led to violence.

Crispus Attucks, a sailor of African-American and Native American ancestry, was an early hero of America's struggle for freedom.

1 The Townshend Acts Are Passed

After the uproar over the Stamp Act, Britain hoped to avoid further conflict. Even so, it still needed to raise money to pay for troops and other expenses in America. The Quartering Act was not working. Most of the British army was in New York, and New York saw that as an unfair burden. Its assembly refused to pay to house the troops.

The king's finance minister, Charles Townshend, told Parliament that he had a way to raise revenue in the colonies. So in 1767, Parliament passed his plan, known as the **Townshend Acts.**

The first of the Townshend Acts suspended New York's assembly until New Yorkers agreed to provide housing for the troops. The other acts placed duties, or import taxes, on various goods brought into the colonies, such as glass, paper, paint, lead, and tea. Townshend thought that duties, which were collected before the goods entered the colonies, would anger the colonists less than the direct taxes of the Stamp Act. The money raised would be used to pay the salaries of British governors and other officials in the colonies. To enforce the acts, British officers

SECTION OBJECTIVES

1. To explain the Townshend Acts
2. To describe why and how the colonists protested the Townshend Acts
3. To explain the Boston Massacre
4. To summarize the Tea Act and the Boston Tea Party

CRITICAL THINKING

Making Inferences, p. 148
Recognizing Propaganda, p. 149
Drawing Conclusions, pp. 150, 151
Recognizing Effects, p. 151

Why It Matters Now
- Politics and Protest, pp. 11–12

FOCUS & MOTIVATE

5-MINUTE WARM-UP

Evaluating Answering these questions will help students understand how colonial resentment toward the British grew.

1. Look at the engraving on page 149. Based on this picture, who appears to be at fault for the Boston Massacre?
2. Why might colonial leaders interested in independence want to blame the massacre on the British?

Warm-Up Transparency WT6

INSTRUCT

INSTRUCT: OBJECTIVE 1
The Townshend Acts Are Passed

- What were the Townshend Acts?
- Why did the British think the acts would anger the colonists less than the Stamp Act did?
- How did the British attempt to enforce the Townshend Acts?

In-Depth Resources: Unit 2
- Guided Reading, p. 4
- Building Vocabulary, p. 8

RECOMMENDED RESOURCES

In-Depth Resources: Unit 2
- Guided Reading, p. 4
- Building Vocabulary, p. 8
- Skillbuilder Practice, p. 9

Reading Study Guide (Spanish and English), pp. 49–50

Why It Matters Now
- Politics and Protest, pp. 11–12

Formal Assessment
- Section Quiz, p. 101

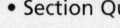

Integrated Assessment
- Rubrics, 3.6, 5.4

Access for Students Acquiring English/ESL
- Guided Reading, p. 33
- Skillbuilder Practice, p. 47

INTEGRATED TECHNOLOGY

Humanities Transparency HT12
- *The Copley Family*

Electronic Teacher Tools

classzone.com

TEST-TAKING RESOURCES

Strategies for Test Preparation

Test Practice Transparencies, TT21

Online Test Practice

INSTRUCT: OBJECTIVE 2

The Reasons for Protest/Tools of Protest

- Why did the writs of assistance anger the colonists?
- What methods did the colonists use to protest the Townshend Acts?

daily*life*

Women and Protest

Colonial women took very seriously their boycott of British items such as tea. On one occasion, for example, a young woman named Susan Boudinot was offered a cup of tea while visiting the home of New Jersey governor William Franklin. She politely accepted the drink and then threw it out of the window.

Some women even put their commitment to the struggle above their social relationships. In Mecklenburg, North Carolina, a group of women signed a pledge to allow only men who had signed up for military service to court them.

Humanities Transparency HT12
• *The Copley Family*

would use **writs of assistance,** or search warrants, to enter homes or businesses to search for smuggled goods.

2 The Reasons for Protest

Protests immediately broke out at news of the Townshend Acts. New Yorkers were angry that their elected assembly had been suspended. People throughout the colonies were upset that Britain was placing new taxes on them. "The issue," said John Dickinson, an important Pennsylvania lawyer, was "whether Parliament can legally take money out of our pockets without our consent." He explained his opposition to the Townshend Acts in essays called *Letters from a Farmer in Pennsylvania,* published in 1767.

A. Answer
He says that happiness depends on freedom, which depends on security of property. Taxes imposed without consent take away that security and should be opposed.

Reading **History**

A. Making Inferences Why does Dickinson believe that taxes interfere with happiness?

daily *life*

WOMEN AND PROTEST

Women were not allowed to participate in political life in the colonies. So their role in protesting British actions was not as prominent as that of men. However, women made their beliefs known by taking part in demonstrations.

Also, some women formed the Daughters of Liberty. This was a patriotic organization that joined in the boycott of British tea and other goods. The refusal of these colonial women to use British imports caused them personal hardship. They were forced to make many of the boycotted items, such as clothing, themselves.

A VOICE FROM THE PAST

Let these truths be . . . impressed on our minds—that we cannot be happy without being free—that we cannot be free without being secure in our property—that we cannot be secure in our property if without our consent others may . . . take it away—that taxes imposed on us by Parliament do thus take it away—that duties laid for the sole purpose of raising money are taxes—that attempts to lay such duties should be instantly and firmly opposed.

John Dickinson, quoted in *A New Age Now Begins* by Page Smith

The colonists were also angry about the writs of assistance. Many believed, as James Otis had argued (see page 143), that the writs went against their natural rights. These rights had been described by English philosopher John Locke during the Enlightenment. The law of nature, said Locke, teaches that "no one ought to harm another in his life, health, liberty, or possessions." The colonists felt that the Townshend Acts were a serious threat to their rights and freedoms.

Tools of Protest

To protest the Townshend Acts, colonists in Boston announced another boycott of British goods in October 1767. The driving force behind this protest was **Samuel Adams,** a leader of the Boston Sons of Liberty. Adams urged colonists to continue to resist British controls.

The boycott spread throughout the colonies. The Sons of Liberty pressured shopkeepers not to sell imported goods. The Daughters of Liberty called on colonists to weave their own cloth and use American products. As a result, trade with Britain fell sharply.

Colonial leaders asked for peaceful protests. Articles in the *Boston Gazette* asked the people to remain calm—

ACTIVITY OPTIONS

INDIVIDUAL NEEDS: GIFTED AND TALENTED

IMPACT OF THE INDIVIDUAL

Class Time One class period

Task Creating a profile of Revolutionary leaders

Purpose To describe the personal characteristics and leadership qualities of Revolutionary leaders

Supplies Needed
- Reference materials on patriots of the Revolutionary War
- Internet access for additional resources

Activity Have small groups of students select at least three of the individuals named in this section. They should prepare a profile of each individual by using the information from the text and outside references. Then they should present their profiles as a "Who Am I?" challenge, without revealing the name of the person to the class. After the correct answer has been given, the small group should be prepared to tell the class how that individual influenced the colonists' move toward independence.

This engraving, *The Bloody Massacre Perpetrated in King Street* by Boston silversmith Paul Revere, appeared in the *Boston Gazette.*

"no mobs. . . . Constitutional methods are best." However, tempers were running high. When customs officers in Boston tried to seize the American merchant ship *Liberty,* which was carrying smuggled wine, a riot broke out. The rioters forced the customs officers to flee.

Fearing a loss of control, officials called for more British troops. A defiant Samuel Adams replied, "We will destroy every soldier that dares put his foot on shore. . . . I look upon them as foreign enemies."

INTERNET ACTIVITY CLASSZONE.COM

The Boston Massacre ❸

In the fall of 1768, 1,000 British soldiers (known as redcoats for their bright red jackets) arrived in Boston under the command of General Thomas Gage. With their arrival, tension filled the streets of Boston.

Since the soldiers were poorly paid, they hired themselves out as workers, usually at rates lower than those of American workers. Resentment against the redcoats grew. Soldiers and street youths often yelled insults at each other. "Lobsters for sale!" the youths would yell, referring to the soldiers' red coats. "Yankees!" the soldiers jeered. *Yankee* was supposed to be an insult, but the colonists soon took pride in the name.

On March 5, 1770, tensions finally exploded into violence. A group of youths and dockworkers—among them Crispus Attucks—started trading insults in front of the Custom House. A fight broke out, and the soldiers began firing. Attucks and four laborers were killed.

The Sons of Liberty called the shooting the **Boston Massacre.** They said that Attucks and the four others had given their lives for freedom. The incident became a tool for anti-British propaganda in newspaper articles, pamphlets, and posters. The people of Boston were outraged.

Meanwhile, the redcoats who had fired the shots were arrested for murder. **John Adams,** a lawyer and cousin of Samuel Adams, defended them in court. Adams was criticized for taking the case. He replied that the law should be "deaf . . . to the clamors of the populace." He supported

Reading **History**

B. Recognizing Propaganda How did the use of the word *massacre* show an anti-British view?

B. Answer
A massacre is a mass killing, often planned; this was not a massacre.

MORE ABOUT . . .

The Boston Massacre

Much about Paul Revere's famous Boston Massacre engraving is less than accurate. The work depicts only seven British musket men, while eight were charged in the incident. Furthermore, Crispus Attucks, reportedly the first man killed in the shootings, does not appear in the engraving.

Even Revere's claim as the artist of the engraving is a bit misleading. Revere borrowed heavily from a piece done by Henry Pelham. He rushed his work to the public ahead of Pelham's. By the time Pelham could protest, Revere's now-famous work was going up on walls throughout Boston.

INSTRUCT: OBJECTIVE ❸

The Boston Massacre

- Why did colonists in Boston resent the presence of so many British soldiers?
- How did the Boston Massacre begin? What was the outcome?
- Why was the massacre an important event in the cause for independence?

ACTIVITY OPTIONS

SKILLBUILDER LESSON: RECOGNIZING PROPAGANDA

Explaining the Skill Propaganda is verbal or visual communication that aims to influence people's opinions, emotions, or actions. Visual propaganda often employs symbols or images to grab attention. Wartime propaganda often seeks to portray the home country as especially good.

Applying the Skill The Boston Massacre—especially as it was portrayed in articles and paintings—was considered an effective tool of anti-British propaganda. Examine the image of the massacre, as well as the text describing it on page 165, and answer the following questions.

1. Why might this engraving have stirred anti-British feeling among colonists? *(It shows British soldiers shooting colonists.)*
2. Based on the text, what aspect of the incident does the engraving leave out? *(the fact that the colonists had been taunting and fighting with the soldiers before the shooting began)*
3. How might an engraving of the massacre have differed? *(It might have shown the soldiers shooting in self-defense.)*

In-Depth Resources: Unit 2
• Skillbuilder Practice, p. 9

AMERICA'S HISTORY MAKERS

John and Samuel Adams

Though different in ages and personalities—John was cautious and reasonable, Samuel was fiery and boisterous—the two cousins got along rather well. However, the two men's relationship collapsed over the issue of politics. In 1796, John ran for president as a member of the Federalist Party—a party Samuel considered elitist and an enemy of the common people. Samuel accused John of betraying "the principles of '75," and he campaigned vigorously against his cousin. Nonetheless, John Adams and the Federalists won the election. Disgusted, Samuel retired from political life. He died in 1803.

Answer: Samuel used fiery speeches and propaganda, while John believed in moderate but steady resistance.

AMERICA'S HISTORY MAKERS

SAMUEL ADAMS
1722–1803

Samuel Adams was a Harvard graduate. But unlike his cousin John, also a Harvard graduate, he showed little skill for the law. Later, when he took control of the family business, he lost his father's fortune. Yet he succeeded in one important undertaking—moving America toward independence.

Adams's true talent lay in rousing people to action in support of a cause. A fiery orator and a master of propaganda, he used words as a weapon. One British official said that "every dip of his pen stings."

JOHN ADAMS
1735–1826

John Adams, unlike Samuel, was considered a moderate in the struggle against Britain. He was an important voice of reason and at first opposed resisting by force.

Adams believed in the rule of law. He called his defense of the soldiers in the Boston Massacre "one of the best pieces of service I ever rendered my country."

Eventually, Adams became convinced that only outright resistance would gain liberty for America. He said, "Britain has at last driven America, to the last Step, a compleat Seperation from her."

How did the cousins John and Samuel Adams differ in the way they protested British actions?

the colonial cause but wanted to show that the colonists followed the rule of law. Adams argued that the soldiers had acted in self-defense. The jury agreed. To many colonists, however, the Boston Massacre would stand as a symbol of British tyranny.

4 The Tea Act

The colonists were unaware that on the day of the Boston Massacre, Parliament proposed the repeal of the Townshend Acts. One month later, all the acts except the tax on tea were repealed. The colonial boycott had been effective—British trade had been hurt. But Parliament kept the tea tax to show that it still had the right to tax the colonists. For most Americans, the crisis was over.

Samuel Adams, however, wanted to make sure people did not forget the cause of liberty. He started a drive to form **committees of correspondence** in various towns in Massachusetts. These groups exchanged letters on colonial affairs. Before long, committees throughout Massachusetts were corresponding with one another and with committees in other colonies.

Then, in 1773, Parliament opened up old wounds when it passed the Tea Act. Tea was very popular in the colonies, but much of it was smuggled in from Holland. The Tea Act gave the British East India Company control over the American tea trade. The tea would arrive in the colonies only in the trading company's ships and be sold there by its merchants. Colonists who had not been paying any tax on smuggled tea would now have to pay a tax on this regulated tea. This enraged colonial shippers and merchants. The colonists wondered what Parliament would do next.

Reading **History**

C. Drawing Conclusions Why did Samuel Adams think that the colonists might forget the cause of liberty?

C. Possible Answer Adams may have thought that since there was no crisis, the colonists would just go back to being involved in their daily lives.

INSTRUCT: OBJECTIVE 4

The Tea Act/The Boston Tea Party

- For what reason did the British repeal the Townshend Acts?
- Why did the Tea Act upset the colonists?
- What was the Boston Tea Party?

ACTIVITY OPTIONS

INTERDISCIPLINARY LINK: LANGUAGE ARTS — BLOCK SCHEDULING

COMMITTEES OF CORRESPONDENCE

Class Time One class period

Task Writing a letter from a committee of correspondence

Purpose To identify and explain the issues that concerned the colonists

Supplies Needed
- Reference materials on colonial objections to British policies
- Internet access for additional resources

Activity Have students break into small groups, each representing a committee of correspondence from a particular colony. Have each group draft a letter to another colony's committee discussing the issues of the day. Letters should display the committee's feelings as well as suggest a possible course of action. Tell students to use whatever style of writing they wish to most effectively convey their message. Have a member from each group read the group's letter before the class.

The Boston Tea Party

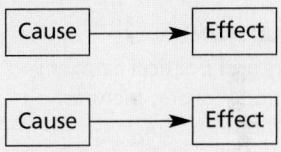

Colonists dumped hundreds of chests of tea into Boston Harbor in 1773 to protest the Tea Act.

Protests against the Tea Act took place all over the colonies. In Charleston, South Carolina, colonists unloaded tea and let it rot on the docks. In New York City and Philadelphia, colonists blocked tea ships from landing. In Boston, the Sons of Liberty organized what came to be known as the **Boston Tea Party.**

*Reading*History
D. Reading a Map Find Boston Harbor on the map on page 156.

On the evening of December 16, 1773, a group of men disguised as Native Americans boarded three tea ships docked in Boston Harbor. One of the men, George Hewes, a Boston shoemaker, later recalled the events.

> *A VOICE FROM THE PAST*
>
> We then were ordered by our commander to open the hatches and take out all the chests of tea and throw them overboard. . . . In about three hours from the time we went on board, we had thus broken and thrown overboard every tea chest to be found on the ship, while those in the other ships were disposing of the tea in the same way, at the same time.
>
> **George Hewes,** quoted in *A Retrospect of the Boston Tea-Party*

E. Possible Answer Britain wanted repayment for the destroyed tea and wanted those involved brought to trial.

That night, Hewes and the others destroyed 342 chests of tea. Many colonists rejoiced at the news. They believed that Britain would now see how strongly colonists opposed taxation without representation.

Others doubted that destroying property was the best way to settle the tax debate. Some colonial leaders offered to pay for the tea if Parliament would repeal the Tea Act. Britain rejected the offer. It not only wanted repayment, but it also wanted the men who destroyed the tea to be brought to trial. The British reaction to the Boston Tea Party would fan the flames of rebellion in the 13 colonies, as you will read in the next section.

*Reading*History
E. Recognizing Effects How did Britain react to the Tea Party?

Section 2 Assessment

1. Terms & Names

Explain the significance of:
- Crispus Attucks
- Townshend Acts
- writs of assistance
- Samuel Adams
- Boston Massacre
- John Adams
- committee of correspondence
- Boston Tea Party

2. Taking Notes

Create a time line like the one below to show the significant people and events described in this section.

1767 ——————— 1773

Which event do you think was the most important? Explain.

3. Main Ideas

a. Why did colonists oppose the Townshend Acts?

b. Why were British troops sent to Boston?

c. What prompted the Boston Tea Party?

4. Critical Thinking

Drawing Conclusions
Do you think colonial outrage over the Boston Massacre was justified? Explain.

THINK ABOUT
- how the British troops were taunted
- whether troops have the right to fire on citizens

ACTIVITY OPTIONS

SPEECH
TECHNOLOGY

Read more about the Boston Massacre or the Boston Tea Party. Present an **oral report** or plan a **multimedia presentation** about the event.

MORE ABOUT . . .

The Boston Tea Party

The day after the Tea Party, news of the incident spread. It stirred both outrage and admiration. John Adams praised his fellow colonists' actions. "There is a dignity, a majesty, a sublimity, in this last effort of the patriots that I greatly admire," he wrote. However, Benjamin Franklin condemned the act and suggested that Boston repay the ship owners for their lost tea. The fiery Samuel Adams curtly dismissed Franklin's words. "Franklin may be a good philosopher," Adams said, "but he is a bungling politician."

ASSESS & RETEACH

Setting the Stage Have students fill in the next four boxes on the chapter graphic organizer.

Formal Assessment
- Section Quiz, p. 101

RETEACHING ACTIVITY

Help students focus on the cause and effect relationships in this section. Students should copy the graphic below and fill it in with Townshend Acts, Tea Act, Boston Massacre, and Boston Tea Party. When they finish, have them write a paragraph describing the connections between the acts and the events.

Cause → Effect

Cause → Effect

In-Depth Resources: Unit 2
- Reteaching Activity, p. 19

Section 2 Assessment

1. Terms & Names

Crispus Attucks, p. 147
Townshend Acts, p. 147
writs of assistance, p. 148
Samuel Adams, p. 148
Boston Massacre, p. 149
John Adams, p. 149
committee of correspondence, p. 150
Boston Tea Party, p. 151

2. Taking Notes

1767: Townshend Acts passed; October 1767: Boston boycotts British goods; March 1770: Boston Massacre; 1773: Tea Act passed; Dec. 1773: Boston Tea Party

Students' responses will vary but should include support from the chapter.

3. Main Ideas

a. because the acts suspended the New York assembly, imposed new taxes, and called for the use of writs of assistance **b.** to keep order after the riot over the merchant ship *Liberty* **c.** the Tea Act of 1773

4. Critical Thinking

Opinions will vary. Justified: soldiers have no right to fire on unarmed citizens; Not Justified: the soldiers were acting in self-defense.

ACTIVITY OPTIONS

Integrated Assessment
- Rubric for an oral report, 3.6
- Rubric for a presentation, 5.4

Interdisciplinary **CHALLENGE**

OBJECTIVE

Students work cooperatively to express persuasive ideas through artwork, words, and statistics that justify the American colonists' goal of independence.

BLOCK SCHEDULING

PROCEDURE

Gather supplies that students might need, such as posterboard, colored markers, and graph paper. For each challenge, have students form groups of three or four. Ask group members to divide the work among themselves. Then have them choose an option for presenting their solution.

ART CHALLENGE

Class Time 50 minutes

To help students present their viewpoints visually, suggest they consider using these kinds of pictures in their posters or political cartoons:

- *symbols*—images that represent concepts or issues
- *caricatures*—drawings that exaggerate or distort characters to convey a message

POSSIBLE SOLUTIONS

Students' posters and political cartoons might feature the following pictures:

- a shattered teapot
- a scene from the Boston Tea Party
- caricatures of penniless American tea sellers, unpopular tax collectors, or tyrannical Parliament members

Interdisciplinary **CHALLENGE**

Fight for Representative Government!

You are a colonist living in Boston on the eve of the American Revolution. Nearly a decade of protest against British policies has failed to secure American rights. Redcoats continue to be quartered in the city. The Tea Act still stands. Now the dumping of tea in Boston Harbor by some Patriots has charged the atmosphere with tension. Trouble lies ahead, but you are determined to fight for a government that will protect your rights.

COOPERATIVE LEARNING On this page are two challenges that you face as the conflict with Britain unfolds. Working with a small group, decide how to deal with each challenge. Choose an option, assign a task to each group member, and do the activity. You will find useful information in the Data File. Present your solutions to the class.

ART CHALLENGE

"Do not . . . sip the accursed, dutied STUFF"

People all over Boston are worried about the Tea Act. It taxes tea, but it also lets the British East India Company sell tea through its own agents. In time, the plan could drive American tea sellers out of business. How can you protest these threats to American commerce and liberty? Present your viewpoint using one of these options:

- **Design an anti–Tea Act poster.**
- **Draw a political cartoon showing the dangers of the Tea Act.**

152

STANDARDS FOR EVALUATION

ART CHALLENGE

Option 1 Posters should

- depict the injustices of the Tea Act.
- convince colonists to take action.

Option 2 Political cartoons should

- portray historical figures, events, or objects related to the Tea Act.
- include a descriptive caption.

MATH CHALLENGE

Option 1 Graphs (bar or line) should

- have clearly labeled axes.
- show the correlation between boycotts and British exports.

Option 2 Editorials should

- state the viewpoint clearly.
- use supporting facts and evidence.

CIVICS CHALLENGE

Option 1 Debate should

- include reasons for or against the tactics.
- include supporting evidence.
- rebut the opposing arguments.

Option 2 Proposal should

- be specific and concrete.
- provide a clear guide to citizen action.

MATH CHALLENGE

"Wear none but your own country linen"

Years of struggle have taken their toll on Boston. People are tired of soldiers and of boycotting British goods, such as clothing. But the Tea Act presents a huge threat. The Boston Tea Party took care of only one shipment. How can you help encourage the boycott of other British goods, such as clothing? Look at the Data File for help. Present your appeal using one of these options:

- **Make a graph showing the effect of colonial boycotts on imports of British goods to America.**
- **Write an editorial using statistics to show how American boycotts have hurt the British.**

ACTIVITY WRAP-UP

Present to the Class **Meet as a group to review your responses to British attacks on American liberty. Pick the most creative solution for each challenge and present these solutions to the class.**

DATA FILE

Population in 1774–1775

Britain: 7,860,000
London: 700,000

The 13 colonies: 2,350,000
Philadelphia: 33,000
New York: 22,000
Boston: 16,000

North American Imports from Britain

(in millions of pounds sterling)

1763	1.6	1770	1.9
1764	2.3	1771	4.2
1765	1.9	1772	3.0
1766	1.8	1773	2.1
1767	1.9	1774	2.6
1768	2.2	1775	0.2
1769	1.3	1776	0.1

North American Exports to Britain

(in millions of pounds sterling)

1763	1.1	1770	1.0
1764	1.1	1771	1.3
1765	1.2	1772	1.3
1766	1.0	1773	1.4
1767	1.1	1774	1.4
1768	1.3	1775	1.9
1769	1.1	1776	0.1

Key Boycott Dates

1764 Boycott after passage of Sugar Act
1765 Boycott after passage of Stamp Act
1766 Boycott relaxed after Stamp Act repealed
1767 Boycott after passage of Townshend Acts
1770 Townshend Acts repealed
1774 Boycott after passage of Intolerable Acts

Sales and Consumption of Tea at the Time of the Boston Tea Party

British sales: fourth most important product shipped to America
American consumption: 1.2 million pounds per year

For more on Revolutionary America . . .

RESEARCH LINKS
CLASSZONE.COM

MATH CHALLENGE

Class Time 50 minutes

Suggest that students look at current newspaper editorials and graphs to use as models. Ask them to consider how statistics can make ideas more meaningful and paint a clearer picture of an event.

POSSIBLE SOLUTION

Students might convert facts and figures from the Data File into a line graph organized as follows:

- Vertical axis scale ranges from 0 to 4.5 (in millions of pounds sterling) to indicate North American Imports from Britain.
- Dates on the horizontal axis range from 1763 to 1776. Callouts identify the years that correspond to Key Policy Dates listed in the Data File.
- Points plotted on the line graph correspond to the numbers listed by year in the Data File.

ALTERNATIVE CHALLENGE

CIVICS CHALLENGE

"The destruction of the Tea"

After the Boston Tea Party, John Adams writes in his diary, "The destruction of the Tea is so bold and it must have so important Consequences." You and other colonists wonder if this protest by the Sons of Liberty was too bold. Was the Boston Tea Party an act of patriotism or terrorism? Present your position using one of these options:

- **Stage a debate in which you argue for or against the tactics used by the Sons of Liberty.**
- **Write a proposal explaining what citizens should do about unjust laws.**

ACTIVITY WRAP-UP

To help student groups evaluate the creativity of their challenge solutions, ask them to make a grid with criteria like the one shown. Then have them rate each solution on a scale from 1 to 5.

Originality	1	2	3	4	5
Persuasive appeal	1	2	3	4	5
Audience impact	1	2	3	4	5
Overall effectiveness	1	2	3	4	5

SECTION OBJECTIVES

1. To describe the Intolerable Acts
2. To explain how the colonies wavered between war and peace
3. To profile the Midnight Ride
4. To describe the battles of Lexington and Concord

SKILLBUILDER

Interpreting Charts, p. 155
Interpreting Maps: Location, Movement, p. 156

CRITICAL THINKING

Evaluating, p. 156
Recognizing Effects, p. 156
Drawing Conclusions, p. 157
Supporting Opinions, p. 157

FOCUS & MOTIVATE

5-MINUTE WARM-UP

Drawing Conclusions To help students understand the coming war between Britain and America, have them answer these questions.

1. Look at the map on page 156. What were the British forced to do after Concord?
2. What might the British action indicate about the colonists' chances in a war against Britain?

Warm-Up Transparency WT6

INSTRUCT

INSTRUCT: OBJECTIVE 1

The Intolerable Acts

- What were the Intolerable Acts?
- What effect did the Intolerable Acts have on the colonies?
- How did the colonies come to the aid of Massachusetts?

In-Depth Resources: Unit 2
- Guided Reading, p. 5

Reading Study Guide (Spanish and English), pp. 51–52

3 The Road to Lexington and Concord

TERMS & NAMES
militia
Minuteman
Intolerable Acts
First Continental Congress
Paul Revere
Lexington and Concord
Loyalist
Patriot

MAIN IDEA	WHY IT MATTERS NOW
The tensions between Britain and the colonies led to armed conflict in Massachusetts.	Americans at times still find themselves called upon to fight for their principles.

This statue of Captain John Parker stands in Lexington, Massachusetts.

ONE AMERICAN'S STORY

At dawn on April 19, 1775, some 70 militiamen gathered on the grassy common at the center of Lexington, Massachusetts, a small town near Boston. Captain John Parker, a veteran of the French and Indian War, was their commander. The <u>militia</u> was a force of armed civilians pledged to defend their community. About one-third of the Lexington militia were <u>Minutemen</u>, trained to be "ready to act at a minute's warning." Everyone had heard the news—the British were coming!

Each militiaman was equipped with a musket, a bayonet, and ammunition. Parker had spent months drilling his troops, but they had never faced British soldiers. Soon they would meet the British on Lexington Green in the first battle of the Revolutionary War. According to tradition, Parker told his men, "Stand your ground; don't fire unless fired upon, but if they mean to have war, let it begin here."

In this section, you will read how colonial protests eventually turned into violent revolution.

1 The Intolerable Acts

The Boston Tea Party had aroused fury in Britain. One British official said that the people of Boston "ought to be knocked about their ears." King George III declared, "We must master them or totally leave them to themselves and treat them as aliens." Britain chose to "master" the colonies.

In 1774, Parliament passed a series of laws to punish the Massachusetts colony and to serve as a warning to other colonies. The British called these laws the Coercive Acts, but they were so harsh that the colonists called them the **<u>Intolerable Acts.</u>**

One of the acts would close the port of Boston until colonists paid for the destroyed tea. Others banned committees of correspondence, allowed Britain to house troops wherever necessary, and let British officials accused of crimes in the colonies stand trial in Britain. To enforce the acts, Parliament appointed General Thomas Gage governor of Massachusetts.

In 1773, Sam Adams had written, "I wish we could arouse the continent." The Intolerable Acts answered his wish. Other colonies

RECOMMENDED RESOURCES

In-Depth Resources: Unit 2
- Guided Reading, p. 5
- Building Vocabulary, p. 8
- Literature Selection: "Paul Revere's Ride," pp. 14–17

Reading Study Guide (Spanish and English), pp. 51–52

Formal Assessment
- Section Quiz, p. 102

Integrated Assessment
- Rubrics, 2.1, 2.2

Access for Students Acquiring English/ESL
- Guided Reading, p. 34

INTEGRATED TECHNOLOGY

Critical Thinking Trans. CT17

Electronic Teacher Tools

classzone.com

immediately offered Massachusetts their support. They sent food and money to Boston. The committees of correspondence also called for a meeting of colonial delegates to discuss what to do next.

2 The First Continental Congress Meets

In September 1774, delegates from all the colonies except Georgia met in Philadelphia. At this meeting, called the **First Continental Congress,** delegates voted to ban all trade with Britain until the Intolerable Acts were repealed. They also called on each colony to begin training troops. Georgia agreed to be a part of the actions of the Congress even though it had voted not to send delegates.

The First Continental Congress marked a key step in American history. Although most delegates were not ready to call for independence, they were determined to uphold colonial rights. This meeting planted the seeds of a future independent government. John Adams called it "a nursery of American statesmen." The delegates agreed to meet in seven months, if necessary. By that time, however, fighting with Britain had begun.

*Reading***History**
A. Evaluating Why do you think the First Continental Congress was important?
A. Possible Answer It was important because it showed that colonists were determined to uphold colonial rights.

Between War and Peace

The colonists hoped that the trade boycott would force a repeal of the Intolerable Acts. After all, past boycotts had led to the repeal of the Stamp Act and the Townshend Acts. This time, however, Parliament stood firm. It even increased restrictions on colonial trade and sent more troops.

By the end of 1774, some colonists were preparing to fight. In Massachusetts, John Hancock headed the Committee of Safety, which had the power to call out the militia. The colonial troops continued to train.

CAUSE AND EFFECT: *Growing Conflict Between Britain and America*

DATE	BRITISH ACTION	COLONIAL REACTION
1763	Proclamation of 1763 issued	Proclamation leads to anger
1765	Stamp Act passed	Boycott of British goods; Stamp Act Resolves passed
1766	Stamp Act repealed; Declaration Act passed	Boycott ended
1767	Townshend Acts passed	New boycotts; Boston Massacre (March 1770)
1770	Townshend Acts repealed (April)	Tension between colonies and Britain reduced
1773	Tea Act passed	Boston Tea Party
1774	Intolerable Acts passed	First Continental Congress bans trade; militias organized
1775	Troops ordered to Lexington and Concord, Massachusetts	Militia fights British troops; Second Continental Congress; Continental Army established

SKILLBUILDER **Interpreting Charts**
1. *What British action caused the first violence in the growing conflict between Britain and America?*
2. *How might the Intolerable Acts be seen as a reaction as well as an action?*

Skillbuilder Answers
1. The Townshend Acts led to the Boston Massacre.
2. The Intolerable Acts were passed as a result of the Boston Tea Party, and they caused the calling of the First Continental Congress.

INSTRUCT: OBJECTIVE 2

The First Continental Congress Meets/ Between War and Peace

- What happened at the First Continental Congress?
- How did the colonists protest the Intolerable Acts? How successful were they?
- What did most colonial leaders think about the prospect of war with Britain?

MORE ABOUT . . .

First Continental Congress
In the first session of the Continental Congress, the delegates rejected, by a vote of six to five, Pennsylvania delegate Joseph Galloway's plan to create a union of the colonies. Galloway's Plan of Union included a Grand Council with delegates from all the colonies that would deal with issues affecting more than one colony. Legislation would be subject to Parliament's approval. The council would also have the right to reject Parliament's legislation.

HISTORY FROM VISUALS

Interpreting the Chart Have students note the span of years on the chart, and explain that the graphic shows how British-American tension built up over time and did not stem from one or two incidents. Ask students how colonial leaders might use this chart to defend their desire to break free from Britain. **Possible Response** Colonial leaders might use the chart to emphasize Britain's pattern of injustice and to show how the colonies have been enduring such injustice for too long.

Extension Have students work in pairs to create a different way of showing the same information.

Critical Thinking Transparency CT17
- Cause and Effect: Growing Conflict Between Britain and America

ACTIVITY OPTIONS

INTERDISCIPLINARY LINK: MATH — BLOCK SCHEDULING

EFFECTS OF A BOYCOTT

Class Time 30 minutes

Task Determining a boycott's economic impact

Purpose To understand the effectiveness of boycotting as a form of protest

Supplies Needed
- Scratch paper and pencils
- Calculators

Activity Divide students into groups representing British colonial businesses (tea, woolens, foodstuffs, tinware, glass and pottery, textiles). Provide each group with a figure that represents the business's average monthly earnings (e.g., $50,000). Have each group determine the economic impact of a six-month boycott against its products by using several different assigned loss percentages (2 percent, 5 percent, 10 percent, etc.). Each group should share its findings with the class and discuss how the losses would affect the political views of the British businessmen.

INSTRUCT: OBJECTIVE 3

The Midnight Ride

- What was the role of spies in the pre-revolutionary period?
- Why did Britain's General Gage send troops to Lexington and Concord?
- What was the mission of the midnight riders?

In-Depth Resources: Unit 2
- Literature Selection: "Paul Revere's Ride," pp. 14–17

MORE ABOUT . . .

A Revolutionary Spy
One of the most shocking spy cases of the Revolutionary period involved Dr. Benjamin Church, the colonial army's surgeon general. Church was a member of the inner circle of patriot leaders—and a British agent. Church's spying days ended after a coded message ended up in the hands of colonial leaders. This particular memo described the strength and movement of colonial troops. After serving some time in prison, Church was released due to ill health and allowed to sail to the West Indies. His ship sank during the trip, and he was lost at sea.

HISTORY FROM VISUALS

Reading the Map Point out to students the number of riders, as well as the routes each one took. Ask them who appeared to take the longest route to Lexington. **Answer** William Dawes

Extension Have students imagine they are a midnight rider, and ask them to write a brief diary entry about their ride.

Most colonial leaders believed that any fight with Britain would be short. They thought that a show of force would make Britain change its policies. Few expected a war. One who did was Patrick Henry.

A VOICE FROM THE PAST

Gentlemen may cry peace, peace—but there is no peace. The war is actually begun! The next gale that sweeps from the north will bring to our ears the clash of resounding arms! Our brethren are already in the field! Why should we idle here? . . . I know not what course others may take. But as for me, give me liberty or give me death.

Patrick Henry, quoted in *Patriots* by A. J. Langguth

Henry delivered what became his most famous speech in the Virginia House of Burgesses in March 1775.

3 The Midnight Ride

Meanwhile, spies were busy on both sides. Sam Adams had built a spy network to keep watch over British activities. The British had their spies too. They were Americans who were loyal to Britain. From them, General Gage learned that the Massachusetts militia was storing arms and ammunition in Concord, about 20 miles northwest of Boston. He also heard that Sam Adams and John Hancock were in Lexington. On the night of April 18, 1775, Gage ordered his troops to arrest Adams and Hancock in Lexington and to destroy the supplies in Concord.

The Sons of Liberty had prepared for this moment. **Paul Revere,** a Boston silversmith, and a second messenger, William Dawes, were charged with spreading the news about British troop movements. Revere had arranged a system of signals to alert colonists in Charlestown, on the shore opposite Boston. If one lantern burned in the Old North Church steeple, the British troops were coming by land; if two, they were coming by water. Revere would go across the water from Boston to Charlestown and ride to Lexington and Concord from there. Dawes would take the land route.

Reading **History**
B. Recognizing Effects What effect might spying have had on the people of Boston?
B. Possible **Answer** It might have turned them against one another.

Background
The signals were a backup system in case Revere was captured.

Skillbuilder Answers
1. Lexington and Concord
2. About six miles

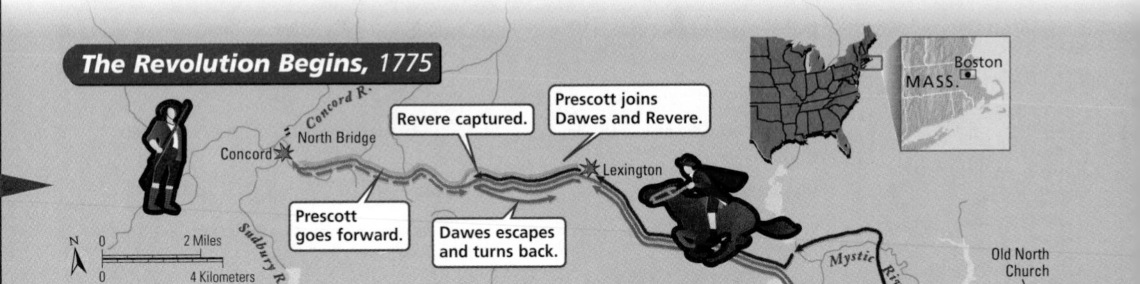

GEOGRAPHY SKILLBUILDER
Interpreting Maps
1. **Location** *Where were battles fought?*
2. **Movement** *What was the distance between Lexington and Concord?*

156

ACTIVITY OPTIONS

INDIVIDUAL NEEDS

STUDENTS ACQUIRING ENGLISH/ESL

Social Studies Vocabulary To help students understand the many social studies concept vocabulary words in this section, have the students add the following list to their personal dictionaries: *militia, musket, intolerable, committees, correspondence, continental, congress, delegate, boycott, repeal.*

Next have students look up the words in a dictionary. Help them understand each word by discussing its meaning and use. Then have them write a definition of the term in their own words in their personal dictionaries.

Have the students find the words in a sentence in the text. (The words listed are in order according to appearance.) Ask them to read the sentence aloud and explain what the sentence means. Finally, have the students write a sentence using the term.

When the British moved, so did Revere and Dawes. They galloped over the countryside on their "midnight ride," spreading the news. In Lexington, they were joined by Dr. Samuel Prescott. When Revere and Dawes were stopped by a British patrol, Prescott broke away and carried the message to Concord.

4 Lexington and Concord

At dawn on April 19, some 700 British troops reached Lexington. They found Captain John Parker and about 70 militiamen waiting. The British commander ordered the Americans to drop their muskets. They refused. No one knows who fired first, but within a few minutes eight militiamen lay dead. The British then marched to Concord, where they destroyed military supplies. A battle broke out at a bridge north of town, forcing the British to retreat.

Nearly 4,000 Minutemen and militiamen arrived in the area. They lined the road from Concord to Lexington and peppered the retreating redcoats with musket fire. "It seemed as if men came down from the clouds," one soldier said. Only the arrival of 1,000 more troops saved the British from destruction as they scrambled back to Boston.

Lexington and Concord were the first battles of the Revolutionary War. As Ralph Waldo Emerson later wrote, colonial troops had fired the "shot heard 'round the world." Americans would now have to choose sides and back up their political opinions by force of arms. Those who supported the British were called **Loyalists.** Those who sided with the rebels were **Patriots.** The conflict between the two sides divided communities, families, and friends. The war was on!

C. Possible Answer
The American revolt stunned the world.

Background
British losses totaled 273 soldiers compared to 95 militiamen.

Reading **History**
C. Drawing Conclusions
Why did Emerson call it the "shot heard 'round the world"?

Now and then

PATRIOTS' DAY

The "shot heard 'round the world" is celebrated every year in Massachusetts and Maine. Patriots' Day, as it is called, is the third Monday of April. In Concord and nearby towns, modern-day Minutemen like those below reenact the battle that began the Revolution on April 19, 1775. The Boston Marathon is also run on Patriots' Day.

Section 3 Assessment

1. Terms & Names

Explain the significance of:
- militia
- Minuteman
- Intolerable Acts
- First Continental Congress
- Paul Revere
- Lexington and Concord
- Loyalist
- Patriot

2. Taking Notes

Use a diagram like the one below to show events that led to the Revolutionary War.

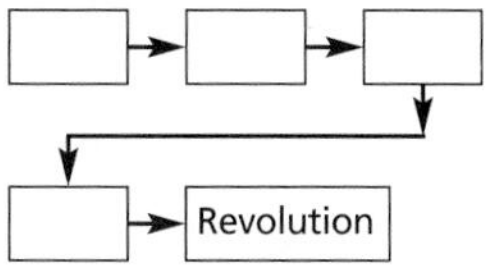

3. Main Ideas

a. Why did Britain pass the Intolerable Acts?

b. Who took part in the First Continental Congress?

c. What was the purpose of the "midnight ride"?

4. Critical Thinking

Supporting Opinions
Do you think the fighting between Britain and the colonies could have been avoided? Why or why not?

THINK ABOUT
- Britain's attitude toward the colonies
- colonial feelings about Britain

ACTIVITY OPTIONS

GEOGRAPHY
MATH

Research the Battles of Lexington and Concord. Draw a **map** of key events or create a **chart** showing statistics from the battles.

INSTRUCT: OBJECTIVE 4

Lexington and Concord

- What happened at the battles of Lexington and Concord?
- Who were the Loyalists and Patriots?

MORE ABOUT . . .

Lexington and Concord

The last person said to die in the battles of Lexington and Concord was not a Minuteman or redcoat—but a teenage boy. As the British fought their way back from Concord to Boston, they passed through Charlestown, home of 14-year-old Edward Barber. Barber rushed to his window to watch the fighting. By this time, British troops had endured numerous hit-and-run attacks from colonists. As a result, they considered anyone moving in a house to be a possible sniper. A British soldier aimed his musket at the Barber home and killed young Edward with one shot.

ASSESS & RETEACH

Setting the Stage Have students fill in the next three boxes on the chapter graphic organizer.

Formal Assessment
- Section Quiz, p. 102

RETEACHING ACTIVITY

Divide students into groups of five. Have each group create a section review, with each member of the group writing a one- or two-sentence summary of a subsection. Have each member read the summary sentence to the rest of the group.

In-Depth Resources: Unit 2
- Reteaching Activity, p. 20

Section 3 Assessment

1. Terms & Names

militia, p. 154
Minuteman, p. 154
Intolerable Acts, p. 154
First Continental Congress, p. 155
Paul Revere, p. 156
Lexington and Concord, p. 157
Loyalist, p. 157
Patriot, p. 157

2. Taking Notes

Intolerable Acts; First Continental Congress; troop training; battles of Lexington and Concord

3. Main Ideas

a. to punish Massachusetts for the Boston Tea Party **b.** delegates from all the colonies except Georgia **c.** to warn Lexington and Concord that British troops were coming

4. Critical Thinking

Students might say the fighting was inevitable; there was little room for compromise; tensions had been building; each side believed it was right.

ACTIVITY OPTIONS

Integrated Assessment
- Rubrics for a map, 2.1
- Rubrics for a chart, 2.2

Literature *Connections*

OBJECTIVE

Students analyze a passage from historical fiction that imaginatively depicts issues about the battles of Lexington and Concord during the American Revolution.

BLOCK SCHEDULING

FOCUS & MOTIVATE

Making Inferences To help the students picture the events of *Johnny Tremain,* have them study the image on page 159 and answer the following questions.

1. What information can you gather about the event shown in the picture?
2. How do you think news of this event will reach those who were not present?

MORE ABOUT . . .

Johnny Tremain

Set in Boston from 1773 to 1775, *Johnny Tremain* tells the story of a young silversmith apprentice and his role in events, such as the Boston Tea Party and the battles of Lexington and Concord, that lead to the Revolutionary War. The fictional characters in the novel become involved with actual historical figures, including Paul Revere, William Dawes, General Thomas Gage, John Hancock, and Samuel Adams.

From

JOHNNY TREMAIN

by Esther Forbes

In 1775, 16-year-old Johnny Tremain lives in Boston and works as a delivery boy for a newspaper. Because he travels so much around the city, he is able to help the Patriots gather information about what the British are doing.

On the night of April 18, Johnny learns that British troops will be leaving on an expedition to seize the gunpowder at Lexington and Concord. He rushes to tell this news to Dr. Joseph Warren, who is a Patriot. Then Johnny goes to bed, wondering if the war has started and worried about his friend Rab, who has gone to join the Minutemen at Lexington.

So Johnny slept. It was daylight when he woke with Warren's hand upon his shoulder. Outside on Tremont Street he could hear the clumping of army boots. A sergeant was swearing at his men. The soldiers were paraded so close to the house, which stood **flush**[1] with the sidewalkless street, that Johnny at first thought they must be in the room.

Doctor Warren dared speak no louder than a whisper.

"I'm going now."

"Something's happened?"

"Yes." He motioned Johnny to follow him into the kitchen. This room was on the back of the house. They could talk without danger of being overheard by the troops in the street.

Doctor Warren had on the same clothes as the day before. He had not been to bed. But now his hat was on his head. His black bag of instruments and medicines was packed and on the table. Silently he put milk, bread, herrings beside it, and gestured to Johnny to join him.

"Where did it begin?" asked Johnny.

"Lexington."

"Who won?"

"They did. Seven hundred against seventy. It wasn't a battle. It was . . . just target practice . . . for them. Some of our men were killed and the British **huzzaed**[2] and took the road to Concord."

"And did they get our supplies there?"

"I don't know. Paul Revere sent for me just after the firing on Lexington Green."

The young man's usually fresh-colored face was **haggard**.[3] He knew the seriousness of this day for himself and for his country.

"But everywhere the alarm is spreading. Men are grabbing their guns—marching for Concord. Paul Revere did get through in time last night. Billy Dawes a little later. Hundreds—maybe thousands—of Minute Men are on the march. Before the day's over, there'll be real fighting—not target practice. But Gage doesn't know that it's begun. You see, long before Colonel Smith got to Lexington—just as soon as he heard that Revere had warned the country—he sent back for reinforcements. For Earl Percy. You and I, Johnny, are just about the only people in Boston who know that blood has already been shed."

"Were many killed—at Lexington?"

"No, not many. They stood up—just a handful. The British fired on them. It was dawn."

Johnny licked his lips. "Did they tell you the names of those killed?"

1. **flush:** in a line with.
2. **huzzaed:** cheered.
3. **haggard:** tired.

ACTIVITY OPTIONS

INDIVIDUAL NEEDS

LESS PROFICIENT READERS

Building Language Skills Call on some fluent readers to perform an oral reading of the passage from *Johnny Tremain* for small groups of less proficient readers. In each group, have two students read aloud the dialogue between Johnny and Doctor Warren. Coach the readers to express the emotions conveyed in the characters' spoken words.

After the oral reading, have the less proficient readers in each group dramatize moments from the scene they have just listened to. Assuming the role of either Johnny or Doctor Warren, they can take turns retelling parts of the conversation. As an alternative, student groups can create a comic strip version of the passage, using speech balloons to retell the discussion between Johnny and Doctor Warren.

"No. Did Rab get out in time?"

"Yes. Last Sunday."

The Doctor's clear blue eyes darkened. He knew what was in Johnny's mind. He picked up his bag. "I've got to get to them. They'll need surgeons. Then, too, I'd rather die fighting than on a gallows. Gage won't be so **lenient**[4] now—soon as he learns war has begun."

"Wait until I get my shoes on."

"No, Johnny, you are to stay here today. Pick up for me any information. For instance, out of my bedroom window I can see soldiers standing the length of the street 'way over to the Common. You find out what regiments are being sent—and all that. And today go about and listen to what folk are saying. And the names of any the British arrest. We know Gage expects to move his men back here tonight. If so, there'll be a lot of confusion getting them into town. You watch your chance and slip out to me."

"Where'll I find you?"

" . . . Ask about."

"I will do so."

"They've begun it. We'll end it, but this war . . . it may last quite a long time."

They shook hands silently. Johnny knew that Warren was always conscious of the fact that he had a crippled hand. Everybody else had accepted and forgotten it. The back door closed softly. Warren was gone.

Johnny went to the **surgery**,[5] put on his boots and jacket. The wall clock said eight o'clock. It was time to be about. There was no leaving by the front door. The soldiers were leaning against it. Through the curtains of the windows he could see the muskets. He noticed the facings on their uniforms. The Twenty-Third Regiment. The narrow course of Tremont Street was filled to the brim and overflowing with the waiting scarlet-coated men. Like a river of blood. He left by the kitchen.

4. **lenient:** not strict.
5. **surgery:** operating room.

CONNECT TO HISTORY

1. **Recognizing Effects** What was Johnny's reaction to the news about Lexington? Discuss what roles Johnny and Dr. Warren were to play in the early days of the Revolutionary War.

See Skillbuilder Handbook, page R11.

CONNECT TO TODAY

2. **Researching** Where are there revolutions in the world today?

For more about revolutions . . .

RESEARCH LINKS CLASSZONE.COM

British troops fire on the Lexington militia on April 19, 1775. The war begins here!

INSTRUCT

- What issues about the battles of Lexington and Concord do Johnny and Doctor Warren discuss?
- How are the British portrayed in this reading selection? Do you think the account is one-sided? Explain.
- What do you predict will happen next in the story?

MAKING PERSONAL CONNECTIONS

Ask students to think about ways in which young people can contribute to political causes today. What roles might they play to promote America's ideals of freedom? What individual rights would they consider defending?

VOCABULARY ACTIVITY

Ask students to tell or write a sentence of their own, using each of the words defined on the bottom of pages 158 and 159.

HISTORY FROM VISUALS

Interpreting the Painting Have students cite details from the painting that illustrate Doctor Warren's account of the battle of Lexington on page 158. **Possible Responses** British troops won a quick victory because they appeared well organized and better prepared to fight. They outnumbered the Minutemen, who are pictured as easy targets.

CONNECT TO HISTORY

1. **Recognizing Effects Possible Responses** Johnny shows deep personal concern and recognizes the political consequences of the battle at Lexington. Johnny will continue to report and gather information about the British, while Doctor Warren will treat Patriot soldiers wounded in battle.

CONNECT TO TODAY

2. **Researching** Using the Internet or a current encyclopedia, students should find out about independence movements today. Examples include the Basques in Spain, groups in Wales and Scotland, people in Corsica, the people in Kosovo, and the Tamil people of Sri Lanka. Have students create an annotated map that identifies both the location and the goals of various modern independence movements.

SECTION OBJECTIVES

1. To describe the early skirmishes between the Continental and British armies
2. To profile British and American responses to the deepening conflict
3. To summarize Thomas Paine's *Common Sense*
4. To explain how colonial leaders officially declared their independence from Britain

CRITICAL THINKING

Analyzing Points of View, p. 162
Forming Opinions, p. 163
Summarizing, p. 165
Drawing Conclusions, p. 165

FOCUS & MOTIVATE

5-MINUTE WARM-UP

Interpreting a Painting These questions will help students see art as a source of information.

1. Look at the picture on page 161. Based on the artist's view, who do you think won the Battle of Bunker Hill?
2. What information about both armies can you learn from studying the painting?

Warm-Up Transparency WT6

INSTRUCT

INSTRUCT: OBJECTIVE 1

The Continental Army Is Formed/ The Battle of Bunker Hill

- For what reasons did General Gage move his troops to Boston after the battles at Lexington and Concord?
- What did the Second Continental Congress accomplish?
- Why was the Battle of Bunker Hill considered an important one for the colonists?

In-Depth Resources: Unit 2
- Guided Reading, p. 6
- Primary Source: Letter from Abigail Adams, p. 13

America's History Makers
- Abigail Adams, pp. 23–24

4 Declaring Independence

TERMS & NAMES
Ethan Allen
artillery
Second Continental Congress
Continental Army
Benedict Arnold
Declaration of Independence
Thomas Jefferson

MAIN IDEA	WHY IT MATTERS NOW
Fighting between American and British troops led the colonies to declare their independence.	The United States of America was founded at this time.

ONE AMERICAN'S STORY

In May 1775—one month after the battle at Lexington and Concord—Abigail Adams wrote to her husband, John Adams. "The house is a Scene of Confusion," she said. Colonial militiamen were camped outside. Everyone was preparing for war. John Adams was away in Philadelphia at the time, meeting with other Patriot leaders at the Second Continental Congress.

Abigail and John Adams would spend most of the Revolutionary War apart. In his absence, she ran the household and farm in Braintree, Massachusetts, and raised their four children. During their separation, they exchanged many letters. Abigail was a very sharp observer of the political scene. In one letter, she shared her concerns about the future of the American government.

Abigail Adams was an early advocate of women's rights and one of the great letter writers in history.

A VOICE FROM THE PAST

If we separate from Britain, what Code of Laws will be established? How shall we be governed so as to retain our Liberties? Can any government be free which is not administered by general stated Laws? Who shall frame these Laws? Who will give them force and energy?

Abigail Adams, quoted in *Abigail Adams: Witness to a Revolution* by Natalie S. Bober

These questions would be answered later. First, a war had to be fought and won.

1 The Continental Army Is Formed

After the fighting at Lexington and Concord, militiamen from Massachusetts and other colonies began gathering around Boston. Their numbers eventually reached some 20,000. General Gage decided to move his soldiers from the peninsula opposite Boston to the city itself. Boston was nearly surrounded by water. This fact, he thought, made a colonial attack by land almost impossible.

Not long after, on May 10, 1775, Americans attacked Britain's Fort Ticonderoga on the New York side of Lake Champlain. **Ethan Allen** led

RECOMMENDED RESOURCES

In-Depth Resources: Unit 2
- Geo. Application, pp. 10–11
- Primary Source: Letter from Abigail Adams, p. 13
- Enrichment Activity, p. 22
- History Workshop, p. 23

America's History Makers
- Abigail Adams, pp. 23–24
- Thomas Paine, pp. 25–26

Reading Study Guide, pp. 53–54

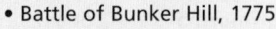

Formal Assessment
- Section Quiz, p. 103

Integrated Assessment
- Rubrics, 1.7, 4.3

Access for Students Acquiring English/ESL
- Guided Reading, p. 35
- Geo. Application, pp. 38–39

INTEGRATED TECHNOLOGY

Geography Transparency GT6
- Battle of Bunker Hill, 1775

Electronic Teacher Tools

classzone.com

TEST-TAKING RESOURCES

Strategies for Test Preparation

Test Practice Transparencies, TT23

Online Test Practice

this band of backwoodsmen known as the Green Mountain Boys. They captured the fort and its large supply of **artillery**—cannon and large guns. These guns would be used later to drive the British from Boston.

Also on May 10, the **Second Continental Congress** began meeting in Philadelphia. Delegates included John and Samuel Adams, John Hancock, Benjamin Franklin, George Washington, and Patrick Henry. They agreed to form the **Continental Army.** Washington, who was from Virginia, was chosen as its commanding general. He had served as a colonial officer with the British during the French and Indian War. Congress also authorized the printing of paper money to pay the troops. It was beginning to act as a government.

The Battle of Bunker Hill

Background
The battle was called Bunker Hill because the original plan was to fight the battle there.

Meanwhile, tensions were building in Boston in June 1775. Militiamen seized Bunker Hill and Breed's Hill behind Charlestown. They built fortifications on Breed's Hill. Alarmed, the British decided to attack.

"Don't fire until you see the whites of their eyes!"
Colonel William Prescott

General William Howe crossed the bay with 2,200 British soldiers. Forming in ranks, they marched up Breed's Hill. On the hilltop, the militia waited. According to the legend, Colonel William Prescott ordered, "Don't fire until you see the whites of their eyes!" When the British got close, the militia unleashed murderous fire. The British fell back and then charged again. Finally, they forced the militia off the hill.

The redcoats had won the Battle of Bunker Hill, but at tremendous cost. More than 1,000 were killed or wounded, compared with some 400 militia casualties. "The loss we have sustained is greater than we can bear," wrote General Gage. The inexperienced colonial militia had held its own against the world's most powerful army.

The bloody fighting between militiamen and British troops is shown in *The Death of General Warren at Bunker Hill* by John Trumbull (1786).

MORE ABOUT . . .

General Washington

George Washington did not become commander of the Continental Army without some reservations. Colonial leaders from New England, for example, voiced concerns about handing the army over to a Southerner—Washington was from Virginia.

Washington himself questioned his own abilities. He ultimately accepted the post, but he declared, "I feel great distress from a consciousness that my abilities and military experience may not be equal to the extensive and important trust."

MORE ABOUT . . .

The Battle of Bunker Hill

Questionable tactics and overconfidence may have played a role in Britain's difficulty in taking Breed's Hill. British troops moved in tight formation, wearing roughly 125 pounds of gear each. Positioned so close together and slowed by their added weight, the redcoats made easy targets for the colonials shooting at them from above. When the bloody battle had ended, a British officer stated, "from an absurd and destructive confidence, carelessness or ignorance, we have lost a thousand of our best men and officers."

Geography Transparency GT6
• Battle of Bunker Hill, 1775

ACTIVITY OPTIONS

INDIVIDUAL NEEDS

LESS PROFICIENT READERS

Creating a Time Line To help less proficient readers keep track of events leading up to the adoption of the Declaration of Independence, have them create a time line such as the one to the right and mark the key events of the section. Students should begin with the formation of the Second Continental Congress and end with the signing of the Declaration. After students have completed their time lines, have them discuss which event they think played the greatest role in prompting the colonists to declare their independence from Britain.

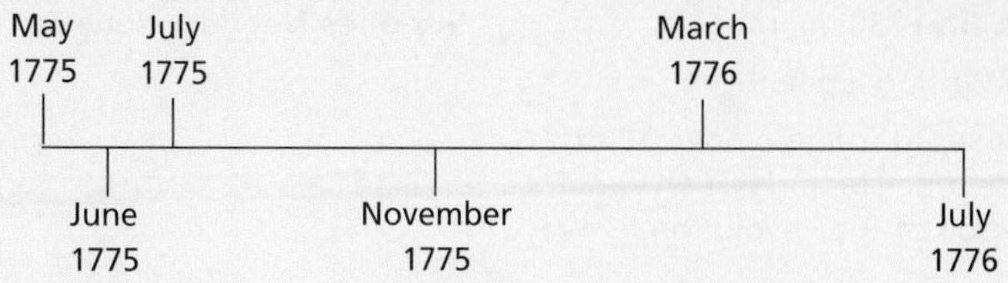

INSTRUCT: OBJECTIVE 2

A Last Attempt at Peace/ The British Retreat from Boston

- What was the purpose and outcome of the Olive Branch Petition?
- What was the purpose and outcome of the colonial attack on Quebec? on Boston?
- Why did so many Loyalists flee Boston with the British?

In-Depth Resources: Unit 2
- Geography Application: Historic Boston—1775 and Today, pp. 10–11

Connections TO *LITERATURE*

Phillis Wheatley

From a very early age, Wheatley showed herself to have an extraordinary gift for words. With no formal schooling, she mastered the English language just 16 months after arriving from Africa. She wrote her first poem at the age of 14 and soon gained international acclaim for her work. The French writer and philosopher Voltaire commented about Wheatley, "There is right now a Negress who writes excellent verse in English." Wheatley's poetry often dealt with the colonists' struggle against Britain.

Connections TO *LITERATURE*

PHILLIS WHEATLEY

Phillis Wheatley was America's first important African-American poet. She was born in Africa about 1753 and sold into slavery as a child. She was a household servant for the Wheatley family of Boston but was raised and educated as a family member.

Some of Wheatley's poems were about the Patriot cause. Of George Washington, she wrote:

Proceed, great chief, with
virtue on thy side,
Thy ev'ry action let the
goddess guide.
A crown, a mansion, and
a throne that shine,
With gold unfading,
Washington! be thine.

In other poems, Wheatley connected America's fight against British oppression with the struggle for freedom for enslaved African Americans.

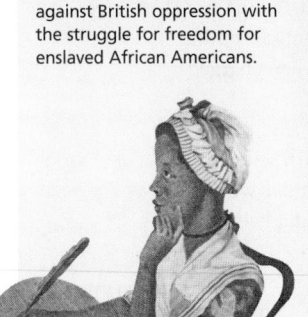

2 A Last Attempt at Peace

Despite this deepening conflict, most colonists still hoped for peace. Even some Patriot leaders considered themselves loyal subjects of the king. They blamed Parliament for the terrible events taking place.

In July 1775, moderates in Congress drafted the Olive Branch Petition and sent it to London. This document asked the king to restore harmony between Britain and the colonies. Some members opposed the petition but signed it anyway as a last hope.

Background
The olive branch is considered a symbol of peace.

The king rejected the petition, however, and announced new measures to punish the colonies. He would use the British navy to block American ships from leaving their ports. He also would send thousands of hired German soldiers, called Hessians, to fight in America. "When once these rebels have felt a smart blow, they will submit," he declared.

***Reading*History**
A. Analyzing Points of View Why did King George reject the petition?
A. Possible Answer He was not used to having his authority questioned. He felt that he had a right to demand obedience.

The colonial forces were not going to back down, though. They thought they were equal to the British troops. George Washington knew otherwise. The British soldiers were professionals, while the colonial troops had little training and were poorly equipped. The Massachusetts militia barely had enough gunpowder to fight one battle.

During the summer of 1775, Washington arrived at the militia camp near Boston. He immediately began to gather supplies and train the army. In the fall, Washington approved a bold plan. Continental Army troops would invade Quebec, in eastern Canada. They hoped to defeat British forces there and draw Canadians into the Patriot camp. One of the leaders of this expedition was **Benedict Arnold.** He was an officer who had played a role in the victory at Fort Ticonderoga.

After a grueling march across Maine, Arnold arrived at Quebec in November 1775. By that time, however, winter had set in. Under harsh conditions, the Americans launched their attack but failed. After several months, they limped home in defeat.

The British Retreat from Boston

In Massachusetts, the Continental Army had surrounded British forces in Boston. Neither side was able or willing to break the standoff. However, help for Washington was on the way. Cannons were being hauled from Fort Ticonderoga. This was a rough job, since there were no roads across the snow-covered mountains. It took soldiers two months to drag the 59 heavy weapons to Boston, where they arrived in January 1776.

ACTIVITY OPTIONS

MULTIPLE LEARNING STYLES: LINGUISTIC — **BLOCK SCHEDULING**

WRITING A REVOLUTIONARY POEM

Class Time 30 minutes

Task Writing a poem

Purpose To create a poem illustrating an understanding of an event or person of the Revolutionary War period

Supplies Needed None

Activity Remind students that poetry attempts to re-create emotions and experiences. Students should select a person or event about which to write. Have them brainstorm adjectives describing the event or person. Remind them that they also may rely more on the sounds of words and less on fixed rhythms and rhyme schemes. Tell students they may write their poems in any style they wish. They also may work with a partner. When they are finished, have a poetry reading, and have the group discuss the meaning of each work.

Armed with these cannons, Washington moved his troops to Dorchester Heights, overlooking Boston. The Americans threatened to bombard the city. General Howe, who was now in charge of the British forces, decided to withdraw his troops. On March 17, about 9,000 British soldiers departed Boston in more than 100 ships. Boston Patriots joyfully reclaimed their city. Although the British had damaged homes and destroyed possessions, Boston was still standing.

More than 1,000 Loyalist supporters left along with the British troops. Anti-British feeling in Boston was so strong that the Loyalists feared for their safety. Some Patriots even called for Loyalists to be hanged as traitors. This did not happen, but Loyalists' homes and property were seized.

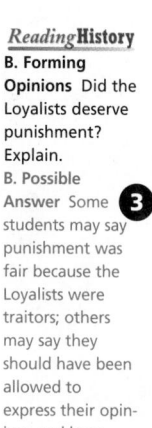

Reading **History**

B. Forming Opinions Did the Loyalists deserve punishment? Explain.

B. Possible Answer Some students may say punishment was fair because the Loyalists were traitors; others may say they should have been allowed to express their opinions and keep their possessions.

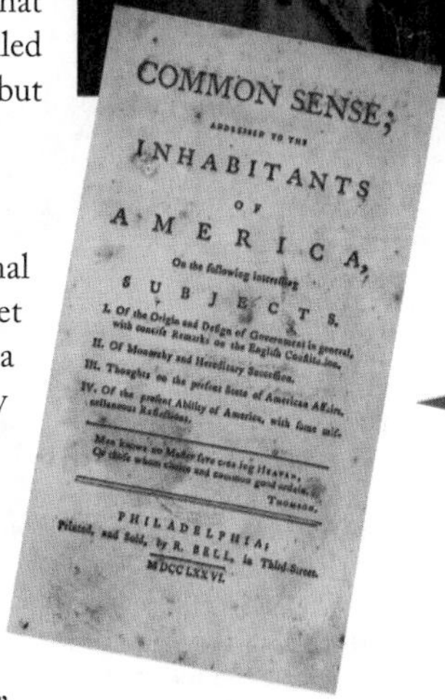

This is the front page of *Common Sense* by Thomas Paine (above). It was one of the most influential political documents in history.

3 *Common Sense* Is Published

In early 1776, most Americans still wanted to avoid a final break with Britain. However, the publication of a pamphlet titled *Common Sense* helped convince many Americans that a complete break with Britain was necessary. Written by Thomas Paine, a recent immigrant from England, this pamphlet made a strong case for American independence.

Paine ridiculed the idea that kings ruled by the will of God. Calling George III "the Royal Brute," Paine argued that all monarchies were corrupt. He also disagreed with the economic arguments for remaining with Britain. "Our corn," he said, "will fetch its price in any market in Europe." He believed that America should follow its own destiny.

A VOICE FROM THE PAST

Everything that is right or natural pleads for separation. The blood of the slain, the weeping voice of nature cries, "'Tis time to part." Even the distance at which the Almighty has placed England and America is a strong and natural proof that the authority of the one over the other was never the design of heaven.

Thomas Paine, *Common Sense*

Common Sense was an instant success. Published in January, it sold more than 100,000 copies in three months. The call for independence had become a roar.

4 A Time of Decision

The Continental Congress remained undecided. A majority of the delegates still did not support independence. Even so, in May 1776, Congress adopted a resolution authorizing each of the 13 colonies to establish its own government.

On June 7, Richard Henry Lee of Virginia introduced a key resolution. It called the colonies "free and independent states" and declared

INSTRUCT: OBJECTIVE 3

***Common Sense* Is Published**

- What points does Thomas Paine make in *Common Sense?*
- What impact did Paine's pamphlet have on the colonies?

America's History Makers
- Thomas Paine, pp. 25–26

MORE ABOUT . . .

Common Sense

Some historians credit *Common Sense,* more than any other document, with generating popular support of the Declaration of Independence. About *Common Sense* Benjamin Rush said it was "read by public men, repeated in clubs, spouted in schools." However, not everyone found the arguments satisfactory. None other than John Adams attacked the ideas about government in the document as either "honest ignorance or knavish hypocrisy." In response to Paine's pamphlet, Adams wrote a response entitled *Thoughts on Government.*

INSTRUCT: OBJECTIVE 4

A Time of Decision/ The Declaration Is Adopted

- Why did colonial leaders choose Thomas Jefferson to write the Declaration of Independence?
- What is the core idea of the Declaration of Independence?
- Which parts of the population does the Declaration neglect?

ACTIVITY OPTIONS

INTERDISCIPLINARY LINK: CIVICS

B BLOCK SCHEDULING

CREATING A NEW *COMMON SENSE*

Class Time 30 minutes

Task Creating a political pamphlet

Purpose To understand the colonists' feelings about the war

Supplies Needed
- Drawing paper, markers
- Word processors, if available

Activity Divide the class into small groups. Have each group produce a pamphlet designed to persuade the colonists to accept the Patriot or Loyalist position. Tell students that the pamphlet should use persuasive language to express the Loyalist or Patriot point of view. It also should express the views of the day and end with some kind of call to action. Suggest that students include an eye-catching front page, with hand-drawn illustrations or other art forms. Have the groups share their work with the class.

HISTORY through ART

Interpreting the Painting The artist John Trumbull produced more than 200 works about the American Revolution. One of his most famous paintings, shown here, is entitled *The Declaration of Independence.*

In 1786, Thomas Jefferson urged Trumbull to depict the famous event to help ensure that it lived on in the nation's memory. Jefferson even supplied Trumbull with a rough sketch of the scene from which the artist could work.

Trumbull took seven years to complete the work, painstakingly painting 48 of the Congress members from life portraits.

Possible Response: By presenting a dark scene with somber-looking men, the artist conveys the gravity and seriousness of declaring independence from a ruling country.

MORE ABOUT . . .

A New Home for Old Documents

Known as the Charters of Freedom, the Declaration of Independence, the U.S. Constitution, and the Bill of Rights are on display at the National Archives in Washington, D.C.

The documents are moved to a bombproof vault every day at closing time. Over time, the outside elements have invaded the glass cases that contain them. As a result, the documents are beginning to show slight signs of decay.

A team of scientists, engineers, designers, and archivists is working to create an advanced, airtight encasement for the documents by 2003.

HISTORY through ART

The Declaration of Independence is presented for adoption to the Continental Congress by John Adams, Roger Sherman, Robert Livingston, Thomas Jefferson, and Benjamin Franklin (left to right). John Trumbull painted this work many years after the adoption of the Declaration on July 4, 1776.

What is the artist trying to show about the mood of the American leaders as they declare independence?

that "all political connection between them and the state of Great Britain is . . . totally dissolved."

Congress debated the resolution, but not all the delegates were ready to vote on it. They did, however, appoint a committee to draft a **Declaration of Independence.** The committee included Benjamin Franklin, John Adams, Roger Sherman, Robert Livingston, and **Thomas Jefferson.**

The group chose Jefferson to compose the Declaration. Two reasons for selecting Jefferson were that he was an excellent writer and that he came from Virginia. The members knew that no independence movement could succeed without Virginia's support. Jefferson immediately went to work. In two weeks, he had prepared most of the Declaration. (See pages 166–169.) On July 2, 1776, Congress considered Lee's resolution again. Despite some strong opposition, the measure passed. From this point forward, the colonies considered themselves independent.

The Liberty Bell was rung to announce the first public reading of the Declaration of Independence, in Philadelphia on July 8, 1776.

The Declaration Is Adopted

Two days later, on July 4, 1776, Congress adopted the document that proclaimed independence—the Declaration of Independence. John Hancock, the president of the Congress, was the first to sign the Declaration. According to tradition, he wrote in large letters and commented, "There, I guess King George will be able to read that." The core idea of the Declaration is based on the philosophy of John Locke. This idea is that people have unalienable rights, or rights that government

ACTIVITY OPTIONS

INDIVIDUAL NEEDS: GIFTED AND TALENTED

DEBATING INDEPENDENCE

Class Time 30 minutes

Task Re-creating the debate over the Declaration of Independence

Purpose To understand the different views on severing ties with Great Britain

Supplies Needed

- Resource materials on the views of Patriots and Loyalists concerning independence from Great Britain

Activity Have students act as congressional delegates debating independence. Those favoring independence should note the core ideas of the Declaration of Independence, as well as the events and acts of the chapter that support their stance. Those opposing independence should focus on the consequences of severing ties with Britain (such as a war), as well as what difficulties the colonists might face in trying to create a new country (no government, no currency, etc.).

In-Depth Resources: Unit 2
- Enrichment Activity, p. 22

cannot take away. Jefferson stated this belief in what was to become the Declaration's best-known passage.

A VOICE FROM THE PAST

We hold these truths to be self-evident, that all men are created equal, that they are endowed by their Creator with certain unalienable Rights, that among these are Life, Liberty and the pursuit of Happiness.

Thomas Jefferson, The Declaration of Independence

If a government disregards these rights, Jefferson explained, it loses its right to govern. The people then have the right to abolish that government, by force if necessary. They can form a new government that will protect their rights. When Jefferson spoke of "the people," however, he meant only free white men. Women and enslaved persons were left out of the Declaration.

The Declaration also explained the reasons for breaking with Britain. It then declared the colonies to be free and independent states. This was a very serious action—treason from the British point of view—and the delegates knew it. John Hancock urged the delegates to stand together in mutual defense. Each realized that if the war were to be lost, they would most likely be hanged.

The Declaration closed with this pledge: "And for the support of this Declaration, with a firm reliance on the protection of divine Providence, we mutually pledge to each other our Lives, our Fortunes, and our sacred Honor."

Americans had declared independence. Now they had to win their freedom on the battlefield.

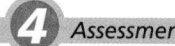

***Reading*History**

C. Summarizing When does the Declaration say it is right to overthrow an established government?

C. Possible Answer People can abolish a government when it disregards their rights.

AMERICA'S HISTORY MAKERS

THOMAS JEFFERSON
1743–1826

Jefferson was just 33 when chosen to write the Declaration of Independence. He was already a brilliant thinker and writer and a highly respected political leader. Jefferson came from a wealthy Virginia family. As a child, he was interested in everything, and he became an inventor, scientist, and architect, among other things. In 1769, he began his political career in the House of Burgesses.

Jefferson felt that writing the Declaration was a major achievement of his life. He had that fact carved on his tombstone.

Why do you think Jefferson felt the Declaration was one of his greatest achievements?

Section 4 Assessment

1. Terms & Names

Explain the significance of:
- Ethan Allen
- artillery
- Second Continental Congress
- Continental Army
- Benedict Arnold
- Declaration of Independence
- Thomas Jefferson

2. Taking Notes

Use the chart below to explain colonial views for and against independence.

Views About Independence

For	
Against	

What is the strongest reason for independence? against independence?

3. Main Ideas

a. What challenges did George Washington face in forming the army?

b. What forced the British to leave Boston?

c. What is *Common Sense*?

4. Critical Thinking

Drawing Conclusions Why did it take colonists so long to declare independence?

THINK ABOUT
- the colonists' British traditions
- the risk of revolution

ACTIVITY OPTIONS

ART
LANGUAGE ARTS

Find out more about a person discussed in this section. Create a **trading card** or write a **biography** of that person.

AMERICA'S HISTORY MAKERS

Thomas Jefferson

Jefferson was a "silent member" of the Continental Congress. He had great difficulty speaking in public. In fact, during the entire session of the Second Continental Congress he never gave a speech. Jefferson, of course, let his writing speak for him. In insisting that Jefferson craft the Declaration of Independence, John Adams pointed to his fellow delegate's "peculiar felicity of expression" when it came to the written word.

Possible Response: The Declaration inspired Americans to work for and, ultimately, to win their freedom.

ASSESS & RETEACH

Setting the Stage Have students fill in the next three boxes on the graphic organizer.

Formal Assessment
- Section Quiz, p. 103

Critical Thinking Transparency CT16
- Setting the Stage

RETEACHING ACTIVITY

Have students pretend they are reporters for a colonial newspaper, and have them write an article chronicling one of three events: the Battle of Bunker Hill; the publishing of *Common Sense;* the signing of the Declaration of Independence.

In-Depth Resources: Unit 2
- Reteaching Activity, p. 21

Section 4 Assessment

1. Terms & Names

Ethan Allen, p. 160
artillery, p. 161
Second Continental Congress, p. 161
Continental Army, p. 161
Benedict Arnold, p. 162
Declaration of Independence, p. 164
Thomas Jefferson, p. 164

2. Taking Notes

For: blood had been spilled; wanted new kind of government
Against: still felt British; loyal to king

Student answers may vary but should include support from the chapter.

3. Main Ideas

a. creating a trained force and getting enough supplies **b.** colonial artillery fire from Dorchester Heights **c.** a pamphlet written by Thomas Paine that gave arguments for independence

4. Critical Thinking

The colonists were used to British rule, had a habit of loyalty, and knew that revolution would be bloody and they might lose.

ACTIVITY OPTIONS

Integrated Assessment
- Rubrics for a trading card, 1.7
- Rubrics for a biography, 4.4

INTERACTIVE PRIMARY SOURCE

OBJECTIVE
Student will be able to identify colonial grievances against the British and explain why independence was declared.

Primary Source Explorer
- *The Declaration of Independence*

The Explorer will help students select and produce their own presentations.

Specific information about the document can be found in **A Closer Look.** To learn more about key people and events of the time, students should click on **Life in These Times. What Happened Next** will show the student the impact of the document both at home and abroad, and tie the document to today.

FOCUS & MOTIVATE

Finding Main Ideas To help students understand the main ideas of the Declaration, write the blue headings on the board. Then ask the students what kind of information they would expect to find in each section. Write that information under each heading. After reading, check to see how accurate the predictions were.

In-Depth Resources: Unit 2
- Guided Reading, p. 7

Access for Students Acquiring English/ESL
- Guided Reading, p. 36

MORE ABOUT . . .

The Declaration of Independence
The Declaration is divided into five parts: a preamble that announces the reason for the document; a section that explains the political principles underlying the rights of the people; a list of the unfair acts of the British king; a list of actions the colonials took to redress the problems; and the actual declaration of independence from Britain.

Note: The headings shown in the document are to aid student learning and do not appear in the original document.

INTERACTIVE PRIMARY SOURCE

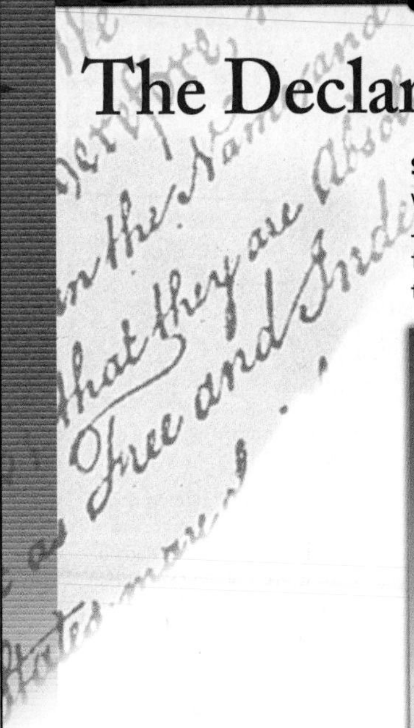

The Declaration of Independence

Setting the Stage On July 4, 1776, the Second Continental Congress adopted what became one of America's most cherished documents. Written by Thomas Jefferson, the Declaration of Independence voiced the reasons for separating from Britain and provided the principles of government upon which the United States would be built. **See Primary Source Explorer**

[Preamble]

When in the Course of human events, it becomes necessary for one people to dissolve the political bands which have connected them with another, and to assume among the powers of the earth, the separate and equal station to which the Laws of Nature and of Nature's God entitle them, a decent respect to the opinions of mankind requires that they should declare the causes which impel them to the separation.

[The Right of the People to Control Their Government]

We hold these truths to be self-evident, that all men are created equal, that they are **endowed**[1] by their Creator with certain **unalienable**[2] Rights, that among these are Life, Liberty and the pursuit of Happiness; that, to secure these rights, Governments are instituted among Men, deriving their just powers from the consent of the governed; that whenever any Form of Government becomes destructive of these ends, it is the Right of the People to alter or to abolish it, and to institute new Government, laying its foundation on such principles and organizing its powers in such form, as to them shall seem most likely to effect their Safety and Happiness. Prudence, indeed, will dictate that Governments long established should not be changed for light and transient causes; and accordingly all experience hath shewn that mankind are more disposed to suffer, while evils are sufferable, than to right themselves by abolishing the forms to which they are accustomed. But when a long train of abuses and **usurpations,**[3] pursuing invariably the same Object, evinces a design to reduce them under absolute **Despotism,**[4] it is their right, it is their duty, to throw off such Government, and to provide new Guards for their future security.

Such has been the patient sufferance of these Colonies; and such is now the necessity which constrains them to alter their former Systems of Government. The history of the present King of Great Britain is a history of repeated injuries and usurpations, all having in direct object the establishment of an absolute Tyranny over these States. To prove this, let facts be submitted to a **candid**[5] world.

A CLOSER LOOK

RIGHTS OF THE PEOPLE

The ideas in this passage reflect the views of John Locke. Locke was an English philosopher who believed that the natural rights of individuals came from God, but that a government's power comes from the consent of the governed. This belief is the foundation of modern democracy.

1. In what way can American voters bring about changes in their government?

1. **endowed:** provided.
2. **unalienable:** unable to be taken away.
3. **usurpations:** unjust seizures of power.
4. **Despotism:** rule by a tyrant with absolute power.
5. **candid:** fair, impartial.

166

TEACHING STRATEGY

Analyzing Causes To help students understand the events and causes that led to the demand for independence, have them copy the graphic shown. Use the information in the *Efforts of the Colonies* section (p. 168) to identify actions taken by the colonists and the responses by the British.

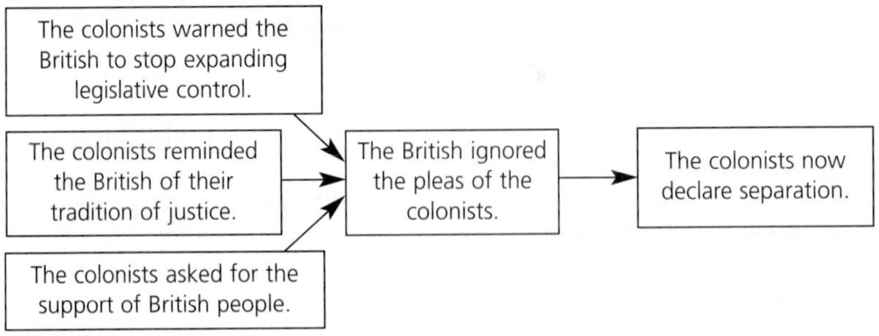
The colonists warned the British to stop expanding legislative control.
The colonists reminded the British of their tradition of justice.
The colonists asked for the support of British people.
The British ignored the pleas of the colonists.
The colonists now declare separation.

[Tyrannical Acts of the British King]

He has refused his Assent to Laws, the most wholesome and necessary for the public good.

He has forbidden his Governors to pass Laws of immediate and pressing importance, unless suspended in their operation till his assent should be obtained; and, when so suspended, he has utterly neglected to attend to them.

He has refused to pass other Laws for the accommodation of large districts of people, unless those people would **relinquish**[6] the right of Representation in the Legislature, a right inestimable to them, and formidable to tyrants only.

He has called together legislative bodies at places unusual, uncomfortable, and distant from the depository of their public Records, for the sole purpose of fatiguing them into compliance with his measures.

He has dissolved Representative Houses repeatedly, for opposing with manly firmness his invasions on the rights of the people.

He has refused for a long time, after such dissolutions, to cause others to be elected; whereby the Legislative powers, incapable of Annihilation, have returned to the people at large for their exercise; the State remaining in the mean time exposed to all the dangers of invasions from without, and **convulsions**[7] within.

He has endeavoured to prevent the population of these States; for that purpose obstructing the Laws for **Naturalization**[8] of Foreigners; refusing to pass others to encourage their migration hither, and raising the conditions of new Appropriations of Lands.

He has obstructed the Administration of Justice, by refusing his Assent to Laws for establishing Judiciary powers.

He has made Judges dependent on his Will alone, for the **tenure**[9] of their offices, and the amount and payment of their salaries.

He has erected a multitude of New Offices, and sent hither swarms of Officers to harass our people and **eat out their substance.**[10]

He has kept among us, in times of peace, Standing Armies, without the Consent of our legislatures.

He has affected to render the Military independent of and superior to the Civil power. He has combined with others to subject us to a jurisdiction foreign to our constitution and unacknowledged by our laws; giving his Assent to their Acts of pretended Legislation:

For **quartering**[11] large bodies of armed troops among us;

For protecting them, by a mock Trial, from punishment for any Murders which they should commit on the Inhabitants of these States;

For cutting off our Trade with all parts of the world;

6. **relinquish:** give up.
7. **convulsions:** violent disturbances.
8. **Naturalization:** process of becoming a citizen.
9. **tenure:** term.
10. **eat out their substance:** drain their resources.
11. **quartering:** housing or giving lodging to.

A CLOSER LOOK

GRIEVANCES AGAINST BRITAIN

The list contains 27 offenses by the British king and others against the colonies. It helps explain why it became necessary to seek independence.

2. Which offense do you think was the worst? Why?

A CLOSER LOOK

LOSS OF REPRESENTATIVE GOVERNMENT

One of the Intolerable Acts of 1774 stripped the Massachusetts Legislature of many powers and gave them to the colony's British governor.

3. Why was this action so "intolerable"?

A CLOSER LOOK

QUARTERING TROOPS WITHOUT CONSENT

The Quartering Act of 1765 required colonists to provide housing and supplies for British troops in America.

4. Why did colonists object to this act?

INSTRUCT

- Why do you think the colonists believed they had to explain their actions?
- According to the Declaration of Independence, when is it right to overthrow a government?
- In what ways did the acts of the king prove he was becoming a despot?
- Which acts are related to actions of the military, and why do you think they are cited by the colonists as problems?

MORE ABOUT . . .

Tyrannical Acts of the British King

The Declaration picked up on Thomas Paine's ideas in *Common Sense.* Before Paine's publication, colonists' anger had been focused against the Parliament. Appeals to the king to intercede were made to no avail. In fact, the king favored the use of force to bring the colonies back into line.

The Declaration cleared the air for many colonists. Joseph Barton of Delaware wrote on July 9, 1776, "I could hardly own the King and fight against him at the same time, but now these matters are cleared up Heart and hand shall move together."

VOCABULARY ACTIVITY

Have students substitute the definitions for the highlighted words in the sentences in which they are found. Have them read the sentence aloud to see if it makes the sentence meaning more clear. Then have them rewrite each sentence in their own words.

TEACHING STRATEGY

Recognizing Tone To help students understand the tone of accusation of the document, have volunteers read aloud from the list of grievances using the beginning word *he.* Have the students read only the first three words of each grievance, for example: *He has refused; He has forbidden; He has dissolved.* Also point out how the parallel sentence structure reinforces the tone of the document. Review the strong verbs used by the writer of the Declaration. Ask students how this language helps the reader understand the tone of the message. Discuss how substituting the weaker verbs would change the impact of the document. For example: "He has refused to pass other laws" reads differently from "He failed to pass other laws."

INSTRUCT

- Why did the actions listed on this page cause increased tension between Britain and the colonists?
- Do you believe that the actions of the colonists were reasonable? Support your opinion.
- Why do you think the British government took the actions it did?

MORE ABOUT . . .

Further Grievances Against the King

In this section of the grievances against the king, the Declaration refers to actions by the British military against colonists. Falmouth (now Portland), Maine, was burned in 1775, and the coast of Virginia was attacked in the same year. These actions reinforced the colonists' belief that Britain would not resolve differences with the colonies.

Furthermore, Virginia's Governor Dunmore was inciting Ohio Valley Indians on the frontiers of Virginia. Rumors were flying about the hiring of mercenaries to attack the colonies.

A CLOSER LOOK

TAXATION WITHOUT REPRESENTATION

The colonists believed in the long-standing British tradition that Parliament could tax only those citizens it represented—and the colonists claimed to have no representation in Parliament.

5. How do persons today give consent to taxation?

For imposing Taxes on us without our Consent;

For depriving us, in many cases, of the benefits of Trial by Jury;

For transporting us beyond Seas to be tried for pretended offenses;

For abolishing the free System of English Laws in a neighboring Province, establishing therein an **Arbitrary**[12] government, and enlarging its Boundaries so as to render it at once an example and fit instrument for introducing the same absolute rule into these Colonies;

For taking away our Charters, abolishing our most valuable laws, and altering fundamentally the Forms of our Governments;

For suspending our own Legislatures, and declaring themselves invested with power to legislate for us in all cases whatsoever.

He has **abdicated**[13] Government here, by declaring us out of his Protection and waging War against us.

He has plundered our seas, ravaged our Coasts, burnt our towns, and destroyed the lives of our people.

He is at this time transporting large Armies of **foreign Mercenaries**[14] to compleat the works of death, desolation, and tyranny, already begun with circumstances of Cruelty & **perfidy**[15] scarcely paralleled in the most barbarous ages, and totally unworthy the Head of a civilized nation.

He has constrained our fellow Citizens, taken Captive on the high Seas, to bear Arms against their Country, to become the executioners of their friends and Brethren, or to fall themselves by their Hands.

He has excited **domestic insurrections**[16] amongst us, and has endeavoured to bring on the inhabitants of our frontiers the merciless Indian Savages, whose known rule of warfare is an undistinguished destruction of all ages, sexes and conditions.

A CLOSER LOOK

PETITIONING THE KING

The colonists sent many petitions to King George III. In the Olive Branch Petition of 1775, the colonists expressed their desire to achieve "a happy and permanent reconciliation." The king rejected the petition.

6. Why did the colonists at first attempt to solve the dispute and remain loyal?

[Efforts of the Colonies to Avoid Separation]

In every stage of these Oppressions We have **Petitioned for Redress**[17] in the most humble terms; Our repeated Petitions have been answered only by repeated injury. A Prince, whose character is thus marked by every act which may define a Tyrant, is unfit to be the ruler of a free people.

Nor have We been wanting in attentions to our British brethren. We have warned them from time to time of attempts by their legislature to extend an unwarrantable jurisdiction over us. We have reminded them of the circumstances of our emigration and settlement here. We have appealed to their native justice and **magnanimity**,[18] and we have conjured them by the ties of our common kindred, to disavow these usurpations, which would inevitably interrupt our connections and correspondence. They too have been deaf to

12. **Arbitrary:** not limited by law.
13. **abdicated:** given up.
14. **foreign Mercenaries:** professional soldiers hired to serve in a foreign army.
15. **perfidy:** dishonesty, disloyalty.
16. **domestic insurrections:** rebellions at home.
17. **Petitioned for Redress:** asked for the correction of wrongs.
18. **magnanimity:** generosity, forgiveness.

TEACHING STRATEGY

The Colonists' Responses Remind the students that the tension between the colonies and Britain was caused by the actions of both. Use the graphic to help students review the responses of the colonists to the actions of the king. For example: imposing taxes without consent was met by the Stamp Act Congress and the boycott and protests by the colonists. Ask the students to think of other action-reaction situations.

British Action	Colonial Response
Imposing taxes without consent	Stamp Act Congress; boycotts; protest

the voice of justice and of **consanguinity**.[19] We must, therefore, **acquiesce**[20] in the necessity, which denounces our Separation, and hold them, as we hold the rest of mankind, Enemies in War, in Peace Friends.

[The Colonies Are Declared Free and Independent]

We, therefore, the Representatives of the United States of America, in General Congress, Assembled, appealing to the Supreme Judge of the world for the **rectitude**[21] of our intentions, do, in the name, and by the Authority of the good People of these Colonies solemnly publish and declare, That these United Colonies are, and of Right ought to be, Free and Independent States; that they are Absolved from all Allegiance to the British Crown, and that all political connection between them and the State of Great Britain is, and ought to be, totally dissolved; and that as Free and Independent States, they have full Power to levy War, conclude Peace, contract Alliances, establish Commerce, and do all other Acts and Things which Independent States may of right do.

And for the support of this Declaration, with a firm reliance on the protection of divine Providence, we mutually pledge to each other our Lives, our Fortunes, and our sacred Honor. [Signed by]

John Hancock *President, from Massachusetts*
[Georgia] Button Gwinnett; Lyman Hall; George Walton
[Rhode Island] Stephen Hopkins; William Ellery
[Connecticut] Roger Sherman; Samuel Huntington; William Williams; Oliver Wolcott
[North Carolina] William Hooper; Joseph Hewes; John Penn
[South Carolina] Edward Rutledge; Thomas Heyward, Jr.; Thomas Lynch, Jr.; Arthur Middleton
[Maryland] Samuel Chase; William Paca; Thomas Stone; Charles Carroll
[Virginia] George Wythe; Richard Henry Lee; Thomas Jefferson; Benjamin Harrison; Thomas Nelson, Jr.; Francis Lightfoot Lee; Carter Braxton
[Pennsylvania] Robert Morris; Benjamin Rush; Benjamin Franklin; John Morton; George Clymer; James Smith; George Taylor; James Wilson; George Ross
[Delaware] Caesar Rodney; George Read; Thomas McKean
[New York] William Floyd; Philip Livingston; Francis Lewis; Lewis Morris
[New Jersey] Richard Stockton; John Witherspoon; Francis Hopkinson; John Hart; Abraham Clark
[New Hampshire] Josiah Bartlett; William Whipple; Matthew Thornton
[Massachusetts] Samuel Adams; John Adams; Robert Treat Paine; Elbridge Gerry

19. **consanguinity:** relationship by a common ancestor; close connection.
20. **acquiesce:** accept without protest.
21. **rectitude:** moral uprightness.

A CLOSER LOOK

POWERS OF AN INDEPENDENT GOVERNMENT

The colonists identified the ability to wage war and agree to peace; to make alliances with other nations; and to set up an economic system as powers of a free and independent government.

7. What other powers are held by an independent government?

A CLOSER LOOK

DECLARATION SIGNERS

The Declaration was signed by 56 representatives from the 13 original states.

8. Which signers do you recognize? Write one line about each of those signers.

Interactive Primary Source Assessment

1. Main Ideas

a. What is the purpose of the Declaration of Independence as stated in the Preamble?

b. What are the five main parts of the Declaration?

c. What are three rights that all people have?

2. Critical Thinking

Drawing Conclusions Why did the colonies feel that they had to declare their independence?

THINK ABOUT

- colonial grievances against Britain
- Britain's response to these grievances

169

INSTRUCT

- By whose authority is independence declared? Why would that group be chosen?
- Why do you think the signers pledged everything they had in support of the Declaration?
- How do you think this document was viewed by the British king and Parliament?

MAKING PERSONAL CONNECTIONS

Have the entire class read aloud the final paragraph of the Declaration. Ask them to discuss what the pledge means. Then ask them if there are any causes that they feel so strongly about that they would make a similar pledge. If the answer is no, ask them why they would not take this kind of a pledge.

MORE ABOUT . . .

Lesser-Known Signers

Elbridge Gerry served as vice-president under James Madison. Richard Stockton was captured by the British and treated so harshly he became an invalid. Thomas Lynch, Jr., signed the Declaration but did little else in the Revolution. He disappeared at sea with his wife. Button Gwinett was killed in a duel during the Revolutionary War. Charles Carroll was the only Roman Catholic to sign the Declaration and the last signer to die, living until 1832.

Interactive Primary Source Assessment

1. Main Ideas

a. to explain why the colonists declared independence

b. Preamble, The Right of the People to Control Their Government, Tyrannical Acts of the British King, Efforts of the Colonies to Avoid Separation, The Colonies Are Declared Free and Independent

c. life, liberty, and the pursuit of happiness

2. Critical Thinking

The colonists believed that the British government had abused its powers by taking away their rights, and it had ignored their pleas to settle grievances.

A CLOSER LOOK

1. The people can vote elected officials out of office by casting their ballots for other candidates.
2. Answers will vary, but each answer should include an explanation.
3. The people of Massachusetts found this action intolerable because it took away their only representation in government.
4. The people believed that this act violated their freedom.
5. Citizens elect representatives to the legislative bodies that enact taxes.
6. Many colonists viewed themselves as British citizens and thus had difficulty separating from Great Britain.
7. the ability to make laws and to seek membership in world organizations
8. Student responses will vary.

TERMS & NAMES

1. **Stamp Act,** p. 144
2. **Sons of Liberty,** p. 145
3. **writs of assistance,** p. 145
4. **Samuel Adams,** p. 148
5. **Boston Tea Party,** p. 151
6. **militia,** p. 154
7. **Lexington and Concord,** p. 157
8. **Loyalist,** p. 157
9. **Declaration of Independence,** p. 164
10. **Thomas Jefferson,** p. 164

REVIEW QUESTIONS

Possible Responses

1. They worsened as Britain tried to impose controls on the colonies.
2. to earn revenue to pay debts carried over from the French and Indian War and to pay for housing troops in the colonies
3. because they felt they should not be taxed without representation in Parliament
4. They organized a boycott of British goods and held peaceful protests. Sometimes they reacted violently.
5. The Sons of Liberty exaggerated the incident to raise anti-British feelings.
6. Groups of leaders in various towns and colonies exchanged letters and shared information.
7. to plan a response to the Intolerable Acts
8. the ride of Paul Revere, William Dawes, and Samuel Prescott to warn Lexington and Concord that British troops were coming to seize Patriot war supplies
9. It was a battle on the hills above Charlestown, across the bay from Boston, in which the British defeated the militia but suffered high casualties in their victory.
10. the idea of natural rights: that people have basic rights that governments cannot and should not take away

VISUAL SUMMARY

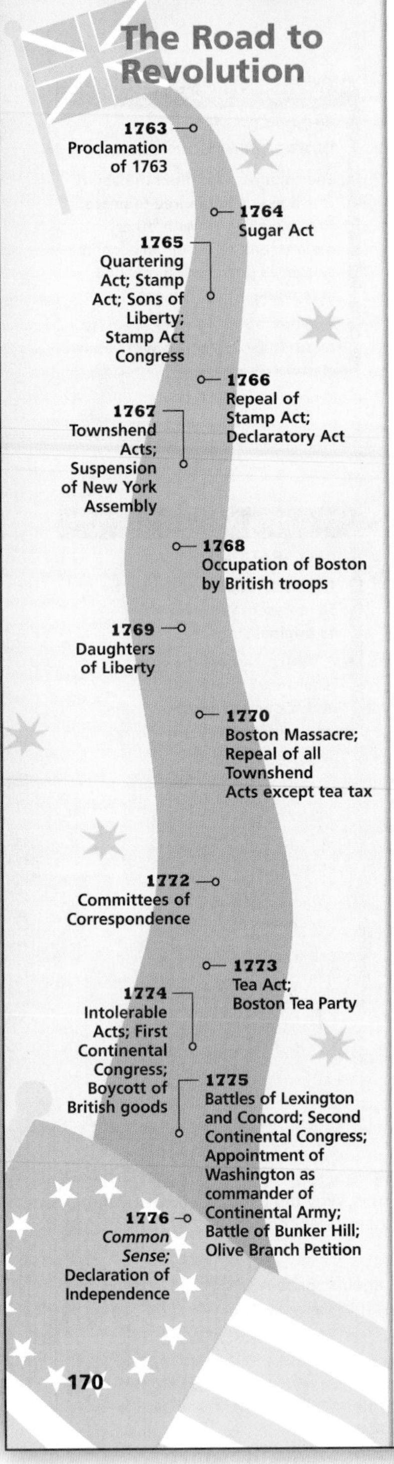

Chapter 6 ASSESSMENT

TERMS & NAMES

Briefly explain the significance of each of the following.

1. Stamp Act
2. Sons of Liberty
3. writs of assistance
4. Samuel Adams
5. Boston Tea Party
6. militia
7. Lexington and Concord
8. Loyalist
9. Declaration of Independence
10. Thomas Jefferson

REVIEW QUESTIONS

Tighter British Control (pages 143–146)

1. How did relations between Britain and the colonies change after the Seven Years' War?
2. Why did Britain try to tax the colonies?
3. Why did the colonists cry, "No taxation without representation"?

Colonial Resistance Grows (pages 147–153)

4. How did the colonists protest the Townshend Acts?
5. How was the Boston Massacre used for propaganda purposes?
6. How did the committees of correspondence help keep people informed?

The Road to Lexington and Concord (pages 154–159)

7. Why was the First Continental Congress held?
8. What was the Midnight Ride?

Declaring Independence (pages 160–169)

9. What was the Battle of Bunker Hill?
10. What was the core idea of the Declaration of Independence?

CRITICAL THINKING

1. USING YOUR NOTES

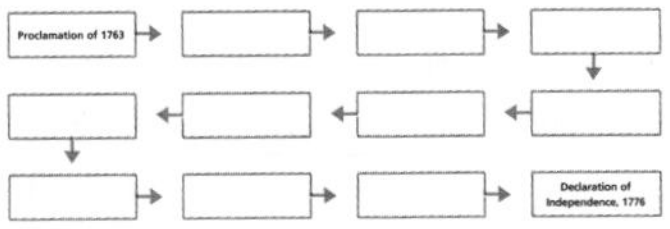

Using your completed chart, answer the questions below.

a. What city was the site of early protest activity?

b. What event happened after the Tea Act?

2. ANALYZING LEADERSHIP

How did colonial leaders differ in their methods of defending and securing basic rights for the colonies?

3. APPLYING CITIZENSHIP SKILLS

Did colonial leaders have a responsibility to include women, African Americans, and other groups in the Declaration of Independence? Explain.

4. THEME: IMPACT OF THE INDIVIDUAL

How did John Adams's role as lawyer for the British soldiers involved in the Boston Massacre help set a tone for the Revolutionary cause?

5. DRAWING CONCLUSIONS

What factors and events led the colonies to seek independence?

6. SUPPORTING OPINIONS

Do you think the American Revolution would have occurred if Britain had not taxed the colonies? Why or why not?

Interact *with* History

Now that you have read about the road to revolution, do you consider your decision made at the beginning of the chapter to join or not join the protest a wise choice or a poor choice? Explain.

CRITICAL THINKING

Possible Responses

1. **USING YOUR NOTES** **a.** Boston **b.** Boston Tea Party
2. **ANALYZING LEADERSHIP** Some leaders were quite radical, even violent. Others were very moderate, not wishing to offend Britain.
3. **APPLYING CITIZENSHIP SKILLS** Students may say leaving them out denied them full rights, or that including them might have jeopardized approval of the Declaration.
4. **THEME: IMPACT OF THE INDIVIDUAL** He showed that colonists could seek their rights and oppose British policy in a lawful, nondestructive way.
5. **DRAWING CONCLUSIONS** Taxes and other restrictive policies. Their protests brought even more controls from Britain and led to armed conflict.
6. **SUPPORTING OPINIONS** It might have been delayed, but eventually the colonists would probably have found other reasons to resist British rule.

Interact *with* History Answers will vary depending on whether students chose to join the protest or not. In their responses, they should show understanding of the events in the chapter.

HISTORY SKILLS

1. INTERPRETING MAPS: Location

Study the map and then answer the questions.

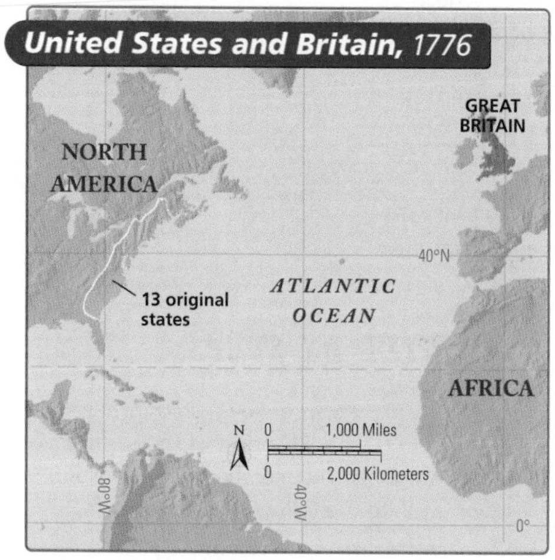

United States and Britain, 1776

Basic Map Elements

a. What is the subject of the map?

b. What do the colors yellow and orange represent?

Interpreting the Map

c. What is the approximate distance between Great Britain and the United States?

d. Who do you think had the advantage in a war fought on the North American mainland?

2. INTERPRETING PRIMARY SOURCES

This British political cartoon is titled *Poor Old England Endeavoring to Reclaim His Wicked Children*. Study the cartoon carefully. Answer the questions.

a. How is England pictured? America?

b. Does the cartoon suggest England will be successful? Explain.

ALTERNATIVE ASSESSMENT

1. INTERDISCIPLINARY ACTIVITY: World History

Giving a Report Do research about another country, colony, or region of the world during the 1760s and 1770s. Give a brief oral report, comparing and contrasting events and conditions there with those in the British colonies.

2. COOPERATIVE LEARNING ACTIVITY

Debating During discussion of the Declaration of Independence, members of the Continental Congress held heated debates on the issue of independence and whether to abolish the slave trade. Imagine that you and your classmates are delegates to the Congress. Hold a debate on these issues, choosing one of the following roles to play:

- a strong supporter of independence and of an end to the slave trade (such as Samuel Adams or John Adams)
- a supporter of independence but an opponent of ending the slave trade (such as George Washington)
- an independence opponent (such as John Dickinson)

3. PRIMARY SOURCE EXPLORER

Writing a Play The Declaration of Independence announced to the world that the colonies had chosen independence and why. Using the CD-ROM, your textbook, and library research, find out more about the Declaration and the people and events surrounding it. Then write a one-act play using the suggestions below. Be sure to use standard grammar, spelling, sentence structure, and punctuation in your play.

- Set the play after the Declaration has been drafted.
- Have Thomas Jefferson, as the author, answer questions about what he included and perhaps did not include in the Declaration.
- Have Jefferson questioned by delegates to the Congress, or have him appear before a town meeting of ordinary citizens.
- Prepare introductory material to describe the setting and write dialogue for the characters.

4. HISTORY PORTFOLIO

Review your section and chapter assessment activities. Select one that you think was your best work. Then give consideration to suggestions made by your teacher or classmates and revise your work. Add it to your portfolio.

Additional Test Practice, pp. S1–S33

TEST PRACTICE CLASSZONE.COM

ALTERNATIVE ASSESSMENT

1. INTERDISCIPLINARY ACTIVITY: World History

Each student's report should
- be well organized and clearly stated.
- provide evidence and factual support.
- present the information in a lively and interesting style.

2. COOPERATIVE LEARNING ACTIVITY

Debate should
- clearly state a position.
- present and support main points.
- refute the ideas of the opposition.

3. PRIMARY SOURCE EXPLORER

A play should
- accurately portray the event.
- exhibit creativity in creating the scene.
- clearly portray all sides of the issue.

4. HISTORY PORTFOLIO

Revised section or chapter assessment activities should
- address teacher and peer responses to the selected work.
- solve problems present in the first versions of the work.

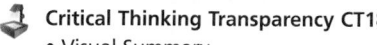

Critical Thinking Transparency CT18
- Visual Summary

Formal Assessment
- Chapter Test, Forms A, B, and C, pp. 104–118

HISTORY SKILLS

Possible Responses

1. INTERPRETING MAPS

Basic Map Elements

a. the United States and Britain in 1776

b. yellow for 13 original states, orange for Great Britain, and green for all other areas

Interpreting the Map

c. about 3,000 miles

d. the United States, because the war was being fought on its own territory whereas Britain had to bring soldiers and supplies from 3,000 miles away

2. INTERPRETING PRIMARY SOURCES

a. England is an old man trying to get his wicked children back; America is pictured as his children pulling away.

b. No, England is too weak to get America back.

HISTORY WORKSHOP

OBJECTIVE
Students role-play activities, re-create cultural artifacts, and present issues related to the declaring of independence during the American Revolution.

BLOCK SCHEDULING

PROCEDURE

Gather the materials listed in the "Toolbox." Divide the class into groups of four or five. Then review the steps for raising the liberty pole and for preparing a persuasive speech.

In-Depth Resources: Unit 2
- History Workshop Resources, p. 23

MORE ABOUT . . .

The Liberty Tree
The Sons of Liberty met at the Liberty Tree in Boston to sing songs, condemn the British government, and stage imaginary hangings of hated officials. In 1775, British soldiers cut the tree down and turned it into firewood.

Each of the 13 colonies had its own Liberty Tree. The last surviving Liberty Tree, a 400-year-old tulip poplar in Maryland, had to be cut down after it suffered great damage in a 1999 hurricane.

HISTORY FROM VISUALS

Interpreting the Painting Have students point out images from the painting that convey the country's patriotic spirit in July 1776. **Possible Responses** the liberty pole; the recruiting station and recruiting sign; the drummer with the red sash; the gestures of the men, women, and children

Raise the Liberty Pole

In 1765, the Sons of Liberty gathered around a huge elm tree in Boston that they named the Liberty Tree. It became a meeting place where people voiced their protests against British policies. Replicas of the Liberty Tree—giant poles sometimes decorated with the flags of the colonies—were raised throughout the colonies. These liberty poles represented the unity of the American colonies as they struggled to break away from British rule.

ACTIVITY Like the American Patriots, each group of students will raise its own liberty pole. Each group also will write and deliver a persuasive speech supporting the cause of the American colonies.

TOOLBOX

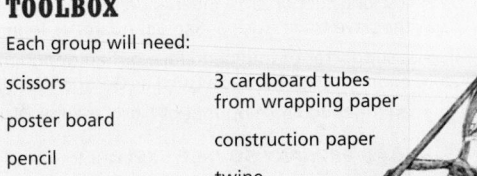

Each group will need:

- scissors
- poster board
- pencil
- markers
- masking tape
- 3 cardboard tubes from wrapping paper
- construction paper
- twine
- stapler

STEP BY STEP

1 Form groups. Each group should consist of four or five students. The members of your group will do the following jobs:

- research each colony
- design and create flags
- construct a pole
- write and deliver a speech

2 Do research on the 13 colonies. For each colony, your group should find a person, place, or object that represents that colony. For example, a Pilgrim's hat might represent Massachusetts. The 13 colonies are listed below.

New England Colonies	Middle Colonies	Southern Colonies
Massachusetts (including Maine)	New York	North Carolina
New Hampshire	Delaware	Virginia
Connecticut	New Jersey	Maryland
Rhode Island	Pennsylvania	South Carolina
		Georgia

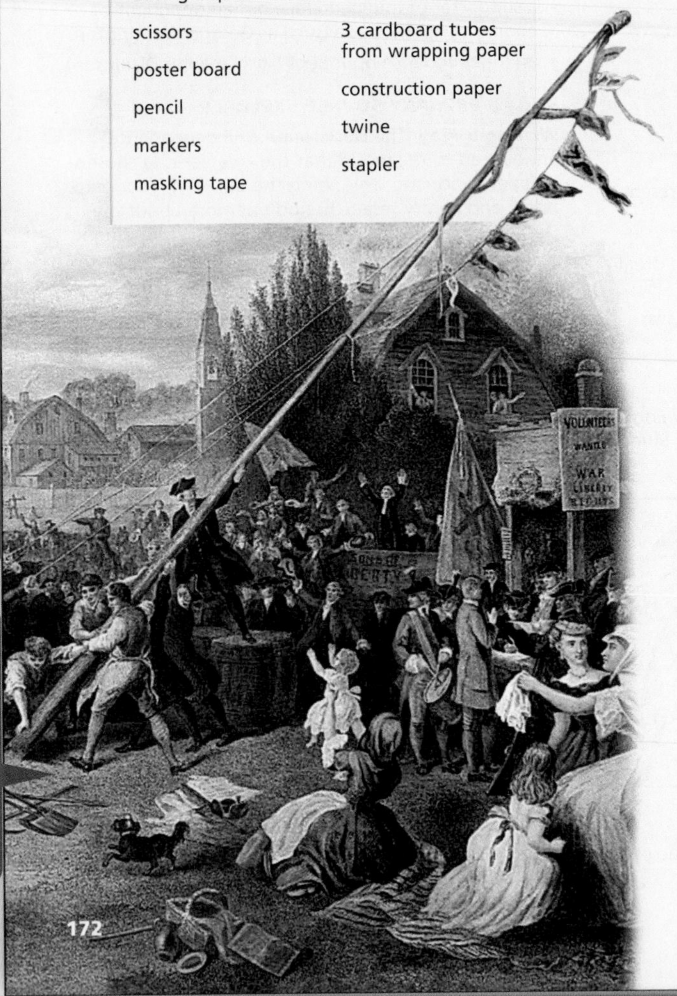

Members of the Sons of Liberty raise a liberty pole in July 1776 to celebrate America's independence.

172

RECOMMENDED RESOURCES

JOURNALS AND BOOKS FOR THE TEACHER

Kreamer, Todd Alan. "Sons of Liberty: Patriots or Terrorists?" ***The Early America Review. A Journal of People, Issues, and Events in 18th Century America.*** Washington: DEV Communications, Inc., Fall 1996.

Shearer, Benjamin F. and Barbara S. Shearer. ***State Names, Seals, Flags, and Symbols.*** Greenwood Publishing Group, 1994.

VIDEOS

LIBERTY! The American Revolution. PBS Home Video. 1997. Three-part documentary covering the years 1763–1791.

To Keep Our Liberty. National Park Service. Dramatic portrayal of the early revolutionary period, 1763–1775.

BOOKS FOR THE STUDENTS

Bloss, Janet Adele. ***State Flags.*** Willowisp Press, 1996.

Langguth, A. J. ***Patriots: The Men Who Started the American Revolution.*** Touchstone, 1989.

3 Design and create 13 flags for the colonies. Decide what person, place, or object you will use on your flag for each colony. Cut each flag out of the poster board. Sketch your design on the flag with a pencil. Then use markers to decorate it. On the back of each flag, explain how your design portrays the characteristics of that colony.

4 Construct the pole. Using masking tape, fasten the three cardboard tubes together to form one long tube. Then reinforce the tube by taping construction paper around it.

5 String the flags on the pole. Feed a piece of twine through the open ends of the long tube. Tie the ends of the twine together to form a tight loop. Now staple all 13 flags to the twine.

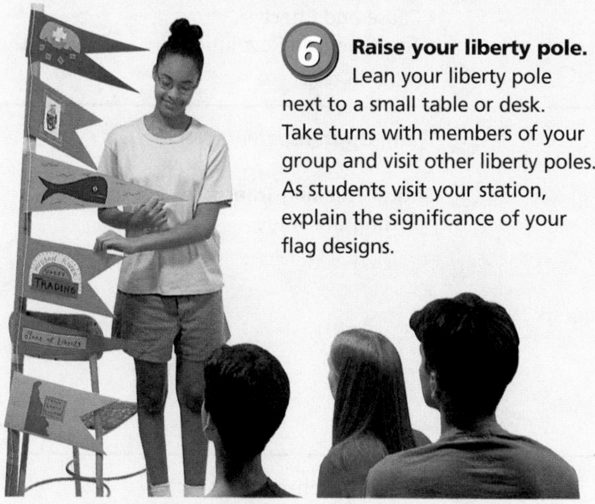

6 Raise your liberty pole. Lean your liberty pole next to a small table or desk. Take turns with members of your group and visit other liberty poles. As students visit your station, explain the significance of your flag designs.

WRITE AND SPEAK

Write a persuasive speech to recruit others to join the cause of liberty. In your speech, explain what is wrong with British policies. Give reasons why the colonies should become independent. Then read your speech to the other groups as part of the recruitment process.

HELP DESK

For related information on the Liberty Tree, see pages 145–146 in Chapter 6.

Researching Your Project

- *The Revolutionary War* by Bart McDowell
- *The American Revolutionaries* edited by Milton Meltzer

For more about the American Revolution . . .

RESEARCH LINKS
CLASSZONE.COM

Did You Know?

The numbers 45 and 92 played an important part in the history of these liberty poles. The 45th issue of a British newspaper openly criticized the king in 1763 and was reprinted in the colonies. In 1768, 92 members of the Massachusetts General Assembly voted against canceling a letter to the other 12 colonies that called for action against Britain. To represent the numbers, 92 members of the Sons of Liberty would often raise liberty poles to a height of about 45 feet.

REFLECT & ASSESS

- **How well do your flags represent the colonies?**
- **How clearly does your speech explain grievances against the British?**
- **Why do you think the practice of raising liberty poles spread to many of the colonies?**

MORE ABOUT . . .

Protest Symbols Today

Many people still rely on images and artworks as expressions of protest. For example, a blue ribbon symbolizes freedom of speech, while raised fists, featured in many outdoor murals, often represent the fight against social injustices. Have the class brainstorm visual symbols of protest they have observed, such as graffiti, bumper stickers, hairstyles, compact disc covers, and so on.

REFLECT & ASSESS

1. Ask students to defend their choices of symbols by referring to the written explanations on the back of each flag.
2. Have students work with a peer editor who comments on the clarity of the grievances.
3. Have students imagine members of the Sons of Liberty from different colonies writing letters to one another.

STANDARDS FOR EVALUATION

HISTORY WORKSHOP

Liberty poles should

- appear well-constructed and realistic.
- include flags that are symbolic of the 13 colonies.
- show evidence of research.

WRITE AND SPEAK

Persuasive speeches should

- state opinions clearly.
- include historical details about unfair British policies.
- present convincing reasons for supporting the colonies' goal of independence.

CHAPTER 7 PLANNING GUIDE

The American Revolution 1776–1783

	CHAPTER OVERVIEW	COPYMASTERS	INTEGRATED TECHNOLOGY
CHAPTER RESOURCES	The chapter describes the battles, people, strategies, and hardships involved in fighting the American Revolution. It also discusses the aftermath of the war and how the newly independent United States will govern itself.	**In-Depth Resources: Unit 2** • Tracing Themes: Citizenship, p. 25 • Building Vocabulary, p. 30 **Interdisciplinary Projects,** pp. 37–42	• eEdition Plus Online • EasyPlanner Plus Online • eTest Plus Online • eEdition • Power Presentations • EasyPlanner • Electronic Library of Primary Sources • Test Generator • Reading Study Guide • America's Music
SECTION 1 **The Early Years of the War** **pp. 177–183**	**KEY IDEAS** • Americans are divided on the question of independence, making it difficult for Washington to raise an army. • Britain seeks to control the Middle Colonies and Hudson River Valley. • The Battles of Saratoga turn the tide of the war.	**In-Depth Resources: Unit 2** • Setting the Stage, p. 24 • Guided Reading, p. 26 • Skillbuilder Practice, p. 31 • Literature Selection, pp. 36–38 • Reteaching Activity, p. 39 **America's History Makers** • George Washington, pp. 27–28 • Haym Salomon, pp. 29–30 **Citizenship Today,** pp. 3–4	**Humanities Transparency HT13** • *Battle of Saratoga* **Humanities Transparency HT14** • *The Spirit of '76* **Geography Transparency GT7** • Final Battle of Saratoga, 1777 **Critical Thinking Transparency CT20** • Cause and Effect: The American Revolution classzone.com
SECTION 2 **The War Expands** **pp. 184–189**	• France enters the war on the American side, preventing the British from concentrating their strength. • The Continental Army endures a harsh winter at Valley Forge, but Americans win key victories on the frontier. • American privateers wage war at sea, disrupting British trade.	**In-Depth Resources: Unit 2** • Setting the Stage, p. 24 • Guided Reading, p. 27 • Primary Source, p. 34 • Reteaching Activity, p. 40 **American History Plays** • *Fires at Valley Forge* by Barrett H. Clark	**Warm-Up Transparency WT7** **Critical Thinking Transparency CT19** • Setting the Stage classzone.com
SECTION 3 **The Path to Victory** **pp. 190–194**	• Britain moves the war to the Southern colonies, seeking Loyalist support. • After several British victories, Americans turn to guerrilla warfare. • The American army and French fleet surround the British at Yorktown, Virginia, forcing British leader, Cornwallis, to surrender.	**In-Depth Resources: Unit 2** • Setting the Stage, p. 24 • Guided Reading, p. 28 • Geography Application: Cornwallis Is Trapped at Yorktown, 1781, pp. 32–33 • Reteaching Activity, p. 41	**Warm-Up Transparency WT7** **Critical Thinking Transparency CT19** • Setting the Stage classzone.com
SECTION 4 **The Legacy of the War** **pp. 195–199**	• Factors in the American victory are better leadership, aid from abroad, knowledge of the land, and motivation. • The Treaty of Paris acknowledges American independence and boundaries, and defines the terms of peace. • The United States institutes a republican form of government.	**In-Depth Resources: Unit 2** • Setting the Stage, p. 24 • Guided Reading, p. 29 • Primary Source, p. 35 • Reteaching Activity, p. 42 **Economics in History** • Independence and Free Enterprise, p. 7 **Why It Matters Now** • Democracy in South Africa, pp. 13–14 **Outline Map Activities** • North America, 1783, pp. 13–14	**Warm-Up Transparency WT7** **Critical Thinking Transparency CT19** • Setting the Stage **Critical Thinking Transparency CT21** • Visual Summary classzone.com

Pupil's Edition | Overhead Transparency | CD-ROM
Copymaster | Audio Library | Internet

ASSESSMENT OPTIONS

- **Chapter Assessment,** pp. 200–201
- **Formal Assessment**
  - Chapter Tests, Forms A, B, and C, pp. 123–134
- **Test Generator**
- **Online Test Practice**
- **Strategies for Test Preparation**

- **Section Assessment,** p. 183
- **Formal Assessment,** Quiz, p. 119
- **Integrated Assessment Book**
  - Rubrics, 4.4, 1.7
- **Test Generator**
- **Test Practice Transparencies,** TT24

- **Section Assessment,** p. 189
- **Formal Assessment,** Quiz, p. 120
- **Integrated Assessment Book**
  - Rubrics, 1.3, 3.4
- **Test Generator**
- **Test Practice Transparencies,** TT25

- **Section Assessment,** p. 194
- **Formal Assessment,** Quiz, p. 121
- **Integrated Assessment Book**
  - Rubrics, 5.1, 4.8
- **Test Generator**
- **Test Practice Transparencies,** TT26

- **Section Assessment,** p. 199
- **Formal Assessment,** Quiz, p. 122
- **Integrated Assessment Book**
  - Rubrics, 3.6, 2.3
- **Test Generator**
- **Test Practice Transparencies,** TT27

CUSTOMIZING FOR INDIVIDUAL NEEDS

Students Acquiring English/ESL

- **Reading Study Guide** (English and Spanish), pp. 59–68
- **Access for Students Acquiring English/ESL:** Spanish Translations, pp. 40–46
- **Chapter Summaries on CD** (English and Spanish)
- **Modified Lesson Plans for English Learners**

Less Proficient Readers

- **Reading Study Guide** (English and Spanish), pp. 59–68
- **Chapter Summaries on CD** (English and Spanish)

Gifted and Talented Students

- **In-Depth Resources: Unit 2**
  - Enrichment Activity, p. 43
- **America's History Makers**
  - George Washington, pp. 27–28
  - Haym Salomon, pp. 29–30

CROSS-CURRICULAR CONNECTIONS

Culture

Cox, Clinton. ***Come All You Brave Soldiers: Blacks in the Revolutionary War.*** New York: Cartwheel Books, 1999. A factual, easy-to-read account of African-American contributions to the Revolution.

Geography

King, David C. ***Saratoga.*** Battlefields Across America series. Fairfield, IA: Twenty-First Century, 1998. Information on this battle is well presented in maps, text, and historic images.

Interdisciplinary Projects, pp. 37–42

- Math: Calculating the Value of Currency
- Science: Chemical Reactions
- Language Arts: Broadsides
- Health: Health and Nutrition in the Army

Primary Sources

Meltzer, Milton, ed. ***The American Revolutionaries: A History in Their Own Words, 1750–1800.*** New York: Harper Trophy, 1993. Chronological collection of first-person accounts.

Humanities: Music

McNeil, Rusty. ***Colonial & Revolution Songs.*** WEM, 1989. Two audiocassettes and a songbook.

Literature

Collier, James. ***My Brother Sam Is Dead.*** New York: S&S, 1984. Prize-winning, fact-based story of one family's wrenching experience in the Revolution.

O'Dell, Scott. ***Sarah Bishop.*** A girl's father and brother take opposite sides in the Revolution.

Yates, Elizabeth. ***Amos Fortune: Free Man.*** New York: Dutton, 1967. The life of an 18th-century prince who is captured by slavers and lives in Massachusetts as a slave during the Revolution.

ENRICHMENT ACTIVITIES

- **Pupil's Edition, pp. 174–201**
  - **Interact with History,** p. 175
  - **Citizenship Today,** p. 182
  - **Technology of the Time,** p. 192
  - **Economics in History,** p. 198
- **In-Depth Resources: Unit 2**
  - Geography Application: Cornwallis Is Trapped at Yorktown, 1781, pp. 32–33
  - Primary Source: from *Private Yankee Doodle,* p. 34
  - Primary Source: An African-American Petition for Freedom, p. 35
  - Literature Selection: from *Citizen Tom Paine,* pp. 36–38
- **America's History Makers**
  - George Washington, pp. 27–28
  - Haym Salomon, pp. 29–30
- **Outline Map Activities**
  - North America, 1783, pp. 13–14
- **Why It Matters Now**
  - Democracy in South Africa, pp. 13–14

BLOCK SCHEDULING — LESSON PLAN OPTIONS (90-MINUTE PERIOD)

DAY 1

Interact with History, p. 175
Class Time 20 Minutes

Options for pacing and variety:
- **Role-Playing** Have students assume the role of Mrs. Schuyler and write a letter from Mrs. Schuyler to her husband explaining why she set fire to the fields and how she felt as the British approached. **Class Time** 20 minutes

Setting the Stage, p. 176
Class Time 20 minutes

Options for pacing and variety:
- **Time Saver** For a homework assignment, have students preview the section, looking at subsection heads and illustrations. Then students can make a list of "What Do You Want to Know?" questions for the section. **Class Time** 5 minutes

Section 1, pp. 177–183
Class Time 50 minutes

Options for pacing and variety:
- **History on Film** Extend students' background knowledge of the American Revolution by viewing *The American Revolution.* Schlesinger, 1996. **Class Time** 35 minutes
- **Team Teaching** Invite a music teacher to talk to the class about the instruments used in Revolutionary War bands and to play some popular music of the war years. **Class Time** 30 minutes

DAY 2

Section 2, pp. 184–189
Class Time 45 minutes

Options for pacing and variety:
- **Internet** Extend students' background knowledge of the American Revolution by visiting classzone.com. **Class Time** 20 minutes
- **Time Saver** For a homework assignment, have students answer the Reading History questions. **Class Time** 5 minutes

Section 3, pp. 190–194
Class Time: 45 minutes

Options for pacing and variety:
- **Peer Teaching** Have pairs of students choose two events in this chapter and write news headlines for them. Then have student pairs exchange headlines and write short news articles to go with the ones they receive. **Class Time** 40 minutes
- **Peer Evaluation** Have small groups of students work together to answer the Section Assessment Critical Thinking question and create a cause-and-effect graphic organizer to show their conclusions. **Class Time** 20 minutes

DAY 3

Section 4, pp. 195–199
Class Time 45 minutes

Options for pacing and variety:
- **Peer Evaluation** Have students work in pairs to answer the Connect to History and Connect to Today questions in the Economics in History feature on page 198. **Class Time** 20 minutes
- **Time Saver** As a homework assignment after completing the Economics in History feature, have students answer Critical Thinking question 3 in the chapter assessment on page 200. **Class Time** 10 minutes

Chapter 7 Assessment, pp. 200–201
Class Time 40 minutes

Options for pacing and variety:
- **Peer Evaluation** Have students prepare a summary of the chapter using the words in the Terms & Names in the Chapter Assessment. Have them exchange papers and evaluate each other's summaries. **Class Time** 20 minutes
- **Peer Teaching** Have pairs of students make up five questions based on the Visual Summary on page 200. **Class Time** 20 minutes

TEACHER-TESTED ACTIVITY **Barbara Kennedy, Sylvan Middle School, Citrus Heights, California**

MEDIA INTERVIEW SKITS

Class Time Two class periods for preparation and two for presentation

Task Creating a videotape to present arguments for and against war with Britain

Purpose To understand the beliefs of Americans on both sides of the debate over the Revolution

Supplies Needed
- Reference materials and Internet resources on the American Revolution
- Costumes supplied by students
- Video camera and tapes

Activity Divide the class into small groups. Within groups, students should choose roles such as camera person, producer, interviewer, pro-Revolution and anti-Revolution colonists, Native Americans, enslaved African Americans, or free black colonists. Have each group write a script for the "person-on-the-street" interview, making sure that interviews capture multiple points of view. Students may use cue cards to help them with their presentations while filming. Have them practice their skits before taping them.

VIDEO SKETCHES OF HEROES

Producing a short video sketch on the life of a hero of the American Revolution will require a variety of student talents and skills. Another advantage of this activity is that the products can be shared with other students in the school or even other schools. If the technological capability exists to port the video to the World Wide Web, students could also build a Web site to share their video sketches with a wider audience.

ACTIVITY OUTLINE

Objective Developing biographical sketches of selected heroes of the Revolution will help students understand the role of the individual in shaping history.

Task Students will research the background of an individual, write a short script, select an actor or narrator to tell the individual's story, gather visual materials, and videotape the sketch.

Class Time Two class periods

DIRECTIONS

1. Have the class review people mentioned in the text or people they already know who played a significant role in the American Revolution. Next, conduct a "brain-storming" session to compile a list of favorite heroes. (Suggested people: George Washington, John Paul Jones, George Clark, Francis Marion, Marquis de Lafayette, Molly Pitcher, Nancy Hart, Haym Salomon, Thomas Paine, James Forten, Elizabeth Freeman, Benjamin Franklin, Nathanael Greene, Baron de Kalb, Baron von Steuben, Thomas Jefferson, John and Abigail Adams, James Madison, John Hancock, Alexander Hamilton)

2. Divide students into groups of about five students.

3. Assign each group an individual to focus on. Each group will then research its assigned hero. Students should use the school library or the sites listed at classzone.com to find additional information about that person. Research can be conducted outside of class, if necessary.

4. Remind students to look for the following information:
   - family life and work life
   - age at the time of the Revolution
   - contribution to the Revolution
   - interesting and little-known facts

5. After each group has completed its research, group members should write a script for the video sketch. Remind students that one written page of script will equal about one minute of video. All members of the group should participate in the scriptwriting. Instruct the groups to choose whether they want their script to be narrated in first person or in third person. This decision could influence the choice of a narrator or performer and what that person will wear for the taping.

6. When scripts have been completed, narrations or performances rehearsed, costumes arranged, and all materials and equipment made available, have each group tape its video. Team members not "on camera" should help with filming.

7. After all the groups have completed the taping, arrange a class showing of the video sketches.

CHAPTER 7 OBJECTIVE

The student will organize events of the American Revolution in chronological sequence and analyze the causes that led to an American victory.

HISTORY FROM VISUALS

Interpreting the Painting Ask students to read the caption on page 174, then to study the painting of the Patriot troops at Valley Forge. Ask them to describe the weather and the men's clothing and physical condition. **Possible Responses** The weather appears cold and snowy. The mounted men are heavily cloaked, but the men on foot are less warmly dressed. They have no cloaks, hats, or gloves. One soldier is wounded and is being helped by another. The soldier in front is acknowledging Washington. The soldier standing at the horse's head appears to be talking with the officers on horseback.

Extension Ask students to write three things the soldier in the coat may be reporting to General Washington and his aides.

CRITICAL THINKING ACTIVITY

Making Inferences Ask students to make inferences about the physical and mental condition of both the troops and the officers. Encourage them to discuss the relationship between morale and physical conditions such as being cold, hungry, tired, or injured. Ask them to explain the adage, attributed to Napoleon not long after the American Revolution, "An army marches on its stomach." How might physical hardship affect a soldier's loyalty as well as his ability to fight?

Class Time 10 minutes

CHAPTER 7

The American Revolution 1776–1783

This painting shows General Washington and his ragged troops traveling to their winter camp at Valley Forge.

174

RECOMMENDED RESOURCES

BOOKS FOR THE TEACHER

Bobrick, Benson. ***Angel in the Whirlwind: The Triumph of the American Revolution.*** New York: Simon and Schuster, 1997. Packed with human drama.

Flexner, James T. ***Washington: The Indispensable Man.*** New York: Little, Brown, 1974. Shorter version of the authoritative biography.

Franklin, Benjamin. ***Autobiography & Other Writings.*** Ormond Seavey, ed. New York: Oxford, 1999. Observations from America's scientist, sage, and diplomat.

SOFTWARE

American Leaders Series. Decision Development Corp. Sortable, searchable, and highly graphic biographies.

VIDEO

The American Revolution: Two Views. Queue, 1994. Unusual presentation of both sides in the war.

INTERNET

For more about the Revolutionary War, visit . . .

classzone.com

Interact *with* History

The British army is on the other side of this hill and coming fast.
These are the family and servants of the American general Philip Schuyler.
Mrs. Schuyler sets fire to her harvest to prevent the British from taking it.

It is 1777. Your brother is an American soldier. In his last letter to you, he wrote that the army has no shoes or bullets and little food. But he plans to keep fighting.

Now, a British army is coming toward your farm. You hear that the soldiers are stealing crops to feed themselves and their horses.

What Do You Think?

- **What sacrifices do civilians like Mrs. Schuyler make during wartime?**
- **What sacrifices do soldiers make?**
- **Is it worth such sacrifices to win independence for your country? Why or why not?**

What would you sacrifice to win freedom?

USA

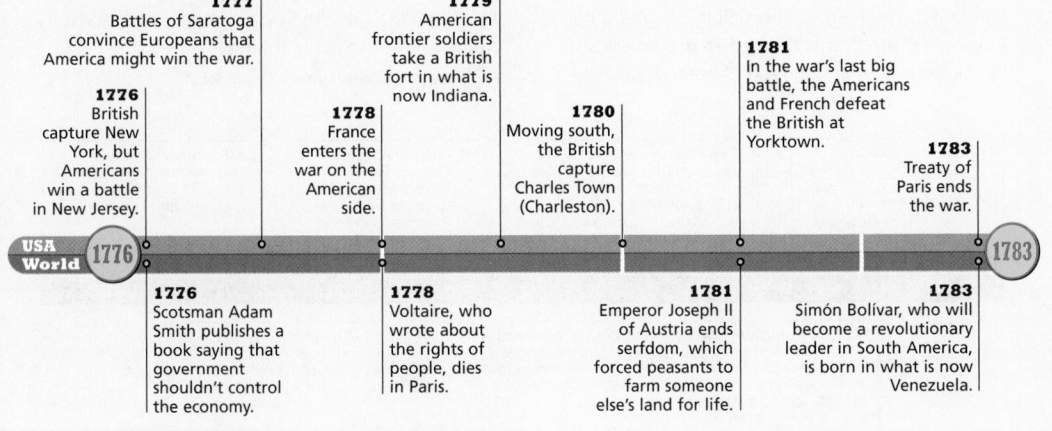

- **1776** British capture New York, but Americans win a battle in New Jersey.
- **1777** Battles of Saratoga convince Europeans that America might win the war.
- **1778** France enters the war on the American side.
- **1779** American frontier soldiers take a British fort in what is now Indiana.
- **1780** Moving south, the British capture Charles Town (Charleston).
- **1781** In the war's last big battle, the Americans and French defeat the British at Yorktown.
- **1783** Treaty of Paris ends the war.

World

- **1776** Scotsman Adam Smith publishes a book saying that government shouldn't control the economy.
- **1778** Voltaire, who wrote about the rights of people, dies in Paris.
- **1781** Emperor Joseph II of Austria ends serfdom, which forced peasants to farm someone else's land for life.
- **1783** Simón Bolívar, who will become a revolutionary leader in South America, is born in what is now Venezuela.

Interact *with* History

OBJECTIVES

- To describe the harsh conditions that many soldiers and civilians faced during the Revolution
- To identify physical hardships and material sacrifices that students might endure for the sake of freedom

What Do You Think?

1. Ask students to think about the role of civilians in wartime. Discuss how war affects civilians, whether or not they are near the battlefield.
2. Besides the obvious risk of death, suggest that students also think about the hardships of a soldier's daily life.
3. Discuss the various meanings that independence might have had in the 1770s for the members of the Schuyler household. Remind students that independence did not bring the same political rights for women and African Americans that it did for white men. Still, everyone in the picture will share in the hardships of the war.

What would you sacrifice to win freedom?

Ask students to predict the consequences of Mrs. Schuyler's action for herself and her family, as well as what she hopes to accomplish with her act.

MAKING PERSONAL CONNECTIONS

Have students think about the meaning of freedom in their own lives. Ask them to consider which of their personal possessions they would be willing to sacrifice to preserve their freedom. Ask them to consider recent events in the news that relate to the issue of political independence, and ask which event they found most gripping or personally touching.

TIME LINE DISCUSSION

Remind students that the battles of Lexington and Concord began in 1775, and the signing of the Declaration of Independence took place in 1776.

- Ask students how many different years are represented on the time line. **Answer** Eight, 1776–1783 inclusive. Have them compare the period covered by this time line to several from earlier chapters. Ask why this time line might show such a short period.

Possible Response These are very important years in U.S. history, and crucial events during these years should be studied very closely.

- Ask students what reaction American Patriots might have had to Adam Smith's book.

Possible Response Given that much of the conflict between Britain and the colonies arose over trade regulation, colonial Patriots would probably have agreed with Smith.

BEFORE YOU READ

Previewing the Theme: Citizenship

Ask students to think about why the Patriots persisted in declaring independence, even though they knew it would lead to a war they might not win.

What Do You Know?

Students often forget that Washington and other Patriots could not be certain that the colonists would win the war. In the event of capture or defeat, American leaders faced execution as traitors to the British Crown. Understanding that it was as difficult to predict the outcome of events in 1776 as it is today is one of the most important historical lessons that students can learn.

In-Depth Resources: Unit 2
- Tracing Themes: Citizenship, p. 25

READ AND TAKE NOTES

Reading Strategy: Sequencing Events
Tell students that sequencing events in the chapter will help them relate events to one another. Viewing events on a time line will help students develop such critical thinking skills as recognizing cause and effect. When the time line is completed, students should be able to use it to identify key events in the early years of the war in chronological order.

In-Depth Resources: Unit 2
- Setting the Stage, p. 24

Critical Thinking Transparency CT19
- Setting the Stage

Chapter 7 SETTING THE STAGE

BEFORE YOU READ

This Patriot has climbed a flagpole to tear down the British flag and replace it with an American one.

Previewing the Theme

Citizenship During the Revolution, many Americans saw themselves as citizens of a new country—the United States. They made great sacrifices and risked their lives and fortunes to win independence. This chapter explains how those Patriots overcame enormous odds to defeat the powerful British Empire.

What Do You Know?

What stories do you know about the people or events of the Revolution? How do people display courage and self-sacrifice during wartime?

THINK ABOUT
- what you've learned about the American Revolution from books, movies, and other classes
- news stories you've heard about revolutions or civil wars in other countries today

What Do You Want to Know?

What would you like to learn about the steps that people took to win the American Revolution? In your notebook, record what you hope to learn from this chapter.

READ AND TAKE NOTES

Reading Strategy: Sequencing Events To sequence is to put events in the order in which they happened. You learned this skill in Chapter 6 by sequencing the events that led to the American Revolution. Now as you read Chapter 7, practice sequencing again. Put the major battles and events of the war in order by recording them on a time line. Copy the time line below in your notebook. You may want to make it bigger.

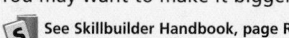

See Skillbuilder Handbook, page R4.

1776 | 1777 | 1778 | 1779 | 1780 | 1781 | 1782 | 1783

- 1776 British forced Washington from New York. Washington surprised Hessians at Trenton.
- 1777 Washington won at Princeton. Burgoyne lost at Saratoga. Americans suffer at Valley Forge.
- 1778 France became America's ally. Clark captured Kaskaskia. British captured Savannah.
- 1779 Clark captured Vincennes. Jones defeated the *Serapis.*
- 1780 British captured Charles Town. British defeated Gates at Camden. Americans won at Kings Mountain.
- 1781 Americans and French forced Cornwallis to surrender at Yorktown.
- 1783 Americans and British signed the Treaty of Paris ending the war.

TEACHING STRATEGY

READING THE CHAPTER

This is a chronological chapter focusing on the events in the early years of the American Revolution. Encourage students to relate the events to one another and look for events that led to the war. Encourage them also to look for causes and effects of these events. Pause after each section to review the chronology of the key events described.

ALTERNATIVE ASSESSMENT

The Chapter Assessment describes three activities for alternative assessment on page 201. You may wish to have students work on these activities during the course of the chapter and then present them at the end.

1 The Early Years of the War

TERMS & NAMES
George Washington
mercenary
strategy
rendezvous
Battles of Saratoga

MAIN IDEA	WHY IT MATTERS NOW
The American desire to gain rights and liberties led them to fight for independence from Britain.	Today those same rights and liberties are protected by the U.S. Constitution.

ONE AMERICAN'S STORY

In search of liberty, Haym Salomon moved from eastern Europe to America sometime between 1764 and 1775. He was a Jew from Poland. Arriving in New York City, Salomon soon became a successful merchant and banker. After the war broke out, Salomon supported the Patriot cause.

When the British captured New York in 1776, many Patriots fled but Salomon stayed. The British arrested him as a spy. Salomon spoke many languages. The British thought he could help their supply officers deal with foreign merchants, so they let him out of prison. Salomon used this opportunity to help other prisoners escape.

In 1778, the British wanted to arrest Salomon again, so he fled to Philadelphia. His earlier time in the cold, damp prison had permanently damaged his health. Even so, he continued to aid the Patriots. He loaned the new government more than $600,000, which was never repaid.

Like Salomon, many people made hard choices about which side to support during the Revolutionary War. This section discusses those choices and the obstacles Americans faced in the war's early years.

Haym Salomon sacrificed his health and his fortune to help his new country.

1 Americans Divided

The issue of separating from Great Britain divided American society. Opinion polls did not exist in the 1700s, so we don't know exactly how many people were on each side. But historians estimate that roughly 20 to 30 percent of Americans were Loyalists, roughly 40 to 45 percent were Patriots, and the rest remained neutral. Most Americans did not support the Revolution.

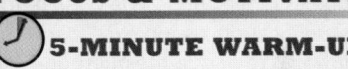

Both Patriots and Loyalists came from all walks of life and all parts of America. In general, New England and Virginia had high numbers of Patriots. Loyalists were numerous in cities, in New York State, and in the

Choosing Sides

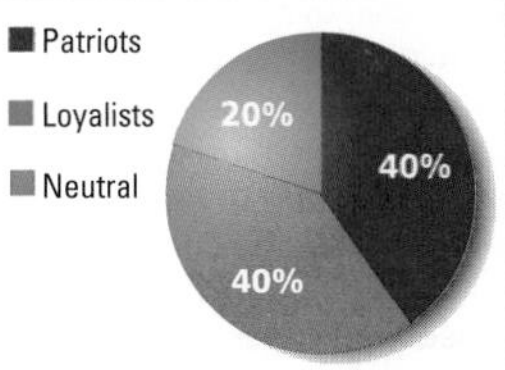

Source: *Blackwell Encyclopedia of the American Revolution*

SECTION OBJECTIVES

1. To describe colonial opinions on American independence
2. To explain the importance of the mid-Atlantic coastal cities
3. To analyze early British strategy
4. To summarize the causes and effects of the Battles of Saratoga

SKILLBUILDERS
Interpreting Maps: Place, Movement, pp. 179, 181

CRITICAL THINKING
Analyzing Causes, p. 178
Solving Problems, p. 179
Recognizing Propaganda, p. 180
Evaluating, p. 181
Forming and Supporting Opinions, p. 183
Contrasting, p. 183

FOCUS & MOTIVATE

5-MINUTE WARM-UP

Making Inferences The questions will help students understand important early battles.

1. Look at the map on page 189. Where are the earliest battles of the Revolution?
2. What major city did the British win?

Warm-Up Transparency WT7

INSTRUCT

INSTRUCT: OBJECTIVE 1

Americans Divided/Creating an Army

- What were the major positions among colonists concerning independence?
- How did the issue of revolution affect Native Americans and African Americans?
- What problems challenged Washington in raising an army?

In-Depth Resources: Unit 2
- Guided Reading, p. 26

America's History Makers
- Haym Salomon, pp. 29–30

RECOMMENDED RESOURCES

In-Depth Resources: Unit 2
- Guided Reading, p. 26
- Skillbuilder Practice, p. 31
- Literature Selection, pp. 36–38

Reading Study Guide (Spanish and English), pp. 59–60

America's History Makers
- George Washington, pp. 27–28
- Haym Salomon, pp. 29–30

Citizenship Today, pp. 3–4

Formal Assessment
- Section Quiz, p. 119

Integrated Assessment
- Rubrics, 4.4, 1.7

Access for Students Acquiring English/ESL
- Guided Reading, p. 40
- Skillbuilder Practice, p. 44

INTEGRATED TECHNOLOGY

Humanities Trans. HT13, HT14
- *Battle of Saratoga*
- *The Spirit of '76*

Geography Transparency GT7
- Final Battle of Saratoga, 1777

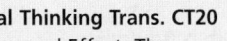

Critical Thinking Trans. CT20
- Cause and Effect: The American Revolution

TEST-TAKING RESOURCES

Strategies for Test Preparation

Test Practice Transparencies, TT24

Online Test Practice

HISTORY FROM VISUALS

Reading the Chart (p. 177) Point out that fewer than half the colonists supported the Revolution. Ask students how the large number of people who were neutral might have affected the independence movement. **Possible Response** Patriots might not get as many volunteers as they needed for soldiers or enough supplies to support the army.

Extension Have students make inferences as to what kinds of practical support Loyalists might have given to Great Britain.

Critical Thinking Transparency CT20
• Cause and Effect: The American Revolution

AMERICA'S HISTORY MAKERS

George Washington
According to Thomas Jefferson, George Washington rarely spoke in political discussion except to "the main point which was to decide the question." Yet Washington's actions spoke volumes. As tensions mounted between the Crown and the colonies, Washington took to wearing his uniform from the French and Indian War. Scholars think he wore it on purpose—to indicate his opinion that it was time for military action and to remind Congress of his soldiering experience.

Possible Responses: He learned to handle hardship and live outdoors. He learned to fight and discovered his own bravery. He led soldiers.

America's History Makers
• George Washington, pp. 27–28

South. Many Loyalists worked for the British government or were clergy in the Church of England. Some Quakers were Loyalists, although many wanted peace. (Their faith taught that war was wrong.)

The war divided Native Americans, too. For instance, some Iroquois nations fought with the British and others with the Americans. Those Native Americans who joined the British feared that if the Americans won, they would take Native American land. Some Native Americans who lived near colonists and interacted with them sided with the Americans.

Background
The Iroquois League had generally kept peace among the Iroquois nations for about 200 years—until the American Revolution.

African Americans also fought on both sides. At first, slave owners feared that African Americans who had guns might lead slave revolts. Therefore, few states allowed African Americans to enlist, or sign up with the army. Then a British governor offered freedom to any enslaved person who joined the British army. Many slaves ran away to fight for the British. In response, most states began to accept African-American soldiers. In all, about 5,000 African Americans served in the Continental Army. Many African Americans who did so hoped that American independence would bring greater equality.

Differences over the war split families, too. For example, Benjamin Franklin's son William took Britain's side. The father and son stopped speaking.

AMERICA'S HISTORY MAKERS

GEORGE WASHINGTON
1732–1799

At the age of 16, George Washington worked as a surveyor, setting land boundaries in the wilderness. He learned to handle hardship by hunting for food and sleeping outdoors.

In the French and Indian War, Washington had many brushes with death. Yet he wrote, "I heard the bullets whistle, and, believe me, there is something charming in the sound."

That war made him the most famous American officer. People loved him for his courage. As commander of the Continental Army, Washington's popularity helped unite Americans.

How did Washington's early life prepare him to lead the army?

Creating an Army

Because not everyone supported the war, raising an army was difficult. The army also faced other problems. In June 1775, **George Washington** became the commander of the Continental Army. At first, this new national army was formed from state militias, made up of untrained and undisciplined volunteers.

Reading **History**
A. Analyzing Causes Why would the lack of agreement about the war make it hard to raise an army?
A. Possible Responses Only Patriots would join the army, and they were a minority. Some Patriots might hesitate to join if most of their neighbors were Loyalists.

After Congress created the Continental Army, men began to enlist, but most of them didn't stay long. At the start of the war, Congress asked men to enlist only for one year. Later Congress did lengthen the term of service. When the soldiers' time was up, they went home. As a result, Washington's army never numbered more than 17,000 men.

Congress's inability to supply the army also frustrated Washington. The soldiers needed everything—blankets, shoes, food, and even guns and ammunition. Angrily, Washington wrote, "Could I have foreseen what I have, and am likely to experience, no consideration upon earth should have induced [persuaded] me to accept this command."

Many women tried to help the army. Martha Washington and other wives followed their husbands to army camps. The women cooked, did laundry, and

ACTIVITY OPTIONS

SKILLBUILDER LESSON: CREATING A MULTIMEDIA PRESENTATION

BLOCK SCHEDULING

Explaining the Skill Explain to students that a multimedia presentation involves using a variety of media that could include any of the following: primary source materials; visual material such as photographs, paintings, charts, maps; electronic materials such as quick time clips, film clips, music or other recordings, or videotaped presentations.

Applying the Skill With the class, identify and list on the board several topics that seem suitable for a presentation that combines several media. Possibilities include public opinion, forming an army, or Washington's role. Then discuss possible formats—a radio interview, a videotaped news report, a press conference, and so on. Be sure that students understand that they will need to incorporate a variety of components to make the presentation multimedia. Encourage students to work together in small groups to choose a topic and plan their presentation. Remind students that further research may be necessary to make their presentations effective.

In-Depth Resources: Unit 2
• Skillbuilder Practice, p. 31

nursed sick or wounded soldiers. A few women even helped fight. Mary Hays earned the nickname "Molly Pitcher" by carrying water to tired soldiers during a battle. Deborah Sampson dressed as a man, enlisted, and fought in several engagements.

Building an army was crucial to Washington's plan. To the British, the Americans were disorganized, inexperienced rebels. The British thought that if they won a decisive battle, the Americans would give up. By contrast, Washington's main goal was to survive. To do so, he needed to keep an army in the field, win some battles—no matter how small—and avoid a crushing defeat. He knew he could not hope to win a major battle until he had a large, well-equipped army.

*Reading*History

B. Solving Problems How did Washington try to solve the problem of leading a small, inexperienced force against a large professional army?

B. Answer He decided the important thing was to survive, even if he didn't win any big battles. He was buying time until he could build a better army.

These Hessian boots weighed about 12 pounds a pair.

Struggle for the Middle States ❷

As Chapter 6 explains, Washington had forced the British to retreat from Boston in March 1776. He then hurried his army to New York City, where he expected the British to go next. One British goal was to occupy coastal cities so that their navy could land troops and supplies in those cities. From there, they could launch their military campaigns.

Washington's hunch was correct. In July 1776, Britain's General William Howe arrived in New York with a large army. Then in August, more soldiers arrived, including about 9,000 Hessian mercenaries. A **mercenary** is a professional soldier hired to fight for a foreign country. British soldiers usually signed up for life—which discouraged enlistment. So Britain needed mercenaries, whom it hired from the German states.

Background

The British-hired mercenaries came from a part of Germany called Hesse, which is the origin of the term *Hessian.*

For several months, the British and American armies fought for New York State. Finally, the British forced Washington to retreat through New Jersey. By December, when the American army crossed the Delaware River into Pennsylvania, it was in terrible condition. Charles Willson Peale, a Philadelphia painter who watched the crossing, saw one muddy soldier who "had lost all his clothes. He was in an old, dirty blanket jacket, his beard long, and his face so full of sores he could not clean it." To Peale's shock, the soldier called his name. He was Peale's brother!

Political writer Thomas Paine also witnessed the hard conditions and the soldiers' low spirits on the retreat. To

Skillbuilder Answers

1. New Jersey
2. He sailed from New York, down the coast, and then up Chesapeake Bay.

GEOGRAPHY SKILLBUILDER Interpreting Maps

1. **Place** *In what state did the American victories take place?*
2. **Movement** *How did the British general Howe travel from New York to Brandywine?*

INSTRUCT: OBJECTIVE ❷

Struggle for the Middle States

- Why did the British want to occupy the coastal cities of the Middle Atlantic states?
- What course did the war take between July and December 1776?
- What significant gains did the colonial troops make at Trenton?

MORE ABOUT . . .

Howe and Washington

The case of the American army was so desperate at the end of 1776 that Washington is reported to have told his brother, "I think the game is pretty nearly up." If Howe had followed the Americans across the Delaware River and attacked, the British might have won the war within a few weeks. Instead, Howe followed the European military custom of not fighting during winters. He settled down comfortably in New York City and was taken completely by surprise when Washington attacked.

HISTORY FROM VISUALS

Reading the Map Point out that this map shows the location of the battlefront in the first year of the war. Ask students to identify which troops traveled on foot and which by boat. **Answer** American forces traveled on foot; British forces went by boat. Ask how travel by sea might have benefited the British and why American troops did not use the same method. **Possible Responses** British troops could rest aboard ship; they did not have to worry about ambush or attack. The Americans could not travel by sea because of the powerful British navy.

Extension Ask students to speculate how each method of travel might affect the speed of moving men and supplies.

ACTIVITY OPTIONS

INTERDISCIPLINARY LINK: GEOGRAPHY

BLOCK SCHEDULING

TIME AND TRAVEL

Class Time 10–15 minutes

Task Plotting the course of British ships across the Atlantic to the colonies

Purpose To understand the strategic necessity of controlling the coastal cities

Supplies Needed

- Globe, or map of the Atlantic, showing both North America and Europe
- Atlas map of winds and ocean currents

Activity Ask students to locate cities in England and the colonies. In the atlas, they can see wind patterns (the westerlies and trade winds). Have them trace routes between cities and estimate the distances across the ocean. Explain that the trip from London to Boston usually took about four weeks, more if weather was bad. Discuss the problems this might pose for British generals. Why was it essential for the British to hold the port cities? **Possible Response** They relied on troops and supplies that arrived by sea.

MORE ABOUT . . .

Thomas Sully

Thomas Sully was one of the most renowned U.S. portrait artists of the 19th century. He was born in Lincolnshire, England, in 1783, but he moved with his parents to the United States in 1792. After studying painting in London in 1809, Sully made Philadelphia his home. His most admired works were portraits, especially of women. One publication said that Sully "paints exquisitely beautiful portraits of ladies. His praise is in all the parlours."

MORE ABOUT . . .

The Battle of Trenton

The Germans' celebration had consisted of heavy drinking and card playing. They had gone to sleep only a couple of hours before Washington reached Trenton—about 6:30 A.M. The German commander barely had time to dress himself and order his troops into battle. But the Americans had already taken over a number of houses in Trenton, dried their rifles, and positioned themselves at windows in those homes. The German commander fell mortally wounded, the Germans surrendered, and fighting was over by 9:30.

Thomas Sully's *Passage of the Delaware* shows Washington at the Delaware River, leading to the American attack on the British at Trenton, New Jersey.

urge them to keep fighting, Paine published the first in a series of pamphlets called *The American Crisis.*

A VOICE FROM THE PAST

These are the times that try men's souls. The summer soldier and the sunshine patriot will, in this crisis, shrink from the service of their country; but he that stands it *now,* deserves the love and thanks of man and woman.

Thomas Paine, *The American Crisis*

***Reading*History**

C. Recognizing Propaganda How does this passage promote the American cause?

C. Possible Response It says that those who endure hardships deserve to be honored.

Washington hoped a victory would encourage his weary men. He also knew that he must attack the British quickly because most of his soldiers would leave once their enlistments ended on December 31.

Late on December 25, 1776, Washington's troops rowed across the icy Delaware River to New Jersey. From there, they marched in bitter, early-morning cold to Trenton to surprise the Hessians, some of whom were sleeping after their Christmas celebration. The Americans captured or killed more than 900 Hessians and gained needed supplies. Washington's army won another victory at Princeton eight days later. These victories proved that the American general was better than the British had thought. The American army began to attract new recruits.

3 Britain's Strategy

Meanwhile, the British were pursuing a **strategy**—an overall plan of action—to seize the Hudson River Valley. If successful, they would cut off New England from the other states. The strategy called for three armies to meet at Albany, New York. General John Burgoyne would lead a force south from Canada. Lieutenant Colonel Barry St. Leger would lead his army from Lake Ontario down the Mohawk Valley. Burgoyne expected General Howe to follow the Hudson north from New York City.

INSTRUCT: OBJECTIVE 3

Britain's Strategy/ Battles Along the Mohawk

- What was the British strategy in 1777?
- How did Howe and St. Leger fail to follow through with the planned strategy?
- How did Howe's and St. Leger's actions affect Burgoyne?

ACTIVITY OPTIONS

INDIVIDUAL NEEDS

LESS PROFICIENT READERS

Sequencing Events Show students how to construct a chart with the following headings: *Date, Battle, American Leader, British Leader.* Then have students review pages 178–180 and fill in appropriate material. They can continue to fill in the chart as they finish reading the section. Encourage them to use the chart as they work with their sequencing organizer; suggest that they keep the chart current as they continue through the chapter.

Date	Battle	American Leader	British Leader
Dec. 26, 1776	Trenton	Washington	Howe

Burgoyne left Canada in June 1777 with an army that included British, Hessians, and Iroquois. In July, they captured Fort Ticonderoga.

Called "Gentleman Johnny" by his soldiers, Burgoyne enjoyed traveling slowly and throwing parties to celebrate victories. After Ticonderoga, his delays gave the Americans time to cut down trees to block his route. They also burned crops and drove off cattle, leaving the countryside bare of supplies for the British troops.

Things grew rougher during the last 25 miles of Burgoyne's march to Albany. On a map, the route looked easy, but it really crossed a swampy wilderness. The army had to build bridges and roads. Burgoyne took four weeks to reach the Hudson. Still confident, he looked forward to the **rendezvous**, or meeting, with St. Leger and Howe in Albany.

On August 4, Burgoyne received a message from Howe. He would not be coming north, Howe wrote, because he had decided to invade Pennsylvania to try to capture General Washington and Philadelphia—where the Continental Congress met. "Success be ever with you," wrote Howe. Yet Burgoyne needed Howe's soldiers, not his good wishes.

Howe did invade Pennsylvania. In September 1777, he defeated but did not capture Washington at the Battle of Brandywine. Howe then occupied Philadelphia. In October, Washington attacked Howe at Germantown. Washington lost the battle, however, and retreated.

War in the North, 1777

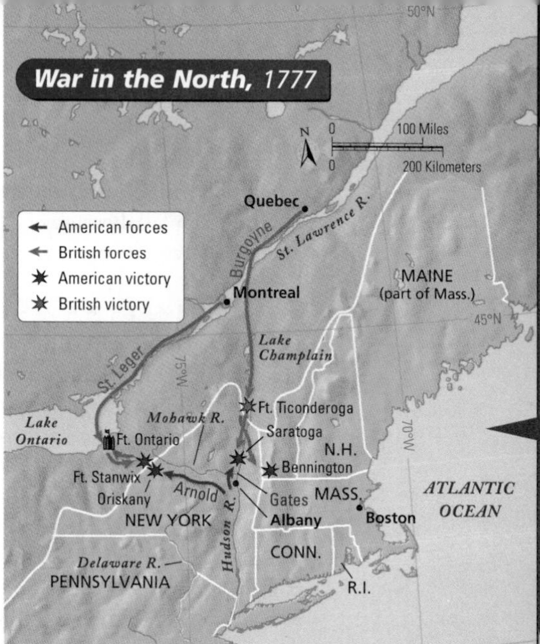

GEOGRAPHY SKILLBUILDER Interpreting Maps

1. **Place** *From which two cities did the British invade the United States?*
2. **Movement** *What did St. Leger want to capture by taking the longer route by way of Lake Ontario?*

Skillbuilder Answers
1. Quebec, Montreal
2. Fort Ontario, Fort Stanwix

Reading **History**
D. Evaluating Review Howe's two goals for his invasion of Pennsylvania. Was he successful?
D. Answer No. He captured Philadelphia but did not capture Washington.

Battles Along the Mohawk

As Burgoyne received Howe's message, St. Leger faced his own obstacle in reaching Albany. In the summer of 1777, he was trying to defeat a small American force at Fort Stanwix in the Mohawk River valley of New York. St. Leger's forces included Iroquois led by Mohawk chief Joseph Brant, also called Thayendanegea (THĪ•ehn•DAHG•ee).

Brant and his sister, Molly, had strong ties to the British. Molly was a British official's wife, and Joseph was a convert to the Church of England. Both Joseph and Molly tried to convince the Iroquois to fight for the British, who upheld Iroquois rights to their land.

Vocabulary
convert: a person who changes religions

During August 1777, American general Benedict Arnold led a small army up the Mohawk River. He wanted to chase the British away from

The Iroquois chief Joseph Brant was a British ally.

HISTORY FROM VISUALS

Reading the Map Point out that the British strategy shifted the battlefront from the coastal cities to the inland frontier. Ask students to tell what other geographical obstacles the troops might encounter, in addition to the "swampy wilderness" mentioned in the text. **Possible Responses** The area was rough and mountainous, and probably much of the region was heavily forested.

Extension Have students do research to determine the following: How might conditions in Europe differ from those on the colonial frontier? Ask students how unfamiliarity with the territory might affect an army's success.

MORE ABOUT . . .

Burgoyne's March

To "take to the field as a gentleman should," Burgoyne traveled with more than 30 wagons full of his personal belongings, wines, and the wardrobe of his lady friend. He also insisted on bringing overland about 140 artillery pieces. To cross 23 miles of swampy New York wilderness with this wagon train, Burgoyne's men laid log roads. Progress was slow—between a half-mile and a mile a day. Patriot general Philip Schuyler sent his woodsmen to harass the British troops, who also suffered from the heat, humidity, and biting swarms of mosquitoes and black flies.

ACTIVITY OPTIONS

MULTIPLE LEARNING STYLES: SPATIAL

BLOCK SCHEDULING

MAKING A BOARD GAME

Class Time One class period

Task Making a board game to show important battles

Purpose To arrange events in the American Revolution in chronological sequence

Supplies Needed
- Posterboard
- Markers, rulers, pens

Activity Students can work in pairs to list the battles in order and then incorporate that information into a board game such as the one shown here. Have students write rules for the game.

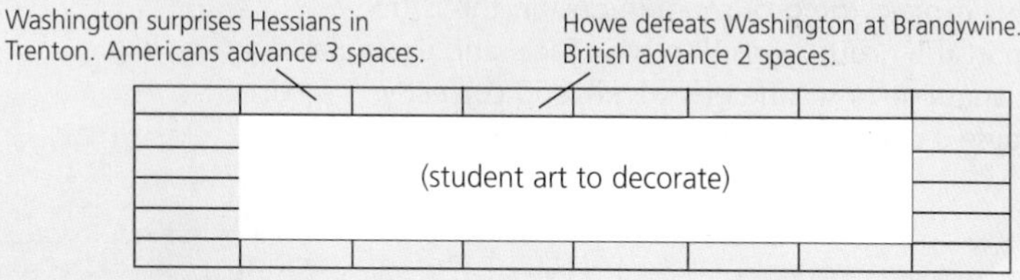

INSTRUCT: OBJECTIVE 4

Saratoga: A Turning Point

- Why did Burgoyne send troops into Vermont?
- What were the two most important results of the colonial victories at the Battles of Saratoga?

Humanities Transparency HT13, HT14
- *Battle of Saratoga*
- *The Spirit of '76*

Geography Transparency GT7
- Final Battle of Saratoga, 1777

Fort Stanwix. Arnold sent a captured Loyalist and some Iroquois who were American allies to spread the rumor that he had a large army.

The trick worked. St. Leger's troops were afraid they were about to be outnumbered. The army retreated so fast that it left behind tents, cannon, and supplies. Because of St. Leger's flight and Howe's refusal to follow the strategy, no one was left to rendezvous with Burgoyne.

4 Saratoga: A Turning Point

By this time, Burgoyne's army was running out of supplies, and it needed horses. The general sent a raiding party into Vermont to see what it could find. The raiding party encountered New England troops, who badly defeated it at the Battle of Bennington on August 16, 1777.

Despite this setback, Burgoyne's army headed slowly toward Albany. On the way, it met a powerful Continental Army force led by General Horatio Gates. Gates's soldiers were waiting on a ridge called Bemis Heights, near Saratoga, New York. There the Americans had created fortifications, or built-up earthen walls, behind which to fight. The Polish engineer Tadeusz Kosciuszko (TAH•deh•oosh KAWSH•choosh•kaw) had helped the Americans do this.

Reading **History**
E. Reading a Map Find Saratoga on the map on page 181. Notice how close it is to Burgoyne's goal of Albany.

Burgoyne would have to break through the fortifications to proceed to Albany. On September 19, he attacked. While Gates commanded the Americans on the ridge, Benedict Arnold led an attack on nearby

CITIZENSHIP TODAY

OBJECTIVE

Students will explain the importance of free speech in both historic and modern American life.

***The American Crisis* Supports Independence**

The American Crisis includes 16 pamphlets written between 1776 and 1783. The first article appeared in the *Pennsylvania Journal* on December 19, 1776, at a time when the Continental Army had just suffered defeat in New York. The article so impressed George Washington that he ordered it read to all his troops with the hope of inspiring them.

Citizenship Today, pp. 3–4

In-Depth Resources: Unit 2
- Literature Selection: from *Citizen Tom Paine* by Howard Fast, pp. 36–38

CITIZENSHIP TODAY

Exercising Free Speech

The British could have charged Thomas Paine with a crime for writing *The American Crisis.* The crime was sedition, or stirring up rebellion. By saying what he thought, Paine risked going to prison. Today U.S. citizens have the right to speak freely without fear of jail.

Like Thomas Paine, some students have used free speech to urge people to take action. For example, the Sidney Lanier Middle School in Houston, Texas, has published its school newspaper on the Internet. In October 1996, one writer urged other students to get involved in that year's election, saying, "Even though you will not be able to vote yet, you can still influence your parents to do so."

These students are working together to produce a school newspaper.

How Do You Exercise Free Speech?

1. Working in a small group, choose an issue that you care about. Look through newsmagazines for ideas.
2. Use a cluster diagram to record your feelings and opinions about the issue.
3. As a group, decide what action you think people should take on the issue.
4. Write an article expressing the group's opinion. Each member should read the article and suggest changes. Revise the article.
5. Send the revised article to the editorial page of your school or local newspaper.

See Citizenship Handbook, page 266.

For more about free speech . . .

RESEARCH LINKS CLASSZONE.COM

STANDARDS FOR EVALUATION: CITIZENSHIP TODAY

Each article should
- focus on a subject that the students care about.
- be directed to an appropriate audience.
- clearly explain the group's opinions on the issue.
- support the group's position with facts and examples.
- use language and tone effectively and correctly.
- propose a course of action.

Freeman's Farm. His men repeatedly charged the British and inflicted heavy casualties. Still, the British held their position.

On October 7, another battle broke out. Again Arnold led daring charges against the British. Although hundreds of muskets were firing at him, he galloped through the battlefield "like a madman," a sergeant later said. Frightened, Burgoyne's Hessian mercenaries began to fall back. Eventually, a bullet tore into Arnold's leg and stopped him. Even so, the Americans forced Burgoyne to retreat.

Burgoyne's army moved slowly through heavy rain to a former army camp at Saratoga. By the time they arrived, the men were exhausted. Some fell in the mud and slept in their wet uniforms. The Continental Army then surrounded Burgoyne's army and fired on it day and night without stopping. Burgoyne decided to surrender. The series of conflicts that led to this surrender is known as the **Battles of Saratoga**.

The Battles of Saratoga had two very different consequences. As Benedict Arnold was recovering from his wound, he married a woman who was a Loyalist. Over time, Arnold came to feel that Congress had not rewarded him enough for his heroic actions at Saratoga and other battles. Influenced by his bitterness and his wife, he betrayed his army. In 1780, he agreed to turn over an American fort to the British. Although his plot was discovered before he could carry it out, he escaped. Even today, the name *Benedict Arnold* is used to mean traitor.

On the positive side, the victory at Saratoga was a turning point in the Revolution. It caused European nations to think that the Americans might win their war for independence. As you will read in Section 2, several European nations decided to help America in its struggle.

America's HERITAGE

THE FIRST FLAG

June 14 is Flag Day in the United States. On June 14, 1777, the Continental Congress adopted the stars and stripes design for the U.S. flag. According to legend, a Philadelphia seamstress named Betsy Ross designed the first flag, illustrated below. Historians have found no evidence to support this legend. However, Ross did make flags for the Pennsylvania navy.

F. Possible Response European help for the United States, because that made up for American weaknesses

Reading **History**

F. Forming and Supporting Opinions Which of the two consequences of the Battles of Saratoga was more significant? Why?

Section 1 Assessment

1. Terms & Names

Explain the significance of:
- George Washington
- mercenary
- strategy
- rendezvous
- Battles of Saratoga

2. Taking Notes

Use a cluster diagram like the one shown to list the difficulties Americans faced in the early years of the war.

Which difficulty do you think was hardest to overcome?

3. Main Ideas

a. How were Americans divided over the issue of separating from Great Britain?

b. Why was it difficult for George Washington to form and keep a large army?

c. How did the Battles of Saratoga mark a turning point in the war?

4. Critical Thinking

Contrasting How did the British and American strategies differ during the early years of the war?

THINK ABOUT
- what the British expected from the Americans
- Washington's main goals for the American army
- why Burgoyne invaded from Canada

ACTIVITY OPTIONS

LANGUAGE ARTS
ART

Learn more about a Revolutionary War leader. Write a brief **biography** or create a **trading card** with a picture on one side and important facts on the other.

America's HERITAGE

The First Flag

The Continental Congress offered this explanation of the design and color choices for the new flag: "that the flag be 13 stripes alternate red and white; that the union be 13 stars, white in a blue field, representing a new constellation. . . . White signifies Purity and Innocence; Red, Hardiness and Valor; Blue signifies Vigilance, Perseverance and Justice."

ASSESS & RETEACH

Setting the Stage Have students complete a sequence of events for 1776 and 1777.

Formal Assessment
- Section Quiz, p. 119

Critical Thinking Transparency CT19
- Setting the Stage

RETEACHING ACTIVITY

Divide students into six teams and furnish each team with a felt-tip marker, a sheet of 11- x 17-inch paper, and a pair of scissors. Assign one part of the section to each team and tell them to compose three cause-and-effect statements on their paper. Have teams cut their statements apart, separating causes from effects, and give both sets to you. Redistribute the effects slips to teams. Then read each cause aloud, letting students identify the correct effect. As each cause is paired with its effect, pin the statement on a bulletin board.

In-Depth Resources: Unit 2
- Reteaching Activity, p. 39

Section 1 Assessment

1. Terms & Names

George Washington, p. 178
mercenary, p. 179
strategy, p. 180
rendezvous, p. 181
Battles of Saratoga, p. 183

2. Taking Notes

divisions in society about the war; short enlistments robbed the army of men; lack of supplies and military experience; brutal conditions

Responses will vary. Make sure the students give reasons why they chose a particular difficulty.

3. Main Ideas

a. Patriots and neutrals were about equal; Loyalists made up only a small percentage. **b.** recruiting difficulties; short enlistment terms; lack of supplies **c.** It kept the British from isolating New England; it gave the Europeans more confidence to aid America.

4. Critical Thinking

The British tried to split the colonies in two to weaken them. Washington tried to survive by winning and retreating.

ACTIVITY OPTIONS

Integrated Assessment
- Rubrics for a biography, 4.4
- Rubrics for a trading card, 1.7

SECTION OBJECTIVES

1. To explain why and how Europeans helped the United States
2. To gain insight into the hardships and sacrifices of the revolutionary forces
3. To describe the war on the frontier
4. To summarize important battles at sea

SKILLBUILDER

Interpreting Maps: Movement, Region, p. 187

CRITICAL THINKING

Recognizing Effects, p. 185
Identifying Facts and Opinions, p. 186
Analyzing Points of View, pp. 187, 189
Making Decisions, p. 188

FOCUS & MOTIVATE

5-MINUTE WARM-UP

Making Inferences To help students understand how the war effort expanded, have them answer the following questions.

1. Read the headings on pages 184–185. Who becomes involved in the Americans' revolt? Why might other countries aid the Patriots?
2. Now read the headings on pages 187–188. Where does the fighting move? When?

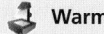

Warm-Up Transparency WT7

INSTRUCT

INSTRUCT: OBJECTIVE 1

Help from Abroad/ Europeans Help Washington

- Why did France and Spain ally themselves with the United States?
- What were Lafayette's early contributions?
- How did Barons de Kalb and von Steuben help General Washington?

In-Depth Resources: Unit 2
- Guided Reading, p. 27
- Building Vocabulary, p. 30

Reading Study Guide (Spanish and English), pp. 61–62

2 The War Expands

TERMS & NAMES
ally
Marquis de Lafayette
bayonet
desert
privateer
James Forten
John Paul Jones

MAIN IDEA	WHY IT MATTERS NOW
Some Europeans decided to help America. As the war continued, it spread to the sea and the frontier.	This was the beginning of the United States' formal relationships with other nations.

ONE AMERICAN'S STORY

To defeat the mighty British Empire, the United States needed a foreign ally. An <u>ally</u> is a country that agrees to help another country achieve a common goal. The ideal ally would share America's goal of defeating Britain. It also had to be able to provide money, troops, and ships. So the United States turned to France—Britain's long-time enemy.

In the fall of 1776, Congress sent Benjamin Franklin to the French capital, Paris. His job was to persuade France to be the ally of the United States. Franklin was already famous for his experiments with electricity. When he reached Paris, he became a celebrity. He wrote to his daughter, saying that medallions with his likeness were popular there.

Franklin's simple Quaker coat and fur hat amused the French. The clothes fit the image they had of him—a wise, noble man from a wild country.

A VOICE FROM THE PAST

These, with the pictures, busts [sculptures of the head and shoulders], and prints (of which copies upon copies are spread everywhere), have made your father's face as well known as that of the moon.

Benjamin Franklin, letter to his daughter Sally

In spite of his popularity, Franklin couldn't convince the French to become America's formal ally until after the victory at Saratoga. Then the French agreed to an alliance. This section explains how the war expanded after foreign allies joined the American side.

1 Help from Abroad

France was still bitter over its defeat by Britain in the French and Indian War, in which France lost its North American colonies. The French hoped to take revenge on the British by helping Britain's American colonies break free. In 1776, France began to give secret aid to the Americans. However, the French didn't want to lose to Britain a second time. That is why they didn't publicly ally themselves with the United States until after the Americans had proved they could win battles.

After hearing of the American victory at Saratoga, King Louis XVI of France recognized U.S. independence. In 1778, France signed two treaties of alliance with the United States. By doing so, France went to

RECOMMENDED RESOURCES

In-Depth Resources: Unit 2
- Guided Reading, p. 27
- Building Vocabulary, p. 30
- Primary Source, p. 34
- Enrichment Activity p. 43

Reading Study Guide (Spanish and English), pp. 61–62

American History Plays
- *Fires at Valley Forge*

Formal Assessment
- Section Quiz, p. 120

Integrated Assessment
- Rubrics, 1.3, 3.6

Access for Students Acquiring English/ESL
- Guided Reading, p. 41

INTEGRATED TECHNOLOGY

Electronic Teacher Tools

classzone.com

TEST-TAKING RESOURCES

Strategies for Test Preparation

Test Practice Transparencies, TT25

Online Test Practice

war with Britain. As part of its new alliance, France sent badly needed funds, supplies, and troops to America.

In 1779, France persuaded its ally Spain to help the Americans. Spain was also Britain's rival. The Spanish governor of Louisiana, General Bernardo de Gálvez, acted quickly. He captured the British strongholds of Natchez and Baton Rouge in the lower Mississippi Valley.

Background Galveston, Texas, is named for Gálvez.

From there, his small army went on to take Mobile, and in 1781 Pensacola in West Florida. These victories prevented the British from attacking the United States from the southwest. In addition, Britain had to keep thousands of troops fighting Gálvez—instead of fighting the Americans. However, like France, Spain's motives were not simply to help the United States. Gálvez's victories helped extend Spain's empire in North America.

A. Answer They forced Britain to spread its troops over many fronts, such as the West Indies.

***Reading*History**
A. Recognizing Effects How did America's allies prevent Britain from focusing all its might on the Americans?

By entering the war on America's side, France and Spain forced the British to fight a number of enemies on land and sea. The British had to spread their military resources over many fronts. For example, they were afraid they might have to fight the French in the West Indies, so they sent troops there. This prevented the British from concentrating their strength to defeat the inexperienced Americans.

Europeans Help Washington

The Americans gained some of the military experience they needed from Europe. Several European military officers came to Washington's aid, including men from France, Poland, and the German states.

Background Many of these European officers were professional soldiers looking for an army that would hire them. Some, like Lafayette, also believed in the American cause.

The **Marquis de Lafayette** (LAF•ee•EHT) was a 19-year-old French nobleman who volunteered to serve in Washington's army. He wanted a military career, and he believed in the American cause. He quickly gained Washington's confidence and was given the command of an army division. Lafayette won respect and love from his men by sharing their hardships. Called "the soldier's friend," he used his own money to buy warm clothing for his ragged troops. Washington regarded him almost as a son.

Lafayette fought in many battles and also persuaded the French king to send a 6,000-man army to America. He became a hero in both France and the United States. Later he took part in France's own revolution.

Along with Lafayette came the Baron de Kalb, a German officer who had served in the French army. He became one of Washington's generals and earned a reputation for bravery. In 1780, he received 11 wounds in the Battle of Camden and died.

Another German, Baron von Steuben, helped turn the inexperienced Americans

Lafayette stands with the slave James Armistead, whose owner allowed him to spy for Lafayette. After the war, the state of Virginia set Armistead free. Armistead then took Lafayette's last name as his own.

MORE ABOUT . . .

Help from France

Secretly, the French and Spanish had been aiding the Americans since May 1776. French Foreign Minister Vergennes, along with the Bourbons of Spain, had set up a "dummy" firm, Rodrigue Hortalez et Cie. Cash, credit, and supplies such as bedding, uniforms, muskets, and high-quality gunpowder came to the Patriots through this fictitious business.

On February 6, 1778, France formally recognized the independence of the United States. Along with supplies, France now offered its powerful fleet, second in size only to Great Britain's. The French also opened their ports to American warships. From these bases the American seamen, especially one Captain John Paul Jones, took great pride in harassing British ships and shipping in the English Channel.

MORE ABOUT . . .

Friedrich von Steuben

Washington put 47-year-old Steuben in charge of training the Americans at Valley Forge in February 1778. Steuben's rigorous military training included only ten command words; the shorter and fewer the commands, the faster the men could obey. Steuben also instilled professional pride in the demoralized troops. He taught them to conduct themselves as if their ragged clothing were full dress uniform. By late March, Washington could write that "our prospects begin to brighten." By the end of the difficult winter, the Continental Army was a cohesive, disciplined fighting force.

ACTIVITY OPTIONS

INDIVIDUAL NEEDS

LESS PROFICIENT READERS

Finding Main Ideas and Details As a way of previewing the section with students, have them read the headings aloud. On the board, write each heading inside a circle. As students read the paragraphs under each heading, ask them to suggest important words and phrases. Write these in smaller circles around each heading to create concept webs. Point out to students that they are supplying details about the main idea inside each circle.

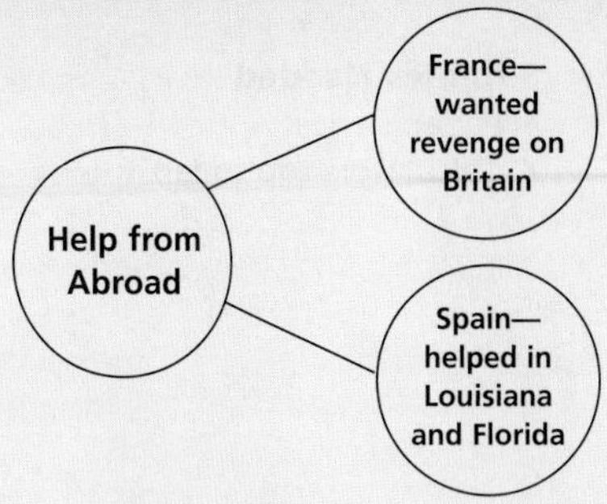
Help from Abroad
France—wanted revenge on Britain
Spain—helped in Louisiana and Florida

MORE ABOUT . . .

Musket Balls

Along with almost all other supplies, the revolutionaries were often short of musket balls (bullets) and the lead from which to make them. At the very beginning of the war, Patriots had a "leaden windfall": in New York City, a crowd toppled the 4,000-pound lead statue of King George III. After breaking it up, they sent the pieces to munitions makers in Connecticut, who produced 42,000 bullets from the former monument to royalty.

INSTRUCT: OBJECTIVE 2

Winter at Valley Forge

- What kinds of help did the Americans need from their European allies?
- What hardships did American troops endure during the winter at Valley Forge?
- How did private citizens help the revolutionary cause?

daily*life*

Camp Life in Winter

Congress had selected Valley Forge as a winter retreat during the summer of 1777. Supplies had been hidden there—thousands of barrels of flour, horseshoes, tools, and other necessities. But British troops under General Howe had come foraging in the autumn. They had found and removed these provisions.

Nearly everything was lacking at Valley Forge—even water. The nearest source of good drinking water was two miles away. Each day, those men who were healthy enough to work had to carry supplies of water back to camp.

When Steuben first saw the troops he was to train, he said, "No European army could have held together in such circumstances."

In-Depth Resources: Unit 2
- Primary Source, p. 34
- Enrichment Activity, p. 43

into a skilled fighting force. Washington asked him to train the army. In 1778, Steuben began by forming a model company of 100 men. Then he taught them how to move in lines and columns and how to handle weapons properly. Under Steuben's direction, the soldiers practiced making charges with **bayonets**—long steel knives attached to the ends of guns. Within a month, the troops were executing drills with speed and precision. Once the model company succeeded, the rest of the army adopted Steuben's methods.

2 Winter at Valley Forge

Help from Europeans came at a time when the Americans desperately needed it. In late 1777, Britain's General Howe forced Washington to retreat from Philadelphia. Beginning in the winter of 1777–1778, Washington and his army camped at Valley Forge in southeast Pennsylvania.

On the march to Valley Forge, Washington's army was so short on supplies that many soldiers had only blankets to cover themselves. They also lacked shoes. The barefoot men left tracks of blood on the frozen ground as they marched. The soldiers' condition did not improve at camp. The Marquis de Lafayette described what he saw.

B. Possible Response He is recounting facts, such as lack of coats, hats, and so on. However, the phrase *unfortunate soldiers* is an opinion.

***Reading*History**

B. Identifying Facts and Opinions Is Lafayette mainly recounting facts or expressing opinions? Explain.

A VOICE FROM THE PAST

> The unfortunate soldiers were in want of everything; they had neither coats, nor hats, nor shirts, nor shoes; their feet and their legs froze till they grew black and it was often necessary to amputate them. . . . The Army frequently passed whole days without food.
>
> **Marquis de Lafayette,** quoted in *Valley Forge: Pinnacle of Courage*

daily*life*

CAMP LIFE IN WINTER

At Valley Forge, soldiers slept in small huts, 12 men to a hut. They slept in shifts so they could take turns using the scarce blankets. The men also shared clothing. If one went on guard duty, the others lent him their clothes and stayed by the fire in the hut until he came back. Guards had to stand in old hats to keep their shoeless feet warm.

The soldiers cooked on hot stones, in iron kettles, or on portable iron braziers. Often the only food they had was fire cakes—a bread made of flour and water paste.

Because of this, the name *Valley Forge* came to stand for the great hardships that Americans endured in the Revolutionary War. Over the winter, the soldiers at Valley Forge grew weak from not having enough food or warm clothing. Roughly a quarter of them died from malnutrition, exposure to the cold, or diseases such as smallpox and typhoid fever.

These iron kettles were so heavy that soldiers often threw them away on a march.

This surgeon's kit includes a saw, used to perform amputations.

Soldiers would place burning coals in braziers like this. Braziers were used to cook food and heat huts.

ACTIVITY OPTIONS

INTERDISCIPLINARY LINK: MATH — BLOCK SCHEDULING

FEEDING THE ARMY

Class Time 15–25 minutes

Task Figuring the daily cost of feeding one soldier

Purpose To gain insight into the supply shortage of the Continental Army

Supplies Needed
- Paper, pencil
- Calculators (optional)

Activity By March 1778, when supplies were more available, each soldier was theoretically entitled to a daily ration of a pound and a half of flour or bread; a pound of beef or fish, or three-fourths pound of pork; half a pint of peas or beans (dried); and a gill (4 ounces) of spirits. Have students work in pairs or small groups to determine how much food Washington would have needed each week, at this rate, to supply the approximately 10,000 soldiers who had survived the winter.

Washington appealed to Congress to send the soldiers supplies, but it was slow in responding. Luckily, private citizens sometimes came to the soldiers' aid. According to one story, on New Year's Day 1778, a group of Philadelphia women drove ten teams of oxen into camp. The oxen were pulling wagons loaded with supplies and 2,000 shirts. The women had the oxen killed to provide food for the men.

Despite the hardships, Washington and his soldiers showed amazing endurance. Under such circumstances, soldiers often **desert,** or leave military duty without intending to return. Some soldiers did desert, but Lieutenant Colonel John Brooks wrote that the army stayed together because of "Love of our Country." The men also stayed because of Washington. Private Samuel Downing declared that the soldiers "loved him. They'd sell their lives for him."

C. Possible Response love of country; love of General Washington

Reading History
C. Analyzing Points of View What are two different explanations for why American soldiers did not desert?

3 War on the Frontier

Elsewhere, other Americans also took on difficult challenges. In 1777, a 24-year-old frontiersman named George Rogers Clark walked into the office of Virginia's governor, Patrick Henry. Clark said he had come to take part in defending the Western frontier. He lived in Kentucky, which was claimed by Virginia. Clark wanted Virginia to defend that region against British soldiers and their Native American allies in what is now Indiana and Illinois. "If a country is not worth protecting," he said, "it is not worth claiming."

> ***"If a country is not worth protecting, it is not worth claiming."***
> George Rogers Clark

Background
In the late 1700s, the Western frontier was the region between the Appalachian Mountains and the Mississippi River.

Clark was difficult to ignore. He stood six feet tall, had red hair, and displayed a dramatic personality. He persuaded Governor Henry that he was right. The governor told Clark to raise an army to capture British posts on the Western frontier.

In May of 1778, Clark and a group of frontiersmen began to travel down the Ohio River. He recruited others on the way, until he had a force of 175 to 200. They went by boat and later on foot to Kaskaskia, a British post on the Mississippi River. They captured Kaskaskia without a fight.

Then they moved east to take Fort Sackville at Vincennes, in present-day Indiana. Earlier, a small force sent by Clark had taken Vincennes, but British forces under Henry Hamilton had recaptured it. Settlers called Hamilton the "Hair Buyer" because he supposedly paid rewards for American scalps.

Skillbuilder Answers
1. Fort Detroit
2. the Ohio and the Mississippi

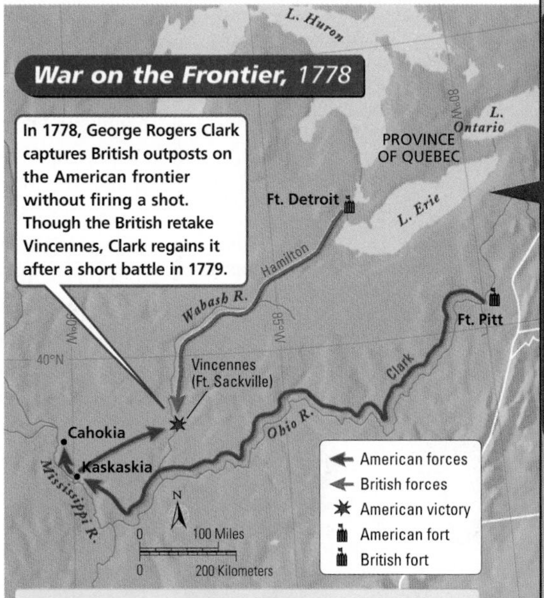

GEOGRAPHY SKILLBUILDER Interpreting Maps
1. **Movement** *From what fort did British general Hamilton travel to Vincennes?*
2. **Region** *What rivers form the boundaries of the region captured by Clark and his men?*

187

MORE ABOUT . . .

Desertions
Soldiers of the militia wanted to stay close to their homes. They were likely to disappear during spring planting or fall harvesting, a source of complaint for Washington and other American officers. However, time and again, the local militia seemed to appear when they were needed in their own region.

INSTRUCT: OBJECTIVE 3

War on the Frontier

- How did Clark justify his request for a command?
- Why was Clark's victory at Vincennes important to the revolutionary cause?

HISTORY FROM VISUALS

Reading the Map Have students study the map to gain clues about broad strategic objectives. Why was the sparsely settled frontier region around Kaskaskia, Cahokia, and Vincennes important to both sides? **Possible Response** The confluence of rivers made this area the key to controlling the entire region drained by the Mississippi, Wabash, and Ohio rivers.

Extension Have the students use an atlas to find out which states are now in the area labeled *frontier* in 1778.

ACTIVITY OPTIONS

INTERDISCIPLINARY LINK: HUMANITIES — BLOCK SCHEDULING

THE REVOLUTION IN ART

Class Time One class period

Task Using paintings as historical documents

Purpose To make inferences about history from art

Supplies Needed
- Sources for paintings on Revolutionary War events (books, museum postcards, Internet sites)
- Construction paper
- Pens and markers

Activity Encourage students to find paintings of events from the Revolutionary War. They can print out material from Web sites or photocopy paintings from books. Tell them to remove and save all captions, numbering them to indicate which painting they go with. Have them mount the pictures on construction paper and display them around the room. Let students see how many battles, events, and leaders they can identify without referring to the captions. What inferences can they make from this art?

MORE ABOUT . . .

George Rogers Clark and the Frontier

Called the "Washington of the West," Clark was one of the intensely patriotic frontiersmen who offered help to fellow soldiers "back east" at the Revolution's start. By capturing British strongholds on the western frontier, Clark not only provided the Americans with a claim to that territory but also opened another front that the British would have to guard—thus forcing them to split their forces and attention.

INSTRUCT: OBJECTIVE 4

War at Sea/A Naval Hero

- Why did the colonists need to challenge Britain's control of the seas?
- What did privateers contribute to the war effort?
- What effects did the victory of John Paul Jones have?

STRANGE *but* True

The First Combat Submarine

Earlier in the war, David Bushnell, designer of the *Turtle,* had tried to blow up British ships by setting afloat kegs filled with explosives. No ships were destroyed, but the attack so alarmed the British that they began shooting at anything that floated. The events inspired Philadelphia politician Francis Hopkinson to write a poem, "The Battle of the Kegs," which became quite popular among Patriots.

Determined to retake Fort Sackville, Clark and his men set out for Vincennes from Kaskaskia in February 1779. Hamilton wasn't expecting an attack because the rivers were overflowing their banks and the woods were flooded. Clark's men slogged through miles of icy swamps and waded through chest-deep water. They caught the British at Vincennes by surprise.

When Hamilton and his troops tried to remain in the fort, Clark pretended to have a larger force than he really had. He also found a way to frighten the British into leaving. Clark and his men had captured several Native Americans, who were allies of the British and had American scalps on their belts. Clark executed some of them in plain view of the fort. He promised to do the same to Hamilton and his men if they didn't surrender immediately. The British gave up.

Clark's victory gave the Americans a hold on the vast region between the Great Lakes and the Ohio River. This area was more than half the total size of the original 13 states. However, Fort Detroit on Lake Erie remained in the hands of the British.

D. Possible Response They had American scalps; it was the only way he could frighten the larger British force into surrendering.

Reading **History**

D. Making Decisions What factors do you think influenced Clark's decision to execute his prisoners?

STRANGE *but* True

THE FIRST COMBAT SUBMARINE

During the Revolution, the Americans built the first combat submarine—the *Turtle,* shown below. It held only a pilot, who steered with one hand and cranked a propeller with the other. To submerge, the pilot used a foot pump to let in water.

In 1776, the *Turtle* failed on its mission to attach a bomb to a British warship in New York harbor. It reached the ship but couldn't drill through its copper-clad hull. The *Turtle* failed at later missions, too.

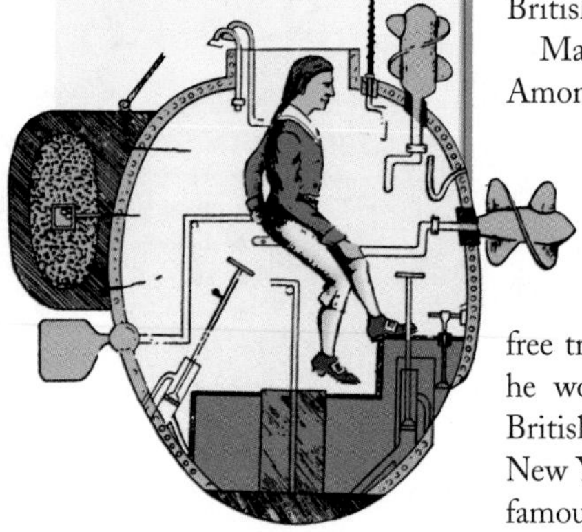

4 War at Sea

The war expanded not only to the frontier but also to the sea. By 1777, Britain had about 100 warships off the American coast. This allowed Britain to control the Atlantic trade routes. There was no way the Americans could defeat the powerful British navy.

But American privateers attacked British merchant ships. A **privateer** is a privately owned ship that a wartime government gives permission to attack an enemy's merchant ships. After capturing a British merchant ship, the crew of a privateer sold its cargo and shared the money. As a result, a desire for profit as well as patriotism motivated privateers. The states and Congress commissioned more than 1,000 privateers to prey on the British. During the war, they captured hundreds of British ships. This disrupted trade, causing British merchants to call for the war to end.

Many men answered the privateers' call for volunteers. Among them was 14-year-old **James Forten,** who was the son of a free African-American sail maker. In 1780, Forten signed up to sail on the *Royal Louis* to earn money for his family after his father died. When a British ship captured the *Royal Louis* in 1781, the British offered Forten a free trip to England. Reportedly, Forten refused, saying he would never betray his country. Released from a British prison after the war, Forten walked barefoot from New York to his home in Philadelphia. He later became famous for his efforts to end slavery.

Vocabulary

merchant ship: a ship used in trade

ACTIVITY OPTIONS

MULTIPLE LEARNING STYLES: INTRAPERSONAL BLOCK SCHEDULING

LETTERS FROM A CAPTIVE

Class Time 15 minutes

Task Writing a letter to express the thoughts of James Forten

Purpose To analyze the major decisions that some young people faced during the Revolution

Supplies Needed

- Paper and pencils

Activity Ask students to consider the hopes and fears that James Forten must have experienced as a powderboy on the *Royal Louis* and as a prisoner of war. Have each student write a letter telling of these events from one of the following points of view: (1) Forten as a war captive, not knowing whether the British will keep him prisoner or sell him as a slave in the West Indies; (2) Forten writing from New York to his family after his release from the British prison; (3) Forten as an old man, looking back on events of his boyhood.

188 CHAPTER 7

A Naval Hero

Though outnumbered, the Continental Navy scored several victories against the British. An officer named **John Paul Jones** won the most famous sea battle.

In 1779, Jones became the commander of a ship named *Bonhomme Richard.* With four other ships, he patrolled the English coast. In September, Jones's vessels approached a convoy in which two British warships were guarding a number of supply ships.

Vocabulary
convoy: a group of ships traveling together for safety

Jones closed in on the *Serapis,* the larger of the two warships. At one point, the *Bonhomme Richard* rammed the better-armed British vessel. As the two ships locked together, the confident British captain demanded that Jones surrender. In words that have become a famous U.S. Navy slogan, Jones replied, "I have not yet begun to fight!"

The two warships were so close together that the muzzles of their guns almost touched. They blasted away, each seriously damaging the other. On the shore, crowds of Britons gathered under a full moon to watch the fighting. After a fierce three-and-a-half-hour battle, the main mast of the *Serapis* cracked and fell. The ship's captain then surrendered. The *Bonhomme Richard* was so full of holes that it eventually sank, so Jones and his crew had to sail away in the *Serapis*!

Jones's success against the best navy in the world angered the British and inspired the Americans. Even so, the Americans knew that the war had to be won on land. The next section discusses the major land battles in the closing years of the war.

AMERICA'S HISTORY MAKERS

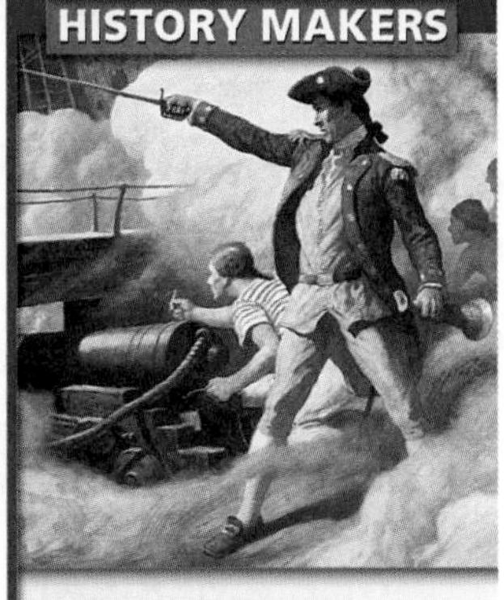

JOHN PAUL JONES
1747–1792

The most famous naval officer of the Revolution is known by a fake name. He was born John Paul in Scotland and first went to sea as a 12-year-old. By age 21, he had command of a merchant ship.

In 1773, Paul killed the leader of a mutiny on his ship. To avoid a murder trial, he fled to America and added Jones to his name.

Bold and daring, Jones scored many victories against the British. But his battle with the *Serapis* is what earned his place in history.

What are the two words that you think best describe Jones's character? Explain.

Section 2 Assessment

1. Terms & Names

Explain the significance of:
- ally
- Marquis de Lafayette
- bayonet
- desert
- privateer
- James Forten
- John Paul Jones

2. Taking Notes

Use this diagram to list the effects of the entry of France and Spain into the war.

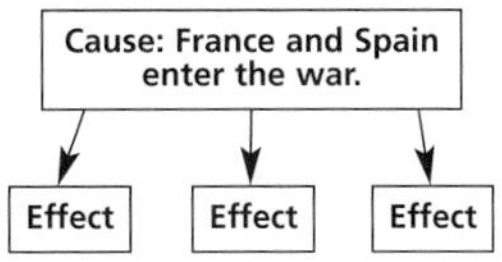

3. Main Ideas

a. What role did Benjamin Franklin play in helping America win the Revolution?

b. How did European officers such as Lafayette aid America in the Revolutionary War?

c. What was John Paul Jones's major contribution during the war, and why was it important?

4. Critical Thinking

Analyzing Points of View
Why do you think George Rogers Clark thought the frontier was important to defend?

THINK ABOUT
- why General Hamilton was called "Hair Buyer"
- why America might have wanted the frontier region after the war

ACTIVITY OPTIONS

ART / **SPEECH** Imagine yourself at Valley Forge in the winter of 1777–1778. Create a **comic strip** or give a **talk** describing your response to the harsh conditions.

AMERICA'S HISTORY MAKERS

John Paul Jones

Under a commission from Ben Franklin, Jones commanded three small warships and an old armed French brigantine (*Bonhomme Richard,* to honor Poor Richard, Franklin's famed almanac character). Jones's raids on the merchant ships in the Channel and on towns along the coastline spread panic and brought the war in the colonies much closer to home than the British people liked. In addition to the *Serapis* incident, Jones's career is notable for a "first" and a "last"—his ship was the first to fly the American colors; and his attack on Whitehaven, a port town in western England, was the last invasion of the British mainland.

Possible Responses: famous, daring, violent, bold, impulsive

ASSESS & RETEACH

Setting the Stage Have students complete the sequence of events for the years 1778 and 1779.

Formal Assessment
- Section Quiz, p. 120

RETEACHING ACTIVITY

Assign pairs of students to review various parts of this section and write three- to five-sentence summaries. (More than one pair will be working with any given part.) When students have completed their summaries, have all pairs assigned to the same section division get together to share and discuss their summaries. Have these larger groups compose a revised, edited summary based on their discussion. Post summaries on the bulletin board.

In-Depth Resources: Unit 2
- Reteaching Activity, p. 40

Section 2 Assessment

1. Terms & Names

ally, p. 184
Marquis de Lafayette, p. 185
bayonet, p. 186
desert, p. 187
privateer, p. 188
James Forten, p. 188
John Paul Jones, p. 189

2. Taking Notes

Effects: France sends troops, funds, and supplies; Spain fights the British in the Mississippi Valley and Florida; Britain sends troops to the West Indies to defend against France.

3. Main Ideas

a. He persuaded France to be America's ally. **b.** They trained special troops; led troops into battle; fought and died; helped attain more foreign aid. **c.** He defeated the British warship *Serapis,* which raised American spirits.

4. Critical Thinking

because more Americans would want to move into that region after the war ended

ACTIVITY OPTIONS

Integrated Assessment
- Rubrics for a comic strip, 1.3
- Rubrics for a speech, 3.6

SECTION OBJECTIVES

1. To explain why the war shifted to the South
2. To analyze fighting methods and their effects
3. To summarize events that led to the war's end

SKILLBUILDER

Interpreting Maps: Place, Movement, p. 193

CRITICAL THINKING

Drawing Conclusions, p. 191
Evaluating, p. 191
Contrasting, p. 193
Analyzing Causes, p. 194

FOCUS & MOTIVATE

5-MINUTE WARM-UP

Making Inferences These questions will help the student understand fighting methods in the war.

1. Look at the picture on page 190. What does the picture suggest about the involvement of civilians in the war?
2. Look at the heading on page 191. What does the word *guerrilla* mean? Given the picture and this word, what changes in the way the war was fought will this section describe?

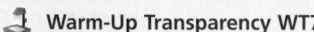

Warm-Up Transparency WT7

INSTRUCT

INSTRUCT: OBJECTIVE 1

Savannah and Charles Town

- Why did their victories in the North bring the British no closer to winning the war?
- What considerations led the British to shift their forces to the South?
- Why was the defeat at Charles Town the worst American disaster of the war?

In-Depth Resources: Unit 2
- Guided Reading, p. 28

Reading Study Guide (Spanish and English), pp. 63–64

3 The Path to Victory

TERMS & NAMES
Lord Cornwallis
guerrillas
pacifist
Battle of Yorktown

MAIN IDEA	WHY IT MATTERS NOW
Seeking Loyalist support, the British invaded the South—but ultimately lost the war there.	For more than two centuries, the American Revolution has inspired other people to fight tyranny.

ONE AMERICAN'S STORY

Patriot Nancy Hart glared at the five armed Loyalists who burst into her Georgia cabin. Tradition says that the men had shot her last turkey and ordered her to cook it for them. Raids like this were common in the South, where feuding neighbors used the war as an excuse to fight each other. Both Patriots and Loyalists took part in the raids. Many women and children had moved out of Georgia, but the six-foot-tall, freckled Hart chose to stay and fight. She could shoot a gun as accurately as any man.

As she prepared the food, Hart planned her attack. When dinner was ready, the men sat down to eat. Seizing one of their muskets, Hart quickly shot and killed one man and wounded another. She kept the gun aimed on the others as her daughter ran for help. A group of nearby Patriots arrived and hanged the Loyalists.

The state of Georgia named a county after Nancy Hart, who is shown here holding Loyalists prisoner.

As Nancy Hart's story demonstrates, the fighting between Patriots and Loyalists in the South was vicious. In this section, you will learn why the British war effort shifted to the South and why it failed.

1 Savannah and Charles Town

The British believed that most Southerners were Loyalists. Because of this, in 1778 the British decided to move the war to the South. After three years of fighting in the North, the British were no closer to victory. Although they had captured Northern cities, they couldn't control the countryside because they did not have enough troops to occupy it. The British believed that if they gained territory in the South, Southern Loyalists would hold it for them.

The British also expected large numbers of Southern slaves to join them because they had promised to grant the slaves freedom. Although thousands of African Americans did run away to join the British, not all of them were set free. Instead, some British officers sold African Americans into slavery in the West Indies.

RECOMMENDED RESOURCES

In-Depth Resources: Unit 2
- Guided Reading, p. 28
- Building Vocabulary, p. 30
- Geography Application: Cornwallis Is Trapped at Yorktown, 1781, pp. 32–33

Reading Study Guide (Spanish and English), pp. 63–64

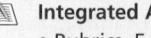

Formal Assessment
- Section Quiz, p. 121

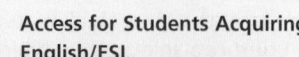

Integrated Assessment
- Rubrics, 5.1, 4.8

Access for Students Acquiring English/ESL
- Guided Reading, p. 42
- Geography Application, pp. 45–46

INTEGRATED TECHNOLOGY

Electronic Teacher Tools
classzone.com

TEST-TAKING RESOURCES

Strategies for Test Preparation
Test Practice Transparencies, TT26
Online Test Practice

Reading **History**

A. Drawing Conclusions Why was it an advantage to be able to move troops between the West Indies and the South?

A. Answer They could cover both areas with a smaller number of troops by shifting them as needed.

Britain's West Indian colonies were a third reason the British invaded the South. Southern seaports were closer to the West Indies, where British troops were stationed. If the British captured Southern ports, they could move troops back and forth between the two regions.

In December 1778, the British captured the port of Savannah, Georgia. Using Savannah as a base, they then conquered most of Georgia. In 1780, a British army led by General Henry Clinton landed in South Carolina. They trapped American forces in Charles Town (now Charleston), which was the largest Southern city. When the city's 5,000 defenders surrendered, the Americans lost almost their entire Southern army. It was the worst American defeat of the war.

2 The Swamp Fox and Guerrilla Fighting

After that loss, Congress assigned General Horatio Gates—the victor at Saratoga—to form a new Southern army. Continental soldiers led by Baron de Kalb formed the army's core. Gates added about 2,000 new and untrained militia. He then headed for Camden, South Carolina, to challenge the army led by the British general **Lord Cornwallis.**

On the way, a band of Patriots from South Carolina approached Gates. "Their number did not exceed 20 men and boys, some white, some black, and all mounted, but most of them miserably equipped," wrote an officer. Their leader was Francis Marion, called the "Swamp Fox." He provided Gates with helpful knowledge of South Carolina's coastal swamplands. Gates sent Marion to destroy boats on the Santee River behind Camden. (See the map on page 193.) This would cut off British communications with Charles Town.

In August 1780, Gates's army ran into British troops outside Camden. The Americans were in no condition to fight. They were out of supplies and half-starved. Even worse, Gates put the inexperienced militia along part of the frontline instead of behind the veterans. When the British attacked, the militia panicked and ran. Gates also fled, but Kalb remained with his soldiers and received fatal wounds. This second defeat in the South ended Gates's term as head of an army and caused American spirits to fall to a new low.

Reading **History**

B. Evaluating What do you think was most responsible for the American loss at Camden?

B. Possible Response Gates's poor decision-making in fighting with weak soldiers and not placing his troops properly

After Camden, a small British force set out for Charles Town with a column of American prisoners. Marion's band overwhelmed the British and freed the prisoners. Fighting from a base in the swamps, Marion's men cut the British supply line that led inland and north from Charles Town. Marion used the methods of a guerrilla. **Guerrillas** are small bands of fighters who weaken the enemy with surprise raids and hit-and-run attacks. Both Patriots and Loyalists formed guerrilla bands in the South. They carried out vicious raids.

Now and then

BATTLE TACTICS

A difference in battle tactics affected future warfare. British soldiers marched shoulder to shoulder in three rows. When they neared the enemy, the first row knelt, the second crouched, and the third remained standing. They all fired without aiming.

The Americans were better shots. They often marched in rows, but sometimes they hid in woods or behind walls to take aim. Guerrillas attacked swiftly, then fled into the countryside. Those tactics succeeded and are still used today. This photograph shows modern U.S. soldiers learning guerrilla tactics.

MORE ABOUT . . .

Loyalist Support

Ever since the beginning of the war, the British had hoped for help from those loyal to the Crown. When Clinton and Cornwallis raised the King's Standard at Savannah, about 2,000 Tories (Loyalists) did indeed enlist. However, such support was rare. Even the stunning British victories at Savannah and Charles Town did not bring Tories flocking to the British cause. Cornwallis, who needed Loyalist enlistment to help him to victory in the South, was finally forced to observe that the Tories' "friendship was only passive."

INSTRUCT: OBJECTIVE 2

The Swamp Fox and Guerrilla Fighting

- What objective did General Gates and Baron de Kalb have?
- Why was the battle at Camden important?
- What contributions did Francis Marion make to the war effort in the South?

Now and then

Battle Tactics

Some scholars have compared the Revolutionary War to the anticolonial wars of the late 20th century. Consider the following parallels. In the Revolution, the world's most powerful nation—Britain—was bogged down in a war against a small guerrilla army—the Patriots. The superpower had to supply its forces from thousands of miles away; the war was unpopular with the British people; and the rebels received aid from the superpower's chief military and political enemy—France.

ACTIVITY OPTIONS

INTERDISCIPLINARY LINK: GOVERNMENT/CIVICS — BLOCK SCHEDULING

GOVERNMENT AND GUERRILLAS

Class Time 15 minutes

Task Differentiating between guerrilla and regular tactics

Purpose To understand the governmental difficulties created by guerrilla warfare

Supplies Needed
- Current newspapers
- Internet access for additional resources

Activity Have students scan current news sources for world situations where guerrilla fighting has escaped from governmental control. Have the class create a chart identifying the locations of the warfare and damage caused by guerrillas. Review the story of Nancy Hart and ask: What problems do civilians face in such circumstances?

Technology OF THE Time

OBJECTIVES

1. To describe the technology used by fighting forces in the Revolutionary War
2. To use illustrations and captions to explain historical details about weaponry in the Revolution

INSTRUCT

- What additional supplies did artillery require armies to carry with them?
- How might the presence of artillery have affected the troops' traveling pace?
- What phrases tell you that fires were part of the necessary equipment in using cannons? What additional supplies would troops have had to collect for the fires?
- How long do you estimate the entire process of loading and firing a cannon might take? Explain.

Technology OF THE Time

Artillery of the Revolution

Artillery—large guns and cannon—played a key role in the American Revolution. The ability of these guns to kill and destroy from a distance made them essential in war. One witness of a battle described the destruction: "Many men were badly injured and mortally wounded by the fragments of bombs, . . . their arms and legs severed or themselves struck dead." Most cannon used in the Revolution were made of cast bronze. During the 1700s, artillery design did not change significantly. However, artillery became more mobile (more easily moved).

After each shot, a soldier sponged the inside of the barrel. This put out sparks and cleaned away any dirt left from the last shot.

A soldier loaded the cannon with gunpowder and a cannonball. He did so by ramming them down the barrel.

Soldiers aimed the gun by turning the entire carriage. An instrument called a quadrant told them how high to raise the barrel to reach their target.

Cannon were classified by the weight of the iron ball they fired. American artillery ranged from 3-pounders to 32-pounders.

Soldiers lit the cannon by applying a red-hot wire or a tube of burning powder to a touchhole drilled through the back of the barrel, where the gunpowder lay. The gunpowder exploded, forcing the projectile out of the open end of the barrel.

In the 1700s, most cannon were accurate at ranges of up to 1,000 yards. That is the length of ten football fields laid end to end.

192

CONNECT TO HISTORY

1. **Recognizing Effects** Why would it be an advantage to an army to have mobile artillery?

See Skillbuilder Handbook, page R11.

CONNECT TO TODAY

2. **Researching** Find information about modern artillery in an encyclopedia or on the Internet. How did artillery change in the 20th century?

For more about artillery . . .

RESEARCH LINKS CLASSZONE.COM

CONNECT TO HISTORY

1. **Recognizing Effects** **Possible Response** The army could move its guns where they were most needed. This would be especially important when using a gun that had short range, because they would need to move close to their target.

CONNECT TO TODAY

2. **Researching** **Possible Response** According to the *World Book Encyclopedia,* big guns have become less important, artillery has become more mobile, and artillery can now fire atomic shells.

❸ The Tide Turns

Even battles in the South sometimes turned vicious. One example was the Battle of Kings Mountain, fought on the border of North and South Carolina in October 1780. After surrounding a force of about 1,000 Loyalist militia and British soldiers, the Americans slaughtered most of them. James P. Collins, a 16-year-old American, described the scene.

> *A VOICE FROM THE PAST*
>
> The dead lay in heaps on all sides, while the groans of the wounded were heard in every direction. I could not help turning away from the scene before me with horror and, though exulting in victory, could not refrain from shedding tears.
>
> **James P. Collins,** quoted in *The Spirit of Seventy-Six*

Many of the dead had been shot or hanged after they surrendered. The Americans killed them in revenge for Loyalist raids and an earlier incident in which the British had butchered Americans. Kings Mountain was one of Britain's first losses in the South. It soon suffered more.

After Gates's defeat at Camden, Washington put a new general, Nathanael Greene, in charge of the Southern army. Greene was one of Washington's most able officers. He had been a Quaker, but his church had cast him out because of his belief in the armed struggle against the British. Most Quakers are **pacifist,** or opposed to war.

Under Greene's command, the American army avoided full-scale battles, in which the British had the edge because of superior firepower. So the American forces let the British chase them around the countryside and wear themselves out. When the Americans did fight, they did their best to make sure the British suffered heavy losses.

As the fighting dragged on into its sixth year, opposition to the war grew in Britain. As a result, some British leaders began to think that American independence would not be so bad.

❹ The End of the War

In 1781, most of the fighting took place in Virginia. In July of that year, the British general Cornwallis set up his base at Yorktown, located on a peninsula in Chesapeake Bay. From there, his army could receive supplies by ship from New York.

Reading **History**

C. Contrasting How did Greene's strategy as a general differ from that of Gates at Camden?

C. Possible Response Greene would not risk his army in a large battle like Camden. He tried to hurt the British with as little harm to his army as possible.

Skillbuilder Answers
1. Charles Town, Savannah
2. Wilmington—Cornwallis; New York—Washington and Rochambeau

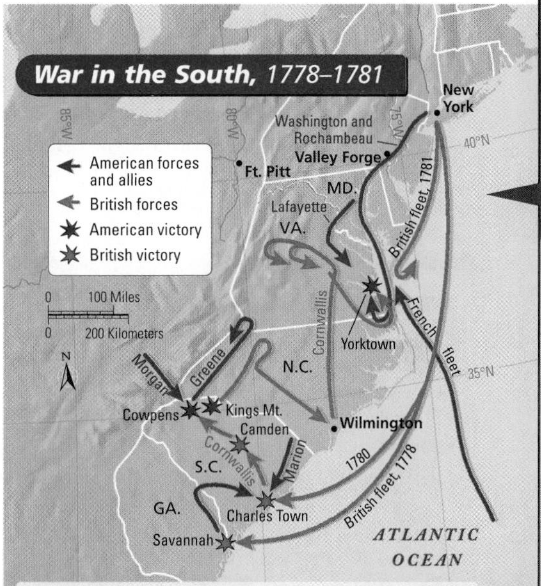

GEOGRAPHY SKILLBUILDER Interpreting Maps
1. **Place** *What ports did the British use to invade the South?*
2. **Movement** *Who traveled from Wilmington to Yorktown, and who traveled from New York?*

INSTRUCT: OBJECTIVE ❸

The Tide Turns

- What factors led Washington to name a new commander in the South?
- Why did Greene avoid full-scale battles with the British?
- How did the course of the war affect public opinion in Britain?

HISTORY FROM VISUALS

Reading the Map Have students read the map carefully, finding text on the page that explains the troop movements. What direction did the French fleet come from? Where did it arrive at the coast? Which side did it support? **Answers** The fleet came from the southeast. It arrived near the Virginia coast. It supported the Americans.

Extension Have students use an atlas to identify some French ports from which the French fleet may have sailed, as well as various routes they might have taken. What danger did the French fleet face as it sailed for the United States?

INSTRUCT: OBJECTIVE ❹

The End of the War

- Why did Cornwallis establish his base of operations at Chesapeake Bay?
- How did the French and the Americans cooperate militarily to defeat Cornwallis?

In-Depth Resources: Unit 2
- Geography Application: Cornwallis Is Trapped at Yorktown, 1781, pp. 32–33

ACTIVITY OPTIONS

INDIVIDUAL NEEDS

STUDENTS ACQUIRING ENGLISH/ESL

Figures of Speech Point out the following figures of speech to students: "the tide turns" (page 193); "wear themselves out" (page 193); and "a golden opportunity" (page 194). Explain what each phrase means, and give students the opportunity to discuss them by asking such questions as:
- What sport or work might you do that would "wear you out"?
- What would you consider a "golden opportunity" in life?

Then ask questions like the following to assess students' comprehension of the section:
- In what way did "the tide turn" for the American army under Nathanael Greene's command?
- How did Cornwallis's decision to set up a base at Yorktown become "a golden opportunity" for Washington?

HISTORY FROM VISUALS

Interpreting the Painting This huge oil painting (12 feet by 18 feet) by John Trumbull hangs in the Capitol Rotunda in Washington, D.C. Although its title is *The Surrender of Cornwallis,* Cornwallis could not bring himself to attend the ceremony in person. He claimed to be sick and sent his aide, General Charles O'Hara, shown on the white horse in the center. O'Hara led the British troops between the two victorious armies—French and American—as British bands played "The World Turned Upside Down."

Ask students what impression the painting creates. What might be the artistic purpose of the dramatic contrasts in the sky? **Possible Responses** The overall impression is one of dignity and formality. The artist may have wanted to highlight George Washington and the American flag.

CRITICAL THINKING ACTIVITY

Evaluating Ask students to define the term *peninsula.* Let a volunteer sketch a peninsula on the board. Discuss the military advantages and disadvantages to such a location. Is it easy to defend against an attack by land? by sea? What are its vulnerabilities? Apply the students' conclusions to Cornwallis's situation.

Class Time 10 minutes

ASSESS & RETEACH

Setting the Stage Have students complete the sequence of events for 1780 and 1781.

Formal Assessment
- Section Quiz, p. 121

RETEACHING ACTIVITY

Have students do mock interviews with Washington, Cornwallis, and a French sea captain to identify the strategies each used.

In-Depth Resources: Unit 2
- Reteaching Activity, p. 41

The victorious American forces accept the British surrender at Yorktown. George Washington is to the left of the American flag.

Washington saw Cornwallis's decision as a golden opportunity. In August 1781, a large French fleet arrived from the West Indies and blocked Chesapeake Bay. These ships prevented the British from receiving supplies—and from escaping. They also allowed Washington to come from the North and trap Cornwallis on the peninsula. Washington had enough men to do this because a large French force led by General Jean Rochambeau had joined his army.

Washington and Rochambeau moved south. When British ships tried to reach Cornwallis, French ships drove them back. In the **Battle of Yorktown,** the American and French troops bombarded Yorktown with cannon fire, turning its buildings to rubble. Cornwallis had no way out. On October 19, 1781, he surrendered his force of about 8,000.

Vocabulary
bombard: to attack with artillery

Although some fighting continued, Yorktown was the last major battle of the war. When the British prime minister, Lord North, heard the news, he gasped, "It is all over!" Indeed, he and other British leaders were soon forced to resign. Britain's new leaders began to negotiate a peace treaty, which is discussed in the next section.

Section 3 Assessment

1. Terms & Names

Explain the significance of:
- Lord Cornwallis
- guerrillas
- pacifist
- Battle of Yorktown

2. Taking Notes

Use a chart like the one below to list the geographic factors that made the British move their war effort to the South.

Physical factors, such as location	Human factors, such as who lived there

Were the human factors as helpful as the British hoped?

3. Main Ideas

a. Why did the fighting between Patriots and Loyalists in the South turn vicious?

b. What type of warfare did Francis Marion and his men employ?

c. How did Gates's errors in leadership contribute to the American loss at Camden?

4. Critical Thinking

Analyzing Causes How did each of the following help bring about the British defeat at Yorktown?

THINK ABOUT
- the location chosen by Cornwallis
- the French fleet
- the French troops under Rochambeau
- Washington's planning

ACTIVITY OPTIONS

TECHNOLOGY
MUSIC

Imagine that Congress has asked you to commemorate the Battle of Yorktown. Design a **Web page** or write a **song** celebrating the U.S. victory.

Section 3 Assessment

1. Terms & Names

Lord Cornwallis, p. 191
guerrilla, p. 191
pacifist, p. 193
Battle of Yorktown, p. 194

2. Taking Notes

Physical factors: nearness to the West Indies; valuable sea ports
Human factors: Loyalist Southerners; enslaved African Americans
No, because the South was more divided in its loyalties than the British thought.

3. Main Ideas

a. Both used the war as an excuse for feuding neighbors to raid each other. **b.** guerrilla warfare **c.** He relied on troops weak with hunger, and he put inexperienced troops on the frontline.

4. Critical Thinking

Student answers should be organized in four parts to cover each point.

ACTIVITY OPTIONS

Integrated Assessment
- Rubrics for a Web page, 5.1
- Rubrics for songs, 4.8

4 The Legacy of the War

TERMS & NAMES
Treaty of Paris of 1783
republicanism
Elizabeth Freeman
Richard Allen

MAIN IDEA
After the war, the new nation faced issues such as a high national debt and calls for equality.

WHY IT MATTERS NOW
To promote liberty, some states passed laws outlawing slavery and protecting religious freedom.

ONE AMERICAN'S STORY

In 1776, 15-year-old Joseph Plumb Martin of Connecticut signed up to fight for the Americans. He stayed with the army until the war ended and rose in rank from private to sergeant. Among his experiences were the terrible winter at Valley Forge and the winning battle at Yorktown.

One of the hardest things Martin faced was leaving the army after the war was over. Many years later, he wrote about that day.

A VOICE FROM THE PAST

There was as much sorrow as joy. . . . We had lived together as a family of brothers for several years, setting aside some little family squabbles, like most other families, had shared with each other the hardships, dangers, and sufferings incident to a soldier's life; had sympathized with each other in trouble and sickness; had assisted in bearing each other's burdens. . . . And now we were to be . . . parted forever.

Joseph Plumb Martin, quoted in *The Revolutionaries*

At war's end, Martin and his country faced an uncertain future. How would the United States recover from the war? What issues would confront the new nation? Section 4 discusses those questions.

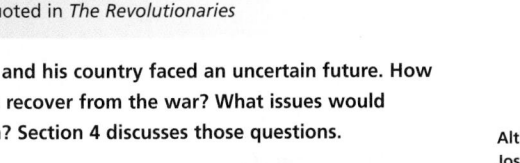

Although this painting is not of Joseph Plumb Martin himself, he may have dressed like this American soldier.

1 Why the Americans Won

In November 1783, the last British ships and troops left New York City, and American troops marched in. As Washington said good-bye to his officers in a New York tavern, he hugged each one. Tears ran down his face. He became so upset that he had to leave the room.

Earlier in the fall, Washington had written a farewell letter to his armies. In it, he praised them by saying that their endurance "through almost every possible suffering and discouragement for the space of eight long years, was little short of a standing miracle."

By their persistence, the Americans won independence even though they faced many obstacles. As you have read, they lacked training and experience. They were often short of supplies and weapons. By contrast, the British forces ranked among the best trained in the world. They were

SECTION OBJECTIVES

1. To evaluate the strengths of the American army in comparison with the British army
2. To summarize the 1783 Treaty of Paris
3. To analyze the costs of the Revolution
4. To identify challenges that the new United States faced after the war

SKILLBUILDERS
Interpreting Charts, p. 197

CRITICAL THINKING
Evaluating, p. 196
Analyzing Causes, p. 197
Solving Problems, p. 199
Recognizing Effects, p. 199

Why It Matters Now
- Democracy in South Africa, pp. 13–14

FOCUS & MOTIVATE

5-MINUTE WARM-UP

Making Generalizations These questions will help students understand the soldiers' life.

1. Read "A Voice from the Past" on page 195. How does Joseph Plumb Martin react to the end of the war? Do you think other soldiers felt as he did?
2. Give an example from your own experience of ties forged through shared difficulties.

Warm-Up Transparency WT7

INSTRUCT

INSTRUCT: OBJECTIVE 1

Why the Americans Won

- What drawbacks did the Americans have to overcome?
- What factors aided the Americans?

In-Depth Resources: Unit 2
- Guided Reading, p. 29

RECOMMENDED RESOURCES

In-Depth Resources: Unit 2
- Guided Reading, p. 29
- Building Vocabulary, p. 30
- Primary Source, p. 35

Reading Study Guide (Spanish and English), pp. 65–66

Economics in History
- Independence and Free Enterprise, p. 7

Outline Map Activities
- North America, 1783, pp. 13–14

Why It Matters Now
- Democracy in South Africa, pp. 13–14

Formal Assessment
- Section Quiz, p. 122

Integrated Assessment
- Rubrics, 3.6, 2.3

Access for Students Acquiring English/ESL
- Guided Reading, p. 43

INTEGRATED TECHNOLOGY

Electronic Teacher Tools

classzone.com

TEST-TAKING RESOURCES

Strategies for Test Preparation

Test Practice Transparencies, TT27

Online Test Practice

INSTRUCT: OBJECTIVE 2

The Treaty of Paris

- What was the most important condition of the Treaty of Paris?
- What provisions benefited the British? the Americans? the Loyalists?

Outline Map Activities
- North America, 1783, pp. 13–14

MORE ABOUT . . .

The Treaty of Paris
Concluding the peace treaty took almost two years—and a lot of talking. At one point, Franklin told the British representatives a tale from ancient Rome. A small state, defeated by the mighty Romans, asked the Roman senate for peace. "How long will the peace last?" the senators asked in response. The country's ambassador replied that the duration of the peace would depend on the conditions Rome set: "If they are reasonable, the peace will be lasting; if not, the peace will be short."

HISTORY through ART

Interpreting the Painting The British did not take losing gracefully. Cornwallis refused to attend the formal surrender ceremony; he pleaded sick and sent his subordinate, Brigadier General Charles O'Hara, to hand over his sword. King George stubbornly refused to believe that the loss at Yorktown meant the loss of his "American farms."

Possible Response: Perhaps the British did not want to appear in a painting that showed American "upstarts" as their equals; the British did not want to be portrayed as defeated. The British were bitter and resentful.

experienced and well-supplied professional soldiers. Yet the Americans had certain advantages that enabled them to win.

1. **Better leadership.** British generals were overconfident and made poor decisions. By contrast, Washington learned from his mistakes. After early defeats, he developed the strategy of dragging out the war to wear down the British. Despite difficulties, he never gave up.
2. **Foreign aid.** Britain's rivals, especially France, helped America. Foreign loans and military aid were essential to America's victory.
3. **Knowledge of the land.** The Americans knew the land where the war took place and used that knowledge well. The British could control coastal cities but could not extend their control to the interior.
4. **Motivation.** The Americans had more reason to fight. At stake were not only their lives but also their property and their dream of liberty.

Reading **History**
A. Evaluating What do you think was Washington's best characteristic as a leader?
A. Possible Responses His courage, his strategy of wearing down the British, his perseverance, his willingness to suffer for his cause, his ability to inspire his men

2 The Treaty of Paris

As the winners, the Americans won favorable terms in the **Treaty of Paris of 1783,** which ended the Revolutionary War. The treaty included the following six conditions:

1. The United States was independent.
2. Its boundaries would be the Mississippi River on the west, Canada on the north, and Spanish Florida on the south.
3. The United States would receive the right to fish off Canada's Atlantic Coast, near Newfoundland and Nova Scotia.
4. Each side would repay debts it owed the other.
5. The British would return any enslaved persons they had captured.
6. Congress would recommend that the states return any property they had seized from Loyalists.

Neither Britain nor the United States fully lived up to the treaty's terms. Americans did not repay the prewar debts they owed British merchants or return Loyalist property. For their part, the British did not return

HISTORY through ART

The American painter Benjamin West began a portrait of the men who negotiated the Treaty of Paris. But the British officials refused to pose, so West never finished the painting. From left to right are the American officials John Jay, John Adams, Benjamin Franklin, and two others.

What does this painting reveal about the British response to losing the war?

196

ACTIVITY OPTIONS

INTERDISCIPLINARY LINK: LANGUAGE ARTS — BLOCK SCHEDULING

COSTS AND BENEFITS OF WAR

Class Time 15–20 minutes

Task Debating the costs and benefits of the Revolutionary War

Purpose To form opinions and provide supporting evidence

Supplies Needed
- Reference materials about the American Revolution

Activity On the board, write the following quotation from a letter by Benjamin Franklin to Josiah Quincy: "There never was a good war or a bad peace." Allow students several moments to think about the quote's meaning. Then ask them to apply it to the Revolutionary War. Divide the class into two teams. Assign one team to argue the affirmative (in support of the statement) and the other to argue the negative. Each team should support its argument with evidence from the text.

runaway slaves. They also refused to give up military outposts in the Great Lakes area, such as Fort Detroit.

Background Even after George Rogers Clark's Western victories, the British stayed at Fort Detroit.

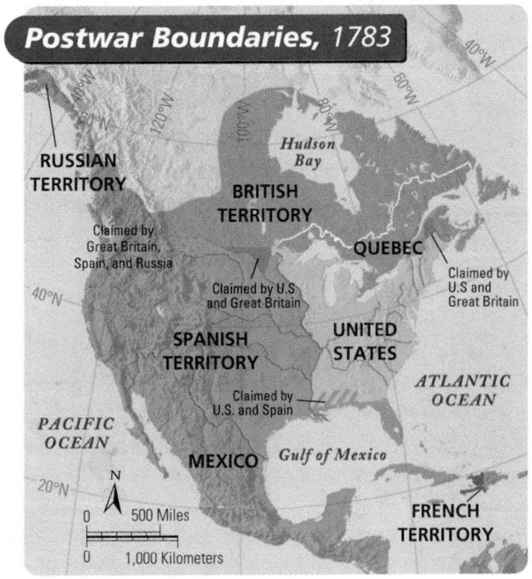

3 Costs of the War

No one knows exactly how many people died in the war, but eight years of fighting took a terrible toll. An estimated 25,700 Americans died in the war, and 1,400 remained missing. About 8,200 Americans were wounded. Some were left with permanent disabilities, such as amputated limbs. The British suffered about 10,000 military deaths.

Many soldiers who survived the war left the army with no money. They had received little or no pay for their service. Instead of back pay, the government gave some soldiers certificates for land in the West. Many men sold that land to get money for food and other basic needs.

Both the Congress and the states had borrowed money to finance the conflict. The war left the nation with a debt of about $27 million—a debt that would prove difficult to pay off.

The losers of the war also suffered. Thousands of Loyalists lost their property. Between 60,000 and 100,000 Loyalists left the United States during and after the war. Among them were several thousand African Americans and Native Americans, including Joseph Brant. Most of the Loyalists went to Canada. There they settled new towns and provinces. They also brought English traditions to areas that the French had settled. Even today, Canada has both French and English as official languages.

B. Possible Responses They were afraid of reprisals; they wanted to remain under British rule.

***Reading*History**
B. Analyzing Causes Why do you think the Loyalists left the United States?

CONNECTIONS TO MATH

Military Deaths in the American Revolution

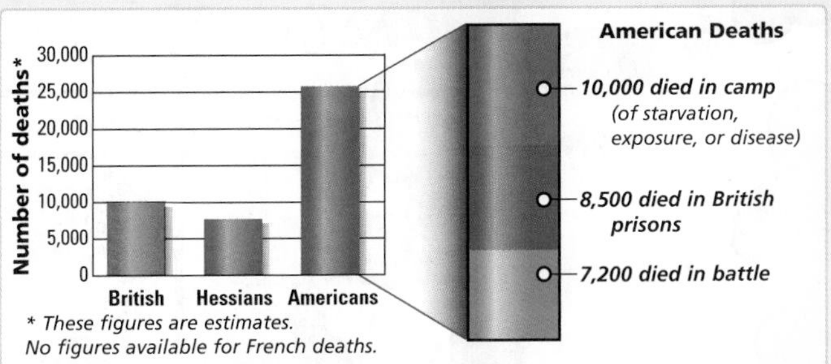

* These figures are estimates.
No figures available for French deaths.

Sources: *World Book Encyclopedia; An Outline History of the American Revolution*

SKILLBUILDER **Interpreting Charts**
1. *How many more deaths did the Americans suffer than the British?*
2. *What percentage of American deaths occurred in battle?*

Skillbuilder Answers
1. about 15,700
2. about 28 percent

INSTRUCT: OBJECTIVE 3
Costs of the War

- What were some of the human costs of the war?
- What financial problems did the war leave for the new nation?
- How did the Loyalists change Canada?

HISTORY FROM VISUALS

Reading the Map Guide students in using the map to summarize the changes in North American territorial claims after the Revolutionary War. Ask: About what fraction of North America theoretically belonged to the United States in 1783? On which border did the British still threaten the United States? What country controlled the largest share of the continent? **Answers** about one-fourth or less; the northern boundary; Spain

Extension Ask students to make inferences about how these territorial arrangements might have affected international relationships. Which countries might the United States have regarded with suspicion?

HISTORY FROM VISUALS

Interpreting the Chart Which category would include the American soldiers who died at Valley Forge? **Answer** died in camp

Remind students that the British and Hessians also lost soldiers from the same causes as the Americans—disease, poor camp conditions, American prisons, and battle.

Extension Have the students illustrate the statistics in the chart in another way, such as a pie chart or table.

ACTIVITY OPTIONS

INDIVIDUAL NEEDS: GIFTED AND TALENTED

THE NATIONAL DEBT

Class Time One class period

Task Preparing and presenting a news broadcast about the U.S. national debt

Purpose To familiarize students with the concept of national debt and its causes

Supplies Needed
- Reference materials such as encyclopedias and almanacs
- Internet access for additional resources

Activity Divide students into groups. Their task is to prepare a newscast segment of 1–3 minutes on the concept of the national debt. Encourage students to use a variety of references to research the U.S. national debt. They should determine when and how much the national debt was and is, and what the causes of national debt are.

INSTRUCT: OBJECTIVE 4

Issues After the War

- Explain the idea of republicanism.
- How did the citizenship obligations of men and women differ?
- How did the new principles of government affect other aspects of American life?

4 Issues After the War

The American Revolution was not just a war, but a change in ideas about government. Before the war, Americans had demanded their rights as English citizens. But after declaring their independence, they replaced that goal with the idea of **republicanism.** This idea stated that instead of a king, the people would rule. The government would obtain its authority from the citizens and be responsible to them.

For this system to work, individuals would have to place the good of the country above their own interests. At first, only men were allowed to take part in governing by voting or holding public office—and not even all men. However, women could help the nation by teaching their children the virtues that benefited public life. Such virtues included honesty, duty, and the willingness to make sacrifices.

Economics *in* History

OBJECTIVE

Students will be able to explain the elements of free enterprise and how the loosening of British economic controls during the war allowed U.S. free enterprise to begin.

The Development of Free Enterprise

Scottish economist Adam Smith outlined his ideas of free enterprise in his book *The Wealth of Nations,* first published in 1776. Smith argued that the world would be a more orderly and progressive place if people were allowed to follow their own interests. He reasoned that sellers made money only by producing things that people wanted to buy. Free enterprise, Smith claimed, would lead to social harmony "as if by an invisible hand." Smith criticized Britain's mercantilist policies and said that a government was necessary only to preserve law and order, defend the country, and provide for a few needs that could not be met by the market.

Economics in History
- Independence and Free Enterprise, p. 7

Economics *in* History

Free Enterprise

One cause of the Revolution was the colonists' resentment of British mercantilism. Parliament passed laws to discourage the colonists from developing their own manufacturing and to force them to buy British goods. During the war, British economic control weakened. British exports of woolens to the colonies dropped from £645,900 in 1774 to only £2,540 in 1776. As a result, the colonists were able to make more economic choices—for example, they could choose to manufacture wool clothing.

The end of Britain's mercantilist control allowed free enterprise to begin to develop in the United States. In a free-enterprise system, business can be conducted freely based on the choices of individuals. The government does not control the system, but only protects and regulates it.

CONNECT TO HISTORY

1. **Analyzing Causes** Why do you think the colonists were able to manufacture their own wool clothing during the war?

See Skillbuilder Handbook, page R11.

CONNECT TO TODAY

2. **Comparing** Think about a mall where you shop. Name examples of businesses that compete with each other. Compare the methods they use to attract customers.

For more about free enterprise . . .

RESEARCH LINKS CLASSZONE.COM

- **A** Competition encourages businesses to improve goods and services and to keep prices down.
- **B** Property is owned by individuals and businesses.
- **C** The desire to make a profit motivates businesspeople.
- **D** Individuals, not the government, decide what to buy and what to manufacture and sell.
- **E** The government protects private property and makes sure businesses operate fairly.

CONNECT TO HISTORY

1. **Analyzing Causes** **Possible Response** Britain had to direct all its energy to fighting the war and was not able to enforce the mercantilist laws that prevented colonial manufacturing.

CONNECT TO TODAY

2. **Comparing** Students should examine the following areas:
   - attractiveness of the store, including cleanliness and store design
   - organization of the products
   - variety of products
   - service
   - prices
   - promotional ideas and advertising

As part of their liberty, Americans called for more religious freedom. Before the war, some laws discriminated against certain religions. Some states had not allowed Jews or Catholics to hold public office. After the war, states began to abolish those laws. They also ended the practice of using tax money to support churches.

Background
Only Northern states ended slavery after the war. In the North, slavery was not as important a part of the economy as in the South.

Many people began to see a conflict between slavery and the ideal of liberty. Vermont outlawed slavery, and Pennsylvania passed a law to free slaves gradually. Individual African Americans also tried to end slavery. For example, **Elizabeth Freeman** sued for her freedom in a Massachusetts court and won. Her victory in 1781 and other similar cases ended slavery in that state. Freeman later described her desire for freedom.

A VOICE FROM THE PAST

Anytime while I was a slave, if one minute's freedom had been offered to me, and I had been told I must die at the end of that minute, I would have taken it—just to stand one minute on God's earth a free woman.

Elizabeth Freeman, quoted in *Notable Black American Women*

Elizabeth Freeman fought a court case that helped end slavery in Massachusetts.

Reading History
C. Solving Problems How did free African Americans take on the responsibility of trying to improve their lives?
C. Possible Response They began self-help organizations and African-American churches.

With freedom, African Americans began to form their own institutions. For example, the preacher **Richard Allen** helped start the Free African Society. That society encouraged African Americans to help each other. Allen also founded the African Methodist Episcopal Church, the first African-American church in the United States.

Perhaps the main issue facing Americans after the war was how to shape their national government. American anger over British taxes, violation of rights, and control of trade had caused the war. Now the United States needed a government that would protect citizens' rights and economic freedom. In Chapter 8, you will read how U.S. leaders worked to create such a government.

Section 4 Assessment

1. Terms & Names

Explain the significance of:
- Treaty of Paris of 1783
- republicanism
- Elizabeth Freeman
- Richard Allen

2. Taking Notes

Use a chart like the one below to classify the terms of the Treaty of Paris according to which side they favored. (Do not list terms that don't favor either side.)

Terms of the Treaty of Paris	
Favorable to America	Favorable to Britain

3. Main Ideas

a. What advantages helped the Americans win the Revolutionary War?

b. How did the end of the war affect Loyalists?

c. What were the economic costs of the war to individuals and to the government?

4. Critical Thinking

Recognizing Effects How did republicanism shape the United States after the war?

THINK ABOUT
- American ideas about government
- the roles men and women could play in public life
- religious freedom
- the antislavery movement

ACTIVITY OPTIONS
SPEECH
MATH

Look up the U.S. population in 1780. Calculate what percentage of American people died in the war. Report your findings in a **speech** or a **pie graph.**

CRITICAL THINKING ACTIVITY

Analyzing Causes Ask students what American statements and ideals from the Revolutionary era conflicted with the institution of slavery. Encourage them to locate specific examples from the documents and quotations in this chapter and the preceding one.

Class Time 15 minutes

In-Depth Resources: Unit 2
- Primary Source: An African-American Petition for Freedom, p. 35

ASSESS & RETEACH

Setting the Stage Have students complete the section of the time line for 1783.

Formal Assessment
- Section Quiz, p. 122

Critical Thinking Transparency CT19
- Setting the Stage

RETEACHING ACTIVITY

Divide the students into four groups and assign a portion of each section to each group. Have each group compose three sentences explaining the connection between their assigned portion and the section's title and main idea. Allow time for sharing, discussing, and editing of students' sentences.

In-Depth Resources: Unit 2
- Reteaching Activity, p. 42

Section 4 Assessment

1. Terms & Names

Treaty of Paris of 1783, p. 196
republicanism, p. 198
Elizabeth Freeman, p. 199
Richard Allen, p. 199

2. Taking Notes

Favorable to America: The United States was independent; its boundaries were the Mississippi River, Canada, and Spanish Florida. Favorable to Britain: The states were to return Loyalist property.

3. Main Ideas

a. better leadership; foreign aid; knowledge of the land; motivation
b. Many lost property; 80,000 to 100,000 left the United States.
c. Many soldiers received no pay and were in debt after the war; the government was $27 million in debt.

4. Critical Thinking

It led Americans to want a government in which authority came from the people, and that fostered personal and economic freedoms.

ACTIVITY OPTIONS

Integrated Assessment
- Rubrics for a speech, 3.6
- Rubrics for a pie graph, 2.3

TERMS & NAMES

1. **George Washington,** p. 178
2. **mercenary,** p. 179
3. **Battles of Saratoga,** p. 183
4. **ally,** p. 184
5. **Marquis de Lafayette,** p. 185
6. **John Paul Jones,** p. 189
7. **Lord Cornwallis,** p. 191
8. **Battle of Yorktown,** p. 194
9. **Treaty of Paris of 1783,** p. 196
10. **republicanism,** p. 198

REVIEW QUESTIONS

Possible Responses

1. The British promised to free them; the Americans because they hoped that independence would bring greater equality
2. They cooked, sewed, and nursed soldiers. They took supplies to Valley Forge. Some even fought in battle.
3. Arnold forced St. Leger to retreat and miss the rendezvous with Burgoyne. Howe refused to rendezvous with Burgoyne. Burgoyne traveled too slowly, ran out of supplies, and was surrounded by the Americans.
4. France sent troops, money, and supplies. Spain fought the British in the Mississippi Valley and Florida.
5. The weather was cold and harsh. The troops did not have enough food, clothing, or supplies. Many died of starvation, exposure, and disease.
6. Savannah and Charles Town
7. The French fleet prevented British ships from assisting Cornwallis. French troops increased the size of Washington's army.
8. for their endurance during suffering
9. all the land between Canada and Spanish Florida, west to the Mississippi
10. Vermont, Pennsylvania, and Massachusetts

Chapter 7 ASSESSMENT

TERMS & NAMES

Briefly explain the significance of each of the following.

1. George Washington
2. mercenary
3. Battles of Saratoga
4. ally
5. Marquis de Lafayette
6. John Paul Jones
7. Lord Cornwallis
8. Battle of Yorktown
9. Treaty of Paris of 1783
10. republicanism

REVIEW QUESTIONS

The Early Years of the War (pages 177–185)

1. What motives led African Americans to fight for the British? The Americans?
2. How did women help the American war effort?
3. What events led to the British defeat at Saratoga?

The War Expands (pages 184–189)

4. What foreign countries helped America? How?
5. What were conditions like at Valley Forge?

The Path to Victory (pages 190–194)

6. What two Southern ports did the British capture?
7. How did America's ally France contribute to the victory at Yorktown?

The Legacy of the War (pages 195–199)

8. For what did Washington praise his army in his farewell letter?
9. What land did the United States acquire from Britain as a result of the Treaty of Paris?
10. What three states outlawed slavery after the war?

CRITICAL THINKING

1. USING YOUR NOTES

Using your completed time line, answer the questions below.

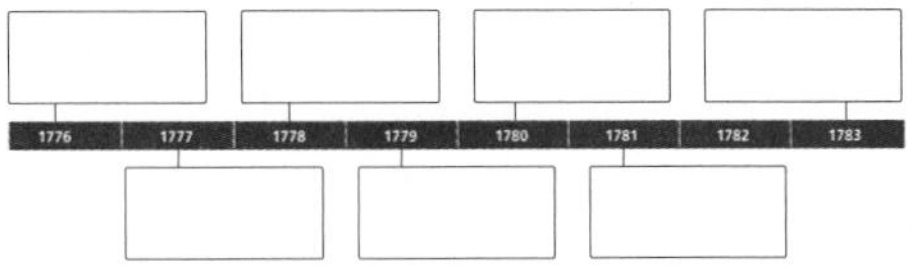

a. What were the main events of 1776 and 1777?

b. While George Rogers Clark was capturing Kaskaskia, what was happening in the South?

2. ANALYZING LEADERSHIP

George Washington was the most beloved American leader of his time. What qualities do you think made him such a respected leader?

3. THEME: CITIZENSHIP

What Revolutionary leaders displayed civic virtue by putting the good of the nation ahead of their own interests? Explain your answer.

4. RECOGNIZING EFFECTS

How did Britain's loss in the war allow free enterprise to develop in the United States?

5. APPLYING CITIZENSHIP SKILLS

How was the writing of *The American Crisis* an example of good U.S. citizenship?

Interact *with* History

How did the sacrifices you discussed before you read the chapter compare with what Patriots really did?

VISUAL SUMMARY

The American Revolution

People and Events of the Revolution

Military		Civilian	
George Washington	commanded the Continental Army.	Haym Salomon	helped finance the war for America.
Marquis de Lafayette	fought for the Americans.	Molly Pitcher	aided soldiers by bringing them water in battle.
John Burgoyne	surrendered to the Americans at Saratoga.	Thomas Paine	wrote *The American Crisis* to inspire Americans.
John Paul Jones	won a major naval victory for America.	Benjamin Franklin	was a diplomat to France and Britain.
George Rogers Clark	helped hold the Western frontier for America.	James Forten	was captured by the British but would not betray America.
Lord Cornwallis	surrendered at Yorktown, ending the war.	Nancy Hart	defended her Georgia home against Loyalist raiders.

CRITICAL THINKING

Possible Responses

1. **USING YOUR NOTES a.** 1776—Washington forced British from Boston; Washington surprised Hessians at Trenton. 1777—Washington won at Princeton; Gates and Arnold defeated Burgoyne at Saratoga. **b.** The British were capturing Savannah.
2. **ANALYZING LEADERSHIP** He suffered with his men, showed caution and courage, and never gave up.
3. **THEME: CITIZENSHIP** Washington gave up running his plantation to fight the war; Salomon and Clark went into debt to help the war effort.
4. **RECOGNIZING EFFECTS** After Britain lost the war, it could no longer impose mercantilist controls on the economy, so Americans were free to make their own economic choices.
5. **APPLYING CITIZENSHIP SKILLS** Paine used that pamphlet to urge people to fight for their country's freedom and not to abandon it just because times were difficult.

Interact *with* History Answers will vary but should include information learned in the chapter.

HISTORY SKILLS

1. INTERPRETING MAPS: Movement

Study the map, then answer the questions.

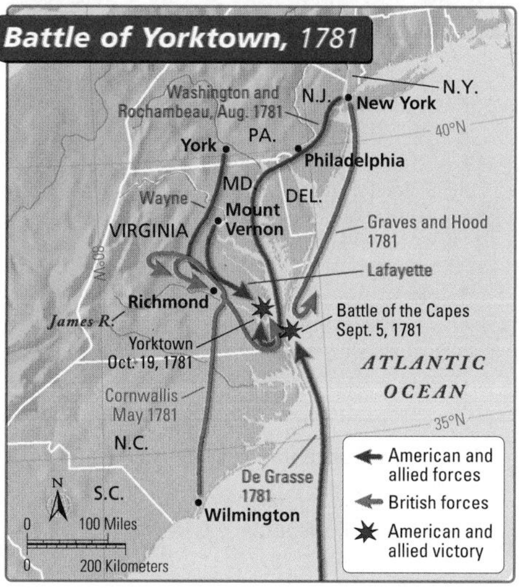

Basic Map Elements

a. In what state was the Battle of Yorktown fought?
b. In what battle did De Grasse's fleet defeat the British fleet led by Graves and Hood?

Interpreting the Map

c. Describe the route Washington took to reach Yorktown.
d. What British force tried to come to Cornwallis's aid?

2. INTERPRETING PRIMARY SOURCES

Read the passage below, which is a longer version of the quotation you read on page 180.

> These are the times that try men's souls. The summer soldier and the sunshine patriot will, in this crisis, shrink from the service of their country; but he that stands it *now,* deserves the love and thanks of man and woman. Tyranny, like hell, is not easily conquered; yet we have this consolation with us, that the harder the conflict, the more glorious the triumph. What we obtain too cheap, we esteem too lightly: it is dearness only that gives everything its value.
>
> **Thomas Paine,** *The American Crisis*

a. In your own words, explain who "the summer soldier and the sunshine patriot" are.
b. What does Paine promise will be the reward of a hard conflict?

ALTERNATIVE ASSESSMENT

1. INTERDISCIPLINARY ACTIVITY: Science

Creating a Poster Two of the diseases that killed American soldiers in camp were typhoid fever and smallpox. Do research to learn the following about one of these diseases: its cause, its symptoms, its treatment, and how common it is today. Use the information to create a public health poster to inform people about the disease.

2. COOPERATIVE LEARNING ACTIVITY

Performing a Talk Show In a small group, prepare to hold a talk show in which the guests discuss which side to take in the Revolutionary War. One member of your group should be the talk show host. The others should play the roles of various Americans. Each person should explain the reasons for his or her position. Perform the talk show before the class. Students might choose from the following roles:

a. the wife of an American soldier
b. an enslaved African American
c. an Iroquois chief
d. a Quaker minister
e. an employee of the British government

3. TECHNOLOGY ACTIVITY

Creating a Multimedia Presentation Use the Internet, books, and other reference materials to create a multimedia presentation on one of the major battles of the Revolution. Consider including the following:

- paintings of the conflict and photographs of artifacts
- quotations from participants and witnesses
- music of the time period
- recorded sound effects
- graphs showing battle statistics

Show your presentation to the class.

For more about Revolutionary battles . . .

INTERNET ACTIVITY
CLASSZONE.COM

4. HISTORY PORTFOLIO

Review this chapter and write a short report identifying the era it covers and describing the era's defining characteristics. Be sure to use standard grammar, spelling, sentence structure, and punctuation in your report. Add your report to your portfolio.

Additional Test Practice, pp. S1–S33

TEST PRACTICE
CLASSZONE.COM

ALTERNATIVE ASSESSMENT

1. INTERDISCIPLINARY ACTIVITY: Science
 Posters should
 - convey a concept through effective visuals.
 - use persuasive language in slogans or memorable sentences.
 - target a specific audience.
 - be presented neatly.

2. COOPERATIVE LEARNING ACTIVITY
 Talk shows should
 - have questions that reflect the focus on positions in the Revolutionary War.
 - have answers that accurately reflect the thoughts and experiences of the subject's life.
 - show evidence of involvement of each person in the group.

3. TECHNOLOGY ACTIVITY
 Presentations should
 - utilize two or more media.
 - clearly present accurate information about a battle.
 - present information about both sides in the battle.
 - show technical proficiency.

4. HISTORY PORTFOLIO
 Short reports should
 - define and characterize the American Revolution.
 - use evidence to develop and support ideas.
 - cite sources of information.
 - use standard grammar, spelling, sentence structure, and punctuation.

Critical Thinking Transparency CT21
- Visual Summary

Formal Assessment
- Chapter Test, Forms A, B, and C, pp. 123–134

HISTORY SKILLS

Possible Responses

1. INTERPRETING MAPS
 Basic Map Elements
 a. Virginia
 b. Battle of the Capes
 Interpreting the Map
 c. He moved south over land until he reached a bay, then traveled by water to Yorktown.
 d. the fleet led by Graves and Hood

2. INTERPRETING PRIMARY SOURCES
 a. They are Americans who will cease to support the war because it is going badly.
 b. a glorious triumph

Confederation to Constitution 1776–1791

	CHAPTER OVERVIEW	COPYMASTERS	INTEGRATED TECHNOLOGY
CHAPTER RESOURCES	The chapter describes the development of the United States government from the Articles of Confederation to the Constitution. It focuses on the debate between the Federalists and the Antifederalists over ratification and a Bill of Rights.	**In-Depth Resources: Unit 2** • Tracing Themes: Democratic Ideals, p. 45 • Building Vocabulary, p. 49 **Interdisciplinary Projects,** pp. 43–48	• eEdition Plus Online • EasyPlanner Plus Online • eTest Plus Online • eEdition • Power Presentations • EasyPlanner • Electronic Library of Primary Sources • Test Generator • Reading Study Guide • America's Music
SECTION 1 **The Confederation Era** **pp. 205–211**	**KEY IDEAS** • The new United States sets up a republic. • The Land Ordinance of 1785 and the Northwest Ordinance set policy for organizing the new western lands. • Poor economic conditions in the 1780s lead to Shays's Rebellion.	**In-Depth Resources: Unit 2** • Setting the Stage, p. 44 • Guided Reading, p. 46 • Primary Source, p. 53 • Reteaching Activity, p. 58 **America's History Makers** • Daniel Boone, pp. 31–32 **Economics in History** • The Value of Land, p. 8	**Warm-Up Transparency WT8** **Geography Transparency GT8** • United States, 1787 **Critical Thinking Transparency CT22** • Setting the Stage **classzone.com**
SECTION 2 **Creating the Constitution** **pp. 212–217**	• James Madison and others propose a new plan of government. • The Great Compromise resolves conflicts among the states over representation. • Debates over slavery conclude with the Three-Fifths Compromise and the temporary extension of the slave trade.	**In-Depth Resources: Unit 2** • Setting the Stage, p. 44 • Guided Reading, p. 47 • Primary Source, p. 54 • Literature Selection, pp. 55–57 • Reteaching Activity, p. 59 **America's History Makers** • James Madison, pp. 33–34 **Citizenship Today,** p. 68	**Humanities Transparency HT15** • George Washington at the Constitutional Convention **Critical Thinking Transparency CT23** • Cause and Effect: The Constitutional Convention **Primary Source Explorer** • *The Federalist,* Number 51 • *Objections to the Constitution* **classzone.com**
SECTION 3 **Ratifying the Constitution** **pp. 218–223**	• Federalists support ratification of the Constitution, while Antifederalists oppose it. • *The Federalist* Papers—essays by Madison, Hamilton, and Jay—win public support for ratification. • The Constitution is ratified, and a Bill of Rights is added to it.	**In-Depth Resources: Unit 2** • Setting the Stage, p. 44 • Guided Reading, p. 48 • Skillbuilder Practice, p. 50 • Geography Application: Ratifying the Constitution, pp. 51–52 • Reteaching Activity, p. 60 **Why It Matters Now** • The Living Constitution, pp. 15–16 **Outline Map Activities** • The Original 13 States, 1790, pp. 15–16	**Warm-Up Transparency WT8** **Humanities Transparency HT16** • Constitution, Page One—A Replica **Critical Thinking Transparency CT22** • Setting the Stage **classzone.com**

Pupil's Edition
Copymaster
Overhead Transparency
Audio Library
CD-ROM
Internet

ASSESSMENT OPTIONS

Chapter Assessment, pp. 224–225

Formal Assessment
- Chapter Tests, Forms A, B, and C, pp. 138–149

Test Generator

Online Test Practice

Strategies for Test Preparation

Section Assessment, p. 209

Formal Assessment, Quiz, p. 135

Integrated Assessment Book
- Rubrics, 4.1, 2.1

Test Generator

Test Practice Transparencies, TT28

Section Assessment, p. 217

Formal Assessment, Quiz, p. 136

Integrated Assessment Book
- Rubrics, 5.3, 1.2

Test Generator

Test Practice Transparencies, TT29

Section Assessment, p. 221

Formal Assessment, Quiz, p. 137

Integrated Assessment Book
- Rubrics, 3.3, 4.5

Test Generator

Test Practice Transparencies, TT30

CUSTOMIZING FOR INDIVIDUAL NEEDS

Students Acquiring English/ESL

Reading Study Guide (English and Spanish), pp. 69–76

Access for Students Acquiring English/ESL: Spanish Translations, pp. 47–52

Chapter Summaries on CD (English and Spanish)

Modified Lesson Plans for English Learners

Less Proficient Readers

Reading Study Guide (English and Spanish), pp. 69–76

Chapter Summaries on CD (English and Spanish)

Gifted and Talented Students

In-Depth Resources: Unit 2
- Enrichment Activity, p. 61

America's History Makers
- Daniel Boone, pp. 31–32
- James Madison, pp. 33–34

CROSS-CURRICULAR CONNECTIONS

Geography

Aylesworth, Thomas G., and Virginia L. Aylesworth. ***Eastern Great Lakes: Indiana, Michigan, Ohio.*** New York: Chelsea House Publishers, 1988. The geography and culture of these states that were carved from the Northwest Territory.

Government

Jaffe, Steven H. ***Who Were the Founding Fathers? Two Hundred Years of Reinventing American History.*** New York: Holt, 1996. A lively look at changing views of historic figures, as seen in contemporary and modern journalism, cartoons, and art.

Interdisciplinary Projects, pp. 43–48
- Math: Finding the Area
- Science: Preserving Important Documents
- Language Arts: Formal English: The Bill of Rights
- Art: Designing the First U.S. Flag

Primary Sources

Viola, Herman J. ***The National Archives of the United States.*** New York: Abrams, 1984. A beautifully illustrated account of the preservation of American records and documents such as the Constitution.

Literature

Irving, Washington. ***The Legend of Sleepy Hollow.*** New York: Tor Books, 1990. The much-loved American classic of life in post-Revolutionary New York State.

Willis, Patricia. ***Danger Along the Ohio.*** Boston: Houghton, 1997. Adventures of the three Dunn children as they struggle to return to their father after being cast ashore on the wild banks of the Ohio River in 1793.

ENRICHMENT ACTIVITIES

Pupil's Edition, pp. 202–225
Interact with History, p. 203
Geography in History, pp. 210–221
Interactive Primary Sources, pp. 222–223

In-Depth Resources: Unit 2
- Geography Application: Ratifying the Constitution, pp. 51–52
- Primary Source: A Letter from Benjamin Lincoln, p. 53
- Primary Source: from *Debates on the Adoption of the Federal Constitution,* p. 54
- Literature Selection: from *Our Independence and the Constitution,* pp. 55–57

America's History Makers
- Daniel Boone, pp. 31–32
- James Madison, pp. 33–34

Outline Map Activities
- The Original 13 States, 1790, pp. 15–16

Primary Source Explorer
- *The Federalist,* Number 51
- *Objections to the Constitution*

Why It Matters Now
- The Living Constitution, pp. 15–16

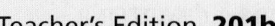

BLOCK SCHEDULING — LESSON PLAN OPTIONS (90-MINUTE PERIOD)

DAY 1

Interact with History, p. 203
Class Time 20 Minutes

Options for pacing and variety:
- **Role-Playing** Have students role-play a dialogue between a newspaper reporter and a delegate to the Constitutional Convention. The reporter can ask the delegate why he or she is there, how decisions will be made, and what the important issues are. After 10 minutes, have students switch roles and resume the conversation.
  Class Time 20 minutes

Setting the Stage, p. 204
Class Time 20 minutes

Options for pacing and variety:
- **Time Saver** For a homework assignment, have students answer the questions "Why do nations have governments?" and "What does the U.S. government do?"
  Class Time 5 minutes

Section 1, pp. 205–211
Class Time 50 minutes

Options for pacing and variety:
- **History on Film** Extend students' background knowledge of trailblazer Daniel Boone by viewing *Daniel Boone and the First American Pioneers,* SVE, 1996. **Class Time** 30 minutes
- **Peer Teaching** Have pairs of students use the graph on page 208 to write a summary of the Continental Congress, describing its successes and failures. **Class Time** 20 minutes

DAY 2

Section 2, pp. 212–217
Class Time 45 minutes

Options for pacing and variety:
- **Peer Teaching** Using the chart The Great Compromise on page 216 as a model, have pairs of students create a chart showing how a compromise was reached on the issue of slavery. Have pairs exchange their charts and evaluate each other's graphics.
  Class Time 10 minutes
- **Internet** Extend students' background knowledge of the creation of the Constitution by having them visit classzone.com.
  Class Time 20 minutes

Section 3, pp. 218–223
Class Time 45 minutes

Options for pacing and variety:
- **Time Saver** Use the chart on page 219 to summarize the differences between the Federalists and the Antifederalists for the class.
  Class Time 10 minutes
- **Role-Playing** Have two students role-play a conversation between a person who favors ratifying the Constitution and one who opposes it. Ask the class to decide which speaker's arguments are more convincing.
  Class Time 10 minutes

Chapter 8 Assessment, pp. 224–225
Class Time 40 minutes

Options for pacing and variety:
- **Peer Evaluation** Have student pairs answer the Critical Thinking questions from the Chapter Assessment. Then have them make up one additional Critical Thinking question to pose to the class. **Class Time** 20 minutes
- **Peer Teaching** Within small groups, have students share their completed Reading Strategy charts from page 204 with the class, explaining the problems and solutions they identified. **Class Time** 30 minutes

TEACHER-TESTED ACTIVITY Paul Beavers, J. T. Moore Middle School, Nashville, Tennessee

NORTH V. SOUTH

Class Time Two class periods

Task Solving conflicts that arose between Northern and Southern delegates at the Constitutional Convention

Purpose To recognize the difficulties that delegates faced in finding compromises on difficult issues

Supplies Needed
- Reference books and Internet sources on the Constitutional Convention

Activity Divide the class into groups of five or six students. Within each group, some students should represent the North and others the South. Have each group make a list of what it hopes to achieve at the convention and identify issues on which it is willing to compromise. With this list as a starting point, have each group create a framework for government that addresses the issues of slavery and protective tariffs. Have each group explain its plan to the class and defend it. Then allow time for other class members to suggest changes in the plan.

INTERNET - SEARCH FOR ROOTS OF THE CONSTITUTION

Internet research can provide students with an overwhelming amount of information on many topics. Students need to know the purpose of the search from the outset, so that they can focus their efforts and locate the desired information quickly. In this activity, students will search documents that preceded and influenced the drafting of the U.S. Constitution.

ACTIVITY OUTLINE

Objective By identifying and researching key ideas that helped to form the Constitution, students will learn more about the Constitution and gain experience with Internet research.

Task Students will use the Internet to research documents that shaped the ideas in the U.S. Constitution. After reviewing these key ideas, students will evaluate the relevance of these ideas to their own lives.

Class Time Two class periods

DIRECTIONS

1. Students will use the Internet to research the ideas that influenced the drafters of the U.S. Constitution. Remind students they may have read about some of the early influences in Chapter 5. Now they will research the actual documents and pick several ideas to compare with the Constitution.

2. Divide the class into small groups. Assign the groups the following topics:
   - the Magna Carta
   - the English Bill of Rights
   - the ideas of English philosopher John Locke
   - the ideas of French political thinker Charles de Montesquieu
   - the ideas of French philosopher Jean-Jacques Rousseau
   - the ideas of English philosopher Thomas Hobbes

3. Have each group begin by reviewing relevant ideas introduced in Chapter 5. Then they should visit the links provided on classzone.com. They should identify one major concept or thought that may have influenced writers of the Constitution.

4. Suggest some tips for doing this type of Internet research.
   - Limit browsing time to about 30 minutes.
   - Since the information they will see is complex and sometimes written in unfamiliar, flowery language, students should first skim the information by looking for headings and introductory sentences.
   - Encourage students to discuss the article and to look for ideas that are similar to those in the Constitution.

5. After each group has completed its research and selected a key idea, ask any groups that searched the same document to work together and combine ideas. Each team should construct a chart that lists key ideas of the U.S. Constitution on one side and key ideas found in their document on the opposite side. Each column should be labeled clearly with the source document's name. Then have students point out the key ideas they found that relate to ideas in the Constitution.

6. Display the charts of each group for the whole class. Finally, have students evaluate key ideas in the Constitution that are most valuable to them in their daily lives. Have each student write a short essay that answers these questions:
   - Which of the ideas in the Constitution are most important to me in my daily life?
   - What would life in the United States be like without the Constitution?

CHAPTER 8 OBJECTIVE

The student will analyze the Articles of Confederation, major issues faced by delegates to the Constitutional Convention of 1787, and the debate over ratifying the Constitution.

HISTORY FROM VISUALS

Interpreting the Painting Ask students to study the scene outside the Pennsylvania State House during the Constitutional Convention of 1787. Ask them to make inferences about what the people in the painting may have been talking about. **Possible Responses** the likelihood of a new form of government, the effects such a government might have on their lives, and the issues involved in establishing that government

Extension Ask students how Americans learn about government activities today.

CRITICAL THINKING ACTIVITY

Identifying and Solving Problems Draw a problem-solution outline on the board for the following problem: "The existing form of government does not meet the needs of the people." Ask students to suggest ways a country can solve this problem. **Possible Responses** A convention of representatives revamps the government, an election changes the government, or a revolution overthrows the government.

Class Time 25 minutes

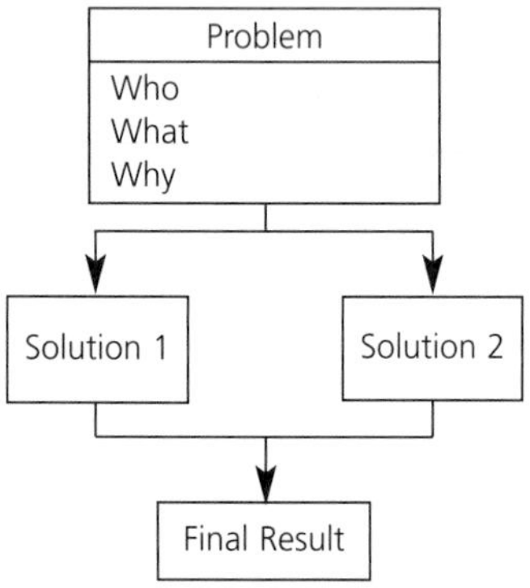

CHAPTER 8

Confederation to Constitution

1776–1791

Delegates to the Constitutional Convention in 1787 gathered in Philadelphia. They held their meetings in the Pennsylvania State House, now known as Independence Hall.

RECOMMENDED RESOURCES

BOOKS FOR THE TEACHER

Boone, Daniel, and Francis Lister Hawks. ***Daniel Boone, His Own Story & The Adventures of Daniel Boone, The Kentucky Rifleman.*** Bedford, MA: Applewood Books, 1995. Two volumes—one by Boone himself and one by an early biographer.

Bowen, Catherine Drinker. ***Miracle at Philadelphia: The Story of the Constitutional Convention.*** Boston: Little, Brown, 1986. Highly readable story of the Convention.

Duncan, Christopher M. ***The Anti-Federalists and Early American Political Thought.*** De Kalb: N. Ill. Univ. Pr., 1995. An argument in favor of the Antifederalists.

SOFTWARE

Decisions, Decisions: The Constitution. Tom Snyder Prod'ns. 1999. Part of an award-winning set of 15 CDs.

VIDEO

Daniel Boone. A&E Biography Series. Moonbeam Pubs.

INTERNET

For more about creating a constitution, visit . . .

classzone.com

Interact *with* History

Delegates kept the windows closed during meetings so that the proceedings would be secret.
Some of the most respected men in the nation served as delegates, including Alexander Hamilton and Benjamin Franklin.
The delegates chose George Washington, hero of the Revolutionary War, to be president of the convention.

The year is 1787, and your young country needs to reform its government. Now everyone is wondering what the new government will be like. You have been called to a convention to decide how the new government should be organized.

What Do You Think?

- What will be your main goal in creating a new government?
- How will you get the people at the convention to agree on important issues?

How do you form a government?

USA

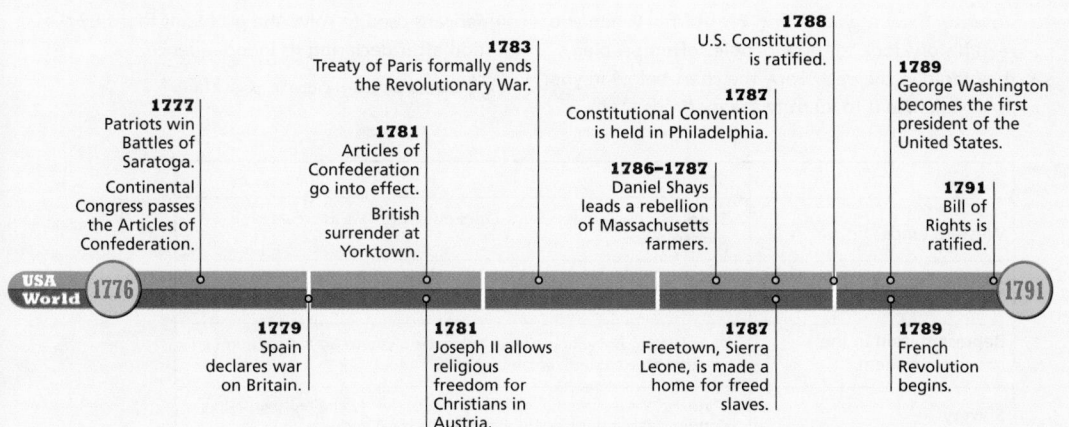

- **1777** Patriots win Battles of Saratoga. Continental Congress passes the Articles of Confederation.
- **1781** Articles of Confederation go into effect. British surrender at Yorktown.
- **1783** Treaty of Paris formally ends the Revolutionary War.
- **1786–1787** Daniel Shays leads a rebellion of Massachusetts farmers.
- **1787** Constitutional Convention is held in Philadelphia.
- **1788** U.S. Constitution is ratified.
- **1789** George Washington becomes the first president of the United States.
- **1791** Bill of Rights is ratified.

World

- **1779** Spain declares war on Britain.
- **1781** Joseph II allows religious freedom for Christians in Austria.
- **1787** Freetown, Sierra Leone, is made a home for freed slaves.
- **1789** French Revolution begins.

1776 — 1791

Interact *with* History

OBJECTIVES

- To help students evaluate the importance of the Constitutional Convention
- To help students make connections with individuals who participated in the Convention

What Do You Think?

1. Ask students to explain how they identified their main goal.
2. Have students explain how they and friends or family members make decisions.

How do you form a government?

Ask students to consider the services a government provides and the services they think it should provide.

MAKING PERSONAL CONNECTIONS

Ask students to think about meetings in which they have participated or that they attended in person. Examples might include student government or special club meetings. Ask: How were those meetings conducted? Did everyone agree on decisions made at the meeting? How did those who presided over the meeting make sure everyone had a chance to express his or her own views on a topic?

TIME LINE DISCUSSION

Remind students that in the 1780s, large areas of the world were still dominated by colonial powers such as Great Britain, Spain, and France. The young United States faced threats from outside powers and tensions at home over difficult issues like slavery and the role of government.

- Ask: How long after independence did the United States experience an internal rebellion? **Answer** Shays's Rebellion occurred in 1786, three years after the Treaty of Paris.
- Ask students to identify an event that occurred in the same year as the Constitutional Convention. **Answer** Freetown, Sierra Leone, becomes a home for freed slaves.
- Ask students to identify an event in Europe after the Constitutional Convention that greatly interested Americans. **Answer** the French Revolution, because France had been a U.S. ally during the American Revolution

BEFORE YOU READ

Previewing the Theme: Democratic Ideals

Ask students why they think the states wanted to form any national government at all. Why didn't the states simply remain 13 independent nations?

Possible Response Much of the world in the late 1700s was dominated by powerful empires. Many Americans feared that each state would be too weak on its own to defend itself against foreign domination. Together, the states could more successfully defend themselves from foreign military or economic threats. However, they struggled to determine what form their national government should take and how powerful it should be.

What Do You Know?

Point out to students that state and local governments are not part of our national government. State and local governments have their own powers and responsibilities in the United States. In this chapter they will learn why this is so.

In-Depth Resources: Unit 2
- Tracing Themes: Democratic Ideals, p. 45

READ AND TAKE NOTES

Reading Strategy: Solving Problems

Explain to students that as they study history, they will read about various kinds of problems faced by Americans and about the ways they tried to solve these problems. Point out that if more than one problem is presented in a chapter, it is a good idea to use a chart to keep track of the problems and their solutions. Ask students to look at the chart on page 204 and identify the four problems listed.

In-Depth Resources: Unit 2
- Setting the Stage, p. 44

Critical Thinking Transparency CT22
- Setting the Stage

Chapter 8 SETTING THE STAGE

BEFORE YOU READ

Previewing the Theme

Democratic Ideals Between 1776 and 1791, the United States struggled to set up a national government. The Articles of Confederation established the first federal government. Chapter 8 explains how the weaknesses of the Articles led Americans to write a new constitution for the United States.

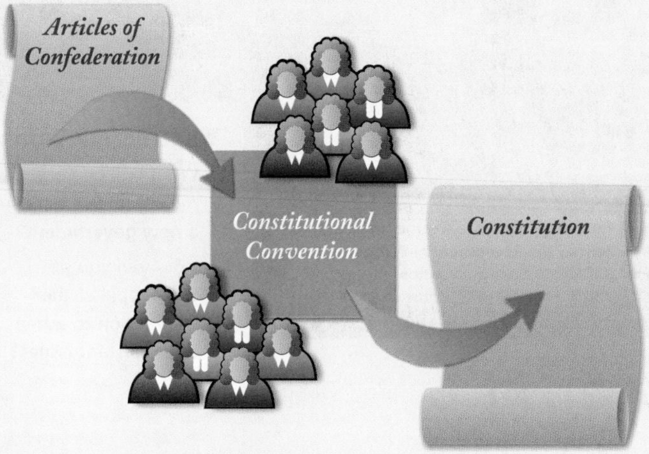

What Do You Know?

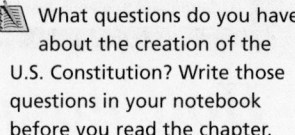

What do you think of when people talk about the U.S. government? Why do nations have governments? What does the U.S. government do?

THINK ABOUT
- what you've learned about the U.S. government from the news or your teachers
- what the purpose of a government is
- how the government affects your everyday life

What Do You Want to Know?

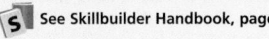

What questions do you have about the creation of the U.S. Constitution? Write those questions in your notebook before you read the chapter.

READ AND TAKE NOTES

Reading Strategy: Solving Problems When you read history, look for how people solved problems they faced in the past. Copy the chart below in your notebook. Use it to identify the methods that Americans used to solve the problems faced by the nation after declaring its independence.

See Skillbuilder Handbook, page R18.

Problems	Solutions
Western lands	States give up Western claims. Congress passes laws to organize the territories.
Postwar depression	Annapolis Convention is called to discuss problems of commerce.
Representation in the new government	Philadelphia convention is held. Delegates agree to Great Compromise to settle issue of state representation.
Slavery	Three-Fifths Compromise addresses issue of slavery and representation. Congress delays discussion of banning the slave trade.

TEACHING STRATEGY

READING THE CHAPTER

This is a chronological chapter focusing on the origins of government in the new nation. Encourage students to identify problems leading to the creation of the Articles of Confederation, the Constitution, and the Bill of Rights. Have students identify events in this period that illustrate political problems and the solutions people devised. Pause at the end of each section to review the events and their relationships.

ALTERNATIVE ASSESSMENT

The Chapter Assessment describes three activities for alternative assessment on page 225. You may wish to have students work on these activities during the course of the chapter and then present them at the end.

1 The Confederation Era

TERMS & NAMES
Wilderness Road
republic
Articles of Confederation
Land Ordinance of 1785
Northwest Territory
Northwest Ordinance
Shays's Rebellion

MAIN IDEA

The Articles of Confederation were too weak to govern the nation after the war ended.

WHY IT MATTERS NOW

The weakness of the Articles of Confederation led to the writing of the U.S. Constitution.

SECTION OBJECTIVES

1. To describe the expansion of the nation and the development of state governments
2. To analyze the strengths and weaknesses of the Articles of Confederation
3. To evaluate the importance of the Northwest Ordinance
4. To identify the causes and effects of Shays's Rebellion

SKILLBUILDER
Interpreting Maps: Location, p. 207
Interpreting Graphs, p. 208

CRITICAL THINKING
Finding Main Ideas, p. 207
Analyzing Causes, p. 208
Forming and Supporting Opinions, p. 209

FOCUS & MOTIVATE

5-MINUTE WARM-UP

Making Inferences The questions below focus on the challenges faced by the new nation.

1. Look at the map on page 207. What kinds of problems do you think might be caused by conflicting state claims to new territories?
2. How do you think those conflicting claims could be resolved?

Warm-Up Transparency WT8

INSTRUCT

INSTRUCT: OBJECTIVE 1
Moving West/New State Governments

- Into which areas did American settlement expand in the late 1700s?
- What kind of governments did the new states create for themselves?
- What is a republic? Why is the United States a republic?

In-Depth Resources: Unit 2
- Guided Reading, p. 46

ONE AMERICAN'S STORY

In 1775, Daniel Boone and 30 woodsmen cut a road over the Appalachian Mountains into Kentucky. They hacked through brush, chopped down trees, and bridged creeks. They labored like this for about 250 miles. Eventually, they arrived in a grassy meadow along the banks of the Kentucky River. Felix Walker, a member of Boone's party, described what they saw.

A VOICE FROM THE PAST

On entering the plain we were permitted to view a very interesting and romantic sight. A number of buffaloes . . . supposed to be between two and three hundred, made off . . . in every direction. . . . Such a sight some of us never saw before, nor perhaps ever may again.

Felix Walker, quoted in *The Life and Adventures of Daniel Boone*

Early travel to Kentucky is shown in this detail of *Daniel Boone Escorting Settlers Through the Cumberland Gap* (1851–1852) by George Caleb Bingham.

Boone was one of the earliest American settlers in Kentucky. In the late 1700s, most Americans thought of Kentucky as the wild frontier. Some, like Boone, looked at the frontier and saw a world of opportunity. Exploring and governing these lands was only one of the many challenges that faced the new government of the United States.

1 Moving West

The trail into Kentucky that Daniel Boone helped build was called the **Wilderness Road.** This road was not easy to travel. It was too narrow for carts or wagons, but it became the main road into Kentucky. The settlers came on foot or on horseback. Settlers were drawn to Kentucky's rich river valleys, where few Native Americans lived. But some Native Americans, such as the Shawnee, did live, hunt, and fish in the area.

Tensions between Native Americans and settlers led to violent confrontations. But the settlers did not stop coming. By the early 1790s, about 100,000 Americans lived there. While settlers headed into the Western territories, the people in the East began to create new state governments.

RECOMMENDED RESOURCES

In-Depth Resources: Unit 2
- Guided Reading, p. 46
- Building Vocabulary, p. 49
- Primary Source, p. 53

Reading Study Guide (Spanish and English), pp. 69–70

Economics in History
- The Value of Land, p. 8

America's History Makers
- Daniel Boone, pp. 31–32

Formal Assessment
- Section Quiz, p. 135

Integrated Assessment
- Rubrics, 4.1, 2.1

Access for Students Acquiring English/ESL
- Guided Reading, p. 47

INTEGRATED TECHNOLOGY

Geography Transparency GT8
- United States, 1787

Electronic Teacher Tools

classzone.com

TEST-TAKING RESOURCES

Strategies for Test Preparation

Test Practice Transparencies, TT27

Online Test Practice

MORE ABOUT . . .

The English Bill of Rights

The English Bill of Rights limited the power of the English monarch. Among other things, it prevented the monarch from suspending the law, levying taxes, and maintaining an army in peacetime without consent of Parliament. It also guaranteed free elections and free speech for members of Parliament (but not for other people).

INSTRUCT: OBJECTIVE 2

The Articles of Confederation

- What issues divided the Continental Congress as it developed a plan for a national government?
- What were the structure and powers of the national government under the Articles of Confederation?
- How did state claims to western lands affect the acceptance of the Articles of Confederation?

CRITICAL THINKING ACTIVITY

Analyzing Points of View Divide the class into pairs of students. Tell one student in each pair to list arguments supporting the views of the large states while the other member of each pair should list the views of the small states, about western land claims and representation in Congress. Tell students to record their lists on a chart like the one below. Allow pairs to use their charts as the basis for a short debate.

Large States	Small States

Class Time 25 minutes

New State Governments

Once the American colonies declared independence, each of the states set out to create its own government. The framers, or creators, of the state constitutions did not want to destroy the political systems that they had had as colonies. They simply wanted to make those systems more democratic. Some states experimented with creating separate branches of government, giving different powers to different branches. By creating separate branches, Americans hoped to prevent the government from becoming too powerful.

Some states included a bill of rights in their constitutions as a way to keep the government under control. The idea of a bill of rights came from the English Bill of Rights of 1689. This was a list of rights that the government guaranteed to English citizens.

Although not all the states had a bill of rights, all of them did have a republican form of government. In a **republic,** the people choose representatives to govern them.

Background
Two states, Connecticut and Rhode Island, kept their old colonial charters as their constitutions. The other 11 states wrote new constitutions.

2 The Articles of Confederation

While the states were setting up their governments, Americans also discussed the form of their national government. During the Revolutionary War, Americans realized that they needed to unite to win the war against Britain. As Silas Deane, a diplomat from Connecticut, wrote, "United we stand, divided we fall."

"United we stand, divided we fall."
Silas Deane

In 1776, the Continental Congress began to develop a plan for a national government. Congress agreed that the government should be a republic. But the delegates disagreed about whether each state should have one vote or voting should be based on population. They also disagreed about whether the national government or the individual states should control the lands west of the Appalachians.

The Continental Congress eventually arrived at a final plan, called the **Articles of Confederation.** In the Articles, the national government had few powers, because many Americans were afraid that a strong government would lead to tyranny, or oppressive rule. The national government was run by a Confederation Congress. Each state had only one vote in the Congress. The national government had the power to wage war, make peace, sign treaties, and issue money.

But the Articles left most important powers to the states. These powers included the authority to set taxes and enforce national laws. The Articles proposed to leave the states in control of the lands west of the Appalachian Mountains.

***Reading*History**
A. Reading a Map Look at the map on page 207 to see which states claimed territories in the West.

ACTIVITY OPTIONS

INDIVIDUAL NEEDS

LESS PROFICIENT READERS

Categorizing To help students understand the purpose and provisions of the Articles of Confederation, create a two-column chart on the board. Add the headings *States* and *National Government* to the chart. Ask students to list the powers of the states and of the central government under the Articles of Confederation. Add student responses to the appropriate column. You may want students to copy and save the chart for future discussion on the weaknesses of the Articles of Confederation.

States	National Government
Set taxes	Wage war
Enforce laws	Make peace
Control western lands	Sign treaties
Have one vote in Congress	Issue money

The Continental Congress passed the Articles of Confederation in November 1777. It then sent the Articles to the states for ratification, or approval. By July 1778, eight states had ratified the Articles. But some of the small states that did not have Western land claims refused to sign.

These states felt that unless the Western lands were placed under the control of the national government, they would be at a disadvantage. The states with Western lands could sell them to pay off debts left from the Revolution. But states without lands would have difficulty paying off the high war debts.

Over the next three years, all the states gave up their claims to Western lands. This led the small states to ratify the Articles. In 1781, Maryland became the 13th state to accept the Articles. As a result, the United States finally had an official government.

*Reading*History
B. Finding Main Ideas Why did the states without Western land claims want the other states to give up their claims?
B. Answer The states without claims feared that the states with claims would be richer and stronger than them.

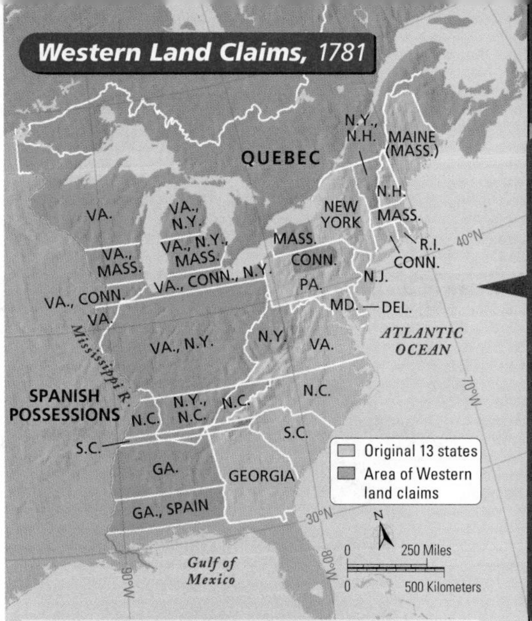

GEOGRAPHY SKILLBUILDER Interpreting Maps
1. **Location** *Which of the original 13 states had Western land claims?*
2. **Location** *To what geographic feature did the Western land claims extend?*

Skillbuilder Answers
1. Virginia, New York, Massachusetts, Connecticut, North Carolina, South Carolina, Georgia, and New Hampshire
2. Mississippi River

❸ The Northwest Ordinance

One of the most important questions that the Confederation Congress faced was what to do with the Western lands that it now controlled. Congress passed important laws on how to divide and govern these lands—the Land Ordinance of 1785 and the Northwest Ordinance (1787). (See Geography in History on pages 210–211.)

The **Land Ordinance of 1785** called for surveyors to stake out six-mile-square plots, called townships, in the Western lands. These lands later became known as the **Northwest Territory**. The Northwest Territory included land that formed the states of Ohio, Indiana, Michigan, Illinois, and Wisconsin and part of Minnesota.

The **Northwest Ordinance** (1787) described how the Northwest Territory was to be governed. As the territory grew in population, it would gain rights to self-government. When there were 5,000 free males in an area, men who owned at least 50 acres of land could elect an assembly. When there were 60,000 people, they could apply to become a new state.

The Northwest Ordinance also set conditions for settlement in the Northwest Territory and outlined the settlers' rights. Slavery was outlawed, and the rivers were to be open to navigation by all. Freedom of religion and trial by jury were guaranteed.

The Northwest Ordinance was important because it set a pattern for the orderly growth of the United States. As the nation grew, it followed this pattern in territories added after the Northwest Territory.

Background
According to the Northwest Ordinance, Native Americans were to be treated fairly, and their lands were not to be taken from them.

HISTORY FROM VISUALS

Reading the Map The western lands of the new United States were vast. Have students list some of the challenges of governing such a large territory.
Possible Answers setting up government divisions, keeping order, defending territories from foreign threats

Extension Have students create a map of what they think the United States would look like today if the original states had not given up their claims to western lands.

Geography Transparency GT8
- United States, 1787

INSTRUCT: OBJECTIVE ❸
The Northwest Ordinance

- How did the Land Ordinance of 1785 state that the western lands should be divided?
- How were the western territories governed under the Northwest Ordinance?
- Why was the Northwest Ordinance important to the growth of the United States?

Economics in History
- The Value of Land, p. 8

MORE ABOUT . . .

Western Land Claims
Western land claims originated in vaguely worded colonial charters that gave some colonies control of territory reaching from the Atlantic to the Pacific ocean. After the Revolution, new states scrambled to claim as much territory as they could.

ACTIVITY OPTIONS
INTERDISCIPLINARY LINK: GOVERNMENT — BLOCK SCHEDULING

BECOMING A STATE

Class Time 30 minutes

Task Making a time line showing the steps toward statehood

Purpose To identify the procedure for territories becoming states

Supplies Needed
- Textbook
- Encyclopedias and other reference books on state history
- Paper and art supplies

Activity Assign each student one of the following states formed (totally or partially) from the Northwest Territory: Wisconsin, Illinois, Indiana, Michigan, Ohio, Minnesota. Direct students to find out when the first settlers arrived in the territory, when it first applied for statehood, and when it became a state. Make a class time line showing these dates for all states.

INSTRUCT: OBJECTIVE 4

Weaknesses of the Articles/ Shays's Rebellion

- Why was debt a critical problem for the national government under the Articles of Confederation?
- Why did the national government get little financial support from the states?
- How did Shays's Rebellion point out the weaknesses of government under the Articles of Confederation?

HISTORY FROM VISUALS

Interpreting the Chart Point out to students that the Confederation Congress had deliberately created a very weak central government. Ask students why they think the states feared a strong central government. **Possible Answers** The states had resented the power of the British monarch over their affairs. They did not want to replace one form of tyranny with what they believed might be another in the form of a strong national government.

Extension Ask students to identify the one duty they believe is most important for a national government. Tell them to explain their choice.

MORE ABOUT . . .

Shays's Rebellion

Thomas Jefferson, author of the Declaration of Independence, was not alarmed by Shays's Rebellion. "I hold it that a little rebellion now and then is a good thing," he said. He added: "The tree of liberty must be refreshed from time to time with the blood of patriots and tyrants. It is its natural manure."

Skillbuilder Answers
1. Possible Response Governing the nation during the Revolutionary War, because if the war was lost, there would be no nation.

Weaknesses of the Articles 4

Aside from its handling of land issues, however, the Confederation Congress had few successes. By the end of the Revolutionary War, the United States faced serious problems, and the Confederation Congress did not have enough power to solve them.

U.S. Government, 1776–1787

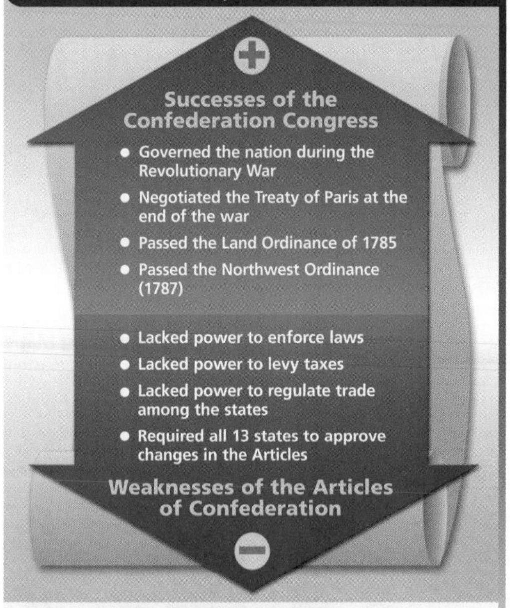

Successes of the Confederation Congress
Governed the nation during the Revolutionary War
Negotiated the Treaty of Paris at the end of the war
Passed the Land Ordinance of 1785
Passed the Northwest Ordinance (1787)
Lacked power to enforce laws
Lacked power to levy taxes
Lacked power to regulate trade among the states
Required all 13 states to approve changes in the Articles
Weaknesses of the Articles of Confederation

SKILLBUILDER **Interpreting Charts**
1. *What do you think was the greatest success of the Confederation Congress?*
2. *What do you think was the greatest weakness of the Articles of Confederation?*

Debt was a critical problem for the government. Congress had borrowed large sums to pay for the Revolutionary War. Much of that money was owed to soldiers of its own army. Upset at not being paid, several hundred soldiers surrounded the Pennsylvania State House where Congress was meeting in June 1783. The soldiers threatened the legislators, thrusting their bayonets through the windows. The delegates were forced to flee the city. The event was a clear sign of Congress's weakness.

Reading **History**
C. Analyzing Causes How did debt cause problems for the U.S. government under the Articles of Confederation?
C. Answer Congress could not raise money to pay its debts, even to the soldiers who had fought the war.

Even if Congress wanted to pay the soldiers, it did not have the power to levy taxes. The national government depended on the states to send money to Congress. But the states sent very little money.

Congress was not alone in facing economic crises. People throughout the nation faced hard times. In Massachusetts, the economy was so bad that people rose up in arms against the government.

2. Possible Responses Some students might say the lack of the power to tax, because it meant the government could not pay for what it wanted to do. Others might say the requirement for all 13 states to agree, because it could paralyze Congress.

Shays's Rebellion

In the mid-1780s, Massachusetts faced economic problems, as did other states. People had little money, but the state continued to levy high taxes. The average family owed $200 in taxes per year—more money than most farmers made. Many Massachusetts farmers fell deeply into debt. Debt laws at the time were strict. Anyone who could not repay his debts would have his property auctioned off. If the auction didn't raise enough money to settle the debts, the debtor could be put in jail. In western Massachusetts, many jails were packed with debtors.

Farmers asked the Massachusetts legislature to provide debt relief. But the legislature refused—and the farmers rebelled. One of the leaders of the rebellion was a Revolutionary War veteran named Daniel Shays. He commanded a group of about 1,500 men.

ACTIVITY OPTIONS

INTERDISCIPLINARY LINK: ART BLOCK SCHEDULING

DRAWING AN EDITORIAL CARTOON

Class Time One class period

Task Drawing an editorial cartoon about the Articles of Confederation

Purpose To understand the concerns over the weaknesses of the Articles of Confederation

Supplies Needed
- Textbook
- Drawing paper

Activity Explain that editorial cartoons express ideas in pictures. Provide some examples of editorial cartoons from local or national newspapers. Then have students draw cartoons about the problems of the United States under the Articles of Confederation. When they have finished their cartoons, invite volunteers to share them with the rest of the class.

Shays's rebels take over a Massachusetts courthouse. A stone marker rests on the spot of the rebellion.

In January 1787, Shays and his men marched on a federal arsenal, a place to store weapons. The arsenal was defended by 900 soldiers from the state militia. The militia quickly defeated Shays's men. But even though the militia put down **Shays's Rebellion,** as the uprising came to be known, the farmers won the sympathy of many people. America's leaders realized that an armed uprising of common farmers spelled danger for the nation.

Background
In 1788, Daniel Shays was pardoned for his actions.

Some leaders hoped that the nation's ills could be solved by strengthening the national government. In the next section, you'll read how Americans held a convention to change the Articles of Confederation.

Section 1 Assessment

1. Terms & Names

Explain the significance of:

- Wilderness Road
- republic
- Articles of Confederation
- Land Ordinance of 1785
- Northwest Territory
- Northwest Ordinance
- Shays's Rebellion

2. Taking Notes

Use a diagram like the one below to list some of the challenges Americans faced in shaping a new government.

Which challenge do you think was the toughest? Why?

3. Main Ideas

a. What issues affected the Western territories between 1775 and 1787?

b. What were three successes of the Continental Congress?

c. What were the strengths and weaknesses of the Articles of Confederation?

4. Critical Thinking

Forming and Supporting Opinions Which side would you have supported during Shays's Rebellion—the farmers or the officials who called out the militia? Why?

THINK ABOUT

- the farmers' problems
- the farmers' march on the arsenal
- the job of the government

ACTIVITY OPTIONS

CIVICS
GEOGRAPHY

Write an **opinion article** about how the United States should govern the Western territories or draw a **map** showing how you would have divided the lands.

MORE ABOUT . . .

Punishing the Rebels
The sentences of Shays and his captured followers stirred up great controversy. After about a dozen of the rebels were sentenced to death, the high sheriff of Pittsfield found a note at his door with this message about the sentences: "I pray have a care that you assist not in the execution of so horrid a crime, for by all that is above, he that condemns and he that executes shall share alike." Two of the rebels were hanged for looting, but all the others, including Shays himself, were pardoned.

In-Depth Resources: Unit 2
- Primary Source: A Letter from Benjamin Lincoln, p. 53

ASSESS & RETEACH

Setting the Stage Have students complete the first row on the graphic organizer on page 204.

Formal Assessment
- Section Quiz, p. 135

Critical Thinking Transparency CT22
- Setting the Stage

RETEACHING ACTIVITY

Organize the class into groups of four. Each group member should be responsible for answering the Key Questions for one section objective. (See pages 221, 222, 223, and 224 for Key Questions.) Then have group members make copies of their Key Questions and answers and distribute their copies to others in the group.

In-Depth Resources: Unit 2
- Reteaching Activity, p. 58

Section 1 Assessment

1. Terms & Names

Wilderness Road, p. 205
republic, p. 206
Articles of Confederation, p. 206
Land Ordinance of 1785, p. 207
Northwest Territory, p. 207
Northwest Ordinance, p. 207
Shays's Rebellion, p. 209

2. Taking Notes

Challenges: postwar depression; debt; weakness of the Articles of Confederation; all 13 states required to approve changes to the Articles. Answers will vary. Be sure students give support for their opinions.

3. Main Ideas

a. who would control the territories; how to divide and govern these lands **b.** created the Articles; settled western land claims; passed the Land Ordinances **c. Strength:** It left important powers to the states. **Weaknesses:** It lacked the power to enforce laws, levy taxes, and regulate trade.

4. Critical Thinking

Responses will vary. Be sure students include support for the side they choose.

ACTIVITY OPTIONS

Integrated Assessment
- Rubrics for an opinion article, 4.1
- Rubrics for a map, 2.1

GEOGRAPHY *in* HISTORY

OBJECTIVE

Students will analyze the government's division of the Northwest Territory and the interaction between settlers and the environment in the region.

BLOCK SCHEDULING

MORE ABOUT . . .

Surveying

A clear and easy-to-understand grid system for dividing land reduced confusion and court cases. New England towns used a grid to divide property before settlers arrived. In New Jersey and other colonies, however, farmers hired private surveyors who drew complicated boundaries to encompass the best farmland. Americans adopted the British system of measuring land, including the furlong (660 feet), the square furlong of 10 acres, and the square mile of 640 acres.

INSTRUCT

- How did the Land Ordinance show a commitment to formal education in the territory?
- What do you suppose life must have been like for early settlers in the Northwest Territory?
- What do you think Native Americans thought about the increasing numbers of American settlers moving westward?

MAP SKILL QUESTIONS

What water routes in the Northwest Territory likely were important for the movement of people and goods?

Into what states was the region eventually divided?

How was land within the territory divided?

GEOGRAPHY *in* HISTORY

REGION AND HUMAN-ENVIRONMENT INTERACTION

The Northwest Territory

The Northwest Territory was officially known as "the Territory Northwest of the River Ohio." In the mid-1780s, Congress decided to sell the land in the territory to settlers. The sale of land solved two problems. First, it provided cash for the government. Second, it increased American control over the land.

The Land Ordinance of 1785 outlined how the land in the Northwest Territory would be divided. Congress split the land into grids with clearly defined boundaries. It created townships that could be divided into sections, as shown on the map below. Each township was six miles by six miles. This was an improvement over earlier methods of setting boundaries. Previously, people had used rocks, trees, or other landmarks to set boundaries. There had been constant fights over disputed claims.

The Land Ordinance of 1785

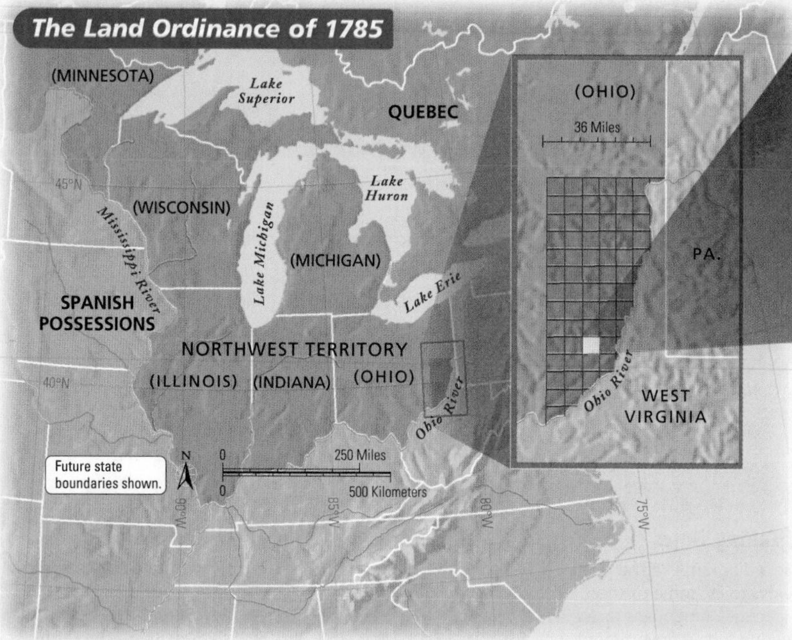

TOWNSHIP, 1785

36	30	24	18	12	6
35	29	23	17	11	5
34	28	22	16	10	4
33	27	21	15	9	3
32	26	20	14	8	2
31	25	19	13	7	1

Each township contained 3 sections. Each section was one square mile.

ARTIFACT FILE

The Theodolite The theodolite is a surveying tool. It consists of a telescope that can be moved from side to side and up and down. A theodolite measures angles and determines alignment. These functions are necessary for land surveyors to establish accurate boundaries for land claims.

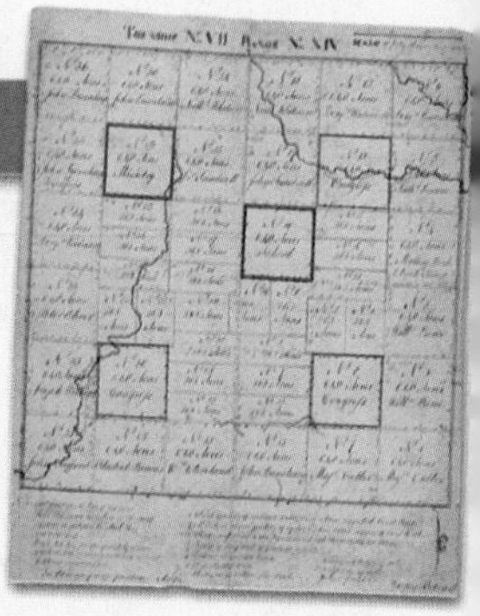

Township Map Congress reserved several plots (outlined on map) for special purposes. A few were set aside for later sale to raise money for the government. One plot was reserved to support a local school.

MUSEUM CONNECTIONS

The Shelby County Historical Society Web site offers interesting insights into town life at various times, including an interview with a woman who moved to the area in 1831. Her father cleared the land, and her family watched as other families settled in the area.

The Web site for the Sidney, Ohio, Historical Society provides a state-by-state listing of historical societies and other museums of interest to a student of history.

Campus Martius: The Museum of the Northwest Territory in Marietta, Ohio, is located on the site of the original fort designed to protect the first organized American settlement in the Northwest Territories. Marietta, Ohio, was organized in 1788.

The Web site for this museum provides more information about life in the Northwest Territory.

1. The first things settlers needed were food and shelter. Cutting trees provided fields for crops and wood for log cabins. The first crop most farmers planted was corn. Even if the land was not fully cleared of trees, farmers planted corn between the stumps.

2. A shortage of labor meant that a farmer working alone was doing well if he cleared several acres a year. As a result, few farms were completely fenced in, and forest covered most of the property. Hogs were allowed to find food in the woods. Farmers collected apples from trees and used sap to make syrup.

3. Over time, families planted fruits and vegetables. Cattle raising also became more common. Beef cattle supplied families with meat. Dairy cattle provided milk. Families could sell extra fruits, vegetables, and dairy products, such as butter and cheese.

CONNECT TO GEOGRAPHY

1. **Region** What was the land in the Northwest Territory like before Americans settled there?
2. **Human-Environment Interaction** How did American settlers affect the landscape in the territory?

See Geography Handbook, pages 4–5.

CONNECT TO HISTORY

3. **Making Inferences** Why did so many people buy land in the new territory?

On-Line Field Trip

The Ohio Historical Society is located in Columbus, Ohio. It maintains a Web site called Ohio History Central that includes information on the Ohio portion of the Northwest Territory.

For more about the Northwest Territory . . .

RESEARCH LINKS
CLASSZONE.COM

CRITICAL THINKING ACTIVITY

Questioning Tell students to look at the inset map on page 210. Ask them to think about a family selecting a plot of land for their farm. Tell students to write as many questions as they can that such a family might have asked before selecting a plot of land. When all the questions are complete, work with the class to create headings for classifying them. **Possible Responses** Students may pose questions about the land itself, including the fertility of the soil, the presence of water, and the kind of trees. Other questions may concern the location of the plot within the township, the neighbors, and other township settlers.

Class Time 20 minutes

MORE ABOUT . . .

Settlers' Rights

The Northwest Ordinance of 1787 included a Bill of Rights that guaranteed settlers freedom of religion and trial by jury, among other rights. The Ordinance also forbade slavery in the territories and stated that "The utmost good faith shall always be observed towards the Indians." The Ordinance states why education is important to the nation in these words: "Religion, morality, and knowledge, being necessary to good government and the happiness of mankind, schools and the means of education shall forever be encouraged."

CONNECT TO GEOGRAPHY

1. **Region** It was mostly wooded. The land was good, so there were many plants in addition to trees. Many things could grow there.
2. **Human-Environment Interaction** **Possible Response** Since the land was divided up by the government, things were more orderly. The land was identified as farmland, so most of the settlers were people interested in putting down roots. Farmers faced problems clearing the land and carving farms out of the land.

CONNECT TO HISTORY

3. **Making Inferences** **Possible Response** Land in the East was more expensive, and the best farmland was already claimed. Western lands were not only cheaper but the land was very fertile. Also, many people saw the land as an opportunity for prosperity and independence.

SECTION OBJECTIVES

1. To identify key events leading to the Constitutional Convention and to identify key delegates
2. To describe the delegates' expectations
3. To analyze the major issues and compromises of the Constitutional Convention
4. To explain the compromises made regarding slavery and trade in the Constitution

SKILLBUILDER

Interpreting Charts, p. 216

CRITICAL THINKING

Evaluating, p. 213
Making Decisions, p. 214
Summarizing, p. 215
Forming and Supporting Opinions, p. 217
Analyzing Points of View, p. 217

FOCUS & MOTIVATE

5-MINUTE WARM-UP

Making Inferences These questions focus on the challenges facing the Constitutional Convention.

1. Read the quotation on page 212. What grave danger did Randolph believe the nation faced?
2. What conflicts had already occurred to make Randolph's worries seem justified?

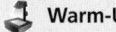

Warm-Up Transparency WT8

INSTRUCT

INSTRUCT: OBJECTIVE 1

A Constitutional Convention Is Called/ The Convention's Delegates

- What events encouraged leaders to call a Constitutional Convention?
- Who were some of the key delegates?
- What groups of Americans were not represented at the Convention?

In-Depth Resources: Unit 2
- Guided Reading, p. 47
- Literature Selection: from *Our Independence and the Constitution* by Dorothy Canfield Fisher, pp. 55–57

2 Creating the Constitution

TERMS & NAMES

Constitutional Convention
James Madison
Virginia Plan
New Jersey Plan
Great Compromise
Three-Fifths Compromise

MAIN IDEA	WHY IT MATTERS NOW
The states sent delegates to a convention to solve the problems of the Articles of Confederation.	The Constitutional Convention formed the plan of government that the United States still has today.

ONE AMERICAN'S STORY

On the afternoon of May 15, 1787, Edmund Randolph, the young governor of Virginia, arrived in Philadelphia for the Constitutional Convention. The young nation faced violence and lawlessness, as Shays's Rebellion had shown. And now delegates from throughout the states were coming to Philadelphia to discuss reforming the government.

Randolph knew the serious task he and the other delegates were about to undertake. Early in the convention, Randolph rose to speak. He looked squarely at the delegates and reminded them of their grave responsibility.

A VOICE FROM THE PAST

Let us not be afraid to view with a steady eye the [dangers] with which we are surrounded. . . . Are we not on the eve of [a civil] war, which is only to be prevented by the hopes from this convention?

Edmund Randolph, quoted in *Edmund Randolph: A Biography*

Edmund Randolph (left) and the other delegates gathered in the Pennsylvania State House (above) to discuss creating a new government for the United States.

Over the next four months, the delegates debated how best to keep the United States from falling apart. In this section, you will read about the Convention of 1787 and the creation of the U.S. Constitution.

1 A Constitutional Convention Is Called

In 1786, a series of events began that would eventually lead to a new form of government for the United States. In September of that year, delegates from five states met in Annapolis, Maryland, to discuss ways to promote trade among their states. At the time, most states placed high taxes on goods from other states. The delegates believed that creating national trade laws would help the economies of all the states.

Making such changes required amending the Articles of Confederation, because the national government had been granted no power to regulate trade among the states. The Annapolis delegates, led by Alexander Hamilton of New York, called for the states to send representatives to

RECOMMENDED RESOURCES

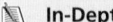

In-Depth Resources: Unit 2
- Guided Reading, p. 47
- Building Vocabulary, p. 49
- Primary Source, p. 54
- Literature Selection, pp. 55–57

Reading Study Guide (Spanish and English), pp. 71–72

America's History Makers
- James Madison, pp. 33–34

Formal Assessment
- Section Quiz, p. 136

Citizenship Today, p. 68

Integrated Assessment
- Rubrics, 5.3, 1.2

Access for Students Acquiring English/ESL
- Guided Reading, p. 48

INTEGRATED TECHNOLOGY

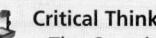

Critical Thinking Trans. CT23
- The Constitutional Convention

Humanities Transparency HT15
- George Washington at the Constitutional Convention

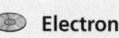

Electronic Teacher Tools

classzone.com

TEST-TAKING RESOURCES

Strategies for Test Preparation

Test Practice Transparencies, TT29

Online Test Practice

Philadelphia the following May to discuss such changes.

At first, many Americans doubted that the national government needed strengthening. But news of Shays's Rebellion in late 1786 and early 1787 quickly changed many people's minds. Fearing that rebellion might spread, 12 states sent delegates to the meeting in Philadelphia in the summer of 1787. Only Rhode Island refused to participate.

Background
Rhode Island did not send delegates because it feared that a strong national government would force people to repay the war debts on difficult terms.

The Convention's Delegates

The 55 delegates to the **Constitutional Convention**, as the Philadelphia meeting became known, were a very impressive group. About half were lawyers. Others were planters, merchants, and doctors. Three-fourths of them had been representatives in the Continental Congress. Many had been members of their state legislatures and had helped write their state constitutions. Along with other leaders of the time, these delegates are called the Founders, or Founding Fathers, of the United States.

America's most famous men were at the Constitutional Convention. George Washington, the hero of the Revolution, came out of retirement for the meeting. Benjamin Franklin, the famous scientist and statesman, lent his wit and wisdom to the convention. One of the ablest delegates was **James Madison.** Madison had read more than a hundred books on government in preparation for the meeting. When Thomas Jefferson, serving as ambassador to France, read the list of delegates, he wrote, "It is really an assembly of demigods."

***Reading*History**
A. Evaluating How well do the characteristics of the Founders serve as models of civic virtue?
A. Possible Response They provide an excellent model of civic virtue because they were educated, well-informed, and actively participated in government.

America's HERITAGE

INDEPENDENCE HALL

The Pennsylvania State House, where the Constitutional Convention took place, is now called Independence Hall. It is protected as part of a national park in Philadelphia.

The State House itself was the site where George Washington received his commission to lead the Continental Army and where the Declaration of Independence was signed. The Liberty Bell is nearby. Many visitors come to Philadelphia to stand in the building where much of America's early history as a nation was made.

Not everyone was at the Constitutional Convention. Thomas Jefferson and John Adams were overseas at their diplomatic posts. But they wrote home to encourage the delegates. Others had a less positive outlook on the convention. For example, Patrick Henry, who had been elected as a delegate from Virginia, refused to attend. He said he "smelled a rat in Philadelphia, tending toward monarchy."

Also, the convention did not reflect the diverse U.S. population of the 1780s. There were no Native Americans, African Americans, or women among the delegates. The nation's early leaders did not consider these groups of people to be citizens and did not invite any of them to attend. However, the framework of government the Founders established is the very one that would eventually provide full rights and responsibilities to all Americans.

2 The Delegates Assemble

Most of the delegates arrived at the Constitutional Convention without a clear idea of what to expect. Some thought they would only draft

America's HERITAGE

Independence Hall
Independence Hall is considered a world cultural treasure. It is a World Heritage site, indicating that it has been judged to have "outstanding universal value" by an international group administered by UNESCO. World Heritage sites include the Acropolis in Greece, Stonehenge in England, and the Taj Mahal in India. There are a total of 22 World Heritage sites in the United States.

MORE ABOUT . . .

Delegates to the Constitution
Most of the delegates to the Constitutional Convention owned property and were men of means, and most had been born in America. They represented a number of occupations, including doctors, merchants, and generals, and 35 were lawyers or had legal training. More than half of the delegates had attended college. The average age of the delegates was 44. Benjamin Franklin was the oldest delegate, at 81 years. The youngest member of the Convention was 26.

INSTRUCT: OBJECTIVE 2

The Delegates Assemble/ The Convention Begins

- What challenge faced the delegates at the Convention?
- Why did the delegates select George Washington as president of the Convention?
- Why did the delegates vote to make discussions at the Convention secret?

Humanities Transparency HT15
- George Washington at the Constitutional Convention

Critical Thinking Trans. CT23
- Cause and Effect: The Constitutional Convention

ACTIVITY OPTIONS

MULTIPLE LEARNING STYLES: INTERPERSONAL — BLOCK SCHEDULING

CONVENTION CROSSWORD

Class Time 30–45 minutes

Task Creating a crossword puzzle

Purpose To help students work together to identify important people discussed in this section

Supplies Needed
- Textbook
- Paper
- Sample crossword puzzle

Activity Have students work in pairs to create a crossword puzzle using the names of people mentioned in this section. Show students a sample crossword puzzle if necessary. Tell partners to list the names of people discussed in the chapter and divide the list in half. Each partner should write clues for half the list. Then the partners should work together to mold their clues into the "Across" and "Down" clues of a good puzzle. Allow pairs to exchange puzzles with one another.

AMERICA'S HISTORY MAKERS

James Madison

Madison himself wrote to an admirer that he could not take credit as "Father of the Constitution." Modestly, Madison said that the Constitution "ought to be regarded as the work of many heads and hands." Although Edmund Randolph presented the Virginia Plan, James Madison had worked it out before the Convention began.

Answer: He kept a record of and was a valuable participant in the proceedings.

America's History Makers
- James Madison, pp. 33–34

MORE ABOUT . . .

Private Sessions

Although today most congressional hearings are open to the public, Congress does have the right to hold sessions in private. One reason for a private session is a threat to national security. At other times, members of Congress, like their predecessors at the Constitutional Convention, hope to reduce political pressure by debating highly controversial issues in private.

INSTRUCT: OBJECTIVE 3

The Virginia Plan/The Great Compromise

- How did the Virginia Plan and New Jersey Plan differ?
- Why did the issue of representation in Congress divide the large states from the smaller states?
- How did the Great Compromise satisfy the concerns of the large and the smaller states?

Citizenship Today, p. 72

AMERICA'S HISTORY MAKERS

JAMES MADISON
1751–1836

James Madison was a short, soft-spoken man, but he may have made the greatest contribution of any of the Founders at the Constitutional Convention. He took thorough notes of the convention's proceedings. His notes are the most detailed picture we have of the debates and drama of the convention.

But Madison did not just observe the convention. He was perhaps the most important participant. One of the other delegates called him "the best informed Man of any point in debate." Madison was so important that he earned the title "Father of the Constitution."

How did Madison contribute to the Constitutional Convention?

amendments to the Articles of Confederation. Others thought they would design an entirely new plan for the government. But they all agreed that the government should protect people's rights.

Back in 1776, many Americans thought that government was the main threat to people's rights. But by 1787, many realized that the people often came into conflict and needed a government that could maintain order. As a result, the government had to be strong enough to protect people's rights but not too strong to be controlled. Madison later wrote about this problem.

A VOICE FROM THE PAST

If men were angels, no government would be necessary. If angels were to govern men, neither external nor internal controls on government would be necessary. In framing a government which is to be administered by men over men, the great difficulty lies in this: you must first enable the government to control the governed; and in the next place oblige it [the government] to control itself.

James Madison, ***The Federalist*** **"Number 51"**

This was the challenge that faced the delegates: how to set up a strong but limited federal government. By May 25, 1787, at least two delegates from each of seven states had arrived in Philadelphia. With 29 delegates in attendance, the convention was officially under way.

The Convention Begins

The first order of business was to elect a president for the convention. Robert Morris of Pennsylvania nominated George Washington. No American was more respected or admired than Washington. Every delegate voted for him. Washington's quiet and dignified leadership set a solemn and serious tone for the convention.

At their next meeting, the delegates decided on the rules for the convention. They wanted to be able to consider all ideas and to be able to change sides in any debate. They did not want to be pressured by the politics of the day. For these reasons, they decided that their discussions would remain secret. To ensure privacy, the windows in their meeting room were kept shut even though it was summer. Guards were posted outside the door. Whenever the door was opened, the delegates stopped talking. With the secrecy rule approved, they got down to business.

3 The Virginia Plan

On May 29, the delegates began the real work of designing a new national government. Presiding over the convention, George Washington

B. Possible Responses The problem is in framing a government that can control itself as well as the governed.

Reading **History**
B. Using Primary Sources According to Madison, what is the central problem in framing a government?

C. Possible Responses Some students might agree because the delegates might not have felt free to have an honest debate without secrecy. Others might disagree because they believe people should have had the right to know what the delegates were doing.

Reading **History**
C. Making Decisions Do you agree with the Founders' decision to keep the convention secret? Why or why not?

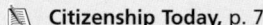

ACTIVITY OPTIONS

INDIVIDUAL NEEDS

STUDENTS ACQUIRING ENGLISH/ESL

Understanding Key Concepts Write the word *compromise* on the board and define it as "an agreement reached by bargaining, with both sides giving up some part of their demands." Discuss examples of compromises reached by students with their friends or family members. Ask students to use a Venn diagram to illustrate one compromise. Then point out *The Great Compromise* chart on page 216. Discuss the terms of each plan agreed upon in the Constitutional Convention. Ask students to tell why they think the delegates at the Convention considered the compromise fair.

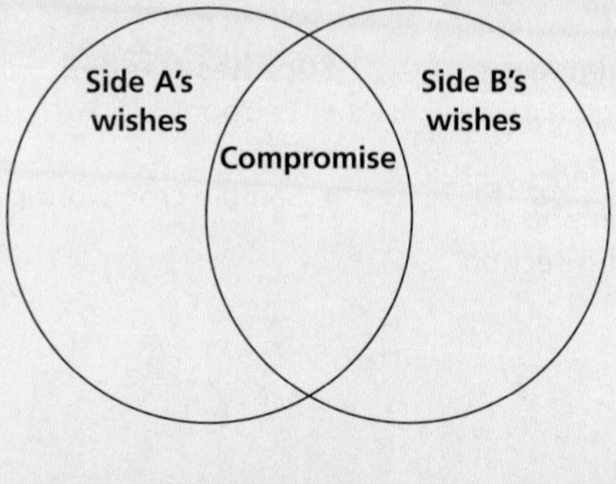

The delegates at the Constitutional Convention debated the Constitution intensely.

recognized Edmund Randolph as the first speaker. Randolph offered a plan for a whole new government. The plan became known as the **Virginia Plan.** Madison, Randolph, and the other Virginia delegates had drawn up the plan while they waited for the convention to open.

The Virginia Plan proposed a government that would have three branches. The first branch of government was the legislature, which made the laws. The second branch was the executive, which enforced the laws. The third branch was the judiciary, which interpreted the laws.

"If men were angels, no government would be necessary."
James Madison

The Virginia Plan proposed a legislature with two houses. In both houses, the number of representatives from each state would be based on the state's population or its wealth. The legislature would have the power to levy taxes, regulate commerce, and make laws "in all cases where the separate states are incompetent [unable]."

*Reading***History**
D. Summarizing What was the Virginia Plan?
D. Answer It was the plan for the legislature offered by the Virginia delegates to the convention. It proposed a legislature with two houses with representation based on population or wealth.

The Virginia Plan led to weeks of debate. Because they had larger populations, larger states supported the plan. It would give them greater representation in the legislature. The smaller states opposed this plan. They worried that the larger states would end up ruling the others. Delaware delegate John Dickinson voiced the concerns of the small states.

A VOICE FROM THE PAST

Some of the members from the small states wish for two branches in the general legislature and are friends to a good [strong] national government; but we would sooner submit [give in] to a foreign power than submit to be deprived, in both branches of the legislature, of an equal suffrage [vote], and thereby be thrown under the domination of the larger states.

John Dickinson, quoted in *Mr. Madison's Constitution*

The Great Compromise

In response to the Virginia Plan, New Jersey delegate William Paterson presented an alternative on June 15. The **New Jersey Plan** called for a legislature with only one house. In it, each state would have one vote. In providing equal representation to each state, the New Jersey Plan was similar to the Articles of Confederation.

Even though the New Jersey Plan gave the legislature the power to regulate trade and to raise money by taxing foreign goods, it did not offer the broad powers proposed by the Virginia Plan. The delegates

CRITICAL THINKING ACTIVITY

Analyzing Points of View After students read the material for Objective 3, have them draw a graphic like the one below. Then have the students fill in the views of large and small states.

	Large States	Small States
Legislative Houses		
Representation in Legislature		
Legislative Powers		

Class Time 25 minutes

MORE ABOUT . . .

Large States and Small States

The most populous states represented at the Constitutional Convention were Virginia, Pennsylvania, North Carolina, and Massachusetts. South Carolina and Georgia tended to side with the large states because their own populations were growing at a rapid pace. The small states were Connecticut, New Jersey, Delaware, and Maryland. New York was somewhere in the middle and tended to side with the smaller states. New Hampshire's delegation arrived too late to take part in debate over the most important issues. Rhode Island refused to participate at all.

In-Depth Resources: Unit 2
- Primary Source: from *Debates on the Adoption of the Federal Constitution,* p. 54

ACTIVITY OPTIONS

INTERDISCIPLINARY LINK: HUMANITIES

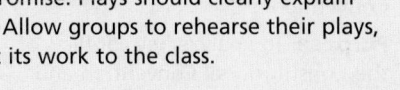

BLOCK SCHEDULING

GREAT COMPROMISE PLAY

Class Time One class period to prepare; one class period to present

Task Producing a short play about the Great Compromise

Purpose To demonstrate knowledge of the Virginia Plan, the New Jersey Plan, and the Great Compromise by producing a short drama summarizing the arguments on all sides

Supplies Needed
- Textbook
- Reference books on the Constitutional Convention

Activity Have groups of students write and produce short plays about the debate in the Constitutional Convention over representation in Congress. Each group should do research on the Convention and assign one or more actors to represent actual delegates who supported the Virginia Plan, the New Jersey Plan, and the Great Compromise. Plays should clearly explain the reasons for supporting each plan. Allow groups to rehearse their plays, and then allow each group to present its work to the class.

HISTORY FROM VISUALS

Interpreting the Chart Point out that in a *compromise* each side gives up some things so that both sides can agree. Ask: What did each side give up in the Great Compromise? **Answer** Supporters of the Virginia Plan conceded that representation in one house of Congress would be equal for all states; supporters of the New Jersey Plan conceded their demand for a one-house legislature and their demand that each state would have equal representation in Congress by allowing representation based on population in one house.

Extension Ask students to draw a chart or sketch showing what representation in Congress today would be under the Virginia Plan or the New Jersey Plan.

MORE ABOUT . . .

Slavery and the Constitution

You might wish to point out to students that some scholars argue that most delegates—from Southern as well as Northern states—believed slavery would eventually fade away. The debate, however, occurred before cotton production and its extensive labor needs became king in the South.

INSTRUCT: OBJECTIVE 4

Slavery and the Constitution/ Regulating Trade

- How did the states resolve the debate over representation for enslaved Americans?
- How did the states compromise over the issue of slave trade?
- What did Southern states give up in debates over trade issues?

The Great Compromise

VIRGINIA PLAN

- The legislative branch would have two houses.
- Both houses in the legislature would assign representatives according to state population or wealth.

NEW JERSEY PLAN

- The legislature would have one house.
- Each state would have one vote in the legislature.

THE GREAT COMPROMISE

- The Senate would give each state equal representation.

The legislature would have two houses.

- The House of Representatives would have representation according to state population.

SKILLBUILDER Interpreting Charts

1. *Which plan appealed more to the small states?*
2. *Did the Great Compromise include more of what the large states wanted or more of what the small states wanted?*

Skillbuilder Answers
1. the New Jersey Plan
2. **Possible Response** It included more of what the large states wanted because there were two houses in the legislature, one of which had representation by population.

voted on these two plans on June 19. The Virginia Plan won and became the framework for drafting the Constitution.

During the rest of June, the delegates argued over representation in the legislature. Emotions ran high as the delegates struggled for a solution. In desperation, the delegates selected a committee to work out a compromise in early July. The committee offered the **Great Compromise.** (Some people also refer to it as the Connecticut Compromise.)

Background Roger Sherman of Connecticut is widely credited with proposing the Great Compromise.

To satisfy the smaller states, each state would have an equal number of votes in the Senate. To satisfy the larger states, the committee set representation in the House of Representatives according to state populations. More than a week of arguing followed the introduction of the plan, but on July 16, 1787, the convention passed it.

4 Slavery and the Constitution

Because representation in the House of Representatives would be based on the population of each state, the delegates had to decide who would be counted in that population. The Southern states had many more slaves than the Northern states. Southerners wanted the slaves to be counted as part of the general population for representation but not for taxation. Northerners argued that slaves were not citizens and should not be counted for representation but should be counted for taxation.

On this issue, the delegates reached another compromise, known as the **Three-Fifths Compromise.** Under this compromise, three-fifths of the slave population would be counted when setting direct taxes on the states. This three-fifths ratio also would be used to determine representation in the legislature.

The delegates had another heated debate about the slave trade. Slavery had already been outlawed in several Northern states. All of the Northern states and several of the Southern states had banned the

ACTIVITY OPTIONS

MULTIPLE LEARNING STYLES: SPATIAL — BLOCK SCHEDULING

MUSEUM EXHIBIT

Class Time One class period

Task Planning a museum exhibit that summarizes important compromises of the Constitutional Convention

Purpose To analyze key conflicts of the Constitutional Convention and to illustrate how they were resolved by compromise

Supplies Needed
- Art supplies (optional)
- Video camera (optional)

Activity Tell students to plan a museum exhibit that illustrates and explains one major conflict of the Constitutional Convention and its resolution through compromise. Students may choose from different media for their exhibit: a poster, a video presentation, or manipulatives. You may want students to continue working on the display during other class periods and display completed projects.

Reading **History**

E. Forming and Supporting Opinions Did the delegates do the right thing in agreeing to the Three-Fifths Compromise? Explain.

E. Possible Responses Some might say no, because the Founders should have abolished slavery. Others might say yes, because otherwise the Southern states might not have ratified the Constitution.

importation of slaves. Many Northerners wanted to see this ban extended to the rest of the nation. But Southern slaveholders strongly disagreed. The delegates from South Carolina and Georgia stated that they would never accept any plan "unless their right to import slaves be untouched." Again, the delegates settled on a compromise. On August 29, they agreed that Congress could not ban the slave trade until 1808.

Regulating Trade

Aside from delaying any ban on the slave trade, the Constitution placed few limits on Congress's power "to regulate commerce with foreign nations, and among the several states, and with the Indian tribes." Most delegates were glad that Congress would regulate—and even promote—commerce. After all, commercial problems were the main cause of the Annapolis Convention in 1786. Southerners, however, succeeded in banning Congress from taxing exports because Southern economies depended on exports. The commerce clause also showed the shadowy status that Native Americans had under the Constitution. They were neither foreign nations nor part of the separate states.

The Constitutional Convention continued to meet into September. On Saturday, September 15, 1787, the delegates voted their support for the Constitution in its final form. On Sunday, it was written out on four sheets of thick parchment. On Monday, all but three delegates signed the Constitution. It was then sent, with a letter signed by George Washington, to the Confederation Congress, which sent it to the states for ratification, or approval. In the next section, you will read about the debate over ratification.

Now and then

PRESERVING THE CONSTITUTION

The National Archives is responsible for preserving the 200-year-old sheets of parchment on which the original Constitution was first written.

The Archives stores the document in an airtight glass case enclosed in a 55-ton vault of steel and concrete. Every few years, scientists examine the pages with the latest technology. For the last examination in 1995, they used fiber-optic light sources and computer-guided electronic cameras designed for space exploration.

Section 2 Assessment

1. Terms & Names

Explain the significance of:
- Constitutional Convention
- James Madison
- Virginia Plan
- New Jersey Plan
- Great Compromise
- Three-Fifths Compromise

2. Taking Notes

Use a chart like the one below to take notes on the contributions made by the leading delegates at the Constitutional Convention.

Delegate	Contribution

3. Main Ideas

a. What was the relationship between the Annapolis Convention and the Constitutional Convention?

b. What is the significance of the date 1787?

c. How did the Constitutional Convention reach a compromise on the issue of slavery?

4. Critical Thinking

Analyzing Points of View How did the delegates at the convention differ on the issue of representation in the new government?

THINK ABOUT
- the large states and the small states
- the Virginia Plan
- the New Jersey Plan
- the Great Compromise

ACTIVITY OPTIONS

TECHNOLOGY / ART Think about the Three-Fifths Compromise. Make an **audio recording** of a speech or draw a **political cartoon** that expresses your views on the issue.

Now and then

Preserving the Constitution

Congress established the National Archives in 1934 as the repository for all federal papers and records of permanent value. However, the National Archives hold much more, from patent drawings to maps, from letters to military service records. The archives hold more than 325 billion documents, more than 5 million photographs, and more than 81 million feet of motion picture film.

CRITICAL THINKING ACTIVITY

Forming and Supporting Opinions To help students understand the dilemmas that faced the delegates, ask students to discuss whether they believe reaching agreement on the Constitution was worth the compromises made on slavery. Point out that without the compromises, the nation may have broken apart. On the other hand, as the students will learn later, deep divisions over slavery later pushed the nation into civil war.

Class Time 20 minutes

ASSESS & RETEACH

Setting the Stage Have students complete the second, third, and fourth rows on the graphic organizer on page 204.

Formal Assessment
- Section Quiz, p. 136

RETEACHING ACTIVITY

Give each student five index cards. Tell students to write one of five different key terms or names from the section (including those listed on page 228) on each of the cards. Then have students exchange cards and write the definitions or significance of each term or name on the back of the card. Students may then use their flash cards to quiz each other about the section.

In-Depth Resources: Unit 2
- Reteaching Activity, p. 59

Section 2 Assessment

1. Terms & Names

Constitutional Convention, p. 213
James Madison, p. 213
Virginia Plan, p. 215
New Jersey Plan, p. 215
Great Compromise, p. 216
Three-Fifths Compromise, p. 216

2. Taking Notes

James Madison—Took notes on the Convention; earned the nickname "Father of the Constitution"
George Washington—Presided over the Convention
Edmund Randolph—Offered the Virginia Plan
William Paterson—Offered the New Jersey Plan

3. Main Ideas

a. No conclusion could be drawn at Annapolis, so the delegates agreed to meet the next year; that meeting created the new Constitution.
b. Delegates voted to support the Constitution. **c.** It did not outlaw slavery, and decided no law could be made until 1808.

4. Critical Thinking

Large states wanted representation by population; small states wanted each state to have one vote.

ACTIVITY OPTIONS

Integrated Assessment
- Rubrics audio recordings, 5.3
- Rubrics for a political cartoon, 1.2

SECTION OBJECTIVES

1. To identify positions of the Federalists and Antifederalists
2. To explain the role of *The Federalist* papers in the ratification process
3. To describe the battle for ratification
4. To summarize efforts to pass and ratify the Bill of Rights

SKILLBUILDER

Interpreting Charts, p. 219

CRITICAL THINKING

Making Inferences, p. 219
Drawing Conclusions, p. 220
Recognizing Propaganda, p. 221

Why It Matters Now
- The Living Constitution, pp. 15–16

FOCUS & MOTIVATE

5-MINUTE WARM-UP

Interpreting Pictures These questions focus on the debate over ratification of the Constitution.

1. Look at the quotation from Hamilton and the illustration on pages 219 and 220. Did Hamilton support or oppose the Constitution?
2. Why does Hamilton think adoption is a good option?

Warm-Up Transparency WT8

INSTRUCT

INSTRUCT: OBJECTIVE 1
Federalists and Antifederalists

- What was the goal of the Federalists?
- Why did Antifederalists oppose the Constitution?
- How did Antifederalists work against ratification?

In-Depth Resources: Unit 2
- Guided Reading, p. 48

Humanities Transparency HT16
- Constitution, Page One—A Replica

3 Ratifying the Constitution

TERMS & NAMES
federalism
Federalists
Antifederalists
The Federalist papers
George Mason
Bill of Rights

MAIN IDEA	WHY IT MATTERS NOW
Americans across the nation debated whether the Constitution would produce the best government.	American liberties today are protected by the U.S. Constitution, including the Bill of Rights.

ONE AMERICAN'S STORY

For a week in early January 1788, a church in Hartford, Connecticut, was filled to capacity. Inside, 168 delegates were meeting to decide whether their state should ratify the U.S. Constitution. Samuel Huntington, Connecticut's governor, addressed the assembly.

A VOICE FROM THE PAST

This is a new event in the history of mankind. Heretofore, most governments have been formed by tyrants and imposed on mankind by force. Never before did a people, in time of peace and tranquillity, meet together by their representatives and, with calm deliberation, frame for themselves a system of government.

Samuel Huntington, quoted in *Original Meanings*

The governor supported the new Constitution and wanted to see it ratified. Not everyone agreed with him. In this section, you will learn about the debates that led to the ratification of the Constitution.

Samuel Huntington

1 Federalists and Antifederalists

By the time the convention in Connecticut opened, Americans had already been debating the new Constitution for months. The document had been printed in newspapers and handed out in pamphlets across the United States. The framers of the Constitution knew that the document would cause controversy. They immediately began to campaign for ratification, or approval, of the Constitution.

The framers suspected that people might be afraid the Constitution would take too much power away from the states. To address this fear, the framers explained that the Constitution was based on federalism. **Federalism** is a system of government in which power is shared between the central (or federal) government and the states. Linking themselves to the idea of federalism, the people who supported the Constitution took the name **Federalists.**

People who opposed the Constitution were called **Antifederalists.** They thought the Constitution took too much power away from the

RECOMMENDED RESOURCES

In-Depth Resources: Unit 2
- Guided Reading, p. 48
- Building Vocabulary, p. 49
- Skillbuilder Practice, p. 50
- Geo. Application, pp. 51–52
- Enrichment Activity, p. 61

Reading Study Guide (Spanish and English), pp. 73–74

Outline Map Activities, pp. 15–16

Why It Matters Now
- The Living Constitution, pp. 15–16

Formal Assessment
- Section Quiz, p. 137

Integrated Assessment
- Rubrics, 3.3, 4.5

Access for Students Acquiring English/ESL
- Guided Reading, p. 49
- Skillbuilder Practice, p. 50
- Geography Application, pp. 51–52

INTEGRATED TECHNOLOGY

Humanities Transparency HT16
- Constitution, Page One—A Replica

TEST-TAKING RESOURCES

Strategies for Test Preparation

Test Practice Transparencies, TT30

Online Test Practice

states and did not guarantee rights for the people. Some were afraid that a strong president might be declared king. Others thought the Senate might turn into a powerful aristocracy. In either case, the liberties won at great cost during the Revolution might be lost.

Vocabulary
aristocracy: a group or class considered superior to others

Antifederalists published their views about the Constitution in newspapers and pamphlets. They used logical arguments to convince people to oppose the Constitution. But they also tried to stir people's emotions by charging that it would destroy American liberties. As one Antifederalist wrote, "After so recent a triumph over British despots [oppressive rulers], . . . it is truly astonishing that a set of men among ourselves should have had the effrontery [nerve] to attempt the destruction of our liberties."

2 *The Federalist* Papers

The Federalists did not sit still while the Antifederalists attacked the Constitution. They wrote essays to answer the Antifederalists' attacks. The best known of the Federalist essays are ***The Federalist* papers.** These essays first appeared as letters in New York newspapers. They were later published together in a book called *The Federalist.*

Three well-known politicians wrote *The Federalist* papers—James Madison, Alexander Hamilton, and John Jay, the secretary of foreign affairs for the Confederation Congress. Like the Antifederalists, the Federalists appealed to reason and emotion. In *The Federalist* papers, Hamilton described why people should support ratification.

A. Possible Response He believes failure to ratify the Constitution will put Americans' liberty, dignity, and happiness at risk.

***Reading*History**
A. Making Inferences What does Hamilton think will happen if the Constitution is not ratified?

A VOICE FROM THE PAST

Yes, my countrymen, . . . I am clearly of opinion it is in your interest to adopt it [the Constitution]. I am convinced that this is the safest course for your liberty, your dignity, and your happiness.

Alexander Hamilton, *The Federalist* "Number 1"

Federalists and Antifederalists

FEDERALISTS	ANTIFEDERALISTS
• Supported removing some powers from the states and giving more powers to the national government	• Wanted important political powers to remain with the states
• Favored dividing powers among different branches of government	• Wanted the legislative branch to have more power than the executive
• Proposed a single person to lead the executive branch	• Feared that a strong executive might become a king or tyrant
	• Believed a bill of rights needed to be added to the Constitution to protect people's rights

John Jay

George Mason

SKILLBUILDER **Interpreting Charts**
1. *Which group wanted a stronger central government?*
2. *If you had been alive in 1787, would you have been a Federalist or an Antifederalist?*

Skillbuilder Answers
1. Federalists
2. Possible Responses Some students may say Federalist because they favor the Constitution. Others may say Antifederalist because they favor individual rights.

MORE ABOUT . . .

Antifederalists
The author of the quotation was Samuel Bryan, who often wrote under the name "Centinel" when he wanted to make controversial statements. Mercy Otis Warren was the only prominent woman to speak out against the Constitution. She believed that the Federalists were destroying the American liberties won by the Revolution. Both Bryan and Warren subscribed to the Antifederalist slogan, Grant Power Cautiously.

INSTRUCT: OBJECTIVE 2

***The Federalist* Papers**

- What were *The Federalist* papers?
- Who wrote *The Federalist* papers?
- In which states was there strong opposition to the Constitution?

HISTORY FROM VISUALS

Interpreting the Chart Divide the class into two groups. Tell one group to read aloud the bulleted points summarizing the positions of the Federalists. Alternate with the other group reading aloud the positions of the Antifederalists. Ask students to identify a position of the Antifederalists that was likely to be accepted by Federalists. **Answer** adding a Bill of Rights

Extension Have students write a letter to the editor expressing their opinion of the Constitution from the point of view of a strong Federalist or a strong Antifederalist.

ACTIVITY OPTIONS

SKILLBUILDER LESSON: ANALYZING POINTS OF VIEW

BLOCK SCHEDULING

Explaining the Skill Analyzing points of view means closely studying the opinions people have on a particular issue. It also means examining the methods and arguments people use to support their particular points of view.

Applying the Skill Have students consider the points of view of the Federalists and the Antifederalists. Remind them that the main issue dividing the two sides was ratification of the Constitution. Ask the following questions:

1. What were four criticisms raised by Antifederalists against the Constitution? *(It took too much power from the states; didn't guarantee citizens' rights; gave too much power to the executive branch and the chief executive.)*
2. How did Federalists address fears about the Constitution? *(They pointed out that power is shared between the central government and the states. They also suggested that a bill of rights could be added later.)*
3. What kinds of arguments did both sides use in the debate? *(They appealed to logic, or reason, as well as to emotions.)*

In-Depth Resources: Unit 2
- Skillbuilder Practice, p. 50

HISTORY through ART

Interpreting the Illustration The debate over ratification of the Constitution gripped the entire nation. Both the Federalists and the Antifederalists poured out newspaper articles and pamphlets stating the arguments for their side and took the streets with parades. Ask students what media politicians use today to gain support for their positions.

Possible Response: It implies that the Constitution was very important to people because thousands attended the parade.

HISTORY *through* ART

Supporters of the Constitution turned out in parades like this one in New York in 1788. The "Ship of State" float has Alexander Hamilton's name on it to celebrate his role in creating the Constitution.

What does the picture indicate about the importance of the Constitution in people's lives?

The Federalists had an important advantage over the Antifederalists. Most of the newspapers supported the Constitution, giving the Federalists more publicity than the Antifederalists. Even so, there was strong opposition to ratification in Massachusetts, North Carolina, Rhode Island, New York, and Virginia. If some of these states failed to ratify the Constitution, the United States might not survive.

INSTRUCT: OBJECTIVE 3

The Battle for Ratification

- When did the first nine states ratify the Constitution?
- What slowed ratification in Virginia and New York?
- What helped to win ratification in New York?

In-Depth Resources: Unit 2
- Geography Application: Ratifying the Constitution, pp. 51–52

3 The Battle for Ratification

The first four state conventions to ratify the Constitution were held in December 1787. It was a good month for the Federalists. Delaware, New Jersey, and Pennsylvania voted for ratification. In January 1788, Georgia and Connecticut ratified the Constitution. Massachusetts joined these states in early February.

By late June, nine states had voted to ratify the Constitution. That meant that the document was now officially ratified. But New York and Virginia had not yet cast their votes. There were many powerful Antifederalists in both of those states. Without Virginia, the new government would lack the support of the largest state. Without New York, the nation would be separated into two parts geographically.

B. Answer Several states refused to ratify the Constitution unless a bill of rights was added.

Reading **History**

B. Drawing Conclusions How did the lack of a bill of rights endanger the Constitution?

Virginia's convention opened the first week in June. The patriot Patrick Henry fought against ratification. **George Mason,** perhaps the most influential Virginian aside from Washington, also was opposed to it. Mason had been a delegate to the Constitutional Convention in Philadelphia, but he had refused to sign the final document. Both Henry and Mason would not consider voting for the Constitution until a bill of rights was added. A bill of rights is a set of rules that defines people's rights.

James Madison was also at Virginia's convention. He suggested that Virginia follow Massachusetts's lead and ratify the Constitution, and he recommended the addition of a bill of rights. With the addition of a bill of rights likely, Virginia ratified the Constitution at the end of June.

ACTIVITY OPTIONS

INDIVIDUAL NEEDS: GIFTED AND TALENTED

BILL OF RIGHTS

Class Time One class period

Task Reading and interpreting the Bill of Rights

Purpose To familiarize students with the Bill of Rights; to analyze the amendments from a historical perspective and to consider which are most applicable today

Supplies Needed
- Textbook

Activity Have students read the Bill of Rights on pages 266–268. Remind students that the Bill of Rights was intended to preserve and protect the rights of individuals. Then ask them to discuss why they think each specific amendment was included. You might prompt discussion with the following questions:
- Which amendment would you have proposed if you were a delegate at the Convention?
- Which amendment do you think is most important today?
- Which amendment, if any, do you think is not necessary today?

In-Depth Resources: Unit 2
- Enrichment Activity, p. 61

The news of Virginia's vote arrived while the New York convention was in debate. The Antifederalists had outnumbered the Federalists when the convention had begun. But with the news of Virginia's ratification, New Yorkers decided to join the Union. New York also called for a bill of rights.

It was another year before North Carolina ratified the Constitution. In 1790, Rhode Island became the last state to ratify it. By then, the new Congress had already written a bill of rights and submitted it to the states for approval.

4 The Bill of Rights

Background
The seven states that asked for a bill of rights were Massachusetts, South Carolina, New Hampshire, Virginia, New York, North Carolina, and Rhode Island.

At the same time that seven of the states ratified the Constitution, they asked that it be amended to include a bill of rights. Supporters of a bill of rights hoped that it would set forth the rights of all Americans. They believed it was needed to protect people against the power of the national government.

Madison, who was elected to the new Congress in the winter of 1789, took up the cause. He proposed a set of changes to the Constitution. Congress edited Madison's list and proposed placing the amendments at the end of the Constitution in a separate section.

The amendments went to the states for ratification. As with the Constitution, three-quarters of the states had to ratify the amendments for them to take effect. With Virginia's vote in 1791, ten of the amendments were ratified and became law. These ten amendments to the U.S. Constitution became known as the **Bill of Rights.** (See the Constitution Handbook, pages 250–252.)

The passage of the Bill of Rights was one of the first acts of the new government. In the next chapter, you will read about other issues that faced the new government.

America's HERITAGE

RELIGIOUS FREEDOM

Freedom of religion was an important part of the First Amendment. Jefferson and Madison believed that government enforcement of religious laws was the source of much social conflict. They supported freedom of religion as a way to prevent such conflict.

Even before Madison wrote the Bill of Rights, he worked to ensure religious liberty in Virginia. In 1786, he helped pass the Virginia Statute for Religious Freedom, originally written by Jefferson in 1777.

Section 3 Assessment

1. Terms & Names

Explain the significance of:
- federalism
- Federalists
- Antifederalists
- *The Federalist* papers
- George Mason
- Bill of Rights

2. Taking Notes

Use a diagram like the one below to compare and contrast the Federalists and the Antifederalists.

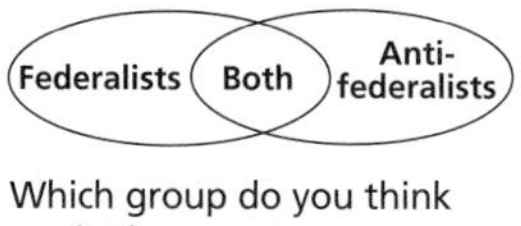

Which group do you think made the stronger argument about ratification? Why?

3. Main Ideas

a. What were Patrick Henry's and George Mason's views on ratification?

b. How did the Federalists and the Antifederalists try to convince people to take their sides in the debate over the Constitution?

c. What was the significance of the Bill of Rights?

4. Critical Thinking

Recognizing Propaganda
Reread the quotation by Hamilton on page 219. Is it an example of propaganda? Why or why not?

THINK ABOUT
- Hamilton's use of the word *countrymen*
- Hamilton's reference to liberty, dignity, and happiness

ACTIVITY OPTIONS

SPEECH
LANGUAGE ARTS

Review the major arguments for and against ratification of the Constitution. Hold a **press conference** or write a **news report** on the ratification debate.

INSTRUCT: OBJECTIVE 4
The Bill of Rights

- What was the purpose of the Bill of Rights?
- What role did James Madison play in adding the Bill of Rights to the Constitution?
- When did the Bill of Rights become part of the Constitution?

Outline Map Activities
- The Original 13 States, 1790, pp. 15–16

America's HERITAGE

Religious Freedom

During colonial times, the Anglican Church was the established religion of the colony. A portion of the taxes paid by the colonists went to support the church. After the Revolution, some Virginians wanted state tax money to support all recognized Christian churches. Madison and Jefferson opposed government support of any religion. They thought that religion was a matter of individual choice and that church and state should be separate.

ASSESS & RETEACH

Setting the Stage Have students create a problem-solution chart such as the one on page 220 for the problems faced by the Federalists in getting the Constitution ratified.

Formal Assessment
- Section Quiz, p. 137

Critical Thinking Transparency CT22
- Setting the Stage

RETEACHING ACTIVITY

Organize a "Meet the Press" discussion about the ratification of the Constitution. Ask for volunteers to represent the Federalists and the Antifederalists. Other class members act as reporters, asking questions about the debates.

In-Depth Resources: Unit 2
- Reteaching Activity, p. 60

Section 3 Assessment

1. Terms & Names

federalism, p. 218
Federalists, p. 218
Antifederalists, p. 218
***The Federalist* papers,** p. 219
George Mason, p. 220
Bill of Rights, p. 221

2. Taking Notes

Federalists: stronger national government; one person to head the executive branch. Both: different branches of the government; supported a bill of rights. Antifederalists: stronger state government; feared a strong executive

Responses will vary.

3. Main Ideas

a. Both men refused to support it until a bill of rights was added.
b. Both sides wrote pamphlets, gave speeches outlining their views, and appealed to reason and emotion.
c. It was key to getting enough support to ensure ratification of the Constitution.

4. Critical Thinking

yes, because his tone and words will stir the emotions of Americans

ACTIVITY OPTIONS

Integrated Assessment
- Rubrics for a press conference, 3.3
- Rubrics for a news report, 4.5

INTERACTIVE PRIMARY SOURCES

OBJECTIVE
Students will compare and evaluate the arguments of two prominent figures, James Madison and George Mason, in the debate over ratification of the Constitution.

Primary Source Explorer
- *The Federalist,* "Number 51"
- *Objections to the Constitution*

The Explorer will help students select and produce their own presentations.

Specific information about the document can be found in **A Closer Look.** To learn more about key people and events of the time, students should click on **Life in These Times. What Happened Next** will show the student the impact of the document and tie it to today.

FOCUS & MOTIVATE

Finding Main Ideas To help students understand the conflicting views of Madison and Mason, direct them to the "A Closer Look" callouts on each page. Read these callouts before the students read the documents themselves. The callouts will provide an overview of the main issues in the documents.

MORE ABOUT . . .

Madison's Opinions
Madison thought that a large republic had a second advantage over a small one. He argued that citizens of a large republic would elect qualified and capable leaders to office, not the poorly qualified and self-interested politicians who often won local elections. Madison believed that petty politicians would not have the broad appeal needed for election from a large constituency.

The Federalist "Number 51"

Setting the Stage James Madison wrote 29 essays in *The Federalist* papers to argue in favor of ratifying the Constitution. In *The Federalist* "Number 51," Madison explains how the government set up by the Constitution will protect the rights of the people by weakening the power of any interest, or group, to dominate the government. **See Primary Source Explorer**

A CLOSER LOOK

MINORITY RIGHTS

In the 1700s, people feared that democratic majorities could turn into mobs that would violate other people's rights. Madison had to explain how the Constitution would prevent this.

1. What two methods does Madison suggest a society can use to protect minority rights?

A CLOSER LOOK

REPUBLICS IN LARGE SOCIETIES

For centuries, people believed that only small societies could be republics. But Madison argues that large societies are more likely to remain republics.

2. Why does Madison believe that a large republic is likely to protect justice?

It is of great importance in a republic not only to guard the society against the oppression of its rulers, but to guard one part of the society against the injustice of the other part. Different interests necessarily exist in different classes of citizens. If a majority be united by a common interest, the rights of the minority will be insecure. There are but two methods of providing against this evil: the one by creating a will in the community independent of the majority—that is, of the society itself; the other, by **comprehending**[1] in the society so many separate descriptions of citizens as will render an unjust combination of a majority of the whole very improbable, if not **impracticable.**[2] . . .

Whilst[3] all authority in it will be derived from and dependent on the society, the society itself will be broken into so many parts, interests and classes of citizens, that the rights of individuals, or of the minority, will be in little danger from interested combinations of the majority. In a free government the security for civil rights must be the same as that for religious rights. It consists in the one case in the multiplicity of interests, and in the other in the **multiplicity of sects.**[4] . . .

In the extended republic of the United States, and among the great variety of interests, parties, and sects which it embraces, a **coalition**[5] of a majority of the whole society could seldom take place on any other principles than those of justice and the general good. . . .

It is no less certain than it is important . . . that the larger the society, provided it lie within a practicable sphere, the more duly capable it will be of self-government. And happily for the republican cause, the practicable sphere may be carried to a very great extent by a **judicious modification**[6] and mixture of the *federal principle.*

—*James Madison*

1. **comprehending:** understanding.
2. **impracticable:** not practical or realistic.
3. **whilst:** while.
4. **multiplicity of sects:** large number of groups.
5. **coalition:** alliance of groups.
6. **judicious modification:** careful change.

222

TEACHING STRATEGY

Comparing Guide students through the two documents by drawing two spider maps on the board, one for the Madison document and one for the Mason document. Label the central circle for the Madison document "Protections for the Rights of Citizens." Label the central circle for the Mason document "Worries About the Constitution." Then read the documents as a class. As you read, ask students to add topics and subtopics to the maps.

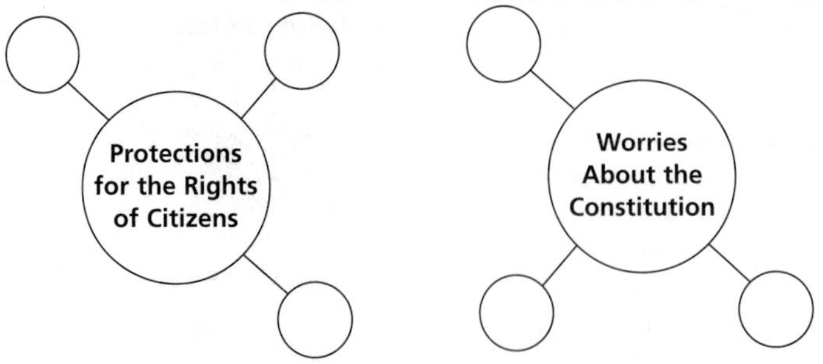

Objections to the Constitution

Setting the Stage George Mason was one of the leading Antifederalists. In "Objections to the Constitution of Government Formed by the Convention," he listed his reasons for opposing ratification. Above all, he feared that the Constitution created a government that would destroy democracy in the young nation. **See Primary Source Explorer**

There is no Declaration of Rights; and the Laws of the general Government being **paramount**[1] to the Laws and Constitutions of the several States, the Declaration of Rights in the separate States are no Security. Nor are the people secured even in the Enjoyment of the Benefits of the common-Law. . . .

In the House of Representatives, there is not the Substance, but the Shadow only of Representation; which can never produce proper Information in the Legislature, or inspire Confidence in the People; the Laws will therefore be generally made by Men little concern'd in, and **unacquainted**[2] with their Effects and Consequences.

The Senate have the Power of altering all Money-Bills, and of originating Appropriations of Money and the **Sallerys**[3] of the Officers of their own Appointment in **Conjunction**[4] with the President of the United States; altho' they are not the Representatives of the People, or **amenable**[5] to them. . . .

The President of the United States has the unrestrained Power of granting Pardon for Treason; which may be sometimes exercised to screen from Punishment those whom he had secretly **instigated**[6] to commit the Crime, and thereby prevent a Discovery of his own Guilt.

This Government will **commence**[7] in a moderate **Aristocracy;**[8] it is at present impossible to foresee whether it will, in [its] Operation, produce a **Monarchy,**[9] or a corrupt oppressive Aristocracy; it will most probably vibrate some Years between the two, and then terminate in the one or the other.

—*George Mason*

1. **paramount:** most important.
2. **unacquainted:** unfamiliar.
3. **sallerys:** salaries.
4. **conjunction:** joining.
5. **amenable:** agreeable.
6. **instigated:** caused.
7. **commence:** begin.
8. **aristocracy:** rule by a few, usually nobles.
9. **monarchy:** rule by one, usually a king.

A CLOSER LOOK

DECLARATION OF RIGHTS

At the time of the ratification debate, Americans across the nation complained that the Constitution did not include a bill of rights.

3. What arguments does Mason make about the lack of a Declaration of Rights?

A CLOSER LOOK

ABUSE OF POWER

Mason believed that presidents might abuse the power to grant pardons for treason in order to protect the guilty.

4. Can you think of any presidents who have granted pardons?

Interactive Primary Sources Assessment

1. Main Ideas

a. Why does Madison believe that a society broken into many parts will not endanger minority rights?

b. What does Mason argue might happen if the president had the power to pardon people?

c. For each writer, what is one example of a fact and one example of an opinion?

2. Critical Thinking

Drawing Conclusions Who do you think makes the stronger argument? Explain your reasons.

THINK ABOUT

- what you know about the history of the United States
- the evidence used by each writer

223

INSTRUCT

- Why was a Declaration of Rights important to Mason?
- Does Madison think that most people work for the common good or for their own interests? Do you agree with his view?
- Why did Madison believe that the government created under the Constitution would not be dominated by an oppressive majority?
- Why did Madison think that a large society could govern itself as a republic?

MORE ABOUT . . .

Mason and the Constitution

Although he himself owned slaves, Mason hated the institution of slavery and hoped that it would be abolished quickly. Mason objected strongly when the Constitutional Convention accepted the compromise that allowed continuation of the slave trade for 20 years.

Interactive Primary Sources Assessment

1. Main Ideas

a. because no group will be strong enough to oppress the others

b. The president could pardon people who had broken the law at his suggestion, hiding his own guilt.

c. All of Madison's statements are opinions. Mason's first sentence is a fact. His last paragraph is an opinion.

2. Critical Thinking

Some students might say Madison because his argument about multiplicity of sects is plausible. Others might say Mason because he discusses specific aspects of the Constitution.

A CLOSER LOOK

1. by creating a will in the community that is not dependent on the majority, and by creating so many different types of citizens to make it impossible for any to create a majority
2. Because there are so many sects, none will be able to oppress the others.
3. There will be no way to protect citizens' rights. The state declarations will lack the power to protect them against the federal government.
4. Some students may know that President Gerald Ford pardoned President Richard Nixon after Watergate.

TERMS & NAMES

1. **republic,** p. 206
2. **Articles of Confederation,** p. 206
3. **Northwest Ordinance,** p. 207
4. **Shays's Rebellion,** p. 209
5. **Constitutional Convention,** p. 213
6. **James Madison,** p. 213
7. **Great Compromise,** p. 216
8. **Federalists,** p. 218
9. **George Mason,** p. 220
10. **Bill of Rights,** p. 221

REVIEW QUESTIONS

Possible Responses

1. It is a road Daniel Boone and his men made. It led into Kentucky from the east.
2. the problems of winning independence and handling the Western territories
3. the power to wage war; make peace; sign treaties; issue money
4. It convinced many people that a new national government, with stronger powers, was needed.
5. Native Americans; African Americans; women
6. The new government should be a republic; it needed to protect people's rights.
7. the Great Compromise and the Three-Fifths Compromise
8. Federalism is a form of government in which power is divided between the central government and the states.
9. because they were large states in the geographic center of the nation
10. because otherwise a tyrannical government might abuse individual liberties

Chapter 8 ASSESSMENT

VISUAL SUMMARY

Confederation to Constitution

1777
Continental Congress passes the Articles of Confederation.

1777–1781
States debate ratification of the Articles of Confederation.

1781
Articles of Confederation go into effect.

1786
Annapolis Convention is held.

1786–1787
Shays's Rebellion occurs.

1787
Constitutional Convention is held in Philadelphia.

1788
U.S. Constitution is ratified.

1789
Government created by the new Constitution takes power.

1791
Bill of Rights is added to the Constitution.

TERMS & NAMES

Briefly explain the significance of each of the following.

1. republic
2. Articles of Confederation
3. Northwest Ordinance
4. Shays's Rebellion
5. Constitutional Convention
6. James Madison
7. Great Compromise
8. Federalists
9. George Mason
10. Bill of Rights

REVIEW QUESTIONS

The Confederation Era (pages 205–211)

1. What is the Wilderness Road, and where did it lead?
2. What problems did the Confederation Congress successfully address?
3. What powers did the government have under the Articles of Confederation?
4. How did Shays's Rebellion affect people's views on the Articles of Confederation?

Creating the Constitution (pages 212–217)

5. What groups of people were not represented at the Constitutional Convention?
6. What were some things the delegates agreed on at the convention?
7. What compromises did the delegates make during the convention?

Ratifying the Constitution (pages 218–223)

8. What is federalism?
9. Why were Virginia and New York important in the battle for ratification of the Constitution?
10. Why did some states think that it was necessary to add a bill of rights to the Constitution?

CRITICAL THINKING

1. USING YOUR NOTES

Problems	Solutions
Western lands	
Postwar depression	
Representation in the new government	
Slavery	

Using your completed chart, answer the questions below.

a. What were the major problems facing the nation during the Confederation Era?

b. How well did the nation solve these problems? Explain.

2. ANALYZING LEADERSHIP

Think about the leaders discussed in this chapter. Based on their actions, which leader do you think made the greatest contribution to the Constitutional Convention? Why?

3. THEME: DEMOCRATIC IDEALS

How do the Articles of Confederation and the Constitution each carry out democratic ideals?

4. APPLYING CITIZENSHIP SKILLS

Do you think the Founders were right to make the compromises they did in the Constitution on the issues of representation and slavery? What might have happened if they had not compromised?

5. RECOGNIZING EFFECTS

How might U.S. history be different if Virginia had refused to ratify the Constitution? If New York had refused? If both had refused?

Interact *with* History

How did your ideas about how you would form a government change after reading this chapter?

CRITICAL THINKING

Possible Responses

1. **USING YOUR NOTES a.** Answers will vary. **b.** All problems in the chart were solved with the exception of slavery.
2. **ANALYZING LEADERSHIP** Students may choose Daniel Boone, James Madison, Daniel Shays, George Mason, or John Jay. Be sure that they discuss contributions made and reasons behind their choice.
3. **THEME: DEMOCRATIC IDEALS** Both documents deal with the national government and worked toward the creation of a republic.
4. **APPLYING CITIZENSHIP SKILLS** Students should discuss the Virginia Plan, the New Jersey Plan, the Great Compromise, and the Three-Fifths Compromise, and how things would have been different without them.
5. **RECOGNIZING EFFECTS** Student responses should include the largeness of these states, their influence over the rest of the country, and their geographic importance. Answers will vary.

Interact *with* History. Students should include the idea of considering many different viewpoints and needs of citizens.

HISTORY SKILLS

1. INTERPRETING MAPS: Region

Study the map and then answer the questions.

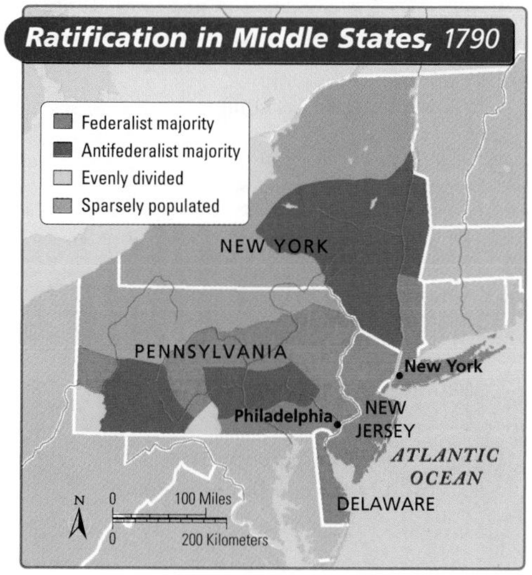

Source: *American Heritage Pictorial Atlas of United States History*

Basic Map Elements

a. Which states are identified on the map?
b. In which states did the Federalists have statewide majorities?

Interpreting the Map

c. Why do you think the two cities on the map were strong Federalist supporters?

2. INTERPRETING PRIMARY SOURCES

The following law was put into effect in Virginia in 1786. Read the law and answer the questions.

> *Be it enacted by the General Assembly,* That no man shall be compelled to frequent or support any religious worship, place, or ministry, whatsoever . . . but that all men shall be free to profess, and by argument maintain, their opinion in matters of religion, and that the same shall in no way diminish, enlarge, or affect their civil capacities.
>
> *The Statute of Virginia for Religious Freedom, 1786*

a. How would you summarize this law?
b. Which right in the Bill of Rights was based on this law?
c. Based on what you know about colonial history, how had American society changed between the early 1600s and the late 1700s?

ALTERNATIVE ASSESSMENT

1. INTERDISCIPLINARY ACTIVITY: Government

Making a Chart Do research to learn how the U.S. Constitution has been used as a model by other nations. Make a chart to summarize the information you find about one specific nation. Include the country, the date the country's constitution was ratified, and two ways in which that nation's constitution is similar to and different from the U.S. Constitution.

2. COOPERATIVE LEARNING ACTIVITY

Staging a Debate Stage a debate between a Federalist and an Antifederalist. Work in small groups to read some of the different arguments each side used. Look for discussions of one or more of the issues listed below. Pick one of the issues and stage a debate, using the strongest arguments from each side. Let the class determine who won the debate and why.

a. the representation of people in Congress
b. the strength of the president and Senate
c. the need for a bill of rights

3. PRIMARY SOURCE EXPLORER

Creating a Museum Exhibit The creation of the U.S. Constitution was one of the most important events in the nation's history. There is a great amount of information about the Constitution. Using the Primary Source Explorer CD-ROM and your local library, collect information on different topics relating to the Constitution.

Create a museum exhibit about the Constitution using the suggestions below.

- Include information on the historical background of the Constitutional Convention, such as Shays's Rebellion and Enlightenment ideas about government.
- Find biographies about the delegates to the convention, including portraits.
- Collect important primary sources, such as Madison's notes and *The Federalist* papers.
- Include photographs or facsimiles of the documents.
- Draw a diagram that shows a layout for the exhibit.

4. HISTORY PORTFOLIO

Review your section and chapter assessment activities. Select one that you think shows your best work. Then use comments made by your teacher or classmates to improve your work and add it to your portfolio.

Additional Test Practice, pp. S1–S33

TEST PRACTICE CLASSZONE.COM

ALTERNATIVE ASSESSMENT

1. INTERDISCIPLINARY ACTIVITY: **Government**

Charts should
- present information accurately.
- present information in a style that will aid the viewer in understanding the information.
- be presented neatly.

2. COOPERATIVE LEARNING ACTIVITY

Debaters should
- have a central question or proposition.
- support their own positions and refute their opponent's position with evidence.
- appropriately respond to each other's statements.

3. PRIMARY SOURCE EXPLORER

Exhibits should
- have a complete introductory overview.
- contain accurate and well-described textual information.
- use a variety of media.

4. HISTORY PORTFOLIO

Revised section or chapter assessment activities should
- address teacher and peer responses to the selected work.
- solve problems present in the first versions of the work.

Critical Thinking Transparency CT24
- Visual Summary

Formal Assessment
- Chapter Test, Forms A, B, and C, pp. 138–139

HISTORY SKILLS

Possible Responses

1. INTERPRETING MAPS

Basic Map Elements

a. New York, Pennsylvania, New Jersey, and Delaware
b. New Jersey and Delaware

Interpreting the Map

c. Cities had a great deal of commerce. New York and Philadelphia would have supported the Constitution because it would have solved some of the commerce problems of the Articles of Confederation.

2. INTERPRETING PRIMARY SOURCES

a. The law says that people shall have freedom of religion.
b. the freedom of religion clause in the First Amendment
c. In the early 1600s, some of the colonies were based on religious beliefs. In the late 1700s, some colonists supported freedom of religion.

HANDBOOKS PLANNING GUIDE

The Constitution and Citizenship Handbook

	HANDBOOK OVERVIEW	COPYMASTERS	INTEGRATED TECHNOLOGY
RESOURCES	The Constitution Handbook discusses the underlying principles of the United States Constitution. It also presents the full text of the document for study. The Citizenship Handbook explains who citizens are, lists their rights and responsibilities, and gives examples of ways to become a model citizen.	**In-Depth Resources: Unit 2** • Guided Readings on the Constitution, pp. 62–65	• eEdition Plus Online • EasyPlanner Plus Online • eTest Plus Online • eEdition • Power Presentations • EasyPlanner • Electronic Library of Primary Sources • Test Generator • Reading Study Guide • America's Music
SECTION 1 **The Seven Principles, Preamble, and Article 1** **pp. 228–239**	**KEY IDEAS** • The Constitution is a living document, based on seven fundamental principles. • The Preamble sets forth the purposes for which the Constitution was written. • Congress makes laws for the nation.	**In-Depth Resources: Unit 2** • Guided Reading, p. 62 **Citizenship Today:** • Simulation 1: Senate Debate of a Bill, pp. 19–28 • Federalism and the Distribution of Power, p. 73 • Separation of Powers and Inefficiency, p. 81	**Warm-Up Transparency WTCON** **Humanities Transparency HT16** • Constitution, Page One—A Replica classzone.com
SECTION 2 **Articles 2 and 3** **pp. 240–245**	• The president enforces the laws and commands the military. • The Constitution creates the Supreme Court, which interprets the laws. • The Constitution also gives Congress the power to create lower-ranking federal courts.	**In-Depth Resources: Unit 2** • Guided Reading, p. 63 **Citizenship Today:** • Simulation 2: Presidential Press Conference, p. 29 • Simulation 3: Mock Trial, pp. 30–41 • Organization of the Executive Branch, p. 54 • Organization of the Judicial Branch, pp. 58–61	**Humanities Transparency HT16** • Constitution, Page One—A Replica **Primary Source Explorer** • *The Constitution* classzone.com
SECTION 3 **Articles 4–7** **pp. 246–249**	• States must honor one another's laws, records, and court rulings. • The Constitution is the supreme law of the land, but it can be changed through amendments. • The Constitution is ratified by 9 of the 13 original states.	**In-Depth Resources: Unit 2** • Guided Reading, p. 64	**Humanities Transparency HT16** • Constitution, Page One—A Replica **Primary Source Explorer** • *The Constitution* classzone.com
SECTION 4 **The Bill of Rights and Amendments** **pp. 250–261**	• The first ten amendments, known as the Bill of Rights, protect such basic liberties as freedom of religion and free speech. • Later amendments help the Constitution adapt to social changes and historical trends.	**In-Depth Resources: Unit 2** • Guided Reading, p. 65 **Citizenship Today:** • Balancing Liberty and National Security, p. 75 • Suspects' Rights Versus Public Protection, p. 76 • Equality: Its Meaning and Application, p. 77 • Minority Rights, p. 79	**Warm-Up Transparency WTCON** **Humanities Transparency HT16** • Constitution, Page One—A Replica **Primary Source Explorer** • *The Constitution* classzone.com
SECTION 5 **Citizenship Handbook** **pp. 264–271**	• A person can become a U.S. citizen by birth or by naturalization. • Citizenship includes many rights and responsibilities. • Being a good citizen involves staying informed, making wise decisions, and participating in the community.	**Citizenship Today:** • The Importance of Juries, pp. 1–2 • Obeying Rules and Laws, pp. 5–6 • Becoming a Citizen, pp. 9–10 • Debating Points of View, pp. 11–12 • Community Service, pp. 13–14 • Detecting Bias in the Media, pp. 15–16 • Writing to Government Officials, pp. 17–18 • Simulation 4: Town Meeting, pp. 42–45	**Warm-Up Transparency WTCON** classzone.com

Pupil's Edition
Copymaster
Overhead Transparency
Audio Library
CD-ROM
Internet

ASSESSMENT OPTIONS

- **Constitution Assessment,** pp. 262–263
- **Formal Assessment**
  - Chapter Tests, Forms A, B, and C, pp. 157–168
- **Test Generator**
- **Online Test Practice**
- **Strategies for Test Preparation**

- **Section Assessment,** pp. 231, 239
- **Formal Assessment,** Quiz, pp. 150–151
- **Test Generator**

- **Section Assessment,** pp. 243, 245
- **Formal Assessment,** Quiz, pp. 152–153
- **Test Generator**

- **Section Assessment,** p. 249
- **Formal Assessment,** Quiz, p. 154
- **Test Generator**

- **Section Assessment,** pp. 252, 261
- **Formal Assessment,** Quiz, pp. 155–156
- **Test Generator**

- **Test Generator**

CUSTOMIZING FOR INDIVIDUAL NEEDS

Students Acquiring English/ESL

- **Reading Study Guide** (English and Spanish), pp. 77–86
- **Access for Students Acquiring English/ESL: Spanish Translations,** pp. 53–56
- **Handbook Summaries on CD** (English and Spanish)
- **Modified Lesson Plans for English Learners**

Less Proficient Readers

- **Reading Study Guide** (English and Spanish), pp. 77–86
- **Handbook Summaries on CD** (English and Spanish)

Gifted and Talented Students

- **America's History Makers**
  - George Washington, pp. 27–28
  - James Madison, pp. 33–34
  - Alexander Hamilton, pp. 35–36
  - Thomas Jefferson, pp. 39–40

CROSS-CURRICULAR CONNECTIONS

Civics

Hjelmeland, Andy. ***Kids in Jail.*** Minneapolis: Lerner, 1992. Gives students a vivid picture of how the justice system works by following a repeat offender from arrest through his time in jail, court appearance, and time spent in a correctional facility.

Lewis, Barbara A. ***The Kid's Guide to Social Action.*** Minneapolis: Free Spirit Pub., 1991. A resource guide for young people learning political action skills.

Geography

Stein, R. Conrad. ***The United States of America (Enchantment of the World).*** Chicago: Children's Press, 1994. Overview of physical and cultural geography of the United States.

Government

Kent, Deborah. ***The Disability Rights Movement.*** New York: Children's Press, 1996. The story of how one group of Americans worked for greater rights and access.

Whitney, Sharon. ***The Equal Rights Amendment: The History and the Movement.*** New York: F. Watts, 1984. An examination of the ERA movement, its criticisms, and defeat.

Mathematics

Ashabranner, Melissa, and Brent Ashabranner. ***Counting America: The Story of the United States Census.*** New York: Putnam, 1989. The story of the decennial census required by the Constitution.

Literature

Rennert, Rick, ed. ***Civil Rights Leaders.*** New York: Chelsea House Pub., 1992. Brief biographies of eight civil rights leaders including James Weldon Johnson; Martin Luther King, Jr.; Jesse Jackson; and Thurgood Marshall.

ENRICHMENT ACTIVITIES

- **Pupil's Edition**
  Constitution Handbook, pp. 226–263
  Citizenship Handbook, pp. 264–271
- **Citizenship Today**
  - Constitution Handbook, pp. 19–28, 30–41, 50, 54–63, 64–67, 69, 70–76, 81–83, 86
  - Citizenship Handbook, pp. 1–2, 5–6, 9, 11–18, 42–45
- **America's History Makers**
  - George Washington, pp. 27–28
  - James Madison, pp. 33–34
  - Alexander Hamilton, pp. 35–36
  - Thomas Jefferson, pp. 39–40
- **Primary Source Explorer**
  - *The Constitution*

BLOCK SCHEDULING — LESSON PLAN OPTIONS (90-MINUTE PERIOD)

DAY 1

History from Visuals, pp. 226–227
Class Time 20 minutes

Options for pacing and variety:
- Peer Teaching Divide students into small groups. Have each group discuss the five events shown on these pages and explain how each event is linked to constitutional decision making. **Class Time** 10 minutes

Principles of the Constitution, pp. 228–232
Class Time 45 minutes

Options for pacing and variety:
- Peer Teaching Have students complete the Interdisciplinary Activity, Art: Presenting the Principles Visually, p. 229 **(TE)**. **Class Time** 30 minutes

Article 1, pp. 233–239
Class Time 50 minutes

Options for pacing and variety:
- Time Saver Use the chart on pages 236–237 to summarize for students Article 1, Section 7, How a Bill Becomes a Law. **Class Time** 10 minutes
- Peer Evaluation Have student pairs provide written answers to A Closer Look questions 6–10 and share their responses with the class. **Class Time** 20 minutes

DAY 2

Article 2, pp. 240–243
Class Time 45 minutes
- Time Saver Use the chart of the electoral college on page 240 to help students understand how the electoral college works. **Class Time** 15 minutes
- Peer Teaching Have students work together to complete the Main Ideas and Critical Thinking questions for the Article 2 Assessment on page 243. **Class Time** 15 minutes

Article 3, pp. 244–245
Class Time 30 minutes

Options for pacing and variety:
- Time Saver Use the chart on Checks and Balances on page 245 to help students understand the relationship of the judiciary to the executive and legislative branches of government. Assign the Skillbuilder: Interpreting Charts questions for homework. **Class Time** 10 minutes

Articles 4–7, pp. 246–249
Class Time 30 minutes

Options for pacing and variety:
- Peer Teaching For a homework assignment have students review the chart on page 246 and bring to class newspaper or newsmagazine articles showing an example of a national power, a shared power, and a state power. Have each student pick one article to summarize for the class. Then create a Constitution database using all students' articles. **Class Time** 25 minutes
- Peer Evaluation Have student pairs answer the Applying Citizenship, Critical Thinking question on page 263 of the Constitution Assessment. **Class Time** 10 minutes

DAY 3

Bill of Rights and Amendments 11–27, pp. 250–261
Class Time 45 minutes

Options for pacing and variety:
- History on Film Extend students' background knowledge of the amendments to the Constitution by showing some of the seven short films in the series *The Amendments to the Constitution.* Cambridge, 1998. **Class Time** 35 minutes

Constitution Assessment, pp. 262–263
Class Time 40 minutes

Options for pacing and variety:
- Peer Evaluation To reinforce students' understanding of the principles of the Constitution, have seven-member groups complete the Seven Principles chart on page 262 of the Constitution Assessment. Within groups, have each student complete a different row of the chart. **Class Time** 15 minutes

Citizenship Handbook, pp. 264–271
Class Time 40 minutes

Options for pacing and variety:
- Peer Teaching Divide students into four groups. Assign each group the information in one of the charts or the diagram on pages 266–267. Have each group create a different way to present this information to the class. **Class Time** 30 minutes
- Peer Evaluation Divide students into three groups. Assign each group one of the three Practicing Citizenship Skills activities on page 271. Work with each group to establish a time line for completion of the group's project and develop a list of criteria for evaluating the project. **Class Time** 25 minutes

TEACHER-TESTED ACTIVITY **Paul Beavers, J. T. Moore Middle School, Nashville, Tennessee**

FEDERALISM AND POWER SHARING

Class Time One class period

Task Debating the division of power between the states and the national government

Purpose To understand the debates that took place following the Constitutional Convention between the Federalists and the Antifederalists

Supplies Needed
- Reference materials and Internet sources on the opinions of the Federalists and the Antifederalists

Activity Review the definition of federalism on page 245. Have students give examples of shared powers, powers delegated to the national government, and powers reserved to the states. Write the following debate topic on the chalkboard: *The states should give up as little power as possible to the central government.* Divide students into small groups. Have half the groups research the Federalists' stand on this topic, while the other half looks at the Antifederalists' position. Pick a panel of three from each side to debate the topic.

CONSTITUTION AND CITIZENSHIP HANDBOOK TECHNOLOGY IN THE CLASSROOM

USING AND CREATING WEB SITES

The Internet provides a wealth of resources for student research, including a good deal of information on the Constitution. Students can use these resources to learn how the Constitution affects them and other people their age. By creating their own Web sites, students are able to showcase what they have learned and express their opinions.

ACTIVITY OUTLINE

Objective Students will use and create Web sites to learn about some of their rights as students and teenagers.

Task Students will use the Internet to research the constitutionality of hypothetical scenarios and then create Web sites showing how the Bill of Rights relates to teenagers.

Class Time Three class periods

DIRECTIONS

1. Have students read the Bill of Rights and list the ways that each right might affect them or other people their age. Discuss their ideas in class.

2. Ask students whether they have the same constitutional rights as adults under all circumstances. When might they not have the same rights?

3. Read the following scenarios to the class. Have students use the Web sites at classzone.com to research each one, and ask the students to state which constitutional right each scenario relates to.

   - You work for the official school newspaper, which the school pays for. You want to write an article on the school's drug education program, but the teacher who helps out with the paper will not let you publish this story.
   - You have not had a haircut in six years, and your hair is now down to your knees. Your friends are very impressed, but the principal of your school has instructed you to cut your hair so it's no longer than your waist.
   - You and a friend want to start a religious club and use one of the school's classrooms to hold meetings.
   - It is midnight, and you and a friend are taking a walk to enjoy what might be the last warm night of the year. A police officer stops you and gives you both tickets for violating the town's curfew. Then he drives you home and gives your parents a warning.

4. Discuss students' findings. What are the purposes of these laws? What are the pros and cons of having these laws? Do they seem fair?

5. Have students create Web sites showing how the Bill of Rights relates to people their age. Each page of the Web site should focus on one of the rights guaranteed by the Bill of Rights. Each page should include the full text of the amendment, explain how the amendment might affect teenagers, describe controversies teenagers may face regarding this right (e.g. curfew and dress codes), and propose things teenagers can do if their legal rights have been violated.

CONSTITUTION HANDBOOK OBJECTIVE

The student will understand the seven principles of government that helped to shape the Constitution.

HISTORY FROM VISUALS

Interpreting the Photographs and Painting Ask students to compare the people shown in the photographs with those in the painting. What groups of people took part in the Constitutional Convention of 1787? What groups were not present? **Possible Responses** The painting shows only white men; they represented various states. In contrast, the photographs show several ethnic groups, women, and young people; members of these groups were not present at the Constitutional Convention. However, over the years, they have won rights as citizens under the Constitution.

Extension Have students write five questions they would ask one or more people in the photographs or painting.

MORE ABOUT . . .

Strict Constructionists and Loose Constructionists
Explain to students that there are different viewpoints toward how to interpret the Constitution. Some people believe in a strict, or narrow, interpretation of the Constitution. Others believe in a loose, or broad, interpretation of the Constitution. Those who favor a strict construction sometimes oppose the idea that the Constitution is open to constant reinterpretation. You may wish to discuss in class these opposing viewpoints on how flexible the Constitution is.

The Living Constitution

The Framers of the Constitution created a flexible plan for governing the United States far into the future. They also described ways to allow changes in the Constitution. For over 200 years, the Constitution has guided the American people. It remains a "living document." The Constitution still thrives, in part, because it echoes the principles the delegates valued. Each generation of Americans renews the meaning of the Constitution's timeless ideas. These two pages show you some ways in which the Constitution has shaped events in American history. **See Primary Source Explorer**

"In framing a system which we wish to last for ages, we should not lose sight of the changes which ages will produce."

—JAMES MADISON, CONSTITUTIONAL CONVENTION

1787

Delegates in Philadelphia sign the Constitution.

1965

Civil rights leaders protest to end the violation of their constitutional rights. Dr. Martin Luther King, Jr., Coretta Scott King, and others march from Selma toward Montgomery, Alabama, to gain voting rights.

RECOMMENDED RESOURCES

BOOKS FOR THE TEACHER

Frost, Elizabeth, and Kathryn Cullen-Dupont. ***Women's Suffrage in America.*** New York: Facts on File, 1992. Primary sources in the struggle for suffrage.

Garraty, John, ed. ***Quarrels That Have Shaped the Constitution.*** New York: Harper, 1988. Landmark cases.

Lusane, Clarence. ***No Easy Victories.*** Danbury, CT: Franklin Watts, 1996. The African-American struggle for the vote.

St. John, Jeffrey. ***Forge of Union, Anvil of Liberty.*** Ottawa, IL: Jameson, 1992. Story of the Bill of Rights and the first election.

VIDEOS

The Congress: The History and Promise of Representative Government. PBS Video, 1988. Part of a series by Ken Burns.

Mr. Smith Goes to Washington. Columbia, 1939. The classic Jimmy Stewart film provides a look at Congress in theory and practice.

SOFTWARE

How a Bill Becomes a Law. Word Associates, 3226 Robincrest Drive, Northbrook, IL 60062.

For a tutorial and tests about the Constitution, visit . . .

classzone.com

1971

The 26th Amendment to the Constitution gives young people "18 years of age or older" the right to vote.

1981

A Supreme Court decision rules that Congress can exclude women from the draft. Still, many women who have joined the armed forces have served in combat.

"All the News That's Fit to Print"

The New York Times

National Edition

ONE DOLLAR

VOL. CXLVIII . . . No. 51,432

SATURDAY, FEBRUARY 13, 1999

CLINTON ACQUITTED DECISIVELY: NO MAJORITY FOR EITHER CHARGE

President Says He Is Sorry And Seeks Reconciliation

CENSURE IS BARRED

But Rebuke From Both Sides of Aisle Dilutes President's Victory

The Fallout Of the Trial

Effects on the Office Are Far From Certain

'Senators, How Say You?'

1999

The Senate tries President Bill Clinton for the impeachment charges brought against him by the House of Representatives. As required by the Constitution, the Senate needs a two-thirds majority vote to convict him. This rule saves his presidency.

TABLE OF CONTENTS

HOW TO READ THE CONSTITUTION

The complete text of the Constitution of the United States begins on page 232. The main column has the actual text. Some of the spellings and punctuation have been updated for easier reading. Headings and subheadings have been added to the Constitution to help you find specific topics. Those parts of the Constitution that are no longer in use have been crossed out. "A Closer Look" notes and charts will help you understand issues related to the Constitution.

CONSTITUTION HANDBOOK

MORE ABOUT . . .

The 26th Amendment

Until 1970, the right to vote was limited to citizens aged 21 and over. The Vietnam War created pressure to grant 18-year-olds the right to vote. People questioned the fairness of sending a young soldier to fight and possibly die when he had no voice in setting national policy.

The Voting Rights Act of 1970 extended the right to vote in national elections to citizens 18 and older. However, many states still kept 21 as the voting age in state and local elections. To avoid the problem of maintaining two sets of voter registration books, Congress passed the 26th Amendment, which took priority over state laws on voting age. The states ratified the new amendment in less than four months.

MORE ABOUT . . .

Women in Combat

During World War II, about 350,000 women joined the military, participating in every type of work except actual combat. By the Gulf War in 1990–1991, more than 35,000 servicewomen served in such combat-related jobs as air traffic controller, reconnaissance aircraft pilot, and equipment mechanic. Two women were taken prisoners of war, and 16 women were killed in the conflict. As more military missions involve peacekeeping or police actions, the distinction between combat and noncombat positions has become less clear.

TEACHING STRATEGY

Comparing Remind the students that the Framers of the Constitution intended it to be flexible enough to deal with unanticipated problems in the new nation. Have them read the quotation from James Madison on page 226 and discuss the meaning of the statement.

Tell the students to study the photographs and captions. Ask: What political changes would Madison notice if he could compare these photographs to the United States of his own time? **Possible Responses** free African Americans demanding voting rights, young people voting, women in the military

Ask the students which of the pictures shows a situation that the Framers of the Constitution anticipated might happen. **Answer** the impeachment of a president

FOCUS & MOTIVATE

5-MINUTE WARM-UP

Finding Main Ideas These questions help students to see that the seven principles of government all relate to questions of power.

1. Read the questions under headings 1–7 on pages 228–231. What important word occurs in five of the questions? Does this word also relate to the other two headings?
2. What events before the Revolution raised questions about the power of government?

Warm-Up Transparency WTCON

INSTRUCT

Seven Principles of the Constitution

- Why do you think the Framers of the Constitution worried about the question of power in government?
- Which of the seven principles of the Constitution deal with governmental power?
- Which principles deal with the rights of the people?

MORE ABOUT . . .

Popular Sovereignty
Popular sovereignty is the idea that the government's authority comes from the people and reflects their will. This philosophy had its roots in classical antiquity but was newly expressed during the Enlightenment by such political writers as John Locke (1632–1704) and Jean-Jacques Rousseau (1712–1778). The Framers were deeply influenced by these ideas.

Constitution Connections
The following are parts of the Constitution that embody the principle of popular sovereignty:
- Preamble
- Article 1, Section 2
- Amendments 10, 14, 15, 19, 26

Seven Principles of the Constitution

The Framers of the Constitution constructed a new system of government. Seven principles supported their efforts. To picture how these principles work, imagine seven building blocks. Together they form the foundation of the United States Constitution. In the pages that follow, you will find the definitions and main ideas of the principles shown in the graphic below.

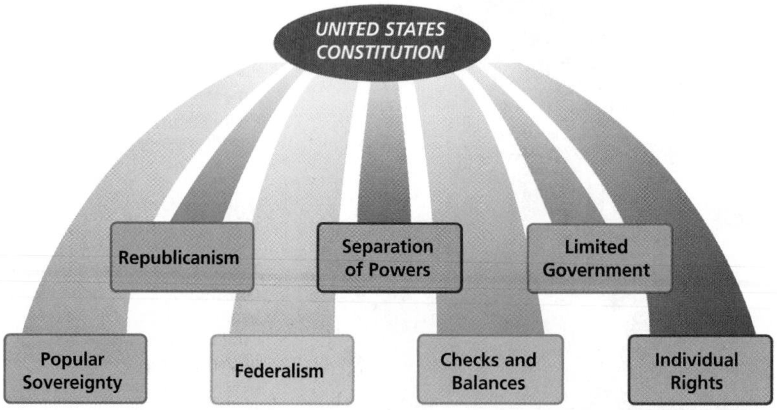

1 Popular Sovereignty
Who Gives the Government Its Power?

"We the people of the United States . . . establish this Constitution for the United States of America." These words from the Preamble, or introduction, to the Constitution clearly spell out the source of the government's power. The Constitution rests on the idea of **popular sovereignty**—a government in which the people rule. As the nation changed and grew, popular sovereignty took on new meaning. A broader range of Americans shared in the power to govern themselves.

In 1987, Americans gathered in Washington, D.C., to celebrate the 200th anniversary of the Constitution. The banner proudly displays that the power to govern belongs to the people.

TEACHING STRATEGY

Using Visual Elements The concepts behind the seven principles are very complex. To help the students build an understanding of the principles, direct the students' attention to the pictures, graphics, and questions shown with each principle. Ask them to look at the picture or graphic and to read the question. Then discuss how the visual element helps to answer the question.

The concepts of federalism, separation of powers, and checks and balances are especially challenging. The graphic organizers should help the students see the differences among these concepts.

In a republican government, voting citizens make their voices heard at the polls. The power of the ballot prompts candidates to listen to people's concerns.

2 Republicanism
How Are People's Views Represented in Government?

The Framers of the Constitution wanted the people to have a voice in government. Yet the Framers also feared that public opinion might stand in the way of sound decision making. To solve this problem, they looked to republicanism as a model of government.

Republicanism is based on this belief: The people exercise their power by voting for their political representatives. According to the Framers, these lawmakers played the key role in making a republican government work. Article 4, Section 4, of the Constitution also calls for every state to have a "republican form of government."

3 Federalism
How Is Power Shared?

The Framers wanted the states and the nation to become partners in governing. To build cooperation, the Framers turned to federalism. **Federalism** is a system of government in which power is divided between a central government and smaller political units, such as states. Before the Civil War, federalism in the United States was closely related to dual sovereignty, the idea that the federal government and the states each had exclusive power over their own spheres.

The Framers used federalism to structure the Constitution. The Constitution assigns certain powers to the national government. These are *delegated powers*. Powers kept by the states are *reserved powers*. Powers shared or exercised by national and state governments are known as *concurrent powers*.

Federalism

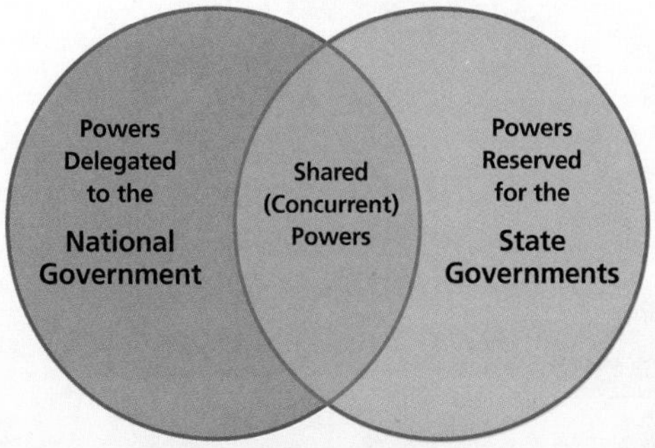

The overlapping spheres of power bind the American people together.

CONSTITUTION HANDBOOK

MORE ABOUT . . .

Republicanism

Students frequently confuse this term with the American political party. To clarify the term, explain that republicanism is usually defined as *representative democracy.* That is, the people elect representatives to make laws and exercise the powers of government. (When the people themselves make laws, as in town meetings, the process is called *direct democracy.*)

At the time of the Revolution, many people considered republican government to be a very radical idea. The Framers of the Constitution, however, believed that voters were capable of making good choices in selecting the leaders who would govern the nation. Procedures for the election of representatives are a part of the Constitution.

Constitution Connections

The following are parts of the Constitution that embody the principle of republicanism:

- Article 1, Section 4
- Article 4, Section 4
- Amendments 12, 20

MORE ABOUT . . .

Federalism

To succeed, federalism requires both a strong central government and vigorous local governments. The idea of federalism is reflected in the motto of the United States, *E pluribus, unum* (From many, one).

Constitution Connections

The following are parts of the Constitution that embody the principle of federalism:

- Article 4
- Article 5
- Article 6
- Amendments 10, 11

Citizenship Today

- Federalism and the Distribution of Power, p. 69
- State Governments, pp. 58–63
- Local Governments, pp. 64–67

ACTIVITY OPTIONS

INTERDISCIPLINARY LINK: ART | BLOCK SCHEDULING

PRESENTING THE PRINCIPLES VISUALLY

Class Time 30 minutes

Task Making a visual representation of the seven principles explained on pages 228–231

Purpose To transform verbal information into a visual representation

Supplies Needed

- Textbook
- Art supplies, including markers, posterboard, and construction paper
- Material suitable for three-dimensional work, such as small boxes, string or yarn, and labels

Activity Divide the class into seven groups and assign each group one of the seven principles. Each group should carefully study the description of its principle in the textbook. Then the group should decide on a two- or three-dimensional way to illustrate the principle. The group should decide who will create the art and who will explain it to the class. Have students present the principles to the class and combine all the illustrations into a single display.

MORE ABOUT . . .

Separation of Powers

The Framers of the Constitution deliberately pitted the branches of government against one another. Although this arrangement lessened the efficiency of government, it also guarded against abuse. James Madison wrote in *Federalist* No. 47, "The accumulation of all powers, legislative, executive, and judiciary, in the same hands, whether one, a few, or many . . . may justly be pronounced the very definition of tyranny."

Constitution Connections

The following are parts of the Constitution that embody the principle of separation of powers:

- Article 1
- Article 2
- Article 3

Citizenship Today

• Separation of Powers and Inefficiency, p. 81

4 Separation of Powers
How Is Power Divided?

The Framers were concerned that too much power might fall into the hands of a single group. To avoid this problem, they built the idea of **separation of powers** into the Constitution. This principle means the division of basic government roles into branches. No one branch is given all the power. Articles 1, 2, and 3 of the Constitution detail how powers are split among the three branches.

Separation of Powers

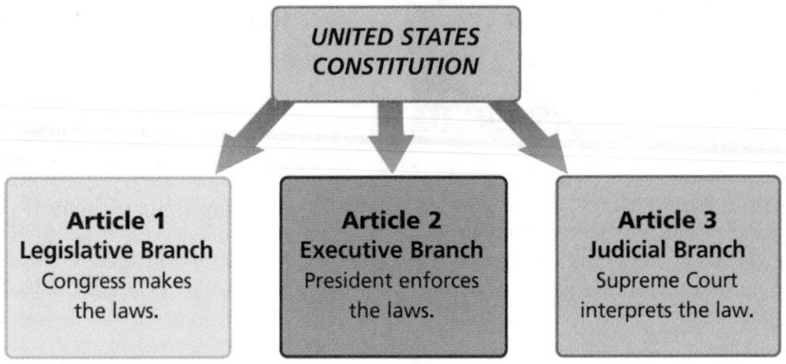

MORE ABOUT . . .

Checks and Balances

Like separation of powers, the principle of checks and balances is a way of limiting the power of government. In *Federalist* No. 51, Madison described this principle as a method of "keeping each other [the three branches] in their proper places."

Constitution Connections

The following are parts of the Constitution that embody the principle of checks and balances:

- Article 1
- Article 2
- Article 3

5 Checks and Balances
How Is Power Evenly Distributed?

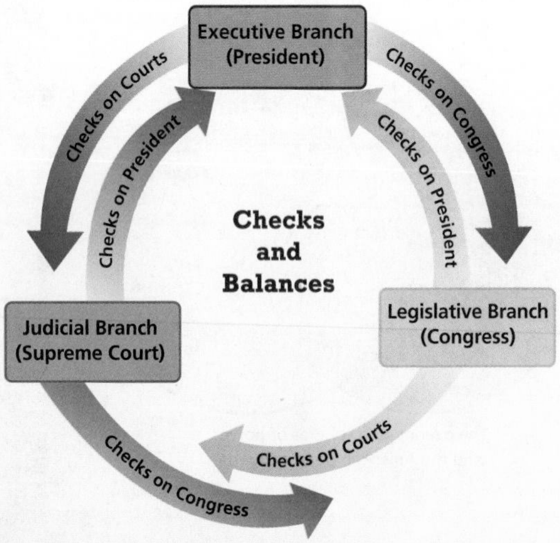

Baron de Montesquieu, an 18th-century French thinker, wrote, "Power should be a check to power." His comment refers to the principle of **checks and balances.** Each branch of government can exercise checks, or controls, over the other branches. Though the branches of government are separate, they rely on one another to perform the work of government.

The Framers included a system of checks and balances in the Constitution to help make sure that the branches work together fairly. For example, only Congress can pass laws. Yet the president can check this power by refusing to sign a law into action. In turn, the Supreme Court can declare that a law, passed by Congress and signed by the president, violates the Constitution.

ACTIVITY OPTIONS

INTERDISCIPLINARY LINK: DRAMA — BLOCK SCHEDULING

CHECKS AND BALANCES

Class Time 30 minutes

Task Dramatizing the concept of checks and balances

Purpose To more clearly understand the ability of each branch to check the powers of the others

Supplies Needed

- Index cards, each labeled with one of the bulleted items in the chart on page 245; cards may be color-coded according to branch of government

Activity Divide the class into three groups. Assign each group one branch of government. Each group should study the powers of its branch in the chart on page 245.

Set up a "power arena" in the room. Have a student draw an index card listing one of the checks on power. Each branch that is affected by this power must then send a representative to the arena to explain how that check limits or enhances its power and influences its relations with the other branches of government. Continue until all the checks have been pulled.

6 Limited Government
How Is Abuse of Power Prevented?

The Framers restricted the power of government. Article 1, Section 9, of the Constitution lists the powers denied to the Congress. Article 1, Section 10, forbids the states to take certain actions.

The principle of **limited government** is also closely related to the "rule of law": In the American government everyone, citizens and powerful leaders alike, must obey the law. Individuals or groups cannot twist or bypass the law to serve their own interests.

In this political cartoon, President Richard Nixon shakes his fist as he defies the "rule of law." Faced with charges of violating the Constitution, Nixon resigned as president in 1974.

Students exercise their right to protest. They urge the community to protect the environment.

7 Individual Rights
How Are Personal Freedoms Protected?

The first ten amendments to the Constitution shield people from an overly powerful government. These amendments are called the Bill of Rights. The Bill of Rights guarantees certain **individual rights,** or personal liberties and privileges. For example, government cannot control what people write or say. People also have the right to meet peacefully and to ask the government to correct a problem. Later amendments to the Constitution also advanced the cause of individual rights.

Assessment: Principles of the Constitution

1. Main Ideas

a. What are the seven principles of government?

b. How does the Constitution reflect the principle of separation of powers?

c. Why did the Framers include a system of checks and balances in the Constitution?

2. Critical Thinking

Forming Opinions How do the rights and responsibilities of U.S. citizenship reflect American national identity?

THINK ABOUT
- what it means to be an American
- the rights and responsibilities of U.S. citizens

MORE ABOUT . . .

Limited Government

Having just won a war against the British monarchy, many Americans in 1787 were concerned that a powerful president might make himself a king. In later years, political opponents accused both John Adams and Andrew Jackson of acting like kings.

In the 20th century, the power of the presidency increased sharply, provoking frequent controversy. Theodore Roosevelt, Woodrow Wilson, Franklin Roosevelt, Lyndon Johnson, Richard Nixon, Ronald Reagan, and Bill Clinton were all accused at times of abusing their power.

Constitution Connections

The following are parts of the Constitution that embody the principle of limited government:
- Article 1
- Article 2
- Article 3

MORE ABOUT . . .

Individual Rights

The principle of individual rights includes both civil liberties and civil rights. While these terms are often used interchangeably, their meanings are slightly different.

Usually, *civil liberties* refers to freedoms protected by limits on government. For example, the First Amendment prohibits government from interfering with freedom of speech and of religion.

Civil rights usually refers to positive acts by government to protect citizens against injustice. An example is the 14th Amendment's promise of "equal protection of the laws."

Constitution Connections

The following are parts of the Constitution that embody the principle of individual rights:
- Article 1, Sections 9, 10
- Article 6, Section 3
- Bill of Rights Amendments 1–10
- Amendments 13, 14, 15, 19, 26

Formal Assessment
- Section Quiz, p. 150

Assessment: Principles of the Constitution

1. Main Ideas

a. popular sovereignty, republicanism, federalism, separation of powers, checks and balances, limited government, individual rights **b.** Articles 1–3 divide roles of government into three branches—legislative, executive, and judicial. **c.** to prevent any one branch from abusing its power

2. Critical Thinking

Possible Response The American national identity is one of individuality and freedom. U.S. citizens have a responsibility to respect and protect the rights of others to exercise their individuality and freedom.

INTERACTIVE PRIMARY SOURCE

OBJECTIVE

Students will be able to identify the basic plan for the structure of the United States government as set forth in the Constitution.

Primary Source Explorer
- *The Constitution*

The Explorer will help students select and produce their own presentations.

Specific information about the document can be found in **A Closer Look.** To learn more about key people and events of the time, students should click on **Life in These Times. What Happened Next** will show the student the impact of the document, both at home and abroad, and tie it to today.

FOCUS & MOTIVATE

5-MINUTE WARM-UP

Finding Main Ideas Have students read aloud the Preamble and study the chart on page 232. Ask the following questions:

1. What other examples can you think of for each of the goals in the Preamble?
2. Why is it important to know what the goals of the Framers were?

Warm-Up Transparency WTCON

MORE ABOUT . . .

Barbara Jordan

In 1974, Jordan was a first-term member of Congress on the House Judiciary Committee, which was investigating the Watergate scandal. In a televised speech on the issue of impeachment, Jordan told the nation, "My faith in the Constitution is whole, it is complete, it is total. I am not going to sit here and be an idle spectator to the diminution, the subversion, the destruction of the Constitution."

The Constitution of the United States

See Primary Source Explorer

"In 1787, I was not included in that 'We the people.' . . . But through the process of amendment, interpretation, and court decision, I have finally been included in 'We the people.'"

—BARBARA JORDAN, 1974
The first African-American congresswoman from the South (Texas)

Preamble. *Purpose of the Constitution*

We the people of the United States, in order to form a more perfect Union, establish justice, insure domestic tranquility, provide for the common defense, promote the general welfare, and secure the blessings of liberty to ourselves and our posterity, do ordain and establish this Constitution for the United States of America.

***A CLOSER LOOK* Goals of the Preamble**

PREAMBLE	EXPLANATION	EXAMPLES
"Form a more perfect Union"	Create a nation in which states work together	• U.S. Postal System • U.S. coins, paper money
"Establish justice"	Make laws and set up courts that are fair	• Court system • Jury system
"Insure domestic tranquility"	Keep peace within the country	• National Guard • Federal marshals
"Provide for the common defense"	Safeguard the country against attack	• Army • Navy
"Promote the general welfare"	Contribute to the happiness and well-being of all the people	• Birth certificate • Marriage license
"Secure the blessings of liberty to ourselves and our posterity"	Make sure future citizens remain free	• Commission on Civil Rights • National Council on Disability

SKILLBUILDER Interpreting Charts

1. *Which goal of the Preamble do you think is most important? Why?*
2. *How does the Preamble reflect the principle of popular sovereignty?*

SKILLBUILDER Possible Responses
1. Students should choose one of the six goals listed and support their choice with convincing reasons.
2. "We the people" expresses that the people are the source of the government's power.

ACTIVITY OPTIONS

INTERDISCIPLINARY LINK: CURRENT EVENTS — BLOCK SCHEDULING

WHAT DOES CONGRESS DO?

Class Time One class period

Task Categorizing congressional activities

Purpose To understand the variety of matters that come before Congress

Supplies Needed
- Newspapers and magazines
- File folders or shoe boxes
- Markers

Activity Label boxes or folders with various areas of congressional responsibility (elections, lawmaking, taxation, commerce, etc.) as outlined on pages 233–238. (Select the headings that pertain to current topics.) Be sure to include a file for the elastic clause. Have students collect news items about current activities in Congress. Tell them to decide which category of congressional responsibility each item falls within and file the article in the appropriate folder. Ask: What activities are hard to categorize? What activities take most of Congress's time?

Article 1. *The Legislature*

MAIN IDEA The main role of Congress, the legislative branch, is to make laws. Congress is made up of two houses—the Senate and the House of Representatives. Candidates for each house must meet certain requirements. Congress performs specific duties, also called delegated powers.

WHY IT MATTERS NOW Representatives in Congress still voice the views and concerns of the people.

Section 1. Congress All legislative powers herein granted shall be vested in a Congress of the United States, which shall consist of a Senate and House of Representatives.

Section 2. The House of Representatives

1. Elections The House of Representatives shall be composed of members chosen every second year by the people of the several states, and the **electors** in each state shall have the qualifications requisite for electors of the most numerous branch of the state legislature.

2. Qualifications No person shall be a Representative who shall not have attained to the age of twenty-five years, and been seven years a citizen of the United States, and who shall not, when elected, be an inhabitant of that state in which he shall be chosen.

3. Number of Representatives Representatives ~~and direct taxes~~ shall be apportioned among the several states which may be included within this Union, according to their respective numbers, ~~which shall be determined by adding to the whole number of free persons, including those bound to service for a term of years, and excluding Indians not taxed, three-fifths of all other Persons.~~ The actual **enumeration** shall be made within three years after the first meeting of the Congress of the United States, and within every subsequent term of ten years, in such manner as they shall by law direct. The number of Representatives shall not exceed one for every thirty thousand, but each state shall have at least one Representative; ~~and until such enumeration shall be made, the state of New Hampshire shall be entitled to choose three, Massachusetts eight, Rhode Island and Providence Plantations one, Connecticut five, New York six, New Jersey four, Pennsylvania eight, Delaware one, Maryland six, Virginia ten, North Carolina five, South Carolina five, and Georgia three.~~

4. Vacancies When vacancies happen in the representation from any state, the executive authority thereof shall issue writs of election to fill such vacancies.

5. Officers and Impeachment The House of Representatives shall choose their Speaker and other officers; and shall have the sole power of **impeachment.**

VOCABULARY

electors voters

enumeration an official count, such as a census

impeachment the process of accusing a public official of wrongdoing

A CLOSER LOOK

ELECTIONS

Representatives are elected every two years. There are no limits on the number of terms a person can serve.

1. What do you think are the advantages of holding frequent elections of representatives?

A CLOSER LOOK

REPRESENTATION

Some delegates, such as Gouvernor Morris, thought that representation should be based on wealth as well as population. Others, such as James Wilson, thought representation should be based on population only. Ultimately, the delegates voted against including wealth as a basis for apportioning representatives.

2. How do you think the United States would be different today if representation were based on wealth?

INSTRUCT

Article 1: The Legislature

- Why do you think the Framers were careful to give different duties to the House and to the Senate?
- Why do you think the Framers required revenue bills to start in the House of Representatives?
- What powers does the Constitution deny to Congress? to the states?

In-Depth Resources: Unit 2
- Guided Reading, p. 62

Reading Study Guide (Spanish and English), pp. 77–78

Access for Students Acquiring English/ESL
- Guided Reading, p. 53

Citizenship Today
- Simulation 1: Senate Debate of a Bill, pp. 19–28

CRITICAL THINKING ACTIVITY

Comparing If your school has an active student government, you may want to discuss how the form of student government is indirectly influenced by the Constitution. Examples could include such things as qualifications for representatives, majority rule, and regular elections. Ask students to list the kinds of decisions that their student government makes. What powers does it have? What are the limits on its powers? How does it interact with other groups within the school, such as clubs, faculty, and administration?

Class Time 10 minutes

A CLOSER LOOK

1. Frequent elections keep representatives more accountable to voters; they make it easier to vote ineffective representatives out of office.
2. The wealthier people would have more representation in Congress, and, therefore, more power to push through legislation than poorer people.

MORE ABOUT . . .

From Senator to Vice-President

The Senate has long been a steppingstone to the vice-presidency. Since World War II, eight senators have served as vice-presidents—Harry Truman, Alben Barkley, Richard Nixon, Lyndon Johnson, Hubert Humphrey, Walter Mondale, Dan Quayle, and Al Gore. Several of these men went on to become president. Although the vice-president is only a heartbeat from the presidency, most of these men agreed that they had more real power as senators than as vice-presidents.

VOCABULARY

pro tempore for the time being

indictment a written statement issued by a grand jury charging a person with a crime

quorum the minimum number of members that must be present for official business to take place

SKILLBUILDER Possible Responses
6-year terms give senators more time and political power to carry out legislative programs and make Congress more stable than the House. Higher qualifications allow for older, more experienced people to serve in the Senate.

Section 3. The Senate

1. Numbers The Senate of the United States shall be composed of two Senators from each state, ~~chosen by the legislature thereof,~~ for six years; and each Senator shall have one vote.

2. Classifying Terms Immediately after they shall be assembled in consequence of the first election, they shall be divided as equally as may be into three classes. The seats of the Senators of the first class shall be vacated at the expiration of the second year, of the second class at the expiration of the fourth year, and of the third class at the expiration of the sixth year, so that one-third may be chosen every second year; ~~and if vacancies happen by resignation, or otherwise, during the recess of the legislature of any state, the executive thereof may make temporary appointments until the next meeting of the legislature, which shall then fill such vacancies.~~

3. Qualifications No person shall be a Senator who shall not have attained to the age of thirty years, and been nine years a citizen of the United States, and who shall not, when elected, be an inhabitant of that state for which he shall be chosen.

A CLOSER LOOK **Federal Office Terms and Requirements**

POSITION	TERM	MINIMUM AGE	RESIDENCY	CITIZENSHIP
Representative	2 years	25	state in which elected	7 years
Senator	6 years	30	state in which elected	9 years
President	4 years	35	14 years in the U.S.	natural-born
Supreme Court Justice	unlimited	none	none	none

SKILLBUILDER **Interpreting Charts**
Why do you think the term and qualifications for a senator are more demanding than for a representative?

4. Role of Vice-President The Vice-President of the United States shall be President of the Senate, but shall have no vote, unless they be equally divided.

5. Officers The Senate shall choose their other officers, and also a President **pro tempore**, in the absence of the Vice-President, or when he shall exercise the office of President of the United States.

6. Impeachment Trials The Senate shall have the sole power to try all impeachments. When sitting for that purpose, they shall be on oath or affirmation. When the President of the United States is tried, the Chief Justice shall preside: and no person shall be convicted without the concurrence of two-thirds of the members present.

7. Punishment for Impeachment Judgment in cases of impeachment shall not extend further than to removal from office, and disqualification to hold and enjoy any office of honor, trust or profit under the United States; but the party convicted shall nevertheless be liable and subject to **indictment**, trial, judgment and punishment, according to law.

MORE ABOUT . . .

Impeachment

Impeachment is a formal accusation of wrongdoing by a public official. It is a legal process that can be used not only against the president of the United States but also against other officials such as federal judges or cabinet officers. To date, 16 federal officials have been impeached by the House of Representatives, of whom seven have then been convicted by the Senate. All of those convicted were federal judges. Two presidents, Andrew Johnson and Bill Clinton, were impeached, but neither was convicted.

A CLOSER LOOK

IMPEACHMENT

The House brings charges against the president. The Senate acts as the jury. The Chief Justice of the Supreme Court presides over the hearings.

3. How many presidents have been impeached?

234 THE LIVING CONSTITUTION

TEACHING STRATEGY

Vocabulary Activities To help students understand the vocabulary words on this page, have them read the words and pronounce them correctly.

Next, discuss the definitions. For the word *indictment,* be sure to explain that a grand jury is not the same as a trial jury. The purpose of a grand jury is to seek information and decide if a crime has been committed. If it concludes that there has been a crime and that there is reason to suspect a particular person, the grand jury can issue an indictment against that person.

Explain to the students that, generally speaking, a *quorum* consists of half the total number of the group, plus one. Thus the Senate, which has 100 members, has a quorum when 51 senators are present.

Finally, have the students find the vocabulary words in the document and read them in context.

Section 4. Congressional Elections

1. Regulations The times, places and manner of holding elections for Senators and Representatives shall be prescribed in each state by the legislature thereof; but the Congress may at any time by law make or alter such regulations, except as to the places of choosing Senators.

2. Sessions The Congress shall assemble at least once in every year, ~~and such meeting shall be on the first Monday in December, unless they shall by law appoint a different day.~~

Section 5. Rules and Procedures

1. Quorum Each house shall be the judge of the elections, returns and qualifications of its own members, and a majority of each shall constitute a **quorum** to do business; but a smaller number may adjourn from day to day, and may be authorized to compel the attendance of absent members, in such manner, and under such penalties as each house may provide.

2. Rules and Conduct Each house may determine the rules of its proceedings, punish its members for disorderly behavior, and, with the concurrence of two-thirds, expel a member.

3. Congressional Records Each house shall keep a journal of its proceedings, and from time to time publish the same, excepting such parts as may in their judgment require secrecy; and the yeas and nays of the members of either house on any question shall, at the desire of one-fifth of those present, be entered on the journal.

4. Adjournment Neither house, during the session of Congress, shall, without the consent of the other, adjourn for more than three days, nor to any other place than that in which the two houses shall be sitting.

Section 6. Payment and Privileges

1. Salary The Senators and Representatives shall receive a compensation for their services, to be ascertained by law, and paid out of the treasury of the United States. They shall in all cases, except treason, felony and breach of the peace, be privileged from arrest during their attendance at the session of their respective houses, and in going to and returning from the same; and for any speech or debate in either house, they shall not be questioned in any other place.

2. Restrictions No Senator or Representative shall, during the time for which he was elected, be appointed to any civil office under the authority of the United States, which shall have been created, or the emoluments whereof shall have been increased during such time; and no person holding any office under the United States, shall be a member of either house during his continuance in office.

A CLOSER LOOK

SENATE RULES

Senate rules allow for debate on the floor. Using a tactic called filibustering, senators give long speeches to block the passage of a bill. Senator Strom Thurmond holds the filibustering record—24 hours, 18 minutes.

4. Why might a senator choose filibustering as a tactic to block a bill?

A CLOSER LOOK

SALARIES

Senators and representatives are paid $136,700 a year. The Speaker of the House is paid $175,400—the same as the vice-president.

5. How do the salaries of members of Congress compare to those of adults you know?

MORE ABOUT . . .

Congressional Meetings

One of the complaints that the colonists voiced against King George III in the Declaration of Independence was that he refused to allow colonial legislatures to meet regularly. The Framers wanted to ensure that the Congress met on a regular basis, so they specified in Section 4 that meetings were to be held every year. The 20th Amendment changed the meeting day for Congress from the beginning of December to January 3.

MORE ABOUT . . .

Congressional Salaries

In 1790, senators and representatives earned six dollars a day. By 1950, they earned a little over $10,000 per year. By 1978, their salaries had risen to about $60,000 per year. In the late 1990s, the salary reached almost $137,000. In the same period, by comparison, salaries and compensation for business leaders rose even more rapidly; hourly wages rose much less sharply.

A CLOSER LOOK

3. two presidents—Andrew Johnson and Bill Clinton
4. to prevent a vote on a bill that the majority supports but the filibustering senator strongly opposes
5. Some students may say that congressional members earn much more than teachers but considerably less than sports superstars. For additional comparisons, suggest that students find the salaries for various occupations published by the U.S. Department of Labor.

MORE ABOUT . . .

Presidential Veto

Often Congress passes a flurry of bills toward the end of a session. The president faces the task of signing or vetoing many bills. One way to block a bill is called a "pocket veto." A pocket veto occurs when the president does not act on a bill within ten days and Congress adjourns during that time. The bill then "dies" even though it has passed both houses. To revive the bill, the House and the Senate must pass it again when Congress reconvenes.

MORE ABOUT . . .

Overriding a Veto

When the president vetoes a bill, Congress has three choices. One is to give up on the bill and let the veto stand. The second is to make changes in the bill so that it is more acceptable to the president and send it back. The third is to try to override the veto. Historically, Congress has found it hard to round up enough votes for an override. Of the 1,470 bills that were vetoed up to mid-1998, Congress succeeded in overriding only 105. But the percentage of successful overrides has risen sharply in recent years, from about 6 percent before 1969 to about 18 percent since then.

VOCABULARY

revenue income a government collects to cover expenses

naturalization a way to give full citizenship to a person of foreign birth

tribunals courts

felonies serious crimes

appropriation public funds set aside for a specific purpose

Section 7. How a Bill Becomes a Law

1. Tax Bills All bills for raising **revenue** shall originate in the House of Representatives; but the Senate may propose or concur with amendments as on other Bills.

2. Lawmaking Process Every bill which shall have passed the House of Representatives and the Senate, shall, before it become a law, be presented to the President of the United States; if he approves he shall sign it, but if not he shall return it, with his objections to that house in which it shall have originated, who shall enter the objections at large on their journal, and proceed to reconsider it. If after such reconsideration two-thirds of that house shall agree to pass the bill, it shall be sent, together with the objections, to the other house, by which it shall likewise be reconsidered, and if approved by two-thirds of that house, it shall become a law. But in all such cases the votes of both houses shall be determined by yeas and nays, and the names of the persons voting for and against the bill shall be entered on the journal of each house respectively. If any bill shall not be returned by the President within ten days (Sundays excepted) after it shall have been presented to him, the same shall be a law, in like manner as if he had signed it, unless the Congress by their adjournment prevent its return, in which case it shall not be a law.

3. Role of the President Every order, resolution, or vote to which the concurrence of the Senate and House of Representatives may be necessary (except on a question of adjournment) shall be presented to the President of the United States; and before the same shall take effect, shall be approved by him, or being disapproved by him, shall be repassed by two-thirds of the Senate and House of Representatives, according to the rules and limitations prescribed in the case of a bill.

SKILLBUILDER Possible Responses
1. By vetoing the bill.
2. President can check Congress's lawmaking power by vetoing a bill; Congress can check president's power by overriding the veto with a two-thirds majority vote. The bill then becomes a law without the president's signature.

A CLOSER LOOK **How a Bill Becomes a Law**

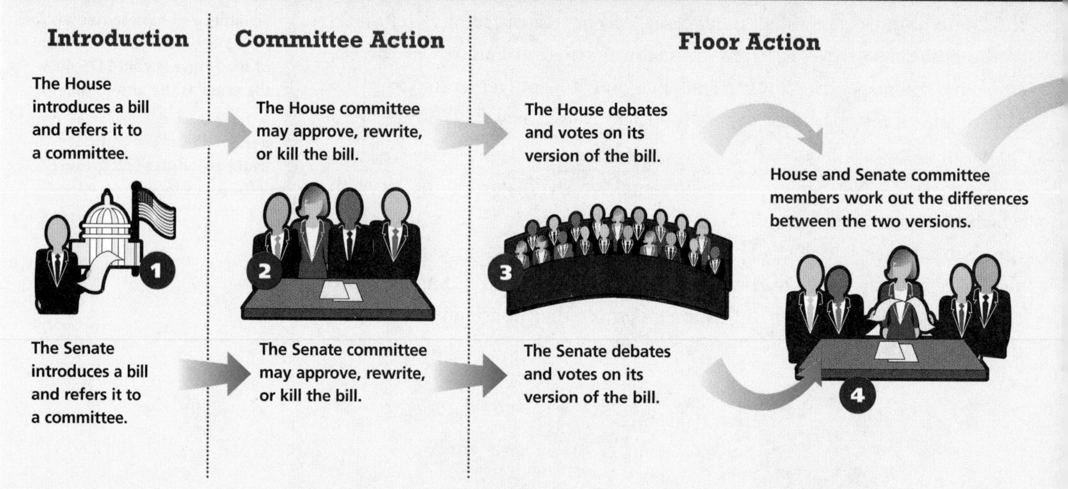

Introduction
Committee Action
Floor Action
The House introduces a bill and refers it to a committee.
The House committee may approve, rewrite, or kill the bill.
The House debates and votes on its version of the bill.
House and Senate committee members work out the differences between the two versions.
1
2
3
4
The Senate introduces a bill and refers it to a committee.
The Senate committee may approve, rewrite, or kill the bill.
The Senate debates and votes on its version of the bill.

ACTIVITY OPTIONS

MULTIPLE LEARNING STYLES: BODILY-KINESTHETIC

BLOCK SCHEDULING

CREATING A PLAY

Class Time One class period

Task Creating a dramatic presentation on lawmaking

Purpose To illustrate an understanding of the process by which a bill becomes a law

Supplies Needed
- Art supplies
- Costumes (optional)

Activity Divide the students into groups. The groups should carefully study the diagram on pages 236–237. Then each group should create a presentation to show an audience of younger students how a bill becomes a law. The group will need to assign the tasks of actor, illustrator, narrator, and scriptwriter. After developing a script, the groups should gather props and rehearse their presentations. Finally, let them present the dramas to a class of younger students.

Section 8. Powers Granted to Congress

1. Taxation The Congress shall have power to lay and collect taxes, duties, imposts and excises, to pay the debts and provide for the common defense and general welfare of the United States; but all duties, imposts and excises shall be uniform throughout the United States;

2. Credit To borrow money on the credit of the United States;

3. Commerce To regulate commerce with foreign nations, and among the several states, and with the Indian tribes;

4. Naturalization, Bankruptcy To establish a uniform rule of **naturalization,** and uniform laws on the subject of bankruptcies throughout the United States;

5. Money To coin money, regulate the value thereof, and of foreign coin, and fix the standard of weights and measures;

6. Counterfeiting To provide for the punishment of counterfeiting the securities and current coin of the United States;

7. Post Office To establish post offices and post roads;

8. Patents, Copyrights To promote the progress of science and useful arts, by securing for limited times to authors and inventors the exclusive right to their respective writings and discoveries;

9. Federal Courts To constitute **tribunals** inferior to the Supreme Court;

10. International Law To define and punish piracies and **felonies** committed on the high seas, and offenses against the law of nations;

11. War To declare war, grant letters of marque and reprisal, and make rules concerning captures on land and water;

12. Army To raise and support armies, but no **appropriation** of money to that use shall be for a longer term than two years;

13. Navy To provide and maintain a navy;

A CLOSER LOOK

REGULATING COMMERCE

Commerce can also apply to travelers crossing state lines. Congress's power to regulate the movement of people from state to state paved the way for the Civil Rights Act of 1964. This act included fair treatment of interstate travelers. People of all races can use public places, such as hotels and bus stations.

6. To what other areas might the commerce clause apply?

A CLOSER LOOK

DECLARING WAR

Only Congress can declare war. Yet in the following "undeclared" wars, Congress bowed to the president's power to take military action and send troops overseas: Korean War (1950–1953), Vietnam War (1957–1975), Persian Gulf War (1991), and Kosovo crisis (1999).

7. Why do you think the Constitution sets limits on the president's war-making powers?

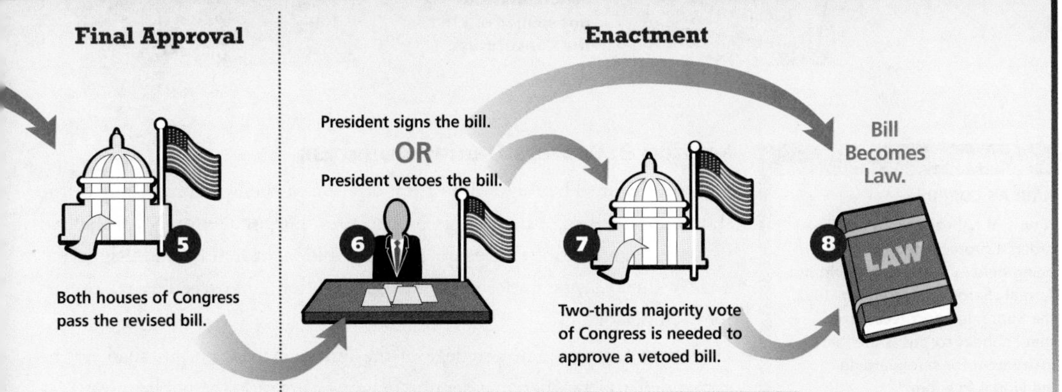

Final Approval
Enactment
Both houses of Congress pass the revised bill.
5
President signs the bill.
OR
President vetoes the bill.
6
7
Two-thirds majority vote of Congress is needed to approve a vetoed bill.
Bill Becomes Law.
8
LAW

SKILLBUILDER **Interpreting Charts**

1. *How can a president block a bill?*
2. *What examples of checks and balances are shown in the chart?*

MORE ABOUT . . .

Market Economy and the Constitution

The Framers of the Constitution included many provisions to support and encourage a market economy. In addition to the commerce clause, Section 8 includes clauses on taxation, bankruptcy, money, and patents and copyrights, as well as the elastic clause. Other parts of the Constitution that support a market economy include Article 1, Sections 9 and 10, and Amendments 4, 5, 9, 10, and 14. Of course, the major purpose of the Constitution is political stability, which is an important precondition for economic growth.

MORE ABOUT . . .

Sacagawea—The New Dollar Coin

In the year 2000, a new coin honoring a Native American woman, Sacagawea, replaced the Susan B. Anthony dollar coin. The design was described as "Liberty . . . inspired by Sacagawea."

Sacagawea was a young Shoshone woman who traveled with the Lewis and Clark expedition and is credited with saving Captain Clark's journals when a boat capsized. She also acted as translator for the expedition and saved the expedition from hostile Native Americans.

The new coin is an alloy of manganese, brass, and copper. It will glitter like a gold coin.

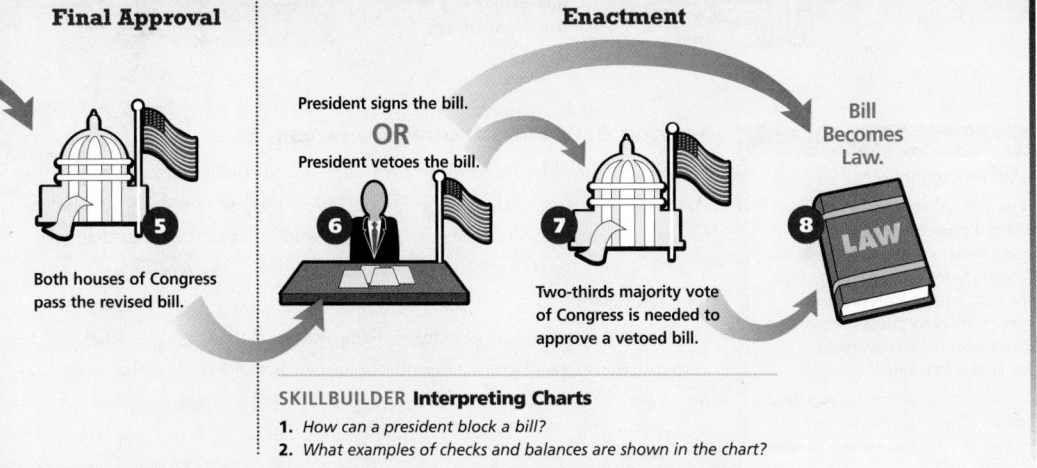

A CLOSER LOOK

6. Commerce can apply to all things that cross state lines, such as goods, modes of transportation (buses, trains, and airplanes), and communications (radio, TV, and the Internet).

7. to provide a check on the president's military power; to prevent the president from becoming a military dictator

VOCABULARY

militia an emergency military force, such as the National Guard, that is not part of the regular army

bill of attainder a law that condemns a person without a trial in court

ex post facto law a law that would make an act a criminal offense after it was committed

tender money

14. Regulation of Armed Forces To make rules for the government and regulation of the land and naval forces;

15. Militia To provide for calling forth the **militia** to execute the laws of the Union, suppress insurrections and repel invasions;

16. Regulations for Militia To provide for organizing, arming, and disciplining the militia, and for governing such part of them as may be employed in the service of the United States, reserving to the states respectively the appointment of the officers, and the authority of training the militia according to the discipline prescribed by Congress;

17. District of Columbia To exercise exclusive legislation in all cases whatsoever, over such district (not exceeding ten miles square) as may, by cession of particular states, and the acceptance of Congress, become the seat of the government of the United States, and to exercise like authority over all places purchased by the consent of the legislature of the state in which the same shall be, for the erection of forts, magazines, arsenals, dockyards, and other needful buildings;—and

18. Elastic Clause To make all laws which shall be necessary and proper for carrying into execution the foregoing powers, and all other powers vested by this Constitution in the government of the United States, or in any department or officer thereof.

MORE ABOUT . . .

The Elastic Clause

Also known as the "necessary and proper" clause, the elastic clause has proven to be one of the most farsighted measures in the Constitution. Broadly interpreted, that clause gave Congress authority to do much more than the simple list of duties in clauses 1–17 of Section 8. And, in the 1819 Court case *McCulloch* v. *Maryland,* Chief Justice John Marshall supported the broad interpretation. (See (Chapter 11, Section 3.) Marshall ruled that Congress could use "all means which are appropriate, . . . which are not prohibited" to fulfill legitimate ends.

Citizenship Today
- *McCulloch* v. *Maryland,* p. 87

A CLOSER LOOK The Elastic Clause

ELASTIC CLAUSE
1787
13 states
• agricultural
• rural
about 4 million people
POP.
The elastic clause allows future generations to expand the meaning of the Constitution. Congress can take action on issues not spelled out in the Constitution.
TODAY
50 states
• industrial
• high-tech
• urban
POP.
about 250 million people

Section 9. Powers Denied Congress

~~**1. Slave Trade** The migration or importation of such persons as any of the states now existing shall think proper to admit, shall not be prohibited by the Congress prior to the year one thousand eight hundred and eight, but a tax or duty may be imposed on such importation, not exceeding ten dollars for each person.~~

2. Habeas Corpus The privilege of the writ of habeas corpus shall not be suspended, unless when in cases of rebellion or invasion the public safety may require it.

A CLOSER LOOK

HABEAS CORPUS

A writ of habeas corpus is a legal order. It protects people from being held in prison or jail without formal charges of a crime. In 1992, the Supreme Court recognized that "habeas corpus is the [basic] instrument for safeguarding individual freedom."

8. How does habeas corpus help ensure fairness and justice?

MORE ABOUT . . .

Habeas Corpus

Habeas corpus is a Latin phrase meaning, "You have the body [of the prisoner in question]." The writ orders a sheriff or other official to present the prisoner before a judge to be charged with a specific crime or to be released. Habeas corpus has been considered part of the bedrock of English liberty since Parliament passed the law in 1679.

A CLOSER LOOK

8. People cannot be held in jail indefinitely without a trial. People who are arrested can demand to be charged with a specific crime or else set free.

9. People are concerned about the amount of taxes and the way government uses tax money. People often object to taxes on personal income that reduce their spending money, but they also expect government to provide the services (enumerated in the Preamble) that taxes support.

10. Senator (and the person's last name); Congressman or Congresswoman (and the person's last name); Mr. President (or Madame President if a woman is elected)

3. Illegal Punishment No bill of attainder or ex post facto law shall be passed.

4. Direct Taxes No capitation, ~~or other direct,~~ tax shall be laid, ~~unless in proportion to the census or enumeration herein before directed to be taken.~~

5. Export Taxes No tax or duty shall be laid on articles exported from any state.

6. No Favorites No preference shall be given by any regulation of commerce or revenue to the ports of one state over those of another: nor shall vessels bound to, or from, one state be obliged to enter, clear, or pay duties in another.

7. Public Money No money shall be drawn from the treasury, but in consequence of appropriations made by law; and a regular statement and account of the receipts and expenditures of all public money shall be published from time to time.

8. Titles of Nobility No title of nobility shall be granted by the United States: and no person holding any office of profit or trust under them shall, without the consent of the Congress, accept of any present, emolument, office, or title, of any kind whatever, from any king, prince, or foreign state.

Section 10. Powers Denied the States

1. Restrictions No state shall enter into any treaty, alliance, or confederation; grant letters of marque and reprisal; coin money; emit bills of credit; make anything but gold and silver coin a tender in payment of debts; pass any bill of attainder, ex post facto law, or law impairing the obligation of contracts, or grant any title of nobility.

2. Import and Export Taxes No state shall, without the consent of the Congress, lay any imposts or duties on imports or exports, except what may be absolutely necessary for executing its inspection laws; and the net produce of all duties and imposts, laid by any state on imports or exports, shall be for the use of the treasury of the United States; and all such laws shall be subject to the revision and control of the Congress.

3. Peacetime and War Restraints No state shall, without the consent of Congress, lay any duty of tonnage, keep troops or ships of war in time of peace, enter into any agreement or compact with another state, or with a foreign power, or engage in war, unless actually invaded, or in such imminent danger as will not admit of delay.

A CLOSER LOOK

DIRECT TAX

In 1913, the 16th Amendment allowed Congress to collect an income tax—a direct tax on the amount of money a person earns. Americans today pay much more in taxes than their ancestors would have imagined.

9. Why do you think the issue of taxes is so important to people?

A CLOSER LOOK

TITLES OF NOBILITY

The Framers disapproved of titles of nobility. The list of grievances in the Declaration of Independence included numerous examples of King George III's abuses of power. Symbols of these abuses included English titles of nobility, such as "king," "queen," and "duke." The Framers said clearly that there would be no such titles in the new republic.

10. How do TV news reporters address members of Congress and the president?

Article 1 Assessment

1. Main Ideas

a. What is the main job of the legislative branch?

b. What role does the vice-president of the United States play in the Senate?

c. Why are there more members in the House of Representatives than the Senate?

d. What is one of the powers denied to Congress?

2. Critical Thinking

Drawing Conclusions How does Article 1 show that the Constitution is a clearly defined yet flexible document?

THINK ABOUT

- the powers of Congress
- the "elastic clause"

MORE ABOUT . . .

Bill of Attainder

The individual rights protected by the bill of attainder clause are among the few cited in the Constitution before the Bill of Rights (Amendments 1–10). The question of attainder has cropped up in some unlikely places. The issue was first tested in court after the Civil War. Southerners who wanted to practice law were required to take an oath that they had not participated in the Confederate rebellion. But the courts struck down that requirement as being a bill of attainder; the would-be lawyers were being deprived of their livelihood without having been convicted of any crime. In 1965, on the same basis, the Supreme Court struck down a law barring a member of the Communist Party from holding office in a labor union.

CRITICAL THINKING ACTIVITY

Identifying Problems Have students study Section 10. Ask them to think about the kinds of problems that would occur if states had the powers listed as "Powers Denied the States."

Class Time 15 minutes

Formal Assessment
- Section Quiz, p. 151

Assessment: Article 1

1. Main Ideas

a. to make laws **b.** acts as president of the Senate **c.** The Framers intended the Senate to be a more select group—older, fewer, serving longer, and presumably wiser. **d.** Under Section 9, Congress cannot suspend habeas corpus, pass bills of attainder and ex post facto laws, favor one state over another, tax any state's exports to another, take public money without appropriation, or grant titles of nobility.

2. Critical Thinking

Possible Responses It is clearly defined in that it specifically explains the organization and procedures of the House and Senate and spells out Congress's powers. It is flexible in its broad application of the commerce clause and especially in the elastic clause.

OBJECTIVE

Students will be able to identify the duties and powers of the executive branch of the United States government.

INSTRUCT

Article 2: The Executive

- What colonial experiences might have influenced the Framers' ideas of duties for the executive branch?
- How is enforcing the laws different from making the laws?
- Who will help the chief executive enforce the laws?

In-Depth Resources: Unit 2
- Guided Reading, p. 63

Reading Study Guide (Spanish and English), pp. 79–80

Access for Students Acquiring English/ESL
- Guided Reading, p. 54

VOCABULARY

natural-born citizen a citizen born in the United States or a U.S. commonwealth, or to parents who are U.S. citizens living outside the country

affirmation a statement declaring that something is true

Article 2. *The Executive*

MAIN IDEA The president and vice-president are the leaders of the executive branch. Their main role is to enforce the laws. The president commands the military and makes foreign treaties with the Senate's approval.

WHY IT MATTERS NOW As the United States has become a world power, the authority of the president has also expanded.

Section 1. The Presidency

1. Terms of Office The executive power shall be vested in a President of the United States of America. He shall hold his office during the term of four years, and, together with the Vice-President, chosen for the same term, be elected, as follows:

2. Electoral College Each state shall appoint, in such manner as the Legislature thereof may direct, a number of electors, equal to the whole number of Senators and Representatives to which the State may be entitled in the Congress; but no Senator or Representative, or person holding an office of trust or profit under the United States, shall be appointed an elector.

A CLOSER LOOK Electoral College *(based on 2000 Census)*

American voters do not choose their president directly. Members of a group called the electoral college actually elect the president. Each state has electors. Together they form the electoral college. In most states, the winner takes all. Except for Maine and Nebraska, all the electoral votes of a state go to one set of candidates.

number of electors for each state = total number of its senators and representatives

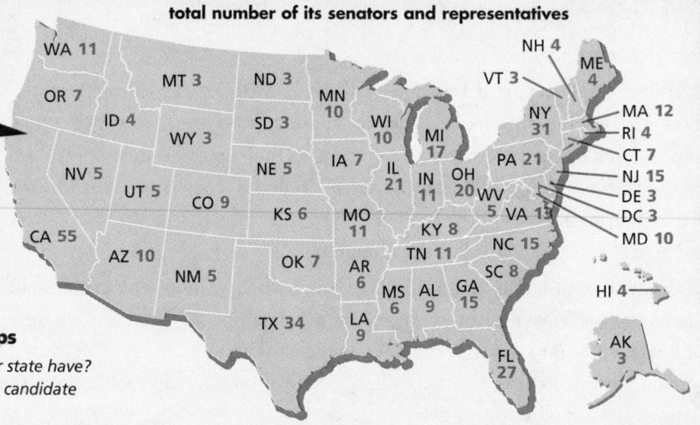

SKILLBUILDER Interpreting Maps

1. *How many electoral votes does your state have?*
2. *In which states would a presidential candidate campaign most heavily? Why?*

SKILLBUILDER Possible Responses
1. Students should locate their state on the map and identify the correct number of electoral votes.
2. California, New York, Texas, Florida Pennsylvania, Illinois, and Ohio—states in the West, East, South, and Midwest with the most electoral votes.

~~**3. Former Method of Electing President** The electors shall meet in their respective states, and vote by ballot for two persons, of whom one at least shall not be an inhabitant of the same state with themselves. And they shall make a list of all the persons voted for, and of the number of votes for each; which list they shall sign and certify, and transmit sealed to the seat of the government of the United States, directed to the President of the Senate. The President of the Senate shall, in the presence of the Senate and House of Representatives, open all the certificates, and the votes shall then be counted. The person having the greatest number of votes shall be the~~

ACTIVITY OPTIONS

INTERDISCIPLINARY LINK: MATH

BLOCK SCHEDULING

THE ELECTORAL COLLEGE

Class Time 30 minutes

Task Creating a table to illustrate the link between popular and electoral votes

Purpose To help students understand the problems with the electoral college

Supplies Needed
- Calculators or pencils and paper
- Voting figures, state by state, from a recent election
- Map with electoral votes (page 240)

Activity Ask students to calculate the number of electoral votes necessary to win the presidency. In pairs or small groups, have students compute the total popular vote and electoral vote for each candidate. Ask students to scan the list for states where the popular vote was close. How many votes would it have taken to change the result in those states? Would such a change have altered the outcome of the national election? Could a candidate have lost the popular vote but won the election?

~~President, if such number be a majority of the whole number of electors appointed; and if there be more than one who have such majority, and have an equal number of votes, then the House of Representatives shall immediately choose by ballot one of them for President; and if no person have a majority, then from the five highest on the list the said House shall in like manner choose the President. But in choosing the President, the votes shall be taken by States, the representation from each state having one vote; a quorum for this purpose shall consist of a member or members from two-thirds of the states, and a majority of all the states shall be necessary to a choice. In every case, after the choice of the President, the person having the greatest number of votes of the electors shall be the Vice-President. But if there should remain two or more who have equal votes, the Senate shall choose from them by ballot the Vice-President.~~

A CLOSER LOOK

Vice-President Lyndon Johnson, next in line of succession, takes the oath of office after the assassination of President John F. Kennedy in 1963. Johnson, like every U.S. president, promises to uphold the Constitution. The 25th Amendment sets up clearer procedures for presidential succession.

4. Election Day The Congress may determine the time of choosing the electors, and the day on which they shall give their votes, which day shall be the same throughout the United States.

5. Qualifications No person except a **natural-born citizen,** ~~or a citizen of the United States at the time of the adoption of this Constitution,~~ shall be eligible to the office of President; neither shall any person be eligible to that office who shall not have attained to the age of thirty-five years, and been fourteen years a resident within the United States.

6. Succession In case of the removal of the President from office, or of his death, resignation, or inability to discharge the powers and duties of the said office, the same shall devolve on the Vice-President, and the Congress may by law provide for the case of removal, death, resignation or inability, both of the President and Vice-President, declaring what officer shall then act as President, and such officer shall act accordingly, until the disability be removed, or a President shall be elected.

7. Salary The President shall, at stated times, receive for his services, a compensation, which shall neither be increased nor diminished during the period for which he shall have been elected, and he shall not receive within that period any other emolument from the United States, or any of them.

8. Oath of Office Before he enter on the execution of his office, he shall take the following oath or **affirmation:**—"I do solemnly swear (or affirm) that I will faithfully execute the office of President of the United States, and will to the best of my ability, preserve, protect and defend the Constitution of the United States."

A CLOSER LOOK

PRESIDENT'S SALARY

The president's yearly salary is $400,000. The president also gets special allowances, such as funds for travel expenses. Here are some other benefits:

- **living in a mansion, the White House**
- **vacationing at Camp David, an estate in Maryland**
- **using *Air Force One*, a personal jet plane**

11. Why do you think the president needs to have a plane and a vacation spot?

HISTORY FROM VISUALS

Interpreting the Photograph Ask the class to study the photograph of Lyndon Johnson taking the oath of office. Ask if they can figure out the location of the ceremony and suggest why it is taking place there. **Possible Response** The ceremony is taking place on an airplane (Air Force One), because it was necessary for the security of the country that the office of the presidency should be filled immediately.

Extension Have the students find out which other vice-presidents have come to power as a result of the assassination of a president.

MORE ABOUT . . .

Presidential Assassinations

John F. Kennedy was the fourth U.S. president to be assassinated. Abraham Lincoln, James A. Garfield, and William McKinley also died at the hands of assassins. Five presidents survived assassination attempts—Andrew Jackson, Franklin Roosevelt, Harry Truman, Gerald Ford, and Ronald Reagan.

A CLOSER LOOK

11. Plane—The president's job requires extensive travel, often on short notice.
Vacation spot—The president may need a restful place; Camp David is also used for meetings with foreign heads of state. Presidential security is also a factor in the need for these benefits.

HISTORY FROM VISUALS

Interpreting the Photographs Ask the students to study the photographs of the various roles the president plays. Then ask them to read the sections of the Constitution on page 243 and find the section that pertains to each role. **Possible Responses** commander in chief—2.1; chief executive—2.1; chief diplomat and chief of state—2.2, 2.3; legislative leader—2.3, 3; head of political party, not mentioned

Extension Have the students read the newspaper and find articles about the president filling some of the roles shown on page 242. Cut out the articles and mount them on the bulletin board. Ask students to write a sentence for each article, describing the role the president is filling.

MORE ABOUT . . .

Power of the President

Most scholars agree that the power of the presidency increased dramatically during the Civil War, when Abraham Lincoln took extraordinary measures during the crisis. However, the greatest expansion of presidential powers occurred during the presidency of Franklin D. Roosevelt. Confronted with both the Great Depression and World War II, Roosevelt took unprecedented steps to save the country. Many of these steps strengthened the executive branch of the government. Since World War II, the emergence of the United States as a world power also increased the power of the American president as a foreign-policy leader.

A CLOSER LOOK Roles of the President

Commander in Chief

As a military leader, President Abraham Lincoln meets with his generals during the Civil War.

Chief Executive

Like a business executive, the president solves problems and makes key decisions. President John F. Kennedy is shown in the oval office in 1962.

Chief Diplomat and Chief of State

As a foreign policy maker, President Richard M. Nixon visits the People's Republic of China in 1972.

Legislative Leader

President Lyndon Johnson signs the Civil Rights Act of 1964. All modern presidents have legislative programs they want Congress to pass.

Head of a Political Party

President Ronald Reagan rallies support at the 1984 Republican Convention. By this time, Reagan had put together a strong bloc of voters who supported the Republican Party's policies. During his presidency (1981–1989), Reagan helped build new unity among party members.

A CLOSER LOOK

12. A candidate often shares the president's basic political views, values, and ideas. Usually the candidate is widely respected in the legal community, with previous judicial experience. The candidate must also be one who can win Senate confirmation.

13. To lead the nation, presidents need widespread support. Effective presidents skillfully use persuasion to "sell" their programs, policies, and decisions to a broad range of people.

Section 2. Powers of the President

1. Military Powers The President shall be commander in chief of the Army and Navy of the United States, and of the militia of the several states, when called into the actual service of the United States; he may require the opinion, in writing, of the principal officer in each of the executive departments, upon any subject relating to the duties of their respective offices, and he shall have power to grant **reprieves** and pardons for offenses against the United States, except in cases of impeachment.

2. Treaties, Appointments He shall have power, by and with the advice and consent of the Senate, to make treaties, provided two-thirds of the Senators present concur; and he shall nominate, and by and with the advice and consent of the Senate, shall appoint ambassadors, other public ministers and consuls, judges of the Supreme Court, and all other officers of the United States, whose appointments are not herein otherwise provided for, and which shall be established by law; but the Congress may by law vest the appointment of such inferior officers, as they think proper, in the President alone, in the courts of law, or in the heads of departments.

3. Vacancies The President shall have power to fill up all vacancies that may happen during the recess of the Senate, by granting commissions which shall expire at the end of their next session.

Section 3. Presidential Duties He shall from time to time give to the Congress information of the State of the Union, and recommend to their consideration such measures as he shall judge necessary and expedient; he may, on extraordinary occasions, **convene** both houses, or either of them, and in case of disagreement between them, with respect to the time of adjournment, he may adjourn them to such time as he shall think proper; he shall receive ambassadors and other public ministers; he shall take care that the laws be faithfully executed, and shall commission all the officers of the United States.

Section 4. Impeachment The President, Vice-President and all civil officers of the United States shall be removed from office on impeachment for, and conviction of, treason, bribery, or other high crimes and **misdemeanors**.

VOCABULARY

reprieves delays or cancellations of punishment

convene call together

misdemeanors violations of the law

A CLOSER LOOK

SUPREME COURT APPOINTMENTS

Recent presidents have used their power of appointment to add minorities and women to the Supreme Court. In 1967, President Lyndon Johnson appointed the first African-American justice, Thurgood Marshall. In 1981, President Ronald Reagan appointed the first woman, Sandra Day O'Connor.

12. What do you think influences a president's choice for a Supreme Court justice?

A CLOSER LOOK

STATE OF THE UNION

Major TV networks broadcast the State of the Union address to the whole nation. In this yearly message, the president urges Congress to achieve certain lawmaking goals. The president's speech also must gain the attention of TV viewers.

13. Why is the president's power to persuade an important political skill?

Article 2 Assessment

1. Main Ideas

a. What is the chief purpose of the executive branch?

b. What are the requirements for becoming president?

c. How does the Constitution limit the president's power to make appointments and treaties?

2. Critical Thinking

Analyzing Issues Why do you think the Constitution states that the president must seek approval from the Senate for most political appointments and treaties?

THINK ABOUT
- the abuse of power
- the will of the voters

MORE ABOUT . . .

Military Powers of the President

The president is the commander in chief of the military, but the president cannot declare war—only Congress can. However, the president can order troops into action without congressional approval.

After Richard Nixon openly defied a request from Congress to be informed about troop deployment, Congress passed the War Powers Resolution. The resolution requires the president to report any combat involvement to the Congress and to end it within 60 or 90 days unless Congress approves a longer time period. Several presidents in the late 20th century have ignored the resolution.

MORE ABOUT . . .

The President's Cabinet

The Constitution does not specifically call for a cabinet of presidential advisers. But it does mention executive departments. The heads of the executive departments become part of the president's advisory board—the cabinet.

George Washington's cabinet consisted of four members—Secretaries of State, Treasury, and War, and the Attorney General. Today's cabinet has the heads of 14 departments. The president may also give cabinet rank to other high-ranking officials whose advice on issues would be valuable.

Citizenship Today
- Organization of the Executive Branch, p. 50

Formal Assessment
- Section Quiz, p. 152

Assessment: Article 2

1. Main Ideas

a. to enforce laws **b.** being a natural-born citizen, at least 35 years old, who has been a resident of the United States for 14 years or more
c. Many presidential appointments and all treaties with foreign powers require the Senate's approval.

2. Critical Thinking

Possible Responses This requirement is one of the checks and balances within the Constitution. It limits the power of the president in making foreign policy and appointing important government officials.

OBJECTIVE

Students will be able to explain the organization and duties of the federal courts.

INSTRUCT

Article 3: The Judiciary

- How is interpreting the laws different from enforcing the laws?
- How do the courts shape government policies?
- How do the courts interact with the other branches of government?

Citizenship Today
- Simulation 3: Mock Trial, pp. 30–41

MORE ABOUT . . .

Federal Courts

The Constitution actually creates only one court—the Supreme Court. It gives Congress the ability to set up "inferior" courts. Today the federal court system consists of three tiers.

At the lowest level are 94 U.S. District Courts. These are the courts where federal trials take place. The second level in the court system includes 13 U.S. Courts of Appeal. These courts hear cases "on appeal." At the third level is the highest court of appeal, the Supreme Court.

Citizenship Today
- Organization of the Judicial Branch, pp. 54–57

MORE ABOUT . . .

Judicial Review

The Constitution does not spell out the power of judicial review. This power emerged primarily from a case called *Marbury* v. *Madison.* That was the first case in which the Supreme Court ruled that an act of Congress was unconstitutional. Chief Justice John Marshall wrote, "It is emphatically the province and duty of the judicial department to say what the law is."

Citizenship Today
- *Marbury* v. *Madison,* p. 83

VOCABULARY

inferior courts courts with less authority than the Supreme Court

appellate having power to review court decisions

A CLOSER LOOK

ORGANIZING FEDERAL COURTS

The Judiciary Act of 1789, passed by the First Congress, included establishing a Supreme Court with a chief justice and five associate justices and other lower federal courts.

14. How many Supreme Court justices are there today?

A CLOSER LOOK

JUDICIAL POWER

Judicial power gives the Supreme Court and other federal courts the authority to hear certain kinds of cases. These courts have the power to rule in cases involving the Constitution, national laws, treaties, and states' conflicts.

15. What federal cases have you seen reported on TV?

Article 3. *The Judiciary*

MAIN IDEA The judicial branch interprets the laws. This branch includes the Supreme Court, the highest court in the nation, and other federal courts.

WHY IT MATTERS NOW Supreme Court rulings can shape government policies on hotly debated issues.

Section 1. Federal Courts and Judges The judicial power of the United States shall be vested in one Supreme Court, and in such **inferior courts** as the Congress may from time to time ordain and establish. The judges, both of the Supreme and inferior courts, shall hold their offices during good behavior, and shall, at stated times, receive for their services a compensation, which shall not be diminished during their continuance in office.

Section 2. The Courts' Authority

1. General Authority The judicial power shall extend to all cases, in law and equity, arising under this Constitution, the laws of the United States, and treaties made, or which shall be made, under their authority;—to all cases affecting ambassadors, other public ministers and consuls;—to all cases of admiralty and maritime jurisdiction;—to controversies to which the United States shall be a party;—to controversies between two or more states;—~~between a state and citizens of another state;—~~between citizens of different states;—between citizens of the same state claiming lands under grants of different states, ~~and between a state, or the citizens thereof, and foreign states, citizens or subjects.~~

A CLOSER LOOK **Judicial Review**

Judicial review allows the Supreme Court and other federal courts to play a key role in lawmaking. The judges examine a law or government activity. They then decide whether it violates the Constitution. The Supreme Court established this important right in the case of *Marbury* v. *Madison* (1803). (See Chapter 10.)

2. Supreme Court In all cases affecting ambassadors, other public ministers and consuls, and those in which a state shall be party, the Supreme Court shall have original jurisdiction. In all the other cases before mentioned, the Supreme Court shall have **appellate** jurisdiction, both as to law and fact, with such exceptions, and under such regulations, as the Congress shall make.

A CLOSER LOOK

14. nine

15. Examples of federal cases include those involving states' rights; acts of terrorism within the United States; protection of constitutional rights, such as freedom of speech and religion; and protection of civil liberties. Be sure students understand that ordinary criminal cases—even those involving major crimes such as murder—fall under the jurisdiction of state courts.

A CLOSER LOOK Checks and Balances

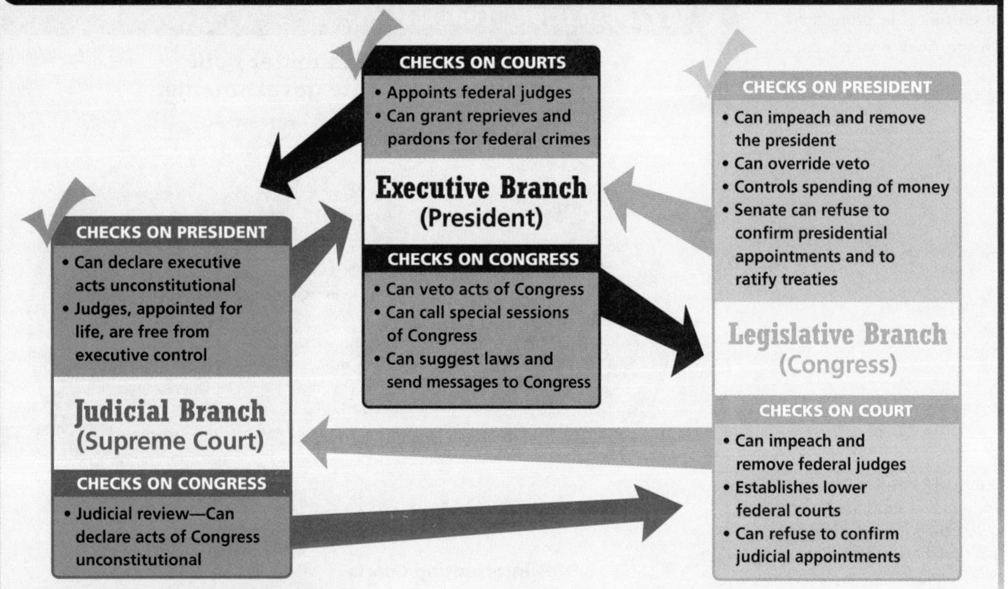

CHECKS ON COURTS
• Appoints federal judges
• Can grant reprieves and pardons for federal crimes
Executive Branch
(President)
CHECKS ON CONGRESS
• Can veto acts of Congress
• Can call special sessions of Congress
• Can suggest laws and send messages to Congress
CHECKS ON PRESIDENT
• Can impeach and remove the president
• Can override veto
• Controls spending of money
• Senate can refuse to confirm presidential appointments and to ratify treaties
Legislative Branch
(Congress)
CHECKS ON COURT
• Can impeach and remove federal judges
• Establishes lower federal courts
• Can refuse to confirm judicial appointments
CHECKS ON PRESIDENT
• Can declare executive acts unconstitutional
• Judges, appointed for life, are free from executive control
Judicial Branch
(Supreme Court)
CHECKS ON CONGRESS
• Judicial review—Can declare acts of Congress unconstitutional

SKILLBUILDER Interpreting Charts

1. *Why is judicial review an important action of the Supreme Court?*
2. *Which check do you think is most powerful? Why?*

3. Trial by Jury The trial of all crimes, except in cases of impeachment, shall be by jury; and such trial shall be held in the state where the said crimes shall have been committed; but when not committed within any state, the trial shall be at such place or places as the Congress may by law have directed.

Section 3. Treason

1. Definition Treason against the United States shall consist only in levying war against them, or in adhering to their enemies, giving them aid and comfort. No person shall be convicted of treason unless on the testimony of two witnesses to the same overt act, or on confession in open court.

2. Punishment The Congress shall have power to declare the punishment of treason, but no attainder of treason shall work corruption of blood, or forfeiture except during the life of the person attained.

SKILLBUILDER Possible Responses

1. Checks the lawmaking powers of Congress; makes sure that laws and government actions do not violate the Constitution.
2. Students should choose one of the checks shown on the chart and support their choice with convincing reasons.

Article 3 Assessment

1. Main Ideas

a. What is the main purpose of the judicial branch?

b. What is judicial review?

c. What are two kinds of cases that can begin in the Supreme Court?

2. Critical Thinking

Drawing Conclusions Why might the Supreme Court feel less political pressure than Congress in making judgments about the Constitution?

THINK ABOUT

- the appointment of Supreme Court justices
- Congress members' obligation to voters

HISTORY FROM VISUALS

Interpreting the Chart Ask students to choose two branches and find the ways they check and balance each other. Remind them that sometimes the powers are clearly stated and other times the answer must be inferred. Continue to compare until all possible pairings have been completed. Help students rephrase in their own words the limitations explained in the chart.

Extension Have students devise a way to present the information in the chart in skit form.

Citizenship Today
• The Role of the Judicial Branch, p. 71

MORE ABOUT . . .

Treason

The Constitution sets a high standard of proof for treason. The Framers knew, from examples in English history, that charges of treason were often politically motivated. Thus, the Constitution requires open acts of treason—not merely disloyal thoughts or words—before a person can be convicted.

The first person to be tried for treason under this law was Aaron Burr, a former vice-president, in 1807. Burr was suspected of trying to found a western empire, taking over part of the United States. But the evidence against him did not meet the high constitutional standard, and he was acquitted.

Formal Assessment
• Section Quiz, p. 153

Assessment: Article 3

1. Main Ideas

a. to interpret laws **b.** the power to examine a law and decide whether or not it violates the Constitution **c.** cases involving the Constitution, national laws, treaties, and state conflicts

2. Critical Thinking

Possible Responses Supreme Court justices are not elected; they are appointed for life. Therefore, they do not need to be concerned with winning voter support for their decisions about the Constitution.

HISTORY FROM VISUALS

Interpreting Graphics Have the students study the national and state powers. Ask students if they think any of the state powers could be handled by the federal government. Then ask why they think those powers were assigned to the states. **Possible Responses** The federal government might set up schools or regulate state commerce, marriages, and corporations. These are areas that do not involve other states or foreign nations, so there is little reason for national involvement. The states wish to maintain local control.

Extension Have the students illustrate a chart showing the national, shared, and state powers.

OBJECTIVES

1. Students will be able to summarize the processes for adding states and for amending the Constitution.
2. Students will be able to describe the nature of the supremacy of the national government.

INSTRUCT

Articles 4–7: States, Amendments, Supremacy, and Ratification

- In what ways should the "united states" cooperate?
- How can the Constitution be changed?
- What does the "supremacy clause" mean?

In-Depth Resources: Unit 2
- Guided Reading, p. 64

Reading Study Guide (Spanish and English), pp. 81–82

Access for Students Acquiring English/ESL
- Guided Reading, p. 55

VOCABULARY

immunities legal protections
suffrage right to vote

A CLOSER LOOK **Federalism**

Americans live under both national and state governments.

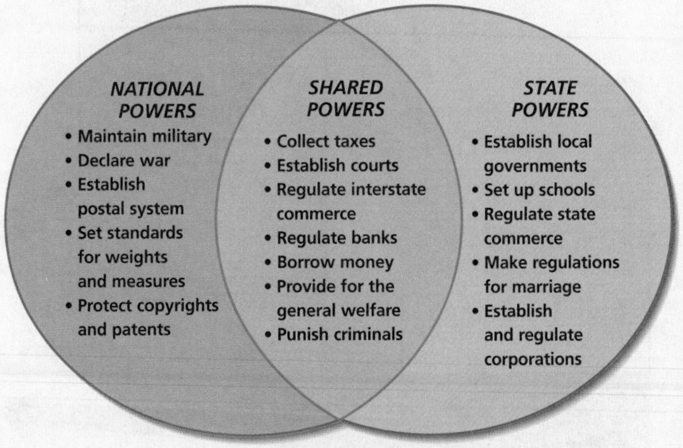

NATIONAL POWERS
• Maintain military
• Declare war
• Establish postal system
• Set standards for weights and measures
• Protect copyrights and patents
SHARED POWERS
• Collect taxes
• Establish courts
• Regulate interstate commerce
• Regulate banks
• Borrow money
• Provide for the general welfare
• Punish criminals
STATE POWERS
• Establish local governments
• Set up schools
• Regulate state commerce
• Make regulations for marriage
• Establish and regulate corporations

SKILLBUILDER **Interpreting Charts**
What do you think is the purpose of dividing the powers between national and state governments?

SKILLBUILDER Possible Responses
Makes national and state governments partners in governing; builds cooperation between national and state governments; gives states local control, while allowing national government to direct issues that affect the whole country.

Article 4. *Relations Among States*

MAIN IDEA **States must honor one another's laws, records, and court rulings.**
WHY IT MATTERS NOW **Article 4 promotes cooperation, equality, and fair treatment of citizens from all the states.**

Section 1. State Acts and Records Full faith and credit shall be given in each state to the public acts, records, and judicial proceedings of every other state. And the Congress may by general laws prescribe the manner in which such acts, records and proceedings shall be proved, and the effect thereof.

Section 2. Rights of Citizens

1. Citizenship The citizens of each state shall be entitled to all privileges and **immunities** of citizens in the several states.

2. Extradition A person charged in any state with treason, felony, or other crime, who shall flee from justice, and be found in another state, shall on demand of the executive authority of the state from which he fled, be delivered up, to be removed to the state having jurisdiction of the crime.

~~**3. Fugitive Slaves** No person held to service or labor in one state, under the laws thereof, escaping into another, shall, in consequence of any law or regulation therein, be discharged from such service or labor, but shall be delivered up on claim of the party to whom such service or labor may be due.~~

A CLOSER LOOK

EXTRADITION

Persons charged with serious crimes cannot escape punishment by fleeing to another state. They must be returned to the first state and stand trial there.

16. Why do you think the Framers included the power of extradition?

ACTIVITY OPTIONS

INTERDISCIPLINARY LINK: GEOGRAPHY — BLOCK SCHEDULING

CREATING NEW STATES

Class Time 30 minutes

Task Creating a map of the United States with new states

Purpose To understand the constitutional procedure for admitting new states

Supplies Needed
- Blank maps of the United States
- Atlas with physical and political maps of the United States
- Tracing paper
- Markers or colored pencils

Activity Divide the class into small groups and give each group a blank map of the United States. Tell them to create a new set of states. They may wish to consult the atlas to consider geographical features. Using tracing paper, draw a map with the current state boundaries. Place the tracing paper over the new states so that students can compare their new states with the old ones. Look at Article 4, Section 3.1. How would the new states have to be admitted?

Section 3. New States

1. Admission New states may be admitted by the Congress into this Union; but no new state shall be formed or erected within the jurisdiction of any other state; nor any state be formed by the junction of two or more states, or parts of states, without the consent of the legislatures of the states concerned as well as of the Congress.

2. Congressional Authority The Congress shall have power to dispose of and make all needful rules and regulations respecting the territory or other property belonging to the United States; and nothing in this Constitution shall be so construed as to prejudice any claims of the United States, or of any particular state.

Section 4. Guarantees to the States

The United States shall guarantee to every state in this Union a republican form of government, and shall protect each of them against invasion; and on application of the legislature, or of the executive (when the legislature cannot be convened) against domestic violence.

Article 5. *Amending the Constitution*

MAIN IDEA **The Constitution can be amended, or formally changed.**

WHY IT MATTERS NOW **The amendment process allows the Constitution to adapt to modern times.**

The Congress, whenever two-thirds of both houses shall deem it necessary, shall propose amendments to this Constitution, or, on the application of the legislatures of two-thirds of the several states, shall call a convention for proposing amendments, which, in either case, shall be valid to all intents and purposes, as part of this Constitution, when ratified by the legislatures of three-fourths of the several states, or by conventions in three-fourths thereof, as the one or the other mode of ratification may be proposed by the Congress; ~~provided that no amendment which may be made prior to the year one thousand eight hundred and eight shall in any manner affect the first and fourth clauses in the ninth section of the first article~~; and that no state, without its consent, shall be deprived of its equal **suffrage** in the Senate.

A CLOSER LOOK **Process for Amending the Constitution**

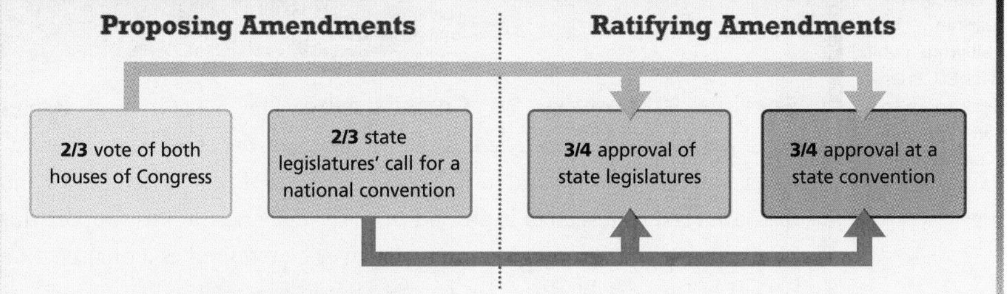

SKILLBUILDER **Interpreting Charts**

Why do you think more votes are needed to ratify an amendment than to propose one?

A CLOSER LOOK

ADMISSION TO STATEHOOD

In 1998, Puerto Ricans voted against their island becoming the 51st state. A lawyer in Puerto Rico summed up a main reason: "Puerto Ricans want to have ties to the U. S., but they want to protect their language and culture." Also, as a U.S. commonwealth, Puerto Rico makes its own laws and handles its own finances.

17. Do you think Puerto Rico should become a state? Why or why not?

SKILLBUILDER Possible Responses
Framers wanted ideas for constitutional changes to be considered but not too easily accepted and approved.

CRITICAL THINKING ACTIVITY

Analyzing Ask students to consider the sentence that begins "Full faith and credit" in Article 4, Section 1. Ask why this is an important statement for relations among the states. In Section 2, why is it important that states grant one another's citizens the same "privileges and immunities"?

Class Time 10 minutes

MORE ABOUT . . .

Unratified Amendments

Twenty-seven amendments have been added to the Constitution since it was ratified in 1789. Other proposed amendments didn't make it. Among the rejected amendments were proposals involving numbers for representation in Congress, slavery, titles of nobility, and child labor. The most widely publicized amendment that failed in recent years was the Equal Rights Amendment, which would have made equality for men and women a part of the Constitution.

HISTORY FROM VISUALS

Interpreting a Chart Have students study the chart and focus on the ways to change the Constitution. Ask students to identify two ways that a new amendment can begin. **Answers** (1) by a two-thirds vote of both houses of Congress; (2) if two-thirds of state legislatures call for a convention

Extension Have students do research to find out which of the above methods has been used most frequently.

A CLOSER LOOK

16. The states involved must negotiate with one another. The state where the suspects are in custody usually has first claim. However, if one crime was much more serious than the others, public pressure might force the other states to turn the suspects over for trial where the most serious crime occurred.

17. Yes—Puerto Rico should take advantage of the economic and political benefits of becoming a state. No—Puerto Rico should maintain its independence and preserve its cultural identity.

MORE ABOUT . . .

Integrating Central High School, 1957

Ordered to allow African Americans to attend Central High School, Arkansas Governor Orval Faubus, a segregationist, refused to maintain law and order. He allowed angry mobs to threaten the nine African-American teenagers at the school. Even after federal troops arrived, the nine students and their families endured death threats, midnight phone calls, and shots through their home windows. Several times, lynch mobs chased and nearly caught the students. At school, for a full year, the students were shoved, pushed down staircases, slapped, spat upon, and cursed. Their bravery in the face of constant danger, day after day, made the nine teenagers heroes in the struggle for civil rights.

HISTORY FROM VISUALS

Interpreting the Photograph Ask the students to examine the photograph and determine what the soldiers are doing. Then ask why they think the soldiers are present. **Possible Responses** The soldiers are protecting the students, watching for danger; they are ordered to be there to prevent violence.

Extension Have the students find out more about the nine students who integrated Central High School in Little Rock, Arkansas.

VOCABULARY

ratification official approval

unanimous consent complete agreement

A CLOSER LOOK

PAYING DEBTS

The U.S. government agreed to pay all debts held under the Articles of Confederation. For example, the United States still owed money from the costs of the Revolutionary War.

18. What problems might arise in a country that has a huge national debt?

Article 6. *Supremacy of the National Government*

MAIN IDEA **The Constitution, national laws, and treaties are the supreme, or highest, law of the land. All government officials must promise to support the Constitution.**

WHY IT MATTERS NOW **The authority of federal laws over state laws helps keep the nation unified.**

Section 1. Valid Debts All debts contracted and engagements entered into, before the adoption of this Constitution, shall be as valid against the United States under this Constitution, as under the Confederation.

Section 2. Supreme Law This Constitution, and the laws of the United States which shall be made in pursuance thereof; and all treaties made, or which shall be made, under the authority of the United States, shall be the supreme law of the land; and the judges in every state shall be bound thereby, anything in the constitution or laws of any state to the contrary notwithstanding.

A CLOSER LOOK

In 1957, the "supreme law of the land" was put to a test. The governor of Arkansas defied a Supreme Court order. The Court ruled that African-American students could go to all-white public schools. President Dwight D. Eisenhower then sent federal troops to protect the first African-American students to enroll in Central High School in Little Rock, Arkansas.

Section 3. Loyalty to Constitution The Senators and Representatives before mentioned, and the members of the several state legislatures, and all executive and judicial officers, both of the United States and of the several states, shall be bound by oath or affirmation to support this Constitution; but no religious test shall ever be required as a qualification to any office or public trust under the United States.

A CLOSER LOOK

18. damage to nation's economy; lack of economic growth; cuts in federal programs; loss of people's confidence in government; fear of national bankruptcy

19. Slavery was not outlawed; slaves were considered three-fifths of a person for the purposes of taxation and representation in Congress; women were denied the right to vote in most places.

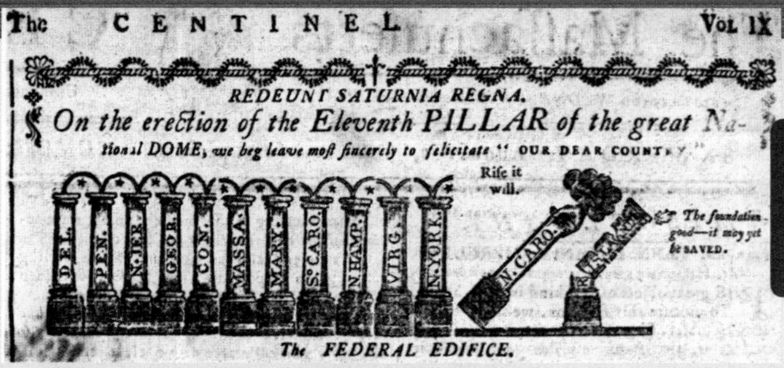
The CENTINEL Vol IX
REDEUNT SATURNIA REGNA.
On the erection of the Eleventh PILLAR of the great National DOME, we beg leave most sincerely to felicitate "OUR DEAR COUNTRY."
Rise it will.
The foundation good—it may yet be SAVED.
DEL.
PENN.
N.JERS.
GEOR.
CON.
MASSA.
MARY.
Sth CARO.
N.HAMP.
VIRG.
N.YORK.
N.CARO.
The FEDERAL EDIFICE.

A CLOSER LOOK

This political cartoon shows that New York was the 11th state to ratify the Constitution. Each of the 13 states is represented by a pillar.

Article 7. *Ratification*

MAIN IDEA Nine of the 13 states had to ratify, or approve, the Constitution before it could go into effect.

WHY IT MATTERS NOW The approval of the Constitution launched a new plan of government still followed today.

The **ratification** of the conventions of nine states shall be sufficient for the establishment of this Constitution between the states so ratifying the same. Done in convention by the **unanimous consent** of the states present, the seventeenth day of September in the year of our Lord one thousand seven hundred and eighty-seven and of the independence of the United States of America the twelfth. In witness whereof we have hereunto subscribed our names.

George Washington—President and deputy from Virginia

New Hampshire: *John Langdon, Nicholas Gilman*

Massachusetts: *Nathaniel Gorham, Rufus King*

Connecticut: *William Samuel Johnson, Roger Sherman*

New York: *Alexander Hamilton*

New Jersey: *William Livingston, David Brearley, William Paterson, Jonathan Dayton*

Pennsylvania: *Benjamin Franklin, Thomas Mifflin, Robert Morris, George Clymer, Thomas FitzSimons, Jared Ingersoll, James Wilson, Gouverneur Morris*

Delaware: *George Read, Gunning Bedford, Jr., John Dickinson, Richard Bassett, Jacob Broom*

Maryland: *James McHenry, Dan of St. Thomas Jenifer, Daniel Carroll*

Virginia: *John Blair, James Madison, Jr.*

North Carolina: *William Blount, Richard Dobbs Spaight, Hugh Williamson*

South Carolina: *John Rutledge, Charles Cotesworth Pinckney, Charles Pinckney, Pierce Butler*

Georgia: *William Few, Abraham Baldwin*

A CLOSER LOOK

THE SIGNERS

The 39 men who signed the Constitution were wealthy and well-educated. About half of them were trained in law. Others were doctors, merchants, bankers, and slaveholding planters. Missing from the list of signatures are the names of African Americans, Native Americans, and women. These groups reflected the varied population of the United States in the 1780s.

19. How do you think the absence of these groups affected the decisions made in creating the Constitution?

Articles 4–7 Assessment

1. Main Ideas

a. What rights does Article 4 guarantee to citizens if they go to other states in the nation?

b. What are two ways of proposing an amendment to the Constitution?

c. What makes up "the supreme law of the land"?

2. Critical Thinking

Forming and Supporting Opinions Should the Framers of the Constitution have allowed the people to vote directly for ratification of the Constitution? Why or why not?

THINK ABOUT

- the idea that the government belongs to the people
- the general public's ability to make sound political decisions

HISTORY FROM VISUALS

Interpreting a Political Cartoon Ask the students to describe the pillars for North Carolina and Rhode Island. What is the cartoonist suggesting about those states? **Possible Response** Those pillars are broken or collapsing. Ratification efforts in those states were apparently not succeeding when the cartoon was drawn.

Extension Have the students find the number of states necessary to ratify the Constitution, as listed in Article 7. Then, using the cartoon, determine which state was the final one needed for the Constitution to go into effect.

MORE ABOUT . . .

The Signers of the Constitution

Of the signers, only one—Roger Sherman—signed all four of the most important documents in the history of the new nation. He signed the Articles of Association (1774), the Declaration of Independence (1776), the Articles of Confederation (1777), and the Constitution (1787).

Many of the signers went on to become senators or representatives; several served in the Supreme Court; and two—Washington and Madison—were elected president.

Formal Assessment

- Section Quiz, p. 154

Assessment: Articles 4–7

1. Main Ideas

a. the privileges and immunities (rights) of the citizens in those states **b.** a two-thirds vote of both houses of Congress; call by two-thirds of state legislatures for national conventions **c.** Constitution, national laws, and treaties

2. Critical Thinking

Possible Responses Yes—People should have had a more direct say because they, in turn, were directly affected by the Constitution. The Preamble states that "We the people . . . establish the Constitution of the United States"; therefore, the people should have been allowed to vote directly on ratification.

No—Too many people lacked the necessary political knowledge, and communication was too slow for a widespread popular vote in 1787–1790.

OBJECTIVES

1. To summarize changes made in the original Constitution
2. To identify rights protected in the Bill of Rights
3. To trace the expansion of rights for all citizens as evidenced in the Constitution

FOCUS & MOTIVATE

5-MINUTE WARM-UP

Recognizing Effects To help students understand how the Bill of Rights has an impact on their lives, have them answer these questions.

1. Look at the chart on page 250. Which of the freedoms shown have you exercised?
2. What do you think would happen if any of those five freedoms were lost or taken away?

Warm-Up Transparency WTCON

INSTRUCT

The Bill of Rights

- What is the Bill of Rights?
- What specific rights does it protect?
- Why do some individual rights need special protection in the Constitution?

In-Depth Resources: Unit 2
- Guided Reading, p. 65

Reading Study Guide (Spanish and English), pp. 83–84

Access for Students Acquiring English/ESL
- Guided Reading, p. 56

Citizenship Today
- Balancing Liberty and National Security, p. 72

The Bill of Rights and Amendments 11–27

In 1787, Thomas Jefferson sent James Madison a letter about the Constitution. Jefferson wrote, "I will now add what I do not like . . . [there is no] bill of rights." He explained his reasons: "A bill of rights is what the people are entitled to against every government on earth . . . and what no just government should refuse." Jefferson's disapproval is not surprising. In writing the Declaration of Independence, he spelled out basic individual rights that cannot be taken way. These are "life, liberty, and the pursuit of happiness." The Declaration states that governments are formed to protect these rights.

Several states approved the Constitution only if a list of guaranteed freedoms was added. While serving in the nation's first Congress, James Madison helped draft the Bill of Rights. In 1791, these first ten amendments became part of the Constitution.

SKILLBUILDER
Possible Responses
1. Preserves democracy by allowing citizens to voice their ideas and views.
2. Diverse American culture of many religious beliefs; greater acceptance of different religions and sometimes mistrust; opportunities for immigrants who come to the U.S. to escape religious persecution.

AMENDMENTS 1–10. *The Bill of Rights*

MAIN IDEA **The Bill of Rights protects citizens from government interference.**
WHY IT MATTERS NOW **Issues related to the Bill of Rights are still being applied, tested, and interpreted.**

AMENDMENT 1. Religious and Political Freedom (1791)

Congress shall make no law respecting an establishment of religion, or prohibiting the free exercise thereof; or **abridging** the freedom of speech, or of the press; or the right of the people peaceably to assemble, and to petition the Government for a redress of grievances.

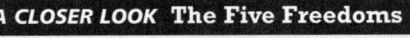

A CLOSER LOOK **The Five Freedoms**

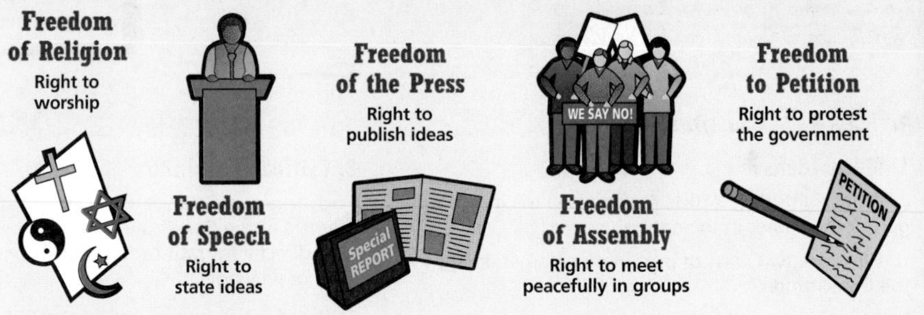

SKILLBUILDER **Interpreting Charts**
1. *Why is freedom of speech and the press important in a democratic society?*
2. *What impact has religious freedom had on the American way of life?*

TEACHING STRATEGY

Restating the Bill of Rights To help students understand the rights and impact of the Bill of Rights on their lives, they need to understand the language of the Constitution. As you cover each of the amendments, have them write out the amendment in their own words. Then have them list one or more ways the amendment affects people's lives today.

You may want to have students keep a scrapbook of print media articles or a log of television reports that relate to the freedoms protected by the Bill of Rights.

AMENDMENT 2. Right to Bear Arms (1791) A well-regulated militia, being necessary to the security of a free state, the right of the people to keep and bear arms, shall not be infringed.

AMENDMENT 3. Quartering Troops (1791) No soldier shall, in time of peace be **quartered** in any house, without the consent of the owner, nor in time of war, but in a manner to be prescribed by law.

AMENDMENT 4. Search and Seizure (1791) The right of the people to be secure in their persons, houses, papers, and effects, against unreasonable searches and seizures, shall not be violated, and no warrants shall issue, but upon probable cause, supported by oath or affirmation, and particularly describing the place to be searched, and the persons or things to be seized.

AMENDMENT 5. Rights of Accused Persons (1791) No person shall be held to answer for a capital, or otherwise infamous crime, unless on a presentment or indictment of a Grand Jury, except in cases arising in the land or naval forces, or in the militia, when in actual service in time of war or public danger; nor shall any person be subject for the same offense to be twice put in jeopardy of life or limb; nor shall be compelled in any criminal case to be a witness against himself, nor be deprived of life, liberty, or property, without **due process of law;** nor shall private property be taken for public use, without just compensation.

AMENDMENT 6. Right to a Speedy, Public Trial (1791) In all criminal prosecutions, the accused shall enjoy the right to a speedy and public trial, by an impartial jury of the State and district wherein the crime shall have been committed, which district shall have been previously ascertained by law, and to be informed of the nature and cause of the accusation; to be confronted with the witnesses against him; to have **compulsory process** for obtaining witnesses in his favor, and to have the assistance of **counsel** for his defense.

VOCABULARY

abridging reducing

quartered given a place to stay

due process of law fair treatment under the law

compulsory process required procedure

counsel a lawyer

A CLOSER LOOK

SEARCHES

Metal detectors at airports search passengers. Airline workers search all carry-on luggage. Do these actions violate the 4th Amendment? The courts say no. They have cited many situations that allow for searches without a warrant, or written order. A person's right to privacy is balanced against the government's need to prevent crime.

20. What does the right to privacy mean to you at home and at school?

A CLOSER LOOK

In 1966, the Supreme Court made a decision based on the 5th and 6th Amendments. The warnings outlined in this ruling are often called "Miranda rights." Miranda rights protect suspects from giving forced confessions. Police must read these rights to a suspect they are questioning. For example:

- "You have the right to remain silent."
- "Anything that you say can and will be used against you in a court of law."
- "You have the right to an attorney."

MORE ABOUT . . .

Locker Searches

Throughout the nation, school officials claim the authority to search student lockers, usually for drugs or weapons. Students often assert that such searches violate their rights under the 4th Amendment.

Most courts have ruled that lockers are the property of the school district; therefore, school officials may legally search lockers. In 1998, the Pennsylvania State Supreme Court ruled that "a school district's interests outweigh a student's privacy rights." Searches, however, cannot be conducted without reasonable grounds. That is, school officials must have reason to believe that there is contraband in the locker.

MORE ABOUT . . .

Miranda Rights

The statement "You have the right to remain silent," often heard in television police programs, is part of the well-known list called "Miranda Rights." Ernesto Miranda was charged with kidnapping and rape. After being questioned by police, he confessed and signed a written statement. However, he had never been told that he had the right to say nothing or to have a lawyer. A jury convicted him, based on his written confession. But in 1966, the Supreme Court ruled that the police had violated Miranda's rights under the 5th and 6th Amendments. Now police must inform suspects of their rights before questioning them.

Citizenship Today
- Suspects' Rights versus Public Protection, p. 73

Citizenship Today
- *Miranda* v. *Arizona,* pp. 81–82

A CLOSER LOOK

20. at home—private phone conversations; at school—no locker searches without good reason

HISTORY FROM VISUALS

Interpreting the Photographs Have the students examine the photographs. Ask them which side of the death penalty controversy they think the pictured people support. Have the students identify the arguments the placards present. **Possible Responses** The young woman at the left represents the anti-death-penalty group; the group of people at the right supports the death penalty. Their arguments include victim rights, political correctness, equality for victims and guilty parties.

Extension Ask students to find the phrase in the 8th Amendment that relates to the debate on the death penalty. **Answer** "cruel and unusual punishments." Have students gather additional information about both sides of the argument and conduct a debate in class.

MORE ABOUT . . .

"Cruel and Unusual"?

Cases involving the death penalty and the 8th Amendment began to arise in the 1970s. In 1972, the Supreme Court ruled that the death penalty itself was not "cruel and unusual" punishment. However, the Court said that the way the death penalty was then administered did violate the Constitution because death sentences were arbitrary and unpredictable. "People live or die," one justice wrote, "dependent on the whim" of a judge or jury.

States quickly revised their laws to meet the Court's objections. In 1976, the Court allowed the death penalty under one of the new laws. Since then, the Court has continued to debate the issue, almost always upholding the death penalty.

Formal Assessment
- Section Quiz, p. 155

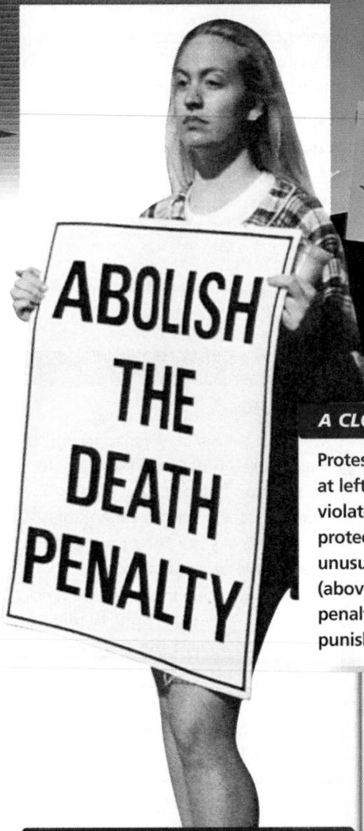

A CLOSER LOOK

Protesters such as the young woman at left claim that the death penalty violates the 8th Amendment, which protects people against "cruel and unusual punishment." Supporters (above) believe that the death penalty is a justly deserved punishment.

AMENDMENT 7. Trial by Jury in Civil Cases (1791) In suits at **common law**, where the value in controversy shall exceed twenty dollars, the right of trial by jury shall be preserved, and no fact tried by a jury, shall be otherwise reexamined in any court of the United States, than according to the rules of the common law.

AMENDMENT 8. Limits of Fines and Punishments (1791) Excessive **bail** shall not be required, nor excessive fines imposed, nor cruel and unusual punishments inflicted.

AMENDMENT 9. Rights of People (1791) The enumeration in the Constitution of certain rights shall not be construed to deny or disparage others retained by the people.

AMENDMENT 10. Powers of States and People (1791) The powers not delegated to the United States by the Constitution, nor prohibited by it to the States, are reserved to the States respectively, or to the people.

A CLOSER LOOK

STATES' POWERS

The 10th Amendment gives the states reserved powers. Any powers not clearly given to the national government by the U.S. Constitution or denied to the states in Article I, Section 10, belong to the states. State constitutions sometimes assume authority in unexpected areas. For example, California's constitution sets rules for governing the use of fishing nets.

21. What are some common areas in which states have authority?

Bill of Rights Assessment

1. Main Ideas

a. Which amendment protects your privacy?

b. Which amendments guarantee fair legal treatment?

c. Which amendment prevents the federal government from taking powers away from the states and the people?

2. Critical Thinking

Forming and Supporting Opinions The 4th, 5th, 6th, 7th, and 8th Amendments protect innocent people accused of crimes. Do you think these five amendments also favor the rights of actual criminals? Explain.

THINK ABOUT
- criminals who go free if valuable evidence is found after their trials
- criminals released on bail

252 THE LIVING CONSTITUTION

Assessment: Bill of Rights

1. Main Ideas

a. 3rd and 4th Amendments **b.** 4th, 5th, 6th, 7th, and 8th Amendments **c.** 9th and 10th Amendments

2. Critical Thinking

Possible Responses Yes—It's too easy for criminals to skirt the law using these amendments. The police need to be able to gather evidence more freely. No—Police have routinely violated the rights of accused persons. These amendments are necessary to protect all people.

Amendments 11–27

MAIN IDEA The Constitution has adapted to social changes and historical trends.

WHY IT MATTERS NOW Amendments 11–27 show that the Constitution is a living document.

AMENDMENT 11. Lawsuits Against States (1798)

Passed by Congress March 4, 1794. Ratified February 7, 1795. Proclaimed 1798.
Note: Article 3, Section 2, of the Constitution was modified by Amendment 11.

The Judicial power of the United States shall not be construed to extend to any suit in law or **equity**, commenced or prosecuted against one of the United States by citizens of another state, or by citizens or subjects of any foreign state.

AMENDMENT 12. Election of Executives (1804)

Passed by Congress December 9, 1803. Ratified June 15, 1804.
Note: Part of Article 2, Section 1, of the Constitution was replaced by the 12th Amendment.

The electors shall meet in their respective states and vote by ballot for President and Vice-President, one of whom, at least, shall not be an inhabitant of the same state with themselves; they shall name in their ballots the person voted for as President, and in distinct ballots the person voted for as Vice-President, and they shall make distinct lists of all persons voted for as President, and of all persons voted for as Vice-President, and of the number of votes for each, which lists they shall sign and certify, and transmit sealed to the seat of the government of the United States, directed to the President of the Senate;—the President of the Senate shall, in the presence of the Senate and House of Representatives, open all the certificates and the votes shall then be counted;—the person having the greatest number of votes for President, shall be the President, if such number be a majority of the whole number of electors appointed; and if no person have such majority, then from the persons having the highest numbers not exceeding three on the list of those voted for as President, the House of Representatives shall choose immediately, by ballot, the President. But in choosing the President, the votes shall be taken by states, the representation from each state having one vote; a quorum for this purpose shall consist of a member or members from two-thirds of the states, and a majority of all the states shall be necessary to a choice. And if the House of Representatives shall not choose a President whenever the right of choice shall devolve upon them, ~~before the fourth day of March next following,~~ then the Vice-President shall act as President, as in the case of the death or other constitutional disability of the President. The person having the greatest number of votes as Vice-President, shall be the Vice-President, if such number be a majority of the whole number of Electors appointed, and if no person have a majority, then from the two highest numbers on the list, the Senate shall choose the Vice-President; a quorum for the purpose shall consist of two-thirds of the whole number of Senators, and a majority of the whole number shall be necessary to a choice. But no person constitutionally ineligible to the office of President shall be eligible to that of Vice-President of the United States.

VOCABULARY

common law a system of law developed in England, based on customs and previous court decisions

bail money paid by arrested persons to guarantee they will return for trial

equity a system of justice not covered under common law

A CLOSER LOOK

SEPARATE BALLOTS

The presidential election of 1800 ended in a tie between Thomas Jefferson and Aaron Burr. At this time, the candidate with the most votes became president. The runner-up became vice-president. The 12th Amendment calls for separate ballots for the president and vice-president. The vice-president is specifically elected to the office, rather than being the presidential candidate with the second-most votes.

22. Why do you think it's important for a presidential election to result in a clear-cut winner?

OBJECTIVES

1. To trace the expansion of voting rights
2. To explain amendments leading to social changes
3. To identify amendments that overturned Supreme Court decisions
4. To summarize changes in election procedures and conditions of office

FOCUS & MOTIVATE

5-MINUTE WARM-UP

Making Generalizations To help students categorize Amendments 11–27, have them answer these questions.

1. Look at the graphic on pages 260–261. Which type of amendment has been the most numerous?
2. Which amendments do you think have had the greatest impact on today's citizens?

Warm-Up Transparency WTCON

INSTRUCT

Amendments 11–27

- How have voting rights expanded?
- Why have few amendments been about social change?
- Why have election procedures and conditions of office needed change?
- How have checks and balances played into constitutional changes?

A CLOSER LOOK

21. Students may list some of the state powers shown in the federalism diagram on page 256.

22. Lack of a clear-cut winner could result in recounts, court cases, and long delays in determining the outcome of an election; this situation could leave the country leaderless in a crisis. Doubts about an election might make citizens mistrustful of the government and insecure about the leadership.

MORE ABOUT . . .

Slavery and the Constitution

The Constitutional Convention struggled with the issue of slavery. Many of the Framers were uneasy about referring openly to slavery in this document, given the ideals of human equality expressed in the Declaration of Independence. So they avoided the word *slave* by using such phrases as "other persons" or "person held to service."

Three places in the body of the Constitution dealt with slavery. Article 1, Section 2, Paragraph 3 established that a slave would count as three-fifths of a person in determining a state's representation in Congress. Article 1, Section 9, Paragraph 1 stated that Congress could not ban the importation of slaves until 1808. And Article 4, Section 2, Paragraph 3 required the return of runaway slaves to their owners. The 13th Amendment overturned all these provisions.

MORE ABOUT . . .

Equality in Sports

Like the Americans with Disabilities Act, the Education Amendments Act of 1972 is based on the 14th Amendment. One of the provisions of the Education Act required schools to provide equal resources for girls and boys in athletics. Known as Title IX, the provision opened up athletics for girls and permanently changed American sports.

Title IX has led to a dramatic increase in the number of girls who participate in high school sports. In 1972, only 1 girl in 27 played sports. By 1999, 1 girl in 3 participated. Many people have said that the U.S. women's victory in the 1999 World Cup Soccer Championship was a direct result of Title IX sports programs.

Citizenship Today

- Equality: Its Meaning and Application, p. 74

VOCABULARY

servitude being under the authority of an owner or master
naturalized granted nationality
insurrection revolt against authority
bounties rewards

AMENDMENT 13. Slavery Abolished (1865)

Passed by Congress January 31, 1865. Ratified December 6, 1865.

Note: A portion of Article 4, Section 2, of the Constitution was superseded by the 13th Amendment.

Section 1. Neither slavery nor involuntary **servitude,** except as a punishment for crime whereof the party shall have been duly convicted, shall exist within the United States, or any place subject to their jurisdiction.

Section 2. Congress shall have power to enforce this article by appropriate legislation.

AMENDMENT 14. Civil Rights (1868)

Passed by Congress June 13, 1866. Ratified July 9, 1868.

Note: Article 1, Section 2, of the Constitution was modified by Section 2 of the 14th Amendment.

Section 1. All persons born or **naturalized** in the United States, and subject to the jurisdiction thereof, are citizens of the United States and of the state wherein they reside. No state shall make or enforce any law which shall abridge the privileges or immunities of citizens of the United States; nor shall any state deprive any person of life, liberty, or property, without due process of law; nor deny to any person within its jurisdiction the equal protection of the laws.

Section 2. Representatives shall be apportioned among the several states according to their respective numbers, counting the whole number of persons in each state, excluding Indians not taxed. But when the right to vote at any election for the choice of electors for President and Vice-President of the United States, Representatives in Congress, the executive and judicial officers of a state, or the members of the legislature thereof, is denied to any of the male inhabitants of such state, being twenty-one years of age, and citizens of the United States, or in any way abridged, except for participation in rebellion, or other crime, the basis of representation therein shall be reduced in the proportion which the number of such male citizens shall bear to the whole number of male citizens twenty-one years of age in such state.

A CLOSER LOOK

The 14th Amendment laid the groundwork for many civil rights laws, such as the Americans with Disabilities Act (1990). This act gave people with mental or physical disabilities "equal protection of the laws." For example, public places had to be designed for wheelchair use. Wider doors and ramps allow disabled people to go in and out of buildings.

254 THE LIVING CONSTITUTION

ACTIVITY OPTIONS

INTERDISCIPLINARY LINK: ART

BLOCK SCHEDULING

CREATING A MURAL

Class Time One class period

Task Creating a design for a mural

Purpose To identify the impact on American society of the 13th, 14th, and 15th Amendments

Supplies Needed

- Drawing paper or graph paper
- Art supplies
- Research materials on the 13th, 14th, and 15th Amendments

Activity Divide the class into small groups and have each group design an outdoor mural to show how the 13th, 14th, and 15th Amendments changed life in the United States even in the 20th century. Then post all the designs and either select one design or create a new design with a combination of ideas from all the plans. The class may wish to paint the design on a large roll of paper.

Section 3. No person shall be a Senator or Representative in Congress, or elector of President and Vice-President, or hold any office, civil or military, under the United States, or under any state, who, having previously taken an oath, as a member of Congress, or as an officer of the United States, or as a member of any state legislature, or as an executive or judicial officer of any state, to support the Constitution of the United States, shall have engaged in **insurrection** or rebellion against the same, or given aid or comfort to the enemies thereof. But Congress may, by a vote of two-thirds of each house, remove such disability.

Section 4. The validity of the public debt of the United States, authorized by law, including debts incurred for payment of pensions and **bounties** for services in suppressing insurrection or rebellion, shall not be questioned. But neither the United States nor any state shall assume or pay any debt or obligation incurred in aid of insurrection or rebellion against the United States, or any claim for the loss or emancipation of any slave; but all such debts, obligations and claims shall be held illegal and void.

Section 5. The Congress shall have power to enforce, by appropriate legislation, the provisions of this article.

AMENDMENT 15. Right to Vote (1870)

Passed by Congress February 26, 1869. Ratified February 3, 1870.

Section 1. The right of citizens of the United States to vote shall not be denied or abridged by the United States or by any state on account of race, color, or previous condition of servitude.

Section 2. The Congress shall have power to enforce this article by appropriate legislation.

A CLOSER LOOK Reconstruction Amendments

The 13th, 14th, and 15th Amendments are often called the Reconstruction Amendments. They were passed after the Civil War during the government's attempt to rebuild the Union and to grant rights to recently freed African Americans.

Amendment 13	Amendment 14	Amendment 15
1865	1868	1870
• Ended slavery in the United States	• Defined national and state citizenship • Protected citizens' rights • Promised "equal protection of the laws"	• Designed to protect African Americans' voting rights

SKILLBUILDER **Interpreting Charts**
What problems did these amendments try to solve?

A CLOSER LOOK

VOTING RIGHTS

The Voting Rights Act of 1965 extended the 15th Amendment. To qualify as voters, African Americans were no longer required to take tests proving that they could read and write. Also, federal examiners could help register voters. As a result, the number of African-American voters rose sharply.

23. What effect do you think the Voting Rights Act had on candidates running for office?

SKILLBUILDER Possible Responses
Corrected unjust treatment of African Americans before the Civil War—enslavement; inequality; denial of citizenship, civil rights, and voting rights.

CRITICAL THINKING ACTIVITY

Recognizing Effects Explain to the class that the 15th Amendment was rarely enforced in the South between 1877 and 1965. Then, in 1965, Congress passed the Voting Rights Act, which provided federal enforcement for African Americans' right to vote.

Write the following statistics on the board or, if possible, on an outline map of the United States. They show the percentage increase in African-American voter registration between 1960 and 1966: Texas, 76.2; Louisiana, 52.8; Mississippi, 695.4; Alabama, 278.8; Georgia, 66.7; Florida, 65.6; Arkansas, 57.5; Tennessee, 21.6; South Carolina, 229.3; North Carolina, 34.3; Virginia, 105.0.

Ask which states had the greatest increase in registration. Then ask students to suggest possible reasons for the greater increases in those states. Finally, ask what other political changes the increase in registered African Americans may have brought about.

Class Time 10 minutes

HISTORY FROM VISUALS

Interpreting the Chart Ask the students to place a sheet of paper over the captions under the three symbols on the chart. Ask them to determine what each of the amendments is about by looking only at the symbols. Then have them read the captions for additional information. **Possible Responses** 13th—freedom; 14th—equality and justice; 15th—voting.

Extension Have the students suggest a way to commemorate the 150th anniversary of these amendments, which will occur in their lifetimes.

Citizenship Today
- Minority Rights, p. 75

A CLOSER LOOK

23. Candidates had to consider the views of increasing numbers of African-American voters; more African-American candidates ran for office.

MORE ABOUT . . .

Income Tax

The Constitution gave the federal government the power to tax, a power it had lacked under the Articles of Confederation. But the Constitution denied the federal government the power to levy a direct tax—that is, a tax paid directly to the government by the taxpayer. For many years, the government received most of its money from tariffs on imported goods. During the Civil War, Congress briefly enacted an income tax to pay war expenses. Then, in 1894, Congress passed a permanent income tax, but the Supreme Court struck it down. The 16th Amendment made it possible for the government to levy a direct tax. By 1917, when the United States entered World War I, the income tax was the largest source of government revenue. It remains so today.

A CLOSER LOOK

INCOME TAX

People below the poverty level, as defined by the federal government, do not have to pay income tax. In 1997, the poverty level for a family of four was $16,400 per year. About 13.3 percent of all Americans were considered poor in 1997.

24. Why do you think people below the poverty level do not pay any income tax?

AMENDMENT 16. Income Tax (1913)

Passed by Congress July 12, 1909. Ratified February 3, 1913.

Note: Article 1, Section 9, of the Constitution was modified by the 16th Amendment.

The Congress shall have power to lay and collect taxes on incomes, from whatever source derived, without apportionment among the several states, and without regard to any census or enumeration.

AMENDMENT 17. Direct Election of Senators (1913)

Passed by Congress May 13, 1912. Ratified April 8, 1913.

Note: Article 1, Section 3, of the Constitution was modified by the 17th Amendment.

Section 1. The Senate of the United States shall be composed of two Senators from each state, elected by the people thereof, for six years; and each Senator shall have one vote. The electors in each state shall have the qualifications requisite for electors of the most numerous branch of the state legislatures.

Section 2. When vacancies happen in the representation of any state in the Senate, the executive authority of such state shall issue writs of election to fill such vacancies: Provided, that the legislature of any state may empower the executive thereof to make temporary appointments until the people fill the vacancies by election as the legislature may direct.

Section 3. This amendment shall not be so construed as to affect the election or term of any Senator chosen before it becomes valid as part of the Constitution.

MORE ABOUT . . .

Prohibition and Bootlegging

One of the effects of the Prohibition Amendment was to create an illegal trade in alcohol. That trade was run by "bootleggers." The term comes from the practice of hiding flasks of liquor in a boot top. Bootleggers developed an entire chain of distribution from distillers or brewers to bars. Those bars were often called "speakeasies," because of the need to speak quietly to avoid attracting police attention. Prohibition was repealed in 1933 by the 21st Amendment.

A CLOSER LOOK

Under Prohibition, people broke the law if they made, sold, or shipped alcoholic beverages. Powerful crime gangs turned selling illegal liquor into a big business. This photo shows federal agents getting ready to smash containers of illegal whiskey. The 21st Amendment ended Prohibition.

AMENDMENT 18. Prohibition (1919)

Passed by Congress December 18, 1917. Ratified January 16, 1919. Repealed by the 21st Amendment.

~~**Section 1.** After one year from the ratification of this article the manufacture, sale, or transportation of intoxicating liquors within, the importation thereof into, or the exportation thereof from the United States and all territory subject to the jurisdiction thereof for beverage purposes is hereby prohibited.~~

~~**Section 2.** The Congress and the several states shall have concurrent power to enforce this article by appropriate legislation.~~

~~**Section 3.** This article shall be inoperative unless it shall have been ratified as an amendment to the Constitution by the legislatures of the several states, as provided in the Constitution, within seven years from the date of the submission hereof to the states by the Congress.~~

ACTIVITY OPTIONS

INTERDISCIPLINARY LINK: WORLD HISTORY

BLOCK SCHEDULING

RESEARCHING SUFFRAGE MOVEMENTS

Class Time One class period

Task Tracing women's suffrage movements in other parts of the world

Purpose To identify the links between the American suffrage movement and similar movements in other countries

Supplies Needed

- Research materials on woman suffrage in the United States and in other nations
- Large sheets of paper
- Markers

Activity Divide students into small groups. They should do research into suffrage movements both in the United States and in other countries. Tell them to look for connections or comparisons among the various movements.

Next, each group should create a graphic to illustrate the information they have found. The graphic could be a time line, a world map, a sequence chart, or another visual method of showing the information.

A CLOSER LOOK

At left, marchers campaign for the 19th Amendment—woman suffrage. Since winning the right to vote in 1920, women have slowly gained political power. Pictured below are Congress members who belong to the Congressional Caucus for Women's Issues.

AMENDMENT 19. Woman Suffrage (1920)

Passed by Congress June 4, 1919. Ratified August 18, 1920.

Section 1. The right of citizens of the United States to vote shall not be denied or abridged by the United States or by any state on account of sex.

Section 2. Congress shall have power to enforce this article by appropriate legislation.

AMENDMENT 20. "Lame Duck" Sessions (1933)

Passed by Congress March 2, 1932. Ratified January 23, 1933.

Note: Article 1, Section 4, of the Constitution was modified by Section 2 of this amendment. In addition, a portion of the 12th Amendment was superseded by Section 3.

Section 1. The terms of the President and Vice-President shall end at noon on the 20th day of January, and the terms of Senators and Representatives at noon on the 3rd day of January, of the years in which such terms would have ended if this article had not been ratified; and the terms of their successors shall then begin.

Section 2. The Congress shall assemble at least once in every year, and such meeting shall begin at noon on the 3rd day of January, unless they shall by law appoint a different day.

Section 3. If, at the time fixed for the beginning of the term of the President, the President elect shall have died, the Vice-President elect shall become President. If a President shall not have been chosen before the time fixed for the beginning of his term, or if the President elect shall have failed to qualify, then the Vice-President elect shall act as President until a President shall have qualified; and the Congress may by law provide for the case wherein neither a President elect nor a Vice-President elect shall have

A CLOSER LOOK

THE EQUAL RIGHTS AMENDMENT

In 1920, the 19th Amendment took effect, guaranteeing women the right to vote. Nevertheless, many women have continued to face discrimination in the United States. In 1923, the National Women's Party supported the passage of an equal rights amendment to protect women. Congress did not pass such an amendment until 1972. In 1982, however, the amendment died after it failed to be ratified by enough states to be added to the Constitution.

25. Why do you think the 19th Amendment failed to create equality for women?

MORE ABOUT . . .

Woman Suffrage

More than a century before the 19th Amendment, a few women in the United States were already voting. After the Revolution, New Jersey granted the vote to all citizens who owned the required amount of property—and some of those property owners were women. But in 1807, New Jersey limited suffrage to white males.

Not until 1890 did another state grant women the right to vote. In that year, Wyoming became the first state to enact a constitution that allowed woman suffrage. By 1918, women could vote in 15 states, mostly in the West.

Citizenship Today

• The Rights of Women, p. 80

MORE ABOUT . . .

Women in Congress

Jeannette Rankin was the first woman elected to Congress. A Republican representative from Montana, she served from 1917 to 1919 and again from 1941 to 1943. Best known for her pacifist stands against both World Wars I and II, she was also a vigorous supporter of social and electoral reforms.

The number of women in Congress increased gradually. By the end of the 1990s, there were 58 women among the 435 representatives in the House and 9 women among the 100 senators. Reflecting the increased participation of women in politics, the Congressional Caucus for Women's Issues informs other members of Congress about such matters as economic equity, education, domestic violence, and family concerns.

A CLOSER LOOK

24. The government recognizes that poor people need to use all their earnings to pay for basic needs—food, clothing, and shelter.

25. The 19th Amendment only dealt with the right to vote. Voting rights alone cannot create equality.

MORE ABOUT . . .

The Repeal of Prohibition

It proved virtually impossible to enforce the Volstead Act (Prohibition). There were only 1,550 federal agents to police the entire country. Although the consumption of alcohol did decline significantly, many people broke the law and patronized speakeasies. Some public officials got rich by taking part in the bootlegging industry they were supposed to prosecute. Organized crime grew by enormous proportions. This widespread disregard for the law led many influential individuals to support repeal. In 1932, the Democratic Party included a call for repeal in its platform.

MORE ABOUT . . .

Roosevelt's Four Terms

When Franklin Roosevelt accepted the nomination for a third term, even some of his strongest supporters objected. His previous vice-president, John Nance Garner, was among those who disagreed. With war raging in Europe and economic depression still a threat in the United States, Roosevelt ran in 1940 on the idea that the country shouldn't "switch horses in the middle of the stream." In 1944, as World War II continued, Roosevelt won a fourth term.

Fearing an "imperial presidency," Congress moved to institutionalize the custom of a two-term presidency. The 22nd Amendment guaranteed that no future president would equal FDR's record.

VOCABULARY

inoperative no longer in force

primary an election in which registered members of a political party nominate candidates for office

qualified, declaring who shall then act as President, or the manner in which one who is to act shall be selected, and such person shall act accordingly until a President or Vice-President shall have qualified.

Section 4. The Congress may by law provide for the case of the death of any of the persons from whom the House of Representatives may choose a President whenever the right of choice shall have devolved upon them, and for the case of the death of any of the persons from whom the Senate may choose a Vice-President whenever the right of choice shall have devolved upon them.

Section 5. Sections 1 and 2 shall take effect on the 15th day of October following the ratification of this article.

Section 6. This article shall be **inoperative** unless it shall have been ratified as an amendment to the Constitution by the legislatures of three-fourths of the several states within seven years from the date of its submission.

AMENDMENT 21. Repeal of Prohibition (1933)

Passed by Congress February 20, 1933. Ratified December 5, 1933.

Section 1. The eighteenth article of amendment to the Constitution of the United States is hereby repealed.

Section 2. The transportation or importation into any state, territory, or possession of the United States for delivery or use therein of intoxicating liquors, in violation of the laws thereof, is hereby prohibited.

Section 3. This article shall be inoperative unless it shall have been ratified as an amendment to the Constitution by conventions in the several states, as provided in the Constitution, within seven years from the date of the submission hereof to the states by the Congress.

A CLOSER LOOK

George Washington set the tradition of limiting the presidency to two terms. Franklin Roosevelt broke this custom when he was elected president four terms in a row—1932, 1936, 1940, and 1944. His record-long presidency led to the 22nd Amendment. A two-term limit, written into the Constitution, checks the president's power.

AMENDMENT 22. Limit on Presidential Terms (1951)

Passed by Congress March 21, 1947. Ratified February 27, 1951.

Section 1. No person shall be elected to the office of the President more than twice, and no person who has held the office of President, or acted as President, for more than two years of a term to which some other person was elected President shall be elected to the office of the President more than once. ~~But this article shall not apply to any person holding the office of President when this article was proposed by the Congress, and shall not prevent any person who may be holding the office of President, or acting as President, during the term within which this article becomes operative from holding the office of President or acting as President during the remainder of such term.~~

Section 2. This article shall be inoperative unless it shall have been ratified as an amendment to the Constitution by the legislatures of three-fourths of the several states within seven years from the date of its submission to the states by the Congress.

258

ACTIVITY OPTIONS

INTERDISCIPLINARY LINK: LANGUAGE ARTS

BLOCK SCHEDULING

DEBATING TERM LIMITS

Class Time Two class periods

Task Debating the idea of term limits

Purpose To pose and answer questions about the proposal to limit the number of terms a person can serve in Congress

Supplies Needed
- Research materials on term limits

Activity Divide the class into two parts. Assign one group to present arguments in favor of term limits and the other, arguments against limits. Have students research their side and write out a minimum of three questions and answers supporting their position.

Next, divide the class into sets of four—two students from the pro side with two students from the con side. Let the students conduct their debates within these small-group settings, using the questions and answers that they generated.

AMENDMENT 23. Voting in District of Columbia (1961)

Passed by Congress June 17, 1960. Ratified March 29, 1961.

Section 1. The district constituting the seat of government of the United States shall appoint in such manner as Congress may direct: a number of electors of President and Vice-President equal to the whole number of Senators and Representatives in Congress to which the district would be entitled if it were a state, but in no event more than the least populous state; they shall be in addition to those appointed by the states, but they shall be considered, for the purposes of the election of President and Vice-President, to be electors appointed by a state; and they shall meet in the district and perform such duties as provided by the twelfth article of amendment.

Section 2. The Congress shall have power to enforce this article by appropriate legislation.

AMENDMENT 24. Abolition of Poll Taxes (1964)

Passed by Congress August 27, 1962. Ratified January 23, 1964.

Section 1. The right of citizens of the United States to vote in any **primary** or other election for President or Vice-President, for electors for President or Vice-President, or for Senator or Representative in Congress, shall not be denied or abridged by the United States or any state by reason of failure to pay any poll tax or other tax.

Section 2. The Congress shall have power to enforce this article by appropriate legislation.

AMENDMENT 25. Presidential Disability, Succession (1967)

Passed by Congress July 6, 1965. Ratified February 10, 1967.

Note: Article 2, Section 1, of the Constitution was affected by the 25th Amendment.

Section 1. In case of the removal of the President from office or of his death or resignation, the Vice-President shall become President.

Section 2. Whenever there is a vacancy in the office of the Vice-President, the President shall nominate a Vice-President who shall take office upon confirmation by a majority vote of both houses of Congress.

Section 3. Whenever the President transmits to the President pro tempore of the Senate and the Speaker of the House of Representatives his written declaration that he is unable to discharge the powers and duties of his office, and until he transmits to them a written declaration to the contrary, such powers and duties shall be discharged by the Vice-President as Acting President.

A CLOSER LOOK

POLL TAX

The poll tax was aimed at preventing African Americans from exercising their rights. Many could not afford to pay this fee required for voting.

26. How do you think the 24th Amendment affected elections?

A CLOSER LOOK

PRESIDENTIAL DISABILITY

President John F. Kennedy's death in 1963 signaled the need for the 25th Amendment. The Constitution did not explain what to do in the case of a disabled president. James Reston, a writer for *The New York Times,* summed up the problem: Suppose Kennedy was "strong enough to survive [the bullet wounds], but too weak to govern." The 25th Amendment provides for an orderly transfer of power.

27. What do you think can happen in a country where the rules for succession are not clear?

MORE ABOUT . . .

Barriers to Voting

Article 1, Section 4 of the Constitution gives the states the right to establish voter qualifications. The poll tax was one of a number of methods that some states used to prevent certain individuals—usually African Americans—from voting. Other barriers to voting included property ownership, literacy tests, residency requirements, and "grandfather" clauses. Grandfather clauses guaranteed the vote to people whose ancestors had voted before 1867—nearly all of whom were white—even if they could not pay the poll tax or pass the literacy test that was required of African Americans.

In addition to the 24th Amendment, the Voting Rights Act of 1965 and two extensions of the act in 1970 and 1975 removed some of the barriers. Supreme Court decisions during the 1960s removed other barriers to voting.

MORE ABOUT . . .

Presidential Succession

Earlier questions about presidential succession arose when Woodrow Wilson had a severe stroke in 1919. Dwight Eisenhower's heart attack brought the issue back into discussion in 1955. What would happen if a president was too ill or badly injured to govern? Finally, John F. Kennedy's death presented the additional problem of how to replace a vice-president. When Lyndon Johnson became president, there was no longer a vice-president to succeed him if he were to die or become unable to govern. The presidency would have passed to the Speaker of the House. The only solution lay in a constitutional amendment.

A CLOSER LOOK

26. More African Americans voted and were elected to office.

27. Political disorder might follow as groups and individuals compete to take over the top leadership position.

MORE ABOUT . . .

A Vice-Presidential Successor

Amendment 25, Section 2 provides a way to replace a vice-president who leaves office before completing the term. The president nominates a new vice-president, who must win confirmation by a majority vote of each house of Congress.

In 1973, Gerald Ford became vice-president in this way after Spiro Agnew resigned. The following year, when Ford became president after Nixon resigned, Nelson Rockefeller became vice-president through the same procedure.

HISTORY FROM VISUALS

Interpreting the Time Line Ask the students to study the time line. Tell them to find the ten-year period in which the greatest number of amendments were passed. Then ask if they can infer reasons why so many amendments were enacted in that decade. **Possible Response** Four amendments were enacted between 1913 and 1923, and four more between 1961 and 1971. Both were periods of great political turbulence and social change.

Extension Have the students create an illustrated time line showing all 27 amendments in a logo form.

A CLOSER LOOK

SUCCESSION

Who takes over if a president dies in office or is unable to serve? The top five in the line of succession follow:

- vice-president
- speaker of the house
- president pro tempore of the Senate
- secretary of state
- secretary of the treasury

28. Why should voters know the views of the vice-president?

Section 4. Whenever the Vice-President and a majority of either the principal officers of the executive departments or of such other body as Congress may by law provide, transmit to the President pro tempore of the Senate and the Speaker of the House of Representatives their written declaration that the President is unable to discharge the powers and duties of his office, the Vice-President shall immediately assume the powers and duties of the office as Acting President. Thereafter, when the President transmits to the President pro tempore of the Senate and the Speaker of the House of Representatives his written declaration that no inability exists, he shall resume the powers and duties of his office unless the Vice-President and a majority of either the principal officers of the executive department[s] or of such other body as Congress may by law provide, transmit within four days to the President pro tempore of the Senate and the Speaker of the House of Representatives their written declaration that the President is unable to discharge the powers and duties of his office. Thereupon Congress shall decide the issue, assembling within forty-eight hours for that purpose if not in session. If the Congress, within twenty-one days after receipt of the latter written declaration, or, if Congress is not in session, within twenty-one days after Congress is required to assemble, determines by two thirds vote of both houses that the President is unable to discharge the powers and duties of his office, the Vice-President shall continue to discharge the same as Acting President; otherwise, the President shall resume the powers and duties of his office.

A CLOSER LOOK Amendments Time Line *1791–1992*

Use the key below to help you categorize the amendments.

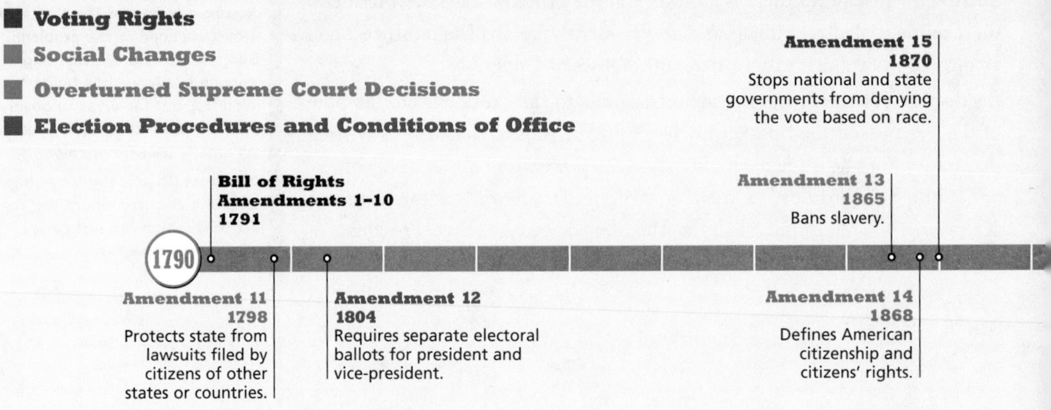

Voting Rights
Social Changes
Overturned Supreme Court Decisions
Election Procedures and Conditions of Office
Amendment 15
1870
Stops national and state governments from denying the vote based on race.
Bill of Rights
Amendments 1–10
1791
Amendment 13
1865
Bans slavery.
1790
Amendment 11
1798
Protects state from lawsuits filed by citizens of other states or countries.
Amendment 12
1804
Requires separate electoral ballots for president and vice-president.
Amendment 14
1868
Defines American citizenship and citizens' rights.

A CLOSER LOOK

28. If the president dies or is unable to serve, the vice-president will become president.

AMENDMENT 26. 18-year-old Vote (1971)

Passed by Congress March 23, 1971. Ratified July 1, 1971.

Note: Amendment 14, Section 2, of the Constitution was modified by Section 1 of the 26th Amendment.

Section 1. The right of citizens of the United States, who are eighteen years of age or older, to vote shall not be denied or abridged by the United States or by any state on account of age.

Section 2. The Congress shall have power to enforce this article by appropriate legislation.

AMENDMENT 27. Congressional Pay (1992)

Passed by Congress September 25, 1789. Ratified May 7, 1992.

No law, varying the compensation for the services of the Senators and Representatives, shall take effect, until an election of Representatives shall have intervened.

ROCK THE VOTE

A CLOSER LOOK

Members of the recording industry founded Rock the Vote. They urge young people to vote in elections.

Amendments 11–27 Assessment

1. Main Ideas

a. Which amendments affected the office of president?

b. Which pair of amendments shows the failure of laws to solve a social problem?

c. Which amendments corrected unfair treatment toward African Americans and women?

2. Critical Thinking

Summarizing What is the purpose of amending the Constitution?

THINK ABOUT

- the purpose of the Constitution
- problems and issues that Americans have faced throughout U.S. history

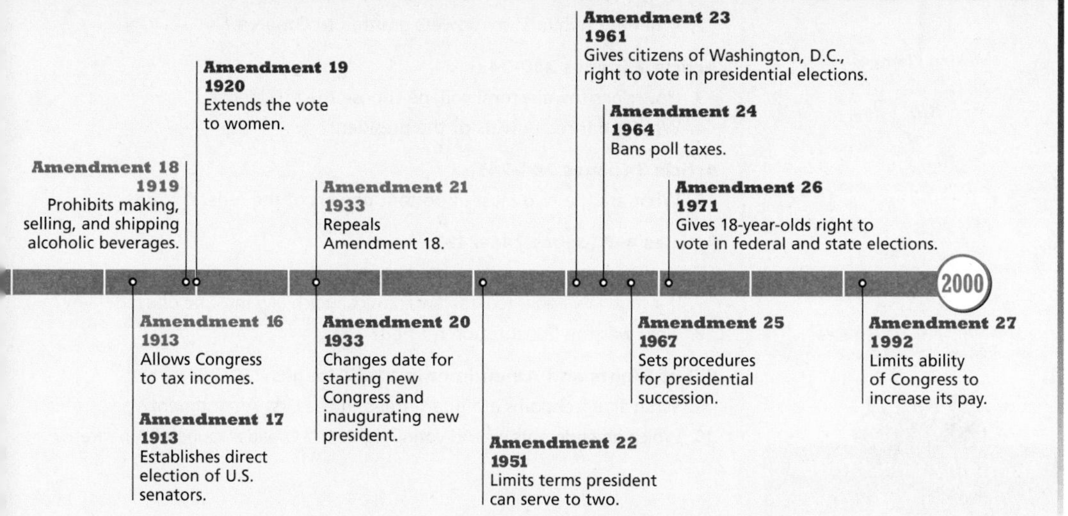

Amendment 18
1919
Prohibits making, selling, and shipping alcoholic beverages.
Amendment 19
1920
Extends the vote to women.
Amendment 21
1933
Repeals Amendment 18.
Amendment 23
1961
Gives citizens of Washington, D.C., right to vote in presidential elections.
Amendment 24
1964
Bans poll taxes.
Amendment 26
1971
Gives 18-year-olds right to vote in federal and state elections.
2000
Amendment 16
1913
Allows Congress to tax incomes.
Amendment 17
1913
Establishes direct election of U.S. senators.
Amendment 20
1933
Changes date for starting new Congress and inaugurating new president.
Amendment 22
1951
Limits terms president can serve to two.
Amendment 25
1967
Sets procedures for presidential succession.
Amendment 27
1992
Limits ability of Congress to increase its pay.

MORE ABOUT . . .

Rock the Vote

Founded in 1990, Rock the Vote has worked to increase the number of young people participating in the political life of their communities. At the end of the 1990s, only about 38 percent of people between the ages of 18 and 29 turned out to vote.

The organization provides information on local issues and elections, as well as tracking voter turnout. It is exploring such ideas as expanding elections to more than one day and using technology to increase the participation and education of voters.

MORE ABOUT . . .

The 27th Amendment

The 27th Amendment is the newest—and oldest—amendment in the Constitution. It was actually proposed on September 25, 1789, one day earlier than the Bill of Rights. But it lay dormant until the 1980s, when an aide to a Texas legislator discovered it and began a campaign to get the amendment adopted. The 27th Amendment was finally ratified more than 200 years after it was introduced.

Citizenship Today

- Constitutional Change and Flexibility, p. 77

Formal Assessment

- Section Quiz, p. 156

Assessment: Amendments 11–27

1. Main Ideas

a. 12th, 20th, 22nd, and 25th Amendments b. 18th and 21st Amendments c. African Americans—13th, 14th, 15th, and 24th Amendments; women—14th and 19th Amendments

2. Critical Thinking

Amending the Constitution helps keep it relevant to the time. As Americans' problems issues change, so should the Constitution.

VOCABULARY

1. **electors,** p. 233
2. **impeachment,** p. 233
3. **naturalization,** p. 236
4. **felonies,** p. 236
5. **bill of attainder,** p. 238
6. **ex post facto law,** p. 238
7. **suffrage,** p. 246
8. **due process of law,** p. 251
9. **servitude,** p. 254
10. **primary,** p. 258

SEVEN PRINCIPLES OF THE CONSTITUTION

Possible Responses

1. government in which the people rule—Preamble ("We the people . . .")
2. people exercise their power by voting for their political representatives—Article 1 (popular election of representatives)
3. states and national government share powers—10th Amendment (powers reserved to the states)
4. division of government roles into branches—Articles 1, 2, 3 (legislative, executive, and judicial branches)
5. each branch of government exercises controls over the other branches—Article 1 (impeachment)
6. restrictions of government powers—Article 1, Section 9 (powers denied Congress)
7. personal liberties and privileges—Bill of Rights

REVIEW QUESTIONS

Possible Responses

1. House—at least age 25; resident of state in which elected; citizen for 7 years

   Senate—at least age 30; resident of state in which elected; citizen for 9 years
2. declare war; raise armies; provide a navy; organize the National Guard (militia)
3. In a presidential election, the "winner takes all"; all the electoral votes of a state (except Maine and Nebraska) go to one set of candidates.

Constitution ASSESSMENT

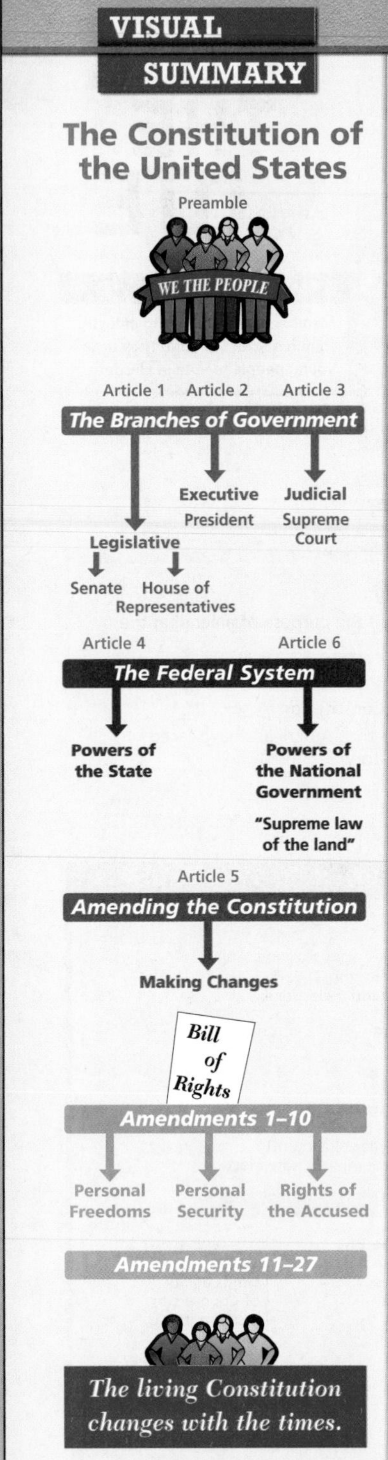

262 THE LIVING CONSTITUTION

VOCABULARY

Briefly explain the significance of each of the following.

1. electors
2. impeachment
3. naturalization
4. felonies
5. bill of attainder
6. ex post facto law
7. suffrage
8. due process of law
9. servitude
10. primary

SEVEN PRINCIPLES OF THE CONSTITUTION

Make a chart like the one shown. Then fill it in with a definition of each principle and an example from the Constitution.

Principle	Definition	Example
1. popular sovereignty		
2. republicanism		
3. federalism		
4. separation of powers		
5. checks and balances		
6. limited government		
7. individual rights		

REVIEW QUESTIONS

Article 1 (pages 233–239)

1. What are the requirements for becoming a member of the House of Representatives and the Senate?
2. What are two military powers granted to Congress?

Article 2 (pages 240–243)

3. How does the electoral college choose the president?
4. What are three powers of the president?

Article 3 (pages 244–245)

5. What are the two most important powers of the federal courts?

Articles 4–7 (pages 246–249)

6. How can the Constitution be changed?
7. If a state law and a federal law conflict, which law must be obeyed? Why?
8. How was the Constitution ratified?

Bill of Rights and Amendments 11–27 (pages 250–261)

9. What five freedoms are guaranteed in the First Amendment?
10. Which amendments extend voting rights to a broader range of Americans?

CRITICAL THINKING

Possible Responses

1. **DRAWING CONCLUSIONS** Proposing—two-thirds of both houses of Congress approve or two-thirds of state legislatures call for national convention. Ratifying—three-fourths of state legislatures approve or three-fourths of state conventions approve. **a.** pressuring senators and representatives to propose amendments **b.** to make sure the Constitution keeps pace with the times; to address unsolved problems (such as slavery) present in the original document
2. **MAKING INFERENCES** The elastic clause suggests that Congress has the power to deal with matters not specifically mentioned in the Constitution.
3. **ANALYZING LEADERSHIP** problem solver; decision maker; effective planner and manager; strong communicator; powerful persuader

CRITICAL THINKING

1. DRAWING CONCLUSIONS

In a two-column chart, summarize the processes for changing the Constitution. Then use your completed chart to answer the questions below.

Proposing Amendments	Ratifying Amendments
1.	1.
2.	2.

a. What role can citizens play in proposing amendments?
b. What do you think are the main reasons for changing the Constitution?

2. MAKING INFERENCES

Explain how the "elastic clause" in Article 1 gives Congress the authority to take action on other issues unknown to the Framers of the Constitution.

3. ANALYZING LEADERSHIP

Think about the president's roles described in the Constitution. What qualities does a president need to succeed as a leader in so many different areas?

4. RECOGNIZING EFFECTS

How would you describe the impact of the 14th, 15th, and 16th Amendments on life in the United States?

5. APPLYING CITIZENSHIP

Suppose you and your family go on a road trip across several states. According to Article 4 of the Constitution, what citizens' rights do you have in the states you are visiting?

HISTORY SKILLS

INTERPRETING PRIMARY SOURCES

In 1937, President Franklin D. Roosevelt gave a speech over the radio. He used interesting comparisons to explain how the government works.

> I described the American form of government as a three-horse team provided by the Constitution to the American people so that their field might be plowed. The three horses are, of course, the three branches of government—the Congress, the Executive, and the Courts. . . . It is the American people themselves who are in the driver's seat. It is the American people themselves who want the furrow plowed.
>
> **Franklin D. Roosevelt,** Radio Address

- How does Roosevelt describe the separation of powers?
- How does Roosevelt explain popular sovereignty?

ALTERNATIVE ASSESSMENT

1. INTERDISCIPLINARY ACTIVITY: Government

Creating a Database Review the grievances against King George III listed in the Declaration of Independence. Then create a database that shows how specific sections of the U.S. Constitution addressed those grievances. Write a brief summary stating how well the Constitution addressed the grievances.

2. COOPERATIVE LEARNING ACTIVITY

Drafting a Constitution Imagine you are asked to write a constitution for a newly formed country. Working with a group, use the outline below to organize and write your constitution.

I. Purpose of the Constitution (Preamble)
II. Making Laws (Legislative Branch)
III. Carrying Out the Laws (Executive Branch)
IV. Making Laws Fair (Judicial Branch)
V. Choosing Leaders
VI. Citizens' Rights (Bill of Rights)

3. PRIMARY SOURCE EXPLORER

Making a Learning Center Creating the U.S. Constitution was one of the most important events in the nation's history. Use the CD-ROM and the library to collect information on different topics related to the Constitution.

Create a learning center featuring the suggestions below.

- Find biographies and portraits of the Framers.
- Collect important primary sources such as James Madison's notes and *The Federalist* papers.
- Gather recent pictures and news articles about the Congress, the president, the Supreme Court, and the Bill of Rights.

4. HISTORY PORTFOLIO

Review your draft of the constitution you wrote for the assessment activity. Choose one of these options below.

Option 1 Use comments made by your teacher or classmates to improve your work.

Option 2 Illustrate your constitution. Add your work to your history portfolio.

Additional Test Practice, pp. S1–S33

TEST PRACTICE CLASSZONE.COM

4. acts as commander in chief of the military; makes treaties and appointments; approves bills passed by Congress
5. interpret laws and judicial review
6. through the amendment process
7. federal law, under the supremacy clause
8. Nine of 13 states had to ratify.
9. religion, speech, press, assembly, petition
10. 15th, 19th, and 26th Amendments

ALTERNATIVE ASSESSMENT

Standards for Evaluation

1. INTERDISCIPLINARY ACTIVITY: Math

Each database should

- present a variety of information from several sources.
- present information accurately.
- clearly identify sources of information.

2. COOPERATIVE LEARNING ACTIVITY

Each constitution should

- have a clear statement of its goals.
- reflect an understanding of the functions of various parts of government.
- follow the rules of spelling, punctuation, and grammar.

3. PRIMARY SOURCE EXPLORER

Learning centers should

- have a clear focus and logical organization.
- use interesting images or audio elements to make points.
- give appropriate background and research information.

4. HISTORY PORTFOLIO

Option 1 Revised assessment activities should

- address teacher and peer response to the selected work.
- solve problems present in the first versions of the work.

Option 2 Illustrated constitutions should

- be creative and neatly presented.
- present information to aid the viewer in understanding the material.
- demonstrate an understanding of methods of governing.

Formal Assessment

- Chapter Test, Forms A, B, and C, pp. 157–168

4. **RECOGNIZING EFFECTS** African Americans slowly gained civil rights and political power. Their example inspired other minorities to demand fair treatment.
5. **APPLYING CITIZENSHIP** the same rights and privileges that citizens of those states have

HISTORY SKILLS

Possible Responses

Roosevelt describes the separation of powers as a "three-horse team provided by the Constitution." The three horses are the three branches of government. He explains popular sovereignty as the "American people . . . in the driver's seat," directing the three-horse team.

CITIZENSHIP HANDBOOK OBJECTIVE

The student will be able to define citizenship and to explain a citizen's rights and responsibilities.

FOCUS & MOTIVATE

5-MINUTE WARM-UP

Categorizing Answering this question will help students to understand that being a citizen has specific requirements.

1. Read the Kennedy quotation on page 264. Why do you think he wanted all persons to be active citizens?
2. How is a citizen different from a person who lives in a country but is not a citizen?

Warm-Up Transparency WTCON

INSTRUCT

What Is a Citizen?

- Why does a country have rules about who is considered a citizen?
- What are two ways to become a United States citizen?
- Why might a person want to change citizenship from one country to another?

The Role of the Citizen

Citizens of the United States enjoy many basic rights and freedoms. Freedom of speech and religion are examples. These rights are guaranteed by the Constitution, the Bill of Rights, and other amendments to the Constitution. Along with these rights, however, come responsibilities. Obeying rules and laws, voting, and serving on juries are some examples.

Active citizenship is not limited to adults. Younger citizens can help their communities become better places. The following pages will help you to learn about your rights and responsibilities. Knowing them will help you to become an active and involved citizen of your community, state, and nation.

In this book you will find examples of active citizenship by young people like yourself. **Look for the Citizenship Today features.**

President John F. Kennedy urged all Americans to become active citizens and work to improve their communities.

The weather was sunny but cold on January 20, 1961—the day that John F. Kennedy became the 35th president of the United States. In his first speech as president, he urged all Americans to serve their country. Since then, Kennedy's words have inspired millions of Americans to become more active citizens.

> *"Ask not what your country can do for you—ask what you can do for your country!"*
>
> —JOHN F. KENNEDY

What Is a Citizen?

A citizen is a legal member of a nation and pledges loyalty to that nation. A citizen has certain guaranteed rights, protections, and responsibilities. A citizen is a member of a community and wants to make it a good place to live.

Today in the United States there are a number of ways to become a citizen. The most familiar are citizenship by birth and citizenship by naturalization. All citizens have the right to equal protection under the law.

TEACHING STRATEGY

CITIZENS

The term *citizen* is often used in a very broad sense to mean a resident of a community. However, the term can also describe a specific legal status. Some students may not easily identify with their legal status as citizens. To help students think about citizenship and its importance for preserving democracy, discuss the meaning of the following quotation: "Whether in private or in public the good citizen does something to support democratic habits and the constitutional order" (Judith Shklar, 1991). Prompt students by asking how the quotation combines the two meanings of *citizen.*

Next, have students look at the graphic on page 264. Ask them how it illustrates the ideas in the quotation. Guide the discussion so that they understand that the information in the graphic exemplifies the "democratic habits" needed to fulfill the role of a citizen in a democracy.

CITIZENSHIP BY BIRTH A child born in the United States is a citizen by birth. Children born to U.S. citizens traveling or living outside the country, such as military personnel, are citizens. Even children born in the United States to parents who are not citizens of the United States are considered U.S. citizens. These children have dual citizenship. This means they are citizens of two countries—both the United States and the country of their parents' citizenship. At the age of 18, the child may choose one of the countries for permanent citizenship.

CITIZENSHIP BY NATURALIZATION A person who is not a citizen of the United States may become one through a process called naturalization. The steps in this process are shown below. To become a naturalized citizen, a person must meet certain requirements.

- Be at least 18 years old. Children under the age of 18 automatically become naturalized citizens when their parents do.
- Enter the United States legally.
- Live in the United States for at least five years immediately prior to application.
- Read, write, and speak English.
- Show knowledge of American history and government.

See Citizenship Today: Becoming a Citizen, p. 411

Steps in the Naturalization Process

1. **File an application.**
2. **Take an examination.**
3. **File a legal petition for naturalization.**
4. **Appear at a court hearing.**
5. **Take an oath of allegiance.**

Hundreds of people become new citizens at a single ceremony in San Antonio, Texas.

MORE ABOUT . . .

Naturalization

Naturalization can occur individually, as described in this handbook, or collectively. In collective naturalization, an entire group of people are naturalized at the same time. This process takes place through treaties, a Joint Resolution of Congress, an act of Congress to acquire new territory, or a constitutional amendment. For example, when the United States passed an act of Congress to acquire the new territory of Puerto Rico in 1917, all of the people of Puerto Rico became naturalized citizens of the United States.

MORE ABOUT . . .

Ethnic Restrictions

For much of the 20th century, the U.S. government used ethnicity to determine the number of people allowed to immigrate to the United States. In 1924, Congress passed the Johnson-Reed Act to preserve the "racial composition" of the country. This act set quotas for immigrants, based on their country of origin. These quotas favored Northern Europeans over Southern and Eastern Europeans. Not until 1965 were ethnic quotas removed from immigration laws. The new law limits each country, regardless of ethnicity, to an annual quota of 20,000 people.

MORE ABOUT . . .

Citizenship Test

The U.S. government's Immigration and Naturalization Service Web site has sample questions for the naturalization test. Have students visit classzone.com for more information.

You may also want students to review the INS site for eligibility standards for immigrants to become citizens.

Citizenship Today
- Becoming a Citizen, p. 9

ACTIVITY OPTIONS

INTERDISCIPLINARY LINK: LANGUAGE ARTS — BLOCK SCHEDULING

INTERVIEW

Class Time 10 minutes for explanation

Task Interviewing adults about citizenship

Purpose To identify the public's view of citizenship

Supplies Needed
- Log book
- Audio or video recording equipment (optional)

Activity Have each student interview five adults. Discuss with students some of the people they may choose to interview. Explain that techniques of a good interviewer include listening carefully, asking open-ended questions, and taking good notes. Have them ask the following questions:
- What does it mean to be a citizen?
- What rights does a citizen have?
- What responsibilities does a citizen have?

Students should write a summary answer to each question that incorporates all their findings and report their findings to the class.

INSTRUCT

What Are Your Rights?/
What Are Your Responsibilities?

- What are the three categories of rights?
- What are the two categories of responsibilities?
- How are rights and responsibilities linked?

MORE ABOUT . . .

Freedom of Speech
No right is absolute or unlimited. The Supreme Court has struggled, for example, with the issue of free speech. Ruling in *Schenck* v. *United States,* Justice Oliver Wendell Holmes, Jr., created what became known as the "clear and present danger" rule. He stated, "The question in every case is whether the words . . . create a clear and present danger that they will bring about the substantive evils that Congress has the right to prevent."

CRITICAL THINKING ACTIVITY

Analyzing Explain that rights are valuable, yet can cause conflict and create debate within society. Have students choose two rights, one from the basic freedoms box and the other from the personal protections box. Then have them create a chart for each right that lists why that right is valuable and how that right can cause debate. After they have completed the charts, have a class discussion about their answers.

Class Time 20 minutes

Why is this right valuable?	How does this right create debate?

What Are Your Rights?

Citizens of the United States are guaranteed rights by the U.S. Constitution, state constitutions, and state and federal laws. All citizens have three kinds of rights: basic freedoms, protection from unfair government actions, and equal treatment under the law.

Citizens' basic rights and freedoms are sometimes called **civil rights**. Some of these rights are personal, and others are political.

The U.S. Constitution grants these five basic freedoms.

BASIC FREEDOMS
- Freedom of religion
- Freedom of speech
- Freedom of the press
- Freedom of peaceful assembly
- Freedom to petition the government for change

The second category of rights is intended to protect citizens from unfair government actions.

PERSONAL PROTECTIONS
- The right to bear arms
- Freedom from being forced to house soldiers
- Protection from unreasonable search and seizure
- The right to a speedy public trial by an impartial jury
- No excessive bail or fines
- Protection from cruel and unusual punishment

Other parts of the Bill of Rights grant these rights.

The third category is the right to equal treatment under the law. The government cannot treat one individual or group differently from another.

Rights of citizenship have expanded over the years.

EQUAL PROTECTION UNDER THE LAW
- No slavery
- The right to vote to all male citizens over 21 years old
- The right to vote to women
- The right to vote to 18 year olds
- The Civil Rights Acts of 1964 protects voting rights and prevents discrimination.
- The Americans with Disabilities Act of 1990 protects the rights of disabled citizens.

LIMITS TO RIGHTS The rights guaranteed to citizens have sensible limits. For example, the right to free speech does not allow a person to falsely shout, "Fire!" at a crowded concert. The government may place limits on certain rights to protect national security or to provide equal opportunities for all citizens. And rights come with responsibilities.

ACTIVITY OPTIONS
MULTIPLE LEARNING STYLES: VISUAL

BLOCK SCHEDULING

CITIZENS' RIGHTS

Class Time 30 minutes

Task Creating a visual representation of citizens' rights

Purpose To explain citizens' rights in an alternative format

Supplies Needed
- Art supplies
- Software to create graphics (optional)

Activity Have students create a visual representation of the information on page 266. Tell them that their representations should be geared toward younger children or people who do not read English. Some ideas may include a poster, a sculpture, or a mobile. If software is available, students can create computer artwork. Then have students present their visual representation to the class.

What Are Your Responsibilities?

For American democracy to work, citizens must carry out important responsibilities. There are two kinds of responsibilities—personal and civic. Personal responsibilities include taking care of yourself, helping your family, knowing right from wrong, and behaving in a respectful way.

Civic responsibilities are those that involve your government and community. They include obeying rules and laws, serving on juries, paying taxes, and defending your country when called upon. One of the most important responsibilities is voting. When you turn 18, you will have that right.

As a young person, you can be a good citizen in a number of ways. You might work with other people in your community to make it a fair and just place to live. Working for a political party or writing to your elected officials about issues that concern you are some other examples.

The chart below shows how responsibilities change with a citizen's age. Notice that all citizens share the responsibility to obey the laws of their communities.

See Citizenship Today: Obeying Rules and Laws, p. 284

Responsibilities of a Citizen

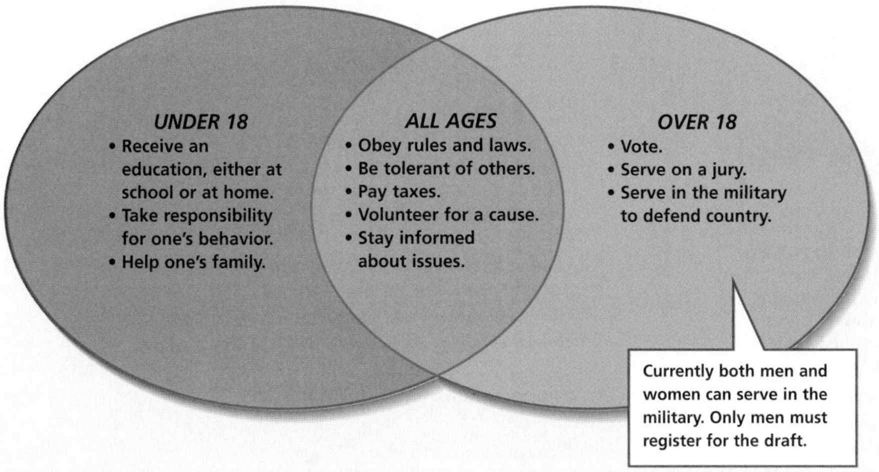

UNDER 18
• Receive an education, either at school or at home.
• Take responsibility for one's behavior.
• Help one's family.
ALL AGES
• Obey rules and laws.
• Be tolerant of others.
• Pay taxes.
• Volunteer for a cause.
• Stay informed about issues.
OVER 18
• Vote.
• Serve on a jury.
• Serve in the military to defend country.
Currently both men and women can serve in the military. Only men must register for the draft.

CITIZENSHIP ACTIVITIES

1. Interview a recently naturalized citizen. Ask about the test he or she took to become a U.S. citizen. Write a report of your findings.
2. Using newspapers or magazines, find examples of citizens using their unalienable rights or practicing responsible citizenship. Cut out five articles to illustrate the points. Mount them and write a one-sentence explanation of each article.

CRITICAL THINKING ACTIVITY

Making Inferences Tell the class that in the presidential election of 1996, less than a third of voters aged 18 and 19 (32.4%) voted versus almost three-fourths of voters aged 65 to 74 (72.6%).

Ask the students why they think the voter turnout is low among young people. How does their not voting affect the lawmaking process? Discuss the reasons given and consider ways to improve voter turnout among young people.

Class Time 20 minutes

Citizenship Today
- Obeying Rules and Laws, pp. 5–6

MORE ABOUT . . .

Juries

Any citizen over 18 can be called to serve on a jury. People are chosen from a list created by jury commissioners. When a person is called, he or she receives a writ of *venire facias,* which means "you must come." Then he or she must go to the designated courthouse to be assigned to a case. Typically, 12 people are selected from a large pool of potential jurors to serve on each trial jury. The chosen juror must sit in the court for the entire length of the trial, which can last from one day to several months, depending on the trial's complexity. A juror's obligation is to hear the evidence and to deliver a verdict.

Citizenship Today
- The Importance of Juries, pp. 1–2

INDIVIDUAL NEEDS: CITIZENSHIP ACTIVITIES

An interview report should
- fully and accurately record the answers to the questions.
- evaluate the information.
- follow the rules of spelling, punctuation, and grammar.

A scrapbook should
- be neatly presented.
- provide a clear summary of the selected article.
- follow the rules of spelling, punctuation, and grammar.

INSTRUCT

How Do You Stay Informed?/ How Do You Make Wise Decisions?/ How Do You Participate in Your Community?

- Why is it important to stay informed about community issues?
- What are some steps involved in making important decisions?
- How can you contribute to your community?

Citizenship Today
- Debating Points of View, pp. 11–12
- Detecting Bias in the Media, pp. 15–16
- Writing Government Officials, pp. 17–18

CRITICAL THINKING ACTIVITY

Identifying Facts and Opinions Find a brief article on a local issue. Reproduce it for each member of the class. Remind the class that a *fact* is a piece of information that can be checked for accuracy, whereas an *opinion* expresses the beliefs, attitudes, or feelings of an individual. Have each student read the article, underlining any facts and circling any opinions. Then divide the class into pairs. Have students compare their answers with those of their partner. Then have a class discussion about how the facts and opinions in the article shaped their understanding of the issue.

Class Time 25 minutes

Building Citizenship Skills

Good citizenship skills include **staying informed, solving problems** or **making decisions,** and **taking action.** Every citizen can find ways to build citizenship skills. By showing respect for the law and for the rights of others in your daily life, you promote democracy. You can also work to change conditions in your community to make sure all citizens experience freedom and justice.

How Do You Stay Informed?

Americans can sometimes feel that they have access to too much information. It may seem overwhelming. Even so, you should stay informed on issues that affect your life. Staying informed gives you the information you need to make wise decisions and helps you find ways to solve problems.

These Texas middle school students are staying informed by talking to their Texas state representative. Many public officials enjoy having students visit and ask them questions about their jobs, and about issues students think are important.

Watch, Listen, and Read

The first step in practicing good citizenship is to know how to find information that you need.

Sources of information include broadcast and print media and the Internet. Public officials and civic organizations are also good sources for additional information. Remember as you are reading to evaluate your sources.

See Citizenship Today: Debating Points of View, p. 456

Evaluate

As you become informed, you will need to make judgments about the accuracy of your news sources. You must also be aware of those sources' points of view and biases. (A bias is a judgment formed without knowing all of the facts.)

You should determine if you need more information. If you do, then decide where to find it. After gathering information, you may be ready to form an opinion or a plan of action to solve a problem.

See Citizenship Today: Detecting Bias in the Media, p. 557

Communicate

To bring about change in their communities, active citizens may need to contact public officials. In today's world, making contact is easy.

You can reach most public officials by telephone, voice mail, fax, or letter. Many public officials also have Internet pages or e-mail that encourages input from the public.

ACTIVITY OPTIONS

INDIVIDUAL NEEDS

STUDENTS ACQUIRING ENGLISH/ESL

This activity provides an opportunity for students who speak a language other than English to develop a brochure in their own language that informs community members of important information.

Pair an English-speaking student with a student acquiring English. Have the pairs identify community services or information they think would benefit members of the community. Then they should plan a brochure by determining a written or visual way to present the information that is appealing and informative. One brochure should be produced in the language of the ESL student as well as one in English. Once the brochures are completed, have the pairs pass them around the class.

How Do You Make Wise Decisions?

Civic life involves making important decisions. As a voter, whom should you vote for? As a juror, should you find the defendant guilty or not guilty? As an informed citizen, should you support or oppose a proposed government action? Unlike decisions about which video to rent, civic decisions cannot be made by a process as easy as tossing a coin. Instead, you should use a problem-solving approach like the one shown in the chart below. Decision making won't always proceed directly from step to step. Sometimes it's necessary to backtrack a little. For example, you may get to the "Analyze the Information" step and realize that you don't have enough information to analyze. Then you can go back a step and gather more information.

Problem-Solving and Decision-Making Process

Problem-solving and decision-making involves many steps. This diagram shows you how to take those steps. Notice that you may have to repeat some steps depending on the information you gather.

IDENTIFY THE PROBLEM Decide what the main issues are and what your goal is.

GATHER INFORMATION Get to know the basics of the problem. Find out as much as possible about the issues.

ANALYZE THE INFORMATION Look at the information and determine what it reveals about solving the problem.

CONSIDER OPTIONS Think of as many ways as possible to solve the problem. Don't be afraid to include ideas that others might think are unacceptable.

CHOOSE A SOLUTION Choose the solution you believe will best solve the problem and help you reach your goal.

IMPLEMENT THE SOLUTION Take action or plan to take action on a chosen solution.

EVALUATE THE SOLUTION Review the results of putting your solution into action. Did the solution work? Do you need to adjust the solution in some way?

Students working on an environmental project are gathering and analyzing information to help them make decisions.

MORE ABOUT . . .

Decision Making
Problem solving and decision making are both public and private processes. Both processes are used in every branch and at every level of government. Some key decisions of the 20th century that have shaped the lives of American citizens include the following:

- Entering World Wars I and II, the Korean War, and the Vietnam War
- Dropping the atomic bombs on Hiroshima and Nagasaki
- Desegregation of all schools
- Financing a space program

CRITICAL THINKING ACTIVITY

Evaluating Have students study each of the steps in the diagram. Then ask them to think about which steps are most often ignored in the decision-making process. Discuss why eliminating steps in the process may lead to poor decisions.

Class Time 10 minutes

ACTIVITY OPTIONS

INTERDISCIPLINARY LINK: CIVICS

BLOCK SCHEDULING

PROBLEM-SOLVING PROCESS

Class Time One class period

Task Using the decision-making model to solve a problem

Purpose To identify a school need and formulate a plan to meet that need

Supplies Needed None

Activity Have the class brainstorm about needs they think the school may have (for example, a recycling program, more choices for lunch, a new playground). Write those ideas on the board. Once students agree on a need, divide them into groups. Using the problem-solving model on page 269, each group should follow the steps necessary to meet that need. When the students feel their solution is sound, have them present it to the principal or another school official to help implement the solution.

MORE ABOUT . . .

Suitcases for Kids

Aubyn Burnside collected 300 suitcases within a few months after she started her project. As of 1999, she had over 17,000 suitcases dropped off at her house. American Airlines and TWA encourage flight attendants to donate their used luggage. Boys and Girls Clubs of America and trucking firms have helped out. Her project has spread to 50 states, Canada, and Russia.

Hoping to inspire other young people to volunteer, Aubyn said, "Age is not a limit. . . . Listen to people when they ask for help. Just try to do stuff, because if you don't try, you're not gonna get anywhere."

Citizenship Today
- Community Service, pp. 13–14
- Simulation 4: Town Meeting, pp. 42–45

CRITICAL THINKING ACTIVITY

Making Inferences Have students look at the picture on this page. Ask them to infer why these students organized the rally. Then ask how this rally reflects the problem-solving model on the previous page.

Class Time 10 minutes

How Do You Participate in Your Community?

Across the country many young people have come up with ways to make their communities better places to live. Thirteen-year-old Aubyn Burnside of Hickory, North Carolina, is just one example. Aubyn felt sorry for foster children she saw moving their belongings in plastic trash bags. She founded Suitcases for Kids. This program provides used luggage for foster children who are moving from one home to another. Her program has been adopted by other young people in several states. Below are some ways in which you can participate in your community.

See Citizenship Today: Community Service, p. 542

Students participate in a rally to promote safety in their school.

Find a Cause

How can you become involved in your community? First, select a community problem or issue that interests you. Some ideas from other young people include starting a support group for children with cancer, publishing a neighborhood newspaper with children's stories and art, and putting on performances to entertain people in shelters and hospitals.

Develop Solutions

Once you have found a cause on which you want to work, develop a plan for solving the problem. Use the decision-making or problem-solving skills you have learned to find ways to approach the problem. You may want to involve other people in your activities.

Follow Through

Solving problems takes time. You'll need to be patient in developing a plan. You can show leadership in working with your group by following through on meetings you set up and plans you make. When you finally solve the problem, you will feel proud of your accomplishments.

CITIZENSHIP ACTIVITIES

1. Use the telephone directory to make a list of names, addresses, and phone numbers of public officials or organizations that could provide information about solving problems in your community.
2. Copy the steps in the problem-solving and decision-making diagram and show how you followed them to solve a problem or make a decision. Be sure to clearly state the problem and the final decision.

INDIVIDUAL NEEDS: CITIZENSHIP ACTIVITIES

The list should
- include information from various levels of government.
- include information from private or nonprofit organizations.
- contain accurate and up-to-date phone numbers and addresses.

The problem-solving report should
- accurately copy the steps of the model.
- clearly state the problem and steps taken to solve it.
- identify the solution.

Practicing Citizenship Skills

You have learned that good citizenship involves three skills: staying informed, solving problems, and taking action. Below are some activities to help you improve your citizenship skills. By practicing these skills you can work to make a difference in your own life and in the lives of those in your community.

CITIZENSHIP ACTIVITIES

Stay Informed

CREATE A PAMPHLET OR RECRUITING COMMERCIAL

Ask your school counselors or write to your state department of education to get information on state-run colleges, universities, or technical schools. Use this information to create a brochure or recruiting commercial showing these schools and the different programs and degrees they offer.

KEEP IN MIND

What's there for me? It may help you think about what areas students are interested in and may want to pursue in later life.

Where is it? You may want to have a map showing where the schools are located in your state.

How can I afford it? Students might want to know if financial aid is available to attend the schools you have featured.

Make Wise Decisions

CREATE A GAME BOARD OR SKIT

Study the decision-making diagram on page 285. With a small group, develop a skit that explains the steps in problem solving. Present your skit to younger students in your school. As an alternative, create a game board that would help younger students understand the steps in making a decision.

KEEP IN MIND

What do children this age understand? Be sure to create a skit or game at an age-appropriate level.

What kinds of decisions do younger students make? Think about the kinds of decisions that the viewers of your skit or players of the game might make.

How can I make it interesting? Use visual aids to help students understand the steps in decision making.

Take Action

CREATE A BULLETIN BOARD FOR YOUR CLASS

Do some research on the Internet or consult the yellow pages under "Social Services" to find the names of organizations that have volunteer opportunities for young people. Call or write for more information. Then create a bulletin board for your class showing groups that would like volunteer help.

KEEP IN MIND

What kinds of jobs are they? You may want to list the types of skills or jobs volunteer groups are looking for.

How old do I have to be? Some groups may be looking for younger volunteers; others may need older persons.

How do I get there? How easy is it to get to the volunteer group's location?

CRITICAL THINKING ACTIVITY

Forming and Supporting Opinions After looking at the diagram, ask students to describe what they think the characteristics of a model citizen are. Make sure the students support their opinions about the characteristics. Then ask if they think young people can be model citizens. They should support this opinion as well.

Class Time 10 minutes

ASSESS & RETEACH

RETEACHING ACTIVITY

Have students copy the graphic on page 264. Working in small groups or pairs, students should write specific information they have learned about each element shown in the ovals. For example, under Know Your Rights, the students should be able to list rights guaranteed to an American citizen.

INDIVIDUAL NEEDS: CITIZENSHIP ACTIVITIES

Stay Informed

The pamphlet or commercial should

- clearly present all information.
- use art that aids the viewer in understanding the information.
- be neatly presented and creative.

Make Wise Decisions

The game should

- have a clear focus and logical organization throughout.
- use pictures, words, and symbols to explain each step in a process.

The skit should

- capture the audience's attention.
- clearly present the concepts.

Take Action

The bulletin board should

- accurately and factually present all information.
- capture the audience's attention with an interesting layout.
- reflect opportunities appropriate for middle-school volunteers.

UNIT 3
The Early Republic
1789–1844

BEFORE YOU READ

Previewing Unit 3

Unit 3 details the struggles of the new nation to meet challenges, both those from within and those from abroad. Political parties develop, and the United States faces another war with Great Britain. The nation almost doubles in size with the purchase of the Louisiana Territory, and the Lewis and Clark expedition brings back exciting information about the vast lands between the Mississippi River and the Pacific Ocean. As the nation's economy develops, sectional divisions also emerge.

"Our country! May she always be in the right; but our country, right or wrong."

—Stephen Decatur

Known as "Old Ironsides," the U.S.S. *Constitution* won more battles than any other early American warship. Today it rests in Boston Harbor.

HISTORY FROM VISUALS

Interpreting the Photograph Ask the class to discuss how the quotation from Stephen Decatur reflects a feeling of nationalism. Then ask students what they think might have inspired Decatur's words. **Possible Response** Perhaps someone had said something to Decatur implying that the United States was at fault for some action or policy. Then ask why a picture of this particular ship was chosen to represent the Early Republic. **Possible Response** The name U.S.S. *Constitution* may point to the way the early republic began.

Extension Ask students to find out when the U.S.S. *Constitution* was built, how it earned its nickname, and how it has been preserved as a national treasure.

CHAPTER 9 PLANNING GUIDE

Launching a New Republic 1789–1800

	CHAPTER OVERVIEW	COPYMASTERS	INTEGRATED TECHNOLOGY
CHAPTER RESOURCES	The chapter discusses Washington's presidency and the difficulties of interpreting the Constitution. It also describes expansion into the Northwest Territory, problems in foreign policy, and the development of political parties during the Adams administration.	**In-Depth Resources: Unit 3** • Tracing Themes: Democratic Ideals, p. 2 • Building Vocabulary, p. 6 **Interdisciplinary Projects,** pp. 49–54	• eEdition Plus Online • EasyPlanner Plus Online • eTest Plus Online • eEdition • Power Presentations • EasyPlanner • Electronic Library of Primary Sources • Test Generator • Reading Study Guide • America's Music
	KEY IDEAS		
SECTION 1 **Washington's Presidency** **pp. 277–281**	• George Washington takes office and appoints his cabinet; Congress sets up a federal court system. • Hamilton develops a financial plan to improve the U.S. economy. • Jefferson and Hamilton clash over how to interpret the Constitution.	**In-Depth Resources: Unit 3** • Setting the Stage, p. 1 • Guided Reading, p. 3 • Primary Source, p. 10 • Reteaching Activity, p. 15 **America's History Makers** • Alexander Hamilton, pp. 35–36 **Economics in History** • Personal Banking, p. 9 **Why It Matters Now** • The Importance of Leadership, pp. 17–18	**Warm-Up Transparency WT9** **Critical Thinking Transparency CT25** • Setting the Stage classzone.com
SECTION 2 **Challenges to the New Government** **pp. 282–286**	• U.S. troops defeat Native Americans at the Battle of Fallen Timbers in the Northwest Territory. • Washington asserts federal authority by using troops to put down the Whiskey Rebellion. • The United States remains neutral in European conflicts.	**In-Depth Resources: Unit 3** • Setting the Stage, p. 1 • Guided Reading, p. 4 • Skillbuilder Practice: Making Inferences, p. 7 • Literature Selection, pp. 12–14 • Reteaching Activity, p. 16 **Citizenship Today,** pp. 5–6	**Warm-Up Transparency WT9** **Geography Transparency GT9** • Trouble Spots in the New Republic 1790–1794 **Critical Thinking Transparency CT25** • Setting the Stage classzone.com
SECTION 3 **The Federalists in Charge** **pp. 287–291**	• After Washington retires, two parties dominate national politics. • During John Adams's presidency, the French Revolution increased political division within the United States. • The Federalists pass the Alien and Sedition Acts, clamping down on freedom of speech and of the press.	**In-Depth Resources: Unit 3** • Setting the Stage, p. 1 • Guided Reading, p. 5 • Geography Application: The Nation's Capital, pp. 8–9 • Primary Source, p. 11 • Reteaching Activity, p. 17 **America's History Makers** • Benjamin Banneker, pp. 37–38 **Outline Map Activities** • The 13 States Become 16, pp. 17–18	**Warm-Up Transparency WT9** **Humanities Transparencies HT17, HT18** • *Abigail Adams* by Gordon Phillips • Engraving of Washington, D.C. **Critical Thinking Transparency CT26** • Cause and Effect: Growth of Political Parties **Critical Thinking Transparency CT27** • Visual Summary

Pupil's Edition · Overhead Transparency · CD-ROM · Copymaster · Audio Library · Internet

ASSESSMENT OPTIONS

Chapter Assessment, pp. 292–293

Formal Assessment
- Chapter Tests, Forms A, B, and C, pp. 172–183

Test Generator

Online Test Practice

Strategies for Test Preparation

Section Assessment, p. 281

Formal Assessment, Quiz, p. 169

Integrated Assessment Book
- Rubrics, 4.1, 1.2

Test Generator

Test Practice Transparencies, TT31

Section Assessment, p. 286

Formal Assessment, Quiz, p. 170

Integrated Assessment Book
- Rubrics, 2.1, 1.3

Test Generator

Test Practice Transparencies, TT32

Section Assessment, p. 291

Formal Assessment, Quiz, p. 171

Integrated Assessment Book
- Rubrics, 5.3, 3.1

Test Generator

Test Practice Transparencies, TT33

CUSTOMIZING FOR INDIVIDUAL NEEDS

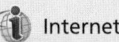

Students Acquiring English/ESL

Reading Study Guide (English and Spanish), pp. 87–94

Access for Students Acquiring English/ESL: Spanish Translations, pp. 57–62

Chapter Summaries on CD (English and Spanish)

Modified Lesson Plans for English Learners

Less Proficient Readers

Reading Study Guide (English and Spanish), pp. 87–94

Chapter Summaries on CD (English and Spanish)

Gifted and Talented Students

In-Depth Resources: Unit 3
- Enrichment Activity, p. 18

America's History Makers
- Alexander Hamilton, pp. 35–36
- Benjamin Banneker, pp. 37–38

CROSS-CURRICULAR CONNECTIONS

Geography

McCall, Edith. ***Biography of a River: The Living Mississippi.*** New York: Walker, 1990. Entertainingly describes the Mississippi as both a natural system and a human highway.

Economics

Whitelaw, Nancy. ***More Perfect Union: The Story of Alexander Hamilton.*** Greensboro, NC: Morgan Reynolds, 1997. Story of the first secretary of the treasury.

Science

Litwin, Laura Baskes. ***Benjamin Banneker: Astronomer and Mathematician.*** Berkeley Heights, NJ: Enslow, 1999. Illustrated biography uses contemporary documents.

Literature

Benet, Stephen Vincent. ***A Book of Americans.*** New York: Holt, 1995. Short, memorable, and sometimes amusing poems about Americans from Thomas Jefferson to Captain Kidd.

Collier, James Lincoln, and Christopher Collier. ***Jump Ship to Freedom.*** New York: Yearling Books, 1987. A young boy headed for a life of slavery in the West Indies escapes to post-Revolutionary New York.

Rinaldi, Ann. ***The Second Bend in the River.*** New York: Scholastic, 1997. Romance between Tecumseh and an Ohio girl. An appended note explains what's factual.

Interdisciplinary Projects, pp. 49–54
- Math: Mathematical Puzzles
- Science: Preserving Food
- Language Arts: Newspaper Editorials
- Art: Neoclassical Architecture of Washington, D.C.

ENRICHMENT ACTIVITIES

Pupil's Edition, pp. 274–293
Interact with History, p. 275
Economics in History, p. 280
Citizenship Today, p. 284

In-Depth Resources: Unit 3
- Geography Application: The Nation's Capital, pp. 8–9
- Primary Source: from *Journal* by William Maclay, p. 10
- Primary Source: "Hail, Columbia" by Joseph Hopkinson, p. 11
- Literature Selection: from *Davy Crockett, Tennessee Settler,* pp. 12–14

America's History Makers
- Alexander Hamilton, pp. 35–36
- Benjamin Banneker, pp. 37–38

Outline Map Activities
- The 13 States Become 16, pp. 17–18

Why It Matters Now
- The Importance of Leadership, pp. 17–18

BLOCK SCHEDULING — LESSON PLAN OPTIONS (90-MINUTE PERIOD)

DAY 1

Interact with History, p. 275
Class Time 20 Minutes

Options for pacing and variety:
- **Role-Playing** Divide students into groups of five students each. Have each group member assume the role of one of the people shown in the Interact with History painting. Have each tell the others why his experience makes him well suited to his job in the new government.
Class Time 20 minutes

Setting the Stage, p. 276
Class Time 20 minutes

Options for pacing and variety:
- **Time Saver** For a homework assignment, have students create their own definitions of *democracy* and *republic* and make a list of three questions they have about the roles of Washington, Jefferson, Hamilton, Randolph, or Knox in the new government.
Class Time 5 minutes

Section 1, pp. 277–281
Class Time 50 minutes

Options for pacing and variety:
- **Peer Teaching** Ask a pair of students to review the Economics in History lesson on page 296 as well as the information at classzone.com on banking. Tell them to create a poster to explain to the class how banks work. **Class Time** 20 minutes
- **Time Saver** Assign the Taking Notes and Critical Thinking questions in the Section Assessment as homework.
Class Time 35 minutes

DAY 2

Section 2, pp. 282–286
Class Time 45 minutes

Options for pacing and variety:
- **Internet** Extend students' background knowledge of George Washington and his Mount Vernon home by visiting classzone.com.
Class Time 20 minutes
- **Peer Teaching** After reading Citizenship Today on page 284, ask a panel of four students to debate the question: Should American communities have curfew laws? Have the rest of the class act as debate judges, deciding which speakers make the most convincing arguments.
Class Time 25 minutes

Section 3, pp. 287–291
Class Time 45 minutes

Options for pacing and variety:
- **Time Saver** Use the chart on page 288 to summarize the differences between the Federalists and the Democratic-Republicans.
Class Time 5 minutes
- **History on Film** Extend students' background knowledge of the Alien and Sedition Acts and many other events in this chapter by viewing *A New Nation.* Schlessinger, 1996.
Class Time 35 minutes

Chapter 9 Assessment, pp. 292–293
Class Time 40 minutes

Options for pacing and variety:
- **Peer Evaluation** Divide students into pairs. Using the information in the Visual Summary on page 292, have students identify two events in each president's term that they consider most important and explain why.
Class Time 20 minutes
- **Peer Teaching** Assign different groups of students each of the four Critical Thinking questions and the Interact with History question on page 292. Have groups answer the question assigned and share their responses with the class.
Class Time 10 minutes

TEACHER-TESTED ACTIVITY **Brent Heath, De Anza Middle School, Ontario, California**

GEORGE WASHINGTON'S FAREWELL

Class Time Two class periods

Task Analyzing George Washington's Farewell Address

Purpose To understand this important speech and its impact on U.S. history

Supplies Needed
- Reference materials and Internet resources on George Washington
- Copies of Washington's Farewell Address

Activity Have each student read through the Farewell Address at his or her own pace, highlighting key ideas, words, or phrases on a copy of the document. Divide students into trios and have them read aloud their marked copies to their group, stopping at each highlighted idea or phrase to discuss with other group members what it means. Then have groups choose three ideas, words, or phrases that they all consider important. Have groups share their choices with the class, explaining why they think these ideas, words, or phrases are important and how these concepts might influence the nation's future history.

POLLING THE SEEDS OF PARTISANSHIP: A ROLE-PLAY

Role-playing is an excellent way to immerse students in the thoughts and emotions of the people from the past. In this activity, students will assume the roles of characters that might have lived during the time of the formation of the American republic. They will participate in a pre-election straw poll.

ACTIVITY OUTLINE

Objective Role-playing and conducting a poll about U.S. politics in the 1790s can help students understand major issues in the new republic.

Task Students will play the roles of different groups in U.S. society in the 1790s and conduct a poll before the 1796 presidential election.

Class Time Two class periods

DIRECTIONS

1. Explain to students that most of them will be playing characters that might have lived in the United States in the 1790s.
2. Divide the number of students by ten, place at least that many copies of each of the following phrases on pieces of paper, and put the pieces into a container. Have each student draw one piece of paper. Women were not allowed to vote at the time, so none are included in the list, but they could be added.
   - Pennsylvania backcountry farmer
   - wealthy eastern Virginia planter
   - Northwest Territory frontiersman/fur trader
   - Boston shopkeeper
   - Philadelphia banker
   - Maryland manufacturer
   - South Carolina lawyer/legislator
   - New York craftsman/tradesman
   - rural South Carolina clergyman
3. The tenth group will be the pollsters. They will devise a short list of questions, a method of tallying results, and a way to report their findings.
   - What do you think is the most important issue you face today?
   - Do you think political parties are a good idea or not?
   - Which party would you support if the election were today?
4. The rest of the students will work with the others who drew the same character and meet to review what they have read in the text about the political tendencies of their character. They will also need to review the factors likely to affect which of the political parties they would likely support.
5. After the groups have completed their research, give them 5–10 minutes to prepare a short role-play to demonstrate the personality of their character. Tell students to think of words or actions that would indicate likely political preferences, concerns, or issues for their group.
6. Have each group perform their role-play for the rest of the class. Then ask the groups to mingle and discuss issues with characters different from themselves. Remind them to stay in character to express their opinions. Some suggested issues would be:
   - Do you believe in states rights or a strong federal government?
   - Do you think the Constitution should be interpreted loosely or strictly?
   - Do you think the economy of the United States should be mostly based on manufacturing and shipping or agriculture?
   - Do you think slavery should be allowed or not?
7. Finally, have the pollsters divide the class into sections of mixed characters for polling. Each pollster should survey one section with the questions they have created and tally the results. Pollsters will then combine the results and calculate percentages of support for the different candidates.

CHAPTER 9 OBJECTIVE

The student will explain how the leaders of the new nation met the challenges of establishing a sound economy and a stable, democratic government.

CHAPTER 9 Launching a New Republic 1789–1800

HISTORY FROM VISUALS

Interpreting the Painting Have students note the expressions on the faces of the people on the shore and Washington's sober, steady gaze. Ask students how the artist suggests the patriotic nature of the event and the seriousness and significance of the occasion. **Possible Responses** *Patriotic:* Students may note the two American flags and the eagle. *Seriousness:* Students may note the expressions on the faces of those on the boat and on the shore and the restrained way in which Washington greets the crowd and the crowd watches Washington.

Extension Have the students pick one of the people waiting on the shore and write a diary entry for April 23, 1789, explaining what he or she hoped the new government would do.

George Washington arrives by boat in New York on April 23, 1789, for his presidential inauguration.

RECOMMENDED RESOURCES

BOOKS FOR THE TEACHER

Levy, L. W. ***Emergence of a Free Press.*** New York: Oxford Univ. Press, 1985. A noted authority takes a fresh look at the topic.

McCoy, Drew R. ***The Elusive Republic: Political Economy in Jeffersonian America.*** Chapel Hill, NC: Univ. of North Carolina Press, 1980. A look at underlying trends and stresses in the period.

Stinchcombe, William. ***The XYZ Affair.*** Westport, CT: Greenwood, 1980. Scholarly but engrossing account of this early cloak-and-dagger episode.

VIDEO

Abigail Adams. American Women of Achievement Video Collection. Schlessinger Media, 1995. Life and times of the second First Lady.

INTERNET

For more about Mt. Vernon and Monticello, visit . . .

classzone.com

Interact *with* History

Alexander Hamilton, brilliant lawyer and economist, becomes secretary of the treasury.
Thomas Jefferson, farmer, diplomat, and principal author of the Declaration of Independence, becomes secretary of state.
Edmund Randolph, attorney general of Virginia, becomes attorney general of the federal government.
Henry Knox, a general of artillery during the Revolution, becomes secretary of war.
George Washington, general and Revolutionary War hero, is president.

The year is 1789, and George Washington has been inaugurated as the first president of the United States. It quickly becomes obvious to you and to others that the president will need help. He chooses people with different talents and experience to help him govern.

What Do You Think?

- Why might you want people with different viewpoints in your government?
- How would you go about setting up a government?
- What do you think your biggest challenges would be?

What kind of person would you choose to help you govern?

USA

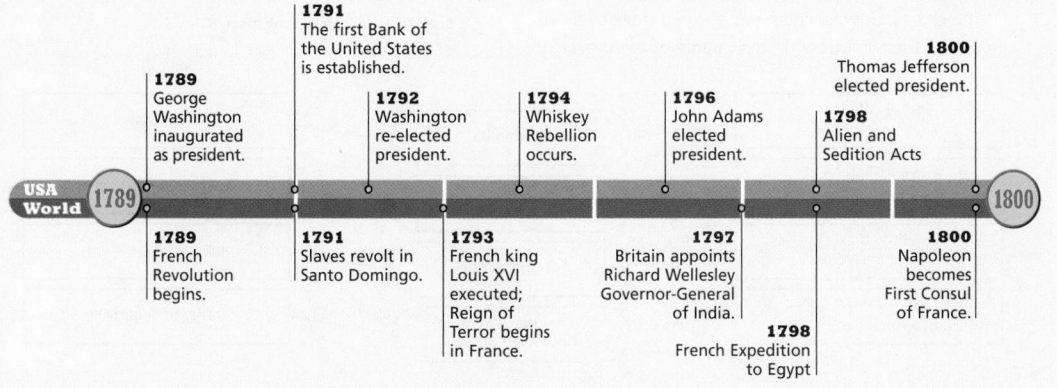

1789 George Washington inaugurated as president.

1791 The first Bank of the United States is established.

1792 Washington re-elected president.

1794 Whiskey Rebellion occurs.

1796 John Adams elected president.

1798 Alien and Sedition Acts

1800 Thomas Jefferson elected president.

World

1789 French Revolution begins.

1791 Slaves revolt in Santo Domingo.

1793 French king Louis XVI executed; Reign of Terror begins in France.

1797 Britain appoints Richard Wellesley Governor-General of India.

1798 French Expedition to Egypt

1800 Napoleon becomes First Consul of France.

Interact *with* History

OBJECTIVES

- To understand the reasons that Washington needed a cabinet
- To speculate on the responsibilities of each cabinet member

What Do You Think?

1. Note that the men shown with Washington formed the first cabinet, which was made up of the attorney general and the secretaries (heads) of the three departments. They advised the president on various issues. Ask why Washington might have felt he needed advisers.
2. Ask students to name some of the responsibilities that they would expect each man to have.
3. Have students list some of the national issues government leaders will have to address: security, finance, domestic and foreign trade, relations with other countries and with Native Americans, law and order, expansion of white settlement.

What kind of person would you choose to help you govern?

Encourage students to think not only about the responsibilities of government but also about the temperament and character of the people they would choose to have as leaders.

MAKING PERSONAL CONNECTIONS

Ask students to think about any groups that they have worked in, perhaps to complete a group project for a class or a club committee. How easy and enjoyable do students find working in a group? What sort of qualities make a good group member?

TIME LINE DISCUSSION

Point out to students that in the 11-year period shown on this time line, the United States was establishing a stable government. Meanwhile, in Europe, there was great upheaval.

- Ask students which events show the United States government was stable. **Answer** the election of three presidents and the establishment of a U.S. bank
- Ask students which events suggest that France experienced great political instability during this time. **Answer** 1789 revolution; 1793 execution of monarch, Reign of Terror; 1800 Napoleon heads new government
- Ask students what differences existed in the ways the French and the Americans chose leaders during this period. **Answer** Americans chose leaders peacefully through the electoral process; French leaders rose and fell through revolution and violent conflict.

BEFORE YOU READ

Previewing the Theme: Democratic Ideals

Have students make a list of what they consider "democratic ideals," or basic beliefs about how the democratic system should function. Have students explain why each ideal is important.

Tell students that Washington and other leaders of the new nation knew how important it was that they make the new government work to solve the nation's problems.

What Do You Know?

Remind students that the Constitution provided only an outline for the government of the nation. It remained for the newly elected officials to put the Constitution to work.

In-Depth Resources: Unit 3
- Tracing Themes: Democratic Ideals, p. 2

READ AND TAKE NOTES

Reading Strategy: Identifying and Solving Problems

Note that identifying problems faced and solutions found will help students gain historical perspective. Point out that the chart on page 292 alerts readers to problems and solutions regarding the major issues of economics, politics, foreign affairs, and relations with Native Americans. Encourage students to identify these problems and solutions as they read the chapter.

In-Depth Resources: Unit 3
- Setting the Stage, p. 1

Critical Thinking Transparency CT25
- Setting the Stage

Chapter 9 SETTING THE STAGE

BEFORE YOU READ

Inaugural coat buttons, 1789, proclaim the beginning of the Washington presidency.

Previewing the Theme

Democratic Ideals During the Federalist era (1789–1801), the leaders of the United States faced many challenges and difficulties. In this chapter, you will see how the way in which they responded to those obstacles and opportunities established a democratic foundation.

What Do You Know?

What do you think of when you hear the words *democracy* and *republic?* Why do you think the citizens and leaders of the new country wanted to establish a republic governed by laws?

THINK ABOUT
- the experience of the colonists under British rule
- the effect of the Revolutionary War and the period immediately after the war

What Do You Want to Know?

What questions do you have about the people who created the U.S. government? Record your questions in your notebook before you read the chapter.

READ AND TAKE NOTES

Reading Strategy: Identifying and Solving Problems As you read history, try to identify problems in past times and the solutions that people came up with to solve their problems. A graphic organizer such as the chart below can help you to keep track of problems and their solutions. In the middle of the chart, four headings categorize the major issues faced by the young nation. Copy the chart into your notebook and then record problems and the proposed solutions in each category.

See Skillbuilder Handbook, page R18.

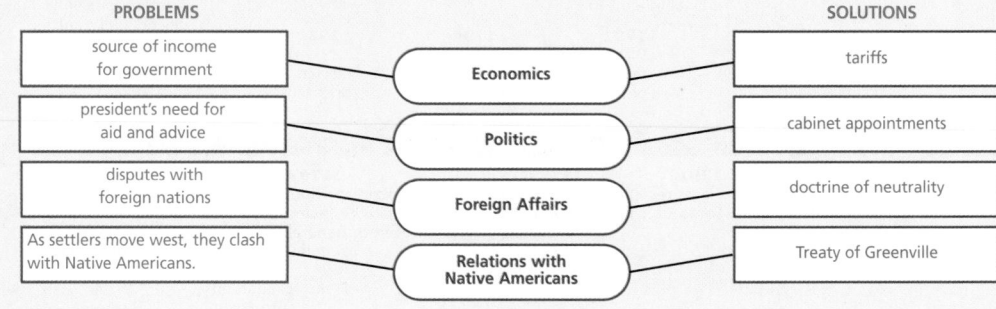

PROBLEMS		SOLUTIONS
source of income for government	Economics	tariffs
president's need for aid and advice	Politics	cabinet appointments
disputes with foreign nations	Foreign Affairs	doctrine of neutrality
As settlers move west, they clash with Native Americans.	Relations with Native Americans	Treaty of Greenville

TEACHING STRATEGY

READING THE CHAPTER

This is a thematic chapter focusing on the work of the government in implementing the Constitution and in dealing with domestic rebellion, relations with Native Americans and foreign nations, and issues of national security. Encourage students to note the obstacles leaders faced and how they attempted to solve those difficulties. You may want to review the problem-solving model found on page 269 in the Citizenship Handbook to compare the steps taken by the leaders to solve problems.

ALTERNATIVE ASSESSMENT

The Chapter Assessment describes three activities for alternative assessment on page 293. You may wish to have students work on these activities during the course of the chapter and then present them at the end.

1 Washington's Presidency

TERMS & NAMES
inaugurate
Federal Judiciary Act
cabinet
tariff

MAIN IDEA
The president and the Congress began to set up the new government.

WHY IT MATTERS NOW
The strength of the U.S. today is due to the decisions of the Founders about how to organize the government.

ONE AMERICAN'S STORY

Charles Thomson had known George Washington for many years. Thomson had served as secretary of the Continental Congress when delegates from the colonies first met in Philadelphia in 1774.

Now, 15 years later, on April 14, 1789, he had a very different job to do. He had come to Mount Vernon in Virginia with a letter for George Washington. Washington knew the reason for the visit. Thomson's letter was to tell him that he had been elected the nation's first president. Before giving Washington the letter, Thomson made a short speech.

Charles Thomson delivers the letter to Washington announcing his election as president.

A VOICE FROM THE PAST

I have now Sir to inform you that . . . your patriotism and your readiness to sacrifice . . . private enjoyments to preserve the liberty and promote the happiness of your Country [convinced the Congress that you would accept] this important Office to which you are called not only by the unanimous votes of the Electors but by the voice of America.

Charles Thomson, quoted in Washington's Papers, Library of Congress

As you will read in this section, Washington accepted the honor and the burden of his new office. He guided the nation through its early years.

1 Washington Takes Office

Washington had been elected only a few months before. Each member of the electoral college had written down two names. The top vote-getter, Washington, became president. The runner-up, John Adams, became vice-president. Washington left Mount Vernon on April 16, 1789. He traveled north through Baltimore and Philadelphia to New York City, the nation's capital. On April 30 at Federal Hall, Washington was **inaugurated,** or sworn in, as president. John Adams of Massachusetts was his vice-president.

SECTION OBJECTIVES

1. To explain how the nation's court system was established
2. To describe the first cabinet
3. To analyze Hamilton's financial plans
4. To identify interpretations of the Constitution and explain how they influenced attitudes toward the national bank

CRITICAL THINKING
Making Inferences, pp. 278, 279
Contrasting, p. 281

Why It Matters Now
- The Importance of Leadership, pp. 17–18

FOCUS & MOTIVATE

5-MINUTE WARM-UP

Making Inferences These questions focus on Washington's choice as the first president.

1. Read "A Voice from the Past" on page 277. According to Thomson, why was Washington chosen as president?
2. What does Thomson mean by the "voice of America"?

Warm-Up Transparency WT9

INSTRUCT

INSTRUCT: OBJECTIVE 1

Washington Takes Office/ Setting Up the Courts

- What does the phrase "[Washington] would set a precedent" mean?
- What decisions about the nation's court system did the Constitution leave to Congress to decide?
- What was the purpose of the Federal Judiciary Act of 1789?

In-Depth Resources: Unit 3
- Guided Reading, p. 3

Reading Study Guide (Spanish and English), pp. 87–88

RECOMMENDED RESOURCES

In-Depth Resources: Unit 3
- Guided Reading, p. 3
- Building Vocabulary, p. 6
- Primary Source: from *Journal,* p. 10

Reading Study Guide (Spanish and English), pp. 87–88

Economics in History
- Personal Banking, p. 9

America's History Makers
- Alexander Hamilton, pp. 35–36

Why It Matters Now
- The Importance of Leadership, pp. 17–18

Formal Assessment
- Section Quiz, p. 169

Integrated Assessment
- Rubrics, 4.1, 1.2

Access for Students Acquiring English/ESL
- Guided Reading, p. 57

INTEGRATED TECHNOLOGY

Electronic Teacher Tools

classzone.com

TEST-TAKING RESOURCES

Strategies for Test Preparation

Test Practice Transparencies, TT31

Online Test Practice

As the nation's first president, Washington faced a difficult task. He knew that all eyes would be on him. His every action as president would set a precedent—an example that would become standard practice. People argued over what to call him. Some, including John Adams, suggested "His Excellency" or "His Highness." Others argued that such titles would suggest that he was a king. The debate tied up Congress for a month. Finally, "Mr. President" was agreed upon. Congress had to settle other differences about how the new government should be run.

*Reading*History

A. Making Inferences Why were people so concerned about how to address the president?

A. Answer They probably believed that the way the president was addressed might affect how the office was perceived—as a monarchy or a democracy.

Setting Up the Courts

The writers of the Constitution had left many matters to be decided by Congress. For example, the Constitution created a Supreme Court but left it to Congress to decide the number of justices. Leaders also argued about how much power the Supreme Court should have. One reason for disagreement was that the states already had their own courts. How would authority be divided between the state and federal courts?

To create a court system, Congress passed the **Federal Judiciary Act** of 1789. This act gave the Supreme Court six members: a chief justice, or judge, and five associate justices. Over time, that number has grown to nine. The act also provided for other lower, less powerful federal courts. Washington appointed John Jay, the prominent New York lawyer and diplomat, as chief justice.

Vocabulary

judiciary: system of courts and judges

INSTRUCT: OBJECTIVE 2

Washington's Cabinet/Economic Problems

- How did the cabinet help the president govern the nation?
- What financial problems did the nation face? How did Hamilton propose to solve them?
- What beliefs influenced Hamilton's financial plans for the nation?

Now *and* then

The President's Cabinet

Each president uses his cabinet differently. Andrew Jackson called his cabinet together only 16 times in 8 years. FDR was the first president to appoint a woman to the cabinet when he made Frances Perkins secretary of labor. Robert Weaver, Lyndon Johnson's secretary of housing and urban development, was the first African American to join a presidential cabinet. President Ronald Reagan set up small groups within his cabinet to deal with specific issues.

Now *and* then

THE PRESIDENT'S CABINET

The president's cabinet has more than tripled in size since it began with the secretaries of state, war, and treasury, and the attorney general. As the nation has faced new challenges, the government has added new departments. In 1977, concerns about oil shortages led to the creation of the Department of Energy. The Department of Veterans' Affairs was added in 1989. Today the cabinet (Clinton's cabinet shown below) includes the heads of 14 departments.

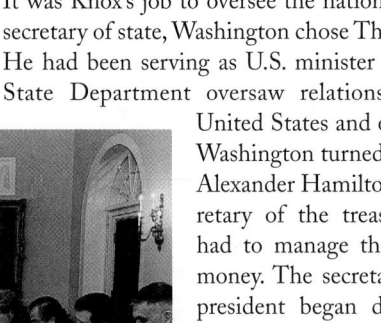

2 Washington's Cabinet

The Constitution also gave Congress the task of creating departments to help the president lead the nation. The president had the power to appoint the heads of these departments, who were to assist the president with the many issues and problems he had to face. These heads of departments became his **cabinet.**

The Congress created three departments. In his first major task as president, Washington chose talented people to run them. For secretary of war, he picked Henry Knox, a trusted general during the Revolution. It was Knox's job to oversee the nation's defenses. For secretary of state, Washington chose Thomas Jefferson. He had been serving as U.S. minister to France. The State Department oversaw relations between the United States and other countries. Washington turned to the brilliant Alexander Hamilton to be the secretary of the treasury. Hamilton had to manage the government's money. The secretary's ties to the president began during the war when he had served as one of Washington's aides. To advise the

ACTIVITY OPTIONS

INTERDISCIPLINARY LINK: CIVICS — BLOCK SCHEDULING

FORMING A CABINET

Class Time One class period

Task Writing job descriptions for cabinet members of a new government

Purpose To understand the challenges of forming a new government and the functions of the executive branch

Supplies Needed

- Civics and/or government textbooks and other reference materials on the executive branch
- Large note cards

Activity Divide the class into groups and have them list the departments they would create if they were in charge of a new government. Have group members write job descriptions for the heads of these departments. Descriptions should include the name and mission of the department, the tasks the head must perform, the qualifications and experience needed, and any benefits or perks of the job. Post finished descriptions on a bulletin board. Have students pick a post they would like and write a letter telling why they would like the job.

government on legal matters, Washington picked Edmund Randolph as attorney general.

These department heads and the attorney general made up Washington's cabinet. The Constitution made no mention of a cabinet. However, Washington began the practice of calling his department heads together to advise him.

Economic Problems

As secretary of the treasury, Alexander Hamilton faced the task of straightening out the nation's finances. First of all, the new government needed to pay its war debts. During the Revolution, the United States had borrowed millions of dollars from France, the Netherlands, and Spain. Within the United States, merchants and other private citizens had loaned money to the government. State governments also had wartime debts to pay back. By 1789, the national debt totaled more than $52 million.

Most government leaders agreed that the nation must repay its debts to win the respect of both foreign nations and its own citizens. Hamilton saw that the new nation must assure other countries that it was responsible about money. These nations would do business with the United States if they saw that the country would pay its debts. If the nation failed to do so, no country would lend it money in the future.

Hamilton came up with a financial plan that reflected his belief in a strong central government. He thought the power of the national government should be stronger than that of the state governments. Hamilton also believed that government should encourage business and industry. He sought the support of the nation's wealthy merchants and manufacturers. He thought that the nation's prosperity depended on them. The government owed money to many of these rich men. By paying them back, Hamilton hoped to win their support for the new government.

AMERICA'S HISTORY MAKERS

ALEXANDER HAMILTON
1755?–1804

Alexander Hamilton was born into poverty in the British West Indies. When he was ten years old, the young Alexander went to work as a clerk. He so impressed his employers that they helped to send him to school at King's College (now Columbia University) in New York.

During the Revolutionary War, he became an aide to General Washington. Hamilton moved up quickly in the army and later in political life. Although of humble origins, Hamilton had little faith in the common people and put his trust in the wealthy and educated to govern.

Why is it odd that Hamilton distrusted the common people to govern?

Reading **History**

B. Making Inferences Why might merchants and manufacturers support a strong central government?

B. Answer
Because a strong central government could encourage the development of business and make it easier to do business and collect debts.

Hamilton's Financial Plan ❸

In 1790, Hamilton presented his plan to Congress. He proposed three steps to improve the nation's finances.

1. paying off all war debts
2. raising government revenues
3. creating a national bank

Hamilton wanted the federal government to pay off the war debts of the states. However, sectional differences arose over repayment of state debts. Virginia, Georgia, and many other Southern states had already repaid their debts and did not like being asked to help Northern states pay theirs.

AMERICA'S HISTORY MAKERS

Alexander Hamilton

Hamilton was the son of a Scottish merchant, James Hamilton. His mother, Rachel Lavine, was a French Huguenot woman who was separated from her husband when she met James Hamilton on the island of St. Croix. In 1765, after living with Lavine for some years, he abandoned the family. Desperately poor with two children, Lavine sent young Alexander to work as a clerk in a counting-house. Three years later his mother died, and he became the ward of her relatives. In 1772, Hamilton's abilities and engaging manner so impressed friends that they paid for him to go to New Jersey for further schooling. He then attended King's College in New York.

Possible Response: Hamilton himself was born in poverty. He came from the common people. He worked hard to become part of the elite.

America's History Makers
- Alexander Hamilton, pp. 35–36

INSTRUCT: OBJECTIVE ❸

Hamilton's Financial Plan

- What were the three steps in Hamilton's financial plan?
- Why did many Southern states object to helping the country pay off its war debts?
- Why did Hamilton favor imposing high tariffs on foreign goods and creating a national bank?

ACTIVITY OPTIONS

INDIVIDUAL NEEDS

LESS PROFICIENT READERS

Creating an Outline Show students how to create an outline using topic sentences from the text as main ideas. After writing the main ideas on the board, ask students to reread the text and identify details to complete the outline. Sample details are given for the first topic sentence below.

I. Hamilton wanted the federal government to pay war debts.
  A. Many Southern states had paid debts.
  B. They did not want to help Northern states repay debts.
  C. In exchange for Southern states helping Northern states repay debts, the capital would be placed in the South.
II. Hamilton favored tariffs.
III. Hamilton called for the creation of a national bank.

Hamilton asked Thomas Jefferson of Virginia to help him gain Southern support. They reached a compromise. In exchange for Southern support of the plan, Northerners agreed to place the new nation's capital in the South. The location chosen was on the Potomac River between Virginia and Maryland.

The secretary of the treasury favored tariffs. A **tariff** is a tax on imported goods. It serves two purposes: raising money for the government and encouraging the growth of American industry. The government placed the highest tariffs on foreign goods—such as shoes and textiles—that Americans bought in great quantities. This ensured a steady flow of income to the government. In addition, since tariffs made foreign goods more expensive, they encouraged people to buy American goods.

Hamilton also called for the creation of a national bank. Such a bank would meet many needs. It would give the government a safe place to keep

Economics *in* History

How Banks Work

Why did Hamilton want to create a national bank? He believed that such a bank could help the economy of the new nation. It would create a partnership between the federal government and American business.

Let's say you deposited money into a bank account. Then you went back another day to withdraw some of the money. What happened in the meantime? Did the money just sit in the bank until you wanted it back? No—the bank used your money, and in doing so, helped fuel economic growth. In this way, money flows in a circular path from people like you into the general economy and back to you again. In the process, money can create goods and services, jobs, and profits, as the diagram explains.

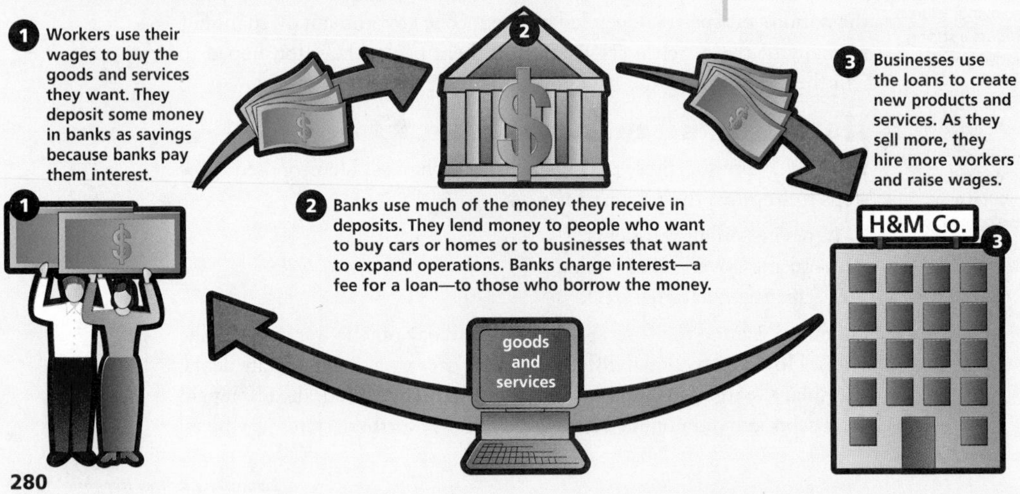

1 Workers use their wages to buy the goods and services they want. They deposit some money in banks as savings because banks pay them interest.
2 Banks use much of the money they receive in deposits. They lend money to people who want to buy cars or homes or to businesses that want to expand operations. Banks charge interest—a fee for a loan—to those who borrow the money.
3 Businesses use the loans to create new products and services. As they sell more, they hire more workers and raise wages.
H&M Co.
goods and services

CONNECT TO HISTORY

1. **Analyzing Points of View** Do you think that the people who feared a strong central government supported Hamilton's idea of a national bank? Why or why not?

See Skillbuilder Handbook, page R9.

CONNECT TO TODAY

2. **Making Inferences** How do banks make money?

For more about banking . . .

RESEARCH LINKS CLASSZONE.COM

280

CRITICAL THINKING ACTIVITY

Analyzing Points of View Tell students that while tariffs raised revenue and encouraged the purchase of American-made goods, they had other consequences as well. Ask students which businesses were likely to be helped by raising tariffs. Which business owners or consumers might be hurt by tariffs? Use a two column chart to help students examine these questions.

Class Time 10 minutes

Economics *in* History

OBJECTIVE

Students will be able to explain how a bank could help the economy of the new nation. They will be able to describe how a commercial bank operates and how a commercial bank can help the general economy.

The Federal Reserve System

The Federal Reserve System is the present-day "national bank." In 1913, Congress passed laws creating the Federal Reserve System, the central banking system of the United States. The system consists of 12 Federal Reserve banks, each of which is owned by the member banks in its district. The 12 banks are regulated by a central board based in the nation's capital and appointed by the president. The board manages the country's money supply, controlling the lending rate to member banks. It tightens lending rates to fight inflation or lowers rates to spur business growth through lending during economic downturns.

Economics in History
- Personal Banking, p. 9

CONNECT TO HISTORY

1. **Analyzing Points of View** They probably did not favor Hamilton's idea of a national bank because it extended the role of government into the economic sector, increasing the power and influence of the federal government on U.S. businesses.

CONNECT TO TODAY

2. **Making Inferences** Banks make money by charging interest on the loans they make to individuals and businesses.

Vocabulary
currency: money

money. It would also make loans to businesses and government. Most important, it would issue bank notes—paper money that could be used as currency. Overall, Hamilton's plan would strengthen the central government. However, this worried Jefferson and Madison.

Two of the first U.S. coins, 1792

4 Interpreting the Constitution

Jefferson and Madison believed that the Constitution discouraged the concentration of power in the federal government. The Constitution's writers had tried to make the document general enough so that it would be flexible. As a result, disagreements sometimes arose over the document's meaning.

The debate over Hamilton's plan for a national bank exposed differences about how to interpret the Constitution. Madison and Jefferson argued that the Constitution did not give the government the power to set up a bank. They believed in the strict construction—narrow or strict interpretation—of the Constitution. They stated that the government has only those powers that the Constitution clearly says it has. Therefore, since the Constitution does not mention a national bank, the government cannot create one.

C. Answer Strict construction favors a narrow interpretation of the Constitution, while loose construction favors a broad interpretation.

Reading **History**
C. Contrasting What is the main difference between strict and loose interpretations of the Constitution?

Hamilton disagreed. He favored a loose construction—broad or flexible interpretation—of the Constitution. Pointing to the elastic clause in the document, he argued that the bank was "necessary and proper" to carry out the government's duties. (See The Living Constitution, page 238.) According to this view, when the Constitution grants a power to Congress, it also grants Congress the "necessary and proper" means to carry out that power. Jefferson and Hamilton argued their positions to Washington. Hamilton won, and the Bank of the United States was set up in 1791. The president, meanwhile, was dealing with other challenges at home and abroad, which you will read about in Section 2.

Section 1 Assessment

1. Terms & Names

Explain the significance of:
- inaugurate
- Federal Judiciary Act
- cabinet
- tariff

2. Taking Notes

In a chart, list members of Washington's cabinet and their responsibilities.

Cabinet member	Responsibilities

Which cabinet member had the greatest responsibilities? Explain.

3. Main Ideas

a. What was the purpose of Washington's cabinet?

b. What economic problems did the new government face?

c. How did Hamilton's financial plan attempt to solve the nation's economic problems?

4. Critical Thinking

Contrasting How did Hamilton and Jefferson differ in their interpretation of the Constitution?

THINK ABOUT
- views on the national bank
- views on the role of government

ACTIVITY OPTIONS

LANGUAGE ARTS
ART

Imagine you oppose or support Hamilton's plan for the nation's finances. Write a **letter to the editor** or draw a **political cartoon** expressing your opinion.

INSTRUCT: OBJECTIVE 4
Interpreting the Constitution

- What are the two major ways of interpreting the Constitution, and how do they differ?
- Why did Madison and Jefferson oppose the creation of a national bank?
- How was the argument over the bank settled?

ASSESS & RETEACH

Setting the Stage Have students fill in the sections on the chapter graphic organizer.

Formal Assessment
- Section Quiz, p. 169

Critical Thinking Transparency CT25
- Setting the Stage

RETEACHING ACTIVITY

Divide the class into groups of three. Have each group member answer one of the review questions for Section 1 in the Chapter Assessment on page 308. Have students share their answers with the group.

In-Depth Resources: Unit 3
- Reteaching Activity, p. 15

Section 1 Assessment

1. Terms & Names

inaugurate, p. 277
Federal Judiciary Act, p. 278
cabinet, p. 278
tariff, p. 280

2. Taking Notes

Hamilton—treasury; managed the nation's money
Jefferson—state; oversaw foreign relations
Knox—war; managed defenses
Randolph—attorney general; advised on legal affairs

Accept reasonable answers supported with evidence.

3. Main Ideas

a. to assist and advise the president on the nation's issues **b.** paying off war debts, creating a financial plan to handle debt agreed to by Congress **c.** He arranged for the government to pay off the state's war debts, argued to raise revenues through tariffs, and supported a national bank.

4. Critical Thinking

Jefferson was a strict constructionist. Hamilton was a loose constructionist.

ACTIVITY OPTIONS

Integrated Assessment
- Rubrics for an opinion article, 4.1
- Rubrics for a cartoon, 1.2

SECTION OBJECTIVES

1. To explain why Washington wanted to secure the Trans-Appalachian West
2. To analyze the causes and outcome of the Battle of Fallen Timbers
3. To identify the reasons for the Whiskey Rebellion
4. To explain how Washington maintained U.S. neutrality

SKILLBUILDER

Interpreting Maps: Region, Location, p. 283

CRITICAL THINKING

Making Inferences, p. 283
Drawing Conclusions, p. 286
Evaluating, p. 286

FOCUS & MOTIVATE

5-MINUTE WARM-UP

Reading a Map These questions focus on the reasons for conflict in the Trans-Appalachian West.

1. Look at the map on page 283. Which states and territory were part of the Trans-Appalachian West?
2. Which natural feature formed the western boundary of the Trans-Appalachian West?

Warm-Up Transparency WT9

INSTRUCT

INSTRUCT: OBJECTIVE 1

Securing the Northwest Territory

- Why was there conflict over the West?
- How did the Battle of Fallen Timbers affect Native American claims to land?
- Why was Washington's treatment of the Whiskey Rebellion important?

In-Depth Resources: Unit 3
- Guided Reading, p. 4
- Building Vocabulary, p. 6

2 Challenges to the New Government

MAIN IDEA

Washington established central authority at home and avoided war with European powers.

WHY IT MATTERS NOW

Washington's policies at home and abroad set an example for later presidents.

TERMS & NAMES

Battle of Fallen Timbers
Treaty of Greenville
Whiskey Rebellion
French Revolution
neutral
Jay's Treaty
Pinckney's Treaty

ONE AMERICAN'S STORY

Pioneers had been moving west since before the Revolution. However, the settlers met fierce resistance from Native Americans. One of their most respected military leaders was Chief Little Turtle of the Miami tribe of Ohio. In 1790 and 1791, he had won decisive victories against U.S. troops.

Now, two years later, the Miami and their allies again faced attack by American forces. At a council meeting, Little Turtle gave a warning to his people about the troops led by General Anthony Wayne.

General Anthony Wayne negotiates with a Miami war chief.

A VOICE FROM THE PAST

We have beaten the enemy twice under different commanders. . . . The Americans are now led by a chief [Wayne] who never sleeps. . . . During all the time he has been marching on our villages . . . we have not been able to surprise him. Think well of it. . . . It would be prudent [wise] to listen to his offers of peace.

Little Turtle, quoted in *The Life and Times of Little Turtle*

While the council members weighed Little Turtle's warning, President Washington was making plans to secure—guard or protect—the western borders of the new nation.

1 Securing the Northwest Territory

As a general, Washington had skillfully waged war. As the nation's president, however, he saw that the country needed peace in order to prosper. But in spite of his desire for peace, he considered military action as trouble brewed in the Trans-Appalachian West, the land between the Appalachian Mountains and the Mississippi River. The 1783 Treaty of Paris had attempted to resolve the claims. The source of the trouble was competing claims for these lands. Some years later, however, Spain, Britain, the United States, and Native Americans claimed parts of the area as their own.

Spain held much of North America west of the Mississippi. It also claimed Florida and the port of New Orleans at the mouth of the

RECOMMENDED RESOURCES

In-Depth Resources: Unit 3
- Guided Reading, p. 4
- Building Vocabulary, p. 6
- Skillbuilder Practice, p. 7
- Literature Selection: from "Davy Crockett, Tennessee Settler," pp. 12–14

Reading Study Guide (Spanish and English), pp. 89–90

Citizenship Today, pp. 5–6

Formal Assessment
- Section Quiz, p. 170

Integrated Assessment
- Rubrics, 2.1, 1.3

Access for Students Acquiring English/ESL
- Guided Reading, p. 58
- Skillbuilder Practice, p. 60

INTEGRATED TECHNOLOGY

Geography Transparency GT9
- Trouble Spots in the New Republic, 1790–1794

Electronic Teacher Tools

classzone.com

TEST-TAKING RESOURCES

Strategies for Test Preparation

Test Practice Transparencies, TT32

Online Test Practice

282 CHAPTER 9

Mississippi. For American settlers in the West, this port was key to trade. They carried their goods to market by flatboat down the Mississippi to New Orleans. They took Spanish threats to close the port very seriously. The Spanish also stirred up trouble between the white settlers and the Creeks, Choctaws, and other Native American groups in the Southeast.

The strongest resistance to white settlement came from Native Americans in the Northwest Territory. This territory was bordered by the Ohio River to the south and Canada to the north. Native Americans in that territory hoped to join together to form an independent Native American nation. In violation of the Treaty of Paris, the British still held forts north of the Ohio River. The British supported Native Americans in order to maintain their access to fur in these territories. Eventually, Native Americans and white settlers clashed over the Northwest Territory.

Reading **History**
A. Making Inferences What expectations might the Native Americans have had of the British as the tribes came into conflict with white settlers?
A. Answer Native Americans probably expected the British to support them in their conflicts with American settlers since both were clashing with American settlers.

Battle of Fallen Timbers ❷

Believing the Northwest Territory was critical to the security and growth of the new nation, Washington sent troops to the Ohio Valley. As you read in One American's Story, this first federal army took a beating from warriors led by Little Turtle in 1790. The chief's force came from many tribes, including the Shawnee, Ottawa, and Chippewa, who joined in a confederation to defeat the federal army.

After a second defeat in 1791 of an army headed by General Arthur St. Clair, Washington ordered another army west. This time Anthony Wayne, known as "Mad Anthony" for his reckless courage, was at its head.

The other chiefs ignored Little Turtle's advice to negotiate. They replaced him with a less able leader. Expecting British help, Native American warriors gathered at British-held Fort Miami. On August 20, 1794, a fighting force of around 2,000 Native Americans clashed with Wayne's troops. The site was covered with trees that had been struck down by a storm. The Native Americans were defeated in what became known as the **Battle of Fallen Timbers.**

Skillbuilder Answers
1. Land surrendered by Native Americans in Treaty of Greenville
2. Rivers and lakes provided an easy way to move troops and supplies.

The Battle of Fallen Timbers memorial sculpture below shows two American soldiers and a Native American.

GEOGRAPHY SKILLBUILDER
Interpreting Maps
1. **Region** *What does the yellow area of the map represent?*
2. **Location** *Why might the British forts be located near water?*

INSTRUCT: OBJECTIVE ❷
Battle of Fallen Timbers

- Why did Washington decide to send troops to the Ohio Valley to fight the force led by Little Turtle?
- What were the results of the Battle of Fallen Timbers for the Native Americans? for the United States?
- Why did the British refuse to help the Native Americans?

MORE ABOUT . . .

Little Turtle
Little Turtle had good reason to think the British would aid his people at the Battle of Fallen Timbers. During the Revolution, the Miami leader had fought alongside the British against the colonists.

HISTORY FROM VISUALS

Reading the Map Have the students draw conclusions about what is happening to Native Americans in the time period from 1791 to 1795. Ask them what they think will happen to the Native Americans after 1795. **Possible Response** The Native Americans are being squeezed out of the area by settlement on both sides of the Appalachians. They will probably move West.

Extension Have students use a current political map to determine which states or parts of states were created from the area turned over to the United States by Native Americans in 1795.

ACTIVITY OPTIONS

SKILLBUILDER LESSON: MAKING INFERENCES | BLOCK SCHEDULING

Explaining the Skill An *inference* is a conclusion drawn from interpretation of facts, data, and other information contained in a reading. Making an inference often requires the reader to derive information from what is implied as well as what is directly stated. It is important to read carefully to understand both the facts and the implications. Forming questions may also help the reader.

Applying the Skill Direct students' attention to the Reading History question on this page. Have them answer this question and questions 1 and 2, which follow.

1. How did the British react to Native American efforts to resist settlement by Americans in the Northwest Territory? Why? *(The British supported Native Americans to maintain the fur trade.)*
2. Given these facts, what can you infer about how Native Americans would expect the British to respond to the conflict with Wayne's troops at Fallen Timbers? *(Native Americans would expect help from the British.)*

In-Depth Resources: Unit 3
- Skillbuilder Practice, p. 7

INSTRUCT: OBJECTIVE 3

The Whiskey Rebellion

- Why were farmers angry about the whiskey tax?
- Why did Washington decide to crush the rebellion and enforce the tax?
- What other options, if any, might Washington have chosen? What might the farmers have chosen?

Geography Transparency GT9
- Trouble Spots in the New Republic, 1790–1794

The Native Americans retreated to Fort Miami. The British, not wanting war with the United States, refused to help them. The Battle of Fallen Timbers crushed Native American hopes of keeping their land in the Northwest Territory. Twelve tribes signed the **Treaty of Greenville** in 1795. They agreed to cede, or surrender, much of present-day Ohio and Indiana to the U.S. government.

Reading **History**

B. Reading a Map Use the map on page 283 to see which two states to the south bordered the land ceded by Native Americans.

3 The Whiskey Rebellion

Not long after the Battle of Fallen Timbers, Washington put another army into the field. The conflict arose over the government's tax on whiskey, part of Hamilton's financial plan. From Pennsylvania to Georgia, outraged farmers resisted the tax. For them, whiskey—and the grain it was made from—were important products.

Because of poor roads, backcountry farmers had trouble getting their grain to market. Crops such as wheat and rye were more easily carried to market in liquid form, so farmers made their grain into whiskey. A farmer's horse could haul only two bushels of rye but could carry two barrels of rye whiskey. This was an amount equal to 24 bushels of the grain. In addition, their customers paid more for whiskey than grain. With little cash to buy goods, let alone pay the tax, farmers often traded whiskey for salt, sugar, and other goods. The farmers used whiskey as money to get whatever supplies they needed.

CITIZENSHIP TODAY

OBJECTIVE

Students will be able to explain some of the issues involved in making and enforcing laws by national and local governments.

Whiskey Rebellion and the Law

The Whiskey Rebellion marked the first major challenge to the authority of the federal government. The revolt was fairly widespread, affecting more than 20 counties in Pennsylvania, Maryland, Virginia, Kentucky, Ohio, and North Carolina. When the armed rebels gathered in Pittsburgh in 1794, they were not only angry about the whiskey tax but about their underrepresentation in state legislatures. Many Backcountry farmers felt the new federal government did not represent or understand their interests any better than had the British Parliament prior to independence.

Citizenship Today, pp. 5–6

CITIZENSHIP TODAY

Obeying Rules and Laws

As the Whiskey Rebellion shows, since the earliest days of the republic our government has made laws and punished those who broke them. These laws affect not only adult citizens, but young people as well.

Today, for example, communities across the country are trying to control the problem of juvenile crime by imposing curfews on young people. These laws require minors to be off the streets after a certain time, often ten or eleven at night. Penalties can be harsh. In certain communities, minors who break curfew laws can be detained, and their parents can be fined.

People who favor curfews believe such laws cut crime. Those who oppose curfews think such limits are the responsibility of parents and not the government.

Why Should You Obey Rules and Laws?

1. What are some arguments in favor of curfew laws? What are arguments against them? Make a list of each.
2. Poll your classmates to see how many agree with each position.
3. Write an essay expressing your opinion on this issue.
4. Brainstorm changes or adaptations to curfew laws that you think would make them more flexible.

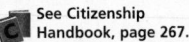

See Citizenship Handbook, page 267.

For more about young people and the law . . .

RESEARCH LINKS CLASSZONE.COM

STANDARDS FOR EVALUATION

CONDUCTING A POLL

Each poll should
- clearly state each position.
- be tabulated correctly.

WRITING AN ESSAY

Each essay should
- concisely state arguments for and against curfews.
- clearly explain the writer's position on this issue.
- provide facts, examples, or reasoned arguments to support the writer's position.
- demonstrate a balanced understanding of the issue.

In the summer of 1794, a group of farmers in western Pennsylvania staged the **Whiskey Rebellion** against the tax. One armed group beat up a tax collector, coated him with tar and feathers, and stole his horse. Others threatened an armed attack on Pittsburgh.

> **"Such a resistance is treason."**
> Alexander Hamilton

Washington, urged on by Hamilton, was prepared to enforce the tax and crush the Whiskey Rebellion. They feared that not to act might undermine the new government and weaken its authority. Hamilton condemned the rebels for resisting the law.

A VOICE FROM THE PAST

> Such a resistance is treason against society, against liberty, against everything that ought to be dear to a free, enlightened, and prudent people. To tolerate it were to abandon your most precious interests. Not to subdue it were to tolerate it.
>
> **Alexander Hamilton,** *The Works of Alexander Hamilton*

In October 1794, General Henry Lee, with Hamilton at his side, led an army of 13,000 soldiers into western Pennsylvania to put down the uprising. As news of the army's approach spread, the rebels fled. After much effort, federal troops rounded up 20 barefoot, ragged prisoners. Washington had proved his point. He had shown that the government had the power and the will to enforce its laws. Meanwhile, events in Europe gave Washington a different kind of challenge.

4 The French Revolution

In 1789, a financial crisis led the French people to rebel against their government. Inspired by the American Revolution, the French revolutionaries demanded liberty and equality. At first, Americans supported the **French Revolution**. By 1792, however, the revolution had become very violent. Thousands of French citizens were massacred. Then, in 1793, Louis XVI, the king of France, was executed.

Other European monarchs believed the revolution threatened their own thrones. France soon declared war on Britain, Holland, and Spain. Britain led the fight against France.

The war between France and Britain put the United States in an awkward position. France had been America's ally in the Revolution against the British.

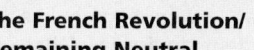

Connections TO WORLD HISTORY

EYEWITNESS TO REVOLUTION

In 1789, an American citizen with a strange first name, Gouverneur Morris, went to Paris as a private business agent. Three years later, President Washington appointed him U.S. minister to France. An eyewitness to the French Revolution, Morris kept a detailed record of what he saw, including the execution of the king and queen by guillotine, as shown below.

Here is part of a letter he wrote on October 18, 1793:

> "Terror is the order of the Day. . . . The Queen was executed the Day before yesterday. Insulted during her Trial and reviled in her last Moments, she behav'd with Dignity throughout."

Connections TO WORLD HISTORY

Marie Antoinette

History has judged Marie Antoinette harshly. Describing her as "frivolous, imprudent, and prodigal," historians have blamed her shallowness and scheming for helping to bring down the French monarchy. Her lavish spending at a time of great financial crisis in France earned her the hatred of the common people. An anecdote of the time tells of the queen asking an official why the poor were protesting. When the official answered that it was because the poor had no bread, the queen callously replied, "Then let them eat cake." Although the story was not true, it was readily believed by Parisians.

INSTRUCT: OBJECTIVE 4

The French Revolution/ Remaining Neutral

- Why did war between France and Britain put the United States in a difficult position?
- How did Jefferson, Hamilton, and Washington think the United States should react to the war?
- What problems did Jay's Treaty and Pinckney's Treaty solve for the United States?

ACTIVITY OPTIONS

INDIVIDUAL NEEDS

STUDENTS ACQUIRING ENGLISH/ESL

Building Vocabulary Point out the word *rebellion* in the heading "The Whiskey Rebellion." Explain that the base word of *rebellion* is *rebel*, which means "to oppose or take arms against a government or ruler," and that a rebellion is armed opposition to authority. Then ask students to read the paragraphs under the heading to identify related words (verb—*rebelled;* noun—*rebels*). Discuss the meanings of those words and ask students to use full sentences to answer questions such as the following:

- In the summer of 1794, who *rebelled* against the tax on whiskey?
- Who condemned the *rebels* for resisting the law?

Then point out the next heading, "The French Revolution." Explain that a *revolution* is a rebellion that results in the overthrow of a government.

MORE ABOUT . . .

Jay's Treaty

The Senate narrowly approved the treaty negotiated by Chief Justice John Jay. The treaty encountered much opposition not only because the British refused to agree to free trade in the British West Indies, but also because the British rejected Jay's proposals that they compensate Americans for slaves abducted during the Revolution. Still, the treaty led to peaceful relations with Britain. It would be 18 years before the United States and Britain were at war again.

ASSESS & RETEACH

Setting the Stage Have students fill in the "Foreign Affairs" and "Relations with Native Americans" sections on the chapter graphic organizer.

Formal Assessment
- Section Quiz, p. 170

RETEACHING ACTIVITY

On the chalkboard create a web diagram like the one below. Ask students to list ways that actions of the United States government affected two groups of Americans.

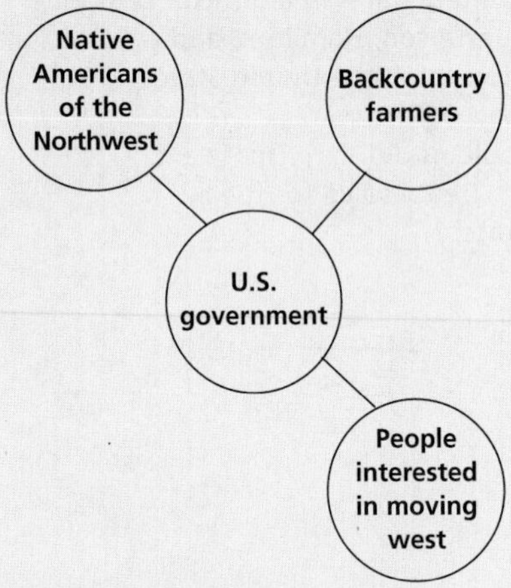

In-Depth Resources: Unit 3
- Reteaching Activity, p. 16

A 1778 treaty still bound the two nations together. In addition, many saw France's revolution as proof that the American cause had been just. Jefferson felt that a move to crush the French Revolution was an attack on liberty everywhere. Hamilton, though, pointed out that Britain was the United States' most important trading partner, and British trade was too important to risk war.

In April 1793, Washington declared that the United States would remain **neutral,** not siding with one country or the other. He stated that the nation would be "friendly and impartial" to both sides. Congress then passed a law forbidding the United States to help either side.

*Reading***History**
C. Drawing Conclusions What sort of U.S. obligation to France did the wartime alliance and treaty of 1778 create?
C. Answer Since France supported the U.S. in its Revolution, many people thought the U.S. should support France.

Remaining Neutral

Britain made it hard for the United States to remain neutral. Late in 1792, the British began seizing the cargoes of American ships carrying goods from the French West Indies.

Washington sent Chief Justice John Jay to England for talks about the seizure of U.S. ships. Jay also hoped to persuade the British to give up their forts on the Northwest frontier. During the talks in 1794, news came of the U.S. victory at the Battle of Fallen Timbers. Fearing another entanglement, the British agreed to leave the Ohio Valley by 1796. In **Jay's Treaty,** the British also agreed to pay damages for U.S. vessels they had seized. Jay failed, however, to open up the profitable British West Indies trade to Americans. Because of this, Jay's Treaty was unpopular.

Like Jay, Thomas Pinckney helped the United States reduce tensions along the frontier. In 1795, **Pinckney's Treaty** with Spain gave Americans the right to travel freely on the Mississippi River. It also gave them the right to store goods at the port of New Orleans without paying customs duties. In addition, Spain accepted the 31st parallel as the northern boundary of Florida and the southern boundary of the United States.

Meanwhile, more American settlers moved west. As you will read in the next section, change was coming back east as Washington stepped down.

D. Answer By remaining neutral, the new nation did not make enemies, did not lose a trading partner, did not become involved in a war.

*Reading***History**
D. Evaluating What were some of the advantages to the new nation of remaining neutral?

Section 2 Assessment

1. Terms & Names

Explain the significance of:
- Battle of Fallen Timbers
- Treaty of Greenville
- Whiskey Rebellion
- French Revolution
- neutral
- Jay's Treaty
- Pinckney's Treaty

2. Taking Notes

Use a chart to record U.S. responses to various challenges.

Challenge	Response
From Spain	
From Britain	
From France	

Which challenge seemed greatest? Why?

3. Main Ideas

a. What military and other actions secured the West for the United States?

b. Why did Washington consider it important to put down the Whiskey Rebellion?

c. How did the French Revolution create problems for the United States?

4. Critical Thinking

Drawing Conclusions Why was neutrality a difficult policy for the United States to maintain?

THINK ABOUT
- ties with France
- ties with Britain
- restrictions on trade

ACTIVITY OPTIONS

GEOGRAPHY / ART Make a **map** that describes the Battle of Fallen Timbers, or draw a **scene** from that battle.

Section 2 Assessment

1. Terms & Names

Battle of Fallen Timbers, p. 283
Treaty of Greenville, p. 284
Whiskey Rebellion, p. 285
French Revolution, p. 285
neutral, p. 286
Jay's Treaty, p. 286
Pinckney's Treaty, p. 286

2. Taking Notes

From Spain—Pinckney's Treaty
From Britain—Jay's Treaty
From France—policy of neutrality

Accept answers that are supported with evidence.

3. Main Ideas

a. Battle of Fallen Timbers; Treaty of Greenville **b.** to uphold the authority of the federal government **c.** The United States became caught in the middle between France and Great Britain.

4. Critical Thinking

The British angered Americans by seizing U.S. shipping.

ACTIVITY OPTIONS

Integrated Assessment
- Rubrics for a map, 2.1
- Rubrics for a scene, 1.3

3 The Federalists in Charge

TERMS & NAMES
foreign policy
political party
XYZ Affair
Alien and Sedition Acts
states' rights

MAIN IDEA	WHY IT MATTERS NOW
The split between Hamilton and Jefferson led to the growth of political parties.	The two-party system is still a major feature of politics in the United States.

ONE AMERICAN'S STORY

In 1796, President George Washington decided that two terms in office was enough. The president was fed up with political quarreling. He wanted to return to Mount Vernon, his estate in Virginia. But as he left office, he feared the development of political parties would split the nation into enemy camps. With Hamilton's help, in 1796 he wrote a final address to the nation.

This painting portrays Mount Vernon in 1792.

A VOICE FROM THE PAST

Let me now . . . warn you . . . against the [harmful] effects of the spirit of party. . . . This spirit, unfortunately . . . exists in different shapes in all governments . . . but in those of the popular form, it is seen in its greatest rankness and is truly their worst enemy.

George Washington, Farewell Address

In his address, Washington warned of the dangers of political division, or what he termed "the spirit of party." As you will see in this section, few people took his advice.

1 Washington Retires

Washington had come to the presidency greatly admired by the American people. Throughout his eight years in office (1789–1797), he had tried to serve as a symbol of national unity. In large part, he succeeded. During his second term, however, opponents of Jay's Treaty led attacks on the president. Thomas Paine called Washington "treacherous in private friendship . . . and a hypocrite in public life" because he failed to support the French Revolution.

Washington saw such attacks as the outcome of political disagreements. In his farewell address, he warned that such differences could weaken the nation. Despite his advice, political parties became a part of American politics.

SECTION OBJECTIVES

1. To explain how political parties developed
2. To identify the problems President John Adams faced with France
3. To describe and evaluate the Alien and Sedition Acts and responses to them
4. To explain how Adams made peace with France

SKILLBUILDER
Interpreting Charts, p. 288

CRITICAL THINKING
Summarizing, p. 288
Drawing Conclusions, p. 290
Making Inferences, p. 291
Evaluating, p. 291

FOCUS & MOTIVATE

5-MINUTE WARM-UP

Drawing Conclusions These questions focus on Washington's opposition to political parties.

1. Read the quotation from Washington's Farewell Address on page 287. What did he mean by the "[harmful] effects of the spirit of party"?
2. Why might Washington's advice to avoid political parties be hard to follow?

Warm-Up Transparency WT9

INSTRUCT

INSTRUCT: OBJECTIVE 1

Washington Retires/ Growth of Political Parties

- What advice did Washington give the nation on foreign affairs?
- Over what issues did political parties develop?
- Who were the leaders and the major groups that supported each party?

In-Depth Resources: Unit 3
- Guided Reading, p. 5

Reading Study Guide (Spanish and English), pp. 91–92

RECOMMENDED RESOURCES

In-Depth Resources: Unit 3
- Guided Reading, p. 5
- Building Vocabulary, p. 6
- Geography Application, pp. 8–9
- Primary Source, p. 11
- Enrichment Activity, p. 18

Reading Study Guide (Spanish and English), pp. 91–92

Outline Map Activities, pp. 17–18

America's History Makers
- Benjamin Banneker, pp. 37–38

Formal Assessment
- Section Quiz, p. 171

Integrated Assessment
- Rubrics, 5.3, 3.1

Access for Students Acquiring English/ESL, pp. 59, 61–62

INTEGRATED TECHNOLOGY

Critical Thinking Trans. CT26
- Cause and Effect: Growth of Political Parties

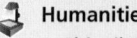

Humanities Trans. HT17
- *Abigail Adams* by Gordon Philips

Humanities Trans. HT18
- Engraving of Washington, D.C.

TEST-TAKING RESOURCES

Strategies for Test Preparation

Test Practice Transparencies, TT33

Online Test Practice

Americans listened more closely to Washington's parting advice on **foreign policy**—relations with the governments of other countries. He urged the nation's leaders to remain neutral and "steer clear of permanent alliances with any portion of the foreign world." He warned that agreements with foreign nations might work against U.S. interests. His advice served to guide U.S. foreign policy into the twentieth century.

Growth of Political Parties

Despite Washington's warning against political parties, Americans were deeply divided over how the nation should be run. During Washington's first term (1789–1792), Hamilton and Jefferson had hotly debated the direction the new nation should take. Then Jefferson returned to Virginia in 1793. During Washington's second term, Madison took Jefferson's place in the debates with Hamilton.

Both sides disagreed on how to interpret the Constitution and on economic policy. Hamilton favored the British government and opposed the French Revolution. Jefferson and Madison were the opposite. Hamilton fought for a strong central government. Jefferson and Madison feared such a government might lead to tyranny. They had different visions of what the nation should become. Hamilton wanted a United States in which trade, manufacturing, and cities grew. Jefferson and Madison pictured a rural nation of planters and farmers.

These differences on foreign and domestic policy led to the nation's first political parties. A **political party** is a group of people that tries to promote its ideas and influence government. It also backs candidates for office. Together, Jefferson and Madison founded the Democratic-Republican Party. The party name reflected their strong belief in democracy and the republican system. Their ideas drew farmers and workers to the new party. Hamilton and his friends formed the Federalist Party. Many Northern merchants and manufacturers became Federalists.

A. Answer The Federalists believed in a strong national government, a national bank, and a loose interpretation of the Constitution. Democratic-Republicans believed in a limited government, an economy based on farming, and a strict interpretation of the Constitution.

***Reading*History**
A. Summarizing What were the major beliefs of each party?

The First Political Parties

FEDERALISTS	DEMOCRATIC-REPUBLICANS
Strong national government	Limited national government
Fear of mob rule	Fear of rule by one person or a powerful few
Loose construction (interpretation) of the Constitution	Strict construction (interpretation) of the Constitution
Favored national bank	Opposed national bank
Economy based on manufacturing and shipping	Economy based on farming
Supporters: lawyers, merchants, manufacturers, clergy	Supporters: farmers, tradespeople

SKILLBUILDER **Interpreting Charts**
1. *Which economic interests were served by the Federalists?*
2. *Which party favored a ruling elite? Which put more trust in the common people?*

Skillbuilder Answers
1. Federalists served the economic interests of business and manufacturing; the propertied classes.
2. Federalists favored a ruling elite; Democratic-Republicans put more trust in the common people.

MORE ABOUT . . .

Democratic-Republicans
The Democratic-Republicans chose the name *Republicans* to stress their commitment to states' rights and to suggest that their party's concern for individual liberties had a link to the ideals of the ancient Roman republic.

HISTORY FROM VISUALS

Interpreting Charts Have students study the chart to identify the differences between the Federalists and the Democratic-Republicans. Each had beliefs about the role of the national government in American life. How were those beliefs reflected in their stands on the issues of constitutional interpretation and the national bank? **Possible Response** The Federalists, who favored a strong national government, supported a national bank and a loose construction of the Constitution, giving the government more power to act on its own. The Democratic-Republicans, who favored limited government, opposed the bank. They were strict constructionists who favored limiting the policy-making power of the government.

Extension Have students research the early history of the two parties to find other differences between them.

Critical Thinking Transparency CT26
• Cause and Effect: Growth of Political Parties

ACTIVITY OPTIONS
MULTIPLE LEARNING STYLES: KINESTHETIC

BLOCK SCHEDULING

POLITICAL PARTIES

Class Time One hour

Task Conducting a press conference for the election of 1796

Purpose To compare and contrast the beliefs and ideas of the first two American political parties

Supplies Needed
- Reference materials on Jefferson, John Adams, the Federalists, the Democratic-Republicans, and the election of 1796

Activity Pick two students to play the roles of John Adams and Thomas Jefferson in the election of 1796. Have the remainder of the class act as members of the press. Allow 15 minutes for candidates to prepare for their roles and for reporters to write questions to ask each candidate. Then hold a forum at which the candidates explain why they think they should be elected. Follow up with questions from reporters about each candidate's stand on such issues as the national bank, relations with France and Britain, the French Revolution, and economic policies.

America's HERITAGE

WASHINGTON, D.C., AND BENJAMIN BANNEKER

Benjamin Banneker was a free African-American farmer. He was a self-taught mathematician and astronomer. He also wrote an almanac (see below). He was named to the survey commission appointed to lay out the boundaries of the nation's new capital. Working with chief planner Pierre L'Enfant, Banneker helped to decide where the White House and Capitol would be located. Their final design is shown at the left.

2 John Adams Takes Office

In 1796, the United States held its first elections in which political parties competed. The Federalists picked Washington's vice-president, John Adams, as their candidate for president. An experienced public servant, Adams had been a leader during the Revolution and at the Continental Congress. He had also been a diplomat in France, the Netherlands, and Britain before serving with Washington. The Democratic-Republicans chose Jefferson.

In the electoral college, Adams received 71 votes and Jefferson 68. The Constitution stated that the runner-up should become vice-president. Therefore, the country had a Federalist president and a Democratic-Republican vice-president. Adams became president in 1797. His chief rival, Jefferson, entered office as his vice-president. In 1800, Adams became the first president to govern from the nation's new capital city, Washington, D.C.

Problems with France

When Washington left office in 1797, relations between France and the United States were tense. With Britain and France still at war, the French began seizing U.S. ships to prevent them from trading with the British. Within the year, the French had looted more than 300 U.S. ships.

Although some Federalists called for war with France, Adams hoped talks would restore calm. To this end, he sent Charles Pinckney, Elbridge Gerry, and John Marshall to Paris. Arriving there, they requested a meeting with the French minister of foreign affairs. For weeks, they were

America's HERITAGE

Washington, D.C., and Benjamin Banneker

L'Enfant was dismissed from his position as chief architect of the new capital of Washington, D.C. The explosive planner left abruptly and took all the plans for the new city with him. Banneker was able to recreate the plans from memory in only two days.

Although Banneker had little formal education and was self-taught in astronomy, he accurately predicted the solar eclipse of 1789. For five years beginning in 1791, he made all the astronomical and tide computations and weather predictions for a yearly almanac.

America's History Makers
- Benjamin Banneker, pp. 37–38

INSTRUCT: OBJECTIVE 2

John Adams Takes Office/ Problems with France

- Why was the election of 1796 different from the previous election?
- How did Thomas Jefferson, Adams's rival for president, become his vice-president?
- What caused the XYZ Affair? How did it affect U.S. relations with France?

In-Depth Resources: Unit 3
- Geography Application: The Nation's Capital, pp. 8–9

Outline Map Activities
- The 13 States Become 16, pp. 17–18

CRITICAL THINKING ACTIVITY

Evaluating Have students explain how John Adams became president in 1796 while his chief rival became his vice-president. What problems might a president face having his political rival as his vice-president? Would there be any advantages?

Class Time 5–10 minutes

ACTIVITY OPTIONS

INDIVIDUAL NEEDS: GIFTED AND TALENTED

GEORGE WASHINGTON

Class Time One class period

Task Planning a televised biography of George Washington

Purpose To familiarize students with the highlights of Washington's life and presidency

Supplies Needed
- Reference materials about George Washington
- Posterboard

Activity Have students plan a 30-minute television program about the life of Washington. Tell students to find visuals and primary source material to include. Tell them to write an outline and then create a storyboard. A storyboard combines small drawings for each image in the program with a short description.

[voice over] "First in war, first in peace, first in the hearts of his countrymen."	➤		➤	

In-Depth Resources: Unit 3
- Enrichment Activity, p. 18

HISTORY through ART

Interpreting the Cartoon After President Adams learned of the French agents' bribery attempt, he stated publicly that he had lost hope in the talks with France. Congress demanded to see the correspondence from Pinckney, Gerry, and Marshall. Adams agreed to give them to Congress, but before he did so, he replaced the names of the French agents with the letters *X, Y,* and *Z.* When American newspapers got hold of the correspondence, they gave the episode the name *XYZ Affair.*

Answer: The cartoonist is critical of France, as is shown by the depiction of the group ruling France as a monster.

CRITICAL THINKING ACTIVITY

Making Inferences Outrage over the XYZ Affair temporarily improved the fortunes of the Federalist party. In the 1798 elections, they gained control of both houses of Congress. Ask students why they think the Federalists became more popular with the public during the conflict with France. Have students consider recent foreign conflicts. Why does the president and the party in power often gain support during times of foreign conflict?

Class Time 5 minutes

INSTRUCT: OBJECTIVE 3

The Alien and Sedition Acts

- Why did Congress pass the Alien and Sedition Acts?
- How were immigrants and members of the press affected by these acts?
- How did the Democratic-Republicans use the theory of states' rights to fight the Alien and Sedition Acts?
- How did Kentucky and Virginia support the Democratic-Republicans' position?

HISTORY *through* ART

American newspapers fueled public anger over the XYZ Affair by publishing editorials and cartoons like this one. Here the five-man group ruling France demands money at dagger point from the three Americans. The American diplomats respond, "Cease bawling, monster! We will not give you sixpence!"

What attitude does the cartoonist have toward France's role in this affair? How can you tell?

ignored. Then three French agents—later referred to as X, Y, and Z—took the Americans aside to tell them the minister would hold talks. However, the talks would occur only if the Americans agreed to loan France $10 million and to pay the minister a bribe of $250,000. The Americans refused. "No, no, not a sixpence," Pinckney shot back.

Adams received a full report of what became known as the **XYZ Affair**. After Congress and an outraged public learned of it, the press turned Pinckney's words into a popular slogan: "Millions for defense, not one cent for tribute!" In 1798, Congress canceled its treaties with France and allowed U.S. ships to seize French vessels. Congress also set aside money to expand the navy and the army.

Reading **History**

B. Drawing Conclusions How did the XYZ Affair show the young nation's growing confidence?

B. Answer The nation was willing to defy French power and to build up its strength.

3 The Alien and Sedition Acts

The conflict with France made Adams and the Federalists popular with the public. Many Democratic-Republicans, however, were sympathetic to France. One Democratic-Republican newspaper called Adams "the blasted tyrant of America." In turn, Federalists labeled Democratic-Republicans "democrats, mobcrats, and other kinds of rats."

Angered by criticism in a time of crisis, Adams blamed the Democratic-Republican newspapers and new immigrants. Many of the immigrants were Democratic-Republicans. To silence their critics, the Federalist Congress passed the **Alien and Sedition Acts** in 1798. These acts targeted aliens—immigrants who were not yet citizens. One act increased the waiting period for becoming a U.S. citizen from 5 to 14 years. Other acts gave the president the power to arrest disloyal aliens or order them out of the country during wartime. A fourth act outlawed sedition, saying or writing anything false or harmful about the government.

With these acts, the Federalists clamped down on freedom of speech and the press. About 25 Democratic-Republican newspaper editors were

ACTIVITY OPTIONS

INTERDISCIPLINARY LINK: LANGUAGE ARTS — BLOCK SCHEDULING

EXPRESSING AN OPINION

Class Time 20 minutes

Task Writing an editorial about the Alien and Sedition Acts

Purpose To express an opinion about the constitutionality of and the need for the Alien and Sedition Acts

Supplies Needed

- Reference materials on the Alien and Sedition Acts
- Editorials from local or national newspapers

Activity Discuss with the class the techniques of persuasive writing or ask the language arts teacher to do so. Have students examine newspaper editorials to find examples of various ways writers argue and support their positions. Then ask each student to write an editorial about the passage of the Alien and Sedition Acts and/or the arrests of Democratic-Republican newspaper editors. Students may write their editorials from the perspective of a Federalist, a Democratic-Republican, or a present-day constitutional scholar.

charged under this act, and 10 were convicted of expressing opinions damaging to the government. A Vermont congressman, Matthew Lyon, was also locked up for saying that the president should be sent "to a mad house." The voters re-elected Lyon while he was in jail.

Reading **History**
C. Making Inferences How might the theory of states' rights undermine the federal government?
C. Answer It might encourage states to try to nullify or ignore federal laws.

The Democratic-Republicans, led by Jefferson and Madison, searched for a way to fight the Alien and Sedition Acts. They found it in a theory called **states' rights**. According to this theory, states had rights that the federal government could not violate. Jefferson and Madison wrote resolutions (or statements) passed by the Kentucky and Virginia legislatures in 1798 and 1799. In the Kentucky Resolutions, Jefferson proposed nullification, the idea that a state could nullify the federal law within the state. In the Virginia Resolutions, Madison said a state could interpose, or place, itself between the federal government and its citizens. These resolutions declared that the Alien and Sedition Acts violated the Constitution. No other states supported Kentucky and Virginia. However, within two years the Democratic-Republicans won control of Congress, and they either repealed the Alien and Sedition Acts or let them expire between 1800 and 1802.

4 Peace with France

While Federalists and Democratic-Republicans battled at home, the United States made peace with France. Although war fever was high, Adams reopened talks with France. This time the two sides quickly signed the Convention of 1800, an agreement to stop all naval attacks. This treaty cleared the way for U.S. and French ships to sail the ocean in peace.

Adams's actions made him enemies among the Federalists. Despite this, he spoke proudly of having saved the nation from bloodshed. "I desire no other inscription over my gravestone than: 'Here lies John Adams, who took upon himself the responsibility of the peace with France in the year 1800.'" Adams lost the presidential election of 1800 to Thomas Jefferson. You will read more about Jefferson in the next chapter.

Section 3 Assessment

1. Terms & Names
Explain the significance of:
- foreign policy
- political party
- XYZ Affair
- Alien and Sedition Acts
- states' rights

2. Taking Notes
Use a cluster diagram to review details about the Alien and Sedition Acts.

What was the worst effect of the Alien and Sedition Acts? Why?

3. Main Ideas
a. What two pieces of advice did Washington give in his Farewell Address?
b. What led to the rise of political parties?
c. Why did Congress pass the Alien and Sedition Acts? How did Kentucky and Virginia respond?

4. Critical Thinking
Evaluating Do you think Washington's warning about political parties was good advice? Explain.
THINK ABOUT
- roles of political parties
- advantages of parties
- disadvantages of parties

ACTIVITY OPTIONS
TECHNOLOGY / SPEECH
Read more about Benjamin Banneker. Plan part of a **video presentation** on him or present **dramatic readings** of excerpts from the almanac he wrote.

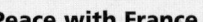

INSTRUCT: OBJECTIVE 4
Peace with France
- How did Adams settle the conflict between the United States and France?

ASSESS & RETEACH

Setting the Stage Have students add to the Politics and Foreign Affairs sections on the chapter graphic organizer.

Formal Assessment
- Section Quiz, p. 171

Critical Thinking Transparency CT25
- Setting the Stage

RETEACHING ACTIVITY
Use the chart on page 288 to reinforce the differences between the Federalists and the Democratic-Republicans. Have students identify the political party of John Adams (Federalist) and Thomas Jefferson (Democratic-Republican).

In-Depth Resources: Unit 3
- Reteaching Activity, p. 17

Section 3 Assessment

1. Terms & Names
foreign policy, p. 288
political party, p. 288
XYZ Affair, p. 290
Alien and Sedition Acts, p. 290
states' rights, p. 291

2. Taking Notes
targeted aliens; increased waiting period for becoming U.S. citizen; president can arrest disloyal aliens; clamped down on freedom of speech; aliens could be ordered out of country during war

Accept all reasonable responses that are supported by evidence.

3. Main Ideas
a. He warned against political parties and divisions and urged the country to remain neutral.
b. disagreements over running the nation; economic policy; Constitutional interpretation
c. to silence critics; passed resolutions that declared that the acts violated the Constitution

4. Critical Thinking
Students may answer that the state of politics today indicates that Washington was right.

ACTIVITY OPTIONS
Integrated Assessment
- Rubrics for a video presentation, 5.3
- Rubrics for a reading, 3.1

TERMS & NAMES

1. **inaugurate,** p. 277
2. **cabinet,** p. 278
3. **tariff,** p. 280
4. **Battle of Fallen Timbers,** p. 283
5. **Whiskey Rebellion,** p. 285
6. **neutral,** p. 286
7. **foreign policy,** p. 288
8. **political party,** p. 288
9. **Alien and Sedition Acts,** p. 290
10. **states' rights,** p. 291

REVIEW QUESTIONS

Possible Responses

1. the number of justices on Supreme Court; how much power the Court should have; at first the Supreme Court had six members, which has grown to nine
2. war debts; lack of revenues; lack of central financial authority
3. Jefferson believed in a strict and narrow interpretation of the Constitution; Hamilton believed in a broad and loose interpretation.
4. He sent troops to the area.
5. Farmers resisted the government's taxation of whiskey.
6. He believed the nation would grow stronger and more prosperous if it avoided foreign entanglements.
7. Jay's Treaty addressed problems between Britain and the United States caused by U.S. neutrality; Pinckney's Treaty addressed problems with Spain about trade on the Mississippi and boundaries between Spanish territory to the south and the new nation.
8. He thought political parties led to political divisions, conflict, and divisiveness.
9. an attempt by French officials to extort a bribe from U.S. ministers in Paris
10. to silence their Democratic-Republican critics; defied the acts and passed Kentucky and Virginia Resolutions

Chapter 9 ASSESSMENT

TERMS & NAMES

Briefly explain the significance of each of the following.

1. inaugurate
2. cabinet
3. tariff
4. Battle of Fallen Timbers
5. Whiskey Rebellion
6. neutral
7. foreign policy
8. political party
9. Alien and Sedition Acts
10. states' rights

REVIEW QUESTIONS

Washington's Presidency (pages 277–281)

1. What questions about the judiciary were left open by the Constitution? How were they answered?
2. What financial problems did the new nation face?
3. How did Hamilton and Jefferson interpret the Constitution differently?

Challenges to the New Government (pages 282–286)

4. What did Washington do to secure the West?
5. What were the major arguments regarding taxation under the new government?
6. Why did Washington favor neutrality in the conflict between France and Britain?
7. What problems did the Jay and Pinckney treaties address?

The Federalists in Charge (pages 287–291)

8. Why did Washington oppose political parties?
9. What was the XYZ Affair?
10. Why did Federalists pass the Alien and Sedition Acts? How did Republicans respond?

CRITICAL THINKING

1. USING YOUR NOTES

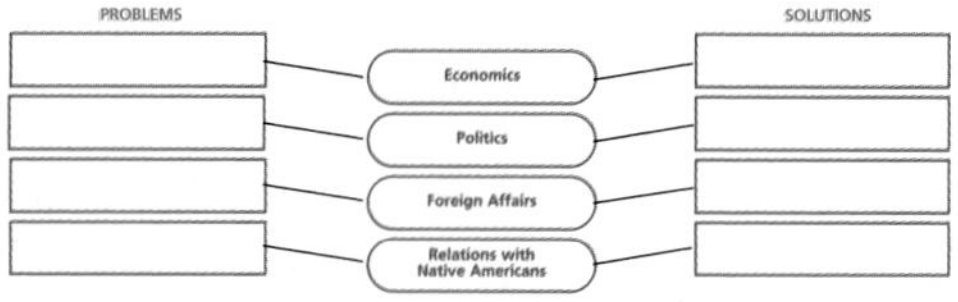

Using your completed chart, answer the questions.

a. What were the problems that characterized the Federalist era?
b. What do the solutions to these problems reveal about the characteristics of the era?

2. ANALYZING LEADERSHIP

How did Washington's efforts to serve as a symbol of national unity help the new nation?

3. APPLYING CITIZENSHIP SKILLS

How might the farmers in the Whiskey Rebellion have expressed their disapproval of the whiskey tax while staying within the law?

4. THEME: DEMOCRATIC IDEALS

Did the formation of political parties make the nation more or less democratic?

Interact *with* History

How did the challenges of setting up a government that you discussed before you read the chapter compare with the actual challenges you read about?

VISUAL SUMMARY

The First Presidents

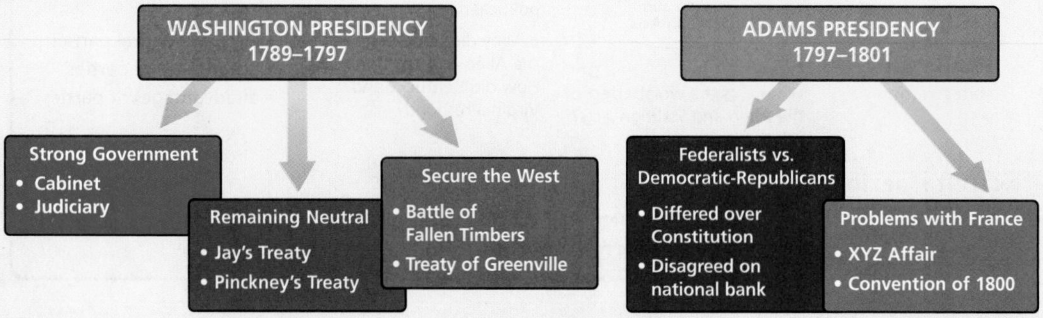

292 CHAPTER 9

CRITICAL THINKING

Possible Responses

1. **USING YOUR NOTES a.** government funding; organization of the government; disputes with foreign nations and Native Americans **b. Possible Response** The era was characterized by the new government taking action to solve problems.
2. **ANALYZING LEADERSHIP** Washington acted wisely and modestly. He helped to establish a democratic government by setting a good example of how a president should behave.
3. **APPLYING CITIZENSHIP SKILLS** They could have sent a delegation to the federal government to express their point of view, written a petition, voted their preferences in the next election, or taken their case to the newspapers.
4. **THEME: DEMOCRATIC IDEALS** probably more democratic, since political parties provided an outlet for different points of view

Interact *with* History Answers will vary, but students should probably note the extreme difficulties involved in setting up a government.

HISTORY SKILLS

1. INTERPRETING CHARTS

The following chart shows the money problems of the new nation between 1789 and 1791. The numbers have been rounded off. Study the chart and then answer the questions.

Financial Problems, *1789–1791*

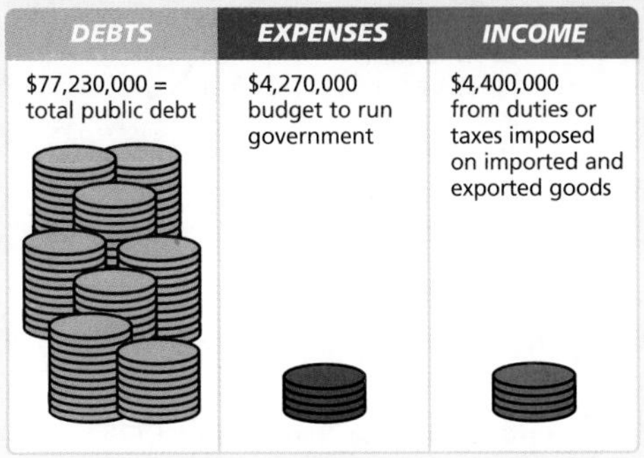

DEBTS
$77,230,000 = total public debt
EXPENSES
$4,270,000 budget to run government
INCOME
$4,400,000 from duties or taxes imposed on imported and exported goods

Source: *Historical Statistics of the United States*

a. What was the government's total income in these years?

b. How much money did the government owe in these same years?

c. How might the government try to raise more money?

2. INTERPRETING PRIMARY SOURCES

In a letter to her sister, John Adams's wife, Abigail, had the following to say about President Washington. Read the quotation and answer the questions.

> He is polite with dignity, affable without familiarity, distant without haughtiness, . . . modest, wise, and good.
>
> **Abigail Adams,** letter of January 5, 1790

a. What qualities seemed to set Washington apart from other political leaders?

b. Is Mrs. Adams's overall impression of Washington positive or negative? Explain your answer.

c. What qualities or characteristics did the people of Washington's time seem to expect in a leader?

ALTERNATIVE ASSESSMENT

1. INTERDISCIPLINARY ACTIVITY: World History

Writing a Letter Imagine that you are a U.S. citizen during the French Revolution. Write a letter to the secretary of state recommending a policy you think the U.S. government should follow. Be sure to use standard grammar, spelling, sentence structure, and punctuation in your letter.

2. COOPERATIVE LEARNING ACTIVITY

Holding a Debate The controversy over the Alien and Sedition Acts deeply divided Federalists and Democratic-Republicans. Were the acts constitutional or an abuse of basic rights? Should criticism of the government be allowed in a time of near war?

Working in three groups, do research on the Alien and Sedition Acts and the positions taken by both political parties on these acts. Then have Federalist and Democratic-Republican groups pick representatives to debate the questions posed above, while the remaining group acts as audience and judge for the debate.

3. TECHNOLOGY ACTIVITY

Creating a Television Commercial People of the eighteenth century had different expectations of their political leaders than do people today. The quotation from Abigail Adams on this page is an example of the different perspective people held in Washington's time. Using the library or the Internet, find pictures of, and quotations about, political leaders of the time.

For more about the first presidents . . .

INTERNET ACTIVITY
CLASSZONE.COM

Create a 30-second television commercial that advertises an American history theme park, using the suggestions below.

- Try to find quotations that suggest the most important qualities of leaders such as Washington, Adams, Hamilton, and Jefferson.
- Try to find more than one image of each leader; find images that suggest different qualities in the person.
- Use quotations from and images of leaders as part of your commercial for a theme park.
- Show your commercial to the class.

4. HISTORY PORTFOLIO

Review your section and chapter assessment activities. Select one that you think is your best work. Then use comments made by your teacher or classmates to improve your work and add it to your portfolio.

Additional Test Practice, pp. S1–S33

TEST PRACTICE
CLASSZONE.COM

ALTERNATIVE ASSESSMENT

1. INTERDISCIPLINARY ACTIVITY: **World History**
   Letters should
   - clearly state a position about the issue.
   - present supporting reasons for the position.
   - clearly rebut other viewpoints.
   - use correct grammar, spelling, and punctuation.

2. COOPERATIVE LEARNING ACTIVITY
   Debates should
   - have a central question or proposition.
   - support a position and refute their opponent's position with evidence.
   - respond appropriately to each other's statements.

3. TECHNOLOGY ACTIVITY
   Commercials should
   - clearly present persuasive reasons for visiting the theme park.
   - utilize a variety of information.
   - use correct grammar in the script or print materials.
   - show technical proficiency.

4. HISTORY PORTFOLIO
   Revised section or chapter assessment activities should
   - address teacher and peer responses to the selected work.
   - solve problems present in the first versions of the work.

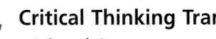

Critical Thinking Transparency CT27
- Visual Summary

Formal Assessment
- Chapter Test, Forms A, B, and C, pp. 172–183

HISTORY SKILLS

Possible Responses

1. INTERPRETING CHARTS
   a. $4,400,000
   b. $77,230,000
   c. by increasing tariffs and taxes

2. INTERPRETING PRIMARY SOURCES
   a. wisdom, seriousness, virtue
   b. Her impression is very positive; she sees him as a model of virtue.
   c. They do not seem to expect their leader to be too much like them; he is to be polite and friendly without being too familiar. Mainly he is expected to fulfill his public role and function with virtue and dignity.

CHAPTER 10 PLANNING GUIDE

The Jefferson Era 1800–1816

	CHAPTER OVERVIEW	COPYMASTERS	INTEGRATED TECHNOLOGY
CHAPTER RESOURCES	The chapter describes Thomas Jefferson's presidency, his philosophy of government, and the Louisiana Purchase. It also describes problems in foreign affairs and the War of 1812.	**In-Depth Resources: Unit 3** • Tracing Themes: Expansion, p. 20 • Building Vocabulary, p. 25 • History Workshop Resources, p. 39 **Interdisciplinary Projects,** pp. 55–60	• eEdition Plus Online • EasyPlanner Plus Online • eTest Plus Online • eEdition • Power Presentations • EasyPlanner • Electronic Library of Primary Sources • Test Generator • Reading Study Guide • America's Music
SECTION 1 **Jefferson Takes Office** **pp. 297–301**	**KEY IDEAS** • Thomas Jefferson becomes president in 1801. • Jefferson believes the United States should be a nation of small, independent farmers. • Chief Justice John Marshall establishes the principle of judicial review in *Marbury* v. *Madison.*	**In-Depth Resources: Unit 3** • Setting the Stage, p. 19 • Guided Reading, p. 21 • Geography Application, pp. 27–28 • Reteaching Activity, p. 34 **America's History Makers** • Thomas Jefferson, pp. 39–40 **Citizenship Today,** pp. 86–87 **Why It Matters Now** • Peaceful Transfers of Power, pp. 19–20	**Warm-Up Transparency WT10** **Critical Thinking Transparency CT28** • Setting the Stage classzone.com
SECTION 2 **The Louisiana Purchase and Exploration** **pp. 302–309**	• Jefferson buys the Louisiana Purchase from France at a bargain price. • Lewis and Clark explore the new territory from the Mississippi River to the Pacific Ocean. • Western exploration leads to better maps and greater knowledge of the continent.	**In-Depth Resources: Unit 3** • Setting the Stage, p. 19 • Guided Reading, p. 22 • Literature Selection, pp. 31–33 • Reteaching Activity, p. 35 **America's History Makers** • Sacagawea, pp. 41–42 **American History Plays** • *Land of the Unknown* **Outline Map Activities** • The Louisiana Purchase, pp. 19–20	**Warm-Up Transparency WT10** **Humanities Transparency HT19** • *Lewis and Clark* **Geography Transparency GT10** • United States, 1803 **Critical Thinking Transparency CT28** • Setting the Stage classzone.com
SECTION 3 **Problems with Foreign Powers** **pp. 310–313**	• Conflicts with Britain and France disrupt American trade. • Despite Tecumseh's efforts to unite the tribes, Native Americans lose more land through treaties and battles. • A group of congressmen known as War Hawks demand war against Britain.	**In-Depth Resources: Unit 3** • Setting the Stage, p. 19 • Guided Reading, p. 23 • Skillbuilder Practice: Analyzing Causes, p. 26 • Primary Source, p. 29 • Reteaching Activity, p. 36	**Warm-Up Transparency WT10** **Critical Thinking Transparency CT28** • Setting the Stage classzone.com
SECTION 4 **The War of 1812** **pp. 314–317**	• The U.S. Navy wins important victories early in the War of 1812. • The Treaty of Ghent ends the war, and Andrew Jackson defeats the British at New Orleans. • The war increases patriotism, bolsters American confidence, and encourages the growth of industry.	**In-Depth Resources: Unit 3** • Setting the Stage, p. 19 • Guided Reading, p. 24 • Primary Source, p. 30 • Reteaching Activity, p. 37 **Economics in History** • The Economic Impact of the War of 1812, p. 10	**Warm-Up Transparency WT10** **Humanities Transparency HT20** • *Constitution and Guerriere* **Critical Thinking Transparency CT29** • Cause and Effect: The War of 1812 **Critical Thinking Transparency CT30** • Visual Summary classzone.com

Pupil's Edition
Copymaster
Overhead Transparency
Audio Library
CD-ROM
Internet

ASSESSMENT OPTIONS

Chapter Assessment, pp. 318–319

Formal Assessment
- Chapter Tests, Forms A, B, and C, pp. 188–199

Test Generator

Online Test Practice

Strategies for Test Preparation

Section Assessment, p. 301

Formal Assessment, Quiz, p. 184

Integrated Assessment Book
- Rubrics, 5.1, 1.10

Test Generator

Test Practice Transparencies, TT34

Section Assessment, p. 307

Formal Assessment, Quiz, p. 185

Integrated Assessment Book
- Rubrics, 2.4, 2.1

Test Generator

Test Practice Transparencies, TT35

Section Assessment, p. 313

Formal Assessment, Quiz, p. 186

Integrated Assessment Book
- Rubrics, 1.3, 3.3

Test Generator

Test Practice Transparencies, TT36

Section Assessment, p. 317

Formal Assessment, Quiz, p. 187

Integrated Assessment Book
- Rubrics, 4.8, 1.10

Test Generator

Test Practice Transparencies, TT37

CUSTOMIZING FOR INDIVIDUAL NEEDS

Students Acquiring English/ESL

Reading Study Guide (English and Spanish), pp. 95–104

Access for Students Acquiring English/ESL: Spanish Translations, pp. 63–69

Chapter Summaries on CD (English and Spanish)

Modified Lesson Plans for English Learners

Less Proficient Readers

Reading Study Guide (English and Spanish), pp. 95–104

Chapter Summaries on CD (English and Spanish)

Gifted and Talented Students

In-Depth Resources: Unit 3
- Enrichment Activity, p. 38

America's History Makers
- Thomas Jefferson, pp. 39–40
- Sacagawea, pp. 41–42

CROSS-CURRICULAR CONNECTIONS

Culture

Hilton, Suzanne. ***A Capital Capital City, 1790–1814.*** New York: Atheneum, 1992. An engaging account of the first 25 years of Washington, D.C.

Geography

Lourie, Peter. ***In the Path of Lewis and Clark: Traveling the Missouri.*** Englewood Cliffs, NJ: Silver Burdett Press, Inc., 1997. Travel-writers Lourie and William Least Heat-Moon retrace the steps of the explorers of the Louisiana Purchase.

Science

Weitzman, David. ***Old Ironsides: Americans Build a Fighting Ship.*** Boston: Houghton Mifflin, 1997. Illustrated with detailed charts and drawings.

Interdisciplinary Projects, pp. 55–60
- Math: Lines of Symmetry
- Science: Taxonomy
- Language Arts: The Poetry of the National Anthem
- Music: Backcountry Folk Music

Literature

Bohner, Charles. ***Bold Journey: West with Lewis and Clark.*** Boston: Houghton Mifflin, 1990. Private Hugh McNeal tells of his travels with Lewis and Clark.

San Souci, Robert D. ***Cut from the Same Cloth: American Women of Myth, Legend, and Tall Tale.*** New York: Putnam, 1992. Folk tales of 15 brave and sometimes outrageous women.

McDougal Littell *The Language of Literature*

Stephen E. Ambrose, from ***Undaunted Courage*** (nonfiction)

McDougall Littell Literature Connections

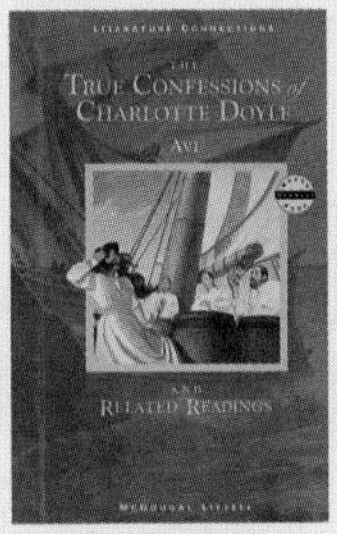

Avi

The True Confessions of Charlotte Doyle

Much-acclaimed story of young Charlotte Doyle's voyage from England to America in the early 19th century.

ENRICHMENT ACTIVITIES

Pupil's Edition, pp. 294–321
Interact with History, p. 295
Geography in History, pp. 308–309
History Workshop, pp. 320–321

In-Depth Resources: Unit 3
- Geography Application: Election of 1800, pp. 27–28
- Primary Source: A Plea for Native American Unity, p. 29
- Primary Source: from *Memoirs and Letters of Dolley Madison,* p. 30
- Literature Selection, pp. 31–33
- History Workshop Resources, p. 39

America's History Makers
- Thomas Jefferson, pp. 39–40
- Sacagawea, pp. 41–42

American History Plays
- *Land of the Unknown*

Outline Map Activities
- The Louisiana Purchase, pp. 19–20

Why It Matters Now
- Peaceful Transfers of Power, pp. 19–20

BLOCK SCHEDULING — LESSON PLAN OPTIONS (90-MINUTE PERIOD)

DAY 1

Interact with History, p. 295
Class Time 20 Minutes

Options for pacing and variety:
- **Role-Playing** Have students work in pairs to create a dialogue between two of the explorers after encountering the bear. The explorers should discuss how to describe the encounter for their expedition's report. **Class Time** 15 minutes

Setting the Stage, p. 296
Class Time 20 minutes

Options for pacing and variety:
- **Time Saver** For a homework assignment, ask students to list the issues a president might consider before making a major land purchase. **Class Time** 10 minutes

Section 1, pp. 297–301
Class Time 50 minutes

Options for pacing and variety:
- **Internet** Extend students' background knowledge of the decisions facing Thomas Jefferson as president and how he made them by visiting classzone.com. **Class Time** 20 minutes
- **Peer Teaching** Working in pairs, students should make a graphic organizer showing how the opinions of Jefferson and Hamilton differed on the public debt. **Class Time** 30 minutes

DAY 2

Section 2, pp. 302–309
Class Time 45 minutes

Options for pacing and variety:
- **History on Film** Extend students' knowledge of the Lewis and Clark expedition with the film *We Proceeded On . . : The Expedition of Lewis and Clark,* Kaw Valley Films. **Class Time** 35 minutes
- **Time Saver** Use the chart on page 307 to summarize the effects of the Lewis and Clark and Pike expeditions. **Class Time** 10 minutes

Section 3, pp. 310–313
Class Time 45 minutes

Options for pacing and variety:
- **Peer Teaching** Have pairs of students review the Main Idea for the section on page 310 and find three details to support it. Then have each pair list two additional important ideas and trade lists with another group to find details. **Class Time** 10 minutes
- **Time Saver** Use the cartoon on page 319 of the Chapter Assessment to introduce the causes of the War of 1812. **Class Time** 10 minutes

DAY 3

Section 4, pp. 314–317
Class Time 45 minutes

Options for pacing and variety:
- **Peer Teaching** Divide students into small groups. Have each group create a cause-and-effect chart for the War of 1812. Then compare their chart to CT29. Discuss the differences. **Class Time** 10 minutes
- **Peer Evaluation** Have students work in groups to answer the Reading History questions. **Class Time** 25 minutes

Chapter 10 Assessment, pp. 318–319
Class Time 40 minutes

Options for pacing and variety:
- **Peer Teaching** Divide students into groups of four. Have each student in a group answer the Review Questions for one of the four sections. Have students share answers within groups. **Class Time** 20 minutes

History Workshop, pp. 320–321
Options for pacing and variety
- **Team Teaching** Invite a science teacher to visit the class to explain to students how botanists and other scientists make and use field notes. **Class Time** 20 minutes

---

TEACHER-TESTED ACTIVITY **Meg Robbins, Wilbraham Middle School, Wilbraham, Massachusetts**

LOUISIANA PURCHASE

Class Time One class period

Task Making a map

Purpose To analyze the physical and economic impact on the United States of the Louisiana Purchase

Supplies Needed
- Reference materials and Internet sources on the Louisiana Purchase
- Political map of the United States about 1800
- Current political map of the United States
- Posterboard
- Markers or colored pencils

Activity Working in pairs, students should create a map showing how the United States would look today if President Jefferson had not purchased the Louisiana Territory from France. Maps should include only the states that already existed or were territories in 1800 and the nations that bordered the United States at that time. Have each pair display its map along with a short essay hypothesizing on the ways in which the United States would be different today if it had not acquired the Louisiana Purchase.

CREATING A DATABASE OF NORTHWEST NATIVE AMERICAN HISTORY

A database is a structured collection of information about a particular subject. A database is useful for compiling information that can be accessed repeatedly. It can be created using database software on a computer, a multi-column table (chart) in a word processor, or simply a paper card file.

ACTIVITY OUTLINE

Objective Creating a database on Native American tribes between 1790 and 1820 will help students understand the situations these tribes faced.

Task In this activity, students will compile information about individual Native American tribes between 1790 and 1820. They will work together to design the fields for the database, conduct research, and enter the data.

Class Time Two class periods

DIRECTIONS

1. Students will build a database of information about Native American tribes between 1790 and 1820. The whole class will need to work as a group to determine the general design of the database. A small team of students who are familiar with the database software will create the database structure on a shared network space or on a classroom computer. Then each student in the class will work with a partner or small group to research individual tribal histories and enter the data into the database.

2. Give students 15–20 minutes to review information in *Creating America.*

3. Discuss with the class the fields that would be needed for the database. Possible fields include:
   - names of tribes
   - leaders or known members of the tribe
   - tribal characteristics
   - types of dress
   - principle sources of food
   - interactions with nonnative peoples
   - population and location in five-year intervals between 1790 and 1820

4. Once the whole class has agreed on the fields, assign some students to be database builders. These should be students who are familiar with database software. They may need to instruct other students on how to enter their data into the database.

5. Explain to students that each record in the database should hold information for only one tribe. Each group will research one tribe. If more than one group works on the same tribe, they can combine information as they enter it into the database.

6. Remind students they will be looking for information to complete the database fields, and that some information may not be readily available. They will need to find out how events, such as the Lewis and Clark Expedition, affected individual tribes at different times

7. The second class period should be spent entering information into the database. Once all data is entered, the database builders should conduct a test to make sure the database functions properly.

8. Students should be encouraged to continue to track the history of their tribe as they learn more about the tribe. They can add fields and additional information, as needed.

CHAPTER 10 OBJECTIVE

The student will understand how the election and presidency of Thomas Jefferson shaped the American system of government and how the Louisiana Purchase and the War of 1812 affected the nation.

HISTORY FROM VISUALS

Interpreting the Painting Ask students to study the painting. Have them describe the various ways Bierstadt emphasizes not only the beauty of the West but its grandeur. Ask students whether they notice the people or the landscape first. To which does Bierstadt give greater importance? Why? **Possible Responses** The artist emphasizes the monumental grandeur of the landscape by making the snowcapped mountains and waterfall focal points of the painting, while the people in the foreground seem small and insignificant by comparison.

Extension Have the students make a list of five adjectives that they would use to describe Bierstadt's painting and write a paragraph using their list to describe the scene.

CHAPTER 10

The Jefferson Era 1800–1816

Section 1 **Jefferson Takes Office**
Section 2 **The Louisiana Purchase and Exploration**
Section 3 **Problems with Foreign Powers**
Section 4 **The War of 1812**

Albert Bierstadt's painting, *The Rocky Mountains* (1863), celebrates the beauty of the American West.

294

RECOMMENDED RESOURCES

BOOKS FOR THE TEACHER

Kessler, Donna J. ***The Making of Sacajawea: A Native American Legend.*** Tuscaloosa: U. of Alabama Press, 1998. Separates the facts from the legend about this extraordinary person.

Larkin, Jack. ***The Reshaping of Everyday Life, 1790–1840.*** New York: HarperCollins, 1988. Readable account of changes in daily life.

Smith, Jean Edward. ***John Marshall: Definer of a Nation.*** New York: Holt, 1998. Acclaimed as an authoritative biography.

Sugden, John. ***Tecumseh: A Life.*** New York: St. Martin's, 1995. A recent biography that looks at both Tecumseh the man and his effort to unite Native Americans in a coherent resistance movement.

SOFTWARE

Critical Decisions of Thomas Jefferson. K–12 MicroMedia, 1996. Allows students to follow historical records day by day.

VIDEO

Lewis & Clark: The Journey of the Corps of Discovery. 2 cassettes. Dir. Ken Burns. PBS Home Video, 1997. Acclaimed, gripping, and filled with magnificent scenery.

INTERNET

For more about the War of 1812, visit . . .

classzone.com

Interact *with* History

This painting gives a more realistic view of the West than that shown at the left.
Explorers often chose to travel by water.
In the early 1800s, it took about 20 seconds to load and fire a gun.
Adult grizzly bears might weigh as much as 900 pounds and run 30 miles per hour.

You have been chosen to participate in an expedition to the West in the early 1800s. You are excited and curious, but also a little scared. You know that you will see and experience many new things. But you know there are risks involved, too.

What Do You Think?

- **Notice the land features in these scenes. What problems might they hold for an explorer?**
- **What other people might you meet on the expedition?**
- **How will you find food during the long winter?**

What dangers will you face on an expedition west?

USA

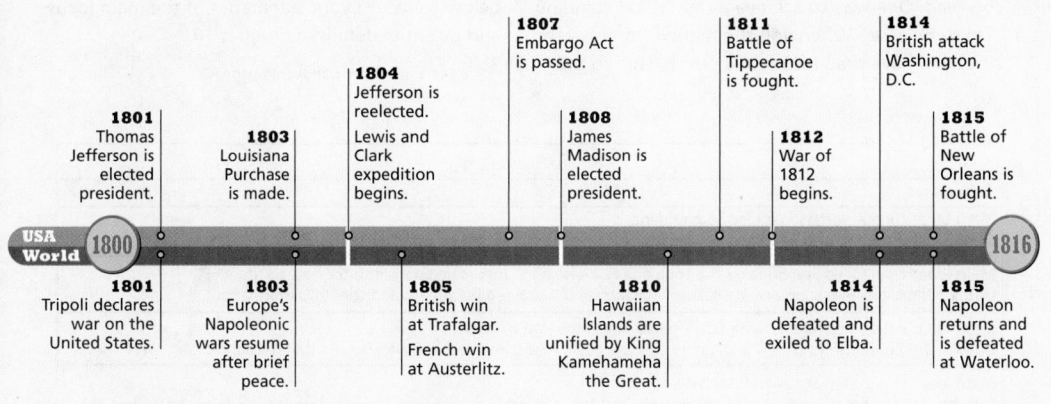

- **1801** Thomas Jefferson is elected president.
- **1803** Louisiana Purchase is made.
- **1804** Jefferson is reelected. Lewis and Clark expedition begins.
- **1807** Embargo Act is passed.
- **1808** James Madison is elected president.
- **1811** Battle of Tippecanoe is fought.
- **1812** War of 1812 begins.
- **1814** British attack Washington, D.C.
- **1815** Battle of New Orleans is fought.

1800 — 1816

World

- **1801** Tripoli declares war on the United States.
- **1803** Europe's Napoleonic wars resume after brief peace.
- **1805** British win at Trafalgar. French win at Austerlitz.
- **1810** Hawaiian Islands are unified by King Kamehameha the Great.
- **1814** Napoleon is defeated and exiled to Elba.
- **1815** Napoleon returns and is defeated at Waterloo.

Interact *with* History

OBJECTIVES

- To help students identify the challenges faced by the early explorers of the West
- To help students connect with the people and events they will study in this chapter

What Do You Think?

1. Students can consider the difficulties of hiking and hauling supplies and boats up and down rugged high-mountain terrain.
2. Students might think about the people living in the West at this time, both Native Americans and people from other nations. Remind students that fur trapping and trading had been important economic activities for both the French and the British.
3. Students might consider that explorers could not carry enough food to stockpile for the winter. They might also consider what wildlife might be available as a source for food.

What dangers will you face on an expedition west?

Encourage students to think about how an expedition to the West in the early 1800s would be different from such a journey today. In addition to facing wild animals, potentially hostile people, and the difficulties of the terrain and the weather, explorers faced challenges in traveling with few or no reliable maps, no personal knowledge of the area, and no way to contact anyone for rescue.

MAKING PERSONAL CONNECTIONS

Ask students to think about how they might prepare for a camping trip to an area they have never visited. Have students list various sources of information they could use to learn more about the place prior to the trip. Then have them cross off their lists any sources of information that did not exist in 1800.

TIME LINE DISCUSSION

Tell students that during this time period European nations were involved in the Napoleonic Wars. Two of the major events on the USA line were related to activities in Europe.

- Ask students to choose the most important event on this time line during Jefferson's first term as president and the most important event during Madison's presidency. **Answer** Louisiana Purchase, War of 1812
- Ask students what event suggests that Americans were already engaged in conflict before the War of 1812 began. **Answer** Battle of Tippecanoe
- Have students determine with what country the Americans were at war. **Answer** Britain

BEFORE YOU READ

Previewing the Theme:

Expansion

Have students examine the map and notice how the size of the United States changed between 1800 and 1816. Have students make inferences about how the nation acquired this additional territory and from what nation the territory might have been acquired. Students might also discuss how they think doubling the size of the United States might affect the wealth and power of the nation.

What Do You Know?

Have students think about the nations and groups that had competed for possession of the Northwest Territory. Which of these groups might have claimed parts of what is now the continental United States? What natural resources of the territory west of the Mississippi did Americans already know about? Have students describe what information they would want to have before purchasing a large parcel of land west of the Mississippi if they had been president in the early 1800s.

In-Depth Resources: Unit 3
- Tracing Themes: Expansion, p. 20

READ AND TAKE NOTES

Reading Strategy: Summarizing

Tell students that summarizing material is a useful way to study. Explain that the process of summarizing helps them pick out the most important parts of what they read. They can use their own summaries for review. Point out that the Reading Strategy chart gives them a format for summarizing.

In-Depth Resources: Unit 3
- Setting the Stage, p. 19

Critical Thinking Transparency CT28
- Setting the Stage

Chapter 10 SETTING THE STAGE

BEFORE YOU READ

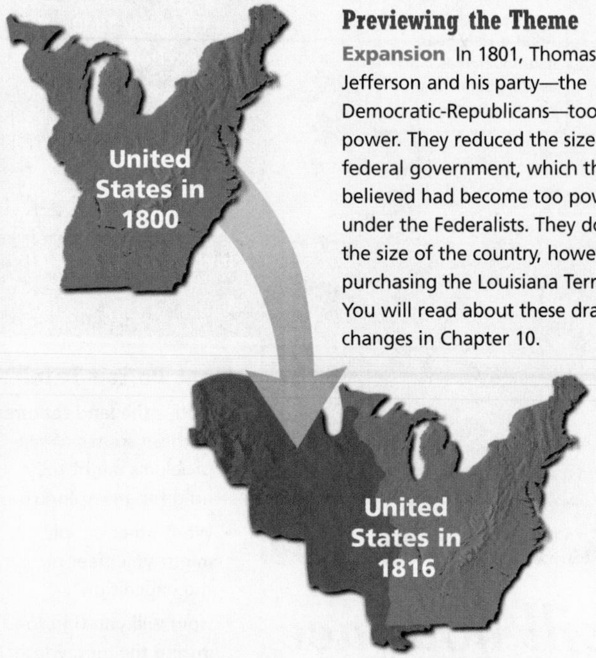

Previewing the Theme

Expansion In 1801, Thomas Jefferson and his party—the Democratic-Republicans—took power. They reduced the size of the federal government, which they believed had become too powerful under the Federalists. They doubled the size of the country, however, by purchasing the Louisiana Territory. You will read about these dramatic changes in Chapter 10.

What Do You Know?

What parts of the United States today were not part of the country in 1800? What should leaders consider before they buy land for their countries?

THINK ABOUT
- where the money for the purchase will come from
- what should be done if people already live on the land

What Do You Want to Know?

What details do you need to help you understand the nation's expansion in the early 1800s? Make a list of information you need in your notebook before you read the chapter.

READ AND TAKE NOTES

Reading Strategy: Summarizing When you study history, it is important to clearly understand what you read. One way to achieve a clear understanding is to summarize. When you summarize, you restate what you have read into fewer words, stating only the main ideas and essential details. It is important to use your own words in a summary. Use the chart below to record your summaries of the main ideas and essential details in Chapter 10.

See Skillbuilder Handbook, page R2.

The Jefferson Era
Summaries
Main Idea: Thomas Jefferson is elected president. **Details:** Jefferson replaces Federalist policies with his own but has problems with the judiciary.
Main Idea: The United States makes the Louisiana Purchase and sends expeditions into the new territory. **Details:** Napoleon sells Louisiana in 1803; Lewis, Clark, and Pike bring back maps and scientific information.
Main Idea: British interference with U.S. affairs leads to the War of 1812. **Details:** Britain interferes with U.S. shipping, kidnaps U.S. citizens, and supports Native American resistance.
Main Idea: The United States wins the War of 1812. **Details:** The war has two phases; U.S. victory weakens Native American resistance and increases patriotism and manufacturing.

TEACHING STRATEGY

READING THE CHAPTER

This is a chronological chapter focusing on the expansion of the nation, conflict among different political parties, and conflict with foreign countries. Encourage students to note differing views on foreign policy and the causes and results of the War of 1812. Remind students to think about how expansion of the nation affects its policies.

ALTERNATIVE ASSESSMENT

The Chapter Assessment describes three activities for alternative assessment on page 319. You may wish to have students work on these activities during the course of the chapter and then present them at the end.

1 Jefferson Takes Office

TERMS & NAMES
- radical
- Judiciary Act of 1801
- John Marshall
- *Marbury* v. *Madison*
- unconstitutional
- judicial review

MAIN IDEA

When Jefferson became president in 1801, his party replaced Federalist programs with its own.

WHY IT MATTERS NOW

Today's Democratic Party traces its roots to the party of Jefferson, the Democratic-Republicans.

ONE AMERICAN'S STORY

Supporters of John Adams and Thomas Jefferson—competitors in the presidential election of 1800—fought for their candidates with nasty personal attacks. Scottish immigrant James Callender, a Jefferson supporter, wrote some of the harshest criticisms. During the campaign, he warned voters not to reelect President John Adams.

A VOICE FROM THE PAST

In the fall of 1796 . . . the country fell into a more dangerous juncture than almost any the old confederation ever endured. The tardiness and timidity of Mr. Washington were succeeded by the rancour [bitterness] and insolence [arrogance] of Mr. Adams. . . . Think what you have been, what you are, and what, under [Adams], you are likely to become.

James Callender, quoted in *American Aurora*

In the presidential election of 1800, Thomas Jefferson was the candidate of the Democratic-Republican Party. John Adams represented the Federalists.

Adams's defenders were just as vicious. One went so far as to claim that if Jefferson won, "the soil will be soaked with blood, and the nation black with crimes." In spite of the campaign's nastiness, the election ended with a peaceful transfer of power from one party to another. The 1800 election was more than a personal battle, though. It was a contest between two parties with different ideas about the role of government.

1 The Election of 1800

The two parties contesting the election of 1800 were the Federalists, led by President John Adams, and the Democratic-Republicans, represented by Thomas Jefferson. Each party believed that the other was endangering the Constitution and the American republic.

The Democratic-Republicans thought they were saving the nation from monarchy and oppression. They argued, again and again, that the Alien and Sedition Acts supported by the Federalists violated the Bill of Rights. (See pages 290–291.) The Federalists thought that the nation was about to be ruined by **radicals**—people who take extreme political positions. They remembered the violence of the French Revolution, in which radicals executed thousands in the name of liberty.

SECTION OBJECTIVES

1. To describe the election of 1800 and explain the role of political parties
2. To identify Jefferson's achievements
3. To analyze Jefferson's philosophy of government
4. To analyze the significance of *Marbury* v. *Madison*

CRITICAL THINKING

Analyzing Points of View, p. 298
Summarizing, p. 299
Analyzing Causes, p. 300
Making Generalizations, p. 301

Why It Matters Now
- Peaceful Transfers of Power, pp. 19–20

FOCUS & MOTIVATE

5-MINUTE WARM-UP

Making Inferences The questions focus on Jefferson's view of politics.

1. Read "A Voice from the Past" on page 299. What does Jefferson urge Americans to do?
2. What might George Washington have said in reply to Jefferson's advice?

Warm-Up Transparency WT10

INSTRUCT

INSTRUCT: OBJECTIVE 1

The Election of 1800/Breaking the Tie

- How did the political positions of the Federalists and Democratic-Republicans differ?
- What was unusual about the 1800 election?
- Why did Hamilton encourage Federalists to vote for Jefferson instead of Burr?

In-Depth Resources: Unit 3
- Guided Reading, p. 21
- Geography Application: Election of 1800, pp. 27–28

Reading Study Guide (Spanish and English), pp. 95–96

RECOMMENDED RESOURCES

In-Depth Resources: Unit 3
- Guided Reading, p. 21
- Building Vocabulary, p. 25
- Geography Application: Election of 1800, pp. 27–28

Reading Study Guide (Spanish and English), pp. 95–96

America's History Makers
- Thomas Jefferson, pp. 39–40

Why It Matters Now
- Peaceful Transfers of Power, pp. 19–20

Citizenship Today, pp. 86–87

Formal Assessment
- Section Quiz, p. 184

Integrated Assessment
- Rubrics, 5.1, 1.10

Access for Students Acquiring English/ESL, pp. 63, 68–69

INTEGRATED TECHNOLOGY

Electronic Teacher Tools

classzone.com

TEST-TAKING RESOURCES

Strategies for Test Preparation

Test Practice Transparencies, TT34

Online Test Practice

STRANGE *but* True

Hamilton-Burr Duel

Although duels were not uncommon in the early 1800s, they were illegal in New York. Burr was vice-president at the time of his duel with Hamilton, which took place in New Jersey. Immediately after the announcement of Hamilton's death, the public turned against Burr. He was indicted for murder in New York and New Jersey. However, public reaction eventually calmed, and Burr returned to Washington to resume his official duties. He completed his term in 1805, but the duel had ended his chances of any further public career.

INSTRUCT: OBJECTIVE 2

The Talented Jefferson/ Jefferson's Philosophy

- In what areas did Jefferson excel besides politics?
- How did Jefferson plan to unite Americans?

America's History Makers
- Thomas Jefferson, pp. 39–40

When election day came, the Democratic-Republicans won the presidency. Jefferson received 73 votes in the electoral college, and Adams earned 65. But there was a problem. Aaron Burr, whom the Democratic-Republicans wanted as vice president, also received 73 votes.

Background
In 1804, the Twelfth Amendment solved this problem by creating separate ballots for president and vice president.

STRANGE *but* True

HAMILTON-BURR DUEL

In 1804, the Democratic-Republicans replaced Aaron Burr as their candidate for vice president. Burr then decided to run for governor of New York.

Alexander Hamilton questioned Burr's fitness for public office. He wrote that Burr was a "dangerous man . . . who ought not to be trusted with the reins of government."

Burr lost the election. Furious, he challenged Hamilton to a duel. Hamilton went to the duel but resolved not to fire. Burr, however, shot Hamilton, who died the next day.

Breaking the Tie

According to the Constitution, the House of Representatives had to choose between Burr and Jefferson. The Democratic-Republicans clearly intended for Jefferson to be president. However, the new House of Representatives, dominated by Jefferson's party, would not take office for some months. Federalists still held a majority in the House, and their votes would decide the winner.

The Federalists were divided. Some feared Jefferson so much that they decided to back Burr. Others, such as Alexander Hamilton, considered Burr an unreliable man and urged the election of Jefferson. Hamilton did not like Jefferson, but he believed that Jefferson would do more for the good of the nation than Burr. "If there be a man in the world I ought to hate," he said, "it is Jefferson. . . . But the public good must be [more important than] every private consideration."

***Reading*History**
A. Analyzing Points of View Why did Hamilton think that Jefferson was the better choice for president?
A. Possible Response He believed that Jefferson would do more for the public good than Burr.

Over a period of seven days, the House voted 35 times without determining a winner. Finally, two weeks before the inauguration, Alexander Hamilton's friend James A. Bayard persuaded several Federalists not to vote for Burr. On the thirty-sixth ballot, Jefferson was elected president. Aaron Burr, who became vice president, would never forget Hamilton's insults.

People were overjoyed by Jefferson's election. A Philadelphia newspaper reported that bells rang, guns fired, dogs barked, cats meowed, and children cried over the news of Jefferson's victory.

2 The Talented Jefferson

In over 200 years, the United States has had more than 40 presidents. Many of them were great leaders. But no president has ever matched Thomas Jefferson in the variety of his achievements.

Jefferson's talents went beyond politics. He was still a young lawyer when he became interested in the architecture of classical Greece and Rome. The look of our nation's capital today reflects that interest. When Washington, D.C., was being built during the 1790s, Jefferson advised its architects and designers.

Jefferson's passion for classical styles can also be seen in his plan of Monticello, his Virginia home. For this elegant mansion, Jefferson designed storm windows, a seven-day clock, and a dumbwaiter—a small elevator that brought bottles of wine from the cellar.

ACTIVITY OPTIONS

INDIVIDUAL NEEDS: GIFTED AND TALENTED

JEFFERSON EXHIBIT

Class Time One class period

Task Planning an exhibit

Purpose To create an exhibit that illustrates Jefferson's life and achievements

Supplies Needed
- Reference materials about Jefferson, Internet access

Activity Tell students to plan an exhibit about Thomas Jefferson suitable for display in elementary schools. The exhibit may contain paintings, artifacts, and large posters containing quotations from Jefferson and others. Have students do research to find the items and quotes they would like to use. Tell them to photocopy pictures of the items or write short descriptions of them. Students should present their final plans with items for the exhibit numbered in order as they would be displayed.

Jefferson was a skilled violinist, horseman, amateur scientist, and a devoted reader, too. His book collection later became the core of the Library of Congress. After his election, Jefferson applied his many talents and ideas to the government of the United States.

Jefferson's Philosophy

The new president had strong opinions about what kind of country the United States ought to be. But his first order of business was to calm the nation's political quarrels.

> *A VOICE FROM THE PAST*
>
> Let us, then, fellow-citizens, unite with one heart and one mind. . . . Every difference of opinion is not a difference of principle. . . . We are all Republicans, we are all Federalists.
>
> **Thomas Jefferson,** First Inaugural Address

Reading **History**
B. Summarizing How did Thomas Jefferson try to unite the nation after he was elected?
B. Possible Response He promoted a common way of life based on a nation of small independent farmers.

One way Jefferson tried to unite Americans was by promoting a common way of life. He wanted the United States to remain a nation of small independent farmers. Such a nation, he believed, would uphold the strong morals and democratic values that he associated with country living. He hoped that the enormous amount of available land would prevent Americans from crowding into cities, as people had in Europe.

As president, Jefferson behaved more like a gentleman farmer than a privileged politician. Instead of riding in a fancy carriage to his inauguration, Jefferson walked the two blocks from his boarding house to the Capitol. Though his chef served elegant meals, the president's guests ate at round tables so that no one could sit at the head of the table.

To the end, Jefferson refused to elevate himself because of his office. For his tombstone, he chose this simple epitaph: "Here was buried

The Talented Jefferson

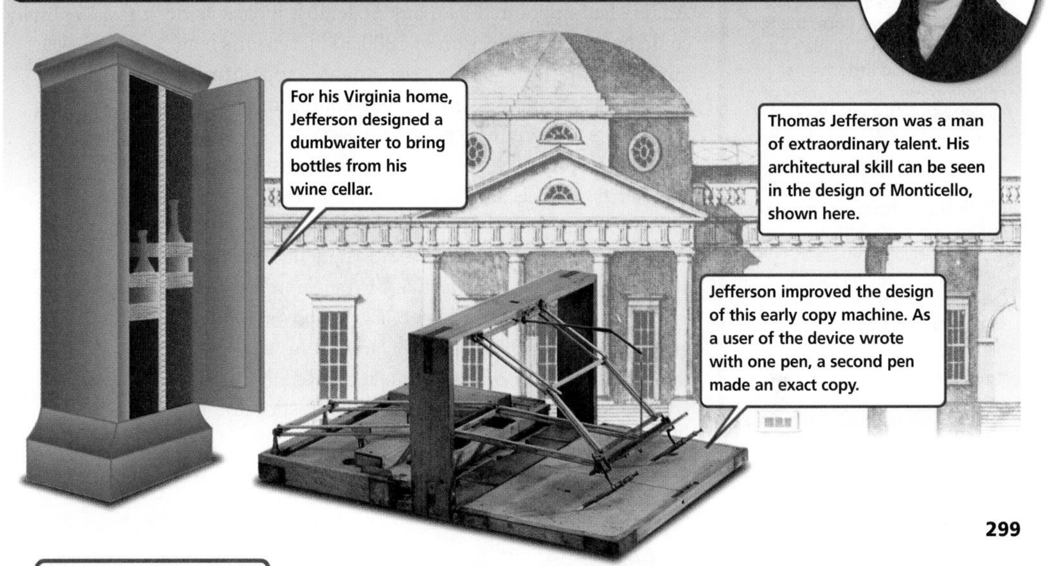
For his Virginia home, Jefferson designed a dumbwaiter to bring bottles from his wine cellar.
Thomas Jefferson was a man of extraordinary talent. His architectural skill can be seen in the design of Monticello, shown here.
Jefferson improved the design of this early copy machine. As a user of the device wrote with one pen, a second pen made an exact copy.

MORE ABOUT . . .

Jefferson and JFK
At a White House dinner for Nobel Prize winners, President John F. Kennedy recalled Jefferson's versatility and brilliance with the following remark. He called his dinner guests "the most extraordinary collection of talents . . . that has ever been gathered together at the White House, with the possible exception of when Thomas Jefferson dined alone." Among Jefferson's many interests were farming, architecture, law, geography, botany, natural history, and fine food and wine. His personal library contained almost 6,500 books. These volumes helped to form the initial collection of the Library of Congress in 1815.

MORE ABOUT . . .

Thomas Jefferson
Jefferson brought a studied informality to the office of president. One morning he shocked a British minister by receiving him while wearing slippers. Jefferson held no formal receptions, and when he entertained guests at meals, he did not seat them according to any system of rank—he would not even single out a guest of honor.

ACTIVITY OPTIONS

MULTIPLE LEARNING STYLES: VISUAL — BLOCK SCHEDULING

JEFFERSON POSTAGE STAMPS

Class Time One class period

Task Creating a postage stamp that commemorates one of Thomas Jefferson's talents, interests, or achievements

Purpose To identify Thomas Jefferson's talents and achievements

Supplies Needed
- Biographies and other reference materials on Jefferson's life and inventions and on Monticello
- Posterboard
- Art supplies
- Envelopes with canceled postage stamps or pictures of stamps

Activity Tell students to design a set of stamps that honor Jefferson's many talents and interests. Divide students into groups. Encourage students to examine some real stamps before beginning so that their stamps will look like actual postage stamps. Remind students that stamps should show at a glance who or what the subject is. Have each group pick one of Jefferson's achievements as the subject of their stamp and prepare a poster-sized rendition of their design. Display the completed stamps.

INSTRUCT: OBJECTIVE 3

Undoing Federalist Programs

- What did Jefferson believe about the role of government?
- How did Jefferson reduce the size and power of government?
- How did Hamilton and Jefferson differ in their views on public debt?

AMERICA'S HISTORY MAKERS

John Marshall

Before Marshall led the Supreme Court, justices had followed the English custom of having each judge deliver an opinion in a major case. Justices sometimes disagreed, so these presentations added little to the authority of the high court. The Marshall Court changed to the present practice, in which the Supreme Court issues only one opinion on a case. Because Marshall wrote many opinions and his opinions were clear, persuasive, and well reasoned, this practice helped the Supreme Court to gain respect and authority.

Possible Response: He had to make many difficult decisions and explain them in written opinions. He wrote 519 out of the 1,000 decisions he participated in.

INSTRUCT: OBJECTIVE 4

Marshall and the Judiciary/ *Marbury* v. *Madison*

- How did John Marshall influence the federal court system?
- How did the case of *Marbury* v. *Madison* establish the principle of judicial review?
- How did Marshall help create a balance of power among the three branches of government?

Citizenship Today, pp. 86–87

Thomas Jefferson, author of the Declaration of American Independence, of the statute of Virginia for religious freedom, and father of the University of Virginia." Jefferson chose not to list his presidency. His belief in a modest role for the central government is reflected in the changes he made during his presidency.

Background
In addition to founding the University of Virginia in 1819, Jefferson designed its buildings and supervised their construction.

3 Undoing Federalist Programs

Jefferson believed that the federal government should have less power than it had had under the Federalists. During his term of office, he sought to end many Federalist programs.

At the president's urging, Congress—now controlled by Democratic-Republicans—allowed the Alien and Sedition Acts to end. Jefferson then released prisoners convicted under the acts—among them, James Callender. Congress also ended many taxes, including the unpopular whiskey tax. Because the loss of tax revenue lowered the government's income, Jefferson reduced the number of federal employees to cut costs. He also reduced the size of the military.

AMERICA'S HISTORY MAKERS

JOHN MARSHALL
1755–1835

John Marshall was born, the first of 15 children, in Virginia's backcountry. He had little formal schooling. He received most of his education from his parents and a minister who lived with the family one year.

Even so, the lasting strength of the U.S. Constitution is partly due to Marshall's brilliant legal mind. In his long tenure as Chief Justice, John Marshall participated in more than 1,000 decisions and wrote 519 of them himself.

How does Marshall's record as Chief Justice demonstrate his decision-making abilities?

Jefferson next made changes to the Federalists' financial policies. Alexander Hamilton had created a system that depended on a certain amount of public debt. He believed that people who were owed money by their government would make sure the government was run properly. But Jefferson opposed public debt. He used revenues from tariffs and land sales to reduce the amount of money owed by the government.

4 Marshall and the Judiciary

Though Jefferson ended many Federalist programs, he had little power over the courts. John Adams had seen to that with the **Judiciary Act of 1801**. Under this act, Adams had appointed as many Federalist judges as he could between the election of 1800 and Jefferson's inauguration in 1801. These last-minute appointments meant that the new Democratic-Republican president would face a firmly Federalist judiciary.

Jefferson often felt frustrated by Federalist control of the courts. Yet because judges received their appointments for life, the president could do little.

Before he left office in 1801, President Adams also appointed a new Chief Justice of the Supreme Court. He chose a 45-year-old Federalist, **John Marshall**. He guessed that Marshall would be around for a long time to check the power of the Democratic-Republicans. He was right. Marshall served as Chief Justice for over three decades. Under Marshall, the Supreme Court upheld federal authority and strengthened federal

***Reading* History**
C. Analyzing Causes Why did the Federalists retain a great deal of power even after they were defeated by the Democratic-Republicans?
C. Possible Response They kept firm control of the judiciary.

ACTIVITY OPTIONS

INTERDISCIPLINARY LINK: LANGUAGE ARTS/CIVICS — BLOCK SCHEDULING

MARSHALL AND THE JUDICIARY

Class Time 30 minutes

Task Writing a eulogy for John Marshall

Purpose To evaluate the impact of John Marshall and the Marshall Court on the federal judicial system

Supplies Needed
- Civics and/or government textbooks and other reference materials on Marshall

Activity Explain to students that a eulogy is a speech or written remarks that praise an individual for his or her character and/or achievements. Often speakers give eulogies at funerals or memorial services. Have students review the reference materials on John Marshall and then prepare a five-minute speech on Marshall's life and accomplishments. When students have completed their eulogies, choose several examples for students to read aloud to the class.

courts. One of the most important decisions of the Marshall Court was ***Marbury* v. *Madison*** (1803).

Marbury v. *Madison*

Vocabulary
justice of the peace: a low-level official with limited authority, including the power to perform marriages

William Marbury was one of Adams's last-minute appointments. Adams had named him as a justice of the peace for the District of Columbia.

Marbury was supposed to be installed in his position by Secretary of State James Madison. When Madison refused to give him the job, Marbury sued. The case went to the Supreme Court, which ruled that the law under which Marbury sued was **unconstitutional**—that is, it contradicted the law of the Constitution.

Although the Court denied Marbury's claim, it did establish the principle of **judicial review**. This principle states that the Supreme Court has the final say in interpreting the Constitution. In his decision, Marshall declared, "It is emphatically the province and duty of the Judicial Department to say what the law is." If the Supreme Court decides that a law violates the Constitution, then that law cannot be put into effect.

Jefferson and Madison were angry when Marshall seized this new power for the Supreme Court, but they could hardly fight his decision. After all, he had decided *Marbury* v. *Madison* in their favor.

By establishing judicial review, Marshall helped to create a lasting balance among the three branches of government. The strength of this balance would be tested as the United States grew. In the next section, you will read about a period of great national growth.

Now and then

THE SUPREME COURT TODAY

The principle of judicial review is still a major force in American society. In June 1999, the Supreme Court used this power to restrict the ability of the federal government to enforce its laws in the 50 states.

In one case, *Alden* v. *Maine*, the Court ruled that employees of a state government cannot sue their state even when the state violates federal labor laws—such as those that set guidelines for overtime wages.

Section 1 Assessment

1. Terms & Names

Explain the significance of:
- radical
- Judiciary Act of 1801
- John Marshall
- *Marbury* v. *Madison*
- unconstitutional
- judicial review

2. Taking Notes

Use a chart like the one below to list some of the changes made by Jefferson and his party.

Changes made by Democratic-Republicans
1.

What branch of government gave Jefferson trouble?

3. Main Ideas

a. How was the tie between Jefferson and Burr settled after the election of 1800?

b. In what ways did Jefferson's talents reach beyond politics?

c. How did the opinions of Jefferson and Hamilton regarding the public debt differ?

4. Critical Thinking

Making Generalizations How was Thomas Jefferson's philosophy reflected in his personal life?

THINK ABOUT
- how he behaved after being elected
- how he felt about his presidency later in life

ACTIVITY OPTIONS

TECHNOLOGY / ART

Read more about Thomas Jefferson. Design Jefferson's **Internet home page** showing his inventions or create a **model** of a building he designed.

Now and then

The Supreme Court Today

Alden v. *Maine* (1999) shows how the Supreme Court continues to wrestle with federalism and with questions about how power should be divided between the states and the federal government. In this case, a group of probation officers employed by the state sued Maine under the federal Fair Labor Standards Act. They charged that the state had violated the overtime pay provisions of this act. The state insisted that it could not be sued under federal law even in state court. The Supreme Court agreed with the state, in a narrow decision: five justices voted in favor of the state's view, four against.

ASSESS & RETEACH

Setting the Stage Have students fill in the first section on the chapter graphic organizer.

Formal Assessment
- Section Quiz, p. 184

Critical Thinking Transparency CT28
- Setting the Stage

RETEACHING ACTIVITY

Working in pairs, have students create outlines of the section. Have students use their outline to write a summary of the chapter.

In-Depth Resources: Unit 3
- Reteaching Activity, p. 34

Section 1 Assessment

1. Terms & Names

radical, p. 297
Judiciary Act of 1801, p. 300
John Marshall, p. 300
***Marbury* v. *Madison*,** p. 301
unconstitutional, p. 301
judicial review, p. 301

2. Taking Notes

He repealed unpopular taxes; reduced the number of federal employees; reduced the size of the military; and replaced Hamilton's financial system.

the judicial branch

3. Main Ideas

a. The House of Representatives broke it. **b.** He was an architect, inventor, violinist, and amateur scientist. **c.** Hamilton thought some public debt gave citizens an interest in good government. Jefferson opposed all public debt.

4. Critical Thinking

He reflected a gentleman-farmer philosophy, and refused to elevate himself because of his office.

ACTIVITY OPTIONS

Integrated Assessment
- Rubrics for a Web page, 5.1
- Rubrics for a model, 1.10

SECTION OBJECTIVES

1. To explain why Jefferson offered to buy New Orleans from France
2. To analyze why Napoleon sold the Louisiana Territory to the United States
3. To summarize the experiences of the Lewis and Clark expedition
4. To evaluate the results of Pike's expedition

SKILLBUILDER

Interpreting Maps: Location, Movement, p. 304
Interpreting Charts, p. 307

CRITICAL THINKING

Making Inferences, pp. 303, 305
Finding Main Ideas, p. 306
Recognizing Effects, p. 307

FOCUS & MOTIVATE

5-MINUTE WARM-UP

Reading a Map These questions focus on the Lewis and Clark expedition.

1. Look at the map on page 304. What might be forms of transportation used by the expedition? How can you tell?
2. What were some problems of travel by foot or on horseback?

Warm-Up Transparency WT10

INSTRUCT

INSTRUCT: OBJECTIVE 1

The West in 1800/ Napoleon and New Orleans

- What four nations claimed parts of the area between the Mississippi and the Pacific?
- How did Jefferson attempt to settle the nation's dispute with France?

In-Depth Resources: Unit 3
- Guided Reading, p. 22
- Building Vocabulary, p. 25

Reading Study Guide (Spanish and English), pp. 97–98

2 The Louisiana Purchase and Exploration

TERMS & NAMES
Louisiana Purchase
Meriwether Lewis
William Clark
Lewis and Clark expedition
Sacagawea
Zebulon Pike

MAIN IDEA	WHY IT MATTERS NOW
Jefferson purchased the Louisiana Territory in 1803 and doubled the size of the United States.	Thirteen more states were eventually organized on the land acquired by the Louisiana Purchase.

ONE AMERICAN'S STORY

In 1790, Captain Robert Gray became the first American to sail around the world. Two years later, Gray explored a harbor in what is now Washington state. This harbor was later named Gray's Harbor, and Washington's largest river was named after Gray's ship, the *Columbia*.

New England merchants like Captain Gray had to sail all the way around South America to reach the profitable trading regions of the Oregon Country. (See the map on page 304.) In spite of the long trip, merchants from Boston soon began to appear there frequently. They appeared so often that the Native Americans they traded with began calling all white people "Bostons."

Gray's explorations helped to establish U.S. claims to the Pacific Northwest. In this section, you will learn how a lucky land purchase and a daring expedition further hastened westward expansion.

Robert Gray sailed his ship *Columbia* on trading voyages to the Northwest and China.

1 The West in 1800

In 1800, when Americans talked about the "West," they meant the area between the Appalachian Mountains and the Mississippi River. Thousands of settlers were moving westward across the Appalachians to settle in this region. Many moved onto land long inhabited by Native Americans. Even so, several U.S. territories soon declared statehood. Kentucky and Tennessee had become states by 1800, and Ohio entered the union in 1803.

Although the Mississippi River was the western border of the United States, there was a great deal of activity further west. In 1800, France and Spain were negotiating for ownership of the Louisiana Territory—the vast region between the Mississippi River and the Rocky Mountains.

The Pacific coast region and the Oregon Country, as you read in One American's Story, also attracted increasing attention. In California, Spain had a chain of 21 missions stretching from San Diego to San Francisco. Starting just north of San Francisco, Russian settlements dotted the Pacific coast all the way to Alaska. Great Britain also claimed land in the region.

RECOMMENDED RESOURCES

In-Depth Resources: Unit 3
- Guided Reading, p. 22
- Literature Selection, pp. 31–33
- Enrichment Activity, p. 38

Reading Study Guide (Spanish and English), pp. 97–98

Outline Map Activities, pp. 19–20

America's History Makers
- Sacagawea, pp. 41–42

American History Plays
- *Land of the Unknown*

Formal Assessment
- Section Quiz, p. 185

Integrated Assessment
- Rubrics, 2.4, 2.1

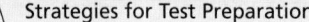

Access for Students Acquiring English/ESL, p. 64

INTEGRATED TECHNOLOGY

Geography Transparency GT10

Humanities Transparency HT19

Electronic Teacher Tools

classzone.com

TEST-TAKING RESOURCES

Strategies for Test Preparation

Test Practice Transparencies, TT35

Online Test Practice

ReadingHistory
A. Reading a Map Use the map on page 304 to find the location of New Orleans.

As the number of Westerners grew, so did their political influence. A vital issue for many settlers was the use of the Mississippi River. Farmers and merchants used the river to move their products to the port of New Orleans, and from there to east coast markets. Threats to the free navigation of the Mississippi and the use of the port at New Orleans brought America to the brink of war.

Napoleon and New Orleans

"There is on the globe one single spot the possessor of which is our natural and habitual enemy," President Jefferson wrote. That spot was New Orleans. This strategic port was originally claimed by France. After losing the French and Indian War, France turned over the Louisiana Territory—including New Orleans—to Spain. But in a secret treaty in 1800, Spain returned Louisiana and the port to France's powerful leader, Napoleon. Now Napoleon planned to colonize the American territory.

Background
In 1799, Napoleon was made the top official of the French Republic. In 1804, he became emperor.

In 1802, these developments nearly resulted in war. Just before turning Louisiana over to France, Spain closed New Orleans to American shipping. Angry Westerners called for war against both Spain and France. To avoid hostilities, Jefferson offered to buy New Orleans from France. He received a surprising offer back. The French asked if the United States wanted to buy all of the Louisiana Territory—a tract of land even larger than the United States at that time.

2 The Louisiana Purchase

A number of factors may have led Napoleon to make his surprising offer. He was probably alarmed by America's fierce determination to keep the port of New Orleans open. Also, his enthusiasm for a colony in America may have been lessened by events in a French colony in the West Indies. There, a revolt led by Toussaint L'Ouverture (too•SAN loo•vehr•TOOR) had resulted in disastrous losses for the French. Another factor was France's costly war against Britain. America's money may have been more valuable to Napoleon than its land.

Jefferson was thrilled by Napoleon's offer. However, the Constitution said nothing about the president's right to buy land. This troubled Jefferson, who believed in the strict interpretation of the Constitution. But he also believed in a republic of small farmers, and that required land. So, on April 30, 1803, the **Louisiana Purchase** was approved for $15 million—about three cents per acre. The purchase doubled the size of the United States. At the time, Americans knew little about the territory. But that would soon change.

B. Possible Response He believed that acquiring land for a republic of small farmers was important.

ReadingHistory
B. Making Inferences Why did Jefferson purchase Louisiana even though the Constitution said nothing about the president's right to buy land?

Connections to WORLD HISTORY

TOUSSAINT L'OUVERTURE

Toussaint L'Ouverture was born in Hispaniola, an island in the West Indies once colonized by both France and Spain. In 1791, L'Ouverture helped to lead a slave revolt against the French-controlled part of Hispaniola. A natural leader, L'Ouverture won admiration when he preached harmony between former slaves and planters.

In 1801, L'Ouverture overran the Spanish part of the island. He then freed all the slaves and put himself in charge of the entire island.

Hoping to regain their territory, the French invaded in 1802. They arrested L'Ouverture but failed to end the rebellion.

INSTRUCT: OBJECTIVE 2

The Louisiana Purchase/ Lewis and Clark Explore

- What caused Jefferson to hesitate before agreeing to purchase the Louisiana Territory?
- How did the Louisiana Purchase change the size of the United States?
- What was the purpose of the Lewis and Clark expedition?

Outline Map Activities
- The Louisiana Purchase, pp. 19–20

Connections TO WORLD HISTORY

Toussaint L'Ouverture

In May 1802, L'Ouverture was forced to surrender after a French invasion overwhelmed his small force. He agreed to lay down his weapons in exchange for a French promise not to restore slavery in Haiti. At first, L'Ouverture was allowed to live peacefully on a plantation in Haiti, but he was later seized by the French and sent to France, where he was imprisoned in a dungeon, interrogated, and died in 1803.

CRITICAL THINKING ACTIVITY

Evaluating Have students review Jefferson's philosophy of government. Did the Louisiana Purchase contradict that philosophy? Why or why not?

Class Time 10 minutes

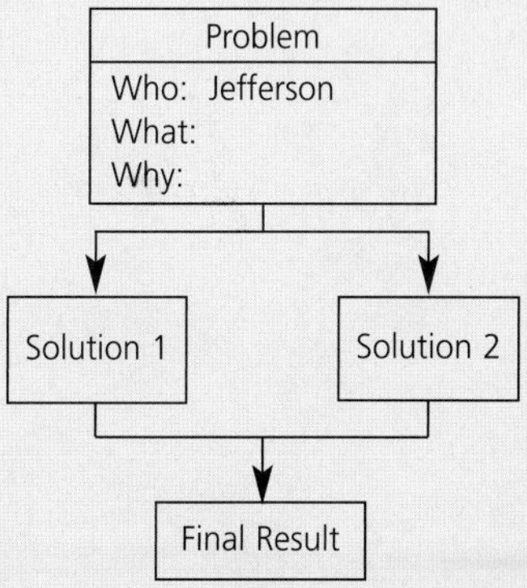

ACTIVITY OPTIONS

INTERDISCIPLINARY LINK: MATHEMATICS — BLOCK SCHEDULING

LOUISIANA PURCHASE WORD PROBLEMS

Class Time 20 minutes

Task Solving math problems using information about the Louisiana Purchase

Purpose To analyze the value of the Louisiana Purchase

Supplies Needed
- Calculator

Activity Put the following information on the chalkboard:
- Louisiana Purchase: approximately 828,000 square miles
- Size of the United States in 1800: 891,000 square miles
- Size of the United States today: 3,787,000 square miles

Have students calculate the following: a) the price per square mile of the Louisiana Territory based on a purchase price of $15 million; b) the percentage of the total land area of the United States today that the Louisiana Purchase represents. Then have students make up one more problem based on these data.

MORE ABOUT . . .

The Lewis and Clark Expedition

The Lewis and Clark expedition consisted of about 40 men in their late twenties or early thirties who were physically fit, experienced outdoorsmen. Expedition members contributed knowledge about many topics to the group, including botany, weather forecasting, zoology, and navigation by the moon and stars. Other members knew some Native American sign language or were skilled at carpentry, gun repair, or piloting boats.

In-Depth Resources: Unit 3
- Enrichment Activity, p. 38

HISTORY FROM VISUALS

Reading the Map Ask students what made St. Louis a good starting point for exploring the West. **Possible Response** It could be reached by the Mississippi River and was located on the Missouri River, providing access to the interior of the Louisiana Territory. Then ask why Pike might have chosen to go south in the Louisiana Territory. **Possible Response** to get information different from that of Lewis and Clark

Extension Have students use a current political map to determine what states or parts of states were created from the Louisiana Purchase.

Geography Transparency GT10
- United States, 1803

Lewis and Clark Explore

Since 1802, Thomas Jefferson had planned an expedition to explore the Louisiana country. Now that the Louisiana Purchase had been made, learning about the territory became even more important.

Jefferson chose a young officer, Captain **Meriwether Lewis,** to lead the expedition. In Jefferson's map-lined study, the two men eagerly planned the trip. Lewis turned to his old friend, Lieutenant **William Clark,** to select and oversee a volunteer force, which they called the Corps of Discovery. Clark was a skilled mapmaker and outdoorsman and proved to be a natural leader. The Corps of Discovery soon became known as the **Lewis and Clark expedition.**

Vocabulary
corps (kor): a number of people acting together for a similar purpose

Clark was accompanied by York, his African-American slave. York's hunting skills won him many admirers among the Native Americans met by the explorers. The first black man that many Indians had ever seen, York became something of a celebrity among them.

Lewis and Clark set out in the summer of 1803. By winter, they reached St. Louis. Located on the western bank of the Mississippi River, St. Louis would soon become the gateway to the West. But in 1803, the city was a sleepy town with just 180 houses. Lewis and Clark spent the winter at St. Louis and waited for the ceremony that would mark the transfer of Louisiana to the United States. In March 1804, the American flag flew over St. Louis for the first time.

Skillbuilder Answers
1. Missouri and Mississippi rivers
2. For part of the trip, Clark took a southerly route along the Yellowstone River.

The Louisiana Purchase and Explorations, 1804–1807

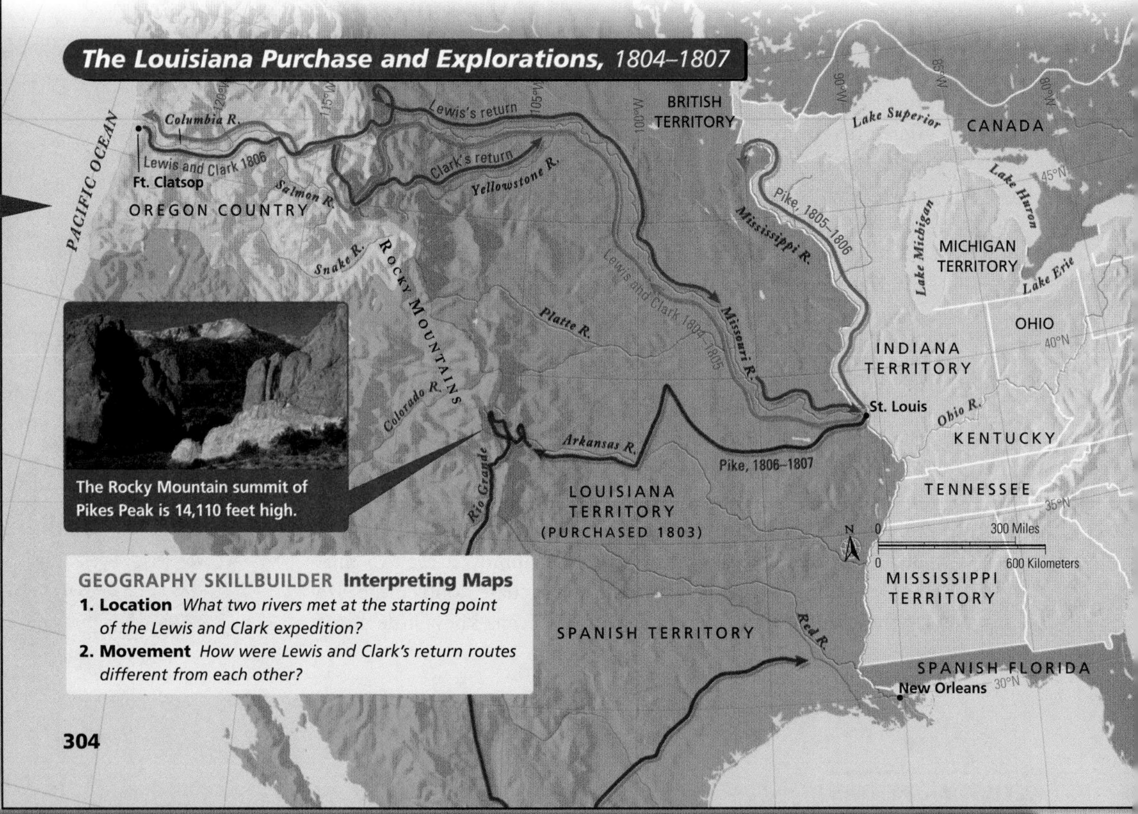

GEOGRAPHY SKILLBUILDER Interpreting Maps
1. **Location** *What two rivers met at the starting point of the Lewis and Clark expedition?*
2. **Movement** *How were Lewis and Clark's return routes different from each other?*

ACTIVITY OPTIONS

INDIVIDUAL NEEDS

LESS PROFICIENT READERS

Sequencing Events To help students follow the sequence of events and understand the importance of the Lewis and Clark expedition, work with them to create a sequence chart. As students read the sections "Lewis and Clark Explore," "Up the Missouri River," and "On to the Pacific Ocean," pause and ask students to identify each new event and its corresponding date. Write students' responses on the board in a chart.

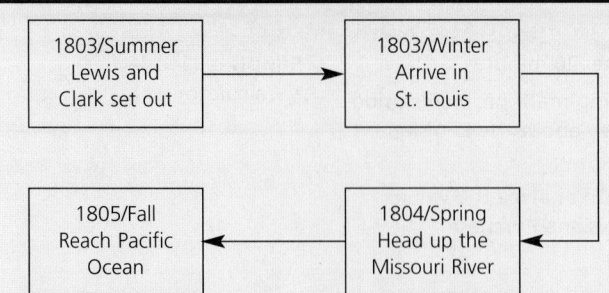

- 1803/Summer Lewis and Clark set out →
- 1803/Winter Arrive in St. Louis →
- 1804/Spring Head up the Missouri River →
- 1805/Fall Reach Pacific Ocean

AMERICA'S HISTORY MAKERS

MERIWETHER LEWIS
1774–1809

Meriwether Lewis was well qualified for the first overland expedition to the Pacific Northwest. In Virginia, he had become an expert hunter. From 1801 to 1803, he worked for President Jefferson, who had him trained in geography, mineralogy, and astronomy.

The journals Lewis kept tell what the West was like in the early 1800s and are still exciting to read. In one entry, dated September 17, 1804, Lewis describes the "immense herds of Buffaloe, deer Elk and Antelopes which we saw in every direction feeding on the hills and plains."

WILLIAM CLARK
1770–1838

William Clark was an army friend of Meriwether Lewis. Lewis personally chose him to be co-captain of the Corps of Discovery.

Clark's experience in his state militia and the U.S. Army had taught him how to build forts, draw maps, and lead expeditions through enemy territory.

He had less formal training than Lewis, but with his six feet of height and muscular build, he was a more rugged explorer.

Clark's leadership skills smoothed disputes. Also, his artistic skills made the expedition's maps and drawings both accurate and beautiful.

What were the different skills of Lewis and Clark that qualified them as co-leaders of the expedition?

3 Up the Missouri River

The explorers, who numbered about 40, set out from St. Louis in May of 1804. They headed up the Missouri River in one shallow-bottomed riverboat and two pirogues—canoes made from hollowed-out tree trunks. They had instructions from President Jefferson to explore the river and hoped to find a water route across the continent. Lewis and Clark were also told to establish good relations with Native Americans and describe the landscape, plants, and animals they saw.

Reading **History**
C. Making Inferences Why did Lewis and Clark travel on the Missouri River?
C. Possible Response They were instructed to explore the river and find a water route across the continent.

The explorers inched up the Missouri. The first afternoon, they traveled only about three miles. Sometimes the men had to pull, rather than row or sail, their boats against the current. In late October, they reached the Mandan Indian villages in what is now North Dakota.

The explorers built a small fort and spent the winter with the friendly Mandan. There, they also met British and French-Canadian trappers and traders. They were not happy to see the Americans. They suspected that the Americans would soon compete with them for the rich trade in beaver furs—and they were right.

In the spring of 1805, the expedition set out again. A French trapper, his 17-year-old-wife, **Sacagawea** (SAK•uh•juh•WEE•uh), and their baby went with them. Sacagawea was a Shoshone woman whose language skills and knowledge of geography would be of great value to Lewis and Clark—especially when they reached the area where she was born.

AMERICA'S HISTORY MAKERS

Meriwether Lewis

Thomas Jefferson said of Lewis that he possessed "a firmness & perseverance of purpose which nothing but impossibilities could divert from its direction." Lewis was Jefferson's private secretary when the president began unofficially training him to lead an expedition to chart the Louisiana Territory. After the expedition, in 1807 Lewis became governor of the Louisiana Territory. Two years later he died in an inn on the Natchez Trace. Historians still debate whether the cause of his death was suicide or murder.

William Clark

After the expedition, Clark became governor of the Missouri Territory. He held this office until his death in 1838. Earlier, he had served as governor of the Missouri Territory and surveyor general for Illinois, Missouri, and Arkansas. Both Lewis and Clark received 1,600 acres of public land for leading the successful expedition.

Possible Responses: Lewis had training in geography, mineralogy, and astronomy. Clark had extensive experience in the military and was a skilled artist.

Humanities Transparency HT19
- *Lewis and Clark*

INSTRUCT: OBJECTIVE 3

Up the Missouri River/ On to the Pacific Ocean

- What goals did Jefferson have for the Lewis and Clark expedition?
- How did the Mandan and Sacagawea help the expedition?
- What did the Lewis and Clark expedition accomplish?

In-Depth Resources: Unit 3
- Literature Selection: from *Streams to the River, River to the Sea*, pp. 31–33

ACTIVITY OPTIONS

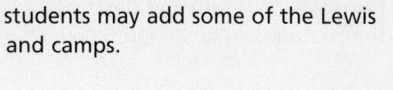

INTERDISCIPLINARY LINK: GEOGRAPHY — BLOCK SCHEDULING

MAPPING THE LEWIS AND CLARK EXPEDITION

Class Time One class period

Task Making a map showing the route of the Lewis and Clark expedition

Purpose To apply map skills and to study parts of the western United States

Supplies Needed
- Atlas map of the western United States
- Reference materials about the Lewis and Clark expedition
- Art supplies

Activity Have students draw their own maps of the Lewis and Clark expedition, using the map on page 304 as a model. Tell students to add present-day state boundaries, state capitals, and other large cities and towns. Tell them to choose one of the following categories to include on their map: state and national parks, mountain ranges and rivers, and Indian groups at the time of the expedition. Motivated students may add some of the Lewis and Clark expedition's stopping places and camps.

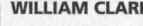

MORE ABOUT . . .

Records of the Expedition

Patrick Gass came to the Lewis and Clark expedition from the army in Illinois. Gass kept a journal that coincides in most details with the journals of Lewis and Clark. Gass paints a poignant picture of the expedition's Christmas celebration on December 24 and 25, 1804. The men feasted on special items including flour, dried apples, and pepper. Captain Clark presented each man a glass of brandy, and later the men danced.

MORE ABOUT . . .

Sacagawea

When the Lewis and Clark expedition reached the area known as the Three Forks of the Missouri in western Montana, Sacagawea recognized her surroundings. Born in what is today Idaho, she was about 12 years old when she was kidnapped by the Hidatsa Sioux and taken from her Shoshone home to a Hidatsa-Mandan village near what is today Bismarck, North Dakota. Later she was bought by Charbonneau, who claimed her as his wife. Sacagawea knew sign language and spoke many Native American dialects. Sacagawea was later reunited with her brother Cameahwait, the Shoshone chief.

America's History Makers
- Sacagawea, pp. 41–42

INSTRUCT: OBJECTIVE 4

Pike's Expedition/The Effects of Exploration

- What area of the Louisiana Purchase did Pike explore?
- What did Pike hope to achieve?
- What were the effects of the explorations of Lewis and Clark and Pike?

Lewis and Clark kept beautiful journals that provided priceless information about the West.

On to the Pacific Ocean

On their way west, the expedition had to stop at the Great Falls of the Missouri. Lewis called this ten-mile-long series of waterfalls "the grandest sight I ever beheld." He described his approach to the falls.

A VOICE FROM THE PAST

I had proceeded on this course about two miles . . . whin my ears were saluted with the agreeable sound of a fall of water and advancing a little further I saw the spray arrise above the plain like a collumn of smoke. . . . (It) soon began to make a roaring too tremendious to be mistaken for any cause short of the great falls of the Missouri.

Meriwether Lewis, quoted in *Undaunted Courage*

To get around the Great Falls, the explorers had to carry their boats and heavy supplies for 18 miles. They built wheels from cottonwood trees to move the boats. Even with wheels, the trek took nearly two weeks. Rattlesnakes, bears, and even a hailstorm slowed their steps.

As they approached the Rocky Mountains, Sacagawea excitedly pointed out Shoshone lands. Eager to make contact with the tribe, Lewis and a small party made their way overland. Lewis soon found the Shoshone, whose chief recognized Sacagawea as his sister. The chief traded horses to Lewis and Clark, and the Shoshone helped them cross the Rocky Mountains.

The explorers then journeyed to the mighty Columbia River, which leads to the Pacific Ocean. In November 1805, Clark wrote in his journal, "Ocian in view! O! The joy." They soon arrived at the Pacific Coast. There, they spent a rain-soaked winter before returning to St. Louis the following year.

The Lewis and Clark expedition brought back a wealth of scientific and geographic information. Though they learned that an all-water route across the continent did not exist, Americans received an exciting report of what lay to the west.

D. Possible Response The explorers brought back important scientific and geographic information about the west.

***Reading*History**

D. Finding Main Ideas Why was the Lewis and Clark expedition valuable?

4 Pike's Expedition

Lewis and Clark explored the northern part of the Louisiana Purchase. In 1806, an expedition led by **Zebulon Pike** left St. Louis on a southerly route. (Refer to the map on page 304.) Pike's mission was to find the sources of the Arkansas and Red rivers. The Red River formed a boundary between Spanish territory and Louisiana.

Background The previous year, Pike had led a 5,000-mile expedition to search for the source of the Mississippi River.

Pike's party of two dozen men headed westward across the Great Plains. When they reached the Arkansas River, they followed it toward the Rocky Mountains. From 150 miles away, Pike spied the Rocky Mountain peak that would later bear his name—Pikes Peak. However, he failed in his attempt to climb it. Then they turned south, hoping that they would eventually run into the Red River. Instead, they ran into the

ACTIVITY OPTIONS

INTERDISCIPLINARY LINK: GEOGRAPHY — BLOCK SCHEDULING

HISTORICAL MARKERS FOR THE PIKE EXPEDITION

Class Time One class period

Task Creating a set of three historical markers for Zebulon Pike's expedition

Purpose To locate and describe the route taken by Zebulon Pike

Supplies Needed
- Reference materials on the Pike expedition
- Detailed map of the route taken by Pike
- Physical and current political maps of the United States
- Posterboard and markers

Activity As a class, compare the map of the route taken by the Pike expedition with a physical map of the United States. Then explain what a historical marker is and give examples of local markers. Have students use the reference materials and map of Pike's route to identify two or three places on the route where they would like to place a marker. The marker should tell when the expedition passed this point and describe anything of interest that took place there. Have each group indicate where on a present-day map of the United States it would be placed.

EFFECTS: *Exploration of the West, 1804–1807*

1. Accurate maps
Lewis and Clark and Pike produced the first good maps of the Louisiana Territory. Later travelers would use these maps to make their way west.

2. Growth of fur trade
Exploration boosted interest in the fur trade. Hunters and trappers would add to the knowledge of the West.

3. Mistaken view of Great Plains
Pike inaccurately described the treeless Great Plains as a desert. This led many Americans to believe that the Plains were useless for farming.

SKILLBUILDER **Interpreting Charts**
Why might Pike's description of the Great Plains have led to the idea that Native Americans east of the Mississippi should be moved there?

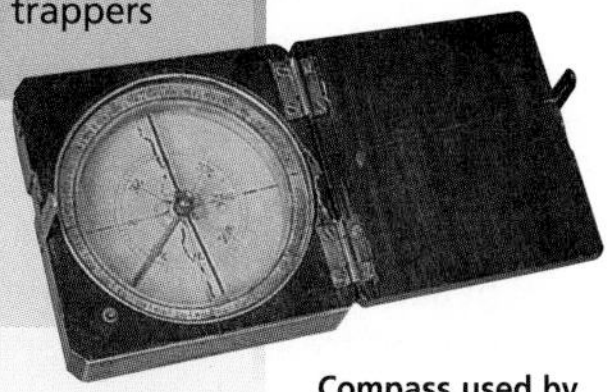

Compass used by Lewis and Clark

Vocabulary
Rio Grande: Spanish for *big river*

Rio Grande, which was in Spanish territory. There, they were arrested by Spanish troops.

The explorers returned to the United States after being released by Spanish officials in 1807. Though Pike and his men never explored the Red River, they did bring back valuable descriptions of the Great Plains and the Rio Grande River Valley.

Skillbuilder Answer
The land of the Great Plains was believed to be less valuable than that of the East.

The Effects of Exploration

The first American explorers of the West brought back tales of adventure as well as scientific and geographical information. As the chart above shows, this information would have long-lasting effects.

Early in Jefferson's presidency, events at home occupied much of the new president's time. In the next section, you will learn about foreign affairs during the same time period.

Section 2 Assessment

1. Terms & Names
Explain the significance of:
- Louisiana Purchase
- Meriwether Lewis
- William Clark
- Lewis and Clark expedition
- Sacagawea
- Zebulon Pike

2. Taking Notes
Use a chart like the one below to record the factors that might have led Napoleon to sell the Louisiana Territory.

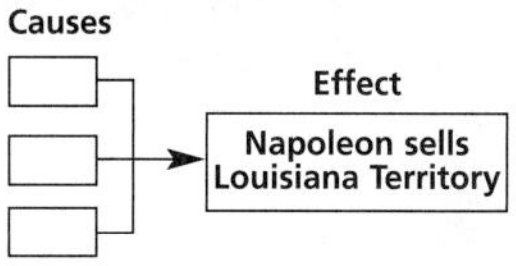

3. Main Ideas
a. What groups might dispute European land claims in the West?
b. Why was New Orleans important to Americans?
c. How did Sacagawea help Lewis and Clark?

4. Critical Thinking
Recognizing Effects What were some of the effects of the explorations of the West in the 1800s?
THINK ABOUT
- how other people might use the information brought back by the explorers
- the economic effects of the expedition

ACTIVITY OPTIONS
WORLD HISTORY
GEOGRAPHY
Read more about New Orleans. Make an illustrated **time line** of the French, Spanish, and U.S. ownership of the city or create a **map** of its port.

HISTORY FROM VISUALS

Interpreting Charts Have students explore how these effects of early explorations both spurred and deterred westward settlement by whites. Ask students what was likely to be the impact of Lewis and Clark's and Pike's explorations on Native American groups living in the Louisiana Purchase.
Possible Response Since accurate maps and the growth of the fur trade would encourage trade and travel by whites, a long-term effect was likely to be white settlement of the area, leading to conflict between Native Americans and whites.

Extension Have students use reference materials to find out why Pike concluded that the Great Plains were useless for farming.

ASSESS & RETEACH

Setting the Stage Have students fill in the second section on the chapter graphic organizer.

Formal Assessment
- Section Quiz, p. 185

RETEACHING ACTIVITY

Have students make a diagram showing three causes of the sale of the Louisiana Territory to the United States and three or more effects of this sale on the history of the United States.

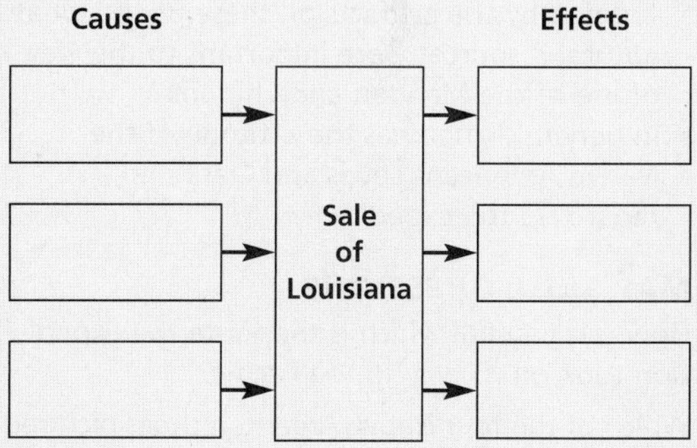

In-Depth Resources: Unit 3
- Reteaching Activity, p. 35

Section 2 Assessment

1. Terms & Names
Louisiana Purchase, p. 303
Meriwether Lewis, p. 304
William Clark, p. 304
Lewis and Clark expedition, p. 304
Sacajawea, p. 305
Zebulon Pike, p. 306

2. Taking Notes
Causes: determination of Americans to use port at New Orleans; losses suffered by France in Caribbean colonies; costly wars in Europe

3. Main Ideas
a. Native Americans **b.** It was an important port for farmers and merchants. **c.** with her knowledge of geography and language skills

4. Critical Thinking
created more detailed maps; boosted interest in the fur trade; led to the mistaken view of the region as useless for farming

ACTIVITY OPTIONS
Integrated Assessment
- Rubrics for a time line, 2.4
- Rubrics for a map, 2.1

GEOGRAPHY *in* HISTORY

OBJECTIVE

Students will analyze and interpret information from a map and paintings to identify Native American groups that Lewis and Clark met along their route. They will note how some of these groups assisted the explorers.

BLOCK SCHEDULING

MORE ABOUT . . .

The Shoshone

The Shoshone lived in a resource-poor area of deserts and salt flats known as the Great Basin, bordered on the east by the Wasatch Mountain Range and on the west by the Sierra Nevada. A nomadic people, they survived by moving from place to place with the seasons, hunting rabbits, and less often, antelope, deer, or sheep. They spent much of their time searching for seeds, berries, nuts, roots, and bulbs. Their diet also consisted of lizards, rats, rabbits, and insects. As hunters and gatherers, they typically traveled in small family bands. They made much of their clothing from rabbit skins.

INSTRUCT

- Judging by the artifacts on these pages, what natural resources were important to the way of life of the Mandan and Chinook?
- In general, what was the attitude of the Native Americans Lewis and Clark met regarding the expedition?

MAP SKILL QUESTIONS

How can you tell which is the route the expedition took on its way to the Pacific?

Which of the four Native American tribes pictured here lived closest to St. Louis? to Fort Clatsop?

Which of the two explorers was more likely to have met the Atsina on his return trip?

GEOGRAPHY *in* HISTORY

PLACE AND LOCATION

Native Americans on the Explorers' Route

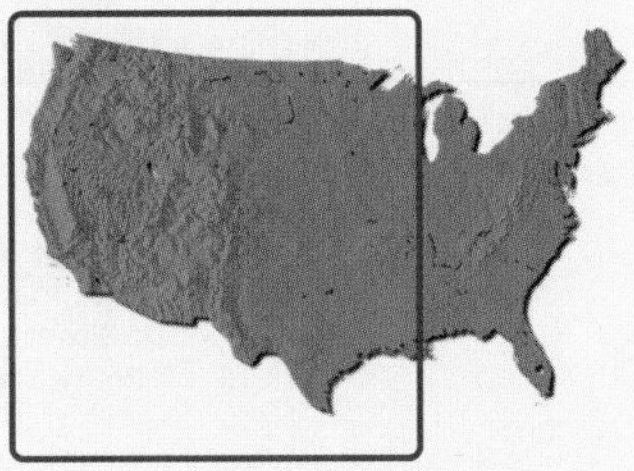

When Thomas Jefferson bought the Louisiana Territory, Native Americans had already been living in that area for thousands of years. Before Lewis and Clark began their trip, Jefferson instructed them to deal with Native Americans in a peaceful manner and to make it clear that the United States wished to be "friendly and useful to them." On their journey, Lewis and Clark met almost 50 different tribes.

Sacagawea

In 1805, the explorers arrived in Shoshone territory near the Rocky Mountains. A Shoshone chief, Cameahwait, confirmed that there was no all-water route to the Pacific. Later, when Cameahwait recognized Sacagawea as his sister, he agreed to sell the explorers the horses they needed to cross the mountains.

1 Oto

In 1804, Lewis and Clark met the Oto, a buffalo-hunting people. This was the first formal meeting of U.S. representatives with western Native Americans. Lewis told the Oto that they were "children" of a new great "father"—President Thomas Jefferson.

ARTIFACT FILE

Buffalo Robe Pictured to the right is a section of a Mandan buffalo robe. On it, a Mandan painted a battle scene between the Mandan and the Sioux.

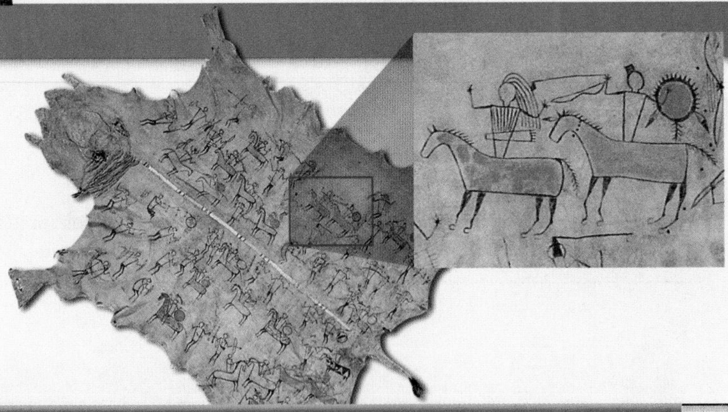

308 CHAPTER 10

MUSEUM CONNECTIONS

Among the on-line exhibits at the Web site of the Peabody Museum of Archaeology and Ethnology is a fascinating look at objects relating to Native Americans collected by Lewis and Clark during their expedition. The exhibit is called "The Ethnology of Lewis and Clark: Native American Objects and the American Quest for Commerce and Science." For more on the Peabody Museum, classzone.com.

The Museum of Westward Expansion is part of the Jefferson National Expansion Memorial in St. Louis, Missouri. Located underneath the soaring Gateway Arch, a memorial to the nation's pioneers, the museum includes an overview of the Lewis and Clark expedition. For an on-line tour of the museum, including an audio presentation of the words of Thomas Jefferson and William Clark, see classzone.com.

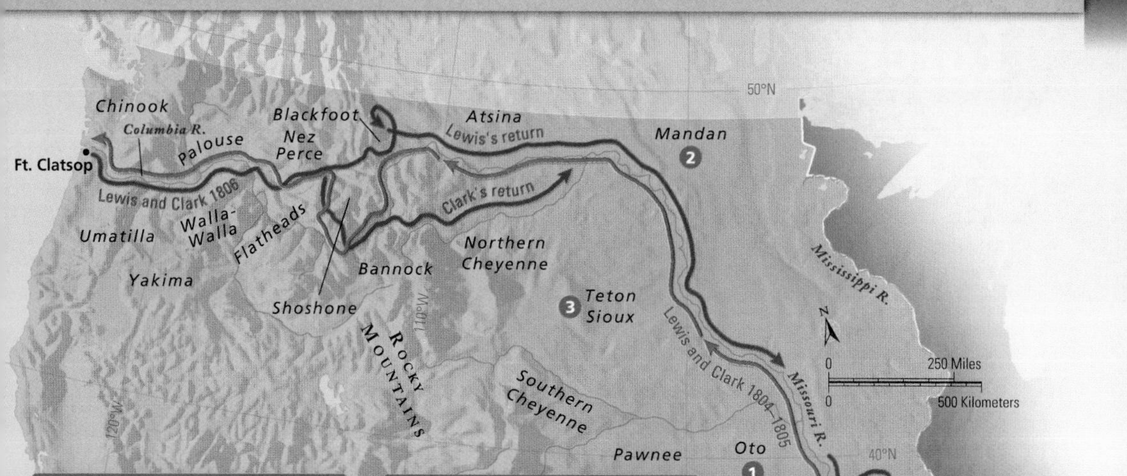

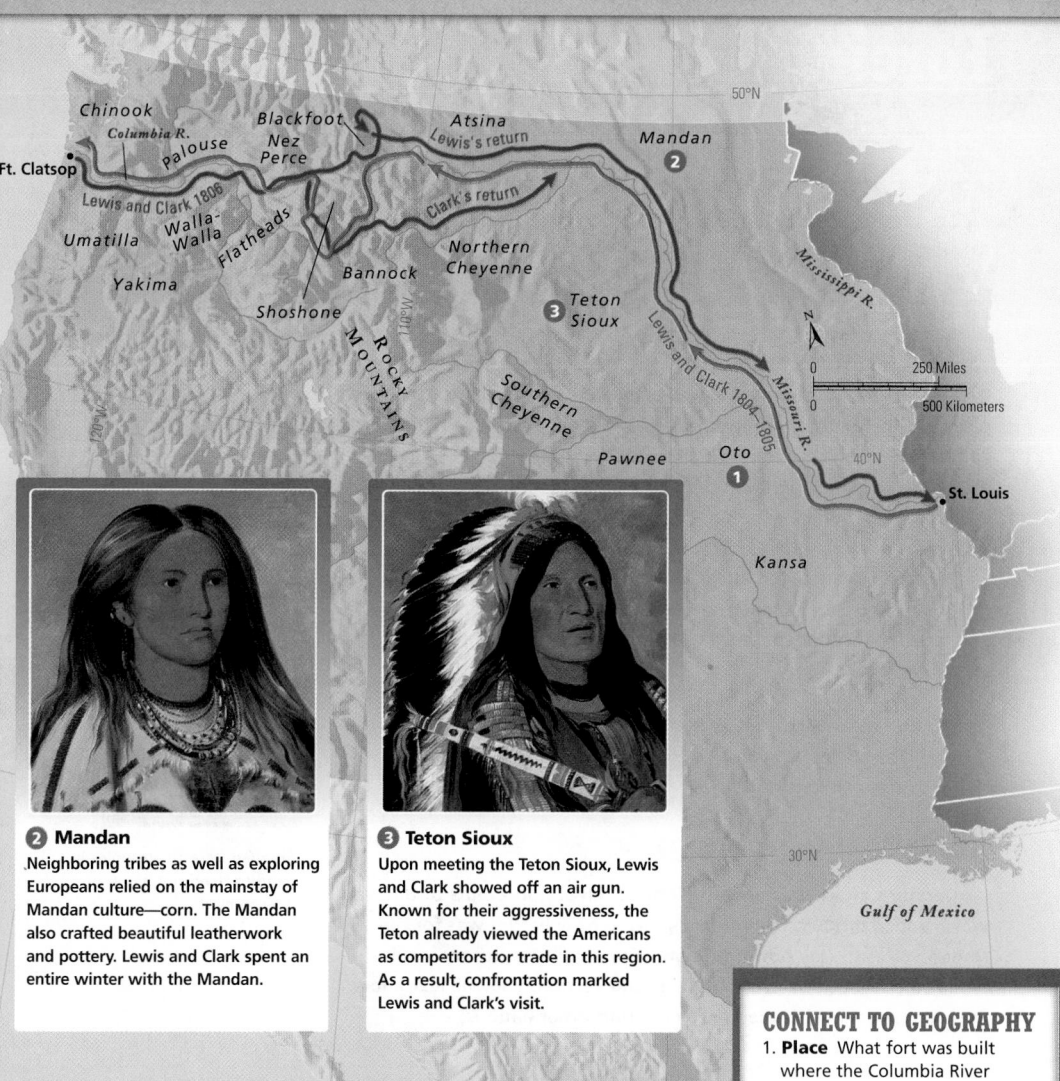

2 Mandan
Neighboring tribes as well as exploring Europeans relied on the mainstay of Mandan culture—corn. The Mandan also crafted beautiful leatherwork and pottery. Lewis and Clark spent an entire winter with the Mandan.

3 Teton Sioux
Upon meeting the Teton Sioux, Lewis and Clark showed off an air gun. Known for their aggressiveness, the Teton already viewed the Americans as competitors for trade in this region. As a result, confrontation marked Lewis and Clark's visit.

On-Line Field Trip

The Peabody Museum in Cambridge, Massachusetts, holds an important collection of Native American artifacts. This rain hat was worn by Chinook whalers of the Northwest. The Chinook made these water-repellent hats out of cedar bark and bear grass.

For more about Native American artifacts . . .

RESEARCH LINKS
CLASSZONE.COM

CONNECT TO GEOGRAPHY

1. **Place** What fort was built where the Columbia River empties into the Pacific Ocean?
2. **Location** In what mountain range did the Shoshone tribe live?

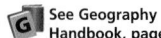

See Geography Handbook, page 4.

CONNECT TO HISTORY

3. **Forming Opinions** What do you think the Native Americans that Lewis and Clark met thought about the explorers?

CRITICAL THINKING ACTIVITY

Forming and Supporting Opinions Ask students to make a graphic like the one below. Then have them read the information about the Shoshone, Oto, Mandan, and Teton Sioux and complete the chart. Have students use the information on the chart to decide how important they think Native Americans were to the success of the Lewis and Clark expedition. Have students give reasons for their opinions.

Native Americans	Response to Lewis and Clark Expedition
Shoshone	
Oto	
Mandan	
Teton Sioux	

Class Time 15 minutes

MORE ABOUT . . .

The Mandan

Lewis and Clark met the Mandan when the expedition crossed the Great Plains in 1804. The Mandan made their home in large, fenced-in villages of earthen lodges along the upper Missouri River. They were one of the first Plains tribes to come into frequent contact with whites. French trappers had visited and traded with them as early as the mid-1700s. In the 1830s, American artist George Catlin and Swiss painter Karl Bodmer made paintings of these early farmers of the Plains, recording their vibrant culture and way of life shortly before they were almost completely wiped out by smallpox.

CONNECT TO GEOGRAPHY

1. **Place** Fort Clatstop
2. **Location** the Rocky Mountains

CONNECT TO HISTORY

3. **Forming Opinions** They had different reactions. Some tribes, like the Mandan, were friendly. Others, like the Teton Sioux, were hostile.

SECTION OBJECTIVES

1. To describe foreign policy challenges that Jefferson faced
2. To describe how Tecumseh attempted to unify Native American peoples
3. To explain why many Americans were War Hawks

SKILLBUILDER
Interpreting Charts, p. 313

CRITICAL THINKING
Analyzing Causes, p. 311
Recognizing Effects, p. 312
Forming Opinions, p. 312
Analyzing Points of View, p. 313

FOCUS & MOTIVATE

5-MINUTE WARM-UP

Drawing Conclusions These questions focus on problems with Britain in the early 1800s.

1. Study the picture on page 311 and read the caption. Where is this kidnapping taking place? Who are the kidnappers?
2. How might Jefferson respond to this hostile action?

Warm-Up Transparency WT10

INSTRUCT

INSTRUCT: OBJECTIVE 1
Jefferson's Foreign Policy

- Why did Jefferson advise against "entangling alliances"?
- Why was the United States likely to have conflicts with other nations?

In-Depth Resources: Unit 3
• Guided Reading, p. 23

Reading Study Guide (Spanish and English), pp. 99–100

3 Problems with Foreign Powers

TERMS & NAMES
impressment
Embargo Act of 1807
Tecumseh
War Hawk

MAIN IDEA	WHY IT MATTERS NOW
Jefferson tried to avoid involvement in the problems of other nations.	British interference with the affairs of the United States led to the War of 1812.

ONE AMERICAN'S STORY

In 1804, U.S. Navy Lieutenant Stephen Decatur was on a daring mission overseas. The United States was at war with Tripoli, a state on the North African coast. The war, which began in 1801, was the result of repeated attacks on American merchant ships by African pirates. Decatur's mission was to destroy the U.S. warship *Philadelphia*—which had been captured by Tripoli—so that it could not be used by the enemy.

Decatur bravely sailed into Tripoli's harbor and set fire to the *Philadelphia.* He then managed to escape under enemy fire with only one man wounded. Decatur later issued this rallying cry for all Americans.

A VOICE FROM THE PAST

Our country! In her [relationships] with foreign nations may she always be in the right; but our country, right or wrong.

Stephen Decatur, 1816

Stephen Decatur struggles in hand-to-hand combat with African pirates.

Decatur's attack was one of the most celebrated events of the war, which ended in 1805. The conflict showed how hard it was for the United States to stay out of foreign affairs while its citizens participated so heavily in overseas trade. In this section, you will learn how President Jefferson handled problems with other nations.

1 Jefferson's Foreign Policy

When Thomas Jefferson took office in 1801, he expected to concentrate on domestic concerns. In his inaugural address, he happily noted that America was "kindly separated by nature and a wide ocean from the exterminating havoc [wars] of one quarter of the globe." Jefferson advised the United States to seek the friendship of all nations, but to enter into "entangling alliances with none."

However, the president's desire to keep the United States separated from other nations and their problems was doomed to fail. For one thing, American merchants were busily engaged in trade all over the world. For

RECOMMENDED RESOURCES

In-Depth Resources: Unit 3
• Guided Reading, p. 23
• Building Vocabulary, p. 25
• Skillbuilder Practice, p. 26
• Primary Source: A Plea for Native American Unity, p. 29

Reading Study Guide (Spanish and English), pp. 99–100

Formal Assessment
• Section Quiz, p. 186

Integrated Assessment
• Rubrics, 1.3, 3.3

Access for Students Acquiring English/ESL
• Guided Reading, p. 65
• Skillbuilder Practice, p. 67

INTEGRATED TECHNOLOGY
Electronic Teacher Tools
classzone.com

TEST-TAKING RESOURCES
Strategies for Test Preparation
Test Practice Transparencies, TT36
Online Test Practice

another, the Louisiana Purchase and the Lewis and Clark expedition were about to open the country to westward expansion. Expansion would bring Americans into closer contact with people from other nations who had already established settlements in the West.

Finally, the United States had little control over the actions of foreign nations—as North African interference with U.S. shipping had shown. Staying out of the ongoing conflict between France and England would be just as difficult.

Reading **History**
A. Analyzing Causes Why was it hard for the United States to avoid other nations' problems?
A. Possible Responses because of the overseas involvement of U.S. merchants, westward expansion, and lack of control over the actions of foreign nations

2 Problems with France and England

For a long time, the United States managed not to get involved in the European wars that followed the French Revolution. At times, the nation even benefited from the conflict. Busy with affairs in Europe, France sold the Louisiana Territory to the United States. And American shippers eagerly took over the trade interrupted by the war.

By 1805, however, the British began to clamp down on U.S. shipping. They did not want Americans to provide their enemies with food and supplies. After the United States threatened to take action, the British decided to set up a partial blockade. This would only allow some American ships to bring provisions to Europe.

This partial blockade angered France, which enacted its own laws to control foreign shipping. These changes put American merchants in a difficult position. If they obeyed the British rules, their ships could be seized by the French. If they obeyed the French rules, their ships could be seized by the British.

Britain also interfered with U.S. trade by the **impressment,** or kidnapping, of American sailors to work on British ships. Between 1803 and 1812, the British impressed about 6,000 American sailors.

One of the most famous incidents occurred in 1807. The British ship *Leopard* attacked an American naval ship, the *Chesapeake,* off the coast of Virginia. Three Americans lost their lives in the battle. The attack aroused widespread anger. Had Congress been in session, America might have declared war. But Jefferson, who had been re-elected in 1804, decided against it. One critic, furious at the president's caution, called Jefferson a "dish of skim milk curdling at the head of our nation."

Trade as a Weapon

Instead of declaring war, Jefferson asked Congress to pass legislation that would stop all foreign trade. "Peaceable coercion," as the president described his policy, would prevent further bloodshed.

Vocabulary
coercion: the practice of forcing someone to act in a certain way by use of pressure or threats

British officers seize an American sailor at gunpoint.

311

INSTRUCT: OBJECTIVE 2

Problems with France and England/ Trade as a Weapon

- What caused conflict between the United States and Britain and France?
- Why did Americans call for war against Britain?
- How did both Jefferson and Madison try to use trade as a weapon against Britain and France? Were they successful?

MORE ABOUT . . .

Impressment

When Britain impressed sailors from American ships, it claimed to take only British subjects, ignoring the fact that many native-born Britons had become naturalized American citizens. Britain adopted its policy of impressment to fill its great need for sailors in the Royal Navy, the largest navy in the world. Few men chose to enlist in the Royal Navy, and many that did enlist deserted. Many British subjects, including some deserters, preferred to work on American merchant ships, rather than on ships of the Royal Navy. Conditions on American vessels were much better than on British ships.

ACTIVITY OPTIONS

INDIVIDUAL NEEDS

STUDENTS ACQUIRING ENGLISH/ESL

Understanding Key Concepts To help students understand the concept of *foreign policy,* write the word *foreign* on the board and define it as "of, from, or having to do with other countries." Then write the phrases *foreign nations* and *foreign policy* on the board. Explain that foreign nations are countries other than one's own, and that foreign policy is the way a government deals with other nations or countries. Ask students to name some of the foreign nations the U.S. government had contact with and some of the problems that resulted.

Extend the discussion by comparing *foreign policy* to *domestic policy.* Point out the statement on page 310, "When Thomas Jefferson took office in 1801, he expected to concentrate on domestic concerns." Help students to see that domestic concerns are those of one's own country. Encourage a discussion about current foreign policies and domestic issues.

INSTRUCT: OBJECTIVE

Tecumseh and Native American Unity 3

- What did Tecumseh hope to achieve by uniting Native Americans?
- What was Tecumseh's response to the Treaty of Fort Wayne?
- How did the Battle of Tippecanoe affect Tecumseh's hopes for unity?

MORE ABOUT . . .

Tecumseh

Tecumseh continues to be one of the most honored Native American leaders. He is revered not only for his gifts as a statesman and a fighter but also for his oratory, his patriotism, and love of his people. In a letter to Sir Isaac Brock, dated August 14, 1812, Tecumseh reflected bitterly on the white man's treatment of his people: "We gave them forest-clad mountains and valleys full of game, and in return what did they give our warriors and our women? Rum, trinkets, and a grave."

In-Depth Resources: Unit 3
- Primary Source: A Plea for Native American Unity by Tecumseh, p. 29

CRITICAL THINKING ACTIVITY

Drawing Conclusions Have students examine Tecumseh's actions. What did he hope to achieve? Why did defeat at Tippecanoe make it more difficult to unite groups of Native Americans? If Native Americans had united, could they have stopped the loss of land? Why or why not?

Class Time 10 minutes

In December, Congress passed the **Embargo Act of 1807**. Now American ships were no longer allowed to sail to foreign ports. The act also closed American ports to British ships.

Jefferson's policy was a disaster. It was more harmful to the United States than to the British and French. American farmers and merchants were especially hard hit. Southern and Western farmers, for example, lost important markets for their grain, cotton, and tobacco. Shippers lost income, and many chose to violate the embargo by making false claims about where they were going. One New Englander said the embargo was like "cutting one's throat to cure the nosebleed."

The embargo became a major issue in the election of 1808. Jefferson's old friend James Madison won the election. By the time he took office, Congress had already repealed the embargo.

Madison's solution to the problem was a law that allowed merchants to trade with any country except France and Britain. Trade with these countries would start again when they agreed to respect U.S. ships. But this law proved no more effective than the embargo.

*Reading*History

B. Recognizing Effects What were the results of the Embargo Act?

B. Possible Response It was damaging to U.S. trade because farmers and merchants lost important markets.

The Shawnee chief Tecumseh led Native American resistance to white rule in the Ohio River Valley.

Tecumseh and Native American Unity 3

British interference with American shipping and impressment of U.S. citizens made Americans furious. They also were angered by Britain's actions in the Northwest. Many settlers believed that the British were stirring up Native American resistance to frontier settlements.

Since the Battle of Fallen Timbers in 1794 (see page 283), Native Americans continued to lose their land. Thousands of white settlers had swarmed into Ohio and then into Indiana.

Tecumseh, a Shawnee chief, vowed to stop the loss of Native American land. He believed that the reason Native Americans continued to lose their land was because they were separated into many different tribes. He concluded that Native Americans had to do what white Americans had done: unite. Events in 1809 proved him right.

That September, William Henry Harrison, governor of the Indiana Territory, signed the Treaty of Fort Wayne with chiefs of the Miami, Delaware, and Potawatomi tribes. They agreed to sell over three million acres of land. But Tecumseh declared the treaty meaningless.

C. Possible Response He believed that land could be sold only when all, not just some, Native Americans gave permission.

*Reading*History

C. Forming Opinions Why did Tecumseh declare the Treaty of Fort Wayne meaningless?

A VOICE FROM THE PAST

[Whites] have taken upon themselves to say this [land] belongs to the Miamis, this to the Delawares and so on. But the Great Spirit intended [Native American land] to be the common property of all the tribes, [and it cannot] be sold without the consent of all.

Tecumseh, quoted in *Tecumseh and the Quest for Indian Leadership*

After the Treaty of Fort Wayne, many Native Americans began to answer Tecumseh's call for unity. But his efforts ultimately failed. In November 1811, while Tecumseh was away recruiting tribes for his alliance, the Shawnee were defeated by Harrison's forces at the Battle of

ACTIVITY OPTIONS

SKILLBUILDER LESSON: ANALYZING CAUSES — BLOCK SCHEDULING

Explaining the Skill When historians analyze events, they not only consider when, where, and how an event happened but they also think about why it occurred. In analyzing causes, it is important to look for the reasons behind an event. Words or phrases such as *because, due to, since,* and *therefore* often indicate cause.

Applying the Skill Direct students to the subsection War Hawks on page 313. Ask these questions:

1. How did Americans react to the British decision to aid Tecumseh? *(This aid fueled anti-British feelings.)*
2. What cause of the war does this reaction suggest? *(American anger over British support of Native Americans)*
3. What clue word in paragraph 3 suggests other causes of the war? *(because)* What causes does it suggest? *(British violations of American rights at sea)*

In-Depth Resources: Unit 3
- Skillbuilder Practice, p. 26

Tippecanoe. It was a severe setback for Tecumseh's movement.

4 War Hawks

After the battle of Tippecanoe, Tecumseh and his warriors found a warm welcome with the British in Canada. At that point, the Native Americans and the British became allies. Tecumseh's welcome in Canada raised even higher the anti-British feelings in the West.

Leaders such as Congressman Henry Clay of Kentucky angrily demanded war against Britain. Westerners who called for war were known as **War Hawks**. They wanted British aid to Native Americans stopped, and they wanted the British out of Canada. Conquering Canada would open up a vast new empire for Americans.

Vocabulary
hawk: a person who favors the use of military force to carry out foreign policy

Other Americans sought war because of the British violations of American rights at sea. Future president Andrew Jackson said hostilities were necessary "for the protection of our maritime citizens impressed on board British ships of war," and to "open a market for the productions of our soil."

Urged on by Jackson and the War Hawks, Congress declared war on Britain on June 18, 1812. In the next section, you will read about the second—and final—war between the United States and Great Britain.

Causes of the War of 1812

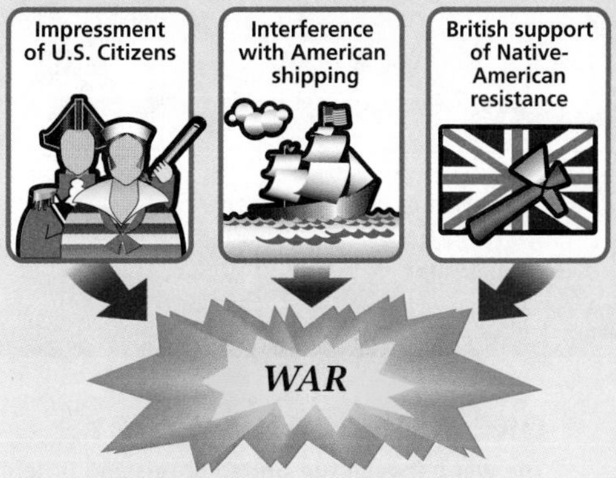

SKILLBUILDER **Interpreting Charts**
Which cause of the War of 1812 was not related to activities on the sea?

Skillbuilder Answer
British support of Native American resistance

Section 3 Assessment

1. Terms & Names

Explain the significance of:
- impressment
- Embargo Act of 1807
- Tecumseh
- War Hawk

2. Taking Notes

Use a chart like the one below to record the effects of Jefferson's Embargo Act.

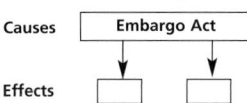

Causes → Embargo Act
Effects → [ ] [ ]

Why didn't the act work?

3. Main Ideas

a. How did the British and French interfere with American shipping?

b. How did Jefferson respond to the interference?

c. Why did the War Hawks favor war?

4. Critical Thinking

Analyzing Points of View
Why did Tecumseh think it was important for Native Americans to unite?

THINK ABOUT
- what he learned about white men
- what Native Americans would lose if they did not act together

ACTIVITY OPTIONS

ART
SPEECH

Do research on the Battle of Tippecanoe. Draw a **comic strip story** of the battle or hold a **press conference** to describe the battle's outcome.

INSTRUCT: OBJECTIVE 4

War Hawks

- Why did War Hawks favor war?
- What were other reasons for war against Britain?
- When did Congress declare war on Britain?

HISTORY FROM VISUALS

Interpreting the Chart Ask students why they think trade issues and interference with American shipping were so important to the United States at this time. Which cause of war had American leaders tried to resolve peacefully? **Answer** Foreign trade was an important part of the American economy. The Embargo Act was Jefferson's attempt at a peaceful solution to the problems of impressment and interference with American shipping.

Extension Have students research the reasons why the War of 1812 is sometimes called the Second War for American Independence.

ASSESS & RETEACH

Setting the Stage Have students fill in the third section on the chapter graphic organizer.

Formal Assessment
- Section Quiz, p. 186

RETEACHING ACTIVITY

Have students write one or two questions for each of the main topics in the section. Ask pairs of students to take turns answering each other's questions and then work together to verify the answers.

In-Depth Resources: Unit 3
- Reteaching Activity, p. 36

Section 3 Assessment

1. Terms & Names

impressment, p. 311
Embargo Act of 1807, p. 312
Tecumseh, p. 312
War Hawk, p. 313

2. Taking Notes

Effects: Lost markets hurt farmers; merchants lost sources of income.

The act hurt the economy of the United States more than the European economies that it targeted.

3. Main Ideas

a. They blockaded and seized U.S. ships and kidnapped American sailors. **b.** He got Congress to pass the Embargo Act of 1807, which stopped all foreign trade. **c.** War was the best way to stop British interference with U.S. shipping and support of Native American resistance.

4. Critical Thinking

because without joining together, they would not be able to prevent the loss of their land

ACTIVITY OPTIONS

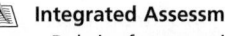

Integrated Assessment
- Rubrics for a comic strip, 1.3
- Rubrics for a press conference, 3.3

SECTION OBJECTIVES

1. To analyze the beginning of the War of 1812
2. To describe the battles of the first phase of the war
3. To describe the fighting in the second phase of the war
4. To evaluate the effects of the war and its legacy

SKILLBUILDER
Interpreting Maps: Location, Movement, p. 315
Interpreting Charts, p. 317

CRITICAL THINKING
Drawing Conclusions, p. 316
Making Inferences, p. 317
Recognizing Effects, p. 317

FOCUS & MOTIVATE

5-MINUTE WARM-UP

Reading a Map These questions focus on battles of the War of 1812.

1. Study the map on page 315. Which battles were fought on water?
2. Which bodies of water were blockaded by the British? How could a successful blockade hurt the American war effort?

Warm-Up Transparency WT10

INSTRUCT

INSTRUCT: OBJECTIVE 1

The War Begins

- Why did Britain try to avoid war? What steps did it take to avoid war?
- What were the two main phases of the war?

In-Depth Resources: Unit 3
- Guided Reading, p. 24
- Primary Source, p. 30

Reading Study Guide (Spanish and English), pp. 101–102

4 The War of 1812

TERMS & NAMES
Oliver Hazard Perry
Battle of the Thames
Francis Scott Key
Treaty of Ghent

MAIN IDEA	WHY IT MATTERS NOW
Angered by Britain's interference in the nation's affairs, the United States went to war.	The War of 1812 showed that the United States was willing and able to protect its national interests.

ONE AMERICAN'S STORY

The war between the United States and Britain had begun in 1812. Two years later, British troops were marching toward Washington, D.C. Dolley Madison, the president's wife, stayed behind until the last minute. With bombs bursting in the distance, she hurried to save important historical objects from the White House.

A VOICE FROM THE PAST

I have had [a wagon] filled with . . . the most valuable portable articles belonging to the house. . . . I insist on waiting until the large picture of General Washington is secured . . . It is done! and the precious portrait placed in the hands of two gentlemen of New York, for safe keeping.

Dolley Madison, from a letter sent to her sister

When the British troops arrived in the city, they set fire to many public buildings, including the White House and the Capitol. The next day, a violent storm caused even more damage. Fortunately, the heavy rains that accompanied the storm helped put out the fires. You will learn about other events of the War of 1812 in this section.

Before British troops set fire to the president's mansion, Dolley Madison saved priceless historical objects.

1 The War Begins

Britain did not really want a war with the United States because it was already involved in another war with France. To try to avoid war, the British announced that they would no longer interfere with American shipping. But the slow mails of the day prevented this news from reaching the United States until weeks after June 18th, when Congress approved Madison's request for a declaration of war.

The War of 1812 had two main phases. From 1812 to 1814, Britain concentrated on its war against France. It devoted little energy to the conflict in North America, although it did send ships to blockade the American coast. The second phase of the war began after the British defeated France in April 1814. With their European war nearly at an end, the British could turn their complete attention to the United States.

RECOMMENDED RESOURCES

In-Depth Resources: Unit 3
- Guided Reading, p. 24
- Building Vocabulary, p. 25
- Primary Source: from *Memoirs and Letters of Dolley Madison,* p. 30
- History Workshop, p. 39

Reading Study Guide (Spanish and English), pp. 101–102

Economics in History
- The Economic Impact of the War of 1812, p. 10

Formal Assessment
- Section Quiz, p. 187

Integrated Assessment
- Rubrics, 1.10, 4.8

Access for Students Acquiring English/ESL, p. 66

INTEGRATED TECHNOLOGY

Critical Thinking Trans. CT29
- Cause and Effect: The War of 1812

Humanities Transparency HT20
- *Constitution and Guerriere*

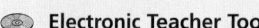

Electronic Teacher Tools

classzone.com

TEST-TAKING RESOURCES

Strategies for Test Preparation

Test Practice Transparencies, TT37

Online Test Practice

The United States military was weak when the war was declared. Democratic-Republicans had reduced the size of the armed forces. When the war began, the Navy had only about 16 ships. The army had fewer than 7,000 men. These men were poorly trained and equipped, and were often led by inexperienced officers. A young Virginia army officer complained that the older officers were victims of "sloth, ignorance, or habits of [excessive] drinking."

2 The First Phase of the War

In spite of its small size, the United States Navy rose to the challenge. Its warships were the fastest afloat. American naval officers had gained valuable experience fighting pirates in the Mediterranean Sea. Early in the war, before the British blockaded the coast, ships such as the *Constitution* and the *United States* won stirring victories. These victories on the high seas boosted American confidence.

The most important U.S. naval victory took place on Lake Erie. In the winter of 1812–1813, the Americans had begun to build a fleet on the shores of Lake Erie. **Oliver Hazard Perry,** an experienced officer, took charge of this infant fleet. In September 1813, the small British force on the lake set out to attack the American ships. Commodore Perry, who had predicted that this would be "the most important day of my life," sailed out to meet the enemy. Perry's ship, the *Lawrence,* flew a banner declaring, "Don't give up the ship."

Skillbuilder Answers
1. in Baltimore, Maryland; near the Chesapeake Bay
2. the Battle of the Thames River

The War of 1812

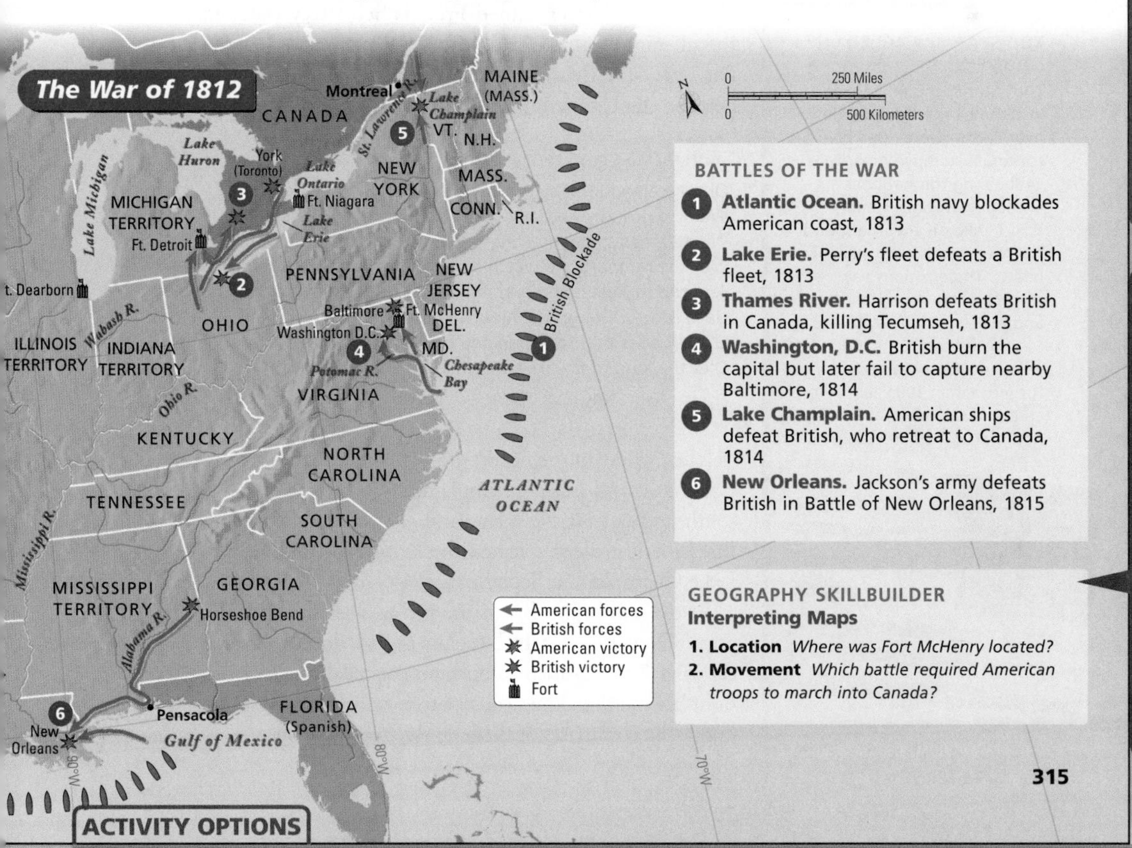

BATTLES OF THE WAR

1. **Atlantic Ocean.** British navy blockades American coast, 1813
2. **Lake Erie.** Perry's fleet defeats a British fleet, 1813
3. **Thames River.** Harrison defeats British in Canada, killing Tecumseh, 1813
4. **Washington, D.C.** British burn the capital but later fail to capture nearby Baltimore, 1814
5. **Lake Champlain.** American ships defeat British, who retreat to Canada, 1814
6. **New Orleans.** Jackson's army defeats British in Battle of New Orleans, 1815

GEOGRAPHY SKILLBUILDER
Interpreting Maps
1. **Location** *Where was Fort McHenry located?*
2. **Movement** *Which battle required American troops to march into Canada?*

315

INSTRUCT: OBJECTIVE 2

The First Phase of the War

- What were the strengths of the U.S. Navy?
- Where did the most important U.S. naval victory take place?
- What were two results of the victory on the Thames River?

MORE ABOUT . . .

Oliver Hazard Perry

Perry continued his message to Harrison with the details of his victory: "We have met the enemy and they are ours—two ships, two brigs, one schooner, and one sloop." He was only 28 years old at the time. Perry came from a family with a strong naval heritage on his father's side. He became a midshipman at the age of 13 and sailed under his father's command to the Caribbean. His career was cut short when he died from yellow fever at the age of 34.

HISTORY FROM VISUALS

Reading the Map After the students have studied the map, ask if they can think of reasons why so many battles took place along the U.S. border. **Possible Response** Canada was controlled by the British, who wanted to keep Americans out of Canada. Then ask students why they think the British wanted to capture New Orleans. **Answer** It was a major port for the United States and would enable the British to control shipping on the Mississippi.

Extension Have students choose one of the battles listed on the map and research the reasons for victory by either the Americans or the British.

ACTIVITY OPTIONS

INDIVIDUAL NEEDS

LESS PROFICIENT READERS

Previewing As a way to preview the chapter "The War of 1812" and to provide students with a strategy for reading, ask them to read the headings and turn each heading into a question. For example, students may formulate questions such as:
- Why did the war begin? When did the war begin?
- What happened in the first phase of the war? Who was successful in the first phase of the war?
- What happened in the second phase of the war?
- What was the legacy of the war? What were the effects of the war in the United States?

Encourage students to look for answers to their questions as they read each section.

INSTRUCT: OBJECTIVE 3

The Second Phase of the War

- What inspired Francis Scott Key to write "The Star-Spangled Banner"?
- What was the outcome of the Battle of Lake Champlain?
- Why was the Battle of New Orleans unnecessary?

Humanities Transparency HT20
• *Constitution and Guerriere*

America's HERITAGE

The Star-Spangled Banner

The national anthem was first published anonymously as a poem with the title "Defence of Fort M'Henry" in the *Baltimore Patriot.* It was soon set to the tune of an English drinking song and quickly gained widespread popularity. The army and navy used it as the national anthem before Congress officially adopted it in 1931. Composer and bandmaster John Philip Sousa prepared the official arrangement of the song. Since Americans and the British have become friends and allies, the second and third verses of the anthem are not usually sung.

CRITICAL THINKING ACTIVITY

Making Inferences Have students make inferences about how the personal fortunes of Andrew Jackson and the history of the United States might have been different if the Battle of New Orleans had not been fought.

Class Time 10 minutes

For two hours, the British and Americans exchanged cannon shots. Perry's ship was demolished and the guns put out of action. He grabbed his ship's banner and leaped into a rowboat. Under British fire, he and four companions rowed to another ship. In command of the second ship, Perry destroyed two of the enemy's ships and soon forced the British to surrender. After the battle, Perry sent a message to General Harrison: "We have met the enemy and they are ours."

"Don't give up the ship."
Banner on Perry's ship, the *Lawrence*

When General Harrison received Perry's note, he set out to attack the British. But when Harrison transported his army across Lake Erie to Detroit, he discovered that the British had retreated into Canada. Harrison pursued the British forces and defeated them at the **Battle of the Thames** in October. This victory put an end to the British threat to the Northwest—and also claimed the life of Tecumseh, who died in the battle fighting for the British.

Reading **History**
A. Drawing Conclusions What was the overall result of the Battle of the Thames?
A. Possible Response The victory put an end to the British threat from the Northwest.

3 The Second Phase of the War

After defeating Napoleon in April 1814, Britain turned its full attention to the United States. As you read in One American's Story, British forces burned the Capitol building and the president's mansion in August. The British then attacked Fort McHenry at Baltimore.

The commander of Fort McHenry had earlier requested a flag "so large that the British will have no difficulty in seeing it." Detained on a British ship, a Washington lawyer named **Francis Scott Key** watched the all-night battle. At dawn, Key discovered that the flag was still flying. He expressed his pride in what became the U.S. national anthem.

America's HERITAGE

THE STAR-SPANGLED BANNER

The "Star-Spangled Banner," inspired by the flag that flew over Fort McHenry (see below), continues to move Americans. On hearing this national anthem, patriotic listeners stand, take off their hats, and put their hands over their hearts. These actions pay respect to the American flag and the song that celebrates it.

Francis Scott Key's song enjoyed widespread popularity for more than 100 years before an act of Congress made it the national anthem in 1931.

A VOICE FROM THE PAST

Oh say can you see by the dawn's early light
What so proudly we hail'd at the twilight's last gleaming,
Whose broad stripes and bright stars through the perilous fight
O'er the ramparts we watch'd were so gallantly streaming?
And the rockets' red glare, the bombs bursting in air,
Gave proof through the night that our flag was still there.
Oh, say does that star-spangled banner yet wave
O'er the land of the free and the home of the brave?

Francis Scott Key, *Star-Spangled Banner*

Meanwhile, in the north, the British sent a force from Canada across Lake Champlain. Its goal was to push south and cut off New England. The plan failed when the American fleet defeated the British in the Battle of Lake Champlain in September 1814.

In the south, the British moved against the strategic port of New Orleans. In December 1814, dozens of ships carrying 7,500 British troops approached Louisiana. To fight them, the Americans patched together an army under the command of General Andrew Jackson.

Reading **History**
B. Reading a Map Locate the battles of the second phase of the war on the map on page 315. Note how far apart the sites were.

ACTIVITY OPTIONS

INTERDISCIPLINARY LINK: HUMANITIES — BLOCK SCHEDULING

NATIONAL ANTHEMS

Class Time 30 minutes

Task Analyzing primary sources

Purpose To compare and contrast two patriotic songs

Supplies Needed
- Lyrics of the "Star-Spangled Banner" and "America the Beautiful"
- Recordings of both songs

Activity Make copies of the lyrics for both the "Star-Spangled Banner" and "America the Beautiful" and distribute them to the class. Play each song as students read the lyrics. Ask students what they think is the purpose of a national anthem. Then ask what makes each song patriotic. Tell students that "America the Beautiful" has often been proposed as a substitute for the "Star-Spangled Banner" as the national anthem. Have volunteers tell which song they prefer and why. Then have the class vote on which song they would rather have as their national anthem.

***Reading* History**

C. Making Inferences Why did Jackson fight the British at New Orleans after a peace treaty was signed?

C. Possible Response because slow mails delayed news of the treaty

The British attacked Jackson's forces on January 8, 1815. Protected by earthworks, American riflemen mowed down the advancing redcoats. It was a great victory for Jackson. American casualties totaled 71, compared to Britain's 2,000. Though the Battle of New Orleans made Jackson a hero, it was unnecessary. Slow mails from Europe had delayed news of the **Treaty of Ghent,** which ended the War of 1812. It had been signed two weeks earlier, on December 24, 1814.

4 The Legacy of the War

The treaty showed that the war had no clear winner. No territory changed hands, and trade disputes were left unresolved. Still, the war had important consequences. First, the heroic exploits of men such as Andrew Jackson and Oliver Perry increased American patriotism. Second, the war broke the strength of Native Americans, who had sided with the British. Finally, when war interrupted trade, the Americans were forced to make many of the goods they had previously imported. This encouraged the growth of U.S. manufactures.

The United States had also proved that it could defend itself against the mightiest military power of the era. For perhaps the first time, Americans believed that the young nation would survive and prosper. You will learn about the country's growing prosperity in Chapter 11.

Skillbuilder Answer U.S. manufacturing grew.

The Effects of the War

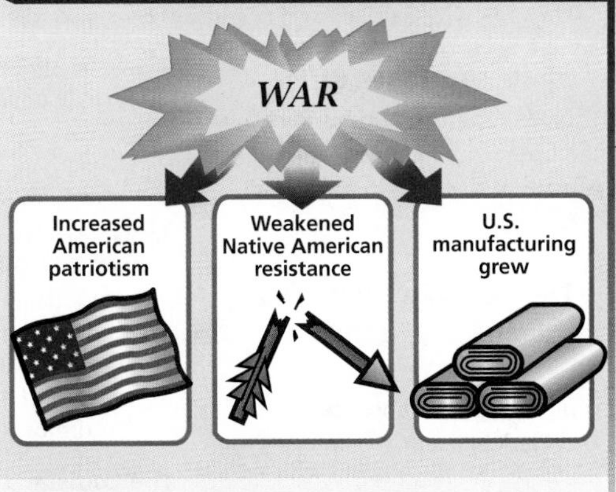

SKILLBUILDER Interpreting Charts
Which effect do you think resulted from the war's interruption of U.S. trade?

Section 4 Assessment

1. Terms & Names

Explain the significance of:
- Oliver Hazard Perry
- Battle of the Thames
- Francis Scott Key
- Treaty of Ghent

2. Taking Notes

Use a chart like the one shown to record military events of the War of 1812.

First Phase of War	Second Phase of War
1.	2.

Why was the war divided into two phases?

3. Main Ideas

a. What was the state of the U.S. military when the war began?

b. What were the results of General Harrison's victory at the Battle of the Thames?

c. Where did the British focus their attacks during the second phase of the war?

4. Critical Thinking

Recognizing Effects What was the legacy of the War of 1812?

THINK ABOUT
- Americans' feelings toward their country
- U.S. relations with Native Americans
- possible economic effects

ACTIVITY OPTIONS

LANGUAGE ARTS
ART

Research the U.S.S. *Constitution.* Write a **poem** to commemorate one of its victories or design a **model** to show its parts.

INSTRUCT: OBJECTIVE 4

The Legacy of the War

- How did the Treaty of Ghent show that the war had no clear winner?
- What were three consequences of the war?
- How did the American victory increase optimism abut the future of the nation?

Economics in History
- The Economic Impact of the War of 1812, p.10

HISTORY FROM VISUALS

Interpreting the Chart Have students identify specific causes for each of these effects. How did the war increase American patriotism? Why did it weaken Native American resistance? How did it help U.S. manufacturing grow? **Answers** Americans felt more pride in their country and its leaders. It made Tecumseh's drive to unite Native Americans more difficult. It forced Americans to buy homemade goods instead of imports.

Extension Have students find out which U.S. industries were helped by the war.

Critical Thinking Transparency CT29
- Cause and Effect: The War of 1812

ASSESS & RETEACH

Setting the Stage Have students fill in the last section on the chapter graphic organizer.

Formal Assessment
- Section Quiz, p. 187

Critical Thinking Transparency CT28
- Setting the Stage

RETEACHING ACTIVITY

Have students create a time line for the years 1812–1815, showing major events of the war and its aftermath. Have students write two or three sentences explaining their effects.

In-Depth Resources: Unit 3
- Reteaching Activity, p. 37

Section 4 Assessment

1. Terms & Names

Oliver Hazard Perry, p. 315
Battle of the Thames, p. 316
Francis Scott Key, p. 316
Treaty of Ghent, p. 317

2. Taking Notes

First Phase: American victories on high seas; Perry defeats British fleet on Lake Erie; Second Phase: British fail to capture Baltimore; American fleet defeats British fleet on Lake Champlain; because the British were also involved in a war with France

3. Main Ideas

a. Poor; the navy had only 16 ships, and the army was small, poorly trained, and led by inexperienced officers. **b.** The victory ended the British threat to the Northwest. Tecumseh was killed. **c.** in the Chesapeake Bay area; near Lake Champlain; and in New Orleans

4. Critical Thinking

It increased American patriotism, weakened Native American resistance, and encouraged the growth of American manufactures.

ACTIVITY OPTIONS

Integrated Assessment
- Rubrics for a poem, 4.8
- Rubrics for a model, 1.10

TERMS & NAMES

1. ***Marbury* v. *Madison*,** p. 301
2. **judicial review,** p. 301
3. **Louisiana Purchase,** p. 303
4. **Lewis and Clark expedition,** p. 304
5. **impressment,** p. 311
6. **Embargo Act of 1807,** p. 312
7. **Tecumseh,** p. 312
8. **War Hawk,** p. 313
9. **Oliver Hazard Perry,** p. 315
10. **Treaty of Ghent,** p. 317

REVIEW QUESTIONS

Possible Responses

1. The Federalists thought the nation was about to be ruined by radicals, and the Democratic-Republicans believed they were saving the country from monarchy and oppression.
2. He believed that the United States should be a democracy of small independent farmers.
3. from the East coast to the territory between the Mississippi River and the Rocky Mountains
4. traveling against strong currents in the Missouri River; stopping for the winter; going around the Great Falls; crossing the Rocky Mountains.
5. He and his men strayed into Spanish territory and were arrested.
6. global activity of American merchants; westward expansion; actions of foreign nations were unpredictable
7. by unifying Native Americans
8. impressment of U.S. citizens; interference with U.S. shipping; British support of Native American resistance
9. Battle of the Thames
10. the British defeat of France in April 1814

Chapter 10 ASSESSMENT

VISUAL SUMMARY

The Jefferson Era

Jefferson Takes Office

Thomas Jefferson and his party, the Democratic-Republicans, win control of the government from the Federalists.

The Louisiana Purchase and Exploration

After Jefferson purchases Louisiana from France, Lewis and Clark are sent to explore the new American territory.

Problems with Foreign Powers

Other countries' interference makes it difficult for Jefferson to stay out of foreign affairs.

The War of 1812

When Britain continues to interfere in American affairs, the two nations battle in the War of 1812.

TERMS & NAMES

Briefly explain the significance of each of the following:

1. *Marbury* v. *Madison*
2. judicial review
3. Louisiana Purchase
4. Lewis and Clark expedition
5. impressment
6. Embargo Act of 1807
7. Tecumseh
8. War Hawk
9. Oliver Hazard Perry
10. Treaty of Ghent

REVIEW QUESTIONS

Jefferson Takes Office (pages 297–301)

1. What were the main parties in the election of 1800, and how did their views differ?
2. How did Jefferson envision the future of America?

The Louisiana Purchase and Exploration (pages 302–309)

3. What was the extent of U.S. territory after the Louisiana Purchase?
4. What difficulties did Lewis and Clark face on their expedition?
5. What troubles did Zebulon Pike have on his 1806-1807 trip?

Problems with Foreign Powers (pages 310–313)

6. Why did Jefferson have difficulty staying out of foreign affairs?
7. How did Tecumseh intend to prevent the loss of Native American land?
8. What were some of the causes of the War of 1812?

The War of 1812 (pages 314–317)

9. Which battle ended the British threat to the U.S. Northwest?
10. What event preceded the second phase of the war?

CRITICAL THINKING

1. USING YOUR NOTES

Using your completed chart, answer the questions below.

The Jefferson Era
Summaries
Main Idea: Thomas Jefferson is elected president. **Details:** Jefferson replaces Federalist policies with his own but has problems with the judiciary.
Main Idea: **Details:**
Main Idea: **Details:**
Main Idea: **Details:**

a. What were the major events of the Jefferson era?

b. Based on these events, how would you describe the characteristics of the era?

2. ANALYZING LEADERSHIP

How do you think Thomas Jefferson's behavior as president might have affected the way future presidents viewed the office?

3. THEME: EXPANSION

How did the expansion of the United States affect its foreign policy?

4. RECOGNIZING PROPAGANDA

Before elections, supporters of different candidates sometimes make outrageous claims. How was the election of 1800 an example of this?

5. APPLYING CITIZENSHIP SKILLS

In what ways did Jefferson's behavior as president reflect his idea of good citizenship?

Interact *with* History

How did the dangers you predicted before you read the chapter compare to those experienced by people on expeditions west?

CRITICAL THINKING

Possible Responses

1. USING YOUR NOTES **a.** 1800—Jefferson elected president; 1803—Louisiana Purchase; 1812—U.S. goes to war against Britain. **b.** The United States expands its claims to the west and solidifies its independence from Britain.
2. ANALYZING LEADERSHIP Responses should include Jefferson's refusal to elevate himself because of his office and how this idea became a model for leaders of democracies.
3. THEME: EXPANSION Expansion brought America into closer contact with other nations who already had establishments in parts of the West.
4. RECOGNIZING PROPAGANDA The campaign of 1800 was fought with nasty personal attacks. One individual said a Jefferson victory would result in a "nation black with crimes."
5. APPLYING CITIZENSHIP SKILLS Jefferson behaved more like a gentleman farmer than a "privileged politician." He refused to elevate himself above other people because of his office.

Interact *with* History Answers will vary, but students should recall the dangers of the expeditions that are shown throughout the chapter.

HISTORY SKILLS

1. INTERPRETING GRAPHS

Study the graph. Answer the questions.

Foreign Trade, *1800–1812*

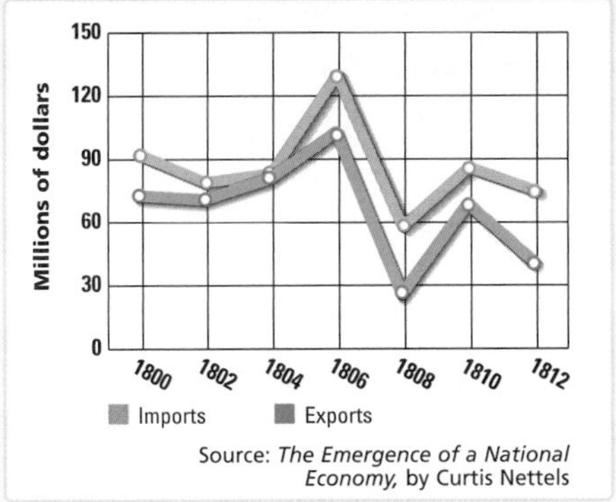

Source: *The Emergence of a National Economy,* by Curtis Nettels

Basic Graph Elements

a. What do the numbers on the left side of the chart indicate?

Interpreting the Graph

b. In what years did the value of U.S. trade decrease dramatically?

c. What was the value of exports in 1806? in 1808?

2. INTERPRETING PRIMARY SOURCES

Examine the cartoon below, which comments on the United States trade policies you read about in Section 3.

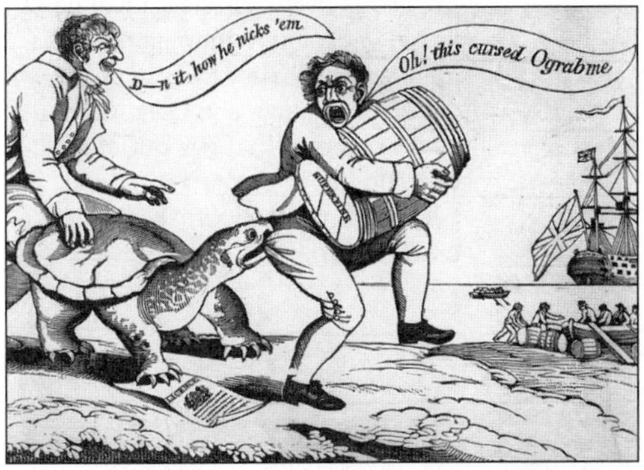

a. What does *Ograbme* spell when written backwards?

b. What other clues tell you that this cartoon is about the embargo against Great Britain?

ALTERNATIVE ASSESSMENT

1. INTERDISCIPLINARY ACTIVITY: Geography

Making an Outline Make an outline of Section 2 of this chapter using the format from page R7. Review your outline with a partner. Organize and interpret the information from both outlines and write a report about the Louisiana Purchase and the Lewis and Clark expedition.

2. COOPERATIVE LEARNING ACTIVITY

Designing a Plan for Economic Action Form a group that will develop a plan to end British interference with U.S. shipping. Select a leader for your group. Then pick one member of your group to represent farmers, another to represent shippers, and another to speak for those who are demanding war. Discuss the interests of all these groups and then write down your policy statement and present it to the class. Use standard grammar, spelling, sentence structure, and punctuation in your policy statement. Be sure to consider:

- the superior power of the British Navy
- where the farmers will sell their products
- how the shippers will earn their money

3. TECHNOLOGY ACTIVITY

Creating a Multimedia Presentation Use the Internet, books, and other reference materials to create a multimedia presentation on one of the major battles of the War of 1812. Consider including the following:

- paintings or written descriptions of the battle
- pictures of the weapons that were used
- music from the time period
- recorded sound effects
- graphs showing battle statistics

For more about the War of 1812 . . .

INTERNET ACTIVITY
CLASSZONE.COM

4. HISTORY PORTFOLIO

Identify the dates that you consider to be the Jefferson Era. Then identify previous eras in American history and place them all in chronological sequence on a time line. Add your time line to your portfolio.

Additional Test Practice, pp. S1–S33

TEST PRACTICE
CLASSZONE.COM

ALTERNATIVE ASSESSMENT

1. INTERDISCIPLINARY ACTIVITY: **Geography**
   Outlines should
   - be organized logically.
   - be reviewed carefully.
   - be interpreted accurately.
   - provide a basis for a well-organized report.

2. COOPERATIVE LEARNING ACTIVITY
   Plans should
   - support positions with evidence or logic.
   - respond to each other's statements.
   - be acceptable to at least two of the parties.

3. TECHNOLOGY ACTIVITY
   Presentations should
   - utilize two or more media.
   - clearly present accurate information about a battle.
   - present information about both sides in the battle.
   - show technical proficiency.

4. HISTORY PORTFOLIO
   Timelines should
   - be organized chronologically.
   - include Jefferson Era and previous eras.
   - be presented neatly.

Critical Thinking Transparency CT30
- Visual Summary

Formal Assessment
- Chapter Test, Forms A, B, and C, pp. 188–199

HISTORY SKILLS

Possible Responses

1. INTERPRETING GRAPHS
   Basic Graph Elements
   a. the value of imports and exports in millions of dollars

   Interpreting the Graph
   b. 1806–1808
   c. about $100 million; about $30 million

2. INTERPRETING PRIMARY SOURCES
   a. embargo
   b. The man is taking his goods to a British ship anchored in the distance.

HISTORY WORKSHOP

OBJECTIVE

Students create a journal of field notes and then write a paragraph comparing their field notes with those of Lewis and Clark.

BLOCK SCHEDULING

PROCEDURE

Have students assemble the materials listed in the "Toolbox." Divide the class into groups of three or four. Then review the steps for assigning tasks within the group, making a journal, and putting the journal together. Have students make notes in their journal as they explore the neighborhood, using the Lewis and Clark journal as a model. Make sure students include a map of their neighborhood walk in their journal.

In-Depth Resources: Unit 3
- History Workshop Resources, p. 39

MORE ABOUT . . .

Instructions from Jefferson

President Jefferson gave Lewis explicit directions about his observations. He told Lewis "your observations are to be taken with great pains and accuracy, to be entered distinctly and intelligibly for others as well as yourself, to comprehend."

HISTORY FROM VISUALS

Interpreting the Field Notes of Lewis and Clark

Ask students why they think the authors of these notes drew such detailed pictures and took so many notes. **Possible Responses** Lewis and Clark knew that they were acting as the "eyes" of many scientists and scholars. They knew that the information they recorded would be of immeasurable assistance to the explorers, scientists, and settlers who would follow them.

Making Explorers' Field Notes

On their expedition in the early 1800s, Lewis and Clark filled their journals with field notes—detailed observations and scientific illustrations of the land, plants, and wildlife they saw. Lewis made drawings of plants and animals. Clark drew detailed maps. For many years, their journals were the main source of information about the West.

ACTIVITY Create a journal of field notes that includes illustrations of plants, animals, and terrain found in your neighborhood. Then write a comparison article between your field notes and those of Lewis and Clark.

TOOLBOX

Each group will need:

drawing paper	ruler
poster board for covers	string
pencil and pen	hole punch and hole reinforcers
scissors	

STEP BY STEP

1 **Form groups.** Each group should consist of 3 to 4 students. The members of your group will do the following tasks:
- design and create a handmade journal
- take a walk in your neighborhood and record observations as field notes
- compare the field notes you have created with those of Lewis and Clark

2 **Make your journal.** Your group will need a journal to make field notes on the nature walk. Each page of the journal should be six inches wide and roughly eight inches long, approximately the size of the one used by Lewis and Clark. Cut 10–15 sheets of that size out of the drawing paper. Create a front and back cover for the journal using the poster board.

The scientific and artistic skills of Lewis and Clark made their journals both accurate and beautiful.

RECOMMENDED RESOURCES

JOURNALS AND BOOKS FOR THE TEACHER

Duncan, Dayton and Ken Burns. ***Lewis & Clark.*** New York: Knopf, 1997.

Fisher, Ron. "Lewis and Clark" ***National Geographic.*** Washington: National Geographic Society, October 1998.

VIDEO

Gone West: The Growth of a Nation. United Learning, 1998. Looks at the Lewis and Clark expedition and the Louisiana Purchase through the use of animated maps and period art.

INTERNET

For more about Lewis and Clark . . .

RESEARCH LINKS
CLASSZONE.COM

BOOKS FOR THE STUDENTS

Calvert, Patricia. ***Great Lives: The American Frontier.*** New York: Atheneum, 1997.

Freedman, Russell. ***An Indian Winter.*** New York: Holiday House, 1992.

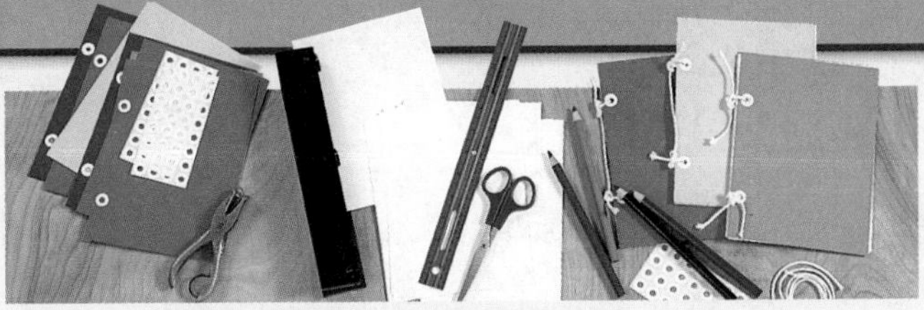

3 **Put your journal together.** Punch three holes in the left side of the pages, including the covers. Place hole reinforcers around the holes to ensure that the pages won't tear. Bind the pages and the covers together with string.

4 **Explore your neighborhood.** Take a walk in your neighborhood, in the area around your school, or in a nearby woods. You might want to divide the tasks of observing, drawing, describing, and mapping among the members of the group.

5 **Model your field notes on those of Lewis and Clark.** In their journals, Lewis and Clark included drawings of animals and plants, as well as detailed observations about them. Remember to draw the plants, insects, and animals as if you have never seen them before.

6 **Make a map of your route.** In addition to the drawings, create a map of your walk. Include any interesting landmarks as well as a detailed description of the terrain. Remember to sketch the route as if it's unexplored territory.

WRITE AND SPEAK

Write and present a paper that compares and contrasts Lewis and Clark's journal with the one your group has completed. Also, explain how your journal might help someone who has just moved to your school or neighborhood.

HELP DESK

For related information, see pages 304–309 in Chapter 10.

Researching Your Project

- You can find copies of Lewis and Clark's journals in many libraries.
- *Undaunted Courage* by Stephen Ambrose gives a fascinating account of the expedition.

For more about Lewis and Clark . . .

RESEARCH LINKS
CLASSZONE.COM

Did You Know?

- The Corps of Discovery sent Jefferson six live specimens of animals, including a prairie dog.
- At one point, the men on the expedition consumed nine pounds of buffalo meat a day.
- Swarms of mosquitoes plagued the expedition. The explorers often found it impossible to eat without inhaling some of the pesky insects.
- Clark estimated that the expedition traveled 4,162 miles. His guess was only 40 miles off the actual distance.

REFLECT & ASSESS

- What process did your group use to observe, draw, and describe your route?
- How did you decide what information to include in your journal?
- How important are the illustrations to understanding the area in which your group took its walk?

MORE ABOUT . . .

Myths About the West

The field notes of Lewis and Clark and the journals of the Corps of Discovery helped dispel many myths about the West. The most widely held myth was the belief that there was a northwest passage, or all-water route, to the Pacific.

MORE ABOUT . . .

Exploration Today

Today scientists, mapmakers, and explorers have not only still cameras, tape recorders, and video cameras but also computers, global positioning satellites, and many other high-tech tools to help them make accurate field notes.

REFLECT & ASSESS

1. Students can make a diagram showing the sequence of steps in the process of observing, drawing, and describing or recording information about their route.
2. Students can explain what they considered to be the goals of the journal writing and what types of information helped them meet these goals.
3. Students may want to pick out one of their illustrations and talk specifically about what it added to their knowledge of the area.

STANDARDS FOR EVALUATION

HISTORY WORKSHOP

Field Notes should

- demonstrate an attempt at careful observation.
- contain a detailed drawing of the plants, animals, or objects identified.
- use the written description that accompanies each drawing to add information about the drawing.
- be simple, clear, and readable.

WRITE AND SPEAK

Comparison should

- clearly state the purpose of the comparison.
- describe the ways the journals are alike and different.

CHAPTER 11 PLANNING GUIDE

National And Regional Growth 1800–1844

	CHAPTER OVERVIEW	COPYMASTERS	INTEGRATED TECHNOLOGY
CHAPTER RESOURCES	The chapter describes the early years of the Industrial Revolution in the North and the cotton boom and spread of slavery in the South. It also discusses the increase in sectionalism and efforts to resolve the conflict over slavery with the Missouri Compromise.	**In-Depth Resources: Unit 3** • Tracing Themes: Science and Technology, p. 41 • Building Vocabulary, p. 45 **Interdisciplinary Projects,** pp. 61–66	• eEdition Plus Online • EasyPlanner Plus Online • eTest Plus Online • eEdition • Power Presentations • EasyPlanner • Electronic Library of Primary Sources • Test Generator • Reading Study Guide • America's Music
	KEY IDEAS		
SECTION 1 **Early Industry and Inventions** **pp. 325–331**	• The Industrial Revolution begins in New England using water-powered factories. • The new factories employ men, women, and often children as well. • Technological breakthroughs improve manufacturing, travel, communication, and agriculture.	**In-Depth Resources: Unit 3** • Setting the Stage, p. 40 • Guided Reading, p. 42 • Primary Source, p. 49 • Literature Selection, pp. 51–53 • Reteaching Activity, p. 54	**Warm-Up Transparency WT11** **Humanities Transparency HT21** • New England Textile Mill **Critical Thinking Transparency CT31** • Setting the Stage **Critical Thinking Transparency CT32** • Cause and Effect: Industrial Revolution **classzone.com**
SECTION 2 **Plantations and Slavery Spread** **pp. 332–337**	• The invention of the cotton gin makes cotton "king" of the Southern economy. • The spread of cotton farming leads to an expansion of slavery. • Enslaved African Americans find strength in family life and religion, and they continue to resist enslavement.	**In-Depth Resources: Unit 3** • Setting the Stage, p. 40 • Guided Reading, p. 43 • Geography Application, pp. 47–48 • Primary Source, p. 50 • Reteaching Activity, p. 55 **America's History Makers** • Eli Whitney, pp. 43–44 • Frederick Douglass, pp. 45–46 **Economics in History,** p. 11	**Warm-Up Transparency WT11** **Humanities Transparency HT22** • A Cotton Plantation **Critical Thinking Transparency CT31** • Setting the Stage **classzone.com**
SECTION 3 **Nationalism and Sectionalism** **pp. 338–345**	• The American System, new transportation links, and several Supreme Court decisions promote national unity. • The Missouri Compromise preserves the balance of power. • The Monroe Doctrine announces that the Americas are closed to further European colonization.	**In-Depth Resources: Unit 3** • Setting the Stage, p. 40 • Guided Reading, p. 44 • Skillbuilder Practice, p. 46 • Reteaching Activity, p. 56 **Citizenship Today,** pp. 87–88 **Why It Matters Now** • Expanding Economies, pp. 21–22 **Outline Map Activities** • Economic Expansion, 1841, pp. 21–22	**Warm-Up Transparency WT11** **Geography Transparency GT11** • Railroads Extend Westward, 1850–1860 **Critical Thinking Transparency CT33** • Visual Summary **Primary Source Explorer** • *The Monroe Doctrine* **classzone.com**

Pupil's Edition | Overhead Transparency | CD-ROM
Copymaster | Audio Library | Internet

ASSESSMENT OPTIONS

- **Chapter Assessment,** pp. 346–347
- **Formal Assessment**
  - Chapter Tests, Forms A, B, and C, pp. 203–217
- **Test Generator**
- **Online Test Practice**
- **Strategies for Test Preparation**

- **Section Assessment,** p. 329
- **Formal Assessment,** Quiz, p. 200
- **Integrated Assessment Book**
  - Rubrics, 3.6, 2.3
- **Test Generator**
- **Test Practice Transparencies,** TT38

- **Section Assessment,** p. 337
- **Formal Assessment,** Quiz, p. 201
- **Integrated Assessment Book**
  - Rubrics, 4.7, 3.6
- **Test Generator**
- **Test Practice Transparencies,** TT39

- **Section Assessment,** p. 343
- **Formal Assessment,** Quiz, p. 202
- **Integrated Assessment Book**
  - Rubrics, 4.1, 1.2
- **Test Generator**
- **Test Practice Transparencies,** TT40

CUSTOMIZING FOR INDIVIDUAL NEEDS

Students Acquiring English/ESL

- **Reading Study Guide** (English and Spanish), pp. 105–112
- **Access for Students Acquiring English/ESL:** Spanish Translations, pp. 70–75
- **Chapter Summaries on CD** (English and Spanish)
- **Modified Lesson Plans for English Learners**

Less Proficient Readers

- **Reading Study Guide** (English and Spanish), pp. 105–112
- **Chapter Summaries on CD** (English and Spanish)

Gifted and Talented Students

- **In-Depth Resources: Unit 3**
  - Enrichment Activity, p. 57
- **America's History Makers**
  - Eli Whitney, pp. 43–44
  - Frederick Douglass, pp. 45–46

CROSS-CURRICULAR CONNECTIONS

Economics

Macaulay, David. ***Mill.*** Boston: Houghton Mifflin, 1983. Detailed drawings illustrate the story of the growth of a Massachusetts mill.

Primary Sources

Deitch, JoAnne W. ***The Lowell Mill Girls: Life in the Factory.*** Carlisle, MA: Discovery Enterprises, 1998. Plentiful primary sources give this account a fine ring of authenticity.

Science

Spangenburg, Ray, and Diane K. Moser. ***The Story of America's Canals.*** New York: Facts on File, 1992. Part of the series called Connecting a Continent, informative, illustrated, and packed with time lines and charts.

Interdisciplinary Projects, pp. 61–66
- Math: Encoding and Decoding Messages
- Science: Scientific Inquiry
- Language Arts: Describing a Place
- Music: Spirituals

Literature

Aiken, Joan. ***Midnight Is a Place.*** New York: Viking, 1974. A brilliant novel about child labor in the Industrial Revolution, set in England.

DeFelice, Cynthia. ***The Apprenticeship of Lucas Whitaker.*** New York: Avon, 1998. Engrossing and sometimes gruesome story about the scourge of tuberculosis in the mid-19th century.

Paterson, Katherine. ***Lyddie.*** New York: Lodestar, 1991. Three years in the life of a Vermont farm girl who goes to work in Lowell.

McDougal Littell Literature Connections

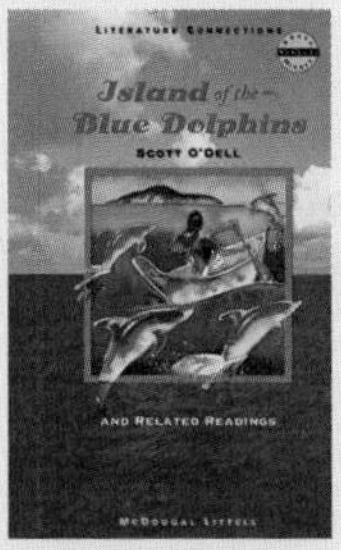

Scott O'Dell
Island of the Blue Dolphins
In this classic novel set in the early 1800s, Karana, a Native American girl, survives 18 years alone on an island off the coast of southern California.

ENRICHMENT ACTIVITIES

- **Pupil's Edition, pp. 322–347**
  Interact with History, p. 323
  Interdisciplinary Challenge, pp. 330–331
  Interactive Primary Source, pp. 344–345

- **In-Depth Resources: Unit 3**
  - Geography Application: The Internal Slave Movement After 1810, pp. 47–48
  - Primary Source: from *Loom and Spindle,* p. 49
  - Primary Source: Wes Brady Describes His Life Under Slavery, p. 50
  - Literature Selection: from *The Clock,* pp. 51–53

- **America's History Makers**
  - Eli Whitney, pp. 43–44
  - Frederick Douglass, pp. 45–46
- **America's Music CD**
- **Outline Map Activities**
  - Economic Expansion, 1841, pp. 21–22
- **Primary Source Explorer**
  - *The Monroe Doctrine*
- **Why It Matters Now**
  - Expanding Economies, pp. 21–22

BLOCK SCHEDULING — LESSON PLAN OPTIONS (90-MINUTE PERIOD)

DAY 1

Interact with History, p. 323
Class Time 20 Minutes

Options for pacing and variety:
- **Peer Teaching** Divide the class into small groups. Have students speculate on how each of the four inventions shown in the Interact with History illustration is likely to change how Americans live. Have groups share their opinions with the class. **Class Time** 15 minutes

Setting the Stage, p. 324
Class Time 20 minutes

Options for pacing and variety:
- **Time Saver** Ask students to come to class with a list of questions to ask people from different regions about their lives in preparation for discussion of "What Do You Want to Know?" **Class Time** 5 minutes

Section 1, pp. 325–331
Class Time 50 minutes

Options for pacing and variety:
- **Peer Teaching** Have students work in small groups to make up three questions: one about an invention, one about an inventor, and one about the effects of an invention. Collect the questions, group them by category, and have a "Jeopardy" quiz bowl. **Class Time** 30 minutes

DAY 2

Interdisciplinary Challenge, pp. 330–331
Class Time 55 minutes

Options for pacing and variety:
- **Team Teaching** Invite a math teacher to your class to coach student groups as they solve the Math Challenge on page 331. **Class Time** 55 minutes

Section 2, pp. 332–337
Class Time 45 minutes

Options for pacing and variety:
- **History on Film** Extend students' knowledge of slavery by viewing *Slavery: America's Peculiar Institution.* The film describes the family life, education, and living conditions of slaves in the South. Zenger Media **Class Time** 30 minutes
- **Time Saver** For a homework assignment, have students complete the Taking Notes and Critical Thinking exercises in the Section Assessment. **Class Time** 15 minutes

Section 3, pp. 338–345
Class Time 50 minutes

Chapter 11 Assessment, pp. 346–347
Class Time 40 minutes

Options for pacing and variety:
- **Peer Evaluation** Have students work in groups to discuss the Interact with History and Critical Thinking questions, page 346. Have groups pick the question they found most interesting and share their response with the class. **Class Time** 20 minutes
- **Peer Teaching** Divide students into small groups. Tell them to study the chart on page 346 and create a different way to present the information to the class. **Class Time** 30 minutes

TEACHER-TESTED ACTIVITY Kelly Ellis, Hamilton Junior High School, Cypress, Texas

ERIE CANAL POSTCARDS

Class Time 30 minutes

Task Creating a postcard featuring the Erie Canal

Purpose To summarize information about the Erie Canal

Supplies Needed
- Illustrated reference materials and Internet sources on the Erie Canal
- Markers or colored pencils
- Posterboard cut into 6" x 8" rectangles

Activity Have each student create a two-sided postcard of the Erie Canal. On the front side, they should draw a picture or diagram of the canal. On the back, they can compose a caption explaining the picture. Then have them use the card to write a message to a friend or relative describing cities along the canal, how the canal operates, types of boats and goods that travel on the canal, or its economic impact on the region. Remind students to include a place for an address and a stamp.

BUILDING AN ELECTRONIC WEB ON THE IMPACT OF TECHNOLOGY

Making a web that connects related concepts can help students understand historical change. In this activity, students will build an electronic web that shows the impact of new technologies introduced during the first half of the 19th century.

ACTIVITY OUTLINE

Objective Creating an electronic web that shows the impact of new technologies on U.S. history will help students understand technological change.

Task This activity can be done with any software program that has the capability to create lines, circles, and text. One way to conduct this activity is to create a document that is stored on a shared classroom network. If a group document is available for classroom-wide access, one person may have to act as a document director to create and name the initial document. This same person can monitor the document's progress and its contents to make sure lines and circles are properly connected. Students can contribute ideas, make connections, or change connections. The web-building process can proceed over several days, while other class activities are going on.

Class Time One to three class periods, intermittently

DIRECTIONS

1. Have students begin by reviewing Chapter 11 of *Creating America.* They should focus on the new technologies of the time, such as canals, the steam engine, cotton gin, and other inventions. Remind students that they will also be trying to establish cause-and-effect connections between these new technologies and their impact on the country.

2. Ask two students to create a file to receive entries for the web. The file can be a blank word processing page, preferably with a landscape layout. The word processor should have the capability to draw circles or ovals, draw connecting lines, and put text into the circles. These students should periodically check the web, make back-up copies, adjust connecting lines, or help solve any technical problems.

3. When the file has been created, students can enter their ideas into the web. If working on a network with access to the shared space, students can enter their ideas over several days or perhaps even from home.

4. Remind students that creating a web in this manner will require them to respect other people's ideas. Tips for making entries to the class web include:
   - Be conscious of the space, adjusting the size of circles and lines to the size of the page.
   - Enter a circle with a word in it and connect it with a line to another circle, or leave it unconnected.
   - Do not erase or delete anyone else's ideas.
   - Do not enter inappropriate words or words that are disrespectful of others.

5. Allow students time over a few class periods to complete the class web. Announce to the class the final time limit for entering ideas into the web. You may want to periodically check the file and print out the web in its various stages.

CHAPTER 11 OBJECTIVE
The student will analyze the ways in which new machines changed American society, encouraged the expansion of slavery, and contributed to both nationalism and sectionalism in the first half of the 1800s.

CHAPTER 11

National and Regional Growth

1800–1844

Section 1 **Early Industry and Inventions**
Section 2 **Plantations and Slavery Spread**
Section 3 **Nationalism and Sectionalism**

HISTORY FROM VISUALS

Interpreting the Painting Have students study the painting, which shows a barge on the Erie Canal. Students may not realize that the canal boat is propelled by mule power. Point out the mules at the lower left. A rope connects them to the boat.

Ask students what they observe about the land and activity along the canal. **Possible Responses** The canal cuts a path through farmland. Crops grow in nearby fields, and farmers tend livestock.

Ask students to keep this scene in mind as they read about the changes that canals and other innovations helped bring about in the United States during the early 1800s.

Extension Ask students to identify major transportation routes and centers (water, air, or land) in their state and explain how they are important to local people and businesses.

The Erie Canal, which opened in 1825, increased western trade and migration.

322

CRITICAL THINKING ACTIVITY

Making Inferences Ask students why canals were preferred routes for transporting farm produce and manufactured goods in the early 1800s. What other ways might goods have been transported to markets in those days? If students do not understand the advantages of water transportation, explain that two or three mules could not move such a heavy load overland; moving heavy goods by water takes much less power.

Class Time 10 minutes

RECOMMENDED RESOURCES

BOOKS FOR THE TEACHER

Cunningham, Noble E., Jr. ***The Presidency of James Monroe.*** Lawrence, KA: Univ. Press of Kansas, 1996. A balanced view of a diligent and influential, but rather uncharismatic, president.

Eisler, Benita. ***The Lowell Offering: Writings by New England Mill Women (1840–1845).*** New York: Norton, 1997. Extraordinary collection of women's writings on laundry, love, food, hope, and work.

Tucker, Barbara M. ***Samuel Slater and the Origins of the American Textile Industry, 1790–1860.*** Ithaca, NY: Cornell Univ. Press, 1984. How an early case of industrial espionage jump-started the U.S. textile industry.

VIDEO

Indians of North America: The Seminole. GPN, 1994. History, culture, and the modern situation.

INTERNET

For more about the Lowell Mills or inventions made by women, visit . . .

classzone.com

Interact *with* History

This Currier and Ives print, *Progress of the Century,* shows some inventions of the 1800s.

From 1790 to 1840, you have seen an explosion of new inventions. These include the cotton gin, the steamboat, the steel plow, and the telegraph. You have also seen neighbors leave their farms to run machines in new factories. You sense that the country is changing.

What Do You Think?

- **What would it mean to be able to grow more grain and cotton?**
- **What would it mean to communicate and travel more quickly?**
- **How might it feel to do factory work instead of farm work?**

How will new inventions change your country?

USA

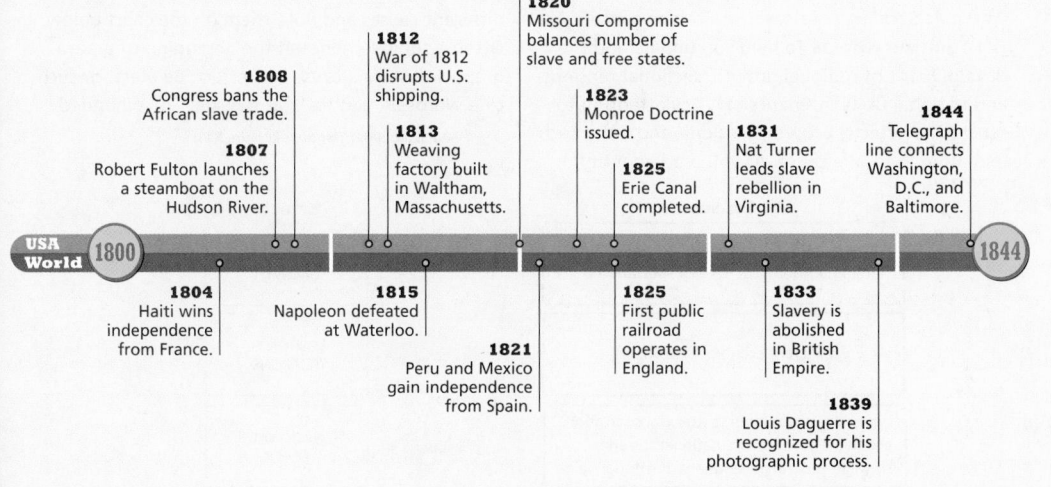

- **1807** Robert Fulton launches a steamboat on the Hudson River.
- **1808** Congress bans the African slave trade.
- **1812** War of 1812 disrupts U.S. shipping.
- **1813** Weaving factory built in Waltham, Massachusetts.
- **1820** Missouri Compromise balances number of slave and free states.
- **1823** Monroe Doctrine issued.
- **1825** Erie Canal completed.
- **1831** Nat Turner leads slave rebellion in Virginia.
- **1844** Telegraph line connects Washington, D.C., and Baltimore.

1800 — 1844

World

- **1804** Haiti wins independence from France.
- **1815** Napoleon defeated at Waterloo.
- **1821** Peru and Mexico gain independence from Spain.
- **1825** First public railroad operates in England.
- **1833** Slavery is abolished in British Empire.
- **1839** Louis Daguerre is recognized for his photographic process.

Interact *with* History

OBJECTIVES

- To identify some important inventions from the period between 1790 and 1840
- To describe how such inventions affected people's lives and businesses

What Do You Think?

1. Ask students to identify the uses of grain and cotton.
2. Ask students how long they think it would take to travel to a nearby town by horseback or wagon. How often might people make such a trip?
3. Have students describe the kinds of things they think farmers and factory workers do during a typical workday. Ask them to consider which kind of work changes more from week to week and which worker has more independence.

How will new inventions change your country?

Suggest that students consider how modern technologies, such as computers and the Internet, are changing life in the United States today.

MAKING PERSONAL CONNECTIONS

Ask students to consider how they might be affected if travel to places far from home were slow or dangerous or if communication with friends and family members who live far away were difficult.

TIME LINE DISCUSSION

In this chapter, issues such as new links between various regions of the nation, challenges to slavery, and relationships with other nations are changing American society.

- Ask students to identify events that probably made it easier to communicate and travel over long distances. **Answer** 1807, Fulton's steamboat; 1825, Erie Canal and first public railroad; 1844, telegraph line
- Ask students to identify events involving slavery. **Answer** 1808, Congress banned African slave trade; 1820, Missouri Compromise; 1831, Turner's rebellion; 1833, slavery abolished in British Empire
- Identify which events occurring in the world might worry Americans and why. **Answer** 1821, independence in Mexico because United States shared a border; 1833, slavery abolished in British Empire because American slaves might want freedom too

BEFORE YOU READ

Previewing the Theme:
Science and Technology
Ask students to explain the links between these inventions and economic growth. Students may note that inventions allowed faster travel or communication and led to increased production.

What Do You Know?

Students may note that today—because of television and other forms of mass communication, national chains of restaurants and stores, and urbanization—fewer differences exist among regions in the United States. However, in the 1800s, regional differences were much more pronounced. People identified themselves more in terms of region than nation. Point out that differing perspectives and personal experiences often influence people's opinions on an issue.

In-Depth Resources: Unit 3
- Tracing Themes: Science and Technology, p. 41

READ AND TAKE NOTES

Reading Strategy: Analyzing Causes and Recognizing Effects
Tell students that analyzing causes and effects in the chapter will help them relate events to one another. Point out the chart on page 340. Help students understand that their purpose for reading this chapter is to identify the causes that brought about regional growth, sectional tensions, and national unity.

In-Depth Resources: Unit 3
- Setting the Stage, p. 40

Critical Thinking Transparency CT31
- Setting the Stage

Chapter 11 SETTING THE STAGE

BEFORE YOU READ

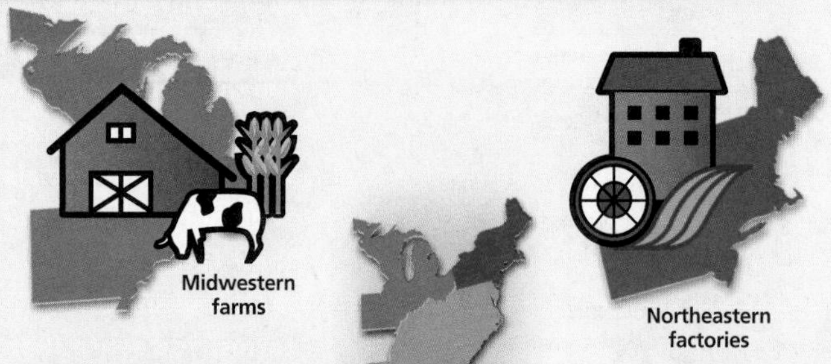

Previewing the Theme
Science and Technology
In this chapter, you will learn how new inventions helped regions of the country grow in the 1800s and also helped pull regions together as a nation. For example, the power loom made the Northeast a cloth manufacturing center. The cotton gin turned the South into a Cotton Kingdom. The telegraph let people communicate instantly across regions.

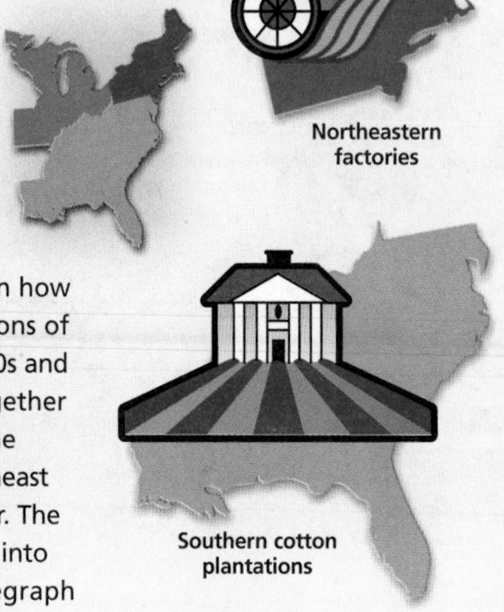

What Do You Know?
What connects you to someone who lives in the same region? When have you felt a bond with someone from a different region?

THINK ABOUT
- the activities of people in different regions
- the things that unite people as a nation

What Do You Want to Know?
What would you ask people from different regions—a factory worker, wheat farmer, plantation owner, or field slave—about their lives in the 1800s? Write these questions in your notebook. Read to see if they are answered in Chapter 11.

READ AND TAKE NOTES

Reading Strategy: Analyzing Causes and Recognizing Effects To help you understand the development of regional growth, sectional tensions, and national unity in Chapter 11, pay attention to causes and effects. Growth, tensions, and unity each had more than one cause. As you read, identify different causes and note them on the chart below. Often a topic sentence at the beginning of a paragraph will state a cause and effect. Be alert for such clue words as "led to," "as a result," or "changed."

See Skillbuilder Handbook, page R11.

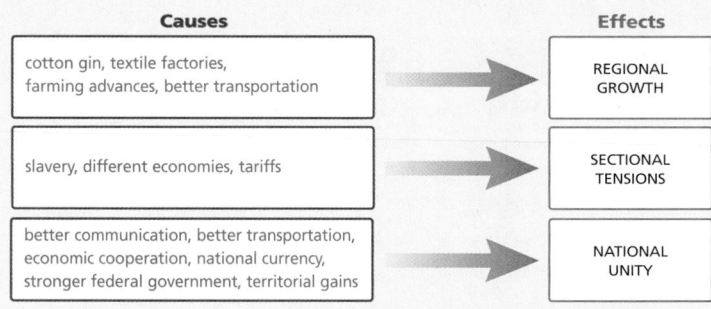

Causes		Effects
cotton gin, textile factories, farming advances, better transportation	→	REGIONAL GROWTH
slavery, different economies, tariffs	→	SECTIONAL TENSIONS
better communication, better transportation, economic cooperation, national currency, stronger federal government, territorial gains	→	NATIONAL UNITY

TEACHING STRATEGY

READING THE CHAPTER
This is a thematic chapter focusing on early industries and inventions that led to national and regional growth. Encourage students to look for cause-and-effect relationships as they read the chapter. Pause after each section to review key events and their impact on the nation or on a particular region.

ALTERNATIVE ASSESSMENT
The Chapter Assessment describes three activities for alternative assessment on page 347. You may wish to have students work on these activities during the course of the chapter and then present them at the end.

1 Early Industry and Inventions

TERMS & NAMES
Samuel Slater
Industrial Revolution
factory system
Lowell mills
interchangeable parts
Robert Fulton
Samuel F. B. Morse

MAIN IDEA	WHY IT MATTERS NOW
New machines and factories changed the way people lived and worked in the late 1700s and early 1800s.	The industrial development that began more than 200 years ago continues today.

ONE AMERICAN'S STORY

In 1789, the Englishman Samuel Slater sailed to the United States under a false name. It was illegal for textile workers like him to leave the country. Britain wanted no other nation to copy its new machines for making thread and cloth. But Slater was going to bring the secret to America. When he got to New York, he wrote a letter to Rhode Island investor Moses Brown.

A VOICE FROM THE PAST

A few days ago I was informed that you wanted a manager of *cotton spinning* . . . in which business I flatter myself that I can give the greatest satisfaction, in making machinery, making good yarn, either for *stockings* or *twist,* as any that is made in England.

Samuel Slater, quoted in *Samuel Slater: Father of American Manufactures*

Samuel Slater's mill was located in Pawtucket, Rhode Island.

With Brown's backing, Slater built the first successful water-powered textile mill in America. You will learn in Section 1 how the development of industries changed the ways Americans lived and worked.

1 Free Enterprise and Factories

The War of 1812 brought great economic changes to the United States. It sowed the seeds for an Industrial Revolution like the one begun in Britain during the late 18th century. During the **Industrial Revolution,** factory machines replaced hand tools, and large-scale manufacturing replaced farming as the main form of work. For example, before the Industrial Revolution, women spun thread and wove cloth at home using spinning wheels and hand looms. The invention of such machines as the spinning jenny and the power loom made it possible for unskilled workers to produce cloth. These workers, who were often children, could produce more cloth, more quickly.

The **factory system** brought many workers and machines together under one roof. Most factories were built near a source of water to power the machines. People left their farms and crowded into cities where the

SECTION OBJECTIVES

1. To explain how the Industrial Revolution began
2. To describe the role of the factory system and interchangeable parts
3. To identify inventions that improved transportation and communication
4. To explain increased farm production

CRITICAL THINKING
Recognizing Effects, pp. 326, 328, 329
Contrasting, p. 327

FOCUS & MOTIVATE

5-MINUTE WARM-UP

Making Generalizations Answering these questions will help students understand the way new machines changed textile production.

1. Look at the illustration on page 327. Why would operating this factory require the efforts of many workers?
2. How do you think this factory could pay for itself over time?

Warm-Up Transparency WT11

INSTRUCT

INSTRUCT: OBJECTIVE 1

Free Enterprise and Factories/ Factories Come to New England

- How did the Industrial Revolution change the way people worked?
- Why was New England a good place to set up factories?

In-Depth Resources: Unit 3
- Guided Reading, p. 42

Reading Study Guide (Spanish and English), pp. 105–106

Critical Thinking Transparency CT32
- Cause and Effect: Industrial Revolution

RECOMMENDED RESOURCES

In-Depth Resources: Unit 3
- Guided Reading, p. 42
- Building Vocabulary, p. 45
- Primary Source: from *Loom and Spindle,* p. 49
- Literature Selection, pp. 51–53

Reading Study Guide (Spanish and English), pp. 105–106

Formal Assessment
- Section Quiz, p. 200

Integrated Assessment
- Rubrics, 3.6, 2.3

Access for Students Acquiring English/ESL
- Guided Reading, p. 70

INTEGRATED TECHNOLOGY

Humanities Transparency HT21
- New England Textile Mill

Critical Thinking Trans. CT32
- Cause and Effect: Industrial Revolution

Electronic Teacher Tools

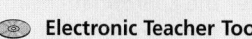

classzone.com

TEST-TAKING RESOURCES

Strategies for Test Preparation

Test Practice Transparencies, TT38

Online Test Practice

CRITICAL THINKING ACTIVITY

Comparing and Contrasting Have students use a two-column chart to contrast Samuel Slater's mill system with Francis Cabot Lowell's mill system. The charts should note the origins of the machinery designs as well as the work performed and source of employees at the different mills.

Class Time 20 minutes

Slater's Mills	Lowell's Mills
children or families as workers	young women as workers
machinery copied from English	power looms copied from English
spinning mill	cotton to yarn wove cloth

Humanities Transparency HT21
- New England Textile Mill

INSTRUCT: OBJECTIVE 2

The Lowell Mills Hire Women/ A New Way to Manufacture

- How did the Lowell mills change the textile industry in the United States?
- How did interchangeable parts change industry and management?

In-Depth Resources: Unit 3
- Literature Selection: from *The Clock* by James Lincoln Collier and Christopher Collier, pp. 51–53

factories were. They worked for wages, on a set schedule. Their way of life changed, and not always for the better.

Many Americans did not want the United States to industrialize. But the War of 1812 led the country in that direction. Because the British naval blockade kept imported goods from reaching U.S. shores, Americans had to start manufacturing their own goods. The blockade also stopped investors from spending money on shipping and trade. Instead, they invested in new American industries. Taking advantage of the country's free enterprise system, American businessmen built their own factories, starting in New England. These businessmen and their region grew wealthier.

Vocabulary
industrialize: to develop factories

Reading History
A. Recognizing Effects How did the War of 1812 cause economic changes in America?
A. Answer It blocked shipping, forcing Americans to manufacture their own goods and to invest in businesses other than shipping.

Factories Come to New England

New England was a good place to set up factories for several reasons. Factories needed water power, and New England had many fast-moving rivers. For transportation, it also had ships and access to the ocean. In addition, New England had a willing labor force. The area's first factory workers were families who were tired of scraping a living from their stony fields.

Samuel Slater built his first spinning mill in Pawtucket, Rhode Island, in 1790. He hired eight children between the ages of 7 and 12, paying them a low wage. Later, he built a larger mill and employed whole families. As Slater influenced others to start mills, his family system of employment spread through Rhode Island, Connecticut, and southern Massachusetts.

2 The Lowell Mills Hire Women

In 1813, the American textile industry leaped forward when Francis Cabot Lowell built a factory in Waltham, in eastern Massachusetts. This factory not only spun raw cotton into yarn, but wove it into cloth on power looms. Lowell had seen power looms in English mills and had figured out how to build them. Like Samuel Slater, he had brought secrets to America.

The Waltham factory was so successful that Lowell and his partners built a new factory town, Lowell, near the Merrimack and Concord rivers. The **Lowell mills,** textile mills in the village, employed farm girls who lived in company-owned boardinghouses. "Lowell girls" worked $12\frac{1}{2}$-hour days in deafening noise.

Background
Founded in 1826, the town was named for Lowell, who died in 1817.

Lowell girls published a literary magazine.

A VOICE FROM THE PAST

At first the hours seemed very long . . . and when I went out at night the sound of the mill was in my ears . . . . You know that people learn to sleep with the thunder of Niagara [falls] in their ears, and a cotton mill is no worse, though you wonder that we do not have to hold our breath in such a noise.

"Letters from Susan," quoted in the *Lowell Offering*

ACTIVITY OPTIONS
INDIVIDUAL NEEDS

STUDENTS ACQUIRING ENGLISH/ESL

Building Vocabulary Help students become more familiar with the specialized vocabulary in this section by having them build a word wall. Write each section heading on a sheet of paper and attach it to a wall or bulletin board. As students read the paragraphs under the headings, have them identify words that are new to them. Write these words on index cards and write out the definition. Then place the cards under the appropriate heading. Encourage students to refer to the wall and use the words frequently in speaking and writing activities.

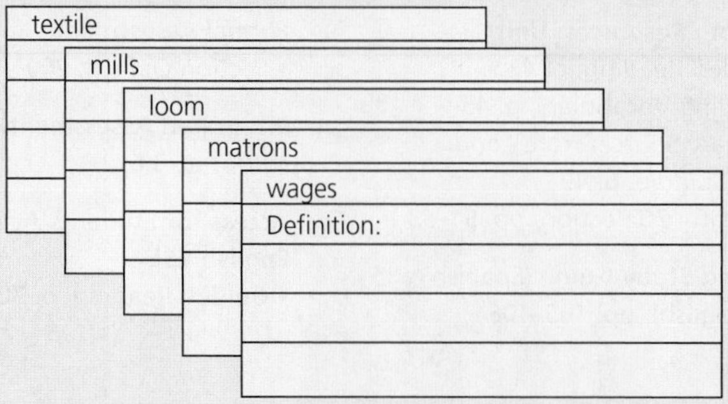

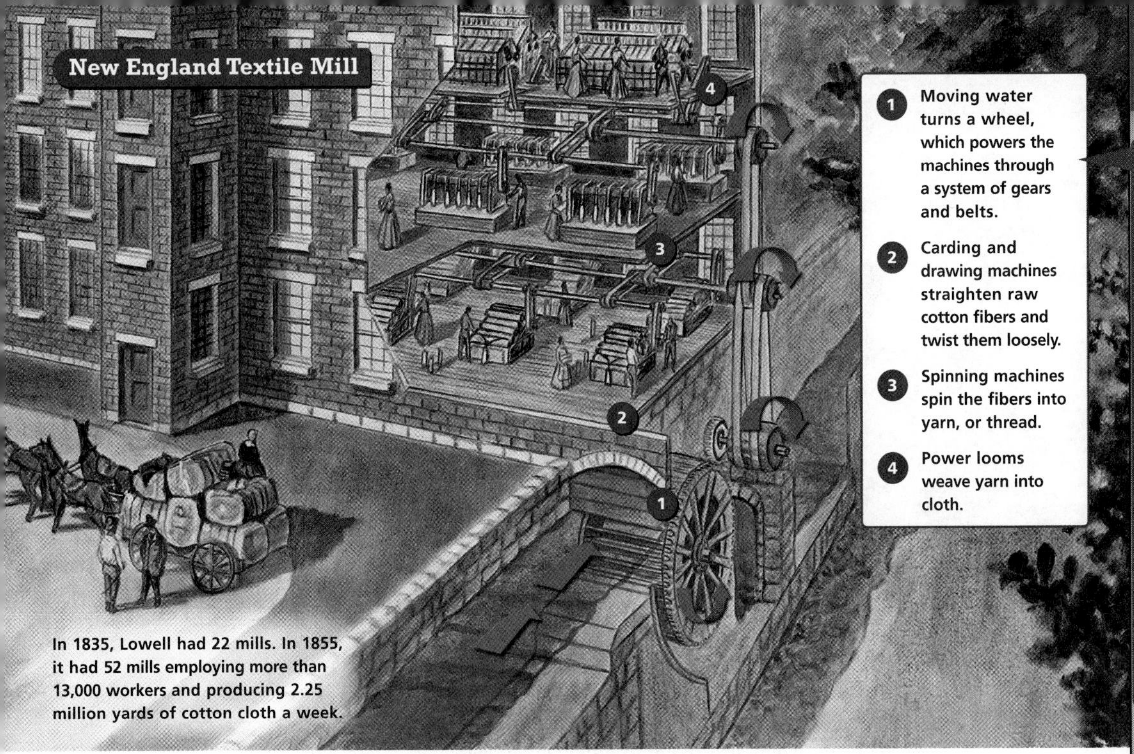
New England Textile Mill
1
2
3
4
1 Moving water turns a wheel, which powers the machines through a system of gears and belts.
2 Carding and drawing machines straighten raw cotton fibers and twist them loosely.
3 Spinning machines spin the fibers into yarn, or thread.
4 Power looms weave yarn into cloth.

In 1835, Lowell had 22 mills. In 1855, it had 52 mills employing more than 13,000 workers and producing 2.25 million yards of cotton cloth a week.

Young women came to Lowell in spite of the noise. In the early years, wages were high—between two and four dollars a week. Older women supervised the girls, making them follow strict rules and attend church. Girls read books, went to lectures, and even published a literary magazine—the *Lowell Offering.* Usually they worked for only a few years, until they married. By the 1830s, however, falling profits meant that wages dropped and working conditions worsened for the Lowell girls.

The Lowell mills and other early factories ran on water power. Factories built after the 1830s were run by more powerful steam engines. Because steam engines used coal and wood, not fast-moving water, factories could be built away from rivers and beyond New England.

Reading **History**

B. Contrasting How did the Lowell mills differ from Slater's mill?

B. Answer Lowell mills wove cloth, employed young women, and were larger than Slater's mill, which only spun thread and employed children and families.

A New Way to Manufacture

New manufacturing methods changed the style of work in other industries besides the textile industry. In 1797, the U.S. government hired the inventor Eli Whitney to make 10,000 muskets for the army. He was to have the guns ready in two years. Before this time, guns were made one at a time by gunsmiths, from start to finish. Each gun differed slightly. If a part broke, a new part had to be created to match the broken one.

Whitney sought a better way to make guns. In 1801, he went to Washington with a box containing piles of musket parts. He took a part from each pile and assembled a musket in seconds. He had just demonstrated the use of **interchangeable parts,** parts that are exactly alike.

HISTORY FROM VISUALS

Reading the Diagram Point out that each step in the textile-production process in this mill was done on a separate floor. Ask students to make inferences about what kinds of workers were necessary to keep such a large mill running. **Possible Responses** maintenance workers to keep machinery operating properly; workers to accept raw materials for production, to operate the machines, to transport finished products from one floor to another; managers to supervise work on each floor; accountants to keep track of expenses and income; shippers to send products to markets

Extension Have students do research to find out how factories are organized today. Help them make connections between a typical modern factory and the textile mill shown here.

MORE ABOUT . . .

Mill Girls on Strike

The textile industry saw the first strikes by women factory workers in the United States. Following wage cuts, women workers at the Boston Manufacturing Company in Waltham went on strike in 1821. The strike shut down factory production for two days. Textile workers later formed the Factory Girls' Association. The organization joined others in pushing for a 10-hour workday.

In-Depth Resources: Unit 3
- Primary Source: from *Loom and Spindle* by Harriet Hanson Robinson, p. 49

ACTIVITY OPTIONS

INTERDISCIPLINARY LINK: ECONOMICS

BLOCK SCHEDULING

A BUSINESS PLAN

Class Time One class period

Task Creating a business plan

Purpose To apply the ideas of industrialism to a new enterprise

Supplies Needed
- Paper and pencils

Activity Have small groups of students create a business plan for a company that sells tools or other manufactured products. On the board, write a sample business plan outline: company name, product, likely customers, methods of production, and employees needed. Discuss whether the product will require interchangeable parts and whether they are suitable for mass production with the factory system. Some students may wish to make a prototype of their group's product.

MORE ABOUT . . .

The *Clermont*

The *Clermont* was about 150 feet long with a single-cylinder engine. Its paddle wheels had diameters of 15 feet. When Fulton began using the *Clermont* commercially, other boats would ram the open paddle wheels, hoping to damage their new rival.

INSTRUCT: OBJECTIVE 3

Moving People, Goods, and Messages

- Why was the steamboat an improvement over earlier forms of river transportation?
- How did the telegraph revolutionize long-distance communication?

MORE ABOUT . . .

Robert Fulton

Robert Fulton also contributed to the future of naval warfare. In 1800, he constructed a novel weapon called a submarine. The plan was for the crew of the *Nautilus* to place explosives under the hulls of British ships. The *Nautilus* did not succeed in sinking an enemy ship, but the submarine became an especially destructive weapon in naval warfare during World Wars I and II.

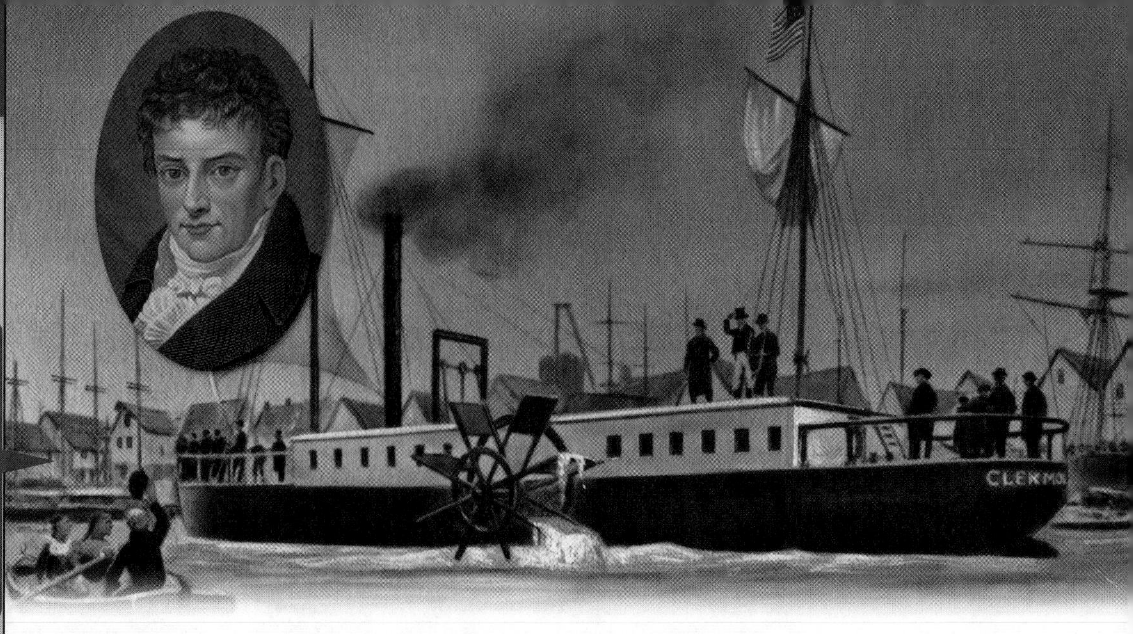

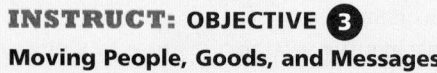

Robert Fulton invented the *Clermont*, a steamboat.

Machines that produced exactly matching parts soon became standard in industries. Interchangeable parts speeded up production, made repairs easy, and allowed the use of lower-paid, less-skilled workers. But the new system also required a new style of management, with inspectors to make sure each piece was uniform. Workers who were used to more independence disliked such close supervision.

Reading **History**

C. Recognizing Effects What were the effects of using interchangeable parts?

C. Answer They made production faster and repairs easier. They allowed the use of less-skilled workers but required the workers to be closely supervised.

3 Moving People, Goods, and Messages

New inventions increased factory production. They also improved transportation and communication. Steamboats carried people and goods farther and faster and led to the growth of cities like New Orleans and St. Louis. **Robert Fulton** invented a steamboat that could move against the current or a strong wind. He launched the *Clermont* on the Hudson River in 1807. Its steam engine turned two side paddle wheels, which pulled the boat through the water.

The *Clermont* was dubbed "Fulton's Folly" and described as "looking precisely like a backwoods saw-mill mounted on a scow [boat] and set on fire." But it made the 300-mile trip from New York to Albany and back in a record 62 hours. Even Fulton had not expected to travel so quickly.

A VOICE FROM THE PAST

I overtook many sloops and schooners, beating to the windward, and parted with them as if they had been at anchor. The power of propelling boats by steam is now fully proved.

Robert Fulton, quoted in *Robert Fulton and the "Clermont"*

In 1811, the first steamship traveled down the Mississippi and Ohio rivers. But its engine was not powerful enough to return upriver, against the current. Henry Miller Shreve, a trader on the Mississippi, designed

ACTIVITY OPTIONS

MULTIPLE LEARNING STYLES: KINESTHETIC — BLOCK SCHEDULING

STEAMSHIP MODELS

Class Time One class period

Task Creating models

Purpose To evaluate the importance of the steamship for river navigation

Supplies Needed

- Illustrated encyclopedias or books on steamships
- Light cardboard or heavy construction paper
- Glue or clear tape
- Fine-tip markers

Activity Students should research the basic designs of the vessels and construct models on a design of their choice. The models need not be intricate or show interior machinery. Students may describe the functions of different parts, such as the smokestack and paddle wheel, by writing small captions on them. Have students write the name of their ship on the bow. Discuss the importance of a boat that could travel upstream on a major waterway such as the Mississippi.

a more powerful engine. He installed it on a double-decker boat with a paddle wheel in the back. In 1816, he sailed this boat up the Mississippi and launched a new era of trade and transportation on the river.

In 1837, **Samuel F. B. Morse** first demonstrated his telegraph. This machine sent long and short pulses of electricity along a wire. These pulses could be translated into letters of a message. With the telegraph, it took only seconds to communicate with someone in another city. In 1844, the first long-distance telegraph line carried news from Baltimore to Washington, D.C., about who had been nominated for president. Telegraph lines spanned the country by 1861, bringing people closer as a nation. Both the telegraph and the steamboat brought more national unity.

Reading **History**

D. Recognizing Effects What made the steamboat and telegraph such important inventions?

D. Answer They increased commerce and communication between regions of the country.

4 Technology Improves Farming

Other new inventions increased farm production. In 1836, the blacksmith John Deere invented a lightweight plow with a steel cutting edge. Older cast-iron plows were designed for the light, sandy soil of New England. But rich, heavy Midwestern soil clung to the bottom of these plows and slowed farmers down. Deere's new plow made preparing ground much less work. As a result, more farmers began to move to the Midwest.

The mechanical reaper and the threshing machine were other inventions that improved agriculture. Cyrus McCormick's reaper, patented in 1834, cut ripe grain. The threshing machine separated kernels of wheat from husks.

Vocabulary

patented: protected by a patent, which gives an inventor the sole right to make, use, or sell an invention

John Deere invented the steel plow.

New technologies linked regions and contributed to national unity. With new farm equipment, Midwestern farmers grew food to feed Northeastern factory workers. In turn, Midwestern farmers became a market for Northeastern manufactured goods. The growth of Northeastern textile mills increased demand for Southern cotton. This led to the expansion of slavery in the South, as you will learn in Section 2.

Section 1 Assessment

1. Terms & Names

Explain the significance of:
- Samuel Slater
- Industrial Revolution
- factory system
- Lowell mills
- interchangeable parts
- Robert Fulton
- Samuel F. B. Morse

2. Taking Notes

On a chart like the one below, note new inventions, their dates, and their effects on the United States.

Invention	Date	Effects

Which inventions did most to link the nation? Explain.

3. Main Ideas

a. Why was New England a good place to build early factories?

b. What were working conditions like in Lowell mills?

c. How were different U.S. regions linked economically?

4. Critical Thinking

Evaluating How would you judge Samuel Slater and Francis Lowell, who brought secrets to the United States illegally?

THINK ABOUT
- what they gained
- how they affected the United States and England
- what you believe about keeping technology secret

ACTIVITY OPTIONS

SCIENCE

SPEECH

Explain how an invention from this chapter works, either in an **oral report** or a **labeled diagram.**

INSTRUCT: OBJECTIVE 4

Technology Improves Farming

- Why was John Deere's new plow an important development?
- What other inventions improved agriculture?
- How did new technologies link regions more closely together?

CRITICAL THINKING ACTIVITY

Analyzing Causes and Recognizing Effects
Have students use an organizer to illustrate how new technologies linked regions of the United States. See example below.

Discuss how the links might have an effect on the balance of power among the regions. **Possible Response** The Northeast had ties to both the South and the Midwest. The Northeast could come to dominate the other regions economically.

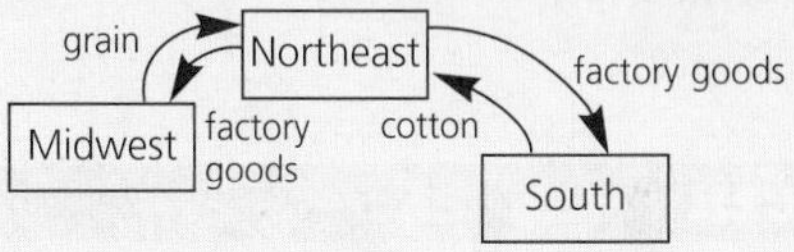

Class Time 10 minutes

ASSESS & RETEACH

Setting the Stage Have students place information about the Industrial Revolution in the first and third cause-and-effect boxes on the graphic.

Formal Assessment
- Section Quiz, p. 200

Critical Thinking Transparency CT31
- Setting the Stage

RETEACHING ACTIVITY

Have students work with partners to create a poster illustrating important inventions or innovations that spurred growth in the United States. Students should write short captions noting the significance of each item.

In-Depth Resources: Unit 3
- Reteaching Activity, p. 54

Section 1 Assessment

1. Terms & Names

Samuel Slater, p. 325
Industrial Revolution, p. 325
factory system, p. 325
Lowell mills, p. 326
interchangeable parts, p. 327
Robert Fulton, p. 328
Samuel F. B. Morse, p. 329

2. Taking Notes

interchangeable parts: 1801, standardized parts; steamboat: 1807, improved river transportation; telegraph: 1837, improved communication; steel plow: 1836, increased food production. The steamboat and telegraph promoted national unity.

3. Main Ideas

a. available water power; good transportation; a willing labor force **b.** noisy; long hours; many women workers **c.** The Midwest and Northeast exchanged food and manufactured goods. The South provided cotton for Northeast textile mills.

4. Critical Thinking

Students may either admire them for enabling America to compete with England or fault them for stealing national secrets for profit.

ACTIVITY OPTIONS

Integrated Assessment
- Rubrics for an oral report, 3.6
- Rubrics for a diagram, 2.3

Interdisciplinary CHALLENGE

OBJECTIVE
Students work cooperatively to analyze and solve technological, economic, and occupational-safety problems in running a New England textile mill.

BLOCK SCHEDULING

PROCEDURE

Assemble the supplies that students may need, such as books about waterwheels, drawing paper, posterboard, markers, pencils, and perhaps calculators. Have students form groups of four or five to complete each challenge. Group members should choose an option and divide the work among themselves.

HEALTH CHALLENGE

Suggest that students ask the human resources department of a local manufacturing plant for a copy of the company safety manual for employees and copies of safety signs posted in the plant. Other sources of information about occupational safety, such as federal rules, can be found at the library.

POSSIBLE SOLUTION
Some Boston mill employers vaccinated employees against smallpox, a disease that could easily spread in a crowded factory. However, many mill owners argued that the health of workers was generally no worse than that of people who did not work at the mills. Accidents were considered the worker's fault. Mill owners had no obligation to compensate workers injured on the job, so there was little financial incentive to improve safety except for the slight cost of training a new worker to replace the injured person.

Interdisciplinary CHALLENGE

Run a Mill Town

You are the owner of a new water-powered textile mill that will soon open in New England. Mills have been around for more than 20 years, and you have studied their operations closely. Even so, you face many problems as you start your business. Machinery failures, labor problems, demanding investors—all will be part of your life from now on.

COOPERATIVE LEARNING On this page are two challenges you face as the owner of a textile mill. Working with a small group, decide how to deal with each challenge. Choose an option, assign a task to each group member, and do the activity. You will find useful information in the Data File. Be prepared to present your solutions to the class.

HEALTH CHALLENGE

"Anna Tripp lost three fingers today."

A neighboring mill owner has just left after sharing some bad news. Today 12-year-old Anna Tripp lost three fingers in one of his machines. Last week, one of his workers was hit and nearly killed by the flying end of a broken belt. Several girls went home because they had trouble breathing. They blamed the closed, damp machine rooms with lint-filled air. How will you reduce the number of costly health problems like these in your mill? Present your plan using one of these options:

- **Write a speech to workers outlining the company's safety measures.**
- **Design a sign for each floor of the mill stating the company's safety rules.**

HEALTH CHALLENGE

Option 1 Speeches should
- identify potential health and safety problems.
- provide clear instructions to promote health and safety.

Option 2 Signs should
- clearly state safety rules.
- explain reasons for the rules.

MATH CHALLENGE

Option 1 Reports should
- explain hiring decisions.
- summarize payroll information.

Option 2 Posters should
- clearly identify the kinds of workers desired.
- include information about wages and open positions.

SCIENCE CHALLENGE

Option 1 Diagrams should
- show how the waterwheel works.
- include labels that clearly explain why that particular wheel is the best choice.

Option 2 Instructions should
- include clear, easy-to-follow directions.
- show how the wheel works.

MATH CHALLENGE

"So many applicants for employment"

To make a profit, you must operate at top capacity for the lowest cost. Your mill generates 2 mill power. This dictates how many spinners you can hire. You need about two-and-a-half times that many weavers. What will be your weekly payroll for spinners and weavers? How many men will you hire? Women? Look at the Data File for help. Present your hiring plan for spinners and weavers using one of these options:

- **Write a report telling investors whom you plan to hire.**
- **Design want-ad posters aimed at the workers you are looking for.**

DATA FILE

Water Power

Potential energy: energy released when water falls from a height.

Kinetic energy: energy provided by fast-moving water.

1 mill power: power produced by 25 cubic feet of water per second dropping over a 30-foot fall; about 60 horsepower.

1 mill power: runs 3,584 spindles.

Waterwheels

Overshot

Undershot

Mid-wheel

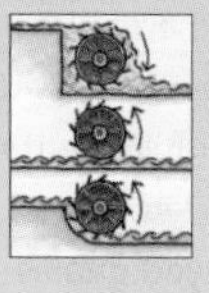

Wage Rates

Men: \$.85–\$2.09 per day, depending on skill

Women: \$.52–\$.78 per day, depending on skill

Positions

Pickers: clean raw cotton.

Carders: feed cotton into machine that makes a thick strand of fibers.

Spinners: operate a machine that twists thick fibers into yarn and winds it on bobbins fastened to moving spindles. One worker operates 128 spindles.

Dressers: treat finished yarn with a starch paste.

Drawing-in hands: attach dressed yarn to the mechanical loom for weavers.

Weavers: weave dressed yarn into finished cloth. One worker operates two looms.

Work Hours

12 hours per day, 6 days per week, 309 days per year with holidays on Fast Day (spring), the Fourth of July, and Thanksgiving

For more about textile mills . . .

RESEARCH LINKS
CLASSZONE.COM

ACTIVITY WRAP-UP

Present to the Class Meet as a group to review your responses to running a mill town. Pick the most creative solution for each challenge and present these solutions to the class.

331

MATH CHALLENGE

Class Time 50 minutes

Students should use information in the Data File to calculate the number of spinners and weavers needed.

POSSIBLE SOLUTION

56 spinners, 140 weavers. Payroll for spinners and weavers will vary depending on whom students employ in those positions. Point out that the most physically demanding jobs were picking and carding.

In general, men held all supervisory jobs. Men also were hired as machinists and for physically demanding jobs that mill owners considered too difficult for women. Women held machine-tending jobs after carding, such as spinning and weaving. Although the great majority of workers were women, men held all the highest-paying jobs.

ALTERNATIVE CHALLENGE

SCIENCE CHALLENGE

"Water power . . . invited the enterprise of manufacturers"

Like other manufacturers, you buy land for your mill along a deep, fast-moving river. The water cascades over a 10-foot falls. You know that the right waterwheel can harness 60 percent of the energy in this falling water. Which kind of wheel will you choose? Look at the Data File for help and do more research on waterwheels. Present your choice using one of these options:

- **Draw a labeled diagram of your waterwheel that explains why it is the most efficient choice.**
- **Create illustrated instructions for your carpenters explaining how the wheel works.**

ACTIVITY WRAP-UP

Presentations should

- clearly identify the problems in each challenge.
- provide clear, effective solutions to each problem.
- evaluate and explain the effectiveness of the solutions.
- explain the originality of the solutions.

SECTION OBJECTIVES

1. To explain the relationship between the cotton boom and slavery
2. To analyze the important divisions within Southern society
3. To describe African-American culture and family life under slavery
4. To summarize information about slave rebellions

SKILLBUILDERS

Interpreting Maps: Human-Environment Interaction, p. 334

CRITICAL THINKING

Recognizing Effects, pp. 333, 336, 337
Analyzing Points of View, p. 334
Contrasting, p. 336
Making Inferences, p. 336
Drawing Conclusions, p. 337

FOCUS & MOTIVATE

5-MINUTE WARM-UP

Making Generalizations These questions focus on the expansion of slavery.

1. Look at the graph on page 334. By how much did cotton growing expand from 1800 to 1860?
2. How does the information on the graph and map support the title of this section?

Warm-Up Transparency WT11

INSTRUCT

INSTRUCT: OBJECTIVE 1

The Cotton Boom/Slavery Expands

- How did the invention of the cotton gin change Southern life?
- How did the rise in cotton production affect slavery?

In-Depth Resources: Unit 3
- Guided Reading, p. 43
- Building Vocabulary, p. 45

2 Plantations and Slavery Spread

TERMS & NAMES
Eli Whitney
cotton gin
spirituals
Nat Turner

MAIN IDEA	WHY IT MATTERS NOW
The invention of the cotton gin and the demand for cotton caused slavery to spread in the South.	The spread of slavery created lasting racial and sectional tensions.

ONE AMERICAN'S STORY

Catherine Beale was born into slavery in 1838. At the age of 91, in 1929, she recalled her childhood on a Virginia plantation. When asked what games she had played, Catherine replied that enslaved children never played games—they were too busy with chores. Among the tasks were picking and cleaning cotton.

A VOICE FROM THE PAST

We had to work in the field in the day and at night we had to pick out the seed before we went to bed. And we had to clean the wool, we had to pick the burrs and sticks out so it would be clean and could be carded and spun and wove.

Catherine Beale, quoted in *Slave Testimony*

Enslaved workers labor in the cotton fields.

Catherine had to clean cotton by hand because the plantation didn't have a cotton gin. This machine made it easier for enslaved workers to clean cotton. But it also made cotton growing and slave owning more profitable. In this section, you will learn how slavery expanded in the South and how it affected the lives of people living under it.

1 The Cotton Boom

Eli Whitney invented a machine for cleaning cotton in 1793, after visiting the Georgia plantation of Catherine Greene, the widow of a Revolutionary War general. Mrs. Greene was struggling to make her plantation profitable. English textile mills had created a huge demand for cotton, but the short-fibered cotton that grew in most parts of the South was hard to clean by hand. A worker could clean just one pound of this cotton in a day.

Whitney's **cotton gin** (short for "engine") made the cotton-cleaning process far more efficient. With the new machine, one worker could now clean as much as 50 pounds of cotton a day. The cotton gin helped set the South on a different course of development from the North. It made

RECOMMENDED RESOURCES

In-Depth Resources: Unit 3
- Guided Reading, p. 43
- Building Vocabulary, p. 45
- Geog. Application, pp. 47–48
- Primary Source: Wes Brady Describes His Life Under Slavery, p. 50

Reading Study Guide (Spanish and English), pp. 107–108

Economics in History, p. 11

America's History Makers, pp. 43–46

Formal Assessment
- Section Quiz, p. 201

Integrated Assessment
- Rubrics, 4.7, 3.6

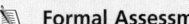

Access for Students Acquiring English/ESL, pp. 71, 74–75

INTEGRATED TECHNOLOGY

Humanities Transparency HT22
- A Cotton Plantation

America's Music CD

Electronic Teacher Tools

classzone.com

TEST-TAKING RESOURCES

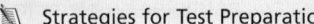

Strategies for Test Preparation

Test Practice Transparencies, TT39

Online Test Practice

The Cotton Gin

1. A hand crank turns a series of rollers.
2. A roller with wire teeth pulls the cotton through slots too narrow for the seeds.
3. The cotton seeds fall into a hopper.
4. A roller with brushes removes the cleaned cotton from the first roller.
5. The cleaned cotton leaves the gin.

short-fibered cotton a commercial product and changed Southern life in four important ways.

1. It triggered a vast move westward. Cotton farming moved beyond the Atlantic coastal states, where long-fibered, easy-to-clean cotton grew. Cotton plantations began to spread into northern Florida, Alabama, and Mississippi. Then they crossed into Louisiana and Arkansas. After 1840, they reached Texas.
2. Because cotton was valuable, planters grew more cotton rather than other goods, and cotton exports increased.
3. More Native American groups were driven off Southern land as it was taken over for cotton plantations.
4. Growing cotton required a large work force, and slavery continued to be important as a source of labor. Many slaves from the east were sold south and west to new cotton plantations.

Reading **History**

A. Reading a Map Use the map on page 334 to find cotton-growing areas in 1840.

Reading **History**

B. Recognizing Effects What impact did the cotton gin have on the South?

B. Answer It allowed cotton farming to move west, made cotton more important than other crops, led to the seizure of more Native American land, and kept slavery important as a labor source.

Slavery Expands

From 1790 to 1860, cotton production rose greatly. So did the number of enslaved people in the South. Using slave labor, the South raised millions of bales of cotton each year for the textile mills of England and the American Northeast. (See the graph on page 334.) In 1820, the South earned $22 million from cotton exports. By the late 1830s, earnings from cotton exports were nearly ten times greater, close to $200 million.

As cotton earnings rose, so did the price of slaves. A male field hand sold for $300 in the 1790s. By the late 1830s, the price had jumped to

MORE ABOUT . . .

The Cotton Gin

Gins in use before Whitney invented his machine were similar to clothes wringers on old washing machines. Friction from the grooved rollers on those gins could remove seeds from long-staple cotton but not from the shorter fibers of the cotton best suited to the South's climate and soil.

America's History Makers
- Eli Whitney, pp. 43–44

HISTORY FROM VISUALS

Reading the Illustration Point out the hand crank shown at the top of the illustration. Tell students that gins varied in size from hand-operated ones like this to larger ones turned by horse power or water power. Ask students how this machine helped determine how labor was distributed in cotton production. **Possible Response** Instead of having many slaves spending time cleaning cotton, cotton producers could use most of their slaves for picking cotton. Only a few workers would be needed to run the machine.

Extension Have students suggest labor-saving machines that are used today. Ask them to speculate about how those machines save time or change work patterns.

Economics in History
- The Economics of Slavery, p. 11

ACTIVITY OPTIONS

INDIVIDUAL NEEDS

LESS PROFICIENT READERS

Analyzing Causes and Recognizing Effects To help students understand the effect of the cotton gin on the South, draw a cause-and-effect chart like the one begun here. Work with students to complete the chart, beginning with Eli Whitney's invention of the cotton gin. Continue with expansion of slavery and new plantations. Point out that an effect can often become a cause that triggers a subsequent event.

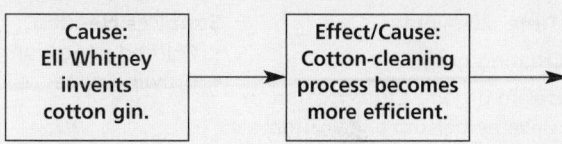

Cause: Eli Whitney invents cotton gin. → Effect/Cause: Cotton-cleaning process becomes more efficient. →

HISTORY FROM VISUALS

Reading the Map Point out that growing and harvesting cotton was very labor-intensive: the more slaves a landowner had, the more land he could farm and the larger his cotton crop. Based on the map information about cotton production, ask students which states probably had the largest concentrations of enslaved African Americans.
Answers States of the lower South—Louisiana, Mississippi, Alabama, Georgia, and South Carolina

Based on the graph information, ask the students how they think the map would look in 1860.
Possible Response More areas of the country would be shown growing cotton.

Extension Have students use almanacs and other classroom and library resources to identify states that are major cotton producers today.

Humanities Transparency HT22
- A Cotton Plantation

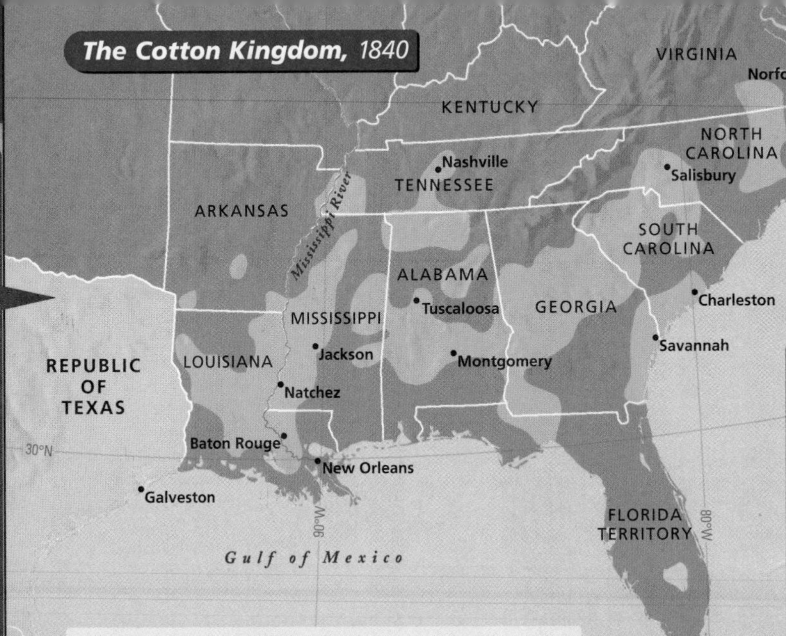

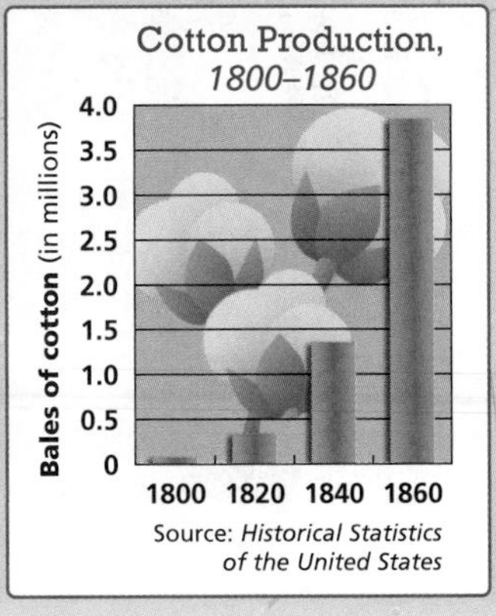

GEOGRAPHY SKILLBUILDER Interpreting Maps
1. **Human-Environment Interaction** *Which five states had the largest areas devoted to growing cotton?*
2. **Human-Environment Interaction** *How far north did people grow cotton?*

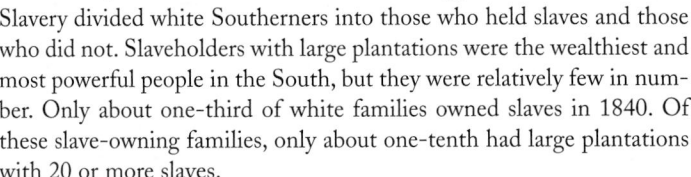

Skillbuilder Answers
1. South Carolina, Georgia, Alabama, Mississippi, and Louisiana
2. southern Virginia

$1,000. After 1808, when it became illegal to import Africans for use as slaves, the trading of slaves already in the country increased.

The expansion of slavery had a major impact on the South's economy. But its effect on the people living there was even greater.

Slavery Divides the South ❷

Slavery divided white Southerners into those who held slaves and those who did not. Slaveholders with large plantations were the wealthiest and most powerful people in the South, but they were relatively few in number. Only about one-third of white families owned slaves in 1840. Of these slave-owning families, only about one-tenth had large plantations with 20 or more slaves.

Most white Southern farmers owned few or no slaves. Still, many supported slavery anyway. They worked their small farms themselves and hoped to buy slaves someday, which would allow them to raise more cotton and earn more money. For both small farmers and large planters, slavery had become necessary for increasing profits.

Reading **History**
C. Analyzing Points of View Why did many white farmers without slaves still support slavery?
C. Answer They hoped to own slaves in the future.

African Americans in the South

Slavery also divided black Southerners into those who were enslaved and those who were free. Enslaved African Americans formed about one-third of the South's population in 1840. About half of them

INSTRUCT: OBJECTIVE ❷

Slavery Divides the South/ African Americans in the South

- How widespread was slaveholding in the South?
- What kinds of work did enslaved African Americans do?
- What was life like for free African Americans in the South?

In-Depth Resources: Unit 3
- Geography Application: The Internal Slave Movement After 1810, pp. 47–48

ACTIVITY OPTIONS

INTERDISCIPLINARY LINK: MATH — BLOCK SCHEDULING

CIRCLE GRAPHS

Class Time 20 minutes

Task Creating graphs

Purpose To organize information about slave ownership and African Americans in the South

Supplies Needed
- Colored pencils or markers
- Drawing paper

Activity Have students create a circle graph titled *White Southern Families in 1840.* Explain that one-third of all white Southern families owned slaves in 1840, so they should make a wedge that takes up about a third of the circle. This wedge should be labeled *Slaveholders.* Students may also create graphs for the proportion of slaveholding families with more than 20 slaves and for the proportion of free African Americans in the South. Students should keep the charts for use as study guides.

worked on large plantations with white overseers. Decades later, a former slave described the routine in an interview.

A VOICE FROM THE PAST

The overseer was 'straddle his big horse at three o'clock in the mornin', roustin' the hands off to the field. . . . The rows was a mile long and no matter how much grass [weeds] was in them, if you [left] one sprig on your row they [beat] you nearly to death.

Wes Brady, quoted in *Remembering Slavery*

Reading History
D. Contrasting How was plantation slavery different from slavery in cities?
D. Answer In cities, slaves had more variety in work and were sometimes allowed to keep part of their earnings.

Not all slaves faced the back-breaking conditions of plantations. In cities, enslaved persons worked as domestic servants, skilled craftsmen, factory hands, and day laborers. Sometimes they were hired out and allowed to keep part of their earnings. Frederick Douglass, an African-American speaker and publisher, once commented, "A city slave is almost a freeman, compared with a slave on the plantation." But they were still enslaved.

In 1840, about 8 percent of African Americans in the South were free. They had either been born free, been freed by an owner, or bought their own freedom. Many free African Americans in the South lived in cities such as Baltimore and Washington, D.C.

Though not enslaved, free blacks faced many problems. Some states made them leave once they gained their freedom. Most states did not permit them to vote or receive an education. Many employers refused to hire them. But their biggest threat was the possibility of being captured and sold into slavery.

daily life

SPIRITUALS

Singing spirituals offered comfort for pain, bound people together at religious meetings, and eased the boredom of daily tasks. This verse came from a spiritual sung by slaves in Missouri.

Dear Lord, dear lord,
when slavery'll cease
Then we poor souls
will have our peace;—
There's a better day a coming,
Will you go along with me?
There's a better day a coming,
Go sound the jubilee!

3 Finding Strength in Religion

An African-American culture had emerged on plantations by the early 1800s. Slaves relied on that culture—with its strong religious convictions, close personal bonds, and abundance of music—to help them endure the brutal conditions of plantation life.

Reading History
E. Making Inferences Why would enslaved African Americans be inspired by the biblical story of Moses?
E. Answer Because they hoped for freedom, and Moses led enslaved people to freedom.

Some slaveholders tried to use religion to make slaves accept their treatment. White ministers stressed such Bible passages as "Servants, obey your masters." But enslaved people took their own messages from the Bible. They were particularly inspired by the story of Moses leading the Hebrews out of bondage in Egypt.

Enslaved people expressed their religious beliefs in **spirituals,** religious folk songs. Spirituals often contained coded messages about a planned escape or an owner's unexpected return. African-American spirituals later influenced blues, jazz, and other forms of American music.

Detail of *Plantation Burial,* (1860), John Antrobus.

MORE ABOUT . . .

African-American Craftsmen

Enslaved African-American craftsmen formed guilds in some large Southern cities, such as Richmond, Virginia, and Charleston, South Carolina. However, white craftsmen then successfully lobbied state and local governments to pass laws restricting the ability of slaves to hire out for work in skilled crafts.

In-Depth Resources: Unit 3
- Primary Source, p. 50

daily life

Spirituals

Many spirituals concerned the desire for freedom from slavery. Often this desire was expressed in symbolic words and phrases, the real meanings of which were known only to the singers and other slaves. For example, Frederick Douglass (to whom students will be introduced on page 352) recalled a spiritual he and other slaves sang as they prepared to escape to the North:

O Canaan, sweet Canaan,
I am bound for the land of Canaan.

In-Depth Resources: Unit 3
- Enrichment Activity, p. 57

INSTRUCT: OBJECTIVE 3

Finding Strength in Religion/ Families Under Slavery

- What role did religion play in the system of slavery?
- What was family life like for enslaved people?
- What forms did resistance to slavery take?

ACTIVITY OPTIONS

INTERDISCIPLINARY LINK: LANGUAGE ARTS

BLOCK SCHEDULING

JOURNAL ENTRY

Class Time One class period

Task Creating a journal entry from a historical perspective

Purpose To describe the experiences of free African Americans before the Civil War

Supplies Needed
- Writing materials

Activity Pose the following scenario: In an old trunk at a flea market, students have found the journal of a free African American from a large Southern city in 1840. Ask them to consider the thoughts and feelings free African Americans might have had at the time: their daily lives, expectations, dreams, and fears. Then have students write entries that such a journal might have contained, telling about a day in their lives. Use the entries to frame a discussion about free African Americans in the pre–Civil War South.

MORE ABOUT . . .

Children Without Parents

Some students might be particularly concerned about the fate of enslaved children separated from their parents. In such cases, West African traditions of large, extended families proved important. Typically, separated children were raised by other relatives. If that was not possible, other adults in the slave community took the responsibility of caring for the children, serving as surrogate grandparents, uncles, and aunts.

America's History Makers
- Frederick Douglass, pp. 45–46

MORE ABOUT . . .

The Slave Trade

Slave owners rarely blamed themselves or the slave system for the breakup of African-American families; instead they blamed the economy or the slave traders who ran auctions, such as the one shown here. Southerners expressed contempt for slave traders and considered them social inferiors. But such attitudes did not stop slaveholders from doing business with the traders.

Slave auctions were part of what is called the domestic slave trade—the buying and selling of slaves within the United States. Federal law ended the foreign slave trade in 1808, but slave traders continued to smuggle enslaved people from Africa and the West Indies into the United States as late as the 1850s.

Families Under Slavery

Perhaps the cruelest part of slavery was the sale of family members away from one another. Although some slaveholders would not part mothers from children, many did, causing unforgettable grief. When enslaved people ran away, it was often to escape separation or to see family again.

When slave families could manage to be together, they took comfort in their family life. They married, though their marriages were not legally recognized. They tried to raise children, despite interference from owners. Most slave children lived with their mothers, who tried to protect them from punishment. Parents who lived on other plantations often stole away to visit their children, even at the cost of a whipping. Frederick Douglass recalled visits from his mother, who lived 12 miles away.

*Reading*History
F. Recognizing Effects How did slavery harm family life?
F. Answer It separated families, did not recognize marriages, and took away parents' authority over their children.

A VOICE FROM THE PAST

I do not recollect of [remember] ever seeing my mother by the light of day. She was with me in the night. She would lie down with me, and get me to sleep, but long before I waked she was gone.

Frederick Douglass, *Narrative of the Life of Frederick Douglass*

Douglass's mother resisted slavery by the simple act of visiting her child. Douglass later rebelled by escaping to the North. Other enslaved people rebelled in more violent ways.

A slave auction threatens to split a family apart.

336

ACTIVITY OPTIONS

INTERDISCIPLINARY LINK: HUMANITIES

BLOCK SCHEDULING

SPIRITUALS

Class Time One class period

Task Analyzing a traditional spiritual

Purpose To understand the ideas expressed in the music of enslaved African Americans

Supplies Needed
- Book of spirituals, such as *Go Down Moses: A Celebration of the African American Spiritual* by Richard Newman
- Recordings of spirituals
- Writing paper
- Drawing materials

Activity Have students, working in pairs, choose a spiritual and then explain the emotions expressed in the lyrics. Ask students to make inferences about the meanings of words or phrases: Were they symbols for something that could not be openly expressed, such as a desire for escape and freedom? Invite singers and musicians in your class to sing their spiritual for the other students. Encourage students to draw a sketch or paint a picture illustrating their spiritual. Display the artwork in the classroom.

America's Music CD

❹ Slave Rebellions

Armed rebellion was an extreme form of resistance to slavery. Gabriel Prosser planned an attack on Richmond, Virginia, in 1800. In 1822, Denmark Vesey planned a revolt in Charleston, South Carolina. Both plots were betrayed, and the leaders were hanged.

The most famous rebellion was led by **Nat Turner** in Virginia in 1831. On August 21, Turner and 70 followers killed 55 white men, women, and children. Later, witnesses claimed that he spoke these words.

> *A VOICE FROM THE PAST*
>
> We do not go forth for the sake of blood and carnage; . . . Remember that ours is not a war for robbery, . . . it is a struggle for freedom.
>
> **Nat Turner,** quoted in *Nat Turner,* by Terry Bisson

G. Answer It made them fearful and vengeful. They killed African Americans and passed new laws to control them.

Reading **History**

G. Recognizing Effects How did Nat Turner's rebellion affect white Southerners?

Most of Turner's men were captured when their ammunition ran out, and 16 were killed. When Turner was caught, he was tried and hanged.

Turner's rebellion spread fear in the South. Whites killed more than 200 African Americans in revenge. State legislatures passed harsh laws that kept free blacks and slaves from having weapons or buying liquor. Slaves could not hold religious services unless whites were present. Postmasters stopped delivering antislavery publications.

After Turner's rebellion, the grip of slavery grew even tighter in the South. Tension over slavery increased between the South and the North, as you will see in the next section.

AMERICA'S HISTORY MAKERS

NAT TURNER
1800–1831

Nat Turner was born on a plantation in Virginia. As a child, Turner learned to read and write. He became an enthusiastic reader of the Bible. Slaves gathered in forest clearings to listen to his powerful sermons. Turner believed that God wanted him to free the slaves, even if by armed rebellion. He defended the justice of his cause in what came to be known as *Confessions of Nat Turner,* which he dictated to a white lawyer before his execution.

How did Turner justify his rebellion?

Section 2 Assessment

1. Terms & Names

Explain the significance of:
- Eli Whitney
- cotton gin
- spirituals
- Nat Turner

2. Taking Notes

In a chart like the one below, note facts about each group of Southerners.

Group	Facts
slaveholding whites	
nonslaveholding whites	
enslaved blacks	
free blacks	

Why do you think many free blacks lived in cities?

3. Main Ideas

a. How did the cotton gin lead to the spread of slavery?

b. How was life different for plantation slaves, city slaves, and free blacks in the South?

c. What were three ways that enslaved people resisted slavery?

4. Critical Thinking

Forming Opinions How do you think slave rebellions affected the institution of slavery?

THINK ABOUT
- Nat Turner's reasons for rebelling
- the reaction of white Southerners and slave owners to Turner's rebellion

ACTIVITY OPTIONS

LANGUAGE ARTS
SPEECH

Write a **book report** on a slave narrative, or perform an **oral interpretation** of a passage from one.

AMERICA'S HISTORY MAKERS

Nat Turner

It is not known for certain how Nat Turner learned to read. Turner claimed that the ability to read came to him in a vision. Some historians have speculated that older slaves, perhaps his grandmother, taught the young Turner how to read. Others have argued that a son of one of Turner's masters did so, despite laws prohibiting this practice.

Answer: Turner led an armed rebellion with other enslaved African Americans because he believed God wanted him to free the slaves.

INSTRUCT: OBJECTIVE ❹

Slave Rebellions

- Who was Nat Turner?
- What were the effects of Turner's rebellion?

ASSESS & RETEACH

Setting the Stage Have students place information about slavery in the second cause-and-effect box on the graphic.

Formal Assessment
- Section Quiz, p. 201

RETEACHING ACTIVITY

Organize the class into small groups. Assign one of the section's illustrations to each group member. Ask each student to write a paragraph about the significance of the subject of that illustration to the section's Main Idea. Have group members compile their paragraphs into a booklet. Make photocopies of the booklets and distribute them to students.

In-Depth Resources: Unit 3
- Reteaching Activity, p. 55

Section 2 Assessment

1. Terms & Names

Eli Whitney, p. 332
cotton gin, p. 332
spirituals, p. 335
Nat Turner, p. 337

2. Taking Notes

slaveholding whites: one-third of population, wealthy, powerful; nonslaveholding whites: small farms, supported slavery; enslaved blacks: one-third of the Southern population, variety of jobs; free blacks: 8 percent of population in the South; most lived in cities, where more work was available

3. Main Ideas

a. more efficient production, larger area to work, need for slaves increased **b.** Plantation slaves were field workers, city slaves held a variety of jobs, free blacks lived in cities. **c.** secret visits, escape, rebellions, antislavery religious beliefs

4. Critical Thinking

Answers will vary. Themes could include freedom or the South's reinforced fear of blacks.

ACTIVITY OPTIONS

Integrated Assessment
- Rubrics for a book report, 4.7
- Rubrics for an oral report, 3.6

SECTION OBJECTIVES

1. To describe efforts to make the United States self-sufficient and to improve transportation
2. To explain the growth of national unity and the settling of boundaries
3. To analyze sectional tensions and the compromises that lessened them
4. To explain the Monroe Doctrine

SKILLBUILDER

Interpreting Maps: Movement, Region, p. 339
Interpreting Maps: Location, Region, pp. 341, 342

CRITICAL THINKING

Recognizing Effects, pp. 339, 343
Finding Main Ideas, p. 340
Analyzing Causes, p. 341
Analyzing Points of View, p. 342

Why It Matters Now
- Expanding Economies, pp. 21–22

FOCUS & MOTIVATE

5-MINUTE WARM-UP

Making Inferences These questions focus on nationalism and sectionalism.

1. Look at "A Voice from the Past" on page 338. What do you think Henry Clay is suggesting?
2. How does Clay think independence is achieved?

Warm-Up Transparency WT11

INSTRUCT

INSTRUCT: OBJECTIVE 1

Nationalism Unites the Country/ Roads and Canals Link Cities

- What was the American System?
- How was transportation improved?

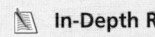

In-Depth Resources: Unit 3
- Guided Reading, p. 44

Reading Study Guide (Spanish and English), pp. 109–110

3 Nationalism and Sectionalism

MAIN IDEA

Patriotic pride united the states, but tension between the North and South emerged.

WHY IT MATTERS NOW

The tension led to the Civil War, and regional differences can still be found in the United States today.

TERMS & NAMES
nationalism
Henry Clay
American System
Erie Canal
James Monroe
sectionalism
Missouri Compromise
Monroe Doctrine

ONE AMERICAN'S STORY

In the early 1800s, as you have read, the North began to industrialize and the South relied more heavily on growing cotton. At the same time, a rising sense of nationalism pulled people from different regions together. Nationalism is a feeling of pride, loyalty, and protectiveness toward your country. The War of 1812 sent a wave of nationalist feeling through the United States.

Representative Henry Clay, from Kentucky, was a strong nationalist. After the war, President James Madison supported Clay's plan to strengthen the country and unify its different regions.

A VOICE FROM THE PAST

Every nation should anxiously endeavor to establish its absolute independence, and consequently be able to feed and clothe and defend itself. If it rely upon a foreign supply that may be cut off . . . it cannot be independent.

Henry Clay, quoted in *The Annals of America*

Henry Clay

In this section, you will learn how nationalism affected U.S. economic growth and foreign policy. You'll also see how Americans were beginning to be torn between the interests of their own regions and those of the country as a whole.

1 Nationalism Unites the Country

In 1815, President Madison presented a plan to Congress for making the United States economically self-sufficient. In other words, the country would prosper and grow by itself, without foreign products or foreign markets.

The plan—which Henry Clay promoted as the **American System**—included three main actions.

1. **Establish a protective tariff,** a tax on imported goods that protects a nation's businesses from foreign competition. Congress passed a tariff in 1816. It made European goods more expensive and encouraged Americans to buy cheaper American-made products.

RECOMMENDED RESOURCES

In-Depth Resources: Unit 3
- Guided Reading, p. 44
- Building Vocabulary, p. 45
- Skillbuilder Practice, p. 46

Reading Study Guide (Spanish and English), pp. 109–110

Outline Map Activities, pp. 21–22

Why It Matters Now, pp. 21–22

Citizenship Today, pp. 90–91

Formal Assessment
- Section Quiz, p. 202

Integrated Assessment
- Rubrics, 4.1, 1.2

Access for Students Acquiring English/ESL, pp. 72–73

INTEGRATED TECHNOLOGY

Geography Transparency GT11
- Railroads Extend Westward, 1850–1860

Electronic Teacher Tools

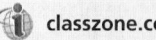

classzone.com

TEST-TAKING RESOURCES

Strategies for Test Preparation

Test Practice Transparencies, TT40

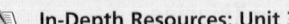

Online Test Practice

Reading **History**

A. Recognizing Effects How would the three parts of the American System help to make the country self-sufficient?

A. Answer A tariff would protect businesses; a national bank and improved transportation would make internal trade easier.

2. **Establish a national bank** that would promote a single currency, making trade easier. (Most regional banks issued their own money.) In 1816, Congress set up the second Bank of the United States.
3. **Improve the country's transportation systems,** which were important for a strong economy. Poor roads made transportation slow and costly.

Roads and Canals Link Cities

Representative John C. Calhoun of South Carolina also called for better transportation systems. "Let us bind the Republic together with a perfect system of roads and canals," he declared in 1817. Earlier, in 1806, Congress had funded a road from Cumberland, Maryland, to Wheeling, Virginia. By 1841, the National Road, designed as the country's main east-west route, had been extended to Vandalia, Illinois.

Water transportation improved, too, with the building of canals. In fact, the period from 1825 to 1850 is often called the Age of Canals. Completed in 1825, the massive **Erie Canal** created a water route between New York City and Buffalo, New York. The canal opened the upper Ohio Valley and the Great Lakes region to settlement and trade. It also fueled nationalism by unifying these two sections of the country.

The Erie Canal allowed farm products from the Great Lakes region to flow east and people and manufactured goods from the East to flow

Skillbuilder Answers
1. a route including Lake Erie, the Erie Canal, and the Hudson River
2. the North

MORE ABOUT . . .

The Erie Canal

Building the Erie Canal took more than eight years. The canal's route crossed 363 miles of wilderness and hilly terrain. Engineers had to construct more than 80 locks to raise and lower ships where elevation changed along the route. When the canal opened, freight rates between Albany and Buffalo dropped from $100 per ton to a mere $9 per ton.

For passengers, traveling by canal boat was more comfortable than traveling by coach over bumpy roads—but not by much. Several times an hour, everyone on the boat had to flop down flat on the deck as they passed under one of the many bridges that crossed the canal. As the folk song about the canal puts it:

Low bridge—everybody down!
Low bridge—'cause we're comin' to a town.

Major Canals, 1840

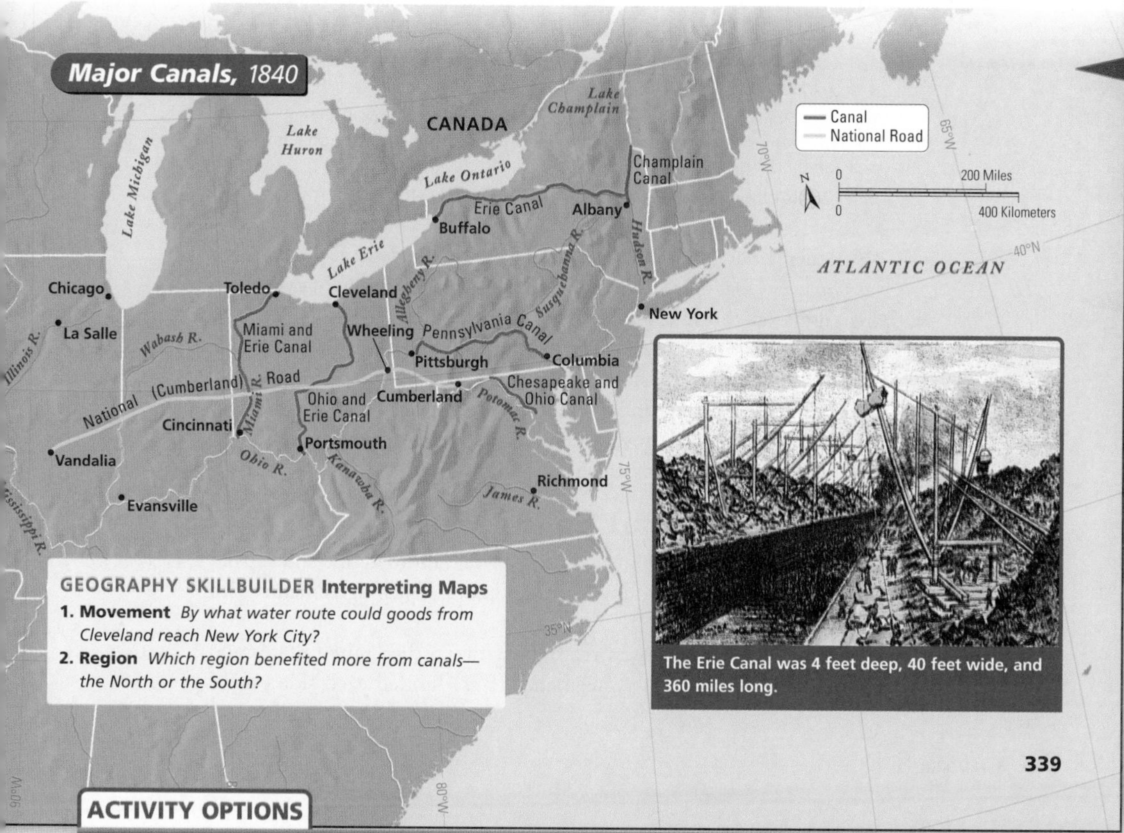

The Erie Canal was 4 feet deep, 40 feet wide, and 360 miles long.

GEOGRAPHY SKILLBUILDER Interpreting Maps
1. **Movement** *By what water route could goods from Cleveland reach New York City?*
2. **Region** *Which region benefited more from canals—the North or the South?*

339

HISTORY FROM VISUALS

Reading the Map Ask students to identify cities that likely developed because of the canal system. **Possible Responses** Buffalo, Cleveland, Toledo, Chicago, Albany, Syracuse, Pittsburgh, Columbia, Portsmouth, Cincinnati, Evansville, La Salle, Richmond. Then ask what impact transportation systems have on the development of cities.

Extension Ask students to compare the interstate highway system built since the 1950s to the canal boom in its effects.

Outline Map Activities
- Economic Expansion, 1841, pp. 21–22

Geography Transparency GT11
- Railroads Extend Westward, 1850–1860

ACTIVITY OPTIONS

INTERDISCIPLINARY LINK: GEOGRAPHY BLOCK SCHEDULING

TRANSPORTATION MAP

Class Time One class period

Task Creating a state transportation map

Purpose To help students explore the importance of efficient transportation networks to unite large areas

Supplies Needed
- Topographic and political maps of your state
- An outline map of your state
- Drawing paper
- Colored pencils or markers

Activity Ask students to suppose that they are planning a transportation network for their state in 1840. Their state is only sparsely settled and has no important roads, canals, and railroads yet. Have students use a topographic map to identify major rivers and other important physical features. Then have them use that information to complete a map showing efficient routes for roads, canals, and railroads. Where might towns develop? Use these maps in discussing how transportation helped unite the young United States.

INSTRUCT: OBJECTIVE 2

The Era of Good Feelings/ Settling National Boundaries

- Why was Monroe's administration called the Era of Good Feelings?
- How did Supreme Court decisions promote national unity?
- How did the United States settle disputes with Britain and Spain in the early 1800s?

MORE ABOUT . . .

John Marshall

John Marshall is a towering figure in the history of the judicial branch of the government. He served as chief justice (1801–1835) longer than any other man. He helped to make the Supreme Court as important as Congress and the presidency. In cases such as *Marbury* v. *Madison* (1803) and *McCulloch* v. *Maryland* (1819), Marshall helped define the power of the Court to determine whether acts of Congress or the president violated the Constitution. It was while tolling for Marshall's funeral in 1835 that the Liberty Bell cracked.

Citizenship Today, pp. 86–87

MORE ABOUT . . .

Gibbons* v. *Ogden

You may wish to point out that in *Gibbons* v. *Ogden*, the Supreme Court was guided by the Commerce Clause (Article I, Section 8) of the Constitution. That clause specifically gives the federal government the power to regulate interstate commerce. Congress also used the Commerce Clause to justify the passage of the Civil Rights Act of 1964. That law banned racial discrimination in hotels, restaurants, theaters, and other public places.

west. Trade stimulated by the canal helped New York City become the nation's largest city. Between 1820 and 1830, its population swelled from less than 125,000 to more than 200,000.

Around the 1830s, the nation began to use steam-powered trains for transportation. In 1830, only about 30 miles of track existed in the United States. But by 1850, the number had climbed to 9,000 miles. Improvements in rail travel led to a decline in the use of canals.

2 The Era of Good Feelings

James Monroe

As nationalist feelings spread, people slowly shifted their loyalty away from state governments and more toward the federal government. Democratic-Republican **James Monroe** won the presidency in 1816 with a large majority of electoral votes. The Federalist Party provided little opposition to Monroe and soon disappeared. Political differences gave way to what one Boston newspaper called the Era of Good Feelings.

During the Monroe administration, several landmark Supreme Court decisions promoted national unity by strengthening the federal government. For example, in *McCulloch* v. *Maryland* (1819), the state of Maryland wanted to tax its branch of the national bank. If this tax were allowed, the states could claim to have power over the federal government. The Court upheld federal authority by ruling that a state could not tax a national bank.

Background
Maryland also argued that Congress had no power to create the bank, but the Court ruled that it did have such power.

A VOICE FROM THE PAST

The States have no power, by taxation or otherwise, to retard, impede, burden, or in any manner control the operations of the constitutional laws enacted by Congress.

Chief Justice John Marshall, *McCulloch* v. *Maryland* (1819)

Another Court decision that strengthened the federal government was *Gibbons* v. *Ogden* (1824). Two steamship operators fought over shipping rights on the Hudson River in New York and New Jersey. The Court ruled that interstate commerce could be regulated only by the federal government, not the state governments.

The Supreme Court under John Marshall clearly stated important powers of the federal government. A stronger federal government reflected a growing nationalist spirit.

***Reading* History**
B. Finding Main Ideas How did the Supreme Court strengthen the federal government?
B. Answer By ruling that states could not interfere with federal laws and that only the federal government could regulate interstate commerce.

Settling National Boundaries

This nationalist spirit also made U.S. leaders want to define and expand the country's borders. To do this, they had to reach agreements with Britain and Spain.

Two agreements improved relations between the United States and Britain. The Rush-Bagot Agreement (1817) limited each side's naval

ACTIVITY OPTIONS

INTERDISCIPLINARY LINK: GOVERNMENT — BLOCK SCHEDULING

BROCHURES

Class Time 20 minutes

Task Creating a brochure

Purpose To show how the actions of all three branches of the federal government contributed to nationalism and a stronger central government

Supplies Needed
- Drawing paper
- Colored pencils or markers

Activity Have pairs of students create a brochure titled "Uniting the Country." In the brochure, students should list and illustrate actions taken by the legislative, executive, and judicial branches that helped unite the nation and strengthen the federal government during the early 1800s.

Answers Legislative: protective tariff, national bank, transportation network. Executive: negotiated foreign agreements that settled national boundaries. Judicial: Supreme Court decisions, such as *McCulloch* v. *Maryland* (1819) and *Gibbons* v. *Ogden* (1824)

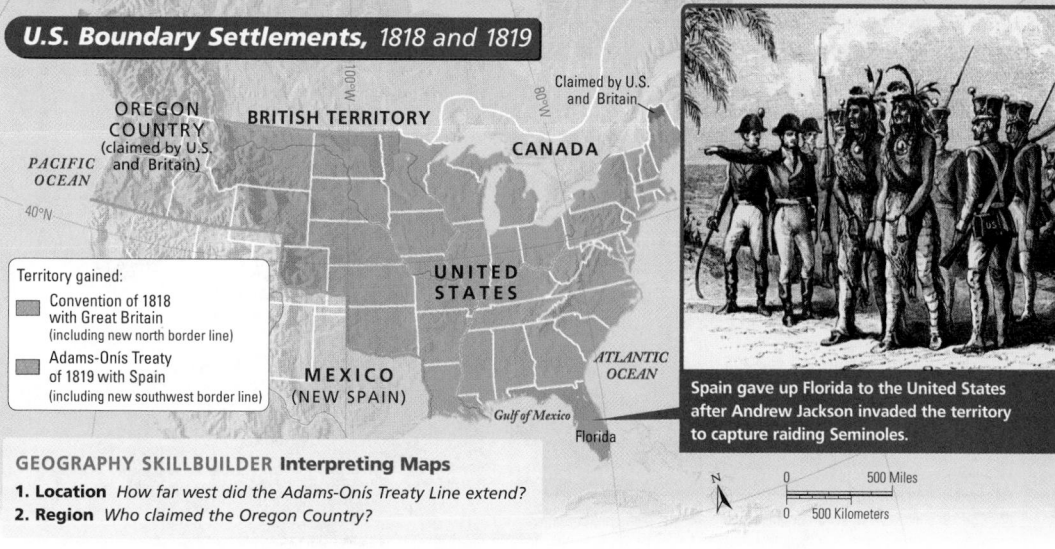

U.S. Boundary Settlements, *1818 and 1819*

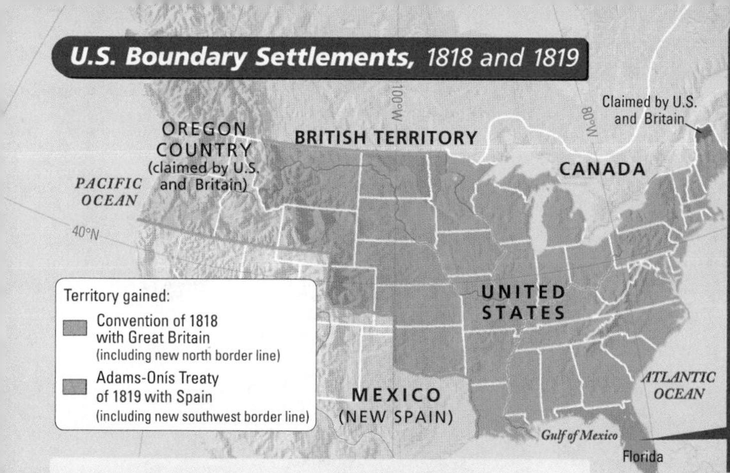

Spain gave up Florida to the United States after Andrew Jackson invaded the territory to capture raiding Seminoles.

GEOGRAPHY SKILLBUILDER Interpreting Maps

1. Location *How far west did the Adams-Onís Treaty Line extend?*
2. Region *Who claimed the Oregon Country?*

forces on the Great Lakes. In the Convention of 1818, the two countries set the 49th parallel as the U.S.-Canadian border as far west as the Rocky Mountains.

But U.S. relations with Spain were tense. The two nations disagreed on the boundaries of the Louisiana Purchase and the ownership of West Florida. Meanwhile, pirates and runaway slaves used Spanish-held East Florida as a refuge. In addition, the Seminoles of East Florida raided white settlements in Georgia to reclaim lost lands.

In 1817, President Monroe ordered General Andrew Jackson to stop the Seminole raids, but not to confront the Spanish. Jackson followed the Seminoles into Spanish territory and then claimed the Floridas for the United States.

Monroe ordered Jackson to withdraw but gave Spain a choice. It could either police the Floridas or turn them over to the United States. In the Adams-Onís Treaty of 1819, Spain handed Florida to the United States and gave up claims to the Oregon Country. The map above shows boundaries drawn and territories gained in 1818 and 1819.

Reading **History**
C. Analyzing Causes Why did Andrew Jackson invade East Florida?
C. Answer President Monroe ordered him to stop the Seminole raids.

Skillbuilder Answers
1. to the Pacific Ocean
2. both the United States and Great Britain

3 Sectional Tensions Increase

At the same time nationalism was unifying the country, sectionalism was threatening to drive it apart. **Sectionalism** is loyalty to the interests of your own region or section of the country, rather than to the nation as a whole. Economic changes had created some divisions within the United States. As you have seen, white Southerners were relying more on cotton and slavery. In the Northeast, wealth was based on manufacturing and trade. In the West, settlers wanted cheap land and good transportation. The interests of these sections were often in conflict.

Sectionalism became a major issue when Missouri applied for statehood in 1817. People living in Missouri wanted to allow slavery in their state. At the time, the United States consisted of 11 slave states and 11

HISTORY FROM VISUALS

Reading the Map Point out that the United States was bounded on three sides by British and Spanish possessions. Ask students why establishing firm boundaries with these powers was important. **Possible Responses** Firm boundaries would limit disputes that might lead to war. They also would make previous U.S. territorial expansion more secure.

Extension Ask students to find state boundaries that, like the U.S.–Canada border, follow parallels of latitude. What is another common way of determining boundaries? **Answer** rivers

INSTRUCT: OBJECTIVE 3

Sectional Tensions Increase/ The Missouri Compromise

- How did economic changes contribute to growing sectionalism?
- Why did the question of admitting Missouri to the Union divide the nation?
- How did the Missouri Compromise address the issue of slavery in U.S. territories and future states?

ACTIVITY OPTIONS

INDIVIDUAL NEEDS: GIFTED AND TALENTED

NATIONALISM/SECTIONALISM

Class Time One class period

Task Creating a political advertisement that expresses a point of view

Purpose To identify and summarize opinions of nationalists and sectionalists

Supplies Needed
- Audio recorder and tapes (optional)
- Video recorder and tapes (optional)

Activity Have individual students adopt the viewpoint of a citizen who supports nationalism (the concept of loyalty to one's nation as a whole) or the viewpoint of a citizen who supports sectionalism (loyalty to one's region or section of the country). Ask students to write radio or TV ads of no longer than 30 seconds that express their points of view. Remind them to include facts and information that could persuade listeners to adopt their viewpoint. Record or videotape their ads so students can listen to themselves.

HISTORY FROM VISUALS

Reading the Map Ask the students how much of the unorganized U.S. territory west of Missouri and Illinois was open to slavery. **Answer** None north of Missouri Compromise line. South of the line was blocked by New Spain. Ask students how those facts might contribute to increasing tensions between slave and free states. **Possible Responses** People in slave states might fear that free states would soon outnumber slave states.

Extension Have students research the history of slavery in Mexico to find when it began and ended. **Answer** Slavery in New Spain dated back to the first decades of the Spanish conquest. However, by the early 1800s, slavery (and Spanish power) was fading in much of Latin America. Mexico abolished slavery in 1829.

MORE ABOUT . . .

The Missouri Compromise

Thomas Jefferson, for one, realized that the Missouri Compromise was a temporary solution to a serious problem. He called it "a fire bell in the night" that filled him with terror. The dispute between North and South, he said, was "a speck on our horizon" that might eventually "burst on us as a tornado." John Quincy Adams called the Missouri Compromise "a mere preamble—a title-page to a great, tragic volume."

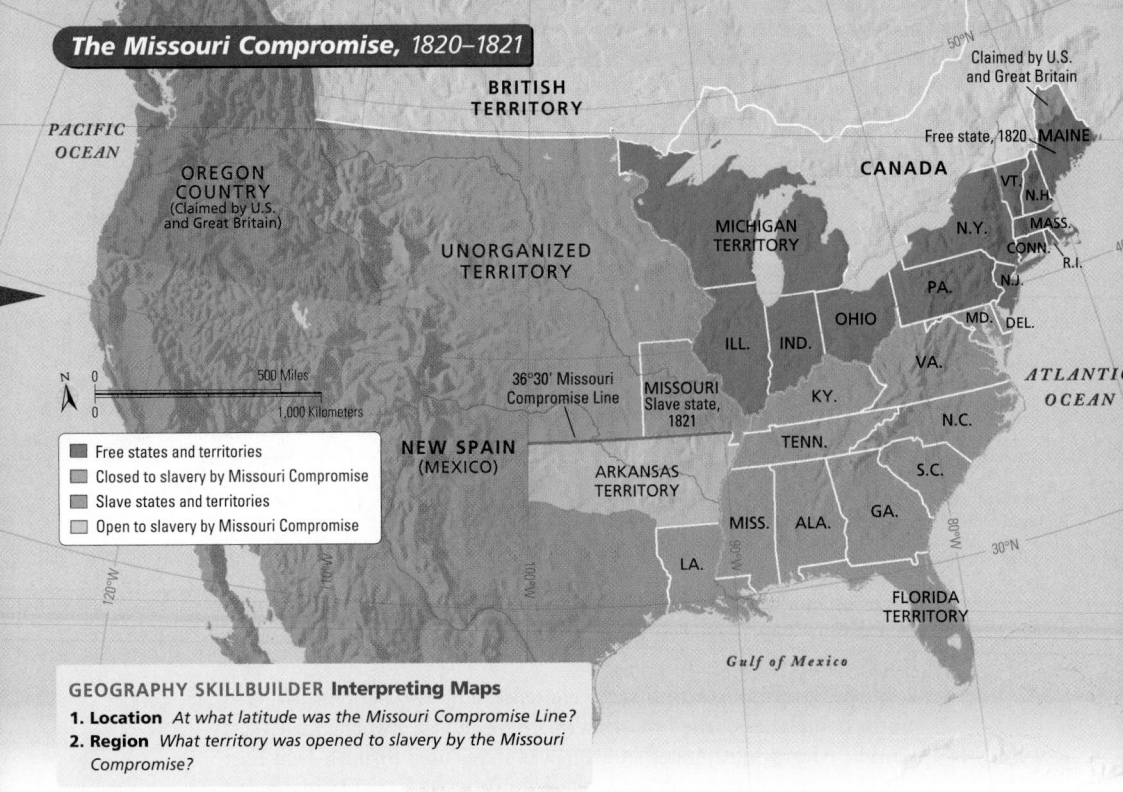

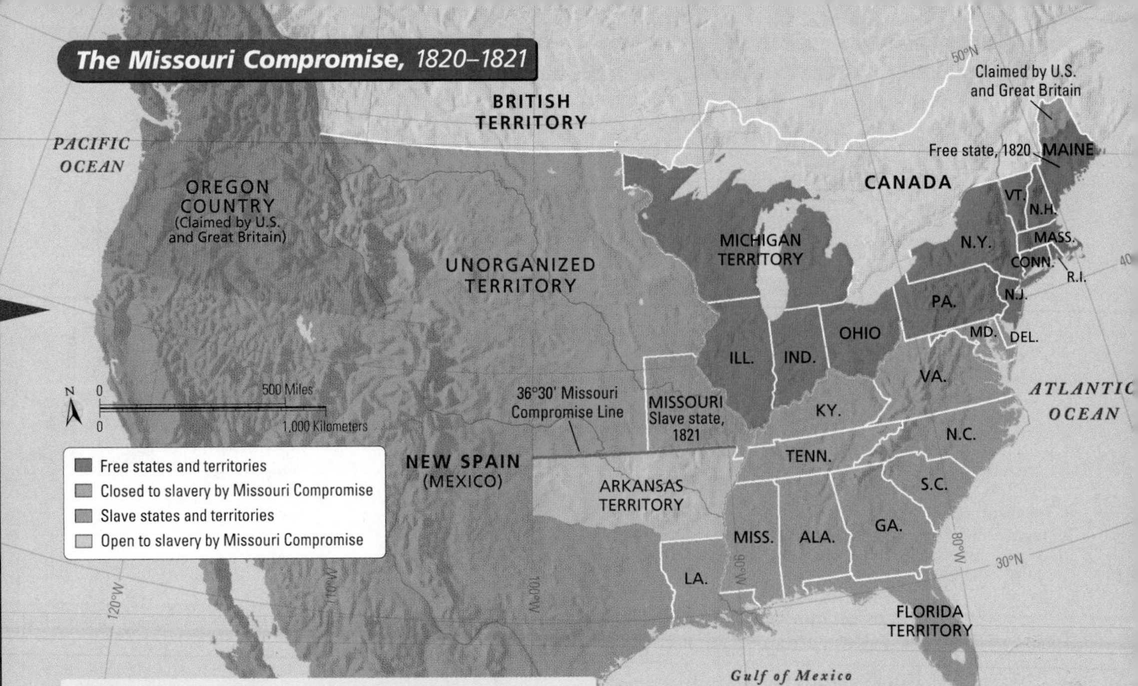

GEOGRAPHY SKILLBUILDER Interpreting Maps

1. **Location** *At what latitude was the Missouri Compromise Line?*
2. **Region** *What territory was opened to slavery by the Missouri Compromise?*

Skillbuilder Answers
1. 36° 30′ N
2. Arkansas Territory

free states. Adding Missouri as a slave state would upset the balance of power in Congress. The question of Missouri soon divided the nation.

The Missouri Compromise

For months, the nation argued over admitting Missouri as a slave state or a free state. Debate raged in Congress over a proposal made by James Tallmadge of New York to ban slavery in Missouri. Angry Southerners claimed that the Constitution did not give Congress the power to ban slavery. They worried that free states could form a majority in Congress and ban slavery altogether. Representative Thomas Cobb of Georgia expressed the Southerners' point of view when he responded to Tallmadge.

Reading **History**
D. Analyzing Points of View Why was it so important to Southerners to admit Missouri as a slave state?
D. Answer They feared that having more free states than slave states would enable Congress to ban slavery and overturn the South's economic system.

A VOICE FROM THE PAST

If you persist, the Union will be dissolved. You have kindled a fire which all the waters of the ocean cannot put out, which seas of blood can only extinguish.

Thomas Cobb, quoted in *Henry Clay: Statesman for the Union*

Meanwhile, Maine, which had been part of Massachusetts, also wanted statehood. Henry Clay, the Speaker of the House, saw a chance for compromise. He suggested that Missouri be admitted as a slave state and Maine as a free state. Congress passed Clay's plan, known as the **Missouri Compromise,** in 1820. It kept the balance of power in the Senate

ACTIVITY OPTIONS

SKILLBUILDER LESSON: COMPARING AND CONTRASTING

BLOCK SCHEDULING

Explaining the Skill Historians compare and contrast events, people, ideas, and other things in order to understand them well. Comparing involves finding similarities and differences between things. Contrasting means examining only the differences between them.

Applying the Skill Ask students to review what they have learned about the North and the South. Then ask the following questions.

1. Contrast the economies of the North and the South. *(North: wealth based on manufacturing and trade; South: relied on cotton and slavery)*
2. Compare the two regions' boundary disputes with foreign powers. *(Similarity: Both had unsettled boundaries with European powers. Difference: The North's dispute was with Britain; the South's, with Spain.)*

In-Depth Resources: Unit 3
- Skillbuilder Practice, p. 46

between the slave states and free states. It also called for slavery to be banned from the Louisiana Territory north of the parallel 36° 30', Missouri's southern border.

Thomas Jefferson, nearing 80 years old and living quietly in Virginia, was troubled by the Missouri Compromise. Worried that sectionalism would destroy the country, Jefferson wrote: "In the gloomiest moment of the Revolutionary War I never had any apprehension equal to what I feel from this source."

> **"If you persist, the Union will be dissolved."**
> Thomas Cobb

4 The Monroe Doctrine

The nation felt threatened not only by sectionalism, but by events elsewhere in the Americas. In Latin America, several countries had successfully fought for their independence from Spain and Portugal. Some European monarchies planned to help Spain and Portugal regain their colonies, hoping to keep the urge to revolt from reaching Europe. U.S. leaders feared that if this happened, their own government would be in danger.

Russian colonies in the Pacific Northwest also concerned Americans. The Russians entered Alaska in 1784. By 1812, their trading posts reached almost to San Francisco.

In December 1823, President Monroe issued a statement that became known as the **Monroe Doctrine.** (See Interactive Primary Source, page 344.) Monroe said that the Americas were closed to further colonization. He also warned that European efforts to reestablish colonies would be considered "dangerous to our peace and safety." Finally, he promised that the United States would stay out of European affairs. The Monroe Doctrine showed that the United States saw itself as a world power and protector of Latin America.

In Chapter 12, you will learn how a new democratic spirit grew—and how Native Americans suffered—during Andrew Jackson's presidency.

Background
Latin America refers to the Spanish- and Portugese-speaking nations of the Western Hemisphere south of the United States.

Background
The ideas in the Monroe Doctrine came from John Quincy Adams, Monroe's secretary of state. Adams delivered a speech against colonization on July 4, 1821—two years before Monroe announced his doctrine.

Section 3 Assessment

1. Terms & Names

Explain the significance of:
- nationalism
- Henry Clay
- American System
- Erie Canal
- James Monroe
- sectionalism
- Missouri Compromise
- Monroe Doctrine

2. Taking Notes

On a diagram like the one below, name things that contributed to national unity in the early 1800s.

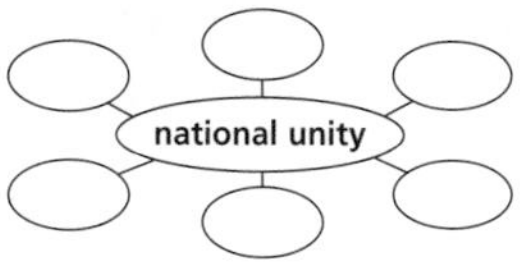

Which of these are still important for national unity?

3. Main Ideas

a. How did the Erie Canal help the nation grow?

b. How did the Missouri Compromise resolve a conflict between the North and South?

c. What was the main message of the Monroe Doctrine, and toward whom was it directed?

4. Critical Thinking

Recognizing Effects If the Supreme Court had decided differently in *Gibbons* v. *Ogden* or *McCulloch* v. *Maryland,* what might be one result today?

THINK ABOUT
- if states could interfere with federal laws
- if states controlled interstate commerce

ACTIVITY OPTIONS

LANGUAGE ARTS / ART In an **editorial** or a **political cartoon,** give your opinion of either the Missouri Compromise or the Monroe Doctrine.

INSTRUCT: OBJECTIVE 4

The Monroe Doctrine

- Why did events in the early 1800s in Latin America concern the United States?
- What was the purpose of the Monroe Doctrine?

MORE ABOUT . . .

The Monroe Doctrine

The Monroe Doctrine has been an important basis for American foreign policy since 1823. At that time, the United States was not in a position to enforce the Monroe Doctrine, as it came to be known some years later. However, in the 1840s, President Polk invoked the doctrine when he warned Britain and Spain not to make settlements in Oregon, California, or in Mexico. President Theodore Roosevelt expanded the Monroe Doctrine in 1904 with the addition of the "Roosevelt Corollary," designed to prevent European nations from using force.

ASSESS & RETEACH

Setting the Stage Have students place information about slavery and foreign relations in the appropriate box on the graphic organizer.

Formal Assessment
- Section Quiz, p. 202

Critical Thinking Transparency CT31
- Setting the Stage

RETEACHING ACTIVITY

Have students write a summary paragraph that uses the section's Main Idea as the topic sentence. The paragraph should identify the things that contributed to a feeling of nationalism and the tensions that over time contributed to sectionalism.

In-Depth Resources: Unit 3
- Reteaching Activity, p. 56

Section 3 Assessment

1. Terms & Names

nationalism, p. 338
Henry Clay, p. 338
American System, p. 338
Erie Canal, p. 339
James Monroe, p. 340
sectionalism, p. 341
Missouri Compromise, p. 342
Monroe Doctrine, p. 343

2. Taking Notes

protective tariffs, national bank, road and canal systems, strong federal government, settled national boundaries

transportation and strong federal government

3. Main Ideas

a. It opened the upper Ohio Valley and Great Lakes regions to settlement and trade. **b.** It kept the balance of slave and free states in the Senate. **c.** Europe should not colonize the Americas; directed toward Europeans

4. Critical Thinking

The federal government would be much weaker, and there would be greater state rivalries.

ACTIVITY OPTIONS

Integrated Assessment
- Rubrics for an editorial, 4.1
- Rubrics for a political cartoon, 1.2

INTERACTIVE PRIMARY SOURCE

OBJECTIVE

Students will understand that the Monroe Doctrine declares that the United States will not interfere with the internal affairs or wars of European countries nor with existing European colonies in the Americas, and that the Western Hemisphere was not open to further colonization.

Primary Source Explorer
- *The Monroe Doctrine*

The Explorer will help students select and produce their own presentations.

Specific information about the document can be found in **A Closer Look.** To learn more about key people and events of the time, students should click on **Life in These Times. What Happened Next** will show the student the impact of the document and tie it to today.

FOCUS & MOTIVATE

Identifying and Solving Problems Ask students to recall the nations that have claims to lands in the Americas. Ask why the United States might view those nations as a threat in 1823. **Possible Answer** Britain, Spain, France, Portugal, and Russia. They were powerful nations and earlier had been fighting each other. Now they were not fighting and wanted land claims in the Americas.

MORE ABOUT . . .

Reasons for Monroe's Statements

Great Britain had sent a proposal to the United States suggesting that the two nations join in issuing a statement condemning European efforts to regain control of former colonies in the Western Hemisphere. John Quincy Adams, secretary of state to Monroe, said, "It would be more candid, as well as more dignified, to avow our principles explicitly to Russia and France, than to come in as a cock-boat [row boat] in the wake of the British man-of-war."

INTERACTIVE PRIMARY SOURCE

The Monroe Doctrine

Setting the Stage On December 6, 1823, President James Monroe gave a State of the Union address. Part of the speech became known as the Monroe Doctrine. The "allied powers" Monroe refers to are Russia, Prussia, Austria, and France. Earlier in the year, these European monarchies had crushed a revolution in Spain and restored the Spanish king to his throne. They were threatening to help Spain regain its Latin American colonies. See **Primary Source Explorer**

A CLOSER LOOK

NO FUTURE COLONIES

Monroe declares that European countries may not start any new colonies in the Americas.

1. Why might it threaten the United States to have new European colonies near them?

A CLOSER LOOK

NEUTRALITY TOWARD EUROPE

Monroe says that the United States will not take sides in European wars.

2. Why might the United States want to remain neutral toward conflicts in Europe?

[T]he occasion has been judged proper for asserting, as a principle in which the rights and interests of the United States are involved, that the American continents, by the free and independent condition which they have assumed and maintain, are henceforth not to be considered as subjects for future colonization by any European powers. . . .

It was stated at the commencement of the last session that great effort was then making in Spain and Portugal to improve the condition of the people of those countries and that it appeared to be conducted with extraordinary moderation. It need scarcely be remarked that the result has been so far very different from what was then anticipated. . . . The citizens of the United States cherish sentiments the most friendly in favor of the liberty and happiness of their fellowmen on that side of the Atlantic. In the wars of the European powers in matters relating to themselves we have never taken any part, nor does it **comport**[1] with our policy so to do. It is only when our rights are invaded or seriously **menaced**[2] that we resent injuries or make preparation for our defense.

With the movements in this hemisphere we are of necessity more immediately connected, and by causes which must be obvious to all enlightened and impartial observers. The political system of the allied powers is essentially different in this respect from that of America. This difference proceeds from that which exists in their respective governments; and to the defense of our own, which has been achieved by the loss of so much blood and treasure, and matured by the wisdom of their most enlightened citizens, and under which we have enjoyed **unexampled felicity**,[3] this whole nation is devoted. We owe it, therefore, to **candor**[4] and to the **amicable**[5] relations existing between the

1. **comport:** agree with.
2. **menaced:** threatened.
3. **unexampled felicity:** the greatest happiness.
4. **candor:** honesty.
5. **amicable:** friendly.

TEACHING STRATEGY

Analyzing Tell students that President Monroe addressed the threat of European nations helping Spain regain its former colonies in South America. Americans strongly supported the new Latin American republics. In addition, Britain seemed interested in taking over Cuba. Read the selection to the class. Pause after every sentence and ask students to explain the sentence in their own words. When you have worked through the document with the class, ask students to identify where in the document Monroe addresses the European threats and American hopes for Latin America. Then complete the cause-and-effect graphic on the right.

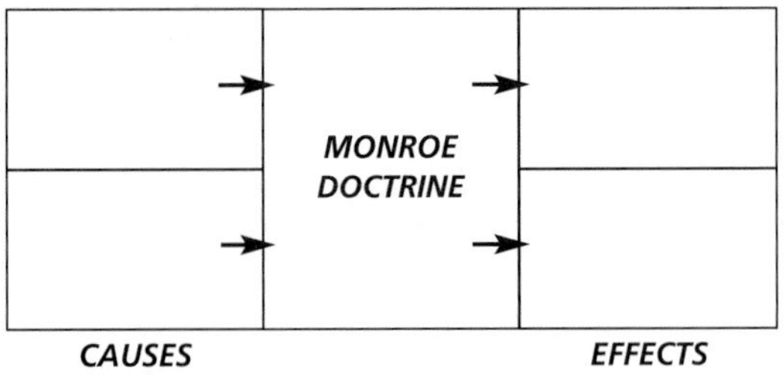

United States and those powers to declare that we should consider any attempt on their part to extend their system to any portion of this hemisphere as dangerous to our peace and safety.

With the existing colonies or dependencies of any European power we have not interfered and shall not interfere. But with the governments who have declared their independence and maintained it, and whose independence we have, on great consideration and on just principles, acknowledged, we could not view any **interposition**[6] for the purpose of oppressing them, or controlling in any other manner their destiny, by any European power in any other light than as the manifestation of an unfriendly disposition toward the United States. In the war between those new governments and Spain we declared our neutrality at the time of their recognition, and to this we have adhered and shall continue to adhere, provided no change shall occur which, in the judgment of the competent authorities of this government, shall make a corresponding change on the part of the United States indispensable to their security.

The late events in Spain and Portugal show that Europe is still unsettled. Of this important fact no stronger proof can be adduced than that the allied powers should have thought it proper, on any principle satisfactory to themselves, to have interposed by force in the internal concerns of Spain. To what extent such interposition may be carried, on the same principle, is a question in which all independent powers whose governments differ from theirs are interested, even those most remote, and surely none more so than the United States.

—*James Monroe*

6. **interposition:** interference.

A CLOSER LOOK

A DIFFERENT SYSTEM

Monroe states that the United States will defend its republican form of government and would be threatened if Europeans set up monarchies in the Americas.

3. Why would U.S. citizens want their government to be a republic and not an absolute monarchy?

A CLOSER LOOK

NO INTERFERENCE

Monroe warns that if Europeans invade the newly independent republics in Latin America, this would be considered hostile to the United States as well.

4. What would the United States have to fear if these republics were overthrown?

Interactive Primary Source Assessment

1. Main Ideas

a. Why might the United States want no more European colonies in the Americas, particularly in Latin America?

b. How would staying neutral in European wars protect the United States?

c. How might the U.S. system of government be threatened if Europeans regained control of former colonies in the Americas?

2. Critical Thinking

Making Inferences For decades, the United States lacked the military power to enforce the Monroe Doctrine and depended on the British navy to keep other European powers out of Latin America. Why, then, did the United States proclaim the Monroe Doctrine?

THINK ABOUT

- what the doctrine shows about the values and wishes of the United States
- what it shows about how the country saw itself or wanted to be seen

345

Interactive Primary Source Assessment

1. Main Ideas

a. The United States might fear colonies in Latin America because of the closeness of borders and because new European colonies might threaten trade or wage war involving the United States.

b. protection from one-sided attack and from committing troops to aid an ally

c. European powers might be tempted to try to take control of the United States.

2. Critical Thinking

The United States wanted respect from other nations, hoped the doctrine would help it negotiate settlements, and wanted to uphold the principles of freedom and independence on which it was founded.

INSTRUCT

- What was the major purpose of Monroe's statements?
- What position does Monroe say that the United States will maintain in European wars?
- What reason does Monroe give for United States concern over events in Latin America?
- How does Monroe say that the United States would view any interference by European nations with the governments of Latin America?

MAKING PERSONAL CONNECTIONS

Ask students whether they are more interested in national or local news. Discuss why events in their own neighborhood are important to them. Use a map to show the Western Hemisphere and reminds students that the nations of the Americas are "neighbors" of the United States.

MORE ABOUT . . .

Invoking the Monroe Doctrine

The United States cited the Monroe Doctrine when it opposed European interest in building a canal across Central America. In 1895, the United States invoked the Monroe Doctrine when it forced Great Britain and Venezuela to arbitrate a dispute about the boundary between Venezuela and British Guiana. The doctrine was also invoked when the United States sent troops to Nicaragua, Haiti, Guatemala, Cuba, the Dominican Republic, Grenada, and Panama to prevent feared Communist takeovers and civil wars.

A CLOSER LOOK

1. New colonies might have boundary conflicts with the United States, interfere with trade, be on land that the United States wants to acquire, or be battlegrounds in future European wars.
2. It might remain neutral to avoid being attacked, to avoid having to commit troops or funds, to be able to trade with both sides, or to better concentrate on its own affairs.
3. because people want to act in their own interest by electing representatives to make decisions for them instead of having decisions made by a hereditary ruler acting in his or her own interest
4. fear that European nations would invade the United States and return it to colonial status, or that European rulers might outlaw U.S. trade with their colonies or have their military forces blockade U.S. ports

TERMS & NAMES

1. **Samuel Slater,** p. 325
2. **Industrial Revolution,** p. 325
3. **Robert Fulton,** p. 328
4. **Eli Whitney,** p. 332
5. **cotton gin,** p.332
6. **Nat Turner,** p. 337
7. **nationalism,** p. 338
8. **sectionalism,** p.341
9. **Missouri Compromise,** p. 342
10. **Monroe Doctrine,** p. 343

REVIEW QUESTIONS

Possible Responses

1. The British blockade forced Americans to develop their own industries.
2. Investments switched from shipping and trade to manufacturing American goods.
3. expanded trade; transportation; national unity
4. sped up production; made repairs easy; allowed use of low-paid, unskilled labor
5. The cotton gin made it easier to raise short-fibered cotton, which grew in many parts of the South. Slavery provided the large work force needed on the plantations.
6. difficult work; severe punishment; separation from family
7. They had faith that God would end slavery. They sang religious spirituals for comfort.
8. It limited state powers by ruling that no state could tax a national bank.
9. Spain gave it to the United States in 1819 with the Adams-Onís Treaty.
10. Maine entered as a free state while Missouri entered as a slave state, and slavery was banned above the 36°30′ parallel.

Chapter 11 ASSESSMENT

VISUAL SUMMARY

Early Industry and Inventions

New machines allowed the Northeast to industrialize and the Midwest to increase farm production.

Plantations and Slavery Spread

The cotton gin led to the expansion of plantations and slavery in the South.

Nationalism and Sectionalism

Nationalism drew regions together. At the same time, economic differences created tension between regions.

TERMS & NAMES

Briefly explain the significance of each of the following.

1. Samuel Slater
2. Industrial Revolution
3. Robert Fulton
4. Eli Whitney
5. cotton gin
6. Nat Turner
7. nationalism
8. sectionalism
9. Missouri Compromise
10. Monroe Doctrine

REVIEW QUESTIONS

Early Industry and Inventions (pages 325–331)

1. How did the War of 1812 push the United States to build factories?
2. How did the War of 1812 and free enterprise affect the U.S. economy?
3. What was one effect of the steamboat?
4. How did interchangeable parts transform the manufacturing process?

Plantations and Slavery Spread (pages 332–337)

5. Why did slavery spread in the South?
6. What were three hardships faced by enslaved people on plantations?
7. How did religion help people endure or resist slavery?

Nationalism and Sectionalism (pages 338–345)

8. How did the Supreme Court's ruling in *McCulloch v. Maryland* strengthen the federal government?
9. How did the United States gain the territory of Florida?
10. What were the terms of the Missouri Compromise?

CRITICAL THINKING

1. USING YOUR NOTES

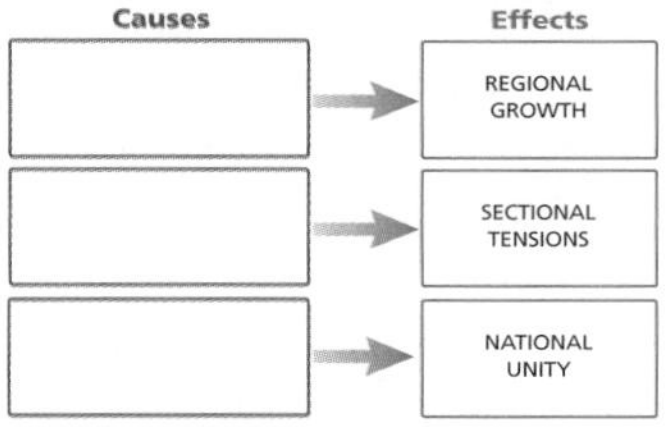

Using your completed chart, answer the questions.

a. What were three causes leading to national unity?
b. What was one cause of sectional tension?

2. THEME: SCIENCE AND TECHNOLOGY

Of all the new inventions mentioned in the chapter, which do you think was most important and why?

3. ANALYZING CAUSES

How did geographic differences between regions lead to economic differences between them?

4. APPLYING CITIZENSHIP SKILLS

Do you think the Missouri Compromise was a wise decision? Consider what might have happened without it, and also why it made Jefferson so uneasy.

5. ANALYZING LEADERSHIP

Think about the Monroe Doctrine and the boundary settlements achieved during the Monroe administration. How would you judge Monroe's foreign policy?

Interact *with* History

Did you predict the ways that new inventions would change the country? What surprised you?

CRITICAL THINKING

Possible Responses

1. USING YOUR NOTES **a.** better communications; better transportation; economic cooperation **b.** slavery
2. THEME: SCIENCE AND TECHNOLOGY Students may choose the cotton gin because it led to the expansion of slavery in the South, or the steamboat and the telegraph because both linked people in different cities.
3. ANALYZING CAUSES Water power from rivers helped build Northeast factories; good soils built the South and West agricultural economies.
4. APPLYING CITIZENSHIP SKILLS Without it, the country might have engaged in civil war sooner. However, it simply prolonged the debate over slavery. Jefferson worried that this type of sectionalism would destroy the nation.
5. ANALYZING LEADERSHIP Students may see Monroe's policy as bold and nationalistic, or aggressive and arrogant.

Interact *with* History Answers will vary based on the student's predictions.

HISTORY SKILLS

1. INTERPRETING MAPS: Region

Study the map. Answer the questions.

Basic Map Elements

a. What region is the subject of the map?

b. What do the dates on the map mean?

Interpreting the Map

c. What countries were independent by 1823, when the Monroe Doctrine was issued?

d. When did Mexico become independent?

2. INTERPRETING PRIMARY SOURCES

The following verse is from a well-known folk song. Read the verse and answer the questions.

> **Low Bridge, Everybody Down**
> I've got a mule and her name is Sal,
> Fifteen miles on the Erie Canal.
> She's a good old worker and a good old pal,
> Fifteen miles on the Erie Canal.
> We've hauled some barges in our day,
> Filled with lumber, coal, and hay,
> And we know every inch of the way
> From Albany to Buffalo.

a. In the song, how is the Erie Canal used?

b. What feeling does the song give you about working on the Erie Canal?

ALTERNATIVE ASSESSMENT

1. INTERDISCIPLINARY ACTIVITY: Science

Making a Presentation Do research to learn how inventions of the early 1800s have been improved upon today. For example, learn what kind of engine powers modern boats, and why it works better than a steam engine. Or find out what modern farmers use instead of the McCormick reaper. Share your findings in an oral presentation with visual aids.

2. COOPERATIVE LEARNING ACTIVITY

Planning an Exhibit As a class, plan a museum exhibit to show what slavery was like on cotton plantations. Break into small groups to research different topics—for example, what enslaved people wore, what their houses were like, what rules they lived under, and what stories they told. Bring back your research and decide how you can best share what you learned with an audience. Part of your exhibit might be a model of a plantation or dramatic readings from slave narratives.

3. PRIMARY SOURCE EXPLORER

Planning Foreign Policy The Monroe Doctrine was President Monroe's outline for U.S. foreign policy early in the 19th century. Using the Primary Source Explorer CD-ROM, library, and Internet, find out more about the Monroe Doctrine.

Imagine that you are president of the United States. Come up with four main principles of foreign policy that this country should follow in the 21st century.

- With classmates, talk about broad principles from the Monroe Doctrine. Keeping out of European conflicts would be one example. Protecting free republics would be another.
- Decide whether you agree or disagree with these principles. Think of current U.S. policies that follow or reject them.
- As president, decide how you will communicate U.S. foreign policy for the 21st century to the public. If you make a televised speech, what facts and visual aids would be most persuasive?

4. HISTORY PORTFOLIO

Review the questions you listed for What Do You Want to Know? on page 340. In a brief report, write what you learned about the lives of people from different regions in the early 1800s. Be sure to use standard grammar, spelling, sentence structure, and punctuation in your report.

Additional Test Practice, pp. S1–S33 TEST PRACTICE CLASSZONE.COM

ALTERNATIVE ASSESSMENT

1. INTERDISCIPLINARY ACTIVITY: Science
   Presentations should
   - present information that reflects the student's research on inventions and improvements.
   - use visual aids to support information.
   - have a clear introduction and conclusion.
   - have adequate delivery and establish rapport with the audience.

2. COOPERATIVE LEARNING ACTIVITY
   Exhibits should
   - have a complete introductory overview.
   - contain accurate and well-described textual information.
   - use a variety of media.
   - be accompanied by well-informed and lively student presenters.

3. PRIMARY SOURCE EXPLORER
   Presentations should
   - clearly state four main principles.
   - present supporting reasons for each position.
   - clearly rebut other viewpoints.
   - include visual aids.
   - use standard grammar, spelling, sentence structure, and punctuation.

4. HISTORY PORTFOLIO
   Option 1 Revised section or chapter assessment activities should
   - address teacher and peer responses to the selected work.
   - solve problems present in the first versions of the work.

   Option 2 Short reports should
   - answer questions about the differences in the regions of the United States in the first half of the 1800s.
   - cite sources of information.
   - use standard grammar, spelling, sentence structure, and punctuation.

Critical Thinking Transparency CT33
- Visual Summary

Formal Assessment
- Chapter Test, Forms A, B, and C, pp. 203–217

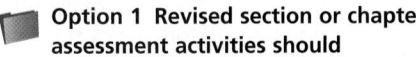

HISTORY SKILLS

Possible Responses

1. INTERPRETING MAPS
   Basic Map Elements
   a. Latin America
   b. date of independence
   Interpreting the Map
   c. Mexico, Haiti, Santo Domingo, Brazil, Paraguay, Argentina, Chile, Peru
   d. 1821

2. INTERPRETING PRIMARY SOURCES
   a. to transport trade goods such as lumber, coal, and hay between Albany and Buffalo
   b. Work was done with a mule and seems to be repetitive.

UNIT 4

A Changing Nation

1810–1860

CHAPTER 12
The Age of Jackson, 1824–1840
CHAPTER 13
Manifest Destiny, 1810–1853
CHAPTER 14
A New Spirit of Change, 1820–1860

BEFORE YOU READ

Previewing Unit 4

Unit 4 examines the many ways the United States grows and changes from the 1820s to the 1850s. During these years, a new spirit of democracy and a great interest in politics spread through the nation. Many Americans believe strongly in their country's manifest destiny—to expand across the continent. The United States goes to war with Mexico and claims California and much of the Southwest as a result. But national expansion comes at the expense of the lives and cultures of Native Americans and Hispanics. Reformers of the day work to improve American society, while women and African Americans work toward the goal of equality under the law.

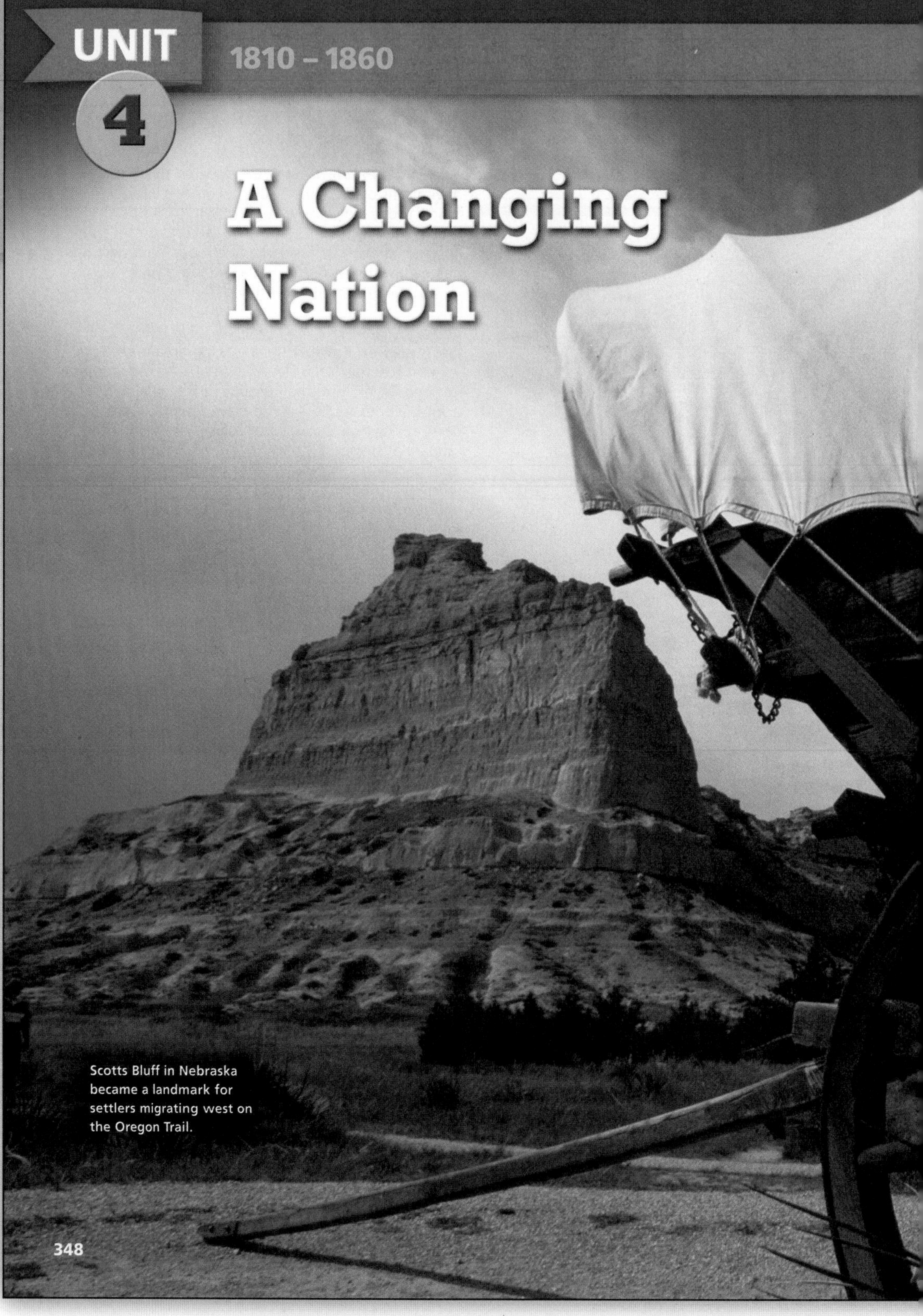

Scotts Bluff in Nebraska became a landmark for settlers migrating west on the Oregon Trail.

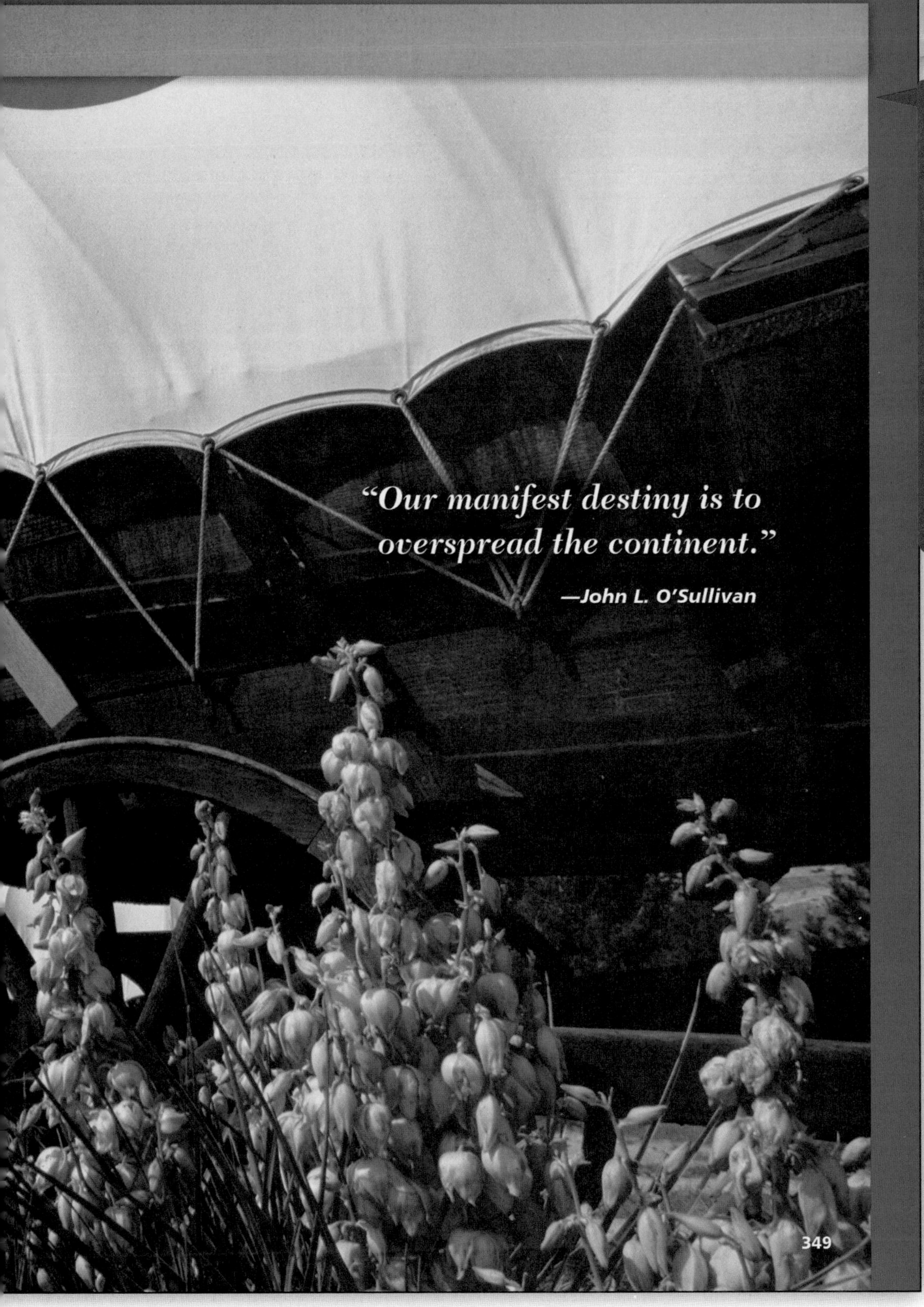

"Our manifest destiny is to overspread the continent."
—John L. O'Sullivan
349

HISTORY FROM VISUALS

Interpreting the Photograph Ask students to think about long trips they have taken by car or bus. Have students brainstorm a list of words and phrases to describe such trips. Write the positive words and phrases in one column on the board and put the negative words and phrases in a second column. Then ask students to make a list of words describing travel in a covered wagon such as the one shown here. Tell students to classify their list into two columns headed *positive aspects* and *negative aspects.* Combine responses on the chalkboard to make a class list.

Extension Ask students to write a short story about a family traveling in a covered wagon along the Oregon Trail. Tell students to use Scotts Bluff as the setting of their story.

CHAPTER 12 PLANNING GUIDE

The Age of Jackson 1824–1840

	CHAPTER OVERVIEW	COPYMASTERS	INTEGRATED TECHNOLOGY
CHAPTER RESOURCES	This chapter describes the presidency of Andrew Jackson and the concept of Jacksonian democracy. It also discusses Jackson's policies on Native Americans, the national bank, and states' rights.	**In-Depth Resources: Unit 4** • Tracing Themes: Economics in History, p. 2 • Building Vocabulary, p. 7 **Interdisciplinary Projects,** pp. 67–72	• eEdition Plus Online • EasyPlanner Plus Online • eTest Plus Online • eEdition • Power Presentations • EasyPlanner • Electronic Library of Primary Sources • Test Generator • Reading Study Guide • America's Music
SECTION 1 **Politics of the People** **pp. 353–357**	**KEY IDEAS** • Andrew Jackson wins the election of 1828, his popularity based on his humble origins and his military record. • Voting rights expand to include most white men, regardless of economic level. • Jackson gives government jobs to his political backers, a process called the spoils system.	**In-Depth Resources: Unit 4** • Setting the Stage, p. 1 • Guided Reading, p. 3 • Geography Application, pp. 9–10 • Literature Selection, pp. 13–15 • Reteaching Activity, p. 16 **America's History Makers** • Andrew Jackson, pp. 47–48 **Citizenship Today,** pp. 7–8 **Why It Matters Now,** pp. 23–24	**Warm-Up Transparency WT12** **Geography Transparency GT12** • State Voting Qualifications, 1828 **Critical Thinking Transparency CT34** • Setting the Stage classzone.com
SECTION 2 **Jackson's Policy Toward Native Americans** **pp. 358–362**	• Native Americans who adopt white ways of life hold much land in the Southeast. • Jackson supports the Indian Removal Act, which forces tribes to move west. • Many Native Americans resist removal, but eventually lose their lands.	**In-Depth Resources: Unit 4** • Setting the Stage, p.1 • Guided Reading, p. 4 • Primary Source, p. 11 • Reteaching Activity, p. 17 **America's History Makers** • Sequoya, pp. 49–50 **Outline Map Activities** • Native American Movement, 1830–1842, pp. 23–24	**Warm-Up Transparency WT12** **Humanities Transparency HT23** • Political Cartoon: Andrew Jackson and Native Americans **Critical Thinking Transparency CT34** • Setting the Stage **Critical Thinking Transparency CT35** • Cause and Effect: Native American Removal classzone.com
SECTION 3 **Conflicts over States' Rights** **pp. 363–367**	• The country argues over the sale of public lands, tariffs, and internal improvements. • Southerner John C. Calhoun proposes the doctrine of nullification, allowing a state to overrule a federal law. • Jackson insists that federal laws will be enforced, and compromise averts the crisis.	**In-Depth Resources: Unit 4** • Setting the Stage, p. 1 • Guided Reading, p. 5 • Primary Source, p. 12 • Reteaching Activity, p. 18 **Economics in History** • Conflict over High Tariffs, p. 12	**Warm-Up Transparency WT12** **Critical Thinking Transparency CT34** • Setting the Stage classzone.com
SECTION 4 **Prosperity and Panic** **pp. 368–371**	• Jackson vetoes the charter of the national bank. • Jackson's economic policies lead to inflation, and an economic depression begins in 1837. • A new political party, the Whig Party, arises and wins the election of 1840.	**In-Depth Resources: Unit 4** • Setting the Stage, p. 1 • Guided Reading, p. 6 • Skillbuilder Practice: Interpreting Political Cartoons, p. 8 • Reteaching Activity, p. 19	**Warm-Up Transparency WT12** **Humanities Transparency HT24** • Whig Rolling Ball, 1840 **Critical Thinking Transparency CT34** • Setting the Stage **Critical Thinking Transparency CT36** • Visual Summary classzone.com

Pupil's Edition | Overhead Transparency | CD-ROM
Copymaster | Audio Library | Internet

ASSESSMENT OPTIONS

Chapter Assessment, pp. 372–373

Formal Assessment
- Chapter Tests, Forms A, B, and C, pp. 222–236

Test Generator

Online Test Practice

Strategies for Test Preparation

Section Assessment, p. 357

Formal Assessment, Quiz, p. 218

Integrated Assessment Book
- Rubrics, 2.1, 2.2

Test Generator

Test Practice Transparencies, TT41

Section Assessment, p. 362

Formal Assessment, Quiz, p. 219

Integrated Assessment Book
- Rubrics for a map, 2.1, 2.2

Test Generator

Test Practice Transparencies, TT42

Section Assessment, p. 367

Formal Assessment, Quiz, p. 220

Integrated Assessment Book
- Rubrics for a speech, 3.6, 5.3

Test Generator

Test Practice Transparencies, TT43

Section Assessment, p. 371

Formal Assessment, Quiz, p. 221

Integrated Assessment Book
- Rubrics, 4.1, 1.1

Test Generator

Test Practice Transparencies, TT44

CUSTOMIZING FOR INDIVIDUAL NEEDS

Students Acquiring English/ESL

Reading Study Guide (English and Spanish), pp. 113–122

Access for Students Acquiring English/ESL: Spanish Translations, pp. 76–82

Chapter Summaries on CD (English and Spanish)

Modified Lesson Plans for English Learners

Less Proficient Readers

Reading Study Guide (English and Spanish), pp. 113–122

Chapter Summaries on CD (English and Spanish)

Gifted and Talented Students

In-Depth Resources: Unit 4
- Enrichment Activity, p. 20

America's History Makers
- Andrew Jackson, pp. 47–48
- Sequoya, pp. 49–50

CROSS-CURRICULAR CONNECTIONS

Culture

Tunis, Edwin. ***Frontier Living.*** New York: Harper/Collins, 1976. Award-winning presentation of daily life and work on the frontier, with details about everything from clothing to tools to transportation to social life.

Economics

Otfinoksi, Steve. ***Kid's Guide to Money.*** New York: Scholastic, 1996. Explains the uses of banks, along with information about how to earn money, save it, and spend it wisely.

Government

Collier, Christopher. ***Andrew Jackson's America, 1824–1850.*** Tarrytown, NY: Benchmark Books, 1999. Examines politics and government in a turbulent time.

Interdisciplinary Projects, pp. 67–72

- Math: Calculating Voter Turnouts
- Science: Veterinary Medicine
- Language Arts: Campaign Literature of 1828
- Art: Political Cartoons

Literature

Cheatham, K. Follis. ***Bring Home the Ghost.*** New York: Harcourt, 1980. A young man and his personal slave return from fighting in the Seminole war to find their home destroyed in an Indian raid. They strike out for the frontier, where the enslaved Jason learns what freedom really means.

Harrell, Beatrice Orcutt and Tony Meers. ***Longwalker's Journey: A Novel of the Choctaw Trail of Tears.*** New York: Dial, 1999. Minko and his family are forced to relocate from Mississippi to Oklahoma.

Holmes, Jean. ***Mornin' Star Risin'.*** Nampa, ID: Pacific Press Publishing Association, 1992. First volume in the highly successful, multigenerational saga of the black and white families whose lives intertwine at the Weldon Oaks Plantation on the Sea Islands of Georgia.

ENRICHMENT ACTIVITIES

Pupil's Edition, pp. 350–373
Interact with History, p. 351
Citizenship Today, p. 356
Economics in History, p. 364

In-Depth Resources: Unit 4
- Geography Application: Election of 1828, pp. 9–10
- Primary Source: A Petition by Cherokee Women, p. 11
- Primary Source: from *Reminiscences and Anecdotes of Daniel Webster*, p. 12
- Literature Selection: from *Jackson* by Max Byrd, pp. 13–15

America's History Makers
- Andrew Jackson, pp. 47–48
- Sequoya, pp. 49–50

Outline Map Activities
- Native American Movement, 1830–1842, pp. 23–24

Why It Matters Now
- Expanding Democracy, pp. 23–24

BLOCK SCHEDULING — LESSON PLAN OPTIONS (90-MINUTE PERIOD)

DAY 1

Interact with History, p. 351
Class Time 20 Minutes

Options for pacing and variety:
- Role-Play Have groups of three students assume the roles of new voters in the election of 1828. Students can take turns explaining to their partners what qualities make a strong leader and identifying earlier presidents they consider strong leaders. Have groups report their conclusions to the class. **Class Time** 20 minutes

Setting the Stage, p. 352
Class Time 20 minutes

Options for pacing and variety:
- Time Saver Ask students to come to class with two lists. One list should describe what they already know about Andrew Jackson and a second list should contain questions they would like answered about his presidency. **Class Time** 5 minutes

Section 1, pp. 353–357
Class Time 50 minutes

Options for pacing and variety:
- Peer Teaching Working in groups, have students prepare media reports on the outcome of the election of 1824 and share them with the class. **Class Time** 20 minutes
- Time Saver Use the chart on page 357 to summarize the section. **Class Time** 10 minutes

DAY 2

Section 2, pp. 358–362
Class Time 45 minutes

Options for pacing and variety:
- Time Saver As a homework assignment, have students answer Critical Thinking question 5 in the Chapter Assessment on page 372. Discuss responses in class. **Class Time** 10 minutes
- Internet Extend students' background knowledge of the Cherokee by learning about Native American languages at classzone.com. **Class Time** 20 minutes

Section 3, pp. 363–367
Class Time 45 minutes

Options for pacing and variety:
- Peer Teaching Ask two volunteers to review Economics in History on page 364 and explain to the class how a protective tariff works. To check student comprehension, the peer teachers can have students give oral answers to the Connect to History and Connect to Today questions for the feature. **Class Time** 15 minutes
- Time Saver For a homework assignment, have students complete the Main Ideas and Critical Thinking questions in the section assessment. **Class Time** 5 minutes

DAY 3

Section 4, pp. 368–371
Class Time 45 minutes

Options for pacing and variety:
- Time Saver Use the cartoon "Jackson Fights the Second Bank" on page 369 to summarize the section. **Class Time** 10 minutes
- History on Film Extend students' background knowledge of Andrew Jackson's presidency by viewing "The Jackson Years: Toward Civil War." Learning Corporation of America. **Class Time** 30 minutes

Chapter 12 Assessment, pp. 372–373
Class Time 40 minutes

Options for pacing and variety:
- Peer Evaluation Working in groups, students should review the Visual Summary on page 388 and explain why each of the topics mentioned became a major issue of Jackson's presidency. Students can also discuss whether they agree with the actions Jackson took in each case. **Class Time** 15 minutes
- Peer Teaching Ask one student to assume the role of a supporter of Jackson and the other a critic. Pair critics and supporters and have each explain to the other how he or she feels about the cartoon "King Andrew the First" in the Chapter Assessment. **Class Time** 10 minutes

TEACHER-TESTED ACTIVITY **Brent Heath, De Anza Middle School, Ontario, California**

THE DOCTRINE OF NULLIFICATION

Class Time Two class periods

Task Presenting a "Face the Nation" talk show on the doctrine of nullification

Purpose To identify and summarize conflicting positions in the states' rights debate on the doctrine of nullification

Supplies Needed
- Reference books and Internet sources on Daniel Webster, John C. Calhoun, and the nullification controversy

Activity Divide students into six-member groups. Within groups, have students assume the following roles: Daniel Webster, John C. Calhoun, host/moderator, newspaper reporters. One member of the group can be the show's producer. Review the positions of Webster and Calhoun on nullification. Then have groups prepare background material for the roles they will play. The host can prepare a short speech introducing each guest, and reporters can make up questions to ask the show's guests. Calhoun and Webster can make short statements about their positions on the issues before questioning by reporters begins.

CHAPTER 12 TECHNOLOGY IN THE CLASSROOM

STATES' RIGHTS CHAT ROOM

Electronic bulletin boards or chat rooms have become hotbeds of activity for the expression of opinions of like-minded groups. There are now electronic bulletin boards for almost every kind of group. Electronic chat rooms can be forums to hold discussions on important issues. Students can create their own electronic chat room for this purpose.

ACTIVITY OUTLINE

Objective Setting up an electronic chat room to debate states' rights and the authority of the federal government will broaden students' understanding of these issues and help familiarize them with the technology of electronic chat rooms.

Task Students will set up an electronic chat room to debate the issue of states' rights and the authority of the federal government.

Class Time One class period

DIRECTIONS

1. Students will begin by studying the issues surrounding the historical debate over states' rights and federal power during the Age of Jackson. Create a history chat room in your school's network where students can sign on at various times throughout the day to debate the issue with other students. Appoint different students to monitor the chat room throughout the day.

2. Give students 15–20 minutes to review the information in Chapter 12 on states' rights. Remind them that this issue was one of the most controversial issues of the day. Also, remind the students that this issue was covered in earlier chapters, too. After a short review, ask students why this issue would lead to heated debates.

3. Ask students to begin to formulate their opinions, taking notes to support one side of the debate or the other. Then have a group of students sign on to the chat room and begin their discussion. Remind them that they need to be prepared to defend their opinions.

4. Set a time limit for students to sign on to the chat room. After the time expires, print a log of the opinions and topics discussed.

5. Conduct a classroom discussion to process the different opinions expressed regarding states' rights and federal power. Ask students:
   - What was the strongest argument supporting states' rights that you read?
   - What was the strongest argument supporting greater federal power?
   - Is this still an important issue today? Explain.

CHAPTER 12 OBJECTIVE

The student will understand the far-reaching consequences of the political and economic decisions made by Andrew Jackson during his two terms as president.

HISTORY FROM VISUALS

Interpreting the Illustration This 1829 print by Robert Cruikshank was originally titled "The President's levee, or all Creation going to the White House." Read students the following pairs of adjectives and ask which word in each pair better describes the crowd in the picture: quiet or noisy; festive or angry; dignified or rowdy.

In supporting their choices, students may notice details like the kicking horse, the boy falling out of the coach, and the brightly colored clothing. Some students may also point out the contrast between the stark, formal White House and the excited, energetic spectators.

Extension Have the students write a dialogue about the presidential inauguration that might be taking place between two people in the crowd.

CRITICAL THINKING ACTIVITY

Making Inferences Point out that Jackson is shown on horseback on both pages 351 and 352. Students may also be familiar with equestrian statues that honor noteworthy leaders from their own region. Discuss the implications of military leadership, social rank, and power that such images present.

Class Time 10 minutes

CHAPTER 12

The Age of Jackson 1824–1840

The people came by the thousands to the White House on Inauguration Day to see their president—Andrew Jackson.

350

RECOMMENDED RESOURCES

BOOKS FOR THE TEACHER

Marszalek, John F. ***The Petticoat Affair: Manners, Sex, & Mutiny in Andrew Jackson's White House.*** New York: Free Press, 1997. Lively account of "the Eaton Affair," in which gossip about a cabinet wife exposed stresses within the administration.

Wallace, Anthony F. C. ***The Long, Bitter Trail: Andrew Jackson and the Indians.*** New York: Hill & Wang, 1993. A succinct account of the politics, ethnic friction, and just plain double-dealing that led to this tragic episode.

Watson, Harry L. ***Andrew Jackson vs. Henry Clay: Democracy and Development in Antebellum America.*** New York: St. Martin's, 1998. Dual biography of these clashing leaders.

VIDEO

Andrew Jackson: A Man for the People. A&E (Moonbeam Pubs.), 1995. Life story of one of our most colorful presidents.

INTERNET

For more about Native American languages, visit . . .

classzone.com

Interact *with* History

General Andrew Jackson commands his troops in battle.

The year is 1828. You will vote for president for the first time. Important economic, social, and political issues face the country. The favored candidate is Andrew Jackson, a military hero. Before you vote, you should decide what qualities make a strong leader.

What Do You Think?

- **What qualities are suggested by this image?**
- **Which earlier presidents would you consider strong leaders and which not?**
- **Would qualities that make a military leader also make a good president? Why or why not?**

What qualities do you think make a strong leader?

USA

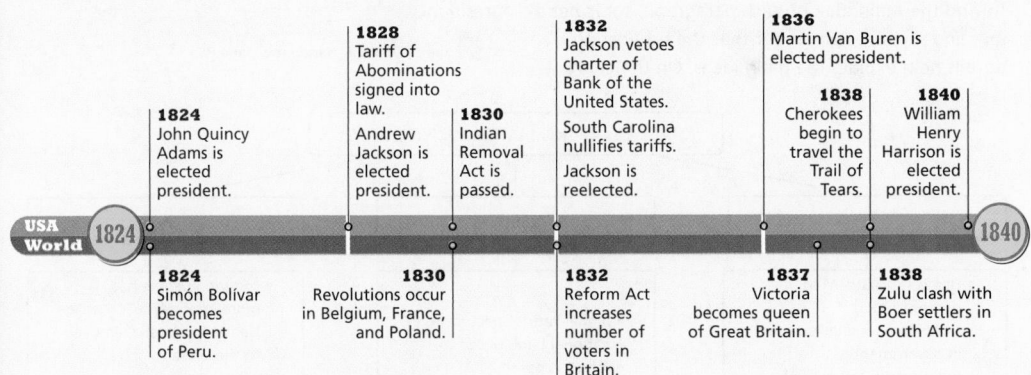

- **1824** John Quincy Adams is elected president.
- **1828** Tariff of Abominations signed into law. Andrew Jackson is elected president.
- **1830** Indian Removal Act is passed.
- **1832** Jackson vetoes charter of Bank of the United States. South Carolina nullifies tariffs. Jackson is reelected.
- **1836** Martin Van Buren is elected president.
- **1838** Cherokees begin to travel the Trail of Tears.
- **1840** William Henry Harrison is elected president.

1824 — 1840

World

- **1824** Simón Bolívar becomes president of Peru.
- **1830** Revolutions occur in Belgium, France, and Poland.
- **1832** Reform Act increases number of voters in Britain.
- **1837** Victoria becomes queen of Great Britain.
- **1838** Zulu clash with Boer settlers in South Africa.

Interact *with* History

OBJECTIVES

- To help students identify the qualities that make a strong leader
- To help students understand the strong feelings—both pro and con—that Jackson aroused

What Do You Think?

1. Students might begin by listing the presidents who preceded Jackson and reviewing how each responded to the challenges he faced.
2. Students can consider both historic and current figures in framing their definitions of leadership.
3. Students can begin to answer this question by looking at the trait suggested in the illustration of Jackson on this page.

What qualities do you think make a strong leader?

Point out that strong leaders have the ability to make others eager to follow them; the word *charisma* refers to this quality. Encourage students to think about decision-making skills as well as personal qualities.

MAKING PERSONAL CONNECTIONS

Ask students to think about adults or peers that they have known through school, camp, youth groups, or other activities that they consider to be strong leaders. What traits made them especially effective?

TIME LINE DISCUSSION

Tell students that during this time period, many people believed democracy was expanding, both in the United States and in other parts of the world.

- Ask students what events in western Europe during this time suggest that democracy was expanding. **Answer** Revolutions in Belgium, France, and Poland; Reform Act in Britain
- What events on the time line suggest that not everyone was a part of expanding democracy? **Answer** Indian Removal Act; Zulu clash with Boer settlers; Cherokee Trail of Tears

BEFORE YOU READ

Previewing the Theme: Economics in History

Have students examine the poster and notice the building in the background. Ask what the building is supposed to be. Next ask what impression the poster gives of Jackson. **Possible Response** The White House. The poster suggests that Jackson is a man of action who will act energetically and that he will bring change.

What Do You Know?

Have students describe causes of earlier conflicts between Native Americans and white settlers. Students might also consider the issues of industrialization, trade, sectionalism, western expansion, and political parties. Encourage them to consider how these matters might develop during the Age of Jackson.

In-Depth Resources: Unit 4
- Tracing Themes: Economics in History, p. 2

READ AND TAKE NOTES

Reading Strategy: Finding Main Ideas

Explain to students that they can organize the main ideas in this chapter into three broad topics. Point out the three categories on the chart—*political, economic,* and *social*—and review these concepts with students. Encourage them to take notes by listing main ideas under these headings as they read the section.

In-Depth Resources: Unit 4
- Setting the Stage, p. 1

Critical Thinking Transparency CT34
- Setting the Stage

Chapter 12 SETTING THE STAGE

BEFORE YOU READ

Previewing the Theme

Economics in History Americans elected Andrew Jackson president in 1828. Many believed that he would bring sweeping changes to the government. This chapter explains how President Jackson made decisions that had far-reaching effects on the American economy and on political life. In fact, because he so dominated the life of the nation, his time in office has been called the Age of Jackson.

What Do You Know?

What do you already know about the issues that faced the nation in the first half of the 19th century? How did presidents before Jackson deal with problems?

THINK ABOUT
- what you have learned about Andrew Jackson from books and movies
- how American life is affected by the actions of a president, by conflicts among different parts of the country, and by the will of the people

What Do You Want to Know?

What questions do you have about Jackson and his presidency? Record them in your notebook before reading the chapter.

READ AND TAKE NOTES

Reading Strategy: Finding Main Ideas To make it easier for you to understand what you read, learn to find the main idea of each paragraph, topic heading, and section. Remember that the supporting details help explain the main ideas. On the chart below, write down the main ideas about the political, economic, and social changes during Jackson's presidency.

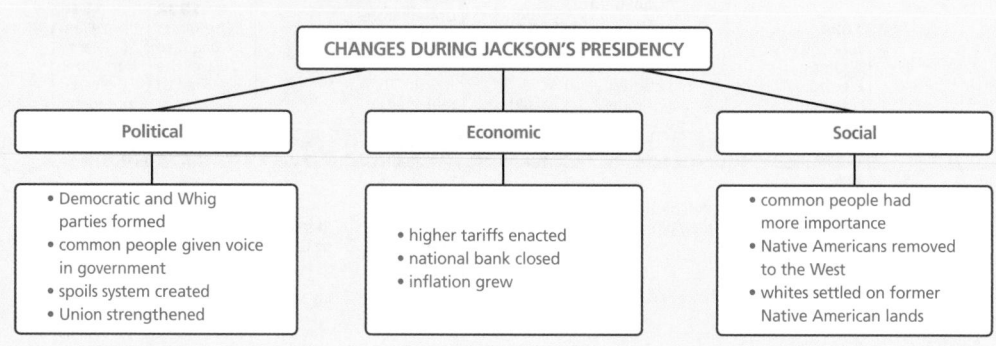

See Skillbuilder Handbook, page R5.

CHANGES DURING JACKSON'S PRESIDENCY

Political	Economic	Social
• Democratic and Whig parties formed • common people given voice in government • spoils system created • Union strengthened	• higher tariffs enacted • national bank closed • inflation grew	• common people had more importance • Native Americans removed to the West • whites settled on former Native American lands

TEACHING STRATEGY

READING THE CHAPTER

This is a thematic chapter focusing on Jackson's presidency and the political, economic, and social changes that took place while he was in office. Encourage students to compare Jackson's policies to those of former presidents John Quincy Adams and Thomas Jefferson. Ask them to note the specific changes Jackson brought to the presidency.

ALTERNATIVE ASSESSMENT

The Chapter Assessment describes three activities for alternative assessment on page 373. You may wish to have students work on these activities during the course of the chapter and then present them at the end.

1 Politics of the People

TERMS & NAMES
John Quincy Adams
Andrew Jackson
Jacksonian democracy
spoils system

MAIN IDEA

Andrew Jackson's election to the presidency in 1828 brought a new era of popular democracy.

WHY IT MATTERS NOW

Jackson's use of presidential powers laid the foundation of the modern presidency.

ONE AMERICAN'S STORY

Margaret Bayard Smith was 22 years old when she married and moved to Washington, D.C., in 1800. For the next 40 years, she and her husband, a government official, were central figures in the political and social life of Washington. They entertained presidents from Jefferson to Jackson.

Smith wrote magazine articles and numerous letters describing life in Washington. In 1824, she described how John Quincy Adams reacted to his election as president.

A VOICE FROM THE PAST

When the news of his election was communicated to Mr. Adams by the Committee . . . the sweat rolled down his face—he shook from head to foot and was so agitated that he could scarcely stand or speak.

Margaret Bayard Smith, *The First Forty Years of Washington Society*

Margaret Bayard Smith wrote about life in the nation's capital in the first half of the 19th century.

Adams had reason to be shaken by his election. It had been hotly contested, and he knew that he would face much opposition as he tried to govern. In this section, you will learn how Adams defeated Andrew Jackson in 1824, only to lose to him four years later.

1 The Election of 1824

In 1824, regional differences led to a fierce fight over the presidency. The Democratic-Republican Party split apart, with four men hoping to replace James Monroe as president. **John Quincy Adams,** Monroe's secretary of state, was New England's choice. The South backed William Crawford of Georgia. Westerners supported Henry Clay, the "Great Compromiser," and **Andrew Jackson,** a former military hero from Tennessee.

Jackson won the most popular votes. But he did not receive a majority of electoral votes. According to the Constitution, if no person wins a majority of electoral votes, the House of Representatives must choose the president. The selection was made from the top three vote getters.

Clay had come in fourth and was out of the running. In the House vote, he threw his support to Adams, who then won. Because Adams

SECTION OBJECTIVES

1. To explain the importance of the 1824 election
2. To analyze Jacksonian democracy and the expansion of voting rights
3. To explain why Jackson was known as "the people's president"
4. To evaluate Jackson's use of the spoils system to begin a new political era

SKILLBUILDER

Interpreting Charts, p. 357

CRITICAL THINKING

Analyzing Causes, p. 354
Recognizing Effects, p. 355
Drawing Conclusions, p. 356
Analyzing Points of View, p. 357

Why It Matters Now
- Expanding Democracy, pp. 23–24

FOCUS & MOTIVATE

5-MINUTE WARM-UP

Comparing These questions will help students compare and contrast Jefferson and Jackson.

1. Look at the chart on page 357. What beliefs did the two leaders share?
2. How might government for the people be different from government by the people?

Warm-Up Transparency WT12

INSTRUCT

INSTRUCT: OBJECTIVE 1

The Election of 1824

- Why was the election of 1824 decided by the House of Representatives?
- How did Clay help Adams win the election?

In-Depth Resources: Unit 4
- Guided Reading, p. 3

Reading Study Guide (Spanish and English), pp. 113–114

RECOMMENDED RESOURCES

In-Depth Resources: Unit 4
- Guided Reading, p. 3
- Building Vocabulary, p. 7
- Geog. Application, pp. 9–10
- Literature Selection, pp. 13–15

Reading Study Guide (Spanish and English), pp. 113–114

America's History Makers, pp. 47–48

Why It Matters Now, pp. 23–24

Citizenship Today, pp. 7–8

Formal Assessment
- Section Quiz, p. 218

Integrated Assessment
- Rubrics, 2.1, 2.2

Access for Students Acquiring English/ESL, pp. 76, 81–82

INTEGRATED TECHNOLOGY

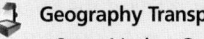

Geography Transparency GT12
- State Voting Qualifications, 1828

Electronic Teacher Tools

classzone.com

TEST-TAKING RESOURCES

Strategies for Test Preparation

Test Practice Transparencies, TT41

Online Test Practice

AMERICA'S HISTORY MAKERS

John Quincy Adams
During his campaign for reelection, Adams refused to defend himself against slurs by Jackson and his followers because he thought it was beneath the dignity of the presidency to take part in political mudslinging.

After his defeat, Massachusetts voters elected Adams to the House of Representatives, a position he held for 17 years. On winning election to the House, he said, "My election as President of the United States was not half so gratifying."

Andrew Jackson
Before becoming president, Jackson's fiery temper involved him in several duels. In an 1806 duel he killed Charles Dickinson, a lawyer who had accused Jackson of being a "worthless scoundrel, a poltroon, and a coward" and had also made insulting remarks about his wife, Rachel.

Possible Answer: Adams was vain, wealthy, and aloof. He came from a privileged background and was unwilling to compromise. Jackson was a war hero with a reputation for toughness. Jackson appealed to common voters because he was a self-made man who had overcome poverty and personal tragedy.

America's History Makers
- Andrew Jackson, pp. 47–48

INSTRUCT: OBJECTIVE 2

Jacksonian Democracy

- How did Jackson portray himself and Adams in the campaign of 1828?
- What does the phrase "Jacksonian democracy" mean?
- How were voting rights still limited?

Geography Transparency GT12
- State Voting Qualifications, 1828

AMERICA'S HISTORY MAKERS

JOHN QUINCY ADAMS
1767–1848
John Quincy Adams was born into wealth and social position. He was the son of President John Adams. Like his father, he had a sharp mind, spoke eloquently, worked tirelessly in public service, and had high principles. But he was sometimes vain, and unwilling to compromise. This made him unpopular with many people and often ineffective. After his presidency, he served with distinction in Congress.

ANDREW JACKSON
1767–1845
Andrew Jackson was the son of a poor farm couple from South Carolina. Orphaned by age 14, he was a wild and reckless youth.

Jackson moved on to become a successful lawyer and plantation owner in Tennessee. But his quick temper still got him into brawls and duels. Bullets in his body from two duels frequently caused him pain.

Jackson's humble background and reputation for toughness endeared him to voters. They considered him one of their own.

Why do you think Jackson was popular but Adams was not?

later named Clay as his secretary of state, Jackson's supporters claimed that Adams gained the presidency by making a deal with Clay. Charges of a "corrupt bargain" followed Adams throughout his term.

Adams had many plans for his presidency. He wanted to build roads and canals, aid education and science, and regulate the use of natural resources. But Congress, led by Jackson supporters, defeated his proposals.

Reading **History**
A. Analyzing Causes What was the main reason John Quincy Adams was not effective as president?
A. Possible Answer His proposals faced opposition from Jackson supporters in Congress, and he was unwilling to bargain.

2 Jacksonian Democracy

Jackson felt that the 1824 election had been stolen from him—that the will of the people had been ignored. Jackson and his supporters were outraged. He immediately set to work to gain the presidency in 1828.

For the next four years, the split in the Democratic-Republican Party between the supporters of Jackson and of Adams grew wider. Jackson claimed to represent the "common man." He said Adams represented a group of privileged, wealthy Easterners. This division eventually created two parties. The Democrats came from among the Jackson supporters, while the National Republicans grew out of the Adams camp.

The election of 1828 again matched Jackson against Adams. It was a bitter campaign—both sides made vicious personal attacks. Even Jackson's wife, Rachel, became a target. During the campaign, Jackson crusaded against control of the government by the wealthy. He promised to look out for the interests of common people. He also promoted the concept of majority rule. The idea of spreading political power to all the people and ensuring majority rule became known as **Jacksonian democracy**.

Actually, the process of spreading political power had begun before Jackson ran for office. When Jefferson was president in the early 1800s,

ACTIVITY OPTIONS
INDIVIDUAL NEEDS

LESS PROFICIENT READERS

Setting a Purpose To help students set a purpose for reading the section and understand how Jackson's policies changed the presidency, prepare a series of questions for students to use as a guide. Write the questions on the board and read them with students. Have students jot down answers to the questions as they read the section. When they have finished reading and answering the questions, encourage students to review and discuss their answers.

You might want to ask questions such as the following:
- What group of people did Jackson represent?
- What is "Jacksonian democracy"?
- How did the expansion of voting rights help Jackson win the election in 1828?
- What experiences in Jackson's life helped prepare him for the presidency?
- What was Jackson's first change to the government?

additional people had gained the right to vote as states reduced restrictions on who could vote. Before, for example, only those who owned property or paid taxes could vote in many states. This easing of voting restrictions increased the number of voters. But voting was still limited to adult white males.

The expansion of voting rights helped Jackson achieve an overwhelming win in the 1828 presidential election. Jackson's triumph was hailed as a victory for common people. Large numbers of Western farmers as well as workers in the nation's cities supported him. Their vote put an end to the idea that the government should be controlled by an educated elite. Now, the common people would be governed by one of their own. (See chart "Changes in Ideas About Democracy," page 357.)

Reading **History**
B. Recognizing Effects What factor made Jackson's appeal to the "common man" especially important in the election of 1828?
B. Answer More people had gained the right to vote, including people without property or much money.

STRANGE *but* True

ADAMS AND JEFFERSON

John Adams and Thomas Jefferson died on the same day—the Fourth of July, 1826, the 50th anniversary of the adoption of the Declaration of Independence.

Both Adams and Jefferson were founders of the nation, signers of the Declaration, and presidents. They were also political enemies who had become friends late in life.

Adams was 90; Jefferson, 83. Adams's last words were "Jefferson still survives." He was unaware that Jefferson had died hours earlier.

The People's President ❸

Jackson's humble background, and his reputation as a war hero, helped make him president. Many saw his rise above hardship as a real American success story. He was the first president not from an aristocratic Massachusetts or Virginia family, and the first from the West.

Jackson indeed had had a hard life. His father died shortly before his birth, and Jackson grew up on a frontier farm in South Carolina. At 13, he joined the militia with his older brother to fight in the Revolutionary War. In 1781, they were taken prisoner by the British. While captive, he allegedly refused when commanded to shine an officer's boots. The officer struck Jackson with a sword, leaving scars on his hand and head. Later, Jackson's mother obtained her sons' release from a military prison, where they had become ill with smallpox. Jackson's brother died, but his mother nursed Jackson back to health. A short time later, she also died. Jackson's experiences during the Revolution left him with a lifelong hatred of the British.

After the war, Jackson moved to the Tennessee frontier. In 1784, he began to study law. He built a successful legal practice and also bought and sold land. Jackson then purchased a plantation near Nashville and ran successfully for Congress. After the War of 1812 broke out, he was appointed a general in the army. At the Battle of New Orleans in 1815, Jackson soundly defeated the British even though his troops were greatly outnumbered. He became a national war hero. He earned the nickname "Old Hickory," after a soldier claimed that he was "tough as hickory."

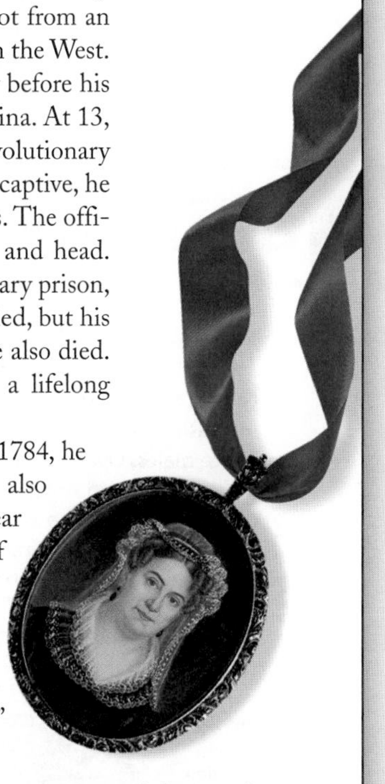

Jackson usually wore this miniature oil portrait of his beloved wife, Rachel, around his neck.

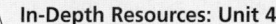

Jackson Takes Office

Jackson's success in the presidential election of 1828 came at a high price. Shortly after he won, his wife, Rachel, died of a heart attack. Jackson believed that the campaign attacks on her reputation had killed her. She was a private woman who preferred a quiet life. In fact, she had

STRANGE *but* True

Adams and Jefferson

Adams and Jefferson met in 1775 and worked together to create the Declaration of Independence. Their friendship cooled sharply after 1790, when they disagreed on how the United States should respond to the French Revolution. As heads of the nation's first political parties, they became bitter rivals. Political differences soured the friendship until a mutual friend brought the two together in 1811. They began a correspondence that lasted the rest of their lives.

INSTRUCT: OBJECTIVE ❸

The People's President/ Jackson Takes Office

- What events in Jackson's past had increased his popularity and made him nationally known?
- How did Jackson's supporters celebrate his inauguration?

In-Depth Resources: Unit 4
- Geography Application: Election of 1828, pp. 9–10
- Literature Selection: from *Jackson* by Max Byrd, pp. 13–15

ACTIVITY OPTIONS

INTERDISCIPLINARY LINK: CIVICS — BLOCK SCHEDULING

JACKSON FOR PRESIDENT

Class Time One class period

Task Planning a political advertisement for Andrew Jackson's 1828 campaign

Purpose To analyze how political ads affect voters' impressions of a candidate

Supplies Needed
- Biographies and other reference materials on Jackson
- Video camera and tapes (optional)

Activity Divide the class into groups. Tell students they are political consultants hired by the Jackson campaign to create three-minute TV ads. The ads should tell viewers about Jackson's political beliefs and his stands on issues. An ad might also include information about his life. Each group should assign members to write, direct, narrate, and act in the video. They might also find music or create slogans. You may want to take other class periods to actually produce the ads. Let groups show their ads to the class. Conclude by discussing whether ads are a good way for voters to learn about candidates.

CRITICAL THINKING ACTIVITY

Forming and Supporting Opinions Many voters supported Andrew Jackson in the election of 1828 because he came from a humble background, had risen above poverty and hardship, and was a war hero. Ask students whether they think these are sound reasons for supporting a candidate for president. Why or why not?

Class Time 10 minutes

said that she would "rather be a doorkeeper in the house of God than . . . live in that palace at Washington." Margaret Bayard Smith described Rachel's importance to Jackson, saying she "not only made him a happier, but a better man."

Jackson looked thin, pale, and sad at his inauguration on March 4, 1829. But the capital was full of joy and excitement. Thousands of people were there. Senator Daniel Webster wrote about the inauguration.

> ***A VOICE FROM THE PAST***
>
> I have never seen such a crowd before. Persons have come five hundred miles to see General Jackson, and they really seem to think that the country has been rescued from some dreadful danger.
>
> **Daniel Webster,** *Correspondence*

C. Possible Answer The common people felt one of their own was now president.

Reading **History**

C. Drawing Conclusions Why did Jackson's supporters react with such enthusiasm at his inauguration?

At the inauguration ceremony, the crowd shouted, waved, applauded, and saluted its hero. He bowed low to the people in turn. A throng followed Jackson to the White House reception. One person described the crowd as containing "all sorts of people, from the highest and most polished, down to the most vulgar and gross in the nation."

The crowd grew rowdy. People broke china and glasses as they grabbed for the food and drinks. The pushing and shoving finally drove the new president to flee the White House. As Supreme Court Justice Joseph Story observed, "The reign of King Mob seemed triumphant."

CITIZENSHIP TODAY

OBJECTIVE

Students will be able to explain the value of mock elections in increasing future voters' political awareness and involvement.

Exercising the Vote

Groups and events such as Kid's Voting, Rock the Vote, and the National Student/Parent Mock Election have an urgent mission to interest young people in voting. The reason for their efforts is the sharp decline in voter turnout that has occurred since the 1960s, particularly among younger voters. In 1960, during the Kennedy-Nixon contest, 62.8 percent of the voting-age population went to the polls. By 1996, when Bill Clinton battled Bob Dole and Ross Perot for the presidency, only 49 percent of possible voters cast their ballots.

Citizenship Today, pp. 7–8

CITIZENSHIP TODAY

Exercising the Vote

During the Age of Jackson, rules on who could vote were eased. This increased the number of voters. But voting was still limited to adult white males. Over the years, other groups gained the right to vote, including African Americans, women, and Native Americans. Today's elections are open to all citizens aged 18 and over.

Future voters can practice casting their votes in mock, or pretend, elections. The National Student/Parent Mock Election teaches students to be informed voters. Mock presidential elections attract coverage by the media. Television stations may even broadcast live from schools, interviewing student voters.

One high school student, Charlie Tran from San Jose, California, said, "Students seem to catch the important political events surrounding them. Some students are taking their views . . . to a new level by campaigning for the candidate they support."

Students register to vote in a mock election.

How Do You Set Up a Mock Election?

1. Choose issues and candidates and then set up a mock election in your classroom. (You could focus on the national, state, or local level.)
2. Create the materials of an election, such as the polling place, ballots, and posters.
3. Campaign for the candidates or the issues you support.
4. Conduct the voting.
5. Prepare mock media reports on the election's outcome. You may want to interview voters.

See Citizenship Handbook, page 267.

For more about citizenship and voting . . .

RESEARCH LINKS CLASSZONE.COM

STANDARDS FOR EVALUATION: CITIZENSHIP TODAY

Each report should

- use simple, easy-to-understand language.
- clearly identify the candidates or summarize the issues to be decided.
- offer a balanced treatment.
- give specific numbers for election results.
- analyze the election results and suggest reasons for the outcome.

Changes in Ideas About Democracy

JEFFERSONIAN DEMOCRACY	JACKSONIAN DEMOCRACY
government for the people by capable, well-educated leaders	government by the people
democracy in political life	democracy in social, economic, and political life
championed the cause of the farmer in a mainly agricultural society	championed the cause of the farmer and the laborer in an agricultural and industrial society
limited government	limited government, but with a strong president

SKILLBUILDER **Interpreting Charts**

1. *What do you think was the most important change in democracy?*
2. *Did Jefferson or Jackson exercise more power?*

❹ A New Political Era Begins

Jackson's inauguration began a new political era. In his campaign, he had promised to reform government. He started by replacing many government officials with his supporters. This practice of giving government jobs to political backers became known as the **spoils system.** The name comes from a statement that "to the victor belong the spoils [possessions] of the enemy." Jackson's opponents charged that the practice was corrupt. But he defended it, noting that it broke up one group's hold on government.

As president, Jackson would face three major issues—the status of Native Americans, the rights of the states, and the role of the Bank of the United States. In the next section, you will learn how Jackson's policies affected Native Americans.

Skillbuilder Answers
1. Some students may say government by the people; others might choose the spread of democracy to social and economic life.
2. Jackson exercised more power because he believed in a strong presidency.

Section 1 Assessment

1. Terms & Names

Explain the significance of:
- John Quincy Adams
- Andrew Jackson
- Jacksonian democracy
- spoils system

2. Taking Notes

Use a chart to identify important biographical information about Andrew Jackson.

Life of Andrew Jackson	
Youthful life	
Road to Congress	
War hero	
Appeal to voters	

3. Main Ideas

a. How did Andrew Jackson react to the election of 1824? Why?

b. What factors helped Jackson win the presidency in 1828?

c. What was the effect of expanding voting rights?

4. Critical Thinking

Analyzing Points of View What are reasons for and against the spoils system?

THINK ABOUT
- the effects of giving government workers lifetime jobs
- the effects of rewarding political supporters

ACTIVITY OPTIONS

GEOGRAPHY / **MATH**

Find out which states Jackson and Adams won in the 1828 election. Show the results on a **map** or **chart** that includes vote totals and percentages.

HISTORY FROM VISUALS

Interpreting Charts Have students examine the differences between Jefferson and Jackson. Then ask students how Jackson's concept of democracy differed from Jefferson's. How were they similar?
Possible Response Jackson had a broader definition of democracy. Jefferson sought to make political life democratic, but was less concerned about expanding economic and social opportunities for ordinary people. Both believed common people were capable of being informed voters and choosing good leaders.

Extension Have students use the information on the chart to write a paper comparing and contrasting Jeffersonian and Jacksonian Democracy.

INSTRUCT: OBJECTIVE ❹

A New Political Era Begins

- What was the spoils system, and why was it controversial?
- What important issues did Jackson face as president?

ASSESS & RETEACH

Setting the Stage Have students classify information in this section according to the categories presented on the graphic organizer on page 352.

Formal Assessment
- Section Quiz, p. 218

Critical Thinking Transparency CT34
- Setting the Stage

RETEACHING ACTIVITY

Working in groups of four, students should write two questions about each of the words or phrases in "Terms & Names" on page 353. Have groups exchange questions, answer each other's questions, and return the answers for checking.

In-Depth Resources: Unit 4
- Reteaching Activity, p. 16

Section 1 Assessment

1. Terms & Names

John Quincy Adams, p. 353
Andrew Jackson, p. 353
Jacksonian democracy, p. 354
spoils system, p. 357

2. Taking Notes

Youthful life: frontier farm, prisoner in Revolutionary War, wild and reckless; Road to Congress: lawyer in Tennessee, bought a plantation, elected to Congress; War hero: defeated British in Battle of New Orleans; Appeal to voters: poor background; military hero; defender of common people

3. Main Ideas

a. outraged because he felt the presidency was stolen from him **b.** his background; his appeal to common people; the expansion of voting rights **c.** the election of a president who was a champion of the common people

4. Critical Thinking

For: it broke up one group's hold on government jobs; Against: it was just a way to reward political supporters

ACTIVITY OPTIONS

Integrated Assessment
- Rubrics for a map, 2.1
- Rubrics for a chart, 2.2

SECTION OBJECTIVES

1. To explain the conflict between whites and Native Americans in the Southeast
2. To evaluate Jackson's removal policy
3. To describe the hardships of the Trail of Tears
4. To explain how Native American groups in the East resisted removal

SKILLBUILDER

Interpreting Maps: Movement, Location, p. 360

CRITICAL THINKING

Drawing Conclusions, p. 360
Recognizing Effects, pp. 361, 362

FOCUS & MOTIVATE

5-MINUTE WARM-UP

Reading a Map These questions focus on Jackson's Indian removal policy.

1. Look at the map on page 360. What Southeastern tribes were affected by Jackson's Indian policy?
2. Judging by the map, what was the purpose of this policy?

Warm-Up Transparency WT12

INSTRUCT

INSTRUCT: OBJECTIVE 1

Native Americans in the Southeast/ The Cherokee Nation

- What were the conflicts between whites and Native Americans in the Eastern states?
- How had the Cherokee adapted to living among white settlers?
- Why did whites pressure the government to force the Cherokee out of Georgia?

In-Depth Resources: Unit 4
- Guided Reading, p. 4
- Building Vocabulary, p. 7

2 Jackson's Policy Toward Native Americans

TERMS & NAMES
Sequoya
Indian Removal Act
Indian Territory
Trail of Tears
Osceola

MAIN IDEA	WHY IT MATTERS NOW
During Jackson's presidency, Native Americans were forced to move west of the Mississippi River.	This forced removal forever changed the lives of Native Americans in the United States.

ONE AMERICAN'S STORY

For 12 years, a brilliant Cherokee named **Sequoya** (sih KWOY uh) tried to find a way to "teach the Cherokees to talk on paper like the white man." In 1821, he reached his goal. Sequoya invented a writing system for the Cherokee language without ever having learned to read or write in any other language. Helped by his young daughter, he identified all the sounds in Cherokee and created 86 characters to stand for syllables.

Using this simple system, the Cherokees soon learned to read and write. They even published a newspaper and books in their own language. A traveler in 1828 marveled at how many Cherokees had learned to read and write without schools or even paper and pens.

A VOICE FROM THE PAST

I frequently saw as I rode from place to place, Cherokee letters painted or cut on the trees by the roadside, on fences, houses, and often on pieces of bark or board, lying about the houses.

Anonymous traveler, quoted in the *Advocate*

Sequoya invented a writing system of 86 characters, shown here, for the Cherokee language.

Sequoya hoped that by gaining literacy—the ability to read and write—his people could share the power of whites and keep their independence. But even Sequoya's invention could not save the Cherokees from the upheaval to come. In this section, you will learn about President Jackson's policy toward Native Americans and its effects.

1 Native Americans in the Southeast

Since the 1600s, white settlers had pushed Native Americans westward as they took more and more of their land. However, there were still many Native Americans in the East in the early 1800s. Some whites hoped that the Native Americans could adapt to the white people's way of life. Others wanted the Native Americans to move. They believed this was the only way to avoid conflict over land. Also, many whites felt that Native Americans were "uncivilized" and did not want to live near them.

By the 1820s, about 100,000 Native Americans remained east of the Mississippi River. The majority were in the Southeast. The major tribes

RECOMMENDED RESOURCES

In-Depth Resources: Unit 4
- Guided Reading, p. 4
- Building Vocabulary, p. 7
- Primary Source: p. 11
- Enrichment Activity, p. 20

Reading Study Guide (Spanish and English), pp. 115–116

Outline Map Activities, pp. 23–24

America's History Makers
- Sequoya, pp. 49–50

Formal Assessment
- Section Quiz, p. 219

Integrated Assessment
- Rubrics, 2.1, 2.2

Access for Students Acquiring English/ESL, p. 77

INTEGRATED TECHNOLOGY

Critical Thinking Trans. CT35

Humanities Transparency HT23
- Political Cartoon: Andrew Jackson and Native Americans

Electronic Teacher Tools

classzone.com

TEST-TAKING RESOURCES

Strategies for Test Preparation

Test Practice Transparencies, TT42

Online Test Practice

Reading **History**

A. Reading a Map Use the map on page 360 to locate Native American lands in the Southeast.

were the Cherokee, Chickasaw, Choctaw, Creek, and Seminole. Whites called them the Five Civilized Tribes because they had adopted many aspects of white culture. They held large areas of land in Georgia, the Carolinas, Alabama, Mississippi, and Tennessee.

The Cherokee Nation

More than any other Southeastern tribe, the Cherokee had adopted white customs, including their way of dressing. Cherokees owned prosperous farms and cattle ranches. Some even had slaves. From Sequoya, they acquired a written language, and they published their own newspaper, the *Cherokee Phoenix*. Some of their children attended missionary schools. In 1827, the Cherokees drew up a constitution based on the U.S. Constitution and founded the Cherokee Nation.

A year after the Cherokees adopted their constitution, gold was discovered on their land in Georgia. Now, not only settlers but also miners wanted these lands. The discovery of gold increased demands by whites to move the Cherokees. The federal government responded with a plan to remove all Native Americans from the Southeast.

2 Jackson's Removal Policy

Andrew Jackson had long supported a policy of moving Native Americans west of the Mississippi. He first dealt with the Southeastern tribes after the War of 1812. The federal government ordered Jackson, then acting as Indian treaty commissioner, to make treaties with the Native Americans of the region. Through these treaties forced on the tribes, the government gained large tracts of land.

Jackson believed that the government had the right to regulate where Native Americans could live. He viewed them as conquered subjects who lived within the borders of the United States. He thought that Native Americans had one of two choices. They could adopt white culture and become citizens of the United States. Or they could move into the Western territories. They could not, however, have their own governments within the nation's borders.

After the discovery of gold, whites began to move onto Cherokee land. Georgia and other Southern states passed laws that gave them the right to take over Native American lands. When the Cherokee and other tribes protested, Jackson supported the states.

To solve the problem, Jackson asked Congress to pass a law that would require Native Americans to either move west or submit to state laws. Many Americans objected to Jackson's proposal. Massachusetts congressman Edward Everett opposed removing Native Americans against their will to a distant land. There, he said, they would face "the

Now and then

CHEROKEE PEOPLE TODAY

Today, there are more than 300,000 Cherokees. They are part of three main groups—the Cherokee Nation of Oklahoma, the United Keetoowah Band in Oklahoma, and the Eastern Band of Cherokee Indians of North Carolina.

Wilma Mankiller, shown below, was the first woman elected principal chief of the Cherokee Nation of Oklahoma. She has said that the "Cherokee people possess an extraordinary ability to face down adversity and continue moving forward. We are able to do that because our culture, though certainly diminished, has sustained us since time immemorial."

Now and then

Cherokee People Today

Wilma Mankiller was elected principal chief of the Cherokee Nation of Oklahoma in 1985. During her years as chief, she has worked for improved health care, better education, and more efficient tribal government. She says that although the Cherokee have many challenges, she is optimistic about the future. "We've had daunting problems in many critical areas," she says, "but I believe in the old Cherokee injunction to be of a good mind. Today it's called positive thinking." Mankiller's last name is a term of respect for warriors who protected villages.

America's History Makers
- Sequoya, pp. 49–50

INSTRUCT: OBJECTIVE 2

Jackson's Removal Policy

- Why did Jackson believe the government had the right to decide where Native Americans could live?
- How did Jackson propose to solve the problem of Native American protests?
- How did the Indian Removal Act affect Native Americans in the Southeast?

Outline Map Activities
- Native American Movement, 1830–1842, pp. 23–24

CRITICAL THINKING ACTIVITY

Analyzing Points of View Ask students why whites called the Cherokee, Chickasaw, Choctaw, Creek, and Seminole the Five Civilized Tribes. What does this name suggest about how most whites at that time viewed Native American cultures? Which of Jackson's criteria for remaining on their land had the Cherokee met? Which had they failed to meet? If the Cherokee had chosen another course of action, would it have changed the outcome?

Class Time 10 minutes

ACTIVITY OPTIONS

INTERDISCIPLINARY LINK: LANGUAGE ARTS/WRITING — BLOCK SCHEDULING

A LETTER TO THE PRESIDENT

Class Time One class period

Task Writing a letter on a public issue

Purpose To evaluate the Indian removal policy from different perspectives

Supplies Needed
- Reference materials on the Indian Removal Act and on the Native American groups affected
- Writing materials

Activity Explain to students that the Indian Removal Act affected peaceful Native American groups that had been considered sovereign nations and that held their lands by treaty with the United States. Then ask students to assume the viewpoints of members of Southeastern tribes and write letters to Jackson expressing their views on the act and describing how it will affect them. Remind them that their purpose is to influence the president, not to antagonize him.

HISTORY FROM VISUALS

Reading the Map Have students identify the Southeastern tribe that was forced to leave Florida. Ask them which group had the largest number of people forced to relocate. **Answers** Seminole; Creeks, over 14,000. Ask students what reason might have been cited to move Native Americans from Wisconsin and Michigan. Ask them why the federal government might have chosen parts of what are now Oklahoma and Kansas for the relocation of Native Americans. **Possible Response** More white settlers were moving into those territories. The area was not considered valuable by white settlers.

Extension Have students pick one of the Southeastern peoples shown on the chart and do research to learn its current size, status, and location.

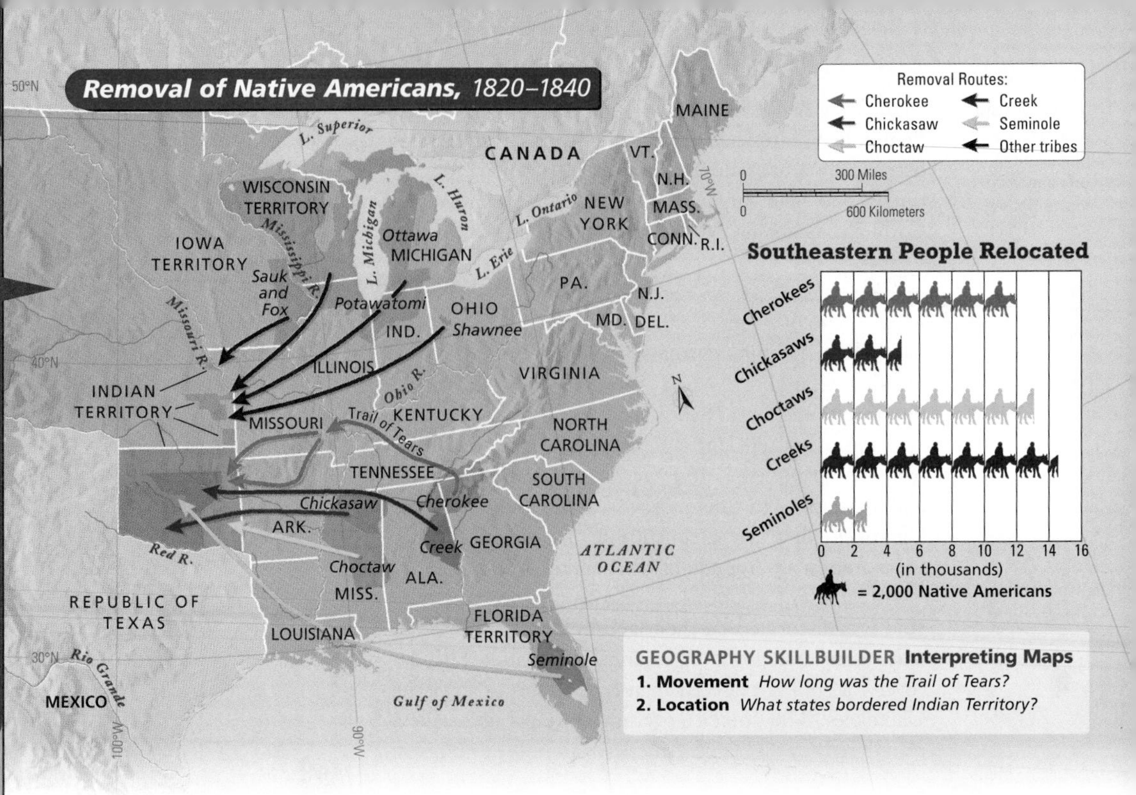

GEOGRAPHY SKILLBUILDER Interpreting Maps
1. **Movement** *How long was the Trail of Tears?*
2. **Location** *What states bordered Indian Territory?*

Skillbuilder Answers
1. about 700 miles
2. Missouri and Arkansas

perils and hardships of a wilderness." Religious groups such as the Quakers also opposed forced removal of Native Americans. After heated debate, Congress passed the **Indian Removal Act** in 1830. The act called for the government to negotiate treaties that would require Native Americans to relocate west.

Jackson immediately set out to enforce the law. He thought his policy was "just and liberal" and would allow Native Americans to keep their way of life. Instead, his policy caused much hardship and forever changed relations between whites and Native Americans.

Reading **History**
B. Drawing Conclusions What were reasons for and against the Indian Removal Act?
B. Possible Answers Reasons for: White settlers wanted Native American land. Relocation would prevent tribes from being wiped out. Reasons against: Native Americans did not want to move, and they had treaties protecting their lands.

3 The Trail of Tears

As whites invaded their homelands, many Native Americans saw no other choice but to sign treaties exchanging their land for land in the West. Under the treaties, Native Americans would be moved to an area that covered what is now Oklahoma and parts of Kansas and Nebraska. This area came to be called **Indian Territory.**

Beginning in the fall of 1831, the Choctaw and other Southeast tribes were removed from their lands and relocated to Indian Territory. The Cherokees, however, first appealed to the U.S. Supreme Court to protect their land from being seized by Georgia. In 1832, the Court, led by Chief Justice John Marshall, ruled that only the federal government, not the states, could make laws governing the Cherokees. This ruling meant that

INSTRUCT: OBJECTIVE 3
The Trail of Tears

- How did the Cherokee fight the takeover of their lands in Georgia?
- How did the Supreme Court rule on the Cherokee case, and why was Jackson able to ignore this ruling?
- Why is the journey of the Cherokee to Indian Territory known as the Trail of Tears?

In-Depth Resources: Unit 4
- Primary Source: A Petition by Cherokee Women, p. 11

Critical Thinking Transparency CT35
- Cause and Effect: Native American Removal

ACTIVITY OPTIONS
MULTIPLE LEARNING STYLES: SPATIAL — BLOCK SCHEDULING

TRAIL OF TEARS MEMORIAL

Class Time One class period

Task Designing a model for a memorial commemorating the Trail of Tears

Purpose To express the hardships of Indian removal for the Cherokee

Supplies Needed
- Reference materials on the Trail of Tears
- Photographs of various public monuments and memorials
- Modeling clay and poster paper

Activity Using the photographs, encourage the class to discuss what makes a monument effective. Then have students work in groups of three to read more about the Trail of Tears and to create a design for a memorial. Have each group use clay to make a model of its monument or use paper to make a drawing. Designs should include an inscription explaining the monument's purpose. Groups can share their models or drawings with the class or post photos on a class Web site.

the Georgia laws did not apply to the Cherokee Nation. However, both Georgia and President Jackson ignored the Supreme Court. Jackson said, "John Marshall has made his decision. . . . Now let him enforce it."

A small group of Cherokees gave up and signed a treaty to move west. But the majority of the Cherokees, led by John Ross, opposed the treaty. Jackson refused to negotiate with these Cherokees.

In 1838, federal troops commanded by General Winfield Scott rounded up about 16,000 Cherokees and forced them into camps. Soldiers took people from their homes with nothing but the clothes on their backs. Over the fall and winter of 1838–1839, these Cherokees set out on the long journey west. Forced to march in the cold, rain, and snow without adequate clothing, many grew weak and ill. One-fourth died. The dead included John Ross's wife. One soldier never forgot what he witnessed on the trail.

Reading **History**

C. Recognizing Effects What happened to the Cherokees as a result of the Indian Removal Act?

C. Possible **Answers** They lost their land, property, and homes. One-fourth of them died on the long journey west. They had to resettle in a strange land.

A VOICE FROM THE PAST

Murder is murder and somebody must answer, somebody must explain the streams of blood that flowed in the Indian country in . . . 1838. Somebody must explain the four-thousand silent graves that mark the trail of the Cherokees to their exile. I wish I could forget it all, but the picture of six-hundred and forty-five wagons lumbering over the frozen ground with their Cargo of suffering humanity still lingers in my memory.

John G. Burnett, quoted in *The Native Americans,* edited by Betty and Ian Ballantine

This harsh journey of the Cherokee from their homeland to Indian Territory became known as the **Trail of Tears.**

HISTORY *through* ART

In 1838, the Cherokees left their homeland by wagon, horse, donkey, and foot, forced to travel hundreds of miles along the Trail of Tears. This painting is by Robert Lindneux, a 20th-century artist.

How does this portrayal of the Trail of Tears reflect continuity and change in 19th-century American life?

361

MORE ABOUT . . .

Jackson and Native Americans

Andrew Jackson's complex and contradictory nature was seldom better illustrated than in his attitudes toward Native Americans. He almost always spoke of them in hostile, contemptuous terms. Yet his troops at the Battle of Horseshoe Bend included Indian allies. And after a battle in 1813, he took under his protection a three-year-old Indian boy whose parents had been killed by Jackson's troops. Jackson, who had been orphaned himself, said he felt "an unusual bond of sympathy" for the child, whom he sent home to Rachel to raise with their other adopted son.

Humanities Transparency HT23
- Political Cartoon: Andrew Jackson and Native Americans

HISTORY *through* ART

Interpreting the Painting About 4,000 Cherokee died on the 116-day march, largely of exposure and starvation. The soldiers that led them refused to slow down or stop so that people could recover from exhaustion or illness before continuing the long journey.

Possible Answer: The artist shows the Native Americans under army guard. Many are forced to walk. They also look cold, tired, and sad.

In-Depth Resources: Unit 4
- Enrichment Activity, p. 20

ACTIVITY OPTIONS

INDIVIDUAL NEEDS: GIFTED AND TALENTED

WRITING HISTORICAL FICTION

Class Time Two class periods

Task Writing an outline for a work of historical fiction

Purpose To familiarize students with the suffering endured by Native Americans as they journeyed west

Supplies Needed
- Reference materials, including primary sources
- For more about Cherokee history, visit classzone.com.

Activity First, have students use encyclopedias, textbooks, and primary sources to familiarize themselves with the Trail of Tears. Encourage them to focus their research on the length of the journey, the means of travel available, the weather and road conditions, the role of troops, and everyday details. Then have them create outlines for fictional stories based on this historical event. Discuss with the class the advantages and drawbacks of using fiction in history.

INSTRUCT: OBJECTIVE 4

Native American Resistance

- How did some Native American groups in the Southeast resist removal?
- What were the causes and the outcome of the Second Seminole War, and what part did Osceola play in Seminole resistance?
- Besides the Southeastern tribes, what other groups were forced to move to Indian Territory?

MORE ABOUT . . .

The Second Seminole War

The Second Seminole War (1835–1842) was the longest and costliest Indian war in American history. It led to the death of 1,500 American soldiers. The number of Native Americans killed in this war is unknown. By 1842, about 3,000 Seminoles had been forced to move to Indian Territory. Another thousand hid in the Florida swamps and Everglades. Today the descendants of the Seminoles who remained in Florida hold three reservations and in 1957 created the Seminole Tribe of Florida, whose members number around 1,200.

ASSESS & RETEACH

Setting the Stage Have students use information in this section to fill in the appropriate sections on the chapter graphic organizer.

Formal Assessment
- Section Quiz, p. 219

RETEACHING ACTIVITY

Have students create a cause-and-effect chart showing the events that were set in motion when gold was discovered in Georgia and white settlers sought control of Native American lands in the Southeast.

In-Depth Resources: Unit 4
- Reteaching Activity, p. 17

Osceola led the Seminoles in their fight against removal.

4 Native American Resistance

Not all the Cherokees moved west in 1838. That fall, soldiers had rounded up an old Cherokee farmer named Tsali and his family, including his grown sons. On the way to the stockade, they fought the soldiers. A soldier was killed before Tsali fled with his family to the Great Smoky Mountains in North Carolina. There they found other Cherokees. The U.S. Army sent a message to Tsali. If he and his sons would give themselves up, the others could remain. They surrendered, and all except the youngest son were shot. Their sacrifice allowed some Cherokees to stay in their homeland.

Other Southeast tribes also resisted relocation. In 1835, the Seminoles refused to leave Florida. This refusal led to the Second Seminole War. One elderly Seminole explained why he could not leave: "If suddenly we tear our hearts from the homes around which they are twined [wrapped around], our heart strings will snap."

Background The Seminoles fought three wars against the U.S. government between 1817 and 1858, when their resistance ended.

One of the most important leaders in the war was **Osceola** (AHS ee OH luh). Hiding in the Everglades, Osceola and his band used surprise attacks to defeat the U.S. Army in many battles. In 1837, Osceola was tricked into capture when he came to peace talks during a truce. He later died in prison. But the Seminoles continued to fight. Some went deeper into the Everglades, where their descendants live today. Others moved west. The Second Seminole War ended in 1842.

Some tribes north of the Ohio River also resisted relocation. The Shawnee, Ottawa, Potawatomi, Sauk, and Fox were removed to Indian Territory. But in 1832, a Sauk chief named Black Hawk led a band of Sauk and Fox back to their lands in Illinois. In the Black Hawk War, the Illinois militia and the U.S. Army crushed the uprising.

In the next section, you will learn about other issues Jackson faced, especially increasing tensions between various sections of the country.

Section 2 Assessment

1. Terms & Names

Explain the significance of:
- Sequoya
- Indian Removal Act
- Indian Territory
- Trail of Tears
- Osceola

2. Taking Notes

Use a chart to list the reasons for Jackson's Native American removal policy.

Reasons Native Americans Were Forced West		
Economic	Political	Social

What do you think was the main reason?

3. Main Ideas

a. How did President Jackson justify the Indian Removal Act?

b. In what ways did Native Americans resist the Indian Removal Act?

c. What were the consequences of the Indian Removal Act?

4. Critical Thinking

Recognizing Effects What were some economic effects of the Indian Removal Act on Native Americans? On whites?

THINK ABOUT
- what the Native Americans lost
- what the white settlers gained

ACTIVITY OPTIONS

GEOGRAPHY
MATH

Use the map on page 376 to estimate the distance traveled by each of the five Southeastern tribes. Show your calculation on a **map** or **chart.**

Section 2 Assessment

1. Terms & Names

Sequoya, p. 358
Indian Removal Act, p. 360
Indian Territory, p. 360
Trail of Tears, p. 361
Osceola, p. 362

2. Taking Notes

Economic: white settlers and miners wanted their land; Political: Native Americans could not maintain independent governments in the United States; Social: many whites considered them uncivilized
Answers will vary but should be supported with information from the chapter.

3. Main Ideas

a. He said Native Americans could either adopt white culture or move out of the United States. **b.** took up arms; fought against relocation; went into hiding; used the courts for help **c.** Native Americans lost land, property, and homes; many died.

4. Critical Thinking

Native Americans became impoverished because they lost all their land and had to move. Whites became richer because they gained land and mined gold.

ACTIVITY OPTIONS

Integrated Assessment
- Rubrics for a map, 2.1
- Rubrics for a chart, 2.2

3 Conflicts Over States' Rights

TERMS & NAMES
John C. Calhoun
Tariff of Abominations
doctrine of nullification
Webster-Hayne debate
Daniel Webster
secession

MAIN IDEA	WHY IT MATTERS NOW
Jackson struggled to keep Southern states from breaking away from the Union over the issue of tariffs.	Disputes about states' rights and federal power remain important in national politics.

ONE AMERICAN'S STORY

Early in his political career, John C. Calhoun was hailed as "one of the master-spirits who stamp their name upon the age in which they live." This was praise indeed for someone from the backwoods of South Carolina who had little formal education before age 18. Elected to the U.S. Congress at 28, Calhoun soon was one of its leaders. He supported the need for a strong central government and became something of a hero to the nation's young people. He spoke out against sectionalism.

A VOICE FROM THE PAST

What is necessary for the common good may apparently be opposed to the interest of particular sections. It must be submitted to [accepted] as the condition of our [nation's] greatness.

John C. Calhoun, quoted in *John C. Calhoun: American Portrait* by Margaret L. Coit

But Calhoun's concern for the economic and political well-being of his home state of South Carolina, and the South in general, later caused him to change his beliefs. He became the foremost champion of states' rights, rigid in his views and increasingly bitter.

In this section, you will learn how two strong-willed men—Calhoun and Jackson—came in conflict over the issue of states' rights.

The bitter debate over states' rights took a physical toll on John C. Calhoun. He is shown here in about 1825 and in 1849.

1 Rising Sectional Differences

Andrew Jackson had taken office in 1829. At the time, the country was being pulled apart by conflicts among its three main sections—the Northeast, the South, and the West. Legislators from these regions were arguing over three major economic issues: the sale of public lands, internal improvements, and tariffs.

The federal government had acquired vast areas of land through conquests, treaties, and purchases. It raised money partly by selling these public lands. However, Northeasterners did not want public lands in the West to be sold at low prices. The cheap land would attract workers who were needed in the factories of the Northeast. But Westerners wanted

SECTION OBJECTIVES

1. To identify the issues that led to rising sectional differences
2. To explain how the "Tariff of Abominations" led to a crisis over nullification
3. To analyze the issues in the debate over states' rights
4. To describe how South Carolina's threat to secede was resolved

CRITICAL THINKING

Analyzing Causes, p. 365
Summarizing, p. 365
Analyzing Points of View, p. 367
Recognizing Effects, p. 367

FOCUS & MOTIVATE

5-MINUTE WARM-UP

Drawing Conclusions These questions focus on some of the causes of sectionalism.

1. Read the quotation from Calhoun on page 363. What did Calhoun mean by "common good," and what was his advice about sectionalism?
2. Why might sectionalism undermine a nation's "greatness"?

Warm-Up Transparency WT12

INSTRUCT

INSTRUCT: OBJECTIVE 1

Rising Sectional Differences

- Why did Northerners and Westerners disagree over the sale of public land?
- What were the differences among the sections on internal improvements and tariffs?

In-Depth Resources: Unit 4
- Guided Reading, p. 5

Reading Study Guide (Spanish and English), pp. 117–118

RECOMMENDED RESOURCES

In-Depth Resources: Unit 4
- Guided Reading, p. 5
- Building Vocabulary, p. 7
- Primary Source: from *Reminiscences and Anecdotes of Daniel Webster,* p. 12

Reading Study Guide (Spanish and English), pp. 117–118

Economics in History
- Westerners and High Tariffs, p. 12

Formal Assessment
- Section Quiz, p. 220

Integrated Assessment
- Rubrics, 3.6, 5.3

Access for Students Acquiring English/ESL, p. 78

INTEGRATED TECHNOLOGY

Electronic Teacher Tools

classzone.com

TEST-TAKING RESOURCES

Strategies for Test Preparation

Test Practice Transparencies, TT43

Online Test Practice

MORE ABOUT . . .

Internal Improvements

Among the most important internal improvements were better roads. Most roads at the time were unpaved paths where wagon wheels sank hub-deep in mud in wet weather and lurched over holes and ruts in dry weather. The new roads, built with both private and public money, were wider, better graded, and better surfaced.

low land prices to encourage settlement. The more people who moved West, the more political power the section would have.

The issue of internal improvements also pulled the sections apart. Business leaders in the Northeast and West backed government spending on internal improvements, such as new roads and canals. Good transportation would help bring food and raw materials to the Northeast and take manufactured goods to Western markets. Southerners opposed more federal spending on internal improvements because the government financed these projects through tariffs, which were taxes on imported goods. The South did not want any increase in tariffs.

Since 1816, tariffs had risen steadily. They had become the government's main source of income. Northerners supported high tariffs because they made imported goods more expensive than American-made goods. The Northeast had most of the nation's manufacturing. Tariffs helped

Background
During the Jackson era, the West included states that are now considered part of the Midwest.

Economics *in* History

OBJECTIVE

Students will be able to distinguish between revenue tariffs and protective tariffs and explain how protective tariffs work.

How Tariffs Work

Throughout much of American history, protective tariffs have sparked political debate. Most manufacturers and their workers, particularly in the North, have favored such tariffs. Farmers and Southern planters, who relied on foreign markets for the sale of their farm products, usually opposed tariffs. As American industries grew stronger, however, support for tariffs weakened. Since 1948, the United States has worked with other nations to lower tariffs on industrial goods. Once highly controversial, by the 1990s, free trade had become the official political position of both Democrats and Republicans.

Economics in History
- Westerners and High Tariffs, p.12

Economics *in* History

How Tariffs Work

Tariffs are taxes added to the cost of goods imported from another country. There are two kinds of tariffs—revenue tariffs and protective tariffs. **Revenue tariffs** are used to raise money, like the sales taxes that states add to purchases today. These tariffs tend to be fairly low. **Protective tariffs** usually are much higher. They have another goal: to persuade consumers to buy goods made in their own country instead of purchasing foreign-made products. Congress passed a protective tariff in 1828 to help American companies.

The illustration shows how a protective tariff works. A British-made teapot sells for $3.50, and a similar teapot made in the United States sells for $4.00. Most shoppers will buy the British teapot and save 50 cents. But when the government adds a 40 percent tariff to British goods, the price of the British teapot soars to $4.90. The result: consumers buy the now-cheaper American teapots.

CONNECT TO HISTORY

1. **Recognizing Effects** Do consumers benefit from high tariffs? Why or why not?

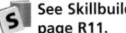

See Skillbuilder Handbook, page R11.

CONNECT TO TODAY

2. **Making Inferences** Today, many leaders around the world promote the idea of "free trade." What do you think "free trade" means?

For more about tariffs . . .

RESEARCH LINKS
CLASSZONE.COM

CONNECT TO HISTORY

1. **Recognizing Effects** **Possible Response** Consumers do not usually benefit because they have to pay higher prices.

CONNECT TO TODAY

2. **Making Inferences** **Possible Response** Free trade means goods are traded between countries without any tariffs.

American manufacturers sell their products at a lower price than imported goods.

The South opposed rising tariffs because its economy depended on foreign trade. Southern planters sold most of their cotton to foreign buyers. They were not paid in money but were given credit. They then used the credit to buy foreign manufactured goods. Because of higher tariffs, these foreign goods cost more. Eventually, the tariff issue would lead to conflict between North and South.

Reading **History**
A. Analyzing Causes Why did the three sections of the country differ on the sale of public lands, internal improvements, and tariffs?
A. Possible Answer The economy of each section was affected differently by these issues.

Tariff of Abominations ❷

In 1828, in the last months of John Quincy Adams's presidency, Congress passed a bill that significantly raised the tariffs on raw materials and manufactured goods. Southerners were outraged. They had to sell their cotton at low prices to be competitive. Yet tariffs forced them to pay high prices for manufactured goods. Southerners felt that the economic interests of the Northeast were determining national policy. They hated the tariff and called it the **Tariff of Abominations** (an abomination is a hateful thing).

Differences over the tariff helped Jackson win the election of 1828. Southerners blamed Adams for the tariff, since it was passed during his administration. So they voted against him.

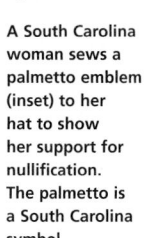

A South Carolina woman sews a palmetto emblem (inset) to her hat to show her support for nullification. The palmetto is a South Carolina symbol.

Crisis over Nullification

The Tariff of Abominations hit South Carolinians especially hard because their economy was in a slump. Some leaders in the state even spoke of leaving the Union over the issue of tariffs. John C. Calhoun, then Jackson's vice-president, understood the problems of South Carolina's farmers because he was one himself. But he wanted to find a way to keep South Carolina from leaving the Union. The answer he arrived at was the **doctrine of nullification.** A state, Calhoun said, had the right to nullify, or reject, a federal law that it considers unconstitutional.

Reading **History**
B. Summarizing How did the issue of tariffs threaten to tear the Union apart?
B. Possible Answers The South resented the Northeast for pushing higher tariffs without regard for the effect on the South's economy. South Carolina threatened to secede over the issue.

Calhoun was not the first person to propose the doctrine of nullification. Thomas Jefferson developed it in 1799 in the Kentucky Resolutions. He argued that the Union was a league of sovereign, or self-governing, states that had the right to limit the federal government. Calhoun extended the doctrine. He said that any state could nullify, or make void, a federal law within its borders. He believed that Congress had no right to impose a tariff that favored one section of the country. Therefore, South Carolina had the right to nullify the tariff. Calhoun's doctrine was an extreme form of states' rights—the theory that states have the right to judge whether a law of Congress is unconstitutional.

In the summer of 1828, Calhoun wrote a document called the "South Carolina Exposition and Protest." It stated his theory. Calhoun allowed the document to be published, but he did not sign his name. He knew his ideas would cause controversy.

Vocabulary
controversy: a public dispute

INSTRUCT: OBJECTIVE ❷

Tariff of Abominations/ Crisis over Nullification

- Why did the tariff of 1828 anger Southerners?
- What was the doctrine of nullification?
- How did Calhoun apply that doctrine to the "Tariff of Abominations"?

MORE ABOUT . . .

Calhoun and Nullification

In the first half of his public career, Calhoun was a strong nationalist who fought for the Second Bank of the United States, a permanent road system, and a standing army. He supported the protective tariff of 1816. Yet by 1828, he led the fight for states' rights. Calhoun favored nullification in part because he feared that the Northern majority in Congress might one day act against the South on the issue of slavery. Calhoun wrote that the tariff was of "vastly inferior importance to the great question to which it has given rise . . . the right of a state to . . . [stop] an unconstitutional act of the General Government."

ACTIVITY OPTIONS

INDIVIDUAL NEEDS

LESS PROFICIENT READERS

Rereading If students have difficulty completing the "Taking Notes" chart on page 367, you might want to provide a strategy for rereading to review and clarify this complex material. Have students reread pages 363–365 and identify the position taken by each region of the United States on each issue. Then work with students to extend the chart to explain why each region held the position it did. You can create a chart on the board similar to the one pictured, with additional categories for internal improvements and high tariffs.

	North	West	South
High prices for public lands	Yes	No	No position shown
Why?	Would lose workers	Would gain political power	
Tariffs			

MORE ABOUT . . .

Daniel Webster

During his lifetime, Daniel Webster was famed for his skill as an orator. Even years after his death, students memorized lines from his speeches. He was best known for the final line of a speech he delivered in the Senate in 1830. "Liberty and Union," he said, "now and forever, one and inseparable." These words became a rallying cry for Union soldiers during the Civil War.

In-Depth Resources: Unit 4
- Primary Source: from *Reminiscences and Anecdotes of Daniel Webster,* p. 12

INSTRUCT: OBJECTIVE 3

The States' Rights Debate

- Why did the theory of nullification develop into a national debate?
- What was the importance of the Webster-Hayne debate in Congress?
- How did the nullification issue make Jackson and Calhoun political enemies?

MORE ABOUT . . .

Robert Hayne

Although John C. Calhoun was the leading advocate of states' rights, he was also vice-president and therefore could not take part in Senate debates. So Robert Hayne spoke for him. Like Calhoun, Hayne was from South Carolina. Born on Pon Pon plantation in 1791, he had studied law and served in the War of 1812. He was elected to the Senate in 1823, where he served until 1832. Then he resigned to become governor of South Carolina and thereafter, mayor of Charleston. He died in 1839.

"Liberty and Union, now and forever, one and inseparable!"
Daniel Webster of Massachusetts
"The measures of the federal government . . . will soon involve the whole South in . . . ruin."
Robert Y. Hayne of South Carolina

Daniel Webster (standing) and Robert Y. Hayne (seated, with hands extended) debated nullification in the U.S. Senate in 1830.

3 The States' Rights Debate

Calhoun was right. His ideas added fuel to the debate over the nature of the federal union. This debate had been going on since independence from Britain. More and more people took sides. Some supported a strong federal government. Others defended the rights of the states. This question would be a major political issue from this time until the Civil War was fought to resolve it some 30 years later.

One of the great debates in American history took place in the U.S. Senate over the doctrine of nullification—the **Webster-Hayne debate** of 1830. On one side was **Daniel Webster,** a senator from Massachusetts and the most powerful speaker of his time. On the other was Robert Y. Hayne, a senator from South Carolina. Hayne defended nullification. He argued that it gave the states a lawful way to protest and to maintain their freedom. He also said that the real enemies of the Union were those "who are constantly stealing power from the States, and adding strength to the Federal Government."

Webster argued that it was the people and not the states that made the Union. In words that were printed and spread across the country, Webster declared that freedom and the Union go together.

A VOICE FROM THE PAST

When my eyes shall be turned to behold for the last time the sun in heaven, may I not see him shining on the broken and dishonored fragments of a once glorious Union. . . . Liberty and Union, now and forever, one and inseparable!

Daniel Webster, a speech in the U.S. Senate, January 26, 1830

Jackson had not yet stated his position on the issue of states' rights, even though Calhoun was his vice-president. He got his chance in April at a dinner in honor of the birthday of Thomas Jefferson. Calhoun and other

ACTIVITY OPTIONS

INTERDISCIPLINARY LINK: GOVERNMENT/CIVICS — BLOCK SCHEDULING

DEBATING STATES' RIGHTS

Class Time One class period

Task Holding a debate on the following statement: *Resolved: Allowing the states to nullify a federal law would destroy the national government's ability to govern.*

Purpose To analyze the effects of the doctrine of nullification

Supplies Needed
- Reference materials on the doctrine of nullification and the Webster-Hayne debate

Activity Divide students into two groups, one to support nullification and another to oppose it. Before the debate begins, members of each group should develop a list of arguments in support of their side's position on the issue. Allow practice time for each group to brainstorm counterarguments for every argument their opponents might present. Agree on rules for the debate.

supporters of nullification planned to use the event to win support for their position. Jackson learned of their plans and went to the dinner prepared.

After dinner, Jackson was invited to make a toast. He stood up, looked directly at Calhoun, and stated bluntly, "Our Federal Union—it must be preserved." As Calhoun raised his glass, his hand trembled. Called on to make the next toast, Calhoun stood slowly and said, "The Union—next to our liberty, the most dear; may we all remember that it can only be preserved by respecting the rights of the states and distributing equally the benefits and burdens of the Union." From that time, the two men were political enemies.

Reading **History**

C. Analyzing Points of View What do you think Calhoun meant by "the benefits and burdens of the Union" should be equally distributed?

C. Possible Answer One section should not benefit at the expense of another.

4 South Carolina Threatens to Secede

Even though Jackson made it clear that he opposed the doctrine of nullification, he did not want to drive the South out of the Union. He asked Congress to reduce the tariff, and Congress did so in 1832. But Southerners thought the reduced rates were still too high. South Carolina nullified the tariff acts of 1828 and 1832 and voted to build its own army. South Carolina's leaders threatened **secession,** or withdrawal from the Union, if the federal government tried to collect tariffs.

Jackson was enraged. He told a South Carolina congressman that if the state's leaders defied federal laws, he would "hang the first man of them I can get my hands on." Jackson ran for reelection in 1832, this time without Calhoun as his running mate. After he won, he made it clear that he would use force to see that federal laws were obeyed and the Union preserved.

In the Senate, Henry Clay came forward with a compromise tariff in 1833. He hoped that it would settle the issue and prevent bloodshed. Congress quickly passed the bill, and the crisis ended. South Carolina stayed in the Union. In the next section, you will read about another issue of Jackson's presidency—his war on the national bank.

Section 3 Assessment

1. Terms & Names

Explain the significance of:
- John C. Calhoun
- Tariff of Abominations
- doctrine of nullification
- Webster-Hayne debate
- Daniel Webster
- secession

2. Taking Notes

Use a chart to indicate how each section stood on these issues.

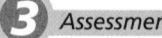

	Northeast	West	South
Sale of public lands			
Internal improvements			
High tariffs			

3. Main Ideas

a. Why did the South oppose high tariffs?

b. What were Calhoun's reasons for proposing the doctrine of nullification?

c. Why did South Carolina threaten secession, and how was the crisis resolved?

4. Critical Thinking

Recognizing Effects In what ways would the doctrine of nullification have made it difficult for the federal government to operate?

THINK ABOUT
- its effect on the enforcement of laws
- its effect on the power of the federal government

ACTIVITY OPTIONS

SPEECH / **TECHNOLOGY** Research Daniel Webster's speech; a part of it appears on page 382. Deliver a **speech** for or against nullification to the class, or record it on an **audiocassette.**

INSTRUCT: OBJECTIVE 4

South Carolina Threatens to Secede

- How did Southerners protest the tariffs?
- What was Jackson's response to South Carolina's threat to secede?
- How was the tariff controversy settled?

MORE ABOUT . . .

Henry Clay

Henry Clay, senator from Kentucky, first gained national attention as a War Hawk urging President Madison to declare war on Britain in 1812. Some years later, however, his sponsorship of a compromise tariff that ended the crisis over the tariff act of 1828 and his efforts to end sectional conflicts earned him the nickname the "Great Compromiser" or the "Great Pacificator." He ran unsuccessfully for president in 1824, 1832, and 1844 and is often remembered for his assertion that he would "rather be right than be president."

ASSESS & RETEACH

Setting the Stage Have students organize the information in this section in the appropriate category on the graphic organizer.

Formal Assessment
- Section Quiz, p. 220

RETEACHING ACTIVITY

Have students make a cluster diagram showing three causes of sectional conflict and the positions each section took on each issue.

In-Depth Resources: Unit 4
- Reteaching Activity, p. 18

Section 3 Assessment

1. Terms & Names

John C. Calhoun, p. 363
Tariff of Abominations, p. 365
doctrine of nullification, p. 365
Webster-Hayne debate, p. 366
Daniel Webster, p. 366
secession, p. 367

2. Taking Notes

Sale of public lands: Northeast against, West for, South no opinion; Internal improvements: Northeast and West for, South against; High tariffs: Northeast for, South against, West no opinion

3. Main Ideas

a. They hurt the economy of the South. **b.** He saw it as a way for the South to avoid paying tariffs and still stay in the Union. **c.** to keep the federal government from collecting the tariffs; resolved by Clay's compromise tariff

4. Critical Thinking

The government could not enforce laws across the nation, making the states more powerful than the federal government.

ACTIVITY OPTIONS

Integrated Assessment
- Rubrics for a speech, 3.6
- Rubrics for audiocassette, 5.3

SECTION OBJECTIVES

1. To explain why conflict erupted over the Second Bank of the United States
2. To describe how Jackson destroyed the bank
3. To analyze how economic prosperity turned into depression
4. To explain how the Whig Party won the election of 1840

CRITICAL THINKING

Analyzing Points of View, p. 369
Recognizing Effects, p. 370
Making Inferences, p. 371
Comparing, p. 371

FOCUS & MOTIVATE

5-MINUTE WARM-UP

Making Inferences These questions focus on economic concepts.

1. Look at the list of terms at the top of page 368. Which terms suggest that this section deals with economic problems?
2. What do you think might occur in an economic panic?

Warm-Up Transparency WT12

INSTRUCT

INSTRUCT: OBJECTIVE 1

Mr. Biddle's Bank

- Why was the Second Bank of the United States important, and what was Nicholas Biddle's role in it?
- Why did Jackson oppose the bank?

In-Depth Resources: Unit 4
- Guided Reading, p. 6

Reading Study Guide (Spanish and English), pp. 119–120

4 Prosperity and Panic

TERMS & NAMES
inflation
Martin Van Buren
Panic of 1837
depression
Whig Party
William Henry Harrison
John Tyler

MAIN IDEA	WHY IT MATTERS NOW
Jackson's policies caused the economy to collapse after he left office and affected the next election.	The condition of the economy continues to affect the outcomes of presidential elections.

ONE AMERICAN'S STORY

Nicholas Biddle was the kind of person that Andrew Jackson neither liked nor trusted. Biddle was wealthy, well educated, and came from a socially prominent Philadelphia family. He was also the influential president of the powerful Second Bank of the United States—the bank that Jackson believed to be a monster of corruption. Jackson declared war on Biddle and the bank during his 1832 reelection campaign. But Biddle felt sure of his political power.

A VOICE FROM THE PAST

I have always deplored making the Bank a [political] question, but since the President will have it so, he must pay the penalty of his own rashness. . . . [m]y hope is that it will contribute to relieve the country of the domination of these miserable [Jackson] people.

Nicholas Biddle, from a letter to Henry Clay dated August 1, 1832

For his part, Jackson vowed to "kill" the bank. In this section, you will read about his war on the bank and its effect on the economy.

Nicholas Biddle was the president of the powerful Second Bank of the United States, located in Philadelphia.

1 Mr. Biddle's Bank

The Second Bank of the United States was the most powerful bank in the country. It held government funds and issued money. As its president, Nicholas Biddle set policies that controlled the nation's money supply.

Although the bank was run efficiently, Jackson had many reasons to dislike it. For one thing, he had come to distrust banks after losing money in financial deals early in his career. He also thought the bank had too much power. The bank made loans to members of Congress, and Biddle openly boasted that he could influence Congress. In addition, Jackson felt the bank's lending policies favored wealthy clients and hurt the average person.

To operate, the bank had to have a charter, or a written grant, from the federal government. In 1832, Biddle asked Congress to renew the bank's charter, even though it would not expire until 1836. Because 1832 was an election year, he thought Jackson would agree to renewal rather than risk angering its supporters. But Jackson took the risk.

RECOMMENDED RESOURCES

In-Depth Resources: Unit 4
- Guided Reading, p. 6
- Building Vocabulary, p. 7
- Skillbuilder Practice, p. 8

Reading Study Guide (Spanish and English), pp. 119–120

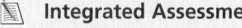

Formal Assessment
- Section Quiz, p. 221

Integrated Assessment
- Rubrics, 4.1, 1.1

Access for Students Acquiring English/ESL
- Guided Reading, p. 79
- Skillbuilder Practice, p. 80

INTEGRATED TECHNOLOGY

Humanities Transparency HT24
- Whig Rolling Ball, 1840

Electronic Teacher Tools

classzone.com

TEST-TAKING RESOURCES

Strategies for Test Preparation

Test Practice Transparencies, TT44

Online Test Practice

2 Jackson's War on the Bank

When Congress voted to renew the bank's charter, Jackson vetoed the renewal. In a strongly worded message to Congress, Jackson claimed the bank was unconstitutional. He said the bank was a monopoly that favored the few at the expense of the many. The Supreme Court earlier had ruled that the bank was constitutional. But Jackson claimed elected officials had to judge the constitutionality of a law for themselves. They did not need to rely on the Supreme Court. His veto message also contained this attack on the bank.

Vocabulary
monopoly: a company or group with complete control over a product or service

A VOICE FROM THE PAST

It is to be regretted that the rich and powerful too often bend the acts of government to their selfish purposes. . . . Distinctions in society will always exist under every just government. . . . [B]ut when the laws undertake to . . . make the rich richer and the potent more powerful, the humble members of society . . . have a right to complain of the injustice of their Government.

Andrew Jackson, veto message, July 10, 1832

Jackson's war on the bank became the main issue in the presidential campaign of 1832. The National Republican Party and its candidate, Henry Clay, called Jackson a tyrant. They said he wanted too much power as president. The Democrats portrayed Jackson as a defender of the people. When he won reelection, Jackson took it as a sign that the public approved his war on the bank.

In his second term, Jackson set out to destroy the bank before its charter ended in 1836. He had government funds deposited in state banks, which opponents called Jackson's "pet banks." Biddle fought back by making it harder for people to borrow money. He hoped the resulting economic troubles would force Jackson to return government deposits to the bank. Instead, the people rallied to Jackson's position. Eventually, the bank went out of business. Jackson had won the war, but the economy would be a victim.

***Reading* History**
A. Analyzing Points of View What reasons did Jackson have for wanting to destroy the Second Bank of the United States?
A. Possible Answer Jackson thought that the bank was too powerful and that its lending policies favored the wealthy and hurt the average person.

Jackson Fights the Second Bank

In this political cartoon, Jackson fights the many-headed monster—the Second Bank of the United States and its branches—with a cane labeled "VETO."

- A President Jackson
- B Cane labeled "VETO"
- C Nicholas Biddle
- D Vice-President Van Buren

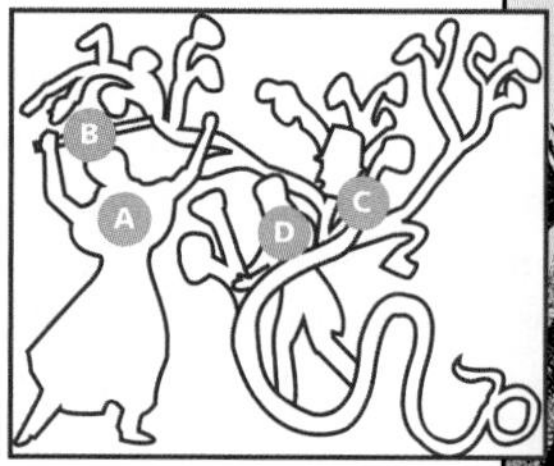

INSTRUCT: OBJECTIVE 2
Jackson's War on the Bank

- How did Jackson justify his veto of the bank charter?
- How did the bank issue affect the presidential campaign of 1832?
- How did Jackson drive the national bank out of business?

CRITICAL THINKING ACTIVITY

Analyzing Ask students to consider Jackson's claim that elected officials should judge a law's constitutionality for themselves. How would such a claim affect the separation of powers? Remind students of Jackson's remark, "John Marshall has made his decision. . . . Now let him enforce it" (page 361). Ask: Which branch is supposed to enforce the laws? **Answer** executive branch

Encourage students to compare Jackson's views on Supreme Court rulings with Calhoun's views on federal laws (nullification). Which branches or levels of government gain power under each man's theory? Which lose power?

Class Time 15 minutes

HISTORY FROM VISUALS

Interpreting Political Cartoons Ask students to look at the cartoon of Jackson fighting the bank. Ask: Why is Nicholas Biddle shown where he is? **Answer** He is the head of the bank. Next, ask: What is Vice-President Van Buren doing? **Possible Response** He seems to be helping Jackson by holding the heads for Jackson to strike.

ACTIVITY OPTIONS

SKILLBUILDER LESSON: INTERPRETING POLITICAL CARTOONS — BLOCK SCHEDULING

Explaining the Skill A political cartoon presents a point of view on a major issue or a political personality. Political cartoons can be valuable historic sources. They provide visual and written clues to public opinion in their time.

Use these steps to analyze a cartoon: (1) Identify the subject of the cartoon. (2) Pick out key symbols and details that help you interpret the cartoon's message. (3) Analyze the cartoonist's point of view on the subject.

Applying the Skill Examine the cartoon on page 369, using these questions to analyze it.

1. What is the cartoon's subject? *(Jackson's war on the bank)*
2. What symbol represents the bank? What does Jackson's cane represent? *(The many-headed monster stands for the bank; the cane, Jackson's veto.)*
3. What is the cartoon's message? *(The bank is a monster that Jackson is struggling to kill with his veto.)*
4. What does the artist think of the bank? *(He opposes it.)*

In-Depth Resources: Unit 4
- Skillbuilder Practice, p. 8

INSTRUCT: OBJECTIVE 3

Prosperity Becomes Panic

- How did Jackson's use of "pet banks" cause inflation?
- How did the Panic of 1837 lead to a nation-wide depression?
- What were the economic consequences of the depression?

***America's* HERITAGE**

Political Parties

The log cabin proved to be such a successful symbol for the Whigs in the 1840 campaign that they built cabins for party rallies, put them on wheels and pulled them in parades, and put them up in every city, town, and village they could find. Whigs distributed log-cabin newspapers and songbooks and sang such ditties as this one, reminding voters that Harrison fought at Tippecanoe:

Farewell, dear Van
You're not our man;
To guide the ship,
We'll try old Tip.

INSTRUCT: OBJECTIVE 4

The Rise of the Whig Party/ The Election of 1840

- How did Clay's and Webster's ideas about the economy differ from Van Buren's?
- What did the Whig Party stand for, and why did Whigs choose Harrison as their candidate?
- How did the Whigs try to win the votes of the common people in 1840?

Humanities Transparency HT24
• Whig Rolling Ball, 1840

3 Prosperity Becomes Panic

Most of the nation prospered during Jackson's last years in office. Because it was easier to borrow money, people took out loans to buy public lands, and the economy boomed. But the "pet banks" issued too much paper money. The rise in the money supply made each dollar worth less. As a result, prices rose. **Inflation,** which is an increase in prices and decrease in the value of money, was the outcome. To fight inflation, Jackson issued an order that required people to pay in gold or silver for public lands.

Jackson left office proud of the nation's prosperity. But it was a puffed-up prosperity. Like a balloon, it had little substance. Because of Jackson's popularity, his vice-president, **Martin Van Buren,** was elected president in 1836. Within a few months after Van Buren took office, a panic—a widespread fear about the state of the economy—spread throughout the country. It became known as the **Panic of 1837.**

People took their paper money to the banks and demanded gold or silver in exchange. The banks quickly ran out of gold and silver. When the government tried to get its money from the state banks, the banks could not pay. The banks defaulted, or went out of business. A **depression,** or severe economic slump, followed.

The depression caused much hardship. Because people had little money, manufacturers no longer had customers for their goods. Almost 90 percent of factories in the East closed in 1837. Jobless workers had no way of buying food or paying rent. People went hungry. They lived in shelters or on the streets, where many froze in the winter. Every section of the country suffered, but the depression hit hardest in the cities. Farmers were hurt less because they could at least grow their own food. The depression affected politics, too.

***America's* HERITAGE**

POLITICAL PARTIES

Today's Democratic and Republican parties were born more than a century ago. Andrew Jackson's supporters first called themselves Democratic-Republicans. But in the 1830s, they became known simply as Democrats. They stood for states' rights and saw themselves as defenders of the common people. The modern Republican Party was formed in 1854 as the successor to the Whig Party, founded in 1834.

In the Jackson era, political parties campaigned for their candidates by staging parades and rallies. Participants often carried banners like the one below with a log cabin, the symbol for the campaign of William H. Harrison in 1840.

***Reading*History**

B. Recognizing Effects What were the short-term and long-term effects of Jackson's war on the bank?

B. Possible Answer In the short run, the economy boomed as credit became easy to get and people borrowed to buy public lands. In the long run, the easy credit and over-printing of money caused inflation and eventually a depression.

4 The Rise of the Whig Party

In the depths of the depression, Senators Henry Clay and Daniel Webster argued that the government needed to help the economy. Van Buren disagreed. He believed that the economy would improve if left alone. He argued that "the less government interferes with private pursuits the better for the general prosperity." Many Americans blamed Van Buren for the Panic, though he had taken office only weeks before it started. The continuing depression made it almost impossible for him to win reelection in 1840.

ACTIVITY OPTIONS

INDIVIDUAL NEEDS

STUDENTS ACQUIRING ENGLISH/ESL

Understanding Specialized Vocabulary To help students understand how Jackson's policies caused the economy to collapse, you might want to point out some of the specialized vocabulary in the section to students before they begin to read. Write some or all of the following words on the board:

economy	*funds*	*deposit*	*loans*
prosperity	*credit*	*borrow*	*lending policies*

Discuss the words with students to see which ones they already understand and which need clarification. In some cases the words may be familiar, but the concepts may still be challenging. Define words as necessary.

After students read the section, ask them questions based on the section content. Encourage them to use the specialized vocabulary in their responses to the questions.

Van Buren faced a new political party in that election. During Jackson's war on the national bank, Clay, Webster, and other Jackson opponents had formed the **Whig Party.** It was named after a British party that opposed royal power. The Whigs opposed the concentration of power in the chief executive—whom they mockingly called "King Andrew" Jackson. In 1840, the Whigs chose **William Henry Harrison** of Ohio to run for president and **John Tyler** of Virginia to run for vice-president.

The Whigs nominated Harrison largely because of his military record and his lack of strong political views. Harrison had led the army that defeated the Shawnees in 1811 at the Battle of Tippecanoe. He also had been a hero during the War of 1812. The Whigs made the most of Harrison's military record and his nickname, "Old Tippecanoe." The phrase "Tippecanoe and Tyler too" became the Whig election slogan.

Reading **History**

C. Making Inferences Why did the Whigs want to nominate a candidate like Harrison, who did not have strong political views?

C. Possible Answer A candidate without strong political views would be less likely to lose votes by taking stands on the issues.

The Election of 1840

During the 1840 election campaign, the Whigs emphasized personalities more than issues. They tried to appeal to the common people, as Andrew Jackson had done. Harrison was the son of a Virginia plantation owner. However, because he had settled on a farm in Ohio, the Whigs said Harrison was a true Westerner. They used symbols of the frontier, such as a log cabin, to represent Harrison. The Whigs contrasted Harrison with the wealthy Van Buren. Harrison won in a close election.

At his inauguration, the 68-year-old president spoke for nearly two hours in cold March weather with no hat or coat. Later, he was caught in the rain. He came down with a cold that developed into pneumonia. On April 4, 1841, one month after being inaugurated, Harrison died—the first president to die in office. Vice-President Tyler became president.

The election of 1840 showed the importance of the West in American politics. In the next chapter, you'll learn more about the lure of the West and the westward expansion of the United States.

Section 4 Assessment

1. Terms & Names

Explain the significance of:
- inflation
- Martin Van Buren
- Panic of 1837
- depression
- Whig Party
- William Henry Harrison
- John Tyler

2. Taking Notes

Use a diagram to list the events that led to the closing of the Second Bank of the United States.

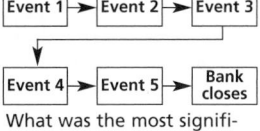

Event 1 → Event 2 → Event 3 → Event 4 → Event 5 → Bank closes

What was the most significant event?

3. Main Ideas

a. Why did Jackson declare war on the Second Bank of the United States?

b. How did Jackson kill the bank?

c. What role did Jackson's popularity play in the elections of 1836 and 1840?

4. Critical Thinking

Comparing What strategy did the Whig Party use in the 1840 election?

THINK ABOUT
- how Harrison was portrayed
- what group of voters it was trying to attract

ACTIVITY OPTIONS

LANGUAGE ARTS

ART

Imagine yourself as a presidential candidate in 1840. Focusing on the economy as an issue, write a campaign **slogan** or create a **banner** to rally support.

CRITICAL THINKING ACTIVITY

Evaluating Have students evaluate the presidency of Andrew Jackson, focusing on his political ideas, his economic policies, his treatment of Native Americans, his attitude toward the Supreme Court, and his handling of states' rights issues. Was Jackson a great president? Have students give reasons for their opinion. Use the chart to help students make their own assessments of his years in office.

	Achievements	Failures
Political Ideas		
National Bank		
Native Americans		
States' Rights		
Supreme Court		

Class Time 15 minutes

ASSESS & RETEACH

Setting the Stage Have students complete the graphic organizer categorizing changes during the Age of Jackson.

Formal Assessment
- Section Quiz, p. 221

Critical Thinking Transparency CT34
- Setting the Stage

RETEACHING ACTIVITY

Give students the following three topics: Jackson's war on the bank; the Panic of 1837; the election of 1840. Ask them to write one sentence about each event, showing how it connects to one of the others.

In-Depth Resources: Unit 4
- Reteaching Activity, p. 19

Section 4 Assessment

1. Terms & Names

inflation, p. 370
Martin Van Buren, p. 370
Panic of 1837, p. 370
depression, p. 370
Whig Party, p. 371
William Henry Harrison, p. 371
John Tyler, p. 371

2. Taking Notes

Event 1: Biddle asks Congress to renew charter in 1832; Event 2: Congress renews charter; Event 3: Jackson vetoes charter; Event 4: Jackson reelected; Event 5: Jackson deposits federal funds in pet banks. Answers will vary, but should include support from information in the chapter.

3. Main Ideas

a. He considered it too powerful and corrupt; he thought it favored wealthy people. **b.** He vetoed the renewal of the bank's charter, withdrew all federal money, and set up state banks. **c.** His vice-president, Van Buren, won election in 1836; Harrison won the 1840 election by running as a Jackson-like candidate.

4. Critical Thinking

They represented Harrison as a man like Jackson and avoided real issues.

ACTIVITY OPTIONS

Integrated Assessment
- Rubrics for leaflet, 1.13
- Rubrics for a poster, 1.1

TERMS & NAMES

1. **John Quincy Adams,** p. 353
2. **Jacksonian democracy,** p. 354
3. **spoils system,** p. 357
4. **Sequoya,** p. 358
5. **Indian Removal Act,** p. 360
6. **Trail of Tears,** p. 361
7. **secession,** p. 367
8. **inflation,** p. 370
9. **depression,** p. 370
10. **Whig Party,** p. 371

REVIEW QUESTIONS

Possible Responses

1. He was not from the East and did not come from an aristocratic family.
2. He portrayed himself as a common person who had worked his way up, a Westerner, a war hero, and a champion of the common people.
3. to make them leave so whites could settle there and mine for gold
4. He considered Native Americans to have no rights to establish an independent government within the borders of the United States and promoted the idea of relocation.
5. They lost everything they owned and suffered a long, harsh journey to a new land; many lost their lives.
6. The North and South had differing opinions. Each region wanted high or low tariffs based on how the tariff would affect the economy of that region.
7. South Carolina threatened to secede; Jackson vowed to use force to see that federal laws were obeyed.
8. Henry Clay proposed a compromise tariff, Congress passed it, and South Carolina stayed in the Union.
9. because he had lost money in financial deals involving banks; he thought the bank was too powerful, corrupt, and favored wealthy people
10. Credit became easy, people borrowed heavily to buy public land, the banks printed too much money, and money began to lose value.

Chapter 12 ASSESSMENT

TERMS & NAMES

Briefly explain the significance of each of the following.

1. John Quincy Adams
2. Jacksonian democracy
3. spoils system
4. Sequoya
5. Indian Removal Act
6. Trail of Tears
7. secession
8. inflation
9. depression
10. Whig Party

REVIEW QUESTIONS

Politics of the People (pages 353–357)

1. How was Jackson different from earlier presidents?
2. How did Jackson appeal to voters in his election campaign of 1828?

Jackson's Policy Toward Native Americans (pages 358–362)

3. What were Georgia's policies toward Native Americans?
4. What was Jackson's position on Native Americans in the United States?
5. How did the Indian Removal Act affect Native Americans?

Conflicts over States' Rights (pages 363–367)

6. How did the issue of tariffs divide the country?
7. Why did nullification threaten the nation?
8. How was the nullification crisis resolved?

Prosperity and Panic (pages 368–371)

9. Why did Jackson oppose the Second Bank of the United States?
10. What were the effects of Jackson's war on the bank?

CRITICAL THINKING

1. USING YOUR NOTES

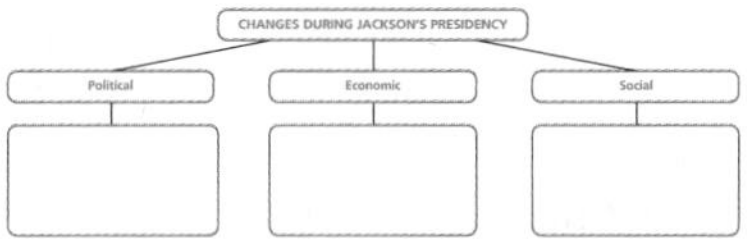

Use your completed chart to answer the questions.

a. What do you think was the most positive change of the Jackson era? Explain.
b. What was the most negative change? Explain.
c. Based on these changes, how would you describe the characteristics of the Jackson era?

2. ANALYZING LEADERSHIP

What was the basis of Andrew Jackson's power as president?

3. APPLYING CITIZENSHIP SKILLS

How did the majority of voters in the presidential elections of 1828 and 1840 exercise their vote in a similar way?

4. THEME: ECONOMICS IN HISTORY

Based on its economic effects, was Jackson's decision to end the national bank a good one? Explain.

5. MAKING INFERENCES

In what ways did Andrew Jackson's policy toward Native Americans reflect bias?

Interact *with* History

Now that you have read the chapter, do you think the qualities that made Jackson a strong military leader made him a good president? Explain your answer.

VISUAL SUMMARY

Major Issues of Jackson's Presidency

POLICY TOWARD NATIVE AMERICANS	CONFLICT OVER STATES' RIGHTS	WAR ON BANK OF THE UNITED STATES
White settlers wanted Native American lands.	Sectional differences developed.	Second Bank of the United States had economic and political power.
Jackson proposed Indian Removal Act of 1830.	Jackson supported strong central government.	Jackson opposed bank and vetoed renewal of its charter.
Thousands of Native Americans removed to Indian Territory.	South Carolina threatened to secede over tariff issue, but compromise reached.	Bank driven out of business, but Jackson's policies eventually led to inflation and depression.

CRITICAL THINKING

Possible Responses

1. **USING YOUR NOTES** **a.** Students might cite the focus on common people gaining a voice in the government because it broadened the base of our democracy. **b.** Students might cite the relocation of Native Americans because it caused so much suffering. **c.** Students might cite the focus on the common man and strengthening of democracy.
2. **ANALYZING LEADERSHIP** his great popularity and public support; the support of the Democratic Party; his lack of fear of using the veto
3. **APPLYING CITIZENSHIP SKILLS** They defeated a president seeking reelection.
4. **THEME: ECONOMICS IN HISTORY** The decision was a poor one because the long-term effects were disastrous for the nation's economy.
5. **RECOGNIZING BIAS** Previous treaties gave the Native Americans the right to their land, but Jackson denied that they had this right. He singled them out as a group and denied their rights.

Interact *with* History Students' responses will vary but should include elements discussed in the chapter.

HISTORY SKILLS

1. INTERPRETING GRAPHS

Study the graph. Answer the questions.

Voter Participation, *1824 & 1828 Elections*

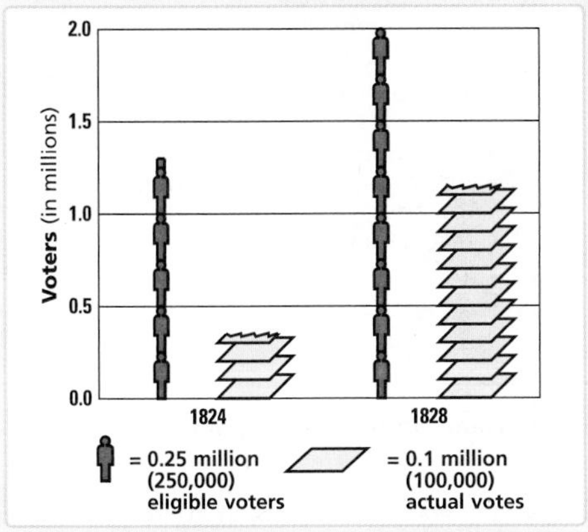

Source: *Historical Statistics of the United States*

Basic Graph Elements

a. What is the subject of the graph?

b. What do the symbols represent?

Interpreting the Graph

c. How many more eligible voters were there in 1828 than in 1824?

d. What percentage of eligible voters cast their ballots in 1824? in 1828?

2. INTERPRETING PRIMARY SOURCES

This is a political cartoon from the 1832 election campaign. It is entitled "King Andrew the First."

a. Is the comparison of Jackson to a king meant as praise or criticism? Explain.

b. What does it mean that he is standing on torn papers entitled "U.S. Constitution" and "U.S. Bank"?

ALTERNATIVE ASSESSMENT

1. INTERDISCIPLINARY ACTIVITY: Speech

Presenting a Debate Working with a partner, take sides on the doctrine of nullification and prepare a debate for the class.

2. COOPERATIVE LEARNING ACTIVITY

Preparing a Problem-Solving Proposal Plan and write a proposal outlining a solution to the problems between white settlers and Native Americans in the Southeast in the early 1800s. Working in a small group, first brainstorm ideas and make a list. Then identify the positives and negatives of each idea. Agree on an outline for a final plan. Then write, revise, and make a final copy of your proposal. Present your proposal to the class and defend it.

3. TECHNOLOGY ACTIVITY

Designing a Political Campaign Web Site Andrew Jackson was one of the more colorful figures in American history. His election as president brought significant changes to the nation. Plan a Web site for candidate Jackson for the 1828 presidential campaign. Use the Internet or search the library for information on Jackson's life before the presidency and on the 1828 election.

For more about Andrew Jackson . . .

INTERNET ACTIVITY
CLASSZONE.COM

Design the Web site using the suggestions below.

- Include biographical facts.
- Select images that tell Jackson's story.
- Present his views on the major issues of the day using quotations from speeches and other documents.
- Locate appropriate links for visitors to your Web site.

4. HISTORY PORTFOLIO

Option 1 Review your section and chapter assessment activities. Select one that you think was your best work. Then use comments made by your teacher or classmates to improve your work and add it to your portfolio.

Option 2 Review the questions that you wrote for What Do You Want to Know? on page 352. Then write a short report in which you explain the answers to your questions. Be sure to use standard grammar, spelling, sentence structure, and punctuation in your report. Add your work to your history portfolio.

Additional Test Practice, pp. S1–S33

TEST PRACTICE
CLASSZONE.COM

ALTERNATIVE ASSESSMENT

1. INTERDISCIPLINARY ACTIVITY: Speech

Debates should
- have a central question or proposition.
- support a position and refute opponent's position with evidence.
- respond appropriately to each other's statements.

2. COOPERATIVE LEARNING ACTIVITY

Proposals should
- reflect the use of a problem-solving technique.
- focus on resolving the problem.
- support positions with evidence or logic.
- reflect the student's research in the presentation.

3. TECHNOLOGY ACTIVITY

Web sites should
- contain at least three links.
- make effective use of pictures and icons.
- contain written summaries that will encourage browsers to visit other Web sites.
- show technical proficiency.

4. HISTORY PORTFOLIO

Option 1 Revised section or chapter assessment activities should
- address teacher and peer responses to the selected work.
- solve problems present in the first versions of the work.

Option 2 Short reports should
- answer questions about the presidency of Andrew Jackson.
- use evidence to develop and support ideas.
- cite sources of information.
- use standard grammar, spelling, sentence structure, and punctuation.

Critical Thinking Transparency CT36
- Visual Summary

Formal Assessment
- Chapter Test, Forms A, B, and C, pp. 222–236

HISTORY SKILLS

Possible Responses

1. INTERPRETING GRAPHS

Basic Graph Elements

a. voter participation in the 1824 and 1828 elections

b. eligible voters and actual votes

Interpreting the Graph

c. about .7 million, or 700,000

d. about 30 percent in 1824, more than 55 percent in 1828

2. INTERPRETING PRIMARY SOURCES

a. Criticism—because a king is not elected, a king is not a democratic ruler.

b. It shows that he was harming the Constitution and the bank.

Manifest Destiny 1810–1853

	CHAPTER OVERVIEW	COPYMASTERS	INTEGRATED TECHNOLOGY
CHAPTER RESOURCES	This chapter discusses the westward migration of the American people and the national belief in Manifest Destiny. It also describes the Texas Revolution, the War with Mexico, and the California gold rush.	**In-Depth Resources: Unit 4** • Tracing Themes: Expansion, p. 22 • Building Vocabulary, p. 27 **Interdisciplinary Projects,** pp. 73–78	• eEdition Plus Online • EasyPlanner Plus Online • eTest Plus Online • eEdition • Power Presentations • EasyPlanner • Electronic Library of Primary Sources • Test Generator • Reading Study Guide • America's Music
	KEY IDEAS		
SECTION 1 **Trails West** **pp. 377–383**	• Mountain men open the Far West, and their reports lure others. • Traders and settlers go west on the Oregon and Santa Fe Trails. • The Mormons go to Utah in search of religious freedom.	**In-Depth Resources: Unit 4** • Setting the Stage, p. 21 • Guided Reading, p. 23 • Primary Source, p. 31 • Reteaching Activity, p. 36 **America's History Makers** • Narcissa Whitman, pp. 51–52 **Outline Map Activities** • The Opening of the West, 1850, pp. 25–26	**Warm-Up Transparency WT13** **Humanities Transparency HT25** • *The Cowboy* **Humanities Transparency HT26** • *On the Trail* **Critical Thinking Transparency CT37** • Setting the Stage classzone.com
SECTION 2 **The Texas Revolution** **pp. 384–389**	• Stephen Austin starts an American colony under Mexican rule in Texas. • Rising tensions eventually lead Texans to revolt against Mexico. • Texans win the Battle of San Jacinto and declare their independence as a republic.	**In-Depth Resources: Unit 4** • Setting the Stage, p. 21 • Guided Reading, p. 24 • Primary Source, p. 32 • Reteaching Activity, p. 37 **America's History Makers** • Juan Seguín, pp. 53–54 **American History Plays** • *Live from the Alamo*	**Warm-Up Transparency WT13** **Geography Transparency GT13** • The Battle of the Alamo, 1836 **Critical Thinking Transparency CT37** • Setting the Stage classzone.com
SECTION 3 **The War with Mexico** **pp. 390–395**	• Many Americans support the idea of Manifest Destiny. • The United States declares war on Mexico, provoking debate over expansion and slavery. • The U.S. victory leads to the acquisition of Texas, California, and a vast area in the Southwest.	**In-Depth Resources: Unit 4** • Setting the Stage, p. 21 • Guided Reading, p. 25 • Skillbuilder Practice, p. 28 • Geography Application, pp. 29–30 • Reteaching Activity, p. 38 **Why It Matters Now** • The Influence of the West, pp. 25–26	**Warm-Up Transparency WT13** **Critical Thinking Transparency CT37** • Setting the Stage classzone.com
SECTION 4 **The California Gold Rush** **pp. 396–401**	• Before 1849, California is home to Native Americans, *Californios*, and some American settlers. • The discovery of gold in California leads to the gold rush of 1849. • The influx of American settlers harms Native Americans and *Californios* but leads to California's statehood.	**In-Depth Resources: Unit 4** • Setting the Stage, p. 21 • Guided Reading, p. 26 • Literature Selection, pp. 33–35 • Reteaching Activity, p. 39 **Economics in History** • Gold Rush Entrepreneurs, p. 13	**Warm-Up Transparency WT13** **Critical Thinking Transparency CT37** • Setting the Stage **Critical Thinking Transparency CT38** • Cause and Effect: U.S. Expansion, 1846–1853 **Critical Thinking Transparency CT39** • Visual Summary classzone.com

Pupil's Edition

Copymaster

Overhead Transparency

Audio Library

CD-ROM

Internet

ASSESSMENT OPTIONS

Chapter Assessment, pp. 402–403

Formal Assessment
- Chapter Tests, Forms A, B, and C, pp. 241–252

Test Generator

Online Test Practice

Strategies for Test Preparation

Section Assessment, p. 381

Formal Assessment, Quiz, p. 237

Integrated Assessment Book
- Rubrics, 4.3, 3.6

Test Generator

Test Practice Transparencies, TT45

Section Assessment, p. 389

Formal Assessment, Quiz, p. 238

Integrated Assessment Book
- Rubrics, 1.7, 4.4

Test Generator

Test Practice Transparencies, TT46

Section Assessment, p. 495

Formal Assessment, Quiz, p. 239

Integrated Assessment Book
- Rubrics, 2.3, 2.1

Test Generator

Test Practice Transparencies, TT47

Section Assessment, p. 401

Formal Assessment, Quiz, p. 240

Integrated Assessment Book
- Rubrics, 4.5, 2.1

Test Generator

Test Practice Transparencies, TT48

CUSTOMIZING FOR INDIVIDUAL NEEDS

Students Acquiring English/ESL

Reading Study Guide (English and Spanish), pp. 123–132

Access for Students Acquiring English/ESL: Spanish Translations, pp. 83–89

Chapter Summaries on CD (English and Spanish)

Modified Lesson Plans for English Learners

Less Proficient Readers

Reading Study Guide (English and Spanish), pp. 123–132

Chapter Summaries on CD (English and Spanish)

Gifted and Talented Students

In-Depth Resources: Unit 4
- Enrichment Activity, p. 40

America's History Makers
- Narcissa Whitman, pp. 51–52
- Juan Seguín, pp. 53–54

CROSS-CURRICULAR CONNECTIONS

Culture

Hoyt, Edwin P. ***The Alamo: An Illustrated History.*** Dallas, TX: Taylor Publishing Company, 1999. Beautiful account of the historic mission.

Geography

Cobb, Hubbard, and Stanley Schuler. ***American Battlefields: A Complete Guide to the Historic Conflicts in Words, Maps, and Photos.*** Foster City, CA: IDG Books Worldwide, 1996. A chronologically organized guide to battles fought in the United States, including the Mexican War.

Humanities: Art

Driesbach, Janice Tolhurst, Harvey Jones and Katherine Church Holland. ***Art of the Gold Rush.*** Los Angeles, CA: Univ. of California Press, 1998. Drawings and paintings of the gold rush era.

Interdisciplinary Projects, pp. 73–78

- Math: The Geometry of Quilts
- Science: Ecosystems Along the Santa Fe Trail
- Language Arts: Tall Tales
- Home Economics: Pioneer Clothing

Literature

Cushman, Karen. ***The Ballad of Lucy Whipple.*** New York: Harpercollins, 1998. Young Lucy writes from the mining frontier to her grandmother in the East in this well-researched novel.

Karr, Kathleen. ***The Great Turkey Walk.*** New York: Farrar, 1998. Based on a true story, the story of a 15-year-old boy who tries to herd a flock of 1,000 turkeys from Missouri to Colorado.

Mayfield, Thomas Jefferson. ***Adopted by Indians: A True Story.*** ed. by Malcolm Margolin. Berkeley, CA: Heyday Books, 1997. After his mother's death in 1850, young Mayfield lived with the Choinumne Indians. This account of his life and the traditional ways of the Choinumne was edited for children.

McDougall Littell Literature Connections

Betsy Byars

Trouble River

Dewey Martin, a 12-year-old boy in the 1800s, is left behind to tend the family farm while his parents go to Hunter City. Fearing an Indian raid, Dewey, his grandmother, and their dog Charlie set off on a small raft on Trouble River.

ENRICHMENT ACTIVITIES

Pupil's Edition, pp. 374–403
Interact With History, p. 375
Interdisciplinary Challenge, pp. 382–383
Technology of the Time, p. 399

In-Depth Resources: Unit 4
- Geography Application: The United States Gains Land from Mexico, pp. 29–30
- Primary Source: from *Luzena Stanley Wilson, '49er,* p. 31
- Primary Source: A Mexican Account of the Battle of the Alamo, p. 32
- Literature Selection: from *Roughing It* by Mark Twain, pp. 33–35

America's History Makers
- Narcissa Whitman, pp. 51–52
- Juan Seguín, pp. 53–54

Outline Map Activities
- The Opening of the West, 1850, pp. 25–26

Why It Matters Now
- The Influence of the West, pp. 25–26

BLOCK SCHEDULING — LESSON PLAN OPTIONS (90-MINUTE PERIOD)

DAY 1

Interact with History, p. 375
Class Time 20 Minutes

Options for pacing and variety:
- Role-Playing In small groups have students assume the roles of a pioneer family going west. Two can be parents, others can be grandparents, unmarried aunts and uncles, or teenagers. Have each tell what they expect to gain and what they fear they might lose by going west. **Class Time** 20 minutes

Setting the Stage, p. 376
Class Time 20 minutes

Options for pacing and variety:
- Time Saver For a homework assignment, have students bring to class the names of movies, books, or television shows that have influenced their views of the West.
Class Time 5 minutes

Section 1, pp. 377–383
Class Time 50 minutes

Options for pacing and variety:
- History on Film Extend students' background knowledge of the westward journey by viewing *The Story of the Oregon Trail.* Boettcher/Trinklein. 1992
Class Time 60 minutes
- Time Saver Use the map of western trails in 1850 on page 379 to summarize the section.
Class Time 20 minutes

DAY 2

Interdisciplinary Challenge, pp. 382–383
Class Time 45 minutes

Options for pacing and variety:
- Team Teaching Invite the science or physics teacher to coach student groups as they solve the Science Challenge on page 382.
Class Time 30 minutes
- Peer Evaluation Write the Standards for Evaluation for the Civics Challenge found on page 382 of the Teacher's Edition on the chalkboard. Have students use these criteria to evaluate one another's role plays or written recommendations.
Class Time 30 minutes

Section 2, pp. 384–389
Class Time 45 minutes

Section 3, pp. 390–395
Class Time 45 minutes

Options for pacing and variety:
- Peer Teaching Assign the content under each heading to a small group of students. Each group is responsible for explaining the information to the class. **Class Time** 30 minutes
- Peer Evaluation Have groups of students perform the Cooperative Learning Activity on page 403. **Class Time** 45 minutes

DAY 3

Section 4, pp. 396–401
Class Time 45 minutes

Options for pacing and variety:
- Time Saver Using Critical Thinking Transparency CT39, ask student volunteers to summarize the chapter.
Class Time 10 minutes
- Internet Extend students' background knowledge of the California gold rush by visiting the Library of Congress American Memory collection at classzone.com.
Class Time 20 minutes

Chapter 13 Assessment, pp. 402–403
Class Time 40 minutes

Options for pacing and variety:
- Peer Teaching Have students prepare a summary of the chapter using the words in the Terms & Names in the Chapter Assessment. Have students exchange papers and evaluate one another's summaries.
Class Time 20 minutes
- Peer Evaluation Have students find partners and compare their Using Your Notes charts, checking each other's charts for completeness and accuracy. **Class Time** 20 minutes

TEACHER-TESTED ACTIVITY **Lisa Williams, Lamberton Middle School, Carlisle, Pennsylvania**

COME TO CALIFORNIA!

Class Time One class period
Task Creating an advertising poster
Purpose To understand the motives that drew people to California and the methods of transportation they used

Supplies Needed
- Research materials on the California gold rush and on transportation
- Construction paper or posterboard
- Colored markers or crayons

Activity Each student should create an advertisement that urges people to join the gold rush to California. The ad should focus on a way of getting to the gold fields and present its advantages. Students should be aware that many people reached California by sailing "around the Horn" or by crossing the Isthmus of Panama. Posters should be persuasive and attractive.

ELECTRONIC POSTER EXHIBIT

Poster art of the 1800s was used to advertise everything from free land to mail-order brides. The railroad industry used posters to entice Americans to move west along the railroad lines. Clipper ship companies used posters to advertise passage to the Oregon Territory and the California gold mines. Territories advertised free passage to anyone who would settle in the territory. Students should enjoy creating posters to advertise the opportunities Americans could find in the West.

ACTIVITY OUTLINE

Objective Creating an electronic poster promoting migration to the West will help students understand the reasons people settled in the American West in the 19th century. It will also help familiarize students with computer technology to display graphic art.

Task Students will study examples of poster art of the early 1800s to gain ideas they will use to produce posters of their own. The posters can be displayed in an electronic slide show.

Class Time One class period

DIRECTIONS

1. Discuss with students who have read Chapter 13 what the phrase "manifest destiny" means. Why did Americans at the time believe the United States would inevitably expand across the continent?

2. Conduct a brainstorming session with students to think of possible subjects for posters. Direct students to think of things that someone of the period might have advertised.

3. Then tell students to pick a subject from the list. Suggest that students study examples of advertising posters in the text and look for examples on some of the Web sites listed on classzone.com. Posters can contain both artwork and text or just text. They should be based on factual information and events.

4. Allow one class period for planning and research. The actual posters can be completed outside of class. When posters have been turned in and displayed, have students scan them to create an electronic copy.

5. When all posters have been scanned, ask for student volunteers to create an electronic slide show of all the posters.

CHAPTER 13 OBJECTIVE
The student will understand westward expansion and its political, economic, and social effects on the development of the nation.

HISTORY FROM VISUALS

Interpreting the Photograph Ask the students to study the photograph of pioneers resting beside their wagons. Ask them to draw conclusions about the lives of the adults and children on the trip west. **Possible Responses** The trip west was not an easy one. The people appear tired and dirty. The wagons look too small to carry both people and equipment. Most pioneers probably walked.

Extension Have the students write five questions to ask the people in the photograph.

CRITICAL THINKING ACTIVITY

Making Inferences Using masking tape, have student teams mark out a 4' x 10' space on the classroom floor. Do as many of these as your classroom will accommodate. Then have students make inferences about how much and what kinds of supplies and personal belongings could fit into the space, which is approximately the size of the floor of a wagon. They may also discuss who would ride and who would walk.

Class Time 15 minutes

CHAPTER 13 Manifest Destiny 1810–1853

Weary from their trip west, this pioneer family stops for a rest.

RECOMMENDED RESOURCES

BOOKS FOR THE TEACHER

Ghent, William J. ***The Road to Oregon.*** London: Longmans, 1929. A noted chronicle of the Oregon Trail.

Lavender, David. ***The Great West.*** New York: Am. Heritage, 1965. A single volume covering exploration and settlement of the West from 1763.

Parkman, Francis. ***The Oregon Trail.*** New York: Viking, 1989. A reprint of Parkman's 1849 chronicle of his journeys in the West.

SOFTWARE

Oregon Trail I and II. MECC, 1993. Award-winning simulation of a covered-wagon journey on the Oregon Trail.

Wagon Train 1848. MECC. Puts users in the shoes of pioneers traveling the Oregon Trail.

VIDEO

The West. PBS Video, 1996. Ken Burns's nine-part look at the American West. See episode two, "Empire upon the Trails."

INTERNET

For more about the West, visit . . .
classzone.com

Interact *with* History

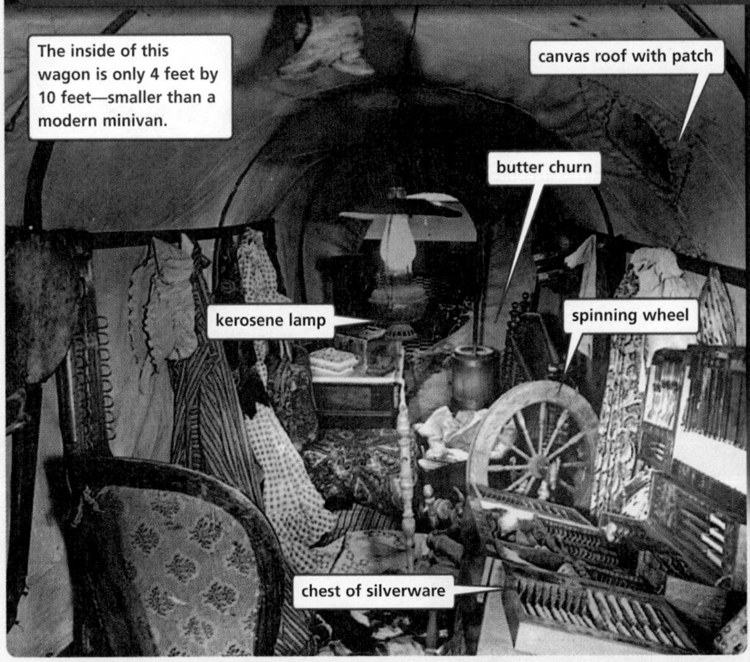

The inside of this wagon is only 4 feet by 10 feet—smaller than a modern minivan.
canvas roof with patch
butter churn
kerosene lamp
spinning wheel
chest of silverware

The year is 1844, and you live on a small rocky farm in Massachusetts. Your family has decided to move to Oregon to gain cheap, fertile land. Your father says this move will make your family better off—and give you a brighter future.

What Do You Think?

- What do you think daily life on the trail west might be like?
- What might be the greatest obstacles that you face?
- Notice the necessities packed in this crowded wagon. What might have been left behind?

What might you gain and lose by going west?

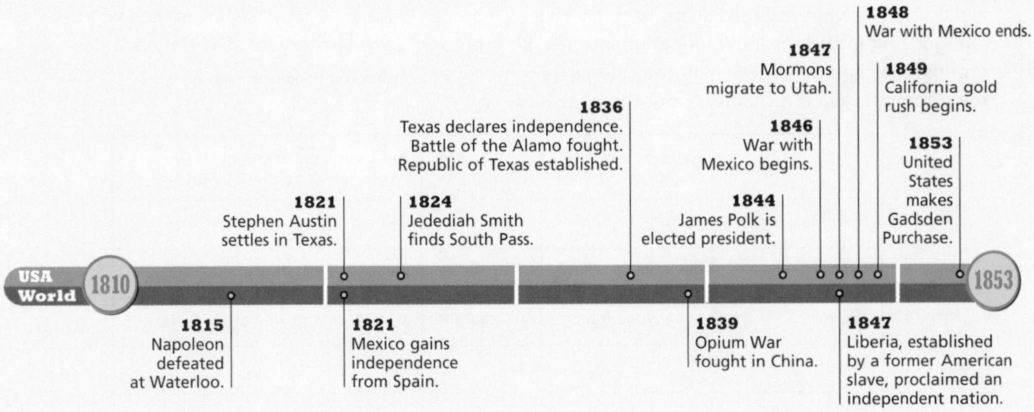

USA
World
1810
1853
1815 Napoleon defeated at Waterloo.
1821 Stephen Austin settles in Texas.
1821 Mexico gains independence from Spain.
1824 Jedediah Smith finds South Pass.
1836 Texas declares independence. Battle of the Alamo fought. Republic of Texas established.
1839 Opium War fought in China.
1844 James Polk is elected president.
1846 War with Mexico begins.
1847 Mormons migrate to Utah.
1847 Liberia, established by a former American slave, proclaimed an independent nation.
1848 War with Mexico ends.
1849 California gold rush begins.
1853 United States makes Gadsden Purchase.

Interact *with* History

OBJECTIVES

- To help students understand the difficulty of moving west
- To help students connect with the people and the events they will study in this chapter

What Do You Think?

1. Ask students why the items they identified would be left behind.
2. Have students think about their daily activities and how those activities would be accomplished on the trail.
3. Ask students to think about the effect of land features, weather, transportation, and other people on the trip.

What might you gain and lose by going west?

Encourage students to think about the jobs, possessions, and people left behind and the challenges of a new life.

MAKING PERSONAL CONNECTIONS

Ask students to think about moves they have made. How would their move compare or contrast to the trip made by these pioneers? Would the reasons for moving be similar or different?

TIME LINE DISCUSSION

Remind the students that in 1803, the United States bought the Louisiana Territory. In this time period (1810–1853), large acquisitions of land would give the United States control of an area of North America that stretched from sea to sea.

- Ask students to identify which decade seems to be filled with the most historical events. **Answer** 1840–1850. Follow up by asking them to hypothesize about why so many events took place between 1840 and 1850. **Possible Response** There was a great demand for land during that time period.
- Have the students look at the time line and find an event in the world that may have had a direct impact on the United States. **Answer** Mexican independence, because Mexico is so near the United States

BEFORE YOU READ

Previewing the Theme: Expansion

Ask the students to think of reasons why the people of the United States might have believed they should take over the entire continent. **Possible Response** Motives for expanding the nation from "sea to sea" ranged from the conviction that the continent needed to become an area of freedom and democracy separate from the dangers of monarchies to support for extending slavery. Still others looked to the lands of the West and the Pacific Coast as areas ready to be developed for agriculture and trade.

What Do You Know?

To avoid confusion, remind students that this movement westward was not the same as the westward movement that occurred after the Homestead Act of 1862 and the Civil War. Many movies about the West took place during that later time.

In-Depth Resources: Unit 4
- Tracing Themes: Expansion, p. 22

READ AND TAKE NOTES

Reading Strategy: Categorizing

Tell students that categorizing information will help them see common characteristics among groups. Knowing that information may help the student accomplish such critical-thinking skills as comparing and contrasting information. For example, by the time the chart is finished, the students should be able to compare the reasons for westward migration.

In-Depth Resources: Unit 4
- Setting the Stage, p. 21

Critical Thinking Transparency CT37
- Setting the Stage

Chapter 13 SETTING THE STAGE

BEFORE YOU READ

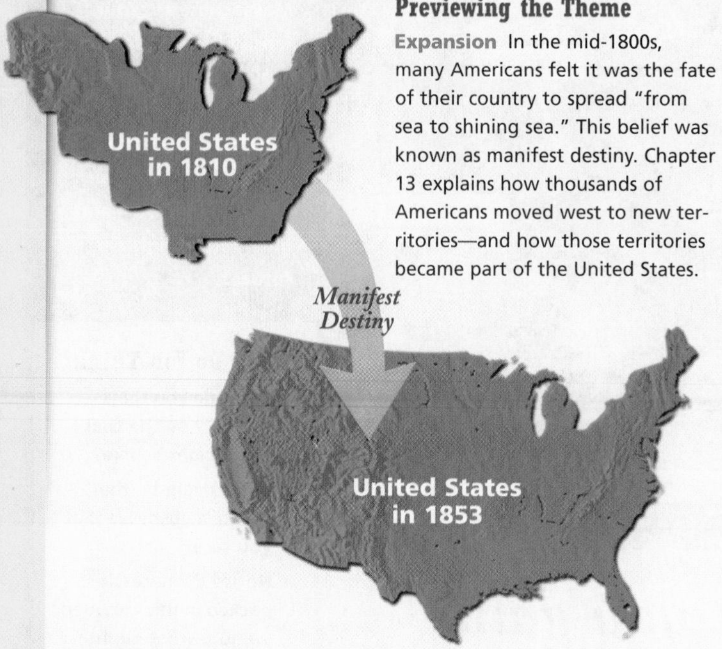

Previewing the Theme

Expansion In the mid-1800s, many Americans felt it was the fate of their country to spread "from sea to shining sea." This belief was known as manifest destiny. Chapter 13 explains how thousands of Americans moved west to new territories—and how those territories became part of the United States.

What Do You Know?

What do you think of when you hear the phrase "the West"? Who do you think moved west in the early 1800s? What do you think drew them to the West?

THINK ABOUT
- what you've learned about the West from movies or travel
- reasons that people move to new places today

What Do You Want to Know?

What questions do you have about the westward movement of the 1800s? Record those questions in your notebook before you read the chapter.

READ AND TAKE NOTES

Reading Strategy: Categorizing To help you make sense of what you read, learn to categorize. Categorizing means sorting information into groups. The chart below will help you categorize the information in this chapter about the westward movement. Use the chart to take notes on what groups went west, why they went, and what events brought each territory into the United States.

See Skillbuilder Handbook, page R6.

	Types of people who traveled there	Why they went there	Key events that brought the territory into the United States
New Mexico	farmers and traders	land or profit	War with Mexico
Utah	Mormons	religious freedom	War with Mexico
Oregon	farmers and traders	land or profit	agreement with Britain
Texas	farmers and ranchers	land	Texas Revolution
California	miners and traders	land or profit	War with Mexico

TEACHING STRATEGY

READING THE CHAPTER

This is a thematic chapter focusing on westward movement of both people and a nation. Encourage students to look for the causes and effects of movement during this time period. Have them think about what is happening in the country that encourages this movement. Pause after each section to review the ideas of cause and effect as illustrated in the section.

ALTERNATIVE ASSESSMENT

The Chapter Assessment describes three activities for alternative assessment on page 403. You may wish to have students work on these activities during the course of the chapter and then present them at the end.

1 Trails West

TERMS & NAMES
Jedediah Smith
mountain man
Jim Beckwourth
land speculator
Santa Fe Trail
Oregon Trail
Mormon
Brigham Young

MAIN IDEA

Thousands of settlers followed trails through the West to gain land and a chance to make a fortune.

WHY IT MATTERS NOW

This migration brought Americans to the territories that became New Mexico, Oregon, and Utah.

ONE AMERICAN'S STORY

The mountain man Jedediah Smith was leading an expedition to find a route through the Rocky Mountains when a grizzly bear attacked. The bear seized Smith's head in its mouth, shredded his face, and partially tore off one ear. Smith's men chased the bear away. Jim Clyman recalled the scene.

A VOICE FROM THE PAST

I asked [Smith] what was best. He said, "One or two go for water and if you have a needle and thread get it out and sew up my wounds around my head." . . . I told him I could do nothing for his ear. "Oh, you must try to stitch it up some way or other," said he. Then I put in my needle and stitched it through and through.

Jim Clyman, quoted in *The West,* by Geoffrey C. Ward

This likeness of Jedediah Smith shows the ruggedness and spirit of the mountain man.

Ten days after this attack, Smith was ready to continue exploring. The following spring, he found what he was looking for—a pass through the Rocky Mountains.

Jedediah Smith was one of the daring fur trappers and explorers known as mountain men. The mountain men opened up the West by discovering the best trails through the Rockies. Later, thousands of pioneers followed these trails. In this section, you will learn about the trails—and why people followed them west.

1 Mountain Men and the Rendezvous

Mountain men survived by being tough and resourceful. They spent most of the year alone, trapping small animals such as beavers. Easterners wanted beaver furs to make the men's hats that were in fashion at the time. To obtain furs, mountain men roamed the Great Plains and the Far West, the regions between the Mississippi River and the Pacific Ocean, and set traps in icy mountain streams.

Because of their adventures, mountain men such as Jedediah Smith and **Jim Beckwourth** became famous as rugged loners. However, they were not as independent as the legends have portrayed them. Instead, they were connected economically to the businessmen who bought their furs.

SECTION OBJECTIVES

1. To explain the role of mountain men in the exploration and expansion of the West
2. To identify reasons people went west
3. To describe the opening of the Santa Fe Trail
4. To describe the impact of "Oregon Fever" on westward expansion
5. To profile the Mormons' westward journey

SKILLBUILDER

Interpreting Maps: Place, Human-Environment Interaction, p. 379

CRITICAL THINKING

Making Inferences, p. 379
Finding Main Ideas, p. 381
Analyzing Causes, p. 381
Drawing Conclusions, p. 381

FOCUS & MOTIVATE

5-MINUTE WARM-UP

Making Inferences Answering these questions will help students understand the impact the settlers had on the lands and people of the West.

1. Look at the map on page 379. What effects might movement of people on the trails have on the land and people living there?
2. Why did Americans going west think the land was largely empty?

Warm-Up Transparency WT13

INSTRUCT

INSTRUCT: OBJECTIVE 1

Mountain Men and the Rendezvous/ Mountain Men Open the West

- What motivated mountain men?
- What information helped mountain men open the West?
- How did their exploration lead to expansion of the West?

In-Depth Resources: Unit 4
- Guided Reading, p. 23

Reading Study Guide (Spanish and English), pp. 123–124

RECOMMENDED RESOURCES

In-Depth Resources: Unit 4
- Guided Reading, p. 23
- Building Vocabulary, p. 27
- Primary Source: from *Luzena Stanley Wilson,* '49er, p. 31

Reading Study Guide (Spanish and English), pp. 123–124

Outline Map Activities
- The Opening of the West, 1850, pp. 25–26

America's History Makers
- Narcissa Whitman, pp. 51–52

Formal Assessment
- Section Quiz, p. 237

Integrated Assessment
- Rubrics, 4.3, 1.3

Access for Students Acquiring English/ESL
- Guided Reading, p. 83

INTEGRATED TECHNOLOGY

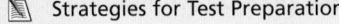

Humanities Transparency HT25
- *The Cowboy*

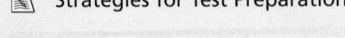

Humanities Transparency HT26
- *On the Trail*

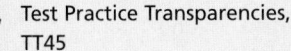

Electronic Teacher Tools

classzone.com

TEST-TAKING RESOURCES

Strategies for Test Preparation

Test Practice Transparencies, TT45

Online Test Practice

AMERICA'S HISTORY MAKERS

Jim Beckwourth

Jim Beckwourth was adopted and taken into a Crow tribe when an old woman claimed he was her long lost son. Named "Morning Star," he quickly became a leader of Crow braves. His prowess as a warrior led to a name change—"Bloody Arm."

Beckwourth left the Crow in 1833. Later, he served as a guide and interpreter for the United States in the wars with Native Americans. Beckwourth's death in 1867 has been attributed to poisoning. Some accounts say it was food poisoning. However, others claim an angry former wife or disgruntled Crow leaders may have poisoned him.

Answer: He discovered a mountain pass into what is now northern California.

INSTRUCT: OBJECTIVE 2

The Lure of the West

- How did some people profit during the westward expansion?
- For what reasons did Americans go west?

Humanities Transparency HT25
- *The Cowboy*

AMERICA'S HISTORY MAKERS

JIM BECKWOURTH
1798–1867

Jim Beckwourth was born in slavery and set free by his owner. At the age of 25, Beckwourth joined a group of fur traders going west and in time became a daring mountain man.

For several years, Beckwourth lived with a Crow tribe. Later, he worked as an army scout and gold prospector. In 1850, he discovered a mountain pass that became the route into present-day northern California. This pass is still called Beckwourth Pass.

What was Beckwourth's most important contribution to the westward movement?

One businessman, William Henry Ashley, created a trading arrangement called the rendezvous system. Under this system, individual trappers came to a prearranged site for a rendezvous with traders from the east. The trappers bought supplies from those traders and paid them in furs. The rendezvous took place every summer from 1825 to 1840. In that year, silk hats replaced beaver hats as the fashion, and the fur trade died out.

Vocabulary
rendezvous (RAHN•day•voo): meeting; from a French word meaning "present yourselves"

Mountain Men Open the West

During the height of the fur trade, mountain men worked some streams so heavily that they killed off the animals. This forced the trappers to search for new streams where beaver lived. The mountain men's explorations provided Americans with some of the earliest firsthand knowledge of the Far West. This knowledge, and the trails the mountain men blazed, made it possible for later pioneers to move west.

For example, thousands of pioneers used South Pass, the wide valley through the Rockies that Jedediah Smith had publicized. Smith learned of this pass, in present-day Wyoming, from Native Americans. Unlike the high northern passes used by Lewis and Clark, South Pass was low, so snow did not block it as often as it blocked higher passes. Also, because South Pass was wide and less steep, wagon trails could run through it.

***Reading* History**
A. Reading a Map Find South Pass on the map on page 379. Notice which two trails used that pass.

Smith wrote to his brother that he wanted to help people in need: "It is for this that I go for days without eating, and am pretty well satisfied if I can gather a few roots, a few snails, . . . a piece of horseflesh, or a fine roasted dog."

2 The Lure of the West

Few of the people who went west shared Smith's noble motive. To many, the West with its vast stretches of land offered a golden chance to make money. The Louisiana Purchase had doubled the size of the United States, and some Americans wanted to take the land away from Native Americans who inhabited this territory.

People called **land speculators** bought huge areas of land. To speculate means to buy something in the hope that it will increase in value. If land value did go up, speculators divided their land holdings into smaller sections. They made great profits by selling those sections to the thousands of settlers who dreamed of owning their own farms.

Manufacturers and merchants soon followed the settlers west. They hoped to earn money by making and selling items that farmers needed. Other people made the trip to find jobs or to escape people to whom they owed money.

ACTIVITY OPTIONS

INTERDISCIPLINARY LINK: ECONOMICS — BLOCK SCHEDULING

LAND SPECULATION

Class Time 20 minutes

Task Determining land values

Purpose To understand how land speculators make money

Supplies Needed
- Envelopes with varying amounts of play money
- Diagram of a large rectangle with river running through it at an angle, and divided into eight plots; each plot is equal to 80 acres

Activity Give each student an envelope with money. Begin an auction for the land plots. Record the price paid for each plot. After the eight plots are sold, discuss the reasons why the plots sold for different prices. Run a second auction for the land. Suggest that the new owners may want to divide their land holdings. After the auction, look at how much profit the owners made from the land sale. Have the students write a paragraph explaining the basic concept of land sales and speculation.

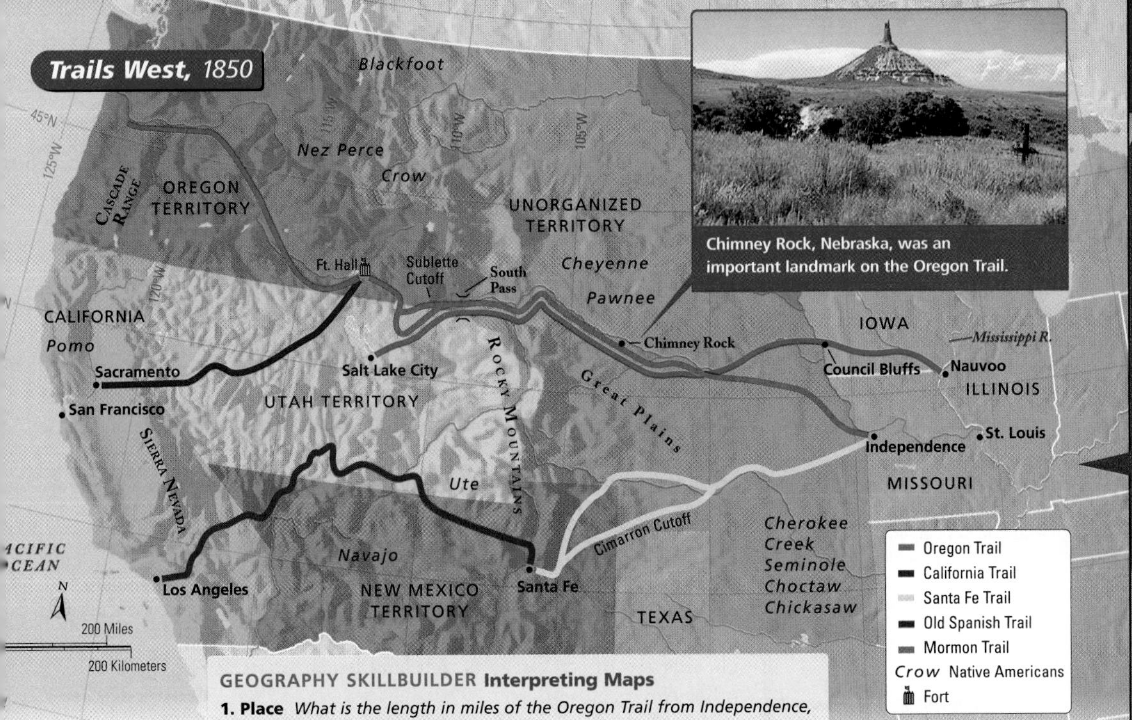

Chimney Rock, Nebraska, was an important landmark on the Oregon Trail.

GEOGRAPHY SKILLBUILDER Interpreting Maps

1. **Place** *What is the length in miles of the Oregon Trail from Independence, Missouri, to Fort Vancouver?*
2. **Human-Environment Interaction** *Why do you think some of the trails ran along rivers?*

❸ The Trail to Santa Fe

Traders also traveled west in search of markets. After Mexico gained independence from Spain in 1821, it opened its borders to American traders, whom Spain had kept out. In response, the Missouri trader William Becknell set out with hardware, cloth, and china for Santa Fe, capital of the Mexican province of New Mexico. By doing so, he opened the **Santa Fe Trail**, which led from Missouri to Santa Fe. Once in Santa Fe, he made a large profit because the New Mexicans were eager for new merchandise.

When Becknell returned to Missouri weeks later, a curious crowd met him. One man picked up one of Becknell's bags and slit it open with a knife. As gold and silver coins spilled onto the street, the onlookers gasped. The news spread that New Mexico was a place where traders could become rich.

The following spring, Becknell headed to Santa Fe again. This time he loaded his trade goods into covered wagons, which Westerners called prairie schooners. Their billowing white canvas tops made them look like schooners, or sailing ships.

Becknell could not haul wagons over the mountain pass he had used on his first trip to Santa Fe. Instead, he found a cutoff, a shortcut that avoided steep slopes but passed through a deadly desert to the south. As his traders crossed the burning sands, they ran out of water. Crazed by

***Reading* History**
B. Making Inferences What do you think other Missourians might decide to do after seeing Becknell's wealth?
B. Possible Answer They might decide to go to Santa Fe to trade and become rich.

Skillbuilder Answers
1. about 1,600 miles
2. Rivers provided water, food, and often ran along valleys, allowing travelers to avoid rugged terrain.

HISTORY FROM VISUALS

Reading the Map Point out different landforms on the map. Have the students discuss how the landforms would affect the progress of the settlers. **Possible Response** Much of the journey passed through mountains, making travel difficult and slow.

Extension Have students use an atlas to determine if any major highways follow the routes of the trails shown on the map.

Outline Map Activities
- The Opening of the West, 1850, pp. 25–26

INSTRUCT: OBJECTIVE ❸

The Trail to Santa Fe

- How did Mexican independence open the New Mexico territory to American traders?
- Who opened the Santa Fe Trail to New Mexico?
- What was important about the Cimarron cutoff?

MORE ABOUT . . .

Traveling the Santa Fe Trail
Council Grove, in present-day Kansas, was the last rendezvous point for joining a caravan to Santa Fe. The complete journey from Missouri to New Mexico took two to three months and covered over 800 miles. However, the return trip might take half as long because of the lighter load. The high point of the trip was the arrival in Santa Fe. The whole town turned out to greet the wagoneers, who were dressed in their best clothes in honor of the occasion.

ACTIVITY OPTIONS

INDIVIDUAL NEEDS

STUDENTS ACQUIRING ENGLISH/ESL

Asking Questions To help students focus before they read, have them preview the section and write questions based on the heads in the section. The questions should ask: Who? What? Where? When? Why? or How? Some sample questions follow, but students should be encouraged to write their own questions.

Who were the mountain men?
What was a rendezvous?
Why was the Santa Fe Trail important?

After students have read the section, they should go back and write answers to the questions they have written. As an alternative, have students work in pairs to write the questions and then discuss their answers with each other.

daily*life*

Dinner on the Trail

The basic diet on the trail was bread, bacon, and coffee. The semi-arid Plains provided little additional food; however, some wild game, fish, berries, and roots were available. The Plains did furnish the principle fuel for fires—buffalo chips. The dried dung of buffalo was picked up along the way. The chips also served another purpose. Children threw them for fun, in a sort of ancestor to the frisbee of today.

Humanities Transparency HT26
- *On the Trail*

INSTRUCT: OBJECTIVE 4

Oregon Fever/One Family Heads West

- What group was among the earliest travelers to the Oregon Territory?
- What kinds of stories encouraged people to make the journey to Oregon?
- What was the journey to Oregon like?

America's History Makers
- Narcissa Whitman, pp. 51–52

In-Depth Resources: Unit 4
- Primary Source, p. 31

daily *life*

DINNER ON THE TRAIL

To add to their limited supplies, pioneers on the trail gathered berries and wild onions. They also hunted buffalo and small game. Below is a recipe that many might have used.

Fricasseed Squirrel
1 squirrel, skinned
3 slices of bacon, chopped
1 tablespoon chopped onions
2 teaspoons lemon juice
⅓ cup water
salt, pepper, & flour
Cut squirrel in pieces. Rub pieces with salt, pepper, and flour. Fry with bacon for 30 minutes. Add onion, lemon juice, and water. Cover tightly. Cook for 1½ hours.

Nebraska Centennial First Ladies Cookbook

thirst, they lopped off mules' ears and killed their dogs to drink the animals' blood. Finally, the men found a stream. The water saved them from death, and they reached Santa Fe.

Becknell returned home with another huge profit. Before long, hundreds of traders and prairie schooners braved the cutoff to make the 800-mile journey from Missouri to New Mexico each year.

4 Oregon Fever

Hundreds of settlers also began migrating west on the **Oregon Trail,** which ran from Independence, Missouri, to the Oregon Territory. The first whites to cross the continent to Oregon were missionaries, such as Marcus and Narcissa Whitman in 1836. At that time, the United States and Britain were locked in an argument about which country owned Oregon. To the Whitmans' great disappointment, they made few converts among the Native Americans. However, their glowing reports of Oregon's rich land began to attract other American settlers.

Vocabulary
converts: people who accept a new religious belief

Amazing stories spread about Oregon. The sun always shone there. Wheat grew as tall as a man. One tale claimed that pigs were "running about, . . . round and fat, and already cooked, with knives and forks sticking in them so you can cut off a slice whenever you are hungry."

Such stories tempted many people to make the 2,000-mile journey to Oregon. In 1843, nearly 1,000 people traveled from Missouri to Oregon. The next year, twice as many came. "The Oregon Fever has broken out," observed a Boston newspaper, "and is now raging."

One Family Heads West

The experiences of the Sager family show how difficult the trail could be. In 1844, Henry Sager, his wife, and six children left Missouri to find cheap, fertile land in Oregon. They had already moved four times in the past four years. Henry's daughter Catherine explained her family's moves.

A VOICE FROM THE PAST

Father was one of those restless men who are not content to remain in one place long at a time. . . . [He] had been talking of going to Texas. But mother, hearing much said about the healthfulness of Oregon, preferred to go there.

Catherine Sager, quoted in *The West,* by Geoffrey C. Ward

The Oregon Trail was dangerous, so pioneers joined wagon trains. They knew their survival would depend on cooperation. Before setting out, the wagon train members agreed on rules and elected leaders to enforce them.

Even so, life on the trail was full of hardship. The Sagers had barely begun the trip when Mrs. Sager gave birth to her seventh child. Two

ACTIVITY OPTIONS

MULTIPLE LEARNING STYLES: MUSICAL — **BLOCK SCHEDULING**

PIONEER SONGS

Class Time 20 minutes

Task Analyzing primary sources

Purpose To gain an understanding of the trip west or reasons people took the journey by studying song lyrics

Supplies Needed
- Songbooks such as *American Ballads and Folk Songs* by Alan Lomax and *The Ballad of America* by John Anthony Scott
- Recordings of ballads or folk songs

Activity Suggest that students research songs sung by the people going west. They may want to consult with a music teacher. Have students study the lyrics to understand the reasons pioneers went west and what their journey was like. The song "Sweet Betsy from Pike" is a good one to start with. Students should provide an explanation of the lyrics to the class and, if possible, perform the songs or find recordings and play them.

months later, nine-year-old Catherine fell under a moving wagon, which crushed her left leg. Later, "camp fever" killed both of the Sager parents.

Even though the Sager parents had died, the other families in the train cooperated to help the Sager orphans make it to Oregon. There, the Whitmans agreed to adopt them. When Narcissa met them, Catherine recalled, "We thought as we shyly looked at her that she was the prettiest woman we had ever seen."

Reading **History**
C. Finding Main Ideas What difficulties did families like the Sagers face?
C. Answer Many faced illness and injury due to harsh conditions.

The Mormon Trail 5

While most pioneers went west in search of wealth, one group migrated for religious reasons. The **Mormons,** who settled Utah, were members of the Church of Jesus Christ of Latter-Day Saints. Joseph Smith had founded this church in upstate New York in 1830. The Mormons lived in close communities, worked hard, shared their goods, and prospered.

The Mormons, though, also made enemies. Some people reacted angrily to the Mormons' teachings. They saw the Mormon practice of polygamy—allowing a man to have more than one wife at a time—as immoral. Others objected to their holding property in common.

In 1844, an anti-Mormon mob in Illinois killed Smith. **Brigham Young,** the next Mormon leader, moved his people out of the United States. His destination was Utah, then part of Mexico. In this desolate region, he hoped his people would be left to follow their faith in peace.

Reading **History**
D. Analyzing Causes Why did Brigham Young lead the Mormons to Utah?
D. Answer so that he and his followers could practice their religion in peace

In 1847, about 1,600 Mormons followed part of the Oregon Trail to Utah. There they built a new settlement by the Great Salt Lake. Because Utah has little rainfall, the Mormons had to work together to build dams and canals. These structures captured water in the hills and carried it to the farms in the valleys below. Through teamwork, they made their desert homeland bloom.

In the meantime, changes were taking place in Texas. As you will read in Section 2, Americans had been moving into that Mexican territory, too.

Section 1 Assessment

1. Terms & Names

Explain the significance of:
- Jedediah Smith
- mountain man
- Jim Beckwourth
- land speculator
- Santa Fe Trail
- Oregon Trail
- Mormon
- Brigham Young

2. Taking Notes

Use a cluster diagram like the one shown to review details about the trails west.

Which trail would you have wanted to travel? Why?

3. Main Ideas

a. How did the mountain men open up the West for later settlement?

b. What are two examples of pioneer groups who used cooperation to overcome hardship?

c. What economic and social forces drew people to the West?

4. Critical Thinking

Drawing Conclusions Of all the hardships faced by people who went west, what do you think was the worst? Explain.

THINK ABOUT
- the mountain men
- William Becknell
- the Sagers
- the Mormons

ACTIVITY OPTIONS

LANGUAGE ARTS / **ART** — Research a pioneer from this section and either write a **letter** from his or her point of view to a friend or illustrate a **journal entry** with sights from your journey.

INSTRUCT: OBJECTIVE 5

The Mormon Trail

- Why did some people oppose the Mormons?
- Why did the Mormons move west?
- Where did the Mormons settle?

ASSESS & RETEACH

Setting the Stage Have students fill in the first two columns for New Mexico, Utah, and Oregon on the chapter graphic organizer.

Formal Assessment
- Section Quiz, p. 237

Critical Thinking Transparency CT37
- Setting the Stage

RETEACHING ACTIVITY

Divide the class into three teams, each representing one of the three trails discussed in this chapter. Each team should create a set of six flash cards that identify key ideas about that trail. Tape the cards to a string and pin the string across the chalkboard or classroom.

In-Depth Resources: Unit 4
- Reteaching Activity, p. 36

Section 1 Assessment

1. Terms & Names

Jedediah Smith, p. 377
mountain men, p. 377
Jim Beckwourth, p. 377
land speculators, p. 378
Santa Fe Trail, p. 379
Oregon Trail, p. 380
Mormons, p. 381
Brigham Young, p. 381

2. Taking Notes

Mormon Trail—followed Oregon Trail to Utah, taken by Mormons; Oregon Trail—from Missouri to Oregon Territory, people went for land; Santa Fe Trail—from Missouri to Santa Fe, New Mexico, attracted many traders. Answers will vary.

3. Main Ideas

a. Mountain men had knowledge of trails and passes in the western lands. **b.** travelers on the Oregon Trail; the Mormons **c.** chance to make a living farming or ranching; lure of gold; religious freedom

4. Critical Thinking

the dangerous, difficult trip; disease; death; bad food and water

ACTIVITY OPTIONS

Integrated Assessment
- Rubrics for a letter, 4.3
- Rubrics for an oral history, 3.6

Interdisciplinary CHALLENGE

OBJECTIVE

Students work cooperatively to solve technological, social, and nutritional problems pioneers faced in adapting to their environment.

BLOCK SCHEDULING

PROCEDURE

For each challenge, have students form groups of four or five. Ask group members to divide the work among themselves. Then have them choose an option for presenting their solution.

SCIENCE CHALLENGE

Class Time 50 minutes

Use the following suggestions to help students figure out how to slow the descent of the wagon.

- Draw a sketch of a wagon on the down slope.
- Test ways of slowing down the speed of a toy car or skateboard going down a ramp.

POSSIBLE SOLUTIONS

Here are ways that pioneers used to slow down a wagon:

- chains wrapped around wagon wheels
- logs jammed under the wagon wheels
- a makeshift windlass, or winch (hauling machine)

Survive the Oregon Trail!

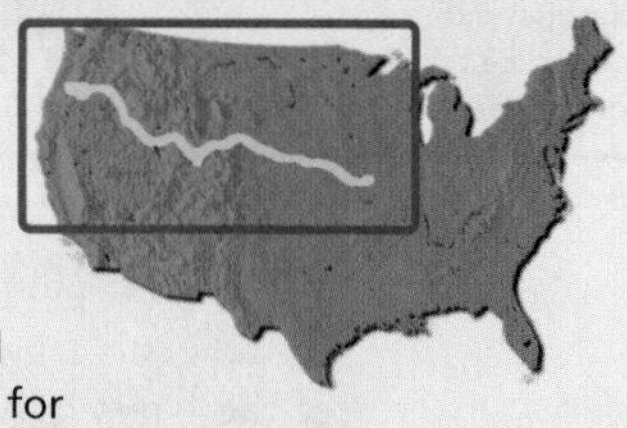

You are part of a wagon train heading west on the Oregon Trail. During your journey, you will cross endless flat prairies and mountains that climb more steeply than a staircase. You will suffer through blazing heat and icy snowstorms. Food is scarce in the land you travel through—and human settlements are even more scarce.

COOPERATIVE LEARNING On this page are three challenges you will face on your journey. Working with a small group, create a solution for each challenge. To help your group work together, assign a task to each group member. You will find helpful information in the Data File. Be prepared to present your solutions to the class.

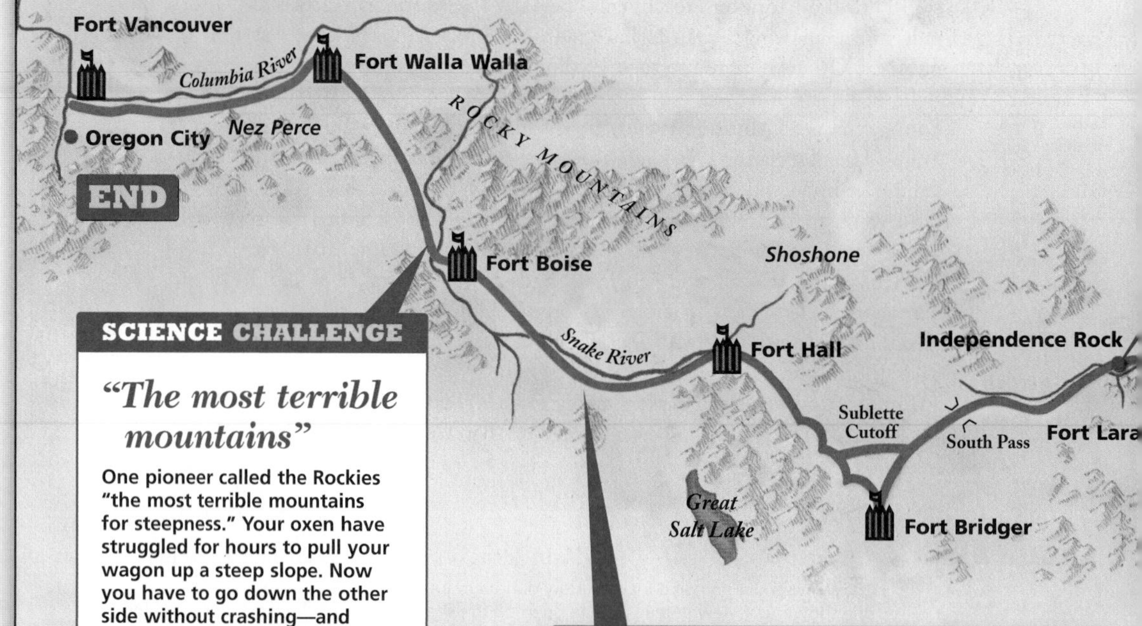

SCIENCE CHALLENGE

"The most terrible mountains"

One pioneer called the Rockies "the most terrible mountains for steepness." Your oxen have struggled for hours to pull your wagon up a steep slope. Now you have to go down the other side without crashing—and wagon wheels have no brakes. How will you slow your descent? Use the Data File for help. Present your ideas using one of these options:

- Write instructions for climbing and descending the mountain.
- Illustrate your solution in a how-to diagram.

CIVICS CHALLENGE

"A thieving scoundrel"

You wake one morning to the sound of shouting. One of the men in the wagon train has been caught stealing another family's ox—to replace an ox that died from drinking bad water. The wagon train leader asks you to help decide how to punish the thief. Present your decision using one of these options:

- As a group, role-play a discussion of what the punishment should be.
- Write an explanation of a punishment to the wagon train leader.

STANDARDS FOR EVALUATION

SCIENCE CHALLENGE

Option 1 Written instructions should
- include clear, easy-to-follow directions.
- present the steps in logical order.

Option 2 How-to diagrams should
- explain a process through the use of arrows, boxes, and other visuals.
- include labels to clarify the sequence of steps.

CIVICS CHALLENGE

Option 1 Role-plays of discussions should
- present different views on the issue.
- include realistic comments.
- reflect sound decision making.

Option 2 Written recommendations should
- describe details of the theft.
- include reasons that justify the punishment.
- reach a logical conclusion.

HEALTH CHALLENGE

Option 1 Food illustrations should
- create a realistic image of a pioneer dish.
- include captions that describe the dish.

Option 2 Recipes should
- list all necessary ingredients.
- describe the preparation in chronological order.

HEALTH CHALLENGE

"A grand blow-out"

On July 4, your wagon train stops near Independence Rock for "a grand blow-out" to celebrate your progress. Each family will bring a dish to the party. What will you cook that is tasty and nutritious? You might use supplies from your wagon and berries or animals from the area. Look at the Data File for help. Present your choice using one of these options:

- **Draw a picture of your dish and describe it.**
- **Write an original recipe.**

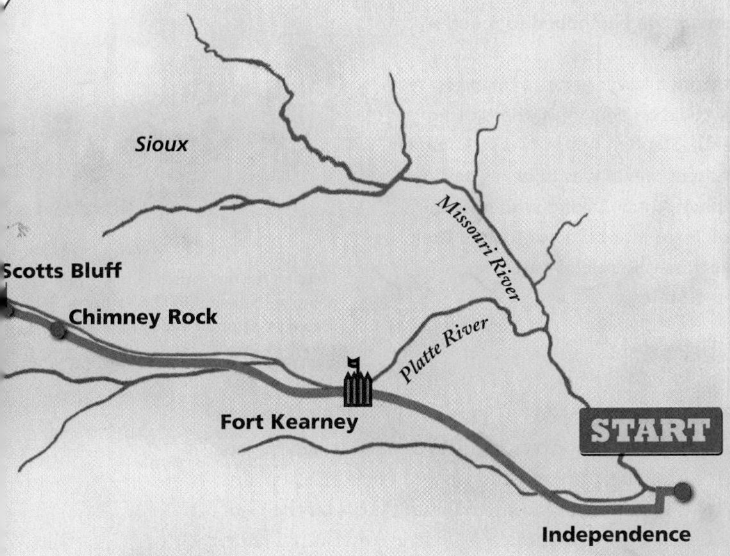

ACTIVITY WRAP-UP

Present to the class Using the model shown here, ask and answer questions about geographic patterns in the West. Choose the best questions to present to the class.

DATA FILE

The Journey

Distance: 2,000 miles

Length: 4–6 months

Average daily distance: 12–15 miles

Best time to travel: April–September

The Wagon

Size of box: 4 x 10 feet

Load: 1,600–2,500 pounds

Oxen needed per wagon: 4–8

Animals Taken

oxen, horses, dairy cows, cattle, chickens, mules, pigs, dogs, cats

Food Supplies

flour, corn meal, salt, baking soda, sugar, crackers, dried beans, rice, dried fruit, bacon, coffee, vinegar

Cooking Equipment

Dutch oven, large kettle, frying pan, bread pan, coffee grinder, rolling pin, tin cups and plates, water kegs, knives, spoons

Other Equipment

bedding, spare wagon parts, tar, rope, chains, pulleys, tools, fishing poles, guns, ammunition, matches, soap, medicines

Trail Hazards

Worst discomforts: heat, cold, wind, rain, dust, mud, mosquitoes, hunger, thirst

Biggest killer: disease

Most common accidents: shooting, drowning, crushing by wagon wheels, injuries from animals

For more about the Oregon Trail . . .

RESEARCH LINKS
CLASSZONE.COM

CIVICS CHALLENGE

Class Time 50 minutes

Suggest that students copy the decision-making chart in the Citizenship Handbook, p. 269, and fill it in to help guide them in choosing a punishment. Ask them to consider a punishment that serves the best interests of the people who belong to the wagon train.

POSSIBLE SOLUTION

A man named "Buckskin Rose" described the punishment administered to horse thieves on his wagon train—they were kicked out. In many wagon trains, justice was swift and the punishment unfair.

HEALTH CHALLENGE

Class Time 50 minutes

Have students look at illustrated cookbooks to use as models for drawing pictures of food or writing a recipe.

POSSIBLE SOLUTION

Pioneers' food choices would not have met today's standards for a well-balanced diet. Bacon, bread, and coffee were generally part of the daily menu.

ACTIVITY WRAP-UP

Presentations should

- pose questions about the model that reflect the most important geographic patterns in the West.
- provide answers based on evidence from the model.

SECTION OBJECTIVES

1. To profile Texas under Spanish rule
2. To explain the tension between Texans and *Tejanos*
3. To summarize the war between Texas and Mexico
4. To explain that Texas became its own country

SKILLBUILDER

Interpreting Maps: Movement, p. 389

CRITICAL THINKING

Analyzing Causes, pp. 385, 386, 389
Summarizing, p. 386
Making Inferences, p. 387
Recognizing Effects, p. 389

FOCUS & MOTIVATE

5-MINUTE WARM-UP

Making Inferences These questions focus on how Americans got involved in the Texas Revolution.

1. Study the poster on page 385. What is being offered to settlers coming to Texas?
2. Why do you think this offer is being made?

Warm-Up Transparency WT13

INSTRUCT

INSTRUCT: OBJECTIVE 1

Spanish Texas

- What made Texas's land so desirable?
- Who are *Tejanos?*
- Why did the Spanish government want to attract settlers to Texas?

In-Depth Resources: Unit 4
- Guided Reading, p. 24
- Building Vocabulary, p. 27

Reading Study Guide (Spanish and English), pp. 125–126

2 The Texas Revolution

TERMS & NAMES
Stephen Austin
Tejano
Antonio López de Santa Anna
Sam Houston
William Travis
Juan Seguín
Battle of the Alamo
Lone Star Republic

MAIN IDEA	WHY IT MATTERS NOW
American and *Tejano* citizens led Texas to independence from Mexico.	The diverse culture of Texas has developed from the contributions of many different groups.

ONE AMERICAN'S STORY

Son of a bankrupt Missouri mine owner, **Stephen Austin** read his mother's letter, written in 1821, in stunned silence. His father, Moses Austin, was dead. In his last moments, she told her son, "He called me to his bedside, . . . he begged me to tell you to take his place . . . to go on . . . in the same way he would have done."

Stephen knew what that meant. Moses Austin had spent the last years of his life chasing a crazy dream. He had hoped to found a colony for Americans in Spanish Texas.

Stephen's dream, though, was to be a lawyer—not a colonizer. Yet as a loving and obedient son, how could he deny his father's dying wish? A week after his father's death, Stephen Austin was standing on Texas soil. From that day on, his father's dream was to be his destiny.

This section explains how Stephen Austin, along with others, worked hard to make the lands of Texas a good place to live. Their spirit would create an independent Texas Republic. Later, Texas would become a state in the United States.

Stephen Austin, shown in this painting, helped fulfill his father's dream by establishing an American colony in Texas.

1 Spanish Texas

The Spanish land called *Tejas* (Tay•HAHS) bordered the United States territory called Louisiana. The land was rich and desirable. It had forests in the east, rich soil for growing corn and cotton, and great grassy plains for grazing animals. It also had rivers leading to natural ports on the Gulf of Mexico. It was home to Plains and Pueblo Native Americans. Even though *Tejas* was a state in the Spanish colony of New Spain, it had few Spanish settlers. Around 1819, Spanish soldiers drove off Americans trying to claim those lands as a part of the Louisiana Purchase.

In 1821, only about 4,000 *Tejanos* (Tay•HAH•nohs) lived in Texas. ***Tejanos*** are people of Spanish heritage who consider Texas their home. The Comanche, Apache, and other tribes fought fiercely against Spanish settlement of Texas. The Spanish officials wanted many more settlers to move to Texas. They hoped that new colonists would help to defend against Native Americans and Americans who illegally sneaked into Texas.

RECOMMENDED RESOURCES

In-Depth Resources: Unit 4
- Guided Reading, p. 24
- Building Vocabulary, p. 27
- Primary Source, p. 32

Reading Study Guide (Spanish and English), pp. 125–126

America's History Makers
- Juan Seguín, pp. 53–54

American History Plays
- *Live from the Alamo*

Formal Assessment
- Section Quiz, p. 238

Integrated Assessment
- Rubrics, 1.7, 5.1

Access for Students Acquiring English/ESL
- Guided Reading, p. 84

INTEGRATED TECHNOLOGY

Geography Transparency GT13
- The Battle of the Alamo, 1836

Electronic Teacher Tools

classzone.com

TEST-TAKING RESOURCES

Strategies for Test Preparation

Test Practice Transparencies, TT46

Online Test Practice

Vocabulary
empresarios: individuals who agreed to recruit settlers for the land

To attract more people to Texas, the Spanish government offered huge tracts of land to *empresarios.* But they were unable to attract Spanish settlers. So, when Moses Austin asked for permission to start a colony in Texas, Spain agreed. Austin was promised a large section of land. He had to agree that settlers on his land had to follow Spanish laws.

TEXAS!!
Emigrants who are desirous of assisting Texas at this important crisis of her affairs may have a free passage and equipments, by applying at the
NEW-YORK and PHILADELPHIA HOTEL,
On the Old Levee, near the Blue Stores.
Now is the time to ensure a fortune in Land:
To all who remain in Texas during the War will be allowed 1280 Acres.
To all who remain Six Months, 640 Acres.
To all who remain Three Months, 320 Acres.
And as Colonists, 4600 Acres for a family and 1470 Acres for a Single Man.
New Orleans, April 23d, 1836.

2 Mexican Independence Changes Texas

Shortly after Stephen Austin arrived in Texas in 1821, Mexico successfully gained its independence from Spain. *Tejas* was now a part of Mexico. With the change in government, the Spanish land grant given to Austin's father was worthless. Stephen Austin traveled to Mexico City to persuade the new Mexican government to let him start his colony. It took him almost a year to get permission. And the Mexican government would consent only if the new settlers agreed to become Mexican citizens and members of the Roman Catholic Church.

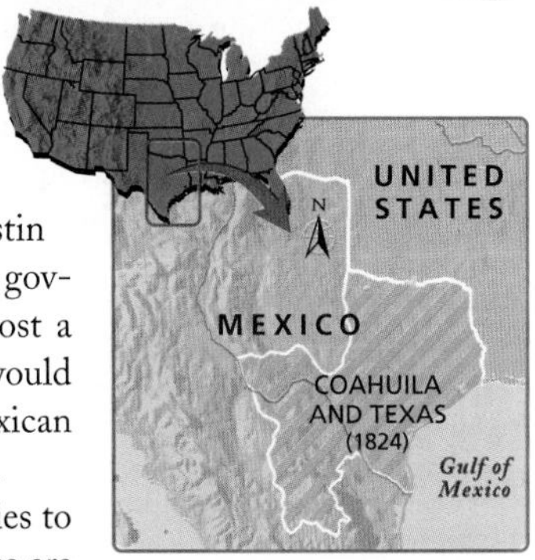

Between 1821 and 1827, Austin attracted 297 families to his new settlement. These original Texas settler families are known as the "Old Three Hundred." He demanded evidence that each family head was moral, worked hard, and did not drink. So law-abiding were his colonists that Austin could write to a new settler, "You will be astonished to see all our houses with no other fastening than a wooden pin or door latch."

Posters such as the one above encouraged Americans from the East to settle in Texas. Some people scrawled G.T.T. on their doors to indicate they had "gone to Texas."

The success of Austin's colony attracted more land speculators and settlers to Texas from the United States. Some were looking for a new life, some were escaping from the law, and others were looking for a chance to grow rich. By 1830, the population had swelled to about 30,000, with Americans outnumbering the *Tejanos* six to one.

A. Answer
Americans had problems adapting to Mexican laws, speaking Spanish, and they wanted slavery to continue.

***Reading* History**
A. Analyzing Causes Why was there growing tension between Americans and *Tejanos?*

Rising Tensions in Texas

As more and more Americans settled in Texas, tensions between them and the *Tejanos* increased. Used to governing themselves, Americans resented following Mexican laws. Since few Americans spoke Spanish, they were unhappy that all official documents had to be in that language. Slave owners were especially upset when Mexico outlawed slavery in 1829. They wanted to maintain slavery so they could grow cotton. Austin persuaded the government to allow slave owners to keep their slaves.

On the other hand, the *Tejanos* found the Americans difficult to live with, too. *Tejanos* thought that the Americans believed they were superior and deserved special privileges. The Americans seemed unwilling to adapt to Mexican laws.

INSTRUCT: OBJECTIVE 2

Mexican Independence Changes Texas/ Rising Tensions in Texas

- How successful was Austin in creating a colony in Texas?
- What was a source of tension between American settlers and *Tejanos?*
- How did the Mexican government respond to the problems between these two groups?

MORE ABOUT . . .

Crossing the Border
In the early 1830s, when Texas was part of Mexico, Mexicans wanted to keep American immigrants out of Texas. Today, the U.S. government patrols the Mexican-American border to keep illegal Mexican immigrants from coming into the United States. In the 1830s, Americans went to Texas for land (economics), while today Mexicans come to the United States for the same reason—greater economic opportunity.

ACTIVITY OPTIONS

INTERDISCIPLINARY LINK: CIVICS

BLOCK SCHEDULING

PROBLEM SOLVING

Class Time 20 minutes

Task Resolving problems between *Tejanos* and Americans

Purpose To use problem-solving skills to find ways that *Tejanos* and Americans could have cooperated in Texas

Supplies Needed
- Textbook
- Copy of problem-solving steps or the transparency of problem-solving steps

Activity Have students work in groups of four. Two students will represent *Tejanos* and the others will be Americans. Hand out a copy of the steps for solving problems or use the overhead transparency. Students should determine the answer to Reading History A. Using those answers as the problems to be solved, the two pairs should use the problem-solving steps to find possible ways the issues could have been solved. Each group should present to the class a solution to one of the problems. The class should discuss which solutions seem most likely to be successful.

INSTRUCT: OBJECTIVE 3

Texans Revolt Against Mexico/ The Fight for the Alamo

- How did Santa Anna react to the letter given to him by Stephen Austin?
- What happened at the Battle of the Alamo?

Geography Transparency GT13
- The Battle of the Alamo, 1836

***America's* HERITAGE**

Remember the Alamo!

Some steps have been taken to combat the moisture problem at the Alamo. Shrubs and grass were removed and replaced with moisture-absorbing gravel and sand. In addition, metal plates were installed underground to block seeping water. One major factor, however, has not been addressed—the breath of the estimated three million tourists that visit the Alamo every year. The tourists' breath brings moisture inside the structure.

In-Depth Resources: Unit 4
- Primary Source: A Mexican Account of the Battle of the Alamo, p. 32

The Mexican government sent an official to Texas to investigate the tensions. He was not happy with what he found. In 1829, he reported to his government, "I am warning you to take timely measures . . . Texas could throw this whole nation into revolution." His advice turned out to be right.

Responding to the warnings, the Mexican government cracked down on Texas. First, it closed the state to further American immigration. Next, it required Texans to pay taxes for the first time. Finally, to enforce these new laws, the government sent more Mexican troops to Texas.

*Reading*History

B. Summarizing What three actions did the Mexican government take to control Texas?

B. Answer The Mexican government stopped American immigration, levied taxes, and sent troops to Texas.

3 Texans Revolt Against Mexico

These actions caused angry protests. Some Texans even talked of breaking away from Mexico. Most, however, listened to Austin, who remained loyal to Mexico. In 1833, Austin set off for Mexico City with a petition. This document listed reforms supported by both Americans and *Tejanos*. The most important request was that Texas become a self-governing state within Mexico.

***America's* HERITAGE**

REMEMBER THE ALAMO!

Today the Alamo, shown below, is again under siege. Moisture seeps into the limestone walls and causes them to crumble. Many people view the mission as a memorial to Americans' willingness to fight for freedom, so a Texas group has begun attempts to preserve the Alamo from further damage. The Alamo looks quite different from the battle site of 1836. The famous bell-shaped front was added in the 1850s.

In Mexico City, Austin met General **Antonio López de Santa Anna,** the Mexican president. At first, the general agreed to most of the reforms in Austin's petition. But then Santa Anna learned of a letter Austin had written. The letter said that if the changes weren't approved Austin would support breaking away from Mexican rule. This was rebellion! The general had Austin jailed for an entire year. The Texans were furious and ready to rebel.

Santa Anna's answer to talk of rebellion was to send more troops to Texas. In late September 1835, Mexican soldiers marched to the town of Gonzales. They had orders to seize a cannon used by the Texans for protection against Native Americans. Texas volunteers had hung a flag on the big gun that said, "Come and Take It."

The Mexican troops failed to capture the cannon. Two months later, Texans drove Mexican troops out of an old mission in San Antonio that was used as a fortress. It was called the Alamo. Among the Texas volunteers were free African Americans such as Hendrick Arnold and Greenbury Logan. Angered by these insults, Santa Anna and 6,000 troops headed for Texas.

*Reading*History

C. Analyzing Causes What Texan actions moved Santa Anna to head toward Texas?

C. Answer American resistance at Gonzales and at San Antonio

The Fight for the Alamo

On March 1–2, 1836, Texans met at a settlement called Washington-on-the-Brazos to decide what to do about Santa Anna's troops. They believed they could do only one thing: to declare Texas a free and independent republic. **Sam Houston,** the only man at the meeting with military experience, was placed in command of the Texas army.

ACTIVITY OPTIONS

INDIVIDUAL NEEDS

LESS PROFICIENT READERS

Sequencing Events Some students may have trouble piecing together the events of the Texas Revolution. To help students understand and remember the events that led to the Texas-Mexican War, have them make a sequence chart like the one at the right.

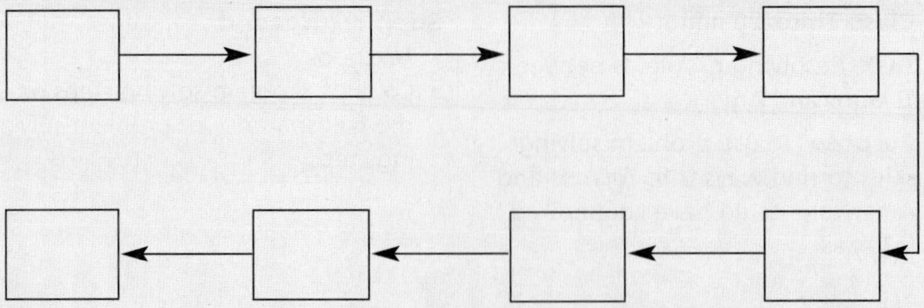

The Texas army hardly existed. At that moment, there were two small forces ready to stand up to Santa Anna's army. One was a company of 420 men, led by James Fannin, stationed at Goliad, a fort in southeast Texas. The second was a company of 183 volunteers at the Alamo. Headed by **William Travis,** this small force included such famous frontiersmen as Davy Crockett and Jim Bowie. In addition, **Juan Seguín** (wahn seh•GEEN) led a band of 25 *Tejanos* in support of revolt.

"Remember the Alamo!"
a Texan soldier

On February 23, 1836, Santa Anna's troops surrounded San Antonio. The next day, Mexicans began their siege of the Alamo. Two nights later, Travis scrawled a message to the world.

Reading **History**
D. Making Inferences Why would William Travis address his message to all Americans?
D. Possible Response Travis wanted to rally support for Texas from all Americans.

A VOICE FROM THE PAST

The enemy has demanded a surrender. . . . I have answered the demand with a cannon shot, and our flag still waves proudly from the walls. I shall never surrender or retreat.

William Travis, "To the People of Texas and all the Americans in the World"

Because Juan Seguín spoke Spanish, he was chosen to carry the plea through enemy lines. Seguín got the message through to other Texas defenders. But when he returned, he saw the Alamo in flames.

The Alamo's defenders held off the Mexican attack for 12 violent days. Travis and the defenders stubbornly refused to surrender. On the 13th day, Santa Anna ordered more than 1,800 men to storm the fortress. The Texans met the attackers with a hailstorm of cannon and gun fire. Then suddenly it became strangely quiet. The Texans had run out of ammunition. At day's end, all but five Texans were dead. The **Battle of the Alamo** was over.

HISTORY through ART

The Battle of the Alamo was so intense that Davy Crockett did not have time to reload his gun, which he called "Betsy." He used it as a club. This print is by a 20th-century illustrator, Frederick Yohn.

What does the print reveal about the battle?

387

MORE ABOUT . . .

William Travis
When Santa Anna arrived in San Antonio with several thousand Mexican troops, he demanded the surrender of the Alamo. As commander, Travis answered Santa Anna with a cannon shot. Inside the Alamo, Travis drew a line in the sand and asked those who wanted to stay and fight to cross the line and join him. All but one person joined him. Some historians dispute this story, but it was related in three separate eyewitness accounts.

HISTORY through ART

Interpreting the Painting The action in the painting is centered on Davy Crockett, and the artist is able to capture the intensity of the hand-to-hand fighting. The Mexican troops are closing in, and the Texans appear to be making their last stand.

Possible Responses: Davy Crockett was courageous, and the battle was very intense.

ACTIVITY OPTIONS

MULTIPLE LEARNING STYLES: KINESTHETIC — BLOCK SCHEDULING

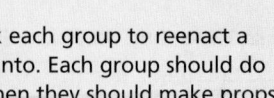

KEY BATTLES OF TEXAS REVOLUTION

Class Time One class period

Task Reenacting key battles of the Texas-Mexican War

Purpose To analyze information and create oral presentations about the Texas Revolution

Supplies Needed
- Reference materials on the Texas Revolution
- Drawing paper or posterboard
- Art supplies

Activity Have students form three groups. Ask each group to reenact a different battle—the Alamo, Goliad, or San Jacinto. Each group should do research on the action in each of the battles. Then they should make props or a map showing the action in the selected battle. Students should focus on showing movement and location during the battle. Have groups present the battles in chronological order. After each presentation, ask the following questions: Which side had more soldiers? What strategies were used? What was the outcome of the battle? What happened as a result of the battle?

AMERICA'S HISTORY MAKERS

Juan Seguín

Because of his goal of a Texas free from Mexico, Juan Seguín got along well with American settlers in Texas. However, he wanted Texas to remain independent and not become part of the United States. He was elected to the Texas Senate in 1838 and was mayor of San Antonio twice. However, Seguín was often betrayed and harassed by Americans. Finally he was forced to leave. In 1846–1848, Senguín fought against Americans in the Mexican War.

America's History Makers
- Juan Seguín, pp. 53–54

Sam Houston

As commander of the Texan forces, Sam Houston developed an unpopular war strategy. To lure the Mexican army deep into Texas, Houston ordered his army to retreat through Texas. Then when he thought the Mexicans were overextended he would attack. Houston's officers doubted he would seek battle. The new president of Texas, David Burnet, said, "the Enemy are laughing at you to scorn . . . You must retreat no farther." However, Houston's win at the Battle of San Jacinto proved his strategy was correct.

Possible Responses: Sequín was a Tejano who fought with Texans. Houston was an American who commanded Texas forces.

INSTRUCT: OBJECTIVE 4

Victory at San Jacinto/Lone Star Republic

- How did the Texans win the Battle of San Jacinto?
- After independence, what did most Texans want from the United States?
- Why did some groups in the United States oppose annexing Texas?

AMERICA'S HISTORY MAKERS

JUAN SEGUÍN
1806–1890

Juan Seguín was a *Tejano* hero of the Texas Revolution. It was Seguín who dashed through enemy lines at the Alamo with a last desperate attempt for aid.

And after the war, it was Seguín who arranged for the remains of the Alamo defenders to be buried with full military honors.

Newcomers to Texas who disliked all *Tejanos* falsely accused Sequín of planning rebellion. Fearing for his life, he fled to Mexico in 1842, there "to seek a refuge amongst my enemies."

SAM HOUSTON
1793–1863

Raised by a widowed mother, Sam Houston grew up in Tennessee. He lived with the Cherokee for about three years. Later, he served in the U.S. Army, in Congress, and as the governor of Tennessee.

"I was a General without an army," wrote Houston, after taking command of the Texas forces in 1836. Yet by the time the war was over, he and his troops had defeated Santa Anna's larger army.

Houston was elected the first president of the Republic of Texas. When Texas became a state, he served as a U.S. senator.

In what ways did the experiences of Seguín and Houston differ?

Those men who had not died in the fighting were executed at Santa Anna's command. A total of 183 Alamo defenders died. A few women and children were not killed. Susanna Dickinson, one of the survivors, was ordered by Santa Anna to tell the story of the Alamo to other Texans. He hoped the story would discourage more rebellion. The slaughter at the Alamo shocked Texans—and showed them how hard they would have to fight for their freedom from Mexico.

4 Victory at San Jacinto

With Santa Anna on the attack, Texans—both soldiers and settlers—fled eastward. Houston sent a message to the men at Goliad, ordering them to retreat. They were captured by Mexican forces, who executed more than 300. The Texans would not soon forget the massacre at Goliad. But even in retreat and defeat, Houston's army doubled. Now it was a fighting force of 800 angry men. It included *Tejanos,* American settlers, volunteers from the United States, and many free and enslaved African Americans.

Reading **History**
E. Reading a Map Use the map on page 389 to see where battles were taking place.

In late April, Santa Anna caught up with Houston near the San Jacinto (san juh•SIN•toh) River. Late in the afternoon of April 21, 1836, the Texans advanced on the Mexican army "with the stillness of death." When close to Santa Anna's camp, they raced forward, rifles ready, screaming "Remember the Alamo!" "Remember Goliad!"

In just 18 minutes, the Texans killed more than half of the Mexican army. Santa Anna was forced to sign a treaty giving Texas its freedom. With the Battle of San Jacinto, Texas was now independent.

ACTIVITY OPTIONS

INTERDISCIPLINARY LINK: LANGUAGE ARTS — BLOCK SCHEDULING

POETRY

Class Time One class period

Task Creating a poem

Purpose To use a poem to describe an individual or a battle from the Texas Revolution

Supplies Needed
- Reference material on the Texas Revolution

Activity Have each student select a person or a battle from the Texas Revolution. Each student should do some research on the topic selected. Ask the language arts teacher to help students understand how to create a poem about an event or person. The poem could be a cinquain, haiku, acrostic, or other form. When students have completed their poems, they may share them with the class.

Skillbuilder Answers
1. about 500 miles
2. The Texans probably had the advantage. Mexican forces traveled much further, which probably caused supply and communication problems.

Lone Star Republic

In September 1836, Texans raised a flag with a single star. They adopted a nickname—**Lone Star Republic**—and proclaimed Texas an independent nation. The new nation set up its own army and navy. Sam Houston was elected president of the Lone Star Republic by a landslide.

Many Texans did not want Texas to remain independent for long. They considered themselves Americans and wanted to be a part of the United States. In 1836, the Texas government asked Congress to annex Texas to the Union.

Vocabulary
annex: to join territory to an existing country

Many Northerners objected. They argued that Texas would become a slave state, and they opposed any expansion of slavery. If Texas joined the Union, slave states would outnumber free states and have a voting advantage in Congress. Other people feared that annexing Texas would lead to war with Mexico.

F. Answer Some worried about the slavery issue and others about a war with Mexico.

In response, Congress voted against annexation. Texas remained an independent republic for almost ten years. In the next section, you will learn that the question of annexing Texas did lead to a war between the United States and Mexico.

*Reading*History
F. Analyzing Causes Why didn't Congress annex Texas?

The Texas Revolution, 1836

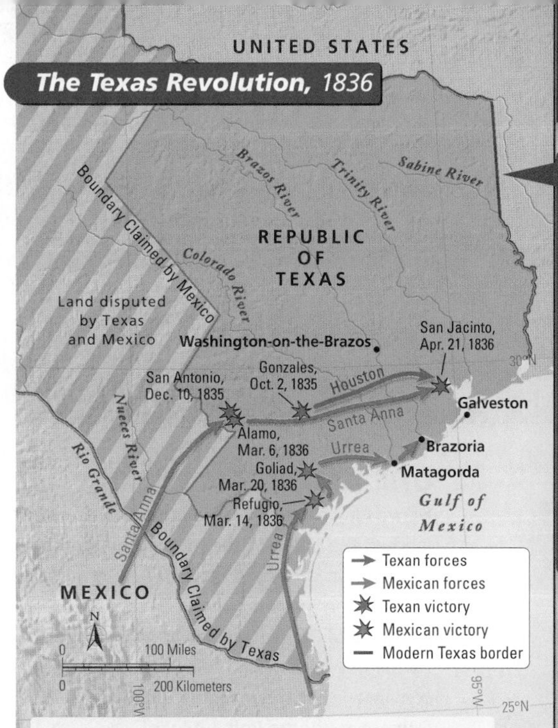

GEOGRAPHY SKILLBUILDER Interpreting Maps
1. **Movement** *About how many total miles did Santa Anna travel from Mexico to San Jacinto?*
2. **Movement** *Look at the distances traveled by Mexican forces and those traveled by the Texans. Which side do you think had an advantage? Explain.*

HISTORY FROM VISUALS

Interpreting the Map The Texas Revolution ended with the defeat of Santa Anna at the Battle of San Jacinto. Ask the students in what way the map suggests that tensions between Texas and Mexico continued after the war. **Possible Responses** Texas and Mexico disagreed over the western and southern boundaries of Texas.

Extension Using the scale, have students calculate how much farther Santa Anna traveled. Have students speculate on how that increased distance may have affected the performance of either army.

ASSESS & RETEACH

Setting the Stage Have students fill in the Texas section on the chapter graphic organizer.

Formal Assessment
- Section Quiz, p. 238

RETEACHING ACTIVITY

Have the students create an annotated time line of the events leading to the creation of the Republic of Texas. The line should begin with Mexican independence in 1821 and have up to ten dates. The annotations should show how each event led toward independence.

In-Depth Resources: Unit 4
- Reteaching Activity, p. 37

Section 2 Assessment

1. Terms & Names

Explain the significance of:
- Stephen Austin
- *Tejano*
- Antonio López de Santa Anna
- Sam Houston
- William Travis
- Juan Seguín
- Battle of the Alamo
- Lone Star Republic

2. Taking Notes

Use a diagram like the one shown to review events that led to Texan independence and put them in order.

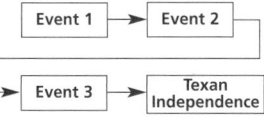

Event 1 → Event 2 → Event 3 → Texan Independence

3. Main Ideas

a. Why did Americans want to move to Texas?

b. How did the Mexican government respond to the Texas rebellion?

c. Why did Congress refuse to annex Texas?

4. Critical Thinking

Recognizing Effects How did losing the Battle of the Alamo help the Texans win their independence?

THINK ABOUT
- the Texans' and Americans' shock over the loss of the battle to the Mexicans
- the need to recruit more forces to fight with the Texas army

ACTIVITY OPTIONS

ART
TECHNOLOGY

Research a figure from the Texas Revolution. Create a **trading card** or design that person's **Web page** for the Internet.

Section 2 Assessment

1. Terms & Names

Stephen Austin, p. 384
Tejano, p. 384
Antonio López de Santa Anna, p. 386
Sam Houston, p. 386
William Travis, p. 387
Juan Seguín, p. 387
Battle of the Alamo, p. 387
Lone Star Republic, p. 389

2. Taking Notes

Event 1: changes in Mexican policy toward Americans; Event 2: imprisonment of Austin; Event 3: Battle of the Alamo or Battle of San Jacinto

3. Main Ideas

a. Land was available for farming or ranching. **b.** They sent troops to Texas and finally signed a treaty giving Texas freedom. **c.** There were questions about slavery and fears of war with Mexico.

4. Critical Thinking

Texans would have to fight hard to win independence, and more than just Americans living in Texas would be required.

ACTIVITY OPTIONS

Integrated Assessment
- Rubrics for a trading card, 1.7
- Rubrics for a Web page, 5.1

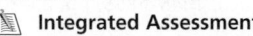

SECTION OBJECTIVES

1. To explain the origins of manifest destiny
2. To describe how the Mexican War began
3. To describe American actions in California, New Mexico, and Mexico
4. To detail the peace agreement with Mexico and territory gained by the United States

SKILLBUILDER

Interpreting Maps: Movement, Location, p. 392
Interpreting Maps: Region, p. 394

CRITICAL THINKING

Drawing Conclusions, p. 391
Analyzing Causes, p. 392
Making Inferences, pp. 393, 395
Finding Main Ideas, p. 395
Comparing, p. 395

Why It Matters Now
- The Influence of the West, pp. 25–26

FOCUS & MOTIVATE

5-MINUTE WARM-UP

Reading a Map These questions focus on the impact of the Mexican War.

1. Study the map on page 410. About how much larger does the United States become as a result of adding Texas and the Mexican Cession?
2. What present-day states were formed from these areas?

Warm-Up Transparency WT13

INSTRUCT

INSTRUCT: OBJECTIVE 1

Americans Support Manifest Destiny

- Why did Americans want to settle the lands in the West?
- What is meant by *manifest destiny?*
- How was the Oregon Territory acquired?

In-Depth Resources: Unit 4
- Guided Reading, p. 25

Reading Study Guide (Spanish and English), pp. 127–128

3 The War with Mexico

TERMS & NAMES
James K. Polk
manifest destiny
Zachary Taylor
Bear Flag Revolt
Winfield Scott
Treaty of Guadalupe Hidalgo
Mexican Cession

MAIN IDEA	WHY IT MATTERS NOW
The United States expanded its territory westward to stretch from the Atlantic to the Pacific coast.	Today, one-third of all Americans live in the areas added to the United States in 1848.

ONE AMERICAN'S STORY

Henry Clay sneered, "Who is **James K. Polk**?" Clay had just learned the name of the man nominated by Democrats to run against him for president in 1844. "A mistake!" answered Washington insiders.

News of Polk's nomination was flashed to the capital by the newly invented telegraph machine. People were convinced that the machine didn't work. How could the Democrats choose Polk? A joke!

Polk was America's first "dark horse," a candidate who received unexpected support. The Democrats had nominated this little-known man only when they could not agree on anyone else.

Still, Polk wasn't a complete nobody. He had been governor of Tennessee and served seven terms in Congress. Polk was committed to national expansion. He vowed to annex Texas and take over Oregon. Americans listened and voted.

When those votes were counted, Clay had his answer. James Knox Polk was the eleventh president of the United States.

During his campaign, Polk's ideas about expanding the country captured the attention of Americans. As you will read in this section, after his election Polk looked for ways to expand the nation.

James Polk's presidential campaign emphasized expansion of the United States.

1 Americans Support Manifest Destiny

The abundance of land in the West seemed to hold great promise for Americans. Although populated with Native Americans and Mexicans, those lands were viewed by white settlers as unoccupied. Many Americans wanted to settle those lands themselves, and they worried about competition from other nations. Mexico occupied the southwest lands, and Britain shared the northwest Oregon Territory with the United States. Many Americans believed that the United States was

RECOMMENDED RESOURCES

In-Depth Resources: Unit 4
- Guided Reading, p. 25
- Building Vocabulary, p. 27
- Skillbuilder Practice, p. 28
- Geography Application: The United States Gains Land from Mexico, 1845–1853, pp. 29–30

Reading Study Guide (Spanish and English), pp. 127–128

Why It Matters Now
- The Influence of the West, pp. 25–26

Formal Assessment
- Section Quiz, p. 239

Integrated Assessment
- Rubrics, 2.3, 2.1

Access for Students Acquiring English/ESL, pp. 85, 87–89

INTEGRATED TECHNOLOGY

Electronic Teacher Tools
classzone.com

TEST-TAKING RESOURCES

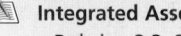

Strategies for Test Preparation
Test Practice Transparencies, TT47
Online Test Practice

destined to stretch across the continent from the Atlantic Ocean to the Pacific Ocean. In 1845, a newspaper editor named John O'Sullivan gave a name to that belief.

A VOICE FROM THE PAST

Our manifest destiny [is] to overspread and possess the whole of the continent which Providence [God] has given us for the development of the great experiment of liberty and . . . self-government.

John O'Sullivan, *United States Magazine and Democratic Review*

Reading **History**

A. Drawing Conclusions What were the positives and negatives of the idea of manifest destiny?

A. Possible Responses Positives include the expansion of democracy on the continent. The negatives include pushing Mexicans and Native Americans out of the territory.

John O'Sullivan used the word *manifest* to mean clear or obvious. The word *destiny* means events sure to happen. Therefore, **manifest destiny** suggested that expansion was not only good but bound to happen—even if it meant pushing Mexicans and Native Americans out of the way. After Polk's election in 1844, manifest destiny became government policy.

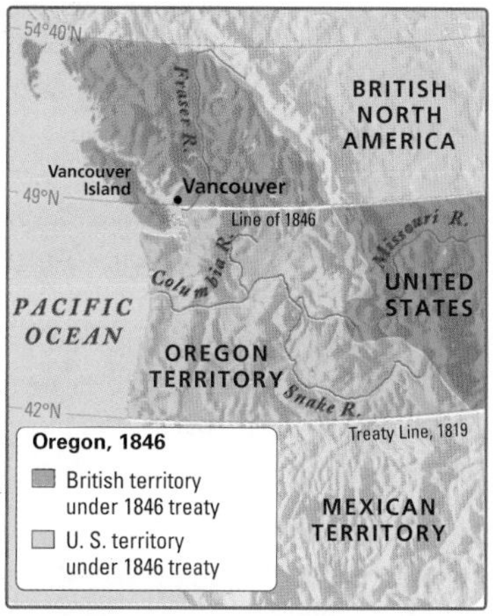

The term "manifest destiny" was new, but the idea was not. By the 1840s, thousands of Americans had moved into the Oregon Territory. Since 1818, Oregon had been occupied jointly by the United States and Britain. In his campaign, Polk had talked of taking over all of Oregon. "Fifty-four forty or fight!" screamed one of his slogans. The parallel of 54° 40' N latitude was the northern boundary of the shared Oregon Territory.

Rather than fight for all of Oregon, however, Polk settled for half. In 1846, the United States and Great Britain agreed to divide Oregon at the 49th parallel. This agreement extended the boundary line already drawn between Canada and the United States. Today this line still serves as the border between much of the United States and Canada.

"Our manifest destiny [is] to . . . possess the whole of the continent."

John O'Sullivan

2 Troubles with Mexico

Polk had good reason for avoiding war with Britain over Oregon. By 1846, he had much bigger troubles brewing with Mexico over Texas.

Reading **History**

B. Reading a Map Use the map on page 392 to find the locations of the disputed border between Texas and Mexico.

In 1845, Congress admitted Texas as a slave state, in spite of Northern objections to the spread of slavery. However, Mexico still claimed Texas as its own. Mexico angrily viewed this annexation as an act of war. To make matters worse, Texas and Mexico could not agree on the official border between them. Texas claimed the Rio Grande, a river south of San Antonio, as its southern boundary. Mexico insisted on the Nueces (noo•AY•sis) River as the border of Texas. The difference in the distance between the two rivers was more than 100 miles at some points. Many thousands of miles of territory were at stake.

Mexico said it would fight to defend its claim. Hoping to settle the dispute peacefully, Polk sent John Slidell, a Spanish-speaking

CRITICAL THINKING ACTIVITY

Analyzing Causes Have students examine the attitude of Americans at this time toward Native Americans, Mexicans, the British, and the Spanish. How did the concept of manifest destiny and these attitudes help bring about American expansion? Use the spider map to help students understand the relationships.

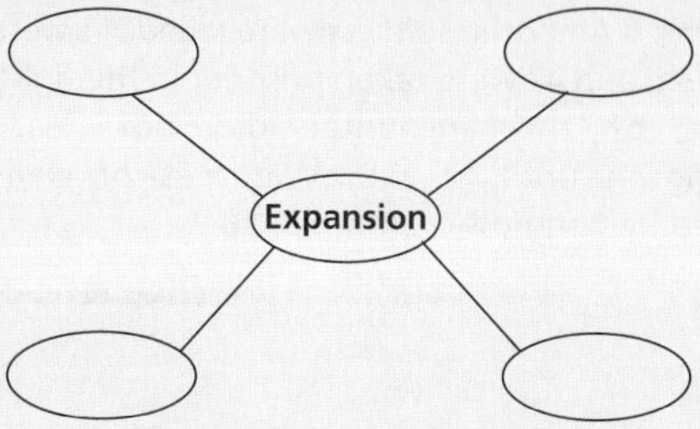

Class Time 10 minutes

INSTRUCT: OBJECTIVE 2

Troubles with Mexico

- How did the annexation of Texas affect U.S.–Mexico relations?
- What did Polk do to avoid war?
- How did the War with Mexico begin?
- How did the American public react to the War with Mexico?

ACTIVITY OPTIONS

INDIVIDUAL NEEDS: GIFTED AND TALENTED

MANIFEST DESTINY

Class Time One class period

Task Analyzing the impact of the doctrine of manifest destiny

Purpose To familiarize the students with an important doctrine that governed American expansionist ideas in the 19th century and determine if it still influences American foreign policy today

Supplies Needed

- Reference materials/primary sources on the idea of manifest destiny
- Newsmagazines or newspapers from recent weeks
- Internet access for additional resources
- Large sheets of paper and markers

Activity Students should begin by familiarizing themselves with the basic concepts of manifest destiny. On a large sheet of paper they should create a list of the basic ideas of the doctrine. Next, students should study current news information to determine if any reasons for U.S. involvement in world events today reflect the reasons listed for manifest destiny. Each article that illustrates this point should be highlighted and saved for the final report.

ambassador, to offer Mexico $25 million for Texas, California, and New Mexico. But Slidell's diplomacy failed.

Believing that the American people supported his expansion plans, Polk wanted to force the issue with Mexico. He purposely ordered General **Zachary Taylor** to station troops on the northern bank of the Rio Grande. This river bank was part of the disputed territory. Viewing this as an act of war, Mexico moved an army into place on the southern bank. On April 25, 1846, a Mexican cavalry unit crossed the Rio Grande. They ambushed an American patrol and killed or wounded 16 American soldiers.

When news of the attack reached Washington, Polk sent a rousing war message to Congress, saying, "Mexico has invaded our territory and shed American blood upon American soil." Two days later, Congress declared war. The War with Mexico had begun. Thousands of volunteers, mostly from western states, rushed to enlist in the army. Santa Anna, who was president of Mexico, built up the Mexican army.

However, Americans had mixed reactions to Polk's call for war. Illinois representative Abraham Lincoln questioned the truthfulness of the president's message and the need to declare war. Northeasterners questioned the justice of men dying in such a war. Slavery became an issue in the debates over the war. Southerners saw expansion into Texas as an opportunity to extend slavery and to increase their power in Congress. To

Reading History

C. Analyzing Causes How did the War with Mexico start?

C. Answer a clash between Mexican and American troops near the Rio Grande

MORE ABOUT . . .

The War with Mexico

The skirmish that started the war happened on April 25, 1846. On that day, a cavalry detachment of Mexicans crossed the Rio Grande. General Taylor sent a 63-man patrol to investigate the reported activities of the Mexican forces. When the Americans encountered the larger force of Mexicans, 5 American soldiers were killed, 11 were wounded, and 47 were taken prisoner in the fight.

News of the encounter did not reach Washington until May 9. War was officially declared by Congress on May 13, 1846.

Skillbuilder Answers

1. about 1,500 miles
2. Texas has only one coast to defend, while Mexico has two.

The War with Mexico, 1846–1847

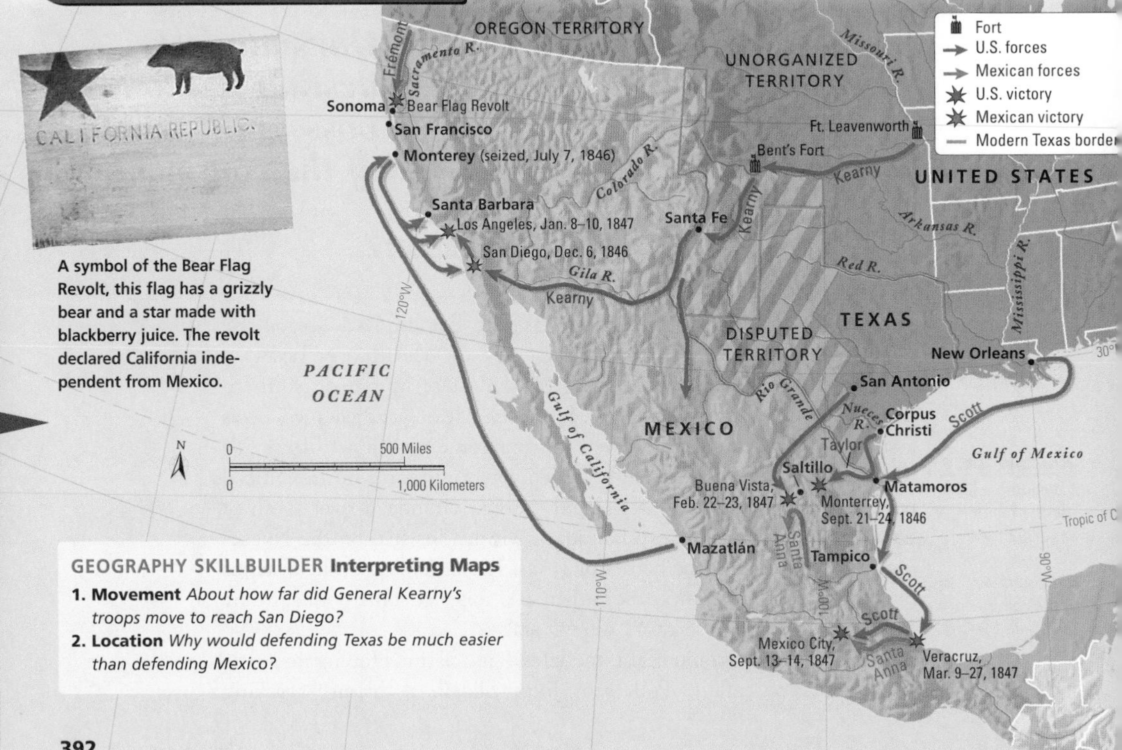

A symbol of the Bear Flag Revolt, this flag has a grizzly bear and a star made with blackberry juice. The revolt declared California independent from Mexico.

GEOGRAPHY SKILLBUILDER Interpreting Maps

1. **Movement** *About how far did General Kearny's troops move to reach San Diego?*
2. **Location** *Why would defending Texas be much easier than defending Mexico?*

392

HISTORY FROM VISUALS

Interpreting the Map Have the students study the map to gain clues about the strategies of war used by the Americans. What tactics did the Americans use to defeat the Mexicans? **Possible Response** The American forces were divided into groups, one moving to California, another moving toward Mexico by water, and one moving toward Mexico by land.

Extension Have students do research to find out why the symbols shown on the flag were chosen.

ACTIVITY OPTIONS

SKILLBUILDER LESSON: READING A SPECIAL PURPOSE MAP

BLOCK SCHEDULING

Explaining the Skill Special purpose maps are created to help the student understand a concept or idea. The map may use traditional political or physical features or may use colors, symbols, or even map distortions to make a point. The title and legend of this type of map need to be examined carefully to gather information that can help in understanding the concept.

Applying the Skill Ask students what the title of the map is and what legend symbols are shown. Then ask the following:

1. On which bodies of water did American forces move? Why do you think they attacked the coastlines? *(Gulf of Mexico and Pacific Ocean; to prevent movement of troops inland to attack American forces)*
2. Which commander's forces divided at Santa Fe, and why do you think that happened? *(Kearny. Forces moved to attack Mexicans and to take California.)*
3. Describe the movements of Santa Anna's troops. *(In February, 1847, Santa Anna moved north to defend Buena Vista. Between March and September, 1847, Santa Anna moved west from Veracruz to defend Mexico City.)*

In-Depth Resources: Unit 4
• Skillbuilder Practice, p. 28

prevent this from happening, antislavery representatives introduced a bill to prohibit slavery in any lands taken from Mexico. Frederick Douglass, the abolitionist, summarized the arguments.

A VOICE FROM THE PAST

The determination of our slaveholding President to prosecute the war, and the probability of his success in wringing from the people men and money to carry it on, is made evident, . . . None seem willing to take their stand for peace at all risks; and all seem willing that the war should be carried on in some form or other.

Frederick Douglass in *The North Star,* January 21, 1848

Despite opposition, the United States plunged into war. In May 1846, General Taylor led troops into Mexico. Many Americans thought it would be easy to defeat the Mexicans, and the war would end quickly.

3 Capturing New Mexico and California

Not long after the war began, General Stephen Kearny (KAHR•nee)—a U.S. Army officer—and his men left Fort Leavenworth, Kansas, with orders to occupy New Mexico. Then they were to continue west to California. As his troops marched along the Santa Fe Trail, they sang songs like this one.

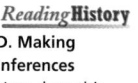

Reading **History**
D. Making Inferences How does this song support the idea of manifest destiny?
D. Possible Response It suggests that America's land should stretch to the Pacific Ocean.

A VOICE FROM THE PAST

Old Colonel Kearny, you can bet,
Will keep the boys in motion,
Till Yankee Land includes the sand
On the Pacific Ocean.

Six weeks and 650 hot and rugged miles later, Kearny's army entered New Mexico. Using persuasion instead of force, he convinced the Mexican troops that he meant to withdraw. This allowed him to take New Mexico without firing a shot. Then Kearny and a small force of soldiers marched on toward California, which had only 8,000 to 12,000 Mexican residents. The remaining force moved south toward Mexico.

In California, Americans led by the explorer John C. Frémont rebelled against Mexican rule in the **Bear Flag Revolt.** They arrested the Mexican commander of Northern California and raised a crude flag showing a grizzly bear sketched in blackberry juice. The rebels declared California independent of Mexico and named it the Republic of California. In the fall, U.S. troops reached California and joined forces with the rebels. Within weeks, Americans controlled all of California.

STRANGE but True

SANTA ANNA'S LOST LEG

Santa Anna lost his left leg in a battle with the French. In 1842, he held a funeral for his severed limb. On that day, church and political officials followed the dictator's leg through the streets of Mexico City to its final resting place—an urn placed on a column.

Two years later, an angry mob broke the urn and threw the leg away. The leg was rescued by a loyal soldier who took it home and hid it.

Thirty years later, that soldier visited Santa Anna and returned the bones of his long-lost leg.

The Invasion of Mexico

The defeat of Mexico proved far more difficult. The Mexican army was much larger, but the U.S. troops

INSTRUCT: OBJECTIVE 3

Capturing New Mexico and California/ The Invasion of Mexico

- How did Stephen Kearny take New Mexico?
- What happened during the Bear Flag Revolt?
- How did the United States defeat Mexico?

MORE ABOUT . . .

The Bear Flag Revolt

In 1846, tensions were running high in California between the 500 Americans and the 8,000 to 12,000 Mexicans living there. Some Americans captured horses that supposedly were being driven to the Mexican militia for use in a possible war against the United States.

Days later, these same men captured Sonoma and declared California the Bear Flag Republic. On July 7, 1846, American naval officer John Sloat bloodlessly captured Monterey and officially raised the American flag over California, ending California's existence as an independent state.

STRANGE *but* True

Santa Anna's Lost Leg

Santa Anna injured his leg when a French cannon shot his horse from under him. The doctors who attended Santa Anna did a poor job, and the bone of the remaining portion of the leg extended two inches beyond the flesh. From that time forward, Santa Anna would use a plain wooden leg for most activities but would replace it with a nice one fitted with a boot for more formal gatherings.

ACTIVITY OPTIONS

INTERDISCIPLINARY LINK: WORLD HISTORY — **BLOCK SCHEDULING**

VIEWPOINTS ON THE WAR WITH MEXICO

Class Time One class period

Task Exploring viewpoints about the War with Mexico

Purpose To help students understand the viewpoints of various groups involved in the conflict

Supplies Needed
- Research materials on the points of view of the groups or persons listed below
- Writing materials or word-processing equipment

Activity Divide the class into groups. Each group should be assigned one of the following roles:
- President Polk and his supporters
- Abraham Lincoln, Frederick Douglass, and the Northeasterners
- Santa Anna and the Mexican government
- the Mexican people living in present-day California and New Mexico

Groups should do research to support their arguments. They should divide tasks of writing, researching, and speaking. Each group should convince the class of its position in an oral presentation.

were led by well-trained officers. American forces invaded Mexico from two directions.

General Taylor battled his way south from Texas toward the city of Monterrey in northern Mexico. On February 22, 1847, his 4,800 troops met General Santa Anna's 15,000 Mexican soldiers near a ranch called Buena Vista. After the first day of fighting, Santa Anna sent Taylor a note offering him a chance to surrender. Taylor declined. At the end of the second bloody day of fighting, Santa Anna reported that "both armies have been cut to pieces." However, it was Santa Anna who retreated after the Battle of Buena Vista. The war in the north of Mexico was over.

In southern Mexico, fighting continued. A second force led by General **Winfield Scott** landed at Veracruz on the Gulf of Mexico and battled inland toward Mexico City. Outside the capital, Scott met fierce resistance at the castle of Chapultepec (chuh•POOL•tuh•pek). About 1,000 soldiers and 100 young military cadets bravely defended the fortress. Despite their determined resistance, Mexico City fell to Scott in September 1847. As he watched, a Mexican officer sighed and said, "God is a Yankee."

Background
General Winfield Scott had become a national hero during the War of 1812.

❹ The Mexican Cession

On February 2, 1848, the war officially ended with the **Treaty of Guadalupe Hidalgo** (gwah•duh•LOOP•ay hih•DAHL•go). In this treaty, Mexico recognized that Texas was part of the United States, and the

Skillbuilder Answers
1. all or part of 14 states
2. Louisiana Purchase

INSTRUCT: OBJECTIVE ❹

The Mexican Cession/ "From Sea to Shining Sea"

- What were the terms of the Treaty of Guadalupe Hidalgo?
- What present-day territory did the United States gain in the Mexican Cession?
- What problems were faced by Mexicans living in the United States after the war?
- What was the last bit of land added after the Mexican War?

In-Depth Resources: Unit 4
- Geography Application: The United States Gains Land from Mexico, 1845–1853, pp. 29–30

Growth of the United States, 1783–1853

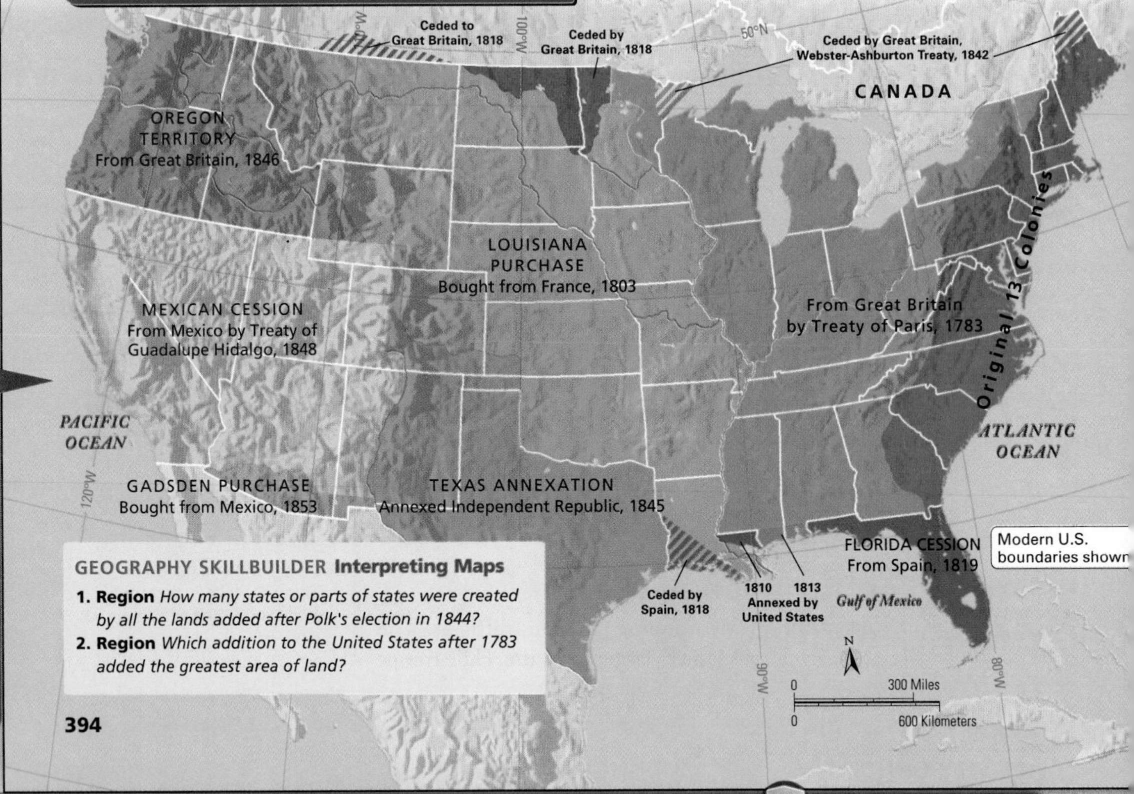

GEOGRAPHY SKILLBUILDER Interpreting Maps
1. **Region** *How many states or parts of states were created by all the lands added after Polk's election in 1844?*
2. **Region** *Which addition to the United States after 1783 added the greatest area of land?*

394

HISTORY FROM VISUALS

Interpreting the Map Have the students construct a time line of the expansion of the United States using the dates found on the map. Ask them in which decade the United States acquired the greatest share of land. **Answer** the 1840s

Extension Using an almanac, have students determine how many people currently live in the states carved out of the lands added in the decade identified above.

ACTIVITY OPTIONS

INTERDISCIPLINARY LINK: LANGUAGE ARTS

BLOCK SCHEDULING

DIARY OF A CADET OF CHAPULTEPEC

Class Time One class period

Task Writing a diary entry of a cadet at the Battle of Chapultepec

Purpose To describe the experiences of a Mexican soldier in the War with Mexico

Supplies Needed
- Reference material on the actions of the cadets of Chapultepec
- Writing materials or word-processing equipment

Activity Ask the language arts teacher to discuss writing diary entries. Then read to or have students read accounts of the attack at Chapultepec and the brave actions of the cadets. Have students write a diary entry of a cadet shortly before the final attack on the castle at Chapultepec. When the students are finished, have them share their entries with one another or bind all of them together as a memory book.

Reading **History**
E. Finding Main Ideas What were the three main parts of the Treaty of Guadalupe Hidalgo?
E. Answer United States would pay $15 million to Mexico, pay $3.25 million in U.S. citizen claims against Mexico, and protect Mexicans in Texas and the Mexican Cession.

Rio Grande was the border between the nations. Mexico also ceded, or gave up, a vast region known as the **Mexican Cession.** This area included the present-day states of California, Nevada, Utah, most of Arizona, and parts of New Mexico, Colorado, and Wyoming. Together with Texas, this land amounted to almost one-half of Mexico. The loss was a bitter defeat for Mexico, particularly because many Mexicans felt that the United States had provoked the war in the hope of gaining Mexican territory.

In return, the United States agreed to pay Mexico $15 million. The United States would also pay the $3.25 million of claims U.S. citizens had against Mexico. Finally, it also promised to protect the approximately 80,000 Mexicans living in Texas and the Mexican Cession.

Mexicans living in the United States saw the conquest of their land differently. Suddenly they were a minority in a nation with a strange language, culture, and legal system. At the same time, they would make important contributions to their new country. They taught new settlers how to develop the land for farming, ranching, and mining. A rich new culture resulted from the blend of many cultures in the Mexican Cession.

Reading **History**
F. Making Inferences Why did the United States pay a large price for the Gadsden Purchase?
F. Answer The land was needed for a transcontinental railroad.

"From Sea to Shining Sea"

The last bit of territory added to the continental United States was a strip of land across what is now southern New Mexico and Arizona. The government wanted the land as a location for a southern transcontinental railroad. In 1853, Mexico sold the land—called the Gadsden Purchase—to the United States for $10 million.

On July 4, 1848, in Washington, President Polk laid the cornerstone of a monument to honor George Washington. In Washington's day, the western border of the United States was the Mississippi River. The United States in 1848 now stretched "from sea to shining sea." In August, Polk learned that gold had been found in California. In the next section, you will read about the California gold rush.

Section 3 Assessment

1. Terms & Names

Explain the significance of:
- James K. Polk
- manifest destiny
- Zachary Taylor
- Bear Flag Revolt
- Winfield Scott
- Treaty of Guadalupe Hidalgo
- Mexican Cession

2. Taking Notes

Review the chapter and find five key events to place on a time line as shown.

War with Mexico

1846 — event — event — event — event — event — 1848

3. Main Ideas

a. How did the acquisitions of Oregon and the Mexican Cession relate to the idea of manifest destiny?

b. Why were some people opposed to the War with Mexico?

c. What does the phrase "sea to shining sea" mean?

4. Critical Thinking

Comparing Compare the different ways land was acquired by the United States in the period of manifest destiny from 1844 to 1853.

THINK ABOUT
- the acquisition of the Oregon Territory
- lands in the Southwest

ACTIVITY OPTIONS

MATH
GEOGRAPHY

In an almanac, find the current population of the states formed from the Mexican Cession. Create a **graph** or a **map** to display the information.

MORE ABOUT . . .

Treatment of Mexicans After the War

Though Mexicans living in the United States after the Mexican Cession were supposed to "enjoy all the rights of citizens of the United States," the reality was much different. As Americans became more dominant, many unfair laws were enacted. For example, the antivagrancy act targeted people with Spanish blood, and the foreign miners' tax of $20 per month was aimed at Mexican miners. Ironically, it was in Mexico that the techniques for extracting gold had been developed.

ASSESS & RETEACH

Setting the Stage Have students fill in the Key Events column for Oregon, New Mexico, and Utah.

Formal Assessment
- Section Quiz, p. 239

RETEACHING ACTIVITY

Have the students look at the Main Idea on page 406. Have them write a summary paragraph that uses the Main Idea as the topic sentence. The paragraph should identify all lands added to the United States and explain how they were acquired.

In-Depth Resources: Unit 4
- Reteaching Activity, p. 38

Section 3 Assessment

1. Terms & Names

James K. Polk, p. 390
manifest destiny, p. 391
Zachary Taylor, p. 392
Bear Flag Revolt, p. 393
Winfield Scott, p. 394
Treaty of Guadalupe Hidalgo, p. 394
Mexican Cession, p. 395

2. Taking Notes

Events could include: attack at the Rio Grande; the fall of New Mexico; the Bear Flag Revolt; the Battle of Buena Vista; the Battle of Veracruz; the Battle of Chapultepec

3. Main Ideas

a. The lands were viewed as a part of the future lands of the United States. **b.** Some questioned the truthfulness of the president, others disliked war, and still others were concerned about slavery in Texas. **c.** the occupation of land from the Atlantic Ocean to the Pacific Ocean

4. Critical Thinking

by treaty (Oregon); by annexation (Texas); by war (Mexican Cession); by purchase (Gadsden Purchase)

ACTIVITY OPTIONS

Integrated Assessment
- Rubrics for a graph, 2.3
- Rubrics for a map, 2.1

SECTION OBJECTIVES

1. To describe California before the gold rush
2. To summarize the activities occurring during the gold rush
3. To describe life in the mining camps
4. To analyze the impact of the gold rush on California

SKILLBUILDER
Interpreting Charts, p. 400

CRITICAL THINKING
Categorizing, p. 397
Making Inferences, p. 398
Analyzing Causes, pp. 398, 400
Recognizing Effects, p. 401

FOCUS & MOTIVATE

5-MINUTE WARM-UP

Recognizing Effects Answering these questions will help students understand the effect the discovery of gold in California had on Americans.

1. Read the James Marshall quote on page 397. What will happen as soon as news of the discovery of gold gets out?
2. What routes might gold seekers take to get to California from the eastern part of the United States? from other countries?

Warm-Up Transparency WT13

INSTRUCT

INSTRUCT: OBJECTIVE 1
California Before the Rush

- Who was living in California before the gold rush?
- What is a *Californio?*
- What role did Marshall and Sutter have in the gold rush?

In-Depth Resources: Unit 4
- Guided Reading, p. 26

4 The California Gold Rush

TERMS & NAMES
forty-niner
Californio
Mariano Vallejo
John Sutter
James Marshall
California gold rush

MAIN IDEA	WHY IT MATTERS NOW
Gold was found in California, and thousands rushed to that territory. California quickly became a state.	The gold rush made California grow rapidly and helped bring about California's cultural diversity.

ONE AMERICAN'S STORY

Luzena Wilson said of the year 1849, "The gold excitement spread like wildfire." The year before, James Marshall had discovered gold in California. Luzena's husband decided to become a forty-niner—someone who went to California to find gold, starting in 1849.

Most forty-niners left their families behind, but Luzena traveled to California with her husband. She later said, "I thought where he could go I could, and where I went I could take my two little toddling babies."

Luzena discovered that women—and their homemaking skills—were rare in California. Shortly after she arrived, a miner offered her five dollars for the biscuits she was baking. Shocked, she just stared at him. He quickly doubled his offer and paid in gold. Luzena realized she could make money by feeding miners, so she opened a hotel.

Like the Wilsons, thousands of people from around the world became forty-niners. In this section, you will read about the forty-niners and what their mining experiences were like. You will learn how the rapid growth of California's population caused problems for the people who lived there before 1849. You will also discover how the gold rush boosted California's economy and changed the nation's history.

This woman is carrying food to miners, just as Luzena Wilson did.

1 California Before the Rush

Before the forty-niners came, California was populated by as many as 150,000 Native Americans and 8,000 to 12,000 ***Californios***—settlers of Spanish or Mexican descent. Most *Californios* lived on huge cattle ranches. They had acquired their estates when the Mexican government took away the land that once belonged to the California missions.

One important *Californio* was **Mariano Vallejo** (mah•RYAH•noh vah•YEH•hoh). A member of one of the oldest Spanish families in America, he owned 250,000 acres of land. Proudly describing the accomplishments of the *Californios*, Vallejo wrote, "We were the pioneers of the Pacific coast . . . while General Washington was carrying on the war of the Revolution." Vallejo himself had been the commander of Northern California when it belonged to Mexico.

RECOMMENDED RESOURCES

In-Depth Resources: Unit 4
- Guided Reading, p. 26
- Building Vocabulary, p. 27
- Literature Selection: from *Roughing It*, pp. 33–35
- Enrichment Activity, p. 40

Reading Study Guide (Spanish and English), pp. 129–130

Economics in History
- Gold Rush Entrepreneurs, p. 13

Formal Assessment
- Section Quiz, p. 240

Integrated Assessment
- Rubrics, 1.5, 5.4

Access for Students Acquiring English/ESL, p. 86

INTEGRATED TECHNOLOGY

Critical Thinking Trans. CT38
- Cause and Effect: U.S. Expansion, 1846–1853

Electronic Teacher Tools

classzone.com

TEST-TAKING RESOURCES

Strategies for Test Preparation

Test Practice Transparencies, TT48

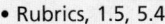

Online Test Practice

Vocabulary
immigration: the movement of people into a country or region where they were not born

When Mexico owned California, its government feared American immigration and rarely gave land to foreigners. But **John Sutter**, a Swiss immigrant, was one exception. Dressed in a secondhand French army uniform, Sutter had visited the Mexican governor in 1839. A charming man, Sutter persuaded the governor to grant him 50,000 acres in the unsettled Sacramento Valley. Sutter built a fort on his land and dreamed of creating his own personal empire based on agriculture.

In 1848, Sutter sent a carpenter named **James Marshall** to build a sawmill on the nearby American River. One day Marshall inspected the canal that brought water to Sutter's Mill. He later said, "My eye was caught by a glimpse of something shining. . . . I reached my hand down and picked it up; it made my heart thump for I felt certain it was gold."

2 Rush for Gold

News of Marshall's thrilling discovery spread rapidly. From all over California, people raced to the American River—starting the **California gold rush.** A gold rush occurs when large numbers of people move to a site where gold has been found. Throughout history, people have valued gold because it is scarce, beautiful, easy to shape, and resistant to tarnish.

Miners soon found gold in other streams flowing out of the Sierra Nevada Mountains. Colonel R. B. Mason, the military governor of California, estimated that the region held enough gold to "pay the cost of the present war with Mexico a hundred times over." He sent this news to Washington with a box of gold dust as proof.

The following year thousands of gold seekers set out to make their fortunes. A forty-niner who wished to reach California from the East had a choice of three routes, all of them dangerous:

1. Sail 18,000 miles around South America and up the Pacific coast—suffering from storms, seasickness, and spoiled food.
2. Sail to the narrow Isthmus of Panama, cross overland (and risk catching a deadly tropical disease), and then sail to California.
3. Travel the trails across North America—braving rivers, prairies, mountains, and all the hardships of the trail.

Because the adventure was so difficult, most gold seekers were young men. "A gray beard is almost as rare as a petticoat," observed one miner. Luzena Wilson said that during the six months she lived in the mining city of Sacramento, she saw only two other women.

HISTORY *through* ART

Clipper ship companies used advertising cards such as this one to convince Easterners that their line provided the fastest, most pleasant voyages.

How has the artist tried to project a positive image for sailing west?

112 DAYS TO
SAN FRANCISCO.
MERCHANTS' EXPRESS LINE OF CLIPPER SHIPS.
Dispatching the Greatest Number of Vessels!
SMALLEST, CHARPEST AND FASTEST VESSEL NOW UP!
THE MAGNIFICENT OUT-AND-OUT CLIPPER SHIP
WHITE SWALLOW
BUNKER, Commander, is now rapidly loading at PIER 16 E. R.
This splendid vessel, having made very short passages, and delivered her cargo in unexceptionable order, has established a reputation that will ensure immediate dispatch.
RANDOLPH M. COOLEY, 88 Wall Street,
(TONTINE BUILDING.)
NESBITT & CO., PRINTERS.

***Reading* History**
A. Categorizing What were the three different types of transportation that people took to get to California?
A. Answer People used ships, horses, riverboats, covered wagons, and they also walked.

MORE ABOUT . . .

John Sutter
Although Sutter had extensive land holdings and other investments in the gold fields, he did not make a profit from the gold rush. In fact, by 1852 he was broke. Squatters took over his lands, killed his cattle, and destroyed his crops. He unsuccessfully petitioned the U.S. Congress for compensation. In June 1880, it appeared Sutter might be successful in getting his money. However, when a senator stopped by to tell him of the news, he found John Sutter dead.

INSTRUCT: OBJECTIVE 2
Rush for Gold

- What is a gold rush?
- How did gold seekers get to the gold fields?
- How difficult was the trip to California?

Economics in History
- Gold Rush Entrepreneurs, p. 13

HISTORY *through* ART

Interpreting the Advertisement Clipper ships provided a faster way to reach California if they didn't get caught in storms or become becalmed. Seasickness, bad food, and endless days of boredom plagued the travelers.

Possible Answer: the use of swallows makes the trip look easy—like flying

ACTIVITY OPTIONS

INTERDISCIPLINARY LINK: GEOGRAPHY — BLOCK SCHEDULING

ROUTES TO CALIFORNIA

Class Time 30 minutes

Task Analyzing routes to California

Purpose To compare the physical geography and hardships of the routes to California

Supplies Needed
- World atlases with physical geography maps
- Copies of a blank map of the western hemisphere

Activity Give each student a blank map. Students may work in pairs. Students should reread the description of the routes to California on page 397, then consult the text map on page 379 and an atlas. The next task is to draw one line on the map for each of the three routes to California. Then have the students label physical features found on the route. Next, using a graphic organizer, they should list physical features for each route and identify the hardships they may have caused. Finally, they should write annotations about the hardships and place them along each of the routes.

Now and then

Levi's Blue Jeans

The term for Levi's pants—*jeans*—comes from the French word for the Italian port of Genoa—Gênes. Working men there wore heavy cotton pants that were a precursor of jeans. The word *denim* also comes from the French. In this case, the phrase *de Nimes,* meaning "from Nimes," was used to identify the tough cotton fabric produced in the French city.

INSTRUCT: OBJECTIVE 3

Life in the Mining Camps/ Miners from Around the World/ Conflicts Among Miners

- What was life like in the mining camps?
- Which countries did non-American miners come from?
- How were foreign miners treated?

In-Depth Resources: Unit 4
- Literature Selection: from *Roughing It* by Mark Twain, pp. 33–35
- Enrichment Activity, p. 40

MORE ABOUT . . .

Foreign Miners

Gold fever reached across the Atlantic. Excitement over the prospect of becoming rich was so great that in France lotteries were held with the winning ticket a guaranteed trip to California. French miners stuck together in the gold fields because they were not able to speak English. Other miners sometimes called them "Keskydees"—a nickname derived from the French expression *"Qu'est-ce qu'il dit?"* or "What is he saying?"

Now and then

LEVI'S BLUE JEANS

Nearly everyone in the United States owns at least one pair of faded, comfortable blue jeans. The first jeans were invented for California miners.

In 1873, a man named Levi Strauss wanted to sell sturdy pants to miners. Strauss made his pants out of the strongest fabric he could buy—cotton denim. He reinforced the pockets with copper rivets so that they could hold heavy tools without ripping.

For more than 125 years, jeans have remained popular. Levi Strauss's pants have proved to be durable in more ways than one.

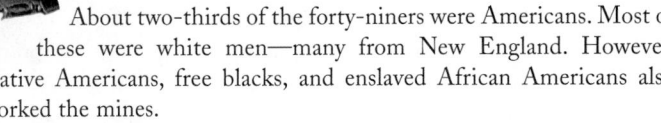

3 Life in the Mining Camps

The mining camps had colorful names like Mad Mule Gulch, Hangtown, and Coyote Diggings. They began as rows of tents along the streams flowing out of the Sierra Nevada. Gradually, the tents gave way to rough wooden buildings that housed stores and saloons.

Mining camps could be dangerous. One woman who lived in the region wrote about camp violence.

A VOICE FROM THE PAST

In the short space of twenty-four days, we have had murders, fearful accidents, bloody deaths, a mob, whippings, a hanging, . . . and a fatal duel.

Louise Clappe, quoted in *Frontier Women*

The mining life was hard for other reasons. Camp gossip told of miners who grew rich overnight by finding eight-pound nuggets, but in reality, such easy pickings were rare. Miners spent their days standing knee-deep in icy streams, where they sifted through tons of mud and sand to find small amounts of gold. Exhaustion, poor food, and disease all damaged the miners' health.

Not only was acquiring gold brutally difficult, but the miners had to pay outrageously high prices for basic supplies. In addition, gamblers and con artists swarmed into the camps to swindle the miners of their money. As a result, few miners grew rich.

Reading **History**

B. Making Inferences Why do you think life in the mining camps was so rough?

B. Possible Responses Mining was dirty and dangerous. It attracted dishonest people.

Miners from Around the World

About two-thirds of the forty-niners were Americans. Most of these were white men—many from New England. However, Native Americans, free blacks, and enslaved African Americans also worked the mines.

Thousands of experienced miners came from Sonora in Mexico. Other foreign miners came from Europe, South America, Australia, and China. Most of the Chinese miners were peasant farmers who fled from a region that had suffered several crop failures. By the end of 1851, one of every ten immigrants was Chinese.

Used to backbreaking labor in their homeland, the Chinese proved to be patient miners. They would take over sites that American miners had abandoned because the easy gold was gone. Through steady, hard work, the Chinese made these "played-out" sites yield profits. American miners resented the success of the Chinese and were suspicious of their different foods, dress, and customs. As the numbers of Chinese miners grew, American anger toward them also increased.

C. Possible Response Americans were unhappy about Chinese success and suspicious of their different customs.

Reading **History**

C. Analyzing Causes Why did some Americans resent Chinese miners?

ACTIVITY OPTIONS

INDIVIDUAL NEEDS

LESS PROFICIENT READERS

Summarizing For Objective 3, pair a less proficient reader with a good reader. Have them read each of the three subheadings under Objective 3 and formulate a question based on the heading. Then they should read to each other. After each of the three subheadings, they should stop to see if the question they created was answered and summarize the information in the paragraphs.

For example:
1. What was life like in the mining camps?
2. Where did miners come from?
3. What kinds of problems were there among miners?

Technology OF THE Time

Surface Mining

Gold is found in cracks, called veins, in the earth's rocky crust. As mountains and other outcrops of rock erode, the gold veins come to the surface. The gold breaks apart into nuggets, flakes, and dust. Flood waters then wash it downhill into stream beds. To mine this surface gold, forty-niners had to use tools designed to separate it from the mud and sand around it. American miners learned some technology from Mexicans who came from the mining region of Sonora.

Miners shoveled dirt into the sluice. The rushing water carried lightweight materials along with it. Heavy gold sank to the bottom and was trapped between the ridges.
A sluice was a series of long boxes with ridges on the bottom. Water ran through the sluice, which angled downward.
Although this photograph shows American and Chinese miners working together, in many places Americans chased the Chinese away.
Mexican miners introduced the use of the pan. A miner would fill a pan with dirt and water. Then he would swirl the pan. Water sloshed over the sides, carrying lightweight minerals with it. Gold settled in the bottom.

CONNECT TO HISTORY

1. **Drawing Conclusions** Which mining method could be used by an individual miner and which needed a group of miners? Explain your answer.

See Skillbuilder Handbook, page R13.

CONNECT TO TODAY

2. **Researching** How is gold mined today?

For more about the California gold rush . . .

RESEARCH LINKS CLASSZONE.COM

399

Technology OF THE Time

OBJECTIVES

1. To use cultural artifacts, such as historical photographs, to acquire information about the United States
2. To explain the technology involved in the process of mining gold in 19th-century America

INSTRUCT

- What precious metals and stones do people mine?
- What kinds of tools are the miners using?
- If you were a forty-niner, which method of surface mining would you prefer—panning for gold or using a sluice? Why?
- What does the photograph show about the relationship among miners from different cultures?

MORE ABOUT . . .

Mexican Miners

Mexican miners skillfully used a *batea,* a pan made out of wood. Besides sharing this method of sifting gravel for gold, Mexican miners also taught American miners Spanish technical terms related to the process. Here are two examples:

- *bonanza,* meaning "a rich deposit of valuable minerals"
- *placer,* meaning "a deposit containing gold dust, flakes, and nuggets"

CONNECT TO HISTORY

1. **Drawing Conclusions** **Possible Answers** Using a pan was a simple manual activity, requiring only one miner. The sluice was a more intricate process of mining for gold and needed the efforts of an entire group, who had to keep shoveling dirt into the row of boxes.

CONNECT TO TODAY

2. **Researching** Students can use an encyclopedia or the Internet to learn about modern gold-mining methods. Suggest that students use a flow chart to summarize their findings. Here is one example.

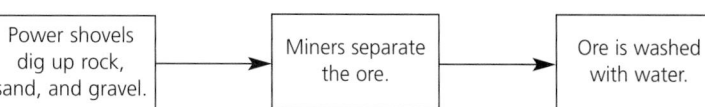

Power shovels dig up rock, sand, and gravel. → Miners separate the ore. → Ore is washed with water.

MORE ABOUT . . .

Miners and Discrimination

The Foreigner Miner Tax laws were mainly aimed at Mexican and, increasingly, Chinese miners. The 1852 law required a three-dollar-per-month payment from every miner who did not want to become a citizen. Chinese people could not become citizens in the United States because that privilege was only for "white" people. The 1852 law, which replaced an 1850 law that had imposed a $20-a-month tax, remained in effect until 1870.

Conflicts Among Miners

A mixture of greed, anger, and prejudice caused some miners to cheat others. For example, I. B. Gilman promised to free an enslaved African American named Tom if he saved enough gold. For more than a year, Tom mined for himself after each day's work was done. When he finally had $1,000, Gilman gave him a paper saying he was free. The next day, the paper suspiciously disappeared. Even though Tom was certain he had been robbed, he couldn't prove it. He had to work for another year before Gilman would free him.

Once the easy-to-find gold was gone, American miners began to force Native Americans and foreigners such as Mexicans and Chinese out of the gold fields to reduce competition. This practice increased after California became a state in 1850. One of the first acts of the California state legislature was to pass the Foreign Miners Tax, which imposed a tax of $20 a month on miners from other countries. That was more than most could afford to pay. As the tax collectors arrived in the camps, most foreigners left.

Driven from the mines, the Chinese opened shops, restaurants, and laundries. So many Chinese owned businesses in San Francisco that their neighborhood was called Chinatown, a name it still goes by today.

D. Answer It passed the Foreign Miners Tax in 1850.

***Reading*History**

D. Analyzing Causes How did the state government make mining harder for foreigners?

INSTRUCT: OBJECTIVE 4

The Impact of the Gold Rush

- What impact did the gold rush have on the economy of California?
- How were the people already living in California affected by the gold rush?
- What impact did the statehood of California have on the slavery issue in the United States?

4 The Impact of the Gold Rush

By 1852, the gold rush was over. While it lasted, about 250,000 people flooded into California. This huge migration caused economic growth that changed California permanently. The port city of San Francisco grew to become a center of banking, manufacturing, shipping, and trade. Its population exploded from around 400 in 1845 to 35,000 in 1850. Sacramento became the center of a productive farming region.

However, the gold rush ruined many *Californios.* The newcomers did not respect *Californios,* their customs, or their legal rights. In many cases,

CAUSE AND EFFECT: *U.S. Expansion, 1846–1853*

CAUSE	EFFECT
Westward trails move thousands to new territories.	Oregon Territory acquired by the United States.
Austin and others colonize Texas.	Texas Revolution
United States annexes Texas.	War with Mexico
Mexican Cession acquired by the United States.	United States expands "sea to sea."
Transcontinental railroad route needed.	Gadsden Purchase
Thousands of gold seekers rush to California.	California becomes a state.

SKILLBUILDER Interpreting Charts

1. *Which two causes are related to transportation?*
2. *Which cause fulfilled the nation's "manifest destiny"?*

Skillbuilder Answers

1. westward trails and transcontinental railroad route
2. Transcontinental railroad route needed.

HISTORY FROM VISUALS

Interpreting the Chart Remind students that there might have been more than one cause, although the chart shows a single cause for an effect. Ask them what impact the idea of manifest destiny had on each one of the causes.

Extension Have the student refer to the time line at the beginning of the chapter and put the effect events in chronological order.

Critical Thinking Transparency CT38
- Cause and Effect: U.S. Expansion, 1846–1853

ACTIVITY OPTIONS

INDIVIDUAL NEEDS

STUDENTS ACQUIRING ENGLISH/ESL

Cause and Effect Pair a proficient student with one learning English. Have the students look at each cause and effect and determine what steps and information are implied in each combination. For example: Oregon was a new territory, thousands move there, the U.S. wants the Oregon Territory, the U.S. makes an agreement with Great Britain over the territory.

Have the students create a three-column, six-row graphic organizer. Place the cause in the left column, the effect in the right column. Use the center column to write out the missing information and steps.

Cause		Effect

Reading History
E. Recognizing Effects What impact did the gold rush have on the people who lived in California before the forty-niners came?
E. Possible Responses *Californios* lost land, and many Native Americans were killed.

Americans seized their property. For example, Mariano Vallejo lost all but 300 acres of his huge estate. Even so, their Spanish heritage became an important part of California culture.

Native Americans suffered even more. Thousands of them died from diseases brought by the newcomers. The miners hunted down and killed thousands more. The reason was the Anglo-American belief that Native Americans stood in the way of progress. By 1870, California's Native American population had fallen from 150,000 to only about 58,000.

A final effect of the gold rush was that by 1849 California had enough people to apply for statehood. Skipping the territorial stage, California applied to Congress for admission to the Union and was admitted as a free state in 1850. Although its constitution outlawed slavery, it did not grant African Americans the vote.

Mariano Vallejo, unhappy that *Californio* culture was ignored in the new American California, named his home "Tear of the Mountain."

For some people, California's statehood proved to be the opportunity of a lifetime. The enslaved woman Nancy Gooch gained her freedom because of the law against slavery. She then worked as a cook and washerwoman until she saved enough money to buy the freedom of her son and daughter-in-law in Missouri. Nancy Gooch's family moved to California to join her. Eventually, they became so prosperous that they bought Sutter's sawmill, where the gold rush first started.

On a national level, California's statehood created turmoil. Before 1850, there was an equal number of free states and slave states. Southerners feared that because the statehood of California made free states outnumber slave states, Northerners might use their majority to abolish slavery. As Chapter 18 explains, conflict over this issue threatened the survival of the Union.

Section 4 Assessment

1. Terms & Names
Explain the significance of:
- forty-niner
- *Californio*
- Mariano Vallejo
- John Sutter
- James Marshall
- California gold rush

2. Taking Notes
Use a chart like the one shown to review and record hardships faced by the forty-niners.

HARDSHIPS	
In the camps	
At work mining	

Which hardships would you have found most difficult?

3. Main Ideas
a. How did the California gold rush get started?

b. Why didn't many forty-niners become rich?

c. How did women and people of different racial, ethnic, or national groups contribute to the California gold rush?

4. Critical Thinking
Recognizing Effects What were some of the effects of the California gold rush?

THINK ABOUT
- changes in San Francisco
- California's bid for statehood

ACTIVITY OPTIONS
SCIENCE / **TECHNOLOGY**
Research the hazards of mining gold and either plan a **science exhibit** or give an **electronic presentation.**

MORE ABOUT . . .

California's Growing Population
California's spectacular growth during the gold rush foreshadowed its growth in the latter half of the 20th century. Between 1980 and 1990, the state grew by more than 25 percent. Currently, California is the most populous state in the nation. Its population is expected to reach 37.8 million by the year 2010. By 2000, more than half of all Californians claimed to be Hispanic or some race other than white.

ASSESS & RETEACH

Setting the Stage Have students fill in the California section on the chapter graphic organizer.

Formal Assessment
- Section Quiz, p. 240

Critical Thinking Transparency CT37
- Setting the Stage

RETEACHING ACTIVITY
Create as many groups of four as possible. Each student within the group should be assigned one of the four objectives in the section. Have all the students in one specific objective meet together. Each objective group should write a three- to five-sentence summary of their part of the section. Then the students should return to their original groups and share their section summaries with other students.

In-Depth Resources: Unit 4
- Reteaching Activity, p. 39

Section 4 Assessment

1. Terms & Names
forty-niner, p. 396
Californio, p. 396
Mariano Vallejo, p. 396
John Sutter, p. 397
James Marshall, p. 397
California gold rush, p. 397

2. Taking Notes
In the camps: poor food, disease, swindlers and crooks
At work mining: cold streams, accidents, exhaustion
Answers will vary.

3. Main Ideas
a. Gold was discovered at Sutter's Mill. **b.** Mining was difficult; prices for basic supplies were high; there was a lot of disease. **c.** It started on a Swiss man's land; Mexicans shared *batea* skills; Chinese, when forced from mining, opened support businesses; women sold supplies.

4. Critical Thinking
California became a state, and San Francisco became a business center.

ACTIVITY OPTIONS
Integrated Assessment
- Rubrics for museum exhibit, 1.5
- Rubrics for electronic presentation, 5.4

TERMS & NAMES

1. **mountain men,** p. 397
2. **Oregon Trail,** p. 380
3. **Stephen Austin,** p. 384
4. ***Tejano,*** p. 384
5. **Antonio López de Santa Anna,** p. 386
6. **manifest destiny,** p. 391
7. **Bear Flag Revolt,** p. 393
8. **Mexican Cession,** p. 395
9. **forty-niner,** p. 396
10. **California gold rush,** p. 397

REVIEW QUESTIONS

Possible Responses

1. to make money speculating land; to own new farms; to find new jobs; to profit from making and selling goods to farmers; to avoid paying debts; to have greater religious freedom
2. Santa Fe Trail, Oregon Trail, and Mormon Trail
3. They built dams and canals to bring water from the hills to their farms below.
4. Texans resented Spanish as the official language and laws against slavery.
5. Battle of the Alamo—raised Texans' awareness of effort needed to win independence; Battle of San Jacinto—marked Mexicans' defeat and Texan Independence
6. Oregon territory, Texas, and the Mexican Cession
7. Americans in California overthrew the Mexicans and secured the land for the United States.
8. Mexican Cession, or the present-day states of California, Nevada, Utah, most of Arizona, and parts of New Mexico, Colorado, and Wyoming
9. white American men; free African Americans; enslaved African Americans; Native Americans; Mexicans; the Chinese
10. economic growth of San Francisco; agricultural development of Sacramento; California statehood; many immigrants settled in California

Chapter 13 ASSESSMENT

VISUAL SUMMARY

Manifest Destiny

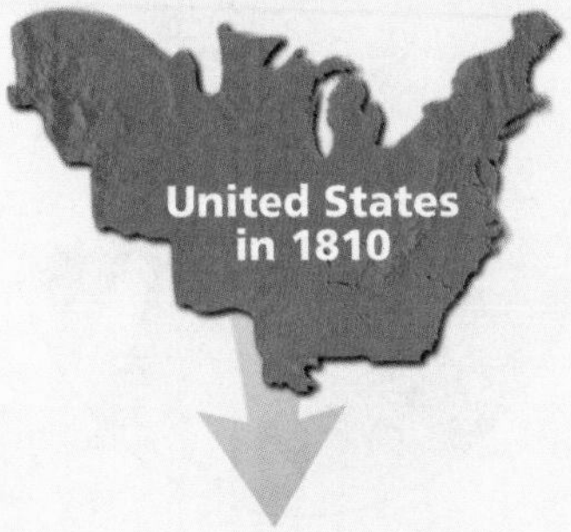

Trails West

Mountain men and traders opened trails in the Far West. Pioneers then went west to gain land, wealth, or religious freedom.

The Texas Revolution

Americans moved into the Mexican territory of Texas. Conflicts led those Americans to revolt, and Texas gained independence.

The War with Mexico

President Polk wanted to expand the nation. He negotiated to gain Oregon. The United States fought Mexico to gain much of the Southwest.

The California Gold Rush

The discovery of gold lured thousands of people to California. California's economy and population grew, resulting in statehood.

TERMS & NAMES

Briefly explain the significance of each of the following.

1. mountain man
2. Oregon Trail
3. Stephen Austin
4. *Tejano*
5. Antonio López de Santa Anna
6. manifest destiny
7. Bear Flag Revolt
8. Mexican Cession
9. forty-niner
10. California gold rush

REVIEW QUESTIONS

Trails West (pages 377–383)

1. What were three reasons why people moved west?
2. What were the three main trails that led to the West?
3. How did the Mormons make the land in Utah productive?

The Texas Revolution (pages 384–389)

4. Why were Texans unhappy with Mexican rule?
5. Why were the battles of the Alamo and San Jacinto important to the Texas Revolution?

The War with Mexico (pages 390–395)

6. What areas did the United States gain as a result of Americans' belief in manifest destiny?
7. How is the Bear Flag Revolt related to the War with Mexico?
8. What lands did the United States acquire as a result of the Treaty of Guadalupe Hidalgo?

The California Gold Rush (pages 396–401)

9. Who were four groups of people who became forty-niners?
10. What were three ways California changed because of the gold rush?

CRITICAL THINKING

1. USING YOUR NOTES

	Types of people who traveled there	Why they went there	Key events that allowed the U.S. to take ownership of the territory
New Mexico			
Utah			
Oregon			
Texas			
California			

Using your completed chart, answer the questions below.

a. In what ways were the reasons people went west similar?
b. Which of the five regions listed on your chart entered the United States peacefully?
c. Which event added the most territory to the United States?

2. ANALYZING LEADERSHIP

Think about the leaders discussed in this chapter. What characteristics did they have that made them good leaders?

3. THEME: EXPANSION

How did the idea of manifest destiny help bring about the expansion of the United States?

4. DRAWING CONCLUSIONS

How did the War with Mexico and the California gold rush contribute to the cultural diversity of the United States?

5. APPLYING CITIZENSHIP SKILLS

What were the different viewpoints that people held about the War with Mexico?

Interact *with* History

Based on this chapter, what do you think you would have gained or lost by going west?

CRITICAL THINKING

Possible Responses

1. **USING YOUR NOTES** **a.** All centered around pursuing a better life. **b.** Oregon **c.** War with Mexico
2. **ANALYZING LEADERSHIP** ability to gain people's respect and confidence; excellent military skills; courage and bravery
3. **THEME: EXPANSION** Under Polk, manifest destiny became government policy; by the 1840s, thousands of Americans had moved westward to the Oregon Territory.
4. **DRAWING CONCLUSIONS** The war with Mexico added lands that were part of Mexico, bringing the customs of those people into the United States. People from all over the world came to California for the gold rush.
5. **APPLYING CITIZENSHIP SKILLS** President Polk and his supporters viewed the War with Mexico as an attempt to extend U.S. lands. Southerners thought it was an opportunity to extend slavery. Northerners thought the war was unnecessary and unjust.

Interact *with* History Answers will vary. Students might say they would have become wealthy, lost relatives, escaped debt, or gained farmland.

HISTORY SKILLS

1. INTERPRETING MAPS: Movement

Study the map. Answer the questions.

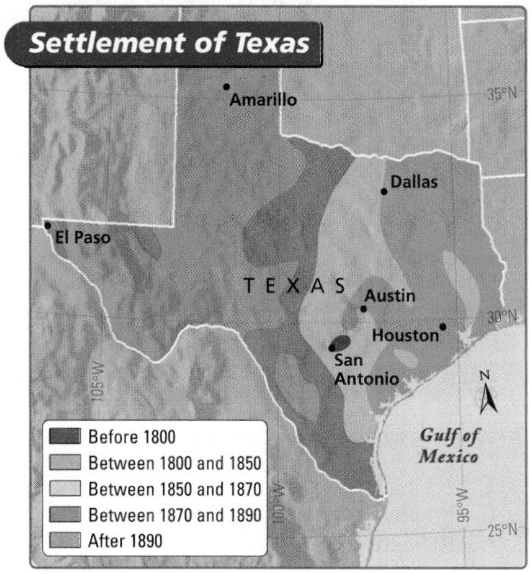

Basic Map Elements

a. What is the subject of the map?
b. What years are covered by the map?
c. What do the colors indicate?

Interpreting the Map

d. Which area of Texas was settled first?
e. In what general direction was Texas settled?

2. INTERPRETING PRIMARY SOURCES

This photograph was taken of a man who planned to go to California to find gold. Study the photo carefully. Answer the questions.

a. What does the photo reveal about the man's expectations of danger?
b. What does the photo suggest about how successful he hopes to be?

ALTERNATIVE ASSESSMENT

1. INTERDISCIPLINARY ACTIVITY: Science

Creating a Diagram Do research to learn how gold is deposited into veins in the earth and how erosion later exposes the gold. Draw diagrams showing the processes of gold vein formation and erosion. Share your diagram with the class.

2. COOPERATIVE LEARNING ACTIVITY

Creating a News Magazine Show With the support of President Polk, Congress declared war on Mexico in 1846. Though many Americans supported the decision, some groups felt that war with Mexico was unnecessary and unjust. Working with a small group, create a news magazine show that explores the different viewpoints surrounding the Mexican War. Research these opinions. Then write and perform the news magazine for the class. One student should be the moderator, while the other students in the group should choose one of the following groups to represent.

a. President Polk and his supporters
b. Northerners, including Abraham Lincoln and Frederick Douglass
c. Southerners

3. TECHNOLOGY ACTIVITY

Making a Class Presentation Life in the mining camps was not like life "back east." Information about the camps comes from primary sources, like diaries and newspaper articles. Using the Internet and library, find sources about life in the mining camps.

For more about gold mining . . .

INTERNET ACTIVITY
CLASSZONE.COM

Your sources might include:

- images of mines, miners, or miners' shacks
- images of items that the general store sold to miners
- tales of the gold fields
- information about the diversity of cultures in the camps

4. HISTORY PORTFOLIO

Review the concept of manifest destiny. Then write a brief report listing the political, economic, and social roots of the concept. Be sure to use standard grammar, spelling, sentence structure, and punctuation in your report. Add your report to your portfolio.

Additional Test Practice, pp. S1–S33

TEST PRACTICE
CLASSZONE.COM

ALTERNATIVE ASSESSMENT

Standards for Evaluation

1. INTERDISCIPLINARY ACTIVITY: Science
   Science diagrams should
   - contain graphic representations of gold vein formation and erosion.
   - depict the sequence of scientific processes.
   - include clear, informative labels and captions.
2. COOPERATIVE LEARNING ACTIVITY
   Shows should
   - include stage directions that describe the setting, cast of characters, and props.
   - contain authentic-sounding dialogue.
   - dramatize the different viewpoints surrounding the war.
3. TECHNOLOGY ACTIVITY
   Class presentations should
   - create oral, visual, or written explanations of social studies material about mining-camp life.
   - reflect the use of primary and secondary sources to acquire information.
4. HISTORY PORTFOLIO
   Short reports should
   - answer questions about manifest destiny.
   - use evidence to develop and support ideas.
   - cite sources of information.
   - use standard grammar, spelling, sentence structure, and punctuation.

Critical Thinking Transparency CT39
- Visual Summary

Formal Assessment
- Chapter Test, Forms A, B, and C, pp. 241–252

HISTORY SKILLS

Possible Responses

1. INTERPRETING MAPS
   Basic Map Elements
   a. the growth of settled areas of Texas during the 1800s
   b. 1800–1890
   c. time spans corresponding to colored regions on the map
   Interpreting the Map
   d. the area around San Antonio
   e. north and east
2. INTERPRETING PRIMARY SOURCES
   a. Carrying two pistols shows that the man fears for his safety.
   b. The sack of gold shows that the man believes his dreams for wealth will come true.

CHAPTER 14 PLANNING GUIDE
A New Spirit of Change 1820–1860

	CHAPTER OVERVIEW	COPYMASTERS	INTEGRATED TECHNOLOGY
CHAPTER RESOURCES	This chapter discusses the surge of immigration to the United States before 1860 and its effects on the population and the culture. It also describes new trends in art and literature as well as a variety of reform movements, including abolitionism and women's rights.	**In-Depth Resources: Unit 4** • Tracing Themes: Impact of the Individual, p. 42 • Building Vocabulary, p. 47 • History Workshop Resources, p. 61 **Interdisciplinary Projects,** pp. 79–84	• eEdition Plus Online • EasyPlanner Plus Online • eTest Plus Online • eEdition • Power Presentations • EasyPlanner • Electronic Library of Primary Sources • Test Generator • Reading Study Guide • America's Music
	KEY IDEAS		
SECTION 1 The Hopes of Immigrants pp. 407–412	• Economic, political, and religious factors motivate thousands of people to leave Europe and come to the United States. • Scandinavians, Germans, and Irish are among the most numerous immigrants. • The influx of immigrants leads to urban overcrowding and nativist opposition.	**In-Depth Resources: Unit 4** • Setting the Stage, p. 41 • Guided Reading, p. 43 • Skillbuilder Practice, p. 48 • Reteaching Activity, p. 56 **Citizenship Today,** pp. 9–10 **Economics in History** • Irish Immigration, p. 14 **Outline Map Activities** • Immigration, Mid-1800s, pp. 27–28	**Warm-Up Transparency WT14** **Geography Transparency GT14** • Settlement of Germans and Irish, 1860 **Critical Thinking Transparency CT40** • Setting the Stage classzone.com
SECTION 2 American Literature and Art pp. 413–416	• American writers and artists celebrate romanticism, the beauties of nature, and their national past. • Transcendentalists such as Emerson, Thoreau, and Fuller argue for the importance of the individual's conscience. • American literature begins to develop its own voice, distinct from Europe's.	**In-Depth Resources: Unit 4** • Setting the Stage, p. 41 • Guided Reading, p. 44 • Reteaching Activity, p. 57	**Warm-Up Transparency WT14** **Humanities Transparency HT27** • Bird of Washington **Critical Thinking Transparency CT40** • Setting the Stage classzone.com
SECTION 3 Reforming American Society pp. 417–423	• The Second Great Awakening brings religious revival and social reform. • Reform movements promote temperance, better working conditions, public education, and care for the needy. • Newspapers and magazines spread new ideas, while some groups start utopian communities.	**In-Depth Resources: Unit 4** • Setting the Stage, p. 41 • Guided Reading, p. 45 • Reteaching Activity, p. 58	**Warm-Up Transparency WT14** **Critical Thinking Transparency CT40** • Setting the Stage **Critical Thinking Transparency CT41** • Cause and Effect: The Reform Movement **Primary Source Explorer** • *Report to the Massachusetts Legislature*
SECTION 4 Abolition and Women's Rights pp. 424–431	• Abolitionists demand an end to slavery. • Eyewitness accounts publicize the evils of slavery, and the Underground Railroad aids those escaping slavery. • Women reformers seek the right to speak in public, the right to own property, the right to vote, and other aspects of legal equality with men.	**In-Depth Resources: Unit 4** • Setting the Stage, p. 41 • Guided Reading, p. 46 • Geography Application, pp. 49–50 • Primary Sources, pp. 51–52 • Literature Selection, pp. 53–55 • Reteaching Activity, p. 59 **America's History Makers,** pp. 55–58 **American History Plays** • *Lucy Stone, Champion of Women's Rights* by Claire Boiko **Why It Matters Now,** pp. 27–28	**Warm-Up Transparency WT14** **Humanities Transparency HT28** • The Fugitive's Song **Critical Thinking Transparency CT40** • Setting the Stage **Critical Thinking Transparency CT42** • Visual Summary classzone.com

Pupil's Edition

Copymaster

Overhead Transparency

Audio Library

CD-ROM

Internet

ASSESSMENT OPTIONS

Chapter Assessment, pp. 432–433

Formal Assessment
- Chapter Tests, Forms A, B, and C, pp. 257–268

Test Generator

Online Test Practice

Strategies for Test Preparation

Section Assessment, p. 412

Formal Assessment, Quiz, p. 253

Integrated Assessment Book
- Rubrics, 5.4, 5.1

Test Generator

Test Practice Transparencies, TT49

Section Assessment, p. 416

Formal Assessment, Quiz, p. 254

Integrated Assessment Book
- Rubrics, 1.3, 5.3

Test Generator

Test Practice Transparencies, TT50

Section Assessment, p. 421

Formal Assessment, Quiz, p. 255

Integrated Assessment Book
- Rubrics, 3.6, 4.3

Test Generator

Test Practice Transparencies, TT51

Section Assessment, p. 429

Formal Assessment, Quiz, p. 256

Integrated Assessment Book
- Rubrics, 5.3, 3.1

Test Generator

Test Practice Transparencies, TT52

CUSTOMIZING FOR INDIVIDUAL NEEDS

Students Acquiring English/ESL

Reading Study Guide (English and Spanish), pp. 133–142

Access for Students Acquiring English/ESL: Spanish Translations, pp. 90–96

Chapter Summaries on CD (English and Spanish)

Modified Lesson Plans for English Learners

Less Proficient Readers

Reading Study Guide (English and Spanish), pp. 133–142

Chapter Summaries on CD (English and Spanish)

Gifted and Talented Students

In-Depth Resources: Unit 4
- Enrichment Activity, p. 60

America's History Makers
- Elizabeth Cady Stanton, pp. 55–56
- Harriet Tubman, pp. 57–58

CROSS-CURRICULAR CONNECTIONS

Culture

Williams, Jean K. ***The Shakers.*** New York: Watts, 1996. A clear and readable history of the Shakers.

Humanities: Art

Driscoll, John Paul. ***All That Is Glorious Around Us: Paintings from the Hudson River School.*** Ithaca, NY: Cornell U. Press, 1997. Examples of the first school of American landscape painting; for advanced students.

Interdisciplinary Projects, pp. 79–84

- Math: Graphing Population Data
- Science: Observations in Space
- Language Arts: Nature Writing
- Art: Audubon's Scientific Illustrations

McDougal Littell *The Language of Literature*

- Emily Dickinson, "Plank to Plank" (poem), Grade 8, Unit 2, Part 2
- Frederick Douglass, "Letter to Harriet Tubman" (letter), Grade 8, Unit 5, Part 1
- Henry Wadsworth Longfellow, "Paul Revere's Ride" (poem), Grade 8, Unit 5, Part 1
- Ann Petry from *Harriet Tubman: Conductor on the Underground Railroad* (biography), Grade 8, Unit 5, Part 1
- Edgar Allan Poe, "The Tell Tale Heart" (story), Grade 8, Unit 4, Part 2

McDougal Littell Literature Connections

Virginia Hamilton

The House of Dies Drear

Acclaimed tale in which a 13-year-old delves into the mysteries of an Ohio house that once formed a part of the Underground Railroad.

ENRICHMENT ACTIVITIES

Pupil's Edition, pp. 404–435
Interact with History, p. 405
Citizenship Today, p. 411
Interactive Primary Source, pp. 422–423
Geography in History, p. 430–431

In-Depth Resources: Unit 4
- Geography Application: King Cotton, pp. 49–50
- Primary Source: from the *Liberator,* p. 51
- Primary Source: The Seneca Falls Declaration and Resolutions, p. 52
- Literature Selection: from *Narrative of the Life of Frederick Douglass,* pp. 53–55
- History Workshop Resources, p. 61

America's History Makers
- Elizabeth Cady Stanton, pp. 55–56
- Harriet Tubman, pp. 57–58

America's Music CD

American History Plays
- *Lucy Stone, Champion of Women's Rights* by Claire Boiko

Outline Map Activities
- Immigration, Mid-1800s, pp. 27–28

Primary Source Explorer
- *Report to the Massachusetts Legislature*

Why It Matters Now
- Working for Change, pp. 27–28

BLOCK SCHEDULING — LESSON PLAN OPTIONS (90-MINUTE PERIOD)

DAY 1

Interact with History, p. 405
Class Time 20 Minutes

Options for pacing and variety:

- Role-Playing Ask students to suppose that they are newspaper reporters who have been assigned to interview the immigrants in this picture. Have each student make a list of questions to ask about the immigrants' lives. **Class Time** 15 minutes

Setting the Stage, p. 406
Class Time 20 minutes

Options for pacing and variety:

- Time Saver Ask students to come to class with a two-column chart. In the first column, have students list what they think were the worst social problems in the United States in the mid-1800s, and in the second column, their ideas about how people at that time might have tried to solve each of these problems. **Class Time** 5 minutes

Section 1, pp. 407–412
Class Time 50 minutes

Options for pacing and variety:

- Peer Teaching After students read Citizenship Today on page 411, divide them into small groups to create the citizenship test suggested for the activity. After administering the test to another group, have students discuss within groups their perceptions of the fairness of the test they took and the one they created. **Class Time** 40 minutes
- Time Saver For a homework assignment, have students complete the Taking Notes diagram and answer the Critical Thinking question in the Section Assessment. **Class Time** 5 minutes

DAY 2

Section 2, pp. 413–416
Class Time 45 minutes

Options for pacing and variety:

- Team Teaching Invite the language arts teacher to your class to talk to your students about James Fenimore Cooper, Henry Wadsworth Longfellow, Ralph Waldo Emerson, and other American writers of this period. **Class Time** 35 minutes
- Time Saver As a homework assignment, ask a group of students to prepare the Interdisciplinary Activity on page 433. Have students present their poems to the class. **Class Time** 10 minutes

Section 3, pp. 417–423
Class Time 45 minutes

Options for pacing and variety:

- History on Film Extend students' knowledge of the Second Great Awakening, temperance, and other reform movements with *Democracy and Reform.* Schlesinger, 1996. **Class Time** 35 minutes
- Time Saver For a homework assignment, have students answer the Reading History questions for the section and then create one Reading History question of their own to share with the class. **Class Time** 10 minutes

DAY 3

Section 4, pp. 424–431
Class Time 45 minutes

Options for pacing and variety:

- Role-Play Ask pairs of students to prepare the Section Assessment Activity Option on page 429 and present their dialogue to the class. **Class Time** 40 minutes
- Internet Extend students' background knowledge of the Underground Railroad by visiting classzone.com. **Class Time** 20 minutes

Chapter 14 Assessment, pp. 432–433
Class Time 40 minutes

Options for pacing and variety:

- Peer Evaluation Working in small groups, students can use the Terms & Names in the Chapter Assessment to write a summary of the chapter. **Class Time** 40 minutes
- Peer Competition Assign each student one of the writers, reformers, abolitionists, or women's rights activists discussed in this chapter. Then have the class play a game of "Twenty Questions," guessing the identity of the historical figure each student has been assigned. **Class Time** 40 minutes

TEACHER-TESTED ACTIVITY Jean Price, T. H. Rogers School, Houston, Texas

REFORM RALLY

Class Time Two class periods for preparation and one for presentation

Task Participating in a rally to promote reform in American society

Purpose To identify and examine goals of the reformers

Supplies Needed

- Reference materials and Internet sources on reformers
- Markers
- Posterboard
- Patriotic music (optional)

Activity Divide the class into groups of four to six students. Assign each group a different reform movement: women's suffrage, temperance, education, treatment of the mentally ill, abolition. Students should design a banner or signs and prepare a slogan for their movement to be used at the rally. Ask each group to prepare a two-minute speech outlining the goals of its movement. On rally day, all groups take part in a short demonstration with slogans, signs, and placards. Following the demonstration, each group gives its speech. After all speakers have finished, ask the class to rank the movements in importance and to justify the rankings.

SEARCH FOR YOUR ANCESTRY

The Internet provides vast resources for tracing genealogy and ancestry. Many Americans can trace family history to another country of origin. Native Americans can trace family history to tribes that may have migrated or been forced to migrate numerous times. Students may not be able to find enough information to complete a family tree for more than three generations, but perhaps they will become interested in using the resources of the Internet to continue to trace their family's heritage, or that of a friend.

ACTIVITY OUTLINE

Objective Students will conduct an Internet search to discover their ancestry. Such a search will help students practice Internet research as well as stimulate interest in history by placing their family in historical context.

Task In this activity, students will interview family members to build a family tree and historical map for their family or that of a close friend.

Class Time One class period to introduce, several weeks to complete outside of class

DIRECTIONS

1. Ask those students who know their country of origin to call out the name of the country. Make a list on the board of all the countries represented in the class. For students who do not know their country of origin, tell them to make an educated guess. Mark all the countries represented on a world map.

2. Tell students they will be using the Internet and interviewing family members over the next few weeks to research their own family's heritage. They will use the information they gather from the Internet and the interviews to build a family tree that goes back at least three generations. Show students an example of a family tree of a famous person, such as that of Franklin Delano Roosevelt, available on classzone.com. Instruct students that the standard way to build a family tree is with the oldest members at the top and the youngest at the bottom.

3. Suggest to students that they begin with family interviews to get some of the information that will be needed in order to take advantage of resources on the Internet. Ask students to think of possible interview questions for parents, grandparents, and other family members or friends. They might want to create an interview sheet, using a word-processing program. Interview questions might include:
   - Where and when were you born?
   - What was your full name at birth?
   - Who were your parents? Grandparents?
   - What do you know about your ancestors?
   - How and why did your ancestors come to the United States?
   - Who else might give me information about my ancestors?

4. After students have gathered initial information from family members or friends, tell them to look at some of the genealogical sources and maps on classzone.com.

5. Students can use a word-processing or graphics program to create their family trees. Ask students to add place of birth to each member of the family tree.

6. After students have determined family members and places of birth, tell them to import a blank map of the United States or of the world into a graphics program and mark the birthplace of each family member. Then they can trace a path from the oldest ancestor to themselves. Students should save the modified maps to use in classroom electronic presentations or wall displays. Encourage students to enhance their family trees and maps with artwork representative of the countries of origin.

7. Allow students several weeks to complete their family trees and maps.

CHAPTER 14 OBJECTIVE

The student will study the era from 1820 to 1860 to identify groups of immigrants who settled in the United States, describe developments in American literature and art, and evaluate the impact of reform movements.

CHAPTER 14 A New Spirit of Change 1820–1860

HISTORY FROM VISUALS

Interpreting the Photograph The photograph shows a poor neighborhood of New York City in 1860. The photographer, Mathew Brady, is one of the most famous American photographers, known for his work on the battlefields of the Civil War. Ask students to examine the photograph, note the living conditions in the neighborhood, and make inferences about what life may have been like for the people who lived there. **Possible Responses** Students should note the lack of open spaces, the poor condition of the streets and buildings, and the crowded, dirty living conditions.

Extension Ask students to identify organizations that work on behalf of the needy in their community. Point out that a number of people and organizations in the early and mid-1800s worked to help the needy in this country.

Mathew Brady took this picture of New York City in 1860. It is one of the earliest photographs of a poor city neighborhood.

CRITICAL THINKING ACTIVITY

Comparing and Contrasting Ask students to compare the neighborhood in the photograph to two different neighborhoods in their community today. What are some of the similarities and differences? Copy the chart below on the board to record responses.

Neighborhood in Photo	Neighborhood A	Neighborhood B

Class Time 15 minutes

RECOMMENDED RESOURCES

BOOKS FOR THE TEACHER

Daniels, Roger. ***Coming to America: A History of Immigration and Ethnicity in American Life.*** New York: Harper-Perennial Library, 1991. Account of the immigrant experience in the United States.

Franklin, John Hope and Loren Schweninger. ***Runaway Slaves: Rebels on the Plantation.*** New York: Oxford University Press, 1999. New analysis of resistance and escape attempts by enslaved Americans.

Gollaher, David L. ***Voice for the Mad: The Life of Dorothea Dix.*** New York: Free Press, 1995. Comprehensive biography of a complicated and sometimes difficult woman.

SOFTWARE

Decisions, Decisions: Immigration. Tom Snyder Productions, 1996. Encourages students to make their own decisions about immigration policy.

VIDEO

Underground Railroad. History Channel, 1998. Tells the exciting story of the movement to liberate enslaved persons.

INTERNET

For more about the Underground Railroad, visit . . .

classzone.com

Interact *with* History

These immigrants live in New York. This one room is their whole apartment.
Women and children have few legal rights. For example, a married woman's earnings are controlled by her husband.
Many people want to outlaw the sale of alcohol. They believe drinking causes poverty.
Many children do not go to school.

You are a writer who moves to New York in the mid-1800s. A newspaper hires you to write about reform. One day, you hear a speaker call for the end of slavery. Another day you talk to a factory worker whose pay has been cut. In the city, you see great poverty and suffering.

What Do You Think?

- How might you persuade Americans to change life in the city?
- What are the problems that you see in these two pictures?
- Should reform come about through new laws or through individual actions?

What reforms do you think will most benefit American society?

USA

1828 Noah Webster publishes the *American Dictionary of the English Language.*

1829 David Walker prints *Appeal,* a pamphlet urging slaves to revolt.

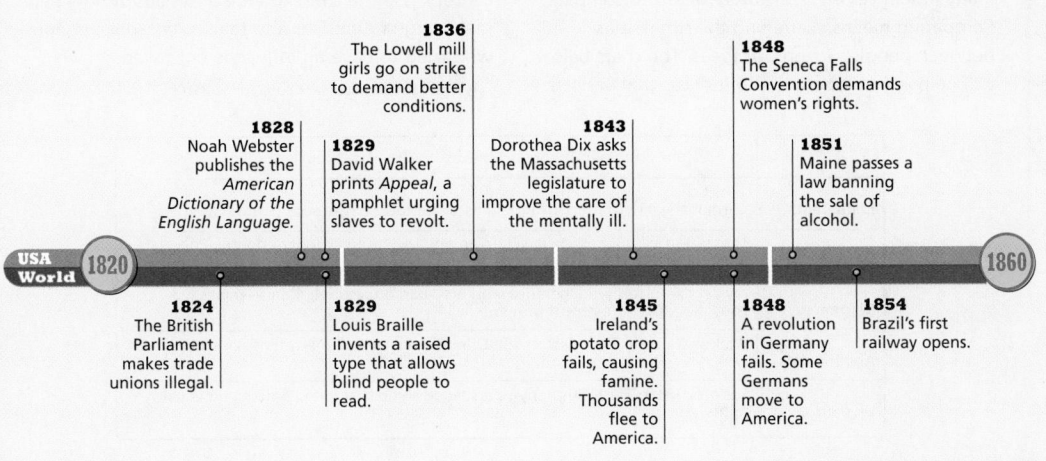

1836 The Lowell mill girls go on strike to demand better conditions.

1843 Dorothea Dix asks the Massachusetts legislature to improve the care of the mentally ill.

1848 The Seneca Falls Convention demands women's rights.

1851 Maine passes a law banning the sale of alcohol.

1820 — **1860**

World

1824 The British Parliament makes trade unions illegal.

1829 Louis Braille invents a raised type that allows blind people to read.

1845 Ireland's potato crop fails, causing famine. Thousands flee to America.

1848 A revolution in Germany fails. Some Germans move to America.

1854 Brazil's first railway opens.

Interact *with* History

OBJECTIVES

- To help students understand some of the problems affecting poor people in the mid-1800s
- To help students understand why Americans worked to reform their society

What Do You Think?

1. Encourage the students to identify not only the highlighted problems but also those that can be inferred, such as unhealthy living conditions.
2. Ask students why laws do not always solve social problems.
3. Ask students why they think it sometimes is difficult for government to pass laws designed to address difficult social problems.

What reforms do you think will most benefit American society?

Encourage students to think about how life could be improved for the family in the visual.

MAKING PERSONAL CONNECTIONS

Ask students whether they, their friends, or family members have ever volunteered to work for an organization that helps needy people. Then ask students what role they think government should have in helping to solve social problems and in meeting the needs that community organizations address.

TIME LINE DISCUSSION

Remind students that the United States was expanding westward in the early and mid-1800s. This territorial expansion was accompanied by growth in immigration and total population. Social and political changes also were sweeping much of Europe.

- Have students identify two events affecting women in the United States. **Answer** Lowell strike in 1836; Seneca Falls Convention in 1848
- Ask students to identify additional events that mark social change. **Possible Response** David Walker's pamphlet; Dorothea Dix's appeal; Maine bans alcohol
- Ask students to identify events in Ireland and Germany that may have encouraged immigration. **Possible Response** the potato famine in Ireland; the revolution in Germany

BEFORE YOU READ

Previewing the Theme:

Impact of the Individual

Ask students to think of ways in which immigrants, artists, and reformers might have shaped American culture in the 1800s. **Possible Response** The many European immigrants who came to the United States helped the nation's cities to grow. They provided labor for new businesses. They brought their religions and customs to their new home. Writers and artists used their talents to explore ideas and communicate them to their audiences. Reformers worked to solve some of the nation's problems.

What Do You Know?

Point out that increasing immigration caused overcrowding in cities and prompted hostility from some native-born Americans. Ask students to speculate about the kinds of problems that may be caused by or worsened by crowded living conditions and by hostility from others in society.

In-Depth Resources: Unit 4
- Tracing Themes: Impact of the Individual, p. 42

READ AND TAKE NOTES

Reading Strategy: Comparing

Tell students that comparing means looking at the similarities among people, actions, or ideas. Explain that examining relationships in this way helps readers build critical-thinking skills as they gain a deeper understanding of the material they read. When the chart is completed, students should be able to use it to compare the influence of groups and individuals on America in the mid-1800s.

In-Depth Resources: Unit 4
- Setting the Stage, p. 41

Critical Thinking Transparency CT40
- Setting the Stage

Chapter 14 SETTING THE STAGE

BEFORE YOU READ

Previewing the Theme

Impact of the Individual In the mid-1800s, millions of Europeans moved to the United States and changed its culture. Writers and artists also shaped American culture. In addition, many individuals worked to reform society in such areas as education and the antislavery movement. Chapter 14 describes how individuals changed America.

This engraving shows a woman teaching a young slave to read, even though it was illegal to do so. The boy grew up, escaped, and became a great reformer—Frederick Douglass.

What Do You Know?

What do you think were the worst problems in the United States in the mid-1800s? How do you think people tried to solve them?

THINK ABOUT
- stories or films that are set in this period
- problems that exist now
- the actions people take to solve today's problems

What Do You Want to Know?

What would you like to learn about the way individuals changed the United States in the mid-1800s? Record your questions in your notebook before you read the chapter.

READ AND TAKE NOTES

Reading Strategy: Comparing To understand the many influences on U.S. culture, learn to compare. Comparing means examining the similarities between people, actions, or ideas. The chart below will help you compare the influences that various people had upon America in the middle of the 19th century. Use the chart to take notes about how people changed America. Also take notes about people who tried to have an influence but failed.

See Skillbuilder Handbook, page R9.

	How People Influenced America in the Mid-1800s
Immigrants	Germans—kindergarten, gymnasiums, some foods; Irish—city politics
Writers	Thoreau—civil disobedience; Whitman and Dickinson—modern poetry; Poe—horror and detective fiction
Reformers	revivalists—reform; temperance workers—ban on alcohol; Mann—public education; Dix—treatment of mentally ill
Abolitionists	Walker, Garrison, Douglass, Truth, Grimkés—convinced many that slavery was wrong
Women	Stanton, Mott, Truth, Anthony—persuaded some that women deserved equal rights

TEACHING STRATEGY

READING THE CHAPTER

This is a thematic chapter focusing on the European immigrants, writers, reformers, abolitionists, and women who shaped the culture of the United States in the mid-1800s. As students read, have them consider the impact of each of these groups. Pause after each section to review the main idea of the section.

ALTERNATIVE ASSESSMENT

The Chapter Assessment describes three activities for alternative assessment on page 433. You may wish to have students work on these activities during the course of the chapter and then present them at the end.

1 The Hopes of Immigrants

MAIN IDEA

In the mid-1800s, millions of Europeans came to the United States hoping to build a better life.

WHY IT MATTERS NOW

These Germans, Irish, and Scandinavians had a strong influence on American culture.

TERMS & NAMES
emigrant
immigrant
steerage
push-pull factor
famine
prejudice
nativist

ONE AMERICAN'S STORY

In June 1831, Gjert Hovland (YEHRT HAHV•LIHND) and his family left Norway for America. After a few years, Hovland wrote to a friend in Norway. He boasted that in the United States a poor man's vote counted as much as a rich man's vote. Americans could travel and work freely. The United States had so much opportunity that Hovland wondered why anyone would choose to stay hungry in Norway.

A VOICE FROM THE PAST

It would greatly please me to learn that all of you who are in need and have little chance of supporting yourselves and your families have decided to leave Norway and come to America; for, even if many more come, there will still be room here for all. Those who are willing to work will not lack employment or business here.

Gjert Hovland, letter to Torjuls Maeland, April 22, 1835

Advertisements for land attracted immigrants, who came to the United States with only what could fit in trunks like the one shown above.

Millions of people like Hovland decided to become emigrants, or people who leave a country. Arriving in the United States, they became immigrants, or people who settle in a new country. This section explains how immigrants enriched the United States with their work and their cultures.

1 Why People Migrated

Most immigrants endured hardships to come to America. Although some, like Hovland, brought their families, many immigrant men came alone and suffered loneliness. Nearly all immigrants made the ocean voyage in **steerage,** the cheapest deck on a ship. In steerage, hundreds of people lived jammed together for ten days to a month. Conditions were filthy. Many passengers became ill or died on the journey.

Despite the hard passage, immigrants flocked to the United States during the mid-1800s. They came from Britain, Ireland, Germany, Scandinavia (Sweden, Denmark, and Norway), and China. Most came from Europe. What made them come to America? Historians talk about

SECTION OBJECTIVES

1. To identify push-pull factors of immigration
2. To summarize reasons for Scandinavian and German immigration and to identify areas where these immigrants settled
3. To describe the experiences of Irish immigrants in the United States
4. To analyze the effects of immigration on U.S. cities and on public opinion

SKILLBUILDER

Interpreting Maps: Place, Region, p. 409

CRITICAL THINKING

Solving Problems, p. 408
Making Inferences, p. 409
Drawing Conclusions, p. 410
Identifying Problems, p. 411
Analyzing Causes, p. 412

FOCUS & MOTIVATE

5-MINUTE WARM-UP

Making Inferences These questions focus on the reasons for immigration.

1. Look at the poster on page 407. What opportunity was being advertised?
2. Why do you suppose such appeals were attractive?

Warm-Up Transparency WT14

INSTRUCT

INSTRUCT: OBJECTIVE 1

Why People Migrated

- What factors pushed emigrants out of their native lands?
- What factors pulled immigrants to the United States?

In-Depth Resources: Unit 4
- Guided Reading, p. 43

Reading Study Guide (Spanish and English), pp. 133–134

RECOMMENDED RESOURCES

In-Depth Resources: Unit 4
- Guided Reading, p. 43
- Building Vocabulary, p. 47
- Skillbuilder Practice, p. 48

Reading Study Guide (Spanish and English), pp. 133–134

Economics in History
- Irish Immigration, p. 14

Outline Map Activities, pp. 27–28

Citizenship Today, pp. 9–10

Formal Assessment, Quiz, p. 253

Integrated Assessment
- Rubrics, 5.4, 5.1

Access for Students Acquiring English/ESL, pp. 90, 94

INTEGRATED TECHNOLOGY

Geography Transparency GT14
- Settlement of Germans and Irish, 1860

Electronic Teacher Tools

classzone.com

TEST-TAKING RESOURCES

Strategies for Test Preparation

Test Practice Transparencies, TT49

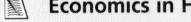

Online Test Practice

HISTORY FROM VISUALS

Reading Charts Help students visualize the concept of push-pull factors by demonstrating how an object, such as your desk or desk chair, can be moved across the floor by pushing, pulling, or by both. The combination creates the strongest force. Ask students whether they think many immigrants would have come to the United States if there had been few "push" factors in their home countries.
Possible Response It is possible that many would-be emigrants might have found leaving families, friends, and familiar lands and customs more difficult if they had not felt "pushed" to leave by other factors.

Extension Ask students which "pull" factors of the 1800s still draw new immigrants today. Have them identify new "pull" factors at work in today's society.

MORE ABOUT . . .

Population Growth
Europe's population nearly doubled between 1750 and 1850, from about 140 million to 265 million people. The growth rate in North America was even faster—from 5 million in 1750 to 39 million by 1850.

INSTRUCT: OBJECTIVE 2

Scandinavians Seek Land/ Germans Pursue Economic Opportunity

- Which of the push-pull factors had the greatest influence on Scandinavians and Germans?
- Where did many Scandinavians and Germans settle in this country?
- How did German immigrant influence American culture?

Geography Transparency GT14
• Settlement of Germans and Irish, 1860

Push–Pull Factors of Immigration

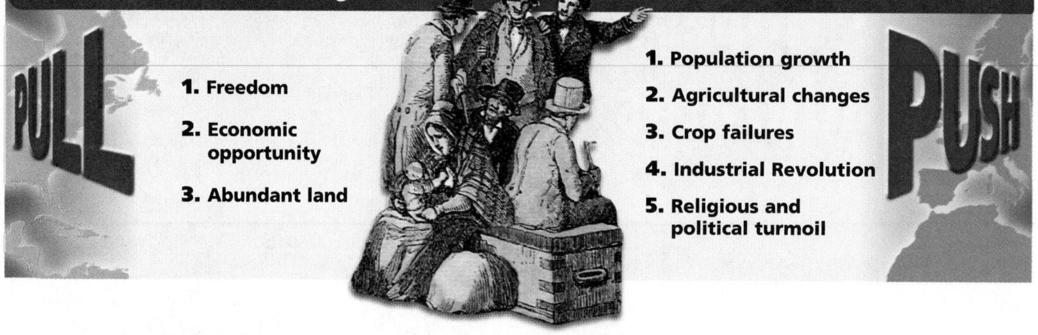

push-pull factors. These forces push people out of their native lands and pull them toward a new place. **Push factors** included the following:

1. **Population growth.** Better food and sanitation caused Europe's population to boom after 1750, and the land became overcrowded.
2. **Agricultural changes.** As Europe's population grew, so did cities. Landowners wanted to make money selling food to those cities. New methods made it more efficient to farm large areas of land than to rent small plots to tenants. So landlords forced tenants off the land.
3. **Crop failures.** Poor harvests made it difficult for small farmers to pay their debts. Some of these farmers chose to start over in America. Crop failures also led to hunger, causing people to emigrate.
4. **Industrial Revolution.** Goods produced in factories became cheaper than goods produced by artisans. Suddenly out of work, some artisans took factory jobs. Others emigrated.
5. **Religious and political turmoil.** To escape religious persecution, Quakers fled Norway and Jews left Germany. Also, many Germans came to America after a revolution in Germany failed in 1848.

Vocabulary
tenant: renter

Vocabulary
artisan: skilled worker

Immigrants chose the United States because of three main **pull factors**:

1. **Freedom.** As Gjert Hovland wrote, "Everyone has the freedom to practice the teaching and religion he prefers."
2. **Economic opportunity.** Immigrants sought a land where they could support their families and have a better future. Immigration often rose during times of U.S. prosperity and fell during hard times.
3. **Abundant land.** The acquisition of the Louisiana Purchase and the Mexican Cession gave the United States millions more acres of land. To land-starved Europeans, America was a land of opportunity.

***Reading* History**
A. Solving Problems Many of the push factors were problems. Which pull factors were solutions to which problems?
A. Possible Responses Freedom—religious and political turmoil; economic opportunity—Industrial Revolution; abundant land—population growth, crop failures, and agricultural changes.

2 Scandinavians Seek Land

Public land in America was sold for $1.25 an acre, which lured thousands of Scandinavians. At first, their governments tried to keep them at home. A Swedish law of 1768 restricted the right to emigrate. But growing poverty in Scandinavia caused officials to cancel this law in 1840.

Scandinavian clergymen also tried to halt the emigration. At first, they warned their church members against leaving the homeland. Eventually, though, the preachers realized their words had little effect. Some of them even went to America themselves.

ACTIVITY OPTIONS

INTERDISCIPLINARY LINK: GEOGRAPHY — BLOCK SCHEDULING

CREATING AN IMMIGRATION MAP

Class Time 30 minutes

Task Creating a map showing European immigration to the United States in the early and mid-1800s

Purpose To analyze and synthesize information about European immigration to the United States

Supplies Needed
- Textbook
- Art supplies
- Outline maps showing North America and Europe (optional)
- Research materials such as a historical statistical abstract (optional)

Activity Divide students into groups. Each group should create a map showing immigration from Scandinavia, Germany, or Ireland to the United States in the early and mid-1800s. The map may be an outline or hand-drawn map. Groups should identify areas from which immigrants came and areas where immigrants settled. The students may want to use arrows to show movement, concentration of immigrants, years, or a combination of information about immigration.

Reading **History**

B. Making Inferences Why do you think Scandinavians moved to places that felt familiar?

B. Possible Responses They knew how to farm in those climates; they thought they would be less homesick there.

In the United States, Scandinavians chose regions that felt familiar. Many settled in the Midwest, especially Minnesota and Wisconsin. These states had lakes, forests, and cold winters like their homelands. A high proportion of Scandinavian immigrants became farmers.

Germans Pursue Economic Opportunity

Like the Scandinavians, many Germans moved to the Midwest. Germans especially liked Wisconsin because the climate allowed them to grow their traditional crop of oats. Some moved to Milwaukee, Wisconsin, because the Catholic bishop there was German. (In the 1800s, German Christian immigrants included both Catholics and Protestants.)

Germans also settled in Texas. In New Braunfels, a group of German nobles bought land and sold it in parcels to German immigrants. The town had to survive poor harvests and conflicts with Native Americans, but it eventually prospered. Germans also founded Fredericksburg, Texas, which still retains its German culture today.

Immigrants from Germany settled in cities as well as on farms or the frontier. German artisans opened businesses as bakers, butchers, carpenters, printers, shoemakers, and tailors. Many German immigrants achieved great success. For instance, in 1853 John Jacob Bausch and Henry Lomb started a firm to make eyeglasses and other lenses. Their company became the world's largest lens maker.

Skillbuilder Answers
1. Massachusetts, Minnesota, New York, Rhode Island, Wisconsin
2. The South already had a cheap labor supply in slaves, so there might be fewer jobs for immigrants.

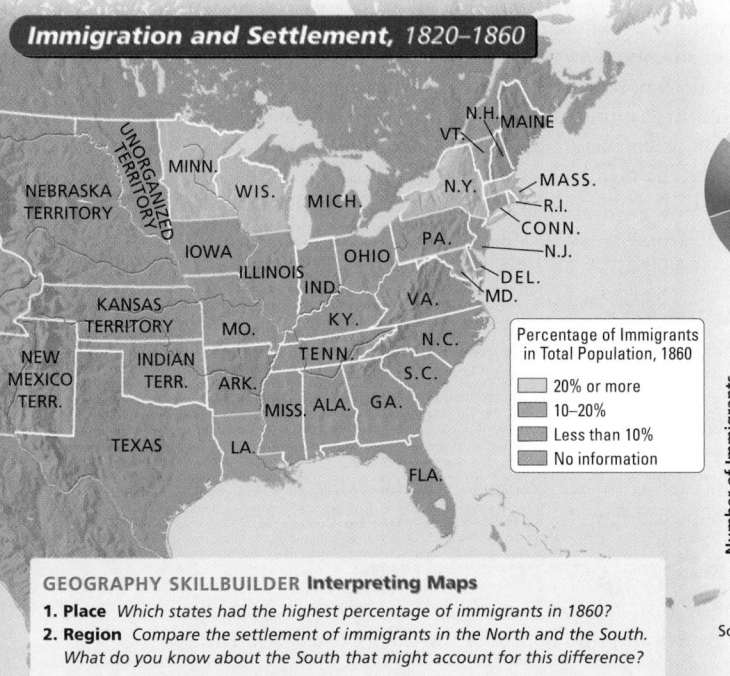

Immigration and Settlement, *1820–1860*

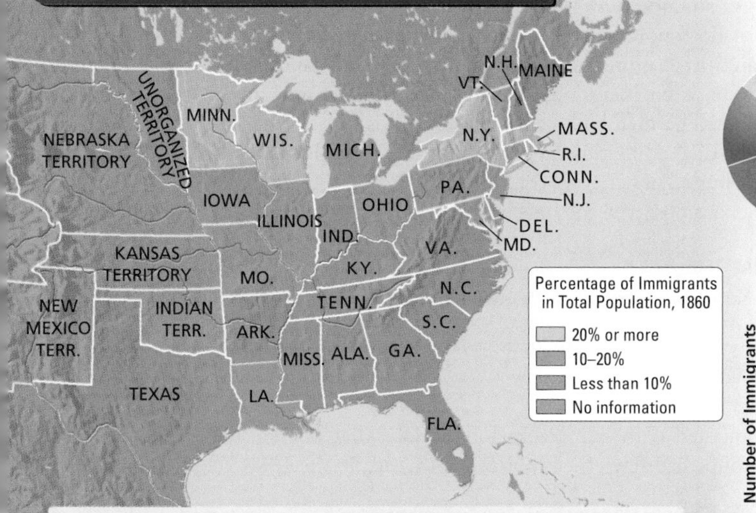

Sources of Immigration, *1820–1860*

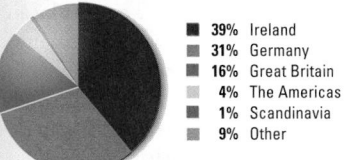

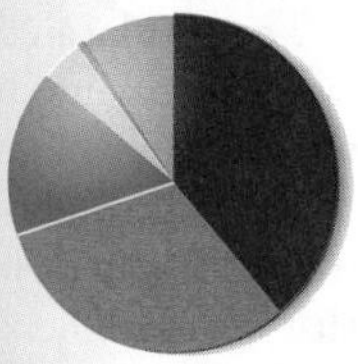

Immigration to the United States *(by decade)*

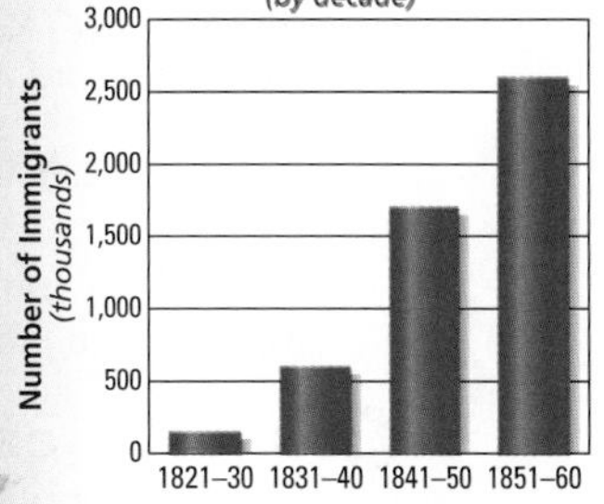

Source: *Historical Statistics of the United States*

GEOGRAPHY SKILLBUILDER Interpreting Maps
1. **Place** *Which states had the highest percentage of immigrants in 1860?*
2. **Region** *Compare the settlement of immigrants in the North and the South. What do you know about the South that might account for this difference?*

MORE ABOUT . . .

Scandinavian Immigrants

One of the best-known literary works about Scandinavian immigrants in the United States is *The Emigrants*, a four-volume epic published between 1949 and 1959 by Swedish author Vilhelm Moberg (1898–1973). The author weaves a story about the experiences of 16 Swedish emigrants who left their small community in Sweden, eventually settling in Minnesota in 1850. *Giants in the Earth* is a famous novel about Norwegian immigrants in the Dakota Territory by O. E. Rölvaag. Rölvaag was himself an emigrant from Norway, and he wrote his novel in Norwegian.

HISTORY FROM VISUALS

Reading the Map Point out that New York, Rhode Island, and Massachusetts had the highest percentage of immigrants of states on the East Coast. Ask the students which cities in those states would be ports of entry. Then ask why many immigrants might have settled there. **Possible Response** New York City and Boston; Immigrants lacked money to move farther west.

Extension Have students use almanacs and other classroom and library resources to identify other major points of entry for immigrants.

Reading the Graphs Copy the bar graph on the board. Place a dot at the top right corner of each bar. Then draw a line connecting the dots. Ask students what the line tells us about the trend in immigration during the period. **Answer** Immigration increased throughout the period but was fastest over the period from 1841 to 1850.

Extension Have students research immigration figures over the past 40 years. Have them note the trend and create pie graphs showing the sources of immigration over this most recent period.

ACTIVITY OPTIONS

SKILLBUILDER LESSON: INTERPRETING GRAPHS

BLOCK SCHEDULING

Explaining the Skill Graphs show statistical information visually. Pie graphs are useful to show relative sizes or proportions of related numbers. The circle represents a whole. The "pie slices" represent parts of the whole. Bar graphs compare numbers. They also can show changes over time.

Applying the Skill Ask students to identify the titles of the graphs. Then ask the following questions:

1. Which nation sent the highest percentage of immigrants to the United States from 1820 to 1860? *(Ireland)*
2. What percentage of immigrants did not come from Ireland, Germany, Great Britain, or Scandinavia? *(13 percent)*
3. In which decade did immigration to the United States increase the most? How much did it increase over the previous decade? *(1841–1850; more than 1 million)*

In-Depth Resources: Unit 4
- Skillbuilder Practice, p. 48

daily*life*

Immigrant Culture

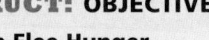

One cultural import that the Irish brought to the United States is the celebration of St. Patrick's Day on March 17. People throughout the United States observe the feast day of Ireland's patron saint, but the parades and other celebrations are largest in cities with significant Irish-American populations. Irish immigrants began the custom of parades on St. Patrick's Day as part of their fight for equal rights to jobs and fair wages. In Ireland, St. Patrick's Day is observed more quietly as a holy day of the Catholic religion. In the past 20 years, however, the day has become increasingly more festive.

INSTRUCT: OBJECTIVE 3

The Irish Flee Hunger

- What factors encouraged Irish immigration to the United States?
- Why did the Irish settle primarily in cities?
- What kinds of work did Irish immigrants find?

Economics in History
- Irish Immigration, p. 14

INSTRUCT: OBJECTIVE 4

U.S. Cities Face Overcrowding/ Some Americans Oppose Immigration

- What were some results of overcrowding in U.S. cities in the early and mid-1800s?
- Why did some native-born Americans oppose immigration?
- What role did the Know-Nothings play in the debate over immigration?

Outline Map Activities
- Immigration, Mid-1800s, pp. 27–28

daily*life*

IMMIGRANT CULTURE

To maintain their culture, immigrants continued many of their traditional activities in the United States. For example, German culture is rich in music. German immigrants put together marching bands, symphony orchestras, and choruses.

In Ireland, many of the Irish had poured their energy into defying the British. This gave them experience with political organization. As a result, Irish immigrants became active in U.S. politics, especially in the cities.

Some German immigrants were Jews. Many of them worked as traveling salespeople. They brought pins, needles, pots—and news—to frontier homes and mining camps. In time, some opened their own general stores. Other Jews settled in cities, where many found success. For example, Alexander Rothschild worked as a grocer upon arriving in Hartford, Connecticut, in the 1840s. By 1851, he ran a popular hotel.

The Germans were the largest immigrant group of the 1800s and strongly influenced American culture. Many things we think of as originating in America came from Germany—the Christmas tree, gymnasiums, kindergartens, and the hamburger and frankfurter.

Background The hamburger and frankfurter are named after the German cities Hamburg and Frankfurt am Main.

3 The Irish Flee Hunger

Most Irish immigrants were Catholic. Protestant Britain had ruled Ireland for centuries—and controlled the Catholic majority by denying them rights. Irish Catholics could not vote, hold office, own land, or go to school. Because of the poverty produced by Britain's rule, some Irish came to America in the early 1800s.

Then, in 1845, a disease attacked Ireland's main food crop, the potato, causing a severe food shortage called a **famine.** The Irish Potato Famine killed 1 million people and forced many to emigrate. By 1854, between 1.5 and 2 million Irish had fled their homeland.

In America, Irish farmers became city-dwellers. Arriving with little or no savings, many of these immigrants had to settle in the port cities where their ships had docked. By 1850, the Irish made up one-fourth of the population of Boston, New York, Philadelphia, and Baltimore.

The uneducated Irish immigrants arrived with few skills and had to take low-paying, back-breaking jobs. Irish women took in washing or worked as servants. The men built canals and railroads across America. So many Irishmen died doing this dangerous work that people said there was "an Irishman buried under every [railroad] tie." In 1841, British novelist Charles Dickens observed the huts in which railroad workers lived.

ReadingHistory
C. Drawing Conclusions How did the effects of British rule make it hard for Irish immigrants to America to find good jobs?
C. Possible Response Because the British made it illegal for the Irish to go to school, they had few skills when they came to America.

A VOICE FROM THE PAST

The best were poor protection from the weather; the worst let in the wind and rain through the wide breaches in the roofs of sodden grass and in the walls of mud; some had neither door nor window; some had nearly fallen down.

Charles Dickens, quoted in *To Seek America*

The Irish competed with free blacks for the jobs that nobody else wanted. Both groups had few other choices in America in the 1800s.

4 U.S. Cities Face Overcrowding

Immigrants like the Irish and Germans flocked to American cities. So did native-born Americans, who hoped for the chance to make a better

ACTIVITY OPTIONS

INDIVIDUAL NEEDS: GIFTED AND TALENTED

COMMUNITY-LEVEL IMMIGRATION

Class Time Three class periods

Task Creating a series of pie graphs showing sources of immigration to your community since 1820

Purpose To use a variety of sources to research immigration data

Supplies Needed
- Reference sources such as almanacs, encyclopedias, and specialized local library holdings
- Internet access

Activity Have students do research about the origins of immigrants to your community since 1820. Direct students to print resources such as encyclopedias, almanacs, the Internet, and specialized references in the local library. If your community has a historical society, suggest that students inquire there for information. Tell students to prepare a series of pie graphs showing the major countries of origin for immigrants to your community for the periods 1820–1860, 1860–1900, 1900–1940, 1940–1980, 1980–present.

living. Between 1800 and 1830, New York's population jumped from 60,489 to 202,589. St. Louis doubled its population every nine years. Cincinnati grew even faster, doubling every seven years.

Rapid urban growth brought problems. Not enough housing existed for all the newcomers. Greedy landlords profited from the housing shortage by squeezing large apartment buildings onto small lots. Using every inch of space for rooms, these cramped living quarters lacked sunlight and fresh air. Their outdoor toilets overflowed, spreading disease. In such depressing urban neighborhoods, crime flourished.

American cities were unprepared to tackle these problems. In fact, before 1845, New York City had no public police force. Until the 1860s, it had only a volunteer fire department. And in 1857, the rapidly growing city had only 138 miles of sewers for 500 miles of streets.

Most immigrant groups set up aid societies to help newcomers from their country. Many city politicians also offered to assist immigrants in exchange for votes. The politicians set up organizations to help new arrivals find housing and work.

D. Possible Responses the problem of immigrants finding housing and work, and the problem of getting themselves (the politicians) elected

Reading **History**
D. Identifying Problems What problems were politicians trying to solve by offering to help new immigrants?

Some Americans Oppose Immigration

Some native-born Americans feared that immigrants were too foreign to learn American ways. Others feared that immigrants might come to outnumber natives. As a result, immigrants faced anger and prejudice. **Prejudice** is a negative opinion that is not based on facts. For example,

CITIZENSHIP TODAY

Becoming a Citizen

Most immigrants who came to America in the 1800s shared one thing: an appreciation for the nation's values and laws. As a result, many chose to become U.S. citizens.

This trend continues today. In recent decades, more than half a million Vietnamese have immigrated to the United States. Many became citizens of their new country. One of them was Lam Ton, who is a successful restaurant owner in Chicago. Ton viewed U.S. citizenship as both a privilege and a duty. "We have to stick to this country and help it do better," he said.

Each year, immigrants from around the world are sworn in as U.S. citizens on Citizenship Day, September 17. But first they must pass a test on English, the U.S. political system, and the rights and duties of citizenship.

This young immigrant proudly holds up his certificate of citizenship.

How Does Someone Become a Citizen?

1. In a small group, discuss what questions you would ask those seeking to become U.S. citizens.
2. Create a citizenship test using your questions.
3. Have another group take the test and record their scores.
4. Use the McDougal Littell Internet site to link to the actual U.S. citizenship test. Compare it to your test.

See Citizenship Handbook, page 265.

For more about becoming a U.S. citizen . . .

RESEARCH LINKS
CLASSZONE.COM

CRITICAL THINKING ACTIVITY

Comparing and Contrasting Have students use a chart such as the one below to compare and contrast the experiences of Scandinavian, German, and Irish immigrants in the early and mid-1800s.

Immigrant Groups	Reasons for Emigrating	Where They Settled	Kind of Work
Scandinavian			
German			
Irish			

Class Time 30–45 minutes

CITIZENSHIP TODAY

OBJECTIVE

Students will be able to explain why it is important that immigrants learn and understand this nation's values and laws before becoming citizens.

Becoming a Citizen

As more and more businesses operate internationally, the number of people who have dual citizenship has increased. For example, a baby born to American parents while they are living in another country is an American citizen. But the baby may also be a citizen of the country where he or she was born.

The Supreme Court has ruled that a person cannot be stripped of his or her U.S. citizenship—even for deserting in wartime. The Court's decision means that almost the only way to lose citizenship is to renounce it voluntarily.

Citizenship Today, pp. 9–10

STANDARDS FOR EVALUATION: CITIZENSHIP TODAY

Each citizenship test should

- allow the test taker to demonstrate understanding of the U.S. political system and the rights and duties of citizenship.
- include clear, focused questions.
- include a key to the correct answers for test questions.
- use correct grammar, usage, capitalization, punctuation, and spelling.

In 1844, a riot took place between Catholics and non-Catholics in Philadelphia. Several people were killed.

some Protestants in the 1800s believed that Catholics threatened democracy. Those Protestants feared that the Pope, the head of the Roman Catholic Church, was plotting to overthrow democracy in America.

Native-born Americans who wanted to eliminate foreign influence called themselves **nativists.** Some nativists refused to hire immigrants and put up signs like "No Irish need apply." In cities like New York and Boston, nativists formed a secret society. Members promised not to vote for any Catholics or immigrants running for political office. If asked about their secret group, they said, "I know nothing about it."

Background
Protestants feared the Pope because in many European countries, the Catholic Church worked closely with the ruling monarchs.

In the 1850s, nativists started a political party. Because of the members' answers to questions about their party, it was called the Know-Nothing Party. It wanted to ban Catholics and the foreign-born from holding office. It also called for a cut in immigration and a 21-year wait to become an American citizen. The Know-Nothings did elect six governors. But they disappeared quickly as a national party. Their northern and southern branches couldn't agree on the issue of slavery.

In spite of such barriers as prejudice, the immigrants of the 1800s had a strong impact on American culture. Writers and artists of the 1800s also shaped American culture. Section 2 discusses their influence.

Section 1 Assessment

1. Terms & Names

Explain the significance of:
- emigrant
- immigrant
- steerage
- push-pull factor
- famine
- prejudice
- nativist

2. Taking Notes

Use a cluster diagram like the one below to record details about immigration, such as which groups came, where they settled, and how they influenced America.

3. Main Ideas

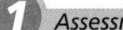

a. What were the push-pull factors that led to immigration?

b. How did the arrival of so many immigrants affect U.S. cities?

c. What was the Know-Nothing Party, and what was its point of view about immigration?

4. Critical Thinking

Analyzing Causes How did the rapid increase in immigration cause conflict?

THINK ABOUT
- why Irish immigrants and free blacks competed for jobs
- the growth of cities and the problems it created
- the prejudices of nativists
- religious differences

ACTIVITY OPTIONS

TECHNOLOGY
ART

Plan a **multimedia presentation** or design a **Web page** that shows immigrants the advantages of settling in the United States.

MORE ABOUT . . .

The Know-Nothing Party
Also called the American Party, the Know-Nothing Party reached its height of national power in 1855, when it had 43 members in Congress. In 1856, the American Party nominated Millard Fillmore for president. As the American Party's nominee, Fillmore carried only one state, Maryland.

ASSESS & RETEACH

Setting the Stage Have students fill in the first row on the graphic organizer.

Formal Assessment
- Section Quiz, p. 253

Critical Thinking Transparency CT40
- Setting the Stage

RETEACHING ACTIVITY

Have students write a summary paragraph that uses the section's Main Idea as the topic sentence: "In the mid-1800s, millions of Europeans came to the United States hoping to build a better life." Student paragraphs should identify the origin of immigrants, briefly explain why they came, and note the effects of their immigration on this country's cities and on public opinion.

In-Depth Resources: Unit 4
- Reteaching Activity, p. 56

Section 1 Assessment

1. Terms & Names

emigrant, p. 407
immigrant, p. 407
steerage, p. 407
push-pull factors, p. 408
famine, p. 410
prejudice, p. 411
nativist, p. 412

2. Taking Notes

Scandinavians, Germans, Irish; Scandinavians settled on farms, in the northern Midwest; Germans settled in cities and farms on the frontier; Irish settled in port cities. Influences include German kindergartens, gymnasiums, musical groups, and food; Irish labor and political activity.

3. Main Ideas

a. pull factors: desire for freedom, economic opportunity, land; push factors: population growth, crop failures, religious and political turmoil **b.** Cities grew rapidly, leading to overcrowding, disease, and crime. **c.** a political party; cut immigration to reduce the influence of foreigners

4. Critical Thinking

Irish competed with blacks for jobs; overcrowding of neighborhoods increased crime; discrimination led to riots.

ACTIVITY OPTIONS

Integrated Assessment
- Rubrics for multimedia presentation, 5.4
- Rubrics for a Web page, 5.1

2 American Literature and Art

TERMS & NAMES
romanticism
Hudson River school
transcendentalism
civil disobedience

MAIN IDEA	WHY IT MATTERS NOW
Inspired by nature and democratic ideals, writers and artists produced some of America's greatest works.	Nineteenth-century writers such as Hawthorne and Thoreau laid the foundation for American literature.

ONE AMERICAN'S STORY

As a young man, Washington Irving published articles that made fun of society in the early 1800s. Although he studied to be a lawyer, he eventually made writing his full-time career.

Irving wrote some of the first stories to describe America. For example, "Rip Van Winkle" tells of a man in New York State. Rip wakes up after a 20-year nap to find everything changed. He goes to the inn, which once had a picture of King George on its sign.

A VOICE FROM THE PAST

> The red coat was changed for one of blue and buff, a sword was held in the hand instead of a sceptre [staff of authority], the head was decorated with a cocked hat, and underneath was painted in large characters, GENERAL WASHINGTON.
>
> **Washington Irving,** "Rip Van Winkle"

While Rip slept, the Americans had fought and won their revolution!

Irving's work helped to win European respect for American writing for the first time. This section discusses other individuals of the 1800s who created uniquely American literature and art.

In another Irving tale, "The Legend of Sleepy Hollow," a spooky creature—perhaps a ghost from the Revolution—chases a teacher.

1 Writing About America

Irving and other writers were influenced by a style of European art called **romanticism**. It stressed the individual, imagination, creativity, and emotion. It drew inspiration from nature. American writers turned their interest in nature into a celebration of the American wilderness.

Many books featured the wilderness. James Fenimore Cooper wrote five novels about the dramatic adventures of wilderness scout Natty Bumppo. One that remains popular is *The Last of the Mohicans.* Francis Parkman wrote a travel book, *The Oregon Trail,* about the frontier trail.

SECTION OBJECTIVES

1. To analyze how writers and artists celebrated the American wilderness
2. To explain the influence of transcendentalism on American writing
3. To analyze how writers shaped American literature

CRITICAL THINKING

Making Inferences, p. 415
Recognizing Effects, p. 416
Evaluating, p. 416

FOCUS & MOTIVATE

5-MINUTE WARM-UP

Making Inferences These questions explore the influence of this country's natural environment on American artists.

1. Look at the painting on page 414. What is the focus of the painting?
2. What can you learn about the artist from the painting?

Warm-Up Transparency WT14

INSTRUCT

INSTRUCT: OBJECTIVE 1

Writing About America/ Creating American Art

- How did romanticism influence the creation of an American style in literature and art?
- How did Noah Webster contribute to a developing American style of writing?
- How did enslaved African Americans contribute to American art?

In-Depth Resources: Unit 4
- Guided Reading, p. 44
- Building Vocabulary, p. 47

Reading Study Guide (Spanish and English), pp. 135–136

RECOMMENDED RESOURCES

In-Depth Resources: Unit 4
- Guided Reading, p. 44
- Building Vocabulary, p. 47

Reading Study Guide (Spanish and English), pp. 135–136

Formal Assessment
- Section Quiz, p. 254

Integrated Assessment
- Rubrics, 1.3, 5.3

Access for Students Acquiring English/ESL
- Guided Reading, p. 91

INTEGRATED TECHNOLOGY

Humanities Transparency HT27
- Bird of Washington

Electronic Teacher Tools

classzone.com

TEST-TAKING RESOURCES

Strategies for Test Preparation

Test Practice Transparencies, TT50

Online Test Practice

HISTORY through ART

Interpreting the Painting Thomas Cole was the first of the Hudson River painters. He spent weeks at a time walking and sketching in the Catskill Mountains, the White Mountains, and other wilderness areas. Asher Durand traveled with Cole in the Catskills. Before he died, Cole lamented that the wilderness was disappearing: "They are cutting down all the trees in the beautiful valley on which I have looked so often with a loving eye. . . ." Durand's painting was commissioned as a tribute to Cole by a wealthy patron who was inspired by Bryant's eulogy for the painter.

Possible Responses: lighter tones, subject is more nature than people, feeling is more of pleasure than work

MORE ABOUT . . .

Noah Webster

Noah Webster (1758–1843) recorded uniquely American words such as *skunk, hickory,* and *chowder.* He also advocated revising the spelling of some words, changing, for example, *musik* to *music* and *plough to plow.* It is because of Webster that Americans write *honor* not *honour,* and *theater* and *center* instead of *theatre* and *centre.*

MORE ABOUT . . .

American Arts and Artists

While the Hudson River school focused on the grandeurs of the landscape, other artists in the 1830s and 1840s depicted the daily life of ordinary people. Such paintings of farmers, fur traders, sailors, and storekeepers fit with the spirit of Jacksonian democracy. Engraved copies of these paintings—far less expensive than originals—allowed many Americans to decorate their homes with images of their nation and its people.

Humanities Transparency HT27
- Bird of Washington

HISTORY through ART

Asher Durand was a founder of the Hudson River school of painting. His best-known work, *Kindred Spirits,* was painted in 1849. This romantic work shows two artists inspired by a beautiful landscape. The figures in the painting are Durand's friends, the poet William Cullen Bryant and the painter Thomas Cole.

Compare this painting to the one on page 164. What, if any, change in style can you see in Durand's painting?

In addition, writers began to use a more American style. A teacher and lawyer named Noah Webster gave guidelines to that style in his *American Dictionary of the English Language.* Webster first published his dictionary in 1828. He later revised it in 1840. The dictionary gave American, not British, spellings and included American slang.

Other writers besides Irving celebrated America's past. Henry Wadsworth Longfellow wrote many poems that retold stories from history. For example, "Paul Revere's Ride" depicted the Revolutionary hero's ride to warn of a British attack. Generations of students memorized lines from the poem, such as, "One if by land, and two if by sea; / And I on the opposite shore will be."

Creating American Art

European styles continued to influence American artists, but some took these styles in new directions. One group of painters influenced by romanticism worked near the Hudson River in New York State. **Hudson River school** artists painted lush natural landscapes. Several members of this school went west for a change of scenery. For example, Albert Bierstadt took several trips to America's mountainous West. He produced huge paintings that convey the majesty of the American landscape. (See page 294.)

ACTIVITY OPTIONS

INDIVIDUAL NEEDS

LESS PROFICIENT READERS

Categorizing To help students understand how the art and literature discussed in the section reflect this period in history, copy the chart on the board before students begin to read. As you read the section with students, discuss each term. Have the students write a definition or description of the term in the first box. Ask students to supply names of writers or artists associated with each word or phrase and add them to the chart under the correct heading. At the end of the section, ask students to quiz each other on the terms.

Romanticism	Hudson River School	Fireside Poets	Transcendentalism

Background The National Audubon Society, whose goal is the protection of wildlife today, is named for John James Audubon.

Other artists also went west. John James Audubon came to the United States from France at age 18. Traveling across the continent, Audubon sketched the birds and animals of his adopted country.

Enslaved African Americans also contributed to American art. They made beautiful baskets, quilts, and pottery. Most of these slaves remained anonymous, but one did not. David Drake worked in a South Carolina pottery factory and signed the pottery he created. He was the only factory worker to do so.

2 Following One's Conscience

By the 1840s, Americans took new pride in their emerging culture. Ralph Waldo Emerson, a New England writer, encouraged this pride. He urged Americans to cast off European influence and develop their own beliefs. His advice was to learn about life from self-examination and from nature as well as books.

> "No law can be sacred to me but that of my nature."
> Ralph Waldo Emerson

Emerson's student, Henry David Thoreau, followed that advice. In 1845, Thoreau moved to a simple cabin he had built by Walden Pond near the town of Concord, Massachusetts. Thoreau furnished it with only a bed, a table, a desk, and three chairs. He wrote about his life in the woods in *Walden.* Thoreau said that people should live by their own individual standards.

***Reading*History**
A. Making Inferences What do you think it means to "hear a different drummer"?
A. Possible Response to have different opinions or ideas than other people

A VOICE FROM THE PAST

If a man does not keep pace with his companions, perhaps it is because he hears a different drummer. Let him step to the music which he hears, however measured or far away.

Henry David Thoreau, *Walden*

Emerson and Thoreau belonged to a group of thinkers with a new philosophy called **transcendentalism.** It taught that the spiritual world is more important than the physical world. It also taught that people can find the truth within themselves—through feeling and intuition.

Because Thoreau believed in the importance of individual conscience, he urged people not to obey laws they considered unjust. Instead of protesting with violence, they should peacefully refuse to obey those laws. This form of protest is called **civil disobedience.** For example, Thoreau did not want to support the U.S. government, which allowed slavery and fought the War with Mexico. Instead of paying taxes that helped to finance the war, Thoreau went to jail.

Another New England transcendentalist, Margaret Fuller, also called for change. In her magazine, *The Dial,* and in her book, *Woman in the Nineteenth Century,* Fuller argued for women's rights.

Connections TO LITERATURE

"CIVIL DISOBEDIENCE"

In his essay "Civil Disobedience," Thoreau wrote that "Under a government which imprisons any unjustly the true place for a just man is also a prison."

Thoreau did land in prison when he refused to pay his taxes. According to legend, Emerson visited Thoreau in jail and asked, "Why are you here?" Thoreau replied, "Why are you not here?"

In the 20th century, Mohandas K. Gandhi of India and Martin Luther King, Jr., of the United States both used civil disobedience to fight injustice.

INSTRUCT: OBJECTIVE 2

Following One's Conscience

- How did the fireside poets popularize American poetry?
- How did Ralph Waldo Emerson and Henry David Thoreau put the philosophy of transcendentalism into practice?

MORE ABOUT . . .

Ralph Waldo Emerson

"The only way to have a friend is to be one." "Hitch your wagon to a star." "Nothing great was ever achieved without enthusiasm." "The reward of a thing well done, is to have done it." These lines from Ralph Waldo Emerson's essays became well-known sayings to later generations of Americans. Emerson advocated nonconformity, self-reliance, and independent thought.

Connections TO *LITERATURE*

"Civil Disobedience"

The unpaid tax that sent Thoreau to jail was a poll tax of $2.00, and he spent one night in jail. Thoreau's nonconformity started early. At Harvard, he flouted the rule requiring students to wear black coats by wearing a green one. In addition to lecturing and writing against slavery, Thoreau also aided African Americans fleeing from slavery along the Underground Railroad.

ACTIVITY OPTIONS

INTERDISCIPLINARY LINK: ART — BLOCK SCHEDULING

CREATING POSTERS

Class Time One class period

Task Creating posters advertising events and individuals featured at an American culture fair in 1850

Purpose To synthesize information about American literature and art in the first half of the 1800s

Supplies Needed
- Poster paper or large sheets of plain paper
- Art supplies
- Textbook

Activity Have students imagine that they are in charge of publicity for a three-day American Culture Fair in 1850. The fair features presentations by poets, writers of fiction and nonfiction, and artists. Students should create posters advertising the fair. Posters should highlight at least one individual who will present his or her work, including biographical information and descriptions or samples of his or her work. Display completed posters.

INSTRUCT: OBJECTIVE 3

Exploring the Human Heart

- How did poets such as Walt Whitman and Emily Dickinson influence American poetry in the early and mid-1800s?
- Which fiction writers helped shape American literature?

STRANGE *but* True

Gifts on Poe's Grave

Poe was originally buried in an unmarked grave in 1849. An attempt to mark the grave in 1860 failed when Poe's stone monument was destroyed in a bizarre accident in which a train jumped the tracks and slammed into the yard where the monument had been created. Poe's remains were moved in 1875 to another spot in the cemetery, where family, friends, and admirers erected a new monument. Still, strange rumors have persisted that Poe's remains were never moved in 1875 and still lie somewhere in an unmarked grave nearby. In death, it seems, Poe remains for some a source of mystery.

ASSESS & RETEACH

Setting the Stage Have students fill in the second row on the graphic organizer.

Formal Assessment
- Section Quiz, p. 254

RETEACHING ACTIVITY

Have students create flash cards using index cards or 3" x 5" sheets of paper. On each card or paper, students should write the name of one writer, poet, or artist from this section. On the back, students should describe the significance or accomplishment of that individual. When they have completed their set of cards, students can use them to quiz each other about material in the section.

In-Depth Resources: Unit 4
- Reteaching Activity, p. 57

STRANGE *but* True

GIFTS ON POE'S GRAVE

Every year a mysterious figure dressed in black celebrates Edgar Allan Poe's birthday. He leaves three roses on the author's Baltimore grave at 3:00 A.M.

The puzzling tradition began in 1949, exactly 100 years after Poe's death. In 1993, a new black-coated visitor took over the tradition. The person who began the ritual was ill—and later died in 1999.

Although many witnesses watch the ritual each year, none ask the visitor his name. Poe's fans have always liked mysteries.

3 Exploring the Human Heart

Like Thoreau, other writers broke with tradition. In 1855, poet Walt Whitman published *Leaves of Grass,* a book that changed American poetry. His bold, unrhymed poems praised ordinary people. Emily Dickinson lived in her family's home almost her entire life. She wrote poems on small pieces of paper that she sewed into booklets. Her subjects include God, nature, love, and death. Most of her 1,775 poems were published only after her death. Both Whitman and Dickinson shaped modern poetry by experimenting with language.

Fiction writers of the 1800s also shaped American literature. Edgar Allan Poe wrote terrifying tales that influence today's horror story writers. He also wrote the first detective story, "The Murders in the Rue Morgue."

Nathaniel Hawthorne depicted love, guilt, and revenge during Puritan times in *The Scarlet Letter.* The novel shows that harsh judgment without mercy can lead to tragedy. Hawthorne may have learned that lesson from his family history. One of his ancestors condemned people at the Salem witchcraft trials.

Herman Melville won fame by writing thrilling novels about his experiences as a sailor. In 1851, Melville published his masterpiece, *Moby Dick.* This novel tells about a man's destructive desire to kill a white whale. Although the novel was not popular when it was published, it is widely read now. Several movie versions exist.

These fiction writers portrayed the harmful effects of cruel actions. Other people thought that individuals could alter society for good. Section 3 describes those reformers.

***Reading*History**

B. Recognizing Effects How did Poe influence the fiction that people read today?

B. Possible Response by influencing horror stories and inventing the detective story

Section 2 *Assessment*

1. Terms & Names

Explain the significance of:
- romanticism
- Hudson River school
- transcendentalism
- civil disobedience

2. Taking Notes

Use a chart like the one below to list important individual writers and artists. For each one, name or describe one of his or her works.

Writer or artist	His or her work

Which one would you like to learn more about? Why?

3. Main Ideas

a. What was romanticism and how did Americans adapt it?

b. What is civil disobedience and what did Thoreau do that is an example of it?

c. How did the writers of the mid-1800s shape modern literature?

4. Critical Thinking

Evaluating Why do you think the literature and art of the mid-1800s are still valued?

THINK ABOUT
- the way they feature U.S. history and culture
- their universal themes—themes that relate to all people in all time periods
- the way they reflect changes happening at that time

ACTIVITY OPTIONS

ART / TECHNOLOGY Choose an American painting, sketch it, and make it into a **jigsaw puzzle;** or make an **audio recording** of a museum guide's description of it.

Section 2 *Assessment*

1. Terms & Names

romanticism, p. 413
Hudson River school, p. 414
transcendentalism, p. 415
civil disobedience, p. 415

2. Taking Notes

Washington Irving: "Rip Van Winkle"; James Fenimore Cooper: *The Last of the Mohicans;* Henry David Thoreau: *Walden;* Margaret Fuller: *Woman in the Nineteenth Century;* Emily Dickinson: poems about God, nature, love, and death. Answers will vary. Encourage students to read more by the author they chose.

3. Main Ideas

a. an art style that stressed the individual, imagination, creativity, and emotion; by celebrating the American wilderness **b.** a peaceful protest in which people refuse to obey laws they consider unjust; he refused to pay taxes **c.** writing that used American dialect; poetry that praised ordinary people; new types of horror

4. Critical Thinking

Students may choose the portrayal of historical events or the universal themes of love, God, death, nature, guilt, and revenge.

ACTIVITY OPTIONS

Integrated Assessment
- Rubrics for an illustration, 1.3
- Rubrics for an audio presentation, 5.3

3 Reforming American Society

MAIN IDEA

In the mid-1800s, several reform movements worked to improve American education and society.

WHY IT MATTERS NOW

Several laws and institutions, such as public schools, date back to this period.

TERMS & NAMES
revival
Second Great Awakening
temperance movement
labor union
strike
Horace Mann
Dorothea Dix

ONE AMERICAN'S STORY

Anne Newport Royall was a travel writer. In her 1830 book *Letters from Alabama,* Royall recorded America's growing interest in religion. She also described hearing a preacher at a Tennessee revival, or meeting to reawaken religious faith.

A VOICE FROM THE PAST

His text was, "He that hath ears to hear, let him hear." The people must have been deaf indeed that could not have heard him. . . . He began low but soon bawled to deafening. He spit in his hands, rubbed them against each other, and then would smite them together, till he made the woods ring.

Anne Newport Royall, *Letters from Alabama*

This revival meeting took place during the Second Great Awakening—a rebirth of religious faith named after the Great Awakening of the 1700s.

Some preachers, like the one Royall saw, were circuit riders. A circuit rider rode from town to town, often holding his meetings in a tent. The preacher gave a sermon urging individuals to give up their sins. This section explains how, in the mid-1800s, many individuals called on Americans to reform, or to improve themselves and their society.

1 A Spirit of Revival

The renewal of religious faith in the 1790s and early 1800s is called the **Second Great Awakening.** Revivalist preachers said that anyone could choose salvation. This appealed to equality-loving Americans. Revivals spread quickly across the frontier. Settlers eagerly awaited the visits of preachers like Peter Cartwright. At the age of 16, Cartwright had given up a life of gambling and joined a Methodist Church. He became a minister and spent more than 60 years preaching on the frontier.

The revival also traveled to Eastern cities. There, former lawyer Charles Grandison Finney held large revival meetings. He preached that "all sin consists in selfishness" and that religious faith led people to help others. Such teaching helped awaken a spirit of reform. Americans began to believe that they could act to make things better.

SECTION OBJECTIVES

1. To describe the spirit of reform of the early and mid-1800s
2. To evaluate the impact of the early labor movement
3. To describe efforts to improve education and to care for the needy
4. To describe the growth of print media and the utopian movement

CRITICAL THINKING

Evaluating, p. 418
Making Inferences, p. 419
Recognizing Effects, pp. 420, 421
Forming and Supporting Opinions, p. 421

FOCUS & MOTIVATE

5-MINUTE WARM-UP

Making Inferences The following questions focus on the goals of the temperance movement.

1. Study the poster on page 418. What pledge are readers asked to take?
2. What reward does the poster's picture suggest for temperance?

Warm-Up Transparency WT14

INSTRUCT

INSTRUCT: OBJECTIVE 1

A Spirit of Revival/Temperance Societies

- How did the Second Great Awakening foster a spirit of reform?
- Why did many women join the temperance movement?
- How successful was the temperance movement?

In-Depth Resources: Unit 4
- Guided Reading, p. 45

Reading Study Guide (Spanish and English), pp. 137–138

RECOMMENDED RESOURCES

In-Depth Resources: Unit 4
- Guided Reading, p. 45
- Building Vocabulary, p. 47
- Enrichment Activity, p. 60

Reading Study Guide (Spanish and English), pp. 137–138

Formal Assessment
- Section Quiz, p. 255

Integrated Assessment
- Rubrics, 3.6, 4.3

Access for Students Acquiring English/ESL
- Guided Reading, p. 92

INTEGRATED TECHNOLOGY

Critical Thinking Trans. CT41
- Cause and Effect: The Reform Movement

Electronic Teacher Tools

classzone.com

TEST-TAKING RESOURCES

Strategies for Test Preparation

Test Practice Transparencies, TT51

Online Test Practice

MORE ABOUT . . .

Contemporary Reform Movements
Various organizations today work for laws designed to prevent drunk driving and to keep alcohol out of the hands of minors. Among those organizations are Mothers Against Drunk Driving (MADD) and Students Against Destructive Decisions (SADD) (formerly Students Against Drunk Driving). SADD asks young adults to sign a Contract for Life, in which the signer pledges to avoid using alcohol and drugs.

Critical Thinking Transparency CT41
- Cause and Effect: The Reform Movement

INSTRUCT: OBJECTIVE 2
Fighting for Workers' Rights

- What were the goals of people who fought for workers' rights?
- How did government and private organizations work for better schools?

MORE ABOUT . . .

Strikes in the New England Mills
When employers in the 1830s and 1840s cut wages, workers felt that their independence was threatened as well as their pay. Striking workers often compared themselves to the American Patriots during the Revolutionary War, 60 years earlier. They called the factory owners "Tories in disguise" and reprinted the Declaration of Independence. One group of workers began their strike on Washington's birthday. The women of the Lowell mills noted that they were "daughters of freemen" whose ancestors had fought British tyranny.

Temperance pledges often displayed inspiring pictures and mottoes.

Temperance Societies

Led by churches, some Americans began the **temperance movement,** which is a campaign to stop the drinking of alcohol. Heavy drinking was common in the early 1800s. Some workers spent most of their wages on alcohol—leaving their families without enough money to live on. As a result, many women joined the temperance movement. "There is no reform in which women can act better or more appropriately than temperance," said Mary C. Vaughan.

Some temperance workers handed out pamphlets urging people to stop drinking. Others produced dramas, such as one entitled *The Drunkard,* to dramatize the evils of alcohol. In addition, temperance speakers traveled widely, asking people to sign a pledge to give up alcohol. By 1838, a million people had signed.

A. Possible Response The temperance movement inspired dramas that addressed issues of drunkenness and temperance.

Reading **History**
A. Evaluating How did the temperance movement affect the development of drama?

Temperance also won the support of business owners. Industry needed workers who could keep schedules and run machines. Alcohol made it hard for workers to do either. New England businessman Neal Dow led the fight to make it illegal to sell alcohol. In 1851, Maine banned the sale of liquor. By 1855, 13 other states passed similar laws. But many people opposed these laws, and most were repealed. Still, the movement to ban alcohol remained strong, even into the 20th century.

Vocabulary
repeal: to cancel

2 Fighting for Workers' Rights

As business owners tried to improve workers' habits, workers called for improvements in working conditions. Factory work was noisy, boring, and unsafe. In the 1830s, American workers began to organize.

The young women mill workers in Lowell, Massachusetts, started a labor union. A **labor union** is a group of workers who band together to seek better working conditions. In 1836, the mill owners raised the rent of the company-owned boarding houses where the women lived. About 1,500 women went on **strike,** stopping work to demand better conditions. Eleven-year-old Harriet Hanson helped lead the strikers.

A VOICE FROM THE PAST

I . . . started on ahead, saying, . . . "I don't care what you do, I am going to turn out, whether anyone else does or not," and I marched out, and was followed by the others. As I looked back at the long line that followed me, I was more proud than I have ever been since.

Harriet Hanson, quoted in *A People's History of the United States*

Other workers called for shorter hours and higher wages. In 1835 and 1836, 140 strikes took place in the eastern United States. Then the Panic

ACTIVITY OPTIONS
INDIVIDUAL NEEDS

STUDENTS ACQUIRING ENGLISH/ESL

Building Vocabulary Copy the graphic shown here on the chalkboard. Pronounce the word *reform* and write its definition, "to improve or make better," on the graphic. Then point out the words *Reforming* in the section title and *reformers* on page 420. Discuss the part of speech and meaning of each word. Ask students to add definitions to the graphic. After students have read the section, ask them to give examples of reform that occurred in the early 1800s and to identify reformers who are associated with this movement.

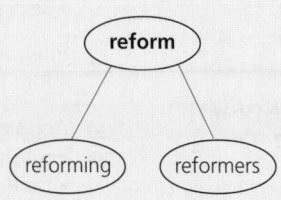

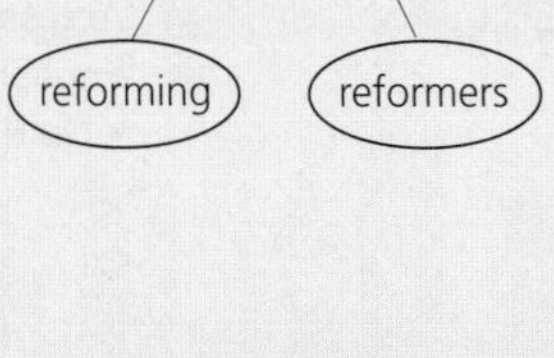

of 1837 brought hard times. Jobs were scarce, and workers were afraid to cause trouble. The young labor movement fell apart. Even so, workers achieved a few goals. For example, in 1840 President Martin Van Buren ordered a ten-hour workday for government workers.

Background
President Van Buren's order reduced the workweek from 70 to 60 hours.

3 Improving Education

In the 1830s, Americans also began to demand better schools. In 1837, Massachusetts set up the first state board of education in the United States. Its head was **Horace Mann.** Mann called public education "the great equalizer." He also argued that "education creates or develops new treasures—treasures never before possessed or dreamed of by any one." By 1850, many Northern states had opened public elementary schools.

Boston opened the first public high school in 1821. A few other Northern cities followed suit. In addition, churches and other groups founded hundreds of private colleges in the following decades. Many were located in states carved from the Northwest Territory. These included Antioch and Oberlin Colleges in Ohio, the University of Notre Dame in Indiana, and Northwestern University in Illinois.

Women could not attend most colleges. One exception was Oberlin. It was the first college to accept women as well as men. In 1849, English immigrant Elizabeth Blackwell became the first woman to earn a medical degree in the United States. Despite such individual efforts, it was rare for a woman to attend college until the late 1800s.

Mary Jane Patterson was the first African-American woman to earn a college degree. She graduated from Oberlin in 1862 and went on to work as a teacher.

African Americans also faced obstacles to getting an education. This was especially true in the South. There, teaching an enslaved person to read had been illegal since the Nat Turner Rebellion in 1831. Enslaved African Americans who tried to learn were brutally punished. Even in the North, most public schools barred African-American children.

Reading **History**
B. Making Inferences Why do you think women and African Americans had a hard time getting an education?
B. Possible Response because of prejudice and discrimination

Few colleges accepted African Americans. Those that did often took only one or two blacks at a time. The first African American to receive a college degree was Alexander Twilight in 1823. John Russwurm received one in 1826 and later began the first African-American newspaper.

Caring for the Needy

As some people promoted education, others tried to improve society's care for its weakest members. In 1841, **Dorothea Dix,** a reformer from Boston, was teaching Sunday school at a women's jail. She discovered some women who were locked in cold, filthy cells

INSTRUCT: OBJECTIVE 3
Improving Education/Caring for the Needy

- What efforts were made to improve educational opportunities for women?
- What obstacles faced African Americans who wanted an education?
- How did Dorothea Dix improve care for people who were mentally ill?

MORE ABOUT . . .

Oberlin College
From its founding in 1833, Oberlin announced that it would admit students regardless of race or sex. At first, Oberlin offered women only a short course in literature, but within a few years women were taking the same courses as men. Still, the college administrators believed that their main goal was to prepare women to be better mothers. Women students with different goals—such as Antoinette Brown, who became a minister, and Lucy Stone, later a suffrage leader—often challenged that point of view, even while they relished the education that Oberlin provided.

ACTIVITY OPTIONS
INTERDISCIPLINARY LINK: GOVERNMENT — BLOCK SCHEDULING

WRITING A RESOLUTION

Class Time One class period

Task Writing a resolution calling for an educational reform

Purpose To formulate ideas for reforming education today and to learn how local governments operate

Supplies Needed
- References on education
- Internet access
- Sample resolutions for models

Activity As a class, brainstorm a list of desirable improvements in your school, such as enhanced computer access. Divide the class into groups and allow each group to select one reform from the list. Tell the groups to do some research on their reform and then write a resolution for the local school board and/or finance committee of your community asking for the improvement. Present your resolution to the class. You may want to contact a school board member about your resolution.

AMERICA'S HISTORY MAKERS

Horace Mann
Mann considered his advocacy for education as a moral vocation. He once described himself as "circuit rider to the next generation," referring to the circuit riders who rode from town to town to preach at revival meetings. In his effort to improve education, Mann visited schools, gave lectures, started a journal, and lobbied the state legislature. His work made the cause of education reform very popular.

Dorothea Dix
Dix traveled around the country to visit places that housed people with mental illnesses. A visit by Dix could cause anxiety for the administrators of these hospitals or asylums. "To have Miss Dix suddenly arrive at your asylum and find anything neglected or amiss, was considerably worse than an earthquake," said one doctor at a mental hospital in Providence, Rhode Island. "Not that she said anything on the spot, but one felt something ominous suspended in the very air."

Answer: Both overcame poor or unhappy backgrounds, perhaps strengthening their identification with the underdog.

INSTRUCT: OBJECTIVE 4

Spreading Ideas Through Print/ Creating Ideal Communities

- How did affordable newspapers and new magazines spread ideas through print?
- For what reasons did some Americans attempt to establish utopias? How successful were they?
- How did Shakers organize their communities?

In-Depth Resources: Unit 4
- Enrichment Activity, p. 60

AMERICA'S HISTORY MAKERS

HORACE MANN
1796–1859
Horace Mann once said in a speech to students, "Be ashamed to die until you have won some victory for humanity." Mann had no reason to be ashamed. As a child, he knew poverty and hardship. He educated himself and later fought for public education for other people.

Toward the end of his life, Mann became president of Antioch College. It committed itself to education for both men and women and equal rights for African Americans.

DOROTHEA DIX
1802–1887
At the age of 12, Dorothea Dix left an unhappy home to go live with her grandparents in Boston. Just two years later, she began teaching little children.

In 1841, Dix saw the harsh treatment of mentally ill women. Society frowned upon women traveling alone, but Dix defied custom. She went by train to several places where the mentally ill were housed.

Dix wrote a report about her research. (See page 422.) That report changed the care of the mentally ill.

How might their backgrounds have motivated Dorothea Dix and Horace Mann to become leaders in reform movements?

simply because they were mentally ill. Visiting other jails, Dix learned that the mentally ill often received no treatment. Instead, they were chained and beaten. Dix pleaded with the Massachusetts Legislature to improve the care of the mentally ill. Later, she traveled all over the United States on behalf of the mentally ill. Her efforts led to the building of 32 new hospitals.

Some reformers worked to improve life for people with other disabilities. Thomas H. Gallaudet started the first American school for deaf children in 1817. Samuel G. Howe founded the Perkins School for the Blind in Boston in the 1830s.

Reformers also tried to improve prisons. In the early 1800s, debtors, lifelong criminals, and child offenders were put in the same cells. Reformers demanded that children go to special jails. They also called for the rehabilitation of adult prisoners. Rehabilitation means preparing people to live useful lives after their release from prison.

Reading **History**
C. Recognizing Effects How did reformers change the treatment of the mentally ill, the disabled, and prisoners?
C. Possible Response The mentally ill were put in hospitals; the deaf and blind had new schools; adult and child prisoners were separated, and reformers tried to rehabilitate prisoners.

4 Spreading Ideas Through Print

During this period of reform, Americans began to receive more information about how they should lead their lives. In the 1830s, cheaper newsprint and the invention of the steam-driven press lowered the price of a newspaper to a penny. Average Americans could afford to buy the "penny papers." Penny papers were also popular because, in addition to serious news, they published gripping stories of fires and crimes.

Hundreds of new magazines also appeared. One was the *Ladies' Magazine.* Its editor was Sarah Hale, a widow who used writing to support her family. The magazine advocated education for women. It also

ACTIVITY OPTIONS
INTERDISCIPLINARY LINK: LANGUAGE ARTS — BLOCK SCHEDULING

DICTIONARY OF REFORMERS

Class Time One class period

Task Creating biographical dictionaries of 19th-century reformers

Purpose To collect and organize information about reformers

Supplies Needed
- Art supplies
- Textbook
- Encyclopedias, biographical dictionaries, Internet access

Activity Have students make lists of reformers mentioned in this chapter and do research to learn about other reformers from this time period, such as Emma Willard. Have students alphabetize the final list of reformers by last name. Divide the list among the class. For each reformer, students should find birth and death dates and major achievements. Students may write their dictionary entries on separate sheets of paper, make a title page, and staple the pages together to make a book.

suggested that men and women were responsible for different, but equally important, areas of life. The magazine taught that a woman's area was the home and the world of "human ties." A man's area was politics and the business of earning a living for his family. Later, Hale edited *Godey's Lady's Book*, which published poems and stories as well as articles.

Creating Ideal Communities

While magazines sought to tell people how to live and reform movements tried to change society, some individuals decided to start over. They aimed to build an ideal society, called a utopia.

Two attempts at utopias were New Harmony, Indiana, and Brook Farm, Massachusetts. In both, residents received food and other necessities of life in exchange for work. However, both utopias experienced conflicts and financial difficulties. They ended after only a few years.

ReadingHistory
D. Forming and Supporting Opinions Why do you think it was hard for utopias to succeed? Give reasons.
D. Possible Responses Members might disagree over rules; the people who live in such communities tend to be dreamers and not financially practical; people are often too selfish to live in an "ideal community."

Religious belief led to some utopias. For example, the Shakers followed the beliefs of Ann Lee. She preached that people should lead holy lives in communities that demonstrate God's love to the world. When a person became a Shaker, he or she vowed not to marry or have children. Shakers shared their goods with each other, believed that men and women are equal, and refused to fight for any reason. Shakers set up communities in New York, New England, and on the frontier.

People called them *Shakers* because they shook with emotion during church services. Otherwise, Shaker life was calm. Shakers farmed and built simple furniture in styles that remain popular today. The childless Shakers depended on converts and adopting children to keep their communities going. In the 1840s, the Shakers had 6,000 members—their highest number. In 1999, only seven Shakers remained.

In the 1840s and 1850s, reform found a new direction. Many individuals began to try to win rights for two oppressed groups—women and enslaved persons. Section 4 discusses these efforts.

Section 3 Assessment

1. Terms & Names

Explain the significance of:
- revival
- Second Great Awakening
- temperance movement
- labor union
- strike
- Horace Mann
- Dorothea Dix

2. Taking Notes

Create a chart like the one below. Use it to list problems identified by reformers and their solutions to them.

Problem	Reformer's Solution

3. Main Ideas

a. How did the Second Great Awakening influence the reform movement?

b. How did labor unions try to force business owners to improve working conditions?

c. What were women's contributions to the reform movement?

4. Critical Thinking

Recognizing Effects What was the long-term impact of the reform movement that took place in the mid-1800s?

THINK ABOUT
- the changes reformers made in education, temperance, prisons, and the care of the disabled
- which of those changes are still in effect today

ACTIVITY OPTIONS

SPEECH
CIVICS

Think of a modern problem that is similar to an issue discussed in this section. Give a **speech** or write a **letter** to a government official suggesting a reform.

MORE ABOUT . . .

The Shakers

Shakers were hard workers and their farms prospered. Shakers actively sought new ways to make their labor efficient and easy. They invented many laborsaving devices, including the buzz saw, a revolving oven, and apple corers and parers. They sold products such as garden seeds, herbs and medicines, baskets, boxes, brooms, and woven goods to the public. They were the first to package seeds in the small paper envelopes still used today.

ASSESS & RETEACH

Setting the Stage Have students fill in the third row on the graphic organizer.

Formal Assessment
- Section Quiz, p. 255

RETEACHING ACTIVITY

Have students use a web such as the one below to organize information about the reform movements discussed in this section.

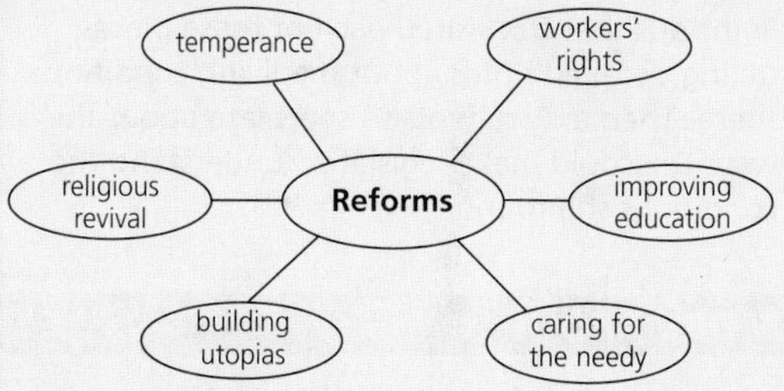

In-Depth Resources: Unit 4
- Reteaching Activity, p. 58

Section 3 Assessment

1. Terms & Names

revival, p. 417
Second Great Awakening, p. 417
temperance movement, p. 418
labor union, p. 418
strike, p. 418
Horace Mann, p. 419
Dorothea Dix, p. 419

2. Taking Notes

poverty caused by drinking—laws that ban alcohol; unsafe work for little pay and long hours—strike; lack of education—public schools and reformed college admittance; mentally ill in jail—hospitals; unorganized prisons—children in special jails and prisoner rehabilitation

3. Main Ideas

a. It urged people to give up their sins and help others. **b.** They went on strike. **c.** temperance workers; women workers went on strike; tried to improve the care of the mentally ill; published a magazine giving women advice

4. Critical Thinking

The creation of public schools, mental hospitals, schools for the deaf and blind, and separate jails for children are all still in existence today.

ACTIVITY OPTIONS

Integrated Assessment
- Rubrics for a speech, 3.6
- Rubrics for a letter, 4.3

INTERACTIVE PRIMARY SOURCE

OBJECTIVE
The student will be able to describe the living conditions of mentally ill people in jails and poorhouses during the early 1800s and the appeals made by Dorothea Dix on their behalf.

Primary Source Explorer
- *Report to the Massachusetts Legislature*

The Explorer will help students select and produce their own presentations.

Specific information about the document can be found in **A Closer Look.** To learn more about key people and events of the time, students should click on **Life in These Times. What Happened Next** will show the student the impact of the document and tie it to today.

FOCUS & MOTIVATE

Evaluating Tell students that personal research is important in developing an understanding of complicated issues. Ask students to evaluate the extent of Dix's research into the problem of poor housing and care for mentally ill people. To help students evaluate the report by Dix, have students identify the locations Dix highlights for legislators. Point out that Dix visited each of these places, taking detailed notes about the living conditions there. Then ask students to speculate about the ways Dix could make legislators understand the conditions she found.

MORE ABOUT . . .

Dix's Investigations
Dorothea Dix spent 18 months touring places in Massachusetts where mentally ill people were confined. Then she visited Western and Southern states as well as Europe in her efforts to improve care for mentally ill people. In Europe, she met with Pope Pius IX and harshly criticized a local asylum. The pope ordered an investigation and then instituted reforms at the hospital.

Report to the Massachusetts Legislature

Setting the Stage After traveling to several places where the mentally ill were kept, Dorothea Dix wrote a report describing the conditions she had discovered. In 1843, she presented her report to lawmakers to alert them to the horrible treatment of the mentally ill. This report has been called the "first piece of social research ever conducted in America." An excerpt from Dorothea Dix's report follows. **See Primary Source Explorer**

Report to the Massachusetts Legislature

Gentlemen: . . . I come to present the strong claims of suffering humanity. I come to place before the Legislature of Massachusetts the condition of the miserable, the desolate, the outcast. I come as the **advocate**[1] of helpless, forgotten, insane, and idiotic men and women; of beings sunk to a condition from which the most unconcerned would start with real horror; of beings wretched in our prisons, and more wretched in our **almshouses.**[2]

I must confine myself to a few examples, but am ready to furnish other and more complete details, if required.

I proceed, gentlemen, briefly to call your attention to the *present* state of insane persons confined within this **Commonwealth,**[3] in *cages, closets, cellars, stalls, pens! Chained, naked, beaten with rods,* and *lashed* into obedience.

I offer the following extracts from my notebook and journal.

Springfield: In the jail, one lunatic woman, furiously mad, a state **pauper,**[4] improperly situated, both in regard to the prisoners, the keepers, and herself. It is a case of extreme self-forgetfulness and oblivion to all the decencies of life, to describe which would be to repeat only the grossest scenes. She is much worse since leaving Worcester. In the almshouse of the same town is a woman apparently only needing **judicious**[5] care and some well-chosen employment to make it unnecessary to confine her in solitude in a dreary unfurnished room. Her appeals for employment and companionship are most touching, but the mistress replied "she had no time to attend to her."

Lincoln: A woman in a cage. *Medford:* One idiotic subject chained, and one in a close stall for seventeen years. *Pepperell:* One often doubly chained, hand and foot; another violent; several peaceable now. *Brookfield:* One man caged, comfortable. *Granville:* One often closely confined, now losing the use of his

A CLOSER LOOK

ADVOCATE OF THE HELPLESS

In earlier times, the term *idiotic* did not mean stupid. It was used to describe someone who was mentally retarded.

1. For what groups of people is Dix pleading for help?

A CLOSER LOOK

JUDICIOUS CARE

Dix describes a woman who needs only some care and a useful task to do.

2. What did the woman's keeper say when Dix pointed that out?

1. **advocate:** a person who pleads another person's cause.
2. **almshouses:** homes for poor people.
3. **Commonwealth:** one of four U.S. states whose constitution uses this term to describe their form of self-government; in this case, Massachusetts.
4. **pauper:** a person who lives on the state's charity.
5. **judicious:** wise and careful.

TEACHING STRATEGY

Finding Main Ideas To help students work through the report, have them copy the graphic shown. In the center circle, write Abuses of People in Asylums. Direct students to put specific examples of abuses in the surrounding circles.

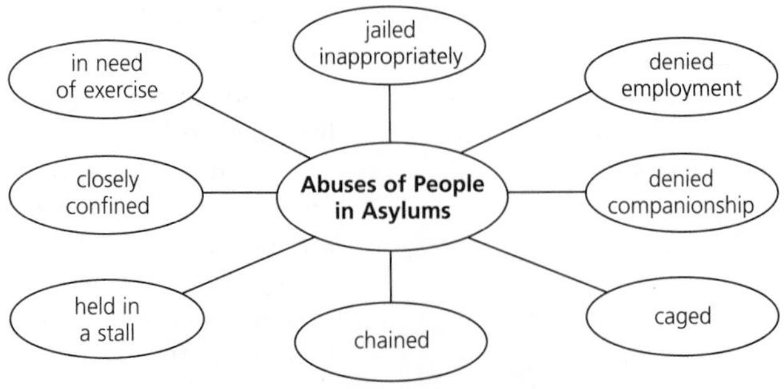

limbs from want of exercise. *Charlemont:* One man caged. *Savoy:* One man caged. *Lenox:* Two in the jail, against whose unfit condition there the jailer protests.

Dedham: The insane **disadvantageously**[6] placed in the jail. In the almshouse, two females in stalls, situated in the main building, lie in wooden bunks filled with straw; always shut up. One of these subjects is supposed curable. The overseers of the poor have declined giving her a trial at the hospital, as I was informed, on account of expense.

Besides the above, I have seen many who, part of the year, are chained or caged. The use of cages is all but universal. Hardly a town but can refer to some not distant period of using them; chains are less common; **negligences**[7] frequent; willful abuse less frequent than sufferings proceeding from ignorance, or want of consideration. I encountered during the last three months many poor creatures wandering reckless and unprotected through the country. . . . But I cannot **particularize.**[8] In traversing the state, I have found hundreds of insane persons in every variety of circumstance and condition, many whose situation could not and need not be improved; a less number, but that very large, whose lives are the saddest pictures of human suffering and degradation.

I give a few illustrations; but description fades before reality. . . .

Men of Massachusetts, I beg, I implore, I demand pity and protection for these of my suffering, outraged sex. . . . Become the benefactors of your race, the just guardians of the solemn rights you hold in trust. Raise up the fallen, **succor**[9] the desolate, restore the outcast, defend the helpless, and for your eternal and great reward receive the benediction, "Well done, good and faithful servants, become rulers over many things!"

6. **disadvantageously:** harmfully.
7. **negligences:** careless actions.
8. **particularize:** to name in detail.
9. **succor:** to give help during a time of need.

A CLOSER LOOK
I HAVE SEEN MANY

Notice that Dix cites evidence from many different towns.

3. Why do you think she includes so many specific details in her report?

A CLOSER LOOK
MEN OF MASSACHUSETTS

When Dix says "Men of Massachusetts," she is still speaking to the members of the state legislature.

4. What does Dix want the Massachusetts Legislature to do?

INSTRUCT

- What role did Dix see for herself regarding the care of mentally ill people?
- Why does Dix offer so many examples of the way people with mental illnesses or mental handicaps are treated?
- What action does Dix want the legislators to take?
- What kind of reward does Dix suggest for those legislators who act to help mentally ill people?

MORE ABOUT . . .

Dix's Career

During the U.S. Civil War, Dix served as the Union's Superintendent of Female Nurses, although she never had any formal training in nursing. Under her leadership, more than 2,000 women served as Union nurses during the war. She, however, was not effective in this post. She often squabbled with the military and ignored administrative details.

Interactive Primary Source Assessment

1. Main Ideas

a. On what evidence did Dorothea Dix base her report about "suffering humanity"?

b. How were the mentally ill treated in Massachusetts?

c. Who did Dorothea Dix ask to help to improve the care of the mentally ill?

2. Critical Thinking

Evaluating Dix succeeded in convincing the legislature to provide funds for new hospitals. What do you think made her report so persuasive?

THINK ABOUT
- the details included in the report
- how Dix got the information to write her report
- the techniques you would use to persuade someone

Interactive Primary Source Assessment

1. Main Ideas

a. on her personal visits to places where mentally ill people were confined and the conditions she witnessed there

b. chained; jailed; beaten; kept naked; kept in solitude; put in cages

c. the Massachusetts Legislature

2. Critical Thinking

Possible Responses Dix made a detailed case based on her own research, providing specific examples of the abuse of mentally ill people. She also appealed to the humanity and good will of the legislators, using emotionally charged language.

A CLOSER LOOK

1. the mentally ill and the mentally retarded
2. She didn't have time to take care of the woman.
3. to persuade the legislature to do something
4. to protect the mentally ill, especially women; to give them aid and to defend them

SECTION OBJECTIVES

1. To describe the development of the abolitionist movement
2. To explain the significance of the Underground Railroad
3. To evaluate the results of the women's rights movement
4. To identify important early leaders in the fight for women's rights

CRITICAL THINKING

Drawing Conclusions, pp. 425, 429
Comparing, p. 425
Forming and Supporting Opinions, p. 406

Why It Matters Now
- Working for Change, pp. 27–28

FOCUS & MOTIVATE

5-MINUTE WARM-UP

Making Inferences These questions deal with pressures for reform.

1. Look at the drawing and read the caption on page 429. What does this suggest about the roles of men and women?
2. What do you think the cartoonist's attitude toward women's rights is?

Warm-Up Transparency WT14

INSTRUCT

INSTRUCT: OBJECTIVE 1

Abolitionists Call for Ending Slavery/ Eyewitnesses to Slavery

- When did the abolitionist movement begin? What success did it have in getting state laws and state constitutions to abolish slavery by 1804?
- Who were some of the prominent abolitionists?
- What roles did former slaves play in the abolitionist movement?

In-Depth Resources: Unit 4
- Guided Reading, p. 46

4 Abolition and Women's Rights

MAIN IDEA

The spread of democracy led to calls for freedom for slaves and more rights for women.

WHY IT MATTERS NOW

The abolitionists and women reformers of this time inspired 20th-century reformers.

TERMS & NAMES

abolition
Frederick Douglass
Sojourner Truth
Underground Railroad
Harriet Tubman
Elizabeth Cady Stanton
Seneca Falls Convention
suffrage

ONE AMERICAN'S STORY

African-American poet Frances Ellen Watkins Harper was free but grew up in the slave state of Maryland. Harper often wrote about the suffering of enslaved persons. For example, the poem excerpt below describes a woman whose child has been taken from her and sold.

A VOICE FROM THE PAST

They tear him from her circling arms,
Her last and fond embrace.
Oh! never more may her sad eyes
Gaze on his mournful face.

No marvel, then, these bitter shrieks
Disturb the listening air:
She is a mother, and her heart
Is breaking in despair.

Frances Ellen Watkins Harper, "The Slave Mother"

Frances Ellen Watkins Harper impressed audiences with her speaking ability as she called for reform.

In the 1850s, Harper lectured against slavery throughout the North. Later in her life, she called for other reforms, such as the right to vote for women. As this section explains, many individuals in the mid-1800s demanded equal rights for African Americans and women.

1 Abolitionists Call for Ending Slavery

Abolition, the movement to end slavery, began in the late 1700s. By 1804, most Northern states had outlawed slavery. In 1807, Congress banned the importation of African slaves into the United States. Abolitionists then began to demand a law ending slavery in the South.

David Walker, a free African American in Boston, printed a pamphlet in 1829 urging slaves to revolt. Copies of this pamphlet, *Appeal . . . to the Colored Citizens of the World,* made their way into the South. This angered slaveholders. When Walker heard that his life was in danger, he refused to run away. Shortly afterward, he died mysteriously.

A few Northern whites also fought slavery. In 1831, William Lloyd Garrison began to publish an abolitionist newspaper, *The Liberator,* in

RECOMMENDED RESOURCES

In-Depth Resources: Unit 4
- Guided Reading, p. 46
- Geog. Application, pp. 49–50
- Primary Sources, pp. 51–52
- Literature Selection, pp. 53–55
- History Workshop, p. 61

Reading Study Guide (Spanish and English), pp. 139–140

America's History Makers, pp. 55–56, 57–58

Why It Matters Now
- Working for Change, pp. 27–28

American History Plays
- *Lucy Stone, Champion of Women's Rights*

Formal Assessment
- Section Quiz, p. 256

Integrated Assessment
- Rubrics, 5.3, 3.1

Access for Students Acquiring English/ESL, pp. 93, 95–96

INTEGRATED TECHNOLOGY

Humanities Transparency HT28
- The Fugitive's Song

Electronic Teacher Tools

TEST-TAKING RESOURCES

Strategies for Test Preparation

Test Practice Transparencies, TT52

Online Test Practice

Boston. Of his antislavery stand, he wrote, "I will not retreat a single inch—AND I WILL BE HEARD." Many people hated his views. In 1834, a furious mob in Boston grabbed Garrison and dragged him toward a park to hang him. The mayor stepped in and saved his life.

Two famous abolitionists were Southerners who had grown up on a plantation. Sisters Sarah and Angelina Grimké believed that slavery was morally wrong. They moved north and joined an antislavery society. At the time, women were not supposed to lecture in public. But the Grimkés lectured against slavery anyway. Theodore Weld, Angelina's husband, was also an abolitionist. He led a campaign to send antislavery petitions to Congress. Proslavery congressmen passed gag rules to prevent the reading of those petitions in Congress.

Reading **History**
A. Drawing Conclusions How would the Grimké sisters' background help them as abolitionist speakers?
A. Possible Response They could give eyewitness testimony of the horrors of slavery.

John Quincy Adams ignored the gag rules and read the petitions. He also introduced an amendment to abolish slavery. Proslavery congressmen tried to stop him. Such efforts, however, only weakened the proslavery cause by showing them to be opponents of free speech. Adams also defended a group of Africans who had rebelled on the slave ship *Amistad.* He successfully argued their case before the U.S. Supreme Court in 1841, and in 1842, the Africans returned home.

Eyewitnesses to Slavery

Two moving abolitionist speakers, **Frederick Douglass** and **Sojourner Truth,** spoke from their own experience of slavery. Douglass's courage and talent at public speaking won him a career as a lecturer for the Massachusetts Anti-Slavery Society. Poet James Russell Lowell said of him, "The very look and bearing of Douglass are an irresistible logic against the oppression of his race."

People who opposed abolition spread rumors that the brilliant speaker could never have been a slave. To prove them wrong, in 1845 Douglass published an autobiography that vividly narrated his slave experiences. Afterwards, he feared recapture by his owner, so he left America for a two-year speaking tour of Great Britain and Ireland. When Douglass returned, he bought his freedom. He began to publish an antislavery newspaper.

Sojourner Truth also began life enslaved. Originally named Isabella, Sojourner Truth was born in New York State. In 1827, she fled her owners and went to live with Quakers, who set her free. They also helped her win a court battle to recover her young son. He had been sold illegally into slavery in the South. A devout Christian, Truth changed her name in 1843 to reflect her life's work: to sojourn (or stay temporarily in a place) and "declare the truth to the people." Speaking for abolition, she drew huge crowds throughout the North.

B. Possible Responses Both were former slaves; both were good speakers.
Reading **History**
B. Comparing How were Frederick Douglass and Sojourner Truth similar as abolitionists?

AMERICA'S HISTORY MAKERS

FREDERICK DOUGLASS
1817–1895

Douglass, born Frederick Bailey, was the son of a black mother and a white father. When he was eight, his owner sent him to be a servant for the Auld family. Mrs. Auld defied state law and taught young Frederick to read.

At the age of 16, Douglass returned to the plantation as a field hand. He endured so many whippings he later wrote, "I was seldom free from a sore back."

In 1838, he escaped to the North by hopping a train with a borrowed pass. To avoid recapture, he changed his last name.

How did Mrs. Auld unknowingly help Douglass become an abolitionist leader? Explain.

MORE ABOUT . . .

Abolition and Early State Constitutions

Antislavery activists succeeded in banning slavery in Northern states in different ways. In 1777, Vermont's constitution banned slavery, but it was the only state constitution to explicitly do so. Other states passed laws for gradual emancipation, including Pennsylvania (1780), Connecticut (1784), Rhode Island (1784), New York (1799), and New Jersey (1804). In Massachusetts, most historians credit a 1783 court case, *Commonwealth* v. *Jennison* (also known as the Quock Walker case) with ending slavery there, although no official document from this case directly banned slavery.

In-Depth Resources: Unit 4
- Primary Source: from the *Liberator,* p. 51

AMERICA'S HISTORY MAKERS

Frederick Douglass

Douglass took his new last name from the hero of *The Lady of the Lake,* a long narrative poem by the Scottish writer Sir Walter Scott. The Douglass in Scott's poem returns home to Scotland years after his entire family has been banished. In 1877, Douglass visited St. Michaels, Maryland, where he had been held as a slave and worked as a field hand. He called on Thomas Auld, his former owner. Auld starved his slaves and gave Douglass many beatings. The elderly Auld apologized for his actions as a slaveholder but also tried to defend them.

Answer: She taught him to read. This is probably one reason for his great skill as a speaker.

In-Depth Resources: Unit 4
- Geography Application, pp. 49–50
- Literature Selection: from *Narrative of the Life of Frederick Douglass,* pp. 53–55

Humanities Transparency HT28
- The Fugitive's Song

ACTIVITY OPTIONS

INTERDISCIPLINARY LINK: SPEECH — BLOCK SCHEDULING

ANALYZING SPEECHES

Class Time One class period

Task Analyzing a speech by Frederick Douglass

Purpose To evaluate a primary source and to appreciate the eloquence of a great orator

Supplies Needed
- Internet access (optional)

Activity Present the following quote from an 1852 speech by Frederick Douglass. Tell students that the speech was in honor of the Fourth of July. "This Fourth [of] July is yours, not mine. You may rejoice, I must mourn . . . above your national, tumultuous joy, I hear the mournful wail of millions!" Ask students to write a short paragraph explaining why Douglass says that he cannot celebrate the Fourth of July. The complete speech and others by Douglass may be found by visiting classzone.com.

INSTRUCT: OBJECTIVE 2

The Underground Railroad/Harriet Tubman

- How did the Underground Railroad operate?
- How did Harriet Tubman fight against slavery?

Now and then

The Underground Railroad

Some historians estimate that somewhere between 30,000 and 100,000 enslaved Americans traveled the Underground Railroad, beginning in the 1830s and ending at the close of the Civil War. The Underground Railroad Network to Freedom Act, passed by Congress in 1998, instructed the National Park Service to identify and locate important places along the Underground Railroad. By mid-1999, about three dozen sites had been located. Each site has a plaque describing its importance to those seeking freedom.

MORE ABOUT . . .

Harriet Tubman

When Harriet Tubman made her escape from the plantation on Maryland's eastern shore where she was a field hand, she was unable to persuade her brothers and her husband to come with her. When she reached Pennsylvania, she said in a later account, she was free, but she was alone—"a stranger in a strange land." Eventually, Tubman helped to guide six of her brothers, her elderly parents, and a number of other relatives to freedom. During the Civil War, Tubman served as a nurse, scout, and spy for the Union army. She also helped locate and free enslaved African Americans living in the path of advancing Union troops.

America's History Makers
- Harriet Tubman, pp. 57–58

2 The Underground Railroad

Some abolitionists wanted to do more than campaign for laws ending slavery. Some brave people helped slaves escape to freedom along the Underground Railroad. Neither underground nor a railroad, the **Underground Railroad** was actually an aboveground series of escape routes from the South to the North. On these routes, runaway slaves traveled on foot. They also took wagons, boats, and trains.

Some enslaved persons found more unusual routes to freedom. For example, Henry Brown persuaded a white carpenter named Samuel A. Smith to pack him in a wooden box and ship him to Philadelphia. The box was only two and one half feet deep, two feet wide, and three feet long. It bore the label "This side up with care." Despite the label, Brown spent several miserable hours traveling head down. At the end of about 24 hours, Henry "Box" Brown climbed out of his box a free man in Philadelphia. Brown eventually made his way to Boston and worked on the Underground Railroad.

On the Underground Railroad, the runaways usually traveled by night and hid by day in places called stations. Stables, attics, and cellars all served as stations. At his home in Rochester, New York, Frederick Douglass hid up to 11 runaways at a time.

Harriet Tubman

The people who led the runaways to freedom were called conductors. One of the most famous conductors was **Harriet Tubman.** Born into slavery in Maryland, the 13-year-old Tubman once tried to save another slave from punishment. The angry overseer fractured Tubman's skull with a two-pound weight. She suffered fainting spells for the rest of her life but did not let that stop her from working for freedom. In 1849, Tubman learned that her owner was about to sell her. Instead, she escaped. She later described her feelings as she crossed into the free state of Pennsylvania: "I looked at my hands to see if I was the same person now that I was free. There was such a glory over everything."

After her escape, Harriet Tubman made 19 dangerous journeys to free enslaved persons. The tiny woman carried a pistol to frighten off slave hunters and medicine to quiet crying babies. Her enemies offered $40,000 for her capture, but no one caught her. "I never run my train off the track and I never lost a passenger," she proudly declared. Among the people she saved were her parents.

Reading **History**

C. Reading a Map The map on page 431 shows the routes of the Underground Railroad. Notice that most of these routes led to Canada.

D. Possible Responses They knew how bad slavery was; they felt grateful to the people who helped them and wanted to repay that kindness by helping others.

Reading **History**

D. Forming and Supporting Opinions Why do you think escaped slaves such as Brown, Douglass, and Tubman risked their lives to help free others?

Now and then

THE UNDERGROUND RAILROAD

In 1996, historian Anthony Cohen took six weeks to travel from Maryland to Canada. Cohen followed the paths runaway slaves had taken 150 years earlier. He is shown below arriving in Canada.

Cohen walked, sometimes as much as 37 miles in a day. He also hitched rides on trains and canal boats.

About those long-ago slaves fleeing toward the hope of freedom, Cohen said, "They had no choice. . . . Nobody would do this if they didn't have to."

ACTIVITY OPTIONS

INTERDISCIPLINARY LINK: LANGUAGE ARTS — BLOCK SCHEDULING

WRITING POEMS

Class Time One class period

Task Creating poems for travelers on the Underground Railroad

Purpose To create a poem showing an understanding of the difficulty and risks of trying to escape from slavery

Supplies Needed
- Words to song "Follow the Drinking Gourd." Visit www.mcdougallitell.com
- Atlases

Activity Read the spiritual "Follow the Drinking Gourd" to the class (or play it) and point out some of the symbols it uses to guide escaping slaves to freedom, such as "drinking gourd" for the Big Dipper. Tell students to write their own poem (or song) offering secret advice to runaways on the Underground Railroad to help them reach freedom. Tell students to use an atlas and the map on page 431 for information about the geographic features of the route they will describe.

Reformers' Hall of Fame

William Lloyd Garrison
Even after being threatened with hanging, Garrison continued to publish his antislavery newspaper, *The Liberator.*

Sojourner Truth and Harriet Tubman
Truth spoke out for both abolition and women's rights. Tubman risked her life leading people to freedom on the Underground Railroad.

Lucretia Mott and Susan B. Anthony
An abolitionist, Mott also helped lead the movement for women's rights. Anthony fought for women's suffrage into the 20th century.

3 Women Reformers Face Barriers

Other women besides the Grimké sisters and Sojourner Truth were abolitionists. Two of these were Lucretia Mott and **Elizabeth Cady Stanton.** Mott and Stanton were part of an American delegation that attended the World Anti-Slavery Convention in London in 1840. These women had much to say about their work. Yet when they tried to enter the convention, they were not allowed to do so. Men angrily claimed that it was not a woman's place to speak in public. Instead, the women had to sit silent behind a heavy curtain.

Vocabulary
delegation: a group that represents a larger group

To show his support, William Lloyd Garrison joined them. He said, "After battling so many long years for the liberties of African slaves, I can take no part in a convention that strikes down the most sacred rights of all women."

Stanton applauded Garrison for giving up his chance to speak on abolition, the cause for which he had fought so long. "It was a great act of self-sacrifice that should never be forgotten by women."

However, most people agreed with the men who said that women should stay out of public life. Women in the 1800s enjoyed few legal or political rights. They could not vote, sit on juries, or hold public office. Many laws treated women—especially married women—as children. Single women enjoyed some freedoms, such as being able to manage their own property. But in most states, a husband controlled any property his wife inherited and any wages she might earn.

As the convention ended, Stanton and Mott decided it was time to demand equality for women. They made up their minds to hold a convention for women's rights when they returned home.

MORE ABOUT . . .

Lucretia Mott
Lucretia Coffin Mott and her husband, James Mott, were ardently opposed to slavery. In the early 1800s, they began to boycott all goods produced by slave labor. The Motts did without sugar and molasses. They gave their children special candy made with free labor, although they all agreed it did not taste very good. However, James Mott was in the cotton business and feared that his family would sink into poverty if he gave it up. In 1830, James Mott finally decided he could no longer deal in cotton. He switched his business to wool and after a few months his business was quite successful. Lucretia Mott spoke in Quaker meetings about her refusal to use slave products. She became known as an abolitionist.

INSTRUCT: OBJECTIVE 3

Women Reformers Face Barriers/ The Seneca Falls Convention

- What barriers to equality did women face in the early and mid-1800s?
- How did the abolitionist movement lay the groundwork for the fight for women's rights?
- What did delegates to the Seneca Falls Convention include in their Declaration of Sentiments and Resolutions?

In-Depth Resources: Unit 4
- Primary Source: The Seneca Falls Declaration and Resolutions, p. 52

ACTIVITY OPTIONS

MULTIPLE LEARNING STYLES: LOGICAL — BLOCK SCHEDULING

BOARD GAME

Class Time One class period

Task Planning board games about the women's rights movement

Purpose To synthesize and analyze information about the women's rights movement

Supplies Needed
- Construction paper
- Markers
- Index cards

Activity Have student groups plan board games about the women's rights movement. The basic rules should require players to move from start to finish along the game route by correctly answering questions about barriers women faced, the Seneca Falls Convention, and important individuals. Students should divide these tasks: writing questions on the fronts of cards, answering questions on the backs of cards, designing the game board, and writing game rules. You may want to take additional class periods to complete the game. Groups may then exchange and play the board games.

AMERICA'S HISTORY MAKERS

Elizabeth Cady Stanton

Stanton's father was a distinguished New York state lawyer. Many of his clients were women facing poverty because the laws gave all their money—whether from inheritances or earnings—to their husbands. Sometimes husbands drank or gambled away the money. Some widows were dependent on their sons for money to live on, even though the money had been theirs to begin with. In addition, women who divorced usually lost the right to visit their children, without regard to their reasons for leaving their husbands. New York state laws gave a father the exclusive guardianship of his children, even if he was a drunkard or abusive. Later in life, Stanton worked to change legislation involving the rights of women.

Possible Response: She was not satisfied with proving that she was as good as men but sought equality for all women.

America's History Makers
- Elizabeth Cady Stanton, pp. 55–56

INSTRUCT: OBJECTIVE 4

Continued Calls for Women's Rights

- How did Maria Mitchell contribute to the women's movement?
- What was Susan B. Anthony's role in the women's movement?
- How successful was the women's movement in the 1800s?

AMERICA'S HISTORY MAKERS

ELIZABETH CADY STANTON
1815–1902

Elizabeth Cady Stanton's first memory was the birth of a sister when she was four. So many people said, "What a pity it is she's a girl!" that Stanton felt sorry for the new baby. She later wrote, "I did not understand at that time that girls were considered an inferior order of beings."

When Stanton was 11, her only brother died. Her father said, "Oh, my daughter, I wish you were a boy!" That sealed Stanton's determination to prove that girls were just as important as boys.

How did Stanton's childhood experiences motivate her to help other people besides herself?

The Seneca Falls Convention

Stanton and Mott held the **Seneca Falls Convention** for women's rights in Seneca Falls, New York, on July 19 and 20, 1848. The convention attracted between 100 and 300 women and men, including Frederick Douglass.

Before the meeting opened, a small group of planners debated how to present their complaints. One woman read aloud the Declaration of Independence. This inspired the planners to write a document modeled on it. The women called their document the Declaration of Sentiments and Resolutions. Just as the Declaration of Independence said that "All men are created equal," the Declaration of Sentiments stated that "All men and women are created equal." It went on to list several complaints or resolutions. Then it concluded with a demand for rights.

A VOICE FROM THE PAST

> Now, in view of this entire disenfranchisement [denying the right to vote] of one-half the people of this country, their social and religious degradation—in view of the unjust laws above mentioned, and because women do feel themselves aggrieved, oppressed, and fraudulently deprived of their most sacred rights, we insist that they have immediate admission to all the rights and privileges which belong to them as citizens of the United States.
>
> Seneca Falls Declaration of Sentiments and Resolutions, 1848

Reading **History**
E. Using Primary Sources Why did the women at the Seneca Falls Convention believe they deserved rights and privileges?
E. Possible Responses because they make up half the population; because they are citizens of the United States

Every resolution won unanimous approval from the group except **suffrage,** or the right to vote. Some argued that the public would laugh at women if they asked for the vote. But Elizabeth Cady Stanton and Frederick Douglass fought for the resolution. They argued that the right to vote would give women political power that would help them win other rights. The resolution for suffrage won by a slim margin.

The women's rights movement was ridiculed. In 1852, the *New York Herald* poked fun at women who wanted "to vote, and to hustle with the rowdies at the polls" and to be men's equals. The editorial questioned what would happen if a pregnant woman gave birth "on the floor of Congress, in a storm at sea, or in the raging tempest of battle."

4 Continued Calls for Women's Rights

In the mid-1800s, three women lent powerful voices to the growing women's movement. Sojourner Truth, Maria Mitchell, and Susan B. Anthony each offered a special talent.

In 1851, Sojourner Truth rose to speak at a convention for women's rights in Ohio. Some participants hissed their disapproval. Because Truth supported the controversial cause of abolition, they feared her

ACTIVITY OPTIONS

INDIVIDUAL NEEDS: GIFTED AND TALENTED

DEBATING WOMEN'S RIGHTS

Class Time Two class periods

Task Debating the issue of women's rights

Purpose To research the complaints and resolutions listed in the Declaration of Sentiments and prepare to debate a related question

Supplies Needed
- Reference materials on the issue of women's rights
- Internet access for additional resources

Activity Have students research some of the issues discussed at the Seneca Falls Convention. Then have them formulate a resolution to debate, such as *Women have equal rights to education,* or *Women should be allowed to own property.* Once students have agreed on a resolution, assign students to argue each side of the issue. Review the rules of debate with the students and set time limits. You might want to have students debate in front of the rest of the class and have the audience vote to determine the winning team.

appearance would make their own cause less popular. But Truth won applause with her speech that urged men to grant women their rights.

A VOICE FROM THE PAST

I have heard much about the sexes being equal. I can carry as much as any man, and can eat as much too, if I can get it. I am as strong as any man. . . . If you have woman's rights give it to her and you will feel better. You will have your own rights, and they won't be so much trouble.

Sojourner Truth, quoted by Marius Robinson, convention secretary

The scientist Maria Mitchell fought for women's equality by helping to found the Association for the Advancement of Women. Mitchell was an astronomer who discovered a comet in 1847. She became the first woman elected to the American Academy of Arts and Sciences.

Susan B. Anthony was a skilled organizer who worked in the temperance and antislavery movements. She built the women's movement into a national organization. Anthony argued that a woman must "have a purse [money] of her own." To this end, she supported laws that would give married women rights to their own property and wages. Mississippi passed the first such law in 1839. New York passed a property law in 1848 and a wages law in 1860. By 1865, 29 states had similar laws. (Anthony also fought for suffrage. See Chapter 22.)

But women's suffrage stayed out of reach until the 1900s, and the U.S. government did not fully abolish slavery until 1865. As you will read in the next chapter, the issue of slavery began to tear the nation apart in the mid-1800s.

This drawing shows a husband and wife fighting over who will "wear the pants in the family"—that is, who will rule the household.

Section 4 Assessment

1. Terms & Names

Explain the significance of:
- abolition
- Frederick Douglass
- Sojourner Truth
- Underground Railroad
- Harriet Tubman
- Elizabeth Cady Stanton
- Seneca Falls Convention
- suffrage

2. Taking Notes

On a time line like the one below, record significant individuals and events in the historical development of the abolition movement.

1807 ——— 1865

Why does the time line end in 1865?

3. Main Ideas

a. Why were freedom of speech and freedom of the press important to the abolitionist movement?

b. What were Frederick Douglass's contributions to the abolitionist movement?

c. What were Elizabeth Cady Stanton's contributions to the women's rights movement?

4. Critical Thinking

Drawing Conclusions Why do you think that many of the people who fought for abolition also fought for women's rights?

THINK ABOUT
- why they opposed slavery
- the social and economic position of women
- what the two causes had in common

ACTIVITY OPTIONS

TECHNOLOGY
DRAMA

With a partner, act out a meeting between a reformer from Section 3 and one from Section 4. **Videotape** their conversation or **perform** it for the class.

MORE ABOUT . . .

Maria Mitchell

Maria Mitchell (1818–1889) was born in the whaling town of Nantucket, Massachusetts. Her father plotted stars for navigation charts, and Maria learned astronomy by working with him. She never attended college because the few colleges open to women had no courses in astronomy.

Mitchell was the first woman elected to the American Academy of Arts and Sciences. She also earned an appointment as a professor of astronomy at Vassar College. In addition to many other accomplishments, Mitchell made important contributions to the study of sun spots.

ASSESS & RETEACH

Setting the Stage Have students fill in the last row on the graphic organizer.

Formal Assessment
- Section Quiz, p. 256

Critical Thinking Transparency CT40
- Setting the Stage

RETEACHING ACTIVITY

Write the section objectives on the board and then organize the class into groups of four. Have group members divide the section objectives among themselves, one per member. Each group member should write a short summary of the main ideas for his or her part of the section. Members should then share their summaries with the rest of the group.

In-Depth Resources: Unit 4
- Reteaching Activity, p. 59

Section 4 Assessment

1. Terms & Names

abolition, p. 424
Frederick Douglass, p. 425
Sojourner Truth, p. 425
Underground Railroad, p. 426
Harriet Tubman, p. 426
Elizabeth Cady Stanton, p. 427
Seneca Falls Convention, p. 428
suffrage, p. 428

2. Taking Notes

1807—Congress outlaws importation of slaves; 1831—Garrison publishes *The Liberator;* 1841—the slaves of the *Amistad* win their freedom; 1845—Douglass publishes his autobiography; 1849—Tubman escapes and begins working on the Underground Railroad; 1865—the government abolishes slavery; because slavery is abolished

3. Main Ideas

a. to speak out against slavery; to publish antislavery newspapers
b. He spoke against slavery, wrote a book about his life as a slave, and worked on the Underground Railroad. **c.** She helped organize the Seneca Falls Convention.

4. Critical Thinking

because both were about gaining freedom and equality for an oppressed group

ACTIVITY OPTIONS

Integrated Assessment
- Rubrics for a video presentation, 5.3
- Rubrics for a scene, 3.1

GEOGRAPHY *in* HISTORY

OBJECTIVE

Students will analyze and interpret information from a map to understand the effects of geographic features on the antislavery effort known as the Underground Railroad.

BLOCK SCHEDULING

MORE ABOUT . . .

The Fugitive Slave Act

After the passage of the Fugitive Slave Act of 1850, movement of slaves to the North and Canada increased dramatically.

The law provided for federal commissioners to help catch runaway slaves and gave big rewards for returning runaways.

In some states, mobs prevented the return of fugitive slaves. Personal liberty laws preventing enforcement of the slave law were passed in other states.

INSTRUCT

- What kind of personal qualities would a person need to travel on the Underground Railroad?
- Which cities or locations might be the most dangerous for an escaped slave?
- Why might cities in the Northeast be a good destination for fugitive slaves?

MAP SKILL QUESTIONS

How can you tell which states are free states and which are slave states?

Which foreign countries were destinations for runaway slaves?

How might weather or time of year affect the movement along the Underground Railroad?

GEOGRAPHY *in* HISTORY

PLACE AND MOVEMENT

The Underground Railroad

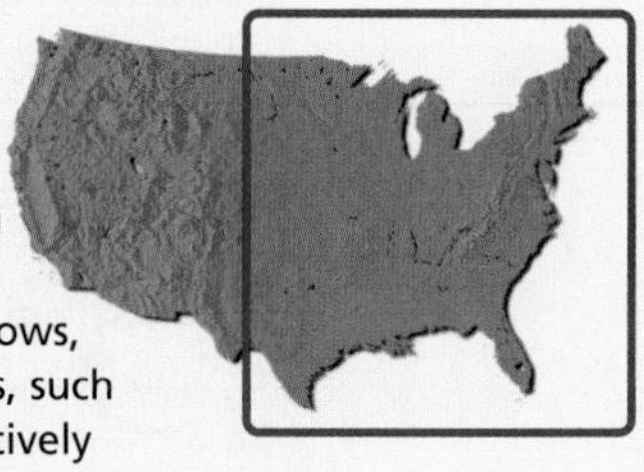

The Underground Railroad was a network of people and places that hid escaping slaves and helped them reach safety in the North or in Canada. One reason slaves often went to Canada is that a U.S. federal law required people to return runaway slaves to their owners. Defying this law, both whites and blacks helped slaves to escape.

The map on page 431 shows the main escape routes. As the map shows, most of the slaves who escaped came from states bordering free states, such as Kentucky and Virginia. Distances from there to the North were relatively short, increasing the chances of reaching freedom. However, the number of slaves who escaped from the Deep South, such as Georgia and South Carolina, was very small, because of the long distances that had to be traveled. While no one knows the exact number, historians estimate that 40,000 to 100,000 people may have used the Underground Railroad on their journey from slavery to freedom.

Among the many people who helped slaves to freedom was former slave Harriet Tubman (far left). She became a well-known guide on the Underground Railroad. She is pictured with her husband (third from left), along with other formerly enslaved people.

ARTIFACT FILE

Identity Tag Enslaved persons were forced to wear tags that identified to whom they belonged.

Freedom Marker The "P" on the rock shown here told slaves that they were in Pennsylvania, a free state.

MUSEUM CONNECTIONS

The Underground Railroad Center will make curricular materials available as well as a genealogy program for tracing African-American heritage.

The National Park Service has published a list of significant Underground Railroad sites and an Underground Railroad Special Resource Study. They can be obtained through the Superintendent of Documents at 202-512-1806.

For more on African-Canadian history and Underground Railroad sites in Canada, visit classzone.com.

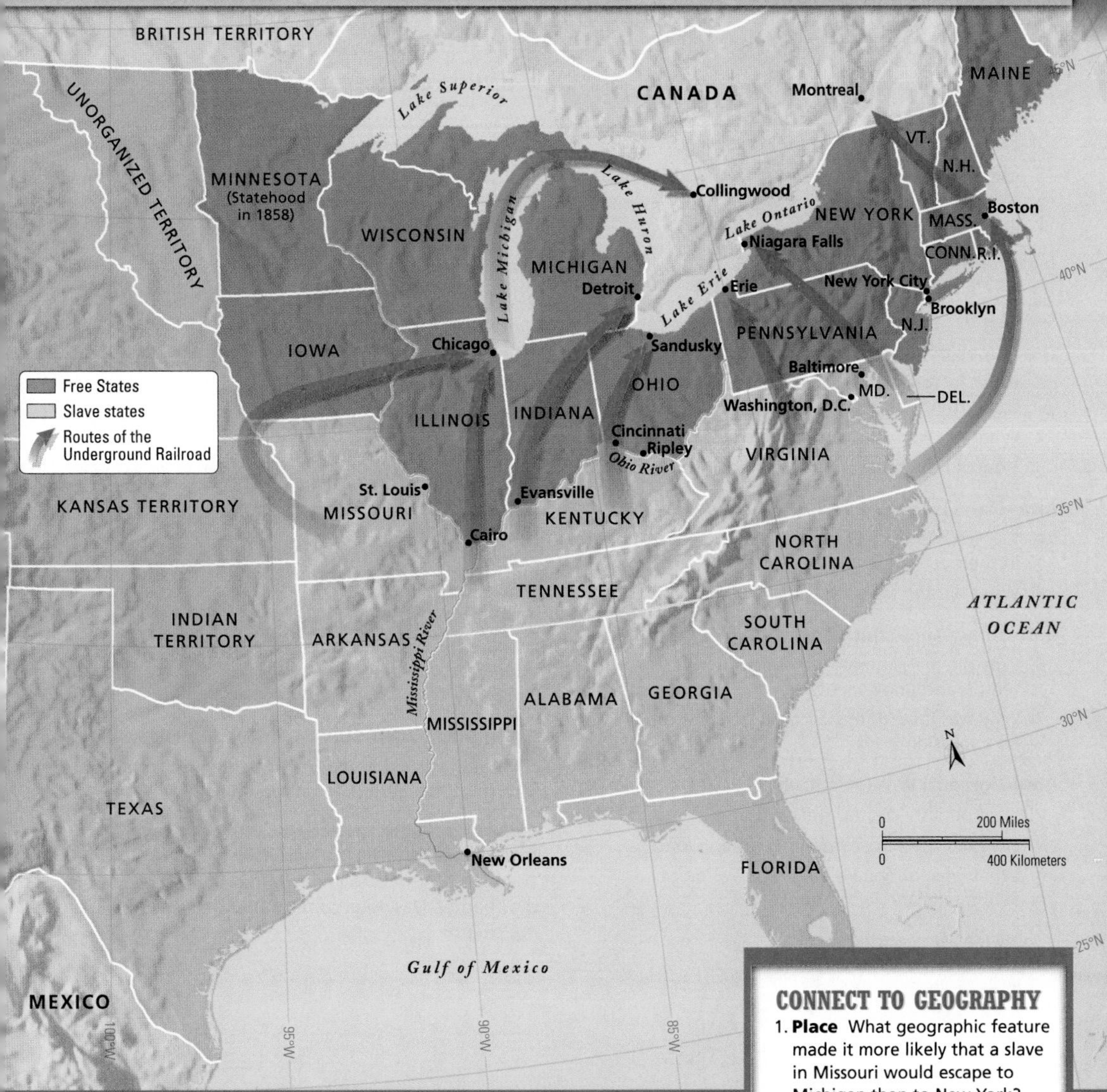

On-Line Field Trip

The National Underground Railroad Freedom Center is being built in Cincinnati, Ohio. Its collections will include artifacts and primary sources like this poster, which shows that substantial rewards were offered for the recapture of slaves.

For more about the Underground Railroad . . .

RESEARCH LINKS CLASSZONE.COM

STOP THE THIEF!

One Hundred Dollars Reward.

Stolen from the Plantation of Mrs. E. S. FARRAR, on the night of Saturday last, two Negro Girls.

One, MARY, low stature, heavy and squarely formed, very straight, black hair—a very bright Mulatto.

The other named CINTA or CINDERILLA, dark Copper, common height, has a flesh mole, near the left ear, and is well formed. Mary is twenty years old and CINTA nineteen.

I will pay a reward of $25 for the apprehension of each, if taken in the State, and $50 if taken out of it.

My address is Howardsville, Albemarle County, or Rockfish Depot, Nelson County.

September 15, 1862. RICHARD T. FARRAR.

CONNECT TO GEOGRAPHY

1. **Place** What geographic feature made it more likely that a slave in Missouri would escape to Michigan than to New York?
2. **Movement** In what way did the Underground Railroad differ from other migrations?

See Geography Handbook, pages 4–5.

CONNECT TO HISTORY

3. **Drawing Conclusions** How did the Underground Railroad reflect the American people's division over slavery?

CRITICAL THINKING ACTIVITY

Recognizing Important Details Have students make a graphic like the one below. Then have them study the map and list the physical features and geographic elements that would either help or hinder the movement of slaves in the Underground Railroad. Some elements may be on both sides. Students should explain the reasons for their choices.

Aid the Escape	Hinder

Class Time 15 minutes

MORE ABOUT . . .

Stations on the Underground Railroad

Escape routes on the Underground Railroad stretched from Topeka, Kansas, in the West to locations along the United States-Canadian border. Buxton, Amherstburg, Chatham, and Sandwich in southwest Ontario were destinations for hundreds of fugitive slaves. Because of the high number of free blacks living in Baltimore, it was a popular location. It was easy for escaped slaves to blend into the population there. Both Harriet Tubman and Frederick Douglass operated out of the Baltimore area.

CONNECT TO GEOGRAPHY

1. **Place** the Mississippi River
2. **Movement** Preparations were made in secret, and travelers were in danger of being caught and sent back.

CONNECT TO HISTORY

1. **Drawing Conclusions** It showed that many Americans opposed slavery and were willing to help slaves escape, despite rewards for their return. It showed that many Northerners opposed slavery and were willing to work against it.

TERMS & NAMES

1. **immigrant,** p. 407
2. **push-pull factors,** p. 408
3. **civil disobedience,** p. 415
4. **revival,** p. 417
5. **Second Great Awakening,** p. 417
6. **labor union,** p. 418
7. **abolition,** p. 424
8. **Underground Railroad,** p. 426
9. **Seneca Falls Convention,** p. 428
10. **suffrage,** p. 428

REVIEW QUESTIONS

Possible Responses

1. to make a better living for themselves and their families; to escape religious or political discrimination
2. the Christmas tree; gymnasiums; kindergartens; hamburgers; hot dogs
3. It devastated Ireland, prompting 1.5 to 2 million Irish people to leave their homeland.
4. They painted the beauty and majesty of the American landscape.
5. that the spiritual world was more important than the physical world and that people can find truth within themselves through feeling and intuition
6. They depended on a sober workforce.
7. Slave codes made it illegal to teach an enslaved person to read. Few states allowed African-American children to attend public schools, and few colleges accepted African Americans.
8. Frances Ellen Watkins Harper; David Walker; William Lloyd Garrison; Frederick Douglass
9. It was a set of escape routes. Runaway slaves traveled by night and hid by day. "Conductors" helped guide the slaves to freedom.
10. It was a document in which women listed a number of complaints and demanded equal rights.

Chapter 14 ASSESSMENT

TERMS & NAMES

Briefly explain the significance of each of the following.

1. immigrant
2. push-pull factors
3. civil disobedience
4. revival
5. Second Great Awakening
6. labor union
7. abolition
8. Underground Railroad
9. Seneca Falls Convention
10. suffrage

REVIEW QUESTIONS

The Hopes of Immigrants (pages 407–412)

1. What factors influenced so many immigrants to come to America in the 1800s?
2. What did Germans contribute to U.S. identity?
3. How did the potato famine affect Irish emigration?

American Literature and Art (pages 413–416)

4. How did American artists display the love of nature in their paintings?
5. What did the transcendentalists believe?

Reforming American Society (pages 417–426)

6. Why did many business owners support the temperance movement?
7. Why was it hard for African Americans to receive an education?

Abolition and Women's Rights (pages 424–431)

8. Who published antislavery writings?
9. How did the Underground Railroad work?
10. What was the Seneca Falls Declaration of Sentiments and Resolutions?

CRITICAL THINKING

1. USING YOUR NOTES

	How People Influenced America in the mid-1800s
Immigrants	
Writers	
Reformers	
Abolitionists	
Women	

Using your chart, answer the questions below.

a. Who influenced America to make reforms?

b. Compare the goals of abolitionists and women. How are they alike?

2. ANALYZING LEADERSHIP

Who is someone from this chapter who exercised leadership by standing up for an unpopular position?

3. THEME: IMPACT OF THE INDIVIDUAL

Judging from what you read in this chapter, what methods can individuals use to influence their society?

4. APPLYING CITIZENSHIP SKILLS

Who in this chapter displayed good citizenship by taking responsibility for their own behavior or by providing for their families? Give examples.

5. FORMING AND SUPPORTING OPINIONS

If someone asked you what was the most important reform of this period, what would you say? Why?

Interact *with* History

Think about the laws you proposed before you read the chapter. Has your opinion changed since you read the chapter?

VISUAL SUMMARY

A New Spirit of Change

The Hopes of Immigrants
Immigrants came to America from many European countries. They strongly influenced American life and culture.
Reforming American Society
Inspired by a religious revival, a reform movement swept the country. It aided schools, the workplace, and the disabled.
IMPACT OF THE INDIVIDUAL
American Literature and Art
American writers and artists of the 1800s produced some of America's greatest works, which are still studied.
Abolition and Women's Rights
Whites and blacks united to fight slavery. Women abolitionists expanded their fight to include women's rights as well.

432 CHAPTER 14

CRITICAL THINKING

Possible Responses

1. **USING YOUR NOTES** **a.** writers; reformers; abolitionists; women **b.** They both sought greater freedom for an oppressed group.
2. **ANALYZING LEADERSHIP** Thoreau disobeyed the law by not paying taxes to support a government he disagreed with. Dix spoke out for the mentally ill even though women were not supposed to speak in public.
3. **THEME: IMPACT OF THE INDIVIDUAL** by creating art; by speaking or writing persuasively for change; by proposing new legislation
4. **APPLYING CITIZENSHIP SKILLS** Immigrants came hoping to provide better lives for their families. People took responsibility for their behavior by signing temperance pledges.
5. **FORMING AND SUPPORTING OPINIONS** labor unions, because they won benefits for workers; public schools, because education is the foundation for progress; laws giving women control of their earnings, because they should be treated the same as men

Interact *with* History Student answers will vary but should be supported with evidence from the chapter.

HISTORY SKILLS

1. INTERPRETING GRAPHS

School Enrollment, *1840–1870*

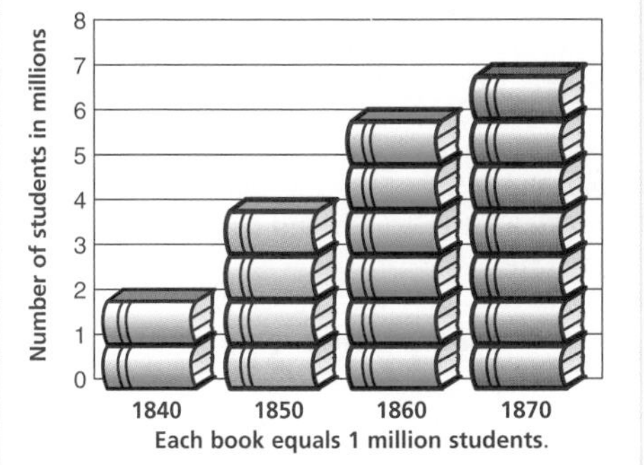

Each book equals 1 million students.

Source: *Census of the United States*

Basic Graph Elements

a. On the graph, what does each book stand for?

Interpreting the Graph

b. How did school enrollment change during the period from 1840 to 1870?

c. What is the difference in school enrollment between 1840 and 1870?

2. INTERPRETING PRIMARY SOURCES

Philip Younger escaped from slavery and eventually went to Canada. He dictated this narrative to Benjamin Drew, who included it in his *A North-Side View of Slavery.*

> I served in slavery fifty-five years, and am now nearly seventy-two years old. . . . I got off by skill. I have children and grandchildren in slavery. I had rather starve to death here, being a free man, than to have plenty in slavery. I cannot be a slave any more—nobody could hold me as a slave now, except in irons. Old as I am, I would rather face the Russian fire, or die at the point of the sword, than go into slavery.
>
> **Philip Younger,** quoted in *A North-Side View of Slavery*

a. What do you think Younger means by saying, "I got off by skill"?

b. How important is his freedom to him?

ALTERNATIVE ASSESSMENT

1. INTERDISCIPLINARY ACTIVITY: Literature

Reading a Poem Aloud Choose a poem by Henry Wadsworth Longfellow that includes references to American history. Research the actual event to which the poem refers. Write an introduction that explains whether the poem portrays history accurately. Practice reading the poem until you are comfortable. Then present the poem to the class.

2. COOPERATIVE LEARNING ACTIVITY

Making an Annotated Map Working in a small group, create an annotated map of the Underground Railroad. Make an enlargement of the map of the Underground Railroad on page 431. Then annotate it, using some of the following suggestions.

- Do research to find the stories of slaves who escaped along the Underground Railroad.
- Put brief, typed summaries of a few stories on the map, with arrows connecting them to the right route.
- Draw illustrations of escape narratives and put them on the map.
- Research to discover appropriate songs and create a recording that can play as people view the map.

3. PRIMARY SOURCE EXPLORER

Preparing a Report Dorothea Dix did not just stand before the legislature and talk about her own opinions. She gathered evidence and then wrote a persuasive report. Using the CD-ROM, library, and Internet, find out more about her report. Plan your own report that you could present to the student government.

- Choose a problem in your school that you think needs addressing.
- Find evidence of the problem. This may involve interviewing other students or observing events.
- Decide what you want the student government or school board to do about the problem.
- Write your report. Make sure to refer to the evidence that you gathered.

4. HISTORY PORTFOLIO

Review the questions that you wrote for What Do You Want to Know? on page 406. Write a short report in which you explain the answers to your questions. Be sure to use standard grammar, spelling, sentence structure, and punctuation in your report. If any questions were not answered, do research to answer them. Add your report to your portfolio.

Additional Test Practice, pp. S1–S33

TEST PRACTICE CLASSZONE.COM

ALTERNATIVE ASSESSMENT

1. INTERDISCIPLINARY ACTIVITY: **Literature**
   Readings should
   - have a clear introduction and conclusion.
   - have adequate delivery and establish rapport with the audience.
2. COOPERATIVE LEARNING ACTIVITY
   Maps should
   - be clearly labeled and neatly presented.
   - include a legend and title.
   - Include either or both physical and political locations.
   - have clearly described events and illustrations.
3. PRIMARY SOURCE EXPLORER
   Reports should
   - state the problem clearly.
   - present supporting reasons for each position.
   - use facts and examples to support major points.
   - Use standard grammar, spelling, sentence structure, and punctuation.
4. HISTORY PORTFOLIO
   Short reports should
   - answer questions about the way individuals changed America in the mid-1800s.
   - use evidence to develop and support ideas.
   - cite sources of information.
   - use standard grammar, spelling, sentence structure, and punctuation.

Critical Thinking Transparency CT42
- Visual Summary

Formal Assessment
- Chapter Test, Forms A, B, and C, pp. 257–268

HISTORY SKILLS

Possible Responses

1. INTERPRETING GRAPHS
   Basic Graph Elements
   a. Each book represents 1 million students.
   Interpreting the Graph
   b. It increased.
   c. 5 million students
2. INTERPRETING PRIMARY SOURCES
   a. He used his wits.
   b. It is more important than his life.

HISTORY WORKSHOP

OBJECTIVE

Students will create artifacts and make decisions in preparing for the journey to the United States as immigrants.

BLOCK SCHEDULING

PROCEDURE

Gather the materials listed in the "Toolbox." Divide the class into groups of four or five. Then review the steps for constructing "trunks" and items students will store in them on their journey to the United States.

In-Depth Resources: Unit 4
- History Workshop Resources, p. 61

MORE ABOUT . . .

Journey Across the Atlantic

Even if immigrants could physically carry more possessions, space was limited on ships. Many immigrants traveled to the United States on freight ships, which usually had room for them on return journeys after delivering timber, cotton, tobacco, and other materials to European ports. The cramped steerage quarters where immigrants stayed were poorly ventilated and often unsanitary. Diseases spread rapidly among the passengers.

Pack Your Trunk

For immigrants, packing up to go to a new land required making hard decisions. Wealthy people could ship belongings ahead. Most immigrants, though, carried their belongings in burlap bags, knotted sheets, large baskets, or small trunks. Even children carried small bundles. Only the very basic items or very precious ones could be taken to the United States. Baggage contained practical items such as tools and household items. But some had personal items such as portraits of loved ones. A few people even carried bags of dirt from their home country!

ACTIVITY Pack a trunk with items needed for a new life in the United States. Explain why you chose the items that you have packed. Finally, write a letter to a friend or relative back in Europe about your journey to the United States.

TOOLBOX

Each group will need:

a shoebox	markers or colored pencils
assorted magazines (optional)	3 x 5 note cards
craft sticks	masking tape
drawing paper or posterboard	styrofoam (optional)

STEP BY STEP

1 Form groups. Each group should consist of about four or five students. Assign group members the following tasks:

- Do research on what people brought with them when immigrating to the United States.
- Choose ten items that you will need for your new life.
- Present your items in class and give reasons for selecting them.

2 Research what immigrants brought with them. In the library or on the Internet (see Researching Your Project on the next page), research what immigrants brought with them to the United States. Make a list of everything you think you'll need for a new life in the United States. Some basic items included

- books
- favorite or special clothing
- toys
- important documents

Real immigrants brought these items to the United States: a mortar and pestle (used to grind spices or medicines), a shoe brush, a coffee grinder, and a paisley shawl.

434

RECOMMENDED RESOURCES

BOOKS FOR THE TEACHER

Ferrie, Joseph P. ***Yankeys Now: Immigrants in the Antebellum United States, 1840–1860.*** New York: Oxford University Press, 1999.

Laxton, Edward. ***The Famine Ships: The Irish Exodus to America.*** New York: Henry Holt, 1998.

VIDEOS

The Irish in America. A&E, 1997. Dramatic re-enactments, illustrations, letters, and other source material.

The Golden Door: Our Nation of Immigrants. Knowledge Unlimited, revised, 1996. A survey of the country's long history of immigration.

BOOKS FOR THE STUDENTS

Freedman, Russell. ***Immigrant Kids.*** New York: Puffin, 1995.

Reimers, David M. ***A Land of Immigrants.*** New York: Chelsea House, 1996.

3 **Create your items.** From your list, choose ten items that you think will be most important to starting a new life. Then draw pictures of the selected items or cut pictures of them out of a magazine. Attach a craft stick to the back of the picture with masking tape.

4 **Write reasons.** Think of why you selected each of the ten items. Write the reasons for each item on a separate 3 x 5 note card. Attach each note card to the back of the corresponding picture.

5 **Decorate the shoebox to look like a trunk.** Using the masking tape, affix your pictures to the rim of the shoebox, or use styrofoam in the bottom of the box to insert the pictures.

6 **Examine other groups' trunks.** Walk around the room and examine the contents of the other groups' trunks. Compare your trunk with that of your classmates. Share your reasons for selecting certain items.

WRITE AND SPEAK

Write a descriptive letter. Use the point of view of an immigrant. Write a letter to someone in your homeland describing your journey to the United States. Your letter might also describe what you miss most (personal belongings or people, for example) since the move. Read the letters to others in your class.

HELP DESK

For related information, see pages 407–412 in Chapter 14.

Researching Your Project

- *They Sought a New World* by William Kurdek and Margaret S. Englehart
- *American Immigration* by Edward G. Hartmann

For more about immigration . . .

RESEARCH LINKS
CLASSZONE.COM

Did You Know?

Most immigrants traveled in **steerage** or third class. It was the lowest area of the ship, where a steering mechanism was located. A family "berth," or space allotted, in steerage was about six feet square.

Before World War I, fares in steerage to the United States from Europe were never more than $35 and by 1900 were as low as $10.

Shipping companies often fed herring (a kind of fish) to the immigrants. Herring was cheap and nourishing. It was also thought to help prevent seasickness.

REFLECT & ASSESS

- What priorities did you use in selecting items for your trunk?
- Which items would have to be left behind if you only had a small bag for your belongings?
- Why do you think other groups selected items different from yours?

MORE ABOUT . . .

An Immigrant Contribution

Immigrants brought more than clothing and other personal possessions. In the 1870s, Mennonites, members of a European Protestant church, emigrated from Russia. They brought hardy wheat strains that would grow well in the plains of the United States.

REFLECT & ASSESS

1. Ask students to consider the usefulness of the items they chose.
2. Students might rank their items by priority, based on what they will need immediately upon arrival in the United States and what items are too personally important to be left behind.
3. Have students interview members of other groups to determine how they set priorities and made their decisions about what items to pack.

Presentations should

- provide a clear, concise statement.
- give a workable solution.
- evaluate the effectiveness of the solution.
- explain the originality of the solution.

MAKING PERSONAL CONNECTIONS

Ask the class to suggest ways they can get involved today to help needy people in their own community. Have students research local organizations that help the needy and report on the kinds of volunteers those organizations need.

STANDARDS FOR EVALUATION

HISTORY WORKSHOP

Trunks should

- include characteristics of common trunks, such as latches and locks.
- include easily identified items.
- include index cards with written reasons why items were selected.

WRITE AND SPEAK

Letters should

- be written from the point of view of an immigrant.
- describe the journey to the United States.
- provide examples or anecdotes about the journey and about the emotions experienced by the immigrant.

UNIT 5

Civil War to Modern America

1846–Present

BEFORE YOU READ

Previewing Unit 5

This unit begins as the sectional rivalry between the North and the South is growing deeper. Gradually the question of slavery—its expansion or its abolition—comes to dominate national politics. When Abraham Lincoln wins the presidency with support only from Northern voters, the Southern states decide to leave the Union. The North wins a long, bloody civil war. After the war, slavery is abolished. African Americans briefly hold many new legal rights—until the federal government stops enforcing civil rights laws.

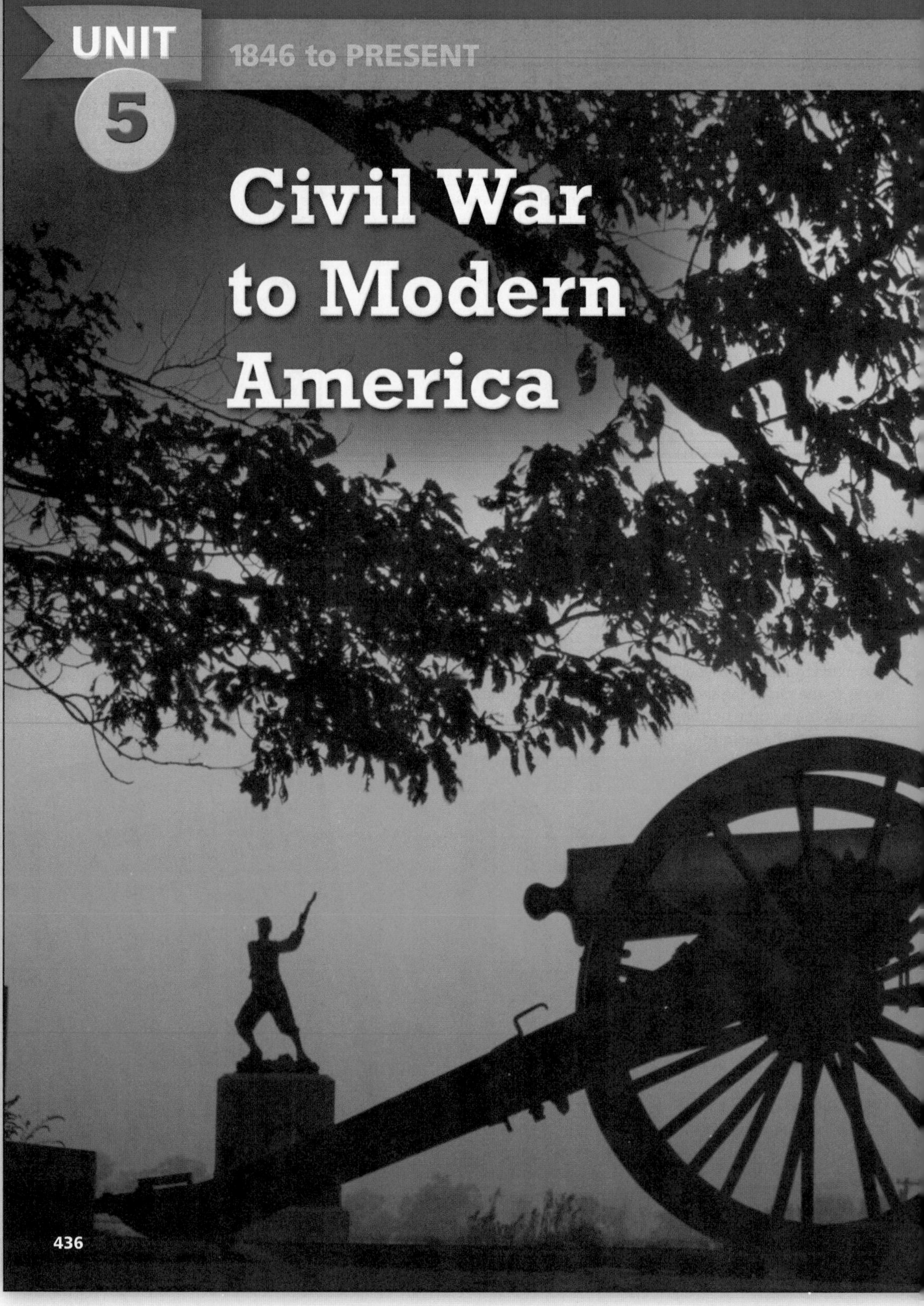

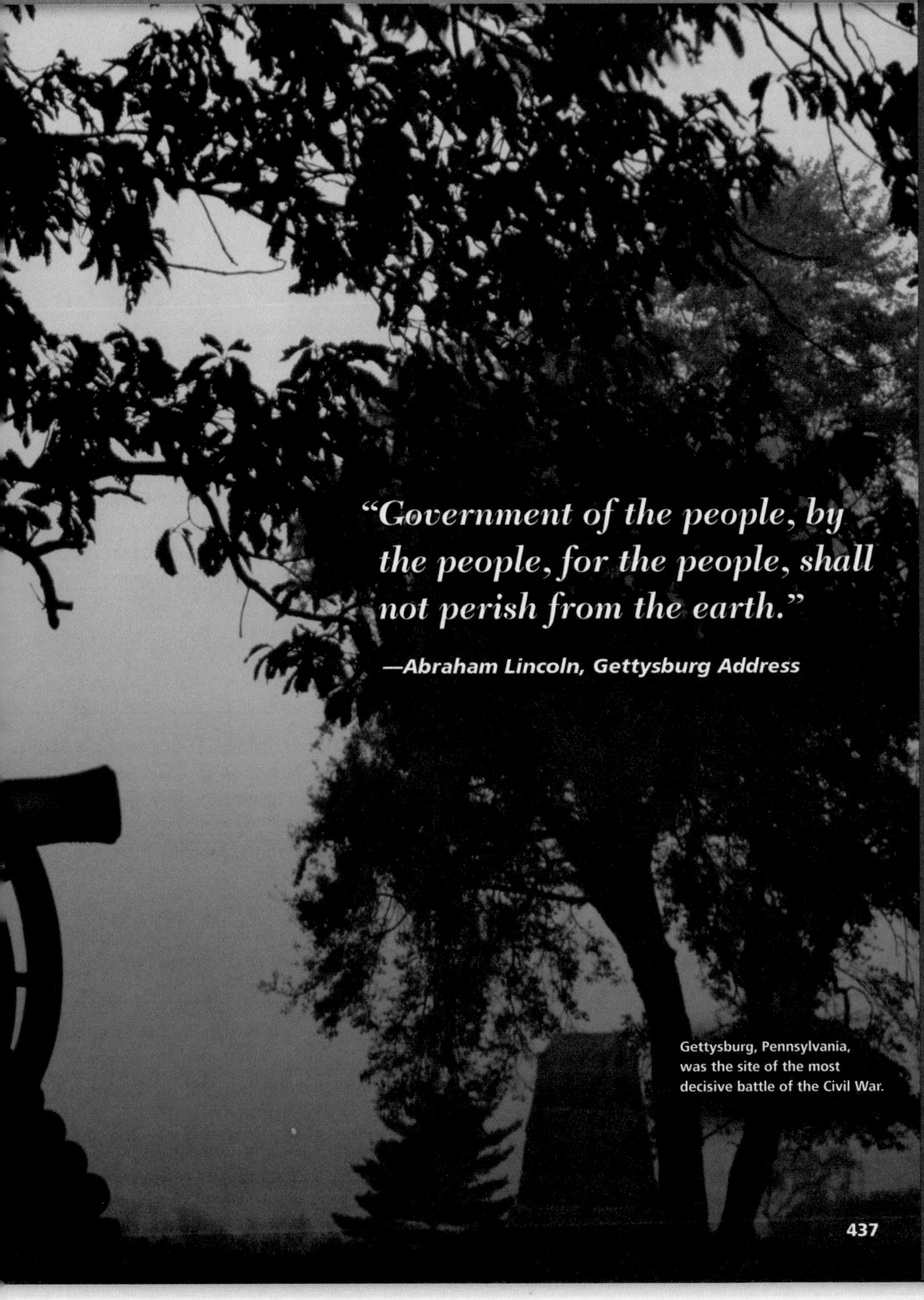

"Government of the people, by the people, for the people, shall not perish from the earth."

—Abraham Lincoln, Gettysburg Address

Gettysburg, Pennsylvania, was the site of the most decisive battle of the Civil War.

HISTORY FROM VISUALS

Interpreting the Photograph The National Military Park at Gettysburg, Pennsylvania, looks peaceful and pleasant in this photograph. Tell students that in 1863, Gettysburg was the site of a three-day battle of the Civil War. More than 50,000 soldiers were killed, wounded, or captured during those three bloody days. Ask students to describe the scene in the photograph using words that appeal to each of the five senses. For example, what sounds might students expect to hear if they were part of the scene photographed? Then ask students to make a second list using words that describe the place during the height of the Battle of Gettysburg.

Extension Ask students to use the words from their two lists to write a poem about Gettysburg.

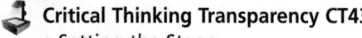

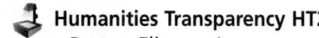

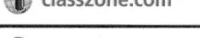

	CHAPTER OVERVIEW	COPYMASTERS	INTEGRATED TECHNOLOGY
CHAPTER RESOURCES	This chapter describes the growing hostility between the North and the South over slavery, especially its extension to new territories in the West. It also describes how this conflict came to dominate national politics, culminating in the secession of the Southern states after the election of Abraham Lincoln in 1860.	**In-Depth Resources: Unit 5** • Tracing Themes: Diversity and Unity, p. 2 • Building Vocabulary, p. 7 **Interdisciplinary Projects,** pp. 85–90	• eEdition Plus Online • EasyPlanner Plus Online • eTest Plus Online • eEdition • Power Presentations • EasyPlanner • Electronic Library of Primary Sources • Test Generator • Reading Study Guide • America's Music
SECTION 1 **Growing Tensions Between North and South** **pp. 441–445**	**KEY IDEAS** • Tensions grow between the North and the South over slavery. • Conflict over extending slavery to the new lands taken from Mexico makes slavery a key issue in national politics. • Congress passes the Compromise of 1850, which settles the problem only temporarily.	**In-Depth Resources: Unit 5** • Setting the Stage, p. 1 • Guided Reading, p. 3 • Reteaching Activity, p. 16 **Economics in History** • King Cotton, p. 15	**Warm-Up Transparency WT15** **Critical Thinking Transparency CT43** • Setting the Stage **Critical Thinking Transparency CT44** • Cause and Effect: The Compromise of 1850 classzone.com
SECTION 2 **The Crisis Deepens** **pp. 446–449**	• The Fugitive Slave Act and the controversial novel *Uncle Tom's Cabin* heighten sectional conflict. • The Kansas-Nebraska Act turns Kansas into a battleground over slavery. • Violence erupts in Congress when a Southerner attacks Senator Charles Sumner, a leading opponent of slavery.	**In-Depth Resources: Unit 5** • Setting the Stage, p. 1 • Guided Reading, p. 4 • Skillbuilder Practice: Sequencing Events, p. 8 • Literature Selection, pp. 13–15 • Reteaching Activity, p. 17 **America's History Makers** • Harriet Beecher Stowe, pp. 59–60	**Warm-Up Transparency WT15** **Humanities Transparency HT29** • Poster: Eliza on Ice **Critical Thinking Transparency CT43** • Setting the Stage classzone.com
SECTION 3 **Slavery Dominates Politics** **pp. 450–454**	• The new Republican Party nominates an antislavery presidential candidate. • In the *Dred Scott* case, the Supreme Court rules that Congress could not ban slavery in the territories. • Abraham Lincoln becomes a national figure as a result of his debates with Stephen Douglas over the slavery issue.	**In-Depth Resources: Unit 5** • Setting the Stage, p. 1 • Guided Reading, p. 5 • Primary Sources, pp. 11–12 • Reteaching Activity, p. 18 **America's History Makers** • Dred Scott, pp. 61–62 **Citizenship Today,** pp. 11–12, 89–90	**Warm-Up Transparency WT15** **Humanities Transparency HT30** • *The Abraham Lincoln Family in 1861* by Francis Carpenter **Geography Transparency GT15** • The Slave Population of the South, 1860 **Critical Thinking Transparency CT43** • Setting the Stage classzone.com
SECTION 4 **Lincoln's Election and Southern Secession** **pp. 455–459**	• The election of 1860 becomes two separate races for president, one in the North and one in the South. • After Lincoln's election, Southern states secede and form the Confederate States of America. • Northerners charge that secession is unconstitutional, and compromise fails.	**In-Depth Resources: Unit 5** • Setting the Stage, p. 1 • Guided Reading, p. 6 • Geography Application, pp. 9–10 • Reteaching Activity, p. 19 **American History Plays** • from *Abe Lincoln in Illinois* by Robert Sherwood **Why It Matters Now,** pp. 29–30 **Outline Map Activities,** pp. 29–30	**Warm-Up Transparency WT15** **Critical Thinking Transparency CT43** • Setting the Stage **Critical Thinking Transparency CT45** • Visual Summary classzone.com

Pupil's Edition | Overhead Transparency | CD-ROM
Copymaster | Audio Library | Internet

ASSESSMENT OPTIONS

Chapter Assessment, pp. 460–461

Formal Assessment
- Chapter Tests, Forms A, B, and C, pp. 273–284

Test Generator

Online Test Practice

Strategies for Test Preparation

Section Assessment, p. 445

Formal Assessment, Quiz, p. 269

Integrated Assessment Book
- Rubric, 5.5, 3.2

Test Generator

Test Practice Transparencies, TT53

Section Assessment, p. 449

Formal Assessment, Quiz, p. 270

Integrated Assessment Book
- Rubrics, 4.7, 1.3

Test Generator

Test Practice Transparencies, TT54

Section Assessment, p. 454

Formal Assessment, Quiz, p. 271

Integrated Assessment Book
- Rubrics, 2.3, 2.1

Test Generator

Test Practice Transparencies, TT55

Section Assessment, p. 459

Formal Assessment, Quiz, p. 272

Integrated Assessment Book
- Rubrics, 3.6, 5.4

Test Generator

Test Practice Transparencies, TT56

CUSTOMIZING FOR INDIVIDUAL NEEDS

Students Acquiring English/ESL

Reading Study Guide (English and Spanish), pp. 143–152

Access for Students Acquiring English/ESL: Spanish Translations, pp. 97–103

Chapter Summaries on CD (English and Spanish)

Modified Lesson Plans for English Learners

Less Proficient Readers

Reading Study Guide (English and Spanish), pp. 143–152

Chapter Summaries on CD (English and Spanish)

Gifted and Talented Students

In-Depth Resources: Unit 1
- Enrichment Activity, p. 20

America's History Makers
- Harriet Beecher Stowe, pp. 59–60
- Dred Scott, pp. 61–62

CROSS-CURRICULAR CONNECTIONS

Geography

St. George, Judith. ***Mason & Dixon's Line of Fire.*** New York: Putnam, 1991. Entertaining and original history of the Pennsylvania-Maryland border.

Civics

Tackach, James. ***The Trial of John Brown.*** San Diego: Lucent, 1998. All the drama of the trial, with background information on Brown's past and his passionate commitment to abolition.

Humanities: Music

Silverman, Jerry. ***Slave Songs (Traditional Black Music).*** Broomal, PA: Chelsea House Pub., 1993. Background information, guitar chords, and piano accompaniment for each of the 30 songs.

Interdisciplinary Projects, pp. 85–90

- Math: Analyzing Data
- Science: The Steam Locomotive
- Language Arts: Political Debates
- Home Economics: Cotton Fabrics

Literature

Rees, Douglas. ***Lightning Time.*** New York: Puffin Books, 1999. Theodore Worth is 14 when he first meets John Brown. Theodore later runs away from his Boston home to follow Brown to Harper's Ferry.

Stowe, Harriet Beecher. ***Uncle Tom's Cabin.*** New York: Modern Library, 1996. The saga of the unforgettable Eliza, Topsy, little Eva, and Uncle Tom. For advanced readers.

McDougal Littell *The Language of Literature*

- Russell Freedman, from ***Lincoln: A Photobiography*** (biography)

McDougal Littell Literature Connections

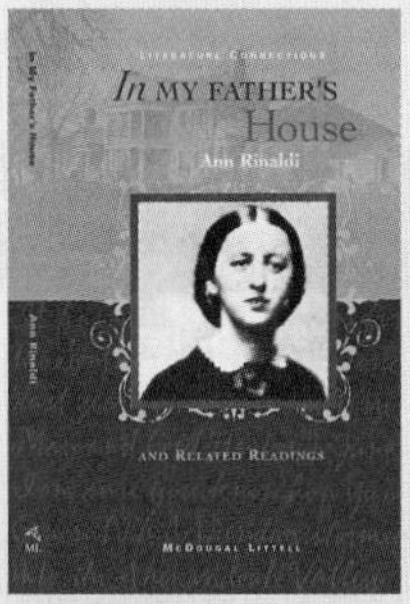

Ann Rinaldi

In My Father's House

This historical novel traces the impact of historical events on one Southern family from 1852 through the Civil War.

ENRICHMENT ACTIVITIES

Pupil's Edition, pp. 438–461
Interact with History, p. 439
Economics in History, p. 442
Citizenship Today, p. 453

In-Depth Resources: Unit 5
- Geography Application: The South Votes to Secede, pp. 9–10
- Primary Source: African-American Protest Against the *Dred Scott* Decision, p. 11
- Primary Source: John Brown's Raid, p. 12
- Literature Selection: from *Uncle Tom's Cabin,* pp. 13–15

America's History Makers
- Harriet Beecher Stowe, pp. 59–60
- Dred Scott, pp. 61–62

American History Plays
- from *Abe Lincoln in Illinois* by Robert Sherwood

Outline Map Activities
- The Election of 1860, pp. 29–30

Why It Matters Now
- Divided Nations, pp. 29–30

BLOCK SCHEDULING — LESSON PLAN OPTIONS (90-MINUTE PERIOD)

DAY 1

Interact with History, p. 439
Class Time 20 Minutes

Options for pacing and variety:
- **Peer Teaching** Working in groups of three, students can answer the "What Do You Think?" questions and share their answer to one of the questions with the class. **Class Time** 15 minutes

Setting the Stage, p. 440
Class Time 20 minutes

Options for pacing and variety:
- **Time Saver** Ask students to come to class with a list of "What Do You Want to Know?" questions. **Class Time** 10 minutes

Section 1, pp. 441–445
Class Time 50 minutes

Options for pacing and variety:
- **Peer Teaching** Have pairs of students create a two column chart comparing the Missouri Compromise and the Compromise of 1850. **Class Time** 30 minutes
- **Time Saver** Have students come to class with answers to the Connect to History and Connect to Today questions for the Economics in History feature on page 442. **Class Time** 5 minutes

DAY 2

Section 2, pp. 446–449
Class Time 45 minutes

Options for pacing and variety:
- **History on Film** Extend students' knowledge of events leading up to the Civil War with *Causes of the Civil War,* Schlesinger, 1996. **Class Time** 35 minutes
- **Time Saver** Use the map on page 448 to summarize the changes taking place in the balance of free states and slave states in the years leading up to war. **Class Time** 10 minutes

Section 3, pp. 450–454
Class Time 45 minutes

Options for pacing and variety:
- **Internet** Extend students' background knowledge of Abraham Lincoln by visiting classzone.com. **Class Time** 20 minutes
- **Time Saver** Assign the Main Ideas and Critical Thinking questions from the Section Assessment for homework. **Class Time** 5 minutes

DAY 3

Section 4, pp. 455–459
Class Time 45 minutes

Options for pacing and variety:
- **Peer Evaluation** Have students work in groups to complete the Taking Notes time line on page 459 of the Section Assessment and then discuss the Taking Notes question. **Class Time** 15 minutes
- **Time Saver** Ask students to bring to class their answers to the Applying Citizenship Skills question in the Critical Thinking section of the Chapter Assessment. **Class Time** 5 minutes

Chapter 15 Assessment, pp. 460–461
Class Time 40 minutes

Options for pacing and variety:
- **Peer Evaluation** Divide students into small groups. Have each group create a cause-and-effect chart or other graphic organizer to show the road to secession. **Class Time** 20 minutes
- **Peer Teaching** Pick eight students and assign each an event on the Visual Summary on page 460. Have students research their events and then make a living time line for the class with each student explaining how his or her event contributed to the dissolution of the Union. **Class Time** 20 minutes

TEACHER-TESTED ACTIVITY Barbara Kennedy, Sylvan Middle School, Citrus Heights, California

THE ABOLITIONIST CAUSE

Class Time 30 minutes

Task Creating an advertisement for *Uncle Tom's Cabin*

Purpose To identify the antislavery message of *Uncle Tom's Cabin* and the audience at which the novel was aimed

Supplies Needed
- Biographical information on Harriet Beecher Stowe and reference material on *Uncle Tom's Cabin*
- Markers, colored pencils
- White art paper

Activity After reviewing information on Harriet Beecher Stowe and *Uncle Tom's Cabin,* divide students into groups to design an advertisement for the book. In planning their ads, groups should identify the target audience for the book and think about the message that will appeal to this audience. The ad should suggest the author's position on slavery and how she hopes readers will react to the book. Students might also include quotes from "book reviews" in their ads. When the ads are completed, students can present them to the class.

VIDEOTAPED NEWS REPORTS AND IN-DEPTH NEWS ANALYSIS

A reporter in the field not only has to report the facts but also understand the complexities of the event that has occurred. He or she must be able to answer questions that might arise regarding the event. Reporters who repeatedly cover a certain type of news become experts in that field and can analyze events based on prior knowledge. To simulate live television news broadcasts, students can videotape both news reports and news analysis discussions.

ACTIVITY OUTLINE

Objective By presenting videotaped news reports on important events as if they were breaking news, students will learn more about the sectional crisis.

Task Students will use techniques of broadcast journalism to produce a news show that includes live reports and a roundtable discussion or analysis of events.

Class Time Two class periods

DIRECTIONS

1. Ask students to think of some of the events they remember reading about in Chapter 15. Assist students in creating a large time line that includes the following events:
   - Compromise of 1850
   - Kansas-Nebraska Act
   - Lincoln-Douglas debates
   - publication of *Uncle Tom's Cabin*
   - violence in the Kansas Territory, Harpers Ferry, and the U.S. Congress
   - *Dred Scott* v. *Sandford*
   - formation of the Republican party
   - 1860 presidential election
   - secession of South Carolina and other Southern states from the Union
2. The time line should be displayed prominently during the rest of the activity, either on the board or as an electronic file that all students can access at any time.
3. Tell students that some of them will be producing short one-minute news reports on each of these events. They will work with partners to research the story, write a reporter's script, and videotape the report.
4. Select five or six students to be news analysts. They will listen to the news reports on each event. After all the news reports are filed, they will do further research in order to be able to make connections between events, find contradictions in decisions and policies (as in the *Dred Scott* case), speculate on possibilities, and make predictions. Then they will conduct a news panel or roundtable discussion to give in-depth analyses of the events.
5. Assign students not serving as news analysts to research and report stories on the time line. Make sure all events are covered. Some reporting teams may need to cover more than one event or combine two events. Any teams that do multiple events should switch the person on- and off-camera for each report. Remind students that they should research their stories thoroughly and be prepared to answer questions.
6. After all reporters have videotaped their reports, arrange a time to broadcast the reports to the class. If possible, combine all videotaped reports into one continuous program.
7. In another class period, provide time for the news panel or roundtable discussion on the events. Remind the analysts that they need to go beyond the straight factual reports they have heard to make connections between events, point out contradictions or bad decisions, and to make predictions about what might happen next. Some of the students not participating in the panel can videotape the discussion.
8. After the completion of the roundtable discussion, ask students in the class to answer these questions:
   - Which event do you think was the most direct cause of secession and the Civil War?
   - What do you think would have been done to prevent the Civil War from starting?

CHAPTER 15 OBJECTIVE

The student will understand the conflicts that pulled the North and South apart and the attempts to resolve the issues dividing the country.

CHAPTER 15 The Nation Breaking Apart

1846–1861

HISTORY FROM VISUALS

Interpreting the Painting Tell students that this painting of one of the Lincoln-Douglas debates is an artist's recreation of the event. Ask students to look at the painting carefully and make some inferences about the artist's opinion of Lincoln. Note that Lincoln is in the center of the painting, standing erect. He wears white. Ask students to notice the kinds of men who make up the audience. Then ask how the artist has painted the audience responding to Lincoln. **Possible Response** The audience looks amused, perhaps in response to some clever words that Lincoln might be saying.

Extension Point out the campaign posters some of the people in the picture are holding. Ask students to comment on the posters, noting that women were not allowed to vote at this time.

Abraham Lincoln and Stephen A. Douglas debate the issue of slavery in the 1858 Senate campaign in Illinois.

438

RECOMMENDED RESOURCES

BOOKS FOR THE TEACHER

Fehrenbacher, Don E. ***The Dred Scott Case: Its Significance in American Law and Politics.*** New York: Oxford UP, 1978. Exhaustive study of this landmark case.

Foner, Eric. ***Free Soil, Free Labor, Free Men: The Ideology of the Republican Party before the Civil War.*** New York: Oxford UP, 1970. Introduction to the ideas behind Republican antislavery.

Potter, David M. ***The Impending Crisis, 1848–1861.*** New York: Harper, 1976. Classic book on the sectional crisis that led to the Civil War.

Stowe, Harriet Beecher. ***Uncle Tom's Cabin, or Life among the Lowly.*** 1852. Classic novel about slavery.

SOFTWARE

African American History: Slavery to Civil War. CD-ROM. Queue, 1995.

VIDEO

The Lincoln-Douglas Debates: The House Divides. Coronet, The Multimedia Co., 1989. Dramatization of the debates.

INTERNET

For more about Abraham Lincoln, visit . . .

classzone.com

Interact *with* History

Disagreements over slavery caused people in the North and the South to lose their tempers. Passions ran so high that fights sometimes broke out between members of Congress.

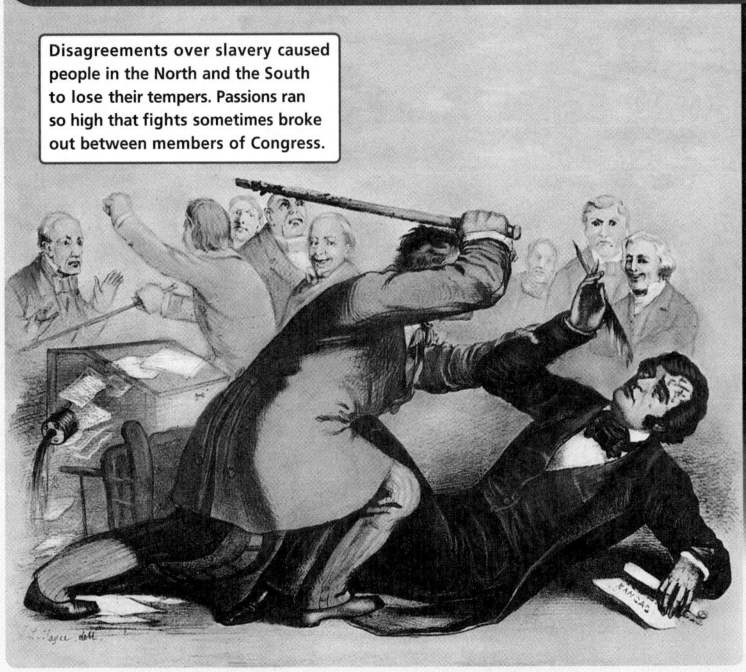

You are a representative in Congress in the 1850s. The issue of slavery is causing heated debates. Tensions over slavery have risen so high that respectable men have turned to violence to settle their differences. You worry that soon this violence may affect the entire nation.

What Do You Think?

- **Why do you think people feel so strongly about slavery?**
- **Do you think debates, such as those between Lincoln and Douglas, could settle emotional issues without leading to violence?**

How would you keep the nation together?

USA

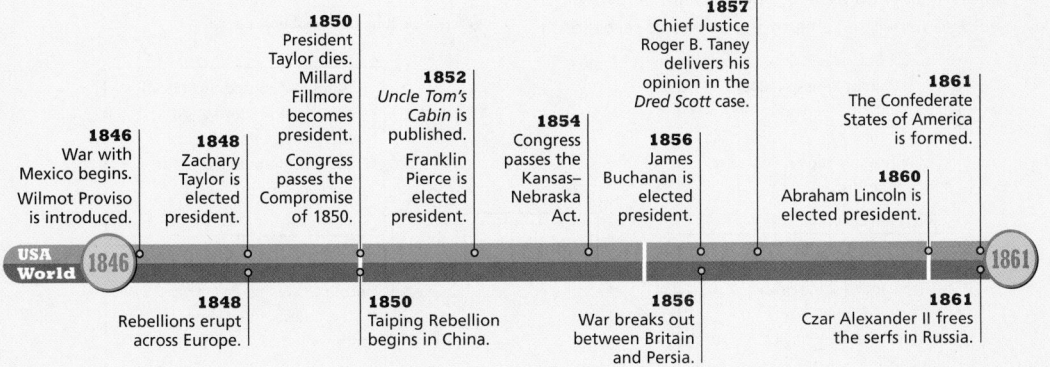

- **1846** War with Mexico begins. Wilmot Proviso is introduced.
- **1848** Zachary Taylor is elected president.
- **1850** President Taylor dies. Millard Fillmore becomes president. Congress passes the Compromise of 1850.
- **1852** *Uncle Tom's Cabin* is published. Franklin Pierce is elected president.
- **1854** Congress passes the Kansas–Nebraska Act.
- **1856** James Buchanan is elected president.
- **1857** Chief Justice Roger B. Taney delivers his opinion in the *Dred Scott* case.
- **1860** Abraham Lincoln is elected president.
- **1861** The Confederate States of America is formed.

World

- **1848** Rebellions erupt across Europe.
- **1850** Taiping Rebellion begins in China.
- **1856** War breaks out between Britain and Persia.
- **1861** Czar Alexander II frees the serfs in Russia.

Interact *with* History

OBJECTIVES

- To help students grasp the intense feelings aroused by the slavery question
- To help students connect with the people and the events in this chapter

What Do You Think?

1. Ask students why members of Congress could get angry about a political issue.
2. Ask students, Do you think debates over slavery made the splitting of the nation more likely?

How would you keep the nation together?

Have students think of different ways of settling arguments, including compromising, using arbitration (an outside group or person asked to hear both sides and give a binding judgment), and by thinking of ways to help those adversely affected.

MAKING PERSONAL CONNECTIONS

Ask students to think of a time when they had a disagreement with a friend. How were they able to resolve the dispute? Did they need to ask other people (parents, friends, counselors) to help find a solution? Did either side have to change his or her position? make accommodations? compromise?

TIME LINE DISCUSSION

Tell students that the issues of slavery and the rights of the states dominated the nation's politics and the attention of the American people during this period.

- Ask students to identify events on the time line that might show peaceful ways to solve the slavery issue. **Answer** 1850 Compromise; Kansas-Nebraska Act; Dred Scott; Lincoln-Douglas debates
- Have students identify an event that signals a violent end to the slavery debate. **Answer** John Brown's raid
- Ask students if they think Lincoln's election could have been a cause of the formation of the Confederate States.

Possible Response Students may already know that Southerners were prepared to secede if Lincoln won the 1860 election.

BEFORE YOU READ

Previewing the Theme:
Diversity and Unity

Ask students to think of values and ideas about government that the North and South shared or that divided them. **Possible Response** Both the North and the South agreed on the ideals of the American Revolution and the basic freedoms set forth in the Bill of Rights. They differed in their view of slavery and which part of government was most important—state government or national government.

What Do You Know?

Remind students that the fertile soil and warm climate of the South made it suitable for plantation crops. The system of slavery provided the large labor force that these crops needed. In the North, industry and trade were important factors in the economy. Immigrants provided a source of cheap labor for growing mills and factories.

In-Depth Resources: Unit 5
- Tracing Themes: Diversity and Unity, p. 2

READ AND TAKE NOTES

Reading Strategy: Analyzing Causes
Explain to students that the causes of historical events are often more complicated than they seem at first. Analysis involves taking a topic apart to discover different ways of looking at it. To understand historical events, a student must use critical-thinking skills, such as analyzing causes and recognizing effects. By the time students finish the chart, they should be able to describe some of the causes that led to secession.

In-Depth Resources: Unit 5
- Setting the Stage, p. 1

Critical Thinking Transparency CT43
- Setting the Stage

Chapter 15 SETTING THE STAGE

BEFORE YOU READ

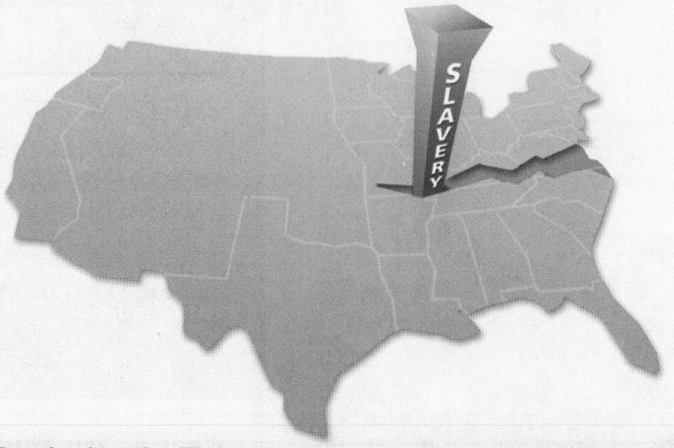

Previewing the Theme

Diversity and Unity As you read in Chapter 14, slavery heightened tensions between Northerners and Southerners. Many people feared that the issue might tear the nation apart. But most Americans hoped that they would be able to solve their problems peacefully. Chapter 15 describes how these tensions led to crisis. It also explains how Americans tried to keep their nation united and how those efforts failed.

What Do You Know?

What do you think about when you hear the terms *slavery* and *abolition?* Why do you think the issue of slavery caused so much anger and resentment?

THINK ABOUT
- what you've learned about differences between the North and the South from books, travel, television, or movies
- reasons people have violent conflicts today

What Do You Want to Know?

What questions do you have about the sectional crisis that led to the Civil War? Record them in your notebook before you read this chapter.

READ AND TAKE NOTES

Reading Strategy: Analyzing Causes Analyzing causes means looking closely at events and describing why they happened. The diagram below will help you analyze some of the causes of secession.

Use the diagram to take notes on how each issue drove the North and the South farther apart.

See Skillbuilder Handbook, page R11.

Wilmot Proviso (1846)
Bill to outlaw slavery in territories taken from Mexico; caused conflict in Congress between Northerners and Southerners

Compromise of 1850
Laws meant to settle problem of slavery; California became free state; new fugitive slave law passed; caused conflict by failing to resolve slavery issue

SECESSION

Kansas–Nebraska Act (1854)
Law to organize Kansas and Nebraska territories; overturned Missouri Compromise; caused violence in Kansas

Election of 1860
Lincoln elected with support only in free states; caused states in Deep South to decide to secede

TEACHING STRATEGY

READING THE CHAPTER

This is a chronological chapter focusing on the widening rift between the North and the South. Encourage students to look for causes and effects of events during this time period. Pause after each section to review the events, their causes, and their effects.

ALTERNATIVE ASSESSMENT

The Chapter Assessment describes three activities for alternative assessment on page 461. You may wish to have students work on these activities during the course of the chapter and then present them at the end.

1 Growing Tensions Between North and South

TERMS & NAMES
Wilmot Proviso
Free-Soil Party
Henry Clay
Daniel Webster
Stephen A. Douglas
Compromise of 1850

MAIN IDEA

Disagreements between the North and the South, especially over the issue of slavery, led to political conflict.

WHY IT MATTERS NOW

Regional differences can make national problems difficult to resolve.

ONE EUROPEAN'S STORY

Alexis de Tocqueville [TOHK•vihl] was a young French government official from a wealthy family. In 1831, he set out to study American prisons and politics.

At one point, Tocqueville traveled in a steamship down the Ohio River. The river was the border between Ohio, a free state, and Kentucky, a slave state. Tocqueville noted what he saw on both sides of the river.

Alexis de Tocqueville

A VOICE FROM THE PAST

The State of Ohio is separated from Kentucky just by one river; on either side of it the soil is equally fertile, and the situation equally favourable, and yet everything is different. Here [on the Ohio side] a population devoured by feverish activity, trying every means to make its fortune. . . . There [on the Kentucky side] are people who make others work for them and show little compassion, a people without energy, mettle or the spirit of enterprise. . . . These differences cannot be attributed to any other cause but slavery. It degrades the black population and enervates [saps the energy of] the white.

Alexis de Tocqueville, *Journey to America*

Tocqueville's comment was aimed not at the Southern people as individuals but at the system of slavery itself. In this section, you will read about the differences between the North and the South. You will also learn how slavery led to political tensions that threatened to tear the nation apart.

1 North and South Take Different Paths

As you read in Chapter 11, the economies of the North and the South developed differently in the early 1800s. Although both economies were mostly agricultural, the North began to develop more industry and commerce. By contrast, the Southern economy relied on plantation farming.

The growth of industry in the North helped lead to the rapid growth of Northern cities. Much of this population growth came from immigration. In addition, immigrants and Easterners moved west and built farms in the new states formed from the Northwest Territory. Most canals and railroads ran east and west, helping the Eastern and

SECTION OBJECTIVES

1. To explain how the abolitionist movement heightened tension between North and South
2. To describe the controversies over slavery in the territories
3. To evaluate how the Wilmot Proviso and potential statehood for California deepened regional divisions
4. To analyze the Compromise of 1850

CRITICAL THINKING

Making Generalizations, p. 442
Recognizing Effects, p. 443
Comparing and Contrasting, p. 445

FOCUS & MOTIVATE

5-MINUTE WARM-UP

Making Inferences These questions explore differences between the North and the South.

1. Look at the chart on page 442. Which region had a more diversified, or varied, economy?
2. Why do you think the South only produced cotton?

Warm-Up Transparency WT15

INSTRUCT

INSTRUCT: OBJECTIVE 1

North and South Take Different Paths

- How did the economies of the North and the South differ?
- What factors caused the rapid growth of Northern cities?
- Why was there so little investment in industry in the South?

In-Depth Resources: Unit 5
- Guided Reading, p. 3

Reading Study Guide (Spanish and English), pp. 143–144

RECOMMENDED RESOURCES

In-Depth Resources: Unit 5
- Guided Reading, p. 3
- Building Vocabulary, p. 7

Reading Study Guide (Spanish and English), pp. 143–144

Economics in History
- King Cotton, p. 15

Formal Assessment
- Section Quiz, p. 269

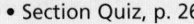

Integrated Assessment
- Rubrics, 5.5

Access for Students Acquiring English/ESL
- Guided Reading, p. 97

INTEGRATED TECHNOLOGY

Critical Thinking Trans. CT44
- Cause and Effect: The Compromise of 1850

Electronic Teacher Tools

classzone.com

TEST-TAKING RESOURCES

Strategies for Test Preparation

Test Practice Transparencies, TT53

Online Test Practice

Economics *in* History

OBJECTIVE
Students will be able to define trade and explain how it works. They will be able to explain how the South and the North benefited from trade with each other.

Trade and Bartering
The concept of trade has its roots in the simpler barter system. In a barter, people exchange items or skills that they have for items or skills that they need or want. No money changes hands, nor is any middle person needed.

As societies become more complicated, bartering does not work well. Systems of trade develop in its place. Trade differs from bartering because money is exchanged instead of goods or skills. In addition, goods may change hands many times, and people are involved in these exchanges.

1. **Solving Problems Possible Responses** Trade helps a country get goods that it wants but cannot produce. A country could try to produce these other goods, but it might be too difficult or expensive.
2. **Comparing Possible Responses** Americans sell many different goods, from farm products and machines to technology to television shows and services. Americans buy many of these same products from other countries.

Economics in History
• King Cotton, p. 15

INSTRUCT: OBJECTIVE 2
Antislavery and Racism

- Why did free workers in the North oppose slavery?
- What reasons did Southern slaveholders offer in defense of slavery?

Economics *in* History

Trade

Trade is based on a simple idea. If you have something someone else needs or wants, and that person has something you need or want, you exchange, or trade, those two things. After the trade, you should both be better off than before.

The concept of trade works similarly for groups of people. For example, in the early 1800s, the South had few factories. Planters who wanted manufactured goods usually had to buy them from manufacturers in the North or in Europe. To have the cash to buy those goods, Southerners sold other goods, such as cotton, to the North and other countries. Each sold the goods they could produce in order to get money to buy the goods they could not make.

CONNECT TO HISTORY
1. **Solving Problems** What problem does trade help a country solve? How else could a country solve this problem?
See Skillbuilder Handbook, page R18.

CONNECT TO TODAY
2. **Comparing** What goods do Americans sell to other countries today? What goods do Americans buy from other countries?

For more about trade . . .
RESEARCH LINKS CLASSZONE.COM

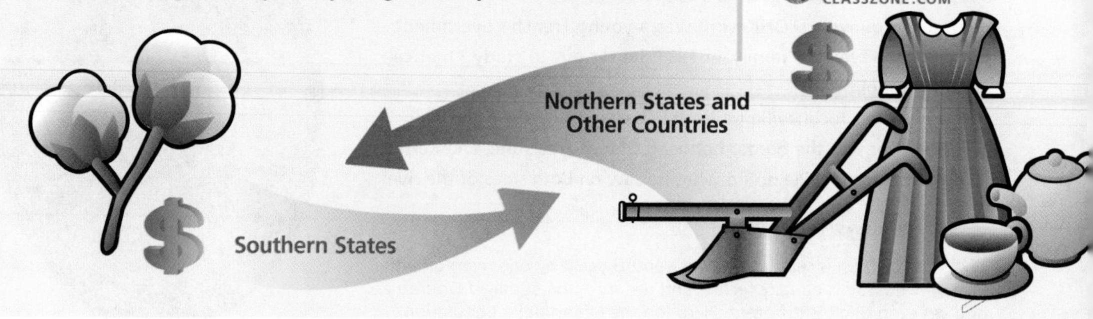

Midwestern states develop strong ties with each other.

The South developed differently than the North. A few wealthy planters controlled Southern society. They made great profits from the labor of their slaves. Much of this profit came from trade. Planters relied on exports, especially cotton. Because these plantations were so profitable, planters invested in slaves instead of industry. As a result, the South developed little industry.

Most Southern whites were poor farmers who owned no slaves. But even many of the nonslaveholding whites supported slavery because it kept them off the bottom of society.

Reading **History**
A. Making Generalizations How did the economies of the North and the South differ?
A. Answer The North was more industrial. The South was more agricultural and used slave labor.

2 Antislavery and Racism

The issue of slavery caused tension between the North and the South. In the North, the antislavery movement had slowly been gaining strength since the 1830s. Abolitionists believed that slavery was unjust and should be abolished immediately. Many Northerners who opposed slavery took a less extreme position. Some Northern workers and immigrants opposed slavery because it was an economic threat to them. Because slaves did not work for pay, free workers feared that managers would employ slaves rather than them. Some workers were even afraid that the expansion of slavery might force workers into slavery to find jobs.

Despite their opposition to slavery, most Northerners, even abolitionists, were racist by modern standards. Many whites refused to go to

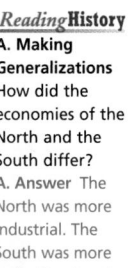

ACTIVITY OPTIONS
INTERDISCIPLINARY LINK: ECONOMICS — BLOCK SCHEDULING

VALUE OF COTTON EXPORTS
Class Time 15 minutes
Task Analyzing data that shows the value of cotton exports and making a graph illustrating the information
Purpose To evaluate the importance of the cotton trade

Supplies Needed
• Art supplies (optional)

Activity Write the following data on the chalkboard.

Cotton Exports		
1836–1840	$321 million	43% of total U.S. exports
1856–1860	$744.6 million	54% of total U.S. exports

Tell students to make pie graphs illustrating cotton's percentage of total U.S. exports for the two periods given. Ask students to explain why cotton exports were important to the nation as a whole. Ask students what factors may have caused the increase in exports over the 20-year period.

school with, work with, or live near African Americans. In most states, even free African Americans could not vote.

Vocabulary
racist: having prejudice based on race

When Northern attacks on slavery increased, slaveholders defended slavery. Most offered the openly racist argument that white people were superior to blacks. Many also claimed that slavery helped slaves by introducing them to Christianity, as well as providing them with food, clothing, and shelter throughout their lives. Slaveholders were determined to defend slavery and their way of life. In this way, the different ideas about slavery brought the North and the South into conflict.

3 The Wilmot Proviso

After the Missouri Compromise in 1820, political disagreements over slavery seemed to go away. But new disagreements arose with the outbreak of the War with Mexico in 1846. Many Northerners believed that Southerners wanted to take territory from Mexico in order to extend slavery. To prevent that, Representative David Wilmot of Pennsylvania proposed a bill, known as the **Wilmot Proviso,** to outlaw slavery in any territory the United States might acquire from the War with Mexico.

But slaveholders believed that Congress had no right to prevent them from bringing slaves into any of the territories. They viewed slaves as property. The Constitution, they claimed, gave equal protection to the property rights of all U.S. citizens. The Wilmot Proviso removed the right of slaveholders to take their slaves, which they regarded as property, anywhere in the United States or its territories. Southerners claimed that the bill was unconstitutional.

The Wilmot Proviso divided Congress along regional lines. The bill passed the House of Representatives. But Southerners prevented it from passing the Senate.

Even though the Wilmot Proviso never became law, it had important effects. It led to the creation of the **Free-Soil Party,** a political party dedicated to stopping the expansion of slavery. The party's slogan expressed its ideals—"Free Soil, Free Speech, Free Labor, and Free Men." The Free-Soil Party won more than ten seats in Congress in the election of 1848. More important, the party made slavery a key issue in national politics. Politicians could ignore slavery no longer.

Connections TO WORLD HISTORY

EXPANDING SLAVERY

William Walker, a Tennessee-born adventurer, wanted to take over land in Central America. In 1855, he joined an army of Nicaraguan rebels and seized power. Walker declared himself president of Nicaragua in 1856. As president, he legalized slavery there.

Troops from nearby countries drove him from power in 1857. The actions of men like Walker helped to convince Northerners that slaveholders were intent on expanding slavery beyond the U.S. South.

Reading **History**
B. Recognizing Effects What were the effects of the Wilmot Proviso?
B. Possible Response It divided Congress along regional lines and led to the formation of the Free-Soil Party.

Controversy over Territories

By 1848, the nation's leaders had begun to debate how to deal with slavery in the lands gained from the War with Mexico. The proposed addition of new states threatened the balance in Congress between North and South. The discovery of gold in California brought thousands of people into that territory. There would soon be enough people in California for it to apply for statehood. Most California residents wanted their state to

INSTRUCT: OBJECTIVE 3

The Wilmot Proviso/ Controversy over Territories

- Why did slaveholders claim that the Wilmot Proviso was unconstitutional?
- Why was the formation of the Free-Soil Party important to national politics?
- What made California's admission as a state controversial?

Connections TO WORLD HISTORY

Slavery in the World Today
Slavery continues to be a threat to poverty-stricken people in some parts of the world. According to a study by the United Nations, about 4 million people are sold into servitude against their will every year. Most are women and girls, although boys and men may also be taken. Many are lured from their homes with false promises of jobs with good pay. Human rights organizations have reported the widespread use of slave labor in China, but the problem is worldwide. In 1998, the U.S. Department of Justice noted that, even in the United States, the problem of enforced servitude is growing worse.

ACTIVITY OPTIONS

INDIVIDUAL NEEDS: GIFTED AND TALENTED

THE SYSTEM OF SERFDOM IN RUSSIA

Class Time Two class periods

Task Preparing a report on serfdom in Russia

Purpose To compare the system of serfdom in Russia to the system of slavery in the United States

Supplies Needed
- Encyclopedias and/or history books
- Internet access (optional)

Activity Have students research the system of serfdom in Russia and write an essay in which they compare the history of serfdom to the history of slavery in the United States. Students should include information about the rights of serfs compared to the rights of slaves; the movement in Russia to end slavery compared to the abolitionist movement; and how the reforms that ended the system of serfdom compared to the way slavery ended in the United States.

be a free state. But this would tip the balance of power clearly in favor of the North. Southerners wanted to divide California in half, making the northern half a free state and the southern half a slave state.

In 1849, President Zachary Taylor—who opposed the extension of slavery—proposed that California submit a plan for statehood that year, without going through the territorial stage. Taylor's plan gave Southern slaveholders little time to move to California with their slaves.

In March 1850, California applied to be admitted as a free state. With California as a free state, slave states would become a minority in the Senate just as they were in the House. Jefferson Davis, a senator from Mississippi, warned, "For the first time, we are about permanently to destroy the balance of power between the sections."

Background
U.S. land gains from the War with Mexico included all or parts of the future states of California, Nevada, Utah, Arizona, New Mexico, and Colorado.

❹ The Compromise of 1850

California could not gain statehood, however, without the approval of Congress. And Congress was divided over the issue. Behind the scenes, statesmen sought compromise. Taking the lead was Senator **Henry Clay**

Henry Clay led the Congress in creating compromises on several important issues during his long career.
John C. Calhoun of South Carolina opposed the Compromise of 1850. He believed the South had no reason to compromise on the issue of slavery.
Daniel Webster spoke eloquently in favor of the compromise.

This engraving dramatically portrays the Senate debate over the Compromise of 1850.

INSTRUCT: OBJECTIVE ❹

The Compromise of 1850

- Why were Southerners opposed to the admission of California to the Union as a free state?
- What compromise allowed California to join the Union? What were its provisions?
- What roles did Henry Clay, Daniel Webster, and Stephen Douglas play in passing the Compromise of 1850?

MORE ABOUT . . .

The Compromise of 1850 Debates

Central roles in the debates were played by Henry Clay, Daniel Webster, and John C. Calhoun. All three men were born during the Revolution, all sought to preserve the nation, and all had once entertained presidential ambitions. Furthermore, all three understood that the Compromise of 1850 represented their last opportunity to shape the future of the country.

Webster and Clay were nationalists who worked to hold the Union together. Calhoun was a states'-rights Southerner who believed the discussion was about property rights. He maintained that Southerners had the constitutional right to take slaves to all territories. If these rights were not protected, Calhoun argued, the South might secede.

Critical Thinking Transparency CT44
• Cause and Effect: The Compromise of 1850

ACTIVITY OPTIONS

INDIVIDUAL NEEDS

LESS PROFICIENT READERS

Finding Main Ideas Students may have difficulty identifying the provisions of proposed laws and understanding how they affected the growing tension between the North and the South. To help students clarify these provisions, have them create webs for the Wilmot Proviso and the Compromise of 1850. Remind students to think of the term in the center as the main idea and to add important details in the surrounding circles.

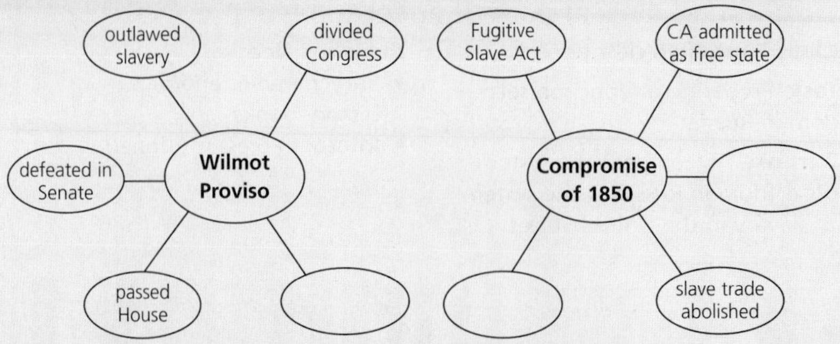

of Kentucky. Clay had helped create the Missouri Compromise in 1820. Now Clay crafted a plan to settle the California problem.

Reading **History**
C. Reading a Map Look at the map on page 448 to see how the Compromise of 1850 affected the territories open to slavery.

1. To please the North, California would be admitted as a free state, and the slave trade would be abolished in Washington, D.C.
2. To please the South, Congress would not pass laws regarding slavery for the rest of the territories won from Mexico, and Congress would pass a stronger law to help slaveholders recapture runaway slaves.

Many people on both sides felt they had to give up too much in this plan. But others were tired of the regional bickering. They wanted to hold the Union together. **Daniel Webster,** senator from Massachusetts, supported the compromise for the sake of the Union.

> *A VOICE FROM THE PAST*
>
> I wish to speak today, not as a Massachusetts man, nor as a Northern man, but as an American. . . . I speak today for the preservation of the Union. Hear me for my cause.
>
> **Daniel Webster,** quoted in *The Annals of America*

The job of winning passage of the plan fell to Senator **Stephen A. Douglas** of Illinois. By the end of September, Douglas succeeded, and the plan, now known as the **Compromise of 1850,** became law.

Some people celebrated the compromise, believing that it had saved the Union. But the compromise would not bring peace. In the next section, you will learn how sectional tensions continued to rise.

AMERICA'S HISTORY MAKERS

STEPHEN A. DOUGLAS
1813–1861

Stephen A. Douglas was one of the most powerful members of Congress in the mid-1800s. In fact, he was called the "Little Giant" because he commanded great respect even though he was only five feet four inches tall.

Perhaps the most important issue that Douglas faced during his career was the expansion of slavery into the territories. Douglas privately hated slavery. But he did not believe a debate on morality would do any good. He suggested that the people of each territory should decide whether or not to allow slavery.

What groups of Americans agreed with Douglas's position on slavery?

Section 1 Assessment

1. Terms & Names

Explain the significance of:
- Wilmot Proviso
- Free-Soil Party
- Henry Clay
- Daniel Webster
- Stephen A. Douglas
- Compromise of 1850

2. Taking Notes

Use a chart like the one below to explain the effects of each cause.

Causes	Effects
Abolitionism	
Wilmot Proviso	
California's application for statehood	

Which issue do you think most threatened national unity?

3. Main Ideas

a. What were two ways that the North and the South differed by the mid-1800s?

b. In what ways was racism common in both the North and the South?

c. How did the War with Mexico lead to conflict between the North and the South?

4. Critical Thinking

Comparing and Contrasting How was the Compromise of 1850 similar to and different from the Missouri Compromise?

THINK ABOUT
- the regional tensions at the time the compromises were proposed
- who proposed each bill
- the provisions of the bills

ACTIVITY OPTIONS

TECHNOLOGY
SPEECH

Imagine you are a television news director. Plan a five-minute **documentary** or organize a **panel discussion** on the Compromise of 1850.

AMERICA'S HISTORY MAKERS

Stephen A. Douglas

Stephen A. Douglas was born in Brandon, Vermont, but migrated to Illinois when he was 20. Douglas became wealthy through land speculation in Illinois. He worked to make Chicago a railroad hub. He believed that great wealth would pour into Illinois when the nation had its first transcontinental railroad. Some historians think that Douglas wanted to settle the issue of slavery in the territories to speed the construction of the railroads.

Douglas died of typhoid fever in 1861. He is buried in Chicago. His tomb bears the words "Tell my children to obey the Laws and uphold the Constitution."

Answer: Southern slaveholders and people who believed each state should make its own laws on slavery

ASSESS & RETEACH

Setting the Stage Have students fill in the boxes for the Wilmot Proviso and the Compromise of 1850 on the graphic organizer.

Formal Assessment
- Section Quiz, p. 269

Critical Thinking Transparency CT43
- Setting the Stage

RETEACHING ACTIVITY

Have one student of a student pair explain the causes and effects of the Wilmot Proviso to his or her partner. Tell the partner to ask questions to clarify the explanation. Then have students switch roles for the Compromise of 1850.

In-Depth Resources: Unit 5
- Reteaching Activity, p. 16

Section 1 Assessment

1. Terms & Names

Wilmot Proviso, p. 443
Free-Soil Party, p. 443
Henry Clay, p. 444
Daniel Webster, p. 445
Stephen A. Douglas, p. 445
Compromise of 1850, p. 445

2. Taking Notes

Abolitionism—Raised tensions among citizens over the morality of slavery; Wilmot Proviso—Caused political conflict over the legality of slavery in the territories; California's application for statehood—Led to the Compromise of 1850
California, because it would give the free states a majority in both houses of Congress

3. Main Ideas

a. The North had an industrial economy, while the South had an agricultural one that relied heavily on slave labor. **b.** feelings of white superiority and black inferiority; discrimination **c.** The land won in the war caused conflict over whether slavery would be legal in these new American territories.

4. Critical Thinking

Similar: both dealt with the issue of slavery in U.S. territories; Different: the 1850 law upset the balance of number of free and slave states

ACTIVITY OPTIONS

Integrated Assessment
- Rubrics, 5.5
- Rubrics, 3.2

SECTION OBJECTIVES

1. To explain how the Fugitive Slave Act and *Uncle Tom's Cabin* affected Northerners
2. To analyze the concept of popular sovereignty
3. To describe the violence in "Bleeding Kansas"
4. To evaluate the attack on Senator Sumner in the Senate

SKILLBUILDER

Interpreting Maps: Region p. 448

CRITICAL THINKING

Analyzing Points of View, p. 447
Sequencing Events, p. 449
Solving Problems, p. 449

FOCUS & MOTIVATE

5-MINUTE WARM-UP

Drawing Conclusions These questions focus on changes in slave and free territory.

1. Look at the maps of the United States on page 448. How many new slave states were added between 1820 and 1854?
2. How much more territory was open to slavery after 1854?

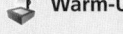

Warm-Up Transparency WT15

INSTRUCT

INSTRUCT: OBJECTIVE 1

The Fugitive Slave Act/*Uncle Tom's Cabin*

- Why did Southerners feel that the Fugitive Slave Act was justified?
- What moral dilemma did the Fugitive Slave Act force Northerners to face?
- Why did white Southerners resent *Uncle Tom's Cabin*?

In-Depth Resources: Unit 5
- Guided Reading, p. 4

America's History Makers
- Harriet Beecher Stowe, pp. 59–60

Reading Study Guide (Spanish and English), pp. 145–146

2 The Crisis Deepens

TERMS & NAMES
Harriet Beecher Stowe
Uncle Tom's Cabin
Fugitive Slave Act
popular sovereignty
Kansas-Nebraska Act
John Brown

MAIN IDEA	WHY IT MATTERS NOW
Turmoil over slavery led to acts of violence.	Violence can make compromise more difficult.

Harriet Beecher Stowe

ONE AMERICAN'S STORY

Harriet Beecher Stowe was outraged when she heard about the part of the Compromise of 1850 that would help slaveholders recapture runaway slaves. She described her feelings about the law.

A VOICE FROM THE PAST

Since the legislative act of 1850, when [I] heard . . . Christian and humane people actually recommending the remanding [returning of] escaped fugitives into slavery, as a duty binding on good citizens, . . . [I] could only think, These men and Christians cannot know what slavery is.

Harriet Beecher Stowe, *Uncle Tom's Cabin*

Stowe's anger motivated her to write *Uncle Tom's Cabin,* a novel that portrayed slavery as brutal and immoral. In this section, you will learn how the Compromise of 1850 deepened the division between the North and the South.

1 The Fugitive Slave Act

The 1850 law to help slaveholders recapture runaway slaves was called the **Fugitive Slave Act**. People accused of being fugitives under this law could be held without an arrest warrant. In addition, they had no right to a jury trial. Instead, a federal commissioner ruled on each case. The commissioner received five dollars for releasing the defendant and ten dollars for turning the defendant over to a slaveholder.

Southerners felt that the Fugitive Slave Act was justified because they considered slaves to be property. But Northerners resented the Fugitive Slave Act. It required Northerners to help recapture runaway slaves. It placed fines on people who would not cooperate and jail terms on people who helped the fugitives escape. In addition, Southern slave catchers roamed the North, sometimes capturing free African Americans.

The presence of slave catchers throughout the North brought home the issue of slavery to Northerners. They could no longer ignore the fact that, by supporting the Fugitive Slave Act, they played an important role in supporting slavery. They faced a moral choice. Should they

RECOMMENDED RESOURCES

In-Depth Resources: Unit 5
- Guided Reading, p. 4
- Building Vocabulary, p. 7
- Skillbuilder Practice, p. 8
- Literature Selection: from *Uncle Tom's Cabin,* pp. 13–15
- Enrichment Activity, p. 20

Reading Study Guide (Spanish and English), pp. 145–146

America's History Makers
- Harriet Beecher Stowe, pp. 59–60

Formal Assessment
- Section Quiz, p. 270

Integrated Assessment
- Rubrics, 4.7, 1.3

Access for Students Acquiring English/ESL, pp. 98, 101

INTEGRATED TECHNOLOGY

Humanities Transparency HT29
- Poster: Eliza on Ice

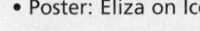

Electronic Teacher Tools

classzone.com

TEST-TAKING RESOURCES

Strategies for Test Preparation

Test Practice Transparencies, TT54

Online Test Practice

obey the law and support slavery, or should they break the law and oppose slavery?

Uncle Tom's Cabin

Stowe published *Uncle Tom's Cabin* in 1852. It dramatically portrayed the moral issues of slavery. In fact, a play based on the book increased the popularity of drama as well as abolitionism. The book's main character was Uncle Tom, a respected older slave. The plot centers on Tom's life under three owners. Two of the owners were kind, but the third was cruel. The novel includes dramatic scenes, such as the dangerous escape of a slave named Eliza and her baby across the Ohio River.

ReadingHistory
A. Analyzing Points of View How did the play *Uncle Tom's Cabin* affect the development of drama in the United States?
A. Possible Response A play based on *Uncle Tom's Cabin* increased the popularity of drama as well as abolitionism.

A VOICE FROM THE PAST

Eliza made her desperate retreat across the river just in the dusk of twilight. The gray mist of evening, rising slowly from the river, enveloped her as she disappeared up the bank, and the swollen current and floundering masses of ice presented a hopeless barrier between her and her pursuer.

Harriet Beecher Stowe, *Uncle Tom's Cabin*

Stowe's book was wildly popular in the North. But white Southerners believed the book falsely criticized the South and slavery.

2 The Kansas–Nebraska Act

While the Fugitive Slave Act and *Uncle Tom's Cabin* heightened the conflicts between the North and the South, the issue of slavery in the territories brought bloodshed to the West. In 1854, Senator Stephen A. Douglas of Illinois drafted a bill to organize territorial governments for the Nebraska Territory. He proposed that it be divided into two territories—Nebraska and Kansas.

To get Southern support for the bill, he suggested that the decision about whether to allow slavery in each of these territories be settled by popular sovereignty. **Popular sovereignty** is a system where the residents vote to decide an issue. If this bill passed, it would result in getting rid of the Missouri Compromise by

Background
The Nebraska Territory was part of the Louisiana Purchase. It lay north of the 36° 30′ line, so the Missouri Compromise banned slavery there.

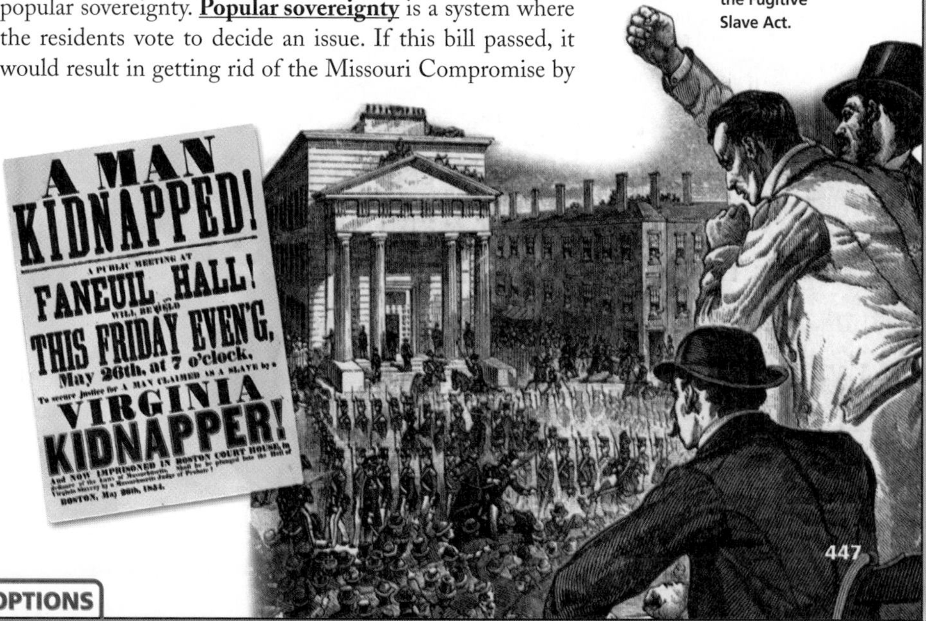

In 1854, Bostonians protested the capture of an African American by federal marshals under the Fugitive Slave Act.

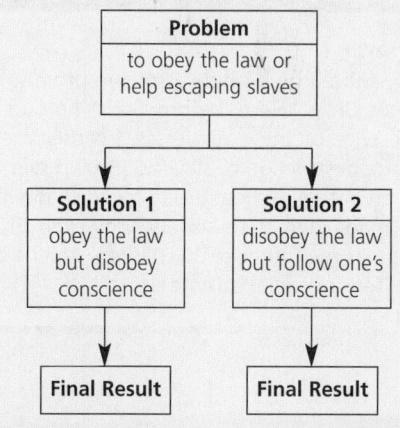

447

MORE ABOUT . . .

Uncle Tom's Cabin

Harriet Beecher Stowe drew on some of her own experiences in writing *Uncle Tom's Cabin.* While living in Cincinnati, she watched her family help runaway slaves from across the Ohio River in Kentucky. Stowe's family was remarkable. Her father, Lyman Beecher, was a famous minister. Her brother, Henry Ward Beecher, was also a preacher and a leading abolitionist. Stowe's sister Catharine worked to improve education for women.

Humanities Transparency HT29
- Poster: Eliza on Ice

INSTRUCT: OBJECTIVE 2

The Kansas-Nebraska Act

- What is popular sovereignty?
- What groups of people supported the Kansas-Nebraska Act? What groups opposed it?
- How did the Kansas-Nebraska Act change decisions about slavery?

CRITICAL THINKING ACTIVITY

Identifying and Solving Problems Have students complete an outline like this one to analyze the problem faced by many abolitionists with the passage of the Fugitive Slave Law.

Problem
to obey the law or help escaping slaves

Solution 1
obey the law but disobey conscience
→ **Final Result**

Solution 2
disobey the law but follow one's conscience
→ **Final Result**

Class Time 15 minutes

ACTIVITY OPTIONS

MULTIPLE LEARNING STYLES: LINGUISTIC | **BLOCK SCHEDULING**

UNCLE TOM'S CABIN

Class Time 30 minutes

Task Reading aloud selected passages from *Uncle Tom's Cabin*

Purpose To familiarize students with an important literary work in the nation's history

Supplies Needed
- Copies of *Uncle Tom's Cabin*

Activity Ask students to practice reading aloud selected sections from *Uncle Tom's Cabin* for presentation to the class. Help students select dramatic scenes, such as Eliza's escape or the death of little Eva. Preview selections for content, language, and dialect appropriate for your class before students begin rehearsing.

In-Depth Resources: Unit 5
- Literature Selection: from *Uncle Tom's Cabin,* pp. 13–15
- Enrichment Activity, p. 20

HISTORY FROM VISUALS

Reading the Map Ask students to point out the differences between the United States at the time of the Missouri Compromise and after the Compromise of 1850. **Possible Responses** Between the Missouri Compromise and the Compromise of 1850, Texas and Florida had become new slave states. Territory in the West, including California, was organized and closed to slavery, while Indian territory and other land in the Southwest were now open to slavery.

Extension Have students draw in the Mason-Dixon Line of the Missouri Compromise on a map showing the United States in 1854. Note how many states or parts of states would have changed status.

INSTRUCT: OBJECTIVE 3

"Bleeding Kansas"

- How did proslavery forces ensure that Kansas would elect a proslavery legislature?
- Why did proslavery forces attack Lawrence, Kansas?
- What effects did John Brown's actions have on the situation in Kansas?

MORE ABOUT . . .

John Brown

In 1837, John Brown made a solemn promise in a church in Ohio. "Here, before God," he said, "in the presence of these witnesses, I consecrate my life to the destruction of slavery." Brown said that seeing a white man beat an enslaved child with a shovel made him hate slavery. However, Brown himself was the father of 20 children, and he beat them often for trivial offenses.

***Free and Slave States and Territories,** 1820–1854*

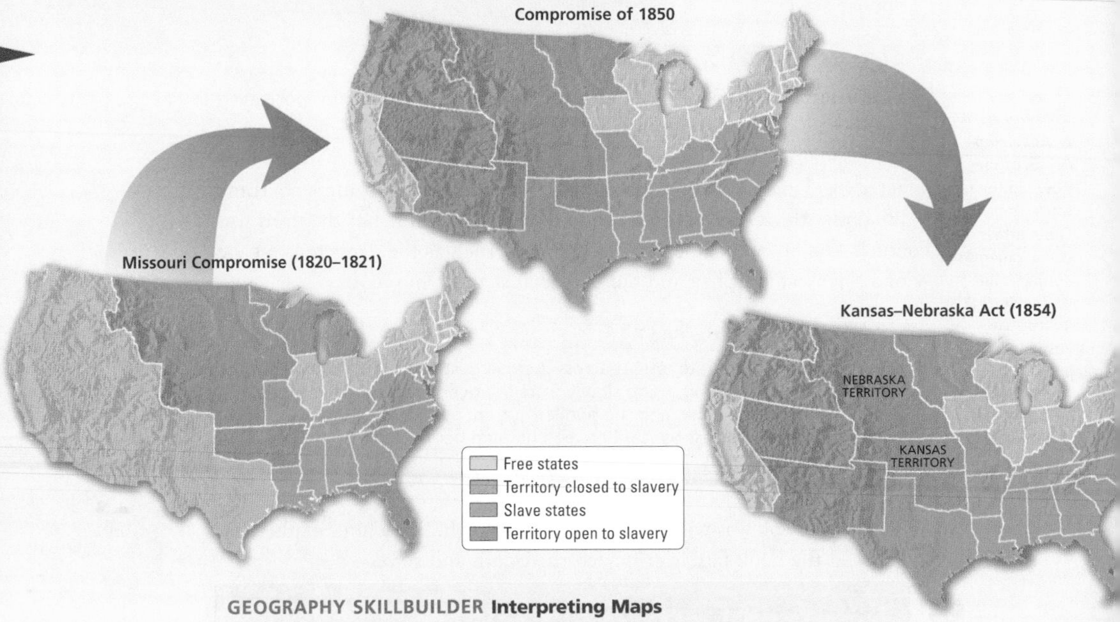

GEOGRAPHY SKILLBUILDER Interpreting Maps

1. **Region** *What new free states and slave states entered the Union between 1820 and 1854?*
2. **Region** *How did the Kansas–Nebraska Act change the amount of territory open to slavery?*

Skillbuilder Answers
1. Free states: Michigan, Wisconsin, Iowa, and California. Slave states: Texas, Arkansas, and Florida
2. The Kansas–Nebraska Act opened new territories to slavery.

allowing people to vote for slavery in territories where the Missouri Compromise had banned it.

As Douglas hoped, Southerners applauded the repeal of the Missouri Compromise and supported the bill. Even though the bill angered opponents of slavery, it passed. It became known as the **Kansas–Nebraska Act.** Few people realized that the act would soon turn Kansas into a battleground over slavery.

3 "Bleeding Kansas"

Proslavery and antislavery settlers rushed into the Kansas Territory, just west of Missouri, to vote for the territorial legislature. At the time of the election in March 1855, there were more proslavery settlers than antislavery settlers in the territory. But the proslavery forces did not want to risk losing the election. Five thousand Missourians came and voted in the election illegally. As a result, the official Kansas legislature was packed with proslavery representatives.

Antislavery settlers boycotted the official government and formed a government of their own. With political authority in dispute, settlers on both sides armed themselves. In May, a proslavery mob attacked the town of Lawrence, Kansas. The attackers destroyed offices and the

Vocabulary
boycott: refuse to participate in

ACTIVITY OPTIONS

SKILLBUILDER LESSON: SEQUENCING EVENTS — BLOCK SCHEDULING

Explaining the Skill Students need to understand the order in which things happen—to put them in sequence—to get an accurate sense of the relationship among events.

Applying the Skill Write the following events on the board: a) Brown leads the Pottawatomie Massacre. b) Missourians vote in the Kansas election. c) The Kansas-Nebraska Act is passed. d) Antislavery forces in Kansas form their own government. e) A proslavery mob attacks Lawrence. Have students put the events in their correct sequence. (1. c 2. b 3. d 4. e 5. a)

After they have finished, discuss the following questions:

1. Why is it important to know that the Kansas-Nebraska Act was passed before Missourians voted in the Kansas election? *(The act said the slavery question would be determined by popular sovereignty. Because the Missourians wanted Kansas to be a slave state, they used numbers to sway the vote.)*
2. Besides numbering events to put them in sequence, how else could you show their chronological order? *(by using a time line)*

In-Depth Resources: Unit 5
- Skillbuilder Practice, p. 8

house of the governor of the antislavery government. This attack came to be known as the Sack of Lawrence.

Onto this explosive scene came **John Brown**, an extreme abolitionist. To avenge the Sack of Lawrence, Brown and seven other men went to the cabins of several of his proslavery neighbors and murdered five people. This attack is known as the Pottawatomie Massacre, after the creek near where the victims were found. As news of the violence spread, civil war broke out in Kansas. It continued for three years, and the territory came to be called "Bleeding Kansas."

Reading **History**
B. Sequencing Events What events in Kansas preceded the Pottawatomie Massacre?
B. Answer Kansas–Nebraska Act (1854); territorial elections (March 1855); Sack of Lawrence (May 1855)

Violence in Congress 4

While violence was spreading in Kansas in the spring of 1856, blood was also being shed in the nation's capital. In late May, Senator Charles Sumner of Massachusetts delivered a speech attacking the proslavery forces in Kansas. His speech was packed with insults. Sumner even made fun of A. P. Butler, a senator from South Carolina.

Preston Brooks, a relative of Butler, heard about Sumner's speech. To defend Butler and the South, he attacked Sumner, who was sitting at his desk. Brooks hit Sumner over the head with his cane. Sumner tried to defend himself, but his legs were trapped. Brooks hit him 30 times or more, breaking his cane in the assault. (The painting on page 439 shows this event.)

Many Southerners cheered Brooks's defense of the South. But most Northerners were shocked at the violence in the Senate. "Bleeding Kansas" and "Bleeding Sumner" became rallying cries for antislavery Northerners and slogans for a new political party. In the next section, you will learn about the creation of the Republican Party.

STRANGE *but* True

PRESTON BROOKS'S CANE

Many Americans, Northerners and Southerners alike, were ashamed of the behavior of Sumner and Brooks. But sectional tensions were so high at the time that a large number of Southerners cheered Brooks for his actions.

A number of Brooks's supporters sent him new canes to replace the one he had broken while hitting Sumner on the head. Some of the canes were inscribed with mottoes such as "Hit Him Again."

Section 2 *Assessment*

1. Terms & Names

Explain the significance of:
- Harriet Beecher Stowe
- *Uncle Tom's Cabin*
- Fugitive Slave Act
- popular sovereignty
- Kansas–Nebraska Act
- John Brown

2. Taking Notes

Use a chart like the one below to compare Northern and Southern views of the issues listed.

Northern View	Issue	Southern View
	Fugitive Slave Act	
	Kansas–Nebraska Act	
	"Bleeding Kansas"	

3. Main Ideas

a. How did the book *Uncle Tom's Cabin* influence national politics?

b. Why was the Kansas–Nebraska Act so controversial?

c. What was the cause of "Bleeding Kansas"?

4. Critical Thinking

Solving Problems What would you have done to prevent the violence in Kansas?

THINK ABOUT
- the repeal of the Missouri Compromise
- popular sovereignty
- the actions of John Brown

ACTIVITY OPTIONS

LITERATURE
ART

Read a chapter of *Uncle Tom's Cabin*. Write a **book review** or make a series of **drawings** illustrating the story.

INSTRUCT: OBJECTIVE 4

Violence in Congress

- How did Northerners react to the beating of Senator Charles Sumner?
- In what ways did the beating of Senator Sumner represent what was happening in the nation?

STRANGE *but* True

Preston Brooks's Cane

A House committee investigated the caning affair and recommended Brooks's expulsion. Nevertheless, the House vote followed party and sectional lines and fell short of the needed two-thirds majority. Brooks resigned his seat and his only punishment was a $300 fine. Brooks was embraced as a hero throughout the South, but Northerners turned Sumner into a martyr. Sumner did not return to his Senate seat for two and a half years.

ASSESS & RETEACH

Setting the Stage Have students fill in the box for the Kansas-Nebraska Act on the graphic organizer.

Formal Assessment
- Section Quiz, p. 270

RETEACHING ACTIVITY

Have students construct a cause-and-effect chain like the one started below to summarize the events surrounding the violence in Kansas.

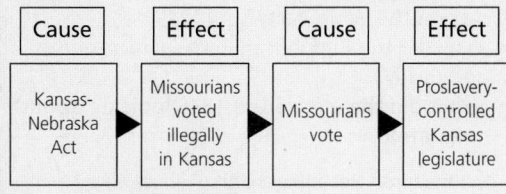

Cause	Effect	Cause	Effect
Kansas-Nebraska Act ▶	Missourians voted illegally in Kansas ▶	Missourians vote ▶	Proslavery-controlled Kansas legislature

In-Depth Resources: Unit 5
- Reteaching Activity, p. 17

Section 2 *Assessment*

1. Terms & Names

Harriet Beecher Stowe, p. 446
Uncle Tom's Cabin, p. 446
Fugitive Slave Act, p. 446
popular sovereignty, p. 447
Kansas-Nebraska Act, p. 448
John Brown, p. 449

2. Taking Notes

Issue 1: North opposed because it forced them to support slavery; South favored because it upheld slavery; Issue 2: North opposed because it allowed slavery in new areas; South supported because it nullified the Missouri Compromise; Issue 3: North blamed proslavery forces; South blamed abolitionists

3. Main Ideas

a. It heightened tensions between North and South. **b.** It scrapped the Missouri Compromise, allowing slavery into areas where it was banned. **c.** Antislavery and proslavery forces clashed over contested elections for the territorial legislature in Kansas.

4. Critical Thinking

Students might suggest keeping the Missouri Compromise or sending the army to keep order.

ACTIVITY OPTIONS

Integrated Assessment
- Rubrics for a book review, 4.7
- Rubrics for an illustration, 1.3

SECTION OBJECTIVES

1. To explain why the Republican Party was formed
2. To summarize the effects of the *Dred Scott* case
3. To analyze the Lincoln-Douglas debates
4. To evaluate the impact of John Brown's raid on Harpers Ferry

CRITICAL THINKING

Summarizing, p. 451
Recognizing Effects, p. 452
Making Inferences, p. 453
Identifying Facts and Opinions, p. 454

FOCUS & MOTIVATE

5-MINUTE WARM-UP

Analyzing Causes and Recognizing Effects
These questions focus on reasons for the creation of the Republican Party.

1. Read the quotation and look at the medal on page 450. What do they tell you about the reasons for starting the new party?
2. Why do you think people wanted to start a new party?

Warm-Up Transparency WT15

INSTRUCT

INSTRUCT: OBJECTIVE 1

The Republican Party Forms/ The Election of 1856

- What was the effect of the Kansas-Nebraska Act on the Whig Party?
- Why did the Republican Party gain strength so quickly?
- What did the election of 1856 indicate about the nation?

In-Depth Resources: Unit 5
- Guided Reading, p. 5

Reading Study Guide (Spanish and English), pp. 147–148

3 Slavery Dominates Politics

MAIN IDEA

Disagreement over slavery led to the formation of the Republican Party and heightened sectional tensions.

WHY IT MATTERS NOW

The Democrats and the Republicans are the major political parties of today.

TERMS & NAMES
Republican Party
John C. Frémont
James Buchanan
Dred Scott v. Sandford
Roger B. Taney
Abraham Lincoln
Harpers Ferry

ONE AMERICAN'S STORY

Joseph Warren, editor of the Detroit *Tribune*, wanted the antislavery parties of Michigan to join forces. In 1854, his newspaper pushed them to unite.

A VOICE FROM THE PAST

[A convention should be called] irrespective of the old party organizations, for the purpose of agreeing upon some plan of action that shall combine the whole anti-Nebraska, anti-slavery sentiment of the State, upon one ticket [set of candidates endorsed by a political party].

Detroit *Tribune*, quoted in *The Origins of the Republican Party*

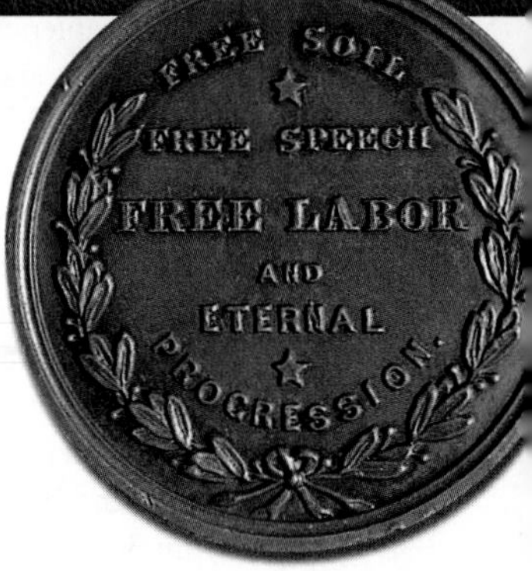

This medal shows an early motto of the Republican Party. It also makes clear the Republican connection to the antislavery position of the Free-Soil Party.

By July, antislavery politicians from various parties, including the Whigs, Free-Soilers, and some Democrats, had settled their differences. On July 6, they met to form a new party "to concentrate the popular sentiment of this state against the aggression of the slave power." In memory of Thomas Jefferson, they called themselves Republicans. In this section, you will learn why the Republican Party was formed and how it changed American politics in the 1850s.

1 The Republican Party Forms

The creation of the Republican Party grew out of the problems caused by the Kansas–Nebraska Act of 1854. The law immediately caused a political crisis for the Whig Party. Southern Whigs had supported the bill for the same reason that Northern Whigs had opposed it: the bill proposed to open new territories to slavery. There was no room for compromise, so the party split.

The Southern Whigs were destroyed by the split. A few joined the Democratic Party. But most searched for leaders who supported slavery and the Union. The Northern Whigs, however, joined with other opponents of slavery and formed the **Republican Party**.

The Republicans quickly gained strength in the North. "Bleeding Kansas" was the key to the Republican rise. Many people blamed the violence on the Democrats. With the 1856 elections nearing, the

RECOMMENDED RESOURCES

In-Depth Resources: Unit 5
- Guided Reading, p. 5
- Primary Sources, pp. 11,12

Reading Study Guide (Spanish and English), pp. 147–148

America's History Makers
- Dred Scott, pp. 61–62

Citizenship Today, pp. 11–12, 90–91

Formal Assessment
- Section Quiz, p. 271

Integrated Assessment
- Rubrics, 2.3, 2.1

Access for Students Acquiring English/ESL, p. 99

INTEGRATED TECHNOLOGY

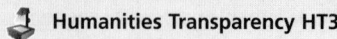

Humanities Transparency HT30

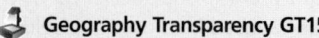

Geography Transparency GT15

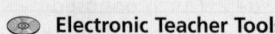

Electronic Teacher Tools

classzone.com

TEST-TAKING RESOURCES

Strategies for Test Preparation

Test Practice Transparencies, TT55

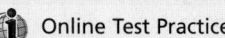

Online Test Practice

Republicans believed that they had an excellent opportunity to gain seats in Congress and win the presidency.

The Republicans needed a strong presidential candidate in 1856 to strengthen their young party. They nominated **John C. Frémont.** Young and handsome, Frémont was a national hero for his explorations in the West, which earned him the nickname the "Pathfinder."

Reading **History**

A. Summarizing Why did the Republicans nominate Frémont for president in 1856?

A. Answer He was a national hero and opposed slavery in Kansas and California.

Republicans liked Frémont for a couple of reasons. He had spoken in favor of admitting both California and Kansas as free states. Also, he had little political experience and did not have a controversial record to defend. Even so, the Republican position on slavery was so unpopular in the South that Frémont's name did not appear on the ballot there.

The Election of 1856

The Democrats nominated **James Buchanan** to run for the presidency in 1856. As minister to Great Britain, he had been in England since 1853 and had spoken neither for nor against the Kansas–Nebraska Act.

Buchanan took advantage of his absence from the country. He said little about slavery and claimed that his goal was to maintain the Union. Buchanan appealed to Southerners, to many people in the upper South and the border states, and to Northerners who were afraid that Frémont's election could tear the nation apart.

The American, or Know-Nothing, Party also nominated a presidential candidate in 1856. They chose Millard Fillmore, who had been president, following the death of Zachary Taylor, from 1850 until 1853. But the Know-Nothings were divided over slavery and had little strength.

The 1856 presidential election broke down into two separate races. In the North, it was Buchanan against Frémont. In the South, it was Buchanan against Fillmore. Buchanan won. He carried all the slave states except Maryland, where Fillmore claimed his only victory. Buchanan also won several Northern states.

Although he lost the election, Frémont won 11 Northern states. These results showed two things. First, the Republican Party was a major force in the North. Second, the nation was sharply split over slavery.

2 The Case of Dred Scott

The split in the country was made worse by the Supreme Court decision in the case of Dred Scott. Scott had been a slave in Missouri. His owner took him to live in territories where slavery was illegal. Then they returned to Missouri. After his owner's death, Scott sued for his freedom. He argued that he was a free man because he had lived in territories where slavery was illegal. His case, ***Dred Scott v. Sandford***, reached the Supreme Court in 1856.

Now and then

THIRD-PARTY CANDIDATES

American politics has usually been dominated by two parties. Most third-party candidates, such as the Republican Frémont in 1856, lose elections. In 1998, Minnesotans broke that pattern when they elected for governor Jesse Ventura of the Reform Party (below).

One reason for Ventura's victory was his celebrity status. He had been a professional wrestler and the host of a popular radio show. His plain speaking appealed to many Minnesotans who felt the major parties were out of touch with the people.

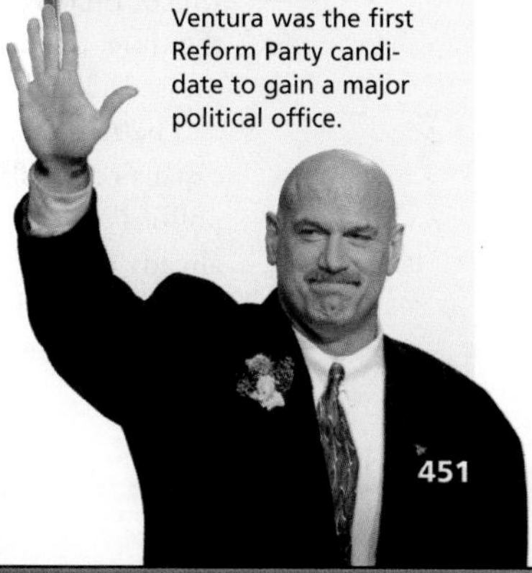

Ventura was the first Reform Party candidate to gain a major political office.

MORE ABOUT . . .

John C. Frémont

Frémont led expeditions to survey and map much of the territory between the Mississippi River and the Pacific Ocean. He joined forces with the famous Kit Carson to complete a survey to the mouth of the Columbia River. His wife, Jessie Benton Frémont, edited her husband's field reports, which were very popular with the public. Frémont was immensely popular in the 1850s and came closer in the election of 1856 than any previous candidate to uniting the antislavery forces.

Now and then

Third-Party Candidates

Third-party candidates work against the odds. Political campaigns are very expensive, and it is harder for a candidate from a minor party to raise money than it is for candidates from one of the two major parties. Independent candidates have no party affiliation at all and, as a result, have an even more difficult time raising funds. One successful independent candidate was Lowell P. Weicker, Jr., governor of Connecticut.

INSTRUCT: OBJECTIVE 2

The Case of Dred Scott

- What reason did Scott give to argue that he was a free man?
- How did Judge Taney counter Scott's argument?
- How did the *Dred Scott* decision affect the Missouri Compromise?

America's History Makers
- Dred Scott, pp. 61–62

In-Depth Resources: Unit 5
- Primary Source: African-American Protest Against the *Dred Scott* Decision, p. 11

ACTIVITY OPTIONS

INDIVIDUAL NEEDS

LESS PROFICIENT READERS

Characterizing Candidates To help less proficient readers keep track of the candidates in the election of 1856, have them fill in a chart such as the one to the right. Have students circle the name of the winning candidate, Buchanan.

Candidates for President, 1856

	Frémont	Buchanan	Fillmore
Party			
Region			
Stand on Slavery			

MORE ABOUT . . .

Dred Scott

By the time the Supreme Court heard Dred Scott's case and ruled against him, Scott was about 65 years old. Manumitted after the decision, he died of tuberculosis after only 16 months of freedom.

Sad as the ruling was for Dred Scott, it was tragic for all African Americans. Not only did Taney's decision allow slavery to spread anywhere in U.S. territory but it also denied the citizenship of free African Americans. Taney wrote that African Americans "had no rights which the white man was bound to respect." Reversing that decision required the Civil War, three constitutional amendments, and a century of activism.

Citizenship Today, pp. 89–90

INSTRUCT: OBJECTIVE 3

Lincoln and Douglas Debate

- How did Lincoln say that the expansion of slavery could be halted?
- How did Douglas's views on the expansion of slavery differ from Lincoln's?
- What effect did the debates have on Lincoln's political career?

MORE ABOUT . . .

The Lincoln-Douglas Debates

Lincoln forced Douglas to explain that his doctrine of popular sovereignty meant that territories could ignore the Supreme Court and keep slavery out. Douglas thus alienated the South. Although he won the Senate seat, he lost his bid to run for president two years later. Lincoln, on the other hand, was invited to speaking engagements throughout the West as a result of the debate. Adding to his fame, 30,000 copies of the transcripts of the debates were sold.

Humanities Transparency HT30
- *The Abraham Lincoln Family in 1861* by Francis Carpenter

Dred Scott (above) first sued for his freedom in 1846. The Supreme Court, led by Chief Justice Roger B. Taney (right), did not rule on the case until 1857.

In 1857, the Court ruled against Scott. Chief Justice **Roger B. Taney** [TAW•nee] delivered his opinion in the case. In it, he said that Dred Scott was not a U.S. citizen. As a result, he could not sue in U.S. courts. Taney also ruled that Scott was bound by Missouri's slave code because he lived in Missouri. As a result, Scott's time in free territory did not matter in his case.

In addition, Taney argued that Congress could not ban slavery in the territories. To do so would violate the slaveholders' property rights, protected by the Fifth Amendment. In effect, Taney declared legislation such as the Missouri Compromise unconstitutional.

Southerners cheered the Court's decision. Many Northerners were outraged and looked to the Republican Party to halt the growing power of Southern slaveholders.

Reading **History**

B. Recognizing Effects How did Taney's opinion affect the Missouri Compromise?

B. Answer The Missouri Compromise had outlawed slavery in territories north of the Missouri Compromise line. Taney said that Congress could not pass laws to ban slavery in the territories.

3 Lincoln and Douglas Debate

After the *Dred Scott* decision, the Republicans charged that the Democrats wanted to legalize slavery not only in all U.S. territories but also in all the states. They used this charge to attack individual Democrats. Stephen A. Douglas, sponsor of the Kansas–Nebraska Act, was one of their main targets in 1858. That year, Illinois Republicans nominated **Abraham Lincoln** to challenge Douglas for his U.S. Senate seat. In his first campaign speech, Lincoln expressed the Northern fear that Southerners wanted to expand slavery to the entire nation. He set the stage for his argument by using a metaphor from the Bible.

A VOICE FROM THE PAST

"A house divided against itself cannot stand." I believe this government cannot endure, permanently half slave and half free. I do not expect the Union to be dissolved—I do not expect the house to fall—but I do expect it will cease to be divided. It will become all one thing, or all the other.

Abraham Lincoln, Springfield, Illinois, June 16, 1858

Later in the year, the two men held formal debates across Illinois. The Lincoln–Douglas debates are now seen as models of political debate. At the time, the debates allowed people to compare the short, stocky, well-dressed Douglas with the tall, thin, gawky Lincoln.

The two men squarely addressed the nation's most pressing issue: the expansion of slavery. For Lincoln, slavery was "a moral, a social and a political wrong." But he did not suggest abolishing slavery where it already existed. He argued only that slavery should not be expanded.

Douglas did not share Lincoln's belief that it was the national government's role to prevent the expansion of slavery. Instead, he argued

ACTIVITY OPTIONS

INTERDISCIPLINARY LINK: CIVICS — BLOCK SCHEDULING

THE *DRED SCOTT* CASE

Class Time Two class periods

Task Presenting a mock hearing of the *Dred Scott* case

Purpose To understand the complexities of the *Dred Scott* case

Supplies Needed
- Encyclopedias and resource material about the *Dred Scott* case

Activity Ask students to do research on the *Dred Scott* case, taking notes on cards emphasizing the most important points of the trial. Form groups and have each group divide up the roles of Dred Scott, his lawyer, opposition lawyers, and Chief Justice Taney. Allow each group to present its mock case, including Chief Justice Taney's handing down of the Court's opinion.

CITIZENSHIP TODAY

Debating Points of View

Debate has long been an important method of exploring public issues. The Lincoln-Douglas debates drew crowds from all over Illinois to hear Lincoln and Douglas discuss the issues of the day. Debates such as these can help people find out about candidates' views.

Today, the National Forensic League (NFL) sponsors Lincoln-Douglas Debates, competitions for high school students. Many judges, actors, news commentators, and talk show hosts began to develop their debating skills in such competitions.

High school students can benefit from learning to defend their positions in debates. One student explained what she learned from NFL debates. "I learned about how to think really fast and how to respond."

Jessica Bailey of Apple Valley High School in Minnesota won second place in the national Lincoln-Douglas Debates competition in 1998.

How Do You Debate an Issue?

1. Choose a debate opponent and an issue to debate. (One NFL topic for national competition was whether the federal government should establish an educational policy to increase academic achievement in secondary schools in the United States.)
2. Research the topic you chose.
3. Agree on a format for your debate—how many minutes for presentation, rebuttal, and closing.
4. Debate your opponent in front of the class.
5. Find out how many students in the audience agree with each side, then ask for their reasons.

See Citizenship Handbook, page 269.

For more about debating . . .

RESEARCH LINKS CLASSZONE.COM

that popular sovereignty was the best way to address the issue because it was the most democratic method to do so.

But popular sovereignty was a problem for Douglas. The Supreme Court decision in the *Dred Scott* case had made popular sovereignty unconstitutional. Why? It said that people could not vote to ban slavery, because doing so would take away slaveholders' property rights. In the debates, Lincoln asked Douglas if he thought people in a territory who were against slavery could legally prohibit it—despite the *Dred Scott* decision.

Douglas replied that it did not matter what the Supreme Court might decide about slavery because "the people have the lawful means to introduce it or exclude it as they please." Douglas won reelection. Lincoln, despite his loss, became a national figure and strengthened his standing in the Republican Party.

Reading **History**

C. Making Inferences Why were popular sovereignty and the opinion in the *Dred Scott* case inconsistent?

C. Answer The *Dred Scott* opinion said that territories could not outlaw slavery. Popular sovereignty said that they could.

4 John Brown Attacks Harpers Ferry

In 1859, John Brown, who had murdered proslavery Kansans three years before, added to the sectional tensions. Brown had a plan. He wanted to inspire slaves to fight for their freedom. To do this, he planned to capture the weapons in the U.S. arsenal at **Harpers Ferry,** Virginia.

On October 16, 1859, Brown and 18 followers—13 whites and 5 blacks—captured the Harpers Ferry arsenal. They killed four people in the raid. Brown then sent out the word to rally and arm local slaves.

Vocabulary

arsenal: stock of weapons

CITIZENSHIP TODAY

OBJECTIVE

Students will be able to explain the importance of debate in exploring public issues in both historic and modern American life.

The Importance of Debate in American Life

Some of the speeches given during the debates over the Compromise of 1850 are the most famous in the history of the Congress. Today, members of Congress still debate new bills presented for their votes. Debates have also become an important part of elections. John F. Kennedy and Richard Nixon, the presidential candidates in 1960, engaged in the first televised presidential debates.

Standards for Evaluation

Each speaker should

- clearly state the problem, position, or topic.
- demonstrate focus and logical organization.
- use appropriate background and research information to defend his or her position.
- conclude with a summarization of the main points and end with an appropriate conclusion.

Citizenship Today, pp. 11–12

INSTRUCT: OBJECTIVE 4

John Brown Attacks Harpers Ferry

- Why did John Brown attack Harpers Ferry?
- What was the reaction of Northerners to Brown's execution?
- How did Southerners react to the raid?

Geography Transparency GT15
- The Slave Population of the South, 1860

In-Depth Resources: Unit 5
- Primary Source: John Brown's Raid, p. 12

ACTIVITY OPTIONS

INDIVIDUAL NEEDS

LESS PROFICIENT READERS

Charting Comparisons Ask students to recall the caning of Charles Sumner (page 449). Then ask them to think about John Brown's attack on Harpers Ferry. In a chart, have them show similarities between the two incidents. Instruct students to concentrate on the reasons for the attacks and their effects.

Similarities Between Charles Sumner and John Brown Incidents

Brooks's Caning of Sumner	Brown's Attack on Harpers Ferry
attack by a Southerner	attack by a Northerner
Brooks thought he was avenging his relative and the honor of the South.	Brown thought he was righting wrong done to slaves.
Southerners thought he was a hero and martyr.	Northerners thought he was a hero and martyr.
incident worsened tensions between North and South	incident worsened tensions between North and South

HISTORY through ART

Interpreting the Painting John Steuart Curry was born in Kansas in 1897. After living in Europe and Connecticut, Curry returned to Kansas in 1937 and spent five years working on a series of murals in the statehouse in Topeka. He used John Brown as his central symbol of the spirit of Kansas. In the image here, Curry shows Brown as one of nature's forces, with a tornado on one side and a prairie fire on the other. Many Kansans were appalled by Curry's murals and by his choice of Brown as their central figure. In 1941, the Kansas legislators refused to allow Curry to finish the murals. In 1992, the Kansas legislature issued an official apology for its treatment of Curry.

Extension Students may wish to view other pictures and paintings of John Brown and compare the portrayals of Brown.

Possible Response: Curry believes Brown caused the Civil War because he shows Brown standing on soldiers' bodies. Brown looks crazy.

ASSESS & RETEACH

Setting the Stage Have students complete the box on the election of 1860 on the chapter graphic organizer.

Formal Assessment
- Section Quiz, p. 271

RETEACHING ACTIVITY

Have students create a time line for the events in this section, beginning with the formation of the Republican Party and ending with John Brown's attack on Harpers Ferry.

In-Depth Resources: Unit 5
- Reteaching Activity, p. 18

HISTORY through ART

John Steuart Curry painted *The Tragic Prelude* between 1937 and 1942. He shows a wild-eyed John Brown standing on the bodies of Civil War soldiers.

What do you think Curry's views were on John Brown's role in U.S. history?

But no slaves joined the fight. The U.S. Marines attacked Brown at Harpers Ferry. Some of his men escaped. But Brown and six others were captured, and ten men were killed.

Brown was then tried for murder and treason. He was convicted and sentenced to hang. On the day he was hanged, abolitionists tolled bells and fired guns in salute. Southerners were enraged by Brown's actions and horrified by Northern reactions to his death.

As the nation headed toward the election of 1860, the issue of slavery had raised sectional tensions to the breaking point. In the next section, you will read about the election of 1860 and its effect on the nation.

Section 3 Assessment

1. Terms & Names

Explain the significance of:
- Republican Party
- John C. Frémont
- James Buchanan
- *Dred Scott v. Sandford*
- Roger B. Taney
- Abraham Lincoln
- Harpers Ferry

2. Taking Notes

Use a chart like the one below to take notes on the major events discussed in this section.

Election of 1856	
Dred Scott v. Sandford	
Lincoln–Douglas debates	
Harpers Ferry	

3. Main Ideas

a. What issues led to the creation of the Republican Party?

b. What consequences did the *Dred Scott* decision have for free blacks?

c. How did John Brown's attack on Harpers Ferry increase tensions between the North and the South?

4. Critical Thinking

Identifying Facts and Opinions How did Lincoln and Douglas disagree about slavery? Which of their views were facts, and which were opinions?

THINK ABOUT
- Lincoln's speech at Springfield in 1858
- Douglas's support of popular sovereignty

ACTIVITY OPTIONS

MATH
GEOGRAPHY

Do research to find election returns from the 1856 presidential election. Make **graphs** or draw a **map** to illustrate the results.

Section 3 Assessment

1. Terms & Names

Republican Party, p. 450
John C. Frémont, p. 451
James Buchanan, p. 451
***Dred Scott* v. *Sandford*,** p. 451
Roger B. Taney, p. 452
Abraham Lincoln, p. 452
Harpers Ferry, p. 453

2. Taking Notes

Event 1: Buchanan won, but the election showed the strength of antislavery forces; Event 2: Supreme Court case that undid the Missouri Compromise; Event 3: a series of debates about slavery in the territories; Event 4: John Brown led an assault for weapons on a U.S. arsenal

3. Main Ideas

a. Slavery in the territories; the Kansas-Nebraska Act; "Bleeding Kansas" **b.** The Supreme Court denied them citizenship. **c.** It contributed to Southerners' fears that Northerners would stop at nothing to destroy slavery.

4. Critical Thinking

Lincoln: Expansion of slavery should be stopped by the national government. Douglas: Popular sovereignty should be used to address slavery. All of their statements were opinions.

ACTIVITY OPTIONS

Integrated Assessment
- Rubrics for a graph, 2.3
- Rubrics for a map, 2.1

4 Lincoln's Election and Southern Secession

TERMS & NAMES
platform
secede
Confederate States of America
Jefferson Davis
Crittenden Plan

MAIN IDEA
The election of Lincoln led the Southern states to secede from the Union.

WHY IT MATTERS NOW
This was the only time in U.S. history that states seceded from the Union.

ONE AMERICAN'S STORY

In May 1860, Murat Halstead, a reporter for the Cincinnati *Commercial,* traveled to Chicago to cover the Republican convention. Most people assumed that William Seward of New York would win the party's presidential nomination. But there were other candidates, too.

Throughout the convention, candidates tried to win away Seward's delegates. As the other candidates hoped, Seward failed to win the nomination on the first ballot. Throughout the tense voting, Abraham Lincoln, a lesser-known candidate from Illinois, gained strength. Halstead described the scene as Lincoln received the winning votes.

In 1860, the Republican delegates met in Chicago at a convention hall known as the Wigwam.

A VOICE FROM THE PAST

There was a moment's silence. The nerves of the thousands, which through the hours of suspense had been subjected to terrible tension, relaxed, and as deep breaths of relief were taken, there was a noise in the Wigwam [convention hall] like the rush of a great wind [just before] a storm—and in another breath, the storm was there. There were thousands cheering with the energy of insanity.

Murat Halstead, *Caucuses of 1860*

Having won the nomination, Lincoln could turn his attention to winning the general election. In this section, you will learn about the election of 1860 and its role in pushing the nation toward civil war.

1 Political Parties Splinter

In April, a few weeks before the Republicans nominated Abraham Lincoln, the Democrats held their convention in Charleston, South Carolina. Northern and Southern Democrats disagreed over what to say about slavery in the party's **platform,** or statement of beliefs.

The Southerners wanted the party to defend slavery in the platform.

SECTION OBJECTIVES

1. To analyze why the Democratic Party split in the election of 1860
2. To identify the issues in the election of 1860
3. To describe the secession of the Southern states from the Union
4. To explain the Union's response to secession

SKILLBUILDER
Interpreting Maps: Region, p. 457

CRITICAL THINKING
Recognizing Effects, p. 456
Making Inferences, p. 459
Analyzing Points of View, p. 459

Why It Matters Now
- Divided Nations, pp. 29–30

FOCUS & MOTIVATE

5-MINUTE WARM-UP

Interpreting Maps These questions focus on the election of 1860.

1. Look at the map on page 457. How many states voted for Lincoln? How many voted for Douglas? for Breckinridge? for Bell?
2. Where did Lincoln have strong support? Where did he have no support?

Warm-Up Transparency WT15

INSTRUCT

INSTRUCT: OBJECTIVE 1
Political Parties Splinter

- What issue split the Democratic Party?
- What was unusual about the number of candidates for president in 1860?
- What was the aim of the Constitutional Union Party?

In-Depth Resources: Unit 5
- Guided Reading, p. 6

Reading Study Guide (Spanish and English), pp. 149–150

RECOMMENDED RESOURCES

In-Depth Resources: Unit 5
- Guided Reading, p. 6
- Building Vocabulary, p. 7
- Geog. Application, pp. 9–10

Reading Study Guide (Spanish and English), pp. 149–150

Outline Map Activities
- The Election of 1860, pp. 29–30

Why It Matters Now
- Divided Nations, pp. 29–30

American History Plays
- from *Abe Lincoln in Illinois* by Robert Sherwood

Formal Assessment
- Section Quiz, p. 272

Integrated Assessment
- Rubrics, 3.6, 5.4

Access for Students Acquiring English/ESL, pp. 100, 102–103

INTEGRATED TECHNOLOGY

Electronic Teacher Tools

classzone.com

TEST-TAKING RESOURCES

Strategies for Test Preparation

Test Practice Transparencies, TT56

Online Test Practice

MORE ABOUT . . .

The Republican Convention of 1860

The convention was held in the cattle-filled streets of the young, rowdy town of Chicago in the newly built, first-of-its-kind convention building, the Wigwam. Although the town boasted 57 hotels, so many Republicans came that many slept on pool tables in hotel billiard rooms. The Republicans were a boisterous group that anticipated a win because of the split in the Democratic Party.

MORE ABOUT . . .

John C. Breckinridge

John Cabell Breckinridge from Kentucky was vice-president of the United States under James Buchanan. When the Civil War began, he joined the Confederacy and served as a general and as Jefferson Davis's secretary of war. At the end of the war, Breckinridge fled abroad where he remained until 1868. Returning to Kentucky, he practiced law and worked for a railroad company.

But Northerners wanted the platform to support popular sovereignty as a way of deciding whether a territory became a free state or a slave state. The Northerners won the platform vote, causing 50 Southern delegates to walk out of the convention.

The remaining delegates tried to nominate a presidential candidate. Stephen A. Douglas was the leading contender, but the Southerners who stayed refused to back him because of his support for popular sovereignty. Douglas could not win enough votes to gain the nomination.

Finally, the Democrats gave up and decided to meet again in Baltimore in June to choose a candidate. But as the Baltimore convention opened, Northerners and Southerners remained at odds. This time, almost all the Southerners left the meeting.

With the Southerners gone, the Northern Democrats nominated Douglas. Meanwhile, the Southern Democrats decided to nominate their own candidate. They chose John Breckinridge of Kentucky, the current vice-president and a supporter of slavery.

As you read in One American's Story on page 455, the Republicans had already nominated Abraham Lincoln. In addition to Lincoln, Douglas, and Breckinridge, a candidate from a fourth party entered the race. This party was called the Constitutional Union Party, and its members had one aim—to preserve the Union. They nominated John Bell of Tennessee to run for president.

Reading **History**

A. Recognizing Effects How did slavery affect U.S. political parties in 1860?

A. Answer It split the Democrats in two and led to the formation of the Constitutional Union Party. It also increased the strength of the Republicans.

2 The Election of 1860

The election of 1860 turned into two different races for the presidency, one in the North and one in the South. Lincoln and Douglas were the only candidates with much support in the North. Breckinridge and Bell competed for Southern votes.

Lincoln and Breckinridge were considered to have the most extreme views on slavery. Lincoln opposed the expansion of slavery into the territories. Breckinridge insisted that the federal government be required to protect slavery in any territory. Douglas and Bell were considered moderates because neither wanted the federal government to pass new laws on slavery.

The outcome of the election made it clear that the nation was tired of compromise. Lincoln defeated Douglas in the North. Breckinridge carried most of the South. Douglas and Bell managed to win only in the states between the North and the Deep South. Because the North had more people in it than the South, Lincoln won the election.

This cartoon of the long-legged Abe Lincoln shows him to be the fittest candidate in the 1860 presidential election.

INSTRUCT: OBJECTIVE 2

The Election of 1860

- How did Breckinridge's stance on the expansion of slavery in the territories differ from Lincoln's?
- Why were Douglas and Bell thought to be moderates?
- What did Southerners fear Lincoln would do after the election?

Outline Map Activities
- The Election of 1860, pp. 29–30

ACTIVITY OPTIONS

INDIVIDUAL NEEDS

STUDENTS ACQUIRING ENGLISH/ESL

Words with Multiple Meanings Point out the word *splinter* in the heading on page 455. Tell students that *splinter* can be used as a verb and as a noun. As a noun, it means "a tiny piece of wood." In the heading *Political Parties Splinter,* it is used as a verb meaning "to break into pieces." Help students understand how the political parties splintered by asking questions such as:

- What issue caused the Democratic Party to splinter?
- How did its division affect the Democratic Party's performance in the election?

You may wish to have students draw political cartoons illustrating the splintering of the Democratic Party.

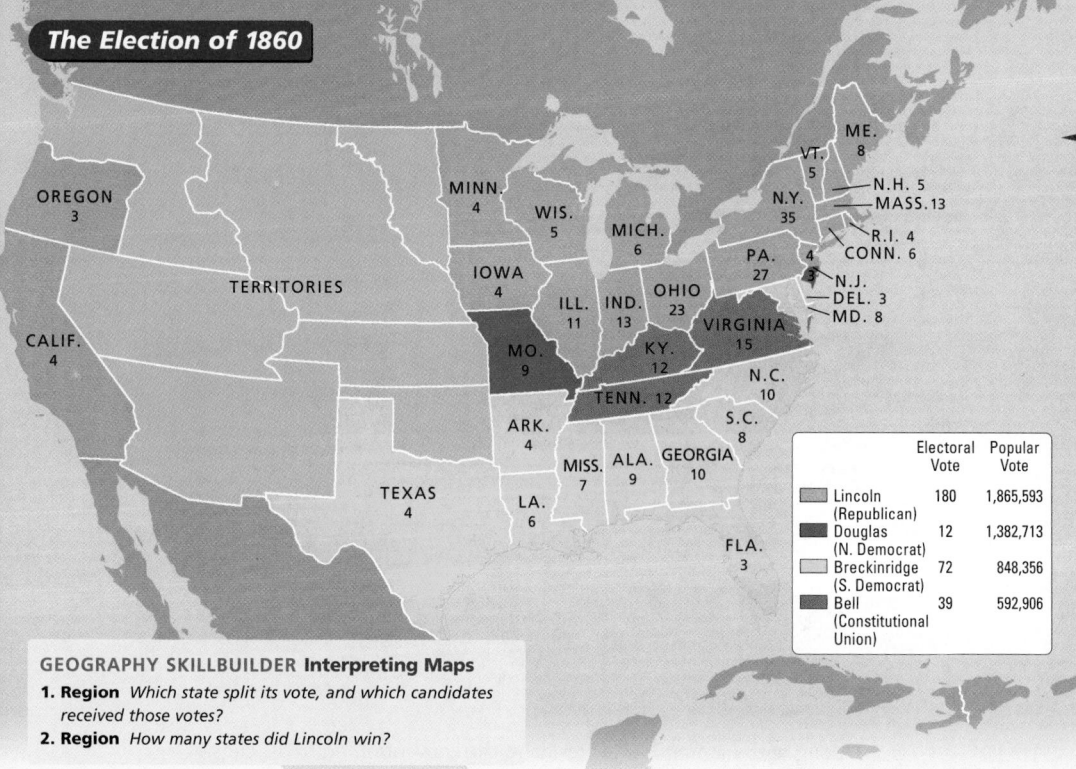

The Election of 1860

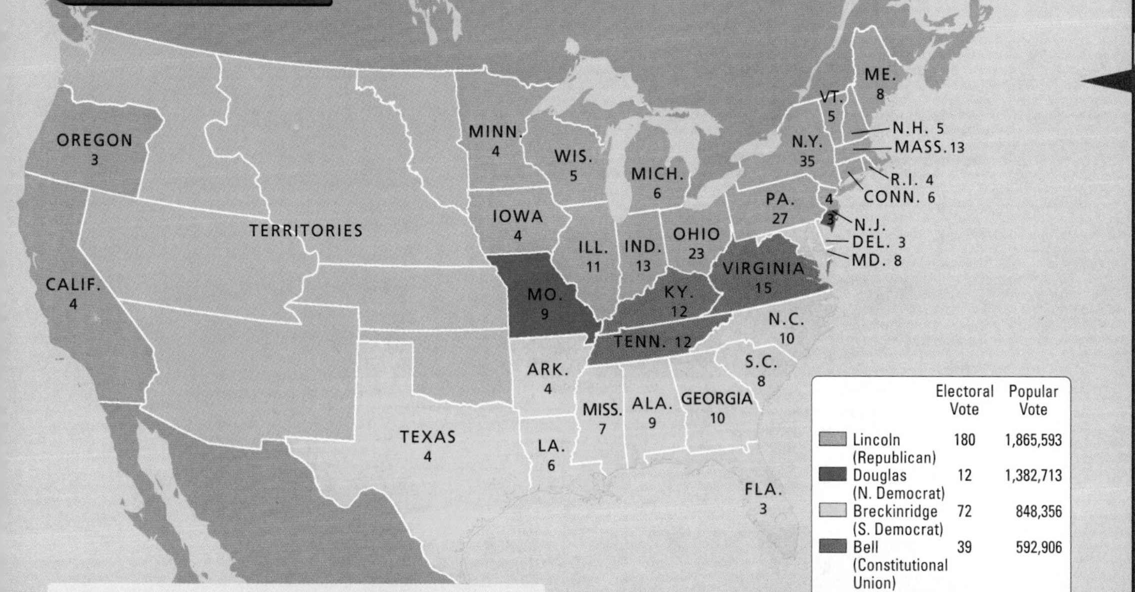

GEOGRAPHY SKILLBUILDER Interpreting Maps

1. **Region** *Which state split its vote, and which candidates received those votes?*
2. **Region** *How many states did Lincoln win?*

Skillbuilder Answers
1. New Jersey; Lincoln 4, Douglas 3
2. 17 and part of New Jersey

Despite Lincoln's statements that he would do nothing to abolish slavery in the South, white Southerners did not trust him. Many were sure that he and the other Republicans would move to ban slavery. As a result, white Southerners saw the Republican victory as a threat to the Southern way of life.

3 Southern States Secede

Before the 1860 presidential election, many Southerners had warned that if Lincoln won, the Southern states would **secede,** or withdraw from the Union. Supporters of secession based their arguments on the idea of states' rights. They argued that the states had voluntarily joined the Union. Consequently, they claimed that the states also had the right to leave the Union.

On December 20, 1860, South Carolina became the first state to secede. Other states in the Deep South, where slave labor and cotton production were most common, also considered secession. During the next six weeks, Mississippi, Florida, Alabama, Georgia, Louisiana, and Texas joined South Carolina in secession.

Background
Before becoming president of the Confederacy, Davis had been a hero during the War with Mexico and a U.S. senator.

In early February 1861, the states that had seceded met in Montgomery, Alabama. They formed the **Confederate States of America.** The convention named **Jefferson Davis** president of the Confederacy.

HISTORY FROM VISUALS

Reading the Map Ask students if the election might have turned out differently if there had been only one Democratic candidate. Tell them to look at the differences in the popular vote and the electoral vote to formulate their answer. **Possible Responses** 1) Probably not, because, although the Democratic candidate might have won the popular vote, the Republicans would have won the electoral vote. 2) Perhaps yes, because it is possible that a single Democratic candidate might have carried some states that went to Lincoln, giving the Democrats enough electoral votes to win.

Extension Have students research the electoral college to understand why Douglas could have won such a large number of popular votes and yet so few electoral votes.

INSTRUCT: OBJECTIVE 3

Southern States Secede

- What argument did some Southerners use to justify secession?
- What were the results of the convention held by the six seceded states?
- How was the Confederate Constitution different from the U.S. Constitution?

In-Depth Resources: Unit 5
- Geography Application, pp. 9–10

MORE ABOUT . . .

Jefferson Davis
The biography of Jefferson Davis contains two small mysteries: his birth date and his middle name. Davis himself was not sure whether he was born in 1807 or 1808. Historians have not been able to verify Davis's middle name, commonly accepted as "Finis." Although records and documents signed by Davis include the middle initial "F," the name is not spelled out on any document. Legend says that Davis's parents named him "Finis," or "the end" because he was their tenth child.

ACTIVITY OPTIONS

INTERDISCIPLINARY LINK: GOVERNMENT

BLOCK SCHEDULING

FORMING A GOVERNMENT

Class Time 45 minutes

Task Forming a new government

Purpose To help students understand the complexities of creating the Confederate government

Supplies Needed
- History and government books on the United States and on the Confederacy; a copy of the Constitution

Activity Challenge students to make some decisions about starting a new government as the secessionists did. Divide the class into groups and ask them to prepare a one-page plan of action for their government that addresses the following questions:
- Brainstorm a list of the first things you will do to start your government.
- What might you follow as a pattern to base your government on? The United States? A different country? What kind of laws will you make and how will you enforce them?

CRITICAL THINKING ACTIVITY

Analyzing Points of View Have students examine Southern justifications of secession and Northern responses by making a spider map. Tell them to write *secession* in the center circle and add information about the two sides on the appropriate lines.

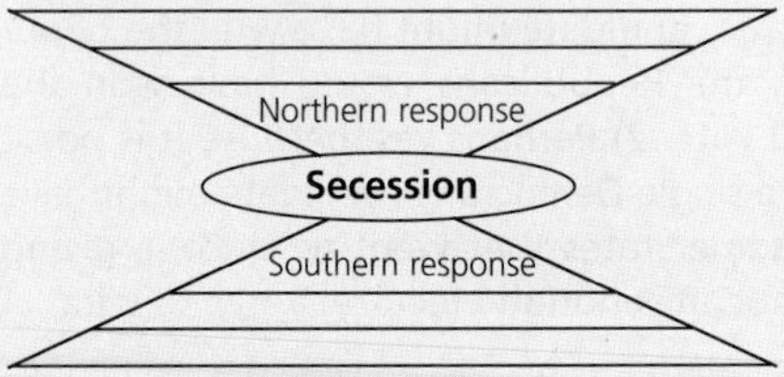

Class Time 15 minutes

MORE ABOUT . . .

James Russell Lowell
Lowell was born in Cambridge, Massachusetts, to an established New England family. He was a crusading reformer, working for abolition, women's rights, temperance, and vegetarianism. He became a professor of literature at Harvard and also served as U.S. ambassador to Spain and to England.

INSTRUCT

INSTRUCT: OBJECTIVE 4

The Union Responds to Secession/ Efforts to Compromise Fail

- How did President Buchanan and other Northerners respond to secession?
- What was the purpose of the Crittenden Plan? Was it successful?
- How did Lincoln try to reassure the South in his First Inaugural Address?

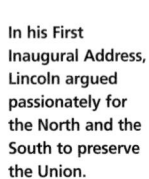

In his First Inaugural Address, Lincoln argued passionately for the North and the South to preserve the Union.

Along with naming Davis president, the convention drafted a constitution. The Confederate Constitution was modeled on the U.S. Constitution. But there were a few important differences. For example, the Confederate Constitution supported states' rights. It also protected slavery in the Confederacy, including any territories it might acquire.

Having formed its government, the Confederate states made plans to defend their separation from the Union. Some believed that war between the states could not be avoided. But everyone waited to see what the Union government would do in response.

4 The Union Responds to Secession

Northerners considered the secession of the Southern states to be unconstitutional. During his last months in office, President James Buchanan argued against secession. He believed that the states did not have the right to withdraw from the Union because the federal government, not the state governments, was sovereign. If secession were permitted, the Union would become weak, like a "rope of sand." He believed that the U.S. Constitution was framed to prevent such a thing from happening.

Vocabulary
sovereign: supreme, self-governing authority

In addition to these issues, secession raised the issue of majority rule. Southerners complained that Northerners intended to use their majority to force the South to abolish slavery. But Northerners responded that Southerners simply did not want to live by the rules of democracy. They complained that Southerners were not willing to live with the election results. As Northern writer James Russell Lowell

ACTIVITY OPTIONS

INTERDISCIPLINARY LINK: SPEECH

BLOCK SCHEDULING

LINCOLN'S FIRST INAUGURAL ADDRESS

Class Time 30 minutes

Task Presenting a portion of the First Inaugural Address

Purpose To familiarize students with one of the nation's famous speeches and to help them understand the role of oratory in the history of the United States

Supplies Needed
- Copies of the First Inaugural Address

Activity Have students work alone or in pairs to read and memorize a section of Lincoln's First Inaugural Address. Have students practice their section out loud and then present it to the class. You may allow students who have difficulty memorizing to prepare a reading of their section. After the presentation, discuss how hearing Lincoln present this speech might have affected the listeners.

wrote, "[The Southerners'] quarrel is not with the Republican Party, but with the theory of Democracy."

Efforts to Compromise Fail

With the states in the lower South forming a new government in Montgomery, Alabama, some people continued to seek compromise. Senator John J. Crittenden of Kentucky developed a compromise plan. The **Crittenden Plan** was presented to Congress in late February 1861, but it did not pass.

"We must not be enemies."
Abraham Lincoln

With the hopes for compromise fading, Americans waited for Lincoln's inauguration. What would the new president do about the crisis? On March 4, Lincoln took the oath of office and gave his First Inaugural Address. He assured the South that he had no intention of abolishing slavery there. But he spoke forcefully against secession. Then he ended his speech with an appeal to friendship.

A VOICE FROM THE PAST

We are not enemies, but friends. We must not be enemies. Though passion may have strained, it must not break our bonds of affection. The mystic chords of memory, stretching from every battle-field and patriot grave, to every living heart and hearthstone, all over this broad land, will yet swell the chorus of the Union, when again touched, as surely they will be, by the better angels of our nature.

Abraham Lincoln, *First Inaugural Address*

*Reading***History**
B. Making Inferences What do you think Lincoln meant by "mystic chords of memory"?
B. Possible Response spiritual attachment that he believed Americans had to their nation's history

Lincoln would not press the South. He wanted no invasion. But he would not abandon the government's property there. Several forts in the South, including Fort Sumter in South Carolina, were still in Union hands. These forts would soon need to be resupplied. Throughout March and into April, Northerners and Southerners waited anxiously to see what would happen next. You will find out in the next chapter.

Section 4 Assessment

1. Terms & Names
Explain the significance of:
- platform
- secede
- Confederate States of America
- Jefferson Davis
- Crittenden Plan

2. Taking Notes
Use a time line to fill in the main events that occurred between April 1860 and March 1861.

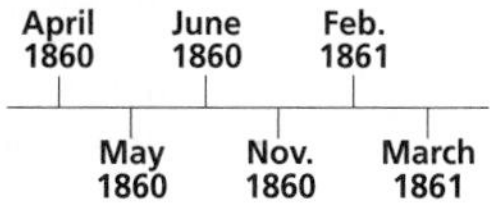

Do you think secession could have been avoided? Why?

3. Main Ideas
a. Who were the candidates in the 1860 presidential election, and what policies did each candidate stand for?
b. Which states seceded right after Lincoln's election? How did they justify this action?
c. What attempts did the North and the South make to compromise? What were the results?

4. Critical Thinking
Analyzing Points of View Do you think the Southern states seceded to protect slavery or states' rights?
THINK ABOUT
- the Southern view of the Fugitive Slave Act
- the Confederate Constitution
- slaveholders' views of the Republican Party

ACTIVITY OPTIONS
SPEECH
TECHNOLOGY
Read Lincoln's First Inaugural Address. Deliver a section of the **speech** before the class or plan an **electronic presentation** about that day and Lincoln's message.

MORE ABOUT . . .

The Crittenden Plan
The Crittenden Plan, or Compromise, as it is sometimes designated, was sponsored by Senator John J. Crittenden of Kentucky. Crittenden proposed that the division established by the Missouri Compromise be extended to the Pacific Ocean. In other words, slavery would be prohibited north of the 36° 30' line set by the Missouri Compromise and protected south of it.

ASSESS & RETEACH

Setting the Stage Have students fill in the box for the Election of 1860 on the graphic organizer on page 440.

Formal Assessment
- Section Quiz, p. 272

Critical Thinking Transparency CT43
- Setting the Stage

RETEACHING ACTIVITY
In small groups, have students use the graphic below to discuss the election of 1860.

In-Depth Resources: Unit 5
- Reteaching Activity, p. 19

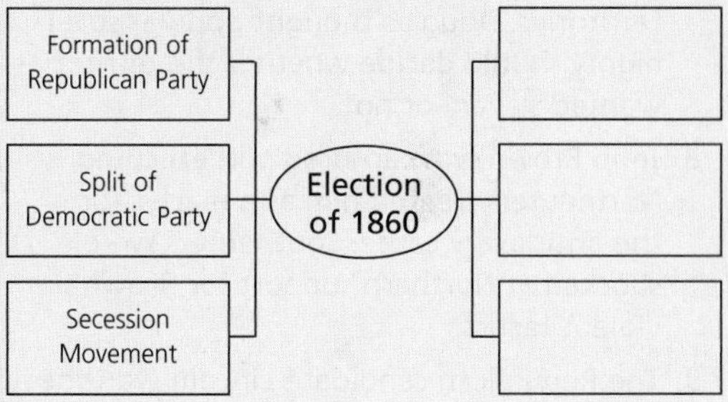

Section 4 Assessment

1. Terms & Names
platform, p. 455
secede, p. 457
Confederate States of America, p. 457
Jefferson Davis, p. 457
Crittenden Plan, p. 459

2. Taking Notes
April 1860: 50 Southern Democrats walk out of the convention; May 1860: Republicans nominate Lincoln; June 1860: Democrats split. November 1860: Lincoln wins election; February 1861: Confederate States of America is formed; March 1861: Lincoln is inaugurated

3. Main Ideas
a. Lincoln: opposed the expansion of slavery; Breckinridge: the federal government should protect slavery; Douglas: popular sovereignty; Bell: preserving the Union **b.** SC, MS, FL, AL, GA, LA, and TX; the Union was voluntary **c.** the Crittenden Plan; it was rejected

4. Critical Thinking
Students might say that they were defending the rights of states or feared the abolition of slavery.

ACTIVITY OPTIONS
Integrated Assessment
- Rubrics for a speech, 3.6
- Rubrics for multimedia, 5.4

TERMS & NAMES

1. **Wilmot Proviso,** p. 443
2. **Compromise of 1850,** p. 445
3. ***Uncle Tom's Cabin,*** p. 446
4. **popular sovereignty,** p. 447
5. **Kansas–Nebraska Act,** p. 448
6. **John Brown,** p. 449
7. **John C. Frémont,** p. 451
8. ***Dred Scott* v. *Sandford,*** p. 451
9. **secede,** p. 457
10. **Confederate States of America,** p. 457

REVIEW QUESTIONS

Possible Responses

1. The North was more industrial while the South remained more agricultural with a heavy reliance on slave labor.
2. They saw it as an attempt to destroy slavery.
3. He worked to get the bill passed by Congress despite regional bickering over the issue.
4. They opposed the law because it forced them to support slavery.
5. The act allowed slavery into territories where it had been banned. Northerners opposed it and Southerners supported it.
6. Democrats took much of the blame for the violence that erupted in Kansas.
7. Lincoln thought that the national government should ban slavery from expanding into new territories. Douglas thought popular sovereignty should decide whether the territories wanted slavery or not.
8. John Brown was captured and executed. Northerners treated him as a martyr for the antislavery cause. Southerners were shocked at Northern support for Brown's violent tactics.
9. The Republican candidate Lincoln won the election of 1860. Southern states feared his motives and seceded from the Union.
10. They argued that they had joined the Union voluntarily and had the right to leave.

Chapter 15 ASSESSMENT

VISUAL SUMMARY

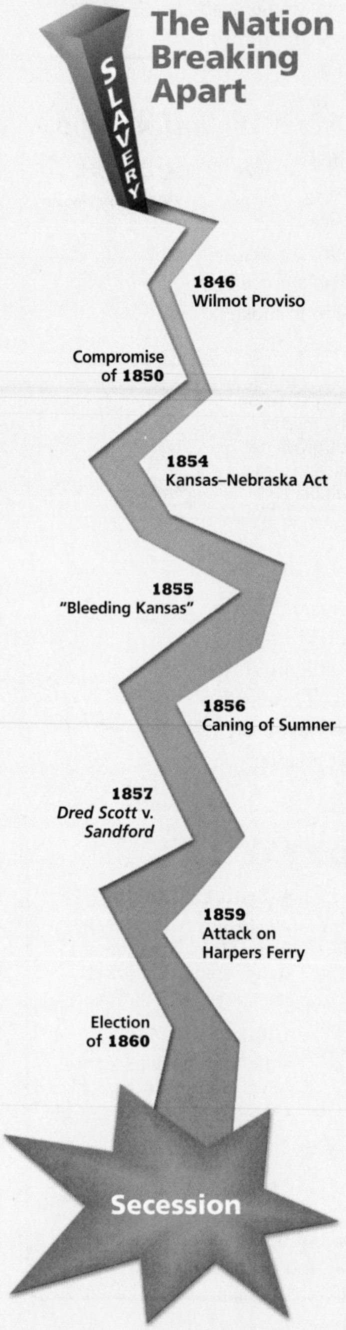

460 CHAPTER 15

TERMS & NAMES

Briefly explain the significance of each of the following.

1. Wilmot Proviso
2. Compromise of 1850
3. *Uncle Tom's Cabin*
4. popular sovereignty
5. Kansas–Nebraska Act
6. John Brown
7. John C. Frémont
8. *Dred Scott* v. *Sandford*
9. secede
10. Confederate States of America

REVIEW QUESTIONS

Growing Tensions Between North and South (pages 441–445)

1. How did the North and the South differ in the 1840s?
2. How did Southerners react to the Wilmot Proviso?
3. What was Stephen A. Douglas's role in passing the Compromise of 1850?

The Crisis Deepens (pages 446–449)

4. How did Northerners react to the Fugitive Slave Act?
5. Why did most Northerners and Southerners disagree about the Kansas–Nebraska Act?
6. How did "Bleeding Kansas" cause problems for Democrats?

Slavery Dominates Politics (pages 450–454)

7. What positions did Lincoln and Douglas take in their debates?
8. What was the result of John Brown's raid on Harpers Ferry?

Lincoln's Election and Southern Secession (pages 455–459)

9. What were the results of the election of 1860, and what did these results show?
10. How did Southerners justify secession?

CRITICAL THINKING

1. USING YOUR NOTES

Using your completed diagram, answer the questions below.

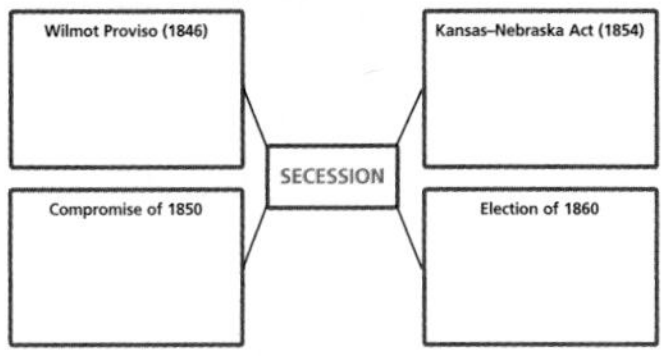

a. What did the Compromise of 1850 and the Kansas–Nebraska Act have in common?

b. Which event do you think caused the most damage to the relationship between the North and the South? Explain.

2. ANALYZING LEADERSHIP

Why were the nation's leaders in 1860 unable to compromise like the leaders in 1820 and 1850? Does their failure to compromise in 1860 mean that they were not as capable as earlier leaders?

3. APPLYING CITIZENSHIP SKILLS

What alternatives did the states in the lower South have to secession? Which of these alternatives do you think would have been the best choice?

4. SOLVING PROBLEMS

How did slavery divide Americans in the 1850s?

5. THEME: DIVERSITY AND UNITY

What could have been done in the 1850s to prevent the Southern states from seceding? What did Americans have in common that could have overcome their differences over slavery?

Interact *with* History

Now that you have read about the sectional crisis of the 1850s, do you think the solution you came up with at the start of the chapter would have helped keep the Union together? Explain.

CRITICAL THINKING

Possible Responses

1. **USING YOUR NOTES a.** Both dealt with the issue of slavery in the territories. **b.** Student responses will vary. Be sure they explain their choice.
2. **ANALYZING LEADERSHIP** In 1860, tensions over slavery were much higher. No, because they faced bigger problems.
3. **APPLYING CITIZENSHIP SKILLS** Student responses will vary. Be sure they give plausible alternatives and explain their choice.
4. **SOLVING PROBLEMS** Many people thought the institution was wrong and inefficient. Others argued that slavery was economically beneficial, that slaves were unfit for freedom, and that it was an important part of Southern culture.
5. **THEME: DIVERSITY AND UNITY** They could have put the issue of slavery to a vote and made a commitment to live with the results. The states had in common a commitment to democracy.

Interact *with* History Responses will vary but should be supported by information in the chapter.

HISTORY SKILLS

1. INTERPRETING MAPS: Region

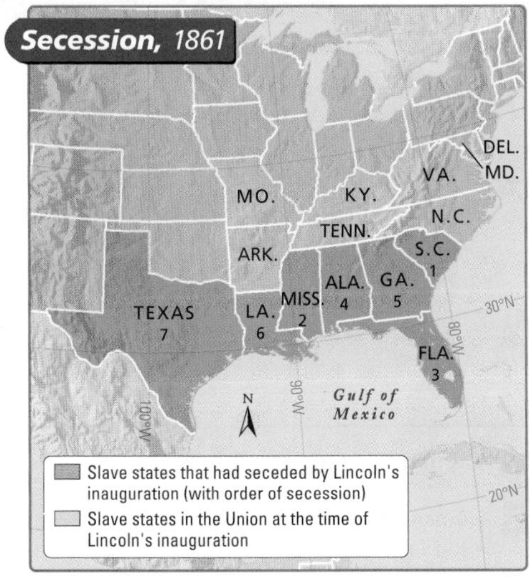

Basic Map Elements

a. Which states seceded before Lincoln's inauguration in March, 1861?

Interpreting the Map

b. What geographical characteristics did these states have in common?

c. Why do you think these states were the first to secede?

2. INTERPRETING PRIMARY SOURCES

A detail of Thomas Hovenden's painting, *The Last Moments of John Brown* (1884), shows Brown being led to the gallows.

a. How does Brown appear in this image?

b. Based on Hovenden's presentation of Brown, what do you think were the artist's views on Brown?

ALTERNATIVE ASSESSMENT

1. INTERDISCIPLINARY ACTIVITY: Language Arts

Conducting an Interview Pick one of the important people in this chapter, such as Stephen A. Douglas or Harriet Beecher Stowe. Think about what questions you would ask that person in an interview. Then research that person's biographies, speeches, or writings to see how he or she might answer your questions. Write the interview in question-and-answer format. Use direct quotes as often as possible.

2. COOPERATIVE LEARNING ACTIVITY

Presenting a Mock Trial The case of Dred Scott went to the Supreme Court. The Court, led by Chief Justice Roger B. Taney, decided against Scott. Did the court reach the right verdict?

Working in a small group, do research on the Dred Scott case. Present a mock trial of the case. Look for information about the roles of Taney, the other justices, Scott, and the other major participants. Have the class render a verdict at the end of the trial. Compare your verdict with the actual historical results.

3. TECHNOLOGY ACTIVITY

Making a Class Presentation American political parties went through extreme changes in the 1840s and 1850s. Using the Internet or the library, find the election returns of the presidential elections from 1848 to 1860.

For more about presidential elections . . .

INTERNET ACTIVITY
CLASSZONE.COM

Use presentation software to teach your class about U.S. presidential elections. Here are some suggestions.

- Use pie charts to show the percentage of votes that went to each party in each election.
- Use bar graphs to show the growth in total popular vote (nationwide) for each party for each election.

4. HISTORY PORTFOLIO

Review the questions that you wrote for What Do You Want to Know? on page 440. Then write a short report in which you explain the answers to your questions. Be sure to use standard grammar, spelling, sentence structure, and punctuation in your report. If any questions were not answered, do research to answer them. Add your report to your portfolio.

Additional Test Practice, pp. S1–S33

TEST PRACTICE
CLASSZONE.COM

ALTERNATIVE ASSESSMENT

1. INTERDISCIPLINARY ACTIVITY: **Language Arts**
   Interviews should
   - reflect the student's understanding of basic concepts relevant to the experiences of the person selected.
   - accurately reflect the thoughts and experiences of the subject's life.
   - use standard grammar, spelling, sentence structure, and punctuation.

2. COOPERATIVE LEARNING ACTIVITY
   Trials should
   - accurately portray the *Dred Scott* trial.
   - have adequate delivery and establish rapport with the audience.
   - show evidence of involvement of each person in the group.

3. TECHNOLOGY ACTIVITY
   Presentations should
   - clearly demonstrate an understanding of the elections of the 1840s and 1850s.
   - utilize several sources of information to create charts and graphs.
   - show proficiency in the use of technology.

4. HISTORY PORTFOLIO
   Option 1 Revised section or chapter assessment activities should
   - address teacher and peer responses to the selected work.
   - solve problems present in the first versions of the work.

   Option 2 Short reports should
   - answer questions about the sectional differences that led to the Civil War.
   - use evidence to develop and support ideas.
   - cite sources of information.
   - use standard grammar, spelling, sentence structure, and punctuation.

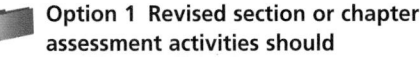

Critical Thinking Transparency CT45
- Visual Summary

Formal Assessment
- Chapter Test, Forms A, B, and C, pp. 273–284

HISTORY SKILLS

Possible Responses

1. INTERPRETING MAPS
   Basic Map Elements
   a. Texas, Louisiana, Mississippi, Alabama, Georgia, South Carolina, and Florida
   Interpreting the Map
   b. These states were the farthest south.
   c. They probably felt they had more in common with one another—slavery—than with states that were to the North.

2. INTERPRETING PRIMARY SOURCES
   a. Brown is shown receiving a kiss from an African-American child. It shows his love for African Americans and his desire to end slavery.
   b. Based on this image, it is likely Hovenden had a positive view of Brown.

CHAPTER 16 PLANNING GUIDE
The Civil War Begins 1861–1862

	CHAPTER OVERVIEW	COPYMASTERS	INTEGRATED TECHNOLOGY
CHAPTER RESOURCES	This chapter describes the start of the Civil War and its early battles. It also examines the horrible conditions of warfare, and the increase in casualties resulting from new weapons.	**In-Depth Resources: Unit 5** • Tracing Themes: Citizenship, p. 22 • Building Vocabulary, p. 26 **Interdisciplinary Projects,** pp. 91–96	• eEdition Plus Online • EasyPlanner Plus Online • eTest Plus Online • eEdition • Power Presentations • EasyPlanner • Electronic Library of Primary Sources • Test Generator • Reading Study Guide • America's Music
SECTION 1 **War Erupts** **pp. 465–471**	**KEY IDEAS** • When Confederates fire on Fort Sumter, Lincoln calls for Union troops. • The border states are of crucial importance and remain in the Union. • The South plans a defensive strategy, while the North takes the offensive, blockading Southern ports.	**In-Depth Resources: Unit 5** • Setting the Stage, p. 21 • Guided Reading, p. 23 • Skillbuilder Practice, p. 27 • Geography Application, pp. 28–29 • Primary Source, p. 30 • Reteaching Activity, p. 35 **America's History Makers,** pp. 63–66 **Economics in History**, p. 16 **Outline Map Activities,** pp. 31–32	**Warm-Up Transparency WT16** **Humanities Transparency HT31** • Robert E. Lee **Humanities Transparency HT32** • Union and Confederate Money **Geography Transparency GT16** • Union and Confederate Resources, 1861
SECTION 2 **Life in the Army** **pp. 472–476**	• Most Civil War soldiers are farmers; many are immigrants; and Union armies eventually accept African-American volunteers. • Army life is filled with hardship and disease. • The development of the rifle and the minié ball increases casualties.	**In-Depth Resources: Unit 5** • Setting the Stage, p. 21 • Guided Reading, p. 24 • Primary Source, p. 31 • Literature Selection, pp. 32–34 • Reteaching Activity, p. 36 **Why It Matters Now** • Modern Warfare, pp. 31–32	**Warm-Up Transparency WT16** **Critical Thinking Transparency CT46** • Setting the Stage **Critical Thinking Transparency CT47** • Cause and Effect: Hardships of Civil War Soldiers **classzone.com**
SECTION 3 **No End in Sight** **pp. 477–483**	• Union forces under Ulysses S. Grant win victories in the West but at a high cost in lives. • A Union fleet captures New Orleans. • Confederate troops under Robert E. Lee dominate the war in the East.	**In-Depth Resources: Unit 5** • Setting the Stage, p. 21 • Guided Reading, p. 25 • Reteaching Activity, p. 37	**Warm-Up Transparency WT16** **Critical Thinking Transparency CT46** • Setting the Stage **Critical Thinking Transparency CT48** • Visual Summary **classzone.com**

Pupil's Edition | Overhead Transparency | CD-ROM
Copymaster | Audio Library | Internet

ASSESSMENT OPTIONS

Chapter Assessment, pp. 482–483

Formal Assessment
- Chapter Tests, Forms A, B, and C, pp. 288–299

Test Generator

Online Test Practice

Strategies for Test Preparation

Section Assessment, p. 469

Formal Assessment, Quiz, p. 285

Integrated Assessment Book
- Rubrics, 4.5, 5.1

Test Generator

Test Practice Transparencies, TT57

Section Assessment, p. 475

Formal Assessment, Quiz, p. 286

Integrated Assessment Book
- Rubrics, 4.3, 2.1

Test Generator

Test Practice Transparencies, TT58

Section Assessment, p. 481

Formal Assessment, Quiz, p. 287

Integrated Assessment Book
- Rubrics, 2.1, 1.3

Test Generator

Test Practice Transparencies, TT59

CUSTOMIZING FOR INDIVIDUAL NEEDS

Students Acquiring English/ESL

Reading Study Guide (English and Spanish), pp. 153–160

Access for Students Acquiring English/ESL: Spanish Translations, pp. 104–109

Chapter Summaries on CD (English and Spanish)

Modified Lesson Plans for English Learners

Less Proficient Readers

Reading Study Guide (English and Spanish), pp. 153–160

Chapter Summaries on CD (English and Spanish)

Gifted and Talented Students

In-Depth Resources: Unit 5
- Enrichment Activity, p. 38

America's History Makers
- Abraham Lincoln, pp. 63–64
- Robert E. Lee, pp. 65–66

CROSS-CURRICULAR CONNECTIONS

Culture

Van Steenwyk, Elizabeth. ***Mathew Brady: Civil War Photographer.*** New York: Franklin Watts, 1997. Describes the early days of photography and Brady's career. Illustrated with Brady photographs.

Humanities: Art

McPherson, James M. ***Images of the Civil War: The Paintings of Mort Künstler.*** New York: Gramercy, 1992. A bare-bones text supports 70 color paintings of Civil War scenes by an artist whose work is so accurate and detailed that Civil War buffs comb them for details as if they were photographs.

Primary Sources

Time-Life Books Editors. ***Soldier Life.*** New York: Time-Life, 1996. Compilation of reminiscences of common soldiers and their families, accompanied by photographs, succeeds in giving a human face to the opposing armies.

Interdisciplinary Projects, pp. 91–96

- Math: Calculating Income Tax
- Science: Filtering Water
- Language Arts: Journalism: The Inverted Pyramid
- Art: Winslow Homer's Civil War Sketches

Literature

The Columbia Book of Civil War Poetry. Richard Marius, ed. New York: Columbia U. Press, 1994. Each poem is introduced by a vignette. Contains songs, famous poems, and rare pieces.

Paulsen, Gary. ***A Soldier's Heart.*** New York: Doubleday, 1998. Unsentimental novel that follows 15-year-old Charley as he joins the Minnesota Volunteers, goes through military training, and encounters the excitement, brutality, and fatigue of war.

Rinaldi, Ann. ***Amelia's War.*** New York: Scholastic, 1999. A young Maryland girl tries not to take sides in the war until troops arrive.

McDougal Littell *The Language of Literature*

- Louisa May Alcott "Civil War Journal" (journal entries)

McDougal Littell Literature Connections

Irene Hunt

Across Five Aprils

This historical novel describes a family with divided loyalties during the Civil War, the sensitive boy left behind to run the farm, and his realization of the horrors of war.

ENRICHMENT ACTIVITIES

Pupil's Edition, pp. 462–483
Interact with History, p. 463
Literature Connections, pp. 470–471
Technology of the Time, pp. 476

In-Depth Resources: Unit 5
- Geography Application: Fort Sumter Falls, 1861, pp. 28–29
- Primary Source: from *Tad Lincoln's Father,* p. 30
- Primary Source: "Battle Cry of Freedom" and "Bonnie Blue Flag," p. 31
- Literature Selection: "An Episode of War," pp. 32–34

America's History Makers
- Abraham Lincoln, pp. 63–64
- Robert E. Lee, pp. 65–66

America's Music CD

Outline Map Activities
- The Divided Union, 1863 pp. 31–32

Why It Matters Now
- Modern Warfare, pp. 31–32

BLOCK SCHEDULING — LESSON PLAN OPTIONS (90-MINUTE PERIOD)

DAY 1

Interact with History, p. 463
Class Time 20 minutes

Options for pacing and variety:
- **Role-Playing** Have pairs of students assume the roles of the two federal artillery officers inside Fort Sumter, one from a Southern state and the other from a Northern state. Have the two discuss the "What Do You Think?" questions and share their conclusions with the class. **Class Time** 10 minutes

Setting the Stage, p. 464
Class Time 20 minutes

Options for pacing and variety:
- **Time Saver** For a homework assignment, have students make a list of what they already know about the Civil War and a list of three questions they have about the outbreak of the war. **Class Time** 10 minutes

Section 1, pp. 465–471
Class Time 50 minutes

Options for pacing and variety:
- **Time Saver** Use the chart on page 468 to summarize the differences in the resources of each side as the Civil War began.
Class Time 5 minutes
- **Internet** Extend students' background knowledge of the Civil War by visiting classzone.com.
Class Time 20 minutes

DAY 2

Section 2, pp. 472–476
Class Time 45 minutes

Options for pacing and variety:
- **Time Saver** For a homework assignment, have students complete the Interdisciplinary Activity on page 483 of the Chapter Assessment. Then have them share their letters and reactions to them with the class.
Class Time 30 minutes
- **Peer Evaluation** Have student pairs answer the Main Ideas and Critical Thinking questions in the Section Assessment. Then have them exchange papers with another team to evaluate their answers.
Class Time 15 minutes

Section 3, pp. 477–481
Class Time 50 minutes

Options for pacing and variety:
- **Team Teaching** Invite a music teacher to come to the class to discuss and play examples of music from the Civil War.
Class Time 20 minutes
- **History on Film** Pick one of the four videos in *The Civil War Legends* series to extend students' knowledge of the roles played by Robert E. Lee, Abraham Lincoln, Stonewall Jackson, or Ulysses S. Grant in the Civil War. Atlas Video.
Class Time 30 minutes

Chapter 16 Assessment, pp. 482–483
Class Time 40 minutes

Options for pacing and variety:
- **Time Saver** For a homework assignment, have students pick two events on the Visual Summary time line and write a paragraph explaining their importance to the war at this point. **Class Time** 5 minutes
- **Peer Evaluation** Have students work in pairs to answer the Using Your Notes question on page 482. **Class Time** 25 minutes

TEACHER-TESTED ACTIVITY Nicholas Sysock, Carteret Middle School, Carteret, New Jersey

TECHNOLOGY OF WAR

Class Time One class period

Task Reporting on how new technology influenced combat and the outcome of the Civil War

Purpose To understand how technology affected the progress and the outcome of the Civil War

Supplies Needed
- Reference books and Internet sources on technology of the Civil War
- Markers, colored pencils
- Posterboard

Activity Divide students into small groups. Assign each group a specific technological advance of the Civil War. Among the topics students might explore are the development of repeating rifles, ironclads, the telegraph, railroads, or improvements in artillery or ammunition. Have students prepare a report that describes the new technology, how it affected the way the war was fought, and its impact on military strategy or on specific land or sea battles. If appropriate, encourage students to make diagrams that show how the technology they have chosen works.

CHAPTER 16 TECHNOLOGY IN THE CLASSROOM

RESEARCHING PERSONAL STORIES

There are countless fascinating stories about the Civil War. The war tore apart the nation, including many communities and even families, during that time. Learning more about the wartime experiences of average Americans can help students understand the Civil War. Students can use a variety of technologies to research and present a specific story that they find meaningful.

ACTIVITY OUTLINE

Objective By researching personal stories from the Civil War, students will gain a deeper understanding of the war.

Task Students will use a variety of technologies.

Class Time Two class periods

DIRECTIONS

1. After students have read Chapter 16, have them write down a topic that they found especially interesting. Then have them use that topic to create a presentation, employing technologies of their choice: videotape, audiotape, electronic presentation tools, electronic spreadsheets, databases, e-mail, or graphics displays. Presentations should be three to five minutes long. Possible presentation topics include:
   - battle descriptions, using graphics and presentation software
   - radio reenactments of a small scene in the life of a soldier or civilian involved in a battle, using audiotape equipment
   - readings of real letters from soldiers, taken from primary source documents
   - stories of prisons and prisoners of war
   - stories of women involved in the war: nurses, spies, and others
   - stories of African Americans in the war: enslaved people who ran away or helped others escape, freedmen who joined the Union army, and others
   - stories of Union or Confederate military leaders
   - videotaped dramatizations of incidents behind the front lines
   - stories of brothers fighting on opposite sides
   - recordings of Civil War songs to accompany a slide show of images of the war
2. Have students write a short proposal for their project topics and their plans for presentation.
3. After the proposal has been approved, students can begin researching their topics and developing their presentations.
4. When presentations have been developed, they should be presented to the class. Ask students viewing the presentations to evaluate the presentations based on the following criteria, and using a rating of one to five, where one is low and five is high:
   - thoroughness of research
   - ability to present the subject at a personal level
   - creativity of presentation
5. Have the presenter do a self-evaluation using the same criteria. Then share evaluations from the class with each presenter.

CHAPTER 16 OBJECTIVE

The student will understand how the Civil War began, its progress during the early years, and its impact on Union and Confederate soldiers.

HISTORY FROM VISUALS

Interpreting the Illustration Have students study the engraving, read the caption, and explain who the people in the crowd are and what they are doing. **Answer** They are South Carolinians looking from the rooftops of city houses at the bombardment of Fort Sumter. Ask students to describe the onlookers' reactions to the event. **Possible Responses** In general, many of the women look frightened or grief-stricken. Most of the men appear riveted by the action.

Extension Have students write a monologue in which one of the people in the illustration tells a grandchild what he or she remembers about standing on the roof on that long-ago day.

CHAPTER 16

The Civil War Begins 1861–1862

In this vivid engraving, South Carolina shore guns fire on Fort Sumter in Charleston's harbor.

462

RECOMMENDED RESOURCES

BOOKS FOR THE TEACHER

McPherson, James M. ***Battle Cry of Freedom: The Civil War Era.*** Classic work on the Civil War.

Olsen, Bernard A. ***Upon the Tented Field.*** Red Bank, NJ: Historic Projs., Inc., 1993. Collection of soldiers' letters paints a gripping picture of what the war was really like.

Wiley, Bell Irvin. ***The Life of Billy Yank: the Common Soldier of the Union*** and ***The Life of Johnny Reb: the Common Soldier of the Confederacy.*** Baton Rouge: Louisiana State UP, 1978. Marvelous works about the experiences of the soldiers on both sides of the war.

VIDEO

The Civil War. Episode 1: "The Cause." Ken Burns, dir. PBS, 1989. Opening salvo in the extremely popular nine-cassette epic.

SOFTWARE

American History Inspirer: The Civil War. Omaha, NE: Educational Software Institute.

INTERNET

For more about the U.S. Civil War, visit . . .

classzone.com

Interact *with* History

This painting shows Fort Sumter from the inside under attack.
damaged fort walls
Federal artillery officers inside Fort Sumter witness bombardment.
stockpile of cannon balls
federal cannon destroyed by Confederate shelling

The date is April 12, 1861. You and other residents of Charleston, South Carolina, watch the bombardment of Fort Sumter by Confederate forces. This event signals the beginning of the Civil War—a war between factions or regions of the same country.

What Do You Think?

- What sort of physical destruction might take place in a civil war?
- What social, political, and economic trouble might be likely to occur in a civil war?
- What might happen when a civil war breaks out?

How might a civil war be worse than other wars?

USA

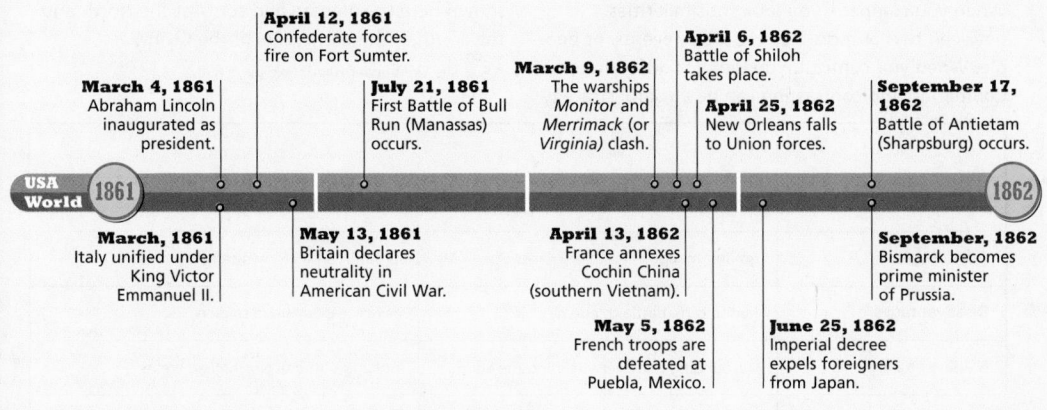

March 4, 1861 Abraham Lincoln inaugurated as president.

April 12, 1861 Confederate forces fire on Fort Sumter.

July 21, 1861 First Battle of Bull Run (Manassas) occurs.

March 9, 1862 The warships *Monitor* and *Merrimack* (or *Virginia)* clash.

April 6, 1862 Battle of Shiloh takes place.

April 25, 1862 New Orleans falls to Union forces.

September 17, 1862 Battle of Antietam (Sharpsburg) occurs.

1861 — 1862

World

March, 1861 Italy unified under King Victor Emmanuel II.

May 13, 1861 Britain declares neutrality in American Civil War.

April 13, 1862 France annexes Cochin China (southern Vietnam).

May 5, 1862 French troops are defeated at Puebla, Mexico.

June 25, 1862 Imperial decree expels foreigners from Japan.

September, 1862 Bismarck becomes prime minister of Prussia.

Interact *with* History

OBJECTIVES

- To help students describe the bombardment of Fort Sumter
- To help students understand the impact of the outbreak of war

What Do You Think?

1. Remind students that the goal of armies is to prevent the enemy's ability to move easily, to have food and supplies, and to produce war goods.
2. Students might think about the war's possible disruption of trade, communication, transportation, agriculture, and education, strains on the health care system, and its impact on families.
3. Students might consider that civil wars are always fought in or near the homes of at least one and usually both sides. Civil wars often divide communities and even families.

How might a civil war be worse than other wars?

Encourage students to think about the ways a civil war might disrupt relationships between neighbors and families or disturb economic and trade relationships.

MAKING PERSONAL CONNECTIONS

Ask students how their lives might be affected if different parts of their town or state went to war. If students could not go to a certain part of town to see friends or relatives, how might they react? How might the economy of their town be affected?

TIME LINE DISCUSSION

Remind students that this time line covers a period of just a little over one year. Point out the number of major battles that took place during this year. Also point out that the activities of European nations diverted them from involvement in the United States.

- Ask how long after Lincoln became president the Civil War began. **Answer** a little over a month
- Ask students which battle of the war shown on this time line was fought at sea. **Answer** March 9, 1862, between the *Monitor* and the *Merrimack*
- Ask students what world event on this time line probably had the greatest impact on the early years of the Civil War. **Answer** Britain's decision to remain neutral

BEFORE YOU READ

Previewing the Theme: Citizenship

Have students examine the photographs and notice the differences in the uniforms and flags. Ask them why flags are often an important part of military activities on the battlefield and in preparing soldiers and civilians for war. Ask students what they can learn about the Confederacy and the Union side from studying their flags.

What Do You Know?

Students might recall some of the devastating civil wars in other parts of the world in the 1990s, such as those in Eastern Europe between Kosovar Albanians and Serbs in Serbia; or among Croats, Serbs, and Muslims in Bosnia. They might also recall the ethnic violence between Hutus and Tutsis that wracked Rwanda in Africa or the massacres in East Timor after that region voted for independence from Indonesia.

In-Depth Resources: Unit 5
- Tracing Themes: Citizenship, p. 22

READ AND TAKE NOTES

Reading Strategy: Comparing and Contrasting

Tell students that comparing and contrasting involves looking for similarities and differences between two or more things. Before students study the chapter, have them read the categories in the first column of the chart. As they read, ask them to keep those categories in mind as they watch for similarities and differences between the North and the South.

In-Depth Resources: Unit 5
- Setting the Stage, p. 21

Critical Thinking Transparency CT46
- Setting the Stage

Chapter 16 SETTING THE STAGE

BEFORE YOU READ

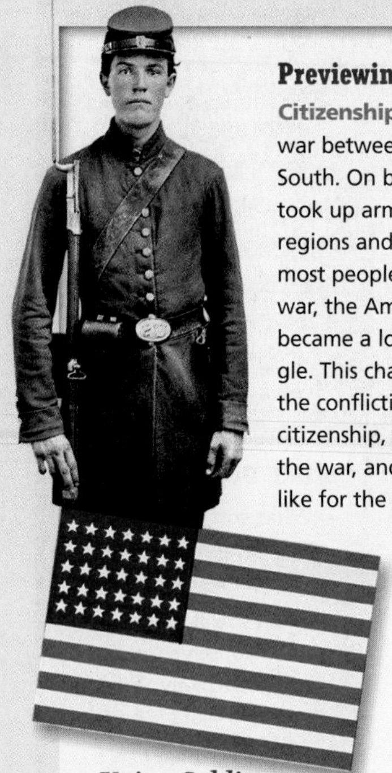

Union Soldier

Previewing the Theme

Citizenship Secession led to war between the North and South. On both sides, citizens took up arms to defend their regions and ideals. Although most people expected a short war, the American Civil War became a long, bloody struggle. This chapter describes the conflicting demands of citizenship, the early years of the war, and what life was like for the soldiers.

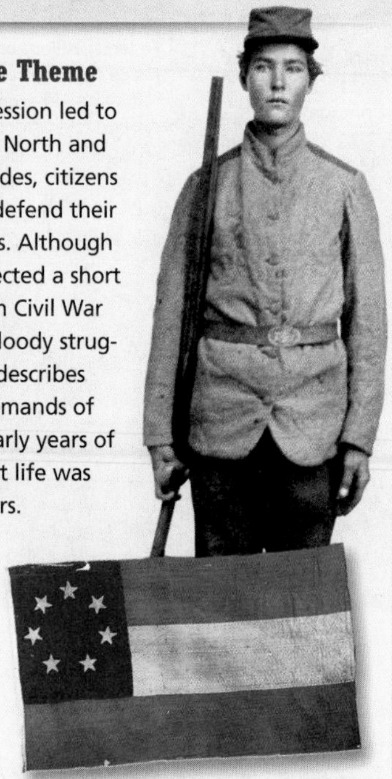

Confederate Soldier

What Do You Know?

What do you think of when you hear the phrase *civil war?* What would it be like to fight in a war of brother against brother? Where and how did the Civil War begin?

THINK ABOUT
- what a civil war is
- what you've learned about the Civil War from movies, television, and books
- reasons that countries threaten to break apart in today's world

What Do You Want to Know?

What details do you need to help you understand the outbreak of the Civil War? Make a list of those details in your notebook before you read the chapter.

READ AND TAKE NOTES

Reading Strategy: Comparing and Contrasting When you compare, you look for similarities between two or more objects, ideas, events, or people. When you contrast, you look for differences. Comparing and contrasting can be a useful strategy for studying the two sides in a war. Use the chart shown here to compare and contrast the North and the South in the early years of the Civil War.

See Skillbuilder Handbook, page R10.

	North	South
Reasons for fighting	to preserve Union	to defend homeland
Advantages	greater manpower and resources	fighting on their own territory
Disadvantages	had to carry battle to enemy	fewer resources and soldiers
Military strategy	surrounding and overwhelming the South	holding out until North grew weary
Battle victories	Shiloh, Antietam	Bull Run, Seven Days' Battles

TEACHING STRATEGY

READING THE CHAPTER

This is a chronological chapter focusing on the early months of the Civil War. It has a section focusing on life in the military. Encourage students to think about how the events of this chapter would affect the soldiers and sailors of the two sides. Ask them to identify other themes that recur throughout the chapter, such as military strategies, division within families, and hardship in the armies.

ALTERNATIVE ASSESSMENT

The Chapter Assessment describes three activities for alternative assessment on page 483. You may wish to have students work on these activities during the course of the chapter and then present them at the end.

1 War Erupts

TERMS & NAMES
Fort Sumter
Robert E. Lee
border state
King Cotton
Anaconda Plan
blockade
First Battle of Bull Run

MAIN IDEA

The secession of the Southern states quickly led to armed conflict between the North and the South.

WHY IT MATTERS NOW

The nation's identity was in part forged by the Civil War.

ONE AMERICAN'S STORY

Two months before the Civil War broke out, 22-year-old Emma Holmes of Charleston began keeping a detailed diary. Like other South Carolinians, Holmes got caught up in the passions that led her state to secede. From a rooftop, she witnessed the event that started the war. She wrote about South Carolina's attack on Fort Sumter, a federal fort in Charleston's harbor, in her diary.

A VOICE FROM THE PAST

[A]t half past four this morning, the heavy booming of cannons woke the city from its slumbers. . . . Every body seems relieved that what has been so long dreaded has come at last and so confident of victory that they seem not to think of the danger of their friends. . . . I had a splendid view of the harbor with the naked eye. We could distinctly see flames amidst the smoke. All the barracks were on fire. . . . With the telescope I saw the shots as they struck the fort and [saw] the masonry crumbling.

Emma Holmes, *The Diary of Emma Holmes 1861–1866*

This photograph of Emma Holmes was taken in 1900.

Many Southerners expected a short war that they would easily win. Northerners expected the same. In this section, you will learn how the war started, how the states divided, and how each side planned to win.

1 First Shots at Fort Sumter

As they seceded from the Union (the states loyal to the United States of America during the Civil War), the Southern states took over most of the federal forts inside their borders. President Abraham Lincoln had to decide what to do about the forts that remained under federal control. Major Robert Anderson and his garrison held on to **Fort Sumter** in the harbor of Charleston, South Carolina, but they were running out of supplies.

If Lincoln supplied the garrison, he risked war. If he ordered the troops to leave the fort, he would be giving in to the rebels. Lincoln informed South Carolina that he was sending supply ships to Fort Sumter. Leaders of the Confederacy (the nation formed by Southern states in 1861) decided to prevent the federal government from holding onto the fort by attacking before the supply ships arrived.

SECTION OBJECTIVES

1. To describe how fighting began at Fort Sumter
2. To analyze the strengths and weaknesses of each side
3. To explain each side's basic strategy
4. To summarize the results of the First Battle of Bull Run

SKILLBUILDER

Interpreting Maps: Location, Region, p. 467
Interpreting Charts, p. 468

CRITICAL THINKING

Comparing, pp. 466, 469
Summarizing, p. 467
Supporting Opinions, p. 468

FOCUS & MOTIVATE

5-MINUTE WARM-UP

Comparing These questions focus on the resources of each side in the war.

1. Look at the chart on page 468. Which side had more people and more factories?
2. Which of the resources do you think would be most critical to winning a war?

Warm-Up Transparency WT16

INSTRUCT

INSTRUCT: OBJECTIVE 1

First Shots at Fort Sumter/ Lincoln Calls Out the Militia

- Why did Lincoln decide to risk war by re-supplying Fort Sumter?
- How did states in the upper South respond to Lincoln's call-up of militia?
- How did Virginia's decision to secede improve the South's chances of winning?

In-Depth Resources: Unit 5
- Guided Reading, p. 23
- Geography Application: Fort Sumter Falls, 1861, pp. 28–29

RECOMMENDED RESOURCES

In-Depth Resources: Unit 5
- Guided Reading, p. 23
- Building Vocabulary, p. 26
- Skillbuilder Practice, p. 27
- Geog. Application, pp. 28–29
- Primary Source, p. 30

Reading Study Guide (Spanish and English), pp. 153–154

Economics in History, p. 16

Outline Map Activities, pp. 31–32

America's History Makers
- Abraham Lincoln, pp. 63–64
- Robert E. Lee, pp. 65–66

Formal Assessment
- Section Quiz, p. 285

Integrated Assessment
- Rubrics, 4.5, 5.1

Access for Students Acquiring English/ESL, pp. 104, 107, 108–109

INTEGRATED TECHNOLOGY

Humanities Transparency HT31
- Robert E. Lee

Humanities Transparency HT32
- Union and Confederate Money

Geography Transparency GT16

TEST-TAKING RESOURCES

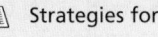

Strategies for Test Preparation

Test Practice Transparencies, TT57

Online Test Practice

AMERICA'S HISTORY MAKERS

Abraham Lincoln
Many historians rate Abraham Lincoln as our greatest president. Although his education was limited to less than a year in a one-teacher school, he held the country together through its most trying time. As commander in chief, Lincoln showed a surprising gift for military strategy. He never wavered in his commitment to preserving the Union.

Possible Response: During a war, citizens are often asked to make great sacrifices. A leader who can inspire others is more likely to unite people for a common purpose.

America's History Makers
- Abraham Lincoln, pp. 63–64

In-Depth Resources: Unit 5
- Primary Source, p. 30

MORE ABOUT . . .

Robert E. Lee
During the Mexican War, Lee served on the staff of General Winfield Scott. General Scott called him the "best soldier I ever saw in the field." Before Lee resigned to lead the Confederate army, President Lincoln offered him a field command of the Union armies. Lee turned the offer down, citing loyalty to Virginia. He was respected and loved by his troops.

America's History Makers
- Robert E. Lee, pp. 65–66

Humanities Transparency HT31
- Robert E. Lee

INSTRUCT: OBJECTIVE 2

Choosing Sides/Strengths and Weaknesses

- Why were the border states important?
- What were the strengths of each side?

Economics in History
- The Value of Border States, p. 16

At 4:30 A.M. on April 12, 1861, shore guns opened fire on the island fort. For 34 hours, the Confederates fired shells into the fort until Anderson was forced to surrender. No one was killed, but the South's attack on Fort Sumter was the beginning of the Civil War.

Lincoln Calls Out the Militia

Two days after the surrender of Fort Sumter, President Lincoln asked the Union states to provide 75,000 militiamen for 90 days to put down the uprising in the South. Citizens of the North responded with enthusiasm to the call to arms. A New York woman wrote, "It seems as if we never were alive till now; never had a country till now."

Background
The state militias were armies of ordinary citizens rather than professional soldiers.

In the upper South, however, state leaders responded with anger. The governor of Kentucky said that the state would "furnish no troops for the wicked purpose of subduing her sister Southern States." In the weeks that followed, Virginia, North Carolina, Tennessee, and Arkansas voted to join the Confederacy.

As each state seceded, volunteers rushed to enlist, just as citizens did in the North. A young Arkansas enlistee wrote, "So impatient did I become for starting that I felt like ten thousand pins were pricking me in every part of the body, and started off a week in advance of my brothers." Some feared the war would be over before they got the chance to fight.

With Virginia on its side, the Confederacy had a much better chance for victory. Virginia was wealthy and populous, and the Confederacy in May of 1861 moved its capital to Richmond. Virginia also was the home of **Robert E. Lee,** a talented military leader. When Virginia seceded, Lee resigned from the United States Army and joined the Confederacy. Although Lee opposed slavery and secession, he explained, "I cannot raise my hand against my birthplace, my home, my children." He eventually became the commanding general of the Army of Northern Virginia.

AMERICA'S HISTORY MAKERS

ABRAHAM LINCOLN
1809–1865

Today, Abraham Lincoln is considered one of the great men of all time. Yet early in his presidency, he was widely criticized and ridiculed. Critics labeled him ignorant, incompetent, and socially crude. As Lincoln grew into his job, however, he gained the respect and affection of many Northerners.

Even as a youth, Lincoln had displayed a gift for public speaking. During the Civil War, through his speeches and writings, Lincoln inspired fellow Americans to "dare to do our duty as we understand it."

Why would the ability to inspire people be important in a wartime leader?

***Reading*History**
A. Comparing Why might citizens in both the North and the South have been eager to fight in the Civil War?
A. Answer Tensions had been brewing a long time, and on both sides people might have been anxious to see the conflict resolved.

2 Choosing Sides

After Virginia seceded, both sides knew that the border states would play a key role in the war's outcome. The **border states**—Delaware, Maryland, Kentucky, and Missouri—were slave states that bordered states in which slavery was illegal. Because of their location and resources, the border states could tip the scales toward one side.

Keeping Maryland in the Union was important for the North. If Maryland seceded, then Washington, D.C., would be cut off from the Union. To hold on to the state, Lincoln considered arresting Maryland lawmakers who backed the South, but he decided against it.

ACTIVITY OPTIONS

INDIVIDUAL NEEDS

STUDENTS ACQUIRING ENGLISH/ESL

Figures of Speech Read aloud the excerpt from Emma Holmes's diary in "A Voice from the Past" on page 465. Explain that writers use figures of speech. A figure of speech is an expression whose meaning goes beyond the dictionary definition of the words being used. Have the students turn to page 484 and look at two of the highlighted words—*King Cotton* and *Anaconda Plan.* Have students find the explanations for these terms. Ask how these are examples of figures of speech. Then explain that figures of speech also make their writing more interesting. As an example, point out the clause, "the heavy booming of cannons woke the city from its slumbers." Ask students questions such as these: *Do cities actually sleep? What do you think Emma Holmes meant when she wrote that sentence in her diary?*

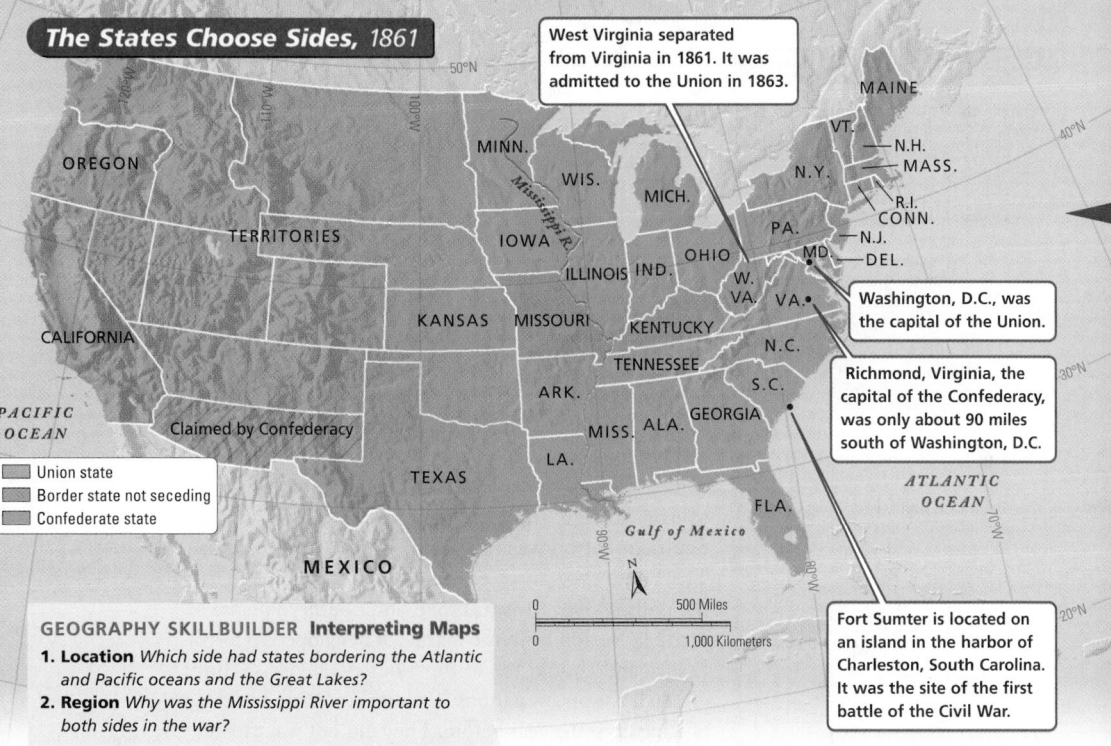

The States Choose Sides, 1861

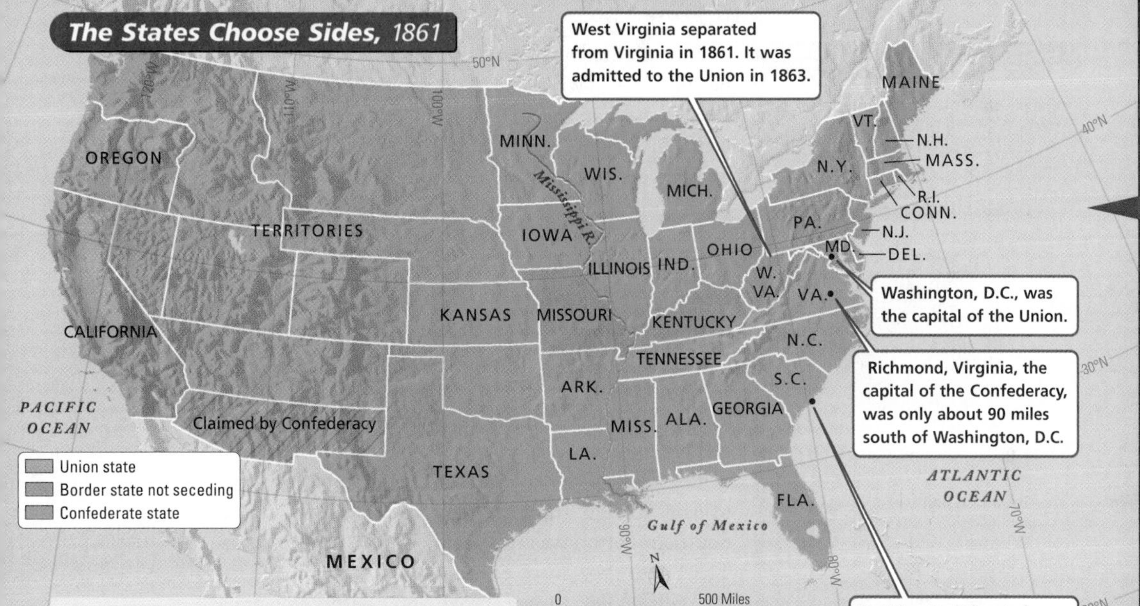

GEOGRAPHY SKILLBUILDER Interpreting Maps

1. **Location** *Which side had states bordering the Atlantic and Pacific oceans and the Great Lakes?*
2. **Region** *Why was the Mississippi River important to both sides in the war?*

Skillbuilder Answers
1. Union
2. It provided a means of transportation, communication, trade, and troop movements.

Pro-Union leaders eventually gained control of the Maryland legislature, and the state stayed in the Union.

Kentucky was also important to both sides because of its rivers. For the Union, the rivers could provide an invasion route into the South. For the South, the rivers could provide a barrier. Kentuckians were deeply divided over secession. However, a Confederate invasion in 1861 prompted the state to stay in the Union.

Reading **History**
B. Summarizing Why were the border states critical to the war's outcome?
B. Answer They were critical because of their location and resources.

Both Missouri and Delaware also stayed in the Union. In Virginia, federal troops helped a group of western counties break away. These counties formed the state of West Virginia and returned to the Union. In the end, 24 states made up the Union and 11 joined the Confederacy.

Strengths and Weaknesses

The Union had huge advantages in manpower and resources. The North had about 22 million people. The Confederacy had roughly 9 million, of whom about 3.5 million were slaves. About 85 percent of the nation's factories were located in the North. The North had more than double the railroad mileage of the South. Almost all the naval power and shipyards belonged to the North.

The Union's greatest asset, however, was President Abraham Lincoln. He developed into a remarkable leader. Lincoln convinced Northerners that democracy depended on preserving the Union.

HISTORY FROM VISUALS

Reading the Maps Ask students to identify the border states. Then have them locate Maryland on the map. Ask why keeping Maryland in the Union was so important to the North. Why might the decision of Missouri and Kentucky to remain in the Union be important? **Possible Responses** Maryland almost surrounded Washington, D.C. Missouri and Kentucky gave Union forces access to the Mississippi River, a key entryway to the South.

Extension Have students pick one of the border states that decided not to secede and report on how state leaders made this decision.

Outline Map Activities
- The Divided Union, 1863, pp. 31–32

Geography Transparency GT16
- Union and Confederate Resources, 1861

MORE ABOUT . . .

West Virginia

Long-standing political and economic differences led Virginia's western counties to form the new state of West Virginia. Few families in the western counties owned slaves, and many opposed slavery. The roads and rivers in this region linked the area's economy more closely with Pennsylvania and Ohio than with the rest of Virginia. However, even though West Virginia joined the Union, people within the new state remained divided in their loyalties. About 32,000 West Virginians joined the Union army, while around 12,800 became Confederate soldiers.

ACTIVITY OPTIONS

INTERDISCIPLINARY LINK: MATH — BLOCK SCHEDULING

RESOURCES OF THE NORTH AND THE SOUTH

Class Time One class period

Task Using data to make graphs on the resources of the North and the South during the Civil War

Purpose To compare resources of the North and the South

Supplies Needed
- Graph paper
- Markers
- Optional: ruler, compass, protractor

Activity Have students review the charts on page 484. Then have them make five more graphs using these data that do not include Missouri, Maryland, or Kentucky. **Agriculture:** Millions of bushels of corn: North 396, South 280. Millions of bales of cotton: North .004, South 5. **Livestock:** Millions of horses: North 3.4, South 1.7. Millions of beef cattle: North 5.4, South 7. **Bank Deposits:** Millions of dollars: North 189, South 47. When graphs are complete, have students identify the resources in which the South had the advantage and assess their importance.

INSTRUCT: OBJECTIVE 3

The Confederate Strategy/ The Union Strategy

- What did the Confederacy expect to gain by withholding cotton from the market?
- What was the goal of the Anaconda Plan, and what were its drawbacks?
- How did each side's strategy change as the war continued?

HISTORY FROM VISUALS

Reading the Charts Have students examine the differences in the resources of the Union and Confederacy. In which area did the North have the greatest advantage? **Answer** Industrial workers. How might the population difference between the two sides help the Union? **Possible Response** The North had more people to serve in the army, to work in factories, and to keep the economy going strong while the soldiers were at war.

Extension Ask students what factors not shown on these charts might be important to each side.

Humanities Transparency HT32
- Union and Confederate Money

CRITICAL THINKING ACTIVITY

Forming and Supporting Opinions After the class discusses the chart, ask: How might the Confederacy compensate for some of its weaknesses? What advantage might Confederates have in battles that were fought on their own territory?

Class Time 10 minutes

Resources, *1860*

The pie charts show the relative strength of the Union and the Confederacy in population and industry.

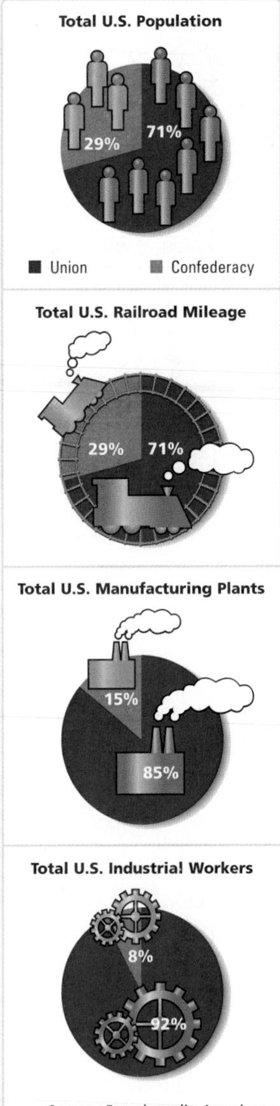

Source: *Encyclopedia Americana*

SKILLBUILDER
Interpreting Charts
1. *Which side had more resources?*
2. *How might the North's railways and factories have helped its armies?*

The Confederacy had some advantages, too. It began the war with able generals, such as Robert E. Lee. It also had the advantage of fighting a defensive war. This meant Northern supply lines would have to be stretched very far. In addition, soldiers defending their homes have more will to fight than invaders do.

3 The Confederate Strategy

At first, the Confederacy took a defensive position. It did not want to conquer the North—it only wanted to be independent. "All we ask is to be let alone," said Confederate President Jefferson Davis. Confederate leaders hoped the North would soon tire of the war and accept Southern independence.

The South also depended on **King Cotton** as a way to win foreign support. Cotton was king because Southern cotton was important in the world market. The South grew most of the cotton for Europe's textile mills. When the war broke out, Southern planters withheld cotton from the market. They hoped to force France and Britain to aid the Confederate cause. But in 1861, European nations had surplus cotton because of a big crop the year before. They did not want to get involved in the American war.

As the war heated up, the South soon moved away from its cautious plans. It began to take the offensive and try for big victories to wreck Northern morale.

The Union Strategy

The North wanted to bring the Southern states back into the Union. To do this, the North developed an offensive strategy based on General Winfield Scott's **Anaconda Plan.** This plan was designed to smother the South's economy like a giant anaconda snake squeezing its prey.

The plan called for a naval blockade of the South's coastline. In a **blockade,** armed forces prevent the transportation of goods or people into or out of an area. The plan also called for the Union to gain control of the Mississippi River. This would split the Confederacy in two.

One of the drawbacks of Scott's plan was that it would take time to work. But many people, eager for action, were calling for an immediate attack on Richmond, the Confederate capital. Lincoln ordered an invasion of Virginia in the summer of 1861.

Reading **History**

C. Supporting Opinions At the beginning of the Civil War, which side would you have predicted to win? Why?

C. Answer Most students will probably pick the North because it had huge advantages in people and resources. Some students might say the South because Southerners were defending their homes.

Skillbuilder Answers
1. the Union
2. The factories produced more supplies that could be delivered by the railways.

ACTIVITY OPTIONS

SKILLBUILDER LESSON: CREATING A DATABASE — BLOCK SCHEDULING

Explaining the Skill A database is a collection of related information, such as census figures, charts, graphs, or pictures. A database can be stored and organized to make the information accessible for users. For example, a database on Civil War battles might allow a user to search for information by name of battle, date of battle, state where a battle took place, or military units involved in it. To create a database, decide what information it will contain and how it will be organized. Then gather the information.

Applying the Skill Divide students into teams and give each team five note cards. Assign each team a topic related to the war. Have each group do research on the topic. The research may include statistical information, pictures, or other data about the topic. Finally, create a directory of the different ways the data in the database might be accessed by users.

In-Depth Resources: Unit 5
- Skillbuilder Practice, p. 27

4 Battle of Bull Run

To take Richmond, the Union army would first have to defeat the Confederate troops stationed at the town of Manassas, Virginia. This was a railway center southwest of Washington, D.C.

Background
In the South, the battle was called the First Battle of Manassas. In most cases, the South named a battle after a nearby town. The North used a landmark near the fighting, usually a stream.

On July 21, 1861, Union forces commanded by General Irvin McDowell clashed with Confederate forces headed by General Pierre Beauregard near a little creek called Bull Run north of Manassas. In the North, this battle came to be known as the **First Battle of Bull Run.**

The Confederate Army passes in review before General Pierre Beauregard.

At one point in the battle, a Confederate officer rallied his troops by pointing his sword toward Southern General Thomas J. Jackson. The officer cried, "There is Jackson standing like a stone wall! Rally behind the Virginians!" From this incident, Jackson won the nickname "Stonewall" Jackson. His men held fast against the Union assault.

As fresh troops arrived, the Confederates equaled the Union forces in number and launched a countercharge. Attacking the Union line, they let out a blood-curdling scream. This scream, later called the "rebel yell," caused the Union troops to panic. They broke ranks and scattered.

The Confederate victory in the First Battle of Bull Run thrilled the South and shocked the North. Many in the South thought the war was won. The North realized it had underestimated its opponent. Lincoln sent the 90-day militias home and called for a real army of 500,000 volunteers for three years. In the next section, you will learn what army life was like.

Section 1 Assessment

1. Terms & Names

Explain the significance of:
- Fort Sumter
- Robert E. Lee
- border state
- King Cotton
- Anaconda Plan
- blockade
- First Battle of Bull Run

2. Taking Notes

Use a Venn diagram to compare and contrast the strengths of the North and the South.

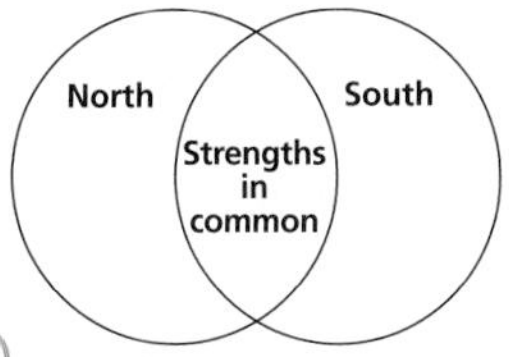

3. Main Ideas

a. How did citizens in the North and the South respond to the outbreak of the Civil War?

b. Why were the border states important to both sides in the Civil War?

c. What kind of military strategy did each side develop?

4. Critical Thinking

Comparing How was the South's situation in the Civil War similar to the situation of the Patriots in the Revolutionary War?

THINK ABOUT
- their reasons for fighting
- their opponents' strengths

ACTIVITY OPTIONS

LANGUAGE ARTS
TECHNOLOGY

Read an account of the First Battle of Bull Run. Use the information to write a **news article** or plan the battle's **home page** for the Internet.

INSTRUCT: OBJECTIVE 4

Battle of Bull Run

- What was the Union army's strategic goal in the summer of 1861?
- What conclusions did each side draw from the Northern defeat at Bull Run?

MORE ABOUT . . .

First Battle of Bull Run

Manassas was so close to Washington that many people came out from the city to watch the battle. They came on horseback or in carriages, bringing their picnic baskets, to watch the battle as if it were a pageant. The onlookers included several senators and congressmen. When Union troops began to retreat and Confederate artillery shells came closer, the spectators suddenly realized that war was dangerous. They joined the withdrawing soldiers, adding greatly to the general confusion, as the retreat became a rout.

ASSESS & RETEACH

Setting the Stage Ask students to fill in the graphic organizer on page 480, based on the information in this section.

Formal Assessment
- Section Quiz, p. 285

Critical Thinking Transparency CT46
- Setting the Stage

RETEACHING ACTIVITY

Ask students to hypothesize that they are advisers to Lincoln or Davis in 1861. Have them write a report describing the strengths and weaknesses of their own side and of the enemy. The report can conclude with an assessment of their chances of winning the war.

In-Depth Resources: Unit 5
- Reteaching Activity, p. 35

Section 1 Assessment

1. Terms & Names

Fort Sumter, p. 465
Robert E. Lee, p. 466
border state, p. 466
King Cotton, p. 468
Anaconda Plan, p. 468
blockade, p. 468
First Battle of Bull Run, p. 469

2. Taking Notes

North: more manpower; 85 percent of nation's factories; double the railroad mileage; almost all naval power and shipyards; South: first-rate generals; defending the homeland; King Cotton; Both: believed in what they were fighting for; many eager volunteers; public support for the war

3. Main Ideas

a. excitement; relief; eagerness
b. Their location and resources made them pivotal in tipping the scales to one side or the other.
c. The South developed a defensive strategy; but it quickly changed to an offensive strategy. The Union developed an offensive strategy.

4. Critical Thinking

Both were fighting more powerful opponents, and both believed they were fighting for freedom.

ACTIVITY OPTIONS

Integrated Assessment
- Rubrics for a news article, 4.5
- Rubrics for a Web page, 5.1

Literature Connections

OBJECTIVE
Students analyze a passage from historical fiction that imaginatively depicts the wrenching conflicts within families that the Civil War caused.

BLOCK SCHEDULING

FOCUS & MOTIVATE

Making Inferences To help students picture the events of *Across Five Aprils,* have students examine the photographs and read the caption on page 471. Then ask the following questions.

1. Can you tell from the photographs that the Terrill brothers fought on different sides in the war?
2. Judging by the memorial built after the deaths of the two brothers, how might this tragedy have affected the Terrill family's views on the war?

MORE ABOUT . . .

Across Five Aprils
This volume of historical fiction was a Newbery Award honor book. It is a historically accurate picture of the heartbreaking choices that many families were forced to make during the Civil War. The Creighton family lived in southern Illinois, where the Confederacy had many sympathizers. The novel describes how Jethro Creighton takes on adult responsibilities when his brother goes to war. His father falls ill, and Jethro must manage the family farm during the war.

Literature Connections

from *Across Five Aprils*

by Irene Hunt

At the beginning of the Civil War, nine-year-old Jethro Creighton and his family live on a farm in southern Illinois. Although Illinois is a free state that remains in the Union, many people in the area have ties to states where slavery is legal. For example, the Creightons have relatives in "Kaintuck," or Kentucky. When this excerpt begins, Jethro has already seen his brother Tom and his cousin Eb go off to fight for the Union. His other brothers, John and Bill, are trying to decide which side to fight for.

A line of wild geese flew southward far overhead, and Jethro stood motionless as he watched them disappear from sight. So **engrossed**[1] he was with the flight of the geese that he did not hear Bill's footsteps until his brother was quite near. He caught his breath at sight of Bill's face, which was swollen and beginning to grow discolored from a deep cut and many bruises.

"What's hurt you, Bill?" he asked, his voice barely **audible,**[2] for he was pretty sure he knew.

"We had a fight, Jeth, about an hour ago. We fit like two madmen, I guess."

"You and John?"

Bill's sigh was almost a moan. "Yes, me and John. Me and my brother John."

Jethro could not answer. He stared at the cut above Bill's right eye, from which blood still trickled down his cheek. Somewhere, far off in another field, a man shouted to his horses, and the shout died away in a cry that ran frightened over the brown water of the creek and into the darkening woods.

He had heard cries often that autumn, all through the countryside. They came at night, wakened him, and then lapsed into silence, leaving him in fear and **perplexity**.[3] Sounds once familiar were no longer as they had seemed in other days—his father calling cattle in from the pasture, the sheep dog's bark coming through the fog, the distant creak of the pulley as Ellen drew water for her chickens—all these once familiar sounds had taken on overtones of wailing, and he seemed to hear an echo of that wailing now. He shivered and looked away from his brother's face.

Bill sat down on the ground beside him. "Did ever Ma tell you, Jeth, about when John and me was little and was goin' to school fer the first time? At night I'd git a book and I'd say to Pa, 'What air that word, Pa?' and when he would tell me, I'd turn to John, jest a scant year older, and I'd say, 'Did Pa call it right, Johnny?' Ma and Pa used to laugh at that, but they was pleased to talk about it. They was always set up at John and me bein' so close."

"I know it." Jethro's words came from a tight throat. "What made you fight, Bill?"

"Hard feelin's that have been buildin' up fer weeks, hard feelin's that fin'ly come out in hard words." He held his hand across his eyes for a minute and then spoke quickly. "I'm leavin', Jeth; it ain't that I want to, but it's that I must. The day is comin' when I've got to fight, and I won't fight fer **arrogance**[4] and big money aginst the southern farmer. I won't do it. You tell Pa that. Tell him, too, that I'm takin' my brown mare—she's mine, and I hev the right. Still, it will leave him short, so you tell him that I'm leavin' money I

---

1. **engrossed:** absorbed; occupied.
2. **audible:** able to be heard.
3. **perplexity:** confusion.
4. **arrogance:** overbearing pride.

470

ACTIVITY OPTIONS
INDIVIDUAL NEEDS

LESS PROFICIENT READERS

Building Language Skills Match each less proficient reader with a more fluent reader. Duplicate copies of the Literature Connection and give each pair a copy and a highlighter. Have groups go through the reading and underline the dialogue between Jethro and Bill, circling any difficult-to-pronounce or unfamiliar words. Pairs can discuss unfamiliar words and their meanings and pronunciations. Then have one person take the part of Bill and the other of Jethro to practice reading the dialogue aloud.

After the oral reading of the dialogue, have pairs highlight a passage in the reading that is *not* dialogue. Ask them to discuss with each other what this section adds to the reading. Have pairs share the passages they chose and their conclusions with the class.

made at the sawmill and at corn shuckin'; it's inside the cover of his Bible. You tell him to take it and buy another horse."

Jethro was crying unashamedly in the face of his grief. "Don't go, Bill. Don't do it," he begged.

"Jeth . . ."

"I don't want you to go, Bill. I don't think I kin stand it."

"Listen to me, Jeth; you're gittin to be a sizable boy. There's goin' to be a lot of things in the years ahead that you'll have to stand. There'll be things that tear you apart, but you'll have to stand 'em. You can't count on cryin' to make 'em right."

The colors were beginning to fade on Walnut Hill. A light wind bent the dried grass and weeds. Jethro felt choked with grief, but he drew a sleeve across his eyes and tried to look at his brother without further weeping.

"Where will you go, Bill?"

"To Kaintuck. I'll go to Wilse's place first. From there—I don't know."

"Will you fight fer the Rebs?"

Bill hesitated a few seconds. "I've studied this thing, Jeth, and I've hurt over it. My heart ain't in this war; I've told you that. And while I say that the right ain't all on the side of the North, I know jest as well that it ain't all on the side of the South either. But if I hev to fight, I reckon it will be fer the South."

Jethro nodded. There were things you had to endure. After a while he asked, "Air you goin' tonight, Bill?"

"Right away. I've had things packed in that holler tree fer a couple days. I've knowed that this was comin' on, but I couldn't make myself leave. Now I'm goin'. The little mare is saddled and tied down at the molasses press. I'll go as fur as Newton tonight; in the morning I'll take out early."

He got to his feet. "There's lots of things I want to say, but I reckon I best not talk." Without looking at Jethro he laid his hand on the boy's shoulder. "Git all the larnin' you kin—and take keer of yoreself, Jeth," he said and turned abruptly away.

"Take keer of yoreself, Bill," Jethro called after him.

Across the prairies, through the woods, over the brown water of the creek, there was a sound of crying. Jethro ran to a tree and hid his face. He had heard his mother say that if you watch a loved one as he leaves you for a long journey, it's like as not to be the last look at him that you'll ever have.

Like the Creighton brothers, the Terrill brothers had different loyalties. William Rufus Terrill (left) fought for the Union as an artillery officer at Shiloh. His brother, James Terrill (right), was the commanding officer of a Virginia infantry regiment. Both men died in the war. William was killed at Perryville, Kentucky, in 1862; James was killed in battle in 1864. After the war, the family built a memorial to the brothers, which contained the words, "God Alone Knows Which Was Right."

CONNECT TO HISTORY

1. **Recognizing Effects** How has the Civil War affected the Creighton family? Discuss how the effect reflects what is happening in the country.

See Skillbuilder Handbook, page R11.

CONNECT TO TODAY

2. **Researching** Where have civil wars or internal rebellions taken place in the recent past?

For more about other civil wars . . .

RESEARCH LINKS CLASSZONE.COM

INSTRUCT

- How does Jethro react when he learns from Bill that his two brothers have been fighting?
- How has the war changed the relationship between Bill and John?
- What factors seem to have influenced Bill in choosing which side to fight for in the war?
- Why does Bill say he "best not talk"?

MAKING PERSONAL CONNECTIONS

Ask students if there are political issues today that might divide families the way the Civil War did. Point out that the Vietnam War often caused conflict between parents and children. What issues might students consider worth fighting for today?

VOCABULARY ACTIVITY

Write the four vocabulary terms on the chalkboard. Have students write four fill-in-the-blank sentences on a sheet of paper with each blank to be completed with one of the vocabulary terms. Be sure students put their answers on their papers. Have students pair up and read their selected sentences aloud, asking their partners to complete the sentences with the correct terms from the list on the board.

CONNECT TO HISTORY

1. **Recognizing Effects** **Possible Responses** The war has torn the Creighton family apart, leading two formerly close brothers to fight. Bill decides to leave home because of the tensions between himself and his brother John. The bitter feuds resulting from divided loyalties tore apart many homes as family members differed on the justice of the Confederate or Union cause.

CONNECT TO TODAY

2. **Researching** Using the *World Almanac,* Internet, or a current encyclopedia, students can find out about recent civil wars or internal rebellions around the world. Civil wars or political unrest have disrupted life in such countries as Sierra Leone, Kenya, Rwanda, Serbia, Indonesia, and Peru. Have students create an annotated map that identifies both the location and causes of recent civil wars or internal unrest.

SECTION OBJECTIVES

1. To explain who joined the armies
2. To describe military training and supplies of the era
3. To summarize the hardships of army life
4. To identify changes in military technology

CRITICAL THINKING

Summarizing, p. 473
Making Inferences, p. 474
Drawing Conclusions, p. 475
Forming and Supporting Opinions, p. 475

Why It Matters Now
- Modern Warfare, pp. 31–32

FOCUS & MOTIVATE

5-MINUTE WARM-UP

Recognizing Effects These questions focus on the difficulty that new recruits faced in adjusting to army life.

1. Read the quotation on page 472. What reasons does the major give for not wanting his brother to enlist?
2. How do you think the major's 18-year-old brother Jim might have responded to his brother's warning?

Warm-Up Transparency WT16

INSTRUCT

INSTRUCT: OBJECTIVE 1

Those Who Fought

- What were the characteristics and background of a typical soldier?
- What obstacles did African Americans face who wanted to serve?
- Why did so many men volunteer?

In-Depth Resources: Unit 5
- Guided Reading, p. 24
- Primary Source: "Battle Cry of Freedom" and "Bonnie Blue Flag," p. 31

2 Life in the Army

TERMS & NAMES
hygiene
rifle
minié ball
ironclad

MAIN IDEA	WHY IT MATTERS NOW
Both Union and Confederate soldiers endured many hardships serving in the army during the Civil War.	The hardships endured led to long-lasting bitterness on both sides.

ONE AMERICAN'S STORY

When the Civil War began, Peter Vredenburgh, Jr., the son of a well-known judge, was working as a lawyer in Eatontown, New Jersey. In 1862, he answered President Lincoln's call for an additional 300,000 soldiers. Nearly 26 years old, Vredenburgh became a major in the 14th Regiment New Jersey Volunteer Infantry. Less than two months after joining the regiment, he wrote a letter urging his parents to keep his 18-year-old brother from enlisting.

A VOICE FROM THE PAST

I am glad that Jim has not joined any Regt. [regiment] and I hope he never will. I would not have him go for all my pay; it would be very improbable that we could both go through this war and come out unharmed. Let him come here and see the thousands with their arms and legs off, or if that won't do, let him go as I did the other day through the Frederick hospitals and see how little account a man's life and limbs are held in by others and what little return he gets in reputation or money for the risk and privations of enlisting and his ideas of the fun of the thing will vanish in thin air.

Major Peter Vredenburgh, Jr., quoted in *Upon the Tented Field*

Major Peter Vredenburgh, Jr., was an officer in the Union army.

On September 19, 1864, Vredenburgh was killed in battle. In this section, you will learn more about other soldiers and what their experiences were like.

1 Those Who Fought

Like Peter Vredenburgh, the majority of soldiers in the Civil War were between 18 and 30 years of age. But both the Confederate and Union armies had younger and older soldiers. Charles Carter Hay was just 11 years old when he joined an Alabama regiment. William Wilkins was 83 when he became one of the Pennsylvania Home Guards.

Farmers made up the largest group among Civil War soldiers. About half the soldiers on both sides came from farms. Having rarely traveled far from their fields, many viewed going off to war as an exciting adventure. Some rode a train for the first time.

RECOMMENDED RESOURCES

In-Depth Resources: Unit 5
- Guided Reading, p. 24
- Building Vocabulary, p. 26
- Primary Source: "Battle Cry of Freedom" and "Bonnie Blue Flag," p. 31
- Literature Selection, pp. 32–34

Reading Study Guide (Spanish and English), pp. 155–156

Why It Matters Now
- Modern Warfare, pp. 31–32

Formal Assessment
- Section Quiz, p. 286

Integrated Assessment
- Rubrics, 4.3, 2.1

Access for Students Acquiring English/ESL
- Guided Reading, p. 105

INTEGRATED TECHNOLOGY

Critical Thinking Trans. CT47
- Cause and Effect: Hardships of Civil War Soldiers

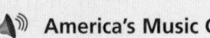

America's Music CD

Electronic Teacher Tools

classzone.com

TEST-TAKING RESOURCES

Strategies for Test Preparation

Test Practice Transparencies, TT58

Online Test Practice

Although the majority of soldiers in the war were born in the United States, immigrants from other countries also served. German and Irish immigrants made up the largest ethnic groups. One regiment from New York had soldiers who were born in 15 foreign countries. The commanding officer gave orders in seven languages.

At the beginning of the war, African Americans wanted to fight. They saw the war as a way to end slavery. However, neither the North nor the South accepted African Americans into their armies. As the war dragged on, the North finally took African Americans into its ranks. Native Americans served on both sides.

In all, about 2 million American soldiers served the Union, and fewer than 1 million served the Confederacy. The vast majority were volunteers. Why did so many Americans volunteer to fight? Many sought adventure and glory. Some sought an escape from the boredom of farm and factory work. Some signed up because their friends and neighbors were doing it. Others signed up for the recruitment money offered by both sides. Soldiers also fought because they were loyal to their country or state.

Reading **History**

A. Summarizing How did most men in the North and the South feel about going off to war?

A. Answer Most were excited by the idea of adventure and committed to doing their duty for their country.

Turning Civilians into Soldiers 2

After enlisting, a volunteer was sent to a nearby army camp for training. A typical camp looked like a sea of canvas tents. The tents were grouped by company, and each tent held from two to twenty men. In winter, the soldiers lived in log huts or in heavy tents positioned on a log base. In the Civil War, Confederate soldiers and soldiers in volunteer units in the Union Army elected their company officers. Both the Union and Confederate armies followed this practice.

A soldier in training followed a set schedule. A bugle or drum awakened the soldier at dawn. After roll call and breakfast, the soldier had the first of several drill sessions. In between drills and meals, soldiers performed guard duty, cut wood for the campfires, dug trenches for latrines (outdoor toilets), and cleaned up the camp.

Shortly after they came to camp, new recruits were given uniforms and equipment. Union soldiers wore

daily *life*

DRILL SESSIONS

"The first thing in the morning is drill. Then drill, then drill again. Then drill, drill, a little more drill. Then drill, and lastly drill." That is the way one soldier described his day in camp.

A soldier in training might have as many as five drill sessions a day, each lasting up to two hours. The soldiers learned to stand straight and march in formation. They also learned to load and fire their guns. Shown drilling below are soldiers of the 22nd New York State Militia near Harpers Ferry, Virginia, in 1862.

473

MORE ABOUT . . .

Native Americans in the Civil War

When the Civil War began, the so-called Five Civilized Tribes, who had been forced to move west in the 1830s, had strong ties to the South. These tribes and others lived in Indian Territory (later Oklahoma). The tribes raised several thousand troops for the South, and the Cherokee Stand Watie became a Confederate brigadier general, commanding the First Indian Cavalry Brigade. However, about an equal number of Native Americans fought for the Union side. Indian Territory was devastated, with up to 25 percent of the Creeks, Seminoles, and Cherokees dead. Nearly every building in the territory was destroyed, and most of the people lost everything they owned.

INSTRUCT: OBJECTIVE 2

Turning Civilians into Soldiers

- What training did soldiers receive?
- Why did both armies have problems providing food, clothing, and shoes for their soldiers?

daily*life*

Drill Sessions

In the 1860s, drilling was a very important part of training because troops were organized into regiments or brigades that were expected to march in formation. To get from a marching formation into a fighting formation required precise, complicated movements. Soldiers who had never worked together as part of a larger unit needed to spend many hours practicing these moves. Otherwise, they risked becoming a mass of confused individuals, rather than a fighting unit, on the battlefield.

ACTIVITY OPTIONS

INTERDISCIPLINARY LINK: MUSIC

BLOCK SCHEDULING

CIVIL WAR SONGS

Class Time One class period

Task Analyzing primary sources

Purpose To gain an understanding of how war songs encouraged patriotism and raised morale

Supplies Needed

- Copies of Civil War songs (See *Folk Song USA* by John and Alan Lomax or *The Ballad of America* by John Anthony Scott.)
- Recordings of Civil War songs (e.g., "John Brown's Body," "Tenting Tonight," "Bonnie Blue Flag")

America's Music CD

Activity Play recordings of a Confederate song and a Union song without identifying them. Have students decide which one is which based on careful listening. Then divide the class in half and give each group Confederate or Union lyrics to analyze. Have students identify patriotic or religious themes in each and suggest reasons why soldiers might like the songs. Make a Venn diagram on the chalkboard and hold a class discussion comparing and contrasting the songs that were popular with each army.

MORE ABOUT . . .

Civil War Surgery

The soft-lead bullets used in Civil War rifles did not chip a bone; they shattered it. As a result, an arm or leg wound often led to the need for amputation. Sometimes, especially in the ill-supplied Confederate army, the doctors had no chloroform to use as an anesthetic for the soldier whose limb they were sawing off. To make matters worse, no one understood why wounds became infected, so doctors saw no need for sterilization or even basic cleanliness. Lacking clean water, some could not even wipe off their bone saws as they went from one patient to the next.

INSTRUCT: OBJECTIVE 3

Hardships of Army Life

- What were the major causes of widespread sickness in army camps?
- How did scientific ignorance contribute to the spread of disease?

In-Depth Resources: Unit 5
- Literature Selection: "An Episode of War" by Stephen Crane, pp. 32–34

Critical Thinking Transparency CT47
- Cause and Effect: Hardships of Civil War Soldiers

STRANGE *but* True

Deadlier than Bullets

Commenting on the level of care received by wounded or ailing soldiers, the Surgeon General of the Union recalled that the war was fought "at the end of the medical middle ages." In one year of the war, Union officials recorded that virtually every soldier in the Union army came down with diarrhea and dysentery. Many men who survived the war suffered the aftereffects of disease for the rest of their lives.

yellowish-brown uniforms. Getting a uniform of the right size was a problem, however. On both sides, soldiers traded items to get clothing that fit properly.

Early in the war, Northern soldiers received clothing of very poor quality. Contractors took advantage of the government's need and supplied shoddy goods. Shoes made of imitation leather, for example, fell apart when they got wet. In the Confederacy, some states had trouble providing uniforms at all, while others had surpluses. Because the states did not always cooperate and share supplies, Confederate soldiers sometimes lacked shoes. Like soldiers in the Revolutionary War, they marched over frozen ground in bare feet. After battles, needy soldiers took coats, boots, and other clothing from the dead.

At the beginning of the war, most soldiers in army camps received plenty of food. Their rations included beef or salt pork, flour, vegetables, and coffee. But when they were in the field, the soldiers' diet became more limited. Some soldiers went hungry because supply trains could not reach them.

Background
Before uniforms became standardized, soldiers dressed in outfits supplied from home. This caused confusion on the battlefield.

STRANGE *but* True

DEADLIER THAN BULLETS

"Look at our company—21 have died of disease, 18 have become so unhealthy as to be discharged, and only four have been killed in battle." So a Louisiana officer explained the high death rate in the Civil War.

More than twice as many men died of disease as died of battle wounds. Intestinal disorders, including typhoid fever, diarrhea, and dysentery, killed the most. Pneumonia, tuberculosis, and malaria killed many others. Bad water and food, poor diet, exposure to cold and rain, unsanitary conditions, and disease-carrying insects all contributed to the high rate of disease.

3 Hardships of Army Life

Civil War soldiers in the field were often wet, muddy, or cold from marching outdoors and living in crude shelters. Many camps were unsanitary and smelled from the odors of garbage and latrines. One Union soldier described a camp near Washington. In the camp, cattle were killed to provide the troops with meat.

A VOICE FROM THE PAST

The hides and [waste parts] of the [cattle] for miles upon miles around, under a sweltering sun and sultry showers, would gender such swarms of flies, armies of worms, blasts of stench and oceans of filth as to make life miserable.

William Keesy, quoted in *The Civil War Infantryman*

Not only were the camps filthy, but so were the soldiers. They often went weeks without bathing or washing their clothes. Their bodies, clothing, and bedding became infested with lice and fleas.

Poor **hygiene**—conditions and practices that promote health—resulted in widespread sickness. Most soldiers had chronic diarrhea or other intestinal disorders. These disorders were caused by contaminated water or food or by germ-carrying insects. People did not know that germs cause diseases. Doctors failed to wash their hands or their instruments. An observer described how surgeons "armed with long, bloody knives and saws, cut and sawed away with frightful rapidity, throwing the mangled limbs on a pile nearby as soon as removed."

B. Answer attention to hygiene in camps by soldiers and doctors

Reading **History**

B. Making Inferences What changes could have helped lower the spread of disease among soldiers?

474

ACTIVITY OPTIONS

INDIVIDUAL NEEDS: GIFTED AND TALENTED

MEDICINE AND DISEASE IN THE CIVIL WAR

Class Time One class period

Task Researching medical aspects of the Civil War

Purpose To understand the connection between the state of medical science and the high death rate in the war

Supplies Needed
- Reference materials on medical history and on the Civil War

Activity Students interested in science or medicine can research one of the diseases that contributed to the high death toll during the Civil War. They might report to the class on how this disease was spread, how it was treated at the time, how it is treated in modern times, or how it is prevented. After each student has made his or her report, the class can discuss how this disease was probably spread on battlefields and in military hospitals and campgrounds during the Civil War.

The naval duel between the Union *Monitor* and the Confederate *Merrimack* (or *Virginia)* took place on March 9, 1862.

4 Changes in Military Technology

While camp life remained rough, military technology advanced. Improvements in the weapons of war had far-reaching effects. Battle tactics changed, and casualties soared.

Rifles that used minié balls contributed to the high casualty rate in the Civil War. A **rifle** is a gun with a grooved barrel that causes a bullet to spin through the air. This spin gives the bullet more distance and accuracy. The **minié ball** is a bullet with a hollow base. The bullet expands upon firing to fit the grooves in the barrel. Rifles with minié balls could shoot farther and more accurately than old-fashioned muskets. As a result, mounted charges and infantry assaults did not work as well. Defenders using rifles could shoot more of the attackers before they got close.

Ironclads, warships covered with iron, proved to be a vast improvement over wooden ships. In the first ironclad battle, the Confederate *Virginia* (originally named the *Merrimack*) battled the Union *Monitor* off the coast of Virginia in 1862. After hammering away for about four hours, the battle ended in a draw. (See page 476 for more information on ironclads.)

Despite new technology and tactics, neither side gained a decisive victory in the first two years of the war, as you will see in the next section.

Vocabulary
casualties: number of people killed or injured

C. Answer Rifles with minié balls increased the casualty rate and changed battle tactics.

Reading History
C. Drawing Conclusions Which changes in military technology had an effect on the average soldier? Why?

Section 2 Assessment

1. Terms & Names

Explain the significance of:
- hygiene
- rifle
- minié ball
- ironclad

2. Taking Notes

Complete the chart below.

The Typical Civil War Soldier	
Age	
Occupation	
Training	
Hardships	

Which hardship do you think would have been most difficult to endure? Why?

3. Main Ideas

a. How were the wartime experiences of Northern and Southern soldiers alike?

b. What factors contributed to the spread of disease among soldiers?

c. How did the use of the rifle and minié ball change combat tactics in the Civil War?

4. Critical Thinking

Forming and Supporting Opinions What were the motives that led individual soldiers to fight in the Civil War?

THINK ABOUT
- the multiple reasons that people had for enlisting
- what you consider valid reasons for fighting

ACTIVITY OPTIONS
LANGUAGE ARTS
ART

Imagine you are a soldier in the Civil War. Write a **letter** home to your parents about your experience or draw an **illustrated map** of your training camp.

MORE ABOUT . . .

Civil War Technology

The Civil War was the first war in which the telegraph and the railroad were vital to a war effort. It was also the first war in which soldiers laid land mines, aimed their rifles with telescopic sites, fired machine guns, and spied on enemy troops from the air—in observation balloons. It was the first war in which soldiers fought from trenches, sometimes using periscopes to peer over the top without making targets of themselves.

INSTRUCT: OBJECTIVE 4

Changes in Military Technology

- What effect did changes in weapons have on the way war was fought?
- What contributed to the high casualty rate in the Civil War?
- Why were ironclads better than wooden warships?

ASSESS & RETEACH

Setting the Stage Tell students to create a diagram like the one on page 480 to compare information about the North and the South for this section.

Formal Assessment
- Section Quiz, p. 286

RETEACHING ACTIVITY

Have students turn each of the subheads in this section into a question. For example, "Hardships of Army Life" becomes "What were the hardships of army life?" Then have students answer the questions they have created.

In-Depth Resources: Unit 5
- Reteaching Activity, p. 36

Section 2 Assessment

1. Terms & Names

hygiene, p. 474
rifle, p. 475
minié ball, p. 475
ironclad, p. 475

2. Taking Notes

Age: between 18 and 30; Occupation: farmer; Training: many long daily drill sessions; Hardships: inadequate food and clothing, crude shelters, dirty camps that stank, poor personal hygiene, chronic sicknesses, poor medical treatment

3. Main Ideas

a. Both endured hunger, cold, dirty living conditions, constant sickness, and poor medical treatment.
b. contaminated water and food; poor diet; exposure to cold and rain; unsanitary conditions
c. Cavalry charges and traditional assaults became outdated.

4. Critical Thinking

the desire for adventure; following the example of others; patriotism

ACTIVITY OPTIONS

Integrated Assessment
- Rubrics for a letter, 4.3
- Rubrics for a map, 2.1

Technology OF THE Time

OBJECTIVES

1. To use the diagram of an ironclad to understand why these ships were a significant technological advance
2. To explain how the introduction of ironclads led to a new era in naval warfare

INSTRUCT

- According to the diagram, what features of the ironclad were geared toward offense? toward defense?
- How do you think the experience of being a sailor on an ironclad would differ from being on another type of ship?
- What aspects of the ironclads reflect the changes in technology that grew out of the Industrial Revolution?
- Judging by the chart, how have warships changed from 1862 to 1972?

MORE ABOUT . . .

Ironclads

The *Merrimack* had been built before the war as a regular 40-gun steam frigate. In April 1861, as Union troops withdrew from the Norfolk Naval Shipyard in Virginia, they sank the *Merrimack* to keep it out of rebel hands. However, Confederate workers repaired the ship, covered it with iron plating, renamed it the *Virginia,* and sent it to sea against the Union blockade. In its first battle, the *Virginia* defeated three Union ships.

Meanwhile, the Union had secretly built its own ironclad, the *Monitor,* which one observer said looked like "a tin can on a shingle." By the end of the war, the U.S. Navy had 626 warships of which 65 were ironclads. Partial ironclads helped Grant in the West in 1862, supporting Union troops on western rivers and the Mississippi.

Technology OF THE Time

Ironclads

They moved through the water, as one observer put it, "like a huge, half-submerged crocodile." To crew members of traditional wooden ships, the ironclads indeed may have seemed like horrible mechanical monsters.

With a powerful iron hull almost entirely under water and a rotating gun turret, or short tower, an ironclad easily destroyed the older vessels it met. When the *Monitor* and the *Merrimack* (or *Virginia*) clashed during the Civil War in the first battle ever waged between ironclads, a new era of naval warfare had begun. Below is a closer look at the Union's *Monitor*.

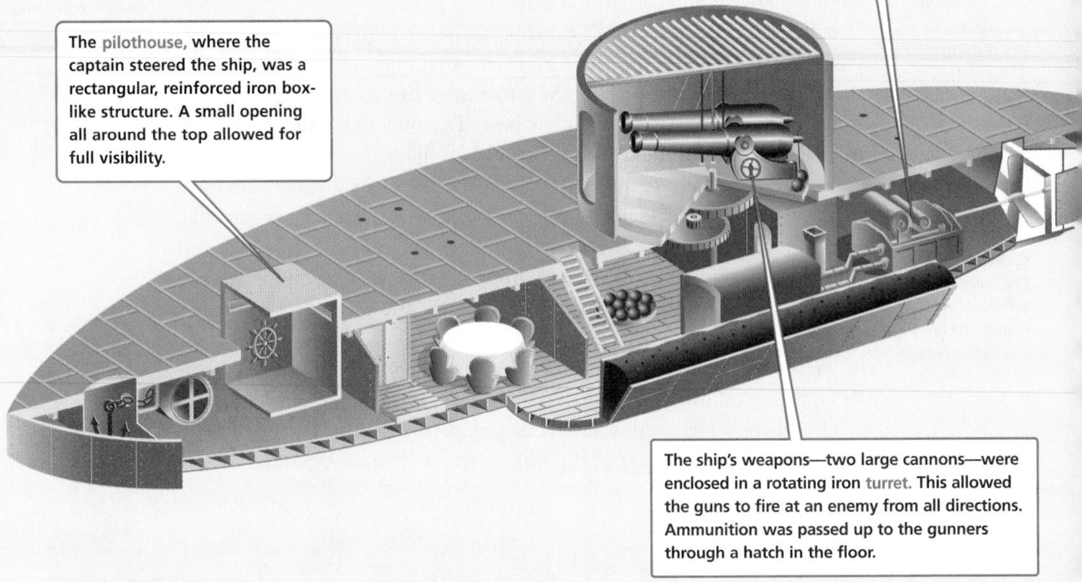
Steam engines powered the ship. They were connected by a propeller shaft to a four-blade propeller. Behind the propeller sat the vessel's rudder. This entire area was heavily protected so the ship could keep moving under heavy fire or ramming.
The pilothouse, where the captain steered the ship, was a rectangular, reinforced iron box-like structure. A small opening all around the top allowed for full visibility.
The ship's weapons—two large cannons—were enclosed in a rotating iron turret. This allowed the guns to fire at an enemy from all directions. Ammunition was passed up to the gunners through a hatch in the floor.

SCALE AND SIZE OF WARSHIPS

Class, Name, Launch Date	Length	Weight	Number of Crew	Weaponry
Ironclad (USS *Monitor*) 1862	172 ft.	987 tons	49	two 11-inch smoothbore cannons
Battleship (USS *Maine*) 1889	319 ft.	6,682 tons	374	four 10-inch guns, six 6-inch guns, seven rapid-fire 6-pounders, four torpedo tubes
Nuclear Submarine (USS *Nautilus*) 1954	324 ft.	4,092 tons	105	six torpedo tubes
Aircraft Carrier (USS *Nimitz*) 1972	1,092 ft.	95,000 tons	6,000	24 F-14A Tomcat warplanes, 16 radar guided missiles, six-barrel, 20-millimeter Gatling gun

CONNECT TO HISTORY

1. **Drawing Conclusions** Why would a rotating gun be an advantage in a naval battle?

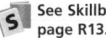

See Skillbuilder Handbook, page R13.

CONNECT TO TODAY

2. **Researching** Find out more about modern battleships or aircraft carriers, and write a brief report about their capabilities in battle.

For more about military ships . . .

RESEARCH LINKS CLASSZONE.COM

476

CONNECT TO HISTORY

1. **Drawing Conclusions Possible Response** As the ship moved during battle, guns could continue to fire at the enemy from any angle. Also the ship could fire at enemy vessels on several sides.

CONNECT TO TODAY

2. **Researching** Students can use an encyclopedia or the Internet to learn about modern naval vessels. One standard reference is *Jane's Fighting Ships.* Students who are interested in building models may be able to show the class examples of aircraft carriers, submarines, battleships, or destroyers from recent years. Some students may be interested in researching other changes in technology that occurred during the Civil War, such as the Gatling gun, and so on.

3 No End in Sight

TERMS & NAMES
Ulysses S. Grant
Battle of Shiloh
cavalry
Seven Days' Battles
Battle of Antietam

MAIN IDEA	WHY IT MATTERS NOW
In the first two years of the war, neither side gained a decisive victory over the other.	A long war can cause much death and destruction and leave a bitter legacy.

ONE AMERICAN'S STORY

In the summer of 1861, President Lincoln gave George McClellan command of the Union army in the East. The army had recently been defeated at Bull Run. McClellan faced the task of restoring the soldiers' confidence while organizing and training an army that could defeat the Confederates.

Within months, McClellan had accomplished the task and won the devotion of his troops. The entire nation expected great things. In November 1861, Lincoln made McClellan general in chief of the entire Union army. But while Lincoln kept urging him to attack Richmond, McClellan kept drilling his troops.

A VOICE FROM THE PAST

[S]oon as I feel that my army is well organized and well disciplined and strong enough, I will advance and force the Rebels to a battle on a field of my own selection. A long time must elapse before I can do that.

General George McClellan, quoted in *Civil War Journal: The Leaders*

President Lincoln (right) meets with General McClellan (left) on the Antietam battlefield in 1862.

Lincoln said McClellan had "the slows." While McClellan was stalling in the East, another general was winning victories in the West.

1 Union Victories in the West

That victorious Union general in the West was <u>**Ulysses S. Grant**</u>. In civilian life, he had failed at many things. But Grant had a simple strategy of war: "Find out where your enemy is, get at him as soon as you can, strike at him as hard as you can, and keep moving on."

In February 1862, Grant made a bold move to take Tennessee. Using ironclad gunboats, Grant's forces captured two Confederate river forts. These were Fort Henry on the Tennessee and Fort Donelson on the nearby Cumberland. (See map on next page.) The seizure of Fort Henry opened up a river highway into the heart of the South. Union gunboats could now travel on the river as far as northern Alabama. When the people of Nashville, Tennessee, heard the forts were lost, they fled the city in panic. A week later, Union troops marched into Nashville.

SECTION OBJECTIVES

1. To analyze the importance of the Union victories in the West
2. To explain how the fall of New Orleans helped the Union
3. To analyze Lee's victories in the East and his decision to invade the North
4. To describe the outcome of the Battle of Antietam

SKILLBUILDER
Interpreting Maps: Location, Region, pp. 478–479

CRITICAL THINKING
Contrasting, p. 478
Recognizing Effects, p. 479
Making Inferences, pp. 480, 481

FOCUS & MOTIVATE

5-MINUTE WARM-UP

Drawing Conclusions These questions focus on regions where fighting took place.

1. Look at the maps on pages 478–479. In what states did most of the battles in the East take place? in the West?
2. Why might so much of the fighting have taken place in or near border states?

Warm-Up Transparency WT16

INSTRUCT

INSTRUCT: OBJECTIVE 1

Union Victories in the West/ The Battle of Shiloh

- Why was control of rivers important?
- How did Shiloh signal a change from earlier battles of the war?
- Why did Lincoln refuse to replace Grant?

In-Depth Resources: Unit 5
- Guided Reading, p. 25

Reading Study Guide (Spanish and English), pp. 157–158

RECOMMENDED RESOURCES

In-Depth Resources: Unit 5
- Guided Reading, p. 25
- Building Vocabulary, p. 26
- Enrichment Activity, p. 38

Reading Study Guide (Spanish and English), pp. 157–158

Formal Assessment
- Section Quiz, p. 287

Integrated Assessment
- Rubrics, 2.1, 1.3

Access for Students Acquiring English/ESL
- Guided Reading, p. 106

INTEGRATED TECHNOLOGY

Electronic Teacher Tools

classzone.com

TEST-TAKING RESOURCES

Strategies for Test Preparation

Test Practice Transparencies, TT59

Online Test Practice

MORE ABOUT . . .

Shiloh Church

Ironically, the Battle of Shiloh, the first bloody battle of the war, took its name from a small Methodist church whose name came from the Hebrew word meaning "place of peace."

In-Depth Resources: Unit 5
- Enrichment Activity, p. 38

The Battle of Shiloh

After Grant's river victories, Albert S. Johnston, Confederate commander on the Western front, ordered a retreat to Corinth, Mississippi. Grant followed. By early April, Grant's troops had reached Pittsburg Landing on the Tennessee River. There he waited for more troops from Nashville. Johnston, however, decided to attack before Grant gained reinforcements. Marching his troops north from Corinth on April 6, 1862, Johnston surprised the Union forces near Shiloh Church. The **Battle of Shiloh** in Tennessee turned into the fiercest fighting the Civil War had yet seen.

Commanders on each side rode into the thick of battle to rally their troops. One Union general, William Tecumseh Sherman, had three horses shot out from under him. General Johnston was killed, and the command passed to General Pierre Beauregard. By the end of the day, each side believed that dawn would bring victory.

That night, there was a terrible thunderstorm. Lightning lit up the battlefield, where dead and dying soldiers lay in water and mud. During the night, Union boats ran upriver to ferry fresh troops to Grant's camp. Grant then led an attack at dawn and forced the exhausted Southern troops to retreat.

The cost of the Union victory was staggering. Union casualties at Shiloh numbered over 13,000, about one-fourth of those who had fought. The Confederates lost nearly 11,000 out of 41,000 soldiers. Describing

A. Answer Grant was a bold and decisive leader while McClellan was slow and cautious.

*Reading***History**

A. Contrasting How did Grant differ from McClellan as a military leader?

HISTORY FROM VISUALS

Reading Maps Have students identify the places on the larger map that each of the three inset maps depicts in greater detail. Then ask students what river both sides were fighting to control. **Answer** the Mississippi River. Ask students to suggest why control of the Mississippi would help the Union. **Possible Response** It would provide a way into the South, making the South a battleground of the war, and would cut off Confederate states west of the Mississippi from those to the east of the river.

Extension Have students pick one of the battles shown on the map and use encyclopedias and other reference materials to learn more about how geographic features of the area affected the outcome.

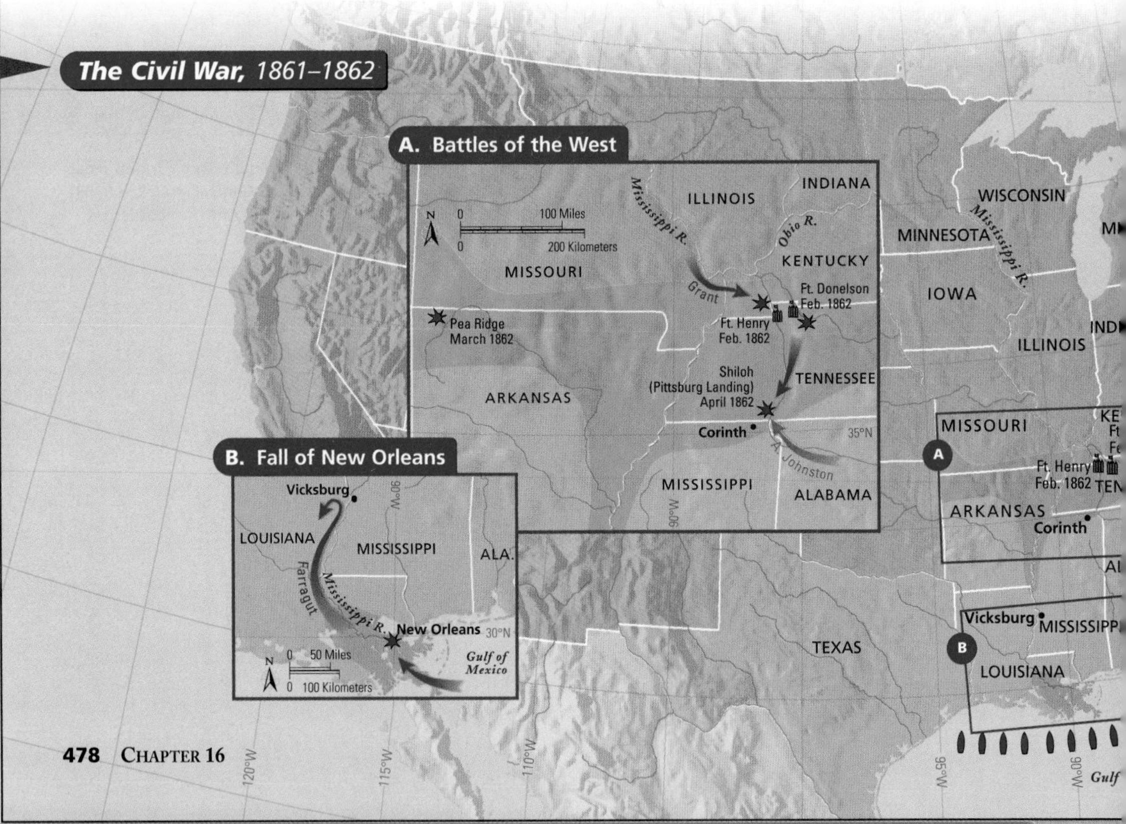

ACTIVITY OPTIONS

INDIVIDUAL NEEDS

LESS PROFICIENT READERS

Sequencing Events Students may have difficulty sequencing the events that occurred in the first two years of the war. To help them focus on the sequence, list the following major events and battles on the board. Have students find the approximate date for each one and then list them in chronological sequence. When the activity is completed, review the section by discussing the significance of each battle or event.

- Battle of Antietam
- Grant captures Fort Henry and Fort Donelson
- Lee crosses Potomac
- Battle of Shiloh
- Seven Days' Battle at Richmond
- Union army captures New Orleans

the piles of mangled bodies, General Sherman wrote home, "The scenes on this field would have cured anybody of war." Congressmen criticized Grant for the high casualties and urged Lincoln to replace him. But Lincoln replied, "I can't spare this man—he fights."

> ***"I can't spare this man—he fights."***
> **Abraham Lincoln, describing General Grant**

2 The Fall of New Orleans

The spring of 1862 brought other bad news for the Confederacy. On April 25, a Union fleet led by David Farragut captured New Orleans, the largest city in the South. Rebel gunboats tried to ram the Union warships and succeeded in sinking one. Farragut's ships had to run through cannon fire and then dodge burning rafts in order to reach the city. Residents stood on the docks and cursed the Yankee invaders, but they were powerless to stop them.

The fall of New Orleans was a heavy blow to the South. Mary Chesnut of South Carolina, the wife of an aide to President Davis, wrote in her diary, "New Orleans gone—and with it the Confederacy. Are we not cut in two?" Indeed, after the victories of General Grant and Admiral Farragut, only a 150-mile stretch of the Mississippi remained in Southern hands. The Union was well on its way to achieving its goal of cutting the Confederacy in two. But guarding the remaining stretch of the river was the heavily armed Confederate fort at Vicksburg, Mississippi.

B. Answer It lowered Southern morale. It helped the North cut the South in two.

***Reading* History**
B. Recognizing Effects Why was the fall of New Orleans significant?

Skillbuilder Answers
1. Early Union victories took place in the West; early Confederate victories took place in the East.
2. because it was near Union and Confederate capitals

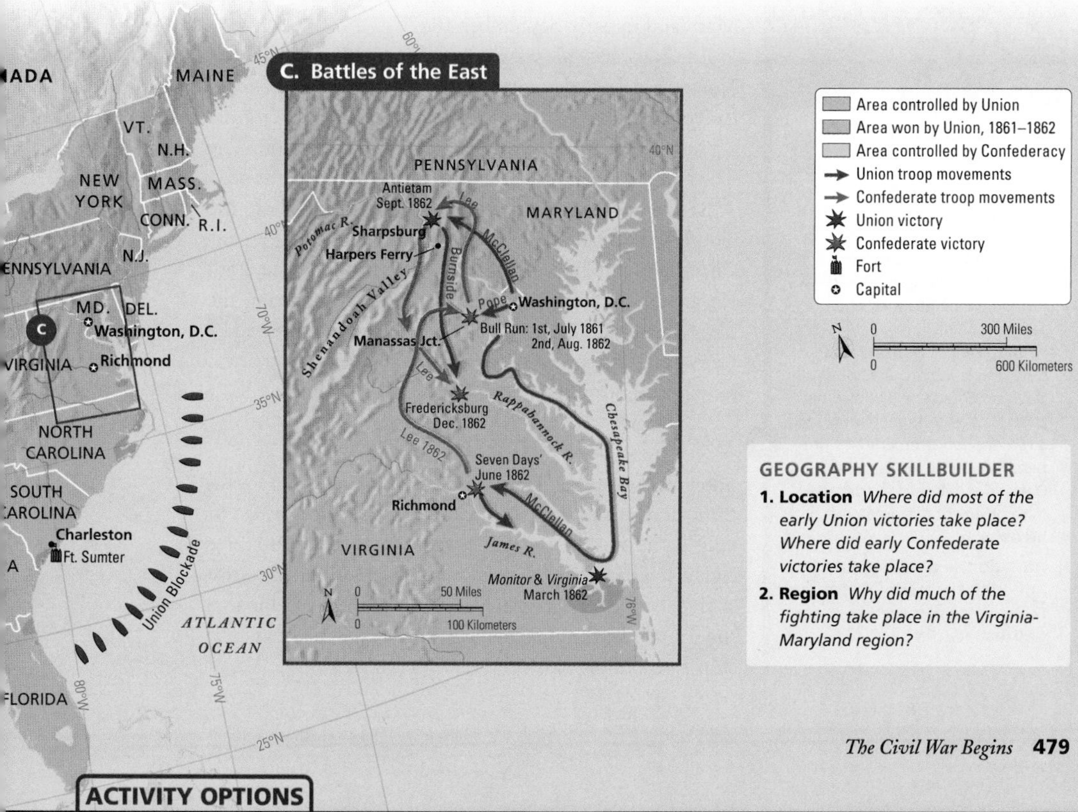

GEOGRAPHY SKILLBUILDER

1. **Location** *Where did most of the early Union victories take place? Where did early Confederate victories take place?*
2. **Region** *Why did much of the fighting take place in the Virginia-Maryland region?*

INSTRUCT: OBJECTIVE 2
The Fall of New Orleans

- Why was naval power crucial in capturing New Orleans?
- How did the fall of New Orleans advance Union strategy?

MORE ABOUT . . .

The Fall of New Orleans
The fall of New Orleans not only devastated Southerners like Mary Chesnut but shocked Europeans as well. Henry Adams reported from London, "People here are quite struck aback at . . . news of the capture of New Orleans. It took them three days to make up their minds to believe it. The division of America had become an idea so fixed that they had about shut out . . . any other."

CRITICAL THINKING ACTIVITY

Recognizing Effects Use the cause-and-effect chart below to help students understand the effects of Union victories on the course of the war. How might the outcome of the conflict in the West have been different if the South had been able to hold Fort Henry in Tennessee? What were the effects of the fall of New Orleans? Which battle was most critical to Union success?

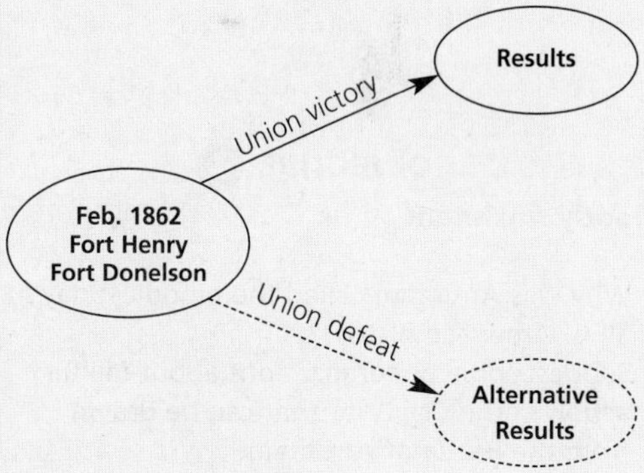

Class Time 10 minutes

ACTIVITY OPTIONS

MULTIPLE LEARNING STYLES: KINESTHETIC — **BLOCK SCHEDULING**

CONDUCT A MILITARY BRIEFING

Class Time One class period

Task Conducting a military-style briefing on war strategies and the outcomes of various battles of 1861–1862

Purpose To analyze the impact of geography on the Union war effort

Supplies Needed
- Reference materials on the battles in 1861–1862
- Wall map of United States
- Pointer

Activity Divide students into three groups. Assign each group a major campaign—western battles, eastern battles, or the capture of New Orleans. Within groups assign students different battles. Have them act as military spokespersons preparing and delivering a briefing to the class. Each group's presentations can summarize battle strategy, highlights, outcome, casualties, and significance to the overall campaign. Presenters can also tell how geography influenced strategy or outcome. Encourage students to use a pointer to note the location of the battle on the wall map, trace troop movements, and indicate rivers and other key features.

INSTRUCT: OBJECTIVE 3

Lee Claims Victories in the East/ Lee Invades the North

- How was Lee able to gain the advantage in the East?
- Why did Lee decide to invade the North?

AMERICA'S HISTORY MAKERS

Jefferson Davis

Despite his devotion and unswerving commitment to the Southern cause, Davis was not well suited to his position as president of the Confederacy. Haughty and narrow-minded, he was highly sensitive to criticism, quarreled often with most of his generals except Robert E. Lee, and showed poor judgment in choosing friends as members of his administration. He also clearly misread the attitudes of the British, French, and other Europeans toward slavery and the Confederate South.

Possible Responses: A military leader must be willing to act decisively and independently to achieve objectives, while a politician must be willing to compromise and be flexible to achieve goals.

INSTRUCT: OBJECTIVE 4

Bloody Antietam

- Why was Antietam called the bloodiest day in all of American history?
- Suggest some generalizations about military action in the Civil War that can be drawn from the Battle of Antietam.
- Why did Lincoln fire McClellan despite the Union victory at Antietam?

3 Lee Claims Victories in the East

Meanwhile, also in the spring of 1862, McClellan finally made his move to try to capture Richmond. He planned to attack the Confederate capital by way of a stretch of land between the York and James rivers. McClellan succeeded in bringing his troops within a few miles of Richmond.

But in June 1862, Robert E. Lee took charge of the Army of Northern Virginia and proceeded to turn the situation around. Lee sent Jeb Stuart and his **cavalry**—soldiers on horseback—to spy on McClellan. With about 1,000 men, Stuart rode around the whole Union army in a few days and reported its size back to Lee. Lee then attacked McClellan's army. The two sides clashed for a week, from June 25 to July 1, 1862, in what became known as the **Seven Days' Battles**. The Army of Northern Virginia suffered heavier losses, but it forced McClellan's army to retreat.

In late August, the Confederates won a second victory at Bull Run, and Union troops withdrew back to Washington. Within just a few months, Lee had ended the Union threat in Virginia.

*Reading*History

C. Making Inferences How was Lee's appointment fortunate for the South?

C. Answer It came at a time when the South appeared to be losing; Lee turned the situation around.

AMERICA'S HISTORY MAKERS

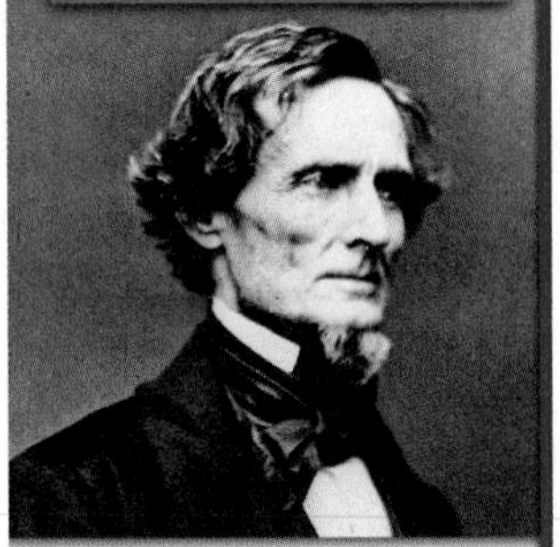

JEFFERSON DAVIS

1808–1889

Jefferson Davis expected to be given a military command when the Confederacy was formed in 1861. But Davis was chosen President of the Confederacy instead, which stunned and saddened him.

Because of his strong sense of duty and loyalty to the South, Davis accepted the unwelcome post. He had to immediately form a national government and prepare for war at the same time. Davis found it hard to compromise or accept disagreement with his opinions.

How do the qualities required in a military leader differ from those required in a political leader?

Lee Invades the North

Riding a wave of victories, General Lee decided to invade the Union. He wrote to tell President Davis of his plan. Lee thought it was a crucial time, with the North at a low point. Without waiting for Davis's response, Lee crossed the Potomac with his army and invaded Maryland in early September 1862.

*Reading*History

D. Reading a Map Use the map on page 479 to follow Lee's movements into the North.

Lee had several reasons for taking the war to the North. He hoped a victory in the North might force Lincoln to talk peace. The invasion would give Virginia farmers a rest from war during the harvest season. The Confederates could plunder Northern farms for food.

Lee hoped the invasion would show that the Confederacy could indeed win the war, which might convince Europe to side with the South. By this time, both Britain and France were leaning toward recognizing the Confederacy as a separate nation. They were impressed by Lee's military successes, and their textile industry was now hurting from the lack of Southern cotton.

4 Bloody Antietam

Soon after invading Maryland, Lee drew up a plan for his campaign in the North. A Confederate officer accidentally left a copy of Lee's battle plans wrapped around three cigars at a campsite. When Union troops stopped to rest at the abandoned campsite, a Union soldier stumbled on the plans. The captured plans gave McClellan a chance to stop Lee and his army.

ACTIVITY OPTIONS

INTERDISCIPLINARY LINKS: LANGUAGE ARTS/WRITING — BLOCK SCHEDULING

NEWS OF WAR

Class Time One class period

Task Writing headlines and news articles on one of the battles or other events discussed in this section

Purpose To describe the war effort from differing perspectives

Supplies Needed

- Reference materials on the Civil War
- Note cards

Activity Divide students into pairs. Have each pair pick one event discussed in the section and write two headlines about this event on a note card. One headline should describe the event as it might have been reported in a Northern paper. The other headline should reflect a Southern perspective. Collect all note cards and redistribute them to different pairs. Have each pair write a two- or three-paragraph article to go along with each headline. Have volunteers read their articles aloud and explain how the language reflects different points of view.

Confederate artillery soldiers lie dead after the Battle of Antietam.

McClellan went on the attack, though he moved slowly as always. On September 17, 1862, at Antietam Creek near Sharpsburg, Maryland, McClellan's army clashed with Lee's. The resulting **Battle of Antietam** was the bloodiest day in all of American history. A Confederate officer later described the battle.

A VOICE FROM THE PAST

Again and again . . . by charges and counter-charges, this portion of the field was lost and recovered, until the green corn that grew upon it looked as if it had been struck by a storm of bloody hail. . . . From sheer exhaustion, both sides, like battered and bleeding athletes, seemed willing to rest.

John B. Gordon, quoted in *Voices of the Civil War*

After fighting all day, neither side had gained any ground by nightfall. The only difference was that about 25,000 men were dead or wounded. Lee, who lost as much as one-third of his fighting force, withdrew to Virginia. The cautious McClellan did not follow, missing a chance to finish off the crippled Southern army. Lincoln was so fed up that he fired McClellan in November, 1862. In the next chapter, you will learn about the historic action Lincoln took after the Battle of Antietam.

Section 3 Assessment

1. Terms & Names

Explain the significance of:
- Ulysses S. Grant
- Battle of Shiloh
- cavalry
- Seven Days' Battles
- Battle of Antietam

2. Taking Notes

Review the section and find five key events to place on a time line as shown.

1860 — event — event — 1863
event — event — event

Which of these events do you think was most important?

3. Main Ideas

a. Why were Union victories in the West and the fall of New Orleans significant to the Union cause?

b. Why did Lee go on the offensive against the North?

c. How did the South's fortunes change after Lee took command of the Army of Northern Virginia?

4. Critical Thinking

Making Inferences What does Lee's invasion of the North suggest about his qualities as a general and a leader?

THINK ABOUT
- Lee's military skills and style
- the North's resources

ACTIVITY OPTIONS

GEOGRAPHY
ART

Develop a new military strategy for either the North or the South. Show your strategy on a **map** or in a **diagram** of troop movements.

MORE ABOUT . . .

George McClellan

McClellan's military career began well. He graduated second in his class at West Point, and early in the war he took charge of making the Army of the Potomac into a sound fighting force. He saw to it that his soldiers were well supplied with food, clothing, and equipment. And he insisted on good training and strict discipline. The soldiers held him in high respect and affection. However, on the battlefield he was slow to make decisions and reluctant to attack. His habit of overestimating the size of the Confederate forces often kept him from acting decisively.

ASSESS & RETEACH

Setting the Stage Fill in the categories in the graphic organizer with the appropriate information from this section.

Formal Assessment
- Section Quiz, p. 287

Critical Thinking Transparency CT46
- Setting the Stage

RETEACHING ACTIVITY

Have students review the battles mentioned in the section. Ask students to pick four battles and write two or three sentences telling how each affected Union and Confederate efforts to win the war.

In-Depth Resources: Unit 5
- Reteaching Activity, p. 37

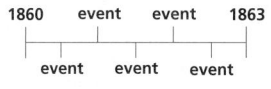

Section 3 Assessment

1. Terms & Names

Ulysses S. Grant, p. 477
Battle of Shiloh, p. 478
cavalry, p. 480
Seven Days' Battles, p. 480
Battle of Antietam, p. 481

2. Taking Notes

Capture of Fort Henry and Fort Donelson, February 1862; Battle of Shiloh, April 6, 1862; Fall of New Orleans, April 25, 1862; Seven Days' Battle, June 25 to July 1, 1862; Battle of Antietam, September 17, 1862

3. Main Ideas

a. They helped the Union to achieve its goal of cutting the Confederacy in two. **b.** victory might force Lincoln to talk peace; give Virginia farmers a rest during the harvest season; convince Europe to side with the South **c.** end of the Union threat in Virginia; took the offensive against the Union army

4. Critical Thinking

Lee was aggressive and willing to take risks. He was a smart leader who planned ahead.

ACTIVITY OPTIONS

Integrated Assessment
- Rubrics for a map, 2.1
- Rubrics for a diagram, 1.3

TERMS & NAMES

1. **Fort Sumter,** p. 465
2. **Robert E. Lee,** p. 466
3. **border state,** p. 466
4. **blockade,** p. 468
5. **hygiene,** p. 474
6. **rifle,** p. 475
7. **ironclad,** p. 475
8. **Ulysses S. Grant,** p. 477
9. **Battle of Shiloh,** p. 478
10. **Battle of Antietam,** p. 481

REVIEW QUESTIONS

Possible Responses

1. April 12, 1861, when the Confederates fired on Fort Sumter
2. more people; 85 percent of the nation's factories; more than double the railroad mileage; almost all the naval power and shipyards, President Lincoln
3. The South planned a defensive war, hoping that the North would give up and King Cotton would cause Europe to aid the Confederacy. The North planned a naval blockade of the South's coastline, a drive to gain control of the Mississippi River, and an attempt to capture the Confederate capital.
4. between 18 and 30 years of age; a farmer; born in the United States; white; patriotic
5. looking for adventure; following what other people were doing; out of a sense of loyalty to their country or state
6. unsanitary living conditions; poor personal hygiene; contaminated water and food; poor diet; exposure to rain, cold, and disease-carrying insects
7. made cavalry charges and traditional assaults outdated
8. cutting the Confederacy in two; by gaining control of forts along the Mississippi
9. McClellan was too cautious.
10. Lee won battles, took the offensive, and turned the war around so that a Confederate victory seemed possible.

Chapter 16 ASSESSMENT

TERMS & NAMES

Briefly explain the significance of each of the following.

1. Fort Sumter
2. Robert E. Lee
3. border state
4. blockade
5. hygiene
6. rifle
7. ironclad
8. Ulysses S. Grant
9. Battle of Shiloh
10. Battle of Antietam

REVIEW QUESTIONS

War Erupts (pages 465–471)

1. How and when did the Civil War start?
2. What advantages did the North have at the beginning of the war?
3. What were the war strategies of the two sides?

Life in the Army (pages 472–476)

4. What was the typical Civil War soldier like?
5. Why did so many people volunteer to fight in the Civil War?
6. Why was the incidence of disease so high among Civil War soldiers?
7. How did the use of rifles and minié balls change war tactics?

No End in Sight (pages 477–481)

8. What goal of the Union strategy did Grant further, and how did he do it?
9. Why did the North have such a hard time capturing Richmond, Virginia?
10. How did Lee's appointment to head the Army of Northern Virginia affect the course of the war?

CRITICAL THINKING

1. USING YOUR NOTES

	North	South
Reasons for fighting		
Advantages		
Disadvantages		
Military strategy		
Battle victories		

Using your completed chart, answer the questions.

a. Which side seemed likelier to win the war? Why?

b. Which side followed more closely its original strategy in the first two years of the war?

2. ANALYZING LEADERSHIP

Think about the leaders discussed in this chapter. Choose one. What character traits helped make him an effective leader?

3. APPLYING CITIZENSHIP SKILLS

Which individuals or groups of people demonstrated good and poor citizenship during the war? Explain your choices.

4. THEME: CITIZENSHIP

How could people on both sides of the Civil War believe that they were being good citizens by fighting?

5. MAKING DECISIONS

In your opinion, was Lincoln correct in deciding to go to war to save the Union? Explain your answer.

Interact *with* History

How did the consequences and effects of civil war that you predicted before you read the chapter compare with the actual conditions you read about?

VISUAL SUMMARY

The Civil War, 1861–1862

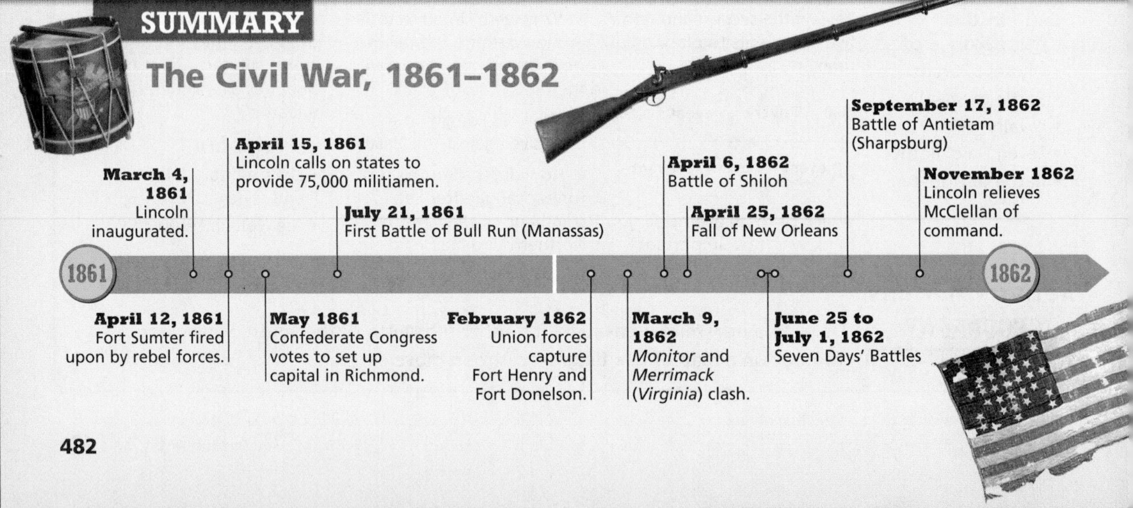
1861
March 4, 1861 Lincoln inaugurated.
April 12, 1861 Fort Sumter fired upon by rebel forces.
April 15, 1861 Lincoln calls on states to provide 75,000 militiamen.
May 1861 Confederate Congress votes to set up capital in Richmond.
July 21, 1861 First Battle of Bull Run (Manassas)
February 1862 Union forces capture Fort Henry and Fort Donelson.
March 9, 1862 Monitor and Merrimack (Virginia) clash.
April 6, 1862 Battle of Shiloh
April 25, 1862 Fall of New Orleans
June 25 to July 1, 1862 Seven Days' Battles
September 17, 1862 Battle of Antietam (Sharpsburg)
November 1862 Lincoln relieves McClellan of command.
1862

CRITICAL THINKING

Possible Responses

1. **USING YOUR NOTES** **a.** Most students would probably favor the North because of its advantages in resources and manpower. **b.** the North
2. **ANALYZING LEADERSHIP** Students might choose Lee, who was brilliant and bold. Or they might choose Grant, who was stubborn and relentless.
3. **APPLYING CITIZENSHIP SKILLS** Students might cite as good the millions of volunteers who fought for their country or the military and civilian leaders who worked to further causes they believed in. They might cite as poor the contractors who sold shoddy military goods to the government.
4. **THEME: CITIZENSHIP** In the North, people believed they were fighting to save the Union and preserve democracy. In the South, people believed they were fighting for the freedom and independence of their state.
5. **MAKING DECISIONS** Students may believe that Lincoln was correct because he succeeded in saving the Union, or Lincoln was wrong because he paid too high a price in human suffering.

Interact *with* History. Students might state that the average soldier found army life more difficult than expected.

HISTORY SKILLS

1. INTERPRETING MAPS: Movement

Study the map and answer the questions.

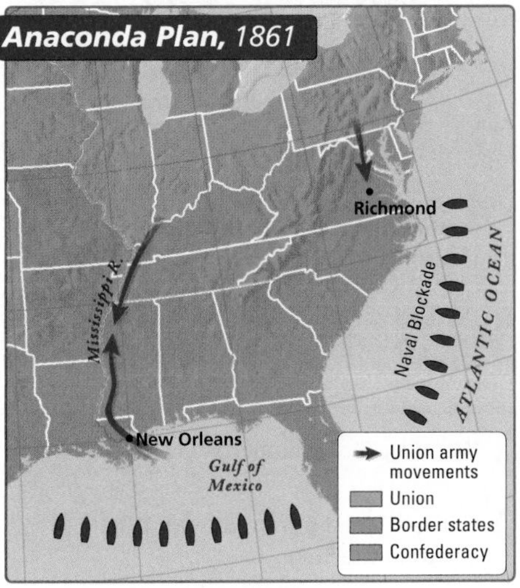

Basic Map Elements

a. What is the subject of the map?

b. What do the colors of the states indicate?

Interpreting the Map

c. What does the arrow in the East indicate?

d. What two bodies of water did the blockade cover?

2. INTERPRETING PRIMARY SOURCES

The following quotation comes from a letter that Robert E. Lee wrote to his sister after Virginia had seceded from the Union and he had resigned from the U.S. Army. Read the quotation and then answer the questions.

> With all my devotion to the Union and the feeling of loyalty and duty of an American citizen, I have not been able to make up my mind to raise my hand against my relatives, my children, my home. I have, therefore, resigned my commission in the Army, and, save in defense of my native state, with the sincere hope that my poor services may never be needed, I hope I may never be called on to draw my sword.
>
> **Robert E. Lee,** quoted in *The Annals of America*

a. What inner conflict does Lee express?

b. What obligation or loyalty does Lee consider greater than his duty to his country?

ALTERNATIVE ASSESSMENT

1. INTERDISCIPLINARY ACTIVITY: Literature

Reading Letters Using the library or the Internet, find firsthand accounts of the Civil War and read some letters written by soldiers. Choose one letter to read aloud to the class. Then, pretend you are the person receiving the letter, and describe your reaction to it.

2. COOPERATIVE LEARNING ACTIVITY

Developing a Peace Proposal The Civil War broke out because the two sides could not reach a compromise. Work in a small group to develop a compromise that would have resolved the conflict between the North and the South. Have one person in the group take the position of a Northerner, another a Southerner, and the third a mediator between the two. Present your proposal to the class for their comments.

3. TECHNOLOGY ACTIVITY

Making a Class Presentation Life in the army training camps during the Civil War was hard. Information about life in the camps comes from primary sources. Using the library and the Internet, find diaries, letters, photographs, and news articles about daily life.

For more about Civil War army camps . . .

INTERNET ACTIVITY
CLASSZONE.COM

Plan an electronic presentation on army life for your class. Use the list of suggested topics below to begin brainstorming.

- Drawings, maps, and photos that show the design of a typical camp
- Items used for cooking, lodging, sanitation, military drilling, and recreation
- Drills and maneuvers soldiers learned
- Personal belongings of the Yankees and rebels
- Firsthand accounts of camp life from letters and diaries
- Changes in camp life as the war dragged on

4. HISTORY PORTFOLIO

Review the questions that you wrote for What Do You Want to Know? on page 464. Then write a short report in which you explain the answers to your questions. Be sure to use standard grammar, spelling, sentence structure, and punctuation in your report. If any questions were not answered, do research to answer them. Add your report to your portfolio.

Additional Test Practice, pp. S1–S33 — TEST PRACTICE CLASSZONE.COM

ALTERNATIVE ASSESSMENT

1. INTERDISCIPLINARY ACTIVITY: **Literature**
   Letters should
   - convey information through performance.
   - be read with creativity.
   - reflect an understanding of the letter's contents.

2. COOPERATIVE LEARNING ACTIVITY
   Proposals should
   - reflect the use of a problem-solving technique.
   - focus on a compromise that would prevent war.
   - support student positions with evidence or logic.

3. TECHNOLOGY ACTIVITY
   Presentations should
   - clearly demonstrate an understanding of life in army training camps.
   - utilize several primary sources of information to create a variety of information.
   - establish a rapport with the audience.
   - show proficiency in the use of technology.

4. HISTORY PORTFOLIO
   Short reports should
   - answer questions about the outbreak of the Civil War.
   - use evidence to develop and support ideas.
   - cite sources of information.
   - use standard grammar, spelling, sentence structure, and punctuation.

Critical Thinking Transparency CT48
- Visual Summary

Formal Assessment
- Chapter Test, Forms A, B, and C, pp. 288–299

HISTORY SKILLS

Possible Responses

1. INTERPRETING MAPS
   Basic Map Elements
   a. the Anaconda Plan of the Union to defeat the Confederacy
   b. Union, border, or Confederacy states
   Interpreting the Map
   c. movement of Union troops toward Confederate capital of Richmond
   d. Gulf of Mexico and Atlantic Ocean

2. INTERPRETING PRIMARY SOURCES
   a. conflict between loyalty to one's family and home and loyalty to one's country
   b. the obligation or loyalty to family and home

CHAPTER 17 PLANNING GUIDE

The Tide of War Turns 1863–1865

	CHAPTER OVERVIEW	COPYMASTERS	INTEGRATED TECHNOLOGY
CHAPTER RESOURCES	This chapter describes the later stages of the Civil War, with its terrible loss of life and the eventual Union victory. It also describes the war's widespread effects on American society and the assassination of President Lincoln.	**In-Depth Resources: Unit 5** • Tracing Themes: Impact of the Individual, p. 40 • Building Vocabulary, p. 45 • History Workshop Resources, p. 59 **Interdisciplinary Projects,** pp. 97–102	• eEdition Plus Online • EasyPlanner Plus Online • eTest Plus Online • eEdition • Power Presentations • EasyPlanner • Electronic Library of Primary Sources • Test Generator • Reading Study Guide • America's Music
SECTION 1 The Emancipation Proclamation pp. 487–490	**KEY IDEAS** • Lincoln issues the Emancipation Proclamation. • The public reaction to the proclamation is divided. • The 54th Massachusetts Regiment organizes as one of the first African-American regiments.	**In-Depth Resources: Unit 5** • Setting the Stage, p. 39 • Guided Reading, p. 41 • Primary Sources, pp. 49–50 • Reteaching Activity, p. 54	**Warm-Up Transparency WT17** **Critical Thinking Transparency CT49** • Setting the Stage **classzone.com**
SECTION 2 War Affects Society pp. 491–495	• As the war drags on, both the North and the South pass draft laws. • The war boosts Northern industry, while the South suffers severe inflation and food shortages. • Women run farms, work in factories, nurse the wounded, and organize relief agencies.	**In-Depth Resources: Unit 5** • Setting the Stage, p. 39 • Guided Reading, p. 42 • Literature Selection, pp. 51–53 • Reteaching Activity, p. 55 **America's History Makers** • Clara Barton, pp. 67–68 **Economics in History** • Financing the Civil War, p. 17	**Warm-Up Transparency WT17** **Critical Thinking Transparency CT49** • Setting the Stage **classzone.com**
SECTION 3 The North Wins pp. 496–503	• The Union victory at Gettysburg is a turning point in the war. • Grant wins control of the Mississippi River, while Sherman wages total war across Georgia. • As Grant closes in on Richmond, Lee surrenders at Appomattox Court House, effectively ending the war.	**In-Depth Resources: Unit 5** • Setting the Stage, p. 39 • Guided Reading, p. 43 • Skillbuilder Practice, p. 46 • Reteaching Activity, p. 56 **America's History Makers** • Ulysses S. Grant, pp. 69–70 **Why It Matters Now** • One Nation, pp. 33–34 **Outline Map Activities,** pp. 33–34	**Warm-Up Transparency WT17** **Humanities Transparency HT33** • Battle of Fredericksburg **Geography Transparency GT17** • Vicksburg Campaign, 1863 **Critical Thinking Transparency CT49** • Setting the Stage **classzone.com**
SECTION 4 The Legacy of the War pp. 504–509	• The Civil War leaves 620,000 dead, and President Lincoln is assassinated soon after Lee's surrender. • The Thirteenth Amendment bans slavery in the United States. • The war enlarges federal power and promotes industry in the North but leaves the South devastated.	**In-Depth Resources: Unit 5** • Setting the Stage, p. 39 • Guided Reading, p. 44 • Geography Application: Booth Assassinates Lincoln, pp. 47–48 • Reteaching Activity, p. 57	**Humanities Transparency HT34** • John Wilkes Booth Poster **Critical Thinking Transparency CT50** • Cause and Effect: The Civil War, 1861–1865 **Critical Thinking Transparency CT51** • Visual Summary **Primary Source Explorer** • *The Gettysburg Address* • *Second Inaugural Address*

Pupil's Edition | Overhead Transparency | CD-ROM
Copymaster | Audio Library | Internet

ASSESSMENT OPTIONS

Chapter Assessment, pp. 510–511

Formal Assessment
- Chapter Tests, Forms A, B, and C, pp. 304–318

Test Generator

Online Test Practice

Strategies for Test Preparation

Section Assessment, p. 490

Formal Assessment, Quiz, p. 300

Integrated Assessment Book
- Rubrics, 5.1, 4.8

Test Generator

Test Practice Transparencies, TT60

Section Assessment, p. 495

Formal Assessment, Quiz, p. 301

Integrated Assessment Book
- Rubrics, 2.1, 3.6

Test Generator

Test Practice Transparencies, TT61

Section Assessment, p. 503

Formal Assessment, Quiz, p. 302

Integrated Assessment Book
- Rubrics, 2.1, 4.5

Test Generator

Test Practice Transparencies, TT62

Section Assessment, p. 507

Formal Assessment, Quiz, p. 303

Integrated Assessment Book
- Rubrics, 2.6, 1.6

Test Generator

Test Practice Transparencies, TT63

CUSTOMIZING FOR INDIVIDUAL NEEDS

Students Acquiring English/ESL

Reading Study Guide (English and Spanish), pp. 161–170

Access for Students Acquiring English/ESL: Spanish Translations, pp. 110–116

Chapter Summaries on CD (English and Spanish)

Modified Lesson Plans for English Learners

Less Proficient Readers

Reading Study Guide (English and Spanish), pp. 160–170

Chapter Summaries on CD (English and Spanish)

Gifted and Talented Students

In-Depth Resources: Unit 5
- Enrichment Activity, p. 58

America's History Makers
- Clara Barton, pp. 67–68
- Ulysses S. Grant, pp. 69–70

CROSS-CURRICULAR CONNECTIONS

Geography

The Conservation Fund, Frances H. Kennedy, ed. ***The Civil War Battlefield Guide.*** Boston: Houghton Mifflin, 1998. New edition of a guide to 384 battles and battlefields with 83 maps.

Health

Wilbur, C. Keith. ***Civil War Medicine, 1861–1865.*** Broomall, PA: Chelsea House Publishing, 1999. Fascinating look at the work and knowledge of doctors and nurses during the war.

Primary Sources

Werner, Emmy E. ***Reluctant Witnesses: Children's Voices from the Civil War.*** Boulder, CO: Westview Press, 1999. A collection of quotations from children, memoirs from adults who were children during the war, and contemporary newspaper articles.

Interdisciplinary Projects, pp. 97–102

- Math: Comparing Data on Bar Graphs
- Science: Make a Pinhole Camera
- Language Arts: Civil War Letters
- Music: Civil War Songs

Literature

Alcott, Louisa May. ***Little Women.*** Boston: Little, Brown, 1968. The much loved classic about a family of girls growing up in New England during the Civil War.

Forrester, Sandra. ***Sound the Jubilee.*** New York: Dutton Lodestar, 1995. Intriguing first novel in which an enslaved family escapes from a plantation to form a community on a Union-held island off the Virginia coast. Based an a historic incident.

Lincoln, Abraham. ***Abraham Lincoln: Speeches and Writings 1859–1865.*** Don E. Fehrenbacher, ed. New York: Literary Classics of United States, 1989. Excellent for browsing or for research.

Morrison, Taylor. ***Civil War Artist.*** Boston: Houghton Mifflin, 1999. Unusual novel about a newspaper artist who follows the Union army at Bull Run.

McDougal Littell
The Language of Literature
Walt Whitman "O Captain! My Captain" (poem)

ENRICHMENT ACTIVITIES

Pupil's Edition, pp. 484–513
Interact with History, p. 485
Geography in History, pp. 498–499
Interactive Primary Sources, pp. 508–509
History Workshop, pp. 512–513

In-Depth Resources: Unit 5
- Geography Application: Booth Assassinates Lincoln, pp. 47–48
- Primary Source: from "Reply to Emancipation Memorial," p. 49
- Primary Source: A Letter from James Henry Gooding, p. 50
- Literature Selection: from *In My Father's House,* pp. 51–53
- History Workshop Resources, p. 59

America's History Makers
- Clara Barton, pp. 67–68
- Ulysses S. Grant, pp. 69–70

America's Music CD

Outline Map Activities
- The End of the Civil War, 1865, pp. 33–34

Primary Source Explorer
- *The Gettysburg Address*
- *Second Inaugural Address*

Why It Matters Now
- One Nation, pp. 33–34

BLOCK SCHEDULING — LESSON PLAN OPTIONS (90-MINUTE PERIOD)

DAY 1

Interact with History, p. 485
Class Time 20 Minutes

Options for pacing and variety:
- **Role-Playing** Divide students into six-member groups. Have three students in each group take the part of Confederate soldiers and the other three the part of Union soldiers. Have each student share with the group how he or she would answer the "What Do You Think?" questions from the perspective of the role assigned. Then have students switch roles and respond to the questions a second time. **Class Time** 15 minutes

Setting the Stage, p. 486
Class Time 20 minutes

Options for pacing and variety:
- **Time Saver** For a homework assignment, have students review Chapter 16 and then answer the "What Do You Know?" questions. **Class Time** 5 minutes

Section 1, pp. 487–490
Class Time 50 minutes

Options for pacing and variety:
- **Time Saver** For a homework assignment, have students write reaction statements that reflect the views of Northern Democrats, Union Soldiers, abolitionists, white Southerners, and enslaved African Americans on news of the Emancipation Proclamation. **Class Time** 15 minutes
- **Peer Teaching** Have students work in pairs to create the graphic organizer for the Section Assessment. Students can use their cluster diagram to answer the Taking Notes questions. **Class Time** 15 minutes

DAY 2

Section 2, pp. 491–495
Class Time 45 minutes

Options for pacing and variety:
- **Peer Teaching** Have students work in pairs to create two math word problems using the information in the Daily Life feature on the impact of inflation on page 493. Collect word problems and ask students to answer selected ones. **Class Time** 15 minutes
- **Internet** Extend students' background knowledge of the Civil War and its aftermath with a look at classzone.com. **Class Time** 20 minutes

Section 3, pp. 496–503
Class Time 45 minutes

Options for pacing and variety:
- **Time Saver** Use the map on page 501 to summarize the final years of the war and the Union's winning strategies. **Class Time** 15 minutes
- **Peer Teaching** Have pairs of student take the On-line Field Trip recommended on page 498 in the Geography in History feature and then answer the Connect to Geography and Connect to History questions for this feature. **Class Time** 25 minutes

DAY 3

Section 4, pp. 504–509
Class Time 45 minutes

Options for pacing and variety:
- **History on Film** Extend students' background knowledge of Lincoln's death by viewing *The Lincoln Assassination.* A&E, 1995. **Class Time** 100 minutes
- **Peer Teaching** Ask a student to summarize the costs of the Civil War for the class using a transparency of the graphs and charts on page 505 as a guide to key points for the presentation. **Class Time** 10 minutes

Chapter 17 Assessment, pp. 510–511
Class Time 40 minutes

Options for pacing and variety:
- **Peer Competition** Divide students into four teams. Have each team create a set of ten questions that can be answered with the Terms & Names from all four sections of the chapter. Collect student questions, arrange them by category, and play two rounds of *Jeopardy,* first with two and then with a second set of teams competing against each other. **Class Time** 30 minutes
- **Peer Teaching** Divide students into an even number of small groups. Have students in each group answer the Critical Thinking questions in the Chapter Assessment and then trade answers with another group to check responses. **Class Time** 15 minutes

History Workshop, pp. 512–513
Class Time 50 minutes

Options for pacing and variety:
- **Time Saver** Have students work on steps 1–5 in Create a Medal of Honor. **Class Time** 40 minutes

TEACHER-TESTED ACTIVITY Ron Campana, Association of Teachers of Social Studies, New York, New York

ANALYZING A CIVIL WAR FILM

Class Time Two or three class periods for viewing films

Task Reviewing a movie about the Civil War

Purpose To analyze a film about the Civil War for historical accuracy

Supplies Needed
- Such films as *Gettysburg, Glory, Gone with the Wind,* or *Red Badge of Courage*
- Videotape player

Activity Select three movies about the Civil War for viewing by students. As a class, develop a list of criteria that can be used to evaluate each film for historical accuracy. Divide students into three groups, and assign each group one of the movies. The group can introduce its movie and create a list of questions for class discussion. At the end of the class discussion, the group in charge can also summarize the class's assessment of the movie in terms of its historical accuracy.

COUNTERFACTUAL HISTORY

Many historical events had more than one possible outcome. An inexplicable change of fortune or some other unforeseen factors might have dramatically changed the course of history. Asking "what if" questions can help students understand such contingency in history. By exploring such counterfactual questions and imagining alternative outcomes, students can better appreciate why certain events played pivotal roles in determining the ultimate Union victory.

ACTIVITY OUTLINE

Objective Posing and answering counterfactual questions about the Civil War can help students understand the outcome of the war.

Task The instructor will supply students with "what if" questions. Students will respond to the questions by developing counterfactual scenarios based on the "what if" questions.

Class Time One class period

DIRECTIONS

1. Ask students to think of a recent event that could have had another outcome. Encourage them to think about how one changed outcome could have rippling affects though history.
2. Ask students to think of some "what if" questions that might have changed the outcome of key events during the Civil War. Explain to students that the events do not necessarily have to be battles. Political, economic, or other events also shaped the outcome of the war. An example: "What if John Wilkes Booth had been apprehended *before* he shot Lincoln?" Brainstorm "what ifs" for a few minutes and have someone record them. Add to the brainstorm list any of the following that were not included:
   - What if McClellan had finished off Lee's army at Antietam?
   - What if the Thirteenth Amendment had passed just after the Emancipation Proclamation instead of two years later?
   - What if the Union hadn't taken Vicksburg and New Orleans?
   - What if the British and/or the French had offered support to the South?
   - What if Maryland, Kentucky, or Missouri had seceded from the Union with the other slave states?
3. Assign questions to students and have them research the question on the Internet or in other library sources.
4. After the students have researched their questions, have them develop their presentations showing how the changed event would have affected the course of history.
5. Final presentations can be done either live or using presentation software. Some presentations may require maps, charts, or other graphics for clarity.
6. After all the presentations have been completed, discuss the following questions with the class:
   - Which alternative turning points were most likely?
   - Which alternative events would have been most crucial?
   - What is the value of studying wars that are in our nation's past?

CHAPTER 17 OBJECTIVE

The student will understand the major events of the Civil War from 1863 to 1865 leading to Union victory and the effect of this conflict on the country.

HISTORY FROM VISUALS

Interpreting the Painting Ask students to study the painting of a cavalry charge at Yellow Tavern, Virginia, on May 11, 1864. Discuss with them how similar the two sides appear to be. Note the two white horses and the flags. Ask students which side appears to be winning. **Possible Response** The Union forces seem more numerous than their opponents, and the Union forces appear to be on the offensive.

Extension Ask students to write a headline for a Confederate and a Union newspaper describing this military action.

CRITICAL THINKING ACTIVITY

Making Inferences Have students think about the title of this chapter. What do they think it means? Discuss the way the ocean tides change. What factors do students think could cause the war to change?

Class Time 10 minutes

CHAPTER 17 The Tide of War Turns 1863–1865

Confederate and Union cavalry clash at Yellow Tavern, Virginia, on May 11, 1864.

RECOMMENDED RESOURCES

BOOKS FOR THE TEACHER

Catton, Bruce. ***Mr. Lincoln's Army; Glory Road: the Bloody Route from Fredericksburg to Gettysburg;*** and ***A Stillness at Appomattox.*** Garden City, NY: Doubleday, 1951–1953. Superb trilogy on the Army of the Potomac.

Foote, Shelby. ***The Civil War: A Narrative.*** 3 vols. New York: Random, 1986. Balanced and fun to read.

Leonard, Elizabeth D. ***All the Daring of the Soldier.*** New York: Norton, 1999. The remarkable stories of women in the war.

VIDEOS

The Fifty-Fourth Massachusetts. A&E Moonbeam, 1996. Documentary history of the black regiment featured in the movie *Glory.*

The Lincoln Assassination. (two cassettes) A&E Moonbeam, 1996. Fascinating minute-by-minute account plus opinions from modern medical and criminal experts.

SOFTWARE

Ulysses S. Grant: Unlikely Hero. Isis Interactive, 1997. Read from Grant's memoirs.

INTERNET

For more about the U.S. Civil War, visit . . .

classzone.com

Interact *with* History

Union soldiers, led by General William Tecumseh Sherman, march through Georgia.
Some soldiers fought to save the Union, others to save the Confederacy.
Many soldiers fought to end slavery. Many fought to save it.
Soldiers often fought alongside their friends and wanted to preserve their honor.

In 1863, you have been a Civil War soldier for two years. The life of a soldier is a hard one. The food is awful. Disease is common. Worst of all is the horrible violence and death. Often you feel the urge to run away and go home.

What Do You Think?

- What would you be willing to sacrifice for your country? What if your country fought for something you did not believe in?
- How would the attitudes of fellow soldiers influence your decision?

What would inspire you to keep fighting?

USA

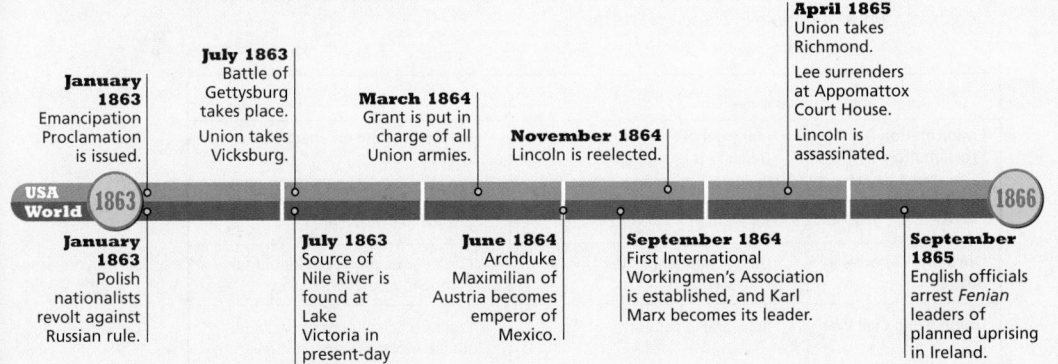

- **January 1863** Emancipation Proclamation is issued.
- **July 1863** Battle of Gettysburg takes place. Union takes Vicksburg.
- **March 1864** Grant is put in charge of all Union armies.
- **November 1864** Lincoln is reelected.
- **April 1865** Union takes Richmond. Lee surrenders at Appomattox Court House. Lincoln is assassinated.

1863 — 1866

World

- **January 1863** Polish nationalists revolt against Russian rule.
- **July 1863** Source of Nile River is found at Lake Victoria in present-day Uganda.
- **June 1864** Archduke Maximilian of Austria becomes emperor of Mexico.
- **September 1864** First International Workingmen's Association is established, and Karl Marx becomes its leader.
- **September 1865** English officials arrest *Fenian* leaders of planned uprising in Ireland.

Interact *with* History

OBJECTIVES

- To help students understand the problems facing both Confederate and Union soldiers
- To help students interact with the people and events they will study in the chapter

What Do You Think?

1. Ask students how they would have responded to soldiers whose attitude about the war differed from theirs.
2. Ask students to discuss the many ways their actions as soldiers might affect the rest of their lives.
3. Have students consider whether refusing to fight for something they don't believe in can be a valid option in wartime.

What would inspire you to keep fighting?

Encourage students to think about the reasons they would continue to fight under difficult conditions.

MAKING PERSONAL CONNECTIONS

Ask students to think about situations where they have taken a stand for something they believed in, even if their friends or classmates made fun of them. Ask if they ever felt like giving up, just as the Civil War soldiers did during this long, difficult conflict. Why did they continue to stand up for their beliefs?

TIME LINE DISCUSSION

Remind students that when the Civil War began, both Northerners and Confederates expected a short war that their side would win easily. Instead, the war dragged on. Many Northerners questioned whether it was worthwhile to fight for a Union that included a slaveholding South.

- Ask students to describe what the European events on the time line have in common. **Answer** All three have to do with revolutionary movements.
- What does the time line tell about Union leadership? **Answer** Grant was put in charge of all Union armies in 1864; Lincoln was reelected in 1864 and assassinated in 1865.
- Which events would lead you to believe the Union is getting closer to victory over the Confederacy? **Answer** victories at Vicksburg and Richmond

BEFORE YOU READ

Previewing the Theme:
Impact of the Individual

Ask students why it is especially important to have outstanding leaders during wartime. **Possible Response** Without strong leaders to inspire them, people may not make the sacrifices required during a war, or they may lose heart when the war continues longer than expected.

What Do You Know?

Remind students that the North was better prepared to fight a long war than the Confederacy. The North had a larger population, more industry, better transportation, a stronger navy, and an astute leader in Abraham Lincoln.

In-Depth Resources: Unit 5
- Tracing Themes: Impact of the Individual, p. 40

READ AND TAKE NOTES

Reading Strategy: Comparing and Contrasting

Explain to students that comparing and contrasting the ways in which the North and the South experienced the war will help them organize the concepts discussed in the chapter. Point out the events listed in the first column of the chart. Encourage students to look for similarities and differences in the ways these events affected the North and the Confederacy and note them on the correct lines.

In-Depth Resources: Unit 5
- Setting the Stage, p. 39

Critical Thinking Transparency CT49
- Setting the Stage

Chapter 17 SETTING THE STAGE

BEFORE YOU READ

Previewing the Theme

Impact of the Individual During the Civil War, thousands of citizens and soldiers acted with great dignity and courage. Leading these men and women were some of the most extraordinary leaders the nation has ever had. You will read more about these citizens and soldiers in Chapter 17.

Robert E. Lee was the military genius at the head of the Confederate armies.

Abraham Lincoln is one of the greatest presidents the United States has ever had.

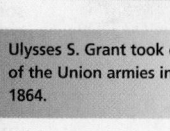

Jefferson Davis, the Confederate president, had the difficult task of keeping the South united.

Ulysses S. Grant took charge of the Union armies in March 1864.

What Do You Know?

What advantages and disadvantages did the North and the South have? Did particular individuals give either side an advantage during the Civil War?

THINK ABOUT
- what qualities contribute to the success of military leaders
- the importance of obeying orders for soldiers even if it might mean death

What Do You Want to Know?

What questions do you have about the later part of the Civil War and how it ended? Make a list of those questions before you read the chapter.

READ AND TAKE NOTES

Reading Strategy: Comparing and Contrasting When you study historical events, it is important to compare and contrast the effects that events had on different individuals and groups. A single event might affect two groups of people in completely different ways. Use the chart below to compare and contrast the impact of events on the Union and the Confederacy in the later years of the Civil War.

See Skillbuilder Handbook, page R10.

	North	South
Emancipation Proclamation	Many people are enthusiastic; Democrats are angered	Most whites are enraged; blacks are elated
War's Impact	Mild inflation; new possibilities for women	Severe inflation; bread riots; new possibilities for women
Northern Victories in Battle	Union confidence rises; Lincoln wins second term	Confederate morale sinks; bid for European recognition is lost
Union Wins Civil War	Industrial expansion	Enslaved persons liberated; widespread economic devastation

TEACHING STRATEGY

READING THE CHAPTER

This is a chronological chapter focusing on the turning points and conclusion of the Civil War. Ask students to note the effects of these events and how each led to the end of the war. The chapter also has a focus on the effect of the war on social, economic, and political life. Encourage students to discuss the costs of the war for the North and for the South.

ALTERNATIVE ASSESSMENT

The Chapter Assessment describes three activities for alternative assessment on page 511. You may wish to have students work on these activities during the course of the chapter and then present them at the end.

The Emancipation Proclamation

TERMS & NAMES
Emancipation Proclamation
54th Massachusetts Regiment

MAIN IDEA	WHY IT MATTERS NOW
In 1863, President Lincoln issued the Emancipation Proclamation, which helped to change the war's course.	The Emancipation Proclamation was an important step in ending slavery in the United States.

ONE AMERICAN'S STORY

During the Civil War, abolitionists like Frederick Douglass continued their fight against slavery. Douglass urged President Lincoln to emancipate, or free, enslaved Americans. "Sound policy . . . demands the instant liberation of every slave in the rebel states," he declared.

A VOICE FROM THE PAST

To fight against slaveholders, without fighting against slavery, is but a half-hearted business, and paralyzes the hands engaged in it. . . . Fire must be met with water. . . . War for the destruction of liberty [by the South] must be met with war for the destruction of slavery.

Frederick Douglass, quoted in *Battle Cry of Freedom*

During the Civil War, Frederick Douglass offered advice to President Lincoln. He urged the president to make the conflict a war against slavery.

Douglass pointed out that the Confederate war effort depended on slave labor. Enslaved Americans worked in Southern mines, fields, and factories. They also built forts and hauled supplies for rebel armies. For both practical and moral reasons, he said, Lincoln should free the slaves. In this section, you will learn how ending slavery became an important goal of the Civil War.

1 Calls for Emancipation

Throughout the war, abolitionists such as Frederick Douglass had been urging Lincoln to emancipate enslaved persons. Many criticized the president for being too cautious. Some even charged that Lincoln's lack of action aided the Confederate cause.

Still, Lincoln hesitated. He did not believe he had the power under the Constitution to abolish slavery where it already existed. Nor did he want to anger the four slave states that remained in the Union. He also knew that most Northern Democrats, and many Republicans, opposed emancipation.

Lincoln did not want the issue of slavery to divide the nation further than it already had. Although he disliked slavery, the president's first priority was to preserve the Union. "If I could save the Union without freeing

SECTION OBJECTIVES

1. To understand the reasons for the call for emancipation
2. To identify the significance of the Emancipation Proclamation
3. To analyze the response to the proclamation
4. To describe the role of African-American soldiers in the war

CRITICAL THINKING

Drawing Conclusions, p. 488
Summarizing, p. 489
Identifying Facts, p. 490
Recognizing Effects, p. 490

FOCUS & MOTIVATE

5-MINUTE WARM-UP

Drawing Conclusions These questions focus on the impact of Confederate and Union leaders.

1. Look at the brief descriptions of the Union and Confederate leaders on page 486. What qualities do you think are most important in a leader?
2. Do you think a president and an outstanding general will possess the same skills and characteristics? Why or why not?

Warm-Up Transparency WT17

INSTRUCT

INSTRUCT: OBJECTIVE 1

Calls for Emancipation

- For what reasons did Lincoln hesitate to abolish slavery?
- What was Lincoln's first priority throughout the war?
- Why did Lincoln decide in favor of emancipation?

In-Depth Resources: Unit 5
- Guided Reading, p. 41

Reading Study Guide (Spanish and English), pp. 161–162

RECOMMENDED RESOURCES

In-Depth Resources: Unit 5
- Guided Reading, p. 41
- Building Vocabulary, p. 45
- Primary Sources, pp. 49–50

Reading Study Guide (Spanish and English), pp. 161–162

Formal Assessment
- Section Quiz, p. 300

Integrated Assessment
- Rubrics, 5.1, 4.8

Access for Students Acquiring English/ESL
- Guided Reading, p. 110

INTEGRATED TECHNOLOGY

Electronic Teacher Tools

classzone.com

TEST-TAKING RESOURCES

Strategies for Test Preparation

Test Practice Transparencies, TT60

Online Test Practice

INSTRUCT: OBJECTIVE 2
The Emancipation Proclamation

- What did the Emancipation Proclamation accomplish, and why was it important?
- Why did Lincoln free slaves only in the South?

In-Depth Resources: Unit 5
- Primary Source: from "Reply to Emancipation Memorial" by Abraham Lincoln, p. 49

MORE ABOUT . . .

The Emancipation Proclamation
Secretary of the Treasury Salmon P. Chase said that when Lincoln read the Emancipation Proclamation to the cabinet (see illustration), he said, "I do not wish your advice about the main matter, that I have determined for myself. . . . I must . . . bear the responsibility of taking the course which I feel I ought to take." Aware of the significance of his action, Lincoln noted that "if my name ever goes into history, it will be for this act."

INSTRUCT: OBJECTIVE 3
Response to the Proclamation

- Why were people living in the North angered by the Emancipation Proclamation?
- Compare the reactions of Union soldiers and white Southerners to the proclamation.

MORE ABOUT . . .

Frederick Douglass
Frederick Douglass (1817–1895), born a slave in Maryland, eventually escaped to the North. Douglass fled to Great Britain for two years to avoid re-enslavement. There he earned enough money to buy his freedom. He returned to the United States where he founded *North Star,* a newspaper he published for 13 years. After the war he held several public offices and campaigned for full civil rights for African Americans and women's suffrage.

any slave I would do it," he declared. "If I could save it by freeing *all* the slaves I would do it; and if I could save it by freeing some and leaving others alone, I would also do that."

By the summer of 1862, however, Lincoln had decided in favor of emancipation. The war was taking a terrible toll. If freeing the slaves helped weaken the South, then he would do it. Lincoln waited, however, for a moment when he was in a position of strength. After General Lee's forces were stopped at Antietam, Lincoln decided to act.

2 The Emancipation Proclamation

On January 1, 1863, Lincoln issued the **Emancipation Proclamation,** which freed all slaves in Confederate territory. The proclamation had a tremendous impact on the public. However, it freed very few slaves. Most of the slaves that Lincoln intended to liberate lived in areas distant from the Union troops that could enforce his proclamation.

Background
In September 1862, Lincoln issued an early proclamation that gave rebellious states a chance to preserve slavery by rejoining the Union.

Lincoln presents the Emancipation Proclamation to his cabinet.

A VOICE FROM THE PAST

On the first day of January, in the year of our Lord one thousand eight hundred and sixty-three, all persons held as slaves within any State or designated part of a State, the people whereof shall then be in rebellion against the United States, shall be then, [thenceforth], and forever free.

Abraham Lincoln, from the *Emancipation Proclamation*

Why, critics charged, did Lincoln free slaves only in the South? The answer was in the Constitution. Because freeing Southern slaves weakened the Confederacy, the proclamation could be seen as a military action. As commander-in-chief, Lincoln had this authority. Yet the Constitution did not give the president the power to free slaves within the Union. But Lincoln did ask Congress to abolish slavery gradually throughout the land.

Reading **History**
A. Drawing Conclusions Why did Lincoln choose to limit his proclamation mostly to rebellious states?
A. Possible Response He believed that he did not have the authority, under the Constitution, to free slaves elsewhere.

Although the Emancipation Proclamation did not free many enslaved people at the time it was issued, it was important as a symbolic measure. For the North, the Civil War was no longer a limited war whose main goal was to preserve the Union. It was a war of liberation.

3 Response to the Proclamation

Abolitionists were thrilled that Lincoln had finally issued the Emancipation Proclamation. "We shout for joy that we live to record this righteous decree," wrote Frederick Douglass. Still, many believed the law should have gone further. They were upset that Lincoln had not freed *all* enslaved persons, including those in the border states.

ACTIVITY OPTIONS
INDIVIDUAL NEEDS

STUDENTS ACQUIRING ENGLISH/ESL

Understanding Key Terms Write the words *emancipation* and *proclamation* on the board and under them write the verbs *emancipate* and *proclaim.* Explain to students that emancipate means to liberate or to free and proclaim means to declare or to announce. Ask students what they think the phrase "emancipation proclamation" means. (an announcement of freedom)

To aid students' understanding of the section, ask questions such as the following and have students answer, using complete sentences.
- What historical document did Lincoln think prevented him from emancipating all the slaves in the nation?
- Did the Emancipation Proclamation actually free the Southern slaves? Why or why not?
- How did abolitionists, Northern Democrats, Union soldiers, and white Southerners react to the Emancipation Proclamation?

Reading **History**

B. Summarizing Why did Northern Democrats oppose the Emancipation Proclamation?

B. Possible Response They were against emancipating Southern slaves and thought that it would prolong the war.

Other people in the North, especially Democrats, were angered by the president's decision. Northern Democrats, the majority of whom were against emancipating even Southern slaves, claimed that the proclamation would only make the war longer by continuing to anger the South. A newspaperman in Ohio called Lincoln's proclamation "monstrous, impudent, and heinous . . . insulting to God as to man."

Most Union soldiers, though, welcomed emancipation. One officer noted that, although few soldiers were abolitionists, most were happy "to destroy everything that . . . gives the rebels strength."

White Southerners reacted to the proclamation with rage. Although it had limited impact in areas outside the reach of Northern armies, many slaves began to run away to Union lines. At the same time that these slaves deprived the Confederacy of labor, they also began to provide the Union with soldiers.

4 African-American Soldiers

In addition to freeing slaves, the Emancipation Proclamation declared that African-American men willing to fight "will be received into the armed service of the United States."

Frederick Douglass had argued for the recruitment of African-American soldiers since the start of the war. He declared, "Once [you] let the black man get upon his person the brass letters, U.S. . . . there is no power on earth which can deny that he has earned the right to citizenship."

Before the proclamation, the federal government had discouraged the enlistment of African Americans, and only a few regiments were formed. After emancipation, African Americans rushed to join the army. By war's end, about 180,000 black soldiers wore the blue uniform of the Union army.

African-American soldiers were organized in all-black regiments, usually led by white officers. They were often given the worst jobs

Thousands of African Americans, such as these men of the 4th U.S. Colored Troops, fought for the Union during the Civil War.

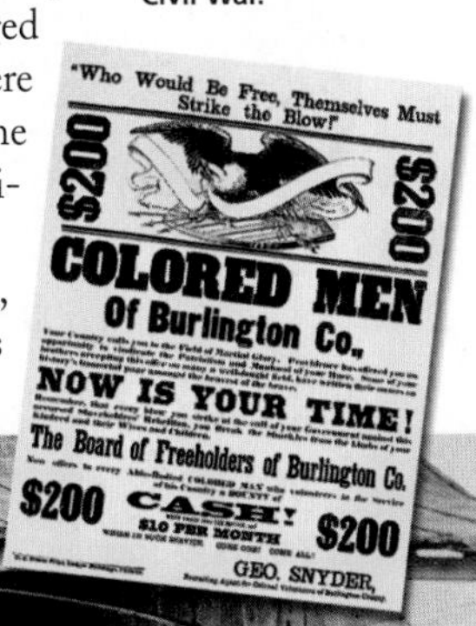

MORE ABOUT . . .

Europe and the Emancipation Proclamation

The Emancipation Proclamation was greeted with enthusiasm in Europe and created a strongly pro-Union atmosphere. Workers in Manchester, England, for example, adopted a resolution expressing their praise of Abraham Lincoln for his "firmness in upholding the proclamation of freedom." The proclamation ended any possibility that France and Britain might recognize Confederate independence.

INSTRUCT: OBJECTIVE 4

African-American Soldiers/ The 54th Massachusetts

- How did the Emancipation Proclamation affect African-American enlistment in the Union army?
- What obstacles did African-American soldiers face?
- Why did the 54th Massachusetts Regiment become famous?

In-Depth Resources: Unit 5

- Primary Source: A Letter from James Henry Gooding, p. 50

MORE ABOUT . . .

African-American Soldiers

William H. Carney of the 54th Massachusetts Regiment won the Medal of Honor. When the soldier carrying the flag fell wounded at the Battle of Fort Wagner, Carney grabbed the flag and kept it aloft despite having received several bullet wounds. Other African Americans who won the Medal of Honor include Powhatan Beatty and Milton M. Holland. These soldiers both took command of their companies when all their officers were dead or wounded. Decatur Dorsey and Aaron Anderson were given Medals of Honor for bravery in battles in 1865.

ACTIVITY OPTIONS

INDIVIDUAL NEEDS

LESS PROFICIENT READERS

Previewing To help students understand how the Civil War affected different aspects of society, have them skim the section, noting the boldfaced headings. Then work with them to turn the headings into questions. Write the questions on the board. Then encourage students to focus their reading in order to answer the questions they have created.

For example, you might want to write the following question for the first heading on the board.

What were the results of disagreement about the war?

- Confederate soldiers went on leave or deserted.
- Northern Democrats became Copperheads, opposing the war.

Now and then

African Americans in the Military

Colin Powell once answered a question about the effect of segregation on his own determination to succeed. Powell cited the Confederate general who pleaded with Jefferson Davis not to allow African Americans to serve in the Confederate army. The general wrote, "Don't let this happen. Whatever you do, don't let this happen. Because if blacks can wear a uniform with brass buttons, and a belt with a brass buckle, and if they go and serve and lay down their lives, they are the equal to us. And if that is the case, the whole theory of the Confederacy is a lie."

ASSESS & RETEACH

Setting the Stage Have students fill in the first section on the chapter graphic organizer on page 486.

Formal Assessment
- Section Quiz, p. 300

Critical Thinking Transparency CT49
- Setting the Stage

RETEACHING ACTIVITY

Divide the class into four groups. Assign each group one of the four objectives in this section. Have each group of students create a poster including the objective, important points about it from the section, and an illustration. Display the posters in class and encourage students to study each one.

In-Depth Resources: Unit 5
- Reteaching Activity, p. 54

Now and then

AFRICAN AMERICANS IN THE MILITARY

During the Civil War, no African-American soldier was promoted above the rank of captain. But times have changed. In 1989, General Colin Powell (shown below) was made a four-star general and named chairman of the Joint Chiefs of Staff—the highest position in the military.

General Powell's appointment was the climax of a long struggle to fully integrate American armed forces. From the Civil War through World War II, African-American soldiers were kept apart from white soldiers and denied equal rights. However, in 1948, President Harry Truman ended segregation in the armed forces. Today the American military is fully integrated.

to do and were paid less than white soldiers. Despite these obstacles, African-American soldiers showed great courage on the battlefield and wore their uniforms with pride. More than one regiment insisted on fighting without pay rather than accepting lower pay than the white soldiers.

Reading **History**

C. Identifying Facts How did many black soldiers protest when they were offered lower pay than white soldiers?

C. Possible Response They insisted on fighting for free rather than take the lower wage.

The 54th Massachusetts

One unit that insisted on fighting without pay was the **54th Massachusetts Regiment,** one of the first African-American regiments organized in the North. The soldiers of the 54th—among whom were two sons of Frederick Douglass—soon made the regiment the most famous of the Civil War.

The 54th Massachusetts earned its greatest fame in July 1863, when it led a heroic attack on Fort Wagner in South Carolina. The soldiers' bravery at Fort Wagner made the 54th a household name in the North and increased African-American enlistment.

The soldiers of the 54th Massachusetts and other African-American regiments faced grave dangers if captured. Rather than take African Americans as prisoners, Confederate soldiers often shot them or returned them to slavery.

The war demanded great sacrifices, not only from soldiers and prisoners, but also from people back home. In the next section, you will read about the hardships that the Civil War placed on the civilian populations in both the North and the South.

Section 1 Assessment

1. Terms & Names

Explain the significance of:
- Emancipation Proclamation
- 54th Massachusetts Regiment

2. Taking Notes

Use a chart to record responses to the Emancipation Proclamation.

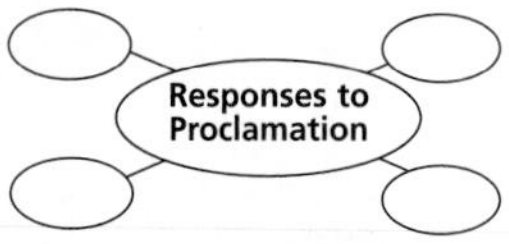

How did the proclamation change Northerners' views of the war?

3. Main Ideas

a. What was Lincoln's reason for not emancipating slaves when the war began?

b. Why was the immediate impact of the Emancipation Proclamation limited?

c. Why did black soldiers often face greater hardships than white soldiers?

4. Critical Thinking

Recognizing Effects How did the Emancipation Proclamation change the role of African Americans in the war?

THINK ABOUT
- how the proclamation changed military policy
- the response of many Southern slaves to the proclamation

ACTIVITY OPTIONS

TECHNOLOGY
MUSIC

Do research on the 54th Massachusetts Regiment. Create a **Web site** for the regiment or write a **song** about the soldiers' heroism at Fort Wagner.

Section 1 Assessment

1. Terms & Names

Emancipation Proclamation, p. 488
54th Massachusetts Regiment, p. 490

2. Taking Notes

Abolitionists were glad it was issued but wished that it had gone further; Northern Democrats were worried it would prolong the war; most Union soldiers welcomed it; white Southerners were outraged; It was no longer a war for limited ends; it was a war of liberation.

3. Main Ideas

a. His first priority was to preserve the Union. **b.** It was effective only in rebellious states and was dependent on the Union army's ability to enforce it. **c.** They were given less pay; when captured they were frequently shot or returned to slavery.

4. Critical Thinking

They ran away to the Union line and became soldiers in large numbers.

ACTIVITY OPTIONS

Integrated Assessment
- Rubrics for a Web site, 5.1
- Rubrics for a song, 4.8

490 CHAPTER 17

2 War Affects Society

TERMS & NAMES
Copperhead
conscription
bounty
income tax
greenback
Clara Barton

MAIN IDEA

The Civil War caused social, economic, and political changes in the North and the South.

WHY IT MATTERS NOW

Some changes, like the growth of industry, affected Americans long after the end of Civil War.

ONE AMERICAN'S STORY

As the Civil War moved into its third year, the constant demand for men and resources began to take its toll back home. Sometimes, the hardships endured by civilians resulted in angry scenes like that witnessed by Agnes, a resident of Richmond, Virginia.

On April 3, 1863, Agnes went for her morning walk and soon came upon a group of hungry women and children, who had gathered in front of the capitol. She described the scene as these women and children were joined by other people who were upset by the shortage of food.

Food became scarce in many places during the Civil War. Here, women demand milk for their hungry families.

A VOICE FROM THE PAST

The crowd now rapidly increased, and numbered, I am sure, more than a thousand women and children. It grew and grew until it reached the dignity of a mob—a bread riot.

Agnes, quoted in *Reminiscences of Peace and War*

The mob then went out of control. It broke into shops and stole food, clothing, and other goods. Only the arrival of Confederate president Jefferson Davis and the threat of force ended the riot.

In this section, you will read more about hardships that the Civil War caused on the home front. These hardships caused changes in civilian society in both the North and the South.

1 Disagreement About the War

In the spring of 1863, riots like the one in Richmond broke out in a number of Southern towns. Southerners were growing weary of the war and the constant sacrifices it demanded.

Confederate soldiers began to leave the army in increasing numbers. By the end of the year, the Confederate army had lost nearly 40 percent of its men. Some of these men were on leave, but many others were deserters.

SECTION OBJECTIVES

1. To analyze discontent with the war
2. To explain anger over the draft laws
3. To identify the economic effects of the war and resistance by enslaved Americans
4. To describe how women aided the war effort and to evaluate conditions in Northern and Southern prison camps

CRITICAL THINKING

Drawing Conclusions, p. 492
Analyzing Causes, p. 493
Summarizing, p. 494
Making Inferences, p. 495
Making Generalizations, p. 495

FOCUS & MOTIVATE

5-MINUTE WARM-UP

Making Generalizations These questions focus on the effect of the Civil War on daily life.

1. Look at the drawing on page 491. Why do you think there wasn't enough milk in Richmond?
2. How would you describe the mood of the people in this illustration?

Warm-Up Transparency WT17

INSTRUCT

INSTRUCT: OBJECTIVE 1

Disagreement About the War

- How did discontent with the war affect the Confederate army?
- How did the principle of states' rights affect the Confederate states?
- Who were the Copperheads? How did Lincoln deal with them?

In-Depth Resources: Unit 5
- Guided Reading, p. 42
- Building Vocabulary, p. 45

Reading Study Guide (Spanish and English), pp. 163–164

RECOMMENDED RESOURCES

In-Depth Resources: Unit 5
- Guided Reading, p. 42
- Building Vocabulary, p. 45
- Literature Selection: from *In My Father's House*, pp. 51–53

Reading Study Guide (Spanish and English), pp. 163–164

Economics in History
- Financing the Civil War, p. 17

America's History Makers
- Clara Barton, pp. 67–68

Formal Assessment
- Section Quiz, p. 301

Integrated Assessment
- Rubrics, 2.1, 3.6

Access for Students Acquiring English/ESL, p. 111

INTEGRATED TECHNOLOGY

Electronic Teacher Tools

classzone.com

TEST-TAKING RESOURCES

Strategies for Test Preparation

Test Practice Transparencies, TT61

Online Test Practice

MORE ABOUT . . .

Copperheads
Another source for the name *Copperheads* is the Indian heads cut from copper pennies that antiwar Democrats wore on their coat lapels. Some Copperheads became part of a fifth column directed by Confederates from bases in Canada. Plots were hatched to burn New York City, to capture a warship on the Great Lakes, and to free captured soldiers in Northern prison camps. None of these plots amounted to anything, but their existence was an open secret that hurt the morale of war-weary Northerners.

INSTRUCT: OBJECTIVE 2

The Draft Laws

- Why did poor Southerners complain that the Civil War was "a rich man's war but a poor man's fight"?
- How were Union and Confederate draft laws similar? How were they different?

MORE ABOUT . . .

Lincoln and the Writ of Habeas Corpus
Lincoln claimed that the "great and dangerous insurrection" justified his suspending the right of habeas corpus during the war. For example, he suspended habeas corpus in Maryland in 1861, as delegates traveled to the session of the legislature that would decide whether Maryland would secede. Delegates from southern Maryland, likely to vote for secession, were impounded, and the remaining delegates voted to remain in the Union.

In this political cartoon, the Union defends itself against "Copperheads." This was the name given to Northerners who sympathized with the South.

Faced with the difficulties of waging war, the Confederate states fell into disagreement. The same principle of states' rights that led them to break with the Union kept them from coordinating their war effort. As one Southern governor put it, "I am *still* a rebel . . . no matter who may be in power."

Disagreements over the conduct of the war also arose in the North. Lincoln's main opponents were the **Copperheads,** Northern Democrats who favored peace with the South. (A copperhead is a poisonous snake that strikes without warning.) Lincoln had protesters arrested. He also suspended the writ of habeas corpus, which prevents the government from holding citizens without a trial.

Vocabulary
writ: a written order issued by a court of law

2 The Draft Laws

As the war dragged on, both the North and the South needed more soldiers. As a result, both sides passed laws of **conscription,** also known as the draft. These laws required men to serve in the military.

The Confederates had been drafting soldiers since the spring of 1862. By 1863, all able-bodied white men between the ages of 18 and 45 were required to join the army. However, there were a number of exceptions. Planters who owned 20 or more slaves could avoid military service. In addition, wealthy men could hire substitutes to serve in their place. By 1863, substitutes might cost as much as $6,000. The fact that wealthy men could avoid service caused poor Southerners to complain that it was a "rich man's war but a poor man's fight."

Reading History
A. Drawing Conclusions Why were many soldiers dissatisfied with the draft laws?
A. Possible Response because it was easier for wealthy men to avoid being conscripted

The Union draft law was passed in March 1863. Like the Confederacy, the Union allowed draftees to hire substitutes. However, the North also offered $300 **bounties,** or cash payments, to men who volunteered to serve. As a result, only a small percentage of men in the North were drafted. Most men volunteered and received the bounty.

ACTIVITY OPTIONS
MULTIPLE LEARNING STYLES: SPATIAL

BLOCK SCHEDULING

A CIVIL WAR RECRUITING POSTER

Class Time One class period

Task Creating a recruiting poster for the Civil War

Purpose To illustrate reasons for enlisting in either the Union army or the Confederate army

Supplies Needed
- Poster paper
- Art supplies

Activity Direct students to review the material about the draft laws on this page. Then tell them to create a poster calling for volunteers for either the Union army or the Confederate forces. Posters should be eye-catching and attractive, and should list at least two reasons for signing up. You might suggest that students direct their posters at potential recruits from their own state or city.

Even so, the draft was extremely unpopular. In July 1863, anger over the draft and simmering racial tensions led to the New York City draft riots. For four days, rioters destroyed property and attacked people on the streets. Over 100 people were killed—many of them African Americans.

3 Economic Effects of the War

Many people suffered economic hardship during the war. The suffering was severe in the South, where most battles were fought, but the North also experienced difficulties.

Food shortages were very common in the South, partly because so many farmers were fighting in the Confederate army. Moreover, food sometimes could not get to market because trains were now being used to carry war materials. The Confederate army also seized food and other supplies for its own needs.

Another problem, especially in the South, was inflation—an increase in price and decrease in the value of money. The average family food bill in the South increased from $6.65 a month in 1861 to $68 by mid–1863. Over the course of the war, prices rose 9,000 percent in the South.

Inflation in the North was much lower, but prices still rose faster than wages, making life harder for working people. Some people took advantage of wartime demand and sold goods for high prices.

Overall, though, war production boosted Northern industry and fueled the economy. In the short term, this gave the North an economic advantage over the South. In the long term, industry would begin to replace farming as the basis of the national economy.

During the war, the federal government passed two important economic measures. In 1861, it established the first **income tax**—a tax on earnings. The following year, the government issued a new paper currency, known as **greenbacks** because of their color. The new currency helped the Northern economy by ensuring that people had money to spend. It also helped the Union to pay for the war.

Some Southerners in the border states took advantage of the stronger Union economy by selling cotton to Northern traders, in violation of Confederate law. "Yankee gold," wrote one Confederate officer, "is fast accomplishing what Yankee arms could never achieve—the subjugation of our people."

Resistance by Slaves

Another factor that affected the South was the growing resistance from slaves. To hurt the Southern economy, slaves slowed their pace of work or stopped working altogether. Some carried out sabotage, destroying crops and farm equipment to hurt the plantation economy. When white

daily*life*

INFLATION IN THE SOUTH

During the Civil War, inflation caused hardship in the North and the South. But inflation was especially severe in the Confederacy, where prices could become outrageously high.

The food prices shown below are from 1864. Consider how many days it took a Confederate soldier to earn enough money to buy each of these foods.

*Reading*History

B. Analyzing Causes Why were economic problems particularly bad in the South?

B. Possible Responses Most battles were fought there; men left their farms to fight; trains were used to carry war materials instead of food; inflation was more severe.

Vocabulary

subjugate: to bring under control or to conquer

MORE ABOUT . . .

Immigrants and Soldiers

Many of the antidraft rioters were immigrants. As poor new arrivals, they especially resented being forced into a war while richer men paid to avoid the battle. Nonetheless, immigrants made up a large part of the Union forces. Approximately 200,000 German immigrants fought for the Union with about 150,000 Irish-born soldiers. One regiment from Illinois was composed of German Jews. Irish and German immigrants also fought for the Confederacy, although fewer immigrants lived in the South.

INSTRUCT: OBJECTIVE 3

Economic Effects of the War/ Resistance by Slaves

- In what ways did the war affect the economy of the South?
- What were the short-term and long-term effects of war production in the North?
- How did slaves damage the Southern economy and sabotage the war effort?

Economics in History
- Financing the Civil War, p. 17

In-Depth Resources: Unit 5
- Literature Selection: from *In My Father's House* by Ann Rinaldi, pp. 51–53

daily*life*

Inflation in the South

The sharp increase in prices for necessary provisions provoked criticism leveled at farmers and planters. The Atlanta *Southern Confederacy* condemned farmers for their exorbitant prices for produce. Provisions cost 200–400 percent more than before the war, despite the fact that food production costs had not increased and crops were abundant.

ACTIVITY OPTIONS

INTERDISCIPLINARY LINK: MATH — BLOCK SCHEDULING

CALCULATING CONFEDERATE COSTS

Class Time 20 minutes

Task Calculating the cost of a simple breakfast in 1864 in the Confederacy

Purpose To use simple math skills to understand the severity of inflation in the South and the hardships it caused for Southerners

Supplies Needed
- Calculators (optional)

Activity Have students use the information in the chart on this page to calculate the cost of this simple breakfast for four people: scrambled eggs, containing 6 eggs; 1 tablespoon of butter (1/32 of a pound); 1 pot of coffee (about 1/25 of a pound); 1 pitcher of milk (1/2 quart). *(Answer: $8.68)* Then have students figure out how much the same breakfast would cost today to prepare at home.

MORE ABOUT . . .

African Americans and Union Forces
At the start of the war, enslaved African Americans began to escape from their owners and seek safety in Union army camps. However, Union soldiers did not know what to do with the refugees. In the border states, the law required that fleeing slaves be returned to their owners, but few Northern soldiers were willing to take on the role of slave catcher. Eventually Union officers found a loophole that justified the presence of escaped slaves in their camps. They termed the slaves *contraband,* meaning property of war seized from the enemy.

INSTRUCT: OBJECTIVE 4

Women Aid the War Effort/ Civil War Prison Camps

- How did the Civil War affect the role of women in society?
- In what ways did women help the war effort?
- How were prisoners of war treated in the North? in the South?

AMERICA'S HISTORY MAKERS

Clara Barton
After the Battle of Bull Run, Clara Barton heard reports of shortages among Union forces. She independently advertised for contributions of foodstuffs and set up an agency to distribute the huge amounts sent in by concerned Northerners. After the war, at President Lincoln's request, she set up a bureau of records to search for soldiers missing in action. Barton threw herself into the creation of the American Red Cross. She was the agency's first president and held that post for 23 years.

Possible Response: by organizing a relief agency to help with the war effort and founding the American Red Cross

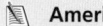

America's History Makers
- Clara Barton, pp. 67–68

planters fled advancing Union armies, slaves often refused to go along. They stayed behind, waiting for Union soldiers to free them.

Some enslaved people even rose up in rebellion against their overseers. More commonly, though, slaves ran away from plantations to join the Union forces as they pushed farther into Confederate territory. One Union officer described a common sight.

A VOICE FROM THE PAST

It was very touching to see the vast numbers of colored [African-American] women following after us with babies in their arms, and little ones like our Anna clinging to their tattered skirts. One poor creature, while nobody was looking, hid two boys, five years old, in a wagon, intending, I suppose that they should see the land of freedom if she couldn't.

Union officer, quoted in *The Civil War*

After Lincoln issued the Emancipation Proclamation, the number of slaves fleeing Southern plantations greatly increased. By the end of the war, as many as half a million had fled to Union lines.

AMERICA'S HISTORY MAKERS

CLARA BARTON
1821–1912
Trained as a schoolteacher, Clara Barton was working for the government when the Civil War began. She organized a relief agency to help with the war effort. "While our soldiers stand and fight," she said, "I can stand and feed and nurse them."

She also made food for soldiers in camp and tended to the wounded and dying on the battlefield. At Antietam, she held a doctor's operating table steady as cannon shells burst all around them. The doctor called her "the angel of the battlefield." After the war, Barton founded the American Red Cross.

How did Clara Barton demonstrate her leadership abilities?

4 Women Aid the War Effort

With so many men away at war, women in both the North and the South assumed increased responsibilities. Women plowed fields and ran farms and plantations. They also took over jobs in offices and factories that had previously been done only by men.

Other social changes came about because of the thousands of women who served on the front lines as volunteer workers and nurses. Susie King Taylor was an African-American woman who wrote an account of her experiences as a volunteer with an African-American regiment. She asked her readers to remember that "many lives were lost,—not men alone but noble women as well."

Relief agencies put women to work washing clothes, gathering supplies, and cooking food for soldiers. Also, nursing became a respectable profession for many women. By the end of the war, around 3,000 nurses had worked under the leadership of Dorothea Dix in Union hospitals. Southern women were also active as nurses and as volunteers on the front.

Women also played a key role as spies in both the North and the South. Harriet Tubman served as a spy for Union forces along the coast of South Carolina. The most famous Confederate spy was Belle Boyd. Although she was arrested six times, she continued her work through much of the war. At one point, she even sent messages from her jail cell by putting them in little rubber balls and tossing them out the window.

Reading **History**
C. Summarizing How did women participate in the Civil War?
C. Possible Responses They worked on farms and in factories, volunteered on the front lines, and worked as nurses and spies.

ACTIVITY OPTIONS

MULTIPLE LEARNING STYLES: INTERPERSONAL — BLOCK SCHEDULING

A CIVIL WAR DIALOGUE

Class Time Two class periods

Task Creating a dialogue about the Civil War from multiple points of view

Purpose To understand the effects of the Civil War on people from different regions and of different backgrounds and occupations

Supplies Needed
- Books and reference materials on popular history of the Civil War

Activity Assign students one of the following roles: drafted Irish immigrant; Confederate deserter; owner of a New England mill; woman managing a farm in Kentucky; nurse on either side; escaped slave with the Union army; soldier in the 54th Massachusetts Regiment; prisoner on either side; spy on either side. Tell students to prepare descriptions of their experiences of the war in their assigned roles. Then allow groups of students to discuss the war from the point of view of their role.

Civil War Prison Camps

Women caught spying were thrown into jail, but soldiers captured in battle suffered far more. At prison camps in both the North and the South, prisoners of war faced terrible conditions.

One of the worst prison camps in the North was in Elmira, New York. Perhaps the harshest feature of a prisoner's life at the camp was the New York winter. One prisoner called Elmira "an excellent summer prison for southern soldiers, but an excellent place for them to find their graves in the winter." In just one year, more than 24 percent of Elmira's 12,121 prisoners died of sickness and exposure to severe weather.

*Reading*History
D. Making Inferences Why were death rates so high at many Civil War prison camps?
D. Possible Response because of poor sanitary conditions and exposure to severe weather

Conditions were also horrible in the South. The camp with the worst reputation was at Andersonville, Georgia. Built to hold 10,000 prisoners, at one point it housed 33,000. Inmates had little shelter from the heat or cold. Most slept in holes scratched in the dirt. Drinking water came from one tiny creek that also served as a sewer. As many as 100 men per day died at Andersonville from starvation, disease, and exposure.

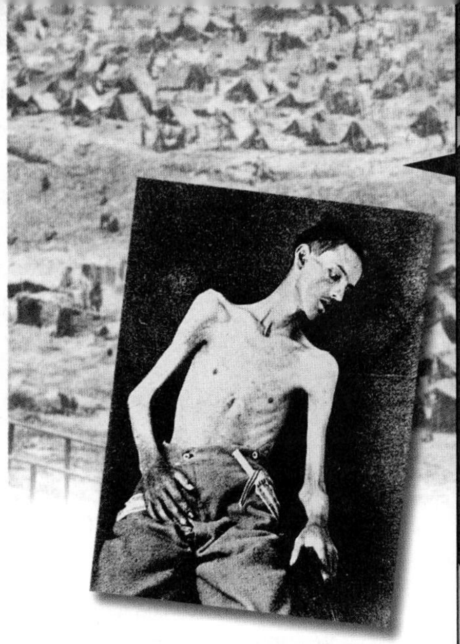

The terrible conditions at Civil War prison camps caused much suffering and death.

People who saw the camps were shocked by the condition of the soldiers. The poet Walt Whitman—who served as a Union nurse—described a group of soldiers who returned from a prison camp. He exclaimed, "Can those be *men?* . . . are they not really mummied, dwindled corpses?"

Around 50,000 men died in Civil War prison camps. But this number was dwarfed by the number of dead on the battlefronts and even more from disease in army camps. In the next section, you will read about the bloody battles that led to the end of the Civil War.

Section 2 Assessment

1. Terms & Names

Explain the significance of:
- Copperhead
- conscription
- bounty
- income tax
- greenback
- Clara Barton

2. Taking Notes

Use a diagram like the one below to compare conditions in the North and South during the later years of war.

Conditions During the War

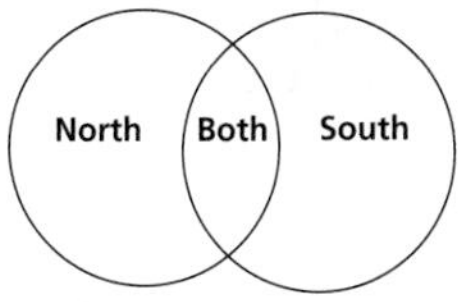

3. Main Ideas

a. How did the South's principle of states' rights undermine the Confederate war effort?

b. How did the draft laws in the North and South differ?

c. What conditions at prison camps caused so many to suffer behind enemy lines?

4. Critical Thinking

Making Generalizations What economic changes took place during the Civil War?

THINK ABOUT
- the war's effect on prices
- industry and agriculture
- new economic measures begun by the government

ACTIVITY OPTIONS

GEOGRAPHY
SPEECH

Study Civil War prison camps. Make a **map** showing where they were located or give a **speech** explaining why prisoners should be treated better.

MORE ABOUT . . .

Treatment of Civil War Prisoners

The conditions at Andersonville caused the death of 13,000 of the 45,000 men imprisoned there. As reports of the terrible conditions at Andersonville arrived in the North, the Union War Department responded. In 1864, it cut the rations for its prisoners to the same level that the Confederacy said it gave to its prisoners. The ration cut, combined with a huge increase in the number of Confederate prisoners, caused conditions in Northern prisons to decline.

ASSESS & RETEACH

Setting the Stage Have students fill in the second section on the chapter graphic organizer.

Formal Assessment
- Section Quiz, p. 301

RETEACHING ACTIVITY

Divide students into two groups. Have students in one group complete the graphic organizer below for the Union while students in the other group complete it for the Confederacy.

In-Depth Resources: Unit 5
- Reteaching Activity, p. 55

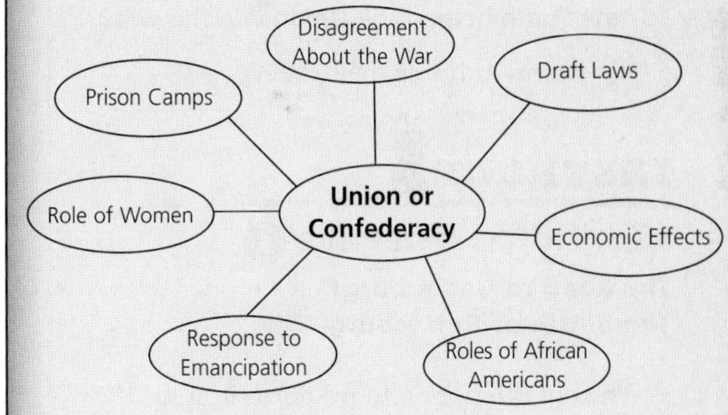

Section 2 Assessment

1. Terms & Names

Copperhead, p. 492
conscription, p. 492
bounty, p. 492
income tax, p. 493
greenback, p. 493
Clara Barton, p. 494

2. Taking Notes

North: Copperheads, draft riots, strong industry; South: food shortages, great hardship, slave resistance; Both: dissent over war and draft laws, inflation, women's key role, harsh prison camps

3. Main Ideas

a. Each state worked in its own interest, preventing the coordination of efforts. **b.** The South required all men between 18 and 45 to enlist, with few exceptions. The North offered a bounty of $300, which led to more volunteers. **c.** exposure to severe weather; poor sanitation

4. Critical Thinking

Inflation became a problem, especially in the South; Northern industry grew; the Union initiated an income tax and paper currency.

ACTIVITY OPTIONS

Integrated Assessment
- Rubrics for a map, 2.1
- Rubrics for a speech, 3.6

SECTION OBJECTIVES

1. To evaluate the importance of the Battle of Gettysburg
2. To evaluate the importance of the siege of Vicksburg and Sherman's march to the coast
3. To trace the Virginia campaign to Appomattox
4. To describe the surrender at Appomattox

SKILLBUILDER

Interpreting Maps: Movement, Location, p. 501

CRITICAL THINKING

Making Inferences, p. 497
Drawing Conclusions, p. 501
Contrasting, p. 503

Why It Matters Now
- One Nation, pp. 33–34

FOCUS & MOTIVATE

5-MINUTE WARM-UP

Making Inferences These questions compare the strengths of the Union and the Confederacy from 1863 to 1865.

1. Study the map on page 501. How does the size of the area controlled by the Union compare with that controlled by the Confederacy?
2. How do you think Sherman's path through the South helped the Union win the war?

Warm-Up Transparency WT17

INSTRUCT

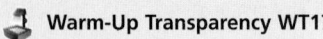

INSTRUCT: OBJECTIVE 1

The Road to Gettysburg/ The Battle of Gettysburg

- Why did Lee decide to go north in June 1863?
- Why was Pickett's charge a mistake?
- Why was the Battle of Gettysburg the turning point of the war?

In-Depth Resources: Unit 5
- Guided Reading, p. 43

3 The North Wins

TERMS & NAMES
Battle of Gettysburg
Pickett's Charge
Ulysses S. Grant
Robert E. Lee
Siege of Vicksburg
William Tecumseh Sherman
Appomattox Court House

MAIN IDEA	WHY IT MATTERS NOW
Thanks to victories, beginning with Gettysburg and ending with Richmond, the Union survived.	If the Union had lost the war, the United States might look very different now.

ONE AMERICAN'S STORY

Joshua Lawrence Chamberlain was a 32-year-old college professor when the war began. Determined to fight for the Union, he left his job and took command of troops from his home state of Maine. Like most soldiers, Chamberlain had to get accustomed to the carnage of the Civil War. His description of the aftermath of one battle shows how soldiers got used to the war's violence.

A VOICE FROM THE PAST

It seemed best to [put] myself between two dead men among the many left there by earlier assaults, and to draw another crosswise for a pillow out of the trampled, blood-soaked sod, pulling the flap of his coat over my face to fend off the chilling winds, and still more chilling, the deep, many voiced moan [of the wounded] that overspread the field.

Joshua Lawrence Chamberlain, quoted in *The Civil War*

During the war, Chamberlain fought in 24 battles. He was wounded six times and had six horses shot out from under him. He is best remembered for his actions at the Battle of Gettysburg, where he courageously held off a fierce rebel attack. In this section, you will read about that battle and others that led to the end of the Civil War.

In 1862, Joshua Chamberlain was offered a year's travel with pay to study languages in Europe. He chose to fight for the Union instead.

1 The Road to Gettysburg

In September 1862, General McClellan stopped General Lee's Northern attack at the Battle of Antietam. But the cautious McClellan failed to finish off Lee's army, which retreated safely to Virginia.

President Lincoln, who was frustrated by McClellan, replaced him with Ambrose Burnside. But Burnside also proved to be a disappointment. At the Battle of Fredericksburg, Virginia, in December 1862, Burnside attacked Confederate troops who had dug trenches. The bloody result was 12,600 Union casualties. This disastrous attack led General Lee to remark, "It is well that war is so terrible—we should grow too fond of it!"

Lincoln replaced Burnside with General Joseph Hooker, who faced Lee the following May at Chancellorsville, Virginia. The result was yet another Union disaster. With half as many men as Hooker, Lee still managed to

RECOMMENDED RESOURCES

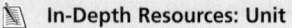

In-Depth Resources: Unit 5
- Guided Reading, p. 43
- Skillbuilder Practice, p. 46

Reading Study Guide (Spanish and English), pp. 165–166

Outline Map Activities
- The End of the Civil War, 1865, pp. 33–34

America's History Makers
- Ulysses S. Grant, pp. 69–70

Why It Matters Now
- One Nation, pp. 33–34

Formal Assessment
- Section Quiz, p. 302

Integrated Assessment
- Rubrics, 2.1, 4.5

Access for Students Acquiring English/ESL, pp. 112, 114

INTEGRATED TECHNOLOGY

Humanities Transparency HT33

Geography Transparency GT17
- Vicksburg Campaign, 1863

Electronic Teacher Tools

TEST-TAKING RESOURCES

Strategies for Test Preparation

Test Practice Transparencies, TT62

Online Test Practice

cut the Union forces to pieces. However, the South paid a high price for its victory. As General "Stonewall" Jackson returned from a patrol on May 2, Confederate guards thought he was a Union soldier and shot him in the arm. Shortly after a surgeon amputated the arm, Jackson caught pneumonia. On May 10, Lee's prized general was dead.

In spite of Jackson's tragic death, Lee decided to head North once again. He hoped that a Confederate victory in Union territory would fuel Northern discontent with the war and bring calls for peace. He also hoped a Southern victory would lead European nations to give diplomatic recognition and aid to the Confederacy.

The Battle of Gettysburg

In late June 1863, Lee crossed into southern Pennsylvania. The Confederates learned of a supply of shoes in the town of Gettysburg and went to investigate. There, on July 1, they ran into Union troops. Both sides called for reinforcements, and the **Battle of Gettysburg** was on.

*Reading*History
A. Reading a Map Use the map and illustration on pages 498–499 to study Gettysburg's geography.

The fighting raged for three days. On the rocky hills and fields around Gettysburg, 90,000 Union troops, under the command of General George Meade, clashed with 75,000 Confederates.

During the struggle, Union forces tried to hold their ground on Cemetery Ridge, just south of town, while rebel soldiers tried to dislodge them. At times, the air seemed full of bullets. "The balls were whizzing so thick," said one Texan, "that it looked like a man could hold out a hat and catch it full."

The turning point came on July 3, when Lee ordered General George Pickett to mount a direct attack on the middle of the Union line. It was a deadly mistake. Some 13,000 rebel troops charged up the ridge into heavy Union fire. One soldier recalled "bayonet thrusts, sabre strokes, pistol shots . . . men going down on their hands and knees, spinning round like tops . . . ghastly heaps of dead men."

Pickett's Charge, as this attack came to be known, was torn to pieces. The Confederates retreated and waited for a Union counterattack. But once again, Lincoln's generals failed to finish off Lee's army. The furious Lincoln wondered when he would find a general who would defeat Lee once and for all.

*Reading*History
B. Making Inferences Why might Lincoln have been disappointed after the Union victory at Gettysburg?
B. Possible Response because General Meade did not finish off the army of General Lee

Even so, the Union rejoiced over the victory at Gettysburg. Lee's hopes for a Confederate victory in the North were crushed. The North had lost 23,000 men, but Southern losses were even greater. Over one-third of Lee's army, 28,000 men, lay dead or wounded. Sick at heart, Lee led his army back to Virginia.

America's HERITAGE

THE GETTYSBURG ADDRESS

On November 19, 1863, President Lincoln spoke at the dedication of a cemetery in Gettysburg for the 3,500 soldiers buried there. His speech was short, and few who heard it were impressed. Lincoln himself called it "a flat failure."

Even so, the Gettysburg Address has since been recognized as one of the greatest speeches of all time. In it, Lincoln declared that the nation was founded on "the proposition that all men are created equal." He ended with a plea to continue the fight for democracy so that "government of the people, by the people, for the people shall not perish from the earth."

See page 508 for the full text of the Gettysburg Address.

MORE ABOUT . . .

The Battle of Chancellorsville

The Battle of Chancellorsville provides the setting for Stephen Crane's famous Civil War novel *The Red Badge of Courage.* The novel tells the story of a raw recruit named Henry Fleming who runs from combat but later rejoins his regiment. Crane never names the battle in the novel, perhaps in part because soldiers like Henry Fleming often did not know their exact location or the name of the battle they were fighting.

Humanities Transparency HT33
- Battle of Fredericksburg

America's HERITAGE

The Gettysburg Address

The featured speaker at the dedication for the cemetery was Edward Everett, the former governor of Massachusetts. His speech lasted almost two hours. While President Lincoln listened, he also edited his own remarks. Although the reporter for the *London Times* said, "The ceremony was rendered ludicrous by . . . the sallies of that poor President Lincoln," Edward Everett disagreed. He wrote the president that "I should be glad if I could flatter myself that I came as near to the central idea of the occasion in two hours as you did in two minutes."

ACTIVITY OPTIONS

INDIVIDUAL NEEDS

LESS PROFICIENT READERS

Finding Main Ideas Students may have difficulty understanding the significance of the key battles that contributed to the Union's victory. To help focus their reading, write the names of the battles on the board and ask students to copy them on a sheet of paper. As you read the section, have students write down the approximate date, significance, and victor in each battle.

Guide students in creating a chart such as the following:

Battle	Date	Significance	Who Won?
Gettysburg			
Vicksburg			
Atlanta			
Richmond			

GEOGRAPHY in HISTORY

OBJECTIVE
Students will analyze and interpret information from a map to understand why Union forces were successful at the Battle of Gettysburg.

B BLOCK SCHEDULING

MORE ABOUT . . .

The Battle of Gettysburg
Some military historians hypothesize that Lee chose to invade Pennsylvania in part because his army was in desperate need of supplies. Years of fighting had depleted Virginia, but Pennsylvania offered fresh supplies of food and other necessities. Lee was headed for Harrisburg, a railroad center, when North and South encountered each other in Gettysburg, a town of about 2,400 people. Lee did not have good information about the location of Union troops. His cavalry chief and "eyes and ears," J. E. B. ("Jeb") Stuart, was somewhere between Harrisburg and Gettysburg when the fighting started and did not arrive until the second day.

INSTRUCT

- Why would moving Confederate troops into Pennsylvania be an advantage for Lee?
- Why did both sides want to control the high ground during the battle?
- How do you think soldiers on both sides were hampered by, and also benefited from, the many trees and small streams on the battlefield?

MAP SKILL QUESTIONS
How can you tell which are the Confederate and which are the Union positions?

Which side controlled Seminary Ridge?

Why did Lee want to break the Union control of Cemetery Ridge?

GEOGRAPHY in HISTORY

PLACE AND HUMAN-ENVIRONMENT INTERACTION

Battle of Gettysburg

A monument stands today near a ridge at the Gettysburg battlefield. Labeled the "High Water Mark of the Rebellion," it shows how far Confederate troops advanced against Union lines. There, on July 3, 1863, the South came closest to winning the Civil War.

The fighting began on July 1. When a Confederate force captured Gettysburg, Union defenders took up new positions in the hills south of town. The next day, Confederate troops attacked across a wheat field and peach orchard in an attempt to seize the hill called Little Round Top. But Union forces held their ground.

July 3 was the decisive day. Lee, having failed to crack the side of General Meade's Union line, attacked its center. In an assault that came to be known as Pickett's Charge, some 13,000 men charged uphill across an open field toward the Union lines along Cemetery Ridge. Union soldiers covered the field with rifle and cannon fire. "Pickett's Charge" was a Confederate disaster.

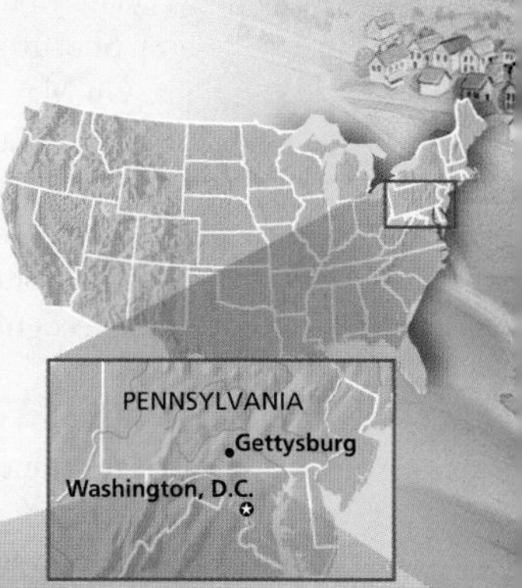

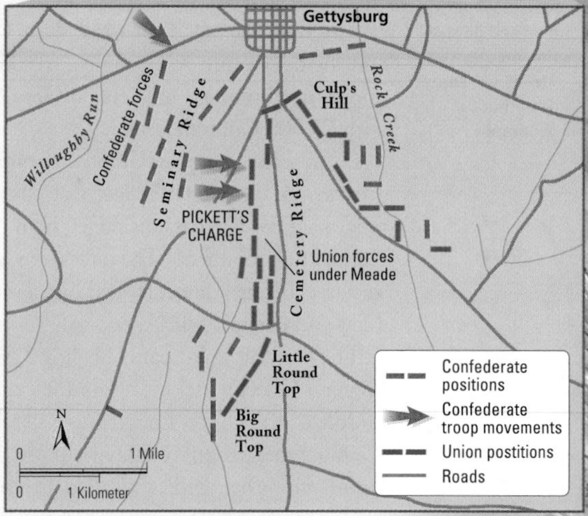

Before beginning the charge named for him, Major General Pickett wrote to his fiancée, "My brave Virginians are to attack in front. Oh, may God in mercy help me."

ARTIFACT FILE

Regimental Flag Flags helped soldiers to identify the different sides during battle. Often, a regiment's flag would show the names of battles it had fought. This flag, which belonged to the 28th North Carolina, was captured at Pickett's Charge.

Soldiers' Diaries Many Civil War soldiers wrote about their wartime experiences in personal diaries, such as this one belonging to Sergeant Alfred S. Rowe of Maryland.

MUSEUM CONNECTIONS
The Gettysburg National Military Park Museum was established by federal law in 1895, and at that time it was administered by Civil War veterans. The museum, a memorial to soldiers from both armies, covers 6,000 acres and 26 miles of park roads. The park contains one of the world's largest collections of outdoor sculpture with some 1,400 statues and monuments. The museum's Web site provides a virtual tour of the battlefield and the museum's holdings. To learn more about Gettysburg National Park, visit classzone.com.

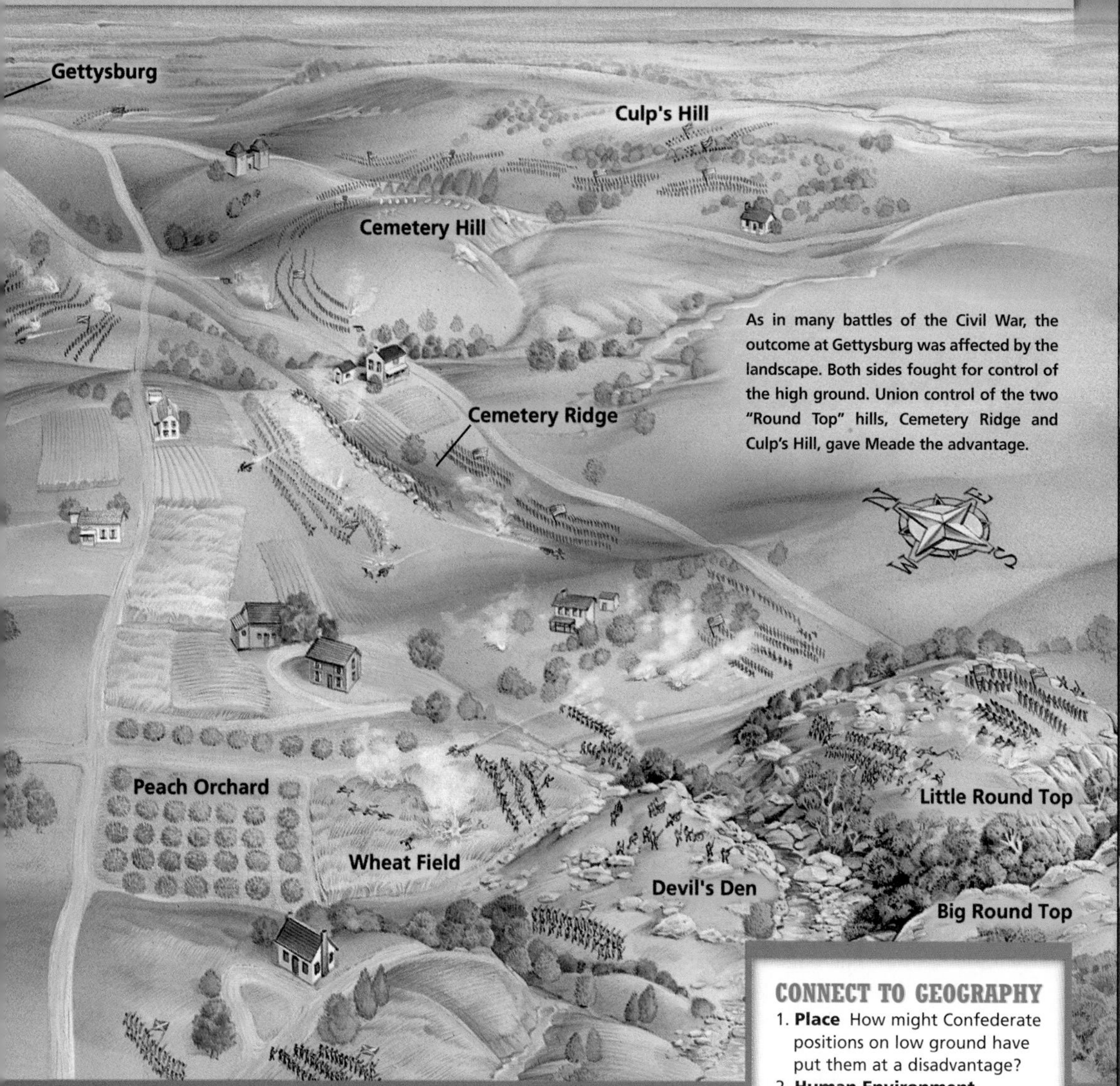

As in many battles of the Civil War, the outcome at Gettysburg was affected by the landscape. Both sides fought for control of the high ground. Union control of the two "Round Top" hills, Cemetery Ridge and Culp's Hill, gave Meade the advantage.

On-Line Field Trip

The Gettysburg National Military Park Museum contains many objects relating to the Battle of Gettysburg, including this federal bass drum. This heavy drum—two feet in diameter—was harnessed to the neck of a soldier, who beat time with leather-covered wooden mallets.

For more about Gettysburg . . .

RESEARCH LINKS CLASSZONE.COM

CONNECT TO GEOGRAPHY

1. **Place** How might Confederate positions on low ground have put them at a disadvantage?
2. **Human-Environment Interaction** How might the attitudes of Union soldiers have been affected by fighting in their own territory?

See Geography Handbook, pages 4–5.

CONNECT TO HISTORY

3. **Asking Questions** Ask and answer a question about how the geographic patterns of the Gettysburg area affected the battle?

The Tide of War Turns 499

CRITICAL THINKING ACTIVITY

Identifying and Solving Problems Have the students study the map and illustration. Notice there are two ridges, each controlled by one of the sides. Divide the class into two sides, Union and Confederate. Have them devise a different battle plan for Gettysburg. Have each side present their plan. Try to determine which side might have been the winner. Ask how geography played into the battle plan they devised.

Class Time 15 minutes

MORE ABOUT . . .

Pickett's Charge

Pickett was 38 years old and engaged to be married. Before the charge, he wrote a note to his fiancée and gave it to General Longstreet to mail. He called to his troops, "Up men, and to your posts! And don't forget that you are from old Virginia." The men followed Pickett cheerfully, one Confederate captain reported. They thought the battle was almost over. A Union officer described their charge: "Right on they move, as with one soul, in perfect order . . . magnificent, grim, irresistible."

MORE ABOUT . . .

Troop Movement at Gettysburg

A Union captain named Federico Fernández Cavada made aerial sketches of Confederate troop movement from hot-air balloons. Cuban-born Cavada was captured at Gettysburg. He described his prison experiences in a book called *Libby Life.* (Libby Prison, in Richmond, Virginia, was another Confederate war prison, comparable to Andersonville.)

CONNECT TO GEOGRAPHY

1. **Place** To defeat the Union army, they would have to fight uphill; this is more strenuous and also makes it difficult to find protective cover; the Union soldiers would have found it easy to aim at the Confederates below.
2. **Human-Environment Interaction** Armies usually feel more motivated to defend their own territory than to seize their enemy's territory.

CONNECT TO HISTORY

3. **Asking Questions** The question should point to important geographic patterns on the model, and the answer should be based on evidence from the model.

AMERICA'S HISTORY MAKERS

Ulysses S. Grant

Geoffrey Perrett, author of *Ulysses S. Grant: Soldier and President,* writes of Grant, "Many who met him were left feeling slightly puzzled; some felt more or less cheated. He did not look like a great general, and did not talk like a great general, did not dress like a great general, and did not even appear to consider himself a great general."

America's History Makers
- Ulysses S. Grant, pp. 69–70

Robert E. Lee

After the war, Lee spent several months recuperating both physically and mentally; however, he never fully regained his health. At 58 he had no means of support and was concerned about the welfare of his seven children. Lee accepted the presidency of Washington College (later called Washington & Lee University) in Lexington, Virginia. Ironically, "the Rebel General" did not believe in slavery and secession and was deeply attached to the Republic.

Possible Responses: Grant's determination to go after Lee even if the costs were high helped the Union win. Lee's belief that siding with Virginia was the honorable decision gave the South its greatest general.

INSTRUCT: OBJECTIVE 2

The Siege of Vicksburg

- How did the citizens of Vicksburg resist Grant's attack?
- What did Grant accomplish for the Union by his victory at Vicksburg?

Geography Transparency GT17
- Vicksburg Campaign, 1863

INSTRUCT: OBJECTIVE 3

Sherman's Total War

- What was Sherman's concept of total war?
- What were the political effects of Sherman's military victories?

AMERICA'S HISTORY MAKERS

ULYSSES S. GRANT
1822–1885

General Ulysses S. Grant was an unlikely war hero. Although educated at West Point Military Academy, he was a poor student and showed little interest in an army career. With his quiet manner and rumpled uniform, he often failed to impress his fellow officers.

Yet on the battlefield, Grant proved to be a brilliant general. Highly focused and cool under fire, he won the first major Union victories of the war.

Grant was willing to fight Lee—even if the costs were high. He told his generals, "Wherever Lee goes, there you will go also."

ROBERT E. LEE
1807–1870

Robert E. Lee seemed destined for greatness. In his crisp uniform and trim, white beard, Lee was a dashing figure on the battlefield.

Born to a leading Virginia family, Lee was a top student at West Point and won praise for his actions in the Mexican War. General Winfield Scott called him "the very best soldier I have ever seen in the field."

Lee did not want to fight the Union, but he felt he had to stand by Virginia. "I did only what my duty demanded," Lee said. "I could have taken no other course without dishonor."

How did the tough decisions made by Grant and Lee affect the Civil War?

2 The Siege of Vicksburg

On July 4, 1863, the day after Pickett's Charge, the Union received more good news. In Mississippi, General Ulysses S. Grant had defeated Confederate troops at the **Siege of Vicksburg**.

Vocabulary
siege: the surrounding of a city, town, or fortress by an army trying to capture it

The previous year, Grant had won important victories in the West that opened up the Mississippi River for travel deep into the South. Vicksburg was the last major Confederate stronghold on the river. Grant had begun his attack on Vicksburg in May 1863. But when his direct attacks failed, he settled in for a long siege. Grant's troops surrounded the city and prevented the delivery of food and supplies. Eventually, the Confederates ran out of food. In desperation, they ate mules, dogs, and even rats. Finally, after nearly a month and a half, they surrendered.

The Union victory fulfilled a major part of the Anaconda Plan. The North had taken New Orleans the previous spring. Now, with complete control over the Mississippi River, the South was split in two.

Background
The Anaconda Plan called for blockading Southern ports, taking control of the Mississippi, and capturing Richmond.

With the victories at Vicksburg and Gettysburg, the tide of war turned in favor of the North. Britain gave up all thought of supporting the South. And, in General Grant, President Lincoln found a man who was willing to fight General Lee.

3 Sherman's Total War

In March 1864, President Lincoln named General Grant commander of all the Union armies. Grant then developed a plan to defeat the Confederacy. He would pursue Lee's army in Virginia, while Union forces under General **William Tecumseh Sherman** pushed through the Deep South to Atlanta and the Atlantic coast.

ACTIVITY OPTIONS

SKILLBUILDER LESSON: INTERPRETING TIME LINES

BLOCK SCHEDULING

Explaining the Skill Time lines depict the chronological order of events. In creating a time line, identify key dates. Then decide on a scale. For example, the time line can be divided into two-, five-, or ten-year intervals. Write key dates below the line and place the events above the line.

Applying the Skill Ask students to make a time line of events from 1862 to 1865, including the following battles and events: Antietam, Fredericksburg, Chancellorsville, death of Jackson, Gettysburg, Vicksburg, fall of Atlanta, fall of Savannah.

1. What key events took place between September 1862 and May 10, 1863? *(General McClellan defeated General Lee at Antietam; Battle of Fredericksburg, 1862; Union defeat at Chancellorsville, Va., May 1863; General Jackson died, May 10, 1863)*
2. Why did the tide of war turn against the Confederacy by July 1863? *(victories at Gettysburg and Vicksburg in July 1863)*
3. What are two events in 1864 that were part of Sherman's campaign of total war? *(Atlanta fell in September 1864; Savannah fell in December 1864)*

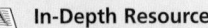

In-Depth Resources: Unit 5
- Skillbuilder Practice, p. 46

Battling southward from Tennessee, Sherman took Atlanta in September 1864. He then set out on a march to the sea, cutting a path of destruction up to 60 miles wide and 300 miles long through Georgia.

Sherman waged total war: a war not only against enemy troops, but against everything that supports the enemy. His troops tore up rail lines, destroyed crops, and burned and looted towns.

Reading **History**
C. Drawing Conclusions How might the political situation in the North have been different if Sherman had not taken Atlanta?
C. Possible Response McClellan might have won the presidency and changed the course of the war.

Sherman's triumph in Atlanta was important for Lincoln. In 1864, the president was running for reelection, but his prospects were not good. Northerners were tired of war, and Democrats—who had nominated George McClellan—stood a good chance of winning on an antiwar platform.

Sherman's success changed all that. Suddenly, Northerners could sense victory. Lincoln took 55 percent of the popular vote and won re-election. In his second inaugural speech, Lincoln hoped for a speedy end to the war: "With malice towards none; with charity for all; . . . let us strive on to finish the work we are in; to bind up the nation's wounds; . . . to do all which may achieve and cherish a just, and a lasting peace." (See page 509 for more of Lincoln's Second Inaugural Address.)

"Let us strive . . . to bind up the nation's wounds."
Abraham Lincoln

In December, Sherman took Savannah, Georgia. He then sent a telegram to Lincoln: "I beg to present you, as a Christmas gift, the city of Savannah, with 150 heavy guns and . . . about 25,000 bales of cotton."

Skillbuilder Answers
1. about 200 miles
2. Petersburg, Virginia

MORE ABOUT . . .

The Battle for Atlanta
Sherman believed "War is cruelty and you cannot refine it." However, he also told Atlanta's mayor, "When peace does come, you may call on me for anything. Then will I share with you the last cracker." After occupying Atlanta, Sherman ordered the civilian population expelled from the city. He believed that Union forces had to undermine the ability of the South to continue the war effort by destroying everything, including the will to resist. His soldiers burned everything of military value in the city before marching out on November 15.

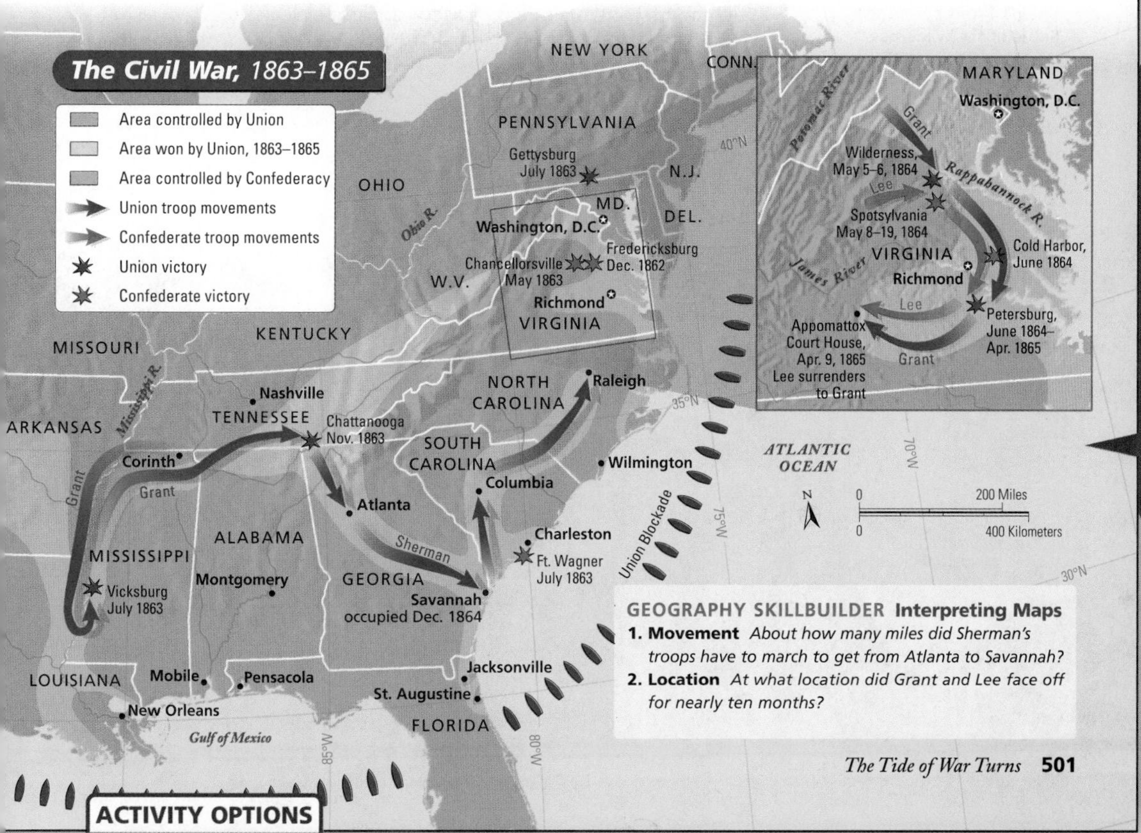

GEOGRAPHY SKILLBUILDER Interpreting Maps
1. **Movement** *About how many miles did Sherman's troops have to march to get from Atlanta to Savannah?*
2. **Location** *At what location did Grant and Lee face off for nearly ten months?*

HISTORY FROM VISUALS

Reading the Map The war ended with the fall of Richmond in 1865. What does the map tell you about Union strategy on land? on sea? **Possible Response** The Union army attacked Confederate cities and controlled land within the Confederacy. At the same time, a Union blockade was in place along the Confederate coast.

Extension Have students work in pairs to create detailed maps of one section of Sherman's march—for example, from Atlanta to Savannah. Maps should be drawn to scale and include towns and dates.

ACTIVITY OPTIONS
INTERDISCIPLINARY LINK: LANGUAGE ARTS

BLOCK SCHEDULING

NEWSPAPER HEADLINES

Class Time One class period

Task Writing newspaper headlines

Purpose To summarize Sherman's progress from Tennessee to Raleigh

Supplies Needed
- Reference materials on Sherman's march
- Internet access

Activity Ask students to research one of the following stops on Sherman's march to the sea: Chattanooga, Atlanta, Savannah, Columbia, and Raleigh. Tell students to summarize their findings about the campaign in a newspaper headline for the day Sherman's troops took the city. Student papers also should include the date that each city fell to the Union.

INSTRUCT: OBJECTIVE 4

Grant's Virginia Campaign/ Surrender at Appomattox

- Why did Grant want to take Richmond?
- What battles were part of the Virginia campaign?

Outline Map Activities
- The End of the Civil War, 1865, pp. 33–34

MORE ABOUT . . .

Petersburg

At Petersburg, Union soldiers from the coal-mining region of Pennsylvania dug a 500-foot tunnel under the Confederate lines and filled it with explosives. The tunnel exploded according to plan, creating an enormous crater and forcing a Confederate retreat. Unfortunately, Union strategy collapsed at this point. Northern soldiers poured into the crater—with no way to climb out. Confederate troops rained fire down on the helpless soldiers. The Union lost about 4,000 soldiers as casualties or prisoners. Southern casualties numbered about 1,300.

HISTORY *through* ART

Interpreting the Photograph This photograph, taken in a Union camp, captures the feeling of camp life during the war. Mathew Brady and his staff photographed Civil War battle scenes as well as more mundane scenes of daily military life. Their cameras were slow, so they did not record action shots. Brady's war photographs were widely reproduced; however, after a series of financial problems, he died in poverty.

Possible Responses: If people were exposed to images of suffering and death caused by war, they might try harder to find peaceful solutions to their problems.

In 1861, Congress created the Medal of Honor to reward individual bravery in combat.

4 Grant's Virginia Campaign

After taking Savannah, Sherman moved north through the Carolinas seeking to meet up with Grant's troops in Virginia. Since May 1864, Grant and his generals had been fighting savage battles against Lee's forces. In battle after battle, Grant would attack, rest, then attack again, all the while moving south toward Richmond.

At the Battle of the Wilderness in May 1864, Union and Confederate forces fought in a tangle of trees and brush so thick that they could barely see each other. Grant lost over 17,000 men, but he pushed on. "Whatever happens," he told Lincoln, "we will not retreat."

At Spotsylvania and Cold Harbor, the fighting continued. Again, the losses were staggering. Grant's attack in June, at Cold Harbor, cost him 7,000 men, most in the first few minutes of battle. Some Union troops were so sure they would die in battle that they pinned their names and addresses to their jackets so their bodies could be identified later.

In June 1864, Grant's armies arrived at Petersburg, just south of Richmond. Unable to break through the Confederate defenses, the Union forces dug trenches and settled in for a long siege. The two sides faced off for ten months.

In the end, though, Lee could not hold out. Grant was drawing a noose around Richmond. So Lee pulled out, leaving the Confederate capital undefended. The Union army marched into Richmond on April 3. One Richmond woman recalled, "Exactly at eight o'clock the Confederate flag that fluttered above the Capitol came

*Reading***History**

D. Reading a Map Use the map on page 501 to find the locations of the major battles of Grant's Virginia campaign.

HISTORY *through* ART

This photograph shows Union officers before the Battle of the Wilderness. Next to the tree on the right is the photographer Mathew Brady. Photography was still a new art when the Civil War began. Brady's Civil War photos represent one of the first examples of photojournalism.

How might people's attitudes toward war be affected when they can see pictures from the front lines?

502

ACTIVITY OPTIONS

MULTIPLE LEARNING STYLES: BODILY-KINESTHETIC

BLOCK SCHEDULING

CIVIL WAR BIOGRAPHIES

Class Time Two class periods

Task Creating a live biographical exhibit about an important figure from the Civil War

Purpose To learn about important leaders in the Civil War

Supplies Needed
- Poster paper
- Art supplies
- Reference materials about the Civil War
- Costume materials (optional)

Activity Have each student select one important figure from this chapter. Students should do research about the person and then create an exhibit about his or her life. Exhibits may include text, music, and illustrations. On an appointed day, have students set up their exhibits throughout the classroom. Each student should assume the role of the person they have studied. Students may wish to wear appropriate costumes. Allow students to take turns visiting one another's exhibits and interviewing one another in their roles.

down and the Stars and Stripes were run up. . . . We covered our faces and cried aloud."

Surrender at Appomattox

From Richmond and Petersburg, Lee fled west, while Grant followed in pursuit. Lee wanted to continue fighting, but he knew that his situation was hopeless. He sent a message to General Grant that he was ready to surrender.

On April 9, 1865, Lee and Grant met in the small Virginia town of **Appomattox Court House** to arrange the surrender. Grant later wrote that his joy at that moment was mixed with sadness.

A VOICE FROM THE PAST

I felt like anything rather than rejoicing at the downfall of a foe who had fought so long and valiantly, and had suffered so much for a cause, though that cause was, I believe, one of the worst for which a people ever fought, and one for which there was the least excuse. I do not question, however, the sincerity of the great mass of those who were opposed to us.

Ulysses S. Grant, *Personal Memoirs*

STRANGE *but* True

WILMER MCLEAN

The first major battle of the Civil War was fought on the property of Wilmer McLean. McLean lived in Manassas, Virginia, the site of the Battle of Bull Run. After the battle, McLean decided to move to a more peaceful place. He chose the village of Appomattox Court House (see map on page 501).

When Lee made the decision to surrender in April 1865, he sent Colonel Charles Marshall to find a location for a meeting with Grant. Marshall stopped the first man he saw in the deserted streets of Appomattox Court House. It was Wilmer McLean.

McLean reluctantly offered his home. Thus, the war that began in McLean's back yard ended in his parlor.

Grant offered generous terms of surrender. After laying down their arms, the Confederates could return home in peace, taking their private possessions and horses with them. Grant also gave food to the hungry Confederate soldiers.

After four long years, the Civil War was coming to a close. Its effects would continue, however, changing the country forever. In the next section, you will learn about the long-term consequences of the Civil War.

Section 3 Assessment

1. Terms & Names

Explain the significance of:
- Battle of Gettysburg
- Pickett's Charge
- Ulysses S. Grant
- Robert E. Lee
- Siege of Vicksburg
- William Tecumseh Sherman
- Appomattox Court House

2. Taking Notes

Use a time line like the one below to record key events from Section 3.

1862 — 1866

Which event is considered the turning point of the war?

3. Main Ideas

a. Why was the Battle of Gettysburg important?

b. Why was Northern success in the Siege of Vicksburg important?

c. How did Grant treat Confederate soldiers after the surrender at Appomattox Court House?

4. Critical Thinking

Contrasting How was the Civil War different from wars that Americans had previously fought?

THINK ABOUT
- the role of civilians
- Sherman's military strategy

ACTIVITY OPTIONS

GEOGRAPHY / LANGUAGE ARTS

Research the Siege of Vicksburg. Make a **topographic map** of the area or write an **article** describing the soldiers' hardships during the siege.

STRANGE *but* True

Wilmer McLean

On the day of the surrender, Lee arrived at McLean's house before Grant. He was dressed in a crisp, gray uniform with an engraved sword by his side. Grant arrived half an hour later. His clothes and sword were spattered with mud. To ease the tension, Grant reminded Lee that they had met during the Mexican War. He later said, "Our conversation grew so pleasant that I almost forgot the object of our meeting."

ASSESS & RETEACH

Setting the Stage Have students fill in the third section of the chart.

Formal Assessment
- Section Quiz, p. 302

RETEACHING ACTIVITY

Have students reread the main idea of the section on page 496. Ask them to use the main idea as the topic sentence of a paragraph. The paragraph should identify the significance of the major campaigns that led to Union victory with the fall of Richmond.

In-Depth Resources: Unit 5
- Reteaching Activity, p. 56

Section 3 Assessment

1. Terms & Names

Battle of Gettysburg, p. 497
Pickett's Charge, p. 497
Ulysses S. Grant, p. 500
Robert E. Lee, p. 500
Siege of Vicksburg, p. 500
William Tecumseh Sherman, p. 500
Appomattox Court House, p. 503

2. Taking Notes

1862: Antietam; Fredericksburg; 1863: Chancellorsville; Gettysburg; Vicksburg; 1864: Grant named head of Union armies; Wilderness; Cold Harbor; Atlanta; Lincoln reelected; Savannah; 1865: Richmond falls; surrender at Appomattox.
Battle of Gettysburg

3. Main Ideas

a. It ended Lee's hopes for a Confederate victory in the North.
b. It would split the South in two and helped propel Grant to the leadership of the Union's armies.
c. respectfully; gave them food; allowed them to take their personal possessions home with them

4. Critical Thinking

They were fighting one another; the civilian population was more heavily involved; anything that supported troops became a potential target.

ACTIVITY OPTIONS

Integrated Assessment
- Rubrics for a map, 2.1
- Rubrics for a news article, 4.5

SECTION OBJECTIVES

1. To analyze the economic, physical, and emotional costs of the Civil War
2. To explain the significance of the Thirteenth Amendment
3. To describe the events related to President Lincoln's assassination
4. To summarize the consequences of the Civil War

SKILLBUILDER
Interpreting Graphs, p. 505
Interpreting Charts, p. 507

CRITICAL THINKING
Contrasting, p. 505
Making Inferences, pp. 505, 507
Summarizing, p. 506

FOCUS & MOTIVATE

5-MINUTE WARM-UP

Drawing Conclusions These questions deal with the costs of the Civil War.

1. Look at the graphs on page 505. Which side lost more soldiers? On which side were there more wounded soldiers?
2. How do you think the number of casualties affected the way Northerners and Southerners felt toward each other after the war?

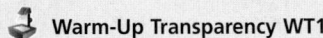

Warm-Up Transparency WT17

INSTRUCT

INSTRUCT: OBJECTIVE 1

Costs of the War

- How did President Lincoln hope to bring the North and South together after the war?
- What were the physical costs of the war?
- What were the economic costs of the war?

In-Depth Resources: Unit 5
- Guided Reading, p. 44

Reading Study Guide (Spanish and English), pp. 167–168

4 The Legacy of the War

TERMS & NAMES
Thirteenth Amendment
John Wilkes Booth

MAIN IDEA	WHY IT MATTERS NOW
The Civil War brought great changes and new challenges to the United States.	The most important change was the liberation of 4 million enslaved persons.

ONE AMERICAN'S STORY

In the spring of 1864, a year before the end of the Civil War, the Union army was running out of cemetery space to bury its war dead. The secretary of war ordered Quartermaster General Montgomery Meigs to find a new site for a cemetery. Without hesitation, Meigs chose Robert E. Lee's plantation in Arlington, Virginia, just across the Potomac River from Washington, D.C. "The grounds about the mansion are admirably adapted to such a use," wrote Meigs in June 1864.

Meigs was from Georgia and had served under Lee in the U.S. Army before the war. Unlike Lee, however, Meigs remained loyal to the Union and disagreed strongly with Lee's decision to join the Confederacy. His decision to turn Lee's plantation into a Union cemetery was highly symbolic. The Union soldiers who died fighting Lee's army would be buried in Lee's front yard. That site became Arlington National Cemetery.

During the Civil War, the government turned Robert E. Lee's Virginia plantation into a graveyard. That graveyard eventually became Arlington National Cemetery.

1 Costs of the War

Many Northerners shared Montgomery Meigs's bitter feelings toward the South. At the same time, many Southerners felt great resentment toward the North. After the war, President Lincoln hoped to heal the nation and bring North and South together again. The generous terms of surrender offered to Lee were part of that effort. Hard feelings remained, however, in part because the costs of the war were so great.

The Civil War was the deadliest war in American history. In four years of fighting, approximately 620,000 soldiers died—360,000 for the Union and 260,000 for the Confederacy. Another 275,000 Union soldiers and 260,000 Confederate soldiers were wounded. Many suffered from their wounds for the rest of their lives.

Altogether, some 3,000,000 men served in the armies of the North and South—around 10 percent of the population. Along with the soldiers, many other Americans had their lives disrupted by the war.

RECOMMENDED RESOURCES

In-Depth Resources: Unit 5
- Guided Reading, p. 44
- Building Vocabulary, p. 45
- Geog. Application, pp. 47–48
- Enrichment Activity, p. 58
- History Workshop, p. 59

Reading Study Guide (Spanish and English), pp. 167–168

Formal Assessment
- Section Quiz, p. 303

Integrated Assessment
- Rubrics, 2.6, 1.6

Access for Students Acquiring English/ESL
- Guided Reading, p. 103
- Geography Application, pp. 115–116

INTEGRATED TECHNOLOGY

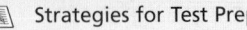

Humanities Transparency HT34

Critical Thinking Trans. CT50
- Cause and Effect: The Civil War, 1861–1865

Electronic Teacher Tools

classzone.com

TEST-TAKING RESOURCES

Strategies for Test Preparation

Test Practice Transparencies, TT63

Online Test Practice

ReadingHistory
A. Contrasting How did government spending during the Civil War compare to that during previous years?
A. Possible Response The amount spent during the war was five times that spent during the previous 80 years.

The war also had great economic costs. Together, the North and South spent more than five times the amount spent by the government in the previous eight decades. Many years after the fighting was over, the federal government was still paying interest on loans taken out during the war.

2 The Thirteenth Amendment

One of the greatest effects of the war was the freeing of millions of enslaved persons. As the Union army moved through the South during and after the war, Union soldiers released African Americans from bondage. One of those released was Booker T. Washington, who later became a famous educator and reformer. He recalled the day a Union officer came to his plantation to read the Emancipation Proclamation.

> **A VOICE FROM THE PAST**
>
> After the reading we were told that we were all free, and could go when and where we pleased. My mother, who was standing by my side, leaned over and kissed her children, while tears of joy ran down her cheeks. She explained to us what it all meant, that this was the day for which she had been so long praying, but fearing that she would never live to see.
>
> **Booker T. Washington,** quoted in his autobiography, *Up from Slavery*

ReadingHistory
B. Making Inferences Why was an amendment needed to free enslaved persons even after the Emancipation Proclamation?
B. Possible Responses Many people were still enslaved in the border states. An amendment would be harder to overturn than a law passed by Congress.

The Emancipation Proclamation applied primarily to slaves in the Confederacy, however. Many African Americans in the border states were still enslaved. In 1864, with the war still under way, President Lincoln had approved of a constitutional amendment to end slavery entirely, but it failed to pass Congress.

In January 1865, Lincoln urged Congress to try again to end slavery. This time, the measure—known as the **Thirteenth Amendment**—passed. By year's end, 27 states, including eight in the South, had ratified the amendment. From that point on, slavery was banned in the United States.

CONNECTIONS TO MATH
Costs of the Civil War

CONFEDERATE CASUALTIES

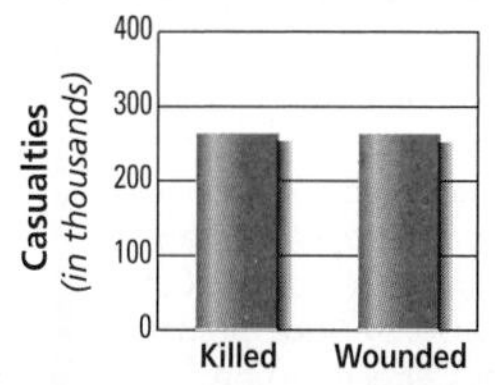

UNION CASUALTIES

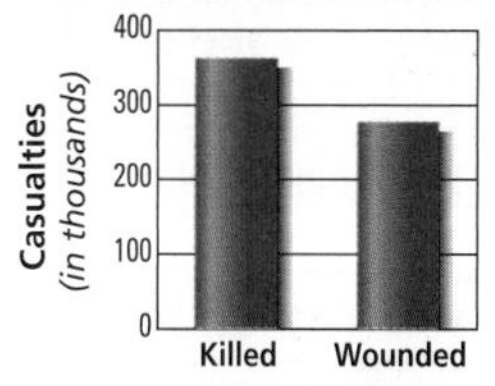

Source: *World Book; Historical Statistics of the United States; The United States Civil War Center*

ECONOMIC COSTS

- Federal loans and taxes to finance the war totaled $2.6 billion.
- Federal debt on June 30, 1865, rose to $2.7 billion.
- Confederate debt ran over $700 million.
- Union inflation reached 182% in 1864 and 179% in 1865.
- Confederate inflation rose to 9,000% by the end of the war.

SKILLBUILDER
Interpreting Graphs
1. *About how many Confederate soldiers were killed in the Civil War?*
2. *Approximately how many soldiers were wounded in the war?*

Skillbuilder Answers
1. 260,000
2. 500,000

3 Lincoln's Assassination

Lincoln did not live to see the end of slavery, however. Five days after Lee's surrender at Appomattox, the president and his wife went to see a play at Ford's Theatre in Washington, D.C. During the play, a Confederate supporter, **John Wilkes Booth,** crept into the balcony where the president sat and shot him in the back of the head. Booth then jumped over the railing and landed on the stage. Although he broke his leg in the leap, he managed to escape the theater.

INSTRUCT: OBJECTIVE 2
The Thirteenth Amendment

- What was required before slavery was abolished throughout the United States?
- When was the Thirteenth Amendment passed?

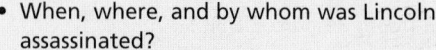

HISTORY FROM VISUALS

Reading the Graphs Have students read the title of the entire visual. Then have them explain the relationship between the information in the graphs and the economic costs. **Possible Response** The costs of the war were not only financial but also human.

Extension Have the students create a different visual to show the information in these graphs.

INSTRUCT: OBJECTIVE 3
Lincoln's Assassination

- When, where, and by whom was Lincoln assassinated?
- How did Lincoln's death affect the nation?

In-Depth Resources: Unit 5
- Geography Application: Booth Assassinates Lincoln, pp. 47–48

Humanities Transparency HT34
- John Wilkes Booth Poster

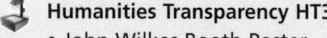

ACTIVITY OPTIONS

INDIVIDUAL NEEDS: GIFTED AND TALENTED

CIVIL WAR ART AND CIVIL WAR PHOTOGRAPHY

Class Time Two class periods

Task Comparing works of art and photographs depicting the Civil War

Purpose To analyze works of art depicting historical events

Supplies Needed
- Books and reference materials with Civil War art and photographs

Activity Have students find both a photograph and a work of art (such as an engraving, drawing, painting, or sculpture) of the same Civil War subject. Then have students do research about the event, the artist, and the photographer. Tell students to prepare an oral presentation in which they discuss both the artwork and the photograph, including an analysis of the purpose of each work, its intended audience, and its medium. Students should also point out any inaccuracies they find in the way the event has been depicted in art.

Connections TO *LITERATURE*

Walt Whitman

Whitman wrote his poem "When Lilacs Last in the Dooryard Bloomed" about the death of Lincoln. Lincoln died in April, and Whitman says in the poem that each year when the lilacs blossom, he will think of the fallen president. Another of Whitman's poems about Lincoln's death is "O Captain! My Captain!"

MORE ABOUT . . .

John Wilkes Booth

Booth was a young, successful actor. Lincoln had seen Booth perform in a play called *The Marble Heart* in November 1863, shortly before the president traveled to Gettysburg where he gave his famous address. In March 1865, Booth and his accomplices tried to kidnap Lincoln at the Soldiers Home outside the city—but Lincoln was not there. Among the people hanged as Booth's accomplices was a woman, Mary Surratt, who ran a boardinghouse in Surrattsville, Md., where the conspirators, including her son John, sometimes met.

INSTRUCT: OBJECTIVE 4

Consequences of the War

- Why did the war change the way people thought about the country?
- How did the war affect the economy in the North and in the South?
- What other challenges did the country face after the war?

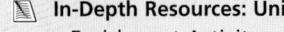

In-Depth Resources: Unit 5
- Enrichment Activity, p. 58

Connections TO *LITERATURE*

WALT WHITMAN
1819–1892

One of the greatest American poets, Walt Whitman (below) was a large, bearded man whose poetry captured the American spirit. His most famous book of poems, *Leaves of Grass,* praised the values of freedom and democracy.

Whitman was 41 when the Civil War began. Too old for the army, he offered his services as a nurse when his younger brother was wounded at Fredericksburg. He stayed on after that to help at hospitals in Washington, D.C.

Whitman wrote a book of poetry about war. Later editions of the book, which appeared after Lincoln's assassination, included several poems about the president.

That same evening, an accomplice of Booth stabbed Secretary of State William Seward, who later recovered. Another man was supposed to assassinate Vice-President Johnson, but he failed to carry out the attack.

Vocabulary
accomplice: someone who aids a lawbreaker

Although Booth had managed to escape after shooting the president, Union troops found and killed him several days later. Soldiers also hunted down Booth's accomplices, whom they either hanged or imprisoned.

After Lincoln was shot, he was carried to a house across the street from the theater. The bullet in his brain could not be removed, however. The next morning, April 15, 1865, the president died. He was the first American president to be assassinated.

Lincoln's murder stunned the nation and caused intense grief. In Washington, D.C., people wept in the streets. One man who mourned the nation's loss was the poet Walt Whitman. In one poem, Whitman considered the president's legacy.

***Reading* History**
C. Summarizing How did Americans react to the assassination of Lincoln?
C. Possible Response People reacted with intense grief and mourning.

A VOICE FROM THE PAST

This dust was once the man,
Gentle, plain, just and resolute, under whose cautious hand,
Against the foulest crime in history known in any land or age,
Was saved the Union of these States.

Walt Whitman, *This Dust Was Once the Man*

The loss of Lincoln's vast experience and great political skills was a terrible setback for a people faced by the challenge of rebuilding their nation. In both the North and the South, life would never be the same after the Civil War.

4 Consequences of the War

In the North, the war changed the way people thought about the country. In fighting to defend the Union, people came to see the United States as a single nation rather than a collection of states. After 1865, people no longer said "the United States *are*" but "the United States *is.*"

The war also caused the national government to expand. Before the war, the government was relatively small and had limited powers. With the demands of war, however, the government grew larger and more powerful. Along with a new paper currency and income tax, the government established a new federal banking system. It also funded railroads, gave western land to settlers, and provided for state colleges. This growth of federal power continued long after the war was over.

Background
In the 1850s, an improved way of making steel—the Bessemer process—had been perfected, allowing for the mass production of steel.

The war also changed the Northern economy. New industries such as steel, petroleum, food processing, and manufacturing grew rapidly. By

ACTIVITY OPTIONS

INTERDISCIPLINARY LINK: LANGUAGE ARTS — BLOCK SCHEDULING

"O CAPTAIN! MY CAPTAIN!"

Class Time 20 minutes

Task Reading a poem by Whitman about Lincoln

Purpose To read a contemporary poem about Lincoln and to understand the effect of his death on the American people

Supplies Needed
- Copies of "O Captain! My Captain!"

Activity Distribute copies of the poem to the class. Have students read it and then ask students to rewrite the first two lines to explain what Whitman means by the ship, the fearful trip, the prize, and the captain. Why does Whitman say that the people should exult and ring bells despite the death of the "captain"?

Then have the students discuss how this poem may reflect the effect of Lincoln's death on the American public. Ask how the poem might have been received by Southerners.

CAUSE AND EFFECT: The Civil War, 1861–1865	
CAUSES	**IMMEDIATE EFFECTS**
Conflict over slavery in territories	Abolition of slavery
Economic differences between North and South	Devastation of South
	Reconstruction of South
Failure of Congress to compromise	**LONG-TERM EFFECTS**
Election of Lincoln as president	Growth of industry
Secession of Southern states	Government more powerful
Firing on Fort Sumter	Nation reunited

SKILLBUILDER Interpreting Charts

1. *What military event is among the causes of the Civil War?*
2. *What effect did the Civil War have on the federal government?*

Skillbuilder Answers
1. firing on Fort Sumter
2. It made federal authority stronger than that of the states.

Background
Some people have called the Civil War the first modern war because of the use of machines, the destructiveness, and the effects on civilians, which would be repeated in later wars.

the late 1800s, industry had begun to replace farming as the basis of the national economy.

For the South, however, the war brought economic disaster. Farms and plantations were destroyed. About 40 percent of the South's livestock was killed. Fifty percent of its farm machinery was wrecked. Factories were also demolished, and thousands of miles of railroad tracks were torn up. Also gone was the labor system that the South had used—slavery.

Before the war, the South accounted for 30 percent of the nation's wealth. After the war it accounted for only 12 percent. These economic differences between the North and the South would last for decades.

The country faced difficult challenges after the war. How would the South be brought back into the Union, and how would four million former slaves be integrated into national life? You will read more about these challenges in the next chapter.

Section 4 Assessment

1. Terms & Names

Explain the significance of:
- Thirteenth Amendment
- John Wilkes Booth

2. Taking Notes

Use a chart like the one below to record the social, economic, and political legacy of the Civil War.

Legacy of the Civil War

Society	Economy	Politics

Is the legacy of the Civil War still apparent today? How?

3. Main Ideas

a. What were some of the human costs of the Civil War?

b. What did the Thirteenth Amendment achieve?

c. What was the state of the Southern economy after the Civil War?

4. Critical Thinking

Making Inferences How do you think the assassination of President Lincoln affected the nation?

THINK ABOUT
- the reaction of ordinary citizens
- its impact on government

ACTIVITY OPTIONS

MATH
TECHNOLOGY

Read about the postwar economy. Create a **database** on industry in the North or make a **storyboard** for a video on the problems in the South.

HISTORY FROM VISUALS

Reading the Chart Point out the relationship between the two parts of the chart. Ask students to identify the results that were positive for the country as a whole. Then ask which results Southerners would have considered positive.
Possible Responses For the country as a whole—the abolition of slavery; reconstruction of the South; a nation reunited; a growth of industry; For the Southerners—the growth of Southern industry

Extension Ask students to divide the causes of the Civil War listed on the chart into "Causes Building Over Time" and "Immediate Causes."

Critical Thinking Transparency CT50
- Cause and Effect: The Civil War, 1861–1865

ASSESS & RETEACH

Setting the Stage Have students fill in the last section on the chapter graphic organizer.

Formal Assessment
- Section Quiz, p. 303

Critical Thinking Transparency CT49
- Setting the Stage

RETEACHING ACTIVITY

Divide the class into four groups. Assign one objective to each student group. Have each group outline the material in the objective using a main idea and supporting detail format. Remind students to title the outlines. Display the completed outlines on a classroom bulletin board.

In-Depth Resources: Unit 5
- Reteaching Activity, p. 57

Section 4 Assessment

1. Terms & Names

Thirteenth Amendment, p. 505
John Wilkes Booth, p. 505

2. Taking Notes

Society: death and injury; disruption of lives; freeing of slaves; Economy: cost of war; Northern industrialization; Southern labor system destroyed; Politics: government expansion; Thirteenth Amendment. Answers will vary but students should be able to explain their responses.

3. Main Ideas

a. Approximately 620,000 casualties, and many lives were disrupted. **b.** It banned slavery in the United States. **c.** economic disaster; much property was destroyed; the traditional labor system, slavery, was abolished

4. Critical Thinking

There was a great sense of tragedy and loss. It would be harder for the nation to confront postwar challenges without his political skills.

ACTIVITY OPTIONS

Integrated Assessment
- Rubrics for a database, 2.6
- Rubrics for a storyboard, 1.6

INTERACTIVE PRIMARY SOURCES

OBJECTIVE
Students will be able to identify the main points of the Gettysburg Address and Lincoln's Second Inaugural Address, and they will gain appreciation for Lincoln's use of language.

Primary Source Explorer
- *The Gettysburg Address*
- *Lincoln's Second Inaugural Address*

The Explorer will help students select and produce their own presentations.

Specific information about the document can be found in **A Closer Look.** To learn more about key people and events of the time, students should click on **Life in These Times. What Happened Next** will show the student the impact of the document, both at home and abroad, and tie the document to today.

FOCUS & MOTIVATE

Making Generalizations Ask students to think about speeches or sermons that they have heard. Tell them to make a list of qualities that they think are important for a speaker to remember. After students have read the Lincoln speeches, ask them to review their lists to find which qualities they contain.

MORE ABOUT . . .

The Gettysburg Address
President Lincoln wrote five different versions of the speech. He also made several changes as he spoke. Probably the most significant change was adding "under God" after the word "nation" in the last sentence. The poetic but simple language of the speech is one reason why it is among the best remembered in American history. The emotional focus of Lincoln's words is on the actions of the soldiers who fought at Gettysburg.

INTERACTIVE PRIMARY SOURCES

The Gettysburg Address (1863)

Setting the Stage On November 19, 1863, officials gathered in Gettysburg, Pennsylvania. They were there to dedicate a national cemetery on the ground where the decisive Battle of Gettysburg had taken place nearly five months earlier. Following the ceremony's main address, which lasted nearly two hours, President Lincoln delivered his Gettysburg Address in just over two minutes. In this famous speech, Lincoln expressed his hopes for the nation. **See Primary Source Explorer**

Four **score**[1] and seven years ago our fathers brought forth on this continent a new nation, conceived in liberty, and dedicated to the proposition that all men are created equal.

Now we are engaged in a great civil war, testing whether that nation or any nation so conceived and so dedicated, can long endure. We are met on a great battlefield of that war. We have come to dedicate a portion of that field, as a final resting place for those who here gave their lives that that nation might live. It is altogether fitting and proper that we should do this.

But, in a larger sense, we cannot dedicate—we can not **consecrate**[2]—we can not hallow—this ground. The brave men, living and dead, who struggled here, have consecrated it, far above our poor power to add or **detract.**[3] The world will little note, nor long remember what we say here, but it can never forget what they did here. It is for us the living, rather, to be dedicated here to the unfinished work which they who fought here have thus far so nobly advanced. It is rather for us to be here dedicated to the great task remaining before us—that from these honored dead we **take increased devotion to**[4] that cause for which they **gave the last full measure of devotion**[5]—that we here highly resolve that these dead shall not have died **in vain**[6]—that this nation, under God, shall have a new birth of freedom—and that government of the people, by the people, for the people, shall not perish from the earth.

A CLOSER LOOK

LINCOLN'S MODESTY
Lincoln claimed that what he said at Gettysburg would not be long remembered. However, the address soon came to be recognized as one of the best speeches of all time.

1. What features of Lincoln's address make it so memorable?

A CLOSER LOOK

FIGHTING FOR A CAUSE
Different people fought for different causes during the Civil War. Sometimes, the causes for which people fought changed over the course of the war.

2. What cause is Lincoln referring to in the Gettysburg Address?

1. **score:** a group of 20.
2. **consecrate:** to declare as sacred.
3. **detract:** to take away from.
4. **take increased devotion to:** work harder for.
5. **gave the last full measure of devotion:** sacrificed their lives.
6. **in vain:** for nothing.

508

TEACHING STRATEGY

Finding Main Ideas To help students understand the main idea of the Gettysburg Address, have them copy the chart shown and match the main ideas it presents with the text.

Main Ideas: The Gettysburg Address
1. Our colonial leaders created a nation based on equality.
2. We are fighting a war to preserve our country.
3. We are here to dedicate a cemetery on a part of the battlefield.
4. What the soldiers who fought at Gettysburg did is the most important thing, not what the living do to honor them now.
5. The living must dedicate themselves to finishing the work of the soldiers to make sure that freedom will survive and that democracy will endure.

Second Inaugural Address (1865)

Setting the Stage President Lincoln delivered his Second Inaugural Address just before the end of the Civil War. In this excerpt, he recalled the major cause of the war and vowed to fight for the restoration of peace and unity. **See Primary Source Explorer**

One-eighth of the whole population were colored slaves. . . . These slaves constituted a peculiar and powerful interest. All knew that this interest was somehow the cause of the war. To strengthen, perpetuate, and extend this interest was the object for which the **insurgents**[1] would rend the Union even by war, while the Government claimed no right to do more than to restrict the territorial enlargement of it. Neither party expected for the war the magnitude or the duration which it has already attained. Neither anticipated that the cause of the conflict might cease with or even before the conflict itself should cease. Each looked for an easier triumph, and a result less fundamental and astounding. Both read the same Bible and pray to the same God, and each invokes His aid against the other. . . . Fondly do we hope, fervently do we pray, that this mighty **scourge**[2] of war may speedily pass away. Yet, if God wills that it continue until all the wealth piled by the **bondsman's**[3] two hundred and fifty years of **unrequited**[4] toil shall be sunk, and until every drop of blood drawn with the lash shall be paid by another drawn with the sword, as was said three thousand years ago, so still it must be said "the judgments of the Lord are true and righteous altogether."

With malice toward none, with charity for all, with firmness in the right as God gives us to see the right, let us strive on to finish the work we are in, to bind up the nation's wounds, to care for him who shall have borne the battle and for his widow and his orphan, to do all which may achieve and cherish a just and lasting peace among ourselves and with all nations.

1. **insurgent:** one that revolts against civil authority.
2. **scourge:** a source of suffering and devastation.
3. **bondsman:** enslaved person.
4. **unrequited:** not paid for.

A CLOSER LOOK

SLAVERY IN TERRITORIES

Before the Civil War, Northern states wanted to prohibit slavery in territories that would eventually become new states. Southern states fought to expand slavery, fearing the prohibition would threaten slavery where it already existed.

1. Why did the Southerners fear that prohibiting slavery in new territories might threaten slavery where it already existed?

A CLOSER LOOK

MALICE TOWARD NONE

As Northerners became more confident in victory, many looked forward to punishing Southerners, whom they blamed for the war. Lincoln, however, urged citizens to care for one another and work for a just and lasting peace.

2. Why do you think that Lincoln believed it would be wiser for Americans not to place blame or seek revenge on one another?

Interactive Primary Sources Assessment

1. Main Ideas

a. Why might President Lincoln have begun the Gettysburg Address by noting that the country was "dedicated to the proposition that all men are created equal"?

b. According to Lincoln's Second Inaugural Address, why did the Confederacy go to war?

c. To what did Lincoln refer with the phrase "the bondsman's two hundred and fifty years of unrequited toil?"

2. Critical Thinking

Making Inferences In 1865, if the South had asked to rejoin the Union without ending slavery, do you think Lincoln would have agreed?

THINK ABOUT
- what Lincoln identifies as the cause of the war
- what might happen if the war ended but slavery did not

INSTRUCT

- What beliefs about the United States does Lincoln express in the Gettysburg Address?
- What is the "unfinished work" that Lincoln believes the living "should dedicate themselves to"?
- In his Second Inaugural Address, what does Lincoln say was the major cause of the war?

MAKING PERSONAL CONNECTIONS

Ask students to reread the last sentence of the Gettysburg Address and the last sentence of the Second Inaugural Address. Ask students if they think Americans are still working to reach the goals set by Lincoln.

MORE ABOUT . . .

The Second Inaugural Address (1865)

Lincoln's second inauguration was on March 4, 1865. It was a cold, windy, rainy day in Washington, D.C. Lincoln stood on the steps of the Capitol Building under its newly completed dome. In the audience stood John Wilkes Booth, an invited guest. Lincoln's tone in the speech is weary and somber. After completing it, Lincoln said, "I am a tired man. Sometimes I think I am the tiredest man on earth."

A CLOSER LOOK

The Gettysburg Address
1. Answers will vary, but each answer should include an explanation.
2. The survival of the United States, whose government was dedicated to the proposition that all men are created equal —a government described by Lincoln as "of the people, by the people, and for the people."

Second Inaugural Address
1. Slave states would have proportionately less representation in the federal government.
2. Lincoln knew that the task of rebuilding the nation after the war would be less difficult if Americans were able to work together.

Interactive Primary Sources Assessment

1. Main Ideas

a. because millions of enslaved men and women were still not recognized as equal
b. to strengthen, perpetuate, and extend slavery against the wishes of the federal government to restrict its territorial enlargement
c. to the work of slaves who had been brought to the United States since the early 1600s

2. Critical Thinking

Lincoln would not have accepted the offer. He saw slavery as the cause of the war. Even if the South had returned to the Union, its system of slavery would have caused the same problems and conflicts again.

TERMS & NAMES

1. **Emancipation Proclamation,** p. 488
2. **54th Massachusetts Regiment,** p. 490
3. **conscription,** p. 492
4. **Battle of Gettysburg,** p. 497
5. **Ulysses S. Grant,** p. 500
6. **Robert E. Lee,** p. 500
7. **Siege of Vicksburg,** p. 500
8. **William Tecumseh Sherman,** p. 500
9. **Appomattox Court House,** p. 503
10. **Thirteenth Amendment,** p. 505

REVIEW QUESTIONS

Possible Responses

1. because he thought that freeing the slaves would weaken the South and help win the war
2. After the Emancipation Proclamation, they enlisted in large numbers. They fought bravely and made a real contribution.
3. There were food riots in the South, and many men deserted the army. "Copperheads" protested against the war in the North, and draft laws resulted in riots in some places.
4. because it was easier for wealthy people to avoid the draft than poor people
5. by slowing down the pace of their work; carrying out sabotage; by joining the Union army
6. It halted Lee's invasion of the North and helped turn the tide of the war.
7. It devastated the South and raised spirits in the North, helping Lincoln get reelected.
8. He kept attacking Lee's forces in Virginia, pushing Lee back and finally forcing his surrender.
9. It freed slaves throughout the United States, not just in the Confederacy, and outlawed slavery in the whole United States.
10. The war encouraged the growth of industry, which began to replace farming as the basis of the national economy.

Chapter 17 ASSESSMENT

TERMS & NAMES

Briefly explain the significance of each of the following.

1. Emancipation Proclamation
2. 54th Massachusetts Regiment
3. conscription
4. Battle of Gettysburg
5. Ulysses S. Grant
6. Robert E. Lee
7. Siege of Vicksburg
8. William Tecumseh Sherman
9. Appomattox Court House
10. Thirteenth Amendment

REVIEW QUESTIONS

The Emancipation Proclamation (pages 487–490)

1. Why did Lincoln issue the Emancipation Proclamation?
2. How did black soldiers aid the war effort?

War Affects Society (pages 491–495)

3. How did events on the home front show the toll that war was taking there?
4. Why did some people say the Civil War was a "rich man's war but a poor man's fight"?
5. How did enslaved persons help the Union?

The North Wins (pages 496–503)

6. Why was the Battle of Gettysburg so important?
7. How did Sherman's march help the Union?
8. How did Grant defeat Lee?

The Legacy of the War (pages 504–507)

9. How was the Thirteenth Amendment different from the Emancipation Proclamation?
10. How did the war change the national economy?

CRITICAL THINKING

1. USING YOUR NOTES

	North	South
Emancipation Proclamation		
War's Impact		
Northern Victories in Battle		
Union Wins Civil War		

a. How did white and black Southerners react to the Emancipation Proclamation?

b. How did inflation affect the North and the South?

2. ANALYZING LEADERSHIP

What qualities made Lincoln an effective leader?

3. THEME: IMPACT OF THE INDIVIDUAL

How did General Grant's actions in the war make a crucial difference to the outcome?

4. FORMING AND SUPPORTING OPINIONS

One Union relief worker said, "The suffering of men in battle is nothing next to the agony that women feel sending forth their loved ones to war." Do you agree with this statement? Explain why or why not.

5. APPLYING CITIZENSHIP SKILLS

How might the behavior of General Grant and President Lincoln toward the Confederacy have helped to begin healing the war-torn nation?

Interact *with* History

Having read about the ferocity of battle during the Civil War, do you still believe that you would be inspired to continue the fighting? Why or why not?

VISUAL SUMMARY

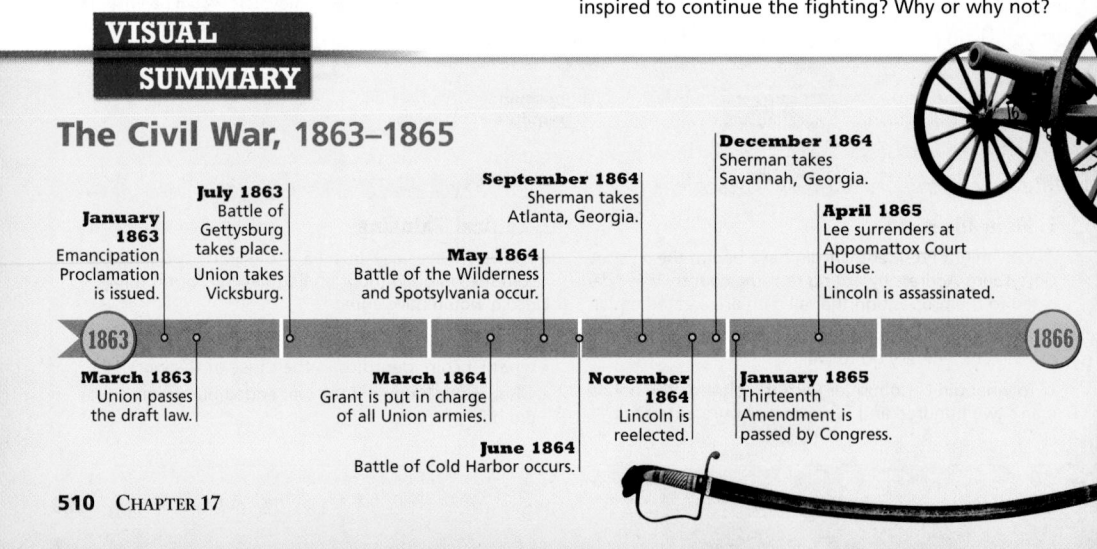

The Civil War, 1863–1865

1863

January 1863 Emancipation Proclamation is issued.

March 1863 Union passes the draft law.

July 1863 Battle of Gettysburg takes place. Union takes Vicksburg.

March 1864 Grant is put in charge of all Union armies.

May 1864 Battle of the Wilderness and Spotsylvania occur.

June 1864 Battle of Cold Harbor occurs.

September 1864 Sherman takes Atlanta, Georgia.

November 1864 Lincoln is reelected.

December 1864 Sherman takes Savannah, Georgia.

January 1865 Thirteenth Amendment is passed by Congress.

April 1865 Lee surrenders at Appomattox Court House. Lincoln is assassinated.

1866

CRITICAL THINKING

Possible Responses

1. **USING YOUR NOTES** **a.** White Southerners reacted with rage. Black Southerners fled to Union lines, depriving the South of labor. Many became Union soldiers. **b.** Inflation had an impact on both the North and South, but it was particularly severe in the South.
2. **ANALYZING LEADERSHIP** He seemed to weigh decisions carefully and keep his goals in mind. He had great strength to persevere when conditions were difficult.
3. **THEME: IMPACT OF THE INDIVIDUAL** Grant was determined to win. He took the offensive regardless of the cost. His attitude played a key role in turning the tide of the war.
4. **FORMING AND SUPPORTING OPINIONS** Answers will vary.
5. **APPLYING CITIZENSHIP SKILLS** Their respect and compassion for fellow citizens helped to reduce the hard feelings among the citizens.

Interact *with* History. Answers will vary. Some will feel that their principles were still worth fighting for, while others will not.

HISTORY SKILLS

1. INTERPRETING MAPS: Location

Study the map. Answer the questions.

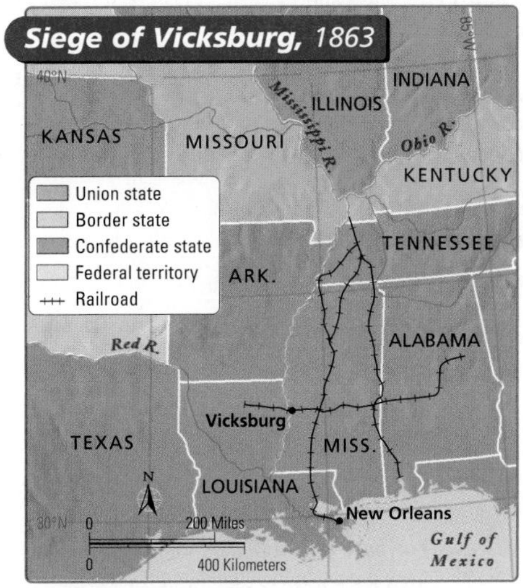

Siege of Vicksburg, 1863

Basic Map Elements

a. Which color represents Confederate states?

Interpreting the Map

b. Next to what river was Vicksburg built?

c. Why might Vicksburg be important for Southerners supplying the Confederacy from Texas?

2. INTERPRETING SECONDARY SOURCES

Historian Bruce Catton describes a brief meeting between two brothers during the Siege of Vicksburg. Read the passage and answer the questions.

> Both boys [were] from Missouri, one of them in Confederate gray and the other in Federal blue. The Confederate had a roll of bills in his hand and gave them to his brother to send to their mother. . . . He couldn't get things out from Vicksburg through the Union lines, Vicksburg being completely surrounded, so he asked his brother to send them to her, and the brother did. There was no shooting while these arrangements were made, then the brothers shook hands and retired to their individual lines, and the shooting started up again.
>
> **Bruce Catton,** from *Reflections on the Civil War*

a. What does this account say about the nature of war?

b. Why might the fact that the brothers came from Missouri pertain to their fighting for different sides?

ALTERNATIVE ASSESSMENT

1. INTERDISCIPLINARY ACTIVITY: Science

Writing a Report Do research on the advances in military technology during the Civil War. Write a report that describes the new or improved weapons that were used during the war. Be sure to use standard grammar, spelling, sentence structure, and punctuation in your report. Present the report to your class with charts that illustrate the changes and innovations that you describe.

2. COOPERATIVE LEARNING ACTIVITY

Creating a Newspaper Work with a group of classmates to produce a simple newspaper that covers a specific period of the Civil War. With your group, choose the period you want to cover and decide whether you will take a Northern or Southern viewpoint. Research events and conditions during that period, then select the topics you will cover in your newspaper. Articles should include descriptions of the characteristics of the Civil War era. Examples include:

- important battles and military strategies
- political news, including government actions and foreign involvement
- social and economic conditions
- profiles of important figures

3. PRIMARY SOURCE EXPLORER

Use the Internet, books, and other resources to do research for a multimedia presentation on a Civil War battle. Using presentation software, consider including the following content:

- paintings or written descriptions of the battle
- images of the destruction caused by the conflict
- music from the time period
- statistics on casualties
- diary and journal entries

4. HISTORY PORTFOLIO

Review your section and chapter assessment activities. Select one that you think is your best work. Then use comments made by your teacher or classmates to improve your work and add it to your portfolio.

Additional Test Practice, pp. S1–S33

TEST PRACTICE CLASSZONE.COM

ALTERNATIVE ASSESSMENT

1. INTERDISCIPLINARY ACTIVITY: **Science**

Reports should
- have a thesis.
- clearly state facts and examples to support major points.
- include illustrations of Civil War military technology.
- have a bibliography.
- use standard grammar, spelling, sentence structure, and punctuation.

2. COOPERATIVE LEARNING ACTIVITY

Newspapers should
- use a journalistic style.
- present information in an unbiased way.
- cover the topic adequately.
- have headlines and present and portray the historical events accurately.
- have a clear and attractive layout.
- use standard grammar, spelling, sentence structure, and punctuation.

3. **PRIMARY SOURCE EXPLORER**

Presentations should
- utilize two or more media.
- clearly demonstrate an understanding of the selected Civil War battle.
- show technical proficiency.

4. HISTORY PORTFOLIO

Revised section or chapter assessment activities should
- address teacher and peer responses to the selected work.
- solve problems present in the first versions of the work.

Critical Thinking Transparency CT51
- Visual Summary

Formal Assessment
- Chapter Test, Forms A, B, and C, pp. 304–305

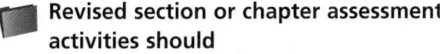

HISTORY SKILLS

Possible Responses

1. INTERPRETING MAPS

Basic Map Elements

a. green

Interpreting the Map

b. Mississippi River

c. because Vicksburg controlled important supply routes across the Mississippi

2. INTERPRETING PRIMARY SOURCES

a. Students might say that war causes such powerful feelings of right and wrong that even brothers are ready to fight against one another for what they believe is right.

b. Missouri was a border state. The state's citizens may have been sympathetic to both sides during the Civil War.

HISTORY WORKSHOP

OBJECTIVE

Students create a cultural artifact, write about a Civil War hero, and role-play activities honoring the hero for his or her actions.

BLOCK SCHEDULING

PROCEDURE

Gather the materials listed in the "Toolbox." Divide the class into groups of two to three students. Then review the steps for identifying a medal recipient, making a medal of honor, writing the letter, and preparing and delivering the speech.

In-Depth Resources: Unit 5
- History Workshop Resources, p. 59

MORE ABOUT . . .

The Medal of Honor

The Medal of Honor is awarded for deeds of bravery that are "beyond the call of duty." That means that if the hero had not performed the deed, he or she would not have been criticized in any way. Strict criteria govern the awarding of a Medal of Honor, including testimony of heroic action by one or more eyewitnesses. Several benefits are attached to the nation's highest military honor, including a monthly stipend for life and the right to burial at Arlington National Cemetery.

Create a Medal of Honor

In 1782, George Washington established the nation's first award to recognize the bravery of American soldiers. It was a purple heart made of cloth and was called the Badge of Military Merit. But the award was not used much after the Revolutionary War. Then, in 1861, Congress created a new award—the Medal of Honor. In the Civil War, 1,520 Union soldiers, including 20 African Americans, received the medal. Today, that medal is the highest United States military award for individual bravery and is commonly referred to as the Congressional Medal of Honor.

ACTIVITY Create a medal of honor for a hero or heroine from either side of the Civil War. Write a letter recommending your hero for the medal. Then read a speech in class as you award your medal to the deserving individual.

TOOLBOX

Each group will need:

- tops of juice cans or cardboard
- aluminum foil
- pieces of ribbon
- safety pins
- glue
- markers
- scissors
- writing paper

STEP BY STEP

1 Form groups. Each group should consist of three or four students. Each group will:

- identify a Civil War hero or heroine
- create a medal
- write a letter explaining why your group considers that person a hero
- award the medal and read a speech in class

2 Research a hero. First, brainstorm characteristics that you think a hero should have. Then, using this chapter, books on the Civil War, or the Internet, select an individual who you think was a hero for either side of the Civil War. Take notes on the actions of the person you selected. The actions should show how that person meets your standards for being a hero.

The Congressional Medal of Honor rewards military personnel who risked their lives, "above and beyond the call of duty." In the Civil War, 1,520 Union soldiers, including 20 African Americans, received the Medal of Honor.

RECOMMENDED RESOURCES

JOURNALS AND BOOKS FOR THE TEACHER

United States of America's Congressional Medal of Honor Recipients and Their Official Citations. Highland House II, Inc., 1994.

deLong, Kent. ***War Heroes: True Stories of Honor Recipients.*** Bergin & Garvey, 1993.

Murphy, Edward. ***Vietnam Medal of Honor Heroes.*** New York: Ballantine Books, 1987.

VIDEOS

Decoration Day. Republic Pictures Home Video. A Hallmark Hall of Fame presentation about a veteran who refuses the Medal of Honor.

Glory: The True Story Continues. Columbia Tristar. Documentary of the 54th Massachusetts.

BOOKS FOR THE STUDENTS

Jacobs, Bruce. ***Heroes of the Army: The Medal of Honor and Its Winners.*** New York: W. W. Norton, 1956.

Doherty, Kiernan. ***Congressional Medal of Honor Recipients.*** Enslow, 1998.

HELP DESK

For related information, see page 502 in Chapter 17.

Researching Your Project

Visit the library to learn more about the history of military awards or go to your local historical museum to examine actual medals.

For more about military awards . . .

RESEARCH LINKS CLASSZONE.COM

Did You Know?

Since the Congressional Medal of Honor was created in 1861, 3,408 persons have received the award. Nineteen persons have received two such awards. Only one woman has received the award.

The Confederate States of America also awarded 43 of its finest men with the Confederate Medal of Honor.

The practice of awarding medals began in Europe during the Middle Ages. Kings realized that giving land to valued knights was too costly, so they gave medals instead.

3 Design your medal. Think about the shape, images, and words that you will use to make your medal of honor. You may want to look at the example from Chapter 17 and in Civil War books. Sketch a design of your medal in pencil.

4 Construct your medal. Using art supplies, construct a medal based on your design. First, construct the medal itself by using a juice can lid or a cardboard pattern. Decorate the medal by using foil and markers. Then add a ribbon and pin.

5 Write a letter. The letter should be addressed to the Congress of the United States of America or the Congress of the Confederate States of America. Your letter should give reasons for recommending your hero based on the person's actions. Carefully recopy your letter after you have made any corrections.

6 Pin up the medal. Create a Medal of Honor board with other groups in your class. Pin up all the medals you have created. Discuss with other groups the standards your group set for calling a person a hero.

REFLECT & ASSESS

- **What requirements did you set for awarding a medal of honor?**
- **What reasons did your letter and speech give for awarding the medal?**
- **What symbols did you use for your medal? Why did you select them?**

WRITE AND SPEAK

Write a Speech As a Civil War military leader, write a speech praising the courage and bravery of the individual who is receiving the medal. Choose another member of your group to act as the recipient of the award. Read your speech to the class as you award the medal to that person.

MORE ABOUT . . .

Congressional Medal of Honor Museums

The Congressional Medal of Honor Museum is located in Mt. Pleasant, South Carolina, on the hangar deck of the U.S.S. *Yorktown.* It is the centerpiece of the Patriot's Point Naval and Maritime Museum. Another museum honoring Medal of Honor winners, the Hall of Heroes, is planned for construction in Pueblo, Colorado.

MORE ABOUT . . .

Dr. Mary Walker (1832–1919)

Dr. Mary Walker is the only woman to receive the Medal of Honor. A surgeon with the Union army during the Civil War, Walker was captured and held prisoner by the Confederates for four months. She was awarded the Medal of Honor for her medical work on the battlefield and in prison camps. After the war, Dr. Walker campaigned for women's suffrage. She also wrote several books about the role of women in society.

REFLECT & ASSESS

1. Ask students to defend their reasons for awarding a Medal of Honor.
2. Have students work with a peer editor who makes suggestions to improve the letter and comments on the validity of the reasons.
3. Have students discuss their symbols and defend their choices.

STANDARDS FOR EVALUATION

HISTORY WORKSHOP

Medals of Honor should
- appear attractive and realistic.
- include symbols that are appropriate.
- show evidence of research.

WRITE AND SPEAK

Letters and speeches should
- state opinions clearly.
- include historic details about the hero's actions.
- present convincing reasons for recommending the hero for a medal.

CHAPTER 18 PLANNING GUIDE

Reconstruction 1865–1877

	CHAPTER OVERVIEW	COPYMASTERS	INTEGRATED TECHNOLOGY
CHAPTER RESOURCES	This chapter focuses on the economic and political effects of Reconstruction in the South, as well as the passage of the 13th, 14th, and 15th Amendments. It also discusses the hardships faced by the newly freed slaves.	**In-Depth Resources: Unit 5** • Tracing Themes: Democratic Ideals, p. 61 • Building Vocabulary, p. 65 **Interdisciplinary Projects,** pp. 103–108	• eEdition Plus Online • EasyPlanner Plus Online • eTest Plus Online • eEdition • Power Presentations • EasyPlanner • Electronic Library of Primary Sources • Test Generator • Reading Study Guide • America's Music
	KEY IDEAS		
SECTION 1 **Rebuilding the Union** **pp. 517–523**	• Southern states enact black codes to limit the freedom of African Americans. • Congress passes the 14th Amendment stating that all people born in the United States are entitled to equal protection under law. • Congress and the president quarrel over Reconstruction.	**In-Depth Resources: Unit 5** • Setting the Stage, p. 60 • Guided Reading, p. 62 • Primary Source, p. 69 • Reteaching Activity, p. 74 **America's History Makers** • Hiram Revels, pp. 71–72 **Why It Matters Now** • The New South, pp. 35–36	**Warm-Up Transparency WT18** **Humanities Transparency HT35** • Political Cartoon: A Carpetbagger Goes South **Geography Transparency GT18** • Southern Military Districts, 1867 **Critical Thinking Transparency CT53** • Cause and Effect: Reconstruction
SECTION 2 **Reconstruction and Daily Life** **pp. 524–528**	• Former slaves seek family members and strive for education. • Lacking land, many African-American and poor white farmers become sharecroppers. • White Southerners form the Ku Klux Klan, which uses violence to support white political power.	**In-Depth Resources: Unit 5** • Setting the Stage, p. 60 • Guided Reading, p. 63 • Geography Application, pp. 67–68 • Primary Source, p. 70 • Literature Selection, pp. 71–73 • Reteaching Activity, p. 75 **America's History Makers** • General Oliver O. Howard, pp. 73–74	**Warm-Up Transparency WT18** **Critical Thinking Transparency CT52** • Setting the Stage classzone.com
SECTION 3 **End of Reconstruction** **pp. 529–533**	• Congress passes the 15th Amendment, giving African-American men the right to vote. • Political scandals and economic depression weaken Grant's presidency. • Reconstruction ends in 1877, leaving the promise of legal equality for African Americans unfulfilled.	**In-Depth Resources: Unit 5** • Setting the Stage, p. 60 • Guided Reading, p. 64 • Skillbuilder Practice: Interpreting Charts, p. 66 • Reteaching Activity, p. 76 **Economics in History** • Understanding the Business Cycle, p. 18 **Outline Map Activities** • Election of 1876, pp. 35–36	**Warm-Up Transparency WT18** **Humanities Transparency HT36** • Parade Celebrating the 15th Amendment **Critical Thinking Transparency CT52** • Setting the Stage **Critical Thinking Transparency CT54** • Visual Summary classzone.com

Pupil's Edition
Copymaster
Overhead Transparency
Audio Library
CD-ROM
Internet

ASSESSMENT OPTIONS

Chapter Assessment, pp. 534–535

Formal Assessment
- Chapter Tests, Forms A, B, and C, pp. 322–333

Test Generator

Online Test Practice

Strategies for Test Preparation

Section Assessment, p. 521

Formal Assessment, Quiz, p. 319

Integrated Assessment Book
- Rubrics, 5.1, 3.6

Test Generator

Test Practice Transparencies, TT64

Section Assessment, p. 528

Formal Assessment, Quiz, p. 320

Integrated Assessment Book
- Rubrics, 3.6, 1.11

Test Generator

Test Practice Transparencies, TT65

Section Assessment, p. 533

Formal Assessment, Quiz, p. 321

Integrated Assessment Book
- Rubrics, 4.1, 4.3

Test Generator

Test Practice Transparencies, TT66

CUSTOMIZING FOR INDIVIDUAL NEEDS

Students Acquiring English/ESL

Reading Study Guide (English and Spanish), pp. 171–178

Access for Students Acquiring English/ESL: Spanish Translations, pp. 117–122

Chapter Summaries on CD (English and Spanish)

Modified Lesson Plans for English Learners

Less Proficient Readers

Reading Study Guide (English and Spanish), pp. 171–178

Chapter Summaries on CD (English and Spanish)

Gifted and Talented Students

In-Depth Resources: Unit 5
- Enrichment Activity, p. 77

America's History Makers
- Hiram Revels, pp. 71–72
- General Oliver O. Howard, pp. 73–74

CROSS-CURRICULAR CONNECTIONS

Culture

Fleischner, Jennifer. ***I Was Born A Slave: The Story of Harriet Jacobs.*** Brookfield, CT: Millbrook, 1997. Based on *Incidents in the Life of a Slave Girl,* this easy-to-read account tells how Jacobs aided former slaves during the Civil War and then became a teacher.

Geography

Savage, Beth L., ed. ***African American Historic Places.*** Washington, D.C.: Preservation Press, 1994. Beautifully illustrated book with information about over 800 historic sites.

Popular Culture

Kalman, Bobbie et al. ***19th Century Clothing (Historic Communities).*** New York: Crabtree Publishing, 1993. What Americans wore, how clothing was made, hairstyles, accessories, and grooming.

Interdisciplinary Projects, pp. 103–108

- Math: Sharecropping Data
- Science: Testing the Soil
- Language Arts: Promoting Literacy
- Art: Reconstruction Era Collage

Primary Sources

Meltzer, Milton. ***The Black Americans: A History in Their Own Words, 1619–1983.*** New York: HarperTrophy, 1987. Letters, speeches, articles, and other primary sources tell a compelling story.

Literature

Fast, Howard. Introduction by Eric Foner. ***Freedom Road (American History through Literature).*** Armonk, NY: M.E. Sharpe, 1995. Re-issue of classic story of Gideon Jackson, a former slave who returns from the Union army to Charleston, South Carolina, and makes his way in the new post war society, becoming a member of Congress.

Nixon, Joan Lowry. ***David's Search.*** New York: Delacorte Press, 1998. This volume in Nixon's saga of the Orphan Train Children sees young David Howard, now living with a Texas family, facing a threat by the KKK to his best friend, an African American and former slave.

Robinet, Harriette Gillem. ***Forty Acres and Maybe a Mule.*** New York: S&S, 1998. Young Pascal joins other former slaves as they search for some land to call their own.

ENRICHMENT ACTIVITIES

Pupil's Edition, pp. 514–535
Interact with History, p. 515
Interdisciplinary Challenge, pp. 522–523

In-Depth Resources: Unit 5
- Geography Application: The Economic Effects of the Civil War, 1860–1880, pp. 67–68
- Primary Source: Report on Freedmen's Bureau, p. 69
- Primary Source: A Letter from Jourdan Anderson, p. 70
- Literature Selection: from *Forty Acres and Maybe a Mule,* pp. 71–73

America's History Makers
- Hiram Revels, pp. 71–72
- General Oliver O. Howard, pp. 73–74

Outline Map Activities
- Election of 1876, pp. 35–36

Why It Matters Now
- The New South, pp. 35–36

BLOCK SCHEDULING — LESSON PLAN OPTIONS (90-MINUTE PERIOD)

DAY 1

Interact with History, p. 515
Class Time 20 minutes

Options for pacing and variety:

- **Role-Playing** Have students imagine they are newly elected African-American members of the House of Representatives representing voters in Southern states during Reconstruction. Have students write short essays describing their thoughts as they watch Congressman Elliott make his speech. **Class Time** 10 minutes

Setting the Stage, p. 516
Class Time 20 minutes

Options for pacing and variety:

- **Time Saver** Assign the "What Do You Know?" and "What Do You Want to Know?" questions for homework. Before students create their "What Do You Want to Know?" questions, have them preview the chapter, looking at headings and illustrations. **Class Time** 10 minutes

Section 1, pp. 517–523
Class Time 50 minutes

Options for pacing and variety:

- **History on Film** Extend students' background knowledge of Reconstruction by having them view *Reconstruction and Segregation,* 1865–1910. Schlessinger Media, 1996. **Class Time** 35 minutes
- **Time Saver** For a homework assignment, have students answer the Critical Thinking question in the Section Assessment. **Class Time** 15 minutes

DAY 2

Interdisciplinary Challenge, pp. 522–523

Options for pacing and variety:

- **Peer Evaluation** Write the standards for evaluating the Arts Challenges that are included in the Teacher's Edition, p. 522, on the chalkboard. As each group presents its model or written proposal of how it would rebuild Richmond, have the other students evaluate the presentations using these guidelines. **Class Time** 30 minutes

Section 2, pp. 524–528
Class Time 45 minutes

Options for pacing and variety:

- **Time Saver** Use the diagram on page 527 to help students understand the cycle of debt and poverty that sharecroppers faced. **Class Time** 10 minutes
- **Internet** Extend students' knowledge of the African-American freedom celebration known as Juneteenth by visiting classzone.com. **Class Time** 20 minutes

Section 3, pp. 529–533
Class Time 45 minutes

Options for pacing and variety:

- **Peer Evaluation** Have students work in pairs to answer the four Reading History questions for the section. **Class Time** 15 minutes

Chapter 18 Assessment, pp. 534–535
Class Time 40 minutes

Options for pacing and variety:

- **Peer Evaluation** Divide the class into three groups to complete the Interdisciplinary Activity on page 535. Ask a third of the class to write a letter about Reconstruction from a member of the old Southern upper class, another third from a newly freed African American, and the remaining third a white Northern carpetbagger. Students should work independently on their letters and then form groups of three to read their letters aloud. **Class Time** 30 minutes
- **Peer Teaching** Within small groups, have students share their completed Reading Strategy charts from page 516, explaining the problems and solutions they identified. **Class Time** 20 minutes

TEACHER-TESTED ACTIVITY Lori Leslie, Cedar Bluff Middle School, Knoxville, Tennessee

DEBATING RECONSTRUCTION

Class Time Two class periods, one for preparation and one for presentation

Task Holding a debate on Reconstruction

Purpose To understand the difficulties the North and the South faced while trying to rebuild the Union

Supplies Needed

- Reference books and Internet sources on the Lincoln/Johnson and the Radical Republican plans for Reconstruction

Activity Divide the class into two groups: those who oppose Radical Reconstruction and those who support it. Each group should choose a speaker and a writer and then create a list of reasons for its position on Radical Reconstruction. For each reason listed, have students brainstorm possible counterarguments their opponents might make. After 20 minutes of preparation, have each speaker give a short statement of his or her position on Reconstruction and then debate the issue.

CHART ANALYSIS: PROBLEMS AND SOLUTIONS OF RECONSTRUCTION

Lincoln's Second Inaugural Address was part of his preparation for the aftermath of the Civil War. His assassination prevented him from implementing his plan. After Lincoln's death, Andrew Johnson became president and developed his own approach to Reconstruction. Students will assist the instructor in building an electronic chart to examine the problems facing the country following the Civil War, efforts to solve those problems, and the success or failure of those efforts.

ACTIVITY OUTLINE

Objective Creating an electronic chart on Reconstruction can help students understand the problems the nation faced following the Civil War.

Task Students will research and analyze the problems of Reconstruction. Then they will combine their analyses into a master chart on Reconstruction.

Class Time Two class periods

DIRECTIONS

1. Ask students to consider the enormity of the problems the nation faced as the war came to an end, including casualties, the destruction of the Southern economy, the poverty of war widows and orphans, the animosity between Northerners and Southerners, and the status of the freed slaves.

2. Allow students time to review Chapter 18, focusing on the problems facing the country after the war. Encourage students to read summaries of the Reconstruction plans of Lincoln and Johnson. These are available on classzone.com.

3. Then, ask students to participate in a 10-minute brainstorming session to list the problems of Reconstruction. First, write several categories on the board, such as: economies, social attitudes, emancipation, and land. As students call out problems, write them under one of the categories.

4. Have students work alone or with a partner to research one of the problems on the board. They will analyze the problem and turn in their analysis to the instructor. Their analysis should include four sections:
   - Problem: a statement of the problem
   - Solution: a description of the solution that was attempted
   - Degree of Success: a brief analysis of whether the solution was successful or not, supported by evidence
   - Other Ideas: ideas that were proposed but not tried, or new ideas that might have worked better

5. When all entries have been received, the class will build a chart, using student entries as data.

6. When the chart is completed, use it as a reference for a classroom discussion about how problems were handled after the war. Ask students:
   - What problems of Reconstruction continue to trouble the United States today?
   - What problems might have been handled differently if Lincoln had not been assassinated?
   - How did politics affect how problems were handled?

CHAPTER 18 OBJECTIVE
The student will describe the political conflict over how to rebuild the South after the Civil War and evaluate the impact of Reconstruction on African Americans and other Southerners.

HISTORY FROM VISUALS

Interpreting the Photograph Ask students what they think freedom was like for the newly freed slaves in the photograph. What problems did these Americans face when the Civil War ended?
Possible Responses Newly freed slaves had to find work, and paid work was scarce in the ruined South. Many newly freed slaves were without the necessities of life—food, clothing, and shelter. Many newly freed slaves wanted to find their families and get an education.

Extension Have students write five questions to ask the people in the photograph about their plans and goals for the future.

CRITICAL THINKING ACTIVITY

Identifying Problems Discuss with students the many different ways the Civil War changed life in the South. Ask students to make two lists of tasks required to rebuild the economy of the South and to rebuild the lives of Southerners. One list should contain items that needed immediate attention. The other list should contain items that could have been dealt with over a period of years.
Class Time 20 minutes

CHAPTER 18

Reconstruction

1865–1877

Section 1 **Rebuilding the Union**
Section 2 **Reconstruction and Daily Life**
Section 3 **End of Reconstruction**

Freed African Americans stand in the ruins of a Southern city after the Civil War.

514

RECOMMENDED RESOURCES

BOOKS FOR THE TEACHER

Campbell, Randolph. ***Grass-Roots Reconstruction in Texas.*** Baton Rouge: Louisiana State U. Pr., 1997. Original research on the economic structures before and after the war.

Foner, Eric. ***Reconstruction: America's Unfinished Revolution, 1863–1877.*** New York: Harper, 1988. Contains new insights into the roles of African Americans in Reconstruction.

Stiles, T. J., compiler and ed. ***In Their Own Words: Robber Barons & Radicals.*** New York: Berkley Pub. Gr., 1997. Varied collection of Reconstruction sources.

SOFTWARE

African-American Experience. CD-ROM. Educational Software Institute.

VIDEOS

Richmond: Historic Sights and Haunts. Spectre Films, 1992. Battlefields, mansions, monuments, and more.

Reconstruction and Segregation, 1870–1910. Schlessinger Media, 1996. From Lincoln's assassination through the Jim Crow laws.

INTERNET

For more about Juneteenth Day, visit . . .
classzone.com

Interact *with* History

In 1874, Congressman Robert B. Elliott of South Carolina made a speech supporting a civil rights bill.
Earlier, former Confederate vice-president Alexander Stephens had spoken against the bill.
Many Southern congressmen ignored Elliott as he spoke.

The Civil War has just ended, and the Southern economy is in ruins. Slavery has been abolished. Northerners and Southerners feel deep anger toward one another. As a member of Congress, you must help rebuild the nation.

What Do You Think?

- What problems would you face in rebuilding the nation?
- How would you ease tensions between North and South?
- How would you help freed African Americans?

How would you rebuild the Union?

USA

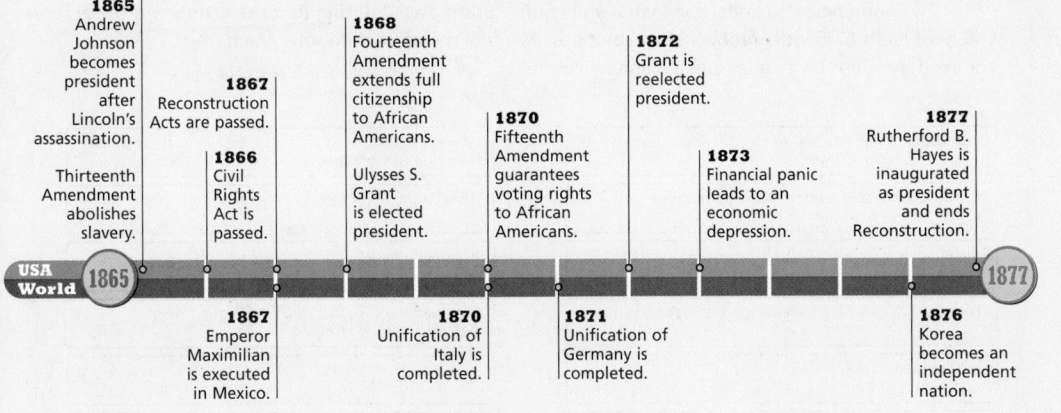

1865 Andrew Johnson becomes president after Lincoln's assassination. Thirteenth Amendment abolishes slavery.

1866 Civil Rights Act is passed.

1867 Reconstruction Acts are passed.

1868 Fourteenth Amendment extends full citizenship to African Americans. Ulysses S. Grant is elected president.

1870 Fifteenth Amendment guarantees voting rights to African Americans.

1872 Grant is reelected president.

1873 Financial panic leads to an economic depression.

1877 Rutherford B. Hayes is inaugurated as president and ends Reconstruction.

1865 — **1877**

World

1867 Emperor Maximilian is executed in Mexico.

1870 Unification of Italy is completed.

1871 Unification of Germany is completed.

1876 Korea becomes an independent nation.

Interact *with* History

OBJECTIVES

- To help students identify divisions in the country over how to begin Reconstruction and rebuild the nation
- To help students describe possible solutions to the problems involved in rebuilding the nation

What Do You Think?

1. Have students consider both the physical damage caused by the Civil War and the fundamental changes in society the war brought to the South.
2. Ask students to suggest issues they believe still divided the nation after the war.
3. Ask students to make inferences about attitudes and prejudices that needed to change after the war.

How would you rebuild the Union?

Point out that differences between Northerners and Southerners were so deep that they led to war. Ask students to consider how those differences could complicate proposals for rebuilding the nation. Discuss how such divisions can be healed.

MAKING PERSONAL CONNECTIONS

Ask students how much they think their opinions about current events and politics are influenced by the region in which they live. Ask them whether they think their opinions might change if they moved to a different region.

TIME LINE DISCUSSION

Point out to students that the time line covers the 12 years following the Civil War, known as Reconstruction. Remind them of the bitter feelings among Northerners and Southerners. Remind them, too, that Lincoln has been assassinated. Point out that big changes are taking place in other parts of the world.

- Ask students to identify the constitutional amendments that resolved the issue of slavery. **Answers** Thirteenth, Fourteenth, and Fifteenth Amendments
- Ask students to identify the year in which federal troops left the South. Then ask students why they think federal troops stayed in the South for ten years. **Answer** 1877; Students may suggest a variety of military or political reasons.
- Ask students to look at the events on the world side of the time line. Ask how the events in Italy and Germany are similar to what has happened in the United States. **Possible Response** Both European nations are now unified, as is the United States.

BEFORE YOU READ

Previewing the Theme:
Democratic Ideals

Remind students that in his Second Inaugural Address (p. 509), President Lincoln had promised "malice toward none and charity for all" and called for Americans to "bind up the nation's wounds." Ask students whether they think that most Americans would be as forgiving as Lincoln toward those who fought for the other side in the Civil War.

Tell students that the United States still faced difficult problems over rebuilding the devastated South, protecting the rights of African Americans, and overcoming the bitterness between Northerners and white Southerners caused by the Civil War.

What Do You Know?

Ask students to define the words *reconstruct* and *reconstruction.* Ask students if something that has been broken can be made exactly the same as it was before. Students may want to know if the North and the South ever did overcome their differences.

In-Depth Resources: Unit 5
- Tracing Themes: Democratic Ideals, p. 61

READ AND TAKE NOTES

Reading Strategy: Identifying and Solving Problems

Tell students that identifying problems and solutions will help them understand the main issues discussed in the chapter. Ask students to create a diagram similar to the one shown to use as they read the chapter. Encourage them to identify the problems and then look for attempts made by the nation to solve them.

In-Depth Resources: Unit 5
- Setting the Stage, p. 60

Critical Thinking Transparency CT52
- Setting the Stage

Chapter 18 SETTING THE STAGE

BEFORE YOU READ

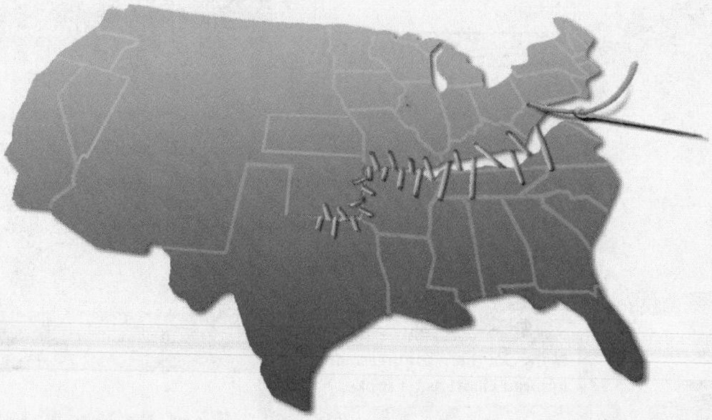

Previewing the Theme

Democratic Ideals After the Union won the war, the nation faced the question of how a democratic government should treat the people who rebelled against it. The Union also faced the question of how to include the millions of freed African Americans in the political process. In this chapter, you will learn how the country struggled to move toward the ideal of equality during Reconstruction.

What Do You Know?

What do you think it means to reconstruct something? What kinds of things did the U.S. government need to reconstruct after the Civil War? Which of these issues do you think was most important?

THINK ABOUT
- what you learned about the Civil War in the last two chapters
- what you've learned about civil rights in the United States from television and movies

What Do You Want to Know?

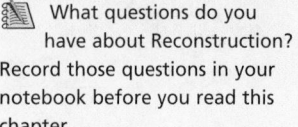

What questions do you have about Reconstruction? Record those questions in your notebook before you read this chapter.

READ AND TAKE NOTES

Reading Strategy: Identifying and Solving Problems Sometimes, to understand what you read, you must learn to identify problems and solutions. As you read through this chapter, use a diagram like the one below to take notes on the problems the United States faced during Reconstruction and the actions the nation took to solve them.

See Skillbuilder Handbook, page R18.

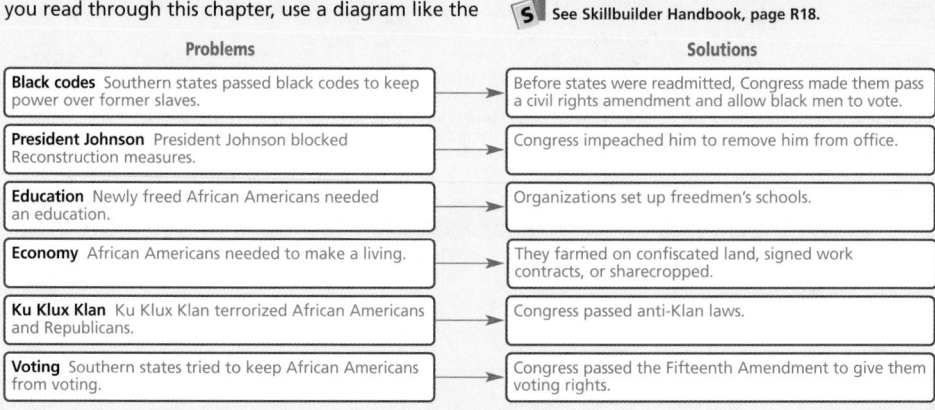

Problems	Solutions
Black codes Southern states passed black codes to keep power over former slaves.	Before states were readmitted, Congress made them pass a civil rights amendment and allow black men to vote.
President Johnson President Johnson blocked Reconstruction measures.	Congress impeached him to remove him from office.
Education Newly freed African Americans needed an education.	Organizations set up freedmen's schools.
Economy African Americans needed to make a living.	They farmed on confiscated land, signed work contracts, or sharecropped.
Ku Klux Klan Ku Klux Klan terrorized African Americans and Republicans.	Congress passed anti-Klan laws.
Voting Southern states tried to keep African Americans from voting.	Congress passed the Fifteenth Amendment to give them voting rights.

TEACHING STRATEGY

READING THE CHAPTER

This is a thematic chapter focusing on the efforts of the United States to rebuild after the Civil War. Encourage students to note positive and negative changes in attitudes among Americans, political efforts made to improve relations between the North and the South, and attempts to guarantee freedom to African Americans.

ALTERNATIVE ASSESSMENT

The Chapter Assessment describes three activities for alternative assessment on page 535. You may wish to have students work on these activities during the course of the chapter and then present them at the end.

1 Rebuilding the Union

TERMS & NAMES
Radical Republicans
Reconstruction
Freedmen's Bureau
Andrew Johnson
black codes
civil rights
Fourteenth Amendment

MAIN IDEA

During Reconstruction, the president and Congress fought over how to rebuild the South.

WHY IT MATTERS NOW

Reconstruction was an important step in the African-American struggle for civil rights.

ONE AMERICAN'S STORY

After the Civil War, Pennsylvania congressman Thaddeus Stevens became a leader of the Radical Republicans. This group of congressmen favored using federal power to create a new order in the South and to promote full citizenship for freed African Americans.

A VOICE FROM THE PAST

The whole fabric of southern society *must* be changed. . . . If the South is ever to be made a safe Republic let her lands be cultivated by the toil of the owners, or the free labor of intelligent citizens.

Thaddeus Stevens, quoted in *The Era of Reconstruction* by Kenneth Stampp

In this section, you will learn how political leaders battled over how to bring the Southern states back into the Union.

Thaddeus Stevens addresses Congress.

1 Reconstruction Begins

After the Civil War ended in 1865, the South faced the challenge of building a new society not based on slavery. The process the federal government used to readmit the Confederate states to the Union is known as **Reconstruction.** Reconstruction lasted from 1865 to 1877.

In his Second Inaugural Address, in March 1865, Lincoln promised to reunify the nation "with malice [harm] toward none, with charity for all." Lincoln's plan included pardoning Confederate officials. It also called for allowing the Confederate states to quickly form new governments and send representatives to Congress.

To assist former slaves, the president established the **Freedmen's Bureau.** This federal agency set up schools and hospitals for African Americans and distributed clothes, food, and fuel throughout the South.

When Lincoln was killed in April 1865, Vice-President **Andrew Johnson** became president. Johnson was a Democrat. The Republicans

SECTION OBJECTIVES

1. To describe why Reconstruction was needed
2. To analyze the conflict that developed over Reconstruction and identify the goals of Radical Republicans
3. To explain the impact of the Civil Rights Act of 1866 and the Fourteenth Amendment
4. To evaluate the effects of Reconstruction

CRITICAL THINKING

Analyzing Causes, p. 518
Making Inferences, p. 519
Finding Main Ideas, p. 520
Drawing Conclusions, p. 521
Evaluating, p. 521

Why It Matters Now
- The New South, pp. 35–36

FOCUS & MOTIVATE

5-MINUTE WARM-UP

Making Inferences These questions focus on the divisions that remained in the country after the Civil War.

1. Read the quote on page 533. Do you think the speaker is a Southerner? Explain.
2. How do you think most white Southerners would respond to the speaker's plans?

Warm-Up Transparency WT18

INSTRUCT

INSTRUCT: OBJECTIVE 1

Reconstruction Begins

- What challenge did the South face after the Civil War?
- What was Reconstruction?
- What were Johnson's Reconstruction policies?

In-Depth Resources: Unit 5
- Guided Reading, p. 62
- Primary Source: Report on the Freedmen's Bureau, p. 69

RECOMMENDED RESOURCES

In-Depth Resources: Unit 5
- Guided Reading, p. 62
- Primary Source, p. 69

Reading Study Guide (Spanish and English), pp. 171–172

America's History Makers
- Hiram Revels, pp. 71–72

Why It Matters Now
- The New South, pp. 35–36

Formal Assessment
- Section Quiz, p. 319

Integrated Assessment
- Rubrics, 5.1, 3.6

Citizenship Today
- Minority Rights, p. 79

Access for Students Acquiring English/ESL
- Guided Reading, p. 117

INTEGRATED TECHNOLOGY

Critical Thinking Trans. CT53
- Cause and Effect: Reconstruction

Humanities Transparency HT35

Geography Transparency GT18

Electronic Teacher Tools

TEST-TAKING RESOURCES

Strategies for Test Preparation

Test Practice Transparencies, TT64

Online Test Practice

AMERICA'S HISTORY MAKERS

Andrew Johnson

Johnson's first career was as a tailor. His wife taught him how to write and do arithmetic, and he was touchy about his humble beginnings. Johnson was serious and intelligent, but he lacked Lincoln's gift of affability. Many people disliked him strongly. Johnson was elected to the U.S. Senate from Tennessee in 1857. Although he was a Democrat and former slaveholder, he was the only Southern senator to remain loyal to the Union. He was selected as Lincoln's running mate in 1864 to increase the appeal of Lincoln's ticket to prowar Democrats.

Possible Response: He may have been sympathetic to Southern slaveholders.

INSTRUCT: OBJECTIVE 2

Rebuilding Brings Conflict

- What policies of new Southern state governments angered Congress?
- How did Congress deal with the Southern states?
- How did the Radical Republicans wish to reorganize the South?

Geography Transparency GT18
- Southern Military Districts, 1867

MORE ABOUT . . .

Confederate Officials

Former Confederate president Jefferson Davis spent two years in prison after the Civil War. On his release, he traveled for two years and then worked in various occupations. He died in 1889, never having taken the oath of allegiance to regain his citizenship. However, Congress restored his citizenship in 1978, nearly a century after his death.

Former Confederate vice-president Alexander Stephens won election to Congress in 1866 but was not seated. He later became a writer and was elected governor of Georgia in 1882. He died in 1883.

AMERICA'S HISTORY MAKERS

ANDREW JOHNSON
1808–1875

Andrew Johnson was a self-educated man whose strong will led to trouble with Congress.

As a former slaveholder from Tennessee, Johnson called for a mild program for bringing the South back into the Union. In particular, he let states decide whether to give voting rights to freed African Americans.

Johnson's policies led to a break with the Radical Republicans in Congress and, finally, to his impeachment trial (see page 521).

Why might Johnson have chosen not to punish the South?

had put him on the ticket in 1864 to help win support in the nation's border states. Johnson was a former slaveholder and, unlike Lincoln, a stubborn, unyielding man.

Johnson believed that Reconstruction was the job of the president, not Congress. His policies were based on Lincoln's goals. He insisted that the new state governments ratify the Thirteenth Amendment, which prohibited slavery. He also insisted that they accept the supreme power of the federal government.

Johnson offered amnesty, or official pardon, to most white Southerners. He promised to return their property. In return, they had to pledge loyalty to the United States. At first, the large plantation owners, top military officers, and ex-Confederate leaders were not included in this offer. But they, too, eventually won amnesty.

Background
Not all Confederate leaders were pardoned. Former Confederate president Jefferson Davis, for example, was imprisoned for two years awaiting trial for treason. But he was never tried.

2 Rebuilding Brings Conflict

As the Southern states rebuilt, they set up new state governments that seemed very much like the old ones. Some states flatly refused to ratify the Thirteenth Amendment. "This is a white man's government," said the governor of South Carolina, "and intended for white men only."

The Southern states passed laws, known as **black codes,** which limited the freedom of former slaves. In Mississippi, for instance, one law said that African Americans had to have written proof of employment. Anyone without such proof could be put to work on a plantation. African Americans were forbidden to meet in unsupervised groups or carry guns. Because of such laws, many people in the North suspected that white Southerners were trying to bring back the "old South."

***Reading* History**
A. Analyzing Causes What was the main reason Southern states passed black codes?
A. Answer They wanted to return former slaves to their low position in society.

When Congress met in December 1865, its members refused to seat representatives from the South. Many of these Southern representatives had been Confederate leaders only months before.

Under the Constitution, Congress has the right to decide whether its members are qualified to hold office. So instead of admitting the Southerners, Congress set up a committee to study conditions in the South and decide whether the Southern states should be represented. By taking such action, Congress let the president know that it planned to play a role in Reconstruction.

Republicans outnumbered Democrats in both houses of Congress. Most Republicans were moderates who believed that the federal government should stay out of the affairs of individuals and the states.

Vocabulary
moderates: people opposed to extreme views

The Radical Republicans, however, wanted the federal government to play an active role in remaking Southern politics and society. Led by Thaddeus Stevens and Massachusetts senator Charles Sumner, the

ACTIVITY OPTIONS

INTERDISCIPLINARY LINK: CIVICS

BLOCK SCHEDULING

POLITICAL CARTOONS

Class Time 45 minutes

Task Creating political cartoons about new Southern governments

Purpose To illustrate the nature of the Southern governments, the people who ran them, and the laws they passed

Supplies Needed
- Art supplies
- Sample political cartoon from a newspaper or magazine

Activity Have students create political cartoons about the Southern governments that formed under President Andrew Johnson's Reconstruction policies. Have students review material in the text about the new governments and decide on a single idea to illustrate before beginning their drawings. Remind students to include a descriptive caption with their cartoon. Individuals depicted in the cartoons should be easily identifiable or labeled.

Radical Republicans pose for a formal portrait. Standing (left to right): James F. Wilson, George S. Boutwell, and John A. Logan. Seated: Benjamin F. Butler, Thaddeus Stevens, Thomas Williams, and John A. Bingham.

group also demanded full and equal citizenship for African Americans. Their aim was to destroy the South's old ruling class and turn the region into a place of small farms, free schools, respect for labor, and political equality for all citizens.

3 The Civil Rights Act

Urged on by the Radicals, Congress passed a bill promoting **civil rights**—those rights granted to all citizens. The Civil Rights Act of 1866 declared that all persons born in the United States (except Native Americans) were citizens. It also stated that all citizens were entitled to equal rights regardless of their race.

Republicans were shocked when President Johnson vetoed the bill. Johnson argued that federal protection of civil rights would lead "towards centralization" of the national government. He also insisted that making African Americans full citizens would "operate against the white race." Congress voted to override Johnson's veto. That is, two-thirds of the House and two-thirds of the Senate voted for the bill after the president's veto, and the bill became law.

The Fourteenth Amendment

Republicans were not satisfied with passing laws that ensured equal rights. They wanted equality to be protected by the Constitution itself. To achieve this goal, Congress proposed the **Fourteenth Amendment** in 1866. It stated that all people born in the United States were citizens and had the same rights. All citizens were to be granted "equal protection of the laws." However, the amendment did not establish black suffrage. Instead, it declared that any state that kept African Americans from voting would lose representatives in Congress. This meant that the Southern states would have less power if they did not grant black men the vote.

*Reading*History

B. Making Inferences How did the Fourteenth Amendment encourage states to give African Americans the vote?

B. Answer It gave the states fewer representatives in Congress if they kept African Americans from voting.

Johnson refused to support the amendment. So did every former Confederate state except Tennessee. This rejection outraged both moderate and Radical Republicans. As a result, the two groups agreed to join forces and passed the Reconstruction Acts of 1867. The passage of these

MORE ABOUT . . .

Thaddeus Stevens

Thaddeus Stevens was a passionate opponent of slavery and supporter of the rights of African Americans. Stevens directed that he be buried among African Americans in a Pennsylvania cemetery after he died. His tombstone carried his own words: "I have chosen this that I might illustrate in my death the principles which I advocated through a long life, Equality of Man before his Creator."

INSTRUCT: OBJECTIVE 3

The Civil Rights Act/
The Fourteenth Amendment

- What were the provisions of the Civil Rights Act of 1866 and the Fourteenth Amendment?
- What was the effect of opposition to civil rights legislation?
- What were the provisions of the Reconstruction Act of 1867?

Citizenship Today
- Minority Rights, p. 79

CRITICAL THINKING ACTIVITY

Comparing Copy the chart below on the board. Ask students to complete it, adding details that explain the differences between Johnson's positions and opinions and those of the Radical Republicans.

	Johnson	Radical Republicans
Role of government in Reconstruction		
Civil Rights Act of 1866		
Fourteenth Amendment		

Class Time 20 minutes

ACTIVITY OPTIONS

MULTIPLE LEARNING STYLES: LINGUISTIC

BLOCK SCHEDULING

"JEOPARDY" QUESTIONS

Class Time One class period

Task Creating questions about Reconstruction immediately after the Civil War

Purpose To synthesize information about the early years of Reconstruction

Supplies Needed
- Index cards

Activity Ask students to write the names of people, events, and concepts on index cards. On the back of each card they should write identifying phrases or definitions for the name or term on the front. Divide the class into teams. Read each definition or phrase. Teams must ask the question for which the phrase or definition is the answer. For example, for "Andrew Johnson," a team might ask, "Who became president after Lincoln?" Students may keep their cards as study aids.

INSTRUCT: OBJECTIVE 4

The New Southern Governments/ Johnson Is Impeached

- What groups controlled the drafting of new state constitutions in the South in 1867?
- What were the effects of the new state constitutions?
- Why was President Johnson impeached? What was the verdict in the impeachment?

Humanities Transparency HT35
- Political Cartoon: A Carpetbagger Goes South

HISTORY through ART

Interpreting the Painting Thomas Waterman Wood (1823–1903) chronicled life in America during a career that spanned the last half of the 1800s. He was fascinated by the growing cultural diversity of the United States, and often included people from a variety of racial and ethnic backgrounds in his paintings. Wood depicted African Americans in a number of his works, as in the one called *To the Polls.* Many of Wood's paintings are exhibited at the T. W. Wood Gallery and Arts Center in Montpelier, Vermont, where he was born.

Possible Responses: hopeful, joyous, serious, nervous, uncertain

MORE ABOUT . . .

Hiram Revels

Revels, a minister and educator, filled the unexpired term of Jefferson Davis in the United States Senate. Opponents tried to block his seating in 1870. They argued that since Revels had only become a citizen with the passage of the Fourteenth Amendment in 1866, he did not meet the nine years of citizenship required by the Constitution. Nevertheless, Revels was seated by a Senate vote of 48 to 8.

America's History Makers
- Hiram Revels, pp. 71–72

acts began a period known as Radical Reconstruction. From this point on, Congress controlled Reconstruction.

One of the Reconstruction Acts of 1867 divided the South into five military districts, each run by an army commander. Members of the ruling class before the war lost their voting rights. The law also stated that before the Southern states could reenter the Union, they would have to do two things:

1. They must approve new state constitutions that gave the vote to all adult men, including African Americans.
2. They must ratify the Fourteenth Amendment.

Background Attempts to secure voting rights for African Americans applied only to men. Women were not allowed to vote until 1919.

4 The New Southern Governments

In 1867, Southern voters chose delegates to draft their new state constitutions. About three-fourths of the delegates were Republicans. Many of the Republicans were poor white farmers. Angry at planters for starting what they called the "rich man's war," these delegates were called scalawags (scoundrels) for going along with Radical Reconstruction.

Another one-fourth of the Republican delegates were known as carpetbaggers—white Northerners who had rushed to the South after the war. Many Southerners accused them, often unfairly, of seeking only to get rich or gain political power.

Background Carpetbaggers were said to have headed south carrying only a cheap suitcase, known as a carpetbag.

African Americans made up the rest of the Republican delegates. Of these, half had been free before the war. Most were ministers, teachers, or skilled workers. About 80 percent of them could read.

HISTORY through ART

His First Vote, an 1868 oil painting by Thomas Waterman Wood, shows a new African-American voter.

How do you think the man felt about voting?

The new constitutions written by these delegates set up public schools and gave the vote to all adult males. By 1870, voters in all the Southern states had approved their new constitutions. As a result, the former Confederate states were let back into the Union and allowed to send representatives to Congress.

During Reconstruction, more than 600 African Americans served in state legislatures throughout the South, and 14 of the new U.S. congressmen from the South were African Americans. Two African Americans served as U.S. senators during this time. One was Hiram Revels of Mississippi, a minister in the African Methodist Episcopal Church. He had recruited African Americans to fight for the Union during the Civil War.

C. Answer Several African Americans were elected to Congress, while hundreds gained seats in state legislatures.

Reading **History**
C. Finding Main Ideas What political gains did African Americans make during Reconstruction?

ACTIVITY OPTIONS

INDIVIDUAL NEEDS: GIFTED AND TALENTED

DEBATING RECONSTRUCTION

Class Time Two class periods

Task Debating the merits of the rival Reconstruction policies

Purpose To analyze rival Reconstruction policies

Supplies Needed
- Reference materials on Reconstruction
- Internet access
- Two podiums, chairs for debaters, desk for moderator

Activity Organize students into two teams, one supporting the Reconstruction policies of President Andrew Johnson and the other supporting the policies of the Radical Republicans. Have students on both teams research specific Reconstruction policies and prepare material for a debate. The teams should debate which policies treated Southern whites and African Americans most fairly and were best for rebuilding the South.

INTERNET ACTIVITY CLASSZONE.COM

Johnson Is Impeached

President Johnson fought against many of Congress's reform efforts during Radical Reconstruction. For instance, he chose people friendly to ex-Confederates to serve as military commanders in the South. The conflict between Johnson and Congress soon brought a showdown.

In 1867, Congress passed the Tenure of Office Act, which prohibited the president from firing government officials without the Senate's approval. In February 1868, Johnson fired his secretary of war, Edwin Stanton, over disagreements about Reconstruction. Three days later, the House of Representatives voted to impeach the president. This means that the House formally accused him of improper conduct while in office. By removing Johnson from office, they hoped to strengthen Congress's role in Reconstruction.

The case moved to the Senate for a trial. After several weeks of testimony, the senators prepared to vote. George Julian, a 20-year congressman from Indiana, recalled the tension in the air.

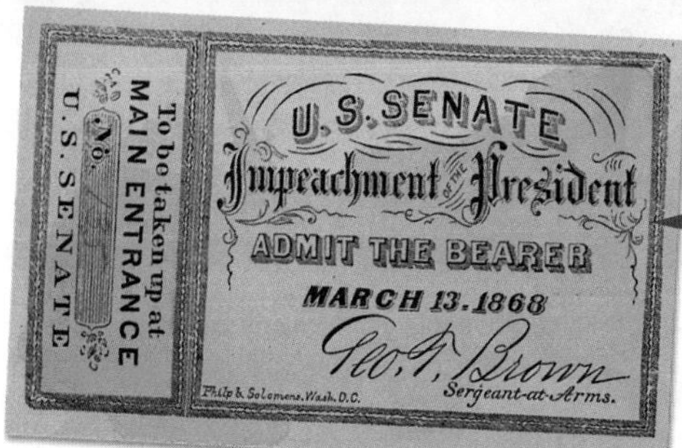

This is a ticket to the 1868 impeachment trial of President Johnson.

***Reading*History**
D. Drawing Conclusions Why did Congress decide to impeach President Johnson?
D. Answer Congress believed that Johnson stood in the way of its Reconstruction plans.

A VOICE FROM THE PAST

The galleries were packed, and an indescribable anxiety was written on every face. Some of the members of the House near me grew pale and sick under the burden of suspense. Such stillness prevailed that the breathing in the galleries could be heard at the announcement of each Senator's voice.

George Julian, quoted in *Grand Inquests*

Vocabulary
acquitted: cleared of a charge

In the end, President Johnson was acquitted by a single vote. But much work remained to be done in rebuilding the South. In the next section, you will learn how African Americans in the South worked to improve their lives.

Section 1 Assessment

1. Terms & Names

Explain the significance of:
- Radical Republicans
- Reconstruction
- Freedmen's Bureau
- Andrew Johnson
- black codes
- civil rights
- Fourteenth Amendment

2. Taking Notes

Use a diagram to review the events that led to Johnson's impeachment.

Event 1 → Event 2 → Event 3 → Event 4

Which event seems most important and why?

3. Main Ideas

a. What was Lincoln's Reconstruction plan?

b. How did white Southerners plan to restore the "old South"?

c. What impact did the Reconstruction Acts of 1867 have on the South?

4. Critical Thinking

Evaluating Do you think the House was justified in impeaching President Johnson? Why or why not?

THINK ABOUT
- the clash over Reconstruction policies
- Congress's motives for impeaching Johnson

ACTIVITY OPTIONS

TECHNOLOGY
SPEECH

Research an African American who served in Congress during Reconstruction. Design his Internet **home page,** or make a **speech** about his accomplishments.

MORE ABOUT . . .

Johnson's Impeachment

The one vote that acquitted Andrew Johnson was cast by Senator Edmund Ross of Kansas, a Republican. Ross voted against his party, along with six other Republicans, and paid the price. Ross was not reelected, and he died in poverty. John F. Kennedy included Ross in his book *Profiles in Courage* and said that Ross "may well have preserved for ourselves and posterity constitutional government in the United States."

MORE ABOUT . . .

Presidential Impeachment

Andrew Johnson's impeachment was the first and only impeachment of a president until 1998, when Congress impeached President Bill Clinton on charges that he had committed perjury in his testimony before a grand jury and obstructed justice in an investigation into his relationship with a former White House intern. As with Johnson in 1868, the Senate failed to convict Clinton in 1999.

ASSESS & RETEACH

Setting the Stage Have students fill in the first two rows of the graphic organizer.

Formal Assessment
- Section Quiz, p. 319

Critical Thinking Transparency CT52
- Setting the Stage

RETEACHING ACTIVITY

Have students create annotated time lines for important events discussed in this section. The time lines should include information about the beginning of Reconstruction, the Civil Rights Act, the Fourteenth Amendment, and the important events and debate over the new order in the South and Johnson's impeachment.

In-Depth Resources: Unit 5
- Reteaching Activity, p. 74

Section 1 Assessment

1. Terms & Names

Radical Republicans, p. 517
Reconstruction, p. 517
Freedmen's Bureau, p. 517
Andrew Johnson, p. 517
black codes, p. 518
civil rights, p. 519
Fourteenth Amendment, p. 519

2. Taking Notes

Event 1: Vetoed Civil Rights Act
Event 2: Did not support Fourteenth Amendment
Event 3: Chose pro-Confederate military commanders
Event 4: Fired Secretary Stanton
Ranking of events will vary.

3. Main Ideas

a. pardoning Confederate officials; allowing Confederate states to form new governments and send officials to Congress **b.** "black codes" or laws to return former slaves to plantation labor **c.** It divided the South into five military districts, and Southern whites lost their voting rights.

4. Critical Thinking

Answers will vary. Be sure students support their opinions.

ACTIVITY OPTIONS

Integrated Assessment
- Rubrics for a Web page, 5.1
- Rubrics for a speech, 3.6

Interdisciplinary CHALLENGE

OBJECTIVE

Students will work cooperatively to solve planning and public safety challenges faced by people in Richmond, Virginia, after the Civil War.

B BLOCK SCHEDULING

PROCEDURE

Gather supplies that students might need, such as posterboard and colored markers. For each challenge, have students form groups of three or four. Ask group members to divide the work among themselves. Then have them choose an option for presenting their solution to each challenge.

ARTS CHALLENGE

Class Time 50 minutes

Suggest that students visit the downtown area of their city or town or one nearby. Tell them to sketch a simple block map for one or two blocks and label the buildings and businesses. As an alternative, encourage students to find library books that have pictures of downtown areas in cities.

POSSIBLE SOLUTIONS

Student models or proposals might include the following:

- A variety of stores and services drawn from the list on page 523
- A system of streets and bridges

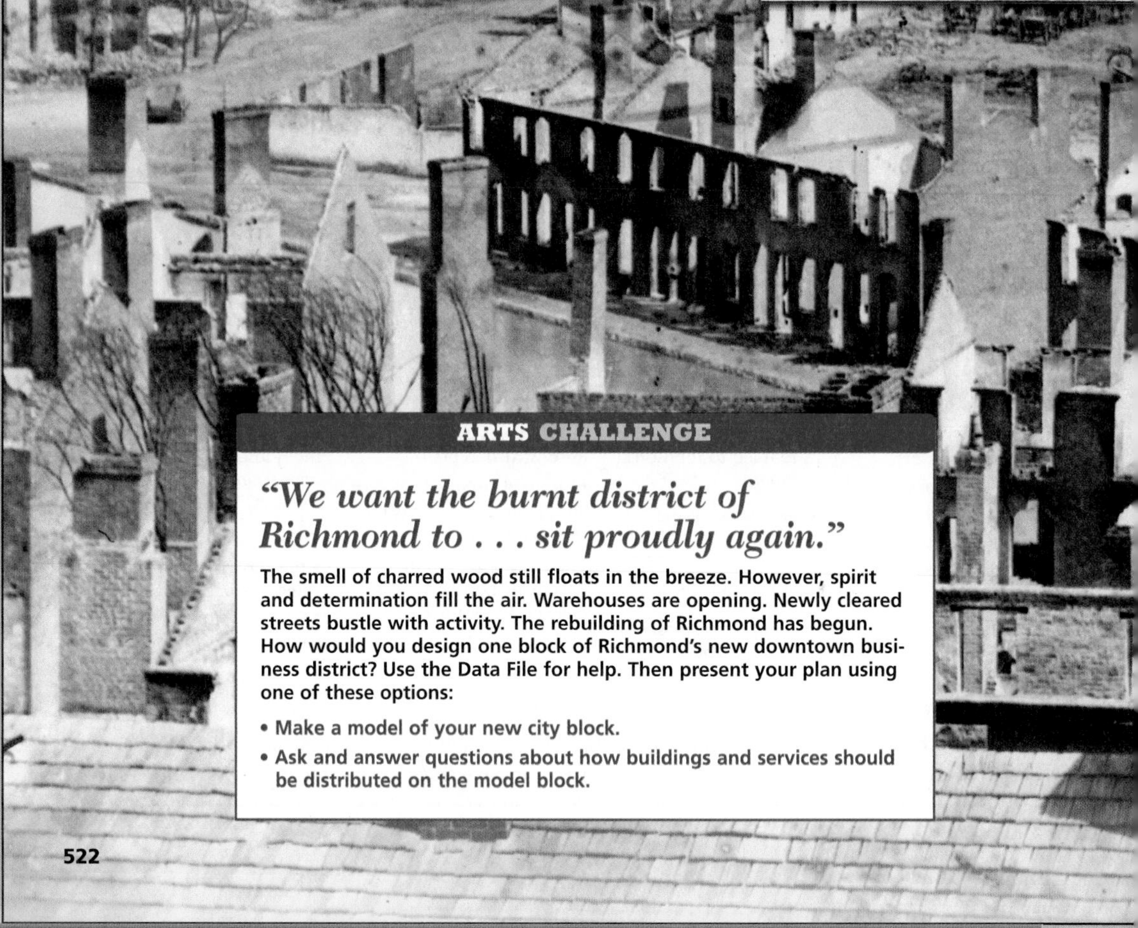

Rebuilding Richmond

You live in Richmond, Virginia, the capital of the Confederacy. It is 1865, and the South faces defeat in the Civil War. On April 2, Confederate officials set fire to supplies in Richmond to prevent the approaching Union army from using them. The fire spreads out of control and destroys downtown Richmond. The next day, Union troops march into the city and take command. You must now help rebuild the city.

COOPERATIVE LEARNING On this page are two challenges you face as a resident of Richmond. Working with a small group, decide how to solve one of these problems. Divide the work among the group members. You will find useful information in the Data File. Be prepared to present your solutions to the class.

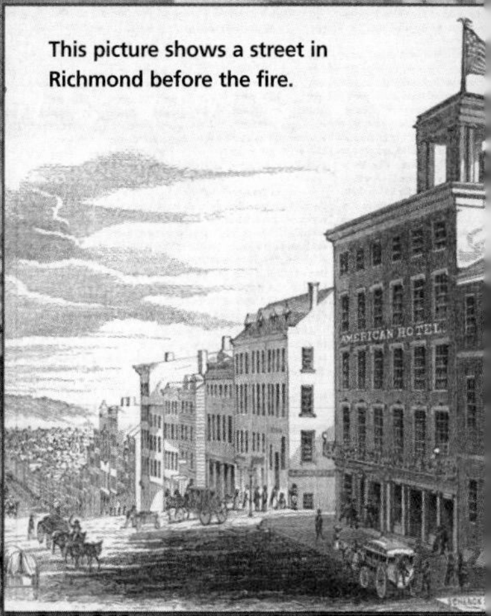

This picture shows a street in Richmond before the fire.

ARTS CHALLENGE

"We want the burnt district of Richmond to . . . sit proudly again."

The smell of charred wood still floats in the breeze. However, spirit and determination fill the air. Warehouses are opening. Newly cleared streets bustle with activity. The rebuilding of Richmond has begun. How would you design one block of Richmond's new downtown business district? Use the Data File for help. Then present your plan using one of these options:

- **Make a model of your new city block.**
- **Ask and answer questions about how buildings and services should be distributed on the model block.**

STANDARDS FOR EVALUATION

ARTS CHALLENGE

Option 1 Models should
- include a variety of buildings and businesses.
- include labels for buildings.

Option 2 Questions and answers should
- consider the range of buildings and services people in a city need.
- consider how a block built on the model would meet those needs.

CIVICS CHALLENGE

Option 1 The town meeting should
- clearly establish the problem.
- provide clear, practical solutions.

Option 2 Emergency laws should
- be practical.
- address specific problems.
- be accompanied by proposals for publicizing them.

HEALTH CHALLENGE

Option 1 Letters should
- include requests for specific food items.
- clearly state the request and describe the need.

Option 2 Flyers should
- state plans clearly.
- be attractive and easy to read.

CIVICS CHALLENGE

"Open robberies have been perpetrated."

Robberies and assaults are commonplace, especially in the burnt area of the downtown. Groups of orphaned children also roam the city, picking pockets to support themselves. Union military police supposedly protect the public. However, soldiers sometimes commit crimes themselves. What would you do to improve public safety? Use the Data File for help. Present your ideas using one of these options:

- Hold a town meeting to explore possible solutions.
- Create a set of emergency laws, with plans for publicizing them.

DATA FILE

THE BURNT DISTRICT

- about $30 million damage
- 20 city blocks destroyed, including 900 buildings

Destroyed Property
all banks, 20 law offices, 24 grocery stores, 36 merchant shops, 2 carriage factories, 2 paper mills, 7 book and stationery stores, 2 train depots, 3 bridges, a church, a machine shop, a tin shop, a pottery factory, several flour mills and printing offices

Surviving Property
capitol and city hall, residential areas, ironworks

EMERGENCY SERVICES

Union Army

- distributes 13,000 food rations
- provides medical help
- guards homes; patrols streets

American Union Commission

- hands out food tickets
- distributes 80,000 pounds of flour; feeds soup to 800 people a day
- provides garden seeds and sells shovels at cost to farmers

REBUILDING

April 1865

- rubble is cleared
- markets sell meat, fish, produce
- hotels and bakeries open
- one bridge is rebuilt

May 1865

- two banks open
- gas and telegraph service is restored
- river opens to steamboat traffic

Summer 1865

- horse-drawn buses operate
- city government is reinstated

Fall 1865

- ironworks reopens
- 100 buildings are now under construction

For more about Reconstruction . . .
RESEARCH LINKS
CLASSZONE.COM

ACTIVITY WRAP-UP

Meet as a group to review your responses to rebuilding Richmond. Pick your most creative solution and present it to the class.

CIVICS CHALLENGE

Class Time 50 minutes

Suggest that students make rules for the town meeting and appoint a moderator. Have them copy the decision-making chart in the Citizenship Handbook, page 269, and use it to help them on needed emergency laws. Remind them that Union troops are the most likely enforcers of the new laws.

POSSIBLE SOLUTIONS

Students' suggestions for town meeting and emergency laws might include the following:

- Appointing city officials
- Curfews to limit the hours people may be on the street
- Supplies of food and clothing for the needy

ALTERNATIVE ACTIVITY

HEALTH CHALLENGE

"there is nothing in the markets but a few small fish"

Thousands of war veterans, former slaves, Yankee traders, and newspaper reporters flood Richmond after the South's defeat. However, 80 percent of the city's food supply is lost in the fire. Now, half of Richmond's residents, including many of these newcomers, rely on charity for food. You want to help the rescue effort. Use the Data File for help. Then present your information using one of these options:

- Write a letter asking for donations, being specific about the kind of food you need.
- Create a flyer describing your plans to distribute food.

ACTIVITY WRAP-UP

To help student groups evaluate the creativity of their models, presentations, and proposals, ask them to make a grid with criteria like the one shown. Then have them rate each solution on a scale from 1 to 5.

• Practicality	1	2	3	4	5
• Effectiveness	1	2	3	4	5
• Creativity	1	2	3	4	5

SECTION OBJECTIVES

1. To describe the responses of African Americans to freedom
2. To trace the establishment of African-American schools
3. To evaluate the impact of land reform, sharecropping, and the contract system
4. To describe the development of the Ku Klux Klan

CRITICAL THINKING

Analyzing Causes, pp. 525, 528
Finding Main Ideas, pp. 525, 528
Analyzing Points of View, p. 526
Recognizing Effects, p. 527

FOCUS & MOTIVATE

5-MINUTE WARM-UP

Making Inferences These questions focus on changes in the lives of African Americans in the South.

1. Look at the "America's Heritage" feature and photograph on page 525. Why do you think building schools was a priority for newly freed African Americans?
2. What other needs do you think African Americans had after slavery ended?

Warm-Up Transparency WT18

INSTRUCT

INSTRUCT: OBJECTIVE 1
Responding to Freedom

- Why did many newly freed African Americans leave plantations?
- How did freedom allow African Americans to strengthen family ties?

In-Depth Resources: Unit 5
- Guided Reading, p. 63
- Building Vocabulary, p. 65

Reading Study Guide (Spanish and English), pp. 173–174

2 Reconstruction and Daily Life

TERMS & NAMES
freedmen's school
sharecropping
Ku Klux Klan
lynch

MAIN IDEA
As the South rebuilt, millions of newly freed African Americans worked to improve their lives.

WHY IT MATTERS NOW
Many important African-American institutions, including colleges, began during Reconstruction.

ONE AMERICAN'S STORY

One day, as the Civil War came to a close, two enslaved women named Mill and Jule saw a fleet of Union gunboats coming up the Mississippi River. Yankee soldiers came ashore and offered them and other slaves passage aboard their boats. On that day, Mill and Jule left the plantation where they had toiled for so long.

A VOICE FROM THE PAST

An' we all got on the boat in a hurry . . . we all give three times three cheers for the gunboat boys, and three times three cheers for big Yankee [soldiers], an' three times three cheers for gov'ment; an' I tell you every one of us, big and little, cheered loud and long and strong, an' made the old river just ring ag'in.

Mill and Jule, quoted in *We Are Your Sisters*

Freed people and a federal soldier pose on a South Carolina plantation.

The Union's victory in the Civil War spelled the end of slavery in America and a new beginning for the nation's millions of newly freed African Americans. In this section, you will learn about the gains and setbacks of former slaves during Reconstruction.

1 Responding to Freedom

African Americans' first reaction to freedom was to leave the plantations. No longer needing passes to travel, they journeyed throughout the region. "Right off colored folks started on the move," recalled one freedman. "They seemed to want to get closer to freedom, so they'd know what it was—like it was a place or a city." Some former slaves returned to the places where they were born. Others went looking for more economic opportunity. Still others traveled just because they could.

African Americans also traveled in search of family members separated from them during slavery. One man walked 600 miles from Georgia to North Carolina to find his family. To locate relatives, people placed advertisements in newspapers. The Freedmen's Bureau helped many families reunite. A Union officer wrote in 1865, "Men are taking

RECOMMENDED RESOURCES

In-Depth Resources: Unit 5
- Guided Reading, p. 63
- Building Vocabulary, p. 65
- Geography Application: The Economic Effects of the Civil War, 1860–1880, pp. 67–68
- Primary Source, p. 70
- Literature Selection, pp. 71–73

Reading Study Guide (Spanish and English), pp. 173–174

America's History Makers
- General Oliver O. Howard, pp. 73–74

Formal Assessment
- Section Quiz, p. 320

Integrated Assessment
- Rubrics, 3.6, 1.11

Access for Students Acquiring English/ESL
- Guided Reading, p. 118
- Geography Application, pp. 121–122

INTEGRATED TECHNOLOGY

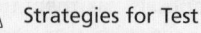

Electronic Teacher Tools

classzone.com

TEST-TAKING RESOURCES

Strategies for Test Preparation

Test Practice Transparencies, TT65

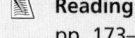

Online Test Practice

Reading **History**

A. Analyzing Causes For what reasons did former slaves move?

A. Answer They moved to find economic opportunity, to locate family members, and merely to experience the freedom of traveling.

their wives and children, families which had been for a long time broken up are united and oh! such happiness."

Freedom allowed African Americans to strengthen their family ties. Former slaves could marry legally. They could raise families without fearing that their children might be sold. Many families adopted children of dead relatives and friends to keep family ties strong.

2 Starting Schools

With freedom, African Americans no longer had to work for an owner's benefit. They could now work to provide for their families. To reach their goal of economic independence, however, most had to learn to read and write. As a result, children and adults flocked to **freedmen's schools** set up to educate newly freed African Americans. Such schools were started by the Freedmen's Bureau, Northern missionary groups, and African-American organizations. Freed people in cities held classes in warehouses, billiard rooms, and former slave markets. In rural areas, classes were held in churches and houses. Children who went to school often taught their parents to read at home.

Reading **History**

B. Finding Main Ideas Why did freed people desire an education?

B. Answer They saw it as a key to economic independence.

In the years after the war, African-American groups raised more than $1 million for education. However, the federal government and private groups in the North paid most of the cost of building schools and hiring teachers. Between 1865 and 1870, the Freedmen's Bureau spent $5 million for this purpose.

Background
Most African Americans were illiterate because teaching slaves to read and write had been illegal.

More than 150,000 African-American students were attending 3,000 schools by 1869. About 10 percent of the South's African-American adults could read. A number of them became teachers. Northern teachers, black and white, also went South to teach freed people. Many white Southerners, however, worked against these teachers' efforts. White racists even killed teachers and burned freedmen's schools in some parts of the South. Despite these setbacks, African Americans kept working toward an education.

America's HERITAGE

BLACK COLLEGES
Some of today's African-American colleges and universities date back to Reconstruction. The Freedmen's Bureau and other societies raised funds to build many of the schools. Howard University, shown in this photograph, opened in 1867. It was named for General Oliver Otis Howard, head of the Freedmen's Bureau. During Reconstruction, these colleges offered courses ranging from basic reading and writing to medicine and law. They also trained much-needed teachers.

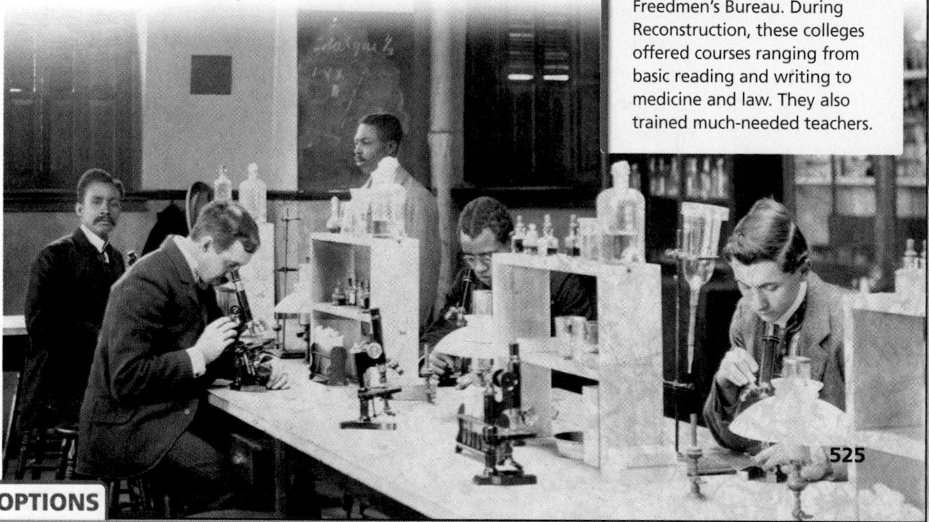

525

MORE ABOUT . . .

Responding to Freedom
Before emancipation, Southern African Americans usually worshiped in separate sections of white churches or held services of their own in secret. Soon after emancipation, African Americans founded their own independent churches, often branches of the Baptist and Methodist churches, throughout the South. Ministers of African-American churches were expected to be community leaders and held great status.

INSTRUCT: OBJECTIVE 2

Starting Schools

- Why was education an important goal for African Americans?
- Who aided and who opposed education for African Americans in the South?

America's HERITAGE

Black Colleges
The first institution of higher education founded for African Americans was Lincoln University in Chester County, Pennsylvania. The first permanent building for African-American education in the South is Jubilee Hall of Fisk University in Nashville, Tennessee. It was paid for by the profits of the Jubilee Singers, a group of student musicians who introduced the spiritual as an art form to audiences around the world.

America's History Makers
- General Oliver O. Howard, pp. 73–74

ACTIVITY OPTIONS

MULTIPLE LEARNING STYLES: INTRAPERSONAL

BLOCK SCHEDULING

A LETTER ABOUT FREEDOM

Class Time 30 minutes

Task Writing a letter from an African American in the South about life after the Civil War

Purpose To apply information about ways the lives of African Americans changed after the war

Supplies Needed
- Writing paper

Activity Have students write a letter from an African American in one part of the South to a friend or relative in another state. Letters should mention emancipation and one or more of the following topics: efforts to locate family members, freedmen's schools, and plans for the future. Have students either read their letters aloud to the class or post them on the bulletin board.

In-Depth Resources: Unit 5
- Primary Source: A Letter to Colonel P. H. Anderson, p. 70

INSTRUCT: OBJECTIVE 3

40 Acres and a Mule/The Contract System/ Sharecropping and Debt

- Why did many Americans want land reform in the South? What happened to proposals for land reform?
- How did the contract system and sharecropping operate?
- What were the drawbacks of the contract system and sharecropping?
- How did reliance on cotton production contribute to poverty in the Deep South?

In-Depth Resources: Unit 5
- Geography Application: The Economic Effects of the Civil War, 1860–1880, pp. 67–68
- Literature Selection: from *Forty Acres and Maybe a Mule* by Harriette Gillem, p. 71

MORE ABOUT . . .

Land in South Carolina

The former owners of plantations on the South Carolina sea islands fled during the war, while their slaves stayed behind. After the war, these former slaves hoped to begin farming on small plots of land. However, when federal agents sold the plantations for back taxes, the land was divided into large and expensive tracts more suitable for growing cotton than for family farms. Investors from the North bought 90 percent of the close to 17,000 acres sold. By pooling their money, African Americans managed to purchase about 2,000 acres.

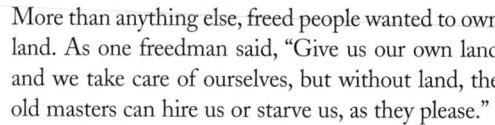

African–American families hoped to own land but were often disappointed.

3 40 Acres and a Mule

More than anything else, freed people wanted to own land. As one freedman said, "Give us our own land and we take care of ourselves, but without land, the old masters can hire us or starve us, as they please."

As the Civil War ended, General William T. Sherman suggested that abandoned land in coastal South Carolina be split into 40-acre parcels and given to freedmen. The rumor then spread that all freedmen would get 40 acres and a mule. Most African Americans thought they deserved at least that much. In the end, however, most freedmen never received land. Those who did often had to return it to its former owners after the owners were pardoned by President Johnson. One freedman, Bayley Wyat, protested.

A VOICE FROM THE PAST

Our wives, our children, our husbands, [have] been sold over and over again to purchase the lands we now [locate] upon; for that reason we have a divine right to the land. . . . And then didn't we clear the land, and raise the crops of corn, of cotton, of tobacco, of rice, of sugar, of everything.

Bayley Wyat, quoted in *Reconstruction: America's Unfinished Revolution*

C. Possible Responses Land would keep them from depending on their former owners; they deserved the land for having worked on it for so long without pay.

Reading **History**

C. Analyzing Points of View What were some arguments in favor of giving land to freed people?

Radical Republican leaders Thaddeus Stevens and Charles Sumner pushed to make land reform part of the Reconstruction Acts of 1867. Stevens proposed a plan to Congress that would have taken land from plantation owners and given it to freed people.

Many moderate Republicans and even some Radicals were against the plan. They believed that new civil and voting rights were enough to give African Americans a better life.

Supporters of the plan argued that civil rights meant little without economic independence. Land could provide that independence, they claimed. However, Congress did not pass the land-reform plan.

The Contract System

Without their own property, many African Americans returned to work on plantations. They returned not as slaves but as wage earners. They and the planters both had trouble getting used to this new relationship. "It seems humiliating to be compelled to bargain and haggle with our own servants about wages," wrote the daughter of a Georgia plantation owner. For their part, many freed workers assumed that wages were extra. They thought that the planters still had to house and feed them.

After the Civil War, planters desperately needed workers to raise cotton, still the South's main cash crop. African Americans reacted to this demand for labor by choosing the best contract offers. The contract system was far better than slavery. African Americans could decide whom to work for, and planters could not abuse them or split up families.

Background Civil War deaths and the departure of slaves from plantations created a labor shortage in the South.

The contract system still had drawbacks, however. Even the best contracts paid very low wages. Workers often could not leave the plantations

ACTIVITY OPTIONS

INTERDISCIPLINARY LINK: LANGUAGE ARTS | **BLOCK SCHEDULING**

A DIALOGUE DURING RECONSTRUCTION

Class Time 30 minutes

Task Writing a dialogue

Purpose To understand the options available to African Americans in the South after the Civil War

Supplies Needed
- Reference materials about Reconstruction

Activity Have students work in pairs to write a dialogue between two African Americans after the Civil War. The dialogue should deal with how the two characters will support themselves. It should mention any skills the characters may possess, any money available to them, where they would like to settle, and where they most likely will go. Have the pairs read their dialogues to the class, then make generalizations about the options available to African Americans after the Civil War.

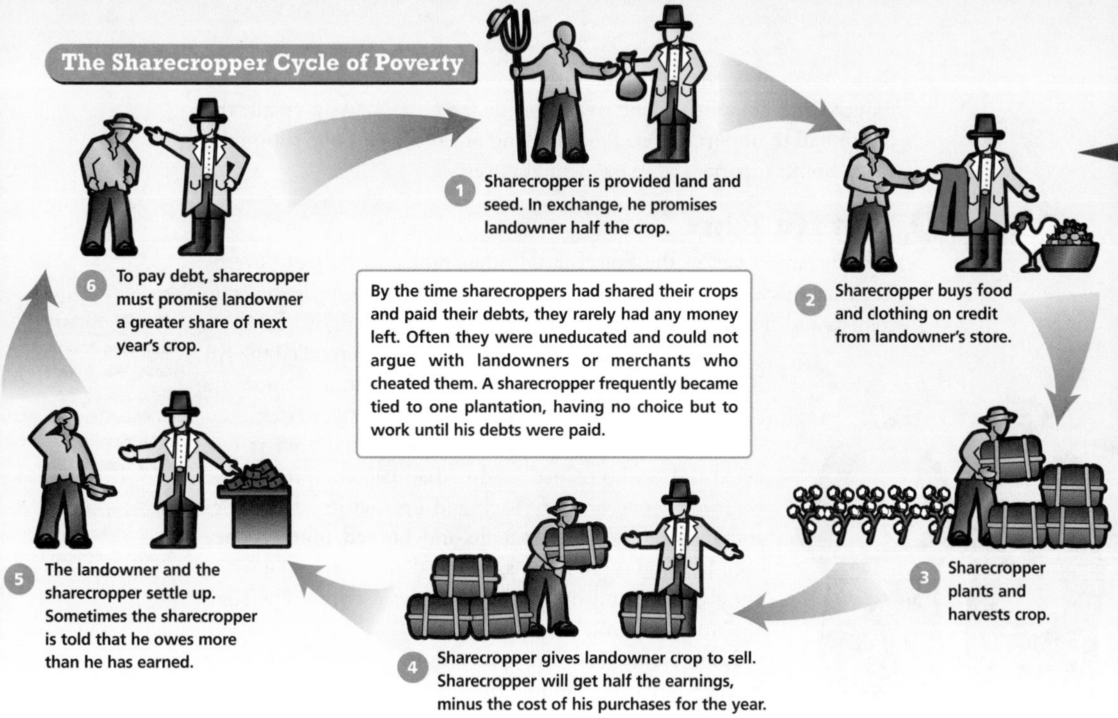

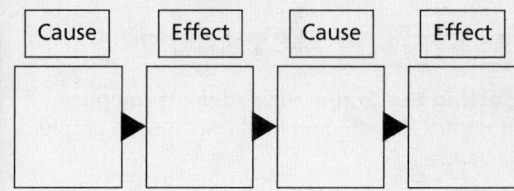

without permission. Many owners cheated workers out of wages and other benefits. Worse yet, laws punished workers for breaking their contracts, even if the plantation owners were abusing or cheating them. These drawbacks made many African Americans turn to sharecropping.

The Sharecropper Cycle of Poverty
1 Sharecropper is provided land and seed. In exchange, he promises landowner half the crop.
2 Sharecropper buys food and clothing on credit from landowner's store.
3 Sharecropper plants and harvests crop.
4 Sharecropper gives landowner crop to sell. Sharecropper will get half the earnings, minus the cost of his purchases for the year.
5 The landowner and the sharecropper settle up. Sometimes the sharecropper is told that he owes more than he has earned.
6 To pay debt, sharecropper must promise landowner a greater share of next year's crop.
By the time sharecroppers had shared their crops and paid their debts, they rarely had any money left. Often they were uneducated and could not argue with landowners or merchants who cheated them. A sharecropper frequently became tied to one plantation, having no choice but to work until his debts were paid.

Sharecropping and Debt

Under the **sharecropping** system, a worker rented a plot of land to farm. The landowner provided the tools, seed, and housing. When harvest time came, the sharecropper gave the landowner a share of the crop. This system gave families without land a place to farm and gave landowners cheap labor.

But problems soon arose with the sharecropping system. One cause of these problems was that farmers and landowners had opposite goals. Farmers wanted to grow food to feed their families, but landowners forced them to grow cash crops, such as cotton. As a result, farmers had to buy food from the local store—which was usually owned by the landlord. Most farmers did not have the money to pay for goods. As a result, many were caught in a cycle of debt, as shown in the diagram above. Often farmers had to use one year's harvest to pay the previous year's bills.

White farmers also became sharecroppers. Many had lost their land in the war. Others had lost it to taxes. By 1880, one-third of the white farmers in the Deep South worked someone else's land.

No matter who worked the plantations, much of what they grew was cotton. After the war, the value of cotton dropped. Southern planters responded by trying to produce more of the cash crop—a move that

Reading **History**

D. Recognizing Effects What were some problems with the sharecropping system?

D. Possible Responses Farmers could not feed themselves under it and were caught in a cycle of debt.

HISTORY FROM VISUALS

Reading the Diagram Ask students how they think this cycle worked to the advantage of plantation owners. Then ask students to explain what happens in the sharecropper cycle of poverty when the crop yield is very low. **Possible Answers** Owners could rely on farmers who were tied to the plantation. Also, owners could shift the cost of supplies to the sharecroppers. Farmers became even poorer.

Extension Ask students to think of ways the sharecroppers might have broken the cycle.

CRITICAL THINKING ACTIVITY

Analyzing Causes and Recognizing Effects
Help students create a cause-and-effect chart on the board to analyze the ways reliance on cotton farming contributed to longtime poverty in the rural South.

Class Time 15 minutes

Cause	Effect	Cause	Effect

ACTIVITY OPTIONS

INDIVIDUAL NEEDS

LESS PROFICIENT READERS

Comparing and Contrasting To help students understand the differences between the contract system and sharecropping, encourage them to look at the benefits and the drawbacks of each system as they read. You might want to guide students in creating a chart such as the one shown.

	Contract System	Sharecropping System
Benefits	Earn wages for work Decide who to work for Families stay together	
Drawbacks	Low wages Can't leave without permission Often cheated, abused by owners	

INSTRUCT: OBJECTIVE 4

The Ku Klux Klan

- What were the goals and tactics of the Ku Klux Klan?
- Why was the Klan successful?
- How did the actions of the Klan benefit the Democratic Party?

MORE ABOUT . . .

The Ku Klux Klan

The Ku Klux Klan was founded at Pulaski, Tennessee, in 1866. Its first leader, called the "Grand Wizard," was Nathan Bedford Forrest, who had been a Confederate general.

Historians believe *klux* is derived from a Greek word—*kyklos*—that means "circle" or "band." The *Ku* and *Klan* apparently were added for the alliteration.

ASSESS & RETEACH

Setting the Stage Have students complete the third, fourth, and fifth rows on the graphic organizer.

Formal Assessment
- Section Quiz, p. 320

RETEACHING ACTIVITY

Copy the graphic organizer below on the board. Have students complete the web with details from the chapter.

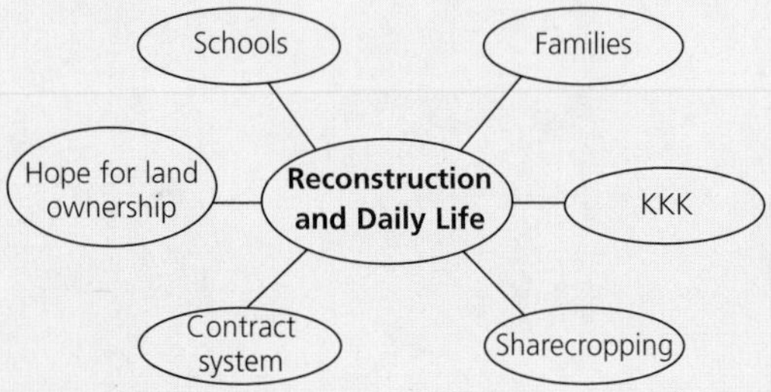

In-Depth Resources: Unit 5
- Reteaching Activity, p. 75

drove down prices even further. Growing cotton exhausted the soil and reduced the amount of land available for food crops. As a result, the South had to import half its food. Relying on cotton was one reason the Deep South experienced years of rural poverty.

4 The Ku Klux Klan

African Americans in the South faced other problems besides poverty. They also faced violent racism. Many planters and former Confederate soldiers did not want African Americans to have more rights. In 1866, such feelings spurred the rise of a secret group called the **Ku Klux Klan.** The Klan's goals were to restore Democratic control of the South and keep former slaves powerless.

The Klan attacked African Americans. Often it targeted those who owned land or had become prosperous. Klansmen rode on horseback and dressed in white robes and hoods. They beat people and burned homes. They even **lynched** some victims, killing them on the spot without a trial as punishment for a supposed crime. The Klan also attacked white Republicans.

Klan victims had little protection. Military authorities in the South often ignored the violence. President Johnson had appointed most of these authorities, and they were against Reconstruction.

The Klan's terrorism served the Democratic Party. As gun-toting Klansmen kept Republicans away from the polls, the Democrats increased their power.

In the next section you will see how planters took back control of the South. You also will learn how they blocked African Americans' attempts to win more rights.

These Ku Klux Klan members were arrested after an 1868 riot in Alabama.

*Reading***History**

E. Finding Main Ideas What were the goals of the Ku Klux Klan?

E. Answer Its goals were to restore Democratic control in the South and keep African Americans from gaining power.

Section 2 Assessment

1. Terms & Names

Explain the significance of:
- freedmen's school
- sharecropping
- Ku Klux Klan
- lynch

2. Taking Notes

Use a cluster diagram like the one below to review details about sharecropping.

For farmers, what were the advantages and disadvantages of sharecropping?

3. Main Ideas

a. How did freedom help strengthen African-American families?

b. How were African Americans educated during Reconstruction?

c. What were the main reasons African Americans wanted their own land?

4. Critical Thinking

Analyzing Causes
Despite greater civil rights, why did African Americans still face difficulty in improving their lives?

THINK ABOUT
- the defeat of the land-reform bill
- the Ku Klux Klan's rise
- the attitude of military authorities in the South

ACTIVITY OPTIONS

SPEECH
ART

Make a **speech** to President Johnson or design a **mural** explaining why land should be given to newly freed African Americans.

Section 2 Assessment

1. Terms & Names

freedmen's school, p. 525
sharecropping, p. 527
Ku Klux Klan, p. 528
lynch, p. 528

2. Taking Notes

family; rent land; tools, seed, housing provided; keep share of crops. Advantages: obtained a plot of land; both the landowner and sharecropper received a share of the crop at harvest time; Disadvantages: forced to grow cash crops, such as cotton; often had to buy their food from a store; got caught in a never-ending cycle of debt

3. Main Ideas

a. Freedmen could marry legally. They could try to locate lost family members. **b.** in freedmen's schools; classes were held in cities and in rural areas **c.** They believed it was their right to own land and wanted to become economically independent and take care of their families.

4. Critical Thinking

because they were unable to own their own land; were afraid to assert their rights for fear of attack by the Ku Klux Klan

ACTIVITY OPTIONS

Integrated Assessment
- Rubrics for a speech, 3.6
- Rubrics for a mural, 1.11

③ End of Reconstruction

TERMS & NAMES
Fifteenth Amendment
Panic of 1873
Compromise of 1877

MAIN IDEA	WHY IT MATTERS NOW
As white Southerners regained power, Reconstruction ended, as did black advances toward equality.	Reforms made during Reconstruction made later civil rights gains possible.

ONE AMERICAN'S STORY

Robert B. Elliott was a U.S. congressman from South Carolina during Reconstruction. In 1874, he made a stirring speech supporting a civil rights bill that would outlaw racial discrimination in public services. (See Interact with History, page 515.)

A VOICE FROM THE PAST

The passage of this bill will determine the civil status, not only of the negro but of any other class of citizens who may feel themselves discriminated against. It will form the capstone of that temple of liberty begun on this continent.

Robert B. Elliott, quoted in *The Glorious Failure*

Robert B. Elliott lost his political office when Reconstruction ended.

Elliott was elected South Carolina's attorney general in 1876. He began his term in 1877, just as Reconstruction was ending. That year, federal troops left the South. White Southerners took back control of the region. Quickly, they forced African Americans, including Elliott, out of office.

In this section, you will learn about the events that ended Reconstruction. You will also see how Reconstruction's end meant setbacks in the fight for civil rights and equality.

❶ The Election of Grant

The Republican Party seemed stronger than ever in 1868. That year, its candidate, General Ulysses S. Grant, won the presidency. During the campaign, the Democrats attacked the Republicans' Reconstruction policies. They blamed the party for granting rights to African Americans.

On Election Day, however, the Republicans won. Grant received 214 electoral votes. His Democratic opponent received only 80. The popular count was much closer. Grant had a majority of only 306,000 votes.

Grant would not have had such a majority without the freedmen's vote. Despite attacks by the Ku Klux Klan, about 500,000 African Americans voted in the South. Most cast their ballots for Grant.

SECTION OBJECTIVES

1. To evaluate the impact of Grant's election and the passage of the Fifteenth Amendment
2. To analyze Grant's administration
3. To explain events that led to the end of Reconstruction
4. To analyze the legacy of Reconstruction

SKILLBUILDER
Interpreting Charts, p. 533

CRITICAL THINKING
Comparing, p. 530
Making Inferences, p. 531
Recognizing Effects, pp. 531, 532
Summarizing, p. 532
Drawing Conclusions, p. 533

FOCUS & MOTIVATE

5-MINUTE WARM-UP

Making Inferences These questions focus on the end of Reconstruction.

1. Look at the illustrations on pages 530 and 532. How do these images of African-American life differ?
2. What inferences can you make about the end of Reconstruction from these illustrations?

Warm-Up Transparency WT18

INSTRUCT

INSTRUCT: OBJECTIVE ❶

The Election of Grant/
The Fifteenth Amendment

- How did Grant's victory in 1868 highlight the role of free African-American voters?
- How did the Fifteenth Amendment protect the rights of African Americans?
- Why did some women protest the passage of the Fifteenth Amendment?

In-Depth Resources: Unit 5
- Guided Reading, p. 64

RECOMMENDED RESOURCES

In-Depth Resources: Unit 5
- Guided Reading, p. 64
- Building Vocabulary, p. 65
- Skillbuilder Practice, p. 66

Reading Study Guide (Spanish and English), pp. 175–176

Economics in History
- Understanding the Business Cycle, p. 18

Outline Map Activities
- Election of 1876, pp. 35–36

Formal Assessment
- Section Quiz, p. 321

Integrated Assessment
- Rubrics, 4.1, 4.3

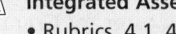

Access for Students Acquiring English/ESL, pp. 119, 120

INTEGRATED TECHNOLOGY

Humanities Transparency HT36
- Parade Celebrating the 15th Amendment

Electronic Teacher Tools

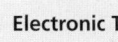

classzone.com

TEST-TAKING RESOURCES

Strategies for Test Preparation

Test Practice Transparencies, TT66

Online Test Practice

Now and then

African Americans in Congress

The increase in the number of African Americans in Congress has not been steady. Only four African Americans held seats in the House from 1901 to 1955. In 1969, the African-American members of the House of Representatives began to organize and formed an organization that, in 1971, became known as the Congressional Black Caucus. This group focuses primarily on issues of particular importance to African Americans. It has at times wielded considerable influence in the formation of policies and legislation.

Humanities Transparency HT36
- Parade Celebrating the 15th Amendment

INSTRUCT: OBJECTIVE 2

Grant Fights the Klan/
Scandal and Panic Weaken Republicans

- How did President Grant and Congress challenge the power of the Ku Klux Klan?
- How did scandals weaken Grant's administration and support for the Republican Party?
- How did economic problems hurt the Republican Party?

MORE ABOUT . . .

The Klan Today

Ku Klux Klan movements have swept the country periodically since the 1870s. A Ku Klux Klan movement rose again in the early 1900s. More than 3 million members made the KKK a powerful political force in a number of states in the Midwest and South. The organization faded in the late 1920s and 1930s. Following World War II, the Klan revived again, especially as the civil rights movement gained momentum. In the 1970s, its membership tripled to around 10,000. Since then, however, it has declined, and when it holds rallies, opponents and spectators frequently outnumber Klan members.

Now and then

AFRICAN AMERICANS IN CONGRESS

Between 1870 and 1877, 16 African Americans served in Congress. Seven are shown in the picture below. Two were senators: Hiram R. Revels and Blanche K. Bruce, both of whom were from Mississippi.

In 1999, there were 38 African Americans in Congress. The longest-serving member was John Conyers, a representative from Michigan elected in 1964. Only two African-American senators were elected in the 20th century. Massachusetts senator Edward W. Brooke served from 1967 to 1979. Illinois senator Carol Moseley-Braun served from 1993 to 1999.

The Fifteenth Amendment

After Grant's victory, Radical Republicans worried that the Southern states might try to keep African Americans from voting in future elections. To prevent this, Radical leaders proposed a new constitutional amendment.

The **Fifteenth Amendment** stated that citizens could not be stopped from voting "on account of race, color, or previous condition of servitude." (This amendment, like the Fourteenth Amendment, did not apply to Native Americans on tribal lands.) The amendment was ratified in 1870.

The Fifteenth Amendment was not aimed only at the South. African-American men could not vote in 16 states. "We have no moral right to impose an obligation on one part of the land which the rest will not accept," one Radical wrote. With the Fifteenth Amendment, the nation again turned toward democracy.

The Fifteenth Amendment did not apply to women. This made many white women angry. Why couldn't they vote when black men—former slaves—could? Suffragist Elizabeth Cady Stanton protested the idea of uneducated immigrants and freedmen "who never read the Declaration of Independence" making laws for educated white women. Most African-American women were not as angry. To Frances E. W. Harper, a black suffragist and writer, it was important for African Americans to gain voting rights, even if that meant only men at first.

*Reading***History**
A. Comparing How was the Fifteenth Amendment a step beyond the Fourteenth Amendment?
A. Answer While the Fourteenth Amendment broadly granted equal rights, the Fifteenth Amendment guaranteed voting rights.

Vocabulary
suffragist: someone who favors equal voting rights, especially for women

2 Grant Fights the Klan

Despite gaining the vote, African Americans in the South continued to be terrorized by the Ku Klux Klan. In 1871, to stop the terror, President Grant asked Congress to pass a tough law against the Klan. Joseph Rainey, a black congressman from South Carolina, had received death threats from the Klan. He urged his fellow lawmakers to support the bill.

A VOICE FROM THE PAST

When myself and colleagues shall leave these Halls and turn our footsteps toward our southern home we know not but that the assassin may await our coming. Be it as it may we have resolved to be loyal and firm, and if we perish, we perish! I earnestly hope the bill will pass.

Joseph Rainey, quoted in *The Trouble They Seen*

Congress approved the anti-Klan bill. Federal marshals then arrested thousands of Klansmen. Klan attacks on African-American voters declined. As a result, the 1872 presidential election was both fair and peaceful in the South. Grant won a second term.

ACTIVITY OPTIONS

INTERDISCIPLINARY LINK: CIVICS

BLOCK SCHEDULING

CAMPAIGN SLOGANS

Class Time 45 minutes

Task Creating a campaign slogan for the 1872 presidential election

Purpose To examine the issues that affected the election

Supplies Needed
- Art supplies (optional)
- Poster paper (optional)

Activity Have students review the material about the effects of the anti-Klan bill and about the scandals that tarnished the Grant administration. Then have them write a slogan for Grant and the Republican Party directed at voters in either the South or the North. Slogans should be no longer than one phrase or sentence. Students may wish to incorporate their slogan into a campaign poster for Grant. Make a list of all slogans, dividing it into those for the North and those for the South. Then have the class select the slogans they think would be most effective and explain why.

Scandal and Panic Weaken Republicans

Under the Grant administration, support for the Republicans and Reconstruction weakened. Scandals hurt the administration and caused divisions in the Republican Party. A financial panic further hurt the Republicans and turned the country's attention away from Reconstruction.

President Grant did not choose his advisers well. He put his former army friends and his wife's relatives in government positions. Many of these people were unqualified. Some Grant appointees took bribes. Grant's private secretary, for instance, took money from whiskey distillers who wanted to avoid paying taxes. Grant's secretary of war, General William Belknap, left office after people accused him of taking bribes.

Such scandals deeply outraged many Republicans. In 1872, some Republican officials broke away and formed the new Liberal Republican Party. The Republicans, no longer unified, became less willing to impose tough Reconstruction policies on the South.

In 1873, political corruption and Republican quarreling gave way to a more serious problem. When several powerful Eastern banks ran out of money after making bad loans, a financial panic swept the country. In the **Panic of 1873,** banks across the land closed. The stock market temporarily collapsed. The panic caused an economic depression, a time of low business activity and high unemployment. The railroad industry, which relied on banks for loans, suffered. Within a year, 89 of the country's 364 railroads went broke. Railroad failures left Midwestern farmers with no way to move their crops, and many farmers were ruined.

The depression, which lasted about five years, touched nearly all parts of the economy. By 1875, more than 18,000 companies had folded. Hundreds of workers had lost their jobs. Many Americans blamed the crisis on the Republicans—the party in power. As a result, Democrats won victories in the 1874 congressional and state elections. In the middle of the depression, Americans grew tired of hearing about the South's problems. The nation was losing interest in Reconstruction.

This cartoon from *Puck* magazine shows President Grant weighed down by corruption in his administration.

Reading History

B. Making Inferences How did Republican scandals hurt Reconstruction?

B. Possible Responses They made the party and its policies seem less moral; they distracted Republican politicians from Reconstruction goals.

C. Answer economic depression, bankrupt railroads, ruined farmers, folded companies, lost jobs, and less interest in Reconstruction

Reading History

C. Recognizing Effects What resulted from the Panic of 1873?

MORE ABOUT . . .

The Election of 1872

President Grant easily defeated *New York Tribune* founder and editor Horace Greeley in the 1872 presidential election. Greeley—a vocal, longtime opponent of slavery and a supporter of the Fourteenth and Fifteenth Amendments—favored a general amnesty for Confederates. He even signed the bail bond that released former Confederate president Jefferson Davis from jail. Greeley was nominated by the Liberal Republican Party and, later, by the Democratic National Convention in 1872. He died less than a month after the election.

MORE ABOUT . . .

Ulysses S. Grant

After he left the presidency, Grant suffered personal financial problems similar to the problems that afflicted his administration. Grant had borrowed money to invest in a firm that was set up by a swindler. The firm collapsed. In order to support his family, Grant began writing magazine articles about the Civil War. Then, already suffering from cancer of the throat, he decided to write his memoirs. Grant finished his autobiography only four days before he died.

CRITICAL THINKING ACTIVITY

Sequencing Events Have students make a time line of the events that weakened the Republican Party during Grant's presidency. Tell them to begin the time line with the election of 1868 and end it with the election of 1876.

Class Time 30 minutes

Economics in History
- Understanding the Business Cycle, p. 18

ACTIVITY OPTIONS

INDIVIDUAL NEEDS

STUDENTS ACQUIRING ENGLISH/ESL

Understanding Literal and Figurative Meanings Ask students to examine the political cartoon on page 531. Point out the caption and read it aloud to students. Ask what students think the phrase *weighed down* means. Elicit or explain that in the literal sense, the phrase means to be burdened with a heavy load. Encourage students to describe objects that weigh people down (heavy backpack, suitcase, uniform, or protective equipment).

Then explain to students that in the figurative sense, the phrase *weighed down* refers to being burdened by issues or problems rather than by objects that you can see or touch. Reread the first three paragraphs in the section "Scandal and Panic Weaken Republicans," and ask students to identify the problems that weighed down President Grant. Then ask students to explain why hiring unqualified people for important jobs and having your employees take bribes would pose problems.

INSTRUCT: OBJECTIVE 3

Supreme Court Reversals/ Reconstruction Ends

- How did Supreme Court decisions affect civil rights for African Americans in the South?
- Why did the presidential election of 1876 lead to the end of Reconstruction?
- What issues were part of the Compromise of 1877?

Outline Map Activities
- Election of 1876, pp. 35–36

MORE ABOUT . . .

The Election of 1876

The electoral votes of Oregon were also disputed. In total there were 20 disputed electoral votes. The Democrats needed only one vote to win, but the Republicans needed all 20. With the electoral votes from the four disputed states, Hayes would have 185 electoral votes—and would win the election. Tilden, however, had won the popular vote. He polled 4,284,020 votes to Hayes's 4,036,572.

The original commission had seven Republicans, seven Democrats, and one Independent. When the Independent resigned to run for Congress, he was replaced with a Republican. Republicans then controlled the commission, and they voted to give Hayes all 20 contested votes. Hayes became president.

3 Supreme Court Reversals

To make matters worse for the Republicans, the Supreme Court began to undo some of the changes that had been made in the South. In an 1876 case, *U.S.* v. *Cruikshank,* the Court ruled that the federal government could not punish individuals who violated the civil rights of African Americans. Only the states had that power, the Court declared. Southern state officials often would not punish those who attacked African Americans. As a result, violence against them increased.

In the 1876 case *U.S.* v. *Reese,* the Court ruled in favor of white Southerners who barred African Americans from voting. The Court stated that the Fifteenth Amendment did not give everyone the right to vote—it merely listed the grounds on which states could not deny the vote. In other words, states could prevent African Americans from voting for other reasons. States later imposed poll taxes and literacy tests to restrict the vote. These Court decisions weakened Reconstruction and blocked African-American efforts to gain full equality.

ReadingHistory
D. Recognizing Effects How did the Reese and Cruikshank rulings affect African Americans' efforts to gain civil rights?
D. Answer One ruling made it easier for attacks against African Americans to go unpunished. The other made it easier to keep them from voting.

Reconstruction Ends

The final blow to Reconstruction came with the 1876 presidential election. The Democrats nominated Samuel J. Tilden, governor of New York. The Republicans chose Rutherford B. Hayes, governor of Ohio. The race was very close. Victory depended on the electoral votes of South Carolina, Louisiana, and Florida. The votes in those states were so close that both the Democrats and the Republicans claimed victory. A special commission of eight Republicans and seven Democrats made a deal. Under the **Compromise of 1877,** Hayes became president. In return, the Republicans compromised with the Southern Democrats on several issues.

This cartoon from *Harper's Weekly* shows a federal soldier as the freedman's only defense against white Southerners.

1. The government would remove federal troops from the South.
2. The government would provide land grants and loans for the construction of railroads linking the South to the West Coast.
3. Southern officials would receive federal funds for construction and improvement projects.
4. Hayes would appoint a Democrat to his cabinet.
5. The Democrats promised to respect African Americans' civil and political rights.

Abolitionist Wendell Phillips was against the compromise. He doubted that the South would respect black rights. "The whole soil of the South is hidden by successive layers of broken promises," he said. "To trust a Southern promise would be fair evidence of insanity."

After the 1876 presidential election, the Reconstruction governments in the South collapsed. The Democrats returned to power, believing that they were the redeemers, or rescuers, of the South.

E. Answer scandals that split the Republican Party, the Panic of 1873, the Reese and Cruikshank Supreme Court rulings, and the Compromise of 1877

ReadingHistory
E. Summarizing What events led to a weakening of support for Reconstruction?

ACTIVITY OPTIONS

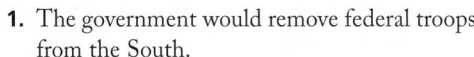

SKILLBUILDER LESSON: INTERPRETING CHARTS — BLOCK SCHEDULING

Explaining the Skill Charts are visual presentations of material. Historians use charts to organize, simplify, and summarize information so that it is easier to understand and to remember. Simple charts summarize information or make comparisons. Tables organize information into columns and rows. Diagrams provide visual clues to the meaning of information they contain.

Applying the Skill Ask students to identify the title of the chart and the kind of information it contains. Then ask the following questions:

1. Which two measures changed the Constitution? *(Fourteenth and Fifteenth Amendments)*
2. Which measures made freed African Americans citizens of the United States? *(Civil Rights Act of 1866 and Fourteenth Amendment)*
3. Which measure was designed to prevent racial discrimination in the courts? Why do you think Congress thought this was important? *(Civil Rights Act of 1875; because it protected African Americans' legal rights)*

In-Depth Resources: Unit 5
- Skillbuilder Practice, p. 66

Reconstruction: Civil Rights Amendments and Laws	
Civil Rights Act of 1866	• Granted citizenship and equal rights to all persons born in the United States (except Native Americans)
Fourteenth Amendment (1868)	• Granted citizenship and equal protection of the laws to all persons born in the United States (except Native Americans)
Fifteenth Amendment (1870)	• Protected the voting rights of African Americans
Civil Rights Act of 1875	• Outlawed racial segregation in public services • Ensured the right of African Americans to serve as jurors

SKILLBUILDER **Interpreting Charts**

1. *Which amendment and law are most similar?*
2. *Which amendment specifically protects voting rights?*

Skillbuilder Answers
1. Civil Rights Act of 1866; Fourteenth Amendment
2. Fifteenth Amendment

4 The Legacy of Reconstruction

Historians still argue about the success of Reconstruction. The nation did rebuild and reunite. However, Reconstruction did not achieve equality for African Americans.

After Reconstruction, most African Americans still lived in poverty. Legally, they could vote and hold public office. But few took part in politics. They continued to face widespread violence and prejudice.

During this period, however, African Americans did make lasting gains. Protection of civil rights became part of the U.S. Constitution. The Fourteenth and Fifteenth amendments would provide a legal basis for civil rights laws of the 20th century. Black schools and churches begun during Reconstruction also endured. Reconstruction changed society, putting African Americans on the path toward full equality. In the next unit, you will learn about other changes in American society after the Civil War.

Section 3 Assessment

1. Terms & Names

Explain the significance of:
- Fifteenth Amendment
- Panic of 1873
- Compromise of 1877

2. Taking Notes

Review the chapter and find five significant individuals and events to place on a time line as shown.

1865 — event — event — event — event — event — 1877

Which event or person was most important and why?

3. Main Ideas

a. What did the Fifteenth Amendment declare?

b. What effect did scandals in the Grant administration have on the Republican Party?

c. What demands did Southern Democrats make in the Compromise of 1877?

4. Critical Thinking

Drawing Conclusions Why do you think the Republicans were willing to agree to the Compromise of 1877 and end Reconstruction?

THINK ABOUT
- the election of 1876
- the Panic of 1873
- the Supreme Court rulings

ACTIVITY OPTIONS

LANGUAGE ARTS / CIVICS Research Ku Klux Klan activities barring African Americans from voting. Then write a protest **letter to the editor** or propose a **law** to protect voting rights.

HISTORY FROM VISUALS

Reading the Chart Have students note the years each measure was passed. (The four measures were passed over the course of less than ten years.) Ask students why Congress saw the need for further legislation to protect the rights of African Americans after the passage of the Civil Rights Act of 1866 and the Fourteenth Amendment in 1868.

Possible Responses Congress saw efforts by white Southerners to ignore the laws and restrict the rights of African Americans. The measures that dealt with voting rights were designed to prevent white Southerners from ending African-American participation and representation in government.

Extension Have students research the legal status of Native Americans at the time the Fourteenth Amendment was passed.

INSTRUCT: OBJECTIVE 4

The Legacy of Reconstruction

- What obstacles did African Americans still face after the end of Reconstruction?
- What lasting gains did African Americans make during Reconstruction?

ASSESS & RETEACH

Setting the Stage Have students complete the last row of the graphic organizer.

Formal Assessment
- Section Quiz, p. 321

Critical Thinking Transparency CT52
- Setting the Stage

RETEACHING ACTIVITY

Have students write a summary paragraph that uses the section's Main Idea as the topic sentence. The paragraphs should note the legacy of Reconstruction, efforts to promote the rights and equality of African Americans, and events that led to the end of Reconstruction.

In-Depth Resources: Unit 5
- Reteaching Activity, p. 76

Section 3 Assessment

1. Terms & Names

Fifteenth Amendment, p. 530
Panic of 1873, p. 531
Compromise of 1877, p. 532

2. Taking Notes

Event 1: Lincoln's death; Event 2: Reconstruction begins; Event 3: Fourteenth Amendment passes; Event 4: Johnson is impeached; Event 5: Grant is elected

Answers will vary as to which event was most important.

3. Main Ideas

a. The right to vote should not be denied on account of race, color, or previous condition of servitude.
b. They helped split the party.
c. the removal of federal troops from the South; land grants and loans to build railroads; money for internal improvements; appointment of a Democrat to the cabinet

4. Critical Thinking

They wanted to retain their hold on the presidency. The nation was in the midst of a depression and had grown weary of Reconstruction.

ACTIVITY OPTIONS

Integrated Assessment
- Rubrics for a letter, 4.1
- Rubrics for a law, 4.3

TERMS & NAMES

1. **Reconstruction,** p. 517
2. **Andrew Johnson,** p. 517
3. **black codes,** p. 518
4. **civil rights,** p. 519
5. **Fourteenth Amendment,** p. 519
6. **sharecropping,** p. 527
7. **lynch,** p. 528
8. **Fifteenth Amendment,** p. 530
9. **Panic of 1873,** p. 531
10. **Compromise of 1877,** p. 532

REVIEW QUESTIONS

Possible Responses

1. a federal agency that assisted former slaves by offering them food and clothing and establishing African-American schools
2. amnesty for most white Southerners; insistence that the new state governments forbid slavery and accept the supreme power of the federal government
3. Scalawags were Southerners who went along with Radical Reconstruction. Carpetbaggers were Northerners who traveled to the South to take part in Reconstruction.
4. He violated the Tenure of Office Act.
5. Congress believed that African Americans' newly gained civil rights were enough to ensure them a better life.
6. the contract system: planters paid former slaves to work their plantations; sharecropping: plantation owners provided farmers with tools and land in exchange for a share of their crops
7. The Klan kept many Republicans away from the polls through violence and intimidation, helping Democrats keep political power.
8. because it gave the right to vote to male immigrants and freedmen but not to women
9. The failure of several powerful banks prompted a financial panic.
10. They took away the federal government's ability to punish civil rights violators, making it easier for whites to deny African Americans the right to vote.

Chapter 18 ASSESSMENT

TERMS & NAMES

Briefly explain the significance of each of the following.

1. Reconstruction
2. Andrew Johnson
3. black codes
4. civil rights
5. Fourteenth Amendment
6. sharecropping
7. lynch
8. Fifteenth Amendment
9. Panic of 1873
10. Compromise of 1877

REVIEW QUESTIONS

Rebuilding the Union (pages 517–523)

1. What was the Freedmen's Bureau?
2. What were the main parts of President Johnson's Reconstruction plan?
3. Who were scalawags and carpetbaggers?
4. What reason did the House give for impeaching President Johnson?

Reconstruction and Daily Life (pages 524–528)

5. Why did Congress not pass a land-reform plan?
6. What new systems of labor developed in the South after the Civil War?
7. How did the Ku Klux Klan serve the Democratic Party?

End of Reconstruction (pages 529–533)

8. Why did the Fifteenth Amendment arouse anger in many women?
9. What caused an economic depression in the 1870s?
10. How did Supreme Court rulings during Reconstruction help weaken African Americans' civil rights?

CRITICAL THINKING

1. USING YOUR NOTES

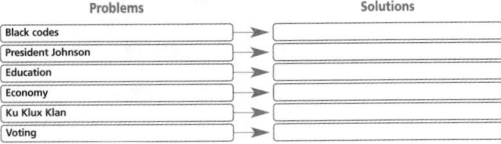

Problems	Solutions
Black codes	
President Johnson	
Education	
Economy	
Ku Klux Klan	
Voting	

Using your diagram, answer the following questions.

a. What was the solution to the problem of educating African Americans?

b. What was the solution to the problem of Ku Klux Klan violence?

2. ANALYZING LEADERSHIP

Why might Reconstruction be considered a time in which the presidency was weak?

3. THEME: DEMOCRATIC IDEALS

How did the Fourteenth and Fifteenth amendments promote greater equality for African Americans? How were the amendments limited?

4. APPLYING CITIZENSHIP SKILLS

What were the different viewpoints of Elizabeth Cady Stanton and Frances E. W. Harper regarding the Fifteenth Amendment's failure to give women an important right of citizenship—the right to vote?

5. ANALYZING CAUSES

What aspect of the Compromise of 1877 likely played the greatest role in ending Reconstruction?

Interact *with* History

How did your solutions to rebuilding the nation compare with the actual solutions carried out?

VISUAL SUMMARY

Reconstruction

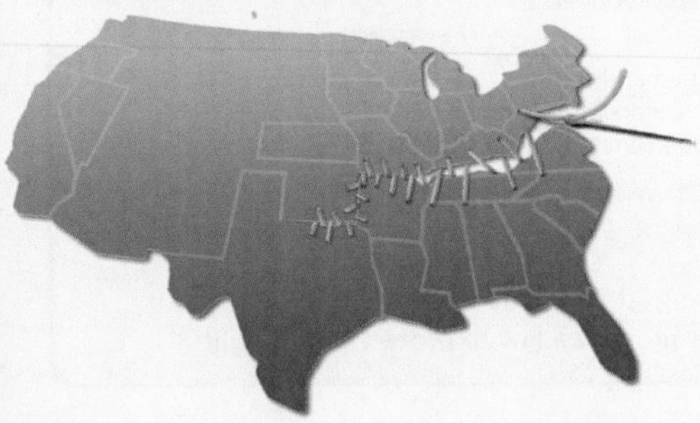

Rebuilding the Union

During Reconstruction, Congress decided how the Southern states would be readmitted to the Union and passed laws to improve conditions for freed people.

Reconstruction and Daily Life

After slavery ended, freed African Americans reunited their families, attended school, and began working for pay. Racist violence and lack of land slowed their progress.

End of Reconstruction

In the 1870s, hostile Supreme Court decisions, the Southern Democrats' return to power, and the withdrawal of federal troops from the South ended Reconstruction.

534 CHAPTER 18

CRITICAL THINKING

Possible Responses

1. USING YOUR NOTES **a.** Freedmen's schools were established. **b.** anti-Klan laws
2. ANALYZING LEADERSHIP because Congress overrode many of Johnson's vetoes, took over Reconstruction, and impeached him; scandals of Grant administration prompted the start of a new Republican Party
3. THEME: DEMOCRATIC IDEALS They gained full rights as citizens and won the right to vote. However, the Supreme Court issued rulings that weakened these amendments.
4. APPLYING CITIZENSHIP SKILLS Stanton criticized the amendment, believing that it was wrong to continue denying the vote to women, many of whom were better educated than former slaves. Harper believed that granting voting rights to male African Americans was a significant step toward full rights for all.
5. ANALYZING CAUSES the removal of federal troops from the South, making it much more difficult for the North to enforce its Reconstruction policies

Interact *with* History Students responses will vary but should include elements from the solutions.

HISTORY SKILLS

1. INTERPRETING MAPS: Region

Study the map and then answer the questions.

Election of 1876

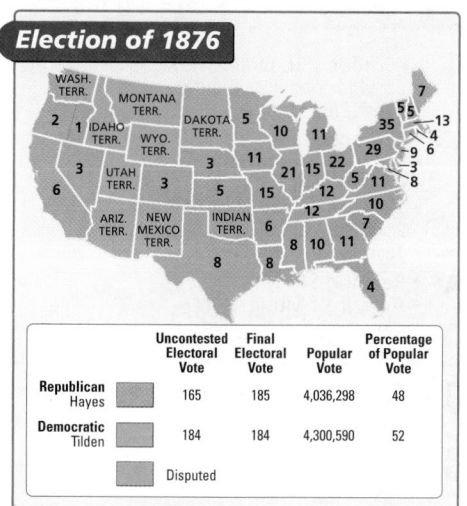

		Uncontested Electoral Vote	Final Electoral Vote	Popular Vote	Percentage of Popular Vote
Republican Hayes		165	185	4,036,298	48
Democratic Tilden		184	184	4,300,590	52
	Disputed				

Basic Map Elements

a. What is the subject of the map?

Interpreting the Map

b. In what region of the country were most of the disputed votes located?

c. What regions voted mostly Republican?

2. INTERPRETING PRIMARY SOURCES

This political cartoon shows the effect of the Ku Klux Klan on African-American families in the South. Study the cartoon carefully and then answer the questions.

a. Based on the cartoon, what were the goals of the Ku Klux Klan?

b. Does the image reflect any bias on the part of the artist? Explain.

ALTERNATIVE ASSESSMENT

1. INTERDISCIPLINARY ACTIVITY: Language Arts

Writing Letters Write letters that you imagine the following three people would write about Reconstruction: 1) a member of the old Southern upper class; 2) a newly freed African American; and 3) a white Northern carpetbagger. Be sure to use standard grammar, spelling, sentence structure, and punctuation in your letters.

2. COOPERATIVE LEARNING ACTIVITY

Conducting an Impeachment Trial The impeachment trial of Andrew Johnson was a dramatic and colorful event. Many officials pleaded their case either for or against the president.

Working in a small group, research the trial using resources such as diaries, journals, autobiographies, letters, and books. Each group member should choose an official who spoke at the trial and collect some of his quotes. The group should then perform its own trial in front of the class, with each member portraying the official he or she chose. Some possible officials include Thaddeus Stevens, Edmund G. Ross, James W. Grimes, Benjamin Butler, and Chief Justice Samuel Chase.

3. TECHNOLOGY ACTIVITY

Making an Electronic Presentation Life under the sharecropping system was not easy. Information about sharecropping comes from a variety of sources. Using the library or the Internet, find diaries, memoirs, images, and news articles about life as a sharecropper.

For more about sharecropping . . .

INTERNET ACTIVITY CLASSZONE.COM

Use presentation software to share your information about sharecropping. Consider the suggestions below to get started.

- images or descriptions of a sharecropper's shack
- examples of the crops that were grown by a sharecropper
- facts and quotations about a sharecropper's life

4. HISTORY PORTFOLIO

Identify the dates that you consider to be the era of Reconstruction. Then identify previous eras in American history and place them all in chronological sequence on a time line. Add your time line to your portfolio.

Additional Test Practice, pp. S1–S33

TEST PRACTICE CLASSZONE.COM

ALTERNATIVE ASSESSMENT

1. INTERDISCIPLINARY ACTIVITY: **Language Arts**
   Letters should
   - accurately reflect the thoughts and experiences of the subject's life.
   - reflect the student's understanding of basic concepts of Reconstruction.
   - use standard grammar, spelling, sentence structure, and punctuation.

2. COOPERATIVE LEARNING ACTIVITY
   Trials should
   - accurately portray the position of the selected official.
   - convey information through performance.
   - have adequate delivery and establish a rapport with the audience.
   - show evidence of involvement of each person in the group.

3. TECHNOLOGY ACTIVITY
   Presentations should
   - utilize two or more media.
   - clearly demonstrate an understanding of the life of a sharecropper.
   - show technical proficiency.

4. HISTORY PORTFOLIO
   Time lines should
   - be organized chronologically.
   - Include the Reconstruction Era and previous eras.
   - be presented neatly.

Critical Thinking Transparency CT54
- Visual Summary

Formal Assessment
- Chapter Test, Forms A, B, and C, pp. 322–333

HISTORY SKILLS

Possible Responses

1. INTERPRETING MAPS
   Basic Map Elements
   a. election of 1876
   Interpreting the Map
   b. the South
   c. the North and West

2. INTERPRETING PRIMARY SOURCES
   a. The Klan's goals were to keep blacks powerless and in fear and to keep whites in power.
   b. By highlighting weapons, such as knives and guns, the cartoon suggests that the Klan intended to use violence to achieve its goals.

CHAPTER 19 EPILOGUE PLANNING GUIDE

The United States, 1860–1920

	EPILOGUE OVERVIEW	COPYMASTERS	INTEGRATED TECHNOLOGY
CHAPTER 19 EPILOGUE RESOURCES	Between 1860 and 1920, the nation expanded its control over the West and experienced rapid industrialization and urbanization. Immigrants increased. Mass culture began to emerge. Racial discrimination persisted. Reform movements addressed the nation's problems. And by winning two wars, the United States became a major world power.	**In-Depth Resources: Unit 5** • Tracing Themes: Expansion, p. 79 • Building Vocabulary, p. 84	• eEdition Plus Online • EasyPlanner Plus Online • eTest Plus Online • eEdition • Power Presentations • EasyPlanner • Electronic Library of Primary Sources • Test Generator • Reading Study Guide • America's Music
	KEY IDEAS		
SECTION 1 A Time of Growth pp. 539–545	• Population in the West increases with the expansion of railroads, mining, and ranching. • Served factors contribute to increased industrialization. • Industrialization and immigration lead to increased urbanization.	**In-Depth Resources: Unit 5** • Setting the Stage, p. 78 • Guided Reading, p. 80 • Geography Application, pp. 86–87 • Reteaching Activity, p. 93 • Enrichment Activity, p. 97	**Warm-Up Transparency WT19EPIL** **Critical Thinking Transparency CT97** • Setting the Stage classzone.com
SECTION 2 Life at the Turn of the Century pp. 546–550	• Life in the West was hard but provided new opportunities for many people, including women. • The nation saw the rise of a mass culture and popular new leisure activities. • Ethnic and racial minorities continued to face discrimination, but they still fought for equality.	**In-Depth Resources: Unit 5** • Setting the Stage, p. 78 • Guided Reading, p. 81 • Reteaching Activity, p. 93 **America's History Makers** • W. E. B. Du Bois, pp. 85–86	**Warm-Up Transparency WT19EPIL** **Critical Thinking Transparency CT97** **Humanities Transparency HT41, HT42** classzone.com
SECTION 3 An Era of Reform PP. 551–555	• Populists address the problems of farmers and Westerners, but the movement stalls after the 1896 elections. • Progressive reformers try to reform governement and expand democracy, promote social welfare, and create economic reform.	**In-Depth Resources: Unit 5** • Guided Reading, p. 82 • Skillbuilder Practice, p. 85 • Primary Source, pp. 88–89 • Literature Selection, pp. 90–92 • Reteaching Activity, p. 94 **America's History Makers** • Jane Addams, pp. 83–84 • Theodore Roosevelt, pp. 87–88	**Warm-Up Transparency WT19EPIL** **Critical Thinking Transparency CT97** **Humanities Transparency HT43, HT44** classzone.com
SECTION 4 Becoming a World Power pp. 556–563	• The U.S. imperialism grows from the nation's efforts to protect its economic interests and military interests as well as from the nation's belief its own cultural superiority. • By helping the Allies win World War I, the United States becomes one of the world's great powers.	**In-Depth Resources: Unit 5** • Guided Reading, p. 83 • Reteaching Activity, p. 95 **Economics in History** • The Economic Causes of Imperialism, p. 23	**Warm-Up Transparency WT19EPIL** **Critical Thinking Transparency CT97** **Humanities Transparency HT46, HT47, HT48** classzone.com

Pupil's Edition
Copymaster
Overhead Transparency
Audio Library
CD-ROM
Internet

ASSESSMENT OPTIONS

Chapter 19 Epilogue Assessment, pp. 564–565

Formal Assessment
- Chapter 19 Epilogue Test, Forms A, B, and C, pp. 338–349

Test Generator

Online Test Practice

Strategies for Test Preparation

Section Assessment, p. 543

Formal Assessment
- Section Quiz, p. 334

Integrated Assessment Book
- Rubrics, 5.6, 2.1

Test Generator

Test Practice Transparencies, TT67–TT74

Section Assessment, p. 550

Formal Assessment
- Section Quiz, p. 335

Integrated Assessment Book
- Rubrics, 4.4, 5.1

Test Generator

Test Practice Transparencies, TT75–TT78

Section Assessment, p. 555

Formal Assessment
- Section Quiz, p. 336

Integrated Assessment Book
- Rubrics, 1.13, 2.1

Test Generator

Test Practice Transparencies, TT79–TT81

Section Assessment, p. 562

Formal Assessment
- Section Quiz, p. 337

Integrated Assessment Book
- Rubrics, 1.10, 2.3

Test Generator

Test Practice Transparencies, TT82–TT88

CUSTOMIZING FOR INDIVIDUAL NEEDS

Students Acquiring English/ESL

Reading Study Guide (English and Spanish), pp. 179–188

Access for Students Acquiring English/ESL: Spanish Translations, pp. 126–132

Chapter Summaries on CD (English and Spanish)

Modified Lesson Plans for English Learners

Less Proficient Readers

Reading Study Guide (English and Spanish), pp. 179–188

Chapter Summaries on CD (English and Spanish)

Gifted and Talented Students

In-Depth Resources: Unit 5
- Enrichment Activity, p. 97

America's History Makers

CROSS-CURRICULAR CONNECTIONS

Civics

Sullivan, George. *The Day the Women Got the Vote: A Photo History of the Women's Rights Movement.* New York: Scholastic, 1994. Aphotographic record of the fight for the vote.

Culture

Freedman, Russell, and **Lewis Hine** (photographer). ***Kids at Work: Lewis Hine and the Crusade Against Child Labor.*** New York: Clarion Books, 1998. Moving photographs by the great reformer with informative, well-written text.

Popular Culture

Alter, Judy. *Vaudeville: The Birth of Show Business.* New York: Franklin Watts, 1998. Short account of the new theater form.

Primary Sources

Brown, Dee, and Amy Ehrlich. ***Wounded Knee: An Indian History of the American West.*** New York: Holt, 1993. Adapted by Ehrlich from Brown's best-selling *Bury My Heart at Wounded Knee;* a poignant illuminating collection of original documents.

Language Arts

Ritchie, Donald A. ***American Journalists: Getting the Story.*** New York: Oxford UP, 1998. The personal and professional lives of 60 American journalists from 1700 to the present.

Interdisciplinary Projects

- Science: Endangered Species
- Language Arts: Mexican Folk Tales of the Southwest
- Art: Comic Strips
- Health: The Flu Epidemic of 1918

Literature

Alger, Horatio. ***Jed, the Poorhouse Boy.*** Mattituck, NY: Amereon, 1976. One of Alger's typical boy heroes rises from famine to fortune by means of good moral character, combined with pluck and luck.

Martinello, Marian L. ***Cedar Fever.*** San Antonio: Corona, 1992. In Texas during World War I, a girl must face the mixed reactions of neighbors to the fact that she is of German descent.

McDougal Littell Literature Connections

Laurence Yep

Dragonwings

A young Chinese immigrant comes to San Francisco at the turn of the century to join his father. They meet dangerous people and new friends and pursue long-held dreams.

ENRICHMENT ACTIVITIES

Pupil's Edition, pp. 536–565
Interact with History, p. 537
Geography in History, pp. 544–545

Economics in History, p. 552

Technology of the Time, p. 559

Interactive Primary Source, p. 563

In-Depth Resources: Unit 5
- Geography Application, pp. 86–87
- Primary Sources, pp. 88–89
- Literature Selection, pp. 90–92

America's History Makers
- Jane Addams, pp. 83–84
- W. E. B. Du Bois, pp. 85–86
- Theodore Roosevelt, pp. 87–88

Chapter Summaries on CD

America's History Plays

Outline Map Activities

BLOCK SCHEDULING — LESSON PLAN OPTIONS (90-MINUTE PERIOD)

DAY 1

Interact with History, p. 537
Class Time 20 minutes

Options for pacing and variety:

- Peer Teaching Have students work in small groups to make a two-column chart showing the four major social problems of the Progressive Era and possible causes of these problems. Then have each group discuss the qualities that would help a leader tackle these problems. **Class Time** 20 minutes

Setting the Stage, p. 538
Class Time 20 minutes

Options for pacing and variety:

- Time Saver For a homework assignment, have students preview the chapter and provide written answers to the "What Do You Know?" and "What Do You Want to Know?" questions. **Class Time** 5 minutes

Section 1, pp. 539–543
Class Time 50 minutes

Options for pacing and variety:

- History on Film Extend students' background knowledge of the West by viewing *Boom or Bust: Mining and the Opening of the West.* United Learning. **Class Time** 25 minutes
- Team Teaching Invite the music teacher to share with the class folk songs about John Henry, Casey Jones, and other railroad workers, including union songs of the day. **Class Time** 30 minutes

Section 2, pp. 546–550

- Internet Extend students' knowledge of the immigrant experience by visiting classzone.com **Class Time** 25 minutes
- Time Saver Assign students the Reading History questions in the section for homework and then have them share their answers in class. **Class Time** 10 minutes

DAY 2

Section 3, pp. 551–555
Class Time 45 minutes

Options for pacing and variety:

- Role-Playing Have small groups of students role-play a conversation among a group of Progressive era leaders, such as Jane Addams, Theodore Roosevelt, and Jacob Riis. The groups should discuss each characters achievements, disappointments, and hopes for the future. **Class Time** 20 minutes
- Time Saver Assign the Critical Thinking question in the Section Assessment on page 555 for homework. **Class Time** 5 minutes

Section 4, pp. 556–562
Class Time 45 minutes

Options for pacing and variety:

- Internet Extend students' background knowledge of imperialism by visiting classzone.com. **Class Time** 20 minutes
- Time Saver Use the map on page 561 to summarize the Allied advances that led to their victory in World War I. **Class Time** 10 minutes

Epilogue Assessment, pp. 564–565
Class Time 40 minutes

Options for pacing and variety:

- Peer Teaching Have students review the chapter for important American leaders around 1900. For each person, have the students identify the role that person played in U.S. history. **Class Time** 20 minutes
- Peer Evaluation Have students review the Interact with History question on page 537, consider their earlier responses, and share their current responses with the class. **Class Time**10 minutes

TEACHER-TESTED ACTIVITY

Brian McKenzie, Dr. Charles Drew Science Magnet School, Buffalo, New York

THE PANAMA CANAL

Class Time Two class periods

Task Creating a map and a journal record of a trip through the Panama Canal

Purpose To identify the location and importance of the Panama Canal to the United States

Supplies Needed

- Outline maps of the world
- Markers or colored pencils
- Globe

Activity Divide the class into four or five groups. Assign each group a journey through the Panama Canal, for example (a) a U.S. naval vessel traveling from Hawaii to Cuba, (b) a U.S. merchant ship traveling from Boston, Massachusetts, to China, or (c) a U.S. passenger vessel traveling from New York to San Francisco. Assign each group member a role such as captain, crew member, or passenger. Passengers can be business leaders, prospectors, politicians, and so on. Each group should map its journey and write three journal entries about the trip, including a description of the passage through the canal.

CHAPTER 19 EPILOGUE TECHNOLOGY IN THE CLASSROOM

PERSUASIVE ESSAYS ON THE LEAGUE OF NATIONS

Woodrow Wilson believed his Fourteen Points and the League of Nations were the tools to build world peace. He traveled the country seeking popular support to ratify the Treaty of Versailles, including a provision for the League of Nations. The U.S. Senate, however, refused to ratify the Treaty. Students can research the Fourteen Points on the *Primary Source Explorer* CD-ROM and interpretations of them on the Internet. Then they can write essays supporting ratification and the League of Nations or taking the side of those who refused to accept Wilson's proposals.

ACTIVITY OUTLINE

Objective By researching and writing persuasive essays, students will better understand contemporary views of the Treaty of Versailles and practice researching on the Internet.

Task Students will write persuasive essays that argue for or against ratification of the Treaty of Versailles.

Class Time One class period

DIRECTIONS

1. Introduce this activity by reminding students that President Woodrow Wilson had resisted entering World War I. Ask students:
   - What events convinced Wilson that the United States needed to enter the war?
   - Do you think Wilson was eager to do this?
   - Did the Congress support the idea of the United States joining the Allies in the war?

2. Tell students that Wilson proposed the Fourteen Points and the League of Nations to the Congress in January 1918, 10 months before the war ended and less than a year after the United States entered the war in the spring of 1917. Ask students to think about what motivated Wilson to make this proposal.

3. Ask students about their reactions to the ideas behind the League of Nations. Do they agree with Wilson that these ideas were essential to create world peace? Or do they agree with Senator Henry Cabot Lodge that the United States should avoid alliances with other countries?

4. Instruct students to do additional research on the pros and cons of the League of Nations, then write short 200–300 word persuasive essays that defend one side or the other. They should find reasons that support their opinions and end with strong concluding statements.

5. Students can use Internet sites listed on classzone.com and the complete Fourteen Points document on the *Primary Source Explorer* CD-ROM for research.

CHAPTER 19 EPILOGUE OBJECTIVE

The student will understand how the nation grew from the Civil War through the end of World War I, dramatically changing the lives of its citizens and its place in the world.

CHAPTER 19 EPILOGUE

The United States, 1860–1920

Section 1 **A Time of Growth**
Section 2 **Life at the Turn of the Century**
Section 3 **An Era of Reform**
Section 4 **Becoming a World Power**

HISTORY FROM VISUALS

Interpreting the Photograph Ask students to study the photograph of people walking along Mulberry Street on New York's Lower East Side around 1900. Have them make inferences about how people lived in this section of New York City at the turn of the century. **Possible Responses** The area looks crowded and busy. People bought produce and other goods at outdoor stalls. Most buildings are four or five stories tall, with shops on the ground floors. The upper floors may be apartments. People travel on foot, and goods move by horse-drawn wagons.

Extension Have students write the headings for five advertising posters that might have been found on Mulberry Street when this photograph was taken.

Crowds of people walk, work, and shop on Mulberry Street in New York's Lower East Side.

536

RECOMMENDED RESOURCES

BOOKS FOR THE TEACHER

Foner, Philip S. ***The Great Labor Uprising of 1877.*** New York: Pathfinder, 1977. Classic work on epic 19th-century labor struggle.

White, Richard. ***"It's Your Misfortune and None of My Own": A New History of the American West.*** Norman, OK: U. of Oklahoma Press, 1993. Groundbreaking work on the movement of Americans into the West.

Williams, William Appleman. ***The Tragedy of American Diplomacy.*** New York: Dell, 1962. Pathbreaking interpretation of American diplomatic history.

SOFTWARE

The Golden Door: The Italian Immigrant Experience in the United States. Social Studies School Service, 1997. Experience Ellis Island and immigrant life in New York around 1900.

VIDEO

Crazy Horse. Time-Life, 1997. Story of the great Oglala Sioux leader.

INTERNET

For more about the United States around 1900, visit . . .

classzone.com

Interact *with* History

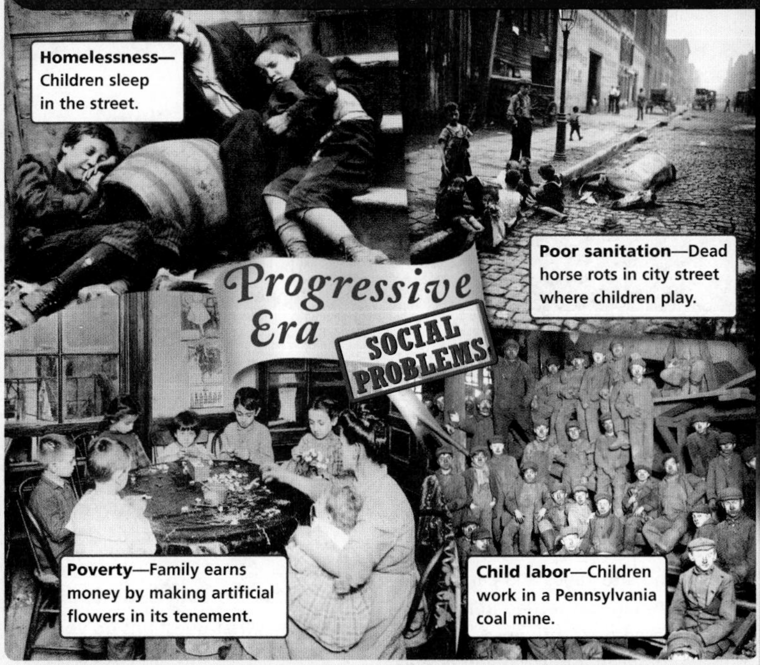

Homelessness—Children sleep in the street.
Poor sanitation—Dead horse rots in city street where children play.
Progressive Era
SOCIAL PROBLEMS
Poverty—Family earns money by making artificial flowers in its tenement.
Child labor—Children work in a Pennsylvania coal mine.

It is 1901, and the nation is at a crossroads. Its population and economy are growing. It is also gaining territories and becoming a world power. But there are serious problems at home. You're anxious to see how your national leaders will address these issues.

What Do You Think?

- Which problem shown in the collage is most important?
- Are domestic issues more important than international ones?
- What should government, business, or other organizations do to address these issues?

How would you solve these problems?

USA

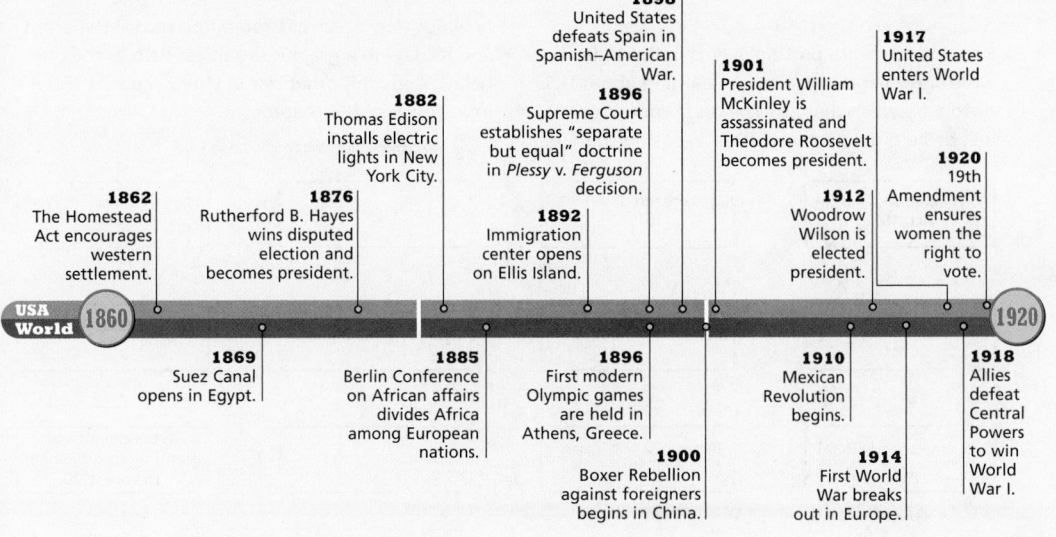

- **1862** The Homestead Act encourages western settlement.
- **1876** Rutherford B. Hayes wins disputed election and becomes president.
- **1882** Thomas Edison installs electric lights in New York City.
- **1892** Immigration center opens on Ellis Island.
- **1896** Supreme Court establishes "separate but equal" doctrine in *Plessy* v. *Ferguson* decision.
- **1898** United States defeats Spain in Spanish-American War.
- **1901** President William McKinley is assassinated and Theodore Roosevelt becomes president.
- **1912** Woodrow Wilson is elected president.
- **1917** United States enters World War I.
- **1920** 19th Amendment ensures women the right to vote.

1860 — 1920

World

- **1869** Suez Canal opens in Egypt.
- **1885** Berlin Conference on African affairs divides Africa among European nations.
- **1896** First modern Olympic games are held in Athens, Greece.
- **1900** Boxer Rebellion against foreigners begins in China.
- **1910** Mexican Revolution begins.
- **1914** First World War breaks out in Europe.
- **1918** Allies defeat Central Powers to win World War I.

537

Interact *with* History

OBJECTIVES

- To help students understand the social problems facing the nation
- To help students identify reform efforts to improve social conditions

What Do You Think?

1. Encourage students to give a reason why the picture they selected was most important to them.
2. Ask students whether they think it is more important to take care of problems at home or to be involved with other nations.
3. Remind students that government, business, and other organizations can set up programs to help people.

How would you solve these problems?

Have students consider why these problems existed and which ones would be most difficult or least difficult to solve. Ask students to consider immediate short-term solutions as well as long-term solutions to these problems.

MAKING PERSONAL CONNECTIONS

Ask students to think about which problems pictured still exist in U.S. cities today. What are some of today's social problems that are not shown in the photographs? Are social problems worse today than a century ago? Explain.

TIME LINE DISCUSSION

From the Civil War through World War I, the nation faced many domestic and international challenges—Western migration, increased immigration, and two wars.

- Ask students what events on the time line suggest U.S. involvement in international affairs. **Answer** Spanish-American War, World War I
- Ask students what events on the time line indicate growth in the U.S. **Possible Responses** Homestead Act encouraged expansion; opening of immigration center on Ellis Island would increase the population.
- Ask students to select one event from the time line and explain the effect it might have on the lives of U.S. citizens. **Possible Responses** Homestead Act would result in more people from the East moving to the West; electric lights in New York City would make life safer and more convenient; wars would result in people losing their lives.

BEFORE YOU READ

Previewing the Theme: Expansion

Ask students to examine the photograph and list the things in the photograph that are related to the theme of expansion. The railroad helped move people to the West. Chinese immigrants in the picture exemplify growing immigration and population. Yet, with immigration came an awareness of increasing social problems and the need for solutions.

What Do You Know?

Students may say "wild west" makes them think of cowboys and Indians and gunfights, which they have seen in Western movies. "Industrialization" may make them think of large factories and machines. "Progressivism" may make them think of progress but not necessarily of social reform. Help them make that connection. "Imperialism" may make them think of empires or emperors, but they may need help seeing the connection to people in distant lands who became subject to imperial rulers.

In-Depth Resources: Unit 5
- Tracing Themes: Expansion, p. 79

READ AND TAKE NOTES

Reading Strategy: Sequencing Events

Explain to students that to sequence events means to list them in chronological order, the order in which they occurred. Explain that the arrows on the chart indicate the order of events. Tell students that using the chart will help them remember the important events in the chapter and what may have happened as a result of each.

In-Depth Resources: Unit 5
Setting the Stage, p. 78

Critical Thinking Transparency, CT97

Chapter 19 Epilogue SETTING THE STAGE

BEFORE YOU READ

The growth of railroads was just one of the factors that spurred the nation's westward expansion and industrial growth, especially after the Civil War.

Previewing the Theme

Expansion This chapter examines the tremendous growth the United States experienced during the late 1800s and early 1900s. The nation expanded physically as Americans settled in the West, built an overseas empire, and increased their influence around the globe. Meanwhile, the nation experienced industrial and population growth, created new ways of life, and renewed efforts to improve conditions for its citizens.

What Do You Know?

What do you think of when you hear the following terms associated with the late 1800s and early 1900s: "wild west," "industrialization," "progressivism," "imperialism?"

THINK ABOUT
- what you already know about these terms from your reading or experience with them from the popular media
- why they might be associated with an era in which America underwent dramatic changes

What Do You Want to Know?

What questions do you have about the United States at the turn of the century? Record these questions in your notebook before you read the chapter.

READ AND TAKE NOTES

Reading Strategy: Sequencing Events
Sequencing means putting events in the order in which they happen in time. In learning about U.S. history between the Civil War and World War I, it will be helpful to list important events in the order in which they occurred. You might record the event and its date in a graphic organizer such as the one below. Copy this organizer in your notebook. Fill it in as you read the chapter.

See Skillbuilder Handbook, page R4.

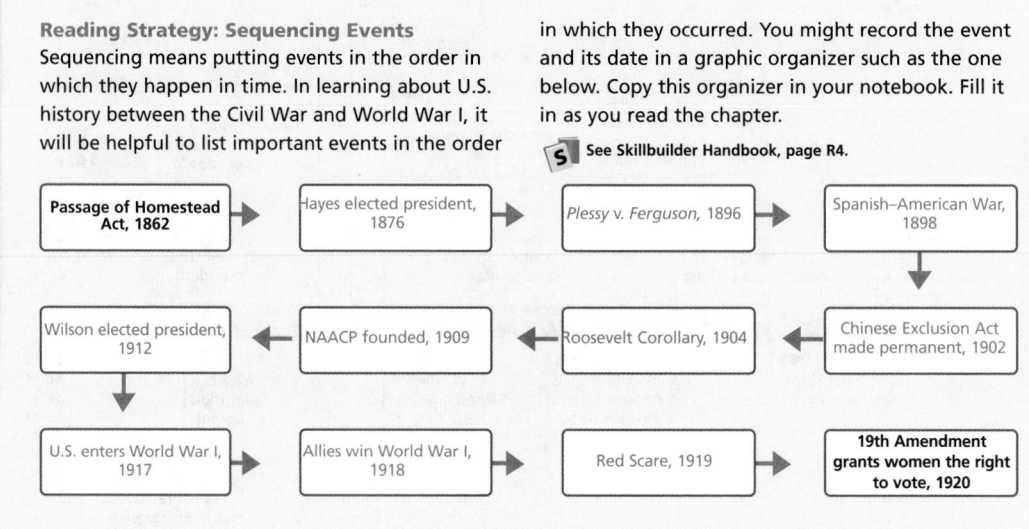

Passage of Homestead Act, 1862 → Hayes elected president, 1876 → *Plessy* v. *Ferguson*, 1896 → Spanish-American War, 1898 → Chinese Exclusion Act made permanent, 1902 → Roosevelt Corollary, 1904 → NAACP founded, 1909 → Wilson elected president, 1912 → U.S. enters World War I, 1917 → Allies win World War I, 1918 → Red Scare, 1919 → **19th Amendment grants women the right to vote, 1920**

TEACHING STRATEGY

READING THE CHAPTER

This is a thematic chapter focusing on the geographic, social, economic, and political growth of the United States. Important changes occur at different rates and with different dynamics. Encourage students to find the connections between the many types of change that take place. They should also look for the problems that arise and the solutions offered to solve those problems.

ALTERNATIVE ASSESSMENT

The Chapter Assessment describes three activities for alternative assessment on page 565. You may wish to have students work on these activities during the course of the chapter and then present them at the end.

1 A Time of Growth

TERMS & NAMES
frontier
Great Plains
Homestead Act
Dawes Act
Gilded Age
urbanization
new immigrants

MAIN IDEA
During the second half of the 19th century, the nation experienced tremendous growth.

WHY IT MATTERS NOW
The changes that the United States underwent helped transform it into the modern nation it is today.

ONE AMERICAN'S STORY

Nat Love was born a slave in Tennessee in 1854. After the Civil War, he was one of thousands of African Americans who left the South and went west. In 1869, Love headed for Dodge City, Kansas. He was 15 and now free.

Love's horse-taming skills landed him a job as a cowhand. For 20 years, he took part in the cattle drives that brought Texas cattle to Kansas stockyards. He became well known for his expert horsemanship. In his autobiography, Love offered a lively but exaggerated account of his life. He told how he braved hailstorms, wild animals, and human attackers.

A VOICE FROM THE PAST

I carry the marks of fourteen bullet wounds on different parts of my body, most any one of which would be sufficient to kill an ordinary man. . . . Horses were shot from under me, men killed around me, but always I escaped with a trifling wound at the worst.

Nat Love, *The Life and Adventures of Nat Love*

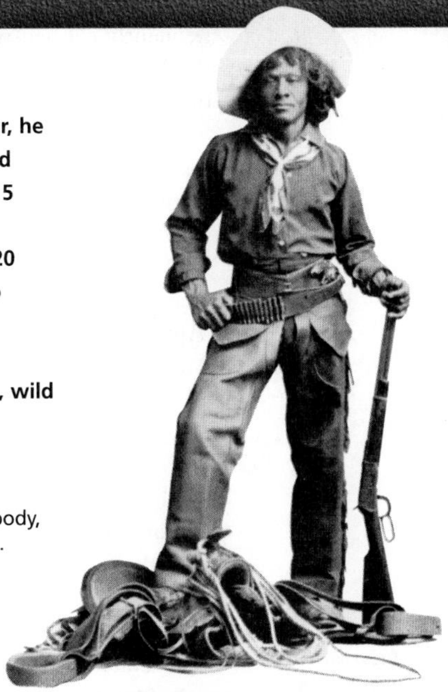

Nat Love was an African-American cowhand who became a rodeo star.

During the second half of the 19th century, the United States underwent a time of tremendous growth. Americans such as Nat Love contributed to this growth.

1 Westward Expansion

In the decades following the Civil War, more Americans began to settle on the **frontier.** The frontier was the sparsely populated area on the western side of the nation. Aside from Native Americans, few people lived there. It included the **Great Plains,** the area from the Missouri River to the Rocky Mountains.

American settlers migrated westward for several reasons. The discovery of gold in California drew numerous fortune seekers to the West. A growing demand for beef in the nation's cities prompted ranchers to seek

SECTION OBJECTIVES

1. To understand the causes and effects of westward expansion
2. To describe U.S. industrialization in the late 19th century
3. To examine the growth and development of U.S. cities
4. To discuss the effects of the new immigrants on American life

SKILLBUILDER
Interpreting Graphs, p. 543

CRITICAL THINKING
Making Inferences, p. 540
Comparing and Contrasting, p. 542
Recognizing Effects, p. 543

FOCUS & MOTIVATE

5-MINUTE WARM-UP

Making Inferences These questions focus on immigration.

1. Look at the graphs on page 543. During which decade did the greatest number of immigrants come to the United States?
2. What part of the world did these immigrants most likely come from?

Warm-Up Transparency, WT19EPIL

INSTRUCT

INSTRUCT: OBJECTIVE 1
Westward Expansion

- Why did many Americans move to the frontier?
- How did the federal government and railroads aid in settling the West?
- What were the causes and consequences of the Dawes Act?

In-Depth Resources: Unit 5
- Guided Reading, p. 80

Reading Study Guide (Spanish and English), pp. 179–180

RECOMMENDED RESOURCES

In-Depth Resources: Unit 5
- Guided Reading, p. 80
- Building Vocabulary, p. 84
- Geog. Application, pp. 86–87
- Reteaching Activity, p. 93
- Enrichment Activity, p. 97

Reading Study Guide (Spanish and English), pp. 179–180

Formal Assessment, Section Quiz, p. 334

Integrated Assessment
- Rubrics, 5.6, 2.1

Access for Students Acquiring English/ESL
- Guided Reading, p. 123
- Geog. Application, pp. 128–129

INTEGRATED TECHNOLOGY
Electronic Teacher Tools
classzone.com

TEST-TAKING RESOURCES
Strategies for Test Preparation
Test Practice Transparencies, TT67–TT74
Online Test Practice

land for raising cattle. In addition, thousands of families sought to start a new life as frontier farmers.

The federal government encouraged western settlement by passing the **Homestead Act** in 1862. This law offered 160 acres of free land to anyone who agreed to live on the land for five years and improve it.

Railroads also played a key role in extending U.S. control over Western lands. Trains carried the natural resources of the West—minerals, timber, crops, and cattle—to markets in the East. In turn, trains brought miners, ranchers, and farmers west to develop these resources further.

This western movement forced changes to Native American ways of life. As white settlers continued to move farther onto the frontier, they frequently clashed with Native Americans over land and resources. By the 1880s, most Native American tribes had been forced onto reservations, land set aside for them by the U.S. government.

Many well-meaning reformers felt that assimilation was the only way for Native Americans to survive. In other words, the reformers wanted Native Americans to adopt the culture of white Americans. Passed in 1887, the **Dawes Act** was intended to encourage Native Americans to give up their traditional cultures and become farmers. The U.S. government sent many Native American children to boarding schools to be "Americanized." In the end, the Dawes Act did little to benefit Native Americans. Not all of them wanted to be farmers. Those who did lacked the tools, money, or other resources to be successful.

Reading **History**

A. Making Inferences Why were railroads so important to the West?

A. Possible Answer They brought Americans to the West and shipped Western products back to the East.

INSTRUCT: OBJECTIVE 2

The Growth of Industry

- What factors helped increase industrialization in the United States?
- Why was the period of the late 1800s called the Gilded Age?
- What tactic helped laborers improve their lot?

2 The Growth of Industry

As thousands of Americans forged new lives in the West, much of the rest of the nation experienced the Industrial Revolution. In the years after the Civil War, a number of factors boosted the pace of industrialization in the United States.

1. **Plentiful natural resources.** The United States had abundant raw materials, including forests, water, coal, iron, copper, silver, and gold.
2. **Improved transportation.** Since the early 1800s, steamboats, canals, and railroads made it ever easier to ship items over long distances.

HISTORY FROM VISUALS

Interpreting the Painting John Ferguson Weir titled this painting *Forging the Shaft.* In his paintings, Weir tried to capture the excitement and dignity of work in heavy industry. Tell students to look closely at the painting. Ask them to make some inferences about the workers who are depicted in the painting and about the kind of work they are doing. **Possible Responses** The work looks like it would be hot, strenuous, and dangerous. Laborers probably were not well paid, but their work required skill as well as strength.

Extension Have students speculate about what the workers in the picture are doing. Ask students what they think the fire is doing to the metal. What might the finished object be used for?

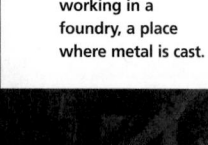

These laborers are working in a foundry, a place where metal is cast.

540

ACTIVITY OPTIONS

INDIVIDUAL NEEDS

BLOCK SCHEDULING

LESS PROFICIENT READERS

Finding Main Ideas As a way to focus students' attention and set a purpose for reading, write the headings from this section on the board and identify them as Main Ideas (MI). As you read the section together, have students identify the important details (D) that support each main idea. Write them in an outline format.

MI: Westward Expansion
- D: Settlers went to the West for gold, beef production, and farming.
- D: The Homestead Act gave settlers a start.
- D: Trains carried people and goods.
- D: Settlers and Native Americans clashed.
- D: The Dawes Act was meant to help Native Americans, but it did not work.

3. **Growing population.** From 1860 to 1900, the U.S. population grew from 31.5 million to 76 million—due in large part to a wave of immigration. This increase provided millions of workers to make products and consumers to buy them.
4. **New inventions.** New technologies and inventions made industry more efficient.
5. **Investment capital.** Banks and wealthy people invested in businesses so they could improve factories and equipment. Such improvements made business more successful. The government also provided help, such as subsidies, to businesses wishing to expand.

Vocabulary
capital: money and property used in a business

Industrialization led to the rise of powerful businessmen. John D. Rockefeller, for example, led the oil industry. Andrew Carnegie controlled the steel industry. They and others made millions—often through ruthless tactics.

The late 1800s become known as the **Gilded Age.** To gild is to coat an object with gold leaf. Gilded decorations were popular during the era. But the name has a deeper meaning. Just as gold leaf can disguise an object of lesser value, so did the wealth of a few people mask society's problems, including corrupt politics and widespread poverty.

Many of the nation's poor were workers who labored in factories. Eventually, angry workers organized to try to improve their lives. They formed labor unions—groups of workers that negotiated with business owners to obtain better wages and working conditions. By standing up to employers, unions won shorter working hours and better pay for workers.

Business leader John D. Rockefeller is shown as a wealthy king. Notice which industries are the "jewels in his crown."

Vocabulary
negotiate: to discuss something in order to reach an agreement

3 Cities Grow and Change

The Industrial Revolution, which transformed how people worked, also changed where people worked. During the late 1800s, more and more people moved to cities to find jobs.

Factories sprouted in cities because they offered good transportation and plentiful workers. Increasing numbers of factory jobs appeared in U.S. cities, followed by more workers to fill those jobs. The growth of cities that resulted from these changes is called **urbanization.**

As people flocked to cities, overcrowding became a serious problem. Many poor families lived in rented apartments or tenements. A tenement is an apartment house that is usually run-down and overcrowded. Many tenements were dangerous and unhealthy places to live.

Many Americans were disgusted by the poverty and slums in the cities. Some people, known as urban reformers, sought changes that could solve these problems. Some reformers helped to ease the problems

MORE ABOUT . . .

Women and Children at Work

The number of women and children in the work force doubled between 1870 and 1890 to 4 million women workers and 1.5 million child workers (ages 10–15). The death rate for female workers was twice that of other workers. Women were paid less than men, were the first to be laid off, and often endured abuse from male coworkers and bosses. Children often earned only pennies, but at best, they received about half the pay of a male adult worker.

INSTRUCT: OBJECTIVE 3

Cities Grow and Change

- Why did people move to the cities during the Industrial Revolution?
- What problems resulted from urbanization?
- How did reformers and political machines address the social problems of the cities?

ACTIVITY OPTIONS

MULTIPLE LEARNING STYLES: SPACIAL — BLOCK SCHEDULING

CITY PLANNING

Class time One class period

Task Designing a plan for a neighborhood of working-class families

Purpose To gain an understanding of the problems faced by late 19th-century working class people

Supplies Needed

- Drawing paper, pens, colored pencils
- Reference materials about 19th-century cities

Activity Suggest that students research living conditions in 19th-century tenements, paying special attention to primary-source photographs of these neighborhoods. Brainstorm the elements in a neighborhood that provide for its citizens' needs. Divide the class into small groups. Each group should draw a street plan for a 19th-century neighborhood of working-class people. Students could also include drawings of the kinds of multifamily or single-family homes they would include in their plan. Display the completed plans in class and discuss them.

CITIZENSHIP TODAY

OBJECTIVE

Students will identify a local community problem and create a plan to solve it.

David Levitt

In addition to collecting food from school cafeterias, Levitt has convinced restaurants to donate food to his project, Food for Thought. Levitt also asked manufacturers to donate containers to store the food he collected. In addition, Levitt worked with a member of the Florida State Legislature on a bill requiring all Florida public schools to donate lunchroom leftovers to food pantries or homeless shelters. The legislation became law in the summer of 1999.

Citizenship Today, pp. 13–14

CITIZENSHIP TODAY

Community Service

Since the United States began, citizens have shared concerns about their communities. Many citizens have identified problems and proposed solutions to them.

In 1993, sixth-grader David Levitt asked his principal if the leftover food from the school cafeteria could be sent to a program to feed needy people. David was told that many restrictions prevented giving away the food.

Determined to get food to people who needed it, David talked to the school board, the state health department, and private companies to convince them to back his program. Today, more than 500,000 pounds of food from schools has been given to hungry people in the Seminole, Florida, area.

David Levitt carries supplies for his food pantry program.

How Do You Participate in Your Community?

1. In a small group, think about problems within your community. Make a list of those problems.
2. Choose one problem to work on.
3. Gather information about the problem. Keep a log of your sources to use again.
4. After you gather information, brainstorm solutions to the problem. Create a plan to carry out one solution.
5. Present the problem and your plan to the class.

See the Citizenship Handbook, page 270.

For more about community service . . .

RESEARCH LINKS CLASSZONE.COM

INSTRUCT: OBJECTIVE 4

The New Immigrants

- How did immigration patterns change at the end of the 19th century?
- How did immigrant cultures become part of American culture?
- What was the purpose of the Chinese Exclusion Act?

of urban life by opening settlement houses. These facilities offered services such as daycare, education, and health care to needy people in slum neighborhoods.

Political machines were another type of organization that addressed the problems of the city. A political machine is an organization that influences enough votes to control a local government. Although often corrupt, political machines did some good things for cities. They built parks, sewers, schools, roads, and orphanages in many cities. In addition, machine politicians often helped city dwellers find jobs or homes.

4 The New Immigrants

Many of those who lived in the nation's growing cities were immigrants. Throughout the late 1800s and early 1900s, the United States experienced a wave of immigration. Until the 1890s, most immigrants to the United States came from northern and western Europe. But after 1900, fewer northern Europeans immigrated, and more southern and eastern Europeans did. This later group of immigrants came to be known as the **new immigrants**.

Immigrants settled where they could find jobs. Many found work in U.S. factories. They tried to assimilate, or become part of American

Reading **History**

B. Comparing and Contrasting How were settlement houses and political machines similar? How were they different?

B. Answer They were similar in that they tried to solve urban problems and help immigrants. They were different in that the political machines were corrupt.

ACTIVITY OPTIONS

STANDARDS FOR EVALUATION: CITIZENSHIP TODAY

BLOCK SCHEDULING

Each plan should

- focus on a community problem.
- be well researched and well organized.
- clearly explain the group's perception of the problem.
- propose a course of action.
- identify the steps the group would take to carry out its solutions.
- use language effectively.

society. At the same time, however, they also were changing America. Immigrants did not give up their cultures right away. Bits and pieces of immigrant languages, foods, and music worked their way into the rest of American culture.

Despite their efforts to assimilate, immigrants faced prejudice from native-born Americans. Many native-born Americans feared they would have to compete with immigrants for jobs. In 1882, Congress passed laws to restrict immigration. Nonwhites faced deeper prejudice than European immigrants did. Asians faced some of the worst prejudice. In 1882, Congress passed the Chinese Exclusion Act. It banned Chinese immigration for ten years. The Chinese Exclusion Act was renewed in 1892. In 1902, Congress made the ban permanent. It was not repealed until 1943.

The Chinese Exclusion Act was not the only example of prejudice in the United States around 1900. As you will read in the next section, racial discrimination was very much a part of life in American society at the dawn of the 20th century.

CONNECTIONS TO MATH

U.S. Immigration, *1841–1900*

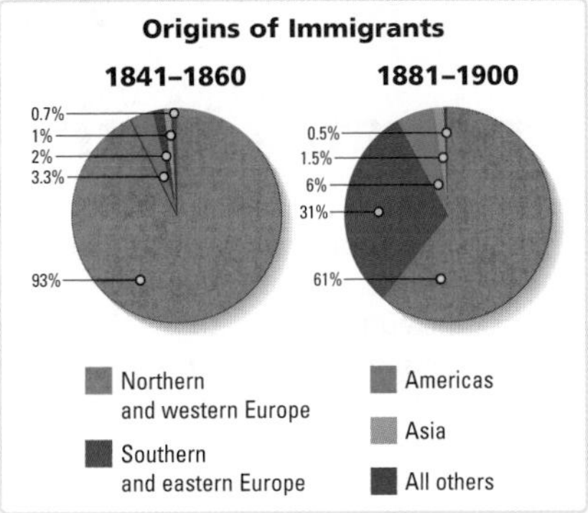

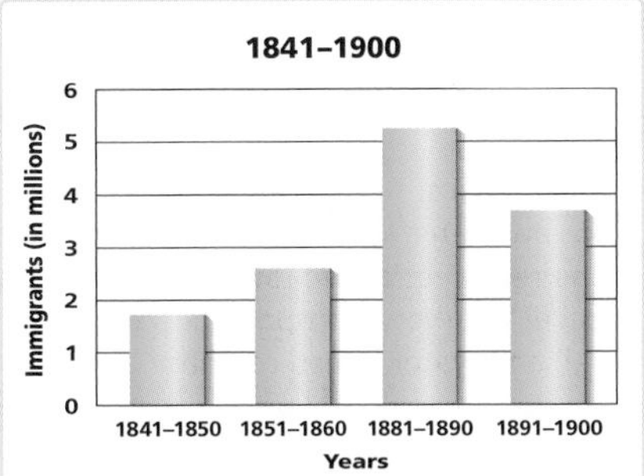

Source: *Historical Statistics of the United States*

SKILLBUILDER **Interpreting Graphs**

1. *About how many immigrants came to the United States from 1841 to 1860?*
2. *About how many southern and eastern European immigrants came to the United States from 1881 to 1900?*

Skillbuilder Answers
1. about 4.3 million
2. about 2.8 million

Section 1 Assessment

1. Terms & Names

Explain the significance of:
- frontier
- Great Plains
- Homestead Act
- Dawes Act
- Gilded Age
- urbanization
- new immigrants

2. Taking Notes

Use a cluster diagram like the one below to list the factors that contributed to industrial growth in the United States.

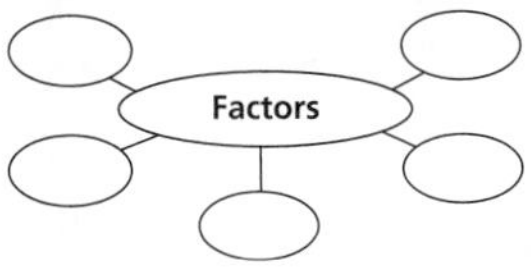

3. Main Ideas

a. What drew large numbers of people to the West in the decades after 1860?

b. What urban problems did reformers try to solve?

c. How were the new immigrants different from earlier immigrants?

4. Critical Thinking

Recognizing Effects How were the effects of the Dawes Act different from what was intended?

THINK ABOUT
- the goals of the act
- the impact on the land use and independence of the Plains people

ACTIVITY OPTIONS

MATH
GEOGRAPHY

Research immigration to your city or state. Create a **spreadsheet** of this information or draw a **map** showing immigration routes.

HISTORY FROM VISUALS

Interpreting the Graphs Point out the different kinds of information presented on the three graphs. Have students discuss how the origins of immigrants changed between 1841–1860 and 1881–1900. Ask: Which two groups showed the greatest increase from the first time period to the second? **Answer** southern and eastern Europe and the Americas. Ask students to summarize the overall changes in immigration that the whole set of graphs depicts. **Possible Responses** Immigration increased tremendously between the 1840s and the 1880s; most immigrants were still coming from Europe, but they came from different regions of Europe.

Extension Using the pie graphs and the bar graph, have students estimate approximately how many millions of immigrants came from northern and western Europe and southern and eastern Europe from 1841 to 1860 and from 1881 to 1900. Ask them to present their answers on a bar graph.

ASSESS & RETEACH

Setting the Stage Have students fill in the appropriate boxes in the graphic organizer.

Formal Assessment
- Section Quiz, p. 334

RETEACHING ACTIVITY

Divide the class into four groups. Assign one section objective to each group. Have the group identify the key concepts in each objective on a graphic organizer, such as a word web, chart, or spider map on a large piece of drawing paper.

In-Depth Resources: Unit 5
- Reteaching Activity, p. 93

Section 1 Assessment

1. Terms & Names

frontier, p. 539
Great Plains, p. 539
Homestead Act, p. 540
Dawes Act, p. 540
Gilded Age, p. 541
urbanization, p. 541
new immigrants, p. 542

2. Taking Notes

Answer: plentiful natural resources; improved transportation; growing population; new inventions; investment capital

3. Main Ideas

a. mining; ranching; farming
b. poverty; crime; sanitation; disease
c. They came from southern and eastern Europe versus the earlier ones who came from northern and western Europe.

4. Critical Thinking

Goal: Better treatment of Native Americans and ensuring their survival. Effect: Native Americans lost their land and culture and were treated with contempt.

ACTIVITY OPTIONS

Integrated Assessment
Rubrics, 5.6, 2.1

GEOGRAPHY *in* HISTORY

OBJECTIVE
Students will analyze and interpret information from a map to understand the effects of geographic features and resources on the development of the Midwest.

BLOCK SCHEDULING

MORE ABOUT . . .

The Canned Food Industry
In 1817, the first canning factories appeared in America. Union soldiers in the Civil War carried canned meat, oysters, and vegetables. After the war, cans were machine-cut. Giant canning factories sprouted up, especially in Chicago, which used assembly lines to mass-produce its food products. The canning industry inspired other inventions, such as a mechanical pea-gathering an shelling machine and a machine to fillet fish.

INSTRUCT

- Why was the Erie Canal important to the growth of the Midwest?
- What caused the boom in industry and manufacturing in the Midwest?
- How did the Midwest's natural resources affect its development?

MAP SKILL QUESTIONS
In the late 1800's what form of transportation would you have used to ship factory parts from Buffalo to Chicago?

Where are most of the sawmill centers located?

Why do you think they were located there?

Which areas in the Midwest had meatpacking?

In what was Chicago connected to other parts of the nation?

GEOGRAPHY *in* HISTORY

REGION AND HUMAN-ENVIRONMENT INTERACTION

Industry in the Midwest

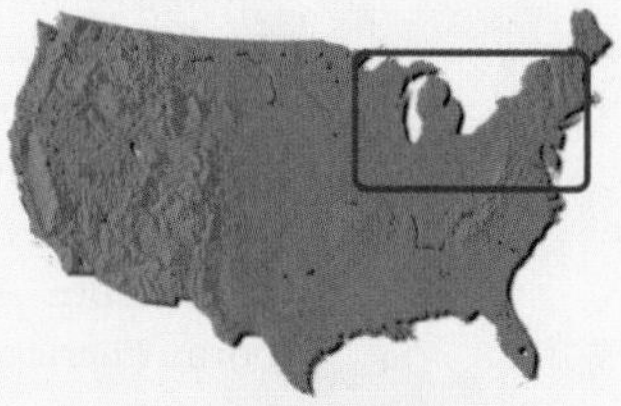

The Midwest is the region around the Great Lakes and the Upper Mississippi Valley. The region saw explosive growth during the 1800s. The first wave came after 1825, when the Erie Canal linked the East with the Great Lakes region. The second wave, caused by investments in products related to the Civil War (1861–1865), saw a boom in mining, farming, forestry, and meat-packing. By 1890, 29 percent of the country's manufacturing employment was in the Midwest, and the next big wave of growth was just beginning. New industries included steel and steel products, such as train rails and skyscraper beams.

Transportation and resources spurred the region's growth. Coal, oil, iron ore, limestone, and lumber were abundant, and the land was fertile. Trains, rivers, and lakes connected the Midwest to markets in the East and South and brought in raw materials from the West. The map on page 545 shows the resources of the lower Great Lakes and how transportation by rail and water joined regions.

The industries of the Midwest used raw materials that came both from their own region and from other regions of the country. For example, the cattle in this photograph of the Chicago stockyards came by rail from the ranches of the West. In contrast, the logs being floated down the river came from the pine forests of Michigan and Wisconsin.

ARTIFACT FILE

A Quick Dinner Midwestern meat-packing companies advertised canned meats as a way to save time feeding a hungry family.

Affordable Housing People began to build with wooden siding over a frame of wooden two-by-fours. These homes were cheap and quick to construct.

MUSEUM CONNECTIONS

The museum of the Chicago Historical Society is dedicated to the multicultural heritage of Chicago and of Illinois. In addition to its extensive collection of research materials about Chicago history, the Society also houses a large collection of material relating to Abraham Lincoln and an outstanding costume collection, as well as paintings, sculpture, and photographs. The Society estimates its collection at about 20 million items.

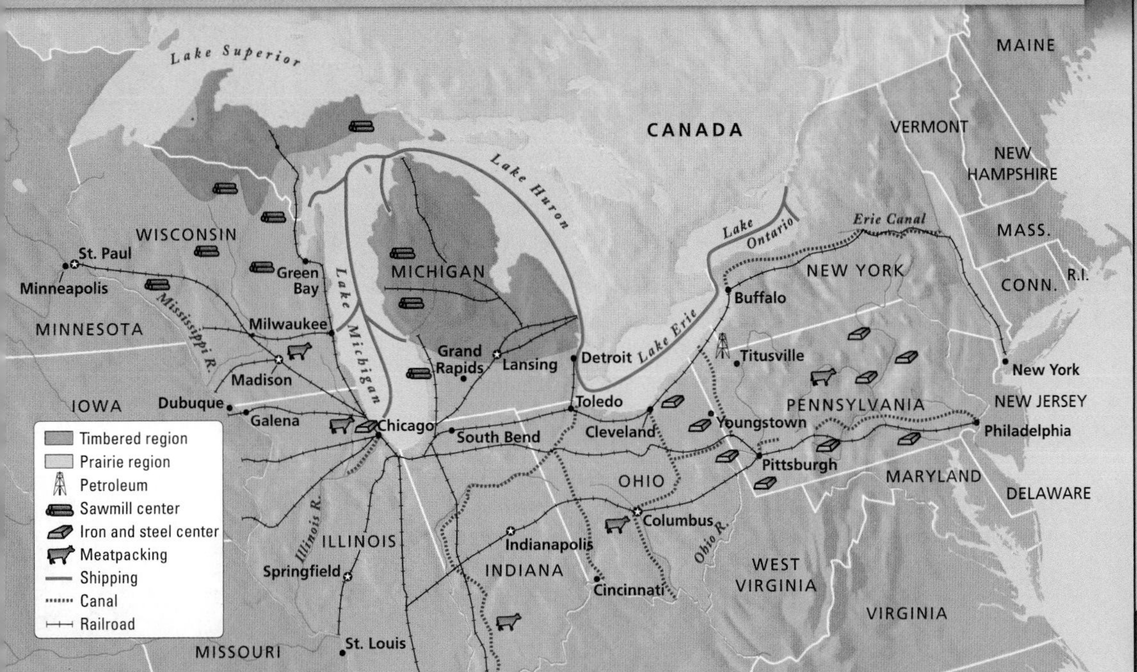

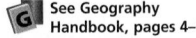

Iron ore from the Lake Superior region and coal from southern Illinois were used to manufacture steel.

On-Line Field Trip

The Chicago Historical Society
in Chicago, Illinois, contains photographs, documents, and artifacts such as this Western Electric typewriter, made in 1900. Typewriters enabled office workers to produce neat, clean documents quickly.

For more about the Midwest . . .

RESEARCH LINKS
CLASSZONE.COM

CONNECT TO GEOGRAPHY

1. **Region** What advantages did the Midwest have that helped it become highly industrialized?
2. **Human-Environment Interaction** How did the development of railroads add to the region's advantages?

See Geography Handbook, pages 4–5.

CONNECT TO HISTORY

3. **Analyzing Causes** Chicago was a big meatpacking center. Why do you think that industry chose to locate there?

CRITICAL THINKING ACTIVITY

Recognizing Important Details Ask students to copy the web below and add resources and details about each category from the feature.

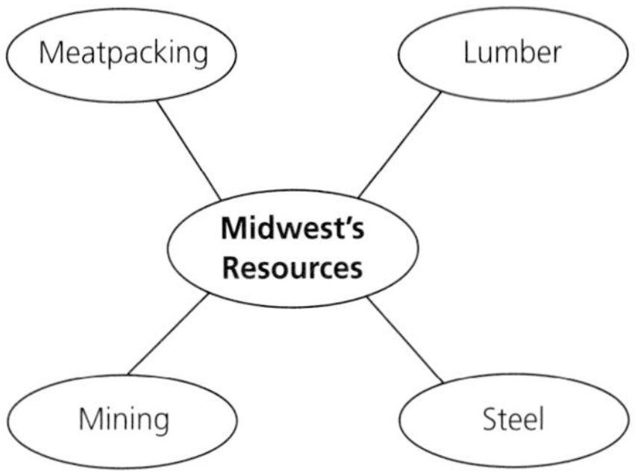

Class Time 20 minutes

MORE ABOUT . . .

Chicago
On October 8, 1871, a fire broke out in the barn behind the O'Leary house in Chicago. One of the family's cows is usually blamed for starting the fire by kicking over a lantern. The fire spread quickly, destroying about 4 square miles of the city and about $200 million in property. After the fire, boosters claimed that Chicago would come back stronger than ever. Investors, recognizing the city's potential for growth, helped the city rebuild. By the end of the 19th century, Chicago had become the nation's second-largest city.

CONNECT TO GEOGRAPHY

1. **Region** The Midwest had abundant natural resources, such as timber, minerals, and oil, as well as rivers and lakes for shipping. The land was fertile for agricultural purposes.
2. **Human-Environment Interaction** The railroads made it easier to ship goods to places where there were no waterways, natural or man-made. Railroads were also able to connect to waterways, so shippers often used both methods.

CONNECT TO HISTORY

3. **Analyzing Causes** Many railroad lines could connect easily with Chicago, which would have made it much easier to bring cattle to market. It also was linked to shipping on the Great Lakes and to the Mississippi River by a canal.

2 Life at the Turn of the Century

TERMS & NAMES
mass culture
leisure
vaudeville
ragtime
Jim Crow
segregation
Plessy v. Ferguson
NAACP

MAIN IDEA	WHY IT MATTERS NOW
Around the turn of the century, mass culture emerged and the nation continued to grapple with racism.	Americans continue to participate in a mass culture and issues of race continue to affect society.

ONE AMERICAN'S STORY

Abigail Scott was born in Illinois in 1834. She was told that her mother remarked at the time, "Poor baby! She'll be a woman some day! . . . A woman's lot is so hard!" At 17, Abigail moved to Oregon by wagon train with her family. Her mother died on the journey. In Oregon, Abigail taught school until she married a farmer named Benjamin Duniway in 1853. When he was disabled in an accident, Abigail assumed the support of her family. She wrote about a day on a pioneer farm with its endless chores.

A VOICE FROM THE PAST

[W]ashing, scrubbing, churning . . . preparing . . . meals in our lean-to kitchen . . . [having] to bake and clean and stew and fry; to be in short, a general pioneer drudge, with never a penny of my own, was not pleasant business.

Abigail Scott Duniway, in her autobiography, *Path Breaking*

Like Abigail Scott Duniway, this pioneer woman worked long and hard. She is shown here with buffalo chips she has collected on the treeless prairie to use as fuel.

The long days of hard work for the frontier pioneers represented only one example of life in the United States at the turn of the 20th century. In the East, industrialization and new technologies were creating a distinct urban culture. At the same time, racial minorities across the country continued to face discrimination.

1 Life in the West

Life in the West was tough. Farmers, such as Abigail Duniway, faced many challenges. The Plains were nearly treeless. Farmers were forced to build their first homes from blocks of sod, or prairie soil. For fuel, the farmers burned corn cobs or "cow chips" (dried manure). In many places, farmers had to dig wells more than 280 feet deep to reach the only water. Blizzards, prairie fires, hailstorms, tornadoes, grasshoppers, and drought added to the misery of life on the plains.

New inventions helped farmers to meet some of these challenges. The steel plow, for example, sliced through the tough sod. Windmills adapted to the plains pumped water from deep wells to the surface. Barbed wire

SECTION OBJECTIVES

1. To describe the challenges and opportunities for Western migrants
2. To identify innovations that shaped mass culture
3. To explain how racism, discrimination, and segregation affected American society

SKILLBUILDER
Interpreting Charts, p. 547

CRITICAL THINKING
Summarizing, p. 547
Making Inferences, pp. 549, 550
Solving Problems, p. 550

FOCUS & MOTIVATE

5-MINUTE WARM-UP

Making Inferences These questions focus on the growth of Western cities.

1. Look at the chart on page 547. Which city was the largest in 1860?
2. How might each of these economic activities—mining, ranching, and farming—contribute to the growth of these cities?

Warm-Up Transparency, WT19EPIL

INSTRUCT

INSTRUCT: OBJECTIVE 1

Life in the West

1. What new inventions helped the farmers meet the challenges of the Plains?
2. What factors led to the rapid growth of Western cities?
3. How would a cowhand's life typically differ from that of a woman in the West?

In-Depth Resources: Unit 5
- Guided Reading, p. 81

Reading Study Guide (Spanish and English), pp. 181–182

RECOMMENDED RESOURCES

In-Depth Resources: Unit 5
- Guided Reading, p. 81
- Building Vocabulary, p. 84
- Reteaching Activity, p. 94

Reading Study Guide (Spanish and English), pp. 181–182

America's History Makers, pp. 85–86

Formal Assessment, Section Quiz, p. 335

Integrated Assessment
- Rubrics, 4.4, 5.1

Access for Students Acquiring English/ESL
- Guided Reading, p. 124

INTEGRATED TECHNOLOGY

Humanities Transparency HT41, HT42
- Edison Concert Phonograph
- Football Game

Electronic Teacher Tools

classzone.com

TEST-TAKING RESOURCES

Strategies for Test Preparation

Test Practice Transparencies, TT75–TT78

Online Test Practice

allowed farmers to fence in land and livestock. Meanwhile, reapers made the harvesting of crops much easier, and threshers helped farmers to separate grain or seed from straw. These inventions also made farm work more efficient. For example, from 1860 to 1890, farmers doubled their production of wheat.

Reading **History**

A. Summarizing What inventions helped farmers to meet the challenges of the prairie?

A. Answer steel plow, windmills, barbed wire, reapers, threshers

The West was also home to numerous cowhands, who helped herd cattle. The cowhands drove the cattle to cow towns, where they would be shipped on trains to the meat markets of the East. Cowhands spent most of their days in the saddle. They ate around campfires and slept under the stars.

In addition to farms and ranches, a number of cities grew in the West. Gold and silver strikes made instant cities of places like Denver in the Colorado Territory and brought new life to sleepy towns like San Francisco in California. These cities prospered while much of the area around them remained barely populated. San Francisco grew from a small town to a city of about 25,000 in just one year following the 1849 gold rush.

The railroads also brought rapid growth to some towns in the West. Omaha, Nebraska, flourished as a meat-processing center for cattle ranches in the region. Portland, Oregon, became a regional market for fish, grain, and lumber.

Skillbuilder Answer San Francisco—142,195 people

Population of Western Cities

CITY	1860	1890
Denver	2,603*	106,713
Omaha	1,883	140,452
Portland	2,874	46,385
San Francisco	56,802	298,997

SKILLBUILDER **Interpreting Charts**

Which city had the largest increase in number of people from 1860 to 1890?

*1861 Territorial Census

Sources: *Population Abstract of the United States; Colorado Republic*

San Francisco, 1847

San Francisco, 1850

❷ Women in the West

Western life provided a few new opportunities for women. Most women who worked held traditional jobs. They were teachers or servants or helped support their families by taking in sewing or laundry. However, a few became sheriffs, gamblers, and even outlaws. In mining camps and cow towns, some women ran dance halls and boarding houses.

Western lawmakers recognized the contributions women made to Western settlement by giving women more legal rights than they had in the East. In most territories, women could own property and control their own money. In addition, in 1869, the Wyoming Territory led the nation in giving women the vote.

HISTORY FROM VISUALS

Reading the Chart Ask students which city had more than 25,000 people in 1860. **Answer** San Francisco. While mining was important to the growth of San Francisco, what evidence suggests that its economic base had become more diversified by 1890? **Possible Response** Its population soared even after the mining boom ended, suggesting that other economic activities continued to provide jobs and draw people there.

Extension Have students locate each city on a U.S. map and write a sentence about how its location contributed to its growth.

INSTRUCT: OBJECTIVE ❷

Women in the West

- What opportunities did life in the West provide for women?
- What political rights did women have in the West?

ACTIVITY OPTIONS

INTERDISCIPLINARY LINK: MATH

BLOCK SCHEDULING

PROFILES OF WESTERN CITIES

Class Time One class period

Task Making a bar graph showing the growth of Western cities between 1860 and 1890

Purpose To analyze and compare growth patterns of Western cities

Supplies Needed

- Graph paper
- Colored markers

Activity Have students make their own population bar graphs by using the information in the pupil edition on page 547, and the information below.

	1860	1890		1860	1890
Des Moines	3,965	50,093	Kansas City	4,418	132,716
Los Angeles	4,385	50,395	San Antonio	8,235	37,673

Then ask: Which cities here have similar rates of growth? *(Des Moines, Los Angeles, and Portland)* Which city grew most rapidly? *(Omaha)*

INSTRUCT: OBJECTIVE 3

Society and Mass Culture/New Leisure Activities

- What medium did advertisers use to influence people?
- Why might spectator sports and other new forms of entertainment develop in urban rather than rural areas?
- How did these new forms of entertainment contribute to the growth of mass culture?

Humanities Transparency HT41, HT42
- Edison Concert Phonograph
- Football Game

MORE ABOUT . . .

Amusement Parks

Trolley companies supported the development of amusement parks at the end of their lines, often by a lake, to encourage people to ride the trolleys on the weekends. These parks usually had picnic tables, dance halls, games, and a few rides. The parks were a huge success. In 1894, Captain Paul Boynton opened the first modern amusement park, Paul Boynton's Water Chutes in Chicago. The Water Chutes charged an entrance fee. It was so successful that Boynton opened another amusement park at Coney Island, on Long Island, in 1895.

Leisure Activities

▼ Coney Island
Visitors to New York's Coney Island cool off in the Steeple-chase Pool.

▼ World's Fair
Visitors to the 1893 world's fair in Chicago saw exotic sights, such as elephants.

▼ Football
Excited fans watch the 1881 Harvard–Yale football game at the Polo Grounds in New York.

Society and Mass Culture 3

Far from the frontier, life for residents of the nation's urban centers was rapidly changing. During the late 1800s, the growth of large cities and other changes helped create an American **mass culture**—a common culture experienced by large numbers of people.

In what became one of the nation's most popular shared activities, more and more Americans began to read newspapers. Newspapers had a wide influence on American life, including the rise of modern advertising. Advertisers used images of celebrities in newspapers and magazines to tempt people to buy products. Advertisements also helped people learn about new products. At the turn of the century, new inventions, such as the electric washing machine, promised to help people do their household chores more easily. Because women did most of these chores as well as most of the shopping, manufacturers marketed these new devices to women.

New Leisure Activities

Advertising and shopping were not the only daily activities changing at this time. **Leisure,** or free time, activities also changed. In cities, new parks provided entertainment for people. The increasing number of people who worked in factories and offices liked to go to parks for sunshine and fresh air. Parks helped bring grass and trees back into city landscapes.

Central Park in New York City is the nation's best-known urban park. Opened in 1876, Central Park was built to look like the country. Trees and shrubs dotted its gently rolling landscape. Winding walkways let city dwellers imagine they were strolling in the woods. People could also ride bicycles and play sports in the park.

In addition to urban parks, amusement parks provided a place people could go for fun. World's fairs provided another wildly popular form of entertainment for Americans. Between 1876 and 1916, several U.S. cities, including Philadelphia, Chicago, St. Louis, and San Francisco, hosted world's fairs.

During this time, spectator sports also became popular entertainment. Baseball, football, boxing, and many other sports drew thousands of people to fields and gymnasiums around the country as spectators as well as participants.

ACTIVITY OPTIONS

INDIVIDUAL NEEDS

BLOCK SCHEDULING

STUDENTS ACQUIRING ENGLISH/ESL

Finding Main Ideas Point out to students the phrase *mass culture* on page 548. Tell them that mass culture is the set of experiences and ideas shared by many Americans across the whole country. Ask them to identify factors in this part of the section that promoted the development of such a shared culture in the early 1900s. Students may recognize the influence of newspapers, spectator sports, and fairs, among other examples. Then ask the class to consider what factors influence American mass culture today. They may suggest such examples as television, nationally known brand names, chain stores, malls, and movies, as well as some of the same factors that shaped life a century ago, such as sports.

In addition to sports, other forms of live entertainment attracted large audiences. **Vaudeville,** for example, featured a mixture of song, dance, and comedy. New types of music also began to be heard. **Ragtime,** a blend of African-American and European musical forms, was an important new type of music. Early in the 20th century, movies began to compete with live entertainment. The first movies were silent and were added as the final feature of a vaudeville show. Soon, storefront theaters appeared that showed only movies.

Reading **History**
B. Making Inferences How do you think movies contributed to mass culture?
B. Answer Unlike live performances, the same movie could be shown all over the country at the same time.

Segregation and Discrimination 4

Many Americans at the turn of the century enjoyed the freedom to participate in the emerging mass culture. For the nation's racial minorities, however, racism and segregation often limited their economic, political, and social freedom. As you read in earlier chapters, racist attitudes had been developing in America for centuries. Such attitudes led whites to discriminate against nonwhites around the country. The most obvious examples of racial discrimination were in the South. African Americans experienced political power in the South during Reconstruction. (See Chapter 18.) But when Reconstruction ended in 1877, Southern states passed laws to restrict African Americans' rights.

Segregation often forced African Americans to use separate entrances from whites.

For example, Southern states passed laws that set up literacy, or reading, tests and poll taxes to prevent blacks from voting. White officials made sure that blacks failed the tests by giving unfair exams. For instance, white officials might give blacks tests written in Latin.

In addition to voting restrictions, African Americans faced **Jim Crow** laws. Jim Crow laws enforced **segregation,** or separation, of white and black people in public places. As a result, separate schools, restrooms, and seating in public places were common throughout the South. In 1896, the Supreme Court upheld the practice of segregation in its decision in ***Plessy v. Ferguson*** by declaring that "separate but equal" facilities did not violate the Fourteenth Amendment.

5 African Americans Organize

A number of African-American leaders worked to overcome discrimination. Booker T. Washington, a former slave, urged blacks to improve their lives by learning trades and gaining economic strength. In 1881, he founded Tuskegee Institute in Alabama to achieve this goal. At Tuskegee, Washington hired talented teachers and scholars, such as George Washington Carver.

To gain white support, Washington did not openly challenge segregation. Some black leaders, however, disagreed with this approach.

MORE ABOUT . . .

Ragtime

Tired of slow waltz music, young people eagerly embraced ragtime around 1900. The name probably came from a description of the rhythm of black dance music as "ragged time." Ragtime's exciting beat inspired the names of such songs as "Irresistible Fox Trot Rag," "That Fascinating Rag," and "That Nifty Rag."

Ragtime had an enormous influence on American music. Throughout the 20th century, American musical styles such as jazz, blues, rock-and-roll, rap, and rhythm-and-blues built on the style of ragtime.

America's Music CD

INSTRUCT: OBJECTIVE

Segregation and Discrimination 4

- How did Southern states restrict African-Americans' rights after Reconstruction?
- What were Jim Crow laws?
- How did *Plessy* v. *Ferguson* affect segregation?

INSTRUCT: OBJECTIVE

African Americans Organize / Discrimination in the West 5

- How did Booker T. Washington and W. E. B. Du Bois differ in their approaches to achieving equality for African Americans?
- What kinds of discrimination did minorities other than African Americans face during this period?
- What groups faced discrimination in the West?

ACTIVITY OPTIONS

INTERDISCIPLINARY LINK: GOVERNMENT/CIVICS

BLOCK SCHEDULING

A TASK FORCE FOR PROGRESS

Class Time One class period

Task Working as a task force to set priorities for a goal

Purpose To analyze the relative importance of three approaches to social change around 1900

Supplies Needed

- Reference material about racial discrimination toward African Americans at the turn of the century
- Information about Booker T. Washington, W. E. B. Du Bois, and Ida B. Wells

Activity Divide the class into three groups. Explain that three leading black activists each gave priority to a different aspect of the struggle for equal rights—economic improvement (Booker T. Washington), political and intellectual activism (W. E. B. Du Bois), and a campaign against violence (Ida B. Wells). Assign each group one of these leaders and tell the group to work as a task force to advocate for that leader's approach. Let each group present its position to the class.

AMERICA'S HISTORY MAKERS

W. E. B. Du Bois

W. E. B. Du Bois was born in Great Barrington, Massachusetts, and graduated from Fisk University. In 1895, he earned a Ph.D. from Harvard University, the first African American to do so. In his 1903 book *The Souls of Black Folk,* Du Bois argued that the greatest force for human progress was "the power of the ballot." Committed to political action, Du Bois criticized Booker T. Washington's approach as a materialistic "gospel of work and money."

Possible Response: Students might suggest that the Talented Tenth would be successful in disproving white stereotypes of most African Americans.

America's History Makers
- W. E. B. Du Bois, pp. 85–86

ASSESS & RETEACH

Setting the Stage Have students review the events from this section that fit on the time line graphic organizer for this section.

Formal Assessment
- Section Quiz, p. 335

RETEACHING ACTIVITY

Divide the class into four teams and assign one of the objectives in the section to each team. Ask each group to make up a series of headlines for newspapers of the period that identifies key events in each objective. Post the headlines on a classroom bulletin board.

In-Depth Resources: Unit 5
- Reteaching Activity, p. 94

AMERICA'S HISTORY MAKERS

W. E. B. DU BOIS
1868–1963

W. E. B. Du Bois grew up in a middle-class home. He went to college and earned his doctorate at Harvard. Du Bois became one of the most distinguished scholars of the 20th century.

Du Bois fought against segregation. He believed that the best way to end it would be to have educated African Americans lead the fight. He referred to this group of educated African Americans as the "Talented Tenth"—the most educated 10 percent of African Americans.

Why do you think Du Bois believed the Talented Tenth should lead the fight against segregation?

W. E. B. Du Bois (doo•BOYS) encouraged African Americans to reject segregation.

A VOICE FROM THE PAST

Is it possible . . . that nine million men can make effective progress in economic lines if they are deprived of political rights? . . . If history and reason give any distinct answer to these questions, it is an emphatic NO.

W. E. B. Du Bois, *The Souls of Black Folk*

Reading **History**

C. Making Inferences In what way did Washington and Du Bois disagree about how to achieve African American progress?

C. Possible Response They were instructed to explore the river and find a water route across the continent.

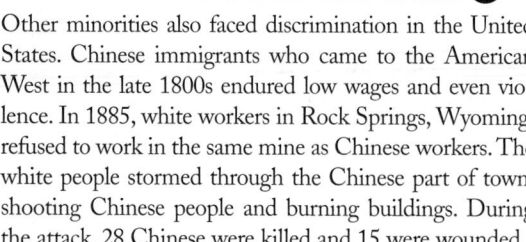

In 1909, Du Bois and other reformers founded the National Association for the Advancement of Colored People, or the **NAACP.** The NAACP played a major role in ending segregation in the 20th century.

Discrimination in the West 5

Other minorities also faced discrimination in the United States. Chinese immigrants who came to the American West in the late 1800s endured low wages and even violence. In 1885, white workers in Rock Springs, Wyoming, refused to work in the same mine as Chinese workers. The white people stormed through the Chinese part of town, shooting Chinese people and burning buildings. During the attack, 28 Chinese were killed and 15 were wounded.

As difficult as life was for the country's minorities, they were not the only ones who struggled. As you will read in the next section, the nation's farmers fought for a stronger voice in government. And a number of Americans strove to improve conditions for workers and reform many of society's ills during the late 1800s and early 1900s.

Section 2 Assessment

1. Terms & Names

Explain the significance of:
- mass culture
- leisure
- vaudeville
- ragtime
- Jim Crow
- segregation
- *Plessy* v. *Ferguson*
- NAACP

2. Taking Notes

Use a diagram such as the one below to note what factors contributed to the emergence of a mass culture at the turn of the century.

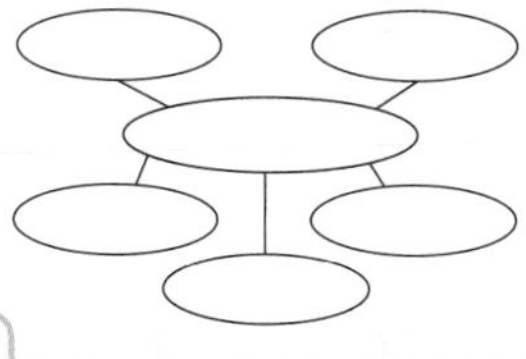

3. Main Ideas

a. How did life on the frontier provide greater opportunities for women?

b. What were Jim Crow laws?

c. What did Chinese immigrants and Mexican immigrants have in common?

4. Critical Thinking

Solving Problems What could have been done to end racial discrimination against nonwhites in the United States around 1900?

THINK ABOUT
- attitudes of whites about nonwhites
- the efforts of nonwhites to find jobs and security
- competition for jobs

ACTIVITY OPTIONS

LANGUAGE ARTS
TECHNOLOGY

Research a civil rights leader from the turn of the century. Write a short **biography** of that person or design a **Web site** devoted to the work of that person.

Section 2 Assessment

1. Terms & Names

mass culture, p. 548
leisure, p. 548
vaudeville, p. 549
ragtime, p. 549
Jim Crow, p. 549
segregation, p. 549
***Plessy* v. *Ferguson*,** p. 549
NAACP, p. 550

2. Taking Notes

newspapers, advertising, urban parks, world's fairs, spectator sports, movies, and shows

3. Main Ideas

a. In addition to more traditional roles, frontier women held numerous jobs normally reserved for men. **b.** laws, mostly in the South, that segregated whites and blacks in public places **c.** Both settled mostly in the West, took low-paying jobs, and faced racial discrimination.

4. Critical Thinking

ACTIVITY OPTIONS

Nonwhites needed to work together to fight against discrimination. Wages for all people needed to be equal to control job competition.

Integrated Assessment
- Rubrics, 4.4, 5.1

3 An Era of Reform

TERMS & NAMES
Populist Party
William Jennings Bryan
progressivism
Theodore Roosevelt
William Howard Taft
Woodrow Wilson

MAIN IDEA
During the late 1800s and early 1900s, Populists and progressives worked for social reform.

WHY IT MATTERS NOW
Many of the reforms supported by Populists and progressives remain in place today.

ONE AMERICAN'S STORY

Journalist Nellie Bly worked for *The New York World.* In 1887, Bly wanted to investigate the Women's Lunatic Asylum in New York City. An asylum is a place where people with an illness can get help. She faked mental illness and fooled doctors so that she could become a patient there. After spending ten days in the asylum, Bly wrote a newspaper article about what she had witnessed. She described being forced to take ice cold baths.

A VOICE FROM THE PAST

My teeth chattered and my limbs were goose-fleshed and blue with cold. Suddenly I got, one after the other, three buckets of water over my head—ice-cold water, too—into my eyes, my ears, my nose and my mouth.

Nellie Bly, quoted in *Nellie Bly: Daredevil, Reporter, Feminist*

Bly also wrote about poor conditions in slums, factories, prisons, and nursing homes—all in an attempt to right the wrongs of American society. She was not alone. During the late 1800s and early 1900s, many Americans worked to reform American institutions and improve life in the United States.

Nellie Bly

1 The Rise of Populism

By the 1870s, many of the nation's farmers faced serious economic problems. Aided by new tools and techniques, farmers grew increasing amounts of food. As supplies of farm products grew, their prices fell. At the same time, farmers had to spend more to run a farm. New farm machinery and railroad rates were especially costly. Railroads, for example, charged the farmers high fees to carry their crops to market.

Farmers eventually began to work together to seek solutions to their problems. In 1890, several farm groups organized to try to gain political power. They formed the **Populist Party**, or People's Party. The Populists wanted the government to adopt a free silver policy, that is, the

SECTION OBJECTIVES

- To identify the factors that gave rise to populism
- To describe the presidential election of 1896
- To detail the goals and tactics of progressive reformers
- To list the progressive actions of U.S. presidents in the early 20th century

CRITICAL THINKING

Recognizing Effects, p. 552
Comparing, p. 552
Analyzing Points of View, p. 553
Finding Main Ideas, p. 553
Drawing Conclusions, p. 555
Recognizing Effects, p. 555

FOCUS & MOTIVATE

5-MINUTE WARM-UP

Drawing Conclusions These questions focus on the progressive policies of Presidents Theodore Roosevelt, Taft, and Wilson.

1. Read "Progressive Presidents" on pages 554–555. What reform programs did these presidents pursue?
2. Which president did the most to advance progressive reform?

Warm-Up Transparency, WT19EPIL

INSTRUCT

INSTRUCT: OBJECTIVE 1

The Rise of Populism

- What economic problems did farmers face in by the 1870s?
- What were the arguments for and against free silver?
- What was the platform of the Populist Party in 1892?

In-Depth Resources: Unit 5
- Guided Reading, p. 81

Reading Study Guide (Spanish and English), pp. 183–184

RECOMMENDED RESOURCES

In-Depth Resources: Unit 5
- Guided Reading, p. 82
- Building Vocabulary, p. 84
- Skillbuilder Practice, p. 85
- Primary Source, pp. 88–89
- Literature Selection, pp. 90–92

Reading Study Guide (Spanish and English), pp. 183–184

America's History Makers, 83–84, 87–88

Formal Assessment, Section Quiz, p. 336

Integrated Assessment
- Rubrics, 1.13, 2.1

Access for Students Acquiring English/ESL, p. 125, 127

INTEGRATED TECHNOLOGY

Humanities Transparency HT43, HT44

Electronic Teacher Tools

classzone.com

TEST-TAKING RESOURCES

Strategies for Test Preparation

Test Practice Transparencies, TT79–TT81

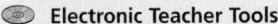

Online Test Practice

unlimited coining of silver. Since silver was plentiful, more money would be put in circulation. Populists believed that increasing the supply of money would raise crop prices. Higher prices would help farmers pay back the money that they had borrowed to improve their farms.

Opponents of free silver wanted to keep the gold standard. Under the gold standard, the government backs every dollar with a certain amount of gold. Since the gold supply is limited, fewer dollars are in circulation. This protects the value of money and keeps prices down.

In 1892, the Populist Party platform called for free silver, government ownership of railroads, shorter working hours, and other economic reforms. The Populist presidential candidate, James B. Weaver won more than a million votes. But he still finished a distant third behind Republican Benjamin Harrison, the incumbent president, and Democrat Grover Cleveland, who won the election.

Economics *in* History

Supply and Demand

Farmers in the West faced serious economic problems in the 1880s. The supply of food was increasing rapidly, but consumer demand was growing slowly. To attract more consumers, farmers had to drop the prices of their products.

The farmers were confronting the **law of supply and demand.** The amount of economic goods available for sale is the **supply.** The willingness and ability of consumers to spend money for goods and services is **demand.** The price of goods is set by the supply of that good and the demand for that good.

At a lower price, businesses produce less of a good because they will make less money. As the price rises, they produce more. Consumer demand works in the opposite way. Consumers want to buy more of the good when the price is lower—after all, it costs them less. They buy less when the price is higher. The actual price of a good results from a compromise—how much consumers are willing to pay and how little businesses are willing to take for the good.

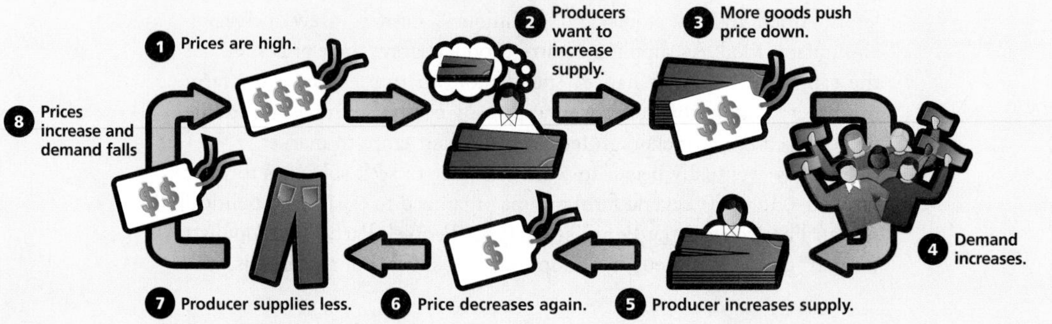

CONNECT TO HISTORY

1. **Recognizing Effects** Suppose farmers found a new market for their wheat—the people in another country, for instance. What effect would that have on price? Why?

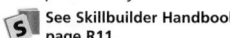

See Skillbuilder Handbook, page R11.

CONNECT TO TODAY

2. **Comparing** How does the price of blue jeans show the law of supply and demand?

For more about supply and demand . . .

RESEARCH LINKS CLASSZONE.COM

Economics *in* History

OBJECTIVE

Students will be able to explain how supply and demand influence production, consumption, and the cost of goods.

Understanding Supply and Demand

By the 1870's, several factors increased the supply of farm products and lowered prices, creating hard times for farmers. During the 1870s, new lands came under cultivation in Canada, Australia, New Zealand, and Argentina, making more food available on world markets. In the United States as well, the number of acres of land devoted to farming more than doubled between 1870 and 1900. Not only was more land farmed but the output per U.S. farm worker also increased as a result of mechanization and improved farming methods. Oversupply pushed prices of crops down to well below the average cost of producing them.

Economics in History
- The Dynamics of Supply and Demand, p. 19

CONNECT TO HISTORY

1. **Recognizing Effects** A new market for wheat means increased demand for this commodity. As demand increases, the price of wheat is likely to rise. As its price goes up, more farmers will decide to grow wheat. Eventually the wheat supply will increase, pushing its price down.

CONNECT TO TODAY

2. **Comparing** Students may discuss the price of designer jeans, with distinctive labels and trademarks, compared to the price of ordinary jeans. Students may note that designers deliberately set a high price for their jeans to make them a status item.

2 The Election of 1896

In 1893, the nation experienced a depression that lasted until 1897. In the face of tough economic times, the Democrats nominated **William Jennings Bryan** of Nebraska for president in 1896. In a speech at the Democratic convention, Bryan urged his listeners to support free silver.

Reading **History**
A. Analyzing Points of View What point was William Jennings Bryan making about the importance of farms?
A. Possible Response Bryan was saying that farms are more important than cities and that without farms the country could not survive.

A VOICE FROM THE PAST

Burn down your cities and leave our farms, and your cities will spring up again as if by magic; but destroy our farms and the grass will grow in the street of every city in the country. . . . [We] . . . answer their demand for a gold standard by saying . . . : You shall not press down upon the brow of labor this crown of thorns. You shall not crucify mankind upon a cross of gold.

William Jennings Bryan, "Cross of Gold" speech, July 8, 1896

The Populists hoped the weak economy would increase support for their candidate in the 1896 presidential election. Because Bryan, the Democratic nominee, supported free silver, the Populists joined the Democrats in supporting Bryan. Meanwhile, the Republicans nominated Ohio governor William McKinley. Although Bryan received heavy support from farmers in the South and the West, McKinley won the election. Bryan's defeat marked the beginning of the end for the Populist Party.

3 Progressivism Emerges

As you saw in Section 1, the rapid growth of cities and industries in the United States at the turn of the century brought many problems. Among them were poverty, the spread of slums, and poor conditions in factories. In addition, corrupt political machines had won control of many city and state governments. Big corporations had gained power over the economy and government. To attack these problems, a varied set of reform movements emerged. These reform movements are commonly grouped under the label **progressivism.**

The progressive reformers shared at least one of three basic goals: first, to reform government and expand democracy; second, to promote social welfare; third, to create economic reform.

In the 1890s and early 1900s, progressive leaders in a number of states sought to expand democracy. They proposed reforms that gave voters more control over their government. For example, an Oregon newspaperman pushed his state to accept three reforms known as the initiative, the referendum, and the recall. The initiative and the referendum allowed voters to propose and pass laws directly without going through the legislature. The

B. Answer They aimed to give voters a larger voice in the government.

Reading **History**
B. Finding Main Ideas What was the main goal behind the progressive reforms of government?

AMERICA'S HISTORY MAKERS

JANE ADDAMS
1860–1935

Jane Addams founded Hull House as an "effort to aid in the solution of the social and industrial problems which are [caused] by the modern conditions of life in a great city."

In addition to her involvement with Hull House, Addams was active in many other areas. She fought for the passage of laws to protect women workers and outlaw child labor. She also worked to improve housing and public health. In 1931, she was awarded a share of the Nobel Peace Prize for her efforts.

Why did Jane Addams found Hull House?

INSTRUCT: OBJECTIVE 2
The Election of 1896

- What was the purpose of William Jennings Bryan's Cross of Gold speech?
- Who were the candidates and winner of the 1896 presidential election?
- What did the election mean for the Populists?

INSTRUCT: OBJECTIVE 3
Progressivism Emerges

- How did the progressive reform movements emerge?
- What basic goals did the progressives share?
- What role did women play in the progressive movement?

AMERICA'S HISTORY MAKERS

Jane Addams

Jane Addams was born in Cedarville, Illinois, to Quaker parents. She traveled to Europe, where she was impressed by a settlement house, Toynbee Hall, in a poor section of London. Addams decided to create a settlement house in Chicago. She also worked for the establishment of juvenile courts, housing codes, factory safety inspections, and workers' compensation. A pacifist, Addams was president of the women's International League for Peace and Freedom from 1915 to 1919.

Answer: to help solve problems caused by industrialization and modern urban life

America's History Makers
- Jane Addams, pp. 83–84

ACTIVITY OPTIONS
INDIVIDUAL NEEDS: GIFTED AND TALENTED — BLOCK SCHEDULING

THE MUCKRAKERS

Class Time Two class periods

Task Researching the work of one muckraking writer and preparing an oral report

Purpose To help students understand the work of the muckrakers and their role in exposing corruption

Supplies Needed
- Reference materials about muckrakers and copies of their books
- Internet access

Activity Divide the students into three groups. Tell students to choose a prominent turn-of-the-century muckraker, such as Ida M. Tarbell, Lincoln Steffens, or Upton Sinclair. Students should research the life and work of the writer they select and read selections from the writer's work. In an oral report, each group should summarize its findings and evaluate the success of its writer in exposing social problems and helping to correct them. Students should submit a bibliography of sources consulted for the report.

INSTRUCT: OBJECTIVE 4

Progressive Presidents

- How did Theodore Roosevelt put his "square deal" program into practice?
- What progressive reforms did Taft promote?
- What two economics-related acts took effect during Wilson's tenure?

MORE ABOUT . . .

Roosevelt and the Trusts

Theodore Roosevelt was known as a "trust buster." One of Roosevelt's targets as a "bad" trust was the Northern Securities Company, a huge railroad conglomerate headed by J. P. Morgan. When the case against Northern Securities began, J. P. Morgan was reported to have approached Roosevelt as he might have approached a business crony. Morgan allegedly said to Roosevelt, "If we have done anything wrong, send your man to my man and they can fix it up."

Humanities Transparency HT44
- Political Cartoon: the Trust Giant's Point of View

AMERICA'S HISTORY MAKERS

Theodore Roosevelt

The outspokenness that endeared Roosevelt to the American public appalled many conservative Republicans. When Roosevelt was nominated for vice-president, Ohio Senator Mark Hanna asked his fellow Republicans, "Don't any of you realize that there's only one life between that madman and the presidency?" When Hanna learned that McKinley had died, he fumed, "Now look! That d----d cowboy is president of the United States!"

Possible Response: Roosevelt was an activist president who promoted reforms and used the power of the government to bring about change.

recall allowed the people to vote an official out of office. In addition, reformers pushed for the direct primary, which allowed voters rather than party conventions, to choose candidates to run for public office.

To promote social welfare, progressives tackled problems such as poverty, unemployment, and poor working conditions. For example, Jane Addams was leader in the settlement house movement. Settlement houses aimed to help people, such as immigrants and the poor, overcome the social problems they faced.

The third progressive goal was to create economic reform. Economic reform often meant limiting the power of big business and regulating its activities. The Sherman Antitrust Act of 1890 made it illegal for corporations to form trusts. Trusts were combinations of businesses that could control a market and squeeze out competition.

An important aspect of progressivism was the role that women played in the movement. Educated middle-class women led many of the social reform movements of the era. As these women worked to better the lives of others, they also sought to improve their own status in society. Many women progressives were active in the struggle for woman suffrage, or the right to vote. They finally achieved this goal in 1920, when the states ratified the Nineteenth Amendment to the Constitution.

AMERICA'S HISTORY MAKERS

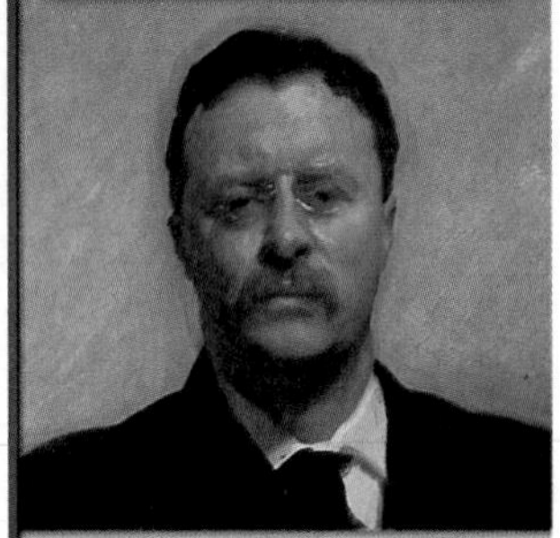

THEODORE ROOSEVELT
1858–1919

From his youth on, Theodore Roosevelt lived what he called the "strenuous life." He rode horses, hiked, boxed, wrestled, and played tennis. In winter, he swam in the icy Potomac River. He hunted rhinoceros in Africa, harpooned devilfish in Florida, and boated down the Amazon.

Americans loved reading of his exploits and affectionately referred to him as "Teddy" or "T.R." Once, on a hunting trip, he refused to shoot a bear cub. News of the event resulted in a new toy—the teddy bear.

How did Roosevelt's active style of living carry over into his presidency?

Progressive Presidents 4

Many Americans supported progressive reforms and they elected presidents who also supported reform. The first progressive president was **Theodore Roosevelt.** Roosevelt saw government as an umpire. Its purpose was to ensure fairness, or a "square deal," for workers, consumers, and business.

Background Theodore Roosevelt became president after McKinley was assassinated in 1901. Roosevelt was reelected in 1904.

Roosevelt began his reforms with an effort to break up trusts. He thought industries should be regulated for the public interest. He acted to regulate the meatpacking industry and signed the Pure Food and Drug Act. This law banned the sale of impure foods and medicines. Roosevelt also fought for conservation to protect America's natural resources. He preserved more than 200 million acres of public lands and doubled the number of national parks in the United States.

Roosevelt's successor, **William Howard Taft,** had a reputation as a conservative. But he also advanced some progressive causes. During his four years in office, Taft pursued almost twice as many antitrust suits as Roosevelt had in nearly eight years in office.

Taft also oversaw the passage of two progressive amendments to the Constitution. The Sixteenth Amendment, passed in 1909 and ratified in 1913, gave Congress the power to establish income taxes. It was

ACTIVITY OPTIONS

SKILLBUILDER LESSON: IDENTIFYING AND SOLVING PROBLEMS — BLOCK SCHEDULING

Explaining the Skill Identifying solutions to problems will help you understand historical events. *Problems* may be defined as obstacles that stop people from reaching their goals. Historical problems may have affected many people or only a few.

Applying the Skill Tell students that solving problems requires identifying problems, understanding what causes the problems, thinking of ways to solve the problems, and implementing the best solution. Draw the flow chart on the board. Tell students to copy it and complete it with information about one of the following problems: limited voter control of government, poverty, unemployment, poor working conditions, control of business by trusts, or impure food. You may want to review the problem-solving steps found on page 269.

In-Depth Resources: Unit 5
- Skillbuilder Practice, p. 85

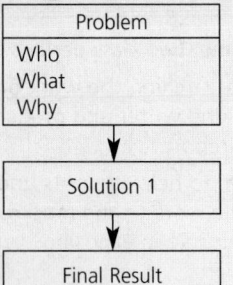

Problem: Who / What / Why
↓
Solution 1
↓
Final Result

Shown at the left is Upton Sinclair's novel, *The Jungle*, which discussed dangerous and unhealthy meat-packing practices. The photograph shows immigrant workers stuffing sausages in a Chicago meat-packing house.

intended to spread the cost of government more fairly among the people. The Seventeenth Amendment also was ratified in 1913. This amendment provided for the direct election of U.S. senators by the voters in each state. It gave people a more direct voice in the government.

Woodrow Wilson was elected president in 1912. He also established a progressive record. At Wilson's urging, Congress passed the Clayton Antitrust Act of 1914. This law banned business practices that reduced competition. In addition, during Wilson's tenure, reform of the nation's financial system took effect. The Federal Reserve Act was passed in 1913. It improved the nation's monetary and banking system.

What Wilson and the other progressive presidents failed to do, however, was try to improve life for African Americans. In fact, Wilson approved the segregation of black and white employees in the federal government. Throughout the Progressive Era, few white politicians promoted civil rights for African Americans.

C. Answer The Sixteenth Amendment helped spread the costs of government more fairly. The Seventeenth Amendment addressed the progressive goal of expanding democracy.

Reading **History**

C. Drawing Conclusions Why are the Sixteenth and Seventeenth amendments considered progressive?

Section 3 Assessment

1. Terms & Names

Explain the significance of:
- Populist Party
- William Jennings Bryan
- progressivism
- Theodore Roosevelt
- William Howard Taft
- Woodrow Wilson

2. Taking Notes

Use a chart to list examples of progressive reforms.

Goals	Reforms
To expand democracy	
To protect social welfare	
To create economic reform	

3. Main Ideas

a. What problems in the late 1800s led farmers to take political action?

b. What did President Roosevelt mean by a "square deal" and how did he try to achieve it?

c. What were three progressive amendments and what did each do?

4. Critical Thinking

Recognizing Effects
In what ways do the reforms that Theodore Roosevelt promoted affect your life today?

THINK ABOUT
- the quality of the food you eat
- natural resources that have been preserved

ACTIVITY OPTIONS

ART / **GEOGRAPHY**

Do research on one of the natural areas that President Roosevelt preserved. Create a **travel brochure** or an **illustrated map** of the area.

MORE ABOUT . . .

The Jungle

Sinclair's novel describes the disgusting conditions in a meat-packing plant in great detail. For example, Sinclair describes thousands of rats scampering over piles of meat in a packing plant. The meat-packers put out poisoned bread for rats and then threw the dead rats and any uneaten bread into the sausage hoppers with the meat. American meat sales fell dramatically immediately after the book's publication.

Humanities Transparency HT43
- Meat Cutters

In-Depth Resources: Unit 5
- Literature Selection: from *The Jungle* by Upton Sinclair, pp. 90–92

ASSESS & RETEACH

Setting the Stage Have students place information in the appropriate boxes on the graphic organizer.

Formal Assessment
- Section Quiz, p. 336

Critical Thinking Transparency CT64
- Setting the Stage

RETEACHING ACTIVITY

Divide students into three groups, and assign one area of American life—government, social welfare, and economy—to each group. Have each group identify reforms, with dates, that affected its area of life. Have students use their lists to create a class time line.

In-Depth Resources: Unit 5
- Reteaching Activity, p. 95

Section 3 Assessment

1. Terms & Names

Populist Party, p. 551
William Jennings Bryan, p. 553
progressivism, p. 553
Theodore Roosevelt, p. 554
William Howard Taft, p. 554
Woodrow Wilson, p. 555

2. Taking Notes

To expand democracy: direct primary; initiative; referendum; recall. To protect social welfare: aid to the unemployed; minimum wage laws. To create economic reform: break up trusts; regulate industry.

3. Main Ideas

a. falling crop prices, high freight rates and grain elevator fees
b. a fair situation for everyone; by breaking up trusts and regulating industries **c.** 16th Amendment—gave Congress power to create income taxes; 17th Amendment—direct election of senators; 19th Amendment—gave women right to vote

4. Critical Thinking

Students consume safer foods and medicines and can enjoy many natural resources.

ACTIVITY OPTIONS

Integrated Assessment
- Rubrics for a brochure, 1.13
- Rubrics for a map, 2.1

SECTION OBJECTIVES

1. To identify the factors that led to U.S. imperialism
2. To trace U.S. involvement in World War I
3. To describe the political and social challenges of postwar America

SKILLBUILDER

- Interpreting Maps: Location, Movement, p. 561

CRITICAL THINKING

- Making Inferences, p. 557
- Finding Main Ideas, p. 558
- Drawing Conclusions, p. 559
- Analyzing Causes, p. 562
- Forming Opinions, p. 562
- Evaluating, p. 563

FOCUS & MOTIVATE

5-MINUTE WARM-UP

Comparing and Contrasting These questions focus on economic and military powers.

1. Read the "One American's Story" about Alfred T. Mahan on this page. How did economic power relate to military power?
2. Why did Mahan encourage U.S. officials to build up the U.S. Navy?

Warm-Up Transparency, WT19EPIL

INSTRUCT

INSTRUCT: OBJECTIVE 1

Growth of U.S. Imperialism

- What is imperialism?
- What factors contributed to the growth of U.S. imperialism?
- How did the United States gain control of Alaska and Hawaii?

4 Becoming a World Power

TERMS & NAMES
- imperialism
- Spanish-American War
- yellow journalism
- Platt Amendment
- Panama Canal
- Roosevelt Corollary
- Fourteen Points
- Great Migration

MAIN IDEA

The United States extended its global influence and fought with the Allies in World War I.

WHY IT MATTERS NOW

The United States continues to be a global power today.

ONE AMERICAN'S STORY

Alfred Thayer Mahan joined the U.S. Navy in the 1850s and served for nearly 40 years. In the 1890s, he made use of his decades of experience to write several books on the historical importance of sea power. In one passage, he discussed the economic importance of trading stations and colonies.

A VOICE FROM THE PAST

The trading-station . . . [was] the same as the . . . colony. In both cases the mother-country had won a foothold in a foreign land, seeking a new outlet for what it had to sell, a new sphere for its shipping, more employment for its people, and more comfort and wealth for itself.

Alfred Thayer Mahan, *The Influence of Sea Power upon History, 1660–1805*

Naval historian Alfred Thayer Mahan at the turn of the century

Mahan encouraged government officials to build up American naval forces so that the United States could compete with other powerful nations. In this section, you will learn how the United States began to extend its influence beyond its boundaries and become a world power.

1 Growth of U.S. Imperialism

By the 1880s, several European nations were expanding their overseas empires. Many Americans believed the United States should also follow a policy of **imperialism**—the policy of extending economic, political, or military control over other nations. Three factors helped to fuel the development of American imperialism.

1. **Economic Interests.** Economic leaders argued that expansion would increase U.S. financial prosperity. Many business leaders saw new colonies as a potential source of cheap raw materials and new markets for their products.
2. **Military Interests.** In his books, Mahan had argued that economic interests went hand-in-hand with military interests. Foreign policy

RECOMMENDED RESOURCES

In-Depth Resources: Unit 5
- Guided Reading, p. 83
- Building Vocabulary, p. 84

Reading Study Guide (Spanish and English), pp. 185–186

Economics in History
- The Economic Causes of Imperialism, p. 23

Formal Assessment
- Section Quiz, p. 337

Integrated Assessment
- Rubrics, 1.10, 2.3

Access for Students Acquiring English/ESL
- Guided Reading, p. 126

INTEGRATED TECHNOLOGY

Humanities Transparency HT46, HT47, HT48

Electronic Teacher Tools

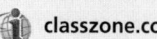

classzone.com

TEST-TAKING RESOURCES

Strategies for Test Preparation

Test Practice Transparencies, TT89–TT95

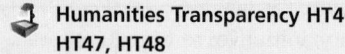

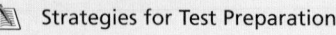

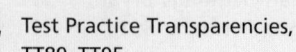

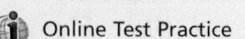

Online Test Practice

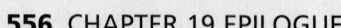

*Reading***History**

A. Making Inferences Why might economic and military interests go hand in hand?

A. Possible Response If a country's economic interests were threatened, the military would be needed to protect them.

experts agreed. They urged U.S. leaders to follow the European example and establish a military presence overseas.

3. **Belief in Cultural Superiority.** Many white Americans believed that their government, religion, and even race were superior to those of other societies. Some people hoped to spread democracy and Christianity overseas.

During the late 19th century, the United States began to gain control over more territories. In 1867, the United States purchased Alaska from Russia. In 1893, U.S. Marines helped American planters in Hawaii overthrow the Hawaiian queen and set up their own government. The United States annexed Hawaii in 1898.

The Spanish-American War 2

America's overseas empire grew dramatically as a result of the **Spanish-American War** of 1898. The war began after Cubans rose up in rebellion against Spain, who had colonized the island. The United States joined the side of the Cuban rebels. Americans were influenced in part by newspaper stories that described—and often exaggerated—news about Spanish cruelty. This sensational style of reporting the news became known as **yellow journalism.**

The war was fought on Spain's colonies in the Caribbean and the Philippine Islands. One of the more famous American fighting units

INSTRUCT: OBJECTIVE 2

The Spanish American War / U.S. Influence Expands

- What factors prompted the United States to declare war against Spain?
- What did the United States gain from its victory in the war?
- What U.S. initiatives influenced its expansion into Latin America and Asia?

Humanities Transparency HT46
- Panama Canal Stamp

CITIZENSHIP TODAY

Detecting Bias in the Media

Modern journalists try to report the news without bias—that is, without letting their personal opinions or those of their employer influence what they write. Unbiased reporting is one of the responsibilities of a free press. It allows citizens to weigh the facts and come to their own understanding of issues and events.

As you have read, journalists and their employers do not always avoid bias. In fact, in the 1890s, journalists were not concerned with bias. Before the United States declared war on Spain in 1898, 'yellow journalists' exaggerated stories to help sell newspapers. These stories helped turn U.S. public opinion in favor of war against Spain. They used words and images to reflect their bias that the United States should declare war on Spain—and sell more papers along the way.

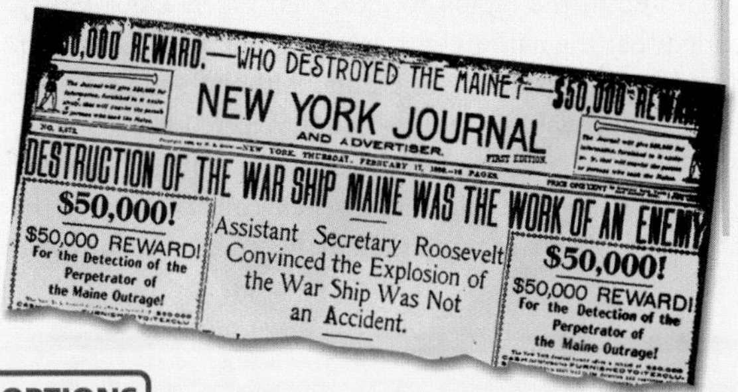

William Randolph Hearst ran this headline in his *New York Journal* before authorities had a chance to determine the cause of the *Maine's* explosion.

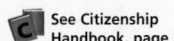

Can You Find Bias in the Media?

1. With a small group, collect news stories from different sources that cover the same issue or event.
2. Record any differences in the way a specific issue or event is covered by the oral, written, or visual sources you have selected.
3. Review the differences and decide whether any of the authors of the sources showed bias in their coverage.
4. Write a report that describes any bias you might detect. Explain why the biased source might have reported the story the way it did.

See Citizenship Handbook, page 268.

For more about the news media . . .

RESEARCH LINKS CLASSZONE.COM

557

CITIZENSHIP TODAY

OBJECTIVE

Students will understand the importance of detecting bias in the media in order to avoid mistaking opinion for fact.

The Legacy of Yellow Journalism

Although the era of yellow journalism instigated by the Hearst-Pulitzer rivalry ended after the turn of the century, many of its trappings linger. Banner headlines, color comics, political cartoons, and copious illustrations have become widespread in the newspaper industry. Yellow journalism's descendants, the tabloids, still depend on sensationalism.

STANDARDS FOR EVALUATION

Each report should
- clearly state its purpose and provide supporting examples from new stories.
- educate the reader on detecting bias in news stories.
- follow the rules of spelling, grammar, and punctuation.

Citizenship Today, pp. 15–16

ACTIVITY OPTIONS

INDIVIDUAL NEEDS: GIFTED AND TALENTED

BLOCK SCHEDULING

COMMENTARY ON THE WAR

Class Time Two class periods

Task Comparing responses of American writers to the Spanish-American War

Purpose To read and compare the writing of Mark Twain, Stephen Crane, and Walt Whitman

Supplies Needed
- Internet access

Activity Direct students to the Library of Congress Web site on the Spanish-American War. Visit classzone.com for the link. Divide the class into three groups and assign each group one of the three writers whose response to the war is discussed and quoted: Twain, Crane, or Whitman. Students should read the material on the writer, summarize it, and select one short representative quotation to read to the class.

MORE ABOUT . . .

The *Maine*

The U.S.S. *Maine* arrived in Havana Harbor on January 25, 1898. Spanish officials came aboard the vessel with the customary welcome. The vessel exploded on February 15 at 9:40 P.M. President McKinley was awakened with the news around 2:00 A.M. About an hour later, the Pulitzer-owned newspaper the *World* had an issue on the streets with a four-column headline trumpeting the news.

MORE ABOUT . . .

The Anti-Imperialist League

U.S. treatment of Spain's former colonies after the Spanish-American War disappointed many Americans, including businessman Andrew Carnegie, reformer Jane Addams, and writer Mark Twain. They helped form the Anti-Imperialist League, which held that Americans should not deny others the right to govern themselves. Their platform included the statement, "We hold that the policy known as imperialism is hostile to liberty," and reaffirmed that "all men, of whatever race or color, are entitled to life, liberty and the pursuit of happiness." The League's voice was lost, however, in the roar of popular approval of the Spanish-American War.

The explosion of the *Maine* and accounts of the event by yellow journalists led many Americans to favor war against Spain.

was known as the Rough Riders. Led by Theodore Roosevelt, its recruits included cowboys, miners, college students, New York policemen, athletes, and Native Americans. The Rough Riders helped the Americans capture Santiago, a key Spanish stronghold in southern Cuba.

Within months, Spain surrendered. As a result of the war, the United States gained the Spanish colonies of Puerto Rico, Guam, and the Philippines. While Cuba won its freedom, the United States insisted that Cubans add the **Platt Amendment** to their constitution. This amendment gave the United States the right to intervene in Cuban affairs anytime the U.S. government believed "life, property, and individual liberty" were in danger.

Some Americans opposed the taking of colonies. They formed the Anti-Imperialist League. Members of the League believed that Americans should not deny other people the right to govern themselves. Most Americans, however, favored the creation of an overseas empire and the power and prestige it brought.

Reading **History**

B. Finding Main Ideas Why did the Anti-Imperialist League oppose U.S. efforts to establish colonies

B. Answer The League believed people should govern themselves.

2 U.S. Influence Expands

In the years following the Spanish-American War, the United States increased its presence on the world stage. It did so by expanding its influence in Asia and Latin America.

During the late 1800s, the United States joined other countries in competing for access to China. In 1899, Secretary of State John Hay asked nations interested in the region to follow an Open Door Policy. This policy intended that the nations with interests in China leave open the door for other nations to trade with China. Although some people did not think Hay's policy would work, no nation rejected it.

Meanwhile, the United States became more involved in the affairs of Latin America. In 1904, the United States began construction of the **Panama Canal** to create a shorter trade route between the Atlantic and

ACTIVITY OPTIONS

INTERDISCIPLINARY LINK: GOVERNMENT/CIVICS — BLOCK SCHEDULING

INTERVENTION ABROAD

Class Time One class period

Task Describing U.S. intervention and its effects

Purpose To understand the intended goal and the effects of U.S. intervention in Latin America

Supplies Needed

- Reference books
- Encyclopedias
- Internet access

Activity Ask students to choose one of the following countries: the Dominican Republic, Cuba, Nicaragua, or Mexico. Tell students to research the reasons for U.S. intervention in their chosen country, the form of the intervention, and its effects. Students may present their findings in a written or oral report. They may also summarize their findings in a graphic organizer. Students may work alone or in groups.

How the Panama Canal Works

Engineers faced a problem in building the Panama Canal. Because of the region's different landscape elevations, no waterway would remain level. They solved this dilemma by building three sets of *locks*—water-filled chambers that raise or lower ships to match a canal's different water levels.

1. The lock gates open on one end to allow the ship to enter.
2. The gates close, and water is pumped in or out depending on whether the ship is moving up or down.
3. Once the water in the chamber and the canal ahead is level, the second gate opens and the ship moves on.

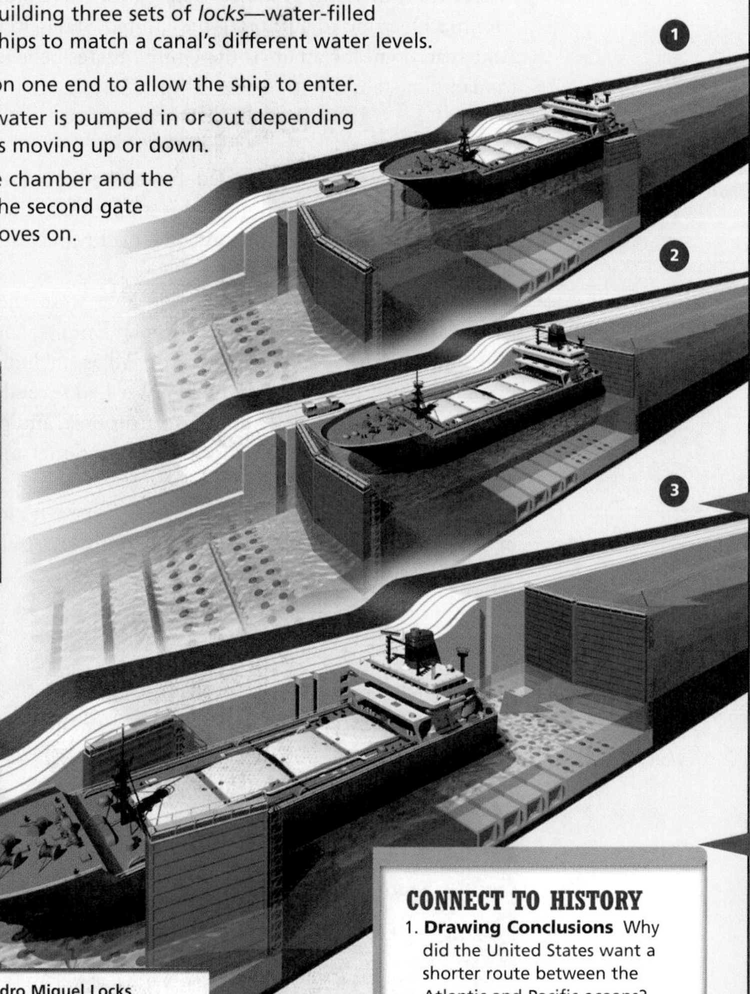

The locks, whose steel gates rise six stories high, can hold as much as 26 million gallons of water—enough to supply a major U.S. city for one day.

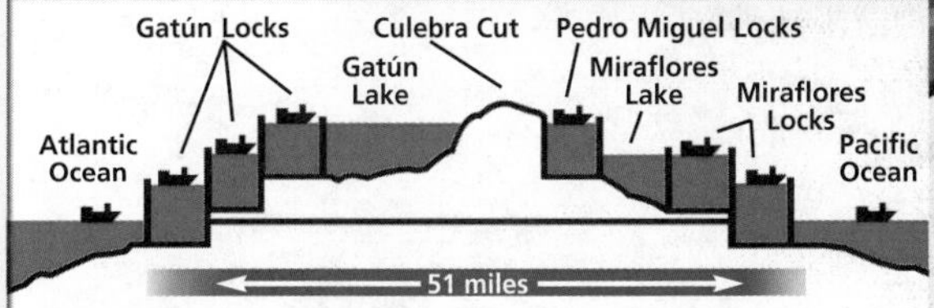

This cross-section shows the different elevations and locks that a ship moves through on the 8–9 hour trip through the canal. Before the canal was built, a trip around South America could take two months.

CONNECT TO HISTORY

1. **Drawing Conclusions** Why did the United States want a shorter route between the Atlantic and Pacific oceans?

CONNECT TO TODAY

2. **Researching** What is the economic and political status of the Panama Canal today?

For more about the Panama Canal . . .

RESEARCH LINKS CLASSZONE.COM

559

Technology OF THE Time

OBJECTIVES

1. To explain the need for a system of locks on the Panama Canal
2. To explain the technology used to build the lock system of the Panama Canal

BLOCK SCHEDULING

INSTRUCT

- What problems did builders of the canal face?
- Look at the first picture. Is the ship going to be moved to a higher or a lower elevation?
- How many different elevations do you see in the diagram?

MORE ABOUT . . .

The History of Locks

In 1373, the Dutch developed the pound (chamber) lock to lift vessels to different elevations, the most significant innovation in canal construction. Leonardo da Vinci is said to have invented a kind of canal gate, designated to withstand more water pressure than previous gates.

MORE ABOUT . . .

Building the Panama Canal

Building the Panama Canal was an enormous feat. When it was completed, the Panama Canal included the world's largest earth dam, the largest system of lock built to that time, and the largest swinging gates ever completed. The most difficult part of the canal to build was the Culebra Cut. One problem in this cut was moving out the dirt and rock that workers loosened. More than 4,000 wagons hauled by 160 locomotives were used to haul out the debris. As the cut deepened, the danger of landslides grew.

CONNECT TO HISTORY

1. **Drawing Conclusions** U.S. interests in Asia demanded easier access to the Pacific; in order to move its naval forces around the world more quickly; to improve trade by providing a shorter route for goods to travel

CONNECT TO TODAY

2. **Researching** Students can use up-to-date encyclopedias or the Internet to learn about the current economic and political status of the canal. Have them write a brief report on their findings.

MORE ABOUT . . .

Globo Cop?

In the early 1900s, the United States used its "police powers" in the Western Hemisphere. Today, U.S. forces participate in police actions all over the globe. This fact has led some journalists to call the United States the "Globo Cop." In the 1990s, U.S. forces helped lead international police actions in Somalia, Yugoslavia, and other areas in crisis. The United States also led the Gulf War forces that liberated Kuwait after it was seized by Iraq. The United States continues to patrol its own hemisphere, too. In 1989, U.S. troops invaded Panama to overthrow dictator Manuel Noriega.

INSTRUCT: OBJECTIVE 3

World War I

- What nations and empires were on each side of World War I before the U.S. joined the effort?
- What were the causes of the war?
- What happened when the United States joined the Allies?

HISTORY FROM VISUALS

Interpreting the Photograph Have students study the photograph on page 560 and read the caption. Explain to the students that this photograph illustrates what was called "going over the top." The smoke is caused by artillery fire from the enemy. Ask students to describe ways this battle scene differs from the paintings that they saw earlier from the American Revolution and the Civil War. **Possible Responses** Students might mention the absence of many elements featured in earlier paintings: colorful flags, officers on horseback, swords, or even a visible enemy. The most striking features in this picture are the trenches and the war-torn earth. Trenches served as a place to live, a staging area for assaults, and protection against enemy fire.

Pacific oceans. In addition, numerous U.S. businesses began establishing relationships with Latin American countries.

As economic interests drew the United States deeper into Latin America, U.S. leaders took a more active role in influencing the region's political affairs. In 1904, President Roosevelt added the **Roosevelt Corollary** to the Monroe Doctrine—the U.S. policy opposing European intervention in Latin America. The Roosevelt Corollary extended the Monroe Doctrine to authorize the United States to intervene in Latin American domestic affairs if the United States believed it was necessary to maintain stability.

Vocabulary
corollary: a statement that follows logically from an earlier statement

3 World War I

By the early 1900s, the United States had become a global power. Perhaps nothing demonstrated this more than the decisive role the nation played in deciding the outcome of the greatest conflict the world had yet seen—World War I.

The war began in 1914. On one side were the Central Powers: Austria-Hungary, Germany, the Ottoman Empire, and Bulgaria. On the other side were the Allied Powers, or Allies, including Serbia, Russia, France, Great Britain, and Italy. The war had several long-term causes. Competition for colonies, an intense arms race, and growing feelings of nationalism had combined to raise international tensions in Europe. These tensions eventually led to war.

Vocabulary
nationalism: devotion to the interests and culture of one's nation

When the war first broke out, the United States announced a policy of neutrality, refusing to take sides in the war. As time passed, many

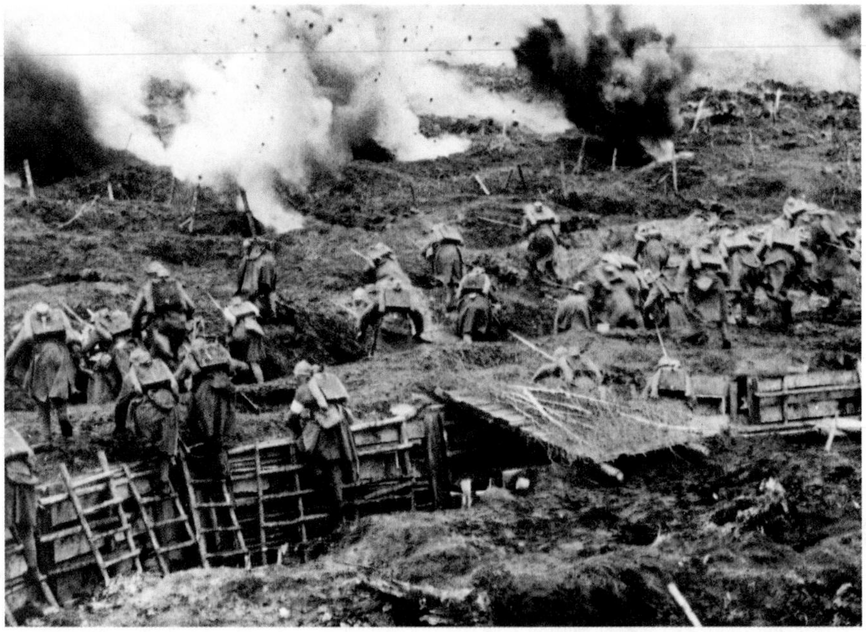

Soldiers scramble out of their trench to attack the enemy during a World War I battle.

ACTIVITY OPTIONS

MULTIPLE LEARNING STYLES: LINGUISTIC

BLOCK SCHEDULING

SIGNING UP THE TROOPS

Class Time One class period

Task Writing a dialogue between an army or navy recruiter and a prospective recruit

Purpose To gain an understanding of the motives that led Americans to join the war effort

Supplies Needed

- Reference materials on the pay, benefits, and duties of the armed forces and the American Red Cross in World War I
- Strips of blank paper and a container

Activity On strips of paper, write the following: *Red Cross worker; sailor in a convoy; combat soldier; military clerical worker; nurse; ambulance driver; entertainer.* Put the strips in a container and divide students into pairs. Have each pair draw a slip and create a dialogue between a prospective recruit and a recruiter looking for someone to fill the position on the slip. The dialogue should include questions and answers about why the recruit should join; what the dangers, duties, and benefits of service are; and what military training or life at the front might be like.

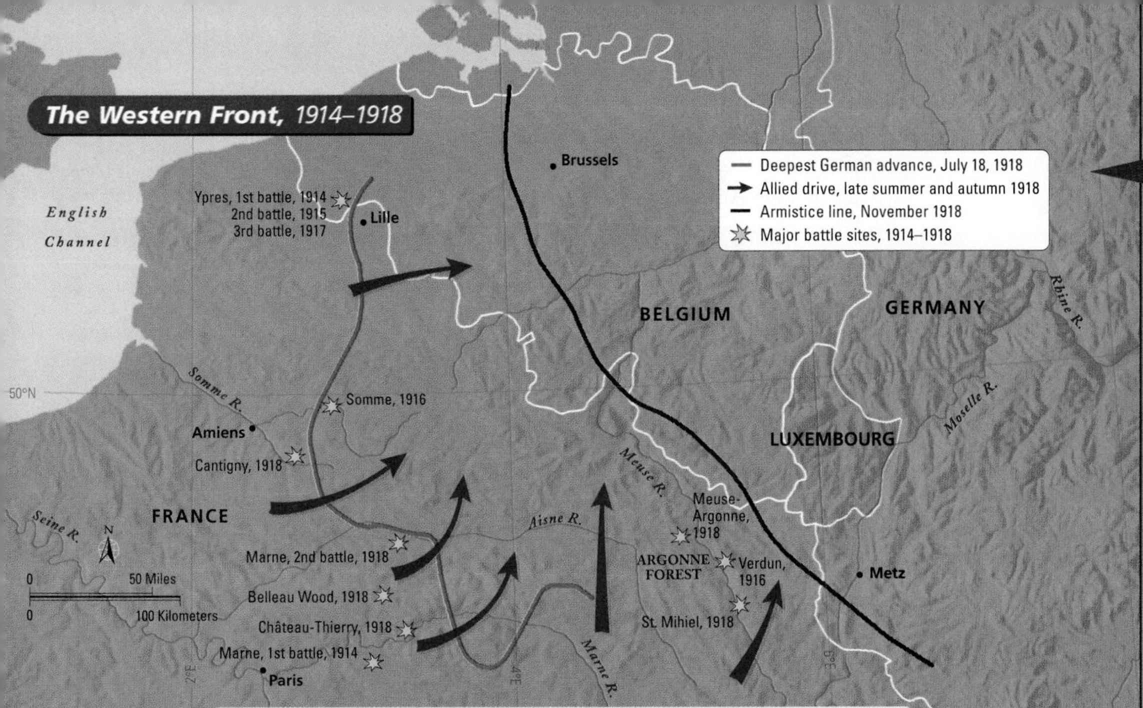

The Western Front, 1914–1918

GEOGRAPHY SKILLBUILDER Interpreting Maps

1. Location *What three battles occurred closest to the Armistice line?*

2. Movement *In what two directions did the Allied drives move?*

Americans developed a greater sympathy for the Allies. And, in 1917, the United States entered the war on the side of the Allies. U.S. forces tipped the balance in favor of the Allies. In 1918, the Allies were clearly winning the war. In November, Germans mutinied and their emperor gave up the throne. The new German government asked for peace.

World War I had been the most devastating conflict the world had yet known. About 8.5 million soldiers died in the war, and about 21 million were wounded. The war also lead to the deaths of millions of civilians in Europe, Asia, and Africa—often due to starvation and disease.

4 Postwar America

During the war, President Woodrow Wilson had announced a plan for a lasting peace. The plan became known as the **Fourteen Points.** Most of the points dealt with specific border placements. Others proposed rules for international relations, such as banning secret agreements. For Wilson, the fourteenth point mattered most. It called for an association of nations to settle disputes peacefully. The other Allied leaders did not support much of Wilson's plan. However, the Treaty of Versailles, which ended the war, still provided for an international organization to address disputes between countries. This organization was called the League of Nations.

Many U.S. citizens and legislators, however, opposed the League. They feared that further involvement in Europe would lead them into

Skillbuilder Answers

1. Meuse-Argonne, Verdun, St. Mihiel
2. east end north

HISTORY FROM VISUALS

Reading the Map Discuss the following questions with the class: How do the dates on the map prove that most of the battles accomplished little? **Possible Response** There was little movement from year to year. For example, there were battles at Ypres in 1914, 1915, and 1917. Why was there no fighting in Germany? **Answer** The armistice was signed before German troops retreated that far.

Extension Have students pick one of the battles on the Western Front and create a map of the battle showing battle lines and troop movements.

INSTRUCT: OBJECTIVE 4

Postwar America

- What did President Wilson try to achieve with his Fourteen Points?
- What caused the Red Scare?
- What were the causes and effects of the Great Migration?

Humanities Transparency HT47, HT48
- The Red Scare
- *The Migrants Arrived in Great Numbers*

ACTIVITY OPTIONS

INTERDISCIPLINARY LINK: GOVERNMENT

BLOCK SCHEDULING

CREATE A CARTOON

Class Time One class period

Task Creating a political cartoon about the Treaty of Versailles

Purpose To contrast the perspectives of various nations on the outcome of the Paris peace conference

Supplies Needed
- Reference material on the Paris peace conference and the Treaty of Versailles
- Markers and posterboard

Activity Divide students into eight groups, six of which represent Britain, France, Germany, Italy, Poland, and Yugoslavia, and two that represent the United States. Have each group prepare a cartoon expressing the opinion of people within that country on the final treaty. One U.S. group should create a cartoon favoring ratification of the treaty, while the other group uses the cartoon to express opposition to it.

Now and then

The Flu Epidemic

To stop contagion, San Francisco officials passed laws requiring residents to wear surgical masks. In Chicago, theater owners refused to let in coughing patrons. Some Americans suspected the Germans of introducing germ warfare. Rumors circulated that German U-boats had brought the flu across the Atlantic. However, such rumors stopped after thousands of Germans also fell sick.

ASSESS & RETEACH

Setting the Stage Have students fill in the graphic organizer for this chapter.

Formal Assessment
- Section Quiz, p. 337

Critical Thinking Transparency CT97

RETEACHING ACTIVITY

Divide the class into four teams and assign one of the objectives in the section to each team. Ask each group to make up a series of headlines for newspapers of the period that identifies key events in each objective. Post the headlines on a classroom bulletin board. For fun, students can make up screaming "yellow journalism" headlines as well.

In-Depth Resources: Unit 5
- Reteaching Activity, p. 96

more conflicts. As a result, the U.S. Senate refused to ratify the Treaty of Versailles. The nation instead made a separate peace agreement with Germany.

After the war, Americans wanted to focus on domestic affairs. Shortly after the war ended, the United States experienced a number of labor strikes. Some Americans saw efforts to organize labor unions as the work of radicals, people who favor extreme measures to bring about change. The strikes sparked fears of a communist revolution. In 1919–1920, this fear created a wave of panic called the Red Scare. (Communists were often called Reds.)

Reading **History**

C. Analyzing Causes Why didn't the United States ratify the Treaty of Versailles?

C. Answer Many Americans feared ratification would force the United States into the League of Nations.

Now and then

THE FLU EPIDEMIC

In 1918, flu victims often came down with pneumonia and died within a week. Today, bacterial infections such as pneumonia resulting from the flu can be controlled with antibiotics.

The 1998 discovery of the frozen remains of a 1918 flu victim in an Alaskan cemetery may one day lead to a better understanding of the virus. Scientists have found a genetic link between the 1918 flu virus and swine flu, a virus first found in pigs. The Alaskan find may help scientists develop vaccines to protect against future flu outbreaks.

Americans also saw a rise in racial tensions after the war. For a few decades, African Americans had been leaving the rural South to escape Jim Crow. During the war, this movement, known as the **Great Migration,** grew as African Americans filled war-related jobs in cities, especially in the North. African Americans enjoyed better-paying jobs and the relative lack of segregation in the North. But in cities where blacks settled in large numbers, racial tensions rose over housing, job competition, and segregation. During the summer of 1919, race riots flared in 25 cities around the country.

By 1920, when the nation held its presidential election, Americans were ready for a break from turmoil at home and abroad. Republican candidate Warren G. Harding of Ohio offered them one. He promised the nation a "return to normalcy" and the voters responded. Harding won a landslide victory. In the next chapter, you will learn about American life in the 1920s and beyond.

Section 4 Assessment

1. Terms & Names

Explain the significance of:
- imperialism
- Spanish-American War
- yellow journalism
- Platt Amendment
- Panama Canal
- Roosevelt Corollary
- Fourteen Points
- Great Migration

2. Taking Notes

Use a chart like the one shown here to record causes of U.S. expansion overseas in the late 1800s.

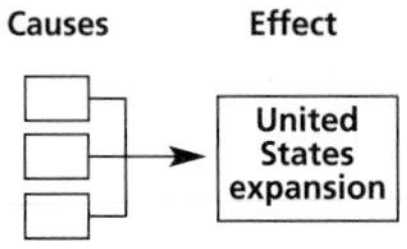

3. Main Ideas

a. How did the Roosevelt Corollary change U.S. foreign policy?

b. What were the long-term causes of World War I?

c. Why did many Americans oppose joining the League of Nations?

4. Critical Thinking

Forming Opinions Did the United States betray its democratic principles when it established overseas colonies?

THINK ABOUT
- the public's response to yellow journalists and U.S. military victories
- the work of the Anti-Imperialist League

ACTIVITY OPTIONS

SCIENCE / **MATH**

Research the Panama Canal. Build a simple **model** of the canal or create a **graph** that shows how many ships use the canal each year.

Section 4 Assessment

1. Terms & Names

imperialism, p. 556
Spanish-American War, p. 557
yellow journalism, p. 557
Platt Amendment, p. 558
Panama Canal, p. 558
Roosevelt Corollary, p. 560
Fourteen Points, p. 561
Great Migration, p. 562

2. Taking Notes

Causes: Americans sought markets and raw materials; they wanted to establish a military presence overseas; belief in the superiority of American culture also fueled expansion.

3. Main Ideas

a. It authorized U.S. intervention into Latin American domestic affairs. **b.** imperialism, nationalism, militarism, and alliances **c.** because they thought joining the League could force the United States to go to war

4. Critical Thinking

Answers will vary but should be supported by evidence in the chapter.

ACTIVITY OPTIONS

Integrated Assessment
- Rubrics for a model, 1.10
- Rubrics for a graph, 2.3

The Fourteen Points

Setting the Stage Nine months after the United States entered World War I, President Wilson delivered to Congress a statement of war aims. This statement became known as the "Fourteen Points." In the speech, President Wilson set forth 14 proposals for reducing the risk of war in the future. Numbers have been inserted to help identify the main points, as well as those omitted. **See Primary Source Explorer**

All the peoples of the world are in effect partners . . . , and for our own part we see very clearly that unless justice be done to others it will not be done to us. The program of the world's peace, therefore, is our program; and that program, . . . as we see it, is this:

[1] Open **covenants**[1] of peace, openly arrived at, after which there shall be no private international understandings of any kind but diplomacy shall proceed always frankly and in the public view.

[2] Absolute freedom of navigation upon the seas . . . in peace and in war. . . .

[3] The removal, so far as possible, of all economic barriers and the establishment of an equality of trade conditions among all the nations. . . .

[4] Adequate guarantees given and taken that national **armaments**[2] will be reduced. . . .

[5] A free, open-minded, and absolutely impartial adjustment of all colonial claims, based upon . . . the principle that . . . the interests of the populations concerned must have equal weight with the . . . claims of the government whose title is to be determined.

[6–13: These eight points deal with specific boundary changes.]

[14] A general association of nations must be formed under specific covenants for the purpose of affording mutual guarantees of political independence and territorial **integrity**[3] to great and small states alike.

—*Woodrow Wilson*

1. **covenants:** binding agreements.
2. **armaments:** weapons and supplies of war.
3. **integrity:** the condition of being whole or undivided; completeness.

A CLOSER LOOK

THE VALUE OF OPENNESS

The first of Wilson's points attempts to solve one of the problems that caused the outbreak of World War I—agreements between nations arrived at in secret.

1. How might agreements arrived at in public prevent another world war?

A CLOSER LOOK

BALANCING CLAIMS

Wilson frequently appeals to fairness, balance, and impartiality in settling competing claims.

2. What might be unusual about a leader such as Wilson calling for an impartial adjustment of colonial claims?

A CLOSER LOOK

LEAGUE OF NATIONS

Wilson proposes that nations join a formal organization to protect one another.

3. Why did Wilson believe that such an organization would benefit the world?

Interactive Primary Source Assessment

1. Main Ideas

a. Why should diplomacy avoid private dealings and proceed in public view?

b. How might equality of trade be important to keeping the peace?

c. What must nations join together to guarantee?

2. Critical Thinking

Evaluating The first five points address issues that Wilson believed had caused the war. How successful do you think Wilson's ideas have been in the rest of the 20th century?

THINK ABOUT
- other conflicts since World War I
- peacekeeping efforts around the world

INTERACTIVE PRIMARY SOURCE

OBJECTIVE

Students will be able to identify and explain the key points from President Wilson's "Fourteen Points" address to Congress.

Primary Source Explorer
- *The Fourteen Points*

The Explorer will help students select and produce their own presentations.

Specific information about the document can be found in **A Closer Look.** To learn more about key people and events of the time, students should click on **Life in These Times. What Happened Next** will show the student the impact of the document and tie it to today.

FOCUS & MOTIVATE

Analyzing Points of View Have the students read the opening paragraph of the document. What view does Wilson have of other nations? What role does he see for the United States?

INSTRUCT

- What point reflects concern about secret alliances? about militarism? about imperialism? about nationalism?
- How is the proposal about a League of Nations related to the above concerns?

A CLOSER LOOK

1. The alliance system before World War I pulled one country after another into the war. Not every country knew all the conditions of various treaties, which made the situation more unstable.
2. Usually leaders of powerful nations argue for their country's narrow interests. Wilson seems willing to consider the claims of others—specifically the colonial populations.
3. He might have thought that nations would be less likely to go to war if they knew that other nations would intervene to keep peace.

Interactive Primary Source Assessment

1. Main Ideas

a. Diplomacy should proceed in public view so that nations will be aware of the consequences of their actions.

b. If nations trade under equal terms, they are less likely to have economic disputes, which could turn into military disputes.

c. Nations must join together to guarantee that they can remain politically independent and not have their territory taken.

2. Critical Thinking

Students may say that Wilson's ideas have not been very successful because after World War I, nations continued to engage in secret dealings, military buildups, and repression of other nations. Other students might say that Wilson's ideas gained more success later with the United Nations and its peacekeeping efforts, arms reduction treaties, and successful movements for national independence.

TERMS & NAMES

1. **frontier,** p. 539
2. **Homestead Act,** p. 540
3. **mass culture,** p. 548
4. **Jim Crow,** p. 549
5. ***Plessy* v. *Ferguson*,** p. 549
6. **Populist Party,** p. 551
7. **progressivism,** p. 553
8. **imperialism,** p. 556
9. **Roosevelt Corollary,** p. 560
10. **Fourteen Points,** p. 561

REVIEW QUESTIONS

Possible Responses

1. control over land and resources
2. Some people grew fabulously wealthy and gilded decorations were popular among the rich. However, gilded also implies that the top layer of wealth hid something less valuable, such as society's problems.
3. southern and eastern Europe
4. a common culture experienced by large numbers of people
5. It held that segregation was constitutional and established the doctrine of "separate but equal."
6. It would cause inflation and thus bring them higher prices for their goods
7. corruption in government; poverty; unemployment; overcrowding; poor working conditions; alcohol abuse; regulating big business
8. other world powers were taking overseas colonies; economic and military interests; a belief in the cultural superiority of the United States
9. Cuba, Puerto Rico, the Philippines, and Guam
10. Many senators feared that if it ratified the treaty and the League of Nations, other countries could force the United States to go to war to settle international disputes.

Chapter 19 EPILOGUE ASSESSMENT

TERMS & NAMES

Briefly explain the significance of each of the following.

1. frontier
2. Homestead Act
3. mass culture
4. Jim Crow
5. *Plessy* v. *Ferguson*
6. Populist Party
7. progressivism
8. imperialism
9. Roosevelt Corollary
10. Fourteen Points

REVIEW QUESTIONS

A Time of Growth (pages 539–545)

1. What caused conflict between Native Americans and white settlers on the Great Plains?
2. Why was the late 1800s known as the Gilded Age?
3. Where did most immigrants to the United States come from around 1900?

Life at the Turn of the Century (pages 546–550)

4. What is mass culture?
5. Why was *Plessy v. Ferguson* an important Supreme Court decision?

An Era of Reform (pages 551–555)

6. Why did farmers favor a free silver policy?
7. What problems did progressivism address?

Becoming a World Power (pages 556–563)

8. Why did Americans become interested in overseas expansion in the late 1800s?
9. What territories did the United States take control of as a result of the Spanish-American War?
10. Why did the U.S. Senate reject the Treaty of Versailles?

CRITICAL THINKING

1. USING YOUR NOTES

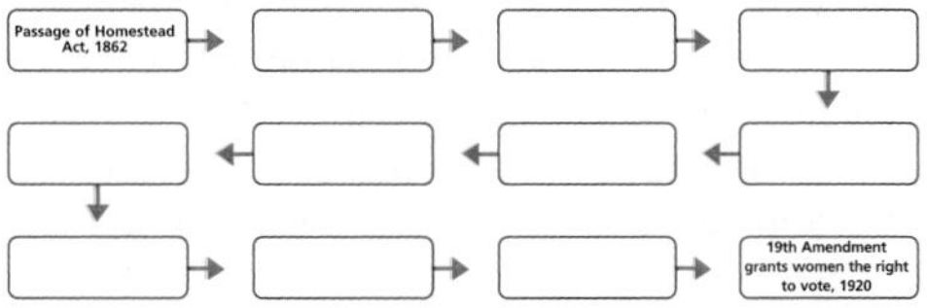

Using your completed chart, answer the questions.

a. Why were the Sixteenth and Seventeenth amendments considered progressive?
b. Why did some Americans oppose the taking of overseas colonies?

2. THEME: EXPANSION

How did U.S. expansion at the end of the 19th century compare with expansion that occurred earlier?

3. ANALYZING LEADERSHIP

Think about the actions of Booker T. Washington and W. E. B. Du Bois. Which approach did each take against discrimination? Whose approach was more effective?

4. APPLYING CITIZENSHIP SKILLS

What issues did progressive reformers address around 1900? What issues would they address today?

5. FORMING OPINIONS

How did "yellow journalism" influence U.S. foreign policy at the turn of the century? How does modern media, such as television, shape public opinion today?

Interact *with* History

How did your solution to one of the problems of the Progressive Era compare with those proposed by reformers?

VISUAL SUMMARY

The United States, 1860–1920

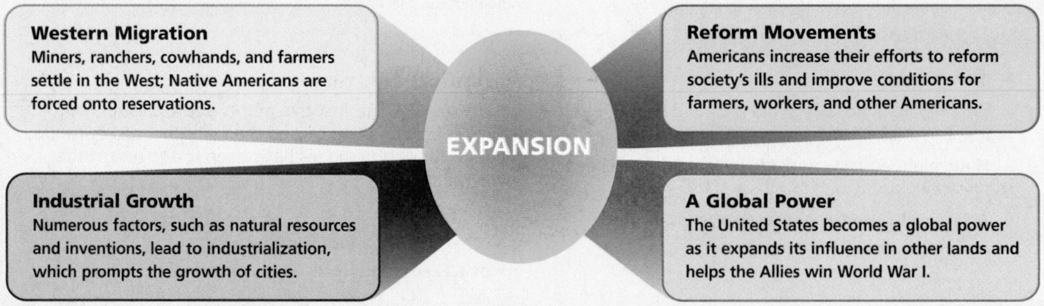

Western Migration
Miners, ranchers, cowhands, and farmers settle in the West; Native Americans are forced onto reservations.
Reform Movements
Americans increase their efforts to reform society's ills and improve conditions for farmers, workers, and other Americans.
EXPANSION
Industrial Growth
Numerous factors, such as natural resources and inventions, lead to industrialization, which prompts the growth of cities.
A Global Power
The United States becomes a global power as it expands its influence in other lands and helps the Allies win World War I.

CRITICAL THINKING

Possible Responses

1. **USING YOUR NOTES** **a.** The 16th Amendment created the income tax and spread the cost of government more evenly. The 17th Amendment provided for the direct elections of senators, giving people a more direct voice in government. **b.** Such action betrayed the ideals of America by denying people the right to govern themselves.
2. **THEME: EXPANSION** Some might say it was similar because it raised issues about the treatment of native people or that it was different because Americans were now expanding onto other continents.
3. **ANALYZING LEADERSHIP** Washington believed that African Americans should concentrate on economic equality before striving for full equality. Du Bois believed that segregation should end immediately.
4. **APPLYING CITIZENSHIP SKILLS** Students might say progressives addressed issues of social welfare, government and economic reform around 1900. They would probably address similar issues today.
5. **FORMING OPINIONS** Answers will vary.

Interact *with* History Student responses will vary but should include information from this chapter and other chapters.

HISTORY SKILLS

1. INTERPRETING GRAPHS

Study the graph below. Then answer the questions that follow.

Election of 1912

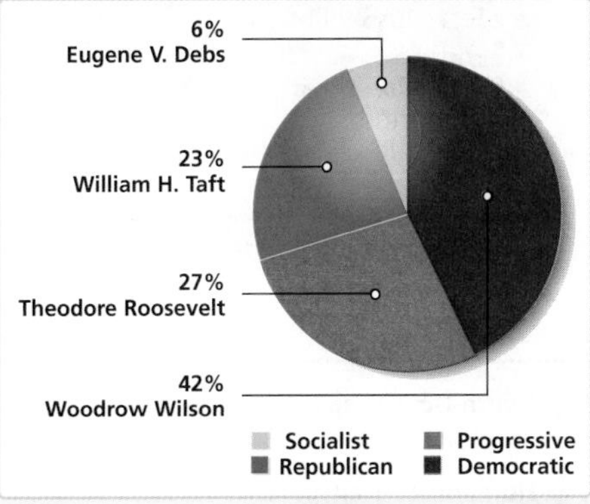

Electoral Vote		Popular Vote*	
Wilson	435	Wilson	6,296,547
Roosevelt	88	Roosevelt	4,118,571
Taft	8	Taft	3,486,720
Debs	0	Debs	900,672

*Other candidates received about 2% of the popular vote.

a. What percentage of the popular vote did Eugene V. Debs win?

b. How many electoral votes did Woodrow Wilson win?

c. Who won the second greatest total of popular votes?

2. INTERPRETING PRIMARY SOURCES

Following is an excerpt from Woodrow Wilson's first inaugural address, delivered on March 4, 1913. Read the excerpt and then answer the questions that follow.

> There can be no equality of opportunity . . . if men and women and children be not shielded in their lives . . . from the consequences of great industrial and social processes which they cannot alter, control, or singly cope with. . . . Sanitary laws, pure-food laws, and laws determining conditions of labor which individuals are powerless to determine for themselves are intimate parts of the very business of justice and legal efficiency.
>
> **Woodrow Wilson,** First Inaugural Address, March 4, 1913

a. What is Wilson promoting in this passage?

b. What values are reflected in this passage?

ALTERNATIVE ASSESSMENT

1. INTERDISCIPLINARY ACTIVITY: Math

Making a Graph Do research to determine the number of immigrants who came from various countries between 1880 and 1914. Find out where immigrants come from today. Make a graph that displays your findings. Explain your graph to the class.

2. COOPERATIVE LEARNING ACTIVITY

Performing Dramatic Readings Drawing on the many journals, diaries, and other primary sources left by sodbusters, create a Voices of the Plains play. Working in small groups, have students research such topics as "the journey west," "first impressions," "dugouts and soddies," "farming the plains," and "women's work and worries." Within groups, members can create presentations using these suggestions.

- Choose and research a topic.
- Select quotations related to the topic.
- Pick writers to compose lines to introduce and make transitions between quotations, and choose readers to perform readings.

3. TECHNOLOGY ACTIVITY

Creating a Multimedia Presentation World War I was the most destructive war the world had yet seen. Use the Internet, books, and other resources to develop a multimedia presentation on the war.

For more information about World War I . . .

INTERNET ACTIVITY
CLASSZONE.COM

Using presentation software, consider including the following content:

- descriptions or images of battles
- the views of American troops as well as the troops of other nations
- public opinion about the war in the United States and other nations
- statistics of casualties suffered by all sides during the conflict

4. HISTORY PORTFOLIO

Review the questions that you wrote for What Do You Want to Know? on page 538. Then write a short report in which you explain the answers to your questions. If any questions were not answered, do research to answer them. Add your answers to your portfolio.

Additional Test Practice, pp. S1–S33

TEST PRACTICE
CLASSZONE.COM

ALTERNATIVE ASSESSMENT

1. INTERDISCIPLINARY ACTIVITY: Math

Graphs should

- present information accurately.
- use bar, line, or pie styles.
- present the information in a style that will aid the viewer in understanding the information.
- be presented neatly.

2. COOPERATIVE LEARNING ACTIVITY

Dramatic reading should

- have a clear focus and be well organized
- include quotations related to the topic
- highlight interesting details of life on the Plains

3. TECHNOLOGY ACTIVITY

Presentations should

- utilize two or more media.
- clearly demonstrate an understanding of World War I.
- show technical proficiency.

4. HISTORY PORTFOLIO

Short reports should

- answer questions about the United States around 1900.
- use evidence to develop and support ideas.
- cite sources of information.
- use standard grammar, spelling, sentence structure, and punctuation.

Critical Thinking Transparency CT97

Formal Assessment

- Chapter Test, Forms A, B, and C, pp. 338–349

HISTORY SKILLS

Possible Responses

1. INTERPRETING GRAPHS

a. six percent

b. 435

c. Theodore Roosevelt

2. INTERPRETING PRIMARY SOURCES

a. He is promoting laws that regulate sanitary working conditions in industry.

b. the value of equal opportunity for all, justice for all, and worth of the individual

CHAPTER 20 EPILOGUE PLANNING GUIDE
The United States Since 1919

	EPILOGUE OVERVIEW	COPYMASTERS	INTEGRATED TECHNOLOGY
CHAPTER 20 EPILOGUE RESOURCES	The Chapter 20 Epilogue describes the history of the nation since the end of World War I. The American people are challenged by the Great Depression, the New Deal, World War II, and the conflicts of the Cold War. Society is changed by new ideas, economic forces, new technology, and new immigrants.	**In-Depth Resources: Unit 5** • Tracing Themes: America in the World, p. 99 • Building Vocabulary, p. 104	• eEdition Plus Online • EasyPlanner Plus Online • eTest Plus Online • eEdition • Power Presentations • EasyPlanner • Electronic Library of Primary Sources • Test Generator • Reading Study Guide • America's Music
SECTION 1 **Prosperity and the Great Depression** **pp. 569–573**	**KEY IDEAS** • The economic boom of the 1920s crashes in 1929. • FDR's New Deal focuses on relief, recovery, and reform. • The New Deal gives the federal government great power.	**In-Depth Resources: Unit 5** • Setting the Stage, p. 98 • Guided Reading, p. 100 • Primary Source: Testimony Before the House Committee on Labor, p. 108 • Literature Selection, pp. 110–112 • Reteaching Activity, p. 113 • Enrichment Activity, p. 117 **America's History Makers** • Franklin Delano Roosevelt, pp. 103–104	**Warm-Up Transparency WT20EPIL** **Humanities Transparency HT51** • Child in the South **Critical Thinking Transparency CT97** • Setting the Stage classzone.com
SECTION 2 **The Rise of Dictators and World War II** **pp. 574–578**	• The rise of dictators leads to World War II. • The attack on Pearl Harbor brings the United States into the war. • The Allies are victorious in Europe and in Asia.	**In-Depth Resources: Unit 5** • Setting the Stage, p. 98 • Guided Reading, p. 101 • Reteaching Activity, p. 114 **America's History Makers** • Dwight D. Eisenhower, pp. 107–108 **Outline Map Activities** • The Axis Powers at Their Peak of Control in Europe, 1942, pp. 49–50	**Warm-Up Transparency WT20EPIL** **Humanities Transparency HT53** • Navajo Code Talkers **Critical Thinking Transparency CT97** • Setting the Stage classzone.com
SECTION 3 **The Cold War** **pp. 579–583**	• The Cold War begins after World War II. • The United States fights the spread of communism in Asia. • The collapse of the Soviet Union ends the Cold War.	**In-Depth Resources: Unit 5** • Setting the Stage, p. 98 • Guided Reading, p. 102 • Skillbuilder Practice, p. 105 • Reteaching Activity, p. 115 **America's History Makers** • John F. Kennedy, pp. 119–120	**Warm-Up Transparency WT20EPIL** **Geography Transparency GT30** • U.S. Troops Around the World, 1975 **Critical Thinking Transparency CT97** • Setting the Stage **Critical Thinking Transparency CT83** • Cause and Effect: The Cold War classzone.com
SECTION 4 **Life in America Since 1945** **pp. 584–589**	• Minorities and women seek greater civil rights. • The Vietnam War splinters society. • New immigrants bring diversity to the United States.	**In-Depth Resources: Unit 5** • Guided Reading, p. 103 • Geography Application: School Integration, 1954–1960, pp. 106–107 • Primary Source, p. 109 **America's History Makers** • Martin Luther King, Jr., pp. 115–116 • Ronald Reagan, pp. 129–130 **Why It Matters Now** • Changes in Modern America, pp. 49–50	**Warm-Up Transparency WT20EPIL** **Critical Thinking Transparency CT97** • Setting the Stage **Critical Thinking Transparency CT98** • Visual Summary classzone.com

Pupil's Edition
Copymaster
Overhead Transparency
Audio Library
CD-ROM
Internet

ASSESSMENT OPTIONS

- **Chapter 20 Epilogue Assessment,** pp. 592–593
- **Formal Assessment**
  - Chapter 20 Epilogue Test, Forms A, B, and C, pp. 354–365
- **Test Generator**
- **Online Test Practice**
- **Strategies for Test Preparation**

- **Section Assessment,** p. 573
- **Formal Assessment**
  - Section Quiz, p. 350
- **Integrated Assessment Book**
  - Rubrics, 4.2, 5.4
- **Test Generator**
- **Test Practice Transparencies,** TT89–TT95

- **Section Assessment,** p. 578
- **Formal Assessment**
  - Section Quiz, p. 351
- **Integrated Assessment Book**
  - Rubrics, 4.3, 5.1
- **Test Generator**
- **Test Practice Transparencies,** TT96–TT100

- **Section Assessment,** p. 583
- **Formal Assessment**
  - Section Quiz, p. 352
- **Integrated Assessment Book**
  - Rubrics, 3.6, 1.3
- **Test Generator**
- **Test Practice Transparencies,** TT101–TT103

- **Section Assessment,** p. 589
- **Formal Assessment**
  - Section Quiz, p. 353
- **Integrated Assessment Book**
  - Rubrics, 2.5, 2.3
- **Test Generator**
- **Test Practice Transparencies,** TT104–TT115

CUSTOMIZING FOR INDIVIDUAL NEEDS

Students Acquiring English/ESL

- **Reading Study Guide** (English and Spanish), pp. 189–198
- **Access for Students Acquiring English/ESL: Spanish Translations,** pp. 130–136
- **Chapter Summaries on CD** (English and Spanish)
- **Modified Lesson Plans for English Learners**

Less Proficient Readers

- **Reading Study Guide** (English and Spanish), pp. 189–198
- **Chapter Summaries on CD** (English and Spanish)

Gifted and Talented Students

- **In-Depth Resources: Unit 7**
  - Enrichment Activity, p. 117
- **America's History Makers**
  - Dwight D. Eisenhower, pp. 107–108
  - Martin Luther King, Jr., pp. 115–116
  - John F. Kennedy, pp. 119–120
  - Ronald Reagan, pp. 129–130

CROSS-CURRICULAR CONNECTIONS

Culture

1,000 Makers of the Millennium: The Men and Women Who Have Shaped the Last 1,000 Years. New York: DK Publishing, 1999. Scientists, explorers, presidents, movie stars, and many more categories.

Economics

Brown, Paul. ***Energy and Resources.*** New York: Franklin Watts, 1998. Discusses the aims of the 1992 Earth Summit and its plan for attaining sustainable development.

Government

Rubel, David. ***Scholastic Encyclopedia of the Presidents and Their Times.*** Scholastic, 1997. An easy-to-use, one-volume reference that catalogs noteworthy events such as election results.

Primary Sources

Levine, Ellen. ***Freedom's Children: Young Civil Rights Activists Tell Their Own Stories.*** New York: Putnam, 1993. First-person accounts by 30 African-American kids who worked for civil rights.

Interdisciplinary Projects

- Math: Analyzing Statistics, p. 145
- Science: Blood Banking, p. 158
- Language Arts: Civil Rights Speech, p. 171
- Art: Latino Art, p. 172

Literature

Conrad, Pam. ***Our House: The Stories of Levittown.*** New York: Scholastic, 1994. A series of stories set in Levittown traces changes in the community.

Hesse, Karen. ***Out of the Dust.*** New York: Scholastic, 1997. Unforgettable, original poems about life on a dried-up Oklahoma wheat farm by a 15-year-old girl named Billie Jo.

Houston, Jeanne Wakatsuki. ***Farewell to Manzanar: A True Story of Japanese American Experience During and After the World War II Internment.*** New York: Bantam Books, 1983. Modern classic tells about life in an internment camp. For advanced readers.

McDougal Littell *The Language of Literature*

- Woody Guthrie. "This Land Is Your Land" (song)

McDougal Littell Literature Connections

Mildred D. Taylor
Roll of Thunder, Hear My Cry
Set in Mississippi during the early years of the Great Depression, Taylor's novel is about the Logan family and their relationships with the land, their neighbors, and each other.

ENRICHMENT ACTIVITIES

- **Pupil's Edition, pp. 566–593**
  Interact with History, p. 567
  Interdisciplinary Challenge, pp. 590–591
- **In-Depth Resources: Unit 7**
  - Geography Application, pp. 106–107
  - Primary Source, p. 108
  - Primary Source, p. 109
  - Literature Selection, pp. 110–112
- **Why It Matters Now**
  - Changes in Modern America, pp. 49–50
- **America's History Makers**
  - Franklin Delano Roosevelt, pp. 103–104
  - Dwight D. Eisenhower, pp. 107–108
  - Martin Luther King, Jr., pp. 115–116
  - John F. Kennedy, pp. 119–120
  - Ronald Reagan, pp. 129–130
- **Outline Map Activities,** pp. 49–50

BLOCK SCHEDULING — LESSON PLAN OPTIONS (90-MINUTE PERIOD)

DAY 1

Interact with History, p. 567
Class Time 20 minutes

Options for pacing and variety:

- **Peer Teaching** Have students work in groups of three to answer the "What Do You Think?" question: "How do you think the 21st century will differ from the 20th century?" Have students write down a list of predictions to share with the class. **Class Time** 15 minutes

Setting the Stage, p. 568
Class Time 20 minutes

Options for pacing and variety:

- **Time Saver** To focus students' responses to the "What Do You Want to Know?" questions, for a homework assignment have them record in their notebooks one question for each of the following decades: 1920s, 1930s, 1960s, and 1990s. **Class Time** 10 minutes

Section 1, pp. 569–573
Class Time 50 minutes

Options for pacing and variety:

- **Time Saver** Use the graph on page 571 to summarize for students the effects of the stock market crash of 1929 on stock prices. **Class Time** 5 minutes
- **History on Film** Extend students' background knowledge of the Great Depression by showing them *The Great Depression and the New Deal.* Schlessinger Media, 1996. **Class Time** 35 minutes

DAY 2

Section 2, pp. 574–578
Class Time 45 minutes

Options for pacing and variety:

- **Peer Teaching** Have student pairs explain how each of the events listed on the time line for 1920–1939 led up to World War II. **Class Time** 15 minutes
- **Internet** Extend students' background knowledge of D-Day events by visiting classzone.com **Class Time** 20 minutes

Section 3, pp. 579–583
Class Time 45 minutes

Options for pacing and variety:

- **Peer Teaching** Ask a student to summarize for the class the causes and effects of the Cold War using the chart on page 582 as a guide. **Class Time** 5 minutes
- **Peer Evaluation** Have student pairs make a Venn diagram showing their responses to the Section Assessment Critical Thinking question. **Class Time** 10 minutes

DAY 3

Section 4, pp. 584–589
Class Time 45 minutes

Options for pacing and variety:

- **Peer Teaching** Have students turn the Critical Thinking Theme question on page 730 into a debate topic: *Does the United States have a special responsibility to intervene in conflicts around the world? Why or why not?* **Class Time** 20 minutes

Interdisciplinary Challenge, pp. 590–591
Class Time 40 minutes

Options for pacing and variety:

- **Team Teaching** Invite a science teacher to assist students in understanding global warming and in solving the Math Challenge. **Class Time** 30 minutes

Epilogue Assessment, pp. 592–593
Class Time 40 minutes

Options for pacing and variety:

- **Peer Teaching** Have students work in groups to complete the Interdisciplinary Activity on page 593 with each group responsible for a different decade of the time line. **Class Time** 50 minutes
- **Peer Competition** Working in small groups, students can write three questions about political events, three about social events, and three about economic events for the period between 1920 and 2000. Questions should be answered with terms or names from the chapter. Collect questions and answers, organize by category, and play a game of *Jeopardy* to review the chapter. **Class Time** 30 minutes

TEACHER-TESTED ACTIVITY Marci Smith, Hurst-Euless-Bedford ISD, Bedford, Texas

HAVE WE REACHED THE DREAM?

Class Time One class period

Task Analyzing and expressing an opinion on changes in race relations

Purpose To evaluate changes in relations among groups within American society since the civil rights movement of the 1960s

Supplies Needed

- Copies of Dr. Martin Luther King, Jr.'s, "I Have a Dream" speech
- Audio-or videotaped version of King's "I Have a Dream" speech
- Two large posterboard signs, one saying "Yes, Completely" and the other saying "No, Not at All"

Activity Write the following question on the chalkboard: *Have we as a nation reached the point where people are judged not by the color of their skin, but by the content of their character?* As the class listens to a recording of King's speech, encourage students to think about the question on the chalkboard. Then place the "Yes, Completely" sign at one end of the room and the "No, Not at All" sign at the other. Tell students to move quietly to the point along the line between the two signs where their opinion lies. Allow each person to make a brief statement in support of his or her opinion. Allow time for rebuttal.

TIME TRAVEL VIDEO PLAYS

Technological change has accelerated in the last 80 years. Two inventions that made those changes possible were the microchip, invented in 1958, and the laser, conceived in 1917 but not produced until around 1960. The microchip made possible the personal computer (PC) revolution. Laser technology and closely related fiber optic technology led to networks (the Internet), microwave technology (cell phones and microwave ovens), and compact disk players. To better understand the speed at which technological change has taken place, students will produce five video plays that examine what life has been like over the past 80 years. In order to make the video plays accurate, each group will research inventions of the specific year they are portraying.

ACTIVITY OUTLINE

Objective By producing video plays about technological change over the past 80 years, students will better understand the ways new technologies have affected people's lives.

Task Students will produce short dramatizations of what life was like at 20-year intervals over the past 80 years.

Class Time Two class periods

DIRECTIONS

1. Ask students what they think the key inventions of the past 80 years have been.

2. Divide students into five groups and assign them a year from 80 years ago to this year. Each group will research technologies that existed during their year. Research can be done on Web sites listed on classzone.com or in the school library.

3. When research is completed, groups will produce short video plays of what life was like during certain years of the recent past. The plays must include only technologies that existed at the time. Scenes in the plays should show life in the following places:
   - at school
   - at home
   - on a trip
   - in a hospital

4. Instruct the groups to plan each scene and the technologies they want to demonstrate. They can pinpoint products and inventions that would have been available or in the news of the time.

5. Tell students they do not have to write a script for the scenes in the play. They should plan the focus for the scene but improvise the action and dialogue. Different members of the group can perform in each scene.

6. After all groups have completed preparation for their video plays, arrange for them to videotape their scenes. The completed video plays should be shown sequentially.

7. After the class has an opportunity to watch the complete set of plays, conduct a class discussion about the rapid rate of technological change and what that seems to indicate for the future.

CHAPTER 20 EPILOGUE OBJECTIVE

The student will understand the challenges faced by the nation during the 20th century and speculate about the challenges of the 21st century.

CHAPTER 20 EPILOGUE

The United States Since 1919

Section 1 **Prosperity and the Great Depression**
Section 2 **The Rise of Dictators and World War II**
Section 3 **The Cold War**
Section 4 **Life in America Since 1945**

HISTORY FROM VISUALS

Interpreting the Photographs Have students look closely at the eight photographs in the film frames and identify those they can (Roaring Twenties' dancers; Great Depression soup kitchen; D-Day invasion during World War II; atomic bomb; Elvis Presley; 1963 March on Washington; Vietnam War; space launch). Have students classify each photograph according to its subject: the nation's political, economic, or social history. Then ask students to use the photographs to construct a generalization about the 20th century. **Possible Response** The 20th century was a time of conflict, social change, and scientific advances.

Extension Ask students to suggest topics for other photographs to represent the last part of the 20th century.

RECOMMENDED RESOURCES

BOOKS FOR THE TEACHER

Coontz, Stephanie. ***The Way We Never Were: American Families and the Nostalgia Trap.*** New York: Basic Books, 1992. A fascinating look at the "good old days."

Galbraith, John K. ***The Great Crash 1929.*** Boston: Houghton, 1997. A pivotal work by one of the nation's most noted economists.

Chafe, William H., and Harvard Sitkoff. ***A History of Our Time: Readings on Postwar America.*** 5th ed. New York: Oxford, 1999. Primary documents and essays on U.S. history since World War II.

SOFTWARE

The Cold War: Decisions, Decisions. CD-ROM. Tom Snyder Productions, 1997. Focuses on foreign policy decisions in the nuclear age.

VIDEO

Four Little Girls. 40 Acres & a Mule Filmworks, 1998. Spike Lee's documentary on the 1963 bombing of the Birmingham, Alabama, church.

INTERNET

For more about Franklin D. Roosevelt, visit . . .

classzone.com

Interact *with* History

During the 20th century, the United States has experienced many challenges. These include war, economic depression, and the struggle for equal rights. New challenges await you in the 21st century. You must decide what they are and how you will respond.

What Do You Think?

- How will technology play a part in your life?
- What are your talents, and how could you use them to benefit yourself and society?
- What do you think the United States and the world need most from your generation?

How do you think the 21st century will differ from the 20th century?

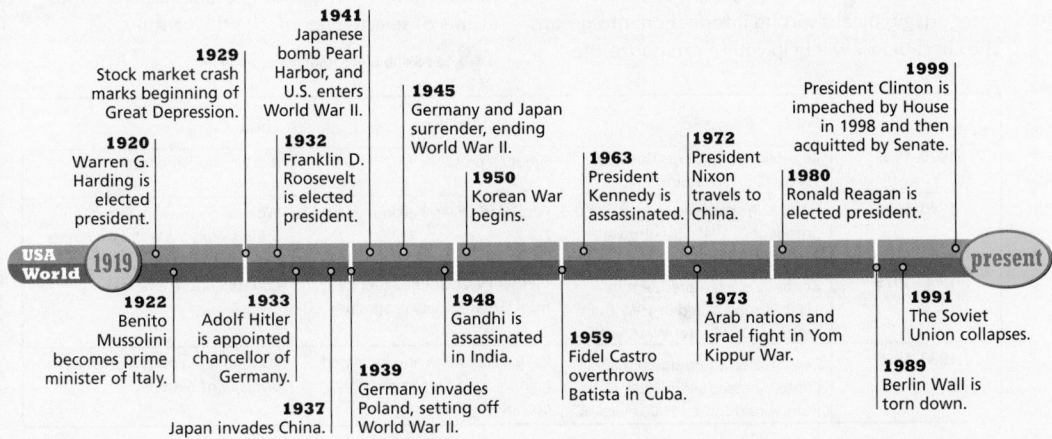

USA
- **1920** Warren G. Harding is elected president.
- **1929** Stock market crash marks beginning of Great Depression.
- **1932** Franklin D. Roosevelt is elected president.
- **1941** Japanese bomb Pearl Harbor, and U.S. enters World War II.
- **1945** Germany and Japan surrender, ending World War II.
- **1950** Korean War begins.
- **1963** President Kennedy is assassinated.
- **1972** President Nixon travels to China.
- **1980** Ronald Reagan is elected president.
- **1999** President Clinton is impeached by House in 1998 and then acquitted by Senate.

World
- **1922** Benito Mussolini becomes prime minister of Italy.
- **1933** Adolf Hitler is appointed chancellor of Germany.
- **1937** Japan invades China.
- **1939** Germany invades Poland, setting off World War II.
- **1948** Gandhi is assassinated in India.
- **1959** Fidel Castro overthrows Batista in Cuba.
- **1973** Arab nations and Israel fight in Yom Kippur War.
- **1989** Berlin Wall is torn down.
- **1991** The Soviet Union collapses.

1919 — present

Interact *with* History

OBJECTIVES
- To help students speculate about the nation's development in the 21st century
- To help students think about their roles as adults in the 21st-century United States

What Do You Think?
1. List all the forms of technology you use in a typical day, from waking to bedtime. What forms of technology do you think Americans will use in the 21st century?
2. Make a lists of jobs you might hold within the next 10 or 15 years. Explain how you could benefit society in each particular occupation.
3. Identify problems that existed in the 20th century. Will those problems need solutions in the 21st century?

How do you think the 21st century will differ from the 20th century?
List on the board some categories for student predictions, such as school, travel, housing, clothing, music, sports, food, foreign relations, and equal rights movements.

MAKING PERSONAL CONNECTIONS
Ask students to choose a single adjective that they hope will describe the 21st century in history books that their children will read in school.

TIME LINE DISCUSSION

Between 1919 and the present, the United States developed into the world's strongest political and economic power. The country and the world survived a deep depression, two world wars, and two wars in Asia. The world's technology moved from horseless carriage to space shuttle.

The nation experienced the assassination of one president, the resignation of another, and the impeachment of a third. Throughout the century, many Americans campaigned for greater rights and for prosperity for all.

- Ask students to look at the events on the time line. What kinds of activities characterized the time from 1919 to the present? **Answer** wars, conflicts
- What does the time line illustrate about the leaders of the United States? **Answer** The government remained stable with legally elected presidents.

BEFORE YOU READ

Previewing the Theme: America in the World

In the cartoon, Uncle Sam says that Europe "ain't what it used to be." Ask the students what changes in the 20th century made Americans want to turn away from affairs in Europe. How does the size of the Atlantic Ocean suggest that isolation from other parts of the world will be unsuccessful?

What Do You Know?

Remind students that helping the Allies win World War II brought the nation out of the economic troubles of the 1930s. It also established the United States as a world leader. A "Cold War" followed the "hot" war and lasted 45 years.

In-Depth Resources: Unit 5
- Tracing Themes: America in the World, p. 99

READ AND TAKE NOTES

Reading Strategy: Categorizing

Remind students that to categorize means to organize ideas or events into groups. The items in each group have something in common. Review the terms *political, economic,* and *social.* Discuss the organization of the chart, and suggest that students use a similar chart to organize the ideas and events they read about in the Chapter 20 Epilogue.

In-Depth Resources: Unit 5
- Setting the Stage, p. 98

Critical Thinking Transparency: **CT97**
- Setting the Stage

Chapter 20 Epilogue SETTING THE STAGE

BEFORE YOU READ

Previewing the Theme

America in the World During the 20th century, the United States took a more prominent place in the world. This chapter explains how the nation's domestic life and politics, as well as its relations with the rest of the world, changed during the century.

In this political cartoon published in the *Washington Post* in the 1930s, Uncle Sam turns his back on Europe.

What Do You Know?

What do you think of when you hear the phrase "the Great Depression"? Who do you think fought in World War II? How can a war be a "Cold War"?

THINK ABOUT
- what you've learned about any of these topics from movies, television, or travel
- how great events shape the lives of individuals

What Do You Want to Know?

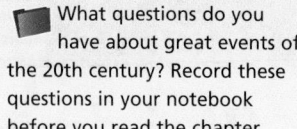

What questions do you have about great events of the 20th century? Record these questions in your notebook before you read the chapter.

READ AND TAKE NOTES

Reading Strategy: Categorizing To help you make sense of what you read, learn to categorize. Categorizing means sorting information into groups. The chart below will help you to categorize the information in this chapter. Use the chart to take notes on important political, economic, and social events of selected decades of this century.

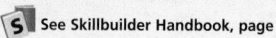

See Skillbuilder Handbook, page R6.

The 20th Century	Political Events	Economic Events	Social Events
1920–1939	Republican presidents dominate 1920s; FDR elected in 1932	Great Depression	Rise of popular entertainment in sports, music, and movies
1940–1959	Harry S. Truman elected president in 1948; Eisenhower elected in 1952	Post-World War II economic boom	Women go to work in factories during World War II; Civil Rights movement grows
1960–1979	Kennedy elected president in 1960; Nixon elected in 1968 then resigns in 1974 after Watergate	Vietnam War drained money from Great Society programs	Counterculture emerges
1980–1999	Reagan elected president in 1980; Clinton impeached in 1998; G. W. Bush wins disputed 2000 election	Reagan cut taxes and increased military spending; strong economic growth	Continuing immigration adds to diversity of nation

TEACHING STRATEGY

READING THE CHAPTER

This is a chronological chapter that summarizes the major events in the United States during the 20th century. It traces the nation's growing leadership in world events and its internal struggles to ensure equal rights for all Americans.

ALTERNATIVE ASSESSMENT

The Chapter 20 Epilogue Assessment describes three activities for alternative assessment on page 593. You may wish to have students work on these activities during the course of the chapter and then present them at the end.

1 Prosperity and the Great Depression

MAIN IDEA

The stock market crash of 1929 and the Great Depression led to Franklin D. Roosevelt's New Deal.

WHY IT MATTERS NOW

The New Deal increased the role of the federal government.

TERMS & NAMES

Warren G. Harding
Calvin Coolidge
jazz
Harlem Renaissance
Great Depression
Franklin D. Roosevelt
New Deal

ONE AMERICAN'S STORY

Louis Armstrong grew up in New Orleans, the birthplace of jazz. As a child, Armstrong often listened to jazz music played at funeral processions, dance halls, saloons, and lawn parties. He learned to play the cornet and trumpet, and became a great jazz musician. In 1922, he accepted a job offer to play jazz with a Chicago band.

A VOICE FROM THE PAST

When I left New Orleans to go up North in 1922 the toughest Negro . . . his name is Slippers . . . he gave me a pep talk. . . . He loved the way I played those Blues. . . . When he found out that I was leaving to go to Chicago, he was the first one to congratulate me. . . . He said, "I love the way you blow that Quail." Of course he meant the cornet.

Louis Armstrong, quoted in *Louis: The Louis Armstrong Story*

Louis Armstrong greatly influenced the development of jazz.

Armstrong and other jazz musicians spread jazz to other parts of the country. In this section, you will read about popular culture, the Harlem Renaissance, the artists of the Lost Generation, and the stock market crash of 1929.

❶ The Roaring Twenties' Business Boom

By the start of the 1920s, Americans were turning away from progressive reforms. World War I was over. Americans were disappointed with the Treaty of Versailles. This, and the terrible human cost of the war, made them unwilling to fight "other people's wars." Now they wanted to help themselves. Americans were ready for a decade-long buying spree.

Earlier in the century, presidents like Roosevelt and Taft had sought to place tighter controls on business. Under presidents **Warren G. Harding** and **Calvin Coolidge,** the government put into practice pro-business policies. These policies made business growth easier and more profitable. President Coolidge came into office in 1923. He spoke for many when he said, "the chief business of the American people is business."

SECTION OBJECTIVES

1. To identify causes of the economic prosperity of the 1920s
2. To describe ways American culture changed during the 1920s
3. To analyze the causes and effects of the Great Depression
4. To evaluate New Deal policies and their lasting effects

SKILLBUILDER

Interpreting Charts, p. 571

CRITICAL THINKING

Analyzing Causes, p. 571
Summarizing, pp. 571, 573
Making Inferences, p. 573

FOCUS & MOTIVATE

5-MINUTE WARM-UP

Recognizing Effects These questions focus on the stock market crash of 1929.

1. Look at the chart on page 571. What years could be described by the words *boom* and *bust?*
2. How might these events affect the average American?

Warm-Up Transparency WT20EPIL

INSTRUCT

INSTRUCT: OBJECTIVE ❶

The Roaring Twenties' Business Boom

- What effect did the pro-business policies of Harding and Coolidge have on the economy?
- Why did Americans have more money to spend and more goods to buy during the Twenties?

In-Depth Resources: Unit 5
- Guided Reading, p. 100

Reading Study Guide (Spanish and English), pp. 189–190

RECOMMENDED RESOURCES

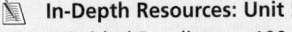

In-Depth Resources: Unit 5
- Guided Reading, p. 100
- Building Vocabulary, p. 104
- Primary Source, p. 108

Reading Study Guide (Spanish and English), pp. 189–190

America's History Makers
- Franklin Delano Roosevelt, pp. 103–104

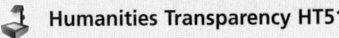

Formal Assessment
- Section Quiz, p. 350

Integrated Assessment
- Rubrics, 4.2, 5.4

Access for Students Acquiring English/ESL
- Guided Reading, p. 130

INTEGRATED TECHNOLOGY

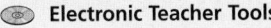

Humanities Transparency HT51

Electronic Teacher Tools

classzone.com

TEST-TAKING RESOURCES

Strategies for Test Preparation

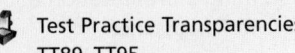

Test Practice Transparencies, TT89–TT95

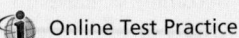

Online Test Practice

MORE ABOUT . . .

Pro-Business Policies

Presidents Harding and Coolidge were both Republicans, and Republicans were the majority party in Congress from 1919 to 1931. Pro-business legislation included lower tax rates for corporations and wealthy individuals and higher tariffs on imports. The Federal Trade Commission and the Interstate Commerce Commission, which regulated corporations, tended to cooperate with business during this decade.

INSTRUCT: OBJECTIVE 2

The Rise of Popular Entertainment

- What is jazz?
- What forms of entertainment were popular in the 1920s?
- What did the term *Harlem Renaissance* symbolize?

In-Depth Resources: Unit 5
- Enrichment Activity, p. 117

MORE ABOUT . . .

More Celebrities of the Twenties

In 1926, Gertrude C. Ederle became the first woman to swim across the English Channel. The record-breaking young swimmer had won one gold and two bronze medals in the 1924 Olympics in Paris.

Another popular sports star was Helen Wills. Wills won the Wimbledon tennis singles championship eight times. She won a total of 31 major tennis titles in her career, including two Olympic gold medals.

Celebrities of the 1920s

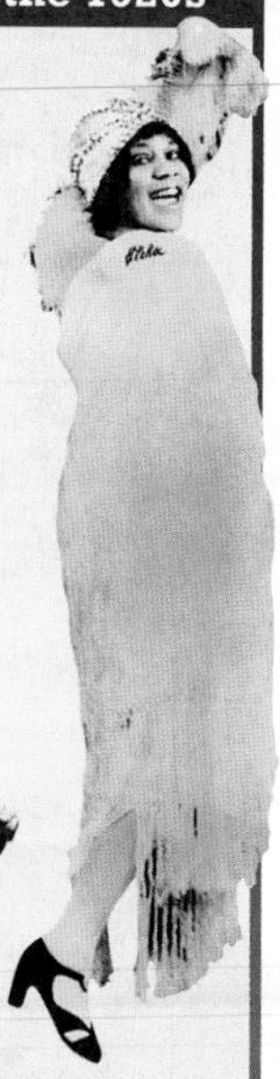

Bessie Smith ▶ Known as "Empress of the Blues," Bessie Smith was perhaps the most outstanding singer of the 1920s.

◀ Babe Ruth Known as the "Sultan of Swat," Babe Ruth hit 60 home runs for the New York Yankees in 1927.

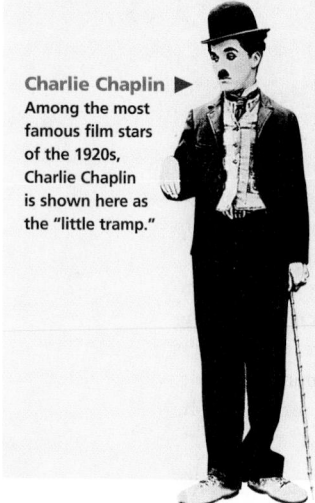

Charlie Chaplin ▶ Among the most famous film stars of the 1920s, Charlie Chaplin is shown here as the "little tramp."

Giant business empires such as the automobile industry made the economy boom. Between 1920 and 1930, the number of cars in the United States almost tripled from about 8 million to 23 million. Car sales fueled demand for steel, oil, rubber, gasoline, and glass. Tourism thrived as more people took vacations by car. Improvements in methods of mass production made it possible to turn out products faster and cheaper. As a result, prices fell for such goods as washing machines and refrigerators. At the same time, the nation's wealth grew. During the 1920s, the income of the average American rose by almost 40 percent. People had both more money to spend and more goods to buy.

The Rise of Popular Entertainment 2

After the sacrifices of World War I, Americans wanted to enjoy themselves. Radio, movies, and sports gained in popularity. Big-city dwellers flocked to nightclubs where they learned hot new dances like the Charleston and the shimmy. The 1920s also introduced more Americans to a musical form called **jazz.** The new jazz music sprang up in cities such as New Orleans and Chicago. It blended African and European musical traditions. Trumpeter Louis Armstrong and composer and bandleader Duke Ellington drew crowds to jazz clubs and speakeasies. Singer Bessie Smith, known as "Empress of the Blues," thrilled audiences wherever she performed.

Vocabulary
speakeasies: places for illegal sale and consumption of alcoholic drinks during the 1920s

Audiences for movies grew throughout the decade. Even small towns had a movie theater. In 1922, people bought tickets to see such stars as Clara Bow and Charlie Chaplin on the silent screen. In 1925, Chaplin charmed audiences with his portrayal of the "little tramp" in silent films such as *The Gold Rush.* Two years later, Al Jolson's *The Jazz Singer* became the first talking picture. By the end of the decade, over 100 million people a year were packing movie theaters for talking pictures.

The growing popularity of radio helped put sports in the spotlight. Radio spread the fame of such teams as the New York Yankees and the Chicago Cubs. It made national heroes out of sports figures like Babe Ruth, who was baseball's home-run king. Baseball, boxing, and football all gained wider audiences.

In literature, such writers as Ernest Hemingway, F. Scott Fitzgerald, and Edna St. Vincent Millay were

ACTIVITY OPTIONS

MULTIPLE LEARNING STYLES: LINGUISTIC

BLOCK SCHEDULING

WRITERS OF THE HARLEM RENAISSANCE

Class Time One class period

Task Creating a presentation about the Harlem Renaissance

Purpose To become familiar with the work of writers of the Harlem Renaissance

Supplies Needed
- Works by writers of the Harlem Renaissance, such as Langston Hughes, Countee Cullen, and Zora Neale Hurston

Activity Divide students into small groups. Have each group research one writer of the Harlem Renaissance and choose one short poem or selection from that writer's works. Representatives of the group should prepare a dramatic reading of the piece to present to the class, while other group members prepare information about the writer's life and literary significance.

able to capture the feelings of disillusionment and rebellion that some young people felt at the end of World War I. In the Harlem section of New York City, the 1920s were a time of great creativity for African-American artists. Writers such as Langston Hughes, Countee Cullen, and Zora Neale Hurston belonged to the cultural movement known as the **Harlem Renaissance.** Hughes used jazz rhythms and dialect in his writings to celebrate black urban life and to call for social change.

3 Stock Market Crash and Great Depression

> ***"The chief business of the American people is business."***
> President Coolidge

During the 1920s, the stock market soared. Ordinary people saw buying stocks as a safe, quick way to get rich. Many ordinary people invested their life savings. Most did not understand the risks of investing. Many investors even borrowed money to buy shares. Then, in October 1929, the stock market crashed.

The crash sparked a chain reaction. First, banks demanded that customers pay back the money they had borrowed to buy stock. When people could not repay these loans, the banks ran short of money. Fearing that banks would close, customers lined up to withdraw their money. Since banks rarely keep enough cash on hand to pay all their customers at once, many banks shut down. The **Great Depression,** a time of great economic hardship, had begun.

As banks failed or cut back on loans to businesses, factories produced fewer goods and therefore laid off workers. With more people out of work, spending declined. Businesses let more workers go and factories closed. By 1932, one-fourth of the nation's workers were jobless.

Everywhere, sales of farm products fell sharply. In the Midwest and Great Plains, farmers not only faced economic losses but also suffered a terrible drought that lasted for years. Poor farming methods and over-farming of the land led to massive soil erosion, making it impossible to grow crops. Winds carried away dry soil over millions of acres, creating the Dust Bowl. Thousands were forced to abandon their farms and leave the Great Plains.

Republican President Herbert Hoover took office early in 1929. When the stock market crashed in October 1929, he urged Americans to be patient. He warned that federal government action would make things worse. Relief, or government aid to the hungry and homeless, would make Americans dependent on government handouts. In the 1932 election, they voted for a leader who promised another way.

Background
The stock market crash came on October 29, 1929. On that day, the prices of stocks fell dramatically.

***Reading* History**
A. Analyzing Causes Why did some banks shut down during the Depression?
A. Answer Banks demanded that customers repay loans. When loans were not repaid, banks ran short of funds.

B. Answer Hoover felt federal aid might make Americans dependent on handouts.

***Reading* History**
B. Summarizing What was Hoover's attitude toward federal aid for the poor?

Stock Prices, *1925–1933*

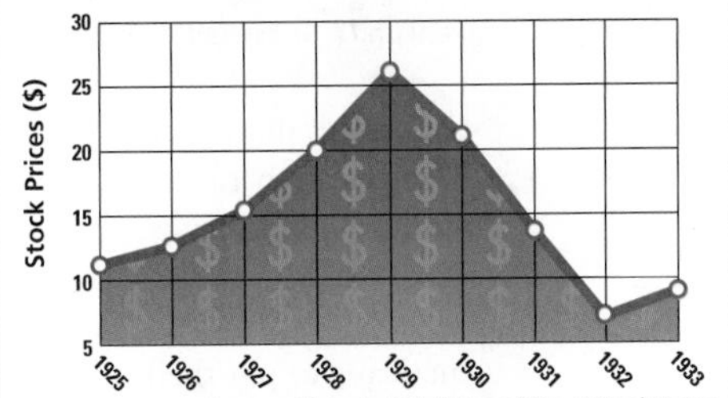

Source: *Historical Statistics of the United States*

SKILLBUILDER Interpreting Charts
1. *In what year did stock prices begin their decline?*
2. *In what year did prices begin to rise again after the crash?*

Skillbuilder Answers
1. 1929
2. 1932

INSTRUCT: OBJECTIVE 3
Stock Market Crash and Great Depression

- What factors led to bank failures after the stock market crash?
- How did the Dust Bowl add to the economic problems of farmers?
- Why was President Hoover reluctant to begin government programs to provide relief for the hungry and homeless?

Humanities Transparency HT51
- Child in the South

In-Depth Resources: Unit 5
- Primary Source, p. 108
- Literature Selection, pp. 110–112

MORE ABOUT . . .

The Stock Market Crash
During the 1920s, stock prices far exceeded their real value. Many stock buyers bought stock on margin, or on money borrowed from the stock broker. When stock prices fell, many investors with margin accounts were forced to sell, driving prices down even further. Stock prices began to fall in September 1929, but October 29, "Black Tuesday," was the worst day in stock market history.

HISTORY FROM VISUALS

Reading the Chart Have students speculate about why it took the economy many years to recover from the crash. **Possible Response** because the Great Depression affected all parts of the economy—business, labor, banks, farms, production

Extension Ask students to create another way to illustrate this information.

ACTIVITY OPTIONS
INDIVIDUAL NEEDS

LESS PROFICIENT READERS

Analyzing Causes and Recognizing Effects Some students may have difficulty understanding the economic problems of the 1920s. On the board, write the following causes and effects in a chart like the one shown here. Read each entry in the chart, and ask students to supply the corresponding cause or effect.

Cause	Effect
Stock prices dropped on October 23.	*<Investors lost money.>*
<People could not repay loans to bank.>	Banks ran short of money.
Businesses sold fewer products.	*<Business fired workers.>*

HISTORY through ART

Interpreting the Painting William Gropper was born in New York City in 1897. His family was extremely poor. Gropper's work reflects his strong social conscience and deep interest in the labor movement. The New Deal sponsored many programs for artists. One such program, called the Fine Arts Section, commissioned art for over 1,000 post offices throughout the country. The Works Progress Administration sponsored art for state and municipal buildings.

Possible Response: The painting shows the dignity and virtue of work.

INSTRUCT: OBJECTIVE 4

Roosevelt's New Deal/ Lasting New Deal Changes

- How did Roosevelt differ from Hoover in his approach to the nation's problems?
- What were the three major goals of the New Deal programs passed during the Hundred Days?
- What lasting changes did the New Deal bring to American society and government?

MORE ABOUT . . .

New Deal Programs

One important New Deal program was the formation of the Tennessee Valley Authority. The goals of the TVA were to prevent flooding in the Tennessee River Valley, to create jobs, and to generate inexpensive electricity for the people of the area.

Another important piece of New Deal legislation was the Social Security Act, passed in 1935. Under the Social Security system, workers and employers make payments into a special fund. When workers retire, they receive a pension from Social Security funds. Laid-off workers, disabled workers, and needy families with dependent children also receive Social Security benefits.

HISTORY through ART

The New Deal's Federal Arts Project commissioned murals for post offices and other public buildings. This mural, entitled *Construction of a Dam,* was painted by William Gropper (1897–1977). It was painted in the Department of the Interior building in Washington, D.C.

What does the painting reveal about the value of work in a time of both economic depression and unemployment?

4 Roosevelt's New Deal

When Democrat **Franklin D. Roosevelt,** also known as FDR, took over as president, millions of families lacked food or shelter. People searched in garbage dumps for food or stood for hours in long lines for soup. Former business executives sold apples on streetcorners. Blaming Hoover for the hard times, the homeless called their tin-and-cardboard shacks "Hoovervilles." Roosevelt set out to restore hope and confidence both in government and in the American economy. His inaugural address expressed his optimism.

A VOICE FROM THE PAST

> This great nation will endure as it has endured, will revive and will prosper. So, first of all, let me assert my firm belief that the only thing we have to fear is fear itself.
>
> **Franklin D. Roosevelt,** Inaugural Address, March 4, 1933

Roosevelt promised immediate action, and he kept his word. His first target was the bank crisis. Calling for a "bank holiday," he ordered a brief shutdown of all banks. Federal officials went to work examining bank records. They decided which ones could reopen at once and which needed government help to do so. FDR's confidence persuaded Americans to put their money back into the banks.

With the public and Congress firmly supporting him, Roosevelt began a bold new program to end the Great Depression. It was called the **New Deal.** During a period known as the "Hundred Days," Congress passed with little debate almost all the bills the White House sent over. Even Republican lawmakers admired FDR's decisiveness.

ACTIVITY OPTIONS

INTERDISCIPLINARY LINK: GOVERNMENT

BLOCK SCHEDULING

A NEW DEAL EXHIBIT

Class Time One class period

Task Preparing an exhibit about New Deal programs

Purpose To learn about the purpose and effects of New Deal legislation

Supplies Needed

- Reference materials on New Deal programs
- Internet access
- Posterboard
- Art supplies

Activity Have students read about New Deal programs in an encyclopedia or a general reference book. Direct each student or small groups of students to select one New Deal program. Students should do more research on their selected program and prepare a poster illustrating the goal of the program, its scope, and its effects. Create a classroom exhibit of the completed posters. Allow the class to tour the exhibit and ask questions about the programs.

Roosevelt's New Deal had three major goals, known as the "three R's":

1. **Relief programs** to help the hungry and jobless
2. **Recovery programs** to help agriculture and industry
3. **Reform of the economy** to ensure that a crisis like the Great Depression did not happen again

Not all of FDR's policies worked, and many angered business leaders because they led to higher taxes. Still, most Americans believed his policies were effective, and they reelected him to office in 1936.

Lasting New Deal Changes

The New Deal made lasting changes in American society and government. It increased the power of the federal government. It encouraged presidents and Congress to practice deficit spending during economic hard times. This means spending more money than the government raises in taxes. Many New Deal programs were financed by deficit spending. The New Deal created Social Security, unemployment insurance, and other federal programs to care for the elderly, jobless, and needy. Roosevelt believed in using the power of government to help those in need. Government-supported social programs were the centerpiece of the New Deal.

Full economic prosperity did not return until the United States entered World War II in 1941. Even so, the New Deal restored Americans' faith in democracy. In the decade ahead, Americans put their lives on the line to preserve democracy abroad.

Reading **History**
C. Summarizing What were some of the accomplishments of the New Deal?
C. Answer Social Security; unemployment insurance; federal programs to care for elderly, jobless, and needy

AMERICA'S HISTORY MAKERS

FRANKLIN DELANO ROOSEVELT
1882–1945

A distant cousin of Theodore Roosevelt, Franklin D. Roosevelt became a New York state senator when he was 29. Later, he served as assistant secretary of the navy.

At the age of 39, FDR caught polio. For the rest of his life, he walked with braces or rode in a wheelchair (see below). Despite this, he continued in politics and was elected New York governor in 1928.

The public rarely saw photos revealing FDR's disability. Even so, many Americans sensed that he understood trouble. This quality helped him as a leader during the Depression.

How would an understanding of trouble help FDR to lead?

Section 1 Assessment

1. Terms & Names

Explain the significance of:
- Warren G. Harding
- Calvin Coolidge
- jazz
- Harlem Renaissance
- Great Depression
- Franklin D. Roosevelt
- New Deal

2. Taking Notes

Fill in the diagram with some causes of the Depression.

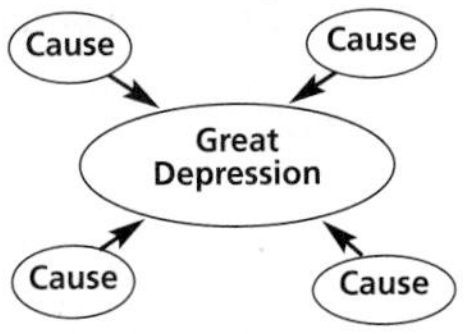

Which cause was most important? Why?

3. Main Ideas

a. How did the boom times of the 1920s lead to the stock market crash?

b. What happened to farm prices during the Great Depression?

c. What were the three goals of FDR's New Deal?

4. Critical Thinking

Making Inferences Why might the Great Depression have caused people to consider changes in the role of government?

THINK ABOUT
- aims of democracy
- fears sparked by the Depression
- attitudes toward government

ACTIVITY OPTIONS

LANGUAGE ARTS
MUSIC

Prepare a short **essay** on a writer of the Harlem Renaissance or make a **class presentation** about jazz of the 1920s in which you play recordings of the music.

AMERICA'S HISTORY MAKERS

Franklin Delano Roosevelt

FDR refused to be an invalid. He began a vigorous exercise program for his upper body. He once said proudly of the results, "Maybe my legs aren't so good, but look at those shoulders." Many people were so captivated by his vigor and confidence that they remained largely unaware of the extent of his dependence on braces and crutches.

Possible Response: Because he had suffered and overcome great difficulties himself, FDR was sensitive to the suffering of others and believed he could help them.

America's History Makers
- Franklin D. Roosevelt, pp. 103–104

ASSESS & RETEACH

Setting the Stage Have students add information about the 1920s to the graphic organizer.

Formal Assessment
- Section Quiz, p. 350

RETEACHING ACTIVITY

Form groups of three. Each student in a group should assume a role: President Coolidge, President Hoover, President Roosevelt. Have each student explain to the group what the person accomplished to help the nation's economy during his term as president.

In-Depth Resources: Unit 5
- Reteaching Activity, p. 113

Section 1 Assessment

1. Terms & Names

Warren G. Harding, p. 569
Calvin Coolidge, p. 569
jazz, p. 570
Harlem Renaissance, p. 571
Great Depression, p. 571
Franklin D. Roosevelt, p. 572
New Deal, p. 572

2. Taking Notes

the stock market crash, bank failures, factory closings, rising unemployment, decline in spending, a fall in farm prices

Answers will vary.

3. Main Ideas

a. Many people, even those who could not afford it, invested all their money in stocks. Some even borrowed money to buy stocks.
b. Prices of farm products fell sharply; economic losses were aggravated by a drought. **c.** relief programs, recovery programs, and economic reform

4. Critical Thinking

The severe economic dislocation caused people to rethink the role of the federal government in creating and monitoring the economy.

ACTIVITY OPTIONS

Integrated Assessment
- Rubrics for an essay, 4.2
- Rubrics for a presentation, 5.4

SECTION OBJECTIVES

1. To identify dictators who took power in the 1930s and to describe the beginning of World War II
2. To explain why the United States entered the war
3. To describe how the war affected American life
4. To trace the war in Europe and the Pacific

SKILLBUILDER
Interpreting Maps: Region, Movement, p. 577

CRITICAL THINKING
Summarizing, p. 577
Analyzing Causes, p. 578

FOCUS & MOTIVATE

5-MINUTE WARM-UP

Drawing Conclusions These questions focus on the beginning of World War II.

1. Look at the time line on page 575. Which three nations began to expand their territories during the 1930s?
2. Look at the map on page 577. What nations formed the Axis Powers? What benefit might they have had in joining forces?

Warm-Up Transparency WT20EPIL

INSTRUCT

INSTRUCT: OBJECTIVE 1

Dictators Take Power/ War Breaks Out in Europe

- How did Mussolini and Hitler appeal to nationalism and racism?
- What actions began World War II?
- What nations made up the Axis Powers? the Allied Powers?

In-Depth Resources: Unit 5
- Guided Reading, p. 101
- Building Vocabulary, p. 104

Outline Map Activities, pp. 49–50

2 The Rise of Dictators and World War II

MAIN IDEA	WHY IT MATTERS NOW
In the 1930s, the rise of dictators and their military aggression led to World War II.	Lessons learned in fighting aggression in World War II continue to influence American foreign policy.

TERMS & NAMES
Benito Mussolini
fascism
Adolf Hitler
Nazi
World War II
Dwight D. Eisenhower
Holocaust

ONE AMERICAN'S STORY

Margaret Bourke-White was a photographer before the era of instant news. Beginning in the 1930s, her powerful pictures in magazines and books helped Americans understand the events of their time. As one of *Life* magazine's first photographers, she traveled to the Dust Bowl in the 1930s to photograph drought victims. During the same decade, she recorded the terrible living conditions of sharecroppers in the South.

As you will read in this section, during the 1940s the United States joined Britain in fighting a war against Nazi Germany. As the first female photographer attached to U.S. forces, Bourke-White risked her life to send home vivid images of combat. At war's end, she crossed into Germany with some of the first U.S. troops. She joined stunned soldiers entering Nazi concentration camps. She became one of the first photographers to record the horrors they saw there.

Margaret Bourke-White (shown above in both pictures) photographed the Manhattan skyline and events of World War II.

1 Dictators Take Power

The Great Depression spread around the world. In Germany and Italy, dictators appealed to desperate citizens by promising to restore prosperity. In Italy, **Benito Mussolini** built a political movement called **fascism**—a system under which the government rules through terror and by appealing to racism and nationalism. Using black-shirted followers to enforce his rule, Mussolini became prime minister in 1922. He won over nationalists by promising to turn Italy into a new Roman Empire. In 1935 his fascist troops invaded Ethiopia in Africa. The League of Nations had been formed to halt such aggression. However, it had little success.

In Germany, **Adolf Hitler** joined the National Socialist German Workers', or **Nazi**, Party. He tapped the bitter anger many Germans felt about the unfairness of the peace agreement ending World War I. The treaty required Germany to pay millions for war damages. Hitler skillfully blamed the nation's economic woes on Jews and other groups. After coming to power in 1933, he jailed critics. His expansion of German territory began with a violation of the World War I peace agreement. He sent troops into the Rhineland, a part of Germany near the French border. In

RECOMMENDED RESOURCES

In-Depth Resources: Unit 5
- Guided Reading, p. 101
- Building Vocabulary, p. 104
- Reteaching Activity, p. 114

Reading Study Guide (Spanish and English), pp. 191–192

Outline Map Activities, pp. 49–50

America's History Makers
- Dwight D. Eisenhower, pp. 107–108

Formal Assessment
- Section Quiz, p. 351

Integrated Assessment
- Rubrics, 4.3, 5.1

Access for Students Acquiring English/ESL
- Guided Reading, p. 131

INTEGRATED TECHNOLOGY

Humanities Transparency HT53

Electronic Teacher Tools

classzone.com

TEST-TAKING RESOURCES

Strategies for Test Preparation

Test Practice Transparencies, TT96–TT100

Online Test Practice

1938, he invaded Austria and attached it to Germany. Prime Minister Neville Chamberlain of Britain met with Hitler in Munich, Germany, in September, 1938. Chamberlain agreed to allow Germany to take parts of Czechoslovakia. In return, Hitler promised not to demand any more land.

During this same period, dictator Joseph Stalin controlled the Soviet Union. Communist parties loyal to the Soviet Union had followers throughout Europe. Both Nazis and Fascists won many supporters by opposing the Communists. People feared Communist governments would seize their businesses and outlaw private property.

In Japan, military leaders held a powerful position in the government. In 1931, Japan invaded Manchuria, a province of China. This signaled the beginning of a planned Asian expansion. The League of Nations did little. In 1940, Japan, Italy, and Germany formed the Axis Powers.

War Breaks Out in Europe

On September 1, 1939, the Nazis invaded Poland. Germany's massive air and ground attack finally made Britain and France understand that Hitler could only be stopped by force. Two days later, Britain and France declared war on Germany. **World War II** had begun.

The early war years were dark ones for the Allies, which included Britain, France, and the Soviet Union, among others. The German military seemed unstoppable. In the spring of 1940, German troops conquered Norway, Denmark, the Netherlands, and Belgium. Paris and much of France fell to the Germans in June.

In 1941, German forces smashed through Eastern Europe and invaded the Soviet Union. Great Britain now stood alone against Hitler. Despite nightly bombings of London and other cities by the Germans, Britain's prime minister, Winston Churchill, inspired Britons to hold on. In the United States, isolationists still urged Americans to stay out of European affairs and avoid war.

***Reading*History**

A. Interpreting Time Lines Which of the steps leading to World War II took place in Asia?

A. Answer Japanese invasions of Manchuria and China

2 Surprise Attack on Pearl Harbor

Roosevelt began his third term in 1941. He was the first and only president to serve more than two terms. He believed that failure to stop the

Steps to World War II, *1920–1939*

1920 — 1930 — 1940 — WWII

- **October 1922** Mussolini takes power in Italy.
- **September 1931** Japan invades Manchuria.
- **January 1933** Hitler becomes chancellor of Germany.
- **October 1935** Italy invades Ethiopia.
- **March 1936** Germany reoccupies the Rhineland.
- **July 1937** Japanese forces move into China.
- **March 1938** Germany annexes Austria.
- **September 1938** Munich Conference
- **August 1939** Nazi-Soviet Pact signed.
- **September 1939** German troops invade Poland.

575

MORE ABOUT . . .

The Axis Powers

An *axis* is a straight line about which a body or geometric object rotates. Earth, for example, revolves on its axis every day, resulting in alternating day and night. Benito Mussolini coined the term *Axis* to refer to the alliance between Italy and Germany formed in October 1936. Hitler and Mussolini expected the rest of Europe to revolve around the "Rome-Berlin Axis." In November 1936, Japan became the third member of the Axis.

MORE ABOUT . . .

Winston Churchill

Winston Churchill (1874–1965) was prime minister of Great Britain from 1940 to 1945 and again from 1951 to 1955. When he first addressed the House of Commons in 1940, he said, "I have nothing to offer but blood, toil, tears, and sweat."

Churchill visited scenes of devastation after air bombings and broadcast radio reports to the nation. His words were inspirational. In 1940, he said of the Royal Air Force: "Never in the field of human conflict was so much owed by so many to so few."

INSTRUCT: OBJECTIVE 2

Surprise Attack on Pearl Harbor

- Why did the United States begin helping the Allies in 1941?
- Why did the United States enter the war?

ACTIVITY OPTIONS

INTERDISCIPLINARY LINK: WORLD HISTORY — BLOCK SCHEDULING

DEBATING THE POLICY OF APPEASEMENT

Class Time One class period

Task Holding a debate on the appeasement of Germany

Purpose To analyze the pros and cons of the policy of appeasement

Supplies Needed

- Reference materials on the policy of appeasement and the positions of Chamberlain and Churchill
- Internet access

Activity Hold a class debate on the following resolution: *Meeting Germany's demands for Czechoslovakia will avert war and end German aggression.* Divide students into two teams, one to support the resolution and the other to oppose it. Agree on rules for the debate. Before the debate begins, students should develop arguments for their side and counterarguments to their opponents' positions.

Now and then

USS *Arizona* Memorial

The *Arizona* was launched in June 1915. The ship served with the Atlantic Fleet during World War I. The *Arizona* was in dry dock at Pearl Harbor for repairs when the Japanese attacked. The *Arizona* became a symbol for Americans at war, especially for those in the navy.

INSTRUCT: OBJECTIVE 3

The Home Front in America

- How did the United States mobilize for war?
- In what ways did wartime conditions affect women and minorities?
- Why were some Japanese Americans sent to internment camps?

MORE ABOUT . . .

Rationing

The complex rationing system for scarce goods during World War II had two purposes. The first purpose was to provide crucial supplies to the war effort. The second purpose was to distribute fairly what goods were available to Americans at home. The first goods to be rationed were automobile tires. A few months later, gasoline was also rationed.

***Now and* then**

U.S.S. *ARIZONA* MEMORIAL

The U.S.S. *Arizona* suffered extensive damage during the attack on Pearl Harbor. The ship sank, and 1,177 of its crew died. The nation chose not to raise the battleship. Instead, officials created a memorial that sits above the sunken hull (see below). The names of all the crewmen who perished are carved on the memorial.

To commemorate the 50th anniversary of the attack against the U.S. naval base at Pearl Harbor, President George Bush visited the site in 1991.

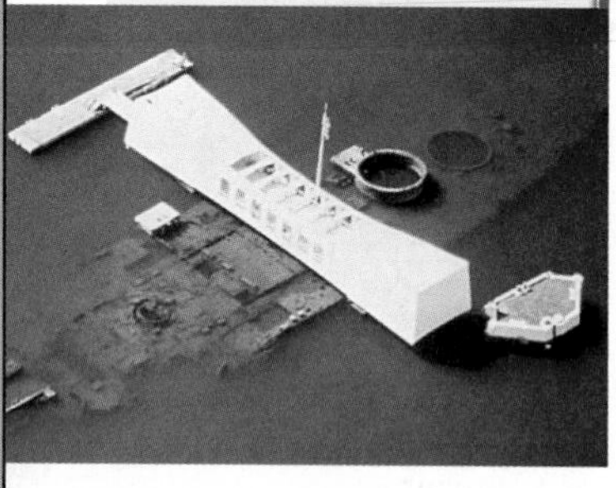

Nazis and Fascists would endanger the United States. In early 1941, he gave a speech to Congress to prepare the public to aid the Allies.

A VOICE FROM THE PAST

> We look forward to a world founded upon four . . . human freedoms. The first is freedom of speech and expression—everywhere in the world. The second is freedom of every person to worship God in his own way. . . . The third is freedom from want. . . . The fourth is freedom from fear . . . anywhere in the world.
>
> **Franklin D. Roosevelt,** State of the Union speech, January 6, 1941

Freedom required arms for its defense. Congress enacted the Lend-Lease Act in 1941. This law allowed the United States to ship arms and supplies, without immediate payment, to Britain and its Allies.

On December 7, 1941, Japan launched an attack against the U.S. naval base in Pearl Harbor, Hawaii. Calling December 7 "a date which will live in infamy," FDR requested and Congress passed a declaration of war against Japan. Japan's allies—Italy and Germany—then declared war on the United States.

In 1942, the Axis Powers (Germany, Italy, Japan) seemed close to victory. By this time, the Soviet Union had joined the Allied Powers, following Germany's invasion of its territory in June 1941.

3 The Home Front in America

Once the United States entered the war, its automobile plants and other factories were turned into defense plants. Airplanes, ships, weapons, and other supplies rolled off production lines at a rapid pace. By 1944, American assembly lines were producing 50 percent more armaments than those in the Axis nations combined.

Poster of factory worker during World War II

Americans put up with wartime shortages so that resources such as steel, tin, and rubber could be redirected to military uses. Gasoline was in short supply. So were meat, butter, coffee, cheese, and sugar. Every family received ration books of stamps to buy goods.

With millions of men at war, women went to work in factories, shipyards, and offices. At first, heavy industries resisted hiring female workers, but by 1944 some 3.5 million stood on assembly lines turning out cargo ships and bombers.

As they had during World War I, hundreds of thousands of African Americans left the South for such cities as Cleveland, Chicago, and Detroit. More than 2 million took jobs in the defense industry. Roosevelt outlawed discrimination in industries with federal contracts.

ACTIVITY OPTIONS

INDIVIDUAL NEEDS

LESS PROFICIENT READERS

Purpose-Setting Questions To help students understand the significance of the events discussed in the heading "War Continues in Europe and Asia," provide them with purpose-setting questions to answer as they read, such as:

- Where and when did the D-Day invasion take place? What was the result of this invasion?
- Who decided to drop the atomic bomb on Hiroshima? Why?
- Who were the victims of the Holocaust?

576 CHAPTER 20 EPILOGUE

*Reading*History

B. Summarizing What were some of the activities and challenges faced by women and minorities on the home front?

B. Answer Women worked in factories; African Americans moved north for jobs in defense industry; Japanese Americans on West Coast were sent to internment camps.

On the home front, Japanese Americans on the West Coast faced harsh treatment. By executive order, over 100,000 loyal Japanese Americans were forced to leave their jobs, businesses, and homes. They were sent to internment (prison) camps throughout the West.

War Continues in Europe and Asia 4

The invasion of Italy got underway with an attack on the island of Sicily in July 1943. The Allies forced the Germans out of Sicily and then swept into Italy. By this time, the Italians had imprisoned Mussolini. The new Italian government surrendered to the Allies in September 1943.

Meanwhile, in August 1942, German forces attacked the Russian city of Stalingrad, an important industrial center. A brutal battle took place. Soviet forces encircled and trapped the German army. As winter approached, the German commander begged Hitler to let him retreat. The *Führer* (or "leader") refused. The trapped Germans had no food or supplies. Each day, thousands of Nazi soldiers froze or starved to death. In late January of 1943, the German troops surrendered. Each side had suffered staggering losses. With its defeat at Stalingrad, Germany's hopes of conquering the Soviet Union ended.

Another turning point in World War II came on June 6, 1944, known as D-Day. About 70,000 American troops crossed the English Channel and landed on the beaches of Normandy in northern France. They were

Skillbuilder Answers
1. Spain, Portugal, Ireland
2. Okinawa

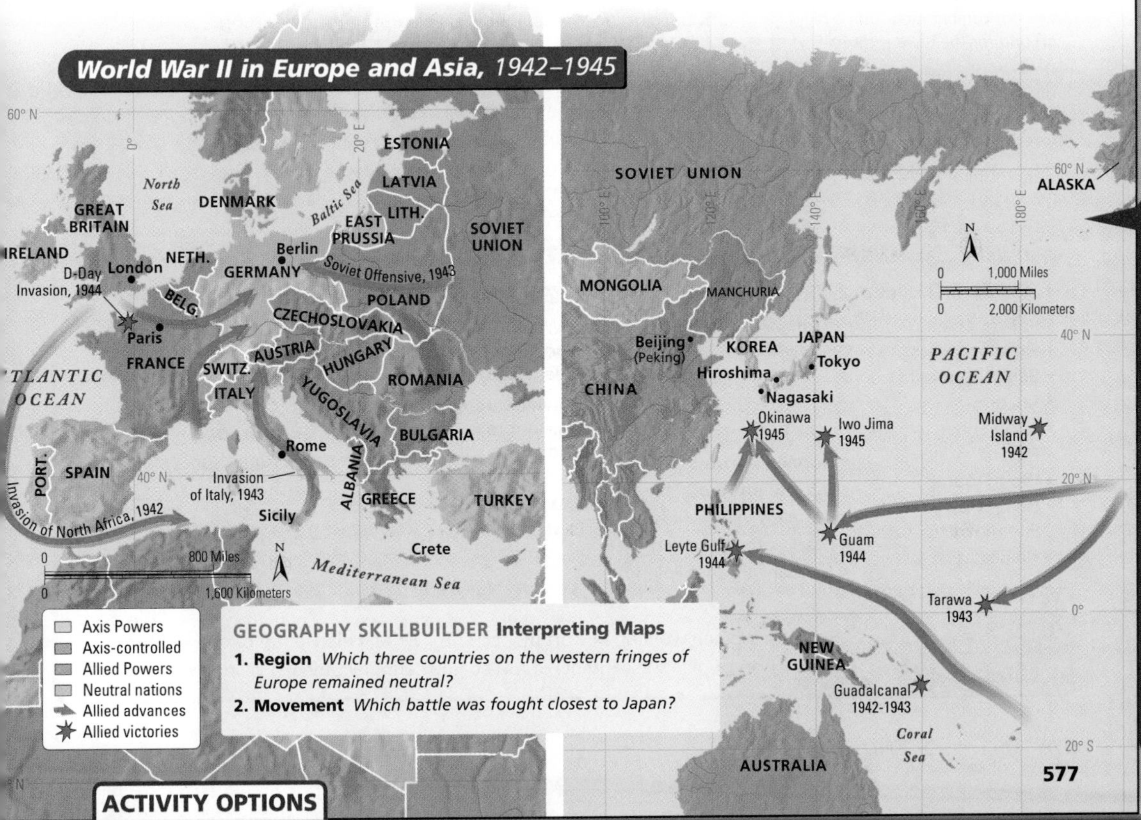

GEOGRAPHY SKILLBUILDER Interpreting Maps

1. **Region** *Which three countries on the western fringes of Europe remained neutral?*
2. **Movement** *Which battle was fought closest to Japan?*

MORE ABOUT . . .

Internment

Even before the United States declared war on Japan, President Roosevelt asked Chicago businessman Curtis Munson to find out if Japanese Americans were a security threat to the country. Munson's report stated that Japanese Americans presented no security threat. Other government officials agreed with his conclusions. However, Lt. General John DeWitt, head of the Western Defense Command, disagreed. DeWitt wanted to clear Japanese Americans from California, Oregon, Washington, and southern Arizona.

INSTRUCT: OBJECTIVE 4

War Continues in Europe and Asia/ The War Is Over

- Why was D-Day the turning point of the war?
- Why did President Truman decide to bomb Hiroshima?
- What was the Holocaust?

Humanities Transparency HT53
- Navajo Code Talkers

HISTORY FROM VISUALS

Reading the Map Ask students to speculate why the Allied Powers were victorious in Europe in 1945. **Possible Response** The Allies attacked the Axis on every front—southern: North Africa (1942) and Italy/Mediterranean Sea (1943); eastern: Soviet offensive (1943); and western: France/D-Day invasion (1944). Then ask how the war in Asia was different from the war in Europe. **Possible Response** Much of the war was fought at sea or on islands.

Extension Have students choose a theater of war—Europe, North Africa, or the Pacific—and research the strategy of the Allies. Then have them write a summary paragraph describing the strategy.

ACTIVITY OPTIONS

INTERDISCIPLINARY LINK: ART

BLOCK SCHEDULING

WARTIME RALLY POSTERS

Class Time One class period

Task Creating a poster urging support on the home front

Purpose To understand how the government used posters to build support for various war efforts

Supplies Needed
- Books with examples of posters from World War II
- Internet access
- Posterboard
- Art supplies

Activity Have students do research to find examples of World War II posters. Discuss some of the posters with the class, pointing out their emotional and visual appeal and their use of slogans. Then tell students to choose a topic relating to support of the war, such as rationing, women joining the work force, conserving resources, or victory gardens. Have students plan and create a poster about their selected topic. Display completed posters and discuss them as a class.

AMERICA'S HISTORY MAKERS

Dwight D. Eisenhower

In World War II, Eisenhower commanded U.S. forces in Great Britain and led the invasion of North Africa and Italy. Later, he was appointed supreme commander of Allied forces in Western Europe and planned the D-Day invasion.

Eisenhower was the Republican Party's presidential candidate in 1952 and was elected president for two terms (1953–1961). He was a popular president who served during a period of domestic and international tension, which included the U.S. civil rights struggle and Cold War conflicts. During his presidency, the United States experienced a period of postwar prosperity and growth.

Answer: They would have appreciated his concern for them and felt that he understood their problems. They probably would have felt greater respect and loyalty for him.

America's History Makers
- Dwight D. Eisenhower, pp. 107–108

AMERICA'S HISTORY MAKERS

DWIGHT D. EISENHOWER
1890–1969

If ever there was a general who cared about his troops, it was General Dwight D. Eisenhower (at left, above). As Allied forces battled in Italy, Ike learned that he and another general were scheduled to stay in two large villas. "That's *not* my villa!" he exploded. "And that's not General Spaatz's villa! None of those will belong to any general as long as I'm Boss around here. This is supposed to be a rest center—for combat men—not a playground for the Brass [officers]!"

How might Eisenhower's concern for the common man have affected his standing with the troops?

part of a vast Allied invasion under the command of American General **Dwight D. Eisenhower.** British and American forces advanced on Germany from the west. The Soviets closed in from the east. In early May of 1945, Germany surrendered.

In the Pacific, the Japanese fought on. After 12 years as president, FDR died suddenly in April 1945, making Harry S. Truman the president. Truman decided to end the war before an invasion of Japan caused huge losses. In August 1945, American bombers dropped atomic bombs on Hiroshima and Nagasaki. In Hiroshima about 70,000 people died instantly. On September 2, 1945, Japan surrendered.

Reading **History**
C. Reading a Map Use the map on page 577 to point out the locations of Hiroshima and Nagasaki on the Japanese mainland.

The War Is Over

World War II had been the costliest and most destructive war in history. Approximately 55 million people died. Among them were some 6 million Jews, or almost two-thirds of Europe's Jews. Victims were shot, gassed, and worked to death in Nazi concentration camps, death camps, and slave labor camps. This systematic mass murder of 6 million Jews and other ethnic minorities by the Nazis became known as the **Holocaust.**

At war's end, the United States joined the United Nations, the international peacekeeping organization that replaced the League of Nations. New York City became its headquarters. The Soviet Union joined as well. Nevertheless, conflict between the former allies would lead to a new era of tension, as you will read in the next section.

Section 2 Assessment

1. Terms & Names

Explain the significance of:
- Benito Mussolini
- fascism
- Adolf Hitler
- Nazi
- World War II
- Dwight D. Eisenhower
- Holocaust

2. Taking Notes

Arrange these events with their dates on a time line:

event 2 event 4

event 1 event 3 event 5

- Normandy Invasion
- U.S. bombs Hiroshima
- Germany invades Russia
- Pearl Harbor bombed
- Germany invades Poland

3. Main Ideas

a. What events following World War I led to the rise of Hitler and Mussolini?

b. Why were Americans reluctant to go to war? What made them change their minds?

c. What ended the war in the Pacific?

4. Critical Thinking

Analyzing Causes What elements in Nazi thinking might have contributed to the Holocaust?

THINK ABOUT
- wartime fears
- attitudes towards minorities
- prejudice

ACTIVITY OPTIONS

LANGUAGE ARTS
TECHNOLOGY

Research women working in wartime factories. Write a **diary entry** of one woman's experiences or plan the contents of a **Web page** about women in World War II.

ASSESS & RETEACH

Setting the Stage Have students add information about the 1940s to the graphic organizer.

Formal Assessment
- Section Quiz, p. 351

RETEACHING ACTIVITY

Divide students into groups of five. Assign one heading from the section to each student in a group. Have each student review his or her section and write three questions about it. Within groups, students should take turns quizzing one another, using their prepared questions.

In-Depth Resources: Unit 5
- Reteaching Activity, p. 114

Section 2 Assessment

1. Terms & Names

Benito Mussolini, p. 574
fascism, p. 574
Adolf Hitler, p. 574
Nazi, p. 574
World War II, p. 575
Dwight D. Eisenhower, p. 578
Holocaust, p. 578

2. Taking Notes

Event 1: 1939 Germany invades Poland; Event 2: June 1941 Germany invades Russia; Event 3: December 1941 Pearl Harbor bombed; Event 4: 1944 Normandy Invasion; Event 5: 1945 U.S. bombs Hiroshima

3. Main Ideas

a. the peace agreement ending World War I and worldwide economic depression **b.** They did not want to get involved in another world war; the Japanese attack on Pearl Harbor **c.** the dropping of the atomic bombs on Hiroshima and Nagasaki

4. Critical Thinking

Hitler blamed the economic woes of Germany on the Jews.

ACTIVITY OPTIONS

Integrated Assessment
- Rubrics for a diary entry, 4.3
- Rubrics for a Web page, 5.1

3 The Cold War

TERMS & NAMES
Harry S. Truman
Cold War
containment
John F. Kennedy
Lyndon B. Johnson
Vietnam War
Richard M. Nixon
Watergate scandal

MAIN IDEA

After World War II, the United States and the Soviet Union entered into a deadly struggle for world power.

WHY IT MATTERS NOW

This struggle affected American foreign policy for almost half a century.

ONE AMERICAN'S STORY

When World War II ended in 1945, Europe lay in ruins. War had destroyed roads, bridges, mines, and railroads. Factories lacked fuel and raw materials. Tensions between the Soviet Union and the United States were rising. U.S. leaders wanted to help the European economies. At the same time, they opposed Communist expansion. George C. Marshall was secretary of state under President Harry S. Truman. Marshall came up with a plan to put Europe back on its feet. The plan offered billions of dollars in aid to Europe.

President Truman and George C. Marshall meet at the White House.

A VOICE FROM THE PAST

[The] United States should do whatever it [can] to assist in the return of . . . economic health in the world, without which there can be no political stability and no. . . peace. Our policy is directed . . . against hunger, poverty, desperation, . . . chaos.

George C. Marshall, speech at Harvard University, June 5, 1947

As you will read in this section, the Marshall Plan helped make Western and Southern Europe stable again.

1 The Cold War Begins

After World War II, fear and mistrust between the superpowers grew. The United States had hoped Eastern European nations would become democracies. Stalin feared that Eastern Europe could again become an invasion route into his country. For this reason, Stalin and the Soviets helped Communist governments come to power throughout Eastern Europe in the late 1940s.

President Truman and his advisers feared the spread of communism and looked for ways to stop it. This struggle marked the start of the **Cold War** between the superpowers. It was called a Cold War because there was no actual, direct fighting between the superpowers. This conflict was waged mainly with threats, spying, propaganda, and war in other countries.

SECTION OBJECTIVES

1. To analyze how the Cold War affected U.S. policies
2. To describe the Cold War conflicts between the superpowers
3. To evaluate the foreign policies of Johnson and Nixon
4. To explain how the Cold War ended

SKILLBUILDER
Interpreting Charts, p. 582

CRITICAL THINKING
Recognizing Effects, p. 580
Summarizing, pp. 581, 582
Comparing, p. 583

FOCUS & MOTIVATE

5-MINUTE WARM-UP

Evaluating These questions focus on the climate of the Cold War.

1. Read the chart on page 582. List words from the chart that indicate competition and tension.
2. What do you think stopped nations from starting a "hot" war?

Warm-Up Transparency WT20EPIL

INSTRUCT

INSTRUCT: OBJECTIVE 1

The Cold War Begins/ The Korean War and McCarthyism

- What were the goals of the containment policy?
- Why did the United States enter the Korean War?
- What was McCarthyism?

In-Depth Resources: Unit 5
- Guided Reading, p. 102

Reading Study Guide (Spanish and English), pp. 193–194

RECOMMENDED RESOURCES

In-Depth Resources: Unit 5
- Guided Reading, p. 102
- Building Vocabulary, p. 104
- Skillbuilder Practice, p. 105

Reading Study Guide (Spanish and English), pp. 193–194

America's History Makers
- John F. Kennedy, pp. 119–120

Formal Assessment
- Section Quiz, p. 352

Integrated Assessment
- Rubrics, 3.6, 1.3

Access for Students Acquiring English/ESL
- Guided Reading, p. 132
- Skillbuilder Practice, p. 134

INTEGRATED TECHNOLOGY

Geography Transparency GT30

Critical Thinking Transparency CT83

Electronic Teacher Tools

TEST-TAKING RESOURCES

Strategies for Taking Tests

Test Practice Transparencies, TT101–TT103

Online Test Practice

CRITICAL THINKING ACTIVITY

Analyzing Causes and Recognizing Effects
Suggest students identify causes and effects of the Korean War using a chart like the one below.

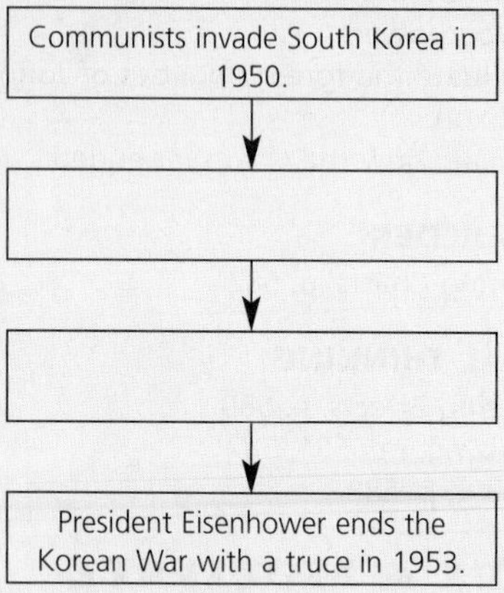
Communists invade South Korea in 1950.
President Eisenhower ends the Korean War with a truce in 1953.

Class Time 15 minutes

MORE ABOUT . . .

Cold War Fears and Spies
Julius and Ethel Rosenberg were the first U.S. civilians to be put to death for espionage. They were convicted of passing data on nuclear weapons to the Soviets. Ethel's brother, David Greenglass, who worked as a machinist at the atomic bomb project at Los Alamos, New Mexico, gave the secret information to the Rosenbergs. He received 15 years in prison after he agreed to become the government's chief witness against his sister and her husband.

INSTRUCT: OBJECTIVE 2

Nuclear Threat and Superpower Conflicts

- What actions began the arms race?
- How did Soviet involvement in Cuba nearly cause war with the United States?
- What were the space-race achievements of the superpowers?

Truman's anti-Soviet policy was called **containment.** It sought to contain, or stop, the Soviet Union from gaining influence outside its borders. Containment became the foundation of American foreign policy.

The Marshall Plan and the North Atlantic Treaty Organization (NATO) were key elements of containment. The Marshall Plan helped pay for Western and Southern Europe's recovery. Under the NATO agreement, Western allies formed a defense pact. The members pledged to protect one another in case of attack. The Soviet Union and its allies formed the Warsaw Pact.

The Korean War and McCarthyism

In 1949, the Communists led by Mao Zedong took power in China. In 1950, troops from Communist North Korea, supplied by the Soviet Union, invaded American-backed South Korea. U.S. troops made up most of a UN force commanded by General Douglas MacArthur. The UN force drove the North Koreans out of the South and back into North Korea.

Fighting continued after General Dwight D. Eisenhower became the new U.S. president in 1953. He soon arranged a truce that ended the three-year war. The national boundaries of the two Koreas had changed very little. However, the United States had shown that the free world would fight Communist aggression.

In the postwar United States, public fears of communism allowed Senator Joseph McCarthy of Wisconsin to gain great power. He claimed that hundreds of government workers were Communists or Communist supporters. His hunt for Communists ruined many lives. A new word—McCarthyism—described the use of unproven charges against opponents and innocent citizens. By 1954, however, the public had turned away in disgust from McCarthy. His power quickly faded.

A. Answer Fear of communism spurred by events in Asia allowed McCarthy to gain power.

Reading **History**
A. Recognizing Effects What effect did the Communist takeover in China and Communist aggression in Korea have on American political life?

2 Nuclear Threat and Superpower Conflicts

In 1945, the United States had dropped two atomic bombs on Japan to end World War II. Four years later, the Soviets built their own atomic bomb. A deadly arms race had begun. Both superpowers stockpiled nuclear weapons. By the end of the decade, both sides were developing missiles to carry bombs to each other's doorsteps.

Vocabulary
stockpiled: maintained a supply for future use

This photograph shows a Soviet ship thought to be carrying nuclear missiles to Cuba.

KASIMOV

Neither superpower wanted to risk an all-out war. Instead, they pursued their rivalry indirectly by supporting opposite sides in conflicts in the Third World. These were the poorer nations of Latin America, Asia, and Africa. One such conflict brought the superpowers to the brink of war. In Cuba, Fidel Castro led a revolution that brought a Communist government to power in 1959. Attempts by the United States to topple Castro failed.

ACTIVITY OPTIONS

SKILLBUILDER LESSON: CATEGORIZING

BLOCK SCHEDULING

Explaining the Skill Facts can be understood and retained more easily if they are organized into categories. By grouping similar events into the same category, one can see the relationships among them. It also becomes easier to compare and contrast events within categories.

Applying the Skill Ask students to think of the various aspects of the Cold War described in this section. Then have them answer the following questions.

1. Into what categories might you divide the events of this section? *(the beginnings, Korean War, Vietnam War threats, super powers, foreign policy)*
2. Choose one of the categories from your answer to the first question above. How does grouping the items in that category help you understand more about each one? *(Categorizing helps clarify the relationships among the various aspects of the Cold War)*

In-Depth Resources: Unit 5
- Skillbuilder Practice, p. 105

Then, in 1962, President **John F. Kennedy** learned that the Soviets were supplying Cuba with missiles. U.S. navy ships blockaded the island. The threat of nuclear war seemed very real. The world waited to see if the Soviets would remove all missiles and missile bases from Cuba. Finally, the Soviet Union agreed to remove them.

By the 1960s the superpowers were in a space race as well as an arms race. Americans were stunned in 1957 when the Soviets sent *Sputnik*, a man-made satellite, into orbit around the earth. Alarm deepened as a Soviet cosmonaut took the first manned space flight. Throughout the 1960s, the two nations raced to see who would be first to put a person on the moon. Americans cheered as Neil Armstrong and Buzz Aldrin made the first lunar landing in 1969.

The U.S. flag is planted on the surface of the moon in July 1969.

*Reading*History
B. Summarizing What are some examples of superpower rivalry?
B. Answer nuclear arms race; third-world conflicts; space race

In 1963, Kennedy was assassinated in Dallas, Texas. Kennedy's vice-president, **Lyndon B. Johnson,** succeeded him as president. Under Johnson, the United States became more deeply involved in conflict in the Southeast Asian countries of North and South Vietnam.

3 War in Vietnam

In 1954, Vietnam was divided in two. The Communists controlled North Vietnam and the non-Communists controlled South Vietnam. The **Vietnam War** began in 1957 when Communist forces attacked the government in the south. American presidents Eisenhower, Kennedy, and Johnson all feared a Communist victory in South Vietnam. Experts argued that if South Vietnam fell to the Communists, other Southeast Asian nations would soon fall.

Background
The idea that if one nation fell to the Communists, others would soon follow, was called the "domino theory."

By 1968, more than 500,000 American troops were serving in Vietnam. U.S. planes dropped thousands of tons of bombs on the North. The large, well-equipped U.S. military faced a disciplined North Vietnamese force. Communist soldiers used hit-and-run guerrilla tactics. They sometimes relied on civilians for shelter and supplies. American soldiers won many battles, but they were stuck in an unwinnable war.

By 1968, the war had divided the United States. Strong criticism of Johnson's Vietnam policy contributed to his decision not to run for reelection. **Richard M. Nixon,** who was elected president in 1968, pledged to end the war. Over the next four years, he expanded the air war into neighboring Cambodia and Laos. At the same time, Nixon withdrew U.S. ground troops from South Vietnam. A 1973 ceasefire brought American troops home. Two years later, South Vietnam fell to the Communists. In 1976, the two Vietnams were united under Communist rule.

daily life

THE "TELEVISION WAR"

The Vietnam War was the first "television war," broadcast each night on the evening news. Reports rarely showed actual battles, partly because much of the fighting occurred off and on and at night, between small units.

Networks also tried to avoid gruesome scenes because they did not want to offend viewers. In addition, the networks agreed not to show any American dead or wounded so that their families would not recognize them on screen. Still, the images of war shocked viewers.

581

MORE ABOUT . . .

Kennedy's Assassination
Kennedy was shot by Lee Harvey Oswald, a political misfit and loner. Two days later, Oswald was shot and killed by Jack Ruby, a nightclub owner. A commission headed by Chief Justice Earl Warren investigated the assassination. The commission concluded that Oswald acted on his own. However, thousands of books and articles have been published since 1963 theorizing about complex plots involving many people in the Kennedy assassination.

America's History Makers
• John F. Kennedy, pp. 119–120

INSTRUCT: OBJECTIVE 3

War in Vietnam/Nixon as President

- Why did Presidents Eisenhower, Kennedy, and Johnson involve the United States in Vietnam?
- How did Nixon improve U.S. relations with China and the Soviet Union?
- Why did Nixon resign?

daily*life*

The "Television War"
After the war, General Westmoreland charged that television and other media coverage had hurt U.S. efforts in Vietnam. For example, he complained that intense and graphic media coverage had made the Tet offensive into a psychological victory for the Viet Cong.

ACTIVITY OPTIONS

INTERDISCIPLINARY LINK: SCIENCE — BLOCK SCHEDULING

SPACE EXPLORATION

Class Time One class period

Task Creating an illustrated time line showing scientific advances in space exploration

Purpose To identify milestones in the exploration of space

Supplies Needed
- Reference materials on space exploration
- Internet access for additional resources
- Oversized sheets of art paper, paints, pencils, and markers

Activity Divide students into five groups. Assign each group a ten-year period from 1957 to the present. Have groups do research and then make illustrated time lines showing key achievements in space research during their decade. Attach completed time lines in chronological order for classroom display.

HISTORY FROM VISUALS

Reading the Chart Have students read aloud each cause of the Cold War, then its immediate effects and its long-term effects. Have them speculate on why the arms race and the rivalry between the two superpowers lasted as long as it did.

Extension Have students look in newsmagazines and other references for characterizations of current U.S. relations with Russia.

MORE ABOUT . . .

Watergate

In the summer of 1973, the Senate committee investigating irregularities in the 1972 election learned that Nixon had installed tape recorders in the White House to record his conversations. Nixon had wanted the tapes to document his place in history. Instead, they destroyed his presidency. When Nixon surrendered the tapes on the order of the Supreme Court, they proved that he had lied about his role in the Watergate cover-up. The content of the tapes shocked the nation because of Nixon's disregard for the law and the Constitution. Many were also bothered by the petty scheming and vulgar language of the president and his aides.

INSTRUCT: OBJECTIVE 4

Foreign Policy of the 1970s and 1980s/ New Threats to the United States

- What were leading foreign policy achievements of Carter and Reagan?
- How did the Cold War end?
- How did terrorism become a serious threat to the United States?

Geography Transparency GT30
- U.S. Troops Around the World, 1975

Critical Thinking Transparency CT83
- Cause and Effect: The Cold War

***CAUSE AND EFFECT:** The Cold War, 1945–1991*

CAUSES		*IMMEDIATE EFFECTS*	*LONG-TERM EFFECTS*
Soviet domination of Eastern Europe	*THE COLD WAR*	Truman Doctrine and Marshall Plan	Arms race between United States and Soviet Union
Communist victory in China		East-West tension	Rivalry between United States and Soviet Union for world power
Distrust between United States and Soviet Union		Founding of NATO and Warsaw Pact	

SKILLBUILDER **Interpreting Charts**

1. *Which of the causes was not centered in Europe?*
2. *Which alliance was founded by the Soviet Union and its allies?*

Skillbuilder Answers
1. Communist victory in China
2. Warsaw Pact

Nixon as President

In the early 1970s, President Nixon took steps to improve relations with the Soviet Union and Communist China. In 1972, Nixon visited China. He reopened direct communication between the two nations after a 21-year break. After Nixon's visit to the Soviet Union, the superpowers signed an agreement limiting nuclear arms.

The **Watergate scandal** took up much of Nixon's second term as president. People who worked for Nixon carried out illegal activities. These included wiretapping telephones and breaking into the Democratic Party headquarters in the Watergate building in Washington, D.C. An investigation showed that Nixon had ordered his staff to cover up White House involvement in these crimes.

In 1974, a congressional committee wanted to impeach Nixon. Rather than face impeachment, Nixon resigned. He became the only U.S. president to do so. Gerald Ford succeeded Nixon as president and eventually pardoned him.

4 Foreign Policy of the 1970s and 1980s

Jimmy Carter won the 1976 presidential election, defeating Gerald Ford. He made human rights a cornerstone of his foreign policy. In 1977, Carter signed a treaty to turn the Panama Canal over to Panama in 2000. Carter also negotiated the Camp David Accords—a peace agreement between Egypt and Israel.

In 1979, the Soviet Union invaded Afghanistan to prop up a pro-Communist government. Ronald Reagan, who became president in 1980, took a tough stance toward the Soviet Union. Reagan increased U.S. defense spending and pledged to oppose communism in Central America. For several years, U.S.-Soviet relations became more tense.

By the late 1980s, however, U.S.-Soviet relations improved. A new Soviet leader, Mikhail Gorbachev, tried to reform the Soviet government and economy. Reagan and Gorbachev signed treaties agreeing to destroy some of their nations' nuclear weapons.

C. Answer
Reagan increased military spending to oppose the spread of communism, but he also negotiated treaties with the Soviets to destroy some nuclear weapons.

*Reading*History
C. Summarizing What were Reagan's policies toward the Soviet Union?

ACTIVITY OPTIONS

INDIVIDUAL NEEDS

STUDENTS ACQUIRING ENGLISH/ESL

Understanding Specialized Vocabulary To help students understand the section, you might want to point out some of the specialized vocabulary to students before they begin to read. Write the following words on the board:

propaganda	*containment*	*superpower*
truce	*rivalry*	*blockade*
guerrilla	*cease-fire*	*wiretapping*
impeach	*terrorism*	*coalition*

Discuss the words with students to see which ones they already understand and which need clarification. In some cases, the words may be familiar, but the concepts may still be challenging. Define words as necessary. Have them write the word and the definition in their notebooks or personal dictionaries.

After students read the section, ask them questions based on the section content. Encourage them to use the specialized vocabulary in their responses.

Meanwhile, many people in Communist nations wanted more freedom. They overthrew Communist rulers and formed democratic governments. In 1991, Communist leaders also lost power in the Soviet Union. The country split into independent states. Russia remained the largest of these states. The collapse of the Soviet Union ended the Cold War.

New Threats to the United States

As the Soviet Union fell apart, the United States stood as the world's only superpower. But major issues still challenged the nation. In 1990, Iraq invaded Kuwait. President George H. W. Bush organized a coalition of nations to drive Iraq out of Kuwait. In 1991, the coalition defeated Iraq in the Persian Gulf War and freed Kuwait of Iraqi control.

Then, in 2001, Americans faced a more direct threat. On September 11, 2001, terrorists hijacked commercial airplanes and crashed them into the World Trade Center in New York City and the Pentagon outside Washington, D.C. Within hours, both World Trade Center towers collapsed. Thousands were buried in the rubble. Meanwhile, the Pentagon was badly damaged. In both attacks, nearly 3,000 people died. Across the nation, Americans mourned for the victims and yearned to bring the terrorists to justice.

Smoke billows from the World Trade Center buildings after the terrorist attack of September 11, 2001.

President George W. Bush vowed to hunt down the attackers and end terrorism. "This battle will take time and resolve," Bush declared. "But make no mistake about it: we will win." Meanwhile, many Americans lost forever their sense of security. As *The New York Times* wrote the next day, "We look back at sunrise yesterday through pillars of smoke and dust, and we understand that everything has changed."

Section 3 Assessment

1. Terms & Names

Explain the significance of:
- Harry S. Truman
- Cold War
- containment
- John F. Kennedy
- Lyndon B. Johnson
- Vietnam War
- Richard M. Nixon
- Watergate scandal

2. Taking Notes

Use a diagram to summarize America's Cold War policy.

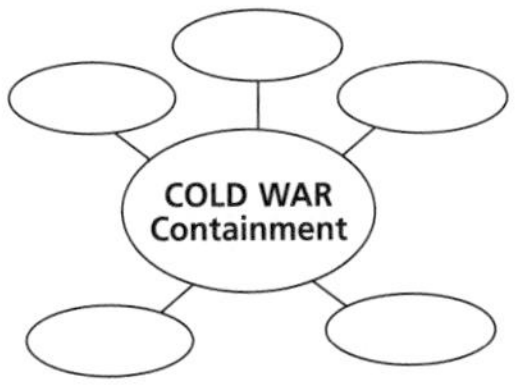

3. Main Ideas

a. How did the goals of the Soviet Union and the United States for Eastern Europe differ after World War II?

b. What were the space race and the arms race?

c. How did the breakup of the Soviet Union change U.S.-Soviet relations?

4. Critical Thinking

Comparing How were the Korean War and the Vietnam War similar and different?

THINK ABOUT
- American goals
- those who fought on each side
- the outcome of each struggle

ACTIVITY OPTIONS

SPEECH
SCIENCE

Give an **oral presentation** on one scientific challenge of landing on the moon or create a **diagram** of the lunar module.

MORE ABOUT . . .

Gorbachev's Reforms

Under Communist rule, the economy of the Soviet Union was centrally controlled. Gorbachev thought that this method contributed to the failure of the Soviet Union to keep pace with capitalist countries in technology and productivity. Gorbachev freed the economy by allowing individuals and families to own businesses. He allowed foreign companies to set up joint ventures in the Soviet Union. In 1989, he permitted farmers to lease land and equipment from the government. Gorbachev also encouraged Soviet citizens to discuss ways to improve their country in a policy of openness called *glasnost.*

ASSESS & RETEACH

Setting the Stage Have students add information about the 1970s to the graphic organizer.

Formal Assessment
- Section Quiz, p. 352

RETEACHING ACTIVITY

Have students form groups of five to discuss the development of the Cold War through each decade: 1940s, 1950s, 1960s, 1970s, 1980s. Ask one student in each group to lead the discussion for one of the five decades. Each student is allowed five minutes to review his or her decade's key Cold War developments.

In-Depth Resources: Unit 5
- Reteaching Activity, p. 115

Section 3 Assessment

1. Terms & Names

Harry S. Truman, p. 579
Cold War, p. 579
containment, p. 580
John F. Kennedy, p. 581
Lyndon B. Johnson, p. 581
Vietnam War, p. 581
Richard M. Nixon, p. 581
Watergate scandal, p. 582

2. Taking Notes

Marshall Plan; NATO; Korean War; Vietnam War; third-world conflicts

3. Main Ideas

a. over the type of governments; the United States wanted democratic; the Soviet Union, Communist **b.** Both were competitions between the U.S. and the Soviet Union—the space race to explore space and reach the moon, the arms race to produce nuclear weapons and the missiles to carry them. **c.** It ended the Cold War.

4. Critical Thinking

Similar: took place in Asia and reached indecisive conclusions; Different: In Korea, South Korea remained free; but in Vietnam, South Vietnam fell under Communist rule.

ACTIVITY OPTIONS

Integrated Assessment
- Rubrics, 3.6, 1.3

SECTION OBJECTIVES

1. To describe the postwar economy and the civil rights movement
2. To explain the achievements of the Great Society and movements for equal rights
3. To evaluate the 1980s conservative movement and the Clinton presidency
4. To describe the diverse U.S. population

SKILLBUILDER

Interpreting Charts, p. 589

CRITICAL THINKING

Recognizing Effects, p. 585
Comparing and Contrasting, p. 586
Summarizing, p. 587
Contrasting, p. 588
Supporting Opinions, p. 589

Why It Matters Now
- Changes in Modern America, pp. 49–50

FOCUS & MOTIVATE

5-MINUTE WARM-UP

Making Generalizations These questions focus on immigrants in the late 20th century.

1. Look at the chart on page 589. How are the immigrants similar to or different from those you read about in earlier chapters?
2. How do you think these immigrants will affect American life?

Warm-Up Transparency WT20EPIL

INSTRUCT

INSTRUCT: OBJECTIVE 1

Economic Boom and Baby Boom/ The Civil Rights Movement

- What characterized the economy of the 1950s?
- What gains did the civil rights movement win?
- What did the Civil Rights Act of 1964 guarantee to Americans?

In-Depth Resources: Unit 5
- Guided Reading, p. 103
- Primary Source, p. 109

4 Life in America Since 1945

TERMS & NAMES
baby boom
Dr. Martin Luther King, Jr.
Great Society
counterculture

MAIN IDEA	WHY IT MATTERS NOW
Since World War II, civil rights, economic growth, and social change have dominated American life.	Prosperity, equality, and rapid change will remain important issues in the 21st century.

ONE AMERICAN'S STORY

When World War II ended, Americans were eager to return to normal life. Couples had put off marrying and having children. Now newlyweds and young families were looking for a way out of crowded city apartments. They wanted cheap single-family houses, and they wanted them fast.

Builder William J. Levitt had the answer. He built cheap houses using assembly-line methods. All of a sudden, many Americans could afford to buy homes. On 1,000 acres of farmland on New York's Long Island, Levitt built more than 17,000 homes in Levittown. It was America's first suburban housing development. As Cold War tensions grew, Levitt liked to brag that his home building was helping to win the war against Communism. "No man who owns his own house and lot," he said, "can be a Communist. He has too much to do." As you will read, in the 1950s a home in the suburbs became a part of the American dream.

William J. Levitt, builder of Levittown, shown above in an aerial view

1 Economic Boom and Baby Boom

After World War II, the U.S. economy boomed. The GI Bill offered returning soldiers schooling and job training. The Veterans Administration provided low-interest mortgages to home buyers. Rising demand for homes made possible the rapid growth of the suburbs. Other home builders were soon copying the building methods pioneered by Levitt. Car sales soared, too. Suburban families needed cars. They drove to work, to shopping centers, to movie theaters, and to restaurants.

During the late 1940s and the 1950s, the population grew rapidly. Americans were having more children, a trend known as the **baby boom.** Many people moved from the cities to the suburbs. They also moved from the Northeast to the Sunbelt—the states of the South and the Southwest.

As Americans earned more, they spent more. Television appeared in almost every home. Americans eagerly bought the cars, electrical appliances, and other goods advertised on television and in magazines.

RECOMMENDED RESOURCES

In-Depth Resources: Unit 5
- Guided Reading, p. 103
- Building Vocabulary, p. 104
- Geography Application, pp. 106–107
- Primary Source, p. 109
- Reteaching Activity, p. 116

Reading Study Guide (Spanish and English), pp. 195–196

Formal Assessment
- Section Quiz, p. 353

Integrated Assessment
- Rubrics, 2.5, 2.3

Access for Students Acquiring English/ESL
- Guided Reading, p. 133
- Geography Application, pp. 135–136

INTEGRATED TECHNOLOGY

America's Music CD

Electronic Teacher Tools

Not all Americans shared in the new prosperity, however. In the 1950s, African Americans and other minorities continued to face discrimination, as did working women. In rural areas and inner cities, many people struggled to survive.

The Civil Rights Movement

In the 1950s, reformers began to win legal victories to end segregation in the South. In 1954, in *Brown* v. *Board of Education of Topeka*, the Supreme Court ruled that segregated public schools were illegal. Two years later, after a black-led boycott of the Montgomery, Alabama, bus system, the Court ruled that segregated public transportation was against the law.

By the early 1960s, a young minister named **Dr. Martin Luther King, Jr.,** led a strong civil rights movement. Despite attacks by whites, the movement for equal rights remained largely nonviolent. At the 1963 March on Washington, King inspired more than 200,000 supporters with his words.

A VOICE FROM THE PAST

I have a dream that my four little children will one day live in a nation where they will not be judged by the color of their skin but by the content of their character. I have a dream today.

Martin Luther King, Jr., "I Have a Dream," August 28, 1963

In 1964, President Johnson pushed a Civil Rights Act through Congress. It banned discrimination in employment and voter registration. It also banned discrimination in public places such as restaurants, motels, and gas stations. Four years later, the Fair Housing Act outlawed discrimination in housing. Many of these changes were inspired by the leadership of Dr. King. King's assassination in Memphis, Tennessee, on April 4, 1968, stunned the nation.

Laws now guarantee African Americans and other minority groups equal treatment. With a growing number of African Americans elected to local, state, and federal offices, they have a greater voice in government.

Reading **History**

A. Recognizing Effects What goals did Dr. Martin Luther King, Jr., help to achieve in civil rights?

A. Answer King led civil rights movement; spoke at March on Washington; helped inspire Civil Rights Acts of the 1960s.

The Great Society ❷

In 1964, President Lyndon B. Johnson convinced Congress to fund his War on Poverty. This effort created many government and private agencies to fight poverty. Some agencies provided job training. Others sent volunteers to teach in poor rural communities and rundown urban neighborhoods. Some programs funded part-time jobs for needy college students. Others offered preschool classes to give poor children a head

AMERICA'S HISTORY MAKERS

DR. MARTIN LUTHER KING, JR.
1929–1968

Dr. King (shown below) became leader of the Montgomery bus boycott. Fresh out of school, he had been in Montgomery about a year. But his courage and eloquence made him the perfect person to lead the movement.

King learned about nonviolence by studying religious writers and thinkers. He came to believe that only love could convert people to the side of justice. He described the power of nonviolent resisters: "We will wear you down by our capacity to suffer. And in winning our freedom . . . we will win you in the process."

How might King's beliefs have supported his leadership of a nonviolent protest?

AMERICA'S HISTORY MAKERS

Dr. Martin Luther King, Jr.

When activists formed the Montgomery Improvement Association to spearhead the Montgomery bus boycott, King became its leader primarily because no one else wanted the job. In King's first speech at an MIA meeting, he said, "We come here tonight to be saved from that patience that makes us patient with anything less than freedom and justice." King clung to his philosophy of love and nonviolence despite threats, bombings, jailings, and scorn from whites and from blacks who thought he moved too slowly.

Possible Response: He had learned nonviolence from religious people whom he respected, and he accepted nonviolence as the best way to stay true to his beliefs and achieve social justice.

America's History Makers
- Martin Luther King, Jr., pp. 115–116

In-Depth Resources: Unit 5
- Geography Application: School Integration, 1954–1960, pp. 106–107

INSTRUCT: OBJECTIVE ❷

The Great Society/Rights for All/ Youth Protests and the Counterculture

- What types of programs were part of the War on Poverty?
- How did Native Americans, Mexican Americans, and women work toward equal rights for their groups?
- How did conflict over the Vietnam War create divisions among Americans?
- How did the values of the counterculture differ from those of the mainstream?

ACTIVITY OPTIONS

MULTIPLE LEARNING STYLES: MUSICAL

BLOCK SCHEDULING

SINGING FOR CIVIL RIGHTS

Class Time One class period

Task Learning songs of the civil rights movement and identifying some of the artists who popularized these songs

Purpose To appreciate a significant part of our musical heritage

Supplies Needed
- Reference materials about the music of the civil rights protests
- CDs or cassettes of civil rights songs such as "We Shall Overcome," "Oh, Freedom," "Blowin' in the Wind," and "I'm on My Way" by performers such as Odetta, Joan Baez, and Peter, Paul, and Mary

Activity Divide the class into groups, including one good singer in each group. Have student groups do research to learn what songs protesters sang during the Freedom Rides and at the March on Washington. Each group should choose one civil rights song and learn it well enough to lead the class in a sing-along. Encourage students to accompany themselves on guitar or piano.

America's Music CD

MORE ABOUT . . .

Women's Rights Advances

Betty Friedan joined with Shirley Chisholm and Bella Abzug to found the National Women's Political Caucus, whose goal was to increase female participation in politics. As a result, in the early 1970s, the number of women attending national party conventions jumped from 13 to 40 percent within the Democratic Party and from 17 to 30 percent in the Republican Party.

CRITICAL THINKING ACTIVITY

Drawing Conclusions Have students choose three organizations from this section and create a chart showing how each group helped fight discrimination.

Organization	How It Helped
NOW	lobbied to help women get equal pay for equal work

Class Time 20 minutes

start on learning. In 1965, Johnson got Congress to set aside millions for health care for the poor, elderly, and disabled. These health-care programs were called Medicare and Medicaid.

Reducing poverty, extending civil rights, and expanding medical care were all parts of Johnson's plan for a better America. He called it the **Great Society**. Like FDR's New Deal, the Great Society reflected Johnson's belief that government can improve people's lives. Johnson's social programs were costly. However, they attempted to reduce the poverty rate during the 1960s. As the U.S. role in the Vietnam War grew, though, fewer dollars were directed to Great Society programs.

Rights for All

In the 1960s, minorities and women struggled for equal rights. Native Americans turned to the courts to fight for their land rights. They held protests highlighting the federal government's failure to honor treaties. One of the most outspoken Native American groups was the American Indian Movement (AIM).

In the early 1960s, César Chávez began organizing poorly paid Mexican-American farm workers in California. He led a five-year-long strike by grape pickers. Then Chávez formed the nation's first successful union of farm workers. It became the United Farm Workers of America. Chávez's success inspired other Mexican Americans to work for change. In 1969–1970, they formed La Raza Unida—"the united people." This group worked to improve the lives of Mexican Americans and others.

César Chávez organized the United Farm Workers of America during the 1960s.

In 1963, Betty Friedan wrote a best-selling book called *The Feminine Mystique.* This book led many women to rethink their roles. In 1966, Friedan and other activists founded the National Organization for Women (NOW). NOW and other women's groups such as Working Women and the American Association of University Women have worked to change laws that discriminate against women. They have helped to reform property rights and hiring. They continue working for equal pay and fair treatment in the workplace.

B. Answer Native Americans, Mexican Americans, and women all struggled for equal rights—Native Americans for land rights, Mexican Americans for better pay and working conditions, and women for equal treatment in the workplace.

***Reading* History**

B. Comparing and Contrasting What was similar and different about the struggles of various groups for their rights?

Youth Protests and the Counterculture

No controversy was more heated than that over the Vietnam War. Opponents of the war argued that it was a civil war between Communists and non-Communists for control of Vietnam. They stated that the United States had no right to interfere. The war's supporters considered these opponents to be traitors who were undermining the war effort. Antiwar protests brought millions of Americans into the streets. Shouting matches and flag burnings followed. Some protests turned violent. Antiwar activists clashed with supporters of the war. At Ohio's Kent State University in 1970, National Guardsmen fired their weapons and killed four students.

ACTIVITY OPTIONS

INDIVIDUAL NEEDS

STUDENTS ACQUIRING ENGLISH/ESL

Building Vocabulary Help students become more familiar with the specialized vocabulary in this section. Have students identify unfamiliar words and phrases. Write these words on index cards and add their definitions. Then post the cards on a bulletin board or on the wall. Ask students to use each word in an original sentence. Encourage students to refer to the wall and use the words frequently when speaking and writing.

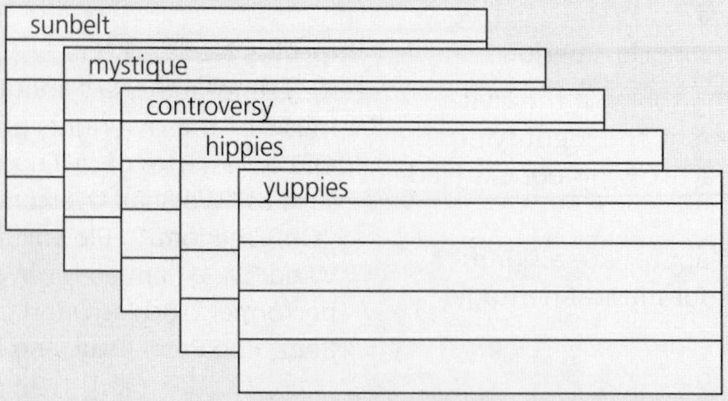

Vietnam widened the gap between younger and older Americans. Differences in beliefs and values between generations eventually gave rise to the **counterculture.** These were groups of people seeking new ways of living. One of the central values for members of the counterculture was a concern for the environment. Environmentalists sought to protect the environment by fighting pollution of the country's natural resources. Some younger Americans had different values from those of the mainstream. "Hippies" emphasized the importance of love and freedom. They celebrated at music festivals such as the one at Woodstock, New York, in 1969. Critics such as President Nixon charged that hippies and antiwar protesters were tearing the nation apart. Many critics spoke out against the way young people questioned American values. Despite such concerns, in 1971 the Twenty-Sixth Amendment lowered the voting age to 18.

Protesters march in 1969 in opposition to the war in Vietnam.

3 Reagan, Bush, and Conservatism

Throughout the 1960s and 1970s, Democratic presidents such as Jimmy Carter had favored a strong role for government in the economy. They favored regulation of big business, support for organized labor, and public spending on the poor.

Ronald Reagan, a former movie actor and governor of California, was elected president in 1980, defeating Jimmy Carter. Reagan wanted to reduce the role of government in American life. "Government," he said, "is not the solution to our problem. Government is the problem." He sharply cut taxes and slashed spending on social programs for the poor. At the same time, he greatly increased military spending.

The tax cuts, coupled with heavy defense spending, caused the national debt to skyrocket. The government was borrowing more money to pay for spending than it was taking in through taxes. As a result, the national debt doubled in size from 1981 through 1986.

Reading **History**
C. Summarizing What are some examples of how Reagan limited the role of government in economic affairs?
C. Answer Reagan slashed taxes and social spending, and abolished many government regulations on business.

Reagan pushed pro-business economic policies. He abolished thousands of government regulations on business. After a recession in 1982, the economy sharply improved. A new wealthy class of young people emerged, whom reporters labeled "yuppies" (from "young urban professionals").

Reagan's successor, George Bush, shared his conservative outlook. In the early 1990s, after his successful management of the Persian Gulf War, Bush's popularity surged. However, when the country headed into a recession, Bush's approval ratings fell sharply. The causes of the weak economy included the nation's growing national debt, rising oil prices as a result of the Persian Gulf War, and shrinking factory production. In 1992, Bush was defeated in his bid for a second term by Bill Clinton, the governor of Arkansas.

INSTRUCT: OBJECTIVE 3

Reagan, Bush, and Conservatism/ The Clinton Presidency

- How did President Reagan reduce the role of government in American life? What effect did his actions have?
- How did President Clinton reduce the federal deficit?
- Why was Clinton impeached?

CRITICAL THINKING ACTIVITY

Contrasting To help students differentiate the policies of Democratic and Republican presidents in the 1970s and 1980s, have them make a chart like the one below. Have students include at least two programs or policies for each president.

President	Dem./Rep.	Domestic	Foreign
Carter			
Reagan			
Bush			
Clinton			

Class Time 20 minutes

MORE ABOUT . . .

Ronald Reagan

One reason for Ronald Reagan's popularity was his unfailing optimism at a time when many Americans felt uncertain. Not even an assassination attempt could dampen his spirits. In 1981, an insane gunman shot the president. When Reagan's wife, Nancy, arrived at the hospital, Reagan told her, "Honey, I forgot to duck." He remarked to the doctors who were about to operate on him, "Please tell me you're Republicans."

America's History Makers
- Ronald Reagan, pp. 129–130

ACTIVITY OPTIONS

INTERDISCIPLINARY LINK: MATHEMATICS — BLOCK SCHEDULING

DEFENSE SPENDING AND THE NATIONAL DEBT

Class Time One class period

Task Making a graph to show the national debt and defense spending from 1981 to 1986

Purpose To compare increases in defense spending and the national debt during the Reagan presidency

Supplies Needed
- Calculator
- Graph paper
- Colored pencils

Activity Give students the following data on the national debt and defense spending:

	1981	1982	1983	1984	1985	1986
Debt	994.8	1,373.3	1,371.7	1,564.7	1,817.5	2,120.6
Defense	157.5	185.3	209.9	227.4	252.7	273.4

(All numbers are in billions of dollars.) Have them make a line graph comparing the data. Ask: (1) How much did the debt increase in these years? Defense spending? (2) How are the two lines on the graph alike? (3) Which increased more rapidly, defense spending or the debt?

(From left) Presidents Clinton, Bush, Reagan, Carter, and Ford at the funeral for President Nixon on April 27, 1994.

The Clinton Presidency

During his first term, Bill Clinton focused on domestic issues. To reduce the deficit, he supported tax increases and spending cuts. To fight crime, he pushed gun-control laws through Congress. Clinton's boldest move was his attempt to overhaul the U.S. health-care system. This effort, led by Hillary Rodham Clinton, failed to pass Congress.

In 1994, the Democrats lost control of Congress to the Republicans. The new Congress pushed for deeper cuts in taxes and social programs than Clinton would support. At first, the two sides failed to reach a budget agreement. Then, a compromise led to deep cuts in some government social programs but protected some spending for education, welfare, and health care programs for the needy. The nation's strong economy helped Clinton win reelection in 1996.

Reading **History**

D. Contrasting What effect did the economy have on the elections of 1992 and 1996?

D. Answer The weak economy of 1992 helped to defeat Bush; the strong economy of 1996 helped to reelect Clinton.

Clinton's second term in office was marred by scandal. An investigation into Clinton's finances revealed that he had had an improper relationship with a White House intern. And he allegedly had lied about it under oath. The charges led to his impeachment in 1998. Despite the charges, Clinton remained popular. The Senate opened its trial of President Clinton in January 1999. Nearly a month later, the Senate acquitted him on both charges, and Clinton remained in office.

4 The 2000 Presidential Election

In 2000, the nation held a presidential election to choose Clinton's successor. The Democrats nominated Vice-President Al Gore as their candidate. The Republicans chose Texas governor George W. Bush, the son of the former president. Gore argued he was the best candidate to keep the nation's economy healthy. Meanwhile, Bush campaigned on a plan to give Americans huge tax cuts.

The 2000 election was one of the closest in U.S. history. By the morning after Election Day, Gore held a narrow lead in the popular vote. However, he did not have enough electoral votes to claim the presidency. Bush led in Florida by a few hundred votes, which promised to give him enough electoral votes to win the election. For five weeks, the two campaigns fought legal battles over recounts of the Florida ballots. Finally, on December 12, the U.S. Supreme Court voted 5 to 4 to stop the recounts, ensuring that Bush would win the presidency.

Immigrants and the New Millennium

From 1981 to 1996, nearly 13.5 million people came to the United States. These new immigrants increased U.S. diversity. Most of the immigrants who arrived in America during earlier periods had come from Europe. Nearly 85 percent of the most recent arrivals came from Latin America or

INSTRUCT: OBJECTIVE 4

The 2000 Presidential Election/Immigrants and the New Millennium

- Who were the major candidates in the 2000 presidential election?
- How was the 2000 presidential election eventually decided?
- How are today's immigrants different from earlier arrivals?
- What are two causes for increased immigration to the United States since 1981?

MORE ABOUT . . .

Hispanic Americans During the 1980s, Hispanic Americans became the fastest-growing U.S. minority. The term *Hispanic* is used for a wide range of peoples. Hispanics include Puerto Ricans, who, as U.S. citizens, travel freely between the mainland and Puerto Rico. Other Hispanics are from Cuba, the Caribbean Islands, and the nations of Central America. Mexican Americans make up two-thirds of all Hispanic Americans. Hispanics are gaining political power, but many still suffer from low pay, unhealthy living conditions, and high unemployment.

ACTIVITY OPTIONS

INDIVIDUAL NEEDS: GIFTED AND TALENTED

COLLECTING ORAL HISTORIES

Class Time One class period

Task Interviewing adults to record their oral histories

Purpose To collect first-hand information about the second half of the 20th century

Supplies Needed
- Tape recorder
- Blank audiotapes

Activity Have students work in pairs to create both introductory and specific questions about the events of each decade. Then ask students to interview two adults about their experiences and memories of events in the 1960s, 1970s, 1980s, and 1990s. Caution students to approach only adults whom they know well. Students should transcribe their interviews, write an overall introduction, and write an introduction to each individual interview.

Asia. The Census Bureau predicts that by 2020 the U.S. Hispanic population will increase from 11 percent to 16 percent. At the same time, the Asian population is expected to climb from 3 percent to nearly 6 percent.

One cause of the recent surge in immigration is the Immigration Act of 1965. It allowed people from a greater variety of countries to enter the United States. The lure of America also plays a role. As with previous waves of immigration, many of the newcomers came to the United States seeking economic opportunity and political freedom.

While immigrants bring their culture to America, they also have embraced many American traditions. Most wear American clothes, adopt American customs, and learn English. Furthermore, they share with other Americans a belief in democracy and freedom.

Citizens of all races and backgrounds will play a vital role in shaping America. So will today's students. You have a part to play in helping the United States embrace people from every culture and land. You are the generation that will create the America of the future.

The American People

Origins of Immigrants, 1981–1996	Numbers of Immigrants*
1. Mexico	3,300,000
2. Philippines	840,000
3. China°	730,000
4. Vietnam	720,000
5. Dominican Republic	510,000
6. India	500,000
7. Korea	450,000
8. Soviet Union†	420,000
9. El Salvador	360,000
10. Jamaica	320,000

* Numbers rounded to nearest 10,000.
° China includes Taiwan.
† The Soviet Union broke apart in 1991. This figure includes the former Soviet republics.

Source: *U.S. Bureau of the Census*

SKILLBUILDER Interpreting Charts

1. *From which European countries were there still substantial numbers of immigrants in the 1980s and 1990s?*
2. *From what regions of the world do most recent immigrants come?*

Skillbuilder Answers
1. the countries that make up the former Soviet Union
2. North America (Mexico); Central America (El Salvador); Asia (Philippines, Vietnam, China, India, Korea); Caribbean (Dominican Republic, Jamaica)

Section 4 Assessment

1. Terms & Names

Explain the significance of:
- baby boom
- Dr. Martin Luther King, Jr.
- Great Society
- counterculture

2. Taking Notes

Use the chart to examine the aims of groups that protested in the 1960s.

	Goal	Success
African Americans		
Mexican Americans		
Native Americans		
Women		

3. Main Ideas

a. How did the civil rights movement of the 1960s lessen discrimination against African Americans?

b. What were the goals of President Johnson's Great Society programs?

c. How did Reagan attempt to reduce the role of government in American life?

4. Critical Thinking

Supporting Opinions Do any youth countercultures exist today? Why or why not?

THINK ABOUT
- music and the arts
- politics
- religion
- values

ACTIVITY OPTIONS

LANGUAGE ARTS
MATH

Find out about voters' attitudes toward politicians. Create a survey, conduct a poll, and either write a **report** or display your results in a **graph**.

HISTORY FROM VISUALS

Interpreting Charts Review with students the continent in which each country is located. Choose five students and assign each the task of totaling the immigration from one continent. Ask which continents are not represented and why there are so few immigrants from those continents. **Possible Response** Africa, South America. People on those continents may be unable or unwilling to migrate to another location.

Extension Using an outline map of the world, have students shade in the countries shown on the chart.

MORE ABOUT . . .

Immigration Acts, 1965–1990

Instead of using national origin, the Immigration Act of 1965 set immigration ceilings by hemisphere. By 1978, these ceilings were replaced by an annual worldwide immigration of no more than 290,000. The ceiling was raised to 540,000 in the 1980s. By 1995, the ceiling was set at 675,000.

ASSESS & RETEACH

Setting the Stage Have students add information on the 1980s to the graphic organizer.

Formal Assessment
- Section Quiz, p. 353

RETEACHING ACTIVITY

Have students work in pairs to write a summary of the section using the "Terms & Names" listed on page 584.

In-Depth Resources: Unit 5
- Reteaching Activity, p. 116

Section 4 Assessment

1. Terms & Names

baby boom, p. 584
Dr. Martin Luther King, Jr., p. 585
Great Society, p. 586
counterculture, p. 587

2. Taking Notes

African Americans: Goal—equality; Success—Civil Rights Act of 1964. Mexican Americans: Goal—better economic opportunity; Success—United Farm Workers. Native Americans: Goal—land rights; Success—AIM drew attention to Native American demands. Women: Goal—equal rights; Success—NOW

3. Main Ideas

a. Dr. Martin Luther King, Jr., led a strong civil rights movement that helped to win passage of the Civil Rights Act in 1964. **b.** reducing poverty, extending civil rights, and expanding medical care **c.** He cut taxes, slashed spending on social programs for the poor, and abolished government regulations on business.

4. Critical Thinking

Answers will vary; students should take into consideration subcultures that might exist in the different areas of music, the arts, politics, and religion.

ACTIVITY OPTIONS

Integrated Assessment
- Rubrics, 2.5, 2.3

Interdisciplinary CHALLENGE

OBJECTIVE

Students will work cooperatively to find solutions to present and future environmental challenges in their community through economics, art, and math activities.

BLOCK SCHEDULING

PROCEDURE

Gather supplies that students might need, such as posterboard, art supplies, annual reports from local manufacturers, and information about environmental groups and recycling programs. For each challenge, have students form groups of three or four. Ask group members to divide the work among themselves. Then have them choose an option for presenting their solution.

ECONOMICS CHALLENGE

Class Time 50 minutes

Tell students that an economic report should include specific numerical data. Such a report may be illustrated and may contain charts and graphs. A proposal may consist of text with an appendix of numerical data.

POSSIBLE SOLUTIONS

Suggest that students do research to find additional examples of corporate conservation.

- Students may use the Internet to find information about ways businesses save money through recycling and reducing waste.
- Students may find information about conservation achievements in annual reports of local companies or through queries by telephone or e-mail to corporate public affairs officers.

Interdisciplinary CHALLENGE

Protecting the Environment

The nation has made great strides over the past several decades in taking better care of the environment. However, much work remains to be done. As the United States embarks on a new century, the country continues to face such controversial issues as global warming, and the problems of water pollution and a growing amount of waste.

COOPERATIVE LEARNING You have recently joined a local organization whose goal is to find solutions to the environmental challenges that affect your community. On these pages are three challenges you face as a member of the organization. Working with a small group, decide how to deal with each challenge. Choose an option, assign a task to each group member, and do the activity. You will find useful information in the Data File. Present your solutions to the class.

ECONOMICS CHALLENGE

"from a feel-good issue to a bottom-line issue"

A growing number of businesses have begun taking steps to curb the amount of trash they produce. These companies have found that scaling back on waste helps to save money. How can you convince businesses in your community to follow this trend? Use the Data File for help. Use one of these options:

- Create an economic report showing companies ways they can cut back on waste while saving money.
- Write a proposal outlining further ways companies can reduce waste.

ART CHALLENGE

"very troubled waters"

In the decades after the Clean Water Act of 1972, many of the nation's rivers grew cleaner. Recently, however, the government has had to name more waterways as unsuitable for fishing or swimming.

The main pollutants include pesticide and sewage runoff from large farms, runoff from city and suburban sewer systems, and chemical waste from mining. How can you alert people in your community to these problems? Use the Data File for help. Present your information using one of these options:

- **Design a poster showing one or more types of pollutants reaching a river.**
- **Create a graphic for town officials that depicts the Data File information about contaminated rivers.**

590

STANDARDS FOR EVALUATION

ECONOMICS CHALLENGE

Option 1 Reports should
- present waste-reduction plans with evidence of dollars saved.
- suggest ways that companies might benefit from adopting new conservation practices.

Option 2 Proposals should
- indicate specific steps to reduce waste.
- identify expected benefits.

ART CHALLENGE

Option 1 Posters should
- use large illustrations and few words to present message clearly.
- demonstrate river pollution in a factual, nonsensational manner.

Option 2 Graphics should
- include clear, legible labels.
- contain accurate data.

MATH CHALLENGE

Option 1 Graphs should
- include clear, legible labels.
- contain accurate data.

Option 2 Reports should
- include realistic suggestions.
- include suggestions for all parts of the house.

MATH CHALLENGE

"the seas would rise . . . and whole forest types could disappear"

Global warming remains a controversial problem. Many—but not all—scientists believe that air pollutants create a ceiling that traps heat near the earth's surface. Foremost among the pollutants is carbon dioxide, which is generated by factories, automobiles, and common household appliances. Help people become more aware of their carbon dioxide output. Use the Data File for help. Present your information using one of these options:

- Make a graph showing the yearly carbon dioxide output of various household items.
- Write a report detailing ways in which a household could reduce its carbon dioxide output.

"Gentlemen, it's time we gave some serious thought to the effects of global warming."

ACTIVITY WRAP-UP

Present to the Class **Meet as a group to review your responses to various environmental challenges. Pick the most creative solution for each challenge and present these solutions to the class.**

DATA FILE

Global Warming

Average U.S. Household's Yearly Output of Carbon Dioxide (in pounds):

Human respiration (2.6 persons)—1,950
Television—510
Range—933
Dishwasher—1,038
Lighting—1,045
Refrigerator—1,136
Dryer—1,177
Washer—1,199
Oil-fired water heater—4,476
Oil-fired space heater—12,958
Car—20,956

What's in Our Dirty Rivers

From a 1998 study: 36 percent of U.S. rivers are contaminated. Percentage of contaminated rivers affected by following pollutants:

- Toxic chemicals—9%
- Waste and chemicals from mining—13%
- City/suburban run-off (trash, chemical fertilizers)—13%
- Treated sewage (nitrogen and phosphorus)—14%
- Silt and sediment (from construction projects)—37%
- Agriculture run-off (dirt, manure, chemical fertilizers)—70%

Corporate Conservation

- Colonial Pacific Leasing Corp. in Oregon cut $5,200 from its yearly electrical bill by using energy-efficient light bulbs.
- Stonyfield Farm Inc. in New Hampshire saved $60,000 one year by reducing the amount of plastic packaging on products.
- Mercer Color Corp. in Ohio made $8,000 one year by selling its waste for recycling.
- Xerox saves more than $200 million a year by reusing print and toner cartridges.

For more about conservation . . .

RESEARCH LINKS
CLASSZONE.COM

ART CHALLENGE

Class Time 50 minutes

To help students focus their poster's message, suggest that they research various contaminants and then select one for the poster. Discuss types of graphs with students who decide to prepare a graphic. Help students select the correct kind of display for the data they wish to illustrate.

POSSIBLE SOLUTIONS

Students' posters and graphics might focus on

- a nearby river or creek.
- one of the U.S. rivers that is in great danger from pollutants.

MATH CHALLENGE

Class Time 50 minutes

Suggest that students research carbon dioxide output and global warming. Then have them brainstorm ways in which they might assess their families' carbon dioxide output before they adopt new practices.

POSSIBLE SOLUTIONS

- Students might make a bar graph illustrating the material in the Data File.
- Students might brainstorm in groups to find suggestions for ways to reduce carbon dioxide output.

ACTIVITY WRAP-UP

To help student groups evaluate the creativity of their challenge solutions, ask them to make a grid with criteria like the one shown. Then have them rate each solution on a scale from 1 to 5.

Originality	1	2	3	4	5
Substantial content	1	2	3	4	5
Presentation	1	2	3	4	5
Audience impact	1	2	3	4	5
Overall effectiveness	1	2	3	4	5

TERMS & NAMES

1. **Great Depression,** p. 571
2. **New Deal,** p. 572
3. **fascism,** p. 574
4. **World War II,** p. 575
5. **Holocaust,** p. 578
6. **Harry S. Truman,** p. 579
7. **Cold War,** p. 579
8. **containment,** p. 580
9. **baby boom,** p. 584
10. **Great Society,** p. 586

REVIEW QUESTIONS

Possible Responses

1. The stock market crash set off a chain reaction of events labeled the Great Depression, a time of economic hardship.
2. to enable federal officials to examine bank records, reopen sound banks, and restore the public's confidence in banks
3. relief programs to aid the hungry and jobless; recovery programs to help agriculture and industry; economic reform
4. Hitler exploited German bitterness at the treaty ending World War I; he blamed Germany's economic woes on the Jews; he expanded German territory
5. The United States began as neutral, but when the Japanese attacked Pearl Harbor in 1941, the United States entered the war.
6. The United States wanted to stop the spread of communism, and the Soviet Union wanted to promote the spread of communism.
7. the Marshall Plan and NATO
8. The rivalry between the superpowers ended, and the United States became the world's only superpower.
9. boycotts, legal victories, marches, and promotion of civil rights legislation
10. Johnson believed that the federal government had an important role to play as a protector of the weak and the poor; Reagan wanted to reduce the role of government in American life.

VISUAL SUMMARY

The United States Since 1919

1920s: Prosperity; increased income and leisure

1930s: Great Depression; New Deal; rise of dictators

1940s: World War II; beginning of Cold War

1950s: Prosperity; growth of suburbs; baby boom

1960s: Civil rights movement; Vietnam War

1970s: Détente; Vietnam War ends; Nixon resigns

1980s: Soaring federal deficit; U.S.-Soviet relations improved

1990s: Collapse of Soviet Union; prosperity

TERMS & NAMES

Briefly explain the significance of each of the following.

1. Great Depression
2. New Deal
3. fascism
4. World War II
5. Holocaust
6. Harry S. Truman
7. Cold War
8. containment
9. baby boom
10. Great Society

REVIEW QUESTIONS

Prosperity and the Great Depression (pages 569–573)

1. What role did the market crash play in the Great Depression?
2. What was the purpose of Roosevelt's bank holiday?
3. What problems did FDR's New Deal address?

The Rise of Dictators and World War II (pages 574–578)

4. How did Hitler and the Nazi Party gain the support of Germans in the 1930s?
5. How did the role of the United States in World War II change between 1939 and 1945?

The Cold War (pages 579–583)

6. What differences between the Soviet Union and the United States fueled the Cold War?
7. What strategies did the United States use to carry out its containment policy?
8. How did the end of the Cold War change the United States' role in world affairs?

Life in America Since 1945 (pages 584–589)

9. What methods did civil rights activists use?
10. How did the views of presidents Johnson and Reagan differ on the role of government?

CRITICAL THINKING

1. USING YOUR NOTES

The 20th Century	Political Events	Economic Events	Social Events
1920–1930			
1940–1950			
1960–1970			
1980–1990			

Using your completed chart, answer the questions below.

a. What was an important political event in the period 1940–1950?

b. What was an important social event in the period 1960–1970?

c. What was an important economic event in the period 1980–1990?

2. APPLYING CITIZENSHIP SKILLS

How has the African-American struggle for civil rights changed since the 1960s?

3. THEME: AMERICA IN THE WORLD

As the world's most powerful nation, does the United States have a special responsibility to intervene in conflicts around the world? Why or why not?

4. ANALYZING LEADERSHIP

How do the leadership skills of a president differ in times of war and in times of peace and prosperity? Explain your answer.

5. FORMING AND SUPPORTING OPINIONS

Should the government's focus today be on domestic issues or on foreign affairs? Explain your answer.

Interact *with* History

Now that you've read the chapter, what are some ways the 21st century may be the same as and different from the 20th century? Explain your ideas.

CRITICAL THINKING

Possible Responses

1. **USING YOUR NOTES** **a.** Harry S. Truman was elected president in 1948. **b.** emergence of a counterculture **c.** Reagan cut taxes.
2. **APPLYING CITIZENSHIP SKILLS** The Civil Rights Acts of the 1960s guaranteed African Americans equal treatment, and many have been elected to local, state, and federal offices.
3. **THEME: AMERICA IN THE WORLD** Answers will vary, but students should consider the consequences of such a responsibility.
4. **ANALYZING LEADERSHIP** Students may feel that during wartime the country requires special skills in a leader, or they may point to Franklin Roosevelt as a leader who excelled during times of both war and peace.
5. **FORMING AND SUPPORTING OPINIONS** Answers will vary. Students should focus on the past few presidencies and consider the different needs each faced. Both areas undoubtedly need constant attention.

Interact *with* History Answers will vary, but students should consider that each generation has different challenges to face.

HISTORY SKILLS

1. INTERPRETING MAPS: Location

Study the map and then answer the questions.

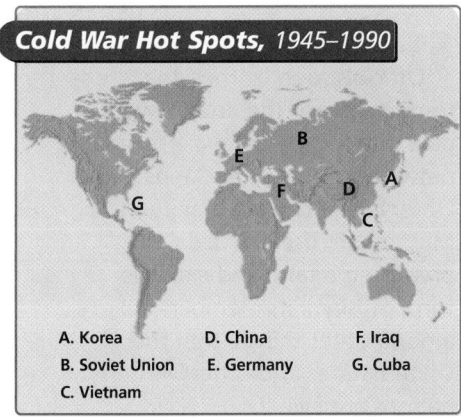

Cold War Hot Spots, *1945–1990*

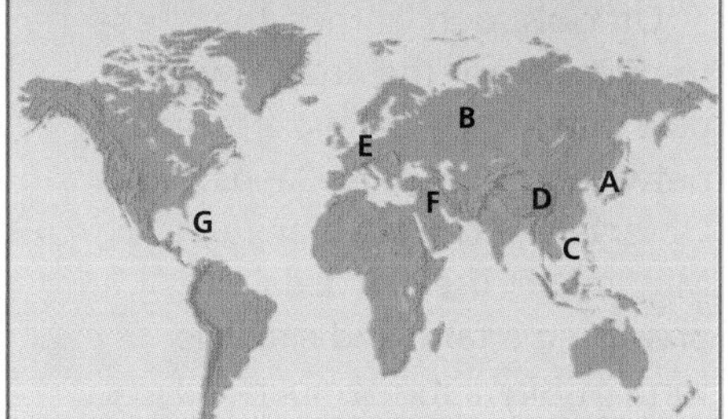

A. Korea
B. Soviet Union
C. Vietnam
D. China
E. Germany
F. Iraq
G. Cuba

Basic Map Elements

a. What is the subject of the map?

b. In which hemisphere are most of these countries located?

Interpreting the Map

c. Why might the United States have been concerned about missiles in Cuba?

d. Which Cold War hot spot was located in Europe?

2. INTERPRETING PRIMARY SOURCES

Ken Burns, a documentary filmmaker, argues that a shared belief in the ideals of democracy and civil rights makes America unique in the world.

> There is no other country on Earth that is configured like ours. Every other nation is there because of race, religion, language, ethnicity, or geography. We are here only because we agreed to subscribe to the words on four pieces of paper—the U.S. Constitution. Unlike every other country, which sees itself as an end unto itself, we see ourselves as evolving. We're not satisfied. We're not willing to rest on our laurels. We think we can get better. We think we've got someplace to go.
>
> **Ken Burns,** quoted in *America West*

a. Does Burns's comment imply a hopeful view of the future? Why or why not?

b. What might be some of the advantages and disadvantages of changing and adapting to meet the future?

ALTERNATIVE ASSESSMENT

1. INTERDISCIPLINARY ACTIVITY: World History

Creating a Linking Time Line Make a dual time line for the period 1920–2000. Divide the time line into eight segments, one for each decade. On one side, list key events from world history during this period. On the other side, note major events from American history. Pick a decade and give a talk explaining how the events on the time line are connected.

2. COOPERATIVE LEARNING ACTIVITY

Analyzing Social Issues Working in groups, make a list of social issues that concern Americans today, such as pollution, drugs, crime, or school violence. Decide which problem the group thinks is most important. Create presentations using these suggestions.

- Research and write a description of the problem.
- Make a list of at least three alternative ways experts suggest for solving the problem.
- Pick the solution your group considers most practical and likely to be effective and write an action statement explaining the reasons for your choice.

3. TECHNOLOGY ACTIVITY

Making an Electronic Presentation During the 1920s, there was a dramatic rise in popular entertainment. Using the library and the Internet, find information about important celebrities of the time, such as Babe Ruth, Bessie Smith, or Charlie Chaplin.

For more about the 1920s . . .

RESEARCH LINKS
CLASSZONE.COM

Use presentation software to create a program about celebrities of the 1920s. Use the suggestions below to get started.

- the 1927 championship boxing match between Jack Dempsey and Gene Tunney
- important events in the baseball career of Ty Cobb or Babe Ruth
- recordings of jazz greats
- facts about movie celebrities of the 1920s

4. HISTORY PORTFOLIO

Review your section and chapter assessment activities. Select one that you think is your best work. Then use comments made by your teacher or classmates to improve your work and add it to your portfolio.

Additional Test Practice, pp. S1–S33

TEST PRACTICE
CLASSZONE.COM

ALTERNATIVE ASSESSMENT

1. INTERDISCIPLINARY ACTIVITY: **World History**
   Time lines should
   - be organized chronologically by decade.
   - clearly describe and illustrate events from both American and world history.
   - be presented neatly.
   - have a clear and logical oral presentation.
2. COOPERATIVE LEARNING ACTIVITY
   Presentations should
   - identify and describe the problem.
   - include at least three ways to solve the problem.
   - contain an action solution for the problem.
   - use standard grammar, spelling, sentence structure, and punctuation.
3. TECHNOLOGY ACTIVITY
   Presentations should
   - utilize two or more media.
   - clearly demonstrate an understanding of the popular entertainment celebrities of the 1920s.
   - show technical proficiency.
4. HISTORY PORTFOLIO
   Option 1 Revised section or chapter assessment activities should
   - address teacher and peer responses to the selected work.
   - solve problems present in the first versions of the work.

   Option 2 Short reports should
   - answer questions about great events of the 20th century.
   - use evidence to develop and support ideas.
   - cite sources of information.
   - use standard grammar, spelling, sentence structure, and punctuation.

Formal Assessment
- Chapter 20 Epilogue Test, Forms A, B, and C, pp. 354–365

HISTORY SKILLS

Possible Responses

1. INTERPRETING MAPS
   Basic Map Elements
   a. the Cold War
   b. eastern (and northern)

   Interpreting the Map
   c. because of Cuba's proximity to the U.S. mainland
   d. Germany

2. INTERPRETING PRIMARY SOURCES
   a. Burns's comment seems hopeful because it suggests that most Americans think the future will be better than the past.
   b. Advantages might be that individuals and society are adaptable and resilient; disadvantages might be that traditional values are neglected.

The Attack: September 11, 2001

Terrorism is the use of violence against people or property to force changes in societies or governments. Acts of terrorism are not new. Throughout history, individuals and groups have used terror tactics to achieve political or social goals.

In recent decades, however, terrorist groups have carried out increasingly destructive and high-profile attacks. The growing threat of terrorism has caused many people to feel vulnerable and afraid. However, it also has prompted action from many nations, including the United States.

Many of the terrorist activities of the late 20th century occurred far from U.S. soil. As a result, most Americans felt safe from such violence. All that changed, however, on the morning of September 11, 2001.

A Surprise Strike

As the nation began another workday, 19 terrorists hijacked four airplanes heading from East Coast airports to California. The hijackers crashed two of the jets into the twin towers of the World Trade Center in New York City. They slammed a third plane into the Pentagon outside Washington, D.C. The fourth plane crashed into an empty field in Pennsylvania after passengers apparently fought the hijackers.

The attacks destroyed the World Trade Center and badly damaged a section of the Pentagon. In all, some 3,000 people died. Life for Americans would never be the same after that day. Before, most U.S. citizens viewed terrorism as something that happened in other countries. Now they knew it could happen on their soil as well.

Officials soon learned that those responsible for the attacks were part of a largely Islamic terrorist network known as al-Qaeda. Observers, including many Muslims, accuse al-Qaeda of preaching a false and extreme form of Islam. Its members believe, among other things, that the United States and other Western nations are evil.

U.S. president George W. Bush vowed to hunt down all those responsible for the attacks. In addition, he called for a greater international effort to combat global terrorism. "This battle will take time and resolve," the president declared. "But make no mistake about it: we will win."

Securing the Nation

As the Bush Administration began its campaign against terrorism, it

Flight Path of the Hijacked Airliners, September 11, 2001

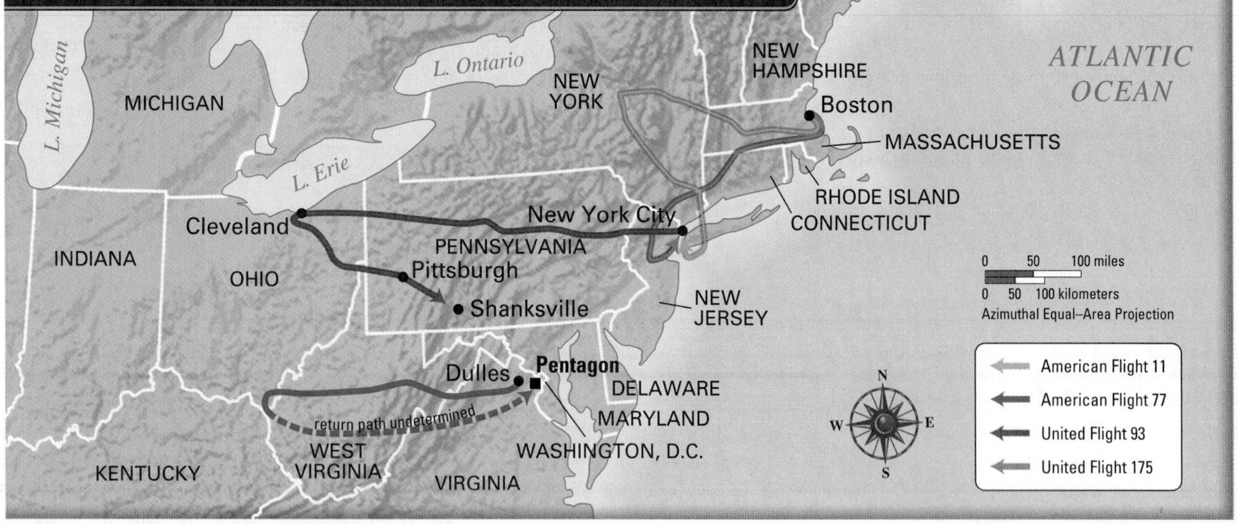

also sought to prevent any further attacks on America. In October 2001, the president signed into law the USA Patriot Act. The law gave the federal government a broad range of new powers to strengthen national security.

The new law enabled officials to detain foreigners suspected of terrorism for up to seven days without charging them with a crime. Officials could also monitor all phone and Internet use by suspects, and prosecute terrorist crimes without any time restrictions or limitations.

In addition, the government created a new cabinet position, the Department of Homeland Security, to coordinate national efforts against terrorism. President Bush named former Pennsylvania governor Tom Ridge as the first Secretary of Homeland Security.

Underneath a U.S. flag posted amid the rubble of the World Trade Center, rescue workers search for survivors of the attack.

Some critics charged that a number of the government's new anti-terrorism measures violated people's civil rights. Supporters countered that occasionally limiting some civil liberties was justified in the name of greater national security.

Stunned bystanders look on as smoke billows from the twin towers of the World Trade Center moments after an airplane slammed into each one.

The federal government also stepped in to ensure greater security at the nation's airports. The September 11 attacks had originated at several airports, with four hijackings occurring at nearly the same time. In November 2001, President Bush signed the Aviation and Transportation Security Act into law. The law put the federal government in charge of airport security. Before, individual airports had been responsible for security. The new law created a federal security force to inspect passengers and carry-on bags. It also required the screening of checked baggage.

While the September 11 attacks shook the United States, they also strengthened the nation's unity and resolve. In 2003, officials approved plans to rebuild on the World Trade Center site and construct a memorial. Meanwhile, the country has grown more unified as Americans recognize the need to stand together against terrorism.

Fighting Back

The attack against the United States on September 11, 2001, represented the single most deadly act of terrorism in modern history. By that time, however, few regions of the world had been spared from terrorist attacks. Today, America and other nations are responding to terrorism in a variety of ways.

The Rise of Terrorism

The problem of modern international terrorism first gained world attention during the 1972 Summer Olympic Games in Munich, Germany. Members of a Palestinian terrorist group killed two Israeli athletes and took nine others hostage. Five of the terrorists, all the hostages, and a police officer were later killed in a bloody gun battle.

Since then, terrorist activities have occurred across the globe. In Europe, the Irish Republican Army (IRA) used terrorist tactics for decades against Britain. The IRA has long opposed British control of Northern Ireland. Since 1998, the two sides have been working toward a peaceful solution to their conflict. In South America, a group known as the Shining Path terrorized the residents of Peru throughout the late 20th century. The group sought to overthrow the government and establish a Communist state.

Africa, too, has seen its share of terrorism. Groups belonging to the al-Qaeda terrorist organization operated in many African countries. Indeed, officials have linked several major attacks against U.S. facilities in Africa to al-Qaeda. In 1998, for example, bombings at the U.S. embassies in Kenya and Tanzania left more than 200 dead and 5,000 injured.

Most terrorists work in a similar way: targeting high profile events or crowded places where people normally feel safe. They include such places as subway stations, bus stops, restaurants, or shopping malls. Terrorists choose these spots carefully in order to gain the most attention and to achieve the highest level of intimidation.

Terrorists use bullets and bombs as their main weapons. In recent years, however, some terrorist groups have used biological and chemical agents in their attacks. These actions involve the release of bacteria or poisonous gas into the air. Gas was the weapon of choice for a radical Japanese religious cult, Aum Shinrikyo. In 1995, cult members released sarin, a deadly nerve gas, in subway stations in Tokyo. Twelve people were killed and more than 5,700 injured. The possibility of this type of terrorism is particularly worrisome, because biochemical agents are relatively easy to acquire.

Terrorism: A Global Problem

PLACE	YEAR	EVENT
Munich, Germany	1972	Palestinians take Israeli hostages at Summer Olympics; hostages and terrorists die in gun battle with police
Beirut, Lebanon	1983	Terrorists detonate truck bomb at U.S. marine barracks, killing 241
Tokyo, Japan	1995	Religious extremists release lethal gas into subway stations, killing 12 and injuring thousands
Omagh, Northern Ireland	1998	Faction of Irish Republican Army sets off car bomb, killing 29
Moscow, Russia	2002	Rebels from Chechnya seize a crowded theater; rescue effort leaves more than 100 hostages and all the terrorists dead

596

Hunting Down Terrorists

Most governments have adopted an aggressive approach to tracking down and punishing terrorist groups. This approach includes spying on the groups to gather information on membership and future plans. It also includes striking back harshly after a terrorist attack, even to the point of assassinating known terrorist leaders.

Another approach that governments use is to make it more difficult for terrorists to act. This involves eliminating a terrorist group's source of funding. President Bush issued an executive order freezing the U.S. assets of alleged terrorist organizations as well as various groups accused of supporting terrorism. President Bush asked other nations to freeze such assets as well. By the spring of 2002, the White House reported, the United States and other countries had blocked nearly $80 million in alleged terrorist assets.

Battling al-Qaeda

In one of the more aggressive responses to terrorism, the United States quickly took military action against those it held responsible for the September 11 attacks.

U.S. officials had determined that members of the al-Qaeda terrorist group had carried out the assault under the direction of the group's leader, Osama bin Laden. Bin Laden was a Saudi Arabian millionaire who lived in Afghanistan. He directed his terrorist activities under the protection of the country's extreme Islamic government, known as the Taliban.

The United States demanded that the Taliban turn over bin Laden. The Taliban refused. In October 2001, U.S. forces began bombing Taliban air defenses, airfields, and command centers. They also struck numerous al-Qaeda training camps. On the ground, the United States provided assistance to rebel groups opposed to the Taliban. By December, the United States had driven the Taliban from power and severely weakened the al-Qaeda network. However, as of 2003, Osama bin Laden was still believed to be at large.

Osama bin Laden delivers a videotaped message from a hidden location shortly after the U.S.-led strikes against Afghanistan began.

Troops battling the Taliban in Afghanistan await transport by helicopter.

The War in Iraq

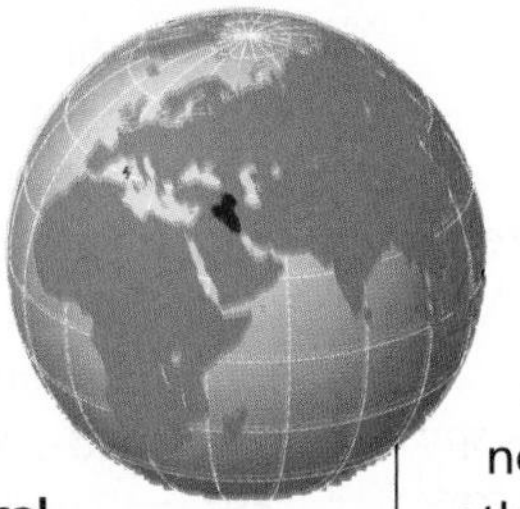

In the ongoing battle against terrorism, the United States confronted the leader of Iraq, Saddam Hussein. The longtime dictator had concerned the world community for years. During the 1980s, Hussein had used chemical weapons to put down a rebellion in his own country. In 1990, he had invaded neighboring Kuwait—only to be pushed back by a U.S.-led military effort. In light of such history, many viewed Hussein as an increasing threat to peace and stability in the world. As a result, the Bush Administration led an effort in early 2003 to remove Hussein from power.

The Path to War

One of the main concerns about Saddam Hussein was his possible development of so-called weapons of mass destruction. These are weapons that can kill large numbers of people. They include chemical and biological agents as well as nuclear devices.

Bowing to world pressure, Hussein allowed inspectors from the United Nations to search Iraq for such outlawed weapons. Some investigators, however, insisted that the Iraqis were not fully cooperating with the inspections.

U.S. and British officials soon threatened to use force to disarm Iraq. During his State of the Union address in January 2003, President Bush declared Hussein too great a threat to ignore in an age of increased terrorism. Reminding Americans of the September 11 attacks, Bush stated, "Imagine those 19 hijackers with other weapons and other plans—this time armed by Saddam Hussein. It would take one vial, one canister, one crate slipped into this country to bring a day of horror like none we have ever known. We will do everything in our power to make sure that day never comes."

Operation Iraqi Freedom

In the months that followed, the UN Security Council debated what action to take. Some countries, such as France and Germany, called for letting the inspectors continue searching for weapons. British prime minister Tony Blair, however, accused the Iraqis of "deception and evasion" and insisted inspections would never work.

On March 17, President Bush gave Saddam Hussein and his top aides 48 hours to leave the country or face a military strike. The Iraqi leader refused. On March 19, a coalition led by the United States and Britain launched air strikes in and around the Iraqi capital, Baghdad. The next day, coalition forces marched into Iraq though Kuwait. The invasion of Iraq to remove Saddam Hussein, known as Operation Iraqi Freedom, had begun.

The military operation met with strong opposition from numerous countries. Russian president Vladimir Putin claimed the invasion could "in no way be justified." He and others criticized the policy of attacking a nation to prevent it from future misdeeds. U.S. and British officials, however, argued that they would not wait for Hussein to strike first.

As coalition troops marched north to Baghdad, they met pockets of stiff resistance and engaged in fierce fighting in several southern cities. Meanwhile, coalition forces parachuted into northern Iraq and began moving south toward the capital city. By early April, Baghdad had fallen and the regime of Saddam Hussein had collapsed. After less than four weeks of fighting, the coalition had won the war.

U.S. Army Specialist Shoshana Johnson was one of several Americans held prisoner and eventually released during the war in Iraq.

598

As the regime of Saddam Hussein collapsed, statues of the dictator toppled.

The Struggle Continues

Despite the coalition victory, much work remained in Iraq. The United States installed a civil administrator, retired diplomat L. Paul Bremer, to help oversee the rebuilding of the nation. With the help of Bremer and others, the Iraqis established their own interim government several months after the war. The new governing body went to work creating a constitution and planning democratic elections.

Meanwhile, numerous U.S. troops had to remain behind to help maintain order and battle pockets of fighters loyal to Saddam Hussein. As for the defeated dictator, intelligence officials searched for clues of his whereabouts. The former Iraqi leader disappeared toward the end of the war, and it was unclear whether he had died or escaped.

Finally, the United States and Britain came under increasing fire for failing to find any weapons of mass destruction in the months after the conflict ended. U.S. and British officials insisted that it would be only a matter of time before they found Hussein's deadly arsenal.

Despite the unresolved issues, coalition leaders declared the defeat of Saddam Hussein to be a victory for global security. In a post-war speech to U.S. troops aboard the aircraft carrier *USS Abraham Lincoln*, President Bush urged the world community to keep moving forward in its battle against terrorism. "We do not know the day of final victory, but we have seen the turning of the tide," declared the president. "No act of the terrorists will change our purpose, or weaken our resolve, or alter their fate. Their cause is lost. Free nations will press on to victory."

President George W. Bush and British prime minister Tony Blair stood together throughout the war.

Special Report Assessment

1. Main Ideas

a. What steps did the U.S. government take to make the nation more secure after the attacks on September 11, 2001?

b. Why did the United States take military action against the Taliban in Afghanistan?

c. What was the result of Operation Iraqi Freedom?

2. Critical Thinking

Analyzing Issues Is it important for the U.S. government to respect people's civil rights as it wages a war against terrorism? Why or why not?

THINK ABOUT
- what steps are necessary to protect the nation
- a government that grows too powerful

Special Report Assessment Answers
Answers will vary. Some students may say maintaining civil rights is very important, or else the government may come to resemble a dictatorship; others might say that maintaining civil rights is not as important as keeping society safe from terrorists attacks.

OBJECTIVE
Students will summarize the issues, decisions, and impact of landmark Supreme Court cases, such as *Marbury* v. *Madison*, *McCulloch* v. *Maryland*, *Gibbons* v. *Ogden*, *Dred Scott* v. *Sandford*, *Plessy* v. *Ferguson*, *Schenck* v. *United States*, *Brown* v. *Board of Education of Topeka*, *Reynolds* v. *Sims*, *Regents of the University of California* v. *Bakke*.

MORE ABOUT . . .

Supreme Court Justices
Between 1789 and 2001, there were 16 chief justices and 97 associate justices who served on the Supreme Court. Four men (John Rutledge, Edward D. White, Harlan F. Stone, and William H. Rehnquist) served as associate justices before becoming chief justice, so 109 men and women had served on the bench by 2001. Of those 109 justices, two have been African Americans (Thurgood Marshall and Clarence Thomas). Two have been women (Sandra Day O'Connor and Ruth Bader Ginsburg). One was president before joining the Supreme Court (William H. Taft). The longest serving chief justice was John Marshall, who served from 1801 to 1835. The longest serving justice of all was William O. Douglas, who was an associate justice from 1939 until 1975.

The Supreme Court

The task of the Supreme Court, according to Chief Justice John Marshall, is "to say what the law is." The Court reviews appeals of decisions by lower courts. It judges whether federal laws or government actions violate the Constitution. And it settles conflicts between state and federal laws.

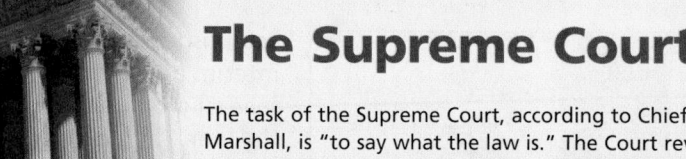

By interpreting the law, the Supreme Court wields great power, for its decisions affect practically every aspect of life in the United States. In the following pages, you'll learn about some of the Supreme Court's landmark cases—decisions that altered the course of history or brought major changes to American life.

"When we have examined . . . the Supreme Court and the [rights] which it exercises, we shall readily admit that a more imposing judicial power was never constituted by any people."

— ALEXIS DE TOCQUEVILLE, *DEMOCRACY IN AMERICA* (1835)

Chief Justice John Marshall established the principle of judicial review.

The development of steamships led to Supreme Court decisions on interstate commerce.

McCulloch v. *Maryland* decided if a state had the power to tax a federal agency.

1803
Marbury* v. *Madison
Judicial Review

1819
McCulloch* v. *Maryland
Powers of Congress and States' Rights

1824
Gibbons* v. *Ogden
State Versus Federal Authority

1857
Dred Scott* v. *Sandford
Citizenship

1896
Plessy* v. *Ferguson
Segregation

RECOMMENDED RESOURCES

BOOKS FOR THE TEACHER
Hall, Kermit L. et al., eds. ***The Oxford Companion to the Supreme Court of the United States.*** New York: Oxford, 1992. Excellent reference work on the Supreme Court and landmark cases.

BOOKS FOR THE STUDENT
Aria, Barbara. ***The Supreme Court.*** New York: Watts, 1994. Basic introduction to the Supreme Court for younger readers.

SOFTWARE
The Supreme Court's Greatest Hits. Evanston, Illinois: Northwestern University Press, 1999. CD-ROM combining abstracts, background information, photographs, and oral arguments and opinions for landmark cases from the last half of the 20th century.

VIDEO
This Honorable Court. Washington, DC: WETA/PBS, 1988. Part 1 is devoted to the Supreme Court's history and landmark cases. Part 2 focuses on how the Court functions and decides cases. Includes a guide.

INTERNET
For more about the Supreme Court, visit . . .
classzone.com

Landmark decisions on school desegregation helped give rise to the civil rights movement.

TABLE OF CONTENTS

BEFORE YOU READ

Think About It Why is there a need for a judicial authority "to say what the law is"? How might the history of the United States have been different if the Supreme Court had not taken on this role?

Find Out About It Use library resources or the Internet to find out what issues the Supreme Court is presently reviewing. How might the Court's decisions on these issues affect you?

For more information on the Supreme Court . . .

RESEARCH LINKS
CLASSZONE.COM

Opinions written by Justice Oliver Wendell Holmes, Jr., helped to set standards for free speech.

The Supreme Court has reviewed several affirmative-action cases in recent years.

1919
Schenck v. *United States*
Freedom of Speech

1954
Brown v. *Board of Education of Topeka*
School Desegregation

1964
Reynolds v. *Sims*
One Person, One Vote

1978
Regents of the University of California v. *Bakke*
Affirmative Action

BEFORE YOU READ

THINK ABOUT IT

Need for judicial authority: Possible Responses Some students may say it is important to have a judicial authority to avoid endless argument and ensure that decisions are made. Others may say confusion will result when no one knows for sure who has ultimate authority.
How U.S. history would be different: Possible Response Congress or the president might have more power than they presently do.

FIND OUT ABOUT IT

Possible Responses Students should find one of two cases recently or currently before the Court. They should offer specific examples of how these cases might affect their lives.

TIME LINE DISCUSSION

Explain to students that the time line shows years when the U.S. Supreme Court decided the cases discussed in this section. These cases are landmarks because they had great influence on life in the United States, including the government, the economy, society, and civil rights. Point out the issues listed with each case, and explain that many, if not all, of these issues are still of great concern, even controversy, in the United States today.

- Ask students which cases focused on state's rights. **Answer** *McCulloch, Gibbons*
- Ask students which of these cases were decided after World War II. **Answer** *Brown, Reynolds, Bakke*
- Ask students to identify the case that immediately followed World War I. **Answer** *Schenck*

OBJECTIVE

Students will describe the basis of Marbury's case, analyze Chief Justice Marshall's opinion, and explain the principle of judicial review.

FOCUS & MOTIVATE

Ask students to review the chart on page 245 and identify which branch of government has the final say on the constitutionality of the actions of the other branches. How important is it for one branch to have ultimate authority in this process?

MORE ABOUT . . .

Types of Jurisdiction

Jurisdiction is the power of a court to try a case and decide it. The court in which a case is first heard is said to have *original jurisdiction,* that is, the power to hear a case before any other court. *Appellate jurisdiction* is the authority of a court to review the decisions of lower courts. Most federal and state courts share the authority to hear certain cases. This shared authority is called *concurrent jurisdiction.*

Marbury v. *Madison* (1803)

THE ISSUE **Judicial Review**

ORIGINS OF THE CASE **In 1801, just before he left office, President John Adams appointed dozens of Federalists as judges. Most of these "midnight justices" took their posts before Thomas Jefferson, Adams's Democratic-Republican successor, took office. Jefferson ordered his secretary of state, James Madison, to block the remaining appointees from taking their posts. One of these appointees, William Marbury, asked the Supreme Court to issue an order forcing Madison to recognize the appointments.**

THE RULING **The Court ruled that the law under which Marbury had asked the Supreme Court to act was unconstitutional.**

LEGAL Sources

U.S. CONSTITUTION/LEGISLATION

Article 3, Section 2 (1789)
"In all cases affecting ambassadors, other public ministers and consuls, and those in which a state shall be party, the Supreme Court shall have original jurisdiction. In all the other cases . . . the Supreme Court shall have appellate jurisdiction."

Judiciary Act, Section 13 (1789)
"The Supreme Court shall . . . have power to issue . . . writs of *mandamus,* in cases warranted by the principles and usages of law."

RELATED CASES

***Fletcher* v. *Peck* (1810)**
For the first time, the Supreme Court ruled a state law unconstitutional.

***Cohens* v. *Virginia* (1821)**
For the first time, the Court overturned a state court decision.

The Legal Arguments

Chief Justice John Marshall wrote the Court's opinion, stating that Marbury had every right to receive his appointment. Further, Marshall noted, the Judiciary Act of 1789 gave Marbury the right to file his claim directly with the Supreme Court. But Marshall questioned whether the Court had the power to act. The answer, he argued, rested on the kinds of cases that could be argued directly in the Supreme Court without first being heard by a lower court.

Article 3 of the Constitution clearly identified those cases that the Court could hear directly. A case like Marbury's was not one of them. The Judiciary Act, therefore, was at odds with the Constitution. Which one should be upheld? Marshall's response was clear:

> **. . . [T]he particular phraseology of the Constitution of the United States confirms and strengthens the principle . . . that a law repugnant to the Constitution is void; and that *courts* . . . are bound by that instrument.**

Since Section 13 of the Judiciary Act violated the Constitution, Marshall concluded, it could not be enforced. The Court, therefore, could not issue the order. With this decision, Marshall appeared to limit the powers of the Supreme Court. In fact, the decision increased the Court's power because it established the principle of judicial review. This holds that the courts—most notably the Supreme Court—have the power to decide if laws are unconstitutional.

William Marbury received his appointment as a reward for his loyal support of John Adams in the 1800 presidential election.

602

ACTIVITY OPTIONS

INDIVIDUAL NEEDS

STUDENTS ACQUIRING ENGLISH/ESL

Learning Common Legal Terms List the following terms on the board: *case, justice, Supreme Court, lower court, ruling, unconstitutional, jurisdiction, act, hear,* and *power.* Have the students add these words to their personal dictionaries. Have students work in pairs to locate these words in the text and write definitions for these words from context or by using a dictionary. Stress that these are legal definitions. Students may add words to the list if they have questions about them. Have the partners create flash cards with a legal term on one side of the card and a simple sentence on the other side that includes that word but leaving a blank where that word should go. Students should test each other with the flash cards periodically.

Why Did It Matter Then?

The principle of judicial review had been set down in earlier state and lower federal court decisions. However, Marshall did not refer to those cases in *Marbury.* Rather, he based his argument on logic.

For a written constitution to have any value, Marshall stated, it is logical that any "legislative act [that is] contrary to the Constitution is not law." Only then could the Constitution be—as Article VI calls it—"the supreme law of the land." Who, then, decides that a law is invalid? Marshall declared that this power rests only with the courts:

> **It is, emphatically, the province and duty of the judicial department to say what the law is. Those who apply the rule to particular cases must of necessity expound and interpret that rule. If [the Constitution and a law] conflict with each other, the courts must decide on the operation of each.**

Not only did the courts have this power, Marshall said, it was "the very essence of judicial duty" for them to exercise it.

Why Does It Matter Now?

Over the years, judicial review has become a cornerstone of American government. The principle plays a vital role in the system of checks and balances that limits the powers of each branch of the federal government. For example, since 1803 the Court has struck down more than 125 acts of Congress as unconstitutional.

The Court has cited *Marbury* more than 250 times to justify its decisions. In *Clinton* v. *Jones* (1997), for example, the Court found that presidents are not protected by the Constitution from lawsuits involving actions in their private lives. The Court supported this finding by pointing to its power "to say what the law is." More recently, in *United States* v. *Morrison* (2000), the Court ruled that Congress went beyond its constitutional bounds by basing a federal law banning violence against women on the Fourteenth Amendment and the Commerce Clause of the Constitution. The opinion pointed out that "ever since *Marbury* this Court has remained the ultimate [explainer] of the constitutional text."

John Marshall, a Federalist, was practically a "midnight justice." John Adams appointed him chief justice in January 1801, just two months before Thomas Jefferson took office.

CONNECT TO HISTORY

1. **Making Decisions** Marshall was a Federalist, and many people expected him to act quickly on Marbury's case. What do you think might have been the consequences if Marshall had found for Marbury?

See Skillbuilder Handbook, page R14.

CONNECT TO TODAY

2. **Researching** Find a recent instance of a law or administrative action that was ruled unconstitutional by the Supreme Court. What were the Court's reasons for the ruling, and what impact did the decision have? Prepare a summary of your findings.

For more information on judicial review . . .

RESEARCH LINKS CLASSZONE.COM

INSTRUCT

- Why did Marbury sue Madison?
- How did the ruling in this case increase the Supreme Court's power?
- How did Chief Justice Marshall logically build his argument?
- What role does judicial review play in the system of checks and balances?

MAKING PERSONAL CONNECTIONS

Have students give examples of a group's rules, codes, and policies that affect them. The group could be a family, school, club, or other organization. Ask them to describe or hypothesize a situation where rules or demands of one group could conflict with another and how a final decision would be made. Does one group's rules always take priority over the rules of the other groups?

CONNECT TO HISTORY

1. **Making Decisions** Possible Responses Some students might say that the Supreme Court would not have the power to strike down unconstitutional laws as it does today. Others might say that judicial review might have been established later in another case.

CONNECT TO TODAY

2. **Researching** Students might use library sources or the Internet to find a recent cases where the Supreme Court found a law or government action unconstitutional. Their summaries should use standard grammar, spelling, sentence structure, and punctuation.

OBJECTIVE

Students will explain the reasoning behind the Court's decision in *McCulloch* v. *Maryland,* and why this case is important today.

FOCUS & MOTIVATE

Have students review Article 6 of the Constitution on page 248 and identify the section that relates to the authority of the U.S. Constitution over state constitutions and laws. Based on this section, have students discuss who has more power, the U.S. Congress or individual states?

MORE ABOUT . . .

The Length of Supreme Court Hearings

The Supreme Court currently has a heavy caseload. Its docket may have up to 7,000 cases per term. When the Court does hear a case, it usually allows no more than an hour to hear arguments, with the time split between the two sides. When the *McCulloch* case was heard, however, there were fewer cases for the Court to handle, and there was more time to hear them. In *McCulloch,* Daniel Webster and William Pinckney argued for the national banks. Luther Martin, Maryland's attorney general, argued on the behalf of his state. Together, the two sides argued for nine days.

McCulloch v. *Maryland* (1819)

THE ISSUES **Balance of power between the federal and state governments**

ORIGINS OF THE CASE **The second Bank of the United States (BUS) was established by an act of Congress in 1816. It set up branches nationwide. But many states objected to the bank's policies and wanted to limit its operations. In fact, Maryland set a tax on the currency issued by the Baltimore branch. The bank could avoid the tax by paying an annual fee of $15,000. However, James McCulloch, the branch cashier, refused to pay either the tax or the fee. The state sued McCulloch, and the Maryland courts ordered him to pay. McCulloch appealed the case to the Supreme Court.**

THE RULING **The Court ruled that Congress had the power to establish a national bank and that the Maryland tax on that bank was unconstitutional.**

The Legal Arguments

The Court first addressed Maryland's argument that the act establishing the BUS was unconstitutional. Chief Justice John Marshall wrote that the Constitution listed the specific powers of Congress. These included collecting taxes, borrowing money, and regulating commerce. In addition, the Elastic Clause gave Congress the authority to make all "necessary and proper" laws needed to exercise those powers. Establishing a bank, he concluded, was necessary for Congress to carry out its powers. The BUS, then, was constitutional.

Next, Marshall addressed whether Maryland had the power to tax the BUS. Marshall acknowledged that the states had the power of taxation. But he said:

> **[T]he constitution and the laws made in pursuance thereof are supreme . . . they control the constitution and laws of the respective states, and cannot be controlled by them.**

So, to give a state the power to tax a federal agency created under the Constitution would turn the Supremacy Clause, Article 6, Section 2, on its head. Further, Marshall observed, "the power to tax involves the power to destroy." If a state could tax one federal agency, it might tax others. This eventually "would defeat all the ends of government." He added that the framers of the Constitution certainly did not intend to make the national government subject to the states:

> **[T]he States have no power, by taxation or otherwise, to retard, impede, burden, or in any manner control, the operations of the constitutional laws enacted by Congress to carry [out its] powers.**

The Maryland tax, therefore, was unconstitutional.

LEGAL *Sources*

U.S. CONSTITUTION/LEGISLATION

Article 1, Section 8 (1789)
"The Congress shall have the power to . . . make all laws which shall be necessary and proper for carrying into execution the [specific powers given to Congress]."

Article 6, Section 2 (1789)
"This Constitution, and the laws of the United States . . . shall be the supreme law of the land; . . . anything in the Constitution or laws of any state to the contrary notwithstanding."

RELATED CASES

***Fletcher* v. *Peck* (1810)**
Noting that the Constitution was the supreme law of the land, the Supreme Court ruled a state law unconstitutional.

***Gibbons* v. *Ogden* (1824)**
The Court ruled that the federal Congress—not the states—had the power to regulate interstate commerce.

ACTIVITY OPTIONS

INTERDISCIPLINARY LINK: ART

***McCULLOCH* EDITORIAL CARTOON**

Class Time 25 minutes

Task Creating an editorial cartoon based on the *McCulloch* case

Purpose To understand and take a position on the major issue of the case

Supplies Needed

- Drawing and writing materials

Activity Have students work in groups to create political cartoons based on the *McCulloch* case. In developing their cartoons, students should focus on the central issue of the case and draw their cartoons to reflect their understanding of the causes and consequences of the case. They should consider whether the Court's decision was a good one or not. If they believe the Court made the wrong decision, they should think about how they could visually show the negative consequences of that decision. If they think the Court made the right decision, they should show the negative consequences that would result if the Court had found for Maryland.

Why Did It Matter Then?

At the time of the *McCulloch* case, there was considerable debate over what powers Congress held. Some people took a very limited view. They suggested that Congress's powers should be restricted to those named in the Constitution. Others pointed out that the Elastic Clause implied that Congress had much broader powers.

The *McCulloch* opinion followed this second view. Marshall wrote:

> **Let the end be [lawful], let it be within the scope of the Constitution, and all means which are appropriate, which are plainly adapted to that end, which are not prohibited, but consist with the letter and spirit of the Constitution, are constitutional.**

In other words, Congress could exercise the powers it considered appropriate to achieve its lawful goals.

Marshall's broad view of congressional power strengthened the federal government. And this stronger government reflected and encouraged the growing nationalist spirit in the early 1800s.

Why Does It Matter Now?

Since Marshall's time, the United States has undergone many changes. Over the course of the 19th and 20th centuries, the country has grown dramatically. The population has increased and moved. In Marshall's day, the United States was predominantly rural. Today, most people live in urban areas, where economic and leisure activities abound.

The economy of the United States, too, has changed. The country has moved from an agricultural economy to one based on industry and, later, service and information.

During this time, the federal government has stretched its powers to meet the needs of the ever-changing American society. Programs like Franklin Roosevelt's New Deal and Lyndon Johnson's Great Society came about through this expanding of powers. Marshall's broad reading of the Elastic Clause in the *McCulloch* opinion, in large part, laid the groundwork for this growth in the size and power of the federal government.

The Bank of the United States had branches throughout the country, including this one in Philadelphia.

CONNECT TO HISTORY

1. **Forming and Supporting Opinions** Chief Justice John Marshall considered the *McCulloch* decision the most important that he made. Why do you think he considered it such an important decision? Give reasons for your answer.

See Skillbuilder Handbook, page R17.

CONNECT TO TODAY

2. **Researching** One issue addressed in *McCulloch* was states' rights and federal authority. Do research to find a recent Supreme Court case that has dealt with this issue. Write a paragraph describing the basis of the case and the Court's decision.

For more information on states' rights and federal authority . . .

RESEARCH LINKS
CLASSZONE.COM

INSTRUCT

- In whose interests did James McCulloch act and why?
- How did Maryland's taxation of the BUS conflict with the Supremacy Clause?
- How did the *McCulloch* ruling reflect the growing nationalist spirit of the times?
- Why would the Elastic Clause be important as the nation grew and changed?

MAKING PERSONAL CONNECTIONS

Ask students to put themselves in the position of James McCulloch. What thoughts do you think he had when he was informed he must pay a tax for the bank? If you were asked to take an action that you feel goes against the rules, how would you handle the situation?

CONNECT TO HISTORY

1. **Forming and Supporting Opinions** Possible **Responses** Some students may say that Marshall knew the Elastic Clause would be necessary for Congress to address issues that would arise as the nation grew and changed. Others might say that it was important for Marshall to defend the supremacy of the federal government.

CONNECT TO TODAY

2. **Researching** Students might use library sources or the Internet to find recent cases where the Supreme Court addressed the issues of states' rights and federal authority. Their paragraphs should use standard grammar, spelling, sentence structure, and punctuation.

OBJECTIVE

Students will discuss the meaning of *commerce* and determine how the *Gibbons* v. *Ogden* ruling established the superiority of federal law over state law regarding interstate commerce.

FOCUS & MOTIVATE

Have students read the legal sources listed on this page. Point out where Article II, Section 8, uses the term *commerce,* and ask the students to define the term. The Coastal Licensing Act, enacted by Congress, refers to *ships, vessels, coasting trade,* and *fisheries.* Ask students what these things have to do with commerce.

MORE ABOUT . . .

A Partnership Gone Sour

Gibbons and Ogden were originally partners in a steamboat company. This was a profitable venture, owing to the lack of bridges over the Hudson and the fact that Ogden held the sole New York rights to operate steamboat ferries between New York and New Jersey.

Gibbons and Ogden, however, had a falling out and fought for control of the company. Armed with a federal permit under the Coastal Licensing Act of 1793, Gibbons split from Ogden and joined forces with capitalist Cornelius Vanderbilt to challenge Ogden's monopoly. After losing their case in the New York state courts, Vanderbilt hired Daniel Webster to argue his appeal in the Supreme Court. Webster was so impressive that Chief Justice Marshall freely borrowed from Webster's argument when writing the opinion of the Court.

Gibbons v. *Ogden* (1824)

THE ISSUE **Federal power to regulate interstate commerce**

ORIGINS OF THE CASE **Aaron Ogden ran steamboats between New York City and New Jersey. The New York state legislature granted him a monopoly—the right to operate this service without any competition. However, Thomas Gibbons ran a competing service. He had a license to sail under the federal Coasting License Act of 1793. Ogden sued Gibbons for violating his monopoly. When the New York state courts found in Ogden's favor, Gibbons appealed to the United States Supreme Court.**

THE RULING **In a unanimous decision, the Court ruled that when state and federal laws on interstate commerce conflict, federal laws are superior.**

LEGAL Sources

U.S. CONSTITUTION/LEGISLATION

Article 1, Section 8 (1789)
"The Congress shall have power to . . . regulate commerce with foreign nations, and among the several states, and with the Indian tribes."

Coasting License Act (1793)
All ships licensed under this act, "and no others, shall be deemed ships or vessels of the United States, entitled to the privileges of ships or vessels employed in the coasting trade or fisheries."

RELATED CASES

***Fletcher* v. *Peck* (1810)**
Citing the Supremacy Clause, the Court ruled that a state law was unconstitutional.

***McCulloch* v. *Maryland* (1819)**
The Court established that states had no authority to tax federal agencies.

The Legal Arguments

Chief Justice John Marshall wrote the Court's unanimous opinion, which found for Gibbons. Since the Constitution gave Congress the power to regulate commerce among the states, Marshall began, it would be useful to decide what the word *commerce* meant. In arguments before the Court, Ogden's lawyers had said that it simply referred to the buying and selling of goods. Marshall disagreed, suggesting that it also included the navigation necessary to move goods from one place to another. He wrote:

> **The word used in the constitution comprehends . . . navigation within its meaning; and a power to regulate navigation is as expressly granted as if that term had been added to the word "commerce."**

Marshall then pointed to the Supremacy Clause of the Constitution. This is Article 6, Section 2, which states, "This Constitution, and the laws of the United States . . . shall be the supreme law of the land."

The New York monopoly law denied Gibbons the right to sail in New York waters. The federal Coasting License Act, however, gave him the right to sail *all* U.S. waters. According to the Supremacy Clause, the Constitution and federal laws were the supreme law of the land. So, Marshall concluded, the Coasting License Act was "the supreme law of the land," and the New York monopoly was void.

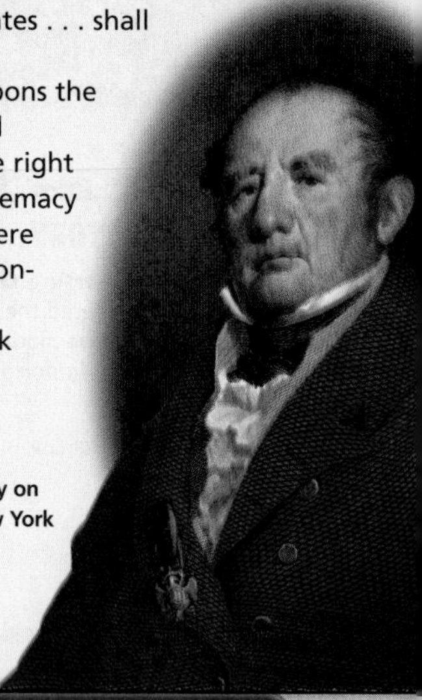

Aaron Ogden obtained a monopoly on steamship operation between New York and New Jersey in 1815.

ACTIVITY OPTIONS

INTERDISCIPLINARY LINK: ECONOMICS

MONOPOLIES

Class Time 30 minutes

Task Playing an uncompetitive card game

Purpose To explain the idea of monopoly and how it relates to the case of *Gibbons* v. *Ogden.*

Supplies Needed

- Deck of cards
- Paper to keep score

Activity Divide the class into groups of five and have each group play a simple card game, such as poker. At the start of each hand, give one player the red aces. This player will have a monopoly on the red aces. Then deal the cards and play the rest of the hand. Have the students record who won each hand. After five hands have been played, add up how many hands each player won and discuss which player benefited from the monopoly. Then give a second player a monopoly on black aces. Play five more hands, recording the winners. Then discuss with students how the new situation affected the competition. Ask them to consider how these card games relate to the situation of Ogden and Gibbons.

Why Did It Matter Then?

At the time of the *Gibbons* case, navigation of the waters around New York was difficult. To encourage companies to provide water transportation, New York granted monopolies to the companies. Some states set up their own. Other states passed laws preventing New York steamboats from entering their waters. Obviously, such a situation was not good for trade among the states. By making it clear that the federal government regulated commerce among the states, the *Gibbons* decision brought order to interstate commerce. And this helped the national economy to grow.

Unlike other decisions of the Marshall Court that strengthened the federal government, *Gibbons* proved popular. Most Americans—even New Yorkers—were opposed to the New York steamboat monopoly. They saw any kind of monopoly as a limit to economic competition. As a result, the *Gibbons* decision was well received throughout the country. One newspaper reported the following incident:

> **Yesterday the Steamboat *United States,* [commanded by] Capt. Bunker, from New Haven, entered New York in triumph, with streamers flying and a large company of passengers [celebrating] the decision of the United States Supreme Court against the New York monopoly. She fired a salute which was loudly returned by [cheers] from the wharves.**

Why Does It Matter Now?

Marshall defined "commerce" very broadly in the *Gibbons* decision. Over the years, Congress has used Marshall's definition to expand its authority over interstate commerce. Today, Congress regulates practically every activity that affects or is connected to commerce.

In 1964, for example, Congress used the Commerce Clause to justify the passage of the Civil Rights Act. This law banned racial discrimination in hotels, restaurants, theaters, and other public places.

The Supreme Court rejected two challenges to the Civil Rights Act—in *Heart of Atlanta Motel, Inc.* v. *United States* (1964) and *Katzenbach* v. *McClung* (1964). In both cases, the Court noted that racial discrimination could harm interstate commerce.

After the first voyage of Robert Fulton's *Clermont* in 1807, it soon became clear that operating steamships could be a profitable business.

CONNECT TO HISTORY

1. **Drawing Conclusions** Many of Chief Justice John Marshall's opinions contributed to the growth of the nationalist spirit in the early 1800s. How do you think the *Gibbons* v. *Ogden* decision might have helped to build national unity?

See Skillbuilder Handbook, page R13.

CONNECT TO TODAY

2. **Researching** Use library resources and the Internet to find recent Supreme Court cases that involved interstate commerce. Write a brief summary of one of these cases, noting whether it expanded or contracted Congress's power to regulate commerce.

For more information on interstate commerce . . .

RESEARCH LINKS CLASSZONE.COM

INSTRUCT

- Why was the definition of the term *commerce* important to this case?
- How did the Marshall Court determine that the federal government should regulate interstate commerce?
- Why did most Americans applaud the ruling in this case?
- How did Congress later associate commerce with the Civil Rights Act?

MAKING PERSONAL CONNECTIONS

Ask students how they buy things. Can they buy things that are made in a different state? What would happen if their ability to buy out-of-state items were restricted because of a shipping monopoly? Do they think that would be fair?

CONNECT TO HISTORY

1. **Drawing Conclusions Possible Response** Orderly interstate commerce would increase the economic links between people of different regions. They could buy and use similar goods. They could also sell their own products throughout the nation, leading to the development of a national economy.

CONNECT TO TODAY

2. **Researching** Students might use library sources or the Internet to find recent cases where the Supreme Court addressed interstate commerce. Their summaries should use standard grammar, spelling, sentence structure, and punctuation.

OBJECTIVE

Students will analyze the ruling in *Dred Scott* v. *Sandford* and identify the context and consequences of the ruling.

FOCUS & MOTIVATE

Have students review the Legal Sources on this page. Point out the term *person* in Article 4, Section 3, of the Constitution and in the Fifth Amendment. Are these two parts of the Constitution in conflict with each other?

MORE ABOUT . . .

The Blow Family

In 1818, Peter Blow moved from Virginia to Alabama, taking his slave Dred Scott with him. At the time, Scott was believed to be "over sixteen years old." In 1830, Blow, along with Scott, moved to St. Louis. Blow died in 1832, and a U.S. Army surgeon named John Emerson bought Scott the following year. Emerson's family owned Scott during the period in which Scott claimed his freedom. Sometime during the 1840s, Scott again came into contact with the sons of Peter Blow. The Blows provided financial help as Scott fought for his freedom. Shortly after Scott lost his case in the Supreme Court in 1857, the Blow family purchased Scott and his family and freed them from slavery.

Dred Scott v. *Sandford* (1857)

THE ISSUE **The definition of citizenship**

ORIGINS OF THE CASE **Dred Scott was an enslaved African American who had lived for a while in Illinois and in the Wisconsin Territory, both of which banned slavery. Scott sued for his freedom, arguing that since he had lived in a free state and a free territory, he was a free man. In 1854, a federal court found against Scott, ruling that he was still a slave. Scott's lawyers appealed to the Supreme Court, which heard arguments in 1856 and delivered its decision the following year.**

THE RULING **The Court ruled that no African American could be a citizen and that Dred Scott was still a slave. The Court also ruled that the Missouri Compromise of 1820 was unconstitutional.**

LEGAL *Sources*

U.S. CONSTITUTION/LEGISLATION

Article 4, Section 3 (1789)
"No person held to service or labor in one state, . . . escaping into another, shall, in consequence of any law or regulation therein, be discharged from such service or labor. . . ."

Fifth Amendment (1791)
"No person shall be . . . deprived of life, liberty, or property, without due process of law."

Missouri Enabling Act (1820)
"[I]n all that territory . . . north of 36° 30' N latitude, . . . slavery . . . shall be . . . forever prohibited." Also known as the Missouri Compromise.

RELATED CASE

***Ableman* v. *Booth* (1858)**
The Court ruled that laws passed in Northern states that prohibited the return of fugitive slaves were unconstitutional.

The Legal Arguments

Chief Justice Roger Taney wrote the majority opinion for the Court. He began by addressing the issue of citizenship. He pointed out that since colonial times African Americans had been looked on as inferior and "had no rights which the white man was bound to respect." Taney added that where African Americans were mentioned in the Constitution, they were referred to as property—slaves. African Americans, whether enslaved or free, he continued:

> **. . . are not included, and were not intended to be included, under the word 'citizens' in the Constitution, and can therefore claim none of the rights and privileges which that instrument provides for and secures to citizens of the United States.**

Since Scott was not a citizen, Taney concluded, he had no right to use the courts to sue for his freedom.

Taney then went further, claiming Scott was still a slave because he had never been free. Congress had gone beyond its power when it passed the Missouri Compromise, he argued. The Constitution guaranteed the right to own property, and slaves were property. By banning slavery from the territories, Congress was, in effect, taking away private property without due process of the law. This action violated the Fifth Amendment. The Missouri Compromise was, Taney charged, "not warranted by the Constitution, and . . . therefore void." As a result, Scott remained a slave, regardless of where he lived.

Two justices disagreed with the majority on both grounds. They pointed to precedents—earlier legal rulings—that indicated that African Americans could, indeed, be citizens. They also argued that the Constitution gave Congress the power to establish rules and regulations for the territories.

ACTIVITY OPTIONS

INTERDISCIPLINARY LINK: GEOGRAPHY

DRED SCOTT'S RESIDENCES

Class Time 30 minutes

Task Creating a map of the places Dred Scott lived

Purpose To use mapping skills to trace movement and show different regions

Supplies Needed

- biographical information on Dred Scott
- maps of the territories of the United States, 1800–1857
- writing and drawing materials

Activity Have students research Scott's biography and draw a map or a series of maps that show the different places that Scott lived. The students' maps should also include information on which territories allowed or prohibited slavery when Scott lived there.

Why Did It Matter Then?

Dred Scott contributed to the growing dispute over slavery that led to the Civil War. White Southerners praised the ruling, seeing it as a spirited defense of their right to own slaves. Many Northerners, however, viewed it with alarm. They feared that if Congress could not ban slavery in the territories, slavery would spread. If this happened, slave states eventually would outnumber free states and would control Congress.

Stephen A. Douglas, a Northern Democrat, disagreed with the Court's finding. He favored leaving the issue of slavery to the voters in each territory. Most Southern Democrats, however, did not agree with him. As a result, the Democratic Party divided along sectional lines in the 1860 presidential election. Northern Democrats supported Douglas, while Southern Democrats backed a proslavery candidate. Because of this split, Abraham Lincoln of the anti-slavery Republican Party won the election. Soon after, many slave states seceded, and the Civil War began.

Why Does It Matter Now?

The issues addressed by *Dred Scott* were resolved by the Thirteenth and Fourteenth amendments to the Constitution. The Thirteenth Amendment, which was ratified in 1865, abolished slavery in the United States. The Fourteenth Amendment, ratified three years later, made it very clear who was a citizen:

> **All persons born or naturalized in the United States, and subject to the jurisdiction thereof, are citizens of the United States and of the state wherein they reside.**

This amendment went on to guarantee all citizens "equal protection of the laws" and the right to due process. These amendments meant the rulings in *Dred Scott* no longer had the force of law.

Today, *Dred Scott* is not used as a precedent. Instead, it is pointed to as an example of how the Supreme Court can make mistakes. In fact, many legal scholars think it is the worst decision the Court has ever handed down.

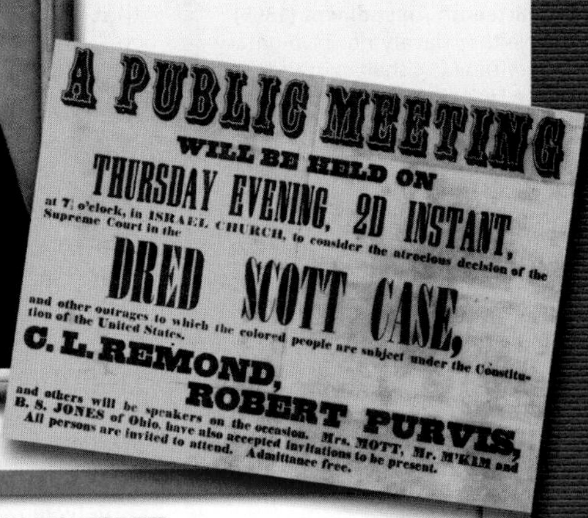

Northern abolitionists held meetings to show their support for Scott (shown here) and their opposition to the Supreme Court decision.

CONNECT TO HISTORY

1. **Forming and Supporting Opinions** The *Dred Scott* decision was just one in a long line of events that led to the Civil War. Write an editorial about the case in which you evaluate its importance in bringing about the war.

See Skillbuilder Handbook, page R17.

CONNECT TO TODAY

2. **Researching** Use library sources and the Internet to research a contemporary Court decision that affects civil rights. Use newspaper indices, periodical guides, and library catalogs, for example, to locate sources of this information. Create a public service brochure to report your findings.

For more information on citizenship . . .

RESEARCH LINKS
CLASSZONE.COM

INSTRUCT

- What was the basis of Scott's argument, and why did the Taney Court disagree?
- What arguments did the two dissenting justices make against the ruling?
- How did Taney justify his position that the Missouri Compromise was unconstitutional?
- How did this ruling affect U.S. politics, including the 1860 presidential election?
- What happened in the 1860s to reverse the *Dred Scott* ruling?

MAKING PERSONAL CONNECTIONS

What does being a U.S. citizen mean to you? Do you know anyone who isn't a citizen? If so, how does this affect him or her? How do you think your life would change if your citizenship were taken away? Is this possible?

CONNECT TO HISTORY

1. **Forming and Supporting Opinions** Editorials should refer to other events that led to the war and take a position on the relative importance of those events. The editorials should also use standard grammar, spelling, sentence structure, and punctuation.

CONNECT TO TODAY

2. **Researching** Students' brochures should include specific references to recent Supreme Court opinions that address civil rights. The brochures should also use standard grammar, spelling, sentence structure, and punctuation.

OBJECTIVE

Students will explain the origins and consequences of *Plessy,* including the "separate but equal" doctrine established by the decision.

FOCUS & MOTIVATE

Have students look at the photograph on the next page and ask them what the sign in the photograph indicates. Then have them read the quotation on this page from the Fourteenth Amendment. Ask them to explain how racial segregation relates to this amendment?

MORE ABOUT . . .

Charles Chesnutt on Segregation

Charles W. Chesnutt (1858–1932) was a Cleveland attorney, a novelist, and an African American. In his 1901 essay, "The White and the Black," he contradicted Justice Henry Brown's opinion that racial inferiority imposed by segregation laws was only a matter of perspective. Chesnutt wrote, "There are separate waiting-rooms at the railway stations. If there is any choice of location the Negro always gets the worst room, and it is seldom so well lighted or clean. . . . In Atlanta the signs read: 'Colored Waiting Room,' 'Waiting Room for Ladies and Gentlemen.' It must be borne in mind that in the South the terms 'gentleman' and 'lady' are reserved, so far as public use of them is concerned, exclusively for white people."

Plessy v. *Ferguson* (1896)

THE ISSUE Segregation

ORIGINS OF THE CASE **By the 1890s, most Southern states had begun to pass laws enforcing segregation—the separation of the races—in public places. One Louisiana law called for "equal but separate accommodations for the white and colored races" on trains. On June 7, 1892, Homer Plessy, who was part African American, took a seat in a train car reserved for whites. When a conductor told him to move, Plessy refused. Plessy was convicted of breaking the "separate car" law. He appealed the case, saying that the law violated his rights under the Thirteenth and Fourteenth amendments.**

THE RULING **The Court ruled that "separate but equal" facilities for blacks and whites did not violate the Constitution.**

LEGAL Sources

U.S. CONSTITUTION/LEGISLATION

Thirteenth Amendment (1865)
"Neither slavery nor involuntary servitude . . . shall exist within the United States, or any place subject to their jurisdiction."

Fourteenth Amendment (1868)
"No state shall make or enforce any law which shall abridge the privileges or immunities of citizens of the United States; nor shall any state deprive any person of life, liberty, or property, without due process of law; nor deny to any person within its jurisdiction the equal protection of the laws."

RELATED CASE

***Cumming* v. *Board of Education of Richmond County* (1899)**
The Court ruled that because education is a local issue, the federal government could not stop school districts from having separate facilities for black and white students.

The Legal Arguments

The Court's opinion, written by Justice Henry Billings Brown, rejected Plessy's appeal. Brown first answered Plessy's claim that the separate car law created a relationship between whites and blacks similar to that which existed under slavery. The Thirteenth Amendment simply ended the ownership of one person by another, Brown wrote. Louisiana's law did not reestablish this system of ownership.

Brown then turned to Plessy's claim that the Fourteenth Amendment was designed to ensure the equality of the races before the law. Brown wrote that the amendment "could not have been intended to abolish distinctions based on color." A law that treated the races differently did not brand one race as inferior. If a law made people feel inferior, it was because they chose to see it that way. Summing up, Brown stated:

> **A [law] which implies merely a legal distinction between the white and colored races . . . has no tendency to destroy the legal equality of the two races.**

Justice John Marshall Harlan strongly disagreed with the majority view. In a bitter dissent, he wrote that the "thin disguise" of separate but equal facilities would fool no one, "nor atone for the wrong this day done."

In his dissent, Justice Harlan stated that "our constitution is color-blind, and neither knows nor tolerates classes among citizens."

ACTIVITY OPTIONS

INTERDISCIPLINARY LINK: LANGUAGE ARTS

WRITING A BIOGRAPHY

Class Time One class period

Task Writing a biography of Homer Plessy, Justice Henry Billings Brown, or Justice John Marshall Harlan

Purpose To analyze the role these people played in the struggle over segregation in the late 19th century.

Supplies Needed
- Research materials, including encyclopedias and the Internet
- Background research on *Plessy* v. *Ferguson*

Activity Have students choose one of these three men and research his life. Using this information, have students write a short biography of that man. Students should try to explain why each man played the role that he did in the case. Students may illustrate their biographies with portraits of their subject or copies of other appropriate illustrations. The biographies should also use standard grammar, spelling, sentence structure, and punctuation.

Why Did It Matter Then?

Plessy was one of several cases in the late 1800s involving the civil rights of African Americans. In these cases, the Court misread the Fourteenth Amendment and let stand state laws that denied African Americans their rights. *Plessy* has come to stand for all of these decisions because it said that "separate but equal" facilities for blacks and whites did not violate the Constitution.

Although the *Plessy* decision dealt only with public transportation, state governments across the South applied it to all areas of life. In time, "Jim Crow" laws forced African Americans to use separate restaurants, hotels, train cars, parks, schools, and hospitals. Signs reading "For Colored Only" and "Whites Only" ruled everyday life in the South for years to come.

Why Does It Matter Now?

After *Plessy,* many African Americans and some whites looked for ways to fight segregation. Some of these people helped to found the National Association for the Advancement of Colored People (NAACP).

Throughout the first half of the 20th century, lawyers working for the NAACP chipped away at segregation laws. Their greatest victory came in 1954, in *Brown* v. *Board of Education of Topeka.* In this decision, the Supreme Court ruled that separate educational facilities were "inherently unequal" and, therefore, unconstitutional. Southern state and local governments had used the *Plessy* decision to build a system of legal segregation. In the same way, civil rights workers used the *Brown* ruling to dismantle it.

After the *Plessy* decision, signs designating separate facilities for whites and African Americans became a common sight throughout the South.

CONNECT TO HISTORY

1. **Drawing Conclusions** Read the section of the Fourteenth Amendment reprinted in the "Legal Sources" section on page 902. Based on that passage, what do you think "equal protection of the laws" means? How does it apply to the *Plessy* case?

See Skillbuilder Handbook, page R13.

CONNECT TO TODAY

2. **Researching** Use library resources and the Internet to find information on Supreme Court cases that dealt with segregation. Present your findings in a three-column chart. Use "Case," "Brief Description of Issues Involved," and "Decision" as column headings.

For more information on segregation and the law . . .

RESEARCH LINKS
CLASSZONE.COM

INSTRUCT

- Why did the Louisiana train conductor ask Homer Plessy to change cars?
- In the context of this case, what does "separate but equal" mean?
- How did Justice Brown interpret *equality* in the Fourteenth Amendment?
- How did the *Plessy* decision uphold Jim Crow laws?
- After *Plessy,* what organization was formed to fight segregation?

MAKING PERSONAL CONNECTIONS

Challenge students to think about situations in their own lives where people are segregated for one reason or another. Have them provide an example where they think segregation is justified—such as different classrooms for students in different grade levels—and an example where it is not justified. Lead a discussion of one or two examples.

CONNECT TO HISTORY

1. **Drawing Conclusions** **Possible Responses** Every U.S. citizen has the same rights and legal protections, regardless of what state they are in. In the *Plessy* case, Justice Brown did not consider separate facilities to be unequal. Thus, he argued they were irrelevant to the equal protection clause.

CONNECT TO TODAY

2. **Researching** Students might use library sources or the Internet to find information about Supreme Court cases that dealt with segregation.

OBJECTIVE

Students will evaluate the decision in *Schenck* v. *United States* and explain some of the complexities of free speech issues.

FOCUS & MOTIVATE

Have students review the First Amendment (page 250). Ask them how important they believe the right to free speech is. Then ask if there are any circumstances in which they feel that people should not be allowed freedom of speech. When might it be important to consider the effects and consequences of a person's speech on the well being of others?

MORE ABOUT . . .

Oliver Wendell Holmes, Jr.

Before serving on the Supreme Court (1902–1922), Boston aristocrat Oliver Wendell Holmes, Jr., attended Harvard Law School. He also fought in the Civil War, which he described as "an organized bore." He did, however, find jurisprudence an intriguing topic. In his landmark book on legal theory, *The Common-Law,* he stated that, "The life of the law has not been logic; it has been experience," meaning that changes in society's attitudes, politics, and prejudices have more affect on determining and interpreting law than does strict reasoning. His "clear and present danger" test is still used in analyzing free speech cases. And, as Holmes would have expected, decisions based on this doctrine have varied according to historical circumstances.

Schenck v. *United States* (1919)

THE ISSUE **Freedom of Speech**

ORIGINS OF THE CASE **In August 1917, Charles Schenck, a Socialist Party official, distributed several thousand antiwar leaflets throughout the city of Philadelphia. The leaflets called the draft a crime and urged people to work for the repeal of the Selective Service Act. Schenck was found guilty of violating the Espionage Act of 1917 and sentenced to prison. He appealed his conviction, arguing that the language in the leaflets was protected by the First Amendment.**

THE RULING **The Court upheld the verdict against Schenck, noting that the leaflets presented "a clear and present danger" to the country during wartime.**

LEGAL Sources

U.S. CONSTITUTION/LEGISLATION

First Amendment (1791)
"Congress shall make no law . . . abridging the freedom of speech, or of the press."

The Espionage Act (1917)
"[Anyone who] shall wilfully obstruct . . . the recruiting or enlistment service of the United States . . . shall be punished by . . . fine . . . or imprisonment . . . or both."

RELATED CASES

***Debs* v. *United States* (1919)**
Upheld the conviction of Socialist Party leader Eugene V. Debs for violating the Espionage Act.

***Frohwerk* v. *United States* (1919)**
Confirmed the guilty verdict against a newspaper publisher for printing articles opposing U. S. involvement in World War I.

***Abrams* v. *United States* (1919)**
Upheld convictions of five people under the Espionage Act. Holmes dissented, arguing that their action did not present "a clear and imminent danger."

The Legal Arguments

Justice Oliver Wendell Holmes, Jr., wrote the Court's unanimous opinion. In ordinary times, Holmes noted, Schenck's claim of First Amendment rights might well be valid. "But the character of every act depends upon the circumstances in which it is done," Holmes added. Schenck distributed the leaflets during wartime, when "many things that might be said in time of peace . . . will not be endured." Holmes suggested that Schenck's "impassioned" appeal for people to oppose the draft was just like someone "falsely shouting fire in a theatre and causing a panic." The First Amendment certainly did not protect such behavior.

Holmes then went on to offer a guide for judging when speech is protected by the First Amendment:

> **The question in every case is whether the words used are used in such circumstances and are of such a nature as to create a clear and present danger that they will bring about the . . . evils that Congress has a right to prevent.**

Schenck's words, Holmes charged, did pose "a clear and present danger" to the United States war effort. Therefore, they did not merit protection under the First Amendment.

Justice Holmes's opinions in the Espionage Act cases set the standard for free speech.

ACTIVITY OPTIONS

INTERDISCIPLINARY LINK: LANGUAGE ARTS

WRITING AN EDITORIAL

Class Time 25 minutes

Task Writing an editorial on the Supreme Court's decision in *Schenck* v. *United States*

Purpose To take a position on the Supreme Court's decision and write an essay explaining that position

Supplies Needed

- Reference material on *Schenck*
- Writing materials or word-processing equipment

Activity Using the Internet and library sources, as well as this textbook, assign students to research *Schenck,* especially Justice Holmes's opinion. Then have them write an editorial that takes a stand on the opinion. When the students are finished, have them read their editorials aloud to the class.

Why Did It Matter Then?

The Supreme Court decisions in *Schenck* and other Espionage Act cases considered the limits of free speech during wartime. In *Schenck,* Justice Holmes stated that speech that presented "a clear and present danger" to the country's well being was not protected. As he looked at other cases, however, Holmes began to refine this view.

In *Frohwerk* v. *United States* (1919), decided just a week after *Schenck,* the Court again upheld a conviction under the Espionage Act. However, Holmes noted that anti-government speech uttered during wartime is not always a crime. "We do not lose our right to condemn either measures or men because the country is at war," he wrote.

Holmes broadened this statement in his dissent to the majority opinion in *Abrams* v. *United States* (1919). The government's power to limit speech during wartime undoubtedly is greater, he noted, "because war opens dangers that do not exist at other times." However, the basic principles of free speech are the same in war as in peace:

> **It is only the present danger of immediate evil or an intent to bring it about that warrants Congress in setting a limit to the expression of opinion.**

All opinions, even ones we find hateful, should be heard, Holmes concluded.

During the Vietnam War, some Americans vigorously challenged government policies.

Why Does It Matter Now?

The Supreme Court has been asked to decide on free speech issues dozens of times since *Schenck.* In making these decisions, the Court has attempted to heed Justice Holmes's words and strike a balance between protecting free speech and maintaining political and social order.

Over the years, the Court has applied this balance test to free speech questions in many settings, including schools. In *Tinker* v. *Des Moines Independent Community School District* (1969), the Court upheld students' right to protest in school. However, the Court added that in certain circumstances school officials might limit the exercise of such rights—if the students' actions disrupt the work of the school, for example.

In two later cases, *Bethel School District No. 403* v. *Fraser* (1986) and *Hazelwood School District* v. *Kuhlmeier* (1988), the Court felt that such circumstances existed. In *Bethel,* the Court upheld the suspension of a student who, during a school assembly, gave a speech that included inappropriate language. The Court ruled that the school could punish behavior that "interferes with the educational process." In *Hazelwood,* the Court ruled that school officials could censor the content of a student newspaper if it was "inconsistent with [the school's] educational mission."

CONNECT TO HISTORY

1. **Making Inferences** The Supreme Court decided *Schenck* and other Espionage Act cases during the Red Scare. Do you think the timing of the cases influenced the Court's decisions? Why or why not?

See Skillbuilder Handbook, page R12.

CONNECT TO TODAY

2. **Researching** Working with a group of two or three other students, identify and research recent court cases involving free speech issues. Present your findings in a brief oral report to the class.

For more information on free speech . . .

RESEARCH LINKS CLASSZONE.COM

INSTRUCT

- Why was Charles Schenck arrested?
- What was Justice Holmes's main argument in the Court's opinion in *Schenck?*
- Why did Justice Holmes disagree with the majority opinion in *Abrams* v. *United States?*
- What criteria did the Court use in deciding the *Tinker, Bethel,* and *Hazelwood* cases?

MAKING PERSONAL CONNECTIONS

Have students review the references to *Tinker, Bethel,* and *Hazelwood* on this page. Ask students to create a list of examples of student expression. Then have them discuss whether any of these examples were inconsistent with or supportive of the school's educational mission or operation. Discuss with them the criteria they would use to categorize acceptable and unacceptable expression.

CONNECT TO HISTORY

1. **Making Inferences Possible Response** The timing was important because the United States had been at war. The Court came to its decision in *Schenck* while national security was a central concern.

CONNECT TO TODAY

2. **Researching** Students' reports should refer to specific free speech cases. The report should be delivered in a logical and coherent fashion.

OBJECTIVE

Students will analyze the *Brown* case and explain its significance for segregation and education in the United States.

FOCUS & MOTIVATE

Ask students to review the quotation on this page from the Fourteenth Amendment. Focus on the words *life, liberty,* and *property.* Ask them which of these concepts was most threatened by segregation. Have them discuss how different interpretations of this amendment might affect school segregation.

MORE ABOUT . . .

Chief Justice Earl Warren
President Dwight Eisenhower appointed Earl Warren as Chief Justice of the Supreme Court in 1953. Warren had been an immensely popular Republican governor, and Eisenhower expected him to act as a moderate conservative judge. However, much to the Eisenhower's disappointment, Warren was more liberal. Warren proved to be an effective leader for the Court. Besides the *Brown* case, he presided over many other landmark decisions during his 16-year tenure. The Warren Court handed down rulings calling for the fair apportionment of state legislative districts *(Reynolds),* and the *Miranda* case, which requires that criminal suspects be informed of their rights before police questioning.

Brown v. *Board of Education of Topeka* (1954)

THE ISSUE **School desegregation**

ORIGINS OF THE CASE **In September 1950, Oliver Brown tried to enroll his seven-year-old daughter, Linda, at the neighborhood grade school. The school principal rejected Brown's request because Linda was an African American. The school was for white students only. Linda ended up attending a school farther away from her home. Brown filed suit against the school board, demanding that Linda be allowed to go to the neighborhood school. The Supreme Court heard arguments in the *Brown* case in 1952 and 1953.**

THE RULING **A unanimous court ruled that segregation in education was unconstitutional.**

LEGAL Sources

U.S. CONSTITUTION/LEGISLATION

Fourteenth Amendment (1868)
"No state shall . . . deprive any person of life, liberty, or property, without due process of law; nor deny to any person within its jurisdiction the equal protection of the laws."

RELATED CASES

***Plessy* v. *Ferguson* (1896)**
Upheld Louisiana laws that segregated railroad passenger cars according to race. Established the doctrine of "separate but equal."

***Brown* v. *Board of Education of Topeka* (May, 1955)**
Ordered that desegregation take place "with all deliberate speed." Often called "*Brown II.*"

The Legal Arguments

Chief Justice Earl Warren wrote the Court's decision. He began by reviewing the history of the Fourteenth Amendment. Its equal protection clause was the basis for the decision. The Court had ruled in *Plessy* v. *Ferguson* (1896) that "separate but equal" facilities for blacks and whites did not violate this amendment. However, Warren pointed out that *Plessy* involved transportation, not education. He then stressed the importance of education for society:

> **It is doubtful that any child may reasonably be expected to succeed in life if he is denied the opportunity of an education.**

Warren went on to suggest that segregation denied African-American children that opportunity. He concluded with *Brown's* most famous statement:

> **. . . [I]n the field of public education the doctrine of "separate but equal" has no place. Separate educational facilities are inherently unequal.**

The Court expected whites in the South, where segregation was dominant, to resist the ruling. Therefore, it delayed orders on how to put the decision into action for several months.

Thurgood Marshall was one of the team of lawyers that represented Oliver Brown. In 1967, Marshall became the first African American appointed as a Supreme Court justice.

ACTIVITY OPTIONS

INTERDISCIPLINARY LINK: SPEECH

CREATING A MOCK NEWS BROADCAST

Class Time One class period

Task Preparing and presenting a news broadcast about the *Brown* case.

Purpose To familiarize students with the people, issues, and actions surrounding this case

Supplies Needed
- Reference materials such as encyclopedias
- Internet access for additional resources
- Video recording equipment

Activity Have students research *Brown* v. *Board of Education of Topeka* to find out about the people involved, the origins of the case, and the case itself. This information will help them produce a script for a news story about the case. Students should cast the roles of significant people to be interviewed, as well as an anchorperson and two or three reporters. Reporters should work with interviewees to create questions and answers explaining their points of view. Other students can participate in man-on-the-street interviews. After the script is written, have the students create a video recording of the story and play it for the class to watch.

Why Did It Matter Then?

The Fourteenth Amendment had guaranteed African Americans equal rights as citizens. In the late 1800s, however, many Southern states passed "Jim Crow" laws, which enforced separation of the races in public places. In 1896, the Supreme Court upheld a "Jim Crow" law in *Plessy* v. *Ferguson.* In the Court's view, "separate but equal" rail cars did not violate the Fourteenth Amendment.

Brown, however, stated that segregated schools denied African Americans the "equal protection of the laws" guaranteed by the Fourteenth Amendment. Segregation, therefore, had no place in school systems.

As the Court expected, the decision met opposition. One Southern politician accused the Court of "a flagrant abuse of judicial power." Even after *Brown II,* many school districts, particularly in the South, dragged their feet on desegregation. Some 10 years later, segregation was still the rule in most Southern school districts. Even so, the impact of the *Brown* decision on American society was immense. It marked the beginning of the civil rights movement, which you read about in Chapter 29.

Why Does It Matter Now?

Throughout the 1960s and 1970s, the Supreme Court continued to review the issue of school segregation. In *Green* v. *New Kent County* (1968), the Court called for the end of the dual school system—one white and one black. This involved integrating not only students, but also teachers, support staff, and services.

In *Swann* v. *Charlotte-Mecklenburg Board of Education* (1971), the Court ruled that busing could be used to achieve school desegregation. Later, in *Milliken* v. *Bradley* (1974), the Court ruled that students might be bused between school districts to achieve this goal. However, this step could be taken only in very exceptional circumstances.

In recent years, the Court has moved away from enforcing desegregation. Still, the *Brown* decision brought about far-reaching changes. The statement that separate facilities are "inherently unequal" proved a powerful weapon against segregation in all areas of American life. Indeed, the Court's opinion in *Brown* provided the basis for most of the civil rights laws passed in the late 1950s and 1960s.

The *Brown* decision was a front-page story in newspapers across the United States.

CONNECT TO HISTORY

1. **Analyzing Points of View** Chief Justice Earl Warren wanted the *Brown* opinion to be unanimous. He even pressured Justice Stanley Reed, a southerner, not to file a dissenting opinion. Why do you think Warren insisted that all the justices agree to the *Brown* decision?

See Skillbuilder Handbook, page R9.

CONNECT TO TODAY

2. **Researching** Working with a group of two or three other students, conduct research to find out about efforts to desegregate another part of American society, such as the military, the workplace, or colleges. Report your findings to the class.

For more information on civil rights today . . .

RESEARCH LINKS CLASSZONE.COM

BROWN V. BOARD OF EDUCATION OF TOPEKA

INSTRUCT

- What led to the case of *Brown* v. *Board of Education of Topeka?*
- What distinction did Chief Justice Warren make between the *Plessy* and *Brown* cases?
- How did opponents to this decision respond, particularly in the South?

MAKING PERSONAL CONNECTIONS

Ask students to think about seven-year-old Linda Brown, whose father attempted to enroll her in a school restricted to whites. Ask students how they would feel if they were in her position. Then ask what challenges and opportunities such a situation might create.

CONNECT TO HISTORY

1. **Analyzing Points of View** The Court's unanimous opinion would send a strong message that school segregation was unquestionably unconstitutional.

CONNECT TO TODAY

2. **Researching** Students' reports should include specific information on the topic chosen and provide references to the sources used.

OBJECTIVE

Students will summarize the ruling in *Reynolds* v. *Sims* and explain the significance of the concept of "one person, one vote" for American democracy.

FOCUS & MOTIVATE

Refer students to the chart on page 611. How many people did Bullock County voters elect to represent them in the state legislature? Compare the population of Bullock County to Mobile County. How many legislators represented Mobile County? Does this seem fair? Explain.

MORE ABOUT . . .

Gerrymandering

When Massachusetts's governor Elbridge Gerry ran for reelection in 1812, his party rearranged district boundaries. Their plan was to establish their party's strength in as many districts as possible and ensure a victory for Gerry. The redrawn district map resembled the silhouette of a salamander. Thus, Gerry's opponents derisively named such a political maneuver a *gerrymander.* Though the term is usually disparaging, the practice is sometimes defended as the best way to achieve fair representation for minorities.

Reynolds v. *Sims* (1964)

THE ISSUE **One Person, One Vote**

ORIGINS OF THE CASE **Most state constitutions require a redrawing of legislative districts every 10 years, based on the latest U.S. Census figures. By the 1960s, however, many states had not redrawn their districts for decades. For example, Alabama's last redrawing—in 1901—did not reflect the great population changes that had taken place. In 1962, a group of Alabama voters sued to have their legislative map redrawn. When a federal court found for the voters, the Alabama state legislature appealed to the Supreme Court.**

THE RULING **The Court firmly established the principle of "one person, one vote." It ruled that Alabama must redraw its legislative districts so that each district had about the same number of people.**

LEGAL Sources

U.S. CONSTITUTION/LEGISLATION

Fourteenth Amendment (1868)
"No state shall . . . deprive any person of life, liberty, or property, without due process of law; nor deny to any person within its jurisdiction the equal protection of the laws."

Alabama Constitution, Article 9, Section 198 (1901)
"The members of the house of representatives shall be apportioned by the legislature among the several counties of the state, according to the number of inhabitants in them, respectively, as ascertained by the decennial census of the United States."

RELATED CASES

***Baker* v. *Carr* (1962)**
Ruled that federal courts could intervene in state legislative districting issues.

***Gray* v. *Sanders* (1963)**
Ruled that when counting votes in primary elections, states should follow the principle of "one person, one vote."

The Legal Arguments

The Court's ruling, written by Chief Justice Earl Warren, clearly stated the issue:

> **The right to vote freely for the candidate of one's choice is of the essence of a democratic society, and any restrictions on that right strike at the heart of representative government.**

Chief Justice Earl Warren considered *Reynolds* v. *Sims* one of the most important opinions he had written.

Weakening the power of an individual's vote, Warren added, was as much a restriction as preventing that individual from voting.

"Legislators represent people, not trees or acres," Warren continued. Population, therefore, had to be the determining factor in redrawing legislative districts. Warren based his argument squarely on the Fourteenth Amendment:

> **We hold that as a basic constitutional standard, the Equal Protection Clause requires that seats in . . . a . . . state legislature must be apportioned on a population basis. . . . [T]he Equal Protection Clause requires that a State make an honest and good faith effort to construct districts . . . as nearly of equal population as is practicable.**

John Marshall Harlan—the grandson of the justice who wrote the famous dissent to *Plessy* v. *Ferguson*—dissented. He claimed that the Constitution did not give the Court the power to interfere in how states decide on their legislative districts.

ACTIVITY OPTIONS

INTERDISCIPLINARY LINK: MATH/GEOGRAPHY

MAPPING MOCK LEGISLATIVE DISTRICTS

Class Time 30 minutes

Task To create a map of legislative districts

Purpose To grasp the relationship between population and the size and shape of voting districts

Supplies Needed

- Census data for your state
- A map of your state
- The number of representatives in your state legislature

Activity Have students divide the population of their state by the number of state representatives in the state. Explain to the students that this number is the number of people each legislator represents. Then take the population of each county and figure out how many representatives it would have based on its population. Have students create a legislative map (by combining or dividing counties) so that every legislator has a district and every district has about the same number of people. Then have the students create a poster-sized version of their map.

Why Did It Matter Then?

Reynolds was one of several voting rights cases that the Court heard in the 1960s. In the first, *Baker* v. *Carr* (1962), the Court broke with past decisions and said that federal courts had the power to make sure that states drew legislative districts fairly. A year later, in *Gray* v. *Sanders* (1963), the Court applied the principle of "one person, one vote" for the first time. The Court observed that the vote of someone living in one part of a state should count as much as that of someone living in another part.

In *Reynolds,* the court extended the "one person, one vote" principle to the drawing of state legislative districts. In time, the *Reynolds* ruling forced most states to draw new district boundaries. As a result, there was a shift in political power in state legislatures. The number of state representatives from cities, which had larger populations, increased. In contrast, the number from rural areas, where fewer people lived, declined.

Why Does It Matter Now?

During the 1990s, the Court faced a new redistricting issue. The Voting Rights Act of 1965 urged states to increase minority representation in the legislatures. To do so, many states created districts where minorities made up a voting majority. However, some white voters challenged these districts under the Fourteenth Amendment.

In several cases—*Bush* v. *Vera* (1996), for example—the Court ruled that such districts were unconstitutional. Since these districts were drawn *solely* based on race, the Court said, they violated the Fourteenth Amendment's equal protection clause. In *Lawyer* v. *Department of Justice* (1997), the Court upheld a Florida district drawn to include several African-American communities. The Court found that in this case, race was only one of several factors used to draw district boundary lines.

After the U.S. Census of 2000, the states began a new round of redistricting. As a result, the Supreme Court probably will revisit this issue over the next few years.

Representation in the Alabama State Legislature, 1962

COUNTY	POPULATION	NUMBER OF HOUSE REPRESENTATIVES
Bullock	13,462	2
Henry	15,286	2
Mobile	314,301	3
Jefferson	634,864	7

Source: *U.S. Supreme Court,* Reynolds v. Sims, *377 U.S. 533 (1964)*

In 1962, the rural counties of Bullock and Henry had less than one-thirtieth of the population of the urban counties of Mobile and Jefferson. Even so, they returned close to half as many state representatives as did the two urban counties.

CONNECT TO HISTORY

1. **Finding Main Ideas** Use library or Internet resources to locate a copy of the majority opinion in *Reynolds* v. *Sims.* Make a chart listing the main idea and details for each part of the opinion. Make a similar chart for Harlan's dissenting opinion in this case.

See Skillbuilder Handbook, page R5.

CONNECT TO TODAY

2. **Researching** Conduct research to find news stories about a recent Supreme Court decision on the issue of redistricting. Write a summary of the background of the case, the ruling the Court made, and the legal reasoning behind that ruling.

For more information on the Supreme Court and redistricting . . .

RESEARCH LINKS
CLASSZONE.COM

REYNOLDS V. SIMS

INSTRUCT

- What is the principle behind "one person, one vote?"
- How was the Equal Protection Clause used to support the *Reynolds* ruling?
- How did the ruling affect the balance of representation between urban and rural areas?
- What made the difference in the rulings in the cases of *Bush* and *Lawyer?*

MAKING PERSONAL CONNECTIONS

Ask students how they would feel if their vote counted less than other people's votes. Would they support reform to make their vote equivalent to other people's votes? What if their vote counted more than other people's votes? Would they support reforms that would decrease the power of their vote so that it would be the same as the votes of other people?

CONNECT TO HISTORY

1. **Finding Main Ideas** Students' charts should accurately identify the main idea of the majority and dissenting opinions. The charts should also give several examples of details that support the main ideas of each opinion.

CONNECT TO TODAY

2. **Researching** Students' summaries should make specific references to the case discussed. The summaries should also use standard grammar, spelling, sentence structure, and punctuation.

OBJECTIVE

Students will analyze the conflict between equal protection and affirmative action in the *Bakke* case.

FOCUS & MOTIVATE

Refer to the photo on page 613. The students in this picture are arguing over a college admissions policy based on race. Have students discuss whether a person's race should be considered as part of admission to a school. Then ask them if it is good for schools to have racially and ethnically diverse student bodies.

MORE ABOUT . . .

Affirmative Action in University Admissions

Much of the focus on the issue of affirmative action and university admissions centers on the admission of racial and ethnic minorities. Scholars William Bowen and James Shulman point out, however, that university admissions offices are more likely to take affirmative action on behalf of the children of alumni and athletes than for minorities. Athletes had a 48 percent "admissions advantage" over other applicants. Children of alumni had a 25 percent advantage. The advantage for minorities was 18 percent.

Regents of the University of California v. *Bakke* (1978)

THE ISSUE **Affirmative action**

ORIGINS OF THE CASE **In 1970, the medical school of the University of California at Davis adopted an "affirmative action" admissions policy. The policy set a quota calling for 16 percent of each year's incoming students to be minority students. Allan Bakke, a white applicant, had better test scores and grades than most of the students accepted under the affirmative-action plan. However, he was not admitted. Bakke sued, arguing that he had been rejected because of his race. The California Supreme Court ordered the school to admit Bakke. The school appealed the case to the U.S. Supreme Court.**

THE RULING **The Court ruled that the school could use race as one of several factors in making admissions decisions but that setting racial quotas was unconstitutional.**

LEGAL Sources

U.S. CONSTITUTION/LEGISLATION

Fourteenth Amendment (1868)
"No state shall . . . deprive any person of life, liberty, or property, without due process of law; nor deny to any person within its jurisdiction the equal protection of the laws."

Civil Rights Act, Title VI (1964)
"No person in the United States shall, on the ground of race, color, or national origin, be excluded from participation in . . . any program or activity receiving Federal financial assistance."

RELATED CASE

***Fullilove* v. *Klutznick* (1980)**
The Court upheld the Public Works Employment Act of 1977, which required that minority-owned businesses receive 10 percent of all federal funds for public works projects.

The Legal Arguments

The Court upheld the California Supreme Court decision in a 5–4 vote. Four of the five majority justices maintained that holding a set number of admission slots for minority students violated the Civil Rights Act of 1964. The fifth justice, Justice Lewis Powell, noted that racial quotas violated the Fourteenth Amendment. Powell wrote:

> **The guarantee of equal protection cannot mean one thing when applied to one individual and something else when applied to a person of another color. If both are not accorded the same protection, then it is not equal.**

However, the Court did not reject affirmative action completely. By a different 5-4 majority, the Court ruled that race could be used as one of several factors in college admissions. Powell, who again provided the deciding vote, thought that race should be considered in order to promote a "diverse student body."

Allan Bakke graduated from the University of California at Davis with a medical degree in 1982.

618

ACTIVITY OPTIONS

INDIVIDUAL NEEDS: GIFTED AND TALENTED

DEBATING AFFIRMATIVE ACTION

Class Time One class period

Task Debating affirmative action

Purpose To gain an understanding of the arguments for and against affirmative action

Supplies Needed

- Reference materials on affirmative action

Activity Divide the class into small groups and have them research the history of affirmative action in the United States. Based on their research, half the groups should develop a case in favor of affirmative action. The other half should develop the case against affirmative action. Choose the two best groups, one pro and one con, to debate the issue, "Resolved: Affirmative action is necessary to increase equality in the United States." Choose one student to be a moderator and another to be a timekeeper.

Why Did It Matter Then?

African Americans made many gains in civil rights during the 1950s and 1960s. President Lyndon Johnson, however, thought more needed to be done. He explained why:

> **You do not take a person who for years has been hobbled by chains and . . . bring him up to the starting line of a race and then say, "you are free to compete with all the others" and still justly believe that you have been completely fair.**

In 1965, Johnson urged companies to increase the hiring and promoting of minorities.

In time, many businesses, colleges, and other organizations set up affirmative-action programs. Not everyone was happy with this development, however. Some whites felt that affirmative action amounted to little more than "reverse discrimination." That is, they felt that they would be denied jobs or college places because of their race.

With the Bakke ruling, the Supreme Court took a compromise position on affirmative-action programs. They were acceptable, the Court said, as long as they did not use strict racial quotas.

The affirmative-action debate, at times, has been quite bitter. Here, supporters and opponents of affirmative action confront each other at a demonstration on the campus of the University of California at Berkeley.

Why Does It Matter Now?

Since *Bakke,* the Court has ruled on several affirmative-action cases. In *Metro Broadcasting* v. *Federal Communications Commission* (1990), for example, the Court upheld a policy that gave preference to minority broadcasters. However, in *Adarand Constructors, Inc.* v. *Peña* (1995), the Court struck down a similar affirmative-action program.

The standing of affirmative action in college admissions is somewhat clearer, however. Some states have abandoned the policy altogether. In California, for example, voters approved a 1996 referendum banning the state's universities from using affirmative action in admissions.

Washington voters passed a similar measure in 1998. These and other states are looking for new ways to help minority students attend college. One method—adopted by California, Florida, and Texas—guarantees admission to state universities for the top students from each high school graduating class.

CONNECT TO HISTORY

1. **Making Inferences** In the *Bakke* case, the Supreme Court issued six separate opinions. Also, the voting on the two issues in the case was 5-4. From this information, what inferences can you draw on the Court's attitudes on affirmative action?

See Skillbuilder Handbook, page R12.

CONNECT TO TODAY

2. **Researching** The state university system of Michigan recently has faced court challenges to its affirmative-action program. Track the progress of these challenges and write a few paragraphs comparing the arguments and court findings in Michigan to those in the *Bakke* case.

For more information on affirmative action . . .

RESEARCH LINKS CLASSZONE.COM

REGENTS OF THE UNIVERSITY OF CALIFORNIA V. BAKKE

INSTRUCT

- What was Bakke's complaint regarding the university's affirmative-action policy?
- How did the Court use the concept of equal protection in the *Bakke* ruling?
- How has affirmative action changed since the *Bakke* ruling?

MAKING PERSONAL CONNECTIONS

Ask students to think about the diversity of a group to which they belong. How can diversity bring strength to that group?

CONNECT TO HISTORY

1. **Making Inferences** **Possible Response** The Supreme Court justices had very little agreement on affirmative action.

CONNECT TO TODAY

2. **Researching** Students' paragraphs should include specific information on the Michigan case and use standard grammar, spelling, sentence structure, and punctuation.

RAND McNALLY

World Atlas

CONTENTS

Complete Legend for Physical and Political Maps

Symbols

Symbol	Meaning
	Lake
	Salt Lake
	Seasonal Lake
	River
\	Waterfall
	Canal
△	Mountain Peak
▲	Highest Mountain Peak

Cities

Symbol	Meaning
■ Los Angeles	City over 1,000,000 population
▣ Calgary	City of 250,000 to 1,000,000 population
• Haifa	City under 250,000 population
⊛ *Paris*	National Capital
★ Vancouver	Secondary Capital (State, Province, or Territory)

Type Styles Used to Name Features

CHINA	Country
O N T A R I O	State, Province, or Territory
PUERTO RICO (U.S.)	Possession
A T L A N T I C O C E A N	Ocean or Sea
A l p s	Physical Feature
Borneo	Island

Boundaries

Symbol	Meaning
	International Boundary
	Secondary Boundary

Land Elevation and Water Depths

Land Elevation

Meters	Feet
3,000 and over	9,840 and over
2,000 - 3,000	6,560 - 9,840
500 - 2,000	1,640 - 6,560
200 - 500	656 - 1,640
0 - 200	0 - 656

Water Depth

Meters	Feet
Less than 200	Less than 656
200 - 2,000	656 - 6,560
Over 2,000	Over 6,560

A1

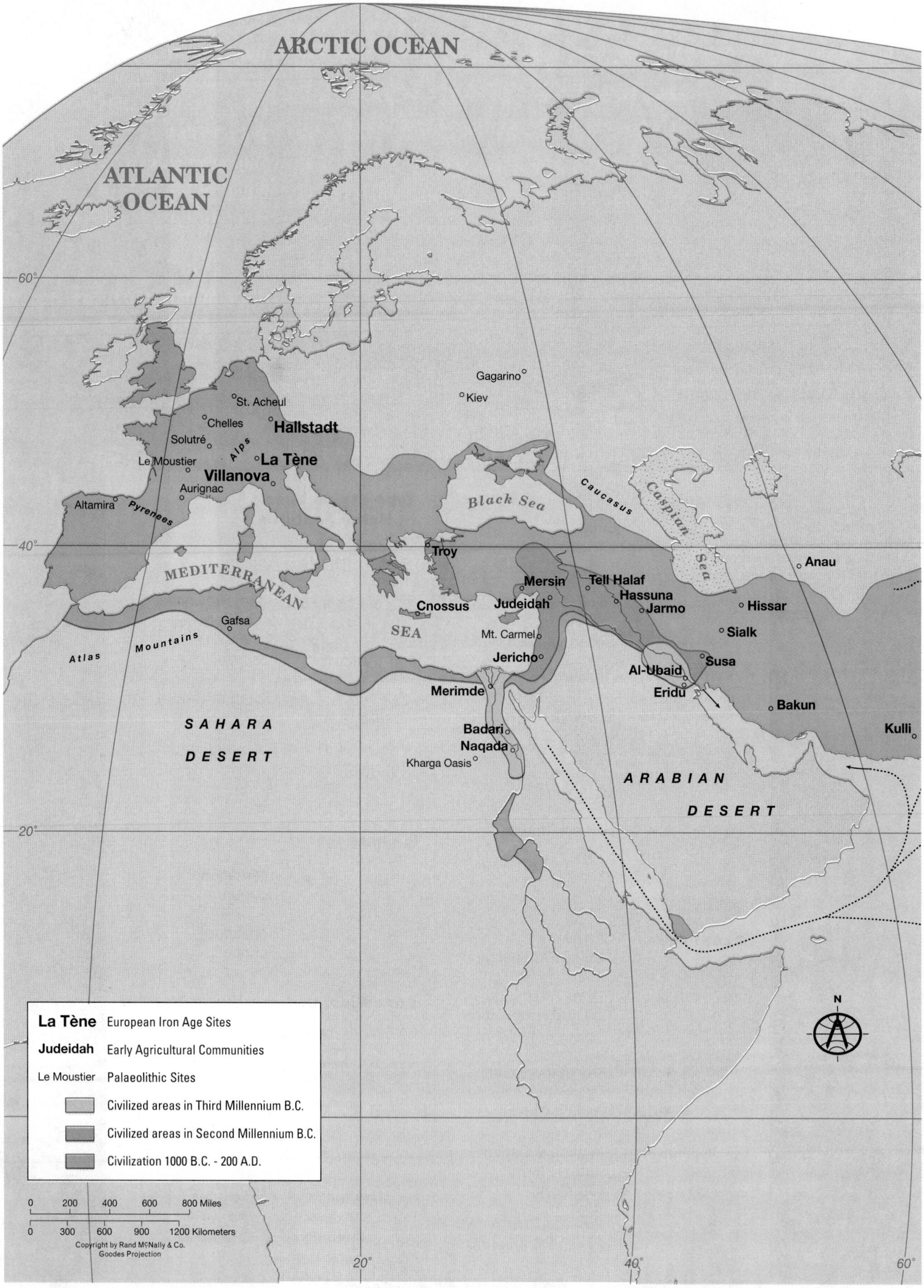
ARCTIC OCEAN
ATLANTIC OCEAN
60°
40°
20°
Gagarino
Kiev
St. Acheul
Chelles
Hallstadt
Solutré
Alps
La Tène
Le Moustier
Villanova
Aurignac
Altamira
Pyrenees
Black Sea
Caucasus
Caspian Sea
Troy
Anau
MEDITERRANEAN SEA
Mersin
Tell Halaf
Hassuna
Jarmo
Hissar
Cnossus
Judeidah
Gafsa
Sialk
Mt. Carmel
Atlas Mountains
Jericho
Susa
Al-Ubaid
Merimde
Eridu
Bakun
SAHARA DESERT
Badari
Kulli
Naqada
Kharga Oasis
ARABIAN DESERT
N
La Tène European Iron Age Sites
Judeidah Early Agricultural Communities
Le Moustier Palaeolithic Sites
Civilized areas in Third Millennium B.C.
Civilized areas in Second Millennium B.C.
Civilization 1000 B.C. - 200 A.D.
0 200 400 600 800 Miles
0 300 600 900 1200 Kilometers
Copyright by Rand McNally & Co.
Goodes Projection
20°
40°
60°

A2

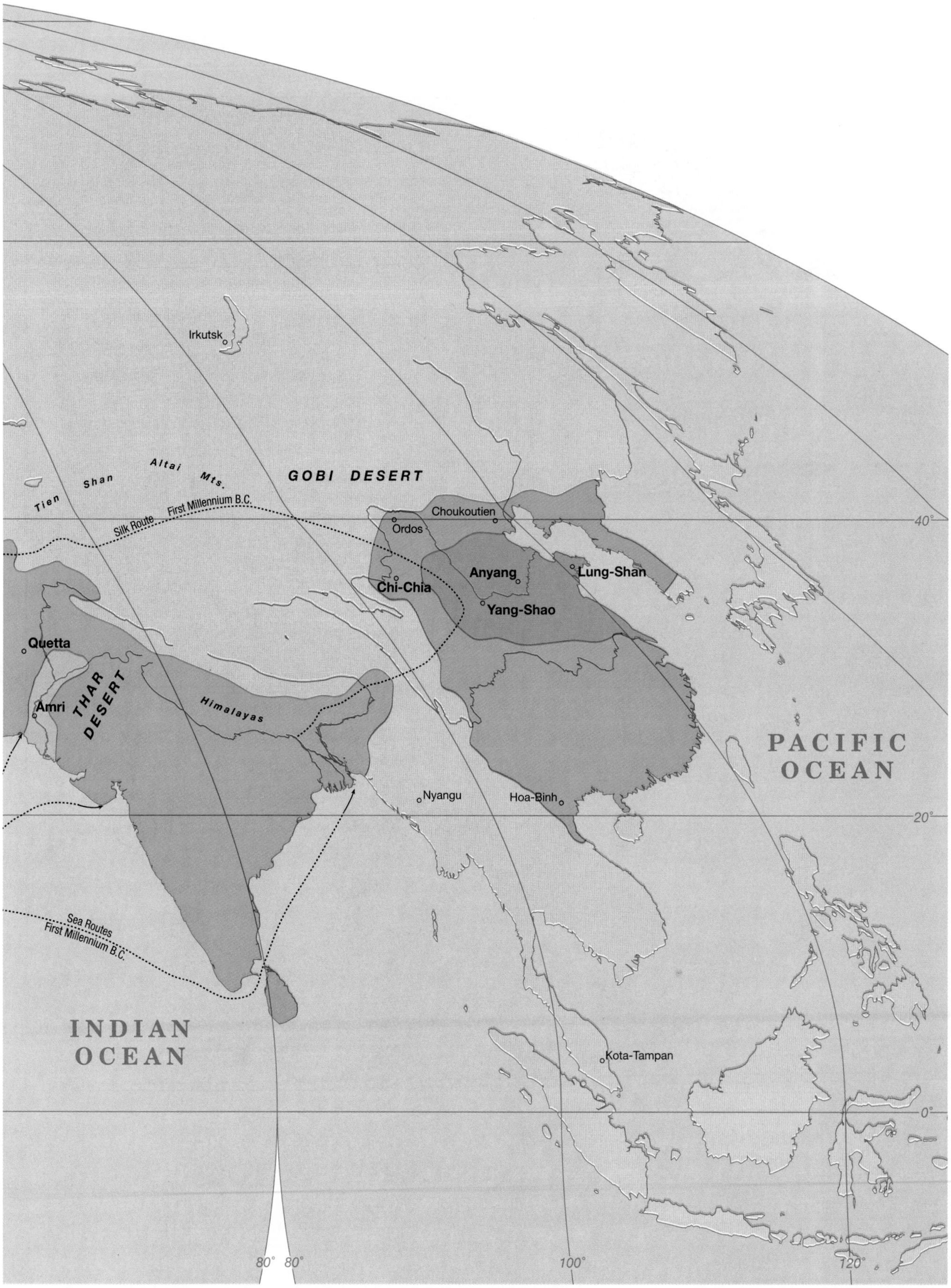
Irkutsk
Tien Shan
Altai Mts.
GOBI DESERT
Silk Route First Millennium B.C.
Choukoutien
Ordos
Anyang
Lung-Shan
Chi-Chia
Yang-Shao
Quetta
THAR DESERT
Amri
Himalayas
PACIFIC OCEAN
Nyangu
Hoa-Binh
Sea Routes First Millennium B.C.
INDIAN OCEAN
Kota-Tampan
40°
20°
0°
80° 80°
100°
120°

A3

ARCTIC OCEAN
GREENLAND (Den.)
Baffin Bay
Arctic Circle
ICELAND
FAROE IS. (Den.)
UNITED KINGDOM
IRELAND
London
FRANCE
PORTUGAL
Madrid
SPAIN
Casablanca
MOROCCO
W. SAHARA
MAURITANIA
MALI
SENEGAL
GAMBIA
GUINEA-BISSAU
GUINEA
SIERRA LEONE
LIBERIA
COTE D'IVOIRE
BURK. FASO
GHANA
Niger
CAPE VERDE
Azores (Port.)
Canary Islands (Sp.)
RUSSIA
ALASKA
Yukon
(U.S.)
Anchorage
Aleutian Islands
CANADA
Hudson Bay
Newfoundland
Vancouver
Missouri
Montréal
Ottawa
Chicago
New York
Washington D.C.
UNITED STATES
Colorado
Mississippi
Los Angeles
Houston
Gulf of Mexico
MEXICO
Mexico City
BAHAMAS
CUBA
HAITI
DOM. REP.
PUERTO RICO (U.S.)
JAMAICA
BELIZE
GUAT.
HOND.
EL SAL.
NIC.
COSTA RICA
PANAMA
Caribbean Sea
Caracas
TRINIDAD AND TOBAGO
VENEZUELA
GUYANA
SURINAME
FRENCH GUIANA
COLOMBIA
ECUADOR
Amazon
BRAZIL
PERU
Lima
BOLIVIA
PARAGUAY
Rio de Janeiro
ARGENTINA
CHILE
Santiago
URUGUAY
Buenos Aires
FALKLAND IS. (U.K.)
South Georgia (U.K.)
South Orkney Is. (U.K.)
South Shetland Is. (U.K.)
Weddell Sea
Antarctic Circle
ATLANTIC
OCEAN
ST. HELENA (U.K.)
N
MIDWAY IS. (U.S.)
Tropic of Cancer
Hawaiian Islands (U.S)
PACIFIC
OCEAN
Equator
KIRIBATI
Galapagos Islands (Ecuador)
SAMOA
AMERICAN SAMOA
COOK ISLANDS (N.Z.)
TONGA
FRENCH POLYNESIA
Tropic of Capricorn
Easter Island (Chile)
0 1000 2000 Miles
0 1000 2000 3000 Kilometers
Copyright by Rand McNally & Co.
Robinson Projection
180° 165° 150° 135° 120° 105° 90° 75° 60° 45° 30° 15°
75° 60° 45° 30° 15° 0° 15° 30° 45° 60° 75°

A4

⊛	National Capital
•	Major Cities

RAND McNALLY

A5

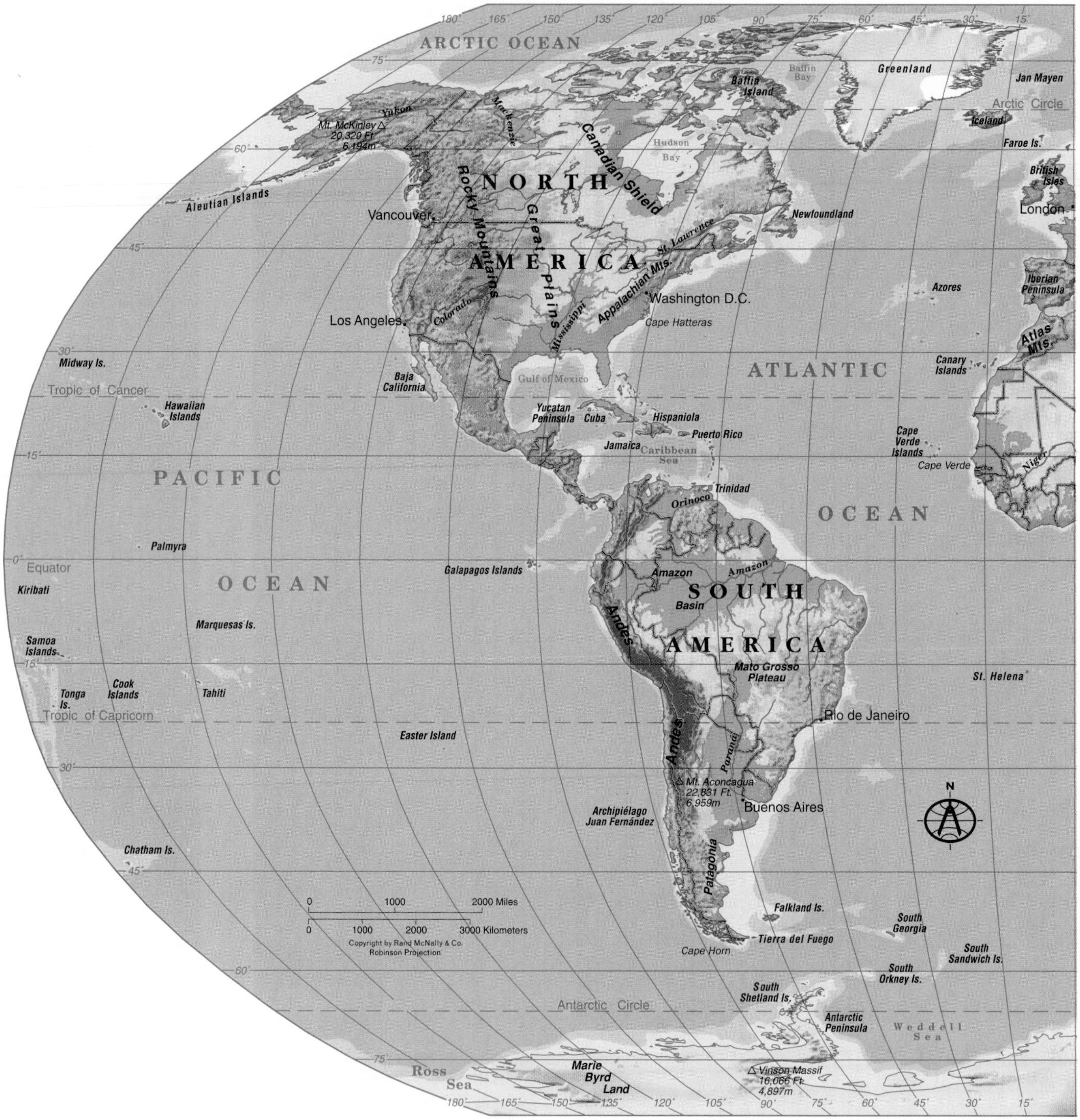
ARCTIC OCEAN
Baffin Island
Baffin Bay
Greenland
Jan Mayen
Arctic Circle
Iceland
Faroe Is.
British Isles
London
Yukon
Mackenzie
Mt. McKinley △ 20,320 Ft. 6,194m
Canadian Shield
Hudson Bay
NORTH AMERICA
Rocky Mountains
Great Plains
Aleutian Islands
Vancouver
Newfoundland
St. Lawrence
Appalachian Mts.
Mississippi
Colorado
Washington D.C.
Cape Hatteras
Los Angeles
Azores
Iberian Peninsula
Atlas Mts.
Midway Is.
Tropic of Cancer
Baja California
Gulf of Mexico
ATLANTIC
Canary Islands
Hawaiian Islands
Yucatan Peninsula
Cuba
Hispaniola
Puerto Rico
Jamaica
Caribbean Sea
Cape Verde Islands
Cape Verde
Niger
PACIFIC
Trinidad
Orinoco
OCEAN
Palmyra
Equator
Galapagos Islands
OCEAN
Kiribati
Amazon
Amazon Basin
SOUTH AMERICA
Andes
Marquesas Is.
Samoa Islands
Mato Grosso Plateau
St. Helena
Tonga Is.
Cook Islands
Tahiti
Tropic of Capricorn
Rio de Janeiro
Easter Island
Paraná
△ Mt. Aconcagua 22,831 Ft. 6,959m
Buenos Aires
Archipiélago Juan Fernández
Chatham Is.
Patagonia
N
0 1000 2000 Miles
0 1000 2000 3000 Kilometers
Copyright by Rand McNally & Co.
Robinson Projection
Falkland Is.
South Georgia
Tierra del Fuego
Cape Horn
South Sandwich Is.
South Orkney Is.
South Shetland Is.
Antarctic Circle
Antarctic Peninsula
Weddell Sea
Ross Sea
Marie Byrd Land
△ Vinson Massif 16,066 Ft. 4,897m
180° 165° 150° 135° 120° 105° 90° 75° 60° 45° 30° 15°
75° 60° 45° 30° 15° 0° 15° 30° 45° 60° 75°

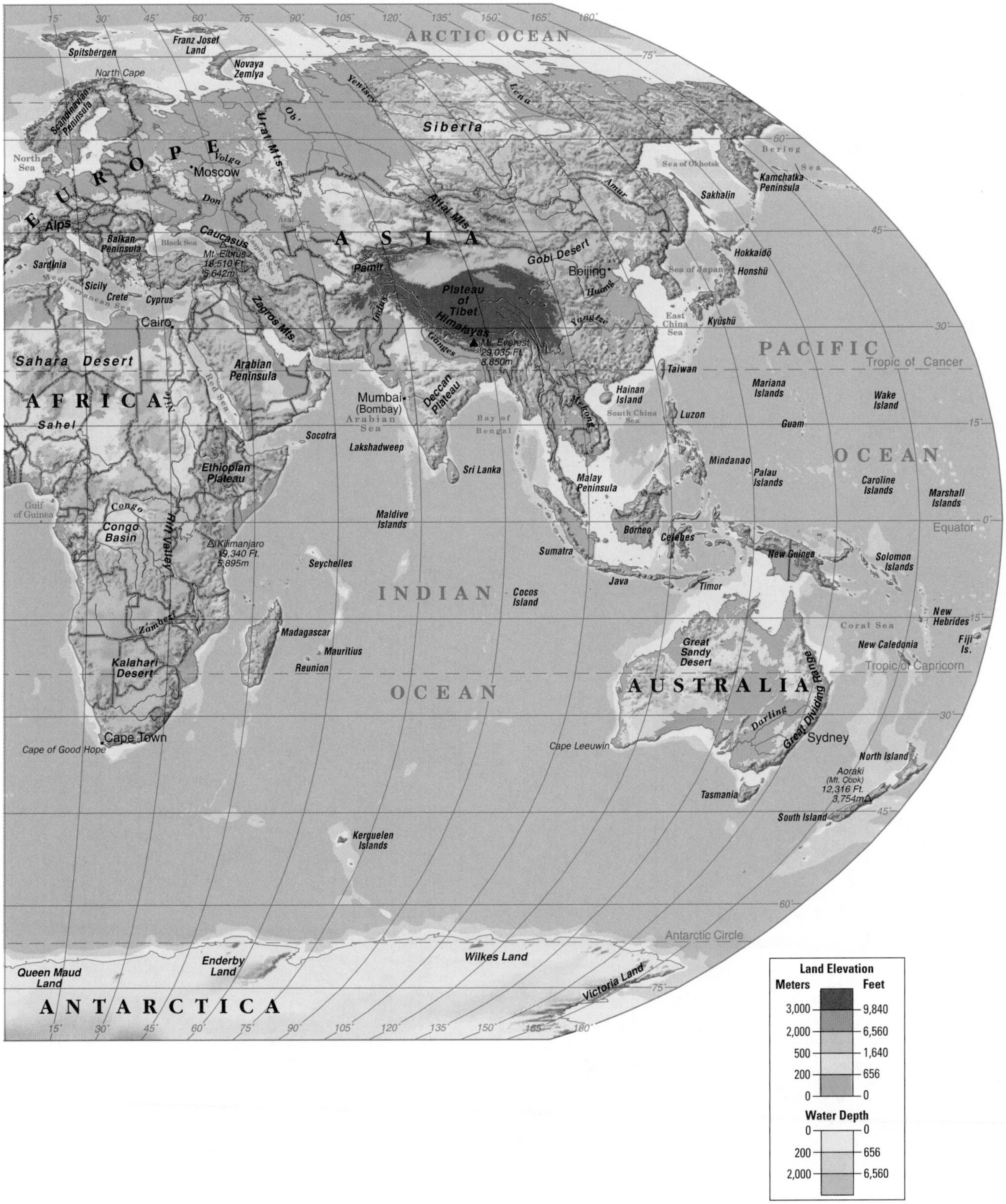
ARCTIC OCEAN
Spitsbergen
Franz Josef Land
North Cape
Novaya Zemlya
Scandinavian Peninsula
North Sea
EUROPE
Moscow
Volga
Ural Mts.
Ob'
Yenisey
Lena
Siberia
Bering Sea
Sea of Okhotsk
Kamchatka Peninsula
Sakhalin
Amur
Don
Alps
Altai Mts.
ASIA
Balkan Peninsula
Black Sea
Caucasus
Mt. Elbrus 18,510 Ft. 5,642m
Aral Sea
Caspian Sea
Sardinia
Sicily
Crete
Cyprus
Mediterranean Sea
Pamir
Gobi Desert
Beijing
Huang
Hokkaidō
Honshū
Sea of Japan
Kyūshū
East China Sea
Plateau of Tibet
Himalayas
Mt. Everest 29,035 Ft. 8,850m
Indus
Ganges
Yangtze
Zagros Mts.
Cairo
Sahara Desert
Arabian Peninsula
Red Sea
Nile
AFRICA
Sahel
Mumbai (Bombay)
Deccan Plateau
Arabian Sea
Bay of Bengal
PACIFIC
Tropic of Cancer
Taiwan
Hainan Island
South China Sea
Mekong
Luzon
Mariana Islands
Wake Island
Guam
Socotra
Lakshadweep
Sri Lanka
Ethiopian Plateau
Mindanao
Palau Islands
OCEAN
Caroline Islands
Marshall Islands
Malay Peninsula
Gulf of Guinea
Congo
Congo Basin
Rift Valley
Maldive Islands
Borneo
Celebes
Equator
Kilimanjaro 19,340 Ft. 5,895m
Seychelles
Sumatra
New Guinea
Solomon Islands
Java
Timor
INDIAN
Cocos Island
Zambezi
Madagascar
Mauritius
Reunion
Coral Sea
New Hebrides
Great Sandy Desert
New Caledonia
Fiji Is.
Kalahari Desert
Tropic of Capricorn
OCEAN
AUSTRALIA
Great Dividing Range
Darling
Cape Town
Cape of Good Hope
Cape Leeuwin
Sydney
North Island
Aoraki (Mt. Cook) 12,316 Ft. 3,754m
Tasmania
South Island
Kerguelen Islands
Antarctic Circle
Queen Maud Land
Enderby Land
Wilkes Land
Victoria Land
ANTARCTICA
15° 30° 45° 60° 75° 90° 105° 120° 135° 150° 165° 180°
75° 60° 45° 30° 15° 0° 15° 30° 45° 60° 75°
Land Elevation
Meters Feet
3,000 9,840
2,000 6,560
500 1,640
200 656
0 0
Water Depth
0 0
200 656
2,000 6,560

A7

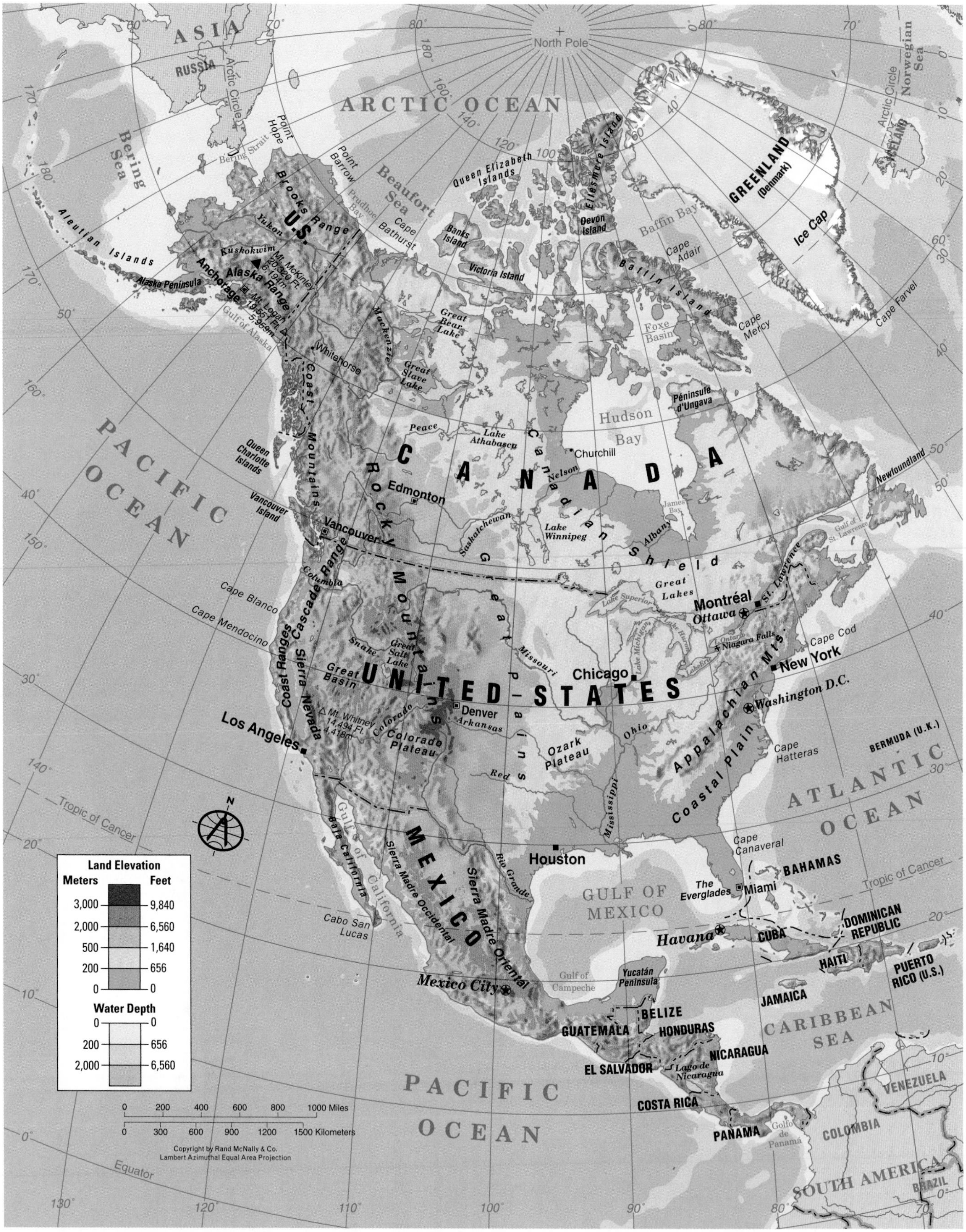
ASIA
RUSSIA
Arctic Circle
North Pole
ARCTIC OCEAN
Bering Sea
Bering Strait
Point Hope
Point Barrow
Beaufort Sea
Prudhoe Bay
Cape Bathurst
Queen Elizabeth Islands
Ellesmere Island
Devon Island
Banks Island
Victoria Island
Baffin Bay
Cape Adair
Baffin Island
GREENLAND (Denmark)
Ice Cap
Norwegian Sea
ICELAND
Cape Farvel
Cape Mercy
Foxe Basin
Aleutian Islands
Alaska Peninsula
Brooks Range
U.S.
Yukon
Kuskokwim
Mt. McKinley 20,320 Ft. 6,194m
Alaska Range
Anchorage
Mt. Logan 19,551 Ft. 5,959m
Gulf of Alaska
Whitehorse
Mackenzie
Great Bear Lake
Great Slave Lake
Péninsule d'Ungava
Hudson Bay
Churchill
Peace
Lake Athabasca
CANADA
Nelson
Canadian Shield
James Bay
Newfoundland
Gulf of St. Lawrence
Queen Charlotte Islands
Coast Mountains
Rocky Mountains
Edmonton
Saskatchewan
Lake Winnipeg
Albany
PACIFIC OCEAN
Vancouver Island
Vancouver
Cascade Range
Columbia
Great Plains
Great Lakes
Lake Superior
Montréal
Ottawa
St. Lawrence
Cape Blanco
Cape Mendocino
Snake
Great Salt Lake
Missouri
Lake Michigan
Lake Huron
Lake Ontario
Lake Erie
Niagara Falls
Cape Cod
New York
Chicago
Great Basin
UNITED STATES
Coast Ranges
Sierra Nevada
Mt. Whitney 14,494 Ft. 4,418m
Colorado
Colorado Plateau
Denver
Arkansas
Ohio
Washington D.C.
Appalachian Mts.
Los Angeles
Ozark Plateau
Red
Mississippi
Coastal Plain
Cape Hatteras
BERMUDA (U.K.)
ATLANTIC OCEAN
Tropic of Cancer
Gulf of California
Baja California
Sierra Madre Occidental
MEXICO
Rio Grande
Sierra Madre Oriental
Houston
Cape Canaveral
BAHAMAS
The Everglades
Miami
GULF OF MEXICO
Cabo San Lucas
Havana
CUBA
DOMINICAN REPUBLIC
HAITI
PUERTO RICO (U.S.)
Gulf of Campeche
Yucatán Peninsula
Mexico City
JAMAICA
BELIZE
GUATEMALA
HONDURAS
CARIBBEAN SEA
NICARAGUA
Lago de Nicaragua
EL SALVADOR
COSTA RICA
PANAMA
Golfo de Panamá
VENEZUELA
COLOMBIA
SOUTH AMERICA
BRAZIL
Equator
Land Elevation
Meters
Feet
3,000
9,840
2,000
6,560
500
1,640
200
656
0
0
Water Depth
0
0
200
656
2,000
6,560
0 200 400 600 800 1000 Miles
0 300 600 900 1200 1500 Kilometers
Copyright by Rand McNally & Co.
Lambert Azimuthal Equal Area Projection

A8

GULF OF MEXICO
NORTH AMERICA
CUBA
Greater Antilles
HAITI
DOMINICAN REPUBLIC
JAMAICA
PUERTO RICO (U.S.)
Lesser Antilles
MEXICO
BELIZE
Gulf of Honduras
HONDURAS
GUATEMALA
CARIBBEAN SEA
EL SALVADOR
NICARAGUA
COSTA RICA
PANAMA
Gulf of Panama
ATLANTIC OCEAN
Cristóbal Colón Peak 18,948 Ft. 5,775m
Caracas
TRINIDAD AND TOBAGO
Orinoco
Llanos
VENEZUELA
Magdalena
Bogotá
COLOMBIA
GUYANA
SURINAME
FRENCH GUIANA
Cape Orange
Galapagos Islands (Ec.)
ECUADOR
Chimborazo 20,703 Ft. 6,310m
Putumayo
Japurá
Negro
Manaus
Amazon
Ilha de Marajó
Belém
Equator
Amazon Basin
Juruá
Madeira
Tapajós
Tocantins
Selvas
BRAZIL
Ucayali
Andes
PERU
Recife
Mt. Huascarán 22,133 Ft. 6,746m
Lima
Mato Grosso Plateau
Mt. Illampu 21,066 Ft. 6,421m
Lake Titicaca
BOLIVIA
Cordillera Oriental
Brasília
São Francisco
Serra do Espinhaço
Mt. Sajama 21,463 Ft. 6,542m
Gran Chaco
Paraná
PARAGUAY
São Paulo
Rio de Janeiro
Atacama Desert
Tropic of Capricorn
Isla San Ambrosio (Chile)
Mt. Ojos del Salado 22,615 Ft. 6,893m
Isla San Felix (Chile)
ARGENTINA
PACIFIC OCEAN
Archipiélago Juan Fernández (Chile)
URUGUAY
Mt. Aconcagua 22,831 Ft. 6,959m
Santiago
Buenos Aires
Río de la Plata
Pampas
CHILE
N
Land Elevation
Meters Feet
3,000 9,840
2,000 6,560
500 1,640
200 656
0 0
Water Depth
0 0
200 656
2,000 6,560
San Matías Gulf
Península Valdés
Chiloé
Patagonia
ATLANTIC OCEAN
San Jorge Gulf
Point Medanoso
Grand Bay
FALKLAND ISLANDS (U.K.)
West Falkland
East Falkland
Strait of Magellan
Tierra del Fuego
Cape Horn
South Georgia (U.K.)
0 200 400 600 800 1000 Miles
0 300 600 900 1200 1500 Kilometers
Copyright by Rand McNally & Co.
Lambert Azimuthal Equal Area Projection
Drake Passage
South Shetland Islands (U.K.)
South Orkney Islands (U.K.)
South Sandwich Islands (U.K.)

A9

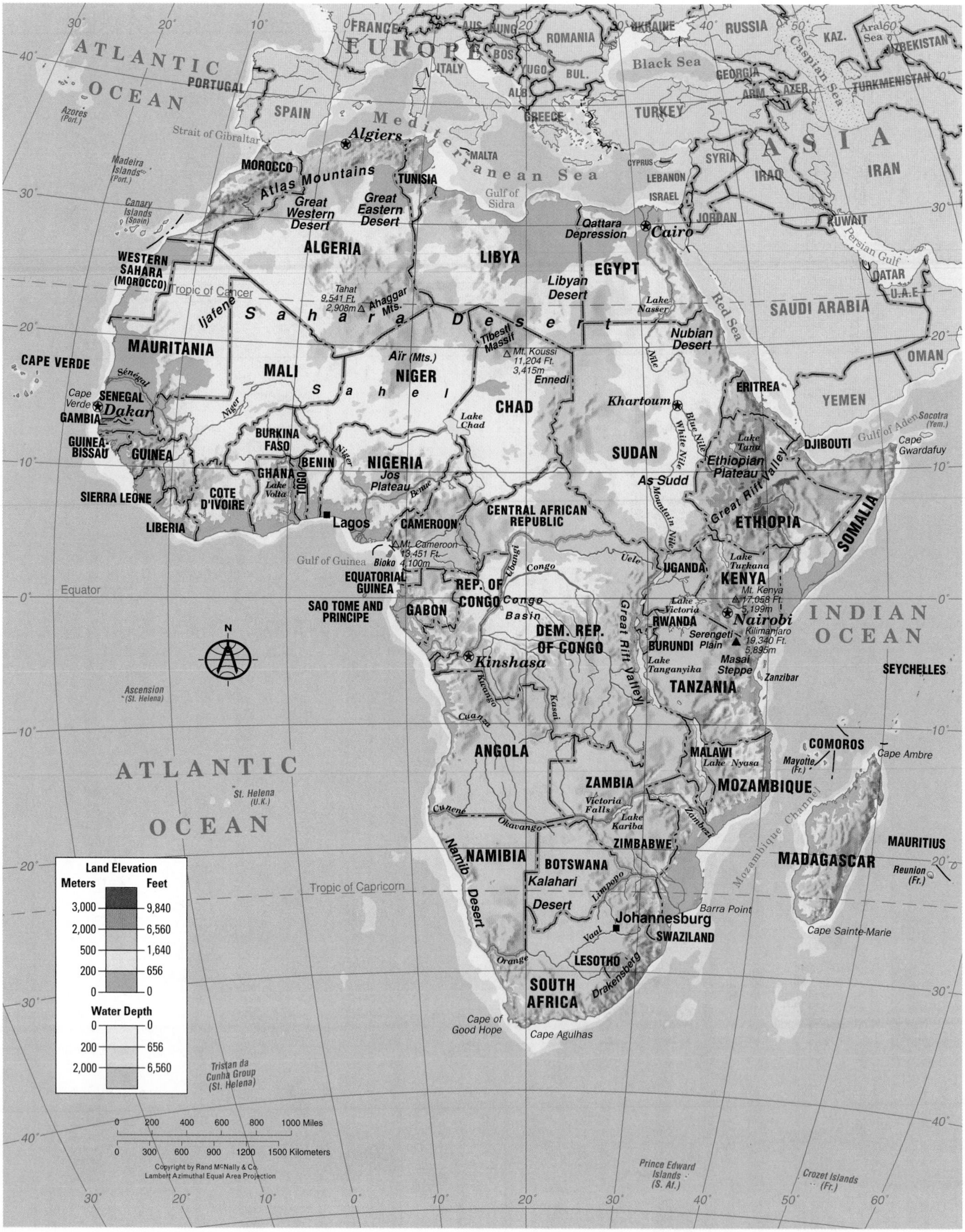
ATLANTIC OCEAN
EUROPE
FRANCE
AUS.
HUNG.
ROMANIA
UKRAINE
RUSSIA
KAZ.
Aral Sea
UZBEKISTAN
PORTUGAL
SPAIN
ITALY
BOS.
YUGO.
BUL.
Black Sea
GEORGIA
Caspian Sea
TURKMENISTAN
ARM.
AZER.
ALB.
GREECE
TURKEY
Azores (Port.)
Strait of Gibraltar
Algiers
Mediterranean Sea
MALTA
CYPRUS
SYRIA
ASIA
IRAN
IRAQ
LEBANON
ISRAEL
JORDAN
KUWAIT
Persian Gulf
QATAR
U.A.E.
Madeira Islands (Port.)
MOROCCO
Atlas Mountains
TUNISIA
Gulf of Sidra
Canary Islands (Spain)
Great Western Desert
Great Eastern Desert
Qattara Depression
Cairo
WESTERN SAHARA (MOROCCO)
ALGERIA
LIBYA
EGYPT
Tropic of Cancer
Tahat 9,541 Ft. 2,908m
Ahaggar Mts.
Libyan Desert
Lake Nasser
Red Sea
SAUDI ARABIA
Ijafene
Sahara Desert
Tibesti Massif
Mt. Koussi 11,204 Ft. 3,415m
Nubian Desert
OMAN
MAURITANIA
CAPE VERDE
Sénégal
Aïr (Mts.)
MALI
NIGER
Ennedi
Nile
ERITREA
YEMEN
Cape Verde
SENEGAL
Dakar
GAMBIA
Sahel
Lake Chad
CHAD
Khartoum
Blue Nile
White Nile
Gulf of Aden
Socotra (Yem.)
Cape Gwardafuy
GUINEA-BISSAU
GUINEA
BURKINA FASO
Niger
BENIN
NIGERIA
SUDAN
Lake Tana
DJIBOUTI
Ethiopian Plateau
SIERRA LEONE
GHANA
Lake Volta
TOGO
COTE D'IVOIRE
Jos Plateau
Benue
As Sudd
Great Rift Valley
LIBERIA
Lagos
CAMEROON
CENTRAL AFRICAN REPUBLIC
Mountain Nile
ETHIOPIA
SOMALIA
Mt. Cameroon 13,451 Ft. 4,100m
Gulf of Guinea
Bioko
Ubangi
Uele
UGANDA
Lake Turkana
KENYA
EQUATORIAL GUINEA
Congo
Equator
REP. OF CONGO
Congo Basin
Lake Victoria
Mt. Kenya 17,058 Ft. 5,199m
INDIAN OCEAN
SAO TOME AND PRINCIPE
GABON
DEM. REP. OF CONGO
RWANDA
Nairobi
Great Rift Valley
Kilimanjaro 19,340 Ft. 5,895m
Serengeti Plain
BURUNDI
Kinshasa
Lake Tanganyika
Masai Steppe
Zanzibar
SEYCHELLES
Ascension (St. Helena)
TANZANIA
Kwango
Kasai
Cuanza
COMOROS
Cape Ambre
MALAWI
Lake Nyasa
Mayotte (Fr.)
ANGOLA
ATLANTIC OCEAN
ZAMBIA
MOZAMBIQUE
St. Helena (U.K.)
Victoria Falls
Lake Kariba
Cunene
Okavango
Zambezi
Mozambique Channel
ZIMBABWE
MAURITIUS
NAMIBIA
BOTSWANA
MADAGASCAR
Reunion (Fr.)
Namib Desert
Kalahari Desert
Limpopo
Tropic of Capricorn
Barra Point
Johannesburg
Vaal
SWAZILAND
Cape Sainte-Marie
Orange
LESOTHO
Drakensberg
SOUTH AFRICA
Cape of Good Hope
Cape Agulhas
Tristan da Cunha Group (St. Helena)
Land Elevation
Meters
Feet
3,000
9,840
2,000
6,560
500
1,640
200
656
0
0
Water Depth
0
0
200
656
2,000
6,560
0 200 400 600 800 1000 Miles
0 300 600 900 1200 1500 Kilometers
Copyright by Rand McNally & Co.
Lambert Azimuthal Equal Area Projection
Prince Edward Islands (S. Af.)
Crozet Islands (Fr.)

A10

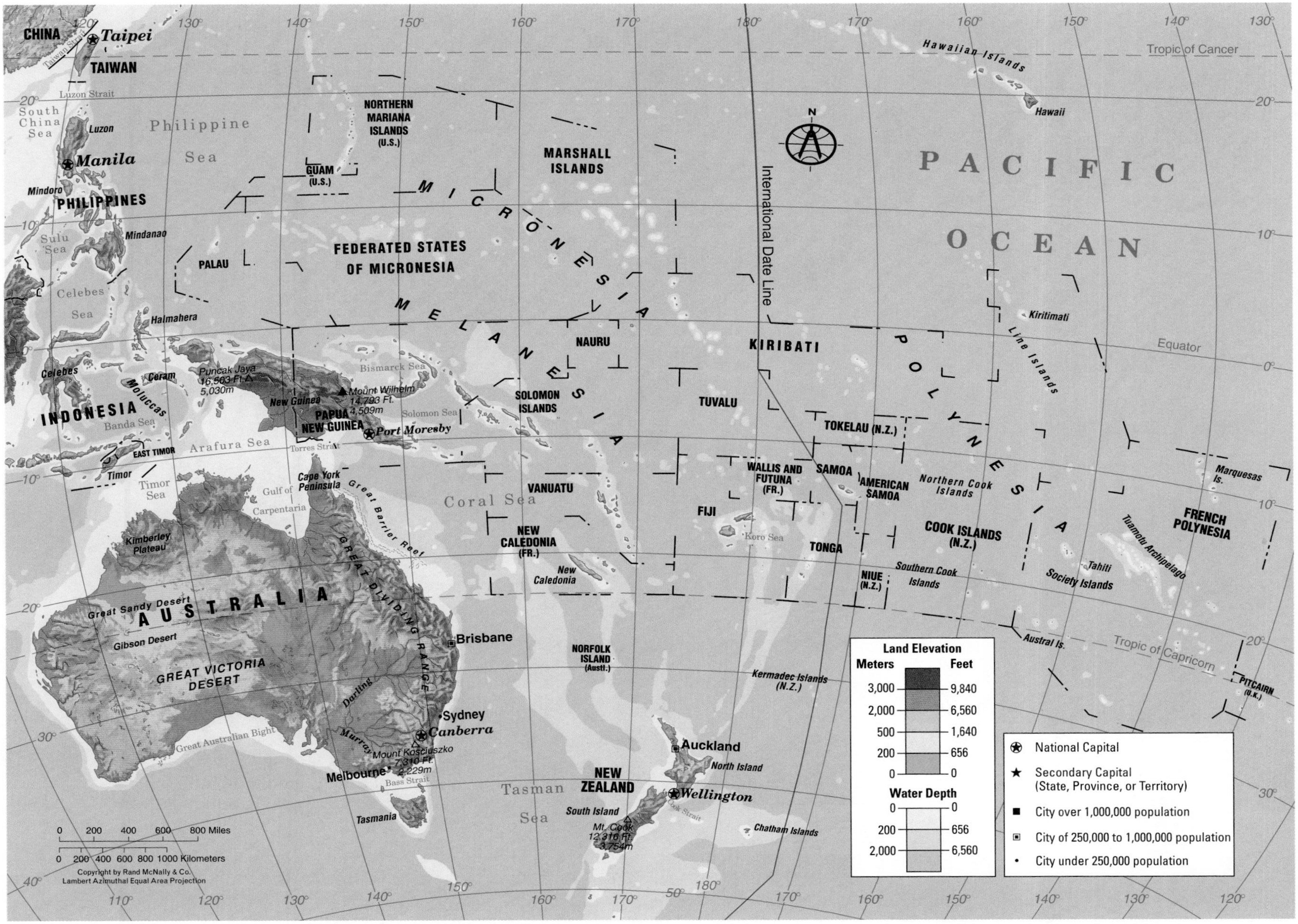
PACIFIC
OCEAN
CHINA
Taipei
TAIWAN
Luzon Strait
South China Sea
Luzon
Manila
Mindoro
PHILIPPINES
Philippine
Sea
Sulu Sea
Mindanao
Celebes
Sea
Halmahera
Celebes
Ceram
Moluccas
INDONESIA
Banda Sea
EAST TIMOR
Timor
Timor Sea
Arafura Sea
PALAU
NORTHERN MARIANA ISLANDS (U.S.)
GUAM (U.S.)
MARSHALL ISLANDS
MICRONESIA
FEDERATED STATES OF MICRONESIA
MELANESIA
POLYNESIA
NAURU
KIRIBATI
TUVALU
Puncak Jaya 16,503 Ft. 5,030m
New Guinea
Mount Wilhelm 14,793 Ft. 4,509m
PAPUA NEW GUINEA
Port Moresby
Bismarck Sea
Solomon Sea
SOLOMON ISLANDS
Torres Strait
Gulf of Carpentaria
Cape York Peninsula
Great Barrier Reef
Coral Sea
VANUATU
NEW CALEDONIA (FR.)
New Caledonia
FIJI
Koro Sea
WALLIS AND FUTUNA (FR.)
SAMOA
AMERICAN SAMOA
TOKELAU (N.Z.)
TONGA
NIUE (N.Z.)
Northern Cook Islands
COOK ISLANDS (N.Z.)
Southern Cook Islands
Hawaiian Islands
Hawaii
Kiritimati
Line Islands
Marquesas Is.
FRENCH POLYNESIA
Tuamotu Archipelago
Tahiti
Society Islands
Austral Is.
PITCAIRN (U.K.)
International Date Line
Tropic of Cancer
Equator
Tropic of Capricorn
Kimberley Plateau
Great Sandy Desert
AUSTRALIA
Gibson Desert
GREAT VICTORIA DESERT
GREAT DIVIDING RANGE
Darling
Murray
Brisbane
Sydney
Canberra
Mount Kosciuszko 7,310 Ft. 2,229m
Melbourne
Bass Strait
Great Australian Bight
Tasmania
Tasman Sea
NORFOLK ISLAND (Austl.)
Kermadec Islands (N.Z.)
NEW ZEALAND
Auckland
North Island
Wellington
Cook Strait
South Island
Mt. Cook 12,316 Ft. 3,754m
Chatham Islands
Land Elevation
Meters
Feet
3,000
9,840
2,000
6,560
500
1,640
200
656
0
0
Water Depth
0
0
200
656
2,000
6,560
National Capital
Secondary Capital (State, Province, or Territory)
City over 1,000,000 population
City of 250,000 to 1,000,000 population
City under 250,000 population
0 200 400 600 800 Miles
0 200 400 600 800 1000 Kilometers
Copyright by Rand McNally & Co.
Lambert Azimuthal Equal Area Projection

A11

ICELAND
Surtsey
Horn
Fontur
Arctic Circle
NORWEGIAN SEA
ATLANTIC OCEAN
FAROE ISLANDS (Den.)
Lofoten Islands
Kebnekaise 6,926 Ft. 2,111m
Lap
Scandinavian Peninsula
NORWAY
SWEDEN
Galdhøpiggen 8,100 Ft. 2,469m
Gulf of Bothnia
Hebrides
Orkney Islands
Grampian Mts.
UNITED KINGDOM
Cheviot Hills
NORTH SEA
DENMARK
Skagerrak
Stockholm
Vänern
Vättern
Öland
BALTIC SEA
IRELAND
Irish Sea
St. George's Channel
Great Britain
Thames
London
Bornholm (Den.)
RUSSIA
NETHERLANDS
Northern Europ
Elbe
Berlin
Oder
POLAND
Wisła
GERMANY
BELGIUM
Rhine
English Channel
Strait of Dover
LUX.
Paris
Paris Basin
Seine
Loire
CZECH REPUBLIC
Bohemian Forest
Black Forest
SLOVAKIA
Danube
FRANCE
Saone
Jura
SWITZERLAND
LIECH.
AUSTRIA
HUNGARY
Great Hungarian Plain
Bay of Biscay
Cantabrian Mts.
Mt. Blanc 15,771 Ft. 4,808m
Massif Central
Dordogne
Rhône
Alps
SLOVENIA
Drava
CROATIA
Po
Douro
Duero
Iberian Mts.
Ebro
Pyrenees
ANDORRA
SAN MARINO
BOSNIA AND HERZEGOVINA
Dinaric Alps
Apennines
MONACO
ADRIATIC SEA
Lisbon
PORTUGAL
Iberian Peninsula
Tagus
SPAIN
Sierra Morena
Corsica (Fr.)
Balkan
YUGOSLAVIA
Rome
ITALY
ALBANIA
MACEDONIA
Balearic Islands
Minorca
Majorca
Ibiza
Sardinia (It.)
Vesuvius 4,190 Ft. 1,277m
Pindus Mts.
Strait of Gibraltar
GIBRALTAR (U.K.)
TYRRHENIAN SEA
Mt. Etna 10,902 Ft. 3,323m
Sicily
IONIAN SEA
Algiers
MEDITERRANEAN
AFRICA
ALGERIA
MOROCCO
TUNISIA
MALTA
Land Elevation
Meters
Feet
3,000 — 9,840
2,000 — 6,560
500 — 1,640
200 — 656
0 — 0
Water Depth
0 — 0
200 — 656
2,000 — 6,560
0 100 200 300 400 Miles
0 200 400 600 Kilometers
Copyright by Rand McNally & Co.
Lambert Conformal Conic Projection

A12

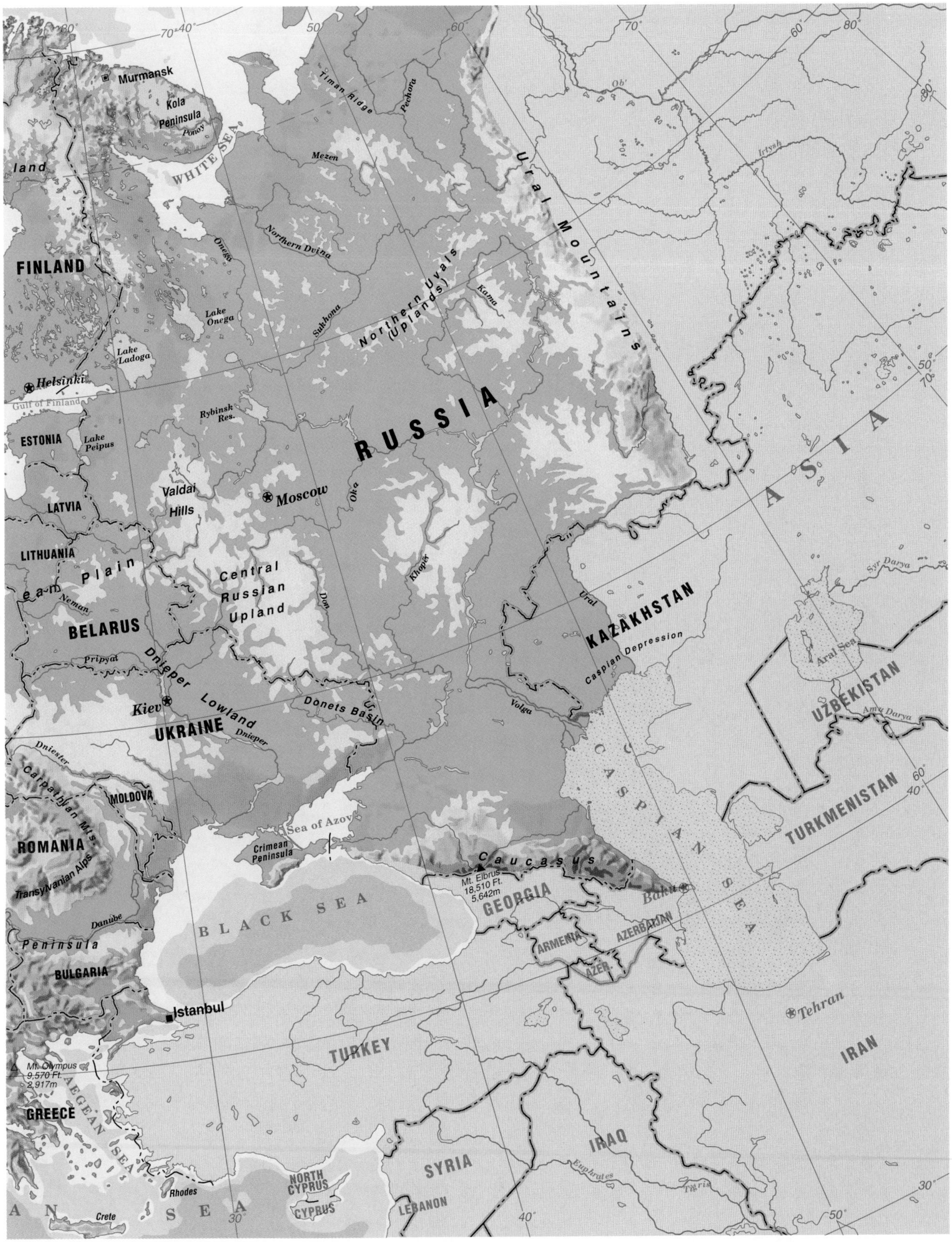
Murmansk
Kola
Peninsula
Ponoy
WHITE SEA
land
Timan Ridge
Pechora
Mezen
Ural Mountains
Northern Dvina
Onega
FINLAND
Northern Uvals (Uplands)
Kama
Sukhona
Lake Onega
Lake Ladoga
Helsinki
Gulf of Finland
RUSSIA
Rybinsk Res.
ESTONIA
Lake Peipus
ASIA
Valdai Hills
Moscow
Oka
LATVIA
LITHUANIA
Plain
Central Russian Upland
Neman
Don
Khoper
Ural
KAZAKHSTAN
Caspian Depression
BELARUS
Pripyat
Dnieper Lowland
Aral Sea
UZBEKISTAN
Amu Darya
Syr Darya
Kiev
Donets Basin
Volga
UKRAINE
Dnieper
Dniester
Carpathian Mts.
MOLDOVA
CASPIAN SEA
TURKMENISTAN
ROMANIA
Sea of Azov
Crimean Peninsula
Caucasus
Transylvanian Alps
Mt. Elbrus 18,510 Ft. 5,642m
GEORGIA
Baku
BLACK SEA
Danube
ARMENIA
AZERBAIJAN
AZER.
Peninsula
BULGARIA
Tehran
Istanbul
TURKEY
IRAN
Mt. Olympus 9,570 Ft. 2,917m
AEGEAN SEA
GREECE
IRAQ
SYRIA
Euphrates
Tigris
Rhodes
NORTH CYPRUS
CYPRUS
LEBANON
Crete
SEA
Ob'
Irtysh
70°
60°
50°
40°
30°
80°

A13

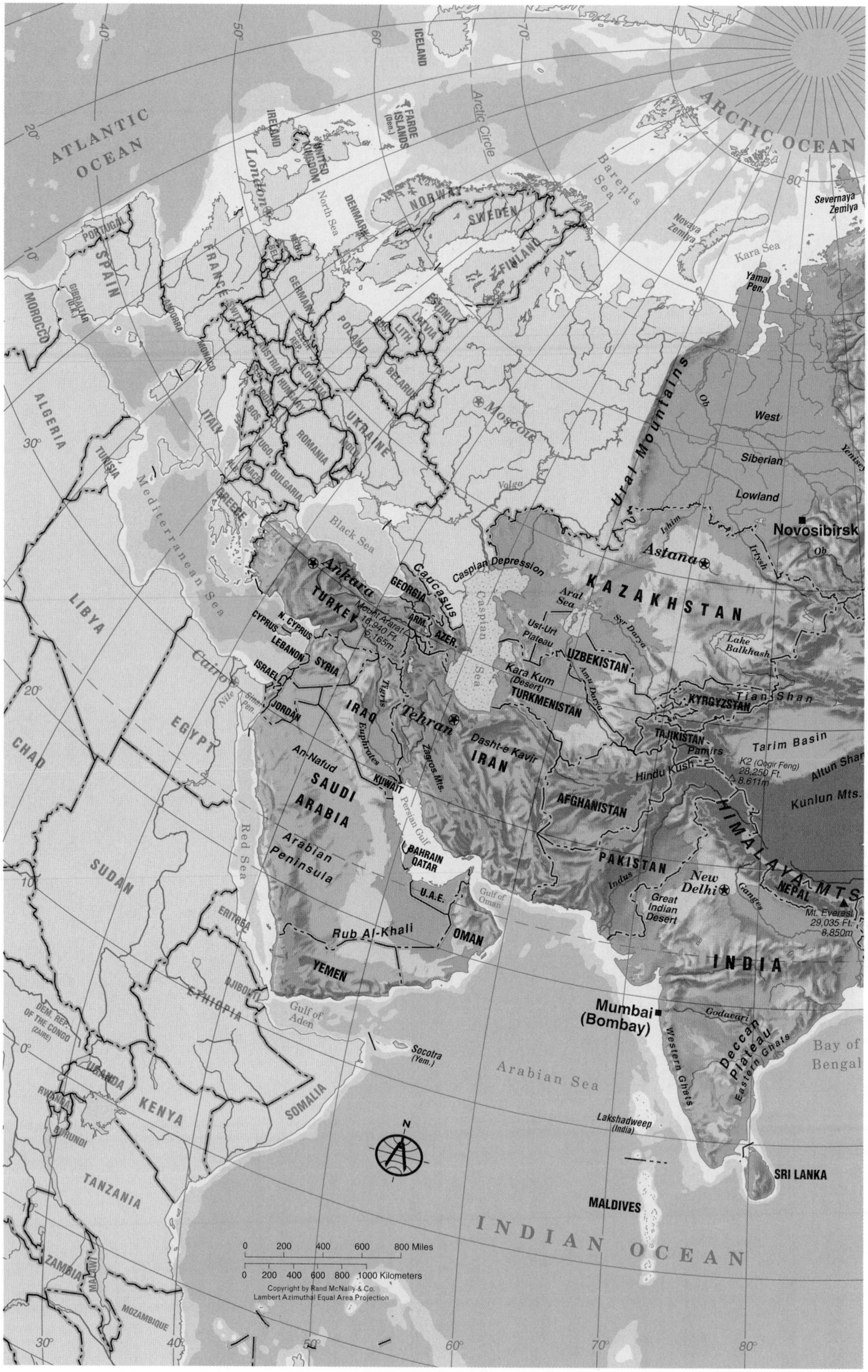
ATLANTIC OCEAN
ARCTIC OCEAN
ICELAND
FAROE ISLANDS (Den.)
IRELAND
UNITED KINGDOM
London
North Sea
DENMARK
NORWAY
SWEDEN
FINLAND
Arctic Circle
Barents Sea
Novaya Zemlya
Severnaya Zemlya
Kara Sea
Yamal Pen.
PORTUGAL
SPAIN
GIBRALTAR (U.K.)
MOROCCO
ANDORRA
FRANCE
MONACO
GERMANY
POLAND
LITH.
LATVIA
ESTONIA
BELARUS
AUSTRIA
HUNGARY
SLOVAKIA
ITALY
ROMANIA
UKRAINE
MOL.
BULGARIA
GREECE
Moscow
Volga
Ural Mountains
Ob
West Siberian Lowland
Yenisey
Ishim
Irtysh
Novosibirsk
Astana
ALGERIA
TUNISIA
Mediterranean Sea
Black Sea
Caucasus
GEORGIA
ARM.
AZER.
Ankara
TURKEY
Mount Ararat 16,940 Ft. 5,165m
N. CYPRUS
CYPRUS
LEBANON
SYRIA
ISRAEL
JORDAN
Caspian Depression
Caspian Sea
Aral Sea
Ust-Urt Plateau
KAZAKHSTAN
Syr Darya
Lake Balkhash
UZBEKISTAN
Kara Kum (Desert)
Amu Darya
TURKMENISTAN
KYRGYZSTAN
Tian Shan
TAJIKISTAN
Pamirs
Tarim Basin
K2 (Qogir Feng) 28,250 Ft. 8,611m
Altun Shan
Kunlun Mts.
Hindu Kush
LIBYA
Cairo
Nile
Sinai Pen.
EGYPT
IRAQ
Tigris
Euphrates
Tehran
Zagros Mts.
Dasht-e Kavir
IRAN
AFGHANISTAN
An-Nafud
SAUDI ARABIA
KUWAIT
Persian Gulf
Arabian Peninsula
BAHRAIN
QATAR
U.A.E.
Gulf of Oman
OMAN
Rub Al-Khali
YEMEN
PAKISTAN
Indus
New Delhi
Great Indian Desert
Ganges
HIMALAYA MTS.
NEPAL
Mt. Everest 29,035 Ft. 8,850m
INDIA
CHAD
SUDAN
Red Sea
ERITREA
DJIBOUTI
ETHIOPIA
Gulf of Aden
Socotra (Yem.)
SOMALIA
DEM. REP. OF THE CONGO (ZAIRE)
UGANDA
KENYA
RWANDA
BURUNDI
TANZANIA
ZAMBIA
MALAWI
MOZAMBIQUE
Mumbai (Bombay)
Godavari
Western Ghats
Deccan Plateau
Eastern Ghats
Bay of Bengal
Arabian Sea
Lakshadweep (India)
MALDIVES
SRI LANKA
INDIAN OCEAN
N
0 200 400 600 800 Miles
0 200 400 600 800 1000 Kilometers
Copyright by Rand McNally & Co.
Lambert Azimuthal Equal Area Projection
10°
20°
30°
40°
50°
60°
70°
80°

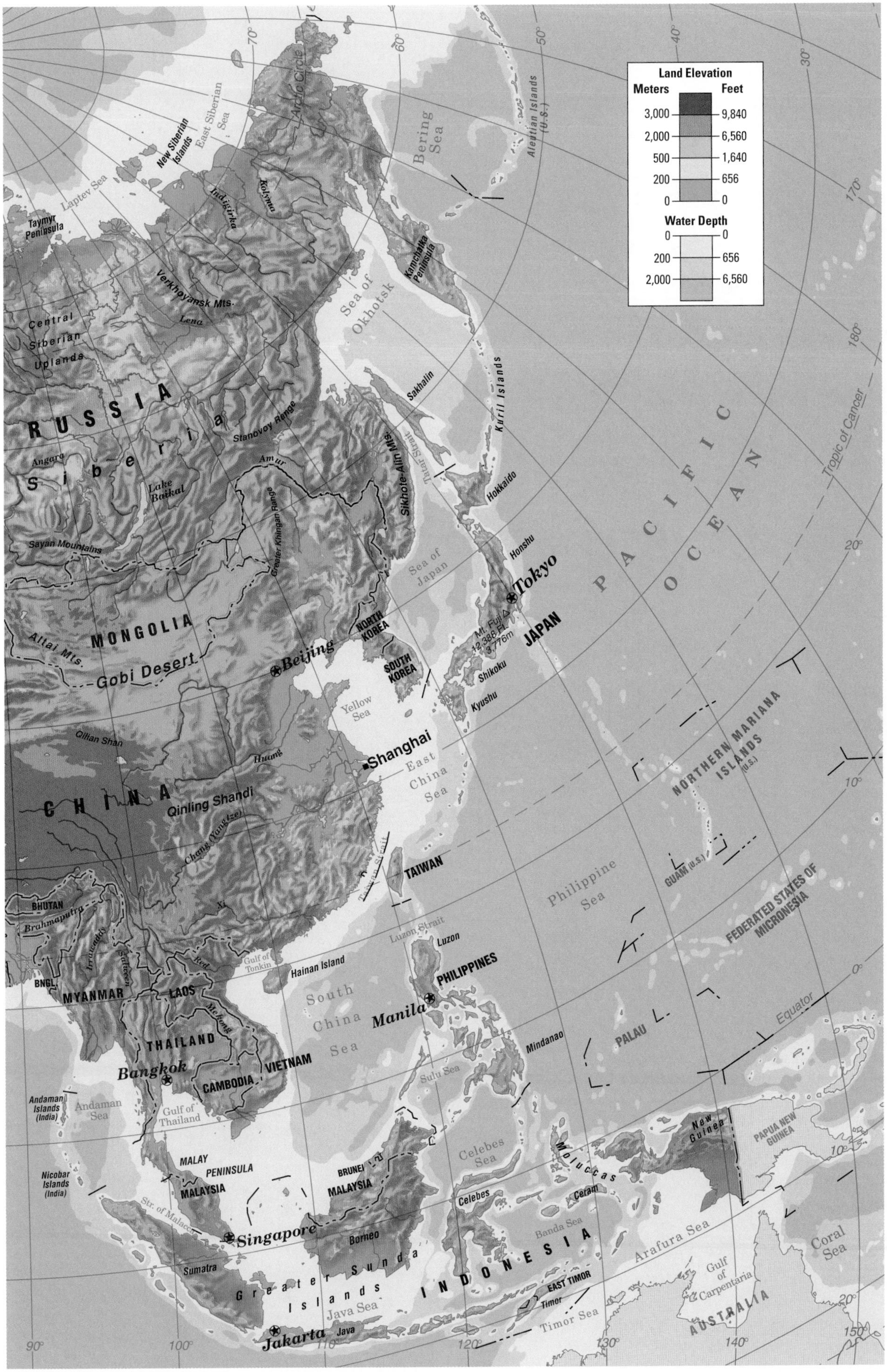
Land Elevation
Meters
Feet
3,000
9,840
2,000
6,560
500
1,640
200
656
0
0
Water Depth
0
0
200
656
2,000
6,560
New Siberian Islands
East Siberian Sea
Arctic Circle
Bering Sea
Aleutian Islands (U.S.)
Laptev Sea
Taymyr Peninsula
Indigirka
Kolyma
Kamchatka Peninsula
Verkhoyansk Mts.
Lena
Sea of Okhotsk
Central Siberian Uplands
RUSSIA
Siberia
Stanovoy Range
Sakhalin
Kuril Islands
Tatar Strait
Sikhote-Alin Mts.
Amur
Angara
Lake Baikal
Greater Khingan Range
Hokkaido
Honshu
Sayan Mountains
Sea of Japan
Tokyo
Mt. Fuji
12,388 ft.
3,776m
JAPAN
PACIFIC OCEAN
Tropic of Cancer
MONGOLIA
NORTH KOREA
SOUTH KOREA
Altai Mts.
Gobi Desert
Beijing
Shikoku
Kyushu
Yellow Sea
Qilian Shan
Huang
Shanghai
East China Sea
NORTHERN MARIANA ISLANDS (U.S.)
CHINA
Qinling Shandi
Chang (Yangtze)
Taiwan Strait
TAIWAN
GUAM (U.S.)
Philippine Sea
FEDERATED STATES OF MICRONESIA
BHUTAN
Brahmaputra
Irrawaddy
Salween
Xi
Red
Luzon Strait
Luzon
Gulf of Tonkin
Hainan Island
PHILIPPINES
BNGL.
MYANMAR
LAOS
South China Sea
Manila
Mekong
Equator
THAILAND
PALAU
Mindanao
Bangkok
VIETNAM
CAMBODIA
Sulu Sea
Andaman Islands (India)
Andaman Sea
Gulf of Thailand
New Guinea
PAPUA NEW GUINEA
Celebes Sea
MALAY PENINSULA
Moluccas
Nicobar Islands (India)
MALAYSIA
BRUNEI
MALAYSIA
Celebes
Ceram
Str. of Malacca
Singapore
Borneo
Banda Sea
Arafura Sea
Coral Sea
Sumatra
Greater Sunda Islands
INDONESIA
EAST TIMOR
Gulf of Carpentaria
Java Sea
Timor
Timor Sea
Jakarta
Java
AUSTRALIA
90°
100°
110°
120°
130°
140°
150°
70°
60°
50°
40°
30°
20°
10°
0°
170°
180°

A15

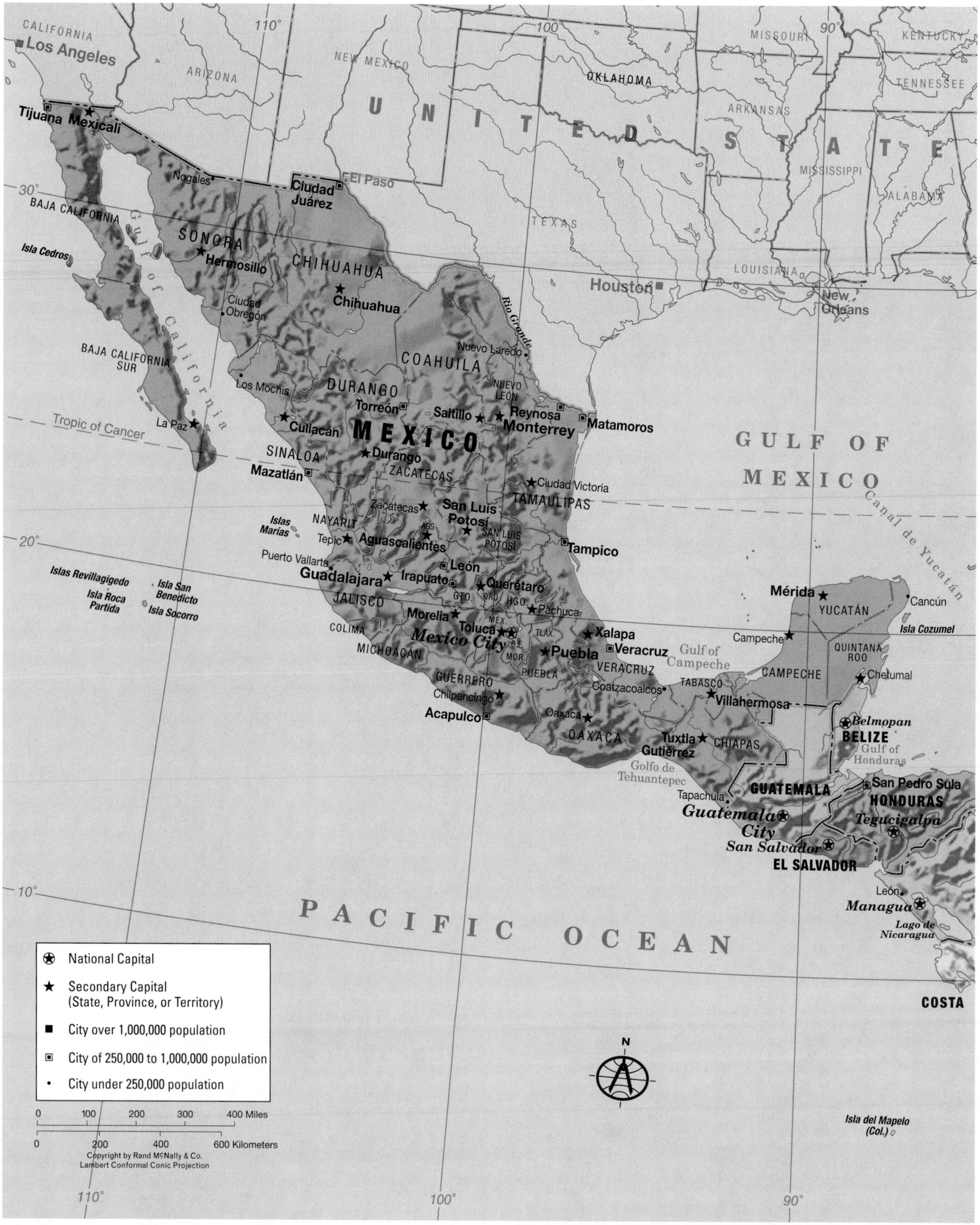
CALIFORNIA
Los Angeles
ARIZONA
NEW MEXICO
OKLAHOMA
MISSOURI
KENTUCKY
TENNESSEE
ARKANSAS
UNITED STATES
MISSISSIPPI
ALABAMA
TEXAS
LOUISIANA
Houston
New Orleans
El Paso
Tijuana
Mexicali
Nogales
Ciudad Juárez
BAJA CALIFORNIA
Isla Cedros
SONORA
Hermosillo
CHIHUAHUA
Chihuahua
Ciudad Obregón
Gulf of California
BAJA CALIFORNIA SUR
Rio Grande
Nuevo Laredo
COAHUILA
Los Mochis
DURANGO
NUEVO LEÓN
Torreón
Saltillo
Reynosa
Monterrey
Matamoros
La Paz
Tropic of Cancer
Culiacán
MEXICO
SINALOA
Durango
Mazatlán
ZACATECAS
Ciudad Victoria
TAMAULIPAS
Zacatecas
San Luis Potosí
Islas Marías
NAYARIT
AGS.
SAN LUIS POTOSÍ
Tepic
Aguascalientes
Tampico
Puerto Vallarta
León
Guadalajara
Irapuato
Querétaro
Islas Revillagigedo
Isla San Benedicto
Isla Roca Partida
Isla Socorro
JALISCO
GTO.
QRO.
HGO.
Pachuca
Morelia
MÉX.
COLIMA
Toluca
TLAX.
Xalapa
Mexico City
D.F.
Puebla
Veracruz
MICHOACÁN
MOR.
PUEBLA
VERACRUZ
Gulf of Campeche
GUERRERO
Chilpancingo
Coatzacoalcos
TABASCO
Villahermosa
Acapulco
Oaxaca
OAXACA
Tuxtla Gutiérrez
CHIAPAS
Golfo de Tehuantepec
GULF OF MEXICO
Canal de Yucatán
Mérida
YUCATÁN
Cancún
Isla Cozumel
Campeche
QUINTANA ROO
CAMPECHE
Chetumal
Belmopan
BELIZE
Gulf of Honduras
Tapachula
GUATEMALA
San Pedro Sula
HONDURAS
Guatemala City
Tegucigalpa
San Salvador
EL SALVADOR
León
Managua
Lago de Nicaragua
COSTA
PACIFIC OCEAN
Isla del Mapelo (Col.)
110°
100°
90°
30°
20°
10°
National Capital
Secondary Capital (State, Province, or Territory)
City over 1,000,000 population
City of 250,000 to 1,000,000 population
City under 250,000 population
0 100 200 300 400 Miles
0 200 400 600 Kilometers
Copyright by Rand McNally & Co.
Lambert Conformal Conic Projection
N

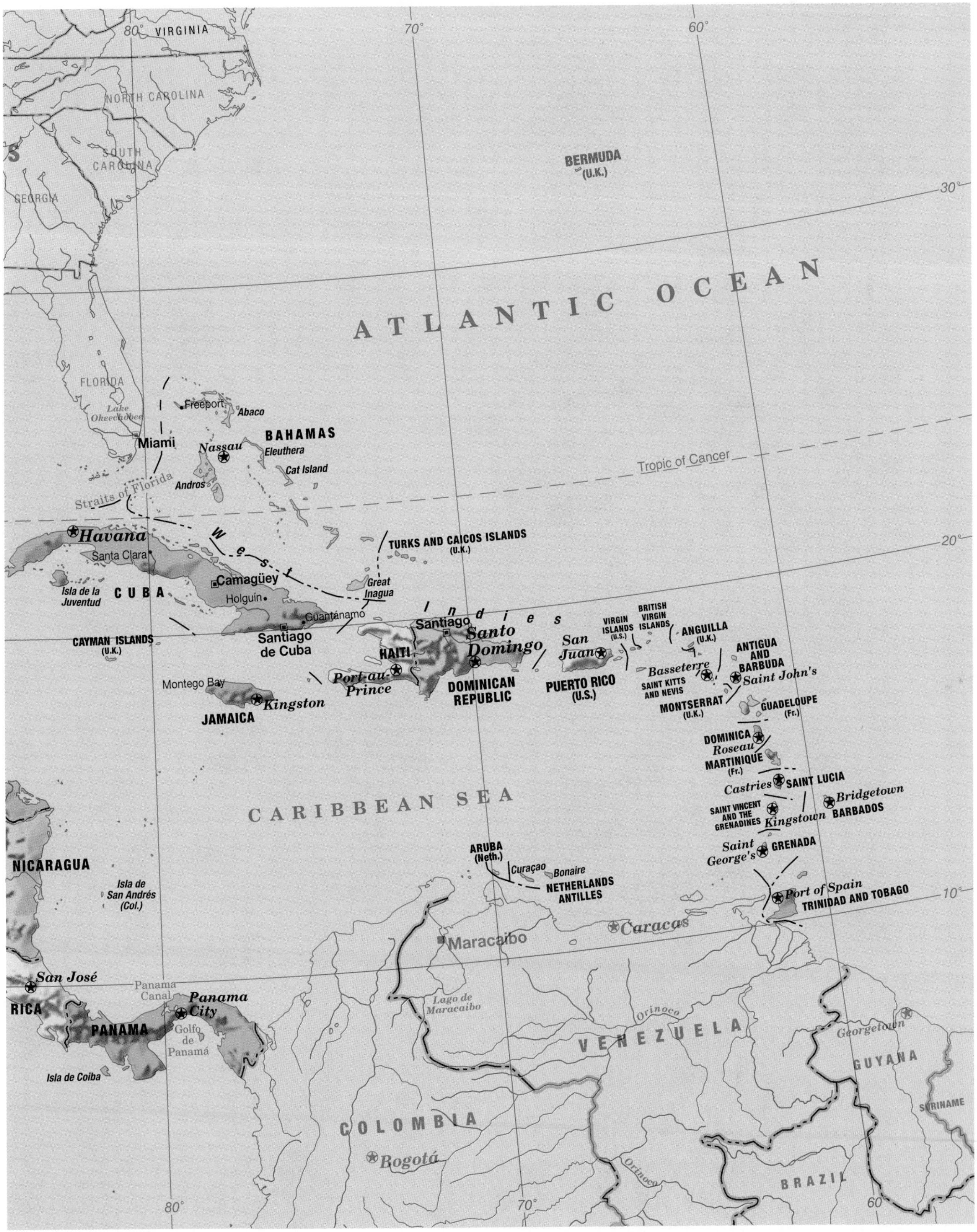

VIRGINIA
NORTH CAROLINA
SOUTH CAROLINA
GEORGIA
FLORIDA
Lake Okeechobee
BERMUDA (U.K.)
ATLANTIC OCEAN
Tropic of Cancer
Freeport
Abaco
BAHAMAS
Nassau
Eleuthera
Cat Island
Miami
Andros
Straits of Florida
West Indies
TURKS AND CAICOS ISLANDS (U.K.)
Havana
Santa Clara
Isla de la Juventud
CUBA
Camagüey
Holguín
Great Inagua
Guantánamo
Santiago de Cuba
CAYMAN ISLANDS (U.K.)
Santiago
Santo Domingo
HAITI
Port-au-Prince
DOMINICAN REPUBLIC
San Juan
PUERTO RICO (U.S.)
VIRGIN ISLANDS (U.S.)
BRITISH VIRGIN ISLANDS
ANGUILLA (U.K.)
ANTIGUA AND BARBUDA
Saint John's
Basseterre
SAINT KITTS AND NEVIS
MONTSERRAT (U.K.)
GUADELOUPE (Fr.)
DOMINICA
Roseau
MARTINIQUE (Fr.)
Castries
SAINT LUCIA
Bridgetown
BARBADOS
SAINT VINCENT AND THE GRENADINES
Kingstown
Saint George's
GRENADA
Montego Bay
Kingston
JAMAICA
CARIBBEAN SEA
NICARAGUA
Isla de San Andrés (Col.)
ARUBA (Neth.)
Curaçao
Bonaire
NETHERLANDS ANTILLES
Port of Spain
TRINIDAD AND TOBAGO
Caracas
Maracaibo
Lago de Maracaibo
San José
RICA
Panama Canal
Panama City
PANAMA
Golfo de Panamá
Isla de Coiba
Orinoco
VENEZUELA
Georgetown
GUYANA
SURINAME
COLOMBIA
Bogotá
BRAZIL
80°
70°
60°
30°
20°
10°

RAND McNALLY

A17

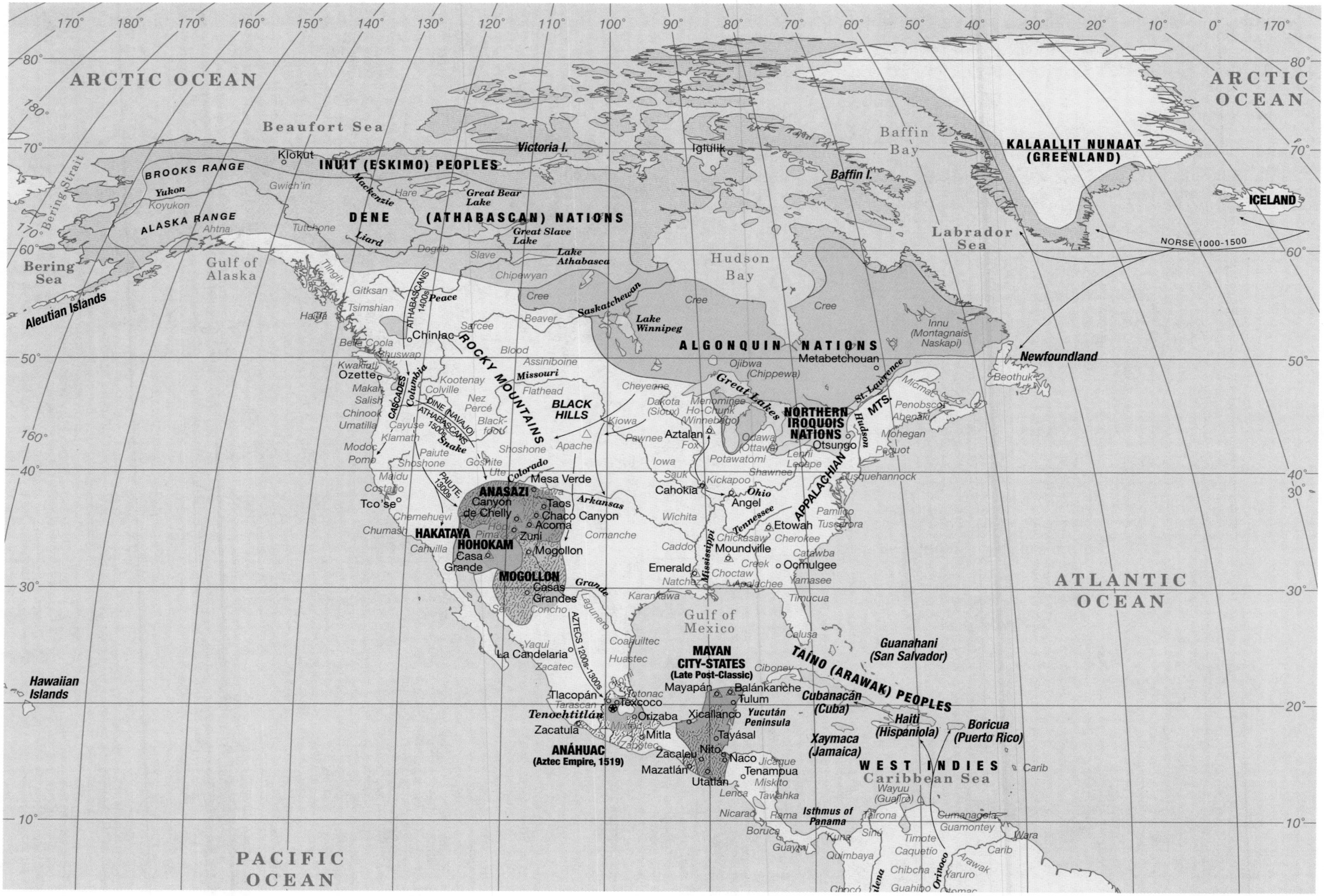
ARCTIC OCEAN
Beaufort Sea
Baffin Bay
Labrador Sea
Hudson Bay
Bering Sea
Gulf of Alaska
Gulf of Mexico
Caribbean Sea
ATLANTIC OCEAN
PACIFIC OCEAN
KALAALLIT NUNAAT (GREENLAND)
ICELAND
NORSE 1000-1500
Newfoundland
Baffin I.
Victoria I.
Aleutian Islands
Bering Strait
Hawaiian Islands
BROOKS RANGE
ALASKA RANGE
Yukon
INUIT (ESKIMO) PEOPLES
DENE (ATHABASCAN) NATIONS
ALGONQUIN NATIONS
NORTHERN IROQUOIS NATIONS
TAÍNO (ARAWAK) PEOPLES
MAYAN CITY-STATES (Late Post-Classic)
ANÁHUAC (Aztec Empire, 1519)
AZTECS 1200s-1300s
ATHABASCANS 1400s
ATHABASCANS 1500s
DINE (NAVAJO)
PAIUTE 1300s
ANASAZI
HOHOKAM
HAKATAYA
MOGOLLON
ROCKY MOUNTAINS
CASCADES
BLACK HILLS
APPALACHIAN MTS.
Klokut
Iglulik
Chinlac
Ozette
Tco'se
Metabetchouan
Otsungo
Aztalan
Cahokia
Angel
Etowah
Moundville
Ocmulgee
Emerald
Mesa Verde
Taos
Chaco Canyon
Canyon de Chelly
Acoma
Zuni
Mogollon
Casa Grande
Casas Grandes
La Candelaria
Tlacopán
Texcoco
Tenochtitlán
Zacatula
Orizaba
Mitla
Xicallanco
Mayapán
Balánkanche
Tulum
Tayásal
Nito
Naco
Tenampua
Zacaleu
Mazatlán
Utatlán
Yucután Peninsula
Guanahani (San Salvador)
Cubanacán (Cuba)
Xaymaca (Jamaica)
Haiti (Hispaniola)
Boricua (Puerto Rico)
WEST INDIES
Isthmus of Panama
Mackenzie
Liard
Peace
Great Bear Lake
Great Slave Lake
Lake Athabasca
Lake Winnipeg
Saskatchewan
Columbia
Snake
Missouri
Colorado
Arkansas
Grande
Mississippi
Ohio
Tennessee
Great Lakes
St. Lawrence
Hudson
Orinoco
Gwich'in
Koyukon
Ahtna
Tutchone
Hare
Dogrib
Slave
Chipewyan
Cree
Tlingit
Haida
Gitksan
Tsimshian
Bella Coola
Shuswap
Kwakiutl
Makah
Salish
Chinook
Umatilla
Cayuse
Klamath
Modoc
Pomo
Maidu
Costano
Chemehuevi
Chumash
Cahuilla
Kootenay
Colville
Nez Percé
Blackfoot
Sarcee
Beaver
Blood
Assiniboine
Flathead
Paiute
Shoshone
Goshute
Ute
Tewa
Hopi
Pima
Apache
Comanche
Wichita
Caddo
Kiowa
Cheyenne
Pawnee
Iowa
Dakota (Sioux)
Menominee
Ho-Chunk (Winnebago)
Fox
Sauk
Kickapoo
Potawatomi
Odawa (Ottawa)
Ojibwa (Chippewa)
Innu (Montagnais-Naskapi)
Beothuk
Micmac
Penobscot
Abenaki
Mohegan
Pequot
Lenni Lenape
Shawnee
Susquehannock
Pamlico
Tuscarora
Cherokee
Catawba
Chickasaw
Creek
Choctaw
Yamasee
Apalachee
Natchez
Timucua
Calusa
Karankawa
Coahuiltec
Huastec
Totonac
Tarascan
Mixtec
Zapotec
Seri
Yaqui
Concho
Lagunero
Zacatec
Ciboney
Jicaque
Miskito
Lenca
Tawahka
Nicarao
Rama
Boruca
Guaymi
Kuna
Sinú
Tairona
Wayuu (Guajiro)
Cumanagoto
Guamontey
Timote
Caquetío
Chibcha
Guahibo
Quimbaya
Chocó
Yaruro
Arawak
Carib
Wara

A18

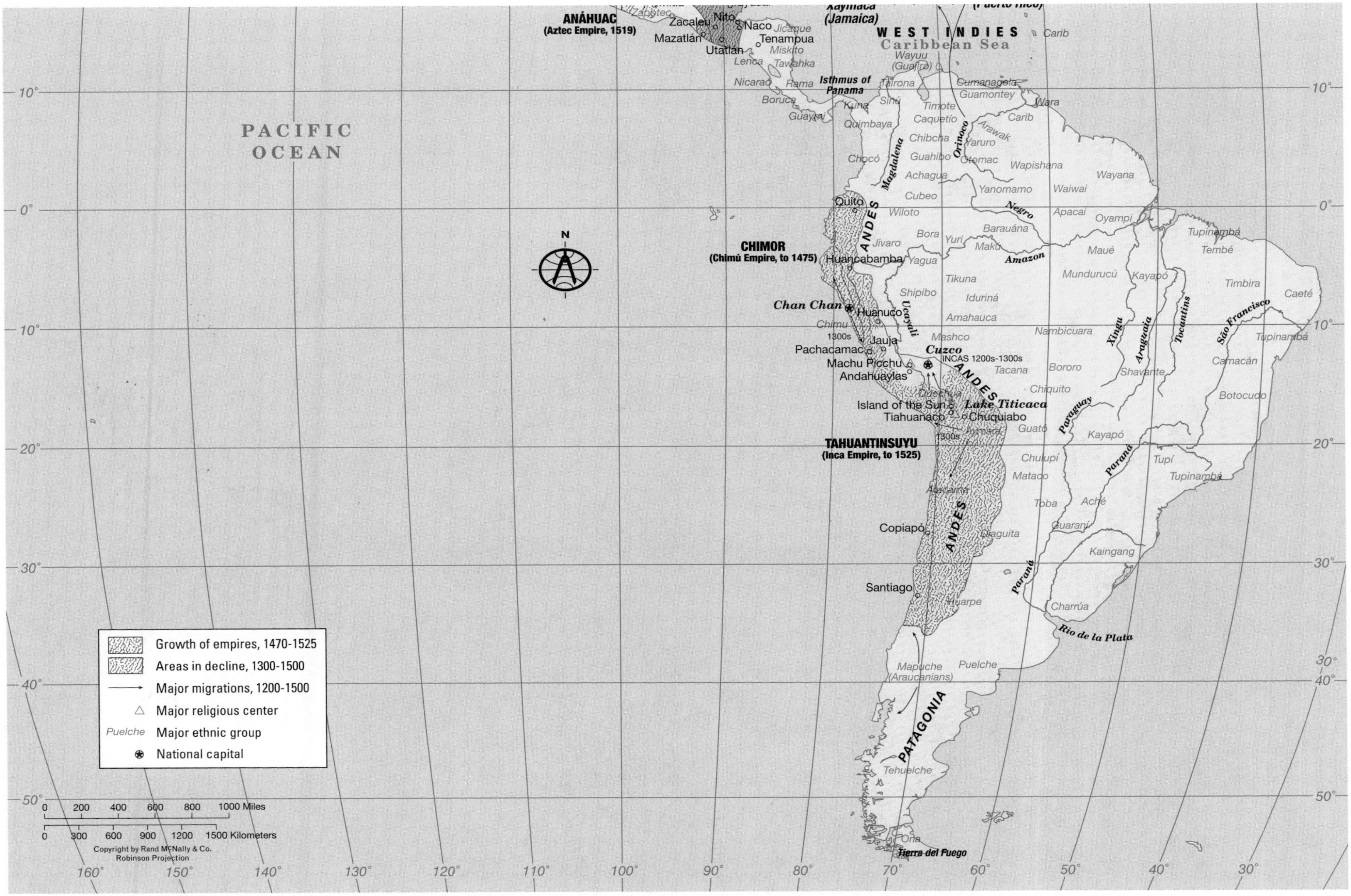

PACIFIC OCEAN
ANÁHUAC (Aztec Empire, 1519)
Zacaleu
Nito
Naco
Mazatlán
Utatlán
Tenampua
Jicaque
Miskito
Lenca
Tawahka
Nicarao
Rama
Boruca
Guaymí
Xaymaca (Jamaica)
WEST INDIES
Caribbean Sea
Carib
Wayuu (Guajiro)
Isthmus of Panama
Tairona
Cumanagota
Guamontey
Wara
Kuna
Sinú
Timote
Caquetío
Quimbaya
Chibcha
Arawak
Yaruro
Orinoco
Magdalena
Chocó
Guahibo
Otomac
Wapishana
Wayana
Achagua
Yanomamo
Waiwai
Cubeo
Quito
Wiloto
Negro
Apacai
Oyampi
Tupinambá
Tembé
CHIMOR (Chimú Empire, to 1475)
ANDES
Jivaro
Bora
Yuri
Barauána
Makú
Maué
Amazon
Huancabamba
Yagua
Tikuna
Mundurucú
Kayapó
Timbira
Caeté
Shipibo
Iduriná
Chan Chan
Huanuco
Ucayali
Amahauca
Chimu
1300s
Jauja
Mashco
Nambicuara
Xingu
Araguaia
Tocantins
São Francisco
Tupinambá
Pachacamac
Cuzco
INCAS 1200s-1300s
Machu Picchu
Andahuaylas
Tacana
Bororo
Shavante
Camacán
Chiquito
Botocudo
Quechua
Island of the Sun
Lake Titicaca
Tiahuanaco
Chuquiabo
Paraguay
Guató
1300s
Aymara
Kayapó
TAHUANTINSUYU (Inca Empire, to 1525)
Chulupí
Tupí
Mataco
Paraná
Tupinambá
Atacama
Toba
Aché
Copiapó
Diaguita
Guaraní
Kaingang
Paraná
Santiago
Huarpe
Charrúa
Río de la Plata
Mapuche (Araucanians)
Puelche
PATAGONIA
Tehuelche
Ona
Tierra del Fuego
Growth of empires, 1470-1525
Areas in decline, 1300-1500
Major migrations, 1200-1500
Major religious center
Puelche Major ethnic group
National capital
0 200 400 600 800 1000 Miles
0 300 600 900 1200 1500 Kilometers
Copyright by Rand McNally & Co.
Robinson Projection
10° 0° 10° 20° 30° 40° 50°
160° 150° 140° 130° 120° 110° 100° 90° 80° 70° 60° 50° 40° 30°

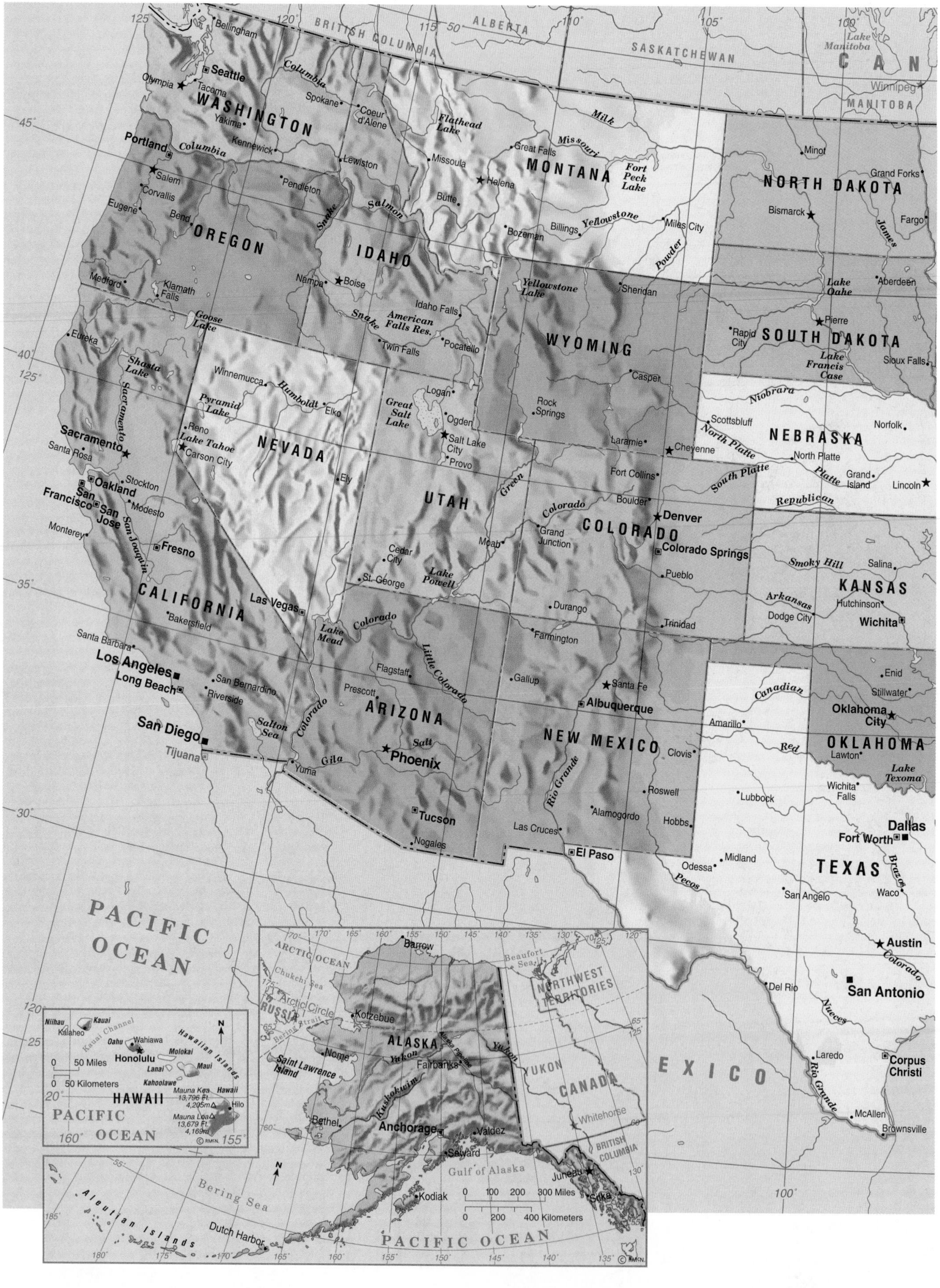
BRITISH COLUMBIA
ALBERTA
SASKATCHEWAN
MANITOBA
Lake Manitoba
Winnipeg
C A N
WASHINGTON
Bellingham
Seattle
Olympia
Tacoma
Yakima
Spokane
Coeur d'Alene
Kennewick
Columbia
Portland
Salem
Corvallis
Eugene
Bend
Pendleton
OREGON
Medford
Klamath Falls
Goose Lake
Lewiston
Snake
Salmon
IDAHO
Nampa
Boise
Idaho Falls
American Falls Res.
Pocatello
Twin Falls
Flathead Lake
Missoula
Helena
Butte
Bozeman
Great Falls
Missouri
Milk
MONTANA
Fort Peck Lake
Billings
Yellowstone
Miles City
Powder
Minot
Grand Forks
NORTH DAKOTA
Bismarck
Fargo
James
Lake Oahe
Aberdeen
Pierre
Rapid City
SOUTH DAKOTA
Lake Francis Case
Sioux Falls
Yellowstone Lake
Sheridan
WYOMING
Casper
Rock Springs
Laramie
Cheyenne
Eureka
Shasta Lake
Sacramento
Santa Rosa
Oakland
San Francisco
San Jose
Stockton
Modesto
Monterey
San Joaquin
Fresno
CALIFORNIA
Bakersfield
Santa Barbara
Los Angeles
Long Beach
San Bernardino
Riverside
San Diego
Tijuana
Salton Sea
Winnemucca
Humboldt
Pyramid Lake
Elko
Reno
Lake Tahoe
Carson City
NEVADA
Ely
Las Vegas
Lake Mead
Great Salt Lake
Logan
Ogden
Salt Lake City
Provo
UTAH
Green
Cedar City
St. George
Lake Powell
Moab
Grand Junction
Colorado
Fort Collins
Boulder
Denver
COLORADO
Colorado Springs
Pueblo
Durango
Trinidad
Scottsbluff
North Platte
NEBRASKA
Niobrara
Norfolk
Platte
Grand Island
Lincoln
South Platte
Republican
Smoky Hill
Salina
KANSAS
Arkansas
Hutchinson
Dodge City
Wichita
Flagstaff
Little Colorado
Prescott
ARIZONA
Gila
Salt
Phoenix
Yuma
Tucson
Nogales
Farmington
Gallup
Santa Fe
Albuquerque
NEW MEXICO
Rio Grande
Clovis
Roswell
Alamogordo
Hobbs
Las Cruces
El Paso
Enid
Stillwater
Canadian
Oklahoma City
OKLAHOMA
Amarillo
Red
Lawton
Lake Texoma
Wichita Falls
Lubbock
Dallas
Fort Worth
Odessa
Midland
TEXAS
Brazos
Pecos
San Angelo
Waco
Austin
Colorado
San Antonio
Del Rio
Nueces
Laredo
Corpus Christi
McAllen
Brownsville
EXICO
PACIFIC OCEAN
Niihau
Kauai
Kalaheo
Kauai Channel
Oahu
Wahiawa
Honolulu
Hawaiian Islands
Molokai
Lanai
Maui
Kahoolawe
Hawaii
Mauna Kea 13,796 Ft. 4,205m
Hilo
Mauna Loa 13,679 Ft. 4,169m
HAWAII
0 50 Miles
0 50 Kilometers
PACIFIC OCEAN
© RMN.
ARCTIC OCEAN
Chukchi Sea
Arctic Circle
RUSSIA
Bering Strait
Barrow
Beaufort Sea
NORTHWEST TERRITORIES
Kotzebue
ALASKA
Nome
Saint Lawrence Island
Yukon
Fairbanks
YUKON
CANADA
Kuskokwim
Bethel
Anchorage
Valdez
Seward
Whitehorse
BRITISH COLUMBIA
Gulf of Alaska
Juneau
Sitka
Kodiak
Bering Sea
Aleutian Islands
Dutch Harbor
PACIFIC OCEAN
0 100 200 300 Miles
0 200 400 Kilometers
© RMN.

A20

ONTARIO
QUÉBEC
NEW BRUNSWICK
Lake Winnipeg
Lake of the Woods
Lake Nipigon
International Falls
Isle Royale
Lake Superior
Lake Michigan
Lake Huron
Georgian Bay
Lake Ontario
Lake Erie
Lake Champlain
Moosehead Lake
Gulf of Maine
ATLANTIC OCEAN
GULF OF MEXICO
Montréal
Ottawa
Toronto
Sault Ste. Marie
MINNESOTA
Duluth
St. Cloud
Minneapolis
St. Paul
Mankato
Rochester
WISCONSIN
Eau Claire
Green Bay
Appleton
OshKosh
Sheboygan
Milwaukee
Madison
Racine
MICHIGAN
Marquette
Traverse City
Saginaw
Flint
Lansing
Grand Rapids
Detroit
Kalamazoo
Ann Arbor
IOWA
Sioux City
Waterloo
Dubuque
Cedar Rapids
Des Moines
Davenport
ILLINOIS
Rockford
Aurora
Chicago
Moline
Peoria
Bloomington
Springfield
Decatur
INDIANA
Gary
South Bend
Fort Wayne
Muncie
Indianapolis
Terre Haute
Bloomington
Evansville
OHIO
Toledo
Cleveland
Akron
Youngstown
Lima
Columbus
Springfield
Dayton
Cincinnati
PENNSYLVANIA
Erie
Oil City
Scranton
Allentown
Harrisburg
Pittsburgh
Philadelphia
NEW YORK
Watertown
Rochester
Syracuse
Buffalo
Albany
Binghamton
New York
VERMONT
Burlington
Montpelier
NEW HAMPSHIRE
Concord
Manchester
MAINE
Bangor
Augusta
Portland
MASSACHUSETTS
Boston
Worcester
CONNECTICUT
Hartford
Bridgeport
R.I.
Providence
Nantucket Island
Long Island
NEW JERSEY
Newark
Trenton
Wilmington
DELAWARE
Dover
Delaware Bay
MARYLAND
Baltimore
Annapolis
Washington D.C.
WEST VIRGINIA
Charleston
Huntington
VIRGINIA
Richmond
Newport News
Norfolk
Virginia Beach
Roanoke
Albemarle Sound
Pamlico Sound
NEBRASKA
Omaha
KANSAS
Kansas City
Topeka
Emporia
MISSOURI
St. Joseph
Kansas City
Columbia
Jefferson City
St. Louis
Springfield
Cape Girardeau
KENTUCKY
Louisville
Frankfort
Lexington
Owensboro
TENNESSEE
Clarksville
Nashville
Knoxville
Johnson City
Chattanooga
Memphis
Kentucky Lake
NORTH CAROLINA
Winston-Salem
Greensboro
Durham
Raleigh
Asheville
Charlotte
Wilmington
SOUTH CAROLINA
Greenville
Columbia
Charleston
OKLAHOMA
Tulsa
Muskogee
ARKANSAS
Fayetteville
Fort Smith
Jonesboro
Little Rock
Pine Bluff
Texarkana
LOUISIANA
Shreveport
Monroe
Toledo Bend Res.
Baton Rouge
Lake Charles
Lafayette
New Orleans
TEXAS
Tyler
Sam Rayburn Res.
Beaumont
Houston
Galveston
MISSISSIPPI
Jackson
Hattiesburg
Gulfport
ALABAMA
Huntsville
Birmingham
Tuscaloosa
Montgomery
Dothan
Mobile
GEORGIA
Athens
Atlanta
Augusta
Macon
Columbus
Albany
Savannah
FLORIDA
Pensacola
Tallahassee
Jacksonville
Gainesville
Daytona Beach
Orlando
Tampa
St. Petersburg
Lakeland
Lake Okeechobee
Fort Myers
West Palm Beach
Fort Lauderdale
Miami
Key West
Mississippi
Missouri
Ohio
Illinois
Wabash
Cumberland
Tombigbee
Chattahoochee
Altamaha
Savannah
Hudson
Susquehanna
Connecticut
St. Lawrence
Arkansas
Ouachita
Red
Trinity
Des Moines
Roanoke
ATLANTIC OCEAN
San Juan
Arecibo
Mayagüez
Ponce
Caguas
PUERTO RICO (U.S.)
Caribbean Sea
0 25 50 Miles
0 25 50 Kilometers
National Capital
Secondary Capital (State, Province, or Territory)
City over 1,000,000 population
City of 250,000 to 1,000,000 population
City under 250,000 population
0 100 200 300 Miles
0 100 200 300 400 Kilometers
Copyright by Rand McNally & Co.
Albers Conic Equal Area Projection

A21

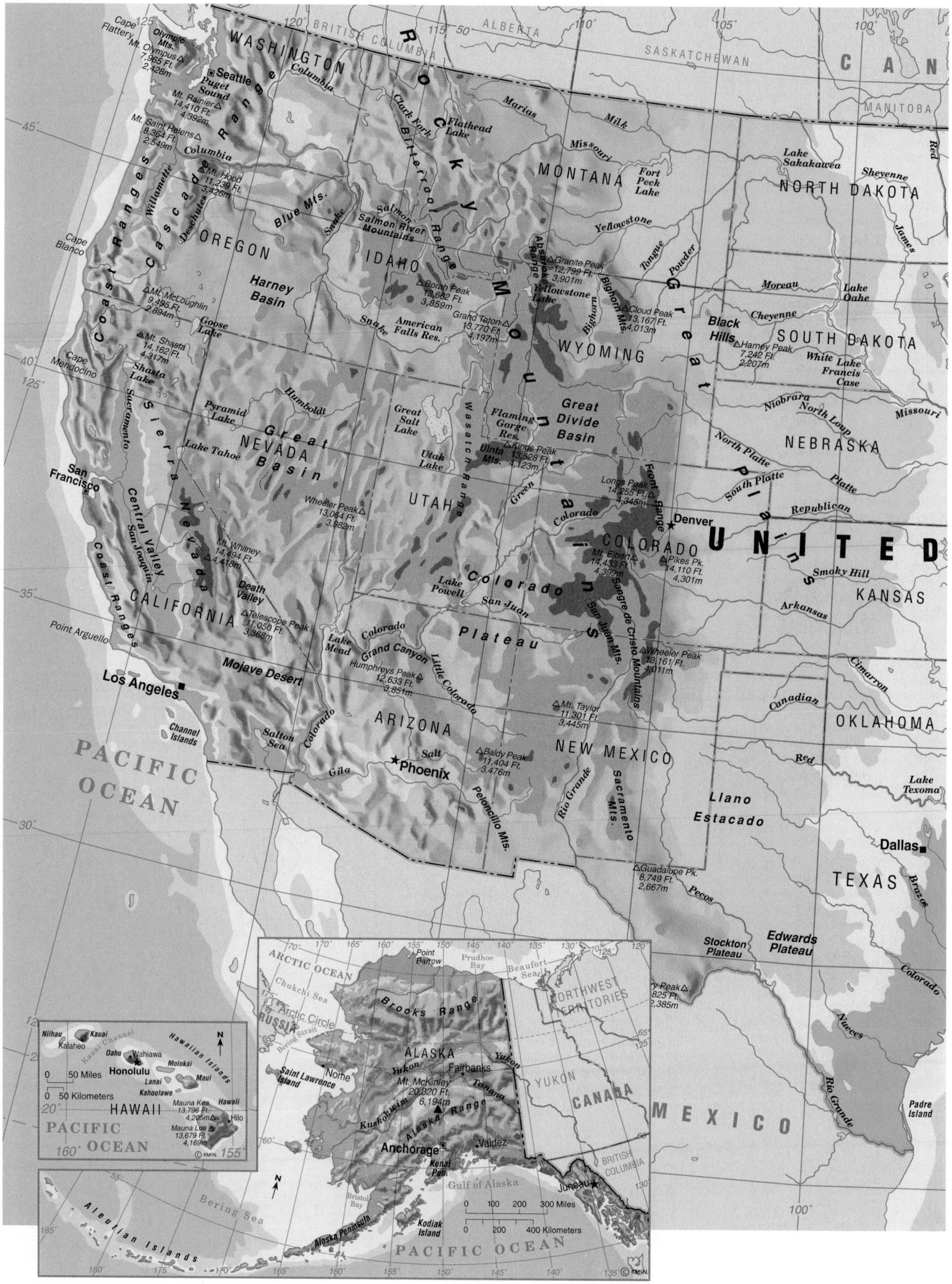
WASHINGTON
OREGON
IDAHO
MONTANA
WYOMING
NORTH DAKOTA
SOUTH DAKOTA
NEBRASKA
KANSAS
OKLAHOMA
TEXAS
COLORADO
UTAH
NEVADA
CALIFORNIA
ARIZONA
NEW MEXICO
UNITED
CAN
MEXICO
BRITISH COLUMBIA
ALBERTA
SASKATCHEWAN
MANITOBA
PACIFIC OCEAN
Rocky Mountains
Great Plains
Great Basin
Great Divide Basin
Colorado Plateau
Cascade Range
Coast Ranges
Sierra Nevada
Olympic Mts.
Mt. Olympus 7,965 Ft. 2,428m
Cape Flattery
Seattle
Puget Sound
Mt. Rainier 14,410 Ft. 4,392m
Mt. Saint Helens 8,364 Ft. 2,549m
Columbia
Mt. Hood 11,239 Ft. 3,426m
Willamette
Deschutes
Cape Blanco
Blue Mts.
Snake
Harney Basin
Mt. McLoughlin 9,495 Ft. 2,894m
Goose Lake
Mt. Shasta 14,162 Ft. 4,317m
Cape Mendocino
Shasta Lake
Sacramento
Pyramid Lake
Humboldt
Lake Tahoe
San Francisco
Central Valley
San Joaquin
Mt. Whitney 14,494 Ft. 4,418m
Death Valley
Telescope Peak 11,050 Ft. 3,368m
Point Arguello
Mojave Desert
Los Angeles
Channel Islands
Salton Sea
Clark Fork
Flathead Lake
Bitterroot Range
Salmon River Mountains
Borah Peak 12,662 Ft. 3,859m
American Falls Res.
Grand Teton 13,770 Ft. 4,197m
Marias
Milk
Missouri
Fort Peck Lake
Yellowstone
Absaroka Range
Granite Peak 12,799 Ft. 3,901m
Yellowstone Lake
Bighorn
Bighorn Mts.
Cloud Peak 13,167 Ft. 4,013m
Tongue
Powder
Great Salt Lake
Wasatch Range
Utah Lake
Flaming Gorge Res.
Uinta Mts.
Kings Peak 13,528 Ft. 4,123m
Green
Wheeler Peak 13,064 Ft. 3,982m
Longs Peak 14,255 Ft. 4,345m
Front Range
Denver
Mt. Elbert 14,433 Ft. 4,399m
Pikes Pk. 14,110 Ft. 4,301m
Colorado
Lake Powell
San Juan
San Juan Mts.
Sangre de Cristo Mountains
Wheeler Peak 13,161 Ft. 4,011m
Lake Mead
Grand Canyon
Humphreys Peak 12,633 Ft. 3,851m
Little Colorado
Mt. Taylor 11,301 Ft. 3,445m
Gila
Salt
Phoenix
Baldy Peak 11,404 Ft. 3,476m
Peloncillo Mts.
Rio Grande
Sacramento Mts.
Guadalupe Pk. 8,749 Ft. 2,667m
Pecos
Llano Estacado
Stockton Plateau
Edwards Plateau
Lake Sakakawea
Sheyenne
James
Red
Moreau
Lake Oahe
Cheyenne
Black Hills
Harney Peak 7,242 Ft. 2,207m
White
Lake Francis Case
Niobrara
North Loup
North Platte
South Platte
Platte
Republican
Smoky Hill
Arkansas
Cimarron
Canadian
Lake Texoma
Dallas
Brazos
Colorado
Nueces
Padre Island
Missouri
ARCTIC OCEAN
Chukchi Sea
Arctic Circle
RUSSIA
Bering Strait
Point Barrow
Prudhoe Bay
Beaufort Sea
Brooks Range
NORTHWEST TERRITORIES
ALASKA
YUKON
CANADA
Yukon
Fairbanks
Tanana
Saint Lawrence Island
Nome
Mt. McKinley 20,320 Ft. 6,194m
Kuskokwim
Alaska Range
Anchorage
Valdez
Kenai Pen.
Gulf of Alaska
Bristol Bay
Juneau
Kodiak Island
Alaska Peninsula
Bering Sea
Aleutian Islands
PACIFIC OCEAN
0 100 200 300 Miles
0 200 400 Kilometers
Niihau
Kauai
Kalaheo
Kauai Channel
Oahu
Wahiawa
Honolulu
Molokai
Lanai
Maui
Kahoolawe
Hawaiian Islands
HAWAII
Hawaii
Mauna Kea 13,796 Ft. 4,205m
Mauna Loa 13,679 Ft. 4,169m
Hilo
0 50 Miles
0 50 Kilometers
PACIFIC OCEAN
© RMcN.

A22

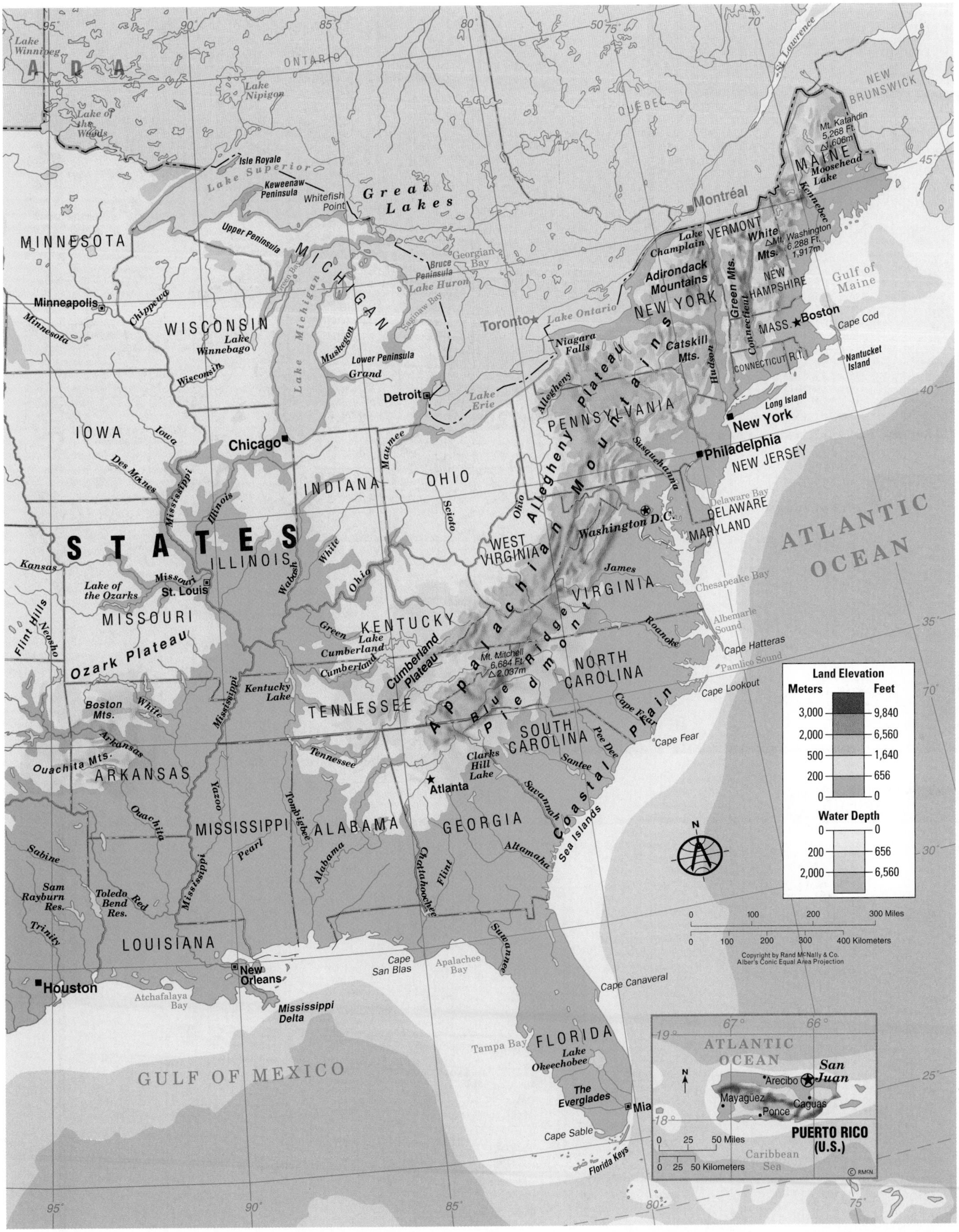
Lake Winnipeg
ONTARIO
Lake Nipigon
Lake of the Woods
QUÉBEC
NEW BRUNSWICK
St. Lawrence
Mt. Katahdin 5,268 Ft. 1,606m
MAINE
Moosehead Lake
Kennebec
Isle Royale
Lake Superior
Keweenaw Peninsula
Whitefish Point
Great Lakes
Montréal
MINNESOTA
Upper Peninsula
MICHIGAN
Bruce Peninsula
Georgian Bay
Lake Huron
Saginaw Bay
Lake Champlain
VERMONT
White Mts.
Mt. Washington 6,288 Ft. 1,917m
Adirondack Mountains
NEW HAMPSHIRE
Gulf of Maine
Minneapolis
Chippewa
Minnesota
WISCONSIN
Lake Winnebago
Green Bay
Lake Michigan
Muskegon
Lower Peninsula
Grand
Toronto
Lake Ontario
NEW YORK
Green Mts.
Connecticut
MASS.
Boston
Cape Cod
Niagara Falls
Catskill Mts.
Hudson
CONNECTICUT
R.I.
Nantucket Island
Wisconsin
Detroit
Lake Erie
Allegheny
Allegheny Plateau
Appalachian Mountains
Long Island
New York
IOWA
Iowa
Chicago
Maumee
PENNSYLVANIA
Susquehanna
Philadelphia
NEW JERSEY
Des Moines
Mississippi
Illinois
INDIANA
OHIO
Scioto
Ohio
Delaware Bay
DELAWARE
Washington D.C.
MARYLAND
ATLANTIC OCEAN
UNITED STATES
Kansas
Missouri
ILLINOIS
Wabash
White
WEST VIRGINIA
James
Chesapeake Bay
Lake of the Ozarks
St. Louis
VIRGINIA
MISSOURI
Flint Hills
Neosho
Green
KENTUCKY
Lake Cumberland
Cumberland
Cumberland Plateau
Blue Ridge
Piedmont
Roanoke
Albemarle Sound
Cape Hatteras
Pamlico Sound
Ozark Plateau
Mt. Mitchell 6,684 Ft. 2,037m
NORTH CAROLINA
Kentucky Lake
Boston Mts.
White
TENNESSEE
Cape Fear
Coastal Plain
Cape Lookout
Arkansas
Ouachita Mts.
ARKANSAS
Tennessee
SOUTH CAROLINA
Pee Dee
Santee
Clarks Hill Lake
Atlanta
Savannah
Yazoo
Tombigbee
Ouachita
MISSISSIPPI
ALABAMA
GEORGIA
Sea Islands
Land Elevation
Meters
Feet
3,000
9,840
2,000
6,560
500
1,640
200
656
0
0
Water Depth
0
0
200
656
2,000
6,560
N
Sabine
Pearl
Alabama
Chattahoochee
Flint
Altamaha
Sam Rayburn Res.
Toledo Bend Res.
Red
Trinity
Mississippi
LOUISIANA
Suwannee
0 100 200 300 Miles
0 100 200 300 400 Kilometers
Copyright by Rand McNally & Co.
Alber's Conic Equal Area Projection
Houston
New Orleans
Cape San Blas
Apalachee Bay
Atchafalaya Bay
Mississippi Delta
Cape Canaveral
FLORIDA
Tampa Bay
Lake Okeechobee
GULF OF MEXICO
The Everglades
Miami
Cape Sable
Florida Keys
ATLANTIC OCEAN
San Juan
Arecibo
Mayagüez
Ponce
Caguas
PUERTO RICO (U.S.)
0 25 50 Miles
0 25 50 Kilometers
Caribbean Sea
© RMcN.
95°
90°
85°
80°
75°
70°
50°
45°
40°
35°
30°
25°
19°
18°
67°
66°

A23

Guam

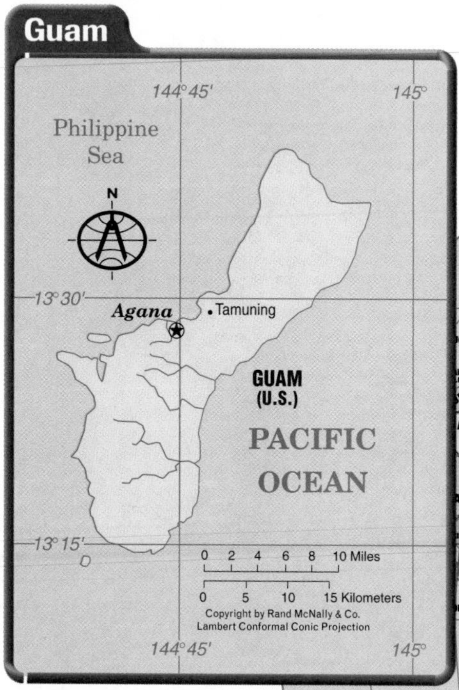

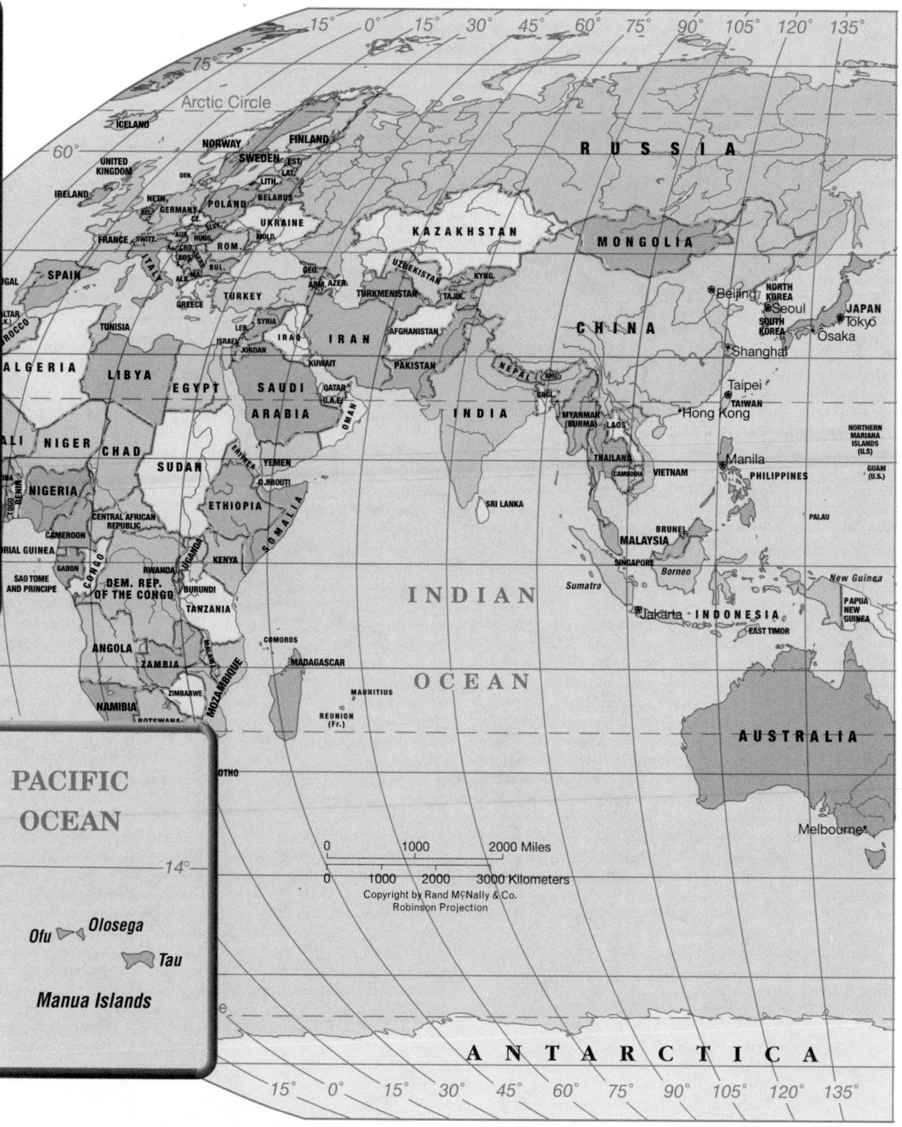

Samoa

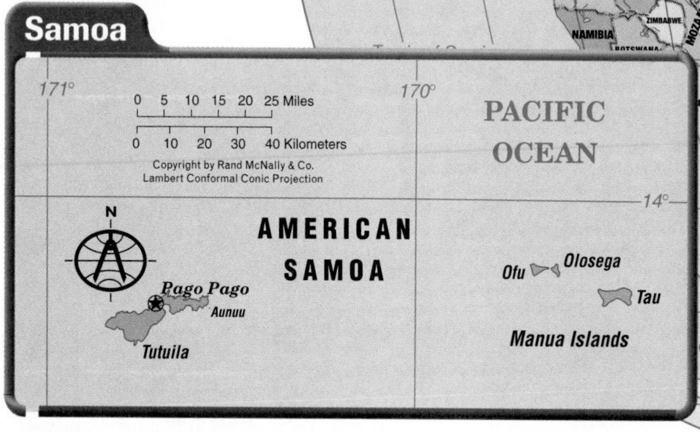

Pacific Islands

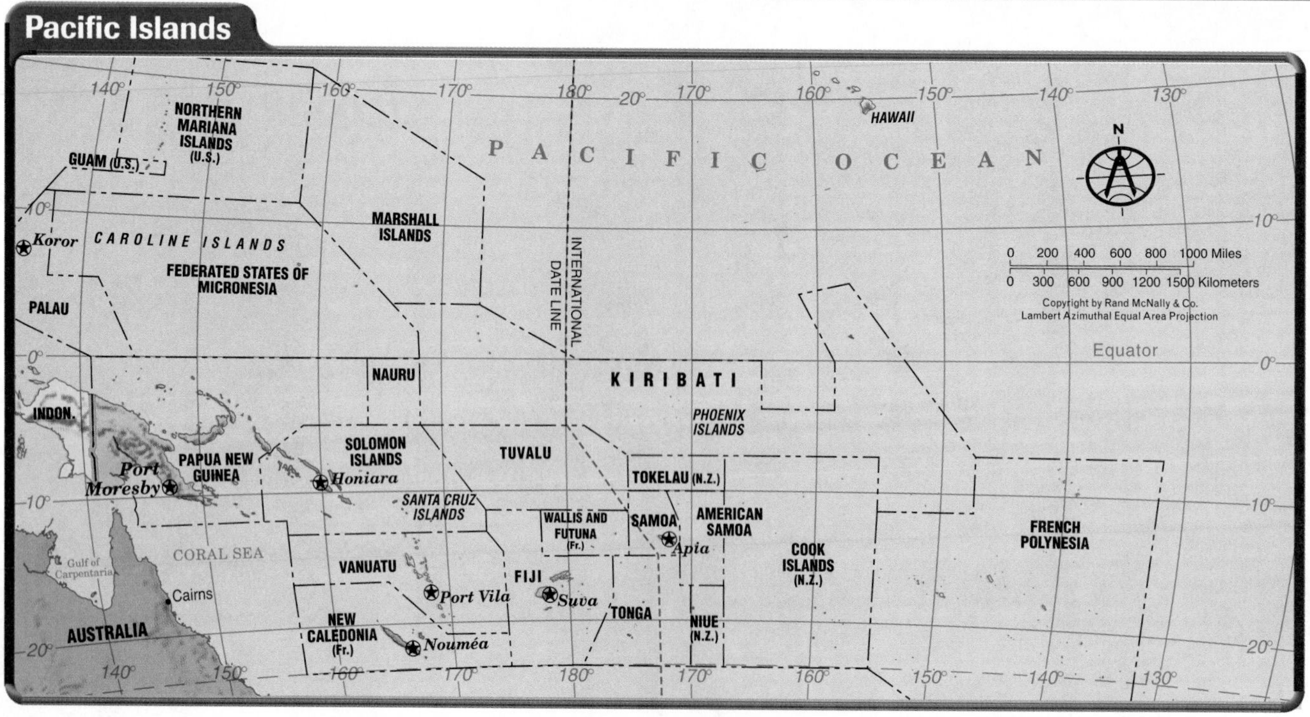

A24

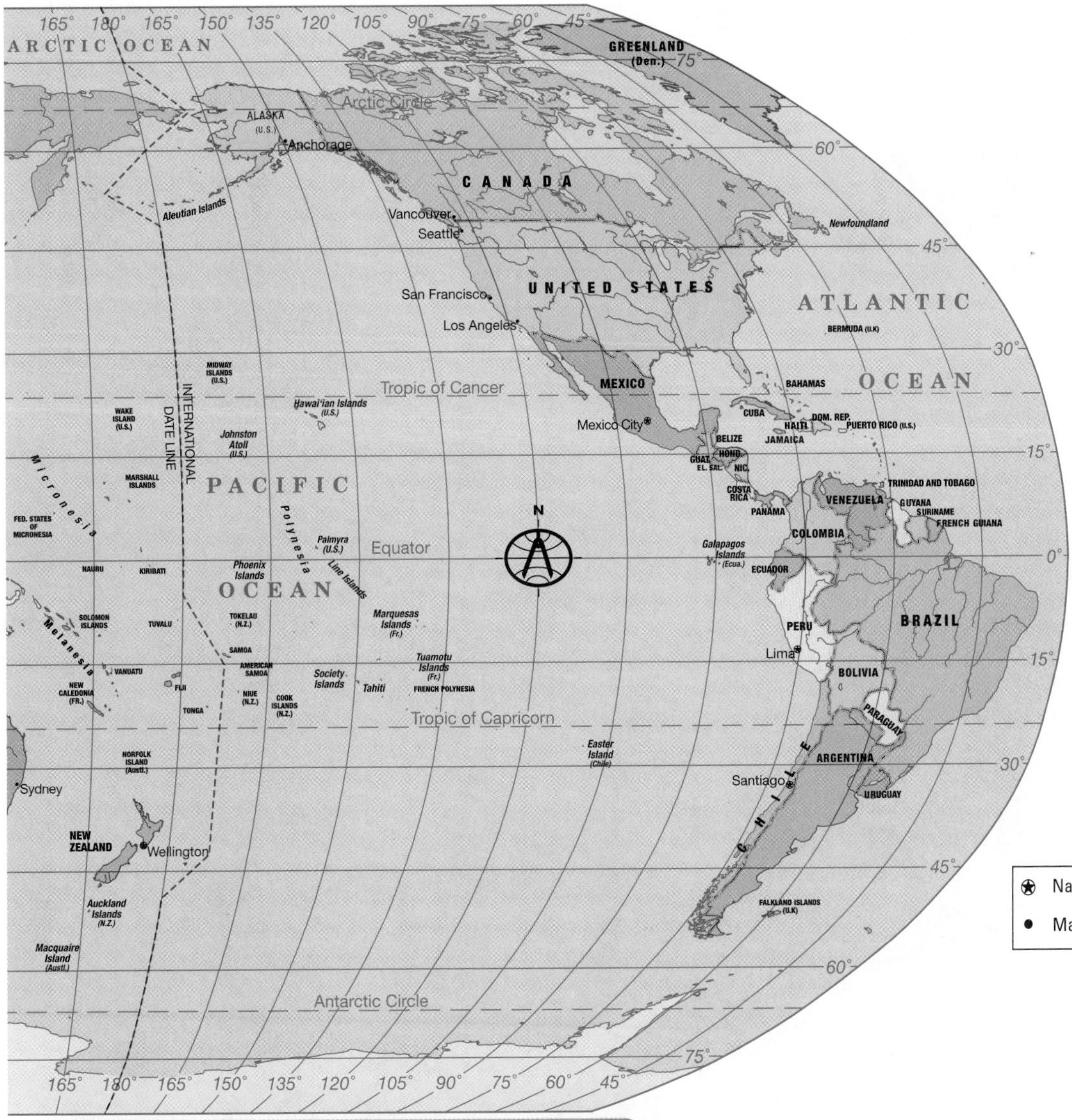

Puerto Rico and the U.S. Virgin Islands

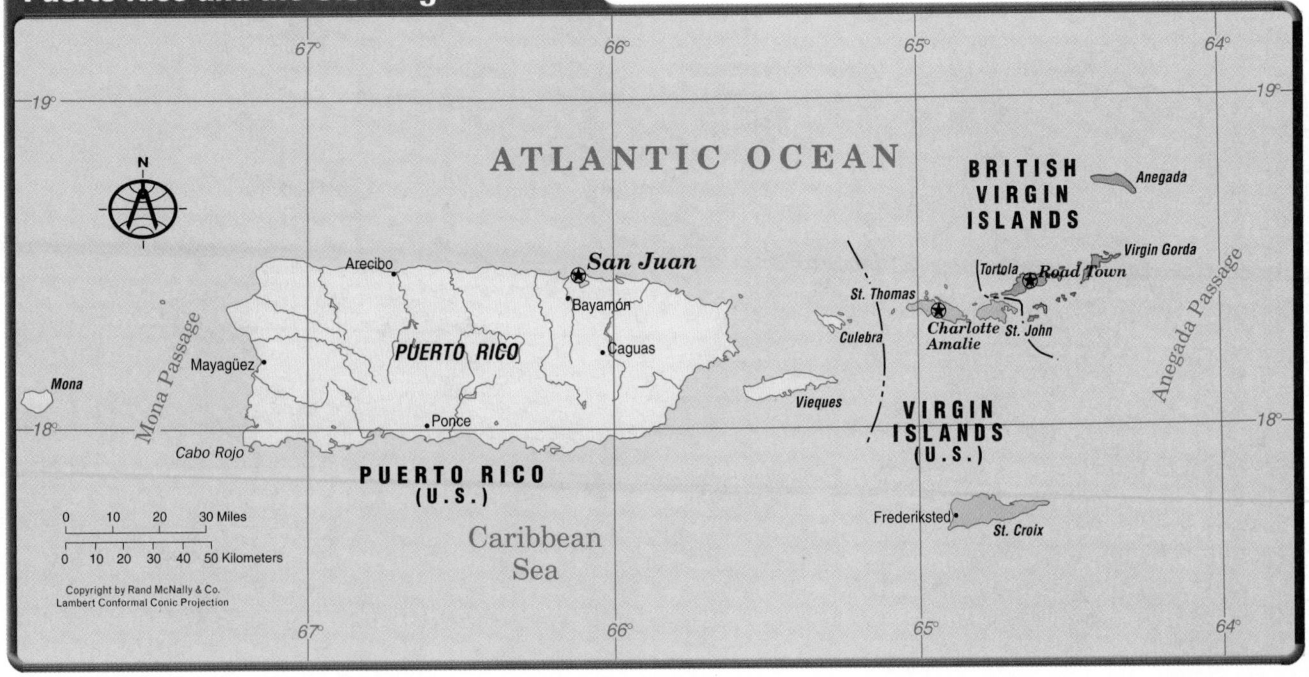

A26

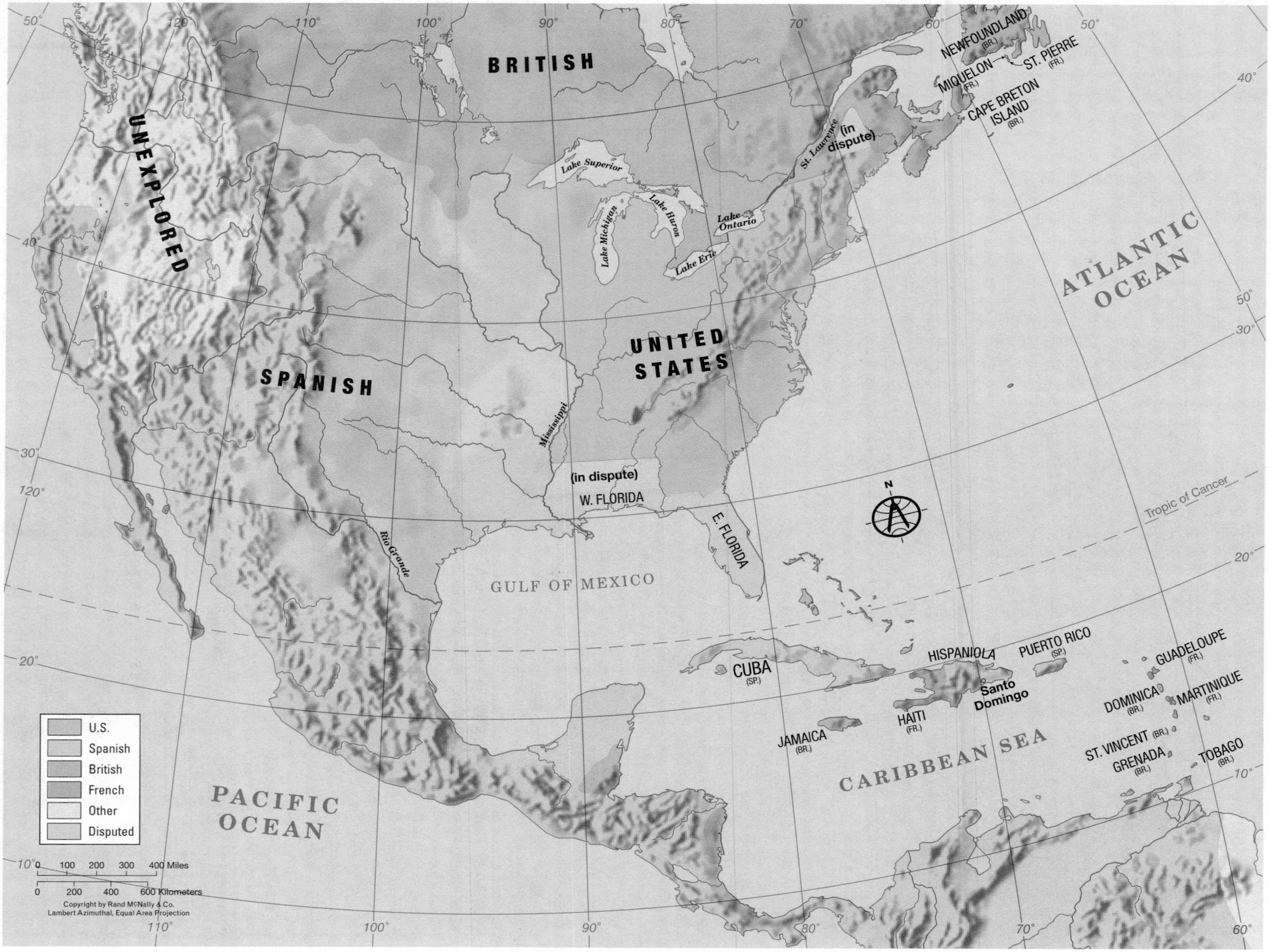
BRITISH
UNEXPLORED
SPANISH
UNITED STATES
NEWFOUNDLAND (BR.)
MIQUELON (FR.)
ST. PIERRE (FR.)
CAPE BRETON ISLAND (BR.)
St. Lawrence
(in dispute)
Lake Superior
Lake Michigan
Lake Huron
Lake Ontario
Lake Erie
ATLANTIC OCEAN
Mississippi
(in dispute)
W. FLORIDA
E. FLORIDA
Rio Grande
GULF OF MEXICO
Tropic of Cancer
N
CUBA (SP.)
HISPANIOLA
PUERTO RICO (SP.)
GUADELOUPE (FR.)
Santo Domingo
HAITI (FR.)
JAMAICA (BR.)
DOMINICA (BR.)
MARTINIQUE (FR.)
ST. VINCENT (BR.)
GRENADA (BR.)
TOBAGO (BR.)
CARIBBEAN SEA
PACIFIC OCEAN
U.S.
Spanish
British
French
Other
Disputed
0 100 200 300 400 Miles
0 200 400 600 Kilometers
Copyright by Rand McNally & Co.
Lambert Azimuthal, Equal Area Projection
50°
40°
30°
20°
10°
120°
110°
100°
90°
80°
70°
60°

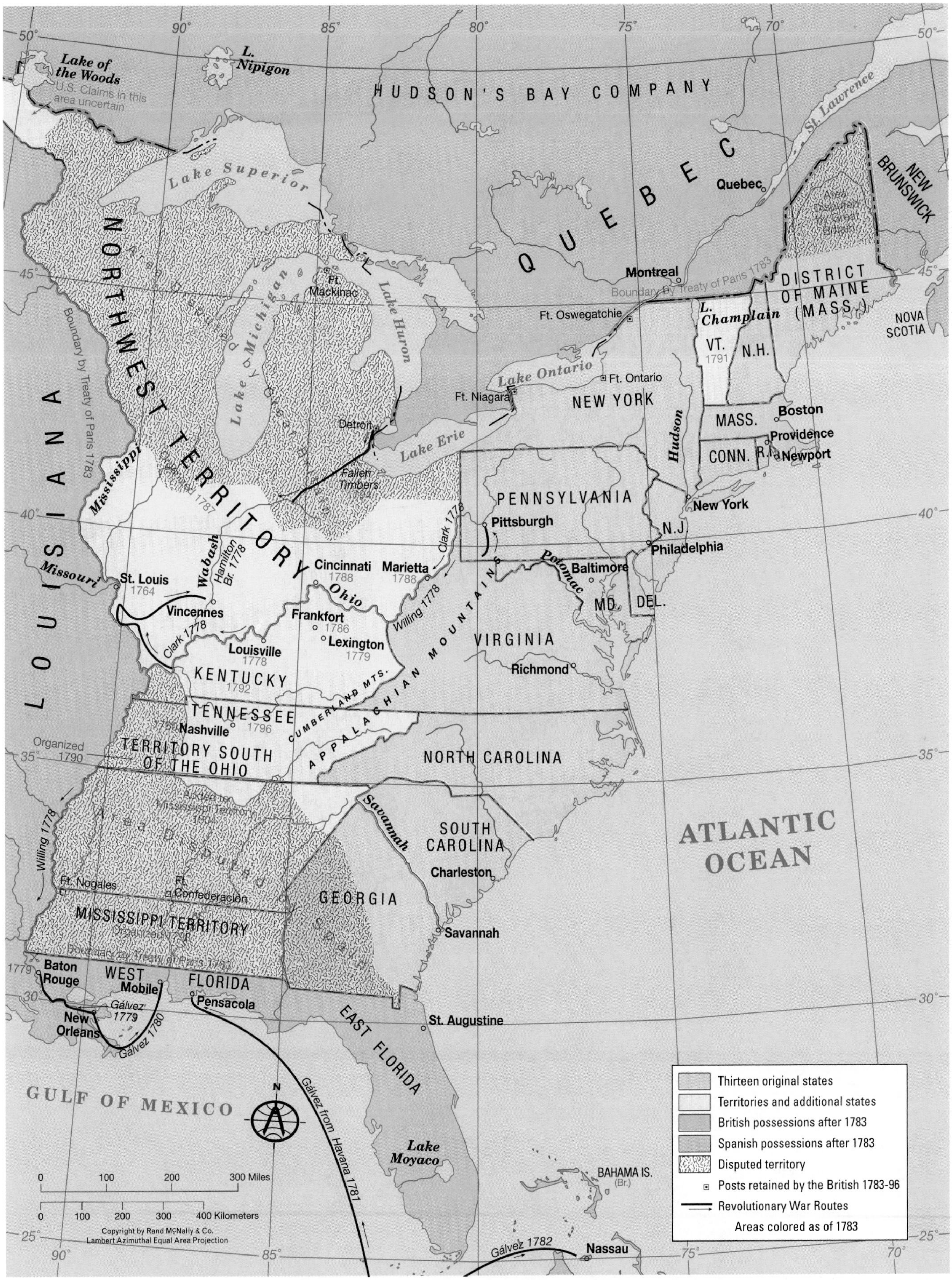
Lake of the Woods
U.S. Claims in this area uncertain
L. Nipigon
HUDSON'S BAY COMPANY
St. Lawrence
Lake Superior
QUEBEC
Quebec
NEW BRUNSWICK
NORTHWEST TERRITORY
Ft. Mackinac
Lake Huron
Lake Michigan
Montreal
Boundary by Treaty of Paris 1783
DISTRICT OF MAINE (MASS.)
Ft. Oswegatchie
L. Champlain
NOVA SCOTIA
Boundary by Treaty of Paris 1783
VT. 1791
N.H.
Lake Ontario
Ft. Ontario
Ft. Niagara
NEW YORK
LOUISIANA
MASS.
Boston
Detroit
Hudson
Providence
Lake Erie
CONN.
R.I.
Newport
Mississippi
Fallen Timbers 1794
1787
PENNSYLVANIA
New York
Clark 1778
Pittsburgh
N.J.
Philadelphia
Wabash
Hamilton Br. 1778
Missouri
St. Louis 1764
Cincinnati 1788
Marietta 1788
Potomac
Baltimore
Ohio
Vincennes
MD.
DEL.
Willing 1778
Frankfort 1786
Clark 1778
Lexington 1779
APPALACHIAN MOUNTAINS
VIRGINIA
Louisville 1778
Richmond
KENTUCKY 1792
CUMBERLAND MTS.
TENNESSEE 1796
Nashville
Organized 1790
TERRITORY SOUTH OF THE OHIO
NORTH CAROLINA
Savannah
Willing 1778
SOUTH CAROLINA
ATLANTIC OCEAN
Charleston
Ft. Nogales
Ft. Confederación
GEORGIA
MISSISSIPPI TERRITORY
Savannah
1779
Baton Rouge
WEST FLORIDA
Mobile
Pensacola
Gálvez 1779
Gálvez 1780
New Orleans
St. Augustine
EAST FLORIDA
GULF OF MEXICO
N
Gálvez from Havana 1781
Lake Moyaco
BAHAMA IS. (Br.)
Gálvez 1782
Nassau
0 100 200 300 Miles
0 100 200 300 400 Kilometers
Copyright by Rand McNally & Co.
Lambert Azimuthal Equal Area Projection
Thirteen original states
Territories and additional states
British possessions after 1783
Spanish possessions after 1783
Disputed territory
Posts retained by the British 1783-96
Revolutionary War Routes
Areas colored as of 1783
50° 90° 85° 80° 75° 70° 45° 40° 35° 30° 25°

A27

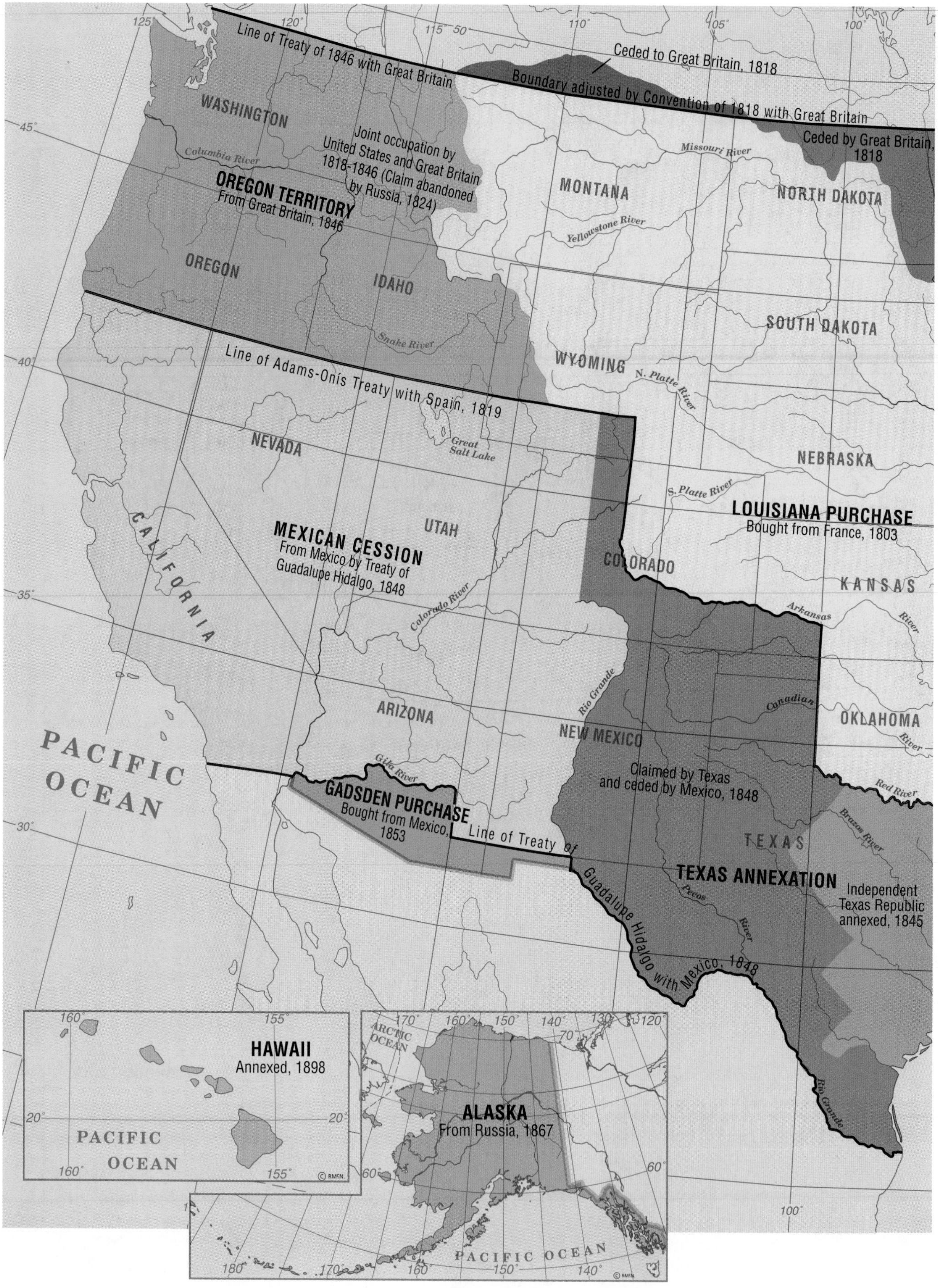
Line of Treaty of 1846 with Great Britain
Ceded to Great Britain, 1818
Boundary adjusted by Convention of 1818 with Great Britain
Ceded by Great Britain, 1818
WASHINGTON
Joint occupation by United States and Great Britain 1818-1846 (Claim abandoned by Russia, 1824)
OREGON TERRITORY
From Great Britain, 1846
Columbia River
MONTANA
NORTH DAKOTA
Missouri River
Yellowstone River
OREGON
IDAHO
Snake River
SOUTH DAKOTA
WYOMING
N. Platte River
Line of Adams-Onís Treaty with Spain, 1819
Great Salt Lake
NEVADA
NEBRASKA
S. Platte River
LOUISIANA PURCHASE
Bought from France, 1803
UTAH
MEXICAN CESSION
From Mexico by Treaty of Guadalupe Hidalgo, 1848
CALIFORNIA
COLORADO
KANSAS
Arkansas River
Colorado River
Rio Grande
Canadian River
ARIZONA
NEW MEXICO
OKLAHOMA
PACIFIC OCEAN
Gila River
Claimed by Texas and ceded by Mexico, 1848
Red River
GADSDEN PURCHASE
Bought from Mexico, 1853
Line of Treaty of Guadalupe Hidalgo with Mexico, 1848
TEXAS
Brazos River
TEXAS ANNEXATION
Independent Texas Republic annexed, 1845
Pecos River
HAWAII
Annexed, 1898
PACIFIC OCEAN
ARCTIC OCEAN
ALASKA
From Russia, 1867
PACIFIC OCEAN
© RMN.

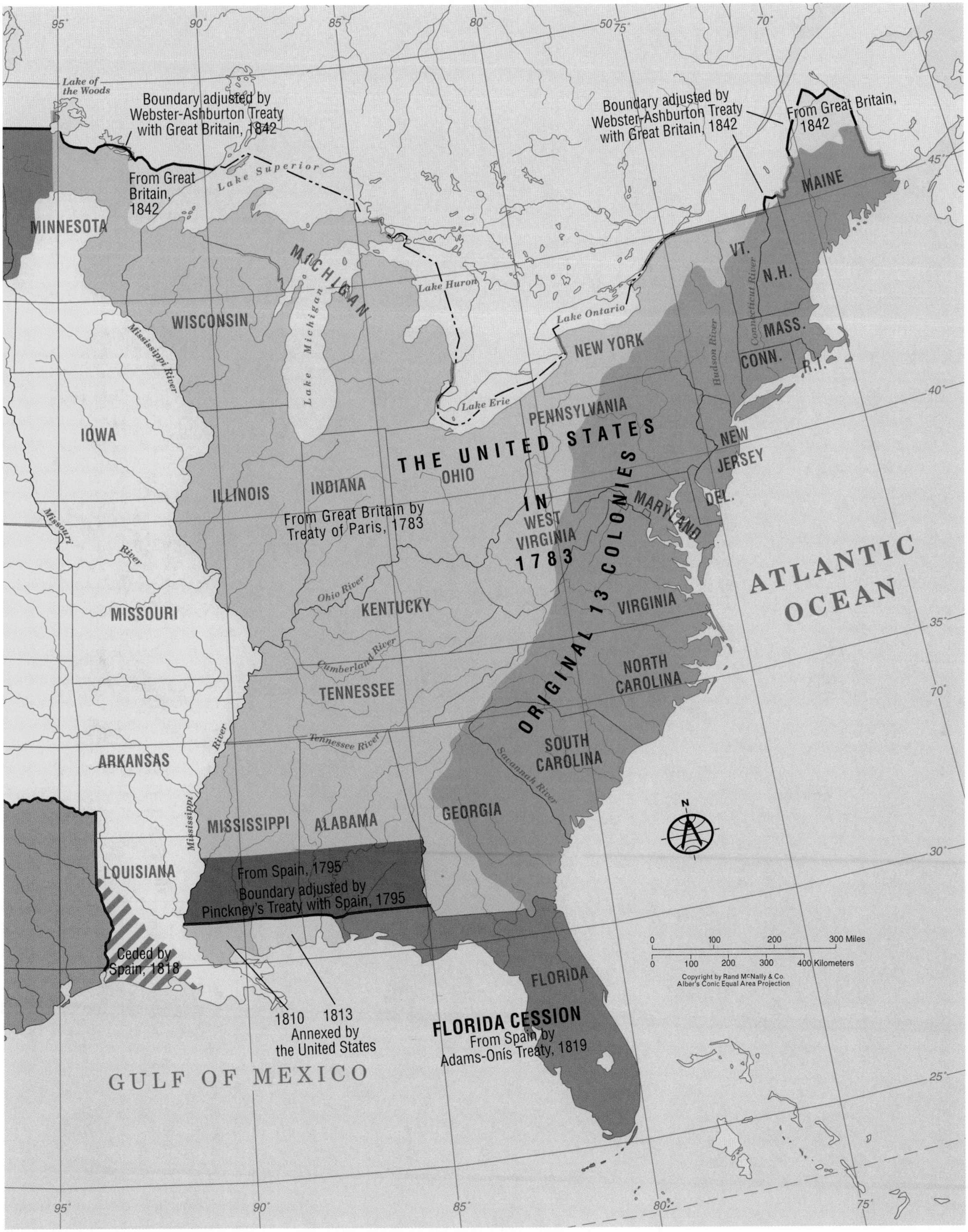
Lake of the Woods
Boundary adjusted by Webster-Ashburton Treaty with Great Britain, 1842
From Great Britain, 1842
MINNESOTA
Lake Superior
MICHIGAN
Lake Huron
Lake Michigan
WISCONSIN
Mississippi River
Lake Ontario
Lake Erie
NEW YORK
Boundary adjusted by Webster-Ashburton Treaty with Great Britain, 1842
From Great Britain, 1842
MAINE
VT.
N.H.
MASS.
CONN.
R.I.
Connecticut River
Hudson River
PENNSYLVANIA
NEW JERSEY
DEL.
MARYLAND
IOWA
ILLINOIS
INDIANA
OHIO
THE UNITED STATES IN 1783
ORIGINAL 13 COLONIES
WEST VIRGINIA
From Great Britain by Treaty of Paris, 1783
Missouri River
Ohio River
MISSOURI
KENTUCKY
VIRGINIA
Cumberland River
TENNESSEE
NORTH CAROLINA
Tennessee River
SOUTH CAROLINA
Savannah River
ARKANSAS
MISSISSIPPI
ALABAMA
GEORGIA
ATLANTIC OCEAN
LOUISIANA
From Spain, 1795
Boundary adjusted by Pinckney's Treaty with Spain, 1795
Ceded by Spain, 1818
1810
1813
Annexed by the United States
FLORIDA
FLORIDA CESSION
From Spain by Adams-Onís Treaty, 1819
GULF OF MEXICO
N
0 100 200 300 Miles
0 100 200 300 400 Kilometers
Copyright by Rand McNally & Co.
Alber's Conic Equal Area Projection
95° 90° 85° 80° 75° 70° 50° 45° 40° 35° 30° 25°

A29

A30

CANADA
WASHINGTON TERRITORY
Free by Oregon Act 1848
Open to Slavery by Dred Scott Decision 1857
Olympia
Columbia
Salem
OREGON
Free by Oregon Act 1848
Snake
(UNORGANIZED)
Free by Missouri Compromise 1820
Open to Slavery by Dred Scott Decision 1857
MINNESOTA
St. Paul
WISCONSIN
Milwaukee
Lake Superior
Lake Michigan
Lake Huron
MICHIGAN
Detroit
NEBRASKA TERRITORY
Free by Missouri Compromise 1820
Open to Slavery by Kansas-Nebraska Act 1854
Yankton
Missouri
Omaha
IOWA
Des Moines
Chicago
ILLINOIS
INDIANA
Indianapolis
OHIO
Cincinnati
Ohio
Cleveland
Lake Erie
Lake Ontario
Buffalo
Albany
NEW YORK
MAINE
Portland
V.T.
N.H.
MASS.
Boston
CONN.
R.I.
New York
NEW JERSEY
PENNSYLVANIA
Pittsburgh
Philadelphia
Baltimore
DEL.
MARYLAND
Washington
Carson City
Sacramento
San Francisco
Salt Lake City
UTAH TERRITORY
Open to Slavery by Compromise of 1850
Denver City
CALIFORNIA
Topeka
KANSAS TERRITORY
Free by Missouri Compromise 1820
Open to Slavery by Kansas-Nebraska Act 1854
St. Louis
Jefferson City
MISSOURI
Louisville
Lexington
KENTUCKY
VIRGINIA
Richmond
Norfolk
Colorado
Missouri Compromise line 1820 36° 30'
Los Angeles
Santa Fe
NEW MEXICO TERRITORY
Open to Slavery by Compromise of 1850
INDIAN TERRITORY
ARKANSAS
Memphis
Mississippi
TENNESSEE
Nashville
NORTH CAROLINA
Wilmington
Little Rock
Atlanta
SOUTH CAROLINA
Charleston
PACIFIC OCEAN
Tucson
MISSISSIPPI
ALABAMA
GEORGIA
Savannah
ATLANTIC OCEAN
Shreveport
TEXAS
Mobile
St. Augustine
San Antonio
New Orleans
LOUISIANA
GULF OF MEXICO
FLORIDA
MEXICO
50% and over Slaves
1% to 50% Slaves
Open to Slavery
Free States
Railroad
Tobacco
Cotton
Sugar
Rice
Abolitionist Incidents
Slave Revolts
0 100 200 300 400 Miles
0 100 200 300 400 500 600 Kilometers
Copyright by Rand McNally & Co.
Alber's Conic Equal Area Projection
N

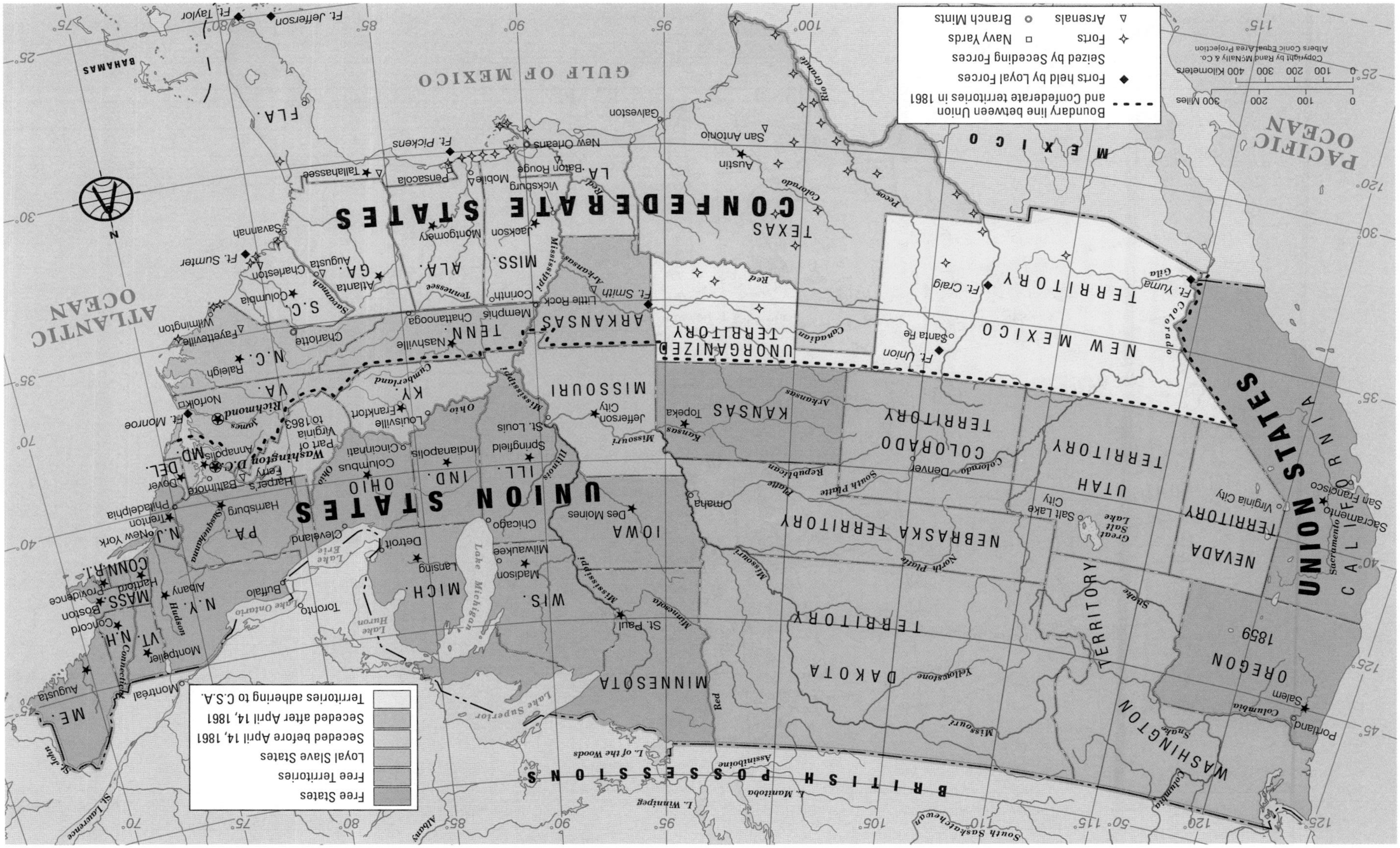
Free States
Free Territories
Loyal Slave States
Seceded before April 14, 1861
Seceded after April 14, 1861
Territories adhering to C.S.A.
Boundary line between Union and Confederate territories in 1861
Forts held by Loyal Forces
Seized by Seceding Forces
Forts
Navy Yards
Arsenals
Branch Mints
0 100 200 300 Miles
0 100 200 300 400 Kilometers
Copyright by Rand McNally & Co.
Albers Conic Equal Area Projection
UNION STATES
CONFEDERATE STATES
BRITISH POSSESSIONS
MEXICO
GULF OF MEXICO
ATLANTIC OCEAN
PACIFIC OCEAN
BAHAMAS
WASHINGTON TERRITORY
OREGON 1859
CALIFORNIA
NEVADA TERRITORY
UTAH TERRITORY
NEW MEXICO TERRITORY
COLORADO TERRITORY
NEBRASKA TERRITORY
DAKOTA TERRITORY
KANSAS
UNORGANIZED TERRITORY
TEXAS
MINNESOTA
IOWA
MISSOURI
ARKANSAS
LA.
WIS.
ILL.
MISS.
MICH.
IND.
KY.
TENN.
ALA.
OHIO
GA.
FLA.
S.C.
N.C.
VA.
PA.
N.Y.
N.J.
DEL.
MD.
VT.
N.H.
MASS.
CONN.
R.I.
ME.
Washington D.C.
Richmond
Part of Virginia to 1863
Ft. Sumter
Ft. Monroe
Ft. Pickens
Ft. Taylor
Ft. Jefferson
Ft. Smith
Ft. Union
Ft. Craig
Ft. Yuma

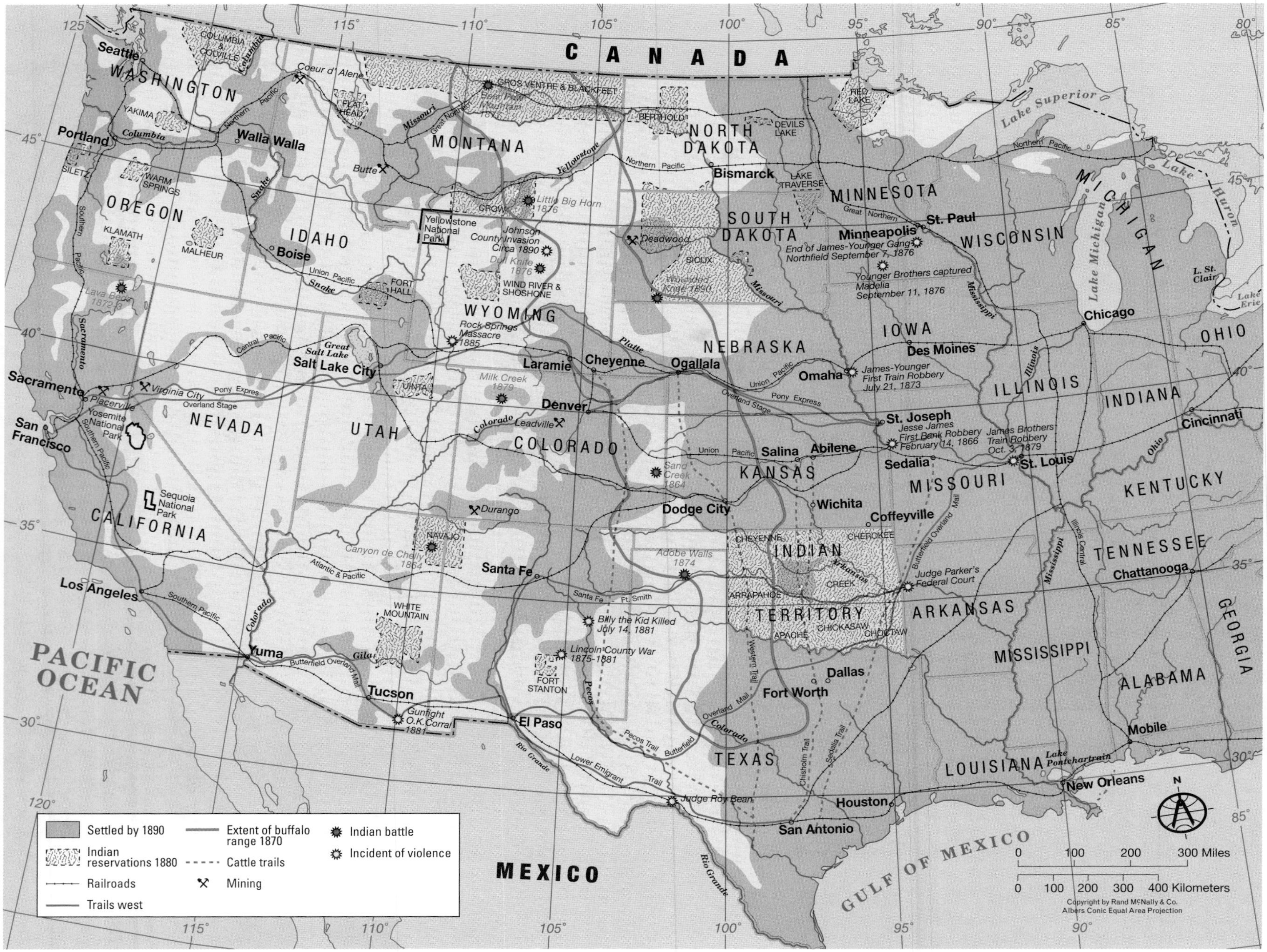
CANADA
MEXICO
PACIFIC OCEAN
GULF OF MEXICO
WASHINGTON
OREGON
CALIFORNIA
NEVADA
IDAHO
MONTANA
WYOMING
UTAH
COLORADO
NORTH DAKOTA
SOUTH DAKOTA
NEBRASKA
KANSAS
INDIAN TERRITORY
TEXAS
MINNESOTA
IOWA
MISSOURI
ARKANSAS
LOUISIANA
WISCONSIN
ILLINOIS
MICHIGAN
INDIANA
OHIO
KENTUCKY
TENNESSEE
MISSISSIPPI
ALABAMA
GEORGIA
Seattle
Portland
Walla Walla
Boise
Butte
Coeur d' Alene
Sacramento
San Francisco
Placerville
Virginia City
Los Angeles
Yuma
Tucson
El Paso
Santa Fe
Salt Lake City
Laramie
Cheyenne
Denver
Leadville
Durango
Ogallala
Dodge City
Salina
Abilene
Wichita
Coffeyville
Omaha
St. Joseph
Sedalia
St. Louis
Des Moines
Bismarck
Deadwood
Minneapolis
St. Paul
Chicago
Cincinnati
Chattanooga
Mobile
New Orleans
Dallas
Fort Worth
Houston
San Antonio
COLUMBIA & COLVILLE
YAKIMA
SILETZ
WARM SPRINGS
KLAMATH
MALHEUR
FLAT HEAD
GROS VENTRE & BLACKFEET
BERTHOLD
DEVILS LAKE
RED LAKE
LAKE TRAVERSE
SIOUX
CROW
FORT HALL
WIND RIVER & SHOSHONE
UINTA
NAVAJO
WHITE MOUNTAIN
FORT STANTON
CHEYENNE
ARAPAHOE
APACHE
CHEROKEE
CREEK
CHICKASAW
CHOCTAW
Yellowstone National Park
Yosemite National Park
Sequoia National Park
Lava Beds 1872-73
Little Big Horn 1876
Johnson County Invasion Circa 1890
Dull Knife 1876
Rock Springs Massacre 1885
Milk Creek 1879
Sand Creek 1864
Wounded Knee 1890
Canyon de Chelly 1864
Adobe Walls 1874
Billy the Kid Killed July 14, 1881
Lincoln County War 1875-1881
Gunfight O.K. Corral 1881
Judge Roy Bean
Judge Parker's Federal Court
End of James-Younger Gang Northfield September 7, 1876
Younger Brothers captured Madelia September 11, 1876
James-Younger First Train Robbery July 21, 1873
Jesse James First Bank Robbery February 14, 1866
James Brothers Train Robbery Oct. 3, 1879
Northern Pacific
Great Northern
Union Pacific
Central Pacific
Southern Pacific
Atlantic & Pacific
Illinois Central
Pony Express
Overland Stage
Butterfield Overland Mail
Overland Mail
Santa Fe
Ft. Smith
Western Trail
Chisholm Trail
Sedalia Trail
Pecos Trail
Lower Emigrant Trail
Columbia
Snake
Missouri
Yellowstone
Platte
Colorado
Gila
Pecos
Rio Grande
Arkansas
Mississippi
Illinois
Ohio
Sacramento
Great Salt Lake
Lake Superior
Lake Michigan
Lake Huron
Lake Erie
L. St. Clair
Lake Pontchartrain
Settled by 1890
Indian reservations 1880
Railroads
Trails west
Extent of buffalo range 1870
Cattle trails
Mining
Indian battle
Incident of violence
0 100 200 300 Miles
0 100 200 300 400 Kilometers
N
Copyright by Rand McNally & Co.
Albers Conic Equal Area Projection
125° 120° 115° 110° 105° 100° 95° 90° 85° 80°
45° 40° 35° 30°

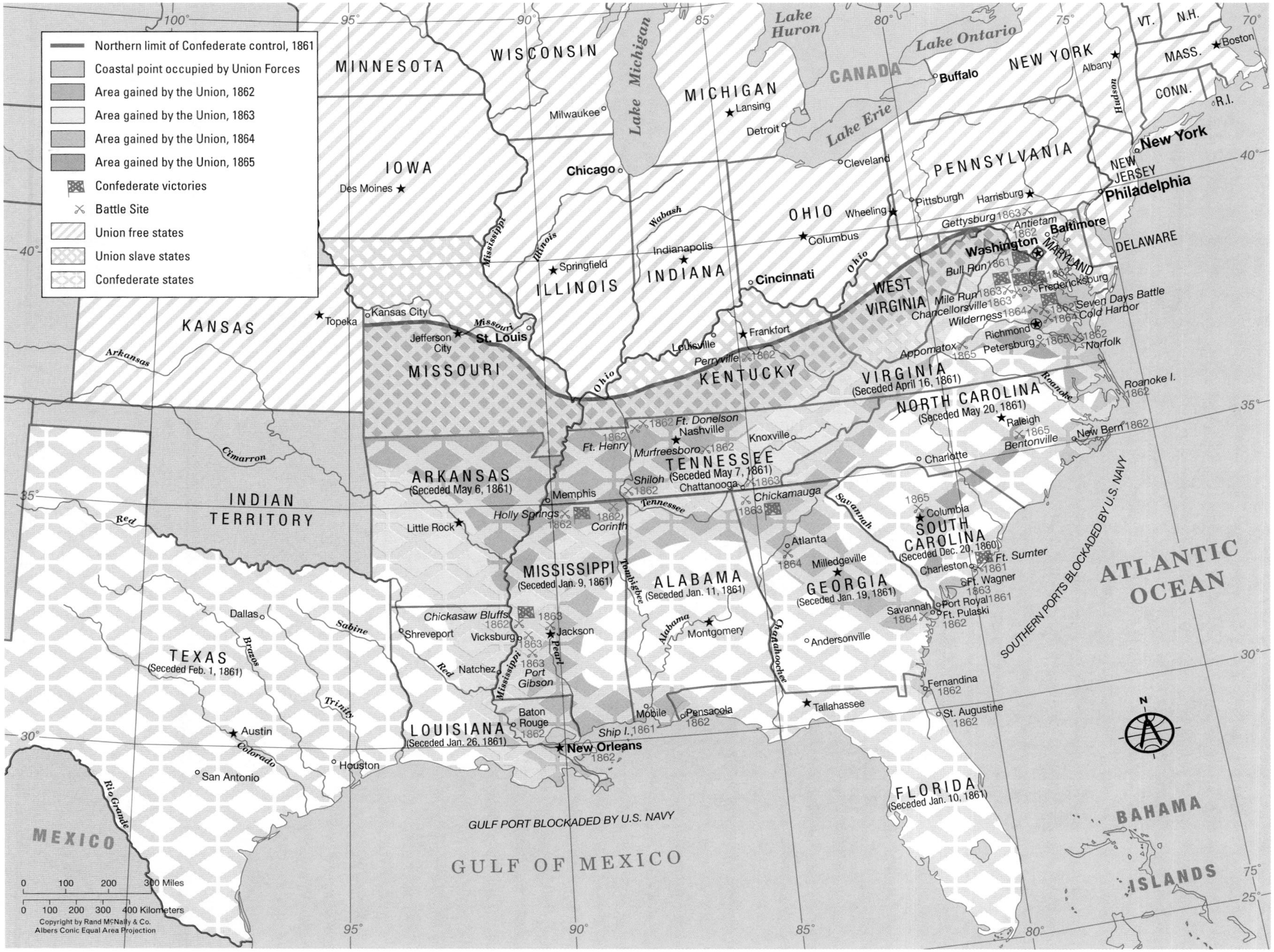
Northern limit of Confederate control, 1861
Coastal point occupied by Union Forces
Area gained by the Union, 1862
Area gained by the Union, 1863
Area gained by the Union, 1864
Area gained by the Union, 1865
Confederate victories
Battle Site
Union free states
Union slave states
Confederate states
MINNESOTA
WISCONSIN
MICHIGAN
IOWA
ILLINOIS
INDIANA
OHIO
PENNSYLVANIA
NEW YORK
VT.
N.H.
MASS.
CONN.
R.I.
NEW JERSEY
DELAWARE
MARYLAND
KANSAS
MISSOURI
KENTUCKY
WEST VIRGINIA
VIRGINIA (Seceded April 16, 1861)
NORTH CAROLINA (Seceded May 20, 1861)
TENNESSEE (Seceded May 7, 1861)
SOUTH CAROLINA (Seceded Dec. 20, 1860)
GEORGIA (Seceded Jan. 19, 1861)
ALABAMA (Seceded Jan. 11, 1861)
MISSISSIPPI (Seceded Jan. 9, 1861)
ARKANSAS (Seceded May 6, 1861)
LOUISIANA (Seceded Jan. 26, 1861)
TEXAS (Seceded Feb. 1, 1861)
FLORIDA (Seceded Jan. 10, 1861)
INDIAN TERRITORY
CANADA
MEXICO
Lake Huron
Lake Michigan
Lake Ontario
Lake Erie
ATLANTIC OCEAN
GULF OF MEXICO
BAHAMA ISLANDS
SOUTHERN PORTS BLOCKADED BY U.S. NAVY
GULF PORT BLOCKADED BY U.S. NAVY
Boston
Albany
Buffalo
New York
Philadelphia
Harrisburg
Pittsburgh
Gettysburg 1863
Antietam 1862
Baltimore
Washington
Bull Run 1861
Fredericksburg 1862
Seven Days Battle 1862
Cold Harbor 1864
Mile Run 1863
Chancellorsville 1863
Wilderness 1864
Richmond
Petersburg 1865
Appomattox 1865
Norfolk 1862
Roanoke I. 1862
New Bern 1862
Raleigh
Bentonville 1865
Charlotte
Columbia 1865
Charleston
Ft. Sumter 1861
Ft. Wagner 1863
Port Royal 1861
Ft. Pulaski 1862
Savannah 1864
Fernandina 1862
St. Augustine 1862
Tallahassee
Andersonville
Milledgeville
Atlanta 1864
Chickamauga 1863
Chattanooga 1863
Knoxville
Nashville
Murfreesboro 1862
Ft. Donelson 1862
Ft. Henry 1862
Shiloh 1862
Memphis
Holly Springs 1862
Corinth 1862
Montgomery
Mobile
Pensacola 1862
Ship I. 1861
New Orleans 1862
Baton Rouge 1862
Port Gibson 1863
Natchez
Jackson 1863
Vicksburg 1863
Chickasaw Bluffs 1862
Shreveport
Little Rock
Dallas
Austin
Houston
San Antonio
Frankfort
Perryville 1862
Louisville
Cincinnati
Columbus
Wheeling
Cleveland
Detroit
Lansing
Chicago
Milwaukee
Indianapolis
Springfield
St. Louis
Jefferson City
Kansas City
Topeka
Des Moines
Mississippi
Missouri
Ohio
Illinois
Wabash
Tennessee
Tombigbee
Alabama
Chattahoochee
Savannah
Roanoke
Hudson
Pearl
Red
Sabine
Trinity
Brazos
Colorado
Rio Grande
Arkansas
Cimarron
0 100 200 300 Miles
0 100 200 300 400 Kilometers
Copyright by Rand McNally & Co.
Albers Conic Equal Area Projection

A33

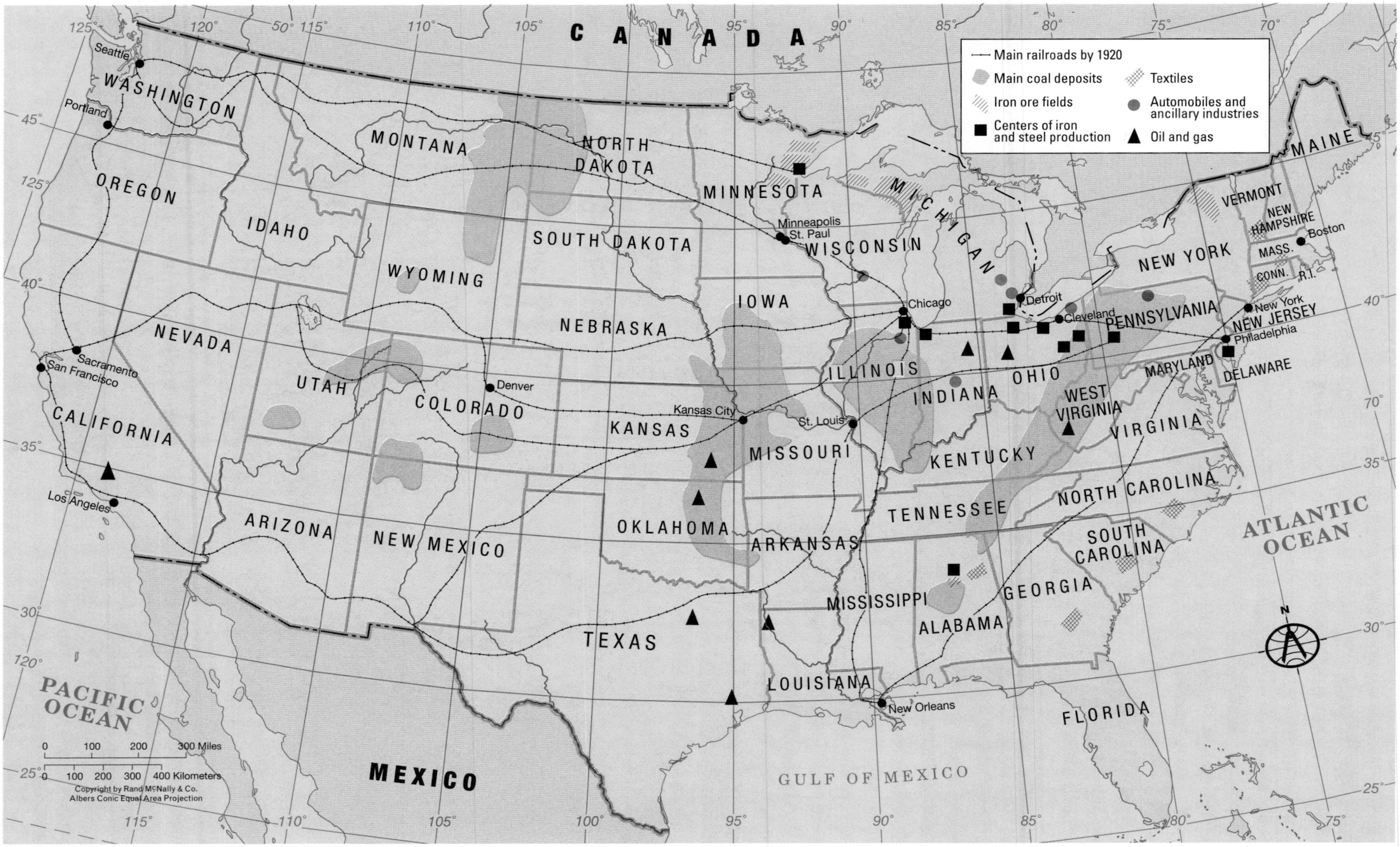
Main railroads by 1920
Main coal deposits
Iron ore fields
Centers of iron and steel production
Textiles
Automobiles and ancillary industries
Oil and gas
CANADA
MEXICO
PACIFIC OCEAN
ATLANTIC OCEAN
GULF OF MEXICO
WASHINGTON
OREGON
CALIFORNIA
NEVADA
IDAHO
MONTANA
WYOMING
UTAH
COLORADO
ARIZONA
NEW MEXICO
NORTH DAKOTA
SOUTH DAKOTA
NEBRASKA
KANSAS
OKLAHOMA
TEXAS
MINNESOTA
IOWA
MISSOURI
ARKANSAS
LOUISIANA
WISCONSIN
ILLINOIS
MICHIGAN
INDIANA
OHIO
KENTUCKY
TENNESSEE
MISSISSIPPI
ALABAMA
GEORGIA
FLORIDA
SOUTH CAROLINA
NORTH CAROLINA
VIRGINIA
WEST VIRGINIA
MARYLAND
DELAWARE
PENNSYLVANIA
NEW JERSEY
NEW YORK
CONN.
R.I.
MASS.
VERMONT
NEW HAMPSHIRE
MAINE
Seattle
Portland
Sacramento
San Francisco
Los Angeles
Denver
Kansas City
St. Louis
Minneapolis
St. Paul
Chicago
Detroit
Cleveland
New York
Philadelphia
Boston
New Orleans
N
0 100 200 300 Miles
0 100 200 300 400 Kilometers
Copyright by Rand McNally & Co.
Albers Conic Equal Area Projection

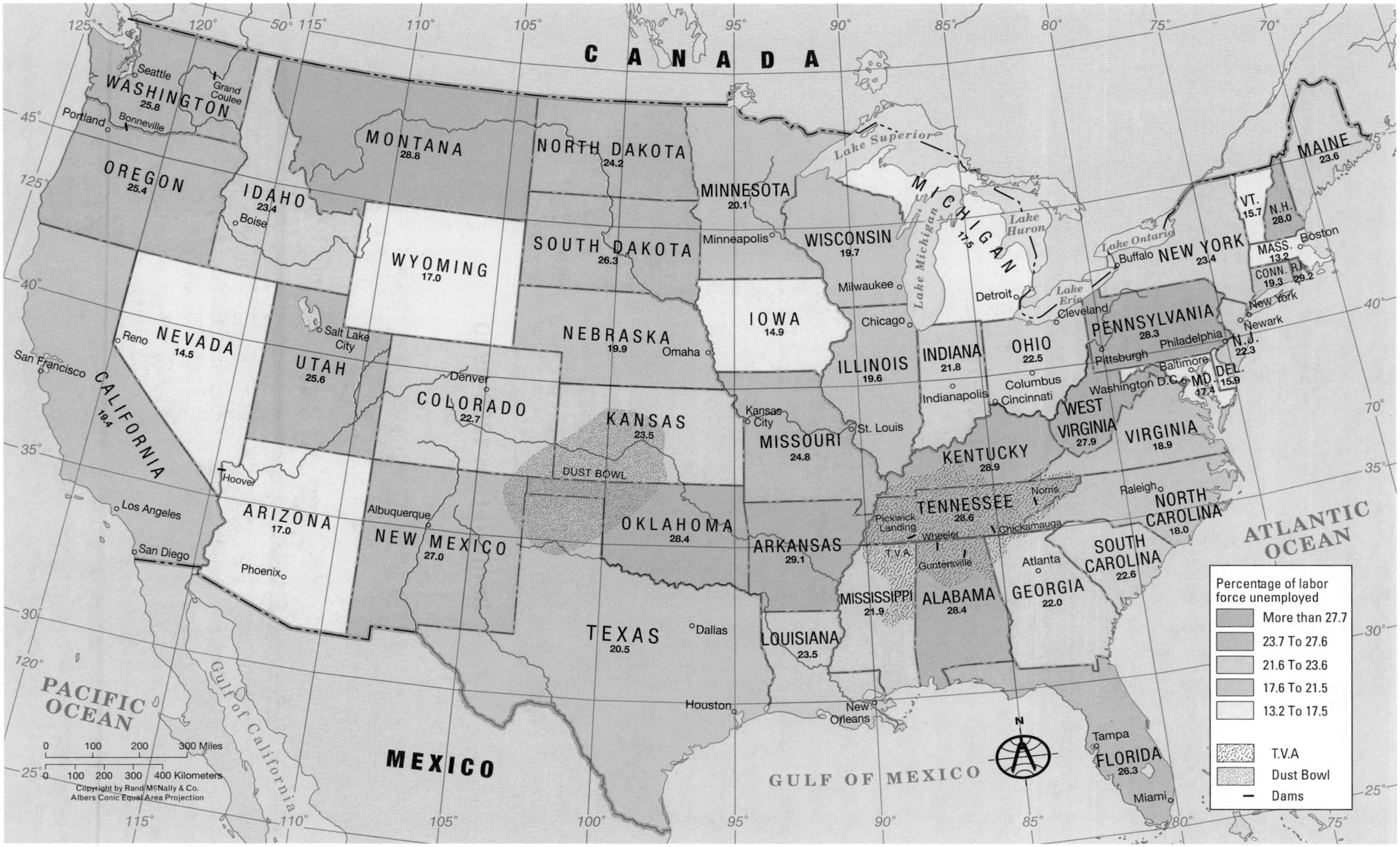
CANADA
MEXICO
PACIFIC OCEAN
ATLANTIC OCEAN
GULF OF MEXICO
Gulf of California
Lake Superior
Lake Michigan
Lake Huron
Lake Erie
Lake Ontario
WASHINGTON 25.8
OREGON 25.4
CALIFORNIA 19.4
NEVADA 14.5
IDAHO 23.4
MONTANA 28.8
WYOMING 17.0
UTAH 25.6
ARIZONA 17.0
COLORADO 22.7
NEW MEXICO 27.0
NORTH DAKOTA 24.2
SOUTH DAKOTA 26.3
NEBRASKA 19.9
KANSAS 23.5
OKLAHOMA 28.4
TEXAS 20.5
MINNESOTA 20.1
IOWA 14.9
MISSOURI 24.8
ARKANSAS 29.1
LOUISIANA 23.5
WISCONSIN 19.7
ILLINOIS 19.6
MICHIGAN 17.5
INDIANA 21.8
OHIO 22.5
KENTUCKY 28.9
TENNESSEE 28.6
MISSISSIPPI 21.9
ALABAMA 28.4
GEORGIA 22.0
FLORIDA 26.3
SOUTH CAROLINA 22.6
NORTH CAROLINA 18.0
VIRGINIA 18.9
WEST VIRGINIA 27.9
PENNSYLVANIA 28.3
NEW YORK 23.4
MD. 17.4
DEL. 15.9
N.J. 22.3
CONN. 19.3
R.I. 29.2
MASS. 13.2
VT. 15.7
N.H. 28.0
MAINE 23.6
Seattle
Portland
Bonneville
Grand Coulee
Boise
San Francisco
Reno
Los Angeles
San Diego
Hoover
Phoenix
Salt Lake City
Denver
Albuquerque
Omaha
Dallas
Houston
Minneapolis
Kansas City
St. Louis
Milwaukee
Chicago
Indianapolis
Detroit
Cleveland
Columbus
Cincinnati
New Orleans
Pickwick Landing
Wheeler
T.V.A.
Guntersville
Chickamauga
Norris
Atlanta
Tampa
Miami
Raleigh
Washington D.C.
Baltimore
Pittsburgh
Philadelphia
Buffalo
Newark
New York
Boston
DUST BOWL
Percentage of labor force unemployed
More than 27.7
23.7 To 27.6
21.6 To 23.6
17.6 To 21.5
13.2 To 17.5
T.V.A
Dust Bowl
Dams
N
0 100 200 300 Miles
0 100 200 300 400 Kilometers
Copyright by Rand McNally & Co.
Albers Conic Equal Area Projection

A35

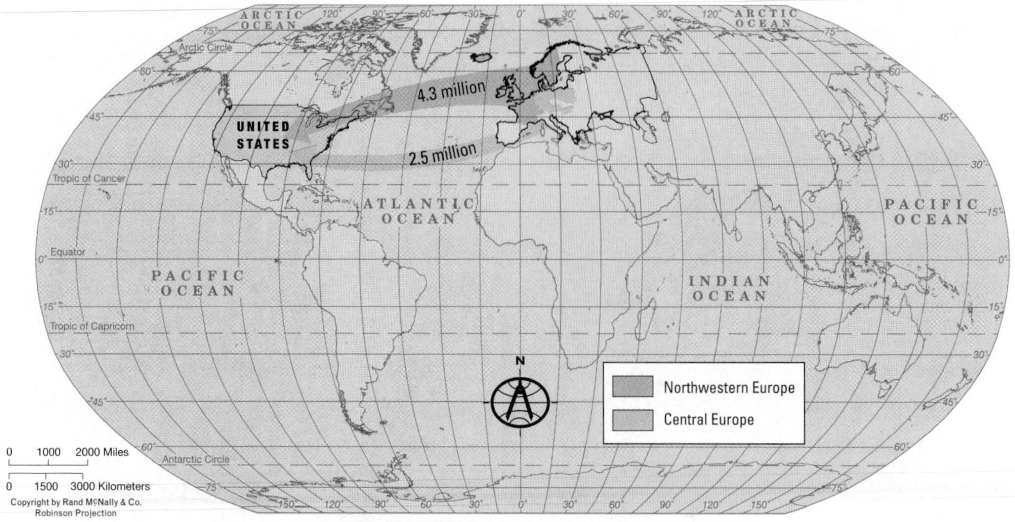

Immigration 1820–1870

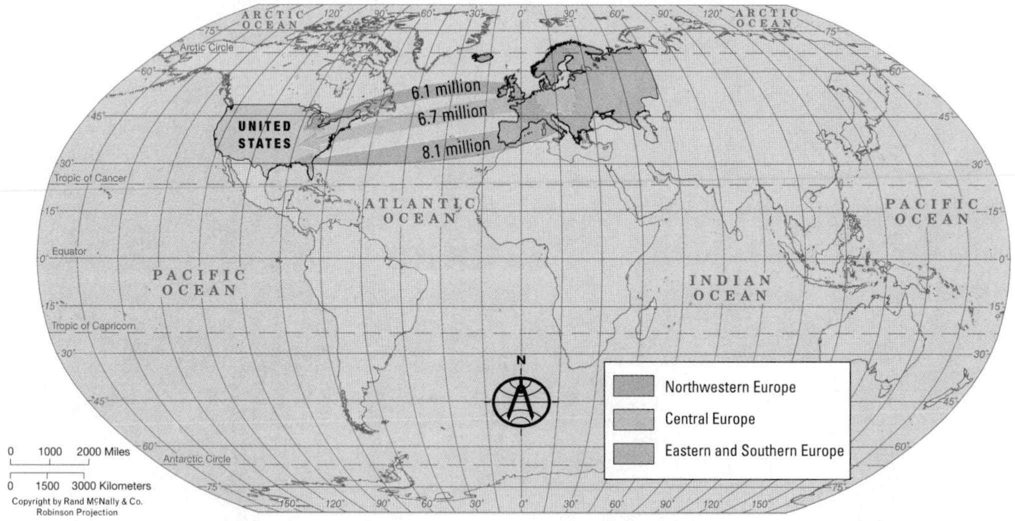

Immigration 1880–1920

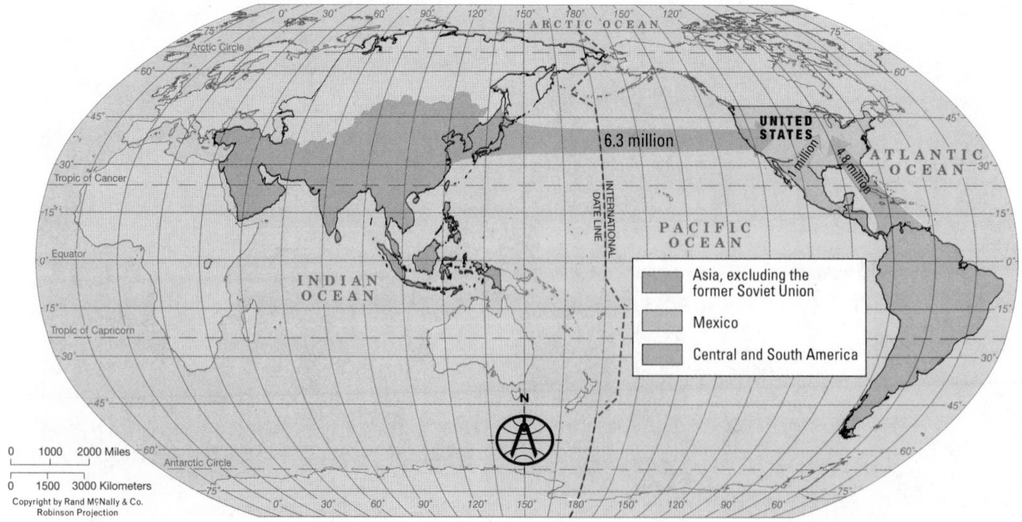

Immigration 1960s–1990s

A36

Immigration's Impact 1910

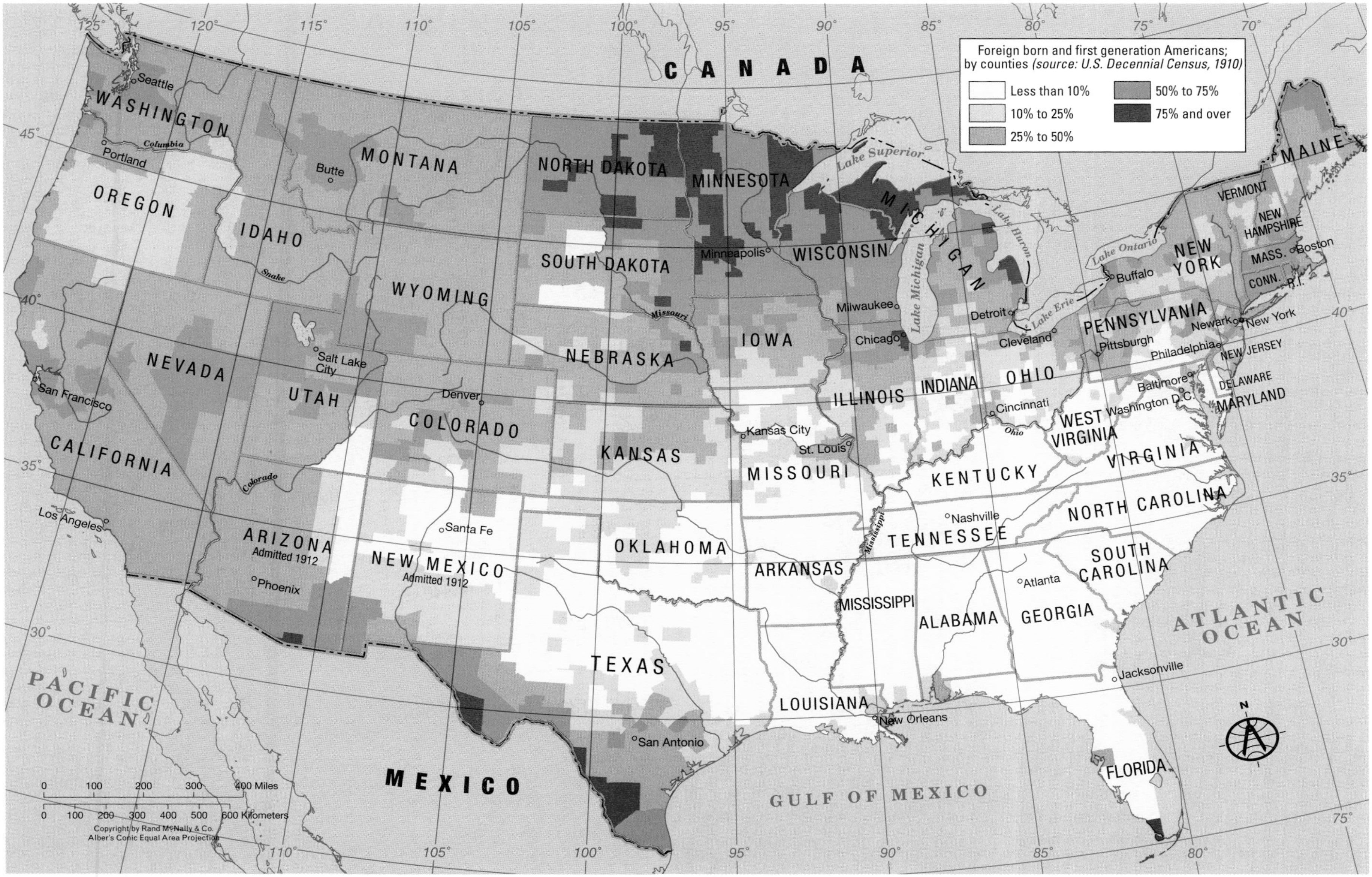

A37

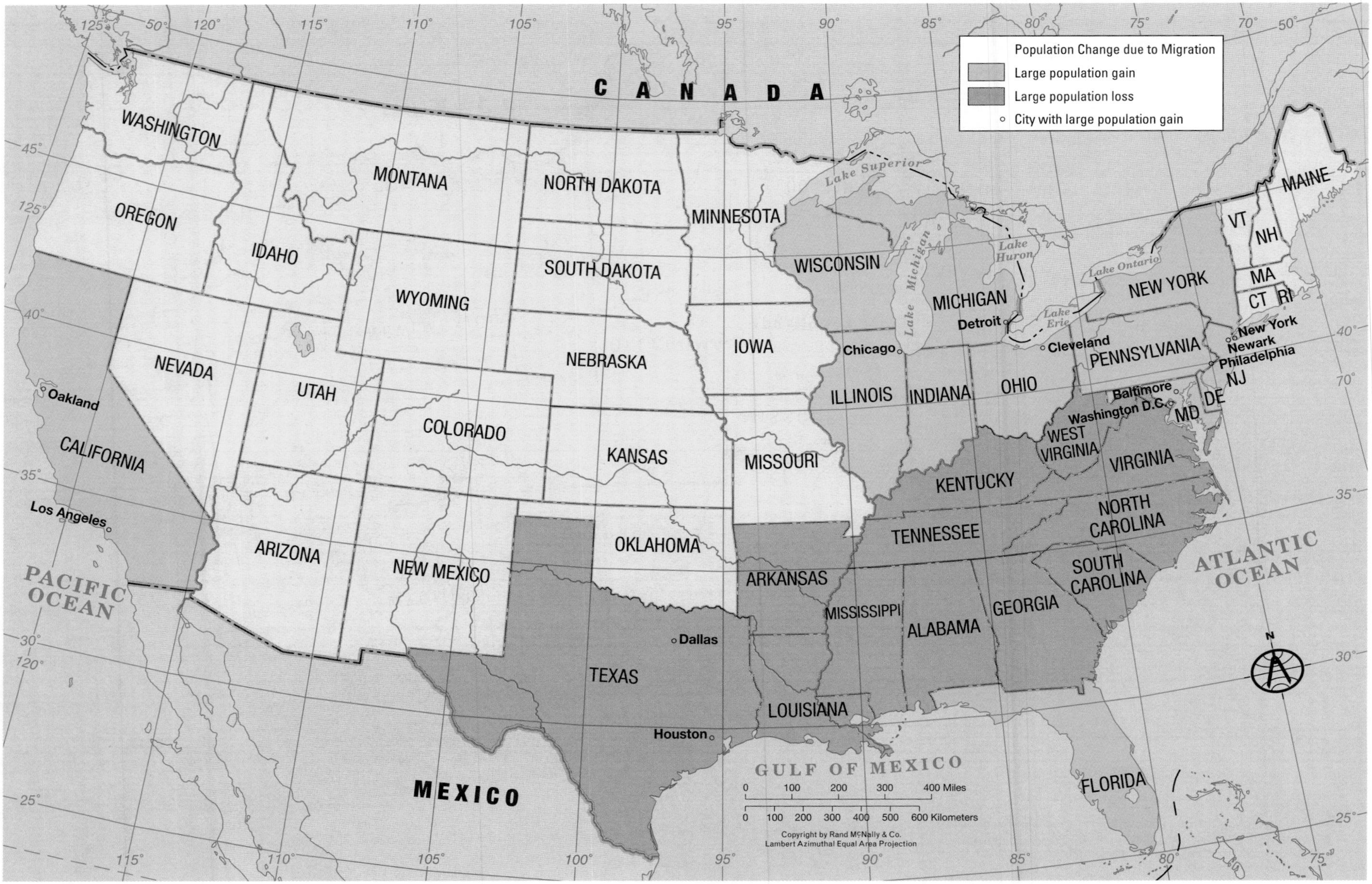
Population Change due to Migration
Large population gain
Large population loss
City with large population gain
CANADA
MEXICO
PACIFIC OCEAN
ATLANTIC OCEAN
GULF OF MEXICO
WASHINGTON
OREGON
CALIFORNIA
NEVADA
IDAHO
MONTANA
WYOMING
UTAH
ARIZONA
COLORADO
NEW MEXICO
NORTH DAKOTA
SOUTH DAKOTA
NEBRASKA
KANSAS
OKLAHOMA
TEXAS
MINNESOTA
IOWA
MISSOURI
ARKANSAS
LOUISIANA
WISCONSIN
ILLINOIS
MICHIGAN
INDIANA
OHIO
KENTUCKY
TENNESSEE
MISSISSIPPI
ALABAMA
GEORGIA
FLORIDA
SOUTH CAROLINA
NORTH CAROLINA
VIRGINIA
WEST VIRGINIA
PENNSYLVANIA
NEW YORK
MD
DE
NJ
CT
RI
MA
VT
NH
MAINE
Lake Superior
Lake Michigan
Lake Huron
Lake Erie
Lake Ontario
Oakland
Los Angeles
Dallas
Houston
Chicago
Detroit
Cleveland
Baltimore
Washington D.C.
Philadelphia
Newark
New York
N
0 100 200 300 400 Miles
0 100 200 300 400 500 600 Kilometers
Copyright by Rand McNally & Co.
Lambert Azimuthal Equal Area Projection

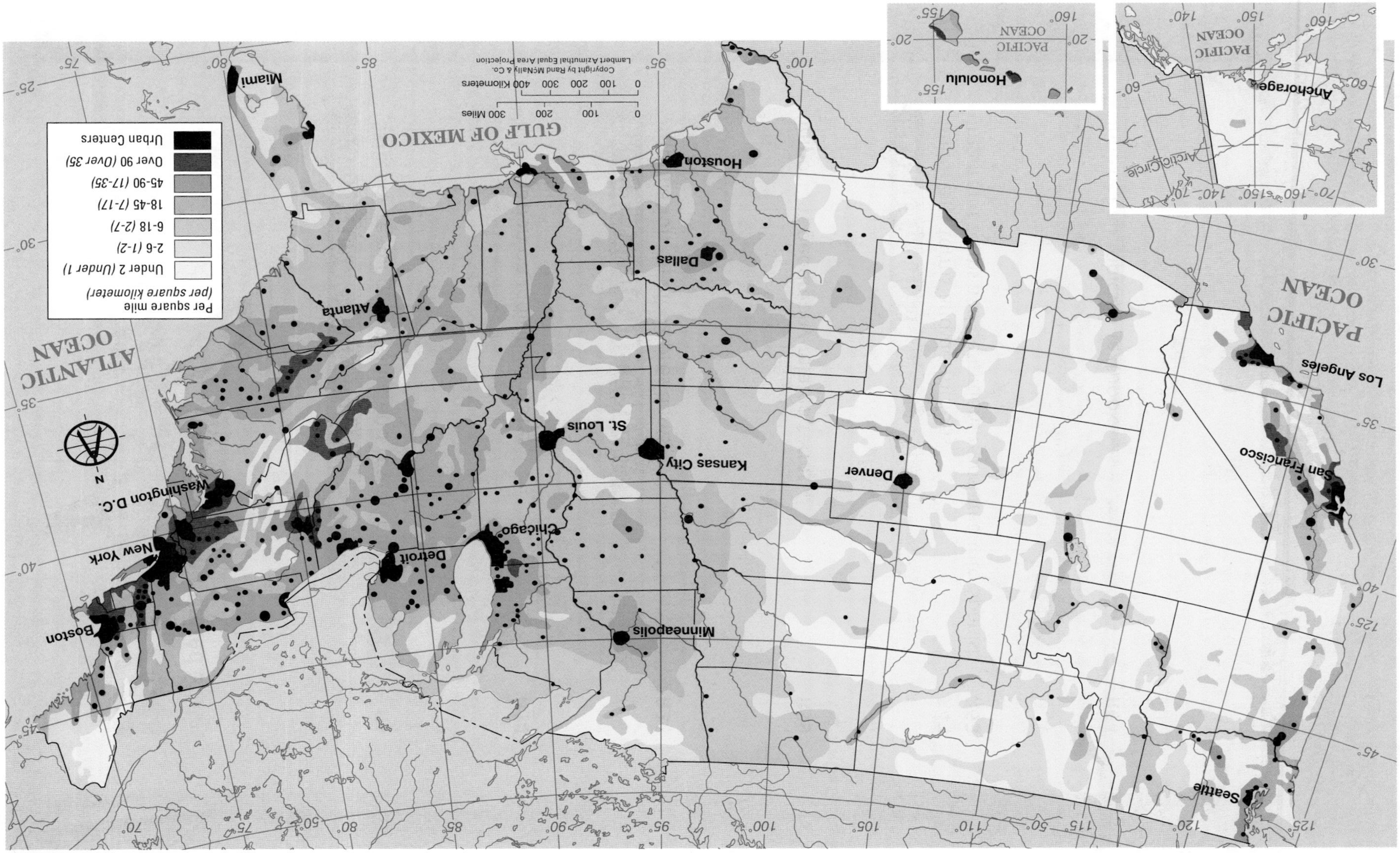
Per square mile
(per square kilometer)
Under 2 (Under 1)
2-6 (1-2)
6-18 (2-7)
18-45 (7-17)
45-90 (17-35)
Over 90 (Over 35)
Urban Centers
ATLANTIC OCEAN
GULF OF MEXICO
PACIFIC OCEAN
Boston
New York
Washington D.C.
Atlanta
Miami
Detroit
Chicago
St. Louis
Minneapolis
Kansas City
Dallas
Houston
Denver
Los Angeles
San Francisco
Seattle
Honolulu
Anchorage
Arctic Circle
0 100 200 300 Miles
0 100 200 300 400 Kilometers
Copyright by Rand McNally & Co.
Lambert Azimuthal Equal Area Projection

Reference Section

Creating America

A History of the United States

Table of Contents

R1

1.1 Summarizing

Defining the Skill

When you **summarize,** you restate a paragraph, passage, or chapter in fewer words. You include only the main ideas and most important details. It is important to use your own words when summarizing.

Applying the Skill

The passage below tells about Harriet Tubman, a prominent member of the Underground Railroad. She helped runaway slaves to freedom. Use the strategies listed below to help you summarize the passage.

How to Summarize

Strategy ❶ Look for topic sentences stating the main idea. These are often at the beginning of a section or paragraph. Briefly restate each main idea—in your own words.

Strategy ❷ Include key facts and any numbers, dates, amounts, or percentages from the text.

Strategy ❸ After writing your summary, review it to see that you have included only the most important details.

HARRIET TUBMAN

❶ One of the most famous conductors on the Underground Railroad was Harriet Tubman. ❷ Born into slavery in Maryland, the 13-year-old Tubman once tried to save another slave from punishment. The angry overseer fractured Tubman's skull with a two-pound weight. She suffered fainting spells for the rest of her life but did not let that stop her from working for freedom. When she was 25, Tubman learned that her owner was about to sell her. Instead, ❷ she escaped.

After her escape, ❷ Harriet Tubman made 19 dangerous journeys to free enslaved persons. The tiny woman carried a pistol to frighten off slave hunters and medicine to quiet crying babies. Her enemies offered $40,000 for her capture, but ❷ no one caught her. "I never run my train off the track and I never lost a passenger," she proudly declared. Among the people she saved were her parents.

Write a Summary

You can write your summary in a paragraph. The paragraph at right summarizes the passage you just read.

❸ *Harriet Tubman was one of the most famous conductors on the Underground Railroad. She had been a slave, but she escaped. She later made 19 dangerous journeys to free other slaves. She was never captured.*

Practicing the Skill

Turn to Chapter 6, Section 2, "Colonial Resistance Grows." Read "The Boston Tea Party" and write a paragraph summarizing the passage.

1.2 Taking Notes

Defining the Skill

When you **take notes,** you write down the important ideas and details of a paragraph, passage, or chapter. A chart or an outline can help you organize your notes to use in the future.

Applying the Skill

The following passage describes President Washington's cabinet. Use the strategies listed below to help you take notes on the passage.

How to Take and Organize Notes

Strategy ❶ Look at the title to find the main topic of the passage.

Strategy ❷ Identify the main ideas and details of the passage. Then summarize the main idea and details in your notes.

Strategy ❸ Identify key terms and define them. The term *cabinet* is shown in boldface type and underlined; both techniques signal that it is a key term.

Strategy ❹ In your notes, use abbreviations to save time and space. You can abbreviate words such as *department (dept.), secretary (sec.), United States (U.S.),* and *president (pres.)* to save time and space.

❶ WASHINGTON'S CABINET

❷ The Constitution gave Congress the task of creating departments to help the president lead the nation. The ❷ president had the power to appoint the heads of these departments, which became his ❸ **cabinet.**

Congress created three departments. Washington chose talented people to run them. ❷ For secretary of war, he picked Henry Knox, a trusted general during the Revolution. ❷ For secretary of state, Washington chose Thomas Jefferson. He had been serving as ambassador to France. The State Department oversaw U.S. foreign relations. For secretary of the treasury, Washington turned to the brilliant ❷ Alexander Hamilton.

Make a Chart

Making a chart can help you take notes on a passage. The chart below contains notes from the passage you just read.

❷ *Item*	*Notes*
1. ❸ cabinet	*heads of ❹ depts.; ❹ pres. appoints heads*
a. War Dept.	*Henry Knox; ❹ sec. of war; former Revolutionary War general*
b. State Dept.	*Thomas Jefferson; sec. of state; oversees relations between ❹ U.S. and other countries*
c. Treasury Dept.	*Alexander Hamilton; sec. of the treasury*

Practicing the Skill

Turn to Chapter 3, Section 3, "Founding the Middle and Southern Colonies." Read "Maryland and the Carolinas" and use a chart to take notes on the passage.

R3

1.3 Sequencing Events

Defining the Skill

Sequence is the order in which events follow one another. By being able to follow the sequence of events through history, you can get an accurate sense of the relationship among events.

Applying the Skill

The following passage describes the sequence of events involved in Britain's plan to capture the Hudson River Valley during the American Revolution. Use the strategies listed below to help you follow the sequence of events.

How to Find the Sequence of Events

Strategy ❶ Look for specific dates provided in the text. If several months within a year are included, the year is usually not repeated.

Strategy ❷ Look for clues about time that allow you to order events according to sequence. Words such as *day, week, month,* or *year* may help to sequence the events.

BRITAIN'S STRATEGY

Burgoyne captured Fort Ticonderoga in ❶ July 1777. From there, it was 25 miles to the Hudson River, which ran to Albany. ❷ Burgoyne took three weeks to reach the Hudson. On ❶ August 3, Burgoyne received a message from Howe. He would not be coming north, Howe wrote, because he had decided to invade Pennsylvania to try to capture Philadelphia and General Washington. "Success be ever with you," Howe's message said. But General Burgoyne needed Howe's soldiers, not his good wishes. Howe did invade Pennsylvania. In ❶ September 1777, he defeated —but did not capture—Washington at the Battle of Brandywine.

Make a Time Line

Making a time line can help you sequence events. The time line below shows the sequence of events in the passage you just read.

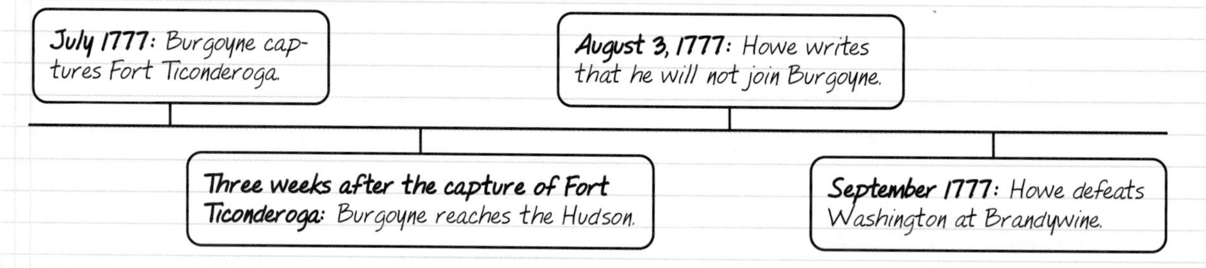

July 1777: Burgoyne captures Fort Ticonderoga.
Three weeks after the capture of Fort Ticonderoga: Burgoyne reaches the Hudson.
August 3, 1777: Howe writes that he will not join Burgoyne.
September 1777: Howe defeats Washington at Brandywine.

Practicing the Skill

Turn to Chapter 10, Section 4, "The War of 1812." Read the section and make a time line showing the sequence of major events in the war.

1.4 Finding Main Ideas

Defining the Skill

The **main idea** is a statement that summarizes the main point of a speech, an article, a section of a book, or a paragraph. Main ideas can be stated or unstated. The main idea of a paragraph is often stated in the first or last sentence. If it is the first sentence, it is followed by sentences that support that main idea. If it is the last sentence, the details build up to the main idea. To find an unstated idea, you must use the details of the paragraph as clues.

Applying the Skill

The following paragraph describes the role of women in the American Revolution. Use the strategies listed below to help you identify the main idea.

How to Find the Main Idea

Strategy ❶ Identify what you think may be the stated main idea. Check the first and last sentences of the paragraph to see if either could be the stated main idea.

Strategy ❷ Identify details that support that idea. Some details explain the main idea. Others give examples of what is stated in the main idea.

WOMEN IN THE REVOLUTION

❶ Many women tried to help the army. Martha Washington and other wives followed their husbands to army camps. ❷ The wives cooked, did laundry, and nursed sick or wounded soldiers. ❷ A few women even helped to fight. ❷ Mary Hays earned the nickname "Molly Pitcher" by carrying water to tired soldiers during a battle. ❷ Deborah Sampson dressed as a man, enlisted, and fought in several engagements.

Make a Chart

Making a chart can help you identify the main idea and details in a passage or paragraph. The chart below identifies the main idea and details in the paragraph you just read.

Main Idea: *Women helped the army during the Revolution.*

Detail: *They cooked and did laundry.*
Detail: *They nursed the wounded and sick soldiers.*
Detail: *They helped to fight.*
Detail: *One woman, Molly Pitcher, carried water to soldiers during battles.*

Practicing the Skill

Turn to Chapter 5, Section 1, "Early American Culture." Read "Women and the Economy" and create a chart that identifies the main idea and the supporting details.

R5

1.5 Categorizing

Defining the Skill

To **categorize** is to sort people, objects, ideas, or other information into groups, called categories. Historians categorize information to help them identify and understand patterns in historical events.

Applying the Skill

The following passage contains information about the reasons people went west during the mid-1800s. Use the strategies listed below to help you categorize information.

How to Categorize

Strategy ❶ First, decide what kind of information needs to be categorized. Decide what the passage is about and how that information can be sorted into categories.

For example, find the different motives people had for moving west.

Strategy ❷ Then find out what the categories will be. To find why many different groups of people moved west, look for clue words such as *some, other,* and *another.*

Strategy ❸ Once you have chosen the categories, sort information into them. Of the people who went west, which ones had which motives?

THE LURE OF THE WEST

❶ People had many different motives for going west. ❷ One motive was to make money. ❷ *Some* people called speculators bought huge areas of land and made great profits by selling it to thousands of settlers. ❷ *Other* settlers included farmers who dreamed of owning their own farms in the West because land was difficult to acquire in the East. ❷ *Another* group to move west was merchants. They hoped to earn money by selling items that farmers needed. Finally, ❷ *some* people went west for religious reasons. These people included ❷ missionaries, who wanted to convert the Native Americans to Christianity, and Mormons, who wanted a place where they could practice their faith without interference.

Make a Chart

Making a chart can help you categorize information. You should have as many columns as you have categories. The chart below shows how the information from the passage you just read can be categorized.

❸

Motives	Money	Land	Religion
Groups	• speculators • merchants	• farmers	• missionaries • Mormons

Practicing the Skill

Turn to Chapter 14, Section 3, "Reforming American Society." Read "Improving Education" and make a chart in which you categorize the changes happening in elementary, high school, and college education.

1.6 Making Public Speeches

Defining the Skill

A speech is a talk given in public to an audience. Some speeches are given to persuade the audience to think or act in a certain way, or to support a cause. You can learn how to **make public speeches** effectively by analyzing great speeches in history.

Applying the Skill

The following is an excerpt from the "I Have a Dream" speech delivered by Martin Luther King, Jr., in 1963 in Washington, D.C. Use the strategies listed below to help you analyze King's speech and prepare a speech of your own.

How to Analyze and Prepare a Speech

Strategy ① Choose one central idea or theme and organize your speech to support it. King organized his speech around his dream of equality.

Strategy ② Use words or images that will win over your audience. King referred to the Declaration of Independence when he used the words "all men are created equal."

Strategy ③ Repeat words or images to drive home your main point—as if it is the "hook" of a pop song. King repeats the phrase "I have a dream."

I HAVE A DREAM

① I have a dream that one day this nation will rise up and live out the true meaning of its creed—we hold these truths to be ② self-evident that all men are created equal.

③ I have a dream that one day on the red hills of Georgia the sons of former slaves and the sons of former slave owners will be able to sit down together at the table of brotherhood.

③ I have a dream that my four little children will one day live in a nation where they will not be judged by the color of their skin but by the content of their character.

③ I have a dream today!

Make an Outline

Making an outline like the one to the right will help you make an effective public speech.

Title: I Have a Dream

I. *Introduce Theme:* I have a dream
   A. This nation will live up to its creed
   B. Quote from the Declaration of Independence: that all men are created equal

II. *Repeat theme:* I have a dream
   A. Sons of former slaves and slave owners will sit together in brotherhood
   B. My four children will be judged by their character, not by their skin color

III. *Conclude:* I have a dream

Practicing the Skill

Turn to Chapter 12, Section 2, "Jackson's Policy Toward Native Americans." Read the section and choose a topic for a speech. First, make an outline like the one to the right to organize your ideas. Exchange your outline with a partner. Organize and interpret information from that outline to write a speech.

1.7 Writing for Social Studies

Defining the Skill

Writing for social studies requires you to describe an idea, situation, or event. Often, social studies writing takes a stand on a particular issue or tries to make a specific point. To successfully describe an event or make a point, your writing needs to be clear, concise, and factually accurate.

Applying the Skill

The following passage describes Stephen A. Douglas. Notice how the strategies below helped the writer explain Douglas's historical importance.

How to Write for Social Studies

Strategy ❶ Focus on your topic. Be sure that you clearly state the main idea of your piece so that your readers know what you intend to say.

Strategy ❷ Collect and organize your facts. Collect accurate information about your topic to support the main idea you are trying to make. Use your information to build a logical case to prove your point.

Strategy ❸ To express your ideas clearly, use standard grammar, spelling, sentence structure, and punctuation when writing for social studies. Proofread your work to make sure it is well organized and grammatically correct.

STEPHEN A. DOUGLAS, 1813–1861

❶ Stephen A. Douglas was one of the most powerful members of Congress in the 1850s. In fact, ❷ he was called the "Little Giant" because he commanded great respect even though he was only five feet four inches tall. The most important issue that Douglas faced in his career was slavery in the territories. ❷ He played a key role in the passage of the Compromise of 1850 as well as the Kansas–Nebraska Act, which addressed this issue. In 1858, his famous debates with Abraham Lincoln also focused on slavery in the territories. ❷ When Douglas ran for president in 1860, his position on slavery was critical to his defeat.

Practicing the Skill

Turn to Chapter 15, Section 1, "Growing Tensions Between North and South." Read the section and use the strategies above to write your answer to Question 4 in the Chapter 15 Section 1 Assessment.

2.1 Analyzing Points of View

Defining the Skill

Analyzing points of view means looking closely at a person's arguments to understand the reasons behind that person's beliefs. The goal of analyzing a point of view is to understand a historical figure's thoughts, opinions, and biases about a topic.

Applying the Skill

The following passage describes the Panic of 1837 and two politicians' points of view about it. Use the strategies listed below to help you analyze their points of view.

How to Analyze Points of View

Strategy ❶ Look for statements that show you a person's view on an issue. For example, Van Buren said he believed the economy would improve if he took no action. Clay thought the government should do something to help the people.

Strategy ❷ Use information about people to validate them as sources and understand why they might disagree. What do you know about Clay and Van Buren that might explain their own biases and disagreements with each other?

Strategy ❸ Write a summary that explains why different people took different positions on the issue.

THE PANIC OF 1837

The Panic of 1837 caused severe hardship. People had little money, so manufacturers had few customers for their goods. Almost 90 percent of factories in the East closed. Jobless workers could not afford food or rent. Many people went hungry.

❶ Whig senator Henry Clay wanted the government to do something to help the people. ❶ President Van Buren, a Democrat, disagreed. He believed that the economy would improve if left alone. He argued that "the less government interferes with private pursuits the better for the general prosperity." Many Americans blamed Van Buren for the Panic, though he had taken office only weeks before it started. The continuing depression made it difficult for him to win reelection in 1840.

Make a Diagram

Using a diagram can help you analyze points of view. The diagram below analyzes the views of Clay and Van Buren in the passage you just read.

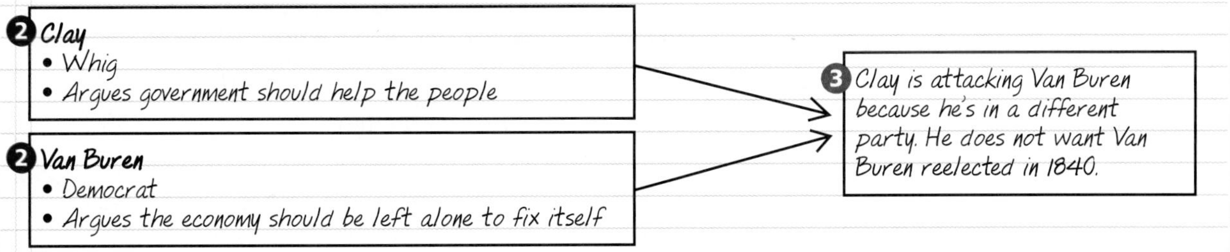

❷ Clay
• Whig
• Argues government should help the people
❷ Van Buren
• Democrat
• Argues the economy should be left alone to fix itself
❸ Clay is attacking Van Buren because he's in a different party. He does not want Van Buren reelected in 1840.

Practicing the Skill

Turn to the Interactive Primary Sources at the end of Chapter 8, Section 3. Read the selections by James Madison and George Mason. Use their language, information from other sources, and information about each man to validate them as sources. Then make a chart to analyze their different points of view on the Constitution.

2.2 Comparing and Contrasting

Defining the Skill

Comparing means looking at the similarities and differences between two or more things. **Contrasting** means examining only the differences between them. Historians compare and contrast events, personalities, behaviors, beliefs, and situations in order to understand them.

Applying the Skill

The following paragraph describes the American and British troops during the Revolutionary War. Use the strategies listed below to help you compare and contrast these two armies.

How to Compare and Contrast

Strategy ❶ Look for two aspects of the subject that may be compared and contrasted. This passage compares the British and American troops to show why the Americans won the war.

Strategy ❷ To contrast, look for clue words that show how two things differ. Clue words include *by contrast, however, except,* and *yet.*

Strategy ❸ To find similarities, look for clue words indicating that two things are alike. Clue words include *both, like, as,* and *similarly.*

WHY THE AMERICANS WON

❶ By their persistence, the Americans defeated the British even though they faced many obstacles. The Americans lacked training and experience. They were often short of supplies and weapons. ❷ *By contrast,* the British forces ranked among the best trained in the world. They were experienced and well-supplied professional soldiers. ❷ *Yet,* the Americans also had advantages that enabled them to win. These advantages over the British were better leadership, foreign aid, a knowledge of the land, and motivation. Although ❸ *both* the British and the Americans were fighting for their lives, ❷ the Americans were also fighting for their property and their dream of liberty.

Make a Venn Diagram

Making a Venn diagram will help you identify similarities and differences between two things. In the overlapping area, list characteristics shared by both subjects. Then, in the separate ovals, list the characteristics of each subject not shared by the other. This Venn diagram compares and contrasts the British and American soldiers.

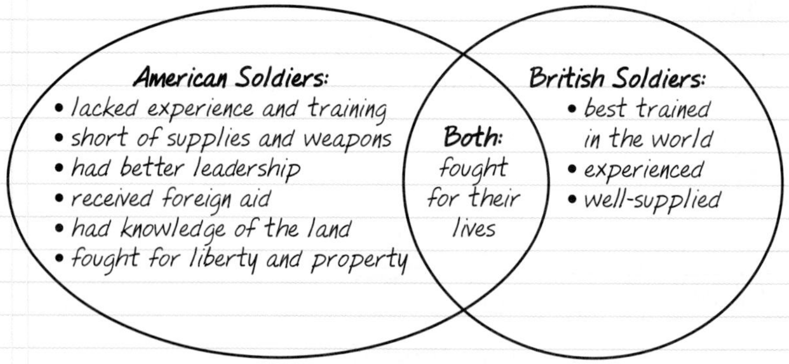
American Soldiers:
• lacked experience and training
• short of supplies and weapons
• had better leadership
• received foreign aid
• had knowledge of the land
• fought for liberty and property
Both:
fought for their lives
British Soldiers:
• best trained in the world
• experienced
• well-supplied

Practicing the Skill

Turn to Chapter 5, Section 1, "Early American Culture." Read "Young People at Work" and make a Venn diagram showing the similarities and differences between the roles of boys and girls in colonial America.

2.3 Analyzing Causes; Recognizing Effects

Defining the Skill

A **cause** is an action in history that makes something happen. An **effect** is the historical event that is the result of the cause. A single event may have several causes. It is also possible for one cause to result in several effects. Historians identify cause-and-effect relationships to help them understand why historical events took place.

Applying the Skill

The following paragraph describes events that caused changes in Puritan New England. Use the strategies listed below to help you identify the cause-and-effect relationships.

How to Analyze Causes and Recognize Effects

Strategy ❶ Ask why an action took place. Ask yourself a question about the title and topic sentence, such as, "What caused changes in Puritan society?"

Strategy ❷ Look for effects. Ask yourself, "What happened?" (the effect). Then ask, "Why did it happen?" (the cause). For example, What caused the decline of Puritan religion in New England?

Strategy ❸ Look for clue words that signal causes, such as *cause* and *led to.*

Strategy ❹ One way to practice recognizing effects is to make predictions about the consequences that will result from particular actions. Then, as you read, look to see if your predictions were accurate.

❶ CHANGES IN PURITAN SOCIETY

❶ The early 1700s saw many changes in New England society. ❷ One of the most important changes was the gradual decline of the Puritan religion in New England. There were a number of reasons for that decline.

❸ One *cause* of this decline was the increasing competition from other religious groups. Baptists and Anglicans established churches in Massachusetts and Connecticut, where Puritans had once been the most powerful group. ❸ Political changes also *led to* a weakening of the Puritan community. In 1691, a new royal charter for Massachusetts granted the vote based on property ownership instead of church membership.

Make a Diagram

Using a diagram can help you understand causes and effects. The diagram below shows two causes and an effect for the passage you just read.

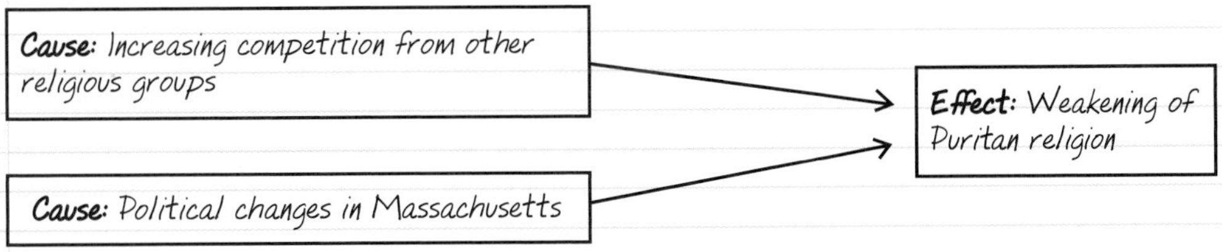

Practicing the Skill

Turn to Chapter 13, Section 3, "The War with Mexico." Read the section and make a diagram about the causes and effects of the war.

R11

2.4 Making Inferences

Defining the Skill

Inferences are ideas that the author has not directly stated. **Making inferences** involves reading between the lines to interpret the information you read. You can make inferences by studying what is stated and using your common sense and previous knowledge.

Applying the Skill

The passage below describes the strengths and weaknesses of the North and the South as the Civil War began. Use the strategies listed below to help you make inferences from the passage.

How to Make Inferences

Strategy ❶ Read to find statements of facts and ideas. Knowing the facts will give you a good basis for making inferences.

Strategy ❷ Use your knowledge, logic, and common sense to make inferences that are based on facts. Ask yourself, "What does the author want me to understand?" For example, from the facts about population, you can make the inference that the North would have a larger army than the South. See other inferences in the chart below.

ADVANTAGES OF THE NORTH AND THE SOUTH

The North had more people and resources than the South. ❶ The North had about 22 million people. ❶ The South had roughly 9 million, of whom about 3.5 million were slaves. In addition, ❶ the North had more than 80 percent of the nation's factories and almost all of the shipyards and naval power. The South had some advantages, too. ❶ It had able generals, such as Robert E. Lee. ❶ It also had the advantage of fighting a defensive war. Soldiers defending their homes have more will to fight than invaders do.

Make a Chart

Making a chart will help you organize information and make logical inferences. The chart below organizes information from the passage you just read.

❶ *Stated Facts and Ideas*	❷ *Inferences*
The North had about 22 million people. *The Confederacy had about 9 million, less the 3.5 million slaves.*	*The North would have a larger army than the South.*
The North had more factories, naval power, and shipyards.	*The North could provide more weapons, ammunition, and ships for the war.*
The Confederacy had excellent generals.	*The Confederacy had better generals, which would help it overcome other disadvantages.*
The Confederacy was fighting a defensive war.	*Confederate soldiers would fight harder because they were defending their homes and families.*

Practicing the Skill

Turn to Chapter 11, Section 1, "Early Industry and Inventions." Read "Free Enterprise and Factories" and use a chart like the one above to make inferences about early industry.

2.5 Drawing Conclusions

Defining the Skill

Drawing conclusions means analyzing what you have read and forming an opinion about its meaning. To draw conclusions, look at the facts and then use your own common sense and experience to decide what the facts mean.

Applying the Skill

The following passage presents information about the Intolerable Acts and the colonists' reactions to them. Use the strategies listed below to help you draw conclusions about those acts.

How to Draw Conclusions

Strategy ❶ Read carefully to identify and understand all the facts, or statements, that can be proven true.

Strategy ❷ List the facts in a diagram and review them. Use your own experiences and common sense to understand how the facts relate to each other.

Strategy ❸ After reviewing the facts, write down the conclusion you have drawn about them.

THE INTOLERABLE ACTS

❶ In 1774, Parliament passed a series of laws to punish the Massachusetts colony and serve as a warning to other colonies. ❶ These laws were so harsh that colonists called them the **Intolerable Acts.** One of the acts closed the port of Boston. Others banned committees of correspondence and allowed Britain to house troops wherever necessary.

In 1773, Sam Adams had written, "I wish we could arouse the continent." ❶ The Intolerable Acts answered his wish. Other colonies immediately offered Massachusetts their support.

Make a Diagram

Making a diagram can help you draw conclusions. The diagram below shows how to organize facts and inferences to draw a conclusion about the passage you just read.

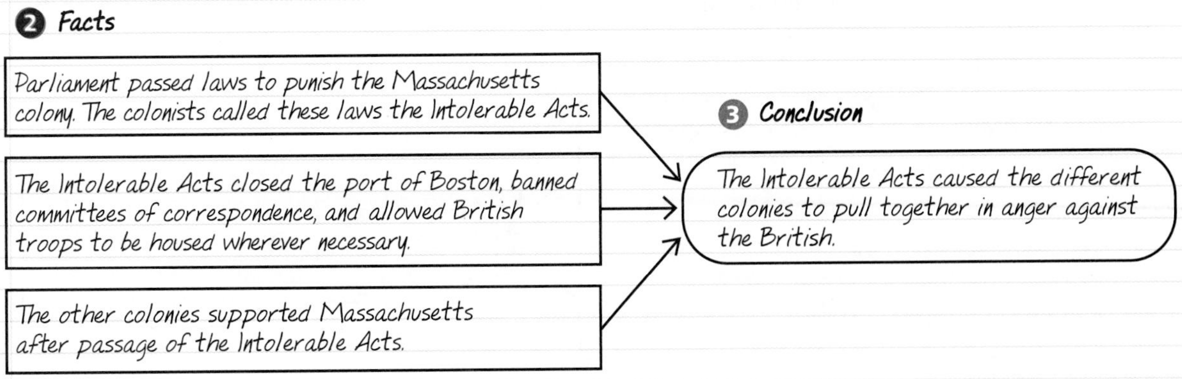

❷ Facts
Parliament passed laws to punish the Massachusetts colony. The colonists called these laws the Intolerable Acts.
The Intolerable Acts closed the port of Boston, banned committees of correspondence, and allowed British troops to be housed wherever necessary.
The other colonies supported Massachusetts after passage of the Intolerable Acts.
❸ Conclusion
The Intolerable Acts caused the different colonies to pull together in anger against the British.

Practicing the Skill

Turn to Chapter 3, Section 2, "New England Colonies." Read "The Salem Witchcraft Trials" and use the diagram above as a model to draw conclusions about the trials.

2.6 Making Decisions

Defining the Skill

Making decisions involves choosing between two or more options, or courses of action. In most cases, decisions have consequences, or results. Sometimes decisions may lead to new problems. By understanding how historical figures made decisions, you can learn how to improve your decision-making skills.

Applying the Skill

The following passage describes Lincoln's decisions regarding federal forts after the Southern states seceded. Use the strategies listed below to help you analyze his decisions.

How to Make Decisions

Strategy 1 Identify a decision that needs to be made. Think about what factors make the decision difficult.

Strategy 2 Identify possible consequences of the decision. Remember that there can be more than one consequence to a decision.

Strategy 3 Identify the decision that was made.

Strategy 4 Identify actual consequences that resulted from the decision.

FIRST SHOTS AT FORT SUMTER

1 Lincoln had to decide what to do about the forts in the South that remained under federal control. A Union garrison still held **Fort Sumter**, but it was running out of supplies. 2 If Lincoln supplied the garrison, he risked war. 2 If he withdrew the garrison, he would be giving in to the rebels. 3 Lincoln informed South Carolina that he was sending supply ships to Fort Sumter. 4 Confederate leaders decided to prevent the federal government from holding on to the fort by attacking before the supply ships arrived. No one was killed, but 4 the South's attack on Fort Sumter signaled the beginning of the Civil War.

Make a Flow Chart

A flow chart can help you identify the process of making a decision. The flow chart below shows the decision-making process in the passage you just read.

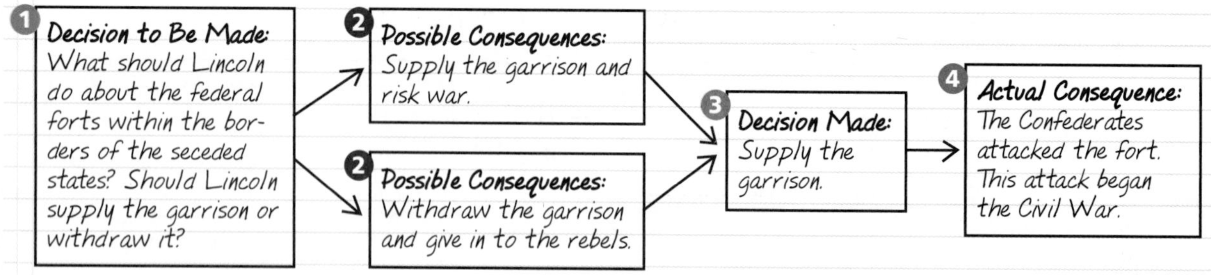

1
Decision to Be Made: What should Lincoln do about the federal forts within the borders of the seceded states? Should Lincoln supply the garrison or withdraw it?
2
Possible Consequences: Supply the garrison and risk war.
2
Possible Consequences: Withdraw the garrison and give in to the rebels.
3
Decision Made: Supply the garrison.
4
Actual Consequence: The Confederates attacked the fort. This attack began the Civil War.

Practicing the Skill

Turn to Chapter 6, Section 1, "Tighter British Control." Read "The Colonies Protest the Stamp Act" and make a flow chart to identify a decision and its consequences described in that section.

2.7 Recognizing Propaganda

Defining the Skill

Propaganda is communication that aims to influence people's opinions, emotions, or actions. Propaganda is not always factual. Rather, it uses one-sided language or striking symbols to sway people's emotions. Modern advertising often uses propaganda. By thinking critically, you will avoid being swayed by propaganda.

Applying the Skill

The following political cartoon shows Andrew Jackson dressed as a king. Use the strategies listed below to help you understand how it works as propaganda.

How to Recognize Propaganda

Strategy ❶ Identify the aim, or purpose, of the cartoon. Point out the subject and explain the point of view.

Strategy ❷ Identify those images on the cartoon that viewers might respond to emotionally and identify the emotions.

Strategy ❸ Think critically about the cartoon. What facts has the cartoon ignored?

BORN TO COMMAND.
OF VETO MEMORY.
HAD I BEEN CONSULTED.
KING ANDREW THE FIRST.

Make a Chart

Making a chart will help you think critically about a piece of propaganda. The chart below summarizes the information from the anti-Jackson cartoon.

❶	*Identify Purpose*	*The cartoon portrays Jackson negatively by showing him as a king.*
❷	*Identify Emotions*	*The cartoonist knows that Americans like democracy. So he portrays Jackson as a king because kings are not usually supporters of democracy. He also shows Jackson standing on a torn U.S. Constitution—another thing that Americans love.*
❸	*Think Critically*	*The cartoon shows Jackson vetoing laws. But it ignores the fact that those actions were not against the Constitution. The president has the power to veto legislation. In this case, Jackson was exercising the power of the presidency, not acting like a king.*

Practicing the Skill

Turn to Chapter 6, Section 2, "Colonial Resistance Grows," and look at the engraving *The Bloody Massacre* on the third page of the section. Use a chart like the one above to think critically about the engraving as an example of propaganda.

2.8 Identifying Facts and Opinions

Defining the Skill

Facts are events, dates, statistics, or statements that can be proved to be true. **Opinions** are the judgments, beliefs, and feelings of a writer or speaker. By identifying facts and opinions, you will be able to think critically when a person is trying to influence your own opinion.

Applying the Skill

The following passage tells about the Virginia Plan for legislative representation offered at the Constitutional Convention of 1787. Use the strategies listed below to help you distinguish facts from opinions.

How to Recognize Facts and Opinions

Strategy ❶ Look for specific information that can be proved or checked for accuracy.

Strategy ❷ Look for assertions, claims, and judgments that express opinions. In this case, one speaker's opinion is expressed in a direct quote.

Strategy ❸ Think about whether statements can be checked for accuracy. Then, identify the facts and opinions in a chart.

ANTIFEDERALIST VIEWS

❶ Antifederalists published their views about the Constitution in newspapers and pamphlets. ❶ They thought the Constitution took too much power away from the states and did not protect the rights of the people. They charged that the Constitution would destroy American liberties. As one Antifederalist wrote, ❷ "It is truly astonishing that a set of men among ourselves should have had the [nerve] to attempt the destruction of our liberties."

Make a Chart

The chart below analyzes the facts and opinions from the passage above.

Statement	❸ *Can It Be Proved?*	❸ *Fact or Opinion*
Antifederalists published their views in newspapers and pamphlets.	*Yes. Check newspapers and other historical documents.*	*Fact*
They thought the Constitution took too much power away from the states.	*Yes. Check newspapers and other historical documents.*	*Fact*
It is astonishing that some Americans would try to destroy American liberties.	*No. This cannot be proved. It is what one speaker believes.*	*Opinion*

Practicing the Skill

Turn to Chapter 11, Section 3, and read the section entitled "The Missouri Compromise." Make a chart in which you analyze key statements to determine whether they are facts or opinions.

2.9 Forming and Supporting Opinions

Defining the Skill

When you **form opinions,** you interpret and judge the importance of events and people in history. You should always **support your opinions** with facts, examples, and quotes.

Applying the Skill

The following passage describes events that followed the gold rush. Use the strategies listed below to form and support your opinions about the events.

How to Form and Support Opinions

Strategy ❶ Look for important information about the events. Information can include facts, quotations, and examples.

Strategy ❷ Form an opinion about the event by asking yourself questions about the information. For example, How important was the event? What were its effects?

Strategy ❸ Support your opinions with facts, quotations, and examples. If the facts do not support the opinion, then rewrite your opinion so it is supported by the facts.

THE IMPACT OF THE GOLD RUSH

By 1852, the gold rush was over. ❶ While it lasted, about 250,000 people flooded into California. ❶ This huge migration caused economic growth that changed California. ❶ The port city San Francisco grew to become a center of banking, manufacturing, shipping, and trade. ❶ However, the gold rush ruined many *Californios*. *Californios* are the Hispanic people of California. The newcomers did not respect *Californios,* their customs, or their legal rights. ❶ In many cases, Americans seized their property.

Native Americans suffered even more. ❶ Thousands died from diseases brought by the newcomers. ❶ Miners hunted down and killed thousands more. ❶ By 1870, California's Native American population had fallen from 150,000 to only about 30,000.

Make a Chart

Making a chart can help you organize your opinions and supporting facts. The following chart summarizes one possible opinion about the impact of the gold rush.

❷ *Opinion*	*The effects of the gold rush were more negative than positive.*
❸ *Facts*	*Californios were not respected, and their land was stolen.* *Many Native Americans died from diseases, and others were killed by miners. Their population dropped from 150,000 to about 30,000.*

Practicing the Skill

Turn to Chapter 11, Section 3, "Nationalism and Sectionalism." Read "The Missouri Compromise" and form your own opinion about the compromise and its impact. Make a chart like the one above to summarize your opinion and the supporting facts and examples.

R17

2.10 Identifying and Solving Problems

Defining the Skill

Identifying problems means finding and understanding the difficulties faced by a particular group of people during a certain time. **Solving problems** means understanding how people tried to remedy those problems. By studying how people solved problems in the past, you can learn ways to solve problems today.

Applying the Skill

The following paragraph describes problems that the Constitutional Convention faced on the issues of taxation, representation, and slavery. Use the strategies listed below to help you see how the Founders tried to solve these problems.

How to Identify Problems and Solutions

Strategy ❶ Look for the difficulties, or problems, people faced.

Strategy ❷ Consider how the problem affected people with different points of view. For example, the main problem described here was how to count the population of each state.

Strategy ❸ Look for solutions people tried to deal with each problem. Think about whether the solution was a good one for people with differing points of view.

SLAVERY AND THE CONSTITUTION

Because the House of Representatives would have members according to the population of each state, ❶ the delegates had to decide who would be counted in the population of each state. The Southern states had many more slaves than the Northern states had. ❷ Southerners wanted the slaves to be counted as part of the general population for representation but not for taxation. ❷ Northerners argued that slaves were not citizens and should not be counted for representation, but that slaves should be counted for taxation. ❸ The delegates decided that three-fifths of the slave population would be counted in the population to determine both representation and taxes.

Make a Chart

Making a chart will help you identify and organize information about problems and solutions. The chart below shows problems and solutions included in the passage you just read.

❶ *Problem*	❷ *Differing Points of View*	❸ *Solution*
Northerners and Southerners couldn't agree on how to count population because of slavery in the South.	*Southerners wanted slaves counted for representation but not for taxation. Northerners wanted slaves counted for taxation but not for representation.*	*Delegates decided that three-fifths of the slave population should be counted.*

Practicing the Skill

Turn to Chapter 8, Section 2, "Creating the Constitution." Read "The Delegates Assemble" and "The Virginia Plan." Then make a chart that summarizes the problems faced by the delegates at the Constitutional Convention and the solutions they agreed on.

2.11 Evaluating

Defining the Skill

To **evaluate** is to make a judgment about something. Historians evaluate the actions of people in history. One way to do this is to examine both the positives and negatives of a historical action, then decide which is stronger—the positive or the negative.

Applying the Skill

The following passage describes Susan B. Anthony's fight for women's rights. Use the strategies listed below to evaluate how successful she was.

How to Evaluate

Strategy ❶ Before you evaluate a person's actions, first determine what that person was trying to do. In this case, think about what Anthony wanted to accomplish.

Strategy ❷ Look for statements that show the positive, or successful, results of her actions. For example, Did she achieve her goals?

Strategy ❸ Also look for statements that show the negative, or unsuccessful, results of her actions. Did she fail to achieve something she tried to do?

Strategy ❹ Write an overall evaluation of the person's actions.

SUSAN B. ANTHONY

❶ Susan B. Anthony was a skilled organizer who fought for women's rights. ❷ She successfully built the women's movement into a national organization. Anthony believed that a woman must have money of her own. To this end, she supported laws that would give married women rights to control their own property and wages. ❷ Mississippi passed the first such law in 1839. New York passed a property law in 1848 and a wages law in 1860. ❸ Anthony also wanted to win the vote for women but failed to convince lawmakers to pass this reform in her lifetime. This reform did go through in 1920, 14 years after her death.

Make a Diagram for Evaluating

Using a diagram can help you evaluate. List the positives and negatives of the historical person's actions and decisions. Then make an overall judgment. The diagram below shows how the information from the passage you just read can be diagrammed.

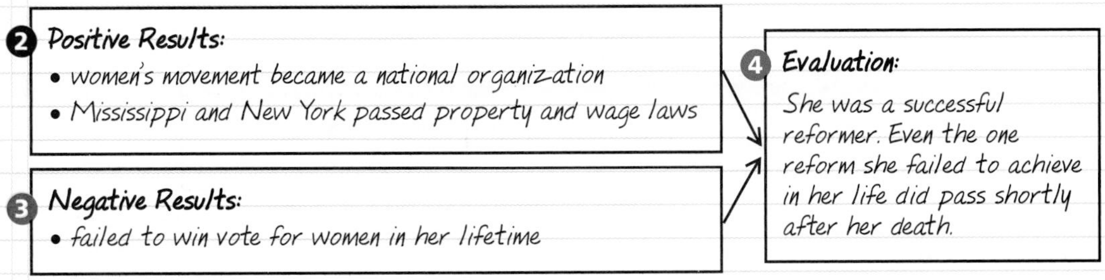

❷ Positive Results:
• women's movement became a national organiz-ation
• Mississippi and New York passed property and wage laws
❸ Negative Results:
• failed to win vote for women in her lifetime
❹ Evaluation:
She was a successful reformer. Even the one reform she failed to achieve in her life did pass shortly after her death.

Practicing the Skill

Turn to Chapter 18, Section 3, "The End of Reconstruction." Read the section and make a diagram in which you evaluate Grant's presidency.

R19

2.12 Making Generalizations

Defining the Skill

To **make generalizations** means to make broad judgments based on information. When you make generalizations, you should gather information from several sources.

Applying the Skill

The following three passages contain different views on George Washington. Use the strategies listed below to make a generalization about these views.

How to Make Generalizations

Strategy ❶ Look for information that the sources have in common. These three sources all discuss George Washington's ability as a military leader.

Strategy ❷ Form a generalization that describes Washington in a way that all three sources would agree with. State your generalization in a sentence.

WASHINGTON'S LEADERSHIP

❶ Washington learned from his mistakes. After early defeats, he developed the strategy of dragging out the war to wear down the British. ❶ Despite difficulties, he never gave up.

—*Creating America*

❶ [Washington] was no military genius. . . . But he was a great war leader. Creating an army out of unpromising material, he kept it in being against great odds.

—*The Limits of Liberty*

❶ [Washington] certainly deserves some merit as a general, that he . . . can keep General Howe dancing from one town to another for two years together, with such an army as he has.

—*The Journal of Nicholas Cresswell, July 13, 1777*

Make a Chart

Using a chart can help you make generalizations. The chart below shows how the information you just read can be used to generalize about people's views of Washington.

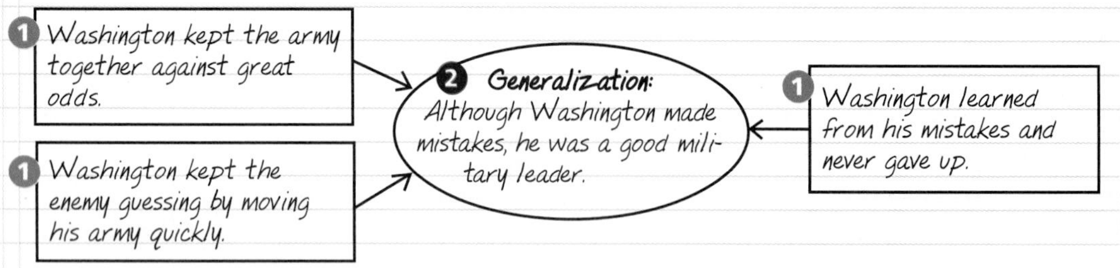

1 Washington kept the army together against great odds.
1 Washington kept the enemy guessing by moving his army quickly.
2 Generalization: Although Washington made mistakes, he was a good military leader.
1 Washington learned from his mistakes and never gave up.

Practicing the Skill

Turn to Chapter 16, Section 1, "War Erupts." Read "Choosing Sides." Also read the excerpt from *Across Five Aprils* at the end of Section 1. Then use a chart like the one above to make a generalization about how the outbreak of the Civil War affected Americans.

3.1 Using Primary and Secondary Sources

Defining the Skill

Primary sources are materials written or made by people who lived during historical events and witnessed them. Primary sources can be letters, journal entries, speeches, autobiographies, or artwork. Other kinds of primary sources are government documents, census surveys, and financial records. **Secondary sources** are materials written by people who did not participate in an event. History books are secondary sources.

Applying the Skill

The following passage contains both a primary source and a secondary source. Use the strategies listed below to help you read them.

How to Read Primary and Secondary Sources

Strategy ❶ Distinguish secondary sources from primary sources. The first paragraph is a secondary source. The Declaration of Independence is a primary source. The secondary source explains something about the primary source.

Strategy ❷ Analyze the primary source and consider why the author produced it. Consider what the document was supposed to achieve and who would read it.

Strategy ❸ Identify the author of the primary source and note when and where it was written.

❶ The core idea of the Declaration is based on the philosophy of John Locke. This idea is that people have unalienable rights, or rights that government cannot take away. Jefferson stated this belief in what was to become the Declaration's best-known passage.

> ❷ We hold these truths to be self-evident, that all men are created equal, that they are endowed by their Creator with certain unalienable Rights, that among these are Life, Liberty and the pursuit of Happiness.
>
> ❸ —Thomas Jefferson, *The Declaration of Independence,* 1776

Make a Chart

Making a chart will help you summarize information from primary sources and secondary sources. The chart below summarizes the information from the passage you just read.

Author	*Thomas Jefferson*
Document	*The Declaration of Independence*
Notes on Primary Source	*The Declaration says that "all men are created equal." It also says that people have "unalienable rights." These rights include the right to life and the right to liberty, as well as a right to pursue happiness.*
Notes on Secondary Source	*Jefferson based his ideas on those of John Locke. Locke had written about rights that governments could not take away from the people.*

Practicing the Skill

Turn to Chapter 6, Section 3, "The Road to Lexington and Concord." Read "Between War and Peace" and make a chart like the one above to summarize the information in the primary source and the secondary source.

R21

3.2 Interpreting Graphs

Defining the Skill

Graphs use pictures and symbols, instead of words, to show information. Graphs are created by taking information and presenting it visually. The graph on this page takes numerical information on immigration and presents it as a bar graph. There are many different kinds of graphs. Bar graphs, line graphs, and pie graphs are the most common. Bar graphs compare numbers or sets of numbers. The length of each bar shows a quantity. It is easy to see how different categories compare on a bar graph.

Applying the Skill

The bar graph below shows numbers of immigrants coming to the United States between 1821 and 1860. Use the strategies listed below to help you interpret the graph.

How to Interpret a Graph

Strategy 1 Read the title to identify the main idea of the graph. Ask yourself what kinds of information the graph shows. For example, does it show chronological information, geographic patterns and distributions, or something else?

Strategy 2 Read the vertical axis (the one that goes up and down) on the left side of the graph. This one shows the number of immigrants in thousands. Each bar represents the number of immigrants during a particular decade.

Strategy 3 Read the horizontal axis (the one that runs across the bottom of the graph). This one shows the four decades from 1821 to 1860.

Strategy 4 Summarize the information shown in each part of the graph. Use the title to help you focus on what information the graph is presenting.

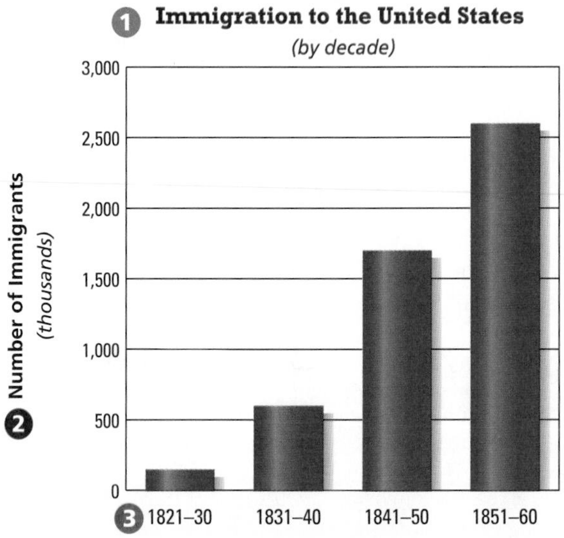

Write a Summary

Writing a summary will help you understand the information in the graph. The paragraph to the right summarizes the information from the bar graph.

4

Immigration to the United States increased between 1821 and 1860. Between 1821 and 1830, fewer than 200,000 immigrants arrived. In the next decade, more than 500,000 immigrants came. During the 1840s, more than 1.5 million immigrants arrived, and that number increased to more than 2.5 million in the 1850s.

Practicing the Skill

Turn to Chapter 16, Section 1, "War Erupts." Look at the graphs entitled "Resources, 1860." Write a paragraph in which you summarize what you learned from these graphs.

3.3 Interpreting Charts

Defining the Skill

Charts, like graphs, present information in a visual form. Charts are created by organizing, summarizing, and simplifying information and presenting it in a format that makes it easy to understand. Tables and diagrams are examples of commonly used charts.

Applying the Skill

The chart below shows the number of slaves who were imported to the Americas between 1601 and 1810. Use the strategies listed below to help you interpret the information in the chart.

How to Interpret a Chart

Strategy 1 Read the title. It will tell you what the chart is about. Ask yourself what kinds of information the chart shows. For example, does it show chronological information, geographic patterns and distributions, or something else?

Strategy 2 Read the labels to see how the information in the chart is organized. In this chart, it is organized by region and years.

Strategy 3 Study the data in the chart to understand the facts that the chart intends to show.

Strategy 4 Summarize the information shown in each part of the chart. Use the title to help you focus on what information the chart is presenting.

1601–1810

1 **Slaves Imported to the Americas** *(in thousands)*

2 *REGION/COUNTRY*	*1601–1700*	*1701–1810*
3 British N. America	*	348
British Caribbean	263.7	1,401.3
French Caribbean	155.8	1,348.4
Spanish America	292.5	578.6
Dutch Caribbean	40	460
Danish Caribbean	4	24
Brazil (Portugal)	560	1,891.4

*= less than 1,000

Source: Philip D. Curtin, *The Atlantic Slave Trade*

Write a Summary

Writing a summary can help you understand the information given in a chart. The paragraph to the right summarizes the information in the chart "Slaves Imported to the Americas, 1601–1810."

4 *The chart shows how many slaves were imported to the Americas between 1601 and 1810. It divides the Americas into seven regions. It also divides the time period into two parts: 1601–1700 and 1701–1810. The number of slaves imported increased greatly from the 1600s to the 1700s. More slaves were imported to Brazil than to any other region.*

Practicing the Skill

Turn to Chapter 17, Section 4, and look at the charts entitled "Costs of the Civil War." Study the charts and ask yourself what geographic patterns and distributions are shown on them. Then write a paragraph in which you summarize what you learned from the charts.

3.4 Interpreting Time Lines

Defining the Skill

A **time line** is a visual list of events and dates shown in the order in which they occurred. Time lines can be horizontal or vertical. On horizontal time lines, the earliest date is on the left. On vertical time lines, the earliest date is often at the top.

Applying the Skill

The time line below lists dates and events during the presidencies of John Adams, Andrew Jackson, and Martin Van Buren. Use the strategies listed below to help you interpret the information.

How to Read a Time Line

Strategy ❶ Read the dates at the beginning and end of the time line. These will show the period of history that is covered. The time line below is a dual time line. It includes items related to two topics. The labels show that the information covers U.S. events and world events.

Strategy ❷ Read the dates and events in sequential order, beginning with the earliest one. Pay particular attention to how the entries relate to each other. Think about which events caused later events.

Strategy ❸ Summarize the focus, or main idea, of the time line. Try to write a main idea sentence that describes the time line.

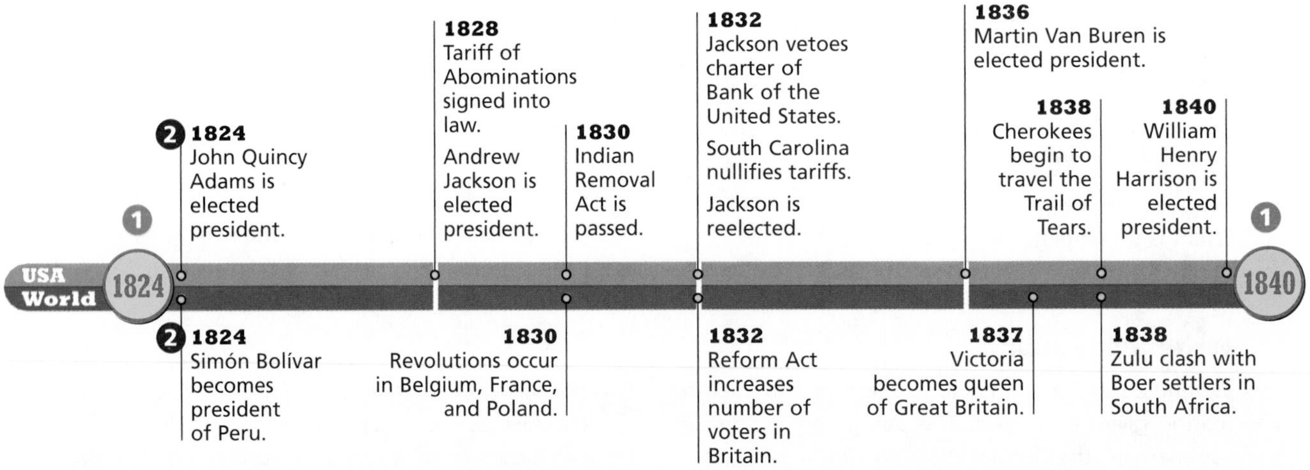

USA
World
1824
1840
❶
❶
❷ 1824 John Quincy Adams is elected president.
1828 Tariff of Abominations signed into law.
Andrew Jackson is elected president.
1830 Indian Removal Act is passed.
1832 Jackson vetoes charter of Bank of the United States.
South Carolina nullifies tariffs.
Jackson is reelected.
1836 Martin Van Buren is elected president.
1838 Cherokees begin to travel the Trail of Tears.
1840 William Henry Harrison is elected president.
❷ 1824 Simón Bolívar becomes president of Peru.
1830 Revolutions occur in Belgium, France, and Poland.
1832 Reform Act increases number of voters in Britain.
1837 Victoria becomes queen of Great Britain.
1838 Zulu clash with Boer settlers in South Africa.

Write a Summary

Writing a summary can help you understand information shown on a time line. The summary to the right states the main idea of the time line and tells how the events are related.

❸ *The time line covers the period between 1824, when John Quincy Adams was elected president, and 1840, when William Henry Harrison was elected president. During that period of time, Andrew Jackson and Martin Van Buren also served as president. The time line shows that the important issues in the United States were tariffs, banking, and relations with Native Americans.*

Practicing the Skill

Turn to Chapter 15 and look at the time line at the beginning of the chapter. Then write a summary of the information shown on the time line.

3.5 Reading a Map

Defining the Skill

Maps are representations of features on the earth's surface. Some maps show political features, such as national borders. Other maps show physical features, such as mountains and bodies of water. By learning to use map elements and math skills, you can better understand how to read maps.

Applying the Skill

The following map shows the Battle of Yorktown during the Revolution. Use the strategies listed below to help you identify the elements common to most maps.

How to Read a Map

Strategy ❶ Read the title. This identifies the main idea of the map.

Strategy ❷ Look for the grid of lines that forms a pattern of squares over the map. These numbered lines are the lines of latitude (horizontal) and longitude (vertical). They indicate the location of the area on the earth.

Strategy ❸ Read the map key. It is usually in a box. This will give you the information you need to interpret the symbols or colors on the map.

Strategy ❹ Use the scale and the pointer, or compass rose, to determine distance and direction.

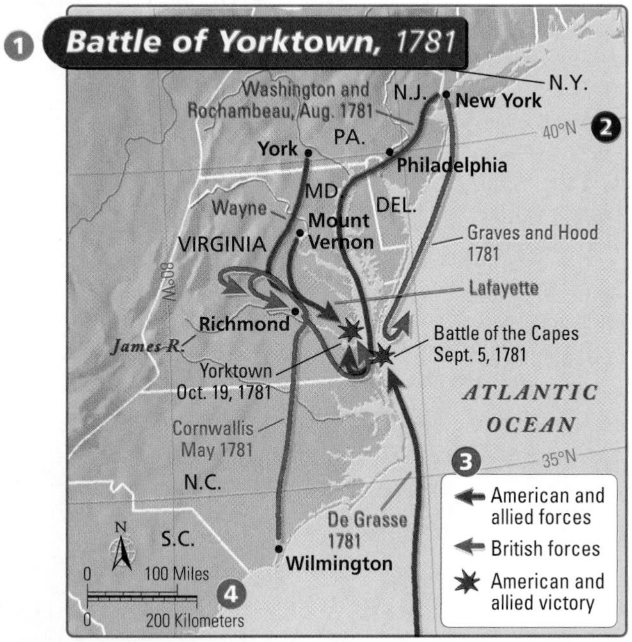

Make a Chart

A chart can help you organize information given on maps. The chart below summarizes information about the map you just studied.

Title	Battle of Yorktown, 1781
Location	between latitude 40° N and 35° N, just east of longitude 80° W
Map Key Information	blue = American and allied forces, red = British forces
Scale	7/16 in. = 100 miles, 9/16 in. = 200 km
Summary	British commanders Graves and Hood sailed south from New York. They were defeated by De Grasse at the Battle of the Capes. British commander Cornwallis marched north from Wilmington, North Carolina, to Virginia, where he was defeated by American forces.

Practicing the Skill

Turn to Chapter 7, Section 1, "The Early Years of the War." Read the map entitled "War in the Middle States, 1776–1777" and make a chart to identify information on the map.

3.6 Reading a Special-Purpose Map

Defining the Skill

Special-purpose maps help people focus on a particular aspect of a region, such as economic development in the South. These kinds of maps often use symbols to indicate information.

Applying the Skill

The following special-purpose map indicates the products of the Southern colonies. Use the strategies listed below to help you identify the information shown on the map.

How to Read a Special-Purpose Map

Strategy ❶ Read the title. It tells you what the map is intended to show.

Strategy ❷ Read the legend. This tells you what each symbol stands for. This legend shows the crops that were grown in various Southern colonies.

Strategy ❸ Look for the places on the map where the symbols appear. These tell you the places where each crop was grown.

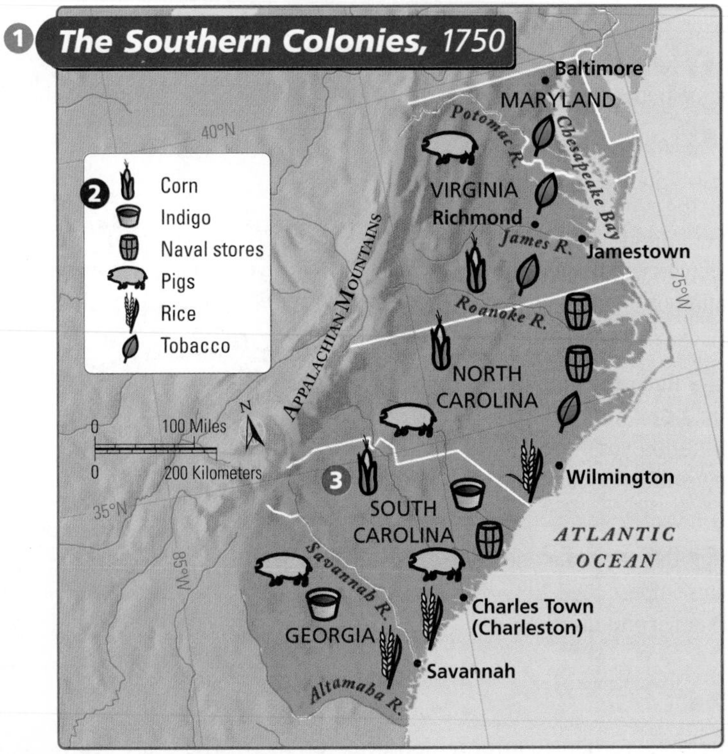

Make a Chart

A chart can help you understand special-purpose maps. The chart below shows information about the special-purpose map you just studied.

	Corn	Indigo	Naval stores	Pigs	Rice	Tobacco
Maryland						x
Virginia	x			x		x
North Carolina	x		x	x	x	x
South Carolina	x	x	x	x	x	
Georgia		x		x	x	

Practicing the Skill

Turn to Chapter 4, Section 1, "New England: Commerce and Religion." Look at the special-purpose map entitled "The New England Colonies, 1750" and make a chart that shows information about products from New England.

3.7 Creating a Map

Defining the Skill

Creating a map involves representing geographical information. When you draw a map, it is easiest to use an existing map as a guide. On the map you draw, you can show geographical information. You can also show other kinds of information, such as data on climates, population trends, resources, or routes. Often, this data comes from a graph or a chart.

Applying the Skill

Below is a map that a student created to show information about the number of slaves in 1750. Read the strategies listed below to see how the map was created.

How to Create a Map

Strategy 1 Select a title that identifies the geographical area and the map's purpose. Include a date in your title.

Strategy 2 Draw the lines of latitude and longitude using short dashes.

Strategy 3 Create a key that shows the colors.

Strategy 4 Draw the colors on the map to show information.

Strategy 5 Draw a compass rose and scale.

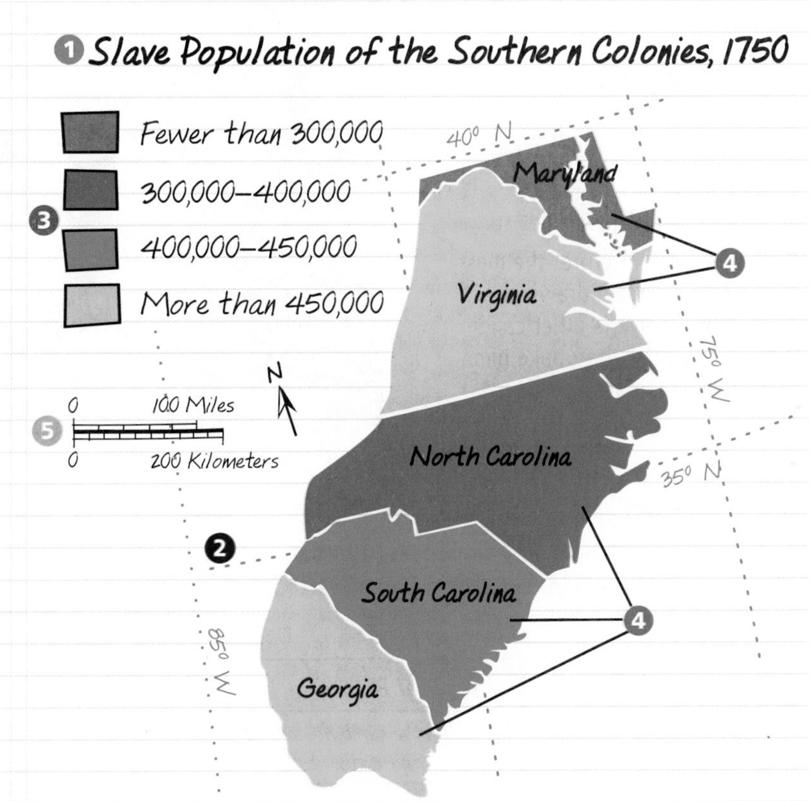

Practicing the Skill

Make your own map. Turn to the Chapter 3 Assessment and study the chart entitled "The 13 Colonies." Use the strategies described above to create a map that shows the 13 colonies and the dates that they were founded.

R27

3.8 Interpreting Political Cartoons

Defining the Skill

Political cartoons are cartoons that use humor to make a serious point. Political cartoons often express a point of view on an issue better than words do. Understanding signs and symbols will help you to interpret political cartoons.

Applying the Skill

The cartoon below shows Abraham Lincoln and the other candidates running for the presidency in 1860. Use the strategies listed below to help you understand the cartoon.

How to Interpret a Political Cartoon

Strategy ❶ Identify the subject by reading the title of the cartoon and looking at the cartoon as a whole.

Strategy ❷ Identify important symbols and details. The cartoonist uses the image of a running race to discuss a political campaign. The White House is the finish line.

Strategy ❸ Interpret the message. Why is Lincoln drawn so much taller than the other candidates? How does that make him the fittest candidate?

Make a Chart

Making a chart will help you summarize information from a political cartoon. The chart below summarizes the information from the cartoon above.

Subject	*"A Political Race" (The Election of 1860)*
Symbols and Details	*Running is a symbol for a political campaign. Lincoln is the tallest and fastest candidate.*
Message	❸ *Lincoln is pulling ahead of the other candidates in the campaign for the presidency.*

Practicing the Skill

Turn to Chapter 18, Section 3, "End of Reconstruction." Look at the political cartoon under "Scandal and Panic Weaken Republicans." It shows a cartoonist's view of corruption in President Grant's administration. Use a chart like the one above and the strategies outlined to interpret the cartoon.

3.9 Creating a Model

Defining the Skill

When you **create a model,** you use information and ideas to show an event or a situation in a visual way. A model might be a poster or a diagram that explains how something happened. Or, it might be a three-dimensional model, such as a diorama, that depicts an important scene or situation.

Applying the Skill

The following sketch shows the early stages of a model of three ways that people could have traveled from the eastern United States to California during the gold rush. Use the strategies listed below to help you create your own model.

How to Create a Model

Strategy 1 Gather the information you need to understand the situation or event. In this case, you need to be able to show the three routes and their dangers.

Strategy 2 Visualize and sketch an idea for your model. Once you have created a picture in your mind, make an actual sketch to plan how it might look.

Strategy 3 Think of symbols you may want to use. Since the model should give information in a visual way, think about ways you can use color, pictures, or other visuals to tell the story.

Strategy 4 Gather the supplies you will need and create the model. For example, you will need a globe and art supplies, such as yarn, for this model.

Strategy 5 Write and answer a question about the California gold rush, as shown in this model.

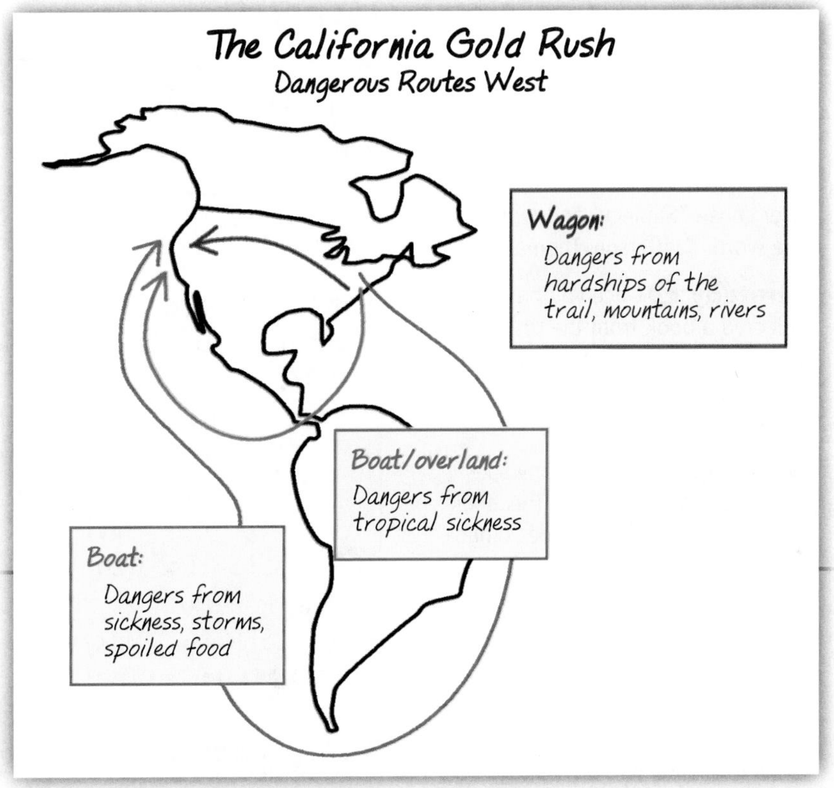

Practicing the Skill

Read the History Workshop called "Pack Your Trunk" at the end of Chapter 14. Follow the step-by-step directions to create a model of a trunk that shows what immigrants might have decided to bring with them when they came to America.

R29

4.1 Using an Electronic Card Catalog

Defining the Skill

An **electronic card catalog** is a library's computerized search program that will help you find information about the books and other materials in the library. You can search the catalog by entering a book title, an author's name, or a subject of interest to you. The electronic card catalog will give you information about the materials in the library. This information is called bibliographic information. You can use an electronic card catalog to create a bibliography (a list of books) on any topic you are interested in.

Applying the Skill

The screen shown below is from an electronic search for information about Thomas Jefferson. Use the strategies listed below to help you use the information on the screen.

How to Use an Electronic Card Catalog

Strategy 1 Begin searching by choosing either subject, title, or author, depending on the topic of your search. For this search, the user chose "Subject" and typed in the words "Jefferson, Thomas."

Strategy 2 Once you have selected a book from the results of your search, identify the author, title, city, publisher, and date of publication.

Strategy 3 Look for any special features in the book. This book is illustrated, and it includes bibliographical references and an index.

Strategy 4 Locate the call number for the book. The call number indicates the section in the library where you will find the book. You can also find out if the book is available in the library you are using. If not, it may be in another library in the network.

```
Search Request:
(1) Subject          Title          Author
-------------------------------------------------------
Find  Options  Locations  Backup  Startover  Help

(2) Miller, Douglas T. Thomas Jefferson and the
creation of America. New York: Facts on File,
1997.
          AUTHOR:  Miller, Douglas T.
      (2)  TITLE:  Thomas Jefferson and the
                   creation of America/Douglas T.
                   Miller.
   (2) PUBLISHED:  New York: Facts on File, ©1997.
      (3) PAGING:  vi, 122p. : ill ; 24 cm.
          SERIES:  Makers of America.
       (3) NOTES:  Includes bibliographical
                   references (p. 117-118) and index.
 (4) CALL NUMBER:  1. 973.46 N61T 1997-Book Available-
```

Practicing the Skill

Turn to Chapter 10, "The Jefferson Era," and find a topic that interests you, such as the Federalists, the Louisiana Purchase, the Lewis and Clark expedition, or the War of 1812. Use the SUBJECT search on an electronic card catalog to find information about your topic. Make a bibliography of books about the subject. Be sure to include the author, title, city, publisher, and date of publication for all the books included.

4.2 Creating a Database

Defining the Skill

A **database** is a collection of data, or information, that is organized so that you can find and retrieve information on a specific topic quickly and easily. Once a computerized database is set up, you can search it to find specific information without going through the entire database. The database will provide a list of all information in the database related to your topic. Learning how to use a database will help you learn how to create one.

Applying the Skill

The chart below is a database for the significant battles of the Civil War. Use the strategies listed below to help you understand and use the database.

How to Create a Database

Strategy 1 Identify the topic of the database. The keywords, or most important words, in this title are "Civil War" and "Battles." These words were used to begin the research for this database.

Strategy 2 Ask yourself what kind of data you need to include. For example, what geographic patterns and distributions will be shown? Your choice of data will provide the column headings for your database. The key words "Battle," "Date," "Location," and "Significance" were chosen to focus the research.

Strategy 3 Identify the entries included under each heading.

Strategy 4 Use the database to help you find information quickly. For example, in this database you could search for "Union victories" to find a list of significant battles won by the North.

1 LOCATION OF SIGNIFICANT CIVIL WAR BATTLES

2 BATTLE	DATE	2 LOCATION	SIGNIFICANCE
3 Fort Sumter	April 12, 1861	Charleston, SC	Beginning of the Civil War
First Battle of Bull Run (Manassas)	July 21, 1861	Virginia	Confederate victory
Shiloh	April 6–7, 1862	Tennessee (near Shiloh Church)	4 Union victory
Antietam	September 17, 1862	Sharpsburg, MD	No clear victory; considered bloodiest battle of war
Gettysburg	July 1–3, 1863	Gettysburg, PA	Retreat of Confederacy
Vicksburg	Three-month siege ending July 3, 1863	Vicksburg, MS	Union gained control of Mississippi River
Chattanooga	November 23–25, 1863	Chattanooga, TN	4 Union victory
Atlanta	September 2, 1864	Atlanta, GA	4 Union victory; helped convince Confederacy of defeat

Practicing the Skill

Create a database for U.S. presidents through the Civil War that shows each president's home state, political party, and years served as president. Use the information in "Presidents of the United States" at the end of the book to provide the data. Use a format like the one above for your database.

4.3 Using the Internet

Defining the Skill

The Internet is a computer network that connects to universities, libraries, news organizations, government agencies, businesses, and private individuals throughout the world. Each location on the Internet has a home page with its own address, or URL (universal resource locator). With a computer connected to the Internet, you can reach the home pages of many organizations and services. The international collection of home pages, known as the World Wide Web, is a good source of up-to-date information about current events as well as research on subjects in history.

Applying the Skill

The Web page below shows the links for Chapter 6 of *Creating America.* Use the strategies listed below to help you understand how to use the Web page.

How to Use the Internet

Strategy ❶ Go directly to a Web page. For example, type classzone.com in the box at the top of the screen and press ENTER (or RETURN). The Web page will appear on your screen. Then click on the link to *Creating America.*

Strategy ❷ Explore the *Creating America* links. Click on any one of the links to find out more about a specific subject. These links take you to other pages at this Web site. Some pages include links to related information that can be found at other places on the Internet.

Strategy ❸ When using the Internet for research, you should confirm the information you find. Web sites set up by universities, government agencies, and reputable news sources are more reliable than other sources. You can often find information about the creator of a site by looking for copyright information.

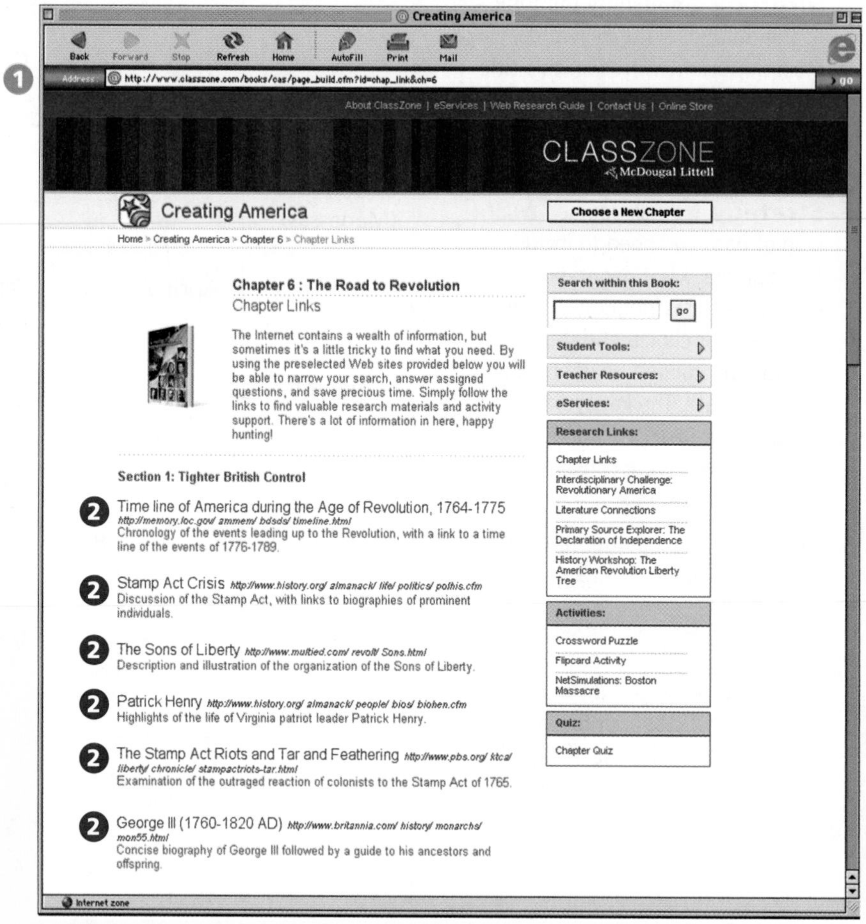

Practicing the Skill

Turn to Chapter 14, Section 2, "American Literature and Art." Read the section and make a list of topics you would like to research. If you have Internet access, go to classzone.com. There you will find links that provide more information about the topics in the section.

4.4 Creating a Multimedia Presentation

Defining the Skill

Movies, CD-ROMs, television, and computer software are different kinds of media. To **create a multimedia presentation,** you need to collect information in different media and organize them into one presentation.

Applying the Skill

The scene below shows students using computers to create a multimedia presentation. Use the strategies listed below to help you create your own multimedia presentation.

How to Create a Multimedia Presentation

Strategy ❶ Identify the topic of your presentation and decide which media are best for an effective presentation. For example, you may want to use slides or posters to show visual images of your topic. Or, you may want to use CDs or audiotapes to provide music or spoken words.

Strategy ❷ Research the topic in a variety of sources. Images, text, props, and background music should reflect the historical period of the event you choose.

Strategy ❸ Write the script for the oral portion of the presentation. You could use a narrator and characters' voices to tell the story. Primary sources are an excellent source for script material. Make sure the recording is clear so that the audience will be able to understand the oral part of the presentation.

Strategy ❹ Videotape the presentation. Videotaping the presentation will preserve it for future viewing and allow you to show it to different groups of people.

Practicing the Skill

Turn to Chapter 15, "The Nation Breaking Apart." Choose a topic from the chapter and use the strategies listed above to create a multimedia presentation about it.

R33

FACTS About the STATES

Alabama
4,486,508 people
52,218 sq. mi.
Rank in area: 30
Entered Union in 1819

Alaska
643,786 people
616,240 sq. mi.
Rank in area: 1
Entered Union in 1959

Arizona
5,456,453 people
113,998 sq. mi.
Rank in area: 6
Entered Union in 1912

Arkansas
2,710,079 people
53,178 sq. mi.
Rank in area: 28
Entered Union in 1836

California
35,116,033 people
158,854 sq. mi.
Rank in area: 3
Entered Union in 1850

Colorado
4,506,542 people
104,093 sq. mi.
Rank in area: 8
Entered Union in 1876

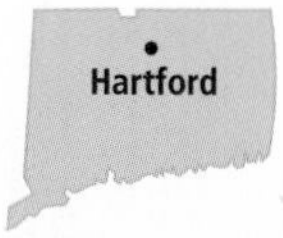

Connecticut
3,460,503 people
5,543 sq. mi.
Rank in area: 48
Entered Union in 1788

Delaware
807,385 people
2,396 sq. mi.
Rank in area: 49
Entered Union in 1787

District of Columbia
570,898 people
68 sq. mi.

Florida
16,713,149 people
59,909 sq. mi.
Rank in area: 23
Entered Union in 1845

Georgia
8,560,310 people
58,970 sq. mi.
Rank in area: 24
Entered Union in 1788

Hawaii
1,244,898 people
6,641 sq. mi.
Rank in area: 47
Entered Union in 1959

Idaho
1,341,131 people
83,570 sq. mi.
Rank in area: 14
Entered Union in 1890

Illinois
12,600,620 people
57,914 sq. mi.
Rank in area: 25
Entered Union in 1818

Indiana
6,159,068 people
36,418 sq. mi.
Rank in area: 38
Entered Union in 1816

Iowa
2,936,760 people
56,271 sq. mi.
Rank in area: 26
Entered Union in 1846

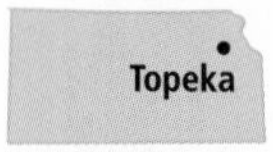

Kansas
2,715,884 people
82,276 sq. mi.
Rank in area: 15
Entered Union in 1861

Kentucky
4,092,891 people
40,409 sq. mi.
Rank in area: 37
Entered Union in 1792

Louisiana
4,482,646 people
49,650 sq. mi.
Rank in area: 31
Entered Union in 1812

Maine
1,294,464 people
33,738 sq. mi.
Rank in area: 39
Entered Union in 1820

Maryland
5,458,137 people
12,297 sq. mi.
Rank in area: 42
Entered Union in 1788

Massachusetts
6,427,801 people
9,240 sq. mi.
Rank in area: 45
Entered Union in 1788

Michigan
10,050,446 people
96,716 sq. mi.
Rank in area: 11
Entered Union in 1837

Minnesota
5,019,720 people
86,938 sq. mi.
Rank in area: 12
Entered Union in 1858

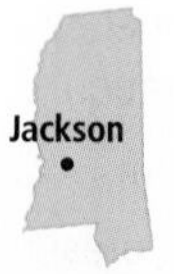

Mississippi
2,871,782 people
48,282 sq. mi.
Rank in area: 32
Entered Union in 1817

Missouri
5,672,579 people
69,704 sq. mi.
Rank in area: 21
Entered Union in 1821

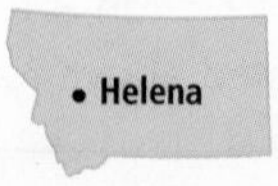

Montana
909,453 people
147,042 sq. mi.
Rank in area: 4
Entered Union in 1889

Sources: U.S. Bureau of the Census, July 1 2002 population estimates.
World Almanac and Book of Facts, 2003
Statistical Abstract of the United States, 2002

Nebraska
1,729,180 people
77,353 sq. mi.
Rank in area: 16
Entered Union in 1867

Ohio
11,421,267 people
44,825 sq. mi.
Rank in area: 34
Entered Union in 1803

Texas
21,779,893 people
267,256 sq. mi.
Rank in area: 2
Entered Union in 1845

Nevada
2,173,491 people
110,560 sq. mi.
Rank in area: 7
Entered Union in 1864

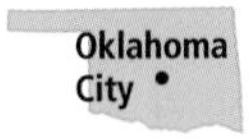

Oklahoma
3,493,714 people
69,898 sq. mi.
Rank in area: 20
Entered Union in 1907

Utah
2,316,256 people
84,898 sq. mi.
Rank in area: 13
Entered Union in 1896

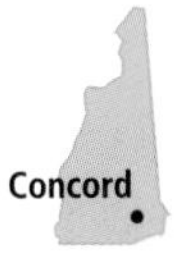

New Hampshire
1,275,056 people
9,282 sq. mi.
Rank in area: 44
Entered Union in 1788

Oregon
3,521,515 people
97,126 sq. mi.
Rank in area: 10
Entered Union in 1859

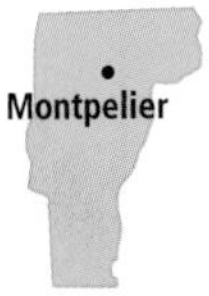

Vermont
616,592 people
9,614 sq. mi.
Rank in area: 43
Entered Union in 1791

New Jersey
8,590,300 people
8,214 sq. mi.
Rank in area: 46
Entered Union in 1787

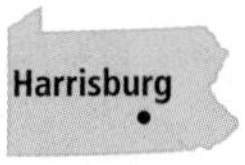

Pennsylvania
12,335,091 people
46,055 sq. mi.
Rank in area: 33
Entered Union in 1787

Virginia
7,293,542 people
42,328 sq. mi.
Rank in area: 35
Entered Union in 1788

New Mexico
1,855,059 people
121,589 sq. mi.
Rank in area: 5
Entered Union in 1912

Rhode Island
1,069,725 people
1,231 sq. mi.
Rank in area: 50
Entered Union in 1790

Washington
6,068,996 people
70,634 sq. mi.
Rank in area: 19
Entered Union in 1889

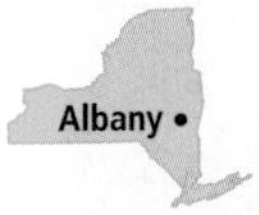

New York
19,157,532 people
54,077 sq. mi.
Rank in area: 27
Entered Union in 1788

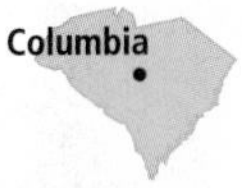

South Carolina
4,107,183 people
31,190 sq. mi.
Rank in area: 40
Entered Union in 1788

West Virginia
1,801,873 people
24,230 sq. mi.
Rank in area: 41
Entered Union in 1863

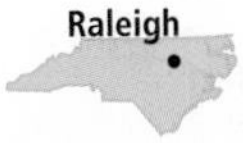

North Carolina
8,320,146 people
52,670 sq. mi.
Rank in area: 29
Entered Union in 1789

South Dakota
761,063 people
77,116 sq. mi.
Rank in area: 17
Entered Union in 1889

Wisconsin
5,441,196 people
65,498 sq. mi.
Rank in area: 22
Entered Union in 1848

North Dakota
634,110 people
70,699 sq. mi.
Rank in area: 18
Entered Union in 1889

Tennessee
5,797,289 people
42,143 sq. mi.
Rank in area: 36
Entered Union in 1796

Wyoming
498,703 people
97,813 sq. mi.
Rank in area: 9
Entered Union in 1890

United States: *Major Dependencies*

- American Samoa—68,688 people; 90 sq. mi.
- Guam—160,796 people; 217 sq. mi.
- Commonwealth of Puerto Rico—3,957,988 people; 5,324 sq. mi.
- Virgin Islands of the United States—123,498 people; 171 sq. mi.
- Midway Atoll—no indigenous inhabitants; 2 sq. mi.
- Wake Atoll—no indigenous inhabitants; 3 sq. mi.

R35

PRESIDENTS of the UNITED STATES

Here are some little-known facts about the presidents of the United States:

- Only former president to serve in Congress: John Quincy Adams
- First president born in the new United States: Martin Van Buren (eighth president)
- Only president who was a bachelor: James Buchanan
- First left-handed president: James A. Garfield
- Largest president: William H. Taft (6 feet 2 inches, 326 pounds)
- Youngest president: Theodore Roosevelt (42 years old)
- Oldest president: Ronald Reagan (77 years old when he left office in 1989)
- First president born west of the Mississippi River: Herbert Hoover (born in West Branch, Iowa)
- First president born in the 20th century: John F. Kennedy (born May 29, 1917)

1 **George Washington**
1789–1797
No Political Party
Birthplace: Virginia
Born: February 22, 1732
Died: December 14, 1799

2 **John Adams**
1797–1801
Federalist
Birthplace: Massachusetts
Born: October 30, 1735
Died: July 4, 1826

3 **Thomas Jefferson**
1801–1809
Democratic-Republican
Birthplace: Virginia
Born: April 13, 1743
Died: July 4, 1826

4 **James Madison**
1809–1817
Democratic-Republican
Birthplace: Virginia
Born: March 16, 1751
Died: June 28, 1836

5 **James Monroe**
1817–1825
Democratic-Republican
Birthplace: Virginia
Born: April 28, 1758
Died: July 4, 1831

6 **John Quincy Adams**
1825–1829
Democratic-Republican
Birthplace: Massachusetts
Born: July 11, 1767
Died: February 23, 1848

7 **Andrew Jackson**
1829–1837
Democrat
Birthplace: South Carolina
Born: March 15, 1767
Died: June 8, 1845

8 **Martin Van Buren**
1837–1841
Democrat
Birthplace: New York
Born: December 5, 1782
Died: July 24, 1862

9 **William H. Harrison**
1841
Whig
Birthplace: Virginia
Born: February 9, 1773
Died: April 4, 1841

10 **John Tyler**
1841–1845
Whig
Birthplace: Virginia
Born: March 29, 1790
Died: January 18, 1862

11 **James K. Polk**
1845–1849
Democrat
Birthplace: North Carolina
Born: November 2, 1795
Died: June 15, 1849

12 **Zachary Taylor**
1849–1850
Whig
Birthplace: Virginia
Born: November 24, 1784
Died: July 9, 1850

13 Millard Fillmore
1850–1853
Whig
Birthplace: New York
Born: January 7, 1800
Died: March 8, 1874

14 Franklin Pierce
1853–1857
Democrat
Birthplace: New Hampshire
Born: November 23, 1804
Died: October 8, 1869

15 James Buchanan
1857–1861
Democrat
Birthplace: Pennsylvania
Born: April 23, 1791
Died: June 1, 1868

16 Abraham Lincoln
1861–1865
Republican
Birthplace: Kentucky
Born: February 12, 1809
Died: April 15, 1865

17 Andrew Johnson
1865–1869
National Union
Birthplace: North Carolina
Born: December 29, 1808
Died: July 31, 1875

18 Ulysses S. Grant
1869–1877
Republican
Birthplace: Ohio
Born: April 27, 1822
Died: July 23, 1885

19 Rutherford B. Hayes
1877–1881
Republican
Birthplace: Ohio
Born: October 4, 1822
Died: January 17, 1893

20 James A. Garfield
1881
Republican
Birthplace: Ohio
Born: November 19, 1831
Died: September 19, 1881

21 Chester A. Arthur
1881–1885
Republican
Birthplace: Vermont
Born: October 5, 1829
Died: November 18, 1886

22 24 Grover Cleveland
1885–1889, 1893–1897
Democrat
Birthplace: New Jersey
Born: March 18, 1837
Died: June 24, 1908

23 Benjamin Harrison
1889–1893
Republican
Birthplace: Ohio
Born: August 20, 1833
Died: March 13, 1901

25 William McKinley
1897–1901
Republican
Birthplace: Ohio
Born: January 29, 1843
Died: September 14, 1901

26 Theodore Roosevelt
1901–1909
Republican
Birthplace: New York
Born: October 27, 1858
Died: January 6, 1919

27 William H. Taft
1909–1913
Republican
Birthplace: Ohio
Born: September 15, 1857
Died: March 8, 1930

28 Woodrow Wilson
1913–1921
Democrat
Birthplace: Virginia
Born: December 28, 1856
Died: February 3, 1924

29 Warren G. Harding
1921–1923
Republican
Birthplace: Ohio
Born: November 2, 1865
Died: August 2, 1923

R37

PRESIDENTS of the UNITED STATES

30 Calvin Coolidge
1923–1929
Republican
Birthplace: Vermont
Born: July 4, 1872
Died: January 5, 1933

31 Herbert C. Hoover
1929–1933
Republican
Birthplace: Iowa
Born: August 10, 1874
Died: October 20, 1964

32 Franklin D. Roosevelt
1933–1945
Democrat
Birthplace: New York
Born: January 30, 1882
Died: April 12, 1945

33 Harry S. Truman
1945–1953
Democrat
Birthplace: Missouri
Born: May 8, 1884
Died: December 26, 1972

34 Dwight D. Eisenhower
1953–1961
Republican
Birthplace: Texas
Born: October 14, 1890
Died: March 28, 1969

35 John F. Kennedy
1961–1963
Democrat
Birthplace: Massachusetts
Born: May 29, 1917
Died: November 22, 1963

36 Lyndon B. Johnson
1963–1969
Democrat
Birthplace: Texas
Born: August 27, 1908
Died: January 22, 1973

37 Richard M. Nixon
1969–1974
Republican
Birthplace: California
Born: January 9, 1913
Died: April 22, 1994

38 Gerald R. Ford
1974–1977
Republican
Birthplace: Nebraska
Born: July 14, 1913

39 James E. Carter, Jr.
1977–1981
Democrat
Birthplace: Georgia
Born: October 1, 1924

40 Ronald W. Reagan
1981–1989
Republican
Birthplace: Illinois
Born: February 6, 1911

41 George H. W. Bush
1989–1993
Republican
Birthplace: Massachusetts
Born: June 12, 1924

42 William J. Clinton
1993–2001
Democrat
Birthplace: Arkansas
Born: August 19, 1946

43 George W. Bush
2001–
Republican
Birthplace: Connecticut
Born: July 6, 1946

GAZETTEER

The Gazetteer identifies important places and geographical features in this book. Entries include a short description, often followed by two page numbers. The first number refers to a text page on which the entry is discussed, and the second, in italics, refers to a map where the place appears. (The reference *Atlas* is to the section of U.S. and world maps on pages A1–A21.) In addition, some entries include rounded-off geographical coordinates. There are entries for all U.S. states (with capital cities).

Africa world's second largest continent. *Atlas*

Alabama 22nd state. Capital: Montgomery. *Atlas*

Alamo Texas mission in San Antonio captured by Mexico in 1836. (29°N 98°W), 387, *m389*

Alaska 49th state. Capital: Juneau. *Atlas*

Antarctica continent at the South Pole. *Atlas*

Antietam Maryland creek; site of bloodiest day's fighting in the Civil War. (39°N 77°W), 481, *m479*

Appalachian Mountains mountain range running from Alabama into Canada. 110, *m111*

Appomattox Court House town near Appomattox, Virginia, where Lee surrendered to Grant on April 9, 1865. (37°N 79°W), 503, *m511*

Arizona 48th state. Capital: Phoenix. *Atlas*

Arkansas 25th state. Capital: Little Rock. *Atlas*

Asia world's largest continent. *Atlas*

Atlantic Ocean ocean forming east boundary of the United States. *Atlas*

Australia island country between Indian and Pacific oceans; also the world's smallest continent. *Atlas*

Austria-Hungary one of the Central Powers in World War I; after the war, divided into smaller countries. 560

Aztec Empire former region of Mexico once under Aztec control. 30, *m30*

Backcountry identification for former undeveloped region beginning in the Appalachian Mountains and extending west. 110, *m111*

Baltimore Maryland city on Chesapeake Bay. (39°N 77°W), 316, *m315*

Bay of Pigs (Bahía de Cochinos) inlet on south coast of Cuba; site of 1961 ill-fated, U.S.-backed Cuban invasion attempt. (22°N 81°W), 822

Beringia former land bridge connecting Asia with North America and now under waters of Bering Strait. (66°N 169°W), 27

Berlin capital of Germany; divided into East and West Berlin, 1948–1989. (53°N 13°E), *m577*

Boston capital of Massachusetts; site of early colonial unrest and conflict. (42°N 71°W), 149, *m156*

Bull Run stream 30 miles southwest of Washington, D.C.; site of first land battle of Civil War. (39°N 78°W), 469, *m479*

Bunker Hill hill now part of Boston; its name misidentifies Revolutionary War battle fought at nearby Breed's Hill. (42°N 71°W), 161

Cahokia Illinois Mound Builders site; village taken from British by Clark in 1778. (39°N 90°W), *m187*

California 31st state. Capital: Sacramento. *Atlas*

Canada nation sharing northern U.S. border. *Atlas*

Caribbean Sea expanse of the Atlantic Ocean between the Gulf of Mexico and South America. *Atlas*

Central America area of North America between Mexico and South America. *m60, Atlas*

Charleston as Charles Town, largest Southern colonial city; South Carolina site of first Civil War shots, at offshore Fort Sumter. (33°N 80°W), 465, *m467*

Charlestown former town, now part of Boston; site of both Bunker and Breed's hills. (42°N 71°W), 161, *m156*

Chicago large Illinois city on Lake Michigan. (42°N 88°W), 544, *m545, Atlas*

China large nation in Asia. *Atlas*

Colorado 38th state. Capital: Denver. *Atlas*

Concord Massachusetts city and site of second battle of the Revolutionary War. (42°N 71°W), 156, *m156*

Confederate States of America nation formed by 11 Southern states during the Civil War. Capital: Richmond, Virginia. 457, 466, *m467*

Connecticut 5th state. Capital: Hartford. *Atlas*

Cuba Caribbean island south of Florida. 558, *Atlas*

Delaware 1st state. Capital: Dover. *Atlas*

District of Columbia (D.C.) self-governing federal district between Virginia and Maryland, made up entirely of the city of Washington, the U.S. capital. (39°N 77°W), 289, *Atlas*

Dominican Republic nation sharing the island of Hispaniola with Haiti. *Atlas*

England southern part of Great Britain. *Atlas*

English Channel narrow waterway separating Great Britain from France. 57

Erie Canal all-water channel dug out to connect the Hudson River with Lake Erie. 339, *m339*

Europe second smallest continent, actually a peninsula of the Eurasian landmass. *Atlas*

Florida 27th state. Capital: Tallahassee. *Atlas*

Fort McHenry fort in Baltimore harbor where 1814 British attack inspired U.S. national anthem. (39°N 77°N), 316, *m315*

Fort Sumter fort in Charleston, South Carolina, harbor where 1861 attack by Confederates began the Civil War. (33°N 80°W), 465, *m467*

France nation in western Europe; it aided America in the Revolutionary War. *Atlas*

Gadsden Purchase last territory (from Mexico, 1853) added to continental United States. 395, *m394*

Georgia 4th state. Capital: Atlanta. *Atlas*

Germany nation in central Europe; once divided into West and East Germany, 1949–1990. *Atlas*

Gettysburg Pennsylvania town and site of 1863 Civil War victory for the North that is considered war's turning point. (40°N 77°W), 497, *m498*

Ghana first powerful West African trading empire. 34, *m34*

Great Britain European island nation across from France; it consists of England, Scotland, and Wales. *Atlas*

Great Lakes five connected lakes—Ontario, Erie, Huron, Michigan, and Superior—on the U.S. border with Canada. 339, *m339*

Great Plains vast grassland region in the central United States. 377, *m379*

Gulf of Mexico body of water forming southern U.S. boundary from east Texas to west Florida. *Atlas*

Haiti nation sharing the island of Hispaniola with Dominican Republic. *Atlas*

Harpers Ferry village today in extreme eastern West Virginia where John Brown raided stored U.S. weapons in 1859. (39°N 78°W), 453, *m479*

Hawaii 50th state. Capital: Honolulu. *Atlas*

Hiroshima Japanese city destroyed by U.S. atomic bomb dropped to end World War II. (34°N 132°E), 578, *m577*

Hispaniola West Indies island (shared today by Dominican Republic and Haiti) that Columbus mistook for Asia. 42, *m41*

Hudson River large river in eastern New York. 84, *m79*

Idaho 43rd state. Capital: Boise. *Atlas*

Illinois 21st state. Capital: Springfield. *Atlas*

Indiana 19th state. Capital: Indianapolis. *Atlas*

Indian Territory area, mainly of present-day Oklahoma, that in the 1800s became land for relocated Native Americans. 360, *m360*

Iowa 29th state. Capital: Des Moines. *Atlas*

Iran Middle East nation. *Atlas*

Iraq Middle East nation whose 1990 invasion of Kuwait led to the Persian Gulf War. *Atlas*

Ireland island country west of England whose mid-1800s famine caused more than one million people to emigrate to America. 410, *Atlas*

Israel Jewish nation in the Middle East. *Atlas*

Italy nation in southern Europe. *Atlas*

Jamestown community in Virginia that was the first permanent English settlement in North America. 71, *m71*

Japan island nation in east Asia. *Atlas*

Kansas 34th state. Capital: Topeka. *Atlas*

Kentucky 15th state. Capital: Frankfort. *Atlas*

Kosovo province of the Yugoslavian republic of Serbia. *Atlas*

Kuwait tiny, oil-rich Middle East nation. *Atlas*

Latin America region made up of Mexico, Caribbean Islands, and Central and South America, where Latin-based languages of Spanish, French, or Portuguese are spoken. 343

Lexington Massachusetts city and site of first Revolutionary War battle in 1775. (42°N 71°W), 157, *m156*

Little Rock capital of Arkansas and site of 1957 school-desegregation conflict. *Atlas*

Los Angeles 2nd largest U.S. city, on California's coast. *Atlas*

Louisiana 18th state. Capital: Baton Rouge. *Atlas*

R40

Louisiana Purchase land west of the Mississippi River purchased from France in 1803. 303, *m314*

Lowell Massachusetts city built in early 1800s as planned factory town. (43°N 71°W), 326

Maine 23rd state. Capital: Augusta. *Atlas*

Mali early West African trading empire succeeding Ghana empire. 34, *m35*

Maryland 7th state. Capital: Annapolis. *Atlas*

Massachusetts 6th state. Capital: Boston. *Atlas*

Mexico nation sharing U.S. southern border. *Atlas*

Michigan 26th state. Capital: Lansing. *Atlas*

Minnesota 32nd state. Capital: St. Paul. *Atlas*

Mississippi 20th state. Capital: Jackson. *Atlas*

Mississippi River second longest U.S. river, south from Minnesota to the Gulf of Mexico. 130, *m137*

Missouri 24th state. Capital: Jefferson City. *Atlas*

Missouri River longest U.S. river, east from the Rockies to the Mississippi River. 305, *m304*

Montana 41st state. Capital: Helena. *Atlas*

Montgomery Alabama capital and site of 1955 African-American bus boycott. (32°N 86°W), *m334*

Nagasaki Japanese port city, one-third of which was destroyed by U.S. atomic bomb dropped to end World War II. (33°N 130°E), 578, *m577*

Nebraska 37th state. Capital: Lincoln. *Atlas*

Nevada 36th state. Capital: Carson City. *Atlas*

New England northeast U.S. region made up of Maine, New Hampshire, Vermont, Massachusetts, Rhode Island, and Connecticut. 93, *m94*

New France first permanent French colony in North America. 58, *m132*

New Hampshire 9th state. Capital: Concord. *Atlas*

New Jersey 3rd state. Capital: Trenton. *Atlas*

New Mexico 47th state. Capital: Santa Fe. *Atlas*

New Netherland early Dutch colony that became New York in 1664. 58

New Orleans Louisiana port city at mouth of the Mississippi River. *Atlas*

New Spain former North American province of the Spanish Empire, made up mostly of present-day Mexico and the southwest United States. 59, *m60*

New York 11th state. Capital: Albany. *Atlas*

New York City largest U.S. city, at the mouth of the Hudson River; temporary U.S. capital, 1785–1790. *Atlas*

Normandy region of northern France where Allied invasion in 1944 turned tide of World War II. 577

North America continent of Western Hemisphere north of Panama-Colombia border. *Atlas*

North Carolina 12th state. Capital: Raleigh. *Atlas*

North Dakota 39th state. Capital: Bismarck. *Atlas*

North Korea Communist country in Asia, bordering eastern China. *Atlas*

North Vietnam northern region of Vietnam, established in 1954; reunified with South Vietnam in 1975 after Vietnam War. 581

Northwest Territory U.S. land north of the Ohio River to the Great Lakes and west to the Mississippi River; acquired in 1783. 207, *m210*

Ohio 17th state. Capital: Columbus. *Atlas*

Ohio River river that flows from western Pennsylvania to the Mississippi River. *Atlas*

Oklahoma 46th state. Capital: Oklahoma City. *Atlas*

Oregon 33rd state. Capital: Salem. *Atlas*

Oregon Country former region of northwest North America claimed jointly by Britain and the United States until 1846. 302, *m304*

Oregon Trail pioneer wagon route from Missouri to the Oregon Territory in the 1840s and 1850s. 380, *m379*

Pacific Ocean world's largest ocean, on the west coast of the United States. *Atlas*

Panama Canal ship passageway cut through Panama in Central America, linking Atlantic and Pacific oceans. (8°N 80°W), 558, 559

Pearl Harbor naval base in Hawaii; site of surprise Japanese aerial attack in 1941. (21°N 158°W), 575–576

Pennsylvania 2nd state. Capital: Harrisburg. *Atlas*

Persian Gulf waterway between Saudi Arabia and Iran, leading to Kuwait and Iraq. 587, *Atlas*

Philadelphia large port city in Pennsylvania; U.S. capital, 1790–1800. (40°N 76°W), 213, *Atlas*

Philippine Islands Pacific island country off the southeast coast of China. 557, *Atlas*

Plymouth town on Massachusetts coast and site of Pilgrim landing and colony. (42°N 71°W), 77, *m79*

Portugal nation in southwestern Europe; leader in early oceanic explorations. 39, *m41*

Potomac River historic river separating Virginia from Maryland and Washington, D.C. 480, *m479*

Puerto Rico Caribbean island that has been U.S. territory since 1898. 558, *Atlas*

R41

Quebec major early Canadian city; also a province of eastern Canada. 130, *m132*

Rhode Island 13th state. Capital: Providence. *Atlas*

Richmond Virginia capital that was also the capital of the Confederacy. (38°N 77°W), 466, *m467*

Rio Grande river that forms part of the border between the United States and Mexico. *Atlas*

Roanoke Island island off the coast of North Carolina; 1585 site of the first English colony in the Americas. (36°N 76°W), 69, *m71*

Rocky Mountains mountain range in the western United States and Canada. *Atlas*

Russia large Eurasian country, the major republic of the former Soviet Union (1922–1991). *Atlas*

St. Augustine oldest permanent European settlement (1565) in the United States, on Florida's northeast coast. (30°N 81°W), 56, 57, *m56*

St. Lawrence River Atlantic-to-Great Lakes waterway used by early explorers of mid-North America. 130, *m132*

St. Louis Missouri city at the junction of the Missouri and Mississippi rivers. (39°N 90°W), 304, *Atlas*

San Antonio Texas city and site of the Alamo. (29°N 99°W), 386, *m389*

San Francisco major port city in northern California. (38°N 123°W), 400, *Atlas*

San Salvador West Indies island near the Bahamas where Columbus first landed in the Americas. (24°N 74°W), 42, *m41*

Santa Fe Trail old wagon route from Missouri to Santa Fe in Mexican province of New Mexico. 379, *m379*

Songhai early West African trading empire succeeding Mali empire. 34–35, *m34*

South America continent of Western Hemisphere south of Panama-Colombia border. *Atlas*

South Carolina 8th state. Capital: Columbia. *Atlas*

South Dakota 40th state. Capital: Pierre. *Atlas*

South Korea East Asian country bordering North Korea. *Atlas*

South Vietnam southern region of Vietnam, established in 1954; reunified with North Vietnam in 1975 after Vietnam War. 581

Soviet Union country created in 1922 by joining Russia and other republics; in 1991, broken into independent states. 576, *m577*

Spain nation in southwestern Europe; early empire builder in the Americas. 40, *m41*

Tennessee 16th state. Capital: Nashville. *Atlas*

Tenochtitlán Aztec Empire capital; now site of Mexico City. 53, *m56*

Texas 28th state. Capital: Austin. *Atlas*

Utah 45th state. Capital: Salt Lake City. *Atlas*

Valley Forge village in southeast Pennsylvania and site of Washington's army camp during winter of 1777–1778. (40°N 75°W), 186, *m193*

Vermont 14th state. Capital: Montpelier. *Atlas*

Vicksburg Mississippi River site of major Union victory (1863) in Civil War. (32°N 91°W), 500, *m501*

Vietnam country in Southeast Asia; divided into two regions (1954–1975), North and South, until end of Vietnam War. 581, *Atlas*

Virginia 10th state. Capital: Richmond. *Atlas*

Washington 42nd state. Capital: Olympia. *Atlas*

Washington, D.C. capital of the United States since 1800; makes up whole of District of Columbia (D.C.). (39°N 77°W), 289, *Atlas*

West Africa region from which most Africans were brought to the Americas. 33, *m34*

Western Hemisphere the half of the world that includes the Americas. 62, *m62*

West Indies numerous islands in the Caribbean Sea, between Florida and South America. 95, *m95*

West Virginia 35th state. Capital: Charleston. *Atlas*

Wisconsin 30th state. Capital: Madison. *Atlas*

Wyoming 44th state. Capital: Cheyenne. *Atlas*

Yorktown Virginia village and site of American victory that sealed British defeat in Revolutionary War. (37°N 77°W), 193, *m193*

GLOSSARY

A

abolition (AB uh LIHSH uhn) *n.* the movement to end slavery. (p. 424)

abridge (uh BRIHJ) *v.* to reduce. (p. 250)

affirmation (AF uhr MAY shuhn) *n.* a statement declaring that something is true. (p. 241)

African Diaspora (AF rih kuhn dy AS puhr uh) *n.* the forced removal of Africans from their homelands to serve as slave labor in the Americas. (p. 61)

Albany Plan of Union *n.* the first formal proposal to unite the American colonies, put forth by Benjamin Franklin. (p. 133)

Alien and Sedition (si DISH uhn) **Acts** *n.* a series of four laws enacted in 1798 to reduce the political power of recent immigrants to the United States. (p. 290)

ally (AL eye) *n.* a country that agrees to help another country achieve a common goal. (p. 184)

American System *n.* a plan introduced in 1815 to make the United States economically self-sufficient. (p. 338)

Anaconda (AN uh KAHN duh) **Plan** *n.* a strategy by which the Union proposed to defeat the Confederacy in the Civil War. (p. 468)

Antifederalist (AN tee FED uhr uh list) *n.* a person who opposed the ratification of the U.S. Constitution. (p. 218)

Appalachian (AP uh LAY chee uhn) **Mountains** *n.* a mountain range that stretches from eastern Canada south to Alabama. (p. 110)

appellate (uh PEL it) *adj.* having power to review court decisions. (p. 244)

Appomattox (AP uh MAT uhks) **Court House** *n.* the Virginia town where Robert E. Lee surrendered to Ulysses S. Grant in 1865, ending the Civil War. (p. 503)

apprentice (uh PREN tis) *n.* a beginner who learns a trade or a craft from an experienced master. (p. 121)

appropriation (uh PROH pree AY shuhn) *n.* public funds set aside for a specific purpose. (p. 237)

Articles of Confederation *n.* a document, adopted by the Continental Congress in 1777 and finally approved by the states in 1781, that outlined the form of government of the new United States. (p. 206)

artillery (ahr TIL uhr ee) *n.* a cannon or large gun. (p. 161)

artisan (AHR ti zuhn) *n.* a skilled worker, such as a weaver or a potter, who makes goods by hand; a craftsperson. (p. 101)

B

baby boom *n.* the term for the generation born between 1946 and 1961, when the U.S. birthrate sharply increased following World War II. (p. 584)

Backcountry *n.* a colonial region that ran along the Appalachian Mountains through the far western part of the New England, Middle, and Southern colonies. (p. 93)

Bacon's Rebellion *n.* a revolt against powerful colonial authority in Jamestown by Nathaniel Bacon and a group of landless frontier settlers that resulted in the burning of Jamestown in 1676. (p. 73)

bail (bayl) *n.* money paid as security by arrested persons to guarantee they will return for trial. (p. 252)

Battle of Antietam (an TEE tuhm) *n.* a Civil War battle in 1862 in which 25,000 men were killed or wounded. (p. 481)

Battle of Fallen Timbers *n.* in 1794, an American army defeated 2,000 Native Americans in a clash over control of the Northwest Territory. (p. 283)

Battle of Gettysburg (GET eez BURG) *n.* an 1863 battle in the Civil War in which the Union defeated the Confederacy, ending hopes for a Confederate victory in the North. (p. 497)

Battle of Quebec (kwi BEK) *n.* a battle won by the British over the French, and the turning point in the French and Indian War. (p. 134)

Battle of Shiloh (SHY loh) *n.* an 1862 battle in which the Union forced the Confederacy to retreat in some of the fiercest fighting in the Civil War. (p. 478)

Battle of Yorktown *n.* the last major battle of the Revolutionary War, which resulted in the surrender of British forces in 1781. (p. 194)

Battle of the Alamo (AL uh MOH) *n.* in 1836, Texans defended a church called the Alamo against the Mexican army; all but five Texans were killed. (p. 387)

Battle of the Thames (temz) *n.* an American victory over the British in the War of 1812, which ended the British threat to the Northwest Territory. (p. 316)

Battles of Saratoga (SAR uh TOH guh) *n.* a series of conflicts between British soldiers and the Continental Army in 1777 that proved to be a turning point in the Revolutionary War. (p. 183)

bayonet (BAY uh net) *n.* a long steel knife attached to the end of a gun. (p. 186)

Bear Flag Revolt *n.* the 1846 rebellion by Americans against Mexican rule in California. (p. 393)

bill of attainder (uh TAYN duhr) *n.* a law that condemns a person without a trial in court. (p. 239)

Bill of Rights *n.* the first ten amendments to the U.S. Constitution, added in 1791, and consisting of a formal list of citizens' rights and freedoms. (p. 221)

black code *n.* a law passed by Southern states that limited the freedom of former slaves. (p. 518)

blockade *n.* when armed forces prevent the transportation of goods or people into or out of an area. (p. 468)

border state *n.* a slave state that bordered states in which slavery was illegal. (p. 466)

Boston Massacre (MAS uh kuhr) *n.* a clash between British soldiers and Boston colonists in 1770, in which five of the colonists, including Crispus Attucks, were killed. (p. 149)

Boston Tea Party *n.* the dumping of 342 chests of tea into Boston Harbor by colonists in 1773 to protest the Tea Act. (p. 151)

bounty (BOWN tee) *n.* a reward or cash payment given by a government. (pp. 255, 492)

boycott (BOI KOT) *n.* a refusal to buy certain goods. (p. 145)

buck *n.* a buckskin from an adult male deer was a unit of money for settlers. (p. 111)

C

cabinet *n.* a group of department heads who serve as the president's chief advisers. (p. 278)

California gold rush *n.* in 1849, large numbers of people moved to California because gold had been discovered there. (p. 397)

caravel (KAR uh VEL) *n.* a ship with triangular sails that allowed it to sail into the wind and with square sails that carried it forward when the wind was at its back. (p. 39)

cash crop *n.* a crop grown by a farmer to be sold for money rather than for personal use. (p. 99)

cavalry *n.* soldiers on horseback. (p. 480)

charter *n.* a written contract issued by a government giving the holder the right to establish a colony. (p. 71)

checks and balances *n.* the ability of each branch of government to exercise checks, or controls, over the other branches. (p. 230)

civil disobedience (DIS uh BEE dee uhns) *n.* peacefully refusing to obey laws one considers unjust. (p. 415)

civilization (SIV uh li ZAY shuhn) *n.* a form of culture characterized by city trade centers, specialized workers, organized forms of government and religion, systems of record keeping, and advanced tools. (p. 28)

civil rights *n.* rights granted to all citizens. (p. 519)

clan *n.* a large group of families that claim a common ancestor. (p. 111)

Cold War *n.* the state of hostility, without direct military conflict, that developed between the United States and the Soviet Union after World War II. (p. 579)

Columbian (kuh LUM bee uhn) **Exchange** *n.* the transfer of plants, animals, and diseases between the Western and the Eastern hemispheres. (p. 62)

committee of correspondence *n.* a group of people in the colonies who exchanged letters on colonial affairs. (p. 150)

common law *n.* a system of law developed in England, based on customs and previous court decisions. (p. 252)

Compromise of 1850 *n.* a series of Congressional laws intended to settle the major disagreements between free states and slave states. (p. 445)

Compromise of 1877 *n.* the agreement that resolved an 1876 election dispute: Rutherford B. Hayes became president and then removed the last federal troops from the South. (p. 532)

compulsory process *n.* a required procedure. (p. 251)

Conestoga (KON i STOW guh) **wagon** *n.* a vehicle with wide wheels, a curved bed, and a canvas cover used by American pioneers traveling west. (p. 101)

Confederate States of America *n.* the confederation formed in 1861 by the Southern states after their secession from the Union. (p. 457)

conquistador (kon KWIS tuh DAWR) *n.* a Spaniard who traveled to the Americas as an explorer and a conqueror in the 16th century. (p. 53)

conscription (kuhn SKRIP shuhn) *n.* a law that required men to serve in the military or be drafted. (p. 492)

Constitutional Convention *n.* a meeting held in 1787 to consider changes to the Articles of Confederation; resulted in the drafting of the Constitution. (p. 213)

containment (kuhn TAYN muhnt) *n.* the blocking by one nation of another nation's attempts to spread influence—especially the efforts of the United States to block the spread of Soviet Communism during the late 1940s and early 1950s. (p. 580)

Continental Army *n.* a colonial force authorized by the Second Continental Congress in 1775, with George Washington as its commanding general. (p. 161)

convene (kuhn VEEN) *v.* to call together. (p. 243)

Copperheads *n.* Abraham Lincoln's main political opponents; they favored peace with the South. (p. 492)

cotton gin *n.* a machine invented in 1793 that cleaned cotton much faster and far more efficiently than human workers. (p. 332)

counterculture (KOWN tuhr KUL chuhr) *n.* a group of young people with values and lifestyles in opposition to those of the established culture. (p. 587)

Crittenden (KRIT uhn duhn) **Plan** *n.* a compromise introduced in 1861 that might have prevented secession. (p. 459)

Crusades (kroo SAYDZ) *n.* a series of wars to capture the Holy Land, launched in 1096 by European Christians. (p. 36)

culture (KUL chuhr) *n.* a way of life shared by people with similar arts, beliefs, and customs. (p. 28)

D

Dawes (dawz) **Act** *n.* a law, enacted in 1887, that distributed reservation land to individual owners. (p. 540)

Declaration of Independence *n.* the document, written in 1776, in which the colonies declared independence from Britain. (p. 164)

depression *n.* a severe economic slump. (p. 370)

desert (di ZURT) *v.* to leave military duty without intending to return. (p. 187)

diversity (di VUR si tee) *n.* a variety of people. (p. 101)

doctrine of nullification (NUL uh fi KAY shuhn) *n.* a right of a state to reject a federal law that it considers unconstitutional. (p. 365)

domestication (doh MES ti KAY shuhn) *n.* the practice of breeding plants or taming animals to meet human needs. (p. 28)

Dred Scott* v. *Sandford *n.* an 1856 Supreme Court case in which a slave, Dred Scott, sued for his freedom because he had been taken to live in territories where slavery was illegal; the Court ruled against Scott. (p. 451)

due process of law *n.* fair treatment under the law. (p. 251)

E

elector *n.* a voter. (p. 233)

Emancipation (i MAN suh PAY shuhn) **Proclamation** *n.* an executive order issued by Abraham Lincoln on January 1, 1863, freeing the slaves in all regions in rebellion against the Union. (p. 488)

Embargo (em BAHR goh) **Act of 1807** *n.* an act that stated that American ships were no longer allowed to sail to foreign ports, and it also closed American ports to British ships. (p. 312)

emigrant (EM i gruhnt) *n.* a person who leaves a country. (p. 407)

encomienda (en koh mee YEN duh) *n.* a grant of Native American labor. (p. 233)

English Bill of Rights *n.* an agreement signed by William and Mary to respect the rights of English citizens and of Parliament, including the right to free elections. (p. 128)

enlightenment (en LYT n muhnt) *n.* an 18th-century movement that emphasized the use of reason and the scientific method to obtain knowledge. (p. 124)

enumeration (i NOO muh RAY shuhn) *n.* an official count, such as a census. (p. 124)

equity (EK wi tee) *n.* a system of justice not covered under common law. (p. 253)

Erie (EER ee) **Canal** *n.* completed in 1825, this waterway connected New York City and Buffalo, New York. (p. 339)

European Middle Ages *n.* a period from the late 400s to about the 1300s, during which Europeans turned to feudalism and the manor system. (p. 35)

ex post facto (EKS pohst FAK toh) **law** *n.* a law that would make an act a criminal offense after it was committed. (p. 239)

F

factory system *n.* a method of production that brought many workers and machines together into one building. (p. 325)

fall line *n.* the point at which a waterfall prevents large boats from moving farther upriver. (p. 110)

famine (FAM in) *n.* a severe food shortage. (p. 410)

fascism (FASH iz uhm) *n.* a political philosophy that advocates a strong, centralized, nationalistic government headed by a powerful dictator. (p. 574)

federalism *n.* a system of government where power is shared among the central (or federal) government and the states. (pp. 218, 229)

Federalists *n.* supporters of the Constitution. (p. 218)

Federalist Papers *n.* a series of essays defending and explaining the Constitution. (p. 219)

Federal Judiciary (joo DISH ee ER ee) **Act** *n.* it helped create a court system and gave the Supreme Court six members. (p. 278)

felony (FEL uh nee) *n.* a serious crime. (p. 237)

feudalism (FYOOD l IZ uhm) *n.* a political system in which the king allows nobles the use of his land in exchange for their military service and their protection of people living on the land. (p. 35)

Fifteenth Amendment *n.* passed in 1870, this amendment to the U.S. Constitution stated that citizens could not be stopped from voting "on account of race, color, or previous condition of servitude." (p. 530)

54th Massachusetts Regiment *n.* one of the first African-American regiments organized to fight for the Union in the Civil War. (p. 490)

First Battle of Bull Run *n.* an 1861 battle of the Civil War in which the South shocked the North with a victory. (p. 469)

foreign (FAWR in) **policy** *n.* relations with the governments of other countries. (p. 288)

Fort Sumter *n.* a federal fort located in the harbor of Charleston, South Carolina; the Southern attack on Fort Sumter marked the beginning of the Civil War. (p. 465)

forty-niner *n.* a person who went to California to find gold, starting in 1849. (p. 396)

Fourteen Points *n.* President Woodrow Wilson's goals for peace after World War I. (p. 561)

Fourteenth Amendment *n.* an amendment to the U.S. Constitution, passed in 1868, that made all persons born or naturalized in the United States—including former slaves—citizens of the country. (p. 519)

First Continental Congress *n.* a meeting of delegates in 1774 from all the colonies except Georgia to uphold colonial rights. (p. 155)

Freedmen's Bureau *n.* a federal agency set up to help former slaves after the Civil War. (p. 517)

freedmen's school *n.* a school set up to educate newly freed African Americans. (p. 525)

Free Soil Party *n.* a political party dedicated to stopping the expansion of slavery. (p. 443)

French and Indian War *n.* a conflict in North America from 1754 to 1763 that was part of a worldwide struggle between France and Britain; Britain defeated France and gained French Canada. (p. 131)

frontier (frun TEER) *n.* unsettled or sparsely settled area occupied largely by Native Americans. (p. 539)

Fugitive Slave Act *n.* an 1850 law to help slaveholders recapture runaway slaves. (p. 446)

French Revolution *n.* in 1789, the French launched a movement for liberty and equality. (p. 285)

Fundamental Orders of Connecticut *n.* a set of laws that were established in 1639 by a Puritan congregation who had settled in the Connecticut Valley and that expanded the idea of representative government. (p. 79)

G

Gilded (gil did) **Age** *n.* an era during the late 1800s of fabulous wealth. (p. 541)

"Glorious Revolution" *n.* the overthrow of English King James II in 1688 and his replacement by William and Mary. (p. 128)

Great Awakening *n.* a revival of religious feeling in the American colonies during the 1730s and 1740s. (p. 123)

Great Compromise *n.* the Constitutional Convention's agreement to establish a two-house national legislature, with all states having equal representation in one house and each state having representation based on its population in the other house. (p. 216)

Great Depression *n.* a period, lasting from 1929 to 1941, in which the U.S. economy was in severe decline and millions of Americans were unemployed. (p. 571)

Great Migration *n.* the movement of Puritans from England to establish settlements around the world, including 20,000 who sailed for America (p. 78); the movement of African Americans between 1910 and 1920 to northern cities from the South. (p. 562)

Great Society *n.* a program started by President Lyndon Johnson that provided help to the poor, the elderly, and women, and also promoted education and outlawed discrimination. (p. 586)

greenback *n.* paper currency issued by the federal government during the Civil War. (p. 493)

gristmill (GRIST MIL) *n.* a mill in which grain is ground to produce flour or meal. (p. 99)

guerrilla (guh RIL uh) *n.* a soldier who weakens the enemy with surprise raids and hit-and-run attacks. (p. 191)

H

Harlem Renaissance *n.* a flowering of African-American artistic creativity during the 1920s, centered in the Harlem community of New York City. (p. 571)

Harpers Ferry *n.* a federal arsenal in Virginia that was captured in 1859 during a slave revolt. (p. 469)

Holocaust (HOL uh KAWST) *n.* the systematic killing by Germany during World War II of about six million Jews as well as millions from other ethnic groups. (p. 578)

Homestead Act *n.* passed in 1862, this law offered 160 acres of land free to anyone who agreed to live on and improve the land for five years. (p. 540)

House of Burgesses *n.* created in 1619, the first representative assembly in the American colonies. (p. 72)

Hudson River school *n.* a group of artists living in the Hudson River Valley in New York. (p. 414)

hygiene (HY JEEN) *n.* conditions and practices that promote health. (p. 474)

I

immigrant *n.* a person who settles in a new country. (p. 407)

immunity *n.* legal protection. (p. 246)

impeachment *n.* the process of accusing a public official of wrongdoing. (p. 233)

imperialism *n.* the policy by which stronger nations extend their economic, political, or military control over weaker nations or territories. (p. 556)

impressment *n.* the act of seizing by force. (p. 311)

inaugurate (in AW gyuh RAYT) *v.* to swear in or induct into office in a formal ceremony. (p. 277)

income tax *n.* a tax on earnings. (p. 493)

indentured servant *n.* a person who sold his or her labor in exchange for passage to America. (p. 72)

Indian Removal Act *n.* this 1830 act called for the government to negotiate treaties that would require Native Americans to relocate west. (p. 360)

Indian Territory *n.* present-day Oklahoma and parts of Kansas and Nebraska to which Native Americans were moved under the Indian Removal Act of 1830. (p. 360)

indictment (in DYT muhnt) *n.* a written statement issued by a grand jury charging a person with a crime. (p. 234)

indigo *n.* a plant grown in the Southern colonies that yields a deep blue dye. (p. 105)

individual right *n.* a personal liberty and privilege guaranteed to U.S. citizens by the Bill of Rights. (p. 231)

Industrial Revolution *n.* in late 18th-century Britain, factory machines began replacing hand tools and manufacturing replaced farming as the main form of work. (p. 325)

inferior court *n.* a court with less authority than the Supreme Court. (p. 244)

inflation *n.* an increase in the price of goods and services and a decrease in the value of money. (p. 370)

inoperative *adj.* no longer in force. (p. 258)

insurrection (IN suh REK shuhn) *n.* open revolt against a government. (p. 255)

interchangeable part *n.* a part that is exactly like another part. (p. 327)

Intolerable Acts *n.* a series of laws enacted by Parliament in 1774 to punish Massachusetts colonists for the Boston Tea Party. (p. 154)

ironclad *n.* a warship covered with iron. (p. 475)

Iroquois (IR uh KWOH) **League** *n.* a 16th-century alliance of the Cayuga, Mohawk, Oneida, Onondaga, and Seneca Native American groups living in the eastern Great Lakes region. (p. 31)

Islam (is LAHM) *n.* a religion founded by the prophet Muhammad in the 600s, which teaches that there is one God, named Allah. (p. 34)

J

Jacksonian democracy *n.* the idea of spreading political power to all the people, thereby ensuring majority rule. (p. 354)

Jamestown *n.* the first permanent English settlement in North America. (p. 71)

Jay's Treaty *n.* the agreement that ended dispute over American shipping during the French Revolution. (p. 286)

jazz *n.* a new kind of music in the 1920s that captured the carefree spirit of the times. (p. 570)

Jim Crow *n.* laws meant to enforce separation of white and black people in public places in the South. (p. 549)

joint-stock company *n.* a business in which investors pool their wealth in order to turn a profit. (p. 70)

judicial (joo DISH uhl) **review** *n.* the principle that the Supreme Court has the final say in interpreting the Constitution. (p. 301)

Judiciary (joo DISH ee ER ee) **Act of 1801** *n.* a law that increased the number of federal judges, allowing President John Adams to fill most of the new spots with Federalists. (p. 300)

K

Kansas-Nebraska Act *n.* an 1854 law that established the territories of Kansas and Nebraska and gave their residents the right to decide whether to allow slavery. (p. 448)

King Cotton *n.* cotton was called king because cotton was important to the world market, and the South grew most of the cotton for Europe's mills. (p. 468)

King Philip's War *n.* a war between the Puritan colonies and Native Americans in 1675–1676. (p. 80)

Ku Klux Klan *n.* a group formed in 1866 that wanted to restore Democratic control of the South and to keep former slaves powerless. (p. 528)

L

labor union *n.* a group of workers who band together to seek better working conditions. (p. 418)

Land Ordinance of 1785 *n.* a law that established a plan for surveying and selling the federally owned lands west of the Appalachian Mountains. (p. 207)

land speculator *n.* a person who buys huge areas of land for a low price and then sells off small sections of it at high prices. (p. 378)

leisure (LEE zhuhr) *n.* free time. (p. 548)

Lewis and Clark expedition *n.* a group led by Meriwether Lewis and William Clark who explored the lands of the Louisiana Purchase beginning in 1803. (p. 304)

Lexington and Concord *n.* sites in Massachusetts of the first battles of the American Revolution. (p. 157)

limited government *n.* the principle that requires all U.S. citizens, including government leaders, to obey the law. (p. 231)

Lone Star Republic *n.* the nickname of the republic of Texas, given in 1836. (p. 389)

Louisiana (loo EE zee AN uh) **Purchase** *n.* the 1803 purchase of the Louisiana Territory from France. (p. 303)

Lowell mills *n.* textile mills located in the factory town of Lowell, Massachusetts, founded in 1826. (p. 326)

Loyalist *n.* an American colonist who supported the British in the American Revolution. (p. 157)

M

Magna Carta *n.* "Great Charter;" a document guaranteeing basic political rights in England, approved by King John in 1215. (p. 125)

manifest destiny *n.* the belief that the United States was destined to stretch across the continent from the Atlantic Ocean to the Pacific Ocean. (p. 391)

Marbury* v. *Madison *n.* an 1803 case in which the Supreme Court ruled that it had the power to abolish laws by declaring them unconstitutional. (p. 301)

mass culture *n.* a common culture experienced by large numbers of people. (p. 548)

Mayflower Compact *n.* an agreement established by the men who sailed to America on the *Mayflower,* which called for laws for the good of the colony and set forth the idea of self-government. (p. 77)

mercantilism (MUHR kuhn tee LIZ uhm) *n.* an economic system in which nations increase their wealth and power by obtaining gold and silver and by establishing a favorable balance of trade. (p. 51)

mercenary (MUR suh NER ee) *n.* a professional soldier hired to fight for a foreign country. (p. 179)

Mexican Cession (sesh uhn) *n.* a vast region given up by Mexico after the War with Mexico; it included the present-day states of California, Nevada, Utah, most of Arizona, and parts of New Mexico, Colorado, and Wyoming. (p. 395)

middle passage *n.* the middle leg of the triangular trade route—the voyage from Africa to the Americas—that brought captured Africans into slavery. (p. 61)

militia (muh LISH uh) *n.* a force of armed civilians pledged to defend their community during the American Revolution. (p. 154); an emergency military force that is not part of the regular army. (p. 238)

minié (MIN ee) **ball** *n.* a bullet with a hollow base. (p. 475)

Minuteman *n.* a member of the colonial militia who was trained to respond "at a minute's warning." (p. 154)

misdemeanor (mis di MEE nuhr) *n.* a violation of the law. (p. 243)

Missouri Compromise *n.* a series of laws enacted in 1820 to maintain the balance of power between slave states and free states. (p. 342)

Monroe Doctrine *n.* a policy of U.S. opposition to any European interference in the Western Hemisphere, announced by President Monroe in 1823. (p. 343)

Mormon *n.* a member of a church founded by Joseph Smith in 1830. (p. 381)

Mound Builder *n.* an early Native American who built large earthen structures. (p. 29)

mountain man *n.* a fur trapper or explorer who opened up the West by finding the best trails through the Rocky Mountains. (p. 377)

Muslim (MUZ luhm) *n.* a follower of Islam. (p. 34)

N

nationalism *n.* a feeling of pride, loyalty, and protectiveness toward one's country. (p. 338)

nativist *n.* a native-born American who wanted to eliminate foreign influence. (p. 412)

natural-born citizen *n.* a citizen born in the United States or a commonwealth of the United States or to parents who are U.S. citizens living outside the country. (p. 241)

naturalization *n.* a way to give full citizenship to a person born in another country. (pp. 237, 254)

Navigation Acts *n.* a series of laws passed by Parliament, beginning in 1651, to ensure that England made money from its colonies' trade. (p. 96)

navigator *n.* a person who plans the course of a ship while at sea. (p. 39)

Nazi (NAHT see) **Party** *n.* the National Socialist German Workers' Party; came to power under Adolf Hitler in the 1930s. (p. 574)

neutral (NOO truhl) *adj.* not siding with one country or the other. (p. 288)

New Deal *n.* President Franklin Roosevelt's programs to fight the Great Depression. (p. 572)

New France *n.* a fur-trading post established in 1608 that became the first permanent French settlement in North America. (p. 58)

new immigrant *n.* a person from southern or eastern Europe who entered the United States after 1900. (p. 542)

New Jersey Plan *n.* a plan of government proposed at the Constitutional Convention in 1787 that called for a one-house legislature in which each state would have one vote. (p. 215)

Northwest Ordinance *n.* it described how the Northwest Territory was to be governed and set conditions for settlement and settlers' rights. (p. 207)

Northwest Territory *n.* territory covered by the Land Ordinance of 1785, which included land that formed the states of Ohio, Indiana, Michigan, Illinois, Wisconsin, and part of Minnesota. (p. 207)

O

Oregon Trail *n.* a trail that ran westward from Independence, Missouri, to the Oregon Territory. (p. 380)

overseer *n.* a worker hired by a planter to watch over and direct the work of slaves. (p. 106)

P

pacifist (PAS uh fist) *n.* a person morally opposed to war. (p. 193)

Panama (PAN uh MAH) **Canal** *n.* a shortcut through Panama that connects the Atlantic and the Pacific oceans. (p. 558)

Panic of 1837 *n.* a financial crisis in which banks closed and the credit system collapsed. (p. 370)

Panic of 1873 *n.* a financial crisis in which banks closed and the stock market collapsed. (p. 531)

Parliament (PAHR luh muhnt) *n.* England's chief lawmaking body. (p. 126)

Patriot *n.* an American colonist who sided with the rebels in the American Revolution. (p. 157)

patroon (puh TROON) *n.* a person who brought 50 settlers to New Netherland and in return received a large land grant and other special privileges. (p. 85)

Pickett's Charge *n.* General George Pickett led a direct attack on Union troops during the 1863 Civil War battle at Gettysburg; the attack failed. (p. 497)

piedmont *n.* a broad plateau that leads to the foot of a mountain range. (p. 110)

Pilgrim *n.* a member of the group that rejected the Church of England, sailed to America, and founded the Plymouth Colony in 1620. (p. 76)

Pinckney's (PINGK neez) **Treaty** *n.* a 1795 treaty with Spain that allowed Americans to use the Mississippi River and to store goods in New Orleans; made the 31st parallel the southern U.S. border. (p. 286)

plantation *n.* a large farm that raises cash crops. (p. 60)

platform *n.* a statement of beliefs. (p. 455)

Platt Amendment *n.* a result of the Spanish-American War, which gave the United States the right to intervene in Cuban affairs when there was a threat to "life, property, and individual liberty." (p. 558)

Plessy* v. *Ferguson *n.* an 1896 case in which the Supreme Court ruled that separation of the races in public accommodations was legal. (p. 549)

Pontiac's (PON tee AKS) **Rebellion** *n.* a revolt against British forts and American settlers in 1763, led in part by Ottawa war leader Pontiac, in response to settlers' claims of Native American lands and to harsh treatment by British soldiers. (p. 135)

popular sovereignty (SOV uhr in tee) *n.* a government in which the people rule (p. 228); a system in which the residents vote to decide an issue. (p. 135)

Populist Party *n.* also known as the People's Party and formed in the 1890s, this group wanted a policy that would raise crop prices. (p. 551)

prejudice (PREJ uh dis) *n.* a negative opinion that is not based on facts. (p. 411)

privateer (PRY vuh TEER) *n.* a privately owned ship that has government permission during wartime to attack an enemy's merchant ships. (p. 188)

Proclamation (PRAHK luh MAY shuhn) **of 1763** *n.* an order in which Britain prohibited its American colonists from settling west of the Appalachian Mountains. (p. 135)

progressivism (pruh GREHS ih VIHZ uhm) *n.* an early 20th-century reform movement seeking to return control of the government to the people, to restore economic opportunities, and to correct injustices in American life. (p. 553)

proprietary (pruh PRY ih TEHR ee) **colony** *n.* a colony with a single owner. (p. 85)

pro tempore (proh TEHM puh ree) *adv.* Latin phrase meaning "for the time being." (p. 234)

Puritan *n.* a member of a group from England that settled the Massachusetts Bay Colony in 1630 and sought to reform the practices of the Church of England. (p. 78)

R49

push-pull factor *n.* a factor that pushes people out of their native lands and pulls them toward a new place. (p. 408)

Q

Quaker (KWAY kuhr) *n.* a person who believed all people should live in peace and harmony; accepted different religions and ethnic groups. (p. 85)

quarter *v.* to give a place to stay. (p. 251)

Quartering Act *n.* a law passed by Parliament in 1765 that required the colonies to house and supply British soldiers. (p. 144)

quorum (KWAWR uhm) *n.* the minimum number of members that must be present for official business to take place. (p. 235)

R

racism (RAY SIHZ uhm) *n.* the belief that some people are inferior because of their race. (p. 62)

radical (RAD ih kuhl) *n.* a person who takes extreme political positions. (p. 297)

Radical Republican (rih PUHB lih kuhn) *n.* a congressman who, after the Civil War, favored using the government to create a new order in the South and to give African Americans full citizenship and the right to vote. (p. 517)

ratification (RAT uh fih KAY shuhn) *n.* official approval. (p. 248)

Reconstruction *n.* the process the U.S. government used to readmit the Confederate states to the Union after the Civil War. (p. 517)

Reformation *n.* a 16th-century religious movement to correct problems in the Roman Catholic Church. (p. 37)

Renaissance (REHN ih SAHNS) *n.* a period of European history, lasting from the 1300s to 1600, that brought increased interest in art and learning. (p. 36)

rendezvous (RAHN day VOO) *n.* a meeting. (p. 181)

reprieve (rih PREEV) *n.* a delay or cancellation of punishment. (p. 243)

republic (rih PUHB lihk) *n.* a government in which people elect representatives to govern for them. (p. 206)

republicanism (rih PUHB lih keh NIHZ uhm) *n.* the belief that government should be based on the consent of the people; people exercise their power by voting for political representatives. (pp. 198, 229)

Republican Party *n.* the political party formed in 1854 by opponents of slavery in the territories. (p. 450)

revenue (REHV uh noo) *n.* income a government collects to cover expenses. (pp. 144, 236)

revival (rih VY vuhl) *n.* a meeting designed to reawaken religious faith. (p. 417)

rifle *n.* a gun with a grooved barrel that causes a bullet to spin through the air. (p. 475)

robber baron *n.* a business leader who became wealthy through dishonest methods. (p. 578)

romanticism (roh MAN tih SIHZ uhm) *n.* a European artistic movement that stressed the individual, imagination, creativity, and emotion. (p. 413)

Roosevelt Corollary (KAWR uh lehr ee) *n.* a 1904 addition to the Monroe Doctrine allowing the United States to be the "policeman" in Latin America. (p. 560)

royal colony *n.* a colony ruled by governors appointed by a king. (p. 87)

S

salutary (SAL yuh TEHR ee) **neglect** *n.* a hands-off policy of England toward its American colonies during the first half of the 1700s. (p. 128)

Santa Fe (SAN tuh FAY) **Trail** *n.* a trail that began in Missouri and ended in Santa Fe, New Mexico. (p. 379)

secede (sih SEED) *v.* to withdraw. (p. 457)

secession (sih SEHSH uhn) *n.* withdrawal. (p. 367)

Second Continental Congress *n.* a governing body whose delegates agreed, in May 1775, to form the Continental Army and to approve the Declaration of Independence. (p. 161)

Second Great Awakening *n.* the renewal of religious faith in the 1790s and early 1800s. (p. 417)

sectionalism (SEHK shuh nuh LIHZ uhm) *n.* the placing of the interests of one's own region ahead of the interests of the nation as a whole. (p. 341)

segregation (SEHG rih GAY shuhn) *n.* separation, especially of races. (p. 549)

Seneca (SEHN ih kuh) **Falls Convention** *n.* a women's rights convention held in Seneca Falls, New York, in 1848. (p. 428)

separation of powers *n.* the division of basic government roles into branches. (p. 230)

servitude (SUR vih TOOD) *n.* a state of belonging to an owner or master. (p. 254)

Seven Days' Battles *n.* an 1862 Civil War battle in which the Confederacy forced the Union to retreat before it could capture the Southern capital of Richmond. (p. 480)

sharecropping *n.* a system in which landowners gave farm workers land, seed, and tools in return for a part of the crops they raised. (p. 527)

Shays's (SHAY zuhz) **Rebellion** *n.* an uprising of debt-ridden Massachusetts farmers in 1787. (p. 209)

Siege (seej) **of Vicksburg** *n.* an 1863 Union victory in the Civil War that enabled the Union to control the entire Mississippi River. (p. 500)

slash-and-burn agriculture (ag rih kuhl chuhr) *n.* a farming method in which people clear fields by cutting and burning trees and grasses, the ashes of which fertilize the soil. (p. 31)

slavery *n.* the practice of holding a person in bondage for labor. (p. 60)

smuggle *v.* to illegally import or export goods. (p. 96)

Sons of Liberty *n.* a group of colonists who formed a secret society to oppose British policies at the time of the American Revolution. (p. 145)

Spanish-American War *n.* a war in 1898 that began when the United States demanded Cuba's independence from Spain. (p. 557)

Spanish Armada (ahr MAH duh) *n.* a fleet of ships sent in 1588 by Philip II, the Spanish king, to invade England and restore Roman Catholicism. (p. 57)

spiritual *n.* a religious folk song. (p. 335)

spoils system *n.* the practice of winning candidates giving government jobs to political backers or supporters. (p. 357)

Stamp Act *n.* a 1765 law passed by Parliament that required all legal and commercial documents to carry an official stamp showing a tax had been paid. (p. 144)

states' rights *n.* theory that said that states had the right to judge when the federal government had passed an unconstitutional law. (p. 291)

steerage *n.* the cheapest deck or place on a ship. (p. 407)

Stono (STOH noh) **Rebellion** *n.* a 1739 uprising of slaves in South Carolina, leading to the tightening of already harsh slave laws. (p. 107)

strategy *n.* an overall plan of action. (p. 180)

strike *v.* to stop work to demand better working conditions. (p. 418)

subsistence farm *n.* a farm that produces enough food for the family with a small additional amount for trade. (p. 94)

suffrage *n.* the right to vote. (pp. 246, 428)

Sugar Act *n.* a law passed by Parliament in 1764 that placed a tax on sugar, molasses, and other products shipped to the colonies; also called for harsh punishment of smugglers. (p. 144)

T

tariff *n.* a tax on imported goods. (p. 280)

Tariff of Abominations *n.* an 1828 law that raised the tariffs on raw materials and manufactured goods; it upset Southerners who felt that economic interests of the Northeast were determining national economic policy. (p. 365)

technology *n.* the use of tools and knowledge to meet human needs. (p. 29)

Tejano (tuh HAH noh) *n.* a person of Spanish heritage who considered Texas his or her home. (p. 384)

temperance movement *n.* a campaign to stop the drinking of alcohol. (p. 418)

tender *n.* money. (p. 239)

Thirteenth Amendment *n.* an amendment to the U.S. Constitution, adopted in 1865, banning slavery and involuntary servitude in the United States. (p. 505)

Three-Fifths Compromise *n.* the Constitutional Convention's agreement to count three-fifths of a state's slaves as population for purposes of representation and taxation. (p. 216)

Townshend (TOWN zuhnd) **Acts** *n.* a series of laws passed by Parliament in 1767 that suspended New York's assembly and established taxes on goods brought into the British colonies. (p. 147)

Trail of Tears *n.* the tragic journey of the Cherokee people from their homeland to Indian Territory between 1838 and 1839; thousands of Cherokee died. (p. 361)

transcendentalism (TRAN sen DEN tl IZ uhm) *n.* a 19th-century philosophy that taught the spiritual world is more important than the physical world and that people can find truth within themselves through feeling and intuition. (p. 415)

Treaty of Ghent (gent) *n.* treaty, signed in 1814, which ended the War of 1812; no territory exchanged hands and trade disputes were not resolved. (p. 317)

Treaty of Greenville *n.* a 1795 agreement in which 12 Native American tribes surrendered much of present-day Ohio and Indiana to the U.S. government. (p. 284)

Treaty of Guadalupe Hidalgo (GWAHD loop hi DAH goh) *n.* the 1848 treaty ending the U.S. war with Mexico; Mexico ceded nearly one-half of its land to the United States. (p. 394)

R51

Treaty of Paris *n.* the 1763 treaty that ended the French and Indian War; Britain gained all of North America east of the Mississippi River. (p. 134)

Treaty of Paris of 1783 *n.* the treaty that ended the Revolutionary War, confirming the independence of the United States and setting the boundaries of the new nation. (p. 196)

Treaty of Tordesillas (TAWR duh SEE uhs) *n.* the 1494 treaty in which Spain and Portugal agreed to divide the lands of the Western Hemisphere between them and moved the Line of Demarcation further west. (p. 51)

triangular trade *n.* the transatlantic system of trade in which goods, including slaves, were exchanged between Africa, England, Europe, the West Indies, and the colonies in North America. (p. 95)

tribunal (try BYOO nuhl) *n.* a court. (p. 237)

U

unanimous (yoo NAN uh muhs) **consent** *n.* complete agreement. (p. 248)

Uncle Tom's Cabin *n.* a novel published by Harriet Beecher Stowe in 1852, which portrayed slavery as brutal and immoral. (p. 446)

unconstitutional *n.* something that contradicts the law of the Constitution. (p. 301)

Underground Railroad *n.* a series of escape routes used by slaves escaping the South. (p. 426)

urbanization *n.* growth of cities resulting from industrialization. (p. 541)

V

vaudeville (VAWD vil) *n.* a form of live stage entertainment with a mixture of songs, dance, and comedy. (p. 549)

Vietnam War (vee ET NAHM) *n.* a military conflict from 1957 to 1975 between the North Vietnam Communists and the non-Communist forces of South Vietnam supported by the United States. (p. 581)

vigilante (vij uh LAN tee) *n.* a person willing to take the law into his or her own hands. (p. 545)

Virginia Plan *n.* a plan proposed by Edmund Randolph, a delegate to the Constitutional Convention in 1787, that proposed a government with three branches and a two-house legislature in which representation would be based on a state's population or wealth. (p. 215)

W

War Hawk *n.* a westerner who supported the War of 1812. (p. 313)

Watergate scandal *n.* a scandal resulting from the Nixon administration's attempt to cover up its involvement in the 1972 break-in at the Democratic National Committee headquarters in the Watergate apartment complex in Washington, D.C. (p. 582)

Webster-Hayne debate *n.* an 1830 debate between Daniel Webster and Robert Hayne over the doctrine of nullification. (p. 366)

Whig (hwig) **Party** *n.* a political party organized in 1834 to oppose the policies of Andrew Jackson. (p. 371)

Whiskey Rebellion *n.* a 1794 protest against the government's tax on whiskey, which was valuable to the livelihood of backcountry farmers. (p. 285)

Wilderness Road *n.* the trail into Kentucky that woodsman Daniel Boone helped to build. (p. 205)

Wilmot (WIL muht) **Proviso** (pruh VY zoh) *n.* an 1846 proposal that outlawed slavery in any territory gained from the War with Mexico. (p. 443)

World War II *n.* a war fought from 1939 to 1945, in which Great Britain, France, the Soviet Union, the United States, and other allies defeated Germany, Italy, and Japan. (p. 575)

writ (rit) **of assistance** *n.* a search warrant that allowed British officers to enter colonial homes or businesses to search for smuggled goods. (p. 148)

X

XYZ Affair *n.* a 1797 incident in which French officials demanded a bribe from U.S. diplomats. (p. 290)

Y

yellow journalism *n.* a style of journalism that exaggerates and sensationalizes the news. (p. 557)

SPANISH GLOSSARY

A

abolition [abolición] *s.* movimiento para eliminar la esclavitud. (p. 424)

abridge [abreviar] *v.* reducir. (p. 250)

affirmation [afirmación] *s.* declaración de que algo es cierto. (p. 241)

African Diaspora [diáspora africana] *s.* traslado forzado de los africanos, desde su patria a las Américas para trabajar allí como esclavos. (p. 61)

Albany Plan of Union [Plan de la Unión de Albany] s. primera propuesta formal para unir las colonias norteamericanas, presentado por Benjamín Franklin. (p. 133)

Alien and Sedition Acts [leyes de Extranjeros y Sedición] *s.* serie de cuatro leyes promulgadas en 1798 para reducir el poder político de inmigrantes recién llegados a Estados Unidos. (p. 290)

ally [aliado] *s.* país que acuerda ayudar a otro país a alcanzar un objetivo común. (p. 184)

American System [Sistema Americano] *s.* plan presentado en 1815 para hacer autosuficiente a Estados Unidos. (p. 338)

Anaconda Plan [Plan Anaconda] *s.* estrategia de tres pasos mediante la cual la Unión se proponía derrotar a la Confederación durante la guerra civil estadounidense. (p. 468)

Antifederalist [antifederalista] *s.* persona que se oponía a la ratificación de la Constitución de los Estados Unidos. (p. 218)

Appalachian Mountains [montes Apalaches] *s.* cadena de montañas que se extiende desde el este de Canadá hacia el sur, hasta Alabama. (p. 110)

appellate [de apelación] *adj.* que tiene el poder de reexaminar decisiones de las cortes. (p. 244)

Appomattox Court House [Appomattox] *s.* pueblo de Virginia donde Robert E. Lee se rindió a Ulysses s. Grant en 1865, finalizando así la guerra civil. (p. 503)

apprentice [aprendiz] *s.* joven que aprende un oficio o una artesanía de un maestro experto. (p. 121)

appropiation [apropiación] *s.* fondos públicos que se reservan para un propósito específico. (p. 237)

Articles of Confederation [Artículos de Confederación] *s.* documento, adoptado por el Congreso Continental en 1777 y finalmente aprobado por los estados en 1781, que delineaba la forma de gobierno de los nuevos Estados Unidos. (p. 206)

artillery [artillería] *s.* cañon o arma grande. (p. 161)

artisan [artesano] *s.* obrero especializado, como un tejedor a telar o un alfarero, que hace artículos a mano; artífice. (p. 101)

B

baby boom *s.* término para la generación que nació en Estados Unidos entre 1946 y 1961, cuando el índice de natalidad aumentó marcadamente después de la segunda guerra mundial. (p. 584)

Backcountry [tierras fronterizas] *s.* región colonial que se extendía a lo largo de los montes Apalaches a través de la sección oeste de Nueva Inglaterra y las colonias del centro y del sur. (p. 93)

Bacon's Rebellion [Rebelión de Bacon] *s.* levantamiento contra la poderosa autoridad colonial de Jamestown por Nathaniel Bacon y un grupo de habitantes de la frontera que resultó en la quema de Jamestown en 1676. (p. 73)

bail [fianza] *s.* dinero que pagan como fianza las personas arrestadas para garantizar que van a regresar para el juicio. (p. 252)

Battle of Antietam [batalla de Antietam] *s.* batalla de la guerra civil, en 1862, en que murieron o resultaron heridos 25,000 hombres. (p. 481)

Battle of Fallen Timbers *s.* en 1794 el ejército estadounidense derrotó a 2,000 amerindios en un enfrentamiento por el control del territorio del Noroeste. (p. 283)

Battle of Gettysburg [batalla de Gettysburg] *s.* batalla de 1863 de la guerra civil en que la Unión derrotó a la Confederación, poniendo fin a la esperanza de una victoria confederada en el Norte. (p. 497)

Battle of Quebec [batalla de Quebec] *s.* batalla en la que los británicos derrotaron a los franceses y cambio decisivo en la guerra Francesa y Amerindia. (p. 134)

Battle of Shiloh [batalla de Shiloh] *s.* batalla de 1862 en que la Unión obligó a la Confederación a retroceder; fue una de las batallas más encarnizadas de la guerra civil. (p. 478)

Battle of Yorktown [batalla de Yorktown] *s.* última batalla importante de la guerra Revolucionaria que resultó en la capitulación de las fuerzas británicas en 1781. (p. 194)

Battle of the Alamo [batalla de El Álamo] *s.* en 1836 los texanos defendieron contra el ejército mexicano una misión llamada El Álamo; sobrevivieron sólo cinco texanos (p. 387)

Battle of the Thames [batalla de Thames] *s.* victoria estadounidense sobre los británicos en la guerra de 1812 que puso fin a la amenaza británica en el Territorio del Noroeste. (p. 316)

Battles of Saratoga [batallas de Saratoga] *s.* serie de conflictos en 1777, entre soldados británicos y el Ejército Continental que resultó en un cambio decisivo en la guerra Revolucionaria. (p. 183)

bayonet [bayoneta] *s.* largo cuchillo de acero colocado en el extremo de un arma de fuego. (p. 186)

Bear Flag Revolt [revuelta de la Bandera del Oso] *s.* rebelión de 1846 por los estadounidenses contra el dominio mexicano en California. (p. 393)

bill of attainder [decreto de proscripción] *s.* ley que condena a una persona sin juicio ante un tribunal. (p. 239)

Bill of Rights [Carta de Derechos] *s.* diez primeras enmiendas a la Constitución de Estados Unidos, adoptadas en 1791, que consisten en una lista formal de los derechos y libertades de los ciudadanos. (p. 221)

black code [código negro] *s.* ley pasada por los estados sureños que limitaba la libertad de los antiguos esclavos. (p. 518)

blockade [bloqueo] *s.* acción de las fuerzas armadas que impide la entrada o salida de mercaderías o personas. (p. 468)

border state [estado fronterizo] *s.* estados esclavistas fronterizos a estados en que la esclavitud era ilegal. (p. 466)

Boston Massacre [Matanza de Boston] *s.* choque en 1770 entre soldados británicos y colonos de Boston en que perecieron cinco de los colonistas, incluso Crispus Attucks. (p. 149)

Boston Tea Party [Motín del Té de Boston] *s.* como protesta contra el Acta del té, en 1773 los colonos arrojaron al puerto de Boston 342 cajones de té. (p. 151)

bounty [gratificación] *s.* recompensa o pago en dinero que da un gobierno. (pp. 255, 492)

boycott [boicot] *v.* negarse a comprar ciertos productos. (p. 145)

buck [ciervo] gamuza obtenida de la piel de un ciervo adulto, o unidad de dinero de los colonos. (p. 111)

C

cabinet [gabinete ministerial] *s.* grupo de ministros que actúan como los asesores princpales del presidente. (p. 278)

California gold rush [fiebre del oro de California] *s.* en 1849 gran cantidad de gente se fue a California porque allí se había descubierto oro. (p. 397)

caravel [carabela] *s.* barco con velas triangulares que le permitían navegar hacia el viento y con velas cuadradas que lo llevaban hacia delante cuando soplaba viento en popa. (p. 39)

cash crop [cultivo comercial] *s.* cultivo que produce un agricultor para venderlo por dinero y no para su uso personal. (p. 99)

cavalry [caballería] *s.* soldados montados a caballo. (p. 480)

charter [cédula] *s.* contrato escrito que concede un gobierno otorgando al que lo recibe el derecho a establecer una colonia. (p. 71)

checks and balances [frenos y cortapisas] *s.* capacidad de cada rama del gobierno de usar frenos o controles sobre las otras ramas. (p. 230)

civil disobedience [desobediencia civil] *s.* negarse pacíficamente a obedecer leyes que uno considera injustas. (p. 415)

civilization [civilización] *s.* forma de cultura caracterizada por ciudades con centros de comercio, trabajadores especializados, formas de gobierno y religión organizadas, sistemas de mantener registros, y herramientas avanzadas. (p. 28)

civil rights [derechos civiles] *s.* derecho otorgado a todos los ciudadanos. (p. 519)

clan [clan] *s.* grupo grande de familias procedentes de un antepasado común. (p. 111)

Cold War [guerra fría] *s.* estado de hostilidad, sin conflicto militar directo, que se desarrolló entre Estados Unidos y la Unión Soviética después de la segunda guerra mundial. (p. 579)

Columbian Exchange [transferencia colombina] *s.* transferencia de plantas, animales y enfermedades entre el hemisferio occidental y el oriental. (p. 62)

committee of correspondence [comité de correspondencia] *s.* grupo de personas de las colonias que se intercambiaban cartas sobre asuntos coloniales. (p. 150)

common law [derecho consuetudinario] *s.* sistema de leyes desarrollado en Inglaterra, basado en costumbres y decisiones jurídicas anteriores. (p. 252)

Compromise of 1850 [Acuerdo de 1850] *s.* serie de medidas del Congreso para resolver los desacuerdos principales entre los estados libres y los esclavistas. (p. 445)

Compromise of 1877 [Acuerdo de 1877] *s.* acuerdo que resolvió la disputa sobre las elecciones de 1876: se declaró presidente a Rutherford B. Hayes, quien entonces retiró las tropas federales que quedaban en el Sur. (p. 532)

compulsory process [proceso obligatorio] *s.* procedimiento requerido. (p. 251)

Conestoga wagon [carreta conestoga] *s.* vehículo que tenía ruedas anchas, caja de carro curvada y capota de lona y se usaba para transportar gente y artículos. (p. 101)

Confederate States of America [Estados Confederados de América] *s.* confederación constituida en 1861 por los estados sureños después de separarse de la Unión. (p. 457)

conquistador [conquistador] *s.* español que en el siglo XVI viajó a las Américas para explorar y conquistar. (p. 53)

conscription [conscripción] *s.* ley que requería que los hombres sirvieran en las fuerzas armadas o que fueran reclutados. (p. 492)

Constitutional Convention [Convención Constitucional] *s.* reunión realizada en 1787 para considerar cambios a los Artículos de Confederación, que resultó en la redacción de la Constitución. (p. 217)

containment [contención] *s.* bloqueo de una nación en la expansión de la influencia de otras naciones, especialmente los esfuerzos de Estados Unidos por bloquear la expansión de la influencia soviética hacia fines de los años cuarenta y comienzos de los cincuenta. (p. 580)

Continental Army [Ejército Continental] *s.* fuerzas coloniales autorizadas en 1775 por el segundo Congreso Continental, con George Washington como su comandante en jefe. (p. 161)

convene [convocar] v. llamar a reunión. (p. 243)

Copperheads [víboras cobrizas] *s.* los principales adversarios políticos de Abraham Lincoln; abogaban por la paz con el Sur. (p. 508)

cotton gin [desmontadora de algodón] *s.* máquina inventada en 1793 que limpiaba el algodón con mucha más rapidez y eficiencia que los obreros humanos. (p. 332)

counterculture [contracultura] *s.* grupo de jóvenes con valores morales y modos de vida contrarios a los de la cultura establecida. (p. 587)

Crittenden Plan [Plan de Crittenden] *s.* acuerdo presentado en 1861 que podría haber evitado la secesión. (p. 459)

Crusades [cruzadas] *s.* serie de guerras para capturar la Tierra Santa, iniciada en 1096 por cristianos europeos. (p. 36)

culture [cultura] *s.* manera de vida compartida por gente que tiene artes, creencias y costumbres semejantes. (p. 28)

D

Dawes Act [ley Dawes] *s.* ley, aprobada en 1887, que distribuía la tierra de las reservas amerindias a dueños individuales. (p. 540)

Declaration of Independence [Declaración de Independencia] *s.* documento, escrito en 1776, en que las colonias declararon su independendia de Gran Bretaña. (p. 164)

depression [depresión] *s.* aguda crisis económica. (p. 370)

desert [desertar] *v.* abandonar el servicio militar sin intenciones de regresar. (p. 187)

diversity [diversidad] *s.* variedad de gente. (p. 101)

doctrine of nullification [doctrina de la invalidación] *s.* derecho de un estado a rechazar una ley federal que considerase inconstitucional. (p. 365)

domestication [domesticación] *s.* práctica de criar plantas o amansar animales para satisfacer las necesidades humanas. (p. 28)

Dred Scott* v. *Sandford [Dred Scott contra Sandford] *s.* caso de 1865 de la Corte Suprema en que un esclavo, Dred Scott, entabló juicio por su libertad porque su amo lo había llevado a vivir en territorios donde la esclavitud era ilegal; la Corte dictaminó contra Scott. (p. 451)

due process of law [proceso legal debido] *s.* tratamiento justo bajo la ley. (p. 251)

E

elector [elector] *s.* votante. (p. 233)

Emancipation Proclamation [Proclama de Emancipación] *s.* orden ejecutiva dictada por Abraham Lincoln el 1.° de enero de 1863, que liberaba a los esclavos de todas las regiones insurgentes contra la Unión. (p. 504)

Embargo Act of 1807 [ley de Embargo de 1807] *s.* ley que dictaminaba que los barcos estadounidenses ya no estaban autorizados para ir a puertos extranjeros y que también cerraba los puertos de Estados Unidos a los barcos británicos. (p. 488)

emigrant [emigrante] *s.* persona que abandona un país. (p. 407)

encomienda [encomienda] *s.* concesión del trabajo de los amerindios. (p. 60)

English Bill of Rights [Carta de Derechos Ingleses] *s.* acuerdo firmado por Guillermo y María por el que prometían respetar los derechos del Parlamento y los ciudadanos ingleses, incluso el derecho a elecciones libres. (p. 128)

enlightenment [Ilustración] *s.* movimiento del siglo XVIII que enfatizaba el uso de la razón y el método científico para obtener conocimiento. (p. 124)

enumeration [enumeración] *s.* recuento oficial, como un censo. (p. 233)

equity [equidad] *s.* sistema de justicia no cubierto bajo la ley común. (p. 253)

Erie Canal [canal de Erie] *s.* completado en 1825, esta vía navegable conectaba a la ciudad de Nueva York con Buffalo, New York. (p. 339)

European Middle Ages [Edad Media europea] *s.* período desde fines del siglo V hasta aproximadamente el siglo XIV, durante el cual los europeos adoptaron el feudalismo y el sistema señorial. (p. 35)

ex post facto law [ley ex post facto] *s.* ley que hace que un acto sea una ofensa criminal aprobada después de cometido el acto. (p. 239)

F

factory system [sistema fabril] *s.* un método de producción que juntó a obreros y máquinas en el mismo edificio. (p. 325)

fall line *s.* punto a partir del cual una catarata impide que los barcos grandes continúen río arriba. (p. 110)

famine [hambruna] *s.* severa escasez de alimentos. (p. 410)

fascism [fascismo] *s.* filosofía política que propugna un fuerte gobierno nacionalista centralizado, con un dictador poderoso a la cabeza. (p. 574)

federalism [federalismo] *s.* sistema de gobierno en que el poder está dividido entre el gobierno central (o federal) y los estados. (pp. 218, 229)

Federalists [federalistas] *s.* partidarios de la Constitución. (p. 218)

Federalist Papers [El federalista] *s.* serie de ensayos que defienden y explican la Constitución, escritos por Alexander Hamilton, James Madison y John Jay. (p. 219)

Federal Judiciary Act [ley de la Judicatura Federal] *s.* ayudó a establecer un sistema de tribunales; le dio al Tribunal Supremo seis miembros. (p. 278)

felony [felonía] *s.* delito grave. (p. 237)

feudalism [feudalismo] *s.* sistema político en que el rey concedía a sus nobles el uso de sus tierras a cambio de su prestación militar y la protección de la gente que vivía en esas tierras. (p. 35)

Fifteenth Amendment [Enmienda Decimoquinta] *s.* aprobada en 1870, esta enmienda a la Constitución de Estados Unidos declaraba que a los ciudadanos no se les podía impedir que votaran "por motivo de raza, color ni condición anterior de esclavitud". (p. 530)

54th Massachusetts Regiment [54.° Regimiento de Massachusetts] *s.* regimientos afroamericano organizado para luchar por la Unión en la guerra civil. (p. 490)

First Battle of Bull Run [primera batalla de Bull Run] *s.* una batalla de la guerra civil, de 1861, en que el Sur horrorizó al Norte con una victoria. (p. 469)

foreign policy [política exterior] *s.* relaciones con los gobiernos de otros países. (p. 288)

Fort Sumter [fuerte Sumter] *s.* fuerte federal ubicado en el puerto de Charleston, Carolina del Sur; el ataque sureño al fuerte Sumter marcó el comienzo de la guerra civil. (p. 465)

forty-niner [buscador de ventura del 49] *s.* persona que fue a California en búsqueda de oro, empezando en 1849. (p. 396)

Fourteen Points [Catorce puntos] *s.* los objetivos del presidente Woodrow Wilson para la paz que siguió a la primera guerra mundial. (p. 561)

Fourteenth Amendment [Enmienda Decimocuarta] *s.* enmienda a la Constitución de Estados Unidos, aprobada en 1868, que hizo ciudadanos del país a todas las personas nacidas en Estados Unidos o naturalizadas, incluso a los antiguos esclavos. (p. 519)

First Continental Congress [primer Congreso Continental] *s.* reunión en 1774 de delegados de todas las colonias, excepto Georgia, para defender los derechos coloniales. (p. 155)

Freedmen's Bureau [Agencia de Manumisos] *s.* agencia federal establecida para ayudar a los antiguos esclavos después de la guerra civil. (p. 517)

freedmen's school [escuela para los manumisos] *s.* escuela establecida por la Agencia de Manumisos para educar a los recientes libertos afroamericanos. (p. 525)

Free Soil Party [Partido del Suelo Libre] *s.* partido político dedicado a parar la expansión de la esclavitud. (p. 443)

French and Indian War [guerra Francesa y Amerindia] *s.* conflicto en Norteamérica, entre 1754 y 1763, que fue parte de una lucha mundial entre Francia y Gran Bretaña y que terminó con la derrota de Francia y el traspaso del Canadá francés a Gran Bretaña. (p. 131)

frontier [frontera] *s.* región sin o con muy pocos asentamientos ocupada mayormente por amerindios. (p. 539)

Fugitive Slave Act [ley de los Esclavos Fugitivos] *s.* ley de 1850 para ayudar a los dueños de esclavos a recapturar los esclavos fugados. (p. 446)

French Revolution [Revolución francesa] *s.* en 1789 los franceses iniciaron un movimiento por la libertad y la igualdad. (p. 285)

Fundamental Orders of Connecticut [Órdenes Fundamentales de Connecticut] *s.* conjunto de leyes establecidas en 1639 por una congregación puritana que se había asentado en el valle del río Connecticut y que ampliaban la idea de un gobierno representativo. (p. 79)

G

Gilded Age [Edad Dorada] *s.* época de fines del siglo XIX de fabulosa riqueza. (p. 541)

"Glorious Revolution" [Revolución gloriosa] *s.* derrocamiento, en 1688, del rey inglés Jacobo II y su substitución por Guillermo y María. (p. 128)

Great Awakening [Gran Despertar] *s.* renovación del sentimiento religioso en las colonias norteamericanas durante las décadas de 1730 a 1750. (p. 123)

Great Compromise [Gran Compromiso] *s.* acuerdo en la Convención Constitucional que estableció una legislatura nacional de dos cámaras; en una de estas cámaras, todos los estados tendrían representación igual, en la otra, cada estado tendría representación basada en su población. (p. 216)

Great Depression [gran depresión] *s.* período que duró desde 1929 hasta 1941, en que la economía de Estados Unidos declinó severamente y millones de estadounidenses estaban sin empleo. (p. 571)

Great Migration [Gran Emigración] *s.* movimiento de puritanos que salieron de Inglaterra para establecer asentamientos por todo el mundo, incluyendo a 20,000 que partieron para América (p. 78); el movimiento de afroamericanos entre 1910 y 1920 del Sur hacia las ciudades del Norte. (p. 562)

Great Society [gran sociedad] *s.* programa iniciado por Lyndon Johnson para ayudan a los pobres, los ancianos y las mujeres y también promovía la educación, prohibía la discriminación racial y protegía el medio ambiente. (p. 586)

greenback [billete verde] *s.* papel moneda emitido por el gobierno federal durante la guerra civil. (p. 493)

gristmill [molino harinero] *s.* molino en que el grano se muele para producir cualquier tipo de harina. (p. 99)

guerrilla [guerrillero] *s.* soldado que debilita al enemigo con asaltos inesperados y ataques relámpagos. (p. 191)

H

Harlem Renaissance [renacimiento de Harlem] *s.* florecimiento de la creatividad artística afroamericana durante los años veinte, centrada en la comunidad de Harlem de la ciudad de Nueva York. (p. 571)

Harpers Ferry *s.* arsenal federal en Virginia, capturado en 1859 durante un levantamiento de esclavos. (p. 469)

Holocaust [Holocausto] *s.* matanza sistemática en Alemania, durante la segunda guerra mundial, de unos seis millones de judíos así como millones de otros grupos étnicos. (p. 578)

Homestead Act [ley de Residencia] *s.* aprobada en 1862, esta ley ofrecía 160 acres de tierra gratis a cualquiera que acordara ocuparla y trabajarla por cinco años. (p. 540)

House of Burgesses [Cámara de los Burgueses] *s.* creada en 1619, la primera asamblea representativa de las colonias norteamericanas. (p. 72)

Hudson River school [Escuela del río Hudson] *s.* grupo de artistas que vivían en el valle del río Hudson del estado de New York. (p. 414)

hygiene [higiene] *s.* condiciones y prácticas que fomentan la buena salud. (p. 474)

I

immigrant [inmigrante] *s.* persona que se establece en un país nuevo. (p. 407)

immunity [inmunidad] *s.* protección legal. (p. 246)

impeachment [imputación] *s.* proceso de acusar a un funcionario público de un delito en el desempeño de sus funciones. (p. 233)

imperialism [imperialismo] *s.* política por la cual las naciones más poderosas extienden su control económico, político o militar sobre territorios o naciones más débiles. (p. 556)

impressment [secuestro] *s.* el acto de capturar personas a la fuerza. (p. 311)

inaugurate [investir] *v.* conferir un cargo oficial en una ceremonia formal. (p. 277)

income tax [impuesto sobre la renta] *s.* impuesto sobre los ingresos. (p. 493)

indentured servant [siervo escriturado] *s.* persona que vendía su trabajo a cambio de pasaje a Norteamérica. (p. 72)

Indian Removal Act [ley del Traslado de los Indígenas] *s.* esta ley de 1830 requería que el gobierno negociara tratados para el traslado de los amerindios al oeste. (p. 360)

Indian Territory [territorio Indio] *s.* lo que hoy son Oklahoma y partes de Kansas y Nebraska a la cual se trasladó a los amerindios bajo la ley del Traslado de los Indígenas de 1830. (p. 360)

indictment [acusación] *s.* declaración escrita dictada por un jurado de acusación que inculpa a una persona de un delito. (p. 234)

indigo [añil] *s.* planta que cultivaban las colonias sureñas de la cual se obtiene un colorante azul oscuro. (p. 105)

individual right [derecho individual] *s.* libertad y privilegio personal que garantiza a los ciudadanos estadounidenses la Carta de Derechos. (p. 231)

Industrial Revolution [revolución industrial] *s.* en la Inglaterra de fines del siglo XVIII, las maquinarias de fábrica empezaron a reemplazar las herramientas manuales, y la producción de bienes manufacturados reemplazó la agricultura como el principal modo de trabajo. (p. 325)

inferior court [tribunal inferior] *s.* corte con autoridad menor que la del Tribunal Supremo. (p. 244)

inflation [inflación] *s.* subida en el precio de los productos y los servicios y disminución del valor del dinero. (p. 370)

inoperative [inoperante] *adj.* que no está vigente. (p. 258)

insurrection [insurrección] *s.* levantamiento abierto contra un gobierno. (p. 255)

interchangeable part [parte intercambiable] *s.* parte que es exactamente igual a otra parte. (p. 327)

Intolerable Acts [leyes Intolerables] *s.* serie de leyes aprobadas en 1774 por el Parlamento para castigar a Massachusetts por el Motín del Té de Boston. (p. 154)

ironclad [acorazado] *s.* buque de guerra cubierto de hierro. (p. 475)

Iroquois League [Liga Iroquesa] *s.* alianza del siglo XVI entre los pueblos amerindios cayuga, mohawk, oneida, onondaga y seneca, que vivían en la región oriental de los Grandes lagos. (p. 31)

Islam [islam] *s.* religión fundada por el profeta Mahoma en el siglo VII, que enseña que hay un solo Dios: Alá. (p. 34)

J

Jacksonian Democracy [democracia jacksoniana] *s.* idea de extender el poder político a toda la gente asegurando de ese modo el gobierno de la mayoría. (p. 354)

Jamestown *s.* primer asentamiento inglés permanente en Norteamérica. (p. 71)

Jay's Treaty [Tratado de Jay] *s.* el acuerdo que puso fin a la disputa sobre los derechos marítimos estadounidenses durante la Revolución francesa. (p. 286)

jazz [jazz] *s.* tipo nuevo de música en los años veinte que capturó el despreocupado espíritu de la época. (p. 570)

Jim Crow [ley Jim Crow] *s.* ley que imponía la separación entre la gente blanca y la de piel negra en los lugares públicos del Sur. (p. 549)

joint-stock company [sociedad por acciones] *s.* empresa en que los inversionistas colocan su dinero en un fondo común con la intención de sacar ganancias. (p. 70)

judicial review [revisión judicial] *s.* principio de que el Tribunal Supremo tiene la última palabra en la interpretación de la Constitución. (p. 301)

Judiciary Act of 1801 [ley Judicial de 1801] *s.* ley que aumentó el número de jueces federales, permitiéndole al presidente John Adams cubrir la mayoría de los puestos nuevos con federalistas. (p. 300)

K

Kansas-Nebraska Act [ley de Kansas-Nebraska] *s.* ley de 1854 que estableció los territorios de Kansas y Nebraska y otorgó a sus habitantes el derecho a decidir si querían o no permitir la esclavitud. (p. 448)

King Cotton [rey Algodón] *s.* al algodón se lo llamaba rey porque era importante en el mercado mundial y el Sur cultivaba la mayor parte del algodón que usaban las fábricas textiles de Europa. (p. 468)

King Philip's War [guerra del rey Felipe] *s.* guerra entre las colonias puritanas y los amerindios que se libró entre 1675 y 1676. (p. 80)

Ku Klux Klan *s.* grupo constituido en 1866 que quería restaurar el control del Sur a los demócratas y mantener sumisos a los antiguos esclavos. (p. 528)

L

labor union [sindicato laboral] *s.* obreros que se unen para tratar de conseguir mejores condiciones de trabajo. (p. 418)

Land Ordinance of 1785 [Ordenanza de Tierras de 1785] *s.* ley que establecía un plan para la agrimensura y venta de las tierras públicas al oeste de los montes Apalaches. (p. 207)

land speculator [especulador en tierras] *s.* persona que compra grandes extensiones de terreno a precio bajo y luego vende secciones pequeñas a precios altos. (p. 378)

leisure *s.* tiempo libre. (p. 548)

Lewis and Clark expedition [expedición de Lewis y Clark] *s.* grupo dirigido por Meriwether Lewis y William Clark que exploró las tierras de la Compra de Luisiana empezando en 1803. (p. 304)

Lexington and Concord *s.* escenarios, en Massachusetts, de las primeras batallas de la Revolución norteamericana. (p. 157)

limited government [gobierno limitado] *s.* principio que requiere que todos los ciudadanos estadounidenses, incluso los líderes gubernamentales, obedezcan la ley. (p. 231)

Lone Star Republic [República de la Estrella Solitaria] *s.* apodo de la República de Texas, que se le dio en 1836. (p. 389)

Louisiana Purchase [Compra de Luisiana] *s.* en 1803, la compra a Francia del Territorio de Luisiana. (p. 303)

Lowell mills [fábricas de Lowell] *s.* fábricas textiles ubicadas en el pueblo manufacturero de Lowell, Massachusetts, fundado en 1826. (p. 326)

Loyalist [realista]. *s.* colono norteamericano que apoyaba a los británicos durante la Revolución norteamericana. (p. 157)

M

Magna Carta [Carta Magna] *s.* "Gran Cédula Real"; documento que garantizaba los derechos políticos básicos en Inglaterra, aprobada por el rey Juan en el año 1215. (p. 125)

manifest destiny [destino manifiesto] *s.* creencia de que era el destino de Estados Unidos extenderse por todo el continente, desde al océano Atlántico al océano Pacífico. (p. 391)

Marbury* v. *Madison [Marbury contra Madison] *s.* caso de 1803 en que el Tribunal Supremo dictaminó que tenía el poder de invalidar leyes declarándolas inconstitucionales. (p. 301)

mass culture [cultura de masas] *s.* cultura común compartida por grandes números de personas. (p. 548)

Mayflower Compact [Pacto del Mayflower] *s.* acuerdo firmado por los hombres que viajaron a América en el Mayflower, que requería leyes para el bien de la colonia y establecía el concepto de autogobierno. (p. 77)

mercantilism [mercantilismo] *s.* sistema económico en que las naciones tratan de aumentar su riqueza y poder obteniendo oro y plata y estableciendo una balanza comercial favorable. (p. 51)

mercenary [mercenario] *s.* soldado profesional contratado para luchar por un país extranjero. (p. 179)

Mexican Cession [Cesión mexicana] *s.* extensa región cedida por México después de la guerra con México; incluía los actuales estados de California, Nevada, Utah, la mayor parte de Arizona y partes de Nuevo México, Colorado y Wyoming. (p. 395)

middle passage [travesía intermedia] *s.* parte intermedia de la ruta del comercio triangular (el viaje de África a las Américas) que traía africanos capturados a la esclavitud. (p. 61)

militia [milicia] *s.* fuerza de civiles armados comprometidos a defender su comunidad durante la Revolución norteamericana. (p. 154); fuerza militar de emergencia, que no es parte del ejército profesional. (p.238)

minié ball [bala minié] *s.* bala con base hueca. (p. 475)

Minuteman [minutero] *s.* miembro de la milicia colonial entrenado para responder "con un minuto de aviso". (p. 154)

misdemeanor [fechoría] *s.* violación de la ley. (p. 243)

Missouri Compromise [Acuerdo de Missouri] *s.* serie de leyes aprobadas en 1820 para mantener el equilibrio del poder político entre los estados esclavistas y los libres. (p. 342)

Monroe Doctrine [Doctrina Monroe] *s.* política de oposición estadounidense a cualquier interferencia europea en el hemisferio occidental, proclamada por el presidente Monroe en 1823. (p. 347)

Mormon [mormón] *s.* miembro de una iglesia fundada por Joseph Smith en 1830. (p. 381)

Mound Builder [constructor de túmulos] *s.* amerindio primitivo que construía grandes estructuras de tierra. (p. 29)

mountain man [hombre de las montañas] *s.* trampero o explorador que abrió el oeste hallando sendas a través de las montañas Rocosas. (p. 377)

Muslim [musulmán] *s.* adherente del islam. (p. 34)

N

nationalism [nacionalismo] *s.* sentido de orgullo, lealtad y protección hacia el país de uno. (p. 338)

nativist [nativista] *s.* estadounidense nativo que quería eliminar toda influencia extranjera. (p. 412)

natural-born citizen [ciudadano nato] *s.* ciudadano nacido en Estados Unidos o en un estado asociado o dependencia de Estados Unidos, o a padres que son ciudadanos estadounidenses que viven fuera del país. (p. 241)

naturalization [naturalización] *s.* manera de darle ciudadanía completa a una persona nacida en otro país. (pp. 237,254)

Navigation Acts [Actas de Navegación] *s.* serie de leyes aprobadas por el Parlamento, empezando en 1651, para asegurarse Inglaterra de que el comercio de sus colonias le rindiera ganancias económicas. (p. 96)

navigator [oficial de derrota] *s.* persona que planea el rumbo de un barco mientras está en el mar. (p. 39)

Nazi Party [Partido Nazi] *s.* partido Alemán Nacionalsocialista de los Trabajadores, llegó al poder bajo Adolfo Hitler en 1930. (p. 574)

neutral [neutral] *adj.* que no apoya ni a un país ni al otro. (p. 288)

New Deal [Nuevo Trato] *s.* programas de Franklin Roosevelt para luchar contra la depresión. (p. 572)

New France [Nueva Francia] *s.* puesto para el comercio de las pieles establecido en 1608 que se convirtió en el primer asentamiento francés permanente en Norteamérica. (p. 58)

new immigrant [inmigrante nuevo] *s.* persona del sur y el este de Europa que entró a Estados Unidos después de 1900. (p. 542)

New Jersey Plan [Plan de Nueva Jersey] *s.* plan de gobierno propuesto en 1787 en la Convención Constitucional que proponía una cámara legislativa única en que cada estado tendría un solo voto. (p. 215)

Northwest Ordinance [Ordenanza del Noroeste] *s.* describe cómo se iba a gobernar el territorio del Noroeste y establecía las condiciones para el asentamiento, así como los derechos de los colonos. (p. 207)

Northwest Territory [territorio del Noroeste] *s.* territorio organizado por la Ordenanza de Tierras de 1785, que incluía tierras que formaron los estados de Ohio, Indiana, Michigan, Illinois, Wisconsin y parte de Minnesota. (p. 207)

O

Oregon Trail [Camino de Oregón] *s.* camino hacia el oeste que iba de Independence, Missouri, al territorio de Oregón. (p. 380)

overseer [capataz] *s.* persona contratada por el dueño de una plantación para vigilar a los esclavos y dirigir su trabajo. (p. 106)

P

pacifist [pacifista] *s.* persona moralmente opuesta a la guerra. (p. 193)

Panama Canal [canal de Panamá] *s.* atajo a través de Panamá que conecta los oceános Atlántico y Pacífico. (p. 558)

Panic of 1837 [pánico de 1837] *s.* crisis financiera con clausura de bancos y colapso del sistema crediticio, que resultó en muchas quiebras y serio desempleo. (p. 370)

Panic of 1873 [pánico de 1873] *s.* crisis financiera en que los bancos se clausuraron y la bolsa de comercio se derrumbó. (p. 531)

Parliament [Parlamento] *s.* el cuerpo legislativo principal de Inglaterra. (p. 126)

Patriot [patriota] *s.* colono norteamericano que durante la Revolución norteamericana estaba a favor de los rebeldes. (p. 157)

patroon [patrono] *s.* persona que traía 50 colonos a Nueva Holanda y a cambio recibía una gran concesión de tierras y otros privilegios especiales. (p. 85)

Pickett's Charge [carga de Pickett] *s.* en 1863 el general George Pickett dirigió una carga frontal contra las fuerzas de la Unión durante la batalla de la guerra civil en Gettysburg; el ataque fracasó. (p. 497)

piedmont [tierras bajas] *s.* ancha extensión de tierra llana al pie de una cadena de montañas. (p. 110)

Pilgrim [peregrino] *s.* miembros del grupo que rechazó la Iglesia de Inglaterra, viajó a América y fundó la colonia de Plymouth en 1620. (p. 76)

Pinckney's Treaty [Tratado de Pinckney] *s.* tratado de 1795 con España que otorgaba a Estados Unidos el uso del río Mississippi y el derecho a depositar bienes en Nueva Orleans; creó el paralelo 31 como el límite sur de Estados Unidos. (p. 286)

plantation [plantación] *s.* finca grande para cultivos comerciales. (p. 60)

platform [plataforma] *s.* declaración de creencias. (p. 455)

Platt Amendment [Enmienda Platt] *s.* resultado de la guerra entre Estados Unidos y España, dio a Estados Unidos el derecho a intervenir en los asuntos de Cuba cuando existiera amenaza a la "vida, propiedad y libertad individual". (p. 558)

Plessy* v. *Ferguson [Plessy contra Ferguson] *s.* caso de 1896 en que el Tribunal Supremo dictaminó que la separación de las razas en las instalaciones públicas era legal. (p. 549)

Pontiac's Rebellion [rebelión de Pontiac] *s.* rebelión de 1763 contra los fuertes británicos y los colonos norteamericanos, dirigida en parte por el líder ottawa Pontiac, en reacción a los colonos que demandaban las tierras de los amerindios, así como a la severidad con que trataban a éstos los soldados británicos. (p. 135)

popular sovereignty [soberanía popular] *s.* gobierno en que gobierna la gente (p. 228); sistema en que los ciudadanos votan para decidir un asunto. (p. 447)

Populist Party [Partido Populista] *s.* también conocido como el Partido del Pueblo y constituido en 1890, este grupo quería una política que aumentara el precio de lo que cultivaban los granjeros. (p. 551)

prejudice [prejuicio] *s.* opinión negativa no basada en los hechos. (p. 411)

privateer [corsario] *s.* barco de propiedad particular autorizado por un gobierno que está en guerra a atacar los barcos de la marina mercante enemiga. (p. 188)

Proclamation of 1763 [Proclama de 1763] *s.* orden por la cual Gran Bretaña les prohibía a los colonos norteamericanos establecer asentamientos al oeste de los montes Apalaches. (p. 135)

progressivism [progresismo] *s.* movimiento reformista de principios del siglo XX que buscaba devolver el control del gobierno al pueblo, restablecer oportunidades económicas y corregir las injusticias de la vida estadounidense. (p. 553)

proprietary colony [colonia de proprietario] *s.* colonia de un único dueño. (p. 85)

pro tempore *adv.* latín para "por el momento". (p. 234)

Puritan [puritano] *s.* miembro de un grupo de Inglaterra que se asentó en la Colonia de la bahía de Massachusetts en 1630 y trató de reformar las prácticas de la Iglesia de Inglaterra. (p. 78)

push-pull factor *s.* factor que empuja a la gente a irse de su tierra natal y las atrae a un lugar nuevo. (p. 408)

Q

Quaker [cuáquero] *s.* persona que creía que todas las personas debieran vivir en paz y armonía; aceptaba a religiones y grupos étnicos diferentes. (p. 85)

quarter [acuartelar] *v.* dar alojamiento. (p. 251)

Quartering Act [ley de Acuartelamiento] *s.* ley aprobada por el Parlamento en 1765 que requería que las colonias alojaran a los soldados británicos y los aprovisionaran. (p. 144)

quorum [quórum] *s.* número mínimo de miembros que deben estar presentes para que pueda empezar a deliberar oficialmente una asamblea. (p. 235)

R

racism [racismo] *s.* creencia de que alguna gente es inferior a causa de su raza. (p. 62)

radical [radical] *s.* persona que adopta posiciones políticas extremas. (p. 297)

Radical Republican [republicano radical] *s.* diputado que después de la guerra civil estaba a favor de usar el gobierno para crear un nuevo orden en el Sur y dar la ciudadanía total y derecho al voto a los afroamericanos. (p. 517)

ratification [ratificación] *s.* aprobación oficial. (p. 248)

Reconstruction [Reconstrucción] *s.* proceso que usó el gobierno de Estados Unidos para readmitir a los estados confederados a la Unión después de la guerra civil. (p. 517)

Reformation [Reforma] *s.* movimiento religioso del siglo XVI para corregir los problemas de la Iglesia Católica Romana. (p. 37)

Renaissance [Renacimiento] *s.* período de la historia europea que duró desde el siglo XIV hasta comienzos del XVII y que acrecentó el interés por el arte y el saber. (p. 36)

rendezvous [encuentro] *s.* reunión. (p. 181)

reprieve [indultar] *n.* cancelación de un castigo. (p. 243)

republic [república] *s.* gobierno en que el pueblo elige representantes para que lo gobiernen. (p. 206)

republicanism [republicanismo] *s.* creencia de que el gobierno se debe basar en el consentimiento del pueblo; el pueblo ejercita su poder votando por representantes políticos. (pp. 198, 229)

Republican Party [Partido Republicano] *s.* el partido político constituído en 1854 por los que se oponían a la esclavitud en los territorios. (p. 450)

revenue [rentas públicas] *s.* entradas que recibe un gobierno para cubrir sus gastos. (pp. 144, 236)

revival [renacimiento religioso] *s.* reunión diseñada para revivir la fe religiosa. (p. 417)

rifle [rifle] *s.* arma de barril estriado que hace que la bala vaya girando por el aire. (p. 475)

robber baron [capitalista inescrupuloso] *s.* líder industrial que se hizo acaudalado usando medios deshonestos. (p. 578)

romanticism [romanticismo] *s.* movimiento artístico europeo que acentuaba al individuo, la imaginación, la creatividad y la emoción. (p. 413)

Roosevelt Corollary [Corolario de Roosevelt] *s.* la adición en 1904 a la Doctrina Monroe permitiendo a los Estados Unidos a actuar de "policía" en Latinoamérica. (p. 560)

royal colony [colonia real] *s.* colonia regida por gobernadores nombrados por un rey. (p. 87)

S

salutary neglect [indiferencia beneficiosa] *s.* política de no interferir Inglaterra en los asuntos de sus colonias norteamericanas durante la primera mitad del siglo XVIII. (p. 128)

Santa Fe Trail [Camino de Santa Fe] *s.* camino hacia el oeste que iba de Missouri a Santa Fe, New Mexico. (p. 379)

secede [separarse] *v.* retirarse. (p. 457)

secession [secesión] *s.* separarse como parte de Estados Unidos. (p. 367)

Second Continental Congress [segundo Congreso Continental] *s.* organismo de gobierno cuyos delegados acordaron en mayo de 1775 organizar el Ejército Continental y aprobar la Declaración de Independencia. (p. 161)

Second Great Awakening [segundo Gran Despertar] *s.* renovación de la fe religiosa durante fines del siglo XVIII y comienzos del XIX. (p. 417)

sectionalism [seccionalismo] *s.* colocar los intereses de la región propia por encima de los de la nación como unidad. (p. 341)

segregation [segregación] *s.* separación. (p. 549)

Seneca Falls Convention [convención de Seneca Falls] *s.* convención sobre los derechos de la mujer llevada a cabo en Seneca Falls, New York, en 1848. (p. 428)

separation of powers [separación de poderes] *s.* división de las funciones básicas del gobierno en tres ramas. (p. 230)

servitude [servitud] *s.* práctica de pertenecer a un dueño o amo. (p. 254)

Seven Days' Battles [batallas de los Siete Días] *s.* batalla de 1862 de la guerra civil en que la Confederación forzó a la Unión a retroceder después de un intento fracasado de capturar la capital sureña de Richmond. (p. 480)

sharecropping [aparcería] *s.* sistema en que los terratenientes daban a los agricultores tierra, semilla y herramientas a cambio de parte de la cosecha. (p. 527)

Shays's Rebellion [revuelta de Shay] *s.* sublevación de granjeros adeudados de Massachusetts en 1787. (p. 209)

Siege of Vicksburg [sitio de Vicksburg] *s.* victoria unionista de 1863, durante la guerra civil que le permitió a la Unión controlar todo el río Misisipí. (p. 500)

slash-and-burn agriculture [agricultura de corte y quema] *s.* método agrícola en que la gente preparaba los campos cortando y quemando árboles y pastos, cuyas cenizas fertilizaban la tierra. (p. 31)

slavery [esclavitud] *s.* sistema de servidumbre humana involuntaria. (p. 60)

smuggle [contrabandear] *v.* importar o exportar mercancías ilegalmente. (p. 96)

Sons of Liberty [Hijos de la Libertad] *s.* grupo de colonos que formaron una sociedad secreta para oponerse a las políticas británicas en los tiempos de la revolución norteamericana. (p. 145)

Spanish-American War *s.* guerra de 1898 que comenzó cuando Estados Unidos demandó que España le concediera la independencia a Cuba. (p. 557)

Spanish Armada [Armada española] *s.* flota de buques enviada en 1588 por el rey español Felipe Segundo para invadir a Inglaterra y restaurar allí el catolicismo romano. (p. 57)

spiritual [canción espiritual] *s.* canción folklórica religiosa. (p. 335)

spoils system [sistema de prebendas] *s.* práctica de otorgar los candidatos elegidos empleos gubernamentales a los simpatizantes políticos. (p. 357)

Stamp Act [ley del Timbre] *s.* ley aprobada por el Parlamento en 1765 que requería que todos los documentos comerciales y legales llevaran un timbre oficial que indicaba que se había pagado un impuesto. (p. 144)

states' rights [derechos estatales] *s.* teoría que sostenía que los estados tenían el derecho a decidir cuándo el gobierno federal había pasado una ley inconstitucional. (p. 291)

steerage [tercera clase] *s.* nivel o lugar más barato de un barco. (p. 407)

Stono Rebellion [Rebelión de Stono] *s.* sublevación de esclavos de 1739, en Carolina del Sur, que resultó en que se hicieran aún más estrictas las leyes que controlaban a los esclavos. (p. 107)

strategy [estrategia] *s.* plan general de acción. (p. 180)

strike [declararse en huelga] *v.* suspender los obreros el trabajo para tratar de conseguir condiciones de trabajo mejores. (p. 418)

subsistence farm *v.* una granja que produce bastante alimento para la familia con sólo una pequeña cantidad para vender. (p. 94)

suffrage [sufragio] *s.* derecho a votar. (pp. 246, 428)

Sugar Act [ley del Azúcar] *s.* ley aprobada por el Parlamento en 1764 que impuso impuestos al azúcar, la melaza y otros productos que llegaban a las colonias; también establecía severos castigos para los contrabandistas. (p. 144)

T

tariff [arance aduanero] *s.* impuesto a las mercancías importadas. (p. 280)

Tariff of Abominations [arancel de las Abominaciones] *s.* ley de 1828 que subió los aranceles de las materias primas y las manufacturas; alteró a los sureños, quienes sentían que la política económica nacional la estaban determinando los intereses económicos del noreste. (p. 365)

technology [tecnología] *s.* uso de herramientas y conocimiento para satisfacer las necesidades humanas. (p. 29)

Tejano [tejano] *s.* persona de ascendencia española que consideraba a Texas su hogar. (p. 384)

temperance movement [movimiento de la templanza] *s.* campaña para acabar con el consumo de las bebidas alcohólicas. (p. 418)

tender *s.* dinero (p. 239)

Thirteenth Amendment [Enmienda Decimotercera] *s.* enmienda a la Constitución de Estados Unidos adoptada en 1865 que abolía la esclavitud y la servidumbre involuntaria en Estados Unidos. (p. 505)

Three-Fifths Compromise [Acuerdo de los Tres Quintos] *s.* acuerdo de la Convención Constitucional que establecía que, para efectos de la representación y del cobro de impuestos, se contarían como parte de la población tres quintos de los esclavos de un estado. (p. 216)

Townshend Acts [leyes de Townshend] *s.* serie de leyes aprobadas por el Parlamento en 1767 que suspendieron la Asamblea de Nueva York y establecieron impuestos a las mercancías importadas a las colonias británicas. (p. 147)

Trail of Tears [Sendero de las Lágrimas] *s.* trágica marcha del pueblo cherokee desde sus tierras hasta el Territorio Indio, entre 1838 y 1839; miles de cherokees murieron. (p. 361)

transcendentalism [trascendentalismo] *s.* filosofía del siglo XIX que enseñaba que el mundo espiritual es más importante que el mundo físico y que las personas pueden hallar la verdad dentro de sí mismas mediante los sentimientos y la intuición. (p. 415)

Treaty of Ghent [Tratado de Gante] *s.* tratado firmado en 1814 que puso fin a la guerra de 1812; no cambió de dueño ningún territorio ni se resolvieron los conflictos comerciales. (p. 317)

Treaty of Greenville [Tratado de Greenville] *s.* acuerdo de 1795 por el cual 12 tribus amerindias cedieron al gobierno de Estados Unidos gran parte de lo que hoy son los estados de Ohio e Indiana. (p. 284)

Treaty of Guadalupe Hidalgo [Tratado de Guadalupe Hidalgo] *s.* tratado de 1848 que puso fin a la guerra estadounidense con México; México cedió California y Nuevo México a los Estados Unidos. (p. 394)

Treaty of Paris [Tratado de París] *s.* tratado de 1763 que puso fin a la guerra Francesa y Amerindia; Inglaterra entregó toda norteamérica del este del río Mississippi. (p. 134)

Treaty of Paris of 1783 [Tratado de París de 1783] *s.* tratado que puso fin a la guerra Revolucionaria, confirmó la independencia de Estados Unidos y estableció los límites de la nueva nación. (p. 196)

Treaty of Tordesillas [Tratado de Tordesillas] *s.* tratado de 1494 por el cual España y Portugal acordaron repartirse las tierras del hemisferio occidental y movieron la línea de demarcación hacia el oeste. (p. 51)

triangular trade [comercio triangular] *s.* sistema de comercio transatlántico en que se intercambiaban mercancías, incluso esclavos, entre África, Inglaterra, Europa, las Antillas y las colonias de Norte América. (p. 95)

tribunal [tribunal] *s.* corte. (p. 237)

U

unanimous consent [consentimiento unánime] *s.* acuerdo completo. (p. 248)

Uncle Tom's Cabin [La cabaña del tío Tom] *s.* novela publicada por Harriet Beecher Stowe en 1852, que mostraba la esclavitud como brutal e inmoral. (p. 446)

unconstitutional [inconstitucional] *adj.* que contradice la ley de la constitución. (p. 301)

Underground Railroad [ferrocarril clandestino] *s.* serie de rutas de escape que usaban los esclavos para escaparse del Sur. (p. 426)

urbanization [urbanización] *s.* crecimiento de las ciudades como resultado de la industrialización. (p. 541)

V

vaudeville [vodevil] *s.* tipo de espectáculo teatral en vivo con mezcla de canciones, baile y comedia. (p. 549)

Vietnam War [guerra de Vietnam] *s.* conflicto militar que duró desde 1954 hasta 1975, entre el Vietnam del Norte comunista, apoyado por China y la Unión Soviética y las fuerzas no comunistas de Vietnam del Sur, apoyadas por Estados Unidos. (p. 581)

vigilante [vigilante] *s.* persona dispuesta a tomar la ley en sus propias manos. (p. 545)

Virginia Plan *s.* plan presentado por Edmund Randolph, delegado a la Convención Constitucional de 1787, que proponía un gobierno de tres ramas y una legislatura bicameral en la que la representación se basaría en la población o la riqueza de un estado. (p. 215)

W

War Hawk *s.* habitante de las regiones del oeste que apoyaba la guerra de 1812. (p. 313)

Watergate Scandal [escándalo de Watergate] *s.* escándalo que resultó de los esfuerzos del gobierno de Nixon por encubrir su participación en el allanamiento de la Sede Central del Partido Demócrata en el edificio de apartamentos Watergate. (p. 582)

Webster-Hayne debate [debate Webster-Hayne] *s.* debate de 1830 entre Daniel Webster y Robert Hayne sobre la doctrina de la invalidación. (p. 366)

Whig Party [Partido Whig] *s.* partido político organizado en 1834 en oposición a las políticas de Andrew Jackson. (p. 371)

Whiskey Rebellion [rebelión del Whisky] *s.* protesta de 1794 contra el impuesto que impuso el gobierno al whisky, valioso medio económico de los granjeros de la frontera. (p. 285)

Wilderness Road [Camino al Desierto] *s.* sendero a Kentucky que ayudó a construir el pionero Daniel Boone. (p. 205)

Wilmot Proviso [Claúsula de Wilmot] *s.* propuesta de 1846 que excluía la esclavitud de cualquier territorio adquirido como resultado de la guerra con México. (p. 443)

World War II [segunda guerra mundial] *s.* guerra que se libró entre 1939 y 1945, en que Gran Bretaña, Francia, la Unión Soviética, Estados Unidos, China y otros aliados derrotaron a Alemania, Italia y Japón. (p. 575)

writ of assistance [mandato judicial de transferencia] *s.* orden de registro que permitía a los oficiales británicos entrar en los hogares o comercios coloniales en busca de contrabando. (p. 148)

X

XYZ Affair [asunto XYZ] *s.* incidente de 1797 en que funcionarios franceses demandaron que los diplomáticos estadounidenses les pagaran un soborno. (p. 290)

Y

yellow journalism [periodismo amarillo] *s.* estilo de periodismo que usa la exageración y el sensacionalismo para presentar las noticias. (p. 557)

INDEX

An *i* preceding a page reference in italics indicates that there is an illustration, and usually text information as well, on that page. An *m* or a *c* preceding an italic page reference indicates a map or a chart, as well as text information on that page.

A

R64

R65

C

R66

R67

D

E

F

R69

G

H

R71

M

N

O

R77

Q

R

R78

S

R79

T

R81

U

V

W

ACKNOWLEDGMENTS

TEXT ACKNOWLEDGMENTS

Chapter 6, pages 174–175: Excerpt from *Johnny Tremain* by Esther Forbes. Copyright © 1943 by Esther Forbes Hoskins, copyright renewed by Linwood M. Erskine, Jr., executor of the Estate of Esther Forbes Hoskins. Reprinted by permission of Houghton Mifflin Company. All rights reserved.

Chapter 9, page 300: "Obeying Rules and Laws," from *Government in America* by Richard J. Hardy. Copyright © 1995 by Houghton Mifflin Company. All rights reserved. Reprinted by permission.

Chapter 16, pages 486–487: Excerpt from *Across Five Aprils* by Irene Hunt. Copyright © 1964 by Irene Hunt. All rights reserved. Reprinted by permission of Shirley Beem on behalf of the author.

Chapter 17, pages 508, 509, 510, 512, 513, 516, 518, 519: Excerpts from *The Civil War* by Kenneth Burns, Ric Burns, and Geoffrey Ward. Copyright © 1990 by American Documentaries, Inc. Reprinted by permission of Alfred A. Knopf, a division of Random House, Inc.

Chapter 20 Epilogue, page 585: Excerpt from "I Have a Dream" by Martin Luther King, Jr. Copyright © 1963 by Martin Luther King, Jr., copyright renewed 1991 by Coretta Scott King. Reprinted by arrangement with The Heirs to the Estate of Martin Luther King, Jr., c/o Writers House, Inc., as agent for the proprietor.

page 593: Quote by Ken Burns from "Of documentaries and storytelling, historical awareness and arrogance, heroes and villains . . . a conversation with Ken Burns" by Sam Stall, *America West Airlines Magazine,* November 1997. Reprinted by permission of America West Airlines Magazine and Sam Stall.

ART CREDITS

Cover and Frontispiece

cover background Copyright © Bob Gelberg/SharpShooters.

frontispiece background The Granger Collection, New York.

Abraham Lincoln: The Library of Congress.

Zitkala-Să: Negative no. Mss 299, William F. Hansen Collection, Photographic Archives, Harold B. Lee Library, Brigham Young University, Provo, Utah.

Sam Houston: The Texas State Library and Archives Commission.

Abigail Adams: *Portrait traditionally said to be Abigail Adams* (about 1795), artist unknown. Oil on canvas, 30 1/4″ × 26 1/2″, N-150.55. Photo by Richard Walker. Copyright © New York State Historical Association, Cooperstown, New York.

Juan Seguín: Detail of *Juan Seguin* (1838), Jefferson Wright. Texas State Library and Archives Commission.

Harriet Tubman: James Gensheimer/NGS Image Collection.

Elizabeth Cady Stanton: The Granger Collection, New York.

Crispus Attucks: Copyright © Stock Montage.

Andrew Jackson: *Andrew Jackson* (1845), Thomas Sully. The Granger Collection, New York.

George Washington: Corbis.

Table of Contents

viii–xvii *background* The Granger Collection, New York; **viii** *top* Smithsonian Institution, Washington, D.C.; *bottom* The Granger Collection, New York; **ix** *top* Copyright © Michael Gadomski/Photo Researchers, Inc.; *center* The Granger Collection, New York; *bottom* Library of Congress; **x** *top* Copyright © R. Kord/H. Armstrong Roberts; *center George Washington in the Uniform of a British Colonial Colonel,* 1772, by Charles Willson Peale. Washington-Custis-Lee Collection, Washington and Lee University, Lexington, VA; *bottom* Illustration by Bill Cigliano; **xi** *bottom right* Copyright © John E. Fletcher & Arlan R. Wiler/NGS Image Collection; *bottom* Corbis; **xii** *top* Copyright © 1998 North Wind Pictures; *center* National Museum of American History, Smithsonian Institution; *bottom* Illustration by Patrick Whelan; **xiii** *top* From the collections of the Minnesota Historical Society; *bottom left* Copyright © 1998 Louis Psihoyos/Matrix; *bottom right* The Granger Collection, New York; **xiv** *top* Copyright © George Peter Alexandre Healy/Wood River Gallery/PNI; *center* Courtesy of Stamatelos Brothers Collection. Photo by Larry Sherer. Copyright © 1991 Time-Life Books Inc.; *bottom* The Granger Collection, New York; **xv** top, *Northern Pacific Railroad. The Pioneer Route to Fargo Moorhead Town Bismark Dakota and Montana and the Famous Valley of the Yellowstone* (about 1885), Creator–Poole Brothers, Printers. Broadside. Chicago Historical Society; *bottom left* NASA; *bottom right* From the Collection of David J. and Janice L. Frent.

Voices from the Past

xix *left The Last Voyage of Henry Hudson,* (1881) John Collier. Tate Gallery, London/Art Resource, NY; *right* The Granger Collection, New York; **xx** Copyright © 1999 North Wind Pictures; **xxi** *top left* Corbis; *bottom left* Illustration from *The Headless Horseman* by Natalie Standiford. Illustration Copyright © 1992 by Donald Cook, Reprinted by permission of Random House, Inc.; *right* Corbis/Bettmann; *right* Library of Congress; **xxii** *top left* National Archives; *center right* Copyright © 1963 Bob Adelman/Magnum Photos; *bottom right* Survey Compass, accession number 1982–145. Colonial Williamsburg Foundation.

Themes of American History

xxviii *top* Copyright © 1999 PhotoDisc, Inc.; *center* Photo by Howard Sochrer/*Life* Magazine, Copyright © Time Inc.; *bottom* Michael S. Yamashita/Corbis; **xxix** *top* Library of Congress; *bottom* National Museum of American History/Smithsonian Institution.

Geography Handbook

2 *top right* Copyright © H. Abernathy/H. Armstrong Roberts; *center left* Copyright © Warren Morgan/H. Armstrong Roberts; *bottom* Copyright © 1996 Denver A. Bryan; **3** *top* Copyright © Nathan Benn/Stock Boston; *bottom right* Copyright © Andy Sacks/Tony Stone Images; **4–5** The Granger Collection, New York; **4** *top* Copyright © 1997 David Noble/FPG International; **5** *top* Copyright © John Coletti/Stock Boston; *center* Copyright © Bill Horsman/Stock Boston; **6** *top* Copyright © George Mobley/NGS Image Collection; *center* Copyright © Lowell Georgia/NGS Image Collection; *bottom left* The Granger Collection, New York; **10** *top* Copyright © T. Algire/H. Armstrong Roberts; *bottom* Copyright © Ken Graham/Tony Stone Images; **11** *top* Copyright © SuperStock; *bottom* Copyright © Tom Dietrich/Tony Stone Images; **12** *top* Copyright © Zane Williams/Tony Stone Images; *bottom* Copyright © Eastcott/Momatiuk/Tony Stone Images; **13** *top* Copyright © SuperStock; *bottom* Copyright © F. Sieb/H. Armstrong Roberts; **14–15** Illustration by Ken Goldammer; **16** *top* Copyright © M. Schneiders/H. Armstrong Roberts; *bottom* Copyright © D. Frazier/H. Armstrong Roberts; **17** *top left* Copyright © Ron Levy/Liaison Agency; *top right,* center right, *bottom right* Copyright © Steve Adams/NGS Image Collection; *bottom left* Copyright © Cathlyn Melloan/Tony Stone Images; **18** *bottom* Copyright © J. Marshall/The Image Works; **19** *left* Culver Pictures; *right* Copyright © Santi Visalli/The Image Bank.

Unit 1

22–23 Copyright © R. Kord/H. Armstrong Roberts.

Chapter 1

24, 25 The Granger Collection, New York; **26** *top* Werner Forman/Art Resource, New York; *center* Copyright © Aldona Sabalis/Photo Researchers, Inc.; *bottom* Copyright © Stuart Dee/The Image Bank; **27** Courtesy of Rock Art Foundation, San Antonio, Texas; **28** Copyright © Francois Gohier/Photo Researchers, Inc.; **29** Smithsonian Institution, Washington, D.C.; **33** Copyright © Thomas D. W. Friedmann/Photo Researchers, Inc.; **34** *left* Copyright © Aldona Sabalis/Photo Researchers, Inc.; **35** PNI; **37** *School of Athens* (1508), Raphael (Raffaello Santi). Stanza della Segnatura, Vatican City, Vatican. Photo copyright © Erich Lessing/Art Resource, New York; **39** Detail of *St. Vincent Polyptych*

(date unknown), Nuno Gonçalves. Museu Nacional de Arte Antiga, Lisbon, Portugal. Copyright © Scala/Art Resource, New York;
40 *Portrait of a Man, Called Christopher Columbus* (1519), Sebastiano del Piombo. Oil on canvas, 42″ × 34 3/4″. The Metropolitan Museum of Art, gift of J. Pierpont Morgan, 1900;
42 Archivio Fotografico del Museo Preistorico Etnografico L. Pigorini, Rome. Photo by Lorenzo de Masi;
43 Cliché Bibliothèque nationale de France, Paris; **45** *bottom* Courtesy of John Goss; **46** Copyright © Francois Gohier/Photo Researchers, Inc.; **47** Photos by Sharon Hoogstraten.

Chapter 2

48, 49 The Granger Collection, New York; **51** Detail of *Pope Alexander VI Borgia Kneeling in Prayer* (date unknown), Bernardino Pinturicchio. Sala die Misteri della Fede, Appartamento Borgia, Vatican Palace, Vatican State/Scala/Art Resource, New York; **53** Corbis; **54** The Granger Collection, New York; **55** *top, The Last Voyage of Henry Hudson* (1881), John Collier. Tate Gallery, London/Art Resource, New York;
57 PNI; **59** The Granger Collection, New York; **61** *right* The Newberry Library, Chicago; *left, Slaves Below Deck of Albanez* (date unknown), Francis Meynell. Copyright © National Maritime Museum Picture Library, London.

Chapter 3

66 The Granger Collection, New York; **67** Colonial Williamsburg Foundation; **69** British Museum; **71** AP/Wide World Photos; **72** *Pocahontas* (1616), Simon van de Passe. Engraving, 6 7/8″ × 4 3/4″ (17.5 cm × 12 cm). Published in the *Baziliologia,* London, 1618. National Portrait Gallery, Smithsonian Institution/Art Resource, New York; **73** The Granger Collection, New York; **74-75** Illustration by Ivan Lapper. Copyright © The Reader's Digest Association; **76** The Granger Collection, New York; **77** *The Mayflower in Plymouth Harbor* (1882), William Halsall. Courtesy of the Pilgrim Society, Plymouth, Massachusetts; **78** *top* Copyright © SuperStock; *bottom* Copyright © Andrew J. Martinez/Photo Researchers, Inc.; **79** *bottom* The Granger Collection, New York; **80** *left* Courtesy of American Antiquarian Society; *right* The New York Public Library; **81** *Trial of George Jacobs for Witchcraft, 1692* (1855), T. H. Matteson. Oil on canvas, acc. #1246. Peabody Essex Museum, Salem, Massachusetts. Photo by Mark Sexton; **84** Detail of *Peter Stuyvesant and the Trumpeter (The Wrath of Peter Stuyvesant)* (1835), Asher B. Durand. Oil on canvas, 24 1/4″ × 30 1/4″, accession no. 1858.28. Copyright © Collection of The New-York Historical Society; **85** Copyright © Tom Dietrich/Tony Stone Images; **87** Brown Brothers;
89 Colonial Williamsburg Foundation.

Chapter 4

90, 91 The Granger Collection, New York; **93** *Sperm Whaling: No. 2, The Capture* (1862), A. Van Best and R. S. Gifford. Lithograph by Endicott and Company, corrected by Benjamin Russell, 16 3/4 × 25 3/4″ (43 cm × 65 cm). N.M.A.H., Harry Peters "America on Stone" Lithography Collection; **94** *right* Copyright © Thomas Neill; **96** North Carolina Collection, University of North Carolina Library at Chapel Hill; **98** Detail of *Quaker Meeting* (date unknown), Egbert Van Heemskerk. The Quaker Collection, Haverford (Pennsylvania) College Library; **99** *right* Historic Hudson Valley, Tarrytown, New York; **100** The Granger Collection, New York; **102** Library of Congress; **103** Detail of *George Mason* (1811), Dominic W. Boudet. Oil on canvas, 30″ × 25″ (76.2 cm × 63.5 cm). Virginia Museum of Fine Arts, Richmond. Gift of David K. E. Bruce. Photo by Ron Jennings. Copyright © Virginia Museum of Fine Arts; **104** *right* Copyright © Chip Henderson/Tony Stone Images; **105** Virginia Historical Society, Richmond, Virginia; **106** The Granger Collection, New York; **108** *bottom left* Smithsonian Institution, Washington, D.C.; *bottom right background* Photo copyright © Dorothy Miller; *bottom right* foreground Copyright © The New York Botanical Garden; **109** *bottom center* Copyright © Old Dartmouth Historical Society, New Bedford (Massachusetts) Whaling Museum; **110** The Granger Collection, New York; **111** *right* Copyright © Michael Gadomski/Photo Researchers, Inc.; **112** Copyright © Mark McGehearty/AllSport; **113** *Catching the Wild Horse* (date unknown), George Catlin. Oil on canvas, 12 1/4″ × 16 1/4″. The Thomas Gilcrease Institute of American History and Art, Tulsa, Oklahoma.

Chapter 5

116 Virginia Historical Society, Richmond, Virginia; **117** Library of Congress; **120, 122** The Granger Collection, New York;
124 Corbis; **125** Detail of *Increase Mather* (1688), John Vander Spriett. Courtesy of the Massachusetts Historical Society;
126 Courtesy of Knox County, Illinois Teen Court; **127** The Granger Collection, New York; **129** *left* Corbis; *right* The Newberry Library, Chicago; **130** Detail of *Braddock's Defeat* (1903), Edward Deming. State Historical Society of Wisconsin Museum Collection; **131** Library of Congress; **133, 135** The Granger Collection, New York.

Unit 2

138–139 Copyright © William Johnson/Stock Boston.

Chapter 6

140, 141 The Granger Collection, New York; **142** *top* Colonial Williamsburg Foundation; *center* Detail of *The Battle of Princeton* (date unknown), William Mercer. The Historical Society of Pennsylvania; *bottom* The Granger Collection, New York; **143** *James Otis Arguing Against the Writs of Assistance in the Old Towne House* (1901), Robert Reid. Courtesy Commonwealth of Massachusetts Art Commission; **144** *top* Rare Books Division, The New York Public Library. Astor, Lenox, and Tilden Foundations; *bottom* Emmet Collection, Manuscripts and Archives Division, The New York Public Library. Astor, Lenox, and Tilden Foundations;
145, 146 The Granger Collection, New York; **147** Copyright © Stock Montage; **148** Copyright © Collection of The New-York Historical Society; **149** The Granger Collection, New York;
150 *left* The Granger Collection, New York; *right, John Adams* (date unknown), John Trumbull. National Portrait Gallery, Smithsonian Institution/Art Resource, New York; **151** The Granger Collection, New York; **152–153** Copyright © McDougal Littell Inc.;
154 Copyright © Paul Mozell/Stock Boston;
157 Copyright © Charles Winters/Stock Boston; **158** Copyright © McDougal Littell Inc.; **159** The Granger Collection, New York; **160** *Portrait traditionally said to be Abigail Adams* (about 1795), artist unknown. Oil on canvas, 30 1/4″ × 26 1/2″, N-150.55. Photo by Richard Walker. Copyright © New York State Historical Association, Cooperstown, New York;
161 Detail of *The Death of General Warren at the Battle of Bunker's Hill, 17 June 1775* (date unknown), John Trumbull. Oil on canvas. Yale University Art Gallery, Trumbull Collection; **162** Library of Congress; **163** *top* The Granger Collection, New York; *bottom* Library of Congress; **164** *top Detail of The Declaration of Independence, 4 July 1776* (date unknown), John Trumbull. Oil on canvas. Yale University Art Gallery, Trumbull Collection; *bottom* Copyright © R. Kord/H. Armstrong Roberts; **165, 166** The Granger Collection, New York; **171** *bottom* Clement Library, University of Michigan;
172 The Granger Collection, New York; **173** Photos by Sharon Hoogstraten.

Chapter 7

174 *March to Valley Forge* (1883), William B. T. Trego. Courtesy of Stacey Swigart, The Valley Forge Historical Society; **175, 176** The Granger Collection, New York; **177** Haym Salomon Home for Nursing and Rehabilitation, Brooklyn, New York. Courtesy of American Jewish Historical Society, Waltham, Massachusetts, and New York, New York; **178** *George Washington in the Uniform of a British Colonial Colonel* (1772), Charles Willson Peale. Washington-Custis-Lee Collection. Washington and Lee University, Lexington, Virginia; **179** *top* From *American Story: The Revolutionaries.* Courtesy of the Jamestown-Yorktown Educational Trust. Photo by Katherine Wetzel. Copyright © 1996 Time-Life Books Inc.; **180** *Washington Crossing the Delaware* (1851), Emanuel Gottlieb Leutze. Oil on canvas, 149″ × 255″. The Metropolitan Museum of Art, gift of John S. Kennedy, 1897; **181** *bottom* The Granger Collection, New York; **182** Copyright © Michael Newman/PhotoEdit/PNI; **183** *Two American Flags Flown*

R85

by John Paul Jones in 1779 (date unknown), unknown Dutch artist. Watercolor. Chicago Historical Society; **184, 185** The Granger Collection, New York; **186** From *American Story: The Revolutionaries.* Courtesy of the Jamestown-Yorktown Educational Trust. Photo by Katherine Wetzel. Copyright © 1996 Time-Life Books Inc.; **189** The Granger Collection, New York; **190** Library of Congress; **191** Defense Visual Information Center, Linda Delatorre, Researcher; **192** Illustration by Bill Cigliano; **194** *Surrender of Lord Cornwallis at Yorktown* (date unknown), John Trumbull. Yale University Art Gallery, Trumbull Collection; **195** Private collection; **196** The Granger Collection, New York; **199** Courtesy of the Massachusetts Historical Society; **200** Private collection.

Chapter 8

202 The Granger Collection, New York; **203** *The Signing of the Constitution* (date unknown), H. C. Chandler. Art Resource, New York; **205** Detail of *Daniel Boone Escorting Settlers Through the Cumberland Gap* (1851–1852), George Caleb Bingham. Oil on canvas, 36 1/2″ × 50 1/4″. Washington University Gallery of Art, St. Louis (Missouri). Gift of Nathaniel Phillips, 1890; **206, 209** top The Granger Collection, New York; **209** *bottom* Copyright © Thad Samuels Abell II/NGS Image Collection; **210** *bottom left* Copyright © John E. Fletcher & Arlan R. Wiler/NGS Image Collection; *bottom right* William L. Clements Library, Map Division, University of Michigan;

211 *top* The Granger Collection, New York; *bottom* Courtesy of the Shelby County (Ohio) Historical Society; **212** Corbis; *inset* Library of Congress; **213** Copyright © Joseph Nettis/Tony Stone Images; **214** The Granger Collection, New York; 231 PNI; **218** The Granger Collection, New York; **219** *left, Portrait of John Jay* (c. 1783, 1804–1808), Gilbert Stuart, believed to have been begun by and finished by John Trumbull. National Portrait Gallery, Smithsonian Institution/Art Resource, New York; **219** *right,* **220** The Granger Collection, New York.

Constitution Handbook

226 *left* The Granger Collection, New York; *right* Copyright © Ivan Massar/Black Star; **227** *top* Copyright © Bob Daemmrich/The Image Works; *center* Copyright © Topham/The Image Works; *bottom* Courtesy of The New York Times; **228** *bottom* Copyright © J. L. Atlan/Sygma; **229** *top* Copyright © Robert E. Daemmrich/Tony Stone Images; **231** *top* Copyright © 1973 Engelhardt in the *St. Louis Post-Dispatch*/Reprinted with permission; *bottom* Copyright © Patrick Forden/Sygma; **232** *background* The Granger Collection, New York; **232** *inset,* **241** AP/Wide World Photos; **242** *top right* Copyright © Archive Photos; *top left* Culver Pictures; *center right* Copyright © 1972 Magnum Photos, Inc.; *center left* AP/Wide World Photos; *bottom right* Courtesy Ronald Reagan Library; **248** AP/Wide World Photos;

249 Copyright © Collection of The New-York Historical Society; **251** Copyright © Baron Wolman/ Tony Stone Images; **252** *left* Copyright © Jean-Marc Giboux/Liaison Agency; *right* Copyright © Bob Dremmrich/Sygma; **254** Copyright © 1993 Ron Rovtar/FPG International; 272 The Granger Collection, New York; **257** *left* Copyright © 1998 FPG International; *right* Copyright © Cynthia Johnson/Liaison Agency; **258** Franklin D. Roosevelt Library; **261** Copyright © Rock the Vote Inc.

Citizenship Handbook

264 AP/Wide World Photos; **265** *background* Copyright © Bob Daemmrich; *foreground* Copyright © 1994 Mark Harmel/FPG International; **268** Copyright © Bob Daemmrich/The Image Works; **269** Copyright © David Young-Wolff/Tony Stone Images; **270** AP/Wide World Photos.

Unit 3

272–273 Copyright © Marvin E. Newman/The Image Bank.

Chapter 9

274 The Granger Collection, New York; **275** *Washington's First Cabinet* (date unknown), Alonzo Chappel. Courtesy of CNA; **276** Washington inaugural buttons, 1789. National Museum of American History, Smithsonian Institution; **278** AP/Wide World Photos; **279** *Portrait of Alexander Hamilton* (about 1796), James Sharples (the Elder). National Portrait Gallery, Smithsonian Institution/Art Resource, New York;

281 Copyright © Larry Stevens/Nawrocki Stock Photo Inc.; **282** Chicago Historical Society; **283** *right* Ohio Historical Society; **285** *Execution of Louis XVI* (18th century), anonymous. Colored engraving. Musée de la Ville de Paris, Musée Carnavalet, Paris, France/Giraudon/Art Resource, NY; **287** Mount Vernon Ladies Association; **289** *top* The Granger Collection, New York; *center right* Maryland Historical Society; **290** The Granger Collection, New York.

Chapter 10

294 *The Rocky Mountains, Lander's Peak* (1863), Albert Bierstadt (1830–1902). Oil on canvas, 73 1/2″ × 120 3/4″. The Metropolitan Museum of Art, Rogers Fund, 1907 (07.123). Photograph copyright © 1979 The Metropolitan Museum of Art; **295** From the Collection of Gilcrease Museum, Tulsa;

297 *left, Thomas Jefferson* (date unknown), Rembrandt Peale. Copyright © Collection of the New-York Historical Society; *right* Boston Athenaeum; **298** The Granger Collection, New York; **299** *center right* Kirby Collection of Historical Paintings, Lafayette College; *bottom background* Monticello/Thomas Jefferson Memorial Foundation, Inc.; *bottom center* Polygraph, 1806. John Isaac Hawkins, Charles Willson Peale. University of Virginia. Photo courtesy of Monticello/Thomas Jefferson Memorial Foundation, Inc.; **300** Boston Athenaeum; **301** Copyright © James Blair/NGS Image Collection; **302, 303** The Granger Collection, New York; **304** *inset* Copyright © Addison Geary/Stock Boston/PNI; **305** *Lewis and Clark at Three Forks* (date unknown), E. S. Paxson. Mural in the Montana State Capitol. Courtesy of the Montana Historical Society. Photo by John Reddy; **306** Copyright © 1998 North Wind Pictures; **307** National Museum of American History, Smithsonian Institution; **308** *center left* Copyright © Stock Montage; *center right, The Surrounder, Chief of the Tribe* (1833), George Catlin. Oto tribe. National Museum of American Art, Smithsonian Institution/Art Resource, New York; *bottom center, bottom right* Peabody Museum of Archeology and Ethnology, Harvard University. Copyright © President and Fellows of Harvard College. Photo by Hillel Burger; **309** *center left, Mink, a Pretty Girl* (1832), George Catlin. National Museum of American Art, Smithsonian Institution/Art Resource, New York; *center right, Steep Wing, a Brave of the Bad Arrow Points Band* (1832), George Catlin. Teton Dakota (Western Sioux). National Museum of American Art, Smithsonian Institution/Art Resource, New York; *bottom* Whaling Chief's Hat, Makah or Nootka. Cedar bark, bear grass, unidentified mammal hair, remnant feathers, leather thong. H 22 cm, D 27 cm. PM# 99-12-10/53080. Peabody Museum of Archeology and Ethnology, Harvard University. Copyright © President and Fellows of Harvard College. Photo by Hillel Burger; **310** Detail of *Decatur Boarding the Tripolitan Gunboat* (date unknown), Dennis Malone Carter. Oil on canvas. Courtesy of the Naval Historical Foundation; **311** Library of Congress; **312** The Granger Collection, New York; **314** *left* White House Collection. Copyright © White House Historical Association; *right* The Granger Collection, New York; **316** National Museum of American History, Smithsonian Institution; **318** *top, Thomas Jefferson* (date unknown), Rembrandt Peale. Copyright © Collection of the New-York Historical Society; *bottom* National Museum of American History, Smithsonian Institution; **319** "Ograbme, or, The American Snapping Turtle" (1807), D. Longworth. Negative no. 7278. Copyright © Collection of The New-York Historical Society; **320** *left* Elk skin bound journal (1805), William Clark. Ink on paper. Missouri Historical Society; *right, bottom* Copyright © 1998 North Wind Pictures;

321 Photos by Sharon Hoogstraten.

Chapter 11

322, 323, 325 Corbis-Bettmann; **326** The Granger Collection, New York; **327** Illustration by Patrick Whelan; **328** Corbis-Bettmann; **329** Copyright © Stock Montage;

330–331 Illustrations by Randal Birkey; **332** The Granger Collection, New York; **333** Illustration by Patrick Whelan; **335**

Detail of *Plantation Burial* (1860), John Antrobus. Williams Research Center, The Historic New Orleans Collection. Photo copyright © Jan White Brantley; **336** Corbis-Bettmann; **337** The Granger Collection, New York; **338** Corbis-Bettmann; **339** *right inset* The Granger Collection, New York; **340, 341** *right inset* Corbis-Bettmann.

Unit 4

348–349 Layne Kennedy/Corbis.

Chapter 12

350 The Granger Collection, New York; **351** Chicago Historical Society; **352** Copyright © Collection of the New-York Historical Society; **353** Redwood Library and Athenaeum, Newport, Rhode Island; **354** *left, John Quincy Adams* (1858), George Healy. Oil on canvas, 62″ × 47″. White House Collection. Copyright © White House Historical Association; *right, Andrew Jackson* (1845), Thomas Sully. The Granger Collection, New York; **355** The Hermitage: Home of President Andrew Jackson, Nashville, Tennessee. Photo of ribbon by Sharon Hoogstraten; **356** Copyright © *The News-Sentinel,* Fort Wayne, Indiana; **357** *left* The Granger Collection, New York; *right* Culver Pictures; **358** *Sequoyah, Indian Statesman* (date unknown), anonymous, after Charles Bird King. Hand-colored lithograph, J. T. Bowen lithography company. National Portrait Gallery, Smithsonian Institution/Art Resource, New York; **359** Copyright © J. Pat Carter/Liaison Agency; **361** *The Trail of Tears* (date unknown), Robert Lindneux. Woolaroc Museum, Bartlesville, Oklahoma; **362** The Granger Collection, New York; **363** *top, John Caldwell Calhoun* (about 1818–1825), attributed to Charles Bird Kind. Oil on canvas, 76.2 cm × 63.5 cm. National Portrait Gallery, Smithsonian Institution/Art Resource, New York; **363** *bottom,* **365** *top* The Granger Collection, New York; *bottom* The Museum of the Confederacy, Richmond, Virginia. Photo by Katherine Wetzel; **366** Detail of *Webster's Reply to Hayne* (date unknown), George Healy. Courtesy Boston Art Commission; **368** *top* The Granger Collection, New York; *bottom inset, Nicholas Biddle* (1839), Henry Inman. Oil on canvas [1978.2]. The Historical Society of Pennsylvania; **369** The Granger Collection, New York; **370** Copyright © Collection of The New-York Historical Society; **373** Library of Congress.

Chapter 13

374 Denver Public Library, Western History Department; **375** National Archives; **376** *Jedediah Smith in the Badlands* (date unknown), Harvey Dunn. The South Dakota Art Museum Collection; **378** Copyright © United States Postal Service;
379 *inset* Copyright © Ric Ergenbright; **380** Skillet, negative no. OrHi 97119. Oregon Historical Society; **384** The Granger Collection, New York; **385** *top* Broadsides Collection, The Center for American History, The University of Texas at Austin; **386** Copyright © Bob Daemmrich/Stock Boston/PNI; **387** *The Battle of the Alamo* (about 1913), Frederick C. Yohn. Courtesy Continental Insurance; **388** *left* Texas State Library and Archives Commission; **388** *right,* **390** The Granger Collection, New York; **392** *inset,* **396** Courtesy of the California History Room, California State Library, Sacramento, California;
397 Copyright © Collection of The New-York Historical Society; **398** Courtesy of Levi Strauss Company; **399, 401** Courtesy of the California History Room, California State Library, Sacramento, California; **403** *bottom* From the collections of the Minnesota Historical Society.

Chapter 14

404 Courtesy Meserve-Kunhardt Collection, Mount Kisco, New York; **405** The Granger Collection, New York; **406** The New York Public Library; **407** *background* From the collections of the Minnesota Historical Society; *foreground* Copyright © Collection of The New-York Historical Society; **408** *center* The Granger Collection, New York; **411** Michael S. Yamashita/Corbis; **412** The Granger Collection, New York;
413 From *The Headless Horseman* by Natalie Standiford, illustrated by Donald Cook. Illustration copyright © 1992 Donald Cook. Reprinted by permission of Random House, Inc.;
414 The Granger Collection, New York; **416** *background* Photo by Simon Marsden/The Marsden Archive; **417** The Granger Collection, New York; 434 Copyright © Archive Photos; **419** Department of Archives, Oberlin (Ohio) College; **420, 424** The Granger Collection, New York; **425** Chester County Historical Society, West Chester, Pennsylvania; **426** Copyright © 1996 Wayne Sorce; **427** *from left to right* The Granger Collection, New York; The Granger Collection, New York; The Granger Collection, New York; The Granger Collection, New York; Corbis-Bettmann; **428** The Granger Collection, New York;
429 *The Discord* (1885), F. Heppenheimer. Color lithograph, negative no. 51038. Copyright © Collection of The New-York Historical Society; **430** *center* Sophia Smith Collection, Smith College; *bottom right, bottom left* Copyright © 1998 Louis Psihoyos/Matrix; **431** *bottom* From the Collections of the National Underground Railroad Freedom Center, Cincinnati, Ohio; **434** From the collections of the Minnesota Historical Society; **435** Photos by Sharon Hoogstraten.

Unit 5

436–437 Corbis.

Chapter 15

438, 439, 441, 444 The Granger Collection, New York;
445 Corbis; **446** Hulton-Deutsch Collection/Corbis; **447** *left* The Granger Collection, New York; *right* Corbis-Bettmann;
450 From the Collection of David J. and Janice L. Frent;
451 AFP/Corbis; **452, 455** The Granger Collection, New York; **456** Lloyd Ostendorf Collection; **458** *background* Hulton-Deutsch Collection/Corbis; *inset* Copyright © George Peter Alexandre Healy/Wood River Gallery/PNI; **461** *The Last Moments of John Brown* (1884), Thomas Hovenden. Oil on canvas, 77 3/8″ × 63 1/4″. The Metropolitan Museum of Art, gift of Mr. and Mrs. Carl Stoeckel, 1897. Photograph copyright © 1982 The Metropolitan Museum of Art.

Chapter 16

462, 463 The Granger Collection, New York; **464** *top left, top right* Library of Congress; *bottom left, bottom right* The Granger Collection, New York; **466** The Lincoln Museum, Fort Wayne, Indiana. #0-43; **469** Copyright © H. Armstrong Roberts; **470** Copyright © McDougal Littell Inc.; **471** *left* Courtesy of Brian C. Pohanka; *right* Massachusetts Commandery Military Order of the Loyal Legion and the U.S. Army Military History Institute; **472** Bureau of Archives and History, New Jersey State Library; **473** Corbis-Bettmann;
474 Culver Pictures; **475** The Granger Collection, New York; **476** Illustration by Alexander Verbitsky; **477** Library of Congress; **478** U.S. Signal Corps photo no. 111-B-4146 (Brady Collection) in the National Archives; **481** Chicago Historical Society; **482** *left, center* Photos by Larry Sherer. Copyright © Time-Life Books Inc.; *bottom right* Fort Sumter National Park.

Chapter 17

484 *Cavalry Charge at Yellow Tavern, Virginia, May 11, 1864* (1871), H. W. Chaloner. Oil on canvas, 31″ × 47 7/8″. Garbisch no. 61.1, purchased from Kenneth E. Snow by Garbisches (1961). Presented by the Estate of Edgar William and Bernice Chrysler Garbisch. Photo by West Point Museum Collections, United States Military Academy; **485** Corbis-Bettmann; **486** *top left, top right, bottom left* Library of Congress; *bottom right* The Granger Collection, New York; **487** Corbis; **488** The Granger Collection, New York; **489** *top* Copyright © Archive Photos; *bottom* Library of Congress; **490** Defense Visual Information Center, Linda Delatorre, Researcher; **491** Culver Pictures; **492** The Granger Collection, New York; **494** American Red Cross; **495** *background* Corbis; *foreground* Massachusetts Commandery Military Order of the Loyal Legion and the U.S. Army Military History Institute; **496** The Pejepscot Historical Society; **497** Copyright © 1994 Kunio Owaki/The Stock Market; **498–499** *background* Illustration by Ken Goldammer; **498** *center* Library of Congress; *bottom left* From *Echoes of Glory: Arms & Equipment of The Union.* Photo by Larry Sherer. Copyright © 1991 Time-Life Books Inc.; *bottom right* The Museum of the Confederacy, Richmond, Virginia. Photo by Katherine Wetzel; **499** *bottom* From *Echoes of Glory: Arms & Equipment of The Union.* Photo by Larry Sherer. Copyright ©

R87

1991 Time-Life Books Inc.; **500** Library of Congress; **502** *top left* Courtesy of Stamatelos Brothers Collection. Photo by Larry Sherer. Copyright © 1991 Time-Life Books Inc.; *bottom* Courtesy Meserve-Kunhardt Collection, Mount Kisco, New York; **504** Copyright © Robert M. Anderson/Uniphoto, Inc.; **506** National Archives; **510** *top right* Manassas National Battlefield Park, National Park Service. Photo by Larry Sherer; *bottom right* Collection of Old Capitol Museum of Mississippi History; **512** *center left, center* High Impact Photography/Copyright © Time-Life Books Inc.; *center right* Courtesy of Stamatelos Brothers Collection. Photo by Larry Sherer. Copyright © 1991 Time-Life Books Inc.; **513** Photos by Sharon Hoogstraten.

Chapter 18

514 Corbis-Bettmann; **515** *The Shackle Broken—by the Genius of Freedom.* Color lithograph. Pub. by E. Sachs & Co., Baltimore, 1874. Chicago Historical Society; **517, 518** The Granger Collection, New York; **519** Corbis; **520** *His First Vote* (1868), Thomas Waterman Wood. Oil on board. Cheekwood Museum of Art, Nashville, Tennessee; **521, 522–523** *background* The Granger Collection, New York; **522** *top right,*
524, 525 Corbis; **526** Library of Congress; **528** The Granger Collection, New York; **529** Library of Congress; **530, 531** The Granger Collection, New York; **532** Library of Congress; **535** *bottom* The Granger Collection, New York.

Chapter 19 Epilogue

536 The Granger Collection, New York; **537** *top left, Street Arabs in Sleeping Quarters at Night* (date unknown), photo by Jacob A. Riis. The Jacob A. Riis collection, Museum of the City of New York; *top right* Library of Congress; *bottom left, Family Making Artificial Flowers* (about 1910), photo by Jessie Tarbox Beals. The Jacob A. Riis Collection, Museum of the City of New York; *bottom right* Library of Congress; **538** Special Collections Division, University of Washington Libraries. Negative no. 2315; **539** Denver Public Library; **540** Detail of *Forging the Shaft* (1874–1877), John Ferguson Weir. Oil on canvas, 52″ x 73 1/4″ (132.1 cm × 186.1 cm). Painted at West Point Foundry at Cold Spring, New York. The Metropolitan Museum of Art, Purchase, Lyman G. Bloomingdale Gift, 1901 (01.7.1). Photograph copyright © 1983 The Metropolitan Museum of Art; **541** The Newberry Library, Chicago; **544** *top right* Library of Congress; *center left* Chicago Historical Society; *bottom right* Library of Congress; **544** *bottom left,* **545** *center left* Corbis-Bettmann; *bottom* Chicago Historical Society; **546** The Kansas State Historical Society, Topeka, Kansas; **547** *top, View of San Francisco [Formerly Yerba Buena]* (1847), attributed to Victor Prevost. Oil on canvas, 25″ x 30″. California Historical Society, gift of the Ohio Historical Society; *bottom* The Bancroft Library, University of California, Berkeley; **548** *top* Lake County Museum/Corbis; *center, bottom* The Granger Collection, New York; **549** Joseph Schwartz Collection/Corbis; **550** Library of Congress; **551** Library of Congress; **553** Corbis-Bettmann; **554** *Theodore Roosevelt* (date unknown), John Singer Sargent. White House Collection. Copyright © 1992 White House Historical Association; **555** *right* Brown Brothers; *left inset* Doubleday, Page and Company, New York, 1906, second issue; **556** Corbis; **557** The Granger Collection, New York; **558** Chicago Historical Society; **559** Illustration by Nick Rotando; *center left* Corbis-Bettmann; **560** The Granger Collection, New York.

Chapter 20 Epilogue

566 *top, left to right* Copyright © Illustration House, Inc.; The Granger Collection, New York; National Archives; U.S. Air Force Photo; *bottom, left to right* Elvis Presley Enterprises, Inc. Used by permission; Copyright © James Blair/NGS Image Collection; Photo by Larry Burrows/*Life* Magazine, copyright © Time Inc.; Copyright © Sentinel Star/Sygma; **567** *top left* Corbis-Bettmann; *top right* Copyright © H. Armstrong Roberts; *center left, center right* Copyright © 1999 Werner Wolff/Black Star; **568** Copyright © The Washington *Post.* Reprinted with permission; **569** Brown Brothers; **570** *top* Culver Pictures; center Copyright © Blank Archives/Archive Photos; *bottom* Movie Still Archives; **572** National Museum of American Art, Smithsonian Institution/Art Resource, New York; **573** Photo by Margaret Suckley/Franklin D. Roosevelt Library; **574** *top* Photo courtesy of Margaret Bourke-White Estate/*Life* Magazine, copyright © 1934 Time Inc.; *bottom* Photo courtesy of Margaret Bourke-White Estate/*Life* Magazine, copyright © Time Inc.; **575** Copyright © Hulton Getty/Liaison Agency; **576** *top* Copyright © 1999 Owen H. K./Black Star; *bottom* The Granger Collection, New York; **578** UPI/Corbis-Bettmann; **579** AP/Wide World Photos; **580** U.S. Air Force Photo; **581** top NASA; *bottom* UPI/Corbis-Bettmann; **583** Patrick Sison/AP/Wide World Photos; **584** *top* Copyright © 1970 Elliott Erwitt/Magnum Photos, Inc.; *bottom* AP/Wide World Photos; **585** Copyright © 1963 Bob Adelman/Magnum Photos, Inc.; **586** Copyright © 1978 George Ballis/Take Stock; **587** *top* Wally McNamee/Corbis; *bottom* From the Collection of David J. and Janice L. Frent; **588** AP/Wide World Photos; **589** Copyright © Robert Brenner/PhotoEdit/PNI; **590–591** *background* NASA; **590** *top right* Copyright © 1996 Tom Stewart/The Stock Market; *bottom left* Copyright © Scott McKlernan/Zuna Images/The Stock Market; **591** *center* Copyright © The New Yorker Collection 1999 Mick Stevens from cartoonbank.com. All rights reserved.

Special Report

595 *top, bottom* AP/Wide World Photos; **597** *top, bottom* AP/Wide World Photos; **598** AP/Wide World Photos; **599** *left* © Mario Tama/Getty Images; *right* © Reuters NewMedia Inc./Corbis.

Supreme Court

600 *top left* Corbis; *bottom left* Copyright © 1994 North Wind Pictures; *bottom center* The Granger Collection, New York; *bottom right* Copyright © 1999 North Wind Pictures; **601** *top* Corbis; *bottom left* Corbis-Bettmann; *bottom right* AP/Wide World Photos; **602** *top left* Corbis; *bottom right* The Granger Collection, New York; **603** Copyright © 1994 North Wind Pictures; **604** Corbis; **605** *left* Culver Pictures; *right* The Granger Collection, New York; **606** Corbis; *bottom right* The Granger Collection, New York; **607** Copyright © 1999 North Wind Pictures; **608** Corbis; **609** *left* The Granger Collection, New York; *right* Lincoln University Archives, Langston Hughes Memorial Library, Lincoln University, Penn.; **610** *top left* Corbis; *bottom right* The Granger Collection, New York; **611** AP/Wide World Photos; **612** *top left* Corbis; **613** Wally Mcnamee/Corbis; **614** *top left* Corbis; *bottom right* AP/Wide World Photos; **615** Corbis; **616** *top left* Corbis; *bottom right* Corbis-Bettmann; **618** *top left* Owen Franken/Corbis; *bottom right* AP/Wide World Photos; **619** AP/Wide World Photos.

SkillBuilder Handbook

R15 Library of Congress; **R28** Courtesy of the Lloyd Ostendorf Collection.

Presidents of the United States

R36–R38 The Oval Office Collection™ except Clinton AP/Wide World Photos, George W. Bush Bush-Cheney 2000, Inc.

Maps created by Mapping Specialists

McDougal Littell has made every effort to locate the copyright holders of all copyrighted material in this book and to make full acknowledgment for its use.

1 2 3 4 5 6 7 8 9 – DWO – 07 06 05 04